psychology and life

psychology

and life

SIXTEENTH EDITION

■

Richard J. Gerrig

State University of New York
at Stony Brook

■

Philip G. Zimbardo

Stanford University

ALLYN AND BACON
Boston
London
Toronto
Sydney
Tokyo
Singapore

Executive Editor: Rebecca Pascal

Development Editor: Lisa McLellan

Senior Editorial-Production Administrator: Joe Sweeney

Editorial-Production Service: Heckman & Pinette Editorial Services

Composition Buyer: Linda Cox

Manufacturing Buyer: Megan Cochran

Cover Administrator: Linda Knowles

Text Designs: Seventeenth Street Studios

Photo Research: Image Quest

Text Composition: Omegatype Typography, Inc.

Allyn and Bacon
A Pearson Education Company
75 Arlington Street
Boston, MA 02116

Internet: www.ablongman.com

Between the time Website information is gathered and
published, some sites may have closed. Also, the transcription
of URLs can result in typographical errors. The publisher
would appreciate notification where these occur so that they
may be corrected in subsequent editions.

ISBN 0-205-33511-X

Brief Contents

Chapter 1
The Science of Psychology in Your Life — 1

Chapter 2
Research Methods in Psychology — 18

Chapter 3
The Biological Bases of Behavior — 47

Chapter 4
Sensation — 82

Chapter 5
Perception — 115

Chapter 6
Mind, Consciousness, and Alternate States — 152

Chapter 7
Learning and Behavior Analysis — 179

Chapter 8
Memory — 215

Chapter 9
Cognitive Processes — 252

Chapter 10
Intelligence and Intelligence Assessment — 289

Chapter 11
Human Development across the Life Span — 317

Chapter 12
Motivation — 362

Chapter 13
Emotion, Stress, and Health — 392

Chapter 14
Understanding Human Personality — 430

Chapter 15
Psychological Disorders — 466

Chapter 16
Therapies for Personal Change — 502

Chapter 17
Social Processes and Relationships — 534

Chapter 18
Social Psychology, Society, and Culture — 564

Contents

Preface   xvii

To the Student   xxv

Chapter 1

The Science of Psychology in Your Life   1

What Makes Psychology Unique?   3

Definitions   3

The Goals of Psychology   4

■ PSYCHOLOGY IN YOUR LIFE:
Why Study Psychology?   7

The Evolution of Modern Psychology   8

Psychology's Historical Foundations   8

Current Psychological Perspectives   10

What Psychologists Do   14

■ PSYCHOLOGY IN THE 21ST CENTURY:
The Future Is Now   16

Recapping Main Points   17

Key Terms   17

Chapter 2

Research Methods in Psychology   18

The Context of Discovery   19

The Context of Justification: Safeguards for Objectivity   21

Observer Biases and Operational Definitions   21

Experimental Methods: Alternative Explanations and the Need for Controls   23

Correlational Methods   27

Subliminal Influence?   28

Psychological Measurement   30

Achieving Reliability and Validity   30

Self-Report Measures   30

Behavioral Measures and Observations   31

Ethical Issues in Human and Animal Research   32

Informed Consent   32

Risk/Gain Assessment   33

Intentional Deception   33

Debriefing   33

Issues in Animal Research: Science, Ethics, Politics   33

Becoming a Wiser Research Consumer   34

■ PSYCHOLOGY IN THE 21ST CENTURY:
Psychological Research and the Information Explosion   35

Recapping Main Points   36

Key Terms   36

Statistical Supplement:
Understanding Statistics: Analyzing Data and Forming Conclusions   37

Analyzing the Data   39

Descriptive Statistics   40

Inferential Statistics   43

Becoming a Wise Consumer of Statistics   46

Chapter 3

The Biological Bases of Behavior   47

Heredity and Behavior   49

Evolution and Natural Selection   49

Variation in the Human Genotype   53

Biology and Behavior   55

Eavesdropping on the Brain   56

The Nervous System   58

Brain Structures and Their Functions   60

Hemispheric Lateralization   66

The Endocrine System   69

The Nervous System in Action   71

The Neuron   71

■ PSYCHOLOGY IN THE 21ST CENTURY:
Advances in Localizing Brain Function   72

Action Potentials   75

Synaptic Transmission 77

Neurotransmitters and Their Functions 78

■ PSYCHOLOGY IN YOUR LIFE:
How Do Life Experiences Affect Your Brain? 79

Recapping Main Points 80

Key Terms 81

Chapter 4

Sensation 82

Sensory Knowledge of the World 84

Psychophysics 84

From Physical Events to Mental Events 88

The Visual System 89

The Human Eye 89

The Pupil and the Lens 90

The Retina 90

Pathways to the Brain 92

Seeing Color 93

■ PSYCHOLOGY IN THE 21ST CENTURY:
Can Technology Restore Sight? 94

Complex Visual Analysis 98

Hearing 100

The Physics of Sound 100

Psychological Dimensions of Sound 100

The Physiology of Hearing 102

Your Other Senses 106

Smell 106

Taste 107

Touch and Skin Senses 108

The Vestibular and Kinesthetic Senses 110

Pain 111

■ PSYCHOLOGY IN YOUR LIFE
Why Is "Hot" Food Painful? 112

Recapping Main Points 113

Key Terms 114

Chapter 5

Perception 115

Sensing, Organizing, Identifying,
and Recognizing 117

The Proximal and Distal Stimuli 118

Reality, Ambiguity, and Illusions 120

■ PSYCHOLOGY IN THE 21ST CENTURY:
Virtual Reality 124

Approaches to the Study of Perception 125

Attentional Processes 126

Selective Attention 126

Attention and Objects in
the Environment 129

Organizational Processes in Perception 131

Figure, Ground, and Closure 131

Principles of Perceptual Grouping 132

Spatial and Temporal Integration 133

Motion Perception 133

Depth Perception 136

Perceptual Constancies 139

■ PSYCHOLOGY IN YOUR LIFE:
How Do You Catch a Fly Ball? 141

Identification and Recognition Processes 144

Bottom-Up and Top-Down Processes 145

Object Recognition 146

The Influence of Contexts and
Expectations 148

Final Lessons 149

Recapping Main Points 150

Key Terms 151

Chapter 6

Mind, Consciousness, and Alternate States 152

The Contents of Consciousness 154

Awareness of Consciousness 154

Accessibility to Consciousness 155

Studying the Contents of Consciousness 156

The Functions of Consciousness 157

The Uses of Consciousness 157

Studying the Functions of Consciousness 159

■ PSYCHOLOGY IN YOUR LIFE:
When Do Children Acquire
Consciousness? 160

Sleep and Dreams 161

Circadian Rhythms 161

The Sleep Cycle 162

Why Sleep? 163

Sleep Disorders 164

Dreams: Theater of the Mind 165

■ PSYCHOLOGY IN THE 21ST CENTURY:
The 24/7 Lifestyle and Sleep 166

Altered States of Consciousness 168

Lucid Dreaming 169

Hypnosis 169

Meditation 172

Hallucinations 172

Religious Ecstasy 173

Mind-Altering Drugs 174

Recapping Main Points 178

Key Terms 178

Chapter 7
Learning and Behavior Analysis 179

The Study of Learning 181

What Is Learning? 181

Behaviorism and Behavior Analysis 182

Classical Conditioning: Learning
Predictable Signals 183

Pavlov's Surprising Observation 183

Processes of Conditioning 184

Focus on Acquisition 188

Applications of Classical Conditioning 190

Operant Conditioning:
Learning about Consequences 194

The Law of Effect 194

Experimental Analysis of Behavior 195

Reinforcement Contingencies 195

Properties of Reinforcers 199

■ PSYCHOLOGY IN YOUR LIFE:
Spare the Rod, Spoil the Child? 200

Schedules of Reinforcement 202

Shaping 204

Biology and Learning 205

Instinctual Drift 206

Taste-Aversion Learning 206

Cognitive Influences on Learning 208

Animal Cognition 209

Observational Learning 211

Recapping Main Points 213

Key Terms 214

Chapter 8
Memory 215

What Is Memory? 217

Ebbinghaus Quantifies Memory 217

Types of Memory 218

An Overview of Memory Processes 220

Sensory Memory 221

Iconic Memory 222

Echoic Memory 223

Short-Term Memory and Working Memory 223

The Capacity Limitations of STM 224

Accommodating to STM Capacity 224

Working Memory 226

Long-Term Memory:
Encoding and Retrieval 228

Context and Encoding 228

Retrieval Clues 231

The Processes of Encoding and Retrieval 234

Improving Memory for Unstructured
Information 236

Metamemory 237

■ PSYCHOLOGY IN YOUR LIFE:
How Can Memory Research Help
You Prepare for Exams? 238

Structures in Long-Term Memory 239

Memory Structures 239

■ PSYCHOLOGY IN THE 21ST CENTURY:
Human Memory Searches and Web Searches 242

Using Memory Structures 243

Remembering as a Reconstructive Process 244

Biological Aspects of Memory 247

Searching for the Engram 247

Amnesia 248

Brain Imaging 249

Recapping Main Points 250

Key Terms 251

Chapter 9
Cognitive Processes 252

Studying Cognition 254

Discovering the Processes of Mind 254

Mental Processes and Mental Resources	255
Language Use	**258**
Language Production	258
Language Understanding	262
Language, Thought, and Culture	265
■ PSYCHOLOGY IN YOUR LIFE: Can Nonhuman Animals Learn Language?	266
Visual Cognition	**267**
Using Visual Representations	268
Combining Verbal and Visual Representations	269
Problem Solving and Reasoning	**271**
Problem Solving	272
Deductive Reasoning	276
Inductive Reasoning	277
■ PSYCHOLOGY IN THE 21ST CENTURY: Expert Systems and Medicine	280
Judging and Deciding	**280**
Heuristics and Judgment	281
The Psychology of Decision Making	284
Recapping Main Points	**288**
Key Terms	288

Chapter 10
Intelligence and Intelligence Assessment | **289**

What Is Assessment?	**290**
History of Assessment	291
Basic Features of Formal Assessment	292
Intelligence Assessment	**295**
The Origins of Intelligence Assessment	295
IQ Tests	296
■ PSYCHOLOGY IN THE 21ST CENTURY: Assessment on the World Wide Web	299
Theories of Intelligence	**299**
Psychometric Theories of Intelligence	299
Sternberg's Triarchic Theory of Intelligence	301
Gardner's Multiple Intelligences and Emotional Intelligence	302
The Politics of Intelligence	**304**
The History of Group Comparisons	304
Heredity and IQ	305
Environments and IQ	307

Culture and the Validity of IQ Tests	309
Creativity	**311**
Assessing Creativity and the Link to Intelligence	312
Exceptional Creativity and Madness	313
Assessment and Society	**314**
Recapping Main Points	**315**
Key Terms	316

Chapter 11
Human Development across the Life Span | **317**

Studying and Explaining Development	**319**
Documenting Development	319
Explaining Development	321
Physical Development across the Life Span	**321**
Prenatal and Childhood Development	322
Physical Development in Adolescence	326
Physical Changes in Adulthood	327
Cognitive Development across the Life Span	**328**
Piaget's Insights into Mental Development	328
Contemporary Perspectives on Early Cognitive Development	331
Cognitive Development in Adulthood	334
Acquiring Language	**336**
Perceiving Speech and Perceiving Words	336
Learning Word Meanings	337
Acquiring Grammar	338
Social Development across the Life Span	**340**
Erikson's Psychosocial Stages	341
Social Development in Childhood	342
■ PSYCHOLOGY IN YOUR LIFE: How Does Day Care Affect Children's Development?	346
Social Development in Adolescence	347
Social Development in Adulthood	350
Gender Development	**354**
Sex and Gender	354
The Acquisition of Gender Roles	356
Moral Development	**357**
Kohlberg's Stages of Moral Reasoning	357

Gender and Cultural Perspectives on Moral Reasoning 358

Learning to Age Successfully 360

Recapping Main Points 360

Key Terms 361

Chapter 12
Motivation 362

Understanding Motivation 364

Functions of Motivational Concepts 364

Sources of Motivation 364

Eating 369

The Physiology of Eating 369

The Psychology of Eating 370

■ PSYCHOLOGY IN THE 21ST CENTURY:
Genes and Obesity 371

Sexual Behaviors 375

Nonhuman Sexual Behaviors 375

Human Sexual Arousal and Response 376

The Evolution of Sexual Behaviors 378

Sexual Norms 379

Homosexuality 381

Motivation for Personal Achievement 383

Need for Achievement 384

Attributions for Success and Failure 385

Work and Organizational Psychology 387

A Hierarchy of Needs 388

■ PSYCHOLOGY IN YOUR LIFE:
Can Psychology Help Me Find
a Career? 389

Recapping Main Points 391

Key Terms 391

Chapter 13
Emotion, Stress, and Health 392

Emotions 394

Basic Emotions and Culture 394

Theories of Emotion 397

Functions of Emotion 402

Stress of Living 405

Physiological Stress Reactions 406

Psychological Stress Reactions 408

Coping with Stress 414

Health Psychology 419

The Biopsychosocial Model of Health 419

Health Promotion 420

■ PSYCHOLOGY IN THE 21ST CENTURY:
Healthy People 2010 422

Treatment 423

Job Burnout and the Health-Care System 425

A Toast to Your Health 426

■ PSYCHOLOGY IN YOUR LIFE:
Does Your Personality Affect Your Health? 427

Recapping Main Points 428

Key Terms 429

Chapter 14
Understanding Human Personality 430

Type and Trait Personality Theories 432

Categorizing by Types 433

Describing with Traits 434

Traits and Heritability 436

Do Traits Predict Behaviors? 437

■ PSYCHOLOGY IN YOUR LIFE:
Why Are Some People Shy? 439

Evaluation of Type and Trait Theories 440

Psychodynamic Theories 440

Freudian Psychoanalysis 440

Evaluation of Freudian Theory 444

Post-Freudian Theories 445

Humanistic Theories 446

Features of Humanistic Theories 446

Evaluation of Humanistic Theories 447

Social-Learning and Cognitive Theories 448

Mischel's Cognitive-Affective Personality Theory 449

Bandura's Cognitive Social-Learning Theory 450

Cantor's Social Intelligence Theory 452

Evaluation of Social-Learning and Cognitive Theories 453

Self Theories 453

Dynamic Aspects of Self-Concepts 453

Self-Esteem and Self-Presentation 454

The Cultural Construction of Self   456

Evaluation of Self Theories   458

■ PSYCHOLOGY IN THE 21ST CENTURY:
The Self on the Internet   459

Comparing Personality Theories   459

Assessing Personality   460

Objective Tests   460

Projective Tests   462

Recapping Main Points   464

Key Terms   465

Chapter 15

Psychological Disorders   466

The Nature of Psychological Disorders   467

Deciding What Is Abnormal   468

The Problem of Objectivity   469

Historical Perspectives   470

The Etiology of Psychopathology   472

Classifying Psychological Disorders   474

Goals of Classification   474

DSM-IV-TR   474

■ PSYCHOLOGY IN YOUR LIFE:
Is "Insanity" Really a Defense?   476

Major Types of Psychological Disorders   477

Anxiety Disorders: Types   478

Anxiety Disorders: Causes   481

Mood Disorders: Types   482

Mood Disorders: Causes   484

Gender Differences in Depression   487

Suicide   488

Personality Disorders   489

Dissociative Disorders   490

■ PSYCHOLOGY IN THE 21ST CENTURY:
Does "Internet Addiction" Exist?   492

Schizophrenic Disorders   493

Major Types of Schizophrenia   493

Causes of Schizophrenia   494

The Stigma of Mental Illness   498

Recapping Main Points   500

Key Terms   501

Chapter 16

Therapies for Personal Change   **502**

The Therapeutic Context   503

Goals and Major Therapies   504

Therapists and Therapeutic Settings   505

Historical and Cultural Contexts   506

Psychodynamic Therapies   508

Freudian Psychoanalysis   508

Neo-Freudian Therapies   509

■ PSYCHOLOGY IN YOUR LIFE:
Are Lives Haunted by Repressed Memories?   510

Behavior Therapies   512

Counterconditioning   512

Contingency Management   514

Social-Learning Therapy   515

Generalization Techniques   517

Cognitive Therapies   517

Cognitive Behavior Modification   518

Changing False Beliefs   519

Existential-Humanistic Therapies   520

■ PSYCHOLOGY IN THE 21ST CENTURY:
Therapy in the Age of Computers   521

Client-Centered Therapy   522

Gestalt Therapy   522

Group Therapies   523

Marital and Family Therapy   523

Community Support Groups   524

Biomedical Therapies   525

Psychosurgery and Electroconvulsive Therapy   525

Drug Therapy   526

Does Therapy Work?   529

Evaluating Therapeutic Effectiveness   529

Treatment Evaluations   530

Prevention Strategies   531

Recapping Main Points   532

Key Terms   533

Chapter 17
Social Processes and Relationships — 534

The Power of the Situation	536
Roles and Rules	536
Social Norms	538
Conformity	539
■ PSYCHOLOGY IN YOUR LIFE: How Do Groups Affect Decision Making?	542
Situational Power: *Candid Camera* Revelations	543
Constructing Social Reality	544
The Origins of Attribution Theory	545
The Fundamental Attribution Error	545
Self-Serving Biases	547
Expectations and Self-Fulfilling Prophecies	548
Behaviors That Confirm Expectations	549
Attitudes, Attitude Change, and Action	550
Attitudes and Behaviors	550
Processes of Persuasion	552
Persuasion by Your Own Actions	554
Compliance	556
Social Relationships	558
Liking	558
Loving	560
■ PSYCHOLOGY IN THE 21ST CENTURY: Relationships and the Internet	562
Recapping Main Points	563
Key Terms	563

Chapter 18
Social Psychology, Society, and Culture — 564

Altruism and Prosocial Behavior	566
The Roots of Altruism	566
Motives for Prosocial Behavior	568
The Effects of the Situation on Prosocial Behavior	569
Aggression	571
Evolutionary Perspectives	571
Individual Differences	572
Situational Influences	573
Cultural Constraints	576
Prejudice	578
Origins of Prejudice	579
Effects of Stereotypes	581
Reversing Prejudice	582
The Psychology of Conflict and Peace	583
■ PSYCHOLOGY IN THE 21ST CENTURY: The World Grows Smaller	584
Obedience to Authority	584
■ PSYCHOLOGY IN YOUR LIFE: Why Do People Join Cults?	588
The Psychology of Genocide and War	589
Peace Psychology	591
A Personal Endnote	594
Recapping Main Points	595
Key Terms	595
Glossary	G-1
References	R-1
Name Index	N-1
Subject Index	S-1
Credits	C-1

Preface

Teaching introductory psychology is one of the greatest challenges facing any academic psychologist. Indeed, because of the range of our subject matter, it is probably the most difficult course to teach effectively in all of academia. We must cover both the micro-level analyses of nerve cell processes and the macro-level analyses of cultural systems; both the vitality of health psychology and the tragedy of lives blighted by mental illness. Our challenge in writing this text—like your challenge in teaching—is to give form and substance to all this information: to bring it to life for our students.

More often than not, students come into our course filled with misconceptions about psychology that they have picked up from the infusion of "pop psychology" into our society. They also bring with them high expectations about what they want to get out of a course in psychology—they want to learn much that will be personally valuable, that will help them improve their everyday lives. Indeed, that is a tall order for any teacher to fill. But we believe that *Psychology and Life* can help you to fill it.

Our goal has been to design a text that students will enjoy reading as they learn what is so exciting and special about the many fields of psychology. In every chapter, in every sentence, we have tried to make sure that students will want to go on reading. At the same time, we have focused on how our text will work within the syllabi of instructors who value a research-centered, applications-relevant approach to psychology.

This 16th edition of *Psychology and Life* is the third collaboration between Philip Zimbardo and Richard Gerrig. Our partnership was forged because we shared a commitment to teaching psychology as a science relevant to human welfare. We both could bring our teaching experience to bear on a text that balances scientific rigor with psychology's relevance to contemporary life concerns. Furthermore, Richard's expertise in cognitive psychology provided an important complement to Phil's expertise in social psychology. With Richard as a coauthor, *Psychology and Life* has been able to keep pace with rapid changes in psychology, particularly in areas such as cognitive neuroscience. To signal his increasing involvement with the text, on this edition Richard has served as lead author. Even so, *Psychology and Life* remains a collaboration of like minds: Together, we celebrate both an ongoing tradition and a continued vision of bringing the most important psychological insights to bear on your students' lives. The 16th edition is a product of this fine collaboration.

Text Theme: The Science of Psychology

The aim of *Psychology and Life* is to use solid scientific research to combat psychological misconceptions. In our experience as teachers, one of the most reliable occurrences on the first day of introductory psychology is the throng of students who push forward at the end of class to ask, in essence, "Will this class teach me what I need to know?":

- My mother is taking Prozac: Will we learn what it does?
- Are you going to teach us how to study better?
- I need to put my son in day care to come back to school. Is that going to be all right for him?
- What should I do if I have a friend talking about suicide?

We take comfort that each of these questions has been addressed by rigorous empirical research. *Psychology and Life* is devoted to providing students with scientific analyses of their foremost concerns. As a result, the features of *Psychology and Life* support a central theme: psychology as a science, with a focus on *applying* that science to your students' lives.

How We Know

An important goal of *Psychology and Life* is to teach the scientific basis of psychological reasoning. When our students ask us questions—what they need to know—they quite often have acquired partial answers based on the types of information that are available in the popular media. Some of that information is accurate, but often students do not know how to make sense of it. How do they learn to interpret and evaluate what they hear in the media? How can they become wiser consumers of the overabundance of research studies and surveys cited? How can they judge the credibility of these sources? To counteract this infusion of so-called reliable research, we provide students with the scientific tools to scrutinize effectively the information with which they are surrounded and to draw generalizations appropriate to the goals and methods of research.

With a feature we call **"How We Know,"** we seek several times in each chapter to confront students directly with the experimental basis of critical conclusions. We give

Chapter 8). There is considerable clinical evidence to support this view, notably from studies of a patient, H.M., perhaps psychology's most famous subject:

HOW WE KNOW

SOME CONSEQUENCES OF HIPPOCAMPAL DAMAGE When he was 27, H.M. underwent surgery in an attempt to reduce the frequency and severity of his epileptic seizures. During the operation, parts of his hippocampus were removed. As a result, H.M. could only recall the very distant past; his ability to put new information into long-term memory was gone. Long after his surgery, he continued to believe he was living in 1953, which was the year the operation was performed.

Damage to the hippocampus does not, on the other hand, impair the ability to acquire *implicit* memories, outside of conscious awareness. Thus, H.M. was able to

each "How We Know" study a title—"Friendship and Self-Serving Biases," "Behavioral Treatments for Drug Addiction," "Mood Effects on Language Use"—so that students can access them easily. Nearly 200 "How We Know" studies appear throughout the text. Our intention is not to maintain that each of these studies is the definitive answer to a particular research area but rather that each opens the door for further questions. Our mission is to reinvent the use of primary research in psychology and describe methodologies clearly, in language accessible to your students. In this way, your students have repeated opportunities to understand how progress is made in psychological research.

Psychology in the 21st Century

At the beginning of the 21st century, our students feel as if they are living in very special times—times that are bringing with them rapid changes. Those changes provide researchers in psychology and related fields with a host of new topics to address as well as a range of new techniques to do so. To reflect these new realities, in this edition of *Psychology and Life* we have added a special feature, boxes we call **"Psychology in the 21st Century."** These boxes cover a diversity of topics, all at the cutting edge: "Can Technology Restore Sight?," "Relationships and the Internet," "Expert Systems and Medicine." Each Psychology in the 21st Century box demonstrates the flexibility with which psychological research tackles new issues and creates new applications.

Psychology in Your Life

The questions we cited earlier are real questions from real students, and your students will find the answers throughout the book. These questions represent data we collected from students over the years. We asked them, "Tell us what you need to know about psychology," and we have placed those questions—your students' own

PSYCHOLOGY IN THE 21ST CENTURY

VIRTUAL REALITY

Here is a plot device that has become commonplace in TV shows and movies at the turn of the century: The hero and heroine becomes immersed in some *virtual world*—a world generated by a computer—with dramatic consequences. For example, in *The Matrix* (spoiler: don't read the rest of this sentence if you haven't seen the movie) the hero discovers that everything that he took to be "real" is actually a highly elaborate *virtual reality*, enacted by the supercomputers that have come to dominate the planet. Fortunately, the versions of virtual re-

ronment. *Presence* has been defined along several different dimensions, including the virtual world's ability to draw participants into a socially rich

How does this apply in virtual environments? The researchers found that participants' lane-keeping per-

PSYCHOLOGY IN YOUR LIFE

WHEN DO CHILDREN ACQUIRE CONSCIOUSNESS?

It seems very likely that at some point in your life you've looked down into a crib at a newborn, or very young child, and wondered to yourself: "What's going on in this child's head?" Often, this question translates into an issue of consciousness: When does the child become conscious of him- or herself as a *self*? Research has suggested that children acquire, in turn, a subjective self and then an objective self (Lewis, 1991; 1999):

■ Children have acquired a *subjective self*, or *subjective self-awareness*, when they have come to the real-

do they realize that the image in the mirror is them? To answer this question, researchers asked mothers to put a small dot of rouge on their children's noses, without allowing the children to know that they were being marked—this is the *nose dot* test. Children understand some of the properties of mirrors at a fairly young age. For example, as early as 6 months, children will reach out and touch some parts of the image in the mirror. However, it isn't until about age 18 months that most children touch their noses in response to the dot of rouge (Bertenthal & Fischer, 1978). Apparently, it is not

an experimenter secretly put a stic in the child's hair. Some of the chil were shown videotape of themsel with the sticker in a *live* recording: They could see the sticker in their hair while they were doing the thi they were doing. The other half of the children watched a videotape about a three-minute *delay*: They watching a tape of themselves, wi sticker in their hair, carrying out ac ties from the recent past. About tv thirds of the children in the *live* gro reached up to the stickers, but onl about one-third of the children did the *delay* group. In fact, it was onl

voices—directly into the text in the form of **"Psychology in Your Life"** boxes. Each chapter includes a box that addresses questions such as "Why Study Psychology?" (Chapter 1), "When Do Children Acquire Consciousness?" (Chapter 6), and "Why Do People Join Cults?" (Chapter 18). Our hope is that your students will see, in each instance, exactly why psychological knowledge is directly relevant to the decisions they make every day of their lives.

Text Organization

Psychology is a field that continues to evolve. We intend the revised organization of this edition of *Psychology and Life* to reflect the way in which psychological research is configured at the turn of the 21st century. Our text organization also incorporates feedback from the text's reviewers and users—both students and professors. They have helped us devise an organization that provides even more support to our theme of psychology as a science.

For example, this edition of *Psychology and Life* features a separate chapter (Chapter 2) on research methods. The goal of that chapter is to acquaint your students with the challenges that researchers face when they attempt to answer important questions and the methods those researchers have devised to overcome those challenges. We also hope that this chapter will inspire your students to undertake the type of critical thinking that we encourage throughout the text. Also new to this edition is a separate chapter on intelligence and intelligence testing (Chapter 10). We found in our own teaching of introductory psychology that the domain of intelligence was one about which students often had the most questions before they enrolled in our courses. To address students' concerns, we now highlight that material in a separate chapter.

Because professors have responded with consistent enthusiasm, other aspects of *Psychology and Life* have remained unchanged. For example, we retain two chapters to cover material on sensation (Chapter 4) and perception (Chapter 5). Students have great intrinsic interest in the processes that make the external world accessible to internal processing. These two chapters are rich with descriptions and demonstrations that allow students to rethink their experience of the world. Similarly, we retained separate chapters on social processes and relationships (Chapter 17) and social psychology, society, and culture (Chapter 18). Researchers in the field of social psychology have most often assumed the burden of tackling the new research issues that arise from different historical circumstances. We have divided the social psychological material into two chapters to enable us to show students how this type of research can have broad

implications for their most pressing issues at both personal and societal levels.

Pedagogical Features

Psychology and Life has maintained a reputation for presenting the science of psychology in a way that is challenging, yet accessible, to a broad range of students, and the 16th edition is no exception. To enhance students' experience with the book, we include several pedagogical features:

- *Chapter-opening vignettes.* Each chapter opens with a brief vignette designed to draw students into the chapter content. We have drawn from sources as diverse as Helen Keller's *The Story of My Life,* for the cognitive chapter, and Colin Turnbull's observations in the African plains for the perception chapter.

- *Summing Up.* In each chapter, *Summing Up* sections are located at the end of each major section. These summaries provide students with a quick check of the main points as they read, and help students locate key ideas in later review.

- *Recapping Main Points.* Each chapter concludes with a chapter summary, *Recapping Main Points,* which summarizes the chapter content and is organized according to major section headings.

- *Key Terms.* Key terms are boldfaced in the text as they appear and are listed, with page references, at the end of each chapter for quick review.

- *New marginal glossary.* In addition to our end-of-text glossary, which functions as a minidictionary of psychology to provide students with a comprehensive resource they can use now and in future courses, we have added a marginal glossary in this edition. The marginal glossary allows students to check their understanding of key concepts as they read the text.

Also, your students can learn how to get the most out of their text by consulting "To the Student: How to Use This Book," which begins on page xxv.

Genotype The genetic structure an organism inherits from its parents.
Phenotype The observable characteristics of an organism, resulting from the interaction between the organism's genotype and its environment.

New in the 16th Edition

In addition to the new features mentioned earlier, *Psychology and Life* is fresh with the most up-to-date coverage and brimming with over 300 new references. Our goal is to be the most current, most accurate, and most accessible treatment of our discipline today. The 16th edition of *Psychology and Life* also incorporates new research on the diversity of people's life experiences. We intend our book to have meaning for the whole range of students who enroll in introductory psychology—men and women, members of diverse cultural and racial groups, traditional and nontraditional students. Wherever possible, we have brought new research to bear on cultural issues.

We have already noted organizational changes we undertook in response to feedback from our users: We have separate chapters on research methods and intelligence. In addition, the 16th edition of *Psychology and Life* has been streamlined to be slimmer than its predecessors. We have sought and used much careful advice to make the book briefer without shirking either classic or cutting-edge research. Finally, *Psychology and Life* is now the sole, premiere text accompanying the revised *Discovering Psychology* telecourse. This course supplement, which includes 26 half-hour video programs, study and faculty guides, and a coordinated Web site, is a landmark educational resource that reveals psychology's contribution not only to understanding the puzzles of behavior but also to identifying solutions and treatments to ease the problems of mental disorders.

Specific Content Changes

- Our expanded **cultural coverage** looks to the past, present, and future. For example, in Chapter 1 we include expanded discussion of the contributions made by women in psychology's early history. In Chapter 13, we describe important new research on gender differences in physiological responses to stress. In Chapter 18, the "Psychology in the 21st Century" box discusses consequences of the way in which the Internet has made the world seem smaller.

- We examine the **impact of technology on psychological research.** Chapter 3 provides information on the very newest techniques that are being used to localize function in the brain. We also consider advances in knowledge based on genetic analyses. For example, in Chapter 12 we describe research that examines genes and obesity.

- Several of our "Psychology in the 21st Century" boxes document the **impact of technology on people's lives.** For example, in Chapter 14 we describe

how people can explore different "possible selves" on the Internet. Similarly, in Chapter 17 we describe cutting-edge research on the impact the Internet has on social relationships.

- Our coverage of **psychopathology and treatment** includes the latest version of the *DSM—DSM-IV-TR.* In addition, we have enhanced our coverage of sociocultural perspectives on psychopathology. Our "Psychology in the 21st Century" boxes discuss the diagnosis of "Internet addiction" (Chapter 15) and the prospects for therapy and self-help on the World Wide Web (Chapter 16).

- We have enhanced our coverage of **intelligence assessment** with new examples of test questions and an analysis of assessment on the World Wide Web (Chapter 10). We have moved coverage of **personality assessment** to the chapter on personality (Chapter 14) to facilitate greater integration of topics.

The Total *Psychology and Life* Teaching Program

A good textbook is only one part of the package of educational materials that makes an introductory psychology course valuable for students and effective for instructors. To make the difficult task of teaching introductory psychology easier for you and more interesting for your students, we have prepared a number of valuable ancillary materials in both electronic and print form.

- *Instructor's Manual.* Written by John Boyd, this unique instructor's manual offers both general teaching strategies and specific tactics that have been class-tested and are known to succeed. For each chapter of the text, you will find detailed learning objectives and outlines, innovative lecture ideas and discussion topics, student activities and demonstrations, biographical profiles, comprehensive timelines, suggestions for further reading, and a complete media resource section.

- *Test Bank.* Written by John Caruso of the University of Massachusetts, Dartmouth, this test bank includes more than 2,000 multiple-choice and essay items. Each question is page-referenced; keyed according to chapter, type, topic, and skill level (factual, applied, or conceptual); and cross-referenced to the Study Guide.

- *Allyn and Bacon Test Manager—Computerized Test Bank.* (Available for Windows and Macintosh; DOS disk available upon request.) Allyn and Bacon *Test Manager* is an integrated suite of testing and assessment tools for Windows and Macintosh. You can use *Test Manager* to create professional-looking exams in just minutes by building tests from the existing database of questions, editing questions, or adding your own. Course management features include a class roster, gradebook, and item analysis. *Test Manager* also has everything you need to create and administer online tests. For first-time users, there is a guided tour of the entire *Test Manager* system and screen wizards to walk you through each area.

- *Allyn and Bacon Transparencies for Introductory Psychology, 2001.* A full set of color acetate transparencies is available to enhance classroom lectures and discussion. These images come from a wide range of sources, to support and extend teaching and learning.

- *Discovering Psychology Telecourse Videos.* Written, designed, and hosted by Philip Zimbardo, this set of 26 half-hour videos is available for class use from the Annenberg/CPB collection. Revised for 2001, the collection includes two completely new programs and more than 15 new sequences that bring students up-to-date on some of the latest developments in the field. A perfect complement to *Psychology and Life,* this course supplement has won numerous prizes and is widely used in the United States and internationally. Contact 1-800-LEARNER for more information.

- *Discovering Psychology Telecourse Study Guide.* In consultation with Phil Zimbardo, Nancy Franklin of the State University of New York at Stony Brook authors the fully revised *Telecourse Study Guide* and *Telecourse Faculty Guide.* In this *Telecourse Study Guide,* each chapter corresponds to one program, expands upon the material covered in the program, specifies appropriate reading assignments, and reviews material covered in the text. In addition, the study guide includes learning objectives; reading assignments; key people and terms; video program summaries and test questions with answer key; textbook test questions with answer key; essay questions; student activities; additional book, article, and film resources and annotated Web sites. All vocabulary and review questions are keyed to *Psychology and Life.*

- *Discovering Psychology Telecourse Faculty Guide.* The *Telecourse Faculty Guide* provides guidelines for using *Discovering Psychology* as a resource within your course. Keyed directly to *Psychology and Life,* the faculty guide includes the complete *Telecourse Study Guide* plus suggested activities; suggested essays; cited studies; instructional resources including books, articles, films, and Web sites; video program test questions with answer key; textbook test questions with answer key; and a key-term glossary.

- *Student Study Guide with Practice Tests.* Authored by Richard Gerrig, this innovative workbook provides students with a variety of dynamic activities designed to strengthen the learning experience. Each chapter begins with an outline and "what you need to know" questions for each major topic. Next, a "Guided Study" section directs the students' learning by providing a variety of questions and exercises. Each chapter also includes suggestions "For Group Study" in which students are encouraged to master and extend course material with the help of their classmates. Finally, the *Study Guide* provides students with two practice multiple-choice tests and answers for each chapter.

- *Practice Test Booklet.* This booklet, written by Marjorie Hardy at Eckerd College, provides 25 multiple-choice questions for each chapter, allowing students to practice what they have learned using a simulated classroom quiz. The booklet also includes answers and page references to the text.

- *Gerrig and Zimbardo PowerPoint Presentation CD-ROM.* This book-specific presentation provides detailed outlines of key points for each chapter, supported by charts, graphs, diagrams, and other visuals from the textbook. Resources from the *Gerrig and Zimbardo Companion Web Site* are also integrated for easy access to this Web site from your classroom as well as the full set of electronic instructor's manual files. This material is also available in a Web format accessible at www.abacon.com/ppt.

- *Companion Web Site.* The companion Web site for *Psychology and Life,* which can be accessed at www.ablongman.com/gerrig, offers a wide range of resources for both instructors and students. Each chapter contains learning objectives, annotated Web-links, Web activities, interactive online quizzes, labeling activities, and multiple-choice practice tests.

- *Mind Matters CD-ROM.* Developed by James Hilton, University of Michigan, and Charles Perdue, West Virginia State College, Mind Matters provides an in-depth, interactive experience in psychology that will enhance students' success in the introductory course. This engaging CD-ROM presents and integrates concepts in ways that invite students to explore the "science of the mind" in an environment that combines text, graphics, humor, and interactivity. Rather than rewarding memorization, Mind Matters nurtures exploration and integration by means of a series of self-contained units. Flexibly organized, it can be used in conjunction with any introductory text. This CD is accompanied by a Faculty Guide with detailed descriptions and test questions.

- *Psychology on the Net, 2002.* Updated to reflect the most current URLs related to the study of psychology, this easy-to-read guide helps point you and your students in the right direction when looking at the tremendous array of information related to psychology on the Internet.

Additional Resources

- *How to Think Straight about Psychology, 6th edition.* This well-known critical thinking manual by Keith Stanovich helps students become educated consumers of psychological information, particularly those topics they may encounter in the media or self-help literature.

- *Diversity Activities for Psychology.* This student manual, developed by Valerie Whittlesey, offers a wide variety of hands-on activities to help incorporate issues of diversity into your classroom. Activities are correlated with all major areas of psychological research, making it easy to assign this supplement with the Gerrig and Zimbardo textbook.

- *Ask Dr. Mike: Frequently Asked Questions about Psychology.* Developed by Mike Atkinson, author of the popular "Ask Dr. Mike" column on the Psychology Place™ Web site, this manual contains a collection of commonly asked student questions with in-depth answers, organized by major topics in the introductory psychology course.

- *Evaluating Psychological Information: Sharpening Your Critical Thinking Skills, 3rd edition.* Developed by James Bell, this workbook focuses on helping students to evaluate psychological research systematically and to improve their critical thinking skills.

- *Tools of Critical Thinking.* This critical thinking text by David A. Levy provides tools and skills for approaching all forms of problem solving, particularly in psychology.

- *Handbook for Psychology.* This helpful handbook, created by Drew Appleby, provides students with a wide array of information ranging from majoring in psychology to graduate school and job opportunities with a psychology degree.

- *How to Write Psychology Papers, 2nd edition.* Les Parrott provides a brief overview for writing APA-style psychology papers, including information on overcoming paper panic, using the Internet, preparing a working reference list, avoiding plagiarism, and using inclusive language.

Personal Acknowledgments

Although the Beatles may have gotten by with a little help from their friends, we have survived the revision and production of this edition of *Psychology and Life* only with a great deal of help from many colleagues and friends. We especially thank Brenda Anderson, Susan Brennan, Edward Carr, Emily Durbin, Nancy Franklin, William Horton, Donna Kat, Daniel Klein, Sheri Levy, Katelyn McKenna, Timothy Peterson, Deborah Prentice, Suparna Rajaram, David Rapp, Arthur Samuel, Pat Whitaker, and Gregory Zelinsky.

We would like to thank the following instructors of both this edition and previous ones, who read drafts of the manuscript and provided valuable feedback

Reviewers for the 16th Edition

Lori L. Badura, State University of New York at Buffalo
Darryl K. Beale, Cerritos College
James F. Calhoun, University of Georgia
Charles F. Levinthal, Hofstra University
Michael R. Markham, Florida International University
Brady J. Phelps, South Dakota State University

Reviewers for Previous Editions

Robert M. Arkin, Ohio State University
Gordon Atlas, Alfred University
N. Jay Bean, Vassar College
Michael Bloch, University of San Francisco
Richard Bowen, Loyola University
Mike Boyes, University of Calgary
James Calhoun, University of Georgia
Timothy Cannon, University of Scranton
John Caruso, University of Massachusetts–Dartmouth
Dennis Cogan, Texas Tech University
Randolph R. Cornelius, Vassar College
Lawrence Dachowski, Tulane University
Mark Dombeck, Idaho State University
Victor Duarte, North Idaho College
Tami Egglesten, McKendree College
Mark B. Fineman, Southern Connecticut State University
Kathleen A. Flannery, Saint Anselm College
Rita Frank, Virginia Wesleyan College
Eugene H. Galluscio, Clemson University
Preston E. Garraghty, Indiana University
W. Lawrence Gulick, University of Delaware
Pryor Hale, Piedmont Virginia Community College
Dong Hodge, Dyersburg State Community College
Mark Hoyert, Indiana University Northwest
Richard A. Hudiburg, University of North Alabama
James D. Jackson, Lehigh University
Seth Kalichman, Georgia State University
Stephen La Berge, Stanford University
Leonard S. Mark, Miami University
Michael McCall, Ithaca College
David McDonald, University of Missouri

Greg L. Miller, Stanford University School of Medicine
Karl Minke, University of Hawaii–Honolulu
Charles D. Miron, Catonsville Community College
J. L. Motrin, University of Guelph
William Pavot, Southwest State University
Gregory R. Pierce, Hamilton College
William J. Pizzi, Northeastern Illinois University
Mark Plonsky, University of Wisconsin–Stevens Point
Bret Roark, Oklahoma Baptist University
Cheryl A. Rickabaugh, University of Redlands
Rich Robbins, Washburn University
Daniel N. Robinson, Georgetown University
Mary Schild, Columbus State University
Norman R. Simonsen, University of
    Massachusetts–Amherst
Peggy Skinner, South Plains College
R. H. Starr, Jr., University of Maryland–Baltimore

Douglas Wardell, University of Alberta
Linda Weldon, Essex Community College
Paul Whitney, Washington State University
Allen Wolach, Illinois Institute of Technology
Jim Zacks, Michigan State University

The enormous task of writing a book of this scope was possible only with the expert assistance of all these friends and colleagues and that of the editorial staff of Allyn and Bacon. We gratefully acknowledge their invaluable contributions at every stage of this project, collectively and, now, individually. We thank the following people at Allyn and Bacon: Rebecca Pascal, Executive Editor; Lisa McLellan, Development Editor; Caroline Croley, Senior Marketing Manager; Joe Sweeney, Editorial Production Supervisor; Sarah Evertson, Photo Researcher; and Margaret Pinette, Project Manager.

■ To the Student

■ How to Use This Book

You are about to embark with us on an intellectual journey through the many areas of modern psychology. Before we start, we want to share with you some important information that will help guide your adventures. "The journey" is a metaphor used throughout *Psychology and Life;* your teacher serves as the tour director, the text as your tour book, and we, your authors as your personal tour guides. The goal of this journey is for you to discover what is known about the most incredible phenomena in the entire universe: the brain, the human mind, and the behavior of all living creatures. Psychology is about understanding the seemingly mysterious processes that give rise to your thoughts, feelings, and actions.

This guide offers general strategies and specific suggestions about how to use this book to get the quality grade you deserve for your performance and to get the most from your introduction to psychology.

■ Study Strategies

1. **Set aside sufficient time** for your reading assignments and review of class notes. This text contains much new technical information, many principles to learn, and a new glossary of terms to memorize. To master this material, you will need at least three hours reading time per chapter.

2. **Keep a record of your study time** for this course. Plot the number of hours (in half-hour intervals) you study at each reading session. Chart your time investment on a cumulative graph. Add each new study time to the previous total on the left-hand axis of the graph and each study session on the baseline axis. The chart will provide visual feedback of your progress and show you when you have not been hitting the books as you should.

3. **Be an active participant.** Optimal learning occurs when you are actively involved with the learning materials. That means reading attentively, listening to lectures mindfully, paraphrasing in your own words what you are reading or hearing, and taking good notes. In the text, underline key sections, write notes to yourself in the margins, and summarize points that you think might be included on class tests.

4. **Space out your studying.** Research in psychology tells us that it is more effective to do your studying regularly rather than cramming just before tests. If you let yourself fall behind, it will be difficult to catch up with all the information included in introductory psychology at last-minute panic time.

5. **Get study-centered.** Find a place with minimal distractions for studying. Reserve that place for studying, reading, and writing course assignments—and do nothing else there. The place will come to be associated with study activities, and you will find it easier to work whenever you are seated at your study center.

6. **Encode reading for future testing.** Unlike reading magazines and watching television (which you do usually for their immediate impact), reading textbooks demands that you process the material in a special way. You must continually put the information into a suitable form (encode it) that will enable you to retrieve it when you are asked about it later on class examinations. Encoding means that you summarize key points, rehearse sections (sometimes aloud), and ask questions you want to be able to answer about the contents of a given section of a chapter as you read.

   You should also take the teacher's perspective, anticipating the kinds of questions she or he is likely to ask, and then making sure you can answer them. Find out what kind of tests you will be given in this course—essay, fill-in, multiple choice, or true–false. That form will affect the extent to which you focus on the big ideas and/or on details. Essays and fill-ins ask for recall-type memory, while multiple-choice and true–false tests ask for recognition-type memory. (Ask the teacher for a sample test to give you a better idea of the kinds of questions for which you need to prepare.)

■ Study Tactics

1. Review the **outline of the chapter.** It shows you the main topics to be covered, their sequence, and their relationship, giving you an overview of what is to come. The outline at the start of each chapter contains first-level and second-level headings of the major topics. The section headings indicate the structure of the chapter, and they are also convenient break points, or time-outs, for each of your study periods.

2. Jump to the end of the chapter to read the "Recapping Main Points" section. There you will find the main ideas of the chapter organized under each of the first-level headings, which will give you a clear sense of what the chapter will be covering.

3. Skim through the chapter to get the gist of its contents. Don't stop, don't take notes, and read as quickly as you can (one hour maximum time allowed).

4. Finally, dig in and master the material by actively reading, underlining, taking notes, questioning, rehearsing, and paraphrasing as you go (two hours minimum time expected). Pay particular attention to the "Summing Up" paragraphs that appear at the end of each section. They serve as an outline of the entire chapter.

■ Special Features

1. Each chapter opens with a brief **vignette** designed to draw you into the chapter content. These openings have two purposes: to grab and focus your attention and to show you the broader relevance of the material to be covered. These openings underscore a basic theme of the chapter. Be especially alert when we refer back to them, because we'll use them to tie together the loose ends of the chapter.

2. The purpose of the **"How We Know"** feature is to help you see the direct link between the experiments researchers conduct and the conclusions they draw. This feature allows you to see the close relationship between psychological research and application.

3. The **"Psychology in Your Life"** boxes also present applications of psychological research to your everyday life. Each of these boxes presents an answer to a question that we have been asked in class by our own students and that we imagine you might ask us.

4. The **"Psychology in the 21st Century"** boxes describe topics and techniques for research that are on the cutting edge at the beginning of the new century. Each box presents applications of psychological research relevant to your experience of these swiftly changing times.

5. **Key terms** and **major contributors** are highlighted within the chapter in **boldface type** so they will stand out for you to notice. When you study for a test, be sure you can define each term and identify each major researcher. In addition, all key terms are listed alphabetically at the end of the chapter.

6. A definition for each key term is provided in a **marginal glossary.** You should use these definitions to test your understanding of these important concepts as your read the text. These key terms are also gathered together in the **glossary,** found at the end of

the text. The glossary provides formal definitions of all key terms that appear in the text, and the page numbers on which they appear. Use it to refresh your memory while studying for tests.

7. The **"Summing Up"** sections encapsulate the key points that you should know before going ahead to the next section. Review the summaries as you finish your in-depth reading of each main section. If you don't understand a summary point, plunge back into the text and reread the appropriate material until you feel confident that you understand. Similarly, use these summaries as a starting point for your studying before tests.

8. The **references,** also at the end of the text, present bibliographic information on every book, journal article, or media source cited in the text. They are a valuable resource in case you wish to find out more about some topic for a term paper in this or another course or just for your personal interest. A name and date set off by parentheses in the text—(Freud, 1923)—identifies the source and publication date of the citation. You will then find the full source information in the references section. Citations with more than two authors list the senior author followed by the notation *et al.,* which means "and others."

9. The **Name Index** and **Subject Index,** also at the end of the text, provide you with alphabetized listings of all terms, topics, and individuals that were covered in the text, along with their page citations.

10. Finally, your study and test performance is likely to be enhanced by using the ***Student Study Guide and Practice Tests*** that accompanies *Psychology and Life.* It was prepared to give students a boost in studying more efficiently and taking tests more effectively. The *Study Guide* contains helpful tips for mastering each chapter, sample practice tests and answers, and interesting experiments and demonstrations (especially valuable if your course has sections or a laboratory component).

So, there you have it—some helpful hints to increase your enjoyment of this special course and to help you get the most out of it. Our text will demand concentrated attention when you are studying to master its wealth of information. Other texts may seem to be easier because they do not give you as much depth as *Psychology and Life,* but then less in means less out.

We appreciate the opportunity your teacher has provided in selecting *Psychology and Life.* You will find it a source of valuable knowledge about a wide range of topics. Many students have reported that *Psychology and Life* has proven to be an excellent reference manual for term papers and projects in other courses as well. You might consider keeping it in your personal library of valuable resources. However, we must begin at the beginning, with the first steps in our journey.

A Final Request

Throughout this book, and through many previous editions, we have tried to make *Psychology and Life* interesting and relevant to you. We have done our best to show you the link between psychological research and your daily life—to show you that what happens in a psychologist's laboratory or clinic explains and elucidates the everyday mysteries of your mind. To do this, we have described why people react the way they do to horror movies, why some people like to eat hot peppers, and why many messages have multiple meanings. As you read, we would like you to think of relevant and interesting examples from your own life, and to send them to us (use the student feedback form on our Web site at www.ablongman.com/gerrig). We might even ask to **publish your examples in future editions of this book!**

We invite you to become part of *Psychology and Life* with us. And we can't wait to start on our journey with you.

Richard J Gerrig
rgerrig@psych1.psy.sunysb.edu

Philip G. Zimbardo
zim@psych.stanford.edu

About the Authors

Richard J. Gerrig is a professor of psychology at the State University of New York at Stony Brook. Before joining the Stony Brook faculty, Gerrig taught at Yale University, where he was awarded the Lex Hixon Prize for teaching excellence in the social sciences. Gerrig's research on cognitive psychological aspects of language use has been widely published. One line of work examines the mental processes that underlie efficient communication. A second research program considers the cognitive and emotional changes readers experience when they are transported to the worlds of stories. His book *Experiencing Narrative Worlds* was published by Yale University Press. Gerrig is a Fellow of the division of experimental psychology of the American Psychological Association.

Gerrig is the proud father of Alexandra, who at age 10 provides substantial and valuable advice about many aspects of psychology and life in the 21st century. Life on Long Island is greatly enhanced by the guidance and support of Timothy Peterson.

Philip G. Zimbardo is professor of psychology at Stanford University, where he has taught since 1968, after earlier teaching at Yale University, New York University, and Columbia University. His dedication to both undergraduate and graduate teaching, as well as his charismatic teaching style, has earned him many awards for distinguished teaching. Zimbardo has been a prolific, innovative researcher across a number of fields in social psychology, with more than 200 professional articles and chapters and 20 books to his credit. To recognize the breadth of his research achievements, the American Psychological Association presented Zimbardo with the Hilgard Award for lifetime contributions to general psychology. In addition, he has "crossed over" into the popular realm to introduce psychology to the general public through his best-selling trade books on shyness and his *Discovering Psychology* video series. Zimbardo was recently elected President of the American Psychological Association.

Zimbardo is the proud father of Adam, Zara, and Tanya. His wife, Christina Maslach, is a professor of psychology at the University of California, Berkeley, and also an award-winning distinguished teacher.

A Final Request

Throughout this book, and through many previous editions, we have tried to make *Psychology and Life* interesting and relevant to you. We have done our best to show you the link between psychological research and your daily life—to show you that what happens in a psychologist's laboratory or clinic explains and elucidates the everyday mysteries of your mind. To do this, we have described why people react the way they do to horror movies, why some people like to eat hot peppers, and why many messages have multiple meanings. As you read, we would like you to think of relevant and interesting examples from your own life, and to send them to us (use the student feedback form on our Web site at www.ablongman.com/gerrig). We might even ask to **publish your examples in future editions of this book**!

We invite you to become part of *Psychology and Life* with us. And we can't wait to start on our journey with you.

Richard J. Gerrig
rgerrig@notes.cc.sunysb.edu

Philip G. Zimbardo
zim@psych.stanford.edu

About the Authors

Richard J. Gerrig is a professor of psychology at the State University of New York at Stony Brook. Before joining the Stony Brook faculty, Gerrig taught at Yale University, where he was awarded the Lex Hixon Prize for teaching excellence in the social sciences. Gerrig's research on cognitive psychological aspects of language use has been widely published. One line of work examines the mental processes that underlie efficient communication. A second research program considers the cognitive and emotional changes readers experience when they are transported to the worlds of stories. His book *Experiencing Narrative Worlds* was published by Yale University Press. Gerrig is a Fellow of the division of experimental psychology of the American Psychological Association.

Gerrig is the proud father of Alexandra, who at age 10 provides substantial and valuable advice about many aspects of psychology and life in the 21st century. Life on Long Island is greatly enhanced by the guidance and support of Timothy Peterson.

Philip G. Zimbardo is professor of psychology at Stanford University, where he has taught since 1968, after earlier teaching at Yale University, New York University, and Columbia University. His dedication to both undergraduate and graduate teaching, as well as his charismatic teaching style, has earned him many awards for distinguished teaching. Zimbardo has been a prolific, innovative researcher across a number of fields in social psychology, with more than 200 professional articles and chapters and 20 books to his credit. To recognize the breadth of his research achievements, the American Psychological Association presented Zimbardo with the Hilgard Award for lifetime contributions to general psychology. In addition, he has "crossed over" into the popular realm to introduce psychology to the general public through his best-selling trade books on shyness and his *Discovering Psychology* video series. Zimbardo was recently elected President of the American Psychological Association.

Zimbardo is the proud father of Adam, Zara, and Tanya. His wife, Christina Maslach, is a professor of psychology at the University of California, Berkeley, and also an award-winning distinguished teacher.

psychology and life

the science of psychology in your life

1

■ **WHAT MAKES PSYCHOLOGY UNIQUE?**
Definitions • The Goals of Psychology

■ **PSYCHOLOGY IN YOUR LIFE: WHY STUDY PSYCHOLOGY?**

■ **THE EVOLUTION OF MODERN PSYCHOLOGY**
Psychology's Historical Foundations • Current Psychological Perspectives

■ **WHAT PSYCHOLOGISTS DO**

■ **PSYCHOLOGY IN THE 21ST CENTURY: THE FUTURE IS NOW**

■ **RECAPPING MAIN POINTS**
Key Terms

I N 1954, the United States Supreme Court handed down a judgment, in the case known as *Brown v. Board of Education of Topeka*, that made segregated schools for black and white children illegal. The Supreme Court's decision was influenced in no small part by the testimony of psychologists and other social scientists who presented research on the psychological harm done to black school children by segregation. Here is the testimony given by one research psychologist, **Kenneth Clark**, in a case that led up to *Brown*—Clark is reporting his research with a group of young black children (Whitman, 1993, pp. 49–51):

> *I made these tests on Thursday and Friday of this past week at your request, and I presented it to children in the Scott's Branch Elementary school, concentrating particularly on the elementary group. I used these methods which I told you about—the Negro and White dolls—which were identical in every respect save skin color. And, I presented them with a sheet of paper on which there were these drawings of dolls…*
>
> *I presented these dolls to them and I asked them the following questions in the following order: "Show me the doll that you like best or that you'd like to play with," "Show me the doll that is the 'nice' doll," "Show me the doll that looks 'bad,'"…*

> *I found that of the children between the ages of six and nine whom I tested, which were a total of sixteen in number, that ten of those children chose the white doll as their preference; the doll which they liked best. Ten of them also considered the white doll a "nice" doll. And, I think you have to keep in mind that these two dolls are absolutely identical in every respect except skin color. Eleven of these sixteen children chose the brown doll as the doll which looked "bad." This is consistent with previous results which we have obtained testing over three hundred children, and we interpret it to mean that the Negro child accepts as early as six, seven or eight the negative stereotypes about his own group….*
>
> *The conclusion which I was forced to reach was that these children in Clarendon County, like other human beings who are subjected to an obviously inferior status in the society in which they live, have been definitely harmed in the development of their personalities; that the signs of instability in their personalities are clear, and I think that every psychologist would accept and interpret these signs as such.*

Can you see why this testimony—a straightforward narration of psychological research—had a great impact on the Supreme Court and the nation's understanding of the psychological costs of segregation?

Kenneth Clark's testimony demonstrates the potential impact of psychological research on both individual lives and the life of our society. You see in this example the main purposes of *Psychology and Life:* to take you on a journey in which rigorous research reveals the intricacies of your human experience; to give you greater control over the forces that shape your life. *Psychology and Life* will lead you from the inner spaces of brain and mind to the outer dimensions of human behavior. We will investigate the processes that provide meaningful structure to your experiences, such as how you perceive the world, communicate, learn, think, and remember. We will try to understand the more dramatic expressions of human nature, such as how and why people dream, fall in love, feel shy, act aggressively, and become mentally ill. Finally, we will demonstrate how psychological knowledge can be used to understand and—in instances such as segregation—change cultural forces at work in our lives.

As authors of *Psychology and Life,* we believe in the power of psychological expertise. The appeal of psychology has grown personally for us over our careers as educators and researchers. In recent years, there has been a virtual explosion of new information about the basic mechanisms that govern mental and behavioral processes. As new ideas replace or modify old ideas, we are continually intrigued and challenged by the many fascinating pieces of the puzzle of human nature. We hope that, by the end of this journey, you too will cherish your store of psychological knowledge.

Foremost in the journey will be a scientific quest for understanding. We shall inquire about the how what, when, and why of human behavior and about the causes and consequences of behaviors you observe in yourself, in other people, and in animals. We will explain why you think, feel, and behave as you do. What makes you uniquely different from all other people? Yet why do you often behave so much like others? Are you molded by heredity, or are you shaped more by personal experiences? How can aggression and altruism, love and hate, and madness and creativity exist side by side in this complex creature—the human animal? In this opening chapter, we consider how and why all these types of questions have become relevant to psychology's goals as a discipline.

What Makes Psychology Unique?

To appreciate the uniqueness and unity of psychology, you must consider the way psychologists define the field and the goals they bring to their research and applications. By the end of the book, we will encourage you to think like a psychologist. In this first section, we'll give you a strong idea of what that might mean.

Definitions

Many psychologists seek answers to the fundamental question: What is human nature? Psychology answers this question by looking at processes that occur within individuals as well as the forces that arise within the physical and social environment. In this light, we formally define **psychology** as the scientific study of the behavior of individuals and their mental processes. Let's explore the critical parts of this definition: *scientific, behavior, individual,* and *mental.*

The scientific aspect of psychology requires psychological conclusions to be based on evidence collected according to the principles of the scientific method. The **scientific method** consists of a set of orderly steps used to analyze and solve problems. This method uses objectively collected information as the factual basis for drawing conclusions. We will elaborate on the features of the scientific method more fully in Chapter 2, when we consider how psychologists conduct their research.

Behavior is the means by which organisms adjust to their environment. Behavior is action. The subject matter of psychology is largely the observable behavior of humans and other species of animals. Smiling, crying, running, hitting, talking, and touching are some obvious

examples of behavior you can observe. Psychologists examine what the individual does and how the individual goes about doing it within a given behavioral setting and in the broader social or cultural context.

The subject of psychological analysis is most often an *individual*—a newborn infant, a teenage athlete, a college student adjusting to life in a dormitory, a man facing a midlife career change, or a woman coping with the stress of her husband's deterioration from Alzheimer's disease. However, the subject might also be a chimpanzee learning to use symbols to communicate, a white rat navigating a maze, or a sea slug responding to a danger signal. An individual might be studied in its natural habitat or in the controlled conditions of a research laboratory.

Many researchers in psychology also recognize that they cannot understand human actions without also understanding *mental processes,* the workings of the human mind. Much human activity takes place as private, internal events—thinking, planning, reasoning, creating, and dreaming. Many psychologists believe that mental processes represent the most important aspect of psychological inquiry. As you shall soon see, psychological investigators have devised ingenious techniques to study mental events and processes—to make these private experiences public.

The combination of these concerns defines psychology as a unique field. Whereas psychologists focus largely on behavior in individuals, sociologists study the behavior of people in groups or institutions, and anthropologists focus on the broader context of behavior in different cultures. Even so, psychologists draw broadly from the insights of other scholars. As one of the *social sciences,* psychology draws from economics, political science, sociology, and cultural anthropology. Psychologists share many interests with researchers in *biological sciences,* especially with those who study brain processes and the biochemical bases of behavior. As part of the emerging area of *cognitive science,* psychologists' questions about how the human mind works are related to research and theory in computer science, artificial intelligence, and applied mathematics. As a *health science*—with links to medicine, education, law, and environmental studies—psychology seeks to improve the quality of each individual's and the collective's well-being. Psychology also retains ties to philosophy and areas in the humanities and the arts, such as literature, drama, and religion.

Although the remarkable breadth and depth of modern psychology are a source of delight to those who become psychologists, these same attributes make the field a challenge to the student exploring it for the first time.

Psychology The scientific study of the behavior of individuals and their mental processes.

Scientific method The set of procedures used for gathering and interpreting objective information in a way that minimizes error and yields dependable generalizations.

Behavior The actions by which an organism adjusts to its environment.

Most psychological study focuses on individuals—usually human ones, but sometimes those of other species. What aspects of your own life would you like psychologists to study?

There is so much more to the study of psychology than one expects initially—and, because of that, there will also be much of value that you can take away from this introduction to psychology. The best way to learn about the field is to learn to share psychologists' goals. Let's consider those goals.

The Goals of Psychology

The goals of the psychologist conducting basic research are to describe, explain, predict, and control behavior. The applied psychologist has a fifth goal—to improve the quality of human life. These goals form the basis of the psychological enterprise. What is involved in trying to achieve each of them?

DESCRIBING WHAT HAPPENS

The first task in psychology is to make accurate observations about behavior. Psychologists typically refer to such observations as their *data* (*data* is the plural, *datum* the singular). **Behavioral data** are reports of observations about the behavior of organisms and the conditions under which the behavior occurs. When researchers undertake data collection, they must choose an appropriate

level of analysis and devise measures of behavior that ensure *objectivity*.

In order to investigate an individual's behavior, researchers may use different *levels of analysis*—from the broadest, most global level down to the most minute, specific level. Suppose, for example, you were trying to describe a painting you saw at a museum (see **Figure 1.1**). At a global level, you might describe it by title, *Bathers*, and by artist, "Georges Seurat." At a more specific level, you might recount features of the painting: Some people are sunning on a riverbank, while others are enjoying the water, and so on. At a very specific level, you might describe the technique Seurat used—tiny points of paint—to create the scene. The description at each level would answer different questions about the painting.

Different levels of psychological description also address different questions. At the broadest level of psychological analysis, researchers investigate the behavior of the whole person within complex social and cultural contexts. At this level, researchers might study cross-cultural differences in violence, the origins of prejudice,

Behavioral data Observational reports about the behavior of organisms and the conditions under which the behavior occurs or changes.

FIGURE 1.1

Levels of Analysis

Suppose you wanted a friend to meet you in front of this painting. How would you describe it? Suppose your friend wanted to make an exact copy of the painting. How would you describe it?

and the consequences of mental illness. At the next level, psychologists focus on narrower, finer units of behavior, such as speed of reaction to a stop light, eye movements during reading, and grammatical errors made by children acquiring language. Researchers can study even smaller units of behavior. They might work to discover the biological bases of behavior by identifying the places in the brain where different types of memories are stored, the biochemical changes that occur during learning, and the sensory paths responsible for vision or hearing. Each level of analysis yields information essential to the final composite portrait of human nature that psychologists hope ultimately to develop.

However tight or broad the focus of the observation, psychologists strive to describe behavior *objectively*. Collecting the facts as they exist, and not as the researcher expects or hopes them to be, is of utmost importance. Because every observer brings to each observation his or her *subjective* point of view—biases, prejudices, and expectations—it is essential to prevent these personal factors from creeping in and distorting the data. As you will see in the next chapter, psychological researchers have developed a variety of techniques to maintain objectivity.

EXPLAINING WHAT HAPPENS

While *descriptions* must stick to perceivable information, *explanations* deliberately go beyond what can be observed. In many areas of psychology, the central goal is to find regular patterns in behavioral and mental processes. Psychologists want to discover *how* behavior works. Why do you laugh at situations that differ from your expectations of what is coming next? What conditions could lead someone to attempt suicide or commit rape?

Explanations in psychology usually recognize that most behavior is influenced by a combination of factors. Some factors operate within the individual, such as genetic makeup, motivation, intelligence level, or self-esteem. These inner determinants of behavior are called **organismic variables.** They tell something special about

the organism. In the case of humans, these determinants are known as **dispositional variables.** Some factors, however, operate externally. Suppose, for example, that a child tries to please a teacher in order to win a prize or that a motorist trapped in a traffic jam becomes frustrated and hostile. These behaviors are largely influenced by events outside the person. External influences on behavior are known as **environmental** or **situational variables.** When psychologists seek to explain behavior, they almost always consider both types of explanation. Suppose, for example, psychologists want to explain why some people start smoking. Researchers might examine the possibility that some individuals are particularly prone to risk taking (a dispositional explanation) or that some individuals experience a lot of peer pressure (a situational explanation)—or that both a disposition toward risk taking and situational peer pressure are necessary (a combined explanation).

Often a psychologist's goal is to explain a wide variety of behavior in terms of one underlying cause. Consider a situation in which your teacher says that to earn a good grade, each student must participate regularly in class discussions. Your roommate, who is always well prepared for class, never raises his hand to answer questions or volunteer information. The teacher chides him for being unmotivated and assumes he is not bright. That same roommate also goes to parties but never asks anyone to dance, doesn't openly defend his point of view when it is challenged by someone less informed, and rarely engages in small talk at the dinner table. What is your diagnosis? What underlying cause might account for this range of

Organismic variables The inner determinants of an organism's behavior.
Dispositional variables The organismic variables, or inner determinants of behavior, that occur within human and nonhuman animals.
Environmental variables External influences on behavior.
Situational variables External influences on behavior.

behavior? How about *shyness?* Like many other people who suffer from intense feelings of shyness, your roommate is unable to behave in desired ways (Cheek, 1989; Zimbardo, 1990). We can use the concept of shyness to explain the full pattern of your roommate's behavior.

To forge such causal explanations, researchers must often engage in a creative process of examining a diverse collection of data. Master detective Sherlock Holmes drew shrewd conclusions from scraps of evidence. In a similar fashion, every researcher must use an informed imagination, which creatively *synthesizes* what is known and what is not yet known. A well-trained psychologist can explain observations by using her or his insight into the human experience along with the facts previous researchers have uncovered about the phenomenon in question. Much psychological research attempts to determine which of several explanations most accurately accounts for a given behavioral pattern.

A psychological prediction

PREDICTING WHAT WILL HAPPEN

Predictions in psychology are statements about the likelihood that a certain behavior will occur or that a given relationship will be found. Often an accurate explanation of the causes underlying some form of behavior will allow a researcher to make accurate predictions about future behavior. Thus, if we believe your roommate to be shy, we could confidently predict that he would be uncomfortable when asked to have a conversation with a stranger. When different explanations are put forward to account for some behavior or relationship, they are usually judged by how well they can make accurate and comprehensive predictions. If your roommate were to blossom in contact with a stranger, we would be forced to rethink our diagnosis.

Just as observations must be made objectively, scientific predictions must be worded precisely enough to enable them to be tested, and rejected if the evidence is not supportive. A *scientific prediction* is based on an understanding of the ways events relate to one another, and it suggests what mechanisms link those events to certain predictors. A *causal prediction* specifies the conditions under which behaviors will change. For example, the presence of a stranger reliably causes human and monkey babies, beyond a certain age, to respond with signs of anxiety. Changes in the observed behavior, however, may depend on variations in the exact situation—such as the extent of strangeness. Would there be fewer signs of anxiety in a human or a monkey baby if the stranger were also a baby rather than an adult, or if the stranger were of the same species rather than of a different one? To improve a causal prediction, a researcher would create systematic variations in environmental conditions and observe their influence on the baby's response.

CONTROLLING WHAT HAPPENS

For many psychologists, control is the central, most powerful goal. Control means making behavior happen or not happen—starting it, maintaining it, stopping it, and influencing its form, strength, or rate of occurrence. A causal explanation of behavior is convincing if it can create conditions under which the behavior can be controlled.

The ability to control behavior is important because it gives psychologists ways of helping people improve the quality of their lives. Throughout *Psychology and Life*, you will see examples of the types of *interventions* psychologists have devised to help people take control over problematic aspects of their lives. Chapter 16, for example, discusses treatments for mental illness. We also describe how people can harness psychological forces to eliminate unhealthy behaviors like smoking and initiate healthy behaviors like regular exercise (see Chapter 13). You will learn what types of parenting practices can help parents maintain solid bonds with their children (Chapter 11); you will learn what forces make strangers reluctant to offer assistance in emergency situations and how those forces can be overcome (Chapter 18). These are just a few examples of the broad range of circumstances in which psychologists use their knowledge to control and improve people's lives. In this respect, psychologists are a rather optimistic group; many believe that virtually any undesired behavior pattern can be modified by the proper intervention. *Psychology and Life* shares that optimism.

It is interesting to note that understanding—rather than control—tends to be the ultimate goal of psychologists in many Asian and African countries (Nobles, 1980; Triandis, 1990). Critics have argued that the focus on control in Western psychology represents a cultural bias that emerged from industrialization and colonialism by Europeans and from the mentality of conquest of the frontier in the United States. The control focus of Western psychology has also been depicted as a more typically male perspective that might not have dominated if women had been more prominent in the development of psychology (Bornstein & Quina, 1988; Riger, 1992).

What causes people to smoke? Can psychologists create conditions under which people will be less likely to engage in this behavior?

SUMMING UP

In this introductory chapter, we are going to take a moment to introduce some special features of *Psychology and Life*—features we have designed to allow you to learn more effectively from the text. A *Summing Up* section will follow the major portions of each chapter. You can use these summaries to help assess your understanding of the key points of the preceding material. Each chapter also ends with a section called *Recapping Main Points.* You should use these summaries to test your comprehension of the text. If you don't understand a summary point, plunge back into the text and reread the appropriate material until you feel confident that you understand. You can use the interim summaries and recapping sections as a starting point for your studying before tests. Here's the first *Summing Up.*

SUMMING UP

Psychologists use the scientific method to draw conclusions about the behavior and mental processes of individuals. Psychologists have several goals: to describe behavior objectively

---

PSYCHOLOGY IN YOUR LIFE

WHY STUDY PSYCHOLOGY?

As you read this opening chapter, the question we pose as the title of this box may have come to mind once or twice: Why study psychology? Our answer to that question is quite straightforward: We believe that psychological research has immediate and crucial applications to important issues of everyday experience. One of the foremost goals of *Psychology and Life* is to highlight the personal relevance and social significance of psychological expertise.

Every semester when we begin to teach, we are faced with students who enter an introductory psychology class with some very specific questions in mind. Sometimes those

questions emerge from their own experience ("What should I do if I think my mother is mentally ill?" "Will this course teach me how to improve my grades?"); sometimes those questions emerge from the type of psychological information that is communicated through the popular press ("Is it true that oldest children are the most conservative?" "Are women really always better parents than men?"). The challenge for us of teaching the course is to bring the products of scientific research to bear on questions that matter to our students.

Almost every section of *Psychology and Life* addresses concerns that our students have brought directly to us. In

this edition, we have also included a special feature, boxes we call ***Psychology in Your Life*** (like this one!). Each of these boxes answers a question we have heard repeatedly both from our own students and from students who used earlier editions of this text. We hope as you read each ***Psychology in Your Life*** box that the questions your peers have posed will strike you as important and relevant to your own life. Please read these boxes carefully. Our aim has been to bring scientific evidence to bear on some of the issues that matter most to students like you. We hope that you will agree that the study of psychology will enrich your life experiences.

and at an appropriate level, to explain the forces that give rise to behaviors, to predict when behaviors will occur, and to control behavior so as to improve the quality of life.

The Evolution of Modern Psychology

In the 21st century, it is relatively easy for us to define psychology and to state the goals of psychological research. As you begin to study psychology, however, it is important to understand the many forces that led to the emergence of modern psychology. At the core of this historical review is one simple principle: *Ideas matter.* Much of the history of psychology has been characterized by heated debates about what constitutes the appropriate subject matter and methodologies for a science of mind and behavior.

Our historical review will be carried out at two levels of analysis. In the first section, we will consider the period of history in which some of the critical groundwork for modern psychology was laid down. This tight focus will enable you to witness at close range the battle of ideas. In the second section, we describe in a broader fashion seven perspectives that have emerged in the modern day. For both levels of focus, you should allow yourself to imagine the intellectual passion with which the theories evolved.

Psychology's Historical Foundations

"Psychology has a long past, but only a short history," wrote one of the first experimental psychologists, **Hermann Ebbinghaus** (1908). Scholars had long asked im-

In 1879, Wilhelm Wundt founded the first formal laboratory devoted to experimental psychology. Suppose you decided to found your own psychology laboratory. What types of issues would you study?

portant questions about human nature—about how people perceive reality, the nature of consciousness, and the origins of madness—but they did not possess the means to answer them. Consider the fundamental questions posed in the fourth and fifth centuries B.C. by the classical Greek philosophers Socrates, Plato, and Aristotle. Although forms of psychology existed in ancient Indian Yogic traditions, Western psychology traces its origin to these great thinkers' dialogues about how the mind works, the nature of free will, and the relationship of individual citizens to their community or state. Toward the end of the 19th century, psychology began to emerge as a discipline when researchers applied the laboratory techniques from other sciences—such as physiology and physics—to the study of these fundamental questions from philosophy.

A critical figure in the evolution of modern psychology was **Wilhelm Wundt,** who, in 1879 in Leipzig, Germany, founded the first formal laboratory devoted to experimental psychology. Although Wundt had been trained as a physiologist, over his research career his interest shifted from questions of body to questions of mind: He wished to understand basic processes of sensation and perception as well as the speed of simple mental processes. By the time he established his psychology laboratory, Wundt had already accomplished a range of research and published the first of several editions of *Principles of Physiological Psychology* (Kendler, 1987). Once Wundt's laboratory was established at Leipzig, he began to train the first graduate students specifically devoted to the emerging field of psychology. Those students often became founders of their own psychology laboratories around the world.

As psychology became established as a separate discipline, psychological laboratories began to appear in universities throughout North America, the first at Johns Hopkins University in 1883. These early laboratories often bore Wundt's impact. For example, after studying with Wundt, **Edward Titchener** became one of the first psychologists in the United States, founding a laboratory at Cornell University in 1892. However, at around the same time, a young Harvard philosophy professor who had studied medicine and had strong interests in literature and religion developed a uniquely American perspective. **William James,** brother of the great novelist Henry James, wrote a two-volume work, *The Principles of Psychology* (1890/1950), which many experts consider to be the most important psychology text ever written. Shortly after, in 1892, G. Stanley Hall founded the American Psychological Association. By 1900 there were more than 40 psychological laboratories in North America (Hilgard, 1986).

Almost as soon as psychology emerged, a debate arose as to the proper subject matter and methods for the new discipline. This debate isolated some of the issues that still loom large in psychology. We will describe, specifically, the tension between structuralism and functionalism.

STRUCTURALISM: THE CONTENTS OF THE MIND

Psychology's potential to make a unique contribution to knowledge became apparent when psychology became a laboratory science organized around experiments. In Wundt's laboratory, experimental participants made simple responses (saying yes or no, pressing a button) to stimuli they perceived under conditions varied by laboratory instruments. Because the data were collected through systematic, objective procedures, independent observers could replicate the results of these experiments. Emphasis on the scientific method, concern for precise measurement, and statistical analysis of data characterized Wundt's psychological tradition.

When Titchener brought Wundt's psychology to the United States, he advocated that such scientific methods be used to study consciousness. His method for examining the elements of conscious mental life was *introspection,* the systematic examination by individuals of their own thoughts and feelings about specific sensory experiences. Titchener emphasized the "what" of mental contents rather than the "why" or "how" of thinking. His approach came to be known as **structuralism,** the study of the structure of mind and behavior.

Structuralism was based on the presumption that all human mental experience could be understood as the combination of basic components. The goal of this approach was to reveal the underlying structure of the human mind by analyzing the constituent elements of sensation and other experience that form an individual's mental life. Many psychologists attacked structuralism on three fronts: (1) It was *reductionistic,* because it reduced all complex human experience to simple sensations; (2) it was *elemental,* because it sought to combine parts, or elements, into a whole rather than study complex, or whole, behaviors directly; and (3) it was *mentalistic,* because it studied only verbal reports of human conscious awareness, ignoring the study of individuals who could not describe their introspections, including animals, children, and the mentally disturbed.

One important alternative to structuralism, pioneered by the German psychologist **Max Wertheimer,** focused on the way in which the mind understands many experiences as *gestalts*—organized wholes—rather than as the sums of simple parts: Your experience of a painting, for example, is more than the sum of the individual daubs of paint. As we shall see in Chapter 5, *Gestalt psychology* continues to have an impact on the study of perception.

A second major opposition to structuralism, which we shall discuss here, came under the banner of *functionalism.*

FUNCTIONALISM: MINDS WITH A PURPOSE

William James agreed with Titchener that consciousness was central to the study of psychology; but for James, the study of consciousness was not reduced to elements, contents, and structures. Instead, consciousness was an ongoing stream, a property of mind in continual interaction with the environment. Human consciousness facilitated one's adjustment to the environment; thus, the acts and *functions* of mental processes were of significance, not the contents of the mind.

Functionalism gave primary importance to learned habits that enable organisms to adapt to their environment and to function effectively. For functionalists, the key question to be answered by research was "What is the function or purpose of any behavioral act?" The founder of the school of functionalism was the American philosopher **John Dewey.** His concern for the practical uses of mental processes led to important advances in education. Dewey's theorizing provided the impetus for *progressive education* in his own laboratory school and more generally in the United States: "Rote learning was abandoned in favor of learning by doing, in expectation that intellectual curiosity would be encouraged and understanding would be enhanced" (Kendler, 1987, p. 124).

Although James believed in careful observation, he put little value on the rigorous laboratory methods of Wundt. In James's psychology, there was a place for emotions, self, will, values, and even religious and mystical experience. His "warm-blooded" psychology recognized a uniqueness in each individual that could not be reduced to formulas or numbers from test results. For James, explanation rather than experimental control was the goal of psychology (Arkin, 1990).

THE LEGACY OF THESE APPROACHES

Despite their differences, the insights of the practitioners of both structuralism and functionalism created an intellectual context in which contemporary psychology could flourish. Psychologists currently examine *both* the structure and the function of behavior. Consider the process of speech production. Suppose you want to invite a friend to the movies. To do so, the words you speak must serve the right function—*Star Wars, with me, tonight*—but also have the right structure: It wouldn't do to say, "Would go *Star Wars* me to with tonight you to like?" To understand how speech production works, researchers study the way that speakers fit meanings (functions) to the grammatical structures of their languages (Bock, 1990). (We will describe some of the processes of language production in Chapter 9.) Throughout *Psychology and Life,* we will emphasize both structure and function, as we review both classic and contemporary research. Psychologists continue to employ a great variety

Structuralism The study of the structure of mind and behavior; the view that all human mental experience can be understood as a combination of simple elements or events.

Functionalism The perspective on mind and behavior that focuses on the examination of their functions in an organism's interactions with the environment.

of methodologies to study the general forces that apply to all humans as well as unique aspects of each individual.

Current Psychological Perspectives

This section outlines the perspectives, or conceptual approaches, that dominate contemporary psychology. Each perspective—biological, psychodynamic, behaviorist, humanistic, cognitive, evolutionary, and cultural—defines points of view and sets of assumptions that influence both what psychologists will study and how: Do people have free will, or do they simply act out a script imposed by their heredity (biological determinism) or their environment (environmental determinism)? Are organisms basically active and creative or reactive and mechanical? Can psychological and social phenomena be explained in terms of physiological processes? Is complex behavior simply the sum of many smaller components, or does it have new and different qualities? A psychologist's perspective determines what to look for, where to look, and what methods to employ. As you read each of the sections that follow, note how each perspective defines the causes and consequences of behavior.

A note of caution: Although each perspective represents a different approach to the central issues of psychology, you should come to appreciate why most psychologists borrow and blend concepts from more than one of these perspectives. Each perspective enhances the understanding of the entirety of human experience. In the chapters that follow, we will elaborate in some detail on the contributions of each approach, because, taken together, they represent what contemporary psychology is all about.

BIOLOGICAL PERSPECTIVE

The **biological perspective** guides psychologists who search for the causes of behavior in the functioning of genes, the brain, the nervous system, and the endocrine system. An organism's functioning is explained in terms of underlying physical structures and biochemical processes. Experience and behaviors are largely understood as the result of chemical and electrical activities taking place within and between nerve cells.

Researchers who take the biological perspective generally assume that psychological and social phenomena can be ultimately understood in terms of biochemical processes: Even the most complex phenomena can be understood by analysis, or reduction, into ever smaller, more specific units. They might, for example,

Biological perspective The approach to identifying causes of behavior that focuses on the functioning of the genes, the brain, the nervous system, and the endocrine system.

Psychodynamic perspective A psychological model in which behavior is explained in terms of past experiences and motivational forces; actions are viewed as stemming from inherited instincts, biological drives, and attempts to resolve conflicts between personal needs and social requirements.

try to explain how you are reading the words of this sentence with respect to the exact physical processes in cells in your brain. In this perspective, behavior is determined by physical structures and hereditary processes. Experience can modify behavior by altering these underlying biological structures and processes. Researchers might ask, "What changes in your brain occurred while you learned to read?" The task of psychobiological researchers is to understand behavior at the most precise level of analysis.

While many such researchers work in university and medical school laboratories, others work in clinical settings. The former might study whether memory in elderly rats can be improved by grafting tissue from the brains of rat fetuses. The latter might study patients suffering a memory loss following an accident or disease. The unifying concern of these researchers is the aspects of behavior that originate from biological forces.

PSYCHODYNAMIC PERSPECTIVE

According to the **psychodynamic perspective,** behavior is driven, or motivated, by powerful inner forces. In this view, human actions stem from inherited instincts, biological drives, and attempts to resolve conflicts between personal needs and society's demands. Deprivation states, physiological arousal, and conflicts provide the power for behavior just as coal fuels a steam locomotive. In this model, the organism stops reacting when its needs are satisfied and its drives reduced. The main purpose of action is to reduce tension.

Psychodynamic principles of motivation were most fully developed by the Viennese physician **Sigmund Freud** in the late 19th and early 20th centuries. Freud's ideas grew out of his work with mentally disturbed patients, but he believed that the principles he observed applied to both normal and abnormal behavior. Freud's psychodynamic theory views a person as pulled and pushed by a complex network of inner and outer forces. Freud's model was the first to recognize that human nature is not always rational, that actions may be driven by motives that are not in conscious awareness. Many psychologists since Freud have taken the psychodynamic model in new directions. Freud himself emphasized early childhood as the stage in which personality is formed. Neo-Freudian theorists have broadened Freud's theory to include social influences and interactions that occur over the individual's entire lifetime.

Freud's ideas have had a great influence on many areas of psychology. You will encounter different aspects of his contributions as you read about child development, dreaming, forgetting, unconscious motivation, personality, and psychoanalytic therapy. But you may be surprised to discover that his ideas were never the result of systematic scientific research. Instead, they were the product of an exceptionally creative mind obsessed with unraveling the deeper mysteries of human thoughts, feelings, and actions.

Sigmund Freud, photographed with his daughter, Anna, on a trip to the Italian Alps in 1913. Freud suggested that behavior is often driven by motives outside of conscious awareness. What implications does that perspective have for the ways in which you make life choices?

BEHAVIORIST PERSPECTIVE

Those who take the **behaviorist perspective** seek to understand how particular environmental stimuli control particular kinds of behavior. First, behaviorists analyze the *antecedent* environmental conditions—those that precede the behavior and set the stage for an organism to make a response or withhold a response. Next, they look at the *behavioral response,* which is the main object of study—the action to be understood, predicted, and controlled. Finally, they examine the observable *consequences* that follow from the response. A behaviorist, for example, might be interested in the way in which speeding tickets of varying sizes (consequences) change the likelihood that motorists will drive with caution or abandon (behavioral responses).

Behaviorists typically collect their data from controlled laboratory experiments; they may use electronic apparatuses and computers to introduce stimuli and record responses. They insist on precise definitions of the phenomena studied and on rigorous standards of evidence, usually in quantifiable form. Often, they have studied nonhuman animals (mostly pigeons and rats) because researchers can control the conditions much more completely than with human participants. Behaviorists assume that the basic processes they investigate with nonhuman animals represent general principles that hold true for different species.

Behaviorism has yielded a critical practical legacy. Its emphasis on the need for rigorous experimentation and carefully defined variables has influenced most areas of psychology. Although behaviorists have conducted much basic research with nonhuman animals, the principles of behaviorism have been widely applied to human problems. Behaviorist principles have yielded a more humane approach to educating children (through the use of positive reinforcement rather than punishment), new therapies for modifying behavior disorders, and guidelines for creating model utopian communities.

HUMANISTIC PERSPECTIVE

Humanistic psychology emerged in the 1950s as an alternative to the psychodynamic and the behaviorist models. In the humanistic view, people are neither driven by the powerful, instinctive forces postulated by the Freudians nor manipulated by their environments, as proposed by the behaviorists. Instead, people are active creatures who are innately good and capable of choice. According to the **humanistic perspective,** the main task for humans is to strive for growth and development of their potential.

Humanistic psychologists study behavior, but not by reducing it to components, elements, and variables in laboratory experiments. Instead, they look for patterns in life histories of people. In sharp contrast to the behaviorists, humanistic psychologists focus on the subjective world experienced by the individual, rather than on the objective world seen by external observers and researchers. To that extent, they are also considered to be *phenomenologists,* those who study the individual actor's personal view of events. Humanistic psychologists also try to deal with the whole person, practicing a holistic approach to human psychology. They believe that true understanding requires integrating knowledge of the individual's mind, body, and behavior with an awareness of social and cultural forces.

The humanistic approach expands the realm of psychology to include valuable lessons from the study of literature, history, and the arts. In this manner, psychology becomes a more complete discipline. Humanists suggest that their view is the yeast that helps psychology rise above its focus on negative forces and on the animal-like aspects of humanity. As we shall see in Chapter 16, the humanistic perspective had a major impact on the development of new approaches to psychotherapy.

COGNITIVE PERSPECTIVE

The cognitive revolution in psychology emerged as another challenge to the limits of behaviorism. The centerpiece of

Behaviorist perspective The psychological perspective primarily concerned with observable behavior that can be objectively recorded and with the relationships of observable behavior to environmental stimuli.

Behaviorism A scientific approach that limits the study of psychology to measurable or observable behavior.

Humanistic perspective A psychological model that emphasizes an individual's phenomenal world and inherent capacity for making rational choices and developing to maximum potential.

the **cognitive perspective** is human thought and all the processes of knowing—attending, thinking, remembering, and understanding. From the cognitive perspective, people act because they think, and people think because they are human beings, exquisitely equipped to do so.

In the cognitive model, behavior is only partly determined by preceding environmental events and past behavioral consequences, as behaviorists believe. Some of the most significant behavior emerges from totally novel ways of thinking, not from predictable ways used in the past. The ability to imagine options and alternatives that are totally different from what is or was enables people to work toward futures that transcend current circumstances. An individual responds to reality not as it is in the objective world of matter, but as it is in the *subjective reality* of the individual's inner world of thoughts and imagination. Cognitive psychologists view thoughts as both results and causes of overt actions. Feeling regret when you've hurt someone is an example of thought as a result. But apologizing for your actions after feeling regret is an example of thought as a cause of behavior.

Cognitive psychologists study higher mental processes such as perception, memory, language use, problem solving, and decision making at a variety of levels. They may examine patterns of blood flow in the brain during different types of cognitive tasks, a student's recollection of an early childhood event, or changes in memory abilities across the lifespan. Because of its focus on mental processes, many researchers see the cognitive perspective as the dominant one in psychology today.

EVOLUTIONARY PERSPECTIVE

The **evolutionary perspective** seeks to connect contemporary psychology to a central idea of the life sciences, Charles Darwin's theory of evolution by natural selection. The idea of natural selection is quite simple: Those organisms that are better suited to their environments tend to produce offspring (and pass on their genes) more successfully than those organisms with poorer adaptations. Over many generations, the species changes in the direction of the privileged adaptation. The evolutionary perspective in psychology suggests that *mental abilities* evolved over millions of years to serve particular adaptive purposes, just as physical abilities did.

To practice evolutionary psychology, researchers focus on the environmental conditions in which the human brain evolved. Humans spent 99 percent of their evolutionary history as hunter–gatherers living in small groups during the Pleistocene era (the roughly 2-million-year period ending 10,000 years ago). Evolutionary psychology uses the rich theoretical framework of evolutionary biology to identify the central adaptive problems that faced this species: avoiding predators and parasites, gathering and exchanging food, finding and retaining mates, and raising healthy children. After identifying the adaptive problems that these early humans faced, evolutionary psychologists generate inferences about the sorts of men-

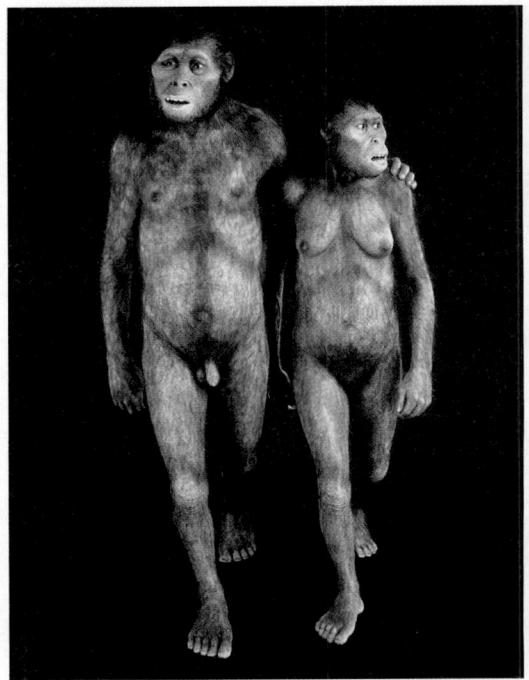

What mental abilities were needed by the *Australopithecus afarensis* of 4 million years ago, and how might these abilities have evolved to the present day?

tal mechanisms, or psychological adaptations, that might have evolved to solve those problems.

Evolutionary psychology differs from other perspectives most fundamentally in its temporal focus on the extremely long process of evolution as a central explanatory principle. Evolutionary psychologists, for example, attempt to understand the different sex roles assumed by men and women as products of evolution, rather than as products of contemporary societal pressures. Because evolutionary psychologists cannot carry out experiments that vary the course of evolution, they must be particularly inventive to provide evidence in favor of their theories.

CULTURAL PERSPECTIVE

Psychologists who take a **cultural perspective** study *cross-cultural* differences in the causes and consequences of behavior. The cultural perspective is an important response to the criticism that psychological research has too often been based on a Western conception of human nature

---

Cognitive perspective The perspective on psychology that stresses human thought and the processes of knowing, such as attending, thinking, remembering, expecting, solving problems, fantasizing, and consciousness.

Evolutionary perspective The approach to psychology that stresses the importance of behavioral and mental adaptiveness, based on the assumption that mental capabilities evolved over millions of years to serve particular adaptive purposes.

Cultural perspective The psychological perspective that focuses on cross-cultural differences in the causes and consequences of behavior.

and had as its subject population only white, middle-class Americans (Gergen et al., 1996). A proper consideration of cultural forces may involve comparisons of groups within the same national boundaries. For example, researchers may compare the prevalence of eating disorders for white American versus African American teenagers within the United States (see Chapter 12). Cultural forces may also be assessed across nationalities, as in comparisons of moral judgments in the United States and India (see Chapter 11). Cross-cultural psychologists want to determine whether the theories researchers have developed apply to all humans, or only to more narrow, specific populations.

A cross-cultural perspective can be brought to bear on almost every topic of psychological research: Are people's perceptions of the world affected by culture? Do the languages people speak affect the way they experience the world? How does culture affect the way children develop toward adulthood? How do cultural attitudes shape the experience of old age? How does culture affect our sense of self? Does culture influence an individual's likelihood to engage in particular behaviors? Does culture affect the way individuals express emotions? Does culture affect the rates at which people suffer from psychological disorders?

By asking these types of questions, the cultural perspective often yields conclusions that directly challenge those generated from the other perspectives. Researchers have claimed, for example, that many aspects of Freud's psychodynamic theories cannot apply to cultures that are very different from Freud's Vienna. This concern was raised as early as 1927 by the anthropologist Bronislaw Malinowski (1927), who soundly critiqued Freud's father-centered theory by describing the family practices of the Trobriand Islanders of New Guinea, for whom family authority resided with mothers rather than with fathers. The cultural perspective, therefore, suggests that some universal claims of the psychodynamic perspective are incorrect. The cultural perspective poses a continual, important challenge to generalizations about human experience that ignore the diversity and richness of culture.

COMPARING PERSPECTIVES: FOCUS ON AGGRESSION

Each of the seven perspectives rests on a different set of assumptions and leads to a different way of looking for answers to questions about behavior. **Table 1.1** summarizes the perspectives. As an example, let's briefly compare how psychologists using these models might deal with the question of why people act aggressively. All of the approaches have been used in the effort to understand the nature of aggression and violence. For each perspective, we give examples of the types of claims researchers might make and experiments they might undertake.

- *Biological.* Study the role of specific brain systems in aggression by stimulating different regions and then recording any destructive actions that are elicited. Also analyze the brains of mass murderers for abnormalities; examine female aggression as related to phases of the menstrual cycle.

TABLE 1.1

Comparison of Seven Perspectives in Contemporary Psychology

Perspective	View of Human Nature	Determinants of Behavior	Focus of Study	Primary Research Topics
Biological	Passive Mechanistic	Heredity Biochemical processes	Brain and nervous system processes	Biochemical basis of behavior and mental processes
Psychodynamic	Instinct-driven	Heredity Early experiences	Unconscious drives Conflicts	Behavior as overt expression of unconscious motives
Behaviorist	Reactive to stimulation Modifiable	Environment Stimulus conditions	Specific overt responses	Behavior and its stimulus causes and consequences
Humanistic	Active Unlimited in potential	Potentially self-directed	Human experience and potentials	Life patterns Values Goals
Cognitive	Creatively active Stimulus reactive	Stimulus conditions Mental processes	Mental processes Language	Inferred mental processes through behavioral indicators
Evolutionary	Adapted to solving problems of the Pleistocene era	Adaptations for survival	Evolved psychological adaptations	Mental mechanisms in terms of evolved adaptive functions
Cultural	Modifiable by culture	Cultural norms	Cross-cultural patterns of attitudes and behaviors	Universal and culture-specific aspects of human experience

- *Psychodynamic.* Analyze aggression as a reaction to frustrations caused by barriers to pleasure, such as unjust authority. View aggression as an adult's displacement of hostility originally felt as a child against his or her parents.

- *Behaviorist.* Identify reinforcements of past aggressive responses, such as extra attention given to a child who hits classmates or siblings. Assert that children learn from physically abusive parents to be abusive with their own children.

- *Humanistic.* Look for personal values and social conditions that foster self-limiting, aggressive perspectives instead of growth-enhancing, shared experiences.

- *Cognitive.* Explore the hostile thoughts and fantasies people experience while witnessing violent acts, noting both aggressive imagery and intentions to harm others. Study the impact of violence in films and videos, including pornographic violence, on attitudes toward gun control, rape, and war.

- *Evolutionary.* Consider what conditions would have made aggression an adaptive behavior for early humans. Identify psychological mechanisms capable of selectively generating aggressive behavior under those conditions.

- *Cultural.* Consider how members of different cultures display and interpret aggression. Identify how cultural forces affect the likelihood of different types of aggressive behavior.

It is not only professional psychologists who have theories about why people do what they do. You probably have some convictions about whether behavior is influenced more by heredity or by environment, whether people are basically good or evil, and whether or not humans have free will. As you read about the findings based on these perspectives, keep checking psychologists' conclusions against your own views. Examine where your personal convictions come from and think about some ways you might want to broaden or modify them.

■ What Psychologists Do

You now know enough about psychology to formulate questions that span the full range of psychological inquiry. If you prepared such a list of questions, you would be likely to touch on the areas of expertise of the great variety of individuals who call themselves psychologists. In **Table 1.2**, we provide our

TABLE 1.2

The Diversity of Psychological Inquiry

The Question	Who Addresses It?
How can people cope better with day-to-day problems?	Clinical psychologists Counseling psychologists Community psychologists Psychiatrists
How do memories get stored in the brain?	Biological psychologists Psychopharmacologists
How can you teach a dog to follow commands?	Experimental psychologists Behavior analysts
Why can't I always recall information I'm *sure* I know?	Cognitive psychologists Cognitive scientists
What makes people different from one another?	Personality psychologists Behavioral geneticists
How does "peer pressure" work?	Social psychologists
What do babies know about the world?	Developmental psychologists
Why does my job make me feel so depressed?	Industrial psychologists Human factors psychologists
How should teachers deal with disruptive students?	Educational psychologists School psychologists
Why do I get sick before every exam?	Health psychologists
Was the defendant insane when she committed the crime?	Forensic psychologists
Why do I always choke during important basketball games?	Sports psychologists

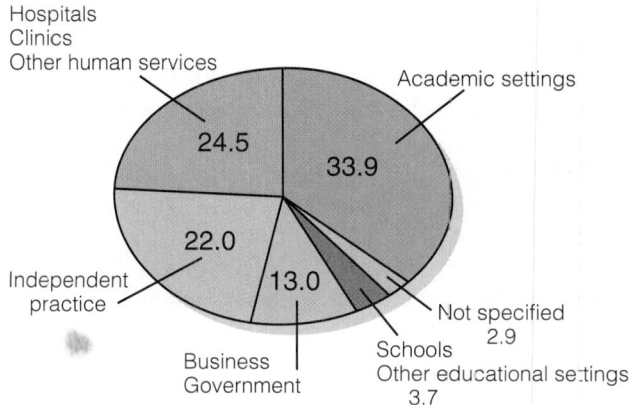

FIGURE 1.2

Work Settings of Psychologists

Shown are percentages of psychologists working in particular settings, according to a survey of American Psychological Association (APA) members holding doctoral degrees in psychology.

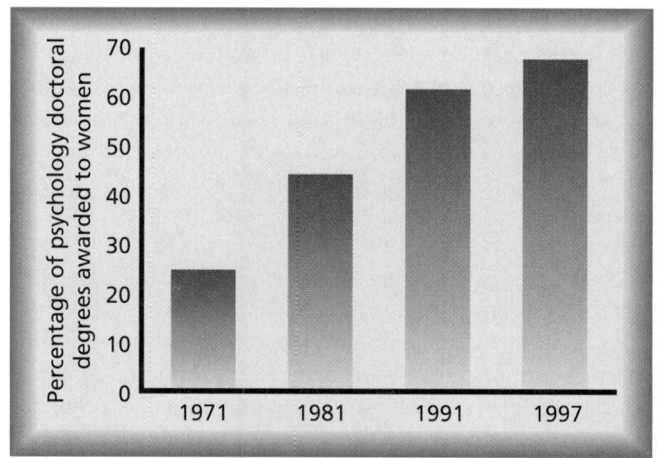

FIGURE 1.3

Percentage of Doctoral Degrees in Psychology Awarded to Women

Over the last 30 years, women have become the majority PhD recipients in psychology.

own version of such questions and indicate to you what sort of psychologist might address each one. If you have the time, make a list of your own questions. Cross off each question as *Psychology and Life* answers it. If, at the end of the course, you still have unanswered questions, please send them to us! **We have provided a response form at the back of the book for you to do so.**

Have you begun to wonder exactly how many practicing psychologists there are in the world? Surveys suggest that the number is well over 500,000. Of that number, approximately 62,000 to 82,000 work at psychological research (see **Figure 1.2**). Although the percentage of psychologists in the population is greatest in Western industrialized nations, interest in psychology continues to increase in many countries. The International Union of Psychological Science draws together member organizations from 64 countries (Rosenzweig, 1999a). The American Psychological Association (APA), an organization that includes psychologists from all over the world, had 155,000 members at the end of 1998 (Fowler, 1999). A second international organization, the American Psychological Society, with more than 16,000 members, focuses more on scientific aspects of psychology and less on the clinical, or treatment, side.

It probably won't surprise you to learn that, early in its history, research and practice in psychology were dominated by men. Even when they were still few in numbers, however, women made substantial contributions to the field (Russo & Denmark, 1987; Scarborough & Furomoto, 1987). In 1894, **Margaret Washburn** graduated from Cornell University to become the first woman to receive a PhD in psychology. She went on to write an influential early textbook, *The Animal Mind.* In 1895,

Mary Calkins completed all the requirements for a Harvard PhD with an exceptional record. Even so, the Harvard administration refused to grant a PhD to a woman. Despite this insult, Calkins became a successful researcher and the first woman president of the American Psychological Association. **Anna Freud,** whom we pictured earlier vacationing with her father, brought about important advances in the practice of *psychoanalysis,* a form of therapy based on the psychodynamic

Developmental psychologists may use puppets or other toys in their study of how children behave, think, or feel. Why might it be easier for a child to express his or her thoughts to a puppet than to an adult?

perspective. We will highlight the work of pioneering women researchers throughout *Psychology and Life.*

In contemporary psychology, women and men jointly share the rewards of furthering theory and applications. As shown in **Figure 1.3,** the majority of doctoral degrees (PhDs) in psychology—the advanced research degree earned by most college faculty—are now awarded to women (Pion et al., 1996). The trend toward higher percentages of degrees going to women holds steady at the turn of the 21st century (Murray & Williams, 1999). As psychology continues to contribute to the scientific and human enterprise, more people—women and men, and members of all segments of society—are being drawn to it as a career.

You're on your way. We hope *Psychology and Life* will be a worthwhile journey, full of memorable moments and unexpected pleasures. Let's go, or, as the Italians say, "Andiamo!"

SUMMING UP

Early psychologists demonstrated that psychological processes are governed by the doctrine of determinism—

mental and physical events are determined by specific causal factors. One early approach, structuralism, focused on mental contents and the structure of behavior; a second approach, functionalism, focused on the functions of behaviors.

Contemporary psychology incorporates seven major perspectives: the biological perspective studies relationships between behavior and brain mechanisms; the psychodynamic perspective looks at behavior as driven by conscious and unconscious motivations; the behaviorist perspective views behavior as determined by external stimulus conditions; the humanistic perspective emphasizes an individual's inherent capacity to achieve personal growth; the cognitive perspective stresses mental processes that affect behavioral responses; the evolutionary perspective looks at behavior as having evolved as an adaptation for survival in the environment; and the cultural perspective examines behavior and its interpretation in cultural contexts.

Psychologists address a diverse set of questions. The profession of psychology has changed over the last few decades to become more international in scope and to include even more women.

PSYCHOLOGY IN THE 21ST CENTURY

THE FUTURE IS NOW

In this edition of *Psychology and Life,* we have added a special feature: brief essays that discuss transitions in the discipline of psychology as we enter the 21st century. In the current chapter, we have given you a brief account of how the discipline has changed, particularly with respect to theoretical perspectives, over the past 100 years. What will the next 100 years bring? It is easy to foresee changes in both the content and practice of psychology.

Although some of the topics psychologists seek to answer are timeless, such as the basic processes of language acquisition, other questions arise because of particular circumstances of human history. For example, much of the social psychological research we will review in Chapters 17 and 18 was initiated by scholars who were trying to understand the forces that gave rise to the horrors of World War II. We cannot foretell what

major social movements will grip the globe in the 21st century, but we can be reasonably certain that psychologists will respond immediately to study the origins and implications of those movements. Psychological research is also very likely to be influenced by the technologies that are shrinking the distances between individuals in diverse cultures and locations. With the World Wide Web giving people instant access to information from all over the world, questions of cultural differences and similarities are likely to loom very large in 21st century psychology.

Even as technological innovations influence the questions psychologists wish to answer, those advances will also change the way in which researchers are able to answer those questions. In the 20th century, the advent of computers and brain imaging devices revolutionized the study of mental processes in ways that Wundt

and his colleagues in early experimental psychology could hardly have imagined. With further technological refinement, researchers may be able to pinpoint the relationship between ongoing mental processes and brain activity with amazing accuracy. Similarly, advances in the technological tools of genetics research may swiftly change the ways in which researchers tease apart the influences of nature and nurture on each individual's life course.

These are the types of issues—innovations in the content and practice of psychology—that we will address in this special feature, ***Psychology in the 21st Century.***

Web sites:

■ www.apa.org, the Web site for the American Psychological Association

■ www.psychologicalscience.org, the Web site for the American Psychological Society

RECAPPING MAIN POINTS

What Makes Psychology Unique?

- Psychology is the scientific study of the behavior and the mental processes of individuals.
- The goals of psychology are to describe, explain, predict, and help control behavior.

The Evolution of Modern Psychology

- Structuralism emerged from the work of Wundt and Titchener. It emphasized the structure of the mind and behavior built from elemental sensations.
- Functionalism, developed by James and Dewey, emphasized the purpose behind behavior.
- Taken together, these theories created the agenda for modern psychology.
- Each of the seven contemporary approaches to studying psychology differs in its view of human nature, the determinants of behavior, the focus of study, and the primary research approach.
- The biological perspective studies relationships between behavior and brain mechanisms.
- The psychodynamic perspective looks at behavior as driven by instinctive forces, inner conflicts, and conscious and unconscious motivations.
- The behaviorist perspective views behavior as determined by external stimulus conditions.
- The humanistic perspective emphasizes an individual's inherent capacity to make rational choices.
- The cognitive perspective stresses mental processes that affect behavioral responses.
- The evolutionary perspective looks at behavior as having evolved as an adaptation for survival in the environment.
- The cultural perspective examines behavior and its interpretation in cultural context.

What Psychologists Do

- Psychologists work in a variety of settings and draw on expertise from a range of specialty areas. Almost any question that can be generated about real-life experiences is addressed by some member of the psychological profession.
- At the start of the 21st century, the profession of psychology has become more international in scope and more diverse in the composition of its practitioners and researchers

Key Terms

Key terms are highlighted within the chapter in boldface type so they will stand out for you to notice. As you can see here, they are listed again at the end of the chapter with the page number on which they first appeared. When you study for a test, be sure you can define each term. In addition, all key terms are listed alphabetically and defined in the **Glossary** at the end of the book. The glossary provides definitions of the key terms, and the page numbers on which they appear. You can use it to refresh your memory while studying.

behavior (p. 3)
behavioral data (p. 4)
behaviorism (p. 11)
behaviorist perspective (p. 11)
biological perspective (p. 10)
cognitive perspective (p. 12)
cultural perspective (p. 12)
dispositional variables (p. 5)
environmental variables (p. 5)
evolutionary perspective (p. 12)
functionalism (p. 9)
humanistic perspective (p. 11)
organismic variables (p. 5)
psychodynamic perspective (p. 10)
psychology (p. 3)
scientific method (p. 3)
situational variables (p. 5)
structuralism (p. 9)

■ **THE CONTEXT OF DISCOVERY**

■ **THE CONTEXT OF JUSTIFICATION: SAFEGUARDS FOR OBJECTIVITY**
Observer Biases and Operational Definitions • Experimental Methods: Alternative Explanations and the Need for Controls • Correlational Methods • Subliminal Influence?

■ **PSYCHOLOGICAL MEASUREMENT**
Achieving Reliability and Validity • Self-Report Measures • Behavioral Measures and Observations

■ **ETHICAL ISSUES IN HUMAN AND ANIMAL RESEARCH**
Informed Consent • Risk/Gain Assessment • Intentional Deception • Debriefing • Issues in Animal Research: Science, Ethics, Politics

■ **BECOMING A WISER RESEARCH CONSUMER**

■ **PSYCHOLOGY IN THE 21ST CENTURY: PSYCHOLOGICAL RESEARCH AND THE INFORMATION EXPLOSION**

■ **RECAPPING MAIN POINTS**
Key Terms

In his autobiography, *Surely You're Joking, Mr. Feynman* (1985), Nobel prize winning physicist Richard Feynman described an informal program of research on the navigational ability of ants (pp. 93–95):

> In my rooms at Princeton I had a bay window with a U-shaped windowsill. One day some ants came out on the windowsill and wandered around a little bit. I got curious as to how they found things. I wondered, how do they know where to go? Can they tell each other where food is, like bees can? Do they have any sense of geometry?
>
> This is all amateurish: everybody knows the answer, but I didn't know the answer…
>
> In [one] experiment, I laid out a lot of glass microscope slides, and got the ants to walk on them, back and forth, to some sugar I put on the windowsill. Then, by replacing an old slide with a new one, or by rearranging the slides, I could demonstrate that the ants had no sense of geometry: they couldn't figure out where something was. If they went to the sugar one way, and there was a shorter way back, they would never figure out the short way.
>
> It was also pretty clear from rearranging the glass slides that the ants left some sort of trail. So then came a lot of easy experiments to find out how long it takes a trail to dry up, whether it can be easily wiped off, and so on. I also found out the trail wasn't directional. If I'd pick up an ant on a piece of paper, turn him around and around, and then put him back onto the trail, he wouldn't know that he was going the wrong way until he met another ant.

Feynman's simple but clever experiments allowed him, in a rigorous fashion, to satisfy his curiosity about ant behavior.

Although you may never have wondered about the ways in which ants communicate, you probably have formulated other questions about human or animal behavior to which you would like to have a compelling answer: You may recall that in Chapter 1 we asked you to compose a list of questions that you would like to have answered by the end of *Psychology and Life*. In this chapter, we describe how psychologists generate answers to these questions that matter most to you. We focus on the special way in which psychology applies the scientific method to its domain of inquiry. We want you to understand how psychologists design their research: How can solid conclusions ever be drawn from the complex and often fuzzy phenomena that psychologists study—how you think, feel, and behave?

Even if you never do any scientific research in your life, mastering the information in this section will be useful. The underlying purpose here is to help improve your *critical thinking skills* by teaching you how to ask the right questions and evaluate the answers about the causes, consequences, and correlates of psychological phenomena. The mass media constantly release stories that begin with, "Research shows that…" By sharpening your intelligent skepticism, we will help you become a more sophisticated consumer of the research-based conclusions that confront you in everyday life. We will show you how to settle arguments with "facts rather than polemics" (Miller, 1992).

The Context of Discovery

The research process in psychology can be divided into two major categories that usually occur in sequence: forming an idea (*discovery*) and then testing it (*justification*). The **context of discovery** is the initial phase of research during which observations, beliefs, information, and general knowledge lead someone to come

Context of discovery The initial phase of research, in which observations, beliefs, information, and general knowledge lead to a new idea or a different way of thinking about some phenomenon.

up with a new idea or a different way of thinking about a phenomenon. Where do researchers' questions originate? Some come from direct observations of events, humans, and nonhumans in the environment. Other research addresses traditional parts of the field: Some issues are considered to be "great unanswered questions" that have been passed down from earlier scholars. Often, researchers combine old ideas in unique ways that offer an original perspective. The hallmark of the truly creative thinker is the discovery of a new truth that moves science and society in a better direction.

Psychological theories, in general, attempt to understand how brain, mind, behavior, and environment function and how they may be related. A **theory** is an organized set of concepts that *explains* a phenomenon or set of phenomena. At the common core of most psychological theories is the assumption of **determinism,** the idea that all events—physical, mental, and behavioral—are the result of, or determined by, specific causal factors. These causal factors are limited to those in the individual's environment or within the person. Researchers also assume that behavior and mental processes follow *lawful patterns* of relationships, patterns that can be discovered and revealed through research. Psychological theories are typically claims about the causal forces that underlie such lawful patterns.

When a theory is proposed in psychology, it is generally expected both to account for known facts and to generate new ideas and hypotheses. A **hypothesis** is a tentative and testable statement about the relationship between causes and consequences. Hypotheses are often stated as if-then predictions, specifying certain outcomes from specific conditions. We might predict, for example, that *if* children view a lot of violence on television, *then* they will engage in more aggressive acts toward their peers. Research is required to verify the if-then link. Theories are of fundamental importance for generating new hypotheses. When scientific data do not bear out a hypothesis, researchers must rethink aspects of their theories. There is, therefore, continual interaction between theory and research.

Another important part of the context of discovery is the special attitudes and values required for participation in research. Science demands an open-minded—critical and skeptical—attitude toward any conclusion until it has been accepted by independent investigators. Open-

Scientific theories undergo rigorous testing, whose results must be replicated by independent investigators before the theories are recognized as proven.

mindedness serves two purposes. First, it makes truth provisional, ever ready to be modified by new data. Second, an open-minded orientation makes researchers willing to evaluate seriously claims for phenomena that they may not personally believe or accept, such as ESP, extrasensory perception (Bem & Honorton, 1994).

Scientific practice is based on respect for evidence obtained through controlled observation and careful measurement. In the realms of science, when good data clash with the opinions of experts, data win. Secrecy is banned from the research procedure because all data and methods must eventually be open for *public verifiability;* that is, other researchers must have the opportunity to inspect, criticize, replicate, or disprove the data and methods. Descriptions of the data, results, and the methods for collecting the data are kept separate from any inferences and conclusions about the meaning of the evidence. In scientific publications, each part of an investigation is reported in a distinct section, to allow readers to distinguish the objective features of the data from subjective interpretation by the researchers. Finally, there is a demand that research be published, to add to the cumulative body of knowledge about the topic studied, as well as to enable other investigators to replicate the findings.

Theory An organized set of concepts that explains a phenomenon or set of phenomena.

Determinism The doctrine that all events—physical, behavioral, and mental—are determined by specific causal factors that are potentially knowable.

Hypothesis A tentative and testable explanation of the relationship between two (or more) events or variables; often stated as a prediction that a certain outcome will result from specific conditions.

SUMMING UP

The context of discovery is the research phase in which researchers use observations, beliefs, information, and general knowledge to formulate new ideas and theories. Psychological theories are attempts to understand the deterministic relationships among the brain, mind, behavior, and the environment.

The Context of Justification: Safeguards for Objectivity

In most cases, researchers proceed from the discovery to the testing of theories. The **context of justification** is the research phase in which evidence is brought to bear on hypotheses. Psychologists face a difficult challenge when they try to get reliable evidence that will generate valid conclusions. They rely on one ally to make success possible: the **scientific method.** The scientific method is a general set of procedures for gathering and interpreting evidence in ways that limit sources of errors and yield dependable conclusions. Psychology is considered a science to the extent that it follows the rules established by the scientific method.

Because subjectivity must be minimized in the data collection and analysis phases of scientific research, procedural safeguards are used to increase objectivity. One of these safeguards needs no explanation: Researchers must keep complete records of observations and data analyses in a form that other researchers can understand and evaluate. For other aspects of the scientific method, we wish to emphasize why a particular procedure is so critical. Accordingly, each of the next two sections begins with a *challenge to objectivity* and then describes the *remedy* prescribed by the scientific method.

Observer Biases and Operational Definitions

When different people observe the same events, they don't always "see" the same thing. In this section, we describe the problem of *observer bias* and the steps researchers take as remedies.

THE CHALLENGE TO OBJECTIVITY *missing link*
An **observer bias** is an error due to the personal motives and expectations of the viewer. At times, people see and hear what they expect rather than what is. Consider a rather dramatic example of observer bias. Around the beginning of the 20th century, a leading psychologist, Hugo Munsterberg, gave a speech on peace to a large audience that included many reporters. He summarized the news accounts of what they heard and saw in this way:

The reporters sat immediately in front of the platform. One man wrote that the audience was so surprised by my speech that it received it in complete silence; another wrote that I was constantly interrupted by loud applause and that at the end of my address the applause continued for minutes. The one wrote that during my opponent's speech I was constantly smiling; the other noticed that my face re-

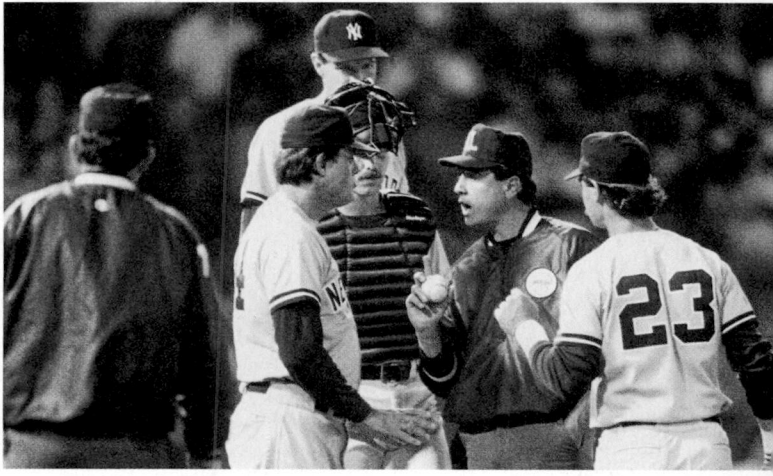

Participants, as well as spectators and broadcast viewers, are subject to observer bias. How can you determine what *really* happened?

mained grave and without a smile. The one said that I grew purple-red from excitement; and the other found that I grew chalk-white. (1908, pp. 35–36)

It would be interesting to go back to the original newspapers, to see how the reporters' accounts were related to their political views—then we might be able to understand why the reporters "saw" what they did.

In a psychology experiment, we wouldn't expect differences between observers to be quite as radical as those reported by Munsterberg. Nonetheless, the example demonstrates how the same evidence can lead different observers to different conclusions. The biases of the observers act as *filters* through which some things are noticed as relevant and significant, and others are ignored as irrelevant and not meaningful.

We'd like you now to try the demonstration in **Figure 2.1,** to illustrate how easy it is to create an observer bias. This quick demonstration gives you an idea of how the experiences you have prior to making an observation can influence how you interpret what you see.

Let's apply this lesson to what happens in psychology experiments. Researchers are often in the business of making observations. Given that every observer brings a different set of prior experiences to making those observations—and often those experiences include a commitment to a particular theory—you can see why observer

Context of justification The research phase in which evidence is brought to bear on hypotheses.
Scientific method The set of procedures used for gathering and interpreting objective information in a way that minimizes error and yields dependable generalizations.
Observer bias The distortion of evidence because of the personal motives and expectations of the viewer.

Look at the glass in this illustration. How would you answer the classic question: Is the glass half empty or half full?

Now suppose you watched this sequence in which water is poured into the glass. Wouldn't you be likely to describe the glass as half full?

Suppose you watched the sequence in which water is removed. Now doesn't the glass seem half empty?

FIGURE 2.1

Observer Bias

Is the glass half empty or half full?

biases could pose a problem. What can researchers do to ensure that their observations are minimally affected by prior expectations?

THE REMEDY

To minimize observer biases, researchers rely on standardization and operational definitions. **Standardiza-**

Standardization A set of uniform procedures for treating each participant in a test, interview, or experiment or for recording data.

Operational definition A definition of a variable or condition in terms of the specific operation or procedure used to determine its presence.

Variable In an experimental setting, a factor that varies in amount and kind.

Independent variable In experimental settings, the stimulus condition whose values are free to vary independently of any other variable in the situation.

Dependent variable In an experimental setting, any variable whose values are the results of changes in one or more independent variables.

tion means using uniform, consistent procedures in all phases of data collection. All features of the test or experimental situation should be sufficiently standardized so that all research participants experience exactly the same experimental conditions. Standardization means asking questions in the same way and scoring responses according to preestablished rules. Having results printed or recorded helps ensure their comparability in different times and places and with different participants and researchers.

Observations themselves must also be standardized: Scientists must solve the problem of how to translate their theories into concepts with consistent meaning. The strategy for standardizing the meaning of concepts is called *operationalization*. An **operational definition** standardizes meaning within an experiment, by defining a concept in terms of specific operations or procedures used to measure it or to determine its presence. All the variables in an experiment must be given operational definitions. A **variable** is any factor that varies in amount or kind. In experimental settings, the stimulus condition whose values are free to vary independently of any other variable in the situation is known as the **independent variable.** Any variable whose values are the results of changes in one or more independent variables is known as a **dependent variable**—they *depend* on variations in the stimulus conditions.

Imagine, for example, that you wished to test the hypothesis we mentioned earlier: that children who view a lot of violence on television will engage in more aggressive acts toward their peers. You could devise an experiment in which you manipulated the amount of violence each participant viewed (the independent variable) and then assessed how much aggression he or she displayed (the dependent variable). An important part of your experimental design would be to operationalize both the amount of violence contained in various television programs and the amount of aggression the participants in your experiments displayed. Think for a moment. What procedures could you develop to make both of these measures precise?

Psychologists are often faced with the problem of operationalizing variables that are quite complex. How, for example, do you operationalize the quality of a relationship a child has with his or her mother? (You'll see an answer in Chapter 11.) Psychologists must also operationalize variables that cannot be directly observed. How do you operationalize self-esteem? (Look to Chapter 14.) If you are a psychological researcher, all other researchers might not agree that you have operationalized a variable successfully—they might believe that you have failed to capture the essence of self-esteem—but if you have offered a precise operational definition, they will know how to judge and replicate your work. Take a moment to see how you might operationalize the concept of happiness with respect to the photographs in **Figure 2.2.**

FIGURE 2.2

Operational Definitions

Suppose you were interested in quantifying how happy each individual is, based only on these photographs. What factors would you take into consideration?

Experimental Methods: Alternative Explanations and the Need for Controls

You know from day-to-day experience that people can suggest many causes for the same outcome. Psychologists face this same problem when they try to make exact claims about causality. To overcome causal ambiguity, researchers use **experimental methods:** They manipulate an independent variable to look for an effect on a dependent variable. The goal of this method is to make strong causal claims about the impact of one variable on the other. In this section, we describe the problem of *alternative explanations* and some steps researchers take to counter the problem.

THE CHALLENGE TO OBJECTIVITY

When psychologists test a hypothesis, they most often have in mind an explanation for why change in the independent variable should affect the dependent variable in a particular way. For example, you might predict, and demonstrate experimentally, that the viewing of television violence leads to high levels of aggression. But how can you know that it was precisely the viewing of *violence* that produced aggression? To make the strongest possible case for their hypotheses, psychologists must be very sensitive to the existence of possible *alternative explanations*. The more alternative explanations there might be for a given result, the less confidence there is in the initial hypothesis. When something other than what an experimenter purposely introduces into a research setting

changes a participant's behavior and adds confusion to the interpretation of the data, it is called a **confounding variable.** When the real cause of some observed behavioral effect is *confounded*, the experimenter's interpretation of the data is put at risk. Suppose, for example, that violent television scenes are louder and involve more movement than do most nonviolent scenes. In that case, "violence" and superficial aspects of the scenes are confounded. The researcher is unable to specify which factor uniquely produces aggressive behavior.

Although each different experimental method potentially gives rise to a unique set of alternative explanations, we can identify two types of confounds that apply to almost all experiments, which we will call *expectancy effects* and *placebo effects.* Unintentional **expectancy effects** occur

Experimental methods Research methodologies that involve the manipulation of independent variables in order to determine their effects on the dependent variables.

Confounding variable A stimulus other than the variable an experimenter explicitly introduces into a research setting that affects a participant's behavior.

Expectancy effects Results that occur when a researcher or observer subtly communicates to participants the kind of behavior he or she expects to find, thereby creating that expected reaction.

Is violent behavior caused by viewing violence on television? How could you find out?

when a researcher or observer subtly communicates to the research participants the behaviors he or she expects to find—thereby producing the desired reaction. Under these circumstances, the experimenter's expectations, rather than the independent variable, actually help trigger the observed reactions.

Robert Rosenthal has studied the phenomenon of expectancy bias and how it can distort research results (Rosenthal, 1966):

HOW WE KNOW

RATS WILL MEET YOUR EXPECTATIONS

Throughout *Psychology and Life,* we will be sharing with you the results from psychological research. Often, our conclusions will be based on studies conducted by several different teams of researchers, at sites all over the world. The purpose of the *How We Know* feature is to give you regular opportunities to make contact with individual experiments that directly answer specific questions. Each *How We Know* gives you the opportunity to see a precise relationship between experiment and insight. For this first *How We Know,* we briefly describe a study that vividly demonstrates the way in which expectations can affect an experiment's outcome.

In a classic experiment, 12 students were given groups of rats that were going to be trained to run a maze. Half of the students were told that their rats were from a special *maze-bright* breed. The other students were told that their rats were bred to be *maze-dull.* As you might guess, their rats were actually all the same. Nonetheless, the students' results corresponded with their expectations for their rats. The rats labeled bright were found to be much better learners than those that had been labeled as dull (Rosenthal & Fode, 1963).

How do you suppose the students communicated their expectations to their rats? Do you see why you should worry even more about expectancy effects when an experiment is carried out within species—with a human experimenter and human participants? Expectation effects distort the content of discovery.

A **placebo effect** occurs when experimental participants change their behavior in the *absence* of any kind of experimental manipulation. This concept originated in medicine to account for cases in which a patient's health improved after he or she had received medication that was chemically inert or a treatment that was nonspecific. The placebo effect refers to an improvement in health or well-being due to the individual's *belief* that the treatment will be effective. Some treatments with no genu-

ine medical effects have been shown, even so, to produce good or excellent outcomes for 70 percent of the patients on whom they were used (Roberts et al., 1993).

In a psychological research setting, a placebo effect has occurred whenever a behavioral response is influenced by a person's expectation of what to do or how to feel, rather than by the specific intervention or procedures employed to produce that response. Recall your experiment relating television viewing to later aggression. Suppose we discovered that experimental participants who hadn't watched any television at all also showed high levels of aggression. We might conclude that these individuals, by virtue of being put in a situation that allowed them to display aggression, would expect that they were *supposed* to behave aggressively and would go on to do so. Experimenters must always worry that participants change the way they behave simply because they are aware of being observed or tested. For example, participants may feel special about being chosen to take part in a study and thus act differently than they would ordinarily. Such effects can compromise an experiment's results.

THE REMEDY

Because human and animal behaviors are complex and often have multiple causes, good research design involves anticipating possible confounds and devising strategies for eliminating them. Similar to defensive strategies in sports, good research designs anticipate what the other team might do and make plans to counteract it. Researchers' strategies are called **control procedures**—methods that attempt to hold constant all variables and conditions other than those related to the hypothesis being tested. In an experiment, instructions, room temperature, tasks, the way the researcher is dressed, time allotted, the way the responses are recorded, and many other details of the situation must be similar for all participants, to ensure that their experience is the same. The only differences in participants' experiences should be those introduced by the independent variable. Let us look at remedies for the specific confounding variables, expectancy and placebo effects.

Imagine, for example, that you enriched the aggression experiment to include a treatment group that watched comedy programs. You'd want to be careful not to treat your comedy and violence participants in different ways based on your expectations. Thus, in your experiment, we would want the research assistant who

Placebo effect A change in behavior in the absence of an experimental manipulation.

Control procedures Consistent procedures for giving instructions, scoring responses, and holding all other variables constant except those being systematically varied.

greeted the participants and later assessed their aggression to be unaware of whether they had watched a violent program or a comedy. In the best circumstances, bias can be eliminated by keeping *both* experimental assistants and participants unaware of, or *blind* to, which participants get which treatment. This technique is called a **double-blind control.** For many sorts of research designs, no one who knows the hypothesis is allowed to participate in data collection.

To account for placebo effects, researchers generally include an experimental condition in which the treatment is not administered. We call this a **placebo control.** Placebo controls fall into the general category of controls by which experimenters assure themselves that they are making appropriate comparisons. Consider the story of a young girl who, when asked if she loved her older sister, replied, "Compared to what?" That question is one that must be asked—and satisfactorily answered—before you can really understand what a research finding means. Suppose you read that a study shows that "more than three-quarters of a group of people trying to quit smoking were able to win with the help of nicotine patches" (Andrews, 1990). Compared to what? What about the control group? In this study's placebo control group, which wore nicotine-free patches, a full 39 percent also stopped smoking! Moreover, the longer they wore those medically useless patches, the more likely they were to quit smoking (Abelin et al., 1989). So the nicotine patch was an effective treatment, but more than half of its effectiveness was due to the placebo effect of expecting that it would work. The data from control conditions provide an important baseline against which the experimental effect is evaluated.

In some research designs, which are referred to as **between-subjects designs,** different groups of participants are *randomly assigned,* by chance procedures, to an experimental condition (exposed to one or more experimental treatments) or to a control condition (not exposed to an experimental treatment). Random assignment is one of the major steps researchers take to eliminate confounding variables that relate to individual differences among potential research participants. This is the design we had in mind for the aggression experiment. The random assignment to experimental and control conditions makes it quite likely that the two groups will be similar in important ways at the start of an experiment, because each participant has the same probability of being in a treatment condition as in a control condition. We shouldn't have to worry, for example, that everyone in the experimental group loves violent television and everyone in the control group hates it. Random assignment should mix both types of people together in each group. If outcome differences are found between conditions, we can be more confident that the differences were caused by a treatment or intervention rather than by preexisting differences.

Researchers also try to approximate randomness in the way they bring participants into the laboratory. Typically, psychology experiments use between 20 and 100 participants—but experimenters would often like to generalize from this **sample** to the full **population** from which the sample is drawn. Suppose you would like to test the hypothesis that 6-year-old children are more likely to lie than 4-year-old children. You can only bring some very small subset of all of the world's 4- and 6-year-olds into your laboratory. To generalize beyond your samples, you need to have confidence that your particular 4- and 6-year-olds are comparable to any other randomly selected groups of children. A sample is a **representative sample** of a population if it closely matches the overall characteristics of the population with respect, for example, to the distribution of males and females, racial and ethnic groups, and so on. You can only generalize from your sample to the population it adequately represents. If you only had boys as participants in your lying study, you'd be incorrect to draw conclusions about girls' probable behavior.

Another type of experimental design—a **within-subjects design**—uses each participant as his or her own control. For example, the behavior of an experimental participant before getting the treatment might be compared with behavior after. In what is known as an **A-B-A design,** participants first experience the

Double-blind control An experimental technique in which biased expectations of experimenters are eliminated by keeping both participants and experimental assistants unaware of which participants have received which treatment.

Placebo control An experimental condition in which treatment is not administered; it is used in cases where a placebo effect might occur.

Between-subjects design A research design in which different groups of participants are randomly assigned to experimental conditions or to control conditions.

Sample A subset of a population selected as participants in an experiment.

Population The entire set of individuals to which generalizations will be made based on an experimental sample.

Representative sample A subset of a population that closely matches the overall characteristics of the population with respect to the distribution of males and females, racial and ethnic groups, and so on.

Within-subjects design A research design that uses each participant as his or her own control; for example, the behavior of an experimental participant before receiving treatment might be compared to his or her behavior after receiving treatment.

A-B-A design Experimental design in which participants first experience the baseline condition (A), then experience the experimental treatment (B), and then return to the baseline (A).

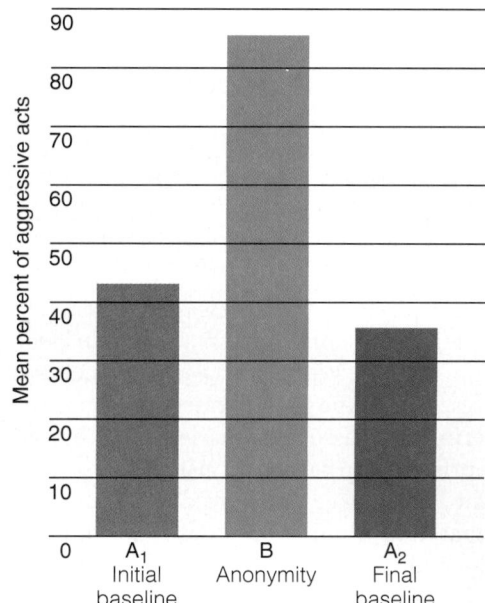

When schoolchildren attended a Halloween party (that was also part of an experiment), they engaged in significantly more aggressive play when they were anonymous than when they were identifiable. Can you think of situations in your own life in which anonymity has changed your behavior?

baseline condition (A), then experience the experimental treatment (B), and then go back to the baseline (A):

HOW WE KNOW

CHILDREN'S AGGRESSIVE PLAY IN AN A-B-A DESIGN An A-B-A design was used by an investigator who wanted to test the hypothesis that making children feel anonymous would increase their level of aggression when the situation provided an opportunity. Grade-school children were invited to a Halloween party where a variety of games were available, both those that invited aggressive play and those that invited nonaggressive play. In the baseline condition (A_1), the children played without wearing Halloween costumes. Then in the treatment condition (B), they put on costumes and continued to play the games of their choice. Finally, in a return to the baseline condition (A_2), they were told the costumes had to be returned but they could continue playing without them. The results supported the experimenter's hypothesis, as you can see in **Figure 2.3**. Across the three conditions that were otherwise constant, the same children were much more aggressive when they were anonymous (B) than when they were identifiable (A_1 or A_2) (Fraser, 1974).

The return to the baseline (the second "A" period) allowed the researcher to be quite confident that the treatment brought about the change and not some confounding variable, like the passage of time.

The research methodologies we have described so far all involve the manipulation of an independent

FIGURE 2.3

Anonymity-Induced Aggression

The effects of being anonymous are dramatic: Aggression is much higher for the same children in the anonymous condition than before and again after they put on Halloween costumes.

variable to look for an effect on a dependent variable. Although this experimental method often allows researchers to make the strongest claims about causal relations among variables, several conditions can make this method less desirable. First, during an experiment, behavior is frequently studied in an artificial environment, one in which situational factors are controlled so heavily that the environment may itself distort the behavior from the way it would occur naturally. Critics claim that much of the richness and complexity of natural behavior patterns is lost in controlled experiments, sacrificed to the simplicity of dealing with only one or a few variables and responses. Second, research participants typically know they are in an experiment and are being tested and measured. They may react to this awareness by trying to please the researcher, attempting to "psych out" the research purpose, or changing their behavior from what it would be if they were unaware of being monitored. Third, there are some important research problems that are not amenable to ethical experimental treatment. We could not, for example, try to discover whether the tendency toward child abuse is transmitted from generation to generation by creating an experimental group of children who would be abused and a control group of children who would not be. In the next section, we turn to a type of research method that often addresses these concerns.

Correlational Methods

Is intelligence associated with creativity? Are optimistic people healthier than pessimists? Is there a relationship between experiencing child abuse and later mental illness? These questions involve variables that a psychologist could not easily or ethically manipulate. To answer these questions, as we will in later chapters, requires research based on **correlational methods.** Psychologists use correlational methods when they want to determine to what extent two variables, traits, or attributes are related.

To determine the precise degree of correlation that exists between two variables, psychologists compute a statistical measure known as the **correlation coefficient (r).** This value can vary between +1.0 and −1.0, where +1.0 indicates a perfect positive correlation, −1.0 indicates a perfect negative correlation, and 0.0 indicates there is no correlation at all. A positive correlation coefficient means that as one set of scores increases, a second set also increases. The reverse is true with negative correlations; the second set of scores goes in the opposite direction to the values of the first scores (see **Figure 2.4**).

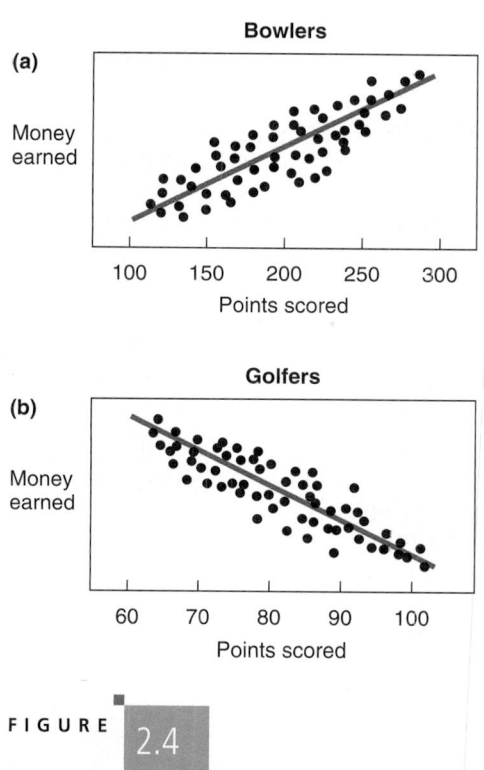

(a)

Bowlers

Money earned

100 150 200 250 300

Points scored

(b)

Golfers

Money earned

60 70 80 90 100

Points scored

FIGURE 2.4

Positive and Negative Correlations

These imaginary data display the difference between positive and negative correlations. Each point represents a single bowler or golfer. (a) In general, the more points a professional bowler scores, the more money he or she will earn. Thus, there is a positive correlation between those two variables. (b) The correlation for golf is negative, because golfers earn more money when they score fewer points.

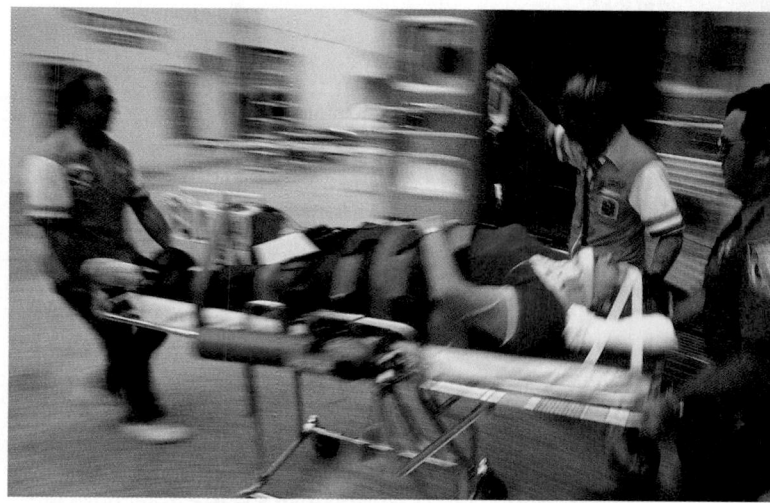

To study the relationship between stress and job performance, researchers must devise methods of measuring both factors. What should the researchers conclude if they find a positive correlation?

Correlations that are closer to zero mean that there is a weak relationship or no relationship between scores on two measures. As the correlation coefficient gets stronger, closer to the ±1.0 maximum, predictions about one variable based on information about the other variable become increasingly more accurate.

For example, a researcher exploring the relationship between worker productivity and stress might measure how much stress people are experiencing in their lives and how well they are performing at work. *Stress* might be operationally defined as a particular score on a stress questionnaire. *Job productivity* might be defined as the number of units of a given product a worker produces each day. The researcher could then measure each variable for many different workers and compute the correlation coefficient between them. A strongly negative score would mean that as stress goes up, productivity goes down. Knowing someone's life stress score would then allow the researcher to make a reasonable prediction about that person's productivity.

The researcher might want to take the next step and say that the way to increase productivity would be to lower stress. This assessment is incorrect. A strong correlation indicates only that two sets of data are related in a systematic way; the correlation does not ensure that one causes the other. *Correlation does not imply causation.* The correlation could reflect any one of several cause-and-effect possibilities, or none. For example, a negative stress

■ **Correlational methods** Research methodologies that determine to what extent two variables, traits, or attributes are related.
■ **Correlation coefficient (r)** A statistic that indicates the degree of relationship between two variables.

and productivity correlation might mean that (1) stress at home carries over to cause people to do poorly at work, (2) poor job productivity makes people experience more stress, or (3) those with a certain personality style are more likely to experience stress and also to perform poorly on the job. Note that in the last case, a third variable is causing the other two to vary. Consider a final scenario. Suppose that new technology leads to much more noise in a particular job setting. More noise could lead to greater stress (because workers can't think) and also lower productivity (because workers can't communicate). The correlation would still be in place—high stress co-occurs with lowered productivity—but there is no causal relationship at all.

Correlations may also be spurious because researchers did not make the appropriate control comparisons. Consider the supposed connection between the power blackout in New York City in 1965 and the reported jump in the birthrate nine months later. "New Yorkers are very romantic. It was the candlelight," said one new father. An official for a planned parenthood group offered the explanation that, because of the blackout, "all the substitutes for sex—meetings, lectures, card parties, theaters, saloons—were eliminated that night. What else could they do?" (*The New York Times,* 8/11/1966). The same kind of correlation is often reported after major blizzards and other disasters in many parts of the world. "Quake May Have Caused Baby Boom in Bay Area" was a more recent headline in the *San Francisco Chronicle* (Chen, 1990). However, when anyone takes the time to compare these apparently dramatic birthrate increases with the ordinary seasonal variations, the correlation turns out to be coincidence masquerading as causation. That is, there is a real correlation between *season* and birthrate—this is the control comparison for the coincidental "disaster" correlation. Clearly, we must apply the same caution to correlational results as we apply to research results that emerge from experimental methods.

We don't want to leave you with the impression that correlational methods aren't valuable research tools. Throughout *Psychology and Life,* we will see many correlational studies that have led to important insights. We'll offer just one example here to whet your appetite:

HOW WE KNOW

THE ORIGINS OF CONDUCT PROBLEMS IN YOUNG BOYS What environmental factors explain why, even by age 5, some boys are displaying conduct problems while others are not? A team of researchers sought to demonstrate that this difference among boys arises, in part, from the varying amount of *destructive sibling conflict* the boys experience with their brothers and sisters (Garcia et al., 2000). The researchers reasoned that high levels of conflict with siblings might reinforce the boys' tendency

toward aggressive or inappropriate responses to life situations. To measure destructive sibling conflict, the researchers videotaped hour-long play sessions between each of 180 boys and his sibling while they were playing together with different sets of toys. The videotaped play sessions were evaluated on such dimensions as the number of conflicts between the children and the intensity of those conflicts. Correlational analyses strongly supported the prediction that boys who experienced high levels of sibling conflict would also be most likely to display aggressive and delinquent behaviors.

Can you see why a correlational design is required to address this prediction? You can't randomly assign children to have a little or a lot of conflict with their siblings. You must wait to see what differences emerge after children are in one situation or the other.

Subliminal Influence?

To close out this section, we offer one concrete example of how psychological research has been used to assess the vigorous claims of advertisers anxious to make you believe in their products. You almost certainly have been subjected to commercials for audiotapes that promise to change your life with messages outside conscious awareness—*subliminal* messages: It's cassette magic! One tape guarantees a better sex life; another provides a quick cure for low self-esteem; a third promises safe and effective weight loss. How? All you have to do is *listen*—in bed, while jogging, when doing your homework—to the "restful splash of ocean waves breaking on sandy shores."

"Subliminal" influence has a long history. Although it was almost certainly a hoax, a 1957 study made headlines when the "inventor" of subliminal advertising claimed that the message "Buy Popcorn" flashed on the screen during a movie yielded a 58 percent increase in popcorn sales (Rogers, 1993)! *The Wall Street Journal* once reported that a New Orleans supermarket significantly decreased stealing and cashier shortages after piping the following subliminal message into its Muzak system: "If I steal, I will go to jail." A telephone survey in Toledo, Ohio, showed that nearly 75 percent of the 400 adults surveyed were familiar with subliminal advertising (Rogers & Smith, 1993). Of that group, again nearly 75 percent believed that subliminal advertising was used successfully by marketers. In general, the better educated the respondents, the more likely they were to believe in the effectiveness of subliminal advertising.

You now have the knowledge to address the critical question: Do subliminal audiotapes really influence mental states and behavior as their advocates claim? Our answer comes from an application of the experimental methods we have described (see **Figure 2.5**).

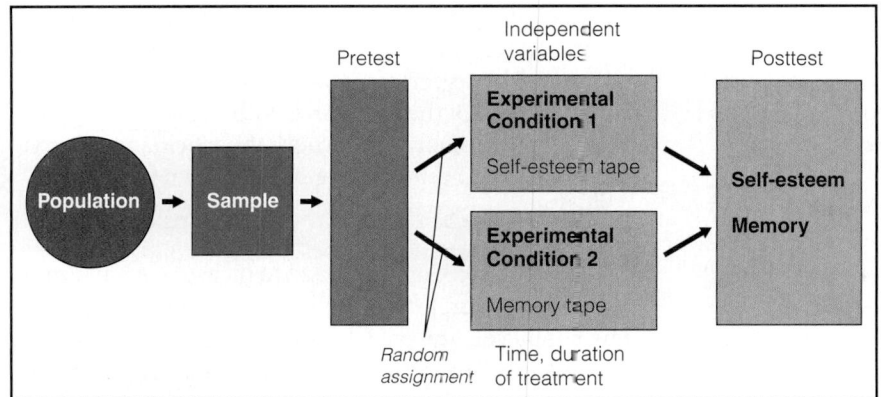

Independent variables · Pretest · Posttest

Population → Sample → [Pretest] → Experimental Condition 1 / Self-esteem tape → Self-esteem Memory

Experimental Condition 2 / Memory tape

Random assignment · Time, duration of treatment

FIGURE 2.5

Experimental Design for Testing Hypotheses about the Effectiveness of Subliminal Audiotapes

In this simplified version of the experiment, a sample of people is drawn from a larger, general population. They are given a series of pretest measures and randomly assigned to receive subliminal tapes with either memory or self-esteem messages. They are then given posttests that objectively assess any changes in the dependent variables: memory and self-esteem. The study found no significant effects of subliminal persuasion.

HOW WE KNOW

EVALUATING SUBLIMINAL EFFECTS A team of experimenters set out to determine the effectiveness of listening to commercially available audiotapes designed to improve self-esteem or memory. The participants were 237 men and women volunteers, ranging from 18 to 60 years of age. After a pretest session in which their initial self-esteem and memory were measured on standard psychological tests and questionnaires, the participants were randomly assigned to two conditions. Half of them received subliminal memory tapes, and the others received subliminal self-esteem tapes. They listened regularly to the tapes for a five-week period and then returned to the laboratory for a posttest session to evaluate their memories (using four memory tests) and self-esteem (using three self-esteem scales). The researchers were blind to which participants received which treatment (Greenwald et al., 1991).

Did the tapes boost self-esteem and enhance memory? The results from this controlled experiment indicate that there was no significant improvement shown on any of the objective measures of either self-esteem or memory. However, one very powerful effect did emerge: the placebo effect of expecting to be helped. Anticipating this placebo effect, the researchers had added another independent variable. Half

the participants in each group received memory tapes that were mismarked "self-esteem" and the others received self-esteem tapes in "memory boxes." Participants *believed* their self-esteem improved if they received tapes with that label or felt that their memory improved if their tapes were labeled "memory"—even when they had been listening to the other tape!

This rigorous experiment allows for some very concrete advice: Save your money; subliminal self-help tapes offer nothing more than placebo effects. An important goal of *Psychology and Life* is to provide you with such concrete conclusions based on solid experimental methods.

This experiment also gives you a specific example of the types of variables that psychologists measure—in this case, it was participants' beliefs about improvements in self-esteem and memory as well as objective measures of self-esteem and memory. In the next section, we discuss more generally the way in which psychologists measure important processes and dimensions of experience.

SUMMING UP

The second phase in the research process is justification. For this, psychologists rely on the scientific method. Observer biases are overcome when researchers standardize procedures for data collection and use operational definitions for concepts. The experimental method allows researchers to make claims about cause-effect relationships.

Researchers must be wary of alternative explanations, including expectancy effects and placebo effects. To safeguard their conclusions, they use procedures such as double-blind controls and placebo controls. Random assignment is an important means of control for between-subjects designs that helps ensure similarity between the control and experimental groups. Within-subjects designs include A-B-A designs, in which participants serve as their own controls. Researchers use correlational methods to determine the extent to which two variables are related. An important limitation of correlation is that it does not imply causation. Experimental methods can be applied to examine real-world claims such as the effects of subliminal audiotapes.

Psychological Measurement

Because psychological processes are so varied and complex, they pose major challenges to researchers who want to measure them. Although some actions and processes are easily seen, many, such as anxiety or dreaming, are not. Thus, one task for a psychological researcher is to make the unseen visible, to make internal events and processes external, and to make private experiences public. You have already seen how important it is for researchers to provide operational definitions of the phenomena they wish to study. Those definitions generally provide some procedure for assigning numbers to, or *quantifying,* different levels, sizes, intensities, or amounts of a variable. Many measurement methods are available, each with its particular advantages and disadvantages.

Our review of psychological measurement begins with a discussion of the distinction between two ways of gauging the accuracy of a measure: reliability and validity. We then review different measurement techniques for data collection. By whatever means psychologists collect their data, they must use appropriate statistical methods to verify their hypotheses. A description of how psychologists analyze their data is given in the Statistical Supplement, which follows this chapter. You should read it in conjunction with this chapter.

Achieving Reliability and Validity

The goal of psychological measurement is to generate findings that are both reliable and valid. **Reliability** refers to the consistency or dependability of behavioral data resulting from psychological testing or experimental research. A reliable result is one that will be repeated under similar conditions of testing at different times. A reliable measuring instrument yields comparable scores when employed repeatedly (and when the thing being measured does not change). Consider the experiment we just

described that showed that subliminal audiotapes generate only placebo effects. That experiment used 237 participants. The experimenters' claim that the result was "reliable" means that they should be able to repeat the experiment with any new group of participants of comparable size and generate the same pattern of data.

Validity means that the information produced by research or testing accurately measures the psychological variable or quality it is intended to measure. A valid measure of *happiness,* for example, should allow us to predict how happy you are likely to be in particular situations. A valid experiment means that the researcher can generalize to broader circumstances, often from the laboratory to the real world. When we gave you advice based on the audiotapes experiment, we were accepting the researchers' claim that the results are valid. Tests and experiments can be reliable without being valid. We could, for example, use your shoe size as an index of your happiness. This would be reliable (we'd always get the same answer), but not valid (we'd learn very little about your day-to-day happiness level).

As you now read about different types of measures, try to evaluate them in terms of reliability and validity.

Self-Report Measures

Often researchers are interested in obtaining data about experiences they cannot directly observe. Sometimes these experiences are internal psychological states, such as beliefs, attitudes, and feelings. At other times, these experiences are external behaviors but—like sexual activities or criminal acts—not generally appropriate for psychologists to witness. In these cases, investigations rely on self-reports. **Self-report measures** are verbal answers, either written or spoken, to questions the researcher poses. Researchers devise reliable ways to quantify these self-reports so they can make meaningful comparisons between different individuals' responses.

Self-reports include responses made on questionnaires and during interviews. A *questionnaire* or *survey* is a written set of questions, ranging in content from questions of fact ("Are you a registered voter?"), to questions about past or present behavior ("How much do you smoke?"), to questions about attitudes and feelings ("How satisfied are you with your present job?"). *Open-*

Reliability The degree to which a test produces similar scores each time it is used; stability or consistency of the scores produced by an instrument.

Validity The extent to which a test measures what it was intended to measure.

Self-report measures The self-behaviors that are identified through a participant's own observations and reports.

ended questions allow respondents to answer freely in their own words. Questions may also have a number of *fixed alternatives* such as *yes, no,* and *undecided.*

An *interview* is a dialogue between a researcher and an individual for the purpose of obtaining detailed information. Instead of being completely standardized, as a questionnaire is, an interview is *interactive.* An interviewer may vary the questioning to follow up on something the respondent said. Good interviewers are also sensitive to the process of the social interaction as well as to the information revealed. They are trained to establish *rapport,* a positive social relationship with the respondent that encourages trust and the sharing of personal information.

Although researchers rely on a wide variety of self-report measures, there are limits to their usefulness. Obviously, many forms of self-report cannot be used with preverbal children, illiterate adults, speakers of other languages, some mentally disturbed people, and nonhuman animals. Even when self-reports can be used, they may not be reliable or valid. Participants may misunderstand the questions or not remember clearly what they actually experienced. Furthermore, self-reports may be influenced by social desirability—people may give false or misleading answers to create a favorable (or, sometimes, unfavorable) impression of themselves. They may be embarrassed to report their true experiences or feelings. If respondents are aware of a questionnaire's or interview's purpose, they may lie or alter the truth to get a job, to get discharged from a mental hospital, or to accomplish any other goal. An interview situation also allows personal biases and prejudices to affect how the interviewer asks questions and how the respondent answers them.

Behavioral Measures and Observations

As a group, psychological researchers are interested in a wide range of behaviors. They may study a rat running a maze, a child drawing a picture, a student memorizing a poem, or a worker repeatedly performing a task. **Behavioral measures** are ways to study overt actions and observable and recordable reactions.

One of the primary ways to study what people do is *observation.* Researchers use observation in a planned, precise, and systematic manner. Observations focus on either the *process* or the *products* of behavior. In an experiment on learning, for instance, a researcher might observe how many times a research participant rehearsed a list of words (process) and then how many words the participant remembered on a final test (product). For *direct observations,* the behavior under investigation must be clearly visible and overt and easily recorded. For example, in a laboratory experiment on emotions, a researcher could observe a participant's facial expressions as the individual looked at emotionally arousing stimuli.

By watching from behind a one-way mirror, a researcher can record observations of a child without influencing or interfering with the child's behavior. Have you ever changed your behavior when you knew you were being watched?

A researcher's direct observations are often augmented by technology. For example, contemporary psychologists often rely on computers to provide very precise measures of the time it takes for research participants to perform various tasks, such as reading a sentence or solving a problem. Although some forms of exact measurement were available before the computer age, computers now provide extraordinary flexibility in collecting and analyzing precise information. In Chapter 3, we will describe the newest types of technologies that allow researchers to produce behavioral measures of a remarkable kind: pictures of the brain at work.

In *naturalistic observations,* some naturally occurring behavior is viewed by a researcher, who makes no attempt to change or interfere with it. For instance, a researcher behind a one-way mirror might observe the play of children who are not aware of being observed. Some kinds of human behavior can be studied only through naturalistic observation, because it would be unethical or impractical to do otherwise. For example, it would be unethical to experiment with severe deprivation in early life to see its effects on a child's later development.

When studying behavior in a laboratory setting, a researcher is unable to observe the long-term effects that one's natural habitat has in shaping complex patterns of behavior. One of the most valuable examples of naturalistic observation conducted in the field is the work of **Jane Goodall** (1986, 1990; Peterson & Goodall, 1993). Goodall has spent more than 30 years studying patterns of behavior among chimpanzees in Gombe, on Lake Tanganyika in Africa. Goodall notes that had she ended

Behavioral measures Overt actions and reactions that are observed and recorded, exclusive of self-reported behavior.

31

Jane Goodall has spent most of her adult life making naturalistic observations of chimpanzees. What has she discovered that she couldn't have discovered if the animals were not in their natural habitat?

her research after 10 years—as she originally planned—she would not have drawn the correct conclusions:

> We would have observed many similarities in their behavior and ours, but we would have been left with the impression that chimpanzees were far more peaceable than humans. Because we were able to continue beyond the first decade, we could document the division of a social group and observe the violent aggression that broke out between newly separated factions. We discovered that in certain circumstances the chimpanzees may kill and even cannibalize individuals of their own kind. On the other side of the coin, we have learned of the extraordinarily enduring affectionate bonds between family members...advanced cognitive abilities, [and the development of] cultural traditions.... (Goodall, 1986, pp. 3–4)

In the early stages of an investigation, naturalistic observation is especially useful. It helps researchers to discover the extent of a phenomenon or to get an idea of what the important variables and relationships might be. The data from naturalistic observation often provide clues for an investigator to use in formulating a specific hypothesis or research plan.

Before we leave the topic of psychological measurement, we must emphasize that many research projects combine both self-report measures and behavioral observations. Researchers may, for example, specifically look for a relationship between how people report they

Case study Intensive observation of a particular individual or small group of individuals.

will behave and how they actually behave (see Chapter 17). In addition, rather than involving large numbers of participants, some research projects will focus all their measures on a single individual in a **case study**. Intensive analyses of particular individuals can sometimes yield important insights into general features of human experience. For example, in Chapter 3 you will learn that careful observations of single patients with brain damage provided the basis for important theories of the localization of language functions in the brain.

We have now described several types of procedures and measures that researchers use. In the next section, we consider the ethical standards that govern the uses of these procedures and measures.

◼ Ethical Issues in Human and Animal Research

In the study that tested the effectiveness of subliminal messages, the researchers deceived the participants by mislabeling the tapes. They did so to see if the participants' expectations would lead them to believe that the messages were helpful even if objective measures of memory and self-esteem showed no improvement. Deception is always ethically suspect, but in this case, how else could researchers assess the placebo effect of false beliefs held by the participants? How should the *potential gains* of a research project be weighed against the *costs* it incurs to those who are subjected to procedures that are risky, painful, stressful, or deceptive? Psychologists ask themselves these questions on an ongoing basis (Rosenthal, 1994).

Respect for the basic rights of humans and animals is a fundamental obligation of all researchers. To guarantee that these rights are honored, special committees oversee every research proposal, imposing strict guidelines issued by the U.S. Department of Health and Human Services. Universities and colleges, hospitals, and research institutes each have *review boards* that approve and reject proposals for human and animal research. The American Psychological Association (1992) has established detailed guidelines for ethical standards for researchers. What are some of those guidelines and ethical concerns?

Informed Consent

At the start of nearly all laboratory research with human subjects, participants are given a description of the procedures, potential risks, and expected benefits they will experience. Participants are assured that their privacy is protected: All records of their behavior are kept strictly confidential; they must approve any public sharing of them. Participants are asked to sign statements indicating that they have been *informed* about these matters, and *consent* to continue. The participants are assured in advance that they may leave an experiment any time they wish, without penalty, and are given the names and phone numbers of officials to contact if they have any grievances.

Risk/Gain Assessment

Most psychology experiments carry little risk to the participants, especially where participants are merely asked to perform routine tasks. However, some experiments that study more personal aspects of human nature—such as emotional reactions, self-images, conformity, stress, or aggression—can be upsetting or psychologically disturbing. Therefore, whenever a researcher conducts such a study, risks must be minimized, participants must be informed of the risks, and suitable precautions must be taken to deal with strong reactions. Where any risk is involved, it is carefully weighed by each institutional review board in terms of its necessity for achieving the benefits to the participants of the study, to science, and to society.

Intentional Deception

For some kinds of research, it is not possible to tell the participants the whole story in advance without biasing the results. If you were studying the effects of violence on television on aggression, for example, you would not want your participants to know your purpose in advance. But is your hypothesis enough to justify the deception? Some researchers have argued that any type of deception is incompatible with the basic right of informed consent (Korn, 1987). The American Psychological Association's (1992) guidelines about deception in research are quite clear: (1) The study must have sufficient scientific and educational importance to warrant deception; (2) researchers must demonstrate that no equally effective procedures excluding deception are available; (3) participants may never be deceived about aspects of the experiment that would affect their willingness to participate; (4) the deception must be explained to the participants by the conclusion of the research. In experiments with deception, a review board may impose constraints, insist on monitoring initial demonstrations of the procedure, or deny approval (Steininger et al., 1984).

Debriefing

Participation in psychological research should always be a mutual exchange of information between researcher and participant. The researcher may learn something new about a behavioral phenomenon from the participant's responses, and the participant should be informed

of the purpose, hypothesis, anticipated results, and expected benefits of the study. At the end of an experiment, each participant must be given a careful **debriefing**, in which the researcher provides as much information about the study as possible and makes sure that no one leaves feeling confused, upset, or embarrassed. If it was necessary to mislead the participants during any stage of the research, the experimenter carefully explains the reasons for the deception. Finally, participants have the right to withdraw their data if they feel they have been misused or their rights abused in any way.

Issues in Animal Research: Science, Ethics, Politics

Should animals be used in psychological and medical research? This question has often produced very polarized responses. On one side are researchers who point to the very important breakthroughs research with animals has allowed in several areas of science (Domjan & Purdy, 1995; Petrinovich, 1998). The benefits of animal research have included discovery and testing of drugs that treat anxiety and mental illnesses as well as important knowledge about drug addiction (Miller, 1985). Animal research benefits animals as well. For example, psychological researchers have shown how to alleviate the stresses of confinement experienced by zoo animals. Their studies of animal learning and social organization have led to the improved design of enclosures and animal facilities that promote good health (Nicoll et al., 1988).

To defenders of animal rights, this list of achievements does not undercut the deep error of believing that there is a "morally relevant difference separating Homo sapiens from other creatures" (Bowd & Shapiro, 1993, p. 136; see also Shapiro, 1998). To remedy this error, ethicists argue for "a shift from laboratory-based invasive research to minimally manipulative research conducted in naturalistic and semi-naturalistic settings" (Bowd & Shapiro, 1993, p. 140). Each animal researcher must judge his or her work with heightened scrutiny.

Surveys of 1,188 psychology students and 3,982 American Psychological Association members on their attitudes toward animal research support a criterion of heightened scrutiny (Plous, 1996a, 1996b):

- Roughly 80 percent of the people surveyed believed that observational studies in naturalistic settings were appropriate. Smaller numbers (30 to 70 percent) supported studies involving caging or confinement,

Debriefing A procedure conducted at the end of an experiment in which the researcher provides the participant with as much information about the study as possible and makes sure that no participant leaves feeling confused, upset, or embarrassed.

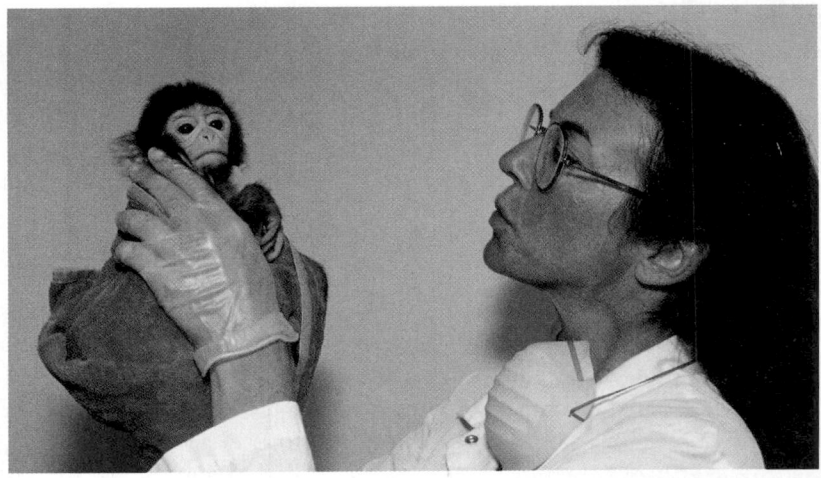

Researchers who use animal subjects are required to provide a humane environment. Do you think scientific gains justify the use of nonhuman animals in research?

depending in part on the type of animal (for example, rats, pigeons, dogs, or primates). Both students and their professors disapproved of studies involving physical pain or death.

- A majority of both groups (roughly 60 percent) supported the use of animals in undergraduate psychology courses, but only about a third of each group felt that laboratory work with animals should be a required part of an undergraduate psychology major.

How do your beliefs compare to those of your peers? How would you make decisions about the costs and benefits of animal research?

SUMMING UP

Psychological measurement must produce findings that are both reliable and valid. Self-report measures are obtained through questionnaires and interviews. Depending on the behavior of interest, a psychologist will use behavioral measures such as direct observation or naturalistic observation. Important ethical issues in human research include informed consent, an assessment of the risks and benefits of the research, the use of intentional deception, and the necessity for debriefing. Researchers must examine carefully the ethical consequences of research with non-human animals.

Becoming a Wiser Research Consumer

In our final section of this chapter, we will focus on the kinds of critical thinking skills you need to become a wiser consumer of psychological knowledge. Honing these thinking tools is essential for any respon-

sible person in a dynamic society such as ours—one so filled with claims of truth, with false "commonsense" myths, and with biased conclusions that serve special interests. To be a *critical thinker* is to go beyond the information as given and to delve beneath slick appearances, with the goal of understanding the substance without being seduced by style and image.

Psychological claims are an ever present aspect of the daily life of any thinking, feeling, and acting person in this psychologically sophisticated society. Unfortunately, much information on psychology does not come from the books, articles, and reports of accredited practitioners. Rather, this information comes from newspaper and magazine articles, TV and radio shows, pop psychology and self-help books. Return to the idea of subliminal mind control. Although it began as a hoax propagated by profit-minded marketing consultant James M. Vicary (Rogers, 1993)—and, as we have seen, has been rigorously discredited in the laboratory—the idea of subliminal influences on overt behavior continues to exert a pull on people's beliefs—and their wallets!

Studying psychology will help you make wiser decisions based on evidence gathered either by you or by others. You should always try to apply the insights you derive from your formal study of psychology to the informal psychology that surrounds you: Ask questions about your own behavior or that of other people, seek answers to these questions with respect to rational psychological theories, and check out the answers against the evidence available to you.

Here are some general rules to keep in mind in order to be a more sophisticated shopper as you travel through the supermarket of knowledge:

- Avoid the inference that correlation is causation.

- Ask that critical terms and key concepts be defined operationally so that there can be consensus about their meanings.

- Consider first how to disprove a theory, hypothesis, or belief before seeking confirming evidence, which is easy to find when you're looking for a justification.

- Always search for alternative explanations to the obvious ones proposed, especially when the explanations benefit the proposer.

- Recognize how personal biases can distort perceptions of reality.

- Be suspicious of simple answers to complex questions or single causes and cures for complex effects and problems.

- Question any statement about the effectiveness of some treatment, intervention, or product by finding the comparative basis for the effect: compared to what?

- Be open-minded yet skeptical: Recognize that most conclusions are tentative and not certain; seek new evidence that decreases your uncertainty while keeping yourself open to change and revision.

- Challenge authority that uses personal opinion in place of evidence for conclusions, and is not open to constructive criticism.

We want you to apply open-minded skepticism while you read *Psychology and Life*. We don't want you to view your study of psychology as the acquisition of a list of facts. Instead, we hope you will participate in the joy of observing and discovering and putting ideas to the test.

PSYCHOLOGY IN THE 21ST CENTURY

PSYCHOLOGICAL RESEARCH AND THE INFORMATION EXPLOSION

If you access the World Wide Web, you will discover an amazing range of sites devoted to topics in psychology. For example, the morning we wrote these paragraphs, one Web search engine turned up 83,760 pages mentioning schizophrenia (see Chapter 15); a second search engine turned up 63,812 pages. No doubt these numbers will grow even higher during the short interval the publisher needs to turn our paragraphs into your textbook. These two data points make it clear why many people characterize the time in which we live as a time of *information explosion*. The challenge for all of us is to become wise consumers of all that information. How can you determine which information posted on the Web arises from legitimate sources and which does not?

In a physical library, it's much easier to determine the source of information. Most psychological research appears in *journals* that are published by organizations such as the *American Psychological Association* or the *American Psychological Society*. When research manuscripts are submitted to most journals, they undergo a process of *peer review*. Each manuscript is typically sent to between two and five experts in the field. Those experts provide detailed analyses of the manuscript's rationale, methodology, and results. Only when those experts have been sufficiently satisfied do manuscripts become journal articles. This is a rigorous process. For example, in 1998, journals published by the American Psychological Association (1999) rejected, on average, 69 percent of the manuscripts submitted to them. The process of peer review isn't perfect—no doubt some worthy research projects are overlooked, and some uneven ones slip through—but, in general, this process ensures that the research you read in the vast majority of journals has met high standards.

In this context, it's easy to identify the problem with much of the information on the Web: You often can't tell who, if anyone, has evaluated the advice a Web page offers or the claims it makes. When you accept information from a Web page, you need to assure yourself that the source is legitimate. One good approach is to look for on-line versions of the journals available in the library. Also, look for the Web pages researchers now often maintain that summarize their projects and list relevant publications. If the information you find on those or any other Web pages interests you, try to find the references and publications they list. In general, you should have the greatest confidence in the information provided on a Web site when the authors of the site are able to point you toward the research sources for that information. You can have confidence in the conclusions we draw throughout *Psychology and Life* because we provide research citations for each of our claims. Make sure to hold Web pages to the same standard!

A news interview with an expert may include misleading sound bites taken out of context, or oversimplified "nutshell" descriptions of research conclusions. How could you become a wiser consumer of media reports?

RECAPPING
MAIN POINTS

The Context of Discovery

■ In the discovery phase of research, observations, beliefs, information, and general knowledge lead to a new way of thinking about a phenomenon. The researcher formulates a theory and generates hypotheses to be tested.

The Context of Justification: Safeguards for Objectivity

■ Justification is the phase in which ideas are tested and proven or disproven to some degree of certainty.

■ To test their ideas, researchers use the scientific method, a set of procedures for gathering and interpreting evidence in ways that limit errors.

■ Researchers combat observer biases by standardizing procedures and using operational definitions.

■ Experimental research methods determine whether causal relationships exist between variables specified by the hypothesis being tested.

■ Researchers rule out alternative explanations by using appropriate control procedures.

■ Correlational research methods determine if and how much two variables are related. Correlations do not imply causation.

Psychological Measurement

■ Researchers strive to produce measures that are both reliable and valid.

■ Psychological measurements include self-reports and behavioral measures.

Ethical Issues in Human and Animal Research

■ Respect for the basic rights of human and animal research participants is the obligation of all researchers. A variety of safeguards have been enacted to guarantee ethical and humane treatment.

Becoming a Wiser Research Consumer

■ Becoming a wise research consumer involves learning how to think critically and knowing how to evaluate claims about what research shows.

Key Terms

A-B-A design (p. 26)
behavioral measures (p. 30)
between-subjects design (p. 25)
case study (p. 32)
confounding variable (p. 23)
context of discovery (p. 19)
context of justification (p. 21)
control procedures (p. 24)
correlation coefficient (*r*) (p. 27)
correlational methods (p. 27)
debriefing (p. 33)
dependent variable (p. 22)
determinism (p. 20)
double-blind control (p. 25)
expectancy effects (p. 23)
experimental methods (p. 23)
hypothesis (p. 20)
independent variable (p. 22)
observer bias (p. 21)
operational definition (p. 22)
placebo control (p. 25)
placebo effect (p. 24)
population (p. 25)
reliability (p. 30)
representative sample (p. 25)
sample (p. 25)
scientific method (p. 21)
self-report measures (p. 30)
standardization (p. 22)
theory (p. 20)
validity (p. 30)
variable (p. 22)
within-subjects design (p. 26)

statistical supplement

understanding statistics:
analyzing data and forming conclusions

■ **ANALYZING THE DATA**
Descriptive Statistics •
Inferential Statistics

■ **BECOMING A WISE
CONSUMER OF STATISTICS**
Key Terms

As we noted in Chapter 2, psychologists use statistics to make sense of the data they collect. They also use statistics to provide a quantitative basis for the conclusions they draw. Knowing something about statistics, therefore, can help you appreciate the process by which psychological knowledge is developed. On a more personal level, having a basic understanding of statistics will help you make better decisions when people use data to try to sway your opinions and actions.

Most students perceive statistics as a dry, uninteresting topic. However, statistics have many vital applications in your life. To demonstrate this point, we will follow a single project from its real-world inspiration to the statistical arguments that were used to bolster general conclusions. The project began in response to the types of stories that appear on newspaper front pages, about shy individuals who became *sudden murderers*. Here's an example:

Fred Cowan was described by relatives, co-workers, and acquaintances as a "nice, quiet man," a "gentle man who loved children," and a "real pussycat." The principal of the parochial school Cowan had attended as a child reported that his former student had received A grades in courtesy, cooperation, and religion. According to a co-worker, Cowan "never talked to anybody and was someone you could push around." Cowan, however, surprised everyone who knew him when, one Valentine's Day, he strolled into work toting a semiautomatic rifle and shot and killed four co-workers, a police officer, and, finally, himself.

This story has a common plot: A shy, quiet person suddenly becomes violent, shocking everyone who knows him. What did Fred Cowan have in common with other people who are suddenly transformed from gentle and caring into violent and ruthless? What personal attributes might distinguish them from us?

A team of researchers had a hunch that there might be a link between shyness and other personal characteristics and violent behavior (Lee et al., 1977). Therefore, they began to collect some data that might reveal such a connection. The researchers reasoned that seemingly nonviolent people who suddenly commit murders are probably typically shy, nonaggressive individuals who keep their passions in check and their impulses under tight control. For most of their lives, they suffer many silent injuries. Seldom, if ever, do they express anger, regardless of how angry they really feel. On the outside, they appear unbothered, but on the inside they may be fighting to control furious rages. They give the impression that they are quiet, passive, responsible people, both as children and as adults. Because they are shy, they probably do not let others get close to them, so no one knows how they really feel. Then, suddenly, something explodes. At the slightest provocation—one more small insult, one more little rejection, one more bit of social pressure—the fuse is lit, and they release the suppressed violence that has been building up for so long. Because they did not learn to deal with interpersonal conflicts through discussion and verbal negotiation, these sudden murderers act out their anger physically.

The researchers' reasoning led them to the hypothesis that shyness would be more characteristic of *sudden murderers*—people who had engaged in homicide without any prior history of violence or antisocial behavior—than it would of *habitual criminal murderers*—those who had committed homicide but had had a previous record of violent criminal behavior. In addition, sudden murderers should have higher levels of control over their impulses than habitually violent people. Finally, their passivity and dependence would be manifested in more feminine and androgynous (both male and female) characteristics, as measured on a standard sex-role inventory, than those of habitual criminals.

To test their ideas about sudden murderers, the researchers obtained permission to administer psychological questionnaires to a group of inmates serving time for murder in California prisons. Nineteen inmates (all male) agreed to participate in the study. Prior to committing murder, some had committed a series of crimes, whereas the other part of the sample had had no previous criminal record. The researchers collected three kinds of data from these two types of participants: shyness scores, sex-role identification scores, and impulse control scores.

Shyness scores were collected using the Stanford Shyness Survey. The most important item on this questionnaire asked if the individual was shy; the answer could be either yes or no. Other items on the scale tapped degree and kinds of shyness and a variety of dimensions related to origins and triggers of shyness.

The second questionnaire was the Bem Sex-Role Inventory (BSRI), which presented a list of adjectives, such as *aggressive* and *affectionate,* and asked how well each adjective described the individual (Bem, 1974, 1981). Some adjectives were typically associated with being "feminine," and the total score of these adjectives was an individual's femininity score. Other adjectives were considered "masculine," and the total score of those adjectives was an individual's masculinity score. The final sex-role score, which reflected the difference between an individual's femininity and masculinity, was calculated by subtracting the masculinity score from the femininity score. A combination of the masculinity and femininity scores shows up as an individual's androgyny score.

The third questionnaire was the Minnesota Multiphasic Personality Inventory (MMPI), which was designed to measure many different aspects of personality (see Chapter 14). The study used only the "ego-overcontrol" scale, which measures the degree to which a person acts out or controls impulses. The higher the individual's score on this scale, the more ego overcontrol the individual exhibits.

The researchers predicted that, compared with murderers with a prior criminal record, sudden murderers would (1) more often describe themselves as shy on the shyness survey; (2) select more feminine traits than masculine ones on the sex-role scale; and (3) score higher in ego overcontrol. What did they discover?

Before you find out, you need to understand some of the basic procedures that were used to analyze these data. The actual sets of data collected by the researchers will be used as the source material to teach you about some of the different types of statistical analyses and also about the kinds of conclusions they make possible.

Analyzing the Data

For most researchers in psychology, analyzing the data is an exciting step—statistical analysis allows researchers to discover if their predictions were correct. In this section, we will work step by step through an analysis of some of the data from the Sudden Murderers Study. If you have looked ahead, you will have seen

Raw Data from the Sudden Murderers Study

Inmate	Shyness	BSRI Femininity-Masculinity	MMPI Ego Overcontrol
Group 1: Sudden Murderers			
1	Yes	+5	17
2	No	−1	17
3	Yes	+4	13
4	Yes	+61	17
5	Yes	+19	13
6	Yes	+41	19
7	No	−29	14
8	Yes	+23	9
9	Yes	−13	11
10	Yes	+5	14
Group 2: Habitual Criminal Murderers			
11	No	−12	15
12	No	−14	11
13	Yes	−33	14
14	No	−8	10
15	No	−7	16
16	No	+3	11
17	No	−17	6
18	No	+6	9
19	No	−10	12

numbers and equations. Keep in mind that mathematics is a tool; mathematical symbols are a shorthand for representing ideas and conceptual operations.

The *raw data*—the actual scores or other measures obtained—from the 19 inmates in the Sudden Murderers Study are listed in **Table S.1.** As you can see, there were ten inmates in the sudden murderers group and nine in the habitual criminal murderers group. When first glancing at these data, any researcher would feel what you probably feel: confusion. What do all these scores mean? Do the two groups of murderers differ from one another on these various personality measures? It is difficult to know just by examining this disorganized array of numbers.

Psychologists rely on two types of statistics to help make sense of and draw meaningful conclusions from the data they collect: descriptive and inferential. **Descriptive statistics** use mathematical procedures in an

Descriptive statistics Statistical procedures that are used to summarize sets of scores with respect to central tendencies, variability, and correlations.

objective, uniform way to describe different aspects of numerical data. If you have ever computed your grade-point average, you already have used descriptive statistics. **Inferential statistics** use probability theory to make sound decisions about which results might have occurred simply through chance variation.

Descriptive Statistics

Descriptive statistics provide a summary picture of patterns in the data. They are used to describe sets of scores collected from one experimental participant or, more often, from different groups of participants. They are also used to describe relationships among variables. Thus, instead of trying to keep in mind all the scores obtained by each of the participants, researchers get indexes of the scores that are most *typical* for each group. They also get measures of how *variable* the scores are with respect to the typical score—whether the scores are spread out or clustered closely together. Let's see how researchers derive these measures.

FREQUENCY DISTRIBUTIONS

How would you summarize the data in Table S.1? To present a clear picture of how the various scores are distributed, we can draw up a **frequency distribution**—a summary of how frequently each of the various scores occurs. The shyness data are easy to summarize. Of the 19 scores, there are 9 *yes* and 10 *no* responses; almost all the *yes* responses are in Group 1, and almost all the *no* responses are in Group 2. However, the ego-overcontrol and sex-role scores do not fall into easy *yes* and *no* categories. To see how frequency distributions of numerical responses can allow informative comparisons between groups, we will focus on the sex-role scores.

Consider the sex-role data in Table S.1. The highest score is +61 (most feminine) and the lowest is −33 (most masculine). Of the 19 scores, 9 are positive and 10 negative—this means that 9 of the murderers described themselves as relatively feminine and 10 as relatively masculine. But how are these scores distributed between the groups? The first step in preparing a frequency distribution for a set of numerical data is to *rank order* the scores from highest to lowest. The rank ordering for the sex-role scores is shown in **Table S.2**. The second step is to group these rank-ordered scores into a smaller number of categories called *intervals*. In this study, 10 categories were used, with each cat-

TABLE S.2

Rank Ordering of Sex-Role Difference Scores

Highest	+61	−1	
	+41	−7	
	+23	−8	
	+19	−10	
	+6	−12	
	+5	−13	
	+5	−14	
	+4	−17	
	+3	−29	
		−33	Lowest

Note: + scores are more feminine; − scores are more masculine.

egory covering 10 possible scores. The third step is to construct a frequency distribution table, listing the intervals from highest to lowest and noting the *frequencies*—the number of scores within each interval. Our frequency distribution shows us that the sex-role scores are largely between −20 and +9 (see **Table S.3**). The majority of the inmates' scores did not deviate much from zero. That is, they were neither strongly positive nor strongly negative.

The data are now arranged in useful categories. The researchers' next step was to display the distributions in graphic form.

TABLE S.3

Frequency Distribution of Sex-Role Difference Scores

Category	Frequency
+60 to +69	1
+50 to +59	0
+40 to +49	1
+30 to +39	0
+20 to +29	1
+10 to +19	1
0 to +9	5
−10 to −1	4
−20 to −11	4
−30 to −21	1
−40 to −31	1

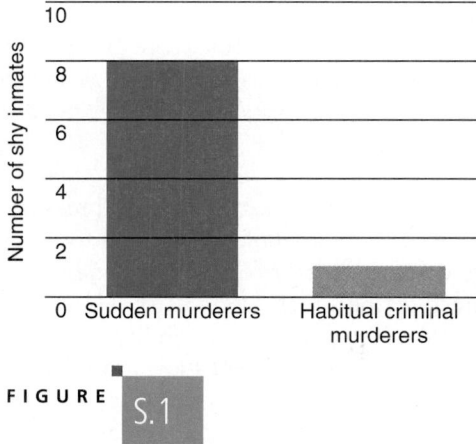

Shyness for Two Groups of Murderers (a Bar Graph)

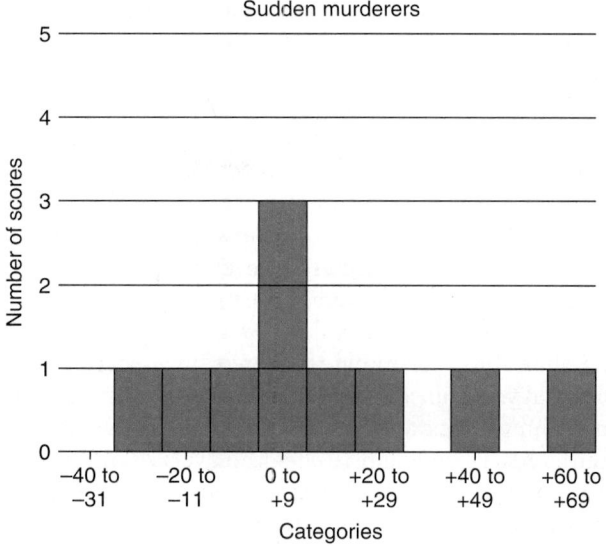

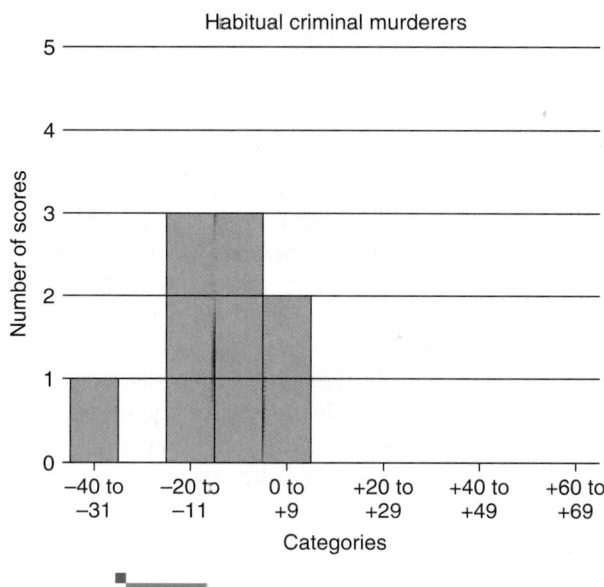

FIGURE S.2

Sex-Role Scores (Histograms)

GRAPHS

Distributions are often easier to understand when they are displayed in graphs. The simplest type of graph is a *bar graph*. Bar graphs allow you to see patterns in the data. We can use a bar graph to illustrate how many more sudden murderers than habitual criminal murderers described themselves as shy (see **Figure S.1**).

For more complex data, such as the sex-role scores, we can use a *histogram,* which is similar to a bar graph except that the categories are intervals—number categories instead of the name categories used in the bar graph. A histogram gives a visual picture of the number of scores in a distribution that are in each interval. It is easy to see from the sex-role scores shown in the histograms (in **Figure S.2**) that the distributions of scores are different for the two groups of murderers.

You can see from Figures S.1 and S.2 that the overall distributions of responses conform to two of the researcher's hypotheses. Sudden murderers were more likely to describe themselves as shy and were more likely to use feminine traits to describe themselves than were habitual criminal murderers.

MEASURES OF CENTRAL TENDENCY

So far, we have formed a general picture of how the scores are *distributed.* Tables and graphs increase our general understanding of research results, but we want to know more—for example, the one score that is most typical of the group as a whole. This score becomes particularly useful when we compare two or more groups; it is much easier to compare the typical scores of two groups than their entire distributions. A single, *representative* score that can be used as an index of the most typical score obtained by a group of participants is called a **measure of central tendency.** (It is located in the center of the distribution, and other scores tend to cluster around it.) Typically, psychologists use three different measures of central tendency: the *mode,* the *median,* and the *mean.*

The **mode** is the score that occurs more often than any other. For the measure of shyness, the modal response of

the sudden murderers was *yes*—eight out of ten said they were shy. Among habitual criminal murderers, the modal response was *no.* The sex-role scores for the sudden murderers had a mode of +5. Can you figure out what the mode of their ego-overcontrol scores is? The mode is the easiest index of central tendency to determine, but it is often the least useful. You will see one reason for this relative lack of usefulness if you notice that only one overcontrol

Measure of central tendency A statistic, such as a mean, median, or mode, that provides one score as representative of a set of observations.

Mode The score appearing most frequently in a set of observations; a measure of central tendency.

score lies above the mode of 17, and six lie below it. Although 17 is the score obtained most often, it may not fit your idea of "typical" or "central."

The **median** is more clearly a central score; it separates the upper half of the scores in a distribution from the lower half. The number of scores larger than the median is the same as the number that are smaller. When there are an odd number of scores, the median is the middle score; when there are an even number of scores, researchers most often average the two scores at the middle. For example, if you rank-order the sex-role scores of only the habitual criminal murderers on a separate piece of paper, you will see that the median score is –10, with four scores higher and four scores lower. For the sudden murderers, the median is +5—the average of the fifth and sixth scores, each of which happens to be +5. The median is not affected by extreme scores. For example, even if the sudden murderers' highest sex-role score had been +129 instead of +61, the median value would still have been +5. That score would still separate the upper half of the data from the lower half. The median is quite simply the score in the middle of the distribution.

The **mean** is what most people think of when they hear the word *average*. It is also the statistic most often used to describe a set of data. To calculate the mean, you add up all the scores in a distribution and divide by the total number of scores. The operation is summarized by the following formula:

$$M = (\Sigma X)/N$$

In this formula, M is the mean, X is each individual score, Σ (the Greek letter sigma) is the summation of what immediately follows it, and N is the total number of scores. Because the summation of all the sex-role scores (ΣX) is 115, and the total number of scores (N) is 10, the mean (M) of the sex-role scores of the sudden murderers would be calculated as follows:

$$M = 115/10 = 11.5$$

Try to calculate their mean overcontrol scores yourself. You should come up with a mean of 14.4.

Unlike the median, the mean *is* affected by the specific values of all scores in the distribution. Changing the value of an extreme score does change the value of the mean. For example, if the sex-role score of inmate 4 were +101 instead of +61, the mean for the whole group would increase from 11.5 to 15.5.

VARIABILITY

In addition to knowing which score is most representative of the distribution as a whole, it is useful to know how representative that measure of central tendency really is. Are most of the other scores fairly close to it or widely spread out? **Measures of variability** are statistics that describe the distribution of scores around some measure of central tendency.

Can you see why measures of variability are important? An example may help. Suppose you are a grade-school teacher. It is the beginning of the school year, and you will be teaching reading to a group of 30 second-graders. Knowing that the average child in the class can now read a first-grade-level book will help you to plan your lessons. You could plan better, however, if you knew how *similar* or how *divergent* the reading abilities of the 30 children were. Are they all at about the same level (low variability)? If so, then you can plan a fairly standard second-grade lesson. What if several can read advanced material and others can barely read at all (high variability)? Now the mean level is not so representative of the entire class, and you will have to plan a variety of lessons to meet the children's varied needs.

The simplest measure of variability is the **range,** the difference between the highest and the lowest values in a frequency distribution. For the sudden murderers' sex-role scores, the range is 90: (+61) – (–29). The range of their overcontrol scores is 10: (+19) – (+9). To compute the range, you need to know only two of the scores: the highest and the lowest.

The range is simple to compute, but psychologists often prefer measures of variability that are more sensitive and that take into account *all* the scores in a distribution, not just the extremes. One widely used measure is the **standard deviation (SD),** a measure of variability that indicates the *average* difference between the scores and their mean. To figure out the standard deviation of a distribution, you need to know the mean of the distribution and the individual scores. The general procedure involves subtracting the value of each individual score from the mean and then determining the average of those mean deviations. Here is the formula:

You should recognize most of the symbols from the formula for the mean. The expression ($X – M$) means "individual score minus the mean" and is commonly called the *deviation score.* The mean is subtracted from each score, and each resulting score is squared (to eliminate negative values). Then the mean of these deviations is calculated by summing them up (Σ) and dividing by the

Median The score in a distribution above and below which lie 50 percent of the other scores; a measure of central tendency.

Mean The arithmetic average of a group of scores; the most commonly used measure of central tendency.

Measures of variability A statistic, such as a range or standard deviation, that indicates how tightly the scores in a set of observations cluster together.

Range The difference between the highest and the lowest scores in a set of observations; the simplest measure of variability.

Standard deviation (SD) The average difference of a set of scores from their mean; a measure of variability.

Calculating the Standard Deviation of Sudden Murderers' Ego-Overcontrol Scores

Score (X)	Deviation (score minus mean) (X – M)	Deviations Squared (score minus mean)² (X – M)²
17	2.6	6.76
17	2.6	6.76
13	–1.4	1.96
17	2.6	6.76
13	–1.4	1.96
19	4.6	21.16
14	–.4	.16
9	–5.4	29.16
11	–3.4	11.56
14	–.4	.16

$$\text{Standard deviation} = SD = \sqrt{\frac{\Sigma (X - M)^2}{N}} \qquad 86.40 = \Sigma (X - M)^2$$

$$\sqrt{\frac{86.40}{10}} = \sqrt{8.64} = 2.94$$

$$SD = 2.94$$

number of observations (N). The symbol $\sqrt{\ }$ tells you to take the square root of the enclosed value to offset the previous squaring. The standard deviation of the over-control scores for the sudden murderers is calculated in **Table S.4.** Recall that the mean of these scores is 14.4. This, then, is the value that must be subtracted from each score to obtain the corresponding deviation scores.

The standard deviation tells us how variable a set of scores is. The larger the standard deviation, the more spread out the scores are. The standard deviation of the sex-role scores for the sudden murderers is 24.6, but the standard deviation for the habitual criminals is only 10.7. This shows that there was less variability in the habitual criminals group. Their scores clustered more closely about their mean than did those of the sudden murderers. When the standard deviation is small, the mean is a good representative index of the entire distribution. When the standard deviation is large, the mean is less typical of the whole group.

CORRELATION

Another useful tool in interpreting psychological data is the **correlation coefficient,** a measure of the nature and strength of the relationship between two variables (such as height and weight or sex-role score and ego-overcontrol score). It tells us the extent to which scores on one measure are associated with scores on the other. If peo-

ple with high scores on one variable tend to have *high* scores on the other variable, then the correlation coefficient will be positive (greater than 0). If, however, most people with high scores on one variable tend to have *low* scores on the other variable, then the correlation coefficient will be negative (less than 0). If there is *no* consistent relationship between the scores, the correlation will be close to 0 (see also Chapter 2).

Correlation coefficients range from +1 (perfect positive correlation) through 0 to –1 (perfect negative correlation). The further a coefficient is from 0 in *either* direction, the more closely related the two variables are, positively or negatively. Higher coefficients permit better predictions of one variable, given knowledge of the other.

In the Sudden Murderers Study, the correlation coefficient (symbolized as *r*) between the sex-role scores and the overcontrol scores turns out to be +0.35. The sex-role scores and the overcontrol scores are, thus, positively correlated—in general, individuals seeing themselves as more feminine also tend to be higher in overcontrol. However, the correlation is modest, compared with the highest possible value, +1.00, so we know that there are many exceptions to this relationship. If we had also measured the self-esteem of these inmates and found a correlation of –0.68 between overcontrol scores and self-esteem, it would mean that there was a negative correlation. If this were the case, we could say that the individuals who had high overcontrol scores tended to be lower in self-esteem. It would be a stronger relationship than the relationship between the sex-role scores and the overcontrol scores, because –0.68 is farther from 0, the point of no relationship, than is +0.35.

Inferential Statistics

We have used a number of descriptive statistics to characterize the data from the Sudden Murderers Study, and now we have an idea of the pattern of results. However, some basic questions remain unanswered. Recall that the research team hypothesized that sudden murderers would be shyer, more overcontrolled, and more feminine than habitual criminal murderers. After we have used descriptive statistics to compare average responses and variability in the two groups, it appears that there are some differences between the groups. But how do we know if the differences are large enough to be meaningful? If we repeated this study, with other sudden murderers and other habitual criminal murderers, would we expect to find the same pattern of results, or could these results have been an outcome of chance? If we could somehow measure the entire population of sudden murderers and habitual criminal murderers, would the

Correlation coefficient (r) A statistic that indicates the degree of relationship between two variables.

means and standard deviations be the same as those we found for these small samples?

Inferential statistics are used to answer these kinds of questions. They tell us which inferences we *can* make from our samples and which conclusions we can legitimately draw from our data. Inferential statistics use probability theory to determine the likelihood that a set of data occurred simply by chance variation.

THE NORMAL CURVE

In order to understand how inferential statistics work, we must look first at the special properties of a distribution called the *normal curve*. When data on a variable (for example, height, IQ, or overcontrol) are collected from a large number of individuals, the numbers obtained often fit a curve roughly similar to that shown in **Figure S.3.** Notice that the curve is symmetrical (the left half is a mirror image of the right) and bell shaped—high in the middle, where most scores are, and lower the farther you get from the mean. This type of curve is called a **normal curve,** or *normal distribution.* (A *skewed* distribution is one in which scores cluster toward one end instead of around the middle.)

Normal curve The symmetrical curve that represents the distribution of scores on many psychological attributes; allows researchers to make judgments of how unusual an observation or result is.

In a normal curve, the median, mode, and mean values are the same. A specific percentage of the scores can be predicted to fall under different sections of the curve. Figure S.3 shows IQ scores on the Stanford-Binet Intelligence Test. These scores have a mean of 100 and a standard deviation of 16. If you indicate standard deviations as distances from the mean along the baseline, you find that a little over 68 percent of all the scores are between the mean of 100 and 1 standard deviation above and below—between IQs of 84 and 116. Roughly another 27 percent of the scores are found between the first and second standard deviations below the mean (IQ scores between 68 and 84) and above the mean (IQ scores between 116 and 132). Less than 5 percent of the scores fall in the third standard deviation above and below the mean, and very few scores fall beyond—only about one-quarter of 1 percent.

Inferential statistics indicate the probability that the particular sample of scores obtained are actually related to whatever you are attempting to measure or whether they could have occurred by chance. For example, it is more likely that someone would have an IQ of 105 than an IQ of 140, but an IQ of 140 is more probable than one of 35.

A normal curve is also obtained by collecting a series of measurements whose differences are due only to chance. If you flip a coin 10 times in a row and record the number of heads and tails, you will probably get 5

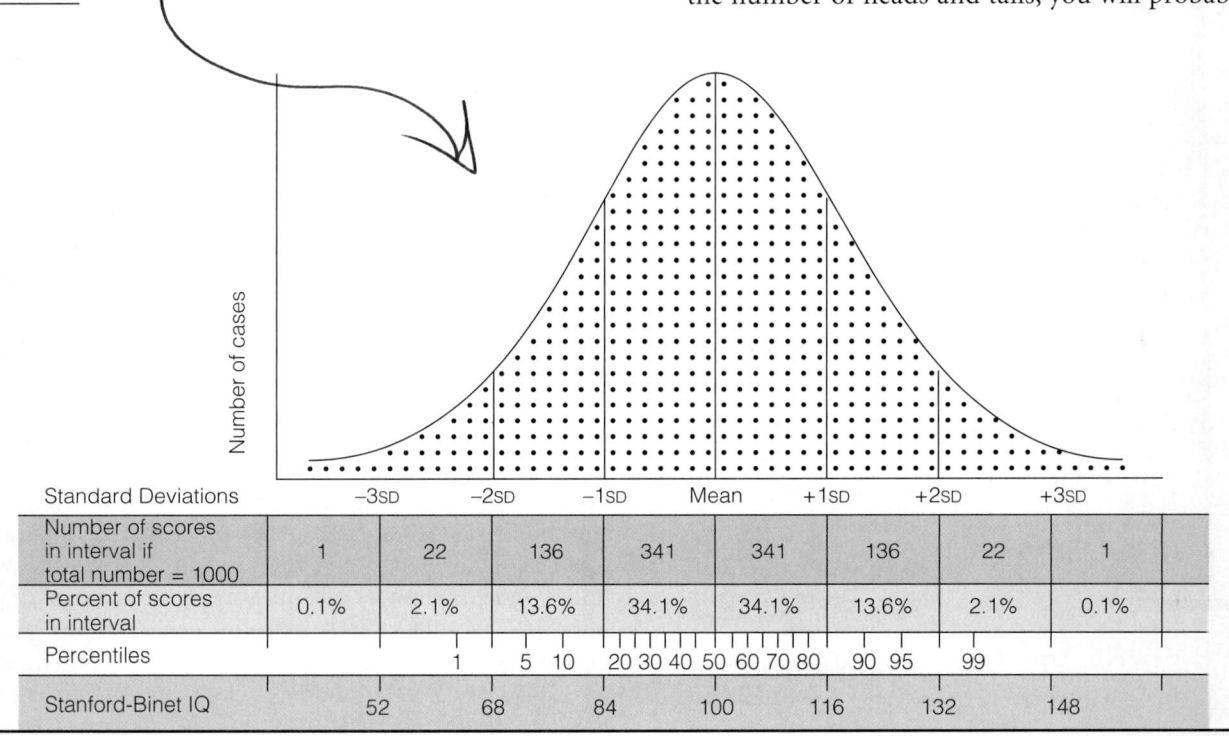

Standard Deviations	–3SD	–2SD	–1SD	Mean	+1SD	+2SD	+3SD	
Number of scores in interval if total number = 1000	1	22	136	341	341	136	22	1	
Percent of scores in interval	0.1%	2.1%	13.6%	34.1%	34.1%	13.6%	2.1%	0.1%	
Percentiles			1	5 10	20 30 40 50 60 70 80	90 95	99		
Stanford-Binet IQ		52	68	84	100	116	132	148	

FIGURE S.3

A Normal Curve

of each—most of the time. If you keep flipping the coin for 100 sets of 10 tosses, you probably will get a few sets with all heads or no heads, more sets where the number is between these extremes, and, most typically, more sets where the number is about half each way. If you made a graph of your 1,000 tosses, you would get one that closely fits a normal curve, such as the one in the figure.

STATISTICAL SIGNIFICANCE

A researcher who finds a difference between the mean scores for two samples must ask if it is a *real* difference or if it occurred simply because of chance. Because chance differences have a normal distribution, a researcher can use the normal curve to answer this question.

A simple example will help to illustrate the point. Suppose your psychology professor wants to see if the gender of a person proctoring a test makes a difference in the test scores obtained from male and from female students. For this purpose, the professor randomly assigns half of the students to a male proctor and half to a female proctor. The professor then compares the mean score of each group. The two mean scores would probably be fairly similar; any slight difference would most likely be due to chance. Why? Because if only chance is operating and both groups are from the same population (no difference), then the means of male proctor and female proctor samples should be fairly close most of the time. From the percentages of scores found in different parts of the normal distribution, you know that less than a third of the scores in the male proctor condition should be greater than one standard deviation above or below the female proctor mean. The chances of getting a male proctor mean score more than three standard deviations above or below most of your female proctor means would be very small. A professor who *did* get a difference that great would feel fairly confident that the difference is a real one and is somehow related to the gender of the test proctor. The next question would be *how* that variable influences test scores.

If male and female students were randomly assigned to each type of proctor, it would be possible to analyze whether an overall difference found between the proctors was consistent across both student groups or was limited to only one sex. Imagine the data show that male proctors grade female students higher than do female proctors, but both grade male students the same. Your professor could use a statistical inference procedure to estimate the probability that an observed difference could have occurred by chance. This computation is based on the size of the difference and the spread of the scores.

By common agreement, psychologists accept a difference as "real" when the probability that it might be due to chance is less than 5 in 100 (indicated by the notation

$p < .05$). A **significant difference** is one that meets this criterion. However, in some cases, even stricter probability levels are used, such as $p < .01$ (less than 1 in 100) and $p < .001$ (less than 1 in 1000).

With a statistically significant difference, a researcher can draw a conclusion about the behavior that was under investigation. There are many different types of tests for estimating the statistical significance of sets of data. The type of test chosen for a particular case depends on the design of the study, the form of the data, and the size of the groups. We will mention only one of the most common tests, the *t-test*, which may be used when an investigator wants to know if the difference between the means of two groups is statistically significant.

We can use a *t*-test to see if the mean sex-role score of the sudden murderers is significantly different from that of the habitual criminal murderers. The *t*-test uses a mathematical procedure to confirm the conclusion you may have drawn from Figure S.2: The distributions of sex-role scores for the two groups is sufficiently different to be "real." If we carry out the appropriate calculations—which evaluate the difference between the two means as a function of the variability around those two means—we find that there is a very slim chance, less than 5 in 100 ($p < .05$), of obtaining such a large *t* value if no true difference exists. The difference is, therefore, statistically significant, and we can feel more confident that there is a real difference between the two groups. The sudden murderers *did* rate themselves as more feminine than did the habitual criminal murderers. On the other hand, the difference between the two groups of murderers in overcontrol scores turns out not to be statistically significant ($p < .10$), so we must be more cautious in talking about this difference. There is a trend in the predicted direction—the difference is one that would occur by chance only 10 times in 100. However, the difference is not within the standard 5-in-100 range. (The difference in shyness, analyzed using another statistical test for frequency of scores, is highly significant.) So, by using inferential statistics, we are able to answer some of the basic questions with which we began, and we are closer to understanding the psychology of people who suddenly change from mild-mannered, shy individuals into sudden murderers. Any conclusion, however, is only a statement of the *probable* relationship between the events that were investigated; it is never one of certainty. Truth in science is provisional, always open to revision by later data from better studies, developed from better hypotheses.

Significant difference A difference between experimental groups or conditions that would have occurred by chance less than an accepted criterion; in psychology, the criterion most often used is a probability of less than 5 times out of 100, or p < .05.

■ Becoming a Wise Consumer of Statistics

Now that we have considered what statistics are, how they are used, and what they mean, we should briefly talk about how they can be misused. Many people accept unsupported "facts" that are bolstered by the air of authority of a statistic. Others choose to believe or disbelieve what the statistics say without having any idea of how to question the numbers that are presented in support of a product, politician, or proposal. At the end of Chapter 2, we gave you some suggestions about how you can become a wiser research consumer. Based on this brief survey of statistics, we can extend that advice to situations in which people make specific statistical claims.

There are many ways to give a misleading impression using statistics. The decisions made at all stages of research—from who the participants are to how the study is designed, what statistics are selected, and how they are used—can have a profound effect on the conclusions that can be drawn from the data.

The group of participants can make a large difference that can easily remain undetected when the results are reported. For example, a survey of views on abortion rights will yield very different results if conducted in a small fundamentalist community in the South rather than at a university in New York City. Likewise, a pro-life group surveying the opinions of its membership will very likely arrive at conclusions that differ from those obtained by the same survey conducted by a pro-choice group.

Even if the participants are randomly selected and not biased by the methodology, the statistics can produce misleading results if the assumptions of the statistics are violated. For example, suppose 20 people take an IQ test; 19 of them receive scores between 90 and 110, and 1 receives a score of 220. The mean of the group will be strongly elevated by that one outlying high score. With this sort of a data set, it would be much more accurate to present the median or the mode, which would accurately report the group's generally average intelligence, rather than the mean, which would make it look as if the average member of this group was of high IQ. This sort of bias is especially powerful in a small sample. If, on the other hand, the number of people in this group were 2,000 instead of 20, the one extreme outlier would make virtually no difference, and the mean would be a legitimate summary of the group's intelligence.

One good way to avoid falling for this sort of deception is to check on the size of the sample—large samples are less likely to be misleading than small ones. Another check is to look at the median or the mode as well as the mean—the results can be interpreted with more confidence if they are similar than if they are different. You should always closely examine the methodology and results of the research reported. Check to see if the experimenters report their sample size, measures of variability, and significance levels. Try to find out if the methods they used measure accurately and consistently whatever they claim to be investigating.

Statistics are the backbone of psychological research. They are used to understand observations and to determine whether the findings are, in fact, correct. Through the methods we have described, psychologists can prepare a frequency distribution of data and find the central tendencies and variability of the scores. They can use the correlation coefficient to determine the strength and direction of the association between sets of scores. Finally, psychological investigators can then find out how representative the observations are and whether they are significantly different from the general population. Statistics can also be used poorly or deceptively, misleading those who do not understand them. But when statistics are applied correctly and ethically, they allow researchers to expand the body of psychological knowledge.

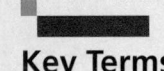

Key Terms

correlation coefficient *(r)* (p. 43)
descriptive statistics (p. 39)
frequency distribution (p. 40)

inferential statistics (p. 40)
mean (p. 42)
measure of central tendency (p. 41)
measures of variability (p. 42)
median (p. 42)

mode (p. 41)
normal curve (p. 44)
range (p. 42)
significant difference (p. 45)
standard deviation (SD) (p. 42)

the biological bases of behavior

3

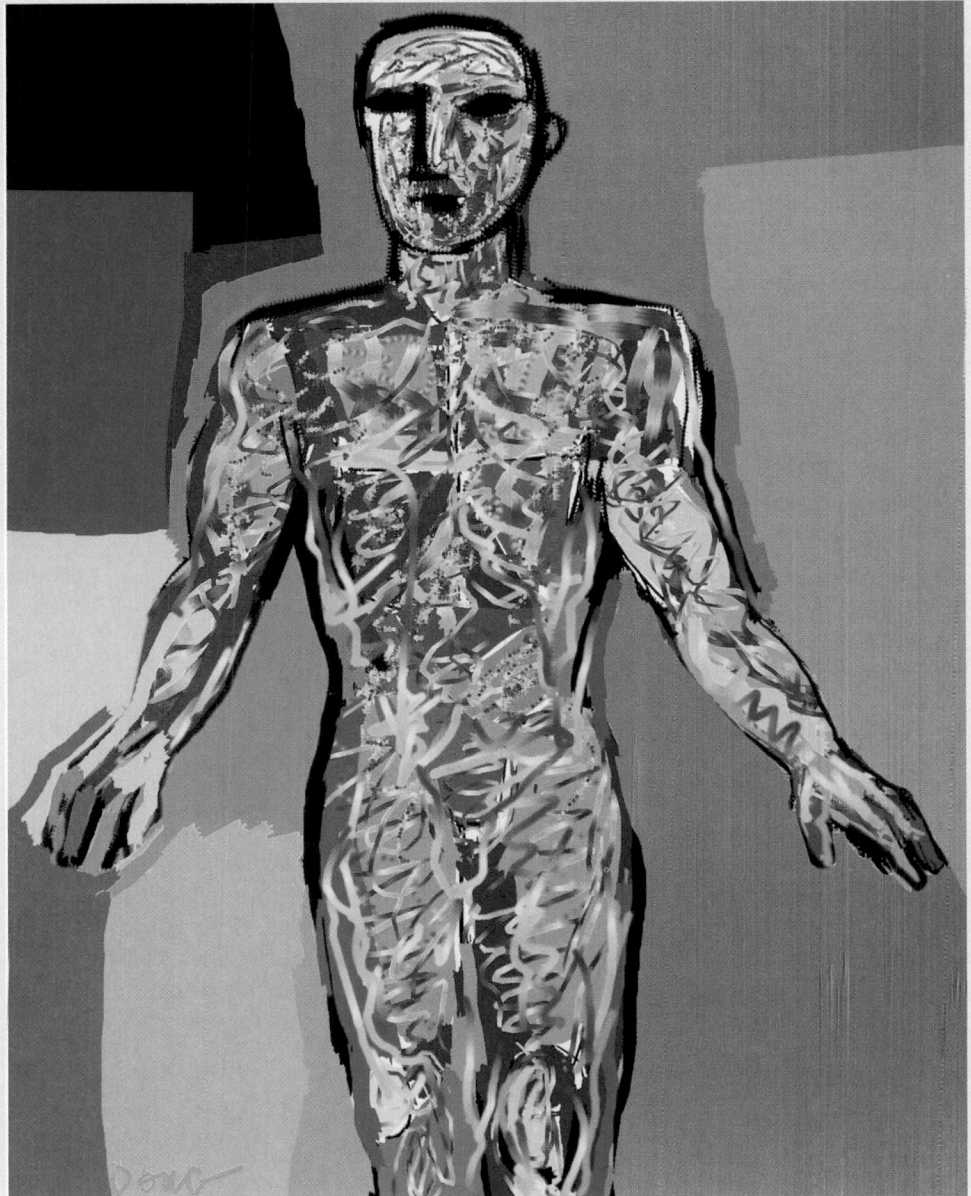

■ **HEREDITY AND BEHAVIOR**
Evolution and Natural
Selection • Variation in the
Human Genotype

■ **BIOLOGY AND BEHAVIOR**
Eavesdropping on the Brain
• The Nervous System •
Brain Structures and Their
Functions • Hemispheric
Lateralization • The Endocrine
System

■ **PSYCHOLOGY IN
THE 21ST CENTURY:
ADVANCES IN LOCALIZING
BRAIN FUNCTION**

■ **THE NERVOUS SYSTEM
IN ACTION**
The Neuron • Action
Potentials • Synaptic
Transmission •
Neurotransmitters
and Their Functions

■ **PSYCHOLOGY IN YOUR
LIFE: HOW DO LIFE
EXPERIENCES AFFECT
YOUR BRAIN?**

■ **RECAPPING MAIN POINTS**
Key Terms

ON SEPTEMBER 13, 1848, a railroad foreman, Phineas P. Gage, suffered an accident in which a 3-foot, 7-inch-long pole was blown, as the result of an unexpected explosion, through his head. Still conscious, Gage was taken by wagon to his hotel, where he was able to walk upstairs. Although Gage was near death for the next two to three weeks, by the middle of October he was recovering steadily. John M. Harlow, the doctor who reported the case to the Massachusetts Medical Society in 1868, was clear that Gage's survival was considered a medical miracle:

> The case occurred nearly twenty years ago, in an obscure town (Cavendish, Vt.), was attended and reported by an obscure country physician, and was received by Metropolitan Doctors with several grains of caution, insomuch that many utterly refused to believe that the man had risen, until they had thrust their fingers into the hole in his head.... (Harlow, 1868, p. 329)

In fact, Gage's physical impairment was remarkably slight: He lost vision in his left eye, and the left side of his face was partially paralyzed, but his posture, movement, and speech were all unimpaired. Yet, psychologically, he was a changed man, as his doctor's account made clear:

> The equilibrium or balance, so to speak, between his intellectual faculties and animal propensities seems to have been destroyed. He is fitful, irreverent, indulging at times in the grossest profanity (which was not previously his custom), manifesting but little deference for his fellows, impatient of restraint or advice when it conflicts with his desires, at times pertinaciously obstinate, yet capricious and vacillating, devising many plans of future operation, which are no sooner arranged than they are abandoned in turn for others appearing more feasible. A child in his intellectual capacity and manifestations, he has the animal passions of a strong man. Previous to his injury, though untrained in schools, he possessed a well-balanced mind, and was looked upon by those who knew him as a shrewd, smart businessman, very energetic and persistent in executing all his plans of operation. In this regard his mind was radically changed, so decidedly that his friends and acquaintances said he was "no longer Gage." (pp. 339–340)

Gage's injury came at a time when scientists were just beginning to form hypotheses about the links between brain functions and complex behavior. Although no one would seek Gage's type of fame, Gage's story remains with us because he provided the earliest documented evidence for a brain basis for psychological processes.

What makes you a unique individual? From the tale of Phineas Gage, you learn that the answer to this question resides, in part, in your brain—and, more generally, in your biological makeup. To help you understand what makes you different from the people around you, we will describe the role that heredity plays in shaping your life and in forming the brain that controls your experiences. Of course, you can only appreciate these differences against the background of what you have in common with all other people. You might, therefore, think of this as a chapter about biological potential: What possibilities for behavior define the human species, and how do those possibilities emerge for particular members of that species?

In a way, this chapter stands as proof of one remarkable aspect of your biological potential: Your brain is sufficiently complex to carry out a systematic examination of its own functions. Why is this so remarkable? The human brain is sometimes likened to a spectacular computer: At only three pounds, your brain contains more cells than there are stars in our entire galaxy—over 100 billion cells that communicate and store information with astonishing efficiency. But even the world's mightiest computer is incapable of reflecting on the rules that guide its own operation. You are, thus, much more than a computer; your consciousness allows you to put your vast computational power to work trying to determine your species' own rules for operation. The research we describe in this chapter arose from the special human desire for self-understanding.

For many students, this chapter will pose a greater challenge than the rest of *Psychology and Life*. It requires that you learn some anatomy and many new terms that seem far removed from the information you may have expected to get from an introduction to psychology. However, understanding your biological nature will enable you to appreciate more fully the complex interplay among the brain, mind, behavior, and environment that creates the unique experience of being human.

Our goal for this chapter is to allow you to understand how biology contributes to the creation of unique individuals against a shared background potential. To approach this goal, we first describe how evolution and heredity determine your biology and behavior. We then see how laboratory and clinical research provides a view into the workings of the brain, the nervous system, and the endocrine system. We next examine some intriguing relationships between these biological functions and some aspects of life experiences. Finally, we consider differences among individuals in the relationship of brain to behavior.

■ Heredity and Behavior

In Chapter 1, we defined one of the major goals of psychology to be the discovery of the causes underlying the variety of human behavior. An important dimension of causal explanation within psychology is defined by the end points of *nature* versus *nurture,* or *heredity* versus *environment.* Consider, as we did in Chapter 1, the question of the roots of aggressive behavior. You might imagine that individuals are aggressive by virtue of some aspect of their biological makeup: They may have inherited a tendency toward violence from one of their parents. Alternatively, you might imagine that all humans are about equally predisposed to aggression and that the degree of aggression individuals display arises in response to features of the environment in which they are raised. The correct answer to this question has a profound impact on how society treats individuals who are overly aggressive—by focusing resources on changing certain environments or on changing aspects of the people themselves. You need to be able to discriminate the forces of heredity from the forces of environment.

Because the features of environments can be directly observed, it is often easier to understand how they affect people's behavior. You can, for example, actually watch a parent acting aggressively toward a child and wonder what consequences such treatment might have on the

The physical characteristics determined by heredity are often relatively easy to observe. Can you find physical similarities across generations in your own family?

child's later tendency toward aggression; you can observe the overcrowded and impoverished settings in which some children grow up and wonder whether these features of the environment lead to aggressive behaviors. The biological forces that shape behavior, by comparison, are never plainly visible to the naked eye. To make the biology of behavior more comprehensible to you, we will begin by describing some of the basic principles that shape a species's potential repertoire of behaviors—elements of the theory of evolution—and then describe how behavioral variation is passed from generation to generation.

Evolution and Natural Selection

In 1831, **Charles Darwin,** fresh out of college with a degree in theology, set sail from England on HMS *Beagle,* an ocean research vessel, for a five-year cruise to survey the coast of South America. During the trip, Darwin collected everything that crossed his path: marine animals, birds, insects, plants, fossils, seashells, and rocks. His extensive notes became the foundation for his books on topics ranging from geology to emotion to zoology. The book for which he is most remembered is *The Origin of Species,* published in 1859. In this work, Darwin set forth science's grandest theory: the evolution of life on planet Earth.

NATURAL SELECTION

Darwin developed his theory of evolution by reflecting on the species of animals he had encountered while on his voyage. One of the many places *Beagle* visited was the Galápagos Islands, a volcanic archipelago off the west coast of South America. These islands are a haven for diverse forms of wildlife, including 13 species of finches, now known as Darwin's finches. Darwin wondered how so many different species of finches could have come to inhabit the islands. He reasoned that they couldn't have migrated from the mainland, because those species didn't exist there. He suggested, therefore, that the variety of species reflected the operation of a process he came to call **natural selection.**

Darwin's theory suggests that each species of finch emerged from a common set of ancestors. Originally, a small flock of finches found their way to one of the islands; they mated among themselves and eventually their number multiplied. Over time, some finches migrated to different islands in the archipelago. What happened next was the process of natural selection. Food resources and living conditions—*habitats*—vary considerably from island to island. Some of the islands are lush with berries and seeds, others are covered with cacti, and others have plenty of insects. At first, the populations on different islands were similar—there was *variation* among the groups of finches on each island.

> **Natural selection** Darwin's theory that favorable adaptations to features of the environment allow some members of a species to reproduce more successfully than others.

However, because food resources on the islands were limited, birds were most likely to survive and reproduce if the shape of their beak was well suited to the food sources available on the island. For example, birds that migrated to islands rich in berries and seeds were more likely to survive and reproduce if they had thick beaks. On those islands, birds with thinner, more pointed beaks, unsuitable for crushing or breaking open seeds, died. The environment of each island determined which among the original population of finches would live and reproduce and which would more likely perish, leaving no offspring. Over time, this led to very different populations on each island and permitted the different species of Darwin's finches to evolve from the original ancestral group.

In general, the theory of natural selection suggests that organisms well adapted to their environment, whatever it happens to be, will produce more offspring than those less well adapted. Over time, those organisms possessing traits more favorable for survival will become more numerous than those not possessing those traits. In evolutionary terms, an individual's success is measured by the number of offspring he or she produces.

Contemporary research has shown that natural selection can have dramatic effects, even in the short run. In a series of studies by **Peter** and **Rosemary Grant** (Grant & Grant, 1989; Grant, 1986; Weiner, 1994), involving several species of Darwin's finches, records were kept of rainfall, food supply, and the population size of these finches on one of the Galápagos Islands. In 1976, the population numbered well over 1,000 birds. The following year brought a murderous drought that wiped out most of the food supply. The smallest seeds were the first to be depleted, leaving only larger and tougher seeds. That year the finch population decreased by more than 80 percent. However, smaller finches with smaller beaks died at a higher frequency than larger finches with thicker beaks. Consequently, as Darwin would have predicted, the larger birds became more numerous in the following years. Why? Because only they, with their larger bodies and thicker beaks, were fit enough to respond to the environmental change caused by the drought. Interestingly, in 1983, rain was plentiful, and seeds, especially the smaller ones, became abundant. As a result, smaller birds outsurvived larger birds, probably because their beaks were better suited for pecking the smaller seeds. The Grants' study shows that natural selection can have noticeable effects even over short periods. Researchers continue to document the impact of environments on natural selection in diverse species, including the European fruit fly (Huey et al., 2000) and the stickleback fish (Rundle et al., 2000).

GENOTYPES AND PHENOTYPES

The example of the ebb and flow of finch populations demonstrates why Darwin characterized the course of evolution as *survival of the fittest.* Imagine that each environment poses some range of difficulties for each species of living beings. Those members of the species who possess the range of physical and psychological attributes best adapted to the environment are most likely to survive. To the extent that the attributes that foster survival can be passed from one generation to another—and stresses in the environment endure over time—the species is likely to evolve.

To examine the process of natural selection in more detail, we must introduce some of the vocabulary of evolutionary theory. Let us focus on an individual finch. At conception, that finch inherited a **genotype,** or genetic structure, from its parents. In the context of a particular environment, this genotype determined the finch's development and behavior. The outward appearance and repertoire of behaviors of the finch are known as its **phenotype.** For our finch, its genotype may have interacted with the environment to yield the phenotype of *small beak* and *able to peck smaller seeds.* If seeds of all types were plentiful, this phenotype would have no particular bearing on the finch's survival. If, however, only small seeds were available, our finch would be at a *selective advantage* with respect to finches with large beaks. If only large seeds were available, our finch would be at a disadvantage.

Only finches that survive can reproduce. Only those animals that reproduce can pass on their genotypes. Therefore, if the environment continued to provide only small seeds, over several generations the finches would probably come to have almost exclusively small beaks—with the consequence that they would be almost exclu-

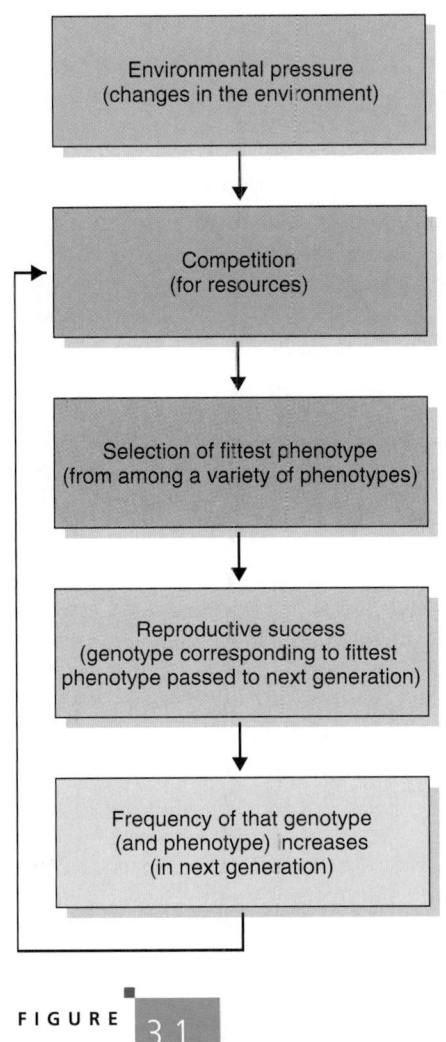

FIGURE 3.1

How Natural Selection Works

Environmental changes create competition for resources among species members. Only those individuals possessing characteristics instrumental in coping with these changes will survive and reproduce. The next generation will have a greater number of individuals possessing these genetically based traits.

sively capable of eating only small seeds. In this way, forces in the environment can shape a species's repertoire of possible behaviors. **Figure 3.1** provides a simplified model of the process of natural selection. Let us now apply these ideas to human evolution.

Genotype The genetic structure an organism inherits from its parents.

Phenotype The observable characteristics of an organism, resulting from the interaction between the organism's genotype and its environment.

By looking backward to the circumstances in which the human species evolved, you can begin to understand why certain physical and behavioral features are part of the biological endowment of the entire human species. In the evolution of our species, natural selection favored two major adaptations—bipedalism and encephalization. Together, they made possible the rise of human civilization. *Bipedalism* refers to the ability to walk upright, and *encephalization* refers to increases in brain size. These two adaptations are responsible for most, if not all, of the other major advances in human evolution, including cultural development (see **Figure 3.2**). As our ancestors evolved the ability to walk upright, they were able to explore new environments and exploit new resources. As brain size increased, our ancestors became more intelligent and developed capacities for complex thinking, reasoning, remembering, and planning. (However, the evolution of a bigger brain did not guarantee that humans would become more intelligent—what was important was the kind of tissue that developed and expanded within the brain.) The genotype coding for intelligent and mobile phenotypes slowly squeezed out other, less well-adapted genotypes from the human gene pool, affording only intelligent bipeds the opportunity to reproduce.

After bipedalism and encephalization, perhaps the most important evolutionary milestone for our species was the advent of *language* (Bickerton, 1990; Holden, 1998). Think of the tremendous adaptive advantages that language conferred on early humans. Simple instructions for making tools, finding a good hunting or fishing spot, and avoiding danger would save time, effort, and lives. Instead of learning every one of life's lessons firsthand, by trial and error, humans could benefit from experiences shared by others. Conversation, even humor, would strengthen the social bonds among members of a naturally gregarious species. Most important, the advent of language would provide for the transmission of accumulated wisdom, from one generation to future generations.

Language is the basis for *cultural evolution,* which is the tendency of cultures to respond adaptively, through learning, to environmental change. Cultural evolution has given rise to major advances in toolmaking, to improved agricultural practices, and to the development and refinement of industry and technology. Cultural evolution allows our species to make very rapid adjustments to changes in environmental conditions. Adaptations to the use of personal computers, for example, have arisen in only the last 20 years. Even so, cultural evolution could not occur without genotype coding for the capacities to learn and to think abstractly. Culture—including art, literature, music, scientific knowledge, and philanthropic activities—is possible only because of the potential of the human genotype.

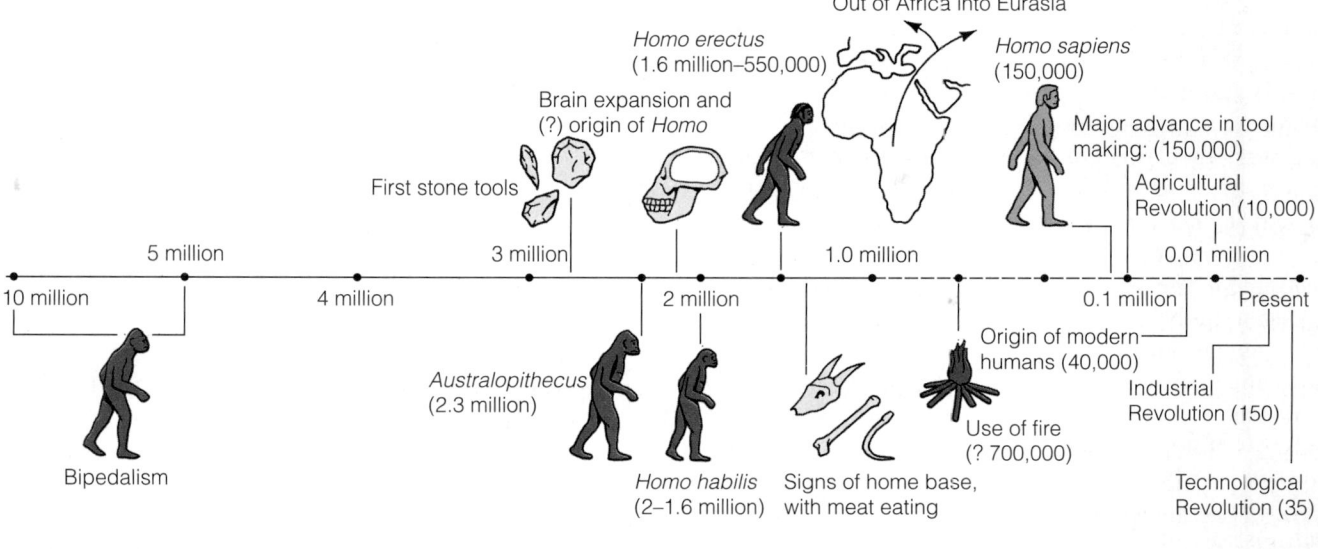

FIGURE 3.2

Approximate Time Line for the Major Events in Human Evolution

Bipedalism freed the hands for grasping and tool use. Encephalization provided the capacity for higher cognitive processes such as abstract thinking and reasoning. These two adaptations probably led to the other major advances in human evolution.

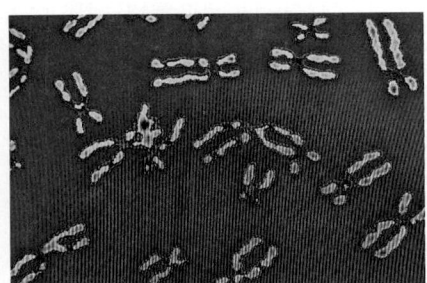

Human chromosomes—at the moment of conception, you inherited 23 from your mother and 23 from your father.

Variation in the Human Genotype

You have seen that the conditions in which humans evolved favored the evolution of important shared biological potential: for example, bipedalism and the capacity for thought and language. There remains, however, considerable variation within that shared potential. Your mother and father have endowed you with a part of what their parents, grandparents, and all past generations of their family lines have given them, resulting in a unique biological blueprint and timetable for your development. The study of the mechanisms of **heredity**—the inheritance of physical and psychological traits from ancestors—is called **genetics.**

BASIC GENETICS

In the nucleus of each of your cells is genetic material called **DNA** (deoxyribonucleic acid). DNA is organized into tiny units, called **genes.** The exact number of genes in the human genome (collection of genes) is still unknown; estimates vary widely from about 30,000 to about 150,000 (Pennisi, 2000). Genes contain the instructions for the production of proteins. These proteins regulate the body's physiological processes and the expression of phenotypic traits: body build, physical strength, intelligence, and many behavior patterns.

Heredity The biological transmission of traits from parents to offspring.

Genetics The study of the inheritance of physical and psychological traits from ancestors.

DNA (deoxyribonucleic acid) The physical basis for the transmission of genetic information.

Genes The biological units of heredity; discrete sections of chromosomes responsible for transmission of traits.

Sex chromosomes Chromosomes that contain the genes that code for the development of male or female characteristics.

Human behavior genetics The area of study that evaluates the genetic component of individual differences in behaviors and traits.

Genes are found on rodlike structures, known as *chromosomes.* At the very instant you were conceived, you inherited from your parents 46 chromosomes—23 from your mother and 23 from your father. Each of these chromosomes contains thousands of genes—the union of a sperm and an egg results in only one of many billion possible gene combinations. The **sex chromosomes** are those that contain genes coding for development of male or female physical characteristics. You inherited an X chromosome from your mother and either an X or a Y chromosome from your father. An XX combination codes for development of female characteristics; an XY combination codes for development of male characteristics.

Although, on average, you have 50 percent of your genes in common with your brothers or sisters, your set of genes is unique unless you have an identical twin. The difference in your genes is one reason why you differ, physically and behaviorally, from your brothers and sisters. The other reason is that you do not live in exactly the same environment as they do. An important goal of psychology, once again, is to understand the balance between these two sources of influence.

GENES AND BEHAVIOR

We have seen that evolutionary processes have allowed a considerable amount of variation to remain in human genotypes; the interactions of these genotypes with particular environments produces variation in human phenotypes. Researchers in the field of **human behavior genetics** unite genetics and psychology to explore the causal link between inheritance and behavior (Maccoby, 2000; Plomin & Rende, 1991; Plomin et al., 1994).

To explore the logic of behavioral genetics, we will describe one surprising finding: Your baseline level of subjective well-being—the *average* happiness you will experience across your lifespan—may have a genetic component.

HOW WE KNOW

THE HERITABILITY OF HAPPINESS To examine the genetic component of happiness, researchers used a classic methodology in behavior genetics: They examined the extent to which *monozygotic (MZ)* twins (those who are genetically identical) and *dizygotic (DZ)* twins (so-called fraternal twins who, like siblings, share only half their genes) showed similar patterns on the behavior of interest—in this case, reports of well-being. The twins' happiness levels were measured by questionnaires that asked them to respond to statements such as, "Taking the good with the bad, how happy and contented are you on the average now, compared with other people?"

The researchers examined two sets of responses from MZ and DZ twins, obtained when they were roughly 20 and 30 years old. They performed a "cross-twin, cross-time" analysis (see **Figure 3.3**): They calculated the extent to which one twin's happiness as a 30-year-old was correlated with his or her brother's or sister's happiness at age 20. The researchers found that there was virtually no relationship for the DZ twins. However, for the MZ twins, 80 percent of the relationship in the ratings from ages 20 to 30 could be explained by this cross-twin analysis. The researchers suggested that this pattern within the pairs of MZ twins is best explained if baseline happiness—the average amount of happiness each person will experience across the lifespan—has a strong genetic component (Lykken & Tellegen, 1996).

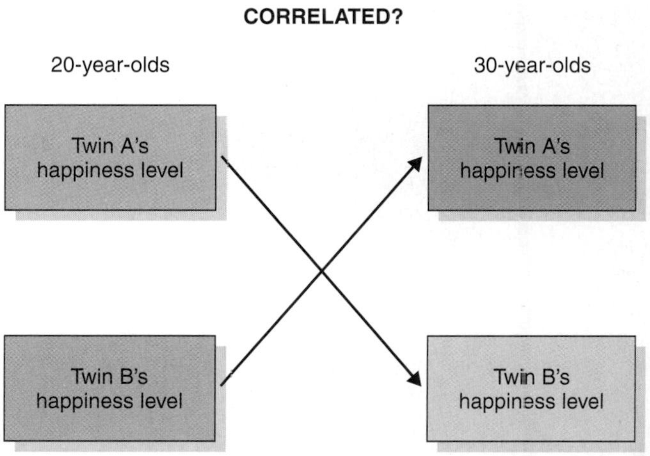

Are you surprised by the claim that average happiness has a strong genetic component? You might think that your happiness would be more strongly affected by the environment: Are you in a romantic relationship? How hard are your courses? What are the obstacles in your life? The researchers propose that such environmental events cause variation around an average level of happiness that was "set" at birth. As an analogy, think of the way the thermostat in your home works. Suppose you set it to 68°F—environmental events will cause variation around this temperature, but on average the temperature should be 68°F. The research on happiness suggests that each of us has a set happiness level—analogous, for example, to 48°F, 68°F, or 88°F—which remains our average in the face of life's ups and downs.

But is it necessarily the case that there is a gene (or genes) specifically for *happiness*? Remember from Chapter 2 that "correlation is not causation." It could be the case that some other aspects of an individual's behaviors or experiences mediate the genetic influence on happiness: The different pattern for identical and fraternal twins tells us only that some elements of the genome come to have an influence on happiness. Suppose that your genetic endowment determined, in part, how you interpret the events that happen to you—so that your brother or sister would be genetically more likely than you to be bothered by minor hassles. You might be happier on the whole, but genetics would affect your interpretations of the world; those interpretations would

Sociobiology A research field that focuses on evolutionary explanations for the social behavior and social systems of humans and other animal species.

FIGURE 3.3

A Research Design to Study the Genetic Basis of Happiness

Researchers examined the correlation between one twin's happiness level at age 20 and the other twin's happiness level at age 30.

give rise to happiness differences. Or, it could be the case that average well-being represents a balance between genes that affect positive and negative emotions (Hamer, 1996). Whatever its exact origin, the existence of this relationship, and others like it, suggests that the genes you receive from your parents have much broader effects than just determining your eye color or height.

Remember, though, that genes do not code for destinies. Just because you're tall doesn't mean you will play basketball. Just because you're a woman doesn't mean you will bear children. Also keep in mind that genotypes are expressed in particular contexts. Physical size, for example, is determined jointly by genetic factors and nutritional environment. Physical strength can be developed in both males and females through special exercise programs. Intellectual growth is determined by both genetic potential and educational experiences. Neither genes nor the environment alone determines who you are or what kind of person you ultimately become.

The study of human behavior genetics most often focuses on the origins of individual differences: What factors in your individual genetic inheritance help to explain the way you think and behave? Researchers in the field of **sociobiology** attempt to answer that question with respect to broader patterns of behavior: This field focuses on evolutionary explanations for the social behavior and social systems of humans and other animal species. Let's consider happiness some more. We just described a behavior genetics study that examined individual differences in happiness, but how might an evolutionary perspective explain the human species's general ability to experience

How does research in behavior genetics affect your beliefs about the effects of environmental events on lifelong happiness?

happiness? Buss (2000) suggests that some limits are placed on human happiness by the "discrepancies between modern and ancestral environments" (p. 15). For example, although humans evolved in the context of small groups, many people now live in large urban environments in which they are mostly surrounded by large numbers of total strangers. We no longer have close bonds to the group of individuals that share our space—the types of bonds that could help us weather crises to experience happy lives. What can be done? Although you cannot turn back the tide of cultural evolution that has brought these changes about, you can try to counteract these changes by increasing your closeness to your family members and to your friends (Buss, 2000). Can you see the contrast between the sociobiological emphasis on the human species in a particular environment versus the behavior genetic emphasis on variation within general species patterns?

SUMMING UP

Species originate and change over time because of natural selection, which is the tendency of organisms to reproduce at different rates due to the interaction of phenotypic traits with the environment. The two most important adaptations in the evolution of humans were bipedalism and encephalization. The development of language allowed for rapid cultural evolution.

Researchers in human behavior genetics explore the link between the genes people inherit and their behavior. Researchers in sociobiology use evolutionary explanations to analyze broader patterns of a species's social behavior.

Biology and Behavior

We turn our attention now to the remarkable products of the human genotype: the biological systems that make possible the full range of thought and performance. Long before Darwin made preparations for his trip aboard *Beagle*, scientists, philosophers, and others debated the role that biological processes play in everyday life. One of the most important figures in the history of brain studies was the French philosopher **René Descartes** (1596–1650). Descartes proposed what at that time was a very new and very radical idea: The human body is an "animal machine" that can be understood scientifically—by discovering natural laws through empirical observation. Descartes argued that human action is a mechanical reflex to environmental stimulation. He proposed that physical energy excites a sense organ. When stimulated, the sense organ transmits the excitation to the brain in the form of "animal spirits." The brain then transmits the animal spirits to the appropriate set of muscles, setting in motion a reflex response.

Descartes's notion of the reflex did not have valid scientific support until 1906, when **Sir Charles Sherrington** discovered that reflexes are composed of direct connections between sensory and motor nerve fibers at the level of the spinal cord. Sherrington also developed the idea that the nervous system involves both *excitatory* (increasing neural activity) and *inhibitory* (decreasing neural activity) processes. It was also not until the beginning of the 20th century that scientists knew anything at all about the basic unit of the nervous system, the *neuron*. **Santiago Ramón y Cajal** detected the physical gaps between adjacent neurons and theorized about the flow of information from one neuron to the next. Fifty years later, with the aid of the electron microscope, other scientists proved his ideas. In 1948, **Donald Hebb** proposed that the brain is not merely a mass of tissue but a highly integrated series of structures, or "cell assemblies," that perform specific functions.

Researchers in the tradition we have traced back to Descartes now call themselves *neuroscientists*. Today, **neuroscience** is one of the most rapidly growing areas of research. Important discoveries come with astonishing regularity. Our discussion of neuroscience begins with an overview of the techniques researchers use to hasten

Neuroscience The scientific study of the brain and of the links between brain activity and behavior.

new discoveries. We then offer a general description of the structure of the nervous system, followed by a more detailed look at the brain itself. Finally, we discuss the activity of the endocrine system, a second biological control system that works in cooperation with your nervous system and brain.

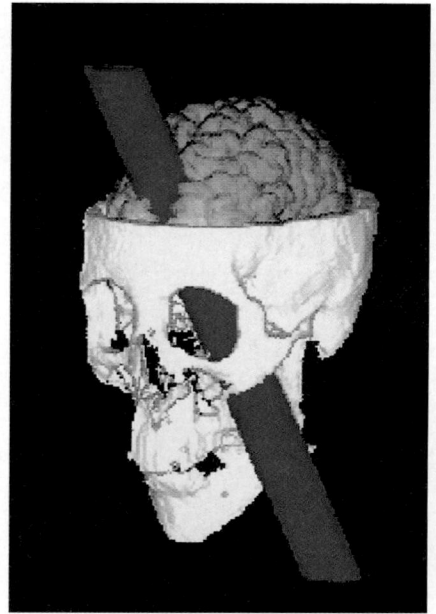

Phineas Gage's skull is preserved in the collections of the Warren Anatomical Museum, Harvard University Medical School. Why were doctors so fascinated by Gage's changes in personality?

Eavesdropping on the Brain

Neuroscientists seek to understand how the brain works at a number of different levels—from the operation of large structures visible to the naked eye to the properties of individual nerve cells visible only under powerful microscopes. The techniques researchers use are suited to their level of analysis. Here, we discuss the techniques that have been used most often to attribute functions and behaviors to particular regions of the brain.

INTERVENTIONS IN THE BRAIN

Several research methods in neuroscience involve direct intervention with structures in the brain. These methods find their historical roots in circumstances like the story of Phineas Gage, with which we opened the chapter. Gage's behavioral changes following the dramatic piercing of his brain prompted his doctor to hypothesize brain bases for aspects of personality and rational behavior. At about the same time that Gage was convalescing from his injury, **Paul Broca** was studying the brain's role in language. His first research in this area involved an autopsy of a man whose name was derived from the only word he had been able to speak, "Tan." Broca found that the left front portion of Tan's brain had been severely damaged. This finding led Broca to study the brains of other persons who suffered from language impairments. In each case, Broca's work revealed similar damage to the same area of the brain, a region now known as **Broca's area.** As you shall see as *Psychology and Life* unfolds, contemporary researchers still attempt to correlate patterns of behavior change or impairment with the sites of brain damage.

The problem with studying accidentally damaged brains, of course, is that researchers have no control over the location and extent of the damage. To produce a well-founded understanding of the brain and its relationship to behavioral and cognitive functioning, scientists need methods that allow them to specify precisely the brain tissue that has been incapacitated. Researchers have developed a variety of techniques to produce **lesions,** highly localized brain injuries. They may, for

example, surgically remove specific brain areas, cut the neural connections to those areas, or destroy those areas through application of intense heat, cold, or electricity. As you would guess, experimental work with lesions is carried out exclusively with nonhuman animals. (Recall our discussion in Chapter 2 that the ethics of this type of animal research has now come under heightened scrutiny.) Our conception of the brain has been radically changed as researchers have repeatedly compared and coordinated the results of lesioning experiments on animals with the growing body of clinical findings on the effects of brain damage on human behavior.

Under some circumstances, neuroscientists can learn about the function of brain regions by directly *stimulating* them. For example, in the mid-1950s, **Walter Hess** pioneered the use of electrical stimulation to probe structures deep in the brain. For example, Hess put electrodes into the brains of freely moving cats. By pressing a button, he could then send a small electrical current to the point of the electrode. Hess carefully recorded the behavioral consequences of stimulating each of 4,500 brain sites in nearly 500 cats. Hess discovered that, depending on the location of the electrode, sleep, sexual arousal, anxiety, or terror could be provoked by the flick of the switch—and turned off just as abruptly. For example, electrical stimulation of certain regions of the brain led the otherwise gentle cats to bristle with rage and hurl themselves upon a nearby object.

Broca's area The region of the brain that translates thoughts into speech or sign.

Lesions Injuries to or destruction of brain tissue.

RECORDING AND IMAGING BRAIN ACTIVITY

Other neuroscientists map brain function by using electrodes to record the electrical activity of the brain in response to environmental stimulation. The brain's electrical output can be monitored at different levels of precision. At the most specific, researchers can insert ultrasensitive microelectrodes into the brain to record the electrical activity of a single brain cell. Such recordings can illuminate changes in the activity of individual cells in response to stimuli in the environment.

For human subjects, researchers often place a number of electrodes on the surface of the scalp to record larger, integrated patterns of electrical activity. These electrodes provide the data for an **electroencephalogram** (**EEG**), or an amplified tracing of the brain activity. EEGs can be used to study the relationship between psychological activities and brain response. For example, in one experiment, participants were asked to view a series of faces and make judgments about whether they thought they would be able to recognize each face in a later memory task. The EEGs revealed a distinctive pattern of brain activity, at the time the participants made their judgments, that predicted those instances in which the participants were, in fact, later able to recognize the faces (Sommer et al., 1995).

Some of the most exciting technological innovations for studying the brain are machines originally developed to help neurosurgeons detect brain abnormalities, such as damage caused by strokes or diseases. These devices produce images of the living brain without invasive pro-

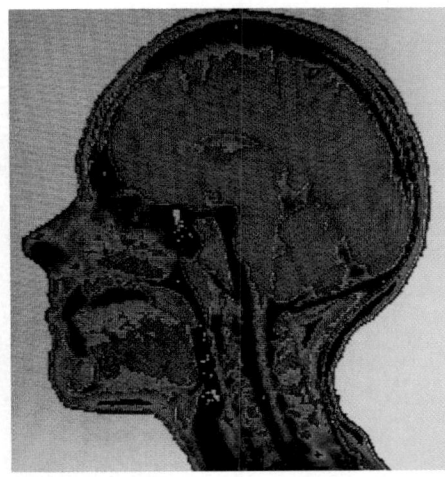

Magnetic resonance imaging (MRI) produces this color-enhanced profile of a normal brain. What is the purpose of trying to identify brain regions that underlie particular functions?

cedures that risk damaging brain tissue. Brain imaging is a promising tool for achieving a better understanding of both normal and abnormal brain function (Barinaga, 1997; Posner, 1993).

In research with positron-emission tomography, or **PET scans**, subjects are given different kinds of radioactive (but safe) substances that eventually travel to the brain, where they are taken up by active brain cells. Recording instruments outside the skull can detect the radioactivity emitted by cells that are active during different cognitive or behavioral activities. This information is then fed into a computer that constructs a dynamic portrait of the brain, showing where different types of psychological activity are actually occurring (see **Figure 3.4**).

Magnetic resonance imaging, or **MRI**, uses magnetic fields and radio waves to generate pulses of energy within the brain. As the pulse is tuned to different frequencies, some atoms line up with the magnetic field. When the magnetic pulse is turned off, the atoms vibrate (resonate) as they return to their original positions. Special radio receivers detect this resonance and channel information to a computer, which generates images of the locations of different atoms in areas of the brain. By looking at the image, researchers can link brain structures to psychological processes.

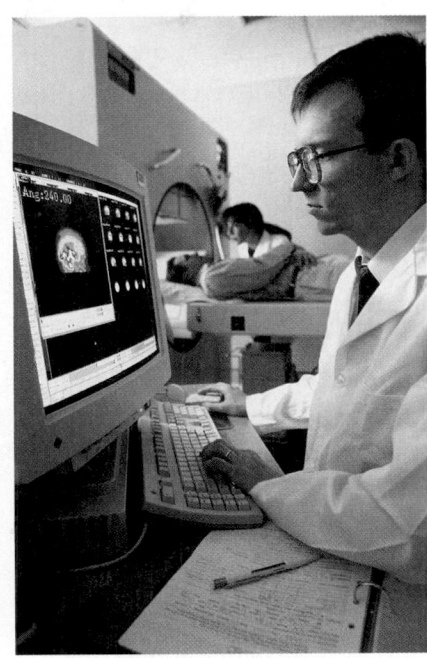

How have new imaging techniques expanded the range of questions researchers can ask?

Electroencephalogram (EEG) A recording of the electrical activity of the brain.

PET scans Brain images produced by a device that obtains detailed pictures of activity in the living brain by recording the radioactivity emitted by cells during different cognitive or behavioral activities.

Magnetic resonance imaging (MRI) A technique for brain imaging that scans the brain using magnetic fields and radio waves.

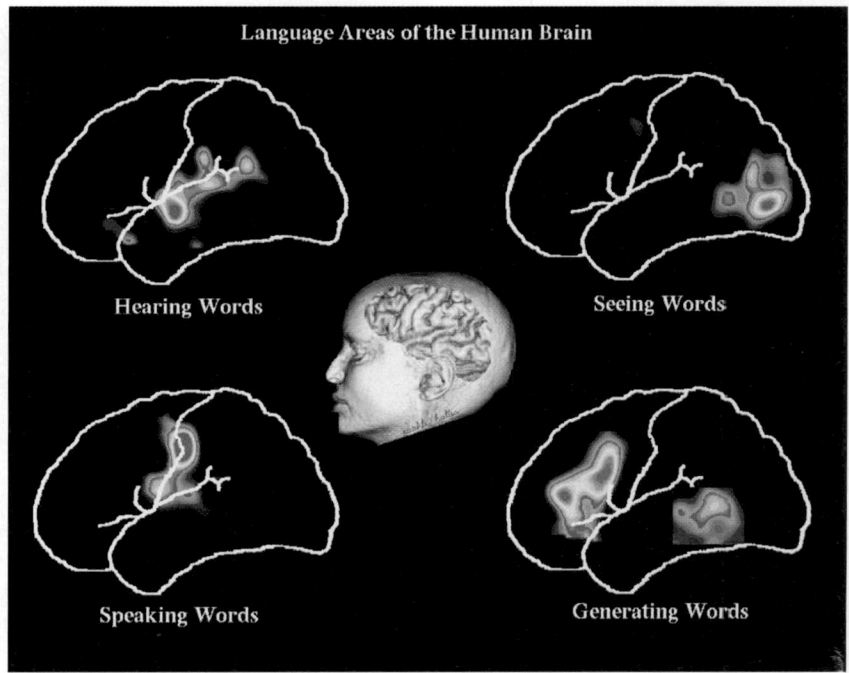

FIGURE 3.4

PET Scans of the Brain at Work

These PET scans show that different tasks stimulate neural activity in distinct regions of the brain.

MRI is most useful for providing clear images of anatomical details; PET scans provide better information about function. A new technique called **functional MRI, or fMRI,** combines some of the benefits of both techniques by detecting magnetic changes in the flow of blood to cells in the brain; fMRI allows more precise claims about both structure and function. Researchers have begun to use fMRI to discover the distributions of brain regions responsible for many of your most important cognitive abilities such as attention, perception, language processing, and memory (Cabeza & Nyberg, 2000).

More than 300 years have passed since Descartes sat in his candlelit study and mused about the brain; over 100 years have passed since Broca discovered that brain regions seem to be linked to specific functions. In the time since these developments, cultural evolution has provided neuroscientists with the technology necessary to reveal some of your brain's most important secrets. The remainder of this chapter describes some of those secrets.

Functional MRI (fMRI) A brain imaging technique that combines benefits of both MRI and PET scans by detecting magnetic changes in the flow of blood to cells in the brain.

Central nervous system (CNS) The part of the nervous system consisting of the brain and spinal cord.

Peripheral nervous system (PNS) The part of the nervous system composed of the spinal and cranial nerves that connect the body's sensory receptors to the CNS and the CNS to the muscles and glands.

The Nervous System

The nervous system is composed of billions of highly specialized nerve cells, or *neurons,* that constitute the brain and the nerve fibers that are found throughout the body. The nervous system is subdivided into two major divisions: the **central nervous system (CNS)** and the **peripheral nervous system (PNS).** The CNS is composed of all the neurons in the brain and spinal cord; the PNS is made up of all the neurons forming the nerve fibers that connect the CNS to the body. **Figures 3.5** and **3.6** show the relationship of the CNS to the PNS.

The job of the CNS is to integrate and coordinate all bodily functions, process all incoming neural messages, and send out commands to different parts of the body. The CNS sends and receives neural messages through the *spinal cord,* a trunk line of neurons that connects the brain to the PNS. The trunk line itself is housed in a hollow portion of the vertebral column, called the spinal column. Spinal nerves branch out from the spinal cord between each pair of vertebrae in the spinal column, eventually connecting with sensory receptors throughout the body and with muscles and glands. The spinal cord coordinates the activity of the left and right sides of the body and is responsible for simple, fast action reflexes that do not involve the brain. For example, an organism whose spinal cord has been severed from its brain can still withdraw its limb from a painful stimulus. Though an intact brain would normally be notified of such action, the organism can complete the action without directions from above. Damage to the nerves of the spinal

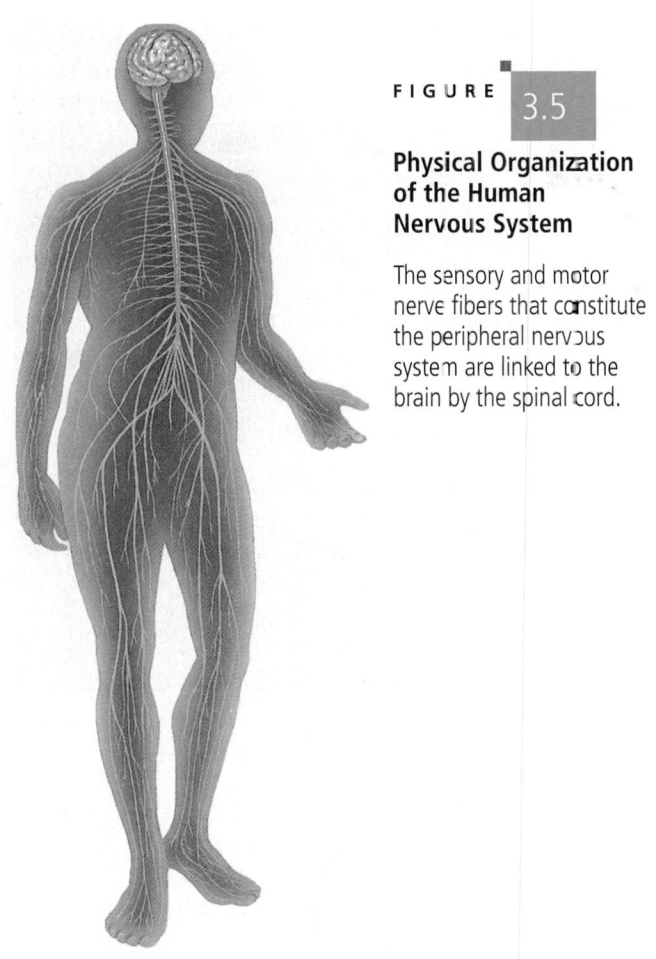

Physical Organization of the Human Nervous System

The sensory and motor nerve fibers that constitute the peripheral nervous system are linked to the brain by the spinal cord.

Despite its commanding position, the CNS is isolated from any direct contact with the outside world. It is the role of the PNS to provide the CNS with information from sensory receptors, such as those found in the eyes and ears, and to relay commands from the brain to the body's organs and muscles. The PNS is actually composed of two sets of nerve fibers (see Figure 3.6). The **somatic nervous system** regulates the actions of the body's skeletal muscles. For example, imagine you are typing a letter. The movement of your fingers over the keyboard is managed by your somatic nervous system. As you decide what to say, your brain sends commands to your fingers to press certain keys. Simultaneously, the fingers send feedback about their position and movement to the brain. If you strike the wrong key (th**w**), the somatic nervous system informs the brain, which then issues the necessary correction, and, in a fraction of a second, you delete the mistake and hit the right key (th**e**).

The other branch of the PNS is the **autonomic nervous system (ANS)**, which sustains basic life processes. This system is on the job 24 hours a day, regulating bodily functions that you usually don't consciously control, such as respiration, digestion, and arousal. The ANS must work even when you are asleep, and it sustains life

■ **Somatic nervous system** The subdivision of the peripheral nervous system that connects the central nervous system to the skeletal muscles and skin.

■ **Autonomic nervous system (ANS)** The subdivision of the peripheral nervous system that controls the body's involuntary motor responses by connecting the sensory receptors to the central nervous system (CNS) and the CNS to the smooth muscle, cardiac muscle, and glands.

cord can result in paralysis of the legs or trunk, as seen in paraplegic individuals. The extent of paralysis depends on how high up on the spinal cord the damage occurred; higher damage produces greater paralysis.

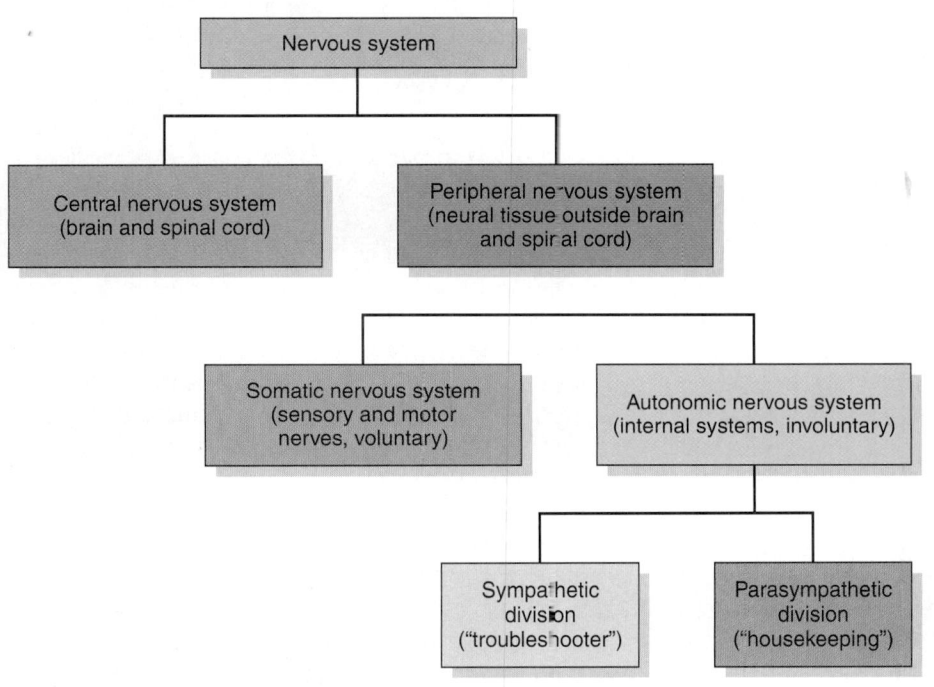

Hierarchical Organization of the Human Nervous System

The central nervous system is composed of the brain and the spinal cord. The peripheral nervous system is divided according to function: The somatic nervous system controls voluntary actions, and the autonomic nervous system regulates internal processes. The autonomic nervous system is subdivided into two systems: The sympathetic nervous system governs behavior in emergency situations, and the parasympathetic nervous system regulates behavior and internal processes in routine circumstances.

BIOLOGY AND BEHAVIOR

59

processes during anesthesia and prolonged coma states. The autonomic nervous system deals with survival matters of two kinds: those involving threats to the organism and those involving bodily maintenance. To carry out these functions, the autonomic nervous system is further subdivided into the sympathetic and parasympathetic nervous system (see Figure 3.6). These divisions work in opposition to accomplish their tasks. The **sympathetic division** governs responses to emergency situations; the **parasympathetic division** monitors the routine operation of the body's internal functions. The sympathetic division can be regarded as a troubleshooter—in an emergency or stressful situation, it arouses the brain structures for "fight or flight." Digestion stops, blood flows away from internal organs to the muscles, oxygen transfer increases, and heart rate increases. After the dan-

ger is over, the parasympathetic division takes charge to decelerate these processes, and the individual begins to calm down. Digestion resumes, heartbeat slows, and breathing is relaxed. The parasympathetic division carries out the body's nonemergency housekeeping chores, such as elimination of bodily wastes, protection of the visual system (through tears and pupil constriction), and long-term conservation of body energy. The separate duties of the sympathetic and parasympathetic nervous systems are illustrated in **Figure 3.7**.

Brain Structures and Their Functions

The brain is the most important component of your central nervous system. The brains of human beings have

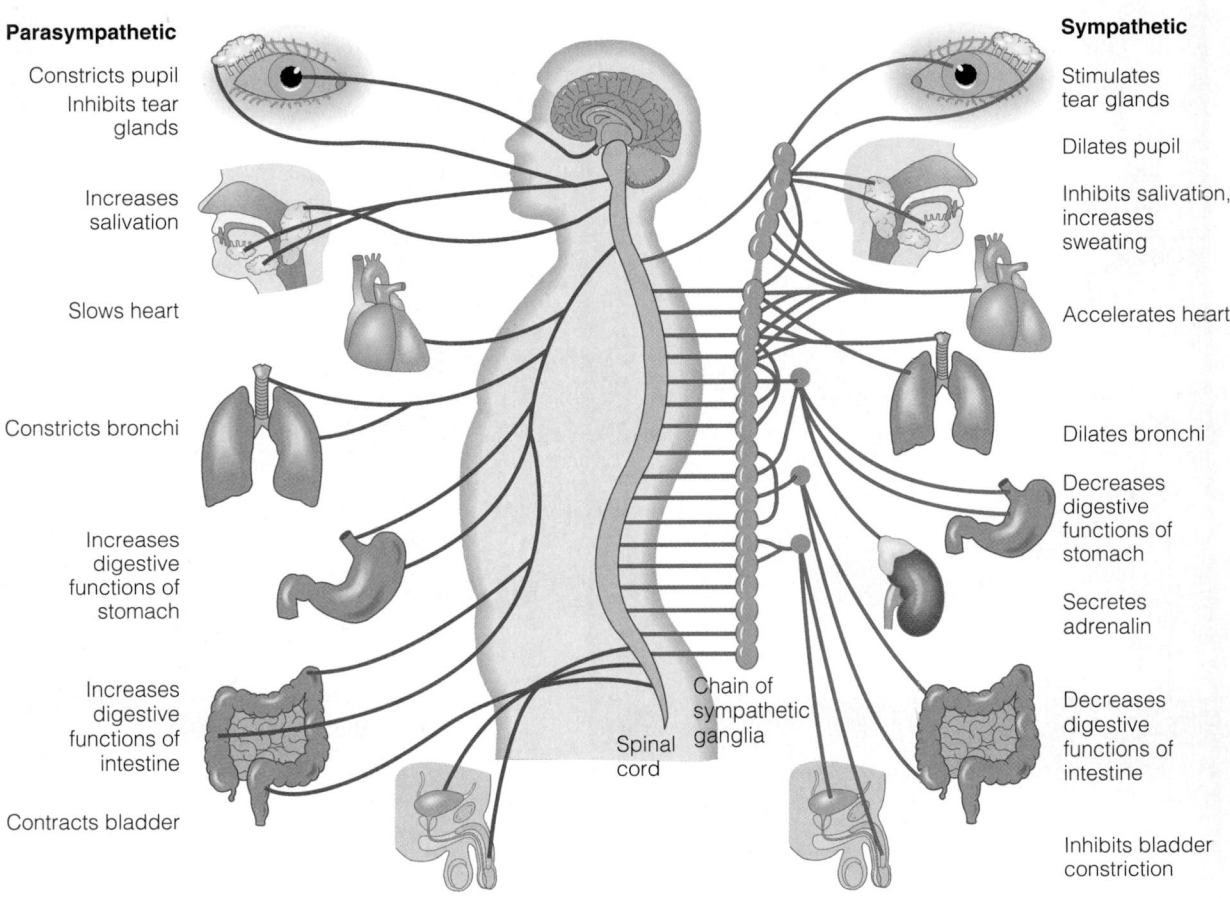

Parasympathetic

Constricts pupil
Inhibits tear glands

Increases salivation

Slows heart

Constricts bronchi

Increases digestive functions of stomach

Increases digestive functions of intestine

Contracts bladder

Sympathetic

Stimulates tear glands

Dilates pupil

Inhibits salivation, increases sweating

Accelerates heart

Dilates bronchi

Decreases digestive functions of stomach

Secretes adrenalin

Decreases digestive functions of intestine

Inhibits bladder constriction

Spinal cord

Chain of sympathetic ganglia

FIGURE 3.7

The Autonomic Nervous System

The parasympathetic nervous system, which regulates day-to-day internal processes and behavior, is shown on the left. The sympathetic nervous system, which regulates internal processes and behavior in stressful situations, is shown on the right. Note that on their way to and from the spinal cord, the nerve fibers of the sympathetic nervous system innervate, or make connections with, ganglia, which are specialized clusters of neuron chains.

three interconnected layers. In the deepest recesses of the brain, in a region called the *brain stem*, are structures involved primarily with autonomic processes such as heart rate, breathing, swallowing, and digestion. Enveloping this central core is the *limbic system,* which is involved with motivation, emotion, and memory processes. Wrapped around these two regions is the *cerebrum*. The universe of the human mind exists in this region. The cerebrum, and its surface layer, the *cerebral cortex,* integrates sensory information, coordinates your movements, and facilitates abstract thinking and reasoning (see **Figure 3.8**). Let's look more closely at the functions of the three major brain regions, beginning with the brain stem, thalamus, and cerebellum.

THE BRAIN STEM, THALAMUS, AND CEREBELLUM

The **brain stem** is found in all vertebrate species. It contains structures that collectively regulate the internal state of the body (see **Figure 3.9**). The **medulla**, located at the very top of the spinal cord, is the center for breathing, blood pressure, and the beating of the heart. Because these processes are essential for life, damage to the medulla can be fatal. Nerve fibers ascending from the body and descending from the brain cross over at the medulla, which means that the left side of the body is linked to the right side of the brain and the right side of the body is connected to the left side of the brain.

Directly above the medulla is the **pons,** which provides inputs to other structures in the brain stem and to the cerebellum (*pons* is the Latin word for bridge). The **reticular formation** is a dense network of nerve cells that serves as the brain's sentinel. It arouses the cerebral cortex to attend to new stimulation and keeps the brain alert even during sleep (Kinomura et al., 1996). Massive damage to this area often results in a coma.

Sympathetic division The subdivision of the autonomic nervous system that deals with emergency response and the mobilization of energy.

Parasympathetic division The subdivision of the autonomic nervous system that monitors the routine operation of the body's internal functions and conserves and restores body energy.

Brain stem The brain structure that regulates the body's basic life processes.

Medulla The region of the brain stem that regulates breathing, waking, and heartbeat.

Pons The region of the brain stem that connects the spinal cord with the brain and links parts of the brain to one another.

Reticular formation The region of the brain stem that alerts the cerebral cortex to incoming sensory signals and is responsible for maintaining consciousness and awakening from sleep.

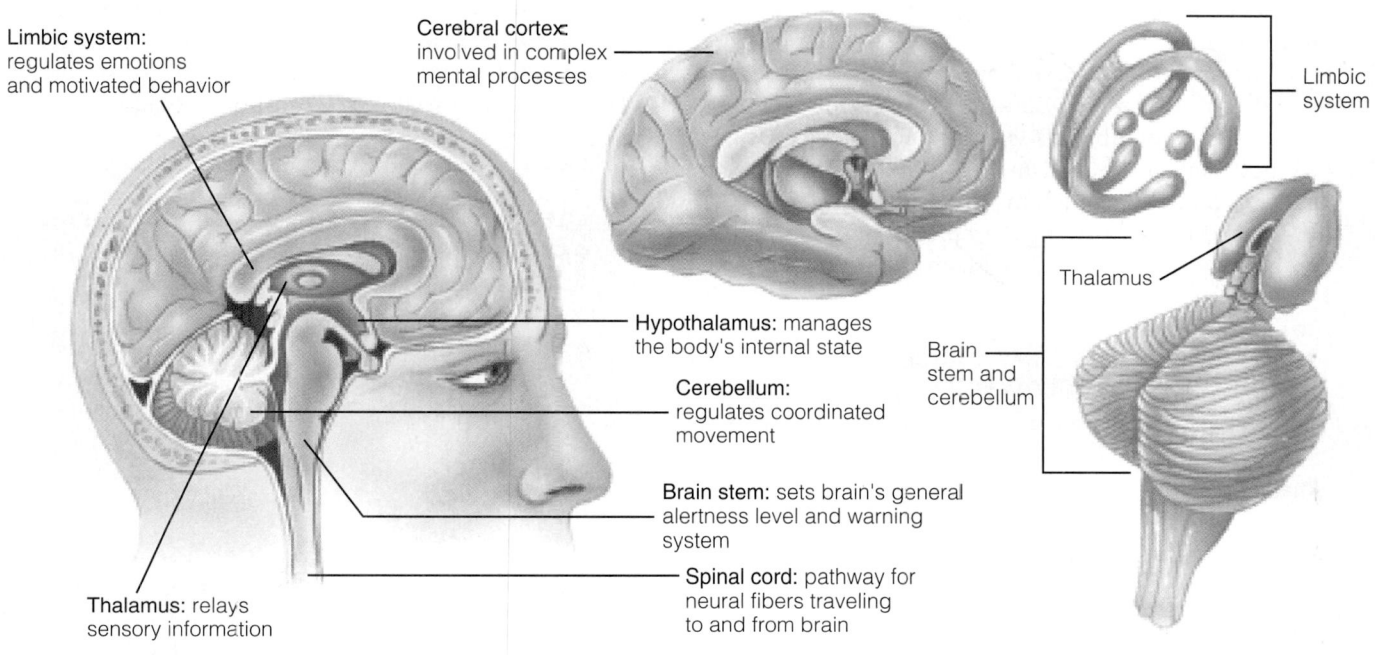

Limbic system: regulates emotions and motivated behavior

Cerebral cortex: involved in complex mental processes

Limbic system

Thalamus

Brain stem and cerebellum

Hypothalamus: manages the body's internal state

Cerebellum: regulates coordinated movement

Brain stem: sets brain's general alertness level and warning system

Spinal cord: pathway for neural fibers traveling to and from brain

Thalamus: relays sensory information

FIGURE

Brain Structures

The brain contains several major components, including the brain stem, cerebellum, limbic system, and cerebral cortex, all of which fit together in an intricate design.

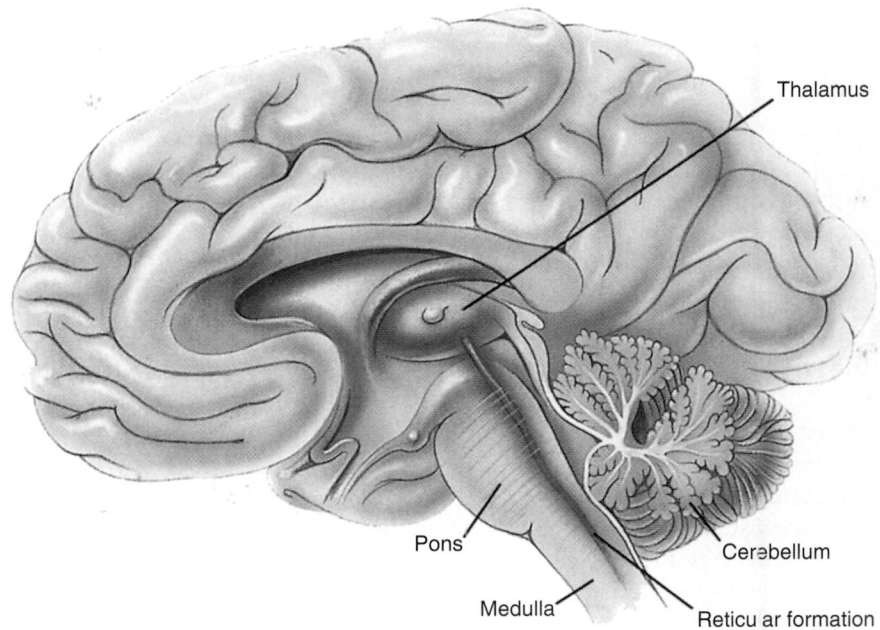

FIGURE 3.9

The Brain Stem, Thalamus, and Cerebellum

These structures are primarily involved in basic life processes: breathing, pulse, arousal, movement, balance, and simple processing of sensory information.

The reticular formation has long tracts of fibers that run to the **thalamus,** which channels incoming sensory information to the appropriate area of the cerebral cortex, where that information is processed. For example, the thalamus relays information from the eyes to cortical areas for vision.

Neuroscientists have long known that the **cerebellum,** attached to the brain stem at the base of the skull, coordinates bodily movements, controls posture, and maintains equilibrium. Damage to the cerebellum interrupts the flow of otherwise smooth movement, causing it to appear uncoordinated and jerky. More recent research suggests that the cerebellum also plays an important role in the ability to learn, for example, the control of body movements (Barinaga, 1996; Raymond et al., 1996).

THE LIMBIC SYSTEM

The **limbic system** mediates motivated behaviors, emotional states, and memory processes. It also regulates body temperature, blood pressure, and blood-sugar level

Thalamus The brain structure that relays sensory impulses to the cerebral cortex.

Cerebellum The region of the brain attached to the brain stem that controls motor coordination, posture, and balance as well as the ability to learn control of body movements.

Limbic system The region of the brain that regulates emotional behavior, basic motivational urges, and memory, as well as major physiological functions.

Hippocampus The part of the limbic system that is involved in the acquisition of explicit memory.

Amygdala The part of the limbic system that controls emotion, aggression, and the formation of emotional memory.

and performs other housekeeping activities. The limbic system comprises three structures: the hippocampus, amygdala, and hypothalamus (see **Figure 3.10**).

The **hippocampus,** which is the largest of the limbic system structures, plays an important role in the acquisition of *explicit* memories (Eichenbaum, 1999; Squire, 1992)—memories that you are aware of retrieving (see Chapter 8). There is considerable clinical evidence to support this view, notably from studies of a patient, H.M., perhaps psychology's most famous subject:

HOW WE KNOW

SOME CONSEQUENCES OF HIPPOCAMPAL DAMAGE When he was 27, H.M. underwent surgery in an attempt to reduce the frequency and severity of his epileptic seizures. During the operation, parts of his hippocampus were removed. As a result, H.M. could only recall the very distant past; his ability to put new information into long-term memory was gone. Long after his surgery, he continued to believe he was living in 1953, which was the year the operation was performed.

Damage to the hippocampus does not, on the other hand, impair the ability to acquire *implicit* memories, outside of conscious awareness. Thus, H.M. was able to acquire new skills. If you were in an accident and sustained damage to your hippocampus, you would still be able to learn some new tasks, but you would not be able to remember having done so! (We will return to the brain bases of memory in Chapter 8.)

The **amygdala** plays a role in emotional control and the formation of emotional memories. Because of this

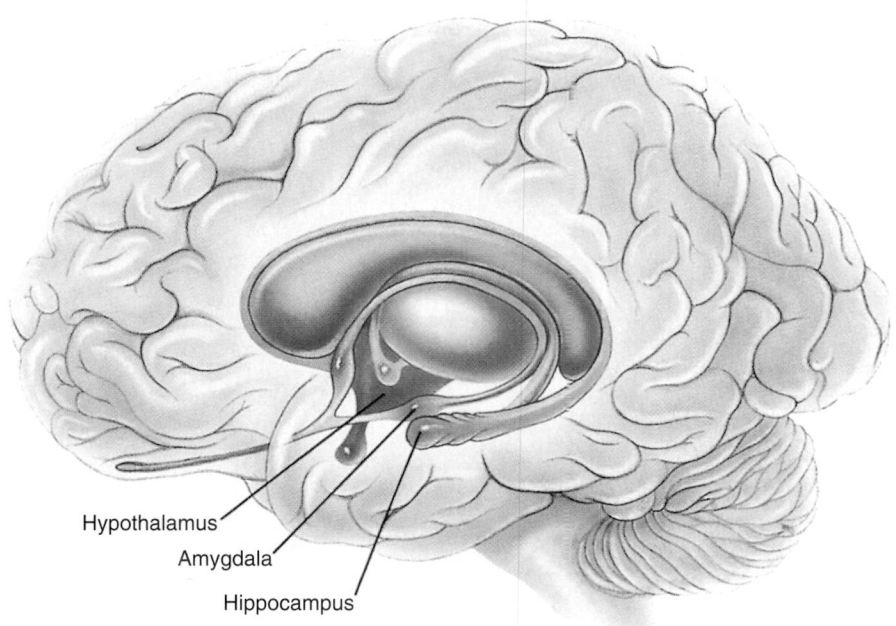

FIGURE 3.10

The Limbic System

The structures of the limbic system, which are present only in mammals, are involved in motivated behavior, emotional states, and memory processes.

Hypothalamus

Amygdala

Hippocampus

control function, damage to areas of the amygdala may have a calming effect on otherwise mean-spirited individuals. (We discuss *psychosurgery* in Chapter 16.) However, damage to some areas of the amygdala also impairs the ability to recognize the emotional content of facial expressions (Adolphs et al., 1994). Those individuals who have suffered amygdala damage are most impaired with respect to negative emotional expressions, especially fear. Researchers speculate that the amygdala may play a special role in people's acquisition and use of knowledge related to threat and danger (Adolphs et al., 1999).

The **hypothalamus** is one of the smallest structures in the brain, yet it plays a vital role in many of your most important daily actions. It is actually composed of several nuclei, small bundles of neurons that regulate physiological processes involved in motivated behavior (including eating, drinking, temperature regulation, and sexual arousal). The hypothalamus maintains the body's internal equilibrium, or **homeostasis.** When the body's energy reserves are low, the hypothalamus is involved in stimulating the organism to find food and to eat. When body temperature drops, the hypothalamus causes blood-vessel constriction, or minute involuntary movements you commonly refer to as the "shivers." The hypothalamus also regulates the activities of the endocrine system.

THE CEREBRUM

In humans, the **cerebrum** dwarfs the rest of the brain, occupying two-thirds of its total mass. Its role is to regulate the brain's higher cognitive and emotional functions. The outer surface of the cerebrum, made up of billions of cells in a layer about a tenth of an inch thick, is called the **cerebral cortex.** The cerebrum is also divided into two almost symmetrical halves, the **cerebral hemispheres** (we

discuss the two hemispheres at length in a later section of this chapter). The two hemispheres are connected by a thick mass of nerve fibers, collectively referred to as the **corpus callosum.** This pathway sends messages back and forth between the hemispheres.

Neuroscientists have mapped each hemisphere, using two important landmarks as their guides. One groove, called the *central sulcus,* divides each hemisphere vertically, and a second similar groove, called the *lateral fissure,* divides each hemisphere horizontally (see **Figure 3.11**). These vertical and horizontal divisions help to define four areas, or brain lobes, in each hemisphere. The **frontal lobe,** which is involved in motor control and cognitive activities, such as planning, making decisions, and setting goals, is located above the lateral fissure and in front of the central sulcus. Accidents that damage the frontal lobes can have devastating effects on human action and personality. This was the location of the injury

Hypothalamus The brain structure that regulates motivated behavior (such as eating and drinking) and homeostasis.

Homeostasis Constancy or equilibrium of the internal conditions of the body.

Cerebrum The region of the brain that regulates higher cognitive and emotional functions.

Cerebral cortex The outer surface of the cerebrum.

Cerebral hemispheres The two halves of the cerebrum, connected by the corpus callosum.

Corpus callosum The mass of nerve fibers connecting the two hemispheres of the cerebrum.

Frontal lobe Region of the brain located above the lateral fissure and in front of the central sulcus; involved in motor control and cognitive activities.

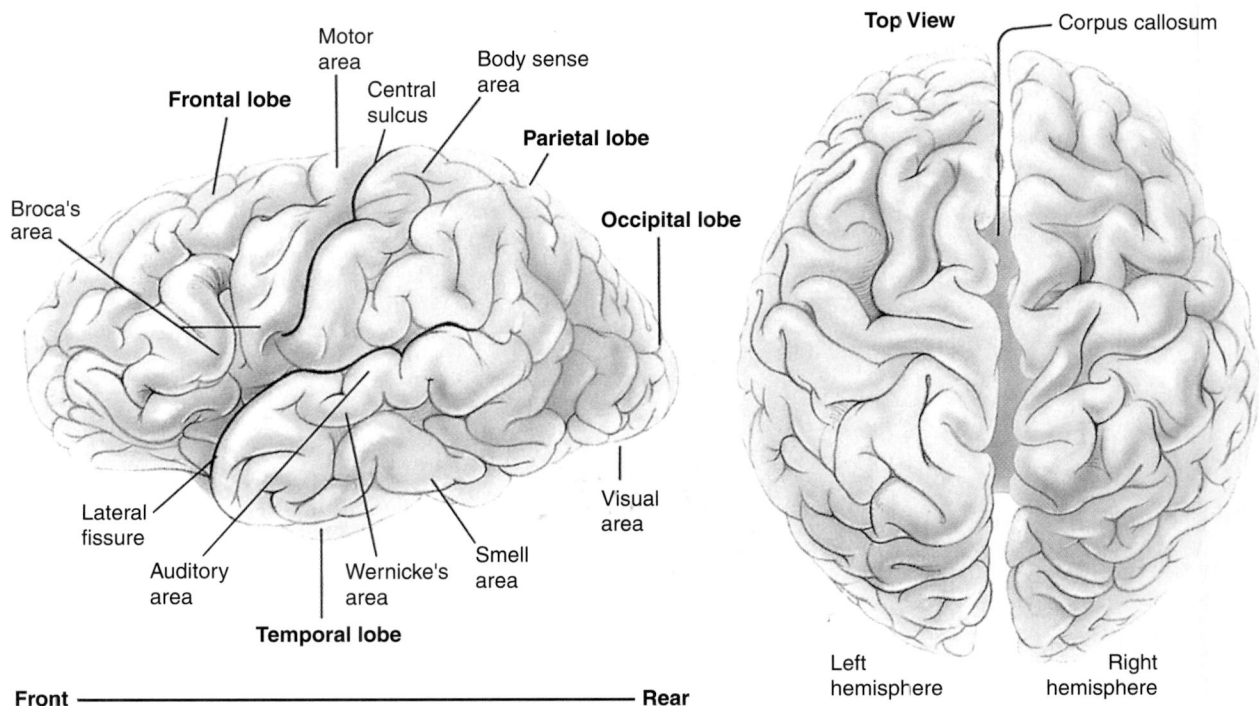

Labels on figure: Motor area, Central sulcus, Body sense area, Frontal lobe, Parietal lobe, Broca's area, Occipital lobe, Top View, Corpus callosum, Lateral fissure, Visual area, Auditory area, Smell area, Wernicke's area, Temporal lobe, Front, Rear, Left hemisphere, Right hemisphere

FIGURE

The Cerebral Cortex

Each of the two hemispheres of the cerebral cortex has four lobes. Different sensory and motor functions have been associated with specific parts of each lobe.

3.11

that brought about such a dramatic change in Phineas Gage (Damasio et al., 1994). The **parietal lobe** is responsible for sensations of touch, pain, and temperature and is located directly behind the central sulcus. The **occipital lobe,** the final destination for visual information, is located at the back of the head. The **temporal lobe,** which is responsible for the processes of hearing, is found below the lateral fissure, on the sides of each cerebral hemisphere.

It would be misleading to say that any lobe alone controls any one specific function. The structures of the brain perform their duties in concert, working smoothly as an integrated unit, similar to a symphony orchestra. Whether you are doing the dishes, solving a calculus

Parietal lobe Region of the brain behind the frontal lobe and above the lateral fissure; contains somatosensory cortex.

Occipital lobe Rearmost region of the brain; contains primary visual cortex.

Temporal lobe Region of brain found below the lateral fissure; contains auditory cortex.

Motor cortex The region of the cerebral cortex that controls the action of the body's voluntary muscles.

problem, or carrying on a conversation with a friend, your brain works as a unified whole, each lobe interacting and cooperating with the others. Nevertheless, neuroscientists can identify areas of the four lobes of the cerebrum that are necessary for specific functions, such as vision, hearing, language, and memory. When they are damaged, their functions are disrupted or lost entirely.

The actions of the body's voluntary muscles, of which there are more than 600, are controlled by the **motor cortex,** located just in front of the central sulcus in the frontal lobes. Recall that commands from one side of the brain are directed to muscles on the opposite side of the body. Also, muscles in the lower part of the body— for example, the toes—are controlled by neurons in the top part of the motor cortex. Muscles in the upper part of the body, such as the throat, are controlled by neurons in the lower part of the motor cortex. As you can see in **Figure 3.12,** the upper parts of the body receive far more detailed motor instructions than the lower parts. In fact, the two largest areas of the motor cortex are devoted to the fingers—especially the thumb—and to the muscles involved in speech. Their greater brain area reflects the importance in human activity of manipulating objects, using tools, eating, and talking.

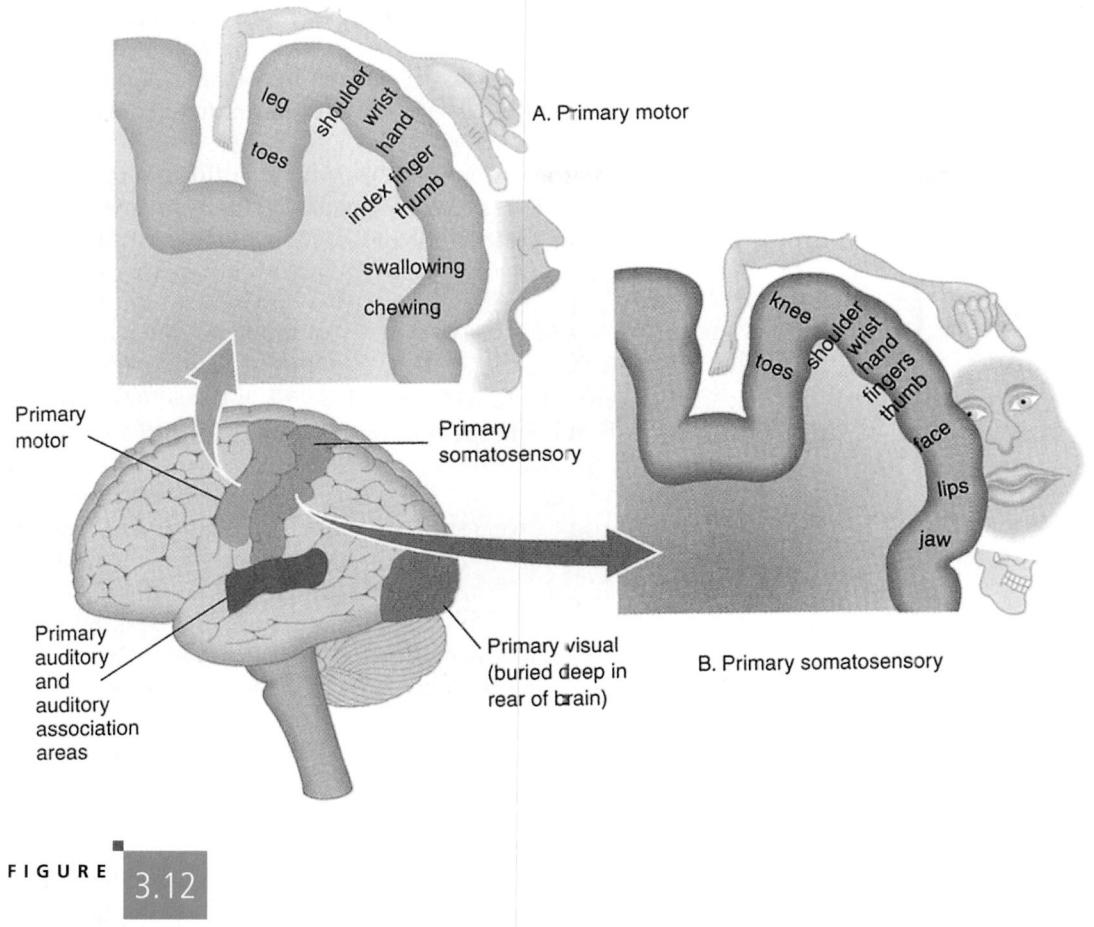

A. Primary motor

Primary
motor

Primary
somatosensory

Primary
auditory
and
auditory
association
areas

Primary visual
(buried deep in
rear of brain)

B. Primary somatosensory

FIGURE 3.12

Motor and Somatosensory Cortex

Different parts of the body are more or less sensitive to environmental stimulation and brain control. Sensitivity in a particular region of the body is related to the amount of space in the cerebral cortex devoted to that region. In this figure, the body is drawn so that the size of body parts is relative to the cortical space devoted to them. The larger the body part in the drawing, the greater its sensitivity to environmental stimulation and the greater the brain's control over its movement.

The **somatosensory cortex** is located just behind the central sulcus in the left and right parietal lobes. This part of the cortex processes information about temperature, touch, body position, and pain. Similar to the motor cortex, the upper part of the sensory cortex relates to the lower parts of the body, and the lower part to the upper parts of the body. Most of the area of the sensory cortex is devoted to the lips, tongue, thumb, and index fingers—the parts of the body that provide the most important sensory input (see Figure 3.12). And like the motor cortex, the right half of the somatosensory cortex communicates with the left side of the body, and the left half communicates with the right side of the body.

Auditory information is processed in the **auditory cortex,** which is in the two temporal lobes. The auditory cortex in each hemisphere receives information from *both* ears. One area of the auditory cortex is in-volved in the production of language, and a different area is involved in language comprehension. Visual input is processed at the back of the brain in the **visual cortex,** located in the occipital lobes. Here the greatest area is devoted to input from the center part of the retina, at the back of the eye, the area that transmits the most detailed visual information.

Not all of the cerebral cortex is devoted to processing sensory information and commanding the muscles to action. In fact, the majority of it is involved in *interpreting*

Somatosensory cortex The region of the parietal lobes that processes sensory input from various body areas.

Auditory cortex The area of the temporal lobes that receives and processes auditory information.

Visual cortex The region of the occipital lobes in which visual information is processed.

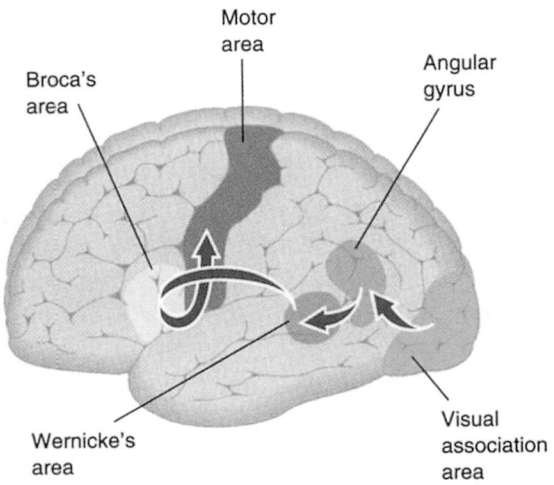

Motor
area

Broca's
area

Angular
gyrus

Wernicke's
area

Visual
association
area

Speaking a written word

FIGURE 3.13

How a Written Word Is Spoken

Nerve impulses, laden with information about the written word, are sent by the retinas to the visual association area of the cortex via the thalamus. The visual cortex sends the nerve impulses to an area in the rear of the temporal lobe, the angular gyrus, where visual coding for the word (the arrangement of letters and their shapes, etc.) is compared with its acoustical coding (the way it sounds). Once the proper acoustical code is found, it is relayed to an area of the auditory cortex known as Wernicke's area. Here it is encoded and interpreted. Nerve impulses are sent to Broca's area, which sends the message to the motor cortex. The motor cortex puts the word in your mouth by stimulating the lips, tongue, and larynx to act in synchrony.

and *integrating* information. Processes such as planning and decision making are believed to occur in **association cortex.** Association areas are distributed to several areas of the cortex—one region is labeled in Figure 3.12. Association cortex allows you to combine information from various sensory modalities to plan appropriate responses to stimuli in the environment.

How do these different areas of the brain work in unison? Consider, as an example, what happens in your brain when you speak a written word (see **Figure 3.13**). Imagine that your psychology instructor hands you a piece of paper with the word *chocolate* written on it and asks you to say the word aloud. The biological processes involved in this action are surprisingly subtle and com-

Association cortex The parts of the cerebral cortex in which many high-level brain processes occur.

plex. Neuroscience can break down your verbal behavior into numerous steps. First, the visual stimulus (the written word *chocolate*) is detected by the nerve cells in the retinas of your eyes, which send nerve impulses to the visual cortex (via the thalamus). The visual cortex then sends nerve impulses to an area in the rear of the temporal lobe (called the angular gyrus) where visual coding for the word is compared with its acoustical coding. Once the proper acoustical code is located, it is relayed to an area of the auditory cortex known as *Wernicke's area,* where it is decoded and interpreted: "Ah! Chocolate! I'd like some now." Nerve impulses are then sent to Broca's area, which, in turn, sends a message to the motor cortex, stimulating the lips, tongue, and larynx to produce the word *chocolate.*

That's a lot of mental effort for just one word. Now imagine what you require of your brain every time you read aloud a book or even a billboard. The truly amazing thing is that your brain responds effortlessly and intelligently, translating thousands of marks on paper into a neurological code, informing other brain areas about what's going on, and, finally, putting words in your mouth.

We have now reviewed the many important structures in your nervous system. When we began to talk about the cerebrum, we noted that each cerebral structure is represented in both hemispheres of your brain. However, the structures in those two hemispheres play somewhat different functions with respect to many types of behavior. We turn now to those differences between your brain's two hemispheres.

Hemispheric Lateralization

What types of information originally led researchers to suspect that there are differences in the functions of the brain's two hemispheres? Recall that when Paul Broca carried out his autopsy on Tan, he discovered damage in the left hemisphere. As he followed up this original discovery, Broca found that other patients who showed similar disruption of their language abilities—a pattern now known as *Broca's aphasia*—also had damage on the *left* side of their brains. Damage to the same areas on the *right* side of the brain did not have the same effect. What should one conclude?

The chance to investigate hemispheric differences first arose in the context of a treatment for severe epilepsy in which surgeons sever the corpus callosum—the bundle of about 200 million nerve fibers that transfers information back and forth between the two hemispheres (see **Figure 3.14**). The goal of this surgery is to prevent the violent electrical activity that accompany epileptic seizures from crossing between the hemispheres. The operation is usually successful, and a patient's subsequent behavior in most circumstances appears normal.

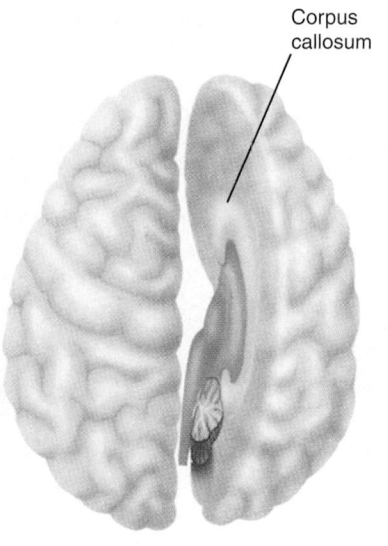

FIGURE 3.14

The Corpus Callosum

The corpus callosum is a massive network of nerve fibers that channels information between the two hemispheres. Severing the corpus callosum impairs this communication process.

Patients who undergo this type of surgery are often referred to as *split-brain* patients.

To test the capabilities of the separated hemispheres of epileptic patients, **Roger Sperry** (1968) and **Michael Gazzaniga** (1970) devised situations that could allow visual information to be presented separately to each hemisphere. Sperry and Gazzaniga's methodology relies on the anatomy of the visual system (see **Figure 3.15**). For each eye, information from the *right visual field* goes to the left hemisphere, and information from the *left visual field* goes to the right hemisphere. Ordinarily, information arriving from both hemispheres is shared very quickly across the corpus callosum. But because these pathways have been severed in split-brain patients, information presented to the right or left visual field may remain only in the left or right hemisphere (see **Figure 3.16**).

Because for most people speech is controlled by the left hemisphere, the left hemisphere could "talk back" to the researchers whereas the right hemisphere could not. Communication with the right hemisphere was achieved by confronting it with manual tasks involving identification, matching, or assembly of objects —tasks that did not require the use of words. Consider the following demonstration of a split-brain subject using his left half brain to account for the activity of

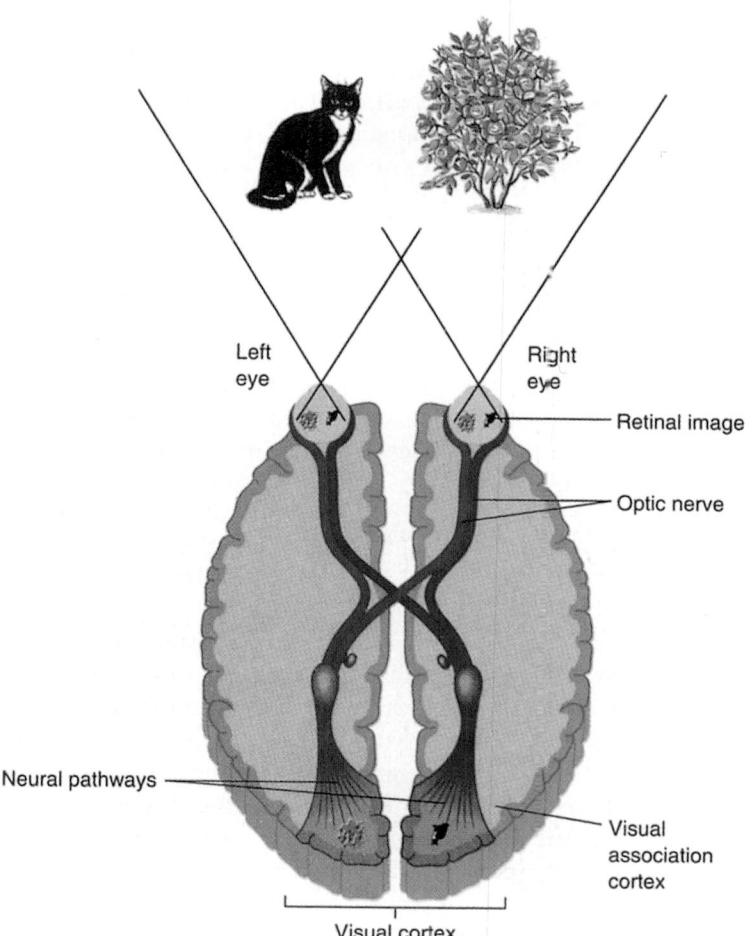

FIGURE 3.15

The Neural Pathways for Visual Information

The neural pathways for visual information coming from the inside portions of each eye cross from one side of the brain to the other at the corpus callosum. The pathways carrying information from the outside portions of each eye do not cross over. Severing the corpus callosum prevents information selectively displayed in the right visual field from entering the right hemisphere, and left visual field information cannot enter the left hemisphere.

BIOLOGY AND BEHAVIOR

his left hand, which was being guided by his right half brain:

HOW WE KNOW

TWO HEMISPHERES IN ACTION A snow scene was presented to the right hemisphere and a picture of a chicken claw was simultaneously presented to the left hemisphere. The subject selected, from an array of objects, those that "went with" each of the two scenes. With his right hand, the patient pointed to a chicken head; with his left hand, he pointed to a shovel. The patient reported that the shovel was needed to clean out the chicken shed (rather than to shovel snow). Since the left brain was not privy to what the right brain "saw" because of the severed corpus callosum, it needed to explain why the left hand was pointing at a shovel when the only picture the left hemisphere was aware of seeing was a chicken claw. The left brain's cognitive system provided a theory to make sense of the behavior of different parts of its body (Gazzaniga, 1985).

From a variety of research methods in addition to split-brain studies, we now know that, for most people, many language-related functions are *lateralized* to the left hemisphere. A function is considered lateralized when one cerebral hemisphere plays the primary role in accomplishing that function. Speech—the ability to produce coherent spoken language—is perhaps the most highly lateralized of all functions. Neuroscientists have found that only about 5 percent of right-handers and 15 percent of left-handers have speech controlled by the right hemisphere, while another 15 percent of left-handers have speech processes occurring in both sides of the brain (Rasmussen & Milner, 1977). For most people, therefore, speech is a left-hemisphere function. As a consequence, damage to the left

side of most people's brains can cause speech disorders. What is interesting is that for users of languages like American Sign Language—which use systems of intricate hand positions and movements to convey meaning—left-brain damage is similarly disruptive (Corina, 1999; Hickok et al., 1996; Poizner et al., 1991). What is lateralized, therefore, is not speech as such but, rather, the ability to produce the sequences of gestures—either vocal or manual—that encode communicative meaning.

You should not conclude that the left hemisphere is somehow "better" than the right hemisphere. Researchers have suggested that each hemisphere has a different "style" for processing the same information. The left hemisphere tends to be more *analytical:* It processes information bit by bit. The right hemisphere tends to be more *holistic:* It processes information with respect to global patterns. It is the combined action of the right and left hemispheres—each with its particular processing style—that gives fullness to your experiences. For example, you wouldn't be surprised to learn that the left hemisphere, with its attention to fine detail, plays a key role in most forms of problem solving. However, the function of the right hemisphere becomes more apparent when problems require creative solutions or bursts of insight—the right hemisphere helps problem solvers do the broader searches of memory that these types of problems require (Bowden & Beeman, 1998). (If you want to put your right hemisphere to work, you can skip ahead to try some of these types of problems on p. 273 in Chapter 9).

Although researchers can confidently make claims about the way in which functions are lateralized in the "average" brain, as with all aspects of human experience there are measurable differences among individuals. When we introduced the lateralization of speech, we also introduced a first individual difference in brain function: Left-handers are somewhat more likely to have speech dominated by their right hemisphere or equally present in both hemispheres. Another distinction that appears to matter greatly

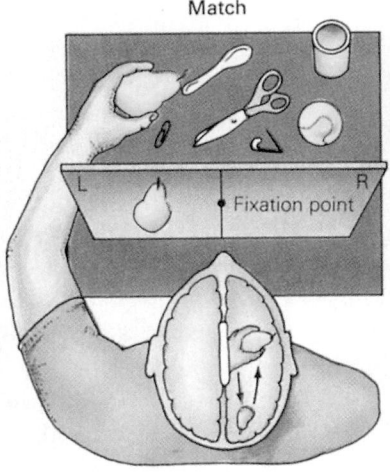 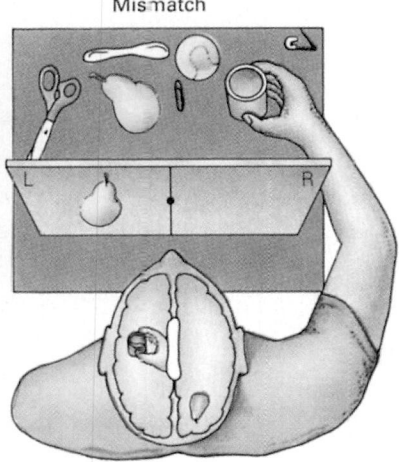

Match   Mismatch

L   R   L   R
· Fixation point

FIGURE 3.16

Coordination between Eye and Hand

Coordination between eye and hand is normal if a split-brain patient uses the left hand to find and match an object that appears in the left visual field, because both are registered in the right hemisphere. However, when asked to use the right hand to match an object seen in the left visual field, the patient cannot do so, because sensory messages from the right hand are going to the left cerebral hemisphere, and there is no longer a connection between the two hemispheres. Here the cup is misperceived as matching the pear.

with respect to brain lateralization is male versus female: There are general differences in the way that male and female brains carry out their functions (Breedlove, 1994; Kimura, 1999). With brain-imaging techniques, it has become relatively easy to look for differences in the regions of men's and women's brains that are brought into action for different tasks. For example, one team of researchers used functional MRI to demonstrate that the brains of men and women become activated in different ways when they make judgments based on language sounds (e.g., Does *sud* rhyme with *wud*?). The brain activity in men was largely localized in the left hemisphere, whereas this task was more likely to engage both left- and right-brain activity for women (Shaywitz et al., 1995). Results like this one return us to the issue of *nature* versus *nurture*. Do males and females come into the world with different brains, or do life experiences modify their brains along the way? The techniques of contemporary neuroscience should allow for a rigorous answer to this question over the next several years.

We have now reviewed the many important structures of your nervous system. Let's now consider the endocrine system, a bodily system that functions in close cooperation with the nervous system to regulate bodily functions.

The Endocrine System

The human genotype specifies a second highly complex regulatory system, the **endocrine system,** to supplement the work of the nervous system. The endocrine system is a network of glands that manufacture and secrete chemical messengers called **hormones** into the bloodstream (see **Figure 3.17**). Hormones are important in everyday functioning, although they are more vital at some stages of life and in some situations than others. Hormones influence your body growth. They initiate, maintain, and stop development of primary and secondary sexual

characteristics; influence levels of arousal and awareness; serve as the basis for mood changes; and regulate metabolism, the rate at which the body uses its energy stores. The endocrine system promotes the survival of an *organism* by helping fight infections and disease. It advances the survival of the *species* through regulation of sexual arousal, production of reproductive cells, and production of milk in nursing mothers. Thus, you could not survive without an effective endocrine system.

Endocrine glands respond to the levels of chemicals in the bloodstream or are stimulated by other hormones or by nerve impulses from the brain. Hormones are then secreted into the blood and travel to distant target cells that have specific receptors; hormones exert their influence on the body's program of chemical regulation only at the places that are genetically predetermined to respond to them. In influencing diverse, but specific, target organs or tissue, hormones can regulate such an enormous range of biochemical processes that they have been called "the messengers of life" (Crapo, 1985). This multiple-action communication system allows for control of slow, continuous processes such as maintenance of blood-sugar levels and calcium levels, metabolism of carbohydrates, and general body growth. But what happens during crises? The endocrine system also releases the hormone adrenaline into the bloodstream; adrenaline energizes your body so that you can respond quickly to challenges.

As we mentioned earlier, the brain structure known as the *hypothalamus* serves as a relay station between the endocrine system and the central nervous system. Specialized

Endocrine system The network of glands that manufacture and secrete hormones into the bloodstream.

Hormones The chemical messengers, manufactured and secreted by the endocrine glands, that regulate metabolism and influence body growth, mood, and sexual characteristics.

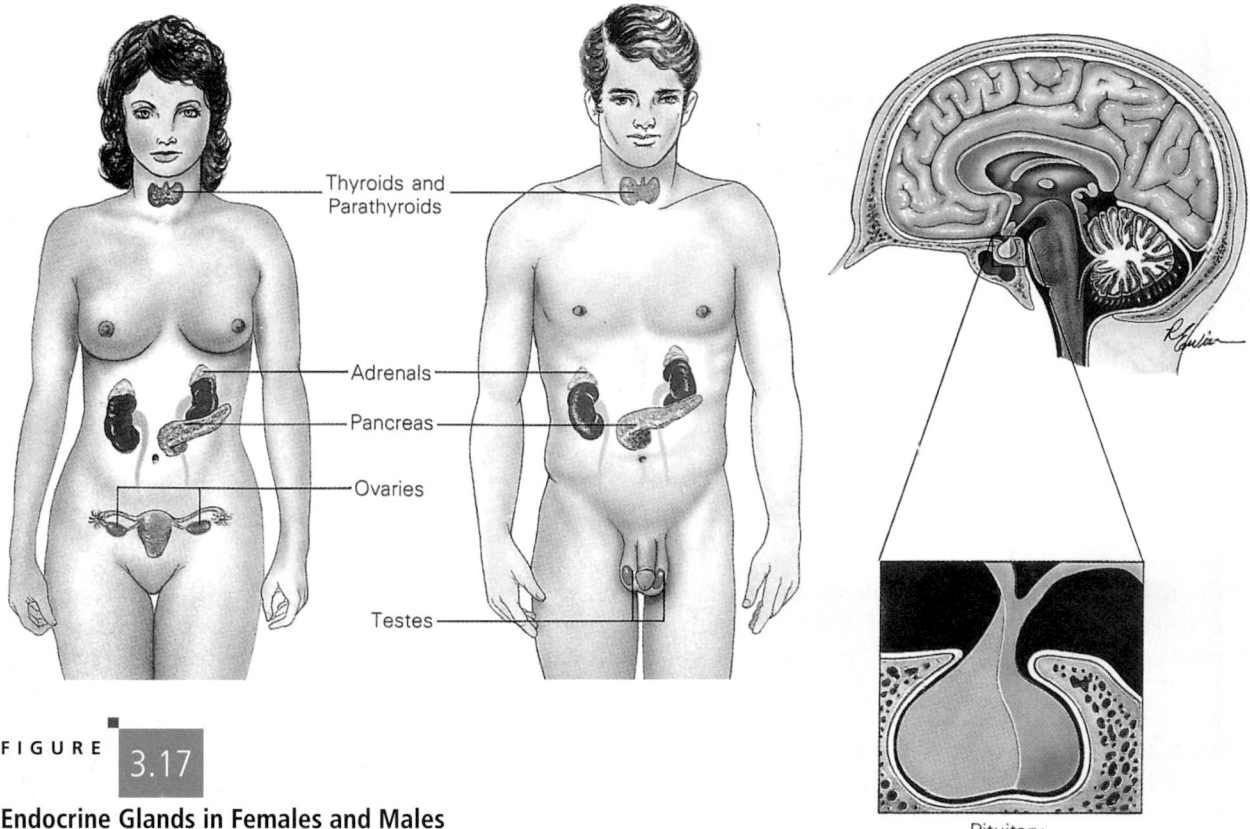

FIGURE 3.17

Endocrine Glands in Females and Males

The pituitary gland is shown at the far right; it is the master gland that regulates the glands shown at the left. The pituitary gland is under the control of the hypothalamus, an important structure in the limbic system.

Pituitary

cells in the hypothalamus receive messages from other brain cells commanding it to release a number of different hormones to the pituitary gland, where they either stimulate or inhibit the release of other hormones. Hormones are produced in several different regions of the body. These "factories" make a variety of hormones, each of which regulates different bodily processes, as outlined in **Table 3.1.** Let's examine the most significant of these processes.

The **pituitary gland** is often called the "master gland," because it produces about ten different kinds of hormones that influence the secretions of all the other endocrine glands, as well as a hormone that influences growth. The absence of this growth hormone results in

dwarfism; its excess results in gigantic growth. In males, pituitary secretions activate the testes to secrete **testosterone,** which stimulates production of sperm. The pituitary gland is also involved in the development of male secondary sexual characteristics, such as facial hair, voice change, and physical maturation. Testosterone may even increase aggression and sexual desire. In females, a pituitary hormone stimulates production of **estrogen,** which is essential to the hormonal chain reaction that triggers the release of ova from a woman's ovaries, making her fertile. Certain birth-control pills work by blocking the mechanism in the pituitary gland that controls this hormone flow, thus preventing the ova from being released.

Pituitary gland Located in the brain, the gland that secretes growth hormone and influences the secretion of hormones by other endocrine glands.

Testosterone The male sex hormone, secreted by the testes, that stimulates production of sperm and is also responsible for the development of male secondary sex characteristics.

Estrogen The female sex hormone, produced by the ovaries, that is responsible for the release of eggs from the ovaries as well as for the development and maintenance of female reproductive structures and secondary sex characteristics.

SUMMING UP

Neuroscience is the contemporary embodiment of the age-old quest to understand the relationship between brain and behavior. Neuroscientists use a variety of methods to eavesdrop on the brain: They study patients with brain damage, they create lesions at specific brain sites, they stimulate brain sites, they record brain activity, and they produce computer-driven images of the brain at work.

The nervous system divides into the peripheral nervous system and the central nervous system. The central ner-

TABLE  3.1

Major Endocrine Glands and the Functions of the Hormones They Produce

These Glands:	Produce Hormones That Regulate:
Hypothalamus	Release of pituitary hormones
Anterior pituitary	Testes and ovaries Breast milk production Metabolism Reactions to stress
Posterior pituitary	Water conservation Breast milk excretion Uterus contraction
Thyroid	Metabolism Growth and development
Parathyroid	Calcium levels
Gut	Digestion
Pancreas	Glucose metabolism
Adrenals	Fight or flight responses Metabolism Sexual desire in women
Ovaries	Development of female sexual traits Ova production
Testes	Development of male sexual traits Sperm production Sexual desire in men

vous system consists of the brain and the spinal cord. The peripheral nervous system consists of the somatic nervous system and the autonomic nervous system.

The brain can be subdivided into the brain stem and cerebellum, the limbic system, and the cerebrum. The brain stem largely maintains basic life functions such as breathing, heart rate, and digestion. The cerebellum coordinates bodily movements and affects some forms of learning. The limbic system plays an important role in motivation, emotion, and memory. The cerebrum is responsible for the higher processes of language and thought.

Research suggests that the two cerebral hemispheres play different roles in most day-to-day tasks. For example, in most individuals the left hemisphere is specialized for speech processing. In general, the right hemisphere is more holistic in style; the left hemisphere is more analytic. General conclusions about the functions of the two hemispheres must be interpreted in light of individual differences, including sex differences.

The endocrine system is a network of glands that secrete hormones to regulate many life processes.

Neuron A cell in the nervous system specialized to receive, process, and/or transmit information to other cells.

The Nervous System in Action

One of the major goals of early physiologists was to better understand how the nervous system operates. Modern neuroscientists have made steady progress toward this goal, but they continue to work on solving more fine-grained pieces of the puzzle. Our objective in this section is to analyze and understand how the information available to your senses is ultimately communicated throughout your body and brain by nerve impulses. We begin by discussing the properties of the basic unit of the nervous system, the neuron.

The Neuron

A **neuron** is a cell specialized to receive, process, and/or transmit information to other cells within the body. Neurons vary in shape, size, chemical composition, and function—over 200 different types have been identified in mammal brains—but all neurons have the same basic structure (see **Figure 3.18**). There are between 100 billion and 1 trillion neurons in your brain.

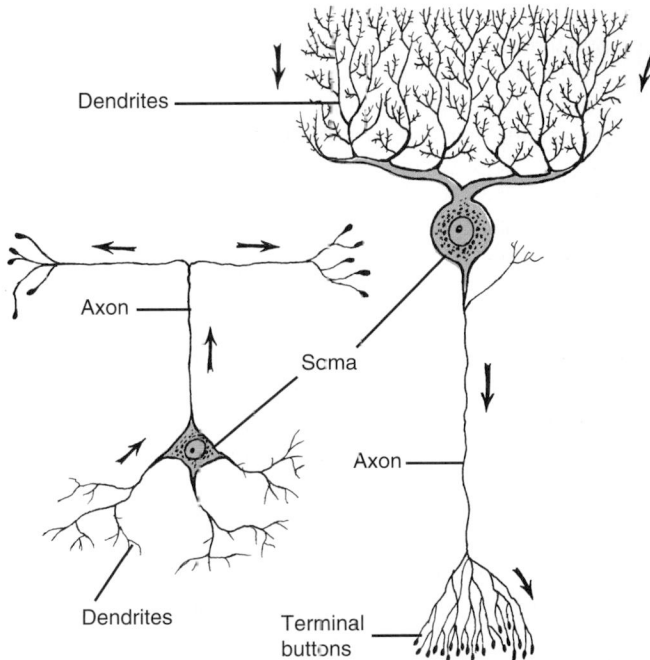

Dendrites · Axon · Soma · Axon · Dendrites · Terminal buttons

FIGURE 3.18

Two Types of Neurons

Note the differences in shape and dendritic branching. Arrows indicate directions to which information flows. Both cells are types of interneurons.

ADVANCES IN LOCALIZING BRAIN FUNCTION

Take a moment to fix your eyes on an object in your environment; perhaps a tree out a window or the computer on your desk. Now close your eyes and form a mental image of that same object. What happened in your brain during these two activities? How likely do you think it is that some of the same brain regions are involved in both real acts of perception and in visual imagination? Technological advances have allowed neuroscientists to answer this interesting question in a rigorous fashion.

As you'll see in Chapter 4, researchers have made great strides in understanding the brain bases of vision: They can trace the transformations of visual information from its beginning at the retinas of your eyes to its destination at primary visual cortex in your occipital lobes. How might researchers discover if the same areas of visual cortex are involved when people engage in visual imagery rather than visual perception? A team of researchers led by **Stephen Kosslyn** (Kosslyn et al., 1999) used two methods: PET scans, to which we have already introduced you, and *repetitive transcranial magnetic stimulation* (rTMS), which is a new technology that has only

quite recently been applied to human cognitive neuroscience.

In this set of studies, participants were asked to memorize four quadrant displays and then visualize them with their eyes closed. The participants' task was to answer questions

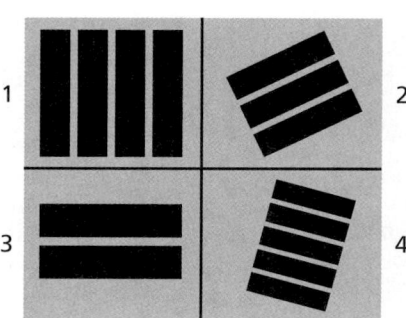

about, for example, the relative length or width of the stripes in the different quadrants. This task was designed so that participants were obliged to form visual images. In the PET studies, participants' brains were scanned while they carried out this task. The scans showed that the same areas of visual cortex were active that would be active if the participants were actually looking at the displays. Recall from Chapter 2,

however, that correlation is not causation: Just because the same areas of the brain are active in both instances doesn't mean the same function is being carried out.

This is where rTMS comes in: rTMS allows stronger causal claims to be made. This new technique uses pulses of magnetic stimulation to create temporary, reversible "lesions": Without any damage being done to tissue, brain regions can be briefly inactivated. What happens when participants attempt to carry out the stripe comparison task after the researchers have used rTMS to "lesion" primary visual cortex? Just as in the cases in which they are making the quadrant comparisons with their eyes wide open, performance is consistently disrupted in circumstances of visual imagery. This finding strongly suggests that primary visual cortex is actively engaged when you form visual images.

Does that finding surprise you? What questions do *you* have about how functions are distributed in your brain? As researchers continue to invent and apply new technologies, it becomes ever more likely that your questions can be brought to definitive answers.

Neurons typically take in information at one end and send out messages from the other. The part of the cell that receives incoming signals is a set of branched fibers called **dendrites**, which extend outward from the cell body. The basic job of the dendrites is to receive stimulation from sense receptors or other neurons. The cell body, or **soma**, contains the nucleus of the cell and the cytoplasm that sustains its life. The soma integrates information about the stimulation received from the dendrites (or in some cases received directly from another neuron) and passes it on to a single, extended fiber, the **axon**. In turn, the axon conducts this information along its length—which, in the spinal cord, can be several feet and, in the brain, less than a millimeter. At the other end of axons are swollen, bulblike structures called **terminal buttons**, through which the neuron is able to stimulate nearby glands, muscles, or other neurons. Neurons gen-

Dendrites The branched fibers of neurons that receive incoming signals.

Soma The cell body of a neuron, containing the nucleus and cytoplasm.

Axon The extended fiber of a neuron through which nerve impulses travel from the soma to the terminal buttons.

Terminal buttons The bulblike structures at the branched endings of axons that contain vesicles filled with neurotransmitters.

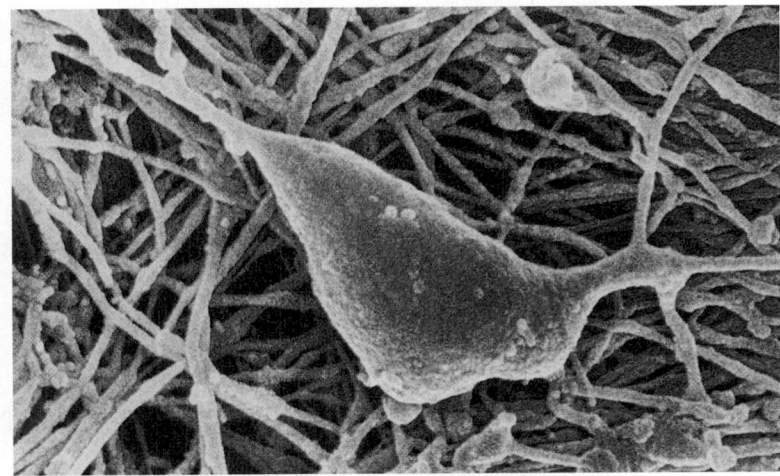

A neuron that affects contractions in the human intestine. What are the roles of the dendrites, soma, and axons in neural transmission?

erally transmit information in only one direction: from the dendrites through the soma to the axon to the terminal buttons (see **Figure 3.19**).

There are three major classes of neurons. **Sensory neurons** carry messages from sense receptor cells *toward* the central nervous system. Receptor cells are highly specialized cells that are sensitive, for example, to light, sound, and body position. **Motor neurons** carry messages *away* from the central nervous system toward the muscles and glands. The bulk of the neurons in the brain are **interneurons,** which relay messages from sensory neurons to other interneurons or to motor neurons. For every motor neuron in the body there are as many as

5,000 interneurons in the great intermediate network that forms the computational system of the brain (Nauta & Feirtag, 1979).

As an example of how these three kinds of neurons work together, consider the pain withdrawal reflex (see

- **Sensory neurons** The neurons that carry messages from sense receptors toward the central nervous system.
- **Motor neurons** The neurons that carry messages away from the central nervous system toward the muscles and glands.
- **Interneurons** Brain neurons that relay messages from sensory neurons to other interneurons or to motor neurons.

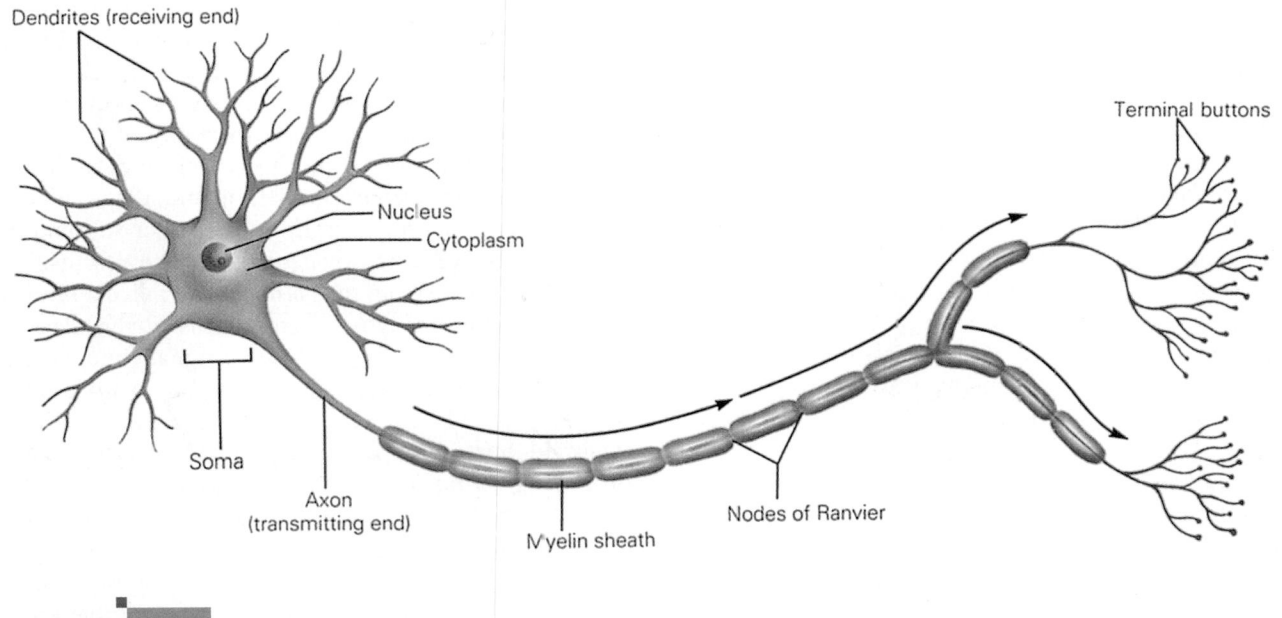

FIGURE 3.19

The Major Structures of the Neuron

The neuron receives nerve impulses through its dendrites. It then sends the nerve impulses through its axon to the terminal buttons, where neurotransmitters are released to stimulate other neurons.

The Pain Withdrawal Reflex

The pain withdrawal reflex shown here involves only three neurons: a sensory neuron, a motor neuron, and an interneuron.

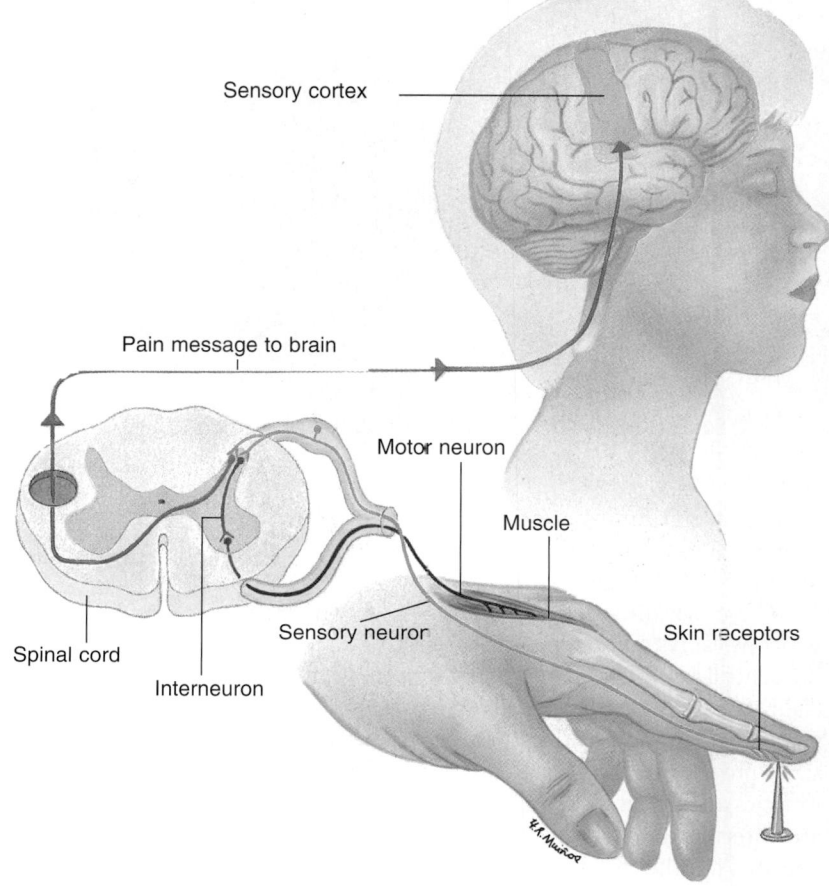

Sensory cortex

Pain message to brain

Motor neuron

Muscle

Spinal cord

Sensory neuron

Skin receptors

Interneuron

Figure 3.20). When pain receptors near the skin's surface are stimulated by a sharp object, they send messages via sensory neurons to an interneuron in the spinal cord. The interneuron responds by stimulating motor neurons, which, in turn, excite muscles in the appropriate area of the body to pull away from the pain-producing object. It is only *after* this sequence of neuronal events has taken place, and the body has been moved away from the stimulating object, that the brain receives information about the situation. In cases such as this, where survival depends on swift action, your perception of pain often occurs after you have physically responded to the danger. Of course, then the information from the incident is stored in the brain's memory system so that the next time you will avoid the potentially dangerous object altogether, before it can hurt you.

Interspersed among the brain's vast web of neurons are about five to ten times as many glial cells (**glia**). The word *glia* is derived from the Greek word for *glue*, which gives you a hint of one of the major duties performed by these cells: They hold neurons in place. In vertebrates, glial cells have several other important functions. A first function applies during development. Glial cells help guide newborn neurons to appropriate locations in the brain. A second function is housekeeping. When neurons are damaged and die, glial cells in the area multiply and clean up the cellular junk left behind; they can also take up excess neurotransmitters and other substances at the gaps between neurons. A third function is insulation. Glial cells form an insulating cover, called a *myelin sheath*, around some types of axons. This fatty insulation greatly increases the speed of nerve signal conduction. A fourth function of glial cells is to prevent toxic substances in the blood from reaching the delicate cells of the brain. Specialized glial cells, called astrocytes, make up a *blood–brain barrier*, forming a continuous envelope of fatty material around the blood vessels in the brain. Substances that are not soluble in fat do not dissolve through this barrier, and because many poisons and other harmful substances are not fat soluble, they cannot penetrate the barrier to reach the brain. Finally, neuroscientists have come to believe that glia may play an active role in affecting neural communication by affecting the concentrations of ions that allow for the transmission of nerve impulses.

Glia The cells that hold neurons together and facilitate neural transmission, remove damaged and dead neurons, and prevent poisonous substances in the blood from reaching the brain.

Excitatory inputs Information entering a neuron that signals it to fire.

Action Potentials

So far, we have spoken loosely about neurons "sending messages" or "stimulating" each other. The time has come to describe more formally the kinds of electro-chemical signals used by the nervous system to process and transmit information. It is these signals that are the basis of all you know, feel, desire, and create.

The basic question asked of each neuron is: Should it or should it not *fire*—produce a response—at some given time? In loose terms, neurons make this decision by combining the information arriving at their dendrites and soma (cell body) and determining whether those inputs are predominantly saying "fire" or "don't fire." More formally, each neuron will receive a balance of **excitatory**—fire!—and **inhibitory**—don't fire!—**inputs**. In neurons, the right pattern of excitatory inputs over time or space will lead to the production of an *action potential:* The neuron fires.

THE BIOCHEMICAL BASIS OF ACTION POTENTIALS

To explain how an **action potential** works, we need to describe the biochemical environment in which neurons draw together incoming information. All neural communication is produced by the flow of electrically charged particles, called *ions*, through the neuron's membrane, a thin "skin" separating the cell's internal and external environments. Think of a nerve fiber as a macaroni, filled with saltwater, floating in a salty soup. The soup and the fluid in the macaroni both contain ions—atoms of sodium (Na^+), chloride (Cl^-), calcium (Ca^+), and potassium (K^+)—that have either positive (+) or negative (−) charges (see **Figure 3.21**). The membrane, or the surface of the macaroni, plays a critical role in keeping the ingredients of the two fluids in an appropriate balance. When a cell is inactive, or in a *resting state,* there are about ten times as many potassium ions inside as there are sodium ions outside. The membrane is not a perfect barrier; it "leaks" a little, allowing some sodium ions to slip in while some potassium ions slip out. To correct for this, nature has provided transport mechanisms within the membrane that pump out sodium and pump in potassium. Successful operation of these pumps leaves the fluid inside a neuron with a slightly negative voltage (70/1,000 of a volt) relative to the fluid outside. This means that the fluid inside the cell is *polarized* with respect to the fluid outside the cell. This slight polarization is called the **resting potential**. It provides the electrochemical context in which a nerve cell can produce an action potential.

Inhibitory inputs Information entering a neuron signaling it not to fire.

Action potential The nerve impulse activated in a neuron that travels down the axon and causes neurotransmitters to be released into a synapse.

Resting potential The polarization of cellular fluid within a neuron, which provides the capability to produce an action potential.

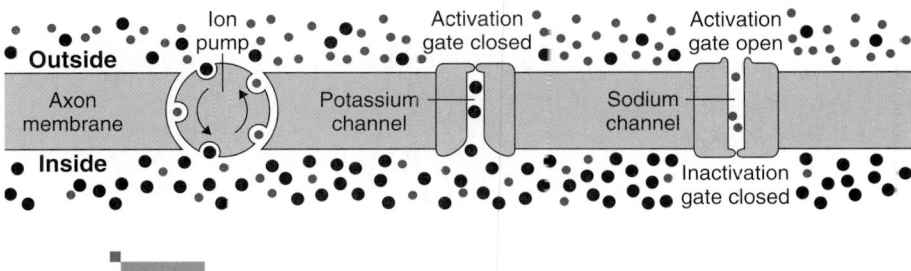

FIGURE 3.21

The Biochemical Basis of Action Potentials

The axon membrane separates fluids that differ greatly in their content of sodium ions (colored dots) and potassium ions (black dots). The exterior fluid is about 10 times richer in sodium ions than in potassium ions; in the interior fluid, the ratio is the reverse. The membrane is penetrated by proteins that act as selective channels for preferentially passing either sodium or potassium ions. In the resting state, when no nerve impulse is being transmitted, the two types of channel are closed and an ion pump maintains the ionic disequilibrium by pumping out sodium ions in exchange for potassium ions. The interior of the axon is normally about 70 millivolts negative with respect to the exterior. If this voltage difference is reduced by the arrival of a nerve impulse, the sodium channel opens, allowing sodium ions to flow into the axon. An instant later, the sodium channel closes and the potassium channel opens, allowing an outflow of potassium ions. The sequential opening and closing of the two kinds of channels effect the propagation of the nerve impulse.

The nerve cell begins the transition from a resting potential to an action potential in response to the pattern of inhibitory and excitatory inputs. Each kind of input affects the likelihood that the balance of ions from the inside to the outside of the cell will change. They cause changes in the function of **ion channels,** excitable portions of the cell membrane that selectively permit certain ions to flow in and out. Inhibitory inputs cause the ion channels to work harder to keep the inside of the cell negatively charged—this will keep the cell from firing. Excitatory inputs cause the ion channels to begin to allow sodium ions to flow in—this will allow the cell to fire. Because sodium ions have a positive charge, their influx can begin to change the relative balance of positive and negative charges across the cell membrane. An action potential begins when the excitatory inputs are sufficiently strong with respect to inhibitory inputs to *depolarize* the cell from –70 millivolts to –55 millivolts: Sufficient sodium has entered the cell to effect this change.

Once the action potential begins, sodium rushes into the neuron. As a result, the inside of the neuron becomes positive relative to the outside, meaning the neuron has become fully depolarized. A domino effect now propels the action potential down the axon. The leading edge of depolarization causes ion channels in the adjacent region of the axon to open and allow sodium to rush in. In this way—through successive depolarization—the signal passes down the axon (see Figure 3.21).

How does the neuron return to its original resting state of polarization after it fires? When the inside of the neuron becomes positive, the channels that allow sodium to flow in close and the channels that allow potassium to flow out open. The outflow of potassium ions restores the negative charge of the neuron. Thus, even while the signal is reaching the far end of the axon, the portions of the cell in which the action potential originated are being returned to their resting balance, so that they can be ready for their next stimulation.

PROPERTIES OF THE ACTION POTENTIAL

The biochemical manner in which the action potential is transmitted leads to several important properties. The action potential obeys the **all-or-none law:** The size of the action potential is unaffected by increases in the intensity of stimulation beyond the threshold level. Once excitatory inputs sum to reach the threshold level, a uniform action potential is generated. If the threshold is not reached, no action potential occurs. An added consequence of the all-or-none property is that the size of the action potential does not diminish along the length of the axon. In this sense, the action potential is said to be *self-propagating;* once started, it needs no outside stimulation to keep itself moving. It's similar to a lit fuse on a firecracker.

Different neurons conduct action potentials along their axons at different speeds; the fastest have signals that move at the rate of 200 meters per second, the slowest plod along at 10 centimeters per second. The axons of the faster neurons are covered with a tightly wrapped myelin sheath—consisting, as we explained earlier, of glial cells—making this part of the neuron resemble short tubes on a string. The tiny breaks between the tubes are called *nodes of Ranvier* (see Figure 3.19). In neurons having myelinated axons, the action potential literally skips along from one node to the next—saving the time and energy required to open and close ion channels at every location on the axon. Damage to the myelin sheath throws off the delicate timing of the action potential and causes serious problems. Multiple sclerosis (MS) is a devastating disorder caused by deterioration of the myelin sheath. It is characterized by double vision, tremors, and eventually paralysis. In MS, specialized cells from the body's immune system actually attack myelinated neurons, exposing the axon and disrupting normal synaptic transmission (Joyce, 1990).

After an action potential has passed down a segment of the axon, that region of the neuron enters a **refractory period** (see **Figure 3.22**). During the *absolute refractory*

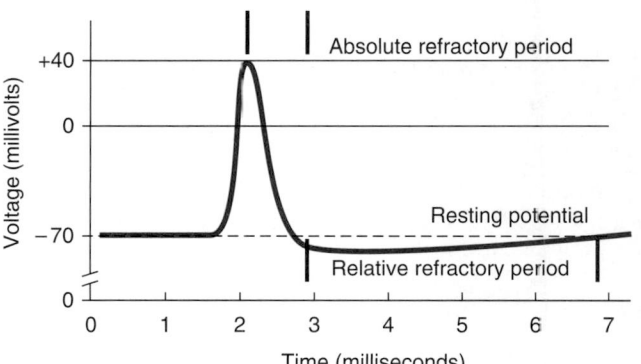

FIGURE 3.22

Timetable for Electrical Changes in the Neuron during an Action Potential

Sodium ions entering the neuron cause its electrical potential to change from slightly negative during its polarized, or resting, state to slightly positive during depolarization. Once the neuron is depolarized, it enters a brief refractory period during which further stimulation will not produce another action potential. Another action potential can occur only after the ionic balance between the inside and the outside of the cell is restored.

Ion channels The portions of neurons' cell membranes that selectively permit certain ions to flow in and out.

All-or-none law The rule that the size of the action potential is unaffected by increases in the intensity of stimulation beyond the threshold level.

Refractory period The period of rest during which a new nerve impulse cannot be activated in a segment of an axon.

period, further stimulation, no matter how intense, cannot cause another action potential to be generated; during the *relative refractory period,* the neuron will only fire in response to a stimulus stronger than what is ordinarily necessary. Have you ever tried to flush the toilet while it is filling back up with water? There must be a critical level of water for the toilet to flush again. Similarly, in order for a neuron to be able to generate another action potential, it must "reset" itself and await simulation beyond its threshold. The refractory period ensures, in part, that the action potential will only travel in one direction down the axon: It cannot move backward, because "earlier" parts of the axon are in a refractory state.

Synaptic Transmission

When the action potential completes its leapfrog journey down the axon to a terminal button, it must pass its information along to the next neuron. But no two neurons ever touch: They are joined at a **synapse,** with a small gap between the *presynaptic membrane* (the terminal button of the sending neuron) and the *postsynaptic membrane* (the surface of a dendrite or soma of a receiving neuron). When the action potential reaches the terminal button, it sets in motion a series of events called **synaptic transmission,** which is the relaying of information from one neuron to another across the synaptic gap (see **Figure 3.23**). Synaptic transmission begins when the arrival of the action potential at the terminal button causes small round packets, called *synaptic vesicles,* to move toward and affix themselves to the interior membrane of the terminal button. Inside each vesicle are **neurotransmitters,** biochemical substances that stimulate other neurons. The

Synapse The gap between one neuron and another.
Synaptic transmission The relaying of information from one neuron to another across the synaptic gap.
Neurotransmitters Chemical messengers released from neurons that cross the synapse from one neuron to another, stimulating the postsynaptic neuron.

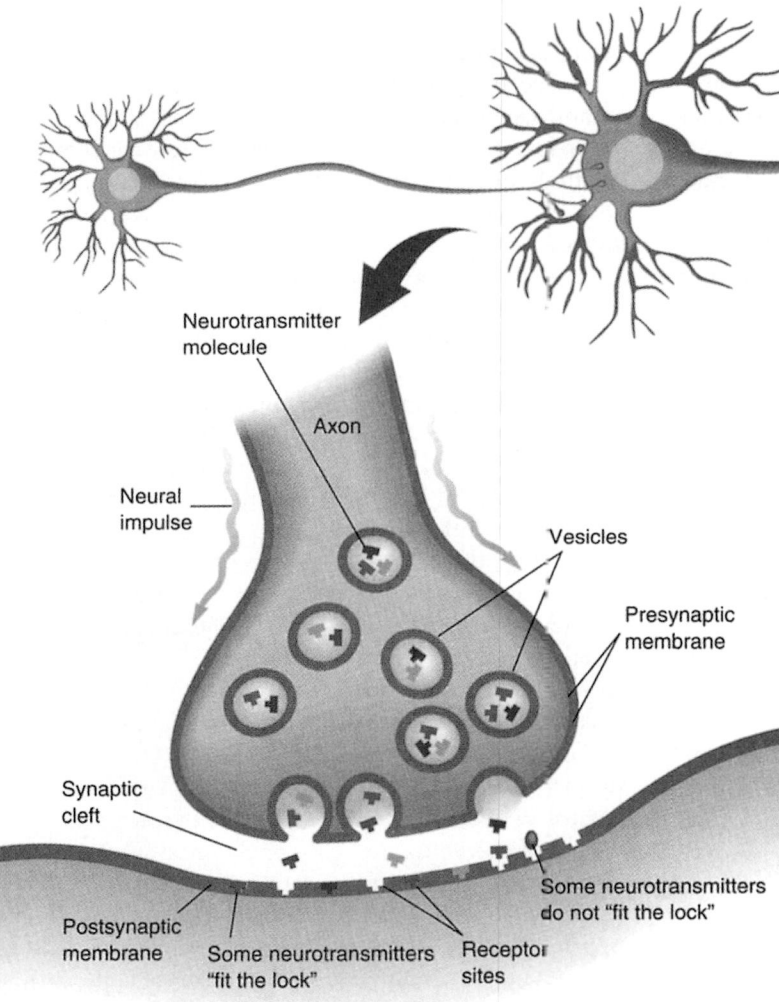

FIGURE 3.23

Synaptic Transmission

The action potential in the presynaptic neuron causes neurotransmitters to be released into the synaptic gap. Once across the gap, they stimulate receptor molecules embedded in the membrane of the postsynaptic neuron. Multiple neurotransmitters can exist within the same cell.

Neurotransmitter molecule

Axon

Neural impulse

Vesicles

Presynaptic membrane

Synaptic cleft

Some neurotransmitters do not "fit the lock"

Postsynaptic membrane

Some neurotransmitters "fit the lock"

Receptor sites

Dendrite

THE NERVOUS SYSTEM IN ACTION

77

action potential also causes ion channels to open that admit calcium ions into the terminal button. The influx of calcium ions causes the rupture of the synaptic vesicles and the release of whatever neurotransmitters they contain. Once the synaptic vesicles rupture, the neurotransmitters are dispersed rapidly across the *synaptic cleft* to the postsynaptic membrane. To complete synaptic transmission, the neurotransmitters attach to *receptor molecules* embedded in the postsynaptic membrane.

The neurotransmitters will bind to the receptor molecules under two conditions. First, no other neurotransmitters or other chemical substances can be attached to the receptor molecule. Second, the shape of the neurotransmitter must match the shape of the receptor molecule—as precisely as a key fits into a keyhole. If neither condition is met, the neurotransmitter will not attach to the receptor molecule. This means that it will not be able to stimulate the postsynaptic membrane. If the neurotransmitter does become attached to the receptor molecule, then it may provide "fire" or "don't fire" information to this next neuron. Once the neurotransmitter has completed its job, it detaches from the receptor molecule and drifts back into the synaptic gap. There it is either decomposed through the action of enzymes or reabsorbed into the presynaptic terminal button for quick reuse.

Depending on the receptor molecule, a neurotransmitter will have either an excitatory or an inhibitory effect. That is, the same neurotransmitter may be excitatory at one synapse but inhibitory at another. Each neuron integrates the information it obtains at synapses with between 1,000 and 10,000 other neurons to decide whether it ought to initiate another action potential. It is the integration of these thousands of inhibitory and excitatory inputs that allows all-or-none action potentials to provide the foundation for all human experience.

You may be wondering why we have taken you so deep into the nervous system. After all, this is a psychology course, and psychology is supposed to be about behavior and thinking and emotion. In fact, synapses are the biological medium in which all of these activities occur. If you change the normal activity of the synapse, you change how people behave, how they think, and how they feel. Understanding the functioning of the synapse has led to tremendous advances in the understanding of learning and memory, emotion, psychological disorders, drug addiction, and, in general, the chemical formula for mental health. You will use the knowledge you have acquired in this chapter throughout *Psychology and Life*.

Neurotransmitters and Their Functions

More than 60 different chemical substances are known or suspected to function as neurotransmitters in the brain. The neurotransmitters that have been studied most intensively meet a set of technical criteria. Each is manufactured in the presynaptic terminal button and is released when an action potential reaches that terminal. The neurotransmitter's presence in the synaptic cleft produces a biological response in the postsynaptic membrane, and, if its release is prevented, no subsequent responses can occur. To give you a sense of the effects different neurotransmitters have on the regulation of behavior, we will discuss a set that has been found to play an important role in the daily functioning of the brain. This brief discussion will also enable you to understand many of the ways in which neural transmission can go awry.

ACETYLCHOLINE

Acetylcholine is found in both the central and peripheral nervous systems. Memory loss among patients suffering from Alzheimer's disease, a degenerative disease that is increasingly common among older persons, is believed to be caused by the deterioration of neurons that secrete acetylcholine. Acetylcholine is also excitatory at junctions between nerves and muscles, where it causes muscles to contract. A number of toxins affect the synaptic actions of acetylcholine. For example, botulinum toxin, often found in food that has been preserved incorrectly, poisons an individual by preventing release of acetylcholine in the respiratory system. This poisoning, known as *botulism*, can cause death by suffocation. Curare, a poison Amazon Indians use on the tips of their blowgun darts, paralyzes lung muscles by occupying critical acetylcholine receptors, preventing the normal activity of the transmitter.

GABA

GABA (gamma-aminobutyric acid) is the most common inhibitory neurotransmitter in the brain. GABA may be used as a messenger in as many as a third of all brain synapses. Neurons that are sensitive to GABA are particularly concentrated in brain regions such as the thalamus, hypothalamus, and occipital lobes. GABA appears to play a critical role in some forms of psychopathology by inhibiting neural activity; when levels of this neurotransmitter in the brain become low, people may experience the extra neural activity as feelings of anxiety (Paul et al., 1986). Anxiety disorders are often treated with *benzodiazepine* drugs, such as *Valium* or *Xanax*, that increase GABA activity (Ballenger, 1999). The *benzodiazepine* drugs do not attach directly to GABA receptors. Instead they allow GABA itself to bind more effectively to postsynaptic receptor molecules.

DOPAMINE, NOREPINEPHRINE, AND SEROTONIN

The *catecholamines* are a class of chemical substances that include two important neurotransmitters, *dopamine* and *norepinephrine*. Both have been shown to play prominent roles in psychological disorders, such as mood disturbances and schizophrenia. Norepinephrine appears to be involved in some forms of depression: Drugs that increase brain levels of this neurotransmitter elevate mood and re-

HOW DO LIFE EXPERIENCES AFFECT YOUR BRAIN?

As you read this chapter, you are acquiring new information—does that mean your brain is changing? It should be! Students who are for the first time encountering contemporary neuroscience often come to wonder about the ways in which life experiences affect their brain.

One classic series of studies, carried out by **Mark Rosenzweig** and his colleagues, demonstrated the consequences for rats of being raised in impoverished or enriched environments (for reviews, see Rosenzweig, 1996, 1999b). For the impoverished environments, the rats were kept alone in their cages; for the enriched environments, the rats shared a large cage with several other rats and had playthings changed daily. After periods varying from a few days to several months, the experimenters examined the rats' brains. The results were dramatic. The average cortex of the rats with experience in the enriched environments was heavier and thicker—positive attributes—than that of their impoverished littermates. Measurable differences emerged even when the rats had been in the enriched environments for only a few days. The differences also emerged in rats beyond their "childhood." That is, even older rats obtained a benefit when they were transferred to enriched environments. Although these studies were carried out with rats, researchers believe the results apply to humans as well: Enriched environments have a positive impact on brain development and function.

With brain imaging techniques, it is possible to measure very specific brain differences related to individuals' life experiences. Consider those musicians who play the violin. They are required to control the fingers of their left hands with an extremely delicate touch. If you refer back to Figure 3.12, you'll see that a good deal of sensory cortex is devoted to the fingers. Brain scans reveal that the representation of fingers of the left hand is even more enhanced for violin players as compared to nonplayers (Elbert et al., 1995). No such increase is found for fingers of the right hand, which do not have as great a sensory role in violin play. The extra represen- tation of the left fingers was greatest for violinists who took up the instrument before age 12.

You have probably already guessed that some life experiences can also have a negative impact on your brain's ability to function. Consider the brain structure called the *hippocampus,* which we described earlier as a critical structure for the acquisition of explicit memories. Researchers have demonstrated that chronic stress—an enduring state in which an organism's physical and psychological resources are taxed to the limit (see Chapter 13)—causes dendrites on the neurons in the hippocampus to atrophy (McEwen, 1999; Sapolsky, 1996). The consequence, as you might anticipate, is that some memory abilities become impaired. Rats, for example, lose some of their ability to learn to navigate mazes successfully after chronic stress (Conrad et al., 1996). An important goal of contemporary research in neuroscience is to devise methods for counteracting the brain consequences of negative life experiences. Such research should benefit us all!

---

lieve depression. Conversely, higher-than-normal levels of dopamine have been found in persons with schizophrenia. As you might expect, one way to treat people with this disorder is to give them a drug that decreases brain levels of dopamine. In the early days of drug therapy, an interesting but unfortunate problem arose. High doses of the drug used to treat schizophrenia produced symptoms of Parkinson's disease, a progressive and ultimately fatal disorder involving disruption of motor functioning. (Parkinson's disease is caused by deterioration of neurons that manufacture most of the brain's dopamine.) This finding led to research that improved drug therapy for schizophrenia and to research that focused on drugs that could be used in the treatment of Parkinson's disease.

All the neurons that produce *serotonin* are located in the brain stem, which is involved in arousal and many autonomic processes. The hallucinogenic drug LSD (ly- sergic acid diethylamide) appears to produce its effects by suppressing the effects of serotonin neurons. These serotonin neurons normally inhibit other neurons, but the lack of inhibition produced by LSD creates vivid and bizarre sensory experiences, some of which last for hours. Many antidepressant drugs, such as Prozac, enhance the action of serotonin by preventing it from being removed from the synaptic cleft (Barondes, 1994).

ENDORPHINS

The *endorphins* are a group of chemicals that are usually classified as neuromodulators. A **neuromodulator** is any substance that modifies or modulates the activities of

Neuromodulator Any substance that modifies or modulates the activities of the postsynaptic neuron.

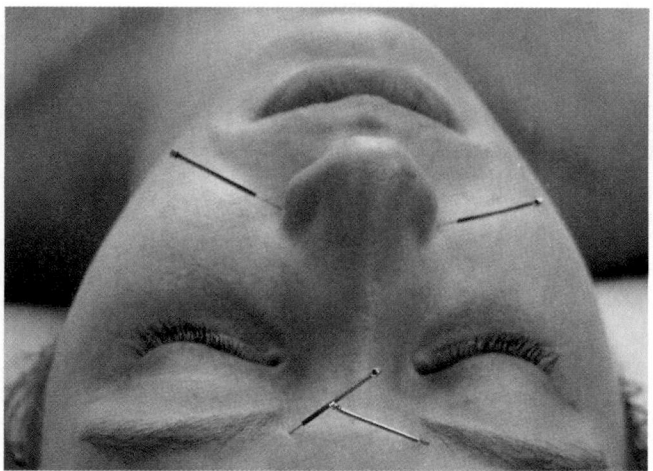

Why do patients experience pain relief from acupuncture?

the postsynaptic neuron. Endorphins (short for *endogenous morphines*) play an important role in the control of emotional behaviors (anxiety, fear, tension, pleasure) and pain—drugs like opium and morphine bind to the same receptor sites in the brain. Endorphins have been called the "keys to paradise" because of their pleasure–pain controlling properties. Researchers have examined the possibility that endorphins are at least partially responsible for the pain-reducing effects of acupuncture and placebos (Fields & Levine, 1984; Murray, 1995; Watkins & Mayer, 1982). Such tests rely on the drug *naloxone*, whose only known effect is to block morphine and endorphins from binding to receptors. Any procedure that reduces pain by stimulating release of endorphins becomes ineffective when naloxone is administered. With the injection of naloxone, acupuncture and placebos do, in fact, lose their power—suggesting that, ordinarily, endorphins help them do their work.

Researchers have also documented that gases like *carbon monoxide* and *nitric oxide* can function as neurotransmitters (Barinaga, 1993). What is most surprising about this new class of neurotransmitters is that they violate many of the normal expectations about synaptic transmission. For example, rather than binding to receptor molecules, as do the other neurotransmitters we have discussed, these gaseous transmitters appear to pass directly through the receptor cell's outer membrane. This surprising discovery should reinforce your impression that the brain possesses many secrets yet to be revealed.

In this chapter, we have taken a brief peek at the marvelous 3-pound universe that is your brain. It is one thing to recognize that the brain controls behavior and your mental processes but quite another to understand how the brain serves all those functions. Neuroscientists are engaged in the fascinating quest to understand the interplay among brain, behavior, and environment. You now have the type of background that will allow you to appreciate new knowledge as it unfolds.

SUMMING UP

Three major types of neurons are sensory neurons, motor neurons, and interneurons. Most of the neurons in the brain are interneurons, held in place by glial cells. Neurons fire when they receive the right balance of excitatory and inhibitory inputs. Neurons send messages in an all-or-none fashion through action potentials traveling down the axon. Neurotransmitters are released into the synaptic cleft and pass on information by binding with receptor molecules on the adjacent neuron. Many life processes depend on the action of important neurotransmitters such as acetylcholine, dopamine, and serotonin.

RECAPPING
MAIN POINTS

Heredity and Behavior

- Species originate and change over time because of natural selection.

- In the evolution of humans, bipedalism and encephalization were responsible for subsequent advances, including language and culture.

- The basic unit of heredity is the gene. Genes determine the range of effects that environmental factors can have in influencing the expression of phenotypic traits.

Biology and Behavior

- Neuroscientists use several methods to research the relation between brain and behavior: studying brain-damaged patients, producing lesions at specific brain sites, electrically stimulating the brain, recording brain activity, and imaging the brain with computerized devices.

- The brain and the spinal cord make up the central nervous system (CNS).

- The peripheral nervous system (PNS) is composed of all neurons connecting the CNS to the body. The PNS consists of the somatic nervous system, which regulates the body's skeletal muscles, and the autonomic nervous system (ANS), which regulates life-support processes.

- The brain consists of three integrated layers: the brain stem, limbic system, and cerebrum.
- The brain stem is responsible for breathing, digestion, and heart rate.
- The limbic system is involved in long-term memory, aggression, eating, drinking, and sexual behavior.
- The cerebrum controls higher mental functions.
- Some functions are lateralized to one hemisphere of the brain. For example, most individuals have speech localized in the left hemisphere.
- Although the two hemispheres of the brain work smoothly in concert, they typically embody different styles of processing: The left hemisphere is more analytic, while the right hemisphere is more holistic.
- Individual differences can modify these general conclusions. For example, males and females have somewhat different patterns of lateralization.
- The endocrine system produces and secretes hormones into the bloodstream.
- Hormones help regulate growth, primary and secondary sexual characteristics, metabolism, digestion, and arousal.
- The hypothalamus controls the endocrine system by stimulating the pituitary gland.

The Nervous System in Action

- The neuron, the basic unit of the nervous system, receives, processes, and relays information to other cells, glands, and muscles.
- Neurons relay information from the dendrites through the cell body (soma) to the axon to the terminal buttons.

- Sensory neurons receive messages from specialized receptor cells and send them toward the CNS. Motor neurons direct messages from the CNS to muscles and glands. Interneurons relay information from sensory neurons to other interneurons or to motor neurons.
- Once the summation of inputs to a neuron exceeds a specific threshold, an action potential is sent along the axon to the terminal buttons.
- All-or-none action potentials are created when the opening of ion channels allows an exchange of ions across the cell membrane.
- Neurotransmitters are released into the synaptic gap between neurons. Once they diffuse across the gap, they lodge in the receptor molecules of the postsynaptic membrane.
- Whether these neurotransmitters excite or inhibit the membrane depends on the nature of the receptor molecule.

Key Terms

action potential (p. 75)
all-or-none law (p. 76)
amygdala (p. 62)
association cortex (p. 66)
auditory cortex (p. 65)
autonomic nervous system (ANS) (p. 59)
axon (p. 72)
brain stem (p. 61)
Broca's area (p. 56)
central nervous system (CNS) (p. 58)
cerebellum (p. 62)
cerebral cortex (p. 63)
cerebral hemispheres (p. 63)
cerebrum (p. 63)
corpus callosum (p. 63)
dendrites (p. 72)
DNA (deoxyribonucleic acid) (p. 53)
electroencephalogram (EEG) (p. 57)
endocrine system (p. 69)
estrogen (p. 70)
excitatory inputs (p. 74)

frontal lobe (p. 63)
functional MRI (fMRI) (p. 58)
genes (p. 53)
genetics (p. 53)
genotype (p. 51)
glia (p. 74)
heredity (p. 53)
hippocampus (p. 62)
homeostasis (p. 63)
hormones (p. 69)
human behavior genetics (p. 53)
hypothalamus (p. 63)
inhibitory inputs (p. 75)
interneurons (p. 73)
ion channels (p. 76)
lesions (p. 56)
limbic system (p. 62)
magnetic resonance imaging (MRI) (p. 57)
medulla (p. 61)
motor cortex (p. 64)
motor neurons (p. 73)
natural selection (p. 50)
neuromodulator (p. 79)
neuron (p. 71)
neuroscience (p. 55)
neurotransmitters (p. 77)
occipital lobe (p. 64)
parasympathetic division (p. 61)
parietal lobe (p. 64)
peripheral nervous system (PNS) (p. 58)
PET scans (p. 57)
phenotype (p. 51)
pituitary gland (p. 70)
pons (p. 61)
refractory period (p. 76)
resting potential (p. 75)
reticular formation (p. 61)
sensory neurons (p. 73)
sex chromosomes (p. 53)
sociobiology (p. 53)
soma (p. 72)
somatic nervous system (p. 59)
somatosensory cortex (p. 65)
sympathetic division (p. 61)
synapse (p. 77)
synaptic transmission (p. 77)
temporal lobe (p. 64)
terminal buttons (p. 72)
testosterone (p. 70)
thalamus (p. 62)
visual cortex (p. 65)

4

■ **SENSORY KNOWLEDGE OF THE WORLD**
Psychophysics • From Physical Events to Mental Events

■ **THE VISUAL SYSTEM**
The Human Eye • The Pupil and the Lens • The Retina • Pathways to the Brain • Seeing Color • Complex Visual Analysis

■ **PSYCHOLOGY IN THE 21ST CENTURY: CAN TECHNOLOGY RESTORE SIGHT?**

■ **HEARING**
The Physics of Sound • Psychological Dimensions of Sound • The Physiology of Hearing

■ **YOUR OTHER SENSES**
Smell • Taste • Touch and Skin Senses • The Vestibular and Kinesthetic Senses • Pain

■ **PSYCHOLOGY IN YOUR LIFE: WHY IS "HOT" FOOD PAINFUL?**

■ **RECAPPING MAIN POINTS**
Key Terms

onathan I. was a painter who, throughout his successful artistic career, produced abstract canvases with great mixtures of vivid colors. At age 65, he suffered brain damage that left him completely color blind. When he looked at his own artwork, all he could see was gray, black, and white; where formerly he had seen colors with rich personal associations, now he saw splotches that were "dirty" or "wrong." And it wasn't just his art. In his day-to-day life, for example, he began to limit his diet to black foods and white foods—black olives and white rice still looked right to him, whereas colored foods now appeared disturbingly gray and unpalatable.

Jonathan I.'s story, however, is ultimately not a tragic one. Over time, as he recovered from his initial sense of dislocation, Mr. I. began to explore the artistic possibilities of painting in black and white. People who admired his work saw this as a new and interesting phase of his career, without knowing that a brain injury had dictated the direction. Mr. I. felt that his sudden color blindness had opened new aspects of the visual world to his examination: "Although Mr. I. does not deny his loss, and at some level still mourns it, he has come to feel that his vision has become 'highly refined,' 'privileged,' that he sees a world of pure form, uncluttered by color" (Sacks, 1995, p. 38). Thus, despite the loss of color vision, Mr I.'s sensory processes still provide him with a version of the world he can appreciate and transform as art.

How does Mr. I.'s story make you feel about your own sensory abilities? Have you ever wondered how your brain—locked in the dark, silent chamber of the skull—experiences the blaze of color in a Van Gogh painting, the driving melodies and rhythms of rock 'n' roll, the refreshing taste of watermelon on a hot day, the soft touch of a child's kiss, or the fragrance of wildflowers in the springtime? Our task in this chapter is to explain how your body and brain make sense of the buzz of stimulation—sights, sounds, and so on—constantly around you. You will see how evolution has equipped you with the capability to detect many different dimensions of experience. You will discover that the senses you most often take for granted involve a remarkably intricate set of mechanisms.

This chapter deals with the basic biological elements of experience: **Sensation** is the process by which stimulation of *sensory receptors*—the structures in our eyes, ears, and so on—produces neural impulses that represent experiences inside or outside the body. By contrast, Chapter 5 deals with the processes associated with higher-level activity of the central nervous system, the perceptual processes—the identification, interpretation, integration, and classification of sensory experiences. By the end of the next chapter, you should understand how your brain ultimately recombines those different types of information to give you a coherent experience of the world.

Sensuality is the enjoyment of sensory experiences. What is the relationship between sensuality and survival?

Sensation The process by which stimulation of a sensory receptor gives rise to neural impulses that result in an experience, or awareness of, conditions inside or outside the body.

However, before starting this journey into the world of sensation, let's pause to reflect on the dual functions of your senses: *survival* and *sensuality*. Your senses help you survive by sounding alarms of danger, priming you to take swift action to ward off hazards, and directing you toward agreeable sensations. Your senses also provide you with sensuality. Sensuality is the quality of being devoted to the gratification of the senses; it entails enjoying the experiences that appeal to your various senses of sight, sound, touch, taste, and smell. As you read this chapter, you might consider how knowledge of the mechanisms of sensation can help you discover the healthy pleasures of sensuality and teach you to take new delight in the world of sounds, colors, smells, tastes, and touch.

■ Sensory Knowledge of the World

Your experience of external reality must be relatively accurate and error free. If not, you couldn't survive. You need food to sustain you, shelter to protect you, interactions with other people to fulfill social needs, and awareness of danger to keep out of harm's way. To meet these needs, you must get reliable information about the world. All species have developed some kinds of specialized mechanisms to gather information. The human species does not specialize in one particular sensory domain: You lack the acute vision of hawks, hearing of bats, and sense of smell of rodents. Instead, humans are equipped with sensory mechanisms that enable them to process a wide variety of complex sensory input.

Because of the importance of sensory processes, sensation has endured as a prominent topic across the whole history of psychological research. While laying down the foundations of experimental psychology, Wundt (1907) proposed that sensations and feelings are the elementary processes from which complex experiences are built. Titchener (1898) brought this view to the United States, giving sensation a central place in his introspective examination of the contents of consciousness. As we shall see next, the earliest psychological research on sensation examined the relationship between events in the environment and people's experience of those events.

Psychophysics The study of the correspondence between physical stimulation and psychological experience.

Absolute threshold The minimum amount of physical energy needed to produce a reliable sensory experience; operationally defined as the stimulus level at which a sensory signal is detected half the time.

Psychometric function A graph that plots the percentage of detections of a stimulus (on the vertical axis) for each stimulus intensity (on the horizontal axis).

■ Psychophysics

How loud must a fire alarm at a factory be in order for workers to hear it over the din of the machinery? How bright does a warning light on a pilot's control panel have to be to appear twice as bright as the other lights? How much sugar do you need to put in a cup of coffee before it begins to taste sweet? To answer these questions, we must be able to measure the intensity of sensory experiences. This is the central task of **psychophysics,** the study of the relationship between physical stimuli and the behavior or mental experiences the stimuli evoke. Psychophysics is the oldest field within the science of psychology (Levine & Shefner, 1981).

The most significant figure in the history of psychophysics was the German physicist **Gustav Fechner** (1801–1887). Fechner coined the term *psychophysics* and provided a set of procedures to relate the intensity of a physical stimulus—measured in physical units—to the magnitude of the sensory experience—measured in psychological units (Fechner, 1860/1966). Fechner's techniques are the same whether the stimuli are for light, sound, taste, odor, or touch: Researchers determine thresholds and construct psychophysical scales relating strength of sensation to strength of stimuli.

ABSOLUTE THRESHOLDS AND SENSORY ADAPTATION

What is the smallest, weakest stimulus energy that an organism can detect? How soft can a tone be, for instance, and still be heard? These questions refer to the **absolute threshold** for stimulation—the minimum amount of physical energy needed to produce a sensory experience. Researchers measure absolute thresholds by asking vigilant observers to perform detection tasks, such as trying to see a dim light in a dark room or trying to hear a soft sound in a quiet room. During a series of many trials the stimulus is presented at varying intensities, and on each trial the observers indicate whether they were aware of it. (If you've ever had your hearing evaluated, you participated in an absolute threshold test.)

The results of an absolute threshold study can be summarized in a **psychometric function:** a graph that shows the percentage of detections (plotted on the vertical axis) at each stimulus intensity (plotted on the horizontal axis). A typical psychometric function is shown in **Figure 4.1.** For very dim lights, detection is at 0 percent; for bright lights, detection is at 100 percent. If there were a single, true absolute threshold, you would expect the transition from 0 to 100 percent detection to be very sharp, occurring right at the point where the intensity reached the threshold. But this does not happen, for at least two reasons: Viewers themselves change slightly each time they try to detect a stimulus (because of changes in attention, fatigue, and so on), and viewers sometimes respond even in the absence of a stimulus

Can you hear the tone? Hearing evaluation is usually done with an absolute threshold test. Why do these tests require multiple trials?

(the type of false alarm we will discuss shortly, when we describe signal detection theory). Thus, the psychometric curve is usually a smooth S-shaped curve, in which there is a region of transition from no detection to occasional detection to detection all the time.

Because a stimulus does not suddenly become clearly detectable at all times at a specific intensity, the operational definition of absolute threshold is *the stimulus level at which a sensory signal is detected half the time.*

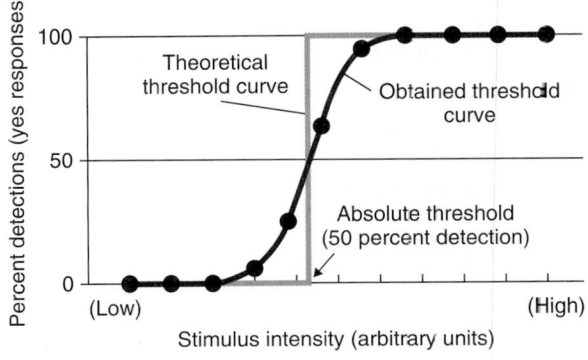

FIGURE 4.1

Calculation of Absolute Thresholds

Because a stimulus does not become suddenly detectable at a certain point, absolute threshold is defined as the intensity at which the stimulus is detected half of the time over many trials.

TABLE 4.1

Approximate Thresholds of Familiar Events

Sense Modality	Detection Threshold
Light	A candle flame seen at 30 miles on a dark, clear night
Sound	The tick of a watch under quiet conditions at 20 feet
Taste	One teaspoon of sugar in 2 gallons of water
Smell	One drop of perfume diffused into the entire volume of a three-room apartment
Touch	The wing of a bee falling on your cheek from a distance of 1 centimeter

Thresholds for different sense modalities can be measured using the same procedure, simply by changing the stimulus dimension. **Table 4.1** shows absolute threshold levels for several familiar natural stimuli.

Although it is possible to identify absolute thresholds for detection, it is also important to note that your sensory systems are more sensitive to *changes* in the sensory environment than to steady states. The systems have evolved so that they favor new environmental inputs over old through a process called adaptation. **Sensory adaptation** is the diminishing responsiveness of sensory systems to prolonged stimulus input. You may have noticed, for example, that sunshine seems less blinding after a while outdoors. People often have their most fortunate experiences of adaptation in the domain of smell: You walk into a room, and something really has a rank odor; over time, however, as your smell system adapts, the odor fades out of awareness. Your environment is always full of a great diversity of sensory stimulation. The mechanism of adaptation allows you to notice, and react, more quickly to the challenges of new sources of information.

RESPONSE BIAS AND SIGNAL DETECTION THEORY

In our discussion so far, we have assumed that all observers are created equal. However, threshold measurements can also be affected by **response bias**, the systematic tendency for an observer to favor responding in a particular way because of factors unrelated to the sensory features of the stimulus. Suppose, for example, you are in an experiment in which you must detect a weak light. In the first phase of the experiment, the researcher gives you $5 when

Sensory adaptation A phenomenon in which receptor cells lose their power to respond after a period of unchanged stimulation; allows a more rapid reaction to new sources of information.

Response bias The systematic tendency as a result of nonsensory factors for an observer to favor responding in a particular way.

you are correct in saying, "yes, a light was there." In the second phase, the researcher gives you $5 when you are correct in saying, "no, there wasn't any light." In each phase, you are penalized $2 any time you are incorrect. Can you see how this reward structure would create a shift in response bias from phase one to phase two? Wouldn't you say "yes" more often in the first phase—with the same amount of certainty that the stimulus was present?

Signal detection theory (SDT) is a systematic approach to the problem of response bias (Green & Swets, 1966). Instead of focusing strictly on sensory processes, signal detection theory emphasizes the process of making a *judgment* about the presence or absence of stimulus events. Whereas classical psychophysics conceptualized a single absolute threshold, SDT identifies two distinct processes in sensory detection: (1) an initial *sensory process,* which reflects the observer's sensitivity to the strength of the stimulus; and (2) a subsequent separate *decision process,* which reflects the observer's response biases.

SDT offers a procedure for evaluating both the sensory process and the decision processes at once. The measurement procedure is actually just an extension of the idea of catch trials. The basic design is given in **Figure 4.2.** A weak stimulus is presented in half the trials; no stimulus is presented in the other half. In each trial, observers respond by saying *yes* if they think the signal was present and *no* if they think it wasn't. As shown in matrix A of the figure, each response is scored as a hit, a miss, a false alarm, or a correct rejection, depending on

whether a signal was, in fact, presented and whether the observer responded accurately.

An observer who is a *yea sayer* (chronically answers *yes*) will give a high number of hits but will also have a high number of false alarms, as shown in matrix B. One who is a *nay sayer* (chronically answers *no*) will give a lower number of hits but also a lower number of false alarms, as shown in matrix C. Working with the percentages of hits and false alarms, researchers use mathematical procedures to calculate separate measures of observers' sensitivity and response biases. This procedure makes it possible to find out whether two observers have the same sensitivity despite large differences in response criterion. By providing a way of separating sensory process from response bias, the theory of signal detection allows an experimenter to identify and separate the roles of the sensory stimulus and the individual's criterion level in producing the final response.

The SDT approach provides a model of decision making that can be used in other contexts as well. Many everyday decisions involve different rewards for every hit and correct rejection and penalties for every miss and false alarm. For example, if you decline an invitation to the movies, will you be avoiding a dull evening (a correct rejection) or eliminating the chance for a lifetime of love (a miss)? Your decisions are likely to be biased by the schedule of anticipated gains and losses. Such a detection matrix is called a *payoff matrix.* If, for example, saying *no* when a stimulus is present (a miss) is more costly than saying *yes* when it is absent (a false alarm), a yes bias will rule. Surgeons are often in this situation. They usually prefer to operate when they are not entirely certain a tumor is malignant, thereby risking a false alarm, rather than risking a missed malignancy—and failing to prevent a death. In general, decision makers must consider the available evidence, the relative costs of each type

> **Signal detection theory (SDT)** A systematic approach to the problem of response bias that allows an experimenter to identify and separate the roles of sensory stimuli and the individual's criterion level in producing the final response.

A. Response given

Stimulus signal		Yes	No
	On	Hit	Miss
	Off	False alarm	Correct rejection

B. "Yea sayer" responses

		Yes	No
	On	92%	8%
	Off	46%	54%

C. "Nay sayer" responses

		Yes	No
	On	40%	60%
	Off	4%	96%

FIGURE 4.2

The Theory of Signal Detection

Matrix A shows the possible outcomes when a subject is asked if a target stimulus occurred on a given trial. Matrixes B and C show the typical responses of a *yea sayer* (biased toward saying yes) and a *nay sayer* (biased toward saying no).

of error, and the relative gains from each type of correct decision. Signal detection theory provides an important tool for analyzing decisions.

DIFFERENCE THRESHOLDS

Imagine you have been employed by a beverage company that wants to produce a cola product that tastes noticeably sweeter than existing colas, but (to save money) the firm wants to put as little extra sugar in the cola as possible. You are being asked to measure a **difference threshold,** the smallest physical difference between two stimuli that can still be recognized as a difference. To measure a difference threshold, you use pairs of stimuli and ask your observers whether they believe the two stimuli to be the same or different.

For the beverage problem, you would give your observers two colas on each trial, one of some standard recipe and one just a bit sweeter. For each pair, the individual would say *same* or *different*. After many such trials, you would plot a psychometric function by graphing the percent of *different* responses on the vertical axis as a function of the actual differences, plotted on the horizontal axis. The difference threshold is operationally defined as *the point at which the stimuli are recognized as different half of the time.* This difference threshold value is known as a **just noticeable difference, or JND.** The JND is a quantitative unit for measuring the magnitude of the psychological difference between any two sensations.

In 1834, **Ernst Weber** pioneered the study of JNDs and discovered the important relationship that we illustrate in **Figure 4.3.** Suppose you perform a difference threshold experiment with a standard bar length of 10 millimeters. To carry out this experiment, you present participants with pairs of bars in which one bar is the 10-millimeter standard length and the second bar varies by some small amount from that standard. The participants' task is to say whether the two bars are the same or different. You find the difference threshold to be about 1 millimeter—you know that a 10-millimeter bar will be detected as different from an 11-millimeter bar 50 percent of the time. With a 20-millimeter standard bar, however, a 1-millimeter increment is not enough. To get a just noticeable difference, you need to add about 2 millimeters. With a bar of 40 millimeters, you would need to add 4 millimeters. Figure 4.3 shows that JNDs increase steadily as the length of the standard bar increases.

What remains the same for both long and short bars is the *ratio* of the size of the increase that produces a just noticeable difference to the length of the standard bar. For example, *1 mm/10 mm = 0.1; 2 mm/20 mm = 0.1.* This relationship is summarized as **Weber's law:** *The JND between stimuli is a constant fraction of the intensity of the standard stimulus.* Thus, the bigger or more intense the standard stimulus, the larger the increment needed to get a just

Difference threshold The smallest physical difference between two stimuli that can still be recognized as a difference; operationally defined as the point at which the stimuli are recognized as different half of the time.

Just noticeable difference (JND) The smallest difference between two sensations that allows them to be discriminated.

Weber's law An assertion that the size of a difference threshold is proportional to the intensity of the standard stimulus.

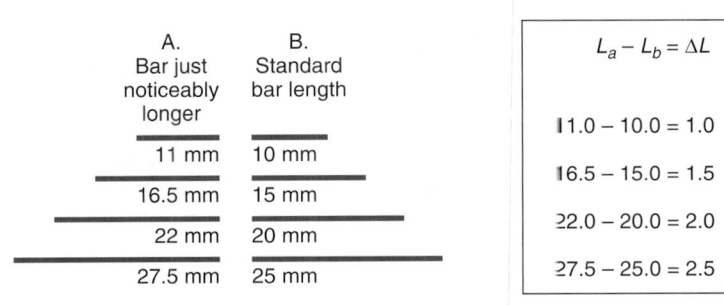

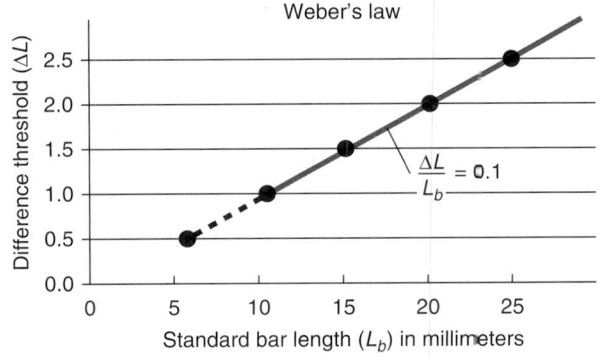

FIGURE 4.3

Just Noticeable Differences and Weber's Law

The longer the standard bar, the greater the amount you must add (ΔL) to see a just noticeable difference. The difference threshold is the added length detected on half the trials. When these increments are plotted against standard bars of increasing length, the proportions stay the same—the amount added is always one-tenth of the standard length. The relationship is linear, producing a straight line on the graph. We can predict that the ΔL for a bar length of 5 will be 0.5.

noticeable difference. This is a very general property of all sensory systems. The formula for Weber's law is $\Delta I / I = k$, where I is the intensity of the standard; ΔI, or delta I, is the size of the increase that produces a JND. Weber found that each stimulus dimension has a characteristic value for this ratio. In this formula, k is that ratio, or *Weber's constant*, for the particular stimulus dimension. (Work through the bar length example plotted in Figure 4.3 to be sure you understand what a JND is, what Weber's law is, and how they are related.) Weber's law provides a good approximation, but not a perfect fit to experimental data, of how the size of JND increases with intensity (most problems with the law arise when stimulus intensities become extremely high).

You see in **Table 4.2** that Weber's constant (k) has different values for different sensory dimensions—smaller values mean that people can detect smaller differences. So this table tells you that you can differentiate two sound frequencies more precisely than light intensities, which, in turn, are detectable with a smaller JND than odor or taste differences are. Your beverage company would need a relatively large amount of extra sugar to produce a noticeably sweeter cola!

From Physical Events to Mental Events

Our review of psychophysics has made you aware of the central mystery of sensation: How do physical energies give rise to particular psychological experiences? How, for example, do the various physical wavelengths of light give rise to your experience of a rainbow? Before we consider specific sensory domains, we wish to give you an overview of the flow of information from physical events—waves of light and sound, complex chemicals, and so on—to mental events—your experiences of sights, sounds, tastes, and smells.

Sensory physiology is the study of the way biological mechanisms convert physical events into neural events. The goal of this field is to discover what happens at a neural level in the chain of events from physical energy to sensory experience. The conversion of one form of physical energy, such as light, to another form, such as neural impulses, is called **transduction.**

Because all sensory information is transduced into identical types of neural impulses, your brain differentiates sensory experiences by devoting special areas of cortex to each sensory domain. For each domain, researchers try to discover how the transduction of physical energy into the electrochemical activity of the nervous system

Sensory physiology The study of the way in which biological mechanisms convert physical events into neural events.

Transduction Transformation of one form of energy into another; for example, light is transformed into neural impulses.

Sensory receptors Specialized cells that convert physical signals into cellular signals that are processed by the nervous system.

TABLE 4.2

Weber's Constant Values for Selected Stimulus Dimensions

Stimulus Dimension	Weber's Constant (k)
Sound frequency	.003
Light intensity	.01
Odor concentration	.07
Pressure intensity	.14
Sound intensity	.15
Taste concentration	.20

gives rise to sensations of different quality (red rather than green) and different quantity (loud rather than soft).

Sensory systems share the same basic flow of information. The trigger for any sensing system is the detection of an environmental event, or *stimulus*. Environmental stimuli are detected by specialized **sensory receptors** (for examples, see **Table 4.3**). Sensory receptors convert the physical form of the sensory signal into cellular signals that can be processed by the nervous system. These cellular signals contribute information to higher-level neurons that integrate information across different detector units. At this stage, neurons extract information about the basic qualities of the stimulus, such as its size, intensity, shape, and distance. Deeper into the sensory systems, information is combined into even more complex codes that are passed on to specific areas of the sensory and association cortex of the brain.

Table 4.3 summarizes the stimuli and receptors for each of the human senses. As we move now to specific sensory domains, you can use the table to preview the rest of the chapter.

SUMMING UP

Researchers in the field of psychophysics study the relationships between physical events in the environment and observers' psychological experiences of those events. An observer's threshold to detect a stimulus event depends on the strength of the stimulus and local circumstances such as the observer's level of sensory adaptation—the definition of the absolute threshold reflects variability in performance. Signal detection theory was developed to separate out sensory processes from response biases in observers' performance. Researchers in psychophysics are also interested in characterizing how much the magnitude of a stimulus must increase or decrease before observers can perceive a difference. Weber's law captures the relationships between changes in physical stimulation and observers' perceptions.

A goal of research on sensory physiology is to discover the ways in which physical events are converted into events

TABLE 4.3

Human Sensory System: Fundamental Features

Sense	Stimulus	Sense Organ	Receptor	Sensation
Sight	Light waves	Eye	Rods and cones of retina	Colors, patterns, textures, motion, depth in space
Hearing	Sound waves	Ear	Hair cells of the basilar membrane	Noises, tones
Skin sensations	External contact	Skin	Nerve endings in skin (Ruffini corpuscles, Merkel disks, Pacinian corpuscles)	Touch, pain, warmth, cold
Smell	Volatile substances	Nose	Hair cells of olfactory epithelium	Odors (musky, flowery, burnt, minty)
Taste	Soluble substances	Tongue	Taste buds of tongue	Flavors (sweet, sour, salty, bitter)
Vestibular sense	Mechanical and gravitational forces	Inner ear	Hair cells of semicircular canals and vestibule	Spatial movement, gravitational pull
Kinesthesis	Body movement	Muscles, tendons, and joints	Nerve fibers in muscles, tendons, and joints	Movement and position of body parts

in the brain. Researchers have characterized the typical flow of information from sensory receptors to areas of the cerebral cortex.

The Visual System

Vision is the most complex, highly developed, and important sense for humans and most other mobile creatures. Animals with good vision have an enormous evolutionary advantage. Good vision helps animals detect their prey or predators from a distance. Vision enables humans to be aware of changing features in the physical environment and to adapt their behavior accordingly. Vision is the most studied of all the sense modalities.

The Human Eye

The eye is the camera for the brain's motion pictures of the world (see **Figure 4.4**). A camera views the world through a lens that gathers and focuses light. The eye also gathers and focuses light—light enters the *cornea*, a transparent bulge on the front of the eye. Next it passes through the *anterior chamber*, which is filled with a clear liquid called the *aqueous humor*. The light then passes through the *pupil*, an opening in the opaque *iris*. To focus a camera, you move its lens closer to or further from the object viewed. To focus light in the eye, a bean-shaped crystalline *lens* changes its shape, thinning to focus on distant objects and thickening to focus on near ones. To control the amount of light coming into a camera, you

Visual acuity enables predatory animals to detect potential prey from a distance. What range of functions did evolution provide for the human visual system?

FIGURE 4.4

Structure of the Human Eye

The cornea, pupil, and lens focus light onto the retina. Nerve signals from the retina are carried to the brain by the optic nerve.

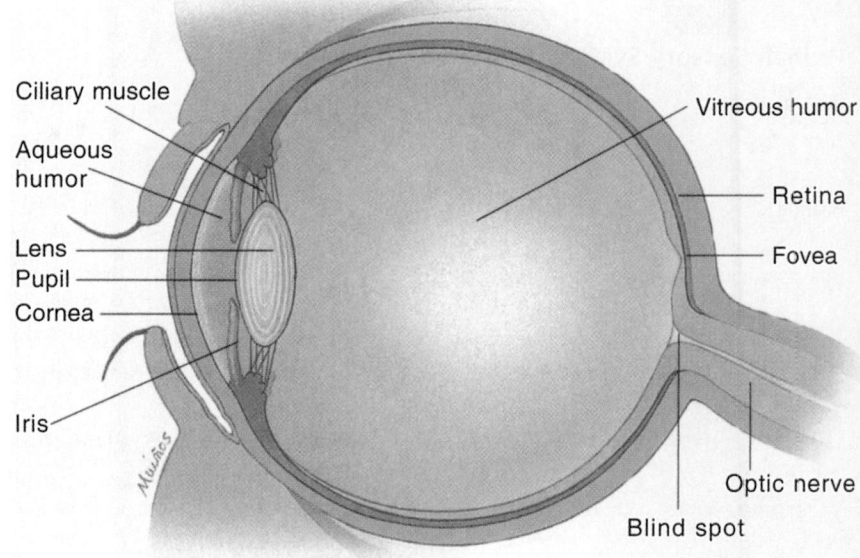

Ciliary muscle
Aqueous humor
Lens
Pupil
Cornea
Iris
Vitreous humor
Retina
Fovea
Optic nerve
Blind spot

vary the opening of the lens. In the eye, the muscular disk of the iris changes the size of the pupil, the aperture through which light passes into the eyeball. At the back of a camera body is the photosensitive film that records the variations in light that have come through the lens. Similarly, in the eye, light travels through the *vitreous humor,* finally striking the *retina,* a thin sheet that lines the rear wall of the eyeball.

As you can see, the features of a camera and the eye are very similar. Now let's examine the components of the vision process in more detail.

The Pupil and the Lens

The pupil is the opening in the iris through which light passes. The iris makes the pupil dilate or constrict to control the amount of light entering the eyeball. Light passing through the pupil is focused by the lens on the retina; the lens reverses and inverts the light pattern as it does so. The lens is particularly important because of its variable focusing ability for near and far objects. The ciliary muscles can change the thickness of the lens and, hence, its optical properties in a process called **accommodation.**

People with normal accommodation have a range of focus from about 3 inches in front of their nose to as far

Accommodation The process by which the ciliary muscles change the thickness of the lens of the eye to permit variable focusing on near and distant objects.

Retina The layer at the back of the eye that contains photoreceptors and converts light energy to neural responses.

Photoreceptors Receptor cells in the retina that are sensitive to light.

as they can see. However, many people suffer from accommodation problems. For example, people who are nearsighted have their range of accommodation shifted closer to them with the consequence that they cannot focus well on distant objects; those who are farsighted have their range of accommodation shifted farther away from them so that they cannot focus normally on nearby objects. Aging also leads to problems in accommodation. The lens starts off as clear, transparent, and convex. As people age, however, the lens becomes more amber-tinted, opaque, and flattened, and it loses its elasticity. The effect of some of these changes is that the lens cannot become thick enough for close vision. When people age past the 45-year mark, the *near point*—the closest point at which they can focus clearly—gets progressively farther away.

The Retina

You look with your eyes but see with your brain. The eye gathers light, focuses it, and starts a neural signal on its way toward the brain. The eye's critical function, therefore, is to convert information about the world from light waves into neural signals. This happens in the **retina,** at the back of the eye. Under the microscope, you can see that the retina has several highly organized layers of different types of neurons.

The basic conversion from light energy to neural responses is performed in your retina by *rods* and *cones*—receptor cells sensitive to light. These **photoreceptors** are uniquely placed in the visual system between the outer world, ablaze with light, and the inner world of neural processing. Because you sometimes operate in near darkness and sometimes in bright light, nature has provided two ways of processing light, rods and cones

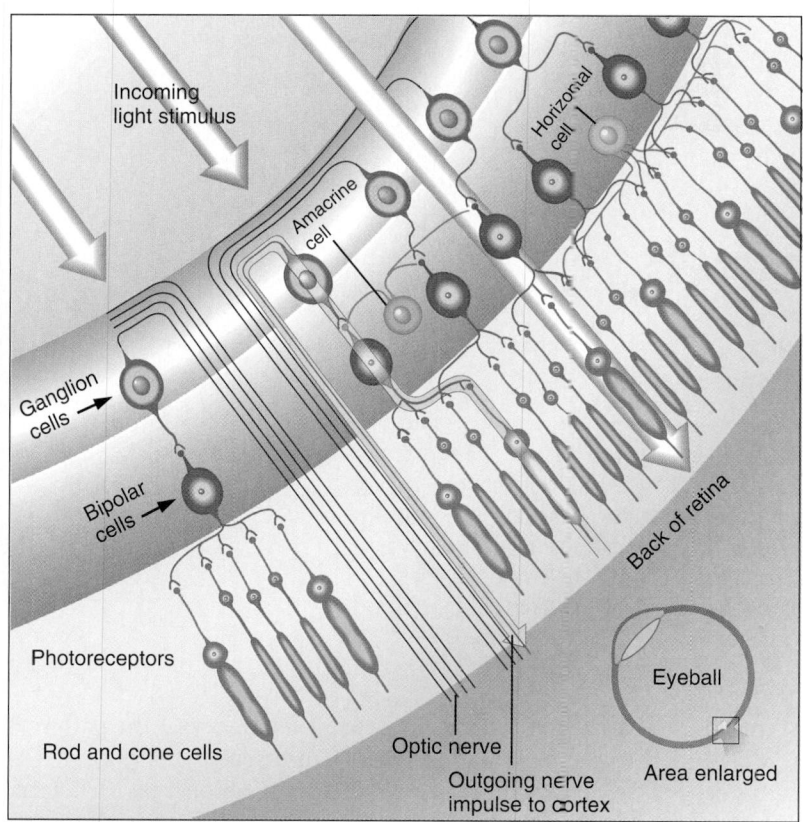

FIGURE 4.5

Retinal Pathways

This is a stylized and greatly simplified diagram showing the pathways that connect three of the layers of nerve cells in the retina. Incoming light passes through all these layers to reach the receptors, at the back of the eyeball, that are pointed away from the source of light. Note that the bipolar cells gather impulses from more than one receptor cell and send the results to ganglion cells. Nerve impulses (blue arrow) from the ganglion cells leave the eye via the optic nerve and travel to the next relay point.

(see **Figure 4.5**). The 120 million thin **rods** operate best in near darkness. The 7 million fat **cones** are specialized for the bright, color-filled day.

You experience differences between the functions of your rods and cones each time you turn off the lights to go to sleep at night. You have noticed many times that at first it seems as though you can't see much of anything in the dim light that remains, but over time your visual sensitivity improves again. You are undergoing the process of **dark adaptation**—the gradual improvement of the eyes' sensitivity after a shift in illumination from light to near darkness. Dark adaptation occurs because, as time passes in the dark, your rods become more sensitive than your cones; over time, your rods are able to respond to less light from the environment than your cones are.

Near the center of the retina is a small region called the **fovea**, which contains nothing but densely packed cones—it is rod-free. The fovea is the area of your sharpest vision—both color and spatial detail are most accurately detected there. Other cells in your retina are responsible for integrating information across regions of rods and cones. The **bipolar cells** are nerve cells that combine impulses from many receptors and send the results to ganglion cells. Each **ganglion cell** then integrates the impulses from one or more bipolar cells into a single firing rate. The cones in the central fovea send their impulses to the ganglion cells in that region while, farther out on the periphery of the retina, rods and cones converge on the same bipolar and ganglion cells. The axons of the ganglion cells make up the optic nerve, which carries this visual information out of the eye and back toward the brain.

Your **horizontal cells** and **amacrine cells** integrate information across the retina. Rather than send signals toward the brain, horizontal cells connect receptors to each other, and amacrine cells link bipolar cells to other bipolar cells and ganglion cells to other ganglion cells.

An interesting curiosity in the anatomical design of the retina exists where the optic nerve leaves each eye. This region, called the optic disk, or *blind spot*, contains no receptor cells at all. You do not experience blindness there, except under very special circumstances, for two

Rods Photoreceptors concentrated in the periphery of the retina that are most active in dim illumination; rods do not produce sensation of color.

Cones Photoreceptors concentrated in the center of the retina that are responsible for visual experience under normal viewing conditions and for all experiences of color.

Dark adaptation The gradual improvement of the eyes' sensitivity after a shift in illumination from light to near darkness.

Fovea Area of the retina that contains densely packed cones and forms the point of sharpest vision.

Bipolar cells Nerve cells in the visual system that combine impulses from many receptors and transmit the results to ganglion cells.

Ganglion cells Cells in the visual system that integrate impulses from many bipolar cells in a single firing rate.

Horizontal cells The cells that integrate information across the retina; rather than sending signals toward the brain, horizontal cells connect receptors to each other.

Amacrine cells Cells that integrate information across the retina; rather than sending signals toward the brain, amacrine cells link bipolar cells to other bipolar cells and ganglion cells to other ganglion cells.

FIGURE 4.6

Find Your Blind Spot

To find your blind spot, hold this book at arm's length, close your right eye, and fixate on the bank figure with your left eye as you bring the book slowly closer. When the dollar sign is in your blind spot, it will disappear, but you will experience no gaping hole in your visual field. Similarly, if you use the same procedure to focus on the plus sign, the line will appear whole when the gap is in your blind spot. In both cases, your visual system fills in the background whiteness of the surrounding area so you "see" the whiteness, which isn't there.

reasons: First, the blind spots of the two eyes are positioned so that receptors in each eye register what is missed in the other; second, the brain "fills in" this region with appropriate sensory information from the surrounding area.

To find your blind spot, you will have to look at **Figure 4.6** under special viewing conditions. Hold this book at arm's length, close your right eye, and fixate on the bank figure with your left eye as you bring the book slowly closer. When the dollar sign is in your blind spot, it will disappear, but you will experience no gaping hole in your visual field. Instead, your visual system fills in this area with the background whiteness of the surrounding area so you "see" the whiteness, which isn't there, while failing to see your money, which you should have put in the bank before you lost it!

For a second demonstration of your blind spot, use the same procedure to focus on the plus sign in Figure 4.6. As you pull the book closer to you, do you see the gap disappear and the line become whole?

Pathways to the Brain

The ultimate destination of much visual information is the part of the occipital lobe of the brain known as primary **visual cortex**. However, most information leaving the retinas passes through other brain regions before it

arrives at the visual cortex. Let's trace out the pathways visual information takes (Van Essen et al., 1992).

The million axons of the ganglion cells that form each **optic nerve** come together in the *optic chiasma*, which resembles the Greek letter χ (*chi*, pronounced *kye*). The axons in each optic nerve are divided into two bundles at the optic chiasma. Half of the fibers from each retina remain on the side of the body from which they originated. The axons from the inner half of each eye cross over the midline as they continue their journey toward the back of the brain (see **Figure 4.7**).

These two bundles of fibers, which now contain axons from both eyes, are renamed *optic tracts*. The optic tracts deliver information to two clusters of cells in the brain. Research supports the theory that visual analysis is separated into pathways for *pattern recognition*—how things look—and *place recognition*—where things are (Rao et al., 1997; Wilson et al., 1993). The separation of visual functions has been observed most dramatically when individuals have lost portions of their visual cortex through injury or surgery. Consider this case study.

HOW WE KNOW

THE SEPARATION OF VISUAL FUNCTIONS From the age of 14, Don had severe, prolonged headaches and incapacitating sensory difficulties in his left visual field. When Don was 34, in an attempt to correct the problem, he decided to have an operation in which a neurosurgeon would remove a small portion of his right occipital cortex. The surgery permanently cured Don's headaches, but he was left totally blind in the left half of his visual field because the region removed contained

Visual cortex The region of the occipital lobes in which visual information is processed.
Optic nerve The axons of the ganglion cells that carry information from the eye toward the brain.

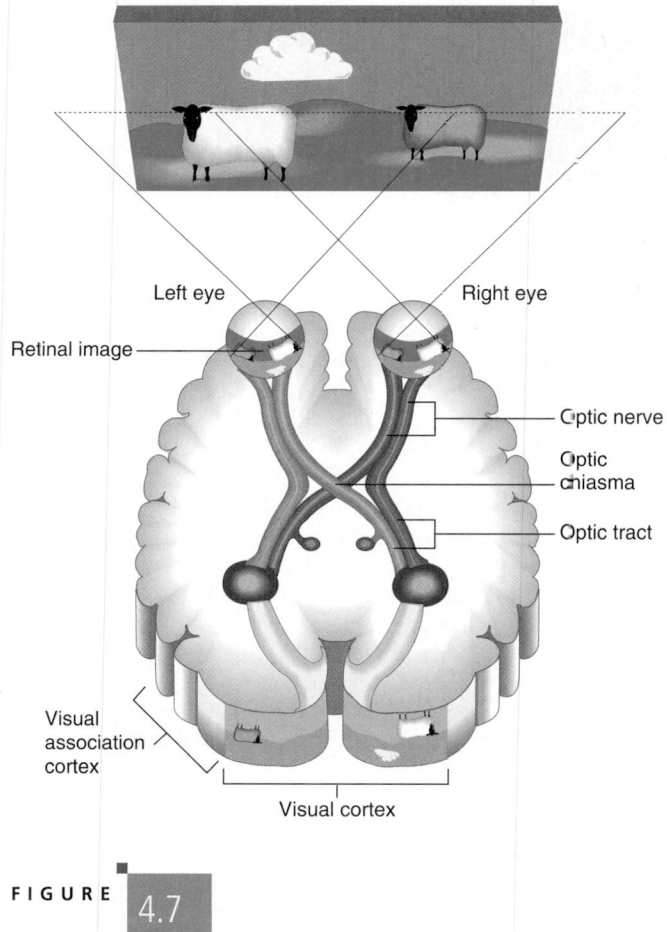

Left eye · Right eye · Retinal image · Optic nerve · Optic chiasma · Optic tract · Visual association cortex · Visual cortex

FIGURE 4.7

Pathways in the Human Visual System

The diagram shows the way light from the visual field projects onto the two retinas and shows the routes by which neural messages from the retina are sent to the two visual centers of each hemisphere.

primary visual cortex. For example, when a bright spot of light was shown directly to the left of his fixation point—a center point on which he was asked to focus his eyes—Don was simply unaware of its presence.

On an informed hunch, however, a group of psychologists asked Don to guess the location of the spot of light by pointing with his left index finger. The results were remarkable. Don was nearly as accurate at locating the spot in this "blind" left field as he was at locating spots in the "sighted" right visual field! Further experiments showed that he could also guess whether a line in his "blind" field was vertical or horizontal and whether a figure presented there was an X or an O. Throughout the tests, Don was completely unaware of the presence of the spots, lines, or figures. He claimed he was merely guessing.

When shown videotapes of his testing, Don was openly astonished to see himself pointing to lights he hadn't seen (Weiskrantz et al., 1974).

Don's "vision" was aptly dubbed *blindsight*: His behavior was visually guided in the absence of conscious visual awareness of an object. Comparable results have been found in tests on several other patients with similar damage in the visual cortex. This pattern of performance has been interpreted as evidence that subcortical structures that remain intact even when cortex is destroyed provide a level of visual analysis appropriate for these tasks—but outside of awareness. This conclusion, however, remains controversial, in large part because of the multiple pathways the brain uses to encode visual information (Gazzaniga et al., 1994; Weiskrantz, 1995). Whatever the neural mechanisms, however, blindsight demonstrates that accurate visual performance can occur outside of consciousness.

You have now learned the basics of how visual information is distributed from the eyes to various parts of the brain. Researchers still have more to learn: There are roughly 30 anatomical subdivisions of primate visual cortex, and theories vary about the pattern of communication among those areas (Hilgetag et al., 1996). For now, we turn to particular aspects of the visual world. One of the most remarkable features of the human visual system is that your experiences of form, color, position, and depth are based on processing the same sensory information in different ways. How do the transformations occur that enable you to see these different features of the visual world?

Seeing Color

Physical objects seem to have the marvelous property of being painted with color. You most often have the impression of brightly colored objects—red valentines, green fir trees, or blue robins' eggs—but your vivid experience of color relies on the rays of light these objects reflect onto your sensory receptors. One of the first to argue this view was Sir Isaac Newton in 1671:

> *For the rays [of light], to speak properly, are not colored. In them there is nothing else than a certain power and disposition to stir up a sensation of this or that color. For as sound, in a bell or musical string or other sounding body, is nothing but a trembling motion, and in the air nothing but that motion propagated from the object,... so colors in the object are nothing but a disposition to reflect this or that sort of ray more copiously than the rest....*

Color is created when your brain processes the information coded in the light source.

THE VISUAL SYSTEM

93

CAN TECHNOLOGY RESTORE SIGHT?

IN DECEMBER 1999 several news agencies reported that Stevie Wonder, the pop star who had been blind nearly from birth, was hoping to undergo an experimental surgical procedure that would restore his sight. In the procedure, developed by **Wentai Liu, Mark Humayun,** and their team of researchers (Liu et al., 2001), a small microchip is connected directly to the retina to replace the function of rods and cones that have been incapacitated by disease. Unfortunately, because of the length of time for which he has been blind, Wonder proved not to be a good candidate for this procedure. However, the technique holds out real promise for those individuals for whom more of the circuitry of the visual system is still intact.

Most blind people have become blind because the receptor cells in their retinas—the rods and cones—succumb to a degenerative disease. (Wonder's blindness was a consequence of too much oxygen being delivered to the incubator in which he was placed shortly after birth.) Even when the sensory receptors cease to function, however, the other cells in the visual pathway—such as bipolar and ganglion cells—survive at high rates. Given the structure of the retina (see Figure 4.5), these other cells are accessible for direct electrical stimulation. The microchip developed by Liu, Humayun, and their colleagues does exactly that: It provides a pattern of electrical stimulation that replaces input from the nonfunctioning rods and cones.

The full system, known as the *multiple-unit artificial retina chipset* (MARC), has several components that function both outside and inside the eyeball. For example, a miniature video camera captures images from the environment. These images are processed and delivered to the microchip surgically implanted on the retina at the back of the eye. The microchip stimulates the ganglion cells in a grid that functions in a way comparable to the operation of a TV or computer screen: Each element of the array—each *pixel*—can take on different values of gray to provide a range of visual sensations.

As you might infer, the MARC procedure will not restore full sight in the way implied by the articles about Stevie Wonder. The amount of information the device provides is quite limited compared to what you ordinarily obtain through your vast number of rods and cones. However, participants in experimental trials of the MARC have been able to identify simple images and shapes. The hope is that the MARC would restore visual function at least to the point at which people could navigate through their environment and read large-print texts. For the millions of people worldwide affected by diseases that cause degeneration of rods and cones, evolving technologies like MARC may very well provide an ingenious means to help preserve visual function.

Web site:

- www.ece.ncsu.edu/erl/erl_eye.html

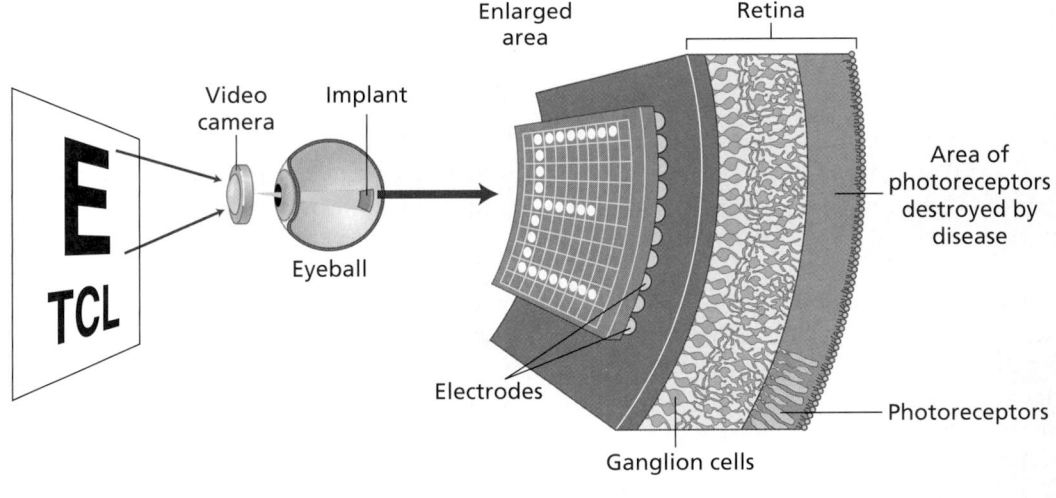

WAVELENGTHS AND HUES

The light you see is just a small portion of a physical dimension called the *electromagnetic spectrum* (see **Figure 4.8**). Your visual system is not equipped to detect other types of waves in this spectrum, such as X rays, microwaves, and radio waves. The physical property that distinguishes types of electromagnetic energy, including light, is *wavelength*, the distance between the crests of

What three dimensions underlie experiences of color?

two adjacent waves. Wavelengths of visible light are measured in *nanometers* (billionths of a meter). What you see as light is the range of wavelengths from 400 to about 700 nanometers. Light rays of particular physical wavelengths give rise to experiences of particular colors—for example, violet-blue at the lower end and red-orange at the higher end. Thus, light is described physically in terms of wavelengths, not colors; colors exist only in your sensory system's interpretation of the wavelengths.

All experiences of color can be described in terms of three basic dimensions: hue, saturation, and brightness. **Hue** is the dimension that captures the qualitative experience of the color of a light. In pure lights that contain only one wavelength (such as a laser beam), the psychological experience of hue corresponds directly to the physical dimension of the light's wavelength. **Figure 4.9** presents the hues arranged in a color circle. Those hues

perceived to be most similar are in adjacent positions. This order mirrors the order of hues in the spectrum. **Saturation** is the psychological dimension that captures the purity and vividness of color sensations. Undiluted colors have the most saturation; muted, muddy, and pastel colors have intermediate amounts of saturation; and grays have zero saturation. **Brightness** is the dimension of color experience that captures the intensity of light. White has the most brightness; black has the least. When colors are analyzed along these three dimensions, a remarkable finding emerges: Humans are capable of visually discriminating about 7 million different colors! However, most people can label only a small number of those colors.

Let's explain some facts about your everyday experience of color. At some point in your science education, you may have repeated Sir Isaac Newton's discovery that sunlight combines all wavelengths of light: You repeated Newton's proof by using a prism to separate sunlight into the full rainbow of colors. What the prism tells you is that the right combination of wavelengths will yield white light. The combination of wavelengths is called *additive color mixture.* Take another look at Figure 4.9. Wavelengths that

Hue The dimension of color space that captures the qualitative experience of the color of a light.

Saturation The dimension of color space that captures the purity and vividness of color sensations.

Brightness The dimension of color space that captures the intensity of light.

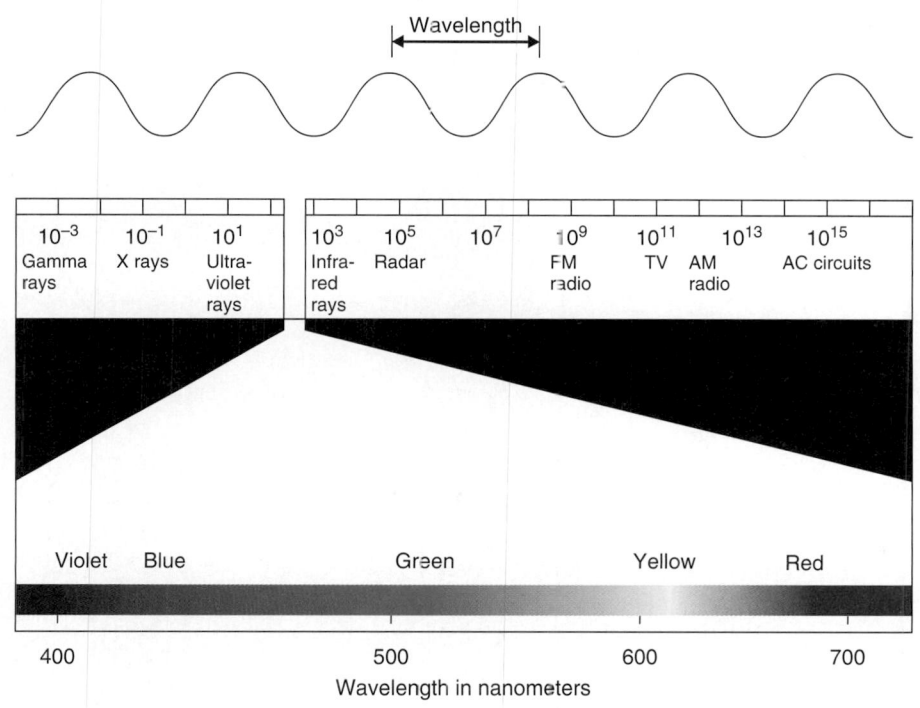

FIGURE 4.8

The Electromagnetic Spectrum

Your visual system can sense only a small range of wavelengths in the electromagnetic spectrum. You experience that range of wavelengths, which is enlarged in the figure, as the colors violet through red.

FIGURE 4.9

The Color Circle

Colors are arranged by their similarity. Complementary colors are placed directly opposite each other. Mixing complementary colors yields a neutral gray or white light at the center. The numbers next to each hue are the wavelength values for spectral colors, those colors within the region of visual sensitivity. Nonspectral hues are obtained by mixing short and long spectral wavelengths.

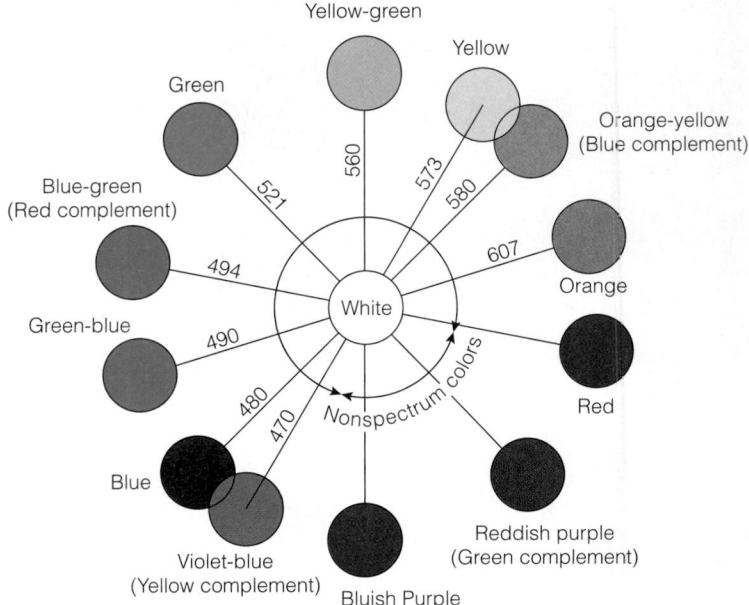

appear directly across from each other on the color circle—called **complementary colors**—will create the sensation of white light when mixed. Do you want to prove to yourself the existence of complementary colors? Consider **Figure 4.10**. The green-yellow-black flag should give you the experience of a *negative afterimage* (the afterimage is called "negative" because it is the opposite of the original color). For reasons that we will explain when we consider theories of color vision, when you stare at any color long enough to partially fatigue your photoreceptors, looking at a white surface will allow you to experience the complement of the original color.

Complementary colors Colors opposite each other on the color circle; when additively mixed, they create the sensation of white light.

You have probably noticed afterimages from time to time in your everyday exposure to colors. Most of your experience with colors, however, does not come from complementary lights. Instead, you have probably spent your time at play with colors combining crayons or paints of different hues. The colors you see when you look at a crayon mark, or any other colored surface, are the wavelengths of light that are not absorbed by the surface. Although yellow crayon looks mostly yellow, it lets some wavelengths escape that give rise to the sensation of green. Similarly, blue crayon lets wavelengths escape that give rise to the sensations of blue and some green. When yellow and blue crayon are combined, yellow absorbs blue and blue absorbs yellow—the only wavelengths that are not absorbed look green! This phenomenon is called *subtractive color mixture*. The remaining wavelengths

FIGURE 4.10

Color Afterimages

Stare at the dot in the center of the green, black, and yellow flag for at least 30 seconds. Then fixate on the center of a sheet of white paper or a blank wall. Try this aftereffect illusion on your friends.

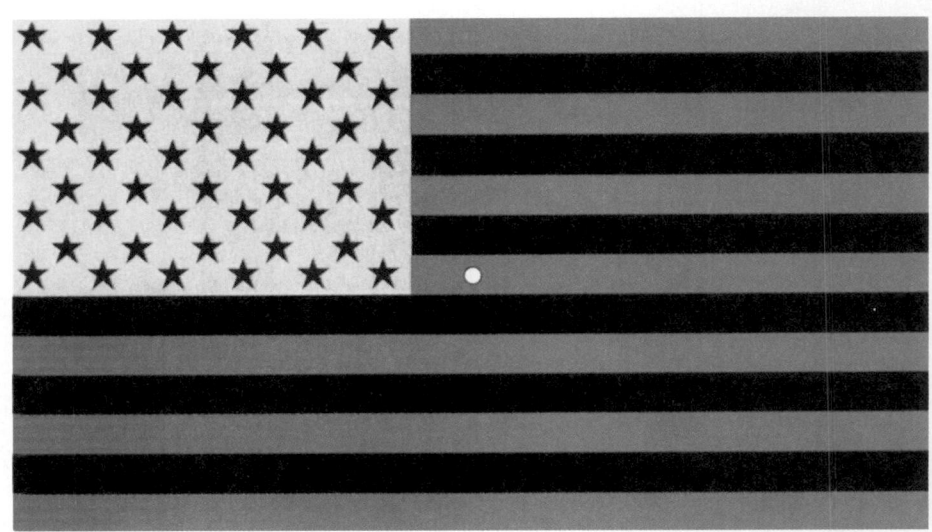

that are not absorbed—the wavelengths that are reflected—give the crayon mixture the color you perceive.

Some of these rules about the experience of color do not apply to those people born with a color deficiency. *Color blindness* is the partial or total inability to distinguish colors. The negative afterimage effect of viewing the green, yellow, and black flag will not work if you are color blind. Color blindness is usually a sex-linked hereditary defect associated with a gene on the X chromosome. Because males have a single X chromosome, they are more likely to show this recessive trait than females. Females would need to have a defective gene on both X chromosomes to be color blind. An estimate for color blindness among Caucasian males is about 8 percent, but less than 0.5 percent among females (Coren et al., 1999).

Most color blindness involves difficulty distinguishing red from green, especially at weak saturations. More rare are people who confuse yellows and blues. Rarest of all are those who see no color at all, only variations in brightness. (Mr. I., at the beginning of the chapter, is quite unusual because brain damage completely deprived him of color vision at age 65.) To see whether you have a color deficiency, look at **Figure 4.11.** If you see the numbers 1 and 5 in the pattern of dots, your color vision is probably normal. If you see something else, you may be at least partially color-blind. (Try the test on others as well—particularly people you know who are color-blind—to find out what they see.) Let's now see how scientists have explained such facts about color vision as complementary colors and color blindness.

THEORIES OF COLOR VISION

The first scientific theory of color vision was proposed by **Sir Thomas Young** around 1800. He suggested that there were three types of color receptors in the normal human eye that produced psychologically primary sensations: red, green, and blue. All other colors, he believed, were additive or subtractive combinations of these three primaries. Young's theory was later refined and extended by **Hermann von Helmholtz** and came to be known as the Young-Helmholtz **trichromatic theory.**

Trichromatic theory provided a plausible explanation for people's color sensations and for color blindness (according to the theory, color-blind people had only one or two kinds of receptors). However, other facts and observations were not as well explained by the theory. Why did adaptation to one color produce color afterimages that had the complementary hue? Why did color-blind people always fail to distinguish pairs of colors: red and green or blue and yellow?

Trichromatic theory The theory that there are three types of color receptors that produce the primary color sensations of red, green, and blue.

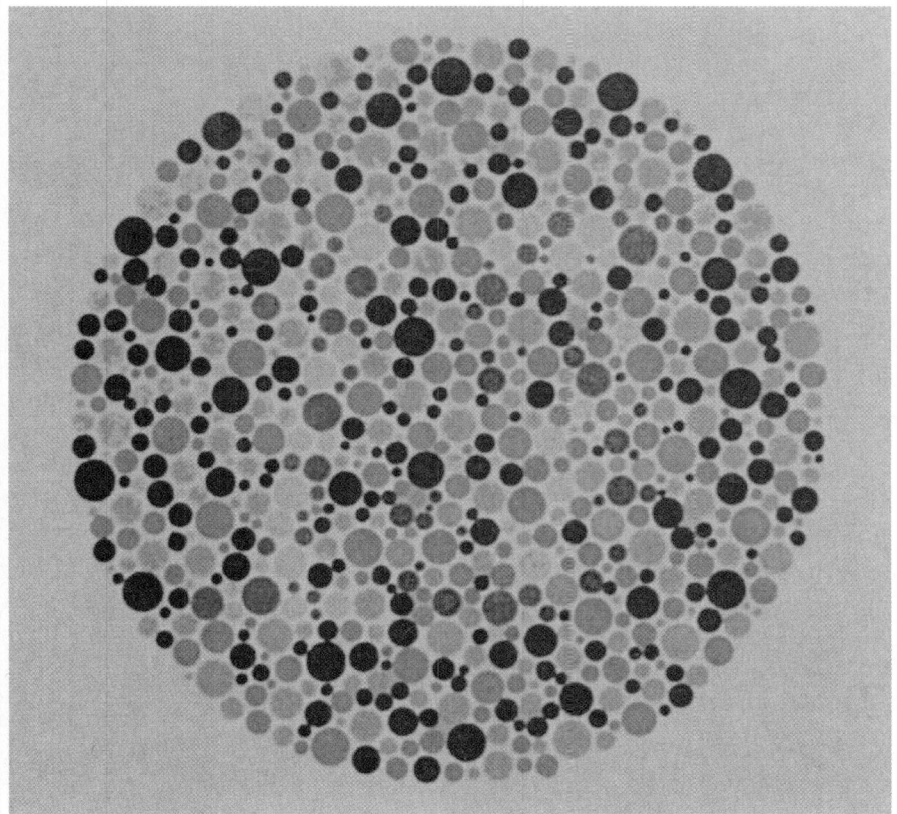

FIGURE 4.11

A Color Blindness Test

A person who cannot discriminate between red and green colors will not be able to identify the number hidden in the figure. What do you see? If you see the number 17 in the dot pattern, your color vision is probably normal.

Answers to these questions became the cornerstones for a second theory of color vision proposed by **Ewald Hering** in the late 1800s. According to his **opponent-process theory,** all color experiences arise from three underlying systems, each of which includes two opponent elements: red versus green, blue versus yellow, or black (no color) versus white (all colors). Hering theorized that colors produced complementary afterimages because one element of the system became fatigued (from overstimulation) and thus increased the relative contribution of its opponent element. In Hering's theory, types of color blindness came in pairs because the color system was actually built from pairs of opposites, not from single primary colors.

For many years, scientists debated the merits of the theories. Eventually, scientists recognized that the theories were not really in conflict; they simply described two different stages of processing that corresponded to successive physiological structures in the visual system (Hurvich & Jameson, 1974). We now know, for example, that there are, indeed, three types of cones. Although the three types of cones each respond to a range of wavelengths, they are each *most* sensitive to light at a particular wavelength.

HOW WE KNOW

CONES HAVE WAVELENGTH PREFERENCES

Vision researchers have developed a technique for analyzing the electrical activity of a single cone. Single-cone cells from macaque monkeys were "sucked up" into a special hollow glass tube that is less than 1/25th the diameter of a human hair. Light of various wavelengths was shone on the tube, and the strength of electrical signals emitted from the cone cell was amplified and measured. Using this technique, the researchers found that some cells were tuned to respond maximally to light wavelengths of 435 nanometers (nm) ("blue" cells), others to 535 nm ("green" cells), and others to 570 nm ("red" cells) (Baylor, 1987).

The responses of these cone types confirm Young and Helmholtz's prediction that color vision relies on three types of color receptors. People who are color blind lack one or more of these types of receptor cones.

We also now know that the retinal ganglion cells combine the outputs of these three cone types in accordance with Hering's opponent-process theory (De Valois & Jacobs, 1968). According to the contemporary version of opponent-process theory, as supported by **Leo Hurvich** and

Opponent-process theory The theory that all color experiences arise from three systems, each of which includes two "opponent" elements (red versus green, blue versus yellow, and black versus white).

Receptive field The visual area from which a given ganglion cell receives information.

Dorothea Jameson (1974), the two members of each color pair work in opposition (are opponents) by means of neural inhibition. Some ganglion cells receive excitatory input from lights that appear red and inhibitory input from lights that appear green. Other cells in the system have the opposite arrangement of excitation and inhibition. Together, these two types of ganglion cells form the physiological basis of the red/green opponent-process system. Other ganglion cells make up the blue/yellow opponent system. The black/white system contributes to your perception of color saturation and brightness.

Complex Visual Analysis

Seeing the world of color is only a small part of the complex task facing your visual system. If you want to catch a football or avoid a hornet's nest, you must also detect the form or shape of objects, their depth or distance, and their movement in space. Your visual system consists of several separate and independent subsystems that analyze different aspects of the same retinal image. Distinct sets of neurons have unique properties that generate the perceptions of color, form, contrast, movement, and texture (Livingstone & Hubel, 1988; Vinje & Gallant, 2000). Although your final perception is of a unified visual scene, your vision of it is accompanied by a host of pathways in your visual system that, under normal conditions, are exquisitely coordinated (Merigan & Maunsell, 1993).

You can start to understand how complex visual analysis works by knowing a single fact: The cells at each level in the visual pathway respond *selectively* only to a particular part of the visual field. For example, we noted earlier that each retinal ganglion cell integrates information about light patterns from many receptor cells. The **receptive field** of a cell is the area in the visual field from which it receives stimulation.

Receptive fields of retinal ganglion cells are of two types (see parts A and B of **Figure 4.12**): (1) those in which stimulation in the center of the field excites the cell, and stimulation in the surrounding part inhibits it; and (2) those with the opposite organization—an inhibitory center and an excitatory surround. Ganglion cells respond to the *differences* in stimulation coming from their center and the surround. They are most excited by *stimulus contrast;* those with *on* centers fire most strongly to a bright spot surrounded by a dark border, and those with *off* centers fire most vigorously to a dark spot surrounded by a light border. Uniform illumination causes the center and surround to cancel each other's activity—the cell is not as excited by uniform illumination as it is by a spot or bar of light.

You have now learned some of the properties of visual processing at your receptor and ganglion cells. But what happens at higher levels in your visual system? Pioneering work on this question was done by **David Hubel** and **Torsten Wiesel**, sensory physiologists who won a

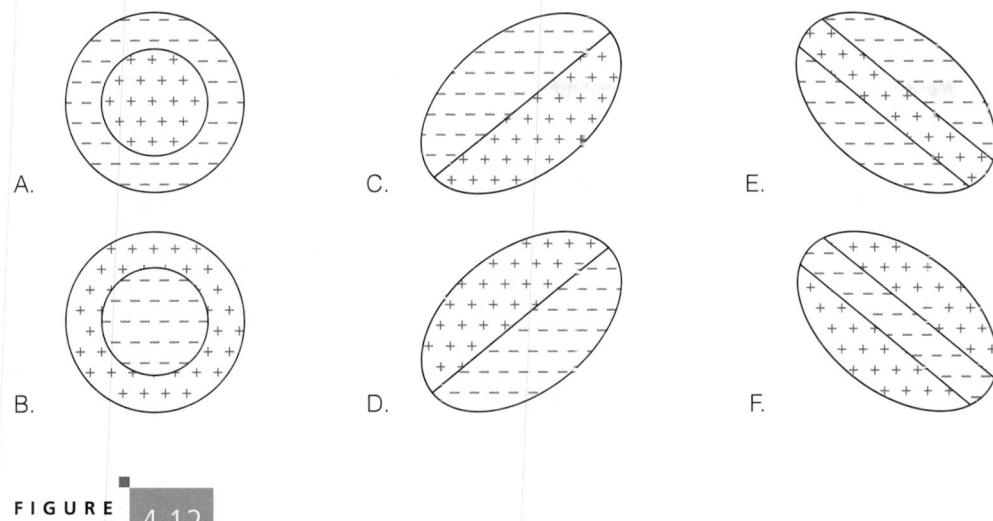

FIGURE 4.12

Receptive Fields of Ganglion and Cortical Cells

The receptive field of a cell in the visual pathway is the area in the visual field from which it receives stimulation. The receptive fields of the ganglion cells in the retina are circular (A, B); those of the simplest cells in the visual cortex are elongated in a particular orientation (C, D, E, F). In both cases, the cell responding to the receptive field is excited by light in the regions marked with plus signs and inhibited by light in the regions marked with minus signs. In addition, the stimulus that most excites the cell is one in which areas where light is excitatory (marked with plus signs) are illuminated, but areas where light is inhibitory (marked by minus signs) are in darkness.

Nobel Prize in 1981 for their studies of receptive fields of cells in the visual cortex. Hubel and Wiesel recorded the firing rates from single cells in the visual cortex of cats in response to moving spots and bars in the visual field. When Hubel and Wiesel mapped out the receptive fields of these cortical cells, they found an organization of cells that had successively more narrow constraints on the visual stimuli that were most likely to cause them to fire (Hubel & Wiesel, 1962, 1979). One type of cortical cell, *simple* cells, responded most strongly to bars of light in their "favorite" orientation (see Figure 4.12). *Complex* cells also each have a "favorite" orientation, but they require as well that the bar be moving. *Hypercomplex* cells require moving bars of a particular length or moving corners or angles. The cells provide types of information to higher visual centers in the brain that ultimately allows the brain to recognize objects in the visual world.

In this section we have focused on the visual system's response to simulation from the external environment. In Chapter 5, we will see that people's perceptions of the world often represent combinations of external information—the waves of light that arrive at the eyes—with internal sources of competing information—knowledge already stored in the brain.

We turn now from the world of sight to the world of sound.

SUMMING UP

The human eye functions much like a camera: Light is focused by the lens onto the retina. The basic conversion of light energy to neural activity occurs in the retina, where the rods specialize in vision in near darkness and the cones specialize in color and spatial detail. Information from the retina makes its way to the brain through a series of levels of processing that extract information about how things look and where they are. The phenomenon of blindsight provides evidence for different types of visual analysis.

The perception of color begins with different wavelengths of light and can be divided into the dimensions of hue, saturation, and brightness. Combinations of wavelengths produce distinctive colors through either additive or subtractive color mixing. People experience color blindness to different degrees; it is quite rare to experience a complete loss of color vision. Research on color vision supports features of both trichromatic theory and opponent-process theory. The visual system has three types of cones with preferences for different wavelength light. These three types of cones combine at a higher level of processing to give rise to opponent processing phenomena.

Some types of visual analysis rely on the receptive fields of ganglion cells. Other types of visual analyses rely on the preferences—for location, orientation, and motion—of cells at higher levels of neural processing.

Hearing

Hearing and vision play complementary functions in your experience of the world. You often hear stimuli before you see them, particularly if they take place behind you or on the other side of opaque objects such as walls. Although vision is better than hearing for identifying an object once it is in the field of view, you often see the object only because you have used your ears to point your eyes in the right direction. To begin our discussion of hearing, we describe the types of physical energy that arrive at your ears.

The Physics of Sound

Clap your hands together. Whistle. Tap your pencil on the table. Why do these actions create sounds? The reason is that they cause objects to vibrate. The vibrational energy is transmitted to the surrounding medium—usually air—as the vibrating objects push molecules of the medium back and forth. The resulting slight changes in pressure spread outward from the vibrating objects in the form of a combination of *sine waves* traveling at a rate of about 1,100 feet per second (see **Figure 4.13**). Sound cannot be created in a true vacuum (such as outer space) because there are no air molecules in a vacuum for vibrating objects to move.

A sine wave has two basic physical properties that determine how it sounds to you: frequency and amplitude. *Frequency* measures the number of cycles the wave completes in a given amount of time. A cycle, as indicated in Figure 4.13, is the left-to-right distance from the peak in one wave to the peak in the next wave. Sound frequency is usually expressed in *hertz* (Hz), which measures cycles per second. *Amplitude* measures the physical property of strength of the sound wave, as shown in its peak-to-valley height. Amplitude is defined in units of sound pressure or energy.

Psychological Dimensions of Sound

The physical properties of frequency and amplitude give rise to the three psychological dimensions of sound: pitch, loudness, and timbre. Let's see how these phenomena work.

Pitch Sound quality of highness or lowness; primarily dependent on the frequency of the sound wave.

Loudness A perceptual dimension of sound influenced by the amplitude of a sound wave; sound waves with large amplitudes are generally experienced as loud and those with small amplitudes as soft.

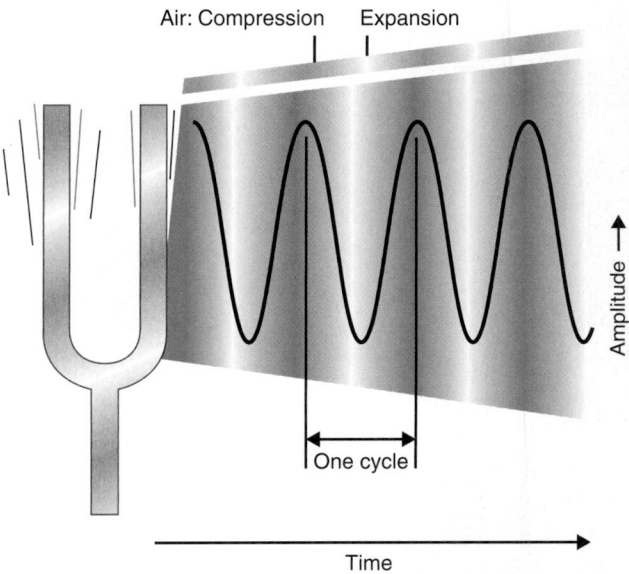

FIGURE 4.13

An Idealized Sine Wave

The two basic properties of sine waves are their *frequency*—the number of cycles in a fixed unit of time—and their *amplitude*—the vertical range of their cycles.

PITCH

Pitch is the highness or lowness of a sound determined by the sound's frequency; high frequencies produce high pitch, and low frequencies produce low pitch. The full range of human sensitivity to pure tones extends from frequencies as low as 20 Hz to frequencies as high as 20,000 Hz. (Frequencies below 20 Hz may be experienced through touch as vibrations rather than as sound.) You can get a sense of how big this range is by noting that the 88 keys on a piano cover only the range from about 30 to 4,000 Hz.

As you might expect from our earlier discussion of psychophysics, the relationship between frequency (the physical reality) and pitch (the psychological effect) is not a linear one. At the low end of the frequency scale, increasing the frequency by just a few hertz raises the pitch quite noticeably. At the high end of frequency, you require a much bigger increase in order to hear the difference in pitch. For example, the two lowest notes on a piano differ by only 1.6 Hz, whereas the two highest ones differ by 235 Hz. This is another example of the psychophysics of just noticeable differences.

LOUDNESS

The **loudness,** or physical intensity, of a sound is determined by its amplitude; sound waves with large amplitudes are experienced as loud and those with small amplitudes as soft. The human auditory system is sensi-

CHAPTER FOUR / SENSATION

What physical properties of sounds allow you to pick out the timbres of individual instruments from the musical ensemble of a band?

tive to an enormous range of physical intensities. At one limit, you can hear the tick of a wristwatch at 20 feet. This is the system's absolute threshold—if it were more sensitive, you would hear the blood flowing in your ears. At the other extreme, a jetliner taking off 100 yards away is

so loud that the sound is painful. In terms of physical units of sound pressure, the jet produces a sound wave with more than a billion times the energy of the ticking watch.

Because the range of hearing is so great, physical intensities of sound are usually expressed in ratios rather than absolute amounts; sound pressure—the index of amplitude level that gives rise to the experience of loudness—is measured in units called decibels (dB). **Figure 4.14** shows the decibel measures of some representative natural sounds. It also shows the corresponding sound pressures for comparison. You can see that two sounds differing by 20 dB have sound pressures in a ratio of 10 to 1. Note that sounds louder than about 90 dB can produce hearing loss, depending on how long you are exposed to them.

TIMBRE

The **timbre** of a sound reflects the components of its complex sound wave. Timbre is what sets apart, for example, the sound of a piano and the sound of a flute. A small number of physical stimuli, such as a tuning fork, produce pure tones consisting of a single sine wave. A *pure tone* has only one frequency and one amplitude. Most sounds in the real world are not pure tones. They are complex waves, containing a combination of frequencies and amplitudes.

Timbre The dimension of auditory sensation that reflects the complexity of a sound wave.

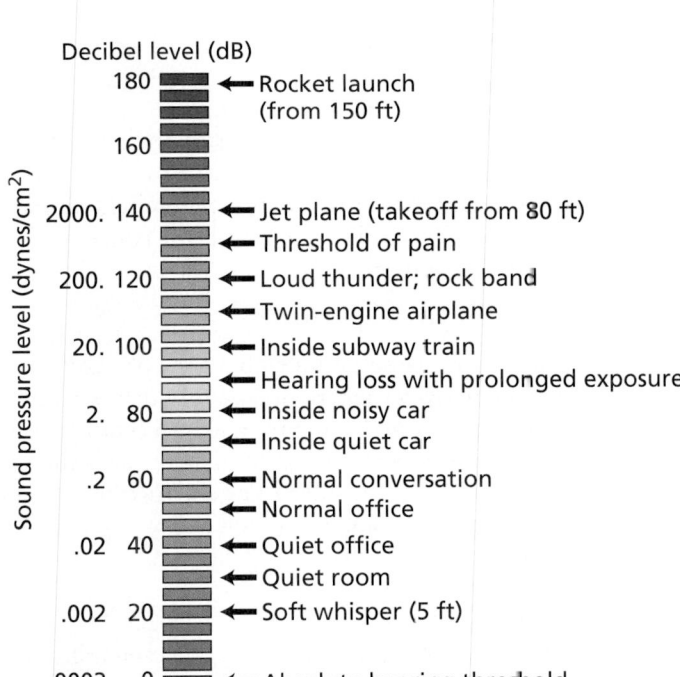

FIGURE 4.14

Decibel Levels of Familiar Sounds

This figure shows the range in decibels of the sounds to which you respond from the absolute threshold for hearing to the noise of a rocket launch. Decibels are calculated from sound pressure, which is a measure of a sound wave's amplitude level and generally corresponds to what you experience as loudness.

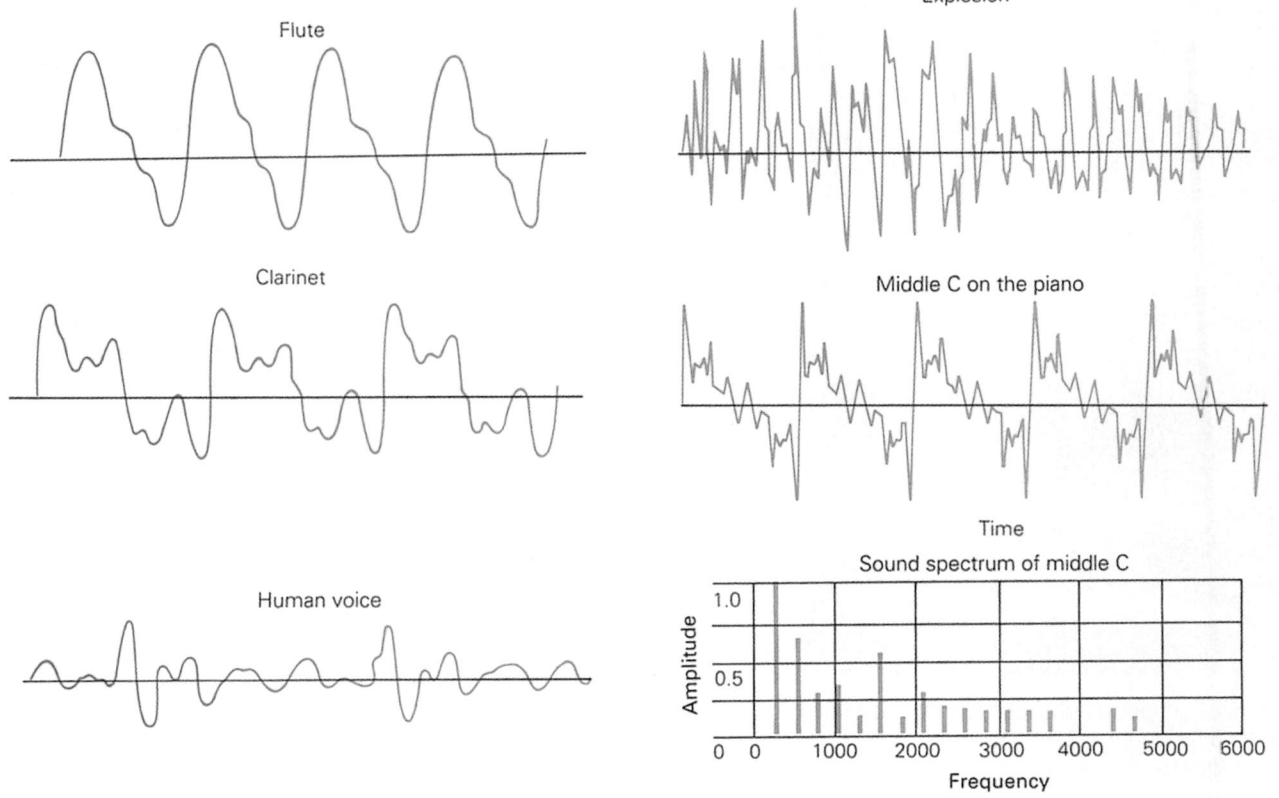

FIGURE 4.15

Waveforms of Familiar Sounds

This figure shows the complex waveforms of familiar sounds and the sound spectrum for middle C on the piano. The basic wavelength is produced by the fundamental, in this case 256 cycles, but the piano's strings are also vibrating at several higher frequencies (known as overtones, or harmonics) that produce the jaggedness of the wave pattern. These additional frequencies are identified in the sound spectrum.

Figure 4.15 displays the complex waveforms that correspond to several familiar sounds. The graph in the figure shows the sound spectrum for middle C on a piano—the range of all the frequencies actually present in that note and their amplitudes.

In a complex tone such as middle C, the lowest frequency (about 256 Hz) is responsible for the pitch you hear; it is called the *fundamental.* The higher frequencies are called *harmonics,* or overtones, and are simple multiples of the fundamental. The complete sound you hear is produced by the total effect of the fundamental and the harmonics shown in the spectrum. If pure tones at these frequencies and intensities were added together, the result would sound the same to you as middle C on a piano.

The sounds that you call *noise* do not have the clear, simple structures of fundamental frequencies and harmonics. Noise contains many frequencies that are not systematically related to each other. For instance, the static noise you hear between radio stations contains energy at all audible frequencies; you perceive it as having no pitch because it has no fundamental frequency.

The Physiology of Hearing

Now that you know something about the physical bases of your psychological experiences of sound, let's see how those experiences arise from physiological activity in the auditory system. First, we will look at the way the ear works. Then we will consider some theories about how pitch experiences are coded in the auditory system and how sounds are localized.

THE AUDITORY SYSTEM

You have already learned that sensory processes transform forms of external energy into forms of energy within your brain. For you to hear, as shown in **Figure 4.16,** four basic energy transformations must take place: (1) Airborne sound waves must get translated into *fluid* waves within the *cochlea* of the ear, (2) the fluid waves must then stimulate mechanical vibrations of the *basilar membrane,* (3) these vibrations must be converted into electrical impulses, and (4) the impulses must travel to the *auditory cortex.* Let's examine each of these transformations in detail.

In the first transformation, vibrating air molecules enter the ears (see Figure 4.16). Some sound enters the external canal of the ear directly and some enters after having been reflected off the *external ear, or pinna.* The sound wave travels along the canal through the outer ear until it reaches the end of the canal. There it encounters a thin membrane called the eardrum, or *tympanic membrane.* The sound wave's pressure variations set the eardrum into motion. The eardrum transmits the vibrations from the outer ear into the middle ear, a chamber that contains the three smallest bones in the human body: the *hammer,* the *anvil,* and the *stirrup.* These bones form a mechanical chain that transmits and concentrates the vibrations from the eardrum to the primary organ of hearing, the *cochlea,* which is located in the *inner ear.*

In the second transformation, which occurs in the cochlea, the airborne sound wave becomes "seaborne." The

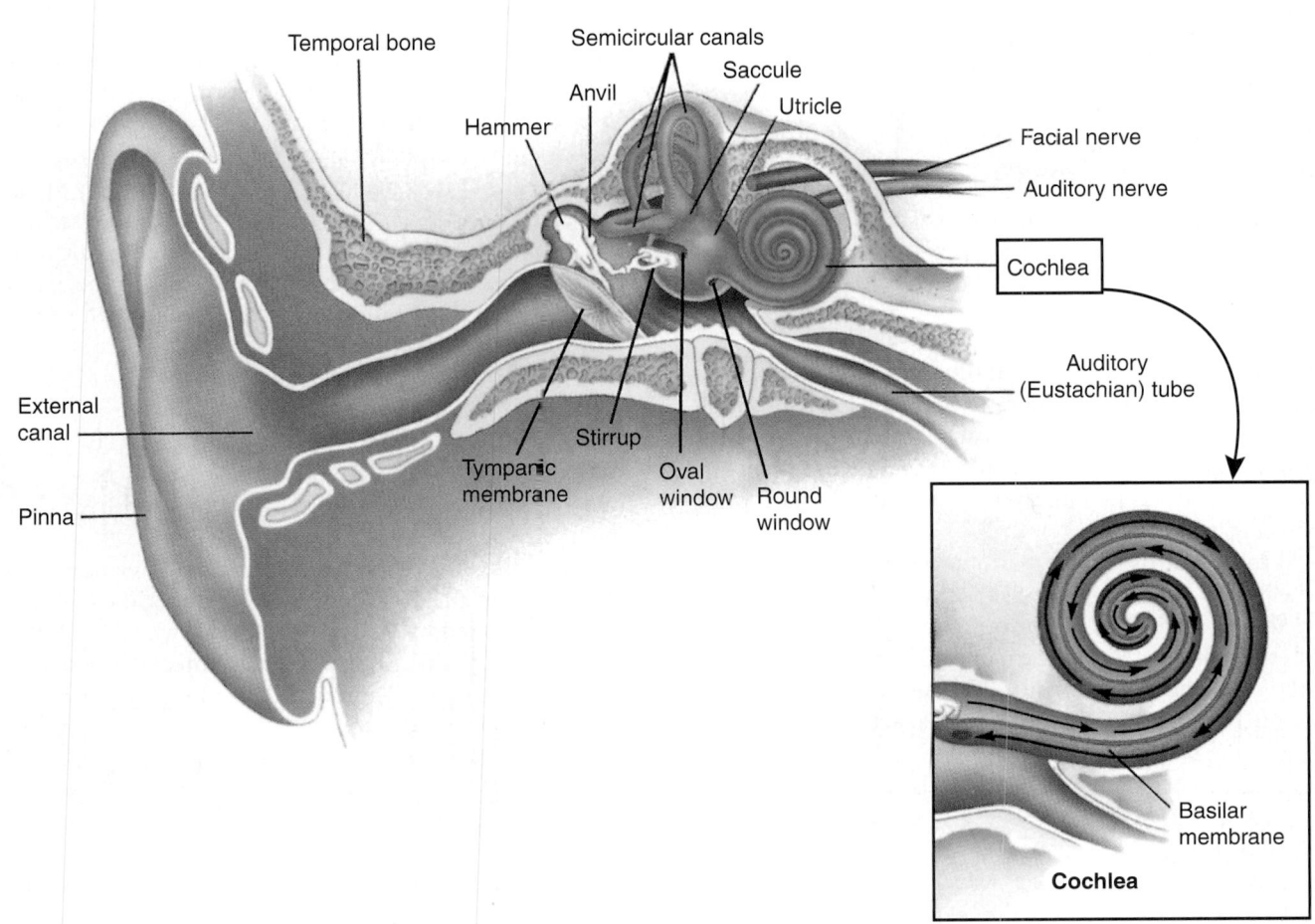

FIGURE 4.16

Structure of the Human Ear

Sound waves are channeled by the external ear, or pinna, through the external canal, causing the tympanic membrane to vibrate. This vibration activates the tiny bones of the inner ear—the hammer, anvil, and stirrup. Their mechanical vibrations are passed along from the oval window to the cochlea, where they set in motion the fluid in its canal. Tiny hair cells lining the coiled basilar membrane within the cochlea bend as the fluid moves, stimulating nerve endings attached to them. The mechanical energy is then transformed into neural energy and sent to the brain via the auditory nerve.

Sustained exposure to loud noise can lead to hearing loss. What can people do to avoid such losses?

cochlea is a fluid-filled, coiled tube that has a membrane, known as the **basilar membrane,** running down its middle along its length. When the stirrup vibrates against the oval window at the base of the cochlea, the fluid in the cochlea causes the basilar membrane to move in a wavelike motion (hence, "seaborne").

In the third transformation, the wavelike motion of the basilar membrane bends the tiny hair cells connected to the membrane. The hair cells are the receptor cells for the auditory system. As the hair cells bend, they stimulate nerve endings, transforming the mechanical vibrations of the basilar membrane into neural activity.

Cochlea The primary organ of hearing; a fluid-filled coiled tube located in the inner ear.

Basilar membrane A membrane in the cochlea that, when set into motion, stimulates hair cells that produce the neural effects of auditory stimulation.

Auditory nerve The nerve that carries impulses from the cochlea to the cochlear nucleus of the brain.

Auditory cortex The area of the temporal lobes that receives and processes auditory information.

Place theory The theory that different frequency tones produce maximum activation at different locations along the basilar membrane, with the result that pitch can be coded by the place at which activation occurs.

Frequency theory The theory that a tone produces a rate of vibration in the basilar membrane equal to its frequency, with the result that pitch can be coded by the frequency of the neural response.

Finally, in the fourth transformation, nerve impulses leave the cochlea in a bundle of fibers called the **auditory nerve.** These fibers meet in the *cochlear nucleus* of the brain stem. Similar to the crossing over of nerves in the visual system, stimulation from one ear goes to both sides of the brain. Auditory signals pass through a series of other nuclei on their way to the **auditory cortex,** in the temporal lobes of the cerebral hemispheres. Higher-order processing of these signals begins in the auditory cortex. (As you will learn shortly, other parts of the ear labeled in Figure 4.16 play roles in your other senses.)

The four transformations occur in fully functioning auditory systems. However, millions of people suffer from some form of hearing impairment. There are two general types of hearing impairment, each caused by a defect in one or more of the components of the auditory system. The less serious type of impairment is *conduction deafness,* a problem in the conduction of the air vibrations to the cochlea. Often in this type of impairment, the bones in the middle ear are not functioning properly, a problem that may be corrected in microsurgery by insertion of an artificial anvil or stirrup. The more serious type of impairment is *nerve deafness,* a defect in the neural mechanisms that create nerve impulses in the ear or relay them to the auditory cortex. Damage to the auditory cortex can also create nerve deafness.

THEORIES OF PITCH PERCEPTION

To explain how the auditory system converts sound waves into sensations of pitch, researchers have outlined two distinct theories: place theory and frequency theory.

Place theory was initially proposed by Hermann von Helmholtz in the 1800s and was later modified, elaborated, and tested by **Georg von Békésy,** who won a Nobel Prize for this work in 1961. Place theory is based on the fact that the basilar membrane moves when sound waves are conducted through the inner ear. Different frequencies produce their most movement at particular locations along the basilar membrane. For high-frequency tones, the wave motion is greatest at the base of the cochlea, where the oval and round windows are located. For low-frequency tones, the greatest wave motion of the basilar membrane is at the opposite end. So place theory suggests that perception of pitch depends on the specific location on the basilar membrane at which the greatest stimulation occurs.

The second theory, **frequency theory,** explains pitch by the rate of vibration of the basilar membrane. This theory predicts that a sound wave with a frequency of 100 Hz will set the basilar membrane vibrating 100 times per second. The frequency theory also predicts that the vibrations of the basilar membrane will cause neurons to fire at the same rate, so that rate of firing is the neural code for pitch. One problem with this theory is that individual neurons cannot fire rapidly enough to repre-

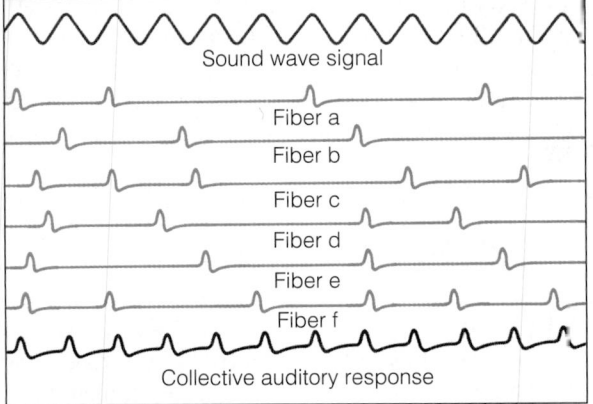

Sound wave signal

Fiber a

Fiber b

Fiber c

Fiber d

Fiber e

Fiber f

Collective auditory response

FIGURE 4.17

The Volley Principle

The total collective activity of the auditory (black) nerve cells has a pattern that corresponds to the input sound wave (red), even though each individual fiber may not be firing fast enough to follow the sound wave pattern.

sent high-pitched sounds, because none of them can fire more than 1,000 times per second. This limitation makes it impossible for one neuron to distinguish sounds above 1,000 Hz—which, of course, your auditory system can do quite well. The limitation might be overcome by the **volley principle**, which explains what might happen at such high frequencies. As shown in **Figure 4.17**, several neurons in a combined action, or volley, could fire at the frequency that matched a stimulus tone of 2,000 Hz, 3,000 Hz, and so on (Wever, 1949).

As with the trichromatic and opponent-process theories of color vision, the place and frequency theories each successfully account for different aspects of your experience of pitch. Frequency theory accounts well for coding frequencies below about 5,000 Hz. At higher frequencies, neurons cannot fire quickly and precisely enough to code a signal adequately, even in volley. Place theory accounts well for perception of pitch at frequencies above 1,000 Hz. Below 1,000 Hz, the entire basilar membrane vibrates so broadly that it cannot provide a signal distinctive enough for the neural receptors to use as a means of distinguishing pitch. Between 1,000 and 5,000 Hz, both mechanisms can operate. A complex sensory task is divided between two systems that, together,

Volley principle An extension of frequency theory which proposes that when peaks in a sound wave come too frequently for a single neuron to fire at each peak, several neurons fire as a group at the frequency of the stimulus tone.

offer greater sensory precision than either system alone could provide. We will next see that you also possess two converging neural systems to help you localize sounds in the environment.

SOUND LOCALIZATION

Porpoises and bats do not use vision to locate objects in dark waters or dark caves. Instead, they use *echolocation*—they emit high-pitched sounds that bounce off objects, giving them feedback about the objects' distances, locations, sizes, textures, and movements. One species of bat is able to use echolocation to differentiate between objects that are just 0.3 millimeter apart (Simmons et al., 1998). Although humans lack this special ability, you do use sounds to determine the location of objects in space, especially when seeing them is difficult. You do so through two mechanisms: assessments of the relative timing and relative intensity of the sounds that arrive at each ear (Middlebrooks & Green, 1991; Phillips, 1993).

The first mechanism involves neurons that compare the relative times at which incoming sound reaches each ear. A sound off to your right side, for example, reaches your right ear before your left (see point B in **Figure 4.18**). Neurons in your auditory system are specialized to fire most actively for specific time delays between the two ears. Your brain uses this information about disparities in arrival time to make precise estimates for the likely origins of a sound in space.

The second mechanism relies on the principle that a sound has a slightly greater intensity in the first ear at which it arrives—because your head itself casts a *sound shadow* that weakens the signal. These intensity differences depend on the relative size of the wavelength of a

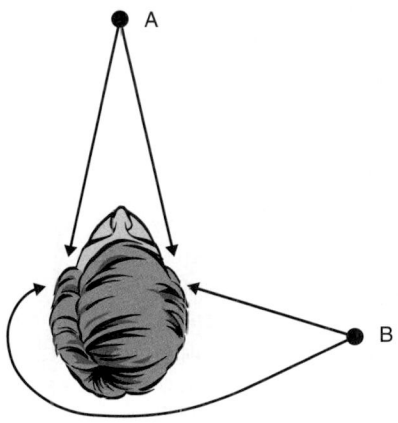

FIGURE 4.18

Time Disparity and Sound Localization

The brain uses differences in the time course with which sounds arrive at the two ears to localize the sounds in space.

Why might bats have evolved the ability to use echolocation to navigate through their environment?

tone with respect to your head. Large-wavelength, low-frequency tones show virtually no intensity differences, whereas small-wavelength, high-frequency tones show measurable intensity differences. Your brain, once again, has specialized cells that detect intensity differences in the signals arriving at your two ears.

But what happens when a sound creates neither a timing nor an intensity difference? In Figure 4.18, a sound originating at point A would have this property. With your eyes closed, you cannot tell its exact location. So you must move your head—to reposition your ears—to break the symmetry and provide the necessary information for sound localization.

SUMMING UP

Combinations of the frequencies and amplitudes of sound waves give rise to perceptions of pitch, loudness, and timbre. Auditory information goes through several transformations from the ear to the brain: Sound waves become fluid waves, and fluid waves produce patterns of neural response. Pitch perception is explained by the combination of two mechanisms: Place theory suggests that different pitches produce movement at particular locations along the basilar membrane; frequency theory suggests that different pitches produce characteristic rates of vibration of the basilar membrane. Sound localization also involves at least two processes: The brain has cells that detect the relative timing and relative intensity of sounds arriving at the two ears.

■ Your Other Senses

We have devoted the most attention to vision and hearing because scientists have studied them most thoroughly. However, your ability both to survive in and to enjoy the external environment relies on your full repertory of senses. We will close our discussion of sensation with brief analyses of several of your other senses.

Smell

You can probably imagine circumstances in which you'd be just as happy to give up your sense of smell: Did you ever have a family dog who lost a battle with a skunk? But to avoid that skunk experience, you'd also have to give up the smells of fresh roses, hot buttered popcorn, and sea breezes. Odors—both good and bad—first make their presence known by interacting with receptor proteins on the membranes of *olfactory cilia* (see **Figure 4.19**). It takes only eight molecules of a substance to initiate one of these nerve impulses, but at least 40 nerve endings must be stimulated before you can smell the substance. Once initiated, these nerve impulses convey odor information to the **olfactory bulb,** located just above the receptors and just below the frontal lobes of the cerebrum. Odor stimuli start the process of smell by stimulating an influx of chemical substances into ion channels in olfactory neurons, an event that, as you may recall from Chapter 3, triggers an action potential (Restrepo et al., 1990). Your sense of smell is one of very few neural systems in which you acquire new neurons on an ongoing basis. When your olfactory neurons age and die, they are replaced by new cells that form their own connections to the olfactory bulb (Farbman, 1992).

Smell presumably evolved as a system for detecting and locating food (Moncrieff, 1951). For many species, smell is also used to detect potential sources of danger. It serves this function well because organisms do not have to come into direct contact with other organisms in order to smell them. In addition, smell can be a powerful form of active communication. Members of some species communicate with each other by secreting and detecting chemical signals called pheromones. **Pheromones** are chemical substances used within a given species to signal sexual receptivity, danger, territorial boundaries, and food sources. For example, male members of various insect species pro-

■**Olfactory bulb** The center where odor-sensitive receptors send their signals, located just below the frontal lobes of the cortex.
■**Pheromones** Chemical signals released by organisms to communicate with other members of the species; often serve as long-distance sexual attractors.

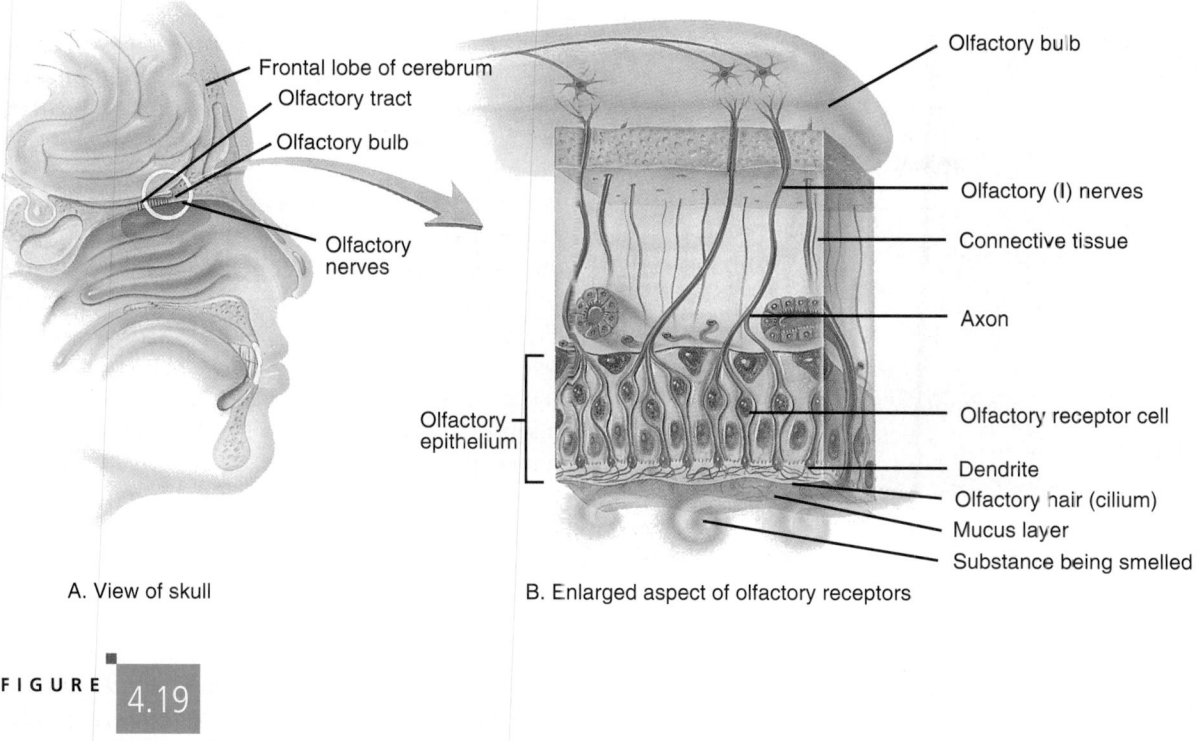

A. View of skull

B. Enlarged aspect of olfactory receptors

Labels for image:
Frontal lobe of cerebrum
Olfactory tract
Olfactory bulb
Olfactory nerves
Olfactory epithelium
Olfactory bulb
Olfactory (I) nerves
Connective tissue
Axon
Olfactory receptor cell
Dendrite
Olfactory hair (cilium)
Mucus layer
Substance being smelled

FIGURE 4.19

Receptors for Smell

The olfactory receptor cells in your nasal cavities are stimulated by chemicals in the environment. They send information to the olfactory bulb in your brain.

duce sex pheromones to alert females of the species that they are available for mating (Farine et al., 1996; Minckley et al., 1991).

The significance of the sense of smell varies greatly across species. Dogs, rats, insects, and many other creatures for whom smell is central to survival have a far keener sense of smell than humans do. Relatively more of their brains is devoted to smell. Humans seem to use the sense of smell primarily in conjunction with taste to seek and sample food, but there is some evidence that humans may also secrete and sense pheromone-like substances (Jacob & McClintock, 2000). Suggestive evidence comes, for example, from the fact that, over time, menstrual cycles of close friends in women's dormitories have been shown to fall into a pattern of synchrony (McClintock, 1971; Stern & McClintock, 1998). This synchronization has been attributed to chemical signals carried through the sense of smell (Cutler et al., 1986; Preti et al., 1986). Research also suggests that smell might play a role in people's readiness to engage in sexual activity.

HOW WE KNOW

DOES SMELL PLAY A ROLE IN HUMAN SEXUAL BEHAVIOR? In a rating study, 289 women provided their reactions to the odor of *androstenone*, a main component of male sweat. Mostly, the women found the odor "unpleasant" and "unattractive." The exception to this general finding occurred in women who were ovulating, whose ratings were more neutral with respect to the odor. What is the implication? The researcher speculated that women who are ovulating—and, thus, most likely to become pregnant—are least likely to resist men's sexual advances because of their natural unpleasant odor (Grammer, 1993).

Are you surprised that odor may play this role in human sexual response?

Taste

Although food and wine gourmets are capable of making remarkably subtle and complex taste distinctions, many of their sensations are really smells and not tastes. Taste and smell work together closely when you eat. In fact, when you have a cold, food seems tasteless, because your nasal passages are blocked and you can't smell the food. Demonstrate this principle for yourself: Hold your nose and try to tell the difference between foods of similar texture but different tastes, such as pieces of apple and raw potato. Some students living in dormitories with notoriously bad food have reported that wearing nose plugs to meals makes everything taste uniformly bland—which is better than the usual taste!

Why would a man with chronic sinus trouble be ill-advised to take up wine tasting?

the flavor of monosodium glutamate (MSG), the chemical that is often added to Asian foods and occurs naturally in foods rich in protein such as meat, seafood, and aged cheese. Although receptor cells for the five qualities may produce small responses to other tastes, the "best" response most directly encodes quality. There appear to be separate transduction systems for each of the basic classes of taste (Bartoshuk & Beauchamp, 1994).

Taste receptors can be damaged by many things you put in your mouth, such as alcohol, cigarette smoke, and acids. Fortunately, your taste receptors get replaced every few days—even more frequently than smell receptors. Indeed, the taste system is the most resistant to damage of all your sensory systems; it is extremely rare for anyone to suffer a total, permanent taste loss (Bartoshuk, 1990).

Touch and Skin Senses

The skin is a remarkably versatile organ. In addition to protecting you against surface injury, holding in body fluids, and helping regulate body temperature, it contains nerve endings that produce sensations of pressure, warmth, and cold. These sensations are called the **cutaneous senses** (skin senses).

Because you receive so much sensory information through your skin, many different types of receptor cells operate close to the surface of the body (see **Figure 4.21**). Each of the types of receptors pictured responds to some-

The surface of your tongue is covered with *papillae,* which give it a bumpy appearance. Many of these papillae contain clusters of taste receptor cells called the *taste buds* (see **Figure 4.20**). Single-cell recordings of taste receptors show that individual receptor cells respond best to one of the four primary taste qualities: sweet, sour, bitter, and saline (salty) (Frank & Nowlis, 1989). In recent years, researchers have found receptors for a fifth basic taste quality, *umami* (Chaudhari et al., 2000). Umami is

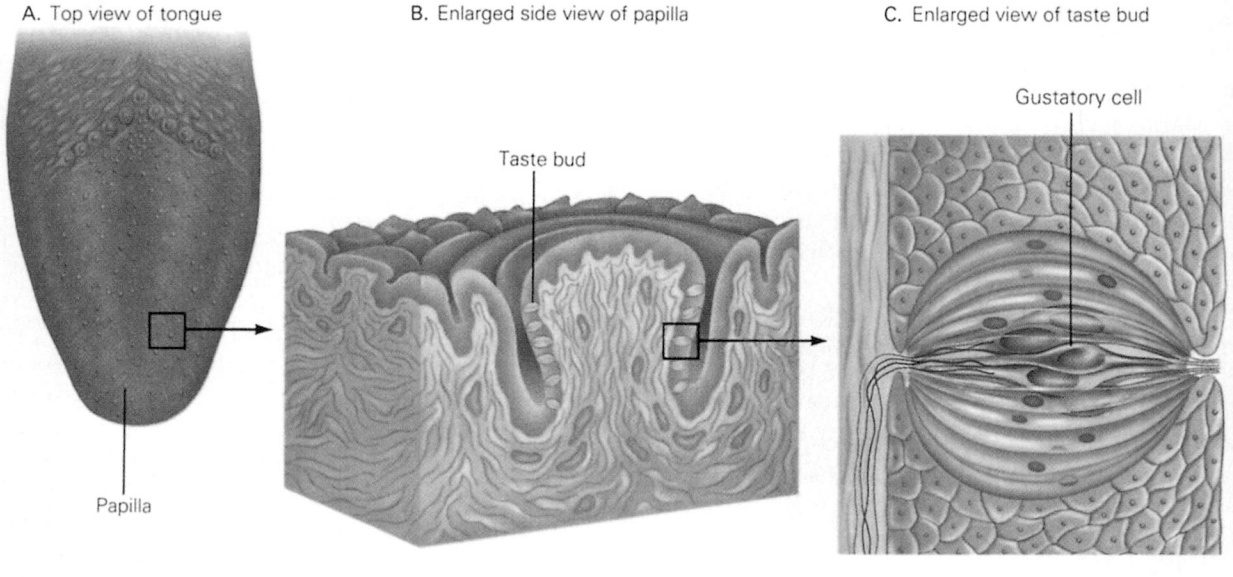

A. Top view of tongue   B. Enlarged side view of papilla   C. Enlarged view of taste bud

Gustatory cell

Taste bud

Papilla

FIGURE 4.20

Receptors for Taste

Part A shows the distribution of the papillae on the upper side of the tongue.
Part B shows a single papilla enlarged so that the individual taste buds are visible.
Part C shows one of the taste buds enlarged.

CHAPTER FOUR / SENSATION

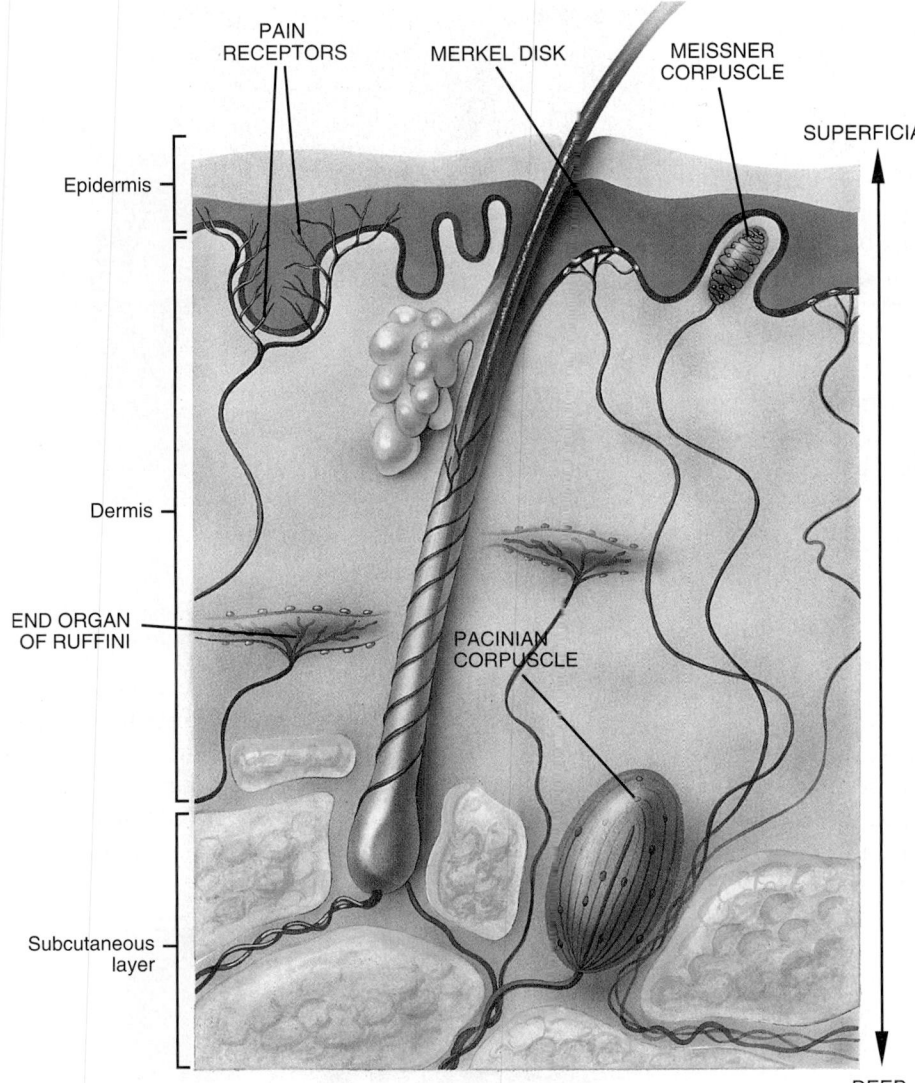

PAIN RECEPTORS

MERKEL DISK

MEISSNER CORPUSCLE

SUPERFICIAL

Epidermis

Dermis

END ORGAN OF RUFFINI

PACINIAN CORPUSCLE

Subcutaneous layer

DEEP

Section of skin and subcutaneous layer

FIGURE 4.21

Receptors for the Cutaneous Senses

Several different types of receptors are responsible for the experience of cutaneous sensations such as pressure, warmth, and cold. For example, *Meissner corpuscles* respond best when something rubs against the skin, and *Merkel disks* are most active when a small object exerts steady pressure against the skin.

what different patterns of contact with the skin (Sekuler & Blake, 1994). As two examples, *Meissner corpuscles* respond best when something rubs against the skin, and *Merkel disks* are most active when a small object exerts steady pressure against the skin. You may be surprised to learn that you have separate receptors for warmth and coolness. Rather than having one type of receptor that works like a thermometer, your brain integrates separate warm and cool signals to monitor changes in environmental temperature.

The skin's sensitivity to pressure varies tremendously over the body. For example, you are ten times more accurate in sensing the position of stimulation on your fingertips than on your back. The variation in sensitivity of different body regions is shown by the greater density of nerve endings in these regions and also by the greater amount of sensory cortex devoted to them. In Chapter 3, you learned that your sensitivity is greatest where you need it most—on your face, tongue, and hands. Precise

sensory feedback from these parts of the body permits effective eating, speaking, and grasping.

One aspect of cutaneous sensitivity plays a central role in human relationships: touch. Through touch, you communicate to others your desire to give or receive comfort, support, love, and passion. However, where you get touched or touch someone else makes a difference; those areas of the skin surface that give rise to erotic, or sexual, sensations are called **erogenous zones.** Other touch-sensitive erotic areas vary in their arousal potential for different individuals, depending on learned associations and the concentration of sensory receptors in the areas.

Cutaneous senses The skin senses that register sensations of pressure, warmth, and cold.

Erogenous zones Areas of the skin surface that are especially sensitive to stimulation and that give rise to erotic or sexual sensations.

YOUR OTHER SENSES

Touch may also play a role in survival. For example, premature babies who were massaged for 45 minutes a day during their hospital stays not only grew faster than untouched preemies, but their mental development was also enhanced by the touch (Field & Schanberg, 1990). Comparable research with rats shows that vigorous stimulation releases growth hormones and activates the growth enzyme ODC (onithine decarboxylase) in the brain and other vital organs. Rat pups that were handled daily in their early lives showed a lifelong enhancement of many aspects of their health. Compared to control animals, the stimulated pups were more resistant to stress and grew old more gracefully, sustaining more brain cells and better memory than unstimulated pups (Meany et al., 1988). The practical message is clear: Touch those you care about often and encourage others to touch you—it not only feels good, it's healthy for you and for them (Montague, 1986).

Why would riding in the front seat of a roller coaster be less likely to make you nauseated than riding in the rear?

The Vestibular and Kinesthetic Senses

The next pair of senses we will describe may be entirely new to you, because they do not have receptors you can see directly, like eyes, ears, or noses. Your **vestibular sense** tells you how your body—especially your head—is oriented in the world with respect to gravity. The receptors for this information are tiny hairs in fluid-filled sacs and canals in the inner ear. The hairs bend when the fluid moves and presses on them, which is what happens when you turn your head quickly. The *saccule* and *utricle* (shown in Figure 4.16) tell you about acceleration or deceleration in a straight line. The three canals, called the *semicircular canals,* are at right angles to each other and, thus, can tell you about motion in any direction. They inform you how your head is moving when you turn, nod, or tilt it.

People who lose their vestibular sense because of accidents or disease are initially quite disoriented and prone to falls and dizziness. However, most of these people eventually compensate by relying more heavily on visual information. *Motion sickness* can occur when the signals from the visual system conflict with those from the vestibular system. People feel nauseated when reading in a moving car because the visual signal is of a stationary object, while the vestibular signal is of movement. Drivers rarely get motion sickness because they are both seeing and feeling motion.

Whether you are standing erect, drawing pictures, or making love, your brain needs to have accurate informa-

tion about the current positions and movement of your body parts relative to each other. The **kinesthetic sense** (also called *kinesthesis*) provides constant sensory feedback about what the body is doing during motor activities. Without it, you would be unable to coordinate most voluntary movements.

What role does the kinesthetic sense play in the performance of skilled athletes?

Vestibular sense The sense that tells how one's own body is oriented in the world with respect to gravity.

Kinesthetic sense Sense concerned with bodily position and movement of the body parts relative to each other.

You have two sources of kinesthetic information: receptors in the joints and receptors in the muscles and tendons. Receptors that lie in the joints respond to pressures that accompany different positions of the limbs and to pressure changes that accompany movements of the joints. Receptors in the muscles and tendons respond to changes in tension that accompany muscle shortening and lengthening.

The brain often integrates information from your kinesthetic sense with information from touch senses. Your brain, for example, can't grasp the full meaning of the signals coming from each of your fingers if it doesn't know exactly where your fingers are in relation to each other. Imagine that you pick up an object with your eyes closed. Your sense of touch may allow you to guess that the object is a stone, but your kinesthetic sense will enable you to know how large it is.

Pain

Earlier we reviewed the beneficial aspects of touch. You know, however, that certain forms of physical contact can lead to pain. **Pain** is the body's response to stimulation from noxious stimuli—those that are intense enough to cause tissue damage or threaten to do so. Are you entirely happy that you have such a well-developed pain sense? Your answer probably should be "yes and no." On the "yes" side, your pain sense is critical for survival. People born with congenital insensitivity to pain feel no hurt, but their bodies often become scarred and their limbs deformed from injuries that they could have avoided had their brains been able to warn them of danger (Larner et al., 1994). Their experience makes you aware that pain serves as an essential defense signal—it warns you of potential harm. On the "no" side, there are certainly times when you would be happy to be able to turn your pain sense off. More than 50 million people in the United States suffer from chronic, persistent pain. Medical treatment for pain and the workdays lost because of pain are estimated to cost more than $70 billion annually in the United States (Turk, 1994). Severe depression can result from the seemingly endless nagging of chronic pain and the ways in which chronic pain causes sufferers to negatively evaluate their lives (Banks & Kerns, 1996). You can see why researchers wish to have a better understanding of the mechanisms that produce sensations of pain—so that they can find more efficient techniques to alleviate suffering.

PAIN MECHANISMS
Almost all animals are born with some type of pain defense system that triggers automatic withdrawal reflexes to certain stimulus events. When the stimulus intensity reaches threshold, organisms respond by escaping—if they can. In addition, they quickly learn to identify painful stimulus situations, avoiding them whenever possible.

People can suffer from two kinds of pain: *nociceptive* and *neuropathic*. **Nociceptive pain** is the negative feeling induced by a noxious external stimulus; for example, the feeling you have when you touch a hot stove with your hand. Specialized nerve endings in the skin send the pain message up your arm, through the spinal cord, and into your brain. By withdrawing, you can make this type of pain stop. **Neuropathic pain** is caused by the abnormal functioning or overactivity of nerves. It comes from injury or disease of nerves caused by accidents or cancer, for example. Drugs and other therapies that calm the nerves can relieve much of this type of pain.

Scientists have begun to identify the specific sets of receptors that respond to pain-producing stimuli. They have learned that some receptors respond only to temperature, others to chemicals, others to mechanical stimuli, and still others to combinations of pain-producing stimuli. This network of pain fibers is a fine meshwork that covers your entire body. Peripheral nerve fibers send pain signals to the central nervous system by two pathways: a fast-conducting set of nerve fibers that are covered with myelin and slower, smaller nerve fibers without any myelin coating. Starting at the spinal cord, the impulses are relayed to the thalamus and then to the cerebral cortex, where the location and intensity of the pain are identified, the significance of the injury is evaluated, and action plans are formulated.

THE PSYCHOLOGY OF PAIN
Your emotional responses, context factors, and your interpretation of the situation can be as important as actual physical stimuli in determining how much pain you experience (Price, 2000; Turk, 1994). The importance of psychological processes in the experience of pain is shown in two extreme cases—one in which there is pain but there is no physical stimulus for it and another in which there is no pain but there is an intensely painful stimulus. For example, up to 10 percent of people who have limbs amputated report extreme or chronic pain in the limb that is no longer there—the **phantom limb phenomenon** (Melzack, 1992). In contrast, some individuals who take part in religious rituals are able to block out pain while participating in activities involving intense stimulation, such as walking on a bed of hot coals or having their bodies pierced with needles.

Pain The body's response to noxious stimuli that are intense enough to cause, or threaten to cause, tissue damage.

Nociceptive pain Pain induced by a noxious external stimulus; specialized nerve endings in the skin send this pain message from the skin, through the spinal chord, into the brain.

Neuropathic pain Pain caused by abnormal functioning or overactivity of nerves; it results from injury or disease of nerves.

Phantom limb phenomenon As experienced by amputees, extreme or chronic pain in a limb that is no longer there.

WHY IS "HOT" FOOD PAINFUL?

Have you ever had this experience? You are eating a very "hot" dish in a Chinese or Mexican restaurant and you accidentally bite directly into a chili pepper. In just moments you go from enjoyment to intense pain. If this has happened, then you know that, in the realm of taste, there is a fine line between what gives pleasure and what gives pain. Let's explore this relationship.

Physiologically, it's easy to explain why hot pepper can cause you pain. On your tongue, your taste buds have associated with them nociceptive pain fibers (Bartoshuk, 1993). Thus, the very same chemical that can stimulate the receptors in your taste buds can stimulate the closely allied pain fibers (Caterina et al., 2000). In the case of hot pepper, this chemical is *capsaicin*. If you want to enjoy a spicy meal, you have to keep the concentration of capsaicin in your meal sufficiently low so that your taste receptors are more active than your pain receptors.

But why, you might wonder, do different people have such obvious differences in their preferences for hot food? People often find it very difficult to understand how their friends can or cannot eat food that is very spicy. Again, we can look to physiology to explain these differences. The figure shows photographs of tongues from two individuals studied by **Linda Bartoshuk** and her colleagues. You can see that one tongue has considerably more taste buds than the other. If there are more taste buds, there will be more pain receptors. Therefore, people with more taste buds are more

likely to get a strong pain response from capsaicin. The group of individuals who have more taste buds have been dubbed *supertasters* (Bartoshuk, 1993). They form a sharp contrast, in the extremes of their sensory experiences, to *nontasters*. For many taste sensations, these two groups are equivalent—you wouldn't know at most times whether you were a supertaster, a nontaster, or somewhere in between. The differences arise only for certain chemicals—capsaicin is an excellent example.

The variations in the density of taste buds on different people's tongues appear to be genetic (Bartoshuk et al., 1994). Women are much more likely to be supertasters than are men. Supertasters generally have more sensitivity to bitter chemicals—a sensory quality shared by most poisons. You can imagine that if women generally were responsible for nurturing and feeding offspring over the course of evolution, the children

of women with greater taste sensitivity would be more likely to survive. Because taster status is genetic, you can find preference differences among children at very young ages (Anliker et al., 1991). Five- to seven-year-old supertasters preferred milk to cheddar cheese. This preference was reversed for nontasters. Why? The supertasters may perceive the milk as sweeter and the cheese as more bitter than do the nontasters. Thus, genetic differences may help explain why some young children have such strong (and vocal) taste preferences.

But let's return to the restaurant meal at which you have had your painful accident. What you might have noticed is that the sensation of pain fades over time. In this respect, the pain receptors in your mouth act like other sensory receptors: Over time, you adapt to a constant stimulus. That's good news! You should be glad that your sensory processes offer built-in relief.

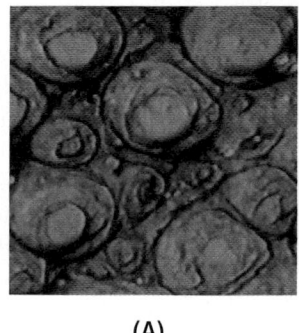 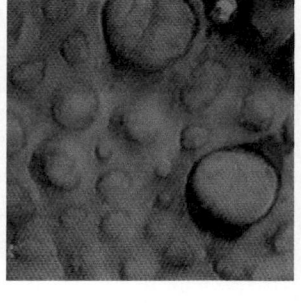

(A)   (B)

(A) The tongue of a supertaster. (B) The tongue of a nontaster

In general, the pain one feels is affected by the context in which it occurs and by learned habits of response. Because pain is in part a psychological response, it can be modified by treatments that make use of mental processes, such as hypnosis, deep relaxation, and thought-distraction procedures. For example, the Lamaze method of preparation for childbirth without anesthetics attempts to reduce the woman's intense labor pains by combining several of these methods. Lamaze breathing exercises aid relaxation and focus attention away from the pain area. The use of distracting, pleasant images, massage that creates gentle counterstimulation, and social support from a coaching spouse or friend all work to give the prospective mother a greater sense of control over this painful situation.

How are pain sensations affected by the psychological context? One theory about the way pain may be modulated is known as the **gate-control theory,** developed by **Ronald Melzack** (1973, 1980). This theory suggests that cells in the spinal cord act as neurological gates, interrupting and blocking some pain signals and letting others get through to the brain. The brain and receptors in the skin send messages to the spinal cord to open or close those gates. It is the messages descending from the brain that provide the psychological context in which you experience pain. In recent years, Melzack (1999) has proposed an updated *neuromatrix theory* of pain that incorporates the reality that people often experience pain with little or no physical cause: In these cases, the experience of pain originates wholly in the brain.

The way you perceive pain, what you communicate about it to others, and even the way you respond to pain-relieving treatments may reveal more about your psychological state than about the intensity of the pain stimulus. What you perceive may be different from, and even independent of, what you sense—as you will see in Chapter 5, in our study of the psychology of perception.

Individuals taking part in religious rituals, such as walking on a bed of hot coals, are able to block out pain. What does that tell you about the relationship between the physiology and psychology of pain?

SUMMING UP

The nerve impulses for your sense of smell begin when chemicals in the air interact with olfactory cilia. Across different species, smell plays a role in regulating sexual behavior and other important functions. The smell and taste systems conspire to produce your experience of most food. Tastes represent mixtures of sweet, sour, bitter and salty responses from appropriate taste buds.

You experience sensations of pressure, warmth, and cold through receptor cells located in your skin. Touch plays an important role in communication and survival. Your vestibular sense keeps track of the orientation of your head and body with respect to gravity. Your kinesthetic sense tracks the positions of your body parts and helps coordinate voluntary motor movements.

You experience nociceptive pain in response to noxious stimuli and neuropathic pain in response to abnormal functioning of nerves. The psychological context determines, in part, how much pain you will experience.

Gate-control theory A theory about pain modulation that proposes that certain cells in the spinal cord act as gates to interrupt and block some pain signals while sending others on to the brain.

RECAPPING
MAIN POINTS

Sensory Knowledge of the World

- Because of the importance of sensory processes for providing information about the world, researchers have studied sensation from the earliest days of psychology.

- Psychophysics investigates psychological responses to physical stimuli. Researchers measure absolute thresholds and just noticeable differences between stimuli.

- Signal detection allows researchers to separate sensory acuity from response biases.

- Researchers in psychophysics have captured the relationship between physical intensity and psychological effect with mathematical functions.

- Sensation translates the physical energy of stimuli into neural codes via transduction.

- Researchers try to trace the flow of information from sensory receptors to areas of the cerebral cortex.

The Visual System

- Photoreceptors in the retina, called rods and cones, convert light energy into neural impulses.
- Ganglion cells in the retina integrate input from receptors and bipolar cells. Their axons form the optic nerves that meet at the optic chiasma.
- Visual information is distributed to several different areas of the brain that process different aspects of the visual environment such as how things look and where they are.
- The wavelength of light is the stimulus for color.
- Color sensations differ in hue, saturation, and brightness.
- Color vision theory combines the trichromatic theory of three color receptors with the opponent-process theory of color systems composed of opponent elements.
- Detection of stimulus features occurs through the action of cells in the retina and higher visual centers.

Hearing

- Hearing is produced by sound waves that vary in frequency, amplitude, and complexity.
- In the cochlea, sound waves are transformed into fluid waves that move the basilar membrane. Hairs on the basilar membrane stimulate neural impulses that are sent to the auditory cortex.
- Place theory best explains the coding of high frequencies, and frequency theory best explains the coding of low frequencies.
- To compute the direction from which the sound is arriving, two types of neural mechanisms compute the relative intensity and timing of sounds coming to each ear.

Your Other Senses

- Smell and taste respond to the chemical properties of substances and work together when people are seeking and sampling food.
- Olfaction is accomplished by odor-sensitive cells deep in the nasal passages.
- Taste receptors are taste buds embedded in papillae, mostly in the tongue.
- The cutaneous (skin) senses give sensations of pressure and temperature.
- The vestibular sense gives information about the direction and rate of body motion.
- The kinesthetic sense gives information about the position of body parts and helps coordinate motion.
- Pain is the body's response to potentially harmful stimuli.
- The physiological response to pain involves sensory response at the site of the pain stimulus and nerve impulses moving between the brain and the spinal cord.
- Pain is in part a psychological response that can be modified by treatments that emphasize mental processes and thought distraction.

Key Terms

absolute threshold (p. 84)
accommodation (p. 90)
amacrine cells (p. 92)
auditory cortex (p. 104)
auditory nerve (p. 104)
basilar membrane (p. 104)
bipolar cells (p. 91)
brightness (p. 95)
cochlea (p. 104)
complementary colors (p. 96)
cones (p. 91)
cutaneous senses (p. 109)
dark adaptation (p. 91)
difference threshold (p. 87)
erogenous zones (p. 109)
fovea (p. 91)
frequency theory (p. 104)
ganglion cells (p. 91)
gate-control theory (p. 113)
horizontal cells (p. 92)
hue (p. 95)
just noticeable difference (JND) (p. 87)
kinesthetic sense (p. 110)
loudness (p. 100)
neuropathic pain (p. 111)
nociceptive pain (p. 111)
olfactory bulb (p. 106)
opponent-process theory (p. 98)
optic nerve (p. 92)
pain (p. 111)
phantom limb phenomenon (p. 111)
pheromones (p. 106)
photoreceptors (p. 91)
pitch (p. 100)
place theory (p. 104)
psychometric function (p. 84)
psychophysics (p. 84)
receptive field (p. 98)
response bias (p. 85)
retina (p. 90)
rods (p. 91)
saturation (p. 95)
sensation (p. 83)
sensory adaptation (p. 85)
sensory physiology (p. 88)
sensory receptors (p. 88)
signal detection theory (SDT) (p. 86)
timbre (p. 101)
transduction (p. 88)
trichromatic theory (p. 97)
vestibular sense (p. 110)
visual cortex (p. 92)
volley principle (p. 105)
Weber's law (p. 87)

perception

5

■ **SENSING, ORGANIZING, IDENTIFYING, AND RECOGNIZING**
The Proximal and Distal Stimuli • Reality, Ambiguity, and Illusions • Approaches to the Study of Perception

■ **PSYCHOLOGY IN THE 21ST CENTURY: VIRTUAL REALITY**

■ **ATTENTIONAL PROCESSES**
Selective Attention • Attention and Objects in the Environment

■ **ORGANIZATIONAL PROCESSES IN PERCEPTION**
Figure, Ground, and Closure • Principles of Perceptual Grouping • Spatial and Temporal Integration • Motion Perception • Depth Perception • Perceptual Constancies

■ **PSYCHOLOGY IN YOUR LIFE: HOW DO YOU CATCH A FLY BALL?**

■ **IDENTIFICATION AND RECOGNITION PROCESSES**
Bottom-Up and Top-Down Processes • Object Recognition • The Influence of Contexts and Expectations • Final Lessons

■ **RECAPPING MAIN POINTS**
Key Terms

Consider the experience of a man named Kenge of the equatorial Africa Pygmy culture. Kenge had lived in dense tropical forests all his life. He had occasion, one day, to travel by car for the first time across an open plain with anthropologist Colin Turnbull. Later, Turnbull described Kenge's reactions.

> Kenge looked over the plains and down to where a herd of about a hundred buffalo were grazing some miles away. He asked me what kind of insects they were, and I told him they were buffalo, twice as big as the forest buffalo known to him. He laughed loudly and told me not to tell such stupid stories, and asked me again what kind of insects they were. He then talked to himself, for want of more intelligent company, and tried to liken the buffalo to the various beetles and ants with which he was familiar.
>
> He was still doing this when we got into the car and drove down to where the animals were grazing. He watched them getting larger and larger, and though he was as courageous as any Pygmy, he moved over and sat close to me and muttered that it was witchcraft.... Finally, when he realized that they were real buffalo he was no longer afraid, but what puzzled him still was why they had been so small, and whether they really had been small and had so suddenly grown larger, or whether it had been some kind of trickery. (Turnbull, 1961, p. 305)

Kenge's tale illustrates quite clearly the influence your experiences in the world exert on your perceptions. Because Kenge had lived his life in a tropical forest, he didn't have the prior knowledge to interpret immediately the sensory information—light reflected from objects at a distance—arriving at his eyes. In this chapter, you will learn how your own knowledge affects what you can and do perceive.

In Chapter 4, you learned that your environment is filled with waves of light and sound—and it is—but that's not the way in which you experience the world. You don't "see" waves of light; you see a poster on the wall. You don't "hear" waves of sound; you hear music from a nearby radio. Sensation is what gets the show started, but something more is needed to make a stimulus meaningful and interesting and, most important, to make it possible for you to respond to it effectively. **Perception** is the set of processes that organize information in the sensory image and interpret that information as having been produced by objects or events in the external world. These processes provide the extra layers of interpretation that enable you to navigate successfully through your environment.

Perception The processes that organize information in the sensory image and interpret it as having been produced by properties of objects or events in the external, three-dimensional world.

We can offer a simple demonstration to help you think about the relationship between sensation and perception. Hold your hand as far as you can in front of your face. Now move it toward you. As you move your hand toward your eyes, it will take up more and more of your visual field. You may no longer be able to see the poster on the wall in back of your hand. How can your hand block out the poster? Has your hand gotten bigger? Has the poster gotten smaller? Your answer must be, "Of course not!" This demonstration tells you something about the difference between sensation and perception. Your hand can block out the poster because, as it comes closer to your face, the hand projects an increasingly larger image on your retina. It is your perceptual processes that allow you to understand that despite the change in the size of the projection on your retina, your hand—and the poster behind it—do not change in actual size.

We might say that the role of perception is to make sense of sensation. Perceptual processes extract meaning from the continuously changing, often chaotic, sensory input and organize it into stable, orderly percepts A *percept* is what is perceived—the phenomenological, or experienced, outcome of the process of perception. It is *not* a physical object or its image in a receptor but, rather, the psychological product of perceptual activity. Thus, your percept of your hand remains stable over changes in the size of the image because your interpretation is governed by stable perceptual activities. Most of the time, sensing and perceiving occur so effortlessly, continuously, and automatically that you take them for granted. It is our goal in this chapter to allow you to understand and appreciate the processes that afford you a suitable account of the world, with such apparent ease. We begin with an overview of perceptual processes in the visual domain.

■ Sensing, Organizing, Identifying, and Recognizing

The term *perception,* in its broad usage, refers to the overall process of apprehending objects and events in the environment—to sense them, understand them, identify and label them, and prepare to react to them. The process of perception is best understood when we divide it into three stages: sensation, perceptual organization, and identification/recognition of objects.

As we saw in Chapter 4, *sensation* refers to conversion of physical energy into the neural codes recognized by the brain. For example, sensation provides the basic facts of the visual field. Your retinal cells are organized to emphasize edges and contrasts while reacting only weakly to unchanging, constant stimulation. Cells in your brain's cortex extract preliminary features from this retinal input.

Perceptual organization refers to the next stage, in which an internal representation of an object is formed and a percept of the external stimulus is developed. The representation provides a working description of the perceiver's external environment. With respect to vision, perceptual processes provide estimates of an object's likely size, shape, movement, distance, and orientation. Those estimates are based on mental computations that integrate your past knowledge with the present evidence received from your senses and with the stimulus within its perceptual context. Perception involves *synthesis* (integration and combination) of simple sensory features, such as colors, edges, and lines, into the percept of an object that can be recognized later. These mental activities most often occur swiftly and efficiently, without conscious awareness.

To understand the difference between these first two stages more clearly, consider the case study of Dr. Richard, whose brain damage left his sensation intact but altered his perceptual processes.

There was nothing wrong with Dr. Richard's eyes or with his ability to *analyze* the properties of stimulus objects—he saw the parts and qualities of objects accurately. Rather, his problem lay in synthesis—putting the bits and pieces of sensory information together properly to form a unified, coherent perception of a single event in the visual scene. His case makes salient the distinction between sensory and perceptual processes. It also serves

Perceptual organization The processes that put sensory information together to give the perception of a coherent scene over the whole visual field.

to remind you that both sensory analysis and perceptual organization must be going on all the time even though you are unaware of the way they are working or even that they are happening.

Identification and recognition, the third stage in this sequence, assigns meaning to percepts. Circular objects "become" baseballs, coins, clocks, oranges, and moons; people may be identified as male or female, friend or foe, relative or rock star. At this stage, the perceptual question "What does the object look like?" changes to a question of identification—"What is this object?"—and to a question of recognition—"What is the object's function?" To identify and recognize what something is, what it is called, and how best to respond to it involves higher-level cognitive processes, which include your theories, memories, values, beliefs, and attitudes concerning the object.

We have now given you a brief introduction to the stages of processing that enable you to arrive at a meaningful understanding of the perceptual world around you. Because Chapter 4 focused on sensation, we will devote the bulk of our attention here to aspects of perception beyond the initial transduction of physical energy. In everyday life, perception seems to be entirely effortless. We will try, beginning in the next section, to convince you that you actually do quite a bit of sophisticated processing, a lot of mental work, to arrive at this "illusion of ease."

The Proximal and Distal Stimuli

Imagine you are the person in **Figure 5.1A,** surveying a room from an easy chair. Some of the light reflected from the objects in the room enters your eyes and forms images on your retinas. **Figure 5.1B** shows what would appear to your left eye as you sit in the room. (The bump on the right is your nose, and the hand and knee at the bottom are your own.) How does this retinal image compare with the environment that produced it?

One very important difference is that the retinal image is *two-dimensional,* whereas the environment is *three-dimensional.* This difference has many consequences. For instance, compare the shapes of the physical objects in Figure 5.1A with the shapes of their corre-

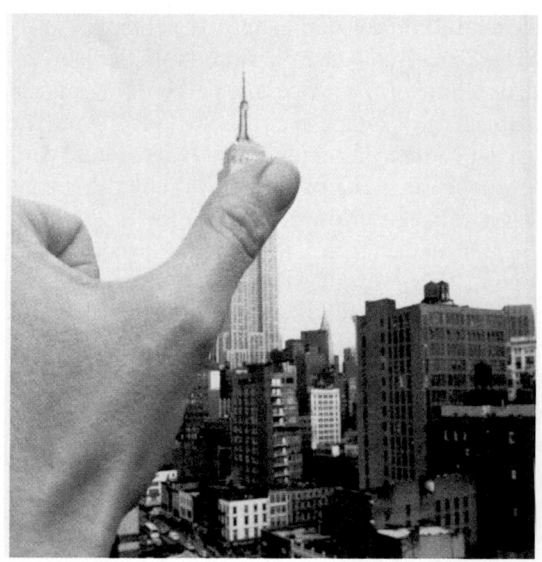

How can one person's thumb wipe out the Empire State Building?

sponding retinal images (**Figure 5.1C**). The table, rug, window, and picture in the real-world scene are all rectangular, but only the image of the window actually produces a rectangle in your retinal image. The image of the picture is a trapezoid, the image of the table top is an irregular four-sided figure, and the image of the rug is actually three separate regions with more than 20 different sides! Here's our first perceptual puzzle: How do you manage to perceive all of these objects as simple, standard rectangles?

The situation is, however, even a bit more complicated. You can also notice that many parts of what you perceive in the room are not actually present in your retinal image. For instance, you perceive the vertical edge between the two walls as going all the way to the floor, but your retinal image of that edge stops at the table top. Similarly, in your retinal image parts of the rug are hidden behind the table; yet this does not keep you from correctly perceiving the rug as a single, unbroken rectangle. In fact, when you consider all the differences between the environmental objects and the images of them on your retina, you may be surprised that you perceive the scene as well as you do.

The differences between a physical object in the world and its optical image on your retina are so profound and important that psychologists distinguish carefully between them as two different stimuli for perception. The physical object in the world is called the **distal stimulus** (distant from the observer) and the optical image on the retina is called the **proximal stimulus** (proximate, or near, to the observer), as shown in **Figure 5.2.**

The critical point of our discussion can now be restated more concisely: What you wish to *perceive* is the *distal stimulus*—the "real" object in the environment—

Identification and recognition Two ways of attaching meaning to percepts.

Distal stimulus In the processes of perception, the physical object in the world, as contrasted with the proximal stimulus, the optical image on the retina.

Proximal stimulus The optical image on the retina; contrasted with the distal stimulus, the physical object in the world.

A. Physical object (distal stimulus)

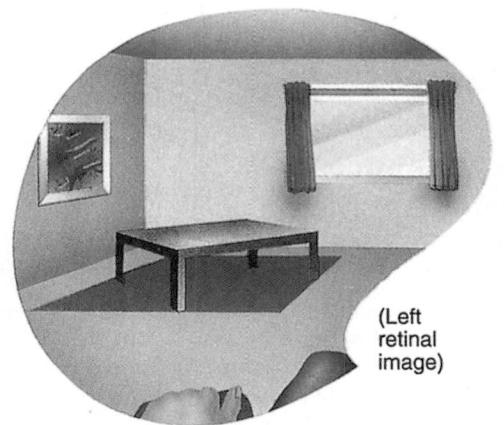

(Left retinal image)

B. Optical image (proximal stimulus)

(Picture)

(Window)

(Table top)

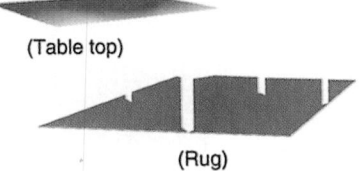

(Rug)

FIGURE 5.1

Interpreting Retinal Images

The major task of visual perception is to interpret or identify the distal stimulus, the actual object in the environment, using the information from the proximal stimulus, the retinal image produced by the object.

whereas the stimulus from which you must derive your information is the *proximal stimulus*—the image on the retina. The major computational task of perception can be thought of as the process of determining the distal

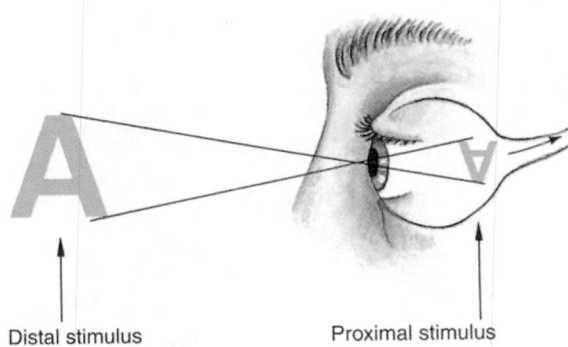

Distal stimulus

Proximal stimulus

FIGURE 5.2

Distal and Proximal Stimuli

The distal stimulus is the physical stimulus in the environment. The proximal stimulus is the pattern of sensory activity that is determined by the distal stimulus. As illustrated here, the proximal stimulus may resemble the distal stimulus, but they are separate events.

stimulus from information contained in the proximal stimulus. This is true across perceptual domains. For hearing, touch, taste, and so on, perception involves processes that use information in the proximal stimulus to tell you about properties of the distal stimulus.

To show you how the distal stimulus and proximal stimulus fit with the three stages in perceiving, let's examine one of the objects in the scene from Figure 5.1: the picture hanging on the wall. In the sensory stage, this picture corresponds to a two-dimensional trapezoid in your retinal image; the top and bottom sides converge toward the right, and the left and right sides are different in length. This is the proximal stimulus. In the perceptual organization stage, you see this trapezoid as a rectangle turned away from you in three-dimensional space. You perceive the top and bottom sides as parallel, but receding into the distance toward the right; you perceive the left and right sides as equal in length. Your perceptual processes have developed a strong *hypothesis* about the physical properties of the distal stimulus; now it needs an identity. In the recognition stage, you identify this rectangular object as a picture. **Figure 5.3** is a flowchart illustrating this sequence of events. The processes that take information from one stage to the next are shown as arrows between the boxes. By the end of this chapter, we will explain all the interactions represented in this figure.

FIGURE
5.3

Sensation, Perceptual Organization, and Identification/ Recognition Stages

The diagram outlines the processes that give rise to the transformation of incoming information at the stages of sensation, perceptual organization, and identification/recognition. Bottom-up processing occurs when the perceptual representation is derived from the information available in the sensory input. Top-down processing occurs when the perceptual representation is affected by an individual's prior knowledge, motivations, expectations, and other aspects of higher mental functioning.

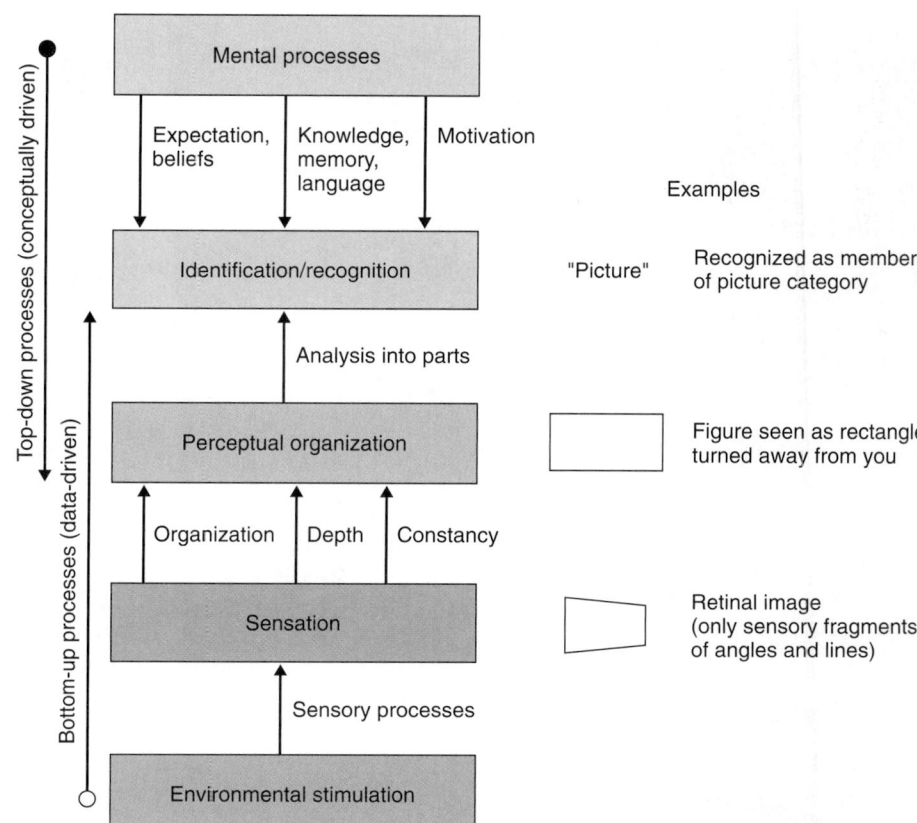

Reality, Ambiguity, and Illusions

We have defined the task of perception as the identification of the distal stimulus from the proximal stimulus. Before we turn to some of the perceptual mechanisms that make this task successful, we want to discuss a bit more some other aspects of stimuli in the environment that make perception complex: *ambiguous* stimuli and perceptual *illusions*.

AMBIGUITY

A primary goal of perception is to get an accurate "fix" on the world. Survival depends on accurate perceptions of objects and events in your environment—Is that motion in the trees a tiger?—that are not always easy to read. Take a look at the photo of black-and-white splotches in **Figure 5.4.** What is it? Try to extract the stimulus figure from the background. Try to see a dalmatian taking a walk. The dog is hard to find because it blends with the background, so its boundaries are not clear. (*Hint:* The dog is on the right side of the figure, with its head pointed toward the center.) This figure is *ambiguous* in

Ambiguity A perceptual object that may have more than one interpretation.

the sense that critical information is missing, elements are in unexpected relationships, and usual patterns are not apparent. **Ambiguity** is an important concept in understanding perception because it shows that a single

FIGURE
5.4

An Ambiguous Picture

What do you see in this picture? Try to see a Dalmatian taking a walk.

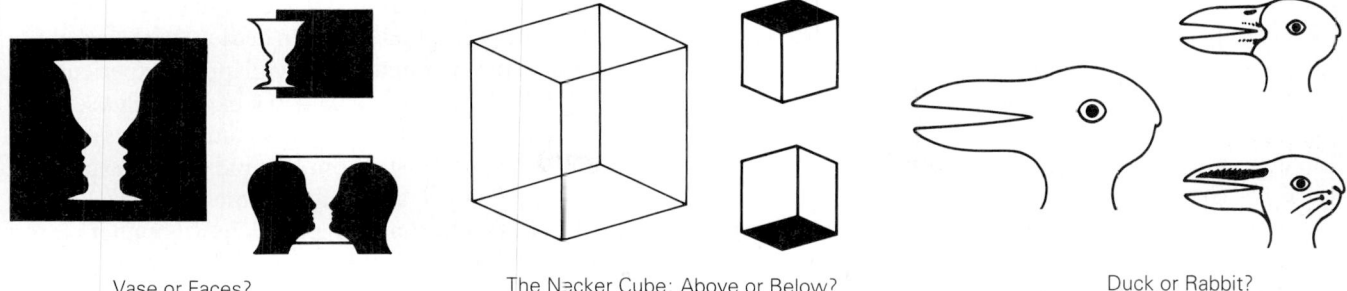

Vase or Faces? The Necker Cube: Above or Below? Duck or Rabbit?

FIGURE 5.5

Perceptual Ambiguities

Each example allows two interpretations, but you cannot experience both at the same time. Do you notice your percept flipping back and forth between each pair of possibilities?

image at the sensory level can result in *multiple interpretations* at the perceptual and identification levels.

Figure 5.5 shows three examples of ambiguous figures. Each example permits two unambiguous but conflicting interpretations. Look at each image until you can see the two alternative interpretations. Notice that once you have seen both of them, your perception flips back and forth between them as you look at the ambiguous figure. This perceptual *instability* of ambiguous figures is one of their most important characteristics.

The vase/faces and the Necker cube are examples of ambiguity in the perceptual organization stage. You have two different perceptions of the same objects in the environment. The vase/faces can be seen as either a central white object on a black background or as two black objects with a white area between them. The Necker cube can be seen as a three-dimensional hollow cube either below you and angled to your left or above you and angled toward your right. With both vase and cube, the ambiguous alternatives are different physical arrangements of objects in three-dimensional space, both resulting from the same stimulus image.

The duck/rabbit figure is an example of ambiguity in the recognition stage. It is perceived as the same physical shape in both interpretations. The ambiguity arises in determining the kind of object it represents and in how best to classify it, given the mixed set of information available.

Many prominent artists have used perceptual ambiguity as a central creative device in their works. **Figure 5.6** presents *Slave Market with the Disappearing Bust of Voltaire*, by Salvador Dali. This work reveals a complex ambiguity in which a whole section of the picture must be radically reorganized and reinterpreted to allow perception of the "hidden" bust of the French philosopher-writer Voltaire. The white sky under the lower arch is Voltaire's forehead and hair; the white portions of the two ladies' dresses are his cheeks, nose, and chin. (If you

have trouble seeing him, try squinting, holding the book at arm's length, or taking off your glasses.) Once you have seen the bust of Voltaire in this picture, however, you will never be able to look at it without knowing where this Frenchman is hiding.

One of the most fundamental properties of normal human perception is the tendency to transform ambiguity and uncertainty about the environment into a clear interpretation that you can act upon with confidence. In a world filled with variability and change, your perceptual system must meet the challenges of discovering invariance and stability.

FIGURE 5.6

Ambiguity in Art

This painting by Salvador Dali is called *Slave Market with the Disappearing Bust of Voltaire.* Can you find Voltaire? Dali is one of a large number of modern and contemporary artists who have exploited ambiguity in their work.

ILLUSIONS

Ambiguous stimuli present your perceptual systems with the challenge of recognizing one unique figure out of several possibilities. One or another interpretation of the stimulus is correct or incorrect with respect to a particular context. When your perceptual systems actually deceive you into experiencing a stimulus pattern in a manner that is demonstrably incorrect, you are experiencing an **illusion**. The word *illusion* shares the same root as *ludicrous*—both stem from the Latin *illudere*, which means "to mock at." Illusions are shared by most people in the same perceptual situation because of shared physiology in sensory systems and overlapping experiences of the world. (As we shall explain in Chapter 6, this sets illusions apart from hallucinations. Hallucinations are nonshared perceptual distortions that individuals experience as a result of unusual physical or mental states.) Examine the classic illusions in **Figure 5.7**. Although it is most convenient for us to present you with visual illusions, illusions also exist in other sensory modalities such as

A. Use a ruler to answer each question.

Which is larger: the brim or the top hat?

Top Hat Illusion

Is the diagonal line broken?

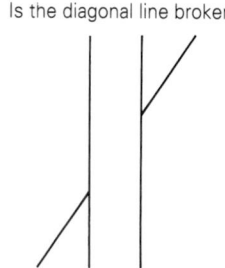

Poggendorf Illusion

B. Which of the boxes are the same size as the standard box? Which are definitely smaller or larger? Measure them to discover a powerful illusory effect.

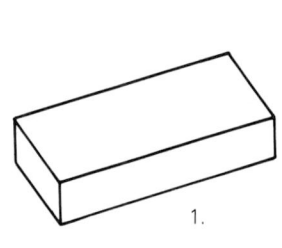

1.

2.

Which central circle is bigger?

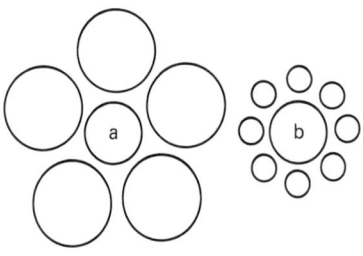
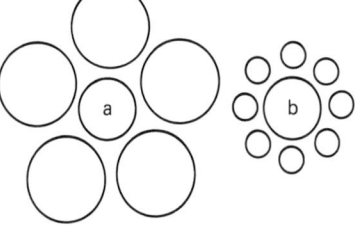

Ebbinghaus Illusion

Standard

Which horizontal line is longer?

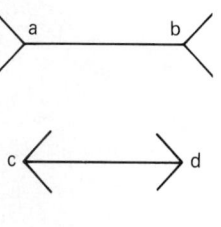

Müller–Lyer Illusion

Are the vertical lines parallel?

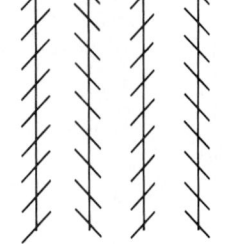

Zöllner Illusion

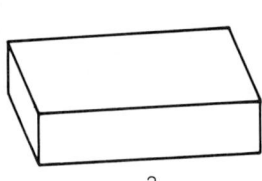

3.

4.

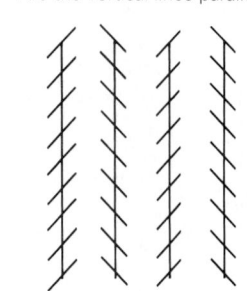

FIGURE 5.7

Five Illusions to Tease Your Brain

Each of these illusions represents circumstances in which perception is demonstrably incorrect. Researchers often use illusions to test their theories. These theories explain why perceptual systems that generally function quite accurately yield illusions in special circumstances.

hearing (Bregman, 1981; Saberi, 1996; Shepard & Jordan, 1984) and taste (Todrank & Bartoshuk, 1991).

Since the first scientific analysis of illusions was published by J. J. Oppel in 1854–1855, thousands of articles have been written about illusions in nature, sensation, perception, and art. Oppel's modest contribution to the study of illusions was a simple array of lines that appeared longer when divided into segments than when only its end lines were present:

| | | | | | | | | | | | | | | |

versus

| |

Oppel called his work the study of *geometrical optical illusions.* Illusions point out the discrepancy between percept and reality. They can demonstrate the abstract conceptual distinctions among sensation, perceptual organization, and identification and can help you understand some fundamental properties of perception.

Researchers often invent new illusions or reconceive old ones to demonstrate important features of perceptual processing. Consider the many versions of the *Müller-Lyer illusion,* presented in **Figure 5.8.** Version A was first given as an illustration by Franz Müller-Lyer in an 1889 work on optical illusions. The other versions were invented before 1900 by Müller-Lyer and others. In each case, the lengths of the "shafts" (or in version D, the distances between the vertices of the angles) are equal.

People are often astonished by this fact—you should take a moment to measure. Despite the age of this illusion, and the research effort devoted to it, several theories of its origin have come and gone (Greene & Nelson, 1997). Its robustness—that is, the ease with which the illusion of greater length can be produced—provides a continuing challenge to theorists in the area of visual processing. This example suggests that illusions are not mere oddities. They provide important data to psychological theories. Researchers, therefore, are not so much impressed by illusions themselves as much as by the knowledge illusions provide about the vast majority of circumstances in which perception provides accurate information about the world.

ILLUSIONS IN EVERYDAY LIFE

Illusions are also a basic part of your everyday life. Consider your day-to-day experience of your home planet, Earth. You've seen the sun "rise" and "set" even though you know that the sun is sitting out there in the center of the solar system as decisively as ever. You can appreciate why it was such an extraordinary feat of courage for Christopher Columbus and other voyagers to deny the obvious illusion that Earth was flat and sail off toward

Illusion An experience of a stimulus pattern in a manner that is demonstrably incorrect but shared by others in the same perceptual environment.

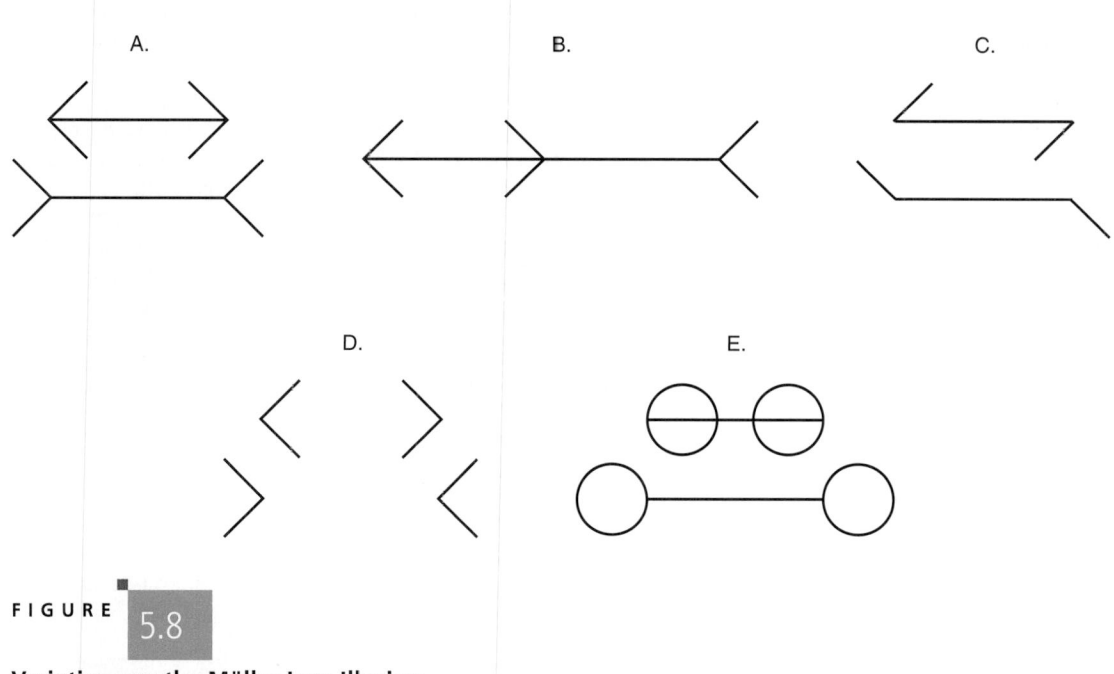

FIGURE 5.8

Variations on the Müller-Lyer Illusion

Each of these variations on the Müller-Lyer illusion was created before 1900. Do you perceive a length difference in each case? Researchers in perception have sought to develop theories that explain why the illusion is so easy to obtain.

one of its apparent edges. Similarly, when a full moon is overhead, it seems to follow you wherever you go even though you know the moon isn't chasing you. What you are experiencing is an illusion created by the great distance of the moon from your eye. When they reach Earth, the moon's light rays are essentially parallel and perpendicular to your direction of travel, no matter where you go.

People can control illusions to achieve desired effects. Architects and interior designers use principles of perception to create objects in space that seem larger or smaller than they really are. A small apartment becomes more spacious when it is painted with light colors and sparsely furnished with low, small couches, chairs, and tables in the center of the room instead of against the walls. Psychologists working with NASA in the U.S. space program have researched the effects of environment on perception in order to design space capsules that have pleasant sensory qualities. Set and lighting directors of movies and theatrical productions purposely create illusions on film and on stage.

Despite all of these illusions—some more useful than others—you generally do pretty well getting around the environment. That is why researchers typically study illusions to help explain how perception ordinarily works so well. The illusions themselves suggest, however, that your perceptual systems cannot perfectly carry out the task of recovering the distal stimulus from the proximal stimulus.

PSYCHOLOGY IN THE 21ST CENTURY

VIRTUAL REALITY

Here is a plot device that has become commonplace in TV shows and movies at the turn of the century: The hero and heroine become immersed in some *virtual* world—a world generated by a computer—with dramatic consequences. For example, in *The Matrix* (spoiler: don't read the rest of this sentence if you haven't seen the movie) the hero discovers that everything that he took to be "real" is actually a highly elaborate *virtual reality*, enacted by the supercomputers that have come to dominate the planet. Fortunately, the versions of virtual reality that are available to most of us, at least so far, are considerably more innocuous; we can escape quite readily from the virtual environments we experience in arcades and amusement park rides. Improvements in the quality of those experiences often rely on researchers' ability to devise new means to fool our perceptual systems: The individuals who design virtual reality systems attempt to transform knowledge from basic research on perceptual processes into vivid experiences of whole new worlds.

The goal of many virtual reality systems is to create for the participant a sense of *presence* in the virtual environment. *Presence* has been defined along several different dimensions, including the virtual world's ability to draw participants into a socially rich or interactive narrative (Lombard & Ditton, 1997). However, with respect to perception, feelings of presence typically rely on immersion in a virtual world that seems perceptually real. Over the last few years, researchers have begun to examine systematically the types of perceptual information virtual worlds require to produce the highest levels of presence. To assess presence, researchers often measure how well people can perform tasks in virtual environments with different perceptual configurations (Nash et al., 2000; Nichols et al., 2000).

Consider a project that examined the way in which visual displays affect participants' ability to steer successfully in a simulation of driving—a task the researchers called *lane keeping* (Kappé et al., 1999). Participants' lane-keeping performance was improved by display changes that provided interesting approximations to perceptual processing in the real world. Recall that when you experience the real world, you obtain information both from your center of attention and from the periphery.

How does this apply in virtual environments? The researchers found that participants' lane-keeping performance was improved when the displays provided peripheral information. However, in analogy to your real-world experiences, that peripheral information didn't need to be very highly detailed. This finding has immediate consequences for the ways in which people design visual displays. This type of experiment suggests that only the center of the visual field needs to be highly detailed. Peripheral information is important, but it can be filled in with coarser visual grain.

Over the next several years, virtual environments will no doubt become ever more compelling: Researchers and inventors will learn ever more about how to convince your perceptual processes that what the computer provides is "real."

Web sites:

■ www.hitl.washington.edu/projects/ knowledge_base/onthenet.html, a site that gathers together Web resources on virtual reality

■ www.vrs.org.uk, the home page for the Virtual Reality Society

Approaches to the Study of Perception

You now are acquainted with some of the major questions of perception: How does the perceptual system recover the structure of the environment? How is ambiguity resolved? Why do illusions arise? Before we move on to answer these questions, we need to give you more of a background in the types of theories that have dominated research on perception.

Many of the differences between these theories can be captured by the distinction between *nature* and *nurture* we introduced in Chapter 3. At issue is how much of a head start you have in dealing with the perceptual world, by virtue of your possession of the human genotype. Do you, as a *nativist* might argue, come into the world with some types of innate knowledge or brain structures that aid your interpretation of the environment? Or do you, as an *empiricist* might assert, come into the world with a relatively blank slate, ready to learn what there is to learn about the perceptual world? Most modern theorists agree that your experience of the world consists of a combination of nature and nurture. We will see, however, that these theorists disagree on the balance that makes up this combination.

HELMHOLTZ'S CLASSICAL THEORY

In 1866, **Hermann von Helmholtz** argued for the importance of experience—or nurture—in perception. His theory emphasized the role of mental processes in interpreting the often ambiguous stimulus arrays that excite the nervous system. By using prior knowledge of the environment, an observer makes hypotheses, or inferences, about the way things really are. For instance, you would be likely to interpret your brief view of a four-legged creature moving through the woods as a dog rather than as a wolf. Perception is thus an *inductive* process, moving from specific images to inferences about the general class of objects or events that the images might represent. Since this process takes place out of your conscious awareness, Helmholtz termed it **unconscious inference.** Ordinarily, these inferential processes work well. However, perceptual illusions can result when unusual circumstances allow multiple interpretations of the same stimulus or favor an old, familiar interpretation when a new one is required.

Helmholtz's theory broke perception down into two stages. In the first, *analytic* stage, the sense organs analyze the physical world into fundamental sensations. In the second, *synthetic* stage, you integrate and synthesize these sensory elements into perceptions of objects and their properties. Helmholtz's theory proposes that you learn how to interpret sensations on the basis of your experience with the world. Your interpretations are, in effect, informed guesses about your perceptions.

THE GESTALT APPROACH

Gestalt psychology, founded in Germany in the second decade of the 20th century, put greater emphasis on the role of innate structures—nature—in perceptual experience. The main exponents of Gestalt psychology, like **Kurt Koffka** (1935), **Wolfgang Köhler** (1947), and **Max Wertheimer** (1923), maintained that psychological phenomena could be understood only when viewed as organized, structured *wholes* and not when broken down into primitive perceptual elements. The term *Gestalt* roughly means "form," "whole," "configuration," or "essence." Gestalt psychology challenged atomistic views of psychology by arguing that the whole is more than the sum of its parts. For example, when you listen to music, you perceive whole melodies even though they are composed of separate notes. Gestalt psychologists argued that the holistic perception of the world arises because the cortex is organized to function that way. You organize sensory information the way you do because it is the most economical, simple way to organize the sensory input, given the structure and physiology of the brain. (Many of the examples of perceptual organization we will discuss in a later section were originated by the Gestaltists.)

GIBSON'S ECOLOGICAL OPTICS

James Gibson (1966, 1979) and **Eleanor Gibson** proposed a very influential approach to perception. Instead of trying to understand perception as a result of an organism's structure, Gibson suggested that it could be better understood through an analysis of the immediately surrounding environment (or its ecology). As one writer put it, Gibson's approach was, "Ask not what's inside your head, but what your head's inside of" (Mace, 1977). In particular, Gibson's **theory of ecological optics** focused attention on properties of external stimuli rather than on the mechanisms by which you perceive the stimuli. This approach was a radical departure from all previous theories. Gibson's ideas emphasized perceiving as *active exploration* of the environment. When an observer is *moving* in the world, the pattern of stimulation on the retina is constantly changing over time as well as over space. The theory of ecological optics tried to specify the information about the environment that was available to the eyes of a moving observer. Theorists in Gibson's

Unconscious inference Helmholtz's term for perception that occurs outside of conscious awareness.

Gestalt psychology A school of psychology that maintains that psychological phenomena can be understood only when viewed as organized, structured wholes, not when broken down into primitive perceptual elements.

Theory of ecological optics A theory of perception that emphasizes the richness of stimulus information and views the perceiver as an active explorer of the environment.

The theory of ecological optics deals with invariant properties of the visual world. What information might a nature guide obtain from this view of a herd of wildebeests?

tradition agree that perceptual systems evolved in organisms who were active—seeking food, water, mates, and shelter—in a complex and changing environment (Gibson, 1979; Greeno, 1994; Nakayama, 1994).

According to Gibson, the answer to the question "How do you learn about your world?" is simple. You directly pick up information about the *invariant,* or stable, properties of sensory information available from the environment. There is no need to hypothesize higher-level systems of perceptual inference—*perception is direct.* Although the retinal size and shape of each environmental object change depending on the object's distance and on the viewing angle, these changes are not random. The changes are systematic, and certain properties of the light reflected by objects remain invariant under all such changes of viewing angles and viewing distances. Your visual system is tuned to detect such invariances because humans evolved in the environment in which perception of invariances was important for survival.

You now have an understanding of the types of theories researchers have developed to explain perceptual processes. We now begin our discussion of those perceptual processes by considering what it means to select,

Attention A state of focused awareness on a subset of the available perceptual information.

Goal-directed selection A determinant of why people select some parts of sensory input for further processing; it reflects the choices made as a function of one's own goals.

Stimulus-driven capture A determinant of why people select some parts of sensory input for further processing; occurs when features of stimuli—objects in the environment—automatically capture attention, independent of the local goals of a perceiver.

or attend to, only a small subset of the information the world makes available.

SUMMING UP

The overall process of perception can be broken down into the three stages of sensation, perceptual organization, and identification/recognition. The major task of visual perception is to identify and interpret the distal stimulus—the actual object in the environment—using the information from the proximal stimulus—the retinal image produced by the object. Ambiguous figures have a single interpretation at the sensory level, but multiple possible interpretations at the levels of organization and identification. Illusions provide constraints on theories about the operation of perceptual processes.

Theories of perception typically agree that perceptual abilities are the products of both nature and nurture, but they disagree on the balance between the two. Helmholtz argued for the importance of experience and proposed that much of perception requires unconscious inference. The Gestalt approach emphasized that perceptual experiences must be viewed as wholes and supported the role of innate processes in perception. James Gibson's approach to perception emphasized the role of the observer as an active explorer and focused on invariant information reflected from the stimulus environment.

Attentional Processes

Take a moment now to find ten things in your environment that had not been, so far, in your immediate awareness. Had you noticed a spot on the wall? Had you noticed the ticking of a clock? If you start to examine your surroundings very carefully, you will discover that there are literally thousands of things on which you could focus your **attention.** Generally, the more closely you attend to some object or event in the environment, the more you can perceive and learn about it. That's why attention is an important topic in the study of perception: Your focus of attention determines the types of information that will be most readily available to your perceptual processes. As you will now see, researchers have tried to understand what types of environmental stimuli require your attention and how attention contributes to your experience of those stimuli. We will start by considering how attention functions to selectively highlight objects and events in your environment.

Selective Attention

We began this section by asking that you try to find—to bring into attention—several things that had, up to that point, escaped your notice. This thought experiment illustrated an important function of attention: to select some part of the sensory input for further processing. Let us see how you make decisions about the subset of the world to which you will attend and what consequences those decisions have for the information readily available to you.

DETERMINING THE FOCUS OF ATTENTION

What forces determine the objects that become the focus of your attention? The answer to this question has two components, which we will call goal-directed selection and stimulus-driven capture (Yantis, 1993). **Goal-directed selection** reflects the choices that you make about the objects to which you'd like to attend, as a function of your own goals. You are probably already comfortable with the idea that you can explicitly choose objects for particular scrutiny. **Stimulus-driven capture** occurs when features of the stimuli—objects in the environment—themselves automatically capture your attention, independent of your local goals as a perceiver. You've experienced stimulus-driven capture, for example, if you've ever been daydreaming at a stoplight while out for a drive. The stoplight's abrupt change from red to green will often capture your attention even if you were not particularly focused on it.

You might wonder what the relationship is between these two processes: Research suggests that, at least under some circumstances, stimulus-driven capture wins out over goal-directed selection.

HOW WE KNOW

COMPETITION BETWEEN PROCESSES THAT DETERMINE FOCUS OF ATTENTION

Researchers created visual displays that put goal-directed selection and stimulus-driven capture into competition (Theeuwes et al., 1998). As shown in Part A of **Figure 5.9**, each trial of an experiment began with a visual display of six gray circles filled with six dim figure eights. After one second, the display changed. In half the trials, as shown in Part B, all but one of the circles changed from gray to red. The participants' task was to shift their eyes to the remaining gray circle and respond whether the character inside was either a forward or a backward letter c. When they carry out this task, participants are using goal-directed selection: They are purposefully shifting their attention to the remaining gray circle.

Now consider Part C of Figure 5.9. In this instance, which represents the remaining half of the trials, a new element is added to the visual array—a new red circle. New objects are the type of visual stimulus that typically engage stimulus-

driven capture. Under ordinary circumstances, we'd expect participants to shift their eyes to that new object. However, in this particular experiment, the participants don't want their eyes to be pulled to that object: They are still asked to report only the contents of the single gray circle. So what happens? Can the participants stop themselves from moving their attention to the new red circle? In fact, on most occasions, the new object automatically drew the participants' attention—even though it was entirely irrelevant to the goal the experimenters had set for them.

You can recognize this phenomenon as stimulus-driven capture, because it works in the opposite direction of the perceiver's goals. Because, that is, the participants would perform the task better if they ignored the new red circle, they must be unable to ignore it (because

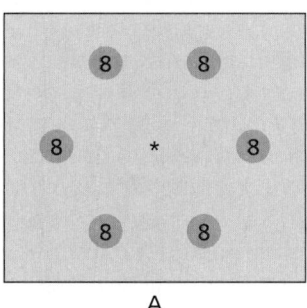

A

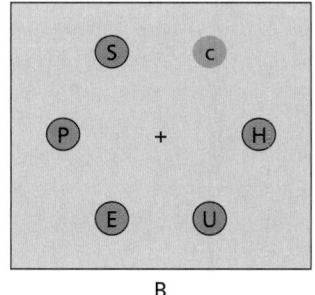

B

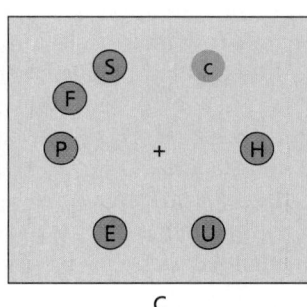

C

FIGURE 5.9

Processes That Select Attention

At the beginning of each trial of this experiment, participants viewed a display with six gray circles (Part A). When the display changed, the participants' task was to report whether the "c" in the one remaining gray circle was forward or backward. On half of the trials, the displays did not introduce new objects (Part B); on the other half of the trials, they did (Part C). Although the participants' goal was to attend to the single gray circle, the new objects—when they occurred—automatically drew their attention.

experimental participants almost always prefer to perform as well as possible on the tasks researchers assign them). The important general conclusion is that your perceptual system is organized so that your attention is automatically drawn to objects that are new to an environment (Yantis & Jonides, 1996).

THE FATE OF UNATTENDED INFORMATION

If you have selectively attended to some subset of a perceptual display—by virtue of your own goals or of properties of the stimuli—what is the fate of the information to which you did *not* attend? Imagine listening to a lecture while people on both sides of you are engaged in conversations. How are you able to keep track of the lecture? What do you notice about the conversations? Could anything appear in the content of one or the other conversation to divert your attention from the lecture?

This constellation of questions was first explored by **Donald Broadbent** (1958), who conceived of the mind as a communications channel—similar to a telephone line or a computer link—that actively processes and transmits information. According to Broadbent's theory, as a communications channel, the mind has only *limited capacity* to carry out complete processing. This limit requires that attention strictly regulate the flow of information from sensory input to consciousness. Attention creates a bottleneck in the flow of information through the cognitive system, filtering out some information and allowing other information to continue. The *filter theory* of attention asserted that the selection occurs early on in the process, before the input's meaning is accessed.

To test the filter theory, researchers re-created the real-life situation of multiple sources of input in the laboratory with a technique called **dichotic listening.** In this paradigm, a participant wearing earphones listens to two tape-recorded messages played at the same time—a different message is played into each ear. The participant is instructed to repeat only one of the two messages to the experimenter, while ignoring whatever is presented to the other ear. This procedure is called *shadowing* the attended message (see **Figure 5.10**).

The strongest form of filter theory was challenged when it was discovered that some listeners were recalling things they would not have been able to recall if attention had been totally filtering all ignored material (Cherry, 1953). Consider, for example, your own name. People often report that they hear their name being mentioned in a noisy room, even when they are engaged in their own conversation. This is often called the *cocktail party phenomenon.*

Dichotic listening An experimental technique in which a different auditory stimulus is simultaneously presented to each ear.
Preattentive processing Processing of sensory information that precedes attention to specific objects.

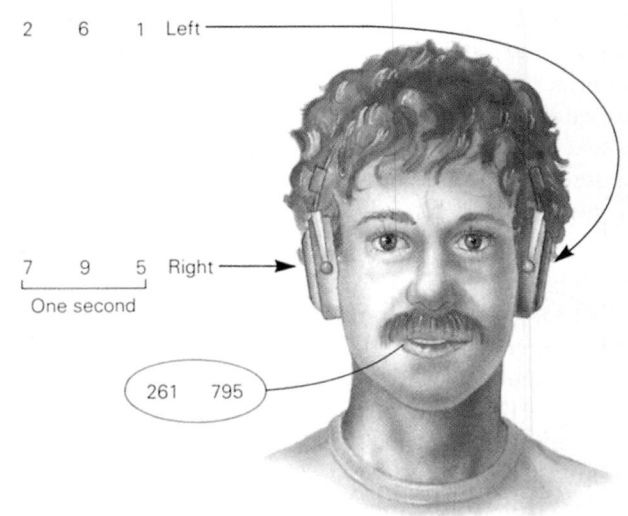

FIGURE 5.10

Dichotic Listening Task

A subject hears different digits presented simultaneously to each ear: 2 (left), 7 (right), 6 (left), 9 (right), 1 (left), and 5 (right). He reports hearing the correct sets—261 and 795. However, when instructed to attend only to the right-ear input, the subject reports hearing only 795.

HOW WE KNOW

DO YOU NEED TO ATTEND TO "HEAR" YOUR NAME? Participants listened to two voices—one male and one female—reading a list of one-syllable words. They were instructed to attend only to their right ear and repeat as accurately as possible (shadow) the words coming to that ear. At some point during the experiment, each participant (except for those in the control group) had his or her name presented in the unattended ear. Did they notice? About one-third (34.6%) of the participants whose names were presented reported hearing them. They did not report hearing any other name, nor did participants in the control group (to whom no names had been presented) report hearing any. Also, the shadowing performance of participants who reported hearing their names (and just that group) was disrupted momentarily just after their names occurred (Wood & Cowan, 1995a).

These results suggest that it is not inevitable that your own name will draw your attention—two-thirds of the listeners failed to notice their names. Even so, the results argue strongly that some meaningful analysis of the ignored channel must have been taking place—otherwise, the one-third of the listeners would never have had attention drawn to their names.

Based on experiments of this type, researchers believe that information in the unattended channel is processed to some extent—but not sufficiently to reach conscious awareness (Wood & Cowan, 1995b). Only if properties of the unattended information are sufficiently distinctive—by virtue, for example, of being a listener's name—will the information become the focus of conscious attention. (We will return to the relationship between attention and consciousness in Chapter 6.) The general rule is that unattended information will not make its presence known. You can see, therefore, why it's dangerous to let yourself become distracted from your immediate task or goal. If you fail to pay attention to some body of information—your professor's lecture, perhaps—the material won't just sink in of its own accord!

Let's move now to the role attention plays in allowing you to find and correctly identify objects in your environment.

■
Attention and Objects in the Environment

One of the main functions of attention is to help you find particular objects in a noisy visual environment. To get a sense of how this works, you can carry out a very simple experiment. Put your book down for a minute and try this:

- Try to find something that is red. Now try to find something that is magenta.
- Try to find something that is a square. Now try to find something that is round.
- Try to find something that is blue. Now try to find something that is both round and blue.

Which did you find harder in each case? Research suggests that you should find it easier to locate something magenta rather than something red (Treisman & Gormican, 1988), something square rather than something round (Kim & Cave, 1995), and something that is defined by one feature rather than two (Treisman & Sato, 1990). Why do you think that is so? You have just discovered some of the features of *preattentive processing* versus processing that requires attention.

Even though conscious memory and recognition of objects require attention, quite complex processing of information goes on without attention and without awareness (Kubovy et al., 1999). This earlier stage of processing is called **preattentive processing** because it operates on sensory inputs before you attend to them, as they first come into the brain from the sensory receptors.

Preattentive processing is quite skilled at finding objects in the environment that can be defined by single features (Treisman & Sato, 1990; Wolfe, 1992). Look at part A of **Figure 5.11**. Can you find the white T? This is a comparable exercise to finding a blue object in the room

A.
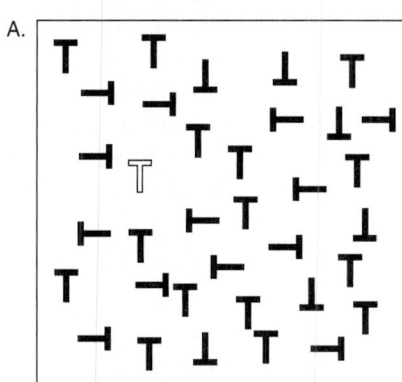

B.
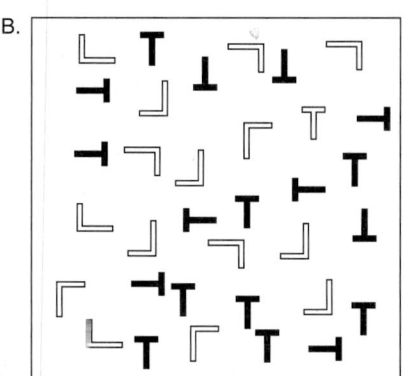

C.
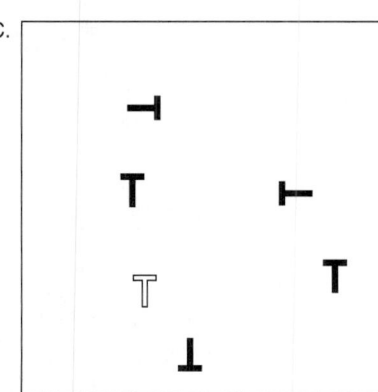

D.
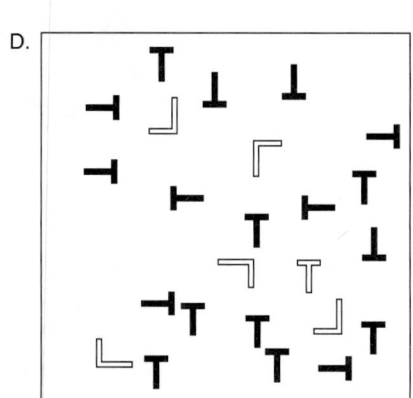

FIGURE 5.11

Attention and Visual Search

(A) To find an object that differs on one salient feature, you can use parallel search.
(B) To find an object based on the conjunction of features, you must use serial search.
(C) Because parallel search is used, there is no difference in search time for this small array of distractors, as compared with the large array in part A.
(D) With serial search, the size of the array of distractors does make a difference. Search in D is faster than search in B.

around you. Preattentive processing allows you to search the environment in parallel for a single salient feature. This means that you can search all locations in the display at the same time: As a product of this parallel search, your attention is directed to the one correct object. Note, however, that not all single features are equally salient. Most people find it easier to find squares than circles—perhaps because the square's angles are distinctive (Kim & Cave, 1995). Most people find it easier to find colors that deviate from a central color, in the way that magenta deviates from red—perhaps because the color departs from an environmental norm (Treisman & Gormican, 1988).

However, despite these salience differences among single features, you'll still find it harder to detect combinations of features. Consider part B of Figure 5.11. Try, once again, to find the white T. Didn't it seem harder? In this case, your attentional system is not equipped to differentiate white T's from white L's in a parallel search. You can still use your capability for parallel search to ignore all the black T's, but you must then consider each white symbol one by one, or serially. This experience is comparable to finding something in your environment that is both red and a circle. Preattentive processing allows you swiftly to find things that are red or things that are circles—preattentive processing allows a **guided search** of your environment (Wolfe, 1994; Wolfe & Gancarz, 1996). At that point, however, you need to attend to each object individually to determine whether it fits the conjunction of the two features, round and red.

Researchers recognize the difference between a parallel and a serial search by determining how hard it is to find a target as a function of the number of distractors.

Guided search In visual perception, a parallel search of the environment for single, basic attributes that guides attention to likely locations of objects with more complex combinations of attributes.

Suppose we ask you to find a white T in a display with five black T's (as in part C of Figure 5.11) versus a display with 34 black T's (as in part A). Because you can carry out this task in parallel, it will take you roughly the same amount of time to find the white T in each case. On the other hand, when you move from part B to part D of this figure, you can sense that you're much quicker to find the white T in part D. You have to attend to each white element serially, so each white element you look at (until you find the right one) adds a separate increment of time.

Researchers can use this logic to discover other aspects of the perceptual world that can be processed preattentively. Consider **Figure 5.12.** In part A, try to find the yellow-and-blue item. In part B, try to find the yellow house with blue windows. Wasn't this second task much easier? Performance is much less affected by extra distractors when the two colors are organized into *parts* and *wholes* (Wolfe et al., 1994). Demonstrations of this sort suggest that preattentive processing provides you with relatively sophisticated assistance in finding objects in your environment.

We are now ready to make the transition from processing of simple features to the perception of whole objects and scenes.

SUMMING UP

You attend selectively to stimuli in the environment either because you choose to—goal-directed selection—or because something about the stimulus captures your attention—stimulus-driven capture. Filter theories of attention conceive of the mind as having limited capacity. Unattended information rarely comes into conscious awareness. Preattentive processing allows you to find objects in the environment that can be identified by a single salient feature.

FIGURE  5.12

Search for the Conjunction of Two Colors

(A) Find the yellow-and-blue item.
(B) Find the yellow house with blue windows.
(A) Search is very inefficient when the conjunction is between the colors of two parts of a target.
(B) However, search is much easier when the conjunction is between the color of the whole item and the color of one of its parts.

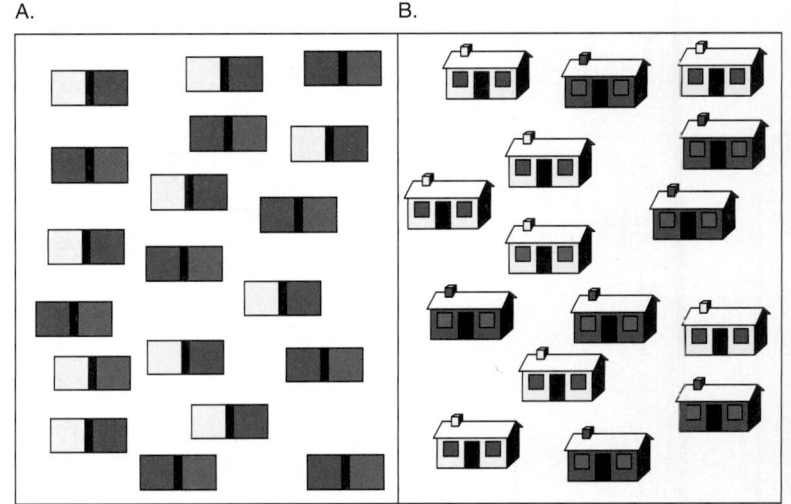

A.

B.

Organizational Processes in Perception

Imagine how confusing the world would be if you were unable to put together and organize the information available from the output of your millions of retinal receptors. You would experience a kaleidoscope of disconnected bits of color moving and swirling before your eyes. The processes that put sensory information together to give you the perception of coherence are referred to collectively as processes of perceptual organization. You have seen that what a person experiences as a result of such perceptual processing is called a *percept*.

For example, your percept of the two-dimensional geometric design in **Figure 5.13** is probably three diagonal rows of figures, the first being composed of squares, the second of arrowheads, and the third of diamonds. This probably seems unremarkable—but we have suggested in this chapter that all the seemingly effortless aspects of perception are made easy by sophisticated processing. Many of the organizational processes we will be discussing in this section were first described by Gestalt theorists who argued that what you perceive depends on laws of organization, or simple rules by which you perceive shapes and forms.

Figure, Ground, and Closure

Why do you perceive Figure 5.13 in the way that you do? Early in the perception of this display, an organizational process divides the display into figures and background. A **figure** is seen as an objectlike region in the forefront,

Suppose you were driving on this street and discovered you had passed your destination and needed to turn around. What features of this noisy environment would your attention seek out?

and **ground** is seen as the backdrop against which the figures stand out. In Figure 5.13, you probably see the dark regions as figures and the light region as ground. However, you can also see this stimulus pattern differently by reversing figure and ground, much as you did with the ambiguous vase/faces drawing. To do this, try to see the white region as a large white sheet of paper that has nine holes cut in it through which you can see a black background.

The tendency to perceive a figure as being in front of a ground is very strong. In fact, you can even get this effect in a stimulus when the perceived figure doesn't actually exist! In the first image of **Figure 5.14,** you probably perceive a fir tree set against a ground containing several red circles on a white surface. Notice, however, that there is no fir tree shape; the figure consists only of three solid red figures and a base of lines. You see the illusory white triangle in front because the straight edges of the red shapes are aligned in a way that suggests a solid white triangle. The other image in Figure 5.14 gives you the illusion of one complete triangle superimposed on another, although neither is really there.

In this example, there seem to be three levels of figure/ground organization: the white fir tree, the red circles, and the larger white surface behind everything else. Notice that, perceptually, you divide the white area in the stimulus into two different regions: the white triangle and the white ground. Where this division occurs,

FIGURE 5.13

Percept of a Two-Dimensional Geometrical Design

What is your percept of the geometrical design?

Figure Objectlike regions of the visual field that are distinguished from background.

Ground The backdrop or background areas of the visual field, against which figures stand out.

ORGANIZATIONAL PROCESSES IN PERCEPTION

131

FIGURE 5.14

Subjective Contours That Fit the Angles of Your Mind

Do you see a fir tree and one triangle superimposed on another? Convince yourself that the triangles are not really there by covering over two of the corners with your thumbs. Processes of perceptual organization devoted to sorting out figure and ground give rise to these subjective contours.

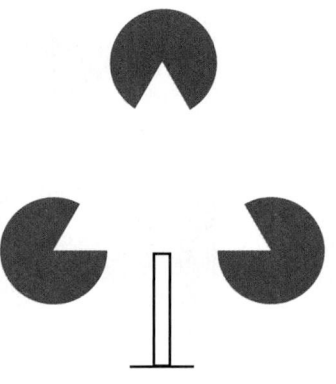

you perceive **illusory contours** that, in fact, exist not in the distal stimulus but only in your subjective experience. Illusory contours were first described in 1900, but have not yet given up all their secrets to researchers (Lesher, 1995).

Your perception of the white triangle in these figures also demonstrates another powerful organizing process: closure. **Closure** makes you see incomplete figures as complete. Though the stimulus gives you only the angles, your perceptual system supplies the edges in between that make the figure a complete fir tree. Closure processes account for your tendency to perceive stimuli as complete, balanced, and symmetrical, even when there are gaps, imbalance, or asymmetry.

Principles of Perceptual Grouping

In Figure 5.13, you perceived the nine figural regions as being grouped together in three distinct rows, each composed of three identical shapes placed along a diagonal line. How does your visual system accomplish this perceptual grouping, and what factors control it?

The problem of grouping was first studied extensively by Gestalt psychologist Max Wertheimer (1923). Wertheimer presented viewers with arrays of simple geometric figures. By varying a single factor and observing how it affected the way people perceived the structure of the array, he was able to formulate a set of

Illusory contours Contours perceived in a figure when no contours are physically present.

Closure A perceptual organizing process that leads individuals to see incomplete figures as complete.

Law of proximity A law of grouping that states that the nearest, or most proximal, elements are grouped together.

Law of similarity A law of grouping that states that the most similar elements are grouped together.

Law of common fate A law of grouping that states that elements moving in the same direction at the same rate are grouped together.

laws of grouping. Several of these laws are illustrated in **Figure 5.15**. In part A, there is an array of equally spaced circles that is ambiguous in its grouping—you can see it equally well as either rows or columns of dots. However, when the spacing is changed slightly so that the horizontal distances between adjacent dots are less than the vertical distances, as shown in B, you see the array unambiguously as organized into horizontal rows; when the spacing is changed so that the vertical distances are less, as shown in C, you see the array as organized into vertical columns. Together, these three groupings illustrate Wertheimer's **law of proximity:** All else being equal, the nearest (most proximal) elements are grouped together. The Gestaltists interpreted such results to mean that the whole stimulus pattern is somehow determining the organization of its own parts; in other words, the *whole percept* is different from the mere collection of its *parts*.

In D, the color of the dots instead of their spacing has been varied. Although there is equal spacing between the dots, your visual system automatically organizes this stimulus into rows because of their *similar color*. You see the dots in E as being organized into columns because of *similar size*, and you see the dots in F as being organized into rows because of *similar shape* and *orientation*. These grouping effects can be summarized by the **law of similarity:** All else being equal, the most similar elements are grouped together.

When elements in the visual field are moving, similarity of motion also produces a powerful grouping. The **law of common fate** states that, all else being equal, elements moving in the same direction and at the same rate are grouped together. If the dots in every other column of G were moving upward, as indicated by the blurring, you would group the image into columns because of their similarity in motion. You get this effect at a ballet when several dancers move in a pattern different from the others. Remember Dr. Richard's observation that an object in his visual field became organized properly when it moved as a whole. His experience was evidence of the powerful organizing effect of common fate.

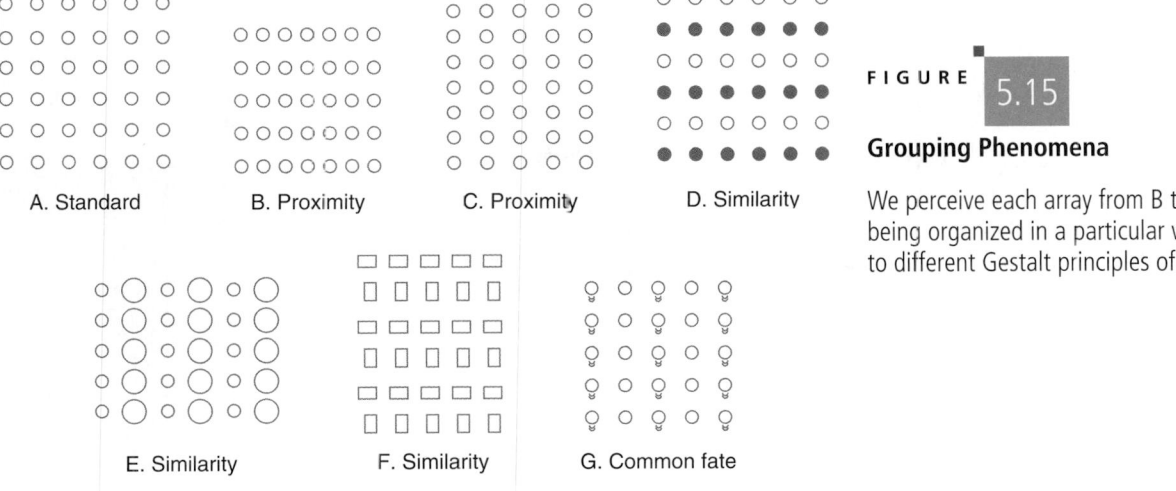

FIGURE 5.15

Grouping Phenomena

We perceive each array from B through G as being organized in a particular way, according to different Gestalt principles of grouping.

Spatial and Temporal Integration

All the Gestalt laws we have presented to you so far should have convinced you that a lot of perception consists of putting the pieces of your world together in the "right way." Often, however, you can't perceive an entire scene in one glance, or *fixation* (recall our discussion of attention). What you perceive at a given time is often a restricted glimpse of a large visual world extending in all directions to unseen areas of the environment. To get a complete idea of what is around you, you must combine information from fixations of different spatial locations—*spatial integration*—at different moments in time—*temporal integration*.

What may surprise you is that your visual system does not work very hard to create a moment-by-moment, integrated picture of the environment. Research suggests that your visual memory for each fixation on the world does not preserve precise details (Carlson-Radvansky & Irwin, 1995; Irwin, 1991; Simons, 2000). In fact, viewers are sometimes unable to detect when a whole object has changed from one fixation to the next.

Many people find this result surprising. How could it be that you have so few processing resources devoted to preserving the details of a scene over time—so that you wouldn't notice that a stapler has turned into a set of keys? Part of the answer might be that the world itself is generally a stable source of information (O'Regan, 1992). It is simply unnecessary to commit to memory information that remains steadily available in the external environment—and so you don't have processes that ordinarily allow you to do so.

One interesting consequence of the way you treat the information from different fixations is that you are taken in by illusions called "impossible" objects, such as those in **Figure 5.17**. For example, each fixation of corners and sides provides an interpretation that is consistent with an object that seems to be a three-dimensional triangle (image A); but when you try to integrate them into a coherent whole, the pieces just don't fit together properly (image B). Image C has two arms that somehow turn into three prongs right before your vigilant gaze, and the perpetual staircase in image D forever ascends or descends.

Motion Perception

One type of perception that does require you to compare across different glimpses of the world is motion perception. Consider the two images given in **Figure 5.18.**

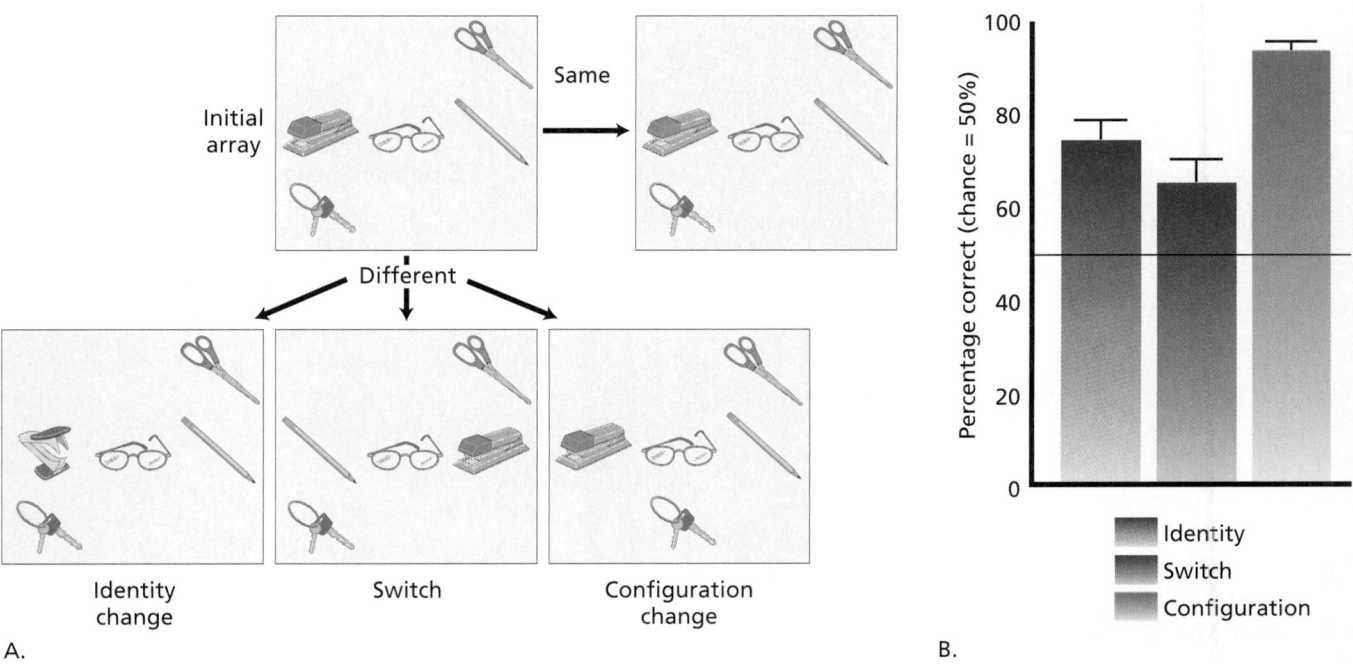

A.

B.

FIGURE 5.16

Change Blindness

(A) Experimental participants were asked to respond whether a second display was the "same as" or "different from" the initial array. (B) When the identity of an object was changed or two objects were switched, participants often were unable to detect the difference. Only when the whole configuration changed were participants nearly always correct.

Suppose that this individual has stood still while you have walked toward him. The size of his image on your retina has expanded as you have drawn near. The rate at which this image has expanded gives you a sense of how quickly you have been approaching (Gibson, 1979).

Suppose, however, you are still but other objects are in motion. The perception of motion, like the perception of shape and orientation, often depends on a reference frame. If you sit in a darkened room and fixate on a stationary spot of light inside a lighted rectangle that is moving very slowly back and forth, you will perceive instead a *moving* dot going back and forth within a *stationary* rectangle. This illusion, called **induced motion,**

> **Induced motion** An illusion in which a stationary point of light within a moving reference frame is seen as moving and the reference frame is perceived as stationary.
>
> **Apparent motion** A movement illusion in which one or more stationary lights going on and off in succession are perceived as a single moving light; the simplest form of apparent motion is the phi phenomenon.
>
> **Phi phenomenon** The simplest form of apparent motion, the movement illusion in which one or more stationary lights going on and off in succession are perceived as a single moving light.

occurs even when your eyes are quite still and fixated on the dot. Your motion-detector cells are not firing at all in response to the stationary dot but presumably are firing in response to the moving lines of the rectangle. To see the dot as moving requires some higher level of perceptual organization in which the dot and its supposed motion are perceived within the reference frame provided by the rectangle.

There seems to be a strong tendency for the visual system to take a larger, surrounding figure as the reference frame for a smaller figure inside it. You have probably experienced induced motion many times without knowing it. The moon (which is nearly stationary) frequently looks as if it is moving through a cloud, when, in fact, it is the cloud that is moving past the moon. The surrounding cloud induces perceived movement in the moon just as the rectangle does in the dot (Rock, 1983, 1986). Have you ever been in a train that started moving very slowly? Didn't it seem as if the pillars on the station platform or a stationary train next to you might be moving backward instead?

Another movement illusion that demonstrates the existence of higher-level organizing processes for motion perception is called **apparent motion.** The simplest form

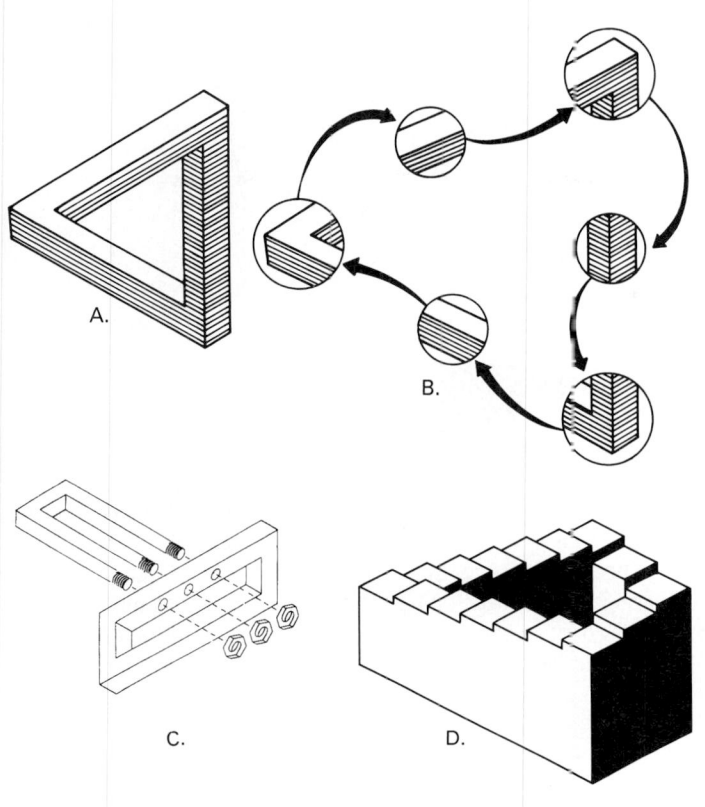

FIGURE 5.17

Impossible Figures

When you look at these figures, each individual fixation suggests that the object is a possible three-dimensional object. It is only when you try to integrate across the different fixations that you discover the objects are impossible.

A.

B.

C.

D.

of apparent motion, the **phi phenomenon,** occurs when two stationary spots of light in different positions in the visual field are turned on and off alternately at a rate of about four to five times per second. This effect occurs on outdoor advertising signs and in disco light displays. Even at this relatively slow rate of alternation, it appears that a single light is moving back and forth between the two spots. There are multiple ways to conceive of the

path that leads from the location of the first dot to the location of the second dot. Yet human observers normally see only the simplest path, a straight line (Cutting & Proffitt, 1982; Shepard, 1984). This straight-line rule is violated, however, when viewers are shown alternating views of a human body in motion. Then the visual system fills in the paths of normal biological motion (Shiffrar, 1994; Stevens et al., 2000).

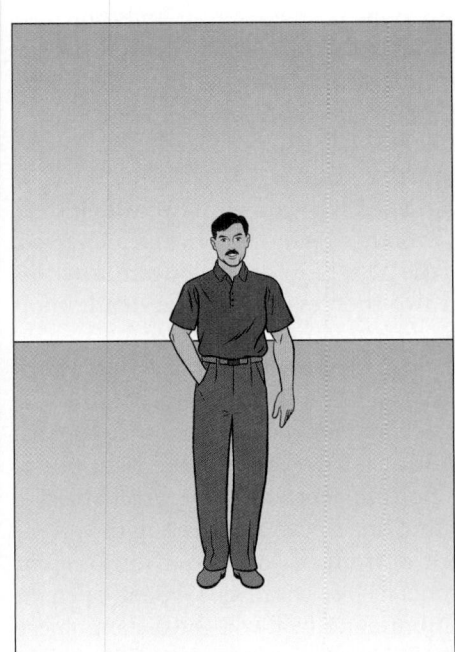

FIGURE 5.18

Approaching a Man

The size of an image expands on your retina as you draw nearer to the stimulus.

What makes you aware that the "protagonist" in this photo is moving—and in what direction is the motion?

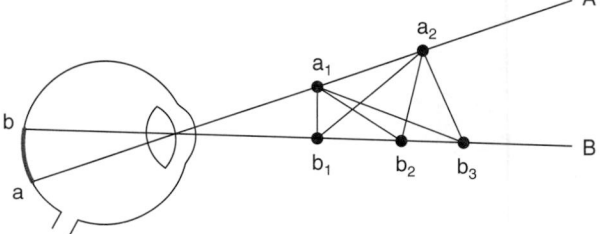

FIGURE  5.19

Depth Ambiguity

Any position on line *A* projects to the same point *a* on the retina; positions along line *B* all project to point *b*. Furthermore, any line segment connecting points on lines *A* and *B* would produce an identical image on the retina. You can see from this figure why depth ambiguity arises: Objects at various distances produce identical images on the retina.

Depth Perception

Until now, we have considered only two-dimensional patterns on flat surfaces. Everyday perceiving, however, involves objects in three-dimensional space. Perceiving all three spatial dimensions is absolutely vital for you to approach what you want, such as interesting people and good food, and avoid what is dangerous, such as speeding cars and falling pianos. This perception requires accurate information about *depth* (the distance from you to an object) as well as about its *direction* from you. Your ears can help in determining direction, but they are not much help in determining depth.

When you think about depth perception, keep in mind that the visual system must rely on retinal images that have only two spatial dimensions—vertical and horizontal. To illustrate the problem of having a two-dimensional retina doing a three-dimensional job, consider the situation shown in **Figure 5.19.** When a spot of light stimulates the retina at point *a*, how do you know whether it came from position a_1 or a_2? In fact, it could have come from *anywhere* along line *A*, because light from any point on that line projects onto the same retinal cell. Similarly, all

points on line *B* project onto the single retinal point *b*. To make matters worse, a straight line connecting any point on line *A* to any point on line *B* (a_1 to b_2 or a_2 to b_1, for example) would produce the same image on the retina. The net result is that the image on your retina is ambiguous in depth: It could have been produced by objects at any one of several different distances.

The two possible views of the Necker cube from Figure 5.5 result from this ambiguity in depth as well. The fact that you can be fooled under certain circumstances shows that depth perception requires an *interpretation* of sensory input and that this interpretation can be wrong. (You already know this if you've ever swung at a tennis ball and come up only with air.) Your interpretation of depth relies on many different information sources about distance (often called *depth cues*)—among them binocular cues, motion cues, and pictorial cues.

BINOCULAR AND MOTION CUES

Have you ever wondered why you have two eyes instead of just one? The second eye is more than just a spare—it provides some of the best, most compelling information about depth. The two sources of binocular depth information are *retinal disparity* and *convergence*.

Because the eyes are about 2 to 3 inches apart horizontally, they receive slightly different views of the world. To convince yourself of this, try the following experiment. First, close your left eye and use the right one to line up your two index fingers with some small object in the distance, holding one finger at arm's length and the other about a foot in front of your face. Now, keeping your fingers stationary, close your right eye and open the left one while continuing to fixate on the distant object. What happened to the position of your two fingers? The

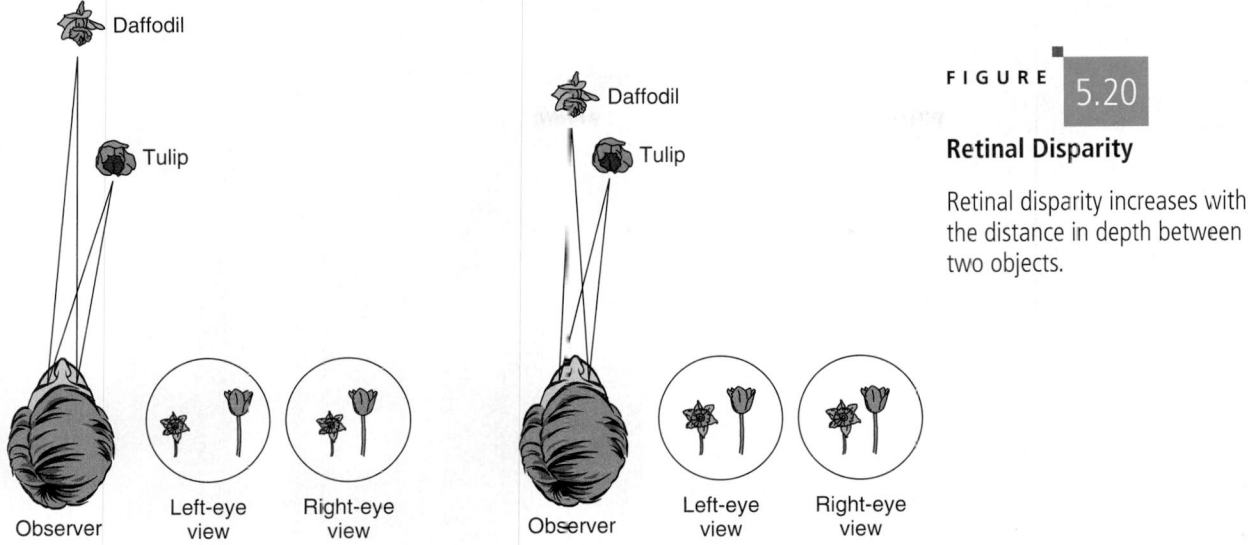

FIGURE 5.20

Retinal Disparity

Retinal disparity increases with the distance in depth between two objects.

second eye does not see them lined up with the distant object because it gets a slightly different view.

This displacement between the horizontal positions of corresponding images in your two eyes is called **retinal disparity**. It provides depth information because the amount of disparity, or difference, depends on the relative distance of objects from you (see **Figure 5.20**). For instance, when you switched eyes, the closer finger was displaced farther to the side than was the distant finger.

When you look at the world with both eyes open, most objects that you see stimulate different positions on your two retinas. If the disparity between corresponding images in the two retinas is small enough, the visual system is able to fuse them into a perception of a single object in depth. (However, if the images are too far apart, as when you cross your eyes, you actually see the double images.) When you stop to think about it, what your visual system does is pretty amazing: It takes two different retinal images, compares them for horizontal displacement of corresponding parts (binocular disparity), and produces a unitary perception of a single object in depth. In effect, the visual system interprets horizontal displacement between the two images as depth in the three-dimensional world.

Other binocular information about depth comes from **convergence**. The two eyes turn inward to some extent whenever they are fixated on an object (see **Figure 5.21**). When the object is very close—a few inches in front of your face—the eyes must turn toward each other quite a bit for the same image to fall on both foveae. You can actually see the eyes converge if you watch a friend focus first

on a distant object and then on one a foot or so away. Your brain uses information from your eye muscles to make judgments about depth. However, convergence information from the eye muscles is useful for depth perception only up to about 10 feet. At greater distances, the angular

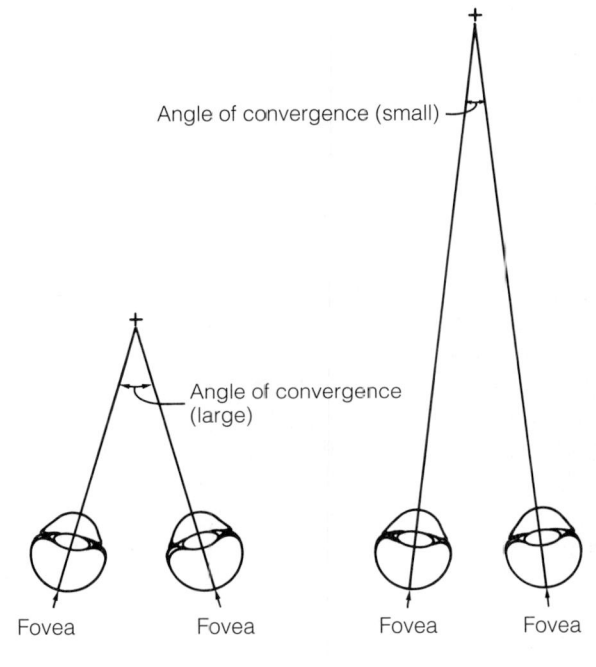

FIGURE 5.21

Convergence Cues to Depth

When an object is close to you, your eyes must converge more than when an object is at a greater distance. Your brain uses information from your eye muscles to use convergence as a cue to depth.

■ **Retinal disparity** The displacement between the horizontal positions of corresponding images in the two eyes.
■ **Convergence** The degree to which the eyes turn inward to fixate on an object.

●ORGANIZATIONAL PROCESSES IN PERCEPTION

137

differences are too small to detect, because the eyes are nearly parallel when you fixate on a distant object.

To see how *motion* is another source for depth information, try the following demonstration. As you did before, close one eye and line up your two index fingers with some distant object. Then move your head to the side while fixating on the distant object and keeping your fingers still. As you move your head, you see both your fingers move, but the close finger seems to move farther and faster than the more distant one. The fixated object does not move at all. This source of information about depth is called **relative motion parallax**. Motion parallax provides information about depth because, as you move, the relative distances of objects in the world determine the amount and direction of their relative motion in your retinal image of the scene. Next time you are a passenger on a car trip, you should keep a watch out the window for motion parallax at work. Objects at a distance from the moving car will appear much more stationary than those closer to you.

PICTORIAL CUES

But suppose you had vision in only one eye. Would you not be able to perceive depth? In fact, further information about depth is available from just one eye. These sources are called pictorial cues, because they include the kinds of depth information found in pictures. Artists who create images in what appear to be three dimensions (on the two dimensions of a piece of paper or canvas) make skilled use of pictorial cues.

Interposition, or *occlusion,* arises when an opaque object blocks out part of a second object (see **Figure 5.22**). Interposition gives you depth information indicating that the occluded object is farther away than the occluding one. Occluding surfaces also block out light, creating shadows that can be used as an additional source of depth information.

Three more sources of pictorial information are all related to the way light projects from a three-dimensional world onto a two-dimensional surface such as the retina: relative size, linear perspective, and texture gradients. *Relative size* involves a basic rule of light projection: Objects of the same size at different distances project images of different sizes on the retina. The closest one projects the largest image and the farthest one the smallest image. This rule is called the *size/distance relation.* As you can see in **Figure 5.23**, if you look at an array with identical objects, you interpret the smaller ones to be further away.

Linear perspective is a depth cue that also depends on the size/distance relation. When parallel lines (by definition separated along their lengths by the same distance) recede

FIGURE 5.22

Interposition Cues to Depth

What are the visual cues that tell you whether this woman is behind the bars?

into the distance, they converge toward a point on the horizon in your retinal image (see **Figure 5.24**). A way to depict this important fact was rediscovered for the first time since classical times in 1425 by Italian Renaissance artists, who were then able to paint depth compellingly (Vasari, 1568/1967). Prior to their discovery, artists had incorporated in their paintings information from interposition, shadows, and relative size, but they had been unable to depict realistic scenes that showed objects at various depths.

Your visual system's interpretation of converging lines gives rise to the Ponzo illusion (also shown in Figure 5.24). The upper line looks longer because you interpret the converging sides according to linear perspective as parallel lines receding into the distance. In this context, you interpret the upper line as though it were farther away, so you see it as longer—a farther object would have to be longer than a nearer one for both to produce retinal images of the same size.

Texture gradients provide depth cues because the density of a texture becomes greater as a surface recedes in depth. The wheat field in **Figure 5.25** is an example

Relative motion parallax A source of information about depth in which the relative distances of objects from a viewer determine the amount and direction of their relative motion in the retinal image.

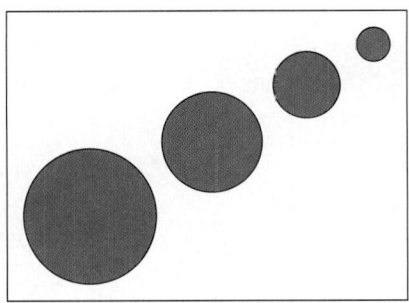

FIGURE  5.23

Relative Size as a Depth Cue

Objects that are closer project larger images on the retina. As a consequence, when you look at an array with identical objects you interpret the smaller ones to be at a greater distance.

of the way texture is used as a depth cue. You can think of this as another consequence of the size/distance relation. In this case, the units that make up the texture become smaller as they recede into the distance, and your visual system interprets this diminishing grain as greater distance in three-dimensional space. Gibson (1966, 1979) suggested that the relationship between texture and depth is one of the invariants available in the perceptual environment.

By now, it should be clear that there are many sources of depth information. Under normal viewing conditions, however, information from these sources comes together in a single, coherent three-dimensional interpretation of the environment. You experience depth, not the different cues to depth that existed in the proximal stimulus. In other words, your visual system uses cues like differential motion, interposition, and relative size automatically, without your conscious awareness, to make the complex computations that give you a perception of depth in the three-dimensional environment.

Perceptual Constancies

To help you discover another important property of visual perception, we are going to ask you to play a bit with your textbook. Put your book down on a table, then move your head closer to it so that it's just a few inches away. Then move your head back to a normal reading distance. Although the book stimulated a much larger part of your retina when it was up close than when it was far away, didn't you perceive the book's size to remain the same? Now set the book upright and try tilting your head clockwise. When you do this, the image of the book rotates counterclockwise on your retina, but didn't you still perceive the book to be upright?

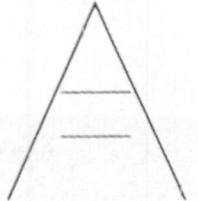

FIGURE  5.24

The Ponzo Illusion

The converging lines add a dimension of depth, and, therefore, the distance cue makes the top line appear larger than the bottom line, even though they are actually the same length.

In general, you see the world as *invariant, constant,* and *stable* despite changes in the stimulation of your sensory receptors. Psychologists refer to this phenomenon as **perceptual constancy.** Roughly speaking, it means that you perceive the properties of the distal stimuli, which are usually constant, rather than the properties of proximal stimuli, which change every time you move your eyes or head. For survival, it is critical that you perceive constant and stable properties of objects in the world despite the enormous variations in the properties of the light patterns that stimulate your eyes. The critical task of perception is to discover *invariant* properties of your environment despite the variations in your retinal impressions of them. We will see how this works for size, shape, and orientation.

SIZE AND SHAPE CONSTANCY

What determines your perception of the size of an object? In part, you perceive an object's actual size on the

Perceptual constancy The ability to retain an unchanging percept of an object despite variations in the retinal image.

ORGANIZATIONAL PROCESSES IN PERCEPTION

139

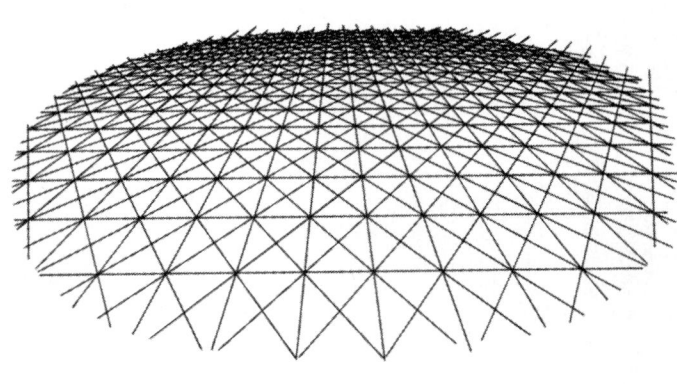

FIGURE 5.25

Examples of Texture as a Depth Cue

The wheat field is a natural example of the way texture is used as a depth cue. Notice the way wheat slants. The geometric design uses the same principles.

basis of the size of its retinal image. However, the demonstration with your book shows that the size of the retinal image depends on both the actual size of the book and its distance from the eye. As you now know, information about distance is available from a variety of depth cues. Your visual system combines that information with retinal information about image size to yield a perception of an object size that usually corresponds to the actual size

How convincing is the perspective in each of these frescoes? Note the difference in the dates when they were created. (*Left:* Duccio, *Maesta: Christ Before Anna and the Denial of St. Peter.* 1308–1311. *Above:* Perugino, *Delivering the Keys of the Kingdom to St. Peter.* 1481–1483. *Both:* Scala/Art Resource, New York.)

HOW DO YOU CATCH A FLY BALL?

Have you ever had this experience: You're standing in deep left field when you hear the distinct crack of a bat, and see a baseball or softball hurtling toward you. What do you do next? How do you *know* where you should run to catch the ball? If you've never played outfield yourself, you've probably still had opportunities to be amazed by someone else's spectacular catches. How did he or she get to the right place at the right time?

The situation of catching a fly ball is one that perception scientists quite reasonably describe as difficult: "The ball's approach pattern renders essentially all major spatial location and depth cues unusable until the final portion of the [ball's path]" (McBeath et al., 1995, p. 569). However, people are quite good at shagging fly balls. The goal of researchers has been to provide a theory that bridges the gap between computational complexity and practical ease. (Recall that at the chapter's outset, we set as our foremost goal to help you understand how perceptual processes afford you such an illusion of ease.)

What types of visual cues might allow you to find your way to the ball? Researchers have proposed two types of *invariant* cues provided by the ball in motion (see the earlier discussion of invariants in Gibson's approach to perception). One group of theorists

What types of visual cues allow a fielder to catch a fly ball?

has suggested that fielders select a path that keeps their visual experience of the ball's speed in the vertical dimension constant as they run (Dannemiller et al., 1996). Another group of theorists suggests that fielders select a path that allows them to keep the angle at which the ball moves relative to the background constant as they run (McBeath et al., 1995, 1996). How do researchers test these theories? Typically, they have launched fly balls and videotaped fielders as they attempted to catch

them. The next research step is to fit mathematical functions to the fielders' performance to see which aspect of their visual experience of the ball's flight they attempt to keep constant. (Perhaps at this moment you feel fortunate that you don't have to understand the mathematics of a perceptual problem to know how to get it right in the real world!)

Research reveals that fielders most often split catching the ball into two phases (Jacobs et al., 1996; McBeath et al., 1996). The first phase is the one we have considered so far—running hard to get to the right place. In the second phase, fielders slow down and may completely stop. The second phase allows location and depth cues to come into play, as the ball swiftly approaches the glove. And once fielders have the ball in their gloves, they are often not completely done: They must typically get the ball back into the infield as quickly as possible, to try to keep runners from advancing or scoring. Therefore, fielders are often performing the perceptually complex feat of catching fly balls while attending, at the same time, to other important aspects of their environment.

Can you take a bit of time off from your studies to play a game of catch? That should allow you to develop your own ideas about this special problem of perception.

---

of the distal stimulus. **Size constancy** refers to your ability to perceive the true size of an object despite variations in the size of its retinal image.

If the size of an object is perceived by taking distance cues into account, then you should be fooled about size whenever you are fooled about distance. One such illusion occurs in the Ames room shown in **Figure 5.26.** In comparison to his 4-foot daughter, Tanya Zimbardo, your 6-foot-tall author looks quite short in the left corner of this room, but he looks enormous in the right corner. The reason for this illusion is that you perceive

the room to be rectangular, with the two back corners equally distant from you. Thus, you perceive Tanya's actual size as being consistent with the size of the images on your retina in both cases. In fact, Tanya is not at the same distance, because the Ames room creates a clever illusion. It appears to be a rectangular room, but it is actually made from nonrectangular surfaces at odd angles in

Size constancy The ability to perceive the true size of an object despite variations in the size of its retinal image.

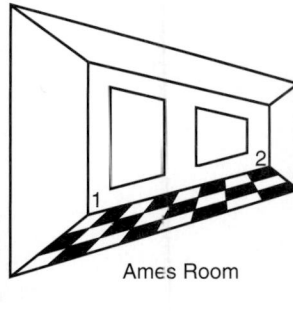

Ames Room

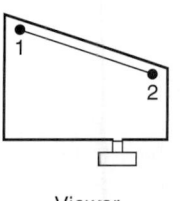

Viewer

FIGURE 5.26

The Ames Room

The Ames room is designed to be viewed through a peephole with one eye—that is the vantage point from which these photographs are taken. The Ames room is constructed from nonrectangular surfaces at odd angles in depth and height. However, with only the view from the peephole, your visual system interprets it as an ordinary room and makes some unusual guesses about the relative heights of the occupants.

depth and height, as you can see in the drawings that accompany the photos. Any person on the right will make a larger retinal image, because he or she is twice as close to the observer. (By the way, to get the illusion you must view the display with a single eye through a peephole—that's the vantage point of the photographs in Figure 5.26. If you could move around while viewing the room, your visual system would acquire information about the unusual structure of the room.)

Another way that the perceptual system can infer objective size is by using prior knowledge about the characteristic size of similarly shaped objects. For instance, once you recognize the shape of a house, a tree, or a dog, you have a pretty good idea of how big each is, even without knowing its distance from you. When past experience does not give you knowledge of what familiar objects look like at extreme distances, size constancy may break down. You have experienced this problem if you have looked down at people from the top of a skyscraper and thought that they resembled ants.

This is also the experience at the core of the story we related at the beginning of the chapter, about Kenge from equatorial Africa. Recall that Kenge, who had lived in dense forests all his life, couldn't make sense of the sight of buffalo grazing at a distance. In the unfamiliar

Shape constancy The ability to perceive the true shape of an object despite variations in the size of the retinal image.
Orientation constancy The ability to perceive the actual orientation of objects in the real world despite their varying orientation in the retinal image.

perceptual environment, Kenge first tried to fit his novel perceptions into a familiar context, by assuming the tiny, distant specks he saw were insects. With no previous experience seeing buffalo at a distance, he had no basis for size constancy, and as the fast-moving car approached them and Kenge's retinal images got larger and larger, he had the frightening illusion that the animals were changing in size. We can assume that, over time, Kenge would have come to see them as Turnbull did. The knowledge he acquired would allow him to arrive at an appropriate perceptual interpretation for his sensory experience.

Shape constancy is closely related to size constancy. You perceive an object's actual shape correctly even when the object is slanted away from you, making the shape of the retinal image substantially different from that of the object itself. For instance, a rectangle tipped away projects a trapezoidal image onto your retina; a circle tipped away from you projects an elliptical image (see **Figure 5.27**). Yet you usually perceive the shapes accurately as a circle and a rectangle slanted away in space. When there is good depth information available, your visual system can determine an object's true shape simply by taking into account your distance from its different parts.

ORIENTATION CONSTANCY

When you tilted your head to the side in viewing your book, the world did not seem to tilt; only your own head did. **Orientation constancy** is your ability to recognize the true orientation of the figure in the real world, even though its orientation in the retinal image is changed. Orientation constancy relies on output from the vestibular system in your inner ear (discussed in Chapter 4)—which

Shape Constancy

As a coin is rotated, its image becomes an ellipse that grows narrower and narrower until it becomes a thin rectangle, an ellipse again, and then a circle. At each orientation, however, it is still perceived as a circular coin.

makes available information about the way in which your head is tilted. By combining the output of the vestibular system with retinal orientation, your visual system is usually able to give you an accurate perception of the orientation of an object in the environment.

In familiar environments, prior knowledge provides additional information about objective orientation. However, you may not be good at recognizing complex and unfamiliar figures when they are seen in unusual orientations. Can you recognize the shape in **Figure 5.28?** When a figure is complex and consists of subparts, you must adjust for the orientation of each part separately (Rock, 1986). So, while you rotate one part to its proper orientation, other parts are still perceived as unrotated. Look at the two upside-down pictures of the pop star Madonna. You can probably tell that one of them has been altered slightly around the eyes and mouth, but the two pictures look pretty similar. Now turn the book upside down and look again. The same pictures look extraordinarily different now. One is still Madonna, but the

other is a ghoulish monster that not even her mother could love! Your failure to see that obvious difference before turning the book upside down may be due to your inability to rotate all of the parts of the face at the same time. It is also a function of years of perceptual training to see the world right side up and to perceive faces in their usual orientation.

LIGHTNESS CONSTANCY

Consider the photograph in **Figure 5.29.** When you look at the brick wall in this picture, you don't perceive some of the bricks to be light red and some of them to be dark red—instead, you perceive this as a wall in which all the bricks are equally light or dark, but some of them are in shadow (Goldstein, 1999). This is an example of lightness constancy: **Lightness constancy** is your tendency to

Lightness constancy The tendency to perceive the whiteness, grayness, or blackness of objects as constant across changing levels of illumination.

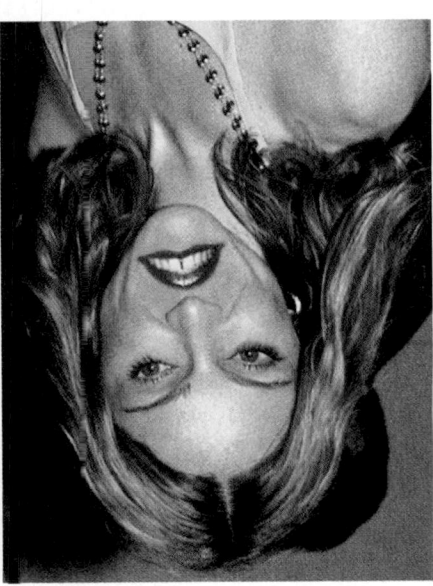

Which of these portraits might express Madonna's feelings after MTV rejects her latest video?

ORGANIZATIONAL PROCESSES IN PERCEPTION

143

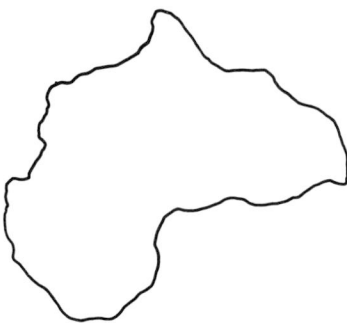

FIGURE 5.28

Africa Rotated 90 Degrees

Did you recognize the rotated continent of Africa? It is often difficult to recognize less familiar figures when they are in unusual orientations.

FIGURE 5.29

Lightness Constancy

Lightness constancy helps explain why you perceive all the bricks in the wall to be made of the same material.

perceive the whiteness, grayness, or blackness of objects as constant across changing levels of illumination.

As with the other constancies we have described, you experience lightness constancy quite frequently in everyday life. Suppose, for example, you are wearing a white T-shirt and walk from a dimly lit room outside into a bright sunny day. In bright sunshine, the T-shirt reflects far more light into your eyes than it does in the dim room, yet it looks about equally light to you in both contexts. In fact, lightness constancy works because the *percentage* of light an object reflects remains about the same even as the *absolute* amount of light changes. Your bright white T-shirt is going to reflect 80 to 90 percent of whatever light is available; your black jeans are going to reflect only about 5 percent of the available light. That's why—when you see them in the same context—the T-shirt will always look lighter than the jeans.

In this section, we have described a number of organizational processes in perception. In the final section of the chapter, we consider the identification and recognition processes that give meaning to objects and events in the environment.

SUMMING UP

The tendency to perceive a figure as being in front of a ground is so strong that it gives rise to the perception of illusory contours. Gestalt psychologists identified several principles of perceptual grouping, including proximity, similarity, and common fate.

Perceptual processes get new information from the world in each fixation. Patterns of stimulation on your retina provide cues to motion. Depth perception arises from a number of converging sources of information. Binocular disparity and convergence are binocular depth cues result-

ing from the horizontal positioning of the eyes. Relative motion parallax provides information about the relative distances of objects. Artists use pictorial depth cues such as interposition, linear perspective, and texture gradients to create the appearance of a third dimension in two-dimensional drawings and paintings.

You perceive size constancy by using distance cues and prior knowledge about size of familiar objects. Shape constancy is aided by good depth information. Orientation constancy relies on the vestibular sense, and prior knowledge about the objective orientation of the observed object. Lightness constancy occurs because objects reflect more or less the same percentage of light whatever the level of illumination.

■ Identification and Recognition Processes

You can think of all the perceptual processes described so far as providing reasonably accurate knowledge about physical properties of the distal stimulus—the position, size, shape, texture, and color of objects in a three-dimensional environment. However, you would not know what the objects were or whether you had seen them before. Your experience would resemble a visit to an alien planet where everything was new to you; you wouldn't know what to eat, what to put on your head, what to run away from, or what to date. Your environment appears nonalien because you are able to recognize and identify most objects as things you have seen before and as members of the meaningful categories that you know about from experience. Identification and recognition attach meaning to percepts.

Bottom-Up and Top-Down Processes

When you identify an object, you must match what you see against your stored knowledge. Taking sensory data in from the environment and sending it toward the brain for extraction and analysis of relevant information is called bottom-up processing. **Bottom-up processing** is anchored in empirical reality and deals with bits of information and the transformation of concrete, physical features of stimuli into abstract representations. This type of processing is also called *data-driven processing*, because your starting point for identification is the sensory evidence you obtain from the environment—the data.

In many cases, however, you can use information you already have about the environment to help you make a perceptual identification. If you visit a zoo, for example, you might be a little more ready to recognize some types of animals than you otherwise would be. You are more likely to hypothesize that you are seeing a tiger there than you would be in your own backyard. When your expectations affect perception, the phenomenon is called top-down processing. **Top-down processing** involves your past experiences, knowledge, motivations, and cultural background in perceiving the world. With top-down processing, higher mental functioning influences how you understand objects and events. Top-down processing is also known as conceptually driven (or hypothesis-driven) processing, because the concepts you have stored in memory are affecting your interpretation of the sensory data. The importance of top-down processing can be illustrated by drawings known as droodles (Price, 1953/1980). Without the labels, these drawings are meaningless. However, once the drawings are identified, you can easily find meaning in them (see **Figure 5.30**).

For a more detailed example of top-down versus bottom-up processing, we turn to the domain of speech perception. You have undoubtedly had the experience of trying to carry on a conversation at a very loud party. Under those circumstances, it's probably true that not all of the physical signal you are producing arrives unambiguously at your acquaintance's ears: Some of what you had to say was almost certainly obscured by coughs, thumping music, or peals of laughter. Even so, people rarely realize that there are gaps in the physical signal they are experiencing. This phenomenon is known as *phonemic restoration* (Warren, 1970). As we explain more fully in Chapter 11, *phonemes* are the minimal, meaningful units of sound in a language; phonemic restoration occurs when people use top-down processes to fill in missing phonemes. Listeners often find it difficult to tell whether they are hearing a word that has a noise replacing part of the original speech signal or whether they are hearing a word with a noise just superimposed on the intact signal (see part A of **Figure 5.31**) (Samuel, 1981, 1991).

Part B of Figure 5.31 shows how bottom-up and top-down processes could interact to produce phonemic res-

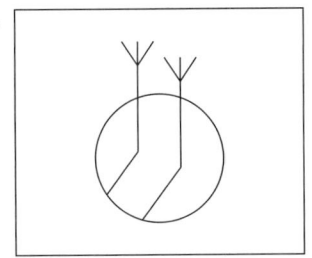

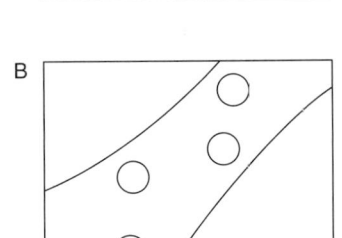

FIGURE 5.30

Droodles

What are these animals? Do you see in (A) an early bird who caught a very strong worm and in (B) a giraffe's neck? Each of these figures can be seen as representing something familiar to you, although this perceptual recognition usually does not occur until some identifying information is provided.

toration (McClelland & Elman, 1986). Suppose part of what your friend says at a noisy party is obscured so that the signal that arrives at your ears is "I have to go home to walk my (noise)og." If noise covers the /d/, you are likely to think that you actually heard the full word *dog*. But why? In Figure 5.31, you see two of the types of information relevant to speech perception. We have the individual sounds that make up words, and the words themselves. When the sounds /o/ and /g/ arrive in this system, they provide information—in a bottom-up fashion—to the word level (we have given only a subset of the words in English that end with /og/). This provides you with a range of candidates for what your friend might have said. Now top-down processes go to work—the context helps you select *dog* as the most likely word to appear in this utterance. When all of this happens swiftly enough—bottom-up identification of a set of candidate words and top-down selection of the likely correct candidate—you'll never know that the /d/ was missing. Your perceptual processes believe that the word was intact (Samuel, 1997). The next time you're in a noisy environment, you'll be glad your perceptual processes fill sounds in so efficiently!

As a final example of top-down processing, consider the people portrayed in **Figure 5.32**. If their fame has not been too fleeting, you should be able to recognize each of these individuals. But is this what they really look like? Probably not, at least on their good days. Your skill at identifying each of these caricatures suggests that your

Bottom-up processing Perceptual analyses based on the sensory data available in the environment; results of analyses are passed upward toward more abstract representations.

Top-down processing Perceptual processes in which information from an individual's past experience, knowledge, expectations, motivations, and background influence the way a perceived object is interpreted and classified.

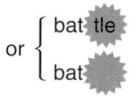

FIGURE 5.31

Phonemic Restoration

(A) Even when a sound is replaced by noise, listeners tend to "hear" the missing information. (B) In this example, noise obscured the /d/ when your friend said dog. Based only on the environmental input, your perceptual system can come up with several hypotheses: dog, log, fog, and so on. However, top-down information from the context—"I have to go home and walk my..."—supports the hypothesis that your friend said dog.

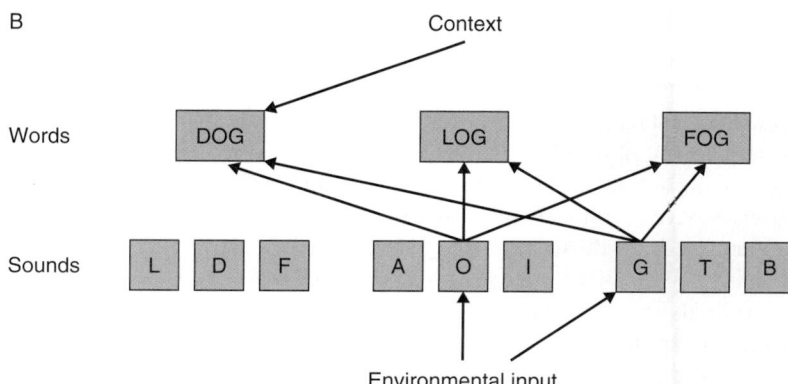

A

The soldier's thoughts of the dangerous

or {
bat⸱tle (Noise added to signal; subject hears both "tle" and noise)

bat⸱ (Noise replaces signal; subject hears only noise)
}

made him very nervous.

B

Context · Words · DOG · LOG · FOG · Sounds · L D F A O I G T B · Environmental input

perception of the world relies on more than just the bottom-up information arriving at your sensory receptors. Your ability to have what you know interact top-down with what you see allows you to recognize Eddie Murphy and Hillary Clinton from these exaggerated portraits. In fact, research has suggested that caricatures may be easier to recognize than more "accurate" representations of famous individuals, because the caricatures emphasize the features that make the individuals distinctive (Mauro & Kubovy, 1992; Rhodes et al., 1997).

Object Recognition

From the example of speech perception, we can derive a general approach that researchers bring to the bottom-up study of recognition: They try to determine the building blocks that perceptual systems use to recognize whole percepts. For language, your speech perception processes combine environmental information about series of sounds to recognize individual words. What are the units from which you construct your representations of objects in the world? How, for example, do you decide that a gray, oddly shaped, medium-size, furry thing is actually a cat? Presumably, you have a memory representation of a cat. The identification process consists in matching the information in the percept to your memory representation of the cat. But how are these matches accomplished? One possibility is that the memory representations of various objects consist of components and information about the way these components are attached to each other (Marr & Nishihara, 1978). **Irving**

FIGURE 5.32

What Enables You to Recognize These Celebrities?

Do you recognize each of these people? You rely on prior acquaintance with these faces—top-down information—to be able to recover the "true" face from the caricature.

Biederman (1987; Hummel & Biederman, 1992) has proposed that all objects can be assembled from a set of *geometrical ions,* or *geons.* Geons are not a large or arbitrary set of shapes. Biederman argued that a set of 36 geons can be defined by following the rule that each three-dimensional geon creates a unique pattern of stimulation on the two-dimensional retina. This uniqueness rule would allow you to work backward from a pattern of sensory stimulation to a strong guess at what the environmental object was like. **Figure 5.33** gives examples of the way in which objects can be assembled from this collection of standard parts.

Researchers have shown that such parts do, in fact, play a role in object recognition. They have done so by presenting viewers with degraded pictures of objects that either do or do not leave parts intact (Biederman, 1987; Biederman & Cooper, 1991). The first column of **Figure 5.34** shows line drawings of common objects.

The middle column shows those same objects with only information deleted that still allows you to recover what the parts are and how they are combined. The right-hand column presents deletions that disrupt your ability to recover the identities of the components and the relationships between them. Do you agree that it would be hard for you to recognize some of these objects based just on the drawings in the third column? The contrast here suggests that you can recognize objects with limited information (just as you can restore missing phonemes), but not if that information disrupts critical components.

Recovery of components alone, however, will not always be sufficient to recognize an object (Hayward & Williams, 2000; Tarr, 1994). One difficulty, as shown in **Figure 5.35**, is that you often see objects from radically different perspectives. The appearance of the parts that make up the object may be quite different from each of these perspectives. As a hedge against this difficulty, you must store separate memory representations for each of the major perspectives from which you view

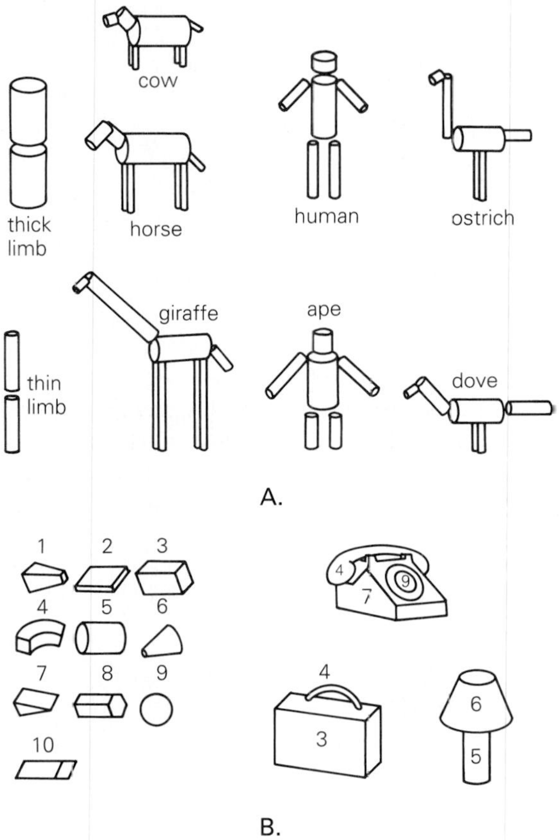

FIGURE 5.33

Recognition by Components

Suggested components of three-dimensional objects and examples of how they may combine. In the top half of the figure, each three-dimensional object is constructed of cylinders of different sizes. In the bottom half of the figure, several different building blocks are combined to form familiar objects.

FIGURE 5.34

Role of Parts in Object Recognition

The deletions of visual information in the middle column leave the parts intact. In the right-hand column, the deletions disrupt the parts. Do you agree that the objects are easier to recognize in the middle versions?

FIGURE
5.35

Looking at the Same Object from Different Perspectives

You see different parts of an object when you view it from different perspectives. To overcome this difficulty, you store multiple views of complex objects in memory.

B.

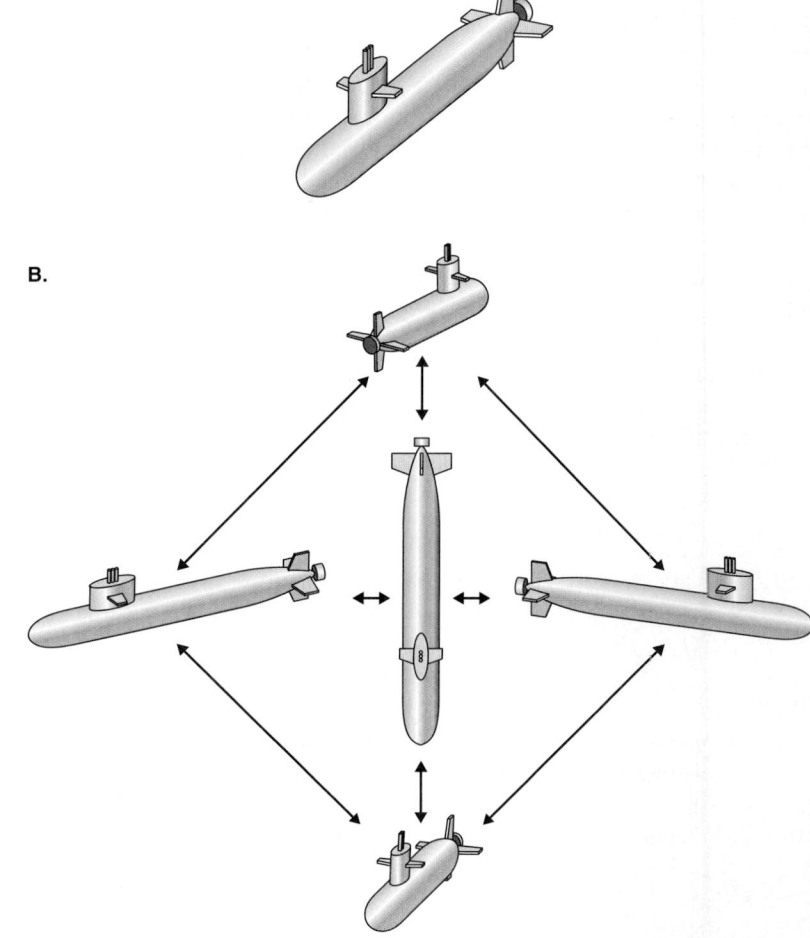

standard objects (Tarr & Pinker, 1989). When you encounter an object in the environment, you may have to mentally transform the percept to determine if it correctly matches one of those views. Thus to recognize a gray, oddly shaped, medium-size, furry thing as a cat, you must recognize it both as an appropriate combination of geons and as that appropriate combination of geons from a specific viewpoint.

The Influence of Contexts and Expectations

What also might help you recognize the cat, however, is to find that gray, oddly shaped, medium-size, furry thing in its accustomed place in your home. This is the top-down aspect of perception: Expectations can influence your hypotheses about what is out there in the world. Have you ever had the experience of seeing people you knew in places where you didn't expect to see them, such as in a different city or a different social group? It takes much longer to recognize them in such situations, and sometimes you aren't even sure that you really know them. The problem is not that they look any different but

that the *context* is wrong; you didn't *expect* them to be there. The spatial and temporal context in which objects are recognized provides an important source of information, because from the context you generate expecta-

FIGURE
5.36A

A Young Beauty

tions about what objects you are and are not likely to see nearby.

Perceptual identification depends on your expectations as well as on the physical properties of the objects you see—object identification is a constructive, interpretive process. Depending on what you already know, where you are, and what else you see around you, your identification may vary. Read the following words:

THE CAT

They say THE CAT, right? Now look again at the middle letter of each word. Physically, these two letters are exactly the same, yet you perceived the first as an H and the second as an A. Why? Clearly, your perception was affected by what you know about words in English. The context provided by T_E makes an H highly likely and an A unlikely, whereas the reverse is true of the context of C_T (Selfridge, 1955).

Researchers have often documented the effects of context and expectation on your perception (and response) by studying set. **Set** is a temporary readiness to perceive or react to a stimulus in a particular way. There are three types of set: motor, mental, and perceptual. A *motor set* is a readiness to make a quick, prepared response. A runner trains by perfecting a motor set to come out of the blocks as fast as possible at the sound of the starting gun. A mental set is a readiness to deal with a situation, such as a problem-solving task or a game, in a way determined by learned rules, instructions, expectations, or habitual tendencies. A *mental set* can actually prevent you from solving a problem when the old rules don't seem to fit the new situation, as we'll see when we study problem solving in Chapter 9. A *perceptual set* is a readiness to detect a particular stimulus in a given context. A new mother, for example, is perceptually set to hear the cries of her child.

Often a set leads you to change your interpretation of an ambiguous stimulus. Consider these two series of words:

FOX; OWL; SNAKE; TURKEY; SWAN; D?CK

BOB; RAY; DAVE; BILL; HENRY; D?CK

Did you read through the lists? What word came to mind for D?CK in each case? If you thought DUCK and DICK, it's because the list of words created a set that directed your search of memory in a particular way.

Labels can provide a context that gives a perceptual set for an ambiguous figure. You have seen how meaningless droodles turn into meaningful objects. Look carefully at the picture of the woman in **Figure 5.36A** on the previous page; have a friend (but not you) examine **Figure 5.36B** on this page. Next, together look at **Figure 5.36C** on page 150—what does each of you see? Did the prior exposure to the unambiguous pictures with

FIGURE 5.36B

An Old Woman

their labels have any effect on perception of the ambiguous image? You can replicate the experiment with a series of friends, to see if you get a consistent difference.

All the effects of context on perception clearly require that your memory be organized in such a fashion that information relevant to particular situations becomes available at the right times. In other words, to generate appropriate (or inappropriate) expectations, you must be able to make use of prior knowledge stored in memory. Sometimes you "see" with your memory as much as you see with your eyes. In Chapter 8, we will discuss the properties of memory that make context effects on perception possible.

Final Lessons

To solidify all that you have learned in this chapter, we suggest that you take a look back at Figure 5.3—you now have the knowledge necessary to understand the whole flowchart. Examination of Figure 5.3 will also confirm that the important lesson to be learned from the study of perception is that a perceptual experience in response to a stimulus event is a response of the whole person. In addition to the information provided when your sensory receptors are stimulated, your final perception depends on who you are, whom you are with, and what you expect, want, and value. A perceiver often plays two different roles that we can compare to gambling and interior design. As a gambler, a perceiver is willing to bet that the present input can be understood in terms of past knowledge and personal theories. As a compulsive interior decorator, a perceiver is constantly rearranging the stimuli

Set A temporary readiness to perceive or react to a stimulus in a particular way.

FIGURE 5.36C

Now What Do You See?

so that they fit better and are more coherent. Incongruity and messy perceptions are rejected in favor of those with clear, clean, consistent lines.

If perceiving were completely bottom-up, you would be bound to the same mundane, concrete reality of the here and now. You could register experience but not profit from it on later occasions, nor would you see the world differently under different circumstances. If perceptual processing were completely top-down, however, you could become lost in your own fantasy world of what you expect and hope to perceive. A proper balance between the two extremes achieves the basic goal of perception: to experience what is out there in a way that optimally serves your needs as a biological and social being, moving about and adapting to your physical and social environment.

SUMMING UP

Identification and recognition involve both bottom-up and top-down processing, which work together to provide a coherent understanding of the world. Object recognition begins with the decomposition of objects into their component parts, or geons. Knowledge of parts must often be combined with knowledge of specific viewpoints to yield object recognition. The spatial and temporal context in which an object is seen creates expectations that influence your ability to recognize the object. Researchers have documented the effects of context on perception by studying set effects.

RECAPPING
MAIN POINTS

Sensing, Organizing, Identifying, and Recognizing

- Your perceptual systems do not simply record information about the external world but actively organize and interpret information as well.
- Perception is a three-stage process consisting of a sensory stage, a perceptual organization stage, and an identification and recognition stage.
- At the sensory level of processing, physical energy is detected and transformed into neural energy and sensory experience.

- At the organizational level, perceptual processes organize sensations into coherent images and give you perception of objects and patterns.
- At the level of identification and recognition, percepts of objects are compared with memory representations to be recognized as familiar and meaningful objects.
- The task of perception is to determine what the distal (external) stimulus is from the information contained in the proximal (sensory) stimulus.
- Ambiguity may arise when the same sensory information can be organized into different percepts.

- Knowledge about perceptual illusions can provide constraints on ordinary perceptual processes.

Attentional Processes

- Attention refers to your ability to select part of the sensory input and disregard the rest.
- Both your personal goals and the properties of objects in the world determine where you will focus your attention.
- The information to which you do not attend has a very limited impact on your ongoing experience.

- Preattentive processing enables you to search the visual environment efficiently.

Organizational Processes in Perception

- Organizational processes provide percepts consistent with the sensory data.
- These processes organize percepts into figures that stand out against the ground.
- You tend to see incomplete figures as wholes and group items by similarity.
- You tend to organize and interpret parts in relation to the spatial and temporal context in which you experience them.
- You also tend to see a reference frame as stationary and the parts within it as moving, regardless of the actual sensory stimulus.
- In converting the two-dimensional information on the retina to a perception of three-dimensional depth, the visual system uses information such as object size and distance.

- You tend to perceive objects as having stable size, shape, orientation, and lightness.

Identification and Recognition Processes

- During the final stage of perceptual processing—identification and recognition of objects—percepts are given meaning through processes that combine bottom-up and top-down influences.
- Context, expectations, and perceptual sets may guide recognition of incomplete or ambiguous data in one direction rather than another, equally possible one.
- Perception thus depends on what you know and expect as well as on the sensory stimulus.

Key Terms

ambiguity (p. 120)
apparent motion (p. 134)
attention (p. 126)
bottom-up processing (p. 145)
closure (p. 132)

convergence (p. 137)
dichotic listening (p. 128)
distal stimulus (p. 118)
figure (p. 131)
Gestalt psychology (p. 125)
goal-directed selection (p. 126)
ground (p. 131)
guided search (p. 130)
identification and recognition (p. 118)
illusion (p. 123)
illusory contours (p. 132)
induced motion (p. 134)
law of common fate (p. 132)
law of proximity (p. 132)
law of similarity (p. 132)
lightness constancy (p. 143)
orientation constancy (p. 142)
perception (p. 116)
perceptual constancy (p. 139)
perceptual organization (p. 117)
phi phenomenon (p. 134)
preattentive processing (p. 128)
proximal stimulus (p. 118)
relative motion parallax (p. 138)
retinal disparity (p. 137)
set (p. 149)
shape constancy (p. 142)
size constancy (p. 141)
stimulus-driven capture (p. 126)
theory of ecological optics (p. 125)
top-down processing (p. 145)
unconscious inference (p. 125)

mind, consciousness, and alternate states

6

■ **THE CONTENTS OF CONSCIOUSNESS**
Awareness and Consciousness • Accessibility to Consciousness • Studying the Contents of Consciousness

■ **THE FUNCTIONS OF CONSCIOUSNESS**
The Uses of Consciousness • Studying the Functions of Consciousness

■ **PSYCHOLOGY IN YOUR LIFE: WHEN DO CHILDREN ACQUIRE CONSCIOUSNESS?**

■ **SLEEP AND DREAMS**
Circadian Rhythms • The Sleep Cycle • Why Sleep? • Sleep Disorders • Dreams: Theater of the Mind

■ **PSYCHOLOGY IN THE 21ST CENTURY: THE 24/7 LIFESTYLE AND SLEEP**

■ **ALTERED STATES OF CONSCIOUSNESS**
Lucid Dreaming • Hypnosis • Meditation • Hallucinations • Religious Ecstasy • Mind-Altering Drugs

■ **RECAPPING MAIN POINTS**
Key Terms

onsider the case of N. N., a young man from Canada who suffered a head injury as a result of a traffic accident. As described by psychologist Endel Tulving (1985), N. N.'s injury left him without the ability to have many of the experiences we will come in this chapter to characterize as *consciousness*. For example, although N. N. "knows a few things about his past—for instance, what year the family moved into the house where they live now, the names of the schools he went to, or where he spent his summers in his teens—he cannot recall a single event or incident from the past" (p. 4). Tulving continues:

> N. N. has no difficulty with the concept of chronological time. He knows the units of time and their relations perfectly well, and he can accurately represent chronological time graphically. But in stark contrast to his abstract knowledge of time, his awareness of subjective time seems to be severely impaired. When asked what he did the day before, he says that he does not know. When asked what he will be doing when he leaves "here," or what he will be doing "tomorrow," he says he does not know....
>
> When asked, on different occasions, to describe the "blankness" that characterizes his state of mind when he tries to think about "tomorrow," he says that it is "like being asleep" or that "it's a big blankness sort of thing." When asked to give an analogy, to describe what it is like, he says, "It's like being in a room with nothing there and having a guy tell you to go find a chair, and there's nothing there." On another occasion he says, "It's like swimming in the middle of a lake. There's nothing there to hold you up or do anything with." When asked to compare his state of mind when he thinks about what he did yesterday, he says it is the "same kind of blankness." N. N. makes all these observations calmly and serenely, without showing any emotion. Only when he is asked whether he is not surprised that there is "nothing there" when he tries to think about yesterday or tomorrow, does he display slight agitation for a moment and utter a soft exclamation of "Wow!"

Can you imagine what it would be like to be N. N.—to try to think about your past or future and only have an experience of "blankness"? Take a moment now to think about a favorite past event; now think about what you'd like to have happen tomorrow or the next day. Where did these memories of the past and projections into the future *come* from and where did they *arrive*? Although you obviously have a vast body of information stored in your brain, it is very unlikely that the thoughts we asked you to have were "in mind" just as you were sitting down to read your psychology text. Therefore, you might feel comfortable saying that the thoughts arrived in your consciousness—and that they came from some part of your brain that was not then conscious. But how did these particular thoughts come to mind? Did you actually consider several different memories or options for the future? That is, were you consciously aware of making a choice? Or did thoughts somehow just emerge—by virtue of some set of unconscious operations—into your consciousness? What capacities do you have that N. N., tragically, has lost?

If you have introspected carefully about what for normal individuals is a simple act of formulating thoughts, you already have an intuitive grasp of the major topics of Chapter 6. In this chapter, we will address a series of questions: What is ordinary conscious awareness? What determines the contents of your consciousness? Why do you need consciousness? Can unconscious mental events really influence your thoughts, emotions, and behavior? How does consciousness change over the course of a day–night cycle, and how can you intentionally alter your state of consciousness? The budding psychologist in you should also want to know how aspects of mind can be studied scientifically. How can you externalize the internal, make public the private, and measure precisely subjective experiences?

Our analysis will begin with an exploration of the contents and functions of consciousness. Along the way, we will turn our spotlight on the human mind. We will help you understand an age-old problem for philosophers, psychologists, and neuroscientists: What is the relationship between brain and mind? Then we will shift to the regular mental changes you all experience during daydreaming, fantasizing, sleeping, and night dreaming. Finally, we will look at how consciousness is altered dramatically by hypnosis, meditation, religious rituals, and drugs.

The Contents of Consciousness

We must start by admitting that the term **consciousness** is ambiguous. We can use the term to refer to a general state of mind *or* to its specific contents: Sometimes you say you were "conscious" in contrast to being "unconscious" (for example, being under anesthesia or asleep); at other times, you say you were conscious—*aware*—of certain information or actions. There is, in fact, a certain consistency here—to be conscious of any particular information, you must be conscious. In this chapter, when we speak of the *contents* of consciousness, we mean the body of information of which you are aware.

Awareness and Consciousness

Some of the earliest research in psychology concerned the contents of consciousness. As psychology gradually diverged from philosophy in the 1800s, it became the science of the mind. Wundt and Titchener used introspection to explore the contents of the conscious mind, and William James observed his own stream of consciousness (see Chapter 1). In fact, on the very first page of his classic 1892 text, *Psychology,* James endorsed as a definition of psychology *"the description and explanation of states of consciousness as such."*

Ordinary waking consciousness includes your perceptions, thoughts, feelings, images, and desires at a given moment—all the mental activity on which you are focusing your attention. You are conscious of both what you are doing and also of the fact that you are doing it. At times, you are conscious of the realization that others are observing, evaluating, and reacting to what you are doing. A *sense of self* comes out of the experience of watching yourself from this privileged "insider" position. Taken together, these various mental activities form the contents of consciousness—all the experiences you are consciously aware of at a particular time (Natsoulas, 1998).

We can define, more formally, three different levels of consciousness. They correspond roughly to (1) a basic level, an awareness of the inner and outer world; (2) a second level, a reflection on what you are aware of; and (3) a top level, an awareness of yourself as a conscious, reflective individual. At the basic level, consciousness is the awareness that you are perceiving and reacting to available perceptual information. At this level, you become aware of a clock ticking in the background or your feelings of hunger. At the second level, consciousness relies on symbolic knowledge to free you from the constraints of real objects and present events. At this level, you can contemplate and manipulate objects in their absence, visualize new forms and uses for the familiar, or plan utopias. The top level of consciousness is **self-awareness,** cognizance (or awareness) that personally experienced events have an *autobiographical* character. Self-awareness gives you your sense of personal history and identity. At this level of consciousness, if you have personally experienced a fairly orderly, predictable world, you come to expect it, and this expectation equips you to choose the best present actions

Why is self-awareness considered to be such an important aspect of consciousness?

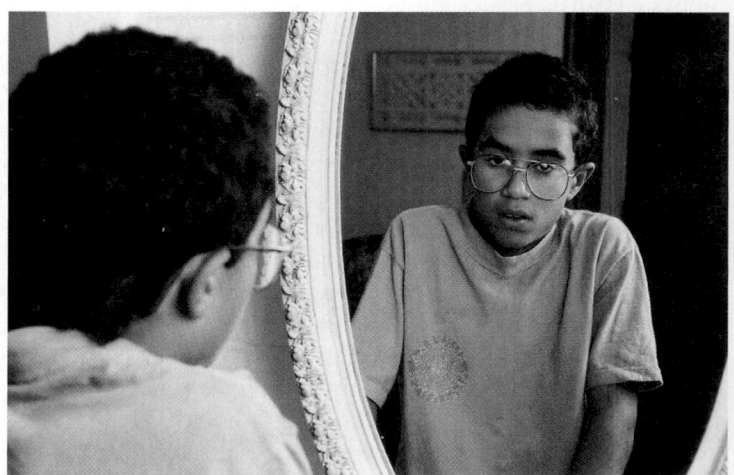

and plans for the future. Recall that we began the chapter with the case of N. N., whose head injury left him with an almost total absence of self-awareness (Tulving, 1985). N. N. had no sense of personal time perspective—no awareness of his own autobiography over time.

Accessibility to Consciousness

We have defined the general types of information that *might* be conscious at a particular place and time, but what determines what is conscious right now? Were you, for example, aware of your breathing just now? Probably not; its control is part of *nonconscious processes*. Were you thinking about your last vacation, or about the author of *Hamlet*? Again, probably not; control of such thoughts are part of *preconscious memories*. Were you aware of background noises, such as a clock ticking, traffic, or a fluorescent light buzzing? It would be difficult to be aware of all this and still pay full attention to the meaning of the material in this chapter; these stimuli are part of *unattended information*. Finally, there may be types of information that are *unconscious*—not readily accessible to conscious awareness—such as the set of grammatical rules that enable you to understand this sentence. Let's examine each of these types of awareness.

NONCONSCIOUS PROCESSES

There is a range of **nonconscious** bodily activities that rarely, if ever, impinge on consciousness. An example of nonconscious processes at work is the regulation of blood pressure. Your nervous system monitors physiological information to detect and act on changes continually, without your awareness. At certain times, some ordinarily nonconscious activities can be made conscious: You can, for example, choose to exercise conscious control over your pattern of breathing. Even so, your nervous system takes care of many important functions without requiring conscious resources.

PRECONSCIOUS MEMORIES

Memories accessible to consciousness only after something calls your attention to them are known as **preconscious memories**. The storehouse of memory is filled with an incredible amount of information, such as your general knowledge of language, sports, or geography and recollections of your personally experienced events. Preconscious memories function silently in the background of your mind until a situation arises in which they are consciously necessary (as when we asked you to call to mind a favorite past event). Memory will be discussed in detail in Chapter 8.

Consciousness A state of awareness of internal events and of the external environment.

Self-awareness The top level of consciousness; cognizance of the autobiographical character of personally experienced events.

Nonconscious Information not typically available to consciousness or memory.

Preconscious memories Memories that are not currently conscious but that can easily be called into consciousness when necessary.

At any given time, thoughts about your job, your parents, or your hungry pet may flow below the level of consciousness until something occurs to focus your attention on one of these topics. Why are these memories considered preconscious, not unconscious?

UNATTENDED INFORMATION

At any given time, you are surrounded by a vast amount of stimulation. As we described in Chapter 5, you can focus your attention only on a small part of it. What you focus on, in combination with the memories it evokes, will determine, to a large extent, what is in consciousness. Nevertheless, you sometimes have an unconscious representation of the information that is not in the focus of your attention. Recall this scenario from Chapter 5: At a noisy party, you try to focus attention on your attractive date and remain seemingly oblivious to a nearby conversation—until you overhear your name mentioned. Suddenly you are aware that you must have been monitoring the conversation—in some unconscious way—to detect that special signal amid the noise (Wood & Cowan, 1995a).

THE UNCONSCIOUS

You typically recognize the existence of *unconscious* information when you cannot explain some behavior by virtue of forces that were conscious at the time of the behavior. An initial theory of unconscious forces was developed by **Sigmund Freud,** who argued that certain life experiences—traumatic memories and taboo desires— are sufficiently threatening that special mental processes (that we will describe in Chapter 14) permanently banish them from consciousness. Freud believed that when the content of original, unacceptable ideas or motives is *repressed*—put out of consciousness—the strong feelings associated with the thoughts still remain and influence behavior. Freud's "discovery" of the unconscious contradicted a long tradition of Western thought. From the time the English philosopher John Locke (1690/1975) wrote his classic text on the mind, *An Essay Concerning Human Understanding,* most thinkers firmly believed that rational beings had access to all the activities of their own minds. Freud's initial hypothesis about the existence of unconscious mental processes was considered outrageous by his contemporaries (Dennett, 1987). (We will revisit Freud's ideas when we discuss the origin of your unique personality in Chapter 14.)

Many psychologists now use the term *unconscious* to refer to information and processes that are more benign than the types of thoughts Freud suggested must be repressed (Baars & McGovern, 1996; Westen, 1998). For example, many types of ordinary language processing

rely on unconscious processes. Consider this sentence (Vu et al., 2000):

> *She investigated the bark.*

How did you interpret this sentence? Did you picture some woman looking after a dog or examining a tree? Because the word *bark* is ambiguous—and the sentence context provides little help—you can only guess at what the writer meant. Now consider the same sentence in a slightly larger context:

> *The botanist looked for a fungus. She investigated the bark.*

Did you find the sentence easier to understand in this context? If you did, it's because your unconscious language processes used the extra context to make a very swift choice between the two meanings of *bark*.

With this example, we demonstrate that processes that operate below the level of consciousness often affect your behavior—in this case, the ease with which you came to a clear understanding of the sentence. We have, thus, shifted subtly from discussing the contents of consciousness to discussing the functions of consciousness. Before we take up that topic in detail, however, we will briefly describe two ways in which the contents of consciousness can be studied.

Studying the Contents of Consciousness

To study consciousness, researchers have had to devise methodologies to make deeply private experiences overtly measurable. One method is a new variation on Wundt and Titchener's practice of introspection. Experimental participants are asked to speak aloud as they work through a variety of complex tasks. They report, in as much detail as possible, the sequence of thoughts they experience while they complete the tasks. The participants' reports, called **think-aloud protocols,** are used to document the mental strategies and representations of knowledge that the participants employ to do the task. These protocols also allow researchers to analyze the discrepancies between task performance and awareness of how it is carried out (Ericsson & Simon, 1993).

In the **experience-sampling method,** participants wear devices that signal them when they should provide reports about what they are feeling and thinking. For example, in one methodology, participants wear electronic pagers. A radio transmitter activates the pager at various random times each day for a week or more. Whenever the pager signals, participants may also be asked to respond to questions, such as "How well were you concentrating?" In this way, researchers can keep a running record of participants' thoughts, awareness, and focuses of attention as they go about their everyday lives (Csikszentmihalyi, 1990).

Think-aloud protocols Reports made by experimental participants of the mental processes and strategies they use while working on a task.

Experience-sampling method An experimental method that assists researchers in describing the typical contents of consciousness; participants are asked to record what they are feeling and thinking whenever signaled to do so.

Think back to your days as an adolescent. What topics were most likely to be occupying your consciousness? To answer that question, a team of researchers outfitted a group of 218 students with electronic pagers that randomly signaled them to answer a series of questions about their thoughts and feelings (Richards et al., 1998). The students' experiences were sampled twice, four years apart: The first time, the students were in grades 5 through 8; the second time, they were in grades 9 through 12. This experimental design allowed the researchers to see how the contents of the adolescents' consciousness changed as they grew older. The researchers were particularly interested in peer companionship during adolescence, so they closely examined how often the students were thinking about friends. The researchers' analyses suggested that increasing age brought with it a shift toward more thoughts about the opposite sex. Whereas fifth and sixth graders were only thinking about the opposite sex 1.0% of the time, for eighth graders this figure was 5.8%. The analyses also revealed an interesting difference between girls and boys: Even when, at the moment the pager sounded, they were not in their friends' immediate company, girls were more likely than boys to be thinking about their friends of both sexes. The researchers suggest that this sex difference foreshadows the greater thought women give to interpersonal relationships across adulthood.

You can see from this example how researchers can use experience-sampling methods to piece together a descriptive account of the typical contents of consciousness.

SUMMING UP

Consciousness can be defined at three levels: an awareness of the inner and outer world, an ability to reflect on that awareness, and a sense of self as an aware, reflective individual. Many bodily processes, such as breathing, are ordinarily nonconscious. You possess a large amount of information in memory that is preconscious—it can be brought into consciousness on demand. Unattended information is the large amount of environmental stimulation to which you are not consciously attending. Although Freud associated the unconscious with repressed memories, contemporary researchers have a broader conceptualization of the unconscious that involves many types of information and processes. Psychologists use techniques like think-aloud protocols and experience sampling to study the contents of consciousness.

■ The Functions of Consciousness

When we address the question of the *functions* of consciousness, we are trying to understand why we *need* consciousness—what does it add to our human experience? The case of N. N. that we described at the chapter's outset provides some strong hints toward an answer. Without a sense of past or future—without the full use of consciousness—important aspects of N. N.'s life were simply a blank. In this section, we will more fully develop such observations about the importance of consciousness to human survival and social function.

The Uses of Consciousness

Human consciousness was forged in the crucible of competition with the most hostile force in its evolutionary environment—other humans. The human mind may have evolved as a consequence of the extreme *sociability* of human ancestors, which was perhaps originally a group defense against predators and a means to exploit resources more efficiently. However, close group living then created new demands for cooperative as well as competitive abilities with other humans. Natural selection favored those who could think, plan, and imagine alternative realities that could promote both bonding with kin and victory over adversaries. Those who developed language and tools won the grand prize of survival of the fittest mind—and, fortunately, passed it on to us (Donald, 1995; Mcphail, 1998).

Because consciousness evolved, you should not be surprised that it provides a range of functions that aid in the survival of the species (Baars, 1997; Baars & McGovern, 1994; Cheney & Seyfarth, 1990; Ornstein, 1991). Consciousness also plays an important role in allowing for the construction of both personal and culturally shared realities.

AIDING SURVIVAL

From a biological perspective, consciousness probably evolved because it helped individuals to make sense of environmental information and to use that information in planning the most appropriate and effective actions. Usually, you are faced with a sensory-information overload. William James described the massive amount of information that strikes the sensory receptors as a "blooming, buzzing confusion" assailing you from all sides. Consciousness helps you adapt to your environment by making sense of this profusion of confusion in three ways.

First, it reduces the flow of stimulus input by restricting what you notice and what you pay attention to. This *restrictive function* of consciousness tunes out much of the information that is not relevant to your immediate goals and purposes. All that is evaluated as "irrelevant" becomes background noise to be ignored while you focus conscious awareness on "relevant" input, the signal you wish to process and respond to.

Second, consciousness performs a *selective storage function*. After the stream of all sensory input is perceptually processed into a smaller number of recognizable patterns and categories, consciousness allows you to selectively store stimuli you want to analyze, interpret, and act on in the future. Consciousness allows you to classify events and experiences as relevant or irrelevant to personal needs by selecting some and ignoring others.

The third function of consciousness is to make you stop, think, consider alternatives based on past knowledge, and imagine various consequences. This *planning* or *executive control function* enables you to suppress strong desires when they conflict with moral, ethical, or practical concerns. Without this kind of consciousness, you might try to steal an apple if you were hungry and it was the first food you saw. Because consciousness gives you a broad time perspective in which to frame potential actions, you can call on abstract representations of the past and the future to influence your current decisions. For all these reasons, consciousness gives you great potential for flexible, appropriate responses to the changing demands in your life.

PERSONAL AND CULTURAL CONSTRUCTIONS OF REALITY

No two people interpret a situation in exactly the same way. Your *personal construction of reality* is your unique interpretation of a current situation based on your general knowledge, memories of past experiences, current needs, values, beliefs, and future goals. Each person attends more to certain features of the stimulus environment than to others precisely because his or her personal construction of reality has been formed from a selection of unique inputs. When your personal construction of reality remains relatively stable, your *sense of self* has continuity over time.

Individual differences in personal constructions of reality are even greater when people have grown up in different cultures, lived in different environments within a culture, or faced different survival tasks. The opposite is also true—because the people of a given culture share many of the same experiences, they often have similar constructions of reality. *Cultural constructions of reality* are ways of thinking about the world that are shared by most

What is your unique way of viewing the world around you? Artist David Hockney created this collage entitled *George, Blanche, Celia, Albert and Percy, London, Jan. 1983* from Polaroid photographs.

members of a particular group of people. When a member of a society develops a personal construction of reality that fits in with the cultural construction, it is affirmed by the culture and, at the same time, it affirms the cultural construction. This mutual affirmation of conscious constructions of reality is known as **consensual validation.**

HOW WE KNOW

THE FUNCTION OF CONSENSUAL VALIDATION German citizens were stopped on a street, either directly in front of a funeral home or about 100 meters from a funeral home. The researchers believed that the vivid presence of the funeral home would make people aware of their mortality and, as a consequence, make them more likely to seek comfort in consensual validation. When, that is, people are in a state that the researchers characterized as "existential terror," the theory suggests that they are consoled by shared cultural beliefs and attitudes. A consequence of this claim is that the vivid presence of the funeral home should prompt individuals to believe that their attitudes are more in line with cultural norms. In this study, participants were asked to estimate the extent to which other German citizens would share their opinions about a change in immigration policy. Those individuals in the minority on the issue increased their estimates of consensus by over 10 percent when they were directly in front of the funeral home versus 100 meters away (Pyszczynski et al., 1996).

Consensual validation The mutual affirmation of conscious views of reality.

This study supports the prediction that individuals need more consensual validation when feelings of mortality impinge on their consciousness. A conscious assertion of agreement with cultural beliefs and attitudes helps to moderate these feelings.

Studying the Functions of Consciousness

Many of the functions of consciousness include implicit comparisons with what remains unconscious. That is, conscious processes often affect or are affected by unconscious processes. To study the functions of consciousness, researchers often study the relationship between conscious and unconscious influences on behavior. Researchers have now developed a variety of ways to demonstrate that unconscious processes can affect conscious behavior (Nelson, 1996; Westen, 1998).

For example, researchers have used the *SLIP* (*Spoonerisms of Laboratory-Induced Predisposition*) technique to determine the way in which unconscious forces affect the probability of making a speech error (Baars et al., 1992). The SLIP procedure enables an experimenter to induce slips of the tongue by setting up expectations for certain patterns of sound. Thus, after pronouncing

a series of word pairs like *ball doze, bell dark,* and *bean deck,* a participant might mispronounce *darn bore* as *barn door.* Experimenters can assess conscious or unconscious influences on the probability of such sound exchanges by altering circumstances external to the task. For instance, participants were more likely to make the error *bad shock* (from *shad bock*) when they believed they might receive a painful electric shock sometime during an experiment (Motley & Baars, 1979). Similarly, male participants who performed the SLIP task in the presence of a provocative female experimenter were more likely to err in producing *good legs* (from *lood gegs*). These results suggest an unconscious contribution to the production of speech errors.

Another way to study the relationship between conscious and unconscious processes is by putting them in opposition (Jacoby et al., 1999). Let's look at a study that creates such an opposition.

HOW WE KNOW

CONSCIOUS AND UNCONSCIOUS PROCESSES IN OPPOSITION Consider the experiment presented in **Figure 6.1.** In this situation, participants are asked to judge a name

Heard → 6 5 19 28 11 17 41 12 . . .

Phase 1:

The participants read out loud a computer-presented list of nonfamous names, while at the same time trying to detect sequences of three odd numbers within a list of numbers presented auditorily.

Phase 2:

Participants are asked to judge a list of names as famous or nonfamous.

They are told that all the names they read previously were nonfamous.

Therefore, if they remember that a name was on the list, they should say **nonfamous:** If they have a <u>conscious</u> memory of the name, they will know it couldn't be famous.

When they say **famous** to a name that was on the list, that must be because the <u>unconscious</u> memory of the name makes it seem familiar.

Participants often <u>will</u> say **famous,** demonstrating the influence of <u>unconscious</u> memories.

FIGURE 6.1

The Influence of Unconscious Memories on "Fame" Judgments

In this experiment, researchers demonstrated the influence of unconscious memories by creating circumstances in which conscious and unconscious processes lead to opposing—"famous" versus "nonfamous"—responses.

WHEN DO CHILDREN ACQUIRE CONSCIOUSNESS?

It seems very likely that at some point in your life you've looked down into a crib at a newborn, or very young child, and wondered to yourself: "What's going on in this child's head?" Often, this question translates into an issue of consciousness: When does the child become conscious of him- or herself as a *self*? Research has suggested that children acquire, in turn, a subjective self and then an objective self (Lewis, 1991; 1999):

- Children have acquired a *subjective self,* or *subjective self-awareness,* when they have come to the realization that they are separate from others. The child is able to *subject* the external world to conscious scrutiny.

- Children have acquired an *objective self,* or *objective self-awareness,* when they can turn their consciousness on themselves—when they can make themselves the *object* of their own conscious analysis. Children are able to reflect on what they "know that they know" or "remember that they remember."

Classic research on children's acquisition of objective self-awareness has relied on their performance in front of mirrors. Researchers wondered: When do they realize that the image in the mirror is them? To answer this question, researchers asked mothers to put a small dot of rouge on their children's noses, without allowing the children to know that they were being marked—this is the *nose dot* test. Children understand some of the properties of mirrors at a fairly young age. For example, as early as 6 months, children will reach out and touch some parts of the image in the mirror. However, it isn't until about age 18 months that most children touch their noses in response to the dot of rouge (Bertenthal & Fischer, 1978). Apparently, it is not until that age that children can think (in some form), "That's me in the mirror—and what's that strange red mark on my nose?"

Even when children can pass the *nose dot* test, they are not finished acquiring a sense of self. Children must still acquire the idea of the objective self having a time component: so they can think of themselves as continuously existing in the past, present, and future. An adaptation of the nose dot procedure allowed researchers to examine children's acquisition of the temporal continuity of the self (Povinelli et al., 1996). In this study, children ranging in age from 30 to 42 months were being videotaped while an experimenter secretly put a sticker in the child's hair. Some of the children were shown videotape of themselves with the sticker in a *live* recording: They could see the sticker in their hair while they were doing the things they were doing. The other half of the children watched a videotape after about a three-minute *delay:* They were watching a tape of themselves, with a sticker in their hair, carrying out activities from the recent past. About two-thirds of the children in the *live* group reached up to the stickers, but only about one-third of the children did in the *delay* group. In fact, it was only at around age 4 years that children were reliably able to watch a delayed videotape of their activities and make a connection to the sticker. Apparently, it's reasonably difficult for children to reason from representations of their past—even the pretty immediate past—to what's happening now.

Do these results surprise you? If you've spent time with two- and three-year-old children, you know that they seem to have a pretty good idea of who they are and what they are up to. The research results suggest how much there really is for children to learn—and, therefore, how complex your adult experience of consciousness really is.

such as "Adrian Marr" as famous or nonfamous. Prior to making these judgments, participants read a long list of names aloud (including "Adrian Marr") in circumstances that did not allow them to concentrate all their attention on the names. When they performed the fame judgments, the participants were warned that all of the names they had read on the earlier list were not famous—thus, if they came upon a name that they recognized from the list, they should say that the person wasn't famous. Suppose, now, that participants get to the name "Adrian Marr." If they are able to find a conscious memory for this name, they will know that it appeared on the earlier list—and, therefore, they will say that "Adrian Marr" is not famous. If they can't find a conscious memory, they might instead have the general feeling that "they've heard this name before" and say that "Adrian Marr" is famous. This phenomenon is an opposition between conscious ("Say no!") and unconscious ("Say yes!") processes. In fact, participants are likely to say that "Adrian Marr" is famous, providing evidence that an unconscious memory influences their judgments (Jacoby et al., 1989).

While the daydreaming of a Little Leaguer may serve different functions from that of a major-league baseball player, daydreaming can have value for both. What functions does daydreaming fill in your day-to-day life?

We have seen how the contents and functions of consciousness are defined and studied. We turn now to ordinary and then extraordinary alterations in consciousness.

SUMMING UP

Consciousness aids survival by reducing the flow of stimulus input, determining which stimuli will be stored, and allowing actions to be planned with consideration of their consequences. Consciousness also mediates people's personal and cultural constructions of reality. To study the functions of consciousness, researchers often invert paradigms that assess the relationship between conscious and unconscious processes.

Sleep and Dreams

Almost every day of your life you experience a rather profound change in consciousness: When you decide it's time to end your day, you will surrender yourself to sleep—and while you sleep you will undoubtedly dream. A third of your life is spent sleeping, when your muscles are in a state of "benign paralysis" and your brain is humming with varied activity. We begin this section by considering the general biological rhythms of wakefulness and sleeping. We then focus more directly on the physiology of sleeping. Finally, we examine the major mental activity that accompanies sleep—dreaming—and explore the role dreams play in human psychology.

Circadian Rhythms

All creatures are influenced by nature's rhythms of day and night. Your body is attuned to a time cycle known as a **circadian rhythm:** Your arousal levels, metabolism, heart rate, body temperature, and hormonal activity ebb and flow according to the ticking of your internal clock

(Moore-Ede et al., 1982). For the most part, these activities reach their peak during the day—usually during the afternoon—and hit their low point at night while you sleep. Research suggests that the clock your body uses is not exactly in synchrony with the clock on the wall: Without the corrective effects of external time cues, the human internal "pacemaker" establishes a 24.18-hour cycle (Czeisler et al., 1999). The exposure to sunlight that you get each day helps you make the small adjustment to a 24-hour cycle. Information about sunlight is gathered through your eyes, but receptors for regulation of circadian rhythms are not the same receptors as allow you to see the world: Animals without rods and cones (see Chapter 4) still sense light in a way that enables them to maintain their circadian rhythms (Freedman et al., 1999).

Changes that cause a mismatch between your biological clock and environmental clocks affect how you feel and act (Moore-Ede, 1993). Perhaps the most dramatic example of how such mismatches arise comes from long-distance air travel. When people fly across time zones, they may experience *jet lag*, a condition whose symptoms include fatigue, irresistible sleepiness, and subsequent unusual sleep–wake schedules. Jet lag occurs because the internal circadian rhythm is out of phase with the normal temporal environment (Redfern et al., 1994). For example, your body says it's 2 A.M.—and thus is at a low point on many physiological measures—when local time requires you to act as if it is noon. Jet lag, a special problem for flight crews, contributes to pilot errors that cause airplane accidents (Coleman, 1986).

What variables influence jet lag? The direction of travel and the number of time zones passed through are the most important variables. Traveling eastbound creates greater jet lag than does westbound flight, because your biological clock can be more readily extended than shortened, as required on eastbound trips (it is easier to stay awake longer than it is to fall asleep sooner). When

Circadian rhythm A consistent pattern of cyclical body activities, usually lasting 24 to 25 hours and determined by an internal biological clock.

healthy volunteers were flown back and forth between Europe and the United States, their peak performance on standard tasks was reached within two to four days after westbound flights but nine days after eastbound travel (Klein & Wegmann, 1974).

The Sleep Cycle

About a third of your circadian rhythm is devoted to that period of behavioral quiescence called *sleep*. Most of what is known about sleep concerns the electrical activities of the brain. The methodological breakthrough for the study of sleep came in 1937 with the application of a technology that records brain wave activity of the sleeper in the form of an electroencephalogram (EEG). The EEG provided an objective, ongoing measure of the way brain activity varies when people are awake or asleep. With the EEG, researchers discovered that brain waves change in form at the onset of sleep and show further systematic, predictable changes during the entire sleep period (Loomis et al., 1937). The next significant discovery in sleep research was that bursts of **rapid eye movements (REM)** occur at periodic intervals during sleep (Aserinsky & Kleitman, 1953). The time when a sleeper is not showing REM is known as **non-REM (NREM) sleep.** We will see in a later section that REM and NREM sleep have significance for one of the night's major activities—dreaming.

Let us track your brain waves through the night. As you prepare to go to bed, an EEG records that your brain waves are moving along at a rate of about 14 cycles per second (cps). Once you are comfortably in bed, you begin to relax, and your brain waves slow down to a rate of about 8 to 12 cps. When you fall asleep, you enter your *sleep cycle*, each of whose stages shows a distinct EEG pattern. In Stage 1 sleep, the EEG shows brain waves of about 3 to 7 cps. During Stage 2, the EEG is characterized by *sleep spindles*, minute bursts of electrical activity of 12 to 16 cps. In the next two stages (3 and 4) of sleep, you enter into a very deep state of relaxed sleep. Your brain waves slow to about 1 to 2 cps, and your breathing and heart rate decrease. In a final stage, the electrical activity of your brain increases; your EEG looks very similar to those recorded during stages 1 and 2. It is during this stage that you will experience REM sleep, and you will begin to dream (see **Figure 6.2**). (Because the EEG pattern during REM sleep resembles that of an awake person, REM sleep was originally termed *paradoxical sleep*.)

Rapid eye movements (REM) A behavioral sign of the phase of sleep during which the sleeper is likely to be experiencing dreamlike mental activity.

Non-REM (NREM) sleep The period during which a sleeper does not show rapid eye movement; characterized by less dream activity than REM sleep.

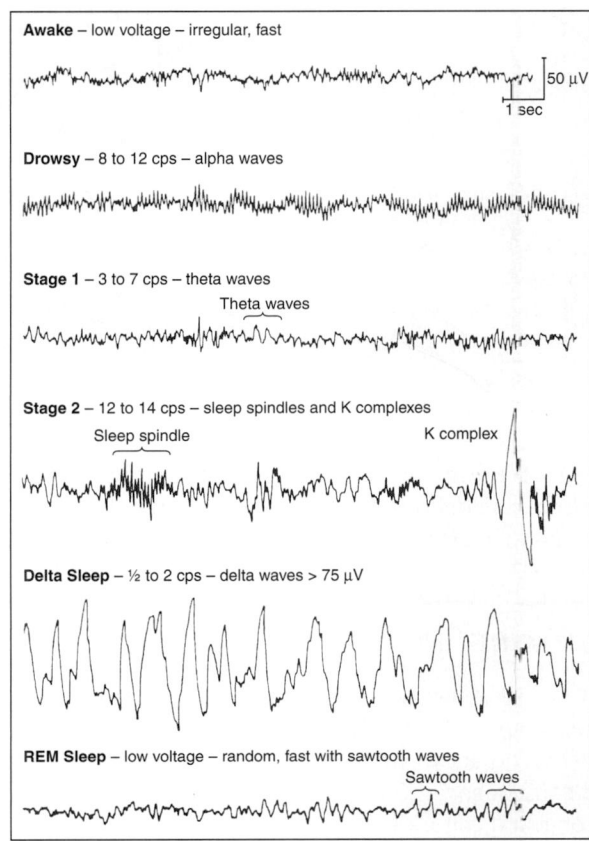

FIGURE 6.2

EEG Patterns Reflecting the Stages of a Regular Night's Sleep

Each sleep stage is defined by characteristic patterns of brain activity.

Cycling through the first four stages of sleep, which are NREM sleep, requires about 90 minutes. REM sleep lasts for about 10 minutes. Over the course of a night's sleep, you pass through this 100-minute cycle four to six times (see **Figure 6.3**). With each cycle, the amount of time you spend in deep sleep (stages 3 and 4) decreases, and the amount of time you spend in REM sleep increases. During the last cycle, you may spend as much time as an hour in REM sleep. NREM sleep accounts for 75 to 80 percent of total sleep time, and REM sleep makes up 20 to 25 percent of sleep time.

Not all individuals sleep for the same amount of time. Although there is a genetic sleep need programmed into the human species, the actual amount of sleep each individual obtains is highly affected by conscious actions. People actively control sleep length in a number of ways, such as by staying up late or using alarm clocks. Sleep duration is also controlled by circadian rhythms; that is, when one goes to sleep influences sleep duration. Getting adequate amounts of NREM and REM sleep

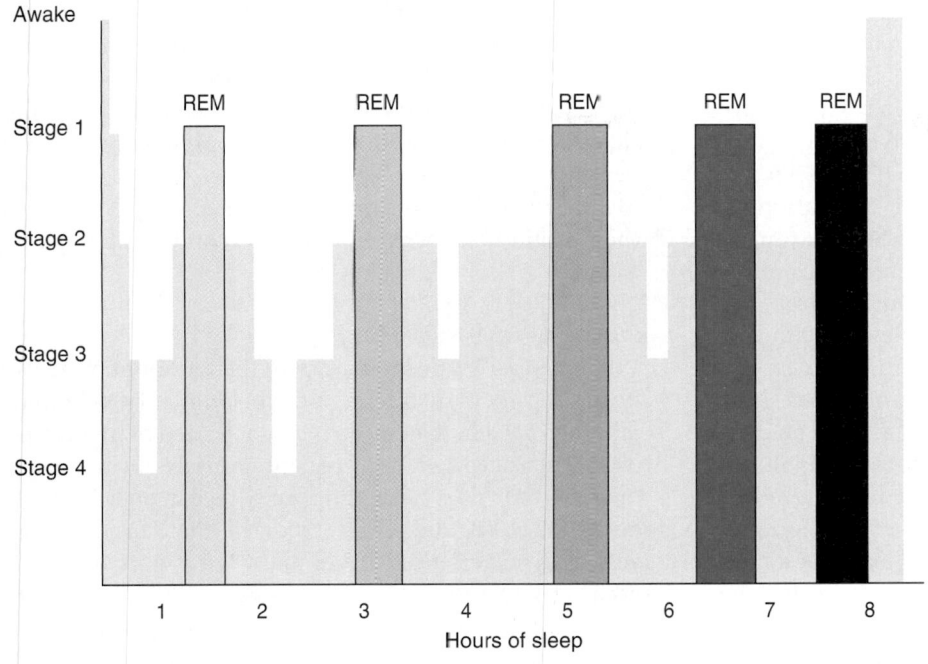

Awake

Stage 1

Stage 2

Stage 3

Stage 4

REM REM REM REM REM

1 2 3 4 5 6 7 8
Hours of sleep

FIGURE 6.3

Stages of Sleep

A typical pattern of the stages of sleep during a single night includes deeper sleep in the early cycles but more time in REM in the later cycles.

is only likely when you standardize your bedtime and rising time across the entire week, including weekends. In that way, the time you spend in bed is likely to correspond closely to the sleepy phase of your circadian rhythm.

Of further interest is the dramatic change in patterns of sleep that occurs over an individual's lifetime (shown in **Figure 6.4**). You started out in this world sleeping for about 16 hours a day, with nearly half of that time spent in REM sleep. By age 50, you may sleep only 6 hours and spend only about 20 percent of the time in REM sleep.

Young adults typically sleep 7 to 8 hours, with about 20 percent REM.

Why Sleep?

The orderly progression of stages of sleep in humans and other animals suggests that there is an evolutionary basis and a biological need for sleep. People function quite well when they get the time-honored seven to eight hours of sleep a night (Harrison & Horne, 1996). Why do humans

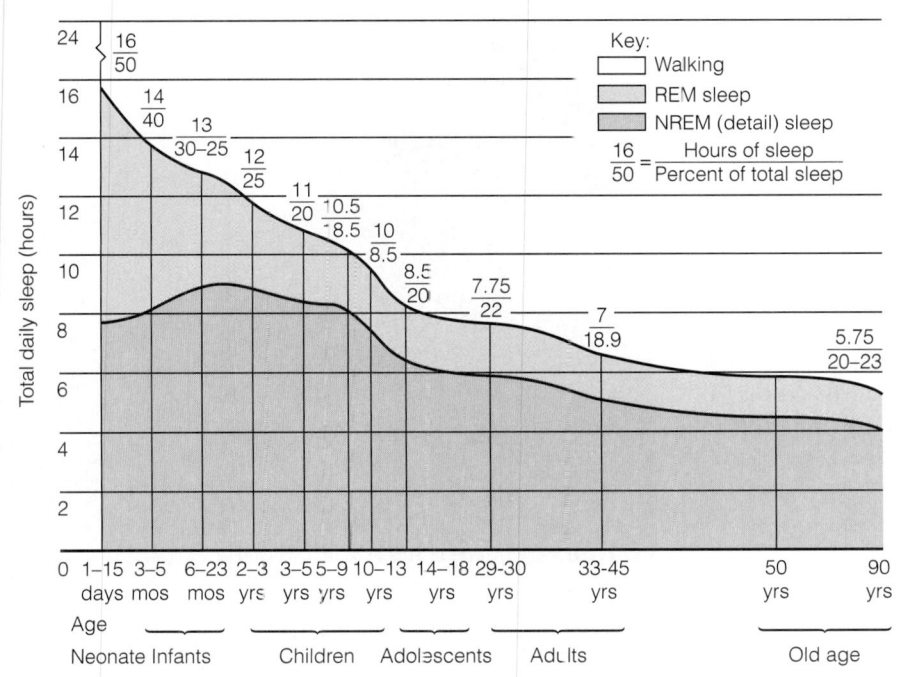

FIGURE 6.4

Patterns of Human Sleep Over a Lifetime

The graph shows changes with age in total amounts of daily REM sleep and NREM sleep and percentage of REM sleep. Note that the amount of REM sleep decreases considerably over the years, and NREM diminishes less sharply.

sleep so much and what functions do types of sleep— NREM and REM—serve?

The two most general functions for NREM sleep may be *conservation* and *restoration*. Sleep may have evolved because it enabled animals to conserve energy at times when there was no need to forage for food, search for mates, or work (Allison & Cicchetti, 1976; Cartwright, 1982; Webb, 1974). On the other hand, sleep also enables the body to engage in housekeeping functions and to *restore* itself in any of several ways. During sleep, neurotransmitters and neuromodulators may be synthesized to compensate for the quantities used in daily activities, and postsynaptic receptors may be returned to their optimal level of sensitivity (Porkka-Heiskanen et al., 1997; Rainnie et al., 1994). Research evidence also suggests that the brain's energy supply is replenished during NREM sleep (Benington & Heller, 1995).

If you were to be deprived of REM sleep for a night, you would have more REM sleep than usual the next night, suggesting that REM sleep also serves some necessary functions. A number of interesting, but not yet fully demonstrated, benefits have been attributed to REM sleep (Moffitt et al., 1993). For example, it appears that, during infancy, REM sleep is responsible for establishing the pathways between your nerves and muscles that enable you to move your eyes. REM sleep may establish functional structures in the brain, such as those involving the learning of motor skills. REM sleep can also play a role in the maintenance of mood and emotion, and it may be required for storing memories and fitting recent experiences into networks of previous beliefs or memories (Cartwright, 1978; Dement, 1976). On the physiological side, researchers have suggested that REM sleep may be necessary to restore the brain's balance after NREM sleep: The unusual type of brain activity characteristic of NREM sleep may, for example, change the balance of brain function in ways that must be returned to normal by REM sleep (Benington & Heller, 1994).

Sleep Disorders

It would be nice if you could always take a good night's sleep for granted. Unfortunately, many people suffer from sleep disorders that pose a serious burden to their personal lives and careers. Disordered sleep can also have societal consequences. Of those individuals whose work schedules include night shifts, more than half nod off at least once a week on the job. Some of the world's most serious industrial accidents—Three Mile Island,

Chernobyl, Bhopal, and the *Exxon Valdez* disaster—have occurred during late evening hours. People have speculated that these accidents occurred because key personnel failed to function optimally as a result of insufficient sleep. Because sleep disorders are important in many students' lives, we will review them here. As you read, remember that sleep disorders vary in severity. Similarly, their origins vary between biological and psychological forces.

INSOMNIA

When people are dissatisfied with their amount or quality of sleep, they are suffering from **insomnia**. This chronic failure to get adequate sleep is characterized by an inability to fall asleep quickly, frequent arousals during sleep, or early-morning awakening. In a recent poll, 58% of adults ages 18 and older reported that, in the past year, they experienced insomnia a few nights or more each week (National Sleep Foundation, 2000). Insomnia is a complex disorder caused by a variety of psychological, environmental, and biological factors (Spielman & Glovinsky, 1997). However, when insomniacs are studied in sleep laboratories, the objective quantity and quality of their actual sleep varies considerably, from disturbed sleep to normal sleep. Research has revealed that many insomniacs who complain of lack of sleep actually show completely normal physiological patterns of sleep—a condition described as subjective insomnia. Equally curious is the finding that some people who show detectable sleep disturbances report no complaints of insomnia (Trinder, 1988). The discrepancies may result from dif-

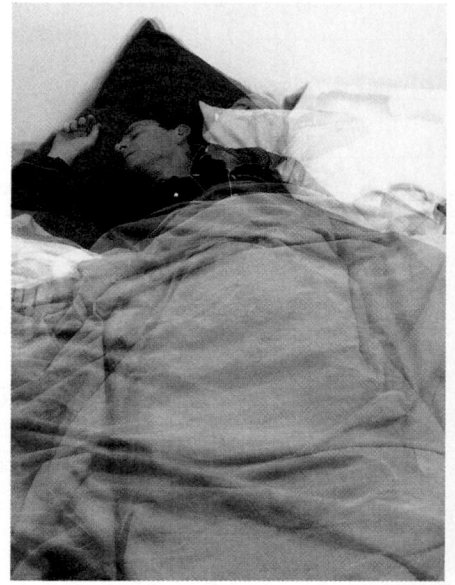

What is the relationship between actual sleep patterns and people's perceptions of insomnia?

Insomnia The chronic inability to sleep normally; symptoms include difficulty in falling asleep, frequent waking, inability to return to sleep, and early-morning awakening.

ferences in the way people recall and interpret a state of light sleep. For example, they may recall light sleep as much more frequent and distressing than it was and have no memory of having slept deeply.

NARCOLEPSY

Narcolepsy is a sleep disorder characterized by periodic sleep during the daytime (Aldrich, 1992). It is often combined with *cataplexy,* muscle weakness or a loss of muscle control brought on by emotional excitement (such as laughing, anger, fear, surprise, or hunger) that causes the afflicted person to fall down suddenly. When they fall asleep, narcoleptics enter REM sleep almost immediately. This rush to REM causes them to experience—and be consciously aware of—vivid dream images or sometimes terrifying hallucinations. Narcolepsy affects about 1 of every 2,000 individuals. Because narcolepsy runs in families, scientists believe the disease has a genetic basis (Mignot, 1998). Narcolepsy often has a negative social and psychological impact on sufferers, because of their desire to avoid the embarrassment of sudden bouts of sleep (Broughton & Broughton, 1994). Narcoleptics can benefit from recognizing the nature of their disease and belonging to social support groups.

SLEEP APNEA

Sleep apnea is an upper-respiratory sleep disorder in which the person stops breathing while asleep. When this happens, the blood's oxygen level drops and emergency hormones are secreted, causing the sleeper to awaken and begin breathing again. Although most people have a few such apnea episodes a night, someone with sleep apnea disorder can have hundreds of such cycles every night. Sometimes apnea episodes frighten the sleeper, but often they are so brief that the sleeper fails to attribute accumulating sleepiness to them (Orr, 1997). Consider, for example, the case of a famous psychologist who, as a product of undetected sleep apnea, could not stay awake during research meetings and lectures. When his wife made him aware of his disturbing nighttime behavior, he went to a sleep disorder clinic that was able to provide a successful treatment that reinvigorated his career (Zimbardo, personal communication, 1991). In other similar cases, people have lost their jobs, friends, and even spouses because their daytime behavior was so disrupted by their nighttime disorder.

Apnea during sleep is also frequent in premature infants, who sometimes need physical stimulation to start breathing again. Because of their underdeveloped respiratory system, these infants must remain attached to monitors in intensive care nurseries as long as the problem continues.

DAYTIME SLEEPINESS

The major complaint of the majority of patients evaluated at U.S. sleep disorder centers is excessive daytime sleepiness. Among a sample of over 1,154 adults in the United States, 43% indicated that a few days or more each month they are so sleepy that their daily activities are disturbed; 20% indicated that daytime sleepiness has a negative impact on their daily activities a few days or more each *week* (National Sleep Foundation, 2000). Excessive sleepiness causes diminished alertness, delayed reaction times, and impaired performance on motor and cognitive tasks. In earlier research, nearly half the patients with excessive sleepiness reported having been involved in automobile accidents, and more than half have had job accidents, some serious (Roth et al., 1989).

In preparing *Sleep Alert,* a documentary film on this sleep deprivation disorder, psychologist **James Maas** reported that "there are some people who are literally walking zombies" (Maas, 1998). He learned of airline pilots who told of falling asleep on the job for short naps, only to find the rest of the crew napping when they awoke. According to Maas, as many as 30 percent of high school students fall asleep in class once a week. Some degree of sleepiness is to be expected when individuals' lifestyles or job requirements prohibit them from getting sufficient nocturnal sleep. Excessive sleepiness, however, often has physiological roots, and sufferers should seek medical attention (White & Mitler, 1997).

Dreams: Theater of the Mind

During every ordinary night of your life, you enter into the complex world of dreams. Once the province only of prophets, psychics, and psychoanalysts, dreams have become a vital area of study for scientific researchers. Much dream research begins in sleep laboratories, where experimenters can monitor sleepers for REM and NREM sleep. Although individuals report more dreams when they are awakened from REM periods—on about 82 percent of their awakenings—dreaming also takes place during NREM periods—on about 54 percent of awakenings (Foulkes, 1962). Dreaming associated with NREM states is less likely to contain story content that is emotionally involving. It is more akin to daytime thought, with less sensory imagery. However, NREM dreaming is enhanced in those with sleep disorders and in normal sleepers during the very late morning hours (Kondo et al., 1989).

Narcolepsy A sleep disorder characterized by an irresistible compulsion to sleep during the daytime.

Sleep apnea A sleep disorder of the upper respiratory system that causes the person to stop breathing while asleep.

Daytime sleepiness The experience of excessive sleepiness during daytime activities; the major complaint of patients evaluated at sleep disorder centers.

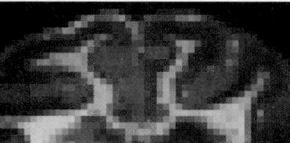

THE 24/7 LIFESTYLE AND SLEEP

Ten or twenty years ago there was very little to do after midnight. When students had finished with their schoolwork, they could pretty much choose between watching late-night television or rolling into bed. By contrast, the last decade of the 20th century brought into existence the World Wide Web and, along with it, a 24/7 supply of stimulation. At any time of day or night, you can cruise the Web or join a chat room. You can finish your midnight snack in Berlin, Connecticut, at the same time you chat with someone eating an early breakfast in Berlin, Germany.

The growth of the internet has amplified what we might characterize as many people's love-hate relationship with sleep. People love to sleep because being rested feels good (and being sleepy feels awful). As we've seen in this chapter, your body *needs* sleep to function effectively. However, people hate to sleep because there are so many enjoyable things to do while they are awake. The World Wide Web increases substantially the range of enjoyable things to do. Your textbook authors are willing to admit that they have purposefully lost sleep rather than discontinue cruising the Web.

From the point of view of many researchers, the 24/7 availability of the Web has only made a bad situation worse. They have been worried for several years that adolescents and college students do not get nearly enough sleep (Dement & Vaughan, 1999; Wolfson & Carskadon, 1998). Although experts recommend that everyone get 8 hours of sleep, a year-2000 poll carried out by the National Sleep Foundation (2000) suggests that the average 18- to 29-year old never meets this standard. During weekdays, the average duration of sleep for individuals in this age range is 6.8 hours; on weekends, this increases to 7.8 hours. No doubt many college students lose sleep because of the stresses associated with studying for exams and writing papers (Murphy & Archer, 1996). However, 55% of the poll participants in the 18-to-29 range agreed to the statement that they "of-ten stay up later than they should because they are watching TV or are on the Internet." Does this apply to you?

We are not trying to discourage you from using the Internet. We are simply offering the observation that new technologies often seem to bring with them new reasons for people to lose sleep. Sleepiness has many serious consequences: lower grades, work problems, and car accidents are just a few. So far, scientists have been able to invent pills that can stop you from sleeping—but none that can stop you from *needing* sleep. You should determine what personal steps you can take so that the 21st century doesn't become your Century of Sleeplessness.

Web sites:

- www.sleepfoundation.org, the home page for the National Sleep Foundation
- www.stanford.edu/~dement, a page created William Dement, a pioneering sleep researcher, that provides a good deal of basic information and links about sleep

---

Because dreams have such prominence in people's mental lives, virtually every culture has arrived at the same question: Do these dreams have significance? The answer that has almost always emerged is "yes." That is, most cultures encode the belief that, in one way or another, dreams have important personal and cultural meaning. We now review some of the ways in which cultures attach meaning to dreams.

FREUDIAN DREAM ANALYSIS

The most prominent theory in modern Western culture was originated by Sigmund Freud. Freud called dreams "transient psychoses" and models of "everynight madness." He also called them "the royal road to the unconscious." He made the analysis of dreams the cornerstone of psychoanalysis with his classic book *The Interpretation of Dreams* (1900/1965). Freud saw dream images as symbolic expressions of powerful, unconscious, repressed wishes. These wishes appear in disguised form because they harbor forbidden desires, such as sexual yearning for the parent of the opposite sex. The two dynamic forces operating in dreams are, thus, the *wish* and the *censorship,* a defense against the wish. The censor transforms the hidden meaning, or **latent content,** of the dream into **manifest content,** which appears to the dreamer after a distortion process that Freud referred to as **dream work.** The manifest content is the acceptable version of the story; the latent content represents the socially or personally unacceptable version but also the true, "uncut" one.

According to Freud, the interpretation of dreams requires working backward from the manifest content to the latent content. To the psychoanalyst who uses dream analysis to understand and treat a patient's problems,

Latent content In Freudian dream analysis, the hidden meaning of a dream.

Manifest content In Freudian dream analysis, the surface content of a dream, which is assumed to mask the dream's actual meaning.

Dream work In Freudian dream analysis, the process by which the internal censor transforms the latent content of a dream into manifest content.

dreams reveal the patient's unconscious wishes, the fears attached to those wishes, and the characteristic defenses the patient employs to handle the resulting psychic conflict between the wishes and the fears. Freud believed in both idiosyncratic—special to particular individuals—and universal meanings—many of a sexual nature—for the symbols and metaphors in dreams:

> Boxes, cases, chests, cupboards and ovens represent the uterus, and also hollow objects, ships, and vessels of all kinds. Rooms in dreams are usually women; if the various ways in and out of them are represented, this interpretation is scarcely open to doubt.... A dream of going through a suite of rooms is a brothel or harem dream.... It is highly probable that all complicated machinery and apparatus occurring in dreams stand for the genitals (and as a rule male ones)....(Freud, 1900/1965, pp. 389–391)

Freud's theory of dream interpretation related dream symbols to his explicit theory of human psychology. Although researchers have not found evidence to support Freud's theory of latent and manifest content, his emphasis on the psychological importance of dreams pointed the way to contemporary examinations of dream content (Domhoff, 1996; Fisher & Greenberg, 1996).

NON-WESTERN APPROACHES TO DREAM INTERPRETATION

Many people in Western societies may never think seriously about their dreams until they become students of psychology or enter therapy. By contrast, in many non-Western cultures, dream interpretation is part of the very fabric of the culture (Lewis, 1995; Tedlock, 1987). Consider the daily practice of the Archur Indians of Ecuador (Schlitz, 1997, p. 2):

> Like every other morning, the men [of the village] sit together in a small circle.... They share their dreams from the night before. This daily ritual of dream-sharing is vital to the life of the Archur. It is their belief that each individual dreams, not for themselves, but for the community as a whole. Individual experience serves collective action.

During these morning gatherings, each dreamer tells his dream story and the others offer their interpretations, hoping to arrive at some consensus understanding of the meaning of the dream. Contrast the belief that individuals dream "for the community as a whole" with the view articulated by Freud, that dreams are the "royal road" to the individual unconscious.

In many cultures, specific groups of individuals are designated as possessing special powers to assist with dream interpretation. Consider the practices of Mayan Indians who live in various parts of Mexico, Guatemala, Belize, and Honduras. In the Mayan culture, *shamans* function as dream interpreters. In fact, among some subgroups of Mayans, the shamans are selected for these roles when they have dreams in which they are visited by deities who announce the shaman's calling. Formal instruction about religious rituals is also provided to these newly selected shamans by way of dream revelation. Although the shamans, and other religious figures, have special knowledge relevant to dream interpretation, ordinary individuals also recount and discuss dreams. Dreamers commonly wake their spouses in the middle of the night to narrate dreams; mothers in some communities ask their children each morning to talk about their dreams. In contemporary times, the Mayan people have been the victims of civil war in their homelands; many people have been killed or forced to flee. One important response, according to anthropologist **Barbara Tedlock,** has been "an increased emphasis on dreams and visions that enable them to stay in touch with their ancestors and the sacred earth on which they live" (Tedlock, 1992, p. 471).

The cultural practices of many non-Western groups with respect to dreams also reflect a fundamentally different time perspective. Freud's theory had dream interpretation looking backwards in time, toward childhood experiences and repressed wishes. In many other cultures, dreams are believed instead to present a vision of the future (Basso, 1987). For example, among the people of the Ingessana Hills, a region along the border of Ethiopia and the Sudan, the timing of festivals is determined by dream visions (Jedrej, 1995). The keepers of religious shrines are visited in their dreams by their fathers and other ancestors who instruct them to "announce the festival." Other groups have culturally given systems of relationships between dream symbols and meanings. Consider these interpretations from the Kapolo Indians of central Brazil (Basso, 1987, p. 104):

> When we dream we are burnt by fire, later we will be bitten by a wild thing, by a spider or a stinging ant, for example.
> When [we dream] we are making love to women, we will be very successful when we go fishing.
> When a boy is in seclusion and he dreams of climbing a tall tree, or another one sees a long path, they will live long. This would also be true if we dreamt of crossing a wide stream in a forest.

Note how each of these interpretations looks to the future. The future orientation of dream interpretation is an important component of a rich cultural tradition.

PHYSIOLOGICAL THEORIES OF DREAM CONTENT

The cornerstone of both Western and non-Western approaches to dream interpretation is that dreams provide information that is of genuine value to the person or community. This view has faced a challenge from biologically based theories. Recall that some researchers believe that you have a physiological need for REM sleep to offset the brain changes of NREM sleep (Benington & Heller, 1994). Are dreams merely the side effects of other brain activities—with no special meaning of their own? Consider the *activation-synthesis model* proposed by **J. Allan Hobson** and **Robert McCarley** (1977; Hobson, 1988). This model suggests that neural signals emerge from the brain stem and then stimulate areas of the brain's cortex. These electrical discharges occur automatically about every 90 minutes and stay activated for 30 minutes or so—accounting for the cyclic alternation of REM and NREM sleep periods. These discharges activate the forebrain and association areas of the cortex; at that point, they trigger memories and connections with the dreamer's past experiences. According to Hobson and McCarley's view, there are no logical connections, no intrinsic meaning, and no coherent patterns to these random bursts of electrical "signals."

The idea that dreams originate from random signals, however, is contradicted by studies of dream content (Domhoff, 1999). Those studies suggest, first, that the content of dreams shows a good deal of continuity with dreamers' waking concerns. Recall, for example, the study we cited earlier that reported gender differences between boys' and girls' thoughts about their same-sex and opposite-sex friends (Richards et al., 1998). Dream studies with 9- to 15-year olds demonstrate similar gender differences in dream content about peers (Strauch & Lederbogen, 1999). A second type of finding also challenges the suggestion that dreams are merely random signals: Across adulthood, the overall content of individuals' dreams stays very much the same. Dream expert **William Domhoff** (1999, p. 207) concludes that "the consistency of dream content over years and decades in adults are not findings that fit easily into a theory that sees dreams as the best that the cortex can do in reaction to periodic bombardments by random stimuli from the pontine region of the brainstem." You might consider keeping your own dream log—try to write down dreams as soon as you wake up each morning—to see both how your own dreams relate to daily concerns and how your dream content changes or remains stable over time.

Another interesting aspect of dreams: Over time, many people have reported that the solutions to important problems or interesting new ideas came to them in their dreams (Shepard, 1978). We offer a small number of examples. Friedrich Kekulé reported that he discovered the elusive chemical structure of benzene in a dream: A snakelike molecule chain suddenly grabbed its own tail, thus forming a ring. Elias Howe had a dream—he was being attacked with spears with holes through their points—that allowed him to perfect his invention of the sewing machine. Composers such as Mozart and Schumann have reported that important musical ideas came to them in their dreams.

NIGHTMARES

When a dream frightens you by making you feel helpless or out of control, you are having a *nightmare*. For most people nightmares are relatively infrequent. In one sample of 220 undergraduates who kept daily dream logs,

the average frequency of nightmares (projected from a two-week sample period) was about 24 a year (Wood & Bootzin, 1990). However, some people experience nightmares more frequently, sometimes as often as every night. Children, for example, are more likely to experience nightmares than are adults (Mindell, 1997). Also, people who have experienced traumatic events, such as rape or war, may have repetitive nightmares that force them to relive some aspects of their trauma. College students who experienced a major earthquake in the San Francisco Bay area were about twice as likely to experience nightmares as a matched group of students who hadn't experienced an earthquake—and, as you might imagine, many of the nightmares were about the devastating effects of earthquakes (Wood et al., 1992).

We can consider nightmares to be at the outer limit of sleep as an everyday change in consciousness. We turn now to circumstances in which individuals deliberately seek to go beyond those everyday experiences.

SUMMING UP

Circadian rhythms reflect the operation of a biological clock. Patterns of brain activity change dramatically over the course of a night's sleep, with the percentage of REM sleep (versus NREM sleep) in each cycle increasing toward morning. The amount of sleep people need, and the ratio of REM to NREM sleep, changes both in response to aging and life circumstances. Sleep serves conservation and restoration functions. Millions of people suffer from the sleep disorders of insomnia, narcolepsy, sleep apnea, and daytime sleepiness. Many cultures believe in the importance of the content of dreams. Sigmund Freud proposed the best known Western theory of dream interpretation. Dream interpretation in non-Western cultures is quite common, with dream symbols often interpreted as providing information about the dreamer's future. Some physiological researchers have suggested that the origin of dream content is initially random signals in the brain, but those suggestions are contradicted by analyses of dream content. Nightmares are particularly frightening dreams.

Altered States of Consciousness

In every culture, people have been dissatisfied with ordinary transformations of their waking consciousness. They have developed practices that take them beyond familiar forms of consciousness to experiences of altered states of consciousness. Some of these practices are individual, such as taking recreational drugs. Others, such as certain religious practices, are shared attempts to transcend the normal boundaries of conscious experience. We survey a variety of such practices in which altered states of consciousness are induced by a range of procedures.

Lucid Dreaming

Is it possible to be aware that you are dreaming while you are dreaming? Proponents of the theory of **lucid dreaming** have demonstrated that being consciously aware that one is dreaming is a learnable skill—perfected with regular practice—that enables dreamers to control the direction of their dreams (Gackenbach & LaBerge, 1988; LaBerge & DeGarcia, 2000).

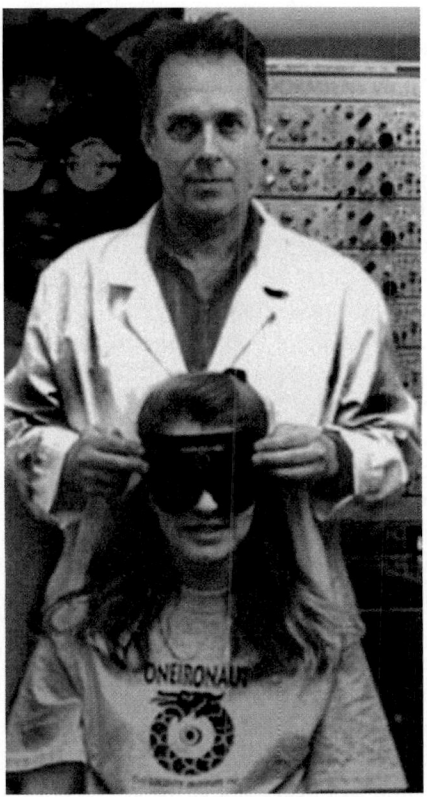

Researcher Stephen LaBerge adjusts the special goggles that will alert the sleeping participant that REM sleep is occurring. The individual is trained to enter into a state of lucid dreaming, being aware of the process and content of dream activity. If you had the ability to experience lucid dreaming, in what ways would you shape your dreams?

HOW WE KNOW

THE EXPERIMENTAL REALITY OF LUCID DREAMING Stephen LaBerge and his colleagues devised a methodology that enabled them to test the reality of reports of lucid dreaming. The demonstration relied on previous research that had shown that some of the eye movements of REM sleep correspond to the reported direction of the dreamer's gaze. The researchers therefore asked experienced lucid dreamers to execute distinctive patterns of *voluntary* eye movements when they realized that they were dreaming. The prearranged eye movement signals appeared on the polygraph records during REM, thus demonstrating that the participants had indeed been lucid during REM sleep (LaBerge et al., 1981).

A variety of methods have been used to induce lucid dreaming. For example, in some lucid dreaming research, sleepers wear specially designed goggles that flash a red light when they detect REM sleep. The participants have learned previously that the red light is a cue for becoming consciously aware that they are dreaming (LaBerge & Levitan, 1995). Once aware of dreaming, yet still not awake, sleepers move into a state of lucid dreaming in which they can take control of their dreams, directing them according to their personal goals and making the dreams' outcomes fit their current needs. The ability to have lucid dreams reportedly increases when sleepers firmly believe that such dreams are possible and regularly practice the induction techniques (LaBerge & Rheingold, 1990). Researchers such as Stephen LaBerge argue that gaining control over the "uncontrollable" events of dreams is healthy because it enhances self-confidence and generates positive experiences for the individual. However, some therapists who use dream analysis as part of their understanding of a patient's problems oppose such procedures because they feel that they distort the natural process of dreaming.

Hypnosis

As portrayed in popular culture, hypnotists wield vast power over their witting or unwitting participants. Is this view of hypnotists accurate? What is hypnosis, what are its important features, and what are some of its valid psychological uses? The term **hypnosis** is derived from Hypnos, the name of the Greek god of sleep. Sleep, however,

Lucid dreaming The theory that conscious awareness of dreaming is a learnable skill that enables dreamers to control the direction and content of their dreams.

Hypnosis An altered state of awareness characterized by deep relaxation, susceptibility to suggestions, and changes in perception, memory, motivation, and self-control.

plays no part in hypnosis, except that people may in some cases give the *appearance* of being in a deeply relaxed, sleeplike state. (If people were really asleep, they could not respond to hypnosis.) A broad definition of hypnosis is that it is an alternative state of awareness characterized by the special ability some people have of responding to suggestion with changes in perception, memory, motivation, and sense of self-control (Orne, 1980). In the hypnotic state, participants experience heightened responsiveness to the hypnotist's suggestions—they often feel that their behavior is performed without intention or any conscious effort (Hilgard, 1968).

Researchers have often disagreed about the psychological mechanisms involved in hypnosis (Kirsch & Lynn, 1995, 1998). Some early theorists suggested that hypnotized individuals enter into a *trance* state, far different from waking consciousness. Others argued that hypnosis was nothing more than heightened motivation. Still others believed it to be a type of social role playing, a kind of *placebo* response of trying to please the hypnotist (see Chapter 2). In fact, research has largely ruled out the idea that hypnosis involves a special, trancelike change in consciousness. However, even though nonhypnotized individuals can produce some of the same patterns of behavior as hypnotized individuals, there appear to be some added effects of hypnosis—beyond motivational or placebo processes. After we discuss hypnotic induction and hypnotizability, we describe some of those effects.

HYPNOTIC INDUCTION AND HYPNOTIZABILITY

Hypnosis begins with a *hypnotic induction,* a preliminary set of activities that minimizes external distractions and encourages participants to concentrate only on suggested stimuli and believe that they are about to enter a special state of consciousness. Induction activities involve suggestions to imagine certain experiences or to visualize events and reactions. When practiced repeatedly, the induction procedure functions as a learned signal so that participants can quickly enter the hypnotic state. The typical induction procedure uses suggestions for deep relaxation, but some people can become hypnotized with an active, alert induction—such as imagining that they are jogging or riding a bicycle (Banyai & Hilgard, 1976).

Stage performances of hypnosis give the impression that the power of hypnosis lies with the hypnotist. However, the single most important factor in hypnosis is a participant's ability or "talent" to become hypnotized. **Hypnotizability** represents the degree to which an individual is responsive to standardized suggestions to experience hypnotic reactions. There are wide individual differences in susceptibility, varying from a complete lack of responsiveness to total responsiveness.

Hypnotizability The degree to which an individual is responsive to standardized hypnotic suggestion.

Figure 6.5 shows the percentage of college-age individuals at various levels of hypnotizability the first time they were given a hypnotic induction test. What does it mean to have scored "high" or "very high" on this scale? When the test is administered, the hypnotist makes a series of posthypnotic suggestions, dictating the experiences each individual might have. When the hypnotist suggested that their extended arms had turned into bars of iron, highly hypnotizable individuals were likely to find themselves unable to bend those arms. With the appropriate suggestion, they were likely to brush away a nonexistent fly. As a third example, highly hypnotizable individuals probably couldn't nod their heads "no" when the hypnotist suggested they had lost that ability. Students who scored "low" on the hypnotizability scale experienced few if any of these reactions.

Hypnotizability is a relatively stable attribute. An adult's scores remain about the same when measured various times over a 10-year period (Morgan et al., 1974). In fact, when 50 men and women were retested 25 years after their college hypnotizability assessment, the results indicated a remarkably high correlation coefficient of .71 (Piccione et al., 1989). Children tend to be more suggestible than adults; hypnotic responsiveness peaks just before adolescence and declines thereafter. There is some evidence for genetic determinants of hypnotizability, because the scores of identical twins are more similar than are those of fraternal twins (Morgan et al., 1970). Although hypnotizability is relatively stable, it is not correlated with any personality trait like gullibility or conformity (Fromm & Shor, 1979; Kirsch & Lynn, 1995). Rather, hypnotizability reflects a unique cognitive ability to become completely absorbed in an experience.

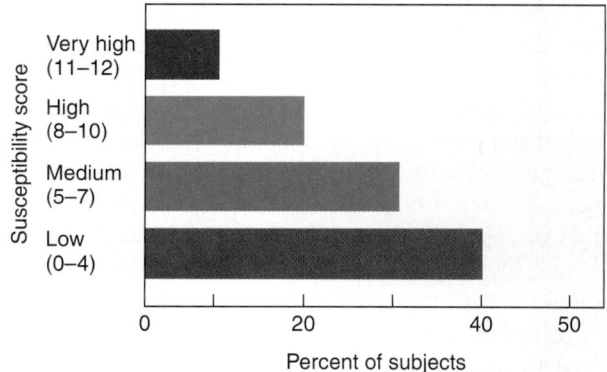

FIGURE 6.5

Level of Hypnosis at First Induction

The graph shows the results for 533 individuals hypnotized for the first time. Hypnotizability was measured on the Stanford Hypnotic Susceptibility Scale, which consists of 12 items.

In describing the way in which hypnotizability is measured, we already mentioned some of the standard effects of hypnosis: While under hypnosis, individuals respond to suggestions about motor abilities (for example, their arms become unbendable) and perceptual experiences (for example, they hallucinate a fly). How can we be sure, however, that these behaviors arise from special properties of hypnosis and not just a strong willingness on participants' part to please the hypnotist? To address this important question, researchers have often conducted experiments that contrast the performance of truly hypnotized individuals to that of *simulators*.

HOW WE KNOW

HYPNOSIS IS MORE THAN SIMULATION

Two groups of students participated in an experiment. One group was truly hypnotized. The other group was instructed to *simulate* hypnosis: They were instructed by a first experimenter that it was their task to fool a second experimenter into believing that they were, in fact, hypnotized. Both groups were then exposed to a series of tones, and asked to judge their loudness. An important part of the experiment was a *demand* instruction, in which the participants were told what they *should* experience (Reed et al., 1996, p. 143):

> People who are exposed to the tone more than once tend to drift back into hypnosis, and this greatly reduces the intensity of the sound that they hear. You probably drifted back into hypnosis on this last trial, and for this reason, heard very little of the tone. Perhaps you didn't hear it at all.

If all the effects of hypnosis can be attributed to participants' desire to respond correctly to experimenter demands, we would expect hypnotized and simulating participants to respond in the same way to this demand. In fact, they do not. Truly hypnotized individuals gave a wider variety of reports: They told something closer to their true experiences, rather than inventing something they thought the experimenter wanted to hear (Reed et al., 1996).

In this case, simulators presumably guess incorrectly what they would be experiencing were they truly hypnotized. From experiments of this type, we can learn exactly what independent contribution hypnosis makes to people's experiences.

An undisputed value of hypnosis is its ability to reduce pain (*hypnotic analgesia*). Your mind can amplify pain stimuli through anticipation and fear; you can diminish this psychological effect with hypnosis (Chaves, 1999.) Pain control is accomplished through a variety of hypnotic suggestions: imagining the part of the body in pain as nonorganic (made of wood or plastic) or as separate from the rest of the body, taking one's mind on a vacation from the body, and distorting time in various ways. People can control pain through hypnosis even when they banish all thoughts and images from consciousness (Hargadon et al., 1995). Hypnosis has proven especially valuable to surgery patients who cannot tolerate anesthesia, to mothers in natural childbirth, and to cancer patients learning to endure the pain associated with the disease and its treatment. Self-hypnosis (*autohypnosis*) is the best approach to controlling pain because patients can then exert control whenever pain arises. In a study of 86 women with metastatic cancer, those using self-hypnosis for pain control reported having only half as much pain as others (Spiegel et al., 1989).

Researchers have used pain reduction to demonstrate that hypnosis produces effects beyond the willingness of participants to play along with what they or the experimenter expects.

HOW WE KNOW

HYPNOSIS REDUCES PAIN Excruciating muscle pain was delivered to volunteers. The individuals' ability to tolerate the pain was measured during three experimental sessions: (1) with highly motivating instructions; (2) following the induction of hypnotic analgesia; and (3) after ingesting a placebo capsule described as painkilling medication. The contrast between (1) and (2) allows for an assessment of the effects of hypnosis beyond the participants' desire to do well in the experiment. The contrast between (2) and (3) allows for a demonstration that hypnosis is more than a placebo effect. The experimenter who actually tested people did not know which had ingested the placebo pill and was misled to believe that hypnotic analgesia worked for all of them. In fact, half of the 24 participants were highly hypnotizable, and the other half scored low on the scale.

The placebo pill significantly reduced pain in all participants, beyond the level of the motivating instructions. In addition, expecting hypnosis to reduce pain also had a significant effect on all participants—a placebo expectancy effect. However, pain tolerance for the highly hypnotizable participants during the hypnotic analgesia induction period was significantly greater than for the low hypnotizables and for any of the other conditions—hypnosis is not just a placebo (McGlashan et al., 1978).

For highly hypnotizable individuals, pain reduction is achieved more efficiently through hypnotic suggestion than through other pain reduction techniques (Miller & Bowers, 1993).

One final note on hypnosis: The power of hypnosis does *not* reside in some special ability or skill of the hypnotist, but rather it resides in the relative hypnotizability of the person or persons being hypnotized. Being hypnotized does not involve giving up one's personal control; instead, the experience of being hypnotized allows an individual to learn new ways to exercise control that the hypnotist—as coach—can train the subject—as performer—to enact. You should keep all of this in mind if you watch a stage show in which people perform outlandish acts under hypnosis: Stage hypnotists make a living entertaining audiences by getting highly exhibitionist people to do things in public that most others could never be made to do. As used by researchers and therapists, hypnosis is a technique with the potential to allow you to explore and modify your sense of consciousness.

Meditation

Many religions and traditional psychologies of the East work to direct consciousness away from immediate worldly concerns. They seek to achieve an inner focus on the mental and spiritual self. **Meditation** is a form of consciousness change designed to enhance self-knowledge and well-being by achieving a deep state of tranquility. During meditation, a person may focus on and regulate breathing, assume certain body positions (yogic positions), minimize external stimulation, generate specific mental images, or free the mind of all thought.

There is some controversy over the measurable effects of meditation. Critics have suggested that there are few physiological differences between a normal "eyes-closed" resting state and the special procedures of meditation (Holmes, 1984). However, advocates of meditation suggest that the true physiology of meditation can be characterized as *restful alertness,* a state of lower bodily arousal but heightened awareness (Dillbeck & Orme-Johnson, 1987; Morrell, 1986). Thus, meditation will at least reduce anxiety, especially in those who function in stress-filled environments (Anderson et al., 1999; Shapiro et al., 1998). The goal, however, is for meditative practices to be more than just time-outs from tension. Practicers of meditation have suggested that, when practiced regularly, some forms of meditation can heighten consciousness, help achieve *enlightenment* by enabling

How does meditation create an altered state of consciousness?

the individual to see familiar things in new ways, and free perception and thought from the restrictions of automatic, well-learned patterns. Some researchers have suggested that the regular practice of meditation moves the mind beyond the limits recognized by Western psychology—and may even result in increases in measured intelligence (IQ; see Chapter 10) and cognitive performance (Cranson et al., 1991). A foremost Buddhist teacher of meditation, Nhat Hanh (1991), recommends awareness of breathing and simple appreciation of your surroundings and minute daily acts as a path to psychological equilibrium.

Hallucinations

Under unusual circumstances, a distortion in consciousness occurs during which an individual sees or hears things that are not actually present. **Hallucinations** are vivid perceptions that occur in the absence of objective stimulation; they are a mental construction of an individual's altered reality. They differ from illusions, which are perceptual distortions of real stimuli. Consider **Figure 6.6.** Most people see a triangle in this figure, although it is not "really" there. However, we would not want to call this a hallucination, because, as we explained in Chapter 5, the triangle "appears" because of the normal processes you use to perceive the world. You could not make this illusory triangle disappear by reminding

■ **Meditation** A form of consciousness alteration designed to enhance self-knowledge and well-being through reduced self-awareness.
■ **Hallucinations** False perceptions that occur in the absence of objective stimulation.

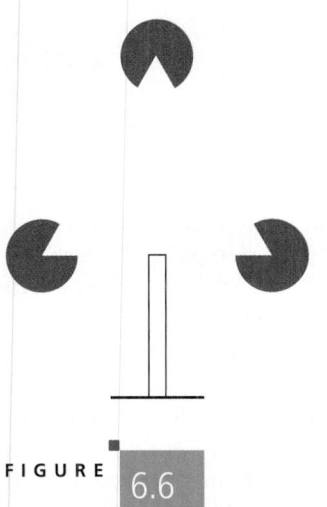

FIGURE 6.6

An Illusion, Not a Hallucination!

Although it is not really there, most people see a triangle in this figure. When people hallucinate, they also have experiences that are not really there. However, the hallucinations arise from individuals' altered states of consciousness rather than from shared perceptual processes.

yourself that it is not real. By contrast to illusions, hallucinations are individual experiences, not shared by others in a situations. Some hallucinations are short-lived; if individuals can swiftly demonstrate to themselves the unreality of a hallucination—by evaluating it against reality—the experience can come to an end. In some cases, however, individuals cannot dispel the "reality" of their hallucinations, and the hallucinations wield an influence on their lives (Siegel, 1992).

Hallucinations are fostered by heightened arousal, states of intense need, or the inability to suppress threatening thoughts. They also occur when the brain experiences an unusual type of stimulation—during, for example, high fevers, epileptic seizures, and migraine headaches—or in patients with severe mental disorders, who respond to private mental events as if they were external sensory stimuli. Hallucinations are also frequently induced by psychoactive drugs, such as LSD and peyote, as well as by withdrawal from alcohol in severe cases of alcoholism (these hallucinations are known as *delirium tremens*, "the DTs"). These chemically induced hallucinations are prompted by direct effects of the drugs on the brain.

In some cultural or religious settings, hallucinations are a desirable and important occurrence (Siegel, 1992). In these circumstances, hallucinations are interpreted as mystical insights that confer special status on the visionary. So, in different settings, the same vivid perception of direct contact with spiritual forces may be deprecated as a sign of mental illness or respected as a sign of special gifts. Evaluation of such mental states often depends as much on the judgment of observers as on the content of the perceptual experience itself.

Religious Ecstasy

Meditation, prayer, fasting, and spiritual communication all contribute to intense *religious experiences*. For William James (1902), religious experiences constituted unique psychological experiences characterized by a sense of oneness and relatedness of events, of realness and vividness of experiences, and an inability to communicate, in ordinary language, the nature of the whole experience. For many people, religious experiences are clearly not part of their ordinary consciousness.

There are few religious experiences more intense than those of the Holy Ghost people of Appalachia. Their beliefs and practices create a unique form of consciousness that enables them to do some remarkable things. At church services, they handle deadly poisonous snakes, drink strychnine poison, and handle fire. To prepare for these experiences, they listen to long sermons and participate in loud, insistent singing and wild spinning and dancing:

> *The enthusiasm may verge on violence.... Members wail and shake and lapse into the unintelligible, ecstatic "new tongues" of glossolalia [artificial speech with no linguistic content].... The ecstasy spreads like contagion.... Their hands are definitely cold, even after handling fire. This would correspond with research in trance states involved in other religious cultures. It would also account for the vagueness of memory,*

The Holy Ghost people of Appalachia and other religious sects engage in such practices as snake handling to prove faith and achieve changes in consciousness. Rayford Dunn was bitten on the hand by this cottonmouth snake moments after this picture was taken in Kingston, Georgia. Although he behaved normally afterward—going out to eat and returning to church the next day to handle snakes again—some believers have died from poisonous snake bites. Have you ever been in a situation in which the strength of your beliefs led you to experience an altered state of consciousness?

almost sensory amnesia, that researchers have reported in serpent handlers as well as fire handlers. (Watterlond, 1983, pp. 53, 55)

Psychological research on serpent-handling religious-group members has found them to be generally well-adjusted people who receive powerful social and psychological support from being part of the group. Participating in the "signs of the spirits" gives them a "personal reward equaled in no other aspect of their lives" (Watterlond, 1983).

Mind-Altering Drugs

Since ancient times, people have taken drugs to alter their perception of reality. There is archaeological evidence for the uninterrupted use of sophora seed (mescal bean) for over 10,000 years in the southwestern United States and Mexico. The Ancient Aztecs fermented mescal beans into a beer. From ancient times, individuals in North and South America also ingested *teonanacatl*, the Psilocybe mushroom also known as "the flesh of the gods," as parts of rituals. Small doses of these mushrooms produce vivid hallucinations.

In Western cultures, drugs are associated less with sacred communal rituals than with recreation. Individuals throughout the world take various drugs to relax, cope with stress, avoid facing the unpleasantness of current realities, feel comfortable in social situations, or experience an alternate state of consciousness. Over a hundred years ago, William James—whom we have cited several times as a founder of psychology in the United States—reported on his experiments with a mind-altering drug. After inhaling nitrous oxide, James explained that "the keynote of the experience is the tremendously exciting sense of intense metaphysical illumination. Truth lies open to the view in depth beneath depth of almost blinding evidence. The mind sees all the logical relations of being with an apparent subtlety and instantaneity to which its normal consciousness offer no parallel" (James, 1882, p. 186). Thus, James's interest in the study of consciousness extended to the study of self-induced alternate states.

Psychoactive drugs Chemicals that affect mental processes and behavior by temporarily changing conscious awareness of reality.

Tolerance A situation that occurs with continued use of a drug in which an individual requires greater dosages to achieve the same effect.

Physiological dependence The process by which the body becomes adjusted to and dependent on a drug.

Addiction A condition in which the body requires a drug in order to function without physical and psychological reactions to its absence; often the outcome of tolerance and dependence.

Psychological dependence The psychological need or craving for a drug.

Using drugs to alter consciousness was popularized by the publication of *The Doors of Perception* by Aldous Huxley (1954). Huxley took mescaline as an experiment on his own consciousness. A few decades after Huxley's book appeared, 6.2 percent of U.S. citizens, in a 1998 survey with nearly 25,500 respondents age 12 and older, reported using one or more illicit drugs during the past year (Substance Abuse and Mental Health Services Administration [SAMHSA], 1999). The rate was much higher for people in their late teen years—16.4 percent of 16- to 17-year-olds and 19.9 percent of 18- to 20-year-olds reported some type of drug use. In addition, 51.7 percent of the individuals in the sample consumed alcohol sometime in the year before the survey and 27.7 percent smoked cigarettes. These figures suggest why an understanding of the causes and consequences of drug use is such an urgent part of researchers' agendas.

DEPENDENCE AND ADDICTION

Psychoactive drugs are chemicals that affect mental processes and behavior by temporarily changing conscious awareness. Once in the brain, they attach themselves to synaptic receptors, blocking or stimulating certain reactions. By doing so, they profoundly alter the brain's communication system, affecting perception, memory, mood, and behavior. However, continued use of a given drug creates **tolerance**—greater dosages are required to achieve the same effect. (We describe some of the psychological roots of tolerance in Chapter 7.) Hand in hand with tolerance is **physiological dependence,** a process in which the body becomes adjusted to and dependent on the substance, in part because neurotransmitters are depleted by the frequent presence of the drug. The tragic outcome of tolerance and dependence is **addiction.** A person who is addicted requires the drug in his or her body and suffers painful withdrawal symptoms (shakes, sweats, nausea, and, in the case of alcohol withdrawal, even death) if the drug is not present.

When an individual finds the use of a drug so desirable or pleasurable that a *craving* develops, with or without addiction, the condition is known as **psychological dependence.** Psychological dependence can occur with any drug. The result of drug dependence is that a person's lifestyle comes to revolve around drug use so wholly that his or her capacity to function is limited or impaired. In addition, the expense involved in maintaining a drug habit of daily—and increasing—amounts often drives an addict to robbery, assault, prostitution, or drug peddling. One of the gravest dangers currently facing addicts is the threat of getting AIDS by sharing hypodermic needles—intravenous drug users can unknowingly share bodily fluids with those who have this deadly immune deficiency disease.

Teenagers who use illicit drugs to relieve emotional distress and to cope with daily stressors suffer long-term negative consequences.

THE CONSEQUENCES OF DRUG ABUSE An eight-year study of teenage drug use starting in 1976, with 1,634 junior high school students from Los Angeles, collected complete annual data on 739 participants. While fewer than 10 percent of those studied were regular or chronic drug users, fewer than 10 percent reported not using any drugs. The results can be grouped into four major findings (Newcomb & Bentler, 1988; Stacy et al., 1991).

- Daily drug use had a negative impact on personal and social adjustment, disrupting relationships, reducing educational potential, increasing nonviolent crime, and encouraging disorganized thinking.

- Hard drugs, such as stimulants and narcotics, increased suicidal and self-destructive thoughts while reducing social support, thereby promoting loneliness.

- Drug effects varied with type of drug and mixed use of drugs, so that cocaine increased confrontations and weakened close relationships, but the combination of hard drugs and cigarettes was most damaging to psychological and physical health.

- Surprisingly, teenagers who used alcohol moderately and no other drugs showed increased social integration and increased self-esteem. These students may have been better adjusted to begin with than their peers.

VARIETIES OF PSYCHOACTIVE DRUGS

Common psychoactive drugs are listed in **Table 5.1.** (In Chapter 16, we will discuss other types of psychoactive drugs that are used to relieve mental illness.) We will briefly describe how each class of drugs achieves its physiological and psychological impact. We also note the personal and societal consequences of drug use.

The most dramatic changes in consciousness are produced by drugs known as *hallucinogens* or *psychedelics;* these drugs alter both perceptions of the external environment and inner awareness. As the name implies, these drugs often create hallucinations and a loss of the boundary between self and nonself. The four most commonly known hallucinogens are *mescaline* (from cactus plants), *psilocybin* (from a mushroom), and *LSD* and *PCP,* which are synthesized in laboratories. PCP, or *angel dust,* produces a particularly strange dissociative reaction in which the user becomes insensitive to pain, becomes confused, and feels apart from his or her surroundings. Hallucinogenic drugs act in the brain at specific receptor sites for the chemical neurotransmitter serotonin (Aghajanian & Marek, 1999).

Cannabis is a plant with psychoactive effects. Its active ingredient is THC, found in both *hashish* (the solidified resin of the plant) and *marijuana* (the dried leaves and flowers of the plant). The experience derived from inhaling THC depends on its dose—small doses create mild, pleasurable highs, and large doses result in long hallucinogenic reactions. Regular users report euphoria, feelings of well-being, distortions of space and time, and, occasionally, out-of-body experiences. However, depending on the context, the effects may be negative—fear, anxiety, and confusion. Researchers have known for several years that *cannabinoids,* the active chemicals in marijuana, bind to specific receptors in the brain—these cannabinoid receptors are particularly common in the hippocampus, the brain region involved in memory. Only in the last decade, however, has research uncovered *anandamide,* a neurotransmitter that binds to the same receptors (Di Marzo et al., 1994; Stahl, 1998). That is, cannabinoids achieve their mind-altering effects at brain sites sensitive to anandamide, a naturally occurring substance in the brain. Scientists have also discovered that *chocolate* contains substances that affect the brain's use of anandamide (di Tomaso et al., 1996)! Molecules in chocolate may either bind to cannabinoid receptors or influence the size of neural responses. These molecules are not found in white chocolate—which may explain why people crave milk chocolate and dark chocolate more often.

Opiates, such as *heroin* and *morphine,* suppress physical sensation and response to stimulation. The initial effect of an intravenous injection of heroin is a rush of pleasure—feelings of euphoria supplant all worries and awareness of bodily needs. Heroin use often leads to addiction. In Chapter 3, we noted that the brain contains endorphins (short for *endogenous morphines*) that generate powerful effects on mood, pain, and pleasure. Drugs like opium and morphine bind to the same receptor sites in the brain (Harrison et al., 1998; Reisine, 1995). Thus, both opiates and, as we described in the previous paragraph, marijuana achieve their effects because they have active components that have similar chemical properties to substances that naturally occur in the brain. When the neural receptors are artificially stimulated by mind-altering drugs, the brain loses its subtle balance.

The *depressants* include *barbiturates* and, most notably, *alcohol.* These substances tend to depress (slow down) the mental and physical activity of the body by inhibiting or decreasing the transmission of nerve impulses in the central nervous system. Depressants achieve this effect, in part, by facilitating neural communication at synapses that use the neurotransmitter GABA (Delaney & Sah, 1999; Malizia & Nutt, 1995). GABA often functions to inhibit neural transmission, which explains depressants' inhibiting outcomes. Barbiturates can be quite dangerous. In a 15-year study, barbiturates were responsible for roughly half of all drug overdoses (Howard, 1984). Commonly prescribed depressants, such as *Valium* and *Xanax,* have

TABLE 6.1

Psychoactive Drugs: Medical Uses, Duration, and Dependencies

	Medical Uses	Duration of Effect (hours)	Dependence Psychological	Physiological
Opiates (Narcotics)				
Morphine	Painkiller	3–6	High	High
Heroin	Under investigation	3–6	High	High
Codeine	Painkiller, cough suppressant	3–6	Moderate	Moderate
Hallucinogens				
LSD	None	8–12	None	Unknown
PCP (Phencyclidine)	Veterinary anesthetic	Varies	Unknown	High
Mescaline (Peyote)	None	8–12	None	Unknown
Psilocybin	None	4–6	Unknown	Unknown
Cannabis (Marijuana)	Nausea associated with chemotherapy	2–4	Low–Moderate	Unknown
Depressants				
Barbiturates (for example, Seconal)	Sedative, sleeping pill, anesthetic, anticonvulsant	1–16	Moderate–High	Moderate–High
Benzodiazepines (for example, Valium)	Antianxiety, sedative, sleeping pill, anticonvulsant	4–8	Low–Moderate	Low–Moderate
Alcohol	Antiseptic	1–5	Moderate	Moderate
Stimulants				
Amphetamines	Hyperkinesis, narcolepsy, weight control	2–4	High	High
Cocaine	None	1–2	High	High
Nicotine	Nicotine gum for cessation of smoking habit	Varies	Low–High	Moderate–High
Caffeine	Weight control, stimulant in acute respiratory failure, analgesic	4–5	Unknown	Moderate

considerable potential to bring about addiction (Miller, 1999).

Alcohol was apparently one of the first psychoactive substances used extensively by early humans. Under its influence, some people become silly, boisterous, friendly, and talkative; others become abusive and violent; still others become quietly depressed. Researchers still do not understand the exact way in which alcohol wields its effects on the brain, although, as with other depressants, it appears to affect GABA activity (De Witte, 1996). At small dosages, alcohol can induce relaxation and slightly improve an adult's speed of reaction. However, the body can break down alcohol only at a slow rate, and large amounts consumed in a short time period overtax the central nervous system. Driving accidents and fatalities occur six times more often to individuals with 0.10 percent alcohol in their bloodstream than to those with half that amount. Another way alcohol intoxication contributes to accidents is by dilating the pupils of the eyes, thereby causing night vision problems. When the level of alcohol in the blood reaches 0.15 percent, there are gross negative effects on thinking, memory, and judgment, along with emotional instability and loss of motor coordination.

Excess consumption of alcohol is a major social problem in the United States. Alcohol-related automobile accidents are the leading cause of death among people between the ages of 15 and 25. When the amount and frequency of drinking interferes with job performance, impairs social and family relationships, and creates serious health problems, the diagnosis of *alcoholism* is appropriate. Physical dependence, tolerance, and addiction all develop with prolonged heavy drinking. For some individuals, alcoholism is associated with an inability to abstain from drinking. For others, alcoholism manifests itself as an inability to stop drinking once the person takes a few drinks. In the 1998 survey, 13.8 percent of 18- to 25-year-olds reported heavy drinking—defined as drinking five or more drinks on the same occasion on each of five or more days in a 1-month period (SAMHSA, 1999). However, for all ages, the average is much higher for men (9.7 percent) than women (2.4 percent).

Stimulants, such as *amphetamines* and *cocaine,* keep the drug user aroused and induce states of euphoria. Stimulants achieve their effects by increasing the brain levels of neurotransmitters such as norepinephrine, serotonin, and dopamine. For example, stimulants act in the brain to pre-

Why does alcohol remain the most popular way in which college students alter their consciousness?

vent the action of molecules that ordinarily remove dopamine from synapses (Giros et al., 1995). Long-term abuse of cocaine may produce changes in the brain systems that regulate the experience of pleasure (Gawin, 1991). Stimulants have three major effects that users seek: increased self-confidence, greater energy and hyperalertness, and mood alterations approaching euphoria. Heavy users experience frightening hallucinations and develop beliefs that others are out to harm them. These beliefs are known as *paranoid delusions*. A special danger with cocaine use is the contrast between euphoric highs and very depressive lows. This leads users to increase uncontrollably the frequency of drug use and the dosage. A highly purified form of cocaine is *crack*, a particularly destructive street drug. It produces a swift high that wears off quickly. Because it is sold in small, cheap quantities that are readily available to the young and the poor, crack is destroying many social communities.

Two stimulants that you may often overlook as psychoactive drugs are *caffeine* and *nicotine*. As you may know from experience, two cups of strong coffee or tea administer enough caffeine to have a profound effect on heart, blood, and circulatory functions and make it difficult for you to sleep. Nicotine, a chemical found in tobacco, is a sufficiently strong stimulant to have been used in high concentrations by Native American shamans to attain mystical states or trances. Unlike some modern users, however, the shamans knew that nicotine is addictive, and they carefully chose when to be under its influence. Like other addictive drugs, nicotine mimics natural chemicals released by the brain. In fact, research has uncovered common regions of brain activation for addiction to nicotine

and cocaine (Pich et al., 1997). Chemicals in nicotine stimulate receptors that make you feel good whenever you have done something right—a phenomenon that aids survival. Unfortunately, nicotine teases those same brain receptors into responding as if it were good for you to be smoking. It's not. The total negative impact of nicotine on health is greater than that of all other psychoactive drugs combined, including heroin, cocaine, and alcohol. The U.S. Public Health Service attributes 400,000 deaths annually to cigarettes. Although smoking is the leading cause of preventable sickness and death, it is both legal and actively promoted—billions are spent annually on advertising. Although antismoking campaigns have been somewhat effective in reducing the overall level of smoking in the United States, some 60 million Americans still smoke (SAMHSA, 1999). Of the 2.1 million people who start smoking each year, many of them now are under 18. In part, this trend can be traced to targeted advertising that has often focused on youth: Noteworthy increases in teenage smoking have occurred in response to a series of major marketing campaigns (Pierce & Gilpin, 1995).

We began this chapter by asking you to consider the case of N. N.—and then to contrast his experience with your own ability to remember the past and plan for the future. We presented this case to demonstrate how activities that should strike you as quite ordinary would allow us nonetheless to pose some interesting questions about consciousness: Where did your thoughts come from? How did they emerge? Where did they arrive? You've now learned some of the theories that apply to these questions and how it has been possible to test those theories. You've seen that consciousness ultimately allows you to have the full range of experiences that define you as human.

We also asked you to consider some increasingly less ordinary uses of consciousness. Why, we asked, do people become dissatisfied with their everyday working minds and seek to alter their consciousness in so many ways? Ordinarily, your primary focus is on meeting the immediate demands of tasks and situations facing you. However, you are aware of these reality-based constraints on your consciousness. You realize they limit the range and depth of your experience and do not allow you to fulfill your potential. Perhaps, at times, you long to reach beyond the confines of ordinary reality. You seek the uncertainty of freedom instead of settling for the security of the ordinary.

SUMMING UP

Individuals in every culture seek means to alter consciousness. Lucid dreamers become aware that they are dreaming and can control the outcomes of their dreams. People differ with respect to how easy it is for them to become hypnotized. Researchers compare truly hypnotized individuals to simulating individuals to distinguish genuine effects of hypnosis from the responses people give to please the hypnotist. Hypnotism has proved to be a particularly powerful technique for pain reduction. People often have the experience of a "hidden observer," which represents a concealed, nonconscious awareness of experiences while under hypnosis.

Meditation can bring on changes of consciousness and may lead to other types of cognitive advances. Hallucinations represent vivid perceptual experiences in the absence of external stimulation. Some people have religious experiences that are not part of ordinary consciousness. The use of drugs as an extraordinary means of altering consciousness is often a dangerous act that can lead to addiction and even death. Drugs affect the central nervous system by stimulating, depressing, or altering neurotransmission.

RECAPPING
MAIN POINTS

The Contents of Consciousness

- Consciousness is an awareness of the mind's contents.
- Three levels of consciousness are: (1) a basic awareness of the world, (2) a reflection on what you are aware of, and (3) self-awareness.
- The contents of waking consciousness contrast with nonconscious processes, preconscious memories, unattended information, the unconscious, and conscious awareness.
- Research techniques such as think-aloud protocols and experience sampling are used to study the contents of consciousness.

The Functions of Consciousness

- Consciousness aids your survival and enables you to construct both personal and culturally shared realities.
- Researchers have studied the relationship between conscious and unconscious processes.

Sleep and Dreams

- Circadian rhythms reflect the operation of a biological clock.
- Patterns of brain activity change over the course of a night's sleep. REM sleep is signaled by rapid eye movements and accompanied by vivid dreaming. About one-fourth of sleep is REM, coming in four or five separate episodes.

- The amount of sleep and relative proportion of REM to NREM sleep change with age.
- REM and NREM sleep serve different functions, including conservation and restoration.
- Sleep disorders such as insomnia, narcolepsy, and sleep apnea have a negative impact on people's ability to function during waking time. Daytime sleepiness is also a widespread, serious problem.
- Freud proposed that the content of dreams is unconscious material slipped by a sleeping censor.
- In other cultures, dreams are interpreted regularly, often by people with special cultural roles, and they are used to foretell the future.
- Some dream theories have focused on biological explanations for the origins of dreams, but those theories are not entirely consistent with reports of dream content.

Altered States of Consciousness

- Lucid dreaming is an awareness that one is dreaming, in an attempt to control the dream.
- Hypnosis is an alternate state of consciousness characterized by the ability of hypnotizable people to change perception, motivation, memory, and self-control in response to suggestions.
- Meditation changes conscious functioning by ritual practices that focus attention away from external concerns to inner experience.

- Hallucinations are vivid perceptions that occur in the absence of objective stimulation.
- In some cultural groups, people undergo intense religious experiences.
- Psychoactive drugs affect mental processes by temporarily changing consciousness as they modify nervous system activity.
- Among psychoactive drugs that alter consciousness are hallucinogens, opiates, depressants, and stimulants.

Key Terms

addiction (p. 174)
circadian rhythm (p. 161)
consciousness (p. 155)
consensual validation (p. 158)
daytime sleepiness (p. 165)
dream work (p. 166)
experience-sampling method (p. 156)
hallucinations (p. 172)
hypnosis (p. 169)
hypnotizability (p. 170)
insomnia (p. 164)
latent content (p. 166)
lucid dreaming (p. 169)
manifest content (p. 166)
meditation (p. 172)
narcolepsy (p. 165)
nonconscious (p. 155)
non-REM (NREM) sleep (p. 162)
physiological dependence (p. 174)
preconscious memories (p. 155)
psychoactive drugs (p. 174)
psychological dependence (p. 174)
rapid eye movements (REM) (p. 162)
self-awareness (p. 155)
sleep apnea (p. 165)
think-aloud protocols (p. 156)
tolerance (p. 174)

learning and behavior analysis

7

■ **THE STUDY OF LEARNING**
What Is Learning? •
Behaviorism and
Behavior Analysis

■ **CLASSICAL CONDITIONING:
LEARNING PREDICTABLE
SIGNALS**
Pavlov's Surprising
Observation • Processes
of Conditioning • Focus
on Acquisition • Applications
of Classical Conditioning

■ **OPERANT CONDITIONING:
LEARNING ABOUT
CONSEQUENCES**
The Law of Effect •
Experimental Analysis of
Behavior • Reinforcement
Contingencies • Properties
of Reinforcers • Schedules
of Reinforcement • Shaping

■ **PSYCHOLOGY IN YOUR
LIFE: SPARE THE ROD,
SPOIL THE CHILD?**

■ **BIOLOGY AND LEARNING**
Instinctual Drift •
Taste-Aversion Learning

■ **COGNITIVE INFLUENCES
ON LEARNING**
Animal Cognition •
Observational Learning

■ **RECAPPING MAIN POINTS**
Key Terms

In his book *Lorenzo the Magnificent,* writer Robert Franklin Leslie describes the adventures of an injured blue jay, Lorenzo, who became a guest of the Leslie family. In this episode, Lorenzo learns a lesson that may be familiar to many of you (Leslie, 1985, pp. 83–85):

> When Lorenzo reached what we estimated to be adolescence, we pitched a party and invited some of his favorite human fans to what one guest called a jaybird Bar Mitzvah. *Among the goodies, all strong preferences of Lorenzo, we served sacramental wine and lox and bagels. Toward the end of the party, Lea [Leslie's wife] located the suddenly "missing" Lorenzo on the kitchen counter, where he was lapping away at the dregs of the wine glasses. At a call, everyone rushed in to witness a feathered creature plastered to the hilt. His boozy squawk sounded like a tape recording played at too slow a speed. Reeling backwards along the counter, Lorenzo fell heels over appetite into a sink half-full of sudsy detergent. While I held him under the faucet, he "mumbled" feebly and pecked his own toes.*

> *I set the bird on the linoleum floor because I dared not let him try wet wings in his condition. Lea placed a mirror in his path so he could see what he looked like. It was one of those magnifying mirrors men use when they trim a pencil-line mustache. Through droopy eyelids, our wet and miserable Lorenzo took one squinty look, staggered backwards, and crumpled into a fluttering heap of slow-motion blah! Caged immediately, he looked even worse.*

> *Next morning he made not the wheeziest peep. Once more our adventurous bird had acquired practical knowledge. I was ashamed to call the vet for aspirin information, revealing that Lea and I were nursing a bird with a hangover.*

> *Forever afterwards Lorenzo turned up his beak at fancy wines regardless of occasion. He even declined food items on his smorgasbord tray in the outdoor cage if any wine had been used in their preparation—except Lobster Newburg: his abstinence did not include absurdity.*

Why, with the one exception of Lobster Newburg, does Lorenzo avoid wine after this one fateful encounter with its effects? The answer that is probably coming to mind is that Lorenzo had learned a new association—in Leslie's words he "had acquired practical knowledge"—that he could apply later in his life. If you are impressed at how thoroughly Lorenzo learned his lesson, you might start to wonder about the processes at work here: How was Lorenzo able to learn this new association so easily? You can ask the same question with respect to the lessons you've learned in life: How do you acquire new associations? The main topic of Chapter 7 is the way your behavior is influenced by the types of learning that you undergo effortlessly in your day-to-day experience.

Psychologists have long been interested in **conditioning,** or the ways in which events and behavior become associated with one another. In this chapter, we will examine two basic types of conditioning: classical conditioning and operant conditioning. As you shall see, each of these types of conditioning represents a different way in which organisms acquire and use information about the structure of their environments. For each of these forms of conditioning, we will describe both the basic mechanisms that govern its operation in the laboratory and applications to real-life situations.

Before we begin our study in earnest, let's consider the significance of learning from an *evolutionary perspective.* Learning is as much a product of your genetic endowment as any other aspect of your experience. Humans, like other organisms, inherit a particular *capacity* for learning. The capacity for learning varies among animal species according to their genetic blueprint. Some creatures, such as reptiles and amphibians, learn little

■ **Conditioning** The ways in which events, stimuli, and behavior become associated with one another.

from interactions with the environment. Their survival depends on living in a relatively constant habitat, in which their innate responses to specific environmental events bring them to what they need or take them away from what they must avoid. For other animals including humans, genes play much less of a role in determining specific behavior-environment interactions and allow for greater *plasticity*, or variability, in learning. These animals are able to learn according to the ways in which their behavior produces changes in their environment. You should always bear in mind, however, that each of us has inherited only a capacity to learn. Whether that capacity is realized—and to what extent—depends on your personal experiences.

How does consistent form in ballet dancers fit the definition of learning?

The Study of Learning

To begin our exploration of learning, we will first define learning itself and then offer a brief sketch of the history of psychological research on the topic.

What Is Learning?

Learning is a process that results in a relatively consistent change in behavior or behavior potential and is based on experience. Let's look more closely at the three critical parts of this definition.

A CHANGE IN BEHAVIOR OR BEHAVIOR POTENTIAL
It is obvious that learning has taken place when you are able to demonstrate the results, such as when you drive a car or use a microwave oven. You can't directly observe learning itself—you can't ordinarily see the changes in your brain—but learning is apparent from improvements in your *performance*. Often, however, your performance doesn't show everything that you have learned. Sometimes, too, you have acquired general attitudes, such as an *appreciation* of modern art or an *understanding* of Eastern philosophy, that may not be apparent in your measurable actions. In such instances, you have achieved a potential for behavior change, because you have learned attitudes and values that can influence the kind of books you read or the way you spend your leisure time. This is an example of the **learning-performance distinction**—the difference between what has been learned and what is expressed, or performed, in overt behavior.

A RELATIVELY CONSISTENT CHANGE
To qualify as learned, a change in behavior or behavior potential must be relatively consistent over different occasions. Thus, once you learn to swim, you will probably always be able to do so. Note that consistent changes are not always permanent changes. You may, for example, have become quite a consistent dart thrower when you practiced every day. If you gave up the sport, however, your skills might have deteriorated toward their original level. But if you have learned once to be a championship dart thrower, it ought to be easier for you to learn a second time. Something has been "saved" from your prior experience. In that sense, the change may be permanent.

A PROCESS BASED ON EXPERIENCE
Learning can take place only through experience. Experience includes taking in information (and evaluating and transforming it) and making responses that affect the environment. Learning consists of a response influenced by the lessons of memory. Learned behavior does not include changes that come about because of physical maturation or brain development as the organism ages, nor those caused by illness or brain damage. Some lasting changes in behavior require a combination of experience and maturational readiness. For example, consider the timetable that determines when an infant is ready to crawl, stand, walk, run, and be toilet trained. No amount of training or practice will produce those behaviors before the child has matured sufficiently. Psychologists are especially interested in discovering what aspects of behavior can be changed through experience and how such changes come about.

Learning A process based on experience that results in a relatively permanent change in behavior or behavioral potential.
Learning-performance distinction The difference between what has been learned and what is expressed in overt behavior.

Behaviorism and Behavior Analysis

Much of modern psychology's view of learning finds its roots in the work of **John Watson** (1878–1958). Watson founded the school of psychology known as *behaviorism.* For nearly 50 years, American psychology was dominated by the behaviorist tradition expressed in Watson's 1919 book, *Psychology from the Standpoint of a Behaviorist.* Watson argued that introspection—peoples' verbal reports of sensations, images, and feelings—was *not* an acceptable means of studying behavior because it was too subjective. How could scientists verify the accuracy of such private experiences? But once introspection has been rejected, what should the subject matter of psychology be? Watson's answer was *observable behavior.* In Watson's words, "States of consciousness, like the so-called phenomena of spiritualism, are not objectively verifiable and for that reason can never become data for science" (Watson, 1919, p. 1). Watson also defined the chief goal of psychology as "the prediction and control of behavior" (Watson, 1913, p. 158).

B. F. Skinner (1904–1990) adopted Watson's cause and expanded his agenda. Over time, Skinner formulated a position known as *radical behaviorism.* Skinner acknowledged that evolution provided each species with a repertory of behaviors. He argued, most famously in the popular book *Beyond Freedom and Dignity* (1972), that all behavior beyond that repertory could be understood as the products of simple forms of learning.

Skinner began the research that would lead him to formulate this position when, after reading Watson's 1924 book, *Behaviorism,* he began his graduate study in psychology at Harvard. Skinner embraced Watson's complaint against internal states and mental events. However, Skinner focused not so much on their legitimacy as data as on their legitimacy as *causes of behavior* (Skinner, 1990). In Skinner's view, mental events, such as thinking and imagining, do not cause behavior. Rather, they are examples of behavior that are caused by environmental stimuli. Suppose that we deprive a pigeon of food for 24 hours, place it in an apparatus where it can obtain food by pecking a small disk, and find that it soon does so. Skinner would argue that the animal's behavior can be fully explained by environmental events—deprivation and the use of food as reinforcement. The subjective feeling of hunger, which cannot be directly observed or measured, is not a cause of the behavior, but the result of deprivation. It adds nothing to our account to say that the bird pecked the disk because it was hungry or because it wanted to get the food. To explain what the bird does, you need not understand anything about its

Behavior analysis The area of psychology that focuses on the environmental determinants of learning and behavior.

B. F. Skinner expanded on Watson's ideas and applied them to a wide spectrum of behavior. Why did Skinner's psychology focus on environmental events rather than on internal states?

inner psychological states—you need only understand the simple principles of learning that allow the bird to acquire the association between behavior and reward. This is the essence of Skinner's brand of behaviorism (Delprato & Midgley, 1992).

This same brand of behaviorism served as the original philosophical cornerstone of **behavior analysis,** the area of psychology that focuses on discovering environmental determinants of learning and behavior (Grant & Evans, 1994). In general, behavior analysts argue that human nature can be understood by using extensions of the methods and principles of natural science. The task is to discover regularities in learning that are universal, occurring in all types of animal species, including humans, under comparable situations. These researchers generally assume that elementary processes of learning are *conserved across species*—that is, across all animal species, these processes are comparable in their basic features. That is why studies with nonhuman animals have been so critical to progress in this area. Complex forms of learning represent combinations and elaborations of simpler processes and not qualitatively different phenomena. Behavior analysis seeks to identify the orderly principles that underlie changes in people's actions in response to their experience. The primary concern, once again, is the relationship between behavior and environmental events and not the relationship between behavior and mental events.

SUMMING UP

Learning is a process that results in a relatively consistent change in behavior or behavior potential and is based on experience. Behavior analysis follows from the theories of Watson and Skinner and focuses on discovering the environmental determinants of learning and behavior.

Classical Conditioning: Learning Predictable Signals

Imagine that you are in a movie theater watching a horror film. As the hero approaches a closed door, the music on the movie's sound track grows dark and menacing. You suddenly feel the urge to yell, "Don't go through that door!" Meanwhile, you find that your heart is racing, and you're sweating all over the theater's upholstery. But why? Somehow your body has learned to produce a physiological response (a racing heart) when one environmental event (for example, scary music) is associated with another (scary visual events). This type of learning is known as **classical conditioning**, a basic form of learning in which one stimulus or event predicts the occurrence of another stimulus or event. The organism learns a new *association* between two stimuli—a stimulus that did not previously elicit the response and one that naturally elicited the response. As you shall see, the innate capacity to quickly associate pairs of events in your environment has profound behavioral implications.

Pavlov's Surprising Observation

The first rigorous study of classical conditioning was the result of what may well be psychology's most famous accident. The Russian physiologist **Ivan Pavlov** (1849–1936) did not set out to study classical conditioning or any other psychological phenomenon. He happened on classical conditioning while conducting research on digestion, research for which he won a Nobel Prize in 1904.

Pavlov had devised a technique to study digestive processes in dogs by implanting tubes in their glands and digestive organs to divert bodily secretions to containers outside their bodies so that the secretions could be measured and analyzed. To produce these secretions Pavlov's assistants put meat powder into the dogs' mouths. After repeating this procedure a number of times, Pavlov ob-

served an unexpected behavior in his dogs—they salivated *before* the powder was put in their mouths! They would start salivating at the mere sight of the food and, later, at the sight of the assistant who brought the food or even at the sound of the assistant's footsteps. Indeed, any stimulus that regularly preceded the presentation of food came to elicit salivation. Quite by accident, Pavlov had observed that learning may result from two stimuli becoming associated with each other.

Fortunately, Pavlov had the scientific skills and curiosity to begin a rigorous attack on this surprising phenomenon. He ignored the advice of the great physiologist of the time, Sir Charles Sherrington, that he should give up his foolish investigation of "psychic" secretions. Instead, Pavlov abandoned his work on digestion and, in so doing, changed the course of psychology forever (Pavlov, 1928). For the remainder of Pavlov's life, he continued to search for the variables that influence classically conditioned behavior. Classical conditioning is also called *Pavlovian conditioning* because of Pavlov's discovery of the major phenomena of conditioning and his dedication to tracking down the variables that influence it.

Pavlov's considerable research experience allowed him to follow a simple and elegant strategy to discover the conditions necessary for his dogs to be conditioned to salivate. As shown in **Figure 7.1**, dogs in his experiments were first placed in a restraining harness. At regular intervals, a stimulus such as a tone was presented, and a dog was given a bit of food. Importantly, the tone had no prior meaning for the dog with respect to food or salivation. As you might imagine, the dog's first reaction to the tone was only an *orienting response*—the dog pricked its ears and moved its head to locate the source of the sound. However, with *repeated pairings* of the tone and the food, the orienting response stopped and salivation

Classical conditioning A type of learning in which a behavior (conditioned response) comes to be elicited by a stimulus (conditioned stimulus) that has acquired its power through an association with a biologically significant stimulus (unconditioned stimulus).

Physiologist Ivan Pavlov (shown here with his research team) observed classical conditioning while conducting research on digestion. What were some of Pavlov's major contributions to the study of this form of learning?

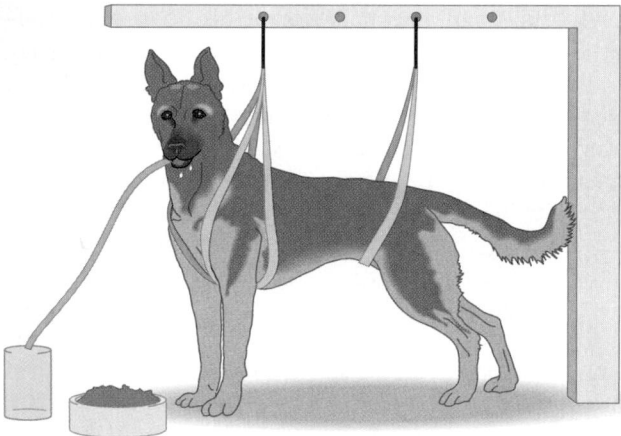

FIGURE 7.1

Pavlov's Original Procedure

In his original experiments, Pavlov used a variety of stimuli such as tones, bells, lights, and metronomes to serve as neutral stimuli. The experimenter presented one of these neutral stimuli and then the food powder. The dog's saliva was collected through a tube.

began. What Pavlov had observed in his earlier research was no accident: The phenomenon could be replicated under controlled conditions. Pavlov demonstrated the generality of this effect by using a variety of other stimuli ordinarily neutral with respect to salivation, such as lights and ticking metronomes.

The main features of Pavlov's classical conditioning procedure are illustrated in **Figure 7.2**. At the core of classical conditioning are reflex responses. A **reflex** is an unlearned response—such as salivation, pupil contraction, knee jerks, or eye blinking—that is naturally elicited by specific stimuli that are biologically relevant for the

Reflex An unlearned response elicited by specific stimuli that have biological relevance for an organism.

Unconditioned stimulus (UCS) In classical conditioning, the stimulus that elicits an unconditioned response.

Unconditioned response (UCR) In classical conditioning, the response elicited by an unconditioned stimulus without prior training or learning.

Conditioned stimulus (CS) In classical conditioning, a previously neutral stimulus that comes to elicit a conditioned response.

Conditioned response (CR) In classical conditioning, a response elicited by some previously neutral stimulus that occurs as a result of pairing the neutral stimulus with an unconditioned stimulus.

Acquisition The stage in a classical conditioning experiment during which the conditioned response is first elicited by the conditioned stimulus.

organism. Any stimulus, such as the food powder used in Pavlov's experiments, that naturally elicits a reflexive behavior is called an **unconditioned stimulus (UCS)**, because learning is not a necessary condition for the stimulus to control the behavior. The behavior elicited by the unconditioned stimulus is called the **unconditioned response (UCR)**.

In a typical classical conditioning experiment, a *neutral stimulus*—a stimulus, such as a light or a tone, that ordinarily has no meaning in the context of the UCS–UCR reflex—is repeatedly paired with the unconditioned stimulus so that the UCS predictably follows the neutral stimulus. The neutral stimulus, like the tone used in Pavlov's experiment, paired with the unconditioned stimulus is called the **conditioned stimulus (CS)**, because its power to elicit behavior like the UCR is *conditioned* on its association with the UCS. After several trials, the CS will produce a response called the **conditioned response (CR)**. Often, the conditioned response is similar to the unconditioned response. For Pavlov's dogs, both responses were salivation. In some cases, however, the CR is more dissimilar to the UCR: The conditioned response is whatever response the conditioned stimulus elicits as a product of learning. Let's review. Nature provides the UCS–UCR connections, but the learning produced by classical conditioning creates the CS–CR connection. The conditioned stimulus acquires some of the power to influence behavior that was originally limited to the unconditioned stimulus. Let's now look in more detail at the basic processes of classical conditioning.

Processes of Conditioning

How does the relative timing of the UCS and CS affect the success of classical conditioning? How fragile is the learning? How precise are the associations? In this section, we review answers to these questions that have emerged from hundreds of different studies across a wide range of animal species.

ACQUISITION AND EXTINCTION

Figure 7.3 displays a hypothetical classical conditioning experiment. The first panel displays **acquisition,** the process by which the CR is first elicited and gradually increases in frequency over repeated trials. In general, the CS and UCS must be paired several times before the CS reliably elicits a CR. With systematic CS–UCS pairings, the CR is elicited with increasing frequency, and the organism may be said to have acquired a conditioned response.

In classical conditioning, as in telling a good joke, *timing* is critical. The CS and UCS must be presented closely enough in time to be perceived by the organism as being related. (We will describe an exception to this rule

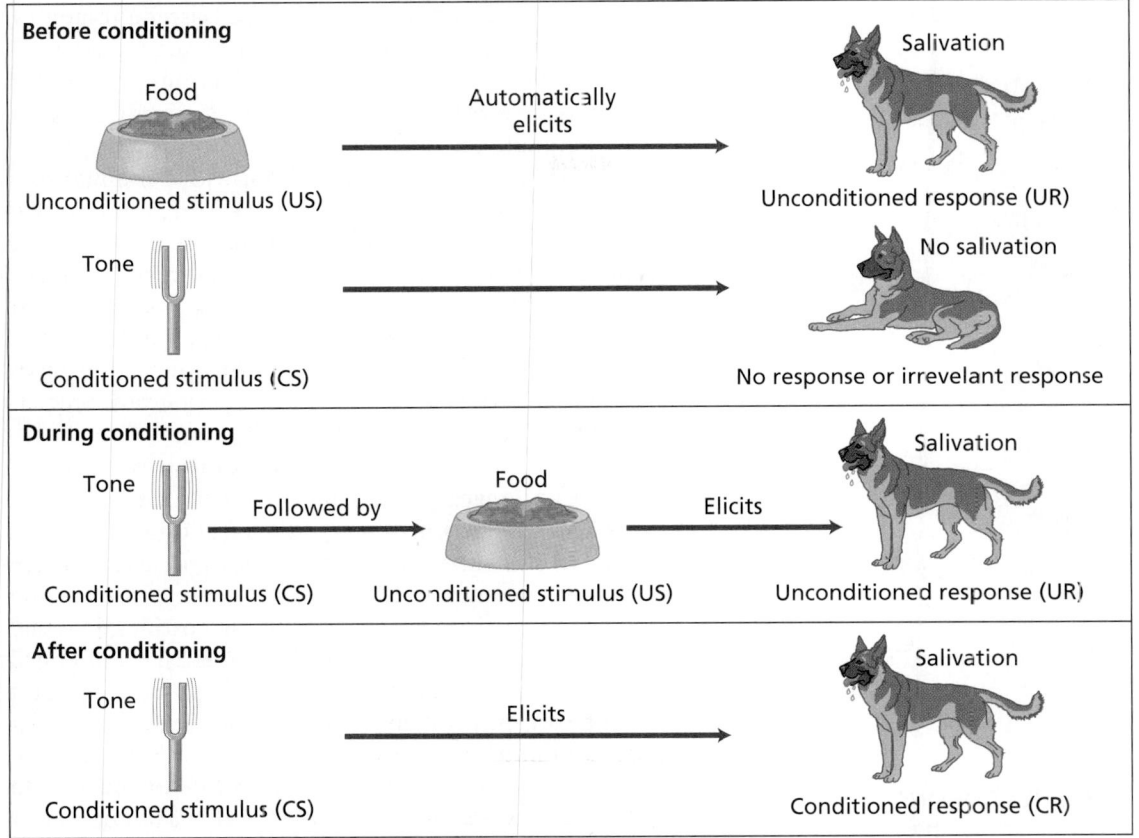

FIGURE 7.2

Basic Features of Classical Conditioning

Before conditioning, the unconditioned stimulus (UCS) naturally elicits the unconditioned response (UCR). A neutral stimulus, such as a tone, has no eliciting effect. During conditioning, the neutral stimulus is paired with the UCS. Through its association with the UCS, the neutral stimulus becomes a conditioned stimulus (CS) and elicits a conditioned response (CR) that is similar to the UCR.

in a later section on *taste-aversion learning*.) Researchers have studied four temporal patterns between the two stimuli, as shown in **Figure 7.4** (Hearst, 1988). The most widely used type of conditioning is called *delayed conditioning*, in which the CS comes on prior to and stays on at least until the UCS is presented. In *trace conditioning*, the CS is discontinued or turned off before the UCS is presented. *Trace* refers to the memory that the

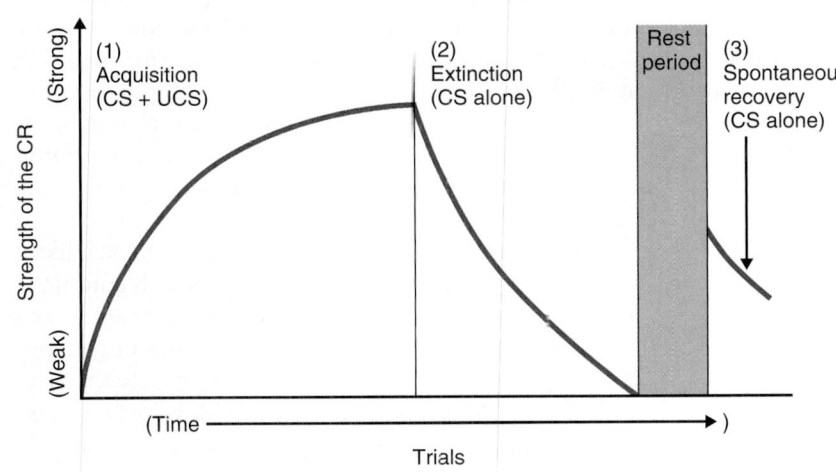

FIGURE 7.3

Acquisition, Extinction, and Spontaneous Recovery in Classical Conditioning

During acquisition (CS + UCS), the strength of the CR increases rapidly. During extinction, when the UCS no longer follows the CS, the strength of the CR drops to zero. The CR may reappear after a brief rest period, even when the UCS is still not presented. The reappearance of the CR is called spontaneous recovery.

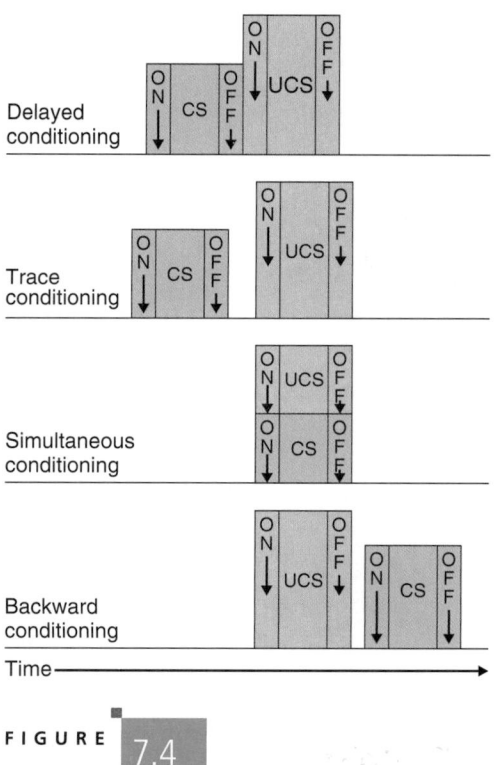

FIGURE 7.4

Four Variations of the CS–UCS Temporal Arrangement in Classical Conditioning

Researchers have explored the four possible timing arrangements between the CS and UCS. Conditioning is generally most effective in a delayed conditioning paradigm with a short interval between the onsets of the CS and UCS.

organism is assumed to have of the CS, which is no longer present when the UCS appears. In *simultaneous conditioning,* both the CS and UCS are presented at the same time. Finally, in the case of *backward conditioning,* the CS is presented after the UCS.

Conditioning is usually most effective in a delayed conditioning paradigm, with a short interval between the onsets of the CS and UCS. However, the exact time interval between the CS and the UCS that will produce optimal conditioning depends on several factors, including the intensity of the CS and the response being conditioned. Let's focus on the response being conditioned. For muscular responses, such as eye blinks, a short in-

Extinction In conditioning, the weakening of a conditioned association in the absence of a reinforcer or unconditioned stimulus.

Spontaneous recovery The reappearance of an extinguished conditioned response after a rest period.

Stimulus generalization The automatic extension of conditioned responding to similar stimuli that have never been paired with the unconditioned stimulus.

terval of a second or less is best. For visceral responses, such as heart rate and salivation, however, longer intervals of 5 to 15 seconds work best. Conditioned fear usually requires a longer interval still, of many seconds or even minutes, to develop.

Conditioning is generally poor with a simultaneous procedure and very poor with a backward procedure. Evidence of backward conditioning may appear after a few pairings of the UCS and CS but disappear with extended training as the animal learns that the CS is followed by a period free of the UCS. In both cases, conditioning is weak because the CS does not actually predict the onset of the UCS. (We will return to the importance of predictability, or *contingency,* in the next section.)

But what happens when the CS (for example, the tone) no longer predicts the UCS (the food powder)? Under those circumstances, the CR (salivation) becomes weaker over time and eventually stops occurring. When the CR no longer appears in the presence of the CS (and the absence of the UCS), the process of **extinction** is said to have occurred (see Figure 7.3, panel 2). Conditioned responses, then, are not necessarily a permanent aspect of the organism's behavioral repertoire. However, the CR will reappear in a weak form when the CS is presented alone again (see Figure 7.3, panel 3). Pavlov referred to this sudden reappearance of the CR after a rest period, or time-out, without further exposure to the UCS as **spontaneous recovery.**

When the original pairing is renewed, postextinction, the CR becomes rapidly stronger. This more rapid relearning is an instance of *savings:* Less time is necessary to reacquire the response than to acquire it originally. Thus, some of the original conditioning must be retained by the organism even after experimental extinction appears to have eliminated the CR. In other words, extinction has only weakened performance, not wiped out the original learning—this is why we made a distinction between learning and performance in our original definition of learning.

STIMULUS GENERALIZATION

Suppose we have taught a dog that presentation of a tone of a certain frequency predicts food powder. Is the dog's response specific to only that stimulus? If you think about this question for a moment, you will probably not be surprised that the answer is no. In general, once a CR has been conditioned to a particular CS, similar stimuli may also elicit the response. For example, if conditioning was to a high-frequency tone, a slightly lower tone could also elicit the response. A child bitten by a big dog is likely to respond with fear even to smaller dogs. This automatic extension of responding to stimuli that have never been paired with the original UCS is called **stimulus generalization.** The more similar the new stimulus is to the original CS, the stronger the response will be. When response strength is measured for each of a series of increasingly

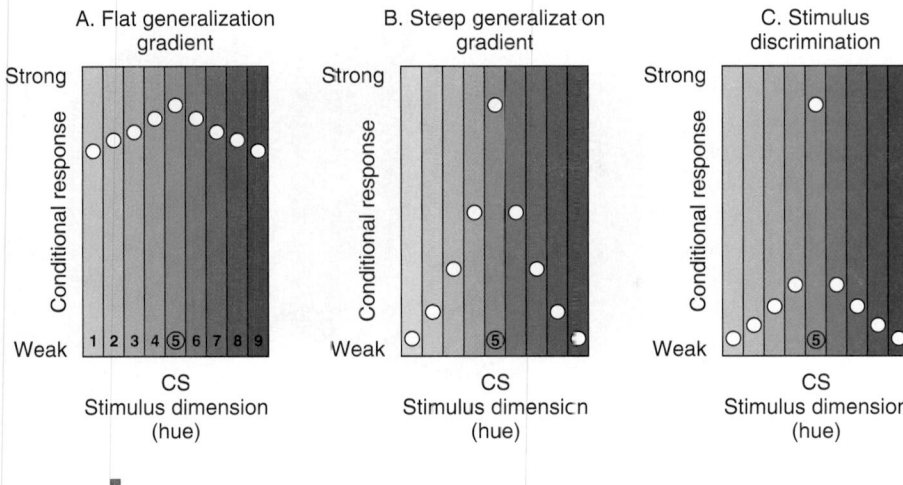

A. Flat generalization gradient

Strong

Conditional response

Weak

| 1 | 2 | 3 | 4 | ⑤ | 6 | 7 | 8 | 9 |

CS
Stimulus dimension
(hue)

B. Steep generalization gradient

Strong

Conditional response

Weak

⑤

CS
Stimulus dimension
(hue)

C. Stimulus discrimination

Strong

Conditional response

Weak

⑤

CS
Stimulus dimension
(hue)

FIGURE 7.5

Stimulus Generalization Gradients

After conditioning to a medium green stimulus, the subject responds almost as strongly to stimuli of similar hues, as shown by the flat generalization gradient in panel A. When the subject is exposed to a broader range of colored stimuli, responses grow weaker as the color becomes increasingly dissimilar to the training stimulus. The generalization gradient becomes very steep, as shown in panel B. The experimenter could change the generalization gradient shown in panel A to resemble the one in panel C by giving the subject discrimination training. In this case, the medium green stimulus would be continually paired with the UCS, but stimuli of all other hues would not.

dissimilar stimuli along a given dimension, as shown in **Figure 7.5**, a *generalization gradient* is found.

The existence of generalization gradients should suggest to you the way classical conditioning serves its function in everyday experience. Because important stimuli rarely occur in exactly the same form every time in nature, stimulus generalization builds in a similarity safety factor by extending the range of learning beyond the original specific experience. With this feature, new but comparable events can be recognized as having the same meaning, or behavioral significance, despite apparent differences. For example, even when a predator makes a slightly different sound or is seen from a different angle, its prey can still recognize and respond to it quickly.

STIMULUS DISCRIMINATION

In some circumstances, however, it is important that a response be made to only a very small range of stimuli. An organism should not, for example, exhaust itself by fleeing too often from animals that are only superficially similar to its natural predators. **Stimulus discrimination** is the process by which an organism learns to respond differently to stimuli that are distinct from the CS on some dimension (for example, differences in hue or in pitch). An organism's discrimination among similar stimuli (tones of 1,000; 1,200; and 1,500 Hz, for example) is sharpened with discrimination training in which only one of them (1,200 Hz, for example) predicts the UCS and in which the others are repeatedly presented without it. Early in conditioning, stimuli similar to the CS will elicit a similar response, though not quite

Why might a child who has been frightened by one dog develop a fear response to all dogs?

> **Stimulus discrimination** A conditioning process in which an organism learns to respond differently to stimuli that differ from the conditioned stimulus on some dimension.

as strong. As discrimination training proceeds, the responses to the other, dissimilar stimuli weaken: The organism gradually learns which event-signal predicts the onset of the UCS and which signals do not.

For an organism to perform optimally in an environment, the processes of generalization and discrimination must strike a balance. You don't want to be overselective—it can be quite costly to miss the presence of a predator—nor do you want to be overresponsive—you don't want to be fearful of every shadow. Classical conditioning provides a mechanism that allows creatures to react efficiently to the structure of their environments (Garcia, 1990).

Focus on Acquisition

In this section, we will examine more closely the conditions that are necessary for classical conditioning to take place: So far, we have *described* the acquisition of classically conditioned responses, but we have not yet *explained* it. Pavlov believed that classical conditioning resulted from the mere pairing of the CS and the UCS. In his view, if a response is to be classically conditioned, the CS and the UCS must occur close together in time—that is, be *temporally contiguous*. As we shall now see, contemporary research has modified that view.

CONTINGENCY

Pavlov's theory dominated classical conditioning until the mid-1960s, when **Robert Rescorla** (1966) conducted a very telling experiment using dogs as subjects. Rescorla designed an experiment that contrasted circumstances in which a tone (the CS) and a shock (the UCS) were merely contiguous—which, if Pavlov was correct, would be sufficient to produce classical conditioning—versus circumstances in which, additionally, the tone reliably predicted the presence of the shock.

HOW WE KNOW

CONTINGENCY MATTERS In the first phase of the experiment, Rescorla trained dogs to jump a barrier from one side of a shuttlebox to the other to avoid an electric shock delivered through the grid floor (see **Figure 7.6**). If the dogs did not jump, they received a shock; if they did jump, the shock was postponed. Rescorla used the frequency with which dogs jumped the barrier as a measure of fear conditioning.

When the dogs were jumping across the barrier regularly, Rescorla divided his subjects into two groups and subjected them to another training procedure. To the random group, the UCS (the shock) was delivered randomly and independently of the CS (the tone) (see **Figure 7.7**). Although the CS and the UCS often occurred close

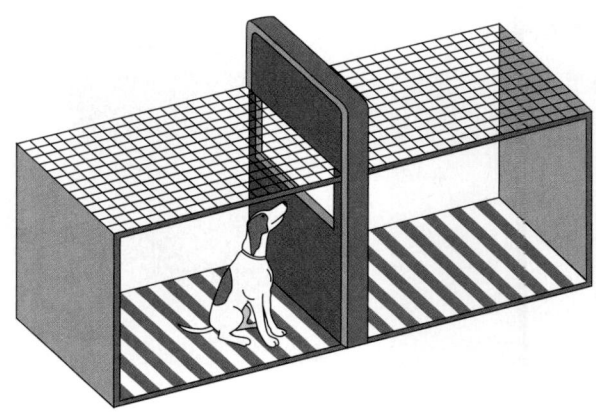

FIGURE 7.6

A Shuttlebox

Rescorla used the frequency with which dogs jumped over a barrier as a measure of fear conditioning.

together in time—they were, by chance, temporally contiguous—the UCS was as likely to be delivered in the absence of the CS as it was in its presence. Thus, the CS had no predictive value. For the contingency group, however, the UCS always followed the CS. Thus, for this group, the sounding of the tone was a reliable predictor of the delivery of the shock.

Once this training was complete, the dogs were put back into the shuttlebox, but this time with a twist. Now the tone used in the second training procedure occasionally sounded, signaling shock. What happened? **Figure 7.8** indicates that dogs exposed to the *contingent* (predictable) CS–UCS relation jumped more frequently in the presence of the tone than did dogs exposed only to the *contiguous* (associated) CS–UCS relation. Contingency was critical for the signal to serve the dogs as a successful cue for the shock.

Thus, in addition to the CS being contiguous—occurring close in time—with the UCS, the CS must also *reliably predict* the occurrence of the UCS in order for classical conditioning to occur (Rescorla, 1988). This finding makes considerable sense. After all, in natural situations, where learning enables organisms to adapt to changes in their environment, stimuli come in clusters and not in neat, simple units, as they do in laboratory experiments.

INFORMATIVENESS

Rescorla's work showed that *contingency* plays a crucial role in classical conditioning. **Leon Kamin** (1969) demonstrated that the CS must also be *informative* (see **Figure 7.9**).

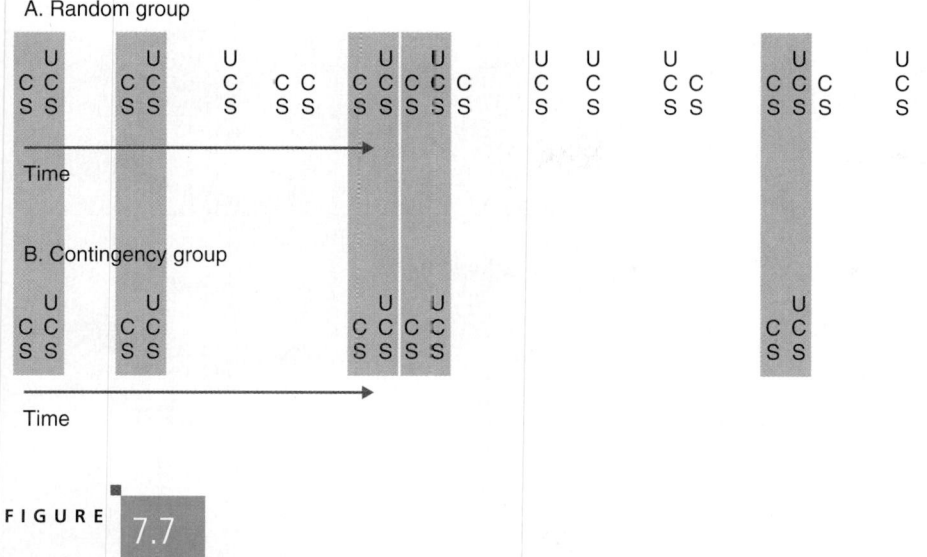

FIGURE 7.7

Rescorla's Procedure for Demonstrating the Importance of Contingency

For the Random group, 5-second tones (the CS) and 5-second shocks (the UCS) were distributed randomly through the experimental period. For the Contingency group, the dogs experienced only the subset of tones and shocks that occurred in a predictive relationship (the onset of the CS preceded the onset of the UCS by 30 seconds or less). Only the dogs in the Contingency group learned to associate the CS with the UCS.

HOW WE KNOW

INFORMATIVENESS ALSO MATTERS
Kamin's study involved two groups of rats. The experimental group was first trained to press a lever in the presence of a tone (CS) to avoid shock (UCS). Next, a second CS—a light—was added; now the UCS was preceded by two CSs: the tone (CS_1) and the light (CS_2). The control group was exposed only to this sequence of tone–light–shock; it never experienced the tone alone as a predictor of shock delivery. Kamin then tested both groups of rats for fear conditioning to the light alone or to the tone alone. If contingency is sufficient to explain classical conditioning, then both groups of rats should have responded in equal amounts to the light and the tone. That is not what Kamin found. The experimental rats responded to the tone but not to the light, whereas control rats responded equally to both the tone and the light (Kamin, 1969).

Kamin explained his results in terms of the *informativeness* of the conditioned stimuli. For experimental rats, the previous conditioning to the tone in the first phase of the experiment *blocked* any subsequent conditioning that could occur to the light. In other words, the previous experience with the tone made the light irrelevant as

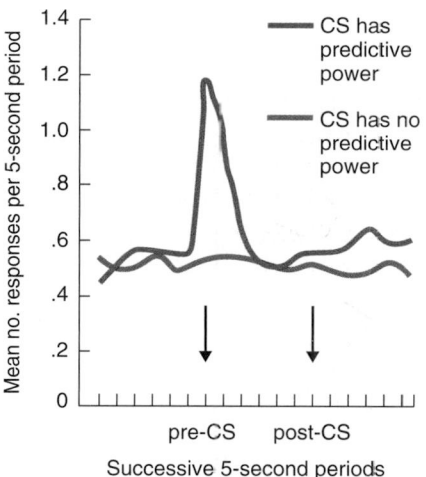

FIGURE 7.8

The Role of Contingency in Classical Conditioning

Rescorla demonstrated that dogs trained under the contingent CS–UCS relation showed more jumping (and thus conditioned fear) than did dogs trained under the contiguous but noncontingent CS–UCS relation. The arrows indicate the onset and offset of the CS tone.

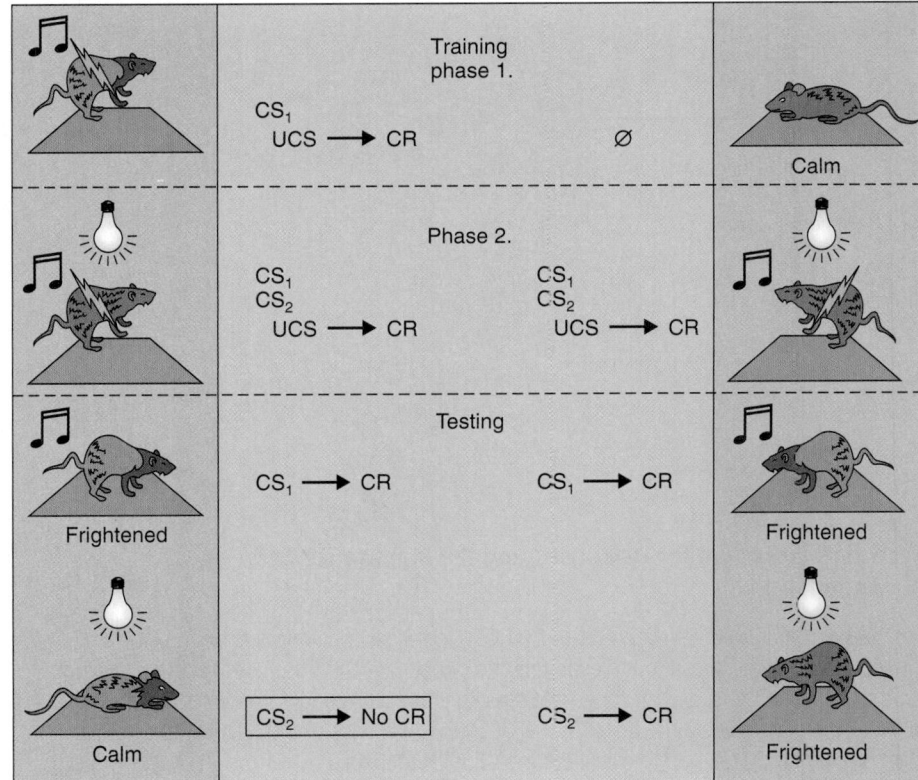

FIGURE 7.9

Kamin's Procedure for Producing the Blocking Effect

Rats in the experimental group were first trained to respond to a tone (CS$_1$). Next, they were trained to respond to both a tone (CS$_1$) and a light (CS$_2$). Rats in the control group were trained only to the compound light and tone (CS). When tested for conditioning to a light alone and a tone alone, only the control rats responded to both stimuli. According to Kamin, experimental rats did not respond to the light because it contained no new information predicting the occurrence of the UCS: The tone's effect blocked the light's effect.

CS$_1$ = tone (♫)   CS$_2$ = light (💡)

a predictor of the UCS. From the rat's point of view, the light may as well not have existed; it provided no additional information beyond that already given by the tone. The ability of the first CS to reduce the informativeness of the second CS because of subjects' previous experience with the UCS is called **blocking**. For control rats, both the light and the tone were equally informative—the rats had no previous experience with either CS, so one did not reduce the informativeness of the other.

The requirement of informativeness explains why conditioning occurs most rapidly when the CS stands out against the many other stimuli that may also be present in an environment. A stimulus is more readily noticed the more *intense* it is and the more it *contrasts* with other stimuli. If you wish to generate good conditioning, you should present either a strong, novel stimulus in an unfamiliar situation or a strong, familiar stimulus in a novel context (Kalat, 1974; Lubow et al., 1976).

You can see that classical conditioning is more complex than even Pavlov originally realized. A neutral stimulus will

Blocking A phenomenon in which an organism does not learn a new stimulus that signals an unconditioned stimulus, because the new stimulus is presented simultaneously with a stimulus that is already effective as a signal.

become an effective CS only if it is both appropriately contingent and informative. But now let's shift your attention a bit. We want to identify real-life situations in which classical conditioning plays a role.

Applications of Classical Conditioning

Your knowledge of classical conditioning can help you understand significant everyday behavior. In this section, we will help you recognize some real-world instances of emotions and preferences as the products of this form of learning. We also explore the role classical conditioning plays in the unfolding of drug addiction. Finally, we describe how classical conditioning is being exploited for its potential to enhance immune function.

EMOTIONS AND PREFERENCES
Earlier we asked you to think about your experience at a horror movie. In that case, you (unconsciously) learned an association between scary music (the CS) and certain likely events (the UCS—the kinds of things that happen in horror movies that cause reflexive revulsion). If you pay careful attention to events in your life, you will discover that there are many circumstances in which you can't quite explain why you are having such a strong emotional reac-

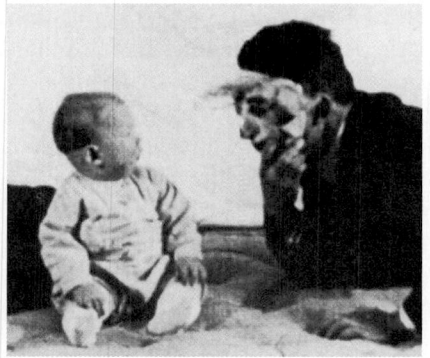

How did John Watson and Rosalie Rayner condition Little Albert to fear small, furry objects?

tion or why you have such a strong preference about something. You might take a step back and ask yourself, Is this the product of classical conditioning?

Consider these situations (Rozin & Fallon, 1987; Rozin et al., 1986):

- Do you think you'd be willing to eat fudge that had been formed into the shape of dog feces?

- Do you think you'd be willing to drink a sugar-water solution if the sugar was drawn from a container that you knew was incorrectly labeled poison?

- Do you think you would be willing to drink apple juice into which a sterilized cockroach had been dipped?

If each of these situations makes you say "no way!" you are not alone. The classically conditioned response—"This is disgusting" or "This is dangerous"—wins out over the knowledge that the stimulus is really okay. Because classically conditioned responses are not built up through conscious thought, they are also hard to eliminate through conscious reasoning!

One of the most extensively studied real-world products of classical conditioning is *fear conditioning*. In the earliest days of behaviorism, John Watson and his colleague Rosalie Rayner sought to prove that many fear responses could be understood as the pairing of a neutral stimulus with something naturally fear-provoking. To test their idea, they experimented on an infant who came to be called Little Albert.

HOW WE KNOW

LITTLE ALBERT'S ACQUIRED FEAR Watson and Rayner (1920) trained Albert to fear a white rat he had initially liked, by pairing its appearance with an aversive UCS—a loud noise just behind him created by striking a large steel bar with a hammer. The unconditioned startle response and the emotional distress to the noxious noise formed the basis of Albert's learning to react with fear

to the appearance of the white rat. His fear was developed in just seven conditioning trials. The emotional conditioning was then extended to behavioral conditioning when Albert learned to escape from the feared stimulus. The infant's learned fear then generalized to other furry objects, such as a rabbit, a dog, and even a Santa Claus mask! (Albert's mother, a wet nurse at the hospital where the study was conducted, took him away before the researchers could remove the experimentally conditioned fear. So we don't know whatever happened to Little Albert [Harris, 1979].)

We know now that conditioned fear is highly resistant to extinction. With the passage of time, an individual may be quite unaware of why a reaction is occurring. Conditioned fear reactions may persist for years, even when the original frightening UCS is never again experienced. For example, researchers demonstrated that, 15 years after the end of World War II, Navy veterans, but not other veterans, still produced a marked response to a "danger signal." During the war, sailors were called to battle stations with a gong that sounded at the rate of 100 rings a minute. That particular auditory pattern—which had been reliably predictive of danger—continued to elicit strong emotional arousal (Edwards & Acker, 1962).

Interestingly, when strong fear is involved, conditioning may take place after only one pairing of a neutral stimulus with the UCS. A single traumatic event can condition you to respond with strong physical, emotional, and cognitive reactions—perhaps for a lifetime. For example, one of our friends was in a bad car accident during a rainstorm. Now every time it begins to rain while he is driving, he becomes panic-stricken, sometimes to the

Fifteen years after World War II was over, Navy veterans still responded as if to current danger signals when exposed to auditory stimuli resembling former battleship gongs. How does classical conditioning explain this response?

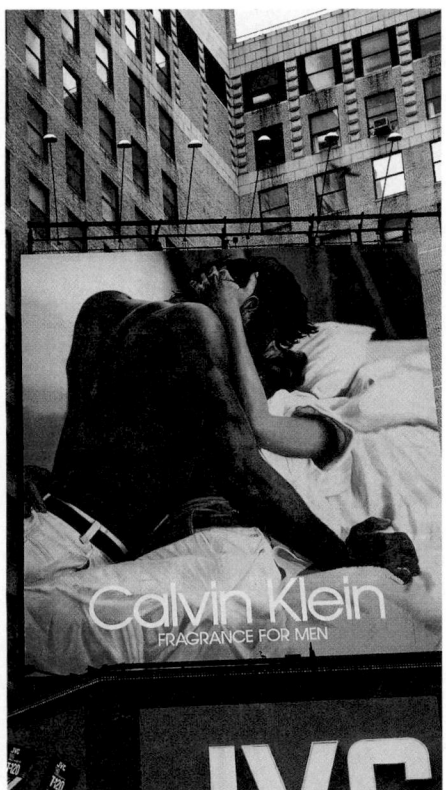

How do advertisers exploit classical conditioning to make you feel "passion" toward their products?

Consider this scenario. A man's body lies in a Manhattan alley, a half-empty syringe dangling from his arm. Cause of death? The coroner called it an overdose, but the man had ordinarily shot up far greater doses than the one that had supposedly killed him. This sort of incident baffled investigators. How could an addict with high drug tolerance die of an overdose when he didn't even get a full hit?

Some time ago, Pavlov (1927) and later his colleague Bykov (1957) pointed out that tolerance to opiates can develop when an individual anticipates the pharmacological action of a drug. Contemporary researcher **Shepard Siegel** refined these ideas. Siegel suggested that the setting in which drug use occurs acts as a conditioned stimulus for a situation in which the body learns to protect itself by preventing the drug from having its usual effect. When people take drugs, the drug (UCS) brings about certain physiological responses to which the body responds with countermeasures intended to reestablish homeostasis (see Chapter 3). The body's countermeasures to the drug are the unconditioned response (UCR). Over time, this *compensatory response* also becomes the conditioned response. That is, in settings ordinarily associated with drug use (the CS), the body physiologically prepares itself (the CR) for the drug's expected effects. Tolerance arises because, in that setting, the individual must consume an amount of the drug that overcomes the compensatory response before starting to get any "positive" effect. Increasingly larger doses are needed as the conditioned compensatory response itself grows.

Siegel tested these ideas in his laboratory by creating tolerance to heroin in laboratory rats.

HOW WE KNOW

CONDITIONED ASPECTS OF DRUG TOLERANCE In one study, Siegel and his colleagues classically conditioned rats to expect heroin injections (UCS) in one setting (CS_1) and dextrose (sweet sugar) solution injections in a different setting (CS_2) (Siegel et al., 1982). In the first phase of training, all rats developed heroin tolerance. On the test day, all animals received a larger-than-usual dose of heroin—nearly twice the previous amount. Half of them received it in the setting where heroin had previously been administered; the other half received it in the setting where dextrose solutions had been given during conditioning. Twice as many rats died in the dextrose-solution setting as in the usual heroin setting—64 percent versus 32 percent!

Presumably, those receiving heroin in the usual setting were more prepared for this potentially dangerous situation, because the context (CS_1) brought about a physi-

extent that he has to pull over and wait out the storm. On one occasion, this rational, sensible man even crawled into the back seat and lay on the floor, face down, until the rain subsided. We will see in Chapter 16 that therapists have designed treatments for these types of fears that are intended to counter the effects of classical conditioning.

We don't want to leave you with the impression that only negative responses are classically conditioned. In fact, we suspect that you will also be able to interpret responses of happiness or excitement as instances of classical conditioning. Certainly, toilers in the advertising industry hope that classical conditioning works as a positive force. They strive, for example, to create associations in your mind between their products (for example, blue jeans, sports cars, and soda pop) and passion. They expect that elements of their advertisements—"sexy" individuals or situations—will serve as the UCS to bring about the UCR—feelings of sexual arousal. The hope then is that the product itself will be the CS, so that the feelings of arousal will become associated with it. To find more examples of the classical conditioning of positive emotions, you should monitor your life for circumstances in which you have a rush of good feelings, when you return, for instance, to a familiar location.

ological response (CR) that countered the drug's typical effects (Poulos & Cappell, 1991).

To find out if a similar process might operate in humans, Siegel and a colleague interviewed heroin addicts who had come close to death from supposed overdoses. In seven out of ten cases, the addicts had been shooting up in a new and unfamiliar setting (Siegel, 1984). Although this natural experiment provides no conclusive data, it suggests that a dose for which an addict has developed tolerance in one setting may become an overdose in an unfamiliar setting. This analysis allows us to suggest that the addict we invoked at the beginning of this section died because he had never shot up before in that alley.

Although we have mentioned research with heroin, classical conditioning is an important component to tolerance for a variety of drugs (Goodison & Siegel, 1995; Poulos & Cappell, 1991; Siegel, 1999). Thus, the same principles Pavlov observed for dogs, bells, and salivation help explain some of the mechanisms underlying human drug addiction.

HARNESSING CLASSICAL CONDITIONING

In the early 1980s, researchers made the rather startling discovery that the body's immune system can be affected by the processes of learning. Historically, it had been assumed that immunological reactions—rapid production of antibodies to counterattack substances that invade and damage the organism—were automatic, biological processes that occurred without any involvement of the central nervous system. Conditioning experiments proved that assumption to be incorrect.

HOW WE KNOW

CLASSICAL CONDITIONING AND IMMUNE FUNCTION Groundbreaking researchers Robert Ader and Nicholas Cohen (1981) taught one group of rats to associate sweet-tasting saccharin (the CS) with cyclophosphamide (CY, the UCS), a drug that weakens immune response. A control group received only the saccharin. Later, when both groups of rats were given only saccharin, the animals that had been conditioned to associate saccharin with CY produced significantly fewer antibodies to foreign cells than those rats in the control group. Thus, the learned association alone was sufficient to elicit suppression of the immune system, making the experimental rats vulnerable to a range of diseases. The learning effect was so powerful that, later in the study, some of the rats died after drinking only the saccharin solution.

Results like this one hold out the promise that classical conditioning can be harnessed to modify the function of the immune system. A new field of study, **psychoneuroimmunology**, has emerged to explore these types of results that involve psychology, the nervous system, and the immune system (Ader & Cohen, 1993; Coe, 1999).

One goal of this new field is to discover techniques that allow conditioning to replace high doses of medications—which often have serious side effects. Ader and his colleague Anthony Suchman, for example, found that patients with high blood pressure (hypertension) who were taken off medication while continuing to be treated with placebos maintained healthy blood pressures longer than patients who did not get placebos (Suchman & Ader, 1989). How could an inert pill cure hypertension? You know the answer from the last section on drug tolerance. Imagine the routine that develops when you take medication on a regular basis. The actual physical ritual involved in taking the drug can serve as the CS, so that when it comes to predict the UCS—the drug—the act can itself elicit the response of lowering blood pressure. In this way,

Psychoneuroimmunology The research area that investigates interactions between psychological processes, such as responses to stress, and the functions of the immune system.

How can classical conditioning be used to change the body's responses to antigens, like the one pictured here?

a placebo—which re-creates the ritual without administering an active substance—can elicit the beneficial bodily reaction. To make this work as a treatment, of course, researchers must ensure that a drug's harsh side effects do not also survive as a product of conditioning.

Researchers hope to develop techniques that will allow for *enhancement*—an increase—of immune response through classical conditioning.

CONDITIONED ENHANCEMENT OF IMMUNE RESPONSE A team of scientists created a conditioning situation in which the taste of saccharin was paired with an injection of hen egg-white lysozyme (HEL), a substance that provokes a response from the rats' immune system. In this paradigm, saccharin served as the CS and HEL as the UCS. The pairing between the CS and UCS was made on only one occasion. Even so, when one group of rats was given water flavored with saccharin, but without an additional injection of HEL, their bodies produced almost as great an immune response as a second group of rats that was actually reinjected with HEL (Alvarez-Borda et al., 1995).

This experiment demonstrates that only a single episode in which the CS was associated with the UCS led to pronounced immune response to the CS alone. Can you start to see the potential for classical conditioning procedures to enhance immune function without a continuous drug regimen?

Before you began to read *Psychology and Life*, you probably knew little about classical conditioning except something vague about Pavlov and his dogs. We hope now that you've now learned enough about this form of learning to appreciate the important role it plays in your day-to-day life. We next discuss a form of learning that you're likely to have thought much more about before you started your psychology course: If you've ever considered how reward and punishment change people's behavior, then you have a head start on the topic of *operant conditioning*.

SUMMING UP

After observing the basic principles of classical conditioning by accident, Pavlov devoted the remainder of his career to determining the specific variables that influence conditioning. In classical conditioning, an unconditioned stimulus naturally elicits a reflexive behavior called an unconditioned response. After pairings of a formerly neutral stimulus—the conditioned stimulus—with the unconditioned stimulus, the conditioned stimulus will come to elicit the conditioned response. Timing is critical to the acquisition of a conditioned response. Stimulus generalization occurs when stimuli similar to the original conditioned stimulus give rise to the conditioned response. Animals can be trained to overcome generalization and discriminate appropriate from inappropriate conditioned stimuli. The acquisition of classically conditioned responses relies on a contingent and informative relationship between the CS and UCS. Real-life instances of classical conditioning are found in the areas of emotions, drug tolerance, and psychoneuroimmunology.

Operant Conditioning: Learning about Consequences

Let's return to the movie theater. The horror film is now over, and you peel yourself off your seat. The friend with whom you saw the movie asks you if you're hoping that a sequel will be made. You respond, "I've learned that I shouldn't go to horror films." You're probably right, but what kind of learning is this? Once again our answer begins around the turn of the 20th century.

The Law of Effect

At about the same time that Pavlov was using classical conditioning to induce Russian dogs to salivate to the sound of a bell, **Edward L. Thorndike** (1898) was watching American cats trying to escape from puzzle boxes (see **Figure 7.10**). Thorndike reported his observations and inferences about the kind of learning he believed was taking place in his subjects. The cats at first only struggled against their confinement, but once some "impulsive" action allowed them to open the door "all the other unsuccessful impulses [were] stamped out and the particular impulse leading to the successful act [was] stamped in by the resulting pleasure" (Thorndike, 1898, p. 13).

What had Thorndike's cats learned? According to Thorndike's analysis, learning was an association between stimuli in the situation and a response that an animal learned to make: a *stimulus-response (S-R) connection*. Thus, the cats had learned to produce an appropriate response (for example, clawing at a button or loop) that in these stimulus circumstances (confinement in the puzzle box) led to a desired outcome (momentary freedom). Note that the learning of these S-R connections occurred gradually and automatically in a mechanistic way as the animal experienced the consequences of its actions through blind *trial and error*. Gradually, the behaviors that had satisfying consequences increased in frequency; they eventually became the dominant response when the animal was placed in the puzzle box. Thorndike referred to this relationship between behavior and its consequences as the **law of effect:** A response that

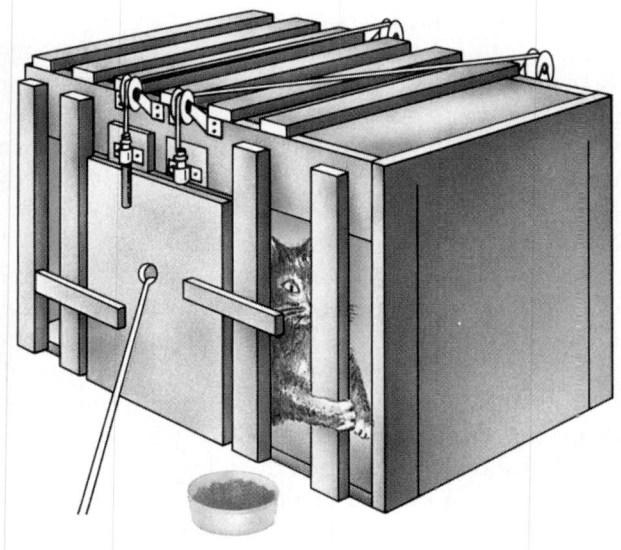

FIGURE 7.10

A Thorndike Puzzle Box

To get out of the puzzle box and obtain food, Thorndike's cat had to manipulate a mechanism to release a weight that would then pull the door open.

is followed by satisfying consequences becomes more probable and a response that is followed by dissatisfying consequences becomes less probable.

Experimental Analysis of Behavior

B. F. Skinner embraced Thorndike's view that environmental consequences exert a powerful effect on behavior. Skinner outlined a program of research, whose purpose was to discover, by systematic variation of stimulus conditions, the ways that various environmental conditions affect the likelihood that a given response will occur:

> A natural datum in a science of behavior is the probability that a given bit of behavior will occur at a given time. An experimental analysis deals with that probability in terms of frequency or rate of responding.... The task of an experimental analysis is to discover all the variables of which probability of response is a function. (Skinner, 1966, pp. 213–214)

Skinner's analysis was experimental rather than theoretical—theorists are guided by derivations and predictions about behavior from their theories, but empiricists, such as Skinner, advocate the bottom-up approach. They start with the collection and evaluation of data within the context of an experiment and are not theory driven.

To analyze behavior experimentally, Skinner developed **operant conditioning** procedures, in which he ma-

nipulated the *consequences* of an organism's behavior in order to see what effect they had on subsequent behavior. An **operant** is any behavior that is *emitted* by an organism and can be characterized in terms of the observable effects it has on the environment. Literally, *operant* means *affecting the environment,* or operating on it (Skinner, 1938). Operants are *not elicited* by specific stimuli, as classically conditioned behaviors are. Pigeons peck, rats search for food, babies cry and coo, some people gesture while talking, and others stutter. The probability of these behaviors occurring in the future can be increased or decreased by manipulating the effects they have on the environment. If, for example, a baby's coo prompts desirable parental contact, the baby will coo more in the future. Operant conditioning, then, modifies the probability of different types of operant behavior as a function of the environmental consequences they produce.

To carry out his new experimental analysis, Skinner invented an apparatus that allowed him to manipulate the consequences of behavior, the *operant chamber.* **Figure 7.11** shows how the operant chamber works. When, after having produced an appropriate behavior defined by the experimenter, a rat presses a lever, the mechanism delivers a food pellet. This device allows experimenters to study the variables that allow rats to learn—or not to learn—the behaviors they define. For example, if a lever press produces a food pellet only after a rat has turned a circle in the chamber, the rat will swiftly learn (through a process called *shaping* that we will consider shortly) to turn a circle before pressing the lever.

In many operant experiments, the measure of interest is how much of a particular behavior an animal carries out in a period of time. Researchers record the pattern and total amount of behavior emitted in the course of an experiment. This methodology allowed Skinner to study the effect of reinforcement contingencies on animals' behavior.

Reinforcement Contingencies

A **reinforcement contingency** is a consistent relationship between a response and the changes in the environment that it produces. Imagine, for example, an experiment

Law of effect A basic law of learning that states that the power of a stimulus to evoke a response is strengthened when the response is followed by a reward and weakened when it is not followed by a reward.

Operant conditioning Learning in which the probability of a response is changed by a change in its consequences.

Operant Behavior emitted by an organism that can be characterized in terms of the observable effects it has on the environment.

Reinforcement contingency A consistent relationship between a response and the changes in the environment that it produces.

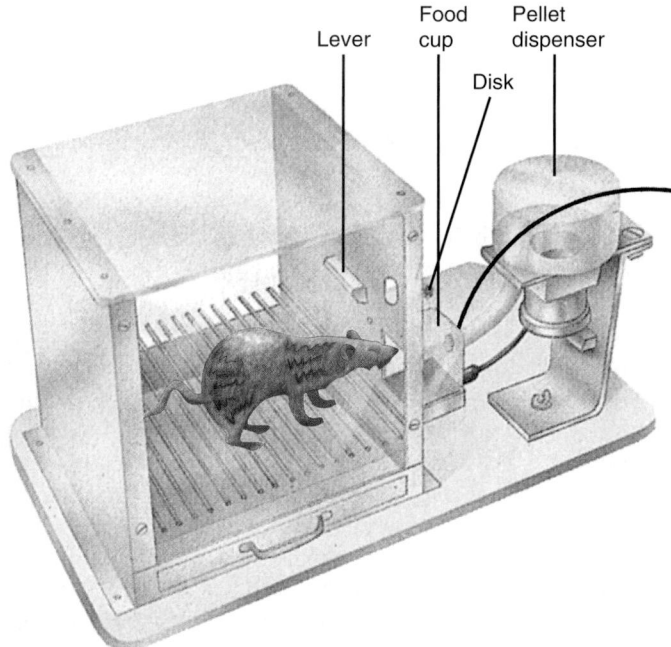

Lever Food cup Pellet dispenser

Disk

FIGURE 7.11

Operant Chamber

In this specially designed apparatus, typical of those used with rats, a press on the lever may be followed by delivery of a food pellet.

in which a pigeon's pecking a disk (the response) is generally followed by the presentation of grain (the corresponding change in the environment). This consistent relationship, or reinforcement contingency, will usually be accompanied by an increase in the rate of pecking. For delivery of grain to increase *only* the probability of pecking, it must be contingent *only* on the pecking response—the delivery must occur regularly after that response but not after other responses, such as turning or bowing. Based on Skinner's work, modern behavior analysts seek to understand behavior in terms of reinforcement contingencies. Let's take a closer look at what has been discovered about these contingencies.

Reinforcer Any stimulus that, when made contingent upon a response, increases the probability of that response.

Positive reinforcement A behavior is followed by the presentation of an appetitive stimulus, increasing the probability of that behavior.

Negative reinforcement A behavior is followed by the removal of an aversive stimulus, increasing the probability of that behavior.

Operant extinction When a behavior no longer produces predictable consequences, its return to the level of occurrence it had before operant conditioning.

Suppose you are now captivated by the idea of getting your pet rat to turn a circle in its cage. To increase the probability of circle-turning behavior you would want to use a *reinforcer*. A **reinforcer** is any stimulus that—when made contingent on a behavior—increases the probability of that behavior over time. *Reinforcement* is the delivery of a reinforcer following a response.

Reinforcers are always defined empirically—in terms of their effects on changing the probability of a response. If you look out at the world, you can probably find three classes of stimuli: those toward which you are neutral, those that you find *appetitive* (you have an "appetite" for them), and those that you find *aversive* (you seek to avoid them). It should be clear that the compositions of these classes of stimuli will not be the same for all individuals: What is appetitive or aversive is defined by the behavior of the individual organism. Consider the strawberry. Although many people find strawberries quite delicious, one of your authors finds strawberries virtually inedible. If you offer that author strawberries contingent on his behavior, his response will be quite different from that of the more commonplace strawberry fans.

When a behavior is followed by the delivery of an appetitive stimulus, the event is called **positive reinforcement.** Your pet rat will turn circles if a consequence of circle turning is the delivery of desirable food. Humans will tell jokes if a consequence of their joke telling is a type of laughter they find pleasurable. When a behavior is followed by the removal of an aversive stimulus, the event is called **negative reinforcement.** Your author, for example, would be more likely to perform a behavior if it would allow him to *avoid* eating strawberries. Using an umbrella to prevent getting wet during a downpour is a common example of a behavior that is maintained by negative reinforcement. The aversive stimulus is getting wet. Using an umbrella allows you to avoid this aversive stimulus. An automobile seat-belt buzzer also serves a negative reinforcing function; its annoying sound is terminated when the driver buckles up.

To distinguish clearly between positive and negative reinforcement, try to remember the following: Both positive reinforcement and negative reinforcement *increase* the probability of the response that precedes them. Positive reinforcement increases response probability by the presentation of an appetitive stimulus following a response; negative reinforcement does the same in reverse, through the removal, reduction, or prevention of an aversive stimulus following a response.

You should recall that for classical conditioning, when the unconditioned stimulus is no longer delivered, the conditioned response suffers extinction. The same rule holds for operant conditioning—if reinforcement is withheld, **operant extinction** occurs. Thus, if a behavior no longer produces predictable consequences, it returns to the level it was at before operant conditioning—it is extinguished. You can probably catch your own behaviors being reinforced and then *extinguished*. Have you ever had the experience of dropping a few coins into a soda machine and getting nothing in return? If you kicked the machine one time and your soda came out, the act of kicking would be reinforced. However, if the next few times your kicking produced no soda, kicking would quickly be extinguished.

POSITIVE AND NEGATIVE PUNISHMENT

You are probably familiar with another technique for decreasing the probability of a response—punishment. A **punisher** is any stimulus that—when it is made contingent on a response—decreases the probability of that response over time. *Punishment* is the delivery of a punisher following a response. Just as we could identify positive and negative reinforcement, we can identify positive punishment and negative punishment. When a behavior is followed by the delivery of an aversive stimulus, the event is called **positive punishment** (you can remember *positive*, because something is added to the situation). Touching a hot stove, for example, produces pain that punishes the preceding response so that you are less likely next time to touch the stove. When a behavior is followed by the removal of an appetitive stimulus, the event is referred to as **negative punishment** (you can remember *negative*, because something is subtracted from the situation). Thus, when a parent withdraws a child's allowance after she hits her baby brother, the child learns not to hit her brother in the future. Which kind of punishment explains why you might stay away from horror movies?

Although punishment and reinforcement are closely related operations, they differ in important ways. A good way to differentiate them is to think of each in terms of its effects on behavior. Punishment, by definition, always *reduces* the probability of a response occurring again; reinforcement, by definition, always *increases* the probability of a response recurring. For example, some people get severe headaches after drinking caffeinated beverages. The headache is the stimulus that positively punishes and reduces the behavior of drinking coffee. However, once the headache is present, people often will take aspirin or another pain reliever to eliminate the headache. The aspirin's analgesic effect is the stimulus that negatively reinforces the behavior of ingesting aspirin.

You are now acquainted with the four basic ways to change the probability of a behavior. **Figure 7.12** shows how you might use them with respect to behaviors in your own life.

DISCRIMINATIVE STIMULI AND GENERALIZATION

You are unlikely to want to change the probability of a certain behavior at all times. Rather, you may want to change the probability of the behavior in a particular context. For example, you often want to increase the probability that a child will sit quietly in class without changing the probability that he or she will be noisy and active during recess. Through their associations with reinforcement or punishment, certain stimuli that precede a particular response—**discriminative stimuli**—come to set the context for that behavior. Organisms learn that, in the presence of some stimuli but not of others, their behavior is likely to have a particular effect on the environment. For example, in the presence of a green street light, the act of crossing an intersection in a motor vehicle is reinforced. When the light is red, however, such behavior may be punished—it may result in a traffic ticket or an accident. Skinner referred to the sequence of discriminative stimulus–behavior–consequence as the **three-term contingency** and believed that it could explain most human action (Skinner, 1953). **Table 7.1** describes how the three-term contingency might explain several different kinds of human behavior.

Under laboratory conditions, manipulating the consequences of behavior in the presence of discriminative stimuli can exert powerful control over that behavior. For example, a pigeon might be given grain after pecking a disk in the presence of a green light but not a red light. The green light is a discriminative stimulus that sets the occasion for pecking; the red is a discriminative stimulus that sets the occasion for not pecking. Organisms learn quickly to discriminate between these conditions, responding regularly in the presence of one stimulus and not responding in the presence of the other. By manipulating the components of the three-term contingency, you can constrain a behavior to a particular context.

Organisms also generalize responses to other stimuli that resemble the discriminative stimulus. Once a response has been reinforced in the presence of one discriminative stimulus, a similar stimulus can become a discriminative stimulus for that same response. For example, pigeons trained to peck a disk in the presence of a green light will also peck the disk in the presence of lights that are lighter or darker shades of green than the original discriminative stimulus. Similarly, you generalize to different shades of green on stop lights as a discriminative stimulus for your "resume driving" behavior.

Punisher Any stimulus that, when made contingent upon a response, decreases the probability of that response.

Positive punishment A behavior is followed by the presentation of an aversive stimulus, decreasing the probability of that behavior.

Negative punishment A behavior is followed by the removal of an appetitive stimulus, decreasing the probability of that behavior.

Discriminative stimuli Stimuli that act as predictors of reinforcement, signaling when particular behaviors will result in positive reinforcement.

Three-term contingency The means by which organisms learn that, in the presence of some stimuli but not others, their behavior is likely to have a particular effect on the environment.

FIGURE 7.12

Operant Conditioning In Your Life

OPERANT CONDITIONING IN YOUR LIFE We want to give you the opportunity to develop your own application for positive and negative reinforcement and positive and negative punishment. Begin by choosing a behavior.

A behavior (of your own, or of someone else) that you'd like to increase in frequency:

Or a behavior that you'd like to decrease in frequency:

Fill in your plan of action for each cell. For example, suppose a behavior you would choose to decrease is your roommate's "staying on the phone" behavior. You might fill in "I would deliver a candy bar each time a phone call lasted less than two minutes" in cell 1 or "I would start slapping my roommate each time a phone call began and only stop when the call was over" in cell 4 (in which case, you'd actually be trying to increase your roommate's "stay off the phone" behavior). Note that, in real life, you might not be able to carry out the actions you invent for each cell!

	APPETITIVE STIMULUS	AVERSIVE STIMULUS
DELIVER	Positive reinforcement (1)	(2) Positive punishment
REMOVE	Negative punishment (3)	(4) Negative reinforcement

USING REINFORCEMENT CONTINGENCIES

Are you ready to put your new knowledge of reinforcement contingencies to work? Here are some considerations you might have:

- *How can you define the behavior that you would like to reinforce or eliminate?* You must always carefully target the specific behavior whose probability you would like to change. Reinforcement should be contingent on exactly that behavior. When reinforcers are presented noncontingently, their presence has little effect on behavior. For example, if a parent praises bad work as well as good efforts, a child will not learn to work harder in school—but, because of the positive reinforcement, other behaviors are likely to increase. (What might those be?)

- *How can you define the contexts in which a behavior is appropriate or inappropriate?* Remember that you rarely want to allow or disallow every instance of a behavior. We suggested earlier, for example, that you might want to increase the probability that a child will sit quietly in class without changing the probability that he or she will be noisy and active during recess. You must define the discriminative stimuli and investigate how broadly the desired response will be generalized to similar stimuli. If, for example, the child learned to sit quietly in class, would that behavior generalize to other "serious" settings?

- *Have you unknowingly been reinforcing some behaviors?* Suppose you want to eliminate a behavior. Before you turn to punishment as a way of reducing its probability (more on that in the *Psychology in Your Life* box), you should try to determine whether you can identify reinforcers for that behavior. If so, you can try to extinguish the behavior by eliminating those reinforcers. Imagine, for example, that a young boy throws a large number of tantrums. You might ask yourself, "Have I been reinforcing those tantrums by paying the boy extra attention when he screams?" If so, you can try to eliminate the tantrums by eliminating the reinforcement. Even better, you can combine extinction with positive reinforcement of more socially approved behaviors.

Behavior analysts assume that any behavior that persists does so because it results in reinforcement. Any behav-

TABLE 7.1

The Three-Term Contingency: Relationships among Discriminative Stimuli, Behavior, and Consequences

	Discriminative Stimulus	Emitted Response	Stimulus Consequence
1. Positive reinforcement: A response in the presence of an effective signal produces the desired consequence. This response increases.	Soft-drink machine	Put coin in slot	Get drink
2. Negative reinforcement (escape): An aversive situation is escaped from by an operant response. This escape response increases.	Heat	Fan oneself	Escape from heat
3. Extinction training: An operant response is not followed by a reinforcer. The response decreases in rate.	None	Clowning behavior	No one notices and response becomes less frequent
4. Positive punishment: A response is followed by an aversive stimulus. The response is eliminated or suppressed.	Attractive matchbox	Play with matches	Get burned or get caught and spanked
5. Negative punishment: A response is followed by the removal of an appetitive stimulus. The response is eliminated or suppressed.	Brussels sprouts	Refusal to eat them	No dessert

How can parents use reinforcement contingencies to affect their children's behavior?

ior, they argue—even irrational or bizarre behavior—can be understood by discovering what the reinforcement or payoff is. For example, symptoms of mental or physical disorders are sometimes maintained because the person gets attention and sympathy and is excused from normal responsibilities. These *secondary gains* reinforce irrational and sometimes self-destructive behavior. Can you see how shy behaviors can be maintained through reinforcement, even though the shy person would prefer not to be shy? It is, of course, not always possible to know what reinforcers are at work in an environment. However, as a behavior becomes more or less probable, you might try to carry out a bit of behavior analysis.

We have recommended that, as much as possible, you use positive reinforcement to change behaviors. Let's now take a look at the ways in which various objects and activities may come to function as reinforcers.

Properties of Reinforcers

Reinforcers are the power brokers of operant conditioning—they change or maintain behavior. Reinforcers have

SPARE THE ROD, SPOIL THE CHILD?

Do you believe the old adage, "Spare the rod, spoil the child"— that children who are not occasionally spanked, for example, will end up being spoiled? If you believe this adage, you are similar to the majority of parents in the United States. In one sample of 991 parents, 35% reported using some form of corporal punishment (e.g., spanking, slapping) on their 1- to 2-year-olds and 94% had used corporal punishment on their 3- to 4-year-olds (Straus & Stewart, 1999). In another sample of 449 parents, 93 percent of them had themselves been spanked—and 87 percent of them approved of it as a form of punishment (Buntain-Ricklefs et al., 1994). You can see that spanking is quite common, and people generally approve of it as a form of punishment. But what are the consequences for children who are spanked?

Researchers have begun to answer this question by examining the link between parents' use of physical punishment and children's aggressive behavior. Contrary to popular wisdom, what many theorists believe is that parents' physical aggression toward their children—even in the context of trying to correct inappropriate behavior—serves as a *model* for children's own responses to situations in which they wish to control other individuals' behavior. That is, children learn from

their parents to use physical aggression. (We will have more to say about learning from models in a later section entitled "Observational Learning.") How might this idea be tested? In one study, involving 273 kindergarten children in Indiana and Tennessee, parents were asked to fill out self-reports about the types of physical punishment they used with their children (Strassberg et al., 1994). We're going to focus on the children's mothers. About 6 percent of the children had mothers who did not use physical punishment. Sixty-eight percent of the children were spanked by their mothers. The remaining 26 percent received more intense forms of physical punishment: Their mothers hit them with fists or closed hands or beat them up.

About six months after the mothers reported on their forms of physical punishment, the children were observed interacting with peers in school. The researchers recorded the children's acts of aggression toward their peers—instances, for example, in which they bullied or became angry and hit another child. Based on these observations, each child earned a score for aggressive acts per hour. The accompanying figure presents the results. As you can see, the more intense the form of the mother's physical punishment, the more aggressive the child. These data suggest rather

strongly that children are learning an aggressive style from their parents. You might be thinking: Maybe kids are being spanked or hit because they were *already* aggressive children. Other developmental evidence suggests that this isn't the case (Chess & Thomas, 1984). Suppose, even so, that there is some truth to the idea that "bad" kids are getting more physical punishment. This study makes it clear that physical punishment is not having the presumably intended effect of teaching bad kids to be better (Mahoney et al., 2000).

If we haven't already convinced you that physical punishment is not an effective parenting strategy, let us report the results from one more study. This analysis was based on a subset of data from an ambitious project that studied 6,002 U.S. families to establish patterns and consequences of family violence. In this instance, the researchers were interested in physical punishment people received during their teenage years as related to later life outcomes (Straus & Kantor, 1994). The results were quite dramatic. Roughly 50 percent of the sample reported having been physically punished as teenagers (58 percent of the boys and 44 percent of the girls). Those individuals who were physically punished were more likely to experience a host of later

---

a number of interesting and complex properties. They can be learned through experience rather than be biologically determined and can be activities rather than objects. In some situations, even ordinarily powerful reinforcers may not be enough to change a dominant

behavior pattern (in this case, we would say that the consequences were not actually reinforcers).

CONDITIONED REINFORCERS

When you came into the world, there were a handful of **primary reinforcers,** such as food and water, whose reinforcing properties were biologically determined. Over time, however, otherwise neutral stimuli have become associated with primary reinforcers and now function as **conditioned reinforcers** for operant responses. Conditioned reinforcers can come to serve as

Primary reinforcers Biologically determined reinforcers such as food and water.

Conditioned reinforcers In classical conditioning, formerly neutral stimuli that have become reinforcers.

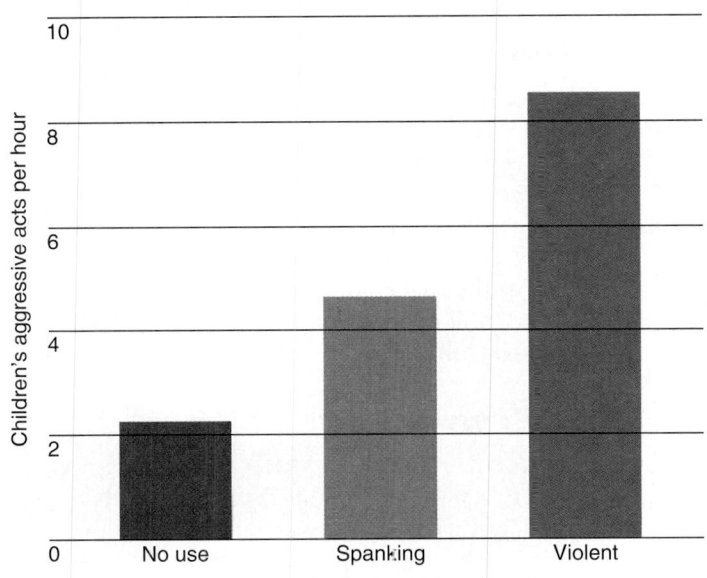

Physical Punishment and Children's Aggression

Children who are spanked by their mothers commit more aggressive acts in the classroom than do their peers who are not spanked. The most aggressive children are those whose mothers use violent punishment—hitting with a fist, closed hand, or object or beating up their children.

problems: They were put at risk for depression, suicide, alcohol abuse, physical abuse of their children, and (for men) wife beating. The researchers conclude that "ending all use of spanking and other corporal punishment can make an important contribution to primary prevention of physical abuse of children and spouses, depression, suicide, and drinking problems" (p. 558). This conclusion is worth serious consideration.

We hope to have convinced you, based on concrete research results, that spanking children is not an appropriate or effective parenting technique. Note, however, that our

intention is not to rule out all forms of punishment. There may well be situations in which, to stop a child's undesirable actions swiftly enough, punishment may become the only alternative. Research shows that punishment should meet a number of conditions (Walters & Grusec, 1977). Punishment should:

- be swift and brief
- be administered right after the response occurs
- be limited in intensity
- be a response to specific undesirable behaviors and never to the person's character

- be limited to the situation in which the response occurs
- consist of penalties instead of physical pain

But beware: The reason many parents use punishment too often is that it can stop a child's unwanted behavior immediately. Because the parents achieve their short-term goal, the children's immediate response reinforces the parents' punishing behavior (Grant & Evans, 1994). But the lesson here is "short-term gain, long-term pain." Parents must patiently forgo that immediate reinforcement to act in the better, long-term interest of their children.

ends in themselves. In fact, a great deal of human behavior is influenced less by biologically significant primary reinforcers than by a wide variety of conditioned reinforcers. Money, grades, smiles of approval, gold stars, and various kinds of status symbols are among the many potent conditioned reinforcers that influence much of your behavior.

Virtually any stimulus can become a conditioned reinforcer by being paired with a primary reinforcer. In one experiment, simple tokens were used with animal learners.

CONDITIONED REINFORCERS FOR CHIMPS
With raisins as primary reinforcers, chimps were trained to solve problems. Then tokens were delivered along with the raisins. When only the tokens were presented, the chimps continued working for their "money" because they could later deposit the hard-earned tokens in a "chimp-o-mat" designed to exchange tokens for the raisins (Cowles, 1937).

Inedible tokens can be used as conditioned reinforcers. In one study, chimps deposited tokens in a "chimp-o-mat" in exchange for raisins. What types of conditioned reinforcers function in your life?

Teachers and experimenters often find conditioned reinforcers more effective and easier to use than primary reinforcers because (1) few primary reinforcers are available in the classroom, whereas almost any stimulus event that is under control of a teacher can be used as a conditioned reinforcer; (2) they can be dispensed rapidly; (3) they are portable; and (4) their reinforcing effect may be more immediate, because it depends only on the perception of receiving them and not on biological processing, as in the case of primary reinforcers.

In some institutions, such as psychiatric hospitals or drug treatment programs, *token economies* have been set up based on these principles. Desired behaviors (grooming or taking medication, for example) are explicitly defined, and token payoffs are given by the staff when the behaviors are performed. These tokens can later be exchanged by the patients for a wide array of rewards and privileges (Kazdin, 1994; Martin & Pear, 1999). These systems of reinforcement are especially effective in modifying patients' behaviors regarding self-care, upkeep of their environment, and, most important, frequency of their positive social interactions.

PROBABLE ACTIVITIES AS POSITIVE REINFORCERS

Suppose you need to get a child to do something. You don't want to pay her or give her a gold star, so instead you strike this bargain: "When you finish your homework, you can play with your video game." Your use of "video game playing" in these circumstances is in keeping with the *Premack principle,* named after its discoverer, **David**

Premack (1965). The Premack principle suggests that a more probable activity (that is, a behavior with a higher probability of occurring under ordinary circumstances) can be used to reinforce a less probable one. In his initial research, Premack found that water-deprived rats learned to increase their running in an exercise wheel when their running was followed by an opportunity to drink. Conversely, exercise-deprived rats learned to increase their drinking when that response was followed by a chance to run. According to the Premack principle, a reinforcer may be any event or activity that is valued by the organism.

The Premack principle has powerful applications. Consider the challenging task of getting nursery-school children to sit quietly and listen to someone talk. Here is one classic solution:

HOW WE KNOW

CHILDREN WILL WORK FOR THE CHANCE TO PLAY Short periods during which the children sat quietly in their chairs facing the blackboard were occasionally followed by the sound of a bell and the instruction "Run and scream." The students immediately jumped out of their chairs and ran around the room screaming and having a good time. After a few minutes, another signal alerted them to stop and return to their chairs. Later in the study, the children were given the opportunity to earn tokens for engaging in low-probability behaviors, such as practicing arithmetic. The children could use the tokens to buy the opportunity to participate in high-probability activities, such as playing with toys. With this kind of procedure, control was virtually perfect after a few days (Homme et al., 1963).

Reprogramming classroom contingencies succeeded where pleas, punishment, and a bit of screaming by the teacher had failed.

You can see how you can apply the Premack principle to get children to engage in low-probability activities. For a socially outgoing child, playing with friends can reinforce the less pleasant task of finishing homework first. For a shy child, reading a new book can be used to reinforce the less-preferred activity of playing with other children. Whatever activity is valued can be used as a reinforcer and thus increase the probability of engaging in an activity that is not currently valued. Over time, there is the possibility that the less favored activities will come to be valued, as exposure to them leads to discovery of their intrinsic worth.

Schedules of Reinforcement

What happens when you cannot, or do not want to, reinforce your pet on every occasion when it performs a special behavior? Consider a story about the young B. F. Skinner. It seems that one weekend he was secluded in his laboratory with not enough of a food-reward supply for his hardworking rats. He economized by giving the rats pellets only after a certain interval of time—no matter how many times they pressed in between, they couldn't get any more pellets. Even so, the rats responded as much with this *partial reinforcement schedule* as they had with continuous reinforcement. And what do you predict happened when these animals underwent extinction training and their responses were followed by no pellets at all? The rats whose lever pressing had been partially reinforced continued to respond longer and more vigorously than did the rats who had gotten payoffs after every response. Skinner was onto something important!

The discovery of the effectiveness of partial reinforcement led to extensive study of the effects of different **schedules of reinforcement** on behavior (see **Figure 7.13**). You have experienced different schedules of reinforcement in your daily life. When you raise your hand in class, the teacher sometimes calls on you and sometimes does not; some slot machine players continue to put coins in the one-armed bandits even though the reinforcers are delivered only rarely. In real life or in the laboratory, reinforcers can be delivered according to either a *ratio schedule*, after a certain number of responses, or an *interval schedule*, after the first response following a specified interval of time. In each case, there can be either a constant, or *fixed*, pattern of reinforcement or an irregular, or *variable*, pattern of reinforcement, making four major types of schedules in all. So far you've learned about the **partial reinforcement effect**: Responses acquired under schedules of partial reinforcement are more resistant to extinction than those acquired with continuous reinforcement (Bitterman, 1975). Let's see what else researchers have discovered about different schedules of reinforcement.

FIXED-RATIO (FR) SCHEDULES

In **fixed-ratio schedules,** the reinforcer comes after the organism has emitted a fixed number of responses. When reinforcement follows one response, the schedule is called an FR-1 schedule (this is the original continuous reinforcement schedule). When reinforcement follows only every twenty-fifth response, the schedule is an FR-25 schedule. FR schedules generate high rates of responding because there is a direct correlation between responding and reinforcement—a pigeon can get as much food as it wants in a period of time if it pecks often enough. Figure 7.13 shows that FR schedules produce a pause after each reinforcer. The higher the ratio, the longer the pause after each reinforcement. Stretching the ratio too thin by requiring a great many responses for reinforcement without first training the animal to emit that many responses may lead to extinction. Many salespeople are on FR schedules: They must sell a certain number of units before they can get paid.

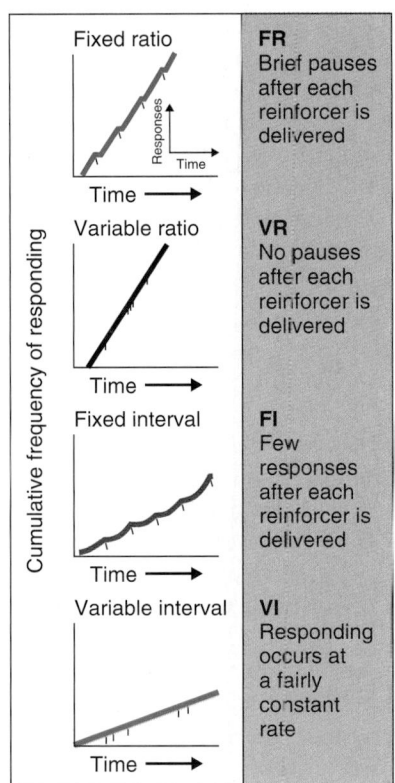

Fixed ratio	**FR** Brief pauses after each reinforcer is delivered	
Variable ratio	**VR** No pauses after each reinforcer is delivered	
Fixed interval	**FI** Few responses after each reinforcer is delivered	
Variable interval	**VI** Responding occurs at a fairly constant rate	

FIGURE 7.13

Reinforcement Schedules

These different patterns of behavior are produced by four simple schedules of reinforcement. The hash marks indicate when reinforcement is delivered.

VARIABLE-RATIO (VR) SCHEDULES

In a **variable-ratio schedule,** the average number of responses between reinforcers is predetermined. A VR-10 schedule means that, on average, reinforcement follows every tenth response, but it might come after only 1 response or after 20 responses. Variable-ratio schedules generate the highest rate of responding and the greatest resistance to extinction, especially when the VR value is

Schedules of reinforcement In operant conditioning, the patterns of delivering and withholding reinforcement.

Partial reinforcement effect The behavioral principle that states that responses acquired under intermittent reinforcement are more difficult to extinguish than those acquired with continuous reinforcement.

Fixed-ratio schedule A schedule of reinforcement in which a reinforcer is delivered for the first response made after a fixed number of responses.

Variable-ratio schedule A schedule of reinforcement in which a reinforcer is delivered for the first response made after a variable number of responses whose average is predetermined.

large. Suppose you start a pigeon with a low VR value (for example, VR-5) and then move it toward a higher value. A pigeon on a VR-110 schedule will respond with up to 12,000 pecks per hour and will continue responding for hours even with no reinforcement. Gambling would seem to be under the control of VR schedules. The response of dropping coins in slot machines is maintained at a high, steady level by the payoff, which is delivered only after an unknown, variable number of coins has been deposited. VR schedules leave you guessing when the reward will come—you gamble that it will be after the next response, not many responses later (Rachlin, 1990).

FIXED-INTERVAL (FI) SCHEDULES

On a **fixed-interval schedule**, a reinforcer is delivered for the first response made after a fixed period of time. On an FI-10 schedule, the subject, after receiving reinforcement, will have to wait 10 seconds before another response can be reinforced—irrespective of the number of responses. Response rates under FI schedules show a scalloped pattern. Immediately after each reinforced response, the animal makes few if any responses. As the payoff time approaches, the animal responds more and more. A monthly paycheck puts you on an FI schedule.

VARIABLE-INTERVAL (VI) SCHEDULES

For **variable-interval schedules,** the average interval is predetermined. For example, on a VI-20 schedule, reinforcers are delivered at an average rate of 1 every 20 seconds. This schedule generates a moderate but very stable response rate. Extinction under VI schedules is gradual and much slower than under fixed-interval schedules. In one case, a pigeon pecked 18,000 times during the first 4 hours after reinforcement stopped and required 168 hours before its responding extinguished completely (Ferster & Skinner, 1957). You have experienced a VI schedule if you've taken a course with a professor who gave occasional, irregularly scheduled pop quizzes. Did you study your notes each day before class?

■

Shaping

As parts of experiments, we have spoken of rats pressing levers to get food. However, even lever pressing is a

learned behavior. When a rat is introduced to an operant chamber, it is quite unlikely that it will ever press the lever spontaneously; the rat has learned to use its paws in many ways, but it probably has never pressed a lever before. How should you go about training the rat to perform a behavior that it would rarely, if ever, produce on its own? You've settled on a reinforcer, food, and a schedule of reinforcement, FR-1, now what? To train new or complex behaviors, you will want to use a method called **shaping by successive approximations**—in which you reinforce any responses that successively approximate and ultimately match the desired response.

Here's how you'd do it. First, you deprive the rat of food for a day. (Without deprivation, food is not likely to serve as a reinforcer.) Then you systematically make food pellets available in the food hopper in an operant chamber so that the rat learns to look there for food. Now you can begin the actual shaping process by making delivery of food contingent on specific aspects of the rat's behavior, such as orienting itself toward the lever. Next, food is delivered only as the rat moves closer and closer to the lever. Soon the requirement for reinforcement is actually to touch the lever. Finally, the rat must depress the lever for food to be delivered. In small increments, the rat has learned that a lever press will produce food. Thus, for *shaping* to work, you must define what constitutes progress toward the target behavior and use *differential reinforcement* to refine each step along the way.

Let's look at another example, in which shaping was used to improve the life of a young autistic child.

HOW WE KNOW

SHAPING WITH AN AUTISTIC CHILD The patient was a 3-year-old boy who was diagnosed as autistic. He lacked normal social and verbal behavior and was given to ungovernable tantrums and self-destructive actions. After a cataract operation, he refused to wear the glasses that were essential for the development of normal vision. So, first, he was given a bit of candy or fruit at the clicking sound of a toy noisemaker; through its association with food, the sound became a conditioned reinforcer. Then training began with empty eyeglass frames. At first, the noisemaker was sounded after the child picked up the glasses. Soon, though, it sounded only when the child held the glasses and, later, only when he carried them. Slowly and through successive approximations, the boy was rewarded for bringing the frames closer to his eyes. After a few weeks, he was putting the empty frames on his head at odd angles, and, finally, he was wearing them in the proper manner. With further training, the child learned to wear his glasses up to 12 hours a day (Wolf et al., 1964).

■ **Fixed-interval schedule** A schedule of reinforcement in which a reinforcer is delivered for the first response made after a fixed period of time.

■ **Variable-interval schedule** A schedule of reinforcement in which a reinforcer is delivered for the first response made after a variable period of time whose average is predetermined.

■ **Shaping by successive approximations** A behavioral method that reinforces responses that successively approximate and ultimately match the desired response.

Let's return to your rat. Recall that we suggested you might wish to teach it to turn circles in its cage. Can you devise a plan, using shaping, to bring about this behavior? What you need to think about is what each successive approximation would be. At the beginning, for example, you might reinforce the rat if it just turned its head in a particular direction. Next, you would only let the rat obtain a food pellet if it turned its whole body in the right direction. What might you do after that?

The two forms of learning we have examined so far—classical conditioning and operant conditioning—have most often been studied with the assumption that processes of learning were consistent across all animals. In fact, we have cited examples from dogs, cats, rats, mice, pigeons, and humans to show exactly such consistency. However, researchers have come to understand that learning is modified in many situations by the particular biological and cognitive capabilities of individual species. We turn now to the processes that limit the generality of the laws of learning.

SUMMING UP

Operant conditioning procedures, pioneered by Thorndike and Skinner, manipulate the consequences of an organism's behavior to affect subsequent behavior. Positive and negative reinforcement increase the probability of a behavior; positive and negative punishment decrease the probability of a behavior. Training with discriminative stimuli reduces generalization beyond target behaviors. Conditioned reinforcers exert more influence than primary reinforcers on many human behaviors. The Premack principle suggests that a more probable activity can be used to reinforce a less probable activity. Different schedules of reinforcement generate distinctive patterns of responses. Shaping requires that successive approximations toward the target behavior be differentially reinforced.

How could you teach an animal friend to waterski using operant conditioning techniques?

Biology and Learning

The contemporary view that a single, general account of the associationist principles of learning is common to humans and all animals was first proposed by English philosopher **David Hume** in 1748. Hume reasoned that "any theory by which we explain the operations of the understanding, or the origin and connexion

This woman, Sue Strong, was assisted by a monkey who had been operantly shaped to comb her hair, feed her, turn book pages, and make other responses she could not do for herself because of paralysis. For each of these behaviors, can you think through the successive approximations you would reinforce to arrive at the end point?

of the passions in man, will acquire additional authority, if we find that the same theory is requisite to explain the same phenomena in all other animals" (Hume, 1748/1951, p. 104).

The appealing simplicity of such a view has come under scrutiny since the 1960s as psychologists have discovered certain constraints, or limitations, on the generality of the findings regarding conditioning (Bailey & Bailey, 1993; Garcia, 1993; Todd & Morris, 1992, 1993). In Chapter 3, we familiarized you with the idea that animals have evolved in response to the need for survival: We can explain many of the differences among species as adaptations to the demands of their particular environmental niches. The same evolutionary perspective applies to a species' capacity for learning (Leger, 1992). **Biological constraints on learning** are any limitations on learning imposed by a species' genetic endowment. These constraints can apply to the animal's sensory, behavioral, and cognitive capacities. We will examine two areas of research that show how behavior–environment relations can be biased by an organism's genotype: instinctual drift and taste-aversion learning.

Instinctual Drift

You have no doubt seen animals performing tricks on television or in the circus. Some animals play baseball or Ping-Pong, and others drive tiny race cars. For years, **Keller Breland** and **Marion Breland** used operant conditioning techniques to train thousands of animals from many different species to perform a remarkable array of behaviors. The Brelands had believed that general principles derived from laboratory research using virtually any type of response or reward could be directly applied to the control of animal behavior outside the laboratory.

At some point after training, though, some of the animals began to "misbehave." For example, a raccoon was trained to pick up a coin, put it into a toy bank, and collect an edible reinforcer. The raccoon, however, would not immediately deposit the coin. Even worse, when there were two coins to be deposited, conditioning broke down completely—the raccoon would not give up the coins at all. Instead, it would rub the coins together, dip them into the bank, and then pull them back out. But is this really so strange? Raccoons often engage in rubbing and washing behaviors as they re-

move the outer shells of a favorite food, crayfish. Similarly, when pigs were given the task of putting their hard-earned tokens into a large piggy bank, they instead would drop the coins onto the floor, root (poke at) them with their snouts, and toss them into the air. Again, should you consider this strange? Pigs root and shake their food as a natural part of their inherited food-gathering repertory.

These experiences convinced the Brelands that, even when animals have learned to make operant responses perfectly, the "learned behavior drifts toward instinctual behavior" over time. They called this tendency **instinctual drift** (Breland & Breland, 1951, 1961). The behavior of their animals is not explainable by ordinary operant principles, but it is understandable if you consider the species-specific tendencies imposed by an inherited genotype. These tendencies override the changes in behavior brought about by operant conditioning.

The bulk of traditional research on animal learning focused on arbitrarily chosen responses to conveniently available stimuli. The Brelands's theory and demonstration of instinctual drift makes it evident that not all aspects of learning are under the control of the experimenters' reinforcers. Behaviors will be more or less easy to change as a function of an animal's normal, genetically programmed responses in its environment. Conditioning will be particularly efficient when you can frame a target response as biologically relevant. For example, what change might you make to get the pigs to place their tokens in a bank? If the token was paired with a water reward for a thirsty pig, it would then not be rooted as food but would be deposited in the bank as a valuable commodity—dare we say a liquid asset?

Taste-Aversion Learning

Your authors have a pair of confessions to make: One of us still gets a bit queasy at the thought of eating pork and beans; the other has the same response, alas, to popcorn. Why? In each case, we became violently ill after eating one of these foods. Although it's very unlikely that it was the food itself that made us sick—and we have tried valiantly, particularly for the popcorn, to convince ourselves of that fact—we nonetheless have this queasy response. We can look to nonhuman animals for a clue to why this is so.

Suppose we asked you to devise a strategy for tasting a variety of unfamiliar substances. If you had the genetic endowment of rats, you would be very cautious in doing so. When presented with a new food or flavor, rats take only a very small sample. Only if it fails to make them sick will they go back for more. To flip that around, suppose we include a substance with the new flavor that does make the rats ill—they'll never consume that fla-

Biological constraints on learning Any limitations on an organism's capacity to learn that are caused by the inherited sensory, response, or cognitive capabilities of members of a given species.

Instinctual drift The tendency for learned behavior to drift toward instinctual behavior over time.

vor again. This phenomenon is known as **taste-aversion learning.** You can see why having this genetic capacity to sample and learn which foods are safe and which are toxic could have great survival value. Remember Lorenzo from the beginning of the chapter? He appears to have become averse to the taste of wine by virtue of the illness he experienced after his binge.

Taste-aversion learning is an enormously powerful mechanism. Unlike most other instances of classical conditioning, taste aversion is learned with only one pairing of a CS (the novel flavor) and its consequences (the result of the underlying UCS—the element that actually brings about the illness). This is true even with a long interval, 12 hours or more, between the time the rat consumes the substance and the time it becomes ill. Finally, unlike many classically conditioned associations that are quite fragile, this one is permanent after one experience. Again, to understand these violations of the norms of classical conditioning, you should consider how dramatically this mechanism aids survival.

John Garcia, the psychologist who first documented taste-aversion learning in the laboratory, and his colleague Robert Koelling used this phenomenon to demonstrate that, in general, animals are biologically prepared to learn certain associations. The researchers discovered that some CS–UCS combinations can be classically conditioned in particular species of animals, but others cannot.

HOW WE KNOW

MATCHES BETWEEN STIMULI AND CONSEQUENCES In phase 1 of Garcia and Koelling's experiment, thirsty rats were first familiarized with the experimental situation in which licking a tube produced three CSs: saccharin-flavored water, noise, and bright light. In phase 2, when the rats licked the tube, half of them received only the sweet water and half received only the noise, light, and plain water. Each of these two groups was again divided: Half of each group was given electric shocks that produced pain, and half was given X-ray radiation that produced nausea and illness.

The amount of water drunk by the rats in phase 1 was compared with the amount drunk in phase 2, when pain and illness were involved (see **Figure 7.14**). Big reductions in drinking occurred when flavor was associated with illness (taste aversion) and when noise and light were associated with pain. However, there was little change in behavior under the other two conditions—when flavor predicted pain or when the "bright-noisy water" predicted illness.

The pattern of results suggests that rats have an inborn bias to associate particular stimuli with particular con-

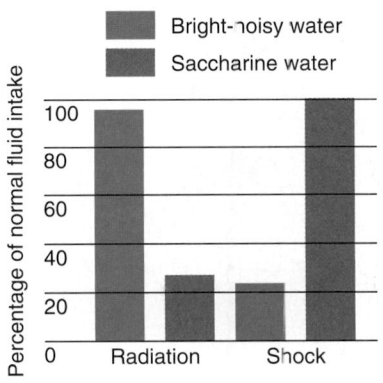

FIGURE 7.14

Inborn Bias

Results from Garcia and Koelling's study (1966) showed that rats possess an inborn bias to associate certain cues with certain outcomes. Rats avoided saccharin-flavored water when it predicted illness but not when it predicted shock. Conversely, rats avoided the "bright-noisy water" when it predicted shock but not when it predicted illness.

sequences (Garcia & Koelling, 1966). Some instances of conditioning, then, depend not only on the relationship between stimuli and behavior but also on the way an organism is genetically predisposed toward stimuli in its environment (Barker et al., 1978). Animals appear to have encoded, within their genetic inheritance, the types of sensory cues—taste, smell, or appearance—that are most likely to signal dimensions of reward or danger. Experimenters who try arbitrarily to break these genetic links will look forward to little success.

Researchers have put knowledge of the mechanisms of taste-aversion learning to practical use. To stop coyotes from killing sheep (and sheep ranchers from shooting coyotes), John Garcia and colleagues have put toxic lamb burgers wrapped in sheep fur on the outskirts of fenced-in areas of sheep ranches. The coyotes who eat these lamb burgers get sick, vomit, and develop an instant distaste for lamb meat. Their subsequent disgust at the mere sight of sheep makes them back away from the animals instead of attacking.

One of the most serious instances of taste aversions in humans occurs when cancer patients become unable to tolerate normal foods in their diets. Their aversions are,

Taste-aversion learning A biological constraint on learning in which an organism learns in one trial to avoid a food whose ingestion is followed by illness.

in part, a consequence of their chemotherapy treatments, which often follow meals and which produce nausea.

HOW WE KNOW

TASTE AVERSIONS IN BREAST CANCER PATIENTS A group of 22 women undergoing treatments for breast cancer provided reports on their food preferences over the course of eight sessions of chemotherapy, each separated by three weeks. The women reported everything they had eaten in the 24-hour periods before and after chemotherapy. They rated each type of food and beverage on a scale from 1 (dislike very much) to 9 (like very much). The researchers considered an aversion to have formed if a participant's rating dropped by 4 points over the course of chemotherapy. Overall, 46 percent of the women developed an aversion to at least one food. However, those aversions formed in the first two sessions of therapy were short-lived. The researchers speculated that, unlike rats and other animals that acquire taste aversions, these women were able to reason that "the chemotherapy caused nausea, not the food." If they tried the food again, the women provided themselves with extinction trials that extinguished the conditioned aversion (Jacobsen et al., 1993).

By showing that aversions are acquired through the mechanisms of classical conditioning, researchers can devise means to counteract them (Bernstein, 1991). Researchers have arranged, for example, for children with cancer not to be given meals just before chemotherapy. They've also created "scapegoat" aversions. The children are given candies or ice cream of unusual flavors to eat before the treatments so that the taste aversion becomes conditioned only to those special flavors and not to the flavors they generally like. Researchers have uncovered other aspects of patients' experiences of chemotherapy that are the product of classical conditioning. Many patients, for example, begin to experience nausea before the chemotherapy sessions—the clinic settings in which they receive treatment begin to function as a conditioned stimulus (Tomoyasu et al., 1996). (This effect should remind you of the studies on drug tolerance.) Once again, understanding the roots of such effects in conditioning allows researchers to design treatments to counteract them.

You have now seen why modern behavior analysts must be attentive to the types of responses each species is best suited to learn (Todd & Morris, 1992). If you want to teach an old dog new tricks, you're best off adapting the tricks to the dog's genetic behavioral repertoire! Our survey of learning is not complete, however, because we have not yet dealt with types of learning that might require more complex cognitive processes. We turn now to those types of learning.

How have researchers used taste-aversion conditioning to prevent coyotes from killing sheep?

SUMMING UP

The phenomenon of instinctual drift suggests that organisms are limited in what they will learn by species-specific instincts. Taste aversion is so powerful in some animals that it is permanently learned after a single pairing of a CS with the consequences of the UCS. Many people who undergo chemotherapy experience conditioned taste aversions. Researchers are trying to devise methods based on classical conditioning to undo or prevent those aversions.

Cognitive Influences on Learning

Our reviews of classical and operant conditioning have demonstrated that a wide variety of behaviors can be understood as the products of simple learning processes. You might wonder, however, if there are certain classes of learning that require more complex, more cognitive types of processes. *Cognition* is any mental activity involved in the representation and processing of knowledge, such as thinking, remembering, perceiving, and language use. In this section, we look at forms of learning in animals and humans that cannot be explained only by principles of classical or operant conditioning. We suggest, therefore, that the behaviors are partially the product of cognitive processes.

Animal Cognition

In this chapter, we have emphasized that, species-specific constraints aside, rules of learning acquired from research on rats and pigeons apply as well to dogs, monkeys, and humans. Researchers who study **animal cognition** have demonstrated that it is not only classical and operant conditioning that generalizes across species (Wasserman, 1993, 1994). In his original formulation of the theory of evolution, Charles Darwin suggested that cognitive abilities evolved along with the physical forms of animals. In this section, we will describe two impressive types of animal performance that indicate further continuity in the cognitive capabilities of nonhuman and human animals.

COGNITIVE MAPS

Edward C. Tolman (1886–1959) pioneered the study of cognitive processes in learning by inventing experimental circumstances in which mechanical, one-to-one associations between specific stimuli and responses could not explain animals' observed behavior. Consider the maze shown in **Figure 7.15**. Tolman and his students demonstrated that, when an original goal path is blocked in a maze, a rat with prior experience in the maze will take the shortest detour around the barrier, even though that particular response was never previously reinforced (Tolman & Honzik, 1930). The rats, therefore, behaved as if they were responding to an internal **cognitive map**—a representation of the overall layout of the maze—rather than blindly exploring different parts of the maze through trial and error (Tolman, 1948). Tolman's results showed that conditioning involves more than the simple formation of associations between sets of stimuli or between responses and reinforcers. It includes learning and representing other facets of the total behavioral context.

Research in Tolman's tradition has consistently demonstrated an impressive capacity for spatial memory in birds, bees, rats, humans, and other animals (Benhamou & Poucet, 1996; Olton, 1992). To understand the efficiency of spatial cognitive maps, consider the functions they serve (Poucet, 1993):

- Animals use spatial memory to recognize and identify features of their environments.

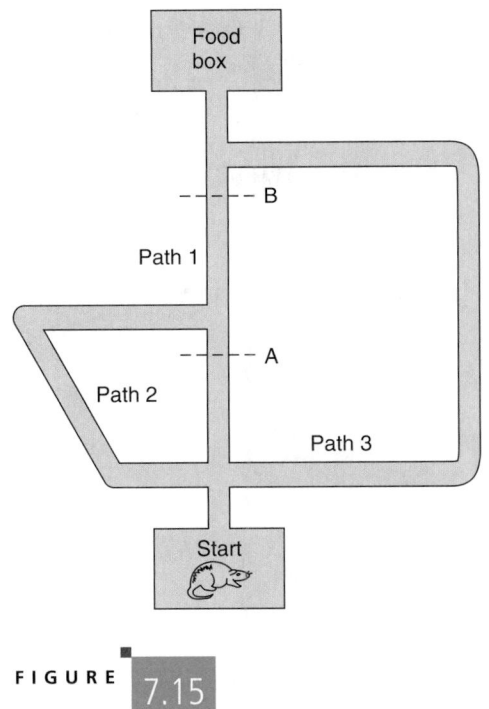

FIGURE 7.15

Use of Cognitive Maps in Maze Learning

Subjects preferred the direct path (Path 1) when it was open. With a block at A, they preferred Path 2. When a block was placed at B, the rats usually chose Path 3. Their behavior seemed to indicate that they had a cognitive map of the best way to get the food.

- Animals use spatial memory to find important goal objects in their environments.

- Animals use spatial memory to plan their route through an environment.

You can see these different functions of cognitive maps at work in the many species of birds that store food over a dispersed area but are able to recover that food with great accuracy when they need it:

Clark's nutcracker is the champion among food storers that have been studied. In the late summer, these birds bury up to 6,000 caches of pine seeds on mountainsides in the American Southwest. They recover the seeds as late as the next spring, when the cached food supports exceptionally early breeding. (Shettleworth, 1993, p. 180)

Animal cognition The cognitive capabilities of nonhuman animals; researchers trace the development of cognitive capabilities across species and the continuity of capabilities from nonhuman to human animals.

Cognitive map A mental representation of physical space.

COGNITIVE INFLUENCES ON LEARNING

209

"Stimulus, response. Stimulus, response! Don't you ever *think?*"

(THE FAR SIDE, by Gary Larson. Copyright © 1986. Universal Press Syndicate. Reprinted with permission. All rights reserved.)

The birds are not just roaming their environment and coming on the seeds through good fortune. They return, with up to 84 percent accuracy, to the thousands of locations at which they buried their seeds (Kamil & Balda, 1990). They are also able to discriminate sites that still have seeds from those that have been emptied (Kamil et al., 1993). Bird species that depend heavily on cached seeds for their food supply outperform other, even closely related, species on laboratory spatial memory tasks (Balda et al., 1997; Olson et al., 1995). No differences correlated with caching behavior are found when the species are compared on nonspatial memory tasks. Note that these birds' caching behaviors are not reinforced when they initially bury their seeds. Only if their cognitive maps remained accurate over the winter can they later recover the seeds and survive to reproduce.

CONCEPTUAL BEHAVIOR

We have seen that cognitive maps, in part, help animals preserve details of the spatial locations of objects in their environments. But what other cognitive processes can animals use to find structure, or categories of experiences, in the diverse stimuli they encounter in their environments? In Chapter 11, we will suggest that one of the challenges of language acquisition is for children to form generalizations about new *concepts* and *categories* they are learning, like the words *dog* and *tree*. Human children, however, are not the only animals capable of facing this challenge. Researchers have demonstrated that pigeons as well have the cognitive ability to make use of *conceptual* distinctions.

HOW WE KNOW

PIGEONS MAKE JUDGMENTS BASED ON CATEGORY STRUCTURE Edward Wasserman and his colleagues (1992) presented pigeons with color photographs of people, flowers, cars, and chairs. For each pigeon, the set of four concepts was divided into two larger categories (see **Figure 7.16**). For example, one pigeon might receive food if it pecked an orange key after viewing a person or a car and if it pecked a red key after viewing a flower or a chair. The pigeons learned to make the appropriate responses around 80 percent of the time or better. In a second training phase of the experiment, the pigeon was trained to provide a new response to only half the members—one smaller category—of each of these larger categories. Thus, the pigeon might be required to peck a green key when it saw a person and a white key when it saw a chair. Once again, performance on this task was about 80 percent accurate or better.

Now what happens when the pigeons are shown a flower or a car and must choose between the green and white keys? They have no history of reinforcement that links these stimuli to these

	Stimulus	Reinforced response
Training phase 1	People or cars	Orange key press
	Flowers or chairs	Red key press
Training phase 2	People	Green key press
	Chairs	White key press

	Stimulus	Category response
Test phase	Cars	Green key press
	Flowers	White key press

FIGURE 7.16

Concept Learning in Pigeons

The first training phase teaches the pigeons which concepts go together into the same larger category. The second training phase teaches a new response for half the members of each category. The test phase demonstrates generalization to the other members of the newly acquired categories. (This is one example of the different combinations of stimuli and responses presented to different pigeons.)

responses, so we can't predict behavior based on simple learning processes. But what would you do if we put you in this situation? In the first phase of the experiment, you would have learned that, for example, flowers and chairs go together. In the second phase of the experiment, you would have learned that you should provide one of two responses to each photo of a flower. When confronted with a chair, and the same choice of responses, you would probably try the response that had applied to flowers. That is, in fact, what pigeons largely did as well. On 60 to 70 percent of test trials, they used "category" information to emit a previously unreinforced behavior.

We already saw that generalization occurs in classical and operant conditioning based on the *perceptual similarity* of stimuli. In this experiment by Wasserman and colleagues, the generalization did not involve perceptual similarity—chairs and flowers, for example, don't look much alike. Instead, the grounds for generalization was the *cognitive similarity* brought about by the newly acquired conceptual structure. Further research suggests that pigeons are able to acquire the abstract concepts of *same* and *different*: They are able to produce distinctive responses when the elements of a test array are all the same (for example, 16 identical pictures of train engines) versus all different (for example, 16 varied pictures) (Wasserman et al., 1995; Young et al., 1997).

We will devote Chapters 8 and 9 to an analysis of cognitive processes in humans. The experiments we have described here, however, should convince you that humans are not the only species with impressive and useful cognitive capabilities. Before we conclude this chapter, let's move to another type of learning that requires cognitive processes.

Observational Learning

To introduce this further type of learning, we'd like you to return for a moment to the comparison of rats' and humans' approaches to sampling new foods. The rats are almost certainly more cautious than you are, but that's largely because they are missing an invaluable source of information—input from other rats. When you try a new food, it's almost always in a context in which you have good reason to believe that other people have eaten and enjoyed the food. The probability of your "food-eating behavior" is thus influenced by your knowledge of patterns of reinforcement for other individuals. This example illustrates your capacity to learn via *vicarious reinforcement* and *vicarious punishment*. You can use your cognitive capacities for memory and

reasoning to change your own behaviors in light of the experience of others.

In fact, much *social learning* occurs in situations where learning would not be predicted by traditional conditioning theory, because a learner has made no active response and has received no tangible reinforcer. The individual, after simply watching another person exhibiting behavior that was reinforced or punished, later behaves in much the same way, or refrains from doing so. This is known as **observational learning.** Cognition often enters into observational learning in the form of expectations. In essence, after observing a model, you may think: If I do exactly what she does, I will get the same reinforcer or avoid the same punisher. A younger child may be better behaved than his older sister because he has learned from the sister's mistakes.

This capacity to learn from watching as well as from doing is extremely useful. It enables you to acquire large, integrated patterns of behavior without going through the tedious trial-and-error process of gradually eliminating wrong responses and acquiring the right ones. You can profit immediately from the mistakes and successes of others. Researchers have demonstrated that observational learning is not special to humans. Among other species, pigeons (Zentall et al., 1996), zebra danio fish (Hall & Suboski, 1995), and even octopuses (Fiorito & Scotto, 1992) are capable of changing their behavior after observing the performance of another member of their species.

A classic demonstration of human observational learning occurred in the laboratory of **Albert Bandura.** After watching adult models punching, hitting, and kicking a large plastic BoBo doll, the children in the experiment later showed a greater frequency of the same behaviors than did children in control conditions who had not observed the aggressive models (Bandura et al., 1963). Subsequent studies showed that children imitated such behaviors just from watching filmed sequences of models, even when the models were cartoon characters.

There is little question now that we learn much—both prosocial (helping) and antisocial (hurting) behaviors—through observation of models, but there are many possible models in the world. What variables are important in determining which models will be most likely to influence you? Research has yielded the following general conclusions (Baldwin & Baldwin, 1973; Bandura, 1977). A model's observed behavior will be most influential when

- it is seen as having reinforcing consequences
- the model is perceived positively, liked, and respected

Observational learning The process of learning new responses by watching the behavior of another.

- there are perceived similarities between features and traits of the model and the observer
- the observer is rewarded for paying attention to the model's behavior
- the model's behavior is visible and salient—it stands out as a clear figure against the background of competing models
- it is within the observer's range of competence to imitate the behavior

To understand this list of findings, you should imagine yourself in modeling situations and see how each item in the list would apply. Imagine, for example, you are watching someone who is learning how to parachute jump. Or consider how someone might learn to be a "good" gang member by observing his or her friends.

Because people learn so efficiently from models, you can understand why a good deal of psychological re-

From top to bottom: Adult models aggression; boy imitates aggression; girl imitates aggression. What does this experiment demonstrate about the role models play in learning?

search has been directed at the behavioral impact of television: Are viewers affected by what they see being rewarded and punished on TV? Attention has focused on the link between televised acts of violence—murder, rape, assault, robbery, terrorism, and suicide—and children's and adolescents' subsequent behavior. Does exposure to acts of violence foster imitation? The conclusion from psychological research is yes—it does for some people, and particularly in the United States (Comstock & Scharrer, 1999). Several decades of research have consistently demonstrated three ways in which television violence has a negative impact on viewers' lives (Smith & Donnerstein, 1998). First, the viewing of television violence brings about, through the mechanisms of observational learning, increases in aggressive behavior. This causal association has particularly important implications for children: Aggressive habits born of heavy television viewing early in life may serve as the basis for antisocial behavior later in life. Second, the viewing of television violence leads viewers to overestimate the occurrences of violence in the everyday world. Television viewers may be unduly afraid of becoming victims of real-world violence. Third, the viewing of television violence may bring about *desensitization*, a reduction in both emotional arousal and distress at viewing violent behavior. Consider a laboratory example of the consequences of desensitization.

HOW WE KNOW

MEDIA VIOLENCE ENHANCES TOLERANCE OF REAL-LIFE AGGRESSION Each student in a group of 42 fourth- and fifth-grade children was brought to an experimental room to watch one of two videotapes: Violent sequences from the movie *The Karate Kid* and nonviolent sports scenes from the 1984 Summer Olympics. After viewing these tapes, the children were led to believe they were watching real-life events unfold over a video hook-up. The events (which were actually on videotape) showed two younger children (6-year-olds) at first playing in a room and then becoming increasingly more aggressive with each other. The older children had been instructed to go get the experimenter if he or she became concerned about the on-camera behavior. Children who had viewed *The Karate Kid* took nearly twice as long to fetch the experimenter as children who had viewed the Olympics. Thus, the researchers concluded that the prior viewing of the violent movie led the children to tolerate the real-world aggression for a longer period of time before they became alarmed (Molitor & Hirsch, 1994).

You may be thinking, "this is a small effect in a laboratory study"—but imagine the cumulative effect of all the violence children have the opportunity to see on TV. Note that research has also shown that children can learn prosocial, helping behaviors when they watch television programs that provide prosocial behavioral models (Rosenkoetter, 1999; Singer & Singer, 1990). You should take seriously the idea that children learn from the television they watch. As a parent or caretaker, you may want to help children select appropriate televised models.

An analysis of observational learning acknowledges both that principles of reinforcement influence behavior and that humans have the capacity to use their cognitive processes to change behaviors with vicarious rewards and punishment. This approach to the understanding of human behavior has proven to be very powerful (Bandura, 1986). In Chapter 16, we will look at successful programs of therapy that have emerged from the cognitive modification of maladaptive patterns of behavior.

Let's close out this chapter by calling back to mind a visit to a horror movie. How can behavior analysis explain your experiences? If you went to the movie because of a friend's recommendation, you have succumbed to vicarious reinforcement. If you made it to the theater, de-

spite havi...
evidence of ...
made you fear ...
fects of classical c...
film made you vow...
you have discovered t...
subsequent behavior.

Are you ready to return ...

SUMMING UP

Researchers have identified cognitive fo... that cannot be explained as instances of class... ant conditioning. Cognitive maps allow animal... tion and survive in complex environments. Pigeons a... to learn to make distinctions based on conceptual dis... tions that are not based on perceptual distinctions. In cir... cumstances of observational learning, humans and other animals acquire new behaviors by virtue of vicarious reinforcement or punishment. People can learn both prosocial and antisocial behaviors from models.

RECAPPING MAIN POINTS

The Study of Learning

- Learning entails a relatively consistent change in behavior or behavior potential based on experience.
- Behaviorists believe that much behavior can be explained by simple learning processes.
- They also believe that many of the same principles of learning apply to all organisms.

Classical Conditioning: Learning Predictable Signals

- In classical conditioning, first investigated by Pavlov, an unconditioned stimulus (UCS) elicits an unconditioned response (UCR). A neutral stimulus paired with the UCS becomes a conditioned stimulus (CS), which elicits a response, called the conditioned response (CR).

- Extinction occurs when the UCS no longer follows the CS.
- Stimulus generalization is the phenomenon whereby stimuli similar to the CS elicit the CR.
- Discrimination learning narrows the range of CSs to which an organism responds.
- For classical conditioning to occur, there must be a contingent and informative relationship between the CS and UCS.
- Classical conditioning explains many emotional responses and drug tolerance. It has also been used to change immune function.

Operant Conditioning: Learning about Consequences

- Thorndike demonstrated that behaviors that bring about satisfying outcomes tend to be repeated.

- Skinner's behavior analytic approach centers on manipulating contingencies of reinforcement and observing the effects on behavior.
- Behaviors are made more likely by positive and negative reinforcement. They are made less likely by positive and negative punishment.
- Contextually appropriate behavior is explained by the three-term contingency of discriminative stimulus-behavior-consequence.
- Primary reinforcers are stimuli that function as reinforcers even when an organism has not had previous experience with them. Conditioned reinforcers are acquired by association with primary reinforcers.
- Probable activities function as positive reinforcers.
- Behavior is affected by schedules of reinforcement that may be varied or fixed and delivered in intervals or in ratios.
- Complex responses may be learned through shaping.

...learning
...by the spe-
...oires of different

...rift may overwhelm
...sponse–reinforcement
...ng.

...ste-aversion learning suggests
that species are genetically prepared for some forms of
associations.

Cognitive Influences on Learning

- Some forms of learning reflect more complex processes than those of classical or operant conditioning.
- Animals develop cognitive maps to enable them to function in a complex environment.
- Conceptual behavior allows animals to form generalizations about the structure of the environment.

- Behaviors can be vicariously reinforced or punished. Humans and other animals can learn through observation.

Key Terms

acquisition (p. 184)
animal cognition (p. 209)
behavior analysis (p. 182)
biological constraints on learning (p. 206)
blocking (p. 190)
classical conditioning (p. 183)
cognitive map (p. 209)
conditioned reinforcers (p. 200)
conditioned response (CR) (p. 184)
conditioned stimulus (CS) (p. 184)
conditioning (p. 180)
discriminative stimuli (p. 197)
extinction (p. 186)
fixed-interval schedule (p. 204)
fixed-ratio schedule (p. 203)
instinctual drift (p. 206)
law of effect (p. 195)
learning (p. 181)
learning-performance distinction (p. 181)

negative punishment (p. 197)
negative reinforcement (p. 196)
observational learning (p. 211)
operant (p. 195)
operant conditioning (p. 195)
operant extinction (p. 196)
partial reinforcement effect (p. 203)
positive punishment (p. 197)
positive reinforcement (p. 196)
primary reinforcers (p. 200)
psychoneuroimmunology (p. 193)
punisher (p. 197)
reflex (p. 184)
reinforcer (p. 196)
reinforcement contingency (p. 195)
schedules of reinforcement (p. 203)
shaping by successive approximations (p. 204)
spontaneous recovery (p. 186)
stimulus discrimination (p. 187)
stimulus generalization (p. 186)
taste-aversion learning (p. 207)
three-term contingency (p. 197)
unconditioned response (UCR) (p. 184)
unconditioned stimulus (UCS) (p. 184)
variable-interval schedule (p. 204)
variable-ratio schedule (p. 203)

memory

8

■ **WHAT IS MEMORY?**
Ebbinghaus Quantifies
Memory • Types of Memory
• An Overview of Memory
Processes

■ **SENSORY MEMORY**
Iconic Memory •
Echoic Memory

■ **SHORT-TERM MEMORY
AND WORKING MEMORY**
The Capacity Limitations
of STM • Accommodating
to STM Capacity • Working
Memory

■ **LONG-TERM MEMORY:
ENCODING AND RETRIEVAL**
Context and Encoding •
Retrieval Cues • The
Processes of Encoding
and Retrieval • Improving
Memory for Unstructured
Information • Metamemory

■ **PSYCHOLOGY IN YOUR
LIFE: HOW CAN MEMORY
RESEARCH HELP YOU
PREPARE FOR EXAMS?**

■ **STRUCTURES IN
LONG-TERM MEMORY**
Memory Structures •
Using Memory Structures •
Remembering as a
Reconstructive Process

■ **PSYCHOLOGY IN THE
21ST CENTURY: HUMAN
MEMORY SEARCHES
AND WEB SEARCHES**

■ **BIOLOGICAL ASPECTS
OF MEMORY**
Searching for the Engram •
Amnesia • Brain Imaging

■ **RECAPPING MAIN POINTS**
Key Terms

AT THE BEGINNING OF HIS AUTOBIOGRAPHY, *Brando,* Marlon Brando shares his earliest memory (Brando, 1994, p. 3):

As I stumble back across the years of my life trying to recall what it was about, I find that nothing is really clear. I suppose the first memory I have was when I was too young to remember how young I was. I opened my eyes, looked around in the mouse-colored light and realized that Ermi [Brando's governess] was still asleep, so I dressed myself as best I could and went down the stairs, left foot first on each step. I had to scuff my way to the porch because I couldn't buckle my sandals. I sat on the one step in the sun at the dead end of Thirty-second Street and waited. It must have been spring because the big tree in front of the house was shedding pods with two wings like a dragonfly. On days when there wasn't any wind, they would spin around in the air as they drifted softly to the ground.

I watched them float all the way down, sitting with my neck craned back until my mouth opened and holding out my hand just in case, but they never landed on it. When one hit the ground I'd look up again, my eyes darting, waiting for the next magical event, the sun warming the yellow hairs on my head.

Waiting like that for the next magic was as good a moment as any other that I can remember in the last sixty-five years.

As you begin this chapter on memory processes, we'd like you to take a moment to recover your own earliest memory. How long ago did the memory originate? Do you recall as clear a scene as Brando described? Has your memory been influenced by other people's recollections of the same event?

Now, a slightly different exercise. We'd like you to imagine what it would be like if you suddenly had no memory of your past—of the people you have known or of events that have happened to you. You wouldn't remember your mother's face, or your tenth birthday, or your senior prom. Without such "time anchors," how would you maintain a sense of who you are—of your self-identity? Or suppose you lost the ability to form any new memories. What would happen to your most recent experiences? Could you follow a conversation or untangle the plot of a TV show? Everything would vanish, as if events had never existed, as if you had never had any thoughts in mind. Is there any activity you can think of that is not influenced by memory?

If you have never given much thought to your memory, it's probably because it tends to do its job reasonably well—you take it for granted, alongside other bodily processes, like digestion or breathing. But as with stomachaches or allergies, the times you notice your memory are likely to be the times when something goes wrong: You forget your car keys, an important date, lines in a play, or the answer to an examination question that you know you "really knew." There's no reason you shouldn't find these occasions irritating, but you should also reflect for a moment on the estimate that the average human brain can store 100 trillion bits of information. The task of managing such a vast array of information is a formidable one. Perhaps you shouldn't be too surprised when an answer is sometimes not available when you need it!

Our goal in this chapter is to explain how you usually remember so much, and why you forget some of what you have known. We will explore how you get your everyday experiences into and out of memory. You will learn what psychology has discovered about different types of memory and about how those memories work. We hope that in the course of learning the many facts of memory, you will gain an appreciation for how wonderful memory is.

One last thing: Because this is a chapter on memory, we're going to put your memory immediately to work. We'd like you to remember the number 37. Do whatever you need to do to remember 37. And yes, there will be a test!

How are actors and actresses able to remember all the different aspects—movements, expressions, and words—of their performances?

What Is Memory?

To begin, we will define **memory** as the capacity to store and retrieve information. In this chapter, we will describe memory as a type of *information processing*. The bulk of our attention, therefore, will be trained on the flow of information in and out of your memory systems. Our examination of the processes that guide the acquisition and retrieval of information will enable you to refine your sense of what *memory* means. Our discussion starts with the earliest formal body of research on memory, published in 1885. We will then introduce you to distinctions among types of memory, carved out by contemporary researchers.

Ebbinghaus Quantifies Memory

See if this statement rings true: "Facts crammed at examination time soon vanish, if they were not sufficiently grounded by other study and later subjected to a sufficient review." In other words, if you cram for a test, you're not likely to remember very much a few days

later. This astute, and very contemporary, observation was made in 1885 by the German psychologist **Hermann Ebbinghaus,** who outlined a series of such phenomena to motivate his new science of memory. Ebbinghaus's observations added up to a convincing argument in favor of an empirical investigation of memory. What was needed was a methodology, and Ebbinghaus invented a brilliant one. Ebbinghaus used nonsense syllables—meaningless three-letter units consisting of a vowel between two consonants, such as *CEG* or *DAX.* He used nonsense syllables, rather than meaningful words, like DOG, because he hoped to obtain a "pure" measure of memory—one uncontaminated by previous learning or associations that a person might bring to the experimental memory task. Not only was Ebbinghaus the researcher, he was also his own subject. He performed the research tasks himself and measured his own performance. The task he assigned himself was memorization of lists of varying length. Ebbinghaus chose to use *rote learning,* memorization by mechanical repetition, to perform the task.

Ebbinghaus started his studies by reading through the items one at a time until he finished the list. Then he read through the list again in the same order, and again, until he could recite all the items in the correct order—the *criterion performance.* Then he distracted himself from rehearsing the original list by forcing himself to learn many other lists. After this interval, Ebbinghaus measured his memory by seeing how many trials it took him to *relearn* the original list. If he needed fewer trials to relearn it than he had needed to learn it initially, information had been *saved* from his original study. (This concept should be familiar from Chapter 7. Recall that there is often a savings when animals relearn a conditioned response.)

HOW WE KNOW

EBBINGHAUS'S FORGETTING CURVE For example, if Ebbinghaus took 12 trials to learn a list and 9 trials to relearn it several days later, his savings score for that elapsed time would be 25 percent (12 trials – 9 trials = 3 trials; 3 trials ÷ 12 trials = 0.25, or 25 percent). Using savings as his measure, Ebbinghaus recorded the degree of memory retained after different time intervals. The curve he obtained is shown in **Figure 8.1.** As you can see, he found a rapid initial loss of memory, followed by a gradually declining rate of loss. Ebbinghaus's curve is typical of results from experiments on rote learning.

Memory The mental capacity to encode, store, and retrieve information.

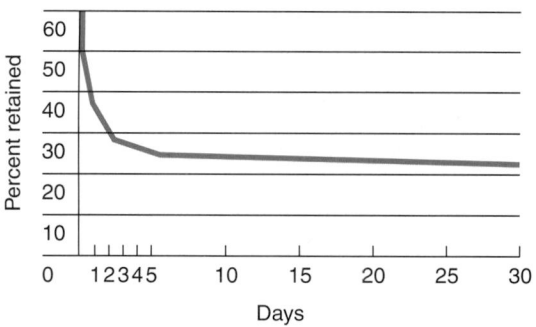

FIGURE 8.1

Ebbinghaus's Forgetting Curve

The curve shows how many nonsense syllables are remembered by individuals using the savings method when tested over a 30-day period. The curve decreases rapidly and then reaches a plateau of little change.

Following Ebbinghaus's lead, psychologists studied verbal learning for many decades by observing participants attempting to learn and recall nonsense syllables. By studying memory in as "pure" a form as possible, uncontaminated by meaning, researchers hoped to find basic principles that would shed light on more complex examples of remembering. Researchers still aspire to discover those basic principles, but they have also turned to

Explicit uses of memory Conscious efforts to recover information through memory processes.

Implicit uses of memory Availability of information through memory processes without the exertion of any conscious effort to encode or recover information.

the study of memory for meaningful material—the type of information you commit to memory on a day-to-day basis.

Types of Memory

When you think about memory, what is most likely to come to mind at first are situations in which you use your memory to recall (or try to recall) specific events or information: your favorite movie, the dates of World War II, or your student ID number. In fact, one of the important functions of memory is to allow you to have conscious access to the personal and collective past. But memory does much more for you than that. It also enables you to have effortless continuity of experience from one day to the next. When you drive in a car, for example, it is this second function of memory that makes the stores along the roadside seem familiar. In defining types of memory, we will make plain to you how hard your memory works to fulfill these functions, often outside of conscious awareness.

IMPLICIT AND EXPLICIT MEMORY

Consider **Figure 8.2**. What's wrong with this picture? It probably strikes you as unusual that there's a bunny rabbit in the kitchen. But where does this feeling come from? You probably didn't go through the objects in the picture one by one and ask yourself, "Does the refrigerator belong?" "Do the cabinets belong?" Rather, the rabbit jumps out at you as being out of place.

This simple example allows you to understand the difference between **explicit** and **implicit uses of memory**. Your discovery of the rabbit is implicit, because your memory processes brought past knowledge of kitchens to bear on your interpretation of the picture without any particular effort on your part. Suppose now we asked

FIGURE 8.2

What's Wrong with This Picture?

Did you think right away, "What's a bunny doing in the kitchen?" If the bunny immediately jumped out at you, it is because your memory processes performed an analysis of the scene outside of consciousness and delivered the bunny as the odd element.

you, "What's missing from the picture?" To answer this second question, you probably have to put explicit memory to work. What appears in the typical kitchen? What's missing? (Did you think of the sink or the stove?) Thus, when it comes to using knowledge stored in memory, sometimes the use will be implicit—the information becomes available without any conscious effort—and sometimes it will be explicit—you make a conscious effort to recover the information.

We can make the same distinction when it comes to the initial acquisition of memories. How do you know what should appear in a kitchen? Did you ever memorize a list of what appears there and what the appropriate configuration should be? Probably not. Rather, it's likely that you acquired most of this knowledge without conscious effort. By contrast, you probably learned the names of many of the objects in the room explicitly. As we shall see in Chapter 11, to learn the association between words and experiences, your younger self needed to engage in explicit memory processes. You learned the word *refrigerator* because someone called your explicit attention to the name of that object.

The distinction between implicit and explicit memory greatly expands the range of questions researchers must address about memory processes (Buchner & Wippich, 2000; Roediger, 1990). In the tradition established by Ebbinghaus, most research concerned the explicit acquisition of information. Experimenters most frequently provided participants with new information to retain, and theories of memory were directed to explaining what participants could and could not remember under those circumstances. However, as you will see in this chapter, researchers have now devised methods for studying implicit memory as well. Thus, we can give you a more complete account of the variety of uses to which you put your memory. We can acknowledge that most circumstances in which you encode or retrieve information represent a mix of implicit and explicit uses of memory (Toth et al., 1994). Let's turn now to a second dimension along which memories are distributed.

DECLARATIVE AND PROCEDURAL MEMORY

Can you whistle? Go ahead and try. Or if you can't whistle, try snapping your fingers. What kind of memory allows you to do these sorts of things? You probably remember having to learn these skills, but now they seem effortless. The examples we gave before of both implicit and explicit memories all involved the recollection of *facts* and *events*, which is called **declarative memory**. Now we see that you also have memories for *how to do things*, which is called **procedural memory**. Because the bulk of this chapter will be focused on how you acquire and use facts, let's take a moment now to consider how you acquire the ability to do things.

Procedural memory refers to the way you remember how things get done. It is used to acquire, retain, and em-

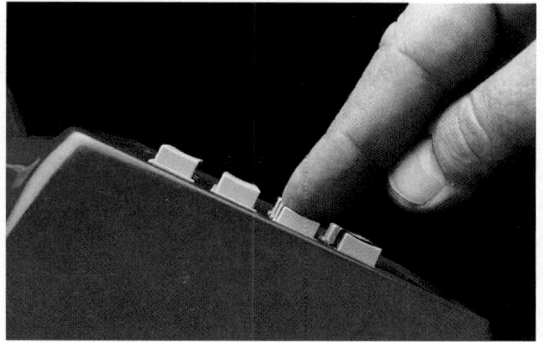

Why does pretending to dial a phone number help you to remember it?

ploy perceptual, cognitive, and motor skills. Theories of procedural memory most often concern themselves with the time course of learning (Anderson, 1996; Anderson et al., 1999): How do you go from a conscious list of declarative facts about some activity to unconscious, automatic performance of that same activity? And why is it that after learning a skill, you often find it difficult to go back and talk about the component declarative facts?

We can see these phenomena at work in even the very simple activity of dialing a phone number that, over time, has become highly familiar. At first, you probably had to think your way through each digit, one at a time. You had to work through a list of declarative facts:

First, I must dial 2,

Next, I must dial 0,

Then I dial 7,

and so on.

However, when you began to dial the number often enough, you could start to produce it as one unit—a swift sequence of actions on the touch-tone pad. The process at work is called *knowledge compilation* (Anderson, 1987). As a consequence of practice, you are able to carry out longer sequences of the activity without conscious intervention. But you also don't have conscious access to the content of these compiled units: Back at the telephone, it's not uncommon to find someone who can't actually remember the phone number without pretending to dial it. In general, knowledge compilation makes it hard to share your procedural knowledge with others. You may have noticed this if your parents tried to teach you to drive. Although they may be good drivers themselves, they may not have been very good at communicating the content of compiled good-driving procedures.

Declarative memory Memory for information such as facts and events.

Procedural memory Memory for how things get done; the way perceptual, cognitive, and motor skills are acquired, retained, and used.

You may also have noticed that knowledge compilation can lead to errors. If you are a skilled typist, you've probably suffered from the *the* problem: As soon as you hit the *t* and the *h* keys, your finger may fly to the *e*, even if you're really trying to type *throne* or *thistle*. Once you have sufficiently committed the execution of *the* to procedural memory, you can do little else but finish the sequence. Without procedural memory, life would be extremely laborious—you would be doomed to go step by step through every activity. However, each time you mistakenly type *the*, you can reflect on the trade-off between efficiency and potential error. Let's continue now to an overview of the basic processes that apply to all these different types of memory.

An Overview of Memory Processes

No matter what the category of memory, being able to use knowledge at some later time requires the operation of three mental processes: encoding, storage, and retrieval. **Encoding** is the initial processing of information that leads to a representation in memory. **Storage** is the retention over time of encoded material. **Retrieval** is the recovery at a later time of the stored information. Simply put, encoding gets information in, storage holds it until you need it, and retrieval gets it out. Let's now expand on these ideas.

Encoding requires that you form *mental representations* of information from the external world. You can understand the idea of mental representations if we draw an analogy to representations outside your head. Imagine we wanted to know something about the best gift you got at your last birthday party. (Let's suppose it's not something you have with you.) What could you do to inform us about the gift? You might describe the properties of the object. Or you might draw us a picture. Or you might pretend that you're using the object. In each case, these are representations of the original object. Although none of the representations is likely to be quite as good as having the real thing present, they should allow us to acquire knowledge of the most important aspects of the gift. Mental representations work much the same way. They preserve the most important features of past experiences in a way that enables you to *re-present* those experiences to yourself.

If information is properly encoded, it will be retained in *storage* over some period of time. Storage requires both short- and long-term changes in the structures of your brain. At the end of the chapter, we will see how

researchers are attempting to locate the brain structures that are responsible for storing new and old memories. We will also see what happens in cases of extreme amnesia, where individuals become incapable of storing new memories.

Retrieval is the payoff for all your earlier effort. When it works, it enables you to gain access—often in a split second—to information you stored earlier. Can you remember what comes before storage: decoding or encoding? The answer is simple to retrieve now, but will you still be able to retrieve the concept of encoding as swiftly and with as much confidence when you are tested on this chapter's contents days or weeks from now? Discovering how you are able to retrieve one specific bit of information from the vast quantity of information in your memory storehouse is a challenge facing psychologists who want to know how memory works and how it can be improved.

Although it is easy to define encoding, storage, and retrieval as separate memory processes, the interaction among the three processes is quite complex. For example, to be able to encode the information that you have seen a tiger, you must first retrieve from memory information about the concept *tiger*. Similarly, to commit to memory the meaning of a sentence such as "He's as honest as Benedict Arnold," you must retrieve the meanings of each individual word, retrieve the rules of grammar that specify how word meanings should be combined in English, and retrieve cultural information that specifies exactly how honest Benedict Arnold—a famous Revolutionary War traitor—was.

We are now ready to look in more detail at the encoding, storage, and retrieval of information. Our discussion will start with short-lived types of memories, beginning with sensory memory, and then move to the more permanent forms of long-term memory (see **Figure 8.3**). We will give you an account of how you remember and why you forget. Our plan is to make you forever self-conscious about all the ways in which you use your capacity for memory. We hope this will even allow you to improve some aspects of your memory skills.

SUMMING UP

Memory is defined as a type of information processing; psychologists study the flow of information in and out of memory systems. Ebbinghaus pioneered memory research by inventing methodologies and producing fundamental findings on the rate of forgetting. Some types of memory retrieval are explicit and some implicit. Some memories include declarative information—knowledge about facts—and some procedural information—compiled knowledge about how tasks are done. The three basic processes of encoding, storage, and retrieval work together in complex interactions to help you form and use new memories.

Encoding The process by which a mental representation is formed in memory.
Storage The retention of encoded material over time.
Retrieval The recovery of stored information from memory.

```
Sensory          →   Working memory        →   Long-term
memory               (includes short-term memory)   memory
                  ←                          ←
```

FIGURE 8.3

The Flow of Information In and Out of Long-Term Memory

Memory theories describe the flow of information to and from long-term memory. The theories address initial encodings of information in sensory and working memory, the transfer of information into long-term memory for storage, and the transfer of information from long-term memory to working memory for retrieval.

Sensory Memory

Let's begin with a demonstration of the impermanence of some memories. In **Figure 8.4** we have provided you with a reasonably busy visual scene. We'd like you to take a quick look at it—about 10 seconds—and then cover it up. Suppose we now ask you a series of questions about the scene:

1. What tool is the little boy at the bottom holding?
2. What is the middle man at the top doing?
3. In the lower right-hand corner, does the woman's umbrella handle hook to the left or to the right?

To answer these questions, wouldn't you be more comfortable if you could go back and have an extra peek at the picture?

Fortunately, the opportunity to have an "extra peek" at the sensory world is built into your memory processes.

FIGURE 8.4

How Much Can You Remember from This Scene?

After viewing this scene for about 10 seconds, cover it up and try to answer the questions in the text. Under ordinary circumstances, iconic memory preserves a glimpse of the visual world for a brief time after the scene has been removed.

Psychologists hypothesize that for each of your sensory modalities, you have a **sensory memory:** Each sensory memory preserves accurate representations of the physical features of sensory stimuli for a few seconds or less. These memories extend the availability of information acquired from the environment. To make this idea more concrete for you, we will describe research on sensory memory in the visual and auditory modalities.

Iconic Memory

Researchers have labeled sensory memory in the visual domain **iconic memory** (Neisser, 1967). Iconic memory allows very large amounts of information to be stored for very brief durations. A visual memory, or icon, lasts about half a second. Iconic memory was first revealed in experiments that required participants to retrieve information from visual displays that were exposed for only one-twentieth of a second.

HOW WE KNOW

ICONIC MEMORY George Sperling (1960, 1963) presented participants with arrays of three rows of letters and numbers.

$$7 \quad 1 \quad V \quad F$$
$$X \quad L \quad 5 \quad 3$$
$$B \quad 4 \quad W \quad 7$$

Participants were asked to perform two different tasks. In a *whole-report procedure,* they tried to recall as many of the items in the display as possible. Typically, they could report only about four items. Other participants underwent a *partial-report procedure,* which required them to report only one row rather than the whole pattern. A signal of a high, medium, or low tone was sounded immediately after the presentation to indicate which row the participants were to report. Sperling found that regardless of which row he asked for, the participants' recall was quite high.

Because participants could accurately report any of the three rows in response to a tone, Sperling concluded that all of the information in the display must have gotten into iconic memory. That is evidence for its large capacity. At the same time, the difference between the whole- and partial-report procedures suggests that the information fades rapidly: The participants in the whole-report procedure were unable to recall all the information present in the icon. This second point was reinforced by experiments in which the identification signal was slightly delayed. **Figure 8.5** shows that as the delay interval increases from zero seconds to one second, the number of items accurately reported declines steadily. Researchers have measured quite accurately the time course with which information must be transferred from the fading icon (Gegenfurtner & Sperling, 1993; Loftus et al., 1992). To take advantage of the "extra peek" at the visual world, your memory processes must very quickly transfer information to more durable stores.

Note that iconic memory is not the same as the "photographic memory" that some people claim to have. The technical term for "photographic memory" is *eidetic imagery:* People who experience eidetic imagery are able to recall the details of a picture, for periods of time considerably longer than iconic memory, as if they were still looking at a photograph. "People" in this case really means children: Researchers have estimated that roughly

■ **Sensory memory** The initial memory processes involved in the momentary preservation of fleeting impressions of sensory stimuli.
■ **Iconic memory** Sensory memory in the visual domain; allows large amounts of information to be stored for very brief durations.

FIGURE 8.5

Recall by the Partial-Report Method

The solid line shows the average number of items recalled using the partial-report method, both immediately after presentation and at four later times. For comparison, the dotted line shows the number of items recalled by the whole-report method. (Adapted from Sperling, 1960.)

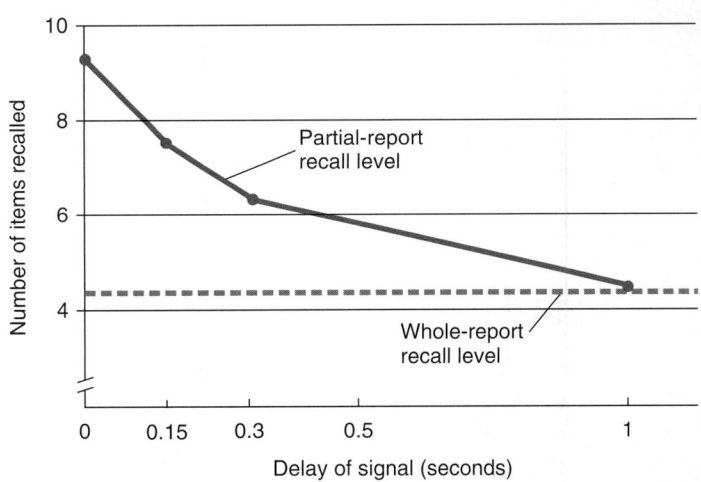

8 percent of preadolescent children are eidetickers, but virtually no adults (Neath, 1998). No satisfactory theory has been proposed for why eidetic imagery fades over time (Crowder, 1992). However, if you are reading this book as a high school or college student, you almost certainly have iconic memory but not eidetic images.

Echoic Memory

Sensory memory for sounds is called **echoic memory**. Just like iconic memory, echoic memory briefly preserves more information than participants can report before it fades away (Crowder & Morton, 1969; Darwin et al., 1972). Echoic memories, however, last longer than iconic memories, perhaps for as long as 5 to 10 seconds. The longer duration of echoic memories may be related to the way in which sounds unfold over time. For example, when you are trying to understand a spoken sentence, increments of sound arrive at your ear one after the other. Echoic memory may help you to gather those increments into coherent wholes.

Research on echoic memory has illustrated another important property of sensory memories: They are easily displaced by new information. If someone reads a list of words to you, each new word will displace the former word in echoic memory. Researchers originally believed that the *physical* similarity of sounds determined whether one stimulus would displace another in echoic memory (Crowder, 1976). However, we know now that the way a listener categorizes an auditory stimulus also matters (Ayres et al., 1979). As you listen to the world, you divide the stream of information arriving at your ears into units—you determine which sounds go together to form a whole. Echoic memory depends on how you group auditory experiences (LeCompte & Watkins, 1995).

HOW WE KNOW

CATEGORIZATION INFLUENCES ECHOIC MEMORY Students participated in a memory experiment in which lists of letters were followed by a *suffix*. The suffix was always the same physical stimulus—it sounded like a sheep's *baa*. However, in one case, participants were led to believe that it was genuinely an animal sound, while in another case, participants believed that it was a *baa* produced by a human trying to sound like a sheep (as it really was). The suffix served to displace information in echoic memory only when the participants believed it to be produced by a human (Neath et al., 1993).

Remember that the actual physical sound was the same in both cases. But only when the participants categorized the list (letters read by a human) and the *baa* (a noise produced by the human) in the same way was echoic

memory disrupted. Thus, even at the earliest stages of the encoding and storage of memories, your *interpretation* of the world becomes important.

You might wonder why sensory memories have the two basic properties of being short-lived and easily displaced. The answer is that these properties fit the facts of your interactions with the environment. You are constantly experiencing new visual and auditory stimulation. This new information must also be processed. Sensory memories are durable enough to give you a sense of the continuity of your world but not sufficiently strong to interfere with new sensory impressions. We now turn to the types of memory processes that enable you to form more durable memories.

SUMMING UP

Sensory memories extend the availability of information acquired from the environment. Iconic memory is a form of visual memory that allows you to store large amounts of information for very brief durations. Echoic memory holds auditory stimuli. Although they have a longer duration than iconic memories, echoic memories are easily displaced by new information.

Short-Term Memory and Working Memory

Before you began to read this chapter, you may not have been aware that you had iconic or echoic memory. It is very likely, however, that you were aware that there are some memories that you possess only for the short term. Consider the common occurrence of consulting a telephone book to find a friend's number and then remembering the number just long enough to dial it. If the number turns up busy, you often have to go right back to the phone book. When you consider this experience, it's easy to understand why researchers have hypothesized a special type of memory called **short-term memory** (STM).

You shouldn't think of short-term memory as a particular place that memories go to, but rather as a built-in mechanism for focusing cognitive resources on some small set of mental representations (Cowan, 1993; Shiffrin, 1993). But the resources of STM are fickle. As even

Echoic memory Sensory memory that allows auditory information to be stored for brief durations.

Short-term memory (STM) Memory processes associated with preservation of recent experiences and with retrieval of information from long-term memory; short-term memory is of limited capacity and stores information for only a short length of time without rehearsal.

your experience with phone numbers shows, you have to take some special care to ensure that memories become encoded into more permanent forms. We will largely focus on the types of short-term memory resources that lead to the acquisition of explicit memories. This focus is necessary because researchers have only just begun to study short-term representations for implicit memories (McKone & Trynes, 1999). Preliminary findings suggest that implicit memories may also pass through a state in which they draw extra short-term resources before passing into more long-term forms of memory.

In this section, we also consider a broader concept of the types of memory processes that provide a foundation for the moment-by-moment fluidity of thought and action: **working memory.** As we shall see, working memory is the memory resource that you use to accomplish tasks such as reasoning and language comprehension (Baddeley, 1986). Suppose you are trying to remember a phone number while you search for a pencil and pad, to write it down. Whereas your short-term memory processes allow you to keep the number in mind, your more general working memory resource allows you to execute the mental operations to accomplish an efficient search. Let's begin with short-term memory.

The Capacity Limitations of STM

The major features of short-term memories are an immediate consequence of the vast amount of information you could potentially make the focus of consciousness. There is always a great amount of new information available. In Chapter 5, we described how your attentional resources are devoted to selecting the objects and events in the external world on which you will expend your mental resources. Just as there are limits on your capacity to attend to more than a small sample of the available information, there are limits on your ability to keep more than a small sample of information active in STM. The limited capacity of STM enforces a sharp focus of mental attention.

To estimate the capacity of STM, researchers at first turned to tests of *memory span.* At some point in your life, you have probably been asked to carry out a task like this one:

> Read the following list of random numbers once, cover them, and write down as many as you can in the order they appear.
>
> 8 1 7 3 4 9 4 2 8 5
>
> How many did you get correct?
>
> Now read the next list of random letters and perform the same memory test.
>
> J M R S O F L P T Z B
>
> How many did you get correct?

If you are like most individuals, you probably could recall somewhere in the range of five to nine items. **George Miller** (1956) suggested that seven (plus or minus two) was the "magic number" that characterized people's memory performance on random lists of letters, words, numbers, or almost any kind of meaningful, familiar item.

Tests of memory span, however, overestimate the true capacity of STM because participants are able to use other sources of information to carry out the task. Remember, for example, that echoic memory will help you to improve your recall on the last few items of a list that is read aloud (at least if there is no suffix). When other sources of memory are factored out, researchers have estimated the pure contribution of STM to your seven (or so) item memory span to be only between two and four items (Crowder, 1976). But if that's all the capacity you have to commence the acquisition of new memories, why don't you notice your limitations more often?

Accommodating to STM Capacity

Despite the capacity limitations of STM, you function efficiently for at least two reasons. First, the encoding of information in STM can be enhanced through rehearsal and chunking. Second, the retrieval of information from STM is quite rapid.

REHEARSAL

You probably know that a good way to keep your friend's telephone number in mind is to keep repeating the digits in a cycle in your head. This memorization technique is called *maintenance rehearsal.* The fate of unrehearsed information was demonstrated in an ingenious experiment.

HOW WE KNOW

WITHOUT REHEARSAL, SHORT-TERM MEMORY FADES Participants heard three consonants, such as F, C, and V. They had to recall those consonants when given a signal after a variable interval of time, ranging from 3 to 18 seconds. To prevent rehearsal, a *distractor task* was put between the stimulus input and the recall signal—the participants were given a three-digit number and told to count backward from it by 3's until the recall signal was presented. Many different consonant sets were given, and several short delays were used over a series of trials with a number of participants.

As shown in **Figure 8.6,** recall became increasingly poorer as the time required to retain the information became longer. After even three seconds, there was considerable memory loss, and by 18 seconds, loss was nearly total. In

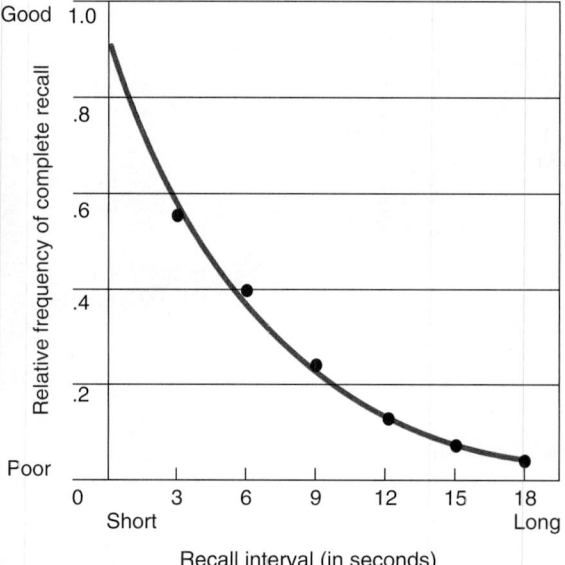

Good ─ 1.0

.8

.6

.4

.2

Poor

Relative frequency of complete recall

0   3   6   9   12   15   18
Short   Long

Recall interval (in seconds)

FIGURE 8.6

Short-Term Memory Recall without Rehearsal

When the interval between stimulus presentation and recall was filled with a distracting task, recall became poorer as the interval grew longer.

the absence of an opportunity to rehearse the information, short-term recall was impaired with the passage of time (Peterson & Peterson, 1959).

Performance suffered because information could not be rehearsed. It also suffered because of interference from the competing information of the distractor task. (We will discuss interference as a cause of forgetting later in this chapter.) You may have noticed how often a new acquaintance says his or her name—and then you immediately forget it. One of the most common reasons for this is that you are distracted from performing the type of rehearsal you need to carry out to acquire a new memory. As a remedy, try to encode and rehearse a new name carefully before you continue with a conversation.

Our conclusion so far is that rehearsal will help you to keep information from fading out of STM. But suppose the information you wish to acquire is, at least at first, too cumbersome to be rehearsed? You might turn to the strategy of chunking.

CHUNKING

A *chunk* is a meaningful unit of information (Anderson, 1996). A chunk can be a single letter or number, a group of letters or other items, or even a group of words or an entire sentence. For example, the sequence 1–9–8–4 consists of four digits that could exhaust your STM capac-

ity. However, if you see the digits as a year or the title of George Orwell's book *1984*, they constitute only one chunk, leaving you much more capacity for other chunks of information. **Chunking** is the process of reconfiguring items by grouping them on the basis of similarity or some other organizing principle, or by combining them into larger patterns based on information stored in long-term memory (Baddeley, 1994).

See how many chunks you find in this sequence of 20 numbers: 19411917186518121776. You can answer "20" if you see the sequence as a list of unrelated digits, or "5" if you break down the sequence into the dates of major wars in U.S. history. If you do the latter, it's easy for you to recall all the digits in proper sequence after one quick glance. It would be impossible for you to remember them all from a short exposure if you saw them as 20 unrelated items.

Your memory span can always be greatly increased if you can discover ways to organize an available body of information into smaller chunks. A famous subject, S. F., was able to memorize 84 digits by grouping them as racing times (S.F. was an avid runner):

HOW WE KNOW

THE BENEFITS OF CHUNKING S. F.'s memory protocols provided the key to his mental wizardry. Because he was a long-distance runner, S. F. noticed that many of the random numbers could be grouped into running times for different distances. For instance, he would recode the sequence 3, 4, 9, 2, 5, 6, 1, 4, 9, 3, 5 as 3:49.2, near record mile; 56:14, 10-mile time; 9:35, slow 2 miles. Later, S. F. also used ages, years of memorable events, and special numerical patterns to chunk the random digits. In this way, he was able to use his long-term memory to convert long strings of random input into manageable and meaningful chunks. S. F.'s memory for letters was still about average, however, because he had not developed any chunking strategies to recall alphabet strings (Chase & Ericsson, 1981; Ericsson & Chase, 1982).

Like S. F., you can structure incoming information according to its personal meaning to you (linking it to the ages of friends and relatives, for example); or you can match new stimuli with various codes that have been stored in your long-term memory. Even if you can't link

Working memory A memory resource that is used to accomplish tasks such as reasoning and language comprehension; consists of the phonological loop, visuospatial sketchpad, and central executive.
Chunking The process of taking single items of information and recoding them on the basis of similarity or some other organizing principle.

How can you put chunking to good use while listening to a lecture?

new stimuli to rules, meanings, or codes in your long-term memory, you can still use chunking. You can simply group the items in a rhythmical pattern or temporal group (181379256460 could become 181, pause, 379, pause, 256, pause, 460). You know from everyday experience that this grouping principle works well for remembering telephone numbers.

RETRIEVAL FROM STM

Rehearsal and chunking both relate to the way in which you encode information to enhance the probability that it will remain or fit in STM. Even without these strategic measures, however, it turns out that retrieval from STM is very efficient. In a series of classic studies, **Saul Sternberg** (1966, 1969) invented a task that enabled him to demonstrate the great speed with which participants could assess which information was in short-term focus.

HOW ▪ WE KNOW

EFFICIENT RETRIEVAL FROM STM On each of many trials, participants were given a memory set consisting of from one to six items—for instance, the digits 5, 2, 9, 4, and 6. From trial to trial, the list would vary in terms of which digits and how many were shown. After presenting each set, Sternberg immediately offered a single test "probe"—a digit that the participants would determine either had or had not been a part of the memory set just shown. The dependent variable was *speed of recognition*. How quickly could participants press a *yes* button to indicate that they had seen the test item in the memory set or a *no* button to indicate they were sure that they had not seen it? Sternberg calculated that it took about 400 milliseconds to encode the test stimulus and make a response and then about 35 milliseconds more to compare the stimulus to each item in the memory set. In a single second, a person could make about 30 such comparisons. Retrieval from STM proved to be extremely efficient.

Although different theories have been offered to explain Sternberg's results (Ratcliff, 1978; Townsend, 1971, 1990), they all agree that retrieval from STM is very swift. Let's draw some conclusions from this finding by making an analogy to a vast research library. Given the abundance of volumes in the library (the abundance of sensory impressions available to you), you would probably be dismayed to discover that the library allowed you to borrow only three books at any given time (the limitations of STM). But suppose each patron could access the information in a book with lightning speed (the speed of retrieval from STM). With this high level of performance, you would use the library and only rarely become aware of the three-book rule. Your short-term memory provides the same trade-off between capacity and efficiency of processing.

Working Memory

Our focus so far has been on short-term memory, and specifically the role that STM plays in the explicit acquisition of new memories. However, as we suggested earlier, you need more memory resources on a moment-by-moment basis than those that allow you to acquire facts. For example, you also need to be able to retrieve preexisting memories. At the start of this chapter, we asked you to commit a number to memory. Can you remember now what it was? If you can remember (if not, peek), you have made your mental representation of that memory active once more—that's another memory function. If we ask you to do something more complicated—suppose we ask you to toss a ball from hand to hand while you count backwards by 3's from 132—you'll put even more demands on your memory resources.

In what ways is retrieval from STM analogous to retrieval from a vast research library?

A Test for Working Memory Span

Read these sentences aloud, and then (without looking back) try to recall the final words of each sentence.

He had patronized her when she was a schoolgirl and teased her when she was a student.

He had an elongated skull which sat on his shoulders like a pear on a dish.

The products of digital electonics will play an important role in your future.

The taxi turned up Michigan Avenue where they had a clear view of the lake.

When at last his eyes opened, there was no gleam of triumph, no shade of anger.

Source: Daneman & Carpenter, 1980.

Based on an analysis of the memory *functions* you require to navigate through life, researchers have articulated theories of working memory that subsume the "classic" short-term memory (Healy & McNamara, 1996). **Alan Baddeley** and his colleagues (Baddeley, 1986, 1992; Baddeley & Andrade, 2000) have provided evidence for three components of working memory:

- A *phonological loop:* This resource holds and manipulates speech-based information. The phonological loop overlaps most with short-term memory, as we have described it in the earlier sections. When you rehearse a telephone number by "listening" to it as you run it through your head you are making use of the phonological loop.

- A *visuospatial sketchpad:* This resource performs the same types of functions as the phonological loop for visual and spatial information. If, for example, someone asked you how many desks there are in your psychology classroom, you might use the resources of the visuospatial sketchpad to form a mental picture of the classroom and then estimate the number of desks from that picture.

- The *central executive:* This resource is responsible for controlling attention and coordinating information from the phonological loop and the visuospatial sketchpad. Any time you carry out a task that requires a combination of mental processes—imagine, for example, you are asked to describe a picture from memory—you rely on the central executive function to apportion your mental resources to different aspects of the task (we return to this idea in Chapter 9).

The incorporation of short-term memory into the broader context of working memory should help rein-force the idea that STM is not a place but a process. To do the work of cognition—to carry out cognitive activities like language processing or problem solving—you must bring a lot of different elements together in quick succession. You can think of working memory as short-term special focus on the necessary elements. If you wish to get a better look at a physical object, you can shine a brighter light on it; working memory shines a brighter mental light on your mental objects—your memory representations. Working memory also coordinates the activities required to take action with respect to those objects.

Researchers have demonstrated that working memory capacity differs among individuals (Daneman & Merikle, 1996; Jenkins et al., 1999). One common measure of these differences is *working memory span.* To determine working memory span, researchers may ask participants to read aloud a series of sentences and then recall the final words. We've given you some sentences to try in **Table 8.1.** It's really not so easy! People are usually considered to be *high span* if they can recall 4 or more words and *low span* if they recall 2.5 or fewer—these are averages across several trials and sets of sentences, so you won't have gotten much information about yourself just by trying Table 8.1. Because working memory span is a measure of the resources individuals have available to carry out short-term cognitive processes, researchers can use it to predict performance on a variety of tasks.

HOW WE KNOW

WORKING MEMORY SPAN AFFECTS MEMORY FOR TEXTS Researchers identified groups of high-, middle-, and low-span individuals. Each participant was asked to read a story about a "fine old home" from either the perspective of a potential homebuyer or a potential burglar. The story contained facts that were more relevant to one or the other perspective: for example, a leaky roof versus a coin collection. The researchers were interested in how much readers' memory representations were affected by the perspective from which they read the story. Participants were asked to recall the story twice: once from their original perspective (that is, homebuyer or burglar) and then a second time from the switched perspective (that is, "Now imagine that you're a…"). High-span readers were able to produce a good deal of information from the "other" perspective; other readers were not (Lee-Sammons & Whitney, 1991).

The researchers concluded that low- and middle-span readers used the perspective to make *choices* about which story information to process extensively; high-span readers were able to process information both relevant and irrelevant to their perspective. Experiments that measure working memory span help to define the ways in which different individuals expend their memory resources.

A final note on working memory: Working memory helps maintain your psychological present. It is what sets a context for new events and links separate episodes together into a continuing story. It enables you to maintain and continually update your representation of a changing situation and to keep track of topics during a conversation. All of this is true because working memory serves as a conduit for information coming and going to long-term memory. Let's turn our attention now to the types of memories that can last a lifetime.

SUMMING UP

A primary function of short-term memory (STM) is to provide the initial encoding for explicit memories. The capacity of STM is two to four items. Rehearsal can maintain information in STM. More information can be accommodated in STM when it is chunked into meaningful units. Information is retrieved from STM with great efficiency. "Classic" research on STM has been subsumed within the broader concept of working memory. The three components of working memory reflect the range of resources people bring to the moment-by-moment experience of the world.

Long-term memory (LTM) Memory processes associated with the preservation of information for retrieval at any later time.

Encoding specificity The principle that subsequent retrieval of information is enhanced if cues received at the time of recall are consistent with those present at the time of encoding.

■ Long-Term Memory: Encoding and Retrieval

How long can memories last? Consider the 90-year-old memories of a woman who vividly recalls the 1906 San Francisco earthquake and subsequent fire. She remembers exactly how she felt as she and the other children scrambled to fetch water from the bay to drench big burlap bags. Her father took the bags she soaked and draped them over the roof, hoping to save their home from the hungry flames. No subsequent memories have displaced the terror and excitement she felt as a young girl watching her city being leveled to the ground.

When psychologists speak of *long-term memory*, it is with the knowledge that memories will often last a lifetime. Therefore, whatever theory explains how memories are acquired for the long term must also explain how they can remain accessible over the life course. **Long-term memory (LTM)** is the storehouse of all the experiences, events, information, emotions, skills, words, categories, rules, and judgments that have been acquired from sensory and short-term memories. LTM constitutes each person's total knowledge of the world and of the self.

Psychologists know that it is often easier to acquire new long-term information when an important conclusion is stated in advance. With that conclusion in place, you have a framework for understanding the incoming information. For memory, the conclusion we will reach is this: Your ability to remember will be greatest when there is a good match between the circumstances in which you encoded information and the circumstances in which you attempt to retrieve it. We will see over the next several sections what it means to have a "good match."

Context and Encoding

To begin our exploration of the match between encoding and retrieval, we want you to consider a phenomenon that you might call "context shock." You see someone across a crowded room, and you know that you know the person but you just can't place her. Finally, after staring for longer than is absolutely polite, you remember who it is—and you realize that the difficulty is that the person is entirely in the wrong context. What is the woman who delivers your mail doing at your best friend's party? Whenever you have this type of experience, you have rediscovered the principle of **encoding specificity**: Memories emerge most efficiently when the context of retrieval matches the context of encoding. Let's see how researchers have demonstrated that principle.

ENCODING SPECIFICITY

What are the consequences of learning information in a particular context? Endel Tulving and Donald Thomson

(1973) first demonstrated the power of encoding specificity by reversing the usual performance relationship between recall and recognition.

ENCODING SPECIFICITY AFFECTS RECALL AND RECOGNITION Participants were asked to learn pairs of words like *train–black*, but they were told that they would be responsible for remembering only the second word of the pair. In a subsequent phase of the experiment, participants were asked to generate four free associates to words like *white*. Those words were chosen so that it was likely that the original to-be-remembered words (like *black*) would be among the associates. The participants were then asked to check off any words on their associates lists that they recognized as to-be-remembered words from the first phase of the experiment. They were able to do so 54 percent of the time. However, when the participants were later given the first words of the pair, like *train*, and asked to recall the associate, they were 61 percent accurate.

After receiving a traffic warning from this man, why might you not recognize him if you ran into him at a party?

Why was recall better than recognition? Tulving and Thomson suggested that what mattered was the change in context. After the participants had studied the word *black* in the context of *train*, it was hard to recover the memory representation when the context was changed to *white*. Given the significant effect of even these minimal contexts, you can anticipate that richly organized real-life contexts would have an even greater effect on your memory.

Researchers have been able to demonstrate rather remarkable effects of context on memory. In one experiment, scuba divers learned lists of words either on a beach or under water. They were then tested for retention of those words, again in one of those two contexts. Performance was nearly 50 percent better when the context at encoding and recall matched—even though the material had nothing at all to do with water or diving (Gooden & Baddeley, 1975). Similarly, people performed better on memory tasks when the tempo of background music remained the same between encoding and recall (Balch & Lewis, 1996). In another study, memory performance was much improved when the smell of chocolate was present at both encoding and recall (Schab, 1990). This research on context-dependent memory with odors has been extended to suggest that the odor must be *distinctive* in the environment.

DISTINCTIVE ODORS SERVE AS CUES What odors are sufficiently distinctive to foster context-dependent memories? A pair of experiments used a scent *novel* for the participants

(*osmanthus*, "an unusual, Asian, floral-fruity scent"; Herz, 1997, p. 375), a familiar scent that was *inappropriate* for a research laboratory (*peppermint*), and a familiar scent *appropriate* for the laboratory (*clean fresh pine*). The hypothesis tested was that only the two odors that called attention to themselves in the environment—by virtue of being novel or inappropriate—would be used for encoding. The results bore out this prediction. Although the encoding and retrieval sessions were 48 hours apart, participants were able to remember reliably more words (from a 20-item list) when the odor in the laboratory room was the same at retrieval as at encoding—but only for osmanthus and peppermint (Herz, 1997).

These studies suggest that not all environmental odors are sufficiently distinctive to provide context for memory encoding. What is distinctive, of course, will vary from context to context. In a candy shop, peppermint might lose its power as a distinctive element of the context.

THE SERIAL POSITION EFFECT

We can also use changes in context to explain one of the classic effects in memory research: the **serial position effect**. Suppose we required you to learn a list of unrelated

Serial position effect A characteristic of memory retrieval in which the recall of beginning and end items on a list is often better than recall of items appearing in the middle.

words. If we asked you to recall those words in order, your data would almost certainly conform to the pattern shown in **Figure 8.7**: You would do very well on the first few words (the **primacy effect**) and very well on the last few words (the **recency effect**) but rather poorly on the middle part of the list. Figure 8.7 shows the generality of this pattern when students are asked to try to remember word lists of varying lengths (6, 10, and 15 words) using either *serial recall* ("Recite the words in the order you heard them") or *free recall* ("Recite as many words as you can") (Jahnke, 1965). Researchers have found primacy and recency in a wide variety of test situations (Crowder, 1976; Neath, 1993). What day is it today? Do you believe that you would be almost a second faster to answer this question at the beginning or end of the week than in the middle (Koriat & Fischoff, 1974)?

The role context plays in producing the shape of the serial position curve has to do with the **contextual distinctiveness** of different items on a list, different experiences in your life, and so on (Knoedler et al., 1999; Marks & Crowder, 1997; Neath & Knoedler, 1994). To under-

stand contextual distinctiveness, you can ask the question, "How different were the contexts in which I learned this information from the context in which I will try to recall it?" Let's focus on recency. **Figure 8.8** is a visual representation of distinctiveness. Imagine, in part A, that you are looking at train tracks. What you can see is that they look as if they clump together at the horizon—even though they are equally spaced apart. We could say that the nearest tracks stand out most—are most distinctive—from your context. Imagine now that you are trying to remember the last ten movies you've seen. The movies are like the train tracks. Under most circumstances, you should remember the last movie best, because you share the most overlapping context with the experience—it is "closest" to the context of your current experiences. This logic suggests that "middle" information will become more memorable if it is made more distinctive. The idea with respect to our analogy, as shown in part B of Figure 8.8, is to make the train tracks seem equally far apart.

- **Primacy effect** Improved memory for items at the start of a list.
- **Recency effect** Improved memory for items at the end of a list.
- **Contextual distinctiveness** The assumption that the serial position effect can be altered by the context and the distinctiveness of the experience being recalled.

HOW WE KNOW

MAKING LIST ITEMS MORE DISTINCTIVE IN CONTEXT To make the train tracks seem evenly spaced, engineers would have to make the more distant ones actually be further apart. Researchers have used the same logic for a

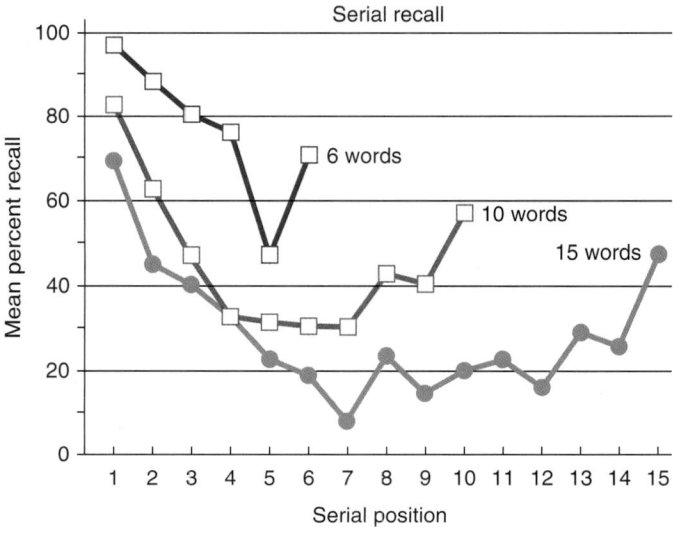

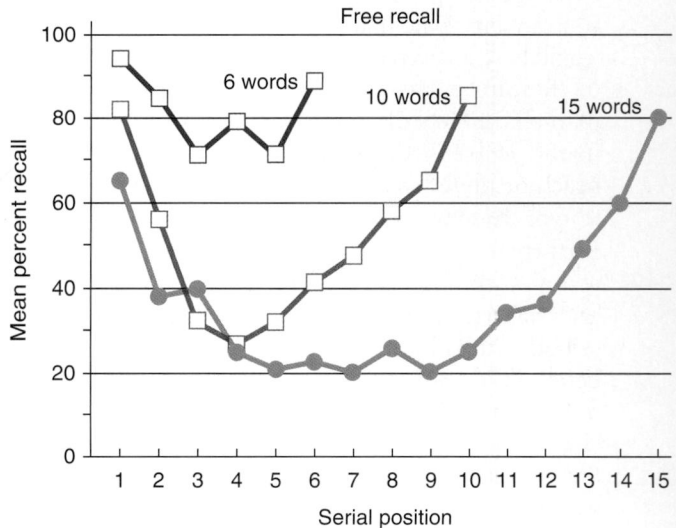

FIGURE 8.7

The Serial Position Effect

This figure shows the generality of the serial position effect. Students were asked to try to remember word lists of varying lengths (6, 10, and 15 words) using either *serial recall* ("Recite the words in the order you heard them") or *free recall* ("Recite as many words as you can"). Each curve shows better memory for both the beginning (the *primacy* effect) and end (the *recency* effect) of the list.

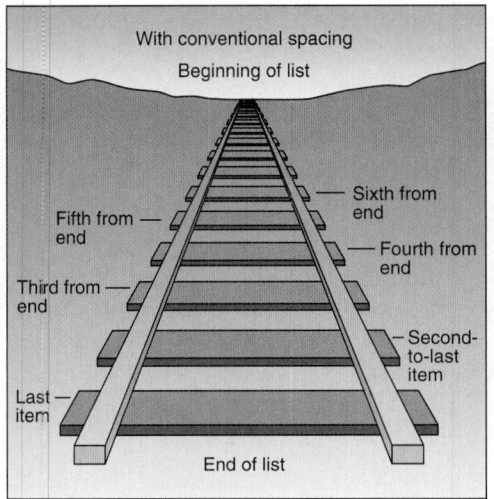

Part A

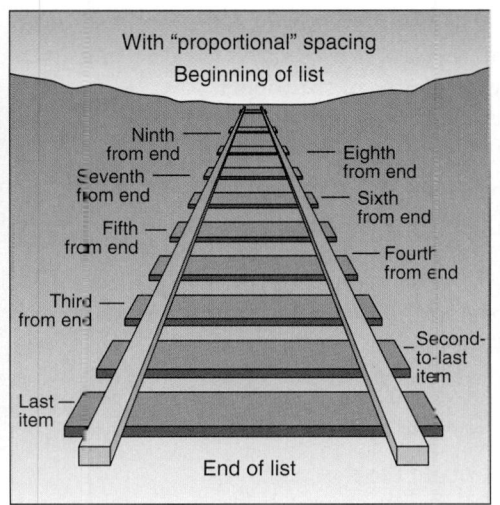

Part B

FIGURE 8.8

Contextual Distinctiveness

You can think of items you put into memory as train tracks. In part A, you can imagine that memories further back in time become blurred together, just like train tracks in the distance. In part B, you see that one way to combat this effect is to make the earlier tracks physically further apart, so the distances look proportional. Similarly, you can make early memories more distinctive by moving them apart psychologically.

memory test, by exploiting the analogy between space and time. They had participants try to learn lists of letters, but they manipulated how far apart in time the letters were made to seem. This manipulation was accomplished by asking participants to read out some number of random digits that appeared on a computer screen between the letters. In the *conventional* condition (like part A of Figure 8.8), each pair of letters was separated by two digits. In the *proportional* condition (like part B), the first pair had four digits and the last pair had zero digits; this should have the effect of making the early digits more distinctive, just like moving distant train tracks farther apart. Participants, in fact, showed better memory for early items on the list when those items had been made more separate (Neath & Crowder, 1990).

This experiment suggests that the standard recency effect arises because the last few items are almost automatically distinctive. The same principle may explain primacy—each time you begin something new, your activity establishes a new context. In that new context, the first few experiences are particularly distinctive. Thus, you can think of primacy and recency as two views of the same set of train tracks—one from each end!

Retrieval Cues

As we continue our exploration of encoding and retrieval, this is a good time to put your memory to work. We will attempt to replicate classic memory experiments by asking you to learn some word pairs. Keep working at it until you can go through the six pairs three times in a row without an error.

Apple–Boat

Hat–Bone

Bicycle–Clock

Mouse–Tree

Ball–House

Ear–Blanket

Now that you've committed the pairs to memory, we want to make the test more interesting. We need to do something to give you a *retention interval*—a period of time over which you must keep the information in memory. Let's spend a moment, therefore, discussing some of the procedures we might use to test your memory. You might assume that you either know something or you don't and that any method of testing what you know will give the same results. Not so. For example, we shall see that tests for implicit and explicit memory can give quite different results. For now, however, let's consider two tests for explicit memory, recall and recognition.

When you **recall**, you reproduce the information to which you were previously exposed. "What is the serial position effect?" is a recall question. **Recognition** refers to the realization that a certain stimulus event is one you have seen or heard before. "Which is the term for a visual sensory memory: (1) echo; (2) engram; (3) icon; or (4) abstract code?" is a recognition question. You can relate recall and recognition to your day-to-day experiences of

Recall A method of retrieval in which an individual is required to reproduce the information previously presented.

Recognition A method of retrieval in which an individual is required to identify stimuli as having been experienced before.

explicit memory. When trying to identify a criminal, the police would be using a recall method if they asked the victim to describe, from memory, some of the perpetrator's distinguishing features: "Did you notice anything unusual about the attacker?" They would be using the recognition method if they showed the victim photos, one at a time, from a file of criminal suspects or if they asked the victim to identify the perpetrator in a police lineup.

Let's now use these two procedures to test you on the word pairs you learned a few moments ago. What words finished the pairs?

    Hat—?   Bicycle—?   Ear—?

Can you select the correct pair from these possibilities?

Apple–Baby	Mouse–Tree	Ball–House
Apple–Boat	Mouse–Tongue	Ball–Hill
Apple–Bottle	Mouse–Tent	Ball–Horn

Was the recognition test easier than the recall test? It should be. Let's try to explain this result with respect to retrieval cues.

Retrieval cues are the stimuli available as you search for a particular memory. These cues may be provided externally, such as questions on a quiz ("What memory principles do you associate with the research of Sternberg and Sperling?"), or generated internally ("Where have I met her before?"). Each time you attempt to retrieve an explicit memory, you do so for some purpose, and that purpose often supplies the retrieval cue. It won't surprise you that memories can be easier or harder to retrieve depending on the quality of the retrieval cue. If a friend asks you, "Who's the one emperor I can't remember?" you're likely to be involved in a guessing game. If she asks instead, "Who was the emperor after Claudius?" you can immediately respond "Nero."

Let's return to recall and recognition. Both memory tests require a search using cues. The cues for recognition, however, are much more useful. For recall, you have to hope that the cue alone will help you locate the information. For recognition, part of the work has been done for you. When you look at the pair *Mouse–Tree,* you only have to answer yes or no to "Did I have this experience?" rather than, in response to *Mouse—?* "What was the experience I had?" In this light, you can see that we made the recognition test reasonably easy for you. Suppose we

had given you, instead, recombinations of the original pairs. Which of these are correct?

    Hat–Clock   Ear–Boat
    Hat–Bone   Ear–Blanket

Now you must recognize not just that you saw the word before, but that you saw it in a particular context. (We will return to the idea of context shortly.) If you are a veteran of difficult multiple-choice exams, you have come to learn how tough even recognition situations can be. However, in most cases, your recognition performance will be better than your recall, because retrieval cues are more straightforward for recognition. Let's look at some other aspects of retrieval cues.

EPISODIC AND SEMANTIC MEMORIES

We have already made a pair of distinctions about types of memories. You have implicit and explicit memories and declarative and procedural memories. We can define another dimension along which declarative memories differ with respect to the cues that are necessary to retrieve them from memory. Canadian psychologist **Endel Tulving** (1972) first proposed the distinction between *episodic* and *semantic* types of declarative memory.

Episodic memories preserve, individually, the specific events that you have personally experienced. For example, memories of your happiest birthday or of your first kiss are stored in episodic memory. To recover such memories, you need retrieval cues that specify something about the time at which the event occurred and something about the content of the events. Depending on how the information has been encoded, you may or may not be able to produce a specific memory representation for an event. For example, do you have any specific memories to differentiate the tenth time ago you brushed your teeth from the eleventh time ago?

Everything you know, you began to acquire in some particular context. However, there are large classes of information that, over time, you encounter in many different contexts. These classes of information come to be available for retrieval without reference to their multiple times and places of experience. These **semantic memories** are generic, categorical memories, such as the meanings of words and concepts. For most people, facts like the formula $E = MC^2$ and the capital of France don't require retrieval cues that make reference to the episodes, the original learning contexts, in which the memory was acquired.

Of course, this doesn't mean that your recall of semantic memories is foolproof. You know perfectly well that you can forget many facts that have become dissociated from the contexts in which you learned them. A good strategy when you can't recover a semantic memory is to treat it like an episodic memory again. By thinking to yourself, "I know I learned the names of the Roman emperors in my Western civilization course," you may be able to provide the extra retrieval cues that will shake loose a memory.

Retrieval cues Internally or externally generated stimuli available to help with the retrieval of a memory.

Episodic memories Long-term memories for autobiographical events and the contexts in which they occurred.

Semantic memories Generic, categorical memories, such as the meanings of words and concepts.

Events of personal importance, like seeing a good friend for the first time after a year's separation, are retained in *episodic* memory. What types of information from *semantic* memory might contribute to a reunion?

INTERFERENCE

When we asked you to learn the paired associates earlier, we were really asking you to acquire new episodic memories. Suppose, now, we ask you to acquire another set of episodic memories. Once again, keep working on these word pairs until you can repeat them three times in a row without an error.

Apple–Robe

Hat–Circle

Bicycle–Roof

Mouse–Magazine

Ball–Baby

Ear–Penny

How did it go? Examine the list. You can see what we've done—each old prompt is paired with a new re-sponse. Was it harder for you to learn these new pairs? Do you think it would now be harder for you to recall the old ones? (Go ahead and try.) The answer in both cases is typically "yes." This brief exercise should give you a sense of another aspect of retrieval cues, interference. **Interference** occurs when retrieval cues do not point effectively to one specific memory. The greater the number of possible responses to a specific retrieval cue, the more difficult it is to retrieve any one response (Bower et al., 1994; Chandler & Gargano, 1995).

We have already given you a real-life example of the problem of interference when we asked you to try to differentiate your recollections of your episodes of tooth-brushing. All of the specific memories interfere with each other. *Proactive interference* (proactive means "forward acting") refers to circumstances in which information you have acquired in the past makes it more difficult to acquire new information. *Retroactive interference* (retroactive means "backward acting") occurs when the acquisition of new information makes it harder for you to remember older information. The word lists we've provided demonstrate both of these types of interference. You've also experienced both proactive and retroactive interference if you've ever moved and had to change your phone number. At first, you probably found it hard to remember the new number—the old one kept popping out (proactive interference). However, after finally being able to reliably reproduce the new one, you may have found yourself unable to remember the old number—even if you had used it for years (retroactive interference).

As with many other memory phenomena, Hermann Ebbinghaus was the first researcher to document interference rigorously through experiments. Ebbinghaus, after learning dozens of lists of nonsense syllables, found himself forgetting about 65 percent of the new ones he was learning. Fifty years later, students at Northwestern University who studied Ebbinghaus's lists had the same

Interference A memory phenomenon that occurs when retrieval cues do not point effectively to one specific memory.

PEANUTS reprinted by permission of United Feature Syndicate, Inc.

experience—after many trials with many lists, what the students had learned earlier interfered proactively with their recall of current lists (Underwood, 1948, 1949).

Remember that the conclusion we are working toward is that the match between encoding and retrieval is critical. From these last two sections, you can see how the pieces fit together to reach that conclusion: The context in which you attempt to retrieve a memory itself acts as a source of retrieval cues. When there is a mismatch between the contexts of encoding and retrieval, the cues provided in the retrieval context cannot help (and may even hurt) your attempt to find the memory you seek.

The Processes of Encoding and Retrieval

We have seen so far that a match between the context of encoding and of retrieval is beneficial to good memory performance. We will now refine this conclusion somewhat by considering the actual processes that are used to get information to and from long-term memory. We will see that memory functions best when encoding and retrieval processes make a good match as well.

LEVELS OF PROCESSING

Let's begin with the idea that the type of processing you perform on information—the type of attention you pay to information at time of encoding—will have an influence on your memory for the information. **Levels-of-processing theory** suggests that the deeper the level at which information was processed, the more likely it is to be committed to memory (Craik & Lockhart, 1972; Lockhart & Craik, 1990). If processing involves more analysis, interpretation, comparison, and elaboration, it should result in better memory.

The depth of processing is often defined by the types of judgments participants are required to make with respect to experimental materials. Consider the word *GRAPE*. We could ask you to make a physical judgment—is the word in capital letters? Or a rhyme judgment—does the word rhyme with tape? Or a meaning judgment—does the word represent a type of fruit? Do you see how each of these questions requires you to think a little bit more deeply about *GRAPE*? In fact, the deeper the original processing participants carry out, the more words they remember (Lockhart & Craik, 1990).

A difficulty of the levels-of-processing theory, however, is that researchers have not always been able to

Levels-of-processing theory A theory that suggests that the deeper the level at which information was processed, the more likely it is to be retained in memory.
Transfer-appropriate processing The perspective that suggests that memory is best when the type of processing carried out at encoding matches the processes carried out at retrieval.

specify exactly what makes certain processes "shallow" or "deep." Even so, results of this sort confirm that the way in which information is committed to memory—the mental processes that you use to encode information—has an effect on whether you can retrieve that information later. However, so far we have discussed only explicit memory. We will now see that the match between processes at encoding and retrieval is particularly critical for implicit memory.

PROCESSES AND IMPLICIT MEMORY

Earlier, we defined the explicit versus implicit dimension for memories as a distinction that applies both at encoding and at retrieval (Roediger, 1990; Schacter et al., 1993). Under many circumstances, for example, you will retrieve implicitly memories that you originally encoded explicitly. This is true when you greet your best friend by name without having to expend any particular mental effort. Even so, implicit memories are often most robust when there is a strong match between the processes at implicit encoding and the processes at implicit retrieval. This perspective is called **transfer-appropriate processing**: Memory is best when the type of processing carried out at encoding *transfers* to the processes required at retrieval (Roediger et al., 1989). To support this perspective, we will first describe some of the methodologies that are used to demonstrate implicit memories. Then we will show how the match between encoding and retrieval processes matters.

Let's consider a typical experiment in which implicit memory is assessed. The researchers presented students with lists of concrete nouns and asked them to judge the pleasantness of each word on a 1 (least pleasant) to 5 (most pleasant) scale (Rajaram & Roediger, 1993). The pleasantness ratings required participants to think about the meaning of a word without explicitly committing it to memory. After this study phase, participants' memory was assessed using one of four implicit memory tasks (suppose that a word on one list was *unicorn*):

- *Word fragment completion.* The participant is given fragments of a word, like __ni__or__, and asked to complete the fragments with the first word that comes to mind.

- *Word stem completion.* The participant is asked to complete a stem, like *uni_____*, with the first word that comes to mind.

- *Word identification.* Words are flashed on a computer screen in such a fashion that participants cannot see them clearly. They must try to guess each word that is flashed. In this case, one of the words would be *unicorn*.

- *Anagrams.* Participants are given a scrambled word, like *corunni,* and asked to give the first unscrambled word that comes to mind.

Just like our example with *unicorn,* correct responses to each of the tasks can be provided by words from the earlier lists. What is critical, however, is that the experimenters have not called attention to the relationship between the words on the earlier list and appropriate responses on these new tasks—that's why the use of memory is implicit.

To assess the degree of implicit memory, the researchers compared the performance of participants who had seen a particular word, like *unicorn,* on the pleasantness lists with those who had not. **Figure 8.9** plots the improvement brought about by implicit memory for a word—percent correct when the word had appeared on the participant's list minus percent correct when it had not. (Different participants experienced different word lists.) You can see that for each task, there was an advantage to having seen a word before, even though participants had been asked only to say whether the word had a pleasant meaning. This advantage is known as **priming,** because the first experience of the word *primes* memory for later experiences. For some memory tasks, like word fragment completion, researchers have found priming effects lasting a week and beyond (Sloman et al., 1988).

Let's turn now to the nature of the match between encoding and retrieval. The four implicit memory tests we've mentioned so far all rely on a *physical* match between the original stimulus and the information given at test. In a sense, whatever processes allow you to encode *unicorn* also make that word available when you are asked to complete the stem *uni_____,* and so on. We can, however, introduce another test, *category association,* that relies on *meaning* or *concepts* instead of on a physical match. Imagine we gave you the category name "mythological creatures" and asked you to name as many members of that category as you could in a short time. You might very well say unicorn. However, if you became more likely to say unicorn because you had seen the word

on an earlier list, in a different context, that would be evidence of implicit memory.

Using two different types of implicit memory tests based on priming—by physical features or by meaning—we can look for a relationship between encoding and retrieval.

PRIMING OCCURS WHEN PROCESSES MATCH Memory researchers designed a levels-of-processing experiment to demonstrate that different implicit memories rely on different types of processes. Participants were given lists of words and asked either to make a *meaning* judgment—how pleasant is the meaning of this word?—or a *physical* judgment—how many consonants does this word have? Recall that the category association test relies on meaning. Accordingly, the researchers predicted that priming on the category association test would occur only when the implicit encoding required an analysis of meaning. The results confirmed their prediction. Similarly, physical judgments produced priming only on implicit memory tests that also relied on physical features (Srinivas & Roediger, 1990).

This type of research supports the idea of transfer-appropriate processing: If you use a certain type of processing—for example, physical or meaning analysis—to encode information, you will retrieve that information most efficiently when the processing uses the same type of analysis (Park & Gabrieli, 1995; Rajaram et al., 1998;

Priming In the assessment of implicit memory, the advantage conferred by prior exposure to a word or situation.

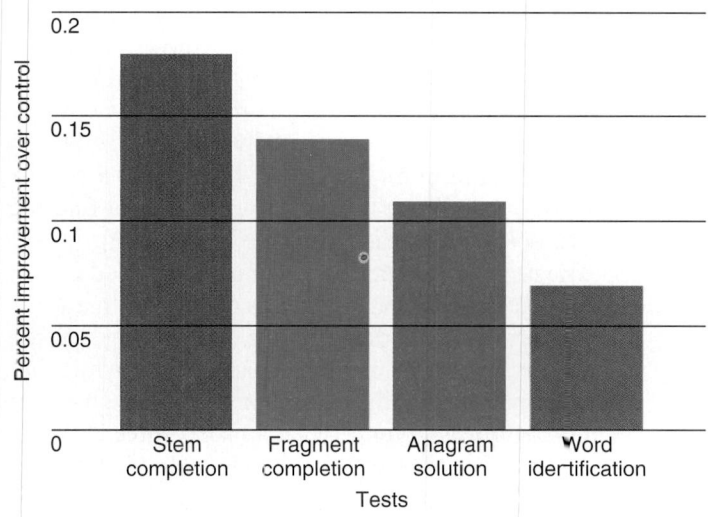

FIGURE 8.9

Priming on Implicit Memory Tests

Priming indicates improvement on the various tasks over performance on control words. Some implicit memory tests demonstrate that priming can last a week or more.

Weldon et al., 1995). Earlier we made this assertion: Your ability to remember will be greatest when there is a good match between the circumstances in which you encode information and the circumstances in which you attempt to retrieve it. This section provided the research evidence for this assertion. Let's now see how we can put theories of encoding and retrieval further to work for you.

Improving Memory for Unstructured Information

After reading this whole section, you should have some concrete ideas about how you could improve your everyday memory performance—how you can remember more and forget less. (The *Psychology in Your Life* box, later in the chapter, will help you solidify those ideas with respect to school work.) You know, especially, that you're best off trying to recover a piece of information in the same context, or by performing the same types of mental tasks, as when you first acquired it. But there's a slightly different problem with which we still must give you some help. It has to do with encoding unstructured or arbitrary collections of information.

For example, imagine that you are working as a clerk in a store. You must try to commit to memory the several items that each customer wants: "The woman in the green blouse wants hedge clippers and a garden hose. The man in the blue shirt wants a pair of pliers, six quarter-inch screws, and a paint scraper." This scenario, in fact, comes very close to the types of experiments in which researchers ask you to memorize paired associates. How did you go about learning the word pairs we presented earlier? The task probably was somewhat of a chore, because the pairs were not particularly meaningful for you—and information that isn't meaningful is hard to remember. To find a way to get the right items to the right customer, you need to make associations seem less arbitrary. Let's explore *elaborative rehearsal* and *mnemonics*.

ELABORATIVE REHEARSAL

A general strategy for improving encoding is called **elaborative rehearsal.** The basic idea of this technique is that while you are rehearsing information—while you are first committing it to memory—you elaborate on the material to enrich the encoding. One way to do this is to invent a relationship that makes an association seem

Elaborative rehearsal A technique for improving memory by enriching the encoding of information.

Mnemonics Strategies or devices that use familiar information during the encoding of new information to enhance subsequent access to the information in memory.

less arbitrary. For example, if you wanted to remember the pair *Mouse–Tree*, you might conjure up an image of a mouse scurrying up a tree to look for cheese. Recall is enhanced when you encode separate bits of information into this type of miniature story line (Bower, 1972). Can you imagine, in the clerk situation, swiftly making up a story to link each customer with the appropriate items? (It will work with practice.) You may have already guessed that it is also often helpful to supplement your story line with a mental picture—a visual image—of the scene you are trying to remember. Visual imagery can enhance your recall because it gives you codes for both verbal and visual memories simultaneously (Paivio, 1986).

Elaborative rehearsal can also help save you from what has been called the *next-in-line effect:* When, for example, people are next in line to speak, they often can't remember what the person directly before them said. If you've ever had a circle of people each give his or her name, you're probably well-acquainted with this effect. What was the name of the person directly in front of you? The origin of this effect appears to be a shift in attention toward preparing to make your own remarks or to say your own name (Bond et al., 1991). To counter this shift, you should use elaborative rehearsal. Keep your attention focused on the person in front of you and enrich your encoding of his or her name: "*Lisa*—she smiles like the *Mona Lisa.*"

MNEMONICS

Another memory-enhancing option is to draw on special mental strategies called *mnemonics* (from the Greek word meaning "to remember"). **Mnemonics** are devices that encode a long series of facts by associating them with familiar and previously encoded information. Many mnemonics work by giving you ready-made retrieval cues that help organize otherwise arbitrary information.

Consider the *method of loci,* first practiced by ancient Greek orators. The singular of *loci* is *locus,* and it means "place." The method of loci is a means of remembering the order of a list of names or objects—or, for the orators, the individual sections of a long speech—by associating them with some sequence of places with which you are familiar. To remember a grocery list, you might mentally put each item sequentially along the route you take to get from home to school. To remember the list later, you mentally go through your route and find the item associated with each spot (see **Figure 8.10**).

The *peg-word method* is similar to the method of loci, except that you associate the items on a list with a series of cues rather than with familiar locations. Typically, the cues for the peg-word method are a series of rhymes that associate numbers with words. For example, you might memorize "one is a *bun,*" "two is a *shoe,*" "three is a *tree,*" and so on. Then you would associate each item on your list interacting with the appropriate cue. For your gro-

FIGURE 8.10

Bread

Orange juice

Ice cream

Bananas

The Method of Loci

In the method of loci, you associate the items you wish to remember (such as the items on a grocery list) with locations along a familiar path (such as your route to and from school).

cery list, you might have the bread nestled among several buns, a shoe filled up with orange juice, a tree with ice cream cones rather than leaves, and so on. You can see that the key to learning arbitrary information is to encode the information in such a fashion that you provide yourself with efficient retrieval cues.

Metamemory

Suppose you're in a situation in which you'd really like to remember something. You're doing your best to use retrieval cues that reflect the circumstances of encoding, but you just can't get the bit of information to emerge. Part of the reason you're expending so much effort is that you're sure that you are in possession of the information. But are you correct to be so confident about the contents of your memory? Questions like this one—about how your memory works or how you know what information you possess—are questions of **metamemory**. One

major question on metamemory has been when and why *feelings-of-knowing*—the subjective sensations that you do have information stored in memory—are accurate.

Research on feelings-of-knowing was pioneered by **J. T. Hart** (1965), who began his studies by asking students a series of general knowledge questions. Suppose, for example, we asked you, "What planet is the largest in our solar system?" Do you know the answer? If you don't, how would you respond to this question: "Even though I don't remember the answer now, do I know the answer to the extent that I could pick the correct answer from among several wrong answers?" This was the question Hart put to his participants. He allowed them to give ratings from 1, to say they were quite sure they wouldn't choose correctly on the multiple choice, to 6, to say they

Metamemory Implicit or explicit knowledge about memory abilities and effective memory strategies; cognition about memory.

HOW CAN MEMORY RESEARCH HELP YOU PREPARE FOR EXAMS?

Among the most frequent questions students ask after they've read about memory research are, "How can I put the information to immediate use? How will this research help me prepare for my next exam?" Let's see what types of advice we can generate from the research conclusions:

- *Encoding specificity.* As you'll recall, the principle of encoding specificity suggests that the context of retrieval should match the context of encoding. In school settings, "context" often will mean "the context of other information." If you always study material in the same context, you may find it difficult to retrieve it in a different context—so, if a professor's questions approach a topic in a slightly unusual way, you might be entirely at a loss. As a remedy, you should change contexts even while you study. Rearrange the order of your notes. Ask yourself questions that mix different topics together. Try to make your own novel combinations. But if you get stuck while you're taking an exam, try to generate as many retrieval cues as you can that reinstate the original context: "Let's see. We heard about this in the same lecture we learned about short-term memory…"

- *Serial position.* You know from the serial position curve that, under

very broad circumstances, information presented in the "middle" is least well remembered. In fact, college students fail more exam items on material from the middle of a lecture than on material from the start or end of the lecture (Holen & Oaster, 1976; Jensen, 1962). When you're listening to a lecture, you should remind yourself to pay special attention in the middle of the session. When it comes time to study, you should devote some extra time and effort to that material—and make sure not to study the material in the same order each time. You might also take note that the chapter you're reading now is about at the middle of *Psychology and Life*. If you have a final examination that covers all the course material, you're going to want to make an especially careful review of this chapter.

- *Elaborative rehearsal and mnemonics.* Sometimes when you study for exams, you will feel as if you are trying to acquire "unstructured information." You might, for example, be asked to memorize the functions of different parts of the brain. Under these circumstances, you need to find ways to provide the structure yourself. Try to form visual images or make up sentences or stories that use the concepts in creative ways. One of your authors still remembers

his mnemonic from introductory psychology to remember the function of the *ventromedial hypothalamus,* which is often abbreviated VMH: Very Much Hungry (however, as you will learn in Chapter 12, research in the 20 intervening years has made that mnemonic less accurate). Elaborative rehearsal allows you to use what you know already to make new material more memorable.

- *Metamemory.* Research on metamemory suggests that people generally have good intuitions about what they know and what they don't know. If you are in an exam situation in which there is time pressure, you should allow those intuitions to guide how you allocate your time. You might, for example, read the whole test over quickly and see which questions give you the strongest feelings-of-knowing. If you are taking an exam on which you lose points for giving wrong answers (which happens, for example, on SAT and some GRE exams), you should be particularly attentive to your metamemory intuitions, so you can avoid answering those questions on which you "sense" you are most likely to be incorrect.

We hope you now have several concrete ideas about how memory research can help you to prepare for your next exam!

---

were quite sure they would choose correctly. What would your rating be? Now here are your alternatives:

a. Pluto

b. Venus

c. Earth

d. Jupiter

If you made an accurate feeling-of-knowing judgment, you should have been less likely to get the correct answer,

d, if you gave a 1 rating than if you gave a 6. (Of course, to have a fair test, we'd want to give you a long series of questions.) Hart found that when participants gave 1 ratings, they answered the questions correctly only 30 percent of the time, whereas 6 ratings predicted 75 percent success. That's pretty impressive evidence that feelings-of-knowing can be accurate.

Research on metamemory focuses on both the processes that give rise to feelings-of-knowing and on how their accuracy is ensured (Koriat & Levy-Sadot, 1999; Metcalfe, 2000):

- The *cue familiarity hypothesis* suggests that people base their feelings-of-knowing on their familiarity with the retrieval cue. Suppose you were asked, "What is the last name of the composer of the 'Maple Leaf Rag'?" If you have prior familiarity with the "Maple Leaf Rag," you might think that you probably would be able to recognize the correct alternative when given the multiple choice (Metcalfe et al., 1993; Reder & Ritter, 1992; Schwartz & Metcalfe, 1992).

- The *accessibility hypothesis* suggests that people base their judgments on the accessibility, or availability, of partial information from memory. Thus, if the question "What is the last name of the composer of the 'Maple Leaf Rag'?" calls quite easily to mind information you believe to be related to the correct answer, you are likely to think that you will be able to recognize the correct answer as well (Koriat, 1993, 1995).

Both of these theories have obtained empirical support—and both suggest that you can generally trust your instincts when you believe that you know something. (Later in the chapter, we will describe research on eyewitness testimony, which provides some exceptions to this general rule.)

You have now learned quite a bit about how you get information in and out of memory. You know what we mean by a "good match" between the circumstances of encoding and of retrieval. In the next section, we will shift our focus from your memory processes to the content of your memories.

SUMMING UP

Theories of long-term memory must explain how memories are acquired and how they are maintained for a lifetime. The encoding specificity principle suggests that memories are best retrieved when the context of retrieval matches the context of encoding. The serial position effect results from the distinctiveness of each experience (word, event, and so on) with respect to the context in which recall occurs.

You search memory with retrieval cues. Performance is often better for recognition tasks than for recall tasks because retrieval cues for recognition provide more information. Episodic memories are encoded with respect to the context of acquisition; semantic memories have lost their encoding with respect to particular episodes. Interference can be proactive, where old information interferes with new information, or retroactive, where new learning interferes with old.

The levels-of-processing theory suggests that more deeply processed information will be better recalled. Research on implicit memory suggests that the match between processes at encoding and processes at retrieval predicts the amount of priming. You can improve memory for unstructured information by using elaborative rehearsal and mnemonics. Metamemory judgments about your knowledge are typically accurate.

Structures in Long-Term Memory

In most of our examples so far, we have asked you to try to acquire and retrieve isolated or unrelated bits of information. What you mostly have represented in memory, however, are large bodies of *organized knowledge*. Recall, for example, that we asked you to consider whether *grape* is a fruit. You could say *yes* very quickly. How about *porcupine*? Is it a fruit? How about *tomato*? In this section, we will examine how the difficulty of these types of judgments relates to the way information is structured in memory. We will also discuss how memory organization allows you to make a best guess at the content of experiences you can't remember exactly.

Memory Structures

An essential function of memory is to draw together similar experiences, to enable you to discover patterns in your interactions with the environment. (Recall a similar description, in Chapter 5, on the functions of perception.) You live in a world filled with countless individual events, from which you must continually extract information to combine them into a smaller, simpler set that you can manage mentally. But apparently you don't need to expend any particular conscious effort to find structure in the world. Just as we suggested when we defined the implicit acquisition of memories, it's unlikely that you ever formally thought to yourself something like, "Here's what belongs in a kitchen." It is through ordinary experience in the world that you have acquired mental structures to mirror environmental structures. Let's look at the types of memory structures you have formed in your moment-by-moment experience of the world.

CATEGORIZATION AND CONCEPTS

We will begin by previewing one of the topics we will discuss in Chapter 11—the mental effort a child must go through to acquire the meaning of a word, such as *doggie*. For this word to have meaning, the child must be able to store each instance in which the word *doggie* is used, as well as information about the context. In this way, the child finds out what common core experience—a furry creature with four legs—is meant by *doggie*. The child must acquire the knowledge that *doggie* applies not just to one particular animal, but to a whole category of creatures. This ability to *categorize* individual experiences—to take the same action toward them or give them the same label—is one of the most basic abilities of thinking organisms (Mervis & Rosch, 1981).

How does the formation of categories—such as what constitutes a healthy head of lettuce, a sweet melon, or a flavorful tomato—help you make daily decisions like what to buy for dinner?

The mental representations of the categories you form are called **concepts.** The concept *doggie,* for example, names the set of mental representations of experiences of dogs that a young child has gathered together in memory. (As we shall see in Chapter 11, if the child hasn't yet refined his or her meaning for *doggie,* the concept might also include features that adults wouldn't consider to be appropriate.) You have acquired a vast array of concepts. You have categories for *objects* and *activities,* such as *barns* and *baseball.* Concepts may also represent *properties,* such as *red* or *large; abstract ideas,* such as *truth* or *love;* and *relations,* such as *smarter than* or *sister of.* Each concept represents a summary unit for your experience of the world.

PROTOTYPES

Given the number of dogs you've seen in your life, what exactly do you think about when, for example, you read a sentence like, "The dog buried the bone"? Do you call

- **Concepts** Mental representations of kinds or categories of items or ideas.
- **Prototype** The most representative example of a category.

to mind some particular dog? Or do you envision some typical dog, averaged across all the dogs you have experienced—your **prototype** for a dog? Let's look at an experiment that helps to address these questions.

In this experiment, participants acted as if they had averaged together all the exemplar faces they had seen to construct the prototypical face.

The prototypes you have for categories are derived from all your experiences with members of that category. For that reason, your prototype shifts subtly every time you encounter a new exemplar of a category. Consequently, researchers believe that you do not actually have a specific mental representation of the prototype for a particular category. Rather, the prototype emerges as an average across your pool of exemplars (Hintzman, 1986; Nosofsky et al., 1992). For example, all the dogs you have encountered to this moment contribute to your notion of the prototypical dog. Moreover, if you go for a walk today and see a dog or two, your prototype will change just the slightest bit.

Being able to find the prototype for a category like *dog* also allows you to recognize some category members as more or less typical—the more features the members share with the prototypical member of the category, the more typical they are likely to be. You can develop this intuition if you think about a category like *bird.* What makes a robin a typical bird, but an ostrich or a penguin atypical? The answer has to do with the degree of match of these creatures to all the other entities that you have classified in memory as birds. The degree of typicality of a category member—the extent to which something

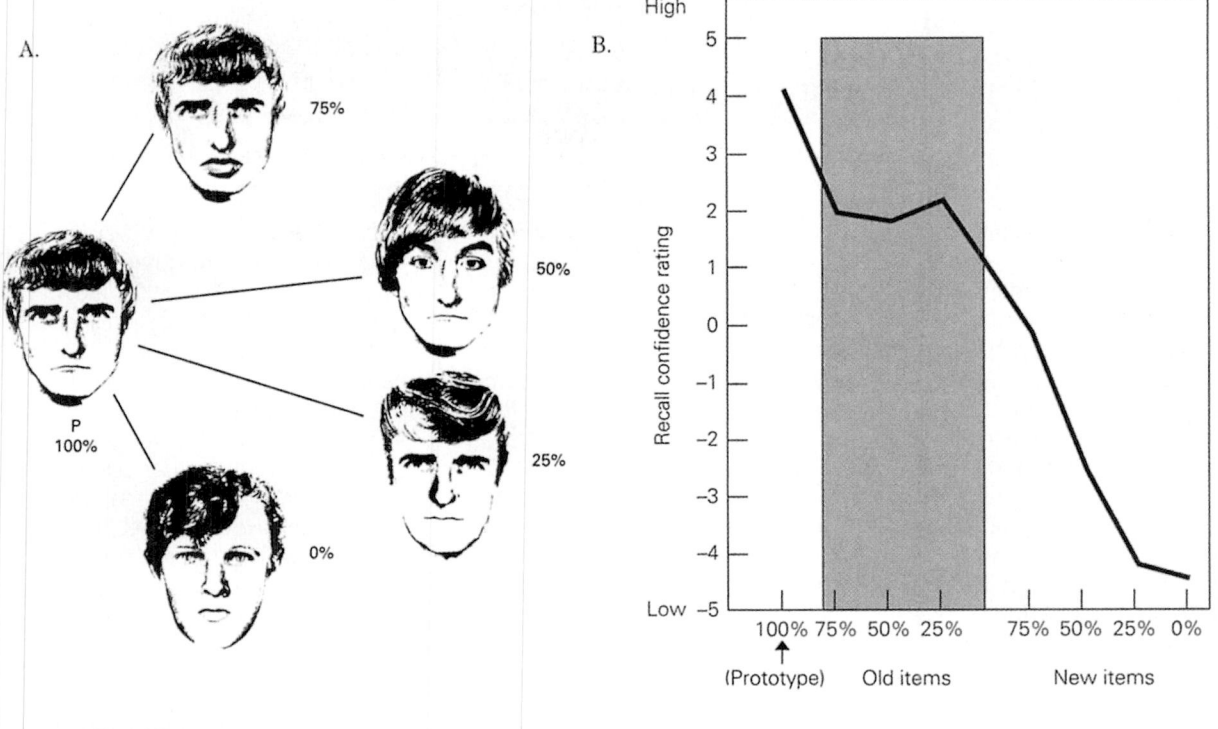

FIGURE 8.11

(A) Prototype Face and Exemplar Faces
(B) Confidence Ratings for Prototype, Old Items, and New Items

(A) The 75-percent face has all the features of the prototype face except the mouth; the 50-percent face has different hair and eyes; the 25-percent face has only the eyes in common; and the 0-percent face has no features in common. (B) Participants were asked to rate how confident they were that they had previously seen a face. Confidence was highest for the prototype face—which they had never actually seen. Confidence was equivalent for old faces. For new faces, participants' confidence dropped as the face grew more distant from the prototype.

matches your prototype—has real-life consequences. Research has shown, for example, that people respond more quickly to typical members of a category than to its more unusual ones. Your reaction time to determine that a robin is a bird would be quicker than your reaction time to determine that an ostrich is a bird (Rosch et al., 1976). This effect arises, once again, because you maintain in memory your history of experiences with the members of the category *bird*. It is easier to find robin experiences than ostrich experiences (unless, of course, you have spent your life among ostriches).

HIERARCHIES AND BASIC LEVELS

Concepts, and their prototypes, do not exist in isolation. As shown in **Figure 8.12**, concepts can often be arranged into meaningful organizations. A broad category like *animal* has several subcategories, such as *bird* and *fish*, which in turn contain exemplars such as *canary, ostrich, shark,* and *salmon.* The animal category

is itself a subcategory of the still larger category of *living beings.* Concepts are also linked to other types of information: You store the knowledge that some birds are *edible,* some are *endangered,* some are *national symbols.*

There seems to be a level in such hierarchies at which people best categorize and think about objects. This has been called the **basic level** (Rosch, 1973, 1978). For example, when you buy an apple at the grocery store, you could think of it as a *piece of fruit*—but that seems imprecise—or a *Golden Delicious*—but that seems too specific or picayune. The basic level is just *apple.* If you were shown a picture of such an object, that's what you'd be likely to call it. You would also be faster to say that it

Basic level The level of categorization that can be retrieved from memory most quickly and used most efficiently.

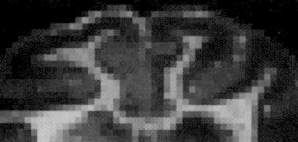

HUMAN MEMORY SEARCHES AND WEB SEARCHES

When people make comparisons between the memory capabilities of humans and computers, it often seems to be the case that computers come out on top. We count on our computers to remember thousands or millions more bits of information than we ourselves could commit to memory. However, there is one feature of human memory that should still make you feel superior to any computer you use: The processes that allow you to retrieve specific information from memory are often far more efficient than comparable Web search procedures.

Suppose, for example, a friend was quizzing you on the content of this chapter and asked, "What researchers originated the concept of *encoding specificity*?" You might give a right answer (Tulving and Thomson), a reasonable wrong answer (Sperling), or you might report that you don't know. You'd be highly unlikely to give an answer that was entirely unrelated to the question. What do you suppose happened when we submitted this question to search engines on the Web? The first Web site suggested by Google.com had the title, "The Isolation of HIV—Has It Been Achieved?" Our second attempt was with AskJeeves.com. That

search engine suggested that we look up the definition of *concept* at Britannica.com. Why are these responses different from the outcome of a human memory search? We will note two properties of human memory searches that give them a potential advantage with respect to Web searches.

First, as you learned earlier in the chapter, human memory searches make efficient use of contextual cues to aid in retrieving information. That makes it quite likely that the information you retrieve will be relevant to the appropriate meaning of the question in context. By contrast, the Web searches most often rely rather narrowly on words rather than contexts. For example, if you use just "encoding specificity" as a search term at either Google or AskJeeves, each immediately gets you to pages that answer the original question. For the Web searches, the parts of the question that were intended to add precision to the context ("what researchers originated") actually had quite a negative impact on the success of the search. For many Web searches, it's hard for searchers to know how to include context in their queries without sending the searches off in undesirable directions.

Second, human memory searches are guided by *concepts* rather than by *words*. When you search your memory for the answer to the question about encoding specificity, it doesn't really matter if you phrase it as "researchers" vs. "experimenters" or "originated" vs. "discovered." It is the concepts each word makes active in working memory that serve as cues for the search. However, Web searches rely heavily on exact words. For example, when we did a Google.com search substituting "discovered" for "originated," we obtained links to appropriate pages on memory theories. However, a change from "researchers" to "experimenters" yielded, as the first link, a page entitled "Waves, Pulses, and the Theory of Neural Masses." This small experiment illustrates how much Web searches, unlike searches of human memory, depend on words rather than concepts.

Do you now feel at least a bit superior to your computer? You might take a few minutes to think about how you could build these features of human memory searches into search engines for the Web.

Web sites:

- www.google.com

- www.AskJeeves.com

---

was an apple than that it was a piece of fruit (Rosch, 1978). The basic level emerges pretty much through the same forces that give rise to the prototype. You have more experience with the term *apple* than with its more or less specific alternatives. If you became an apple grower, however, your basic level would probably shift lower in the hierarchy.

Schemas General conceptual frameworks, or clusters of knowledge, regarding objects, people, and situations; knowledge packages that encode generalizations about the structure of the environment.

SCHEMAS

We have seen that concepts are the building blocks of memory hierarchies. They also serve as building blocks for more complex mental structures. Recall Figure 8.2. Why did you instantly know that the rabbit didn't belong in the kitchen? We suggested earlier that this judgment relied on implicit memory—but we didn't say what type of memory structure you were using. Clearly, what you need is some representation in memory that combines the individual concepts of a kitchen—your knowledge about ovens, sinks, and refrigerators—into a larger unit. We call that larger unit a schema. **Schemas** are conceptual frameworks, or clusters of knowledge, regarding ob-

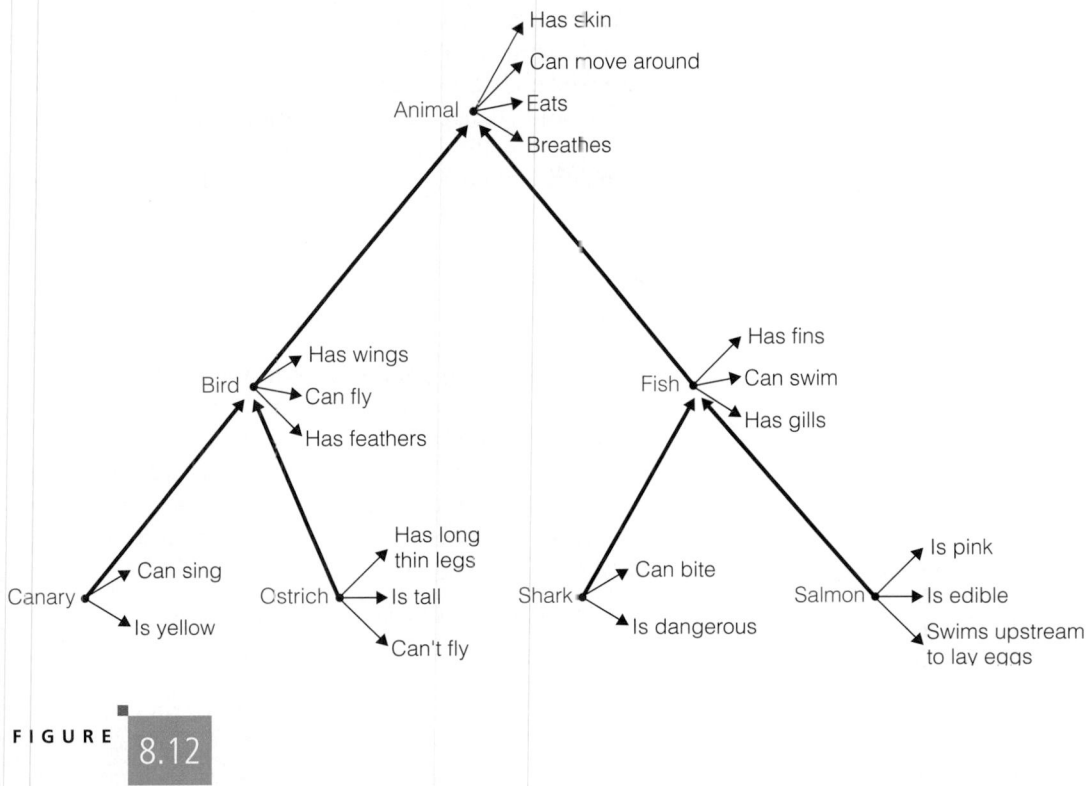

FIGURE 8.12

Hierarchically Organized Structure of Concepts

The category *animal* can be divided into subcategories such as *bird* and *fish;* similarly, each, subcategory can be further divided. Some information (such as *has skin*) applies to all concepts in the hierarchy; other information (such as *can sing*) applies only to concepts at lower levels (for example, a *canary*).

jects, people, and situations. Schemas are "knowledge packages" that encode complex generalizations about your experience of the structure of the environment. You have schemas for kitchens and bedrooms, race car drivers and professors, surprise parties and graduations. You should take a minute right now to think about the types of generalizations you would be willing to offer about each of those categories of experience.

One thing you may have guessed is that your schemas do not include all the individual details of all your varied experiences. Just as a prototype is the average of your experiences of a category, a schema represents your average experience of situations in the environment. Thus, also like prototypes, your schemas are not permanent but shift with your changing life events (Rumelhart et al., 1986). Your schemas also include only those details in the world to which you have devoted sufficient attention. For example, when asked to draw the information on the head sides of U.S. coins, college students virtually never filled in the word *Liberty,* although it appears on every coin (Rubin & Kontis, 1983). Check a coin! Thus, your schemas provide an accurate reflection of what you've *noticed* about the world. Let's now look at all the ways in which you use your concepts and schemas.

Using Memory Structures

Let's consider a couple of instances of memory structures in action. You already saw that your schema for kitchen enables you to determine that the bunny just doesn't belong. For a second example, think back to Chapter 5, where we discussed how prior knowledge has an effect on interpretations of ambiguous stimuli. Do you remember **Figure 8.13?** Do you see a duck or a rabbit? Let's suppose we give you the expectation that you're going to see a duck. If you match the features of the picture against your schematic expectations for the features of a duck, you're likely to be reasonably content. The same thing would happen if we told you to expect a rabbit. You use information from memory to generate—and confirm—expectations.

You also have memory structures that influence what you perceive and remember about people (Cantor & Mischel, 1979; Levy et al., 1999). For example, you have probably acquired the concepts of dentists, cult leaders, environmentalists, and used-car salespeople. If a person you do not know is described as belonging to one of these categories, your stereotypes may lead you to assume that

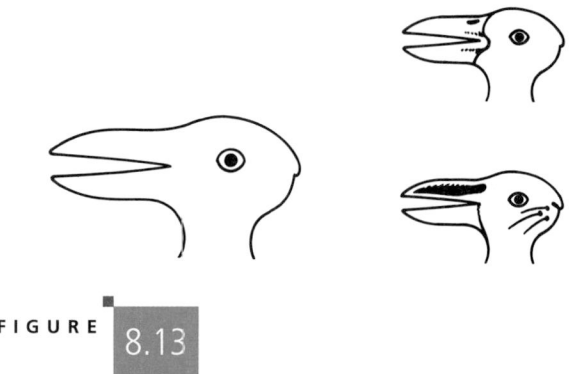

FIGURE 8.13

Recognition Illusion

Duck or rabbit?

the person has particular personality characteristics or behaves in a particular way. Social psychologists have demonstrated that even the words a language makes available can influence this interpersonal use of concepts.

HOW WE KNOW

STEREOTYPES ACROSS LANGUAGES The researchers created descriptions of four individuals, two of whom could easily be labeled by personality-type terms in English, but not in Chinese, and two of whom could easily be labeled in Chinese, but not in English. Consider the term *shì gù*. In Chinese, this term captures an individual who is "worldly, experienced, socially skillful, devoted to his or her family, and somewhat reserved" (Hoffman et al., 1986, p. 1098). In English, no single term or phrase applies to this whole collection of traits. Similarly, no single phrase in Chinese captures the English stereotype of the *artistic type*.

Chinese–English bilinguals read the descriptions in either Chinese or English (half read each description in each language). The researchers predicted that the availability or unavailability of an organized concept in a language would determine whether participants' reasoning was guided by their stereotypes. This expectation was borne out. The impressions participants wrote down for each character were considerably more congruent with a stereotype when the language of processing matched the language in which a concept label was available. For example, a participant might infer that an *artistic-type* person would be *unreliable*—but only when reading the description in English, the language that has the information *artistic* and *unreliable* drawn together as a concept (Hoffman et al., 1986).

This research demonstrates that the availability of memory structures can influence the way you think about the world: Your past experiences color your present experiences and change your expectations for the future. You will see shortly that, for much the same reasons, concepts and schemas can sometimes work against accurate memory.

Remembering as a Reconstructive Process

Let's turn now to another important way in which you use memory structures. In many cases, when you are asked to remember a piece of information, you can't remember the information directly. Instead, you *reconstruct* the information based on more general types of stored knowledge. To experience **reconstructive memory**, consider this trio of questions:

- Did Chapter 3 have the word *the* in it?
- Did 1991 contain the day July 7?
- Did you breathe yesterday between 2:05 and 2:10 P.M.?

You probably were willing to answer "Yes!" to each of these questions without much hesitation, but you almost certainly don't have specific, episodic memories to help you (unless, of course, something happened to fix these events in memory—perhaps July 7 is your birthday or you crossed out all the *the*'s in Chapter 3 to curb your boredom). To answer these questions, you must use more general memories to reconstruct what is likely to have happened. Let's examine this process of reconstruction in a bit more detail.

THE ACCURACY OF RECONSTRUCTIVE MEMORY

If people reconstruct some memories, rather than recovering a specific memory representation for what happened, then you might expect that you could find occasions on which the reconstructed memory differed from the real occurrence—distortions. One of the most impressive demonstrations of memory distortions is also the oldest. In his classic book *Remembering: A Study in Experimental and Social Psychology* (1932), **Sir Frederic Bartlett** undertook a program of research to demonstrate how individuals' prior knowledge influenced the way they remembered new information. Bartlett studied the way British undergraduates remembered stories whose themes and wording were taken from another culture. His most famous story was "The War of the Ghosts," an American Indian tale.

Reconstructive memory The process of putting information together based on general types of stored knowledge in the absence of a specific memory representation.

Bartlett found that his readers' reproductions of the story were often greatly altered from the original. The distortions Bartlett found involved three kinds of reconstructive processes:

- *Leveling*—simplifying the story.

- *Sharpening*—highlighting and overemphasizing certain details.

- *Assimilating*—changing the details to better fit the participant's own background or knowledge.

Thus, readers reproduced the story with words familiar in their culture taking the place of those unfamiliar: *Boat* might replace *canoe* and *go fishing* might replace *hunt seals*. Bartlett's participants also often changed the story's plot to eliminate references to supernatural forces that were unfamiliar in their culture.

Following Bartlett's lead, contemporary researchers have demonstrated a variety of memory distortions that occur when people use constructive processes to reproduce memories (Bergman & Roediger, 1999). For example, one team of researchers produced what they called a "soap opera" effect in story recall (Owens et al., 1979). Here's an example of an episode from one of their stories:

> *Nancy arrived at the cocktail party. She looked around the room to see who was there. She went to talk to her professor. She felt she had to talk to him but was a little nervous about just what to say. A group of people started to play charades. Nancy went over and had some refreshments. The hors d'oeuvres were good but she wasn't interested in talking to the rest of the people at the party. After a while, she decided she'd had enough and left the party.*

Imagine how different it would have been to read that excerpt if you had been among the half of the participants who read this extra introduction to the story:

> *Nancy woke up feeling sick again and she wondered if she really were pregnant. How would she tell the professor she had been seeing? And the money was another problem.*

You might go back now and reread the story excerpt. For the original participants, the presence or absence of the introduction had a dramatic effect on memory performance. When asked to recall the story or to recognize statements from it, readers who had read the extra introductory material—and, thereby, called to mind a schema for an "unwanted pregnancy"—were much more likely to produce or recognize invented statements related to Nancy's pregnancy. The participants' use of the schema led to predictable distortions.

It is important to keep in mind, however, that just as in Chapter 5, when we discussed perceptual illusions, psychologists often infer the normal operation of pro-

Suppose, while you were at this barbecue, someone told you the man on your left was a millionaire. How would this affect your memories for his actions at the barbecue? What if you had been told he only had delusions of being a millionaire?

cesses by demonstrating circumstances in which the processes lead to errors. Just as perceptual illusions don't cause you to walk into walls, memory "illusions" will rarely cause you serious day-to-day worry. You can think of these memory distortions as the consequences of processes that usually work pretty well. In fact, a lot of the time, you don't need to remember the exact details of a particular episode. Reconstructing the gist of events will serve just fine.

Let's explore a bit further the idea that you don't always have to remember particular details. To see how you can reconstruct memories to suit your goal for a particular occasion of memory use, we can look to *quotation*. There are many situations in which you will pepper your own speech with quotations from others' speech. You might, for example, say, "Remember what our psych professor told us, 'Correlation is not causation.'" When you quote someone else's speech, you choose the aspects of that speech that you will reconstruct from memory (Clark & Gerrig, 1990). You may try to reproduce the exact words or just the gist of what was said. You may try to reproduce an accent or a stutter or just speak in your own way. You make these decisions based on your conversational goals. Researchers have demonstrated that the use of memory varies with such goals.

HOW WE KNOW

GOALS AFFECT USES OF MEMORY
Participants watched a videotape of a one-and-a-half minute scene from the movie *Breakfast at Tiffany's* and committed the dialogue to

memory. The memorization took a bit of work—the participants were allowed up to 45 minutes—but over time all the participants were able to reproduce the conversation with near-perfect accuracy. The participants were then divided into two groups. Each participant retold the dialogue to a second student, but half were asked to make the retelling as accurate as possible, while the other half were asked to make the retelling amusing or interesting. Participants with *accuracy* instructions reproduced 99 percent of the original dialogue, word for word. Participants with *interestingness* instructions reproduced only 62 percent of the original dialogue. Because both groups had memorized the conversation nearly perfectly, the interestingness group clearly chose not to reproduce all the dialogue (Wade & Clark, 1993).

This result suggests that the amount of care you take to produce a precise memory will depend on the circumstances. If you are held responsible for exactly what happened, you will produce a precise replica—or perhaps admit that you are unable to do so. In many real-life circumstances, however, it's enough to be able to reconstruct more or less what happened. That's your goal, so that's what you do. There is, however, at least one real-life domain in which you are always held responsible for *exactly* what happened. Let's turn now to eyewitness memory.

EYEWITNESS MEMORY

A witness in a courtroom swears "to tell the truth and nothing but the truth." Throughout this chapter, however, we have seen that whether a memory is accurate or inaccurate depends on the care with which it was encoded and the match of the circumstances of encoding and retrieval. Because researchers understand that people may not be able to report "the truth," even when they genuinely wish to do so, they have focused a good deal of attention on the topic of *eyewitness memory*. The goal is to help the legal system discover the best methods for ensuring the accuracy of witnesses' memories.

Influential studies on eyewitness memory were carried out by **Elizabeth Loftus** (1979, 1992) and her colleagues. The general conclusion from their research was that eyewitnesses' memories for what they had seen were quite vulnerable to distortion from *postevent information*. For example, participants in one study were shown a film of an automobile accident and were asked to estimate the speeds of the cars involved (Loftus & Palmer, 1974). However, some participants were asked, "How fast were the cars going when they smashed into each other?" while others were asked, "How fast were the cars going when they contacted each other?" *Smash* participants estimated the cars'

What postevent factors make it difficult for eyewitnesses to make accurate reports of events?

speed to have been over 40 miles per hour; *contact* participants estimated the speed at 30 miles per hour. About a week later, all the eyewitnesses were asked, "Did you see any broken glass?" In fact, no broken glass had appeared in the film. However, about a third of the *smash* participants reported that there had been glass, while only 14 percent of the *contact* eyewitnesses did so. Thus, postevent information had a substantial effect on what eyewitnesses reported they had experienced.

Postevent information can impair eyewitness memories even when the witnesses are made explicitly aware that the experimenter has attempted to mislead them.

HOW WE KNOW

MEMORY REPORTS ARE INFLUENCED BY POSTEVENT INFORMATION In one experiment, participants viewed a slide show of an office theft. The slide show was accompanied by a tape recording of a woman's voice describing the sequence of events. Immediately after the slide show, the participants heard the woman describe the events again. However, this postevent narrative contained misinformation. For example, for participants who had seen *Glamour* magazine, the tape mentioned *Vogue* instead. Forty-eight hours later, the researcher tested his participants' memory for the information pictured in the slides, but he explicitly informed them that there was no question on the memory test for which the correct answer was mentioned in the postevent narrative. Thus, if participants were able to make a clear distinction in memory between the original events and the postevent information, they should have remained unaffected by that postevent information. That was not the case. Even with fair warning, participants often recalled postevent misinformation rather than real memories (Lindsay, 1990).

The participants had been unable to discriminate between the original sources—event or postevent—of the memory representations (Johnson et al., 1993; Weingardt et al., 1995). As you might expect, when people are repeatedly exposed to the misleading postevent information, they become even more likely to report false memories as real (Mitchell & Zaragoza, 1996). Although some controversy still surrounds the psychological mechanisms that give rise to this memory performance (Lindsay, 1993; Loftus, 1992; Schreiber & Sergent, 1993), the potential for eyewitnesses' reports to be altered in response to postevent information has now been firmly established. This research reinforces the idea that your memories are often collages, reconstructed from different elements of your past experiences.

We have now considered several important features of the encoding, storage, and retrieval of information. In the final section of the chapter, we discuss the brain bases of these memory functions.

SUMMING UP

A primary function of memory is to draw together similar experiences, to find patterns in the environment. Concepts are mental representations of categories. A prototype is derived from all your experiences with members of a category and will, therefore, shift subtly every time you encounter a new exemplar. There appears to be a basic level at which people best categorize and think about objects and entities. Schemas are conceptual frameworks that represent the regularities of larger units of experience than concepts.

When an exact memory cannot be retrieved, a memory is often reconstructed. Reconstructed memories are influenced by schemas. Researchers have demonstrated that the use of memory varies as communication goals vary. Eyewitness testimony presupposes perfect memory for an event, but research has shown that eyewitness testimony is vulnerable to distortion from postevent information. 3

Biological Aspects of Memory

The time has come, once again, for us to ask you to recall the number you committed to memory at the beginning of the chapter. Can you still remember it? What was the point of this exercise? Think for a minute about biological aspects of your ability to look at an arbitrary piece of information and commit it instantly to memory. How can you do that? To encode a memory requires that you instantly change something inside your brain. If you wish to retain that memory for at least the length of a chapter, the change must have the potential

to become permanent. Have you ever wondered how this is possible? Our excuse for having you recall an arbitrary number was so that we could ask you to reflect on how remarkable the biology of memory really is. Let's take a closer look inside the brain.

Searching for the Engram

Let's consider your memory for the number 37 or, more specifically, your memory that the number 37 was the number we asked you to remember. How could we determine where in your brain that memory resides? **Karl Lashley** (1929, 1950), who performed pioneering work on the anatomy of memory, referred to this question as the search for the **engram,** the physical memory representation. Lashley trained rats to learn mazes, removed varying-size portions of their cortexes, and then retested their memories for the mazes. Lashley found that memory impairment from brain lesioning was proportional to the amount of tissue removed. The impairment grew worse as more of the cortex was damaged. However, memory was not affected by *where* in the cortex the tissue was removed. Lashley concluded that the elusive engram did not exist in any localized regions but was widely distributed throughout the entire brain.

Perhaps Lashley could not localize the engram partly because of the variety of types of memory that are called into play even in an apparently simple situation. Maze learning, in fact, involves complex interactions of spatial, visual, and olfactory signals. Neuroscientists now believe that memory for complex sets of information is distributed across many neural systems, even though discrete types of knowledge are separately processed and localized in limited regions of the brain (Markowitsch, 2000; Rolls, 2000).

Four major brain structures are involved in memory:

- The *cerebellum,* essential for procedural memory, memories acquired by repetition, and classically conditioned responses.

- The *striatum,* a complex of structures in the forebrain; the likely basis for habit formation and for stimulus-response connections.

- The *cerebral cortex,* responsible for sensory memories and associations between sensations.

- The *amygdala* and *hippocampus,* largely responsible for declarative memory of facts, dates, and names and also for memories of emotional significance.

Other parts of the brain, such as the thalamus, the basal forebrain, and the prefrontal cortex, are involved also

Engram The physical memory trace for information in the brain.

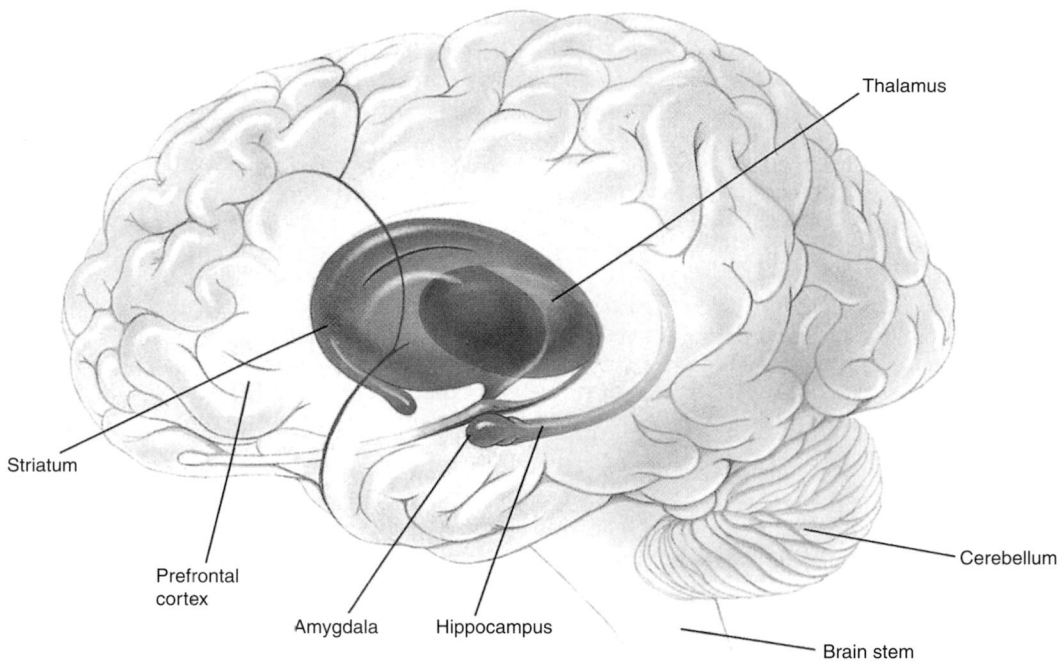

Thalamus

Striatum

Cerebellum

Prefrontal cortex

Amygdala   Hippocampus

Brain stem

FIGURE 8.14

Brain Structures Involved in Memory

This simplified diagram shows some of the main structures of the brain that are involved in the formation, storage, and retrieval of memories.

as way stations for the formation of particular types of memory (see **Figure 8.14**).

In Chapter 3, we focused directly on brain anatomy. Here, let's take a look at the methods that neuroscientists use to draw conclusions about the role of specific brain structures for memory. We will examine two types of research. First, we consider the insights generated by "experiments of nature"—circumstances in which individuals who have suffered brain damage volunteer to further memory research. Second, we describe the ways in which researchers are applying new brain imagining techniques to improve their understanding of memory processes in the brain.

Amnesia

In 1960, Nick A., a young Air Force radar technician, experienced a freak injury that permanently changed his life. Nick had been sitting at his desk while his roommate played with a miniature fencing foil. Then, suddenly,

Nick stood up and turned around—just as his buddy happened to lunge with the sword. The foil pierced Nick's right nostril and continued to cut into the left side of his brain. The accident left Nick seriously disoriented. His worst problem was **amnesia,** the failure of memory over a prolonged period. Because of Nick's amnesia, he forgets many events immediately after they happen. After he reads a few paragraphs of writing, the first sentences slip from his memory. He cannot remember the plot of a television show unless, during commercials, he actively thinks about and rehearses what he was just watching.

Researchers are grateful to patients like Nick for allowing themselves to be studied as "experiments of nature." By relating the locus of brain injuries like Nick's to patterns of performance deficit, researchers have begun to understand the mapping between the types of memory we have introduced you to in this chapter and regions of the brain (Mayes, 2000; Squire et al., 1989). Nick, himself, still remembers how to do things—his procedural knowledge appears to be intact even in the absence of declarative knowledge. So, for example, he remembers how to mix, stir, and bake the ingredients in a recipe, but he forgets what the ingredients are. This selective impairment of explicit memory strongly suggests that different regions of the brain are involved during implicit and explicit retrieval.

Amnesia A failure of memory caused by physical injury, disease, drug use, or psychological trauma.

Let's consider another memory distinction that may be related to different anatomical structures. Researchers have shown that damage to the hippocampus most often impairs explicit, but not implicit, memories (Squire, 1992).

AMNESIA SPARES IMPLICIT MEMORIES
The participants in one series of studies were patients who had suffered hippocampal damage as a consequence of *Korsakoff syndrome,* a product of chronic alcoholism. Both these amnesic patients and a nonamnesic control group were presented with a lists of words and asked to judge how much they liked or disliked each word. To test their memory, participants were provided with word stems, like *uni_____.* In the *cued recall* task, they were told that the stem could be completed with a word that had appeared on the list and that they should try to provide the word. In the *completion task,* they were asked only to provide the first word that came to mind. For the cued recall task, amnesic participants performed considerably less well than the unimpaired control participants. However, their performance on the stem completion task was equivalent to that of the controls (Graf et al., 1984).

This result suggests that the brain damage caused by Korsakoff syndrome affects explicit memory but leaves implicit priming intact. Researchers have demonstrated that such implicit priming can be very long-lived. Both amnesic and unimpaired participants showed implicit memory when naming line drawings on second presentation—even when the initial presentation had been seven days earlier (Cave & Squire, 1992). Implicit memory can be quite impressive even with substantial damage to the hippocampus.

The knowledge that certain forms of brain damage selectively impair explicit but not implicit memory allows researchers to isolate the specific contributions of the two types of memory to encoding and retrieval Consider, for example, the ways in which people form new verbal associations of the type conveyed in a sentence such as "*medicine* cured *hiccup.*" We know, because of the type of research we just described, that individuals with amnesia can acquire knowledge of individual words outside of explicit awareness—but can they also acquire knowledge of associations between words? One answer, from research with an individual known as C. V., whose amnesia stems from damage to the part of his temporal lobe called the medial temporal lobe, is "no" (Rajaram & Coslett, 2000). Although C. V. provided evidence of *perceptual* implicit memory, he provided no evidence

of *conceptual* implicit memory (see page 235). This result suggests that, without explicit memory function, you cannot encode certain types of associations. Studies of this type allow researchers to gain a better understanding of both the brain bases of memory and the organization of memory processes.

Brain Imaging

Psychologists have gained a great deal of knowledge about the relationship between anatomy and memory from the amnesic patients who generously serve as participants in these experiments. However, the advent of brain imaging techniques has enabled researchers to study memory processes in individuals without brain damage (Nyberg & Cabeza, 2000). (You may want to review the section on imaging techniques in Chapter 3.) For example, using positron-emission tomography (PET), Endel Tulving and his colleagues (Nyberg et al., 1996; Tulving et al., 1994) have identified a difference in activation between the two brain hemispheres in the encoding and retrieval of episodic information. Their studies parallel standard memory studies, except that the participants' cerebral blood flow is monitored through PET scans during encoding or retrieval. These researchers discovered disproportionately high brain activity in the left prefrontal cortex (see Figure 8.14) for encoding of episodic information and in the right prefrontal cortex for retrieval of episodic information. Thus, the processes show some anatomical distinctions in addition to the conceptual distinctions made by cognitive psychologists.

Research with functional magnetic resonance imaging (fMRI) has also provided remarkable detail about the way that memory operations are distributed in the brain (Gabrieli et al., 1996, 1997).

THE BRAIN BASIS OF ENCODING OPERATIONS While lying in an MRI device, participants took part in a memory experiment. Words were projected by a magnet-compatible projector onto a screen; participants viewed the images in a mirror mounted above their heads. Each participant was asked to make one of two types of judgments with respect to the words: *semantic* (meaning) *judgments*—"is this word (for example, chair or LOVE) abstract or concrete?"; and *perceptual judgments*—"is this word (for example, TRUST or book) in upper- or lowercase?" The results of the fMRI procedure (see **Figure 8.15**) revealed greater activation in an area of left prefrontal cortex (the nonmotor part of frontal cortex) for semantic than for perceptual encoding (Gabrieli et al., 1996).

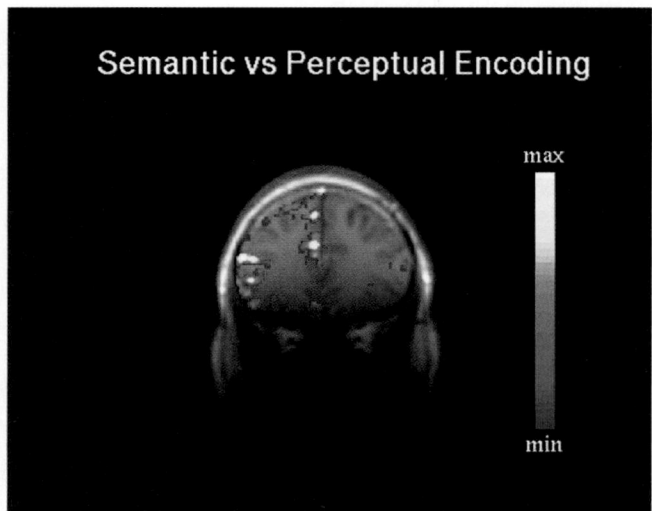

Semantic vs Perceptual Encoding

max

min

FIGURE 8.15

Encoding Operations in the Brain

The figure displays regions of the brain that show extra activity for the semantic task relative to the perceptual task. Note especially the high activity in the left prefrontal cortex—the region of the frontal lobe not involved in motor control—for the semantic task.

The researchers suggest that this region of cortex is particularly activated for semantic encoding because of the link to language functions in the left hemisphere (see Chapter 3).

A recent pair of studies have begun to identify the specific brain regions that are activated when new memories are formed (Brewer et al., 1998; Wagner et al., 1998). In these studies, participants were asked to view scenes or words and make simple judgments (for example, whether the word is abstract or concrete). While they performed these tasks, the participants were undergoing fMRI scans to reveal regions of brain activation. Those fMRI scans uncovered a fascinating pattern: The more strongly that areas in prefrontal cortex and para-hippocampal cortex (a part of cortex close to the hippocampus) were lit up during the scans, the better the participants were later able to recognize the scenes or words. This new research captures the biological basis for the birth of new memories.

The results from imaging studies illustrate why researchers from different disciplines must work closely together in the quest for a full understanding of memory processes. Psychologists provide the data on human performance that become fuel for neurophysiologists' detection of specialized brain structures. At the same time, the realities of physiology constrain psychologists' theories of the mechanisms of encoding, storage, and retrieval. With shared effort, scientists in these fields of research provide great insight into the operation of memory processes.

SUMMING UP

Karl Lashely, who originated the search for the engram, found that memories were widely distributed in the brain. Several brain structures have been implicated for different types of learning and memory processes. Studies with amnesic patients have verified that different brain structures are activated for processes related to implicit and explicit memories. Imaging techniques provide the means to determine the brain bases of memory processes in unimpaired individuals.

RECAPPING MAIN POINTS

What Is Memory?

- Cognitive psychologists study memory as a type of information processing.
- Memories involving conscious effort are explicit. Unconscious memories are implicit.
- Declarative memory is memory for facts; procedural memory is memory for how to perform skills.

- Memory is often viewed as a three-stage process of encoding, storage, and retrieval.

Sensory Memory

- Sensory memory systems have large capacity but very short durations.
- Iconic memory momentarily preserves the visual world.
- Echoic memory holds auditory stimuli.

Short-Term Memory and Working Memory

- Short-term memory (STM) has a limited capacity and lasts only briefly without rehearsal.
- Maintenance rehearsal can extend the presence of material in STM indefinitely.
- STM capacity can be increased by chunking unrelated items into meaningful groups.

- Retrieval from STM is very efficient.
- The broader concept of working memory includes STM.
- The three components of working memory provide the resources for moment-by-moment experiences of the world.

Long-Term Memory: Encoding and Retrieval

- Long-term memory (LTM) constitutes your total knowledge of the world and of yourself. It is nearly unlimited in capacity.
- Your ability to remember information relies on the match between circumstances of encoding and retrieval.
- Similarity in context between learning and retrieval aids retrieval.
- The serial position curve is explained by distinctiveness in context.
- Retrieval cues allow you to access information in LTM.
- Episodic memory is concerned with memory for events that have been personally experienced. Semantic memory is memory for the basic meaning of words and concepts.
- Interference occurs when retrieval cues do not lead uniquely to specific memories.
- Information processed more deeply is typically remembered better.
- For implicit memories, it is important that the processes of encoding and retrieval be similar.
- Memory performance can be improved through elaborative rehearsal and mnemonics.
- In general, feelings-of-knowing accurately predict the availability of information in memory.

Structures in Long-Term Memory

- Concepts are the memory building blocks of thinking. They are formed when memory processes gather together classes of objects or ideas with common properties.
- Prototypes represent the average exemplar of a concept.
- Concepts are often organized in hierarchies, ranging from general, to basic level, to specific.
- Schemas are more complex cognitive clusters.
- All these memory structures are used to provide expectations and a context for interpreting new information.
- Remembering is not simply recording but is a constructive and a selective process.
- Past experiences and goals affect what you remember.
- New information can bias recall, making eyewitness memory unreliable when contaminated by post-event input.

Biological Aspects of Memory

- Different brain structures (including the hippocampus, the amygdala, the cerebellum, and the cerebral cortex) have been shown to be involved in different types of memory.
- Experiments with individuals with amnesia have helped investigators understand how different types of memories are acquired and represented in the brain.
- Brain imaging techniques have extended knowledge about the brain bases of memory encoding and retrieval.

Key Terms

amnesia (p. 248)
basic level (p. 241)
chunking (p. 225)
concepts (p. 240)
contextual distinctiveness (p. 230)
declarative memory (p. 219)
echoic memory (p. 223)
elaborative rehearsal (p. 236)
encoding (p. 220)
encoding specificity (p. 228)
engram (p. 247)
episodic memories (p. 232)
explicit uses of memory (p. 218)
iconic memory (p. 222)
implicit uses of memory (p. 218)
interference (p. 233)
levels-of-processing theory (p. 234)
long-term memory (LTM) (p. 228)
memory (p. 217)
metamemory (p. 237)
mnemonics (p. 236)
primacy effect (p. 230)
priming (p. 235)
procedural memory (p. 219)
prototype (p. 240)
recall (p. 231)
recency effect (p. 230)
recognition (p. 231)
reconstructive memory (p. 244)
retrieval (p. 220)
retrieval cues (p. 232)
schemas (p. 242)
semantic memories (p. 232)
sensory memory (p. 222)
serial position effect (p. 229)
short-term memory (STM) (p. 223)
storage (p. 220)
transfer-appropriate processing (p. 234)
working memory (p. 225)

cognitive processes

9

■ STUDYING COGNITION
Discovering the Processes
of Mind • Mental Processes
and Mental Resources

■ LANGUAGE USE
Language Production •
Language Understanding •
Language, Thought,
and Culture

■ PSYCHOLOGY IN
YOUR LIFE: CAN
NONHUMAN ANIMALS
LEARN LANGUAGE?

■ VISUAL COGNITION
Using Visual Representations
• Combining Verbal and
Visual Representations

■ PROBLEM SOLVING
AND REASONING
Problem Solving • Deductive
Reasoning • Inductive
Reasoning

■ PSYCHOLOGY IN THE
21ST CENTURY: EXPERT
SYSTEMS AND MEDICINE

■ JUDGING AND DECIDING
Heuristics and Judgment •
The Psychology of Decision
Making

■ RECAPPING MAIN POINTS
Key Terms

When I had played with [my new doll] a little while, Miss Sullivan [Helen Keller's teacher] spelled into my hand the word "d-o-l-l." I was at once interested in this finger play and tried to imitate it.... I did not know that I was spelling a word or even that words existed; I was simply making my fingers go in monkey-like imitation.

One day, while I was playing with my new doll, Miss Sullivan put my big rag doll into my lap also, spelled, "d-o-l-l" and tried to make me understand that "d-o-l-l" applied to both. Earlier in the day we had had a tussle over the words "m-u-g" and "w-a-t-e-r." Miss Sullivan had tried to impress upon me that "m-u-g" is mug and that "w-a-t-e-r" is water, but I persisted in confounding the two.....

We walked down the path to the well-house, attracted by the fragrance of the honeysuckle with which it was cov-ered. Someone was drawing water and my teacher placed my hand under the spout. As the cool stream gushed over one hand she spelled into the other the word water, first slowly, then rapidly. I stood still, my whole attention fixed upon the motions of her fingers. Suddenly I felt a misty consciousness as of something forgotten—a thrill of returning thought; and somehow the mystery of language was revealed to me. I knew then that "w-a-t-e-r" meant the wonderful cool something that was flowing over my hand. That living word awakened my soul, gave it light, hope, joy, set it free! There were barriers still, it is true, but barriers that could in time be swept away.

I left the well-house eager to learn. Everything had a name, and each name gave birth to a new thought. As we returned to the house every object which I touched seemed to quiver with life (Keller, 1902/1990, pp. 15–16).

In this excerpt from her autobiography, *The Story of My Life,* Helen Keller reports on her remarkable reawakening of language and thought. As a one-year-old, Keller suffered a mysterious illness that robbed her of her sight and hearing. Three months before her seventh birthday, Anne Sullivan entered her life as a teacher. As you have just read, Sullivan broke through Keller's darkness and allowed her to experience, as Keller put it, "a thrill of returning thought."

You have probably never had cause to express such a dramatic appreciation of your **cognitive processes.** However, the capacity to use language and to think in abstract ways has often been cited as the essence of the human experience. You tend to take cognition for granted because it's an activity you do continually most of your waking hours. Even so, when a carefully crafted speech wins your vote or when you read a detective story in which the sleuth combines a few scraps of apparently trivial clues into a brilliant solution to a crime, you are forced to acknowledge the intellectual triumph of cognitive processes.

Cognition is a general term for all forms of knowing: As shown in **Figure 9.1,** the study of cognition is the study of your mental life. (Note that Chapter 5 already discussed some of the topics shown in Figure 9.1.) Cog-nition includes both contents and processes. The *contents* of cognition are *what* you know—concepts, facts, propositions, rules, and memories: "A dog is a mammal." "A red light means stop." "I first left home at age 18." Cognitive *processes* are *how* you manipulate these mental contents—in ways that enable you to interpret the world around you and to find creative solutions to your life's dilemmas.

Within psychology, the study of cognition is carried out by researchers in the field of **cognitive psychology.** Over the last three decades, the field of cognitive psychology has been supplemented by the interdisciplinary field of **cognitive science** (see **Figure 9.2**). Cognitive science

Cognitive processes Higher mental processes, such as perception, memory, language, problem solving, and abstract thinking.

Cognition Processes of knowing, including attending, remembering, and reasoning; also the content of the processes, such as concepts and memories.

Cognitive psychology The study of higher mental processes such as attention, language use, memory, perception, problem solving, and thinking.

Cognitive science The interdisciplinary field of study of the approach systems and processes that manipulate information.

The Domain of Cognitive Psychology

Cognitive psychologists study higher mental functions with particular emphasis on the ways in which people acquire knowledge and use it to shape and understand their experiences in the world.

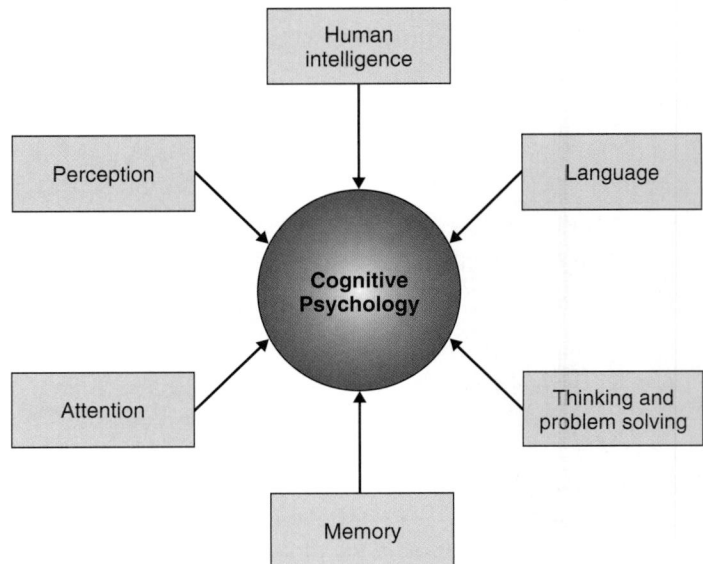

focuses the collected knowledge of several academic specialties on the same theoretical issues. It benefits the practitioners of each of these fields to share their data and insights. You saw this cognitive science philosophy at work in Chapter 8, when we described how studies of the biology of memory can be used to constrain—limit and refine—theories of memory processes. Many of the theories we will describe in this chapter have similarly been shaped through the interactions of researchers from a number of disciplinary perspectives.

We will begin our study of cognition with a brief description of the ways in which researchers try to measure the inner, private processes involved in cognitive functioning. Then we will examine, at some length, topics in cognitive psychology that generate much basic research and practical application: language use, visual cognition, problem solving, reasoning, and judging and decision making.

■ Studying Cognition

How can you study cognition? The challenge, of course, is that it goes on inside the head. You can see the input—for example, a note that says, "Call me"— and experience the output—you make a phone call—but how can you determine the series of mental steps that connected the note to your response? How, that is, can you reveal what happened in the middle—the cognitive processes and the mental representations on which your action relies? In this section, we describe the types of logical analyses that have made possible the scientific study of cognitive psychology.

Discovering the Processes of Mind

One of the fundamental methodologies for studying mental processes was devised, in 1868, by the Dutch physiologist **F. C. Donders.** To study the "speed of mental processes," Donders invented a series of experimental tasks that he believed were differentiated by the mental

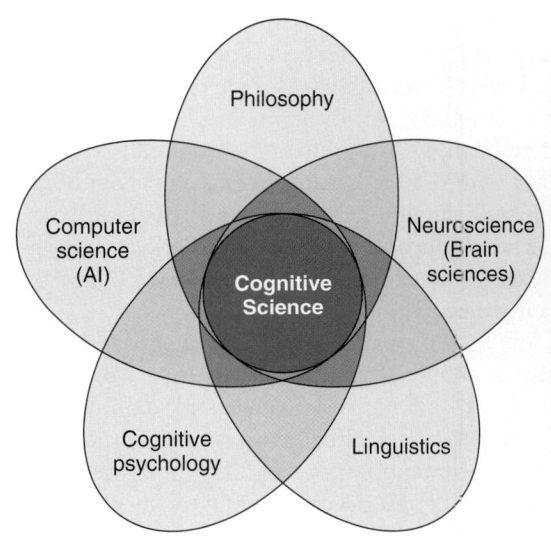

FIGURE 9.2

The Domain of Cognitive Science

The domain of cognitive science occupies the intersection of philosophy, neuroscience, linguistics, cognitive psychology, and computer science (artificial intelligence).

Donders's Analysis of Mental Processes

Note how long (in seconds) it takes you to complete each of these three tasks. Try to complete each task accurately, but as quickly as possible.

Task 1: Draw a C on top of all the capitalized letters:

TO Be, oR noT To BE: tHAT Is thE qUestioN:

WhETher 'Tis noBlEr In tHE MINd tO SuFfER

tHE SLings AnD ARroWS Of OUtrAgeOUs forTUNe,

or To TAke ARmS agaINST a sEa Of tROUBleS,

AnD by oPPOsinG END theM.   TIME: _____

Task 2: Draw a V on top of the capitalized vowels and a C on top of the capitalized consonants:

TO Be, oR noT To BE: tHAT Is thE qUestioN:

WhETher 'Tis noBlEr In tHE MINd tO SuFfER

tHE SLings AnD ARroWS Of OUtrAgeOUs forTUNe,

or To TAke ARmS agaINST a sEa Of tROUBleS,

AnD by oPPOsinG END theM.   TIME: _____

Task 3: Draw a V on top of all the capitalized letters:

TO Be, oR noT To BE: tHAT Is thE qUestioN:

WhETher 'Tis noBlEr In tHE MINd tO SuFfER

tHE SLings AnD ARroWS Of OUtrAgeOUs forTUNe,

or To TAke ARmS agaINST a sEa Of tROUBleS,

AnD by oPPOsinG END theM.   TIME: _____

steps involved for successful performance (Lachman et al., 1979) **Table 9.1** provides a paper-and-pencil experiment that follows Donders's logic. Before reading on, please take a moment to complete each task.

How long did you take to do task 1? Suppose you wanted to give a list of the steps you carried out to perform the task. It might look something like this:

a. Determine whether a character is a capital letter or a small letter.

b. If it is a capital letter, draw a C on top.

How long did you take for task 2? When we have used this exercise, students have often taken an additional half minute or more. You can understand why, once we spell out the necessary steps:

a. Determine whether a character is a capital letter or a small letter.

b. Determine whether each capital letter is a vowel or a consonant.

c. If it is a consonant, draw a C on top. If it is a vowel, draw a V.

Thus, going from task 1 to task 2, we add two mental steps, which we can call *stimulus categorization* (vowel or consonant?) and *response selection* (draw a C or draw a V?). Task 1 requires one stimulus categorization step. Task 2 requires two such categorizations. Task 2 also requires selecting between two responses. Because task 2 requires you to do everything you did for task 1 and more, it takes you more time. That was Donders's fundamental insight: Extra mental steps will often result in more time to perform a task.

(You may be wondering why we included task 3. This is a necessary procedural control for the experiment. We have to ensure that the time difference between tasks 1 and 2 does not stem from the fact that it takes much longer to draw V's than to draw C's. Task 3 should still be much swifter than task 2. Was it?)

Donders originally hoped to use his procedure to obtain precise estimates of the duration of different mental processes. With his subtraction method, you could subtract the time needed to carry out task 1 from the time needed for task 2 and determine how long it takes to perform stimulus categorization and response selection. If you could also develop a task that required stimulus categorization but not response selection (as Donders did), then you could assign numbers—an amount of time—to each individual process. Thus, stimulus categorization might take 100 milliseconds (one-thousandths of a second; abbreviated msec) and response selection 150 msec.

Cognitive psychologists no longer use the subtraction method, because the absolute time for different processes depends so much on the details of each task. Investigators do, however, follow Donders's basic logic. Researchers frequently use *reaction time*—the amount of time it takes experimental participants to perform particular tasks—as a way of testing specific accounts of how some cognitive process is carried out. Donders's basic premise that extra mental steps will result in extra time is still fundamental to a great deal of cognitive psychological research. Let's see how this successful idea has been developed over the past 130 years.

Mental Processes and Mental Resources

When cognitive psychologists break down high-level activities, like language use or problem solving, into their component processes, they often act as if they are playing a game with blocks. Each block represents a different component that must be carried out. The goal is to determine the shape and size of each block and to see how the blocks fit together to form the whole activity. For the Donders tasks, you saw that the blocks can be laid out in a row (see **Figure 9.3,** part A). Each step comes directly after another. The block metaphor allows you to

FIGURE 9.3

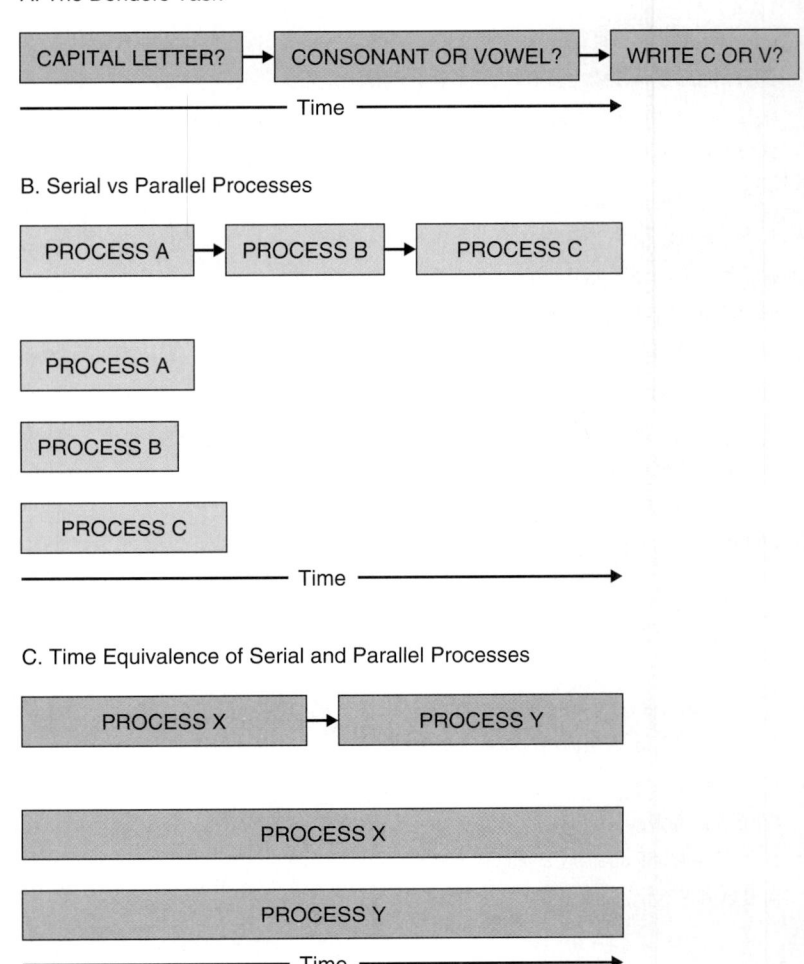

A. The Donders Task

CAPITAL LETTER? → CONSONANT OR VOWEL? → WRITE C OR V?

Time →

B. Serial vs Parallel Processes

PROCESS A → PROCESS B → PROCESS C

PROCESS A
PROCESS B
PROCESS C

Time →

C. Time Equivalence of Serial and Parallel Processes

PROCESS X → PROCESS Y

PROCESS X
PROCESS Y

Time →

Breaking Down High-Level Cognitive Activities

Cognitive psychologists attempt to determine the identity and organization of the mental processes that are the building blocks of high-level cognitive activities.

(A) Our version of the Donders task requires that at least three processes be carried out one after the other.

(B) Some processes are carried out serially, in sequence; others are carried out in parallel, all at the same time.

(C) The time taken to perform a task does not always allow researchers to conclude whether serial or parallel processes were used.

see that we could also stack the blocks so that more than one process occurs simultaneously (part B). These two pictures illustrate a distinction we introduced briefly in Chapter 5, between **serial** and **parallel processes.** You saw there that some kinds of visual searches can be carried out in parallel—all the elements in an array can be examined at the same time—while other kinds of searches require serial processing—each element must be examined separately, one after another.

Cognitive psychologists often use reaction times to determine whether processes are carried out in parallel or serially. However, the examples in part C of Figure 9.3 should convince you that this is a tricky business. Imagine that we have a task that we believe can be decomposed into two processes, *X* and *Y*. If the only information we have is the total time needed to complete

the process, we can never be sure if processes *X* and *Y* happen side by side or one after the other. Much of the challenge of research in cognitive psychology is to invent task circumstances that allow the experimenter to determine which of many possible configurations of blocks is correct. In task 2 of the exercise you just did, we could be reasonably certain that the processes were serial, because some activities logically required others. For example, you couldn't execute your response (prepare to draw a C or a V) until you had determined what the response might be.

In many cases, theorists try to determine if processes are serial or parallel by assessing the extent to which the processes place demands on *mental resources.* Suppose, for example, you are walking to class with a friend. Ordinarily, it should be easy for you to walk a straight path at the same time you carry on a conversation—your navigation processes and your language processes can go on in parallel. But what would happen if you suddenly get to a patch of sidewalk that's dotted with puddles? As you pick your way among the puddles, you may have to stop talking. Now your navigation processes require extra re-

Serial processes Two or more mental processes that are carried out in order, one after the other.

Parallel processes Two or more mental processes that are carried out simultaneously.

Why is it difficult to carry on a conversation while you are trying to avoid puddles?

TABLE 9.2

Number Processing

Your task is to put a check mark on top of the pairs of numbers that are *physically different,* in either numbers or words (that is, you would check both *4–6* and *four–six*). Try to judge which list is harder.

List A

8–8	nine–eight	1–2	eight–eight
2–1	8–9	9–9	2–2
two–two	one–two	nine–nine	eight–nine
one–one	1–1	two–one	9–8

List B

1–1	nine–two	one–one	nine–nine
2–9	eight–two	9–9	1–9
eight–one	8–8	eight–eight	nine–one
2–2	1–8	2–8	two–two

sources for planning, and your language processes are momentarily squeezed out.

A key assumption in this example is that you have *limited* processing resources that must be spread over different mental tasks (Kahneman, 1973; Navon & Gopher, 1979). Your *attentional processes* are responsible for distributing these resources. In Chapter 5, we discussed attention as the set of processes that allow you to select, for particular scrutiny, some small subset of available perceptual information. Our use of *attention* here preserves the idea of selectivity. The decision now, however, concerns which mental processes will be selected as the recipients of processing resources.

We have one more complication to add: Not all processes put the same demands on resources. We can, in fact, define a dimension that goes from processes that are *controlled* to those that are *automatic* (Shiffrin & Schneider, 1977). **Controlled processes** require attention; **automatic processes** generally do not. It is often difficult to carry out more than one controlled process at a time, because they require more resources; automatic processes can often be performed alongside other tasks without interference.

We want to give you an example of an automatic process. To get started, take a moment to carry out the task in **Table 9.2.** Did you find List A somewhat harder than List B?

Controlled processes Processes that require attention; it is often difficult to carry out more than one controlled process at a time.

Automatic processes Processes that do not require attention; they can often be performed along with other tasks without interference.

YOU CAN'T IGNORE THE "MEANING" OF NUMBERS Experimental participants were asked to make the types of judgments illustrated in Table 9.2. The pattern of results suggested that people find it harder to respond *different* when the numbers are close together (for example, 1–2) than when they are far apart (for example, eight–one) irrespective of whether the numbers are rendered as Arabic numerals or written out. Note that List A had "close" different pairs and List B had "far" different pairs, so you should have found it somewhat harder to complete List A. But why should the closeness of the numbers matter for a judgment of *physical* similarity? *One–two* and *one–nine* are about equal on the dimension of *physical* dissimilarity. The researchers suggested that when you look at *2* or *two,* you can't help but think of the quantity it represents—even when the quantity, in this case, impairs performance on the task you've been asked to carry out. That is, you *automatically* access the meaning of a number, even when you don't need (or want) to do so (Dehaene & Akhavein, 1995).

You probably remember, as a small child, having to learn how numbers work. Now the association between numbers and the quantities they represent have become so automatic, you can't shut off the association. This number task illustrates that automatic processes rely heavily on the efficient use of memory (Logan, 1988, 1992). Whether the object in the environment is *2* or *two,* your memory processes swiftly provide information about quantity.

Let's apply this knowledge of controlled and automatic processes back to the situation of walking and talking. When you are walking a straight route, you feel little interference between the two activities, suggesting that maintaining your path and planning your utterances are each relatively automatic activities. The situation changes, however, when the puddles force you to choose between a greater number of options for your path. Now you must select where to go and what to say. Because you can't make both choices simultaneously, you have hit an attentional *bottleneck* (Pashler, 1992, 1994). This example shows why controlled and automatic processes are defined along a dimension, rather than constituting strict categories. When circumstances become challenging, what before seemed automatic now requires controlled attention. Thus, processes may require more or less attention, depending on the context.

You now know a lot about the logic of mental processes. To explain how complex mental tasks are carried out, theorists propose models that combine serial and parallel, and controlled and automatic processes. The goal of much cognitive psychological research is to invent experiments that confirm each of the components of such models. Now that you understand some of the logic behind cognitive psychological research into mental processes, it is time to move to more specific domains in which you put cognitive processes to work. We begin with language use.

SUMMING UP

Cognitive psychologists and cognitive scientists study the mental processes and structures that allow you, for example, to use language, solve problems, and make decisions. Donders pioneered the method of analyzing cognitive tasks into separate component processes. Contemporary researchers examine combinations of serial and parallel processes, as well as processes on a dimension between automatic and controlled, to specify the components of mental activities.

Language Use

It is midnight. There's a knock on your door. When you answer, no one is there, but you see an envelope on the floor. Inside the envelope is a single sheet of paper with a handwritten message: "The cat is on the mat." What do you make of this? What could we do to change the situation so that this message immediately made sense to you? The easiest step we could take would be to introduce appropriate background knowledge. Suppose you are a secret agent who always gets instructions in this curious fashion. You might know that "the cat" is your contact and that "on the mat" means in the wrestling arena. Off you go.

But you don't have to be a spy for "The cat is on the mat" to take on a variety of meanings:

- Suppose your cat waits on a mat by the door when she wants to be let out. When you say to your roommate, "The cat is on the mat," you use those words to communicate, "Could you get up and let the cat out?"

- Suppose your friend is worried about pulling the car out of the driveway because she's uncertain where the cat is. When you say, "The cat is on the mat," you use those words to communicate, "It's safe to pull out of the driveway."

- Suppose you are trying to have a race between your cat and your friend's dog. When you say, "The cat is on the mat," you use those words to communicate, "My cat won't race!"

These examples illustrate the difference between *sentence meaning*—the generally simple meaning of the combined words of a sentence—and *speaker's meaning*—the unlimited number of meanings a speaker can communicate by putting a sentence to good use (Grice, 1968). When psychologists study language use, they want to comprehend both the *production* and the *understanding* of speaker's meaning:

- How do speakers produce the right words to communicate the meaning they intend?

- How do listeners recover the messages the speakers wished to communicate?

We will examine each of these questions in turn.

Language Production

Look at **Figure 9.4.** Try to formulate a few sentences about this picture. What did you think to say? Suppose now we asked you to redescribe the scene for someone who was blind. How would your description change? Does this second description seem to require more mental effort? The study of **language production** concerns both what people say—what they choose to say at a given time—and the processes they go through to produce the message. Note that language users need not produce language out loud. Language production also includes both signing and writing. For convenience, however, we will call language producers *speakers* and language understanders *listeners*.

AUDIENCE DESIGN

We asked you to imagine the different descriptions you'd give of Figure 9.4 to a sighted and a blind person as a way of getting you to think about **audience design** in language production. Each time you produce an utterance, you must have in mind the audience to whom the utterance will be directed, and what knowledge you share with members of that audience (Clark, 1992, 1996). For example, it won't do you the least bit of good to say, "The cat

Among ichthyologists, this is a *Choerodon fasciatus*. What would you call it if you were talking or writing about it to a friend?

Language Production

How would you describe this scene to a friend? How might your description change if your friend were blind?

is on the mat" if your listener does not know that the cat sits on the mat only when she wishes to be let out. An overarching rule of audience design, the *cooperative principle,* was first proposed by the philosopher **H. Paul Grice** (1975). Grice phrased the cooperative principle as an instruction to speakers that they should produce utterances appropriate to the setting and meaning of the ongoing conversation. To expand on this instruction, Grice defined four maxims that cooperative speakers live by. In **Table 9.3,** we present each of those maxims, as well as an invented conversation that illustrates the effect the maxims have on moment-by-moment choices in language production.

As you can see from Table 9.3, being a cooperative speaker depends, in large part, on having accurate expectations about what your listener is likely to know and understand. Thus, you certainly wouldn't tell a friend, "I'm having lunch with Alex" if you didn't have good reason

to believe that your friend knew who Alex was. You also must assure yourself that, of all the Alexes your friend might know and that she knows that you know, only one would come to mind as the specific Alex you would mention in these circumstances. More formally, we can say that there must be some Alex who is prominent in the *common ground*—common knowledge—you share with your friend. **Herbert Clark** and Catherine Marshall (1981) suggested that judgments of common ground are based on three sources of evidence:

- *Community membership.* Language producers often make strong assumptions about what is likely to be mutually known based on shared membership in communities of various sizes.

- *Linguistic copresence.* Language producers often assume that information contained in earlier parts of a conversation (or in past conversations) is part of the common ground.

- *Physical copresence.* Physical copresence exists when a speaker and a listener are directly in the physical presence of objects or situations. This includes both the setting of the conversation and all the people around the conversationalists.

Thus, your use of Alex in "I'm having lunch with Alex" might succeed because your friend and you are part of a small community (for example, roommates) that includes only one Alex (community membership). Or it might succeed because you've introduced the existence of Alex earlier in the conversation (linguistic copresence). Or Alex might be standing right there in the room (physical copresence).

Let's focus a bit more on community membership. Suppose you are meeting a date for the first time. If you want to be a cooperative conversationalist, one of the

Language production What people say, sign, and write, as well as the processes they go through to produce these messages.

Audience design The process of shaping a message depending on the audience for which it is intended.

Grice's Maxims in Language Production

1. *Quantity:* Make your contribution as informative as is required (for the current purposes of the exchange). Do not make your contribution more informative than is required.

   The consequence for the speaker: You must try to judge how much information your audience really needs. Often this judgment will require you to assess what your listener is likely to know already.

2. *Quality:* Try to make your contribution one that is true. Do not say what you believe to be false. Do not say that for which you lack adequate evidence.

   The consequence for the speaker: When you speak, listeners will assume that you can back up your assertions with appropriate evidence. As you plan each utterance, you must have in mind the evidence on which it is based.

3. *Relation:* Be relevant.

   The consequence for the speaker: You must make sure that your listeners will see how what you are saying is relevant to what has come before. If you wish to shift the topic of conversation—so that your utterance is not directly relevant—you must make that clear.

4. *Manner:* Be perspicacious. Avoid obscurity of expression. Avoid ambiguity. Be brief. Be orderly.

   The consequence for the speaker: It is your responsibility to speak in as clear a manner as possible. Although you will inevitably make errors, as a cooperative speaker you must ensure that your listeners can understand your message.

In this conversation, can you see how Chris follows (or violates) Grice's maxims?

What Is Said	What Chris Might Be Thinking
Pat: *Have you ever been to New York City?* Chris: *I was there once in 1992.*	I don't know why Pat is asking me this question, so I probably should say a little more than just "yes."
Pat: *I'm supposed to visit, but I'm worried about being mugged.* Chris: *I think a lot of areas are safe.*	I can't say that he shouldn't worry, because he won't believe me. What can I say that will sound true but make him feel okay?
Pat: *How was your hotel?* Chris: *We didn't stay overnight.*	If I say, "We didn't stay in a hotel," that might suggest we stayed somewhere else. I need to say something relevant that will make clear why I can't answer the question.
Pat: *Would you like to go to New York with me?* Chris: *I'd have to find a way to see if it would be possible for me to leave without it being too impossible.*	I don't want to go, but I don't want to seem rude. Will Pat notice that I'm being evasive in my response?
Pat: *Huh?* Chris: *Well . . .*	Trapped.

first things you must do is to determine the communities to which that individual belongs.

HOW WE KNOW

COMMUNITY MEMBERSHIP AFFECTS LANGUAGE PRODUCTION Researchers created circumstances in which unacquainted students were asked to perform a matching task. The *director* had 16 New York postcards in front of her, laid out in a 4-by-4 array. She had to describe the sights pictured in the postcards so that the *matcher* could recreate the correct 4-by-4 ordering of the pictures. Although the director and the matcher couldn't see each other, they could converse freely. As a consequence, the directors were quickly able to determine whether their matchers were "experts" or "novices" about New York. When they discovered that they were talking to a fellow New Yorker, they were much more likely to use a proper name to pinpoint a postcard—"It's the Citicorp building"—than to give a roundabout description—"It's the tall building with a triangular top" (Isaacs & Clark, 1987).

Thus, speakers adjusted their utterances based on their expectations about what the listener would be able to understand. On the whole, people are pretty accurate at guessing what members of their own communities are likely to know—although they tend to err in the direction of believing other people know the same things they do (Fussell & Krauss, 1992). The accurate guesses make possible appropriate adjustments in language production.

Next time a stranger stops you on the street to ask for directions, pay attention to what you do to figure out how much common ground you share. Do you ask specific questions (for example, "Do you know where the town hall is?")? Do you try to make your best guess from what the stranger is wearing (for example, a campus sweatshirt) or how he or she talks (for example, with a Southern accent in a Midwestern town)?

Our discussion so far has focused on language production at the level of the message: How you shape what you wish to say will depend on the audience to whom you are speaking. Let's turn now to a discussion of the mental processes that allow you to produce these messages.

SPEECH EXECUTION AND SPEECH ERRORS

Would you like to be famous for tripping over your tongue? Consider the Reverend W. A. Spooner of Oxford University, who lent his name to the term *spoonerism:* an exchange of the initial sounds of two or more words in a phrase or sentence. Reverend Spooner came by this honor honestly. When, for example, he was tongue-lashing a lazy student for wasting the term, Reverend Spooner said, "You have tasted the whole worm!" A spoonerism is one of the limited types of speech errors that language producers make. These errors give researchers insight into the planning that goes on as speakers produce utterances. As you can see in **Table 9.4**, you need to plan an utterance at a number of different levels and speech errors give evidence for each of those levels (Bock & Levelt, 1994; Rapp & Goldrick, 2000). What should impress you about all these examples of errors is that they are not just random—they make sense given the structure of spoken English. Thus, a speaker might exchange initial consonants—"tips of the slung" for "slips of the tongue"—but would never say, "tlips of the sung," which would violate the rule of English that "tl" does not occur as an initial sound (Fromkin, 1980).

Given the importance of speech errors to developing theoretical models of speech production, researchers have not always been content just to wait around for errors to happen naturally. Instead, researchers have explored a number of ways to produce artificial errors in controlled experimental settings (Bock, 1996). Those techniques have yielded insights into both the processes and representations that underlie fluent speech production:

- *Processes.* Recall, from Chapter 6, the SLIP (for "spoonerisms of laboratory-induced predisposition") technique that encourages participants to produce spoonerisms (Baars, 1992). In this procedure, participants are asked to read silently lists of word pairs that provide models for the phonetic structure of a target spoonerism: *ball doze, bash door, bean deck, bell dark.* They then are required to pronounce out loud a word pair like *darn bore,* but under the influence of the earlier pairs it will sometimes come out *barn door.*

With this technique, researchers can study the factors that affect the likelihood that speakers will produce errors. For example, a spoonerism is more likely when the error will still result in real words (Baars et al., 1975; Stemberger, 1992). Thus an error on *darn bore* (to produce *barn door*) is more likely than an error on *dart board* (to produce *bart doard*). Findings like this one suggest that while you are producing utterances, some of your cognitive processes are devoted to detecting and editing potential errors. Those processes are reluctant to let you pronounce sounds like *doard,* which are not real English words.

- *Representations.* Another procedure required participants to read pairs of idioms (like *shoot the breeze* and *raise the roof*). After a two-second interval, they were asked to produce one of the idioms from memory, as swiftly as possible. Under this time pressure, participants sometimes produced *blends* of the two idioms, such as *kick the maker* (from *kick the bucket* and *meet your maker*). These blend errors were most likely when the two idioms shared the same underlying meaning (as with *kick the bucket* and *meet your maker*) rather than when they differed in meaning (as with *shoot*

TABLE **9.4**

Errors in Planning Speech Production

Types of planning:

- Speakers must choose the content words that best fit their ideas.

  If the speaker has two words in mind, such as *grizzly* and *ghastly,* a blend like *grastly* might result.

- Speakers must put the chosen words in the right places in the utterance.

  Because speakers plan whole units of their utterances while they produce them, content words will sometimes become misplaced.

  a tank of gas → a gas of tank

  wine is being served at dinner → dinner is being served at wine

- Speakers must fill in the sounds that make up the words they wish to utter.

  Once again, because speakers plan ahead, sounds will sometimes get misplaced.

  left hemisphere → heft lemisphere

  pass out → pat ous

the breeze and *raise the roof*). This result suggests that representations of idioms with similar meanings are linked in memory: As you begin to produce one idiom, a representational link to another with similar meaning may lead to a blend error (Cutting & Bock, 1997). That's the way the cookie bounces!

We have now looked at some of the forces that lead speakers to produce particular utterances and at some of the processes that allow them to do so. We turn next to the listeners, who are responsible for understanding what speakers intend to communicate.

Language Understanding

Suppose a speaker has produced the utterance "The cat is on the mat." You already know that, depending on the context, this utterance can be used to communicate any number of different meanings. How, as a listener, do you settle on just one meaning? We will begin this discussion of language understanding by considering more fully the problem of the ambiguity of meaning.

RESOLVING AMBIGUITY

What does the word *bank* mean? You can probably think of at least two meanings, one having to do with rivers and the other having to do with money. Suppose you hear the utterance "He came from the bank." How do you know which meaning is intended? You need to be able to resolve the *lexical ambiguity* between the two meanings. (*Lexical* is related to *lexicon*, a synonym for *dictionary*.) If you think about this problem, you'll realize that you have some cognitive processes that allow you to use sur-

rounding context to eliminate the ambiguity—to *disambiguate*—the word. Have you been talking about rivers or about money? That broader context should enable you to choose between the two meanings. But how?

Before we answer that question, we'd like to introduce another type of ambiguity. What does this sentence mean: "The mother of the boy and the girl will arrive soon?" You may detect only one meaning right off, but there is a *structural ambiguity* here (Akmajian et al., 1990). Take a look at **Figure 9.5.** Linguists often represent the structure of sentences with tree diagrams to show how the various words are gathered together into grammatical units. In part A, we've shown you an analysis of "The cat is on the mat." The structure is pretty simple: a noun phrase made up of an article and a noun, plus a verb phrase made up of a verb and a prepositional phrase. In the other two parts, you see the more complex structures for the two different meanings of "The mother…" In part B, the analysis shows that the whole phrase "of the boy and the girl" applies to the mother. One person—the mother of two children—will arrive soon. In part C, the analysis shows that there are two noun phrases, "the mother of the boy" and "the girl." There are two people, both of whom will arrive soon. Which understanding of the sentence did you come to when you first read it? Now that you can see that two meanings are possible, we arrive at the same question we did for lexical ambiguity: How does prior context enable you to settle on one meaning when more than one is possible?

Let's return to lexical ambiguity (an ambiguity of word meaning). Consider this sentence:

Nancy watched the ball.

FIGURE 9.5

Sentence Structures

Linguists use tree diagrams to display the grammatical structure of sentences. Part A shows the structure of "The cat is on the mat." Parts B and C show that the sentence "The mother of the boy and girl will arrive soon" can be represented by two different structural analyses. Who will arrive soon, one person (structure B) or two (structure C)?

Art = article
Aux = auxiliary
NP = noun phrase
PP = prepositional phrase
S = sentence
VP = verb phrase

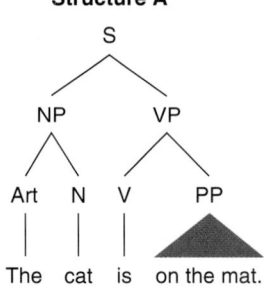

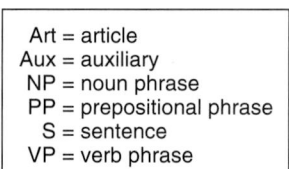

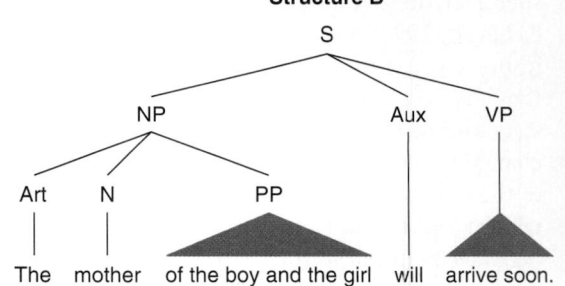

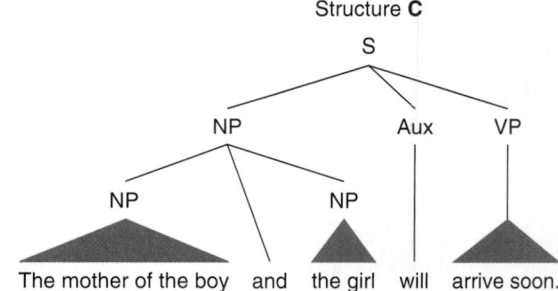

Now that you are looking at a picture of a dancing couple, what comes to mind when you think of the word *ball?*

When you read this sentence, how do you interpret the word *ball?* If you imagine that you have a dictionary in your head, your entry for *ball* might look something like this:

Definition 1. A round object used in a game or sport

Definition 2. A large formal event for dancing

The sentence "Nancy watched the ball" contains no information that allows you to choose between these two definitions. In fact, research suggests that both definitions become accessible in memory after you read this type of sentence (Vu et al., 1998). You need help from surrounding context to determine which ball is which. But how does context help you decide among meanings? Research suggests that context provides a variety of types of evidence (Vu et al., 1998, 2000). Consider these examples:

1. She catered the ball.

2. The juggler watched the ball.

3. The debutante sat by the door. She watched the ball.

In example 1, the verb *catered* helps specify which definition of *ball* is appropriate; in example 2, the noun *juggler* does the work. In example 3, the first sentence evokes a scenario that creates a storylike context for the second sentence, "She watched the ball." These examples suggest that you put various types of evidence to swift and efficient use each time you encounter an ambiguous word: Context immediately affects listeners' consideration of the meanings of ambiguous words (Binder & Morris, 1995; Sereno, 1995). Context wields a similar influence on structural ambiguities (MacDonald, 1993; Shapiro et al., 1993; Trueswell, 1996). Contextual information speeds decisions when you must choose among different possible grammatical structures.

Let us now return to the example with which we began, the considerably ambiguous "The cat is on the mat." In that case, the ambiguity is not in the words or the structure but in the very message itself. Surprisingly, researchers find that the rule of reordering by context applies at this level as well (Gibbs, 1994).

HOW WE KNOW

CONTEXT EASES COMPREHENSION OF NONLITERAL MEANINGS Consider the utterance "Sure is nice and warm in here." What does that mean? As shown in **Table 9.5**, it is possible to write pairs of stories that give very different meanings to simple utterances of this sort. As you can see, the literal version sticks closely to the literal meanings of the words. The nonliteral version uses the same utterance to make a sarcastic request. Let's apply the models we introduced for lexical ambiguity. If readers process along the lines of the constant order model, you might expect that they would always try the literal meaning of an utterance first. Only if the literal meaning failed to fit in the context would readers consider another meaning (Grice, 1975, 1978; Searle, 1979a). If that were true, we would expect that it would take readers more time to understand an utterance that is a request—and a sarcastic one, at that—as compared with just a literal statement. By contrast, suppose the reordering-by-context model is true for whole utterances in the way that it's true for words and structures. Then you'd expect it to be easier to understand the sarcastic request than the literal statement. Indeed, research shows that readers understand the sarcastic requests even more quickly than they understand the literal uses of the same utterances (Gibbs, 1986).

TABLE 9.5

Literal and Sarcastic Interpretations of Ambiguous Utterances

Literal Statement

Martha went over to her sister's house. It was freezing outside and Martha was glad to be inside. She said to her sister, "Your house is very cozy. Sure is nice and warm in here."

Sarcastic Request

Tony's roommate always kept the window open in the living room. He did this even if it was freezing out. Tony kept mentioning this to his roommate, but to no avail. Once it was open and Tony wanted his roommate to shut it. Tony couldn't believe that his roommate wasn't cold. He said to him, "Sure is nice and warm in here."

The overall conclusion you can draw is that your language processes use context powerfully and efficiently to resolve ambiguities. In a way, this shows that there is a good match between production and understanding. When we discussed language production, we emphasized audience design—the processes by which speakers try to make their utterances appropriate in the current context. Our analysis of understanding suggests that listeners expect speakers to have done their jobs well. Under those circumstances, it makes sense for listeners to let context reorder their expectations about what speakers will have meant.

THE PRODUCTS OF UNDERSTANDING

Our discussion of ambiguity resolution focused on the *processes* of understanding. In this section, we shift our attention to the *products* of understanding. The question now is: What *representations* result in memory when listeners understand utterances or texts? What, for example, would be stored in memory when you hear our old standby "The cat is on the mat"? Research has suggested that meaning representation begins with basic units called *propositions* (Clark & Clark, 1977; Kintsch, 1974). Propositions are the main ideas of utterances. For "The cat is on the mat," the main idea is that something is on something else. When you read the utterance, you will extract the proposition *on* and understand the relationship that it expresses between *the cat* and *the mat*. Often propositions are written like this: *ON (cat, mat)*. Many utterances contain more than one proposition. Consider "The cat watched the mouse run under the sofa." We have as the first component proposition *UNDER (mouse, sofa)*. From that, we build up *RUN (mouse, UNDER (mouse, sofa))*. Finally, we get to *WATCH (cat, RUN (mouse, UNDER (mouse, sofa)))*.

How can we test whether your mental representations of meaning really work this way? Some of the earliest experiments in the psychology of language were devoted to showing the importance of propositional representations in understanding (Kintsch, 1974). Research has shown that if two words in an utterance belong to the same proposition, they will be represented together in memory even if they are not close together in the actual sentence.

HOW WE KNOW

PROPOSITIONS STRUCTURE MEMORY

Consider the sentence "The mausoleum that enshrined the tzar overlooked the square." Although *mausoleum* and *square* are far apart in the sentence, a propositional analysis suggests that they should be gathered together in memory in the proposition *OVERLOOKED (mausoleum, square)*. To test this analysis, researchers asked participants to read lists of words and say whether each had appeared in the sentence. Some participants saw *mausoleum* directly after *square* on the list. Others participants saw *mausoleum* after a word from another proposition. The response "Yes, I saw mausoleum" was swifter when *mausoleum* came directly after *square* than when its predecessor came from another proposition. This finding suggests that the concepts *mausoleum* and *square* had been represented together in memory (Ratcliff & McKoon, 1978).

Have you ever noticed how hard it is to remember *exactly* what someone said? You might, for example, have tried to remember a line from a movie word-for-word—but you realized when you got home that you could only remember the general sense of what was said. This experiment indicates why word-for-word memory isn't so good: Because one of the main operations your language processes carry out is the extraction of propositions, the exact form with which those propositions were rendered gets lost pretty quickly (for example, "The cat chased the mouse" versus "The mouse was chased by the cat").

Not all the propositions listeners store in memory are made up of information directly stated by the speaker. Often listeners fill gaps with **inferences**—logical assumptions made possible by information in memory. Consider this pair of utterances:

I'm heading to the deli to meet Donna.

She promised to buy me a sandwich for lunch.

To understand how these sentences go together, you must draw at least two important inferences. You must figure out both who *she* is in the second sentence and how going to a deli is related to a promise to buy a sandwich. Note that a friend who actually uttered this pair of sentences would be confident you could figure these things out. You'd never expect to hear this:

I'm heading to the deli to meet Donna. She— and by she I mean Donna—promised to buy me a sandwich—and a deli is a place where you can buy a sandwich—for lunch.

Speakers count on listeners to draw inferences of this sort.

A great deal of research has been directed toward determining what types of inferences listeners draw on a regular basis (Gerrig, 1993; Graesser et al., 1994; McKoon & Ratcliff, 1992). The number of potential inferences after any utterance is unlimited. For example, because you

Inferences Missing information filled in on the basis of a sample of evidence or on the basis of prior beliefs and theories.

know that Donna is likely to be a human, you could infer that she has a heart, a liver, a pair of lungs, and so on (and on), but it's unlikely that you would feel compelled to call any of those (perfectly valid) inferences to mind when you heard "I'm heading to the deli to meet Donna." Research suggests, in fact, that listeners are reasonably conservative in the inferences they draw. Consider this sentence:

The architect stabbed the man.

When explicitly asked to name what instrument this sentence made them think of, participants most often said *knife*. However, researchers found no evidence that participants, in natural circumstances of reading, called the concept *knife* to mind, or other instruments in similar sentences (Dosher & Corbett, 1982). This finding suggests that you do not automatically draw even some inferences that are pretty safe bets—for instance, that someone who was stabbed was stabbed with a knife. Most of the inferences you habitually draw are like the ones we illustrated before—inferences that capture the relationship between *Donna* and *she* and between *deli* and *sandwich*. These inferences help you form a coherent representation of the information the speaker wishes you to understand; they do not elaborate on it.

Our discussion of language use has demonstrated how much work a speaker does to produce the right sentence at the right time and how much work a listener does to figure out exactly what the speaker meant. You usually aren't aware of all this work! Does this give you a greater appreciation for the elegant design of your cognitive processes?

Language, Thought, and Culture

Have you had the opportunity to learn more than one language? If so, do you believe that you *think* differently in the two languages? Does language affect thought? This question is one that researchers have addressed in a variety of ways. Let us give you a cross-linguistic example to make this question more concrete. Imagine a scene in which a child has watched her father throw a ball. If the child were an English speaker, she might utter the sentence, "Daddy threw the ball." If, by contrast, the child were a Turkish speaker, she would say, "Topu babam atti." Is this just a different collection of words for the same idea? Not entirely: the *-ti* suffix at the end of the Turkish sentence indicates that the event was witnessed by the speaker; if the event hadn't been witnessed by the speaker, a different suffix (*miş*) would be added to *at* (which is the equivalent of *threw*) to form *atmiş*. As an English speaker, you are not required to divide the world into events you witnessed yourself versus those you learned about through other sources; as a Turkish speaker, you would be (Slobin, 1982; Slobin & Aksu,

1982). Could it be the case that the different grammatical requirements of these two languages would affect, in very basic ways, the manner in which people think about the world? No one knows the answer to this specific question about English and Turkish—would you like to carry out appropriate research?—but this distinction provides a good example of why people have so often been intrigued by the question of language's potential influence on thought.

Scholarly work on this question was originated by **Edward Sapir** and his student **Benjamin Lee Whorf,** whose cross-linguistic explorations led them to the somewhat radical conclusion that differences in language would create differences in thought. Here's how Sapir put it:

> *We see and hear and otherwise experience very largely as we do because the language habits of our community predispose certain choices of interpretation. (Sapir, 1941/1964, p. 69)*

For Sapir and Whorf, this conclusion emerged directly from relationships they believed to exist in their own data. Whorf outlined two hypotheses that have collectively come to be called the *Sapir-Whorf hypothesis* (see Brown, 1976):

- *Linguistic relativity.* Structural differences between languages will generally be paralleled by nonlinguistic cognitive differences in the native speakers of the two languages.

- *Linguistic determinism.* The structure of a language strongly influences or fully determines the way its native speakers perceive and reason about the world.

Linguistic determinism is the stronger of the two hypotheses because it asserts a strong causal effect of language on thought. Contemporary researchers in psychology, linguistics, and anthropology have attempted to create rigorous tests of these ideas (Gumperz & Levinson, 1996).

Let's look at one domain in which the influence of language on thought has been studied. You may be surprised to learn that languages of the world differ with respect to the number of basic color terms they use. As determined by linguistic analysis, English has 11 (*black, white, red, yellow, green, blue, brown, purple, pink, orange, and gray)*; some languages of the world, such as the language spoken by the Dani people of Papua New Guinea, have only 2, a simple distinction between *black* and *white* (or *light* and *dark*) (Berlin & Kay, 1969). Whorf had suggested that language users "dissect nature along the lines laid down by [their] native languages" (1956, p. 213): Researchers speculated that the number of color terms (for example, 2 versus 11) might influence the ways in which speakers of different languages were able to think about colors.

CAN NONHUMAN ANIMALS LEARN LANGUAGE?

You have almost certainly seen a movie or television show in which a nonhuman animal carries out a vigorous conversation with a human. Do you remember Mr. Ed, the talking horse? Could this happen in real life? Beginning as early as the 1920s, psychologists tried to address this question by attempting to teach language to chimpanzees. Chimps don't have the appropriate vocal apparatus to produce spoken language, so researchers had to devise other methods of communication. For example, a chimp named Washoe was taught a highly simplified version of American Sign Language (Gardner & Gardner, 1969); a chimp named Sarah was taught to manipulate symbols (which stood for concepts like *apple* and *give*) on a magnetic board (Premack, 1971). The results of these experiments inspired great controversy (Seidenberg & Petitto, 1979). Skeptics asked whether the chimps' occasional combinations of gestures or symbols (for example, *Washoe sorry, You more drink*) constituted any meaningful kind of language use. They also wondered whether most of the meaning attributed to the chimps' utterances wasn't arising in the heads of the humans rather than in the heads of the chimps.

In recent years, **Sue Savage-Rumbaugh** and her colleagues (Savage-Rumbaugh et al., 1998) have conducted research that has provided more solid insights into the language capabilities of chimps. Savage-Rumbaugh works primarily with *bonobos,* a species of great ape that is evolutionarily nearer to humans even than common chimpanzees. Rather remarkably, two of the bonobos in her studies, Kanzi and Mulika, acquired the meanings of plastic symbols *spontaneously:* They received no explicit training; rather, they acquired the symbols

Some bonobos have learned the meanings of words without explicit training. What other abilities must these animals demonstrate before it can be said that they have genuinely acquired a human language?

by observing others (humans and bonobos) using them to communicate. Moreover, Kanzi and Mulika are able to understand some *spoken* English. For example, when Kanzi hears a spoken word, he is able to locate either the symbol for the word or a photograph of the object. This group of researchers has also raised a bonobo and a common chimpanzee together—giving them early language experiences that closely match the circumstances in which humans acquire language (see Chapter 11). This project has demonstrated that even the common chimpanzee, Panpanzee, can acquire the meanings of some spoken English words—although not as many as her companion bonobo, Panbanisha (Brakke & Savage-Rumbaugh, 1995).

The results with bonobos are fascinating. However, there is much more to language than just the use of words. Consider *audience design.* Could nonhuman animals modify their messages based on what members of their audience know? Researchers have set out to answer this question. For example,

Dorothy Cheney and **Robert Seyfarth** (1990) have done extensive research on the communicative capabilities of *vervet monkeys.* Vervet monkeys make distinct *calls* to signal the presence of different dangers, such as leopards, eagles, and snakes. These monkeys are able to modify their calls depending on their audience: Female monkeys gave alarms at much higher rates when they were with their own offspring than when they were with monkeys unrelated to them. However, the vervets do not modify their calls based on what their audience *knows:* In an experimental setting, mother vervets produced the same calls irrespective of whether their offspring had also witnessed the events that evoked the calls. In fact, researchers have suggested that humans may be the only species that can modify its behavior based on someone else's knowledge (Povinelli & Prince, 1998).

You can see from this review that chimpanzees and bonobos possess some but not all of the cognitive capabilities necessary for humanlike language performance.

LANGUAGE AFFECTS COLOR JUDGMENTS

Researchers asked participants to examine triads of color chips all taken from the blue-green continuum. The participants' task was to indicate which of the three hues was most different from the other two. The two groups of participants were speakers of English, a language that includes a lexical distinction between blue and green, and speakers of Tarahumara, a language from Northern Mexico that has only a single lexical item, *siyóname*, that covers both green and blue hues. The researchers suggested that, if the Sapir-Whorf hypothesis is correct, "colors near the *green–blue* boundary will be subjectively pushed apart by English speakers precisely because English has the words *green* and *blue*, while Tarahumara speakers, lacking the lexical distinction, will show no comparable distortion" (Kay & Kempton, 1984, p. 68). The data strongly bore out this prediction: In their judgments of the color triads, English speakers distorted the interhue distances whereas Tarahumara speakers did not.

Further research, however, demonstrated that speakers of the two languages performed the same on a different color judgment task. Thus, the data reject a strong claim of linguistic determinism—language is not destiny—though they support the somewhat weaker claim that language differences yield parallel cognitive differences.

There are thousands of languages in the world, which provide many interesting distinctions: As we indicated for the English–Turkish example with which we started, many interesting hypotheses about the link between language and thought have yet to be tested (Gerrig & Banaji, 1994; Hunt & Agnoli, 1991; Smith, 1996). It is likely to be the case that very many of the lexical and grammatical differences—differences in words and structures—between languages will have no affect on thought. Even so, as we describe cultural differences throughout *Psychology and Life*, it is worth keeping an open mind about linguistic relativity and linguistic determinism. Given the many situations in which members of different cultures speak very different languages, we can wonder to what extent language plays a causal role in bringing about cultural differences.

Let's turn now from circumstances in which meaning is communicated through words to those in which meaning relies also on pictures.

The Dani people of Papua New Guinea speak a language with only two basic color terms—they make a distinction between black and white (or light and dark). English, by comparison, has 11 basic color terms. Could this language difference affect the way people experience the world?

SUMMING UP

When people produce language they try to design their utterances so that they are being cooperative. Appropriate audience design requires that speakers keep in mind the common ground they share with listeners. Spoonerisms and other speech errors provide insights into the planning and editing processes speakers use to produce correct phrases and utterances. Listeners use context to direct their interpretations to different possible meanings of ambiguous words, structures, and utterances. Mental representations are organized around propositions. Listeners must draw inferences to go beyond the information given, but they are fairly conservative about the range of inferences they draw. The Sapir-Whorf hypothesis suggests that the languages people speak affect the way they think about the world. Some support for this hypothesis has been found in the domain of color. Researchers have yet to examine many distinctions among languages that could influence thought.

Visual Cognition

In **Figure 9.6**, we give you two choices for visual representations of the sentence "The cat is on the mat." Which one seems right? If you think in terms of language-based propositions, each alternative captures the right meaning—the cat *is* on the mat. Even so, you're probably happy only with option A, because it matches the scene you likely called to mind when you first read the sentence (Searle, 1979b). How about option B? It probably makes you somewhat nervous because it seems as if the cat is going to tip right over. This anxious feeling must arise because you can think with pictures. In a sense, you can *see* exactly what's going to happen. In this section, we will explore some of the ways in which visual images and visual processes contribute to the way you think.

A

B

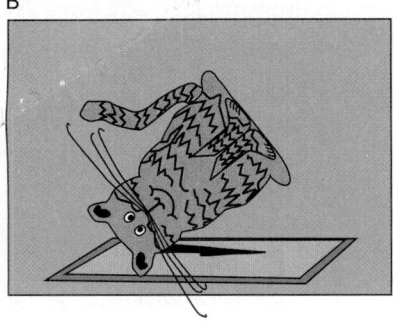

FIGURE 9.6

Visual Representations

Are both of these cats on the mat?

Using Visual Representations

History is full of examples of famous discoveries apparently made on the basis of mental imagery (Shepard, 1978). Recall F. A. Kekulé, whom we mentioned in Chapter 6. Kekulé, the discoverer of the chemical structure of benzene, often conjured up mental images of dancing atoms that fastened themselves into chains of molecules.

His discovery of the benzene ring occurred in a dream in which a snakelike molecule chain suddenly grabbed its own tail, thus forming a ring. Michael Faraday, who discovered many properties of magnetism, knew little about mathematics but he had vivid mental images of the properties of magnetic fields. Albert Einstein claimed to have thought entirely in terms of visual images, translating his findings into mathematical symbols and words only after the work of visually based discovery was finished.

We have given you these examples to encourage you to try to indulge in visual thinking. But even without trying, you regularly use your capabilities for manipulating visual images. Consider a classic experiment in which participants were asked to transform images in their heads.

HOW WE KNOW

MENTAL ROTATION IS LIKE PHYSICAL ROTATION Researchers presented students with examples of the letter R and its mirror image that had been rotated various amounts, from 0 to 180 degrees (see **Figure 9.7**). As the letter appeared, the student had to identify it as either the normal R or its mirror image. The reaction time taken to make that decision was longer in direct proportion to the amount the figure had been rotated. This finding indicated that a subject was imagining the figure in his or her "mind's eye" and rotating the image into an upright position at some fixed rate before deciding whether the figure was an R or a mirror image. The consistency of the rate of rotation suggested that the process of mental rotation was very similar to the process of physical rotation (Shepard & Cooper, 1982).

You put this ability for mental rotation to very good use. As you learned in Chapter 5, you often see objects in

FIGURE 9.7

Rotated R Used to Assess Mental Imagery

Participants presented with these figures in random order were asked to say, as quickly as possible, whether each figure was a normal R or a mirror image. The more the figure was rotated from upright, the longer the reaction time was.

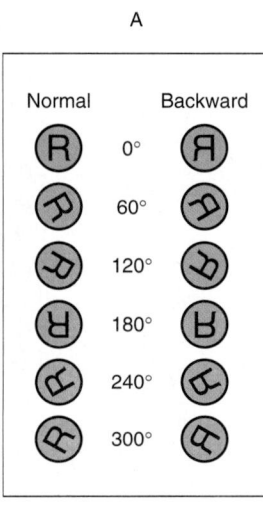

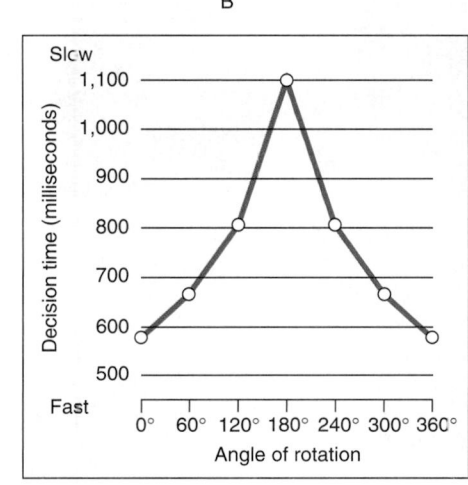

the environment from unfamiliar points of view. Mental rotation enables you to transform the image to one that matches representations stored in memory (Srinivas, 1995; Tarr, 1994; Tarr & Pinker, 1989). For example, in Figure 9.6, you almost certainly had to rotate the image (or did you just tilt your head?) to recognize the object as a cat, on a mat.

You can also use visual images to answer certain types of questions about the world. Suppose, for example, we asked you whether a golf ball is bigger than a Ping-Pong ball. If you can't retrieve that fact directly from memory, you might find it convenient to form a visual image of them side by side. This use of an image, once again, has much in common with the properties of real visual perception.

There are, of course, limits to the use of your visual imagination. Consider this problem:

Imagine that you have a large piece of blank paper. In your mind, fold it in half (making two layers),

fold it in half again (four layers), and continue folding it over 50 times. About how thick is the paper when you are done? (Adams, 1986)

The actual answer is about 50 million miles ($2^{50} \times 0.028$ inches, the thickness of a piece of paper), approximately half the distance between Earth and the sun. Your estimate was probably considerably lower. Your mind's eye was overwhelmed by the information you asked it to represent.

Combining Verbal and Visual Representations

Our discussion so far has largely focused on the types of visual representations that you form by committing to memory—or in the case of imagery, retrieving from memory—visual stimuli from the environment. However, you often form visual images based on verbal descriptions. You can, for example, create a mental picture of a cat with three tails, although you've almost certainly never seen one. The verbal description enables you to form a visual representation. Your ability to produce a mental image of a verbal scene is particularly useful when you read works of fiction that involve spatial details. Consider this passage from the James Bond short story *From a View to a Kill:*

The clearing was about as big as two tennis courts and floored in thick grass and moss. There was one large patch of lilies of the valley and, under the bordering trees, a scattering of bluebells. To one side there was a low mound…completely surrounded and covered with brambles and brier roses now thickly in bloom. Bond walked round this and gazed in

Long image scan

Short image scan

FIGURE 9.8

Visual Scanning of Mental Images

After studying a picture of a boat, subjects were asked to "look at" the motor in their own mental images. They were then asked whether the boat had a windshield or an anchor. The faster response to the windshield, which was closer to the motor than was the anchor, indicated that the subjects were scanning their visual images.

among the roots, but there was nothing to see except the earthy shape of the mound. (Fleming, 1959, pp. 19–20)

Did you try to imagine the scene—and help Bond search for danger? (He will find it.) When you read, you can form a *spatial mental model* to keep track of the where-abouts of characters (Zwaan & Radvansky, 1998). Researchers have often focused on the ways in which spatial mental models capture properties of real spatial experiences (Rinck et al., 1997).

Suppose, for example, you read a passage of a text that places you in the middle of an interesting environment.

> *You are hob-nobbing at the opera. You came to-night to meet and chat with interesting members of the upper class. At the moment, you are standing next to the railing of a wide, elegant balcony overlooking the first floor. Directly behind you, at your eye level, is an ornate lamp attached to the balcony wall. The base of the lamp, which is attached to the wall, is gilded in gold. (Franklin & Tversky, 1990, p. 65)*

In a series of experiments, readers studied descriptions of this sort that vividly described the layout of objects around the viewer (Franklin & Tversky, 1990). The researchers wished to show that readers were faster or slower to access information about the scene depending on where the objects were in the mental space around them. Readers, for example, were quicker to say what object was in front of them in the scene than what object was behind them, even though all objects were introduced equally carefully in the stories (see **Figure 9.9**). It's easiest to understand this result if you believe that the representation you form while reading actually places you, in some sense, in the scene. You are able to transform a verbal experience into a visual, spatial experience.

In general, when you think about the world around you, you are almost always combining visual and verbal representations of information. To prove that to yourself, you can take a minute to draw a map of the world. Go ahead—make a sketch! How do you go about doing this? Some of the things you draw in are probably based on visual experiences—you know the overall shape of Africa only because you have seen it represented in the past. Other features of your drawing will probably rely on verbal information—you are likely to remember that Japan is made up of several islands, even if you don't have a visual representation of quite where they go. In one study, nearly 4,000 students from 71 cities in 49 countries were

FIGURE 9.9

Spatial Mental Models

You can use imagination to project yourself into the middle of a scene. Just as if you were really standing in the room, you would take less time to say what is in front of you (the lamp) than what is behind you (the bust).

asked to carry out the task of drawing a world map (Saarinen, 1987). The goal of the study was to broaden understanding of cultural differences in the way the world is visualized and to promote world peace. The study found that the majority of maps had a Eurocentric worldview. Europe was placed in the center of the map and the other countries were arranged around it, probably due to the dominance for many centuries of Eurocentric representations in geography books. However, the study also yielded many instances of culture-biased maps, such as the one by a Chicago student, in **Figure 9.10**, and that of an Australian student, in **Figure 9.11**. These maps show what happens when a verbal perspective—My home should be in the middle!—is imposed on a visual representation.

In this section, we have seen that you have visual processes and representations to complement your verbal abilities. These two types of access to information give

Problem solving Thinking that is directed toward solving specific problems and that moves from an initial state to a goal state by means of a set of mental operations.

Reasoning The process of thinking in which conclusions are drawn from a set of facts; thinking directed toward a given goal or objective.

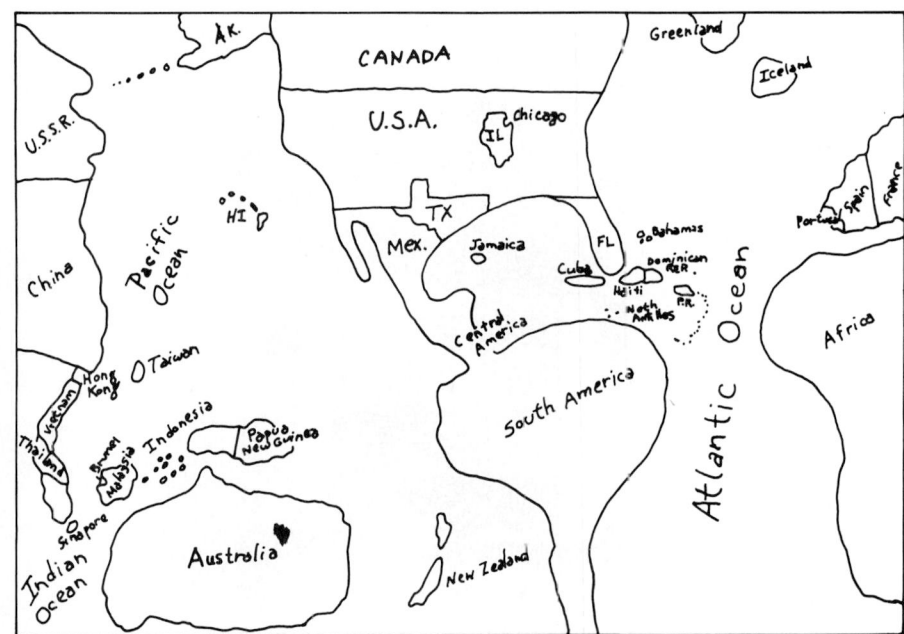

FIGURE 9.10

How does this Chicagocentric view of the world compare with yours?

you extra help in dealing with the demands and tasks of your life. We turn now to domains in which you put both visual and verbal representations to use in coping with your life's complexities: *problem solving* and *reasoning*.

SUMMING UP

People are able to use visual representations to rotate objects mentally. People scan visual images as if they were scanning real objects. By combining verbal and visual information, people can form elaborate mental representations.

■ Problem Solving and Reasoning

Consider a situation that has been all too common in our lives: You've accidentally locked yourself out of your home, room, or car. What do you do next? Reflect for a moment on the types of mental steps you might take to overcome this difficulty. Those mental steps will almost certainly include the cognitive processes that make up **problem solving** and **reasoning**. Both of these activities require you to combine current

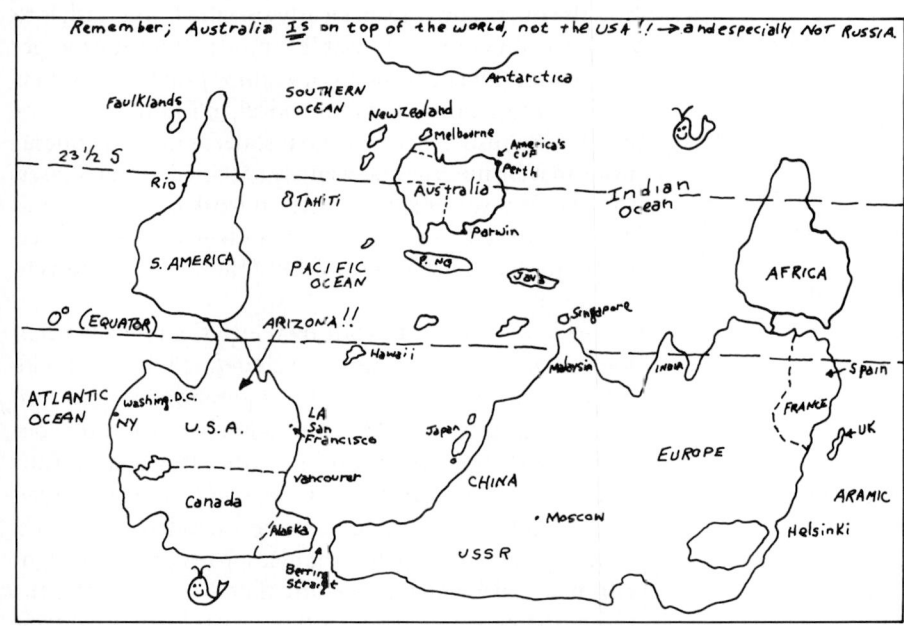

FIGURE 9.11

Look at this Australiocentric view of the world. Now who's down under?

information with information stored in memory to work toward some particular goal: a conclusion or a solution. We will look at aspects of problem solving and at two types of reasoning, deductive and inductive.

Problem Solving

What goes on four legs in the morning, on two legs at noon, and on three legs in the twilight? According to Greek mythology, this was the riddle posed by the Sphinx, an evil creature who threatened to hold the people of Thebes in tyranny until someone could solve the riddle. To break the code, Oedipus had to recognize elements of the riddle as metaphors. Morning, noon, and twilight represented different periods in a human life. A baby crawls and so (effectively) has four legs, an adult walks on two legs, and an older person walks on two legs but uses a cane, making a total of three legs. Oedipus's solution to the riddle was *humans.*

Although your daily problems may not seem as monumental as the one faced by young Oedipus, problem-solving activity is a basic part of your everyday existence. You continually come up against problems that require solutions: how to manage work and tasks within a limited time frame, how to succeed at a job interview, how to break off a relationship, and so on. Many problems involve discrepancies between what you know and what you need to know. When you solve a problem, you reduce that discrepancy by finding a way to get the missing information. To get into the spirit of problem solving, try the problems in **Figure 9.12**. After you're done, we'll see how psychological research can shed light on your performance—and, perhaps, provide some suggestions about how to improve it.

PROBLEM SPACES

How do you define a problem in real-life circumstances? You usually perceive the difference between your current state and a desired goal: for example, you are broke, and you'd like to have some money. You are also usually aware of some of the steps you would be able (or willing) to take to bridge the gap: You will try to get a part-time job, but you won't become a pickpocket. The formal definition of a *problem* captures these three elements (Newell & Simon, 1972). A problem is defined by (1) an *initial state*—the incomplete information or unsatisfac-

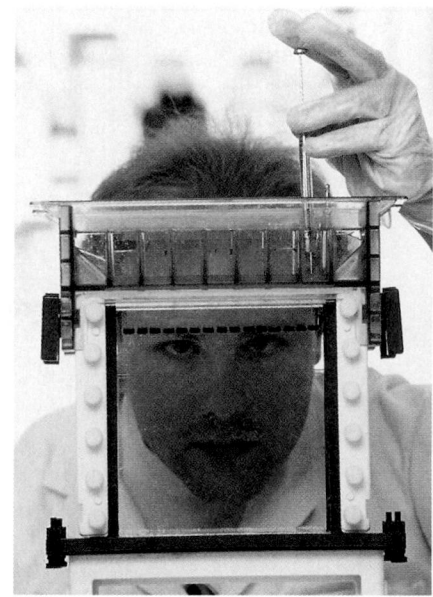

How do scientists approach the ill-defined problem of curing AIDs?

tory conditions you start with; (2) a *goal state*—the information or state of the world you hope to obtain; and (3) a *set of operations*—the steps you may take to move from an initial state to a goal state. Together, these three parts define the **problem space.** You can think of solving a problem as walking through a maze (the problem space) from where you are (the initial state) to where you want to be (the goal state), making a series of turns (the allowable operations).

Much of the initial difficulty in solving a problem will arise if any of these elements are not well-defined (Simon, 1973). A *well-defined problem* is similar to a textbook problem in which the initial state, the goal state, and the operations are all clearly specified. Your task is to discover how to use allowable, known operations to get the answer. By contrast, an *ill-defined problem* is similar to designing a home, writing a novel, or finding a cure for AIDS. The initial state, the goal state, and/or the operations may be unclear and vaguely specified. In such cases, the problem solver's first task is to work out, as much as possible, exactly what the problem is—to make explicit a beginning, an ideal solution, and the possible means to achieve it.

As you know from your own experience, even when the initial and goal states are well defined, it can still be difficult to find the right set of operations to get from the beginning to the end. If you think back to your experience in math classes, you know that this is true. Your teacher gave you a formula like $x^2 + x - 12 = 0$ and asked you to solve for possible values of x. What do you do next? To solve this algebra problem, you can use an **algorithm:** a step-by-step procedure that always provides the right answer for a particular type of problem. If you ap-

Problem space The elements that make up a problem: the initial state, the incomplete information or unsatisfactory conditions the person starts with; the goal state, the set of information or state the person wishes to achieve; and the set of operations, the steps the person takes to move from the initial state to the goal state.

Algorithm A step-by-step procedure that always provides the right answer for a particular type of problem.

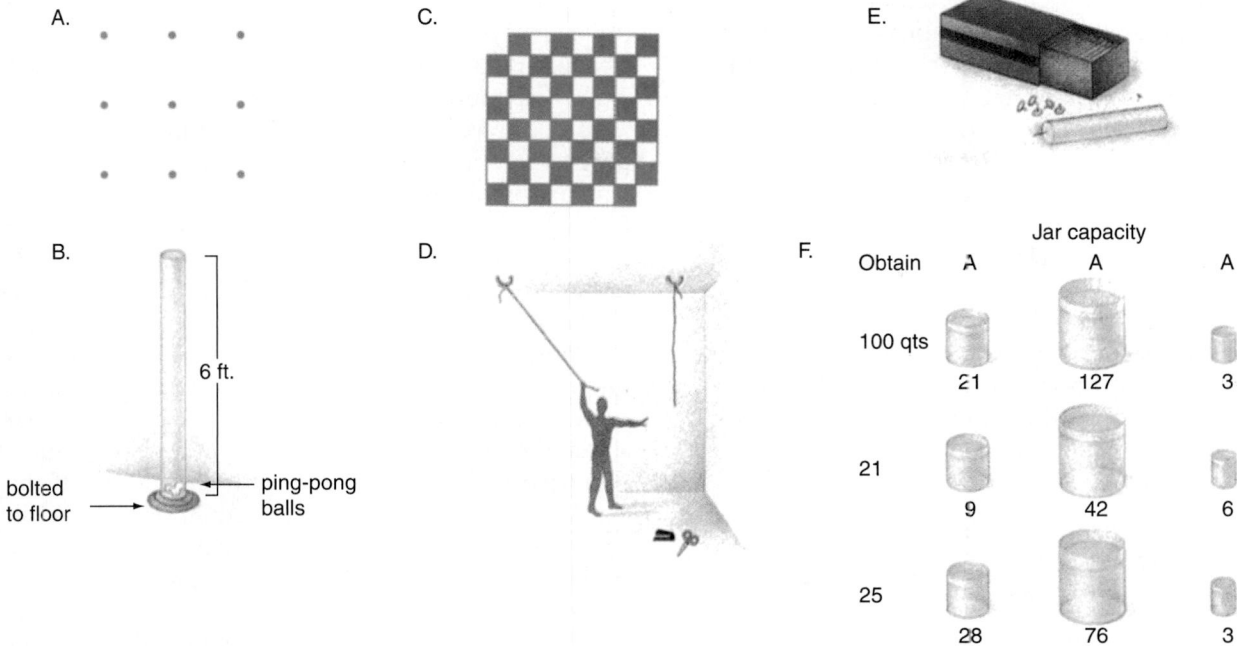

(A) Can you connect all the dots in the pattern by drawing four straight, connected lines without lifting your pen from the paper?

(B) A prankster has put 3 Ping-Pong balls into a 6-foot-long pipe that is standing vertically in the corner of the physics lab, fastened to the floor. How would you get the Ping-Pong balls out?

(C) The checkerboard shown has had 2 corner pieces cut out, leaving 62 squares. You have 31 dominoes, each of which covers exactly 2 checkerboard squares. Can you use them to cover the whole checkerboard?

(D) You are in the situation depicted and given the task of tying the 2 strings together. If you hold one string, the other is out of reach. Can you do it?

(E) You are given the objects shown (a candle, tacks, matches in a matchbox). The task is to mount a lighted candle on a door. Can you do it?

(F) You are given 3 "water-jar" problems. Using only the 3 containers (water supply is unlimited), can you obtain the exact amount specified in each case?

FIGURE 9.12

Can you solve it? (Part I)

Try to solve each of these problems (the answers are in Figure 9.13 on page 275, but don't look until you try to solve them all).

ply the rules of algebra correctly, you are guaranteed to obtain the correct values of x (i.e., 3 and −4). If you've ever forgotten the combination to a lock, you may also have engaged in behavior guided by an algorithm. If you try solutions systematically (e.g., 1, 2, 3; 1, 2, 4) you will definitely arrive at the right combination—though you may be at it for a good long while! Because well-defined problems have clear initial states and goal states, algorithms are more likely to be available for them than for ill-defined problems. When algorithms are unavailable, problem solvers often rely on **heuristics**, which are strat-

egies or "rules of thumb." Suppose, for example, you are reading a mystery and you'd like to solve the problem of who murdered an e-commerce tycoon. You might rule out the possibility that "the butler did it," because you use the heuristic that authors wouldn't use such a trite plot line. As we shall see shortly, heuristics are also a critical aspect of *judging* and *deciding*.

Heuristics Cognitive strategies, or "rules of thumb," often used as shortcuts in solving a complex inferential task.

Researchers have been interested in understanding the way people apply both algorithms and heuristics as they make their way through a problem space. To study the steps problem solvers take, researchers have often turned to **think-aloud protocols.** In this procedure, participants are asked to verbalize their ongoing thoughts (Ericsson & Simon, 1993). For example, a pair of researchers were interested in capturing the mental processes that enable participants to solve the mutilated checkerboard problem that is part C of Figure 9.12 (Kaplan & Simon, 1990). Here is one of their participants having the crucial breakthrough that the problem cannot be solved with only horizontal and vertical placement of pieces (the checkerboard was pink and black):

> *So you're leaving...it's short—how many, you're leaving uhhhh...there's more pinks than black, and in order to complete it you'd have to connect two pinks but you can't because they are diagonally...is that getting close? (Kaplan & Simon, 1990, p. 388)*

The solver has just realized that the goal cannot be accomplished if the dominoes can just be placed horizontally or vertically. Researchers have often used participants' own accounts of their thinking as the starting point for more formal models of problem solving (Simon, 1979, 1989).

IMPROVING YOUR PROBLEM SOLVING

What makes problem solving hard? If you reflect on your day-to-day experience, you might come up with the answer "There are too many things to consider all at once." Research on problem solving has led to much the same conclusion. What often makes a problem difficult to solve is that the mental requirements for solving a particular problem overwhelm processing resources (Kotovsky et al., 1985; Kotovsky & Simon, 1990). To solve a problem, you need to plan the series of operations you will take. If that series becomes too complex, or if each operation itself is too complex, you may be unable to see your way through from the initial state to the goal state. How might you overcome this potential limitation?

An important step in improving problem solving is to find a way to represent a problem so that each operation is possible, given your processing resources. If you must habitually solve similar problems, a useful procedure is to practice each of the components of the solution so that, over time, those components require fewer resources (Kotovsky et al., 1985). Suppose, for example, you were a cab driver in New York City and were faced with daily traffic jams. You might mentally practice your responses to jams at various points in the city, so that

you'd have ready solutions to components of the overall problem of getting your fare from a pickup spot to a destination. By practicing these component solutions, you could keep more of your attention on the road!

You can see an extreme example of the ability to apply past solutions to current problems in the extraordinary performance of world champion chess master Gary Kasparov. Kasparov is able to simultaneously beat several human opponents by recognizing weaknesses in configurations of chess pieces and applying appropriate, practiced solutions (Gobet & Simon, 1996).

Sometimes, finding a useful representation means finding a whole new way to think about the problem. Read the puzzle given in **Table 9.6.** How would you go about offering this proof? Think about it for a few minutes before you read on. How well did you do? If the word *proof* suggested to you something mathematical, you probably didn't make much progress. A better way to think about the problem is to imagine two monks, one starting at the top and another starting at the bottom (Adams, 1986). As one climbs and one descends, it's clear that they will pass at some point along the mountain, right (see **Figure 9.14**)? Now replace the pair of monks with just the one—conceptually it's the same—and there's your proof. What makes this problem suddenly very easy is using the right sort of representation: visual rather than verbal or mathematical.

If you go back to the problems in Figure 9.12 you have other good examples of the importance of an appropriate representation of the problem space. To get the Ping-Pong balls out of the pipe, you had to realize that the solution did not involve reaching into the pipe. To connect the two strings, you had to see one of the tools on the floor as a weight. To mount the candle on the door, you had to alter your usual perspective and perceive the matchbox as a platform instead of as a container, and you had to perceive the candle as a tool as well as the object to be mounted on the door. The last two problems show a phenomenon called functional fixed-

TABLE 9.6

The Monk Puzzle

One morning, exactly at sunrise, a Buddhist monk began to climb a tall mountain. A narrow path, no more than a foot or two wide, spiraled around the mountain to a glittering temple at the summit. The monk ascended at varying rates of speed, stopping many times along the way to rest and eat dried fruit he carried with him. He reached the temple shortly before sunset. After several days of fasting and meditation, he began his journey back along the same path, starting at sunrise and again walking at variable speeds with many pauses along the way. His average speed descending was, of course, greater than his average climbing speed. Prove that there is a spot along the path that the monk will occupy on both trips at precisely the same time of day.

See a "proof" for the Monk Puzzle in Figure 9.14 on the facing page.

Think-aloud protocols Reports made by experimental participants of the mental processes and strategies they use while working on a task.

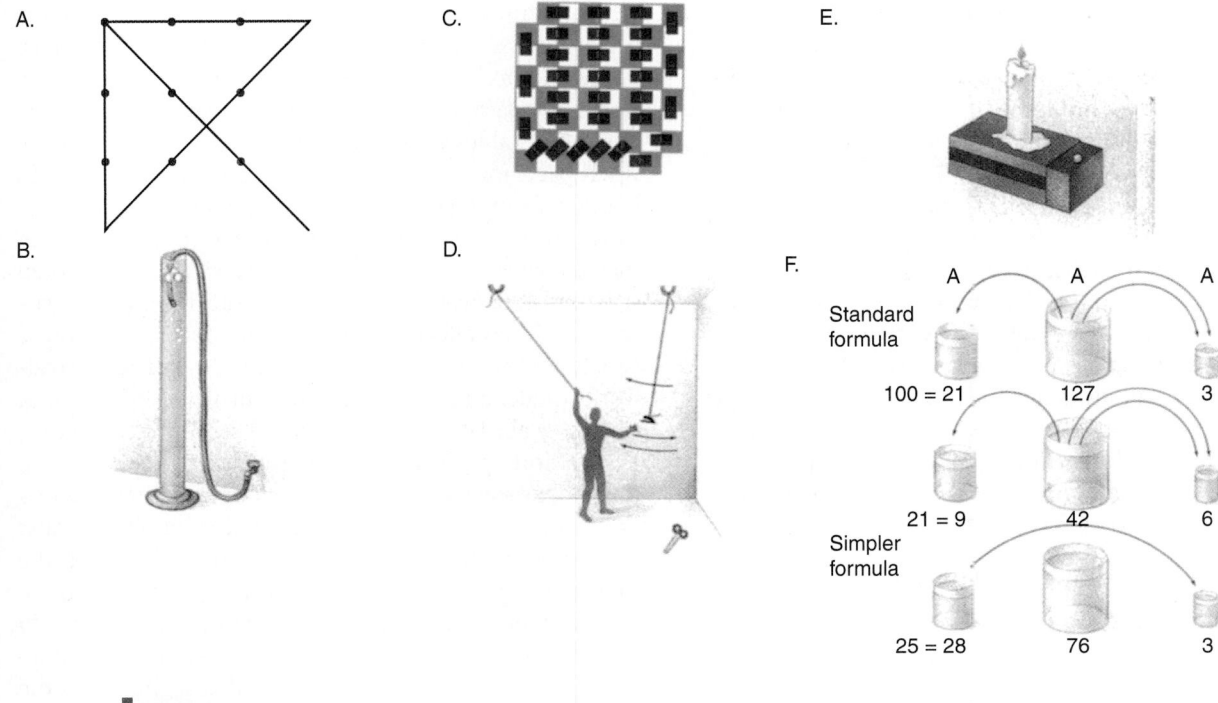

A.

C.

E.

B.

D.

F.

	A	A	A
Standard formula			
	100 = 21	127	3
	21 = 9	42	6
Simpler formula			
	25 = 28	76	3

FIGURE 9.13

Can You Solve It? (Part II)

Here are the solutions to the problems. How did you do? As the section on problem solving and reasoning unfolds, we will talk about what makes these problems hard.

ness (Duncker, 1945; Maier, 1931). **Functional fixedness** is a mental block that adversely affects problem solving by inhibiting the perception of a new function for an object that was previously associated with some other purpose. Whenever you are stuck on a problem, you should ask yourself, "How am I representing the problem? Are there different or better ways that I can think about the problem or components of its solution?" If words don't

work, try drawing a picture. Or try examining your assumptions, and see what "rules" you can break by making novel combinations.

> **Functional fixedness** An inability to perceive a new use for an object previously associated with some other purpose; adversely affects problem solving and creativity.

A

B

FIGURE 9.14

A "Proof" for the Monk Puzzle

Panel A shows two monks, one who starts at the bottom of the mountain and one who starts at the top. Panel B shows that they *must* meet at some time during the day. Replace the two monks with a single monk, and you have your proof!

Often, when you try to solve problems, you engage in special forms of thinking that are called reasoning. Let's turn now to a first type of reasoning you use to solve problems, deductive reasoning.

Deductive Reasoning

Suppose you are on your way to a restaurant and you want to pay for your meal with your only credit card, American Express. You call the restaurant and ask, "Do you accept American Express?" The restaurant's hostess replies, "We accept all major credit cards." You can now safely conclude that they accept American Express. To see why, we can reformulate your interchange to fit the structure of the *syllogism*, introduced by the Greek philosopher Aristotle over 2,000 years ago:

Premise 1. The restaurant accepts all major credit cards.

Premise 2. American Express is a major credit card.

Conclusion. The restaurant accepts American Express.

Aristotle was concerned with defining the logical relationships between statements that would lead to *valid* conclusions. **Deductive reasoning** involves the correct application of such logical rules. We gave the credit-card example to show that you are quite capable of drawing conclusions that have the form of logical, deductive proofs. Even so, psychological research has focused on the question of whether you actually have the formal rules of deductive reasoning represented in your mind (Schaeken et al., 2000). This body of research suggests that you may have some general, abstract sense of formal logic, but your real-world deductive reasoning is affected both by the specific knowledge you possess about the world and the representational resources you can bring to bear on a particular reasoning problem. Let's expand on these conclusions.

How does knowledge influence deductive reasoning? Consider this syllogism:

Premise 1. All things that have a motor need oil.

Premise 2. Automobiles need oil.

Conclusion. Automobiles have motors.

Is this a valid conclusion? According to the rules of logic, it is *not*, because Premise 1 leaves open the possibility that some things that don't have motors will also need oil. The

difficulty for you is that what is invalid in a logic problem is not necessarily untrue in real life. That is, if you take Premises 1 and 2 to be all the information in your possession—as you should if you accept this simply as an exercise in formal logic—the conclusion is not valid. Even so, when participants judge whether the conclusion "follows logically from the premises," they are much more inclined to say yes when the conclusion considers *automobiles* than they are when the nonsense term *oppobines* is substituted (Markovitz & Nantel, 1989). This result illustrates a general **belief-bias effect**—people tend to judge as valid those conclusions for which they can construct a reasonable real-world model and as invalid those for which they cannot (Evans et al., 1983; Janis & Frick, 1943; Newstead et al., 1992). More specifically, if there is a believable conclusion that is consistent with people's mental representations of a problem, they tend to accept that conclusion. In this case, knowledge about automobiles makes it hard to reject the conclusion as invalid. However, when participants were given just the two premises and asked to generate their own conclusions, about half were able to correctly state that no valid conclusion could be reached (that is, based on the two premises, you can't determine whether automobiles have motors). Thus, the belief bias may have a smaller effect on your actual reasoning processes than on your ability to judge someone else's conclusions (Rips, 1990). Formal instruction on logical reasoning, of the sort you are obtaining now, also helps reduce belief bias (Evans et al., 1994).

Experience also improves your reasoning ability. You can see this to be true if you compare performance on an abstract reasoning task with that on a version of the same task that allows you to apply real-world knowledge. Imagine that you are given the array of four cards pic-

Deductive reasoning A form of thinking in which one draws a conclusion that is intended to follow logically from two or more statements or premises.

elief-bias effect A situation that occurs when a person's prior knowledge, attitudes, or values distort the reasoning process by influencing the person to accept invalid arguments.

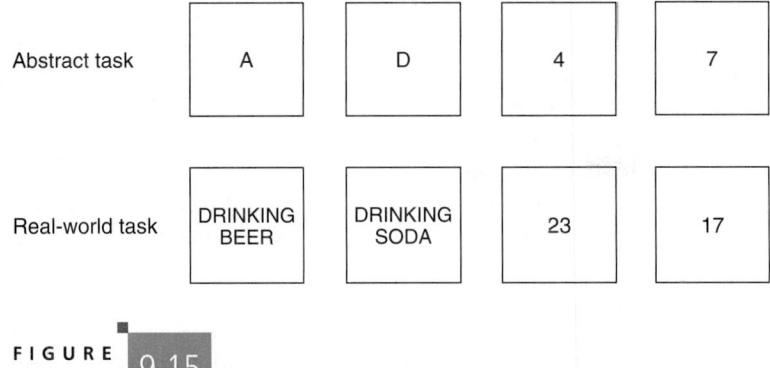

Abstract task	A	D	4	7

Real-world task	DRINKING BEER	DRINKING SODA	23	17

FIGURE 9.15

Abstract versus Real-World Reasoning

In the top row, you are required to say which cards you must turn over to test the rule "If a card has a vowel on one side, then it has an even number on the other side." In the bottom row, you must say which cards you need to turn over to test the rule "If a customer is to drink an alcoholic beverage, then she *must* be at least 18." People typically do better on the second task, which allows them to use real-world strategies.

tured in **Figure 9.15**, which have printed on them *A, D, 4,* and *7.* Your task is to determine which cards you must turn over to test the rule "If a card has a vowel on one side, then it has an even number on the other side" (Johnson-Laird & Wason, 1977). What would you do? Most people say that they would turn over the *A,* which is correct, and the *4*—which is incorrect. No matter what character appears on the flip side of the *4,* the rule will not be invalidated. (Can you see why that is true?) Instead, you must flip the *7.* If you were to find a vowel there, you would have invalidated the rule.

The original research on this task, which is often called the *Wason selection task,* prompted doubts about people's ability to reason effectively. This negative view, however, has been modified in two ways. First, researchers have suggested that participants may follow a nondeductive strategy of examining the cards that will allow them to *confirm* rather than *disconfirm* the generality of the relationship stated in the rule. Although this strategy may lead to the appearance of faulty deductive reasoning, it is a reasonable real-world strategy for learning about associations and making decisions (Oaksford & Chater, 1994; Oaksford et al., 1997).

Second, deductive reasoning is improved when participants are able to apply their real-world knowledge to the Wason task (Holyoak & Spellman, 1993). Suppose you were asked to perform what is a logically comparable task, on the lower set of cards in Figure 9.15. In this case, however, you are asked to evaluate the rule "If a customer is to drink an alcoholic beverage, then she *must* be at least 18" (Cheng & Holyoak, 1985). Now you can probably see immediately which are the correct cards to turn over: *17* and *drinking beer.* When the problem is familiar in real life, you can make use of a *pragmatic reasoning schema.* As we described in Chapter 8, you derive schemas over

the course of your experience in the environment. You have had a good deal of experience in *permission* situations—recall all the times you were given conditions like, "You can't watch television unless you do your homework." Through all those interactions, you derive a reasoning schema. The real-life situation linking age to drinking calls to mind this schema; the arbitrary situation linking even numbers and vowels does not. As a consequence, the arbitrary reasoning task underestimates your ability to make correct deductions.

Note that recent research has proposed an alternative to the view that people *acquire* a schema with respect to permissions. In a version of the card-turning task adapted for children, participants as young as 3 years old could reason successfully about what was and was not permitted by a rule. This result suggests that reasoning about permission situations may be innate (Cummins, 1996). That is, the ability to determine when actions do not follow social norms may be part of the genetic package you inherited as a member of the highly social human species (Cummins, 1999).

To begin this section on deductive reasoning, we described a situation in which you drew a valid deductive inference about your ability to use your American Express card to buy a meal. Unfortunately, life provides many occasions on which you cannot be so certain that you have drawn valid inferences from valid premises. We turn now to a version of the restaurant scenario that requires you to use a different form of reasoning.

Inductive Reasoning

Let's suppose that you have arrived outside the restaurant and only then think to check to see if you have enough cash. Once again you find that you'll want to use your American Express card, but there's no helpful sign on the outside. You peek through the restaurant's windows and see well-dressed clientele. You look at the expensive prices on the menu. You consider the upscale quality of the neighborhood. All these observations lead you to believe that the restaurant is likely to take your credit card. This is not deductive reasoning, because your conclusion is based on probabilities rather than logical certainties. Instead, this is **inductive reasoning**—a form of reasoning that uses available evidence to generate likely, but not certain, conclusions.

Although the name might be new, we have already described to you several examples of inductive reasoning. We saw repeatedly, in Chapters 5 and 8, that people use past information stored as schemas to generate expectations about the present and future. You are using inductive reasoning, for example, if you decide that a certain odor in the air indicates that someone is making popcorn; you are using inductive reasoning if you agree that the words on this page are unlikely to suddenly become invisible (and that, if you study, your knowledge of this material won't become invisible on test day). Finally, earlier in this chapter, we discussed the types of inferences people draw when they use language. Your belief that *she* must be *Donna* in the sequence of utterances we gave you relies on inductive inference.

In real-life circumstances, much of your problem-solving ability relies on inductive reasoning. Return to our opening example: You have accidentally locked yourself out of your home, room, or car. What should you do? A good first step is to call up from memory solutions that worked in the past. This process is called *analogical problem solving:* You establish an analogy between the features of the current situation and the features of previous situations (Holyoak & Nisbett, 1988; Holyoak & Thagard, 1997). In this case, your past experiences of "being locked out" may have allowed you to form the *generalization* "find other people with keys" (Ross & Kennedy, 1990). With that generalization in hand, you can start to figure out who those individuals might be and how to find them. This task might require you to retrieve the method you developed for tracking down your roommates at their afternoon classes. If this problem seems easy to you, it's because you have grown accustomed to letting your past inform your present: Inductive reasoning allows you to access tried-and-true methods that speed current problem solving.

Research on analogical problem solving often has educational implications (Kolodner, 1997). It is likely, for example, that in most of your math and science classes

your teachers and your textbooks provided you with a small number of problems with worked-out solutions and expected you to carry on from there. The expectation built into this educational technique is that you will be able to perform inductive reasoning—you will be able to figure out how past methods can be applied to the new problems. Researchers have tried to determine what circumstances are necessary to enable students to best take advantage of past solutions (Lovett & Anderson, 1994; Novick & Holyoak, 1991). One general conclusion is that students often need help finding the analogy: Extra encouragement is often required, in the form of hints or clues, so that students can see the relevance of past problems to current problems (Ross & Kennedy, 1990). Let's consider an example.

HOW WE KNOW

PEOPLE OFTEN NEED HELP TO FIND ANALOGIES Look at the picture in part A of **Figure 9.16.** Suppose someone were to pour water into the top of the tube so that the water comes out at the lower end. What path will the water take when it exits the tube? You can use the options in part B of Figure 9.16 to make your judgment. Now consider a slight rewording of the question. Suppose someone were to attach a hose to the tube at the top, so that the water would come out at the lower end. Does the mention of *a hose* change your thinking about the problem? Participants in a series of experiments were first asked to draw the path they believed the water would take and then to choose the picture that came closest to capturing their drawings. In one experiment, only 30 percent of participants in the *no-hose* condition chose the right answer (option f), whereas 75 percent of the participants in the *hose* condition chose that answer. What accounts for this difference? Apparently, when they were explicitly reminded about their past experiences— for example, experiences watching water come out of a garden hose—participants were able to engage in appropriate inductive reasoning. However, without the hint about hoses, they defaulted to the "naive physics" view that the circular path would continue when the water left the tube (Catrambone et al., 1995).

This experiment provides an excellent example of circumstances in which most people need an explicit reminding to help them use inductive reasoning for problem solving.

You might be bothered by the conclusion that explicit remindings are often necessary—because teachers and textbooks rarely provide such hints or clues. What can you do? You might try on your own to make the anal-

---

■ **Inductive reasoning** A form of reasoning in which a conclusion is made about the probability of some state of affairs, based on the available evidence and past experience.

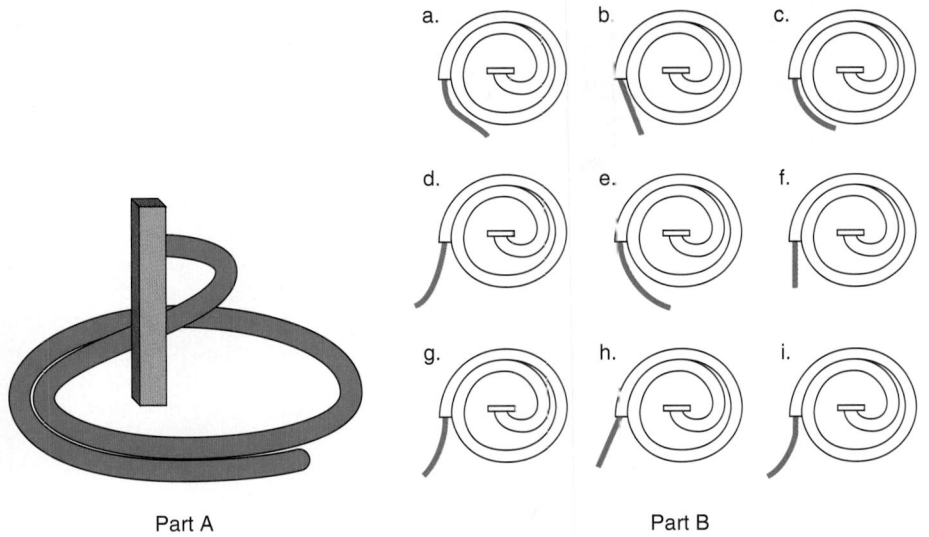

FIGURE 9.16

Part A

Part B

What Path Will the Water Take?

Imagine water is flowing out of the apparatus in Part A. Take a moment to draw the path you think the water will take. After you finish your drawing, choose the option in Part B that is closest to your drawing.

ogies as concrete as possible. Teach yourself to find the underlying structure that makes parts of the problems fill the same roles, and see how the same solution methods can be applied. The more explicit an understanding you have of the components and structure of past problems, the more likely you are to recognize a similarity in a current problem and easily apply a solution technique. (Meanwhile, you should count on experimental psychologists to share their results with the people who teach and write textbooks.)

We have one caution to add about inductive reasoning. Often a solution that has worked in the past can be reused for a successful solution. But sometimes you must recognize that reliance on the past can hamper your problem-solving ability when there is a critical difference between the old and current situations. The water-jar problem given in Figure 9.12 is a classic example of circumstances in which reliance on the past may cause you to miss a solution to a problem (Luchins, 1942). If you had discovered, in the first two problems in part F, the conceptual rule that $B - A - 2(C) = answer$, you probably tried the same formula for the third problem and found it didn't work. Actually, simply filling jar A and pouring off enough to fill jar C would have left you with the right amount. If you were using your initial formula, you probably did not notice this simpler possibility— your previous success with the other rule would have given you a mental set. A **mental set** is a preexisting state of mind, habit, or attitude that can enhance the quality and speed of perceiving and problem solving under some conditions. However, the same set may inhibit or distort the quality of your mental activities at times when old ways of thinking and acting are nonproductive in new situations. When you find yourself frustrated in a problem-solving situation, you might take a step back and ask yourself, "Am I allowing past successes to narrow my fo-

cus too much?" Try to make your problem solving more creative by considering a broader spectrum of past situations and past solutions.

In this section, we have examined a range of types of problem solving and reasoning—and have suggested, in each case, concrete steps you can take to improve your performance in real-world circumstances. We follow the same strategy in the final section of the chapter. We describe some major research findings on the processes of *judgment* and *decision making* and then suggest how you can apply those findings to important situations in your life.

SUMMING UP

A problem space consists of an initial state, a goal state, and a set of operations that allow a problem-solver to move from the initial state to the goal state. Problem solving is improved when people practice components of the solutions and when they find a useful representation. Deductive reasoning yields valid conclusions. Research suggests that people are not always accurate in their deductive reasoning. For example, people succumb to the belief-bias effect. However, deductive reasoning is improved when people reason about situations involving permissions. Inductive reasoning requires generalizations from past experiences. One important use of induction is in analogical problem solving: People solve current problems by forming analogies to prior problems to which they know the solutions.

Mental set The tendency to respond to a new problem in the manner used to respond to a previous problem.

EXPERT SYSTEMS AND MEDICINE

If you've ever had a serious consultation with a medical professional, you've been a participant in a situation in which an individual's ability to reason and problem-solve matters enormously. The person responsible for your health must try to identify the pattern that underlies your constellation of symptoms and infer an underlying cause. Based on his or her causal inferences, the individual must prescribe a plan of action. Given the complexities of this process—just think how hard it is even for you to describe your symptoms accurately, in a way that someone else can understand—it won't surprise you to learn that cognitive scientists have been involved for several years in efforts to provide computer programs that assist doctors and other health-care personnel with diagnosis and treatment planning.

The programs that these researchers have developed are called *expert systems:* An expert system is a computer program that simulates experts' problem-solving performance with respect to an organized body of knowledge. Consider *MYCIN,* a system developed in the mid-1970s that laid the groundwork for much of the research in this area. MYCIN was intended to assist with the diagnosis

and treatment of infectious diseases (Shortliffe, 1976). At the heart of MYCIN was a series of "if-then" rules—rules that related premises to conclusions—that captured heuristic knowledge (i.e., the "rules of thumb") used by experts in this field. As in real medical diagnosis, MYCIN was able to convey the confidence with which premises (e.g., the results of patients' blood tests) are related to particular conclusions (e.g., a diagnosis or a treatment recommendation). The program would also, if asked, reveal the line of reasoning it used to arrive at an ultimate conclusion. Although MYCIN was never implemented in a medical setting, the programs designed by contemporary researchers retain the same basic philosophy of providing users with an understanding of the "reasoning" behind the system's recommendations (Chae, 1998; Hudson & Cohen, 2000).

The ability of these programs to capture reasoning processes is, in fact, an important component of their success or failure. Take the perspective of a doctor interacting with a medical expert system. As a doctor, you might be reluctant to accept the idea that any computer program could outperform your long years of study. What is important to remem-

ber, however, is that expert systems gather together the knowledge of experts in a field. Moreover, these systems incorporate not just facts but the way in which experts reason with respect to those facts. Current research is intended to develop expert systems that provide even more systematic explanations for why a set of facts should lead a healthcare provider to a particular set of conclusions (Chandrasekaran & Mittal, 1999).

Now shift your perspective from doctor to patient. As the 21st century leads to greater improvements in expert systems, it is not unlikely that you will observe a health-care provider entering your case into a computer. You should feel pleased if the doctor is taking a moment to supplement his or her own reasoning skills with those of the collected experts in a field.

Web sites:

- www-camis.stanford.edu
This is the Web site for Stanford Medical Informatics, a research group that carries out a number of projects related to expert systems and medicine.

- www.cis.upenn.edu/~traumaid
TraumAID is a program developed to assist physicians with emergency medicine situations. The Web site includes demonstrations of the expert systems.

Judging and Deciding

We begin this section on *judging* and *deciding* by stating one of the great truths of your day-to-day experience: You live in a world filled with *uncertainty.* Should you spend $9 on a movie you may or may not enjoy? Before an exam, would you better off studying your notes or rereading the chapter? Are you ready to commit yourself to a long-term relationship? Because you can only guess at the future, and because you almost never have full knowledge of the past, very rarely can you be completely certain that you have made a correct judgment or decision. Thus, the processes of judgment and decision mak-

ing must operate in a way that allows you to deal efficiently with uncertainty. As **Herbert Simon,** one of the founding figures of cognitive psychology, put it: because "human thinking powers are very modest when compared with the complexities of the environments in which human beings live" they must be content "to find 'good enough' solutions to their problems and 'good enough' courses of action" (1979, p. 3). In this light, Simon suggested that thought processes are guided by *bounded rationality.* Your judgments or decisions might not be as good—as "rational"—as they always could be, but you should be able to see how they result from your applying limited resources to situations that require swift action.

Before we move to a closer analysis of the products of bounded rationality, let's quickly distinguish between the two processes of judgment and decision making. **Judgment** is the process by which you form opinions, reach conclusions, and make critical evaluations of events and people. You often make judgments spontaneously, without prompting. **Decision making** is the process of choosing between alternatives, selecting and rejecting available options. Judgment and decision making are interrelated processes. For example, you might meet someone at a party and, after a brief discussion and a dance together, *judge* the person to be intelligent, interesting, honest, and sincere. You might then *decide* to spend most of your party time with that person and to arrange a date for the next weekend; decision making is more closely linked to behavioral actions. Let's turn now to research on these two types of thinking.

Heuristics and Judgment

What's the best way to make a judgment? Suppose, for example, you are asked whether you enjoyed a movie. To answer this question, you could fill out a chart with two columns, "What I liked about the movie" and "What I didn't like about the movie," and see which column came out longer. To be a bit more accurate, perhaps you'd weight the entries in each list according to their importance (thus, you might weight "the actors' performances" as more important on the plus side than "the blaring sound track" on the minus side). If you went through this whole procedure, you'd probably be pretty confident of your judgment—but you know already that this is an exercise you rarely undertake. In real-life circumstances, you have to make judgments frequently and rapidly. You don't have the time—and often you don't have sufficient information—to use such a formal procedure. What do you do instead? An answer to this question was pioneered by **Amos Tversky** and **Daniel Kahneman**, who argued that people's judgments rely on heuristics rather than on formal methods of analysis. As we noted in our discussion of problem solving, heuristics are informal rules of thumb that provide shortcuts, reducing the complexity of making judgments.

How do you demonstrate that people are using these mental rules of thumb? As you will soon see, researchers have most often opted to show the circumstances in which the shortcuts lead people to make errors. The logic of these experiments should sound familiar to you by now: Just as you can understand perception by studying perceptual illusion and memory by studying memory failures, you can understand judgment processes by studying judgment errors (Kahneman, 1991). As in those other domains, you have to be careful not to mistake the method for the conclusion. Even though there is a wide range of situations in which

psychologists can show that your perceptual processes can be fooled, you rarely walk into walls. Similarly, despite the errors that arise because your judgment making is implemented by heuristics, you rarely bump against the wall of cognitive limitations.

Does this mean you should be entirely comfortable with these types of errors? Here the analogy to perception breaks down to some extent. Most perceptual illusions are immune to learning. You're always going to perceive the lengths of the lines of the Müller-Lyer illusion (see Chapter 5) to be different, no matter how much you learn about it. By comparison, knowing about judgmental heuristics can enable you to avoid some types of errors. Although general intellectual skills provide no defense against these errors—even the most gifted judgment makers err under some circumstances—specific training can help. Throughout this section, we will point out the ways in which you can improve your judgment making. Let's turn now to three heuristics: availability, representativeness, and anchoring.

AVAILABILITY HEURISTIC

We'll begin by asking you to make a rather trivial judgment. (We know you're likely to give the wrong answer, and we don't want to embarrass you about something important.) If we were to give you a brief excerpt from a novel, do you believe more words in the excerpt would begin with the letter *k* (for example, *kangaroo*) or have *k* in third position (for example, *duke*)? If you are like the participants in a study by Tversky and Kahneman (1973), then you probably judged that *k* is found more often at the beginning of words. In fact, *k* appears about twice as often in the third position.

Why do most people believe that *k* is more likely to appear in first position? The answer has to do with the *availability* of information from memory. It's much easier to think of words that begin with *k* than to think of those in which *k* comes third. Your judgment, thus, arises from use of the **availability heuristic:** You base your judgment on information that is readily available in memory. This heuristic makes sense, because much of the time what is available from memory will lead to accurate judgments. If, for example, you judge bowling to be a less dangerous sport than hang gliding, availability is serving you well. Trouble only arises either when (1) memory processes give rise to a biased sample

---

- **Judgment** The process by which people form opinions, reach conclusions, and make critical evaluations of events and people based on available material; also, the product of that mental activity.
- **Decision making** The process of choosing between alternatives; selecting or rejecting available options.
- **Availability heuristic** A judgment based on the information readily available in memory.

If you were in a happy mood, would you be more likely to remember good times from your younger days?

of information or (2) the information you've stored in memory is not accurate. Let's look at an example of each of these potential problems.

The *k* question is a good example of circumstances in which your memory processes can make an availability-based judgment inaccurate. Given the way words are organized in memory, it's simply easier to find words that begin with a particular letter. Let's consider another case that is closer to the judgments you make in everyday life.

HOW WE KNOW

MOOD AFFECTS THE AVAILABILITY OF MEMORIES Researchers wanted to demonstrate how people's moods influenced their judgments about the likelihood that certain fates would befall them. Participants in their study read statements that put them in either measurably happy or unhappy moods. They then were asked to think of past instances of happy or unhappy events—for example, a welcome invitation or a painful injury—and to estimate how likely it would be that events of this type would happen to them again in the next six months. The participants' ability to recall past events was strongly predicted by their mood—and the availability of mood-congruent memories

predicted judgments about the future. Thus, participants in a happy mood found it easier to recall happy events. But, also, the availability of those happy events led participants to judge that more happy events, and fewer unhappy events, would occur in the future (MacLeod & Campbell, 1992).

This experiment demonstrates how easily judgments can be affected by the type of information that is—for whatever reasons—easily available from memory. You see the implications for your day-to-day life. If you are making important judgments about your future, you should factor in the way mood affects the information available to you. More generally, when it's time to make an important judgment, you can ask yourself, "Is there anything special about my frame of mind that will bias the information coming out of memory?"

A second difficulty with availability as a judgment heuristic arises when the information you have stored in memory has a bias to it. For example, one study examined the relationship between people's television viewing and their estimates about the typical wealth of U.S. citizens (O'Guinn & Shrum, 1997). People who watched more television shows like *Dynasty* and *Dallas* were also more likely to estimate greater numbers of U.S. households that have hot tubs or employ servants. The researchers' explanation for this correlation was that the television programs make unrealistic images of great wealth easily available to heavy viewers. As a second example, consider people's judgments of the populations of various countries (Brown & Siegler, 1992). See if you can order these four countries from smallest to largest population:

a. Sweden

b. Indonesia

c. Israel

d. Nigeria

Researchers demonstrated that, in general, the more participants knew about a country, the higher their population estimates. Furthermore, there was a sizable correlation between participants' rated knowledge about a country and the number of times it had been mentioned in *New York Times* articles in a given year. (The right answer, by the way, is Israel, Sweden, Nigeria, Indonesia. Did availability lead you astray?)

Clearly, you shouldn't feel bad about your cognitive processes because the media have provided you with a flawed database. Even so, you can combat this effect of availability by examining the sources of your information before you make important judgements. How do you know what you think you know?

REPRESENTATIVENESS HEURISTIC

When you make judgments based on the **representativeness heuristic,** you assume that if something has the characteristics considered typical of members of a category, it is, in fact, a member of that category. This heuristic will seem familiar to you because it captures the idea that people use past information to make judgments about similar circumstances in the present. That is the essence of inductive reasoning. Under most circumstances—as long as you have unbiased ideas about the features and categories that go together—making judgments along the lines of similarity will be quite reasonable. Thus, if you are deciding whether to begin a new activity like hang gliding, it makes sense to determine how representative that sport is of the category of activities you have previously enjoyed. Representativeness will lead you astray, however, when it causes you to ignore other types of relevant information, as you will now see (Kahneman & Tversky, 1973).

Consider, for example, the description of a successful attorney, given in **Figure 9.17.**

A successful Jerusalem attorney. Colleagues say his whims prevent him from being a team worker, attributing his success to competitiveness and drive. Slim and not tall, he watches his body and is vain. Spends several hours a week on his favorite sport. What sport is that?

a. Fast walking
b. A ball game
c. Tennis
d. A track and field sport

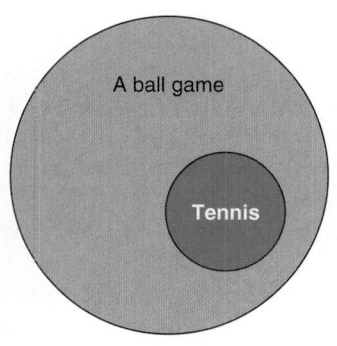

The more inclusive category <u>must</u> be more probable.

FIGURE 9.17

Using the Representativeness Heuristic

When asked to choose the attorney's favorite sport, the representativeness heuristic leads most people to choose "tennis." However, as shown in the bottom part of the figure, the more probable answer is "a ball game," because that includes within it "tennis."

HOW WE KNOW

REPRESENTATIVENESS AFFECTS JUDGMENTS In one experiment, researchers provided their participants with a list of options, including those in Figure 9.17, and gave them the chance to win $45—real money—by ranking the correct option as number 1. Which option seems correct to you? If you're like a majority of the original participants, you'll lose the $45 because you'll say *tennis* rather than *a ball game.* The lower part of Figure 9.17 shows why *tennis* could never be as good a bet: It is included within the category *a ball game.* Participants judge *tennis* to be a better answer because it seems to have all the features of the sport the attorney is likely to play. However, this judgment by representativeness causes participants to neglect another sort of information—category structure. In this case, the measurable cost is $45 (Bar-Hillel & Neter, 1993).

The implication for your day-to-day life is that you should not be fooled into grabbing at a representative alternative before you consider the structure of all the alternatives.

Let's look at a second representativeness example that also might affect the bets you make. Suppose you were given the opportunity to play in a lottery. To win, you must match the three numbers the state draws in the exact order. Which of these numbers would you feel most comfortable betting on?

859	101	333
574	948	772

The question we are really asking you is: Which of these numbers strikes you as most representative of the numbers that win these kinds of lotteries? If you are like most bettors, you will avoid playing numbers that have repeated digits—because those numbers do not seem representative of a random sequence. In fact, 27 percent of the time a three-digit number—with each digit drawn randomly from the pool 0 to 9—will have a repeated numeral. Nevertheless, among individuals who took part in the Indiana Pick-3 lottery in a 15-day period, only 12.6 percent chose to play a number with a repeated digit (Holtgraves & Skeel, 1992). You should be wary, in general, of the way that most gambling situations are constructed. Most often the hope is that you will be guided by representativeness—so you'll choose the options that look like they're more likely to win—rather than by a careful consideration of the odds.

Representativeness heuristic A cognitive strategy that assigns an object to a category on the basis of a few characteristics regarded as representative of that category.

JUDGING AND DECIDING

To introduce you to a third heuristic, we need you to try a thought experiment. First take five seconds to estimate the following mathematical product and write down your answer:

$$1 \times 2 \times 3 \times 4 \times 5 \times 6 \times 7 \times 8 = \underline{\hspace{1.5cm}}$$

In 5 seconds, you can probably make only a couple of calculations. You get a partial answer, perhaps 24, and then adjust up from there. Now try this series of numbers:

$$8 \times 7 \times 6 \times 5 \times 4 \times 3 \times 2 \times 1 = \underline{\hspace{1.5cm}}$$

Even if you notice that this is the same list in reverse, you can see how the experience of carrying out the multiplication would feel quite different. You'd start with 8×7, which is 56, and then attempt 56×6, which already feels quite large. Once again, you can only make a partial guess and then adjust upward. When Tversky and Kahneman (1974) gave these two arrangements of the identical problem to experimental participants, the 1 to 8 order produced median estimates of 512, and the 8 to 1 group produced estimates of 2,250 (*the real answer is 40,320*). Apparently, when participants adjusted up from their five-second estimates, the higher partial solutions led to higher estimates.

Performance on this simple multiplication task provides evidence for an anchoring bias. When you judge the probable value of some event or outcome, a bias based on the **anchoring heuristic** is an insufficient adjustment—either up or down—from an original starting value. In other words, your judgment is "anchored" too firmly to an original guess. The use of an anchor is not costly when the original estimate consists of information genuinely relevant to the judgment at hand. However, people show a strong tendency to be influenced by an anchor, even when the information is clearly of little or no use.

HOW WE KNOW

ARBITRARY ANCHORS CHANGE ESTIMATES
In one study, students in experimental conditions were given an arbitrary identification number (in the range 1,928 to 1,935) that they were instructed to copy onto their questionnaires. (Students in the control group did not receive a number.) The students' attention was called to the number in one of several ways (for example, they were asked to check whether it was higher than 1,940), but the identification numbers were clearly defined as irrelevant to any other answer. Subsequently, the students were asked to estimate the number of physicians listed in the local Yellow Pages. The responses were clearly affected by the totally irrelevant, arbitrary anchor. Students who had their attention called to the arbitrary identification number gave much higher estimates than did students in the control group—631 versus 219. Even when students were specifically warned that the ID number might affect their judgments, they still increased their estimates to 539—well over the control group's 219 estimate (Wilson et al., 1996)!

This last result should give you particular pause: Even a warning didn't help. Salespeople often use anchoring when they are trying to convince you to buy a product. Suppose, for example, you are thinking of buying a new stereo. A salesperson might say, "You'd expect to pay $1,000 or $2,000, wouldn't you?" Once you are anchored on that high estimate, the real price (perhaps $599.99) seems like a good deal. We'd like to think that reading this section will help you to avoid negative anchoring effects, but you are now forewarned that you must be very, very careful.

You employ judgmental heuristics like availability, representativeness, and anchoring because, in most situations, they allow you to make efficient, acceptable judgments. In a sense, you are doing the best you can, given the uncertainties of situations and constraints on your processing resources. We have shown you, however, that heuristics can lead to errors. You should try to use this knowledge to examine your own thought processes when the time comes to make important judgments. You should be especially critical when you feel others might be trying to bias your judgments. Let's move now to the decisions you make, often on the basis of those judgments.

The Psychology of Decision Making

Let us begin with a powerful example of the way that psychological factors affect the decisions people make. Consider the problem given in part 1 of **Table 9.7**. Read the instructions, and then make your choice between Spot A and Spot B. Now read the version of the problem given in part 2. Would you like to change your choice?

In an experiment, students read one version of this problem (Shafir, 1993). When they were asked in part 1 which option they preferred, 67 percent of the students opted for Spot B. However, when students were asked in part 2 to cancel an option, this figure fell to 52 percent (that is, 48 percent said they would cancel Spot B). Why is this change odd? If you take a close look at the "prefer" and "cancel" versions of the problem, you will see that there is no difference in the information available in

Anchoring heuristic An insufficient adjustment up or down from an original starting value when judging the probable value of some event or outcome.

TABLE  9.7

The Effect of Psychological Factors on Decision Making

Part 1: *Prefer Version*	Part 2: *Cancel Version*
1. Imagine that you are planning a week vacation in a warm spot over spring break. You currently have two options that are reasonably priced. The travel brochure gives only a limited amount of information about the two options. Given the information available, which vacation spot would you prefer?	2. Imagine that you are planning a week vacation in a warm spot over spring break. You currently have two options that are reasonably priced, but you can no longer retain your reservation for both. The travel brochure gives only a limited amount of information about the two options. Given the information available, which reservation do you decide to cancel?
Spot A average weather average beaches medium-quality hotel medium-temperature water average nightlife	Spot A average weather average beaches medium-quality hotel medium-temperature water average nightlife
Spot B lots of sunshine gorgeous beaches and coral reefs ultramodern hotel very cold water very strong winds no nightlife	Spot B lots of sunshine gorgeous beaches and coral reefs ultramodern hotel very cold water very strong winds no nightlife

the two cases. On first pass, you might expect that the same information would lead to the same decision. But that's not what people do. It seems that the "prefer" question focuses people's attention on positive features of options—you're gathering evidence in favor of something—whereas the "cancel" question focuses attention on negative features of options—you're gathering evidence against something. Your decision may shift.

This straightforward example demonstrates that the way in which a question is phrased can have great consequences for the decision you will make (Slovic, 1995). This is why you need to understand psychological aspects of decision making: You need to be able to test your own decisions to see whether they hold up under careful analysis. In this case, you might ask yourself, "How would my choice change if I were asked to reject an option rather than to choose one?" If you find that your top preference is also your top candidate for rejection, you will have learned that the option has both many positive and many negative features. Now ask, "Is that acceptable?" This is a key step in developing your critical thinking skills.

THE FRAMING OF DECISIONS

One of the most natural ways to make a decision is to judge which option will bring about the biggest gain or which option will bring about the smallest loss. Thus, if we offer you $5 or $10, you will feel very little uncertainty that the better option is $10. What makes the situation a bit more complicated, however, is that the perception of a gain or a loss often depends on the way in which a deci-

sion is *framed*. A **frame** is a particular description of a choice. Suppose, for example, you were asked how happy you would be to get a $1,000 raise in your job. If you were expecting no raise at all, this would seem like a great gain, and you'd probably be quite happy. But suppose you'd been told several times to expect a raise of $10,000. Now how do you feel? Suddenly, you may feel as if you've lost money, because the $1,000 is less than what you had expected. You're not happy at all! In either case, you'd be getting $1,000 more a year—objectively, you'd be in exactly the same position—but the psychological effect is very different. That's why *reference points* are important in decision making (Kahneman, 1992). What seems like a gain or a loss will be determined in part by the expectations—a $0 raise or a $10,000 raise—to which a decision maker refers. (The decision, in this case, might be whether to stay in the job.)

Let's now take a look at a slightly more complex example in which framing has a sizable impact on the decisions people make. In Table 9.8, you are asked to imagine making a choice between surgery and radiation for treatment of lung cancer. First, read the *survival* frame for the problem and choose your preferred treatment; then read the *mortality* frame and see if you feel like changing your preference. Note that the data are objectively the same in

Frame A particular description of a choice; the perspective from which a choice is described or framed affects how a decision is made and which option is ultimately exercised.

TABLE 9.8

The Effect of Framing

Survival frame

Surgery. Of 100 people having surgery, 90 live through the postoperative period, 68 are alive at the end of the first year, and 34 are alive at the end of five years.

Radiation therapy. Of 100 people having radiation therapy, all live through the treatment, 77 are alive at the end of one year, and 22 are alive at the end of five years.

What do you choose: surgery or radiation?

Mortality frame

Surgery. Of 100 people having surgery, 10 die during surgery or the postoperative period, 32 die by the end of one year, and 66 die by the end of five years.

Radiation therapy. Of 100 people having radiation therapy, none die during treatment, 23 die by the end of one year, and 78 die by the end of five years.

What do you choose: surgery or radiation?

In what ways can salespeople frame their products to get prospective customers to consider them in a positive light?

Even so, participants who read the positive framing recommended an average fine of $40,153, whereas those who read the negative frame recommended a $78,968 fine (Dunegan, 1996). A few words had a major impact!

the two frames. The only difference is whether statistical information about the consequences of each treatment is presented in terms of survival rates or of mortality rates. When this decision was presented to participants, the focus on relative gains and losses had a marked effect on choice of treatment. Radiation therapy was chosen by only 18 percent of the participants who were given the survival frame, but by 44 percent of those given the mortality frame. This framing effect held equally for a group of clinic patients, statistically sophisticated business students, and experienced physicians (McNeil et al., 1982).

What makes this example important is that it shares the uncertainty you frequently have in real life.

HOW WE KNOW

JUDGMENTS ABOUT BAD BUSINESS PRACTICES Suppose you were asked to serve on a disciplinary panel to decide on the size of a fine against a company that had engaged in deceptive advertising practices. Should the way in which the case is framed influence your recommendation? In an experiment, a company's behavior was given either a *positive* spin (for example, "there was a 20 percent chance the organization didn't know its advertising was deceptive") or a *negative* spin (for example, "there was an 80 percent chance the organization knew its advertising was deceptive"). Do you see how both statements convey exactly the same underlying information?

How should you apply results like this one to your own life? Out in the real world, you must often make a decision based on your own, or someone else's, best guess at what likely outcomes will be. In these cases, try to think about the problem with *both* a gain frame and a loss frame. Suppose, for example, you are going to buy a new car. The salesperson will be inclined to frame everything as a gain: "Seventy-eight percent of the Xenons require no repairs in the first year!" You can reframe that to "Twenty-two percent require some repairs in the first year!" Would the new frame change how you feel about the situation? It's an exercise worth trying in real life.

The car salesperson is a good example of a situation in which someone is trying to frame information in a fashion that will have a desired effect on your decision. This, of course, is a regular part of your life. For example, as each election approaches, the two opposing candidates compete to have their framings of themselves and of the issues prevail among the voters. One candidate might say, "I believe in sticking with policies that have been successful." His opponent might counter, "He is afraid of new ideas." One candidate might say, "That policy will bring about economic growth." Her opponent might counter, "That policy will bring about environmental destruction." Often both claims are true—the same policy often will bring about both economic good and environmental harm. In this light, whichever frame seems more compelling may be largely a matter of personal history (Tversky & Kahneman, 1981; Vaughan & Seifert, 1992). Thus, your knowledge of framing effects can help you understand how people can come to such radically different decisions when they are faced with exactly the same evidence. If you want to understand other people's actions, try to think about how those individuals have framed a decision.

TABLE  9.9

Decision Aversion

A. Suppose you are considering buying a compact disk (CD) player, and have not yet decided what model to buy. You pass by a store that is having a 1-day clearance sale. They offer a popular SONY player for just $99, well below the list price. Do you

   1. buy the SONY player

   2. wait until you learn more about the various models

B. Suppose you are considering buying a compact disk (CD) player, and have not yet decided what model to buy. You pass by a store that is having a 1-day clearance sale. They offer a popular SONY player for just $99, and a top-of-the-line AIWA player for just $159, both well below the list price. Do you

   1. buy the AIWA player

   2. buy the SONY player

   3. wait until you learn more about the various models

DECISION AVERSION

Let's suppose that you have worked hard to evaluate a choice from the perspective of different frames. What happens next? You might discover that you have created a situation for yourself in which you will experience **decision aversion:** You might find that you will try hard to avoid making any decision at all. In **Table 9.9,** we provide an example of circumstances that can bring about an increasing unwillingness to make a decision. Consider the scenario in part A. Which would you choose? Researchers found that only 34 percent of their participants said they would wait for more information (Tversky & Shafir, 1992). Now consider the slightly altered scenario given in part B. Do you want to change your choice? In fact, 46 percent of the participants who read this version said they would wait for new information. How could this be? Ordinarily, you would expect that adding an option would decrease the share of the other options. If, for example, a third candidate enters a political race, you would expect that candidate to pull votes away from the original pair. Here, however, the addition of a third possibility increases the share of one of the original choices by 12 percent. What's going on?

The key to obtaining this effect is to make the decision hard. When the researchers tested participants on a version of the problem that provided a low-quality CD player as an extra option, only 24 percent said they would wait for more information—a decrease rather than an increase—which reflects the ease of choosing the Sony. The decision between the less expensive Sony model and the top-quality Aiwa, however, is hard. It's convenient to put the hard decision off, to wait for more information.

Although there are some individual differences, the general tendency to avoid tough decisions is very powerful in most people. Several psychological forces are at work (Beattie et al., 1994):

- People don't like to make decisions that will cause some people to have more and some people to have less of some desired good.

- People are able to anticipate the regret they will feel if the option they choose turns out worse than the option they didn't choose.

- People don't like to be accountable for decisions that lead to bad outcomes.

- People don't like to make decisions for other people.

We can turn this last principle around to define circumstances in which people are *decision seeking:* As much as people are averse to making decisions, they are generally happier to make them themselves than to let other people do so for them. This is something you should bear in mind. Try to avoid letting other people make important decisions for you. Try, as well, not to convince yourself that a decision is so hard that you can't make it at all. In most circumstances, you can count on your cognitive processes to provide you with accurate judgments. Use those judgments to make appropriate choices!

At the chapter's outset, we quoted Helen Keller proclaiming the "thrill of returning thought." As you've considered, in turn, the many types of cognitive processing—language use, visual cognition, problem solving, reasoning, judging, and deciding—we hope you've taken a moment to think about the thrills these capabilities provide to you. Try to learn from Helen Keller's experience not to take your cognitive processes for granted. Every chance you get, give some thought to your thought, reason about your reasoning, and so on. You will be reflecting on the essence of the human experience.

SUMMING UP

Research on judgment demonstrates that people often rely on heuristics rather than on formal analyses. The availability heuristic suggests that people make judgments based on the information most readily available from memory. The representativeness heuristic suggests that people make judgments by determining if an instance is representative of a category. The anchoring heuristic suggests that people make judgments by adjusting estimates from an original starting value. The way in which a question is framed has a major impact on the decisions that people make. Researchers find that difficult decisions are likely to result in decision aversion.

Decision aversion The tendency to avoid decision making; the tougher the decision, the greater the likelihood of decision aversion.

RECAPPING
MAIN POINTS

Studying Cognition

■ Cognitive psychologists study the mental processes and structures that enable you to perceive, use language, reason, solve problems, and make judgments and decisions.

■ Researchers use reaction time measures to decompose complex tasks into underlying mental processes.

Language Use

■ Language users both produce and understand language.

■ Speakers design their utterances to suit particular audiences.

■ Speech errors reveal many of the processes that go into speech planning.

■ Much of language understanding consists of using context to resolve ambiguities.

■ Memory representations of meaning begin with propositions supplemented with inferences.

■ The language individuals speak may play a role in determining how they think.

Visual Cognition

■ Visual representations can be used to supplement propositional representations.

■ Visual representations allow you to think about visual aspects of your environment.

■ People form visual representations that combine verbal and visual information.

Problem Solving and Reasoning

■ Problem solvers must define initial state, goal state, and the operations that get them from the initial to the goal state.

■ Deductive reasoning involves drawing conclusions from premises based on rules of logic.

■ Inductive reasoning involves inferring a conclusion from evidence based on its likelihood or probability.

Judging and Deciding

■ Much of judgment and decision making is guided by heuristics—mental shortcuts that can help individuals reach solutions quickly.

■ Availability, representativeness, and anchoring can all lead to errors when they are misapplied. Decision making is affected by the way in which different options are framed.

■ Because of psychological forces, people have a tendency to avoid making difficult decisions.

Key Terms

algorithm (p. 272)
anchoring heuristic (p. 284)
audience design (p. 259)
automatic processes (p. 257)
availability heuristic (p. 281)
belief-bias effect (p. 276)
cognition (p. 253)
cognitive processes (p. 253)
cognitive psychology (p. 253)
cognitive science (p. 253)
controlled processes (p. 257)
decision aversion (p. 287)
decision making (p. 281)
deductive reasoning (p. 276)
frame (p. 285)
functional fixedness (p. 275)
heuristics (p. 273)
inductive reasoning (p. 278)
inferences (p. 264)
judgment (p. 281)
language production (p. 259)
mental set (p. 279)
parallel processes (p. 256)
problem solving (p. 270)
problem space (p. 272)
reasoning (p. 270)
representativeness heuristic (p. 283)
serial processes (p. 256)
think-aloud protocols (p. 274)

intelligence and intelligence assessment

10

■ **WHAT IS ASSESSMENT?**
History of Assessment •
Basic Features of Formal
Assessment

■ **INTELLIGENCE
ASSESSMENT**
The Origins of Intelligence
Testing • IQ Tests

■ **PSYCHOLOGY IN THE 21ST
CENTURY: ASSESSMENT ON
THE WORLD WIDE WEB**

■ **THEORIES OF
INTELLIGENCE**
Psychometric Theories of
Intelligence • Sternberg's
Triarchic Theory of
Intelligence • Gardner's
Multiple Intelligences
and Emotional Intelligence

■ **THE POLITICS OF
INTELLIGENCE**
The History of
Group Comparisons •
Heredity and IQ •
Environments and IQ •
Culture and the Validity
of IQ Tests

■ **CREATIVITY**
Assessing Creativity and
the Link to Intelligence •
Exceptional Creativity
and Madness

■ **ASSESSMENT AND SOCIETY**

■ **RECAPPING MAIN POINTS**
Key Terms

In earlier, simpler times, you became established in a trade by following a steady path from apprentice to journeyman to master. You matured into a trusted artisan through a natural process, and you did not need to be worried about becoming "certified" and filling in computer-readable answer bubbles with a number-two pencil and responding "true" or "false" on a psychological test to the statement "I prefer tall women." No, a blacksmith was a blacksmith because he was a blacksmith; chandlers chandled and wheelwrights wrought wheels. In today's superrationalized, postindustrial world, however, we trust numbers more than experience, so to qualify for almost any money-making endeavor, from lawyer to interior decorator to cement mason, you may be obliged to take a test....

In an attempt to identify exactly what employers and professional organizations are looking for in their employees and members—and, incidentally, to identify exactly what work I might be suited for other than the underrationalized and basically preindustrial labor of freelance writing—I took thirty-one official or practice tests. The tests ranged from tests for bartenders, postal machine mechanics, radio announcers, and travel agents to tests for addiction specialists, geologists, foreign service officers, and FBI agents.

My results were not always encouraging; I passed only three tests.

In his composition entitled "You'll never groom dogs in this town again!" essayist Henry Alford (1993) describes several of the tests and trials he underwent in search of gainful employment. Anyone who has ever made the rounds, trying to find a job, will find much that is familiar in Alford's humorous accounts. Employers use a wide variety of tests to determine each applicant's "potential." Sometimes it's quite hard to see the relationship between the test and the occupation, but almost always some expert has convinced the company that the test measures relevant differences among candidates.

If you grew up in the United States, it is likely that your "potential" was measured long before you entered the job market: In most school districts, teachers and administrators attempt, very early in your life, to measure your *intelligence*. The goal, most often, is to match students with classroom work that makes appropriate demands. However, as you've almost certainly observed, people's lives often seem to be affected by intelligence testing in areas well outside the classroom.

In this chapter, we will examine the foundations and uses of intelligence assessment. We will review the contributions psychologists have made to the understanding of individual differences in the areas of intelligence. We will also discuss the types of controversies that almost inevitably arise when people begin to interpret these differences. Our focus will be on how intelligence tests work, what makes any test useful, and why they do not always do the job they were intended to do. Finally, we will conclude on a personal note, by considering the role of psychological assessment in society.

We begin now with a brief overview of the general practice of psychological assessment.

▪ What Is Assessment?

Psychological assessment is the use of specified testing procedures to evaluate the abilities, behaviors, and personal qualities of people. Psychological assessment is often referred to as the measurement of *individual differences*, because the majority of assessments specify how an individual is different from or similar to other people on a given dimension. Before we examine in

▪ **Psychological assessment** The use of specified procedures to evaluate the abilities, behaviors, and personal qualities of people.

detail the basic features of psychological testing, let's outline the history of assessment. This historical overview will help you to understand both the uses and limitations of assessment, as well as prepare you to appreciate some current-day controversies.

History of Assessment

The development of formal tests and procedures for assessment is a relatively new enterprise in Western psychology, coming into wide use only in the early 1900s. However, long before Western psychology began to devise tests to evaluate people, assessment techniques were commonplace in ancient China. In fact, China employed a sophisticated program of civil service testing over 4,000 years ago—officials were required to demonstrate their competence every third year at an oral examination. Two thousand years later, during the Han Dynasty, written civil service tests were used to measure competence in the areas of law, the military, agriculture, and geography. During the Ming Dynasty (A.D. 1368–1644), public officials were chosen on the basis of their performance at three stages of an objective selection procedure. During the first stage, examinations were given at the local level. The 4 percent who passed these tests had to endure the second stage: nine days and nights of essay examinations on the classics. The 5 percent who passed the essay exams were allowed to complete a final stage of tests conducted at the nation's capital.

China's selection procedures were observed and described by British diplomats and missionaries in the early 1800s. Modified versions of China's system were soon adopted by the British and later by the Americans for the selection of civil service personnel (Wiggins, 1973).

The key figure in the development of Western intelligence testing was an upper-class Englishman, **Sir Francis Galton.** His book *Hereditary Genius,* published in 1869, greatly influenced subsequent thinking on the methods, theories, and practices of testing. Galton, a half cousin to Charles Darwin, attempted to apply Darwinian evolutionary theory to the study of human abilities. He was interested in how and why people differ in their abilities. He wondered why some people were gifted and successful—like him—while many others were not.

Galton was the first to postulate four important ideas about the assessment of intelligence. First, differences in intelligence were *quantifiable* in terms of degrees of intelligence. In other words, numerical values could be assigned to distinguish among different people's levels of intelligence. Second, differences among people formed a *bell-shaped curve,* or *normal distribution.* On a bell-shaped curve, most people's scores cluster in the middle and fewer are found toward the two extremes of genius and mental deficiency (we return to

What important ideas about the assessment of intelligence are credited to Sir Francis Galton (1822–1911)?

the bell-shaped curve later in the chapter). Third, intelligence, or mental ability, could be measured by objective tests, tests on which each question had only one "right" answer. And fourth, the precise extent to which two sets of test scores were related could be determined by a statistical procedure he called *co-relations,* now known as *correlations.* These ideas proved to be of lasting value.

Unfortunately, Galton postulated a number of ideas that proved considerably more controversial. He believed, for example, that genius was inherited. In his view, talent, or eminence, ran in families; nurture had only a minimal effect on intelligence. In his view, intelligence was related to Darwinian species' fitness and, somehow, ultimately to one's moral worth. Galton attempted to base public policy on the concept of genetically superior and inferior people. He started the *eugenics* movement, which advocated improving the human species by applying evolutionary theory to encouraging biologically superior people to interbreed while discouraging biologically inferior people from having offspring. Galton wrote, "There exists a sentiment, for the most part quite unreasonable, against the gradual extinction of an inferior race" (Galton, 1883/1907, p. 200).

These controversial ideas were endorsed and extended later by many who argued forcefully that the intellectually superior race should propagate at the expense of those with inferior minds. Among the proponents of these ideas were American psychologists Goddard and Terman, whose theories we review later, and, of course, Nazi dictator Adolf Hitler. We will also see later in the chapter that remnants of these elitist ideas are still being proposed today.

Sir Francis Galton's work created a context for contemporary intelligence assessment. Let's now see what features define circumstances of formal assessment.

Basic Features of Formal Assessment

To be useful for classifying individuals or for selecting those with particular qualities, a **formal assessment** procedure should meet three requirements. The assessment instrument should be (1) reliable, (2) valid, and (3) standardized. If it fails to meet these requirements, we cannot be sure whether the conclusions of the assessment can be trusted. Although this chapter focuses on intelligence assessment, formal assessment procedures apply to all types of psychological testing. To ensure that you'll understand the broad application of these principles, we will draw on examples both from intelligence testing and other domains of psychological assessment.

The wrong way to measure split-half reliability.

RELIABILITY

Reliability is the extent to which an assessment instrument can be trusted to give consistent scores. If you stepped on your bathroom scale three times in the same morning and it gave you a different reading each time, the scale would not be doing its job. You would call it *unreliable* because you could not count on it to give consistent results. Of course, if you ate a big meal in between two weighings, you wouldn't expect the scale to produce the same result. That is, a measurement device can be considered reliable or unreliable only to the extent that the underlying concept it is measuring should remain unchanged.

One straightforward way to find out if a test is reliable is to calculate its **test–retest reliability**—a measure of the correlation between the scores of the same people, on the same test, given on two different occasions. A perfectly reliable test will yield a correlation coefficient of +1.00. This means that the identical pattern of scores

emerges both times. The same people who got the highest and lowest scores the first time do so again. A totally unreliable test results in a 0.00 correlation coefficient. That means there is no relationship between the first set of scores and the second set. Someone who initially got the top score gets a completely different score the second time. As the correlation coefficient moves higher (toward the ideal of +1.00), the test is increasingly reliable.

There are two other ways to assess reliability. One is to administer alternate, **parallel forms** of a test instead of giving the same test twice. Using parallel forms reduces the effects of direct practice of the test questions, memory of the test questions, and the desire of an individual to appear consistent from one test to the next. Reliable tests yield comparable scores on parallel forms of the test. The other measure of reliability is the **internal consistency** of responses on a single test. For example, we can compare a person's score on the odd-numbered items of a test with the score on the even-numbered items. A reliable test yields the same score for each of its halves. It is then said to have high internal consistency on this measure of **split-half reliability**.

In most circumstances, not only should the measurement device itself be reliable, but so should the method for using the device. Suppose researchers wished to observe children in a classroom in order to assess different levels of aggressive play. The researchers might develop a *coding scheme* that would allow them to make appropriate distinctions. The scheme would be reliable to the extent that all the people who viewed the same behavior would give highly similar ratings to the same children. This is one of the reasons that quite a bit of training is required before individuals can carry out accurate psychological assessment. They must learn to apply systems of distinctions in a reliable fashion.

VALIDITY

The **validity** of a test is the degree to which it measures what an assessor intends it to measure. A valid test of intelligence measures that trait and predicts performance

- **Formal assessment** The systematic procedures and measurement instruments used by trained professionals to assess an individual's functioning, aptitudes, abilities, or mental states.
- **Reliability** The degree to which a test produces similar scores each time it is used; stability or consistency of the scores produced by an instrument.
- **Test–retest reliability** A measure of the correlation between the scores of the same people on the same test given on two different occasions.
- **Parallel forms** Different versions of a test used to assess test reliability; the change of forms reduces effects of direct practice, memory, or the desire of an individual to appear consistent on the same items.
- **Internal consistency** A measure of reliability; the degree to which a test yields similar scores across its different parts, such as on odd versus even items.
- **Split-half reliability** A measure of the correlation between test takers' performance on different halves (e.g., odd- and even-numbered items) of a test.
- **Validity** The extent to which a test measures what it was intended to measure.

in situations where intelligence is important. Scores on a valid measure of creativity reflect actual creativity, not drawing ability or moods. In general, then, validity reflects a test's ability to make accurate predictions about behaviors or outcomes related to the purpose or design of the test. Three important types of validity are *face validity, criterion validity,* and *construct validity.*

The first type of validity is based on the surface *content* of a test. When test items appear to be directly related to the attribute of interest, the test has **face validity.** Face-valid tests are very straightforward—they simply ask what the test maker needs to know: How anxious do you feel? Are you creative? The person taking the test is expected to answer accurately and honestly. Unfortunately, face validity is often not sufficient to ensure accurate measurement. First, people's perceptions of themselves may not be accurate, or they may not know how they should rate themselves in comparison to other people. Second, a test that too obviously measures some attribute may allow test takers to manipulate the impression they make. Consider the classic case of institutionalized mental patients who did not want to be released from their familiar, structured environment.

How should test-givers choose what types of assessments to use?

HOW WE KNOW

PATIENTS MANIPULATE PSYCHIATRISTS' ASSESSMENTS These long-term schizophrenic patients were interviewed by the staff about how disturbed they were. When they were given a *transfer* interview to assess if they were well enough to be moved to an open ward, these patients gave generally positive self-references. However, when the purpose of the interview was to assess their suitability for *discharge,* the patients gave more negative self-references, because they did not want to be discharged. Psychiatrists who rated the interview data, without awareness of this experimental variation in the purpose of the interview, judged those who gave more negative self-references as more severely disturbed and recommended against their discharge. So the patients achieved the assessment outcome they wanted. The psychiatrists' assessment may also have been influenced by their perspective that anyone who wanted to stay in a mental hospital must be very disturbed (Braginsky & Braginsky, 1967).

This example makes it particularly clear that test givers cannot rely only on measures that have face validity. Let's consider other types of validity that overcome some of these limitations.

To assess the **criterion validity** (also known as **predictive validity**) of a test, psychologists compare a person's score on the test with his or her score on some other standard, or *criterion,* associated with what the test measures. For example, if a test is designed to predict success in college, then college grades would be an appropriate

criterion. If the test scores correlate highly with college grades, then the test has criterion validity. A major task of test developers is to find appropriate, measurable criteria. Once criterion validity has been demonstrated for an assessment device, researchers feel confident using the device to make future predictions. This is the logic college admissions officers use when they ask you for things like SAT scores. In the past, SAT scores have been shown to correlate positively with some aspects of college performance. On that basis, administrators use them to make predictions about your college career.

The conditions under which a test is valid may be very specific, so it is always important to ask about a test, "For what purpose is it valid?" Knowing which other measures a test does and does not correlate with may reveal something new about the measures, the construct, or the complexity of human behavior. For example, suppose you design a test to measure the ability of medical students to cope with stress. You then find that scores on that test correlate well with students' ability to cope with classroom stress. You presume your test will also correlate with students' ability to deal with stressful hospital emergencies, but you discover it does not. Because you have demonstrated some validity, you have learned something both about your test—the circumstances in which it is valid—and about your construct—different categories of stressors have different consequences. You would then modify your test to take account of the kinds of special stressors found in hospital emergencies.

Consider for a moment the relationship between validity and reliability. While reliability is measured by the degree to which a test correlates with itself (administered at different times or using different items), validity is measured

Face validity The degree to which test items appear to be directly related to the attribute the researcher wishes to measure.

Criterion validity The degree to which test scores indicate a result on a specific measure that is consistent with some other criterion of the characteristic being assessed; also known as predictive validity.

Predictive validity See criterion validity.

How would you feel if someone used your adult height to assess intelligence? The measure would be reliable, but would it be valid?

by the degree to which the test correlates with something external to it (another test, a behavioral criterion, or judges' ratings). Usually, a test that is not reliable is also not valid, because a test that cannot predict itself will be unable to predict anything else. For example, if your class took a test of aggressiveness today and scores were uncorrelated with scores from a parallel form of the test tomorrow (demonstrating unreliability), it is unlikely that the scores from either day would predict which students had fought or argued most frequently over a week's time: After all, the two sets of test scores would not even make the same prediction! On the other hand, it is quite possible for a test to be highly reliable without being valid. Suppose, for example, we decided to use your adult height as a measure of intelligence. Do you see why that would be reliable but not valid?

NORMS AND STANDARDIZATION

So we have a reliable and valid test, but we still need *norms* to provide a context for interpreting different test scores. Suppose, for example, you get a score of 18 on a test designed to reveal how depressed you are. What does that mean? Are you a little depressed, not at all depressed, or about averagely depressed? To find out what your score means, you would want to compare your individual score with typical scores, or statistical **norms**, of other students. You would check the test norms to see what the usual range of scores is and what the average is for students of your age and sex. That would provide you with a context for interpreting your depression score.

You probably encountered test norms when you received your scores on aptitude tests, such as the SAT. The

norms told you how your scores compared with those of other students and helped you interpret how well you had done relative to that *normative population*. Group norms are most useful for interpreting individual scores when the comparison group shares important qualities with the individuals tested, such as age, social class, culture, and experience.

For norms to be meaningful, everyone must take the same test under standardized circumstances. **Standardization** is the administration of a testing device to all persons, in the same way, under the same conditions. The need for standardization sounds obvious, but it does not always occur in practice. Some people may be allowed more time than others, be given clearer or more detailed instructions, be permitted to ask questions, or be motivated by a tester to perform better. Consider the experience of one of your authors:

> As a graduate student at Yale, I administered a scale to assess children's degree of test anxiety in grade-school classes. Before starting, one teacher told her class, "We're going to have some fun with this new kind of question game this nice man will play with you." A teacher in another classroom prepared her class for the same assessment by cautioning, "This psychologist from Yale University is going to give you a test to see what you are thinking; I hope you will do well and show how good our class is!" (Zimbardo, personal communication, 1958)

Could you directly compare the scores of the children in these two classes on this "same" test? The answer is no, because the test was not administered in a standardized way. In this case, the children in the second class scored higher on test anxiety. (You're probably not surprised!) When procedures do not include explicit instructions about the way to administer the test or the way to score the results, it is difficult to interpret what a given test score means or how it relates to any comparison group.

We have now reviewed some of the concerns researchers have when they construct a test and find out whether it is indeed testing what they wish to test. They must assure themselves that the test is reliable and valid. They must also specify the standard conditions under which it should be administered, so that resulting norms have meaning. Therefore, you should evaluate any test score you get in terms of the test's reliability and validity, the norms of performance, and the degree of standardization of the circumstances in which you took the test.

We are now ready to turn to the measurement of intelligence.

Norms Standards based on measurements of a large group of people; used for comparing the scores of an individual with those of others within a well-defined group.

Standardization A set of uniform procedures for treating each participant in a test, interview, or experiment, or for recording data.

SUMMING UP

Psychological assessment focuses on individual differences, examining the ways in which an individual is similar to or different from other people. Forms of assessment were developed in ancient China; in the Western world, Sir Francis Galton pioneered the theory and practice of intelligence testing. Unfortunately, he also originated myths about biologically "superior" and "inferior" peoples.

Appropriate tests are both reliable—they assign the same scores to the same people, over time—and valid—they give accurate information about the construct they are intended to measure. It is also important that the administration of tests be standardized and that test scores be compared to relevant population norms.

Intelligence Assessment

How intelligent are you or your friends? To answer this question, you must begin by defining **intelligence**. Doing so is not an easy task, but a group of 52 intelligence researchers concurred on this general definition: "Intelligence is a very general mental capability that, among other things, involves the ability to reason, plan, solve problems, think abstractly, comprehend complex ideas, learn quickly and learn from experience" (Gottfredson, 1997a, p. 13). Given this range of capabilities, it should be clear immediately why controversy has almost always surrounded how intelligence is measured. The way in which theorists conceptualize intelligence and higher mental functioning greatly influences the way they try to assess it (Sternberg, 1994). Some psychologists believe that human intelligence can be quantified and reduced to a single score. Others argue that intelligence has many components that should be separately assessed. Still others say that there are actually several distinct kinds of intelligence, across different domains of experience.

In this section, we will describe how tests of intelligence mesh with these different conceptions of intelligence. Let's begin by considering the historical context in which interest in intelligence and intelligence testing first arose.

The Origins of Intelligence Testing

The year 1905 marked the first published account of a workable intelligence test. **Alfred Binet** had responded to the call of the French minister of public instruction for the creation of more effective teaching methods for developmentally disabled children. Binet and his colleague Theophile Simon believed that measuring a child's intellectual ability was necessary for planning an instructional program. Binet attempted to devise an objective test of intellectual performance that could be used to classify and separate developmentally disabled from normal schoolchildren. He hoped that such a test would reduce the school's reliance on the more subjective, and perhaps biased, evaluations of teachers.

To *quantify*—measure—intellectual performance, Binet designed age-appropriate problems or test items on which many children's responses could be compared. The problems on the test were chosen so that they could be scored objectively as correct or incorrect, could vary in content, were not heavily influenced by differences in children's environments, and assessed judgment and reasoning rather than rote memory (Binet, 1911).

Children of various ages were tested, and the average score for normal children at each age was computed. Then each individual child's performance was compared with the average for other children of his or her age. Test results were expressed in terms of the average age at which normal children achieved a particular score. This measure was called the **mental age.** For instance, when a child's score equaled the average score of a group of 5-year-olds, the child was said to have a *mental age of* 5, regardless of his or her actual **chronological age,** the number of years since birth.

There are four important features of Binet's approach. First, he interpreted scores on his test as an estimate of *current performance* and not as a measure of *innate intelligence.* Second, he wanted the test scores to be used to identify children who needed special help and not to *stigmatize* them. Third, he emphasized that training and opportunity could affect intelligence, and he sought to identify areas of performance in which special education could help disadvantaged children. Finally, he constructed his test empirically—he collected data to see if it was valid—rather than tying it to a particular theory of intelligence.

Binet's successful development of an intelligence test had great impact in the United States. A unique combination of historical events and social-political forces had prepared the United States for an explosion of interest in assessing mental ability. At the beginning of the 20th century, the United States was a nation in turmoil. As a result of global economic, social, and political conditions, millions of immigrants entered the country. New universal education laws flooded schools with students. Some form of assessment was needed to identify, document, and classify immigrant adults and schoolchildren (Chapman, 1988). When World War I began, millions of volunteers marched into recruiting stations. Recruiters needed to determine who of these many people had the ability to learn quickly and benefit from special leadership training. New nonverbal, group-administered tests of mental

Intelligence The global capacity to profit from experience and to go beyond given information about the environment.

Mental age In Binet's measure of intelligence, the age at which a child is performing intellectually, expressed in terms of the average age at which normal children achieve a particular score.

Chronological age The number of months or years since an individual's birth.

ability were used to evaluate over 1.7 million recruits. A group of prominent psychologists, including Lewis Terman, Edward Thorndike, and Robert Yerkes, responded to the wartime emergency and designed these tests in only one month's time (Lennon, 1985).

One consequence of this large-scale testing program was that the American public came to accept the idea that intelligence tests could differentiate people in terms of leadership ability and other socially important characteristics. This acceptance led to the widespread use of tests in schools and industry. Assessment was seen as a way to inject order into a chaotic society and as an inexpensive, democratic way to separate those who could benefit from education or military leadership training from those who could not. To facilitate the wide-scale use of intelligence testing, researchers strove for more broadly applicable testing procedures.

IQ Tests

Although Binet began the standardized assessment of intellectual ability in France, U.S. psychologists soon took the lead. They also developed the IQ, or intelligence quotient. The IQ was a numerical, standardized measure of intelligence. Two families of individually administered IQ tests are used widely today: the Stanford–Binet scales and the Wechsler scales.

THE STANFORD–BINET INTELLIGENCE SCALE

Stanford University's **Lewis Terman,** a former public school administrator, appreciated the importance of Binet's method for assessing intelligence. He adapted Binet's test questions for U.S. schoolchildren, he standardized the administration of the test, and he developed age-level norms by giving the test to thousands of children. In 1916, he published the Stanford Revision of the Binet Tests, commonly referred to as the *Stanford–Binet Intelligence Scale* (Terman, 1916).

With his new test, Terman provided a base for the concept of the **intelligence quotient,** or **IQ** (a term coined by Stern, 1914). The IQ was the ratio of mental age to chronological age multiplied by 100 to eliminate decimals:

$$IQ = \text{mental age} \div \text{chronological age} \times 100$$

A child with a chronological age of 8 whose test scores revealed a mental age of 10 had an IQ of 125 ($10 \div 8 \times 100 = 125$), while a child of that same chronological age who performed at the level of a 6-year-old had an IQ of 75 ($6 \div 8 \times 100 = 75$). Individuals who performed at the mental age equivalent to their chronological age had IQs of 100. Thus, the score of 100 was considered to be the average IQ.

The new Stanford–Binet test soon became a standard instrument in clinical psychology, psychiatry, and educa-

tional counseling. The Stanford–Binet contains a series of subtests, each tailored for a particular mental age. A series of minor revisions were made on these subtests in 1937, 1960, and 1972, to achieve three goals: (1) to extend the range of the test to measure the IQ of very young children and very intelligent adults; (2) to update vocabulary items that had changed in difficulty with changes in society; and (3) to update the norms, or age-appropriate average scores (Terman & Merrill, 1937, 1960, 1972). The most recent, fourth edition of the Stanford–Binet test (Thorndike et al., 1986) furthers the goal of improving the test's validity. This newest Stanford–Binet provides accurate IQ estimates for individuals in the normal range of performance as well as for those individuals who are either mentally impaired or mentally gifted (Laurent et al., 1992).

Note that IQ scores are no longer derived by dividing mental age by chronological age. If you took the test today, your score would be added up and directly compared with the scores of other people your age. An IQ of 100 is "average" and would indicate that 50 percent of those your age had earned lower scores (see **Figure 10.1**). Scores between 90 and 110 are now labeled "normal," and those above 120 are "superior." When individuals below the age of 18 obtain valid IQ scores of 70 to 75 or below, they meet one criterion for a classification of **mental retardation.** However, as shown in **Table 10.1,** to be considered mental retarded, individuals must also demonstrate limitations in their ability to bring *adaptive skills* to bear on life tasks (American Association on Mental Retardation [AAMR], 1992). In earlier times, IQ scores were used to classify mental retardation as "mild," "moderate," "severe," and "profound" (see Figure 10.1). However, the contemporary emphasis on adaptive skills has prompted experts to abandon that terminology in favor of more precise descriptions such as "a person with mental retardation with extensive supports needed in the areas of social skills and self-direction" or "a person with mental retardation who needs limited supports in communication and social skills" (AAMR, 1992, p. 34).

THE WECHSLER INTELLIGENCE SCALES

David Wechsler of Bellevue Hospital in New York set out to correct the dependence on verbal items in the assessment of adult intelligence. In 1939, he published the Wechsler–Bellevue Intelligence Scale, which combined

Intelligence quotient (IQ) An index derived from standardized tests of intelligence; originally obtained by dividing an individual's mental age by chronological age and then multiplying by 100; now directly computed as an IQ test score.

Mental retardation Condition in which individuals have IQ scores 70 to 75 or below and also demonstrate limitations in the ability to bring adaptive skills to bear on life tasks.

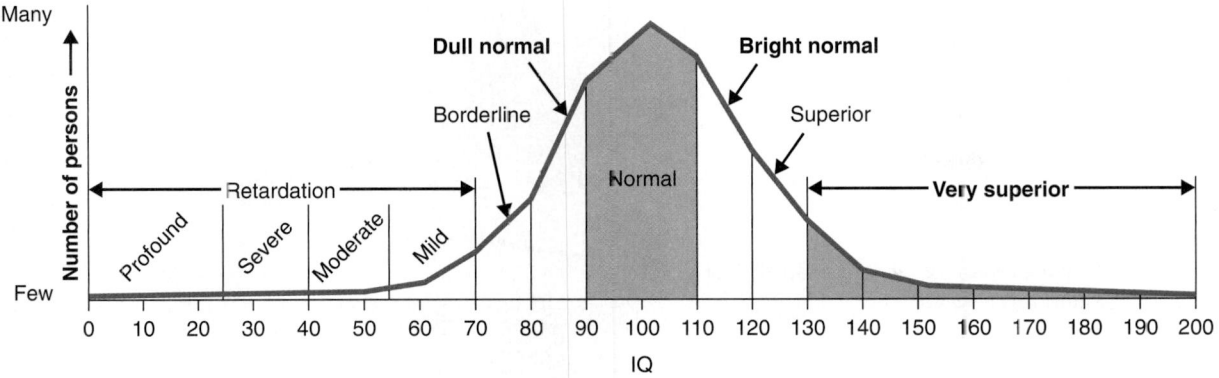

FIGURE  10.1

Distribution of IQ Scores among a Large Sample

IQ scores are normed so that a score of 100 is the population average (as many people score below 100 as score above 100). Scores between 90 and 110 are labeled normal. Scores above 120 are considered to be "superior" or "very superior"; scores below 70 represent increasing levels of mental disability.

verbal subtests with nonverbal, or performance, subtests. Thus, in addition to an overall IQ score, people were given separate estimates of verbal IQ and nonverbal IQ. After a few changes, the test was retitled the *Wechsler Adult Intelligence Scale*—the WAIS in 1955, and the revised WAIS-R today (Wechsler, 1981).

There are six *verbal* subtests of the WAIS-R: Information, Vocabulary, Comprehension, Arithmetic, Similarities (stating how two things are alike), and Digit Span (repeating a series of digits after the examiner). These tests are both written and oral. The five *performance* subtests involve manipulation of materials and have little or

TABLE 10.1

Diagnosis of Mental Retardation

Mental retardation is diagnosed if:

- The individual's IQ is approximately 70 to 75 or below.

- There are significant disabilities in two or more adaptive skill areas:

  Communication. Skills related to the ability to comprehend and express information through linguistic means and nonlinguistic means (for example, facial expressions).

  Self-Care. Skills involved in toileting, eating, dressing, hygiene, and grooming.

  Home Living. Skills related to functioning within a home, such as housekeeping and daily scheduling.

  Social. Skills related to social exchanges with other individuals.

  Community Use. Skills related to the appropriate use of community resources, such as shopping in grocery stores and using public transportation.

  Self-Direction. Skills relating to making choices and seeking appropriate assistance.

  Health and Safety. Skills relating to maintaining one's health and safety.

  Functional Academics. Skills relating to the acquisition of academic subjects (such as reading and mathematics) that contribute to the goal of independent living.

  Leisure. Skills related to the development of leisure and recreational interests.

  Work. Skills related to holding a part- or full-time job or jobs.

- The age of onset is below 18.

Source: Adapted from American Association on Mental Retardation. 1992, pp. 24, 40–41.

TABLE 10.2

Questions and Problems Similar to Those on the WAIS-R

Verbal Subtests

Information	Who wrote *The Great Gatsby?*
Comprehension	What does it mean when people say "Birds of a feather flock together"?
Arithmetic	If you paid $8.50 for a movie ticket and $2.75 for a bucket of popcorn, how much change would you have left from a $20 bill?
Similarities	In what ways are airplanes and submarines alike?
Digit span	Repeat the following numbers: 3 2 7 5 9.
Vocabulary	What does *emulate* mean?

Performance Subtests

Digit Symbol	The examiner presents a key that matches digits (e.g., 1, 2, 3) with symbols (e.g., Φ, Θ, ∀). The test-taker uses the key to complete a chart that gives just digits or symbols.
Picture Completion	The test taker examines a picture and says what is missing (e.g., a horse without a mane).
Block Design	The test taker uses patterned blocks to reproduce designs provided by the examiner.
Picture Arrangement	The test taker puts a series of cartoonlike pictures into order so that they tell a story.
Object Assembly	The examiner gives the test taker a set of cardboard puzzle pieces. The test taker arranges the pieces to form a picture of a common object.

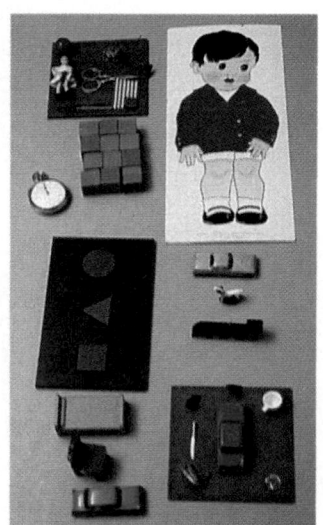

FIGURE 10.2

A psychologist administers an intelligence test to a 4-year-old child. The performance part of the test includes a block design task, an object completion task, and a shape identification task. Why is performance an important component of an IQ assessment?

no verbal content. In the Block Design test, for example, an individual tries to reproduce designs shown on cards by fitting together blocks with colored sides. The Digit Symbol test provides a key that matches nine symbols to nine numeric digits, and the task is to write the appropriate digits under the symbols on another page. Other performance tests include Picture Arrangement, Picture Completion, and Object Assembly. If you were to take the WAIS-R, you would perform all 11 subtests, and receive 3 scores: a Verbal IQ, a Performance IQ, and an overall, or Full Scale, IQ. **Table 10.2** provides examples of the types of questions you would find on the WAIS-R.

The WAIS-R is designed for people 18 years and older, but similar tests have been developed for children (see **Figure 10.2**). The *Wechsler Intelligence Scale for Children— Third Edition* (WISC-III; Wechsler, 1991) is suited for children ages 6 to 17, and the *Wechsler Preschool and Primary Scale of Intelligence—Revised* (WPPSI-R; Wechsler, 1989) for children ages 4 to 6½ years. The recent revisions of both of these tests have made the materials more color-

ful, more contemporary, and more enjoyable for children. Both tests have proven to be reliable and valid measures (Little, 1992; Sattler & Atkinson, 1993).

The WAIS-R, the WISC-III, and the WPPSI-R form a family of intelligence tests that yield a Verbal IQ, a Performance IQ, and a Full Scale IQ at all age levels. In addition, they provide comparable subtest scores that allow researchers to track the development over time of more specific intellectual abilities. For this reason, the Wechsler scales are particularly valuable when the same individual is to be tested at different ages—for example, when a child's progress in response to different educational programs is monitored.

SUMMING UP

Modern intelligence testing originated with Alfred Binet's attempts to identify students who needed extra assistance in school. Binet proposed that each child be classified

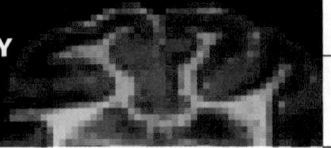

ASSESSMENT ON THE WORLD WIDE WEB

After reading a chapter on intelligence, students often wonder how they would do if they took an IQ test. Nowadays, it's pretty easy for you to visit one of several Web sites to click through a test and get *some* IQ score. Do the numbers you get mean much of anything? We'll answer that question by reviewing some of the concepts we've introduced in this chapter.

To give our analysis, we needed some data—so we asked a friend, whom we'll call Poindexter, to take some on-line IQ tests for us. The first site he visited had four different tests, which gave us the opportunity to assess reliability. Recall that reliability is about consistency: Does each test, which claims to be measuring the same thing, yield very nearly the same score? In fact, Poindexter's four scores were 116, 117, 129, and 130. If you refer back to Figure 10.1, you'll see that all these scores indicate that Poindexter is above average (how nice for Poindexter), but two place him in "bright normal" and two place him right at the border of "superior" and "very

superior." These supposed IQ tests are not particularly reliable.

If the tests aren't reliable, they can't be valid. But let's suppose they were reliable. Let's consider why, in any case, we'd be concerned about their validity: To what extent do the tests measure what they're supposed to measure? The IQ scores at the site Poindexter visited were calculated by comparing his performance (the number he got right out of 20 questions) to the performance of those individuals who had preceded him to the site. By assuming a bell-shaped distribution like the one shown in Figure 10.1, the site estimates IQ. Can you see the problems here? First, we have no reason to believe that, for the people who visit this site, the average IQ (measured by a traditional, reliable off-line test) would be, as it should be, 100. Doesn't it seem likely that there would be self-selection among the people who would be likely to take IQ tests on the Web? Second, we have no reason to believe that everyone took the tests under the same standard circumstances. For example, the tests rely somewhat on vocabu-

lary questions. How can we be sure that people didn't pull out a handy dictionary (or access one on-line) to enhance their scores? ("Look, Ma, I always told you I was a genius!")

The World Wide Web provides a vast number of opportunities for you to assess IQ as well as other performance and personality constructs. You should use the knowledge you've gained in this chapter to do your own careful assessment of the reliability and validity of any scores you obtain on the Web.

Meanwhile, Poindexter has become something of an on-line IQ addict. His best score so far is a 159 on a "European IQ test." Poindexter is convinced that 159 is a valid measure of his IQ. Are you convinced too?

Web sites:

- www.2h.com/Tests/iq.phtml
  A site that gathers together a large number of tests

- www.majon.com/iq.html
  Multiple tests on one site

- cech.cesnet.cz/IQ/index.php
  The European IQ test

---

with respect to his or her mental age. IQ scores are computed as a function of mental age divided by chronological age. Lewis Terman and David Wechsler developed new measures of IQ.

Theories of Intelligence

So far, we have seen some of the ways in which intelligence has been measured. You are now in a position to ask yourself: Do these tests capture everything that is meant by the word *intelligence*? Do these tests capture all abilities you believe constitute your own intelligence? To help you to think about those questions, we now review theories of intelligence. As you read about each theory, ask yourself whether its proponents would be comfortable using IQ as a measure of intelligence.

Psychometric Theories of Intelligence

Psychometric theories of intelligence originated in much the same philosophical atmosphere that gave rise to IQ tests. **Psychometrics** is the field of psychology that specializes in mental testing in any of its facets, including personality assessment, intelligence evaluation, and aptitude measurement. Thus, psychometric approaches are intimately related to methods of testing. These theories examine the *statistical relationships* between different measures of ability, such as the 11 subtests of the WAIS-R, and then make inferences about the nature of human intelligence on the basis of those relationships. The technique used

Psychometrics The field of psychology that specializes in mental testing.

most frequently is called *factor analysis,* a statistical procedure that detects a smaller number of dimensions, clusters, or factors within a larger set of independent variables. The goal of factor analysis is to identify the basic psychological dimensions of the concept being investigated. Of course, a statistical procedure only identifies statistical regularities; it is up to psychologists to suggest and defend interpretations of those regularities.

Charles Spearman carried out an early and influential application of factor analysis in the domain of intelligence. Spearman discovered that the performance of individuals on each of a variety of intelligence tests was highly correlated. From this pattern he concluded that there is a factor of *general intelligence,* or *g,* underlying all intelligent performance (Spearman, 1927). Each individual domain also has associated with it specific skills that Spearman called *s.* For example, a person's performance on tests of vocabulary or arithmetic depends both on his or her general intelligence and on domain-specific abilities.

Raymond Cattell (1963), using more advanced factor analytic techniques, determined that general intelligence can be broken down into two relatively independent

> **g** According to Spearman, the factor of general intelligence underlying all intelligent performance.
>
> **Crystallized intelligence** The facet of intelligence involving the knowledge a person has already acquired and the ability to access that knowledge; measures by vocabulary, arithmetic, and general information tests.
>
> **Fluid intelligence** The aspect of intelligence that involves the ability to see complex relationships and solve problems.

components, which he called crystallized and fluid intelligence. **Crystallized intelligence** involves the knowledge a person has already acquired and the ability to access that knowledge; it is measured by tests of vocabulary, arithmetic, and general information. **Fluid intelligence** is the ability to see complex relationships and solve problems; it is measured by tests of block designs and spatial visualization in which the background information needed to solve a problem is included or readily apparent. Crystallized intelligence allows you to cope well with your life's recurring, concrete challenges; fluid intelligence helps you attack novel, abstract problems.

J. P. Guilford (1961) used factor analysis to examine the demands of many intelligence-related tasks. His *structure of intellect* model specifies three features of intellectual tasks: the *content,* or type of information; the *product,* or form in which information is represented; and the *operation,* or type of mental activity performed.

As shown in **Figure 10.3,** there are five kinds of content in this model—visual, auditory, symbolic, semantic, and behavioral; six kinds of products—units, classes, relations, systems, transformations, and implications; and five kinds of operations—evaluation, convergent production, divergent production, memory, and cognition. Each task performed by the intellect can be identified according to the particular types of content, products, and operations involved. Further, Guilford believes that each content-product-operation combination (each small cube in the model) represents a distinct mental ability. For example, as Figure 10.3 shows, a test of vocabulary would assess your ability for *cognition* of *units* with *semantic content.* Learning a dance routine, on the other hand, requires *memory* for *behavioral systems.*

FIGURE 10.3

The Structure of Intellect

In his structure of intellect model, J. P. Guilford specified three features of intellectual tasks: the *content,* or type of information; the *product,* or form in which information is represented; and the *operation,* or type of mental activity performed. Each task performed by the intellect can be identified according to the particular types of content, products, and operations involved. For example, a test of vocabulary would assess your ability for *cognition* of *units* with *semantic content.*

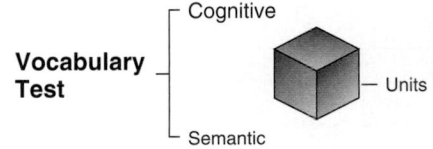

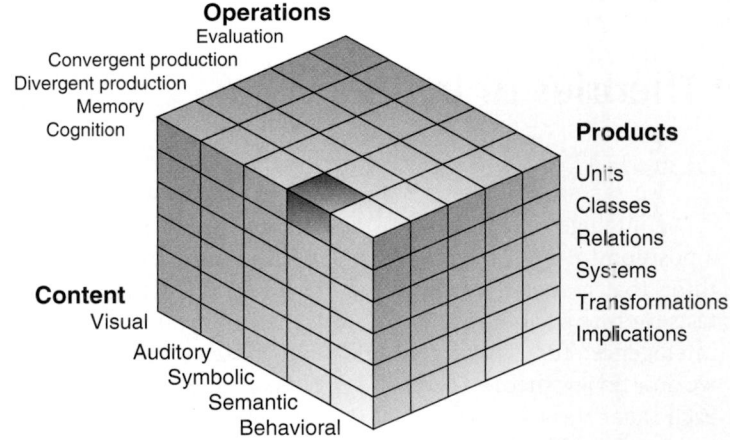

This theoretical model is analogous to a chemist's periodic table of elements. By means of such a systematic framework, intellectual factors, like chemical elements, may be postulated before they are discovered. In 1961, when Guilford proposed his model, nearly 40 intellectual abilities had been identified. Researchers have since accounted for over 100, which shows the predictive value of Guilford's conception of intelligence (Guilford, 1985).

Since Guilford, many psychologists have broadened their conceptions of intelligence to include much more than performance on traditional IQ tests. We now examine two types of theories that go beyond IQ.

Sternberg's Triarchic Theory of Intelligence

Robert Sternberg (1985, 1988) also stresses the importance of cognitive processes in problem solving as part of his more general theory of intelligence. Sternberg outlines a triarchic—three part—theory. His three types of intelligence, componential, experiential, and contextual, all represent different ways of characterizing effective performance.

Componential intelligence is defined by the components, or mental processes, that underlie thinking and problem solving. Sternberg identifies three types of components that are central to information processing: (1) knowledge acquisition components, for learning new facts; (2) performance components, for problem-solving strategies and techniques; and (3) metacognitive components, for selecting strategies and monitoring progress toward success. To put some of your componential intelligence to work, we'd like you now to try the exercise in **Table 10.3.**

TABLE 10.3

Using Componential Intelligence

The following is a list of *anagrams*—scrambled words. As quickly as possible, try to find a solution for each anagram (Sternberg, 1986).

1. H-U-L-A-G   _____
2. P-T-T-M-E   _____
3. T-R-H-O-S   _____
4. T-N-K-H-G-I   _____
5. T-E-W-I-R   _____
6. L-L-A-O-W   _____
7. R-I-D-E-V   _____
8. O-C-C-H-U   _____
9. T-E-N-R-E   _____
10. C-I-B-A-S   _____

Turn to page 316 for the solutions.

How did you do on the anagrams? To solve these anagrams, you mostly needed to use performance components and metacognitive components. The performance components are what allowed you to manipulate the letters in your head; the metacognitive components are what allowed you to have strategies for finding solutions. Consider T-R-H-O-S. How did you mentally transform that into SHORT? A good strategy to get started is to try consonant clusters that are probable in English—such as S-H and T-H. Selecting strategies requires metacognitive components; carrying them out requires performance components. Note that a good strategy will sometimes fail. Consider T-N-K-H-G-I. What makes this anagram hard for many people is that K-N is not a very likely combination to start a word, whereas T-H is. Did you stare at this anagram for a while, trying to turn it into a word beginning with T-H?

By breaking down various tasks into their components, researchers can pinpoint the processes that differentiate the performance outcomes of individuals with different IQs. For example, researchers might discover that the metacognitive components of high-IQ students prompt them to select different strategies, to solve a particular type of problem, than do their lower-IQ peers. The difference in strategy selection accounts for the high-IQ students' greater problem-solving success.

Experiential intelligence captures people's ability to deal with two extremes: novel versus very routine problems. Suppose, for example, a group of individuals found themselves stranded after an accident. You would credit with intelligence the person in the group who could most quickly help the group find its way home. In other circumstances, you would recognize as intelligent the behavior of someone who was able to perform routine tasks automatically. If, for example, a group of people carried out the same tasks day after day, you would be most impressed by the individual who could complete the tasks successfully with the least amount of "new" thought.

Contextual intelligence is reflected in the practical management of day-to-day affairs. It involves your ability to *adapt* to new and different contexts, *select* appropriate contexts, and effectively *shape* your environment to suit your needs. Contextual intelligence is what people sometimes call *street smarts* or *business sense*. Research has shown that people can have high contextual intelligence without having high IQs.

HOW WE KNOW

CONTEXTUAL INTELLIGENCE AT THE RACE TRACK Researchers approached "regulars" at a race track to assess the relationship between IQ and success at handicapping horse races. A group of 30 men was divided into experts and nonexperts, based on their performance at predicting which horses

To what extent does the ability to handicap races correlate with intelligence as it is traditionally measured?

would have the best odds at race time. Although the two groups both had average IQs, right around 100, and there was almost no correlation between IQ and expertise, experts correctly chose the top horse 93 percent of the time, versus 33 percent for nonexperts. The researchers went on to show that the experts were making their quite accurate judgments in a way that mimicked complex statistical procedures (Ceci & Liker, 1986).

Because each horse presents a new combination of variables along a variety of dimensions (lifetime speed, lifetime earnings, track conditions, jockey ability, and several others), the experts' success can't be attributed just to repetition of familiar situations. Rather, they had developed impressive abilities specifically suited to their environment.

Sternberg's triarchic theory recognizes that IQ tests do not capture the full range of intelligent behavior and attempts to do more than label individuals as high or low IQ. Suppose researchers learn, for example, that "unintelligent" people have difficulty with a certain task because they fail to encode all the relevant information. These people can be made to perform in an "intelligent" fashion if they practice that particular component. Thus, componential intelligence can be enhanced. Sternberg believes, similarly, that people can improve experiential and contextual intelligence (Sternberg, 1986). With an appropriate understanding of the component processes that underlie behavior, researchers should be able to devise techniques to make everyone's performance "look intelligent."

Gardner's Multiple Intelligences and Emotional Intelligence

Howard Gardner (1983, 1999) has also proposed a theory that expands the definition of intelligence beyond those skills covered on an IQ test. Gardner identifies numerous intelligences that cover a range of human ex-

perience. The value of any of the abilities differs across human societies, according to what is needed by, useful to, and prized by a given society. As shown in **Table 10.4**, Gardner identified eight intelligences.

Gardner argues that Western society promotes the first two intelligences, while non-Western societies often value others. For example, in the Caroline Island of Micronesia, sailors must be able to navigate long distances without maps, using only their spatial intelligence and bodily kinesthetic intelligence. Such abilities count more in that society than the ability to write a term paper. In Bali, where artistic performance is part of everyday life, musical intelligence and talents involved in coordinating intricate dance steps are highly valued. Interpersonal intelligence is more central to collectivist societies such as Japan, where cooperative action and communal life are emphasized, than it is in individualistic societies such as the United States (Triandis, 1990).

Assessing these kinds of intelligence demands more than paper-and-pencil tests and simple quantified measures. Gardner's theory of intelligence requires that the individual be observed and assessed in a variety of life situations as well as in the small slices of life depicted in traditional intelligence tests.

In recent years, researchers have begun to explore a type of intelligence—*emotional intelligence*—that is related to Gardner's concepts of *interpersonal* and *intrapersonal* intelligence (see Table 10.4). **Emotional intelligence** is defined as having four major components (Mayer & Salovey, 1997; Mayer et al., 2000):

■ The ability to perceive, appraise, and express emotions accurately and appropriately

Emotional intelligence Type of intelligence defined as the abilities to perceive, appraise, and express emotions accurately and appropriately, to use emotions to facilitate thinking, to understand and analyze emotions, to use emotional knowledge effectively, and to regulate one's emotions to promote both emotional and intellectual growth.

Gardner's Eight Intelligences

Intelligence	End States	Core Components
Logical-mathematical	Scientist Mathematician	Sensitivity to, and capacity to discern, logical or numerical patterns; ability to handle long chains of reasoning.
Linguistic	Poet Journalist	Sensitivity to the sounds, rhythms, and meanings of words; sensitivity to the different functions of language.
Naturalist	Biologist Environmentalist	Sensitivity to the differences among diverse species; abilities to interact subtly with living creatures.
Musical	Composer Violinist	Abilities to produce and appreciate rhythm, pitch, and timbre; appreciation of the forms of musical expressiveness.
Spatial	Navigator Sculptor	Capacities to perceive the visual-spatial world accurately and to perform transformations on one's initial perceptions.
Bodily kinesthetic	Dancer Athlete	Abilities to control one's body movements and to handle objects skillfully.
Interpersonal	Therapist Salesperson	Capacities to discern and respond appropriately to the moods, temperaments, motivations, and desires of other people.
Intrapersonal	Person with detailed, accurate self-knowledge	Access to one's own feelings and the ability to discriminate among them and draw upon them to guide behavior; knowledge of one's own strengths, weaknesses, desires, and intelligences.

- The ability to use emotions to facilitate thinking

- The ability to understand and analyze emotions and to use emotional knowledge effectively

- The ability to regulate one's emotions to promote both emotional and intellectual growth

This definition reflects a new view of the positive role of emotion as it relates to intellectual functioning—emotions can make thinking more intelligent, and people can think intelligently about their emotions and those of others.

Consider circumstances in which a teacher asks your class a question, "What was the former name of Istanbul?" Although Tom sees that Pamela has her hand raised, he blurts out the answer, "Constantinople." You understand that Pamela is angry that Tom stole her glory. We might give Tom credit for high IQ, but not high **EQ**—the emotional intelligence counterpart of IQ (Goleman, 1995). Our appreciation of Pamela's feelings is one example of EQ. Researchers have begun to develop measurement devices that they hope will be reliable and valid measures of EQ.

HOW WE KNOW

MEASURING EQ A sample of 503 adults and 229 adolescents completed the *Multifactor Emotional Intelligence Scale*. This scale requires individuals to provide solutions to a series of emotional problems—such as identifying what emotion a situation would generate. Participants' responses were evaluated both against experts' judgments and against the consensus judgments of all the individuals who completed the scale. EQ scores correlated only modestly with IQ scores for both adults and adolescents, suggesting that EQ measures different abilities than do traditional IQ measures. Adults performed at higher levels than did adolescents, suggesting that EQ has an important environmental component. Finally, on this new scale of emotional intelligence, women were significantly superior to men in perceiving emotion (Mayer et al., 1999).

Why do you suppose women would have higher EQs than men? Do you think it has to do with nature—women's evolutionary preparation for certain roles—or nurture—women's socialization to be more emotionally sensitive (Brody, 1997; Eisenberg et al., 1998; LaFrance & Banaji, 1992)?

Our review of intelligence testing and theories of intelligence sets the stage for a provocative discussion of the societal circumstances that make the topic of intelligence so controversial.

EQ The emotional intelligence counterpart of IQ.

Charles Spearman believed that intelligence consists of a general ability he called *g* and domain-specific abilities he called *s*. Other psychometric researchers have attempted to measure further subdivisions of intelligence.

Sternberg proposed that people possess three types of intelligence: componential, experiential, and contextual. Gardner expanded the definition of intelligence to include eight types of intelligence that go beyond skills on traditional IQ tests. Emotional intelligence reflects individuals' ability to use and think about emotions efficiently.

The Politics of Intelligence

We have seen that contemporary conceptions of intelligence reject the narrow linking of a score on an IQ test with a person's intelligence. Even so, IQ tests remain the most frequent measure of "intelligence" in Western society. Because of the prevalence of IQ testing, and the availability of IQ scores, it becomes easy to compare different groups according to their "average" IQ. In the United States, such ethnic and racial group comparisons have often been used as evidence for the innate, genetic inferiority of members of minority groups. We will briefly examine the history of this practice of using IQ test scores to index the alleged mental inferiority of certain groups. Then we will look at current evidence on the nature and nurture of intelligence and IQ test performance. You will see that this is one of the most politically volatile issues in psychology, because public policies about immigration quotas, educational resources, and more may be based on how group IQ data are interpreted.

The History of Group Comparisons

In the early 1900s, psychologist **Henry Goddard** advocated mental testing of all immigrants and the *selective exclusion* of those who were found to be "mentally defective." Such views may have contributed to a hostile national climate against admission of certain immigrant groups (see Cronbach, 1975; McPherson, 1985; Sokal, 1987). Indeed, Congress passed the 1924 Immigration Restriction Act, which made it national policy to administer intelligence tests to immigrants as they arrived at Ellis Island in New York Harbor. Vast numbers of Jewish, Italian, Russian, and immigrants of other nationalities were classified as "morons" on the basis of IQ tests. Some psychologists interpreted these statistical findings as evidence that immigrants from southern and eastern Europe were genetically inferior to those from the hardy northern and western European stock (see Ruch, 1937). However, these "inferior" groups were also least familiar with the dominant language and culture, embedded in the IQ tests, because they had immigrated most recently. (Within a few decades, these group differences completely disappeared from IQ tests, but the theory of racially inherited differences in intelligence persisted.)

Goddard (1917) and others then went beyond merely associating low IQ with hereditary racial and ethnic origins. They added moral worthlessness, mental deficiency, and immoral social behavior to the mix of negatives related to low IQ. Evidence for their view came from case studies of two infamous families: the **Juke family** and the **Kallikak family.** These families allegedly were traced for many generations to show that bad seeds planted in family genes inescapably yield defective human offspring.

Why were IQ tests given to immigrants as they arrived at Ellis Island? How were these tests used to draw conclusions about genetic inferiority?

"GENETICALLY INFERIOR" FAMILIES Over 2,000 members of a New York state family with "Juke's blood" were reported to have been traced (by 1875), because the family had such a notorious record of developmental disability, delinquency, and crime. Of these family members, 458 were found to be developmentally disabled in their school performance, 171 classified as criminals, and hundreds of their kin were labeled as "paupers, intemperates, and harlots." The conclusion reached was that heredity was a dominant factor in the disreputable development of members of this unsavory family.

Goddard drew the same conclusion from his case study of the Kallikaks, a family with one "good seed" side and one "bad seed" side to its family tree. (In his study, Goddard renamed the family Kallikak, which means good-bad in Greek.) Martin Kallikak was a Revolutionary War soldier who had an illegitimate son with a woman described as developmentally disabled. Their union eventually produced 480 descendants. Goddard classified 143 of them as "defective" and only 46 as normal. He found crime, alcoholism, mental disorders, and illegitimacy common among the rest of the family members. By contrast, when Martin Kallikak later married a "good woman," their union produced 496 descendants, only three of whom were classified as "defective." Goddard also found that many offspring from this high-quality union had become "eminent" (Goddard, 1914). Goddard came to believe that heredity determined intelligence, genius, and eminence on the positive side. On the negative side, he arrayed delinquency, alcoholism, sexual immorality, developmental disability, and maybe even poverty (McPherson, 1985).

Goddard's genetic inferiority argument was further reinforced by the fact that, on the World War I Army Intelligence tests, African Americans and other racial minorities scored lower than the white majority. Louis Terman, who as we saw promoted IQ testing in the United States, commented in this unscientific manner on the data he had helped collect on U.S. racial minorities:

> Their dullness seems to be racial.... There seems no possibility at present of convincing society that they should not be allowed to reproduce, although from a eugenics point of view, they constitute a grave problem because of their unusually prolific breeding. (Terman, 1916, pp. 91–92)

The names have changed, but the problem remains the same. In the United States today, African Americans and Latinos score, on average, lower than Asian Americans and whites on standardized intelligence tests. Of course, there are individuals in all groups who score at the highest (and the lowest) extremes of the IQ scale. How should

these group differences in IQ scores be interpreted? The tradition in the United States and Britain has been to attribute these differences to genetic inferiority (nature). After we discuss the evidence for genetic differences in IQ, we will consider a second possibility, that differences in environments (nurture) exert a significant impact on IQ. The validity of either explanation, or some combination of them, has important social, economic, and political consequences.

Heredity and IQ

How can researchers assess the extent to which intelligence is genetically determined? Any answer to this question requires that the researcher choose some measure as an index of intelligence. Thus, the question becomes not whether "intelligence," in the abstract, is influenced by heredity but, in most cases, whether IQs are similar within family trees. To answer this more limited question, researchers need to tease apart the effects of shared genes and shared environment. One method is to compare functioning in identical twins (monozygotic), fraternal twins (dizygotic), and relatives with other degrees of genetic overlap. **Figure 10.4** presents correlations between IQ scores of individuals on the basis of their degree of genetic relationship (Plomin & Petrill, 1997). As you can see, the greater the genetic similarity, the greater the IQ similarity. (You should note in these data that the impact of environment is also revealed in the greater IQ similarities among those who have been reared together.)

Researchers use results of this sort to try to estimate the *heritability* of IQ. A **heritability estimate** of a particular trait, such as intelligence, is based on the proportion of the variability in test scores on that trait that can be traced to genetic factors. The estimate is found by computing the variation in all the test scores for a given population (college students or mental patients, for example) and then identifying what portion of the total variance is due to genetic or inherited factors. This is done by comparing individuals who have different degrees of genetic overlap. Researchers who have reviewed the variety of studies on heritability of IQ conclude that about 50 percent of the variance in IQ scores is due to genetic makeup (Grigorenko, 2000; Neisser et al., 1996; Plomin & Petrill, 1997). What is perhaps even more interesting, however, is that heritability *increases* across the life span: Heritability is about 40 percent for 4- to 6-year-olds but increases to about 60 percent in early adulthood and to about 80 percent in older adults! Many people are surprised by this result, because it seems that

Heritability estimate A statistical estimate of the degree of inheritance of a given trait or behavior, assessed by the degree of similarity between individuals who vary in their extent of genetic similarity.

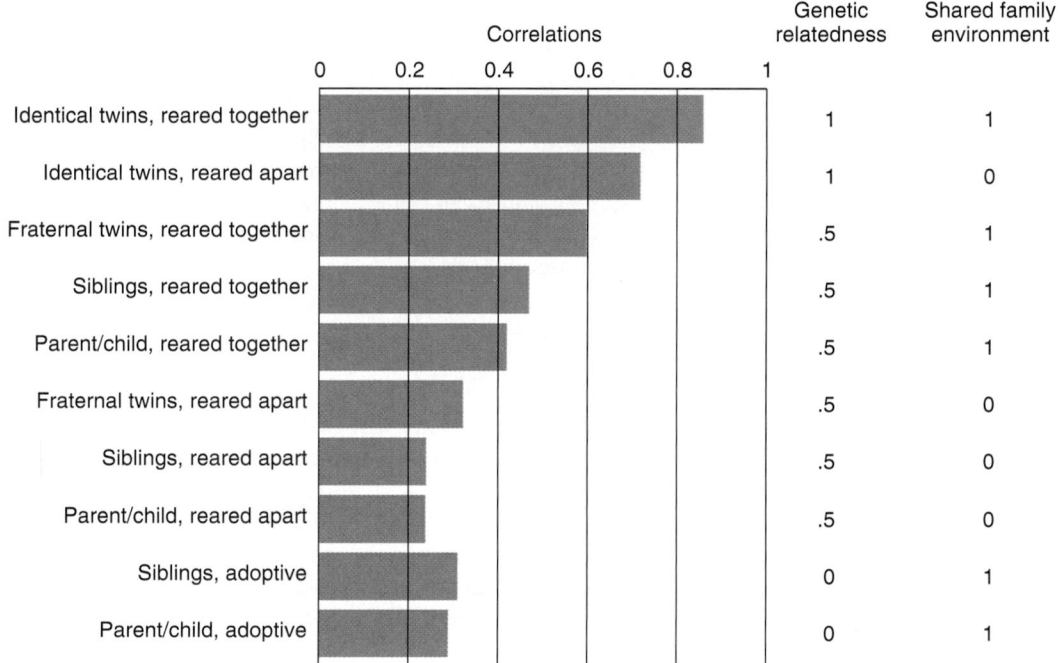

	Correlations	Genetic relatedness	Shared family environment
Identical twins, reared together		1	1
Identical twins, reared apart		1	0
Fraternal twins, reared together		.5	1
Siblings, reared together		.5	1
Parent/child, reared together		.5	1
Fraternal twins, reared apart		.5	0
Siblings, reared apart		.5	0
Parent/child, reared apart		.5	0
Siblings, adoptive		0	1
Parent/child, adoptive		0	1

FIGURE 10.4

IQ and Genetic Relationship

This figure presents the correlations between the IQ scores of identical (monozygotic) and fraternal (dizygotic) twins reared together (in the same home environments) or reared apart (in different home environments). For comparison, it also includes data for siblings (brothers and sisters) and parents and children, both biological and adoptive. The data demonstrate the importance of both genetic factors (the numbers under "genetic relatedness" specify the overlap of genetic material) and environmental factors (the numbers under "shared family environment" indicate whether the environment was the same [1] or different [0]). For example, identical twins show higher correlations between their IQs than do fraternal twins—a genetic influence. However, both types of twins show higher correlations when raised together—an environmental influence.

environments should have more, not less, of an effect as people get older. Here's how researchers explain this counterintuitive finding: "It is possible that genetic dispositions nudge us toward environments that accentuate our genetic propensities, thus leading to increased heritability throughout the life span" (Plomin & Petrill, 1997, p. 61).

Let's return now to the point at which genetic analysis becomes controversial: test score differences between African Americans and white Americans. Although several decades ago, the gap was 15 IQ points, the scores of whites and blacks have been converging over time, so that on a number of contemporary indicators the gap is between 7 and 10 points (Nisbett, 1995, 1998; Williams & Ceci, 1997). Although the close in the gap suggests environmental influences, the lingering difference has prompted many people to suggest that there are unbridgeable genetic differences between the races (Herrnstein & Murray, 1994). However, even if IQ is highly heritable, does this difference reflect genetic in-

feriority of individuals in the lower-scoring group? The answer is no. Heritability is based on an estimate *within* one given group. It cannot be used to interpret differences *between* groups, no matter how large those differences are on an objective test. Heritability estimates pertain only to the average in a given population of individuals. Even though we know that height, for instance, has a high heritability estimate (about 90 percent), you cannot determine how much of your height is due to genetic influences. The same argument is true for IQ; despite high heritability estimates, we cannot determine the specific genetic contribution to any individual's IQ or to mean IQ scores among groups. The fact that on an IQ test one racial or ethnic group scores lower than another group does not mean that the difference between these groups is genetic in origin, even if the heritability estimate for IQ scores is high as assessed within a group.

Another reason that genetic makeup cannot be wholly responsible for group differences in IQ has to do with the *relative* sizes of the differences. There is much

Tiger Woods has ancestors who were white, African American, Thai, Chinese, and Native American. Why is he most often described as African American? What does that suggest about the construct of race in the United States?

overlapping in the distribution of each group's scores despite mean differences: the difference between groups is small compared with the differences among the scores of individuals within each group (Loehlin, 2000; Suzuki & Valencia, 1997). In general, the differences between the gene pools of different racial groups are minute compared with the genetic differences among individual members of the same group (Gould, 1981; Zuckerman, 1990). Furthermore, in the United States, race is often more of a *social* construct than a *biological* construct. Consider the remarkable young golfer Tiger Woods, who has often been labeled—and discriminated against—as African American even though his actual heritage is much more complex (his ancestors were white, black, Thai, Chinese, and Native American). Woods provides an excellent example of the ways in which social judgments do not follow biological reality. As such, there is great danger in treating IQ differences among socially distinct groups as if those differences conform to underlying biology (Suzuki & Valencia, 1997).

Researchers have found ways to put this perspective to a test in a series of studies in which the degree of white or European parentage among blacks is determined. In the United States, the "black" population is estimated to be about 20 to 30 percent European through intermarriages. Does it make a difference in IQ if a "black" person has more or less European genetic stock? The genetic argument holds that it does, but the data suggest the correlation of degree of European ancestry with IQ is very low (on the order of only .15 across

many studies). This is true whether skin color or blood groups are used as the index of racial mixture. Comparisons of German children fathered by African American GI fathers and white GI fathers show no difference in their IQ scores. In addition, children of "black–white" unions have IQs that are seven points higher if the mother is white. This difference is most likely due to the greater contribution of mothers than fathers to a child's intellectual socialization, and, of course, cannot be due to any genetic factor, because each parent contributes equally to the genes of the offspring (Loehlin, 2000; Nisbett, 1998).

Surely genetics plays a sizable role in influencing individuals' scores on IQ tests, as it does on many other traits and abilities. We have argued, however, that heredity does not constitute an adequate explanation for IQ differences between racial and ethnic groups. It has a necessary, but not sufficient, role in our understanding of such performance effects. Let's turn now to the role the environment may play in creating the IQ gap.

Environments and IQ

Because heritability estimates are less than 1.0, we know that genetic inheritance is not solely responsible for anyone's IQ. Environments must also affect IQ. But how can we assess what aspects of the environment are important influences on IQ? What features of your environment affect your potential to score well on an IQ test (Beiser & Gotowiec, 2000; Ceci, 1999; Rowe, 1997; Suzuki & Valencia, 1997)? Environments are complex stimulus packages that vary on many dimensions, both physical and social, and may be experienced in different ways by those within them. Even children in the same family setting do not necessarily share the same critical, psychological environment. Think back to growing up in your family. If you had siblings, did they all get the same attention from parents, did conditions of stress change over the course of time, did the family's financial resources change, did your parents' marital status change? It is obvious that environments are made up of many components that are in a dynamic relationship and that change over time. So it becomes difficult for psychologists to say what kinds of environmental conditions—attention, stress, poverty, health, war, and so on—actually have an impact on IQ.

Researchers have most often focused on more global measures of environment, like the socioeconomic status of the family. For example, in a large-scale longitudinal study of more than 26,000 children, the best predictors of a child's IQ at age 4 were the family's socioeconomic status and the level of the mother's education. This was equally true for African American and Caucasian children (Broman et al., 1975). Similarly, **Figure 10.5** shows an overall impact of social class on IQ.

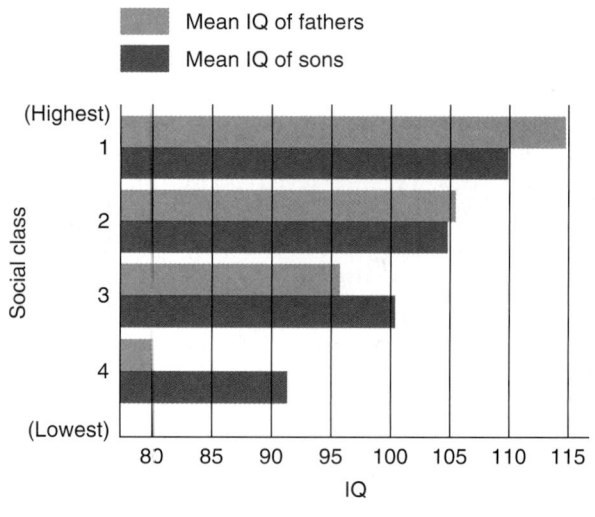

Legend:
- Mean IQ of fathers
- Mean IQ of sons

(Highest) 1 / 2 / 3 / 4 (Lowest)

Social class

IQ: 80 85 90 95 100 105 110 115

FIGURE
10.5

The Relationship among Heredity, Environment, and IQ

This chart shows evidence for the contribution of heredity and environment to IQ scores. There are similar IQs for fathers and sons (influence of heredity), but the IQs of both fathers and sons are related to social class (influence of environment).

Why does social class affect IQ? Wealth versus poverty can affect intellectual functioning in many ways, health and educational resources being two of the most obvious. Poor health during pregnancy and low birth weight are solid predictors of a child's lowered mental ability. Children born into impoverished families often suffer from poor nutrition, many going to school hungry, thus less able to concentrate on learning tasks. Furthermore, impoverished homes may suffer from a lack of books, written media, computers, and other materi-als that add to one's mental stimulation. The "survival orientation" of poor parents, especially in single-parent families, that leaves parents little time or energy to play with and intellectually stimulate their children is detri-mental to performance on tasks such as those on stan-dard IQ tests.

Finally, those living in more impoverished condi-tions are stigmatized in our society, as they are in most countries throughout the world, even in racially homog-enous societies like Japan. For example, the Burakamin of Japan, who are that nation's lowest caste members, have IQs that are 15 points lower than other Japanese (Ogbu, 1987). This social stigma of one's group can exert a negative impact on an individual's sense of self-compe-tence and adversely affect test and school performances. If so, we should see a direct impact on IQ when children are raised in enriched environments.

HOW WE KNOW

THE IMPACT OF ENVIRONMENTS ON IQ A researcher studied two groups of children who were adopted by middle-class white families by the age of 2 (Moore, 1986). One group of nine children had biological parents both of whom were black; a second group of 14 children had one black biological parent and one white biological parent. The Weschler Intelligence Scale for Children was used to estimate each child's IQ sometime between the ages of 7 and 10.

The average IQ for those children for whom both parents were black was 108.7; the average IQ for mixed-race children was 107.2. As shown in **Figure 10.6,** these IQs are well above the average for African Americans (Lynn, 1996).

What is important to note here is that it is not race as such that makes the difference, but the economic, health,

The personal attention children receive can affect their intelligence. In the "separate but equal" schoolroom of 1940s Tennessee shown (at left), African American children received little attention. In contrast, the parent shown (at right) is deeply involved in his children's education. How do these types of environmental differences affect IQ?

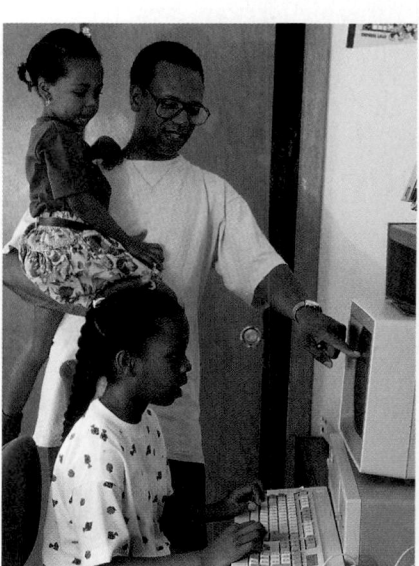

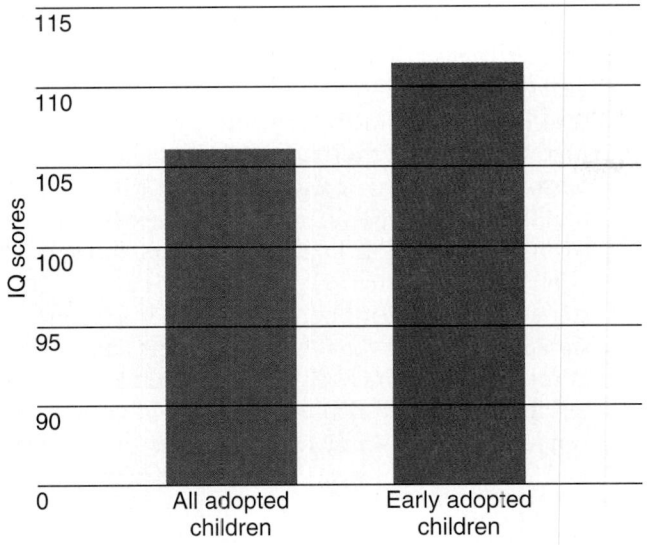

FIGURE 10.6

**IQ Scores of
Adopted Children**

Black and mixed-race children who had been adopted into middle-class white families had IQs that were above average. Because the children come from groups that typically test below average, these data demonstrate the effects of environments on IQ.

and educational resources that are correlated with race in our society and in most countries.

In a sense, researchers have spent the last 30 years attempting to replicate this result at the societal level. The Head Start program was first funded by the federal government in 1965 to address the "physical health, developmental, social, educational, and emotional needs of low-income children and to increase the capacity of the families to care for their children, through empowerment and supportive services" (Kassebaum, 1994, p. 123). The idea of Head Start was not to move children to privileged environments but to improve the environments into which they were born. Children are exposed to special preschool education, they receive decent daily meals, and their parents are given advice on health and other aspects of child rearing. Early assessments of Head Start's effects focused narrowly on improvement on IQ tests and other achievement measures. In fact, after children had been in the program only a few weeks, their IQ scores rose by 10 points. Unfortunately, after they left the program, these IQ gains tended to fade away (Barnett, 1998; Zigler & Muenchow, 1992; Zigler & Styfco, 1994). This pattern yields two lessons: IQ can be affected by the environment, but the enriched environment must be sustained. In any case, more recent assessments of Head Start have overcome the earlier narrow focus on IQ.

> *The empirical literature...delivers good news and bad news. The bad news is that neither Head Start nor any preschool program can inoculate children against the ravages of poverty. Early intervention simply cannot overpower the effects of poor living conditions, inadequate nutrition and health care, negative role models, and substandard schools. But good programs can prepare children for school and possibly help them develop better coping and adaptation skills that will enable better life out-*

> *comes, albeit not perfect ones. (Zigler & Styfco, 1994, p. 129)*

If we use a broader definition of intelligence that goes beyond just verbal and performance tasks on IQ tests, the influence of environment factors becomes clear. An enriched, supportive environment is a good predictor of successful and enhanced intellectual, scholastic, and situationally adaptive performance.

Culture and the Validity of IQ Tests

People would probably care much less about IQ scores if they didn't allow for such useful predictions: Extensive research shows that IQ scores are valid predictors of school grades from elementary school through college, of occupational status, and of performance in many jobs (Brody, 1997b; Gottfredson, 1997b). These patterns of results suggest that IQ tests validly measure intellectual abilities that are very basic and important toward the types of success that are valued in Western cultures—intelligence, as measured by IQ, directly affects success. IQ distinctions can also affect academic and job performance indirectly by changing one's motives and beliefs. Those with higher IQ scores are likely to have had more success experiences in school, become more motivated to study, develop an achievement orientation, and become optimistic about their chances of doing well. Also, children scoring low on IQ tests may get "tracked" into schools, classes, or programs that are inferior and may even be stigmatizing to the student's sense of self-competence. In this way, IQ can be affected by environment and, in turn, can create new environments for the child—some better, some worse. IQ assessment may thus become destiny—whatever the child's underlying genetic endowment for intelligence.

Even though IQ tests have proven to be valid for mainstream uses, many observers still question their validity for comparisons among different cultural and racial groups (Greenfield, 1997; Samuda, 1998; Serpell, 2000). Many forms of tests and testing may not match cultural notions of intelligence or appropriate behavior. Consider one case of negative evaluations in the classroom:

> When children of Latino immigrant parents go to school, the emphasis on understanding rather than speaking, on respecting the teacher's authority rather than expressing one's own opinions leads to negative academic assessment.... Hence, a valued mode of communication in one culture—respectful listening—becomes the basis for a rather sweeping negative evaluation in the school setting where self-assertive speaking is the valued mode of communication. (Greenfield, 1997, p. 1120)

These immigrant children must learn how they must behave in U.S. classrooms to make their teachers believe they are intelligent.

One of the standard concerns about IQ tests is that they are biased toward or against members of different cultures: Critics have argued that group differences in IQ scores are caused by systematic bias in the test questions, making them invalid and unfair for minorities. But even when tests are made more "culture-fair," there remains a racial gap (Neisser et al., 1996). In fact, the issue may be more a problem of the *context* of the test rather than the *content* of the test. **Claude Steele** (1997; Steele & Aronson, 1995, 1998) has argued that people's performance on ability tests is influenced by **stereotype threat** (also known as *stereotype vulnerability*)—the threat of being at risk for confirming a negative stereotype of one's group. Steele's research suggests that the belief that a negative stereotype is relevant in a situation can function to bring about the poor performance encoded in the stereotype.

HOW WE KNOW

THE IMPLICATIONS OF STEREOTYPE THREAT In one study, black and white undergraduates tried to answer very difficult verbal questions of the type found on the Graduate Record Exam. Half of the students were led to believe that performance on the questions was *diagnostic* of their intellectual ability; the other half were only told that the experiment concerned psychological factors involved in solving problems. The theory of stereotype threat suggests that only students for whom the threat of the stereotype is called

into action by the situation—the black students in the *diagnostic* condition—will perform less well on the questions. As you can see in part A of **Figure 10.7,** the results confirmed this prediction. When the black students believed performance could be used to diagnose their intelligence, they performed less well (Steele & Aronson, 1995). The logic of stereotype threat applies to any group for whom there is a stereotype of inferior performance. For example, stereotypes suggest that women are less able at math than are men. As shown in part B of Figure 10.7, a difficult math test produced gender differences only when students had been told that it would (Steele, 1997). That is, prior to attempting the problems, students in the *gender-difference* condition had been told that the test had, in the past, produced gender differences—and so it did, for them.

Note that in each of these studies what matters is how the test takers define the situation. Only when people believe the situation is relevant to the stereotype—because, for example, they believe that the test measures intelligence—does knowledge of the stereotype impair performance. Do you think it would be possible to measure IQ without invoking stereotype threat? If not, researchers may never be able to determine "real" performance.

One final thought on intelligence and culture. Taken as a whole, the United States demonstrates a cultural bias toward genetic explanations of individual differences. **Harold Stevenson** and his colleagues (1993) spent several years tracking the mathematics achievement of Chinese, Japanese, and U.S. children. In 1980, Asian children on the average vastly outperformed their U.S. peers. In 1990, the gap remained: "Only 4.1% of the Chinese children and 10.3% of the Japanese children…had scores as low as those of the average American child" (p. 54). Are Asian children genetically superior? In fact, people in the United States are more likely to answer "yes." When Stevenson and his colleagues asked Asian and U.S. students, teachers, and parents to contrast the importance of "studying hard" versus "innate intelligence," Asian respondents emphasized hard work. U.S. respondents emphasized innate ability. Do you see how this perspective could lead to the conclusion by Americans that Asians must be genetically superior in mathematics? Because such beliefs have public policy implications—how much money should be expended on teaching mathematics if Americans cannot learn math

Stereotype threat The threat associated with being at risk for confirming a negative stereotype of one's group.

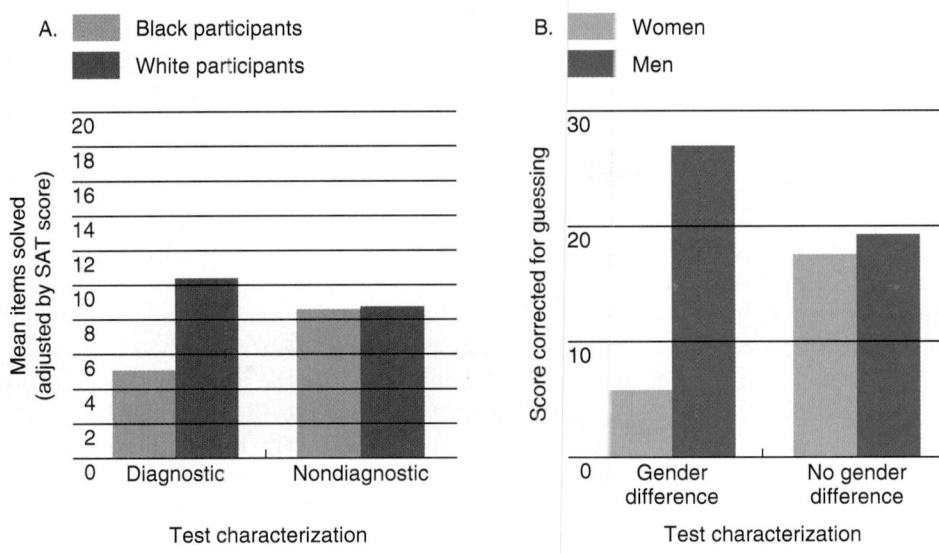

FIGURE 10.7

Stereotype Threat

Stereotype threat occurs when people believe a negative stereotype is relevant to the current testing situation. (A) One study examined the stereotype that African Americans score poorly on intelligence tests. Half of a sample of black and white students were led to believe that a test was diagnostic of their intellectual ability; the other half did not receive this information. When black students believed that the test was diagnostic, their performance was impaired. (Participants' SAT scores were used to eliminate preexisting differences between their expected performance.) (B) A second study examined the stereotype that women score poorly on mathematics exams. Half of a sample of male and female students were told that a math test had previously produced gender differences; the other half did not receive this information. When women believed that the test would produce gender differences, their performance was impaired.

anyway?—it is important to examine rigorous research to sort out what can and cannot be changed with respect to intellectual performance.

SUMMING UP

Goddard helped to initiate the unfortunate tradition of claiming genetic inferiority of some racial and ethnic groups. Behavior genetic analyses reveal a large genetic component to IQ. However, measurement of IQ has often become politically charged because of racial differences in measured IQ. Researchers have identified environmental factors that have important effects on IQ. Although IQ is a valid predictor of such life outcomes as school and job success, its measure may be invalid across different racial and cultural groups. For example, some groups suffer stereotype threat when their intellectual performance is measured.

■ Creativity

Before we leave the area of intelligence and its assessment, we wish to turn the topic of creativity. **Creativity** is an individual's ability to generate ideas or products that are both *novel* and *appropriate* to the circumstances in which they were generated (Sternberg & Lubart, 1999). Consider the invention of the wheel. The device was novel because no one before its unknown inventor had seen the application of rolling objects. It was appropriate because the use to which the novel object could be put was very clear. Without appropriateness, new ideas or objects are often considered strange or irrelevant.

■ **Creativity** The ability to generate ideas or products that are both novel and appropriate to the circumstances.

Our discussion of creativity falls within a chapter on intelligence because many people believe that there is a strong relationship between intelligence and creativity. To determine if this is the case, we need to be able first to test creativity and then to determine the relationship between creativity and intelligence. Thus, we first discuss methods for judging ideas or products to be creative and then look at the link to intelligence. Next, we look at situations of exceptional creativity and evaluate the relationship between creativity and madness. We will see what lessons you can learn from people who are possessed of exceptional creative abilities.

Assessing Creativity and the Link to Intelligence

How might you go about rating individuals as (relatively) creative or uncreative? Many approaches focus on **divergent thinking,** which is defined as the ability to generate a variety of unusual solutions to a problem. Questions that test divergent thinking give the test taker the opportunity to demonstrate *fluid* (swift) and *flexible* thinking (Torrance, 1974; Wallach & Kogan, 1965):

- Name all the things you can think of that are square.

- List as many white, edible things as you can in three minutes.

- List all the uses that you can think of for a *brick*.

> **Divergent thinking** An aspect of creativity characterized by an ability to produce unusual but appropriate responses to problems.

Responses are scored along such dimensions as *fluency,* the overall number of distinct ideas; *uniqueness,* the number of ideas that were given by no other person in an appropriate sample; and *unusualness,* the number of ideas that were given by, for example, less than 5 percent of a sample (Runco, 1991).

When creativity is assessed in this fashion, the test provides a performance index that can be correlated with other measures. On many occasions, researchers have evaluated the relationship between measures of divergent thinking and IQ. A common pattern has emerged: There is a weak or moderate correlation between the two measures up to an IQ level of about 120; above 120, the correlation decreases (Sternberg & O'Hara, 1999). Why might this be so? One researcher suggests that "intelligence appears to enable creativity to some extent but not to promote it" (Perkins, 1988, p. 319). In other words, a certain level of intelligence gives a person the opportunity to be creative, but the person may not avail himself or herself of that opportunity.

Creativity researchers have often been concerned that divergent-thinking tests are too closely tied to the tradition of intelligence testing and to IQ tests themselves (which may explain the correlations up into the 120 IQ range) (Lubart, 1994). A different approach to judging some individuals as creative or uncreative is to ask them specifically to generate a creative product—a drawing, a poem, or a short story. Judges then rate the creativity of each of the products. Consider the two photographs shown in **Figure 10.8.** Which do you think is more creative? Could you explain why you think so? Do you think your friends would agree? Research has shown that agreement is quite high when judges rank products for creativity (Amabile, 1983). People can be reliably identified across judges as being high or low in creativity.

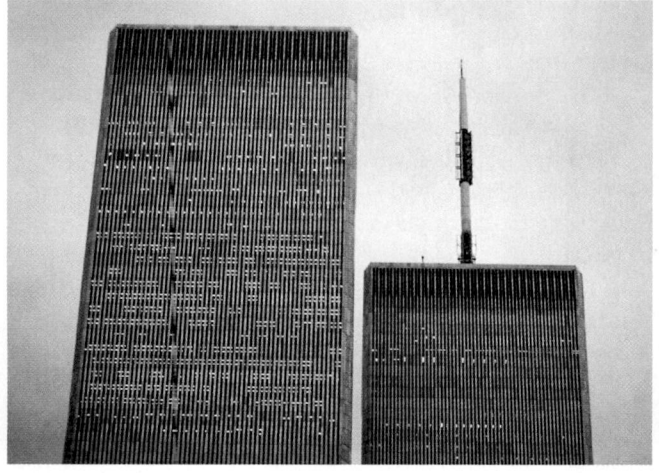

FIGURE 10.8

Hypothetical photography class assignment: take the best picture you can of the World Trade Center. (A) A noncreative response. (B) A creative response.

Exceptional Creativity and Madness

There are some exceptional individuals who would emerge from assessments of creativity as almost off the scale. Who do you think of when you are asked to name someone who is exceptionally creative? Your answer is likely to depend partly on your own areas of expertise and your own preferences. Psychologists might nominate Sigmund Freud. Those people interested in fine art, music, or dance might mention Pablo Picasso, Igor Stravinsky, or Martha Graham. Is it possible to detect the commonalities in the personalities or backgrounds of such individuals that could be predictive of exceptional creativity? Howard Gardner (1993) chose a selection of individuals whose extraordinary abilities were relevant to the eight types of intelligence we described earlier, including Freud, Picasso, Stravinsky, and Graham. Gardner's analysis allows him to yield a portrait of the life experiences of the *exemplary creator*, whom he dubs E.C.:

> E.C. discovers a problem area or realm of special interest, one that promises to [lead] into uncharted waters. This is a highly charged moment. At this point E.C. becomes isolated from her peers and must work mostly on her own. She senses that she is on the verge of a breakthrough that is as yet little understood, even by her. Surprisingly, at this crucial moment, E.C. craves both cognitive and affective support, so that she can retain her bearings. Without such support she might well experience some kind of breakdown. (Gardner, 1993, p. 361)

At the end of this passage, Gardner alludes to one of the most common stereotypes of exemplary creators: their life experiences border on—or include the experience of—madness. The idea that great creativity is intimately related to madness has a history that has been traced as far back as Plato (Kessel, 1989). In more modern times, Kraepelin (1921) argued that the manic phases of individuals who suffer from "manic-depressive insanity," or bipolar disorder, provide a context of free-flowing thought processes that facilitate great creativity. Mania, as we will see in Chapter 15, is characterized by periods of enduring excitedness; the person generally acts and feels elated and expansive. There is little doubt that many great figures in the arts and humanities have suffered from such mood disorders (Keiger, 1993). But how can researchers determine whether these individuals' actual thought processes were affected by their mental illness?

Weisberg's study suggests that madness (in the form of mania) may largely affect motivation. The individual rides the wave of mania to create a great output of work. If the person has a certain level of talent, some, but not all, of that work will reach brilliance—but at a rate no higher than at other times in the artist's life. In general, careful reviews of historical cases find few links between creativity and madness, leading expert **Albert Rothenberg** to conclude, "It is a false and romantic notion that people have to undergo suffering themselves in order to be able to understand the human concerns and suffering of others" (Rothenberg, 1990, p. 164).

What lessons are there for you in tales of exceptional creativity? You can emulate a pattern of *risk taking*. Highly creative individuals are willing to go into "uncharted waters" (Gardner, 1993; Sternberg & Lubart, 1996). There is a pattern of *preparation*. Highly creative individuals typically have spent years acquiring expertise in the domains in which they will excel (Weisberg, 1986).

Art historians have often speculated that Vincent Van Gogh's creativity as an artist was influenced by mental illness. What, in general, have researchers discovered about the link between creativity and madness?

There is a pattern of *intrinsic motivation*. Highly creative individuals pursue their tasks because of the enjoyment and satisfaction they take in the products they generate (Collins & Amabile, 1999). If you can bring all these factors together in your own life, you should be able to increase your personal level of creative performance.

You have now learned some of the ways in which psychologists assess and interpret individual differences in intelligence and creativity. However, as you are certainly aware, there is much more to understanding people than just knowing how intelligent or creative they are. In the next section, we discuss the ways in which psychologists obtain information about the range of personality attributes that make each individual unique.

SUMMING UP

Creativity is typically measured through tests of divergent thinking. Contrary to some claims, there does not appear to be a close association between creativity and madness. However, creativity does require a certain level of risk taking, preparation, and motivation.

Assessment and Society

The primary goal of psychological assessment is to make accurate assessments of people that are as free as possible of errors of assessors' judgments. This goal is achieved by replacing subjective judgments of teachers, employers, and other evaluators with more objective measures that have been carefully constructed and are open to critical evaluation. This is the goal that motivated Alfred Binet in his pioneering work. Binet and others hoped that testing would help democratize society and minimize decisions based on arbitrary criteria of sex, race, nationality, privilege, or physical appearance. However, despite these lofty goals, there is no area of psychology more controversial than assessment. Three ethical concerns that are central to the controversy are the fairness of test-based decisions, the utility of tests for evaluating education, and the implications of using test scores as labels to categorize individuals.

Critics concerned with the fairness of testing practices argue that the costs or negative consequences may be higher for some test takers than for others (Bond, 1995). The costs are quite high, for example, when tests on which minority groups receive low scores are used to keep them out of certain jobs. In some cities, applicants for civil service janitor jobs must pass a verbal test, rather than a more appropriate test of manual skills. According to researcher William Banks, this is a strategy unions use to keep minorities from access to jobs (1990). Sometimes, minority group members test poorly because their scores are evalu-

When schools are rewarded for high scores on standardized tests, are teachers likely to place more emphasis on test-taking skills than on broader learning goals?

ated relative to inappropriate norms. In addition, arbitrary cutoff scores that favor applicants from one group may be used to make selection decisions, when, in reality, a lower cutoff score that is fairer would produce just as many correct hiring decisions. In addition, overreliance on testing may make personnel selection an automatic attempt to fit people into available jobs. Instead, sometimes society might benefit more by changing job descriptions to fit the needs and abilities of people.

A second ethical concern is that testing not only helps evaluate students; it may also play a role in the shaping of education. The quality of school systems and the effectiveness of teachers are frequently judged on the basis of how well their students score on standardized achievement tests. Local support of the schools through tax levies, and even individual teacher salaries, may ride on test scores. The high stakes associated with test scores have led to cheating scandals in several school districts (Kantrowitz & McGinn, 2000). For example, in Potomac, Maryland an elementary school principal resigned when strong evidence suggested that fifth-graders at her school had been given several types of assistance, including extra time and second chances, to improve their test scores (Thomas & Wingert, 2000). The evidence against the school had come from the students themselves. The 10-year-olds reported to their parents that they had been asked or allowed to cheat: They wondered why the adults at the school had insisted that they do so. The children's bewilderment illustrates how damaging it can be when test scores are taken to matter more than education.

A third ethical concern is that test outcomes can take on the status of unchangeable labels. People too often think of themselves as being an IQ of 110 or a B student, as if the scores were labels stamped on their foreheads. Such labels may become barriers to advancement as people come to believe that their mental and personal qualities are fixed and unchangeable—that they cannot improve their lot in life. For those who are negatively assessed, the scores can become self-imposed motivational limits that lower their sense of self-efficacy and restrict the challenges they are willing to tackle. That is another insidious consequence of pronouncements about group deficiencies in IQ. Those stigmatized publicly in this way come to believe what the "experts" are saying about them, and so disidentify with schools and education as means to improve their lives.

This tendency to give test scores a sacred status has societal as well as personal implications. When test scores become labels that identify traits, states, maladjustment, conflict, and pathology within an individual, people begin to think about the "abnormality" of individual children rather than about educational systems that need to modify programs to accommodate all learners. Labels put the spotlight on deviant personalities rather than on dysfunctional aspects of their environment. In societies that have an individualistic orientation, like the United States, people are all too ready to misattribute success and failure to the person, while underestimating the impact of the behavioral setting. We blame the victim for failure and thereby take society off the hook; we give credit to the person for success and thereby do not recognize the many societal influences that made it possible. We need to recognize that what people are now is a product of where they've been, where they think they are headed, and what situation is currently influencing their behavior.

We'd like to conclude this chapter on a personal note from Phil Zimbardo, one that may have some inspirational value to students who do not do well on objective tests:

Although I have gone on to have a successful career as a professional psychologist, the relevant tests I took many years ago would have predicted otherwise. Despite being an Honors undergraduate student, who graduated Summa Cum Laude, I got my only C grade in Introductory Psychology, where grades were based solely on multiple-choice exams. I was initially rejected for graduate training at Yale University; then I became an alternate, and finally, I was accepted reluctantly. This was in part because my GRE math scores were below the psychology department's criterion cutoff level. But I later discovered that it was also due in part to the false assumption of some faculty that I must be Negro—on the basis of the pattern of my answers and other "evidence" revealed in my application and tests. Such data negatively colored their judgments of my potential for a career in psychology. Fortunately, some others were willing to give me a chance when one of their respectable admits (Gordon Bower, now a famous psychologist) went elsewhere to start his graduate training.

Successful performance in a career and in life requires much more than the skills, abilities, and traits measured by standardized tests. While the best tests perform the valuable function of predicting how well people will do on the average, there may be decisional error for any given individual. People can override the pessimistic predictions of their tests scores when ambition, imagination, hope, personal pride, and intense effort empower their performance. Perhaps it is vital to know when you should believe more in yourself than in the results of a test.

SUMMING UP

Although psychological testing often has benefits for the individual, tests are still sometimes used in ways that are irresponsible. Critics worry about the fairness of test-based decisions, the utility of tests for evaluating educational practices, and the implications of using test scores as labels to categorize individuals.

RECAPPING MAIN POINTS

What Is Assessment?

- Psychological assessment has a long history, beginning in ancient China. Many important contributions were made by Sir Francis Galton.

- A useful assessment tool must be reliable, valid, and standardized. A reliable measure gives consistent results. A valid measure assesses the attributes for which the test was designed.

- A standardized test is always administered and scored in the same way; norms allow a person's score to be compared with the averages of others of the same age, sex, and culture.

Intelligence Assessment

- Binet began the tradition of objective intelligence testing in France in the early 1900s. Scores were given in terms of mental ages and were meant to represent children's current level of functioning.
- In the United States, Terman created the Stanford–Binet Intelligence Scale and popularized the concept of IQ.
- Wechsler designed special intelligence tests for adults, children, and preschoolers.

Theories of Intelligence

- Psychometric analyses of IQ suggest that several basic abilities, such as fluid and crystallized aspects of intelligence, contribute to IQ scores.
- Contemporary theories conceive of and measure intelligence very broadly by considering the skills and insights people use to solve the types of problems they encounter.
- Sternberg differentiates componential, experiential, and contextual aspects of intelligence.
- Gardner identifies eight types of intelligence that both include and go beyond the types of intelligence assessed by standard IQ measures. Recent research has focused on emotional intelligence.

The Politics of Intelligence

- Almost from the outset, intelligence tests have been used to make negative claims about ethnic and racial groups.
- Because of the reasonably high heritability of IQ, some researchers have attributed the lower scores of some racial and cultural groups to innate inferiority.
- Environmental disadvantages and stereotype threat appear to explain the lower scores of certain groups. Research shows that group differences can be affected through environmental interventions.

Creativity

- Creativity is often assessed using tests of divergent thinking.
- Exceptionally creative people take risks, prepare, and are highly motivated.
- A link between madness and creativity has not been confirmed.

Assessment and Society

- Though often useful for prediction and as an indication of current performance, test results should not be used to limit an individual's opportunities for development and change.
- When the results of an assessment will affect an individual's life, the techniques used must be reliable and valid for that individual and for the purpose in question.

Key Terms

chronological age (p. 295)
creativity (p. 311)
criterion validity (p. 293)
crystallized intelligence (p. 300)
divergent thinking (p. 312)
emotional intelligence (p. 302)
EQ (p. 303)
face validity (p. 293)
fluid intelligence (p. 300)
formal assessment (p. 292)
g (p. 300)
heritability estimate (p. 305)
intelligence (p. 295)
intelligence quotient (IQ) (p. 296)
internal consistency (p. 292)
mental age (p. 295)
mental retardation (p. 296)
norms (p. 294)
parallel forms (p. 292)
predictive validity (p. 293)
psychological assessment (p. 290)
psychometrics (p. 299)
reliability (p. 292)
split-half reliability (p. 292)
standardization (p. 294)
stereotype threat (p. 310)
test–retest reliability (p. 292)
validity (p. 292)

**Solutions to the anagrams
in Table 10.3:**

1. laugh
2. tempt
3. short
4. knight
5. write
6. allow
7. drive
8. couch
9. enter
10. basic

human development across the life span

11

- **STUDYING AND EXPLAINING DEVELOPMENT**
  Documenting Development • Explaining Development

- **PHYSICAL DEVELOPMENT ACROSS THE LIFE SPAN**
  Prenatal and Childhood Development • Physical Development in Adolescence • Physical Changes in Adulthood

- **COGNITIVE DEVELOPMENT ACROSS THE LIFE SPAN**
  Piaget's Insights into Mental Development • Contemporary Perspectives on Early Cognitive Development • Cognitive Development in Adulthood

- **ACQUIRING LANGUAGE**
  Perceiving Speech and Perceiving Words • Learning Word Meanings • Acquiring Grammar

- **SOCIAL DEVELOPMENT ACROSS THE LIFE SPAN**
  Erikson's Psychosocial Stages • Social Development in Childhood • Social Development in Adolescence • Social Development in Adulthood

- **PSYCHOLOGY IN YOUR LIFE: HOW DOES DAY CARE AFFECT CHILDREN'S DEVELOPMENT?**

- **GENDER DEVELOPMENT**
  Sex and Gender • The Acquisition of Gender Roles

- **MORAL DEVELOPMENT**
  Kohlberg's Stages of Moral Reasoning • Gender and Cultural Perspectives on Moral Reasoning

- **LEARNING TO AGE SUCCESSFULLY**

- **RECAPPING MAIN POINTS**
  Key Terms

I guess my childhood was just what everybody would want. My father was a doctor and my mom's an insurance agent. As far as their economic growth, it's what everybody would want, but it was no family time. You know what I'm saying? Pop's trying to make the dollar so he can buy Mom a Benz, buy her snake-skin shoes and all that, but it was not family time. So you know I learned from my environment. I learned from the kids in the neighborhood.

Because there was no family time, I got whuppings for what I did wrong, but I didn't get rewards for what I did right. So it was always, Well, do something bad so at least they'll hit you, you know? At least you'll get some kind of attention....

What I want to do is start my own school. Ten years from now I see myself in a class, but not a regular classroom. I mean, it's not going to be about surviving in this political and economic system because this politics is evil anyway. It's all about being better than somebody else.

My school is going to be a school of just equal teachers—you know, white, black, Hispanic, Chinese, whatever—'cause it's all about uplifting the heart and liberating the mind and body. Not the money game. Money can buy you the biggest Benz or the biggest house, but if your heart is not satisfied, you're still an upset person.

These are the words of Darryl, a 16-year-old African American adolescent from Atlanta; you learn quite clearly how the events that shaped his past also shape his aspirations for the future (Goodwillie, 1993, pp. 28–29). How did Darryl develop to reach this point? How will he develop over the years to come? In Chapter 11, we seek to understand the forces that shape individuals' lives across their entire life spans.

Imagine you are holding a newborn baby. How might you predict what this child will be like as a 1-year-old? At 5 years? At 15? At 50? At 70? At 90? Your predictions would almost certainly consist of a mixture of the general and the specific—the child is extremely likely to learn a language but might or might not be a gifted author. Your predictions would also rely on considerations of heredity and of environment—if both of the child's parents were gifted authors, you might be willing to guess that the child would also show literary talent; if the child was educated in an enriched environment, you might predict that the child's accomplishments would exceed those of the parents. In this chapter, we describe

the theories of developmental psychology that enable us to think systematically about the types of predictions we can make for the life course of a newborn child.

Developmental psychology is the area of psychology that is concerned with changes in physical and psychological functioning that occur from conception across the entire life span. The task of developmental psychologists is to find out how and why organisms change over time—to *document* and *explain* development. Investigators study the time periods in which different abilities and functions first appear and observe how those abilities are modified. The basic premise is that mental functioning, social relationships, and other vital aspects of human nature develop and change throughout the entire life cycle. Table 11.1 presents a rough guide to the major periods of the life span.

In this chapter we will provide a general account of how researchers document development and the theories they use to explain patterns of change over time. We will then divide your life experiences into different domains and trace development in each domain. Early in the chapter, we focus on physical, cognitive, and language development. We then shift our attention to the changing nature of social relationships over the life span as well as the specific tasks individuals face at different moments in their lives. Let's begin now with the question of what it means to study development.

> ▪ **Developmental psychology** The branch of psychology concerned with interaction between physical and psychological processes and with stages of growth from conception throughout the entire life span.

TABLE 11.1

Stages in Life Span Development

Stage	Age Period
Prenatal	Conception to birth
Infancy	Birth at full term to about 18 months
Early childhood	About 18 months to about 6 years
Late childhood	About 6 years to about 13 years
Adolescence	About 13 years to about 20 years
Early adulthood	About 20 years to about 30 years
Middle adulthood	About 30 years to about 65 years
Late adulthood	About 65 years and older

Studying and Explaining Development

Suppose we ask you to make a list of all the ways in which you believe you have changed in the last year. What sorts of things would you put on the list? Have you undertaken a new physical fitness program? Or have you let an injury heal? Have you developed a range of new hobbies? Or have you decided to focus on just one interest? Have you developed a new circle of friends? Or have you become particularly close to one individual? When we describe development, we will conceptualize it in terms of *change*. We have asked you to perform this exercise of thinking about your own changes to make the point that change almost always involves trade-offs. Often people conceptualize the life span as mostly *gains*—changes for the better—in childhood and mostly *losses*—changes for the worse—over the course of adulthood.

However, the perspective on development we will take here emphasizes that *options*, and therefore gains and losses, are features of all development (Dixon, 1999; Uttal & Perlmutter, 1989). When, for example, people choose a lifetime companion, they give up variety but gain security. When people retire, they give up status but gain leisure time.

It is also important that you not think of development as a *passive* process. You will see that many developmental changes require an individual's *active* engagement with his or her environment (Bronfenbrenner, 1999; Bronfenbrenner & Ceci, 1994).

Let's see how researchers document developmental changes.

Documenting Development

To document change, a good first step is to determine what an average person is like—in physical appearance, cognitive abilities, and so on—at a particular age. **Normative investigations** seek to describe a characteristic of a specific age or developmental stage. By systematically testing individuals of different ages, researchers can determine developmental landmarks. These data provide *norms*, standard patterns of development or achievement, based on observation of many people.

Normative standards allow psychologists to make a distinction between **chronological age**—the number of months or years since a person's birth—and **developmental age**—the chronological age at which most people show the particular level of physical or mental development demonstrated by that child. A 3-year-old child who has verbal skills typical of most 5-year-olds is said to have a developmental age of 5 for verbal skills. Norms provide a standard basis for comparison both between individuals and between groups.

Developmental psychologists use several types of research designs to understand possible mechanisms of change. In a **longitudinal design**, the same individuals are repeatedly observed and tested over time, often for many years. Researchers might, for example, test the same children several times weekly over the course of a few months to catch, as closely as possible, the moment at which each child begins to use a mature strategy to solve arithmetic problems (Siegler & Crowley, 1991). By isolating the moment of change, researchers can gain a better understanding of what circumstances must precede the change. Researchers also often use longitudinal designs to study *individual differences*. To understand the life outcomes of different people, researchers may assess a range of potential causal factors early in life and see how those factors influence each individual's life course.

A general advantage of longitudinal research is that, because the participants have lived through the same socioeconomic period, age-related changes cannot be confused with variations in differing societal circumstances (Schaie, 1989). A disadvantage, however, is that some types of generalizations can be made only to the same *cohort*, the group of individuals born in the same time

Normative investigations Research efforts designed to describe what is characteristic of a specific age or developmental stage.

Chronological age The number of months or years since an individual's birth.

Developmental age The chronological age at which most children show a particular level of physical or mental development.

Longitudinal design A research design in which the same participants are observed repeatedly, sometimes over many years.

In a longitudinal design, observations are made of the same individual at different ages, often for many years. This well-known woman might be part of a longitudinal study of British children born in 1926. How might she be similar to and different from other children in that cohort?

period as the research participants. Also, longitudinal studies are costly because it is difficult to keep track of the participants over extended time, and data are easily lost due to participants' quitting or disappearing.

Most research on development uses a **cross-sectional design,** in which groups of participants, of different chronological ages, are observed and compared at one and the same time. A researcher can then draw conclusions about behavioral differences that may be related to age changes. Researchers might, for example, study changes in the ways friends provide social support across

Cross-sectional design A research method in which groups of participants of different chronological ages are observed and compared at a given time.

the teenage years by having pairs of 11-, 15-, and 19-year-olds engage in the same laboratory task (Denton & Zarbatany, 1996). A disadvantage of cross-sectional designs comes from comparing individuals who differ by year of birth as well as by chronological age. Age-related changes are confounded by differences in the social or political conditions experienced by different *birth cohorts* (people born in the same time period). Thus a study comparing samples of 10- and 18-year-olds now might find that the participants differ from 10- and 18-year-olds who grew up in the 1970s, in ways related to their different eras as well as to their developmental stages.

Each methodology gives researchers the opportunity to document change from one age to another. But how do they explain the overall pattern of changes? We'll consider that question next.

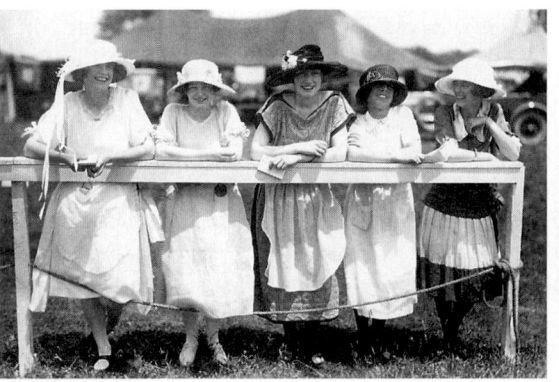

A drawback of cross-sectional research is the cohort effect. What differences might exist between these two groups of women as a result of the era in which they have lived?

Explaining Development

Most children learn to use language, but each child does so at a slightly different rate. Most adolescents reason more efficiently than their younger siblings, but some reason better than others. To explain development, we have to consider both universal, shared aspects of change and the unique aspects of change that characterize each individual.

The sharpest contrast among theories of development has most often applied to changes that occur during childhood. The question is how best to account for the profound differences between a newborn and, for example, a 10-year-old: To what extent is such development determined by heredity (nature), and to what extent is it a product of learned experiences (nurture)? The **nature–nurture controversy** is a long-standing debate among philosophers, psychologists, and educators over the relative importance of heredity versus learning. On one side of this debate are those who believe that the human infant is born without knowledge or skills and that experience, in the form of human learning, etches messages on the blank tablet (in Latin, the *tabula rasa*) of the infant's unformed mind. This view, originally proposed by British philosopher **John Locke,** is known as *empiricism*. It credits human development to experience. Empiricists believe that what directs human development is the stimulation people receive as they are *nurtured*. Among the scholars opposing empiricism was French philosopher **Jean-Jacques Rousseau.** He argued the *nativist* view that *nature*, or the evolutionary legacy that each child brings into the world, is the mold that shapes development.

The debate between empiricists and nativists was intensified by the discovery, in 1798, of a boy who had apparently been raised by animals in the forests around the village of Aveyron, France. This 12-year-old *feral* (wild) child, who became known as the Wild Boy of Aveyron, was thought to hold the answers to profound questions about human nature: Could he, having survived the absence of human contact as a child, become fully human?

A young doctor, **Jean Marc Itard,** accepted the challenge of trying to civilize and educate the Wild Boy of Aveyron, whom he named Victor. At first, Itard's intensive training program seemed to be working; Victor became affectionate and well mannered and learned to follow instructions. After five years, however, progress stopped, and the teacher reluctantly called an end to the experiment (Itard, 1802/1962). Did nature or nurture fail? Perhaps Victor had been abandoned as an infant because he was developmentally disabled. If that was the case, any training could have had only limited success. If not, would modern training procedures have helped the boy develop more fully than Itard's methods? One authority on Victor's story, Harlan Lane (1976, 1986), believes that the case shows clearly the vital role of early social contact on communication and mental growth.

Researchers have now developed a range of techniques to study the effects of nature and nurture without requiring unfortunate *experiments of nature* like Victor's case. We know that the extreme positions of Locke and Rousseau do injustice to the richness of human behavior. Almost any complex action is shaped both by an individual's biological inheritance and by personal experience. We wish you to think about interactions of nature and nurture in this way: Heredity provides potential; experience determines the way in which the potential will be fulfilled. Throughout this chapter, you will see how potential and fulfillment unfold for unique individuals.

SUMMING UP

Developmental psychologists propose theories to explain how and why people change across the life span. Researchers use normative investigations to describe characteristics of specific ages or developmental stages. Longitudinal studies follow the same individuals over time; cross-sectional designs study different age groups at the same time.

Philosophers and psychologists have long debated the relative importance of heredity versus experience in producing developmental change. Most researchers now conceptualize development as interactions of nature and nurture.

Physical Development across the Life Span

Many of the types of development we describe in this chapter require some special knowledge to detect. For example, you might not notice landmarks in social development until you read about them here. We will begin, however, with a realm of development in which changes are often plainly visible to the untrained eye: **physical development**. There is no doubt that you have undergone enormous physical change since you were born. Such changes will continue until the end of your life. Because physical changes are so numerous, we will focus on the types of changes that have an impact on psychological development.

Nature–nurture controversy The debate concerning the relative importance of heredity (nature) and learning or experience (nurture) in determining development and behavior.

Physical development The bodily changes, maturation, and growth that occur in an organism starting with conception and continuing across the life span.

As the brain grows in the developing fetus, it generates 250,000 new neurons per minute. What must the brain be prepared to do, as soon as the child enters the world?

Prenatal and Childhood Development

You began life with unique genetic potential: At the moment of conception a male's sperm cell fertilized a female's egg cell to form the single-cell **zygote;** you received half of the 46 chromosomes found in all normal human body cells from your mother and half from your father. In this section, we outline physical development in the *prenatal period,* from the moment of conception until the moment of birth. We also describe some of the sensory abilities children have obtained even before birth. Finally, we describe the important physical changes that you experienced during childhood.

PHYSICAL DEVELOPMENT IN THE WOMB

The earliest behavior of any kind is the heartbeat. It begins in the *prenatal period,* before birth, when the embryo is about 3 weeks old and a sixth of an inch long. Responses to stimulation have been observed as early as the sixth week, when the embryo is not yet an inch long. Spontaneous movements are observed by the eighth week (Carmichael, 1970; Humphrey, 1970).

After the eighth week, the developing embryo is called a *fetus.* The mother feels fetal movements in about the sixteenth week after conception. At this point, the fetus is about 7 inches long (the average length at birth is 20 inches). As the brain grows in utero, it generates new neurons at the rate of 250,000 per minute, reaching a full complement of over 100 billion neurons by birth (Cowan, 1979). In humans and many other mammals,

Zygote The single cell that results when a sperm fertilizes an egg.

most of this cell proliferation and migration of neurons to their correct locations takes place prenatally, while the development of the branching processes of axons and dendrites largely occurs after birth (Kolb, 1989). The sequence of brain development, from 25 days to 9 months, is shown in **Figure 11.1.**

During the first months of pregnancy, environmental factors such as malnutrition, infection, radiation, or drugs can prevent the normal formation of organs and body structures. For example, when mothers are infected with rubella (German measles) two to four weeks after conception, the probability is roughly 50 percent that the child will suffer negative consequences such as mental retardation, eye damage, deafness, or heart defects. If exposure occurs at other times, the probability of adverse effects is much lower (e.g., 22 percent in the second month; 8 percent in the third month) (Murata et al., 1992). Similarly, mothers who consume certain substances, like alcohol, during sensitive periods put their unborn children at risk for brain damage and other impairment (Goodlett & Johnson, 1999; Jacobson et al., 1993; Roebuck et al., 1999). Facial abnormalities, for example, are most likely to arise from mothers' drinking in the first two months of pregnancy (Coles, 1994). Pregnant women who smoke also put their children at risk, particularly in the second half of pregnancy. Smoking during pregnancy increases the risk of miscarriage, premature births, and low-birth-weight babies. In fact, women who are exposed to secondhand smoke during pregnancy are also more likely to have babies with low birth weights (Dejin-Karlsson et al., 1998).

Some substances may bring about damage at virtually any time during pregnancy. Cocaine, for example, travels through the placenta and can affect fetal development directly. In adults, cocaine causes blood vessels to constrict; in pregnant women, cocaine restricts placental blood flow and oxygen supply to the fetus. If severe oxygen deprivation results, blood vessels in the fetus's brain may burst. Such prenatal strokes can lead to lifelong mental handicaps (Chasnoff et al., 1998; Koren et al., 1998). Research suggests that the brain systems most damaged by cocaine are those responsible for controlling attention: Children exposed to cocaine in the womb may spend their lives overcome by the distractions of irrelevant sights and sounds.

We use these examples to emphasize that nature and nurture interact to shape body and brain even before a child is born.

BABIES PREWIRED FOR SURVIVAL

What capabilities are programmed into this body and brain at birth? We are accustomed to thinking about newborns as entirely helpless. John Watson, the founder of behaviorism, described the human infant as "a lively, squirming bit of flesh, capable of making a few simple responses." If that sounds right, you might be surprised to learn that, moments out of the womb, infants reveal

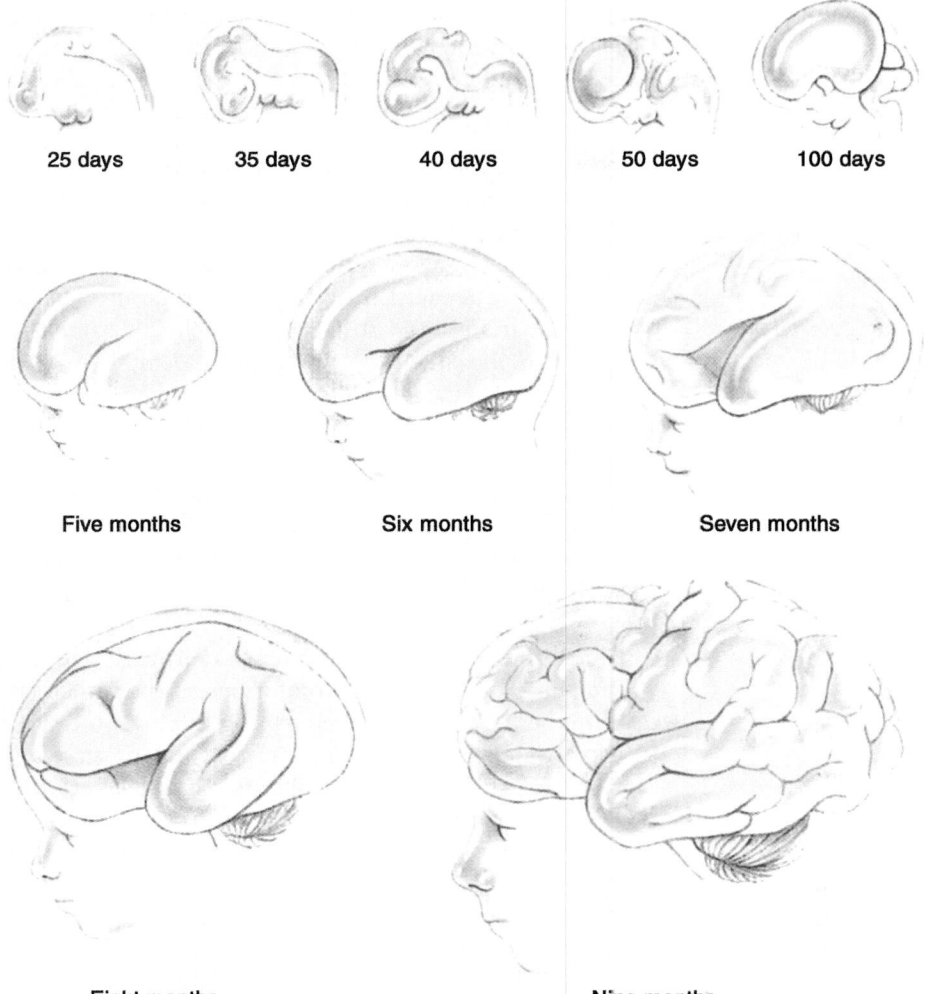

25 days 35 days 40 days 50 days 100 days

Five months Six months Seven months

Eight months Nine months

FIGURE 11.1

The Development of the Human Brain

During the nine months before birth, the brain reaches its complement of over 100 billion neurons.

remarkable abilities to obtain information through their senses and react to it. They might be thought of as *prewired for survival,* well suited to respond to adult caregivers and to influence their social environments.

For example, infants can hear even before birth, so they are prepared to respond to certain sounds when they are born. Newborns prefer to listen to their mothers' voices rather than the voices of other women, suggesting they have learned to recognize their mother's voice while in utero (DeCasper & Fifer, 1980). Researchers have also provided evidence that what newborns recognize, more specifically, is their mothers' voices altered in the way they are altered as the sound passes through the mother's body tissue (i.e., some sound frequencies are filtered out), to reach the child in the uterus (Spence & DeCasper, 1937; Spence & Freeman, 1996). Thus, newborns recognize the sounds closest to their prenatal experience. Unfortunately, they don't seem to have enough auditory experience with their dads: Newborns show no preference for their fathers' voices (DeCasper & Prescott, 1984). Even at age 4 months,

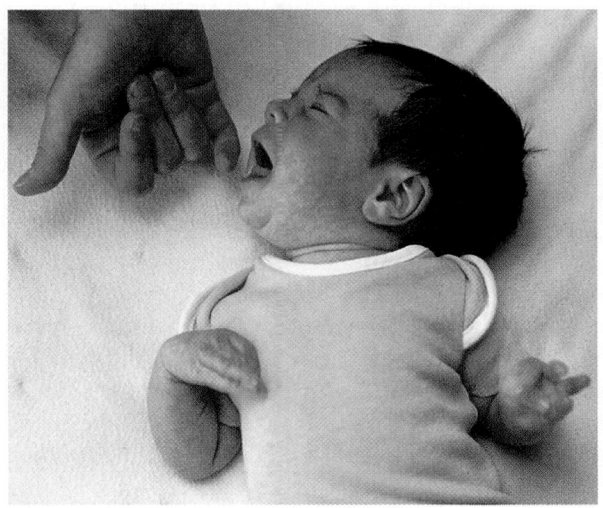

When something touches a newborn's cheek, the rooting reflex prompts the baby to seek something to suck. In what other ways are children prewired for survival?

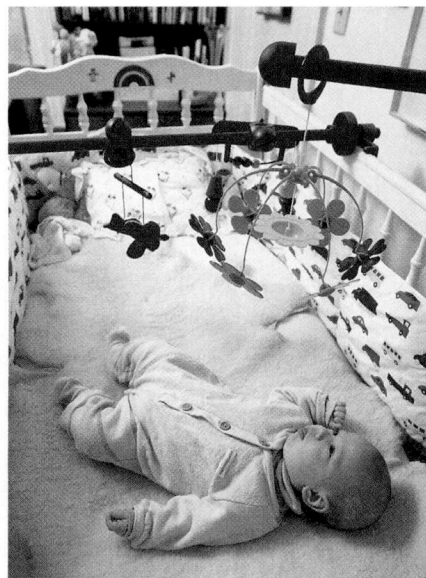

Early on, infants can perceive large objects that display a great deal of contrast. What visual experiences do newborns find particularly appealing?

infants still do not prefer their father's voice to a stranger's voice (Ward & Cooper, 1999).

Infants also put their visual systems to work almost immediately: A few minutes after birth, a newborn's eyes are alert, turning in the direction of a voice and searching inquisitively for the source of certain sounds. Even so, vision is less well developed than the other senses at birth. The visual acuity of adults is roughly 40 times better than the visual acuity of newborns (Sireteanu, 1999). Visual acuity improves rapidly over the first six months of a baby's life. Newborns also are ill equipped to experience the world in three dimensions: It is only at about 4 months of age that children are able to combine information from their two eyes to perceive depth. Good vision—sensitivity to contrast, visual acuity, and color discrimination—requires that a great many photoreceptor cells function in the center of the eye's receptive area and that the optics of the eye develop appropriately (see Chapter 4). Many of these components have yet to mature in the infant's visual system. Good vision also requires that numerous connections between neurons in the brain's visual cortex be made in response to visual experience (Maurer et al., 1999). At birth, not enough of these connections are laid down.

Even without perfect vision, however, children have visual preferences. Pioneering researcher **Robert Fantz** (1963) observed that babies as young as 4 months old preferred looking at objects with contours rather than those that were plain, complex ones rather than simple ones, and whole faces rather than faces with features in disarray. More recent research has confirmed that children prefer human faces to visually similar displays right

from birth (Valenza et al., 1996). In fact, by age 4 days, newborns recognize their own mothers' faces.

This result suggests that at a remarkably early age children have stored important information about their environment: features of their mother's face. You can see why we characterized infants as "prewired for survival."

Once children start to move around in their environment, they quickly acquire other perceptual capabilities. For example, classic research by **Eleanor Gibson** and **Richard Walk** (1960) examined how children respond to depth information. This research used an apparatus called a *visual cliff*. The visual cliff had a board running across the middle of a solid glass surface. As shown in **Figure 11.2**, checkerboard cloth was used to create a deep end and a shallow end. In their original research, Gibson and Walk demonstrated that children would readily leave the center board to crawl across the shallow end, but they were reluctant to crawl across the deep end. Subsequent research has demonstrated that fear of the deep end depends on crawling experience: Children who have begun to crawl experience fear of the deep end, whereas their noncrawling same-age peers do not (Campos et al., 1992). Thus, wariness of heights is not quite "prewired," but it develops quickly as children begin to explore the world under their own power.

GROWTH AND MATURATION IN CHILDHOOD

Newborn infants change at an astonishing rate but, as shown in **Figure 11.3**, physical growth is not equal across all physical structures. You've probably noticed that babies seem to be all head. At birth, a baby's head is already about 60 percent of its adult size and measures a quarter of the whole body length (Bayley, 1956). An infant's body weight doubles in the first six months and triples by the first birthday; by the age of 2, a child's trunk is about half of its adult length. Genital tissue shows little change until the teenage years and then develops rapidly to adult proportions.

For most children, physical growth is accompanied by the maturation of motor ability. **Maturation** refers to

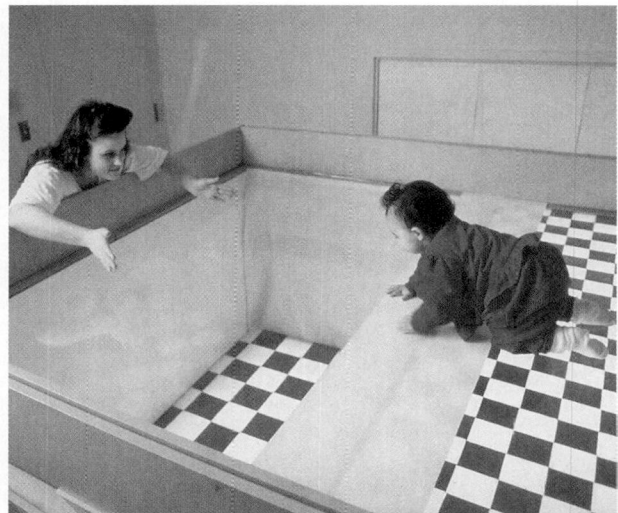

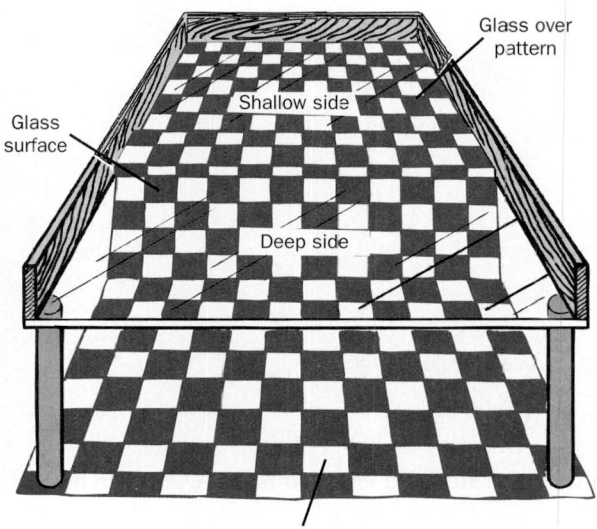

Glass over pattern

Glass surface

Shallow side

Deep side

Floor as seen through glass

FIGURE 11.2

The Visual Cliff

Once children have gained experience crawling around their environment, they show fear of the deep side of the visual cliff.

the process of growth typical of all members of a species who are reared in the species's usual habitat. The characteristic maturational sequences newborns experience are determined by the interaction of inherited biological boundaries and environmental inputs. For example, in the sequence for locomotion, as shown in **Figure 11.4,** a child learns to walk without special training. This se-

Maturation The continuing influence of heredity throughout development; the age-related physical and behavioral changes characteristic of a species.

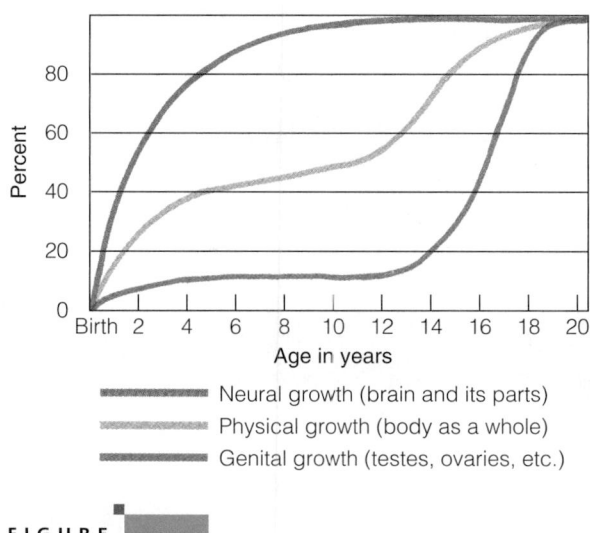

FIGURE 11.3

Growth Patterns across the First Two Decades of Life

Neural growth occurs very rapidly in the first year of life. It is much faster than overall physical growth. By contrast, genital maturation does not occur until adolescence.

quence applies to the great majority of babies; a minority of children skip a step or develop their own original sequences. Even so, in cultures in which there is less physical stimulation, children begin to walk later. The Native American practice of carrying babies in tightly bound back cradles retards walking, but, once released, the child goes through the same sequence. Therefore, you can think of all unimpaired newborn children as possessing the same potential for physical maturation.

What effect does a cradleboard have on the infant's ability to learn to walk?

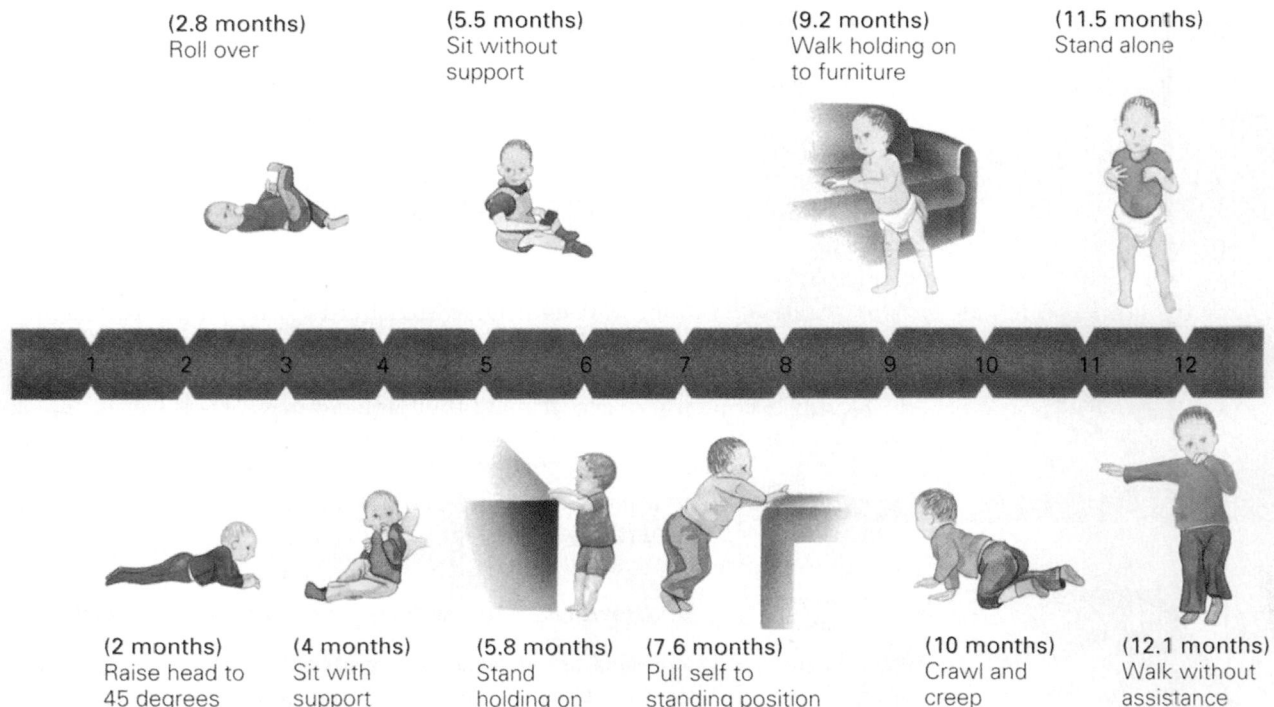

(2.8 months)
Roll over

(5.5 months)
Sit without
support

(9.2 months)
Walk holding on
to furniture

(11.5 months)
Stand alone

1 2 3 4 5 6 7 8 9 10 11 12

(2 months)
Raise head to
45 degrees

(4 months)
Sit with
support

(5.8 months)
Stand
holding on

(7.6 months)
Pull self to
standing position

(10 months)
Crawl and
creep

(12.1 months)
Walk without
assistance

FIGURE 11.4

Maturational Timetable for Locomotion

The development of walking requires no special teaching. It follows a fixed, time-ordered sequence that is typical of all physically capable members of our species. In cultures that provide stimulation for very young children, youngsters begin to walk sooner (Shirley, 1931).

Physical Development in Adolescence

The first concrete indicator of the end of childhood is the *pubescent growth spurt.* At around age 10 for girls and age 12 for boys, growth hormones flow into the bloodstream. For several years, the adolescent may grow three to six inches a year and gain weight rapidly as well. The adolescent's body does not reach adult proportions all at once. Hands and feet grow to full adult size first. The arms and legs come next, with the torso developing most slowly. Thus an individual's overall shape changes several times over the teenage years.

Two to three years after the onset of the growth spurt, **puberty,** or sexual maturity, is reached. (The Latin word *pubertas* means "covered with hair" and signifies the growth of hair on the arms and legs, under the arms, and

Puberty The attainment of sexual maturity; indicated for girls by menarche and for boys by the production of live sperm and the ability to ejaculate.

Menarche The onset of menstruation.

Body image The subjective experience of the appearance of one's body.

in the genital area.) Puberty for males begins with the production of live sperm, while for girls it begins at **menarche,** the onset of menstruation. In the United States, the average time for menarche is between the ages of 12 and 13, although the normal range extends from 11 to 15. For boys, the production of live sperm first occurs, on average, between the ages of 12 and 14, but again there is considerable variation in this timing. These physical changes often bring about an awareness of sexual feelings. In Chapter 12, we will discuss the onset of sexual motivation.

The physical changes of puberty have an impact on other aspects of the adolescent's psychological development. These changes often cause adolescents to focus considerable attention on their physical appearance: Dramatic physical changes and heightened emphasis on peer acceptance exaggerate individuals' concern with their **body image,** their subjective view of their appearance. In data averaged across adolescents from ten countries (including the United States, Bangladesh, Turkey, and Taiwan), 38 percent of the girls and 27 percent of the boys reported feeling ugly and unattractive (Offer et al., 1988). Some girls' exaggerated preoccupation with body image and other aspects of their *social self* can lead to self-destructive behavior (Striegel-Moore & Cachelin,

Why do a significant percentage of adolescents in a variety of cultures report feeling unhappy with their looks?

1999). To achieve their distorted notion of perfection, adolescent females may develop serious eating disorders, such as *anorexia,* which involves self-starvation, and *bulimia,* which involves binging and purging. (We will discuss eating disorders more fully in Chapter 12.) Fortunately, early adolescence appears to be the peak period for this preoccupation. Over time, adolescents become more accepting of their appearances.

With the passing of adolescence, your body once again reaches a period of the life span in which biological change is comparatively minimal. You may affect your body in a variety of ways—by diet and exercise, for example—but the next striking set of changes that are consistent consequences of aging occur in middle and late adulthood.

Physical Changes in Adulthood

Some of the most obvious changes that occur with age concern your physical appearance and abilities. As you grow older, you can expect your skin to wrinkle, your hair to thin and gray, and your height to decrease an inch or two. You can also expect some of your senses to become less acute. These changes do not appear suddenly at age 65. They occur gradually, beginning as soon as early adulthood. However, before we describe some common age-related changes, we want to make a more general point: Many physical changes arise not from aging but from *disuse;* research supports a general belief in the

maxim "Use it or lose it." Older adults who maintain (or renew) a program of physical fitness may experience fewer of the difficulties that are often thought to be inevitable consequences of aging. (Note that we will reach exactly the same conclusion when we discuss cognitive and social aspects of middle and late adulthood.) Let's now look, however, at some changes that are largely unavoidable and frequently have an impact on the way adults think about their lives.

VISION

The vast majority of people over 65 experience some loss of visual function (Carter, 1982; Pitts, 1982). With age, the lenses of people's eyes become yellowed and less flexible. The yellowing of the lens is thought to be responsible for diminished color vision experienced by some older people. Colors of lower wavelengths—violets, blues, and greens—are particularly hard for some older adults to discriminate. The rigidity of the lens can make seeing objects at close range difficult. Lens rigidity also affects dark adaptation, making night vision a problem for older people. Many normal visual changes can be aided with corrective lenses.

HEARING

Hearing loss is common among those 60 and older. The average older adult has difficulty hearing high-frequency sounds (Corso, 1977). This impairment is usually greater for men than for women. Older adults can have a hard time understanding speech—particularly that spoken by high-pitched voices. (Oddly enough, with age, people's speaking voices increase in pitch due to stiffening of the vocal cords.) Deficits in hearing can be gradual and hard for an individual to notice until they are extreme. In addition, even when individuals become aware of hearing loss, they may deny it, because it is perceived as an undesirable sign of aging. Some of the physiological aspects of hearing loss can be overcome with the help of hearing aids. You should also be aware, as you grow older or interact with older adults, that it helps to speak in low tones, enunciate clearly, and reduce background noise.

REPRODUCTIVE AND SEXUAL FUNCTIONING

We saw that puberty marks the onset of reproductive functioning. In middle and late adulthood, reproductive capacity diminishes. Around age 50, most women experience *menopause,* the cessation of menstruation and ovulation. For men, changes are less abrupt, but the quantity of viable sperm falls off after age 40, and the volume of seminal fluid declines after age 60. Of course, these changes are relevant primarily to reproduction. Increasing age and physical change do not necessarily impair other aspects of sexual experience (Levine, 1998; Levy, 1994). Indeed, sex is one of life's healthy pleasures that can enhance successful aging because it is arousing, provides aerobic exercise, stimulates fantasy, and is a vital form of social interaction.

Older adults can and do enjoy the many benefits of intimacy and sexual relationships. Why does this image clash with stereotypes of late adulthood?

You have had a brief review of the landmarks of physical development. Against that background, let's turn now to the ways in which you developed an understanding of the world around you.

SUMMING UP

Babies come into the world with sensory abilities that enable them to acquire information and forge social relationships. Physical growth is usually accompanied by maturation of motor ability.

In adolescence, individuals go through puberty. Adolescents often place exaggerated emphasis on body image. Some physical changes associated with adulthood are the result of disuse rather than the physical processes of aging. However, most adults experience changes in their vision, hearing, and sexual functions.

Cognitive Development across the Life Span

How does an individual's understanding of physical and social reality change across the life span? **Cognitive development** is the study of the processes and products of the mind as they emerge and change over time. Because researchers have been particularly fascinated by the earliest emergence of cognitive capabilities, we will focus much of our attention on the earliest

stages of cognitive development. However, we will also describe some of the discoveries researchers have made about cognitive development across the adult years.

We begin our discussion of cognitive development with the pioneering work of the late Swiss psychologist Jean Piaget.

Piaget's Insights into Mental Development

For nearly 50 years, **Jean Piaget** (1929, 1954, 1977) developed theories about the ways that children think, reason, and solve problems. Perhaps Piaget's interest in cognitive development grew out of his own intellectually active youth: Piaget published his first article at age 10 and was offered a post as a museum curator at age 14 (Brainerd, 1996). Piaget used simple demonstrations and sensitive interviews with his own children and with other children to generate complex theories about early mental development. His interest was not in the amount of information children possessed but in the ways their thinking and inner representations of physical reality changed at different stages in their development.

BUILDING BLOCKS OF DEVELOPMENTAL CHANGE

Piaget gave the name **schemes** to the mental structures that enable individuals to interpret the world. Schemes are the building blocks of developmental change. Piaget characterized the infant's initial schemes as *sensorimotor intelligence*—mental structures or programs that guide sensorimotor sequences, such as sucking, looking, grasping, and pushing. With practice, elementary schemes are combined, integrated, and differentiated into ever-more-complex, diverse action patterns, as when a child pushes away undesired objects to seize a desired one behind him or her. According to Piaget, two basic processes work in tandem to achieve cognitive growth—assimilation and accommodation. **Assimilation** modifies new environmental information to fit into what is already known; the child accesses existing schemes to structure incoming sensory data. **Accommodation** restructures or modifies

Cognitive development The development of processes of knowing, including imagining, perceiving, reasoning, and problem solving.

Schemes Piaget's term for cognitive structures that develop as infants and young children learn to interpret the world and adapt to their environment.

Assimilation According to Piaget, the process whereby new cognitive elements are fitted in with old elements or modified to fit more easily; this process works in tandem with accommodation.

Accommodation According to Piaget, the process of restructuring or modifying cognitive structures so that new information can fit into them more easily; this process works in tandem with assimilation.

the child's existing schemes so that new information is accounted for more completely.

Consider the transitions a baby must make from sucking at a mother's breast, to sucking the nipple of a bottle, to sipping through a straw, and then to drinking from a cup. The initial sucking response is a reflex action present at birth, but it must be modified somewhat so that the child's mouth fits the shape and size of the mother's nipple. In adapting to a bottle, an infant still uses many parts of the sequence unchanged (assimilation) but must grasp and draw on the rubber nipple somewhat differently from before and learn to hold the bottle at an appropriate angle (accommodation). The steps from bottle to straw to cup require more accommodation but continue to rely on earlier skills. Piaget saw cognitive development as the result of exactly this sort of interweaving of assimilation and accommodation. The balanced application of assimilation and accommodation permits children's behavior and knowledge to become less dependent on concrete external reality, relying more on abstract thought.

STAGES IN COGNITIVE DEVELOPMENT

Piaget believed that children's cognitive development could be divided into a series of four ordered, discontinuous stages (see **Table 11.2**). All children are assumed to progress through these stages in the same sequence, although one child may take longer to pass through a given stage than another.

SENSORIMOTOR STAGE The sensorimotor stage extends roughly from birth to age 2. In the early months, much of an infant's behavior is based on a limited array of inborn schemes, like sucking, looking, grasping, and pushing. During the first year, sensorimotor sequences are improved, combined, coordinated, and integrated (sucking and grasping, looking and manipulating, for example). They become more varied as infants discover that their actions have an effect on external events.

The most important cognitive acquisition of the infancy period is the ability to form mental representations of absent objects—those with which the child is not in direct sensorimotor contact. **Object permanence** refers

Object permanence The recognition that objects exist independently of an individual's action or awareness; an important cognitive acquisition of infancy.

Egocentrism In cognitive development, the inability of a young child at the preoperational stage to take the perspective of another person.

Centration A thought pattern common during the beginning of the preoperational stage of cognitive development; characterized by the child's inability to take more than one perceptual factor into account at the same time.

TABLE 11.2

Piaget's Stages of Cognitive Development

Stage/Ages	Characteristics and Major Accomplishments
Sensorimotor (0–2)	Child begins life with small number of sensorimotor sequences. Child develops object permanence and the beginnings of symbolic thought.
Preoperational (2–7)	Child's thought is marked by egocentrism and centration. Child has improved ability to use symbolic thought.
Concrete operations (7–11)	Child achieves understanding of conservation. Child can reason with respect to concrete, physical objects.
Formal operations (11→)	Child develops capacity for abstract reasoning and hypothetical thinking.

to children's understanding that objects exist and behave independently of their actions or awareness. In the first months of life, children follow objects with their eyes, but, when the objects disappear from view, they turn away as if the objects had also disappeared from their minds. At around 3 months of age, however, they keep looking at the place where the objects had disappeared. Between 8 and 12 months, children begin to search for those disappearing objects. By age 2 years, children have no remaining uncertainty that "out of sight" objects continue to exist (Flavell, 1985).

PREOPERATIONAL STAGE The preoperational stage extends roughly from 2 to 7 years of age. The big cognitive advance in this developmental stage is an improved ability to represent mentally objects that are not physically present. Except for this development, Piaget characterizes the preoperational stage according to what the child *cannot* do. For example, Piaget believed that young children's preoperational thought is marked by **egocentrism,** the child's inability to take the perspective of another person. You have probably noticed egocentrism if you've heard a 2-year-old's conversations with other children. Children at this age often seem to be talking to themselves rather than interacting.

Preoperational children also experience **centration**—the tendency to have their attention captured by the more perceptually striking features of objects. Centration is illustrated by Piaget's classic demonstration of a child's inability to understand that the amount of a liquid does not change as a function of the size or shape of its container.

Piaget observed that the typical 6-month-old will attend to an attractive toy (left) but will quickly lose interest if a screen blocks the toy from view (right). What understanding about objects will the child achieve by age 2?

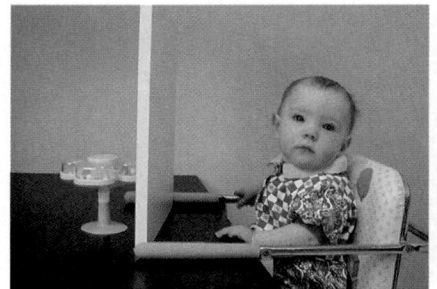 

HOW WE KNOW

PIAGET DEMONSTRATES CENTRATION

When an equal amount of lemonade is poured into two identical glasses, children of ages 5 and 7 report that the glasses contain the same amount. When, however, the lemonade from one glass is poured into a tall, thin glass, their opinions diverge. The 5-year-olds know that the lemonade in the tall glass is the same lemonade, but they report that it now is *more*. The 7-year-olds correctly assert that there is no difference between the amounts.

In Piaget's demonstration, the younger children center on a single, perceptually salient dimension—the height of the lemonade in the glass. The older children take into account both height and width and correctly infer that appearance is not reality. (Do you remember the story at the beginning of Chapter 1? This is the demonstration that student reproduced in his family's kitchen.)

CONCRETE OPERATIONS STAGE   The concrete operations stage goes roughly from 7 to 11 years of age. At this stage, the child has become capable of *mental operations,* actions performed in the mind that give rise to logical thinking. The preoperational and concrete operations stages are often put in contrast because children in the concrete operation stage are now capable of what they failed earlier on. Concrete operations allow children to replace physical action with mental action. For example, if a child sees that Adam is taller than Zara and, later, that Zara is taller than Tanya, the child can reason that Adam is the tallest of the three—without physically manipulating the three individuals. However, the child still cannot draw the appropriate inference ("Adam is tallest") if the problem is just stated with a verbal description. This inability to determine relative heights (and solve similar problems) without direct, physical observation suggests that abstract thought is still in the offing in the period of concrete operations.

The lemonade study illustrates another hallmark of the concrete operations period. The 7-year-olds have mastered what Piaget called **conservation:** They know

■ **Conservation**   According to Piaget, the understanding that physical properties do not change when nothing is added or taken away, even though appearances may change.

This 5-year-old girl is aware that the two containers have the same amount of colored liquid. However, when the liquid from one is poured into a taller container, she indicates that there is more liquid in the taller one. She has not yet grasped the concept of conservation, which she will understand by age 6 or 7. Why wouldn't the 5-year-old child understand the concept, even if she were told the right answer?

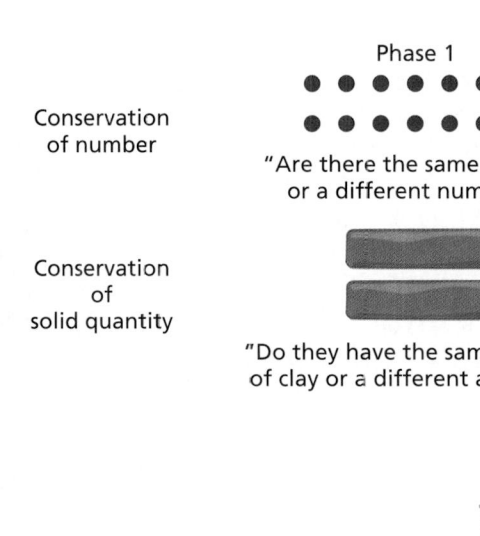

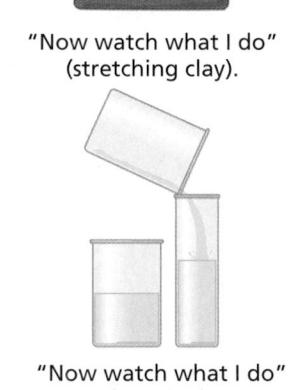
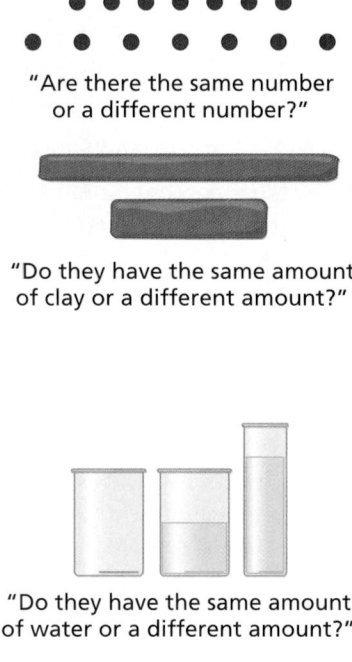

	Phase 1	Phase 2	Phase 3
Conservation of number	"Are there the same number or a different number?"	"Now watch what I do" (spreading).	"Are there the same number or a different number?"
Conservation of solid quantity	"Do they have the same amount of clay or a different amount?"	"Now watch what I do" (stretching clay).	"Do they have the same amount of clay or a different amount?"
Conservation of liquid quantity	"Do they have the same amount of water or a different amount?"	"Now watch what I do" (pouring).	"Do they have the same amount of water or a different amount?"

FIGURE 11.5

Tests of Conservation

that the physical properties of objects do not change when nothing is added or taken away, even though the objects' appearance changes. **Figure 11.5** presents examples of Piaget's tests of conservation for different dimensions. One of the newly acquired operations children can bring to bear on conservation tasks is reversibility. *Reversibility* is the child's understanding that both physical actions and mental operations can be reversed: The child can reason that the amount of lemonade *can't* have changed, because when the physical action is reversed—when the lemonade is poured back into the original glass—the two volumes will once again look identical.

FORMAL OPERATIONS STAGE The formal operations stage covers a span roughly from age 11 on. In this final stage of cognitive growth, thinking becomes abstract. Adolescents can see how their particular reality is only one of several imaginable realities, and they begin to ponder deep questions of truth, justice, and existence. They seek answers to problems in a systematic fashion: Once they achieve formal operations, children can start to play the role of scientist, trying each of a series of possibilities in careful order. Adolescents also begin to be able to use the types of advanced deductive logic we described in Chapter 9. Unlike their younger siblings, adolescents have the ability to reason from abstract premises ("If A, then B" and "not B") to their logical conclusions ("not A").

Contemporary Perspectives on Early Cognitive Development

Piaget's theory remains the classic reference point for the understanding of cognitive development (Flavell, 1996; Lourenço & Machado, 1996, Scholnick et al., 1999). However, contemporary researchers have come up with more flexible ways of studying the development of the child's cognitive abilities. We will now see how a variety of creative new techniques have refined Piaget's conclusions about children's competence.

THE SENSORIMOTOR CHILD REVISITED

Piaget suggested that the development of object permanence is the major accomplishment of the 2-year-old child. However, contemporary research techniques suggest that infants as young as 3 months old, and perhaps younger, have already developed aspects of this concept. They apparently understand the basic principle that solid objects cannot pass through other solid objects. This important finding has been shown with different tasks devised by researcher **Renée Baillargeon** (Buy-ay-zhon) (1987a, 1987b; Baillargeon & DeVos, 1991). During one task, infants demonstrated surprise when observing sequences of events that were impossible.

INFANTS CONTEMPLATE IMPOSSIBLE EVENTS The infants sat in front of a large display box. Directly before them was a small screen; to the left of the screen was a long ramp. The infants watched the following event: The screen was raised (so the infants could see there was nothing behind it) and then lowered; a toy car was pushed onto the ramp; the car rolled down the ramp and across the display box, disappearing as it shot behind the screen, reappearing at the end of the screen, and finally exiting the display box to the right (see **Figure 11.6**).

After the infants became habituated to this event, they saw two test events. (*Habituation* reflects a weakened response when a stimulus is repeated over time.) In both test events, a box was revealed when the screen was raised, but the location of the box differed. In the *possible event,* the box was placed at the back of the display box, behind the tracks of the car, so the car could roll freely through the display. In the *impossible event,* the box was placed on top of the tracks so that it blocked the car's path. Even so, during the event, the car appeared to roll freely across the display. The infants looked longer at the "impossible" event, suggesting that it surprised—dishabituated—them (Baillargeon, 1986).

We can't take the infants' surprise as evidence that they have acquired the full concept of object permanence—they may only know that *something* is wrong without knowing exactly what that something is (Lourenço & Machado, 1996). Even so, Baillargeon's research suggests that even very young children have acquired important knowledge of the physical world.

THE PREOPERATIONAL CHILD REVISITED
Recall that Piaget believed the thinking of preoperational children to be marked by egocentrism. Researchers, however, have demonstrated ways in which children are appropriately sensitive to their audience. For example, children have a pretty good idea of what they know versus what other people know.

YOUNG CHILDREN'S KNOWLEDGE ABOUT OTHERS' KNOWLEDGE Children 4 and 5 years old were asked to consider the knowledge possessed by a 6-month-old baby (Ann), a 4-year-old child (Mary), and an adult (Susan). For each individual, the children were asked questions of the sort, "Does she know what the animal called an elephant looks like?" and "Does she know what the animal called a lemur looks like?" The children were able to differentiate who would know what: The baby would not know about the elephant, but the child would; neither the baby nor the child would know about the lemur; the adult would know about both. This pattern suggests that children don't just make judgments based on what they themselves know (i.e., that they know about elephants, but not lemurs). They are not inevitably egocentric thinkers (Taylor et al., 1991).

Children also can adapt their communication to different types of listeners. When a 4-year-old tells a 2-year-old about a toy, she uses shorter, simpler utterances than she does when telling a peer or adult about that toy (Shatz & Gelman, 1973). Again, this type of adaptation suggests a limit on egocentirsm.

CHILDREN'S FOUNDATIONAL THEORIES
Piaget's theory is built around stages in which landmark changes take place in children's ways of thinking. More

FIGURE 11.6

A Schematic Representation of Habituation and Test Events

In the habituation phase, infants' interest in the event diminished over time. In the test case, their interest was recaptured by the impossible event.

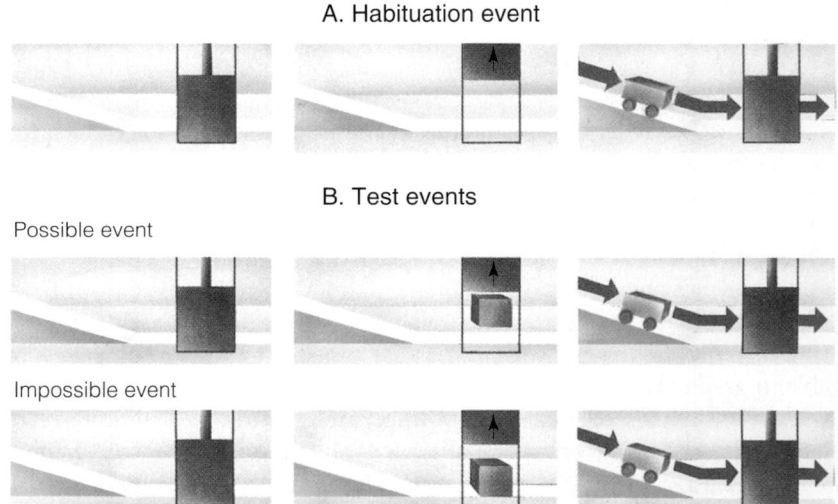

A. Habituation event

B. Test events

Possible event

Impossible event

How do children begin to form generalizations about the world based on what they have experienced and observed?

recently, researchers have explored the idea that changes occur separately, in each of several major domains, as children develop **foundational theories**—frameworks for initial understanding—to explain their experiences of the world (Carey, 1985; Wellman & Gelman, 1992; Wellman & Inagaki, 1997). For example, children accumulate their experiences of the properties of mental states into a *theory of mind,* or naive psychology. By doing so, they are better able to understand the thought processes of themselves and others.

Researchers have formally studied the development of scientific concepts, such as the way in which children project biological properties from one species to another. When asked which of a series of animals sleep or have bones, 4-year-old children were inclined to make their judgments based on their perceptions of the similarity of the animal to humans (Carey, 1985). For example, more 4-year-olds attributed these properties (i.e., "sleep" and "have bones") to dogs than they did to fish, and attributions to fish were, in turn, greater than those to flies. Over time, children must replace a theory based on similarity to humans with one that acknowledges more structure in the animal kingdom—for example, they must acquire the formal distinction between *vertebrates* and *invertebrates* that defines which types of animals have bones. Similarly, 3- and 4-year-old children understand that what is inside objects affects their functions—although they have no clear idea what those insides are (Gelman & Wellman, 1991). Thus, although 3- and 4-year-olds aren't entirely sure what kinds of things are inside dogs, they are quite certain that a dog would cease to be a dog if you removed whatever is inside. In each domain, you see that children begin to develop a general theory and then use a range of new experiences to provide successive refinements.

SOCIAL AND CULTURAL INFLUENCES ON COGNITIVE DEVELOPMENT

In Piaget's theory, much of cognitive development is the product of maturational processes within the child: The environment has very little impact on how the child's cognitive abilities change over time. However, contemporary researchers have begun to focus on the role of social interactions in cognitive development. Much of this research has its origins in the theories of Russian psychologist **Lev Vygotsky.** Vygotsky argued that children develop through a process of **internalization:** They absorb knowledge from their social context that has a major impact on how cognition unfolds over time.

The social theory that Vygotsky pioneered has found support in cross-cultural studies of development. As Piaget's theory initially seized the attention of developmental researchers, many of them sought to use his tasks to study the cognitive achievements of children in diverse cultures (Rogoff & Chavajay, 1995). These studies began to call into question the universality of Piaget's claims because, for example, people in many cultures failed to show evidence that they had acquired formal operations. Late in his life, Piaget himself began to speculate that the specific achievements he characterized as formal operations may rely more on the particular type of science education children obtain rather than on an unfolding of biologically predetermined stages of cognitive development (Lourenço & Machado, 1996).

Vygotsksy's concept of internalization helps to explain the effect culture has on cognitive development. Children's cognition develops to perform culturally valued functions (Serpell & Boykin, 1994; Serpell, 2000). Piaget, for example, invented tasks that reflected his own preconceptions about appropriate and valuable cognitive activities. Other cultures prefer their children to excel in other ways. If Piaget's children had been evaluated with respect to their understanding of the cognitive complexities of weaving, they probably would have appeared to be retarded in their development relative to Mayan children in Guatemala (Rogoff, 1990). Cross-cultural studies of cognitive development have quite often demonstrated that type of schooling plays a large role in determining children's achievement on Piagetian tasks (Rogoff & Chavajay, 1995). Psychologists must use these types of findings to sort out the nature and nurture of cognitive development.

Foundational theories Frameworks for initial understanding formulated by children to explain their experiences of the world.

Internalization According to Vygotsky, the process through which children absorb knowledge from the social context.

The developmental changes we have documented so far are very dramatic. It's easy to tell that a 12-year-old has all sorts of cognitive capabilities unknown to a 1-year-old. We now shift to the more subtle changes that take place throughout adulthood.

Cognitive Development in Adulthood

As we have traced cognitive development across childhood into adolescence, "change" has usually meant "change for the better." When we arrive at the period of late adulthood, though, cultural stereotypes suggest that "change" means "change for the worse" (Parr & Siegert, 1993). However, even when people believe that the course of adulthood brings with it general decline, they still anticipate certain types of gains very late into life (Dixon, 1999). We will look at intelligence and memory to see the interplay of losses and gains.

INTELLIGENCE

There is little evidence to support the notion that general cognitive abilities decline among the healthy elderly. Only about 5 percent of the population experiences major losses in cognitive functioning. When age-related decline in cognitive functioning occurs, it is usually limited to only some abilities. When intelligence is separated into the components that make up your verbal abilities *(crystallized intelligence)* and those that are part of your ability to learn quickly and thoroughly *(fluid intelligence),* fluid intelligence shows the greater decline with age (Baltes & Staudinger, 1993). Much of the decrease in fluidity has

Many prominent figures, such as Nelson Mandela, continue to make important professional contributions through their 70s and beyond. How can some aspects of intellectual performance be kept from decline through late adulthood?

TABLE 11.3

Features of Wisdom

- *Rich factual knowledge.* General and specific knowledge about the conditions of life and its variations

- *Rich procedural knowledge.* General and specific knowledge about strategies of judgment and advice concerning life matters

- *Life span contextualism.* Knowledge about the contexts of life and their temporal (developmental) relationships

- *Uncertainty.* Knowledge about the relative indeterminacy and unpredictability of life and ways to manage it

been attributed to a general slowing down of processing speed: Older adults' performance on intellectual tasks that require many mental processes to occur in small amounts of time is greatly impaired (Salthouse, 1996).

But all change is not in the direction of poorer functioning. For instance, psychologists are now exploring age-related gains in **wisdom**—expertise in the fundamental practices of life (Baltes & Staudinger, 2000). **Table 11.3** presents some of the types of knowledge that define wisdom (Smith & Baltes, 1990). You can see that each type of knowledge is best acquired over a long and thoughtful life. Furthermore, individuals vary greatly in their later-life intellectual performance. Research indicates that older adults who pursue high levels of environmental stimulation tend to maintain high levels of cognitive abilities.

HOW WE KNOW

WHEN PROFESSORS GROW OLD A group of 22 senior professors, ages 60 to 71, from the University of California, Berkeley, were compared in their intellectual functioning to their younger colleagues (ages 30 to 59) and to a control group of older adults in the same age range. The professors performed a variety of tests that tapped different aspects of cognitive functioning. On some of the tests—for example, paired associate learning—the senior professors showed typical patterns of age-related impairment. However, on other measures, the senior professors kept pace with their younger colleagues. For example, they were equally able to listen to tape recordings of brief stories and recall information from those stories. The control group of older adults showed "typical" age-related impairment on this task. How can we explain preserved function for the professors? The researchers suggest that the professors' occupation, which requires them to maintain a high level of mental activity, may protect them from some typical losses of aging (Shimamura et al., 1995).

Does this finding make you want to become a college professor? Other studies suggest that you need not go to that extreme. The important conclusion is that you should keep your mind at work. **Warner Schaie** and his colleagues have even been able to demonstrate that training programs can reverse older adults' decline in some cognitive abilities (Schaie, 1994; Schaie & Willis, 1985). It appears that disuse, rather than decay, may be responsible for the deficits in intellectual performance that are not related to processing speed (Hultsch et al., 1999). As promised, we have again arrived at the conclusion that "Use it or lose it (or seek training to get it back)" is an appropriate motto for the wise older adult.

How can older adults cope successfully with whatever changes inevitably accompany increasing age? Successful aging might consist of making the most of gains while minimizing the impact of the normal losses that accompany aging. This strategy for successful aging, proposed by psychologists **Paul Baltes** and **Margaret Baltes**, is called **selective optimization with compensation** (Baltes et al., 1992; Freund & Baltes, 1998). *Selective* means that people scale down the number and extent of their goals for themselves. *Optimization* refers to people exercising or training themselves in areas that are of highest priority to them. *Compensation* means that people use alternative ways to deal with losses—for example, choosing age-friendly environments. Let's consider an example:

> When the concert pianist [Arthur] Rubinstein was asked, in a television interview, how he managed to remain such a successful pianist in his old age, he mentioned three strategies: (1) In old age he performed fewer pieces, (2) he now practiced each piece more frequently, and (3) he produced more ritardandos [slowings of the tempo] in his playing before fast segments, so that the playing speed sounded faster than it was in reality. These are examples of selection (fewer pieces), optimization (more practice), and compensation (increased use of contrast in speed). (Baltes, 1993, p. 590)

MEMORY

A common complaint among the elderly is the feeling that their ability to remember things is not as good as it used to be. On a number of tests of memory, adults over 60 *do* perform worse than young adults in their 20s (Craik, 1994; Hultsch et al., 1998). People experience memory deficits with advancing age, even when they have been highly educated and otherwise have good intellectual skills (Zelinski et al., 1993). Aging does *not* seem to diminish elderly individuals' ability to access their general knowledge store and personal information about events that occurred long ago. In a study of name and face recognition, middle-aged adults could identify 90 percent of their high school classmates in yearbooks 35 years after graduation, while older adults were still able to recognize 70 to 80 percent of their classmates some 50 years later (Bahrick et al., 1975). However, aging affects the processes that allow new information to be effectively organized, stored, and retrieved (Craik, 1994; Giambra & Arenberg, 1993).

As yet, researchers have been unable to develop a wholly adequate description of the mechanisms that underlie memory impairment in older adults (Craik, 1999). Some theories focus on differences between older and younger people in their efforts to organize and process information. Other theories point to elderly people's reduced ability to pay attention to information. Another type of theory looks to neurobiological changes in the brain systems that produce the physical memory traces. Researchers also believe that older adults' performance may be impaired by their very belief that their memory will be poor (Hertzog et al., 1990; Levy & Langer, 1994). Researchers continue to evaluate the relative contributions of each of these factors.

Some forms of memory impairment are clearly biological. Older adults who suffer from **Alzheimer's disease** experience a gradual loss of memory and deterioration of personality. This disease afflicts about 10 percent of Americans over 65 and perhaps 50 percent of those over 85 (Evans et al., 1989), including, as he made public in November 1994, former president Ronald Reagan. Alzheimer's disease onset is deceptively mild—in early stages the only observable symptom may be memory impairment. However, its course is one of steady deterioration. Victims may show gradual personality changes, such as apathy, lack of spontaneity, and withdrawal from social interactions. In advanced stages, people with Alzheimer's disease may become completely mute and inattentive, even forgetting the names of their spouse and children. Clearly, this form of memory impairment is more profound and tragic than the ordinary memory impairment of late adulthood.

Let's now narrow our focus from general cognitive development to the more specific topic of the acquisition of language.

SUMMING UP

Jean Piaget suggested that children use mental structures called schemes to assimilate and accommodate to information in their environment. Piaget labeled four stages

Wisdom Expertise in the fundamental pragmatics of life.

Selective optimization with compensation A strategy for successful aging in which one makes the most of gains while minimizing the impact of losses that accompany normal aging.

Alzheimer's disease A chronic organic brain syndrome characterized by gradual loss of memory, decline in intellectual ability, and deterioration of personality.

of cognitive development: the sensorimotor stage, in which children achieve object permanence; the preoperational stage, in which children's thought is characterized by egocentrism and centration; the concrete operations stage, in which children become able to conserve and perform concrete mental operations; and the formal operation stage, in which children become able to reason in an abstract and logical fashion.

Contemporary researchers have amended elements of Piaget's theory. For example, children display some aspects of object permanence in their first months; preoperational children are not inevitably egocentric. Researchers also suggest that development may occur separately in different knowledge domains, as children acquire and transform foundational theories. Finally, Piaget's theory needs to be viewed in cultural context. Many cultures value other sorts of cognitive skills than the ones many contemporary cognitive developmentalists study.

Much cognitive decline in adulthood can be traced to a general slowing of cognitive processes. However, people in late adulthood can compensate with the wisdom they have acquired. They can also can preserve a good deal of cognitive functioning by staying mentally active. Most people experience some types of memory loss in adulthood, but those losses are relatively minor compared to the impairments that accompany Alzheimer's disease.

Acquiring Language

Here's a remarkable fact: By the time they are 6 years old, children can analyze language into its units of sound and meaning, use the rules they have discovered to combine sounds into words and words into meaningful sentences, and take an active part in coherent conversations. Children's remarkable language accomplishments have prompted most researchers to agree that the ability to learn language is biologically based—that you are born with an innate language capacity (Pinker, 1994). Even so, depending on where a child happens to be born, he or she may end up as a native speaker of any one of the world's 4,000 different languages. In addition, children are prepared to learn both spoken languages and gestural languages, like American Sign Language. This means that the innate predisposition to learn language must be both quite strong and quite flexible (Meier, 1991).

To explain how it is that infants are such expert language learners, we will describe the evidence that supports the claim of an innate language capacity. We

Phonemes Minimal units of speech in any given language that make a meaningful difference in speech production and reception; *r* and *l* are two distinct phonemes in English but variations of one in Japanese.

TABLE 11.4

The Structure of Language

Grammar is the field of study that seeks to describe the way language is structured and used. It includes several domains:

Phonology—the study of the sounds that are put together to form words.

> A **phoneme** is the smallest unit of speech that distinguishes between any two utterances. For example, *b* and *p* distinguish *bin* from *pin*.
>
> **Phonetics** is the study and classification of speech sounds.

Syntax—the way in which words are strung together to form sentences. For example, subject (*I*) + verb (*like*) + object (*you*) is standard English word order.

> A **morpheme** is the minimum distinctive unit of grammar that cannot be divided without losing its meaning. The word *bins* has two morphemes, *bin* and *s*, indicating the plural.

Semantics—the study of the meanings of words and their changes over time.

> **Lexical meaning** is the dictionary meaning of a word. Meaning is sometimes conveyed by the *context* of a word in a sentence ("Run *fast*" versus "Make the knot *fast*") or the *inflection* with which it is spoken (try emphasizing different words in *white house cat*).

Pragmatics—rules for participation in conversations; social conventions for communicating, sequencing sentences, and responding appropriately to others.

will, however, also discuss the role that the environment plays—after all, children learn the particular languages that are being used in the world around them. Table 11.4 outlines the various types of knowledge children must acquire for their particular signed or spoken language. You might review the language use section of Chapter 9 (pages 258 to 267) to remind yourself how adults put all these types of knowledge to use in fluent conversation.

Perceiving Speech and Perceiving Words

Imagine you are a newborn child, hearing a buzz of noise all around you. How do you start to understand that some of those sounds are relevant to communicating with other people? A child's first step in acquiring a particular language is to take note of the sound contrasts that are used meaningfully in that language. (For signed languages, the child must attend to contrasts in, for example, hand positions.) Each spoken language samples from the set of possible distinctions that can be produced by the human vocal tract; no language uses all of the speech-sound contrasts that can be made. The minimal meaningful units in a language are known as **phonemes.** There are about 45 distinct phonemes in English. Imagine you heard someone speak the words *right* and *light.*

If you are a native speaker of English, you would have no trouble hearing the difference—/r/ and /l/ are different phonemes in English. If, however, your only language experience was with Japanese, you would not be able to hear the difference between these two words, because /r/ and /l/ are not distinct phonemes in Japanese. Do English speakers acquire the ability to make this distinction, or do Japanese speakers lose it?

To answer this type of question, researchers needed to develop methods to obtain linguistic information from prelinguistic children.

COULD YOU PERCEIVE HINDI AT BIRTH?

Using principles of operant conditioning we described in Chapter 6, researchers condition infants to turn their head toward a sound source when they detect a change from one speech sound to another. The reward that reinforces this behavior is an illuminated box that contains a clapping and drumming toy animal. The procedure ensures that, if the children detect changes, they are very likely to turn toward the sound source. To measure the children's ability to perceive a distinction, researchers monitor how frequently the children turn their heads when a change is present.

Janet Werker and her colleagues (Werker, 1991; Werker & Lalond, 1988) have used this technique to examine the innate basis of speech perception abilities—a version of the /r/–/l/ question we posed earlier. Werker studied sound distinctions that are used in Hindi, but not in English—distinctions that make it difficult for adult English speakers to learn Hindi. Werker and her colleagues measured the ability of infants learning English and Hindi, as well as adults who spoke English and Hindi, to hear the differences between the Hindi phonemes. She found that all the infants, regardless of which language they were learning, could hear the differences until the age of 8 months. However, of the infants older than 8 months and of the adults, only the Hindi speakers or speakers-to-be could hear the Hindi contrasts.

Research of this type strongly suggests that you started out with an innate ability to perceive sound contrasts that are important for spoken languages. However, you swiftly lose the ability to perceive some of the contrasts that are not present in the language you begin to acquire (Werker & Tees, 1999).

Along with this biological head start for speech perception, many children also get an environmental head start. When adults in many cultures speak to infants and young children, they use a special form of language that differs from adult speech: an exaggerated, high-pitched intonation known as **child-directed speech,** or less formally as *motherese* or *parentese.* The features that define child-directed speech appear in many but not all cultures (Fernald & Morikawa, 1993; Fernald et al., 1989; Ingram, 1995). Child-directed speech may help infants to acquire language by keeping them interested in and attentive to the things that their parents say to them. The sound patterns of child-directed speech also emphasize emotional content, which might help to forge an emotional bond between infants and their caregivers (Trainor et al., 2000).

At what age are children able to perceive the repetition of patterns of sounds—words—within the stream of speech directed to them? This is the a first big step toward acquiring language: You can't learn that *doggie* has something to do with the shaggy thing in the corner until you recognize that the sound pattern *doggie* seems to recur in that shaggy thing's presence. Infants, on average, appear to gain the insight that repeated sounds have significance somewhere between ages 6 and 7½ months (Jusczyk & Aslin, 1995). For one special word, however, the breakthrough comes a couple of months early: Children at age 4½ months already show a recognition preference for their own names (Mandel et al., 1995)!

Learning Word Meanings

Once you could detect the co-occurrence of sounds and experiences, you were prepared to start learning word meanings. There's no denying that children are excellent word learners. At around 18 months, children's word learning often takes off at an amazing rate. Researchers have called this phase the *naming explosion* because children begin to acquire new words, especially names for objects, at a rapidly increasing rate (see **Figure 11.7**). By the age of 6, the average child is estimated to understand 14,000 words (Templin, 1957). Assuming that most of these words are learned between the ages of 18 months and 6 years, this works out to about nine new words a day or almost one word per waking hour (Carey, 1978). How is this possible?

Imagine a straightforward situation in which a child and her father are walking through a park and the father points and says, "That's a doggie." The child must decide to which piece of the world *doggie* applies. This is no easy feat (Quine, 1960). Perhaps *doggie* means "any creature with four legs" or "the animal's fur" or "the animal's bark" or any of the other large set of meanings that will be true each time someone points toward a dog. Given all

Child-directed speech A special form of speech with an exaggerated and high-pitched intonation that adults use to speak to infants and young children.

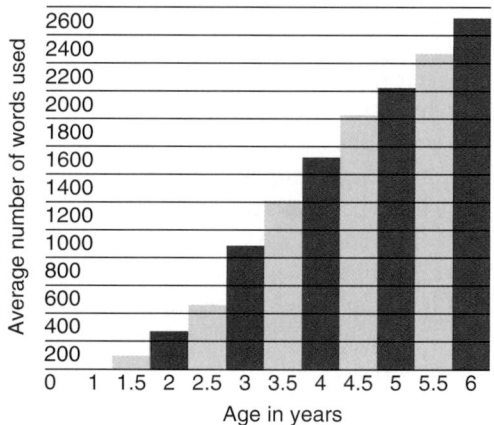

FIGURE 11.7

Children's Growth in Vocabulary

The number of words a child can use increases rapidly between the ages of 18 months and 6 years. This study shows children's average vocabularies at intervals of six months.

(Source: B. A. Moskowitz, 1978. The acquisition of language. Scientific American, Inc. All rights reserved. Reprinted by permission.)

the possibilities, how are children able to fix the meanings of individual words?

We suggest that children act like scientists—developing *hypotheses* about what each new word might mean. You can, for example, see children's scientific minds actively at work when they *overextend* words, using them incorrectly to cover a wide range of objects. They may use the word *doggie* to refer to all animals, or the word *moon* to refer to all round objects, including clocks and coins. Other times, children might *underextend* a word—believing, for example, that *doggie* refers only to their own family dog.

The view that children form hypotheses, however, does not explain why children are vastly more likely to imagine that *doggie* refers to the whole animal and not, for example, to its left front paw. Researchers have suggested that children's hypotheses are *constrained* by principles that may be innate (Clark, 1987, 1993; Markman, 1989). Consider, for example, the principle of *mutual exclusivity,* which suggests that children act as if each object *must* have only one label. How does this principle constrain children's hypotheses? Under normal circumstances, children have a bias toward hypothesizing that a new word applies to a whole object. However, when they already know the name for a whole object, like *telephone,* they apply mutual exclusivity and develop the hypothesis that a word unknown to them, like *receiver,* must label some part of the object (Liittschwager & Markman, 1994; Markman & Wachtel, 1988). The child's hypothesis will most often be correct. Mutual exclusivity explains why a 2-year-old might become irate when his mother calls his fire *engine* a fire *truck!*

Acquiring Grammar

To explain how children acquire meanings, we characterized children as scientists whose hypotheses are constrained by innate principles. We can use the same analogy to describe how children acquire the rules by which units of meaning are combined into larger units—in other words, grammar. The challenge for the child is that different languages follow different rules. For example, in English the typical ordering of units in a sentence is subject-verb-object, but in Japanese the ordering is subject-object-verb. Children must discover what order is present in the language being used around them. How do they do that?

Most researchers now believe that a large part of the answer resides in the human genome. Linguist **Noam Chomsky** (1965, 1975), for example, argued that children are born with mental structures that facilitate the comprehension and production of language. Some of

Children develop linguistic fluency by listening to the speech patterns of those around them. What are the roles of nature and nurture in the acquisition of grammar?

the best evidence for such a biological basis for grammar comes from children who acquire complete grammatical structure in the absence of well-formed input. For example, researchers have studied deaf children whose hearing loss was sufficiently severe that they could not acquire spoken language but whose parents did not expose them to full-fledged signed languages such as American Sign Language (Goldin-Meadow & Mylander, 1990, 1998). These children began to invent signing systems of their own and—despite the lack of environmental support for these invented languages—the gestural systems came to have regular, grammatical structure: "With or without an established language as a guide, children appear to be 'ready' to seek structure at least at word and sentence levels when developing systems for communication" (Goldin-Meadow & Mylander, 1990, p. 351).

But how can researchers go about specifying exactly what knowledge is innately given? The most productive approach to this question is to study language acquisition across many languages—*cross-linguistically.* By examining what is hard and what is easy for children to acquire across the world's many languages, researchers can determine what aspects of grammar are most likely to be supported by innate predispositions.

Here we arrive back at the child as scientist. Children bring innate constraints to the task of learning a particular language. **Dan Slobin** has defined these guidelines as a set of *operating principles* that together constitute the child's **language-making capacity.** According to Slobin's (1985) theory, the operating principles take the form of directives to the child. Here, for example, is an operating principle that helps children discover the words that go together to form a grammatical unit: "store together ordered sequences of word classes and functor classes that co-occur in the expression of a particular proposition type, along with a designation of the proposition type" (p. 1252). In simpler language, this operating principle suggests that children must keep track of the relationship between the order in which words appear and the meanings they express. Slobin derived the operating principles by summarizing across the data provided by a large number of other researchers, who examined a variety of different languages. We will, however, use English examples to demonstrate the principles at work.

Consider what English-speaking children can do when they begin, at about age 2, to use combinations of words—the *two-word stage.* Children's speech at this point has been characterized as *telegraphic* because it is filled with short, simple sequences using mostly nouns and verbs. Telegraphic speech lacks function words, such as *the, and,* and *of,* which help express the relationships between words and ideas. For example, "Allgone milk" is a telegraphic message.

For adults to understand two-word utterances, they must know the context in which the words are spoken.

"Tanya ball," for example, could mean, among other things, "Tanya wants the ball" or "Tanya throws the ball." Even so, children at the two-word stage show evidence that they have already acquired some knowledge of the grammar of English. Operating principles allow them to discover that word order is important in English and that the three critical elements are actor-action-object (subject-verb-object), arranged in that order. Evidence for this "discovery" comes when children misinterpret a sentence such as "Mary was followed by her little lamb to school" as *Mary* (actor) *followed* (action) *her lamb* (object) (see **Figure 11.8**). Over time, children must apply other operating principles to discover that there are exceptions to the actor-action-object rule.

Consider now an operating principle, which Slobin calls *extension,* that requires children to try to use the same unit of meaning, or *morpheme,* to mark the same concept. Examples of such concepts are possession, past tense, and continuing action. In English, each of these concepts is expressed by adding a grammatical morpheme to a content word, such as *-'s* (e.g., *Maria's*), *-ed* (e.g., *called*), and *-ing* (e.g., *laughing*). Note how the addition of each of these sounds to a noun or verb changes its meaning.

Children use operating principles like extension to form hypotheses about how these morphemes work. Because, however, this principle requires that the child try to mark all cases in the same way, the error of **overregularization** often results. For example, once children learn the past-tense rule (adding *-ed* to the verb), they add *-ed* to all verbs, forming words such as *doed* and *breaked.* As children learn the rule for plurals (adding the sound *-s* or *-z* to the end of a word), they again overextend the rule, creating words such as *foots* and *mouses.* Overregularization is an especially interesting error, because it usually appears *after* children have learned and used the correct forms of verbs and nouns. The children first use the correct verb forms (for example, *came* and *went*), apparently because they learned them as separate vocabulary items; but when they learn the general rule for the past tense, they extend it even to verbs that are exceptions to the rule—words that they previously used correctly. Over time, children use other operating principles to overcome this temporary overapplication.

Children's acquisition of language has a major impact on their ability to participate in social interactions. You should keep them in mind as we shift our focus now to social development across the life span.

■ **Language-making capacity** The innate guidelines or operating principles that children bring to the task of learning a language.
■ **Overregularization** A grammatical error, usually appearing during early language development, in which rules of the language are applied too widely, resulting in incorrect linguistic forms.

FIGURE 11.8

Acquiring Grammar

Many toddlers would interpret "Mary was followed by the lamb" and "Mary followed the lamb" to have identical meanings.

SUMMING UP

Most researchers agree that children are born with a biologically based ability to learn language. Support for this idea comes from experiments showing that children have an innate ability to perceive phonemic contrasts—even ones that aren't used in the language around them. By about 7½ months, children recognize recurring sounds. This capability enables them to begin to acquire word meanings. Researchers believe that children learn new word meanings by forming and revising hypotheses that are constrained by innate principles such as mutual exclusivity.

Cross-linguistic studies help researchers determine what aspects of grammar are most likely supported by innate predispositions. The language-making capacity has been characterized as a set of operating principles that guide children's analyses of the language around them.

Social Development across the Life Span

We have seen so far how radically you change as a physical and cognitive being from birth to older adulthood. In this section of the chapter we explore **social development:** how individuals' social interactions and expectations change across the life span. We will see that social and cultural environment interacts with biological aging to provide each period of the life span with its own special challenges and rewards.

As we discuss social development, it is particularly important for you to consider the way in which culture and environment affect certain aspects of our lives. For example, people who live in circumstances of economic hardship undergo types of stress that are absent from the "normal" course of development (Crockett & Silbereisen, 2000; Leventhal & Brooks-Gunn, 2000). Current trends in the United States and in other countries throughout the world make it imperative for developmental psychologists to consider the exceptional circumstances in which many children, adolescents, and adults are forced to live—circumstances that continually put their sanity, safety, and survival at risk (Dryfoos, 1990; Huston et al., 1994; Ladd & Cairns, 1996). U.S. culture also enforces different outcomes for men and for women and for individuals who belong to minority groups. For example, elderly women are more often economically disadvantaged than elderly men; elderly African American women are worse off even than elderly white women (Carstensen & Pasupathi, 1993). These differences are direct products of structural inequities in contemporary U.S. society.

When we draw conclusions about the "average" life course, you should keep in mind that culture dictates that some individuals will depart from this average; as we describe the psychological challenges facing the "ordinary" individual, bear in mind that many individuals face extraordinary challenges. It is the role of researchers to document the impact of contemporary problems—

Social development The ways in which individuals' social interactions and expectations change across the life span.

and to design interventions to alleviate their harshest consequences. Major reforms are clearly needed to institute and coordinate better health care, welfare programs, and social policy. Psychologists will play a role in helping to define what is in the best interest of families and their children (Scarr & Eisenberg, 1993). As we discuss social development, we will have several opportunities to revisit the impact of culture.

As you read the remainder of this chapter, you should keep in mind how the tasks of life are jointly determined by a biological accumulation of years and a social accumulation of cultural experiences. To begin our discussion of social development, we describe Erik Erikson's life span theory which makes explicit the challenges and rewards in each of life's major periods.

Erikson's Psychosocial Stages

Erik Erikson, who was trained by Sigmund Freud's daughter, Anna Freud, proposed that every individual must successfully navigate a series of **psychosocial stages,** each of which presented a particular conflict or crisis. Erikson identified eight stages in the life cycle. At each stage, a particular crisis comes into focus, as shown in Table 11.5. Although each conflict never completely disappears, it needs to be sufficiently resolved at a given stage

if an individual is to cope successfully with the conflicts of later stages.

In Erikson's first stage an infant needs to develop a basic sense of *trust* in the environment through interaction with caregivers. Trust is a natural accompaniment to a strong attachment relationship with a parent who provides food, warmth, and the comfort of physical closeness. But a child whose basic needs are not met, who experiences inconsistent handling, lack of physical closeness and warmth, and the frequent absence of a caring adult, may develop a pervasive sense of mistrust, insecurity, and anxiety.

With the development of walking and the beginnings of language, there is an expansion of a child's exploration and manipulation of objects (and sometimes people). With these activities should come a comfortable sense of *autonomy* and of being a capable and worthy person. Excessive restriction or criticism at this second stage may lead instead to self-doubts, while demands beyond the child's ability, as in too-early or too-severe toilet training,

> **Psychosocial stages** Proposed by Erik Erikson, successive developmental stages that focus on an individual's orientation toward the self and others; these stages incorporate both the sexual and social aspects of a person's development and the social conflicts that arise from the interaction between the individual and the social environment.

TABLE	11.5

Erikson's Psychosocial Stages

Approximate Age	Crisis	Adequate Resolution	Inadequate Resolution
0–1½	Trust vs. mistrust	Basic sense of safety	Insecurity, anxiety
1½–3	Autonomy vs. self-doubt	Perception of self as agent capable of controlling own body and making things happen	Feelings of inadequacy to control events
3–6	Initiative vs. guilt	Confidence in oneself as initiator, creator	Feelings of lack of self-worth
6–puberty	Competence vs. inferiority	Adequacy in basic social and intellectual skills	Lack of self-confidence, feelings of failure
Adolescent	Identity vs. role confusion	Comfortable sense of self as a person	Sense of self as fragmented; shifting, unclear sense of self
Early adult	Intimacy vs. isolation	Capacity for closeness and commitment to another	Feeling of aloneness, separation; denial of need for closeness
Middle adult	Generativity vs. stagnation	Focus of concern beyond onself to family, society, future generations	Self-indulgent concerns; lack of future orientation
Later adult	Ego-integrity vs. despair	Sense of wholeness, basic satisfaction with life	Feelings of futility, disappointment

Erik Erikson's psychosocial stage model is a widely used tool for understanding human development over the life span. What crisis did Erikson suggest dominates individuals of your age?

can discourage the child's efforts to persevere in mastering new tasks.

Toward the end of the preschool period, a child who has developed a basic sense of trust, first in the immediate environment and then in himself or herself, can now *initiate* both intellectual and motor activities. The ways that parents respond to the child's self-initiated activities either encourage the sense of freedom and self-confidence needed for the next stage or produce guilt and feelings of being an inept intruder in an adult world.

During the elementary school years, the child who has successfully resolved the crises of the earlier stages is ready to go beyond random exploring and testing to the systematic development of *competencies*. School and sports offer arenas for learning intellectual and motor skills, and interaction with peers offers an arena for developing social skills. Successful efforts in these pursuits lead to feelings of competence. Some youngsters, however, become spectators rather than performers or experience enough failure to give them a sense of inferiority, leaving them unable to meet the demands of the next life stages.

Erikson believed that the essential crisis of adolescence is discovering one's true *identity* amid the con-

Socialization The lifelong process whereby an individual's behavioral patterns, values, standards, skills, attitudes, and motives are shaped to conform to those regarded as desirable in a particular society.

fusion created by playing many different roles for the different audiences in an expanding social world. Resolving this crisis helps the individual develop a sense of a coherent self; failing to do so adequately may result in a self-image that lacks a central, stable core.

The essential crisis for the young adult is to resolve the conflict between *intimacy* and *isolation*—to develop the capacity to make full emotional, moral, and sexual commitments to other people. Making that kind of commitment requires that the individual compromise some personal preferences, accept some responsibilities, and yield some degree of privacy and independence. Failure to resolve this crisis adequately leads to isolation and the inability to connect to others in psychologically meaningful ways.

The next major opportunity for growth, which occurs during adult midlife, is known as *generativity*. People in their 30s and 40s move beyond a focus on self and partner to broaden their commitments to family, work, society, and future generations. Those people who haven't resolved earlier developmental tasks are still self-indulgent, question past decisions and goals, and pursue freedom at the expense of security.

The crisis in later adulthood is the conflict between *ego-integrity* and *despair*. Resolving the crises at each of the earlier stages prepares the older adult to look back without regrets and to enjoy a sense of wholeness. When previous crises are left unresolved, aspirations remain unfulfilled, and the individual experiences futility, despair, and self-depreciation.

You will see that Erikson's framework is very useful for tracking individuals' progress across the life span. We begin with childhood.

Social Development in Childhood

Children's basic survival depends on forming meaningful, effective relationships with other people. **Socialization** is the lifelong process through which an individual's behavior patterns, values, standards, skills, attitudes, and motives are shaped to conform to those regarded as desirable in a particular society. This process involves many people—relatives, friends, teachers—and institutions—schools, houses of worship—that exert pressure on the individual to adopt socially approved values and standards of conduct. The family, however, is the most influential shaper and regulator of socialization. The concept of family itself is being transformed to recognize that many children grow up in circumstances that include either less (a single parent) or more (an extended household) than a mother, father, and siblings. Whatever the configuration, though, the family helps the individual form basic patterns of responsiveness to others—and these patterns, in turn, become the basis of the individual's lifelong style of relating to other people.

ATTACHMENT

Social development begins with the establishment of a close emotional relationship between a child and a mother, father, or other regular caregiver. This intense, enduring, social-emotional relationship is called **attachment**. Because children are incapable of feeding or protecting themselves, the earliest function of attachment is to ensure survival. In some species, the infant automatically becomes *imprinted* on the first moving object it sees or hears (Johnson & Gottlieb, 1981). **Imprinting** occurs rapidly during a critical period of development and cannot easily be modified. The automaticity of imprinting can sometimes be problematic. Ethologist **Konrad Lorenz** demonstrated that young geese raised by a human will imprint on the human instead of on one of their own kind. In nature, fortunately, young geese mostly see other geese first.

Human infants rely less on instinctive attachment behaviors. Although many hospitals try to foster attachment by placing newborn babies on the mother's stomach, humans rely on more complex signals to solidify adult–child bonding. Infants' *proximity-promoting signals*—such as smiling, crying, and vocalizing—appear to be behaviors built in to signal others to respond to them (Campos et al., 1983). Ten-month-old infants, for example, use smiles selectively to produce an effect on their audience (Jones et al., 1991). Successful attachment, of course, depends not only on an infant's ability to emit signals such as smiles but also on an adult's tendency to respond to the signals. Who can resist a baby's smile? According to **John Bowlby** (1973), an influential theorist on human attachment, infants will form attachments to individuals who consistently and appropriately respond to their signals.

Konrad Lorenz, the researcher who pioneered the study of imprinting, graphically demonstrates what can happen when young animals become imprinted on someone other than their mother. Why is imprinting important for many animal species?

One of the most widely used research procedures for assessing attachment is the *Strange Situation Test,* developed by **Mary Ainsworth** and her colleagues (Ainsworth et al., 1978). In the first of several standard episodes, the child is brought into an unfamiliar room filled with toys. With the mother present, the child is encouraged to explore the room and to play. After several minutes, a stranger comes in, talks to the mother, and approaches the child. Next, the mother exits the room. After this brief separation, the mother returns, there is a reunion with her child, and the stranger leaves. The researchers record the child's behaviors at separation and reunion. Researchers have found that children's responses on this test fall into three general categories (Ainsworth et al., 1978):

- *Securely attached* children show some distress when the parent leaves the room; seek proximity, comfort, and contact upon reunion; and then gradually return to play.

- *Insecurely attached–avoidant* children seem aloof and may actively avoid and ignore the parent upon her return.

- *Insecurely attached–ambivalent/resistant* children become quite upset and anxious when the parent leaves; at reunion, they cannot be comforted, and they show anger and resistance to the parent but, at the same time, express a desire for contact.

In middle-class United States samples, about 70 percent of babies are classified as securely attached; among the insecurely attached children, about 20 percent are classified as avoidant and 10 percent as resistant. Cross-cultural research on attachment relationships—in countries as diverse as Sweden, Israel, Japan, and China—reveals reasonable consistency in the prevalence of types of attachment (van IJzendoorn & Kroonenberg, 1988). In every country, the majority of children are securely attached; most of the cultural differences occur with respect to the prevalence of different types of insecure attachment. Researchers also find a high rate of agreement between attachment classifications made in the Strange Situation and those based on naturalistic observation of children and mothers in their homes (Pederson & Moran, 1996).

Categorizations based on the Strange Situation Test have proven to be highly predictive of a child's later behavior in a wider variety of settings—particularly the overall division between children who are securely and

Attachment Emotional relationship between a child and the regular caregiver.

Imprinting A primitive form of learning in which some infant animals physically follow and form an attachment to the first moving object they see and/or hear.

insecurely attached. For example, longitudinal research revealed that children who showed secure or insecure behavior in the Strange Situation at 15 months differed widely in their school behavior at age 8 to 9 years (Bohlin et al., 2000). Those children who had been securely attached at 15 months were more popular and less socially anxious than their peers who had been insecurely attached. Similar continuity from the quality of attachment to later years has been demonstrated in 10-year-olds (Urban et al., 1991) and adolescents (Weinfield et al., 1997). This suggests that the quality of attachment, as revealed in the Strange Situation, really does have long-term importance. We will see in Chapter 17 that researchers also use attachment measures to predict the quality of adults' loving relationships.

We have seen that attachment relationships are quite important in young lives. Secure attachment to adults who offer dependable social support enables the child to learn a variety of prosocial behaviors, to take risks, to venture into novel situations, and to seek and accept intimacy in personal relationships. We turn now to the question of what parents can do to help bring about these critical secure attachments.

PARENTING STYLES AND PARENTING PRACTICES

Children bring individual temperaments to their interactions with their parents: Parents with more than one child often note how different their children seemed from their very earliest days. Children's temperaments may make parents' best (or worst) efforts at parenting have unexpected consequences. Researchers recognize that children's temperaments and parent's behaviors each influence the other to yield developmental outcomes such as the quality of attachment relationships: As much as parents change their children, children change their parents (Collins et al., 2000).

Even so, against the background of temperamental differences, researchers have located a **parenting style** that is generally most beneficial. This style resides at the intersection of the two dimensions of *demandingness* and *responsiveness* (Maccoby & Martin, 1983): "Demandingness refers to the parent's willingness to act as a socializing agent, whereas responsiveness refers to the parent's recognition of the child's individuality" (Darling & Steinberg, 1993, p. 492). As shown in **Figure 11.9**, *authoritative* parents make appropriate demands on their children—they demand that their children conform to appropriate rules of behavior—but are also responsive to their children—they keep channels of communication

Why is it important for a child to develop a secure attachment to a parent or other caregiver?

open to foster their children's ability to regulate themselves (Gray & Steinberg, 1999). This authoritative style is most likely to produce an effective parent–child bond. The contrast, as seen in Figure 11.9, is to parenting styles that are *authoritarian*—parents apply discipline with little attention to the child's autonomy—or *indulgent*—parents are responsive, but they fail to help children learn about the structure of social rules in which they must live—or *neglecting*—parents neither apply discipline nor are they responsive to their children's individuality.

Even parents with the same overall styles put different priorities on the *socialization goals* they consider important for the children. **Parenting practices** arise in response to particular goals (Darling & Steinberg, 1993). Thus authoritative parents who wish their children to do well in school may create a home environment in which the children come to understand why their parents value that as a goal—and may strive to do well in school because they are effectively socialized toward that goal. However, because not all authoritative parents value school success, you could not predict children's school performance based only on their parents' style (Steinberg et al., 1992). Parents' general attitudes and specific behaviors are both important for charting their children's life course.

A close interactive relationship with loving adults is a child's first step toward healthy physical growth and normal socialization. As the original attachment to the primary caregiver extends to other family members, they too become models for new ways of thinking and behaving. From these early attachments, children develop the ability to respond to their own needs and to the needs of others.

■ **Parenting styles** The manner in which parents rear their children; an authoritative parenting style, which balances demandingness and responsiveness, is seen as the most effective.

■ **Parenting practices** Specific parenting behaviors that arise in response to particular parental goals.

CONTACT COMFORT AND SOCIAL EXPERIENCE

What do children obtain from the attachment bond? Sigmund Freud and other psychologists argued that babies

	Accepting Responsive Child-centered	Rejecting Unresponsive Parent-centered
Demanding, controlling	Authoritative- reciprocal High in bidirectional communication	Authoritarian Power assertive
Undemanding, low in control attempts	Indulgent	Neglecting, ignoring, indifferent, uninvolved

Parent's demandingness

FIGURE 11.9

A Classification of Parenting Styles

Parenting styles can be classifed with respect to the two dimensions of demandingness—the parent's willingness to act as a socializing agent—and responsiveness—the parent's recognition of the child's individuality. The authoritative style is most likely to produce an effective parent–child bond.

become attached to their parents because the parents provide them with food—their most basic physical need. This view is called the *cupboard theory* of attachment. If the cupboard theory were correct, children should thrive as long as they are adequately fed. Does this seem right?

Harry Harlow (1965) did not believe that the cupboard theory explained the importance of attachment. He set out to test the cupboard theory against his own hypothesis that infants might also attach to those who provide **contact comfort** (Harlow & Zimmerman, 1958). Harlow separated macaque monkeys from their mothers at birth and placed them in cages, where they had access to two artificial "mothers": a wire one and a terry cloth

How did Harlow demonstrate the importance of contact comfort for normal social development?

one. Harlow found that the baby monkeys nestled close to the terry cloth mother and spent little time on the wire one. They did this even when only the wire mother gave milk! The baby monkeys also used the cloth mother as a source of comfort when frightened and as a base of operations when exploring new stimuli. When a fear stimulus (for example, a toy bear beating a drum) was introduced, the baby monkeys would run to the cloth mother. When novel and intriguing stimuli were introduced, the baby monkeys would gradually venture out to explore and then return to the terry cloth mother before exploring further.

Further studies by Harlow and his colleagues found that the monkeys' formation of a strong attachment to the mother substitute was not sufficient for healthy social development. At first, the experimenters thought the young monkeys with terry cloth mothers were developing normally, but a very different picture emerged when it was time for the female monkeys who had been raised in this way to become mothers. Monkeys who had been deprived of chances to interact with other responsive monkeys in their early lives had trouble forming normal social and sexual relationships in adulthood.

Primate researcher **Stephen Suomi** (1999; Champoux et al., 1995) has shown that putting emotionally vulnerable infant monkeys in the foster care of supportive mothers virtually turns their lives around. Suomi notes that monkeys put in the care of mothers known to be particularly loving and attentive are transformed from marginal members of the monkey troop into bold, outgoing young males who are among the first to leave the troop at puberty to work their way into a new troop. This *cross-fostering* gives them coping skills and information essential for recruiting support from other monkeys

Contact comfort Comfort derived from an infant's physical contact with the mother or caregiver.

HOW DOES DAY CARE AFFECT CHILDREN'S DEVELOPMENT?

When psychologists first began to study social development, many of the infants on whom they based their conclusions stayed home full time with their mothers. However, societal constraints have shifted over the last few decades, making it necessary for much larger numbers of mothers to work outside the home. As a consequence, many children spend long hours of even the earliest part of their lives outside the influence of their parents. Researchers have reacted to this shift by addressing a pair of questions: In what ways is day care better or worse for the developing child? What is the optimal form of day care?

We have already provided the context in which you can interpret the first question: If the attachments between children and mothers are so critical, shouldn't anything that disrupts the formation of those attachments—such as day care—be necessarily bad for the children? The answer to this question is, "On balance, no" (Scarr, 1998). To arrive at this answer, researchers typically made comparisons between children who stayed at home and those who were placed in day care, on measures of both intellectual and social development. Researchers have found that children placed in day care are often at an *advantage* with respect to these measures, primarily because day care provides more opportunities (Burchinal et al., 1997; Clarke-Stewart, 1991, 1993). Intellectual development

can benefit from a greater range of educational and play activities; social development can benefit from a wider variety of social interactions than would be available in the home.

There are two reasons, however, that the answer "no" must be qualified by "on balance." One is that there are individual differences in the way children respond to care outside the home. The second is that day care takes many forms. Researchers, therefore, have turned their attention away from the "better or worse" question toward the issue of what constitutes quality care for particular children (Zaslow, 1991).

Alison Clarke-Stewart (1993), an expert on day care, has summarized the research literature to provide a series of guidelines for quality day care. Some of her recommendations relate to the physical comfort of the children:

■ The day-care center should be physically comfortable and safe.

■ There should be at least one caretaker for every six or seven children (more for children under age 3).

Other recommendations cover educational and psychological aspects of the day-care curriculum:

■ Children should have a free choice of activities intermixed with explicit lessons.

■ Children should be taught social problem-solving skills.

Clarke-Stewart has also suggested that day-care providers should share the qualities of good parents:

■ Caregivers should be responsive to the children's needs and actively involved in their activities.

■ Caregivers should not put undue restrictions on the children.

■ Caregivers should have sufficient flexibility to recognize differences among the needs of individual children.

If these guidelines are followed, quality day care can be provided to all children whose parents work outside the home. For day care to be truly effective, however, there will have to be changes in the general attitudes of society. First, people must accept the reality that increasing numbers of children will be experiencing day care—and society must direct its resources toward the goal of making all day care quality day care (Fuller et al., 1996; Scarr et al., 1990). Second, people must work to eliminate the stigma associated with "working motherhood" and day care itself (Hoffman, 1989). As psychologists spread the message that day care does not harm, and may even enhance, children's development, parents should feel less distress about the necessity of a dual-career family. Such a reduction in stress could only improve the child's overall psychological environment.

---

and for maintaining a high social status in the group. Let's see now what lessons research with monkeys holds for human deprivation.

HUMAN DEPRIVATION

Tragically, human societies have sometimes created circumstances in which children are deprived of contact comfort. Many studies have shown that a lack of close, loving relationships in infancy affects physical growth

and even survival. In 1915, a doctor at Johns Hopkins Hospital reported that, despite adequate physical care, 90 percent of the infants admitted to orphanages in Baltimore died within the first year. Studies of hospitalized infants over the next 30 years found that, despite adequate nutrition, the children often developed respiratory infections and fevers of unknown origin, failed to gain weight, and showed general signs of physiological deterioration (Bowlby, 1969; Sherrod et al., 1978). Another study of infants in foundling homes in the United States and Canada reported evidence of severe emotional and physical disorders as well as high mortality rates, despite good food and medical care (Spitz & Wolf, 1946).

Negative environments also affect social development. In one study of ten abused toddlers, ages 1 to 3 years, researchers found that the children did not respond appropriately when a peer was in distress. When another child is upset and crying, toddlers will normally show concern, empathy, or sadness. By contrast, the abused children were more likely to respond with fear, anger, or physical attacks (Main & George, 1985). Another study examined the relationship between childhood and adolescent physical and sexual abuse and later-life mental health outcomes. In a sample of 375 young adults, nearly 11 percent reported having endured some type of abuse. Of that group, about 80 percent presented symptoms of one or more psychiatric disorders (Silverman et al., 1996).

Instances of child abuse provide psychologists with a very important agenda: to determine what types of interventions are in the best interest of the child. In the United States, roughly 500,000 children and youths have been removed from their homes and placed in some type of government-funded setting (e.g., a foster home or group residence) (Shealy, 1995). Are these children always happy to be removed from their abusive homes? The answer is complex, because even abused children have often formed an attachment to their caretakers: The children may retain loyalty to their natural family and hope that everything could be put right if they were allowed to return (Poulin, 1985). This is one reason that much research attention is focused on designing intervention programs to preserve or reunite families by changing circumstances that led to abuse (Gillespie et al., 1995; Skibinski, 1995).

In this section, you have seen how experiences during childhood have an impact on later social development. We now shift our focus to later periods of life, beginning with adolescence.

Social Development in Adolescence

Earlier in the chapter, we defined adolescence by physical and cognitive changes. In this section, those changes will serve as background to social experiences. Because the individual has reached a certain level of physical and mental maturity, new social and personal challenges present themselves. We will first consider the general experience of adolescence and then turn to the individual's changing social world.

THE EXPERIENCE OF ADOLESCENCE

The traditional view of adolescence predicts a uniquely tumultuous period of life, characterized by extreme mood swings and unpredictable, difficult behavior: "storm and stress." This view can be traced back to Romantic writers of the late eighteenth and early nineteenth centuries, such as Goethe. The storm-and-stress conception of adolescence was strongly propounded by **G. Stanley Hall**, the first psychologist of the modern era to write at length about adolescent development (1904). Following Hall, the major proponents of this view have been psychoanalytic theorists working within the Freudian tradition (for example, Blos, 1965; Freud, 1946, 1958). Some of them have argued that not only is extreme turmoil a normal part of adolescence but that failure to exhibit such turmoil is a sign of arrested development. **Anna Freud** wrote that "to be normal during the adolescent period is by itself abnormal" (1958, p. 275).

Two early pioneers in cultural anthropology, **Margaret Mead** (1928) and **Ruth Benedict** (1938), argued that the storm-and-stress theory is not applicable to many non-Western cultures. They described cultures in which children gradually take on more and more adult responsibilities without any sudden stressful transition or period of indecision and turmoil. It was not until large studies were undertaken of representative adolescents in Western society, however, that the turmoil theory finally began to be widely questioned within psychology. The results of such studies have been consistent: Few adolescents experience the inner turmoil and unpredictable behavior ascribed to them (Offer & Schonert-Reichl, 1992). **Table 11.6** summarizes key findings from a study of the psychological adjustment of over 20,000 adolescents (Offer et al., 1981a).

Unfortunately, those adolescents who experience maladjustment are likely to continue doing so as they move into adulthood (Offer et al., 1998; Stattin & Magnusson, 1996). Consider the following research that points to a strong link between adolescent conduct problems and subsequent adult criminality.

TABLE 11.6

The Psychological Self of the Normal Adolescent

Item	Percentage of Adolescents Endorsing Each Item
I feel relaxed under normal circumstances.	91
I enjoy life.	90
Usually I control myself.	90
I feel strong and healthy.	86
Most of the time I am happy.	85
Even when I am sad I can enjoy a good joke.	83

CONSEQUENCES OF ADOLESCENT AGGRESSIVENESS A large-scale longitudinal study of adolescents (ages 10 to 13) attending school in a typical Swedish town compared their conduct status (from teachers' reports) and biological functioning with the likelihood of their having criminal records or other adjustment problems as young adults (ages 18 to 26). Among the boys, those who showed early aggressiveness and restlessness (hyperactivity) were significantly more likely to develop into adults who would commit registered criminal offenses. In addition, a more severe pattern of early maladjustment was correlated with other adult adjustment problems as well, such as alcohol abuse and being under psychiatric care. **Figure 11.10** shows the extent to which early aggressiveness is linked to adult criminality (Magnusson, 1987; Magnusson & Bergman, 1990).

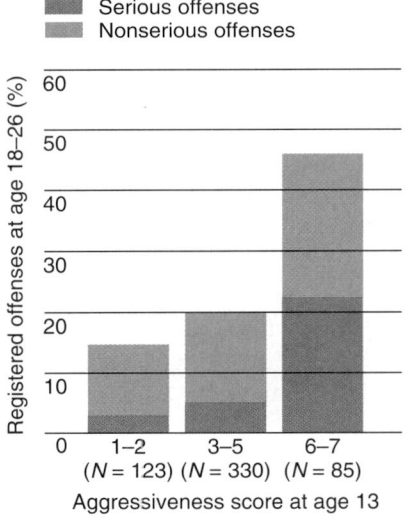

FIGURE 11.10

Adolescent Aggression and Adult Criminality

This chart shows the number of individuals who achieved various ratings of aggressiveness at the age of 13 and the percentages of those individuals who were registered for criminal offenses at the ages of 18 to 26. An offense was regarded as serious if the expected legal sanction was at least one month imprisonment according to Swedish law.

Adolescent problems should not, therefore, be incorrectly attributed to the myth of "storm and stress." Particularly because adolescents are at high risk for suicide (Garland & Zigler, 1993), signs of disturbance should be treated with sincere attention by all those in contact with such adolescents.

Now that we've considered the general adolescent experience, let's shift to aspects of identity formation in adolescence. In Erikson's description of the life span, the essential task of adolescence is to discover one's true identity. We will see how the roles that social relationships and future goals play in the formation of this sense of identity.

SOCIAL RELATIONSHIPS

Much of the study of social development in adolescence focuses on the changing roles of family (or adult caretakers) and friends (Bukowski et al., 1998; Paikoff, 1991). We have already seen that attachments to adults form soon after birth. Children also begin to have friends at very young ages. Adolescence, however, marks the first period in which peers appear to compete with parents to shape a person's attitudes and behaviors. Through interaction with peers, adolescents gradually define the social component of their developing identities, determining the kind of people they choose to be and the kind of relationships they choose to pursue (Berndt, 1992; Hartup, 1996). For this reason, adolescents and their friends are often tightly clustered—for example, with respect to their patterns of drug use (Dinges & Oetting, 1993).

Because peers become an increasingly important source of social support, there is also an increase in anxiety associated with being rejected. As a consequence, conformity to peer values and behaviors—the *peer pressure* that parents fear—rises to a peak around ages 12 and 13 (Brown, 1989). Because of the possibility of peer pressure, parents often worry that they must compete for influence with their children's friends to keep their children from developing harmful attitudes or behaviors. What may be more true, however, is that adolescents generally communicate with their parents and peers about different categories of life experiences. For example, adolescents indicate that they are very likely to discuss with their parents, but not their friends, how well they are doing in school. With their friends, but not their parents, they are likely to discuss their views on dating behavior and sex (Youniss & Smollar, 1985). Thus parents who wish to "compete" with their children's friends in certain domains may have to develop ways to get their adolescents to discuss "friends" topics.

Parents and their adolescent children must also weather a transition in their relationship from one in which a parent has unquestioned authority to one in which the adolescent is granted reasonable independence, or *autonomy,* to make important decisions (Allen & Land, 1999; Holmbeck & O'Donnell, 1991). This transition can be difficult for parents who wish to ac-

How does peer pressure function during adolescence?

knowledge an adolescent's progress toward adulthood by allowing dissent—without allowing improper choices to compromise his or her future.

HOW WE KNOW

ADOLESCENT–PARENT CONFLICTS IN HONG KONG Are the types of conflicts adolescents have with their parents consistent across cultures? Researchers were interested in studying conflicts among Chinese adolescents in Hong Kong, because Chinese culture puts relatively less emphasis on *autonomy* than do Western cultures. (We will expand on this cultural difference in later chapters.) Seventh, ninth, and twelfth graders were asked to generate lists of actual conflicts they had had with their parents, as well as the frequency and severity of those conflicts. The students were also asked to provide justifications for their positions in the conflicts: "Why do you think it is OK for you to do (not do) [this activity]?" The data revealed impressive consistency with the experiences of their Western peers—these Chinese adolescents tended to have conflicts of moderate frequency and severity, mostly with their mothers, about everyday issues such as using the telephone and watching TV. Furthermore, the adolescents' justifications for the conflicts largely reflected the need to assert autonomy or forge an individual identity by making their own decisions. Thus, even in a culture that relatively de-emphasizes individual autonomy, adolescents' conflicts with their parents still often center on the desire to establish a unique identity (Yau & Smetana, 1996).

This study reinforces the idea that parent–child relationships will undergo changes over the period of adoles-cence as children become less reliant on their parents' authority. Although friendships change somewhat over the adolescent years (Shulman, 1993), these changes re-flect greater mutual dependence between friends rather than changes in the equality of the relationship. Parent–child relationships thus may have more built-in potential for conflict than peer relationships.

Identity development ultimately requires the ado-lescent to establish independent commitments that are sensitive to parental and peer environments but are not mere reflections of either. What is important is that ado-lescents find some consistent sources of social support in their environment (Bachar et al., 1997; Fuligni, 1997). Such social support will enable the adolescent to plan for the future, the topic to which we now move.

FUTURE GOALS

Adolescence is the period in which individuals are ex-pected to begin to answer seriously the ever-present ques-tion, "What are you going to be when you grow up?" You might recall that we began the chapter with 16-year-old Darryl's musings about what lay in his future, as a func-tion of his past. The "What are you going to be?" question itself reflects the common assumption that individuals' identities are fixed, in part, by their goals. The selection, for example, of a future occupation involves tasks cen-tral to identity formation: appraisal of one's abilities and interests, awareness of realistic alternatives, and the abil-ity to make and follow through on a choice. Adolescents have concerns about the future at both the personal and societal levels: They worry about their occupations and families as well as global threats of economic collapse or nuclear war (Nurmi, 1991). They also have a keen sense of how their futures should unfold with age. First, ed-ucational goals must be met, followed by occupational goals, and finally family goals. At each juncture, goals are shaped by the constraints of gender roles and family con-text and available resources.

Of course, not all adolescents have the same expectations about what the future will hold. Researchers have studied the social and personal processes that help define how adolescents set goals for themselves.

THE SOCIAL CONTEXT OF ASPIRATIONS AND EXPECTATIONS A group of researchers examined the occupational aspirations and expectations for boys from low-income and middle-income settings: *Aspirations* refer to the job the boys would have if they could have "any job they wanted" when they grew up; *expectations* refer to the job the boys thought they would "probably get" when they grew up. Data were collected from boys in grades 2, 4, 6, and 8 who attended schools either in poor minority neighborhoods or affluent white neighborhoods. **Figure 11.11** displays aspirations and expectations with respect to white-collar occupations (e.g., lawyers or doctors). Although it may not be surprising that inner-city children had lower expectations, note that they also had lower aspirations across this age range. That is, the inner city children didn't even admit to wanting jobs that they didn't believe they could obtain (Cook et al., 1996).

Clearly, if adolescents do not aspire to jobs they will not obtain them. What can be done to change inner-city children's aspirations and expectations? The data from this study suggested that children's expectations were very much influenced by their educational expectations—how far they believed they could get in school. To change these inner-city students' sense of their futures could, therefore, ultimately require educational reforms that would enable all students to believe in the importance and efficacy of their schoolwork.

Choices about educational and occupational goals made in later adolescence can have a profound effect on future options. But, as with all aspects of identity, goal formation is best conceived of in the context of the whole life cycle. The key is a flexibility and a willingness to explore new directions based on a sense of self-confidence developed during successful negotiation through the demands of adolescence. These successes in adolescence set the stage for adult development.

Social Development in Adulthood

Erikson defined two tasks of adulthood to be intimacy and generativity. Freud identified the needs of adulthood to be *Lieben und Arbeiten,* or love and work. Abraham Maslow (1968, 1970) described the needs of this period of life as love and belonging, which, when satisfied, develop into the needs for success and esteem. Other theorists label these needs as affiliation or social acceptance and achievement or competence needs. The shared core of these theories is that adulthood is a time in which both social relationships and personal accomplishments take on special priority. In this section, we track these themes across the breadth of adulthood.

FIGURE 11.11

Career Aspirations and Expectations

Boys from low-income *(inner-city boys)* and middle-income *(other boys)* settings were asked what type of job they would most like to have—their aspirations—and what type of job they thought they would really obtain—their expectations. The results show that the inner-city boys not only have lower expectations, but they also have less ambitious aspirations.

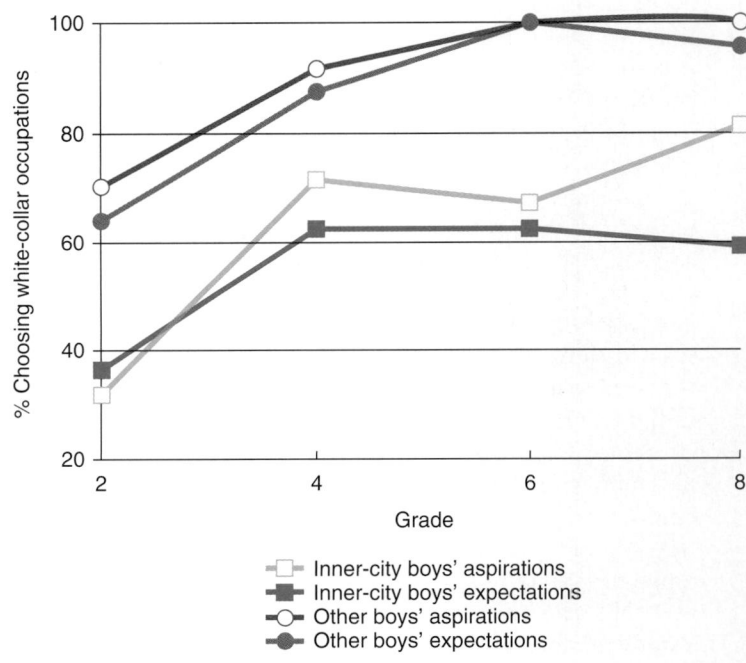

Inner-city boys' aspirations
Inner-city boys' expectations
Other boys' aspirations
Other boys' expectations

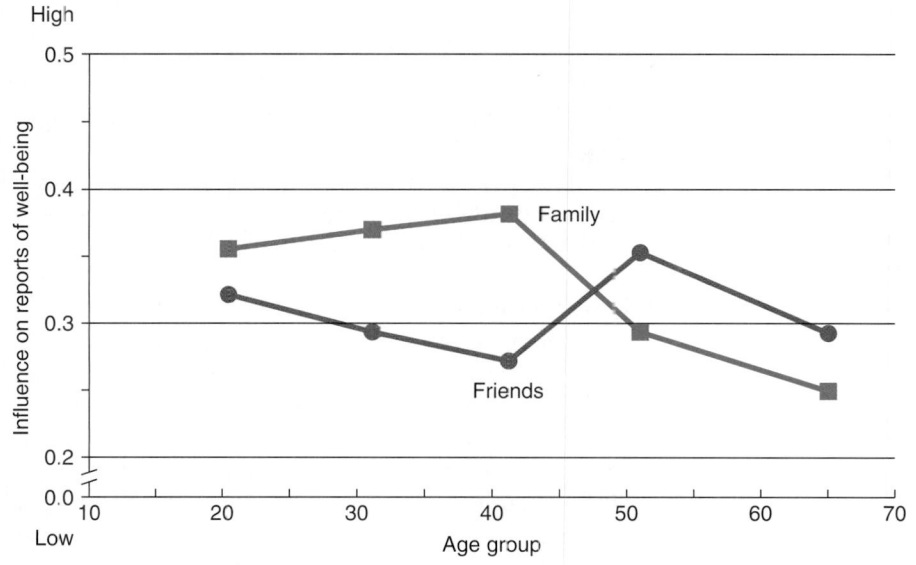

FIGURE  11.12

The Effects of Social Interaction on Well-Being

Across the life span, social interactions with family and friends trade off to provide a fairly constant level of individuals' reports of well-being.

INTIMACY

Erikson described **intimacy** as the capacity to make a full commitment—sexual, emotional, and moral—to another person. Intimacy, which can occur in both friendships and romantic relationships, requires openness, courage, ethical strength, and usually some compromise of one's personal preferences. Research has consistently confirmed Erikson's supposition that social intimacy is a prerequisite for a sense of psychological well-being across the adult life stages (Ishii-Kuntz, 1990). **Figure 11.12** demonstrates that interactions with family and friends trade off over this long span of years to provide a fairly constant level in people's reports of their own well-being. The changes in these sources of support reflect, in part, the life events that are typically correlated with each age. Let's examine these correlations.

Young adulthood is the period in which many people enter into marriage or other stable relationships. The group that counts as family thus will ordinarily grow larger. Historically, most research on relationships and families across adulthood focused on the "standard" configurations of a mother, father, and a house full of children. However, as the realities of people's families have changed, researchers have tried to document and understand the consequences of those changes (Mason et al., 1998). For example, studies now focus on the ways in which homosexual couples enter into and sustain long-term relationships (James & Murphy, 1998). Research suggests that the strategies heterosexuals and homosexuals use to maintain relationships over time have much in common: Both types of couples try to remain close by, for example, sharing tasks and activities together (Haas & Stafford, 1998). However, to combat a lack of social acceptance for gay and lesbian relationships, homosexual couples also need to take special measures to maintain relationships, such as being publicly "out" as a couple. Some heterosexual couples also must persevere in the face of continuing barriers to social acceptance; research suggests that interracial couples also face types of prejudice that have a negative impact on the ability of relationships to endure (Chan & Wethington, 1998; Wilson & Jacobson, 1995).

Each of these types of relationships increases the role of family in adults' social lives. Families also grow when individuals decide to include children in their lives. What

Statistically speaking, which spouse is likely to outlive the other? What effect might the quality of the marriage have on this outcome?

> ■ **Intimacy** The capacity to make a full commitment—sexual, emotional, and moral—to another person.

may surprise you, however, is that the birth of children can often pose a threat to the overall happiness of a couple. Why might that be? Researchers have focused on differences in the way that men and women make the transition to parenthood in heterosexual relationships (Cowan & Cowan, 1998, 2000). In contemporary Western society, marriages are more often founded on notions of equality between men and women than was true in the past. However, children's births can have the effect of pushing husbands and wives in the direction of more traditional gender roles. The wife may feel too much of the burden of child care; the husband may feel too much pressure to support a family. The net effect may be that, following the birth of a child, the marriage changes in ways that both spouses find to be negative (Cowan et al., 1985). Although research on gay male and lesbian couples raising children is far more limited, that research suggests that, as you might expect, concerns about gender roles with respect to parenting have less of a negative impact on homosexual relationships (Patterson, 1995).

For many heterosexual couples, satisfaction with the marriage continues to decline because of conflicts as the child or children pass through their adolescent years. Contrary to the cultural stereotype, many parents look forward to the time when their youngest child leaves home and leaves them with an "empty nest" (Lowenthal & Chiriboga, 1972). Parents may enjoy their children most when they are no longer under the same roof (Levenson et al., 1993). Have we discouraged you from having children? We certainly hope not! Our goal, as always, is to make you aware of research that can help you anticipate and interpret the patterns in your own life. You might think about the steps you could take to ensure that a much-awaited child doesn't undermine relationship satisfaction.

If marriages are, on the whole, happier when the spouses reach late adulthood, should everyone try to stay married late into life? Researchers would like to be able to determine which couples are fundamentally mismatched—with respect, for example, to their patterns of interactions—and which couples could avoid being among the approximately two-thirds of marriages that now end in divorce (Gottman, 1994; Karney & Bradbury 1995). It is clear, however, that the consequences of staying in an unsatisfying marriage are more unfortunate for women than for men.

HOW WE KNOW

THE CONSEQUENCES OF BAD

MARRIAGES Researchers studied 82 middle-aged couples (older spouse between the age of 40 and 50) who had been married for at least 15 years and 74 older couples (older spouse between 60 and 70) who had been married for at least 35 years. Each group of couples was divided into those who

were satisfied with their marriages and those who were dissatisfied. The researchers measured the mental and physical health of all the participants. Results revealed that satisfaction with the marriage did not have much of an impact on the men. For women, however, both physical and mental health was impaired when they were in a dissatisfying marriage (Levenson et al., 1993).

Why are women more affected by bad marriages? The researchers suggest that women bear most of the responsibility for trying to heal ailing marriages, whereas men withdraw from the conflict. As we shall see in Chapter 13, the stress produced by ongoing confrontation can have adverse effects on health. Note that women are also more likely to outlive their husbands. Often this means that they pass from a period in which they must care for an unhealthy elderly husband to a period of mourning and financial insecurity (Carstensen & Pasupathi, 1993). As with other topics of adult development, researchers are only beginning to study issues of intimacy in later adulthood for homosexual and other nonnormative relationships (James & Murphy, 1998).

When we contemplate the death of a spouse or partner, we have come back to one reason that the balance of social interactions shifts somewhat from family to friends late in life (see Figure 11.12). A stereotype about late adulthood is that individuals become more socially isolated. While it is true that older individuals may interact socially with fewer people, the nature of those interactions changes so that intimacy needs continue to be met. This trade-off is captured by the **selective social interaction theory.** This view suggests that, as people age, they become more selective in choosing social partners who satisfy their emotional needs. According to **Laura Carstensen** (1991, 1998), selective interaction may be a practical means by which people can regulate their emotional experiences and conserve their physical energy. Older adults remain vitally involved with some people—particularly family members and longtime friends.

Let's conclude this section where we began, with the idea that social intimacy is a prerequisite for psychological well-being. What matters most is not the quantity of social interaction but the quality (particularly, in U.S. culture, for women). As you grow into older adulthood, you will begin to protect your need for intimacy by selecting those individuals who provide the most direct emotional support.

Let's turn now to a second aspect of adult development, generativity.

Selective social interaction theory The view that suggests that, as people age, they become more selective in choosing social partners who satisfy their emotional needs.

GENERATIVITY

Those people who have established an appropriate foundation of intimate relationships are most often able to turn their focus to issues of **generativity**. This is a commitment beyond oneself to family, work, society, or future generations—typically a crucial step in development in one's 30s and 40s (McAdams & de St. Aubin, 1998). An orientation toward the greater good allows adults to establish a sense of psychological well-being that offsets any longing for youth.

HOW WE KNOW

LIFE OUTCOMES AND GENERATIVITY

George Vaillant studied the personality development of 95 highly intelligent men through interviews and observations over a 30-year period following their graduation from college in the mid-1930s. Many of the men showed great changes over time, and their later behavior was often quite different from their behavior in college. The interviews covered the topics of physical health, social relationships, and career achievement. At the end of the 30-year period, the 30 men with the best outcomes and the 30 with the worst outcomes were identified and compared (see **Table 11.7**). By middle life, the best-outcome men were carrying out generativity tasks, assuming responsibility for others, and contributing in some way to the world. Their maturity even seemed to be associated with the adjustment of their children—the more mature fathers were better able to give children the help they needed in adjusting to the world (Vaillant, 1977).

This study illustrates the prerequisites for generativity: For the best-outcome men, other aspects of their lives were sufficiently stable to allow them to direct their resources outwards, toward generations to come. When asked what it means to be well-adjusted, middle-aged adults (average age 52) and older adults (average age 74) gave the same response as their most frequent answer. Both groups suggested that adjustment relies on being "others oriented"—on being a caring, compassionate person and having good relationships (Ryff, 1989). This is the essence of generativity.

Let us also note that most older adults looking back on their lives do so with a degree of well-being that is unchanged from earlier years of adulthood (Carstensen & Freund, 1994). As we have seen with respect to social relationships, late adulthood is a time when goals are shifted; priorities change when the future does not apparently flow as freely. Across that change in priorities, however, older adults preserve their sense of the value of their lives. Erikson defined the last crisis of adulthood to be the conflict between ego-integrity and despair. The data suggest that

TABLE 11.7

Differences between Best- and Worst-Outcome Subjects on Factors Related to Psychosocial Maturity

	Best Outcomes (30 Men)	Worst Outcomes (30 Men)
Personality integration rated in bottom fifth percentile during college	0%	33%
Dominated by mother in adult life	0%	40%
Bleak friendship patterns at 50	0%	57%
Failure to marry by 30	3%	37%
Pessimism, self-doubt, passivity, and fear of sex at 50	3%	50%
Childhood environment poor	17%	47%
Current job has little supervisory responsibility	20%	93%
Subjects whose career choice reflected identification with father	60%	27%
Children's outcome described as good or excellent	66%	23%

few adults look back over their lives with despair. Most older adults review their lives—and look to the future—with a sense of wholeness and satisfaction.

THE CULTURAL CONSTRUCTION OF LATE ADULTHOOD

Our review of research on the long period of adulthood has emphasized continuities rather than discontinuities; there is no moment at which an individual suddenly becomes old. Even so, it is clear that there are strong cultural beliefs and expectations about the last periods of life (Featherstone & Wernick, 1995). Researchers have documented these expectations by gathering evidence of the stereotypes college-age adults have about the members of their grandparents' generation. These studies suggest that young adults have more than one stereotype of older adults (Brewer et al., 1981; Brewer & Lui, 1989). Attitudes toward older adults vary with these stereotypes. Young adults have relatively positive attitudes toward a "perfect grandparent" and relatively negative attitudes toward a "despondent" older person (Schmidt & Boland, 1986). Even so, the overall stereotype is negative, particularly with respect to declines in physical attractiveness and mental competence (Kite & Johnson, 1988; Sharps et al., 1998).

Generativity A commitment beyond one's self and one's partner to family, work, society, and future generations; typically, a crucial step in development in one's 30s and 40s.

One consequence of this negative stereotype is the particular prejudice against older people, called **ageism.** Ageism leads to discrimination against the elderly that limits their opportunities, isolates them, and fosters negative self-images. Psychologists themselves are often guilty of ageism in the language they use (Schaie, 1993). A survey of 139 undergraduate texts written over the past 40 years revealed that many failed to cover late adulthood or presented stereotypical views of the elderly (Whitbourne & Hulicka, 1990). But a more dramatic instance of ageism is shown in the personal experiences of a reporter who deliberately "turned old" for a while.

HOW WE KNOW

THE EXPERIENCE OF AGEISM Pat Moore disguised herself as an 85-year-old woman and wandered the streets of over 100 American cities to discover what it means to be old in the United States. Clouded contact lenses and earplugs diminished her vision and hearing; bindings on her legs made walking difficult; and taped fingers had the dexterity of arthritic ones. This "little old lady" struggled to survive in a world designed for the young, strong, and agile. She couldn't open jars, hold pens, read labels, or climb up bus steps. The world of speed, noise, and shadows frightened her. When she needed assistance, few ever offered it. She was often ridiculed for being old and vulnerable and was even violently attacked by a gang of adolescents (Moore, 1990).

Moore's experience reinforces the idea that society, in both the physical and social sense, conspires against the elderly.

We have worked our way through the life span by considering social and personal aspects of childhood, adolescence, and adulthood. To close out the chapter, we will trace two particular domains in which experience changes over time, the domains of gender development and moral development.

SUMMING UP

Cultural and historical differences may have a substantial effect on the way in which people experience social aspects of their lives. Erik Erikson conceptualized the life span as a series of crises: Each phase of life presents a dilemma that the individual must successfully resolve to cope effectively with the conflicts of later phases.

Ageism Prejudice against older people, similar to racism and sexism in its negative stereotypes.

Sex differences Biologically based characteristics that distinguish males from females.

Most often, the lifelong process of socialization begins with children's interactions with family members. Human infants respond to and interact with caregivers at very early ages. The Strange Situation was invented to assess children's attachment to their parents. Children who develop secure attachments are more socially competent in later life. Research on parenting styles suggests that the authoritative parenting style is most likely to produce an effective parent–child bond. A lack of attachment experiences has consequences for social development. Harry Harlow's experiments with monkeys demonstrated that motherless monkeys were lacking in social skills. For human children, lack of loving relationships in early life affects physical and social development.

Cross-cultural research suggests that adolescence is not inevitably marked by storm and stress. In adolescence, the views of peers begin to compete with adult influence on many topics. Adolescents must establish their autonomy from the authority of their parents. Adolescents worry about their futures at both the personal level and societal level; future aspirations and expectations are affected by adolescents' personal circumstances.

Adulthood is a time of concern about both relationships and accomplishments. Intimacy can occur in both friendships and romantic relationships—people achieve different balances of social support between family and friends across the life span. As people pass into late adulthood, they become more selective about the social interactions in which they engage. Another task of adulthood is generativity—behaviors devoted to the welfare of others. Overall, college-age adults have a negative stereotype of older adults that may have a harmful impact on late life experiences.

Gender Development

One type of information most children acquire early on is that there are two categories of people in their social world, males and females. Note that, at first, the differences children perceive are entirely social: They begin to sense sex differences well before they understand anything about anatomy. As an adult who both knows about anatomy and understands that sex differences are more than just physical, you can begin to consider why these differences arise. Which differences are indirect consequences of biology? Which are products of socialization? How do boys and girls learn the different expectations their culture has for them?

Sex and Gender

Biologically based characteristics that distinguish males and females are referred to as **sex differences.** These characteristics include different reproductive functions and

How do children form the belief that kitchen work is women's work?

differences in hormones and anatomy. These differences are universal, biologically determined, and unchanged by social influence. Over time, they have also led to the development of some traditional social roles—for example, because women can breast-feed their babies, prehistoric peoples may have determined that women should also remain close to home, caring for children, while the men hunted for food (Rossi, 1984).

Sex differences may also explain the finding that, after infancy, boys are more physically active and aggressive than girls. All over the world, boys are more likely than girls to engage in rough play. This difference is partly related to sex hormones—biological factors can create behavioral dispositions (Collaer & Hines, 1995; Maccoby, 1980). Researchers know that sex hormones affect social play, because observations of young male and female rats and monkeys reveal the same behavioral differences found in humans (Meany et al., 1988). Male animals engage in vigorous forms of physical play that require gross motor activity. Female animals engage in activities that require precise motor skills.

In contrast to biological sex, **gender** is a psychological phenomenon referring to learned, sex-related behaviors and attitudes. Cultures vary in how strongly gender is linked to daily activities and in the amount of tolerance for what is perceived as cross-gender behavior. **Gender identity** is an individual's sense of maleness or femaleness; it includes awareness and acceptance of one's sex. This awareness develops at quite a young age: 10- to 14-month-old children already demonstrate a preference for a video showing the abstract movements of a child of the same sex (Kujawski & Bower, 1993). **Gender roles** are patterns of behavior regarded as appropriate for males and females in a particular society. They provide the basic definitions of masculinity and femininity.

Researchers who study differences between males and females often try to determine which differences should be attributed to nature and nurture—that is, which differences follow from underlying biology and which are consequences of the way in which boys and girls are socialized in particular cultures. Note that young children themselves appear to believe that biology is destiny.

HOW WE KNOW

CHILDREN'S UNDERSTANDING OF SEX DIFFERENCES Groups of children ages 4, 5, 8, 9, and 10 were asked to make predictions about a 10-year-old character named Chris or Pat. The children all believed that the character had been brought up on a beautiful island. However, some of the children were told that Chris or Pat was raised on that isolated island entirely by members of the same sex (e.g., Chris was a boy and all of his caretakers were also male) or entirely by members of the opposite sex (e.g., Chris was a boy and all of his caretakers were female). How did the environment affect the 4- to 10-year-olds' predictions about Chris or Pat's sex-stereotyped behavior? Until age 9, children believed that sex-stereotyped behavior would emerge regardless of the social context. For example, the younger children thought it was equally likely that boy Chris would want to be a firefighter and girl Chris would want to be a nurse, no matter who raised him or her. The older children's judgments were, by contrast, sensitive to the context in which the child was raised: Now Chris's career choice was influenced by his or her caretakers' sex as well as his or her own (Taylor, 1996).

These results suggest that children underestimate the effects environments have on the ways in which boys and girls become different. They are also consistent with the finding that children between the ages of 2 and 6 seem to have more extreme and inflexible perceptions of gender than do adults (Stern & Karraker, 1989). When shown infants dressed in neutral clothing, children of this age are much more consistently affected in their judgments about the infant by an arbitrary label of "male" or "female" than are adults. Younger children's extreme reactions may be linked to the fact that they are at an age when they are trying to establish their own gender identity. They appear, on the whole, to be much more attuned to the "scripts" for gender-appropriate behavior than are their older siblings (Levy & Fivush, 1993).

Gender A psychological phenomenon that refers to learned sex-related behaviors and attitudes of males and females.

Gender identity One's sense of maleness or femaleness; usually includes awareness and acceptance of one's biological sex.

Gender roles Sets of behaviors and attitudes associated by society with being male or female and expressed publicly by the individual.

We have suggested that gender roles are acquired in a cultural context. Let's now consider some of the forces that give rise to those roles.

The Acquisition of Gender Roles

Much of what people consider masculine or feminine is shaped by culture (Leaper, 2000). Many researchers have suggested that gender-role socialization begins at birth. In one study, parents described their newborn daughters, using words such as little, delicate, beautiful, and weak. By contrast, parents described their newborn sons as firm, alert, strong, and coordinated. The babies actually showed no differences in height, weight, or health (Rubin et al., 1974). Parents dress their sons and daughters differently, give them different kinds of toys to play with, and communicate with them differently (Rheingold & Cook, 1974). For children as young as 18 months, parents tend to respond more positively when their children play with sex-appropriate toys. For example, in one experiment fathers gave fewer positive reactions to boys engaging in play with toys typical for girls (Fagot & Hagan, 1991). In general, children receive encouragement from their parents to engage in sex-typed activities (Lytton & Romney, 1991; Witt, 1997).

Parents are not the only socializers of gender roles. **Eleanor Maccoby** (1998) argues, for example, that parents do not merely stamp in gender roles. She has found evidence that play styles and toy preferences are not, in fact, highly correlated with parental preferences or roles. Young children are segregationists—they seek out peers of the same sex even when adults are not su-

How do parents and peers influence children's acquisition of gender roles?

pervising them or in spite of adult encouragement for mixed-group play. Maccoby believes that many of the differences in gender behavior among children are the results of peer relationships.

HOW WE KNOW

THE STRUCTURE OF BOYS' AND GIRLS' PLAY To understand the effects of peer relationships and the acquisition of gender roles, researchers have begun to carry out detailed analyses of the ways in which boys' and girls' play differs. One study examined the extent to which 4- and 6-year-old children in same-sex groups played with one other child—that is, in *dyads*—or engaged in activities involving a larger group of children. The researchers videotaped children at play, and then categorized all the children's interactions. The results revealed that boys and girls are equally likely to play in dyads, although the girls were more likely to play with each peer for a longer period of time (i.e., boys had more different partners), perhaps because girls have longer attention spans. Among these children, only the 6-year-old boys were likely to engage in activities that involved the whole group (Benenson et al., 1997).

The researchers did not offer a full explanation for why 6-year-old boys, but not 6-year-old girls, shift to group play. As always, it's difficult to know whether it is something biological (is it a sex difference?) or something about the expectations adults bring to boys' and girls' play (is it a gender difference?). Even when girls do begin to play in groups, the groups are different. Boys' groups, for example, are more concerned with dominance—who has power over whom—than are girls' groups; girls' groups are typically more interested in consensus than power. Accordingly, boys and girls grow up in different psychological environments that shape their views of the world and their ways of dealing with problems.

We have briefly considered how and why it is that boys and girls experience social development in different fashions. In the next section you will see that some researchers believe that gender also has an impact on moral development.

SUMMING UP

Although sex differences are a matter of biology, cultures also define gender differences. Children acquire knowledge of gender differences very early in life. Some aspects of gender roles are acquired from parents, particularly when parents adhere to traditional patterns of child rearing. Children also are socialized into different gender roles by the different norms of their same-sex peers.

Moral Development

So far we have seen how important it is, across the life span, to develop close social relationships. Let's now consider another aspect of what it means to live as part of a social group: On many occasions you must judge your behavior according to the needs of society, rather than just according to your own needs. This is the basis of *moral behavior*. **Morality** is a system of beliefs, values, and underlying judgments about the rightness or wrongness of human acts. Society needs children to become adults who accept a moral value system and whose behavior is guided by moral principles (Killen & Hart, 1999). As you know, however, what constitutes moral and immoral behavior in particular situations can become a matter of heated public debate. Perhaps it is no coincidence, therefore, that the study of moral development has also proved to be controversial. The controversy begins with the foundational research of Lawrence Kohlberg.

Kohlberg's Stages of Moral Reasoning

Lawrence Kohlberg (1964, 1981) founded his theory of moral development by studying *moral reasoning*—the judgments people make about what courses of action are correct or incorrect in particular situations. Kohlberg's theory was shaped by the earlier insights of Jean Piaget (1965), who sought to tie the development of moral judgment to a child's general cognitive development. In Piaget's view, as the child progresses through the stages of cognitive growth, he or she assigns differing relative weights to the *consequences* of an act and to the actor's *in-*

tentions. For example, to the preoperational child, someone who breaks ten cups accidentally is "naughtier" than someone who breaks one cup intentionally. As the child gets older, the actor's intentions weigh more heavily in the judgment of morality.

Morality A system of beliefs and values that ensures that individuals will keep their obligations to others in society and will behave in ways that do not interfere with the rights and interests of others.

TABLE 11.8

Kohlberg's Stages of Moral Reasoning

Levels and Stages	Reasons for Moral Behavior
I Preconventional morality	
Stage 1 Pleasure/pain orientation	To avoid pain or not to get caught
Stage 2 Cost–benefit orientation; reciprocity—an eye for an eye	To get rewards
II Conventional morality	
Stage 3 Good-child orientation	To gain acceptance and avoid disapproval
Stage 4 Law and order orientation	To follow rules, avoid censure by authorities
III Principled morality	
Stage 5 Social contract orientation	To promote the society's welfare
Stage 6 Ethical principle orientation	To achieve justice and avoid self-condemnation
Stage 7 Cosmic orientation	To be true to universal principles and feel oneself part of a cosmic direction that transcends social norms

These results suggest that as children become more sophisticated cognitively, they are able to shift their focus from just outcomes to consideration of both outcomes and intentions together. However, the difference between acceptability judgments and punishment judgments suggests that some types of moral judgments allow children to consider more factors at an earlier age. As we saw earlier in the chapter, what children are specifically asked to do determines, in part, how "mature" they seem.

Kohlberg expanded Piaget's view to define stages of moral development. Each stage is characterized by a different basis for making moral judgments (see **Table 11.8**). The lowest level of moral reasoning is based on self-interest, while higher levels center on social good, regardless of personal gain. To document these stages, Kohlberg used a series of dilemmas that pit different moral principles against one another:

> In one dilemma, a man named Heinz is trying to help his wife obtain a certain drug needed to treat her cancer. An unscrupulous druggist will only sell it to Heinz for ten times more than what the druggist paid. This is much more money than Heinz has and more than he can raise. Heinz becomes desperate, breaks into the druggist's store, and steals the drug for his wife. Should Heinz have done that? Why? An interviewer probes the participant for the reasons for the decision and then scores the answers.

The scoring is based on the *reasons* the person gives for the decision, not on the decision itself. For example, someone who says that the man should steal the drug because of his obligation to his dying wife or that he should not steal the drug because of his obligation to uphold the law (despite his personal feelings) is expressing concern about meeting established obligations and is scored at Stage 4.

Four principles govern Kohlberg's stage model: (1) an individual can be at only one stage at a given time; (2) everyone goes through the stages in a fixed order; (3) each stage is more comprehensive and complex than the preceding; and (4) the same stages occur in every culture. Kohlberg inherited much of this stage philosophy from Piaget, and, in fact, the progression from Stages 1 to 3 appears to match the course of normal cognitive development. The stages proceed in order, and each can be seen to be more cognitively sophisticated than the preceding. Almost all children reach Stage 3 by the age of 13.

Much of the controversy with Kohlberg's theory occurs beyond Stage 3. In Kohlberg's original view, people would continue their moral development in a steady progression beyond level 3. However, not all people attain Stages 4 to 7. In fact, many adults never reach Stage 5, and only a few go beyond it. The content of Kohlberg's later stages appears to be subjective, and it is hard to understand each successive stage as more comprehen-

sive and sophisticated than the preceding. For example, "avoiding self-condemnation," the basis for moral judgments at Stage 6, does not seem obviously more sophisticated than "promoting society's welfare," the basis for Stage 5. Furthermore, the higher stages are not found in all cultures (Eckensberger & Zimba, 1997). We turn now to extended contemporary critiques of Kohlberg's theory that arise from considerations of gender and culture.

Gender and Cultural Perspectives on Moral Reasoning

Most critiques of Kohlberg's theory take issue with his claims of universality: Kohlberg's later stages have been criticized because they fail to recognize that adult moral judgments may reflect different, but equally moral, principles. In a well-known critique, **Carol Gilligan** (1982) pointed out that Kohlberg's original work was developed from observations only of boys. She argued that this research approach overlooked potential differences between the habitual moral judgments of men and women. Gilligan proposed that women's moral development is based on a standard of *caring for others* and progresses to a stage of self-realization, whereas men base their reasoning on a standard of *justice*. Thus Gilligan's theory broadens Kohlberg's ideas about the range of considerations that may be relevant to moral judgments beyond childhood. Although we can value this contribution, research has suggested that she is incorrect to identify unique styles of moral reasoning for men and women. Let's examine the evidence.

Some studies have indicated that women mold their moral decisions to maintain harmony in their social relationships, whereas men refer more to fairness (Lyons, 1983). Even so, researchers continue to dispute whether gender differences in moral reasoning really exist at all (Baumrind, 1986; Walker, 1984, 1986; Woods, 1996). Although men and women may arrive at their adult levels of moral development through different processes, the actual judgments they make as adults are highly similar (Boldizar et al., 1989). One possibility is that the gender differences are really consequences of the different types of social situations that arise in the lives of men and women. When asked to reason about the same moral dilemmas, men and women gave highly similar patterns of care and justice responses (Clopton & Sorell, 1993).

We can thus characterize adult reasoning about moral dilemmas as a mix between considerations of justice and considerations of caring. This mix will remain in place over most of the life span. However, as you might expect, moral judgments are affected by general changes in adult cognition. One relevant change of late adulthood is that individuals shift the grounds for their judgments away from the details of specific situations toward the use of general principles. Consequently, moral judgments come to be based more on general societal concerns—for example, "What is the law?"—than than on particular dilemmas—for example, "Should an exception be made in this case?" (Pratt et al., 1988).

Note that debates about gender differences in moral reasoning have still mostly been carried out with respect to moral reasoning in Western cultures. Cross-cultural research has provided an important critique of this whole body of research: Comparisons between cultures suggest that it is not even possible to make universal claims about the set of situations to which moral judgments are relevant. Consider this situation: You see a stranger at the side of the road with a flat tire. Should you stop to help? Suppose you say "no." Is that immoral? If you have grown up in the United States, you probably think helping, under these circumstances, is a matter of personal choice—so it isn't immoral; on the other hand, if you had grown up as a Hindu in India, a culture that puts considerably more emphasis on interdependence and mutual assistance, you probably *would* view a failure to help as immoral (Miller et al., 1990).

Let's consider a study that made cross-cultural comparisons of moral reasoning:

HOW WE KNOW

JUSTICE VERSUS INTERPERSONAL RESPONSIBILITIES Participants for a study on moral judgments were recruited from two locations: New Haven, Connecticut, and Mysore, in southern India. These representatives of Western and Hindu cultures were asked to respond to scenarios that made a contrast between *justice* and *interpersonal responsibility*. Suppose, for example, the only way you could deliver the wedding rings to your best friend's wedding was to steal money for a train ticket. The principle of *justice* suggests that you shouldn't steal; the principle of *interpersonal responsibility* suggests that you should honor your interpersonal commitment. If you grew up in a Western culture, you probably don't think of interpersonal responsibility in moral terms: it would be unfortunate, but not immoral, to fail to deliver the wedding rings. However, we noted just earlier that members of the Hindu culture in India do generally consider interpersonal commitments to have a moral character. As a consequence, the researchers predicted that Indian respondents would be more likely to favor interpersonal responsibility than would United States respondents. As shown in **Figure 11.13**, at three different ages Indian respondents were more likely to choose the options that favored interpersonal responsibility (Miller & Bersoff, 1992).

You can see from this example the role that culture plays in defining what is moral or immoral. If you've grown up in the United States, you are probably surprised how strongly individuals from India believe that the commitment to the friend must be honored—it is better to steal than to fail to deliver the rings. Note that this difference in cultural norms most likely applies beyond the two countries of the United States and India. As we shall explore more fully in later chapters, the United States and India are typical of Western and non-Western countries with respect to their emphasis on the individual good versus the collective good.

SUMMING UP

Following Piaget's lead, Kohlberg developed a stage theory of moral development. Gilligan critiqued Kohlberg's theory by suggesting that his approach overlooked basic differences in the moral judgments of men and women.

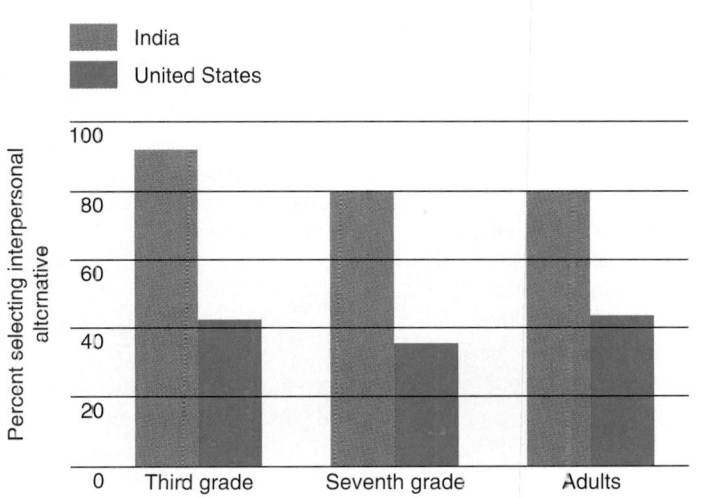

India
United States

FIGURE 11.13

Cross-Cultural Responses to Model Dilemmas

Schoolchildren and adults in India and the United States were asked to choose which courses of action they thought characters should take to resolve moral dilemmas. The participants from India were much more likely to favor interpersonal responsibility options over justice options.

However, subsequent research suggests that most adults produce a mix between considerations of justice and considerations of caring. Cross-cultural research suggests that different cultures have different standards for what types of situations and behaviors count as moral or immoral.

Learning to Age Successfully

Let us now review some of the themes of this chapter, to form a prescription for successful aging. Early in the chapter, we encouraged you to think of development as a type of change that always brings with it gains and losses. In this light, the trick to prospering across the life span is to solidify one's gains and minimize one's losses. We saw that the rule "use it or lose it" applies in both physical and cognitive domains of life. Many of the changes that are stereotypically associated with aging are functions of disuse rather than decay. Our first line of advice is straightforward: Keep at it!

We also suggested that part of successful aging means to employ *selective optimization with compensation* (Baltes et al., 1992; Freund & Baltes, 1998). As you may recall, *selective* means that people choose the most appropriate goals for themselves. *Optimization* refers to people exercising or training themselves in areas that are of highest priority to them. *Compensation* refers to the alternative ways that people use to deal with losses. In this chapter, we saw another good example of this process when we considered the way in which social relationships change during adulthood. Older adults select the goal of having friends who provide optimal levels of emotional support; the choice of friends must change over time to compensate for deaths or other disruptions (Carstensen, 1998; Lang & Carstensen, 1994). Although the selective optimization perspective originated in research on the aging process, it is a good way to characterize the choices you must make throughout your life span. You should always try to select the goals most important to you, optimize your performance with respect to those goals, and compensate when progress toward those goals is blocked. That's our final bit of advice about life span development. We hope you will age wisely and well.

RECAPPING MAIN POINTS

Studying and Explaining Development

- Researchers collect normative, longitudinal, and cross-sectional data to document change.
- Life span development depends on both nature and nurture.

Physical Development across the Life Span

- Environmental factors can affect physical development while a child is still in the womb.
- Newborns and infants possess a remarkable range of capabilities: They are prewired for survival.
- At puberty, adolescents may become overly concerned with their body image.

- Some physical changes in late adulthood are consequences of disuse, not inevitable deterioration.

Cognitive Development across the Life Span

- Piaget's key ideas about cognitive development include development of schemes, assimilation, accommodation, and the four-stage theory of discontinuous development. The four stages are sensorimotor, preoperational, concrete operational, and formal operational.
- Many of Piaget's theories are now being altered by ingenious research paradigms that reveal infants and young children to be more competent than Piaget had thought.
- Researchers suggest that children develop foundational theories, which change over time, in dif-

ferent psychological and physical domains.
- Cross-cultural research has questioned the universality of cognitive developmental theories.
- Age-related declines in cognitive functioning are typically evident in only some abilities. Research suggests that some cognitive deficits are caused by disuse rather than inevitable decay.
- Successful cognitive aging can be defined as people optimizing their functioning in select domains that are of highest priority to them and compensating for losses by using substitute behaviors.

Acquiring Language

- Many researchers believe that humans have an inborn language-making capacity. Even so, interactions with adult speakers is an essential part of the language acquisition process.

- Like scientists, children develop hypotheses about the meanings and grammar of their language. These hypotheses are often constrained by innate principles.

Social Development across the Life Span

- Social development takes place in a particular cultural context.

- Departures from the typical course of developmental change are often products of culturally determined environments.

- Erik Erikson conceptualized the life span as a series of crises with which individuals must cope.

- Socialization is the process whereby children acquire values and attitudes that conform to those considered desirable in society.

- Socialization begins with an infant's attachment to a caregiver.

- Failure to make this attachment leads to numerous physical and psychological problems.

- Lack of nurturing relationships in childhood can impair social development.

- Research shows that most adolescents are satisfied with their lives.

- Adolescents must develop a personal identity by forming comfortable social relationships with parents and peers and by choosing future goals.

- The central concerns of adulthood are organized around the needs of intimacy and generativity.

- People become less socially active as they grow older because they selectively maintain only those relationships that matter most to them emotionally.

- People assess their lives, in part, by their ability to contribute positively to the lives of others.

- Negative stereotypes of older adults lead to ageism.

Gender Development

- Gender is a psychological phenomenon referring to learned, sex-related behavior and attitudes.

- Gender-role socialization begins at birth. A variety of socializing agents reinforce gender stereotypes.

Moral Development

- Kohlberg defined stages of moral development.

- Subsequent research has evaluated gender and cultural differences in moral reasoning.

- Different cultures have different standards for what types of situations and behaviors count as moral or immoral.

Key Terms

accommodation (p. 328)
ageism (p. 354)
Alzheimer's disease (p. 335)
assimilation (p. 328)
attachment (p. 343)
body image (p. 326)

centration (p. 329)
child-directed speech (p. 337)
chronological age (p. 319)
cognitive development (p. 328)
conservation (p. 330)
contact comfort (p. 345)
cross-sectional design (p. 320)
developmental age (p. 319)
developmental psychology (p. 318)
egocentrism (p. 329)
foundational theories (p. 333)
gender (p. 355)
gender identity (p. 355)
gender roles (p. 355)
generativity (p. 353)
imprinting (p. 343)
internalization (p. 333)
intimacy (p. 351)
language-making capacity (p. 339)
longitudinal design (p. 319)
maturation (p. 325)
menarche (p. 326)
morality (p. 357)
nature–nurture controversy (p. 321)
normative investigations (p. 319)
object permanence (p. 329)
overregularization (p. 339)
parenting practices (p. 344)
parenting style (p. 344)
physical development (p. 321)
phonemes (p. 336)
psychosocial stages (p. 341)
puberty (p. 326)
schemes (p. 328)
selective optimization with compensation (p. 335)
selective social interaction theory (p. 352)
sex differences (p. 354)
social development (p. 340)
socialization (p. 342)
wisdom (p. 335)
zygote (p. 322)

motivation

■ **UNDERSTANDING MOTIVATION**
Functions of Motivational Concepts • Sources of Motivation

■ **EATING**
The Physiology of Eating • The Psychology of Eating

■ **PSYCHOLOGY IN THE 21ST CENTURY: GENES AND OBESITY**

■ **SEXUAL BEHAVIORS**
Nonhuman Sexual Behaviors • Human Sexual Arousal and Response • The Evolution of Sexual Behaviors • Sexual Norms • Homosexuality

■ **MOTIVATION FOR PERSONAL ACHIEVEMENT**
Need for Achievement • Attributions for Success and Failure • Work and Organizational Psychology

■ **PSYCHOLOGY IN YOUR LIFE: CAN PSYCHOLOGY HELP FIND ME A CAREER?**

■ **A HIERARCHY OF NEEDS**

■ **RECAPPING MAIN POINTS**
Key Terms

I N HER 1994 BOOK, *On Top of the World*, journalist Rebecca Stephens describes her climb to the top of Mount Everest. Early in the book she explains, very generally, her desire to conquer Everest:

> It was the romance of Everest that I fell in love with. When we were on the mountain, there were at least two, or even three, hundred people of all different colours, creeds and nationalities, each with an unrelenting desire to stand on the summit. Everest's summit is the highest point in the world, and for some unquantifiable reason people are drawn to it, as they are to the North and South Poles, and the deepest ocean. (p. 32)

Later in the book, "romance" gives way to hard reality as the strain and danger of the climb set in. Even so, Stephens comes to a remarkable realization after she suffers an injury to her finger:

> The following morning I had a shock. What had been my little finger was now an ugly fat sausage, like a balloon, taut and full of liquid from the second knuckle to the tip. "That was a…stupid thing to do," snapped [a fellow climber]. How could I have been so careless? So stupid? It was second-degree frostbite.…
>
> I wandered back to my tent, to be alone and sulk. I tried to console myself. "It'll be fine," the doctor had said. But I couldn't help feeling that even if it did heal it would, surely, be more susceptible a second time. This had happened at 20,000 feet. What would happen at 29,000 feet where it was freezing? And the oxygen levels, and therefore my resistance, were low? Was a finger too high a price to pay for the summit? I pondered for a while and concluded, quite calmly, and to my surprise, for I would never have considered this only a month ago, that no, it wasn't too high a price to pay. I could manage without my little finger. (pp. 90–91)

Put yourself in the position of Rebecca Stephens. Could you imagine being so intent on achieving a goal that you would conclude that you could "manage without my little finger"? Is there any goal for which you would give up your life? At least three people died on the icy slopes during the time of Stephens's climb. Why are people willing to take this risk? What determines how dedicated people will be in pursuit of a mountain's summit, a victory, or any other goal? What makes *you* persistently try to attain some goals despite the high effort, pain, and financial costs involved? Why, on the other hand, do you procrastinate too long before attempting to achieve other goals or give in and quit too soon?

Your day-to-day life is filled with circumstances in which people invoke motivational factors to explain events that do and do not take place. You may hear a boss tell her salespeople, "You've got to try harder to sell!" Your friend may reveal that she failed an exam because the professor never motivated her enough. You may read a mystery story and try to figure out the motive for a crime—and by doing so, satisfy your own goal of beating the detective to the identity of the murderer. Like millions of other viewers worldwide, you may glue yourself to soap operas each day to peer into the cauldrons of seething motives like greed, power, and lust.

It is the task of psychological researchers to bring theoretical rigor to such examples of motivation. How might motivational states affect the outcome of a sports competition or an exam? Why do some people become overweight and others starve themselves to death? Are our sexual behaviors determined by our genetic heritage? In this chapter, you will learn that human actions are motivated by a variety of needs—from fundamental physiological needs like hunger and thirst to psychological needs like personal achievement. But you will see that physiology and psychology are often not easy to separate. Even a seemingly biological drive such as hunger competes with an individual's need for personal control and social acceptance to determine patterns of eating.

We begin the chapter by providing you with a framework to understand general issues about the nature and study of motivation. In the second part of the chapter, we will look in depth at three types of motivation, each important in a different way and each varying in the extent to which biological and psychological factors operate. These three are hunger, sex, and personal achievement.

Understanding Motivation

Motivation is the general term for all the processes involved in starting, directing, and maintaining physical and psychological activities. The word *motivation* comes from the Latin *movere*, which means "to move." All organisms move toward some stimuli and activities and away from others, as dictated by their appetites and aversions. Theories of motivation explain both the general patterns of "movement" of each animal species, including humans, and the personal preferences and performances of the individual members of each species. Let's begin our analysis of motivation by considering the different ways in which motivation has been used to explain and predict species and individual behavior.

What different motivational questions might be asked of this individual's behavior?

Functions of Motivational Concepts

Psychologists have used the concept of motivation for five basic purposes:

- *To relate biology to behavior.* As a biological organism, you have complex internal mechanisms that regulate your bodily functioning and help you survive. Why did you get out of bed this morning? You may have been hungry, thirsty, or cold. In each case, internal states of deprivation trigger bodily responses that motivate you to take action to restore your body's balance.

- *To account for behavioral variability.* Why might you do well on a task one day and poorly on the same task another day? Why does one child do much better at a competitive task than another child with roughly the same ability and knowledge? Psychologists use motivational explanations when the variations in people's performance in a constant situation cannot be traced to differences in ability, skill, practice, or chance. If you were willing to get up early this morning to get in some extra studying but your friend was not, we would be comfortable describing you as in a different motivational state than your friend.

- *To infer private states from public acts.* You see someone sitting on a park bench, chuckling. How can you explain this behavior? Psychologists and laypersons are alike in typically moving from observing some behavior to inferring some internal cause for it. People are continually interpreting behavior in terms of likely reasons for why it occurred as it did. The same

rule applies to your own behaviors. You often seek to discover whether your own actions are best understood as internally or externally motivated.

- *To assign responsibility for actions.* The concept of personal responsibility is basic in law, religion, and ethics. Personal responsibility presupposes inner motivation and the ability to control your actions. People are judged less responsible for their actions when (1) they did not intend negative consequences to occur, (2) external forces were powerful enough to provoke the behaviors, or (3) the actions were influenced by drugs, alcohol, or intense emotion. Thus, a theory of motivation must be able to discriminate among the different potential causes of behavior.

- *To explain perseverance despite adversity.* Recall the excerpts we presented at the start of the chapter, from Rebecca Stephens's account of her attempt at Mount Everest. Given that people are often badly or fatally injured, why do people continue to attempt this climb? A final reason psychologists study motivation is to explain why organisms perform behaviors when it might be easier not to perform them. Motivation gets you to work or class on time even when you're exhausted. Motivation helps you persist in playing the game to the best of your ability even when you are losing and realize that you can't possibly win.

You now have a general sense of the circumstances in which psychologists might invoke the concept of motivation to explain and predict behavior. Before we turn to specific domains of experience, let's consider general sources of motivation.

Sources of Motivation

In 1999, cyclist Lance Armstrong won the Tour de France—completing one of the most remarkable comebacks in

Motivation The process of starting, directing, and maintaining physical and psychological activities; includes mechanisms involved in preferences for one activity over another and the vigor and persistence of responses.

What combination of internal and external motivational forces may have helped cyclist Lance Armstrong to overcome cancer and win the Tour de France?

sports history. In 1996, Armstrong had been diagnosed with testicular cancer that had spread to his lungs and brain. After enduring aggressive chemotherapy, Armstrong chose to go back into training. Within three years, he was victorious in his sport's most prestigious event. Armstrong won the Tour de France again in 2000. Detractors had claimed that the field he beat in 1999 was weak; his victory in 2000 proved that he could beat the world's best cyclists.

Could you do what Lance Armstrong did? Could you come back from a serious illness to challenge your body again? Do you think that whatever motivated his behavior was something *internal* to him? Would it take a special set of life experiences for someone to persevere in this manner? Or was it something *external,* something about the situation? Would many or most people behave in this way if they were put in the same situation? Or does his behavior represent an *interaction* of aspects of the person and features of the situation? To help you think about the sources of motivation, we will explore this distinction between internal and external forces. Let's begin with theories that explain certain types of behavior as arising from internal, biological drives.

DRIVES AND INCENTIVES

Some forms of motivation seem very basic: If you feel hungry, you eat; if you feel thirsty, you drink. The theory that much important behavior was motivated by internal drives was most fully developed by theorist **Clark Hull** (1943, 1952). On Hull's view, **drives** are internal states that arise in response to an animal's physiological needs. Organisms seek to maintain a state of equilibrium, or **homeostasis,** with respect to biological conditions such as the body's temperature and energy supply (see Chapter 3, p. 63). Drives are aroused when deprivation creates disequilibrium or *tension*. These drives activate the organism toward *tension reduction;* when the drives are satisfied or reduced—when homeostasis is restored—the organism ceases to act. Thus, according to Hull, when an animal has been deprived of food for many hours, a state of hunger is aroused that motivates food-seeking and eating behaviors. The animal's responses that have led to the food goal will be reinforced because they are associated with the tension reduction that eating produces.

Can tension reduction explain all motivated behavior? Apparently not. Consider groups of rats that have been deprived of food or water. Tension reduction would predict that they would eat or drink at their first opportunity. However, when such rats were placed in a novel environment with plenty of opportunities everywhere to eat or drink, they chose to explore instead. Only after they had first satisfied their curiosity did they begin to satisfy their hunger and thirst (Berlyne, 1960; Fowler, 1965; Zimbardo & Montgomery, 1957). In another series of studies, young monkeys spent much time and energy manipulating gadgets and new objects in their environment, apparently for the sheer pleasure of "monkeying around," without any external rewards (Harlow et al., 1950).

These experiments demonstrate that behavior is not only motivated by internal drives: Behavior is also motivated by **incentives**—external stimuli or rewards that do not relate directly to biological needs. When the rats or monkeys were attuned to objects in the environment rather than to their own internal states, they demonstrated that their behavior was controlled by incentives. Human behavior is also controlled by a variety of incentives. Why do you stay up late cruising the Web instead of getting a good night's sleep? Why do you watch a movie that you know will make you feel anxious or frightened?

Drives Internal states that arise in response to a disequilibrium in an animal's physiological needs.

Homeostasis Constancy or equilibrium of the internal conditions of the body.

Incentives External stimuli or rewards that motivate behavior although they do not relate directly to biological needs.

Why do you eat junk food at a party even when you're already feeling full? In each case, elements of the environment serve as incentives to motivate your behavior.

You can see already that behaviors find their origins in a mixture of internal and external sources of motivation. Even though rats might feel biological pressure to eat or drink, they also indulge an impulse to explore a new environment. We turn now to a contemporary approach to motivation that specifically examines competing motivational states, *reversal theory*.

REVERSAL THEORY

In recent years, **Michael Apter** (1989; see also Frey, 1997) and his colleagues have developed a new theory that also rejects the idea of motivation as tension reduction. Instead, the theory hypothesizes four pairs of *metamotivational states:* states that give rise to distinct patterns of motivation. As shown in **Table 12.1**, the pairs are placed in opposition. The theory claims that, at any given time, only one of the two states in each pair can be operative. If

you work your way through the table, you'll see how each pair defines motivational states that are incompatible. For example, imagine you are in some work-related situation. At a given moment, are you motivated to fit in or to be independent? Are you motivated to be focused on your own feelings or focused on others' feelings? This theory is known as **reversal theory** because it seeks to explain human motivation in terms of *reversals* from one to the other of the opposing states. Consider the contrast between the *paratelic* and the *telic states.* You are in a paratelic state when you engage in an activity with no goal beyond enjoying that particular activity; you are in a telic state when you engage in an activity that is important to you beyond the moment. For example, you are probably in a telic state right now as you read your textbook—you wish to acquire the material so you can do well on an exam. If, however, you take a break from studying to eat a snack or listen to a new CD, you have almost certainly gone into a paratelic state. Reversal theory, in fact, suggests that you are always in one or the other state but never both simultaneously.

At times, you have probably become very aware of the types of reversals predicted by this theory. One particularly dramatic form of reversal occurs in people who engage in high-risk activities, such as parachuting.

TABLE 12.1

Principal Characteristics of the Four Pairs of Metamotivational States

Telic	Paratelic
Serious	Playful
Goal-oriented	Activity-oriented
Prefers planning ahead	Living for the moment
Anxiety-avoiding	Excitement-seeking
Desires progress—achievement	Desires fun and enjoyment

Conformist	Negativistic
Compliant	Rebellious
Wants to keep to rules	Wants to break rules
Conventional	Unconventional
Agreeable	Angry
Desires to fit in	Desires to be independent

Mastery	Sympathy
Power-oriented	Care-oriented
Sees life as struggle	Sees life as cooperative
Tough-minded	Sensitive
Concerned with control	Concerned with kindness
Desires dominance	Desires affection

Autic	Alloic
Primary concern with self	Primary concern with others
Self-centered	Identifiying with other(s)
Focus on own feelings	Focus on others' feelings

HOW WE KNOW

AN ANXIETY TO EXCITEMENT REVERSAL

Why would people voluntarily jump out of airplanes—and claim to do it for fun? It is hard to understand this behavior with respect to tension reduction because the anticipation of jumping out of an airplane increases, rather than reduces, tension. Reversal theory, however, suggests that the experience of parachuting presents a switch from a telic to a paratelic state. In the telic state, high arousal—of the type that would be experienced as you contemplate jumping out of an airplane— leads to feelings of anxiety; in the paratelic state, high arousal is experienced as great excitement. Thus, a reversal from the telic to the paratelic state at the same level of arousal would create an immediate shift from great anxiety to great pleasure. To verify the existence of this immediate shift, researchers gathered data from members of two parachuting clubs. Members of the clubs reported on their feelings of anxiety and excitement in the time before, during, and after their leaps. The data showed a clear reversal: Moments before the leap, they were anxious (but not excited); moments after the parachute opened, they were excited (but not anxious). The arousal did not go away—it took on a different meaning as the parachuter reversed from the telic to the paratelic state (Apter & Batler, 1997).

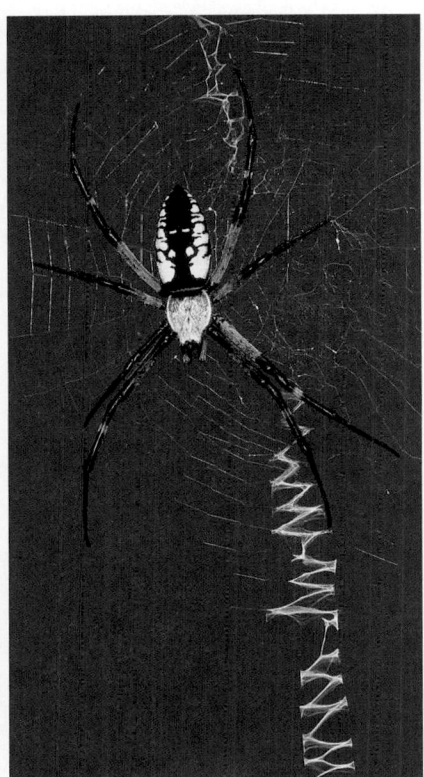

Instinctive behaviors, like the argiope spider's proclivity to build an elaborate capture thread into its web, are motivated by genetic inheritance. What instincts have theorists attributed to the human species?

Do you see how reversal theory explains the self-reports of these parachuters?

Reversal theory provides an interesting general approach to motivation. We move now to a different tradition of research on motivation, one that focuses on species-specific *instinctual* behaviors.

INSTINCTUAL BEHAVIORS AND LEARNING

Why do organisms behave the way they do? Part of the answer is that some aspects of a species's behavior are governed by **instincts**, preprogrammed tendencies that are essential for the survival of their species. Instincts provide repertories of behavior that are part of each animal's genetic inheritance. Salmon swim thousands of miles back to the exact stream where they were spawned, leaping up waterfalls until they come to the right spot, where the surviving males and females engage in ritualized courtship and mating. Fertilized eggs are deposited, the parents die, and, in time, their young swim downstream to live in the ocean until, a few years later, it is time for them to return to complete their part in this continuing drama. Similarly remarkable activities can be reported for most species of animals. Bees communicate the location of food to other bees, army ants go on highly synchronized hunting expeditions, birds build nests, and spiders spin complex webs—exactly as their parents and ancestors did.

Early theories of human function tended to overestimate the importance of instincts for humans. **William James,** writing in 1890, stated his belief that humans rely even more on instinctual behaviors than other animals (although human instincts were generally not carried out with fixed-action patterns). In addition to the biological instincts humans share with animals, a host of social instincts, such as sympathy, modesty, sociability, and love, come into play. For James, both human and animal instincts were *purposive*—they served important purposes, or functions, in the organism's adaptation to its environment.

Sigmund Freud (1915) proposed that humans experience drive states arising from life instincts (including sexuality) and death instincts (including aggression). He believed that instinctive urges direct *psychic energy* to satisfy bodily needs. Tension results when this energy cannot be discharged; this tension drives people toward activities or objects that will reduce the tension. For example, Freud believed that the life and death instincts operated largely below the level of consciousness. However, their consequences for conscious thoughts, feelings, and actions were profound, because of the way the instincts motivated people to make important life choices (we will expand on these ideas in Chapter 14).

By the 1920s, psychologists had compiled lists of over 10,000 human instincts (Bernard, 1924). At this same time, however, the notion of instincts as universal explanations for human behavior was beginning to stagger under the weight of critical attacks. Cross-cultural anthropologists, such as **Ruth Benedict** (1959) and **Margaret Mead** (1939), found enormous behavioral variation between cultures. Their observations contradicted theories that considered only the universals of inborn instincts.

Most damaging to the early instinct notions, however, were behaviorist empirical demonstrations that important behaviors and emotions were learned rather than inborn. These types of demonstrations should be familiar to you from Chapter 7. We saw there that human and nonhuman animals alike are highly sensitive to the ways in which stimuli and responses are associated in the environment. If you want to explain why one animal performs a behavior and another does not, you may need to know nothing more than that one animal's behavior was reinforced and the other's was not. Under those circumstances, you don't need a separate account of motivation at all (that is, it would be a mistake to say that one animal is "motivated" and the other is not).

Reversal theory Theory that explains human motivation in terms of reversals from one to the other opposing metamotivational states.

Instincts Preprogrammed tendencies that are essential to a species's survival.

Recall, however, that in Chapter 7 we also saw that the types of behaviors animals will most readily learn are determined, in part, by species-specific instincts (see page 206). That is, each animal displays a combination of learned and instinctive behaviors. Thus, if you are asked to explain or predict an animal's behavior, you will want to know two things: first, something about the history of its species—what adaptive behaviors are part of the organism's genetic inheritance?—and second, something about the personal history of the animal—what unique set of environmental associations has the organism experienced? In these cases, motivation resides in the effects history has on current behavior.

One final look back to Chapter 7: We saw there that cognitively oriented researchers have challenged the belief that instincts and reinforcement history are sufficient to explain all the details of an animal's behavior. Let's turn now to the role of expectations and cognition in motivation.

EXPECTATIONS AND COGNITIVE APPROACHES TO MOTIVATION

Consider *The Wizard of Oz* as a psychological study of motivation. Dorothy and her three friends work hard to get to the Emerald City, overcoming barriers, persisting against all adversaries. They do so because they expect the Wizard to give them what they are missing. Instead, the wonderful (and wise) Wizard makes them aware that they, not he, always had the power to fulfill their wishes. For Dorothy, *home* is not a place but a feeling of security, of comfort with people she loves; it is wherever her heart is. The courage the Lion wants, the intelligence the Scarecrow longs for, and the emotions the Tin Man dreams of are attributes they already possess. They need to think about these attributes not as internal conditions but as positive ways in which they are already relating to others. After all, didn't they demonstrate those qualities on the journey to Oz, a journey motivated by little more than an *expectation,* an idea about the future likelihood of getting something they wanted? The Wizard of Oz was clearly among the first cognitive psychologists, because he recognized the importance of people's thought processes in determining their goals and behaviors to reach them.

Contemporary psychologists use cognitive analyses to explore the forces that motivate a variety of personal and social behaviors. These psychologists share the Wizard's point of view that significant human motivation comes not from objective realities in the external world but from subjective interpretations of reality. The reinforcing effect of a reward is lost if you don't perceive that your actions obtained it. What you do now is often controlled by what you think was responsible for your past

Social-learning theory The learning theory that stresses the role of observation and the imitation of behaviors observed in others.

successes and failures, by what you believe is possible for you to do, and by what you anticipate the outcome of an action will be. Cognitive approaches explain why human beings are often motivated by expectations of future events.

The importance of *expectations* in motivating behavior was developed by **Julian Rotter** (1954) in his **social-learning theory** (we touched on social learning in our discussion of observational learning in Chapter 7). For Rotter, the probability that you will engage in a given behavior (studying for an exam instead of partying) is determined by your *expectation* of attaining a goal (getting a good grade) that follows the activity and by the *personal value* of that goal. A *discrepancy* between expectations and reality can motivate an individual to perform corrective behaviors (Festinger, 1957; Lewin, 1936). For example, if you find that your own behaviors do not match the standards or values of a group to which you belong, you might be motivated to change your behaviors to achieve a better fit with the group.

How do expectations relate to internal and external forces of motivation? **Fritz Heider** (1958) postulated that the outcome of your behavior (a poor grade, for example) can be attributed to *dispositional forces,* such as lack of effort or insufficient intelligence, or to *situational forces,* such as an unfair test or a biased teacher. These attributions influence the way you will behave. You are likely to try harder next time if you see your poor grade as a result of your lack of effort, but you may give up if you see it as resulting from injustice or lack of ability (Dweck, 1975). Thus, the identification of a source of motivation as internal or external may depend, in part, on your own subjective interpretation of reality.

Let's review the various sources of motivation. We began with the observation that researchers can differentiate internal and external factors that bring about behaviors. Drives, instincts, and histories of learning are all internal sources of motivation that affect behaviors in the presence of appropriate external stimuli. Once organisms begin to think about their behaviors—something humans are particularly prone to do—expectations about what should or should not happen also begin to provide motivation. Thinking animals can choose to attribute some motivations to themselves and others to the outside world.

We have now given you a general framework for understanding motivation. In the remainder of the chapter, we will take a closer look at three different types of behavior that are influenced by interactions of motives: eating, sexual performance, and personal achievement.

SUMMING UP

Psychologists use motivational concepts to relate biology to behavior, to account for behavioral variability, to infer private states from public acts, to assign responsibility for actions, and to explain perseverance despite adversity. Theories of motivation often attempt to identify which motivational forces arise from internal sources, within the organism, and which from external sources, environmental or cultural factors outside of the organism. Drive theory emphasized the importance of tension reduction in motivation. However, behavior is also motivated by external incentives that are unrelated to physiological needs. Reversal theory conceptualizes motivation as being guided by opposing metamotivational states. Species-specific instinctual behaviors are elicited by both internal and external factors. Cognitive theories of motivation focus on people's expectations and on how they sort their world into dispositional versus situational forces.

■ Eating

We'd like to ask you to make a prediction. We are about to offer a slice of pizza to a student enrolled in an introductory psychology course. How likely do you think it is that the student will eat the slice of pizza? Are you willing to make a guess? Your response should probably be, "I need more information." In the last section, we gave you a way of organizing the extra information you need to acquire before making such a prediction. You would want to know about *internal* information. How much has the student eaten already? Is the student trying to diet? You would also want to know about *external* information. Is the pizza tasty? Are friends there to share the pizza and conversation? You can see already that we have some work to do to explain the types of forces that might influence even a simple outcome, such as whether someone is going to eat a slice of pizza. Let's begin with some of the physiological processes that evolution has provided to regulate eating.

■
The Physiology of Eating

When does your body tell you it's time to eat? You have been provided with a variety of mechanisms that contribute to your physical sense of hunger or satiety (Logue, 1991). To regulate food intake effectively, organisms must be equipped with mechanisms that accomplish four tasks: (1) detect internal food need, (2) initiate and organize eating behavior, (3) monitor the quantity and quality of the food eaten, and (4) detect when enough food has been consumed and stop eating. Researchers have tried to understand these processes by relating them either to *peripheral* mechanisms in different parts of the body, such as stomach contractions, or to *central* brain mechanisms, such as the functioning of the hypothalamus. Let's look at these processes in more detail.

PERIPHERAL RESPONSES

Where do sensations of hunger come from? Does your stomach send out distress signals to indicate that it is empty? A pioneering physiologist, **Walter Cannon** (1934), believed that gastric activity in an empty stomach was the sole basis for hunger. To test this hypothesis, Cannon's intrepid student A. L. Washburn trained himself to swallow an uninflated balloon attached to a rubber tube. The other end of the tube was attached to a device that recorded changes in air pressure. Cannon then inflated the balloon in Washburn's stomach. As the student's stomach contracted, air was expelled from the balloon and deflected the recording pen. Reports of Washburn's hunger pangs were correlated with periods when his stomach was severely contracted but not when his stomach was distended. Cannon thought he had proved that stomach cramps were responsible for hunger (Cannon & Washburn, 1912).

Although Cannon and Washburn's procedure was ingenious, later research showed that stomach contractions are not even a necessary condition for hunger. Injections of sugar into the bloodstream will stop the stomach contractions but not the hunger of an animal with an empty stomach. Human patients who have had their stomachs entirely removed still experience hunger pangs (Janowitz & Grossman, 1950), and rats without stomachs still learn mazes when rewarded with food (Penick et al., 1963). So, although sensations originating in the stomach may play a role in the way people usually experience hunger, they do not fully explain how the body detects its need for food and is motivated to eat.

Your empty stomach may not be necessary to feel hungry, but does a "full" stomach terminate eating? Research has shown that gastric distension caused by food—but not by an inflated balloon—will cause an individual to end a meal (Logue, 1991). Thus, the body is sensitive to the source of pressure in the stomach. The oral experience of food also provides a peripheral source of *satiety* cues—cues relevant to feelings of satiation or fullness. You may have noticed that you become less enthusiastic about the tastes of even your favorite foods over the course of a meal, a phenomenon called *sensory-specific satiety*. Foods high in calories and high in protein produce more satiety than do low-calorie and low-protein food (Johnson & Vickers, 1993; Vandewaters & Vickers, 1996). This immediate reduction in "liking" for these types of foods may be one way in which your body regulates intake. However, the "specific" in sensory-specific satiety means that the satiety applies most directly to the actual foods that are eaten. When people are given the opportunity to eat a series of foods with different tastes, rather than sticking with a single, even favorite taste, they eat more food (Rolls et al., 1981). Therefore, variety in food tastes—as is common in many multicourse meals—might counteract other bodily indications that you've already had enough to eat.

Why do people tend to eat more food when a variety of tastes are available?

Let's turn now to the brain mechanisms involved in eating behaviors, where information from peripheral sources is gathered together.

CENTRAL RESPONSES

As is often the case, simple theories about the brain centers for the initiation and cessation of eating have given way to more complex theories. The earliest theories of the brain control of eating were built around observations of the *lateral hypothalamus* (LH) and the *ventromedial hypothalamus* (VMH). (The location of the hypothalamus is shown in Figure 3.10 on page 63.) Research showed that if the VMH was lesioned (or the LH stimulated), the animal consumed more food. If the procedure was reversed, so that the LH was lesioned (or the VMH stimulated), the animal consumed less food. These observations gave rise to the *dual-center model,* in which the LH was thought to be the "hunger center" and the VMH the "satiety center."

Over time, however, the data failed to confirm this theory (Martin et al., 1991; Rolls, 1994). For example, rats with VMH lesions only overeat foods they find palatable; they strongly avoid foods that don't taste good. Thus, the VMH could not just be a simple center for signaling "eat more" or "don't eat more"—the signal depends on the type of food. In fact, destruction of the VMH may, in part, have the effect of exaggerating ordinary reflex responses to food (Powley, 1977). If the rat's reflex response to good-tasting food is to eat it, its exaggerated response will be to overeat. If the rat reflexively avoids bad-tasting food by gagging or vomiting, its exaggerated response could keep the rat from eating altogether.

Let's focus on how the VMH and LH carry out the tasks assigned to them by the brain. Some of the most important information the VMH and LH use to regulate eating comes from your bloodstream (Woods et al., 1998). Sugar (in the form of glucose in the blood) and fat are the energy sources for metabolism. The two basic signals that initiate eating come from receptors that monitor the levels of sugar and fat in the blood. When stored glucose is low or unavailable for metabolism, signals from liver cell receptors are sent to the LH, where neurons acting as glucose detectors change their activity in response to this information. Other hypothalamic neurons may detect changes in free fatty acids and insulin levels in the blood. Together, these neurons appear to activate appetitive systems in the lateral zone of the hypothalamus and initiate eating behavior. Signals that the blood has a high level of glucose or fatty acids are used by the VMH to terminate eating behaviors.

We have seen so far that you have body systems that are dedicated to getting you to start and to stop eating. You almost certainly know, however, from an enormous amount of personal experience, that your need for food depends on more than just the cues generated by your body. Let's look now at psychological factors that motivate you to eat more food or less food.

The Psychology of Eating

You know now that your body is equipped with a variety of mechanisms that regulate the amount of food you eat. But do you eat only in response to hunger? You are likely to respond, "Of course not!" If you think back over the last couple of days, you can probably recall several occasions on which when and what you ate had little to do with hunger. For example, people in the United States typically eat three daily meals at set times; the timing of those meals relies more on social norms than on body cues. Moreover, people often choose what to eat based on social or cultural norms. Would you say "yes" if you were offered a free lobster dinner? Your answer might depend on whether, for example, you are an observant Jew (in which case you would say "no") or a vegetarian (in which case your answer would still depend on whether you are the type of vegetarian who eats seafood). These examples suggest immediately why eating is not just about paying heed to your body's cues.

Beyond social and cultural constraints, why else might your eating be relatively insensitive to feelings of hunger? If you are like most people, you spend quite a bit of time thinking about the consequences of what you eat for your body shape and size. To discuss the psychology of eating, we will focus largely on circumstances in which people try to exercise control over these consequences—to try to reshape their bodies in response to their perceptions of some personal or societal ideal.

Do you worry about your weight? Have you considered going on a diet? If you are a woman, it is more likely that the answer to these questions is yes, but even men in contemporary U.S. society express anxiety about their weight: 52 percent of women and 37 percent of men report that they are overweight (Brownell & Rodin, 1994). In fact, approximately 24 percent of women and 31 percent of men are actually considered to be overweight—so there is a disparity, again, particularly for women, between the

GENES AND OBESITY

The 21st century began with a remarkable announcement from the world of science: Researchers on the *Human Genome Project* reported that they were very close to providing an initial mapping of the chemical bases of the human genome. The ultimate goal of this project is to provide a complete account of the genes that make up that genome. The Human Genome Project has increased scientists' beliefs that they will be able to understand the genetic bases of a large range of disorders that impair the quality of individuals' lives.

One such disorder with a genetic basis is *obesity*. Researchers have provided ample evidence that people are born with innate tendencies to be lighter or heavier. For example, studies of identical twins have revealed great similarity in their overall weight (Allison et al., 1994; Stunkard et al., 1990). Part of this similarity may be explained by the finding that the rate at which an individual's body burns calories to maintain basic functions, the individual's *resting metabolic rate*, is also highly heritable (Bouchard et al., 1989). Thus, some people are innately predisposed to burn a lot of calories just through ordinary day-to-day activities; others are not. Those who are not are more at risk for weight gain.

Recently, researchers have discovered some of the actual genetic mechanisms that may predispose some individuals to obesity (Comuzzie & Allison, 1998; Gura, 2000). For example, a gene has been isolated that appears to control signals to the brain that enough fat has been stored in the body in the course of a meal—so the individual should stop eating (Zhang et al., 1994). If this gene, called *leptin*, is inactive, the individual will continue to eat, with obesity as a potential result. In fact, researchers have discovered small populations of obese individuals with mutations in this gene; the mutation appears to explain their obesity (Jackson et al., 1997; Montague et al., 1997). Because these mutations are extremely rare, they cannot account for the vast majority of cases of obesity. Even so, the confirmation that leptin plays a roll in weight regulation has encouraged researchers' efforts to identify and understand other weight-related genes.

This genetic research holds out the promise of innovative solutions to obesity. Researchers hope, for example, that an understanding of the link between genes and weight regulation will enable them to provide new drug treatments (Campfield et al., 1998).

Some of the early efforts have been discouraging: Research manipulating leptin has yet to show a great impact on weight loss. However, given constant leaps forward in genetic understanding, scientists continue to form new hypotheses about how they might intervene in the body's mechanisms for weight regulation (Gura, 2000). Nonetheless, even the most optimistic researchers provide words of caution: "Innovative drugs will be most effective when they are used as adjuncts to, rather than substitutes for, lifestyle changes to improve the metabolic fitness, health, and quality of life for obese individuals" (Campfield et al., 1998, p. 1387). Put another way, no matter how much we come to understand *nature*, we must always be aware that *nurture* still plays a critical role in our life outcomes.

Web sites:

- www.ornl.gov/hgmis/

This is the U.S. government's extensive Web site about the Human Genome Project.

- www.loop.com/~bkrentzman/ index.html

This site compiles scientific reports on obesity and weight control.

reality of people's bodies and what they perceive those realities to be. In the next section, we will explore some of the roots and consequences of obesity and dieting. We then describe how eating disorders may arise as an extreme response to concerns about body image and weight.

OBESITY AND DIETING

Why do some people become overweight? It probably will not surprise you, as you have seen throughout *Psychology and Life* that the answer lies partly in nature and partly in nurture. This chapter's Psychology in the 21st Century box describes the strong case for "nature": Some people have a genetic predisposition toward obe-sity. However, even a biological predisposition may not be enough to "cause" a particular person to become obese. What matters, in addition, is the way in which an individual *thinks* about food and eating behaviors. Early research on psychological aspects of obesity focused on the extent to which obese individuals are attentive to their bodies' internal hunger cues versus food in the external environment (Schachter, 1971a). The suggestion was that, when food is available and prominent, obese individuals ignore the cues their bodies give them. This theory proved to be insufficient, however, because obesity itself does not always predict eating patterns (Rodin, 1981). That is, not all people who are overweight

■ EATING

have the same psychological makeup with respect to eating behaviors. Let's see why.

Janet Polivy and Peter Herman have proposed that the critical dimension that underlies the psychology of eating behaviors is *restrained* versus *unrestrained* eating (Polivy & Herman, 1975). *Restrained* eaters put constant limits on the amount of food they will let themselves eat: They are chronically on diets; they constantly worry about food. Although obese people may be more likely to report these kinds of thoughts and behaviors, individuals can be restrained eaters whatever their body size. How do people gain weight if they are constantly on a diet? Research suggests that when restrained eaters become *disinhibited*—when life circumstances cause them to let down their restraints—they tend to indulge in high-calorie binges. Disinhibition appears to arise most often when the restrained eaters are made to feel stress about their capabilities and self-esteem (Greeno & Wing, 1994; Tanofsky-Kraff et al., 2000).

THE EFFECTS OF ANXIETY ON RESTRAINED AND UNRESTRAINED EATERS Based on self-evaluations of their behaviors and thoughts with respect to food and dieting, 96 female college students were classified as either restrained (42 women) or unrestrained (54 women) eaters. When they arrived for the experiment, half of the students were told that they would be asked to give a two-minute spontaneous speech, which would give an indication of their verbal fluency. Anticipation of this task provoked high anxiety in these participants. The other half of the participants believed they would be asked to participate in an experiment on their perceptions of fabrics through touch. This provoked low anxiety, and so was considered a control. Next, both groups of participants were asked to perform a preliminary experiment on taste perception. The stimuli for this experiment were both store-bought good-tasting cookies and bad-tasting cookies prepared "by the experimenter's grandmother, against her better judgment" (Polivy et al., 1994, p. 507). Unknown to the participants, the experimenters were recording how many cookies of each type they ate.

The results of the study are shown in **Table 12.2.** When unrestrained eaters became anxious, they ate fewer of both types (good-tasting and bad-tasting) of cookies. Apparently, anxiety suppressed their hunger, to some extent. For restrained eaters, however, anxiety led them to eat more of both types of cookies. Thus, among these women, a state of anxiety created a general disinhibition even for cookies that were rated as not being very tasty (Polivy et al., 1994).

TABLE 12.2

Average Number of Cookies Consumed

	Unrestrained Eaters	Restrained Eaters	Difference
Good-tasting cookies			
Control	6.2	5.1	−1.1
Anxious	5.1	7.6	+2.5
Bad-tasting cookies			
Control	3.0	2.6	−0.4
Anxious	2.7	3.7	+1.0

In this experiment, a minor challenge to self-esteem—the prospect of giving a brief speech that would be evaluated—caused restrained women to eat more than their peers. Research has shown that, in general, restrained eaters are likely to overeat only when they suffer a threat to their psychological well-being; a threat to their physical safety does not have a similar impact (Heatherton et al., 1991). Overeating behavior may allow restrained eaters to distract themselves from the insult to their self-esteem. When restrained eaters were told that they had failed on a problem-solving task, they didn't overeat if they were made to keep focused on the behavior—by watching a videotape of their failure performance (Heatherton et al., 1993). When they weren't made to attend to their failure, the restrained eaters ate twice as much ice cream as they did when they watched the videotape. Note that most of the research on restrained eating has been conducted with women as participants. Less is known about the eating patterns of men (Greeno & Wing, 1994).

The theory of restrained eating suggests why it might be difficult for people to lose weight once they have become overweight. Many overweight people report themselves as constantly on diets—they are often restrained eaters. If stressful life events occur that cause these eaters to become disinhibited, binge eating can easily lead to weight gain. Thus, the psychological consequences of being constantly on a diet can, paradoxically, create circumstances that are more likely to lead to weight gain than to weight loss. In the next section, we will see how these same psychological forces can lead to health- and life-threatening eating disorders.

EATING DISORDERS AND BODY IMAGE

We began this section on psychological aspects of eating by noting that the group of people who believe themselves to be overweight is larger than the group of people who are actually overweight. When the disparity between people's perceptions of their body image and their actual size becomes too large, they may be at risk for *eating disorders*. **Anorexia nervosa** is diagnosed when an individual weighs

What do these photographs of Calista Flockhart and Marilyn Monroe suggest about changes over time in how thin women must be for the media to promote them as sexy?

less than 85 percent of her or his expected weight, but still expresses an intense fear of becoming fat (*DSM-IV*, 1994). The behavior of people diagnosed with **bulimia nervosa** is characterized by binges—periods of intense, out-of-control eating—followed by measures to purge the body of the excess calories—self-induced vomiting, misuse of laxatives, fasting, and so on (*DSM-IV*, 1994). Sufferers from anorexia nervosa may also be bulimic. They may binge and then purge as a way of minimizing calories absorbed. Because the body is being systematically starved, both of these syndromes have serious medical consequences. In the long run, sufferers may starve to death.

In Chapter 11, we noted that adolescent girls are at particular risk for eating disorders (Striegel-Moore & Cachelin, 1999). The prevalence of anorexia among women in late adolescence and early adulthood is about 0.5 to 1.0 percent (*DSM-IV*, 1994). From 1 to 3 percent of the women in this same age group suffer from bulimia (*DSM-IV*, 1994; Rand & Kuldau, 1992). Women suffer from both diseases at approximately ten times the rate of men.

Why do people begin to starve themselves to death, and why are most of those people women? There is some evidence that a predilection toward eating disorders may be genetically transmitted (Strober, 1992). Much research attention, however, has focused on women's expectations for their ideal weight as generated by society and the media (Wertheim et al., 1997). For example, many of the magazines that are marketed specifically to women put great emphasis on weight loss; the same is not true for the magazines that men read (Andersen & DiDomenico, 1992). Thus, women may get more cultural support for their belief that they are overweight than do men. The belief that eating disorders follow, in part, from cultural forces has also received support from a number of analyses that have demonstrated important cultural differences.

Anorexia nervosa An eating disorder in which an individual weighs less than 85 percent of her or his expected weight but still controls eating because of a self-perception of obesity.

Bulimia nervosa An eating disorder characterized by binge eating followed by measures to purge the body of the excess calories.

EATING

FIGURE  12.1

Judgments of Body Size

Which picture do you believe best represents the United States ideal for a woman? For a man?

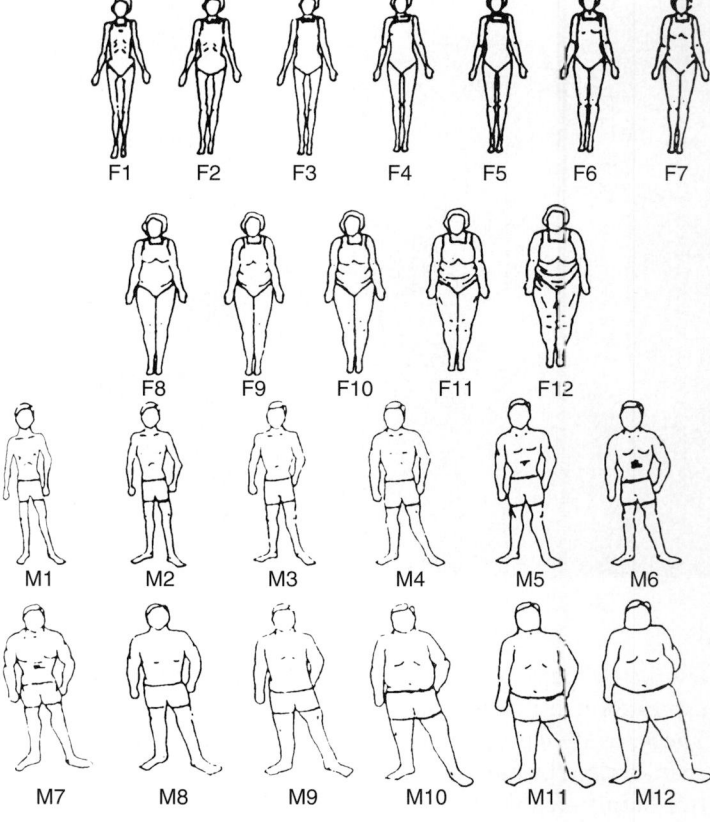

How might these differences be explained? The researchers suggest that in Ghana, as well as in other African countries, not everyone can *afford* to be overweight: "fat is associated with wealth and abundance" (Cogan et al., 1996, p. 98). As you can see in Figure 12.2, the positive association between size and prosperity is particularly applied to women, and particularly by Ghanan men.

Within the United States, it is equally easy to find group differences in judgments about body size. For example, surveys of large groups of adolescent girls consistently reveal that African American girls are more comfortable with their body sizes than are white adolescent girls (Parker et al., 1995; Rand & Kuldau, 1990; Rucker & Cash, 1992). Similarly, when black and white college women rated photographs of thin, average, and large models, only the white women rated the large models lower (compared to the thin and average models) on dimensions such as attractiveness, intelligence, and popularity (Hebl & Heatherton, 1998). Against this background, you will probably not be surprised to learn that white females are also more likely to suffer from eating disorders than are African American females. Although the precise rates at which the two populations experience these disorders is not known, reviews of a large number of studies support the conclusion that African American females suffer less (Crago et al., 1996). Fewer studies have examined other racial and ethnic groups, but evidence to date suggests that eating disturbances are also less frequent in Asian Americans than whites but equally common among Hispanic females as among whites. For each of these findings, researchers try to draw a link between cultural values about body size and dieting behaviors.

A final note: Right now, you're likely to be part of a particular culture that promotes eating disorders. Women in high school and college tend to suffer from anorexia or bulimia more than do nonstudents. In college settings, women may solve the tension between wanting to look attractive and wanting to eat and drink with their friends by bingeing—enjoying the party—and then purging—eliminating the calories (Rand & Kaldau, 1992). You should be aware that college life provides this dangerous potential.

SUMMING UP

Hunger is determined both by peripheral responses, such as sensory-specific satiety, and central responses, such as the activation of areas of the hypothalamus. The tendency to be overweight is influenced by heredity. Psychological forces also play a large role in determining when and how much people will eat. Researchers have described eating behaviors as restrained versus unrestrained; restrained eaters tend to binge when they suffer a threat to their psy-

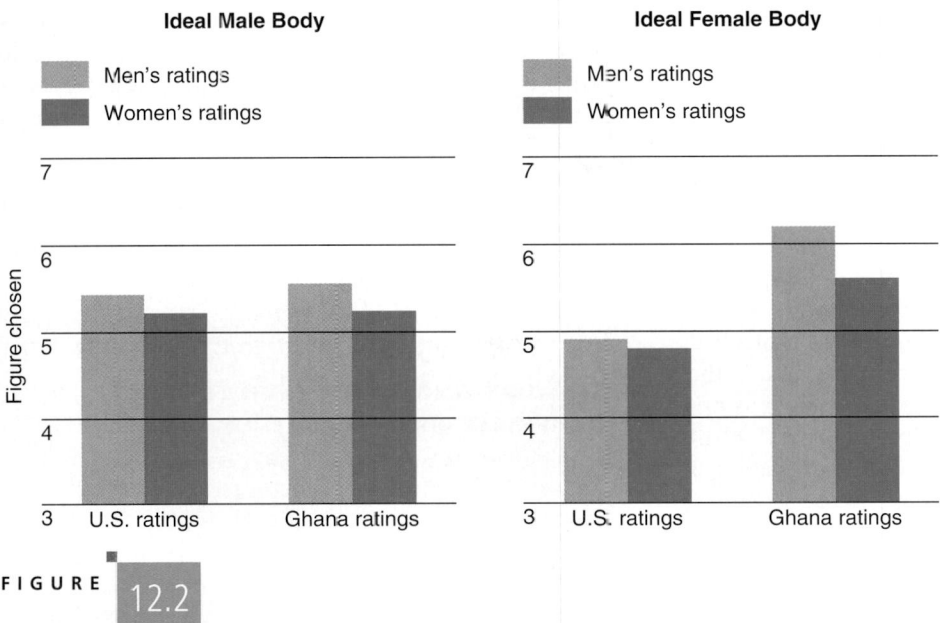

Ideal Male Body

Men's ratings
Women's ratings

Ideal Female Body

Men's ratings
Women's ratings

FIGURE 12.2

Cross-Cultural Perceptions of Body Size

Students from the University of Vermont and the University of Ghana indicated which of the figures from Figure 12.1 best represented what they considered to be the ideal male and female bodies. The students' ratings for male bodies are largely consistent across raters (that is, men and women) and countries. However, the ratings for the ideal woman's body differed from the United States to Ghana by about a full point. Ghanian men gave even higher ratings than Ghanian women.

chological well-being. Eating disorders are most likely to strike adolescent women. However, the rate at which adolescents suffer from eating disorders is affected by their subcultures' attitudes about body image. For example, African American women tend to be more comfortable with their bodies, and they also suffer from fewer eating disorders.

Sexual Behaviors

Your body physiology makes it essential that you think about food every day. But what about sex? It's easy to define the biological function of sex—reproduction—but does that explain the frequency with which you think about sexual behaviors? When asked how often they think about sex, 54 percent of adult men and 19 percent of adult women report they think about sex at least once every day (Michael et al., 1994). How can we explain the frequency with which people think about sex? How do thoughts about sex relate to sexual behaviors?

The question of motivation, once again, is the question of why people carry out certain ranges of behavior. As we already acknowledged, sexual behaviors are biologically necessary only for reproduction. Thus, while eating is essential to individual survival, sex is not. Some

animals and humans remain celibate for a lifetime without apparent detriment to their daily functioning. But reproduction is crucial to the survival of the species as a whole. To ensure that effort will be expended toward reproduction, nature has made sexual stimulation intensely pleasurable. An orgasm serves as the ultimate reinforcer for the energy expended in mating.

This potential for pleasure gives to sexual behaviors motivating power well beyond the need for reproduction. Individuals will perform a great variety of behaviors to achieve sexual gratification. But some sources of sexual motivation are external. Cultures establish norms or standards for what is acceptable or expected sexual behavior. While most people may be motivated to perform behaviors that accord with those norms, some people achieve their sexual satisfaction primarily by violating these norms.

In this section, we will first consider some of what is known about the sex drive and mating behavior in nonhuman animals. Then we shift our attention to selected issues in human sexuality.

Nonhuman Sexual Behaviors

The primary motivation for sexual behaviors in nonhuman animals is reproduction. For species that use sex as a means of reproduction, evolution has generally provided two sexual types, males and females. The female produces relatively large eggs (which contain the energy store for the embryo to begin its growth), and the male produces sperm that are specialized for motility (to move into the eggs). The two sexes must synchronize their activity so that sperm and egg meet under the appropriate conditions, resulting in conception.

Sexual arousal is determined primarily by physiological processes. Animals become receptive to mating largely in response to the flow of hormones controlled by the pituitary gland and secreted from the *gonads,* the sex organs. In males, these hormones are known as *androgens,* and they are continuously present in sufficient supply so that males are hormonally ready for mating at almost any time. In the females of many species, however, the sex hormone *estrogen* is released according to regular time cycles of days or months, or according to seasonal changes. Therefore, the female is not always hormonally receptive to mating.

These hormones act on both the brain and genital tissue and often lead to a pattern of predictable *stereotyped sexual behavior* for all members of a species. If, for example, you've seen one pair of rats in their mating sequence, you've seen them all. The receptive female rat darts about the male until she gets his attention. Then he chases her as she runs away. She stops suddenly and raises her rear, and he enters her briefly, thrusts, and pulls out. She briefly escapes him and the chase resumes—interrupted by 10 to 20 intromissions before he ejaculates, rests awhile, and starts the sex chase again. Apes also copulate only briefly (for about 15 seconds). For sables, copulation is slow and long, lasting for as long as eight hours. Predators, such as lions, can afford to indulge in long, slow copulatory rituals—as much as every 30 minutes over four consecutive days. Their prey, however, such as antelope, copulate for only a few seconds, often on the run (Ford & Beach, 1951).

Sexual arousal is often initiated by stimuli in the external environment. In many species, the sight and sound of ritualized display patterns by potential partners is a necessary condition for sexual response. Furthermore, in species as diverse as sheep, bulls, and rats, the novelty of the female partner affects a male animal's behavior. A male that has reached sexual satiation with one female partner may renew sexual activity when a new female is introduced (Dewsbury, 1981). Touch, taste, and smell can also serve as external stimulants for sexual arousal. As we described in Chapter 4, some species secrete chemical signals, called *pheromones,* that attract suitors, sometimes from great distances (Farine et al., 1996; Minckley et al., 1991). In many species, the female emits pheromones when her fertility is optimal (and hormone level and sexual interest are peaking). These secretions are unconditioned stimuli for arousal and attraction in the males of the species, who have inherited the tendency

to be aroused by the stimuli. When captive male rhesus monkeys smell the odor of a sexually receptive female in an adjacent cage, they respond with a variety of sex-related physiological changes, including an increase in the size of their testes (Hopson, 1979).

Although sexual response in nonhuman animals is largely determined by innate biological forces, this still leaves room for "cultural" aspects to affect choices of mate. Consider the guppy.

Are you surprised to learn that guppies—those innocent fish swimming in aquariums—are paying attention to which other fish have been judged desirable and undesirable? This experiment sets the stage for our discussion of human sexuality. We will soon see that researchers believe that human sexual response is also shaped both by our evolutionary history and the preferences of those around us.

Human Sexual Arousal and Response

Hormonal activity, so important in regulating sexual behavior among other animal species, has little effect on sexual receptiveness or gratification in the vast majority of men and women (Bancroft, 1978). In women, hormones play an important role in controlling the cycles of ovulation and menstruation. However, individual dif-

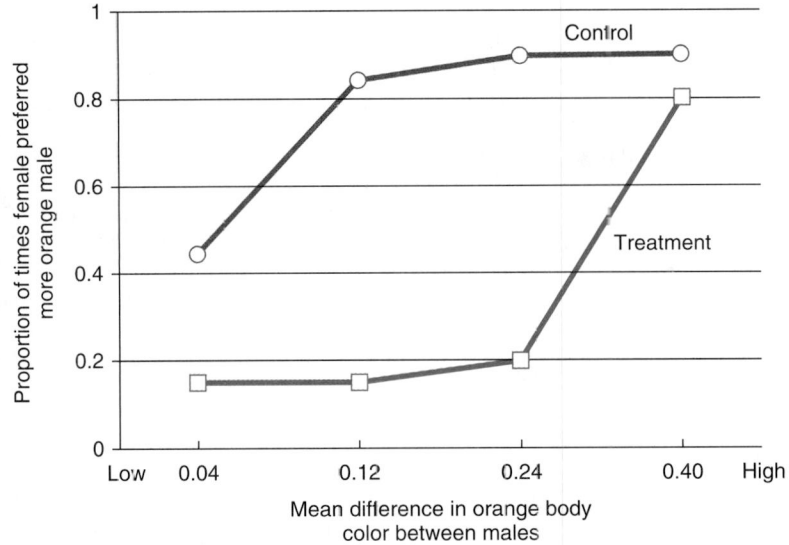

FIGURE 12.3

Female Guppies' Mate Selection

Female guppies in the "treatment" group saw another female near to the less orange male guppy. Female guppies in the "control" group did not observe another female's mate choice. The data suggest a trade-off between nature and nurture. At relatively low discrepancies in coloration, females chose the mate that had been chosen by the other female. However, when the discrepancy became extreme (that is, 40 percent), the females reverted to the choice of "nature," the more orange male.

ferences in hormone levels, within normal limits, are not predictive of the frequency or quality of sexual activity. For men, the hormone *testosterone* is necessary for sexual arousal and performance. Most healthy men from ages 18 to at least 60 have sufficient testosterone levels to experience normal sex drives. Once again, individual variation in these levels among men, within normal limits, is not related to sexual performance.

Sexual arousal in humans is the motivational state of excitement and tension brought about by physiological and cognitive reactions to erotic stimuli. *Erotic stimuli*, which may be physical or psychological, give rise to sexual excitement or feelings of passion. Sexual arousal induced by erotic stimuli is reduced by sexual activities that are perceived by the individual as satisfying, especially by achieving orgasm.

Researchers have studied sexual practices and sexual responses in nonhuman animals for several decades, but for many years studies of similar behaviors in humans were off limits. **William Masters** and **Virginia Johnson** (1966, 1970, 1979) broke down this traditional taboo. They legitimized the study of human sexuality by directly observing and recording, under laboratory conditions, the physiological patterns involved in ongoing human sexual performance. By doing so, they explored not what people said about sex but how individuals actually reacted or performed sexually.

For their direct investigation of the human response to sexual stimulation, Masters and Johnson conducted controlled laboratory observations of thousands of volunteer males and females during tens of thousands of sexual response cycles of intercourse and masturbation. Four of the most significant conclusions drawn from this research are that: (1) Men and women have similar patterns of sexual response; (2) although the sequence of phases of the sexual response cycle is similar in the two sexes, women are more variable, tending to respond more slowly but often remaining aroused longer; (3) many women can have multiple orgasms, whereas men rarely do in a comparable time period; and (4) penis size is generally unrelated to any aspect of sexual performance (except in the male's attitude toward having a large penis).

Four phases were found in the human sexual response cycle: excitement, plateau, orgasm, and resolution (see **Figure 12.4**).

- In the excitement phase (lasting from a few minutes to more than an hour), there are vascular (blood vessel) changes in the pelvic region. The penis becomes erect and the clitoris swells; blood and other fluids become congested in the testicles and vagina; a reddening of the body, or sex flush, occurs.

- During the plateau phase, a maximum (though varying) level of arousal is reached. There is rapidly increased heartbeat, respiration, and blood pressure, increased glandular secretions, and both voluntary and involuntary muscle tension throughout the body. Vaginal lubrication increases, and the breasts swell.

- During the orgasm phase, males and females experience a very intense, pleasurable sense of release from the sexual tension that has been building. Orgasm is characterized by rhythmic contractions that occur approximately every eight-tenths of a second in the genital areas. Respiration and blood pressure reach very high levels in both men and women, and heart rate may double. In men, throbbing contractions lead to ejaculation, an "explosion" of semen.

Sexual arousal The motivational state of excitement and tension brought about by physiological and cognitive reactions to erotic stimuli.

Phases of Human Sexual Response

The phases of human sexual response in males and females have similar patterns. The primary differences are in the time it takes for males and females to reach each phase, and in the greater likelihood that females will achieve multiple orgasms.

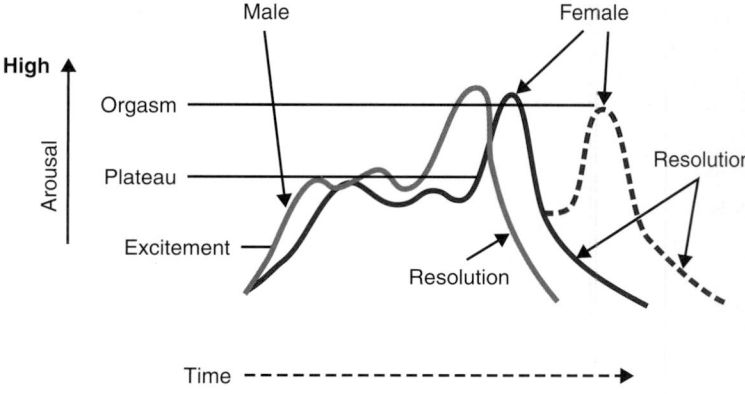

■ During the resolution phase, the body gradually returns to its normal preexcitement state, with both blood pressure and heartbeat slowing down. After one orgasm, most men enter a refractory period, lasting anywhere from a few minutes to several hours, during which no further orgasm is possible. With sustained arousal, some women are capable of multiple orgasms in fairly rapid succession.

Although Masters and Johnson's research focused on the physiology of sexual response, perhaps their most important discovery was the central significance of *psychological* processes in both arousal and satisfaction. They demonstrated that problems in sexual response often have psychological, rather than physiological, origins and can be modified or overcome through therapy. Of particular concern is the inability to complete the response cycle and achieve gratification. Often the source of the inability is a preoccupation with personal problems, fear of the consequences of sexual activity, anxiety about a partner's evaluation of one's sexual performance, or unconscious guilt or negative thoughts. However, poor nutrition, fatigue, stress, and excessive use of alcohol or drugs can also diminish sexual drive and performance.

Although sex fulfills the biological function of reproduction, most humans engage in sex many more times than they reproduce. Even so, how does the evolutionary perspective explain contemporary sexual strategies?

We have now reviewed some physiological aspects of human sexuality and sexual arousal. But we have not yet considered the forces that give rise to *differences* in sexual expression. We begin with the idea that the goal of reproduction ensures different patterns of sexual behavior for men and for women.

The Evolution of Sexual Behaviors

For nonhuman animals, we have already seen that the pattern of sexual behaviors was largely fixed by evolution. The main goal is reproduction—preservation of the species—and sexual behaviors are highly ritualized and stereotyped. Can the same claim be made for general patterns of human sexual behaviors?

Evolutionary psychologists have explored the idea that men and women have evolved to have different *strategies* that underlie sexual behavior (Buss, 1999; Wright, 1994). To describe these strategies, we have to remind you of some of the realities of human reproduction. Human males could reproduce hundreds of times a year if they could find enough willing mates. To produce a child, all they need to invest is a teaspoon of sperm and a few minutes of intercourse. Women can reproduce at most about once a year, and each child then requires a huge investment of time and energy. (Incidentally, the world record for the number of times a woman has given birth falls short of 50, but men have fathered many more children. A Moroccan despot, King Ismail the Bloodthirsty, had over 700 children, and the first Emperor of China is said to have fathered over 3,000; both had large harems.)

Thus, when reproduction is a goal, eggs are the limited resource and males compete for opportunities to fertilize them. The basic problem facing a male animal is to maximize the number of offspring he produces, by mating with the largest number of females possible. But the basic problem facing a female animal is to find a high-quality male to ensure the best, healthiest offspring from her limited store of eggs. Furthermore, human offspring take so long to mature and are so helpless while growing that substantial **parental investment** is required (Trivers, 1972; Wright, 1994). Mothers and fathers must spend time and energy raising the children—unlike fish or spiders, which simply lay eggs and depart. Females thus have the problem of selecting not just the biggest, strongest, smartest, highest-status, most thrilling mate but also the most loyal, committed partner to help raise their children.

One evolutionary psychologist, **David Buss** (1999; Buss & Schmitt, 1993), has suggested that men and women evolved different strategies, emotions, and motivations for *short-term mating* versus *long-term mating*. The male strategy of seducing and abandoning—showing signs of loyalty and commitment and then leaving—is a short-term strategy. The male strategy of staying committed to the female and investing in the offspring is a long-term strategy. The female strategy of attracting a loyal male who will stay to help raise her children is a long-term strategy. There is some controversy about whether women have evolved short-term mating strategies. Some argue that indiscriminate sex never pays for women in an evolutionary sense—they can get pregnant without assurance of male investment later. Women do seem less interested in casual sex than men (Buss & Schmitt, 1993). Others argue that short-term mating with many men—especially older, rich men—in exchange for immediate rewards may pay off by assuring short-term survival.

Researchers have provided a variety of types of evidence to support predictions of evolutionary theory. Consider studies that examined how women's judgments of the attractiveness of male faces was affected by the possibility of conception.

This research examined preferences, rather than actual sexual behavior. Even so, it illustrates how important aspects of human lives may be guided by our evolutionary history.

Although research supports many of the predictions of the evolutionary account of human sexual behaviors, other theorists believe that the account greatly underestimates the role of culture (Angier, 1999). For example, women demonstrate greater *erotic plasticity* than men: Women show greater variation in sexual responses and sexual behaviors than men do (Baumeister, 2000). These variations appear, in large part, to be a consequence of cultural constraints (Hyde & Durik, 2000). Consider the "sexual revolution" of the 1960s: Changes in sexual behavior were brought about by women's increased willingness to engage in casual sexual relations. What had changed was not, of course, women's evolutionary history but, rather, cultural attitudes toward the expression of sexuality.

Although the evolutionary approach explains some aspects of human sexual behavior, the critique calls attention to variability imposed by culture. Norms of sexual behavior are highly sensitive to time and place. We turn now to sexual norms.

Sexual Norms

What is an average sex life like? Scientific investigation of human sexual behavior was given the first important impetus by the work of **Alfred Kinsey** and his colleagues beginning in the 1940s (1948, 1953). They interviewed some 17,000 Americans about their sexual behavior and revealed—to a generally shocked public—that certain behaviors, previously considered rare and even abnormal, were actually quite widespread—or at least were reported to be. In recent years, researchers have conducted surveys about sexual practices with great regularity. The results are often widely trumpeted by the media. In **Table 12.3**, we have provided you with some data from one major effort (Michael et al., 1994). The researchers asked a wide range of questions. We have given you only a small sample of the responses. Can you spot any interesting trends? You might find it noteworthy, for example, that people age 55 to 59 are much more likely to have stuck with one partner since age 18 than are those age 25 to 29. This outcome suggests that the norms for sexual behavior have changed over the last several decades.

Parental investment The time and energy parents must spend raising their offspring.

TABLE 12.3

Sexual Activity of Adult Americans, 1994*

| | Number of Sexual Partners Since Age 18 (Percentage in Each Category) | | | |
	0	1	2–10	10 or More
Men	3	26	44	33
Women	3	31	56	9
Ages 25–29	2	25	53	19
Ages 55–59	1	40	43	15
High school education	3	30	49	17
College education	2	24	50	24

| | Frequency of Sexual Activity in the Past 12 Months (Percentage in Each Category) | | | |
	Not at All	A Few Times per Year	A Few Times per Month	Two or More Times per Week
Men	14	16	37	34
Women	10	18	36	37
Men				
Ages 25–29	7	15	31	47
Ages 55–59	11	22	43	23
Women				
Ages 25–29	5	10	38	47
Ages 55–59	30	22	35	13
Men				
High school	10	15	34	41
Some college	9	18	38	35
Women				
High school	11	16	38	36
Some college	14	17	37	33

*Based on a random survey sample of 3,432 adults, 18 and older.

These sexual norms are part of what you acquire as a member of a culture. We already suggested that some general "male" and "female" aspects of sexual behavior may be products of the evolution of the human species. Even so, different cultures define ranges of behavior that are considered to be appropriate for expressing sexual impulses. **Sexual scripts** are socially learned programs of sexual responsiveness that include prescriptions, usually unspoken, of what to do; when, where, and how to do it; with whom, or with what, to do it; and why it should be done (Gagnon, 1977). Different aspects of these scripts are assembled through social interaction over your lifetime. The attitudes and values embodied in your sexual script are an external source of sexual motivation: The script suggests the types of behaviors you might or should undertake.

Scripts are combinations of prescriptions generated by social norms (what is proper and accepted), individ-

ual expectations, and preferred sequences of behavior from past learning. Your sexual scripts include scenarios not only of what you think is appropriate on your part but also of your expectations for a sexual partner. When

How might instances of sexual harassment arise from conflicting sexual scripts?

Sexual scripts Socially learned programs of sexual responsiveness.

they are not recognized, discussed, or synchronized, differing scripts can create problems of adjustment between partners.

Let's focus more specifically on the sexual practices of college students. Researchers have often been interested in understanding *sexual risk taking:* circumstances in which individuals engage in sexual practices that ignore the risk of pregnancy or sexually transmitted diseases. Given our discussion of evolution and sex differences, you may not be surprised to learn that, on the whole, men are more likely than women to engage in risky behaviors (Poppen, 1995). In one sample of college students, more men than women report that they have gone to bars to meet prospective sex partners (77 vs. 14 percent) and that they have had sex with someone they have just met (47 vs. 24 percent). In addition, slightly more men than women reported having had sex without some form of contraception (78 vs. 64 percent).

Research into the sexual experience of college students has revealed another area in which male and female sexual scripts come into devastating conflict: date rape. **Date rape** applies to circumstances in which someone is coerced into sexual activity by a social acquaintance. In one study, researchers asked 341 women to provide information about their experiences of sexual aggression. In this sample, about 78 percent of the women reported that they had been the victims of some form of sexual aggression; about 15 percent of the women indicated that a date had forced them into sexual intercourse (Muehlenhard & Linton, 1987). When asked to say who was responsible for a date rape, males surveyed tend to blame the victim (that is, the woman who was raped) more than females do (Bell et al., 1994; Ryckman et al., 1998).

Studies of date rape reveal that women and men's sexual scripts differ significantly with respect to the incidence of *token resistance*—a woman's mild resistance to sexual advances despite the intention, ultimately, to allow sexual intercourse. Very few women—about 5 percent—report engaging in token resistance, but about 60 percent of men say that they have, at least once, *experienced* token resistance (Marx & Gross, 1995). The difference between those two figures likely includes many incidents of date rape. Research suggests that some men come to believe that token resistance is part of a sexual game; resistance doesn't signal genuine distress on a woman's part. It is important for men to understand that women, in fact, rarely report themselves to be playing that game—resistance is real.

Throughout most of our discussion of sexual motivation, we have been ignoring a major category of sexual experience: homosexuality. We conclude this section on sexual motivation with a discussion of lesbians and gay men. This discussion will give us another opportunity to see how sexual behavior is controlled by the interplay of internal and external motivational forces.

Homosexuality

Our discussion so far has focused on the motivations that cause people to perform a certain range of sexual behaviors. It is in this same context that we can discuss the existence of homosexuality. That is, rather than presenting homosexuality as a set of behaviors that is "caused" by a deviation from heterosexuality, our discussion of sexual motivation should allow you to see that all sexual behavior is "caused." In this view, homosexuality and heterosexuality result from similar motivational forces. Neither of them represents a motivated departure from the other.

Most surveys of sexual behavior have tried to obtain an accurate estimate of the incidence of homosexuality. In his early research, Alfred Kinsey found that 37 percent of men in his sample had had at least some homosexual experience and that about 4 percent were exclusively homosexual (percentages for women were somewhat smaller). More recent surveys have tried to capture the distinction between having homosexual desires and acting on them. Michael and colleagues (1994) found that about 4 percent of women in their sample were sexually attracted to individuals of the same gender, but only 2 percent of the sample had actually had sex with another woman in the past year. Similarly, 6 percent of the men in their survey were sexually attracted to other men, but again only 2 percent of the sample had actually had sex with another man in the past year. Are these figures correct? As long as there is societal hostility directed toward acting on homosexual desires, it may be impossible to get entirely accurate estimates of the incidence of homosexuality because of people's reluctance to confide in researchers.

In this section we consider the origins of homosexuality and heterosexuality. We also review research on societal and personal attitudes toward homosexual behavior.

THE NATURE AND NURTURE OF HOMOSEXUALITY

After our discussion of evolution and sexual behaviors, it should not surprise you to learn that research evidence suggests that sexual preference has a genetic component. As is often the case, researchers have made this assertion based on studies that compare concordance rates of *monozygotic* (MZ) twins (those who are genetically identical) and *dizygotic* (DZ) twins (those who, like siblings, share only half their genes). When both members of a pair of twins have the same orientation—homosexual or heterosexual—they are concordant. If one twin is homosexual and the other is heterosexual, they are discordant. Studies of both gay men and lesbians have demonstrated

■ **Date rape** Unwanted sexual violation by a social acquaintance in the context of a consensual dating situation.

What evidence suggests that sexual orientation has a genetic component?

considerably higher concordance rates for MZ than for DZ twins (Bailey & Pillard, 1991; Bailey et al., 1993). In these studies, the experimenters searched out individual gay or lesbian twins and then obtained information from them about the sexual orientation of their co-twins or other siblings. The results were startling. Among women, 48 percent of MZ twins were both lesbians, compared with 16 percent of DZ twins (Bailey et al., 1993). Among men, 52 percent of MZ twins were both gay, compared with 22 percent of DZ twins (Bailey & Pillard, 1991). Although MZ twins may also be reared in more similar environments than DZ twins—they may be treated more similarly by their parents—this pattern strongly suggests that sexuality may, in part, be genetically determined. With this knowledge in hand, researchers have started to search for the gene sequences that might control the emergence of homosexuality or heterosexuality (Bailey et al., 1999; Hamer et al., 1993; Rice et al., 1999). So, does biology determine your sexual destiny? Further research may strengthen or weaken the case, but it seems clear that some aspects of homosexuality and heterosexuality emerge in response to purely biological forces (Gladue, 1994; LeVay, 1996).

Social psychologist **Daryl Bem** (1996, 2000) has suggested that biology does not effect sexual preference directly, but rather has an indirect impact by influencing the temperaments and activities of young children. Recall from Chapter 11 that researchers have suggested that boys and girls engage in different activities—boys' play, for example, tends to be more rough-and-tumble. Ac-

cording to Bem's theory, depending on whether they engage in sex-typical or sex-atypical play, children come to feel dissimilar to either their same-sex or opposite-sex peers. In Bem's theory, "exotic becomes erotic": Feelings of dissimilarity lead to emotional arousal; over time this arousal is transformed into erotic attraction. For example, if a young girl feels dissimilar from other girls because she does not wish to engage in girl-typical activities, over time her emotional arousal will be transformed into homosexual feelings. Note that Bem's theory supports the assertion that homosexuality and heterosexuality arise from the same causal forces: In both cases, the gender the child perceives as dissimilar becomes, over time, eroticized. Although Bem provides a range of evidence in favor of his theory, it is still relatively new. We will see in the next several years how it fares when researchers assess its various implications.

SOCIETY AND HOMESEXUALITY

Suppose Bem is correct to argue that childhood experiences matter enormously. Does everyone act on the urgings set down in childhood? What, perhaps, most sets homosexuality apart from heterosexuality is the continuing hostility toward homosexual behaviors in many corners of society (Herek, 1998). In a survey of 363 adults, 68 percent agreed "strongly" or "somewhat" with the statement "Sex between two men is just plain wrong"; 64 percent agreed "strongly" or "somewhat" with the statement "Sex between two women is just plain wrong" (Herek, 1994). Researchers have labeled highly negative attitudes toward gay people *homophobia*. Recent research suggests that some men who present extremely homophobic attitudes are, in fact, aroused by homosexual materials.

HOW WE KNOW

DOES HOMOPHOBIA MASK HOMOSEXUAL INTEREST? Participants in the study were 64 male college students, all of whom rated themselves as "exclusively heterosexual." The students filled out a 25-item scale that measured homophobia. On the basis of this scale, 29 students were identified as nonhomophobic and 35 were identified as homophobic. In the next phase of the experiment, the students were shown erotic videotapes of heterosexual, lesbian, and male homosexual acts. Each student's arousal in response to these videotapes was assessed by a device that monitored changes in the circumference of his penis. The data showed no differences for homophobic and nonhomophobic men's arousal in response to the heterosexual and lesbian videotapes. However, the homophobic men showed reliably greater arousal than did the nonhomophobic men in response to the videotape of male homosexual activity (Adams et al., 1996).

This research suggests that some men's very negative attitudes toward homosexuality may arise, in part, because of an unwillingness by them to confront their own positive sexual responses toward other men.

Most homosexuals come to the realization that they are motivated toward same-sex relationships in the hostile context of societal homophobia—a context that might make it difficult for them to act on those feelings. In fact, many gay men and lesbians experience what has been called *internalized homophobia* or *internalized homonegativity* (Allen & Oleson, 1999; Ross & Rosser, 1996; Shidlo, 1994). In these cases, psychological distress may arise because the gay or lesbian individual has internalized the negative attitudes of society. Moreover, much of lesbians' and gay men's anxiety about homosexuality arises not from being homosexual, but from an ongoing need either to reveal ("come out") or to conceal ("stay in the closet") their sexual identity to family, friends, and co-workers (D'Augelli, 1993). In 1973, the American Psychiatric Association voted to remove homosexuality from the list of psychological disorders; the American Psychological Association followed in 1975 (Morin & Rothblum, 1991). Spurring this action were research reports suggesting that, in fact, most gay men and lesbians are happy, productive human beings who would not change their sexual orientation even if a "magic pill" enabled them to do so (Bell & Weinberg, 1978; Siegelman, 1972). These data suggest that much of the stress associated with homosexuality arises not from the sexual motivation itself—gay people are happy with their orientations—but from the way in which people respond to the revelation of that sexual motivation. As you might expect, gay men and lesbians also spend time worrying about establishing and maintaining loving relationships just as heterosexuals do (D'Augelli, 1993).

The willingness of lesbians and gay men to "come out" may serve as a first step toward decreasing societal hostility. Research has shown that people's attitudes toward gay men and lesbians are much less negative when they actually *know* individuals in these groups; in fact, on average the more gay men and lesbians a person knows, the more favorable is his or her attitude (Herek & Capitanio, 1996). (When we turn to the topic of prejudice in Chapter 18, we will see there again how experiences with members of minority groups can lead to more positive attitudes.) Do you know any gay, lesbian, or bisexual individuals? How have your attitudes been influenced by interactions with gay people? Are you yourself gay, lesbian, or bisexual? How have or could have the attitudes of people around you been affected by knowing that you are gay?

This brief review of homosexuality allows us to reinforce our main conclusions about human sexual motivation. Some of the impetus for sexual behaviors is internal—genetic endowment and species evolution provide internal models for both heterosexual and homosexual behaviors. But the external environment also gives rise to sexual motivation. You learn to find some stimuli particularly alluring and some behaviors culturally acceptable. In the case of homosexuality, external societal norms may work against the internal dictates of nature.

Let's move now to our third example of important motivation: the forces that set an individual's course for relative success or failure.

SUMMING UP

Sexual response in nonhuman animals is largely controlled by hormones. Even so, mate selection is influenced by factors in the environment. Masters and Johnson pioneered the study of sexual response in humans, which can be divided into the excitement, plateau, orgasm, and resolution phases. Evolutionary psychologists have attempted to explain male and female patterns of sexual behavior by reference to the different strategies men and women have with respect to the realities of reproduction. Some of the types of sexual activity in which college students engage put them at risk. Date rape may be one product of men and women's discordant sexual scripts. As with heterosexuality, homosexuality arises from both internal and external motivational forces. The biggest burden for many gay men and lesbians is coping with societal homophobia.

Motivation for Personal Achievement

Why do some people succeed while other people, relatively speaking, fail? Why, for example, are some people able to swim the English Channel, while other people just wave woefully from the shore? You are likely to attribute some of the difference to genetic factors like body type, and you're correct to do so. But

These men are participating in the International Games for the Disabled. How can motivation explain variability among individuals—the fact, for example, that some people do better in competition than others?

you also know that some people are simply much more interested in swimming the English Channel than are others. So we are back at one of our core reasons for studying motivation. We want, in this case, to understand the motivational forces that lead different people to seek different levels of personal achievement. Let's begin with a construct that's actually called the *need for achievement*.

Need for Achievement

As early as 1938, **Henry Murray** had postulated a need to achieve that varied in strength in different people and influenced their tendency to approach success and evaluate their own performances. **David McClelland** and his colleagues (1953) devised a way to measure the strength of this need and then looked for relationships between strength of achievement motivation in different societies, conditions that had fostered the motivation, and its results in the work world. To gauge the strength of the need for achievement, McClelland used his participants' fantasies. On what is called the **Thematic Apperception Test (TAT)**, participants were asked to generate stories in response to a series of ambiguous drawings. Participants shown TAT pictures were asked to make up stories about them—to say what was happening in the picture and describe probable outcomes. Presumably, they projected into the scene reflections of their own values, interests, and motives. According to McClelland: "If you want to find out what's on a person's mind, don't ask him, because he can't always tell you accurately. Study his fantasies and dreams. If you do this over a period of time, you will discover the themes to which his mind returns again and again. And these themes can be used to explain his actions…" (McClelland, 1971, p. 5).

From participant responses to a series of TAT pictures, McClelland worked out measures of several human needs, including needs for power, affiliation, and achievement. The **need for achievement** was designated as *n Ach*. It reflected individual differences in the importance of planning and working toward attaining one's goals. **Figure 12.5** shows an example of how a high *n Ach*

Thematic Apperception Test (TAT) A projective test in which pictures of ambiguous scenes are presented to an individual, who is encouraged to generate stories about them.

Need for achievement (n Ach) An assumed basic human need to strive for achievement of goals that motivates a wide range of behavior and thinking.

FIGURE 12.5

Alternative Interpretations of a TAT Picture

Story Showing High n Ach

This boy has just finished his violin lesson. He's happy at the progress he is making and is beginning to believe that all his progress is making the sacrifices worthwhile. To become a concert violinist, he will have to give up much of his social life to practice for many hours each day. Although he knows he could make more money by going into his father's business, he is more interested in being a great violinist and giving people joy with his music. He renews his personal commitment to whatever it takes to make it.

Story Showing Low n Ach

This boy is holding his brother's violin and wishes he could play it. But he knows it is not worth the time, energy, and money for lessons. He feels sorry for his brother, he has given up all the enjoyable things in life to practice, practice, practice. It would be great to wake up one day and be a top-notch musician, but it doesn't work that way. The reality is boring practice, no fun, and the strong possibility of becoming just another guy playing a musical instrument in a small-town band.

individual and a low *n Ach* individual might interpret a TAT picture. Studies in both laboratory and real-life settings have validated the usefulness of this measure.

For example, high-scoring *n Ach* people were found to be more upwardly mobile than those with low scores; sons who had high *n Ach* scores were more likely than sons with low *n Ach* measures to advance above their fathers' occupational status (McClelland et al., 1976). Men and women who measured high on *n Ach* at age 31 tended to have higher salaries than their low *n Ach* peers by age 41 (McClelland & Franz, 1992). Do these findings indicate that high *n Ach* individuals are always willing to work harder? Not really. In the face of a task that they are led to believe will be difficult, high *n Ach* individuals quit early on (Feather, 1961). What, in fact, seems to typify high *n Ach* individuals is a need for *efficiency*—a need to get the same result for less effort. If they outearn their peers, it might be because they also value concrete feedback on how well they are doing. As a measure of progress, salary is very concrete (McClelland, 1961; McClelland & Franz, 1992).

How does a high need for achievement arise? Researchers have considered whether parenting practices can bring about a high or low need for achievement. Data come from a longitudinal analysis of a group of Boston-area children.

These data suggest that the degree to which you experience a need to achieve may have been established in the first few years of your life.

Attributions for Success and Failure

Need for achievement is not the only variable that affects motivation toward personal success. To see why, let's begin with a hypothetical example. Suppose you have two friends who are taking the same class. On the first midterm, each gets a C. Do you think they would be equally motivated to study hard for the second midterm? Part of

When success comes your way, do you give yourself full credit for the achievement? What type of attributional style would this practice reflect?

the answer will depend on the way in which they each explained the C to themselves.

Consider, for example, the importance of locus of control (Rotter, 1954). A *locus of control orientation* is a belief about whether the outcomes of your actions are contingent on what you do *(internal control orientation)* or on environmental factors *(external control orientation)*. In the case of the C's, your friends might *attribute* their performance to either an external cause (construction noise during the exam) or an internal cause (poor memory). **Attributions** are judgments about the causes of outcomes. (We will develop attribution theory at length in Chapter 17.) In this case, the attributions can have an impact on motivation. If your friends believe they can attribute their performance to construction noise, they are likely to study hard for the next midterm. If they think the fault lies in their poor memory, they're more likely to slack off.

Locus of control is not the only dimension along which attributions can vary (Peterson & Seligman, 1984). We can also ask: "To what extent is a causal factor likely to be stable and consistent over time, or unstable and varying?" The answer gives us the dimension of *stability* versus *instability*. Or we can ask: "To what extent is a causal factor highly specific, limited to a particular task or situation, or global, applying widely across a variety of settings?" This gives us the dimension of *global* versus *specific*.

An example of how locus of control and stability can interact is given in **Figure 12.6**. Let's stay with the example of attributions about exam grades. Your friends can interpret their grades as the result of internal factors, such as ability (a stable personality characteristic) or effort (a varying personal quality). Or they may view the

Attributions Judgments about the causes of outcomes.

Locus of Control

	Internal	External
Stable	Ability	Task difficulty
Unstable	Effort	Luck

Stability

FIGURE 12.6

Attributions Regarding Causes for Behavioral Outcomes

Four possible outcomes are generated with just two sources of attributions about behavior: the locus of control and the situation in which the behavior occurs. Ability attributions are made for the internal-stable combination, effort for the internal but unstable combination, a difficult task (test) when external-stable forces are assumed to be operating, and luck for the unstable-external combination.

TABLE 12.4

Attribution-Dependent Emotional Responses

Your feelings in response to success and failure depend on the kinds of attributions you make regarding the cause of those outcomes. For example, you take pride in success when you attribute it to your ability, but are depressed when you perceive lack of ability to cause failure. Or you feel gratitude when you attribute your success to the actions of others but anger when they are seen as contributing to your failure.

	Emotional Responses	
Attribution	**Success**	**Failure**
Ability	Competence	Incompetence
	Confidence	Resignation
	Pride	Depression
Effort	Relief	Guilt
	Contentment	Shame
	Relaxation	Fear
Action of others	Gratitude	Anger
	Thankfulness	Fury
Luck	Surprise	Surprise
	Guilt	Astonishment

grades as caused primarily by external factors such as the difficulty of the task, the actions of others (a stable situational problem), or luck (an unstable external feature). Depending on the nature of the attribution they make for this success or failure, they are likely to experience one of the emotional responses depicted in **Table 12.4**. What is important here is that the type of interpretation will influence both their emotions and subsequent motivation—to study harder or blow off work—regardless of the true reason for the success or failure.

So far we have been considering the possibility that both of your friends will explain their C's in the same way, but it's very likely that they might arrive at different explanations. One may believe something external ("The professor gave an unfair exam"); the other may believe something internal ("I'm not smart enough for this class"). Researchers have shown that the way people explain events in their lives—from winning at cards to being turned down for a date—can become lifelong, habitual *attributional styles* (Haines et al., 1999). The way you account for your successes and failures can influence your motivation, mood, and even ability to perform appropriately. For several years, researcher **Martin Seligman** has studied the ways in which people's *explanatory style*—their degree of optimism or pessimism—affects activity and passivity, whether they persist or give up easily, take risks, or play it safe (Seligman, 1991).

In Chapter 15, we will see that an internal-global-stable explanatory style ("I never do anything right") puts individuals at risk for depression (and one of the symptoms of depression is impaired motivation). For now, however, let's focus on the way in which explanatory style might lead one of your friends to have an A and the other an F by the end of the semester. Seligman's research team has worked on the problem of explaining one person's ability and another's inability to resist failure. The secret ingredient has turned out to be familiar and seemingly simple: *optimism* versus *pessimism*. Remarkably, these two divergent ways of looking at the world influence motivation, mood, and behavior.

The *pessimistic attributional style* focuses on the causes of failure as internally generated. Furthermore, the bad situation and the individual's role in causing it are seen as stable and global—"It won't ever change and it will affect everything." The *optimistic attributional style* sees failure as the result of external causes—"The test was unfair"—and of events that are unstable or modifiable and specific—"If I put in more effort next time, I'll do better, and this one setback won't affect how I perform any other task that is important to me."

These causal explanations are reversed when it comes to the question of success. Optimists take full, personal internal-stable-global credit for success. However, pessimists attribute their success to external-unstable-global or specific factors. Because they believe themselves to be doomed to fail, pessimists perform worse than others would expect, given objective measures of their talent. A body of research supports these generalizations about optimists and pessimists. For example, one study measured the explanatory styles of 130 male salespeople in a leading United Kingdom insurance company (Corr & Gray, 1996). In the study, salesman with more positive attributional styles were also likely to have higher sales. In everyday life, interpretations of events affect both optimists' and pessimists' levels of motivation for future performance.

To close out this section, let's look at a research example of the powerful impact of causal attributions in an academic setting.

ATTRIBUTIONAL RETRAINING FOR CAREER BELIEFS When you finish college, you're going to want to get the best job possible. But how do you think that's going to happen? Are you going to get a good job because of your own skills and initiative (an internal attribution)? Or because of random circumstances and good luck (an external attribution)? Research suggests that students who believe they have control over career outcomes are more likely to meet their career aspirations. In that context, what can be done to encourage students to change their attributions from external to internal?

A team of researchers developed an intervention that they called *attributional retraining*. Groups of students who indicated that they believed they have little control over their careers viewed a videotaped conversation between a male and female graduate of their university. For the experimental group, part of the graduates' discussion focused on how they made career decisions: "I realized as I was growing up that anything worthwhile in terms of my career was going to take effort and hard work" (Luzzo et al., 1996, p. 417). The control group did not hear this type of information. After this brief intervention, members of the experimental group now indicated a more internal locus of control for career choices and also, as time passed, engaged in more behaviors related to career exploration. The control group did not show these changes (Luzzo et al., 1996).

Because of the way in which attributions affected motivation, a small amount of information about career choices had a profound effect on students' ideas about their futures.

We believe that there is much value to you in this line of psychological research. You can work at developing an optimistic explanatory style for your successes and failures. You can avoid making negative, stable, dis-

positional attributions for your failures by examining possible causal forces in the situation. Finally, don't let your motivation be undermined by momentary setbacks. You can apply this research-based advice to better your life—a recurring theme of *Psychology and Life*.

Work and Organizational Psychology

Now suppose your positive philosophy has helped you to get a job in a big corporation. Can we predict exactly how motivated you'll be just by knowing about you, as an individual—your *n Ach* score or your explanatory style? Your individual level of motivation will depend, in part, on the overall context of people and rules in which you work. Recognizing that work settings are complex social systems, **organizational psychologists** study various aspects of human relations, such as communication among employees, socialization or enculturation of workers, leadership, attitudes and commitment toward a job and/or an organization, job satisfaction, stress and burnout, and overall quality of life at work. As consultants to businesses, organizational psychologists may assist in recruitment, selection, and training of employees. They also make recommendations about job redesign—tailoring a job to fit the person. Organizational psychologists apply theories of management, decision making, and development to improve work settings.

Let's look at a pair of theories organizational psychologists have developed to understand motivation in the workplace. *Equity theory* and *expectancy theory* attempt to explain and predict how people will respond under different working conditions. These theories assume that workers engage in certain cognitive activities, such as assessing fairness through processes of social comparison with other workers or estimating expected rewards associated with their performance.

Equity theory proposes that workers are motivated to maintain fair or equitable relationships with other relevant persons (Adams, 1965). Workers take note of their inputs (investments or contributions they make to their jobs) and their outcomes (what they receive from their jobs), and then they compare these with the inputs and outcomes of other workers. When the ratio of outcomes

Organizational psychologists Psychologists who study various aspects of the human work environment, such as communication among employees, socialization or enculturation of workers, leadership, job satisfaction, stress and burnout, and overall quality of life.

Equity theory A cognitive theory of work motivation that proposes that workers are motivated to maintain fair and equitable relationships with other relevant persons; also, a model that postulates that equitable relationships are those in which the participants' outcomes are proportional to their inputs.

to inputs for Worker A is equal to the ratio for Worker B (outcome A ÷ input A = outcome B ÷ input B), then Worker A will feel satisfied. Dissatisfaction will result when these ratios are not equal. Because feeling this inequity is aversive, workers will be motivated to restore equity by changing the relevant inputs and outcomes. These changes could be behavioral (for example, reducing input by working less, increasing outcome by asking for a raise). Or they could be psychological (for example, reinterpreting the value of the inputs—"My work isn't really that good"—or the value of the outcome—"I'm lucky to have a weekly paycheck I can count on").

Have you noticed the consequences of equity or inequity in your own work situations? Consider a situation in which a coworker leaves for a better job. How does that make you feel? Equity theory suggests that you may feel like you have been unfairly left behind in an undesirable job. In fact, when coworkers leave in circumstances in which they have expressed dissatisfaction, the people remaining tend to become less productive in their jobs—they decrease productivity to restore their sense of equity (Sheehan, 1993). If you end up in a management position, you should try to prevent this pattern by addressing the psychological needs of your employees with respect to equity. For example, keep in mind the benefit of "adequate explanations."

Expectancy theory proposes that workers are motivated when they expect that their effort and performance on the job will result in desired outcomes (Harder, 1991; Porter & Lawler, 1968; Vroom, 1964). In other words, people will engage in work they find attractive (leading to favorable consequences) and achievable. Expectancy theory emphasizes three components: expectancy, instrumentality, and valence. *Expectancy* refers to the perceived likelihood that a worker's efforts will result in a certain level of performance. *Instrumentality* refers to the perception that performance will lead to certain outcomes, such as rewards. *Valence* refers to the perceived attractiveness of particular outcomes. With respect to a particular work situation, you can imagine different probabilities for these three components. You might, for example, have a job in which there is a high likelihood of reward if performance is successful (high instrumentality) but a low likelihood that performance will be successful (low expectancy) or a low likelihood that the reward will be worthwhile (low valence). According to expectancy theory, workers assess the probabilities of these three components and combine them by multiplying their individual values. Highest levels of motivation, therefore, result when all three components have high probabilities, whereas lowest levels result when any single component is zero.

Can you see how an expectancy theory analysis might help you if you were in a management position? You should be able to think more clearly about expectancy, instrumentality, and valence. You should be able

How does expectancy theory explain some players' choice to favor hitting home runs over achieving a higher batting average?

to determine if one piece of the picture is out of kilter. Suppose, for example, your employees came to believe that there wasn't enough of a relationship between their efforts and how much they are rewarded. What could you do to change the workplace to restore high values for instrumentality?

As a conclusion to this section, we offer a cautionary note on achievement and motivation in work settings. When you make a personal choice about how hard you can work at a career, keep a careful watch on other aspects of your life. As we shall see in the next chapter, aggressive striving for success may, in some respects, work counter to the goal of having a long and healthy life.

SUMMING UP

Psychologists measure need for achievement to predict life outcomes. Motivation is influenced by causal attributions that may involve factors that are specific or global, stable or unstable, and internal or external. Research on explanatory style has identified optimistic and pessimistic styles that influence the tasks people undertake and how they persist in those tasks. Organizational psychologists study, in part, motivational forces in the workplace. Equity theory and expectancy theory describe how workers' thoughts about their work situations influence their motivations and outcomes.

A Hierarchy of Needs

In the last three sections, we have focused on specific types of motivation and specific types of behaviors. To close out the chapter, we return to a more global account of motivation. Our intent is to give you a general sense of the forces that could guide your life.

Humanist psychologist **Abraham Maslow** (1970) formulated the theory that basic motives form a **hierar-**

CAN PSYCHOLOGY HELP FIND ME A CAREER?

If you've ever had a job you didn't like, you probably know a lot about what it means to suffer from a lack of motivation: You can hardly stand the idea of reporting to work; every minute seems like an hour. An important part of having a successful career is finding a work setting that provides the types of challenges and rewards that fit your motivational needs. It probably will not surprise you that researchers have studied the match between vocations and people's individual personalities, values, and needs.

To remain motivated for career success, you would like to have a job that suits your interests and serves goals that you consider worthwhile. A widely used test for measuring vocational interests is the *Strong Interest Inventory,* which was originated in 1927 by psychologist **Edward Strong.** To construct the test, Strong first asked groups of men in different occupations to answer items about activities they liked or disliked. Then the answers given by those who were successful in particular occupations were compared with the responses of men in general to create a scale. Subsequent versions of the test, including a 1994 update, have added scales relevant to women and to newer occupations (Harmon et al., 1994). The *Strong Interest Inventory* is quite suc-

cessful at relating people's likes and dislikes to appropriate occupations (Donnay & Borgen, 1996). If you take this test, a vocational counselor could tell you what types of jobs are typically held by people with interests such as yours, because these are the jobs that are likely to appeal to you.

Suppose you have gotten this sort of advice about what career to pursue. How do you select a particular company to join—and how does that company select you? Recently, researchers in *personnel psychology* have focused a good deal of attention on the concept of *person–organization fit*—the goal is to maximize the compatibility between people and the organizations that employ them (Borman et al., 1997; Kristof, 1996; Van Vianen, 2000). One research project has focused on the match between people's personalities and the "culture" of organizations. Consider the personality factor called Agreeableness, which encodes a continuum from "sympathetic and kind" to "cold and quarrelsome" (see Chapter 14). Consider, also, a continuum of organizational cultures from those that are supportive and team-oriented to those that are aggressive and outcome-oriented. Do you see how these dimensions line up? Research suggests that job seekers who score high on Agreeableness will prefer organi-

zations that are culturally supportive and team-oriented (Judge & Cable, 1997). Research of this type suggests why it is not just your own motivational states that matter for career success: The extent to which your preferences for achieving goals match the organization's preferences matters as well.

While you are thinking about the jobs that might keep you motivated to achieve your goals, here's a final factor to consider: As with so many other aspects of life, vocational interests appear to have a genetic component. In one study, researchers asked identical and fraternal twins who had been reared in different homes to complete two vocational interest surveys, like the *Strong Interest Inventory* (Moloney et al., 1991). For the two surveys, the average correlations for the identical twins were .38 and .47; the average correlations for the fraternal twins were only .05 and .06. Remember, these twins were not reared in the same homes! If you have decided to follow in your mother's or father's career path, it might very well not just be the effects of environmental indoctrination.

So, what career path will keep you motivated for success? As with so many of life's dilemmas, psychologists have carried out research that can help you make this important decision.

---

chy of needs, as illustrated in **Figure 12.7.** In Maslow's view, the needs at each level of the hierarchy must be satisfied—the needs are arranged in a sequence from primitive to advanced—before the next level can be achieved. At the bottom of this hierarchy are the basic *biological needs,* such as hunger and thirst. They must be met before any other needs can begin to operate. When biological needs are pressing, other needs are put on hold and are unlikely to influence your actions. When they are reasonably well satisfied, the needs at the next level— *safety needs*—motivate you. When you are no longer concerned about danger, you become motivated by *at-*

tachment needs—needs to belong, to affiliate with others, to love, and to be loved. If you are well fed and safe and if you feel a sense of social belonging, you move up to

■ **Expectancy theory** A cognitive theory of work motivation that proposes that workers are motivated when they expect their efforts and job performance to result in desired outcomes.

■ **Hierarchy of needs** Maslow's view that basic human motives form a hierarchy and that the needs at each level of the hierarchy must be satisfied before the next level can be achieved; these needs progress from basic biological needs to the need for transcendence.

Transcendence
Spiritual needs for
cosmic identification

Self-Actualization
Needs to fulfill potential,
have meaningful goals

Esthetic
Needs for order, beauty

Cognitive
Needs for knowledge,
understanding, novelty

Esteem
Needs for confidence, sense
of worth and competence, self-
esteem and respect of others

Attachment
Needs to belong, to affiliate,
to love and be loved

Safety
Needs for security, comfort,
tranquility, freedom from fear

Biological
Needs for food, water, oxygen, rest,
sexual expression, release from tension

FIGURE 12.7

Maslow's Hierarchy of Needs

According to Maslow, needs at the lower level of the heirarchy dominate an individual's motivation as long as they are unsatisfied. Once these needs are adequately met, the higher needs occupy the individual's attention.

Where does the need to belong, to form attachments and experience love, fit in Maslow's hierarchy?

esteem needs—to like oneself, to see oneself as competent and effective, and to do what is necessary to earn the esteem of others.

Humans are thinking beings, with complex brains that demand the stimulation of thought. You are motivated by strong *cognitive needs* to know your past, to comprehend the puzzles of current existence, and to predict the future. It is the force of these needs that enables scientists to spend their lives in discovering new knowledge. At the next level of Maslow's hierarchy comes the human desire for beauty and order, in the form of *aesthetic needs* that give rise to the creative side of humanity.

At the top of the hierarchy are people who are nourished, safe, loved and loving, secure, thinking, and creating. These people have moved beyond basic human needs in the quest for the fullest development of their potentials, or *self-actualization*. A self-actualizing person is self-aware, self-accepting, socially responsive, creative,

spontaneous, and open to novelty and challenge, among other positive attributes. Maslow's hierarchy includes a step beyond the total fulfillment of individual potential. *Needs for transcendence* may lead to higher states of consciousness and a cosmic vision of one's part in the universe. Very few people move beyond the self to achieve such union with spiritual forces.

Maslow's theory is a particularly upbeat view of human motivation. At the core of the theory is the need for each individual to grow and actualize his or her highest potential. Can we maintain such an unfailingly positive view? The data suggest that we cannot. Alongside the needs Maslow recognized, we find that people express power, dominance, and aggression. You also know from your own experience that Maslow's strict hierarchy breaks down. You're likely, for example, to have ignored hunger on occasion to pursue higher-level needs. Even with these qualifications, however, we hope Maslow's scheme will enable you to bring some order to different aspects of your motivational experiences.

We have come a long way since we asked you to consider Rebecca Stephens's troubled ascent of Mount Everest. We have described the biology and psychology of hunger and eating, and the evolutionary and social dimensions of human sexuality. We have explored individual differences in people's need to achieve and explain personal success. Throughout this discussion, you have seen the intricate interplay of nature and nurture, at the level of both the species and the individual. So, with all this information in hand, what new insights do you have into Stephens's behavior? Do you see more fully why, for some people, a finger might be a small price to pay to achieve a cherished goal?

RECAPPING MAIN POINTS

Understanding Motivation

- Motivation is a dynamic concept used to describe the processes directing behavior.
- Motivational analysis helps explain how biological and behavioral processes are related and why people pursue goals despite obstacles and adversity.
- Drive theory conceptualizes motivation as tension reduction.
- People are also motivated by incentives, external stimuli that are not related to physiological needs.
- Reversal theory posits opposing pairs of metamotivational states.
- Instinct theory suggests that motivation often relies on innate stereotypical responses.
- Social and cognitive psychologists emphasize the individual's perception, interpretation of, and reaction to a situation.

Eating

- The body has a number of mechanisms to regulate the initiation and cessation of eating.
- If obese individuals become restrained eaters, their diets may result in weight gain rather than weight loss.

- Eating disorders are life-threatening illnesses that may arise from cultural pressure and misperceptions of body image.

Sexual Behaviors

- From an evolutionary perspective, sex is the mechanism for producing offspring.
- In animals, the sex drive is largely controlled by hormones.
- The work of Masters and Johnson provided the first hard data on the sexual response cycles of men and women.
- Evolutionary psychologists suggest that much of human sexual behavior reflects different mating strategies for men and women.
- Discrepancies in sexual scripts can lead to serious misunderstandings and even date rape.
- Homosexuality and heterosexuality are determined both by genetics and personal and social environments.

Motivation for Personal Achievement

- People have varying needs for achievement. Motivation for achievement is influenced by how people interpret success and failure.
- Two attributional styles, optimism and pessimism, lead to different attitudes toward achievement and influence motivation.
- Organizational psychologists study human motivation in work settings.

A Hierarchy of Needs

- Abraham Maslow suggested that human needs can be organized hierarchically.
- Although real human motivation is more complex, Maslow's theory provides a useful framework for summarizing motivational forces.

Key Terms

anorexia nervosa (p. 373)
attributions (p. 385)
bulimia nervosa (p. 373)
date rape (p. 381)
drives (p. 365)
equity theory (p. 387)
expectancy theory (p. 389)
hierarchy of needs (p. 389)
homeostasis (p. 365)
incentives (p. 365)
instincts (p. 367)
motivation (p. 364)
need for achievement (p. 384)
organizational psychologists (p. 387)
parental investment (p. 379)
reversal theory (p. 367)
sexual arousal (p. 377)
sexual scripts (p. 380)
social-learning theory (p. 368)
Thematic Apperception Test (TAT) (p. 384)

emotion, stress, and health

13

■ **EMOTIONS**
Basic Emotions and Culture
• Theories of Emotion •
Functions of Emotion

■ **STRESS OF LIVING**
Physiological Stress Reactions
• Psychological Stress
Reactions • Coping
with Stress

■ **HEALTH PSYCHOLOGY**
The Biopsychosocial Model of
Health • Health Promotion •
Treatment • Job Burnout and
the Health-Care System •
A Toast to Your Health

■ **PSYCHOLOGY IN THE
21ST CENTURY:
HEALTHY PEOPLE 2010**

■ **PSYCHOLOGY IN YOUR
LIFE: DOES YOUR
PERSONALITY AFFECT
YOUR HEALTH?**

■ **RECAPPING MAIN POINTS**
Key Terms

A 6-year-old boy, a member of the Warao culture of Venezuela, had fallen ill with a high fever and respiratory congestion. His family attributed his illness to *hebu*, ancestral spirits, and summoned a healer, a *wisidatu*, to extract the *hebu* from the boy's body. The *wisidatu* performed a time-honored ritual, at the center of which was a curing song. This is part of the text the *wisidatu* sang:

You [the hebu] grabbed him, you grabbed him
you grabbed him by the head
with your fevers
with your fevers
with your afflictions, your power for making one crazy
I myself am the one who knows the fevers of the little
   rocks
I myself am the one who knows you
I myself am the one who softens you

I myself am the one who makes you let go
I am immediately grabbing you with my hands
you are immediately falling into my grasp
I am the one who grabs you with my hands
I am grabbing your body, I am making you let go
I am making you let go, I am making [you] let go
I am making you let go, I am making [you] let go all
   along the skin,
between the skin and the flesh, I am making [you] let
   go all along the flesh…
I myself am the one who takes out hebu, I myself am
   the one who takes out hebu
I myself am the one who takes out hebu, I myself am
   the one who makes [you] let go

The fever had broken by the next morning. The family believed the child would have died if the cure had failed (Briggs, 1996).

If you have grown up in a Western culture, you might be reluctant to believe that there was any relationship between the ritual—the *wisidatu*'s communication with the *hebu* spirits—and the child's recovery. We hope, however, by the end of this chapter to make you a bit less skeptical. We wish to expand your ideas about the way in which mind and body interact. You can see in the Warao curing ritual a theme we will emphasize in this chapter: the way in which psychological states, such as strong emotions, can be engaged to affect a state of physical health.

To get started, we ask you to consider a less daunting situation. Suppose we asked you right now, "How are you feeling?" How would you answer that question? There are at least three different types of information you might provide. First, you might reveal to us the mood you are in—the *emotions* you are feeling. Are you happy, because you know you can finish reading this chapter in time to go to a party? Are you angry, because your boss just yelled at you over the telephone? Second, you might tell us something more general about the amount of *stress* you are experiencing. Do you feel as if you can cope with all the tasks you have to get done? Or are you

feeling a bit overwhelmed? Third, you might report on your psychological or physical *health*. Do you feel some illness coming on? Or do you feel an overall sense of wellness?

This chapter will explore interactions among these three ways in which you might answer the question "How are you feeling?"—in relation to your emotions, stress, and health. *Emotions* are the touchstones of human experience. They give richness to your interactions with people and nature and significance to your memories. In this chapter, we will discuss the experience and functions of emotions. But what happens if the emotional demands on your biological and psychological functioning are too great? You may become overwhelmed and unable to deal with the stressors of your life. This chapter will also examine how *stress* affects you and how you can combat it. Finally, we will broaden our focus to consider psychology's contributions to the study of health and illness. *Health psychologists* investigate the ways in which environmental, social, and psychological processes contribute to the development of disease. Health psychologists also use psychological processes and principles to help treat and prevent illness, while also developing strategies to enhance personal wellness. This path from emotions, through stress, to health will create a context in which you can understand the power of the Warao healing ritual.

We begin now by looking at the content and meaning of emotions.

▪ Emotions

Just imagine what your life would be like if you could think and act but not feel. Would you be willing to give up the capacity to experience fear if you would also lose the passion of a lover's kiss? Would you give up sadness at the expense of joy? Surely these would be bad bargains, promptly regretted. We will soon see that emotions serve a number of important functions. Let us begin, however, by offering a definition of emotion and by describing the roots of your emotional experiences.

Although you might be tempted to think of emotion as only a feeling—"I feel happy" or "I feel angry"—we need a more inclusive definition of this important concept that involves both the body and the mind. Contemporary psychologists define **emotion** as a complex pattern of bodily and mental changes that includes physiological arousal, feelings, cognitive processes, and behavioral reactions made in response to a situation perceived as personally significant. To see why all of these components are necessary, imagine a situation that would make you feel very happy. Your physiological arousal might include a gently beating heart. Your feeling would be positive. The associated cognitive processes include interpretations, memories, and expectations that allow you to label the situation as happy. Your overt be-

---

▪ **Emotion** A complex pattern of changes, including physiological arousal, feelings, cognitive processes, and behavioral reactions, made in response to a situation perceived to be personally significant.

---

havioral reactions might be expressive (smiling) and/or action-oriented (embracing a loved one). Our account of emotions will attempt to put all these pieces together—arousal, feelings, thoughts, and actions.

Basic Emotions and Culture

Suppose you could gather together in one room representatives from a great diversity of human cultures. What would be common in their experiences of emotion? For an initial answer, you might look to Charles Darwin's book *The Expression of Emotions in Man and Animals* (1872/1965). Darwin believed that emotions evolved alongside other important aspects of human and nonhuman structures and functions. He was interested in the *adaptive* functions of emotions, which he thought of not as vague, unpredictable, personal states, but as highly specific, coordinated modes of operation of the human brain. Darwin viewed emotions as inherited, specialized mental states designed to deal with a certain class of *recurring situations* in the world. Over the history of our species, humans have been attacked by predators, fallen in love, given birth to children, fought each other, confronted their mates' sexual infidelity, and witnessed the death of loved ones—innumerable times. We might expect, therefore, that certain types of emotional responses would emerge in all members of the human species. Researchers have tested this claim of the *universality of emotions* by looking at the emotional responses of newborn children as well as the consistency of facial expressions across cultures.

ARE SOME EMOTIONAL RESPONSES INNATE?

If the evolutionary perspective is correct, we would expect to find much the same patterns of emotional responses in children all over the world (Izard, 1994). Silvan Tomkins (1962, 1981) was one of the first psychologists to emphasize the pervasive role of immediate, unlearned affective (emotional) reactions. He pointed out that, without prior

Charles Darwin was one of the first to use photographs in the study of emotion. These plates are from *The Expression of Emotions in Man and Animals* (1872/1965). Why did Darwin believe that emotions were the product of evolution?

learning, infants respond to loud sounds with fear or with difficulties in breathing. They seem "prewired" to respond to certain stimuli with an emotional response general enough to fit a wide range of circumstances.

Cross-cultural research has confirmed the expectation that some emotional responses are quite similar in children from very different cultures.

CROSS-CULTURAL EMOTIONAL RESPONSES IN INFANTS Five- and 12-month-old children in the United States and Japan were visited in their homes. The experimenters subjected each child to a procedure in which the infant's wrists were grasped and folded across the infant's stomach. The experimenters videotaped each infant's response. Infants from both cultures moved their facial muscles in the same patterns—resulting in highly similar expressions of distress. Japanese and American infants also showed similar rates of negative vocalization and physical struggling (Camras et al., 1992).

Although this study demonstrates important cross-cultural consistency, more recent research has exposed some differences. In one study, 11-month-old children from China were consistently less emotionally expressive than their age-mates from Japan and the United States (Camras et al., 1998). These results suggest that culture acts very early in life to have an impact on innate emotional responses.

Note that infants also seem to have an innate ability to interpret the facial expressions of others. In one experiment, 4- to 6-month-old infants habituated—they showed decreasing interest—to repeated presentations of adult faces showing a single emotion drawn from the set of surprise, fear, and anger (see Chapter 11 for examples of habituation procedures with children). When the infants were subsequently shown a photograph with a different emotion, they responded with renewed interest—suggesting that surprise, fear, and anger expressions "looked different" to them, even at these very young ages (Serrano et al., 1992). Infants also produce more positive behaviors (for example, approaching movements and smiles) toward happy expressions and more negative behaviors (for example, avoidance movements and frowns) toward angry expressions. This suggests that they not only recognize but also have a very early understanding of the "meaning" of these expressions (Serrano et al., 1995).

ARE EMOTIONAL EXPRESSIONS UNIVERSAL?

We have seen that infants produce and perceive standard emotional expressions. If that is so, we might also expect to find adult members of even vastly different cultures showing reasonable agreement in the way they believe emotion is communicated by facial expressions.

According to **Paul Ekman,** the leading researcher on the nature of facial expressions, all people share an overlap in "facial language" (Ekman, 1984, 1994). Ekman and his associates have demonstrated what Darwin first proposed—that a set of emotional expressions is universal to the human species, presumably because they are innate components of our evolutionary heritage. Before you read on, take a look at **Figure 13.1** to see how well you can identify these seven universally recognized expressions of emotion (Ekman & Friesen, 1986).

There is considerable evidence that these seven expressions are recognized and produced worldwide in response to the emotions of happiness, surprise, anger, disgust, fear, sadness, and contempt. Cross-cultural researchers have

1

2

3

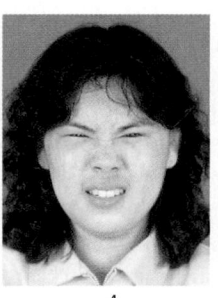
4

5

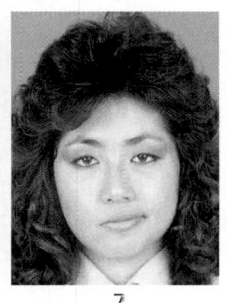
6

7

FIGURE 13.1

Judgments of Emotional Expressions

Match these seven emotion terms with the faces shown at left: fear, disgust, happiness, surprise, contempt, anger, and sadness. The answers are given at the end of the chapter.

asked people from a variety of cultures to identify the emotions associated with expressions in standardized photographs. Individuals are generally able to identify the expressions associated with the seven emotions.

CROSS-CULTURAL RECOGNITION OF FACIAL EXPRESSIONS In one study, members of a preliterate culture in New Guinea (the Fore culture), who had had almost no exposure to Westerners or to Western culture prior to this experiment, accurately identified the emotions expressed in the Caucasian faces shown in Figure 13.1. They did so by referring to situations in which they had experienced the same emotion. For example, photo 5 (fear) suggested being chased by a wild boar when you didn't have your spear, and photo 6 (sadness) suggested your child had died. Their only confusion came in distinguishing surprise, photo 2, from fear, perhaps because these people are most fearful when taken by surprise.

Next, researchers asked other members of the culture (who had not participated in the first study) to model the expressions that they used to communicate six of the emotions (excluding contempt). When U.S. college students viewed videotapes of the facial expressions of the Fore people, they were able to identify their emotions accurately—with one exception. Not surprisingly, the Americans had difficulty distinguishing between the Fore poses of fear and surprise, the same emotions that the Fore had confused in the Western poses (Ekman & Friesen, 1971).

More recent research has compared judgments of facial expressions across individuals in Hungary, Japan, Poland, Sumatra, the United States, and Vietnam—high agreement was found across these diverse populations (Biehl et al., 1997). The general conclusion is that people all over the world, regardless of cultural differences, race, sex, or education, express basic emotions in much the same way and are able to identify the emotions others are experiencing by reading their facial expressions.

Note that the claim of universality is focused on the basic set of seven emotions. Ekman and his colleagues make no claim that all facial expressions are universal or that cultures express all emotions in the same way (Ekman, 1994). In fact, Ekman (1972) called his position on universality the *neuro-cultural* theory, to reflect the joint contributions of the brain (the product of evolution) and of culture in emotional expression. The brain specifies which facial muscles move, to produce a particular expression, when a particular emotion is aroused. Different cultures, however, impose their own constraints beyond universal biology. We reported some cultural effects in the description of the research com-

paring responses of members of the Fore culture and U.S. college students. The six-country comparison we cited earlier also produced some differences among the countries, against the general background of agreement (Biehl et al., 1997). For example, Japanese adults were worse at identifying anger than were U.S., Hungarian, Polish, and Vietnamese adults. Vietnamese adults were worse at identifying disgust than the participants from all the other countries.

Why might these differences arise? Let's now look directly at cultural influences on emotionality.

HOW DOES CULTURE CONSTRAIN EMOTIONAL EXPRESSION?

People all over the world may share a genetic inheritance that specifies a certain range of emotional expression. Even so, different cultures have different standards for how emotion should be managed. Some forms of emotional response, even facial expressions, are unique to each culture. Cultures establish social rules for when people may show certain emotions and for the social appropriateness of certain types of emotional displays by given types of people in particular settings (Mesquita & Frijda, 1992; Ratner, 2000). Let's look at three examples of cultures that express emotions in manners different from the Western norm. We begin with an African culture.

The Wolof people of Senegal live in a society where status and power differences among people are rigidly defined. High-caste members of this culture are expected to show great restraint in their expressions of emotionality; low-caste individuals are expected to be more volatile, particularly a caste called the *griots*. The griots, in fact, are often called upon to express the "undignified" emotions of the nobility.

> One afternoon, a group of women (some five nobles and two griots) were gathered near a well on the edge of town when another woman strode over to the well and threw herself down it. All the women were shocked at the apparent suicide attempt, but the noble women were shocked in silence. Only the griot women screamed, on behalf of all. (Irvine, 1990, p. 146)

Can you imagine how you would respond in this situation? It might be easier to put yourself in the place of the griots rather than in the place of the noble women: How could you help but scream? The answer, of course, is that the noble women have acquired cultural norms for emotional expression that require them not to show any overt response.

A second example of cultural variation in emotional expression arose in the life of one of your authors. At the funeral of an American friend of Syrian descent, he was surprised to see and hear a group of women shrieking and wailing when a visitor entered the funeral parlor. They then stopped just as suddenly until the next visitor arrived, when once again they started their group wail-

In what ways do cultures constrain emotional expressions in situations like funerals?

ing. What is the explanation for this behavior? Because it is difficult for the family members of the deceased to sustain a high emotional pitch over the three days and nights of such wakes, they hire these professional criers to display, on their behalf, appropriately strong emotions to each newcomer. This is an expected practice among a number of Mediterranean and Near Eastern cultures.

For our third example, we need to introduce a distinction between *individualistic* and *collectivist* cultures: Individualistic cultures emphasize individuals' needs, whereas collectivist cultures emphasize the needs of the group (Triandis, 1994, 1995). Whereas individualists look for immediate personal rewards, freedom, equality, personal enjoyment, and a varied, exciting life, collectivists put high value on self-discipline and on accepting one's position in life, honoring parents and other elders, preserving one's image, and working toward long-term goals that benefit the group as a whole. Researchers have suggested that these cultural orientations will affect the expression of emotion.

HOW WE KNOW

EMOTIONAL EXPRESSION IN INDIVIDUALISTIC AND COLLECTIVIST CULTURES What happens when someone expresses a negative emotion toward another person or group of people? Often, the situation will become socially quite awkward. That might be okay if you are a member of an individualistic culture—and are content to use expressions of negative emotions to assert your own independence. If, however, you are a member of a collectivist culture, you may shy away from displays of negative emotions, to avoid causing discord in a group. To test this reasoning, a team of researchers recruited psychology students from universities in the United States (an individualistic culture) and Costa Rica (a collectivist culture)

and asked them how comfortable they would feel *expressing* a range of positive and negative emotions toward another individual, if the individual had "caused them to experience these emotions." **Figure 13.2** displays the results. As you can see, there were no cultural differences for positive emotions. However, as predicted, students in the United States rated themselves considerably more comfortable with expressing negative emotions (Stephan et al., 1996).

Next time you express a negative emotion—for example, anger toward a friend—you should consider how your comfort with that incident reflects cultural values.

When you think about the types of emotional patterns that may have evolved over the course of human experience, you should always bear in mind that culture may have the last word. Western notions of what is necessary or inevitable in emotional expression are as bound to U.S. culture as those of any other societies. Can you see how different standards for emotional expression could cause misunderstandings between people of different cultural origins?

We have seen so far that some physiological responses to emotional situations—such as smiles and grimaces—may be innate. Let's turn now to theories that consider the link between other physiological responses and their psychological interpretations.

Theories of Emotion

Theories of emotion generally attempt to explain the relationship between physiological and psychological aspects of the experience of emotion. We will begin this section by discussing the responses your body gives in emotionally relevant situations. We will then review theories that explore the way these physiological responses contribute to your psychological experience of emotion.

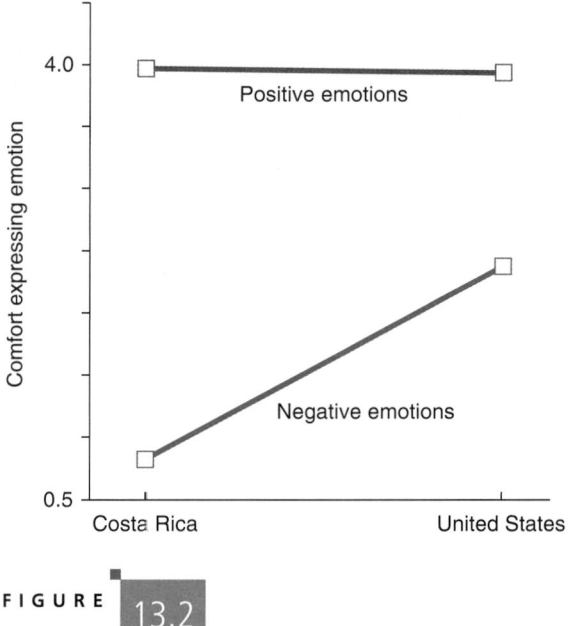

FIGURE **13.2**

Emotional Expression across Cultures

Students from the United States (an individualistic culture) and Costa Rica (a collectivist culture) were asked to indicate how comfortable they would feel expressing positive and negative emotions toward the person who had brought about the emotion. The students made their responses on a scale ranging from 0 (extremely uncomfortable) to 5 (extremely comfortable). Although there were no differences for positive emotions, students from the individualistic culture indicated more comfort with expressing negative emotions.

PHYSIOLOGY OF EMOTION

What happens when you experience a strong emotion? Your heart races, respiration goes up, your mouth dries, your muscles tense, and maybe you even shake. In addition to these noticeable changes, many others occur beneath the surface. All these responses are designed to mobilize your body for action to deal with the source of the emotion. Let's look at their origins.

The *autonomic nervous system* (ANS) prepares the body for emotional responses through the action of both its sympathetic and parasympathetic divisions (see Chapter 3). The balance between the divisions depends on the quality and intensity of the arousing stimulation. With mild, *unpleasant* stimulation, the *sympathetic* division is more active; with mild, *pleasant* stimulation, the *parasympathetic* division is more active. With more intense stimulation of either kind, both divisions are increasingly involved. Physiologically, strong emotions such as fear or anger activate the body's *emergency reaction system*, which swiftly and silently prepares the body for potential danger. The sympathetic nervous system takes charge by directing the release of hormones (epinephrine and norepinephrine) from the adrenal glands, which in turn leads the in-ternal organs to release blood sugar, raise blood pressure, and increase sweating and salivation. To calm you after the emergency has passed, the parasympathetic nervous system inhibits the release of the activating hormones. You may remain aroused for a while after an experience of strong emotional activation, because some of the hormones continue to circulate in your bloodstream.

As we shall see when we describe specific theories of emotion, researchers have debated the question, "Do particular emotional experiences give rise to distinct patterns of activity in the autonomic nervous system?" Cross-cultural research suggests that the answer to the question is "yes."

HOW WE KNOW

DO DIFFERENT EMOTIONS SHOW DIFFERENT PATTERNS OF AUTONOMIC ACTIVITY? Suppose you are feeling surprised, fearful, or disgusted—but you won't tell us which. Could we measure the response of your autonomic nervous system and accurately infer what you are feeling? Paul Ekman and his colleagues (1983) set out to answer this question with a sample of professional actors in the United States. The researchers measured autonomic responses such as heart rate and skin temperature while the actors created emotions and emotional expressions. These measures revealed distinct patterns for different emotions. For example, sadness was marked by high heart rates, whereas happiness was marked by low rates; although both anger and fear produced high heart rates, anger was associated with high skin temperature, whereas fear was associated with low skin temperature.

Do these findings generalize across cultures? The same team of researchers performed another study that compared men and women from the United States to Minangkabau men from West Sumatra. Members of this culture are socialized not to display negative emotions. Would they, even so, show the same underlying autonomic patterns for negative emotions—even when they had little experience displaying the emotions? The data revealed a high level of similarity across the two cultures, leading the researchers to suggest that patterns of autonomic activity are "an important part of our common evolved biological heritage" (Levenson et al., 1992, p. 986).

These experiments suggest that members of different cultures learn to produce different overt responses—when you are angry, do you yell or do you suffer in silence?—for the same underlying bodily experiences.

Let's move now from the autonomic nervous system to the central nervous system. Integration of both the hormonal and the neural aspects of arousal is controlled by the *hypothalamus* and the *limbic system*, control systems for emotions and for patterns of attack, defense, and flight. Neuroanatomy research has particularly focused on the **amygdala** as a part of the limbic system that acts as a gateway for emotion and as a filter for memory. The amygdala does this by attaching significance to the information it receives from the senses. It plays an especially strong role in attaching meaning to negative experiences. For example, when people view pictures of fearful facial expressions, the left amygdala (each side of your brain has a separate amygdala) shows increasing activity as the intensity of the expression increases; by contrast, happy facial expressions produce less activity in the same structure the more intensely happy the face becomes (Morris et al., 1996). Consider also a woman known as D. R., whose left and right amygdalae were lesioned in an effort to control her epilepsy. As a consequence of this surgery, D. R. has great difficulty perceiving emotions of anger or fear when those emotions are presented either by way of facial expressions or tones of voice (Scott et al., 1997). Can you imagine what it would be like to live your life if you couldn't understand when people were trying to communicate negative emotions to you?

The *cortex* is involved in emotional experiences through its internal neural networks and its connections with other parts of the body. The cortex provides the associations, memories, and meanings that integrate psychological experience and biological responses. Research using brain scanning techniques has begun to map out particular responses to different emotions. For example, PET scans (see Chapter 3, page 57) have been used to demonstrate that *happiness* and *sadness* are not just opposite responses in the same portions of the cortex. Rather, these opposite emotions lead to greatest activity in quite different parts of the brain (George et al., 1995). PET scans have also been used to examine the brain consequences of emotional experiences that occur in response to internal stimulation—a person's activa-

tion of emotion-laden memories—versus external stimulation—a person's viewing of films of emotion-laden events (Reiman et al., 1997). These PET scans allow researchers to identify areas of the brain that appear to be active irrespective of the source of emotional stimulation versus those that rely on the particular stimulus that gives rise to the emotional experience. For example, more activity was found in the amygdala for film-generated emotions than for memory-generated emotions. Researchers are still trying to piece together *why* these differences emerge—the PET techniques provide an array of facts that await a unifying theory.

We have seen so far that your body provides many responses to situations in which emotions are relevant. But how do you know which feeling goes with which physiological response? We now review three theories that attempt an answer to this question.

JAMES–LANGE THEORY OF BODY REACTION

You might think, at first, that everyone would agree that emotions precede responses: for example, you yell at someone (response) because you feel angry (emotion). However, over 100 years ago, **William James** argued, as Aristotle had much earlier, that the sequence was reversed—you feel *after* your body reacts. As James put it, "We feel sorry because we cry, angry because we strike, afraid because we tremble" (James, 1890/1950, p. 450). This view that emotion stems from *bodily feedback* became known as the **James–Lange theory of emotion** (Carl Lange was a Danish scientist who presented similar ideas the same year as James). According to this theory, perceiving a stimulus causes autonomic arousal and other bodily actions that lead to the experience of a specific emotion (see **Figure 13.3**). The James–Lange theory is considered a *peripheralist* theory because it assigns the most prominent role in the emotion chain to visceral reactions, the actions of the autonomic nervous system that are peripheral to the central nervous system.

CANNON–BARD THEORY OF CENTRAL NEURAL PROCESSES

Physiologist **Walter Cannon** (1927, 1929) rejected the peripheralist theory in favor of a *centralist* focus on the action of the central nervous system. Cannon (and other critics) raised a number of objections to the James–Lange theory (Leventhal, 1980). They noted, for example, that visceral activity is irrelevant for emotional experience—experimental animals continue to respond emotionally even after their viscera are separated surgically from the CNS. They also argued that ANS responses

What kinds of physiological arousal would you expect to find in a person who is experiencing a high level of frustration?

Amygdala The part of the limbic system that controls emotion, aggression, and the formation of emotional memory.

James–Lange theory of emotion A peripheral-feedback theory of emotion stating that an eliciting stimulus triggers a behavioral response that sends different sensory and motor feedback to the brain and creates the feeling of a specific emotion.

are typically too slow to be the source of split-second elicited emotions. According to Cannon, emotion requires that the brain intercede between the input stimulation and the output response. Signals from the thalamus get routed to one area of the cortex to produce emotional feeling and to another for emotional expressiveness.

Another physiologist, Philip Bard, also concluded that visceral reactions were not primary in the emotion sequence. Instead, an emotion-arousing stimulus has two simultaneous effects, causing both bodily arousal via the sympathetic nervous system and the subjective experience of emotion via the cortex. The views of these physiologists were combined in the **Cannon–Bard theory of emotion.** This theory states that an emotion stimulus produces two concurrent reactions, arousal and experience of emotion, that do not cause each other (see Figure 13.3). If something makes you angry, your heartbeat increases at the same time as you think "I'm ticked off!"—but neither your body nor your mind dictates the way the other responds.

The Cannon–Bard theory predicts independence between bodily and psychological responses. We will see next that contemporary theories of emotion reject the claim that these responses are necessarily independent.

COGNITIVE APPRAISAL THEORIES OF EMOTION

Because arousal symptoms and internal states are similar for many different emotions, it is possible to confuse them at times when they are experienced in ambiguous or novel situations. According to **Stanley Schachter** (1971b), the experience of emotion is the joint effect of physiological arousal and **cognitive appraisal,** with both parts necessary for an emotion to occur. All arousal is assumed to be general and undifferentiated, and arousal is the first step in the emotion sequence. You appraise your physiological arousal in an effort to discover what you are feeling, what emotional label best fits, and what your reaction means in the particular setting in which it is being experienced. **Richard Lazarus** (1991, 1995; Lazarus & Lazarus, 1994), another leading proponent of the cognitive appraisal view, maintains that "emotional experience cannot be understood solely in terms of what happens in the

What emotions would you be likely to feel if people all around you were wildly cheering your favorite team?

person or in the brain, but grows out of ongoing transactions with the environment that are evaluated" (Lazarus, 1984a, p. 124). Lazarus also emphasizes that appraisal often occurs without conscious thought. When you have past experiences that link emotions to situations—here comes that bully I've clashed with before!— you need not explicitly search the environment for an interpretation of your arousal. This position has become known as the **cognitive appraisal theory of emotion** (see Figure 13.3).

To test this theory, experimenters have sometimes created situations in which environmental cues were available to provide a label for an individual's arousal.

HOW WE KNOW

AROUSAL AND EMOTIONAL MISINTERPRETATION A female researcher interviewed male participants who had just crossed one of two bridges in Vancouver, Canada. One bridge was a safe, sturdy bridge; the other was a wobbly, precarious bridge. The researcher pretended to be interested in the effects of scenery on creativity and asked the men to write brief stories about an ambiguous picture that included a woman. She also invited them to call her if they wanted more information about the research. Those men who had just crossed the dangerous bridge wrote stories with more sexual imagery, and four times as many of those men called the female researcher than did those who had crossed the safe bridge. To show that arousal was the independent variable influencing the emotional misinterpretation, the research team also arranged for another group of men to be interviewed 10 minutes or more after crossing the dangerous bridge, enough time for their physical arousal symptoms to be reduced. These nonaroused men did not show the signs of sexual response that the aroused men did (Dutton & Aron, 1974).

Cannon–Bard theory of emotion A theory stating that an emotional stimulus produces two co-occurring reactions—arousal and experience of emotion—that do not cause each other.

Cognitive appraisal With respect to emotions, the process through which physiological arousal is interpreted with respect to circumstances in the particular setting in which it is being experienced; also, the recognition and evaluation of a stressor to assess the demand, the size of the threat, the resources available for dealing with it, and appropriate coping strategies.

Cognitive appraisal theory of emotion A theory stating that the experience of emotion is the joint effect of physiological arousal and cognitive appraisal, which serves to determine how an ambiguous inner state of arousal will be labeled.

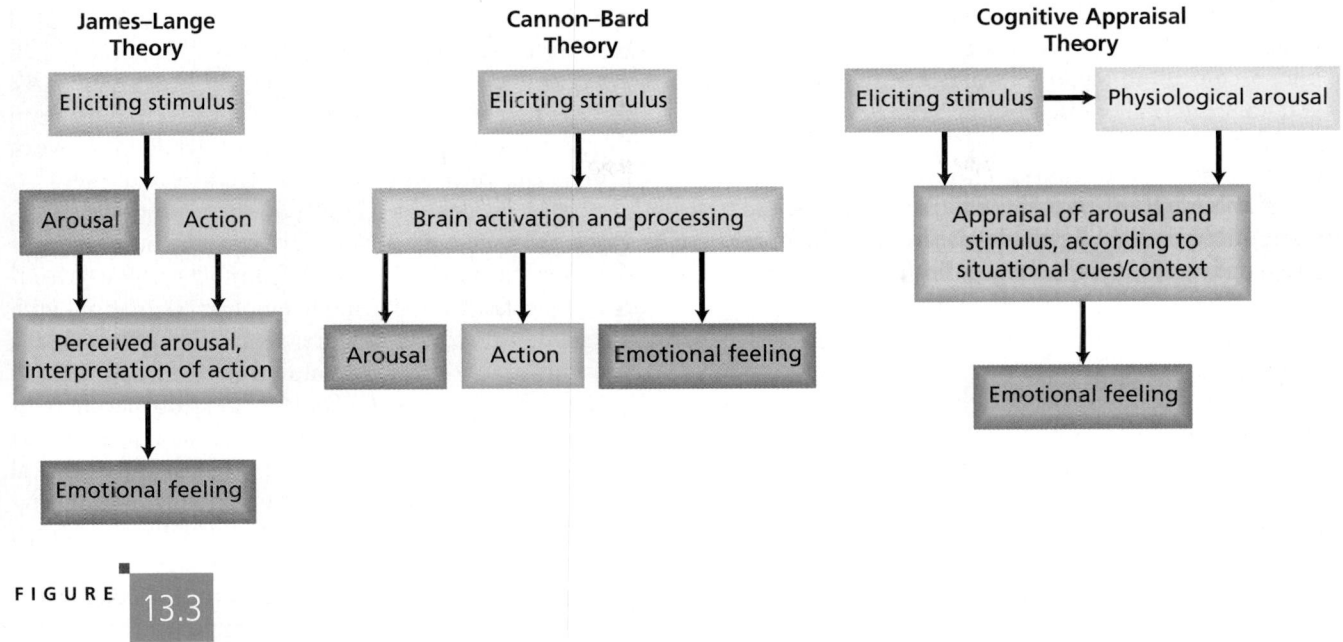

James–Lange Theory

Eliciting stimulus → Arousal, Action → Perceived arousal, interpretation of action → Emotional feeling

Cannon–Bard Theory

Eliciting stimulus → Brain activation and processing → Arousal, Action, Emotional feeling

Cognitive Appraisal Theory

Eliciting stimulus → Physiological arousal → Appraisal of arousal and stimulus, according to situational cues/context → Emotional feeling

FIGURE 13.3

Comparing Three Emotion Theories

These classic theories of emotion propose different components of emotion. They also propose different process sequences by which a stimulus event results in the experience of emotion. In the James–Lange theory, events trigger both autonomic arousal and behavioral action, which are perceived and then result in a specific emotional experience. In the Cannon–Bard theory, events are first processed at various centers in the brain, which then direct the simultaneous reactions of arousal, behavioral action, and emotional experience. In the cognitive appraisal theory, both stimulus events and physiological arousal are cognitively appraised at the same time according to situational cues and context factors, with the emotional experience resulting from the interaction of the level of arousal and the nature of appraisal.

In this situation, the male participants came to an emotional judgment ("I am interested in this woman") based on a *misattribution* of the source of arousal (the woman rather than the danger of the bridge). In a similar experiment, students who performed two minutes of aerobic exercise reported less extreme emotions just after the exercise—when they could easily attribute their arousal to the exercise rather than to an emotional state—by comparison to the emotions they reported after a brief delay that made the exercise seem less relevant to continuing arousal (Sinclair et al., 1994).

Some of the specific aspects of the cognitive appraisal theory have been challenged. For example, you learned earlier that arousal states—the activity of the autonomic nervous system—accompanying different emotions are not identical (Levenson et al., 1992). Therefore, interpretations of at least some emotional experiences may not require appraisal. Furthermore, experiencing strong arousal without any obvious cause does not lead to a neutral, undifferentiated state, as the theory assumes. Stop for a moment and imagine that, right now, your heart suddenly starts beating quickly, your breathing becomes fast and shallow, your chest muscles tighten, and your palms become drenched with sweat. What inter-

pretation would you put on these symptoms? Are you surprised to learn that people generally interpret *unexplained* physical arousal as *negative*, a sign that something is wrong? In addition, people's search for an explanation tends to be biased toward finding stimuli that will explain or justify this negative interpretation (Marshall & Zimbardo, 1979; Maslach, 1979).

Another critique of the cognitive appraisal theory of emotion comes from researcher **Robert Zajonc** (pronounced Zy-Onts), who demonstrates conditions under which it is possible to have preferences without inferences and to feel without knowing why (Zajonc, 1980, 2000). In an extensive series of experiments on the *mere exposure effect,* participants were presented with a variety of stimuli, such as foreign words, Japanese characters, sets of numbers, and strange faces, that were flashed so briefly the items could not be consciously recognized. Participants were still able to express a preference without knowing why they liked some more than others. Those stimuli that were most often repeated produced the strongest liking; yet this increased liking was shown to occur independent of their conscious recognition.

It is probably safest to conclude that cognitive appraisal is an important process of emotional experience,

EMOTIONS

401

but not the only one (Izard, 1993). Under some circumstances, you will, in fact, look to the environment (at least unconsciously) to try to interpret why you feel the way you do. Under other circumstances, however, your emotional experiences may be under the control of the innate links provided by evolution. The physiological response will not require any interpretation. These different routes to emotional experiences suggest that emotions serve a range of functions. We turn now to those functions.

Functions of Emotion

Why do you have emotions? What functions do emotions serve for you? To think about these questions, it might help to review your day and imagine how different it would have been if you couldn't experience or understand emotions. Let's examine some of the roles researchers have suggested that emotion plays in your life.

MOTIVATION AND AROUSAL

The very first time you wear your new sweatshirt, the shoulder seam rips. Why are you likely to storm back to the store and demand a refund? From Chapter 12, you should recognize this as a question about motivation. If you want to answer, "Because I'd be angry" or "Because I'd be disappointed," you can see that emotions often provide the impetus for action. Emotions serve a motiva-

Yerkes–Dodson law A correlation between task performance and optimal level of arousal.

tional function by *arousing* you to take action with regard to some experienced or imagined event. Emotions then *direct* and *sustain* your behaviors toward specific goals. For the love of another person, you may do all you can to attract, be near, and protect him or her. For the love of principle or of country, you may sacrifice your life.

Let's consider cases, however, when emotion may begin to get the better of you. Have you ever been so angry that you felt incapable of taking any action? We have already seen that you respond to emotional situations with physiological arousal. Theorists have suggested that the relationship between arousal and performance follows an *inverted U-shaped function* (∩) (Hebb, 1955). This curve predicts that too little or too much arousal may impair performance. If you have too little physiological stimulation, you may be unable to organize your behaviors effectively (Bexton et al., 1954). If you have too much stimulation, emotion may overwhelm cognition.

Figure 13.4 shows the relationship between arousal and performance. The figure also explores the concept of *optimal arousal level* for best performance. Some tasks are best approached with high levels of arousal and others with more moderate levels. On some tasks, performance is highest when arousal is relatively low. The key to the level of arousal is *task difficulty*. With difficult or complex tasks, the optimal level of arousal for success is on the low end of the continuum. As the difficulty decreases and the task becomes simpler, the optimal level—the level required to perform most effectively—is greater. This relationship has been called the **Yerkes–Dodson law,** which says that performance of difficult tasks decreases as arousal increases, whereas perfor-

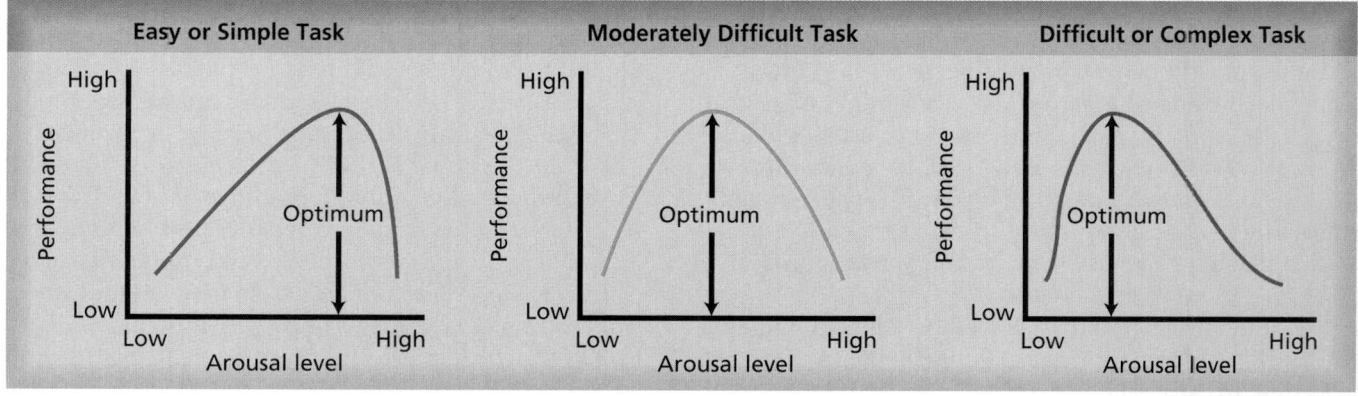

FIGURE 13.4

The Yerkes–Dodson Law

Performance varies with arousal level and task difficulty. For easy or simple tasks, a higher level of arousal increases performance effectiveness. However, for difficult or complex tasks, a lower level of arousal is optimal. A moderate level of arousal is generally best for tasks of moderate difficulty. These inverted U-shaped functions show that performance is worst at both low and high extremes of arousal.

Has a strong emotion, like anger, ever driven you to engage in irrational or destructive behavior?

mance of easy tasks increases as arousal increases (Yerkes & Dodson, 1908).

An important function of emotions, thus, is to get you going—to start you moving toward important goals. The physiological arousal produced by emotional situations may be required to move you toward optimal performance. You should take care, however, that you don't let your emotions become so powerful that they put you on the downward slope of the performance curve.

SOCIAL FUNCTIONS OF EMOTION

On a social level, emotions serve the broad function of regulating social interactions. As a positive social glue, they bind you to some people; as a negative social repellent, they distance you from others. You back off when someone is bristling with anger, and you approach when another person signals receptivity with a smile, dilated pupils, and a "come hither" glance. You might suppress strong negative emotions out of respect for another person's status or power. Recall D. R., the woman who lost the function of her amygdala—and with it the ability to perceive anger and fear (Scott et al., 1997). When we introduced D. R. earlier, we asked you to imagine what life would be like if you couldn't understand when people were trying to communicate negative emotions. For example, what would it be like not to be able to learn from others that a situation was dangerous? Or that your actions had given rise to an angry response? When D. R. lost function in her amygdala, she also lost her ability to function fully in her social world.

The emotions you experience have a strong impact on how you function in social settings. Consider the consequences of people's positive or negative moods on the ways in which they made requests.

HOW WE KNOW

MOOD EFFECTS ON LANGUAGE USE

Participants in an experiment watched short films that put them in happy, neutral, or sad moods. Once the mood was established, the experimenter asked each participant to perform a favor: Would he or she retrieve a stimulus file from a research assistant in the next room? The words the participants used to make the request were recorded. Raters (who did not know which participant had been in which mood) provided ratings of the politeness of each request. As shown in **Figure 13.5**, mood had a large impact on politeness: Sad participants were the most polite. People in sad moods appeared to be cautious about making direct—potentially impolite—demands on other people (Forgas, 1999).

Think about your own life: Are you more risk-taking in social situations when you are in a happy mood? Are you more cautious when you are in a sad mood?

Research also points to the impact of emotion on stimulating prosocial behavior (Hoffman, 1986; Isen, 1984; Schroeder et al., 1995). When individuals are made to feel good, they are more likely to engage in a variety of helping behaviors (Carlson et al., 1988). When research participants were made to feel guilty about a misdeed, they were more likely to volunteer aid in a future situation, presumably to reduce their guilt (Carlsmith & Gross, 1969). Similarly, how people feel depends on how prosocial they have been. For example, when individuals recalled instances in which they had refused to help another person, their moods became more negative (Williamson et al., 1996). This was particularly true when the person they had refused to help was a good friend, family member, or romantic partner. How you feel is greatly affected by how well you are able to carry out your social obligations.

EMOTIONAL EFFECTS ON COGNITIVE FUNCTIONING

Emotions serve cognitive functions by influencing what you attend to, the way you perceive yourself and others, and the way you interpret and remember various features of life situations. Researchers have demonstrated

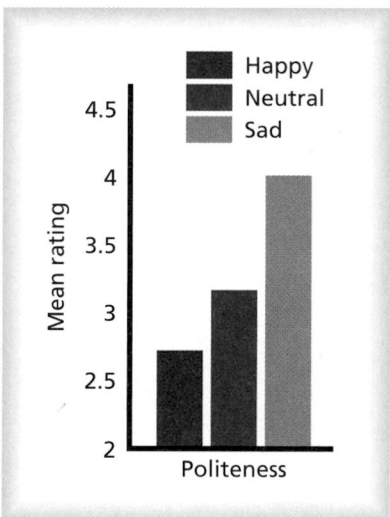

FIGURE 13.5

The Effects of Mood on Request Politeness

Participants in happy, neutral, or negative moods made requests of a stranger. Raters assessed the politeness of each request on a scale ranging from 1 (impolite) to 7 (polite). Participants in sad moods produced requests that were relatively more polite (e.g., "Would you mind getting me the stimulus file?" vs. "I need the stimulus file.").

that emotional states can affect learning, memory, social judgments, and creativity (Bradley, 1994; Forgas, 1995, 2000). Your emotional responses play an important role in organizing and categorizing your life experiences.

Research on the role of emotion in information processing was pioneered by **Gordon Bower** (1981, 1991) and his students. Bower's model proposes that, when a person experiences a given emotion in a particular situation, that emotion is stored in memory along with the ongoing events, as part of the same context. This pattern of memory representation gives rise to mood-congruent processing and mood-dependent memory. *Mood-congruent processing* occurs when people are selectively sensitized to process and retrieve information that agrees with their current mood state. Material that is congruent with one's prevailing mood is more likely to be noticed, attended to, and processed more deeply and with greater elaborative associations (Gilligan & Bower, 1984). *Mood-dependent memory* refers to circumstances in which people find it easier to recall information when their mood at retrieval matches their mood when they first committed the information to memory (Eich, 1995; Eich & Macaulay, 2000).

Let's examine a study that provides an instance both of mood-congruent memory retrieval as well as mood-dependent memory.

MOOD AND AUTOBIOGRAPHICAL MEMORY

This study used upbeat or solemn music to create pleasant and unpleasant moods. Once participants were in an appropriate mood, they were asked to generate autobiographical events from their lives in response to 16 neutral probe words. That is, participants would see a word such as *rose* and try to retrieve a memory from their life as quickly as they could. The data revealed mood-congruent retrieval: Although 72 percent of the memories produced by participants in a pleasant mood were rated as positive memories, only 52 percent of the memories of unpleasant-mood participants were rated as positive events.

To look for mood-dependent memory, the researchers brought the original participants back into the lab two days later. Once again, music was used to create moods in the participants. However, for half of the participants, the moods in the two sessions were matched (for example, they were placed in a pleasant mood on each occasion), whereas the other half of the participants had mismatched moods (for example, they were in an unpleasant mood for the first session and a pleasant mood for the second). If memory is mood-dependent, participants with matched moods should recall more information than participants with mismatched moods. The data revealed exactly that pattern: Participants with matched moods recalled 35 percent of their memories from the earlier session; mismatched participants recalled only 26 percent of their memories (Eich et al., 1994).

Do you recall our discussion of *encoding specificity* in Chapter 8 (see page 228)? These results with mood suggest that we should add emotion to the list of contextual features that are important to the encoding of memories.

One final note about the relationship between mood and cognition. Researchers have consistently demonstrated that positive affect—pleasant moods—produce more efficient and more creative thinking and problem solving (Isen et al., 1987). Consider a study in which physicians were asked to solve problems that required a certain level of creativity. Those who had been placed in a mildly pleasant mood (the experimenters gave the doctors a small gift of candy), performed reliably better on the creativity test than did those doctors in the control group (who got no prior gift) (Estrada et al., 1994). You can see an immediate application of these types of findings: You are likely to carry out your schoolwork more efficiently and creatively if you can maintain a happy mood. You might be thinking, "How am I supposed to stay happy with all the work I have to do?" As we turn now to the topic of stress, and how to cope with it, you will learn how to take cognitive control over how you are "feeling."

SUMMING UP

Charles Darwin originated the idea that emotions evolved in response to classes of recurring situations. Cross-cultural research has supported this evolutionary perspective by providing evidence that some facial expressions are universally produced and recognized. Even so, cultures have different norms for how and when emotions should be displayed. The autonomic nervous system, the limbic system, and areas of cortex all play a role in the physiology of emotion. Theories of emotion typically attempt to specify the causal relationship between physiological arousal and an individual's experience of emotional feelings. Contemporary theories most often assume that cognition, in the form of appraisal, plays a role in the interpretation of feelings. Emotions often serve to motivate people. They also play a role in regulating social relationships and in determining the content and efficiency of cognitive processes.

Stress of Living

Suppose we asked you to keep track of how you are "feeling" over the course of a day. You might report that for brief periods, you felt happiness, sadness, anger, astonishment, and so on. There is one feeling, however, that people often report as a kind of background noise for much of their day-to-day experience, and that is stress (Sapolsky, 1994). Modern industrialized society sets a rapid, hectic pace for living. People often have too many demands placed on their time, are worried about uncertain futures, and have little time for family and fun. But would you be better off without stress? A stress-free life would offer no challenge—no difficulties to surmount, no new fields to conquer, and no reasons to sharpen your wits or improve your abilities. Every organism faces challenges from its external environment and from its personal needs. The organism must solve these problems to survive and thrive.

Stress is the pattern of responses an organism makes to stimulus events that disturb its equilibrium and tax or exceed its ability to cope. The stimulus events include a large variety of external and internal conditions that collectively are called stressors. A **stressor** is a stimulus event that places a demand on an organism for some kind of

Whether at work or play, individuals in contemporary society are likely to encounter a stressful environment. What situations in your life do you find most stressful?

adaptive response: a bicyclist swerves in front of your car, your professor moves up the due date of your term paper, you're asked to run for class president. An individual's response to the need for change is made up of a diverse combination of reactions taking place on several levels, including physiological, behavioral, emotional, and cognitive. What responses might you make to each of the stressors we listed just earlier?

Figure 13.6 diagrams the elements of the stress process. Our goal for this section is to give you a clear understanding of all the features represented in this figure. We will begin by considering general physiological responses to stressors. We then describe the particular effects of different categories of stressors. Finally, we explore different methods you can use to cope with the stress in your life.

Stress The pattern of specific and nonspecific responses an organism makes to stimulus events that disturb its equilibrium and tax or exceed its ability to cope.
Stressor An internal or external event or stimulus that induces stress.

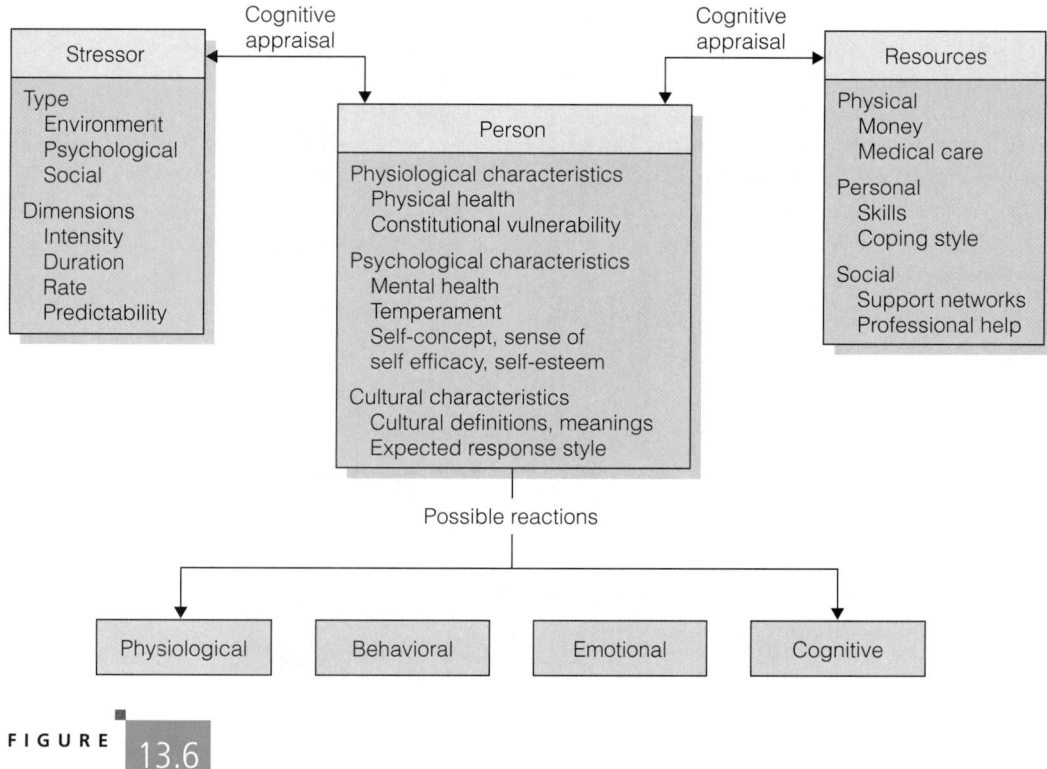

FIGURE 13.6

A Model of Stress

Cognitive appraisal of the stress situation interacts with the stressor and the physical, social, and personal resources available for dealing with the stressor. Individuals respond to threats on various levels: physiological, behavioral, emotional, and cognitive. Some responses are adaptive, and others are maladaptive or even lethal.

Physiological Stress Reactions

How would you respond if you arrived at a class and discovered that you were about to have a pop quiz? You would probably agree that this would cause you some stress, but what does that mean for your body's reactions? Many of the physiological responses we described for emotional situations are also relevant to day-to-day instances of stress. Such transient states of arousal, with typically clear onset and offset patterns, are examples of **acute stress.** Chronic stress, on the other hand, is a state of en-

> **Acute stress** A transient state of arousal with typically clear onset and offset patterns.
>
> **Chronic stress** A continuous state of arousal in which an individual perceives demands as greater than the inner and outer resources available for dealing with them.
>
> **Fight-or-flight response** A sequence of internal activities triggered when an organism is faced with a threat; prepares the body for combat and struggle or for running away to safety; recent evidence suggests that the response is characteristic only of males.

during arousal, continuing over time, in which demands are perceived as greater than the inner and outer resources available for dealing with them. An example of chronic stress might be a continuous frustration with your inability to find time to do all the things you want to do. Let's see how your body responds to these different types of stress.

EMERGENCY REACTIONS TO ACUTE THREATS

In the 1920s, Walter Cannon outlined the first scientific description of the way animals and humans respond to danger. He found that a sequence of activity is triggered in the nerves and glands to prepare the body either to defend itself and struggle or to run away to safety. Cannon called this dual stress response the **fight-or-flight response.** At the center of this stress response is the *hypothalamus,* which is involved in a variety of emotional responses. The hypothalamus has sometimes been referred to as the *stress center* because of its twin functions in emergencies: (1) it controls the autonomic nervous system (ANS) and (2) it activates the pituitary gland.

The ANS regulates the activities of the body's organs. In stressful conditions, breathing becomes faster and deeper, heart rate increases, blood vessels constrict, and blood pressure rises. In addition to these internal changes, muscles open the passages of the throat and nose to allow more air into the lungs while also producing facial expressions of strong emotion. Messages go to smooth muscles to stop certain bodily functions, such as digestion, that are irrelevant to preparing for the emergency at hand.

Another function of the autonomic nervous system during stress is to get adrenaline flowing. It signals the inner part of the adrenal glands, the *adrenal medulla*, to release two hormones, *epinephrine* and *norepinephrine*, which, in turn, signal a number of other organs to perform their specialized functions. The spleen releases more red blood corpuscles (to aid in clotting if there is an injury), and the bone marrow is stimulated to make more white corpuscles (to combat possible infection). The liver is stimulated to produce more sugar, building up body energy.

The *pituitary gland* responds to signals from the hypothalamus by secreting two hormones vital to the stress reaction. The *thyrotrophic hormone* (TTH) stimulates the *thyroid gland*, which makes more energy available to the body. The *adrenocorticotrophic hormone* (ACTH), known as the "stress hormone," stimulates the outer part of the

adrenal glands, the *adrenal cortex*, resulting in the release of hormones that control metabolic processes and in the release of sugar from the liver into the blood. ACTH also signals various organs to release about 30 other hormones, each of which plays a role in the body's adjustment to this call to arms. A summary of this physiological stress response is shown in **Figure 13.7.**

A recent analysis by health psychologist **Shelley Taylor** and her colleagues (2000) suggests that these physiological responses to stress may have different consequences for females than for males. Taylor et al. suggest that females do not experience *fight-or-flight*. Rather, these researchers argue that stressors lead females to experience a **tend-and-befriend response:** In times of stress, females ensure the safety of their offspring by tending to their needs; females befriend other members of their social group with the same goal of reducing the vulnerability of

Tend-and-befriend response A response to stressors that is hypothesized to be typical for females; stressors prompt females to protect their offspring and join social groups to reduce vulnerability.

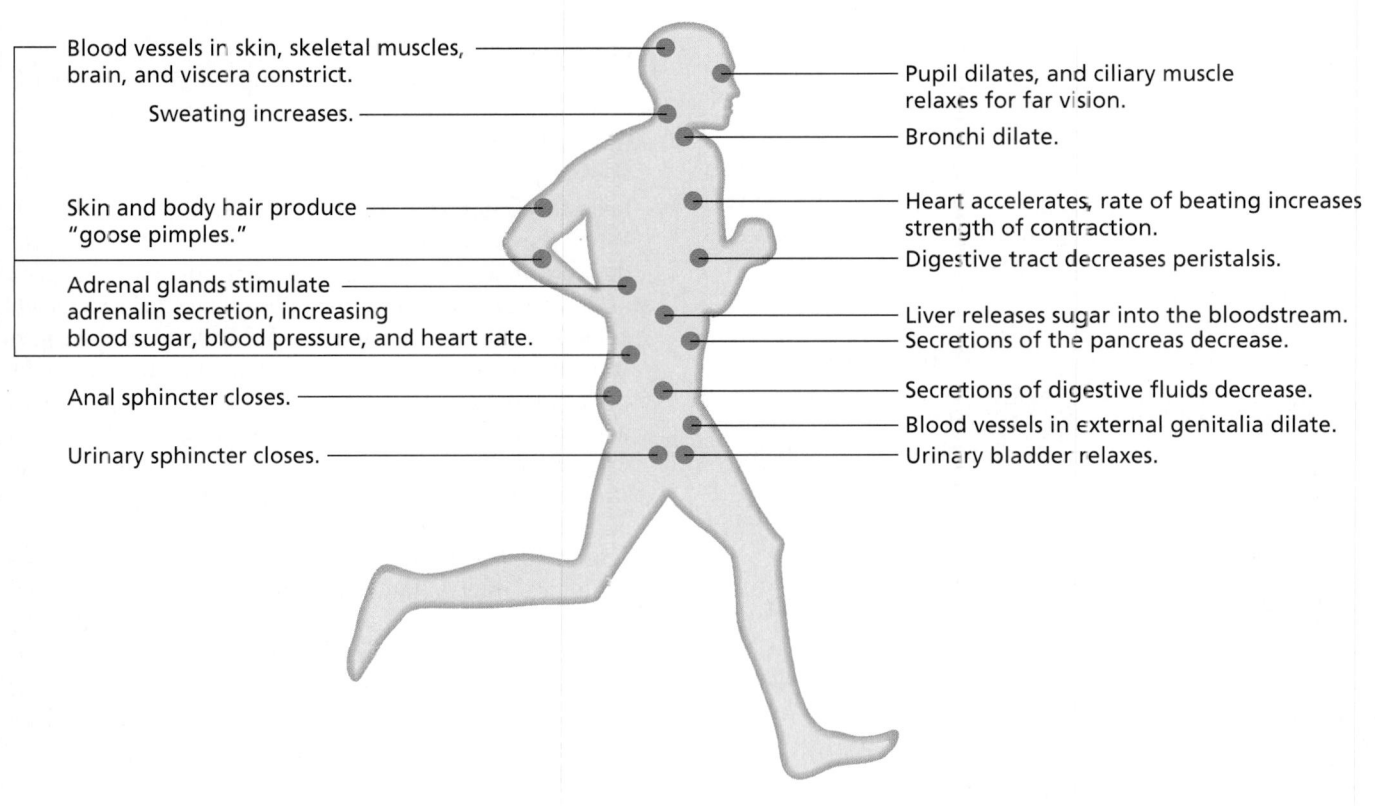

Blood vessels in skin, skeletal muscles, brain, and viscera constrict.

Sweating increases.

Skin and body hair produce "goose pimples."

Adrenal glands stimulate adrenalin secretion, increasing blood sugar, blood pressure, and heart rate.

Anal sphincter closes.

Urinary sphincter closes.

Pupil dilates, and ciliary muscle relaxes for far vision.

Bronchi dilate.

Heart accelerates, rate of beating increases strength of contraction.

Digestive tract decreases peristalsis.

Liver releases sugar into the bloodstream.

Secretions of the pancreas decrease.

Secretions of digestive fluids decrease.

Blood vessels in external genitalia dilate.

Urinary bladder relaxes.

FIGURE 13.7

The Body's Reaction to Stress

Stress produces a wide range of physiological changes in your body.

their offspring. You can see how this analysis of sex differences in stress responses fits with our earlier discussions of evolutionary perspectives on human behavior. For example, when we discussed human sexual behaviors in Chapter 12, we noted that men and women's *mating strategies* differ, in part, because of the relative roles men and women have played—over the course of evolution—in child rearing. The idea here is very much the same: Because of men and women's different evolutionary niches with respect to nurturing offspring, the same initial physiological responses to stress ultimately produce quite different behaviors.

Unfortunately, neither the fight-or-flight nor the tend-or-befriend response is entirely useful for contemporary lives. Many of the stressors both men and women experience on a day-to-day basis make the physiological stress responses fairly maladaptive. Suppose, for example, you are taking a difficult exam and the clock is swiftly ticking away. Although you might value the heightened attentiveness brought about by your stress response, the rest of the physiological changes do you no good: There's no one to fight or to tend, and so on. The responses that developed in the species as adaptive preparations for dealing with external dangers are counterproductive for dealing with many contemporary types of psychological stressors. This is particularly true because, as we shall see next, many people live their lives under circumstances of chronic stress.

THE GENERAL ADAPTATION SYNDROME (GAS) AND CHRONIC STRESS

The first modern researcher to investigate the effects of continued severe stress on the body was **Hans Selye,** a Canadian endocrinologist. Beginning in the late 1930s, Selye reported on the complex response of laboratory animals to damaging agents such as bacterial infections, toxins, trauma, forced restraint, heat, cold, and so on. According to Selye's theory of stress, many kinds of stressors can trigger the same reaction or general bodily response. All stressors call for *adaptation:* An organism must maintain or regain its integrity and well-being by restoring equilibrium, or homeostasis. The response to stressors was described by Selye as the **general adaptation syndrome** (GAS). It includes three stages: an alarm reaction, a stage of resistance, and a stage of exhaustion (Selye, 1976a, 1976b). *Alarm reactions* are brief periods of bodily arousal that prepare the body for vigorous activity. If a stressor is prolonged, the body enters a stage of *resistance*—a state of moderate arousal. During the stage of

What are the physiological consequences of chronic stress?

resistance, the organism can endure and *resist* further debilitating effects of prolonged stressors. However, if the stressor is sufficiently long-lasting or intense, the body's resources become depleted and the organism enters the stage of *exhaustion*. The three stages are diagrammed and explained in **Figure 13.8.**

Selye identified some of the dangers associated with the stage of exhaustion. Recall, for example, that ACTH plays a role in the short-term response to stress. In the long term, however, its action reduces the ability of natural killer cells to destroy cancer cells and other life-threatening infections. When the body is stressed chronically, the increased production of "stress hormones" compromises the integrity of the immune system. This application of the general adaptation syndrome has proven valuable to explain **psychosomatic disorders**—illnesses that could not be wholly explained by physical causes—that had baffled physicians who had never considered stress as a cause for illness and disease. What serves the body well in adapting to acute stress impairs the body's response to chronic stress.

Selye's research makes disease seem an inevitable response to stress. We will see, however, that your psychological interpretation of what is stressful and what is not stressful—the way in which you appraise potentially stressful events—has an impact on your body's physiological response. To give a full account of the effect of stress on your body, we will have to combine Selye's foundational physiological theory with later research on psychological factors.

Psychological Stress Reactions

Your physiological stress reactions are automatic, predictable, built-in responses over which you normally

■ **General adaption syndrome (GAS)** The pattern of nonspecific adaptational physiological mechanisms that occurs in response to continuing threat by almost any serious stressor.
■ **Psychosomatic disorders** Physical disorders aggravated by or primarily attributable to prolonged emotional stress or other psychological causes.

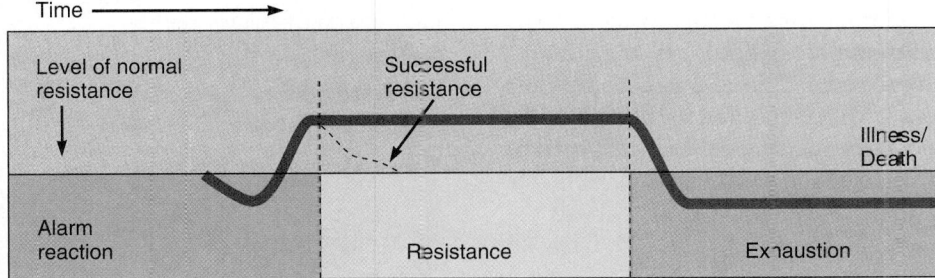

Stage I: Alarm reaction (continuously repeated throughout life)	Stage II: Resistance (continuously repeated throughout life)	Stage III: Exhaustion
• Enlargement of adrenal cortex • Enlargement of lymphatic system • Increase in hormone levels • Response to specific stressor • Epinephrine release associated with high levels of physiological arousal and negative affect • Greater susceptibility to increased intensity of stressor • Heightened susceptibility to illness (If prolonged, the slower components of the GAS are set into motion, beginning with Stage II.)	• Shrinkage of adrenal cortex • Return of lymph nodes to normal size • Sustaining of hormone levels • High physiological arousal • Counteraction of parasympathetic branch of ANS • Enduring of stressor; resistance to further debilitating effects • Heightened sensitivity to stress (If stress continues at intense levels, hormonal reserves are depleted, fatigue sets in, and individual enters Stage III.)	• Enlargement/dysfunction of lymphatic structures • Increase in hormone levels • Depletion of adaptive hormones • Decreased ability to resist either original or extraneous stressors • Affective experience—often depression • Illness • Death

FIGURE 13.8

The General Adaptation Syndrome

Following exposure to a stressor, the body's resistance is diminished until the physiological changes of the corresponding alarm reaction bring it back up to the normal level. If the stressor continues, the bodily signs characteristic of the alarm reaction virtually disappear; resistance to the particular stressor rises above normal but drops for other stressors. This adaptive resistance returns the body to its normal level of functioning. Following prolonged exposure to the stressor, adaptation breaks down; signs of alarm reaction reappear, the stressor effects are irreversible, and the individual becomes ill and may die.

have no conscious control. However, many psychological reactions are learned. They depend on perceptions and interpretations of the world. In this section, we discuss psychological responses to different categories of stressors, such as major life changes and traumatic events.

MAJOR LIFE EVENTS

Major *changes* in life situations are at the root of stress for many people. Even events that you welcome, such as winning the lottery or getting promoted, may require major changes in your routines and adaptation to new requirements. Recall, for example, the pattern of marital well-being we described in Chapter 11. Although the birth of a child is one of the most sought-after changes in a married couple's life, it is also a source of major stress, contributing to reduced marital satisfaction (Cowan & Cowan, 1988; Levenson et al., 1993). Thus, when you try to relate stress to changes in your life, you should consider both positive and negative changes.

The influence of life events on subsequent mental and physical health has been a target of considerable research. It started in the 1960s with the development of the Social Readjustment Rating Scale (SRRS), a simple measure for rating the degree of adjustment required by the various life changes, both pleasant and unpleasant, that many people experience. The scale was developed from the responses of adults, from all walks of life, who were asked to identify from a list those life changes that applied to them. These adults rated the amount of readjustment required for each change by comparing each to marriage, which was arbitrarily assigned a value of 50 life-change units. Researchers then calculated the total number of **life-change units (LCUs)** an individual had undergone,

Life-change units (LCUs) In stress research, the measure of the stress levels of different types of change experienced during a given period.

using the units as a measure of the amount of stress the individual had experienced (Holmes & Rahe, 1967). The SRRS was updated in the 1990s. The researchers used the same procedure of asking participants to rate the stress of life events as compared to marriage (Miller & Rahe, 1997). In this update, the LCU estimates went up 45 percent over the original values—that is, participants in the 1990s reported that they were experiencing overall much higher levels of stress than their peers had in the 1960s. Women in the 1990s also reported experiencing more stress in their lives than did men.

Table 13.1 provides a modification of this scale for college students. Before reading on, take a moment to test your level of stress on the student stress scale. What is your LCU rating? We have provided room for you to carry out this exercise three times, so that you can chart your level of stress across the semester.

Researchers have found a variety of ways to examine the relationship between life events and health outcomes. In one study, participants volunteered to be exposed to viruses that cause the common cold. Those participants who reported a rate of negative life events above the group's average were about 10 percent more likely to actually come down with a cold (Cohen et al., 1993). Consider another study that should have immediate relevance to the choices you make about how to organize your schoolwork.

HOW WE KNOW

THE HEALTH COSTS OF PROCRASTINATION

When a professor gives you an assignment—a stressful life event in every student's life—do you try to take care of it as soon as possible or do you put it off to the very last minute? Psychologists have developed a measurement device called the *General Procrastination Scale* (Lay, 1986) to differentiate those individuals who habitually put things off—*procrastinators*—from those who don't—*nonprocrastinators*. A pair of researchers administered this scale to students in a health psychology course who had a paper due late in the semester. The students were also asked to report, early and late in the semester, how many symptoms of physical illness they had experienced. Not surprisingly, procrastinators, on average, turned their papers in later than did nonprocrastinators; procrastinators also, on average, obtained lower grades on those papers. **Figure 13.9** displays the effect of procrastination on physical health. As you can see, early in the semester, procrastinators reported fewer symptoms, but by late in the semester, they were reporting more symptoms than their nonprocrastinating peers (Tice & Baumeister, 1997).

TABLE

Student Stress Scale

The Student Stress Scale represents an adaptation of Holmes and Rahe's Social Readjustment Rating Scale. Each event is given a score that represents the amount of readjustment a person has to make in life as a result of the change. People with scores of 300 and higher have a high health risk. People scoring between 150 and 300 points have about a 50–50 chance of serious health change within two years. People scoring below 150 have a 1 in 3 chance of serious health change. Calculate your total life-change units (LCUs) three times during the semester and then correlate those scores with any changes in your health status.

Event	Life-Change Units
Death of a close family member	100
Death of a close friend	73
Divorce between parents	65
Jail term	63
Major personal injury or illness	63
Marriage	58
Being fired from job	50
Failing an important course	47
Change in health of family member	45
Pregnancy	45
Sex problems	44
Serious argument with close friend	40
Change in financial status	39
Change of major	39
Trouble with parents	39
New girl- or boyfriend	38
Increased workload at school	37
Outstanding personal achievement	36
First quarter/semester in college	35
Change in living conditions	31
Serious argument with instructor	30
Lower grades than expected	29
Change in sleeping habits	29
Change in social activities	29
Change in eating habits	28
Chronic car trouble	26
Change in number of family get-togethers	26
Too many missed classes	25
Change of college	24
Dropping of more than one class	23
Minor traffic violations	20

My 1st total [＿＿＿＿] (date: ＿＿＿＿)

My 2nd total [＿＿＿＿] (date: ＿＿＿＿)

My 3rd total [＿＿＿＿] (date: ＿＿＿＿)

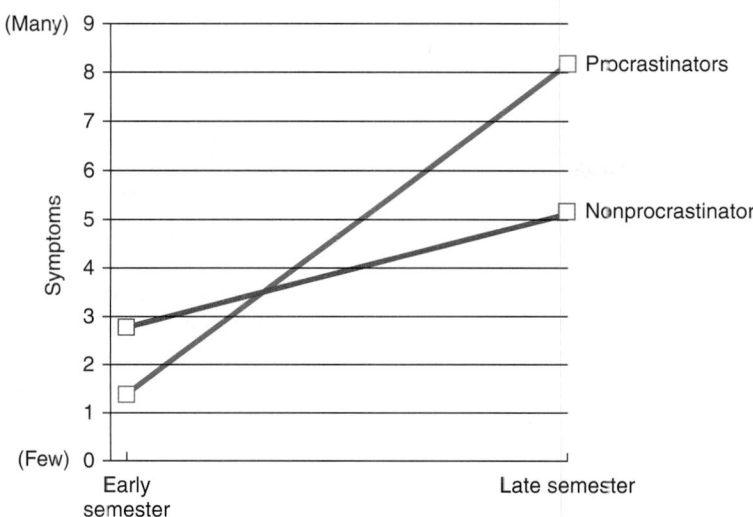

FIGURE 13.9

The Health Costs of Procrastination

Researchers identified students who were, generally, procrastinators and nonprocrastinators. The students were asked to report, early and late in the semester, how many symptoms of physical illness they had experienced. By late in the semester all students showed increases in symptoms. However—as all their work came due—procrastinators were reporting even more symptoms than their nonprocrastinating peers.

You see in this study why not all life events have the same impact on all people. The nonprocrastinators got to work right away and so experienced stress and symptoms early in the semester. However, the consequences for the procrastinators of avoiding the early semester stress was a great increase in physical illness toward the end of the semester. Therefore, they were likely to be feeling ill just at the point in the semester when they needed to be in good health to complete all the work they had put off! You should think about these results as you develop your own plan for navigating each semester. If you believe that you habitually procrastinate, you should consider consulting with a psychologist or school counselor to modify your behavior. Your grades and health are at stake!

CATASTROPHIC AND TRAUMATIC EVENTS

An event that is negative but also uncontrollable, unpredictable, or ambiguous is particularly stressful. These conditions hold especially true in the case of *catastrophic events*. For example, one of your authors, Phil Zimbardo, recalls being at a 1989 World Series game when disaster struck:

> As my three children and I settled into our seats in San Francisco's Candlestick Park, the band started playing. Suddenly, the entire stadium started shaking violently, the lights went out, and the scoreboard turned black. Sixty thousand fans became completely silent.
>
> We had just experienced a major earthquake. The person sitting next to us had a portable TV that showed fires breaking out, a fallen bridge, crushed highways, and numerous deaths.

Shortly after the quake, a team of psychologists began to study how people coped with the catastrophe.

HOW WE KNOW

THE PSYCHOLOGICAL AFTERMATH OF AN EARTHQUAKE For the study, nearly 800 people were chosen randomly from the San Francisco area and from several comparison cities some distance away. They were interviewed once at 1, 2, 3, 6, 8, 16, 28, or 50 weeks after the quake. The participants completed a ten-minute phone survey about their thoughts, social behavior, and health. Three distinct phases of stress reactions were found among the participants who were San Francisco residents. In the emergency phase (first three to four weeks), social contact, anxiety, and obsessive thoughts about the quake increased. The inhibition phase (three to eight weeks) was characterized by a sudden decline in talking and thinking about the quake, but indirect, stress-related reactions increased, such as arguments and earthquake dreams. In the adaptation phase (from two months on), the psychological effects of the catastrophe were over for most people. However, as many as 20 percent of the San Francisco area residents remained distressed about the quake even one year later (Pennebaker & Harber, 1993).

Psychologists attempt to form generalizations from people's responses to catastrophes so that they can alleviate the worst consequences when new catastrophes, such as the bombing in Oklahoma City, present themselves (Krug et al., 1996; Parson, 1995).

Rape and incest victims, survivors of plane and serious automobile crashes, combat veterans, and others who have personally experienced traumatic events may react

STRESS OF LIVING

411

emotionally with **posttraumatic stress disorder** (PTSD). PTSD is a stress reaction in which individuals suffer from persistent reexperiences of the traumatic event in the form, for example, of flashbacks or nightmares (*DSM-IV*, 1994). Sufferers experience an emotional numbing in relation to everyday events and feelings of alienation from other people. Finally, the emotional pain of this reaction can result in an increase in various symptoms, such as sleep problems, guilt about surviving, difficulty in concentrating, and an exaggerated startle response.

Rape victims often show many of the signs of posttraumatic stress (Acierno et al., 1999). In assessments two weeks after being assaulted, 94 percent of rape victims were diagnosed with PTSD; 12 weeks after the assault, 51 percent of the victims still met diagnostic criteria (Foa & Riggs, 1995). The following excerpt of a discussion between two college students about the aftershock of being raped reveals the powerful and enduring emotions.

> *Alice: I was in shock for a pretty long time. I could talk about the fact that I was a rape victim, but the emotions didn't start surfacing until a month later.*
>
> *Beth: During the first two weeks there were people I had chosen to tell who were very, very supportive; but after two weeks, it was like, "Okay, she's over it, we can go on now." But the farther along you get, the more support you need, because, as time passes, you become aware of your emotions and the need to deal with them.*
>
> *Alice: There is a point where you deny it happened. You just completely bury it.*
>
> *Beth: It's so unreal that you don't want to believe that it actually happened or that it can happen. Then you go through a long period of fear and anger.*
>
> *Alice: I'm terrified of going jogging. [Alice had been jogging when she was raped.] I completely stopped any kind of physical activity after I was raped. I started it again this quarter, but every time I go jogging I have a perpetual fear. My pulse doubles. Of course I don't go jogging alone any more, but still the fear is there constantly.*
>
> *Beth: There's also a feeling of having all your friends betray you. I had a dream in which I was being assaulted outside my dorm. In the dream, everyone was looking out their windows—the faces were so clear—every one of my friends lined up against the windows watching, and there were even people two feet away from me. They all saw what was happening and none of them did anything. I woke up and had a feeling of extreme loneliness. (Stanford Daily, 1982)*

The emotional responses of posttraumatic stress can occur in an acute form immediately following a disaster and can subside over a period of several months. These responses can also persist, becoming a chronic syndrome called the **residual stress pattern** (Silver & Wortman, 1980). They can also be delayed for months or even years. Clinicians are still discovering veterans of World War II and the Korean War who are displaying residual or delayed posttraumatic stress disorders (Zeiss & Dickman, 1989). These data suggest that not everyone can "recover" from some types of acute stress (Wortman & Silver, 1989; Wortman et al., 1993).

CHRONIC STRESSORS

In our discussion of physiological responses to stress, we made a distinction between stressors that are acute, with clear onsets and offsets, versus those that are chronic—that is, endure over time. With psychological stressors, it's not always easy to draw a sharp distinction. Suppose, for example, your bicycle is stolen. Originally, this is an acute source of stress. However, if you begin to worry constantly that your new bike will also be stolen, the stress associated with this event can become chronic. Researchers have found this pattern in people who suffer from serious illnesses like cancer (Andersen et al., 1994). The chronic stress of coping with the anxiety of a cancer diagnosis and treatment may impair health more rapidly than the disease alone would.

For many people, chronic stress arises from conditions in society and the environment. What cumulative effect do overpopulation, crime, economic conditions, pollution, AIDS, and the threat of terrorism have on you? How do these and other environmental stressors affect your mental well-being? Some groups of people suffer chronic stress by virtue of their socioeconomic status or racial identity, with stark consequences for overall well-being (Contrada et al., 2000; Stone, 2000; Williams, 1999). African Americans, for example, suffer a much higher rate of heart disease than do white Americans. Research suggests that the underlying cause is not genetic differences. Instead, high blood pressure among African Americans appears to be a consequence of chronic stress caused by the consequences of prejudice: low-status jobs, limited education, fruitless job seeking, and low socioeconomic status (Anderson et al., 1992; Klag et al., 1991). Hypertension results from frustrations in efforts to achieve basic life goals; it is not linked to genetic factors. Similarly, chronic stress among women who are socioeconomically disadvantaged may put them at risk for having premature or low-birth-weight babies (Lobel, 1994; Lobel et al., 1992). Thus children born into poverty or prejudice may start life with greater risks than do their privileged peers.

Posttraumatic stress disorder (PTSD) An anxiety disorder characterized by the persistent reexperience of traumatic events through distressing recollections, dreams, hallucinations, or dissociative flashbacks; develops in response to rapes, life-threatening events, severe injuries, and natural disasters.

Residual stress pattern A chronic syndrome in which the emotional responses of posttraumatic stress persist over time.

These Detroit residents clamoring for post office job applications are likely to have experienced chronic stress due to unemployment or underemployment. What are some likely consequences for their physical and mental health?

THE DEVASTATING EFFECTS OF SUSTAINED ECONOMIC HARDSHIP Most research showing that low income is related to poor health outcomes has measured income at only one time. The correlations obtained may fail to capture the cumulative effect of sustained poverty over many years, and they could also result from reverse causation—poor health may cause poverty. Recent research that measured economic hardships for more than a thousand participants over three decades clearly showed that sustained economic hardship leads to poorer physical, psychological, and cognitive functioning (Lynch et al., 1997).

Economic hardship was defined as household income of less than 200 percent of the federal poverty level. As assessed in 1994, the more periods of economic hardship adults experienced between 1965 and 1983, the more difficulties they had with physical functioning related to basic activities of daily living, such as cooking, shopping, and bathing. Similar effects were found for psychological and cognitive functioning. Compared to those with no period of economic hardship, people with three episodes of poverty were three times more likely to have experienced symptoms of clinical depression, they were more than five times more likely to be assessed as cynically hostile and lacking optimism, and they were more than four times more likely to report difficulties with cognitive functioning. To confirm that these results were caused by economic hardship and not by initial poor health, the researchers demonstrated comparable patterns of disability among those participants whose health at the initial measurement in 1965 had been good or excellent. The researchers concluded that recent economic and political policies are increasing income inequalities and pushing more children into households of sustained poverty, which leave "physical, psychological, and cognitive imprints that decrease the quality of day-to-day life" (p. 1895).

Given these research findings, you will not be surprised to learn that chronic stress can also influence children's intellectual development. Consider a study that assessed the level of stress in a group of 6- to 16-year-old children and also measured their intelligence with an IQ test (see Chapter 10). The data revealed a negative correlation between stress and the Verbal/Comprehension measure on the IQ test: On average, the higher level of stress in the children's lives, the less well they performed on this measure (Plante & Sykora, 1994). Apparently, high levels of chronic stress play a disruptive role in children's cognitive performance. These data also suggest that some of the ill effects of stress need to be counteracted with societal solutions.

DAILY HASSLES

You may agree that the end of a relationship, an earthquake, or prejudice might cause stress, but what about the smaller stressors you experience on a day-to-day basis? What happened to you yesterday? You probably didn't get a divorce or survive a plane crash. You're more likely to have lost your notes or textbook. Perhaps you were late for an important appointment, or you got a parking ticket, or a noisy neighbor ruined your sleep. These are the types of recurring day-to-day stressors that confront most people, most of the time.

In a diary study, a group of white, middle-class, middle-aged men and women kept track of their daily hassles over a one-year period (along with a record of major life changes and physical symptoms). A clear relationship emerged between hassles and health problems: The more frequent and intense the hassles people reported, the poorer was their health, both physical and mental (Lazarus, 1981; 1984b). As daily hassles go down, well-being goes up (Chamberlain & Zika, 1990). Researchers

PEANUTS reprinted by permission of United Feature Syndicate, Inc.

have demonstrated that daily hassles can start to have ill effects quite early in life.

We often think of childhood as a time of innocence. This research suggests, however, that some children already experience a level of stress that is associated with negative outcomes.

We have been focusing largely on day-to-day hassles. It is worth noting, however, that for many people daily hassles may be balanced out by daily positive experiences (Lazarus & Lazarus, 1994). The relative balance of positive and negative experiences may have health consequences. For example, one study asked 96 men to give daily reports of positive and negative events. The men were also tested daily for the strength of their immune response. Results showed that desirable life events were associated with stronger immune response, undesirable events with a weaker response (Stone et al., 1994). There-

fore, if we want to predict your life course based on daily hassles, we also need to know something about the daily pleasures your life provides.

We have just reviewed many sources of stress in people's lives. Psychologists have recognized for quite a long time that the impact of these different types of stressors depends in large part on how effectively people can cope with them. Let's now consider how people cope successfully and unsuccessfully with stress.

Coping with Stress

If living is inevitably stressful, and if chronic stress can disrupt your life and even kill you, you need to learn how to manage stress. **Coping** refers to the process of dealing with internal or external demands that are perceived as straining or exceeding an individual's resources (Lazarus & Folkman, 1984). Coping may consist of behavioral, emotional, or motivational responses and thoughts. We begin this section by describing how cognitive appraisal affects what you experience as stressful. We then consider types of coping responses; we describe both general principles of coping and specific interventions. Finally, we consider some individual differences in individuals' ability to cope with stress.

APPRAISAL OF STRESS
When you cope with stressful situations, your first step is to define in what ways they are, in fact, stressful. *Cognitive appraisal* (see page 400) is the cognitive interpretation and evaluation of a stressor. Cognitive appraisal plays a central role in defining the situation—what the demand is, how big a threat it is, and what resources you have for meeting it (Lazarus, 1993; Lazarus & Lazarus, 1994). Some stressors, such as undergoing bodily injury or finding one's house on fire, are experienced as threats by almost everyone. However, many other stressors can be defined in various ways, depending on your personal life situation, the relation of a particular demand to your central goals, your competence in dealing with the demand, and your self-assessment of that competence. The situation that causes acute distress for another person

Coping The process of dealing with internal or external demands that are perceived to be threatening or overwhelming.

may be all in a day's work for you. Try to notice, and understand, the life events that are different for you and your friends and family: Some situations cause you stress but not your friends and family; other events cause them stress but not you. Why?

Richard Lazarus, whose general theory of appraisal we addressed in our discussion of emotions, has distinguished two stages in the cognitive appraisal of demands. *Primary appraisal* describes the initial evaluation of the seriousness of a demand. This evaluation starts with the questions "What's happening?" and "Is this thing good for me, stressful, or irrelevant?" If the answer to the second question is "stressful," you appraise the potential impact of the stressor by determining whether harm has occurred or is likely to and whether action is required (see **Table 13.2**). Once you decide something must be done, *secondary appraisal* begins. You evaluate the personal and social resources that are available to deal with the stressful circumstance and consider the action options that are needed. Appraisal continues as coping responses are tried; if the first ones don't work and the stress persists, new responses are initiated, and their effectiveness is evaluated.

Cognitive appraisal is an example of a stress moderator variable. **Stress moderator variables** are those variables that change the impact of a stressor on a given type of stress reaction. Moderator variables filter or modify the usual effects of stressors on the individual's reactions. For example, your level of fatigue and general health status are moderator variables influencing your reaction to a given psychological or physical stressor. When you're in

good shape, you can deal with a stressor better than when you aren't. You can see how cognitive appraisal also fits the definition of a moderator variable. The way in which you appraise a stressor will determine the types of coping responses you need to bring to it. Let's now consider general types of coping responses.

TYPES OF COPING RESPONSES

Suppose you have a big exam coming up. You've thought about it—you've appraised the situation—and you're quite sure that this is a stressful situation. What can you do? It's important to note that coping can precede a potentially stressful event in the form of **anticipatory coping** (Folkman, 1984). How do you deal with the stress of the upcoming exam? How do you tell your parents that you are dropping out of school or your lover that you are no longer in love? Anticipating a stressful situation leads to many thoughts and feelings that themselves may be stress inducing, as in the cases of interviews, speeches, or blind dates. You need to know how to cope.

The two main ways of coping are defined by whether the goal is to confront the problem directly—*problem-directed coping*—or to lessen the discomfort associated with the stress—*emotion-focused coping* (Billings & Moos, 1982; Lazarus & Folkman, 1984). Several subcategories of these two basic approaches are shown in **Table 13.3**.

Let's begin with problem-directed coping. "Taking the bull by the horns" is how we usually characterize the strategy of facing up to a problem situation. This approach includes all strategies designed to deal *directly* with the stressor, whether through overt action or through realistic problem-solving activities. You face up to a bully or run away; you try to win him or her over with bribes or other incentives. Your focus is on the problem to be dealt with and on the agent that has induced the stress. You acknowledge the call to action, you appraise the situation and your resources for dealing with it, and you undertake a response that is appropriate for removing or lessening the threat. Such problem-solving efforts are useful for managing *controllable stressors*—those stressors that you can change or eliminate through your actions, such as overbearing bosses or underwhelming grades.

The emotion-focused approach is useful for managing the impact of more *uncontrollable stressors*. Suppose you are responsible for the care of a parent with Alzheimer's. In that situation, there is no "bully" whom you can eliminate from the environment. You cannot look for ways of changing the external stressful situation. Instead, you try to change your feelings and thoughts about it by

TABLE 13.2

Stages in Stable Decision Making/ Cognitive Appraisal

Stage	Key Questions
1. Appraising the challenge	Are the risks serious if I don't change?
2. Surveying alternatives	Is this alternative an acceptable means for dealing with the challenge? Have I sufficiently surveyed the available alternatives?
3. Weighing alternatives	Which alternative is best? Could the best alternative meet the essential requirements?
4. Deliberating about commitment	Shall I implement the best alternative and allow others to know?
5. Adhering despite negative feedback	Are the risks serious if I *don't* change? Are the risks serious if I *do* change?

- **Stress moderator variables** Variables that change the impact of a stressor on a given type of stress reaction.
- **Anticipatory coping** Efforts made in advance of a potentially stressful event to overcome, reduce, or tolerate the imbalance between perceived demands and available resources.

TABLE 13.3

Taxonomy of Coping Strategies

Type of Coping Strategy	Example
Problem-directed coping	
Change stressor or one's relationship to it through direct actions and/or problem-solving activities	Fight (destroy, remove, or weaken the threat)
	Flight (distance oneself from the threat)
	Seek options to fight or flight (negotiating, bargaining, compromising)
	Prevent future stress (act to increase one's resistance or decrease strength of anticipated stress)
Emotion-focused coping	
Change self through activities that make one feel better but do not change the stressor	Somatically focused activities (use of antianxiety medication, relaxation, biofeedback)
	Cognitively focused activities (planned distractions, fantasies, thoughts about oneself)
	Therapy to adjust conscious or unconscious processes that lead to additional anxiety

taking part in a support group for Alzheimer's caregivers or learning relaxation techniques. This approach still constitutes a coping strategy, because you are acknowledging that there is a threat to your well-being and you are taking steps to modify that threat.

Coping is a situation in which the more different strategies you have available to you, the better off you will be (Taylor & Clark, 1986). For coping to be successful, your resources need to match the perceived demand. Thus, the availability of multiple coping strategies is adaptive, because you are more likely to achieve a match and manage the stressful event. Moreover, knowing that you possess a variety of coping strategies can help increase your actual ability to meet environmental demands (Bandura, 1986). Self-confidence can insulate you from experiencing the full impact of many stressors, because believing you have coping resources readily available short-circuits the stressful, chaotic response "What am I going to do?"

Up to now, we have been discussing general approaches to coping with stressors. Now we review specific cognitive and social approaches to successful coping.

MODIFYING COGNITIVE STRATEGIES

A powerful way to adapt to stress is to change your evaluations of stressors and your self-defeating cognitions about the way you are dealing with them. You need to find a different way to think about a given situation, your role in it, and the causal attributions you make to explain the undesirable outcome. Two ways of mentally coping with stress are *reappraising* the nature of the stressors themselves and *restructuring* your cognitions about your stress reactions.

We have already described the idea that people control the experience of stress in their lives in part by the way they appraise life events (Lazarus & Lazarus, 1994). Learning to think differently about certain stressors, to relabel them, or to imagine them in a less-threatening (perhaps even funny) context is a form of cognitive reappraisal that can reduce stress. Worried about giving a speech to a large, forbidding audience? One stressor reappraisal technique is to imagine your potential critics sitting there in the nude—this surely takes away a great deal of their fearsome power. Anxious about being shy at a party you must attend? Think about finding someone who is more shy than you and reducing his or her social anxiety by initiating a conversation.

You can also manage stress by changing what you tell yourself about it and by changing your handling of

Why can speaking directly to a person responsible for a problem, and stating what you want done to resolve it, be an effective means to reduce stress?

it. Cognitive-behavior therapist **Donald Meichenbaum** (1977, 1985, 1993) has proposed a three-phase process that allows for such *stress inoculation*. In Phase 1, people work to develop a greater awareness of their actual behavior, what instigates it, and what its results are. One of the best ways of doing this is to keep daily logs. By helping people redefine their problems in terms of their causes and results, these records can increase their feelings of control. You may discover, for example, that your grades are low (a stressor) because you always leave too little time to do a good job on your class assignments. In Phase 2, people begin to identify new behaviors that negate the maladaptive, self-defeating behaviors. Perhaps you might create a fixed "study time" or limit your phone calls to ten minutes each night. In Phase 3, after adaptive behaviors are being emitted, individuals appraise the consequences of their new behaviors, avoiding the former internal dialogue of put-downs. Instead of telling themselves, "I was lucky the professor called on me when I happened to have read the text," they say, "I'm glad I was prepared for the professor's question. It feels great to be able to respond intelligently in that class."

This three-phase approach means initiating responses and self-statements that are incompatible with previous defeatist cognitions. Once started on this path, people realize that they are changing—and can take full credit for the change, which promotes further successes. **Table 13.4** gives examples of the new kinds of self-statements that help in dealing with stressful situations. *Stress*

TABLE 13.4

Examples of Coping Self-Statements

Preparation
I can develop a plan to deal with it.
Just think about what I can do about it. That's better than getting anxious.
No negative self-statements, just think rationally.

Confrontation
One step at a time; I can handle this situation.
This anxiety is what the doctor said I would feel; it's a reminder to use my coping exercises.
Relax; I'm in control. Take a slow, deep breath.

Coping
When fear comes, just pause.
Keep focused on the present; what is it I have to do?
Don't try to eliminate fear totally; just keep it manageable.
It's not the worst thing that can happen.
Just think about something else.

Self-Reinforcement
It worked; I was able to do it.
It wasn't as bad as I expected.
I'm really pleased with the progress I'm making.

inoculation training has been used successfully in a wide variety of domains.

HOW WE KNOW

STRESS INOCULATION TRAINING FOR PAIN MANAGEMENT This study enrolled 60 male athletes who had undergone knee surgery to repair athletic injuries. Half of the athletes were assigned to a treatment group that received stress inoculation training in addition to their regular program of rehabilitation. The training focused on the types of anxiety and pain the men would experience during their period of recovery, and encouraged them to use cognitive restructuring techniques of the type we described earlier. The other 30 men just underwent the standard course of rehabilitation. All 60 participants were asked to give ratings of their subjective experience of pain before treatment began and then at the beginning of each of ten physical therapy sessions. Although the treatment and control groups did not differ before treatment or at the first test session, over the remaining nine therapy sessions men in the inoculation group reported considerably less pain than did men in the control group (Ross & Berger, 1996).

You might recall that in Chapter 4 we discussed the way in which experiences of pain are determined by both physiological and psychological factors. This experiment with recovering athletes demonstrates how coping techniques can be used to take control of some aspects of the psychological contributions to pain.

Another main component of successful coping is for you to establish **perceived control** over the stressor, a belief that you can make a difference in the course or the consequences of some event or experience (Vaughan, 1993). If you believe that you can affect the course of an illness or the daily symptoms of a disease, you are probably adjusting well to the disorder (Affleck et al., 1987). However, if you believe that the source of the stress is another person whose behavior you cannot influence, or a situation that you cannot change, chances increase for a poor psychological adjustment to your chronic condition (Bulman & Wortman, 1977). Those individuals who are able to maintain perceived control even in the face of fatal diseases like AIDS reap mental and physical health benefits (Thompson et al., 1994).

While you file away these control strategies for future use, we will turn to a final aspect of coping with stress—the social dimension.

Perceived control The belief that one has the ability to make a difference in the course or the consequences of some event or experience; often helpful in dealing with stressors.

Social support refers to the resources others provide, giving the message that one is loved, cared for, esteemed, and connected to other people in a network of communication and mutual obligation (Cohen & Syme, 1985). In addition to these forms of *socioemotional support,* other people may provide *tangible support* (money, transportation, housing) and *informational support* (advice, personal feedback, information). Anyone with whom you have a significant social relationship—such as family members, friends, coworkers, and neighbors—can be part of your social support network in time of need.

Much research points to the power of social support in moderating the vulnerability to stress (Cohen & McKay, 1983). When people have other people they can turn to, they are better able to handle job stressors, unemployment, marital disruption, serious illness, and other catastrophes, as well as their everyday problems of living (Gottlieb, 1981; Pilisuk & Parks, 1986). The positive effects of social support go beyond aiding psychological adjustment to stressful events; they can improve recovery from diagnosed illness and reduce the risk of death from disease (House et al., 1988; Kulik & Mahler, 1989). One study looked at the death rate of patients suffering from severe kidney disease (Christensen et al., 1994). A one-point increase in a measure of family support was associated with a 13 percent decrease in the likelihood of death.

Researchers are trying to identify which types of support are most helpful for specific events (Helgeson & Cohen, 1996; Kuijer et al., 2000).

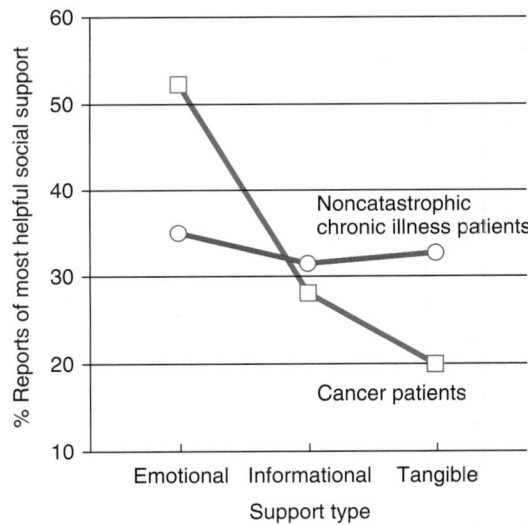

F I G U R E 13.10

The Value of Social Support

Perceived social support as a function of diagnosis.

(From Martin et al., 1994; the data for cancer patients are taken from Dakof & Taylor, 1990.)

chronic headaches and irritable bowel syndrome (Martin et al., 1994). The data suggest, once again, that the optimal type of social support differs for different sources of stress. Can you think of some reasons why emotional support might be more helpful to cancer patients than to patients with noncatastrophic illnesses?

Researchers are also trying to determine when sources of support actually increase anxiety. For example, if someone insisted on accompanying you to a doctor's appointment or to a college interview when you preferred to go alone, you might experience additional anxiety about the situation (Coyne et al., 1988). Similarly, patients with serious diseases may find themselves unable to meet the *expectations* of those individuals in their social circle.

HOW **WE KNOW**

MATCHING SOURCES AND TYPES OF SUPPORT Shelley Taylor and her colleagues have studied the effectiveness of the different types of social support given to cancer patients (Dakof & Taylor, 1990; Taylor, 1986). Patients varied in their assessments of the helpfulness of kinds of support. They thought it was helpful to them for spouses, but not for physicians or nurses, to "just be there." On the other hand, it was important to the patients to receive information or advice from other cancer patients or from physicians, but not from family and friends. Regardless of the source—whether doctors or family or friends—patients did not find helpful forced cheerfulness or attempts to minimize the impact of their disease.

Figure 13.10 provides a comparison of the types of social support that were rated as most helpful for cancer patients versus patients with noncatastrophic illness, such as

HOW **WE KNOW**

EXPECTATIONS AND ADJUSTMENT TO CHRONIC ILLNESS A group of researchers examined the ways in which patients' perceptions of the expectations of the individuals around them affected their adjustment to their illness. The patients were in the final phases of renal disease; all required dialysis. The researchers asked the patients to respond to statements such as "I sometimes feel that my family and friends expect me to cope much better with my illness than I actually can" and "I sometimes think that my family and friends expect me to take more responsibility for my treatment than I can

Social support Resources, including material aid, socioemotional support, and informational aid, provided by others to help a person cope with stress.

manage" on a scale ranging from *strongly disagree* to *strongly agree*. The researchers also obtained measures of how well the patients were coping with their illness. The results revealed consistent positive correlations between expectations and measures of distress. For example, patients who perceived their family and friends' expectations to be excessive were more likely to report depression and low quality of life (Hatchett et al., 1997).

It seems quite likely that these patients' friends and family were doing their best to provide support. Even so, their expectations for the patients increased the patients' distress.

Being part of an effective social support network means that you believe others will be there for you if you need them—even if you don't actually ask for their help when you experience stress. One of the most important take-home messages from *Psychology and Life* is that you should always work at being part of a social support network and never let yourself become socially isolated.

At many points in this discussion of stress, we have noted the effect of stress on physical or psychological well-being. We will now turn directly to the ways in which psychologists apply their research knowledge to issues of illness and health.

SUMMING UP

Stress is brought about by stressors—stimuli that require an organism to respond in some way. Stress brings about physiological responses that prepare the body for action; when those responses are overtaxed, the immune system may be compromised, leading to psychosomatic illnesses. Different types of stressors, such as life changes, daily hassles, and traumatic events, have different psychological effects.

Coping with stress often begins when people appraise the situation to evaluate the demand. People can use either problem-directed coping or emotion-focused coping to address a threat. They can also cope with stress by reappraising the stressor or by restructuring cognitions about reactions to stress. Stress inoculation training is one program for restructuring cognitions. People cope better when they perceive that they have control over a situation. Social support is best when it matches an individual's needs. Social interactions may be negative when they make people feel there are expectations they cannot meet.

■ Health Psychology

How much do your psychological processes contribute to your experiences of illness and wellness? We have already given you reason to believe that the right answer may be "quite a bit." This acknowledgment of the importance of psychological and social factors in health has spurred the growth of a new field, health psychology. **Health psychology** is the branch of psychology that is devoted to understanding the way people stay healthy, the reasons they become ill, and the way they respond when they do get ill (Taylor, 1986, 1990). **Health** refers to the general condition of the body and mind in terms of soundness and vigor. It is not simply the absence of illness or injury, but is more a matter of how well all the body's component parts are working together. We will begin our discussion of health psychology by describing how the field's underlying philosophy departs from a traditional Western medical model of illness. We then consider the contributions of health psychology to the prevention and treatment of illness and dysfunction.

The Biopsychosocial Model of Health

Health psychology is guided by a *biopsychosocial model* of health. We can find the roots of this perspective in many non-Western cultures. To arrive at a definition of the biopsychosocial model, we will start with a description of some of these non-Western traditions.

TRADITIONAL HEALTH PRACTICES

Psychological principles have been applied in the treatment of illness and the pursuit of health for all of recorded time. Many cultures understand the importance of communal health and relaxation rituals in the enhancement of the quality of life. We began the chapter with an example of a healing ceremony from the Warao culture of Venezuela. As we described then, a healer was called on to extract ancestral spirits from an ill boy's body. The healer performed a traditional healing ceremony; the boy's family attributed the cure to the healer's actions (Briggs, 1996).

We can find similar bodies of belief in other cultures. Among the Navajo, for example, disease, illness, and well-being have been attributed to social harmony and mind–body interactions. The Navajo concept of **hozho** (pronounced whoa-zo) means harmony, peace of mind, goodness, ideal family relationships, beauty in arts and crafts, and health of body and spirit. Illness is seen as the outcome of any *disharmony*, caused by evil introduced through violation of taboos, witchcraft, overindulgence, or bad dreams. Traditional healing ceremonies seek to banish illness and restore health, not only through the

Health psychology The field of psychology devoted to understanding the ways people stay healthy, the reasons they become ill, and the ways they respond when they become ill.

Health A general condition of soundness and vigor of body and mind; not simply the absence of illness or injury.

Hozho A Navajo concept referring to harmony, peace of mind, goodness, ideal family relationships, beauty in arts and crafts, and health of body and spirit.

The Navajo, like people in many other cultures around the world, place a high value on aesthetics, family harmony, and physical health. What do the Navajo people consider to be the origins of illness?

medicine of the shaman but also through the combined efforts of all family members, who work together with the ill person to reachieve a state of hozho. The illness of any member of a tribe is seen not as his or her individual responsibility (and fault) but rather as a sign of broader disharmony that must be repaired by communal healing ceremonies. This cultural orientation guarantees that a powerful social support network will automatically come to the aid of the sufferer.

TOWARD A BIOPSYCHOSOCIAL MODEL

We have just seen that healing practices in non-Western cultures often assumed a link between the body and the mind. By contrast, modern Western scientific thinking has relied almost exclusively on a *biomedical model* that has a dualistic conception of body and mind. According to this model, medicine treats the physical body as separate from the psyche; the mind is important only for emotions and beliefs and has little to do with the reality of the body. Over time, however, researchers have begun to document types of interactions that make the strict biomedical model unworkable. You have already seen some of the evidence: Good and bad life events can affect immune function; people are more or less resilient with respect to the negative consequences of stress; adequate social support can decrease the probability of death. These realizations yield the three components of the **biopsychosocial model**. The *bio* acknowledges the reality of biological illness. The *psycho* and the *social* acknowledge the psychological and social components of health.

The biopsychosocial model links your physical health to your state of mind and the world around you. Health psychologists view health as a dynamic, multidimensional experience. Optimal health, or **wellness**, incorporates physical, intellectual, emotional, spiritual, social, and environmental aspects of your life. When you undertake an activity for the purpose of preventing disease or

detecting it in the asymptomatic stage, you are exhibiting *health behavior*. The general goal of health psychology is to use psychological knowledge to promote wellness and positive health behaviors. Let's now consider theory and research relevant to this goal.

Health Promotion

Health promotion means developing general strategies and specific tactics to eliminate or reduce the risk that people will get sick. The prevention of illness in the 21st century poses a much different challenge than it did at the beginning of the 20th century (Matarazzo, 1984). In 1900, the primary cause of death was infectious disease. Health practitioners at that time launched the first revolution in American public health. Over time, through the use of research, public education, the development of vaccines, and changes in public health standards (such as waste control and sewage), they were able to reduce substantially the deaths associated with such diseases as influenza, tuberculosis, polio, measles, and smallpox.

If researchers wish to contribute to the trend toward improved quality of life, they must attempt to decrease those deaths associated with lifestyle factors (see **Table 13.5**). Smoking, being overweight, eating foods high in fat and cholesterol, drinking too much alcohol, driving without seat belts, and leading stressful lives all play a role in heart disease, cancer, strokes, accidents, and suicide. Changing the behaviors associated with these diseases of civilization will prevent much illness and premature death.

Based on this knowledge, it's easy to make some recommendations. You are more likely to stay well if you practice good health habits, such as those listed in **Table 13.6**. Many of these suggestions probably are familiar to you already. However, health psychologists would like to use psychological principles to increase the probability that you will actually do the things you know are good for you. To show you how that works, we now consider a pair of concrete domains: smoking and AIDS.

Biopsychosocial model A model of health and illness that suggests that links among the nervous system, the immune system, behavioral styles, cognitive processing, and environmental factors can put people at risk for illness.

Wellness Optimal health, incorporating the ability to function fully and actively over the physical, intellectual, emotional, spiritual, social, and environmental domains of health.

Health promotion The development and implementation of general strategies and specific tactics to eliminate or reduce the risk that people will become ill.

TABLE 13.5

Leading Causes of Death, United States, 1998

Rank	Percent of Deaths	Cause of Death	Contributors to Cause of Death*
1	31.0	Heart disease	DS
2	23.2	Cancer	DS
3	6.8	Strokes	DS
4	4.8	Obstructive lung diseases	S
5	4.2	All accidents	A
	1.9	Motor vehicle accidents alone	A
6	3.9	Pneumonia and influenza	S
7	2.8	Diabetes	D
8	1.3	Suicide	A
9	1.1	Kidney diseases	
10	1.1	Chronic liver disease and cirrhosis	A

*D = diet; S = smoking; A = alcohol

SMOKING

It would be impossible to imagine that anyone reading this book wouldn't know that smoking is extremely dangerous. Roughly 400,000 people die each year from smoking-related illnesses; tobacco use causes more than 30 percent of cancer deaths in the United States each year (Skaar et al., 1997). Even so, 60 million people in the U.S. still smoke (Substances Abuse and Mental Health Services Administration, 1999). Seventy percent of smokers say they want to quit but are unable to do so (Centers for Disease Control and Prevention, 1997). Health psycholo-

TABLE 13.6

Ten Steps to Personal Wellness

1. Exercise regularly.
2. Eat nutritious, balanced meals (high in vegetables, fruits, and grains; low in fat and cholesterol).
3. Maintain proper weight.
4. Sleep 7 to 8 hours nightly; rest/relax daily.
5. Wear seat belts and bike helmets.
6. Do not smoke or use drugs.
7. Use alcohol in moderation, if at all.
8. Engage only in protected, safe sex.
9. Get regular medical/dental checkups; adhere to medical regimens.
10. Develop an optimistic perspective and friendships.

gists would like to understand both why people begin to smoke—so that the psychologists can help prevent it—and how to assist people in quitting—so they can reap the substantial benefits of becoming ex-smokers.

Analyses of why some people start smoking have focused on personality and social factors. One personality type that has been associated with the initiation of smoking is called *sensation seeking* (Zuckerman, 1988). Individuals characterized as sensation seeking are more likely to engage in risky activities. One study compared personality assessments of men and women in the mid-1960s (1964–1967) with their smoking or nonsmoking behavior in the late 1980s (1987–1991). Both men and women who had revealed themselves to be sensation seeking in the 1960s were more likely to be smoking 20 to 25 years later (Lipkus et al., 1994). These personality factors may go hand in hand with the perception among members of some groups, either in spite of or because of the health risks, that smoking is "cool" (Leary et al., 1994). This may be particularly true for adolescents. Health psychologists understand that successful interventions to prevent the initiation of smoking must attempt to transform smoking into an "uncool" activity.

The best approach to smoking is never to start at all. But for those of you who have begun to smoke, what has research revealed about quitting? Although many people who try to quit have relapses, an estimated 35 million Americans have quit. Ninety percent have done so on their own, without professional treatment programs. Researchers have identified stages people pass through that represent increasing readiness to quit (DiClemente et al., 1991; Prochaska et al., 1993):

- *Precontemplation.* The smoker is not yet thinking about quitting.

- *Contemplation.* The smoker is thinking about quitting but has not yet undertaken any behavioral changes.

- *Preparation.* The smoker is getting ready to quit.

- *Action.* The smoker takes action toward quitting by setting behavioral goals.

- *Maintenance.* The smoker is now a nonsmoker and is trying to stay that way.

This analysis suggests that not all smokers are psychologically equivalent in terms of readiness to quit. Interventions can be designed that nudge smokers up the scale of readiness, until, finally, they are psychologically prepared to take healthy action.

Successful smoking cessation treatment requires that both smokers' physiological and psychological needs be met (Tsoh et al., 1997; U.S. Department of Health and Human Services, 2000). On the physiological side, smokers are best off learning an effective form of *nicotine replacement therapy*, such as nicotine patches or nicotine gum. On the psychological side, smokers must under-

HEALTHY PEOPLE 2010

If you live in the United States, your government has plans for you for the next 10 years: The U.S. Department of Health and Human Services has outlined a program called *Healthy People 2010* that makes concrete recommendations for the behaviors necessary for personal and societal health. The program has two broad goals: (1) to reduce the disparities in health status among different populations, such as the poor, minorities, and children, and (2) to increase the span of healthy life. Psychologists will contribute to both of these goals. With respect to the first goal, *mental health* is included in the category of "health status." For several years now, psychologists have devoted substantial energy in research and practice to improve mental health care for diverse communities. The second goal relates directly to the expertise healthy psychologists bring to the topic of health promotion. The *Healthy People 2010* program wishes people to change their health-relevant behaviors. As we have seen, that's an important topic of health psychology research.

To expand on that claim, let's look at a pair of specific goals from *Healthy People 2010:*

- To reduce the proportion of adults who engage in no leisure-time physical activity from 40 percent to 20 percent.

- To increase the proportion of adults who engage regularly in moderate physical activity (30 minutes, most days) from 15 percent to 30 percent.

You probably know why *Healthy People 2010* wishes you to get regular exercise: Major improvements in health are achieved from such aerobic exercises as bicycling, swimming, running, or even fast walking. These activities lead to increased fitness of the heart and respiratory systems, improvement of muscle tone and strength, and many other health benefits.

So, how can your knowledge of health psychology help people reap these benefits? Researchers are exploring the questions of who exercises regularly and why and are trying to determine what programs or strategies are most effective in getting people to start and continue exercising (Dishman & Buckworth, 1997). In fact, much the same model that we outlined for people's readiness to *quit* smoking applies to people's readiness to *begin* exercising (Myers & Roth, 1997). In the *precontemplation* stage, an individual is still more focused on the barriers to exercise (for example, too little time, no exercise part-

ners) rather than the benefits (for example, helps relaxation, improves appearance). As the individual moves through the *contemplation* and *maintenance* stages toward the *training* stages, the emphasis shifts from barriers to benefits.

If you do not exercise regularly now, how can you get beyond precontemplation? Research suggests that individuals can learn strategies that allow them to overcome obstacles to exercise (Simkin & Gross, 1994). You can treat exercise like any other situation in which you use cognitive appraisal to cope with stress. Try to structure your life so that exercise is a healthy pleasure. You should also be aware that many college students have "rebounds" in both their eating and exercising: When periods of academic stress have passed, they return from poor eating and minimal exercising to healthy behavior (Griffin et al., 1993). How might you structure your thoughts to avoid this pattern? Try to help *Healthy People 2010* meet its goals!

Web site:

- www.health.gov/healthypeople This is the home page for *Healthy People 2010;* you can read about the program's 467 specific objectives.

---

stand that there are huge numbers of ex-smokers and realize that it is possible to quit. Furthermore, smokers must learn strategies to cope with the strong temptations that accompany efforts to quit. Treatments often incorporate the types of cognitive coping techniques we described earlier, which allow people to alleviate the effects of a wide range of stressors. For smoking, people are encouraged to find ways to avoid or escape from situations that may bring on a renewed urge to smoke.

AIDS

AIDS is an acronym for *acquired immune deficiency syndrome.* Although hundreds of thousands are dying from this virulent disease, many more are now living with HIV

infection. **HIV** *(human immunodeficiency virus)* is a virus that attacks the white blood cells (T lymphocytes) in human blood, thus damaging the immune system and weakening the body's ability to fight other diseases. The individual then becomes vulnerable to infection by a

AIDS Acronym for acquired immune deficiency syndrome, a syndrome caused by a virus that damages the immune system and weakens the body's ability to fight infection.

HIV Human immunodeficiency virus, a virus that attacks white blood cells (T lymphocytes) in human blood, thereby weakening the functioning of the immune system; HIV causes AIDS.

host of other viruses and bacteria that can cause such life-threatening illnesses as cancer, meningitis, and pneumonia. The period of time from initial infection with the virus until symptoms occur (incubation period) can be five years or longer. Although most of the estimated millions of those infected with the HIV virus do not have AIDS (a medical diagnosis), they must live with the continual stress that this life-threatening disease might suddenly emerge. At the present time, there are treatments that delay the onset of full-blown AIDS, but there is neither a cure for AIDS nor a vaccine to prevent its spread.

The HIV virus is not airborne; it requires direct access to the bloodstream to produce an infection. The HIV virus is generally passed from one person to another in one of two ways: (1) the exchange of semen or blood during sexual contact and (2) the sharing of intravenous needles and syringes used for injecting drugs. The virus has also been passed through blood transfusions and medical procedures in which infected blood or organs are unwittingly given to healthy people. Many people suffering from hemophilia have gotten AIDS in this way. However, everyone is at risk for AIDS.

The only way to protect oneself from being infected with the AIDS virus is to change those lifestyle habits that put one at risk. This means making permanent changes in patterns of sexual behavior and in use of drug paraphernalia. Health psychologist **Thomas Coates** is part of a multidisciplinary research team that is using an array of psychological principles in a concerted effort to prevent the further spread of AIDS (Catania et al., 1994; Coates, 1990; Ekstrand & Coates, 1990; Kegeles et al., 1996). The team is involved in many aspects of applied psychology, such as assessing psychosocial risk factors, developing behavioral interventions, training community leaders to be effective in educating people toward healthier patterns of sexual and drug behavior, assisting with the design of media advertisements and community information campaigns, and systematically evaluating changes in relevant attitudes, values, and behaviors. Successful AIDS interventions require three components (Fisher et al., 1994, 1996; Yzer et al., 1998):

- *Information.* People must be provided with knowledge about how AIDS is transmitted and how its transmission may be prevented; they should be counseled to practice safer sex (for example, use condoms during sexual contact) and use sterile needles.

- *Motivation.* People must be motivated to practice AIDS prevention.

- *Behavioral skills.* People must be taught how to put the knowledge to use.

Why are all three of these components necessary? People might be highly motivated but uninformed, or vice versa. They may have both sufficient knowledge and sufficient motivation but lack requisite skills. They may not, for example, know exactly how to overcome the social barrier of asking a partner to use a condom (Leary et al., 1994). Psychological interventions can provide role-playing experience, or other behavioral skills, to make that barrier seem less significant.

Treatment

Treatment focuses on helping people adjust to their illnesses and recover from them. We will look at three aspects of treatment. First, we consider the role of psychologists in encouraging patients to adhere to the regimens prescribed by health-care practitioners. Next, we look at techniques that allow people to explicitly use psychological techniques to take control over the body's responses. Finally, we examine instances in which the mind can contribute to the body's cure.

PATIENT ADHERENCE

Patients are often given a *treatment regimen*. This might include medications, dietary changes, prescribed periods of bed rest and exercise, and follow-up procedures such as return checkups, rehabilitation training, and chemotherapy. Failing to adhere to treatment regimens is one of the most serious problems in health care (Clark & Becker, 1998). The rate of patient nonadherence is estimated to be as high as 50 percent for some treatment regimens. Recent research has focused on the types of individual differences that lead some individuals to comply whereas others do not.

HOW WE KNOW

COMPLIANCE FOR PATIENTS ON HEMODIALYSIS A team of researchers examined the relevance of *monitoring attentional style* to patient compliance. When they are ill, some individuals pay close attention to all aspects of the illness—they are called *high monitors*. By contrast, *low monitors* are less likely to focus their attention on their illness. It might not sound dangerous, at first, to be a high monitor. However, because of the tight attentional focus, high monitors tend to overestimate the severity of their illness. As a consequence, high monitors have lower perceived control over their illness—which, the researchers suggested, could undermine their adherence to a treatment regimen. In the current study, the researchers assessed a group of patients for their monitoring attentional style as well as their perceived control and adherence to the regimen. The results fit the pattern the researchers laid out. By comparison to low monitors, high monitors perceived less control over their illness and were also less likely to comply with the regimen specified by their doctors (Christensen et al., 1997).

Why is regular exercise an important component of a life-long plan to reduce stress and preserve health?

Prior to reading about this study, you might have thought that people who are very focused on their illness would be more likely to take good care of themselves. Instead, the data suggest that too tight a focus on an illness can make it seem even worse than it really is—and, therefore, beyond hope of a remedy in a way that discourages patients from taking necessary actions.

Research has shown that health-care professionals can take steps to improve patient adherence. Patients are more satisfied with their health care when they trust that the efficacy of the treatment outweighs its costs. They are also more likely to comply with a regimen when practitioners communicate clearly, make sure that their patients understand what has been said, act courteously, and convey a sense of caring and supportiveness. In addition, health professionals must recognize the role of cultural and social norms in the treatment process and involve family and friends where necessary. Some physicians critical of their profession's outdated reliance on the biomedical model argue that doctors must be taught to care in order to cure (Siegel, 1988). Compliance-gaining strategies developed from psychological research are also being used to help overcome the lack of cooperation between patients and practitioners (Putnam et al., 1994; Zimbardo & Leippe, 1991).

HARNESSING THE MIND TO HEAL THE BODY

More and more often, the treatments to which patients must adhere involve a psychological component. Many investigators now believe that psychological strategies can improve well-being. For example, many people react to stress with tension, resulting in tight muscles and high blood pressure. Fortunately, many tension responses can be controlled by psychological techniques, such as *relaxation* and *biofeedback*.

Relaxation through meditation has ancient roots in many parts of the world. In Eastern cultures, ways to calm the mind and still the body's tensions have been practiced for centuries. Today, Zen discipline and yoga exercises from Japan and India are part of daily life for many people both there and, increasingly, in the West. Growing evidence suggests that complete relaxation is a potent antistress response. The **relaxation response** is a condition in which muscle tension, cortical activity, heart rate, and blood pressure all decrease and breathing slows (Benson & Stuart, 1992; Friedman et al., 1996). There is reduced electrical activity in the brain, and input to the central nervous system from the outside environment is lowered. In this low level of arousal, recuperation from stress can take place. Four conditions are regarded as necessary to produce the relaxation response: (1) a quiet environment, (2) closed eyes, (3) a comfortable position, and (4) a repetitive mental device such as the chanting of a brief phrase over and over again. The first three conditions lower input to the nervous system, while the fourth lowers its internal stimulation.

Biofeedback is a self-regulatory technique used for a variety of special applications, such as control of blood pressure, relaxation of forehead muscles (involved in tension headaches), and even diminishment of extreme blushing. As pioneered by psychologist **Neal Miller** (1978), biofeedback is a procedure that makes an individual aware of ordinarily weak or internal responses by providing clear external signals. The patient is allowed to "see" his or her own bodily reactions, which are monitored and amplified by equipment that transforms them into lights and sound cues of varying intensity. The patient's task is then to control the level of these external cues. Let's consider one application of biofeedback. Have you ever noticed that when you are relaxed your hands get warm and when you are anxious they get cold? In fact, hand temperature is a sign that stress is having an effect on your body. In biofeedback sessions, research participants are given feedback about their hand or finger temperature and asked to try to raise it. For example, in one study men could see their finger temperature on a digital readout; over the course of biofeedback, they were able to raise their average finger temperature from 79.8 to 87.4°F (Roberts & McGrady, 1996). Why does this matter? Research has shown that biofeedback training to prompt skin warming can lead to a sustained reduction in blood pressure (Paran et al., 1996). Researchers are not certain about the physiological mechanism through which biofeedback training for skin temperature decreases blood pressure. They also continue to study why the training works for some individuals but not for others (Lal et al., 1998; Roberts & McGrady, 1996). Even so, if you ever become concerned about high blood pressure, you might seek a course of biofeedback to complement a drug regimen.

Relaxation response A condition in which muscle tension, cortical activity, heart rate, and blood pressure decrease and breathing slows.
Biofeedback A self-regulatory technique by which an individual acquires voluntary control over nonconscious biological processes.

What is the potential for psychological factors—the influence of mind over body—to have an impact on serious illness? Fortunately, research in health psychology paints a rather optimistic picture. Consider a classic study that demonstrated the potential for psychological processes to ease the course of cancer.

HOW WE KNOW

SOCIAL SUPPORT AND CANCER SURVIVAL TIMES Routine medical care was provided to 86 patients with metastatic breast cancer, while an experimental subgroup of 50 also participated in weekly supportive group therapy for one year. These patients met to discuss their personal experiences in coping with the various aspects of having cancer, and they had the opportunity to reveal openly in an accepting environment their fears and other strong emotions.

Although, at the 10-year follow-up, all but three of the total sample had died, there was a significant difference in the survival times between those given the psychological treatment and those given only medical treatment. Those patients who participated in group therapy survived for an average of 36.6 months, compared with the 18.9 months for the control group. This finding in a well-controlled study indicates that psychological treatments can affect the course of disease and the length of life (Spiegel et al., 1989).

Research of this type gives hope that a supportive group environment can add time to cancer patients' lives (Walker et al., 1999). The important insight here is that psychological and biological approaches to healing must work in tandem: Many health psychologists want medical treatments to expand to include psychological practices in addition to traditional treatments.

One last note on treatment. Have you ever had a secret too shameful to tell anyone? If so, talking about the secret could very well improve your health. That is the conclusion from a large body of research by health psychologist **James Pennebaker** (1990, 1997; Petrie et al., 1998), who has shown that suppressing thoughts and feelings associated with personal traumas, failures, and guilty or shameful experiences takes a devastating toll on mental and physical health. Such inhibition is psychologically hard work and, over time, it undermines the body's defenses against illness. Confiding in others neutralizes the negative effects of inhibition. The experience of letting go often is followed by improved physical and psychological health weeks and months later. Consider the effects of emotional disclosure on the functioning of adults with rheumatoid arthritis.

If you disclose your personal thoughts and feelings to a friend, why might that have a positive impact on your health?

HOW WE KNOW

HEALTH BENEFITS OF EMOTIONAL DISCLOSURE Seventy-two adults with rheumatoid arthritis participated in this study. This disease leads to chronic inflammation of the peripheral joints, with accompanying pain and disability. The researchers hypothesized that sessions of emotional disclosure might help alleviate some of the stress associated with the disease and also, therefore, alleviate some of the problems in day-to-day functioning. Half of the patients were assigned to the *disclosure* group and spent 15 minutes on four consecutive days talking to a tape recorder about their deepest feelings surrounding highly stressful life events. The *control* group spent the same amount of time in a neutral task, giving descriptions of color landscapes. In the short run, disclosure patients were a bit worse off—the task stirred up a lot of negative emotions. However, three months after the treatment, the disclosure group was experiencing consistently less physical dysfunction—fewer problems, for example, with walking and bending—than were the members of the control group (Kelley et al., 1997).

For patients in the disclosure group, the relatively simple act of revealing feelings, in private, to a tape recorder brought about measurable improvements in functioning.

Job Burnout and the Health-Care System

One final focus of health psychology is to make recommendations about the design of the health-care system. Researchers, for example, have examined the stress associated with being a health-care provider. Even the most enthusiastic health-care providers run up against the emotional stresses of working intensely with large numbers of

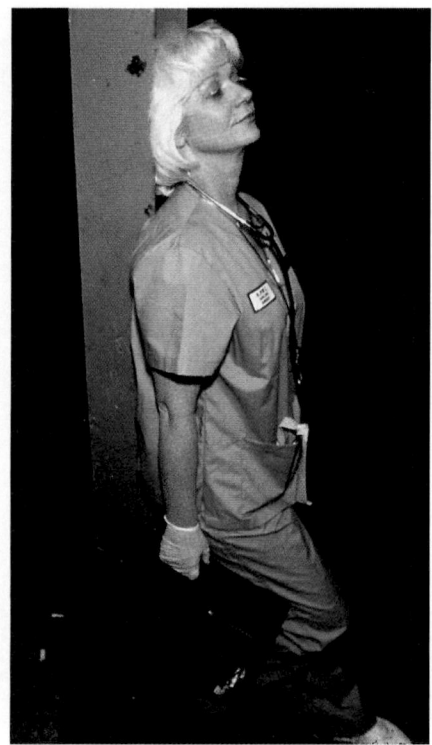

Why are health-care providers particularly prone to job burnout?

people suffering from a variety of personal, physical, and social problems. The special type of emotional stress experienced by these professional health and welfare practitioners has been termed *burnout* by **Christina Maslach,** a leading researcher on this widespread problem. **Job burnout** is a syndrome of emotional exhaustion, depersonalization, and reduced personal accomplishment that is often experienced by workers in professions that demand high-intensity interpersonal contact with patients, clients, or the public. Health practitioners begin to lose their caring and concern for patients and may come to treat them in detached and even dehumanized ways. They feel bad about themselves and worry that they are failures. Burnout is correlated with greater absenteeism and turnover, impaired job performance, poor relations with coworkers, family problems, and poor personal health (Leiter & Maslach, 1988; Maslach, 1982; Maslach & Florian, 1988; Schaufeli et al., 1993). Job burnout in today's workforce is reaching ever higher levels due to the effects of organizational downsizing, job restructuring, and greater concerns for profits than for employee morale and loyalty. Burnout then is not merely a concern of workers and health caregivers, but it also reveals organizational dysfunction that needs to be corrected by reexamining goals, values,

Job burnout The syndrome of emotional exhaustion, depersonalization, and reduced personal accomplishment, often experienced by workers in high-stress jobs.

workloads, and reward structures (Leiter & Maslach, 2000; Maslach & Leiter, 1997).

What recommendations can be made? Several social and situational factors affect the occurrence and level of burnout and, by implication, suggest ways of preventing or minimizing it (Leiter & Maslach, 2000; Prosser et al., 1997). For example, the quality of the patient–practitioner interaction is greatly influenced by the number of patients for whom a practitioner is providing care—the greater the number, the greater the cognitive, sensory, and emotional overload. Another factor in the quality of that interaction is the amount of direct contact with patients. Longer work hours in continuous direct contact with patients are correlated with greater burnout. This is especially true when the nature of the contact is difficult and upsetting, such as contact with patients who are dying (Catalan et al., 1996). The emotional strain of such prolonged contact can be eased by a number of means. For example, practitioners can modify their work schedules in order to withdraw temporarily from such high-stress situations. They can use teams rather than only individual contact. They can arrange opportunities to get positive feedback for their efforts.

A Toast to Your Health

It's time for some final advice. Instead of waiting for stress or illness to come and then reacting to it, you should set goals and structure your life in ways that are most likely to forge a healthy foundation. The following nine steps to greater happiness and better mental health are presented as guidelines to encourage you to take a more active role in your own life and to create a more positive psychological environment for yourself and others. Think of the steps as *year-round resolutions.*

1. Never say bad things about yourself. Look for sources of your unhappiness in elements that can be modified by future actions. Give yourself and others only *constructive criticism*—what can be done differently next time to get what you want?

2. Compare your reactions, thoughts, and feelings with those of friends, coworkers, family members, and others so that you can gauge the appropriateness and relevance of your responses against a suitable social norm.

3. Have several close friends with whom you can share feelings, joys, and worries. Work at developing, maintaining, and expanding your social support networks.

4. Develop a sense of *balanced time perspective* in which you can flexibly focus on the demands of the task, the situation, and your needs; be future oriented when there is work to be done, present oriented when the goal is achieved and pleasure is at hand, and past oriented to keep you in touch with your roots.

DOES YOUR PERSONALITY AFFECT YOUR HEALTH?

Do you know a person like this: someone who is driven to succeed, no matter what obstacles; someone whose high school class voted him or her "Most likely to have a heart attack before age 20"? Are you that person? As you've observed the way in which some people charge through life while others take a more relaxed pace, you may have wondered whether these different personalities affect health. Research in health psychology strongly suggests that the answer is "yes." Let's consider some of the evidence.

In the 1950s, Meyer Friedman and Ray Rosenman reported what had been suspected since ancient times: there was a relationship between a constellation of personality traits and the probability of illness, specifically coronary heart disease (Friedman & Rosenman, 1974). These researchers identified two behavior patterns that they labeled Type A and Type B. The **Type A behavior pattern** is a complex pattern of behavior and emotions that includes being excessively competitive, aggressive, impatient, time urgent, and hostile. Type A people are often dissatisfied with some central aspect of their lives, are highly competitive and ambitious, and often are loners. The **Type B behavior pattern** is everything Type A is not—individuals are less competitive, less hostile, and so on. Friedman and Rosenman reported that people who showed Type A behavior patterns are stricken with coronary heart disease considerably more often than individuals in the general population (Friedman & Rosenman, 1974; Jenkins, 1976).

A great deal of research attention has focused on individuals who are characterized by Type A behavior patterns. Research has related Type A behavior to many subsequent illnesses in addition to heart disease (Suls & Marco, 1990; Vahtera et al., 2000). A current focus is on identifying the specific elements of the Type A behavior pattern that most often put people at risk. The personality trait that has emerged most forcefully as "toxic" is hostility (Carmelli & Swan, 1996; Fredrickson et al., 2000; Smith, 1992). Hostility may affect health for both physiological reasons—by leading to chronic overarousal of the body's stress responses—and psychological reasons—by leading hostile people to practice poor health habits and avoid social support. The good news is that behavioral treatments to reduce Type A reaction patterns have been successful in most cases (Friedman et al., 1986; Thoresen & Powell, 1992). If you recognize yourself in the definition of hostility, you should protect your health by seeking out this type of intervention.

Type A and its opposite, Type B, were originated to account for relationships between behavior and coronary heart disease. More recently, researchers have suggested that a third constellation of behaviors, called the **Type C behavior pattern,** may predict which individuals will be particularly likely to develop cancer or to have their cancer progress quickly (Eysenck, 1994; Temoshok & Dreher,

1992): "Type C coping has been described as being 'nice,' stoic or self-sacrificing, cooperative and appeasing, unassertive, patient, compliant with external authorities, and unexpressive of negative emotions, particularly anger" (Temoshok, 1990, p. 209). Type C behaviors are inconsistent with the "fighting spirit" that may help slow the course of a cancer or other serious illness. Researchers have seen the effect of a fighting spirit, for example, with patients who have been diagnosed with AIDS (Reed et al., 1994). Those individuals who were unwilling to accept the inevitability of their deaths outlived another group of individuals who resigned themselves to their fate.

On the whole, the passive acceptance of the Type C individual is not the best approach to illness. Recall the concept of *optimism* we introduced in Chapter 12. We saw there that optimistic individuals attribute failures to external causes and to events that were unstable or modifiable (Seligman, 1991). This style of coping has a strong impact on the optimist's well-being. Researchers have demonstrated that optimism has an impact on the function of the immune system (Segerstrom et al., 1998). Optimistic people have fewer physical symptoms of illness, are faster at recovering from certain illnesses, are generally healthier, and live longer (Peterson et al., 1988). A positive outlook may both reduce your body's experience of chronic stress and make it more likely that you'll engage in healthy behaviors.

■ **Type A behavior pattern** A complex pattern of behaviors and emotions that includes excessive emphasis on competition, aggression, impatience, and hostility; hostility increases the risk of coronary heart disease.

■ **Type B behavior pattern** As compared to Type A behavior pattern, a less competitive, less aggressive, less hostile pattern of behavior and emotion.

■ **Type C behavior pattern** A constellation of behaviors that may predict which individuals are more likely to develop cancer or to have their cancer progress quickly; these behaviors include passive acceptance and self-sacrifice.

5. Always take full credit for your successes and happiness (and share your positive feelings with other people). Keep an inventory of all the qualities that make you special and unique—those qualities you can offer others. For example, a shy person can provide a talkative person with the gift of attentive listening. Know your sources of personal strength and available coping resources.

6. When you feel you are losing control over your emotions, distance yourself from the situation by physically leaving it, role playing the position of another person in the situation or conflict, projecting your imagination into the future to gain perspective on what seems an overwhelming problem now, or talking to a sympathetic listener. Allow yourself to feel and express your emotions.

7. Remember that failure and disappointment are sometimes blessings in disguise. They may tell you that your goals are not right for you or may save you from bigger letdowns later on. Learn from every failure. Acknowledge setbacks by saying, "I made a mistake," and move on. Every accident, misfortune, or violation of your expectations is potentially a wonderful opportunity in disguise.

8. If you discover you cannot help yourself or another person in distress, seek the counsel of a trained specialist in your student health department or community. In some cases, a problem that appears to be psychological may really be physical, and vice versa. Check out your student mental health services before you need them, and use them without concern about being stigmatized.

9. Cultivate healthy pleasures. Take time out to relax, to meditate, to get a massage, to fly a kite, and to enjoy hobbies and activities you can do alone and by means of which you can get in touch with and better appreciate yourself.

So how are you feeling? If the stressors in your life have the potential to put you in a bad mood, we hope you'll be able to use cognitive reappraisal to minimize their impact. If you are feeling ill, we hope you'll be able to use your mind's healing capacity to speed your way back toward health. Never underestimate the power of these different types of "feelings" to exercise control over your life. Harness that power!

SUMMING UP

Non-Western cultures have a long tradition of using psychological forces to affect the mind. The biopsychosocial model of health reflects all three of the biological, psychological, and social contributions to wellness. Health psychologists seek to use psychological techniques to persuade people to avoid unhealthy behaviors such as smoking. Researchers have also developed complex programs of behavior change to combat AIDS. Health psychological approaches to treatment include analyses of why people do and do not comply with treatment regimens. Research has also demonstrated a number of ways in which the power of the mind to influence the body can be harnessed. Health-care situations must be carefully constructed so that practitioners avoid burnout and remain engaged with their work and clients.

RECAPPING
MAIN POINTS

Emotions

- Emotions are complex patterns of changes made up of physiological arousal, cognitive appraisal, and behavioral and expressive reactions.
- As a product of evolution, all humans may share a basic set of emotional responses.
- Cultures, however, vary in their rules of appropriateness for displaying emotions.
- Classic theories emphasize different parts of emotional response, such as peripheral bodily reactions or central neural processes.

- More contemporary theories emphasize the appraisal of arousal.
- Emotions serve motivational, social, and cognitive functions.

Stress of Living

- Stress can arise from negative or positive events. At the root of most stress is change and the need to adapt to environmental, biological, physical, and social demands.
- Physiological stress reactions are regulated by the hypothalamus and a complex interaction of the hormonal and nervous systems.
- Depending on the type of stressor, and its effect over time, stress can be a mild disruption or lead to health-threatening reactions.
- Cognitive appraisal is a primary moderator variable of stress.
- Coping strategies either focus on problems (taking direct actions) or attempt to regulate emotions (indirect or avoidant).
- Cognitive reappraisal and restructuring can be used to cope with stress.
- Social support is also a significant stress moderator, as long as it is appropriate to the circumstances.

Health Psychology

- Health psychology is devoted to treatment and prevention of illness.
- The biopsychosocial model of health and illness looks at the connections among physical, emotional, and environmental factors in illness.
- Illness prevention in the 21st century focuses on lifestyle factors such as smoking, nutrition, exercise, and AIDS-risk behaviors.
- Psychosocial treatment of illness adds another dimension to patient treatment.
- Individuals who are characterized by Type A (especially hostile), Type B, Type C, and optimistic behavior patterns will experience different likelihoods of illness.
- Health-care providers are at risk for burnout, which can be minimized by appropriate situational changes in their helping environment.

Key Terms

acute stress (p. 406)
AIDS (p. 422)
amygdala (p. 399)
anticipatory coping (p. 415)
biofeedback (p. 424)
biopsychosocial model (p. 420)
Cannon–Bard theory of emotion (p. 400)
chronic stress (p. 406)
cognitive appraisal (p. 400)
cognitive appraisal theory of emotion (p. 400)
coping (p. 414)
emotion (p. 394)
fight-or-flight response (p. 406)
general adaptation syndrome (GAS) (p. 408)
health (p. 419)
health promotion (p. 420)
health psychology (p. 419)
HIV (p. 422)
hozho (p. 419)

James–Lange theory o (p. 399)
job burnout (p. 426)
life-change units (L(
perceived control (p. 417)
posttraumatic stress disorder (PTSD) (p. 412)
psychosomatic disorders (p. 408)
relaxation response (p. 424)
residual stress pattern (p. 412)
social support (p. 418)
stress (p. 405)
stress moderator variables (p. 415)
stressor (p. 405)
tend-and-befriend response (p. 407)
Type A behavior pattern (p. 427)
Type B behavior pattern (p. 427)
Type C behavior pattern (p. 427)
wellness (p. 420)
Yerkes–Dodson law (p. 402)

Answers for Figure 13.1 (p. 395)

First row: Happiness, surprise, anger, disgust

Second row: Fear, sadness, contempt

understanding human personality

14

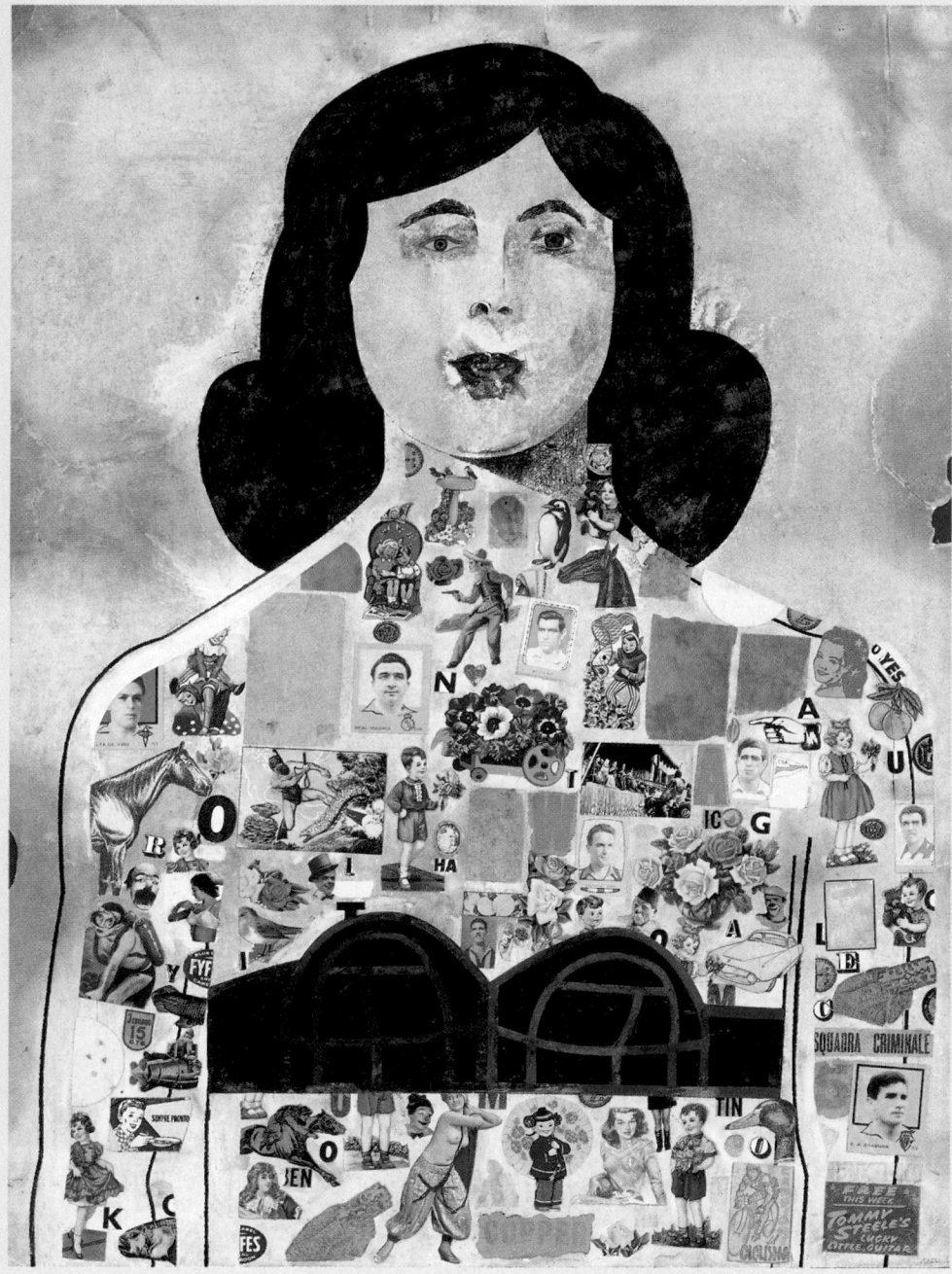

- **TYPE AND TRAIT PERSONALITY THEORIES**
  Categorizing by Types • Describing with Traits • Traits and Heritability • Do Traits Predict Behaviors? • Evaluation of Type and Trait Theories

- **PSYCHOLOGY IN YOUR LIFE: WHY ARE SOME PEOPLE SHY?**

- **PSYCHODYNAMIC THEORIES**
  Freudian Psychoanalysis • Evaluation of Freudian Theory • Post-Freudian Theories

- **HUMANISTIC THEORIES**
  Features of Humanistic Theories • Evaluation of Humanistic Theories

- **SOCIAL-LEARNING AND COGNITIVE THEORIES**
  Mischel's Cognitive-Affective Personality Theory • Bandura's Cognitive Social-Learning Theory • Cantor's Social Intelligence Theory • Evaluation of Social-Learning and Cognitive Theories

- **SELF THEORIES**
  Dynamic Aspects of Self-Concepts • Self-Esteem and Self-Presentation • The Cultural Construction of Self • Evaluation of Self Theories

- **PSYCHOLOGY IN THE 21ST CENTURY: THE SELF ON THE INTERNET**

- **COMPARING PERSONALITY THEORIES**

- **ASSESSING PERSONALITY**
  Objective Tests • Projective Tests

- **RECAPPING MAIN POINTS**
  Key Terms

Do you wonder if you will make a good parent? If you believed a 19th-century theory called *phrenology*, anyone who could feel the shape of your skull could address this concern. The theory behind phrenology was that highly developed organs of the brain would push out against the skull and create protuberances. By assessing the size of the lumps associated with each organ—associated with traits such as *parental love*, *friendship*, and *combativeness*—one could immediately get to know quite a bit about oneself or another person. Here is an account of the manifestations of parental love from a volume entitled *How to Read Character: A New Illustrated Handbook of Phrenology and Physiognomy*, copyrighted by Samuel Wells in 1869:

> The organ of Parental Love or Philoprogenitiveness is situated above the middle part of the cerebellum (2, fig. 23), and about an inch above the occipital protuberance. (p. 42)

Have you located the appropriate spot on your skull? How does it compare to Queen Victoria's or A. Johnson's protuberance shown in the drawings? How does it compare to your friends' skulls? Here's what the *Handbook* predicts about your life as a parent, based on the size of your organ of Parental Love:

> VERY LARGE.—*Your love for children and pets is intense, and as a parent you would idolize your offspring and probably spoil them by pampering and hurtful indulgence, or by allowing them to rule instead of yielding obedience. If you have children, you suffer continual anxiety on their account, especially when absent from them, and the death of one of them would be a blow almost too great to bear.*
>
> FULL.—*You are capable of loving your own children well, and will do and sacrifice much for them,*

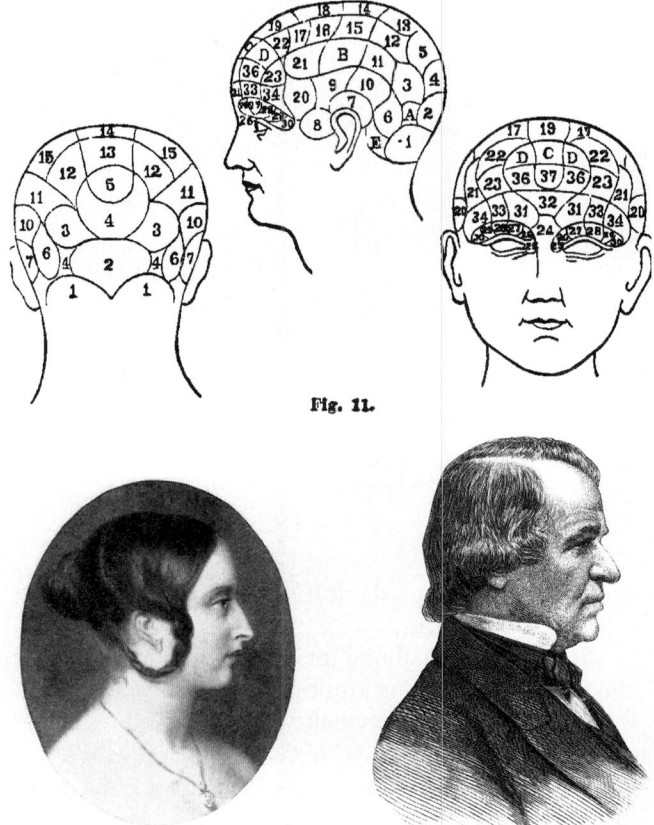

Fig. 11.

> but will not be over-indulgent, and will feel no very strong attraction toward children generally, or toward pets.
>
> MODERATE.—*You are rather indifferent even toward you own children, if you have any, and cold toward all others; can bear little from them, and are not calculated to win their affections. You care nothing for pets.*
>
> SMALL.—*You are inclined to be cold and indifferent toward your own children, and to manifest a positive dislike for all others.* (pp. 160–161)

If you don't see why there should be a relationship between the shape of your skull and your capacity for parental love, you'll be happy to know that phrenology has been thoroughly discredited. However, the impulse behind phrenology is alive and well: Psychologists seek simple but powerful ways to *categorize* people; they want those categorizations to allow them to make *predictions* about how those people will respond and behave in a wide variety of situations. These are the essential goals of theories of *personality*—to specify the differences among

What unexpected consequences may follow from individual differences in personality?

(© The New Yorker Collection 1946 Charles Addams from cartoonbank.com. All Rights Reserved.)

people that allow predictions to be made about their courses through life.

Because of your abundant life experiences, you probably already have strong intuitions about how personality works. What is *your* personality theory? Think of someone you really trust. Now think of someone you know personally who is a role model for you. Imagine the qualities of a person with whom you would like to spend the rest of your life and then of someone you can't stand to be around at all. In each case, what springs to mind immediately are personal attributes, such as honesty, reliability, generosity, aggressiveness, moodiness, or pessimism. Even as a child, you probably developed and put to use your own system for appraising personality. You tried to determine who in a new class would be friend or foe; you worked out techniques for dealing with your parents or teachers based on the way you read their personalities.

Psychologists define personality in many different ways, but common to all of the ways are two basic concepts: *uniqueness* and *characteristic patterns of behavior*. We will define **personality** as the complex set of unique psychological qualities that influence an individual's characteristic patterns of behavior across different situations and over time. Theories of personality are hypothetical statements about the structure and functioning of individual personalities. They help to achieve two

Personality The unique psychological qualities of an individual that influence a variety of characteristic behavior patterns (both overt and covert) across different situations and over time.

of the major goals of psychology: (1) *understanding* the structure, origins, and correlates of personality; and (2) *predicting* behavior and life events based on what we know about personality. Different theories make different predictions about the way people will respond and adapt to certain conditions.

Before we examine some of the major theoretical approaches, we should ask why there are so many different (often competing) theories. Theorists differ in their approaches to personality by varying their starting points and sources of data and by trying to explain different types of phenomena. Some are interested in the structure of individual personality and others in how that personality developed and will continue to grow. Some are interested in what people do, either in terms of specific behaviors or important life events, while others study how people feel about their lives. Finally, some theories try to explain the personalities of people with psychological problems, while others focus on healthy individuals. Thus, each theory can teach something about personality, and together they can teach much about human nature.

Our goal for this chapter will be to provide you with a framework for understanding your everyday experience of personality. However, before we begin, consider this series of questions: If psychologists studied *you*, what portrait of your personality would they draw? What early experiences might they identify as contributing to the way you now act and think? What conditions in your current life exert strong influences on your thoughts and behaviors? What makes you different from other individuals who are functioning in many of the same situations as you? This chapter should help you formulate more specific answers to these questions.

In the next several sections, we consider a series of theoretical approaches to understanding personality: type and trait, psychodynamic, humanistic, social-learning, cognitive, and analyses of the self. We conclude the chapter by describing some of the assessment techniques psychologists use to understand and describe personality.

Type and Trait Personality Theories

Two of the oldest approaches to describing personality involve classifying people into a limited number of *distinct types* and scaling the degree to which they can be described by *different traits*. There seems to be a natural tendency for people to place their own and others' behavior into different categories. Let's examine the formal theories psychologists have developed to capture these differences in types and traits.

Hippocrates theorized that the body contained four essentia fluids, or humors, each associated with a particular temperament. Clockwise: a melancholy patient suffers from an excess of black bile; blood impassions a sanguine lutenist to play; a maiden, dominated by phlegm, is slow to respond to her lover; choler, too much yellow bile, makes an angry master. Do you believe Hippocrates's personality types apply to the people you know?

Categorizing by Types

We are always categorizing people according to distinguishing features. These include college class, academic major, sex, and race. Some personality theorists also group people into distinct, nonoverlapping categories that are called **personality types**. Personality types are all-or-none phenomena, not matters of degree: If a person is assigned to one type, he or she could not belong to any other type within that system. Many people like to use personality types in everyday life because they help simplify the complex process of understanding other people.

One of the earliest type theories was proposed in the fifth century B.C. by **Hippocrates,** the Greek physician who gave medicine the Hippocratic oath. He theorized that the body contained four basic fluids, or *humors,* each associated with a particular *temperament,* a pattern of emotions and behaviors. An individual's personality depended on which humor was predominant in his or her body. Hippocrates paired body humors with personality temperaments according to the following scheme:

- *Blood.* Sanguine temperament: cheerful and active
- *Phlegm.* Phlegmatic temperament: apathetic and sluggish
- *Black bile.* Melancholy temperament: sad and brooding
- *Yellow bile.* Choleric temperament: irritable and excitable

The theory proposed by Hippocrates was believed for centuries, up through the Middle Ages, although it has not held up to modern scrutiny. (We will, however, see a modern echo of Hippocrates's temperaments in Hans Eysenck's trait theory, which we present on p. 435.)

In modern times, **William Sheldon** (1942) originated a type theory that related physique to temperament, a theory that is still touted and reflected in popular media today. He assigned people to three categories based on their body builds: *endomorphic* (fat, soft, round), *mesomorphic* (muscular, rectangular, strong), or *ectomorphic* (thin, long, fragile). Sheldon believed that endomorphs are relaxed, fond of eating, and sociable. Mesomorphs are physical people, filled with energy, courage, and assertive tendencies. Ectomorphs are brainy, artistic, and introverted; they would think about life, rather than consuming it or acting on it. For a period of time, Sheldon's theory was sufficiently influential that nude "posture" photographs were taken of thousands of students at U.S. colleges like Yale and Wellesley to allow researchers to study the relationships between body type and life factors. However, like Hippocrates's much earlier theory, Sheldon's notion of body types has proven to be of very little value in predicting an individual's behavior (Tyler, 1965).

More recently, **Frank Sulloway** (1996) has proposed a contemporary type theory based on *birth order.* Are you the *firstborn* child (or *only* child) in your family, or are you a *laterborn* child? Because you can take on only one of these birth positions, Sulloway's theory fits the criteria for being a type theory. (For people with unusual family constellations—for example, a very large age gap between two children—Sulloway still provides ways of categorizing individuals.) Sulloway makes birth-order predictions based on Darwin's idea that organisms diversify to find niches in which they will survive. According to Sulloway, firstborns have a ready-made niche: They immediately command their parents' love and attention; they seek to maintain that initial attachment by identifying and complying with their parents. By contrast, laterborn children need to find a different niche—one in which they don't so clearly follow their parents' example. As a consequence, Sulloway characterizes laterborns as "born to rebel": "they seek to excel in those domains where older siblings have not already established superiority. Laterborns typically cultivate openness to experience—a useful strategy for anyone who wishes to find a novel and successful niche in life" (p. 353). To test the prediction that laterborns embrace innovation whereas firstborns prefer the status quo, Sulloway examined scientific, historical, and cultural revolutions and determined the birth position of large numbers of historical

Personality types Distinct patterns of personality characteristics used to assign people to categories; qualitative differences, rather than differences in degree, used to discriminate among people.

FIGURE 14.1

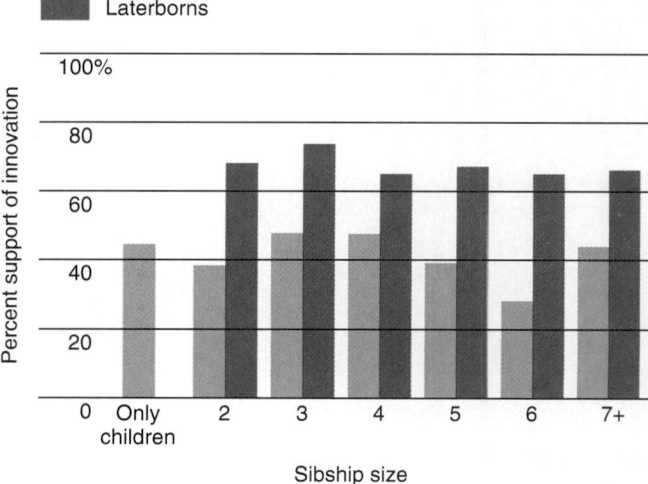

Birth Position and Support for Scientific Innovation

Frank Sulloway examined 23 innovative scientific theories and determined the birth positions of 1,218 scientists who had adopted or rejected those theories. For every family size, laterborns were more likely to adopt the innovative theory than were firstborns.

and contemporary figures who had supported or opposed those revolutions. **Figure 14.1** presents data on the extent to which firstborn and laterborn scientists supported 23 liberal theories in science. As you can see, for all of the family sizes, laterborns were more likely to support the innovative theory than were firstborns. Do you have brothers or sisters? Can you find this pattern in your own family?

Do you know people whom you would label as particular "types"? Does the "type" include all there is to know about the person? Type theories often don't seem to capture more subtle aspects of people's personalities. Let's turn

> **Traits** Enduring personal qualities or attributes that influence behavior across situations.

now to theories that allow more flexibility by differentiating individuals according to traits rather than types.

Describing with Traits

Type theories presume that there are separate, discontinuous categories into which people fit, such as firstborn or laterborn. By contrast, trait theories propose *continuous dimensions,* such as intelligence or friendliness. **Traits** are enduring qualities or attributes that predispose individuals to behave consistently across situations. For example, you may demonstrate honesty on one day by returning a lost wallet and on another day by not cheating on a test. Some trait theorists think of traits as *predispositions* that cause behavior, but more conservative theorists use

In the absence of personality test results, traits can be inferred from observed behavior. For example, Martin Luther King Jr. (top) would be thought to have the cardinal trait of peacefully resisting injustice; honesty would be one of Abraham Lincoln's central traits; and Madonna's predilection for changeable styles would be a secondary trait. What do you think may be your cardinal, central, and secondary traits?

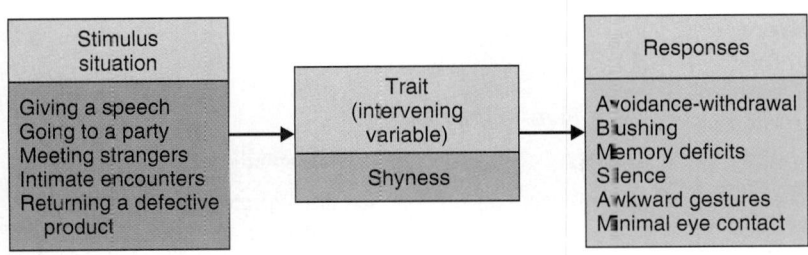

FIGURE 14.2

Shyness as a Trait

Traits may act as intervening variables, relating sets of stimuli and responses that might seem, at first glance, to have little to do with each other

traits only as *descriptive dimensions* that simply summarize patterns of observed behavior. Let's examine prominent trait theories.

ALLPORT'S TRAIT APPROACH

Gordon Allport (1937, 1961, 1966) viewed traits as the building blocks of personality and the source of individuality. According to Allport, traits produce coherence in behavior because they connect and unify a person's reactions to a variety of stimuli. Traits may act as *intervening variables*, relating sets of stimuli and responses that might seem, at first glance, to have little to do with each other (see **Figure 14.2**).

Allport identified three kinds of traits: cardinal traits, central traits, and secondary traits. *Cardinal traits* are traits around which a person organizes his or her life. For Mother Teresa, a cardinal trait might have been self-sacrifice for the good of others. However, not all people develop such overarching cardinal traits. Instead, *central traits* are traits that represent major characteristics of a person, such as honesty or optimism. *Secondary traits* are specific, personal features that help predict an individual's behavior but are less useful for understanding an individual's personality. Food or dress preferences are examples of secondary traits. Allport was interested in discovering the unique combination of these three types of traits that make each person a singular entity and championed the use of case studies to examine these unique traits.

Allport saw *personality structures*, rather than *environmental conditions*, as the critical determiners of individual behavior. "The same fire that melts the butter hardens the egg" was a phrase he used to show that the same stimuli can have different effects on different individuals. Many contemporary trait theories have followed in Allport's tradition.

IDENTIFYING UNIVERSAL TRAIT DIMENSIONS

In 1936, a dictionary search by Gordon Allport and his colleague H. S. Odbert found over 18,000 adjectives in the English language to describe individual differences. Researchers since that time have attempted to identify the fundamental dimensions that underlie that enormous trait vocabulary. They have tried to determine how many dimensions exist and which ones will allow psychologists to give a useful, universal characterization of all individuals.

Raymond Cattell (1979) used Allport and Odbert's list of adjectives as a starting point in his quest to un-

cover the appropriate small set of basic trait dimensions. His research led him to propose that 16 factors underlie human personality. Cattell called these 16 factors *source traits* because he believed that they provide the underlying source for the surface behaviors that we think of as personality. Cattell's 16 factors included important behavioral oppositions such as *reserved* versus *outgoing*, *trusting* versus *suspicious*, and *relaxed* versus *tense*. Even so, contemporary trait theorists argue that even fewer dimensions than 16 capture the most important distinctions among people's personalities.

Hans Eysenck (1973, 1990) derived just three broad dimensions from personality test data: *extraversion* (internally versus externally oriented), *neuroticism* (emotionally stable versus emotionally unstable), and *psychoticism* (kind and considerate versus aggressive and antisocial). As shown in **Figure 14.3**, Eysenck combined the two

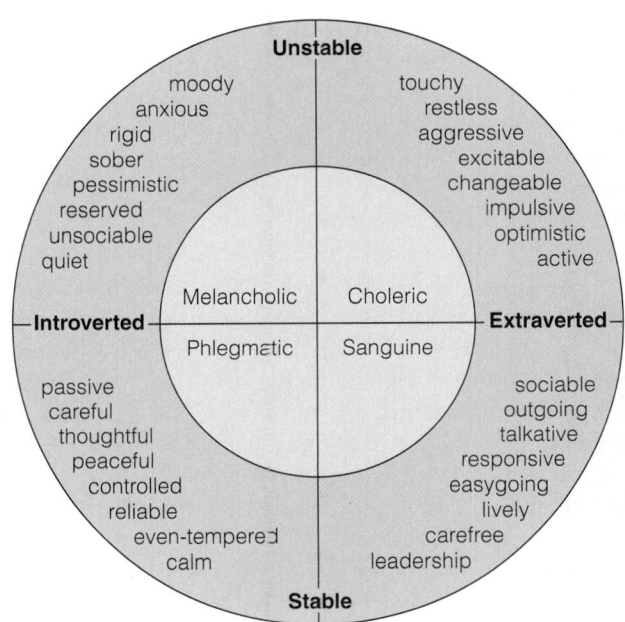

FIGURE 14.3

The Four Quadrants of Eysenck's Personality Circle

The two dimensions of extraversion and neuroticism yield a circular display. Eysenck related each quadrant of the display to one of the four personality types defined by Hippocrates. Eysenck's trait theory, however, allows for individual variation within these categories.

dimensions of extraversion and neuroticism to form a circular display. He suggested that each quadrant of the display represents one of the four personality types identified by Hippocrates. Eysenck's trait theory, however, allows for individual variation within these categories. Individuals can fall anywhere around the circle, ranging from very introverted to very extraverted and from very unstable (neurotic) to very stable. The traits listed around the circle describe people with combinations of these two dimensions. For example, a person who is very extraverted and somewhat unstable is likely to be impulsive.

FIVE-FACTOR MODEL

Research evidence supports many aspects of Eysenck's theory. However, in recent years, a consensus has emerged that *five factors*, which overlap imperfectly with Eysenck's three dimensions, best characterize personality structure (Wiggins & Pincus, 1992). Although these five factors are not accepted by all personality researchers (Block, 1995; Eysenck, 1992; Pervin, 1994), they now serve as a touchstone for most discussions of trait structures.

The movement toward the *five-factor model* represented attempts to find structure among the large list of traits that Allport and Odbert (1936) had extracted from the dictionary. The traits were boiled down into about 200 synonym clusters that were used to form *bipolar* trait dimensions: dimensions that have a high pole and a low pole, such as *responsible* versus *irresponsible*. Next, people were asked to rate themselves and others on the bipolar dimensions, and the ratings were subjected to statistical procedures to determine how the synonym clusters were interrelated. Using this method, several independent research teams came to the same conclusion: that there are only *five basic dimensions* underlying the traits people use to describe themselves and others (Norman, 1963, 1967; Tupes & Christal, 1961).

The five dimensions are very broad, because each brings into one large category many traits that have unique connotations but a common theme. These five dimensions of personality are now called the **five-factor model**, or, more informally, the *Big Five* (McCrae & Costa, 1999). The five factors are summarized in **Table 14.1**. You'll notice again that each dimension is bipolar—terms that are similar in meaning to the name of the dimension describe the high pole, and terms that are opposite in meaning describe the low pole.

The dimensions in the five-factor model were derived from ratings collected in the 1960s, using several different sets of adjectives and many different participant samples and rating tasks. Since then, very similar dimensions have also been found in personality questionnaires, inter-

TABLE 14.1

The Five-Factor Model

Factor	Bipolar Definitions
Extraversion	Talkative, energetic, and assertive versus quiet, reserved, and shy
Agreeableness	Sympathetic, kind, and affectionate versus cold, quarrelsome, and cruel
Conscientiousness	Organized, responsible, and cautious versus careless, frivolous, and irresponsible
Neuroticism	Stable, calm, and contented versus anxious, unstable, and temperamental
Openness to experience	Creative, intellectual, and open-minded versus simple, shallow, and unintelligent

viewer checklists, and other data (Costa & McCrae, 1992a; Digman, 1990; Wiggins & Pincus, 1992). To demonstrate the universality of the five-factor model, researchers have broadened their studies beyond the English language: The five-factor structure has been replicated in a number of languages including German, Portuguese, Hebrew, Chinese, Korean, and Japanese (McCrae & Costa, 1997). The five factors are not meant to replace the many specific trait terms that carry their own nuances and shades of meaning. Rather, they outline a taxonomy—a classification system—that allows you to give a description of all the people you know in ways that captures the important dimensions on which they differ.

It is important to emphasize that the five-factor model is largely descriptive. The factors emerged from statistical analyses of clusters of trait terms, rather than from a theory that said, "These are the factors that must exist" (Ozer & Reise, 1994). Supporters of the five-factor model have begun to address this lack of theoretical grounding by, for example, trying to relate the five dimensions to consistent types of interactions that people had with each other and with the external world over the course of human evolution (Costa & McCrae, 1992a; McCrae et al., 2000). An evolutionary basis would help explain the universality of the five factors across diverse cultures. If this explanation is correct, we might also expect that, like other aspects of human experience that have been shaped by evolution, traits can be passed from one generation to the next. We turn now to that claim.

Traits and Heritability

You've probably heard people say things such as "Jim's artistic, like his mother" or "Mary's as stubborn as her grandfather." Or maybe you've felt frustrated because the characteristics that you find irritating in your siblings are

Five-factor model A comprehensive descriptive personality system that maps out the relationships among common traits, theoretical concepts, and personality scales; informally called the Big Five.

Research with identical twins demonstrates the heritability of personality traits. Are there personality traits you believe run in your family?

those you would like to change in yourself. Let's look at the evidence that supports the heritability of personality traits.

Recall that *behavioral genetics* is the study of the degree to which personality traits and behavior patterns are inherited. To determine the effect of genetics on personality, researchers study the personality traits of family members who share different proportions of genes and who have grown up in the same or different households. For example, if a personality characteristic such as *sociability* is passed on genetically, then sociability should correlate more highly between identical, *monozygotic* twins (who share 100 percent of their genes) than between fraternal, *dizygotic* twins or other siblings (who share, on average, 50 percent of their genes).

Heritability studies show that almost all personality traits are influenced by genetic factors (Loehlin et al., 1998). The findings are the same with many different measurement techniques, whether they measure broad traits, such as extraversion and neuroticism, or specific traits, such as self-control or sociability. Let's consider one sample study.

HOW WE KNOW

THE HERITABILITY OF THE FIVE FACTORS

We just introduced you to the five-factor model of personality. Researchers have turned their attention to the question of whether there is a genetic basis for the factors specified by this model. In one study, a team of researchers from Germany and Poland obtained personality measures for 660 monozygotic twin pairs and 304 dizygotic twin pairs. Data were provided both by self-report (that is, the twins filled out personality inventories of the type we cover

later in the chapter) and by peer report (that is, friends and family members made ratings on one or the other twin). Past research has generally only used self-report data. Critics of heritability research have worried that monozygotic and dizygotic twins may have biases in the way they compare themselves to their twins versus other individuals. The inclusion of peer report eliminates the possibility that high heritability estimates are merely consequences of twins' biases in reporting on themselves. In fact, in all cases, the personalities of monozygotic twins were rated as more similar than those of dizygotic twins. The self-ratings, for example, revealed intertwin correlations of .52 (monzygotic) versus .23 (dizygotic). Using both the self and peer data, these researchers demonstrated substantial heritability estimates for each of the factors defined by the five-factor model (Riemann et al., 1997).

Look back to Table 14.1. Which poles of the five factors seem to apply best to you? Can you find similarities between you and your parents?

Researchers continue to try to improve on the design of heritability studies. For example, because twins and other siblings are usually raised together they share a family environment—which might cause their personalities to be correlated. Thus, *adoption studies* are used to examine the degree to which children's traits correlate with their biological parents' traits, as compared to correlations with their adoptive parents' traits. Adoption studies also reveal sizable genetic contributions to personality traits (Bouchard, 1994).

Do Traits Predict Behaviors?

Suppose we ask you to choose some trait terms that you believe apply particularly well to yourself. You might tell us, for example, that you are *very friendly*. What do we now know? If personality theories allow us to make predictions about behaviors, what can we predict from knowing that you rate yourself as being very friendly? How can we determine the validity of your belief? Let's explore this question.

One idea you might have is that knowing that a person can be characterized by a particular trait would enable you to predict his or her behavior across different *situations*. Thus, we would expect you to produce friendly behaviors in all situations. However, in the 1920s, several researchers who set out to observe trait-related behaviors in different situations were surprised to find little evidence that behavior was consistent across situations. For example, two behaviors presumably related to the trait of honesty—lying and cheating on a test—were only weakly correlated among schoolchildren

(Hartshorne & May, 1928). Similar results were found by other researchers who examined the *cross-situational consistency* for other traits such as introversion or punctuality (Dudycha, 1936; Newcomb, 1929).

If trait-related behaviors are not cross-situationally consistent—that is, if people's behavior changes in different situations—why do you perceive your own and others' personalities to be relatively stable? Even more puzzling, the personality ratings of observers who know an individual from one situation correlate with the ratings of observers who know the individual from another situation. The observation that personality ratings across time and among different observers *are consistent,* while behavior ratings of a person across situations *are not consistent,* came to be called the **consistency paradox** (Mischel, 1968).

The identification of the consistency paradox led to a great deal of research (for a review, see Cervone & Shoda, 1999). Over time, the consensus emerged that the appearance of behavioral inconsistency arose, in large part, because situations had been categorized in the wrong way: The paradox fades away once theorists can provide an appropriate account of the *psychological features* of situations (Mischel & Shoda, 1995, 1999). Suppose, for example, you want to try to assess behavioral consistency by determining if a friend acts in much the same way at every party she attends. You're likely to discover that her behavior varies widely if your level of analysis is just "parties." What you need to determine is what psychologically relevant features separate parties into different categories. Perhaps your friend feels uncomfortable in situations in which she is expected to disclose personal information to strangers. As a consequence, she might seem very unfriendly at some parties (where she is expected to disclose personal information) but quite friendly at others (where she is not). Meanwhile, other situations that require her to be disclosing—such as job interviews—might also bring out negative behaviors. Thus, we find consistency in the way that features of situations elicit people's distinctive responses.

Let's consider a study that examined the psychological features of a variety of situations. The study considered activities children encounter in summer camp.

HOW WE KNOW

CONSISTENCY IN VERBAL AGGRESSION This study was carried out on a group of 6- to 12-year-old children who were referred to a summer camp for children with social adjustment problems. The researchers wished to see how accurately they could predict the situations in which individual children would produce aggressive behavior. To make these predictions, the researchers gathered data on the significant features of different camp situations with respect to the types of demands they put on the child: *cognitive* ("requires the ability to think logically"), *social* ("requires the ability to speak in front of others"), *self-regulatory* ("requires the ability to tolerate frustration"), *physical strength* ("requires physical strength, stamina"), and *motor coordination* ("requires the ability to coordinate arm and body movements"). Swimming, for example, demands physical strength and coordination but relatively little self-regulation. Fishing, by contrast, requires a high level of self-regulation alongside motor coordination.

The children were observed across the full range of camp activities and their incidents of verbal aggression—for example, threatening and teasing—were recorded for each situation. If behavioral consistency depends on the similarities in features of situations, then the higher the level of similarity between two situations the more likely it should be that children will show the same extent of verbal aggression. This prediction was confirmed (Shoda et al., 1993a).

Note the lengths to which the researchers went to derive the relevant features of the situations. This taxonomy allows them to make claims such as, "Sonja has trouble coping with situations that make high cognitive demands—and that's why she's going to be verbally aggressive in such situations." We find consistency when we have the right description of the person ("she can't cope with cognitive demands") and the situation ("this situation creates a cognitive demand").

The consistency debate forced trait theorists to define traits in a more precise way—to outline precisely what classes of behavior should be related to personality traits and in what situations. A trait may be expressed through different behaviors in different situations and at different ages, but, as long as the theory of a trait predicts the way in which psychological features of situations give rise to behavioral expressions, the pattern is coherent. Thus, if you describe yourself as a *very friendly* person, that doesn't mean that we should expect you to perform "friendly" behaviors every moment of your life. Instead, we would expect your friendliness to differ across situa-

Consistency paradox The observation that personality ratings across time and among different observers are consistent, while behavior ratings across situations are not consistent.

Shyness An individual's discomfort and/or inhibition in interpersonal situations that interferes with pursuing interpersonal or professional goals.

WHY ARE SOME PEOPLE SHY?

Recent surveys reveal that more than 50 percent of college students consider themselves to be "currently shy" individuals (Carducci & Zimbardo, 1995). Most of them say that shyness is an undesirable condition that has more negative personal and social consequences than positive effects. Another group of students say that they are "situationally shy," and not "dispositionally shy" like that majority of students. They feel "as if" they were shy in certain situations that are novel, awkward, or socially pressured, such as blind dates, singles bars, being put on the spot to perform in public without preparation. Researchers investigating shyness in adults were surprised to discover that it is the "not shy" person who is the rare, unusual breed in the United States and in every other country surveyed (Zimbardo, 1991).

Shyness may be defined as discomfort and/or inhibition in interpersonal situations that interferes with pursuing one's interpersonal or professional goals. Shyness may be chronic and dispositional, serving as a personality trait that is central in one's self-definition. It can be the mild reticence and social awkwardness many of us feel in new situations, but it can escalate into the extreme of a totally inhibiting fear of people (we will discuss this *social phobia* in Chapter 15). Many shy people are also *introverted;* they have a personal preference for solitary, nonsocial activities and settings. Others are "shy extraverts," publicly outgoing yet privately shy, preferring to engage in social activities, having the social skills to do so effectively, yet doubting that others will really like or respect them (Pilkonis & Zimbardo, 1979).

So why are some people shy, while others are not? One explanation may be *nature.* Research evidence suggests that about 10 percent of infants

are "born shy" (Kagan, 1994). From birth, these children are unusually cautious and reserved when they interact with unfamiliar people or situations. A complementary explanation focuses on *nurture.* As children, some individuals are ridiculed, laughed at, or singled out for public shame for some mistake; others grow up in families that make "being loved" contingent on competitive success in appearance and performance. A third explanation focuses on culture.

Shyness is highest in some Asian countries, notably Japan and Taiwan, and lowest in Israel, among nine countries studied (Zimbardo, 1991). This difference is attributed in part to cultural emphases on shame for social failure and obedience to authority in these Asian countries versus encouragement for taking risks and externalizing blame in Israel (Pines & Zimbardo, 1978). A fourth explanation accounts, in part, for a recent rise in reported prevalence of shyness in the United States: Young people are intensively involved with electronic technology. Spending long hours, typically alone, watching TV, playing video games, surfing the Web, and doing e-mail is socially isolating and reduces daily face-to-face contact. Heavy use of the Internet has the potential to make people feel lonely, isolated, and more shy (Kraut et al., 1998; Nie & Ebring, 2000).

As shyness gets more extreme, it intrudes on ever more aspects of one's life to minimize social pleasures and maximize social discomfort and isolation. There are some simple concepts and tactics we suggest for shy students to think about and try out (see Zimbardo, 1991):

- Realize that you are not alone in your shyness; every other person you see is more like you than different from you in his or her shyness.

- Shyness can be modified, even when there is a genetic component, but it takes dedication and a resolve to change, as with any long-standing habit you want to break.

- Practice smiling and making eye contact with most people you meet.

- Talk up; speak in a loud, clear voice, especially when giving your name or asking for information.

- Be the first to ask a question or make a comment in a new social situation. Be prepared with something interesting to say, and say it first; everyone appreciates an "ice breaker," and then no one will think you are shy.

- Never put yourself down. Instead, think about what you can do next time to gain the outcome you want.

- Focus on making others feel comfortable, especially searching out those other shy people. Doing so lowers your self-consciousness.

- Practice meditation, relaxation, and mental visualization of the ideal scenario before going into a situation that usually triggers your shyness.

If you are shy, we hope you will adopt these suggestions. Other students who have followed them have been released from the prison of shyness into a life filled with newfound liberties. This is one sure benefit of putting some simple psychology to work in your life. If you are not shy, then you can help friends and family who are shy by encouraging them to change their lifestyles in these ways (Henderson & Zimbardo, 1998).

TYPE AND TRAIT PERSONALITY THEORIES

439

Assuming you could afford either one, which of these vacations would you prefer? What might that tell us about the ways in which personality traits interact with features of situations?

tions according to the psychological features of those situations. You may, for example, be very warm with close acquaintances but more formal toward your professors.

Evaluation of Type and Trait Theories

We have seen that type and trait theories allow researchers to give concise descriptions of different people's personalities. These theories have been criticized, however, because they do not generally explain how behavior is generated or how personality develops; they only identify and describe characteristics that are correlated with behavior. Although contemporary trait theorists have begun to address these concerns, trait theories typically portray a *static,* or at least stabilized, view of *personality structure* as it currently exists. By contrast, psychodynamic theories of personality, to which we next turn, emphasize conflicting forces within the individual that lead to change and development.

SUMMING UP

Type theories sort people into nonoverlapping categories (such as firstborns versus laterborns) to make predictions about their personalities. By contrast, trait theories conceptualize personality along continuous dimensions. Contemporary theorists suggest that there are five universal factors that capture the major dimensions of personality cross-culturally: extraversion, agreeableness, conscientiousness, neuroticism, and openness to experience. Research in behavioral genetics suggests that personality traits are highly heritable. Theorists now recognize that the search for consistency in behavior requires an accurate description both of the person and relevant psychological features of situations.

Psychodynamic Theories

Common to all **psychodynamic personality theories** is the assumption that powerful inner forces shape personality and motivate behavior. **Sigmund Freud,** the originator of psychodynamic theories, was characterized by his biographer Ernest Jones as "the Darwin of the mind" (1953). Freud's theory of personality boldly attempts to explain the origins and course of personality development, the nature of mind, aspects of abnormal personality, and the way personality can be changed by therapy. Here we will focus only on normal personality; Freud's views on psychopathology and treatment will be treated in Chapters 15 and 16. After we explore Freud, we will describe some criticisms and reworkings of his theories.

Freudian Psychoanalysis

According to psychoanalytic theory, at the core of personality are events within a person's mind *(intrapsychic events)* that motivate behavior. Often, people are aware of these motivations; however, some motivation also oper-

Psychodynamic personality theories Theories of personality that share the assumption that personality is shaped by and behavior is motivated by powerful inner forces.

Why did Freud believe that eating is motivated not only by the self-preservation drive to satisfy hunger but also by the "erotic" drive to seek oral gratification?

ates at an unconscious level. The *psychodynamic* nature of this approach comes from its emphasis on these inner wellsprings of behavior, as well as the clashes among these internal forces. For Freud, *all behavior was motivated.* No chance or accidental happenings cause behavior; all acts are determined by motives. Every human action has a cause and a purpose that can be discovered through analysis of thought associations, dreams, errors, and other behavioral clues to inner passions. The primary data for Freud's hypotheses about personality came from clinical observations and in-depth case studies of individual patients in therapy. He developed a theory of normal personality from his intense study of those with mental disorders. Let's look at some of the most important aspects of Freud's theory.

DRIVES AND PSYCHOSEXUAL DEVELOPMENT

Freud's medical training as a neurologist led him to postulate a common biological basis for the behavioral pat-

terns he observed in his patients. He ascribed the source of motivation for human actions to *psychic energy* found within each individual. Each person was assumed to have inborn instincts or drives that were *tension systems* created by the organs of the body. These energy sources, when activated, could be expressed in many different ways.

Freud originally postulated two basic drives. One he saw as involved with *self-preservation* (meeting such needs as hunger and thirst). The other he called *Eros*, the driving force related to sexual urges and preservation of the species. Of the two drives, Freud was more interested in the sexual urges. Freud greatly expanded the notion of human sexual desires to include not only the urge for sexual union but all other attempts to seek pleasure or to make physical contact with others. He used the term **libido** to identify the source of energy for sexual urges—a psychic energy that drives us toward sensual pleasures of all types. Sexual urges demand immediate satisfaction, whether through direct actions or through indirect means such as fantasies and dreams.

According to Freud, Eros, as a broadly defined sexual drive, does not suddenly appear at puberty but operates from birth. Eros is evident, he argued, in the pleasure infants derive from physical stimulation of the genitals and other sensitive areas, or *erogenous zones*. Freud's five stages of *psychosexual development* are shown in **Table 14.2**. Freud believed that the physical source of sexual pleasure changed in this orderly progression. One of the major obstacles of psychosexual development, at least for boys, occurs in the phallic stage. Here, the 4- or 5-year-old child must overcome the *Oedipus complex.* Freud named this complex after the mythical figure Oedipus, who unwittingly killed his father and married his

Libido The psychic energy that drives individuals toward sensual pleasures of all types, especially sexual ones.

TABLE 14.2

Freud's Stages of Psychosexual Development

Stage	Age	Erogenous Zones	Major Developmental Task (Potential Source of Conflict)	Some Adult Characteristics of Children Who Have Been Fixated at This Stage
Oral	0–1	Mouth, lips, tongue	Weaning	Oral behavior, such as smoking, overeating; passivity and gullibility
Anal	2–3	Anus	Toilet training	Orderliness, parsimoniousness, obstinacy, or the opposite
Phallic	4–5	Genitals	Oedipus complex	Vanity, recklessness, or the opposite
Latency	6–12	No specific area	Development of defense mechanisms	None: fixation does not normally occur at this stage
Genital	13–18	Genitals	Mature sexual intimacy	Adults who have successfully integrated earlier stages should emerge with a sincere interest in others and a mature sexuality

mother. Freud believed that every young boy has an innate impulse to view his father as a sexual rival for his mother's attentions. Because the young boy cannot displace his father, the Oedipus complex is generally resolved when the boy comes to *identify* with his father's power. (Freud was inconsistent with respect to his theoretical account of the experiences of young girls.)

According to Freud, either too much gratification or too much frustration at one of the early stages of psychosexual development leads to **fixation**, an inability to progress normally to the next stage of development. As shown in Table 14.2, fixation at different stages can produce a variety of adult characteristics. The concept of fixation explains why Freud put such emphasis on early experiences in the continuity of personality. He believed that experiences in the early stages of psychosexual development had a profound impact on personality formation and adult behavior patterns.

PSYCHIC DETERMINISM

The concept of fixation gives us a first look at Freud's belief that early conflicts help *determine* later behaviors. **Psychic determinism** is the assumption that all mental and behavioral reactions (symptoms) are determined by earlier experiences. Freud believed that symptoms were not arbitrary. Rather, symptoms were related in a meaningful way to significant life events.

Freud's belief in psychic determinism led him to emphasize the **unconscious**—the repository of information that is unavailable to conscious awareness. Other writers had discussed this construct, but Freud put the concept of the unconscious determinants of human thought, feeling, and action at center stage in the human drama. According to Freud, behavior can be motivated by drives of which a person is not aware. You may act without knowing why or without direct access to the true cause of your actions. There is a *manifest* content to your behavior—what you say, do, and perceive—of which you are fully aware, but there is also a concealed, *latent* content. The meaning of neurotic (anxiety-based) symptoms, dreams, and slips of the pen and tongue is found at the unconscious level of thinking and information processing. Many psychologists today consider this concept

Fixation A state in which a person remains attached to objects or activities more appropriate for an earlier stage of psychosexual development.

Psychic determinism The assumption that mental and behavioral reactions are determined by previous experiences.

Unconscious The domain of the psyche that stores repressed urges and primitive impulses.

Id The primitive, unconscious part of the personality that operates irrationally and acts on impulse to pursue pleasure.

Superego The aspect of personality that represents the internalization of society's values, standards, and morals.

of the unconscious to be Freud's most important contribution to the science of psychology. Much modern literature and drama, as well, explores the implications of unconscious processes for human behavior.

According to Freud, impulses within you that you find unacceptable still strive for expression. A *Freudian slip* occurs when an unconscious desire is betrayed by your speech or behavior. For example, one of your authors felt obligated to write a thank-you note although he hadn't much enjoyed the weekend he'd spent at a friend's home. He intended to write, "I'm glad we got to spend a chunk of time together." However, in a somewhat testy phone call, the friend informed him that he'd actually written "I'm glad we got to spend a *junk* of time together." Do you see how the substitution of *junk* for *chunk* could be the expression of an unconscious desire? The concept of unconscious motivation adds a new dimension to personality by allowing for greater complexity of mental functioning.

We've now reviewed some basic aspects of Freud's theory. Let's see how they contribute to the structure of personality.

THE STRUCTURE OF PERSONALITY

In Freud's theory, personality differences arise from the different ways in which people deal with their fundamental drives. To explain these differences, Freud pictured a continuing battle between two antagonistic parts of the personality—the *id* and the *superego*—moderated by a third aspect of the self, the *ego*. Although we will refer to these three aspects almost as if they are separate creatures, keep in mind that Freud believed them all to be just different mental *processes*. He did not, for example, identify specific brain locations for the id, ego, and superego.

The **id** is the storehouse of the fundamental drives. It operates irrationally, acting on impulse and pushing for expression and immediate gratification without considering whether what is desired is realistically possible, socially desirable, or morally acceptable. The id is governed by the *pleasure principle*, the unregulated search for gratification—especially sexual, physical, and emotional pleasures—to be experienced here and now without concern for consequences.

The **superego** is the storehouse of an individual's values, including moral attitudes learned from society. The superego corresponds roughly to the common notion of *conscience*. It develops as a child comes to accept as his or her own values the prohibitions of parents and other adults against socially undesirable actions. It is the inner voice of *oughts* and *should nots*. The superego also includes the *ego ideal*, an individual's view of the kind of person he or she should strive to become. Thus, the superego is often in conflict with the id. The id wants to do what feels good, while the superego insists on doing what is right.

The **ego** is the reality-based aspect of the self that arbitrates the conflict between id impulses and superego demands. The ego represents an individual's personal view of physical and social reality—his or her conscious beliefs about the causes and consequences of behavior. Part of the ego's job is to choose actions that will gratify id impulses without undesirable consequences. The ego is governed by the *reality principle,* which puts reasonable choices before pleasurable demands. Thus, the ego would block an impulse to cheat on an exam, because of concerns about the consequences of getting caught, and it would substitute the resolution to study harder the next time or solicit the teacher's sympathy. When the id and the superego are in conflict, the ego arranges a compromise that at least partially satisfies both. However, as id and superego pressures intensify, it becomes more difficult for the ego to work out optimal compromises.

REPRESSION AND EGO DEFENSE

Sometimes this compromise between id and superego involves "putting a lid on the id." Extreme desires are pushed out of conscious awareness into the privacy of the unconscious. **Repression** is the psychological process that protects an individual from experiencing extreme anxiety or guilt about impulses, ideas, or memories that are unacceptable and/or dangerous to express. The ego remains unaware of both the mental content that is censored and the process by which repression keeps information out of consciousness. Repression is considered to be the most basic of the various ways in which the ego defends against being overwhelmed by threatening impulses and ideas.

Ego defense mechanisms are mental strategies the ego uses to defend itself in the daily conflict between id

impulses that seek expression and the superego's demand to deny them (see **Table 14.3**). In psychoanalytic theory, these mechanisms are considered vital to an individual's psychological coping with powerful inner conflicts. By using them, a person is able to maintain a favorable self-image and to sustain an acceptable social image. For example, if a child has strong feelings of hatred toward his father—which, if acted out, would be dangerous—repression may take over. The hostile impulse is then no longer consciously pressing for satisfaction or even recognized as existing. However, although the impulse is not seen or heard, it is not gone; these feelings continue to play a role in personality functioning. For example, by developing a strong *identification* with his father, the child may increase his sense of self-worth and reduce his unconscious fear of being discovered as a hostile agent.

In Freudian theory, **anxiety** is an intense emotional response triggered when a repressed conflict is about

Ego The aspect of personality involved in self-preservation activities and in directing instinctual drives and urges into appropriate channels.

Repression The basic defense mechanism by which painful or guilt-producing thoughts, feelings, or memories are excluded from conscious awareness.

Ego defense mechanisms Mental strategies (conscious or unconscious) used by the ego to defend itself against conflicts experienced in the normal course of life.

Anxiety An intense emotional response caused by the preconscious recognition that a repressed conflict is about to emerge into consciousness.

TABLE 14.3

Major Ego Defense Mechanisms

Denial of reality	Protecting self from unpleasant reality by refusing to perceive it
Displacement	Discharging pent-up feelings, usually of hostility, on objects less dangerous than those that initially aroused the emotion
Fantasy	Gratifying frustrated desires in imaginary achievements ("daydreaming" is a common form)
Identification	Increasing feelings of worth by identifying self with another person or institution, often of illustrious standing
Isolation	Cutting off emotional charge from hurtful situations or separating incompatible attitudes into logic-tight compartments (holding conflicting attitudes that are never thought of simultaneously or in relation to each other); also called *compartmentalization*
Projection	Placing blame for one's difficulties on others or attributing one's own "forbidden" desires to others
Rationalization	Attempting to prove that one's behavior is "rational" and justifiable and thus worthy of the approval of self and others
Reaction formation	Preventing dangerous desires from being expressed by endorsing opposing attitudes and types of behavior and using them as "barriers"
Regression	Retreating to earlier developmental levels involving more childish responses and usually a lower level of aspiration
Repression	Pushing painful or dangerous thoughts out of consciousness, keeping them unconscious; this is considered to be *the most basic of the defense mechanisms*
Sublimation	Gratifying or working off frustrated sexual desires in substitutive nonsexual activities socially accepted by one's culture

to emerge into consciousness. Anxiety is a danger signal: Repression is not working! Red alert! More defenses needed! This is the time for a second line of defense, one or more additional ego defense mechanisms that will relieve the anxiety and send the distressing impulses back down into the unconscious. For example, a mother who does not like her son and does not want to care for him might use *reaction formation,* which transforms her unacceptable impulse into its opposite: "I don't hate my child" becomes "I love my child. See how I smother the dear little thing with love?" Such defenses serve the critical coping function of alleviating anxiety.

If defense mechanisms defend you against anxiety, why might they still have negative consequences for you? Useful as they are, ego mechanisms of defense are ultimately self-deceptive. When overused, they create more problems than they solve. It is psychologically unhealthy to spend a great deal of time and psychic energy deflecting, disguising, and rechanneling unacceptable urges in order to reduce anxiety. Doing so leaves little energy for productive living or satisfying human relationships. Some forms of mental illness result from excessive reliance on defense mechanisms to cope with anxiety, as we shall see in a later chapter on mental disorders.

■■■

Evaluation of Freudian Theory

We have devoted a great deal of space to outlining the essentials of psychoanalytic theory, because Freud's ideas have had an enormous impact on the way many psychologists think about normal and abnormal aspects of personality. However, there probably are more psychologists who criticize Freudian concepts than who support them. What is the basis of some of their criticisms?

First, psychoanalytic concepts are vague and not operationally defined; thus, much of the theory is difficult to evaluate scientifically. Because some of its central hypotheses cannot be disproved, even in principle, Freud's theory remains questionable. How can the concepts of libido, the structure of personality, and repression of infantile sexual impulses be studied in any direct fashion?

A second, related criticism is that Freudian theory is good history but bad science. It does not reliably *predict* what will occur; it is applied *retrospectively*—after events have occurred. Using psychoanalytic theory to understand personality typically involves historical reconstruction, not scientific construction of probable actions and predictable outcomes. In addition, by overemphasizing historical origins of current behavior, the theory directs attention away from the current stimuli that may be inducing and maintaining the behavior.

There are three other major criticisms of Freudian theory. First, it is a developmental theory, but it never included observations or studies of children. Second, it minimizes traumatic experiences (such as child abuse)

by reinterpreting memories of them as fantasies (based on a child's desire for sexual contact with a parent). Third, it has an *androcentric* (male-centered) bias because it uses a male model as the norm without trying to determine how females might be different.

Some aspects of Freud's theory, however, continue to gain acceptance as they are modified and improved through empirical scrutiny. For example, in Chapter 6, we saw that the concept of the unconscious is being systematically explored by contemporary researchers (Baars & McGovern, 1996; Westen, 1998). This research reveals that much of your day-to-day experience is shaped by processes outside of your awareness. These results support Freud's general concept but weaken the link between unconscious processes and psychopathology: Little of your unconscious knowledge will cause you anxiety or distress. Similarly, researchers have found evidence for some of the habits of mind Freud characterized as defense mechanisms (Hentschel et al., 1993; Singer, 1990).

HOW WE KNOW

INDIVIDUAL DIFFERENCES IN THE USE OF DEFENSE MECHANISMS We suggested earlier that individuals are most likely to use defense mechanisms when they are experiencing anxiety. Researchers have tested this hypothesis in a variety of ways. In one study, a researcher examined the extent to which a group of young adults (23-year-olds) had achieved a stable adult identity. (Recall from Chapter 11 that, according to Erik Erikson, forming an identity is a "crisis" individuals are meant to have resolved by the end of adolescence.) Some of the individuals in this group had achieved an identity, whereas others were still in a state of crisis. If this crisis breeds anxiety, we would expect the crisis group to show evidence for more frequent use of defense mechanisms. To test this hypothesis, the researcher asked the young adults to tell stories based on cards from the *Thematic Apperception Test* (see Chapter 12, p. 384). The stories were analyzed for evidence of defense mechanisms such as *denial* and *projection* (see Table 14.3). These analyses supported the hypothesis: Those individuals who had not yet achieved an identity were more likely to show evidence of the use of defense mechanisms (Cramer, 1997).

Some of the styles for coping with stress we described in Chapter 13 fall within the general category of defense mechanisms. You might recall, for example, that inhibiting the thoughts and feelings associated with personal traumas or guilty or shameful experiences can take a devastating toll on mental and physical health (Pennebaker, 1990; Petrie et al., 1998). These findings echo

Freud's beliefs that repressed psychic material can lead to psychological distress.

Freud's theory is the most complex, comprehensive, and compelling view of normal and abnormal personality functioning—even when its predictions prove wrong. However, like any other theory, Freud's theory is best treated as one that must be confirmed or disconfirmed element by element. Freud retains his influence on contemporary psychology because some of his ideas have been widely accepted. Others have been abandoned. Some of the earliest revisions of Freud's theory arose from within his own original circle of students. Let's see how they sought to amend Freud's views.

Post-Freudian Theories

Some of those who came after Freud retained his basic representation of personality as a battleground on which unconscious primal urges conflict with social values. However, many of Freud's intellectual descendants made major adjustments in the psychoanalytic view of personality. In general, these post-Freudians have made the following changes:

- They put greater emphasis on ego functions, including ego defenses, development of the self, conscious thought processes, and personal mastery.

- They view social variables (culture, family, and peers) as playing a greater role in shaping personality.

- They put less emphasis on the importance of general sexual urges, or libidinal energy.

- They have extended personality development beyond childhood to include the entire life span.

We review key features of the theories of Alfred Adler, Karen Horney, and Carl Jung.

Alfred Adler (1929) rejected the significance of Eros and the pleasure principle. Adler believed that as helpless, dependent, small children, people all experience feelings of *inferiority*. He argued that all lives are dominated by the search for ways to overcome those feelings. People compensate to achieve feelings of adequacy or, more often, overcompensate in an attempt to become *superior*. Personality is structured around this underlying striving; people develop lifestyles based on particular ways of overcoming their basic, pervasive feelings of inferiority. Personality conflict arises from incompatibility between external environmental pressures and internal strivings for adequacy, rather than from competing urges within the person.

Karen Horney was trained in the psychoanalytic school but broke from orthodox Freudian theory in several ways. She challenged Freud's phallocentric emphasis on the importance of the penis, hypothesizing that

Jung recognized creativity as a means to release images from both the personal and collective unconscious. Why did Jung believe in the two types of unconscious?

male envy of pregnancy, motherhood, breasts, and suckling is a dynamic force in the unconscious of boys and men. This "womb envy" leads men to devalue women and to overcompensate by unconscious impulses toward creative work. Horney also placed greater emphasis than did Freud on cultural factors and focused on present character structure rather than on infantile sexuality (Horney, 1937, 1939). Because Horney also had influence on the development of humanistic theories, we will return to her ideas in the next section.

Carl Jung (1959) greatly expanded the conception of the unconscious. For him, the unconscious was not limited to an individual's unique life experiences but was filled with fundamental psychological truths shared by the whole human race, a **collective unconscious.** The collective unconscious explains your intuitive understanding of primitive myths, art forms, and symbols, which are the universal archetypes of existence. An **archetype** is a primitive symbolic representation of a particular experience or object. Each archetype is associated with an instinctive tendency to feel and think about it or experience it in a special way. Jung postulated many archetypes from history and mythology: the sun god, the hero, the earth mother. *Animus* was the male archetype, while *anima* was

Collective unconscious The part of an individual's unconscious that is inherited, evolutionarily developed, and common to all members of the species.

Archetype A universal, inherited, primitive, and symbolic representation of a particular experience or object.

the female archetype, and all men and women experienced both archetypes in varying degrees. The archetype of the self is the *mandala,* or magic circle; it symbolizes striving for unity and wholeness (Jung, 1973).

Jung saw the healthy, integrated personality as balancing opposing forces, such as masculine aggressiveness and feminine sensitivity. This view of personality as a constellation of compensating internal forces in dynamic balance was called **analytic psychology.** In addition, Jung rejected the primary importance of libido, so central to Freud's own theory. Jung added two equally powerful unconscious instincts: the need to create and the need to become a coherent, whole individual. In the next section on humanist theories, we will see this second need paralleled in the concept of *self-actualization.*

SUMMING UP

Freud's psychoanalytic theory focuses on the idea that all behavior is motivated and that motivation often operates at an unconscious level. Libido provides an important source of motivation. As a person develops, sexual energy is expressed through a sequence of erogenous zones. After studying patients whose symptoms appeared to reflect earlier life events, Freud developed the theory of psychic determinism. According to Freud's theory, the moral guidance of the superego and the reality base of the ego attempt to moderate the id's relentless search for sexual, emotional, and physical pleasure. Ego defense mechanisms enable a person to cope with the anxiety produced by powerful inner conflicts. Although many aspects of Freud's theory have not withstood critical scrutiny, concepts like the unconscious and defense mechanisms have gained acceptance among many psychologists. Freud's followers, such as Adler, Horney, and Jung suggested a number of corrections and additions to his theory.

Humanistic Theories

Humanistic approaches to understanding personality are characterized by a concern for the integrity of an individual's personal and conscious experience and growth potential. The key feature of all humanistic

Analytic psychology A branch of psychology that views the person as a constellation of compensatory internal forces in a dynamic balance.

Self-actualization A concept in personality psychology referring to a person's constant striving to realize his or her potential and to develop inherent talents and capabilities.

Unconditional positive regard Complete love and acceptance of an individual by another person, such as a parent for a child, with no conditions attached.

theories is an emphasis on the drive toward self-actualization. **Self-actualization** is a constant striving to realize one's inherent potential—to fully develop one's capacities and talents. In this section, you will see how humanist theorists have developed this concept of self-actualization. You will learn, in addition, what additional features set humanistic theories apart from other types of personality theories.

Features of Humanistic Theories

Humanistic personality theorists, such as Carl Rogers, Abraham Maslow, and Karen Horney, believed that the motivation for behavior comes from a person's unique tendencies, both innate and learned, to develop and change in positive directions toward the goal of self-actualization. Recall from Chapter 12 that Maslow placed self-actualization toward the pinnacle of his hierarchy of needs. The striving toward self-fulfillment is a constructive, guiding force that moves each person toward generally positive behaviors and enhancement of the self.

The drive for self-actualization at times comes into conflict with the need for approval from the self and others, especially when the person feels that certain obligations or conditions must be met in order to gain approval. For example, **Carl Rogers** (1947, 1951, 1977) stressed the importance of **unconditional positive regard** in raising children. By this, he meant that children should feel they will always be loved and approved of, in spite of their mistakes and misbehavior—that they do not have to earn their parents' love. He recommended that, when a child misbehaves, parents should emphasize that it is the behavior they disapprove of, not the child. Unconditional positive regard is important in adulthood, too, because worrying about seeking approval interferes with self-actualization. As an adult, you need to give and receive unconditional positive regard from those to whom you are close. Most important, you need to feel unconditional positive *self-regard,* or acceptance of yourself, in spite of the weaknesses you might be trying to change.

Although not often given due credit, Karen Horney was another major theorist whose ideas created the foundation of humanistic psychology (Frager & Fadiman, 1998). Horney came to believe that people have a "real self" that requires favorable environmental circumstances to be actualized, such as an atmosphere of warmth, the goodwill of others, and parental love of the child as a "particular individual" (Horney, 1945, 1950). In the absence of those favorable nurturing conditions, the child develops a basic anxiety that stifles spontaneity of expression of real feelings and prevents effective relations with others. To cope with their basic anxiety, individuals resort to interpersonal or intrapsychic defenses. Interpersonal defenses produce movement toward others (through excessive compliance and self-effacing actions), against others (by aggressive, arrogant, or narcissistic solutions), and away from others (through detachment). Intrapsychic defenses operate to develop for some people an unrealistic idealized self-image that generates a "search for glory" to justify it and a pride system that operates on rigid rules of conduct to live up to a grandiose self-concept. Such people often live by the "tyranny of shoulds," self-imposed obligations, such as "I should be perfect, generous, attractive, brave," and so forth. Horney believed that the goal of a humanistic therapy was to help the individual achieve the joy of self-realization and promote the inherent constructive forces in human nature that support a striving for self-fulfillment.

An important aspect of each of the theories of Maslow, Rogers, and Horney is the emphasis on self-actualization or progress toward the real self. In addition, humanistic theories have been described as being holistic, dispositional, phenomenological, and existential. Let's see why.

Humanistic theories are *holistic* because they explain people's separate acts in terms of their entire personalities; people are not seen as the sum of discrete traits that each influence behavior in different ways. Maslow believed that people are intrinsically motivated toward the upper levels of the hierarchy of needs (discussed in Chapter 12), unless deficiencies at the lower levels weigh them down.

Humanistic theories are *dispositional* because they focus on the innate qualities within a person that exert a major influence over the direction behavior will take. Situational factors are seen as constraints and barriers (like the strings that tie down balloons). Once freed from negative situational conditions, the actualizing tendency should actively guide people to choose life-enhancing situations. However, humanistic theories are not dispositional in the same sense as trait theories or psychodynamic theories. In those views, personal dispositions are recurrent themes played out in behavior again and again. Humanistic dispositions are oriented specifically toward creativity and growth. Each time a humanistic disposition is exercised, the person changes a little, so that the disposition is never expressed in the same way twice. Over time, humanistic dispositions guide the individual toward self-actualization, the purest expression of these motives.

Humanistic theories are *phenomenological* because they emphasize an individual's frame of reference and subjective view of reality—not the objective perspective of an observer or of a therapist. Thus, a humanistic psychologist always strives to see each person's unique point of view. This view is also a present-oriented view; past influences are important only to the extent that they have brought the person to the present situation, and the future represents goals to achieve. Thus, unlike psychodynamic theories, humanistic theories do not see

people's present behaviors as unconsciously guided by past experiences.

Finally, humanistic theories have been described by theorists such as **Rollo May** (1975) as having an *existential perspective*. They focus on higher mental processes that interpret current experiences and enable individuals either to meet or be overwhelmed by the everyday challenges of existence. This existential perspective has its roots in both literary and philosophical traditions that give it a broad appeal to many contemporary scholars and clinicians (Schneider & May, 1995).

The upbeat humanist view of personality was a welcome treat for many psychologists who had been brought up on a diet of bitter-tasting Freudian medicine. Humanistic approaches focus directly on improvement—on making life more palatable—rather than dredging up painful memories that are sometimes better left repressed. The humanist perspective emphasizes each person's ability to realize his or her fullest potential.

Evaluation of Humanistic Theories

Freud's theory was often criticized for providing the too-pessimistic view that human nature develops out of conflicts, traumas, and anxieties. Humanistic theories arose to celebrate the healthy personality that strives for happiness and self-actualization. It is difficult to criticize theories that encourage and appreciate people, even for their faults. Even so, critics have complained that humanistic concepts are fuzzy and difficult to explore in research. They ask, "What exactly is self-actualization?" "Is it an inborn tendency, or is it created by the cultural context?" Humanistic theories also do not traditionally focus on the particular characteristics of individuals. They are more theories about human nature and about qualities all people share than about the individual personality or the basis of differences among people. Other psychologists note that, by emphasizing the role of the self as a source of experience and action, humanistic psychologists neglect the important environmental variables that also influence behavior.

Despite these limitations, a type of contemporary research can be traced in part to the humanist tradition that focuses directly on individual *narratives* or *life stories* (Baumeister, 1994; McAdams, 1996; Rosenwald & Ochberg, 1992). The tradition of using psychological theory to understand the details of an individual's life—to produce a *psychobiography*—can be traced back to Freud's analysis of Leonardo da Vinci (Freud, 1910/1957; see Elms, 1988, for a critique of Freud's work). **Psychobiography** is defined as "the systematic use of psychological

Psychobiography The use of psychological (especially personality) theory to describe and explain an individual's course through life.

(especially personality) theory to transform a life into a coherent and illuminating story" (McAdams, 1988, p. 2). Consider the great artist Pablo Picasso. Picasso suffered a series of traumas as a young child, including a serious earthquake and the death of a young sister. A psychobiography might attempt to explain some of Picasso's vast artistic creativity as the lifelong residue of his responses to these early traumas (Gardner, 1993).

When a well-known or historical figure is the subject of a psychobiography, a researcher may turn to published work, diaries, and letters as sources of relevant data. For more ordinary individuals, researchers may directly elicit narratives of life experiences. The request might be, for example, that the participant talk about a recent peak experience: "What were you thinking and feeling? What might this episode say about who you are, who you were, who you might be, or how you have developed over time?" (McAdams & de St. Aubin, 1992, p. 1010). The characteristic themes that emerge over series of narrative accounts support the holistic and phenomenological version of personality that was put forth by the early humanists: People construct their identities by weaving life stories out of the strands of narrative. Personal accounts provide a window on people's views of themselves and interpersonal relationships (Harvey et al., 1990; Shotter, 1984).

Humanistic theorists emphasized each individual's drive toward self-actualization. This group recognized, however, that people's progress toward this goal is determined, in part, by realities of their environments. We turn now to theories that directly examine how individuals' behaviors are shaped by their environments.

SUMMING UP

Humanistic theorists such as Maslow, Rogers, and Horney believed that behavior is motivated by a basic desire to develop and change in positive ways, moving toward self-actualization. Humanistic theories of personality are holistic, dispositional, phenomenological, and existential. Critics have suggested that some of the central concepts of humanistic theories are ill-defined and that the theories overlook environmental influences on people's lives. By focusing on the way in which individuals create coherent narratives out of the multiple strands of their lives, contemporary theorists carry on the humanist tradition.

Social-Learning and Cognitive Theories

Common to all the theories we have reviewed so far is an emphasis on hypothesized inner mechanisms—traits, instincts, impulses, tendencies toward self-actualization—that propel behavior and form the

basis of a functioning personality. What most of these theories lacked, however, was a solid link between personality and particular behaviors. Psychodynamic and humanistic theories, for example, provide accounts of the total personality but do not predict specific actions. Another tradition of personality theory emerged from a more direct focus on individual differences in behavior. Recall from Chapter 7 that much of a person's behavior can be predicted from contingencies in the environment. Psychologists with a *learning theory* orientation look to the environmental circumstances that control behavior. Personality is seen as the sum of the overt and covert responses that are reliably elicited by an individual's *reinforcement history*. Learning theory approaches suggest that people are different because they have had different histories of reinforcement.

Consider a behaviorist conception of personality developed by a team of Yale University psychologists headed by John Dollard and Neal Miller (1950). Dollard and Miller introduced concepts such as learned drives, inhibition of responses, and learned habit patterns. Similar to Freud, they emphasized the roles of the motivating force of tension and the reinforcing (pleasurable) consequences of *tension reduction*. Organisms act to reduce tension produced by unsatisfied drives. Behavior that successfully reduces such tensions is repeated, eventually becoming a learned habit that is reinforced by repeated tension reduction. Dollard and Miller also showed that one could learn by *social imitation*—by observing the behavior of others without having to actually perform the response. Suppose a youngster sees his older sister given candy when she races to meet their father as he arrives home; the younger brother may begin to carry out the same behavior. The idea of imitation broadened the ways psychologists understood that effective or de-

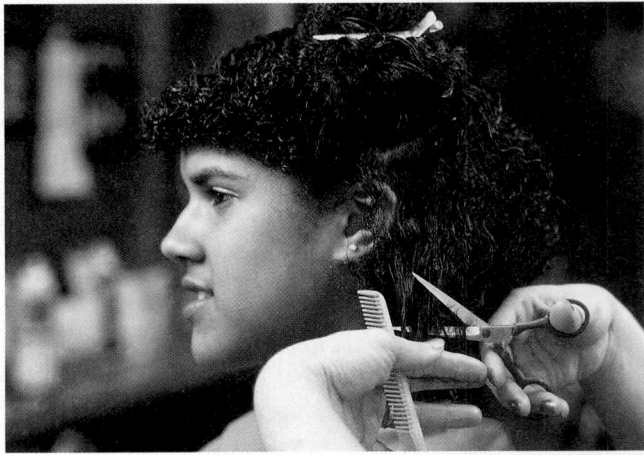

If your parents complimented you every time you got a new haircut, how might that affect your confidence about your appearance and grooming as an adult? Suppose they were regularly critical. What effect could that have?

structive habits are learned. Personality emerges as the sum of these learned habits.

Contemporary social-learning and cognitive theories often share Dollard and Miller's belief that behavior is influenced by environmental contingencies. These theories, however, go one step further to emphasize the importance of cognitive processes as well as behavioral ones, returning a thinking mind to the acting body. Those who have proposed cognitive theories of personality point out that there are important individual differences in the way people think about and define any external situation. Cognitive theories stress the mental processes through which people turn their sensations and perceptions into organized impressions of reality. Like humanistic theories, cognitive theories emphasize that you participate in creating your own personality. For example, you actively *choose* your own environments to a great extent; you do not just react passively. You weigh alternatives and select the settings in which you act and are acted upon—you choose to enter situations that you expect to be reinforcing and to avoid those that are unsatisfying and uncertain. For example, you often choose to return to restaurants where you've had good meals before, rather than always trying someplace new.

Let's look now at more concrete embodiments of these ideas. We examine the theories of Walter Mischel, Albert Bandura, and Nancy Cantor.

Mischel's Cognitive-Affective Personality Theory

Walter Mischel developed an influential theory of the cognitive basis of personality. Mischel emphasizes that people actively participate in the cognitive organization of their interactions with the environment. His approach emphasizes the importance of understanding how behavior arises as a function of interactions between persons and situations (Mischel & Shoda, 1995, 1999). Consider this example:

> *John's unique personality may be seen most clearly in that he is always very friendly when meeting someone for the first time, but that he also predictably becomes rather abrupt and unfriendly as he begins to spend more time with that person. Jim, on the other hand, is unique in that he is typically shy and quiet with people who he does not know well but becomes very gregarious once he begins to know someone well. (Shoda et al., 1993c, p. 1023)*

If we were to average John's and Jim's overall friendliness, we would probably get about the same value on this trait—but that would fail to capture important differences in their behavior. According to Mischel (1973; Mischel & Shoda, 1995), how you respond to a specific environmental input depends on the variables defined in **Table 14.4.** Do you see how each variable listed would affect the way in which a person would behave in particular situations? We have given you examples for each variable. Try to invent a situation in which you would produce behavior different from the characters listed in the table, because you contrast on the particular variable. You may wonder what determines the nature of these variables for a specific individual. Mischel believes that they result from his or her history of observations and interactions with other people and with inanimate aspects of the physical environment (Mischel, 1973).

Mischel and his colleagues have demonstrated the importance of patterns of behavior in their field studies of children's experiences in summer camp.

TABLE 14.4

Person Variables in Mischel's Cognitive-Affective Personality Theory

Variable	Definition	Example
Encodings	The way you categorize information about yourself, other people, events, and situations.	As soon as Bob meets someone, he tries to figure out how wealthy he or she is.
Expectancies and beliefs	Your beliefs about the social world and likely outcomes for given actions in particular situations. Your beliefs about your ability to bring outcomes about.	Greg invites friends to the movies, but he never expects them to say "yes."
Affects	Your feelings and emotions, including physiological responses.	Cindy blushes very easily.
Goals and values	The outcomes and affective states you do and do not value; your goals and life projects.	Peter wants to be president of his college class.
Competencies and self-regulatory plans	The behaviors you can accomplish and plans for generating cognitive and behavioral outcomes.	Jan can speak English, French, Russian, and Japanese and expects to work for the U.N.

Would you feel comfortable making personality judgments about these boys from this one snapshot? Why might you want to know their patterns of behavior across different types of situations?

PATTERNS OF BEHAVIOR We described one study from this project earlier, when we discussed behavioral consistency. Another study focused on children's reactions to different psychological situations, such as having another child initiate positive social contact or being warned by an adult to cease some activity. Children's reactions were coded into categories such as "talked prosocially" or "complied or gave in." In addition, at the end of the summer, camp counselors were asked to label individual children as "aggressive," "withdrawn," or "friendly." What information did they use to make these judgments? Consider the behavior of complying or giving in. Children who were ultimately rated as *friendly* had complied in situations in which they had been given warnings by an adult. Children who were ultimately rated as *withdrawn* had complied in situations in which peers had teased them (Shoda et al., 1993b).

These results suggest that knowing the average rates at which children complied wouldn't tell you very much about their personalities. You would have to know in what situation the compliance took place to understand why one child was labeled as friendly and another as withdrawn. Mischel emphasizes that your beliefs about other people's personalities come not from taking averages but from tracking the way different situations bring out different behaviors (Shoda & Mischel, 1993).

Reciprocal determinism A concept of Albert Bandura's social-learning theory that refers to the notion that a complex reciprocal interaction exists among the individual, his or her behavior, and environmental stimuli and that each of these components affects the others.

Bandura's Cognitive Social-Learning Theory

Through his theoretical writing and extensive research with children and adults, **Albert Bandura** (1986, 1999) has been an eloquent champion of a social-learning approach to understanding personality (recall from Chapter 7 his studies of aggressive behavior in children). This approach combines principles of learning with an emphasis on human interactions in social settings. From a social-learning perspective, human beings are not driven by inner forces, nor are they helpless pawns of environmental influence. The social-learning approach stresses the cognitive processes that are involved in acquiring and maintaining patterns of behavior and, thus, personality.

Bandura's theory points to a complex interaction of individual factors, behavior, and environmental stimuli. Each can influence or change the others, and the direction of change is rarely one way—it is *reciprocal*. Your behavior can be influenced by your attitudes, beliefs, or prior history of reinforcement as well as by stimuli available in the environment. What you do can have an effect on the environment, and important aspects of your personality can be affected by the environment or by feedback from your behavior. This important concept, **reciprocal determinism**, implies that you must examine all components if you want to completely understand human behavior, personality, and social ecology (Bandura, 1999; see **Figure 14.4**). So,

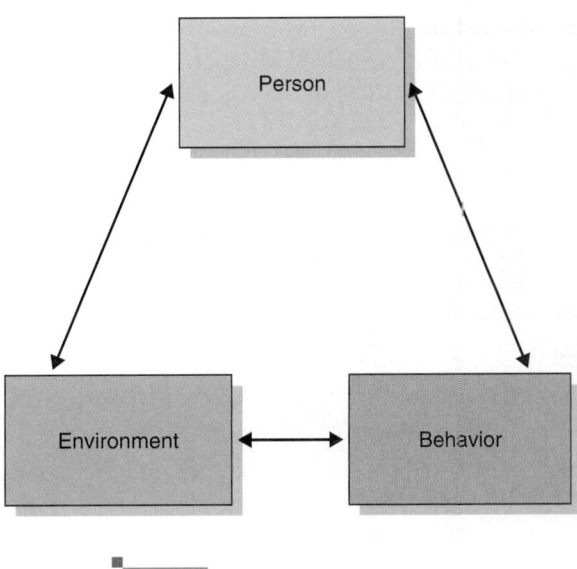

FIGURE 14.4

Reciprocal Determinism

In reciprocal determinism, the individual, the individual's behavior, and the environment all interact to influence and modify the other components.

for example, if you are overweight, you may not choose to be active in track-and-field events, but, if you live near a pool, you may spend time swimming. If you are outgoing, you'll talk to others sitting around the pool and thereby create a more sociable atmosphere, which, in turn, makes it a more enjoyable environment. This is one instance of reciprocal determinism among person, place, and behavior.

You may recall from Chapter 7 that Bandura's social-learning theory emphasizes observational learning as the process by which a person changes his or her behavior based on observations of another person's behavior. Through observational learning, children and adults acquire an enormous range of information about their social environment. Through observation, you learn what is appropriate and gets rewarded and what gets punished or ignored. Because you can use memory and think about external events, you can foresee the possible consequences of your actions without having to actually experience them. You may acquire skills, attitudes, and beliefs simply by watching what others do and the consequences that follow.

As his theory developed, Bandura (1997) elaborated self-efficacy as a central construct. **Self-efficacy** is the belief that one can perform adequately in a particular situation. Your sense of self-efficacy influences your perceptions, motivation, and performance in many ways. You don't even try to do things or take chances when you expect to be ineffectual. You avoid situations when you don't feel adequate. Even when you do, in fact, have the ability—and the desire—you may not take the required action or persist to complete the task successfully, if you think you lack what it takes.

Beyond actual accomplishments, there are three other sources of information for *self-efficacy judgments*.

- vicarious experience—your observations of the performance of others

- persuasion—others may convince you that you can do something, or you may convince yourself

- monitoring of your emotional arousal as you think about or approach a task—for example, anxiety suggests low expectations of efficacy; excitement suggests expectations of success

Self-efficacy judgments influence how much effort you expend and how long you persist when faced with difficulty in a wide range of life situations (Bandura, 1997; Cervone, 2000; Schwarzer, 1992). For example, how vigorously and persistently you study this chapter may depend more on your sense of self-efficacy than on actual ability (Zimmerman et al., 1992). Expectations of success or failure can be influenced by feedback from performance, but they are also likely to create the predicted feedback and thus become self-fulfilling prophecies. Let's apply this insight to academic achievement.

You can see from this study how important it is to believe that you can succeed. Particularly if you plan to be a parent, or if you already have children, you should consider how you can foster your own sense of effective control over your children's learning.

Bandura's theory of self-efficacy also acknowledges the importance of the environment. Expectations of failure or success—and corresponding decisions to stop trying or to persevere—may be based on perceptions of the supportiveness or unsupportiveness of the environment, in addition to perceptions of one's own adequacy or inadequacy. Such expectations are called *outcome-based expectancies*. **Figure 14.5** displays how the parts of Bandura's theory fit together. Behavioral outcomes depend both on people's perceptions of their own abilities and their perceptions of the environment.

Self-efficacy The set of beliefs that one can perform adequately in a particular situation.

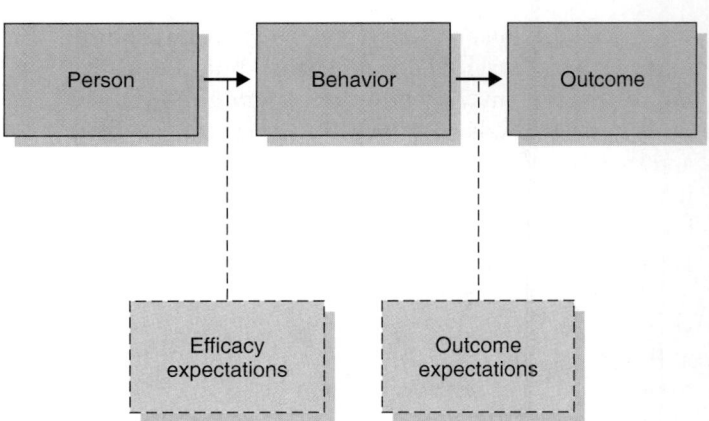

Bandura's Self-Efficacy Model

This model positions efficacy expectations between the person and his or her behavior; outcome expectations are positioned between behavior and its anticipated outcomes.

Cantor's Social Intelligence Theory

Building on these earlier cognitive and social theories, **Nancy Cantor** and her colleagues have outlined a *social intelligence* theory of personality (Cantor & Kihlstrom, 1987; Kilstrom & Cantor, 2000). **Social intelligence** refers to the expertise people bring to their experience of life tasks. The theory defines three types of individual differences:

- *Choice of life goals.* People differ as to which life goals or life tasks are most important to them. For example, college students are often concerned about "getting good grades" or "getting and keeping friends." Is one of these goals more important for you than the other? People's goals may also change over time. Your goals of ten years ago are probably different both from those of today and from those of the future.

- *Knowledge relevant to social interactions.* People differ with respect to the expertise they bring to tasks of social and personal problem solving.

- *Strategies for implementing goals.* People have different characteristic problem-solving strategies.

Can you see how these three dimensions interact to give rise to the different patterns of behavior you would recognize as personality? You might know two people who have the same general life goal—perhaps they both value getting good grades—but, depending on what they know and how they are able to put that knowledge to use, the moment-by-moment decisions they make about how to behave could be very different. One may have been taught explicit strategies for studying, and the other muddles through without special help. The theory of social intelligence gives a new perspective on how person-

Social intelligence A theory of personality that refers to the expertise people bring to their experience of life tasks.

ality predicts consistency: For a given period of time, consistency is found in people's goals, knowledge, and strategies.

Let's examine concrete circumstances in which people's disparate goals yield different outcomes: Researchers have demonstrated that *intimacy goals* have an impact on relationship satisfaction.

HOW WE KNOW

INTIMACY GOALS IN DATING RELATIONSHIPS When some people enter into relationships, their foremost goal is to create intimacy: They wish to experience circumstances in which they can foster interdependence and engage in self-disclosure. Other people are equally interested in having relationships, but for them relationships are more a pathway to desired activities (e.g., parties, sexual relations) rather than to intimacy. To assess these differences in the strength of intimacy goals, researchers asked 60 students to respond to such items as, "In my dating relationships, I try to share my most intimate thoughts and feelings" (Sanderson & Cantor, 1997). The students also reported such factors as, for example, the time they actually spent with their partners in various situations as well as their relationship satisfaction. The data showed a clear pattern: The relationship satisfaction of people with *stronger* intimacy goals was less affected by the amount of time they were able to spend with their partners; their reports of relationship satisfaction were relatively high whether they spent a little or a lot of time. By comparison, the relationship satisfaction of those individuals with weaker intimacy goals was considerably lower when they spent little time with their partners.

Do you see how this pattern could follow from the individuals' goals? People with stronger intimacy goals are highly motivated to make the most of whatever time they can spend with their partners. By comparison, those with weaker intimacy goals may not be able to bring sufficient focus to maintain a satisfying relationship without abundant interactions. In this case, you recognize personality in the consistent way in which people behave in close relationships.

Evaluation of Social-Learning and Cognitive Theories

One set of criticisms leveled against social-learning and cognitive theories is that they often overlook emotion as an important component of personality. In psychodynamic theories, emotions like anxiety play a central role. In social-learning and cognitive theories emotions are perceived merely as by-products of thoughts and behavior or are just included with other types of thoughts rather than being assigned independent importance. For those who feel that emotions are central to the functioning of human personality, this is a serious flaw. Cognitive theories are also attacked for not fully recognizing the impact of unconscious motivation on behavior and affect.

A second set of criticisms focuses on the vagueness of explanations about the way personal constructs and competencies are created. Cognitive theorists have often had little to say about the developmental origins of adult personality; their focus on the individual's perception of the current behavior setting obscures the individual's history. This criticism is leveled particularly at Kelly's theory, which has been described as more of a conceptual system than a theory, because it focuses on structure and processes but says little about the content of personal constructs.

Despite these criticisms, cognitive personality theories have made major contributions to current thinking. Kelly's theory has influenced a large number of cognitive therapists. Mischel's awareness of situation has brought about a better understanding of the interaction between what a person brings to a behavior setting and what that setting brings out of the person. Bandura's ideas have led to improvements in the way teachers educate children and help them achieve as well as new treatments in the areas of health, business, and sports performance. Finally, Cantor's theory shifts the search for personality consistency to the level of life goals and social strategies.

Do these cognitive personality theories provide you with insights about your own personality and behaviors? You can start to see how you define yourself in part through interactions with the environment. We turn now to theories that can add even further to your definition of self.

SUMMING UP

Social-learning and cognitive theories share the view that people's actions are influenced by environmental contingencies. Walter Mischel suggested that people respond to specific environmental inputs based on their encodings, expectancies and beliefs, affects, goals and values, and competencies and self-regulatory plans. Albert Bandura proposed a theory of reciprocal interaction of the person, environment, and behavior; self-efficacy plays a large role in determining the behaviors people undertake. Nancy Cantor's theory suggests that people differ in choice of life goals, in the knowledge they possess, and in the strategies they use to implement their goals.

Self Theories

We have arrived now at theories of personality that are most immediately personal: They deal directly with how each individual manages his or her sense of *self*. What is your conception of your *self*? Do you think of your *self* reacting consistently to the world? Do you try to present a consistent *self* to your friends and family? What impact do positive and negative experiences have on the way you think about your *self*? We will begin our consideration of these questions with a brief historical review.

The concern for analysis of the self found its strongest early advocate in **William James** (1890). James identified three components of self-experience: the *material me* (the bodily self, along with surrounding physical objects), the *social me* (your awareness of how others view you), and the *spiritual me* (the self that monitors private thoughts and feelings). James believed that everything that you associate with your identity becomes, in some sense, a part of the self. This explains why people may react defensively when their friends or family members—a part of the self—have been attacked. The concept of self was also central to psychodynamic theories. Self-insight was an important part of the psychoanalytic cure in Freud's theory, and Jung stressed that to fully develop the self, one must integrate and accept all aspects of one's conscious and unconscious life.

How has the self been treated in contemporary theory? We will first describe cognitive aspects of the self: self-concepts and possible selves. We then examine the way that people present their selves to the world. Finally, we look at the important topic of how views of the self differ across cultures.

Dynamic Aspects of Self-Concepts

The **self-concept** is a dynamic mental structure that motivates, interprets, organizes, mediates, and regulates

Self-concept A person's mental model of his or her abilities and attributes.

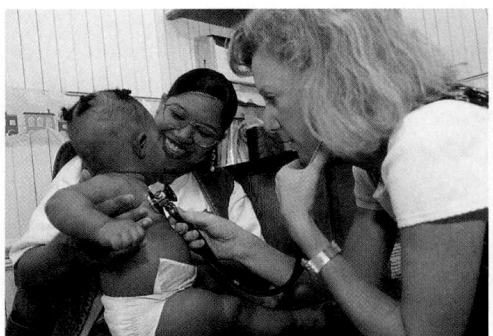

Imagine for a moment your different "possible selves." What effect might consideration of possible selves have on your behavior?

intrapersonal and interpersonal behaviors and processes. The self-concept includes many components. Among them are your memories about yourself; beliefs about your traits, motives, values, and abilities; the ideal self that you would most like to become; the possible selves that you contemplate enacting; positive or negative evaluations of yourself (self-esteem); and beliefs about what others think of you (Brown, 1998; McGuire & McGuire, 1988). In Chapter 8, we discussed *schemas* as "knowledge packages" that embody complex generalizations about the structure of the environment. Your self-concept contains schemas about the self—*self-schemas*—that allow you to organize information about yourself, just as other schemas allow you to manage other aspects of your experience (Markus, 1977). However, self-schemas influence more than just the way you process information about yourself. Research indicates that these schemas, which you frequently use to interpret your own behavior, influence the way you process information about other people as well (Cantor & Kihlstrom, 1987; Markus & Smith, 1981). Thus, you interpret other people's actions in terms of what you know and believe about yourself.

Another important component of your cognitive sense of self may be the other *possible selves* to which you compare your current self-concept. **Hazel Markus** and her colleagues have defined **possible selves** as "the ideal selves that we would very much like to become. They are also the selves we could become, and the selves we are afraid of becoming" (Markus & Nurius, 1986, p. 954). Possible selves play a role in motivating behavior—they spur action by allowing you to consider what directions your "self" could take, for better or for worse.

Consider individuals' ideas about whether they are prepared to become parents.

Possible selves The ideal selves that a person would like to become, the selves a person could become, and the selves a person is afraid of becoming; components of the cognitive sense of self.

Self-esteem A generalized evaluative attitude toward the self that influences both moods and behavior and that exerts a powerful effect on a range of personal and social behaviors.

HOW WE KNOW

POSSIBLE SELF AS PARENT A team of researchers developed an assessment device intended to measure the extent to which young adults could imagine themselves becoming parents (Bloom et al., 1999). The 683 college students who participated in the study responded on a scale of *not at all like me* to *very much like me* to statements such as "In the future I see myself as the kind of person who would get married but choose not to have children." To discourage students from guessing the study's purpose, the items relevant to parenting were dispersed into a longer questionnaire. After completing the questionnaire, each student was assigned a *parent possible-self score* (PPS). On average, men and women did not differ on these scores. However, the researchers defined subsets of both men and women who were particularly high and low on the scale. The individuals in those subsets rated their perceptions of videotaped infants whose behavior ranged from happy to fussy. The high-PPS students gave consistently more favorable ratings to the infants than the low-PPS students did.

Can you think of reasons why a person's ability to envision him- or herself as a parent might have an impact on that person's interpretations of an infant's behavior?

Self-Esteem and Self-Presentation

We have already acknowledged that some people have a negative self-concept, which we could also characterize as low self-esteem. A person's **self-esteem** is a *generalized* evaluation of the self. Self-esteem can strongly influence thoughts, moods, and behavior. Low self-esteem may be characterized, in part, by less certainty about the self. When high- and low-self-esteem individuals were asked to rate themselves along a number of trait dimensions (such as logical, intellectual, and likable), low-self-esteem participants, as you might expect, gave themselves overall lower ratings (Baumgardner, 1990).

However, when they were also asked to provide upper and lower limits for their estimates, the low-self-esteem participants indicated larger ranges: They had a less precise sense of self than their high-self-esteem peers. Thus, part of the phenomenon of low self-esteem may be feeling that you just don't know much about yourself. Lack of self-knowledge makes it difficult to predict that one will make a success of life's endeavors.

Evidence suggests that most people go out of their way to maintain self-esteem and to sustain the integrity of their self-concept (Steele, 1988). People engage in a variety of forms of self-enhancement (Banaji & Prentice, 1994). For example, when you doubt your ability to perform a task, you may engage in **self-handicapping** behavior. You deliberately sabotage your performance! The purpose of this strategy is to have a ready-made excuse for failure that does not imply *lack of ability* (Higgins et al., 1990; Jones & Berglas, 1978). Thus, if you are afraid to find out whether you have what it takes to be premed, you might party with friends instead of studying for an important exam. That way, if you don't succeed, you can blame your failure on low effort, without finding out whether you really had the ability to make it.

Self-handicapping behavior in action: Instead of studying for tomorrow's exam, you fall asleep in the library, thereby enabling yourself to say, "Well, I didn't really study" if you don't ace the test. Are there situations in which you resort to self-handicapping?

HOW WE KNOW

SELF-HANDICAPPING AMONG COLLEGE STUDENTS A pair of researchers asked college students to indicate their agreement with statements that measured self-handicapping: "I would do a lot better if I tried harder"; "I suppose I feel 'under the weather' more often than most"; "I tend to put things off to the last moment." Before their first exam, the students were asked what grade would make them happy. After the exam, they were given false feedback that their score was one-third grade below that "happy" grade (for example, if they had desired a B, they were told they got a B–). At that point, the researchers assessed the students' self-esteem. If self-handicapping protects self-esteem, we would expect high self-handicappers to suffer the least injury to self-esteem when they obtained the dissatisfying grade. That's exactly the pattern that the men in the study showed: High self-handicapping was associated with higher self-esteem. The women students, however, did not show any correlation between self-handicapping and self-esteem. The researchers speculated that men may have a stronger tendency to protect against threats to the self (Rhodewalt & Hill, 1995).

Self-handicapping The process of developing, in anticipation of failure, behavioral reactions and explanations that minimize ability deficits as possible attributions for the failure.

You should think about this study with respect to your own behaviors. Do you indulge in self-handicapping? Even if it protects your self-esteem (particularly if you are male), your grades are still likely to suffer! (By the way, after the study was completed, the researchers thoroughly debriefed the participants—which included explaining the purpose of the deception and giving them their real grades.)

The phenomenon of self-handicapping suggests, as well, that important aspects of self-esteem are related to *self-presentation*. Self-handicapping is more likely when people know that outcomes will be made public (Self, 1990). After all, how can someone think less well of you when your handicap is so obvious? Similar issues of self-presentation help explain behavioral differences between individuals with high and low self-esteem (Baumeister et al., 1989). People with high self-esteem present themselves to the world as ambitious, aggressive risk takers. People with low self-esteem present themselves as cautious and prudent. What is important here is that this stance is for *public* consumption.

HOW WE KNOW

THE PUBLIC FACE OF SELF-ESTEEM Participants high and low in self-esteem were given the opportunity to practice a game for as long as they wanted before undergoing a two-minute timed trial. Half of the participants practiced under the watchful eye of the experimenter; the other half practiced alone. In both cases, the amount of time they spent practicing was measured (explicitly when the experimenter was present and unobtrusively when the experimenter was absent). Results are shown in **Table 14.5**. When they practiced in public,

455

TABLE 14.5

**Mean Duration of Practice for People
with High and Low Self-Esteem**

Self-Esteem	Public	Private
High	123	448
Low	257	387
	−134	+61

Note: Durations are measured in seconds.

> individuals with high self-esteem did so only about
> half as long as their low-self-esteem peers. When
> they practiced in private, the effect was reversed;
> they practiced longer than their low-self-esteem
> peers (Tice & Baumeister, 1990).

We can understand this result in terms of self-presentation. People with high self-esteem may want to appear
to succeed even with very little preparation ("Someone
like me doesn't have to practice!")—and if they fail, they
can fall back on self-handicapping ("You saw how little I
practiced!").

The Cultural Construction of Self

Our discussion so far has focused on constructs relevant
to the self, such as self-esteem and possible selves, that
apply quite widely across individuals. However, researchers on the self have also begun to study the way in which
self-concepts and self-development are affected by differing cultural constraints. If you have grown up in a Western culture, you are likely to be pretty comfortable with
the research we have reviewed so far: The theories and
constructs match the ways that Western cultures conceptualize the *self*. However, the type of culture from
which the Western self emerges—an *individualistic* culture—is in the minority with respect to the world's
population, which includes about 70 percent *collectivist*
cultures. Individualistic cultures emphasize individuals'

Independent construals of self Conceptualization of the self as
an individual whose behavior is organized primarily by reference to
one's own thoughts, feelings, and actions, rather than by reference to
the thoughts, feelings, and actions of others.

Interdependent construals of self Conceptualization of the self
as part of an encompassing social relationship; recognizing that one's
behavior is determined, contingent on, and, to a large extent organized
by what the actor perceives to be the thoughts, feelings, and actions
of others.

In what ways is an individual's sense of self different when
he or she is a member of a culture with an interdependent
construal of self rather than an independent construal of self?

needs, whereas collectivist cultures emphasize the needs
of the group (Triandis, 1994, 1995). This overarching
emphasis has important implications for how each member of these cultures conceptualizes his or her *self*: **Hazel
Markus** and **Shinobu Kitayama** (1991; Kitayama et al.,
1995; Markus et al., 1997) have argued that each culture
gives rise to a different *construal* of the self:

- Individualistic cultures encourage **independent construals of self**—"Achieving the cultural goal of
independence requires construing oneself as an individual whose behavior is organized and made meaningful primarily by reference to one's own internal
repertoire of thoughts, feelings, and action, rather
than by reference to the thoughts, feelings, and actions of others" (Markus & Kitayama, 1991, p. 226).

- Collectivist cultures encourage **interdependent construals of self**—"Experiencing interdependence entails seeing oneself as part of an encompassing social
relationship and recognizing that one's behavior is
determined, contingent on, and, to a large extent
organized by what the actor perceives to be the
thoughts, feelings, and actions of *others* in the relationship" (Markus & Kitayama, 1991, p. 227).

Researchers have documented the reality and implications of these distinctions in a number of ways.

One type of cross-cultural research on the self has
used a measurement device called the *Twenty Statements
Test* (TST) (Kuhn & McPartland, 1954). When they take
this test, participants are asked to give 20 different answers
to the question "Who am I?" As shown in **Table 14.6**, responses to this question typically fall into six different categories. The table also presents the results of a study in
which roughly 300 students from the United States and

India were asked to go through the TST procedure (Dhawan et al., 1995). The greatest difference in the table is the rate at which people gave *self-evaluations*. American students were far more likely to do so—in keeping with their independent sense of self. Indian students gave far fewer self-evaluations and, in keeping with their interdependent sense of self, somewhat more statements about social identity. Note that differences between men and women overall were rather small—culture mattered more. You might wonder how the export of Western culture affects the self-concepts of members of collectivist cultures. One study compared the TST responses of Kenyans who had virtually no exposure to Western culture—members of pastoral Samburu and Maasai tribes—to those who had moved to the Westernized capital city of Nairobi. Roughly 82 percent of the tribe members' responses on the TST were social responses; workers in Nairobi gave only 58 percent social responses, and students at the University of Nairobi gave only 17 percent social responses (Ma & Schoeneman, 1997). This pattern suggests that when a nation imports Western products, they may also import a Western sense of self.

These studies illustrate that the cultures to which people belong have a strong impact on the way they construe their selves. You have already read about the consequences of these construals in earlier chapters. For example, in Chapter 11, you learned that culture affects moral judgments (Miller & Bersoff, 1992); and in Chapter 13, you learned that culture affects emotional expression (Stephan et al., 1996). You will encounter this distinction again later in the book when, for example, we

consider the question of whether ideas about *love* are influenced by construals of the self (see Chapter 17). For now, consider a study that has particular relevance to theories about the self.

HOW WE KNOW

CULTURE, SELF-ENHANCEMENT, AND SELF-CRITICISM Earlier we reviewed evidence that people in Western cultures are concerned with *self-enhancement*—bringing about positive changes in self-esteem. However, this is not typically part of the agenda of a member of a collectivist culture. Instead, having an interdependent construal of self may go hand in hand with *self-criticism*: The individual is concerned with improving the collective by being critical of his or her individual performance. To test these ideas, a team of researchers asked Japanese undergraduates, members of a collectivist culture, and United States undergraduates, members of an individualistic culture, to describe as many situations as possible in which their self-esteem increased or decreased. Success situations were statements such as "When I get an A+ on my paper or final"; failure situations were statements such as "When my favorite baseball team or actress (actor) is overtly criticized." In the next phase, three new groups of students—63 Japanese students in Kyoto, Japan; 88 Japanese students temporarily studying at

TABLE 14.6

Cross-Cultural Comparison of *Twenty Statements Test* Responses—Percent Response in Each Category

Category	Examples	Indian		American	
		Male	Female	Male	Female
Social identity	I'm a student. I am a daughter.	34	28	26	26
Ideological beliefs	I believe that all human beings are good. I believe in God.	2	2	2	1
Interests	I like playing the piano. I enjoy visiting new places.	7	16	6	5
Ambitions	I want to become a doctor. I want to learn more psychology.	11	15	2	2
Self-evaluations	I am honest and hardworking. I am a tall person. I worry about the future.	35	33	64	65
Other	I have noisy friends. I own a dog.	11	6	1	0

the University of Oregon in Eugene, Oregon; and 102 Caucasian students from the University of Oregon—were asked to read the descriptions of the situations and try to visualize themselves in them. They were asked to indicate whether their own self-esteem would be affected by the situation and, if so, in what direction (that is, would it increase or decrease?) and, on a four-point scale, to what extent (1 = "slightly" to 4 = "very much").

The results of the experiment are presented in **Figure 14.6**. Note, first, that the Japanese students—both in Japan and in the United States—were more likely to report decreases in self-esteem. This finding is consistent with the difference we outlined between dependent and interdependent construals of the self. Second, the effects are larger—both self-criticism for the Japanese students and self-enhancement for the U.S. students—when the situation originated, or as the researchers said, was "made," in the matching country. That is, the situations described by U.S. students in the first phase of the project best allowed for U.S. self-enhancement; similarly, the situations described by Japanese students best allowed their peers to be self-critical. Finally, the Japanese students living in the United States were somewhat less self-critical than their peers at home. This could reflect the influence of United States culture on them during their visit to the country or it could reflect self-selection of those students who thought they would fit in during a U.S. visit (Kitayama et al., 1997).

If you have grown up in a Western culture, you might find these results hard to understand. Why would people find it more natural to criticize rather than to enhance their self-esteem? The answer, of course, is that the *self* in self-esteem doesn't have the same meaning: For members of collectivist cultures, what matters is how the self relates to the collective. Over the next few days, you might try to experience both construals of self by trying to attend to how the events that happen around you have an impact both on your self as an individual and your self as a member of a larger social structure.

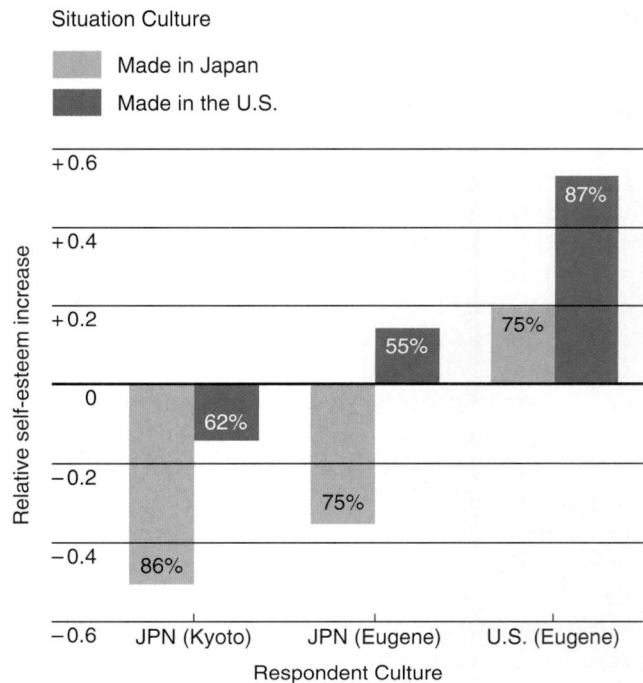

FIGURE 14.6

Culture, Self-Enhancement, and Self-Criticism

In the first phase of the project, U.S. and Japanese students described success and failure situations. The situations that originated in each culture are labeled as "Made in the U.S." and "Made in Japan." In a second phase, students from both cultures, as well as students from Japan visiting the United States, rated how experiencing those situations would affect their self-esteem. On average, Japanese students were more oriented toward self-criticism, with negative changes in self-esteem, whereas U.S. students were more oriented toward self-enhancement, with positive changes in self-esteem. The effects were more powerful when the situations had originated in the respective cultures. The numbers in the bars represent the percentage of students who showed the dominant tendency (for example, 86 percent of the Japanese students displayed self-criticism when responding to Japanese-made situations, whereas 87 percent of the U.S. students showed self-enhancement when responding to U.S.-made situations).

Evaluation of Self Theories

Self theories succeed at capturing people's own concepts of their personalities and the way they wish to be perceived by others. Furthermore, examinations of cross-cultural construals of the self have had great influence on the way psychologists assess the universality of their the-ories. However, critics of self theory approaches to personality argue against its limitless boundaries. Because so many things are relevant to the self and to the self-concept, it is not always clear which factors are most important for predicting behavior. In addition, the emphasis on the self as a social construct is not entirely consistent with evidence that some facets of personality may be inherited. As with the other theories we have described, self theories capture some but not all of what you think of as personality.

Self-concepts are memory structures that include schemas about the self and guide the way people process information about themselves and others. People appear to prefer self-verification even when the self-concept that is verified is negative. People use possible selves to contrast what they are like now to how they could be in the future. Self-esteem provides a general evaluation of the self; it can strongly influence thoughts, mood, and behavior. People engage in self-handicapping to protect self-esteem. Cross-cultural research has focused on the way in which individualistic and collectivist cultures give rise to different construals of self. Members of individualist cultures tend to have independent construals of self, whereas members of collectivist cultures tend to have interdependent construals.

These construals have consequences for the ways in which people make self-evaluations and adjust their self-esteem. Critics of self theories suggest that they do not always allow for precise behavioral predictions and that they do not sufficiently acknowledge genetic aspects of personality.

Comparing Personality Theories

There is no unified theory of personality that a majority of psychologists can endorse. Several differences in basic assumptions have come up repeatedly in our survey of the various theories. It may be helpful to recap five of the most important differences in

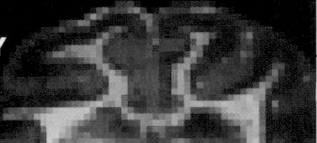

PSYCHOLOGY IN THE 21ST CENTURY

THE SELF ON THE INTERNET

The most pressing question many people ask themselves when they sit down for an Internet session is: Who should I be today? One of the best documented aspects of life on the Internet is that people create new identities for themselves (McKenna & Bargh, 2000; Reid, 1998). When a person enters a chat room, she might decide to be a man rather than a woman, black rather than white, 40 rather than 18, and a successful executive rather than a college sophomore. The Internet brings the concept of *possible selves* very vividly into many people's everyday lives. Let's focus on some positive consequences of these Internet selves.

Something that many people find burdensome in "real" life is that they start to feel as though they are defined rather narrowly: Repeated interactions with family, friends, bosses and co-workers require them to remain consistent in a way that may be at odds with the person they wish to be; it is relatively difficult for people to expand into new realms of experience, given the constraints of their day-to-day social context. The

Internet loosens up that social context (McKenna & Bargh, 2000). People can use the anonymity of the Internet to express new interests or explore new ideas without fear of real-world consequences. Without making radical changes (e.g., claiming to be a woman rather than a man), a person can rehearse possible selves that may be closer to his or her ideal self.

Furthermore, the anonymity of the Internet allows people to reveal more of their selves than they might otherwise be willing to disclose. Recall from Chapter 13 that people obtain positive health benefits when they make emotional disclosures (Pennebaker, 1990). The Internet offers people a broad range of opportunities to engage is such disclosure. People can find specialized chat rooms or newsgroups that explicitly provide forums for such disclosure and social support for the content of the disclosures.

Researchers have demonstrated, in fact, that people's ability to make disclosures about hidden aspects of their self can lead to greater self-acceptance. One study obtained information from people who made postings to

newsgroups intended for people with marginalized sexual identities such as homosexuality. The researchers were able to obtain anonymous data from people who were active participants in those groups (McKenna & Bargh, 1998). The data suggested that newsgroup participation led to greater self-acceptance. In fact, 37 percent of the respondents who provided data had revealed to others the secret of their marginalized identity as a consequence of newsgroup participation.

We have been focusing on the positive aspects of the Internet: People's ability to expand their sense of self and their ability to engage in self-disclosure with consequences for health and self-acceptance. There are, of course, some dangers. Anonymity can lead people to fragment their lives in ways that might lead to maladaptive behaviors (Reid, 1998). We also noted earlier that some researchers attribute a rise in the prevalence of shyness to the availability of the Internet. Still, we hope that most people will benefit from the opportunities the Internet provides to engage, very literally, in self-exploration.

assumptions about personality and the approaches that advance each assumption.

1. *Heredity versus environment.* As you have learned throughout *Psychology and Life,* this difference is also referred to as *nature versus nurture.* What is more important to personality development: genetic and biological factors or environmental influences? Trait theories have been split on this issue; Freudian theory depends heavily on heredity; humanistic, social-learning, cognitive, and self theories all emphasize either environment as a determinant of behavior or interaction with the environment as a source of personality development and differences.

2. *Learning processes versus innate laws of behavior.* Should emphasis be placed on the view that personalities are modified through learning or on the view that personality development follows an internal timetable? Again, trait theories have been divided. Freudian theory has favored the inner determinant view, whereas humanists postulate an optimistic view that experience changes people. Social-learning, cognitive, and self theories clearly support the idea that behavior and personality change as a result of learned experiences.

3. *Emphasis on past, present, or future.* Trait theories emphasize past causes, whether innate or learned; Freudian theory stresses past events in early childhood; social-learning theories focus on past reinforcements and present contingencies; humanistic theories emphasize present reality or future goals; and cognitive and self theories emphasize past and present (and the future if goal setting is involved).

4. *Consciousness versus unconsciousness.* Freudian theory emphasizes unconscious processes; humanistic, social-learning, and cognitive theories emphasize conscious processes. Trait theories pay little attention to this distinction; self theories are unclear on this score.

5. *Inner disposition versus outer situation.* Social-learning theories emphasize situational factors; traits play up dispositional factors; and the others allow for an interaction between person-based and situation-based variables.

Each type of theory makes different contributions to the understanding of human personality. Trait theories provide a catalog that describes parts and structures. Psychodynamic theories add a powerful engine and the fuel to get the vehicle moving. Humanistic theories put a per-

son in the driver's seat. Social-learning theories supply the steering wheel, directional signals, and other regulation equipment. Cognitive theories add reminders that the way the trip is planned, organized, and remembered will be affected by the mental map the driver chooses for the journey. Finally, self theories remind the driver to consider the image his or her driving ability is projecting to backseat drivers and pedestrians.

To complete our discussion of personality, we now consider personality assessment. We will describe some of the ways in which psychologists obtain information about the range of personality attributes that make each individual unique.

SUMMING UP

Personality theories differ with respect to the emphasis they put on heredity versus environment; learning processes versus innate laws of behavior; past causes, present behaviors, or future goals; consciousness versus unconsciousness; and dispositions versus situations. Each theory provides different insights into human personality.

Assessing Personality

Think of all the ways in which you differ from your best friend. Psychologists wonder about the diverse attributes that characterize an individual, set one person apart from others, or distinguish people in one group from those in another (for example, shy people from outgoing or paranoid individuals from normal). Two assumptions are basic to these attempts to understand and describe human personality: first, that there are personal characteristics of individuals that give coherence to their behavior and, second, that those characteristics can be assessed or measured. Personality tests that embody these assumptions can be classified as being either *objective* or *projective.*

Objective Tests

Objective tests of personality are those in which scoring and administration are relatively simple and follow well-defined rules. Some objective tests are scored, and even interpreted, by computer programs. The final score is usually a single number, scaled along a single dimension (such as *adjustment* versus *maladjustment*), or a set of scores on different traits (such as impulsiveness, dependency, or extraversion) reported in comparison with the scores of a normative sample.

A *self-report inventory* is an objective test in which individuals answer a series of questions about their

Personality inventory A self-report questionnaire used for personality assessment that includes a series of items about personal thoughts, feelings, and behaviors.

thoughts, feelings, and actions. One of the first self-report inventories, the *Woodworth Personal Data Sheet* (written in 1917) asked questions such as "Are you often frightened in the middle of the night?" (see DuBois, 1970). Today, a person taking a **personality inventory** reads a series of statements and indicates whether each one is true or typical for himself or herself.

The most frequently used personality inventory is the *Minnesota Multiphasic Personality Inventory,* or MMPI (Dahlstrom et al., 1975). It is used in many clinical settings to aid in the diagnosis of patients and to guide their treatment. After reviewing its features and applications, we will briefly discuss the *NEO Personality Inventory* (NEO-PI), which is used widely with nonpatient populations.

THE MMPI

The MMPI was developed at the University of Minnesota during the 1930s by psychologist Starke Hathaway and psychiatrist J. R. McKinley (Hathaway & McKinley, 1940, 1943). Its basic purpose is to diagnose individuals according to a set of psychiatric labels. The first test consisted of 550 items, which individuals determined to be either true or false for themselves or to which they responded, "Cannot say." From that item pool, scales were developed that were relevant to the kinds of problems patients showed in psychiatric settings.

The MMPI scales were unlike other existing personality tests because they were developed using an *empirical* strategy rather than the intuitive, theoretical approach that dominated at the time. (Recall our discussion earlier of theoretical versus empirical test construction.) Items were included on a scale only if they clearly distinguished between two groups—for example, schizophrenic patients and a normal comparison group. Each item had to demonstrate its validity by being answered similarly by members within each group but differently between the two groups. Thus, the items were not selected on a theoretical basis (what the content seemed to mean to experts) but on an empirical basis (did they distinguish between the two groups?).

The MMPI has 10 *clinical scales,* each constructed to differentiate a special clinical group (such as individuals with schizophrenia) from a normal comparison group. The test also includes *validity scales* that detect suspicious response patterns, such as blatant dishonesty, carelessness, defensiveness, or evasiveness. When an MMPI is interpreted, the tester first checks the validity scales to be sure the test is valid and then looks at the rest of the scores. The pattern of the scores—which are highest, how they differ—forms the "MMPI profile." Individual profiles are compared with those common for particular groups, such as felons and gamblers.

In the mid-1980s, the MMPI underwent a major revision, and it is now called the *MMPI-2* (Butcher et al., 1989; Butcher & Williams, 1992; Greene, 1991). The

TABLE 14.7

MMPI-2 Clinical Scales

Hypochondriasis (Hs): Abnormal concern with bodily functions

Depression (D): Pessimism; hopelessness; slowing of action and thought

Conversion hysteria (Hy): Unconscious use of mental problems to avoid conflicts or responsibility

Psychopathic deviate (Pd): Disregard for social custom; shallow emotions; inability to profit from experience

Masculinity-femininity (Mf): Differences between men and women

Paranoia (Pa): Suspiciousness; delusions of grandeur or persecution

Psychasthenia (Pt): Obsessions; compulsions; fears; guilt; indecisiveness

Schizophrenia (Sc): Bizarre, unusual thoughts or behavior; withdrawal; hallucinations; delusions

Hypomania (Ma): Emotional excitement; flight of ideas; overactivity

Social introversion (Si): Shyness; disinterest in others; insecurity

MMPI-2 has updated language and content to better reflect contemporary concerns, and new populations provided data for norms. The MMPI-2 also adds 15 new *content scales* that were derived using, in part, a theoretical method. For each of 15 clinically relevant topics (such as anxiety or family problems), items were selected on two bases: if they seemed theoretically related to the topic area and if they statistically formed a *homogeneous scale,* meaning that each scale measures a single, unified concept. The clinical and content scales of the MMPI-2 are given in **Table 14.7** and **Table 14.8**. You'll notice that most of the clinical scales measure several related concepts and that the names of the content scales are simple and self-explanatory.

The benefits of the MMPI-2 include its ease and economy of administration and its usefulness for the diagnosis of psychopathology (Butcher & Rouse, 1996). In addition, the item pool can be used for many purposes. For example, you could build a creativity scale by finding creative and noncreative groups of individuals and determining the MMPI items that they answered differently. Over the years, psychologists have developed and validated hundreds of special-purpose scales in this way. For researchers, one of the most attractive characteristics of the MMPI is the enormous archives of MMPI profiles collected over 50 years. Because all of these people have been tested on the same items in a standardized way, they can be compared either on the traditional clinical scales or on special-purpose scales (like our new "creativity" scale). These MMPI archives allow researchers to test hypotheses on MMPIs taken by people many years earlier, perhaps long before the construct being measured was even conceived.

TABLE  14.8

MMPI-2 Content Scales

Anxiety	Antisocial practices
Fears	Type A (workaholic)
Obsessiveness	Low self-esteem
Depression	Social discomfort
Health concerns	Family problems
Bizarre mentation (thoughts)	Work interference
Anger	Negative treatment indicators
Cynicism	(negative attitudes about doctors and treatment)

However, the MMPI-2 is not without its critics. Its clinical scales have been criticized, for example, because they are heterogeneous (they measure several things at once). Researchers have also suggested that the changes from the original MMPI to the revised MMPI-2 were insufficient to recognize advances in personality theory; the test remains close to its empirical origins (Helmes & Reddon, 1993). The MMPI-2 may be criticized in some cases because people try to use it for too many purposes. Some MMPI-2 scales, such as the depression scale, reach acceptable levels of validity (Boone, 1994). The scales devoted to predicting substance abuse, by contrast, are not as valid as more specific assessment devices (Svanum et al., 1994). As with any assessment device, researchers must carefully evaluate the reliability and validity of each special use of the MMPI and MMPI-2 (Greene et al., 1997).

These personality inventories were designed to assess individuals with clinical problems. In the next two sections, we'll describe devices more suited to assess personality in the general, nonpatient population.

THE NEO-PI

The NEO Personality Inventory (NEO-PI) was also designed to assess personality characteristics in nonclinical adult populations. It measures the five-factor model of personality we discussed earlier. If you took the NEO-PI, you would receive a profile sheet that showed your standardized scores relative to a large normative sample on each of the five major dimensions: Neuroticism, Extraversion, Openness, Agreeableness, and Conscientiousness (Costa & McCrae, 1985). A revised version of the NEO-PI assesses 30 separate traits organized within the five major factors (Costa & McCrae, 1992b). For example, the Neu-

Projective test A method of personality assessment in which an individual is presented with a standardized set of ambiguous, abstract stimuli and asked to interpret their meanings; the individual's responses are assumed to reveal inner feelings, motives, and conflicts.

roticism dimension is broken down into six facet scales: Anxiety, Angry hostility, Depression, Self-consciousness, Impulsiveness, and Vulnerability. Much research has demonstrated that the NEO-PI dimensions are homogeneous, highly reliable, and show good criterion and construct validity (Costa & McCrae, 1992a; Furnham et al., 1997). The NEO-PI is being used to study personality stability and change across the life span as well as the relationship of personality characteristics to physical health and various life events, such as career success or early retirement.

A new inventory based on the five-factor model, the *Big Five Questionnaire* (BFQ), was designed to have validity across different cultures. The scale was developed in Italy, but it shows similar psychometric characteristics for U.S. and Spanish populations, and appropriate norms are being established for French, German, Czech, Hungarian, and Polish translations (Barbaranelli et al., 1997; Caprara et al., 1993). Although the BFQ correlates highly with the NEO-PI, it differs in important ways. Factor 1 is labeled Energy or Activity rather than Extraversion (to reduce overlap with the social aspects of Agreeableness). The BFQ includes a scale to see if test takers' responses are biased toward socially desirable responses. It is simpler than the NEO-PI in having only two facets for each of the five factors. For example, Energy is composed of the facets of Dynamism and Dominance. The first is intrapersonal; the second is interpersonal. As psychology becomes more global in its concerns, such assessment instruments that work equally well across language and national boundaries are essential for conducting meaningful cross-cultural research in personality and social psychology.

Projective Tests

Have you ever looked at a cloud and seen a face or the shape of an animal? If you asked your friends to look, too, they may have seen a reclining nude or a dragon. Psychologists rely on a similar phenomenon in their use of projective tests for personality assessment.

As we just saw, objective tests take one of two forms: Either they provide test takers with a series of statements and ask them to give a simple response (such as "true," "false," or "cannot say") or they ask test takers to rate themselves with respect to some dimension (such as "anxious" versus "nonanxious"). Thus, the respondent is constrained to choose one of the predetermined responses. *Projective tests,* by contrast, have no predetermined range of responses. In a **projective test**, a person is given a series of stimuli that are purposely ambiguous, such as abstract patterns, incomplete pictures, or drawings that can be interpreted in many ways. The person may be asked to describe the patterns, finish the pictures, or tell stories about the drawings. Projective tests were first used by psychoanalysts, who hoped that such tests would reveal their patients' unconscious personality dynamics. Because the stimuli are ambiguous, responses to them are determined partly by what the person brings to the situation—namely, inner feelings, personal motives, and conflicts from prior life experiences. These personal, idiosyncratic aspects, which are *projected* onto the stimuli, permit the personality assessor to make various interpretations.

Projective tests are among the assessment devices most commonly used by psychological practitioners (Butcher & Rouse, 1996; Lubin et al., 1984; Piotrowski et al., 1985). They have also been used more often outside the United States, such as in the Netherlands, Hong Kong, and Japan, than objective tests like the MMPI (Piotrowski et al., 1993). Objective tests often fail to be adequately translated or adequately standardized for non-U.S. populations. Projective tests are less sensitive to language variation. However, because projective tests are so widespread, critics have often worried that they are used in ways that are not valid. As we examine two of the most common projective tests, the Rorschach test and the Thematic Apperception Test (TAT), we will discuss those issues of validity.

THE RORSCHACH

In the Rorschach test, developed by Swiss psychiatrist **Hermann Rorschach** in 1921, the ambiguous stimuli are symmetrical inkblots (Rorschach, 1942). Some are black and white and some are colored (see **Figure 14.7**). During the test, a respondent is shown an inkblot and asked, "What might this be?" Respondents are assured that there are no right or wrong answers (Exner, 1974). Testers record verbatim what people say, how much time they take to respond, the total time they take per inkblot, and the way they handle the inkblot card. Then, in a second phase called an *inquiry,* the respondent is reminded of the previous responses and asked to elaborate on them.

The responses are scored on three major features: (1) the *location,* or part of the card mentioned in the response—whether the respondent refers to the whole stimulus or to part of it and the size of the details mentioned; (2) the *content* of the response—the nature of the object and activities seen; and (3) the *determinants*—which aspects of the card (such as its color or shading) prompted the response. Scorers may also note whether responses are original and unique or popular and conforming.

You might think that ambiguous inkblots would give rise to an uninterpretable diversity of responses. In fact, researchers have devised a comprehensive scoring system for Rorschach responses that allows for meaningful comparisons among different test takers (Exner, 1991, 1993; Exner & Weiner, 1994). This scoring system specifies, for example, common categories of content response like *whole human* (the response mentions or implies a whole human form) and *blood* (the response mentions blood, either human or animal). Patterns of responses have been successfully related to normal personality characteristics as well as to psychopathology. Even so, some controversy remains about the validity of the scoring system and the Rorschach test (Exner, 1996; Meyer, 2000; Wood et al., 1996a, 1996b).

THE TAT

In the Thematic Apperception Test, developed by **Henry Murray** in 1938, respondents are shown pictures of ambiguous scenes and asked to generate stories about them, describing what the people in the scenes are doing and thinking, what led up to each event, and how each situation will end (see **Figure 14.8**). The person administering the TAT evaluates the structure and content of the stories as well as the behavior of the individual telling them, in an attempt to discover some of the respondent's major concerns, motivations, and personality characteristics. For example, an examiner might evaluate a person as conscientious if his or her stories concerned people who lived up to their obligations and if the stories were told in a serious, orderly way. Recall from Chapter 12 that the TAT has often been used to reveal individual differences in dominant needs, such as needs for power, affiliation, and achievement (McClelland, 1961). Over several decades of research, the TAT has proven to be a valid measure of the need for achievement (Spangler, 1992).

Let us offer some concluding remarks on the subject of personality assessment. Did you see the relationship between these personality assessment devices and the theories of personality we reviewed earlier? The conclusion we reached was that each of the types of theories illuminated best different aspects of human experience. We can reach much the same conclusions for personality tests: Each has the potential to provide unique insights into an individual's personality. Clinicians most often use a combination of tests when they carry out a personality assessment; the Rorschach and MMPI, for example, may be seen as complementary (Butcher & Rouse, 1996;

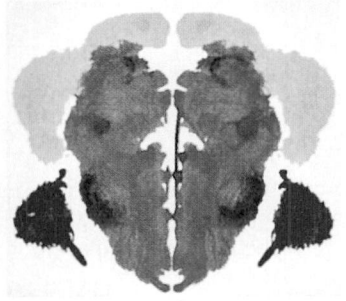

FIGURE 14.7

An Inkblot Similar to Those Used in the Rorschach Test

What do you see? Does your interpretation of this inkblot reveal anything about your personality?

FIGURE 14.8

A Sample Card from the TAT Test

What story do you want to tell? What does your story reveal about your personality?

Lubin et al., 1984; Piotrowksi et al., 1985). Under many circumstances, the profiles that arise from objective, even computer-based analyses may allow accurate predictions to be made for specific outcomes. Under other cir-

cumstances, clinical expertise and skilled intuition must supplement objective norms. In practice, the best predictions are made when the strengths of each approach are combined.

We reminded you at the beginning of the chapter that you couldn't measure personality by feeling bumps on a person's head. However, we also asked you to consider a series of questions: If psychologists studied you, what portrait of your personality would they draw? What early experiences might they identify as contributing to how you now act and think? What conditions in your currrent life exert strong influences on your thoughts and behaviors? What makes you different from other individuals who are functioning in many of the same situations as you? You now can see that each type of personality theory provides a framework against which you can begin to form your answers to these questions. Suppose the time has really come to paint your psychological portrait. Where would you begin?

SUMMING UP

Objective personality tests involve relatively standardized and explicit administration and scoring. The MMPI-2 has updated language and content that reflects advances in clinical theory and assessment. The NEO-PI and BFQ measure aspects of normal personality functioning. Projective tests present individuals with ambiguous stimuli in order to elicit inner feelings, motives, and conflicts. Researchers have developed a comprehensive system for scoring responses to Rorschach ink blots. The TAT provides a valid measure of need for achievement.

RECAPPING
MAIN POINTS

Type and Trait Personality Theories

- Some theorists categorize people by all-or-none types, assumed to be related to particular characteristic behaviors.

- Other theorists view traits—attributes along continuous dimensions—as the building blocks of personality.

- The five-factor model is a descriptive personality system that maps out the relationships among com-

mon trait words, theoretical concepts, and personality scales.

- Twin and adoption studies reveal that personality traits are partially inherited.

- People display behavioral consistency when situations are defined with respect to relevant psychological features.

Psychodynamic Theories

- Freud's psychodynamic theory emphasizes instinctive biological en-

ergies as sources of human motivation.

- Basic concepts of Freudian theory include psychic energy as powering and directing behavior, early experiences as key determinants of lifelong personality, psychic determinism, and powerful unconscious processes.

- Personality structure consists of the id, the superego, and the reconciling ego.

- Unacceptable impulses are repressed and ego defense mechanisms are developed to lessen anxiety and bolster self-esteem.

- Post-Freudians like Adler, Horney, and Jung have put greater emphasis on ego functioning and social variables and less on sexual urges. They see personality development as a lifelong process.

Humanistic Theories

- Humanistic theories focus on self-actualization—the growth potential of the individual.
- These theories are holistic, dispositional, phenomenological, and existential.
- Contemporary theories in the humanist tradition focus on individuals' life stories.

Social-Learning and Cognitive Theories

- Social-learning theorists focus on understanding individual differences in behavior and personality as a consequence of different histories of reinforcement.
- Cognitive theorists emphasize individual differences in perception and subjective interpretation of the environment.
- Walter Mischel explored the origins of behaviors as interactions of persons and situations.
- Albert Bandura described the reciprocal determinism among people, environments, and behaviors.
- Nancy Cantor's theory emphasized the impact of goals, knowledge, and strategies on people's behavior.

Self Theories

- Self theories focus on the importance of the self-concept for a full understanding of human personality.
- The self-concept is a dynamic mental structure that motivates, interprets, organizes, mediates, and regulates personal and interpersonal behaviors and processes.
- Many individual differences are captured by the habitual ways in which people present themselves in social situations.
- Cross-cultural research suggests that individualistic cultures give rise to independent construals of self, whereas collectivist cultures give rise to interdependent construals of self.

Comparing Personality Theories

- Personality theories can be contrasted with respect to the emphasis they put on heredity versus environment; learning processes versus innate laws of behavior; the past, present, or future; consciousness versus unconsciousness; and inner dispositions versus outer situations.
- Each theory makes different contributions to the understanding of human personality.

Assessing Personality

- Personality characteristics are assessed by both objective and projective tests.
- The most common objective test, the MMPI-2, is used to diagnose clinical problems.
- The NEO-PI and BFQ are newer objective personality tests that measure five major dimensions of personality.
- Projective tests of personality ask people to respond to ambiguous stimuli.
- Two important projective tests are the Rorschach test and the TAT.

Key Terms

analytic psychology (p. 446)
anxiety (p. 443)
archetype (p. 445)
collective unconscious (p. 445)
consistency paradox (p. 438)
ego (p. 443)
ego defense mechanisms (p. 443)
five-factor model (p. 436)
fixation (p. 442)
id (p. 442)
independent construals of self (p. 456)
interdependent construals of self (p. 456)
libido (p. 441)
personality (p. 432)
personality inventory (p. 460)
personality types (p. 433)
possible selves (p. 454)
projective test (p. 462)
psychic determinism (p. 442)
psychobiography (p. 447)
psychodynamic personality theories (p. 440)
reciprocal determinism (p. 450)
repression (p. 443)
self-actualization (p. 446)
self-concept (p. 453)
self-efficacy (p. 451)
self-esteem (p. 454)
self-handicapping (p. 455)
shyness (p. 438)
social intelligence (p. 452)
superego (p. 442)
traits (p. 434)
unconditional positive regard (p. 446)
unconscious (p. 442)

psychological disorders

15

■ **THE NATURE OF PSYCHOLOGICAL DISORDERS**
Deciding What Is Abnormal • The Problem of Objectivity • Historical Perspectives • The Etiology of Psychopathology

■ **CLASSIFYING PSYCHOLOGICAL DISORDERS**
Goals of Classification • DSM-IV-TR

■ **PSYCHOLOGY IN YOUR LIFE: IS "INSANITY" REALLY A DEFENSE?**

■ **MAJOR TYPES OF PSYCHOLOGICAL DISORDERS**
Anxiety Disorders: Types • Anxiety Disorders: Causes • Mood Disorders: Types • Mood Disorders: Causes • Gender Differences in Depression • Suicide • Personality Disorders • Dissociative Disorders

■ **PSYCHOLOGY IN THE 21ST CENTURY: DOES "INTERNET ADDICTION" EXIST?**

■ **SCHIZOPHRENIC DISORDERS**
Major Types of Schizophrenia • Causes of Schizophrenia

■ **THE STIGMA OF MENTAL ILLNESS**

■ **RECAPPING MAIN POINTS**
Key Terms

I want to let you know what it is like to be a functional scitzophrenic in these days and times and what someone with my mental illness faces.

I live by myself and am 30. I live on SSI and work part-time as I go through college. Im not allowed to go into Nursing despite past patient care experience and college classes, because of my illness. Im majoring in Human Services to help others with problems, because when I first was sick, I suffered bad and can relate with the suffering.

I live pretty normal and no one can tell Im mentally ill unless I tell them.... My sister (not a twin) has this illness too, for 12 years, and wont take her medicine because she refused to understand she has this illness. Ive had mine for 5 years. I became convinced the 1st year through my suffering by reading the book, "I Never Promised You a Rose Garden." So I improved, thanks to the antipsychotic medicine available. The patient and public, in my opnion needs to be educated about mental illness, because people ridicule

and mistreat, even misunderstand us at crucial times. Like how family, husband, friends, or social services react to what they don't know about us. The medicine works good on some of us.

I can tell the difference between a noise of my illness and a real noise, because Ive studied myself reading about it. There is a common sense rule I use. I just try hard to remember what the world and people are really like. The illness picks such silly nonsense to bother the mind with. The medicine is strong with me and my body chemistry so I don't have too many illness symptoms bothering me....

The delusions before I got my medicine picked any storyline it chose, and changed it at will. As time went by before help, I felt it was taking over my whole brain, and I'd cry wanting my mind and life back....

Everyone that wants to succeed in life needs opportunities for them to prove themself. Im a person besides just a person with an illness.

What are your reactions as you read this young woman's words, an excerpt from a letter to your authors? If they are similar to ours, you feel a mixture of sadness at her plight, of delight in her willingness to do all she can to cope with the many problems her mental illness creates, of anger toward those who stigmatize her because she may act differently at times, and of hope that, with medication and therapy, her condition may improve. These are but a few of the emotions that clinical and research psychologists and psychiatrists feel as they try to understand and treat mental disorders.

This chapter focuses on the nature and causes of psychological disorders: what they are, why they develop, and how we can explain their causes. The next chapter builds on this knowledge to describe the strategies used to treat, and to prevent, mental illness. Research indicates that nearly 50 percent of young and middle adults in the United States have suffered from a psychological disorder at some point in their lives (Kessler et al., 1994). Thus, many of you who read this text are likely to benefit directly from knowledge about psychopathology. Facts

alone, however, will not convey the serious impact psychological disorders have on the everyday lives of individuals and families. Throughout this chapter, as we discuss categories of psychological disorders, try to envision the real people who live with such a disorder every day. We will share with you their words and lives, as we did at the start of the chapter. Let's begin now with a discussion of the concept of abnormality.

■ The Nature of Psychological Disorders

Have you ever worried excessively? Felt depressed or anxious without really knowing why? Been fearful of something you rationally knew could not harm you? Had thoughts about suicide? Used alcohol or drugs to escape a problem? Almost everyone will answer yes to at least one of these questions, which means that almost

What do you imagine the lives of people with mental illnesses are like?

everyone has experienced the symptoms of a psychological disorder. This chapter looks at the range of psychological functioning that is considered unhealthy or abnormal, often referred to as *psychopathology* or *psychological disorder*. **Psychopathological functioning** involves disruptions in emotional, behavioral, or thought processes that lead to personal distress or that block one's ability to achieve important goals. The field of **abnormal psychology** is the area of psychological investigation most directly concerned with understanding the nature of individual pathologies of mind, mood, and behavior.

We begin this section by exploring a more precise definition of abnormality and then look at problems of objectivity. We then examine how this definition evolved over hundreds of years of human history.

Deciding What Is Abnormal

What does it mean to say someone is *abnormal* or *suffering from a psychological disorder*? How do psychologists and other clinical practitioners decide what is abnormal? Is it always clear when behavior moves from the normal to the abnormal category? The judgment that someone has a mental disorder is typically based on the evaluation of the individual's *behavioral* functioning by people with some special authority or power. The terms used to describe these phenomena—mental disorder, mental illness, or abnormality—depend on the particular perspective, training, and cultural background of the evaluator, the situation, and the status of the person being judged.

Let's consider seven criteria you might use to label behavior as "abnormal" (*DSM-IV-TR*, 2000; Rosenhan & Seligman, 1989):

1. *Distress or disability.* An individual experiences personal distress or disabled functioning, which produces a risk of physical or psychological deterioration or loss of freedom of action. For example, a man who cannot leave his home without weeping would be unable to pursue ordinary life goals.

2. *Maladaptiveness.* An individual acts in ways that hinder goals, do not contribute to personal well-being, or interfere strongly with the goals of others and the needs of society. Someone who is drinking so heavily that she cannot hold down a job or who is endangering others through her intoxication is displaying maladaptive behavior.

3. *Irrationality.* An individual acts or talks in ways that are irrational or incomprehensible to others. A man who responds to voices that do not exist in objective reality is behaving irrationally.

4. *Unpredictability.* An individual behaves unpredictably or erratically from situation to situation, as if experiencing a loss of control. A child who smashes his fist through a window for no apparent reason displays unpredictability.

5. *Unconventionality and statistical rarity.* An individual behaves in ways that are statistically rare and that violate social standards of what is acceptable or desirable. Just being statistically unusual, however, does not lead to a psychological judgment of abnormality. For example, possessing genius-level intelligence is extremely rare, but it is also considered desirable. On the other hand, having extremely low intelligence is also rare but is considered undesirable; thus, it has often been labeled abnormal.

6. *Observer discomfort.* An individual creates discomfort in others by making them feel threatened or distressed in some way. A woman walking down the middle of the street, having a loud conversation with herself, creates observer discomfort in motorists trying to drive around her.

7. *Violation of moral and ideal standards.* An individual violates expectations for how one ought to behave with respect to societal norms. By this criterion, people might be considered abnormal by some if they did not wish to work or they did not believe in God. This criterion for abnormality also becomes relevant in legal situations, a topic we address in the Psychology in Your Life box on page 476.

Can you see why most of these indicators of abnormality may not be immediately apparent to all observ-

Psychopathological functioning Disruptions in emotional, behavioral, or thought processes that lead to personal distress or block one's ability to achieve important goals.

Abnormal psychology The area of psychological investigation concerned with understanding the nature of individual pathologies of mind, mood, and behavior.

ers? Consider just the last criterion. Are you mentally ill if you don't wish to work, even if that is abnormal with respect to the norms of society? Or consider a more serious symptom. It is "bad" to have hallucinations in our culture because they are taken as signs of mental disturbance, but it is "good" in cultures in which hallucinations are interpreted as mystical visions from spirit forces. Whose judgment is correct? At the end of this chapter, we will consider some negative consequences and dangers associated with such socially regulated judgments and the decisions based on them.

We are more confident in labeling behavior as "abnormal" when more than just one of the indicators is present and valid. The more extreme and prevalent the indicators are, the more confident we can be that they point to an abnormal condition. None of these criteria is a *necessary* condition shared by all cases of abnormality. For example, during his murder trial, a Stanford University graduate student who had killed his math professor with a hammer, and then taped to his office door a note that read "No office hours today," reported feeling neither guilt nor remorse. Despite the absence of personal suffering, we would not hesitate to label his overall behavior as abnormal. It is also true that no single criterion, by itself, is a *sufficient* condition that distinguishes all cases of abnormal behavior from normal variations in behavior. The distinction between normal and abnormal is not so much a difference between two independent types of behaviors as it is a matter of the degree to which a person's actions resemble a set of agreed-upon criteria of abnormality. Mental disorder is best thought of as a *continuum* that varies between *mental health* and *mental illness*, as shown in **Figure 15.1**.

How comfortable do you feel with these ideas about abnormality? Although the criteria seem fairly clear-cut, psychologists still worry about the problem of objectivity.

The Problem of Objectivity

The decision to declare someone psychologically disordered or abnormal is always a *judgment* about behavior: The goal for many researchers is to make these judgments *objectively*, without any type of bias. For some psychological disorders, like depression or schizophrenia, diagnosis often easily meets the standards of objectivity. Other cases are more problematic. As we have seen throughout our study of psychology, the meaning of behavior is jointly determined by its *content* and by its *context*. The same act in different settings conveys very different meanings. A man kisses another man; it may signify a gay relationship in the United States, a ritual greeting in France, or a Mafia "kiss of death" in Sicily. The meaning of a behavior always depends on context.

Let's see why objectivity is such an important issue. History is full of examples of situations in which judg-

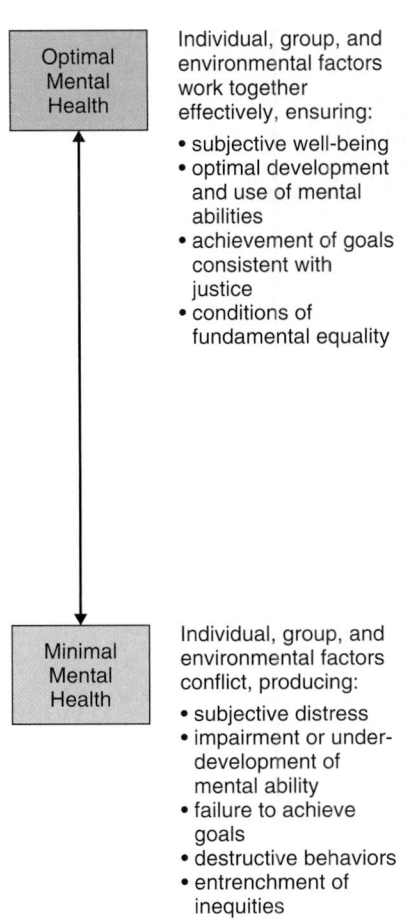

Optimal Mental Health — Individual, group, and environmental factors work together effectively, ensuring:
- subjective well-being
- optimal development and use of mental abilities
- achievement of goals consistent with justice
- conditions of fundamental equality

Minimal Mental Health — Individual, group, and environmental factors conflict, producing:
- subjective distress
- impairment or under-development of mental ability
- failure to achieve goals
- destructive behaviors
- entrenchment of inequities

FIGURE 15.1

Mental Health Continuum

Because the distinction between *normal* and *abnormal* is relative, rather than absolute, it is useful to think of mental health as a continuum. At one end are behaviors that define optimal mental health; at the other end are behaviors that define minimal mental health. In between lie gradual increases in maladaptive behaviors.

ments of abnormality were made by individuals to preserve their moral or political power. Consider an 1851 report, entitled "The Diseases and Physical Peculiarities of the Negro Race," published in a medical journal. Its author, Dr. Samuel Cartwright, had been appointed by the Louisiana Medical Association to chair a committee to investigate the "strange" practices of African American slaves. "Incontrovertible scientific evidence" was amassed to justify the practice of slavery. Several "diseases" previously unknown to the white race were discovered. One finding was that blacks allegedly suffered from a sensory disease that made them insensitive "to pain when being punished" (thus, no need to spare the whip). The committee also invented the disease *drapetomania,* a mania

FIGURE 15.2

The Art of Mihail Chemiakin

Chemiakin was declared insane for painting in a style inconsistent with Soviet doctrine.

to seek freedom—a mental disorder that caused certain slaves to run away from their masters. Runaway slaves needed to be caught so that their illness could be properly treated (Chorover, 1981)!

In more recent history, the leaders of the Soviet Union followed the custom of diagnosing political dissidents as mentally disordered for their unacceptably deviant ideology and sentencing them to long terms in remote mental hospitals. For example, the artist who painted **Figure 15.2,** Mihail Chemiakin, was declared insane and exiled for refusing to paint in the government-approved tradition of Soviet socialist realism.

Once an individual has obtained an "abnormal" label, people are inclined to interpret later behavior to confirm that judgment. **David Rosenhan** (1973, 1975) and his colleagues demonstrated that it may be impossible to be judged "sane" in an "insane place."

HOW WE KNOW

BEING SANE IN AN "INSANE" PLACE
Rosenhan and seven other sane people gained admission to different psychiatric hospitals by pretending to have a single symptom: hallucinations. All eight of these *pseudopatients* were diagnosed on admission as either paranoid schizophrenic or manic-depressive. Once admitted, they behaved normally in every way. Rosenhan observed, however, that when a sane

person is in an insane place, he or she is likely to be judged insane, and any behavior is likely to be reinterpreted to fit the context. If the pseudopatients discussed their situation in a rational way with the staff, they were reported to be using "intellectualization" defenses, while their taking notes of their observations were evidence of "writing behavior." The pseudopatients remained on the wards for almost three weeks, on the average, and not one was identified by the staff as sane. When they were finally released—only with the help of spouses or colleagues—their discharge diagnosis was still "schizophrenia" but "in remission." That is, their symptoms were no longer active.

Rosenhan's research demonstrates how judgments of abnormality rely on factors beyond behavior itself.

In the view of psychiatrist **Thomas Szasz,** mental illness does not even exist—it is a "myth" (1961, 1977, 1995). Szasz argues that the symptoms used as evidence of mental illness are merely medical labels that sanction professional intervention into what are social problems—deviant people violating social norms. Once labeled, these people can be treated either benignly or harshly for their problem "of being different," with no threat of disturbing the existing status quo.

Few clinicians would go this far, in large part because the focus of much research and treatment is on understanding and alleviating personal distress. For most of the disorders we will describe in this chapter, individuals experience their own behavior as abnormal, or poorly adapted to the environment. Even so, this discussion suggests that there can be no altogether objective assessments of abnormality. As we describe each type of psychological disorder, you should try to understand why clinicians believe the cluster of symptoms represents behavior patterns that are more serious for the individual than mere violations of social norms.

To help round out your perspective on the context of psychological disorders, we will now fill in some of the history of the concept of abnormality and the treatment of abnormal behavior. We will then turn to the general causal factors researchers look to as the forces that give rise to abnormality.

Historical Perspectives

Throughout history, humans have feared psychological disorders, often associating them with evil. Because of this fear, people have reacted aggressively and decisively to any behaviors they perceived as bizarre or abnormal. People who have exhibited such behaviors have been imprisoned and made subject to radical medical treatments. Attitudes about the link between mental illness and evil may be as old as human history. Archaeologists have found prehistoric skulls with holes drilled in them. These discoveries might indicate that our ancestors believed such holes would allow the demons that had possessed a loved one to escape.

The following 10th-century invocation was intended to alleviate *hysteria*, an affliction characterized by a cluster of symptoms that included paralysis or pains, dizziness, lameness, and blindness. Hysteria was originally thought to affect only women, and it was believed to be caused by a wandering uterus under the devil's control (Veith, 1965). Notice how the invocation illustrates the role demonic forces were believed to play in psychological disorders.

> *O womb, womb, womb, cylindrical womb, red womb, white womb, fleshy womb, bleeding womb, large womb, neufredic womb, bloated womb, O demoniacal one!...I conjure thee, O womb, in the name of the Holy Trinity to come back to the place from which thou shouldst neither move nor turn away...and to return, without anger, to the place where the Lord has put thee originally. (Zilboorg and Henry, 1941, quoted in Nietzel et al., 1991, p. 19)*

In 1692, in the Massachusetts colony of Salem, numerous young women began experiencing convulsions, nausea, and weakness. They reported sensations of being pinched, pricked, or bitten. Many became temporarily blind or deaf; others reported visions and sensations of flying through the air. Such strange symptoms sparked a frantic search for an explanation. Many people theorized that the symptoms were the work of the devil, who, through the efforts of earthbound witches, had taken over the minds and bodies of the young women. These theories led to a witchcraft panic and to the execution of over 20 women believed to be witches.

Until the end of the 18th century, the mentally ill in Western societies were perceived as mindless beasts who could be controlled only with chains and physical discipline. They were not cared for in hospitals but were incarcerated with criminals. Let's see how that perspective began to change.

EMERGENCE OF THE MEDICAL MODEL

In the latter part of the 18th century, a new perspective about the origins of abnormal behavior emerged—people began to perceive those with psychological problems as *sick*, suffering from illness, rather than as *possessed* or *immoral*. As a result, a number of reforms were gradually implemented in the facilities for the insane. **Philippe Pinel** (1745–1826) was one of the first clinicians to use these ideas to attempt to develop a classification system for psychological difficulties based on the idea that disorders of thought, mood, and behavior are similar in many ways to the physical, organic illnesses. According to such a system, each disorder has a group of characteristic symptoms that distinguishes it from other disorders and from healthy functioning. Disorders are classified according to the patterns of observed symptoms, the circumstances surrounding the onset of the disturbance, the natural course of the disorder, and its response to treatment. Such classification systems are modeled after the biological classification systems naturalists use and are intended to help clinicians identify common disorders more easily.

In 1896, **Emil Kraepelin** (1855–1926), a German psychiatrist, was responsible for creating the first truly comprehensive *classification system* of psychological disorders. Strongly motivated by a belief that there was a physical basis to psychological problems, he gave the process of psychological diagnosis and classification the flavor of medical diagnosis, a flavor that remains today (Rosenhan & Seligman, 1989). His perspective is most readily seen in the terminology used by psychiatrists. They speak of *mental illness,* and *treat* mental *patients* in the hope of *curing* their *diseased* brains.

The Salem witchcraft trials were an outgrowth of a desperate attempt to affix blame for frighteningly bizarre behavior among the Puritan colonists. What general attitudes were common toward the mentally ill in those times?

In this engraving, circa 1780, Franz Mesmer entrances a salon full of fashionable ladies and gentlemen. In what form did "mesmerism" eventually become a useful technique in the treatment of some psychological disorders?

EMERGENCE OF PSYCHOLOGICAL MODELS

An alternative perspective to the medical approach focuses on the psychological causes and treatment of abnormal behavior. This perspective emerged most clearly at the end of the 18th century. It was helped along by the dramatic work of **Franz Mesmer** (1734–1815). Mesmer believed that many disorders, including hysteria, were caused by disruptions in the flow of a mysterious force that he called *animal magnetism*. He unveiled several new techniques to study animal magnetism, including one that eventually became known as *hypnotism* but was originally referred to as *mesmerism* in his honor (Darnton, 1968; Pattie, 1994).

Although Mesmer's general theory of animal magnetism was discredited, his hypnotic techniques were adopted by many researchers, including a prominent French neurologist, **Jean Charcot** (1825–1893). Charcot found that some of the symptoms of hysteria, such as paralysis of a limb, could be eliminated when a patient was under hypnosis. Hypnosis even had the power to *induce*—bring out—the symptoms of hysteria in healthy individuals, dramatically illustrating the potential of *psychological factors* to cause problems that were believed to have an exclusively physical basis.

One of Charcot's students, Sigmund Freud, continued to experiment with hypnosis. Freud used his experiments to elaborate his psychodynamic theories of personality and abnormality, which continue to influence current theories of the nature and causes of psychopathology. (He later abandoned hypnotherapy for psychoanalysis as the treatment for psychological disorders.)

Modern perspectives on abnormality most often combine aspects of both medical and psychological

Etiology The causes of, or factors related to, the development of a disorder.

models of mental illness. We next consider those general types of explanations for the origins or causes of abnormality.

The Etiology of Psychopathology

Etiology refers to the factors that cause or contribute to the development of psychological and medical problems. Knowing why the disorder occurs, what its origins are, and how it affects thought and emotional and behavioral processes may lead to new ways of treating and, ideally, preventing it. An analysis of causality will be an important part of our discussion of each individual disorder. Here we introduce two general categories of causal factors: biological and psychological.

BIOLOGICAL APPROACHES

Building on the heritage of the medical model, modern biological approaches assume that psychological disturbances are directly attributable to underlying biological factors. Biological researchers and clinicians most often investigate structural abnormalities in the brain, biochemical processes, and genetic influences.

The brain is a complex organ whose interrelated elements are held in delicate balance. Subtle alterations in its chemical messengers—the neurotransmitters—or in its tissue can have significant effects. Genetic factors, brain injury, and infection are a few of the causes of these alterations. We have seen in earlier chapters that technological advances in brain imaging techniques allow mental health professionals to view the structure of the brain and specific biochemical processes in living individuals without surgery. Using these techniques, biologically oriented researchers are discovering new links between psychological disorders and specific abnormalities in the brain. In addition, continuing advances in the field of behavioral genetics have improved researchers' abilities to identify the links between specific genes and the presence of psychological disorders. We will look to these different types of biological explanation throughout the chapter as we try to understand the nature of various forms of abnormality.

PSYCHOLOGICAL APPROACHES

Psychological approaches focus on the causal role of psychological or social factors in the development of psychopathology. These approaches perceive personal experiences, traumas, conflicts, and environmental factors as the roots of psychological disorders. We will outline three dominant psychological models of abnormality: the psychodynamic, the behavioral, and the cognitive.

PSYCHODYNAMIC. Like the biological approach, the psychodynamic model holds that the causes of psychopathology are located inside the person. However, according to **Sigmund Freud,** who developed this model, the internal causal factors are psychological rather than biological. As we noted in earlier chapters, Freud believed that many psychological disorders were simply an extension of "normal" processes of psychic conflict and ego defense that all people experience. In the psychodynamic model, early childhood experiences shape both normal and abnormal behavior.

In psychodynamic theory, behavior is motivated by drives and wishes of which people are often unaware. Symptoms of psychopathology have their roots in *unconscious conflict* and thoughts. If the unconscious is conflicted and tension-filled, a person will be plagued by anxiety and other disorders. Much of this psychic conflict arises from struggles between the irrational, pleasure-seeking impulses of the *id* and the internalized social constraints imposed by the *superego.* The *ego* is normally the arbiter of this struggle; however, its ability to perform its function can be weakened by abnormal development in childhood. Individuals attempt to avoid the pain caused by conflicting motives and anxiety with *defense mechanisms,* such as repression or denial. Defenses can become overused, distorting reality or leading to self-defeating behaviors. The individual may then expend so much psychic energy in defenses against anxiety and conflict that there is little energy left to provide a productive and satisfying life.

BEHAVIORAL. Because of their emphasis on observable responses, behavioral theorists have little use for hypothetical psychodynamic processes. These theorists argue that abnormal behaviors are acquired in the same fashion as healthy behaviors—through learning and reinforcement. They do not focus on internal psychological phenomena or early childhood experiences. Instead, they focus on the *current* behavior and the *current* conditions or reinforcements that sustain the behavior. The symptoms of psychological disorders arise because an individual has learned self-defeating or ineffective ways of behaving. By discovering the environmental contingencies that maintain any undesirable, abnormal behavior, an investigator or clinician can then recommend treatment to change those contingencies and extinguish the unwanted behavior. Behaviorists rely on both classical and operant conditioning models (recall Chapter 7) to understand the processes that can result in maladaptive behavior.

COGNITIVE. Cognitive perspectives on psychopathology are often used to supplement behavioral views. The cognitive perspective suggests that the origins of psychological disorders cannot always be found in the objective reality of stimulus environments, reinforcers, and overt responses. What matters as well is the way people perceive or think about themselves and about their relations with other people and the environment. Among the cognitive variables that can guide—or misguide—adaptive responses are a person's perceived degree of control over important reinforcers, a person's beliefs in his or her ability to cope with threatening events, and interpretations of events in terms of situational or personal factors. The cognitive approach suggests that psychological problems are the result of distortions in perceptions of the reality of a situation, faulty reasoning, or poor problem solving.

SOCIOCULTURAL. The sociocultural perspective on psychopathology emphasizes the role culture plays in both the diagnosis and etiology of abnormal behavior. We already gave you a taste of the impact of culture on diagnosis when we described the problem of objectivity. We suggested that behaviors are interpreted in different ways in different cultures: The threshold at which a certain type of behavior will cause an individual problems in adjustment will depend, in part, on how that behavior is viewed in its cultural context. With respect to etiology, the particular cultural circumstances in which people live may define an environment that helps bring about distinctive types or subtypes of psychopathology. We will give you examples of such *culture-bound syndromes* in the next section on classification.

We have now given you a general sense of the types of explanations researchers give for the emergence of mental illness. It is worth noting that contemporary researchers increasingly take an *interactionist* perspective on psychopathology, seeing it as the product of a complex interaction between a number of biological and psychological factors. For example, genetic predispositions may make a person vulnerable to a psychological disorder by affecting neurotransmitter levels or hormone levels, but psychological or social stresses or certain learned behaviors may be required for the disorder to develop fully.

In the next section, we describe the efforts that have been made to classify and describe different categories of disorder.

SUMMING UP

Abnormality is defined with respect to a number of criteria: Distress or disability, maladaptiveness, irrationality, unpredictability, unconventionality and statistical rarity, observer discomfort, and violation of moral and ideal standards. No one of these criteria is necessary or sufficient to define mental illness. A primary goal for researchers is to make objective judgments related to psychological disorders; this goal is complicated because judgments of abnormality are often context-bound. Throughout much of human history, mentally ill individuals were mistreated or incarcerated. More humane treatments were developed when individuals such as Pinel, Mesmer, and Kraepelin began to treat disorders as illnesses that could be categorized and treated. Contemporary researchers generally look to interactions of biological and psychological factors to explain the etiology of mental illness.

Classifying Psychological Disorders

Why is it helpful to have a classification system for psychological disorders? What advantages are gained by moving beyond a global assessment that abnormality exists to distinguish among different types of abnormality? A **psychological diagnosis** is the label given to an abnormality by classifying and categorizing the observed behavior pattern into an approved diagnostic system. Such a diagnosis is in many ways more difficult to make than a medical diagnosis. In the medical context, a doctor can rely on physical evidence, such as X rays, blood tests, and biopsies, to inform a diagnostic decision. In the case of psychological disorders, the evidence for diagnosis comes from interpretations of a person's actions. In order to create greater consistency among clinicians and coherence in their diagnostic evaluations, psychologists have helped to develop a system of diagnosis and classification that provides precise descriptions of symptoms, as well as other criteria to help practitioners decide whether a person's behavior is evidence of a particular disorder.

Psychological diagnosis The label given to psychological abnormality by classifying and categorizing the observed behavior pattern into an approved diagnostic system.

DSM-IV-TR The current diagnostic and statistical manual of the American Psychiatric Association that classifies, defines, and describes mental disorders.

Goals of Classification

To be most useful, a diagnostic system should provide the following three benefits:

- *Common shorthand language.* To facilitate a quick and clear understanding among clinicians or researchers working in the field of psychopathology, practitioners seek a common set of terms with agreed-upon meanings. A diagnostic category, such as *depression,* summarizes a large and complex collection of information, including characteristic symptoms and the typical course of the disorder. In clinical settings, such as clinics and hospitals, a diagnostic system allows mental health professionals to communicate more effectively about the people they are helping. Researchers studying different aspects of psychopathology or evaluating treatment programs must agree on the disorder they are observing.

- *Understanding of etiology.* Ideally, a diagnosis of a specific disorder should make clear the causes of the symptoms. Unfortunately, because there is substantial disagreement or lack of knowledge about the etiology of many psychological disorders, this goal is difficult to meet.

- *Treatment plan.* A diagnosis should also suggest what types of treatment to consider for particular disorders. Researchers and clinicians have found that certain treatments or therapies work most effectively for specific kinds of psychological disorders. For example, drugs that are quite effective in treating schizophrenia do not help and may even hurt people with depression. Further advances in knowledge about the effectiveness and specificity of treatments will make fast and reliable diagnosis even more important.

DSM-IV-TR

In the United States, the most widely accepted classification scheme is one developed by the American Psychiatric Association. It is called the *Diagnostic and Statistical Manual of Mental Disorders.* The revision published 2000 is a "text revision" of the fourth edition (*DSM-IV,* 1994); it is known by clinicians and researchers as *DSM-IV-TR.* It classifies, defines, and describes over 200 mental disorders.

To reduce the diagnostic difficulties caused by variability in approaches to psychological disorders, *DSM-IV-TR* emphasizes the *description* of patterns of symptoms and courses of disorders rather than etiological theories or treatment strategies. The purely descriptive terms allow clinicians and researchers to use a common language to describe problems, while leaving room for disagreement and continued research about which theoretical models best *explain* the problems.

The first version of *DSM,* which appeared in 1952 *(DSM-I),* listed several dozen mental illnesses. *DSM-II,* introduced in 1968, revised the diagnostic system to make it more compatible with another popular system, the World Health Organization's *International Classification of Diseases* (*ICD*). The fourth edition of the *DSM* (*DSM-IV,* 1994) emerged after several years of intense work by committees of scholars. To make their changes (from the *DSM-III-Revised,* which appeared in 1987), these committees carefully scrutinized large bodies of research on psychopathology and also tested proposed changes for workability in actual clinical settings. *DSM-IV* is also fully compatible with the tenth edition of the *ICD. DSM-IV-TR* (2000), the text revision of *DSM-IV,* incorporated new research findings but did not change the classification structure outlined in *DSM-IV.*

To encourage clinicians to consider the psychological, social, and physical factors that may be associated with a psychological disorder, *DSM-IV-TR* uses dimensions, or *axes,* that portray information about all these factors (see **Table 15.1**). Most of the principal clinical disorders are contained on Axis I. Included here are all disorders that emerge in childhood, except for mental retardation. Axis II lists mental retardation as well as personality disorders. These problems may accompany Axis I disorders. Axis III incorporates information about general medical conditions, such as diabetes, that may be relevant to understanding or treating an Axis I or II disorder. Axes IV and V provide supplemental information that can be useful when planning an individual's treatment or assessing the *prognosis* (predictions of future change). Axis IV assesses psychosocial and environmental problems that may explain patients' stress responses or their resources for coping with stress. On Axis V, a clinician evaluates the global level of an individual's

functioning. A full diagnosis in the *DSM-IV-TR* system would involve consideration of each of the axes.

EVOLUTION OF DIAGNOSTIC CATEGORIES

The diagnostic categories and the methods used to organize and present them have shifted with each revision of the *DSM.* These shifts reflect changes in the opinions of a majority of mental health experts about exactly what constitutes a psychological disorder and where the lines between different types of disorders should be drawn. They also reflect changing perspectives among the public about what constitutes *abnormality.*

In the revision process of each *DSM,* some diagnostic categories were dropped and others were added. For example, with the introduction of *DSM-III,* in 1980, the traditional distinction between *neurotic* and *psychotic* disorders was eliminated. **Neurotic disorders,** or *neuroses,* were originally conceived of as relatively common psychological problems in which a person did not have signs of brain abnormalities, did not display grossly irrational thinking, and did not violate basic norms; but he or she did experience subjective distress or a pattern of self-defeating or inadequate coping strategies. **Psychotic disorders,** or *psychoses,* were thought to differ in both quality and severity from neurotic problems. It was believed that psychotic behavior deviated significantly

Neurotic disorders Mental disorders in which a person does not have signs of brain abnormalities and does not display grossly irrational thinking or violate basic norms but does experience subjective distress; a category dropped from *DSM-III.*

Psychotic disorders Severe mental disorders in which a person experiences impairments in reality testing manifested through thought, emotional, or perceptual difficulties; no longer used as a diagnostic category after *DSM-III.*

TABLE 15.1

The Five Axes of *DSM-IV-TR*

Axis	Classes of Information	Description
Axis I	Clinical disorders	These mental disorders present symptoms or patterns of behavioral or psychological problems that typically are painful or impair an area of functioning. Included are disorders that emerge in infancy, childhood, or adolescence.
Axis II	(a) Personality disorders (b) Mental retardation	These are dysfunctional patterns of perceiving and responding to the world.
Axis III	General medical conditions	This axis codes physical problems relevant to understanding or treating an individual's psychological disorders on Axes I and II.
Axis IV	Psychosocial and environmental problems	This axis codes psychosocial and environmental stressors that may affect the diagnosis and treatment of an individual's disorder and the likelihood of recovery.
Axis V	Global assessment of functioning	This axis codes the individual's overall level of current functioning in the psychological, social, and occupational domains.

IS "INSANITY" REALLY A DEFENSE?

On March 30, 1981, the world was shocked when John Hinckley was nearly successful in his attempt to assassinate U.S. president Ronald Reagan. In June 1982, shock turned to outrage when a jury found Hinckley "not guilty by virtue of insanity." Was this outrage appropriate? What does it mean for someone to be *insane*?

Insanity is not defined in *DSM-IV-TR;* there is no accepted clinical definition of insanity. Rather, insanity is a concept that belongs to popular culture and to the legal system. The treatment of insanity in the law dates back to England in 1843, when Daniel M'Naghten was found not guilty of murder by reason of insanity. M'Naghten's intended victim was the British prime minister—M'Naghten believed that God had instructed him to commit the murder. (He accidentally killed the prime minister's secretary instead.) Because of M'Naghten's delusions, he was sent to a mental hospital rather than to prison. The anger surrounding this verdict—even Queen Victoria was infuriated—prompted the House of Lords to articulate a guideline, known as the *M'Naghten rule,* to limit claims of insanity. This rule specifies that a criminal must not "know the nature and quality of the act he was doing; or, if he did know it, that he did not know he was doing what was wrong."

Does the M'Naghten rule seem like a fair test of guilt or innocence?

With advances in the understanding of mental illness, researchers became more aware of circumstances in which a criminal might know right from wrong—a criminal might understand that what he or she was doing was illegal or immoral—but still might not be able to suppress the actions. (We will address this type of dissociation in the discussion of anxiety disorders on page 480.) Often, for example, people with phobias "know" that a spider can do them no harm, but they are unable to suppress panic behaviors in the presence of the spider. This perspective on mental illness was incorporated into the legal standard that was operative at Hinckley's trial. His jury agreed that Hinckley's behavior—arising from his obsession with the actress Jodie Foster—was beyond his control.

Did Hinckley go free? Not at all. He was committed to St. Elizabeth's, a psychiatric hospital in the Washington area—and, as of 2001, remains there. In fact, one of the public's main misconceptions of the insanity defense is that it allows murderers to go free (Caplan, 1992; Silver et al., 1994). Perhaps 90 percent of the individuals acquitted on insanity pleas spend time in psychiatric care after they are found not guilty. In cases like Hinckley's, the individual is released into the community only when he or she is judged by experts no longer to be dangerous—there is often no upper limit placed on psy-

chiatric incarceration as there would be for prison incarceration. In Hinckley's case, how certain do you think a panel of psychiatrists and psychologists would have to feel before they would agree that Hinckley could go free?

In the aftermath of Hinckley's case, many jurisdictions altered their standards for the insanity defense—the general trend was to make it more difficult to obtain a verdict of "not guilty by reason of insanity" (Appelbaum, 1994). Were these changes necessary? On practical grounds, the answer is almost certainly "no." Despite the great attention that insanity pleas receive in the media—and, thus, the public's great awareness of them—such pleas are quite rare (Blau et al., 1993; Lymburner & Roesch, 1999). For example, one study found that in 60,432 indictments in Baltimore, Maryland only 190 defendants (0.31 percent) entered insanity pleas; of the 190 pleas, only 8 (4.2 percent) were successful (Janofsky et al., 1996). Thus, the likelihood that you will ever be asked to sit on a jury and judge another person as sane or insane is quite low. But suppose it did happen. Suppose, for example, you had been on the jury that considered whether Jeffrey Dahmer, who had engaged in cannibalistic rituals, was sane. (The jury rejected the insanity defense.) How might the information you have acquired in this chapter have affected your judgment?

---

from social norms and was accompanied by a profound disturbance in rational thinking and general emotional and thought processes. The *DSM-III* advisory committees felt that the terms neurotic disorders and psychotic disorders had become too general in their meaning to have much usefulness as diagnostic categories (however,

they continue to be used by many psychiatrists and psychologists to characterize the general level of disturbance in a person).

Across the editions of the *DSM*, individual diagnoses have also come and gone. One of the best examples is *homosexuality.* You may recall from Chapter 12 that it was in 1973 that the American Psychiatric Association voted to remove homosexuality from the list of psychological disorders. Until that time, homosexuality appeared in the *DSM* as a bona fide mental illness. What changed the

Insanity The legal (not clinical) designation for the state of an individual judged to be legally irresponsible or incompetent.

opinions of psychiatric experts was research data demonstrating the generally positive mental health of gay men and lesbians. Homosexuality is now simply considered a variant of sexual expression. It is relevant to a diagnosis in *DSM-IV-TR* only if an individual shows "persistent and marked distress about sexual orientation" (*DSM-IV-TR*, 2000, p. 582). That diagnostic criterion could, of course, apply equally well to distressed heterosexuals.

Finally, critics of earlier editions of the *DSM* had been greatly concerned that no attention was paid to cultural variation in the incidence of psychological disorders. In *DSM-IV-TR*, the description of most disorders includes information about "specific culture features." Furthermore, an appendix describes about 25 *culture-bound syndromes*: "recurrent, locality-specific patterns of aberrant behavior and troubling experience that may or may not be linked to a particular *DSM-IV* diagnostic category" (*DSM-IV-TR*, 2000, p. 898). Here are some examples:

- *Boufée delirante.* "A sudden outburst of agitated and aggressive behavior, marked confusion, and psychomotor excitement" (p. 899); reported in West Africa and Haiti.

- *Koro.* "An episode of sudden and intense anxiety that the penis (or, in females, the vulva and nipples) will recede into the body and possibly cause death" (p. 900); reported in south and east Asia.

- *Taijin kyofusho.* "An individual's intense fear that his or her body, its parts or its functions, displease, embarrass, or are offensive to other people in appearance, odor, facial expressions, or movements" (p. 903); reported in Japan

As we describe each major form of psychological disorder, it is important to bear in mind that not all cultures treat the same behaviors as normal or abnormal.

SUMMING UP

The goals of classifying psychological disorders are to provide a common shorthand language for the description and discussion of different disorders as well as to specify an etiology and a treatment plan. *DSM-IV-TR* is the most widely used classification system; information is gathered on five axes. Diagnostic categories have evolved over time to improve the accuracy and usefulness of the system.

Major Types of Psychological Disorders

Now that we have given you a basic framework for thinking about abnormality, we get to the core information that you will want to know—the causes and consequences of major psychological disorders, such as

anxiety, depression, and schizophrenia. For each category, we will begin by describing what sufferers experience and how they appear to observers. Then we will consider how each of the major biological and psychological approaches to etiology explains the development of these disorders.

There are many other categories of psychopathology that we will not have time to examine. However, what follows is a capsule summary of some of the most important we must omit:

- *Substance-use disorders* include both dependence on and abuse of alcohol and drugs. We discussed many issues of substance abuse in the broader context of states of consciousness (see Chapter 6).

- *Somatoform disorders* involve physical (soma) symptoms, such as paralysis or pains in a limb, that arise without a physical cause. This category includes the symptoms of what used to be called hysteria.

- *Sexual disorders* involve problems with sexual inhibition or dysfunction and deviant sexual practices.

- *Disorders usually first diagnosed in infancy, childhood, or adolescence* include mental retardation, communication disorders such as stuttering, and autism.

- *Eating disorders*, such as anorexia and bulimia, were discussed in Chapter 12.

Throughout this chapter, we will provide estimates of the frequency with which individuals experience particular psychological disorders. These estimates arise from research projects in which mental health histories are obtained from large samples of the population, up to 20,000 people. Figures are available for the prevalence of different disorders over one-month, one-year, and lifetime periods (Kessler et al., 1994; Regier et al., 1993a, 1993b). The figures we will generally cite come from the *National Comorbidity Study (NCS)*, which sampled 8,098 U.S. adults ages 15 to 54 years (Kessler et al., 1994). Although we will refer to this sample as "adults," it is important to note that the study included some teenagers and excluded older adults. It is also important to emphasize that often the same individuals have experienced more than one disorder simultaneously at some point in their life span, a phenomenon known as **comorbidity**. (*Morbidity* refers to the occurrence of disease. *Comorbidity* refers to the co-occurrence of diseases.) The NCS found that 56 percent of the people who had experienced one disorder had actually experienced two or more. Researchers have begun to study intensively the patterns of comorbidity of different psychological disorders.

As you read about the symptoms and experiences that are typical of the various psychological disturbances, you may

Comorbidity The experience of more than one disorder at the same time.

begin to feel that some of the characteristics seem to apply to you—at least part of the time—or to someone you know. Some of the disorders that we will consider are not uncommon, so it would be surprising if they sounded completely alien. Many people have human frailties that appear on the list of criteria for a particular psychological disorder. Recognition of this familiarity can further your understanding of abnormal psychology, but you should remember that a diagnosis for any disorder depends on a number of criteria and requires the judgment of a trained mental health professional. Please resist the temptation to use this new knowledge to diagnose friends and family members as pathological. However, if the chapter leaves you uneasy about mental health issues, please note that most colleges and universities have counseling centers for students with such concerns.

We will explore anxiety and depression in depth and more briefly consider personality disorders and dissociative disorders. We then devote a section to schizophrenia.

Anxiety Disorders: Types

Everyone experiences anxiety or fear in certain life situations. For some people, however, anxiety becomes problematic enough to interfere with their ability to function effectively or enjoy everyday life. It has been estimated that almost 25 percent of the adult population has, at some time, experienced symptoms characteristic of the various **anxiety disorders** (Kessler et al., 1994). While anxiety plays a key role in each of these disorders, they differ in the extent to which anxiety is experienced, the severity of the anxiety, and the situations that trigger the anxiety. We will review five major categories: generalized anxiety disorder, panic disorder, phobic disorder, obsessive-compulsive disorder, and posttraumatic stress disorder.

GENERALIZED ANXIETY DISORDER

When a person feels anxious or worried most of the time for at least six months, when not threatened by any specific danger, clinicians diagnose **generalized anxiety disorder.** The anxiety is often focused on specific life circumstances, such as unrealistic concerns about finances or the well-being of a loved one. The way the anxiety is ex-

Anxiety disorders Mental disorders marked by physiological arousal, feelings of tension, and intense apprehension without apparent reason.

Generalized anxiety disorder An anxiety disorder in which an individual feels anxious and worried most of the time for at least six months when not threatened by any specific danger or object.

Panic disorder An anxiety disorder in which sufferers experience unexpected, severe panic attacks that begin with a feeling of intense apprehension, fear, or terror.

Agoraphobia An extreme fear of being in public places or open spaces from which escape may be difficult or embarrassing.

pressed—the specific symptoms—varies from person to person, but for a diagnosis of generalized anxiety disorder to be made, the patient must also suffer from at least three other symptoms, such as muscle tension, fatigue, restlessness, poor concentration, irritability, or sleep difficulties.

Generalized anxiety disorder leads to impaired functioning because the person's worries cannot be controlled or put aside. With the focus of attention on the sources of anxiety, the individual cannot attend sufficiently to social or job obligations. These difficulties are compounded by the physical symptoms associated with the disorder.

PANIC DISORDER

In contrast to the chronic presence of anxiety in generalized anxiety disorder, sufferers of **panic disorder** experience unexpected, severe *panic attacks* that may last only minutes. These attacks begin with a feeling of intense apprehension, fear, or terror. Accompanying these feelings are physical symptoms of anxiety, including autonomic hyperactivity (such as rapid heart rate), dizziness, faintness, or sensations of choking or smothering. The attacks are unexpected in the sense that they are not brought about by something concrete in the situation.

The following comments made during a panic attack will help you appreciate the degree of panic commonly experienced by someone with this disorder:

> Uh, I'm not going to make it. I can't get help, I can't get anyone to understand the feeling. It's like a feeling that sweeps over from the top of my head to the tip of my toes. And I detest the feeling. I'm very frightened.... It feels like I'm going to die or something. (Muskin & Fyer, 1981, p. 81)

A panic disorder is diagnosed when an individual has recurrent unexpected panic attacks and also begins to have persistent concerns about the possibility of having more attacks.

Why might a situation like this one cause difficulty for a person with agoraphobia?

In *DSM-IV-TR*, panic disorder must be diagnosed as occurring with or without the simultaneous presence of agoraphobia. **Agoraphobia** is an extreme fear of being in public places or open spaces from which escape may be difficult or embarrassing. Individuals with agoraphobia usually fear such places as crowded rooms, malls, buses, and freeways. They are often afraid that, if they experience some kind of difficulty outside the home, such as a loss of bladder control or panic attack symptoms, help might not be available or the situation will be embarrassing to them. These fears deprive individuals of their freedom, and, in extreme cases, they become prisoners in their own homes.

Can you see why agoraphobia is related to panic disorder? For some (but not all) people who suffer from panic attacks, the dread of the next attack—the helpless feelings it engenders—can be enough to imprison them. The person suffering from agoraphobia may leave the safety of home but almost always with extreme anxiety.

PHOBIAS

Fear is a rational reaction to an objectively identified external danger (such as a fire in one's home or a mugging attack) that may induce a person to flee or to attack in self-defense. In contrast, a person with a **phobia** suffers from a persistent and irrational fear of a specific object, activity, or situation that is excessive and unreasonable given the reality of the threat.

Many people feel uneasy about spiders or snakes (or even multiple-choice tests). These mild fears do not prevent people from carrying out their everyday activities. Phobias, however, interfere with adjustment, cause significant distress, and inhibit necessary action toward goals. Even a very specific, apparently limited phobia can have a great impact on one's whole life. *DSM-IV-TR* defines two categories of phobias: *social phobias* and *specific phobias* (see **Table 15.2**).

Social phobia is a persistent, irrational fear that arises in anticipation of a public situation in which an individual can be observed by others. A person with a social

What turns a harmless garter snake into a threatening object of phobia?

Fear A rational reaction to an objectively identified external danger that may induce a person to flee or attack in self-defense.
Phobia A persistent and irrational fear of a specific object, activity, or situation that is excessive and unreasonable, given the reality of the threat.
Social phobia A persistent, irrational fear that arises in anticipation of a public situation in which an individual can be observed by others.
Specific phobias Phobias that occur in response to specific types of objects or situations.

TABLE 15.2

Common Phobias

	Sex Difference	Typical Age of Onset
Social phobias (fear of being observed doing something humiliating)	Majority are women	Adolescence
Specific phobias		

Animal type
  Cats (ailurophobia)
  Dogs (cynophobia)
  Insects (insectophobia)
  Spiders (arachnophobia)
  Snakes (ophidiophobia)
  Rodents (rodentophobia)
	Vast majority are women	Childhood

Natural environment type
  Storms (brontophobia)
  Heights (acrophobia)
	Majority or vast majority are women	Childhood

Blood–injection–injury type
  Blood (hemaphobia)
  Needles (belonephobia)
	Majority are women	Any age

Situational type
  Closed spaces
  (claustrophobia)
  Railways
  (siderodromophobia)
	Vast majority are women	Childhood or mid-20s

phobia fears that he or she will act in ways that could be embarrassing. The person recognizes that the fear is excessive and unreasonable yet feels compelled by the fear to avoid situations in which public scrutiny is possible. Social phobia often involves a self-fulfilling prophecy. A person may be so fearful of the scrutiny and rejection of others that enough anxiety is created to actually impair performance. Even when social phobics are successful in social circumstances, they do not allow that success to reflect positively on themselves (Wallace & Alden, 1997). Among U.S. adults, 13.3 percent have experienced a social phobia (Magee et al., 1996).

Specific phobias occur in response to several different types of objects or situations. As shown in Table 15.2, specific phobias are further categorized into several sub-types. For example, an individual suffering from an *animal-type specific phobia* might have a phobic response to spiders. In each case, the phobic response is produced either in the presence of or in anticipation of the feared specific object or situation. Research suggests that 11.3 percent of adults in the United States have experienced a specific phobia (Magee et al., 1996).

OBSESSIVE-COMPULSIVE DISORDERS

Some people with anxiety disorders get locked into specific patterns of thought and behavior.

> *Only a year or so ago, 17-year-old Jim seemed to be a normal adolescent with many talents and interests. Then, almost overnight, he was transformed into a lonely outsider, excluded from social life by his psychological disabilities. Specifically, he developed an obsession with washing. Haunted by the notion that he was dirty—in spite of what his senses told him—he began to spend more of his time cleansing himself of imaginary dirt. At first, his ritual washings were confined to weekends and evenings, but soon they began to consume all his time, forcing him to drop out of school. (Rapoport, 1989)*

Jim is suffering from a condition known as **obsessive-compulsive disorder (OCD)**, which has been estimated to affect 2.5 percent of U.S. adults at some point during their lives (*DSM-IV-TR*, 2000). *Obsessions* are thoughts, images, or impulses (such as Jim's belief that he is unclean) that recur or persist despite a person's efforts to suppress them. Obsessions are experienced as an unwanted invasion of consciousness, they seem to be senseless or repugnant, and they are unacceptable to the person experiencing them. You probably have had some sort of mild obsessional experience, such as the intrusion of petty worries—"Did I really lock the door?"; or "Did I turn off the oven?" The obsessive thoughts of people with obsessive-compulsive disorder are much more compelling, cause much more distress, and may interfere with their social or occupational functioning.

Compulsions are repetitive, purposeful *acts* (such as Jim's washing) performed according to certain rules or in a ritualized manner in response to an obsession. Compulsive behavior is performed to reduce or prevent the discomfort associated with some dreaded situation, but it is either unreasonable or clearly excessive. Typical compulsions include irresistible urges to clean, to check that lights or appliances have been turned off, and to count objects or possessions.

At least initially, people with obsessive-compulsive disorder resist carrying out their compulsions. When they are calm, they view their compulsion as senseless. When anxiety rises, however, the power of the ritual compulsive behavior to relieve tension seems irresistible. Part of the pain experienced by people with this mental problem is created by their frustration at recognizing the irrationality or excessive nature of their obsessions without being able to eliminate them.

POSTTRAUMATIC STRESS DISORDER

In Chapter 13, we presented a discussion between two women who were still grappling with the aftereffects of rape. The conversation portrayed the two women's ongoing anxiety. One reported going through a "long period of fear and anger" and having dreams of being assaulted in front of her dorm, with friends watching without coming to her rescue. The other, who had been raped while jogging, was still afraid to resume running: "Every time I go jogging I have a perpetual fear. My pulse doubles. Of course I don't go jogging alone any more, but still the fear is there constantly." These women suffer from **posttraumatic stress disorder (PTSD)**, an anxiety disorder that is characterized by the persistent reexperience of traumatic events through distressing recollections, dreams, hallucinations, or flashbacks. Individuals may develop PTSD in response to rape, life-threatening events or severe injury, and natural disasters (Davidson et al., 1991; Fairbank et al., 1993; Foa & Riggs, 1995; Green, 1994). People develop PTSD both when they themselves have been the victim of the trauma and when they have witnessed others being victimized. People who suffer from PTSD are also likely to suffer simultaneously from other psychopathologies, such as major depression, substance-abuse problems, and sexual dysfunction.

Research suggests that about 8 percent of adults in the United States will experience PTSD at some point during their lifetime (*DSM-IV-TR*, 2000). Overall, about three-quarters of the general population have experienced an event that could be defined as traumatic, such as a serious accident, a natural disaster, or physical abuse (Green, 1994). In one sample of college students, 84 percent reported that they had experienced at least one traumatic event; roughly one-third reported four or more separate events (Vrana & Lauterbach, 1994). Although men and women experience about the same rate of traumatic events, women are twice as likely to develop PTSD (Breslau et al., 1997). By comparison to men, childhood traumas are particularly likely to give rise to PTSD in women. Researchers are still trying to understand this gender difference.

■ **Obsessive-compulsive disorder (OCD)** A mental disorder characterized by obsessions—recurrent thoughts, images, or impulses that recur or persist despite efforts to suppress them—and compulsions—repetitive, purposeful acts performed according to certain rules or in a ritualized manner.

■ **Posttraumatic stress disorder (PTSD)** An anxiety disorder characterized by the persistent reexperience of traumatic events through distressing recollections, dreams, hallucinations, or dissociative flashbacks.

Posttraumatic stress disorder severely disrupts sufferers' lives. How do researchers go about the complex task of exploring the origins of PTSD and other anxiety disorders? Understanding the origins gives hope to eliminating the psychological distress.

Anxiety Disorders: Causes

How do psychologists explain the development of anxiety disorders? Each of the four etiological approaches we have outlined (biological, psychodynamic, behavioral, and cognitive) emphasizes different factors. Let's analyze how each adds something unique to the understanding of anxiety disorders.

BIOLOGICAL

Various investigators have suggested that anxiety disorders have biological origins. One theory attempts to explain why certain phobias, such as those for spiders or heights, are more common than fears of other dangers, such as electricity. Because many fears are shared across cultures, it has been proposed that, at one time in the evolutionary past, certain fears enhanced our ancestors' chances of survival. Perhaps humans are born with a predisposition to fear whatever is related to sources of serious danger in the evolutionary past. This *preparedness hypothesis* suggests that we carry around an evolutionary tendency to respond quickly and "thoughtlessly" to once-feared stimuli (Öhman, 1986; Seligman, 1971). However, this hypothesis does not explain types of phobias that develop in response to objects or situations that would not have had survival meaning over evolutionary history, like fear of needles or driving or elevators.

The ability of certain drugs to relieve and of others to produce symptoms of anxiety offers evidence of a biological role in anxiety disorders (Holland et al., 1999; Klerman et al., 1994). For example, recall from Chapter 3 that when the level of the neurotransmitter GABA in the brain becomes low, people often experience feelings of anxiety. As we shall see in Chapter 16, drugs that affect GABA levels are used as successful treatments for some of types of anxiety disorders. Researchers are also using imaging techniques to examine the brain bases of these disorders (Malizia, 1999). For example, PET scans have revealed a difference in the function of GABA receptors between the brains of individuals who suffer from panic disorder and those of control individuals (Malizia et al., 1998). These differences may help explain the onset of panic disorder. MRI techniques have revealed very widespread abnormalities in OCD patients brains with respect to a much lower volume of myelinated nerve fibers than in normal brains (Jenike et al., 1996). Researchers are still trying to understand the relationship between these brain abnormalities and the symptoms of OCD.

Finally, research with identical and fraternal twins suggests a genetic basis for the predisposition to experience four of the five categories of anxiety disorders (Skre et al., 1993). For example, the probability that a pair of identical twins both suffered from a panic disorder was twice as great as the probability that both fraternal twins were sufferers. The only type of anxiety disorder that produced no evidence of a genetic contribution were phobias, implicating more purely environmental origins for those disorders.

PSYCHODYNAMIC

The psychodynamic model begins with the assumption that the symptoms of anxiety disorders come from underlying psychic conflicts or fears. The symptoms are attempts to protect the individual from psychological pain. Thus, panic attacks are the result of unconscious conflicts bursting into consciousness. Suppose, for example, a child represses conflicting thoughts about his or her wish to escape a difficult home environment. In later life, a phobia may be activated by an object or situation that symbolizes the conflict. A bridge, for example, might come to symbolize the path that the person must traverse from the world of home and family to the outside world. The sight of a bridge would then force the unconscious conflict into awareness, bringing with it the fear and anxiety common to phobias. Avoiding bridges would be a symbolic attempt to stay clear of anxiety about the childhood experiences at home.

In obsessive-compulsive disorders, the obsessive behavior is seen as an attempt to displace anxiety created by a related but far more feared desire or conflict. By substituting an obsession that symbolically captures the forbidden impulse, a person gains some relief. For example, the obsessive fears of dirt experienced by Jim, the adolescent we described earlier, may have their roots in the conflict between his desire to become sexually active and his fear of "dirtying" his reputation. Compulsive preoccupation with carrying out a minor ritualistic task also allows the individual to avoid the original issue that is creating unconscious conflict.

BEHAVIORAL

Behavioral explanations of anxiety focus on the way symptoms of anxiety disorders are reinforced or conditioned. Investigators do not search for underlying unconscious conflicts or early childhood experiences, because these phenomena can't be observed directly. As we saw in Chapter 7, behavioral theories are often used to explain the development of phobias, which are seen as classically conditioned fears: Recall Little Albert, in whom John Watson and Rosalie Rayner instilled a fear of a white rat (see page 191). The behavioral account suggests that a previously neutral object or situation becomes a stimulus for a phobia by being paired with a frightening experience. For example, a child whose mother yells a warning when he or she approaches a snake may develop a phobia about snakes. After this experience, even thinking about snakes may produce a wave of fear. Phobias continue to be maintained by the reduction in anxiety that occurs when a person withdraws from the feared situation.

A behavioral analysis of obsessive-compulsive disorders suggests that compulsive behaviors tend to reduce the anxiety associated with obsessive thoughts—thus reinforcing the compulsive behavior. For example, if a woman fears contamination by touching garbage, then washing her hands reduces the anxiety and is therefore reinforcing. In parallel to phobias, obsessive-compulsive disorders continue to be maintained by the reduction in anxiety that follows from the compulsive behaviors.

COGNITIVE

Cognitive perspectives on anxiety concentrate on the perceptual processes or attitudes that may distort a person's estimate of the danger that he or she is facing. A person may either overestimate the nature or reality of a threat or underestimate his or her ability to cope with the threat effectively. For example, before delivering a speech to a large group, a person with a social phobia may feed his or her anxiety:

> What if I forget what I was going to say? I'll look foolish in front of all these people. Then I'll get even more nervous and start to perspire, and my voice will shake, and I'll look even sillier. Whenever people see me from now on, they'll remember me as the foolish person who tried to give a speech.

People who suffer from anxiety disorders may often interpret their own distress as a sign of impending disaster. Their reaction may set off a vicious cycle in which the person fears disaster, which leads to an increase in anxiety, which in turn worsens the anxiety sensations and confirms the person's fears (Beck & Emery, 1985).

Psychologists have tested this cognitive account by measuring *anxiety sensitivity*: individuals' beliefs that bodily symptoms—such as shortness of breath or heart palpitations—may have harmful consequences. People high in anxiety sensitivity are likely to agree with statements such as "When I notice that my heart is beating rapidly, I worry that I might have a heart attack." In one study, researchers assessed the anxiety sensitivity of a group of students who were about to undergo a stressful course of U.S. Air Force Academy basic cadet training. Approximately 20 percent of those students who measured above the 90th percentile on anxiety sensitivity experienced panic attacks during the five-week course, compared to 6 percent for the rest of the group (Schmidt

et al., 1997). These data suggest that some individuals may experience panic attacks because they interpret their bodily arousal in a fearful fashion.

Research has also found that anxious patients contribute to the *maintenance* of their anxiety by employing cognitive biases that highlight the threatening stimuli.

PROCESSING OF ANXIETY-RELATED WORDS AND PANIC DISORDER Cognitive theories suggest that people suffering from anxiety disorders should provide evidence of heightened responsiveness to *threat-related* concepts. For individuals who suffer from panic disorders, those concepts include words related to the physiological, body-related symptoms of panic attacks: for example, *dizzy, fainting,* and *breathless.* A team of researchers presented words from this category, as well as a control list of words (for example, *delicate, slow,* and *friendly*) very briefly, for about 1/100th of a second, to individuals suffering from panic disorders. The participants' task was to try to report, on each trial, what word had been presented. Performance of the panic disorder participants was compared to control participants. The cognitive theory predicts that only the panic disorder participants would recognize more words from the body-related list than from the control list. This prediction was confirmed: Panic disorder patients recognized 2.6 more words from the body-related category, whereas healthy controls recognized just 0.7 more words (Pauli et al., 1997).

These results suggest that anxious patients may have a bias in attention or encoding that makes them particularly likely to notice threatening stimuli—even when they last only 1/100th of a second.

Each of the major approaches to anxiety disorders may explain part of the etiological puzzle. Continued research of each approach will clarify causes and, therefore, potential avenues for treatment. Now that you have this basic knowledge about anxiety disorders, we'd like you to consider the next of the three major categories of abnormality we are covering in some detail—*mood disorders.*

Mood Disorders: Types

There have almost certainly been times in your life when you would have described yourself as terribly depressed or incredibly happy. For some people, however, extremes in mood come to disrupt normal life experiences. A **mood disorder** is an emotional disturbance, such as severe depression or depression alternating with mania.

Mood disorder A mood disturbance such as severe depression or depression alternating with mania.

What are some differences between the occasional feelings of unhappiness that most people feel and the symptoms of major depressive disorder?

TABLE 15.3

Characteristics of Major Depressive Disorder

Characteristic	Example
Dysphoric mood	Sad, blue, hopeless; loss of interest or pleasure in almost all usual activities
Appetite	Poor appetite; significant weight loss
Sleep	Insomnia or hypersomnia (sleeping too much)
Motor activity	Markedly slowed down (motor retardation) or agitated
Guilt	Feelings of worthlessness; self-reproach
Concentration	Diminished ability to think or concentrate; forgetfulness
Suicide	Recurrent thoughts of death; suicidal ideas or attempts

Researchers estimate that roughly 19 percent of adults have suffered from mood disorders (Kessler et al., 1994). We will describe two major categories: major depressive disorder and bipolar disorder.

MAJOR DEPRESSIVE DISORDER

Depression has been characterized as the "common cold of psychopathology," both because it occurs so frequently and because almost everyone has experienced elements of the full-scale disorder at sometime in their life. Everyone has, at one time or another, experienced grief after the loss of a loved one or felt sad or upset when failing to achieve a desired goal. These sad feelings are only one symptom experienced by people suffering from a **major depressive disorder** (see Table 15.3).

People diagnosed with depression differ in terms of the severity and duration of their symptoms. While many individuals struggle with clinical depression for only several weeks at one point in their lives, others experience depression episodically or chronically for many years. Estimates of the prevalence of mood disorders reveal that about 21 percent of females and 13 percent of males suffer a major depression at some time in their lives (Kessler et al., 1994).

Depression takes an enormous toll on those afflicted, on their families, and on society. One European study found that people with recurrent depression spend a fifth of their entire adult lives hospitalized, while 20 percent

of sufferers are totally disabled by their symptoms and do not ever work again (Holden, 1986). In the United States, depression accounts for the majority of all mental hospital admissions, but it is still believed to be underdiagnosed and undertreated. Fewer than half of those who suffer from major depressive disorder receive any professional help (Regier et al., 1993b).

BIPOLAR DISORDER

Bipolar disorder is characterized by periods of severe depression alternating with manic episodes. A person experiencing a **manic episode** generally acts and feels unusually elated and expansive. However, sometimes the individual's predominant mood is irritability rather than elation, especially if the person feels thwarted in some way. During a manic episode, a person often experiences an inflated sense of self-esteem or an unrealistic belief that he or she possesses special abilities or powers. The person may feel a dramatically decreased need to sleep and may engage excessively in work or in social or other pleasurable activities. Caught up in this manic mood, the person shows unwarranted optimism, takes unnecessary risks, promises anything, and may give away everything.

Major depressive disorder A mood disorder characterized by intense feelings of depression over an extended time, without the manic high phase of bipolar depression.

Bipolar disorder A mood disorder characterized by alternating periods of depression and mania

Manic episode A component of bipolar disorder characterized by periods of extreme elation, unbounded euphoria without sufficient reason, and grandiose thoughts or feelings about personal abilities.

Sam was a 20-year-old college student experiencing the symptoms of a manic episode:

> *Lately Sam has been feeling fantastic. He has so much energy that he almost never needs to sleep, and he is completely confident that he is the top student at his school. He is bothered that everyone else seems so slow; they don't seem to understand the brilliance of his monologues, and no one seems able to keep up with his pace. Sam has some exciting financial ideas and can't figure out why his friends aren't writing checks to get in on his schemes.*

When the mania begins to diminish, people like Sam are left trying to deal with the damage and predicaments they created during their period of frenzy. Thus manic episodes almost always give way to periods of severe depression.

The duration and frequency of the mood disturbances in bipolar disorder vary from person to person. Some people experience long periods of normal functioning punctuated by occasional, short manic or depressive episodes. A small percentage of unfortunate individuals go right from manic episodes to clinical depression and back again in continuous, unending cycles that are devastating to them, their families, their friends, and their coworkers. While manic, they may gamble away life savings or give lavish gifts to strangers, acts that later add to guilt feelings when they are in the depressed phase. Bipolar disorder is much rarer than major depressive disorder, occurring in about 1.6 percent of adults and distributed equally between males and females (Kessler et al., 1994).

Mood Disorders: Causes

What factors are involved in the development of mood disorders? We will address this question from the biological, psychodynamic, behavioral, and cognitive perspectives. Note that, because of its prevalence, major depressive disorder has been studied more extensively than bipolar disorder. Our review will reflect that distribution of research.

BIOLOGICAL

Several types of research provide clues to the contribution of biology to mood disorders. For example, the ability of different drugs to relieve manic and depressive symptoms provides evidence that different brain states underlie the two extremes of bipolar disorder. Reduced levels of two chemical messengers in the brain, serotonin and norepinephrine, have been linked to depression; increased levels of these neurotransmitters are associated with mania. However, the exact biochemical mechanisms of mood disorders have not yet been discovered (Duman et al., 1997). Researchers have used PET scans to show differences in the way the brain metabolizes cerebral glucose (a type of sugar utilized to produce energy)

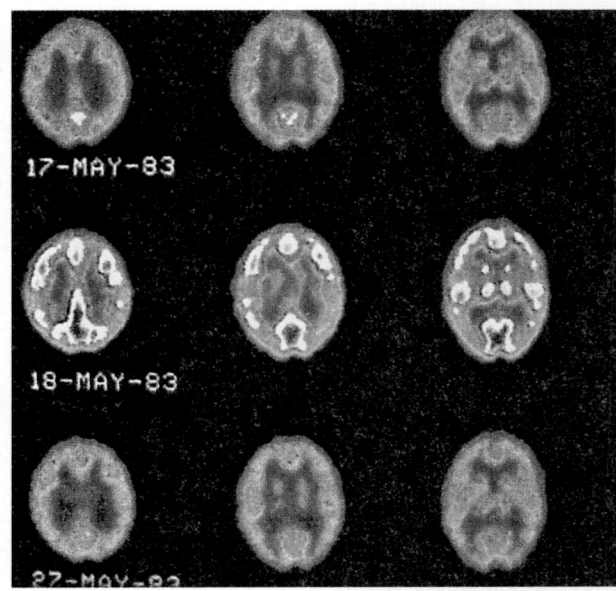

484

FIGURE 15.3

PET Scans of Bipolar Depression

PET scans indicate a higher level of cerebral glucose metabolism during manic phases than during depressive phases. The top and bottom rows show the patient during a depressive phase. The middle row shows the manic phase. The color bar on the right indicates the glucose metabolism rates.

during manic and depressive phases (see **Figure 15.3**), but such differences may be the consequence rather than the cause of the two mood states.

There is growing evidence that the incidence of mood disorder is influenced by genetic factors (McGue & Christensen, 1997). Studies of twins show that when one identical twin is afflicted by a mood disorder, there is a 67 percent chance that the second twin will also have the disorder; the figure for fraternal twins, who do not share identical genetic material, is only 20 percent (Ciaranello & Ciaranello, 1991; Gershon et al., 1987). Given the implication of heredity in the incidence of mood disorders, researchers have attempted to specify the exact locus of the genetic material responsible for transmission across generations.

One series of studies has focused on the pattern of bipolar disorder among the Amish community in Pennsylvania (Egeland et al., 1987). The Amish are ideal participants for such research, because they have large families, keep detailed genealogical records, are genetically isolated, and display few behavioral factors, such as alcoholism or violence, that could confuse the findings. All 15,000 members of the religious sect are descended from just 30 couples who migrated from Europe in the early eighteenth century. There is a tendency for bipolar disorder to run

Because Amish families remain geographically close and can trace their members through several generations, they are ideal participants for the study of hereditary conditions such as bipolar disorder. What goals do researchers bring to such studies?

in some but not other Amish families. This pattern allows researchers to make direct comparisons of the genetic material of individuals who do and do not suffer from the disorder. Although early reports of success in identifying a "bipolar gene" proved to be premature (Kelsoe et al., 1989), investigators remain optimistic that these comparisons will yield the genetic knowledge they seek (Berrettini et al., 1997; Ginns et al., 1992; Kelsoe et al., 1993).

A dramatic example of a biological approach to understanding one type of psychological disorder comes from research on an unusual form of depression. Some people regularly become depressed during the winter months, especially in the long Scandinavian winters when daylight hours are short (see **Figure 15.4**). This disturbance in mood has been appropriately named *seasonal affective disorder,* or *SAD* (Rosenthal et al., 1984; Young et al., 1997). Researchers have devised a therapy that is quite effective at alleviating SAD: patients are systematically exposed to bright white fluorescent light (Blehar & Rosenthal, 1989). Researchers have speculated that the light therapy may affect the activity of the neurotransmitter serotonin which, as we mentioned earlier, has been implicated as a causal factor in depression.

HOW WE KNOW

SEROTONIN AND SEASONAL AFFECTIVE DISORDER Patients suffering from SAD received a course of light therapy—two hours of bright fluorescent light—each evening in their homes. Only patients for whom the light therapy brought about relief (12 out of 14 patients) participated in the second phase of the study, which tested the idea that light therapy affects brain serotonin levels. Patients in an experimental group were put on a diet that was intended to lower the level of brain serotonin; control patients consumed a diet intended to maintain serotonin levels. Patients in the experimental group experienced a relapse of SAD symptoms; control patients did not. This pattern suggests that light therapy was initially responsible for restoring serotonin to levels that allowed patients to experience undepressed affect (Neumesiter et al., 1997).

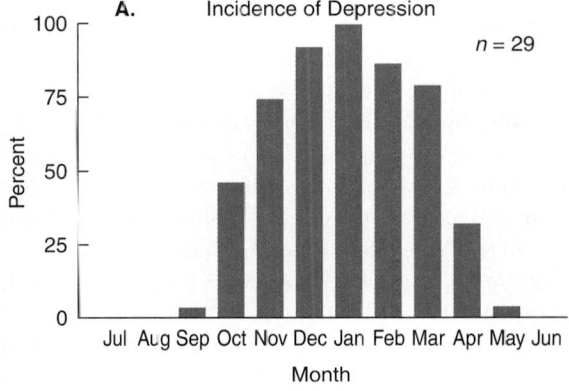

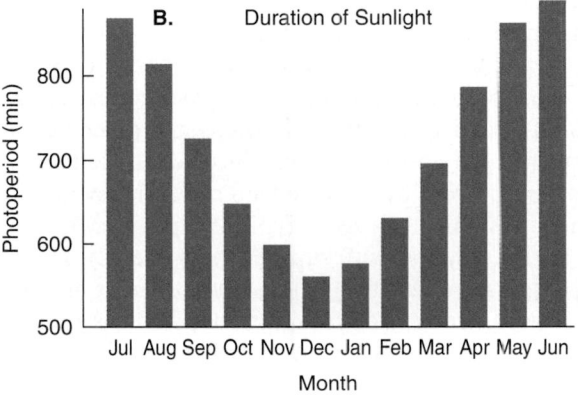

FIGURE 15.4

Seasonal Affective Disorder

People who suffer from seasonal affective disorder experience symptoms of depression during seasons with short sunlight. The figure displays a strong inverse relationship between the incidence of depression (part A) and the duration of sunlight (part B).

You might expect that people would have to take drugs to affect the actions of neurotransmitters in their brains. (We will describe some of these drugs in Chapter 16.) This study suggests, however, that light therapy can have the same effects as some psychoactive drugs. Both types of treatments—drug therapy or light therapy—support the role of a biological imbalance in the etiology of the disorder. Meanwhile, if you recognize yourself in the description of SAD, you should throw some light on the subject—you!

Let's see now what the three major psychological approaches can add to your understanding of the onset of mood disorders.

PSYCHODYNAMIC

In the psychodynamic approach, unconscious conflicts and hostile feelings that originate in early childhood are seen to play key roles in the development of depression. Freud was struck by the degree of self-criticism and guilt that depressed people displayed. He believed that the source of this self-reproach was anger, originally directed at someone else, that had been turned inward against the self. The anger was believed to be tied to an especially intense and dependent childhood relationship, such as a parent–child relationship, in which the person's needs or expectations were not met. Losses, real or symbolic, in adulthood reactivate hostile feelings, now directed toward the person's own ego, creating the self-reproach that is characteristic of depression.

BEHAVIORAL

Rather than searching for the roots of depression in the unconscious, the behavioral approach focuses on the effects of the amount of positive reinforcement and punishments a person receives (Lewinsohn, 1975; Lewinsohn et al., 1985). In this view, depressed feelings result when an individual receives insufficient positive reinforcements and experiences many punishments in the environment following a loss or other major life changes. Without sufficient positive reinforcement, a person begins to feel sad and withdraws. This state of sadness is initially reinforced by increased attention and sympathy from others (Biglan, 1991). Typically, however, friends who at first respond with support grow tired of the depressed person's negative moods and attitudes and begin to avoid him or her. This reaction eliminates another source of positive reinforcement, plunging the person further into depression. Research also shows that depressed people tend to underestimate positive feedback and overestimate negative feedback (Kennedy & Craighead, 1988; Nelson & Craighead, 1977).

Learned helplessness A general pattern of nonresponding in the presence of noxious stimuli that often follows after an organism has previously experienced noncontingent, inescapable aversive stimuli.

COGNITIVE

At the center of the cognitive approach to depression are two theories. One theory suggests that negative *cognitive sets*—"set" patterns of perceiving the world (see Chapter 5)—lead people to take a negative view of events in their lives for which they feel responsible. The second theory, the *explanatory style* model, proposes that depression arises from the belief that one has little or no personal control over significant life events. Each of these models explains some aspects of the experience of depression. Let's see how.

Aaron Beck (1983, 1985, 1988), a leading researcher on depression, has developed the theory of cognitive sets. Beck has argued that depressed people have three types of negative cognitions, which he calls the *cognitive triad* of depression: negative views of themselves, negative views of ongoing experiences, and negative views of the future. Depressed people tend to view themselves as inadequate or defective in some way, to interpret ongoing experiences in a negative way, and to believe that the future will continue to bring suffering and difficulties. This pattern of negative thinking clouds all experiences and produces the other characteristic signs of depression. An individual who always anticipates a negative outcome is not likely to be motivated to pursue any goal, leading to the *paralysis of will* that is prominent in depression.

In the explanatory style view, pioneered by **Martin Seligman** (see Chapter 12), individuals believe, correctly or not, that they cannot control future outcomes that are important to them. Seligman's theory evolved from research that demonstrated depressionlike symptoms in dogs (and later in other species). Seligman and Maier (1967) subjected dogs to painful, unavoidable shocks: no matter what the dogs did, there was no way to escape the shocks. The dogs developed what Seligman and Maier called **learned helplessness.** Learned helplessness is marked by three types of deficits: *motivational deficits*—the dogs were slow to initiate known actions; *emotional deficits*—they appeared rigid, listless, frightened, and distressed; and *cognitive deficits*—they demonstrated poor learning in new situations. Even when put in a situation in which they could, in fact, avoid shock, they did not learn to do so (Maier & Seligman, 1976).

Seligman believed that depressed people are also in a state of learned helplessness: they have an expectancy that nothing they can do matters (Abramson et al., 1978; Peterson & Seligman, 1984; Seligman, 1975). However, the emergence of this state depends, to a large extent, on how individuals explain their life events. As we discussed in Chapter 12, there are three dimensions of explanatory style: *internal-external, global-specific,* and *stable-unstable.* Suppose that you have just received a poor grade on a psychology exam. You attribute the negative outcome on the exam to an internal factor ("I'm stupid"), which makes you feel sad, rather than to an external one ("The

According to cognitive theories, under what circumstances could a poor grade or an unhappy romance lead to major depression?

exam was really hard"), which would have made you angry. You could have chosen a less stable internal quality than intelligence to explain your performance ("I was tired that day"). Rather than attributing your performance to an internal, stable factor that has global or far-reaching influence (stupidity), you could even have limited your explanation to the psychology exam or course ("I'm not good at psychology courses"). Explanatory style theory suggests that individuals who attribute failure to internal, stable, and global causes are vulnerable to depression. This prediction has been confirmed repeatedly (Peterson & Seligman, 1984; Seligman, 1991).

Cognitive theories of depression share the view that the ways in which depressed people think about themselves and the events in their lives are likely to keep them depressed. For example, people have a general tendency toward *self-verification*—they seek information that confirms their self-concept (Swann, 1990, 1997). This tendency has negative consequences for depressed individuals.

HOW WE KNOW

SELF-VERIFICATION AND DEPRESSION

Researchers differentiated three groups of individuals: One group was depressed, the second group was nondepressed but experienced low self-esteem, and the third group was nondepressed and had high self-esteem. The participants in each group completed a packet of questionnaires in preparation for an interview. During the interview, the participants were told that two graduate students had examined those questionnaires and each had written a "personality summary" in advance of a full personality assessment of the individual. In fact, all participants received the same summaries—one was positive ("this person seems well adjusted, self-confident, happy" and so on) and one was negative ("this person seems unhappy, unconfident, uncomfortable around others" and so on). Based on these summaries, participants were asked to choose which full assessment they would like to read. The results are presented in **Table 15.4**. As you can see, depressed individuals were disproportionately interested in reading the negative assessments; individuals with low self-esteem also showed a tendency to prefer negative feedback whereas those with high self-esteem clearly preferred positive feedback. Table 15.4 also provides data for each group on how accurate they believed the positive and negative summaries to be. Note that only depressed participants believed that the negative summary was more accurate (Giesler et al., 1996).

You might have expected that depressed people would try to "pull themselves out of it" by seeking positive feedback. This experiment demonstrates that, instead, they seek information that is consistent with their depression—and almost certainly functions to perpetuate that depression.

In Chapter 16, we will see that insights generated from cognitive theories of depression have given rise to successful forms of therapy. For now, there are two other important aspects of the study of depression that we will review: the large differences between the prevalence of depression in men and women and the link between depression and suicide.

Gender Differences in Depression

One of the central questions of research on depression is why women are afflicted twice as often as men. An insightful proposal by **Susan Nolen-Hoeksema** (1990; Nolen-Hoaksema et al., 1999) points to the response styles

TABLE 15.4

Self-Verification and Depression

	Depressed	Low Self-Esteem	High Self-Esteem
Percent choosing negative assessment	82	64	25
Perceived accuracy of summary[a]			
Positive summary	5.67	6.60	9.70
Negative summary	7.89	6.48	2.45
Difference	−2.22	0.12	7.25

[a]Accuracy ratings were made on an 11-point scale ranging from not at all (1) to very much (11) accurate.

of men and women once they begin to experience negative moods. According to this view, when women experience sadness, they tend to think about the possible causes and implications of their feelings. In contrast, men attempt actively to distract themselves from depressed feelings, either by focusing on something else or by engaging in a physical activity that will take their minds off their current mood state. This model suggests that it is the more thoughtful, *ruminative* response style of women, the tendency to focus obsessively on their problems, that increases women's vulnerability to depression (Butler & Nolen-Hoeksema, 1994). From a cognitive approach, paying attention to your negative moods can increase your thoughts of negative events, which eventually increases the quantity and/or the intensity of negative feelings. Research has confirmed that those individuals who report that they generally ruminate about depression are more likely to suffer severe depressive episodes (Just & Alloy, 1997; Nolen-Hoeksema et al., 1993). The differences in response style between men and women that put women at greater risk for depression emerge in childhood (Nolen-Hoeksema & Girgus, 1994).

A task force of the American Psychological Association that reviewed research on gender differences in depression suggested that women's higher risk for depression can be understood only as the product of an interaction between a number of psychological, social, economic, and biological factors (McGrath et al., 1990). Several of these factors relate to the experience of being female in many cultures, such as women's greater likelihood of experiencing physical or sexual abuse or of living in poverty while being the primary caregiver for children and elderly parents. Such a finding indicates that the causes of depression may be a complex combination of factors and that there are multiple paths from "normal" behavior to depression.

Suicide

"The will to survive and succeed had been crushed and defeated....There comes a time when all things cease to shine, when the rays of hope are lost" (Shneidman, 1987, p. 57). This sad statement by a suicidal young man reflects the most extreme consequence of any psychological disorder—*suicide*. While most depressed people do not commit suicide, analyses suggest that most suicides—perhaps 50 to 80 percent—are attempted by those who are suffering from depression (Shneidman, 1985). In the general U.S. population, the number of deaths officially designated as suicide is around 30,000; because many suicides are attributed to accidents or other causes, the actual rate is probably much higher. Although suicide is the eighth leading cause of death in the United States for all ages, it is third for people ages 15 to 24 (Murphy, 2000). For ev-

Highly successful individuals, like rock star Kurt Cobain, are not immune to the feelings of despair that can trigger suicide. What has research revealed about the relationship between depression and suicide?

ery completed suicide, there may be as many as 8 to 20 suicide attempts. A survey of 694 college freshmen revealed that 26 percent had considered suicide during the past 12 months; 2 percent had actually attempted suicide in the past 12 months; and 10 percent had attempted suicide at some point in their lives (Meehan et al., 1992). Because depression occurs more frequently in women, it is not surprising that women *attempt* suicide about three times more often than men do; attempts by men, however, are more often successful. This difference occurs largely because men use guns more often, and women tend to use less lethal means, such as sleeping pills (Berman & Jobes, 1991).

One of the most alarming social problems in recent decades is the rise of *youth suicide*. Every nine minutes, a teenager attempts suicide; and every 90 minutes, a teenager succeeds. In any one week, 1,000 teenagers will try suicide, and 125 will succeed in killing themselves. Since 1960, the suicide rate among American teenagers has jumped by 200 to 300 percent (Garland & Zigler, 1993). Despite fewer attempts, adolescent boys are over four times more likely to succeed than are adolescent girls (Bingham et al., 1994). Note that the suicide rates for African American youths of both sexes are much lower than those for white youths, although no clear explanation has emerged for this finding (Bingham et al., 1994; Murphy, 2000). These racial differences remain in place across the life span. Elderly white men are at greatest risk for suicide and African American women least, when data are compared across race, gender, and age.

What lifestyle patterns predispose adolescents to attempt suicide? The breakup of a close relationship is a leading traumatic incident for both sexes (Gould et al.,

1996). Other significant incidents that create shame and guilt can overwhelm immature egos and lead to suicide attempts. Such incidents include being assaulted, beaten, raped, or arrested for the first time. Furthermore, gay and lesbian youths are at even higher risk for suicide than are other adolescents (Radkowsky & Siegel, 1997; Remafedi, 1999). These higher suicide rates undoubtedly reflect the relative lack of social support for homosexual orientation. Suicide is an extreme reaction that occurs especially when adolescents feel unable to cry out to others for help.

Youth suicide is not a spur-of-the-moment, impulsive act, but, typically, it occurs as the final stage of a period of inner turmoil and outer distress. The majority of young suicide victims have talked to others about their intentions or have written about them. Thus, talk of suicide should always be taken seriously (Marttunen et al., 1998). Recognizing the signs of suicidal thinking and the experiences that can start or intensify such destructive thoughts is a first step toward prevention. **Edwin Shneidman** (1999), a psychologist who for almost 40 years has studied and treated people with suicidal tendencies, concludes that "suicide is the desperate act of a perturbed and constricted mind, in seemingly unbearable and unresolvable pain.... The fact is that we can relieve the pain, redress the thwarted needs, and reduce the constriction of suicidal thinking" (1987, p. 58). Being sensitive to signs of suicidal intentions and caring enough to intervene are essential for saving the lives of both youthful and mature people who have come to see no exit for their troubles except total self-destruction.

Although, as we noted earlier, suicide rates are generally lower for nonwhites than for whites, there is one startling exception: among Native American youth, suicide is five times greater than among youth of the general population. Suicide is one of several forms of self-destructive behavior seen as part of the ongoing destruction of Native American communities in the United States (Strickland, 1997). **Teresa LaFromboise**, a Native American psychologist who has been studying the problem and developing prevention and treatment strategies, identifies the social causes of youth suicide among her people. With poverty rampant and unemployment high, suicide rates are boosted by "family disruption, pervasive hardship, a severe number of losses (whether through death, desertion, or divorce), substance abuse, the increased mobilities of families, and the incarceration of a significant caretaker" (LaFromboise, 1988, p. 9). In addition, the Native American belief that the living continuously interact with their ancestors in the spiritual world means that death holds little fear.

We have now reviewed two of the major classes of psychopathology: anxiety disorders and mood disorders. Before we turn to the topic of schizophrenia, we briefly consider personality disorders and dissociative disorders.

Personality Disorders

A **personality disorder** is a long-standing (chronic), inflexible, maladaptive pattern of perceiving, thinking, or behaving. These patterns can seriously impair an individual's ability to function in social or work settings and can cause significant distress. They are usually recognizable by the time a person reaches adolescence or early adulthood. There are many types of personality disorders (*DSM-IV-TR* recognizes 10 types). We will discuss four examples: paranoid, histrionic, narcissistic, and antisocial personality disorders.

People with *paranoid personality disorders* show a consistent pattern of distrust and suspiciousness about the motives of the individuals with whom they interact. People who suffer from this disorder suspect that other people are trying to harm or deceive them. They may find hidden unpleasant meanings in harmless situations. They expect their friends and spouses or partners to be disloyal.

Histrionic personality disorder is characterized by patterns of excessive emotionality and attention seeking. People with this disorder always wish to be the center of attention. If they are not, they may do something inappropriate to regain that spot. Sufferers offer strong opinions with great drama but with little evidence to back up their claims. They also react to minor occasions with overblown emotional responses.

People with a *narcissistic personality disorder* have a grandiose sense of self-importance, a preoccupation with fantasies of success or power, and a need for constant admiration. These people often have problems in interpersonal relationships; they tend to feel entitled to special favors with no reciprocal obligations, to exploit others for their own purposes, and to have difficulty recognizing and experiencing how others feel.

Antisocial personality disorder is marked by a long-standing pattern of irresponsible or unlawful behavior that violates social norms. Lying, stealing, and fighting are common behaviors. People with antisocial personality disorder often do not experience shame or remorse for their hurtful actions. Violations of social norms begin early in their lives—disrupting class, getting into fights, and running away from home. Their actions are marked by indifference to the rights of others. Antisocial personality disorder is often comorbid with other pathologies. For example, in one study, about 25 percent of individuals who met criteria for opioid (for example, opium, morphine, and heroin) abuse were also diagnosed with antisocial personality disorder (Brooner et al., 1997).

Personality disorder A chronic, inflexible, maladaptive pattern of perceiving, thinking, and behaving that seriously impairs an individual's ability to function in social or other settings.

In a career where power and financial gain are pursued at all costs, could antisocial personality disorder be an asset?

Although personality disorders have been studied less than other types of disorders, evidence is beginning to accumulate that these disorders have a genetic component (Livesley et al., 1993; Nigg & Goldsmith, 1994). If you recall the discussion in Chapter 14 about the strong heritability of personality traits (see page 437), you might not be surprised that disorders of those traits are also heritable. Research has also focused on the environmental circumstances that give rise to personality disorders (Norden et al., 1995; Paris, 1997). Consider the interactions of genetics and environment that yield antisocial personality disorder.

HOW WE KNOW

GENETICS, ENVIRONMENT, AND ANTISOCIAL PERSONALITY DISORDER A team of researchers recruited a sample of 95 men and 102 women who had been given up for adoption within a few days after birth. Institutional records provided enough information about the biological parents of this group so that the researchers could determine which parents had themselves experienced antisocial personality disorder. These data allowed for an assessment of genetic contributions to the disorder. The researchers also obtained information about the life circumstances of the adoptive families: Through interviews, they determined whether the participants had grown up in adverse environments with adoptive parents who, for example, had marital, legal, or drug and alcohol problems. These data allowed for an assessment of environmental contributions to antisocial personality disorder. The results demonstrated that both types of influences mattered: Individuals whose biological parents were diagnosed with the disorder or who grew up in an adverse environment were more likely, on average, to themselves be diagnosed as having antisocial personality disorder (Cadoret et al., 1995).

We see from this result that either genetics *or* the environment—nature *or* nurture—can put individuals at risk for developing antisocial personality disorder. At the same time, not every individual whose parents suffer from personality disorders or who grew up in a difficult environment develops these disorders. Researchers still wish to understand what makes some individuals vulnerable and others resilient.

Dissociative Disorders

A **dissociative disorder** is a disturbance in the integration of identity, memory, or consciousness. It is important for people to see themselves as being in control of their behavior, including emotions, thoughts, and actions. Essential to this perception of self-control is the sense of selfhood—the consistency of different aspects of the self and the continuity of identity over time and place. Psychologists believe that, in dissociated states, individuals escape from their conflicts by giving up this precious consistency and continuity—in a sense, disowning part of themselves. The forgetting of important personal experiences, a process caused by psychological factors in the absence of any organic dysfunction, called **dissociative amnesia,** is one example of dissociation. Psychologists have begun to document the degree to which such memory dissociation may accompany instances of sexual and physical childhood abuse (Spiegel & Cardeña, 1991). Other types of severe trauma—such as the firestorm that struck Oakland and Berkeley, California, in 1991, resulting in a loss of 25 lives and over a billion dollars damage—also produce dissociative symptoms (Koopman et al., 1996).

Dissociative identity disorder (DID), formerly known as *multiple personality disorder,* is a dissociative

Dissociative disorder A personality disorder marked by a disturbance in the integration of identity, memory, or consciousness.
Dissociative amnesia The inability to remember important personal experiences, caused by psychological factors in the absence of any organic dysfunction.
Dissociative identity disorder (DID) A dissociative mental disorder in which two or more distinct personalities exist within the same individual; formerly known as multiple personality disorder.

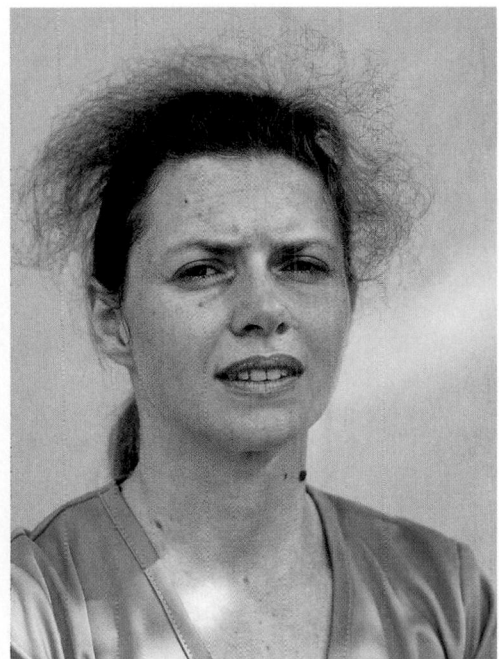

When found in a park in Florida, this woman (dubbed "Jane Doe" by authorities) was emaciated, incoherent, and near death. She was suffering from severe amnesia in which she had lost not only the memory of her name and her past but also the ability to read and write. What types of trauma may lead to dissociative amnesia?

mental disorder in which two or more distinct personalities exist within the same individual. At any particular time, one of these personalities is dominant in directing the individual's behavior. Dissociative identity disorder is popularly known as *split personality*, and sometimes mistakenly called *schizophrenia*, a disorder, as we shall see in the next section, in which personality often is impaired but is not split into multiple versions. In DID, each of the emerging personalities contrasts in some significant way with the original self—they might be outgoing if the person is shy, tough if the original personality is weak, and sexually assertive if the other is fearful and sexually naive. Each personality has a unique identity, name, and behavior pattern. In some cases, dozens of different characters emerge to help the person deal with a difficult life situation. Here is an excerpt from a first-person account of a woman who experiences DID (Mason, 1997, p. 44):

> Just as waves turn the ocean inside out and rearrange the water, different ones of us cycle in and out in an ebb and flow that is sometimes gentle, sometimes turbulent. A child colors with Crayola markers. She moves aside to make way for the administrator, who reconciles the bank statement. A moment later, the dead baby takes over and lies paralyzed on the floor.

> She remains that way for a while, but no one gets upset—it's her turn. The live baby stops in her crawl, engrossed by a speck of dust. The cooker prepares meals for three days and packages each separately—we all have different likes and dislikes. A terrified one screams aloud, a wounded one moans, a grieving one wails.

Can you put yourself in this woman's place, and imagine what it would be like to have this range of "individuals"—the child, the dead baby, the live baby, the cooker, and so on—inside your one head?

Some psychologists believe that multiple personalities develop to serve a vital survival function. DID victims may have been beaten, locked up, or abandoned by those who were supposed to love them—those on whom they were so dependent that they could not fight them, leave them, or even hate them. Instead, the psychodynamic perspective suggests that these victims have fled their terror symbolically through dissociation. They have protected their egos by creating stronger internal characters to help cope with the ongoing traumatic situation. Typically, DID victims are women who report being severely abused physically or sexually by parents, relatives, or close friends for extended periods during childhood. One study obtained questionnaire data from 448 clinicians who had treated cases of dissociative identity disorders and major depressions (used for comparative purposes). As shown in **Table 15.5**, the dominant feature of the 355 DID cases is the almost universal reports of abuse, with incidents often starting around age 3 and continuing for more than a decade. Although the 235 comparison patients with depression disorder also had a high incidence of abuse, it was significantly less than that experienced by those with DID (Schultz et al., 1989).

Although these data—and personal accounts of the type we quoted earlier—seem compelling, many psychologists

TABLE 15.5

Responses to Inquiries Regarding Abuse: Comparing Dissociative Identity Disorder and Depression

Questionnaire Item	DID (%)	Major Depression (%)
Abuse incidence	98	54
Type(s)		
Physical	82	24
Sexual	86	25
Psychological	86	42
Neglect	54	21
All of above	47	6
Physical and sexual	74	14
	(N = 355)	(N = 235)

remain skeptical about the diagnosis of DID (Lilienfeld et al., 1999; Spanos, 1994). No solid data exist about the prevalence of this disorder (*DSM-IV-TR*, 2000). Skeptics have often suggested that therapists who "believe" in DID may create DID—these therapists question their patients, often under hypnosis, in a way that encourages multiple personalities to "emerge." Other psychologists believe that sufficient evidence has accumulated in favor of the DID diagnosis to indicate that it is not just the product of zealous therapists (Gleaves, 1996). The safest conclusion may be that of the group of people diagnosed with DID, some cases are genuine whereas other cases emerge in response to therapists' demands.

SUMMING UP

Anxiety disorders fall into five categories: generalized anxiety disorder, panic disorder, phobias, obsessive-compulsive disorders, and posttraumatic stress disorder. Generalized anxiety disorder is characterized by chronic anxiety, whereas panic disorder is related to acute anxiety. Phobias are characterized by irrational fears so intense that they interfere with adjustment. Obsessions are uncontrollable, disruptive thoughts; compulsions are actions that are similarly uncontrollable. Traumatic events such as rape or severe injury will cause people to suffer from posttraumatic stress disorder. Researchers have demonstrated genetic linkages and brain abnormalities for anxiety disorders. Psychological explanations of these disorders include classical conditioning and cognitive biases.

Mood disorders consist either of major depressive disorder—the most common form of psychopathology—or bipolar disorder. Depression produces changes in mood, cognition, and motivation. People suffering from bipolar disorder experience alternations between periods of depression and mania. Researchers have demonstrated a genetic component for mood disorders as well as changes in

PSYCHOLOGY IN THE 21ST CENTURY

DOES "INTERNET ADDICTION" EXIST?

Do you find yourself spending more time on the Internet than you "should"? Would you rather spend time chatting with friends on the Internet than chatting with friends in person? Do you spend time on the Internet when you should be engaging in other important activities such as studying for exams or sleeping? Is it possible that you are *addicted* to the Internet?

Over the last few years the topic of "Internet addiction" has received a lot of coverage in the popular press: These new stories create images of (most often) adolescent males cutting themselves off from all real-world human contact to disappear into a cyberworld of chat rooms and MUDs. Some researchers have found real-life cases that match these media images. They have embraced the diagnosis of "Internet addiction" (e.g., Young, 1998). Other researchers remain more skeptical of this diagnosis as a unique type of psychopathology. Let's see why.

For each type of psychopathology we have described, we have seen that a diagnosis requires individuals to engage in fairly specific types of maladaptive behaviors, as outlined in *DSM-IV-TR*. However, with respect to the proposed diagnosis of Internet addiction, it is unclear exactly which behaviors of all the behaviors in which people engage on line are maladaptive. In the words of one researcher, "If some people are addicted to the Internet, what are they addicted to?" (Griffiths, 1998, p. 72).

Think about the goals people bring to their Internet use and the variety of activities they engage in while they are on line. For example, people get on the Net to acquire information, to play games, and to seek romantic or sexual partners. Could people become addicted to that general constellation of goals and activities—which is what a diagnosis of "Internet addiction" seems to imply? Or is it more specific aspects of Internet use that cause problems in psychological adjustment? If the latter suggestion is correct, it seems likely that one could find a more specific diagnosis already

recognized by mental health professionals. For example, as we have seen, *DSM-IV-TR* defines the category of *social phobia*. It may be more useful to diagnose someone who limits his or her interactions with other people to Internet interactions as suffering from social phobia rather than from Internet addiction. The particular ways in which people overuse the Internet might be symptoms of recognized disorders; overuse, in and of itself, should not qualify as a disorder.

Note that we are not denying the reality that some small percentage of people use the Internet in ways that are damaging to their personal, social, or professional lives. Research suggests, for example, that some people who use the Internet extensively come to feel isolated and lonely (Kraut et al., 1998; Nie & Erbring, 2000). However, what we want you to contemplate carefully is the idea that there are global properties of the Internet that lead to a specific form of psychopathology that can properly be called "Internet addiction."

brain function associated with depression and mania. Theories of depression often focus on the cognitive interpretations people give to their life experiences. Women's higher rate of serious depression may be related to the different ways in which women and men respond to depression. Depressed individuals quite often contemplate suicide.

Personality disorders are maladaptive forms of thinking and behaving; they may be severe enough to disrupt normal functioning in social or work settings. Dissociative disorders are disturbances in the integration of identity. Although researchers have suggested that childhood sexual abuse is a cause of dissociative identity disorder, the prevalence of the disorder remains controversial.

■ Schizophrenic Disorders

Everyone knows what it is like to feel depressed or anxious, even though most of us never experience these feelings to the degree of severity that constitutes a disorder. Schizophrenia, however, is a disorder that represents a qualitatively different experience from normal functioning. A **schizophrenic disorder** is a severe form of psychopathology in which personality seems to disintegrate, thought and perception are distorted, and emotions are blunted. The person with a schizophrenic disorder is the one you most often conjure up when you think about madness or insanity.

For many of the people afflicted with schizophrenia, the disease is a life sentence without possibility of parole, endured in the solitary confinement of a mind that must live life apart. Although schizophrenia is relatively rare—approximately 0.7 percent of U.S. adults have suffered from schizophrenia at some point in their lives (Kessler et al., 1994)—this figure translates to around two million people affected by this most mysterious and tragic mental disorder. Half of the beds in this nation's mental institutions are occupied by schizophrenic patients, because many spend their entire adult lives hospitalized, with little hope of ever returning to a "normal" existence.

Mark Vonnegut, son of novelist Kurt Vonnegut, was in his early twenties when he began to experience symptoms of schizophrenia. In *The Eden Express* (1975), he tells the story of his break with reality and his eventual recovery. Once, while pruning some fruit trees, his reality became distorted:

> I began to wonder if I was hurting the trees and found myself apologizing. Each tree began to take on personality. I began to wonder if any of them liked me. I became completely absorbed in looking at each tree and began to notice that they were ever so slightly luminescent, shining with a soft inner light that played around the branches. And from out of nowhere came an incredibly wrinkled, iridescent face. Starting as a small point infinitely distant, it rushed forward, becoming infinitely huge. I could see nothing else. My heart had stopped. The moment stretched forever. I tried to make the face go away but it mocked me.... I tried to look the face in the eyes and realized I had left all familiar ground (1975, p. 96).

Vonnegut's description gives you a glimpse at the symptoms of schizophrenia.

In the world of schizophrenia, *thinking* becomes illogical; associations among ideas are remote or without apparent pattern. **Hallucinations** often occur, involving imagined sensory perceptions—sights, smells, or, most commonly, sounds (usually voices)—that patients assume to be real. A person may hear a voice that provides a running commentary on his or her behavior or may hear several voices in conversation. **Delusions** are also common; these are false or irrational beliefs maintained in spite of clear contrary evidence. *Language* may become incoherent—a "word salad" of unrelated or made-up words—or an individual may become mute. *Emotions* may be flat, with no visible expression, or they may be inappropriate to the situation. *Psychomotor behavior* may be disorganized (grimaces, strange mannerisms), or posture may become rigid. Even when only some of these symptoms are present, deteriorated functioning in work and interpersonal relationships is likely as the patient withdraws socially or becomes emotionally detached.

Psychologists divide the symptoms between a positive category and a negative category. During *acute* or *active phases* of schizophrenia, the positive symptoms—hallucinations, delusions, incoherence, and disorganized behavior—are prominent. At other times, the negative symptoms—social withdrawal and flattened emotions—become more apparent. Some individuals, such as Mark Vonnegut, experience only one or a couple of acute phases of schizophrenia and recover to live normal lives. Others, often described as chronic sufferers, experience either repeated acute phases with short periods of negative symptoms or occasional acute phases with extended periods of negative symptoms. Even the most seriously disturbed are not acutely delusional all the time.

Major Types of Schizophrenia

Because of the wide variety of symptoms that can characterize schizophrenia, investigators consider it not a

Schizophrenic disorder Severe form of psychopathology characterized by the breakdown of integrated personality functioning, withdrawal from reality, emotional distortions, and disturbed thought processes.

Hallucinations False perceptions that occur in the absence of objective stimulation.

Delusions False or irrational beliefs maintained despite clear evidence to the contrary.

TABLE 15.6

Types of Schizophrenic Disorders

Types of Schizophrenia	Major Symptoms
Disorganized	Inappropriate behavior and emotions; incoherent language
Catatonic	Frozen, rigid, or excitable motor behavior
Paranoid	Delusions of persecution or grandeur
Undifferentiated	Mixed set of symptoms with thought disorders and features from other types
Residual	Free from major symptoms but evidence from minor symptoms of continuation of the disorder

single disorder but rather a constellation of separate types. The five most commonly recognized subtypes are outlined in **Table 15.6.**

DISORGANIZED TYPE

In this subtype of schizophrenia, a person displays incoherent patterns of thinking and grossly bizarre and disorganized behavior. Emotions are flattened or inappropriate to the situation. Often, a person acts in a silly or childish manner, such as giggling for no apparent reason. Language can become so incoherent, full of unusual words and incomplete sentences, that communication with others breaks down. If delusions or hallucinations occur, they are not organized around a coherent theme.

> *Mr. F. B. was a hospitalized mental patient in his late twenties. When asked his name, he said he was trying to forget it because it made him cry whenever he heard it. He then proceeded to cry vigorously for several minutes. Then, when asked about something serious and sad, Mr. F. B. giggled or laughed. When asked the meaning of the proverb "When the cat's away, the mice will play," Mr. F. B. replied, "Takes less place. Cat didn't know what mouse did and mouse didn't know what cat did. Cat represented more on the suspicious side than the mouse. Dumbo was a good guy. He saw what the cat did, put himself with the cat so people wouldn't look at them as comedians."* (Zimbardo, personal communication, 1957)

Mr. F. B.'s mannerisms, depersonalized, incoherent speech, and delusions are the hallmarks of the disorganized type of schizophrenia.

CATATONIC TYPE

The major feature of the catatonic type of schizophrenia is a disruption in motor activity. Sometimes people with this disorder seem frozen in a stupor. For long periods of time, the individual can remain motionless, often in a bizarre position, showing little or no reaction to anything

in the environment. At other times, these patients show excessive motor activity, apparently without purpose and not influenced by external stimuli. The catatonic type is also characterized by extreme *negativism,* an apparently unmotivated resistance to all instructions.

PARANOID TYPE

Individuals suffering from this form of schizophrenia experience complex and systematized delusions focused around specific themes:

- *Delusions of persecution.* Individuals feel that they are being constantly spied on and plotted against and that they are in mortal danger.

- *Delusions of grandeur.* Individuals believe that they are important or exalted beings—millionaires, great inventors, or religious figures such as Jesus Christ. Delusions of persecution may accompany delusions of grandeur—an individual is a great person but is continually opposed by evil forces.

- *Delusional jealousy.* Individuals become convinced—without due cause—that their mates are unfaithful. They contrive data to fit the theory and "prove" the truth of the delusion.

The onset of symptoms in individuals with paranoid schizophrenia tends to occur later in life than in other schizophrenic types. Individuals with paranoid schizophrenia rarely display obviously disorganized behavior. Instead, their behavior is likely to be intense and quite formal.

UNDIFFERENTIATED TYPE

This is the grab-bag category of schizophrenia, describing a person who exhibits prominent delusions, hallucinations, incoherent speech, or grossly disorganized behavior that fits the criteria of more than one type or of no clear type. The hodgepodge of symptoms experienced by these individuals does not clearly differentiate among various schizophrenic reactions.

RESIDUAL TYPE

Individuals diagnosed as residual type have usually suffered from a major past episode of schizophrenia but are currently free of major positive symptoms such as hallucinations or delusions. The ongoing presence of the disorder is signaled by minor positive symptoms or negative symptoms like flat emotion. A diagnosis of residual type may indicate that the person's disease is entering *remission,* or becoming dormant.

Causes of Schizophrenia

Different etiological models point to very different initial causes of schizophrenia, different pathways along which it develops, and different avenues for treatment. Let's look at the contributions several of these models can make to an understanding of the way a person may develop a schizophrenic disorder.

GENETIC APPROACHES

It has long been known that schizophrenia tends to run in families (Bleuler, 1978; Kallmann, 1946). Three independent lines of research—family studies, twin studies, and adoption studies—point to a common conclusion: Persons related genetically to someone who has had schizophrenia are more likely to become affected than those who are not (Kendler & Diehl, 1993; Tsuang, 2000). A summary of the risks of being affected with schizophrenia through various kinds of relatives is shown in **Figure 15.5.** Schizophrenia researcher **Irving Gottesman** (1991) pooled these data from about 40 reliable studies conducted in Western Europe between 1920 and 1987; he dropped the poorest data sets. As you can see, the data are arranged according to degree of genetic relatedness, which correlates highly with the degree of risk. For example, when both parents have suffered from schizophrenia, the risk for their offspring is 46 percent, as compared with 1 percent in the general population. When only one parent has had schizophrenia, the risk for the offspring drops sharply, to 13 percent. Note also that the probability that identical twins will both have schizophrenia is roughly three times greater than the probability for fraternal twins.

Researchers have also used adoption studies to demonstrate that the etiology of schizophrenia is greatly influenced by genetic factors (Kety et al., 1994). Consider a study that assessed the incidence of thought disorders in biological and adoptive relatives of schizophrenic patients.

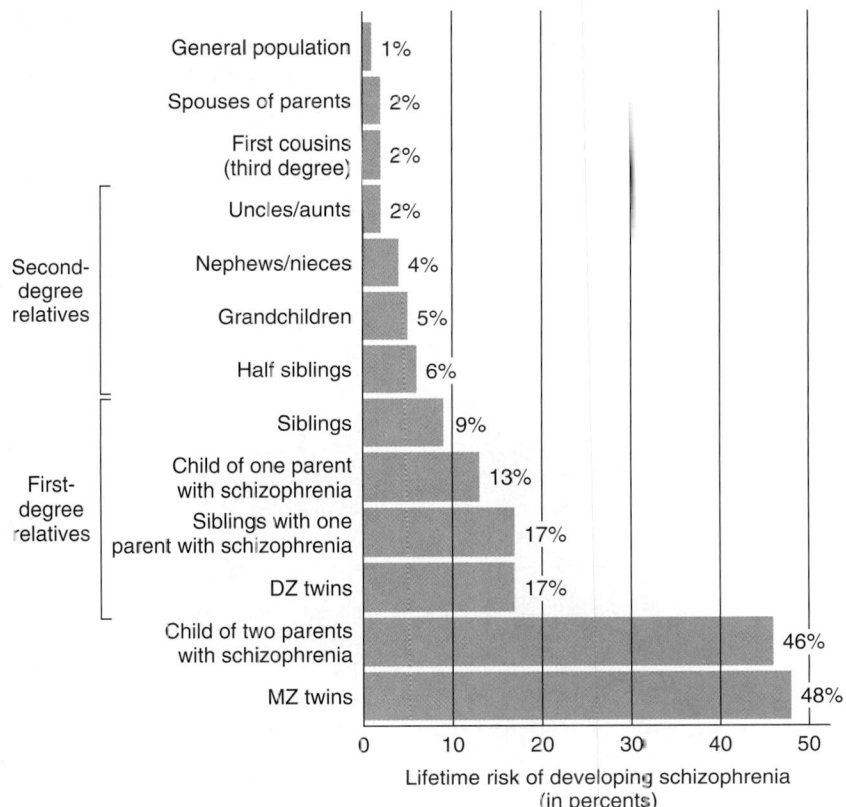

FIGURE 15.5

Genetic Risk of Developing Schizophrenia

The graph shows average risks for developing schizophrenia. Data were compiled from family and twin studies conducted in European populations between 1920 and 1987; the degree of risk correlates highly with the degree of genetic relatedness.

TABLE  15.7

Thought Disorder Scores for Schizophrenic Adoptees, Control Adoptees, and Their Relatives

	Scores on the Thought Disorder Index		
	Schizophrenic Adoptees	Control Adoptees	Difference
The adoptees themselves	4.82	1.15	3.67
All their biological relatives	1.37	0.99	0.38
Their biological siblings and half-siblings	1.44	0.82	0.62
Their adoptive relatives	1.11	1.31	−0.20

indicate that the biological relatives of the schizophrenic adoptees had higher levels of disordered thought than did the biological relatives of control adoptees. However, the adoptive relatives of both groups did not differ in their thought disorders. This pattern of data suggests that genetics matters more than environment in predicting who will experience thought disorders (Kinney et al., 1997).

Almost all the adoptees had been separated from their biological families shortly after birth. Therefore, whatever forces were leading to very high levels of thought disorder in the schizophrenic adoptees and relatively high levels in their biological relatives cannot be attributed to environmental factors.

These different types of evidence converge on the conclusion that some individuals inherit genetic material that puts them at risk for schizophrenia. Researchers who would like to isolate this abnormal genetic material have taken an approach similar to the one we described for studying the genetic origins of bipolar disease in the Amish population. The goal is to isolate portions of genes that set apart those who suffer from the disorder from those who do not. Researchers are making progress at discovering the combination of genes that put individuals at risk for schizophrenia (Brzustowicz et al., 2000).

While there is certainly a strong relationship between genetic similarity and schizophrenia risk, even in the groups with the greatest genetic similarity, the risk factor is less than 50 percent (see **Figure 15.6**). This indicates that, although genes play a role, environmental conditions may also be necessary to give rise to the disorder. A widely accepted hypothesis for the cause of schizophrenia is the *diathesis-stress hypothesis*. According to the **diathesis-stress hypothesis,** genetic factors place the individual at risk, but environmental stress factors must impinge in order for the potential risk to be manifested as a schizophrenic disorder. Once we have considered other biological aspects of schizophrenia, we will review the types of environmental stressors that may speed the emergence of this disorder.

BRAIN FUNCTION AND BIOLOGICAL MARKERS

Another biological approach to the study of schizophrenia is to look for abnormalities in the brains of individuals suffering from the disorder. Much of this research now relies on brain imaging techniques (see Chapter 3), which allow direct comparisons to be made between the structure and functioning of the brains of individuals with schizophrenia and normal control individuals (Gur & Pearlson, 1993; Marsh et al., 1997; Vita et al., 2000). For example, the magnetic resonance procedure has been used to show that the *ventricles*—the brain structures through which cerebrospinal fluid flows—are enlarged in up to 50 percent of individuals with schizophrenia (Degreef et al., 1992). Those individuals who suffer from childhood-onset schizophrenia show progressive

FIGURE 15.6

Genetic Risk for Schizophrenic Disorder

Out of a sample of 100 children of schizophrenic parents, form 10 to 50 percent will have the genetic structure that can lead to schizophrenia. Of these, about 5 percent will develop schizophrenia early and 5 percent later in life. It is important to note that as many as 40 percent of the high-risk subjects will not become schizophrenic.

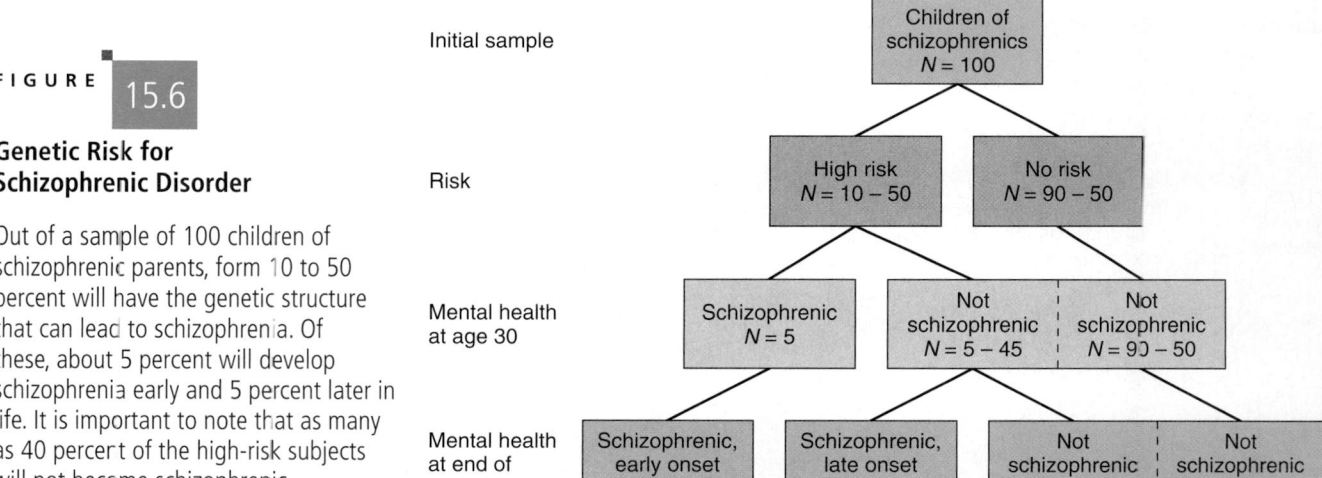

These four genetically identical women each experience a schizophrenic disorder, which suggests that heredity plays a role in the development of schizophrenia. For each of the Genain quadruplets, the disorder differs in severity, duration, and outcome. In general, how do genetics and environment interact to produce instances of schizophrenia?

increases in the size of the ventricles over their adolescent years (Rapoport et al., 1997). Imaging techniques have also revealed that individuals with schizophrenia may have patterns of brain activity different from those of normal controls. For example, one study examined identical twins in which either one or both members of each pair had schizophrenia (Berman et al., 1992). Only those individuals who actually had schizophrenia showed lower activity in the frontal lobes of the brain. This research design allows "genetics" to be held constant, to reveal this other biological aspect of the disorder.

Researchers continue to add to the list of *biological markers* for schizophrenia. A biological marker is a "measurable indicator of a disease that may or may not be causal" (Szymanski et al., 1991, p. 99). In other words, a biological marker may be correlated with a disease, although it does not bring the disease about. At present no known marker perfectly predicts schizophrenia, but markers have great potential value for diagnosis and research. For example, persons with schizophrenia are more likely than normal people to have an eye movement dysfunction when they scan the visual field. This biological marker can be quantified in individuals and is related to the presence of schizophrenia in families (Clementz & Sweeney, 1990; Lencer et al., 2000). Researchers continue to probe to find the specific elements of eye movements that most precisely set individuals with schizophrenia apart from patients with other mental disorders (Katsanis et al., 1997; Sweeney et al., 1994). Precise knowledge of biological markers may help researchers determine what groups of individuals are at risk for developing the disorder.

Diathesis-stress hypothesis A hypothesis about the cause of certain disorders, such as schizophrenia, that suggests that genetic factors predispose an individual to a certain disorder, but that environmental stress factors must impinge in order for the potential risk to manifest itself.

Given the wide range of symptoms of schizophrenia, you are probably not surprised by the comparably wide range of biological abnormalities that may be either causes or consequences of the disorder. What are the ways in which features of the environment may prompt people who are at risk to develop the disease?

FAMILY INTERACTION AS ENVIRONMENTAL STRESSOR

If it is difficult to prove that a highly specific biological factor is a *sufficient* cause of schizophrenia, it is equally hard to prove that a general psychological one is a *necessary* condition. Sociologists, family therapists, and psychologists have all studied the influence of family role relationships and communication patterns in the development of schizophrenia. The hope is to identify environmental circumstances that increase the likelihood of schizophrenia—and to protect at-risk individuals from those circumstances.

Research has provided evidence for theories that emphasize the influence of *deviations* in parental communication on the development of schizophrenia (Milkowitz, 1994; Wearden et al., 2000). These deviations include a

Are there certain destructive or self-contradictory patterns within the family that can contribute to the onset of schizophrenia?

family's inability to share a common focus of attention and parents' difficulties in taking the perspective of other family members or in communicating clearly and accurately. Studies suggest that the speech patterns of families with a schizophrenic member show less responsiveness and less interpersonal sensitivity than those of normal families.

Uncertainty remains over whether deviant family patterns are a cause of schizophrenia, a reaction to an individual's developing symptoms of schizophrenia, or both (Rosenfarb et al., 1995). To help answer this question, researchers undertake *prospective* studies: They measure family function to see which patterns predict who will develop schizophrenia, or experience relapses, in the future. For example, one study focused on the *empathy* skills of patients' relatives with respect to their ability to perceive the patients' mood states (Giron & Gomez-Beneyto, 1998). Over a two-year period, the patients whose relatives had shown low levels of empathy were more likely to suffer relapses in their symptoms of schizophrenia. This study is consistent with other findings that family factors play an important role in influencing the functioning of an individual after the first symptoms appear.

HOW WE KNOW

EXPRESSED EMOTION AND SYMPTOM RELAPSE To examine the role of family communication in schizophrenia, researchers have defined the concept of *expressed emotion*. Families are high on expressed emotion if they make a lot of critical comments about the patient, if they are emotionally overinvolved with the patient (that is, if they are overprotective and intrusive), and if they have a generally hostile attitude toward the patient. One study gathered data on the families of 69 schizophrenic patients who were living at home during a period in which they were considered stable. Each family was evaluated for the extent of its expressed emotion. When the patients' condition was assessed nine months later, 50 percent of the patients from high-expressed-emotion homes had experienced a relapse, whereas only 17 percent of patients from low-expressed-emotion homes had done so. Nonetheless, some aspects of expressed emotion were beneficial to the patients. Those patients whose families were emotionally overinvolved had better social adjustment nine months later. Perhaps the rigid family environment helped the patients make the difficult transition from hospitalization to the outside world (King & Dixon, 1996).

Stigma The negative reaction of people to an individual or group because of some assumed inferiority or source of difference that is degraded.

This study replicates the general pattern that when parents reduce their criticism, hostility, and intrusiveness toward a schizophrenic offspring, the recurrence of acute schizophrenic symptoms and the need for rehospitalization are also reduced (Wearden et al., 2000). The implication is that treatment should be for the entire family as a *system*, to change the operating style toward the disturbed child.

The number of explanations of schizophrenia that we have reviewed—and the questions that remain despite significant research—suggests how much there is to learn about this powerful psychological disorder. Complicating understanding is the likelihood that the phenomenon called schizophrenia is probably better thought of as a group of disorders, each with potentially distinct causes. Genetic predispositions, brain processes, and family interactions have all been identified as participants in at least some cases. Researchers must still determine the exact ways in which these elements may combine to bring about schizophrenia.

SUMMING UP

The symptoms of schizophrenia include illogical thought patterns, hallucinations, delusions, incoherent language, flat emotion, and disorganized psychomotor behavior. The five types of schizophrenia are disorganized type, catatonic type, paranoid type, undifferentiated type, and residual type. There is strong evidence for genetic transmission of schizophrenia. Researchers have also discovered brain abnormalities and other biological markers for the disorder. Particular patterns of family interactions, including expressed emotion, may contribute to the emergence, continuation, or relapse of schizophrenic symptoms.

The Stigma of Mental Illness

One of our most important goals for this chapter has been to demystify mental illness—to help you understand how, in some ways, abnormal behavior is really ordinary. People with psychological disorders are often labeled as *deviant*; society exacts costly penalties from those who deviate from its norms (see **Figure 15.7**). However, the deviant label is not true to prevailing realities: When 50 percent of young and middle-aged adults in the United States report having experienced some psychiatric disorder in their lifetime (Kessler et al., 1994), psychopathology is, at least statistically, relatively normal.

Even given the frequency with which psychopathology touches "normal lives," people who are psychologically disordered are often stigmatized in ways that most physically ill people are not. A **stigma** is a mark or brand of disgrace; in the psychological context, it is a set of

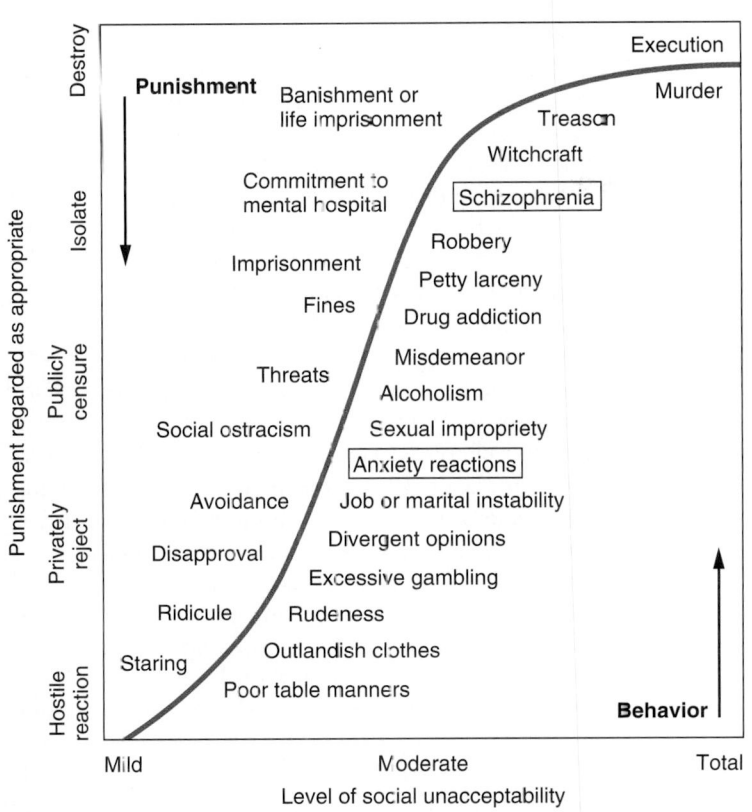

FIGURE 15.7

"Let the Punishment Fit the Crime"

This figure illustrates a continuum of behaviors that are deemed increasingly unacceptable and are responded to with increasing severity. In essence, each reaction is a punishment for deviance. Thus, behavior toward those who suffer from psychopathology can be seen to resemble behavior toward criminals or other deviants.

negative attitudes about a person that places him or her apart as unacceptable (Clausen, 1981). Recall the words we quoted at the beginning of the chapter, "The patient and public, in my [opinion] needs to be educated about mental illness, because people ridicule and mistreat, even misunderstand us at crucial times." Another recovered patient wrote, "For me, the stigma of mental illness was as devastating as the experience of hospitalization itself." She went on to describe her personal experience in vivid terms:

> *Prior to being hospitalized for mental illness, I lived an enviable existence. Rewards, awards, and invitations filled my scrapbook.... The crises of mental illness appeared as a nuclear explosion in my life. All that I had known and enjoyed previously was suddenly transformed, like some strange reverse process of nature, from a butterfly's beauty into a pupa's cocoon. There was a binding, confining quality to my life, in part chosen, in part imposed. Repeated rejections, the awkwardness of others around me, and my own discomfort and self-consciousness propelled me into solitary confinement.*
>
> *My recovery from mental illness and its aftermath involved a struggle—against my own body, which seemed without energy and stamina, and against a society that seemed reluctant to embrace me. (Houghton, 1980, pp. 7–8)*

Negative attitudes toward the psychologically disturbed come from many sources: The mass media portray psychiatric patients as prone to violent crime; jokes about the mentally ill are acceptable; families deny the mental distress of one of their members; legal terminology stresses mental incompetence. People also stigmatize themselves by hiding current psychological distress or a history of mental health care.

Researchers have documented a number of ways in which the stigma of mental illness has a negative impact on people's lives (Farina et al., 1996; Wright et al., 2000). In one sample of 84 men who had been hospitalized for mental illness, 6 percent reported having lost a job because of their hospitalization; 10 percent reported having been denied an apartment or room; 37 percent reported being avoided by others; and 45 percent reported that others had used their history of mental illness to hurt their feelings. Only 6 percent of the men reported no incidents of rejection (Link et al., 1997). This group of men went through a year-long course of treatment that resulted in considerable improvement in their mental health. Even so, at the end of that year, there were no changes in their perception of stigma: Despite their improvements in functioning, the patients did not expect to be treated any more kindly by the world. This type of research shows the great duality of many people's experience with mental disorders: Seeking help—allowing one's problems to be labeled—generally brings both relief *and* stigma; treatment improves quality of life at the same time that stigma degrades it (Rosenfield, 1997).

An added difficulty is that people with mental illness often internalize expectations of rejections that may, in turn, bring about negative interactions (Link et al., 1997). Consider this classic experiment.

EXPECTATIONS OF REJECTION Twenty-nine men who had formerly been hospitalized for mental illness volunteered to participate in this study. They believed that the research concerned the difficulties ex-psychiatric patients have with finding jobs. The participants were informed that they would interact with a personnel trainee recruited from a business establishment. Half of the participants were told that the trainee knew of their status as ex-psychiatric patients; the other half were told that the trainee had been led to believe they had been medical or surgical patients at the hospital. In fact, the "trainee" was a confederate of the experimenter who did not have any prior information about the participants' beliefs about his knowledge. That is, he did not know which participants thought that *he* knew that they were ex-patients. Therefore, any differences in the interactions during the time the participants and confederate spent together can be attributed to the participants' *expectations*. In fact, the participants who believed themselves to have been labeled as ex-psychiatric patients talked less during the session and performed less well on a cooperative task. Furthermore, the confederate rated members of this group as more "tense and anxious" without, again, knowing which group each participant was in (Farina et al., 1971).

The important conclusion here is that people who believe that others have attached the "mental illness" label to them may change their interactions in a way that brings about genuine discomfort: The expectation of rejection can create rejection; mental illness can be another of life's unfortunate self-fulfilling prophecies.

A final note on stigma: Research suggests that people who have had prior contact with individuals with mental illnesses hold attitudes that are less affected by stigma. For example, students who read a vignette about a man named Jim who had recovered from schizophrenia were more optimistic about Jim's future prospects when the students had had prior contact with someone who suffered from a mental illness (Penn et al., 1994). Similarly, students' ratings of the dangerousness of patients with schizophrenia were lower when they had had prior contact (Penn et al., 1999). We hope that one consequence of reading this chapter and the next will be to help modify your beliefs about what it means to be mentally ill and what it means to be "cured"—and to increase your tolerance and compassion for mentally ill individuals.

In making sense of psychopathology, you are forced to come to grips with basic conceptions of normality, reality, and social values. In discovering how to understand, treat, and, ideally, prevent psychological disorders, researchers not only help those who are suffering and losing out on the joys of living, they also expand the basic understanding of human nature. How do psychologists and psychiatrists intervene to right minds gone wrong and to modify behavior that doesn't work? We shall see in the next chapter on therapies.

SUMMING UP

Many people who have been labeled as mentally ill suffer effects of stigma. This stigma can lead to various forms of interpersonal and societal rejection. Even when patients experience relief from treatment of their mental illness, they still suffer from these effects of stigma. Furthermore, patients' expectations of others' responses to them can bring about the negative responses they fear.

RECAPPING
MAIN POINTS

The Nature of Psychological Disorders

- Abnormality is judged by the degree to which a person's actions resemble a set of indicators that include distress, maladaptiveness, irrationality, unpredictability, unconventionality, observer discomfort, and violation of standards or societal norms.

- In earlier times, mentally ill individuals were often treated as possessed by demons or less than human.

- Contemporary approaches to mental illness began with the recognition that mental disorders are illnesses that can be treated.

- There are a number of approaches to studying the etiology of psychopathology.

- The biological approach concentrates on abnormalities in the brain, biochemical processes, and genetic influences.

- Psychological approaches include psychodynamic, behavioral, cognitive, and sociocultural models.

Classifying Psychological Disorders

- Classification systems for psychological disorders should provide a common shorthand for communicating about general types of psychopathology and specific cases.
- The most widely accepted diagnostic and classification system is *DSM-IV-TR*.
- *DSM-IV-TR* uses a multidimensional system of five axes that encourages mental health professionals to consider psychological, physical, and social factors that might be relevant to a specific disorder.

Major Types of Psychological Disorders

- The five major types of anxiety disorders are generalized, panic, phobic, obsessive-compulsive, and posttraumatic stress.
- Mood disorders involve disturbances of emotion. Major depressive disorder is the most common affective disorder, while bipolar disorder is much rarer.
- Suicides are most frequent among people suffering from depression.
- Biological and psychological explanations account for different as-

pects of the etiology of anxiety and mood disorders.

- Personality disorders are patterns of perception, thought, or behavior that are long-standing and inflexible and that impair an individual's functioning.
- Dissociative disorders involve a disruption of the integrated functioning of memory, consciousness, or personal identity.

Schizophrenic Disorders

- Schizophrenia is a severe form of psychopathology that is characterized by extreme distortions in perception, thinking, emotion, behavior, and language.
- The five subtypes of schizophrenia are disorganized, catatonic, paranoid, undifferentiated, and residual.
- Evidence for the causes of schizophrenia has been found in a variety of factors including genetics, brain abnormalities, and family processes.

The Stigma of Mental Illness

- Those with psychological disorders are often stigmatized in ways that most physically ill people are not.
- Although treatment for psychological disorders brings about positive changes the stigma associated

with men...
impact on q...

Key Terms

abnormal psychology (p.
agoraphobia (p. 478)
anxiety disorders (p. 478)
bipolar disorder (p. 483)
comorbidity (p. 477)
delusions (p. 493)
diathesis-stress hypothesis (p. 497)
dissociative amnesia (p. 490)
dissociative disorder (p. 490)
dissociative identity disorder (DID) (p. 490)
DSM-IV-TR (p. 474)
etiology (p. 472)
fear (p. 479)
generalized anxiety disorder (p. 478)
hallucinations (p. 493)
insanity (p. 476)
learned helplessness (p. 486)
major depressive disorder (p. 483)
manic episode (p. 483)
mood disorder (p. 482)
neurotic disorders (p. 475)
obsessive-compulsive disorder (OCD) (p. 480)
panic disorder (p. 478)
personality disorder (p. 489)
phobia (p. 479)
posttraumatic stress disorder (PTSD) (p. 480)
psychological diagnosis (p. 474)
psychopathological functioning (p. 468)
psychotic disorders (p. 475)
schizophrenic disorder (p. 493)
social phobia (p. 479)
specific phobias (p. 479)
stigma (p. 498)

16

■ **THE THERAPEUTIC CONTEXT**
Goals and Major Therapies •
Therapists and Therapeutic
Settings • Historical and
Cultural Contexts

■ **PSYCHODYNAMIC THERAPIES**
Freudian Psychoanalysis •
Neo-Freudian Therapies

■ **PSYCHOLOGY IN YOUR LIFE:
ARE LIVES HAUNTED BY
REPRESSED MEMORIES?**

■ **BEHAVIOR THERAPIES**
Counterconditioning •
Contingency Management •
Social-Learning Therapy •
Generalization Techniques

■ **COGNITIVE THERAPIES**
Cognitive Behavior Modification
• Changing False Beliefs

■ **PSYCHOLOGY IN THE 21ST
CENTURY: THERAPY IN THE
AGE OF COMPUTERS**

■ **EXISTENTIAL-HUMANISTIC
THERAPIES**
Client-Centered Therapy •
Gestalt Therapy

■ **GROUP THERAPIES**
Marital and Family Therapy •
Community Support Groups

■ **BIOMEDICAL THERAPIES**
Psychosurgery and
Electroconvulsive Therapy •
Drug Therapy

■ **DOES THERAPY WORK?**
Evaluating Therapeutic
Effectiveness • Treatment
Evaluations • Prevention
Strategies

■ **RECAPPING MAIN POINTS**
Key Terms

In her autobiography, *The Beast*, Tracy Thompson (1995) describes her 25-year battle with depression, the "Beast" of the title. In this excerpt, Thompson describes her early experiences with the woman who was recommended as a help giver.

> She was a psychotherapist. I will call her Amanda Mayhew. We were to spend much of the next ten years together.
>
> Amanda was a large woman, tastefully dressed, self-consciously poised, and middle-aged, with a soft drawl that, to my trained ears, bespoke an upper-class upbringing or at least faded Southern gentility. Her office was in Buckhead, a fashionable section of Atlanta. On my first visit, she explained the rules: She could see me an hour a week, on Wednesdays, at an hourly fee of fifty-five dollars....
>
> Amanda, despite my initial reservations, seemed wise and competent, capable of rescuing me. But therapy wouldn't be easy, she warned: she foresaw two to five years of intense work ahead of us if I was to get better. Two to five years? It felt like a prison sentence....
>
> In the beginning, in the winter of 1977, my weekly sessions with her were a point of stability, a time when I knew my chaotic feelings would be listened to and taken seriously. Slowly, the depressive episode which had begun the previous spring began to wane. As spring came, and graduation loomed, I felt better—not happy, but at least not preoccupied with thoughts of suicide. Now, I thought, the real work of therapy could begin.
>
> But once this immediate crisis was past, our sessions began to resemble one long mother-daughter fight. With Amanda, I could act out the rebelliousness I felt toward my own mother. I had never felt free to rebel at home; my mother's need for security was so profound that the usual kinds of teenage rebellion—loutish boyfriends, surreptitious pot smoking, profane music—would have shattered her. Amanda became her proxy.... Amanda was getting paid to put up with me—by my mother, who wrote the household checks. It was, in its way, a beautiful system—a kind of passive-aggressive revolt. (pp. 62–65)

In this excerpt, you see represented many salient features of therapies for personal change. Most important, Thompson reports that the course of psychotherapy made her feel better. Even so, this was no quick fix: Thompson's depression was sufficiently disruptive to her life that she required therapy on an ongoing basis. You also see in her narrative that therapeutic relationships are personal relationships. Amanda, the psychotherapist, had a particular collection of attributes that, at first, served Thompson's mental health well but, as therapy proceeded, made her available as a "proxy" for Thompson's mother.

We will return to each of these themes as this chapter unfolds. We will examine the types of therapies that can help restore personal control to individuals with a range of disorders. We address a number of formidable questions: How has the treatment of psychological disorders been influenced by historical, cultural, and social forces? How do theory, research, and practice interact as re-searchers develop and test treatment methods? What can be done to influence a mind ungoverned by ordinary reason, to modify uncontrolled behavior, to alter unchecked emotions, and to correct abnormalities of the brain?

This chapter surveys the major types of treatments currently used by health-care providers: psychoanalysis, behavior modification, cognitive alteration, humanistic therapies, and drug therapies. We will examine the way these treatments work. We will also evaluate the validity of claims about the success of each therapy.

■ The Therapeutic Context

There are different types of therapy for mental disorders, and there are many reasons some people seek help (and others who need it do not). The purposes or goals of therapy, the settings in which therapy occurs, and the kinds of therapeutic helpers also vary. Despite any differences between therapies, however, all are *interventions* into a person's life, designed to change the person's functioning in some way.

Goals and Major Therapies

The therapeutic process can involve four primary tasks or goals:

1. Reaching a *diagnosis* about what is wrong, possibly determining an appropriate psychiatric *(DSM-IV-TR)* label for the presenting problem, and classifying the disorder.

2. Proposing a probable *etiology* (cause of the problem)—that is, identifying the probable origins of the disorder and the functions being served by the symptoms.

3. Making a *prognosis*, or estimate, of the course the problem will take with and without any treatment.

4. Prescribing and carrying out some form of *treatment*, a therapy designed to minimize or eliminate the troublesome symptoms and, perhaps, their sources.

If we think of the brain as a computer, we can say that mental problems may occur either in the brain's hardware or the software that programs its actions. The two main kinds of therapy for mental disorders focus on either the hardware or the software.

Biomedical therapies Treatments for psychological disorders that alter brain functioning with chemical or physical interventions such as drug therapy, surgery, or electroconvulsive therapy.

Psychotherapy Any of a group of therapies, used to treat psychological disorders, that focus on changing faulty behaviors, thoughts, perceptions, and emotions that may be associated with specific disorders.

Biomedical therapies focus on changing the hardware: the mechanisms that run the central nervous system. Practiced largely by psychiatrists and physicians, these therapies try to alter brain functioning with chemical or physical interventions, including surgery, electric shock, and drugs that act directly on the brain–body connection.

Psychological therapies, which are collectively called **psychotherapy,** focus on changing the software—the faulty behaviors people have learned: the words, thoughts, interpretations, and feedback that direct daily strategies for living. These therapies are practiced by clinical psychologists as well as by psychiatrists. There are four major types of psychotherapy: psychodynamic, behavioral, cognitive, and existential-humanistic.

The *psychodynamic* approach views neurotic suffering as the outer symptom of inner, unresolved traumas and conflicts. Psychodynamic therapists treat mental disorder with a "talking cure," in which a therapist helps a person develop insights about the relation between the overt symptoms and the unresolved hidden conflicts that presumably caused them.

Behavior therapy treats the behaviors themselves as disturbances that must be modified. Disorders are viewed as learned behavior patterns rather than as the symptoms of mental disease. Behaviors are transformed in many ways, including changing reinforcement contingencies for desirable and undesirable responding, extinguishing conditioned responses, and providing models of effective problem solving.

Cognitive therapy tries to restructure the way a person thinks by altering the often distorted self-statements a person makes about the causes of a problem. Restructuring cognitions changes the way a person defines and explains difficulties, often enabling the person to cope with the problems.

Therapies that have emerged from the *existential-humanistic tradition* emphasize the patients' values. They are

Cathy □ Cathy Guisewite

Source: CATHY by Cathy Guisewite. Copyright, 1986, Universal Press Syndicate. Reprinted with permission. All rights reserved.

directed toward self-actualization, psychological growth, the development of more meaningful interpersonal relationships, and the enhancement of freedom of choice. They tend to focus more on improving the functioning of essentially healthy people than on correcting the symptoms of seriously disturbed individuals.

Therapists and Therapeutic Settings

When psychological problems arise, most people initially seek out informal counselors who operate in familiar settings. Many people turn to family members, close friends, personal physicians, lawyers, or favorite teachers for support, guidance, and counsel. Those with religious affiliations may seek help from a clergy member. Others get advice and a chance to talk by opening up to bartenders, salesclerks, cabdrivers, or other people willing to listen. In our society, these informal therapists carry the bulk of the daily burden of relieving frustration and conflict. When problems are limited in scope, informal therapists can often help.

Although more people seek out therapy now than in the past, people usually turn to trained mental health professionals only when their psychological problems become severe or persist for extended periods of time. When they do, they can turn to several types of therapists.

A **counseling psychologist** typically provides guidance in areas such as vocation selection, school problems, drug abuse, and marital conflict. Often, these counselors work in community settings related to the problem areas—within a business, a school, a prison, the military service, or a neighborhood clinic—and use interviews, tests, guidance, and advising to help individuals solve specific problems and make decisions about future options.

A **clinical social worker** is a mental health professional whose specialized training in a school of social work prepares him or her to work in collaboration with psychiatrists and clinical psychologists. Unlike many psychiatrists and psychologists, these counselors are trained to consider the social contexts of people's problems, so these practitioners may also involve other family members in the therapy or at least become acquainted with clients' homes or work settings.

A **pastoral counselor** is a member of a religious group who specializes in the treatment of psychological disorders. Often, these counselors combine spirituality with practical problem solving.

A **clinical psychologist** is required to have concentrated his or her graduate school training in the assessment and treatment of psychological problems, completed a supervised internship in a clinical setting, and earned a Ph.D. or Psy.D. These psychologists tend to have a broader background in psychology, assessment, and research than do psychiatrists.

A **psychiatrist** must have completed all medical school training for an M.D. degree and also have undergone some postdoctoral specialty training in mental and emotional disorders. Psychiatrists are trained more in the biomedical basis of psychological problems, and they are currently the only therapists who can prescribe medical or drug-based interventions.

A **psychoanalyst** is a therapist with either an M.D. or a Ph.D. degree who has completed specialized postgraduate training in the Freudian approach to understanding and treating mental disorders.

These different types of therapists practice in many settings: hospitals, clinics, schools, and private offices. Some humanistic therapists prefer to conduct group sessions in their homes in order to work in a more natural environment. Community-based therapies, which take the treatment to the client, may operate out of local storefronts or houses of worship. Finally, therapists who practice *in vivo* therapy work with clients in the life setting that is associated with their problem. For example, they work in airplanes with clients who suffer from flying phobias or in shopping malls with people who have social phobias.

People who enter therapy are usually referred to as either patients or clients. The term **patient** is used by professionals who take a biomedical approach to the treatment of psychological problems. The term **client** is used by professionals who think of psychological disorders as "problems in living" and not as mental illnesses. We will use the preferred term for each approach: *patient* for

Counseling psychologist Psychologist who specializes in providing guidance in areas such as vocational selection, school problems, drug abuse, and marital conflict.

Clinical social worker A mental health professional whose specialized training prepares him or her to consider the social context of people's problems.

Pastoral counselor A member of a religious order who specializes in the treatment of psychological disorders, often combining spirituality with practical problem solving.

Clinical psychologist An individual who has earned a doctorate in psychology and whose training is in the assessment and treatment of psychological problems.

Psychiatrist An individual who has obtained an M.D. degree and also has completed postdoctoral specialty training in mental and emotional disorders; a psychiatrist may prescribe medications for the treatment of psychological disorders.

Psychoanalyst An individual who has earned either a Ph.D. or an M.D. degree and has completed postgraduate training in the Freudian approach to understanding and treating mental disorders.

Patient The term used by those who take a biomedical approach to the treatment of psychological problems to describe the person being treated.

Client The term used by clinicians who think of psychological disorders as problems in living, and not as mental illnesses, to describe those being treated.

biomedical and psychoanalytic therapies and *client* for other therapies.

Before looking at contemporary therapies and therapists in more detail, we will first consider the historical contexts in which treatment of the mentally ill was developed and then broaden the Western perspective with a look at the healing practices of other cultures.

Historical and Cultural Contexts

What kind of treatment might you have received in past centuries if you were suffering from psychological problems? If you had lived in Europe or the United States, chances are the treatment would not have helped and could even have been harmful. In other cultures, treatment of psychological disorders has usually been seen within a broader perspective of religious and social values that yielded more humane treatment.

HISTORY OF WESTERN TREATMENT

Population increases and migration to big cities in 14th-century Western Europe created unemployment and social alienation. These conditions led to poverty, crime, and psychological problems. Special institutions were soon created to warehouse society's three emerging categories of "misfits": the poor, criminals, and the mentally disturbed.

In 1403, a London hospital—St. Mary of Bethlehem—admitted its first patient with psychological problems. For the next 300 years, mental patients of the hospital were chained, tortured, and exhibited to an admission-paying public. Over time, a mispronunciation of Bethlehem—*bedlam*—came to mean *chaos,* because of the horrible confusion reigning in the hospital and the dehumanized treatment of patients there (Foucault, 1975).

It wasn't until the late 18th century that the perception of psychological problems as *mental illness* emerged in Europe. The French physician **Philippe Pinel** wrote in 1801, "The mentally ill, far from being guilty people deserving of punishment, are sick people whose miserable state deserves all the consideration that is due to suffering humanity. One should try with the most simple methods to restore their reason" (Zilboorg & Henry, 1941, pp. 323–324).

In the United States, psychologically disturbed individuals were confined for their own protection and for the safety of the community, but they were given no treatment. However, by the mid-1800s, when psychology as a field of study was gaining some credibility and respectability, "a cult of curability" emerged throughout the country. Insanity was then thought to be related to the environmental stresses brought on by the turmoil of newly developing cities. Eventually, madness came to be viewed as a social problem to be cured through "mental hygiene," just as contagious physical diseases were being treated by physical hygiene.

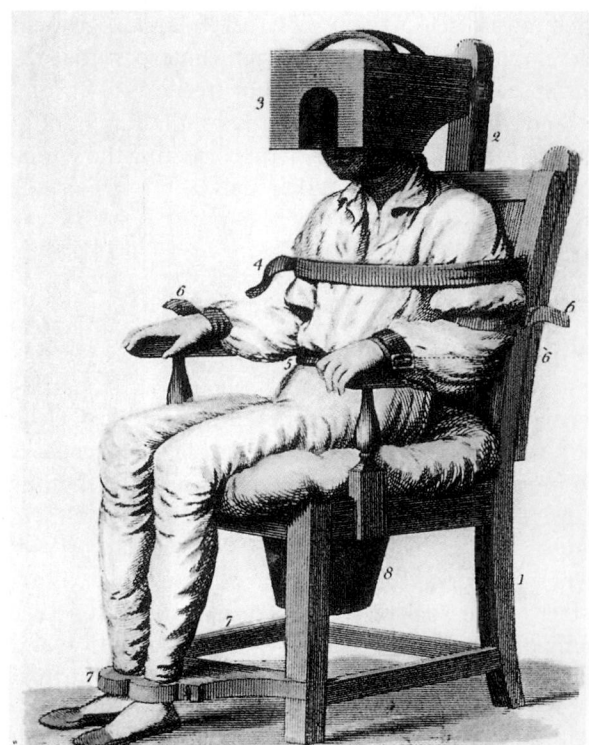

Treatment of mental disorders in the 18th century focused on banishing "ill humors" from the body. Shown here is the "tranquilizing chair" advocated by Philadelphia physician Benjamin Rush. Why did attitudes toward the treatment of the mentally ill change?

In the 1900s, **Clifford Beers** spurred on the mental hygiene movement. Eventually, the confinement of the mentally ill assumed a new *rehabilitative* goal. The *asylum* then became the central fixture of this social-political movement. The disturbed were confined to asylums in rural areas, far from the stress of the city, not only for protection but also for treatment (Rothman, 1971). Unfortunately, many of the asylums that were built became overcrowded. The humane goal of rehabilitation was replaced with the pragmatic goal of *containing* strange people in remote places. These large, understaffed state mental hospitals became little more than human warehouses for disturbed individuals (Scull, 1993). Beginning in the 1960s, reformers began to agitate against these warehouses, in favor of the *deinstitutionalization* of at least those mental patients who could thrive with outpatient treatment and appropriate community supports. Unfortunately, many deinstitutionalized patients do not obtain adequate assistance in their communities. For example, researchers found that 24 percent of a sample of 438 individuals with serious mental illnesses were homeless (Kuno et al., 2000).

CULTURAL SYMBOLS AND RITUALS OF CURING

Our review of these historical trends in the treatment of psychological disorders has been limited to Western views and practices, which emphasize the uniqueness of the individual, independence, and personal responsibility for success and failure. Both demonology and the disease model are consistent with this emphasis, regarding mental disorder as something that happens *inside* a person and as an individual's failure.

This view is not shared by many other cultures (Triandis, 1995). The research of *cultural anthropologists* has provided analyses of the explanations and treatments for psychological disorders across different cultures (Bourguignon, 1979; Evans-Pritchard, 1937; Kluckhohn, 1944; Marsella, 1979). For example, in the African worldview, the emphasis is on cooperation, interdependence, tribal survival, unity with nature, and collective responsibility (Nobles, 1976). It is contrary to the thinking of many non-European cultures to treat mentally ill individuals by *removing* them from society. In many African cultures, healing takes place in a social context, involving a distressed person's beliefs, family, work, and life environment. The African use of group support in therapy has been expanded into a procedure called "network therapy," in which a patient's entire network of relatives, coworkers, and friends becomes involved in the treatment (Lambo, 1978).

In many cultures, the treatment of mental and physical disease is bound up with religion and witchcraft. Certain human beings, called *shamans,* are given special mystical powers to help in the transformation of their distressed fellow beings. **Shamanism** is an ancient and powerful spiritual tradition that has been practiced for close to 30,000 years. In the shamanistic tradition, suffering and disease are diagnosed as powerlessness. This cultural belief system *personalizes* the vague forces of fate or chance that intervene in one's life to create problems. Such personalization permits direct action to be taken against presumed evildoers and direct help to be sought from assumed divine healers (Middleton, 1967). Often, the pathological state that is seen as a result of the spirit possession of the afflicted person is transformed by therapeutic intervention of shaman healers. Drumming, chanting, and other rituals are used to inspire awe and induce altered states of consciousness that facilitate the quest for knowledge and empowerment (Walsh, 1990).

Common to folk-healing ceremonies are the important roles of symbols, myths, and rituals (Lévi-Strauss, 1963). **Ritual healing** ceremonies infuse special emotional intensity and meaning into the healing process. They heighten patients' suggestibility and sense of importance, and, combined with the use of symbols, they connect the individual sufferer, the shaman, and the society to supernatural forces to be won over in the battle against madness (Devereux, 1961). One therapeutic practice used in a number of healing ceremonies is *dissociation of consciousness,* in which the distressed person or a faith healer enters an altered state of consciousness. In Western views, dissociation is itself a symptom of mental disorder to be prevented or corrected; in other cultures,

as consciousness is altered, good spirits are communicated with and evil spirits are exorcised. The use of ceremonial alteration of consciousness can be seen among the cult of Puerto Rican *Espiritistas* in New York City, whose healing ceremonies involve communication with good spirits that are believed to exist outside the person (Garrison, 1977).

Although shamans and other healers play special roles in ritual ceremonies, the healing power most often transcends the individual healer and resides in greater spiritual forces (Katz, 1982, 1993). In describing healing practices in Fiji, psychologist **Richard Katz** writes, "Becoming connected to the spiritual dimension demands commitment to a healing power beyond the self, and entails humility about one's own contribution to healing. The Fijian healer does not claim personal ownership of *mana* [spiritual power derived from the culture's ancestors], or take personal credit for its healing effects" (pp. 327–328). Katz makes an explicit comparison to Western practice: "In contrast, the Western physician is more likely to claim control over, if not ownership of, the ability to cure or heal. Competence—knowing what to do, or at least not revealing that one doesn't know—is stressed over natural human vulnerability" (p. 328).

Some of these non-Western views have begun to work their way into Western practices (Katz, 1982, 1993). The influence of the social-interactive concept and the focus on the *family context* and *supportive community* are evident in newer therapeutic approaches that emphasize social support networks and family therapy. Other Western practitioners work with shamans in an effort to integrate Western psychotherapies that involve self-analysis with the therapies of collectivist societies that view the individual within the current communal context. These attempts at integration make therapies more culturally appropriate to a wider range of clients (Kraut, 1990).

With this brief overview of historical trends and some cultural variations in mind, it is time to investigate in some detail each of the major types of therapies being practiced today.

SUMMING UP

The major goals of the therapeutic context are to determine the causes of mental illness and to provide a plan for treatment. Therapies may be biologically or psychologically oriented. Therapists practice in a variety of settings, and with different specific types of expertise. In Western cultures, mentally ill patients were originally locked away

Shamanism A spiritual tradition that involves both healing and gaining contact with the spirit world.
Ritual healing Ceremonies that infuse special emotional intensity and meaning into the healing process.

from society. The development of models that viewed mental illnesses as diseases to be cured led to more humane treatment. Many non-Western cultures emphasize a larger community and spiritual context in which mental illness develops and is treated. Western practitioners are beginning to adopt some of the community healing models present in these other cultures.

Psychodynamic Therapies

Psychodynamic therapies assume that a patient's problems have been caused by the psychological tension between unconscious impulses and the constraints of his or her life situation. These therapies locate the core of the disorder inside the disturbed person.

Freudian Psychoanalysis

Psychoanalysis, as developed by **Sigmund Freud,** is an intensive and prolonged technique for exploring unconscious motivations and conflicts in neurotic, anxiety-ridden individuals. As we saw in earlier chapters, Freudian theory views anxiety disorders as inabilities to resolve adequately the inner conflicts between the unconscious, irrational impulses of the *id* and the internalized social constraints imposed by the *superego.* The goal of psychoanalysis is to establish intrapsychic harmony that expands awareness of the forces of the *id,* reduces overcompliance with the demands of the *superego,* and strengthens the role of the *ego.*

Of central importance to a therapist is to understand the way a patient uses the process of *repression* to handle conflicts. Symptoms are considered to be messages from the unconscious that something is wrong. A psychoanalyst's task is to help a patient bring repressed thoughts to consciousness and to gain *insight* into the relationship between the current symptoms and the repressed conflicts. In this psychodynamic view, therapy succeeds and patients recover when they are "released from repression" established in early childhood. Because a central goal of a therapist is to guide a patient toward discovering insights into the relationships between present symptoms and past origins, psychodynamic therapy is often called **insight therapy.**

Traditional psychoanalysis is an attempt to reconstruct long-standing repressed memories and then work through painful feelings to an effective resolution. Accordingly, it is a therapy that takes a long time (several years at least, with as many as five sessions a week). It also requires introspective patients who are verbally fluent, highly motivated to remain in therapy, and willing and able to undergo considerable expense. (Newer forms of psychodynamic therapy are making therapy briefer in total duration.) Therapists in the psychodynamic tradition use several techniques to bring repressed conflicts to consciousness and to help a patient resolve them (Henry et al., 1994). These techniques include free association, analysis of resistance, dream analysis, and analysis of transference and countertransference.

FREE ASSOCIATION AND CATHARSIS

The principal procedure used in psychoanalysis to probe the unconscious and release repressed material is called **free association.** A patient, sitting comfortably in a chair or lying in a relaxed position on a couch, lets his or her mind wander freely and gives a running account of thoughts, wishes, physical sensations, and mental images. The patient is encouraged to reveal every thought or feeling, no matter how unimportant it may seem.

Freud maintained that free associations are *predetermined,* not random. The task of an analyst is to track the associations to their source and identify the significant patterns that lie beneath the surface of what are apparently just words. The patient is encouraged to express strong feelings, usually toward authority figures, that have been repressed for fear of punishment or retaliation. Any such emotional release, by this or other processes within the therapeutic context, is called **catharsis.**

Why is psychoanalytic therapy, originally practiced in Freud's study, often called the "talking cure"?

> **Psychoanalysis** The form of psychodynamic therapy developed by Freud; an intensive and prolonged technique for exploring unconscious motivations and conflicts in neurotic, anxiety-ridden individuals.
>
> **Insight therapy** A technique by which the therapist guides a patient toward discovering insights between present symptoms and past origins.
>
> **Free association** The therapeutic method in which a patient gives a running account of thoughts, wishes, physical sensations, and mental images as they occur.
>
> **Catharsis** The process of expressing strongly felt but usually repressed emotions.

RESISTANCE

A psychoanalyst attaches particular importance to subjects that a patient does *not* wish to discuss. At some time during the process of free association, a patient will show **resistance**—an inability or unwillingness to discuss certain ideas, desires, or experiences. Such resistances are conceived of as *barriers* between the unconscious and the conscious. This material is often related to an individual's sexual life (which includes all things pleasurable) or to hostile, resentful feelings toward parents. When the repressed material is finally brought into the open, a patient generally claims that it is unimportant, absurd, irrelevant, or too unpleasant to discuss. The therapist believes the opposite. Psychoanalysis aims to break down resistances and enable the patient to face these painful ideas, desires, and experiences.

DREAM ANALYSIS

Psychoanalysts believe that dreams are an important source of information about a patient's unconscious motivations. When a person is asleep, the superego is presumably less on guard against the unacceptable impulses originating in the id, so a motive that cannot be expressed in waking life may find expression in a dream. In analysis, dreams are assumed to have two kinds of content: *manifest* (openly visible) content that people remember upon awakening and *latent* (hidden) content—the actual motives that are seeking expression but are so painful or unacceptable that they are expressed in disguised or symbolic form. Therapists attempt to uncover these hidden motives by using **dream analysis,** a therapeutic technique that examines the content of a person's dreams to discover the underlying or disguised motivations and symbolic meanings of significant life experiences and desires.

TRANSFERENCE AND COUNTERTRANSFERENCE

During the course of the intensive therapy of psychoanalysis, a patient usually develops an emotional reaction toward the therapist. Often, the therapist is identified with a person who has been at the center of an emotional conflict in the past—most often a parent or a lover. This emotional reaction is called **transference.** Recall from the beginning of the chapter Tracy Thompson's relationship with her therapist Amanda—she explicitly identified Amanda as a "proxy" for her mother. Transference is called *positive transference* when the feelings attached to the therapist are those of love or admiration and *negative transference* when the feelings consist of hostility or envy. Often, a patient's attitude is ambivalent, including a mixture of positive and negative feelings. An analyst's task in handling transference is a difficult one because of the patient's emotional vulnerability; however, it is a crucial part of treatment. A therapist helps a patient to interpret the present transferred feelings by understanding their original source in earlier experiences and attitudes (Henry et al., 1994).

Personal feelings are also at work in a therapist's reactions to a patient. **Countertransference** refers to what happens when a therapist comes to like or dislike a patient because the patient is perceived as similar to significant people in the therapist's life. In working through countertransference, a therapist may discover some unconscious dynamics of his or her own. The therapist becomes a "living mirror" for the patient and the patient, in turn, for the therapist. If the therapist fails to recognize the operation of countertransference, the therapy may not be as effective (Winarick, 1997). Because of the emotional intensity of this type of therapeutic relationship and the vulnerability of the patient, therapists must be on guard about crossing the boundary between professional caring and personal involvement with their patients. The therapy setting is obviously one with an enormous power imbalance that must be recognized, and honored, by the therapist.

Neo-Freudian Therapies

Freud's followers retained many of his basic ideas but modified certain of his principles and practices. In general, these neo-Freudians place more emphasis than Freud did on: (1) a patient's *current* social environment (less focus on the past); (2) the continuing influence of life experiences (not just childhood conflicts); (3) the role of social motivation and interpersonal relations of love (rather than of biological instincts and selfish concerns); (4) the significance of ego functioning and development of the self-concept (less on the conflict between id and superego).

In Chapter 14, we noted two other prominent Freudians, Carl Jung and Alfred Adler. To get a flavor of the more contemporary psychodynamic approaches of the neo-Freudians, here we will look at the work of Harry Stack Sullivan, Melanie Klein, and Heinz Kohut (see Ruitenbeek, 1973, for a look at other members of the Freudian circle).

Harry Stack Sullivan (1953) felt that Freudian theory and therapy did not recognize the importance of social relationships and a patient's needs for acceptance,

Resistance The inability or unwillingness of a patient in psychoanalysis to discuss certain ideas, desires, or experiences.

Dream analysis The psychoanalytic interpretation of dreams used to gain insight into a person's unconscious motives or conflicts.

Transference The process by which a person in psychoanalysis attaches to a therapist feelings formerly held toward some significant person who figured in a past emotional conflict.

Countertransference Circumstances in which a psychoanalyst develops personal feelings about a client because of perceived similarity of the client to significant people in the therapist's life.

ARE LIVES HAUNTED BY REPRESSED MEMORIES?

On September 22, 1969, 8-year-old Susan Nason vanished from her northern California neighborhood. In December 1969, her body was found. For 20 years, no one knew who had murdered her. Then, in 1989, Susan's friend Eileen Franklin-Lipsker contacted county investigators. Eileen told them that, with the help of psychotherapy, she had recalled a long-repressed, horrifying memory about what had happened to Susan. In the fall of 1990, Eileen testified that, over two decades earlier, she had witnessed her father, George Franklin, sexually assault Susan and then bludgeon her to death with a rock (Marcus, 1990; Workman, 1990). Eileen reported that her father had threatened to kill her if she ever told anyone. This testimony was sufficient to have George Franklin convicted of first-degree murder.

How, in theory, had these memories remained hidden for 20 years? The answer to this mystery finds its roots in Sigmund Freud's concept of repressed memories. As we just reminded you, Freud (1923) theorized that some people's memories of life experiences become sufficiently threatening to their psychological well-being that the individuals banish the memories from consciousness—they repress them. Clinical psychologists are often able to help clients take control of their lives by interpreting disruptive life patterns as the consequences of repressed memories; an important goal of therapy is

to achieve catharsis with respect to these repressed memories.

But not all experiences of repressed memories remain in the therapist's office. In recent years, there has been an explosion of mass-media claims for the dramatic recovery of repressed memories. After long intervals of time, individuals report sudden vivid recollections of horrifying events, such as murders or childhood sexual abuse. Could all these claims be real? Our review of memory research in Chapter 8—particularly research on eyewitness memories—provided you with grounds for skepticism (Loftus, 1993; Loftus & Ketcham, 1994; Lynn & Payne, 1997). You might recall from that research that people will report as true memories information that was provided from an artificial source. They will do so even when, as witnesses, they have been specifically warned that they have been misled. Thus, being in confident possession of a memory provides no assurance of the ultimate source of that memory.

In fact, the popular media have in recent years frequently provided reports of repressed memories that can serve as an "artificial source." What an individual saw on TV could be reborn as a personal memory if information about the TV as source somehow got lost. Thus, media descriptions of repressed memories will potentially lead some individuals to "recover" the same memories. Basically, the individual has lost access to the *source* of the memory but held on to the *content* (Johnson et al., 1993).

Clinicians also worry that therapists who believe in repressed memories may, through the mechanisms of psychotherapy, implant those beliefs in their patients (de Rivera, 2000; Sarbin, 1997). For example, researchers have studied women who have ultimately retracted charges of childhood sexual abuse—these women had come to understand that their "memories" of abuse could not have been real. These studies provide evidence that therapists often instigated the patients' efforts to find these memories—and verbally rewarded them when the "memories" came to light (de Rivera, 1997). Cases of this sort have convinced clinicians that they must study the social forces that are at work in therapy, to discover how the therapist's theory is translated into the patient's reality (Lynn et al., 1997).

Belief in the recovery of repressed memories may provide a measurable benefit for patients in psychotherapy. In fact, some portion of recovered memories are valid recollections of earlier traumatic experiences (Schooler & Eich, 2000; Williams, 1995). Even so, if you come to explore the question of whether repressed memories from your past can help explain present discomfort, you should ensure that you are not passively accepting someone else's version of your life. Fortunately for George Franklin, doubts about his daughter's repressed memories led his verdict to be overturned.

---

respect, and love. Mental disorders, he insisted, involve not only traumatic intrapsychic processes but also troubled interpersonal relationships and even strong societal pressures. A young child needs to feel secure and to be treated by others with caring and tenderness. Anxiety and other mental ills arise out of insecurities in relations with parents and significant others. In Sullivan's view, a

self-system is built up to hold anxiety down to a tolerable level. This self-system is derived from a child's interpersonal experiences and is organized around conceptions of the self as the *good-me* (associated with the mother's tenderness), the *bad-me* (associated with the mother's tensions), and the *not-me* (a dissociated self that is unacceptable to the rest of the self).

Therapy based on this interpersonal view involves observing a *patient's feelings* about the *therapist's attitudes*. The therapeutic interview is seen as a social setting in which each party's feelings and attitudes are influenced by the other's. The patient is gently provoked to state his or her assumptions about the therapist's attitudes. Above all, the therapeutic situation, for Sullivan, was one in which the therapist learned and taught lovingly (Wallach & Wallach, 1983).

Melanie Klein (1975) defected from Freud's emphasis on the Oedipus conflict as the major source of psychopathology. Because of Freud's focus on neurotic symptoms arising from the Oedipal period (ages 4 to 5), the task he set for therapeutic intervention was to interpret and illuminate these unconscious sexual conflicts. However, some analytic therapists had difficulty treating patients whose conflicts seemed to arise from earlier times, before they had verbal memory, which often resulted in more extreme pathologies. They often suffered from feelings of unreality, emptiness, and a loss of meaning in life. Klein suggested that primitive forms of the superego appear in the first months of life. Instead of Oedipal sexual conflicts as the most important organizing factors of the psyche, Klein argued that a *death instinct* preceded sexual awareness and led to an innate aggressive impulse that was equally important in organizing the psyche. She contended that the two fundamental organizing forces in the psyche are aggression and love, where aggression *splits* and love *unites* the psyche. Aggressive splitting of the world rejects what is hated and keeps what is desired; love creates unity and wholeness. For Klein, love was not just erotic fulfillment but a true

kindness and authentic caring for others. However, this conscious love is connected to remorse over destructive hate and potential violence toward those we love. Thus, Klein explained "one of the great mysteries that all people face, that love and hate—our personal heaven and hell—cannot be separated from one another" (Frager & Fadiman, 1998, p. 135). Klein's view that the building blocks of how we experience the world emerge from our relations to loved and hated *objects*—significant people in our lives—has become central to a prominent type of psychoanalytic theory and practice called **object relations theory**. Klein also pioneered the use of forceful therapeutic interpretations of both aggressive and sexual drives in analytic patients.

Psychodynamic therapies continue to evolve with a varying emphasis on Freud's constructs. One of the most important new directions for these is the modern concern for the *self* in all its senses, notably the ways one's self-concept emerges, is experienced by the person, and, at times, becomes embattled and requires defending. **Heinz Kohut** (1977; Siegel, 1996) is a leading proponent of this emphasis on the self and founder of the *object relations* school of psychoanalysis. His brand of therapy focuses on how various aspects of the self require *self-objects*, supportive people and significant things everyone needs to maintain optimal personality functioning. This form of self psychology emphasizes the experience of self and especially those experiences that lead to a fragmented self. The therapist's task then is to try as much as possible to empathize with the various psychological states that the client is going through while also accepting the client's view of his or her experiences (Chicago Institute for Psychoanalysis, 1992).

We already noted that psychoanalytic therapy often requires a long period of time to achieve its goals. Often, however, people are suffering from disorders that require more speedy remedies. Behavior therapies, to which we turn next, provide the potential for swift relief from symptoms.

In what ways did the theories of Melanie Klein and Sigmund Freud differ?

SUMMING UP

Psychodynamic therapies originated with Sigmund Freud's theory of unconscious conflict and repression. Therapists use a variety of techniques, including free association, dream analysis, and interpretation of transference to achieve patients' catharsis, a release of psychic energy. Neo-Freudian therapies put more emphasis on a patients' current social environment, the continuing influence of life

Object relations theory Psychoanalytic theory that originated with Melanie Klein's view that the building blocks of how people experience the world emerge from their relations to loved and hated objects (significant people in their lives).

events, the role of social motivation and interpersonal relations, and development of the self-concept.

Behavior Therapies

While psychodynamic therapies focus on presumed inner causes, behavior therapies focus on observable outer behaviors. Behavior therapists argue that abnormal behaviors are acquired in the same way as normal behaviors—through a learning process that follows the basic principles of conditioning and learning. Behavior therapies apply the principles of conditioning and reinforcement to modify undesirable behavior patterns associated with mental disorders.

The terms **behavior therapy** and **behavior modification** are often used interchangeably. Both refer to the systematic use of principles of learning to increase the frequency of desired behaviors and/or decrease that of problem behaviors. The range of deviant behaviors and personal problems that typically are treated by behavior therapy is extensive and includes fears, compulsions, depression, addictions, aggression, and delinquent behaviors. In general, behavior therapy works best with specific rather than general types of personal problems: It is better for a phobia than for unfocused anxiety.

The therapies that have emerged from the theories of conditioning and learning are grounded in a pragmatic, empirical research tradition. The central task of all living organisms is to learn how to adapt to the demands of the current social and physical environment. When organisms do not learn how to cope effectively, their maladaptive reactions can be overcome by therapy based on principles of learning (or relearning). The target behavior is not assumed to be a symptom of any underlying process. The symptom itself is the problem. Psychodynamic therapists predicted that treating only the outer behavior without confronting the true, inner problem would result in *symptom substitution,* the appearance of a new physical or psychological problem. However, research has shown that when pathological behaviors are eliminated by behavior therapy, new symptoms are not substituted (Kazdin, 1982; Wolpe, 1986). "On the contrary, patients whose target symptoms improved often reported improvement in other, less important symptoms as well" (Sloane et al., 1975, p. 219).

Let's look at the different forms of behavior therapies that have brought relief to distressed individuals.

Counterconditioning

Why does someone become anxious when faced with a harmless stimulus, such as a spider, a nonpoisonous snake, or social contact? The behavioral explanation is that the anxiety arises due to the simple conditioning principles we reviewed in Chapters 7 and 15: Strong emotional reactions that disrupt a person's life "for no good reason" are often conditioned responses that the person does not recognize as having been learned previously. In **counterconditioning**, a new response is conditioned to replace, or "counter," a maladaptive response. The earliest recorded use of behavior therapy followed this logic. **Mary Cover Jones** (1924) showed that a fear could be *unlearned* through conditioning. (Compare with the case of Little Albert in Chapter 7.)

> Her patient was Peter, a 3-year-old boy who, for some unknown reason, was afraid of rabbits. The therapy involved feeding Peter at one end of a room while the rabbit was brought in at the other end. Over a series of sessions, the rabbit was gradually brought closer until, finally, all fear disappeared and Peter played freely with the rabbit.

Following in Cover Jones's footsteps, behavior therapists now use several counterconditioning techniques, including systematic desensitization, implosion, flooding, and aversion therapy.

SYSTEMATIC DESENSITIZATION AND OTHER EXPOSURE THERAPIES

The nervous system cannot be relaxed and agitated at the same time, because incompatible processes cannot be activated simultaneously. This simple notion was central to the *theory of reciprocal inhibition,* developed by South African psychiatrist Joseph Wolpe (1958, 1973), who used it to treat fears and phobias. Wolpe taught his patients to *relax* their muscles, and then to *imagine* visually their feared situation. They did so in gradual steps that moved from initially remote associations to direct images. Psychologically confronting the feared stimulus while being relaxed and doing so in a *graduated* sequence is the therapeutic technique known as **systematic desensitization**.

Desensitization therapy involves three major steps. First, the client identifies the stimuli that provoke anxiety and arranges them in a hierarchy ranked from weakest to strongest. For example, a student suffering from severe test anxiety constructed the hierarchy in **Table 16.1.** Note that she rated immediate anticipation of an exami-

Behavior therapy See *behavior modification.*

Behavior modification The systematic use of principles of learning to increase the frequency of desired behaviors and/or decrease the frequency of problem behaviors.

Counterconditioning A technique used in therapy to substitute a new response for a maladaptive one by means of conditioning procedures.

Systematic desensitization A behavioral therapy technique in which a client is taught to prevent the arousal of anxiety by confronting the feared stimulus while relaxed.

TABLE 16.1

Hierarchy of Anxiety-Producing Stimuli for a Test-Anxious College Student (in order of increasing anxiety)

1. A month before an examination.
2. Two weeks before an examination.
3. A week before an examination.
4. Five days before an examination.
5. Four days before an examination.
6. Three days before an examination.
7. Two days before an examination.
8. One day before an examination.
9. The night before an examination.
10. The examination paper face down.
11. Awaiting the distribution of examination papers.
12. Before the unopened doors of the examination room.
13. In the process of answering an examination paper.
14. On the way to the university on the day of an examination.

nation (No. 14) as more stressful than taking the exam itself (No. 13). Second, the client is trained in a system of progressive deep-muscle relaxation. Relaxation training requires several sessions in which the client learns to distinguish between sensations of tension and relaxation and to let go of tension in order to achieve a state of physical and mental relaxation. Finally, the actual process of desensitization begins: The relaxed client vividly imagines the weakest anxiety stimulus on the list. If it can be visualized without discomfort, the client goes on to the next stronger one.

After a number of sessions, the most distressing situations on the list can be imagined without anxiety. Desensitization has been successfully applied to a diversity of human problems, including such generalized fears as stage fright and impotence (Emmelkamp, 1990; Spiegler & Guevremont, 1998). A number of evaluation studies have shown that this behavior therapy works remarkably well with most phobic patients.

Implosion therapy uses an approach that is opposite to systematic desensitization. Instead of experiencing a gradual, step-by-step progression, a client is exposed at the start to the most frightening stimuli at the top of the anxiety hierarchy, but in a safe setting. The therapeutic situation is arranged so that the client cannot run away from the frightening stimulus. The therapist *describes* an extremely frightening situation relating to the client's fear, such as snakes crawling all over his or her body, and urges

the client to *imagine* it fully, experiencing it through all the senses as intensely as possible. Such imagining is assumed to cause an explosion of panic. Because this explosion is an inner one, the process is called *implosion;* hence the term *implosion therapy*. As the situation happens again and again, the stimulus loses its power to elicit anxiety. When anxiety no longer occurs, the maladaptive behavior previously used to avoid it disappears. The idea behind this procedure is that the client is not allowed to deny, avoid, or otherwise escape from experiencing the anxiety-arousing stimulus situations. He or she discovers that contact with the stimulus does not actually have the anticipated negative effects (Stampfl & Levis, 1967).

Flooding is similar to implosion except that it involves clients, with their permission, actually being put into the phobic situation. A person with claustrophobia is made to sit in a dark closet, and a child with a fear of water is put into a pool.

HOW WE KNOW

FLOODING THERAPY FOR BALLOON PHOBIA Bill, a 21-year-old college student, had a phobia of noises that was particularly elicited by balloons—he avoided all situations, such as dances, parties, and athletic events, at which he might hear a balloon pop. Bill agreed to undergo flooding therapy to overcome this phobia. The therapy consisted of three sessions over three consecutive days in which hundreds of balloons were popped. At the beginning of the first session, Bill reported his level of *subjective discomfort* as 100 on a scale ranging from 0 (perfectly calm) to 100 (completely terrified). When the first balloons were popped, Bill was visibly shaking and burst into tears. However, by the end of the third day, Bill reported his subjective discomfort only as 5 on the 100-point scale; he popped the last 115 balloons himself. As a result of the flooding therapy, Bill no longer avoided happy, balloon-filled occasions (Houlihan et al., 1993).

Another form of flooding therapy begins with the use of imagination. In this procedure, the client may listen to a tape that describes the most terrifying version of the phobic fear in great detail for an hour or two. Once the terror subsides, the client is then taken to the feared situation, which, of course, is not nearly as frightening as just imagined. Flooding is more effective than systematic desensitization in the treatment of some behavior

Implosion therapy A behavioral therapeutic technique that exposes a client to anxiety-provoking stimuli, through his or her own imagination, in an attempt to extinguish the anxiety associated with the stimuli.

Flooding A therapy for phobias in which clients are exposed, with their permission, to the stimuli most frightening to them.

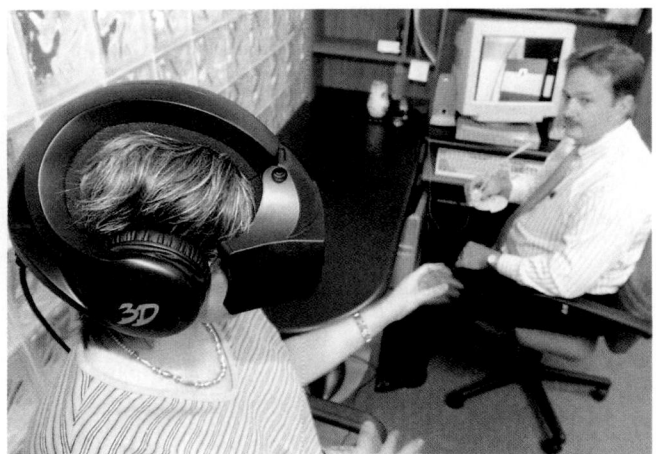

How might a behavior therapist use exposure therapy to help a client overcome a fear of flying?

problems, such as agoraphobia, and treatment gains are shown to be enduring for most clients (Emmelkamp & Kuipers, 1979).

The ingredient common to systematic desensitization, implosion, and flooding therapies is *exposure*. Through imagery, actual contact—or most recently through virtual reality techniques (Rothbaum et al., 1995)—the client is exposed to the object or situation he or she fears. Exposure therapy is also used to combat obsessive-compulsive disorders. For example, one woman who was obsessed with dirt compulsively washed her hands over and over until they cracked and bled. She even thought of killing herself because this disorder totally prevented her from leading a normal life. Under the supervision of a behavior therapist, she confronted the things she feared most—dirt and trash—and eventually even touched them. She gave up washing and bathing her hands and face for five days. Note that behavior therapy here has an added component, *response prevention*. Not only is the client exposed to what is feared (dirt and trash), but she is also prevented from performing the compulsive behavior that ordinarily reduces her anxiety (washing). The therapy teaches the woman to reduce anxiety without engaging her compulsion.

AVERSION THERAPY

The forms of exposure therapy we've described help clients deal directly with stimuli that are not really harmful. What can be done to help those who are *attracted* to stimuli that *are* harmful? Drug addiction, sexual perver-

sions, and uncontrollable violence are human problems in which deviant behavior is elicited by tempting stimuli. **Aversion therapy** uses counterconditioning procedures to pair these stimuli with strong noxious stimuli such as electric shocks or nausea-producing drugs. In time, the same negative reactions are elicited by the tempting stimuli, and the person develops an aversion that replaces his or her former desire. For example, aversion therapy has been used with individuals who engage in *self-injurious behaviors,* such as hitting their heads or banging their heads against other objects. When an individual performs such a behavior, he or she is given a mild electric shock. This treatment effectively eliminates self-injurious behaviors in some, but not all, patients (Duker & Seys, 1996).

In the extreme, aversion therapy resembles torture, so why would anyone submit voluntarily to it? Usually, people do so only because they realize that the long-term consequences of continuing their behavior pattern will destroy their health or ruin their careers or family lives. They may also be coerced to do so by institutional pressures, as has happened in some prison treatment programs. Many critics are concerned that the painful procedures in aversion therapy give too much power to a therapist, can be more punitive than therapeutic, and are most likely to be used in institutional situations in which people have the least freedom of choice about what is done to them. In recent years, use of aversion therapy in institutional rehabilitation programs has become regulated by ethical guidelines and state laws. The hope is that, under these restrictions, it will be therapeutic rather than coercive.

Contingency Management

Counterconditioning procedures are appropriate when one response can be replaced with another. Other behavior modification procedures rely on the principles of operant conditioning that arose in the research tradition pioneered by **B. F. Skinner**. **Contingency management** refers to the general treatment strategy of changing behavior by modifying its consequences. The two major techniques of contingency management in behavior therapy are *positive reinforcement strategies* and *extinction strategies*.

POSITIVE REINFORCEMENT STRATEGIES

When a response is followed immediately by a reward, the response tends to be repeated and to increase in frequency over time. This central principle of operant learning becomes a therapeutic strategy when it is used to modify the frequency of a desirable response as it replaces an undesirable one. Dramatic success has been obtained from the application of positive reinforcement procedures to behavior problems. You might recall two examples from Chapter 7. We described an application

Aversion therapy A type of behavioral therapy used to treat individuals attracted to harmful stimuli; an attractive stimulus is paired with a noxious stimulus in order to elicit a negative reaction to the target stimulus.

Contingency management A general treatment strategy involving changing behavior by modifying its consequences.

of *shaping* to improve the life of an autistic child. The patient was a 3-year-old boy who needed to wear glasses. Therapists used the click of a toy noisemaker as a conditioned reinforcer to move him closer and closer to wearing the glasses. We also described *token economies,* in which desired behaviors (for example, practicing personal care or taking medication) are explicitly defined, and token payoffs are given by institutional staff when the behaviors are performed. These tokens can later be exchanged for an array of rewards and privileges (Kazdin, 1994; Martin & Pear, 1999). These systems of reinforcement are especially effective in modifying patients' behaviors regarding self-care, upkeep of their environment, and frequency of their positive social interactions.

In another approach, therapists differentially reinforce behaviors that are incompatible with the maladaptive behavior. This technique has been used successfully with individuals in treatment for drug addiction.

HOW WE KNOW

BEHAVIORAL TREATMENTS FOR DRUG ADDICTION Researchers recruited 70 men and women who were seeking treatment for cocaine dependence. All the participants received a series of counseling sessions that imparted strategies and skills for overcoming dependence. In addition, 36 participants received vouchers each time they produced a urine specimen that was drug-free. The vouchers were each worth $0.25 and could be used to purchase retail items. The first time participants produced a negative urine specimen, they were given 10 vouchers. As long as they kept producing negative specimens, the number of vouchers on each occasion increased. For these participants, reinforcement with vouchers was *contingent* on being drug free. The remaining 34 participants were also given vouchers; however, their reinforcement was *noncontingent:* Each member of the noncontingent group was yoked to a member of the contingent group so that he or she got the same levels of reinforcement at the same times. Because of this design, we can be confident that any effect of the vouchers was a product of contingency and not reinforcement alone. In fact, contingency had an enduring impact on cocaine use: Both at the end of the study and one year later, participants in the contingent group were consistently more successful at abstaining from cocaine than their peers in the noncontingent group (Higgins et al., 2000).

You might recognize the same philosophy at work here as the one that motivated the counterconditioning procedures we described earlier: Basic principles of learning are used to increase the probability of adaptive behaviors.

EXTINCTION STRATEGIES

Why do people continue to do something that causes pain and distress when they are capable of doing otherwise? The answer is that many forms of behavior have multiple consequences—some are negative, and some are positive. Often, subtle positive reinforcements keep a behavior going despite its obvious negative consequences. For example, children who are punished for misbehaving may continue to misbehave if punishment is the only form of attention they seem to be able to earn.

Extinction strategies are useful in therapy when dysfunctional behaviors have been maintained by unrecognized reinforcing circumstances. Those reinforcers can be identified through a careful situational analysis, and then a program can be arranged to withhold them in the presence of the undesirable response. When this approach is possible, and everyone in the situation who might inadvertently reinforce the person's behavior cooperates, extinction procedures work to diminish the frequency of the behavior and eventually to eliminate the behavior completely. Consider a classroom example. Researchers discovered that attention from their peers was reinforcing the disruptive behavior of four elementary school children. By having their classmates provide attention to appropriate behaviors and ignore disruptive behaviors, the researchers were able to eliminate the children's patterns of misbehavior (Broussard & Northup, 1997).

Even schizophrenic behavior can be maintained and encouraged by unintentional reinforcement. Consider the following circumstances. It is standard procedure in many psychiatric hospitals for the staff to ask patients frequently, as a form of social communication, "How are you feeling?" Patients often misinterpret this question as a request for diagnostic information, and they respond by thinking and talking about their feelings, unusual symptoms, and hallucinations. Such responding is likely to be counterproductive, since it leads staff to conclude that the patients are self-absorbed and not behaving normally. In fact, the more bizarre the symptoms and verbalizations, the more attention the staff members may show to the patient, which reinforces continued expression of bizarre symptoms. In a classic study, dramatic decreases in schizophrenic behavior were observed when hospital staff members were simply instructed to ignore the behavior and to give attention to the patients only when they were behaving normally (Ayllon & Michael, 1959).

Social-Learning Therapy

The range of behavior therapies has been expanded by social-learning theorists who point out that humans learn by observing the behavior of other people. Often, you learn and apply rules to new experiences through symbolic means, such as watching other people's experiences in life, in a movie, or on TV. **Social-learning therapy** is designed to modify problematic behavior patterns by arranging conditions in which a client will observe models being reinforced for a desirable form of responding. This vicarious learning process has been of special value in overcoming phobias and building social skills. We have noted in earlier chapters that this social-learning theory was largely developed through the pioneering research of **Albert Bandura** (1977, 1986). Here we will mention only two aspects of his approach: imitation of models and social-skills training.

IMITATION OF MODELS

Social-learning theory predicts that individuals acquire responses through observation. It should be the case, thus, that people with phobias should be able to unlearn fear reactions through imitation of models. For example, in treating a phobia of snakes, a therapist will first demonstrate fearless approach behavior at a relatively minor level, perhaps approaching a snake's cage or touching a snake. The client is aided, through demonstration and encouragement, to imitate the modeled behavior. Gradually, the approach behaviors are shaped so that the client can pick up the snake and let it crawl freely over him or her. At no time is the client forced to perform any behavior. Resistance at any level is overcome by having the client return to a previously successful, less threatening level of approach behavior.

The power of this form of **participant modeling** can be seen in research comparing this technique with symbolic

> **Social-learning therapy** A form of treatment in which clients observe models' desirable behaviors being reinforced.
>
> **Participant modeling** A therapeutic technique in which a therapist demonstrates the desired behavior and a client is aided, through supportive encouragement, to imitate the modeled behavior.
>
> **Behavioral rehearsal** Procedures used to establish and strengthen basic skills; as used in social-skills training programs, requires the client to rehearse a desirable behavior sequence mentally.

modeling, desensitization, and a control condition. In *symbolic modeling therapy*, individuals who had been trained in relaxation techniques watched a film in which several models fearlessly handled snakes; they could stop the film and try to relax whenever a scene made them feel anxious. In the control condition, no therapeutic intervention was used. As you can see in **Figure 16.1**, participant modeling was clearly the most successful of these techniques. Snake phobia was eliminated in 11 of the 12 individuals in the participant modeling group (Bandura, 1970).

SOCIAL-SKILLS TRAINING

A major therapeutic innovation encouraged by social-learning therapists involves training people with inadequate social skills to be more effective. Many difficulties arise for someone with a mental disorder, or even just an everyday problem, if he or she is socially inhibited, inept, or unassertive. *Social skills* are sets of responses that enable people to effectively achieve their social goals when approaching or interacting with others. These skills include knowing *what* (content) to say and do in given situations in order to elicit a desired response (consequences), *how* (style) to say and do it, and *when* (timing) to say and do it. One of the most common social-skills problems is lack of assertiveness—an inability to state one's own thoughts or wishes in a clear, direct, nonaggressive manner (Alberti & Emmons, 1990; Bower & Bower, 1991). To help people overcome such a problem, many social-learning therapists recommend **behavioral rehearsal**—visualizing how one should behave in a given situation and the desired positive consequences (Yates, 1985). Rehearsal can be used to establish and strengthen any basic skill, from personal hygiene to work habits to social interactions.

Adult pathology is often preceded by deficits in social skills in childhood (Oden & Asher, 1977). Therefore, considerable research and therapy is directed at building competence in withdrawn and disturbed children (Fantuzzo et al., 1996; Pfiffner & McBurnett, 1997).

FIGURE 16.1

Participant Modeling Therapy

The subject shown in the photo first watched a model make a graduated series of snake-approach responses and then repeated them herself. She eventually was able to pick up the snake and let it crawl about on her. The graph compares the number of approach responses subjects made before and after receiving participant modeling therapy (most effective) with the behavior of those exposed to two other therapeutic techniques and a control group.

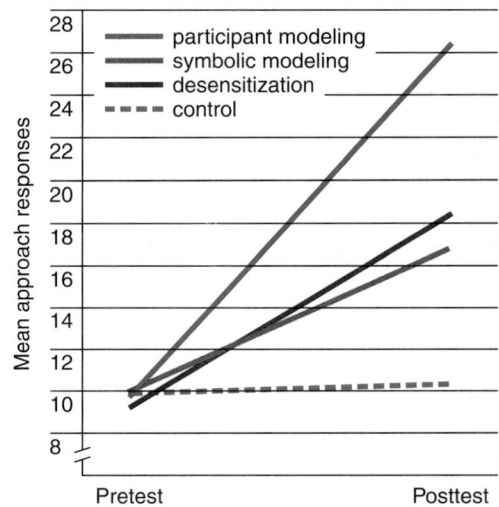

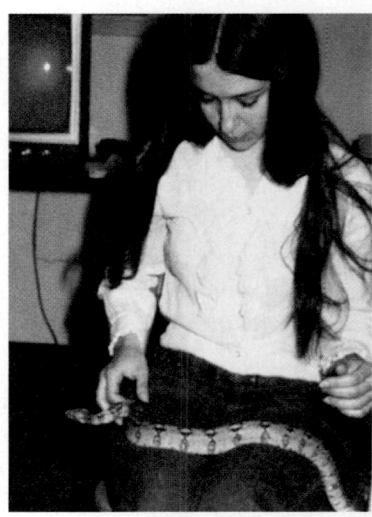

For example, one study demonstrated that preschool-age children diagnosed as *social isolates* could be helped to become sociable in a short training period.

LEARNING TO BE SOCIALLY ASSERTIVE

Twenty-four school children were randomly assigned to one of three play conditions: with a same-age peer, with a peer 1 to 1½ years younger, or with no partner (control condition). The pairs were brought together for ten play sessions, each only 20 minutes long, over a period of about a month. Their classroom behavior before and after this treatment was recorded, and it revealed that the intervention had a strong effect. The opportunity to play with a younger playmate doubled the frequency with which the former social isolates interacted later on with other classmates—bringing them up to the average level of the other children. Playing with a same-age peer also increased children's sociability, but not nearly so much. The researchers concluded that the one-on-one play situation had offered the shy children safe opportunities to be socially assertive. They were able to practice leadership skills with the nonthreatening, younger playmates (Furman et al., 1979).

In another study, social-skills training with a group of hospitalized emotionally disturbed children changed both verbal and nonverbal components of their behavior in social settings (Matson et al., 1980). The children were taught to give appropriate verbal responses in various social situations (giving help or compliments, making requests). They were also taught to display appropriate affect (for example, to smile while giving a compliment) and to make eye contact and use proper body posture (face the person being talked to). These improved social skills generalized outside of training: The children put them into practice on their own when on the ward. These positive effects continued even months later.

Generalization Techniques

An ongoing issue of concern for behavior therapists is whether new behavior patterns generated in a therapeutic setting will actually be used in the everyday situations faced by their clients (Kazdin, 1994). This question is important for all therapies, because any measure of treatment effectiveness must include maintenance of long-term changes that go beyond a therapist's couch, clinic, or laboratory.

When essential aspects of a client's real-life setting are absent from the therapy program, behavioral changes accomplished through therapy may be lost over time after therapy terminates. To prevent this gradual loss, it is becoming common practice to build generalization

techniques into the therapeutic procedure itself. These techniques attempt to *increase* the similarity of target behaviors, reinforcers, models, and stimulus demands between therapy and real-life settings. For example, behaviors are taught that are likely to be reinforced naturally in a person's environment, such as showing courtesy or consideration. Rewards are given on a partial reinforcement schedule to ensure that their effect will be maintained in the real world, where rewards are not always forthcoming. Expectation of tangible extrinsic rewards is gradually *faded out*, while social approval and more naturally occurring consequences, including reinforcing self-statements, are incorporated.

Behavior therapists, for example, used a fading procedure with a 7-year-old boy who frequently stole from his classmates (Rosen & Rosen, 1983). The boy was fined or awarded "points" (which could be exchanged for reinforcers such as extra recess) when a check revealed whether he did or did not have other children's possessions. At first, these checks were made every 15 minutes. Over time, they were faded out to only once every 2 hours. Finally, the possession checks were eliminated. Even after the direct manipulation of reinforcers had been faded out, the boy did not return to stealing.

Before we move on to cognitive therapies, take a few minutes to review the major differences between the two psychotherapies outlined thus far—the psychoanalytic and the behavioral—as summarized in **Table 16.2**.

SUMMING UP

Behavior therapies use principles of learning to increase the frequency of adaptive behaviors and decrease the frequency of maladaptive behaviors. Counterconditioning techniques include systematic desensitization, implosion, and flooding; each therapy has exposure as a critical component. Aversion therapy pairs aversive stimuli with undesirable behaviors. Contingency management uses positive reinforcement and extinction strategies to increase or decrease target behaviors. One application of social-learning therapy is the elimination of phobias; individuals can overcome their fears by imitating models. Therapists also use social-learning techniques to impart social skills.

Cognitive Therapies

Cognitive therapy attempts to change problem feelings and behaviors by changing the way a client thinks about significant life experiences. The underlying

Cognitive therapy A type of psychotherapeutic treatment that attempts to change feelings and behaviors by changing the way a client thinks about or perceives significant life experiences.

TABLE 16.2

Comparison of Psychoanalytic and Behavioral Approaches to Psychotherapy

Issue	Psychoanalysis	Behavior Therapy
Basic human nature	Biological instincts, primarily sexual and aggressive, press for immediate release, bringing people into conflict with social reality.	Similar to other animals, people are born only with the capacity for learning, which follows similar principles in all species.
Normal human development	Growth occurs through resolution of conflicts during successive stages. Through identification and internalization, mature ego controls and character structures emerge.	Adaptive behaviors are learned through reinforcement and imitation.
Nature of psychopathology	Pathology reflects inadequate conflict resolutions and fixations in earlier development, which leave overly strong impulses and/or weak controls. Symptoms are defensive responses to anxiety.	Problematic behavior derives from faulty learning of maladaptive behaviors. The *symptom* is the problem; there is no *underlying disease*.
Goal of therapy	Psychosexual maturity, strengthened ego functions, and reduced control by unconscious and repressed impulses are attained.	Symptomatic behavior is eliminated and replaced with adaptive behaviors.
Psychological realm emphasized	Motives, feelings, fantasies, and cognitions are experienced.	Therapy involves behavior and observable feelings and actions.
Time orientation	The orientation is discovering and interpreting past conflicts and repressed feelings in light of the present.	Concerned only about client's reinforcement history. Present behavior is examined and treated.
Role of unconscious material	This is primary in classical psychoanalysis and somewhat less emphasized by neo-Freudians.	There is no concern with unconscious processes or with subjective experience even in the conscious realm.
Role of insight	Insight is central; it emerges in "corrective emotional experiences."	Insight is irrelevant and/or unnecessary.
Role of therapist	The therapist functions as a *detective*, searching out basic root conflicts and resistances; detached and neutral, to facilitate transference reactions.	The therapist functions as a *trainer*, helping patients unlearn old behaviors and/or learn new ones. Control of reinforcement is important; interpersonal relationship is minor.

assumption of such therapy is that abnormal behavior patterns and emotional distress start with problems in *what* people think (cognitive content) and *how* they think (cognitive process). Cognitive therapies focus on changing different types of cognitive processes and providing different methods of cognitive restructuring. We discussed some of these approaches in Chapter 13 as ways to cope with stress and improve health. In this section, we will describe two major forms of cognitive therapy: cognitive behavior modification (including self-efficacy training) and alteration of false belief systems

(including cognitive therapy for depression and rational-emotive therapy).

Cognitive Behavior Modification

You are what you tell yourself you can be, and you are guided by what you believe you ought to do. This is a starting assumption of **cognitive behavior modification.** This therapeutic approach combines the cognitive emphasis on the role of thoughts and attitudes in influencing motivation and response with the behavioral focus on reinforcement contingencies in the modification of performance. Unacceptable behavior patterns are modified by *cognitive restructuring*—changing a person's negative self-statements into constructive coping statements.

A critical part of this therapeutic approach is the discovery by therapist and client of the way the client thinks

Cognitive behavior modification A therapeutic approach that combines the cognitive emphasis on the role of thoughts and attitudes influencing motivations and response with the behavioral emphasis on changing performance through modification of reinforcement contingencies.

Suppose you were learning to knit. Assuming you wanted to get better at it over time, what would be the best internal message to give yourself about the activity?

about and expresses the problem for which therapy is sought. Once both therapist and client understand the kind of thinking that is leading to unproductive or dysfunctional behaviors, they develop new self-statements that are constructive and minimize the use of self-defeating ones that elicit anxiety or reduce self-esteem (Meichenbaum, 1977, 1985, 1993). For example, they might substitute the negative self-statement "I was really boring at that party; they'll never ask me back" with constructive criticism: "Next time, if I want to appear interesting, I will plan some provocative opening lines, practice telling a good joke, and be responsive to the host's stories." Instead of dwelling on negatives in past situations that are unchangeable, the client is taught to focus on positives in the future.

Cognitive behavior modification builds expectations of being effective. Therapists know that building these expectations increases the likelihood that people will behave effectively. Through setting attainable goals, developing realistic strategies for attaining them, and evaluating feedback realistically, you develop a sense of mastery and *self-efficacy* (Bandura, 1992, 1997). As we saw in Chapter 14, your sense of self-efficacy influences your perceptions, motivation, and performance in many ways. Self-efficacy judgments influence how much effort you expend and how long you persist in the face of difficult life situations (Schwarzer, 1992). The modeling procedures we described earlier allow individuals to increase feelings of *behavioral* self-efficacy: They learn that they can carry out a certain range of behaviors. In contrast, therapy for *cognitive* self-efficacy changes the way clients think about their abilities. For example, in one study, students who believed that a decision-making task would *enhance* their abilities outperformed a second group who thought that the task would only gauge the abilities they already had (Wood & Bandura, 1989). In the study, types of thoughts like "I can learn to do better" actually allowed the students to become better.

Changing False Beliefs

Some cognitive behavior therapists have, as their primary targets for change, beliefs, attitudes, and habitual thought patterns. These cognitive therapists argue that many psychological problems arise because of the way people think about themselves in relation to other people and the events they face. Faulty thinking can be based on (1) unreasonable attitudes ("Being perfect is the most important trait for a student to have"), (2) false premises ("If I do everything they want me to, then I'll be popular"), and (3) rigid rules that put behavior on automatic pilot so that prior patterns are repeated even when they have not worked ("I must obey authorities"). Emotional distress is caused by cognitive misunderstandings and by failure to distinguish between current reality and one's imagination (or expectations).

COGNITIVE THERAPY FOR DEPRESSION

A cognitive therapist helps a patient to correct faulty patterns of thinking by substituting more effective problem-solving techniques. **Aaron Beck** (1976) has successfully pioneered cognitive therapy for the problem of depression. He states the formula for treatment in simple form: "The therapist helps the patient to identify his warped thinking and to learn more realistic ways to formulate his experiences" (p. 20). For example, depressed individuals may be instructed to write down negative thoughts about themselves, figure out why these self-criticisms are unjustified, and come up with more realistic (and less destructive) self-cognitions.

Beck believes that depression is maintained because depressed patients are unaware of the negative automatic thoughts that they habitually formulate, such as "I will never be as good as my brother"; "Nobody would like me if they really knew me"; and "I'm not smart enough to make it in this competitive school." A therapist then uses four tactics to change the cognitive foundation that supports the depression (Beck & Rush, 1989; Beck et al., 1979):

- Challenging the client's basic assumptions about his or her functioning.

- Evaluating the evidence the client has for and against the accuracy of automatic thoughts.

- Reattributing blame to situational factors rather than to the patient's incompetence.

- Discussing alternative solutions to complex tasks that could lead to failure experiences.

This therapy is similar to behavior therapies in that it centers on the present state of the client.

One of the worst side effects of being depressed is having to live with all the negative feelings and lethargy associated with depression. Becoming obsessed with thoughts about one's negative mood brings up memories of all the bad times in life, which worsens the depressive feelings. By filtering all input through a darkly colored lens of depression, depressed people see criticism where there is none and hear sarcasm when they listen to praise—further "reasons" for being depressed. Cognitive therapies arrest depression's downward spiral by helping the client not to become further depressed about depression itself (Teasdale, 1985). Researchers continue to use insights into the experience of depression to refine cognitive therapies (Jacobson et al., 1996; Teasdale et al., 1995). For example, one study provided evidence that a therapy is most effective when its features match the patient's own beliefs about the reasons that they have become depressed (Addis & Jacobson, 1996). Working with these kinds of results, clinicians can tailor appropriate interventions for individual clients.

RATIONAL-EMOTIVE THERAPY

One of the earliest forms of cognitive therapy was the **rational-emotive therapy (RET)** developed by **Albert Ellis** (1962, 1995; Windy & Ellis, 1997). RET is a comprehensive system of personality change based on the transformation of irrational beliefs that cause undesirable, highly charged emotional reactions, such as severe anxiety. Clients may have core values *demanding* that they succeed and be approved, *insisting* that they be treated fairly, and *dictating* that the universe be more pleasant.

Rational-emotive therapists teach clients how to recognize the "shoulds," "oughts," and "musts" that are controlling their actions and preventing them from choosing the lives they want. They attempt to break through a client's closed-mindedness by showing that an emotional reaction that follows some event is really the effect of unrecognized beliefs about the event. For example, failure to achieve orgasm during intercourse (event) is followed by an emotional reaction of depression and self-derogation. The belief that is causing the emotional reaction is likely to be "I am sexually inadequate and may be impotent because I failed to perform as expected." In therapy, this belief (and others) is openly disputed through rational confrontation and examination of alternative reasons for the event, such as fatigue, alcohol, false notions of sexual performance, or reluctance to engage in intercourse at that time or with that particular partner. This confrontation technique is followed by other interventions that replace dogmatic, irrational thinking with rational, situationally appropriate ideas.

Rational-emotive therapy aims to increase an individual's sense of self-worth and the potential to be self-actualized by getting rid of the system of faulty beliefs that block personal growth. As such, it shares much with humanistic therapies, which we consider next.

SUMMING UP

Cognitive therapies attempt to relieve individuals' distress by changing the way they think about life experiences. In cognitive behavior modification, unacceptable behavior patterns are modified by changing a person's negative self-statements into constructive coping statements. Cognitive therapy for depression seeks to eliminate automatic thinking and change clients' thought processes and patterns of attributions. Rational-emotional therapy encourages clients to overcome closed-mindedness and choose the lives they desire.

Existential-Humanistic Therapies

Problems in everyday living, a lack of meaningful human relationships, and an absence of significant goals to strive for are common *existential crises,* according to proponents of humanistic and existentialist perspectives on human nature. These orientations have been combined to form a general type of therapy addressing the basic problems of existence common to all human beings.

As you saw in Chapter 14, at the core of humanistic theories is the concept of a whole person in the continual process of changing and of becoming. Although environment and heredity place certain restrictions, people always remain free to choose what they will become by creating their own values and committing to them through their own decisions. Along with this *freedom to choose,* however, comes the burden of responsibility. Because you are never fully aware of all the implications of your actions, you experience anxiety and despair. You also suffer from guilt over lost opportunities to achieve your full potential. A new clinical version of existential psychology, which integrates its various themes and approaches, assumes that the bewildering realities of modern life give rise to two basic kinds of human maladies. Depressive and obsessive syndromes reflect a retreat from these realities; sociopathic and narcissistic syndromes reflect an exploitation of these realities (Schneider & May, 1995).

Psychotherapies that apply the principles of this general theory of human nature attempt to help clients define their own freedom, value their experiencing selves and the richness of the present moment, cultivate their individuality, and discover ways of realizing their fullest potential (self-actualization). Of importance in the existential perspective is the current life situation as experienced by the person.

Rational-emotive therapy (RET) A comprehensive system of personality change based on changing irrational beliefs that cause undesirable, highly charged emotional reactions such as severe anxiety.

THERAPY IN THE AGE OF COMPUTERS

One of the important goals of a chapter on psychotherapy is to educate students about the effectiveness of therapy: By describing research and practice, we can assure you that help is available to alleviate psychological distress. In fact, the wide availability of computers at the turn of the 21st century has provided an increase in the means psychologists and other mental health practitioners can employ to bring about therapeutic change.

For example, many people now experience the "talking cure"—the type of interactive therapy pioneered by Freud and others in face-to-face settings—through e-mail or the Internet (Fink, 1999; King & Moreggi, 1998). In this type of computer-assisted therapy, individuals often interact with their therapists through exchanges of e-mail. Researchers have been quick to point out both potential dangers and benefits of therapy on the Internet. On the dangers side, researchers worry that patients may be misdiagnosed if they present limited or distorted information without the extra scrutiny that is possible face-to-face (King & Moreggi, 1998). Furthermore, consumers rarely are able to verify the credentials of on-line therapists; in cyberspace anyone can claim to be an expert. Despite these dangers, e-mail therapy may also provide unique opportunities for therapists and their clients. For example, some therapists

believe that the relative anonymity of this form of therapy allows clients to reveal their most pressing problems and concerns more quickly and with less embarrassment; individuals may be more honest when they don't have to worry about their therapist's overt reactions to their difficult confessions (Grohol, 1998). In recognition of both the dangers and benefits of therapy in cyberspace, researchers have formed the *International Society for Mental Health Online*. This organization is devoted to studying practical and ethical constraints for on-line therapy.

Therapists are also inventing new ways to use the Internet and computers to deliver more focused forms of intervention (e.g., Newman et al., 1999; Ström et al., 2000). For example, one team of researchers created a computer program to help achieve cognitive-behavioral treatment of panic disorder (Newman et al., 1997). The study contrasted therapeutic outcomes for a group of participants whose treatment was partially conducted with computer assistance versus a group who received a full course of traditional therapy. The treatment for both groups included a behavioral component—exposure to feared situations and relaxation training—as well as a cognitive component—practice at cognitive restructuring. The therapeutic computer program was loaded onto palmtop computers that, because they weighed less than a pound, the participants

could keep with them at all times. The computer program provided several types of support including a module that displayed a series of self-statements and suggestions to alter thinking as well as one that prompted the practice of breathing retraining. Both computer-assisted and traditional therapy were successful: Six months after the treatment, both groups continued to maintain treatment gains; both treatments, for example, eliminated panic attacks in 67 percent of the participants. Studies of this type hold out the promise that computer-assisted treatments could make therapists available by proxy to clients at all times.

As we've seen in this chapter, most forms of psychotherapy were developed on the assumption that individuals would participate face-to-face with their therapists. At the start of the 21st century, researchers are hard at work trying to define the situations in which computers and the Internet can serve as useful adjuncts to those face-to-face interactions.

Web sites:

- www.ismho.org—The home page for the International Society for Mental Health Online.

- www.metanoia.org/imhs/—A Web site that has taken a lead in trying to provide a list of on-line therapists with appropriate credentials.

The existential-humanistic philosophy also gave rise to the **human-potential movement,** which emerged in the United States in the late 1960s. This movement encompassed methods to enhance the potential of the average human being toward greater levels of performance and greater richness of experience. Through this movement, therapy originally intended for people with psychological disorders was extended to mentally healthy people who wanted to be more effective, more productive, and happier human beings.

Let's examine three types of therapies in the existential-humanistic tradition: person-centered therapy, group therapy, and marital and family therapy.

Human-potential movement The therapy movement that encompasses all those practices and methods that release the potential of the average human being for greater levels of performance and greater richness of experience.

Client-Centered Therapy

As developed by **Carl Rogers** (1951, 1977), *client-centered therapy* has had a significant impact on the way many different kinds of therapists define their relationships to their clients. The primary goal of **client-centered therapy** is to promote the healthy psychological growth of the individual.

The approach begins with the assumption that all people share the basic tendency to self-actualize—that is, to realize their potential. Rogers believed that "it is the inherent tendency of the organism to develop all its capacities in ways which seem to maintain or enhance the organism" (1959, p. 196). Healthy development is hindered by faulty learning patterns in which a person accepts the evaluation of others in place of those provided by his or her own mind and body. A conflict between the naturally positive self-image and negative external criticisms creates anxiety and unhappiness. This conflict, or *incongruence,* may function outside of awareness, so that a person experiences feelings of unhappiness and low self-worth without knowing why.

The task of Rogerian therapy is to create a therapeutic environment that allows a client to learn how to behave in order to achieve self-enhancement and self-actualization. Because people are assumed to be basically good, the therapist's task is mainly to help remove barriers that limit the expression of this natural positive tendency. The basic therapeutic strategy is to recognize, accept, and clarify a client's feelings. This is accomplished within an atmosphere of *unconditional positive regard—* nonjudgmental acceptance and respect for the client. The therapist allows his or her own feelings and thoughts to be transparent to the client. In addition to maintaining this genuineness, the therapist tries to experience the client's feelings. Such total empathy requires that the therapist care for the client as a worthy, competent individual—not to be judged or evaluated but to be assisted in discovering his or her individuality (Meador & Rogers, 1979).

The emotional style and attitude of the therapist is instrumental in *empowering* the client to attend once again to the true sources of personal conflict and to remove the distracting influences that suppress self-actualization. Unlike practitioners of other therapies, who interpret, give answers, or instruct, the client-centered therapist is a supportive listener who reflects and, at times, restates the client's evaluative statements and feelings. Client-centered therapy strives to be *nondirective* by having the therapist merely facilitate the client's search for self-awareness and self-acceptance.

Rogers believed that, once people are freed to relate to others openly and to accept themselves, individuals have the potential to lead themselves back to psychological health. This optimistic view and the humane relationship between therapist-as-caring-expert and client-as-person have influenced many practitioners.

Gestalt Therapy

Gestalt therapy focuses on ways to unite mind and body to make a person whole (recall the Gestalt school of perception, described in Chapter 5). Its goal of self-awareness is reached by helping clients express pent-up feelings and recognize unfinished business from past conflicts that is carried into new relationships and must be completed for growth to proceed. **Fritz Perls** (1969), the originator of Gestalt therapy, asked clients to act out fantasies concerning conflicts and strong feelings and also to re-create their dreams, which he saw as repressed parts of personality. Perls said, "We have to *re-own* these projected, fragmented parts of our personality, and re-own the hidden potential that appears in the dream" (1969, p. 67).

In Gestalt therapy workshops, therapists encourage participants to regain contact with their "authentic inner voices" (Hatcher & Himelstein, 1996). Among the best known methods of Gestalt therapy is the *empty chair technique.* To carry out this technique, the therapist puts an empty chair near the client. The client is asked to imagine that a feeling, a person, an object, or a situation is occupying the chair. The client than "talks" to the chair's occupant. For example, clients would be encouraged to imagine their mother or father in the chair and reveal feelings they might otherwise be unwilling to reveal. The clients can then imagine those feelings in the chair to "talk" to the feelings about the impact they have on the clients' lives. This technique allows clients to confront and explore strong unexpressed feelings that may interfere with psychological well-being.

SUMMING UP

The existential-humanist therapies emphasize the concept of the whole person in the continual process of changing and becoming. Carl Rogers developed client-centered therapy, a treatment aimed at providing a non-directive context in which clients can learn to overcome faulty learning patterns and achieve self-enhancement and self-actualization. Gestalt therapy encourages group participants to express feelings and recognize conflicts as a

Client-centered therapy A humanistic approach to treatment that emphasizes the healthy psychological growth of the individual; based on the assumption that all people share the basic tendency of human nature toward self-actualization.

Gestalt therapy Therapy that focuses on ways to unite mind and body to make a person whole.

way of uniting body and mind. Many people obtain psychological support from self-help groups.

Group Therapies

All the treatment approaches outlined thus far are primarily designed as one-to-one relationships between a patient or client and a therapist. Many people, however, now experience therapy as part of a group. There are several reasons why group therapy has flourished and, in some cases, may even be more effective than individual therapy (Fuhriman & Burlingame, 1994). Some advantages are practical. Group therapy is less expensive to participants and allows small numbers of mental health personnel to help more clients. Other advantages relate to the power of the group setting. The group (1) is a less threatening situation for people who have problems dealing on their own with authority; (2) allows group processes to be used to influence individual maladaptive behavior; (3) provides people with opportunities to observe and practice interpersonal skills within the therapy session; and (4) provides an analogue of the primary family group, which enables corrective emotional experiences to take place.

Some of the basic premises of group therapies differ from those of individual therapy. The social setting of group therapies provides an opportunity to learn how one comes across to others, how the self-image that is projected differs from the one that is intended or personally experienced. In addition, the group provides confirmation that one's symptoms, problems, and "deviant" reactions are not unique but often are quite common. Because people tend to conceal from others negative information about themselves, it is possible for many people with the same problem to believe "It's only me." The shared group experience can help to dispel this pluralistic ignorance in which many share the same false belief about their unique failings. In addition, the group of peers can provide social support outside the therapy setting.

Marital and Family Therapy

Much group therapy consists of strangers coming together periodically to form temporary associations from which they may benefit. Marital and family therapy brings meaningful, existing units into a group therapy setting.

Couples counseling for marital problems seeks to clarify the typical communication patterns of the partners and then to improve the quality of their interaction (Napier, 2000). By seeing a couple together, and often by videotaping and replaying their interactions, a therapist can help them appreciate the verbal and nonverbal styles they use to dominate, control, or confuse each other. Each party is taught how to reinforce desirable responding in the other and withdraw reinforcement for undesirable reactions. They are also taught nondirective listening skills to help the other person clarify and express feelings and ideas. Couples therapy is more effective in resolving marital problems than is individual therapy for only one partner, and it has been shown to reduce marital crises and keep marriages intact (Shadish et al., 1993, 1995).

In *family therapy,* the client is a whole nuclear family, and each family member is treated as a member of a *system* of relationships (Schwebel & Fine, 1994). A family therapist works with troubled family members to help them perceive what is creating problems for one or more of them. The focus is on altering the *psychological spaces* between people and the interpersonal dynamics of people acting as a unit, rather than on changing processes within maladjusted individuals. Consider a family therapy intervention that addressed adolescent drug use.

What are some strengths of group therapies?

HOW WE KNOW

FAMILY THERAPY AND ADOLESCENT DRUG USE A team of researchers took a family therapy approach to reducing adolescent drug use: Their important assumption was that the adolescents in the study were more likely to eliminate drug use if the overall family context was changed. As a consequence, the family therapy was targeted toward improving both the adolescents' functioning and their mothers' and fathers' parenting practices. Early in the six months of therapy, observations of the families indicated that negative parenting practices (for example, expressions of negative emotion, verbal aggression) outnumbered positive ones (for example, optimism, affection)—72 to 53 percent; at the end of therapy, positive practices outnumbered negative ones—77 to 47 percent. Moreover, the children of the parents who showed overall parenting improvement were also likely to have substantially reduced their drug use (Schmidt et al., 1996).

This study illustrates the importance of the family therapy approach. By engaging the whole family, the therapeutic intervention changed environmental factors that may have originally driven the adolescents to initiate drug use and abuse.

Family therapy can reduce tensions within a family and improve the functioning of individual members by helping clients recognize the positive as well as the negative aspects in their relationships. **Virginia Satir** (1967), a developer of family therapy approaches, noted that the family therapist plays many roles, acting as an interpreter and clarifier of the interactions that are taking place in the therapy session and as influence agent, mediator, and referee. Most family therapists assume that the problems brought into therapy represent *situational* difficulties between people or problems of social interaction, rather than *dispositional* aspects of individuals. These difficulties may develop over time as members are forced into or accept unsatisfying roles. Nonproductive communication patterns may be set up in response to natural transitions in a family situation—loss of a job, a child's going to school, dating, getting married, or having a baby. The job of the family therapist is to understand the structure of the family and the many forces acting on it. Then he or she works with the family members to dissolve "dysfunctional" structural elements while creating and maintaining new, more effective structures (Fishman, 1993).

Community Support Groups

A dramatic development in therapy has been the surge of interest and participation in *self-help groups*. It is estimated that about 10 million U.S. adults attend such groups every year (Kessler et al., 1997). These support group sessions are typically free, especially when they are not directed by a health-care professional, and they give people a chance to meet others with the same problems who are surviving and sometimes thriving. The self-help concept applied to community group settings was pioneered by Alcoholics Anonymous (AA), but it was the women's consciousness-raising movement of the 1960s that helped to extend self-help beyond the arena of alcoholism. Now support groups deal with four basic catego-

ries of problems: addictive behavior, physical and mental disorders, life transition or other crises, and the traumas experienced by friends or relatives of those with serious problems. In recent years, people have begun to turn to the Internet as another venue for self-help groups. In general, Internet self-help groups engage the same range of issues as their physical counterparts (Davison et al., 2000). However, the Internet provides a particularly important meeting place for people who suffer from conditions that limit mobility, such as chronic fatigue syndrome and multiple sclerosis: An inability to attend meetings physically no longer denies people the benefits of self-help.

Researchers have begun to investigate what properties of self-help groups can make them most effective. Self-help groups appear to serve a number of functions for their members: For example, they provide people with a sense of hope and control over their problems, they engage social support for people's suffering, and they provide a forum for dispensing and acquiring information about disorders and treatments (Riessman, 1997; Schiff & Bargal, 2000). If you consider joining a self-help group, it is important to note that these groups have the most positive impact on people's feelings of well-being when they are satisfied with the group (Schiff & Bargal, 2000). For example, one study found that individuals who affiliated most strongly with AA after treatment for alcoholism showed the lowest levels of continuing substance abuse. Strong affiliation with AA apparently allowed these individuals to maintain their behavioral self-efficacy with respect to the control of their alcoholism (Morgenstern et al., 1997).

A valuable development in self-help is the application of group therapy techniques to the situations of terminally ill patients. The goals of such therapy are to help patients and their families live lives as fulfilling as possible during their illnesses, to cope realistically with impending death, and to adjust to the terminal illness (Fobair, 1997; LeGrand, 1991). One general focus of such support groups for the terminally ill is to help patients learn how to live fully until they "say goodbye" (Nungesser, 1990).

The group therapies are our final examples of types of therapies that are based purely on psychological interventions—interventions that affect the brain's software. We will now analyze how biomedical therapies work to alter the hardware of the body and brain in order to affect the mind.

SUMMING UP

Group therapies provide both more affordable mental health care and opportunities to observe and practice social behaviors. Marital and family therapy treats individuals' problems in adjustment as consequences of difficulties with systems of relationships. Therapy focuses on changing those systems of relationships in couples or families. Many people obtain psychological support from self-help groups. The groups provide hope, social support, and information to individuals in both physical and cyber settings.

Biomedical Therapies

The ecology of the mind is held in delicate balance. When something goes wrong with the brain, we see the consequences in abnormal patterns of behavior and peculiar cognitive and emotional reactions. Similarly, environmental, social, or behavioral disturbances, such as drugs and violence, can alter brain chemistry and function. Biomedical therapies most often treat mental disorders as "hardware problems" in the brain. We will describe three biomedical approaches to alleviating the symptoms of psychological disorders: psychosurgery, electroconvulsive shock, and drug therapies.

Psychosurgery and Electroconvulsive Therapy

The headline in the *Los Angeles Times* read, "Bullet in the Brain Cures Man's Mental Problem" (2/23/1988). The article revealed that a 19-year-old man suffering from severe obsessive-compulsive disorder had shot a .22-caliber bullet through the front of his brain in a suicide attempt. Remarkably, he survived, his pathological symptoms were cured, and his intellectual capacity was not affected, although some of the underlying causes of his problems remained.

This case illustrates the potential effects of one of the most direct biomedical therapies: surgical intervention in the brain. Such intervention involves lesioning (severing) connections between parts of the brain or removing small sections of the brain. These therapies are often considered methods of last resort to treat psychopathologies that have proven intractable to other, less extreme forms of therapy. **Psychosurgery** is the general term for surgical procedures performed on brain tissue to alleviate psychological disorders. In medieval times, psychosurgery involved "cutting the stone of folly" from the brains of those suffering from madness, as shown vividly in many engravings and paintings from that era.

Modern psychosurgical procedures include severing the fibers of the corpus callosum to reduce violent seizures of epilepsy, as we saw in Chapter 3; severing pathways that mediate limbic system activity (amygdalotomy); and prefrontal lobotomy. The best-known form of psychosurgery is the **prefrontal lobotomy,** an operation that severs the nerve fibers connecting the frontal lobes of the brain with the diencephalon, especially those fibers

of the thalamic and hypothalamic areas. The procedure was developed by neurologist **Egas Moniz,** who, in 1949, won a Nobel Prize for this treatment, which seemed to transform the functioning of mental patients.

The original candidates for lobotomy were agitated schizophrenic patients and patients who were compulsive and anxiety-ridden. The effects of this psychosurgery were dramatic: A new personality emerged without intense emotional arousal and, thus, without overwhelming anxiety, guilt, or anger. However, the operation permanently destroyed basic aspects of human nature: Lobotomized patients lost their unique personality. The lobotomy resulted in inability to plan ahead, indifference to the opinions of others, childlike actions, and the intellectual and emotional flatness of a person without a coherent sense of self. (One of Moniz's own patients was so distressed by these unexpected consequences that she shot Moniz, partially paralyzing him.) Because the effects of psychosurgery are permanent, its negative effects severe and common, and its positive results less certain, its continued use is very limited.

Electroconvulsive therapy (ECT) is the use of electric shock applied to the brain to treat psychiatric disorders such as schizophrenia, mania, and, most often, depression. The technique consists of applying weak electric current (75 to 100 volts) to a patient's temples for a period of time from 1/10 to a full second until a convulsion occurs. The convulsion usually runs its course in 45 to 60 seconds. Patients are prepared for this traumatic intervention by sedation with a short-acting barbiturate and muscle relaxant, which renders the patient unconscious and minimizes the violent physical reactions (Abrams, 1992).

Electroconvulsive therapy has proven extremely successful at alleviating the symptoms of serious depression (Sackheim et al., 2000). ECT is particularly important because it works quickly. Typically, the symptoms of depression are alleviated in a three- or four-day course of treatment, as compared with the one- to two-week time window for drug therapies. Even so, most therapists hold ECT as a treatment of last resort. ECT is often reserved for emergency treatment for suicidal or severely malnourished, depressed patients and for patients who do not respond to antidepressant drugs or can't tolerate their side effects.

Psychosurgery A surgical procedure performed on brain tissue to alleviate a psychological disorder.

Prefrontal lobotomy An operation that severs the nerve fibers connecting the frontal lobes of the brain with the diencephalon, especially those fibers of the thalamic and hypothalamic areas; best-known form of psychosurgery.

Electroconvulsive therapy (ECT) The use of electroconvulsive shock as an effective treatment for severe depression.

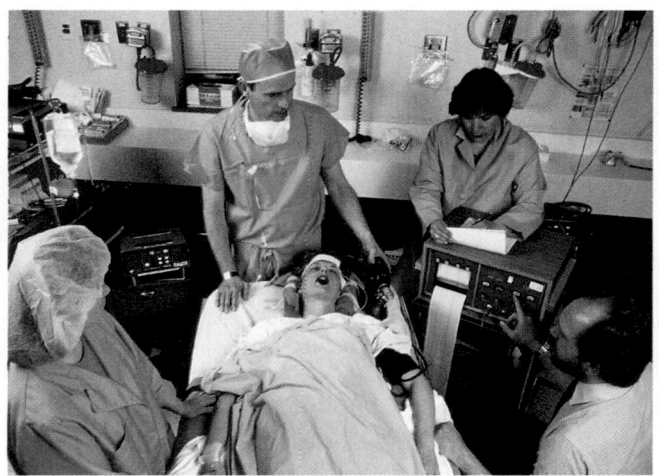
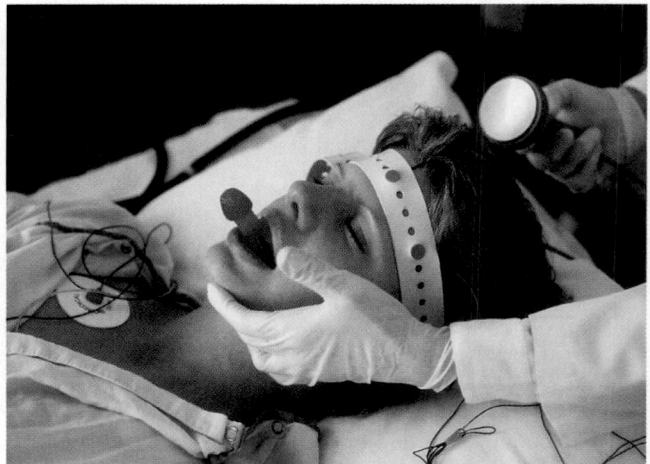

Electroconvulsive therapy has been very effective in cases of severe depression. Why does it remain controversial as a treatment?

If ECT is so effective, why has it so often been demonized? For example, in 1982, the citizens of Berkeley, California, voted to ban the use of electroconvulsive shock in any of their community mental health facilities (the action was later overturned on legal grounds). Scientific unease with ECT centers largely on the lack of understanding of how it works. The therapy was originated when clinicians observed that patients who suffered both from schizophrenia and epilepsy showed improvement in their schizophrenic symptoms after epileptic seizures. The clinicians conjectured that the same effect could be obtained with artificially induced seizures. Although the conjecture proved correct in part—ECT is much more effective at alleviating depression than schizophrenia—researchers have yet to fit a definitive theory to this chance observation.

Critics have also worried about potential side effects of ECT (Breggin, 1979, 1991). ECT produces temporary disorientation and a variety of memory deficits. Patients often suffer amnesia for events in the period of time preceding the treatment; the amnesia becomes more severe the longer the course of treatment. Research has shown, however, that patients generally recover their specific memories within months of the treatment (Cohen et al., 2000). Furthermore, patients who had received a lifetime course of over 100 ECT treatments showed no deficit in functioning compared with a control group of patients who had never received ECT (Devanand et al., 1991). As a way of minimizing even short-term deficits, ECT is now often administered to only one side of the brain so as to reduce the possibility of speech impairment. Such unilateral ECT is an effective antidepressant.

Let's now see why drug therapies have become the most popular form of biomedical interventions for psychopathology.

Psychopharmacology The branch of psychology that investigates the effects of drugs on behavior.

Drug Therapy

In the history of the treatment of mental disorders, nothing has rivaled the revolution created by the discovery of drugs that can calm anxious patients, restore contact with reality in withdrawn patients, and suppress hallucinations in psychotic patients. This new therapeutic era began in 1953 with the introduction of tranquilizing drugs, notably *chlorpromazine,* into hospital treatment programs. Emerging drug therapies gained almost instant recognition and status as an effective way to transform patient behavior. **Psychopharmacology** is the branch of psychology that investigates the effects of drugs on behavior. Researchers in psychopharmacology work to understand the effect drugs have on some biological systems and the consequent changes in responding.

The discovery of *drug therapies* had profound effects on the treatment of severely disordered patients. No longer did mental hospital staff have to act as guards, putting patients in seclusion or straitjackets; staff morale improved as rehabilitation replaced mere custodial care of the mentally ill (Swazey, 1974). Moreover, the drug therapy revolution had a great impact on the U.S. mental hospital population. Over half a million people were living in mental institutions in 1955, staying an average of several years. The introduction of chlorpromazine and other drugs reversed the steadily increasing numbers of patients. By the early 1970s, it was estimated that fewer than half the country's mental patients actually resided in mental hospitals; those who did were institutionalized for an average of only a few months.

Three major categories of drugs are used today in therapy programs: *antipsychotic, antidepressant,* and *antianxiety* compounds. As their names suggest, these drugs chemically alter specific brain functions that are responsible for psychotic symptoms, depression, and extreme anxiety.

ANTIPSYCHOTIC DRUGS

Antipsychotic drugs alter the schizophrenic symptoms of delusions, hallucinations, social withdrawal, and occasional agitation (Dawkins et al., 1999). Antipsychotic drugs work by reducing the activity of the neurotransmitter dopamine in the brain. Drugs like *chlorpromazine* (marketed under the U.S. brand name *Thorazine*) and *haloperidol* (marketed as *Haldol*) block or reduce the sensitivity of dopamine receptors. *Clozapine* (marketed as *Clozaril*), the newest major antipsychotic drug, both directly decreases dopamine activity and increases the level of serotonin activity, which inhibits the dopamine system. Although these drugs function by decreasing the overall level of brain activity, they are not just tranquilizers. For many patients, they do much more than merely eliminate agitation. They also relieve or reduce the positive symptoms of schizophrenia, including delusions and hallucinations.

There are, unfortunately, negative side effects of antipsychotic drugs. Because dopamine plays a role in motor control, muscle disturbances frequently accompany a course of drug treatment. *Tardive dyskinesia* is a particular disturbance of motor control, especially of the facial muscles, caused by antipsychotic drugs. Patients who develop this side effect experience involuntary jaw, lip, and tongue movements. The newer drug clozapine blocks dopamine receptors more selectively, resulting in a lower probability of motor disturbance. Unfortunately, *agranulocytosis*, a rare disease in which the bone marrow stops making white blood cells, develops in 1 to 2 percent of patients treated with clozapine.

Researchers continue to examine the consequences of drug use over long periods of time as well as consequences when patients cease taking the drugs. The rate of relapse when patients go off the drugs is quite high—two-thirds have new symptoms within 18 months—but even patients who remain on the drugs have about a one-third chance of relapse (Gitlin, 1990). Thus, antipsychotic drugs do not cure schizophrenia—they do not eliminate the underlying psychopathology. Fortunately, they are reasonably effective at controlling the disorder's most disruptive symptoms.

ANTIDEPRESSANT DRUGS

Antidepressant drugs work by increasing the activity of the neurotransmitters norepinephrine and serotonin (Holmes, 1994). *Tricyclics*, such as *Tofranil* and *Elavil*, reduce the reuptake of the neurotransmitters from the synaptic cleft. *Prozac*, a *bicyclic*, reduces the reuptake of serotonin. The *monoamine oxidase (MAO) inhibitors* limit the action of the enzyme monoamine oxidase, which is responsible for breaking down (metabolizing) norepinephrine. When MAO is inhibited, more of the neurotransmitter is left available.

Antidepressant drugs are generally successful at relieving the symptoms of depression, although as many as 30 to 40 percent of patients will not show improvement (Hirschfeld, 1999). (Those patients may be candidates for electroconvulsive therapy.) Prozac has been touted as a miracle drug with therapeutic effects more potent than its competitors. Some psychiatrists are great believers in the effectiveness of Prozac. In his best-selling book, *Listening to Prozac* (1993), Peter Kramer, a psychiatrist, describes a number of cases in which patients who were prescribed the drug Prozac underwent startling personality transformations. Consider the case of a woman Kramer calls Tess. Tess presented herself to Kramer and described difficult life circumstances and a history of depression. After two weeks on Prozac, however, Tess was a changed woman.

> Here was a patient whose usual method of functioning changed dramatically. She became socially capable, no longer a wallflower but a social butterfly. Where once she had focused on obligations to others, now she was vivacious and fun-loving. (Kramer, 1993, p. 11)

Tess's relief is quite dramatic. However, critics of Prozac, and other psychoactive drugs, worry that Prozac not only relieves depression but also "relieves" patients of their personality and creativity (Breggin & Breggin, 1994).

Lithium salts have proven effective in the treatment of bipolar disorders (Schou, 1997). People who experience uncontrollable periods of hyperexcitement, when their energy seems limitless and their behavior extravagant and flamboyant, are brought down from their state of manic excess by doses of lithium. Between 60 and 80 percent of patients treated with lithium have a good chance of recovery (Walden et al., 1998). However, for those people suffering from bipolar disorders who cycle frequently between manic episodes and depression, lithium appears to be less effective than other treatments such as the drug *valproate,* which was originally developed as a drug to prevent seizures.

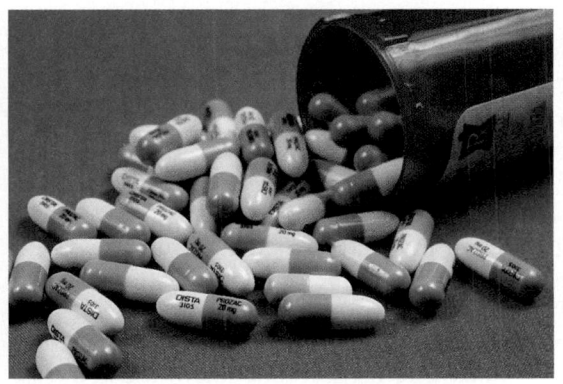

Why has Prozac become the most frequently prescribed antidepressant medication?

527

ANTIANXIETY DRUGS

Like antipsychotic and antidepressant drugs, antianxiety drugs generally have their effect by adjusting the levels of neurotransmitter activity in the brain. Different drugs are most effective at relieving different types of anxiety disorders (Spiegel et al., 2000). Generalized anxiety disorder is best treated with a *benzodiazepine,* such as *Valium* or *Xanax,* which increases the activity of the neurotransmitter GABA. Because GABA regulates inhibitory neurons, increases in GABA activity decrease brain activity in areas of the brain relevant to generalized anxiety responses. Panic disorders, as well as agoraphobia and other phobias, can be treated with antidepressant drugs, although researchers do not yet understand the biological mechanism involved. Obsessive-compulsive disorder, which may arise from low levels of serotonin, responds particularly well to drugs, like Prozac, that specifically affect serotonin function.

PRESCRIPTIONS FOR PSYCHOACTIVE DRUGS

The drugs we have described that alleviate symptoms of various mental disorders are widely prescribed. As mental health care comes increasingly under the direction of health maintenance organizations (HMOs), cost-cutting practices are limiting the number of patients' visits to therapists for psychological therapies while substituting cheaper drug therapies. A recent study of prescribing trends in psychoactive medications reported that in the decade from 1985 to 1994, the number of visits to psychiatrists, primary-care physicians, and other medical specialists in the United States that resulted in some form of drug treatment soared by 20 percent, from 32.7 to 45.6 million (Pincus et al., 1998). Even against this background, some groups of individuals are more likely to receive medication than others. In one five-year study, researchers observed the prescribing practices of mostly Caucasian doctors in the emergency services at four urban general hospitals in California. Those doctors prescribed more antipsychotic medications, at higher doses, to African Americans than to other patients. This was true even though the African American patients were not more dangerous or more severely disturbed than the other patients (Segal et al., 1996). Findings of this sort illustrate why critics of drug treatments believe that they are not always used with purely medical goals.

Given the overall high rate at which psychoactive drugs are prescribed, which particular category is prescribed the most? The answer to this question changed in the period from 1985 to 1994 (Pincus et al., 1998). While prescriptions of antianxiety tranquilizers *decreased* in that decade from 52 to 33 percent of all doctor visits for mental health problems, prescriptions for antidepressant drugs *increased* from 30 to 45 percent. This increase is largely attributable to the introduction of the new class of antidepressant drugs, including Prozac, as well as an increase in the number of patients seeking help for depression (jumping from about 11 million in 1985 to over 20 million in 1994).

WHEN IS DRUG THERAPY NECESSARY?

We have briefly reviewed some of the possibilities of drug therapies for psychological disorders. There are many circumstances in which courses of medication can vastly improve the lives of sufferers. Any course of drug treatment, however, holds out the possibility of physical or psychological addiction and potentially serious side effects. How do people weigh those factors against the probability of relief? We also have noted that drugs may relieve symptoms but may not cure the underlying pathology. How willing should people be to commit themselves to a lifetime course of drugs?

These questions are made even more intriguing by research demonstrating that some forms of therapy have the same effect on the brain as a course of drug treatment.

HOW WE KNOW

BRAIN CHANGES FROM BEHAVIORAL THERAPY A group of patients with obsessive-compulsive disorders chose to undergo either drug therapy (with fluoxetine hydrochloride) or behavior therapy (involving exposure and response prevention). PET scans were performed on the patients' brains before and after treatment. The PET scans detected the same changes in brain function for both forms of therapy (Baxter et al., 1992; Schwartz et al., 1996).

This type of research holds out the exciting possibility that nondrug therapies may have the same healing effect on the brain as drug therapies—without the potential negative aspects of drug therapy.

Choices of one therapy over another often depend on the severity of illness and proven effectiveness of different treatments. For example, whatever their risks, drug treatments for schizophrenia are often essential for patients to have any opportunity for normal living. Let's next examine methods researchers use to assess the effectiveness of different forms of therapy.

SUMMING UP

In contemporary practice, surgical procedures on the brain to alleviate psychological disorders are rare. Electroconvulsive therapy is quite effective at alleviating serious depression. However, because it remains controversial, people still shy away from this treatment. Antipsychotic, antidepressant, and antianxiety drugs generally bring about relief by affecting the activity of neurotransmitters in the brain. The number of prescriptions for drug therapies, especially antidepressants, has risen sharply over the last decade.

Does Therapy Work?

Suppose you have come to perceive a problem in your life that you believe could be alleviated by interaction with a trained clinician. We have mentioned a great variety of types of therapies. How can you know which one of them will work best to relieve your distress? How can you be sure that *any* of them will work? In this section, we examine the projects researchers undertake to test the effectiveness of particular therapies and make comparisons between different therapies. The general goal is to discover the most efficient way to help people overcome distress. We also consider briefly the topic of *prevention:* How can psychologists intervene in people's lives to prevent mental illness before it occurs?

Evaluating Therapeutic Effectiveness

British psychologist **Hans Eysenck** (1952) created a furor some years ago by declaring that psychotherapy does not work at all! He reviewed available publications that reported the effects of various therapies and found that patients who received no therapy had just as high a recovery rate as those who received psychoanalysis or other forms of insight therapy. He claimed that roughly two-thirds of all people with neurotic problems would recover spontaneously within two years of the onset of the problem.

Researchers met Eysenck's challenge by devising more accurate methodologies to evaluate the effectiveness of therapy. What Eysenck's criticism made clear was that researchers needed to have appropriate control groups. For a variety of reasons, *some* percentage of individuals in psychotherapy *does* improve without any professional intervention. This **spontaneous-remission effect** is one *baseline* criterion against which the effectiveness of therapies must be assessed. Simply put, doing something must be shown to lead to a greater percentage of improved cases than doing nothing.

Similarly, researchers generally try to demonstrate that their treatment does more than just take advantage of clients' own expectations of healing. You may recall our earlier discussions of *placebo* effects: In many cases, people's mental or physical health will improve because they expect that it will improve. The therapeutic situation helps bolster this belief by putting the therapist in the specific social role of *healer* (Frank & Frank, 1991). Although the placebo effects of therapy are an important part of the therapeutic intervention, researchers typically wish to demonstrate that their specific form of therapy is more effective than a

"OF COURSE I'VE BECOME MORE MATURE SINCE YOU STARTED TREATING ME. YOU'VE BEEN AT IT SINCE I WAS FOURTEEN YEARS OLD."

placebo therapy (a neutral therapy that just creates expectations of healing) (Enserink, 1999).

In recent years, researchers have evaluated therapeutic effectiveness using a statistical technique called meta-analysis. **Meta-analysis** provides a formal mechanism for detecting the general conclusions to be found in data from many different experiments. In many psychological experiments, the researcher asks, "Did most of my participants show the effect I predicted?" Meta-analysis treats experiments like participants. With respect to the effectiveness of therapy, the researcher asks, "Did most of the outcome studies show positive changes?" The answer to this question is quite strongly "yes" (Lipsey & Wilson, 1993; Shadish et al., 1997). Most courses of therapy appear to bring about at least small positive effects that go beyond "no treatment" or "placebo" effects.

Because of such findings, contemporary researchers are less concerned about asking *whether* psychotherapy works and more concerned about asking why it works and whether any one treatment is most effective for any particular problem and for certain types of patients (Drozd & Goldfried, 1996; Goldfried et al., 1990). It has not always proven easy, however, to make comparisons between studies that report on different therapies. It is hard to control for differences in therapist experience,

Spontaneous-remission effect The improvement of some mental patients and clients in psychotherapy without any professional intervention; a baseline criterion against which the effectiveness of therapies must be assessed.

Placebo therapy A therapy independent of any specific clinical procedures that results in client improvement.

Meta-analysis A statistical technique for evaluating hypotheses by providing a formal mechanism for detecting the general conclusions found in data from many different experiments.

529

duration of therapy, accuracy of the initial diagnosis, type of disorder, differences in the severity and types of patient difficulties, the kinds of outcome measures used, the fit between a patient's expectations and the type of therapy offered, and length of follow-up times, to name but a handful. As we shall see next, researchers have tried to overcome these problems more recently by focusing on direct comparisons of different treatments for depression.

Treatment Evaluations

Because of depression's high incidence (see Chapter 15), many of the studies that compare different types of therapy have drawn on groups of depressed individuals. One particularly ambitious project was coordinated and funded by the National Institutes of Mental Health (NIMH). Its special features included: (1) comparisons of the effectiveness of two different forms of brief psychotherapy, a tricyclic drug treatment, and placebo control; (2) careful definition and standardization of the treatments, accomplished by training 28 therapists in each of the four treatment conditions, with each treatment delivered at three different institutions in different cities; (3) random assignment of 240 outpatients who met standard diagnostic criteria for major depressive disorder; (4) standardized assessment procedures to monitor both the process of the therapy (by analysis of therapy-session videotapes, for example) and a battery of outcome measures administered before treatment began, during the 16-week treatment period, at termination, and 18 months later; and (5) independent assessment of the results at an institution separate from any involved in the training or treatment phases of the study (Elkin et al., 1989).

The psychotherapies evaluated were two that had been developed, or modified, especially for the treatment of depression in people outside a hospital setting. The two brief therapies were cognitive behavior therapy and interpersonal psychotherapy, a psychodynamically oriented therapy that focuses on a patient's current life and interpersonal relationships. *Imipramine,* a tricyclic antidepressant, and a placebo drug control were administered in a double-blind procedure (that is, the experimenters did not know which patients were getting which drugs). Each of the participants in both the real and the placebo drug treatment was seen weekly by a psychiatrist who provided minimal supportive therapy.

One set of results from this model study of therapy outcome is presented in **Figure 16.2.** The graph shows that each of the treatments for severely depressed patients had an effect beyond that of the placebo control, with the antidepressant drug being most effective and the psychodynamic and cognitive therapies having an intermediate level of effectiveness (Klein & Ross, 1993). In

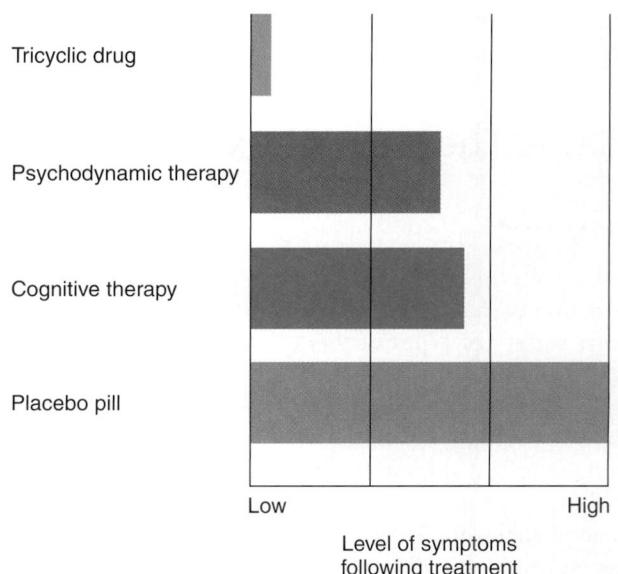

Low   High

Level of symptoms
following treatment

FIGURE 16.2

Depression Therapies

Symptoms of depression are reduced most substantially by drug therapy, but they are also significantly reduced by psychodynamic and cognitive therapies.

more recent projects, researchers have assessed the effectiveness of psychotherapy alone versus psychotherapy combined with drug therapy. One study found that combination therapy was most successful (Keller et al., 2000). Of 519 participants who completed a course of treatment, 55 percent of the participants who received only drug therapy met the study's criterion for symptom relief, as did 52 percent of the participants who received only psychotherapy. For participants who received both drug therapy and psychotherapy, 85 percent showed the same level of improvement.

These studies on treatments for depression demonstrate that both biological and psychological treatments make important contributions to improved mental health. The studies also illustrate the methods researchers can use to determine the optimal therapy for each type of disorder. **Figure 16.3** provides a general flowchart for the way theory, clinical observation, and research all play a role in the development and evaluation of any form of treatment (for both mental and physical disorders). It shows the type of systematic research needed to help clinicians discover if their therapies are making the differences that their theories predict. On one side, you see clinical observation—clinicians' own experience with a new procedure. Typically, new treatments first get tested in the field without rigorous experimental control. On the other side of the figure, you see a theory being developed. The theory makes predictions about what

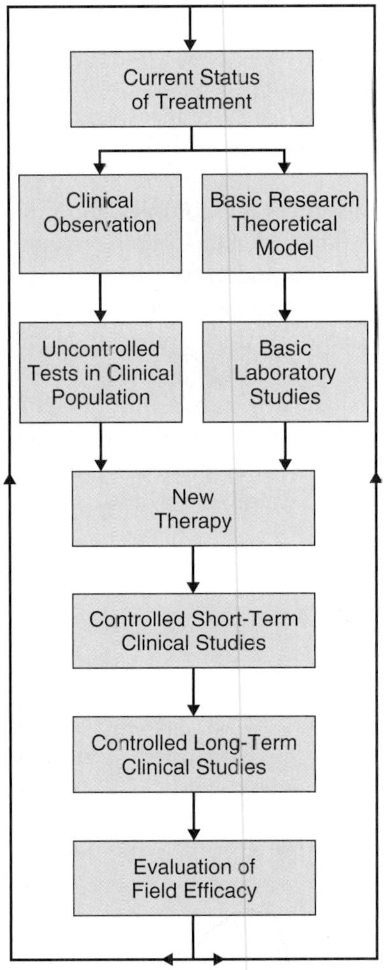
Current Status of Treatment
Clinical Observation
Basic Research Theoretical Model
Uncontrolled Tests in Clinical Population
Basic Laboratory Studies
New Therapy
Controlled Short-Term Clinical Studies
Controlled Long-Term Clinical Studies
Evaluation of Field Efficacy

FIGURE 16.3

Building Better Therapies

Flowchart of stages in the development of treatments for mental/physical disorders.

should work, which may be confirmed in laboratory studies. These two types of insights—clinical and experimental—are combined to yield a new therapy (Goldfried & Wolfe, 1996; Seligman, 1996).

In the final section of this chapter, we reflect on an important principle of life: Whatever the effectiveness of treatment, it is often better to prevent a disorder than to heal it once it arises.

Prevention Strategies

> *Two friends were walking on a riverbank. Suddenly, a child swept downstream in the current. One of the friends jumped in the river and rescued the child. Then the two friends resumed their stroll. Suddenly, another child appeared in the water. The rescuer jumped in and again pulled the victim to safety. Soon, a third drowning child swept by. The still-dry friend began to trot up the riverbank. The rescuer yelled, "Hey, where are you going?" The dry one replied, "I'm going to get the bastard that's throwing them in." (Wolman, 1975, p. 3)*

The moral of this story is clear: *Preventing* a problem is the best solution. The traditional therapies we have examined here share the focus of changing a person who is already distressed or disabled. They begin to do their work after the problem behaviors show up and after the suffering starts. By the time someone elects to go into therapy or is required to, the psychological disorder has "settled in" and had its disruptive effects on the person's daily functioning, social life, job, or career.

The goal of *preventing* psychological problems can be realized at several different levels (Rabins, 1992; Reiss & Price, 1996). *Primary* prevention seeks to prevent a condition before it begins. Steps might be taken, for example, to provide individuals with coping skills so they can be more resilient or to change negative aspects of an environment that might lead to anxiety or depression (Durlak & Wells, 1997; Kaplan, 2000). *Secondary* prevention attempts to limit the duration and severity of a disorder once it has begun. This goal is realized by means of programs that allow for early identification and prompt treatment. *Tertiary* prevention limits the long-term impact of a psychological disorder by seeking to prevent a relapse. Efforts at tertiary prevention require that the causes of a disorder be identified and, as much as possible, eliminated.

The implementation of these three types of prevention has signaled major shifts in the focus and in the basic paradigms of mental health care. The most important of these paradigm shifts are: (1) supplementing treatment with prevention; (2) going beyond a medical disease model to a public health model; (3) focusing on

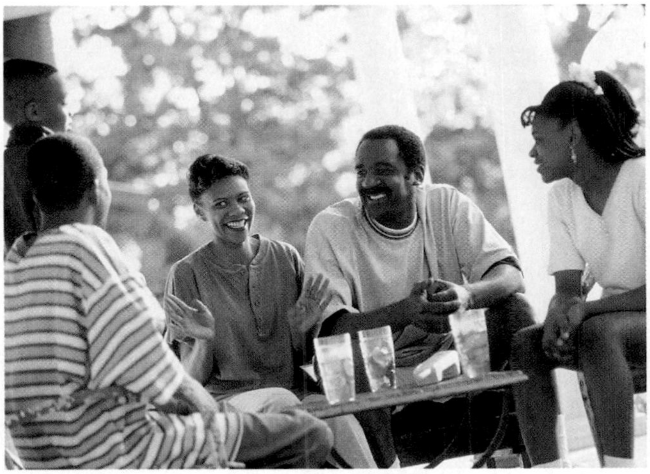

How can prevention strategies encourage people to build "mental hygiene" habits to minimize the need for treatment?

situations and ecologies that put people at risk and away from "at-risk people"; and (4) looking for precipitating factors in life settings rather than for predisposing factors in people (Ammerman & Hersen, 1997; Kendrick et al., 1996).

The medical model is concerned with treating people who are afflicted; a public health model includes identifying and eliminating the causes of disease and illness that exist in the environment. In this approach, an affected individual is seen as the host or carrier—the end product of an existing process of disease. When programs can change the conditions that breed illness, there will be no need to change people later with expensive, extensive treatments. The dramatic reduction of many contagious and infectious diseases, such as tuberculosis, smallpox, and malaria, came about through this approach. With psychopathology, too, many sources of environmental or organizational stress can be identified. Programs can be designed to alleviate them, thus reducing the number of people who will be exposed. The field of **clinical ecology** expands the boundaries of biomedical therapies by relating disorders, such as anxiety and depression, to environmental irritants, such as chemical solvents, noise pollution, seasonal changes, and radiation (Bell, 1982). Some therapists have broadened the definition of environment, as it contributes to psycho-

Clinical ecology A field of psychology that relates disorders such as anxiety and depression to environmental irritants and sources of trauma.

pathology, to include all features of the external environment that interfere with normal adaptations in daily life (Ghadirian & Lehmann, 1993). These include nutritional influences, psychoactive substances, terrorism, natural disasters, and the availability of social support networks.

Preventing mental disorders is a complex and difficult task. It involves not only understanding the relevant causal factors, but overcoming individual, institutional, and governmental resistance to change. A major research effort will be needed to demonstrate the long-range utility of prevention and the public health approach to psychopathology in order to justify the expense in the face of the many other problems that demand immediate solutions. The ultimate goal of prevention programs is to safeguard the mental health of all members of our society.

SUMMING UP

Researchers on psychotherapy seek to determine which therapeutic interventions provide genuine relief. Analyses of large numbers of studies suggest that, in a general sense, psychotherapy is effective. Large-scale studies, such as the depression treatment study coordinated by the NIMH, seek to identify the specific treatments that are most effective for individual disorders. The effort to build better therapies unites insights from laboratory research and clinical practice. A focus on prevention prompts clinicians to attempt to instill skills and change environments to prevent occurrences of disorders and minimize their consequences.

RECAPPING
MAIN POINTS

The Therapeutic Context

- Therapy requires that a diagnosis be made and a course of treatment be established.

- Therapy may be medically or psychologically oriented.

- The four major types of psychotherapy are psychodynamic, behavior, cognitive, and existential-humanist.

- A variety of professionals practice therapy.

- In earlier times, treatment for those with mental problems was often harsh and dehumanizing.

- A disease model of mental illness led to a more humane treatment of patients.

- Cultural anthropology shows that many cultures have ways of understanding and treating mental disorders that can generate important lessons for Western practice.

Psychodynamic Therapies

- Psychodynamic therapies grew out of Sigmund Freud's psychoanalytic theory.

- Freud emphasized the role of unconscious conflicts in the etiol-

ogy of psychopathology. Psychodynamic therapy seeks to reconcile these conflicts.

- Free association, attention to resistance, dream analysis, transference, and countertransference are all important components of this therapy.

- Neo-Freudians place more emphasis on the patient's current social situation, interpersonal relationships, and self-concept.

Behavior Therapies

- Behavior therapies use the principles of learning and reinforcement to modify or eliminate problem behaviors.

- Counterconditioning techniques replace negative behaviors, like phobic responses, with more adaptive behaviors.
- Exposure is the common element in phobia-modification therapies.
- Contingency management uses operant conditioning to modify behavior, primarily through positive reinforcement and extinction.
- Social-learning therapy uses models and social-skills training to help individuals gain confidence about their abilities.

Cognitive Therapies

- Cognitive therapy concentrates on changing negative or irrational thought patterns about the self and social relationships.
- Cognitive behavior modification calls for the client to learn more constructive thought patterns in reference to a problem and to apply the new technique to other situations.
- Cognitive therapy has been used successfully to treat depression.
- Rational-emotive therapy helps clients recognize that their irrational beliefs about themselves interfere with successful life outcomes.

Existential-Humanistic Therapies

- Existential-humanistic therapies work to help individuals become more fully self-actualized.
- Therapists strive to be nondirective in helping their clients establish a positive self-image that can deal with external criticisms.
- Gestalt therapy focuses on the whole person—body, mind, and life setting.

Group Therapies

- Group therapy allows people to observe and engage in social interactions as a means to reduce psychological distress.
- Family and marital therapy concentrates on situational difficulties and interpersonal dynamics of the couple or family group as a system in need of improvement.
- Community and Internet self-help groups allow individuals to obtain information and feelings of control in circumstances of social support.

Biomedical Therapies

- Biomedical therapies concentrate on changing physiological aspects of mental illness.
- Psychosurgery is rarely used because of its radical, irreversible effects.
- Electroconvulsive therapy is highly effective with depressed patients but remains controversial.
- Drug therapies include antipsychotic medications for treating schizophrenia as well as antidepressants and antianxiety drugs.
- Traditional psychotherapies and drug therapies may achieve some of the same changes in the brain.

Does Therapy Work?

- Research shows that many therapies work better than the mere passage of time or nonspecific placebo treatment.
- Evaluation projects, such as the NIMH study of depression therapies, are helping to answer the question of what makes therapy effective.
- Prevention strategies are necessary to stop psychological disorders from occurring and minimize their effects once they have occurred.

Key Terms

aversion therapy (p. 514)
behavioral rehearsal (p. 516)
behavior modification (p. 512)
behavior therapy (p. 512)
biomedical therapies (p. 504)
catharsis (p. 508)
client (p. 505)
client-centered therapy (p. 522)
clinical ecology (p. 532)
clinical psychologist (p. 505)
clinical social worker (p. 505)
cognitive behavior modification (p. 518)
cognitive therapy (p. 517)
contingency management (p. 514)
counseling psychologist (p. 505)
counterconditioning (p. 512)
countertransference (p. 509)
dream analysis (p. 509)
electroconvulsive therapy (ECT) (p. 525)
flooding (p. 513)
free association (p. 508)
Gestalt therapy (p. 522)
human-potential movement (p. 521)
implosion therapy (p. 513)
insight therapy (p. 508)
meta-analysis (p. 529)
object relations theory (p. 511)
participant modeling (p. 516)
pastoral counselor (p. 505)
patient (p. 505)
placebo therapy (p. 529)
prefrontal lobotomy (p. 525)
psychiatrist (p. 505)
psychoanalysis (p. 508)
psychoanalyst (p. 505)
psychopharmacology (p. 526)
psychosurgery (p. 525)
psychotherapy (p. 504)
rational-emotive therapy (RET) (p. 520)
resistance (p. 509)
ritual healing (p. 507)
shamanism (p. 507)
social-learning therapy (p. 516)
spontaneous-remission effect (p. 529)
systematic desensitization (p. 512)
transference (p. 509)

social processes and relationships

17

■ **THE POWER OF THE SITUATION**
Roles and Rules • Social Norms • Conformity • Situational Power: *Candid Camera* Revelations

■ **PSYCHOLOGY IN YOUR LIFE: HOW DO GROUPS AFFECT DECISION MAKING?**

■ **CONSTRUCTING SOCIAL REALITY**
The Origins of Attribution Theory • The Fundamental Attribution Error • Self-Serving Biases • Expectations and Self-Fulfilling Prophecies • Behaviors That Confirm Expectations

■ **ATTITUDES, ATTITUDE CHANGE, AND ACTION**
Attitudes and Behaviors • Processes of Persuasion • Persuasion by Your Own Actions • Compliance

■ **SOCIAL RELATIONSHIPS**
Liking • Loving

■ **PSYCHOLOGY IN THE 21ST CENTURY: RELATIONSHIPS AND THE INTERNET**

■ **RECAPPING MAIN POINTS**
Key Terms

My Sicilian grandfather, Salvatore, loved the opera, but he was too poor ever to go to one in his adopted home, the United States. Instead, every Saturday he listened to the opera from the Met on a little radio in his shoe repair shop in the Bronx. He would play it full blast, and if it were an Italian opera, he would sing along with most of the tenor parts. He also felt he needed to educate "the Americans" to the joys of opera, so he would open his door and let the opera blast out into the streets.

One Saturday his reverie was broken by a gang of toughs who were shouting offensive epithets at him, "dirty wop," "guinea, go back to where you came from," and worse. Their shouting was so loud he could not hear his beloved opera, *La Traviata*. He cursed back, and they laughed and taunted him mercilessly. By the time they left, he could find no joy in listening to the end of the opera.

Next Saturday, like clockwork, the boys returned, shouting and cursing. Grandpa Salvatore now went out front and said to them: "Boys, I did not appreciate what good voices you have. Please continue to shout and scream as loud as you can, and I will give each of you 25

cents for your performance." They did just that, screaming like banshees for nearly half an hour without intermission. He gave them their reward, and they left surprised but happy at this unexpected windfall of money for a movie and a Coke.

On the following Saturday when they returned, Grandpa Salvatore came out and said again how much he loved to hear their voices shouting even louder than the opera or the neighborhood garbage trucks, but since he was only a poor shoe repairman he did not have enough money to pay them what they were worth. For today's show, he could give them only 10 cents each.

"What do you take us for old man, suckers?" "We ain't gonna do no show for you for a measly dime." "Take your money and shove it." With that they sulked away, cursing as usual—but in modulated tones.

Next Saturday and all the ones after that, the ruffians refused to return to curse and shout at the old Italian shoemaker, whom they took for a cheapskate. Grandfather now could listen with undivided attention to his operas every Saturday, play them loud and clear, and not worry about being interrupted and disturbed by this uncouth, prejudiced bunch of kids.

As you admire the ingenuity of Grandpa Salvatore, ask yourself why his actions worked so well. How did his initial payment of 25 cents to each boy transform the situation? Why was the reduction from 25 to 10 cents enough to get the ruffians to leave Salvatore alone with his operas? As you start to formulate answers to these questions, you will be entering the world of *social psychology*—that area of psychology that investigates the ways in which individuals create and navigate social situations.

Social psychology is the study of the ways in which thoughts, feelings, perceptions, motives, and behavior are influenced by interactions and transactions between peo-

ple. Social psychologists try to understand behavior within its social context. This social context is the vibrant canvas on which are painted the movements, strengths, and vulnerabilities of the social animal. Defined broadly, the social context includes the real, imagined, or symbolic presence of other people; the activities and interactions that take place between people; the features of the settings in which behavior occurs; and the expectations and norms that govern behavior in a given setting (Sherif, 1981).

In this chapter and the next, we explore several major themes of social psychological research. In the first part of this chapter, we discuss the power of social situations to control human behavior. We consider a large body of research that shows the surprising extent to which small features of social settings can have a significant impact on what you think and how you act. We next turn to the ways in which people construct social reality and

Social psychology The branch of psychology that studies the effect of social variables on individual behavior, attitudes, perceptions, and motives; also studies group and intergroup phenomena.

▪THE POWER OF THE SITUATION

535

the ways in which attitudes are formed and changed. We then consider the relationships of liking and loving. Throughout this chapter, we illustrate how research in social psychology has immediate applications to your life. As you shall see, in Chapter 18, we extend our analysis of social psychology's relevance beyond the personal to societal concerns. In both chapters, abstract theory meets the stern test of practicality, as we attempt to answer this question: Does psychological knowledge make a difference in the everyday lives of people and society?

The Power of the Situation

Throughout *Psychology and Life,* we have seen that psychologists who strive to understand the causes of behavior look in many different places for their answers. Some look to genetic factors and others to biochemical and brain processes, while still others focus on the causal influence of the environment. Social psychologists believe that the primary determinant of behavior is the nature of the social situation in which that behavior occurs. They argue that social situations exert significant control over individual behavior, often dominating personality and a person's past history of learning, values, and beliefs. As in our opening example of Grandpa Salvatore, situational forces can often work in forceful ways of which we are unaware. In this section, we will review both classic research and recent experiments that together explore the effect of subtle but powerful situational variables on people's behavior.

Roles and Rules

What *social roles* are available to you? A **social role** is a socially defined pattern of behavior that is expected of a person when functioning in a given setting or group. Different social situations make different roles available. When you are at home, you may accept the role of "child" or "sibling." When you are in the classroom, you accept the role of "student." At other times still, you are a "best friend" or "lover." Can you see how these different roles immediately make different types of behaviors more or less appropriate and also available to you?

Situations are also characterized by the operation of **rules,** behavioral guidelines for specific settings. Some rules are *explicitly* stated in signs (DON'T SMOKE, NO EATING IN CLASS), or are explicitly taught to children (Respect

Social role A socially defined pattern of behavior that is expected of a person who is functioning in a given setting or group.
Rules Behavioral guidelines for acting in certain ways in certain situations.

To open or not to open? How do people learn the etiquette for giving and receiving gifts in different cultures?

the elderly, Never take candy from a stranger). Other rules are *implicit*—they are learned through transactions with others in particular settings. How loud you can play your stereo, how close you can stand to another person, when you can call your teacher or boss by a first name, and what is the suitable way to react to a compliment or a gift—all of these actions depend on the situation. For example, the Japanese do not open a gift in the presence of the giver, for fear of not showing sufficient appreciation; foreigners not aware of this unwritten rule will misinterpret the behavior as rude instead of sensitive. Next time you get in an elevator, try to determine what rules you have learned about that situation. Why do people usually speak in hushed tones, or not at all?

Ordinarily, you might not be particularly aware of the effects of roles and rules, but one classic social psychological experiment, the *Stanford Prison Experiment,* put these forces to work with startling results (Haney & Zimbardo, 1977; Zimbardo, 1975; replicated in Australia by Lovibond et al., 1979).

HOW WE KNOW

SOCIAL ROLES IN A SIMULATED PRISON
On a summer Sunday in California, a siren shattered the serenity of college student Tommy Whitlow's morning. A police car screeched to a halt in front of his home. Within minutes, Tommy was charged with a felony, informed of his constitutional rights, frisked, and handcuffed. After he was booked and fingerprinted, Tommy was blindfolded and transported to the Stanford County Prison, where he was stripped, sprayed with disinfectant, and issued a smock-type uniform with an I.D. number on the front and back. Tommy became Prisoner 647. Eight other college students were also arrested and assigned numbers.

Tommy and his cellmates were all volunteers who had answered a newspaper ad and agreed to be participants in a two-week experiment on prison life. By random flips of a coin, some of the volunteers had been assigned to the role of prisoners; the rest became guards. All had been selected from a large pool of student volunteers who, on the basis of extensive psychological tests and interviews, had been judged as law-abiding, emotionally stable, physically healthy, and "normal-average." The prisoners lived in the jail around the clock; the guards worked standard eight-hour shifts.

What happened once these students had assumed their randomly assigned roles? In guard roles, college students who had been pacifists and "nice guys" behaved aggressively—sometimes even sadistically. The guards insisted that prisoners obey all rules without question or hesitation. Failure to do so led to the loss of a privilege. At first, privileges included opportunities to read, write, or talk to other inmates. Later on, the slightest protest resulted in the loss of the "privileges" of eating, sleeping, and washing. Failure to obey rules also resulted in menial, mindless work such as cleaning toilets with bare hands, doing push-ups while a guard stepped on the prisoner's back, and spending hours in solitary confinement. The guards were always devising new strategies to make the prisoners feel worthless.

As prisoners, psychologically stable students soon behaved pathologically, passively resigning themselves to their unexpected fate. Less than 36 hours after the mass arrest, Prisoner 8412, one of the ringleaders of an aborted prisoner rebellion that morning, began to cry uncontrollably. He experienced fits of rage, disorganized thinking, and severe depression. On successive days, three more prisoners developed similar stress-related symptoms. A fifth prisoner developed a psychosomatic rash all over his body when the Parole Board rejected his appeal.

Because of the dramatic and unexpectedly severe emotional and behavioral effects observed, those five prisoners with extreme stress reactions were released early from this unusual prison, and the psychologists were forced to terminate their two-week study after only six days. Although Tommy Whitlow said he wouldn't want to go through it again, he valued the personal experience because he learned so much about himself and about human nature. Fortunately, he and the other students were basically healthy, and they readily bounced back from this highly charged situation. Follow-ups over many years revealed no lasting negative effects. The participants had all contributed to an important lesson: The power of the simulated prison situation had created a

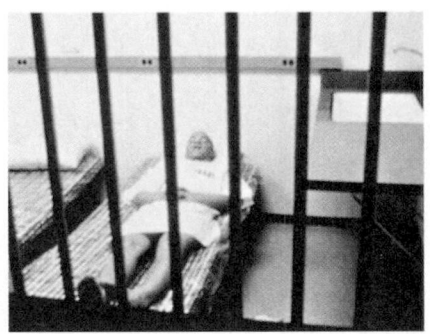

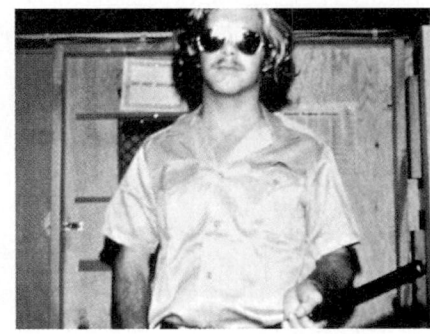

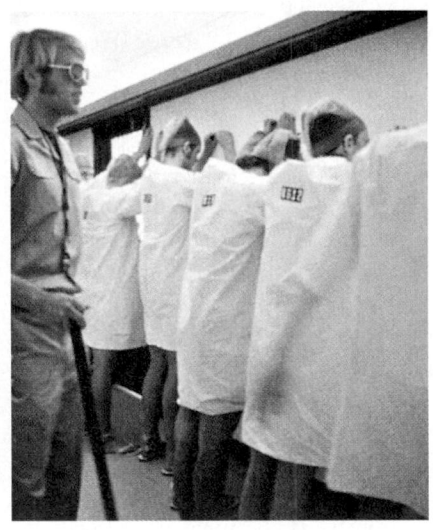

The Stanford Prison Experiment created a new "social reality" in which the norms of good behavior were overwhelmed by the dynamics of the situation. Why did the student guards and inmates adopt their roles so powerfully?

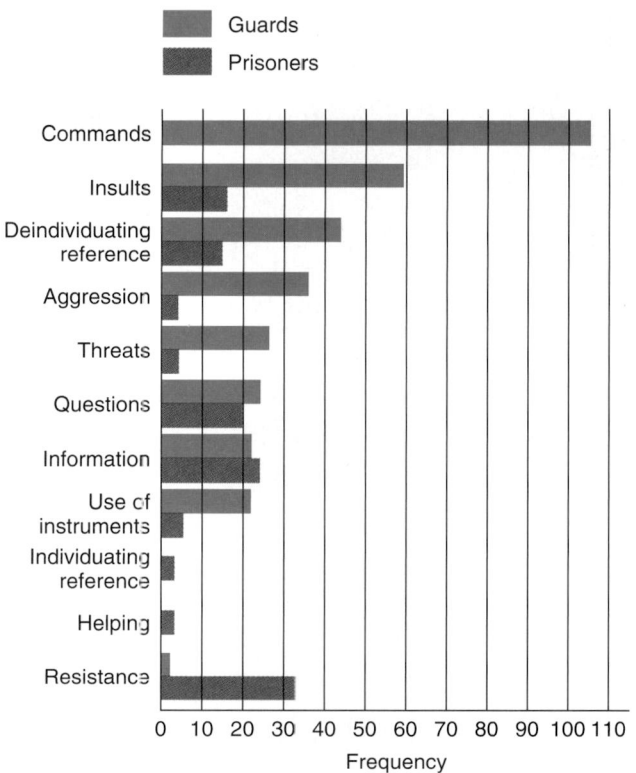

Guards
Prisoners

Frequency

FIGURE 17.1

Guard and Prisoner Behavior

During the Stanford Prison Experiment, the randomly assigned roles of prisoners and guards drastically affected participants' behavior. The observations recorded in the six-day interaction profile show that across 25 observation periods, the prisoners engaged in more passive resistance, while the guards became more dominating, controlling, and hostile.

new *social reality*—a real prison—in the minds of the jailers and their captives.

By the conclusion of the Stanford Prison Experiment, guards' and prisoners' behavior differed from each other in virtually every observable way (see **Figure 17.1**). Yet it was only chance, in the form of random assignment, that had decided their roles—roles that had created status and power differences that were validated in the prison situation. No one taught the participants to play their roles. Without ever visiting real prisons, all the participants learned something about the interaction between the powerful and the powerless (Banuazizi & Movahedi, 1975). A guard type is someone who limits the freedom of prisoner types to manage their behavior and make them

Social norms The expectation a group has for its members regarding acceptable and appropriate attitudes and behaviors.

behave more predictably. This task is aided by the use of *coercive rules,* which include explicit punishment for violations. Prisoners can only *react* to the social structure of a prisonlike setting created by those with power. Rebellion or compliance are the only options of the prisoners; the first choice results in punishment, while the second results in a loss of autonomy and dignity.

The student participants had already experienced such power differences in many of their previous social interactions: parent–child, teacher–student, doctor–patient, boss–worker, male–female. They merely refined and intensified their prior patterns of behavior for this particular setting. Each student could have played either role. Many students in the guard role reported being surprised at how easily they enjoyed controlling other people. Just putting on the uniform was enough to transform them from passive college students into aggressive prison guards. What sort of person do *you* become when you slip in and out of different roles? Where does your sense of personal self end and your social identity begin?

Social Norms

In addition to the expectations regarding role behaviors, groups develop many expectations for the ways their members *should* act. The specific expectations for socially appropriate attitudes and behaviors that are embodied in the stated or implicit rules of a group are called **social norms.** Social norms can be broad guidelines; if you are member of Democrats for Social Action, you may be expected to hold liberal political beliefs, while members of the Young Republicans will advocate more conservative views. Social norms can also embody specific standards of conduct. For example, if you are employed as a waiter or a waitress, you will be expected to treat your customers courteously no matter how unpleasant and demanding they are to you.

Belonging to a group typically involves discovering the set of social norms that regulates desired behavior in the group setting. This adjustment occurs in two ways: You notice the *uniformities* in certain behaviors of all or most members, and you observe the *negative consequences* when someone violates a social norm.

Norms serve several important functions. Awareness of the norms operating in a given group situation helps orient members and regulate their social interaction. Each participant can anticipate how others will enter the situation, how they will dress, and what they are likely to say and do, as well as what type of behavior will be expected of them to gain approval. You often feel awkward in new situations precisely because you may be unaware of the norms that govern the way you ought to act. Some tolerance for deviating from the standard is also part of the norm—wide in some cases, narrow in others. For example, shorts and a T-shirt might be marginally acceptable attire for a religious ceremony; a bathing suit would almost certainly deviate too far from the norm. Group members are usually able to estimate how far they can go before experiencing the coercive power of the group in the form of the three painful R's: *ridicule*, *reeducation*, and *rejection*.

Conformity

When you adopt a social role or bend to a social norm, you are, to some extent, *conforming* to social expectations. **Conformity** is the tendency for people to adopt the behavior and opinions presented by other group members. Why do you conform? Are there circumstances under which you ignore social constraints and act independently? Social psychologists have studied two types of forces that may lead to conformity:

- **Informational** influence processes—wanting to be correct and to understand the right way to act in a given situation.

- **Normative influence** processes—wanting to be liked, accepted, and approved of by others.

We will describe classic experiments that illustrate each type of influence.

When individuals become dependent on a group—such as a religious cult—for basic feelings of self-worth, they are prone to extremes of conformity. Twenty thousand identically dressed couples were married in this service conducted by the Reverend Sun Myung Moon. More recently, in August 1995, Moon simultaneously married 360,000 "Moonie" couples who were linked by satellite in 500 worldwide locations. Why do people find comfort in such large-scale conformity?

INFORMATIONAL INFLUENCE: SHERIF'S AUTOKINETIC EFFECT

Many life situations in which you must make decisions about behaviors are quite ambiguous. Suppose, for example, you are dining at an elegant restaurant with a large group of people. Each place at the table is set with a dazzling array of silverware. How do you know which fork to use when the first course arrives? Typically, you would look to other members of the party to help you make an appropriate choice. This is *informational influence*.

A classic experiment, conducted by **Muzafer Sherif** (1935), demonstrated how informational influence can lead to **norm crystallization**—norm formation and solidification.

HOW WE KNOW

INFORMATIONAL INFLUENCE PRODUCES NORMS Participants were asked to judge the amount of movement of a spot of light, which was actually stationary but that appeared to move when viewed in total darkness with no reference points. This is a perceptual illusion known as the *autokinetic effect*. Originally, individual judgments varied widely. However, when the participants were brought together in a group consisting of strangers and stated their judgments aloud, their estimates began to converge. They began to see the light move in the same direction and in similar amounts. Even more interesting was the final part of Sherif's study—when alone in the same darkened room after the group viewing, these participants continued to follow the group norm that had emerged when they were together.

Once norms are established in a group, they tend to perpetuate themselves. In later research, these autokinetic group norms persisted even when tested a year later and without former group members witnessing the judgments (Rohrer et al., 1954). Norms can be transmitted from one generation of group members to the next and can continue to influence people's behavior long after the original group that created the norm no longer exists (Insko et al., 1980). How do we know that norms can have transgenerational influence? In autokinetic effect

Conformity The tendency for people to adopt the behaviors, attitudes, and values of other members of a reference group.

Informational influence Group effects that arise from individuals' desire to be correct and right and to understand how best to act in a given situation.

Normative influence Group effects that arise from individuals' desire to be liked, accepted, and approved of by others.

Norm crystallization The convergence of the expectations of a group of individuals into a common perspective as they talk and carry out activities together.

studies, researchers replaced one group member with a new one after each set of autokinetic trials until all the members of the group were new to the situation. The group's autokinetic norm remained true to the one handed down to them across several successive generations (Jacobs & Campbell, 1961). Do you see how this experiment captures the processes that allow real-life norms to be passed down across generations?

NORMATIVE INFLUENCE: THE ASCH EFFECT

What is the best way to demonstrate that people will sometimes conform because of *normative influence*—their desire to be liked, accepted, and approved of by others? One of the most important early social psychologists, **Solomon Asch** (1940, 1956), created circumstances in which participants made judgments under conditions in which the physical reality was absolutely clear—but the rest of a group reported that they saw that reality differently. Male college students were led to believe they were in a study of simple visual perception. They were shown cards with three lines of differing lengths and asked to indicate which of the three lines was the same length as the standard line (see **Figure 17.2**). The lines were different enough so that mistakes were rare, and their relative sizes changed on each series of trials.

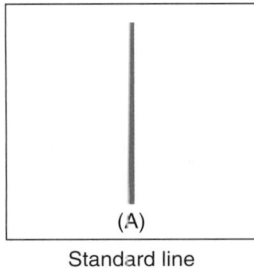

Standard line

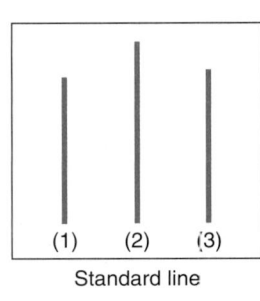

Standard line

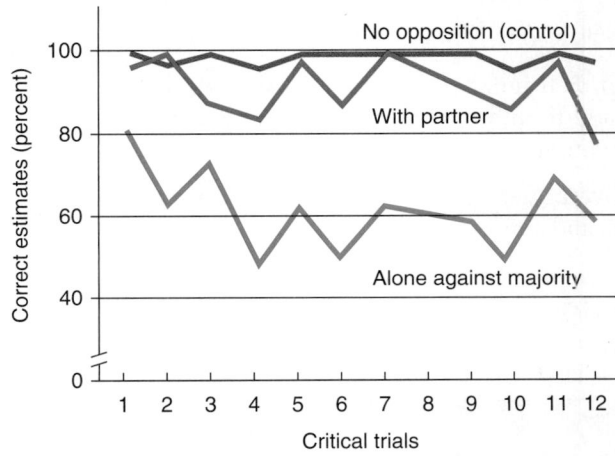

FIGURE 17.2

Conformity in the Asch Experiments

In this photo from Asch's study, it is evident that the naive participant, Number 6, is distressed by the unanimous majority's erroneous judgment. The typical stimulus array is shown at the top left. At top right, the graph illustrates conformity across 12 critical trials when solitary participants were grouped with a unanimous majority, as well as their greater independence when paired with a dissenting partner. A lower percentage of correct estimates indicates the greater degree of an individual's conformity to the group's false estimate.

YIELDING TO LYING LINES? The participants were seated next to last in semicircles of six to eight other students. Unknown to the participants, the others were all experimental confederates—accomplices of the experimenter—who were following a prearranged script. On the first three trials, everyone in the circle agreed on the correct comparison. However, the first confederate to respond on the fourth trial matched two lines that were obviously different. So did all members of the group up to the participant. That student had to decide if he should go along with everyone else's view of the situation and conform or remain independent, standing by what he clearly saw. That dilemma was repeated for the naive participant on 12 of the 18 trials. The participants showed signs of disbelief and obvious discomfort when faced with a majority who saw the world so differently. What did they do?

Roughly one-fourth of the participants remained completely independent—they never conformed. However, between 50 and 80 percent of the participants (in different studies in the research program) conformed with the false majority estimate at least once, while a third of the participants yielded to the majority's wrong judgments on half or more of the critical trials.

Asch describes some participants who yielded to the majority most of the time as "disoriented" and "doubt-ridden"; he states that they "experienced a powerful impulse not to appear different from the majority" (1952, p. 396). Those who yielded underestimated the influence of the social pressure and the frequency of their conformity; some even claimed that they really had seen the lines as the same length, despite their obvious discrepancy.

In other studies, Asch varied three factors: the size of the unanimous majority, the presence of a partner who dissented from the majority, and the size of the discrepancy between the correct physical stimulus comparison and the majority's position. He found that strong conformity effects were elicited with a unanimous majority of only three or four people. However, giving the naive participant a single ally who dissented from the majority opinion had the effect of sharply reducing conformity, as can be seen in Figure 17.2. With a partner, the participant was usually able to resist the pressures to conform to the majority. As you might expect, independence from the majority also increased with the magnitude of the contradiction between one's perception and the group's erroneous judgment. Remarkably, a certain proportion of individuals continued to yield to the group even under the most extreme stimulus discrepancies (Asch, 1955, 1956).

How should we interpret these results? Asch himself was struck by the rate at which participants did *not*

conform (Friend et al., 1990). He reported this research as studies in "independence." In fact, two-thirds of the time, participants gave the correct, nonconforming answer. However, most descriptions of Asch's experiment have emphasized the one-third conformity rate. Accounts of this experiment also often fail to note that not all participants were alike: The number of individuals who never conformed, about 25 percent, was roughly equal to the number who always or almost always conformed. Thus, Asch's experiment teaches two complementary lessons. On the one hand, we find that people are not entirely swayed by normative influence—they assert their independence on a majority of occasions (and some people always do). On the other hand, we find that people will sometimes conform, even in the most unambiguous situations. That potential to conform is an important element of human nature.

CONFORMITY IN EVERYDAY LIFE

Many instances of conformity in everyday life reflect combinations of normative and informational influence: People's desires to be liked or accepted prompts them to turn to a particular reference group to seek information about proper attitudes and correct behavior. Let's look at one experimental example.

TRYING TO CONFORM Students at Texas A&M University were given information about attitudes held by the majority of their peers. For example, they were told that A&M students strongly disagreed with the statement, "I would not approve of a friend who took illegal drugs." (In fact, most students strongly agree with that statement.) The experimental participants were asked to interpret the statement—does "I would not approve" mean that "they would not condone drug use" or that "they would break off the friendship"? The participants then indicated their own agreement with the statement. The participants' patterns of responses depended heavily on whether they reported themselves to be very highly identified as A&M students. Students in the "highly identified" group tended to find a way to interpret the original statement so that they could remain consistent with A&M student norms: That is, they interpreted the statement to mean "I'd break off my friendship" and indicated strong attitudes against that view. Students who were not so closely identified as A&M students did not show such dramatic change in the direction of what they believed the average A&M student thought (Wood et al., 1996).

In this situation, the students for whom it was important to be like other A&M students received information that

HOW DO GROUPS AFFECT DECISION MAKING?

If you've ever tried to make a decision as part of a group, you know that it can be quite torturous. Imagine, for example, that you have just seen a movie with a bunch of friends. Although you thought the movie was "OK," by the end of a postmovie discussion you find yourself agreeing that it was "an incredible piece of trash." Is this change after group discussion typical? Are the judgments groups make consistently different from individuals' judgments? Researchers in social psychology have documented two forces that operate when groups make decisions: *group polarization* and *groupthink*.

Your postmovie experience is an example of **group polarization:** Groups show a tendency to make decisions that are more extreme than the decisions that would be made by the members acting alone. Suppose, for example, you asked each member of the movie group to provide an attitude rating toward the movie; subsequently, as a group you agree on a single value to reflect your group attitude. If the group's rating is more extreme than the average of the individuals' ratings, that would be an instance of polarization. Depending on the initial group tendency—toward caution or risk—group polarization will tend to make a group more cautious or more risky. Researchers have suggested that two types of processes underlie group polarization: the *information-influence* model and the *social comparison* model (Liu & Latané, 1998). The information-influence model suggests that group members contribute different information to a decision. If you and your friends each have a different reason for disliking a movie a little bit, all that information taken together would provide the evidence that you should actually dislike the movie a lot. The social comparison model suggests that group members strive to capture their peers' regard by representing a group ideal that is a bit more extreme than the group's true norm. Thus, if you come to decide that everyone was unhappy with a movie, you could try to present yourself as particularly astute by stating a more extreme opinion. If everyone in a group tries to capture the group's esteem in that same fashion, polarization will result.

Group polarization is one consequence of a general pattern of thought called *groupthink*. **Irving Janis** (1982) coined the term **groupthink** for the tendency of a decision-making group to filter out undesirable input so that a consensus may be reached, especially if it is in line with the leader's viewpoint. Janis's theory of groupthink emerged from his historical analysis of the Bay of Pigs invasion of Cuba in 1960. This disastrous invasion was approved by President Kennedy after Cabinet meetings in which contrary information was minimized or suppressed by those advisors to the president who were eager to undertake the invasion. From his analysis of this event, Janis outlined a series of features that he believed would predispose groups to fall prey to groupthink: He suggested, for example, that groups that were highly cohesive, insulated from experts, and operated under directed leadership would make groupthink decisions. Researchers have attempted to verify Janis's ideas through both further historical analyses and laboratory experiments (Esser, 1998). This body of research suggests that groups are particularly vulnerable to groupthink when they embody a collective desire to maintain a shared positive view of a group (Turner & Pratkanis, 1998). Group members must understand that dissent often improves the quality of a group decisions even if it may detract, on the surface, from the group's positive feel.

The next time you are involved in a group enterprise, see if you can detect these processes at work.

---

made them feel discordant with those fellow students. Normative processes kicked in, prompting them to reconstruct their interpretation of the question so that the information could also be consistent with *their* worldview. You can see from this study that you are more likely to experience informational influence when the information's source is one that is important to you.

MINORITY INFLUENCE AND NONCONFORMITY

Given the power of the majority to control resources and information, it is not surprising that people regularly conform to groups. Yet you know that sometimes individuals persevere in their personal views. How can this happen? How do people escape group domination, and how can anything new (counternormative) ever come about? Are there any conditions under which a small minority

- **Group polarization** The tendency for groups to make decisions that are more extreme than the decisions that would be made by the members acting alone.
- **Groupthink** The tendency of a decision-making group to filter out undesirable input so that a consensus may be reached, especially if it is in line with the leader's viewpoint.

can turn the majority around and create new norms? While researchers in the United States have concentrated their studies on conformity, in part because conformity is intertwined with the democratic process, some European social psychologists have instead focused on the power of the few to change the majority. **Serge Moscovici** of France pioneered the study of minority influence.

Eventually, the power of the many may be undercut by the conviction of the dedicated few (Moscovici, 1980, 1985).

You can conceptualize these effects with respect to the distinction we introduced earlier between normative influence and informational influence (Wood et al., 1994). Minority groups have relatively little normative influence: Members of the majority are typically not particularly concerned about being liked or accepted by the minority. On the other hand, minority groups do have informational influence: Minorities can encourage group members to understand issues from multiple perspectives (Peterson & Nemeth, 1996). Unfortunately, this potential for informational influence may only infrequently allow minorities to overcome majority members' normative desire to distance themselves from deviant or low-consensus views (Wood, 2000).

In society, the majority tends to be the defender of the status quo. Typically, the force for innovation and change comes from the minority members or from individuals who are either dissatisfied with the current system or able to visualize new options and create alternative ways of dealing with current problems. The conflict between the entrenched majority view and the dissident minority perspective is an essential precondition of innovations that can lead to positive social change.

Situational Power: *Candid Camera* Revelations

Social psychologists have attempted to demonstrate the power of social norms and social situations by devising experiments that reveal the ease with which smart, inde-

If you came upon an unattended plate of dollar bills with a sign directing you to TAKE ONE, would you obey it as these *Candid Camera* participants did?

pendent, rational, good people can be led into behaving in ways that are less than optimal. Although social psychologists have shown the serious consequences of situational power such as the social roles that turn ordinary students into aggressive prison guards, it is equally possible to demonstrate this principle with humor. Indeed, *Candid Camera* scenarios, created by intuitive social psychologist **Allen Funt,** have been doing so for nearly 50 years. Funt showed how human nature follows a situational script to the letter. Millions in his TV audiences laughed when a diner stopped eating a hamburger whenever a DON'T EAT counter light flashed; when pedestrians stopped and waited at a red street light above the *sidewalk* on which they were walking; when highway drivers turned back after seeing a road sign that read DELAWARE IS CLOSED; and when customers jumped from one white tile to another in response to a store sign that instructed them not to walk on black tiles. One of the best *Candid Camera* illustrations of the subtle power of implicit situational rules to control behavior is the "elevator caper." A person riding a rigged elevator first obeyed the usual silent rule to face the front, but when a group of other passengers all faced the rear, the hapless victim followed the new emerging group norm and faced the rear as well.

We see in these slice-of-life episodes the minimal situational conditions needed to elicit unusual behaviors in ordinary people. You laugh because people who appear similar to you behave foolishly in response to small modifications in their commonplace situations. You implicitly distance yourself from them by assuming you would not act that way. The lesson of much social psychological research is that, more than likely, you would behave exactly as others have if you were placed in the same situation. Poet John Donne wrote, "No man is an island, entire of itself; every man is a piece of the continent." People are all interconnected by the situations and norms and rules they share. The wise reply to someone who asks how *you* would act if you were in a situation in which people behaved in evil, foolish, or irrational ways is, "I don't know. It depends on how powerful the situation is."

We have reached the important conclusion that situations play a substantial role in determining people's behavior. However, you've almost certainly had real-life experiences in which you have come to understand that you and a friend disagree about exactly what took place—what the situation was. In the next section, we explore the idea that different people interpret the same situations in different ways.

SUMMING UP

Social psychologists often focus on social situations as important determinants of behavior. The Stanford Prison Experiment demonstrated how dramatically social roles can influence people's behavior. Social norms define acceptable attitudes and behaviors. Two types of group influence lead people to conform: informational influence and normative influence. Minorities are more likely to have an effect on majority views through informational influence.

Constructing Social Reality

Suppose you are walking across campus with a friend who has not taken an introductory psychology course. You come upon a police officer yelling at a student. Your friend comments, "That cop doesn't have to be so harsh" but you think to yourself "His behavior is constrained by his social role." Your friend and you, in a sense, are observing the same event but interpreting it in very different ways. That's what we mean by *constructing social reality*. You bring your own knowledge and experience to bear on the interpretation of situations. You construct social reality by the ways you *represent* events cognitively and emotionally.

Let's look at one classic social psychological example in which people's beliefs led them to view the same situation from different vantage points and make contrary conclusions about what "really happened." The study concerned a football game that took place some years ago between two Ivy League teams. An undefeated Princeton team played Dartmouth in the final game of the season. The game, which Princeton won, was rough, filled with penalties and serious injuries to both sides. After the

game, the newspapers of the two schools offered very different accounts of what had happened.

This study makes clear that a complex social occurrence, such as a football game, cannot be observed in an objective, unbiased fashion. Social situations obtain significance when observers *selectively encode* what is happening in terms of what they expect to see and want to see. In the case of the football game, people *looked* at the same activity, but they *saw* two different games.

To explain how the Princeton and Dartmouth fans came to such different interpretations of the football game returns us to the realm of *perception*. Recall from Chapter 5 that you often must put prior knowledge to work to interpret ambiguous perceptual objects. The

Why are fans who watch their favorite team play likely to perceive more instances of unfair play on the part of the opposing team?

principle is the same for the football game—people bring past knowledge to bear on the interpretation of current events—but the objects for perceptual processing are people and situations. **Social perception** is the process by which people come to understand and categorize the behaviors of others. In this section, we will focus largely on two issues of social perception. First, we consider how people make judgments about the forces that influence other people's behavior, their *causal attributions*. Next, we discuss how processes of social perception can sometimes bring the world in line with expectations.

The Origins of Attribution Theory

One of the most important inferential tasks facing all social perceivers is to determine the causes of events. You want to know the why's of life. Why did my girlfriend break off the relationship? Why did he get the job and not I? Why did my parents divorce after so many years of marriage? All such why's lead to an analysis of possible causal determinants for some action, event, or outcome. **Attribution theory** is a general approach to describing the ways the social perceiver uses information to generate causal explanations.

Attribution theory originated in the writings of **Fritz Heider** (1958). Heider argued that people continually make causal analyses as part of their attempts at general comprehension of the social world. People, he suggested, are all *intuitive psychologists* who try to figure out what people are like and what causes their behavior, just as professional psychologists do. Heider believed that the questions that dominate most attributional analyses are whether the cause of a behavior is found in the person (internal or *dispositional* causality) or in the situation (external or *situational* causality) and who is responsible for the outcomes. How do people make those judgments?

Harold Kelley (1967) formalized Heider's line of thinking by specifying the variables that people use to make their attributions. Kelley made the important observation that people most often make causal attributions for events under conditions of *uncertainty*. You rarely, if ever, have sufficient information to know for sure what caused someone to behave in a particular way. Kelley believed that people grapple with uncertainty by accumulating information from multiple events and using the *covariation principle*. The **covariation principle** suggests that people should attribute a behavior to a causal factor if that factor was present whenever the behavior occurred but was absent whenever it didn't occur. Suppose, for example, you are walking down a street and you see a friend pointing at a horse and screaming. What evidence would you gather to decide whether your friend is crazy (a dispositional attribution) or danger is afoot (a situational attribution)?

Kelley suggested that people make this judgment by assessing covariation with respect to three dimensions of information relevant to the person whose acts they are trying to explain: distinctiveness, consistency, and consensus.

- *Distinctiveness* refers to whether the behavior is specific to a particular situation—does your friend scream in response to all horses?

- *Consistency* refers to whether the behavior occurs repeatedly in response to this situation—has this horse made your friend scream in the past?

- *Consensus* refers to whether other people also produce the same behavior in the same situation—is everyone pointing and screaming?

Each of these three dimensions plays a role in the conclusions you draw. Suppose, for example, that your friend was the only one screaming. Would that make you more likely to make a dispositional or a situational attribution?

Thousands of studies have been conducted to refine and extend attribution theory beyond the solid foundation provided by Heider and Kelley (Fiske & Taylor, 1991). Many of those studies have concerned themselves with conditions in which attributions depart from a systematic search of available information. We will describe four types of circumstances in which bias may creep into your attributions.

The Fundamental Attribution Error

Suppose you have made an arrangement to meet a friend at 7 o'clock. It's now 7:30, and the friend still hasn't arrived. How might you be explaining this event to yourself?

- I'm sure something really important happened that made it impossible for her to be here on time.

- What a jerk! Couldn't she try a little harder?

We've given you a choice again between a situational and a dispositional attribution. Research has shown that people are more likely, on average, to choose the second type, the dispositional explanation (Ross & Nisbett, 1991). This tendency is so strong, in fact, that social psychologist **Lee Ross** (1977) labeled it the fundamental attribution error.

Social perception The process by which a person comes to know or perceive the personal attributes of himself or herself and other people.

Attribution theory A social-cognitive approach to describing the ways the social perceiver uses information to generate causal explanations.

Covariation principle A theory that suggests that people attribute a behavior to a causal factor if that factor was present whenever the behavior occurred but was absent whenever it did not occur.

The **fundamental attribution error (FAE)** represents the dual tendency for people to overestimate dispositional factors (blame or credit people) and to underestimate situational factors (blame or credit the environment) when searching for the cause of some behavior or outcome.

Let's look at a laboratory example of the FAE. Ross and his colleagues (1977) created an experimental version of a "College Bowl" type of quiz game in which participants became questioners or contestants by the flip of a coin.

Is this fair? It should be clear that the situation confers a great advantage on the questioner. (Wouldn't you prefer to be the one who gets to ask the questions?) The contes-

Fundamental attribution error (FAE) The dual tendency of observers to underestimate the impact of situational factors and to overestimate the influence of dispositional factors on a person's behavior.

tants' and observers' ratings ignore the way in which the situation allowed one person to look bright and the other to look dull. That's the fundamental attribution error.

You should be on a constant lookout for instances of the FAE. However, this may not always be easy: It often takes a bit of "research" to discover the situational roots of behavior. Situational forces are often invisible. You can't, for example, *see* social norms; you can only see the behaviors they give rise to. What can you do to avoid the FAE? Particularly in circumstances in which you are making a dispositional attribution that is negative ("What a jerk!"), you should take a step back and ask yourself, Could it be something about the situation that is bringing about this behavior? You might think of such an exercise as "attributional charity." Do you see why?

This advice may be particularly important to those of us who live in Western society, because evidence suggests that the FAE is due, in part, to cultural sources (Miller, 1984). Recall the discussion in Chapter 14 of cultural differences in construals of the self. As we explained there, most Western cultures embody *independent construals of self*, whereas most Eastern cultures embody *interdependent construals of self* (Markus & Kitayama, 1991). Research demonstrates that, as a function of the culture of interdependence, members of non-Western cultures are less likely to focus on individual actors in situations. Let's see how this cultural difference affects reporting of news events.

FIGURE 17.3

Ratings of Questioners' and Contestants' General Knowledge

After the quiz game, questioners, contestants, and observers rated each of the participant's general knowledge with respect to a rating of 50 for the average student. Questioners believed that both they and the contestants were average. However, both contestants and observers rated the questioner as much more knowledgeable than the contestant. Furthermore, contestants rated themselves to be a bit below average.

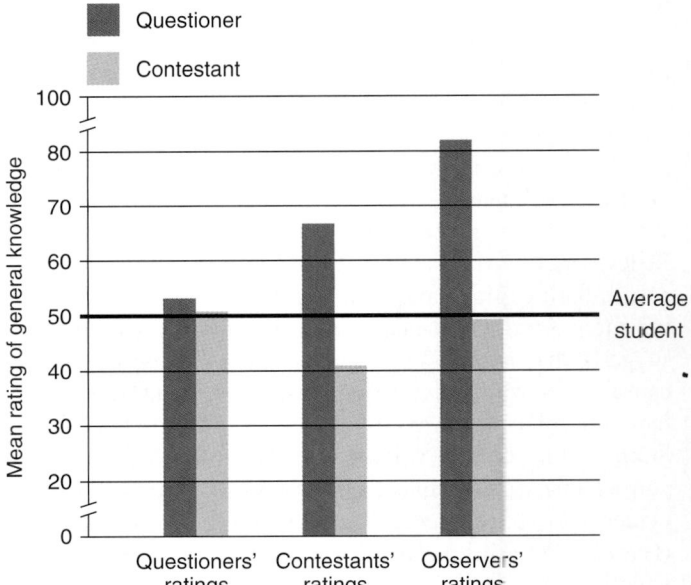

of England's oldest bank, Barings. A research assistant, who was blind to the study's purpose, read each article to extract excerpts in which causal explanations were offered. For each excerpt, another pair of blind research assistants judged whether the explanation offered was dispositional—it attributed blame to an individual—or situational—it attributed blame to an organization. The patterns of attributions were strikingly different for the two sets of articles. U.S. writers tended to make stronger dispositional attributions, whereas Japanese writers made stronger situational attributions (Menon et al., 1999).

An impressive feature of this study is that it captures cultural attributional styles as they are written for newspaper articles. The study makes clear one way in which a cultural style of attribution is transmitted and maintained for all those who are exposed to the media in a particular culture.

Self-Serving Biases

One of the most startling findings in the College Bowl study was the contestants' negative evaluation of their own abilities. This suggests that people will make the FAE even at their own expense. (In fact, you should recall from Chapter 15 that one theory of the origins of depression suggests that depressed people make too many negative attributions to themselves rather than to situational causes.) In many circumstances, however, people do just the opposite—their attributions err in the direction of being self-serving. A **self-serving bias** leads people to take credit for their successes while denying or explaining away responsibility for their failures. In many situations, people tend to make dispositional attributions for success and situational attributions for failure (Gilovich, 1991): "I got the prize because of my ability"; "I lost the competition because it was rigged."

You should look for self-serving biases in other life domains in which you make judgments about your own performance. Consider how you do in your classes. If you get an A, what attributions do you make? How about if you get a C? Research has demonstrated that students tend to attribute high grades to their own efforts and low grades to factors external to themselves (McAllister, 1996). In fact, professors show the same pattern—they make attributions to themselves for students' successes but not their failures. Once again, can you see what impact this pattern of attributions might have on your GPA? If you don't think about the external causes for your successes (for example, "That first exam was easy"), you might fail to study enough the next time; if you

don't think about the dispositional causes for failures (for example, "I shouldn't have stayed so long at that party"), you also might never get around to studying hard enough. We emphasized earlier that you should strive to avoid the FAE when you think about others' behavior. Similarly, you might examine attributions about your own behavior to weed out (non-self-serving) self-serving biases.

People also indulge in self-serving biases when they are members of groups: They are more likely to attribute group successes to themselves and failures to other group members. You may be pleased, however, to learn that friendship puts limits on this effect.

HOW WE KNOW

FRIENDSHIP AND SELF-SERVING BIASES
Experimental participants were asked to engage in a task that measured creativity with either a friend or a stranger. After completing the task, each participant was given feedback on the success of his or her group relative to a large normative sample. Irrespective of their actual performance, half the participants were given *success* feedback (i.e., they were told their performance was in the 93rd percentile); half were given *failure* feedback (i.e., they were told their performance was in the 31st percentile). All the participants were then asked to rate who was more responsible for the test outcome on a scale that ranged from 1 (the other participant) to 10 (myself). As seen in **Figure 17.4**, participants who engaged in the task with a stranger made considerably stronger attributions to themselves for success than for failure (Campbell et al., 2000). Participants' attributions in circumstances of success and failure were more consistent when their partners had been their friends.

Next time you are engaged in a group activity, try to see how this experiment applies to the way in which you make attributions of responsibility to different members of the group.

Why does it matter so much what attributions you make? Recall the example of your tardy friend. Suppose that, because you don't seek information about the situation, you decide that she isn't actually interested in being your friend. Can that incorrect belief actually cause the person to be unfriendly toward you in the future? To address that question, we turn now to the power of beliefs and expectations in constructing social reality.

Self-serving bias A class of attributional biases in which people tend to take credit for their successes and deny responsibility for their failures.

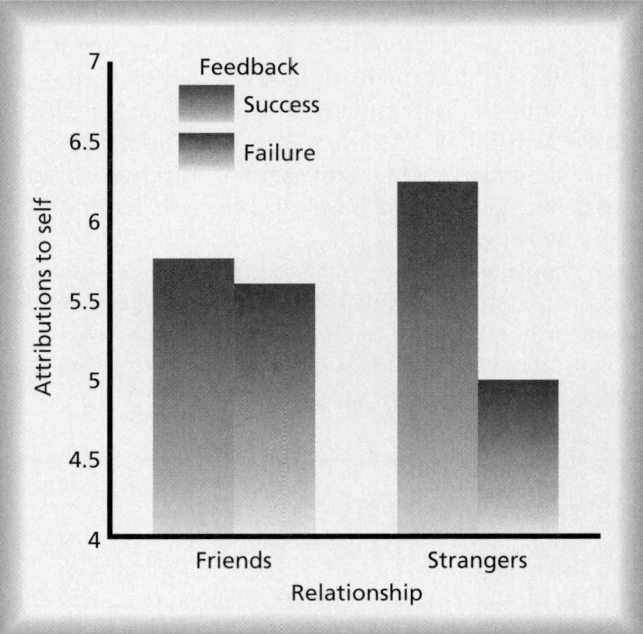

FIGURE 17.4

Patterns of Attributions to Friends and Strangers

Experimental participants were asked to rate who was responsible for their groups' success or failure on a task. With strangers, participants showed a pattern of self-serving biases: They made stronger attributions to themselves when the group had succeeded than when it had failed. Ratings were more consistent when the participants' partners were their friends.

Expectations and Self-Fulfilling Prophecies

Can beliefs and expectations go beyond coloring the way you interpret experiences to actually shape social reality? Much research suggests that the very nature of some situations can be modified significantly by the beliefs and expectations people have about them. **Self-fulfilling prophecies** (Merton, 1957) are predictions made about some future behavior or event that modify behavioral interactions so as to produce what is expected. Suppose, for example, you go to a party expecting to have a great time. Suppose a friend goes expecting it to be boring. Can you imagine the different ways in which the two of you might behave, given these expectations? These alternative ways of behaving may, in turn, alter how others at the party

> **Self-fulfilling prophecy** A prediction made about some future behavior or event that modifies interactions so as to produce what is expected.

behave toward you. In that case, which of you is actually more likely to have a good time at the party?

One of the most powerful demonstrations of self-fulfilling prophecies took its cue from a play by George Bernard Shaw. In Shaw's *Pygmalion* (popularized as the musical *My Fair Lady*), a street waif is transformed into a proper society lady under the intense training of her teacher, Professor Henry Higgins. The effect of social expectancy, or the *Pygmalion effect,* was re-created in a classic experiment by psychologist **Robert Rosenthal** in conjunction with school principal Leonore Jacobson.

HOW WE KNOW

EXPECTATIONS CAN CHANGE IQ Elementary school teachers in Boston were informed by researchers that their testing had revealed that some of their students were "academic spurters." The teachers were led to believe that these particular students were "intellectual bloomers who will show unusual gains during the academic year." In fact, there was no objective basis for that prediction; the names of these late bloomers were chosen randomly. However, by the end of that school year, 30 percent of the children arbitrarily named as spurters had gained an average of 22 IQ points! Almost all of them had gained at least 10 IQ points. Their gain in intellectual performance, as measured by a standard test of intelligence, was significantly greater than that of their control group classmates who had started out with the same average IQ (Rosenthal & Jacobson, 1968).

How did the teachers' false expectations get translated into such positive student performance? Rosenthal (1974) points to at least four processes that were activated by the teachers' expectations (see also Jussim, 1986). First, the teachers acted more warmly and more friendly toward the "late bloomers," creating a climate of social approval and acceptance. Second, they put greater demands—involving both quality and level of difficulty of material to be learned—on those for whom they had high hopes. Third, they gave more immediate and clearer feedback (both praise and criticism) about the selected students' performance. Finally, the teachers created more opportunities for the special students to respond in class, show their stuff, and be reinforced, thus giving them hard evidence that they were indeed as good as the teachers believed they were.

What is unusual, of course, about the situation in the Boston classroom is that the teachers were purposefully given false expectations. This methodology allowed Rosenthal and Jacobson to demonstrate the full potential for self-fulfilling prophecies. In most real-world situations, however, expectations are based on fairly accurate social perceptions (Jussim, 1991). Teachers, for example, expect certain students to do well because those students arrive in the classroom with better qualifications; and those students, typically, do show the best performance. Research has suggested, in fact, that self-fulfilling prophecies have the greatest effect on the lives of low-achieving students (Madon et al., 1997). When teachers expect them to do poorly, they may do even worse; when teachers expect them to do well, that has the potential to turn their school lives around.

In school situations, teachers and professors acquire concrete evidence—from exams and papers—about student performance as a term unfolds. Self-fulfilling prophecies have an ever greater impact in situations that provide little information relevant for a judgment. Let's examine this claim in the context of sex stereotypes.

WHEN DO STEREOTYPES MATTER? An experimenter brought a 9-month-old baby to an undergraduate social psychology class. About half of the students were led to believe that the baby was named Keith; half thought the baby was Karen. The students were asked to give their impressions of the baby with respect to physical attributes, behavior in class, and personality. Ratings for "Keith" and "Karen" did not differ for the two types of judgments for which the situation provided direct evidence: physical attributes and behavior in class. It was only for the domain of personality—which could not be judged based on the baby's behavior in class—that a sex stereotype shone through. "Keith" was rated as more athletic, noisy, active, and rough than was "Karen" (Jussim, 1993).

Expectations did not affect judgments when the environment provided concrete evidence—the students could

What types of judgments would change if you were told this was Baby Keith or Baby Karen?

plainly see what the baby looked like and how the baby behaved. Only when direct evidence was unavailable—the judgments of personality—did stereotypes influence responses. Thus, expectations are most powerful, and self-fulfilling prophecies are most likely to occur, when an individual has not had an opportunity to develop accurate expectations before judgments are made. Of course, in social interactions, "judgments" often give rise to behaviors. Let's see now how a person's choice of behaviors can affect the construction of social reality.

Behaviors That Confirm Expectations

Consider the Boston classroom once again. We have already noted that the teachers performed a series of behaviors that enabled them, in the long run, to confirm their expectations. **Mark Snyder** (1984) introduced the term **behavioral confirmation** to label the process by which someone's expectations about another person actually influence the second person to behave in ways that confirm the original hypothesis. For example, imagine you were about to interview someone, and you were told that the person was shy or *introverted*. Which of these questions might you select to ask (Snyder & Swann, 1978)?

- What would you do if you wanted to liven things up at a party?

- In what situations do you wish you could be more outgoing?

- What factors make it hard for you to really open up to people?

- In what situations are you most talkative?

Suppose you chose the second question—as many experimental participants did when they believed they were going to talk to someone introverted. Isn't it likely that even a very extraverted person could give you reasonable answers to the question? Thus an expectation—"I'm going to talk to someone who is an introvert"—leads to a behavioral choice—"I'm going to ask the kind of question you ask an introverted person"—which leads to potential confirmation of the expectation—"If he could answer this question, I guess he really is introverted."

How powerful are the forces of behavioral confirmation? An initial answer to this question is similar to the one we developed with respect to the likelihood of self-fulfilling prophecies: it depends on the availability of accurate information from the environment.

Behavioral confirmation The process by which people behave in ways that elicit from others specific expected reactions and then use those reactions to confirm their beliefs.

Researchers created circumstances in which one set of undergraduate women, the *perceivers,* were given false expectations about the extraversion or introversion of a second set of women, the *targets.* Each of the targets had, in fact, provided ratings that allowed the experimenters to identify her as an introvert or extravert. However, some of the target women had certain (strong) self-conceptions on this dimension, whereas other of the target women had uncertain (weak) self-conceptions. What happened when the perceivers interacted with the targets? When the targets had uncertain self-conceptions, behavioral confirmation reigned: The perceivers elicited behavior from the targets that confirmed the initial expectation. However, when the targets had more solid and certain self-conceptions, that self-conception shone through contrary to the perceivers' expectations (Swann & Ely, 1984).

Once again you can see that expectations have their greatest effect when the actual state of the world—the "reality" of the target—is ambiguous or uncertain. In those circumstances, you are most likely to go beyond the "data" to make inferences about the underlying reality.

The extent of behavioral confirmation also depends on the motivations the target has with respect to the interaction. In another study, male *perceivers* were led to believe—they were shown photographs—that the female *targets* at the other end of a phone conversation were either of normal weight or obese. In some cases, the women (whose actual weight was unrelated to the photographs) were asked to participate in the conversations to gain knowledge about the personality of the man to whom they were speaking; in other cases, the women's goal was to have a smooth and pleasant interaction with their male partner. In general, this latter situation produced behavioral confirmation: The *targets* were rated as producing behaviors that conformed to an obesity stereotype (for example, they were rated as less sociable and less happy). However, when the *targets* were motivated to obtain knowledge, behavioral confirmation was *not* found (Snyder & Haugen, 1995). This experiment suggests that the normal impulse to have smooth social interactions makes it *more* possible for people to remake the world in line with their own beliefs and attitudes, including stereotypes.

The research we have described in this section leads naturally to the question, How do attitudes and expectations arise? In the experiments we have reviewed, partici-

pants are typically told what to believe. But what happens in the real world, when you arrive at expectations on your own? In the next section, we consider the question of how attitudes are formed and changed—and we examine the links among beliefs, attitudes, and action.

SUMMING UP

The concept of constructing social reality suggests that you bring your own knowledge and experience to bear on the interpretation of situations. Attribution theory attempts to explain how people arrive at judgments about the causes of actions, events, or outcomes. People often underestimate situational causes for behavior and overestimate dispositional causes, a pattern known as the fundamental attribution error. Research suggests that members of nonindividualistic cultures may be less likely to commit this error. People succumb to self-serving biases when they attribute successes to dispositions and failures to situations. Self-fulfilling prophecies occur when people's expectations bring about actual changes in the world. Similarly, behavioral confirmation occurs when people's expectations actually change the nature of other people's behavior. Both of these effects are constrained by the amount of relevant objective information available in the environment.

Attitudes, Attitude Change, and Action

Have you already had a chance today to express an *attitude?* Has someone asked you, "What do you think of my shirt?" or "Was the chicken any good?" An **attitude** is a positive or negative evaluation of people, objects, and ideas. You may have favorable attitudes toward day-care workers, sports cars, and tax cuts, and unfavorable attitudes toward telemarketers, contemporary art, and astrology. This definition of attitude allows for the fact that many of the attitudes you hold are not overt; you may not be consciously aware that you harbor certain attitudes. Attitudes are important because they influence your behavior and how you construct social reality. Recall the Princeton–Dartmouth football game. Those people who favored Princeton "saw" a different game from those people who favored Dartmouth; attributions about events were made in line with their attitudes. What are the sources of your attitudes, and how do they affect your behaviors?

Attitudes and Behaviors

We have already defined attitudes as positive or negative evaluations. We'll begin this section by giving you an op-

Attitude The learned, relatively stable tendency to respond to people, concepts, and events in an evaluative way.

portunity to make an evaluation. To what extent do you agree with this statement? (Circle a number.)

I enjoy movies that star Jim Carrey.

1 —— 2 —— 3 —— 4 —— 5 —— 6 —— 7 —— 8 —— 9

Strongly   Neutral   Strongly
disagree   agree

Let's say that you gave a rating of 3—you disagree somewhat. What is the origin of that judgment? We can identify three types of information that give rise to your attitude:

- *Cognitive.* What thoughts do you have in response to "Jim Carrey"?

- *Affective.* What feelings does the mention of "Jim Carrey" evoke?

- *Behavioral.* How do you behave when, for example, you have the opportunity to see one of Jim Carrey's movies?

Some combination of these types of information most likely guided your hand when you circled "3" (or some other number). Your attitudes also generate responses in the same three categories. If you believe yourself to have a somewhat negative attitude toward Jim Carrey, you might say, "His type of humor is gross" (cognitive), "I don't like looking at his face" (affective), or "I don't want to pay to watch someone fall down" (behavioral).

It isn't too hard to measure an attitude, but is that attitude always an accurate indication of how people will actually behave? You know from your own life experiences that the answer is "no": People will say they dislike Jim Carrey but spend good money to see him anyway. At the same time, sometimes people's behaviors *do* follow their attitudes: They say they won't pay to see Jim Carrey, and they don't. How can you determine when attitudes will or will not predict behavior? Researchers

How does your attitude toward Jim Carrey affect your willingness to watch his movies?

have worked hard to answer that question—to identify the circumstances in which the link is strongest between people's attitudes and how they act (Ajzen & Sexton, 1999; Fazio & Towles-Schwen, 1999).

One property of attitudes that predicts behavior is *accessibility*—the strength of the association between an attitude object and a person's evaluation of that object (Fazio, 1995). When we asked you about Jim Carrey, did an answer rush to mind or did you have to consider the question for a while? Research suggests that behavior is more likely to be consistent with attitudes when the attitude is highly accessible.

An important part of this result is that both the "high accessible" group and the "low accessible" group reported, before the election, that they weren't going to change their minds. That is, attitude accessibility allowed for more valid prediction of eventual voting behavior than the voters' self-reports did!

How do attitudes become highly accessible (Fazio, 1995)? Research suggests that attitudes are more accessible when they are based on *direct experience:* You will have a more accessible attitude about Jim Carrey's movies if you've experienced several of them yourself rather than hearing or reading about them indirectly. Attitudes are also more accessible when they have been rehearsed more often: Just as you might expect, the more often you've formulated an attitude about something (consider "chocolate" versus "kiwi"), the more accessible is the attitude.

Attitudes also are better predictors of behavior when the attitudes and behaviors are measured at the same level of *specificity.* Consider the data presented in **Table 17.1.** In this

Why might someone be able to predict your vote from the speed with which you express an attitude?

study, the researchers were trying to predict the likelihood that members of an initial sample of 270 women, ages 18 to 38, would use birth control pills. You can see in Table 17.1 that the more *specific* the question the women were asked about their attitudes was, the higher was the correlation with their actual specific behavior (Davidson & Jaccard, 1979). (Recall that the closer a correlation is to 1 or –1, the stronger is the relationship.) The concept of specificity also applies to the specific *exemplars* you call to mind when you produce an attitude (Sia et al., 1997). Suppose, for example, we asked you to agree or disagree with the statement "I trust politicians." Your judgment would depend on which politician or politicians came to mind: Was it George Washington, Winston Churchill, Bill Clinton, or George W. Bush? If we asked you the same question in a week, your judgment—your report of your general attitude—might change if some other set of politicians came to mind.

When your attitudes are based on different subsets of information, they may change radically over time: When you gave us your attitude about Jim Carrey, were you

TABLE 17.1

Specificity Improves Attitude-Behavior Correlations

Attitude Measured	Correlation with Behavior of Using Birth Control
Attitude toward birth control	.08
Attitude toward birth control pills	.32
Attitude toward using birth control pills	.52
Attitude toward using birth control pills during the next two years	.57

Specificity (arrow indicating increasing specificity down the list)

Note: Researchers were trying to predict the likelihood that women would use birth control pills in the next two years. The more specific the question the women were asked about their attitudes, the higher was the correlation with their actual behavior.

thinking about the film *Liar, Liar, The Truman Show,* or *The Grinch?* Only when the "evidence" for your attitude remains stable over time can we expect to find a strong relationship between your evaluation (thoughts) and what you do (actions).

Processes of Persuasion

We've just seen that, under appropriate circumstances, attitudes can predict behavior. That's good news for all the people who spend time and money to affect your attitudes. But quite often others *can't* affect your attitudes when they want to do so. You don't change brands of toothpaste each time you see a peppy new commercial with scads of pearly-toothed actors; you don't change your political affiliation each time a candidate looks into the camera and declares sincerely that he or she deserves your vote. Many people in your life indulge in **persuasion**—deliberate efforts to change your attitudes. For persuasion to take place, certain conditions must be met. Let's explore some of those conditions.

To begin, we introduce the **elaboration likelihood model**, a theory of persuasion that defines how likely it is that people will focus their cognitive processes to elaborate upon a persuasive message (Petty & Cacioppo, 1986; Petty & Wegener, 1999). This model makes a critical distinction between *central* and *peripheral routes* to persuasion. The central route represents circumstances in which people think carefully about a persuasive communication so that attitude change depends on the strength of the arguments. When someone is trying to convince you that gasoline should cost $5 a gallon, you are likely to process the information in this careful fashion. The peripheral route represents circumstances in which people do not focus critically on the message but respond to superficial cues in the situation. When a sexy model is placed in front of the product someone wishes you to buy, the seller is hoping you'll avoid critical thought. The central or peripheral route that people take depends in large part on their *motivation* with respect to the message: Are they willing and able to think carefully about the persuasive content?

If you take a close look at the messages that surround you, you will quickly come to the conclusion that advertisers, for example, often count on you to take the peripheral route. Why do advertisers pay celebrities to sell their products? Do you really believe that Hollywood actors worry enormously about which long-distance phone service will produce bigger savings? Presumably, the advertisers hope that you won't evaluate the argu-

Persuasion Deliberate efforts to change attitudes.

Elaboration likelihood model A theory of persuasion that defines how likely it is that people will focus their cognitive processes to elaborate upon a message and therefore follow the central and peripheral routes to persuasion.

Why do advertisers pay celebrities to endorse their products?

ments too closely—instead, they hope you'll let yourself be persuaded by your general feelings of warmth toward the actor hawking the product.

Now ask yourself this question: Under what circumstances are you likely to feel sufficiently motivated to take the central route to persuasion? The answer is important both to people who wish you would (because they think they have strong arguments) and people who wish you wouldn't (because, as we just suggested, they want to persuade you with superficial cues). One example of a characteristic of a persuasive message that prompts you to take the central route is *personal relevance:* You are more likely to evaluate arguments carefully when information is personally relevant (Eagly & Chaiken, 1993). Suppose, for example, you listened to two speeches in succession. The first speaker argued that Hollywood should produce more 3-D movies; the second argued that college tuitions should be raised 50 percent. Which speech would be more likely to engage the central route? Let's look now at an experiment that considers the importance of personal relevance to your experience of fictional worlds.

HOW WE KNOW

PERSONAL RELEVANCE IN FICTIONAL WORLDS Are you persuaded by the information you encounter in fictional worlds—information from the novels you read, the movies you watch, and so on? A team of researchers suggested that the extent to which you will be persuaded depends, in part, on the personal relevance of the fictional setting. Participants in the study were students at Yale and Princeton universities. Some students from each school read a story that was set at Princeton; the remaining students read a story that was identical except that

it was set at Yale. The characters in the stories discussed real-world issues, like whether sunlight is good for the skin or mental illnesses are contagious. The researchers reasoned that participants would be more likely to treat information as personally relevant when they read the story set at their *home* school: For example, a Princeton student reading a story set at Princeton would be more motivated to read the story carefully and consider the characters' arguments. As shown in **Figure 17.5**, the results confirmed this prediction. The students showed attitude change in the direction of the arguments made in the story only when it was set at the *away* school (for example, the Princeton version for Yale students). That is, when the information was not personally relevant, the students failed to carry out central processing to expose the weaknesses in the story information. Without this central processing, the students were persuaded by the story (Prentice et al., 1997).

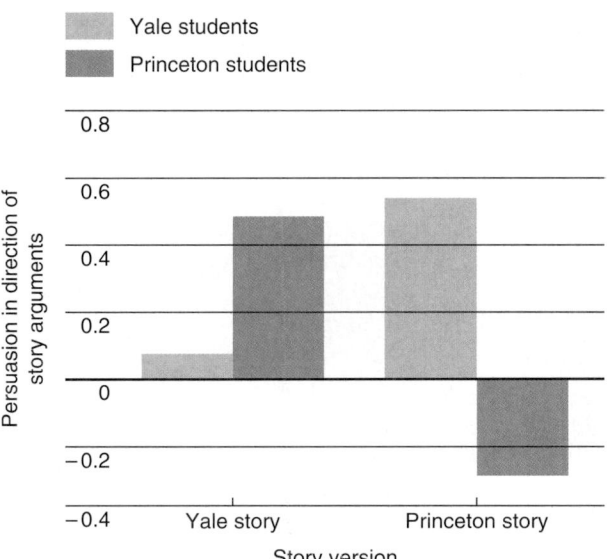

FIGURE 17.5

Persuasion and Personal Relevance

Students read stories that were set either at their "home" school—and therefore were personally relevant—or set at an "away" school. Personal relevance should make it more likely that the students will centrally process the story information and thus be less persuaded by it. In fact, persuasion in the direction of the story only occurred when students read the "away" school versions (for example, when the Yale students read the Princeton version of the story). This finding supports the prediction that the personally relevant "home" school versions led to central processing and rejection of the story arguments, whereas the not personally relevant "away" school versions led to peripheral processing and acceptance of the story arguments.

Note that the two versions of the story were identical, except for their settings. Thus, the difference in persuasion can only be attributed to the extent to which students were motivated to take the central route and evaluate the information carefully (Prentice & Gerrig, 1999). Next time you sit down to watch a TV show, you should consider what types of persuasion might go on via the peripheral route if the content is not personally relevant—by virtue of the setting, characters, and so on—to you.

Another factor that influences your choice of routes is the match between the type of attitude and the type of argument (Ajzen & Sexton, 1999). Earlier, we suggested that both cognitive and affective experiences give rise to attitudes. Research suggests that attitudes are more likely to change when advertisers match cognitive-based arguments to cognitive-based attitudes and affect-based arguments to affect-based attitudes.

HOW WE KNOW

THE MATCH BETWEEN ADVERTISEMENTS AND ATTITUDES What is the basis of your attitudes toward brands of *coffee?* You are likely to make evaluations based on your *cognitive* responses: How do they taste? How much do they cost? Now think about *greeting cards.* For greeting cards, you're more likely to be swayed by *affective* responses: Do they make you smile? Will they capture the right quality relationship? In one experiment, participants were exposed to either cognitive-based or affective-based advertisements for products, including coffee and greeting cards. A cognitive-based ad might read, "The delicious, hearty flavor and aroma of Sterling Blend coffee come from a blend of the freshest coffee beans"; an emotion-based ad might read, "The coffee you drink says something about the type of person you are. It can reveal your rare, discriminating taste." After participants read each of a series of ads, they listed thoughts to indicate how favorably they felt toward the product. As you can see in **Figure 17.6**, there was a strong effect of the match: Participants produced more favorable thoughts when the type of message (for example, cognitive-based ads) matched the type of attitude (for example, cognitive-based attitudes) (Shavitt, 1990).

In your own efforts to change people's attitudes you should also be able to put this result to use: Does the attitude have a strong cognitive component or a strong affective component? How can you tailor your persuasive message accordingly?

Cognitive dissonance The theory that the tension-producing effects of incongruous cognitions motivate individuals to reduce such tension.

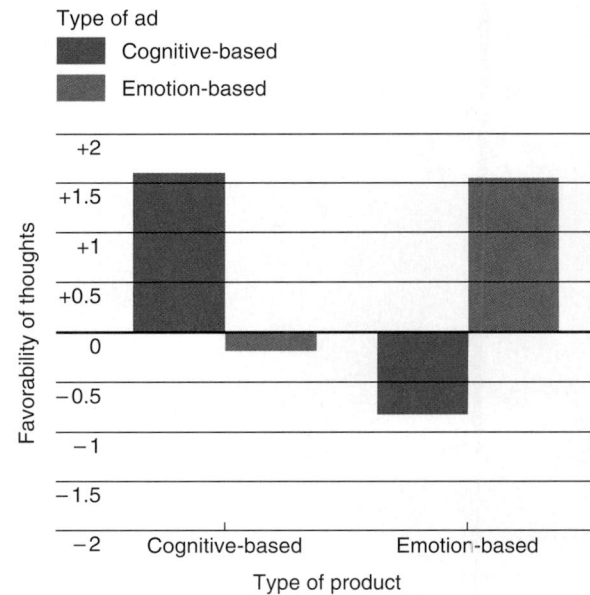

FIGURE 17.6

Emotion- and Cognitive-Based Ads and Products

When the type of advertisement (emotion- or cognitive-based) matched the dimension of evaluation underlying the object—emotions for greeting cards and cognitions for coffee—people reacted more favorably to the product. (The favorability of thoughts was measured on a scale ranging from −3 to +3.)

Persuasion by Your Own Actions

In the last section, we described factors that influence people's ability to change others' attitudes. However, there are forces at work in a number of circumstances that cause people to bring about their *own* attitude change. Imagine a situation in which you've vowed not to eat any extra calories. You arrive at work, and there's a cake for your boss's birthday. You consume a piece. Did you break your vow? That is, should you have a negative attitude about your own behavior? Aren't you likely to think what you did was right? Why? We describe two analyses of self-persuasion, *dissonance theory* and *self-perception theory.*

DISSONANCE THEORY

One of the most common assumptions in the study of attitudes is that people like to believe that their attitudes remain consistent over time (Eagly & Chaiken, 1993). This striving for consistency was explored within the field of social psychology in the theory of *cognitive dissonance,* as developed by **Leon Festinger** (1957). **Cognitive dissonance** is the state of conflict someone experiences *after* making a decision, taking an action, or being ex-

What messages might you give yourself to reduce cognitive dissonance if you were aware of the adverse effects of smoking but continued to smoke?

posed to information that is contrary to prior beliefs, feelings, or values. Suppose, for example, you chose to buy a car against a friend's advice. Why might you be overly defensive about the car? It is assumed that when a person's cognitions about his or her behavior and relevant attitudes are dissonant—they do not follow one to the next—an aversive state arises that the person is motivated to reduce. Dissonance-reducing activities modify this unpleasant state. In the case of your car, being defensive—overstating its value—makes you feel better about going against your friend's advice. (Dissonance also might lead you to think less well of your friend.)

Dissonance has motivational force—it impels you to take action to reduce the unpleasant feeling (Wood, 2000). The motivation to reduce dissonance increases with the magnitude of the dissonance created by a cognitive inconsistency. In other words, the stronger the dissonance, the greater the motivation to reduce it. In a classic dissonance experiment, college students told a lie to other students and came to believe in their lie when they got a small, rather than a large, reward for doing so.

As this experiment shows, under conditions of high dissonance, an individual acts to justify his or her behavior after the fact and engages in self-persuasion. This analysis says that the way to change attitudes is first to change behavior. Ancient biblical scholars knew this principle. They urged rabbis not to insist that people believe before praying but to get them to pray first—and then they would come to believe. Also think back to Grandpa Salvatore, from the beginning of the chapter. Do you see how he cleverly created dissonance in the young ruffians? They responded to conflicting cognitions—"We ought to get 25 cents for shouting" and "He's only going to pay us 10 cents for shouting"—by changing their behavior: They refused to shout.

Hundreds of experiments and field studies have shown the power of cognitive dissonance to change attitudes and behavior (Eagly & Chaiken, 1993; Wicklund & Brehm, 1976). Recently, however, researchers have begun to question whether dissonance effects generalize to other cultures. Consider again the way the concept of *self* changes from culture to culture. As we noted earlier, North Americans typically view themselves as *independent*, distinct from others in the environment; members of Asian cultures typically view themselves as *interdependent*, fundamentally interconnected with others. Does the cultural concept of the self affect the experience of cognitive dissonance?

ratings change from the first to the second time? According to dissonance theory, when you make a tough choice—like the one between your fifth- and sixth-ranked alternatives—you should adjust your attitudes to feel better about the outcome of the choice: "If I chose the Janet Jackson CD [originally No. 5], I must really like it *much* better than the R.E.M. [originally No. 6]." In fact, Canadian participants gave evidence for this change in attitude—the ratings for the chosen CD moved in a positive direction from those for the unchosen CD. Japanese participants, by contrast, showed no effects of dissonance—their choice did not systematically affect their ratings (Heine & Lehman, 1997).

This research suggests that people only experience cognitive dissonance—they only seek to maintain consistency within their self-concept—when they have an *independent* concept of the self. If you are ever in circumstances in which you must make decisions jointly with members of other cultures, you will want to reflect on the culture's impact on the way you all think and act after the decision has been made.

SELF-PERCEPTION THEORY

Dissonance theory describes one way in which people, at least in Western cultures, allow their behaviors ("I chose that CD") to have an impact on their attitudes ("I must like it much better than my other option"). *Self-perception theory,* developed by **Daryl Bem** (1972), identifies other circumstances in which behaviors inform attitudes. According to **self-perception theory,** you infer what your internal states (beliefs, attitudes, motives, and feelings) are or should be by perceiving how you are acting now and recalling how you have acted in the past in a given situation. You use that self-knowledge to reason backward to the most likely causes or determinants of your behavior. For example, the self-perceiver responds to the question, "Do you like psychology?" by saying, "Sure, I'm taking the basic course and it's not required, I do all the readings, I pay attention during lectures, and I'm getting a good grade in the course." In other words, you answer a question about personal preferences by a behavioral description of relevant actions and situational factors—rather than undertaking an intense search of thoughts and feelings.

Self-perception theory lacks the motivational components of dissonance theory. Because self-perception fills in missing attitudes—you look to your behavior to learn how you feel—self-perception processes occur mainly when

Self-perception theory The idea that people observe themselves in order to figure out the reasons they act as they do; people infer what their internal states are by perceiving how they are acting in a given situation.

Compliance A change in behavior consistent with a communication source's direct requests.

you are in ambiguous situations and dealing with unfamiliar events (Fazio, 1987). In these situations, you have a need to discover how you feel about some novel object of attitudinal scrutiny—if you find yourself laughing during your first Jim Carrey movie, you may infer a favorable attitude toward him. One flaw in the process of gaining self-knowledge through self-perception is that people are often insensitive about the extent to which their behavior is influenced by situational forces. You can see this if we return a final time to the College Bowl experiment. Recall that the participants who labored unsuccessfully as contestants rated their own general knowledge relatively low. Imagine what it must have been like to be in their position. Over and over you would hear yourself saying, "I don't know the answer to that question." Can you see how observation of this behavior—the process of self-perception—could give rise to a negative self-evaluation?

Let's return to the attitudes you might express toward yourself if you eat a slice of cake at your boss's birthday party. According to dissonance theory, you need to resolve the inconsistency between your vow ("I won't consume any extra calories") and your behavior (eating a piece of cake). There are many things you can do to avoid feeling bad: Perhaps you'd reason, "I can't afford to have my boss be angry at me by declining a piece of cake." Similarly, according to self-perception theory, you look at your behavior to calculate your attitude. If you think, "Because I ate cake, my boss's birthday must have been very important" you'll also escape any negative impact on your self-esteem. Self-persuasion can sometimes be useful!

Compliance

In this section so far, we have discussed what attitudes are and how they might be changed. It should be clear to you, however, that most often what people want you to do is change your *behavior:* People wish to bring about **compliance**—a change in behavior consistent with their direct requests. When advertisers spend a lot of money for TV commercials, they don't just want you to feel good about their products—they want you to march into a store and buy them. Similarly, doctors want you to follow their medical advice. Social psychologists have extensively studied the way in which individuals bring about compliance with their requests (Cialdini, 2001). We will describe some of those techniques and note how wily salespeople often use them to get you to do things you might not otherwise have done.

RECIPROCITY

One of the rules that dominates human experience is that when someone does something for you, you should do something for that person as well—this is called the **reciprocity norm.** Laboratory research has shown that even very small favors can lead participants to do much larger favors in return (Regan, 1971). Salespeople use reciprocity against you by appearing to do you a favor: "I'll tell you what, I'll take $5 off the price" or "Here's a free sample just for agreeing to talk to me today." This strategy puts you in a position of psychological distress if you don't return the favor and buy the product.

Another compliance technique that arises from the reciprocity norm has often been called the *door-in-the-face technique:* When people say "no" to a large request, they will often say "yes" to a more moderate request.

HOW WE KNOW

THE DOOR-IN-THE-FACE TECHNIQUE In one experiment, students were asked to spend two hours every week for two years as counselors for juvenile delinquents. They all said "no." Next, they were asked if they would serve as chaperones for some of the delinquents on a trip to the zoo. When they had previously said "no" to the large request, 50 percent of the students agreed to this smaller request. When a different group of students was approached, who had never been asked the large request, only 17 percent of them agreed to serve as chaperones (Cialdini et al., 1975).

How does this technique invoke the reciprocity norm? When people making requests go from the large to the moderate request, they have done something for you: Now you must do something for them—or risk violating the norm. You agree to the smaller request!

COMMITMENT

The door-in-the-face technique moves you from a large to a moderate request. Salespeople also know that if they can get you to *commit* yourself to some small concession, they can probably also get you to commit to something larger. In experiments, people who agreed to small requests (for example, signing petitions) were more likely subsequently to agree to a bigger request (for example, putting large signs on their lawn) (Freedman & Fraser, 1966). This is often called the *foot-in-the-door technique:* Once people get a foot in the door, they can use your sense of commitment to increase your later compliance. Salespeople use this technique against you by getting you to make a decision and then subtly changing the deal: "I know this is the car you want to buy, but my manager will only let me give you a $200 discount"; "I know you're the sort of person who buys quality goods, so I know you won't mind paying a little extra." This strategy makes you feel inconsistent or foolish if you don't go through with the purchase.

Reciprocity norm Expectation that favors will be returned—if someone does something for another person, that person should do something in return.

SCARCITY

People dislike feeling that they can't have something (or, from another perspective, people like to have things others can't). Participants, for example, give higher ratings to the taste of chocolate chip cookies that come from a jar with just two cookies than to those that come from a jar of ten (Worchel et al., 1975). How does the principle of *scarcity* apply in the marketplace? Salespeople know that they can increase the likelihood of your purchase if they make goods seem scarce: "This is the last one I have, so I'm not sure you should wait until tomorrow"; "I have another customer who's planning to come back and get this." This strategy makes you feel as if you are missing a critical opportunity by not buying now.

MODELING

For a final example of a technique that will bring about compliance, we return briefly to the idea of conformity. When people conform, they adopt the behavior of a reference group. Thus, one way to get people to comply is to create circumstances of informational influence: People can bring behavior change about by *modeling* the desired behavior.

HOW WE KNOW

MODELING WATER CONSERVATION Administrators at the University of California at Santa Cruz wanted students to conserve energy and water. Because Santa Cruz students claimed to be ardent environmentalists, the bureaucrats believed that displaying a conservation message on signs would lead to significant changes in behavior. A sign on the wall of the men's shower room at the field house encouraged water conservation by urging users to "(1) Wet down. (2) Turn water off. (3) Soap up. (4) Rinse off." Over a period of five days, only 6 percent of the men taking showers followed the suggested routine. When the sign was placed on a tripod and moved to a more prominent spot at the shower room entrance, compliance went up to 19 percent. However, the overall effectiveness of the sign was probably negligible, as some users, resenting the sign, knocked it over and took extra-long showers.

Finally, all signs were removed, and a student modeled appropriate shower-taking behavior. A confederate entered the shower room when it was momentarily empty, turned on the tap, and waited with his back turned to the entrance. As soon as he heard someone enter, he followed the admonition of the sign: He turned off the water, soaped up, rinsed off, and left. Compliance under this approach jumped to 49 percent. When two models were used, 67 percent of those who observed them followed their lead. This is a huge increase from the 6 percent compliance to the original sign (Aronson, 1990).

What can you do if you want to increase the probability that your neighbors will recycle?

Even when there's no explicit model in the situation, salespeople will often try to use both normative and informational influence by telling you how many people of a type to which you should *want* to belong have purchased a product: "I'm only selling these cars to people who are intelligent and confident"; "This is the best-selling model for people who demand excellent stereo speakers."

In explaining these compliance techniques, we have provided a couple of examples of things you might *want* to do: You might want to volunteer your time for good causes or help conserve the earth's resources. However, you can see that much of the time people use these techniques to get you to do things you probably *wouldn't* want to do. How can you defend yourself against wily salespeople and their kin? You should try to catch them using these strategies—and resist their efforts. Try to ignore meaningless favors. Try to avoid foolish consistency. Try to detect false claims of scarcity. Always take time to think and reason before acting. Your knowledge of social psychology can make you an all-round wiser consumer.

Throughout this chapter, we have asked you to imagine situations involving friends. But how and why do some people become your friends? You probably won't be surprised that another important area of social psychological research considers social relationships—the relationships between people and groups of people. We now look at the forces of interpersonal attraction that draw people together.

SUMMING UP

Attitudes are positive or negative evaluations of objects, events, or ideas. When attitudes are highly accessible or specific, there is a stronger link between attitudes and behaviors. According to the elaboration likelihood model, the effectiveness of a persuasive message depends on whether people take a central or peripheral route to persuasion. The central route is more likely when people are motivated by, for example, personal relevance, to weigh arguments carefully. The match between the basis for an attitude and the type of argument also affects the argument's effectiveness. Dissonance theory and self-perception theory suggest that people often change their attitudes in response to their own behaviors. Reciprocity, commitment, scarcity, and modeling are all psychological forces that lead people to comply with requests.

Social Relationships

How do you choose the people with whom you share your life? Why do you seek the company of your friends? Why are there some people for whom your feelings move beyond friendship to feelings of romantic love? Social psychologists have developed a variety of answers to these questions of *interpersonal attraction*. (But don't worry, no one yet has taken all the mystery out of love!)

Liking

Have you ever stopped to examine how and why you acquired each of your friends? The first part of this answer is straightforward: People tend to become attracted to others with whom they are in close *proximity*—you see and meet them because they live or work near you. This factor probably requires little explanation, but it might be worth noting that there is a general tendency for people to like objects and people just by virtue of *mere exposure:* The more you are exposed to something or someone, the more you like it (Zajonc, 1968). This mere exposure effect means that, on the whole, you will come to like more and more the people who are nearby. As we shall see in the Psychology in the 21st Century box, however, the computer age is giving a new meaning to the idea of proximity. Many people now maintain relationships over networks of computers. Although a friend may be geographically quite distant, daily messages appearing on a computer screen can make the person seem psychologically very close. Let's look now at other factors that can lead to attraction and liking.

PHYSICAL ATTRACTIVENESS

For better or worse, *physical attractiveness* often plays a role in the kindling of friendship. There is a strong stereotype in Western culture that physically attractive people are also good in other ways. A review of more than 70 studies suggested that the physical attractiveness stereotype has its largest effect on people's judg-

Why does proximity—in physical space or cyberspace—affect liking?

ments about social competence—people believe that the attractive are likely to be more sociable and extraverted than are the less attractive (Eagly et al., 1991). Attractiveness has a much smaller effect, however, on people's judgments of intelligence or predictions about career success. In light of the social basis of the stereotype, it might not surprise you that physical attractiveness plays a role in liking.

HOW WE KNOW

PURSUING PHYSICALLY ATTRACTIVE PARTNERS In one classic study, researchers randomly assigned incoming University of Minnesota freshmen to couples as blind dates for a large dance. The researchers collected a variety of information about each student along dimensions of intelligence and personality. On the night of the dance and in later follow-ups the students were asked to evaluate their dates and indicate how likely they were to see the individual again. The results were clear, and very similar for both men and women. Beauty mattered more than high IQs, good social skills, or good personalities. Only those matched by chance with beautiful or handsome blind dates wanted to pursue the relationship further (Walster et al., 1966).

Physical attractiveness appears to predict liking in different cultures as well. For example, Chinese 10th- to 12th-graders accorded greater status to their classmates who were physically attractive (Dong et al., 1996). However, as we noted in Chapter 12, cultures differ with respect to their standards for physical beauty. African Americans, for example, associate fewer negative personality traits with obesity than do Anglo-Americans (Hebl & Heatherton, 1998; Jackson & McGill, 1996).

SIMILARITY

A famous adage on *similarity* suggests that "birds of a feather flock together." Is this correct? Research evidence suggests that, under many circumstances, the answer is "yes." Similarity on dimensions such as beliefs, attitudes, and values fosters friendship. Why might that be so? People who are similar to you can provide a sense of personal validation, because a similar person makes you feel that the attitudes, for example, you hold dear are, in fact, the right ones (Byrne & Clore, 1970). Furthermore, dissimilarity often leads to strong repulsion (Rosenbaum, 1986). When you discover that someone holds opinions that are different from yours, you may evoke from memory past instances of interpersonal friction. That will motivate you to stay away—and if you stay away from dissimilar people, only the similar ones will be left in your pool of friends.

If you are living in a dormitory while you attend college, you can look around you to see similarity at work. Do you perceive successful roommates to be similar? Researchers have looked at the similarity of roommates on a variety of dimensions. For example, one study assessed the *communication traits* of pairs of roommates: How similar were they on dimensions such as their willingness to communicate? Roommates who were similar at the positive ends of the trait dimensions (for example, they were both willing to communicate) liked each other more than mismatched pairs or pairs that were both unwilling to communicate (Martin & Anderson, 1995). If you are in a dorm, you can try to confirm this pattern in the field!

RECIPROCITY

Finally, you tend to like people whom you believe like you. Do you recall our discussion of salespeople's use of *reciprocity*? The rule that you should give back what you receive applies to friendship as well. People give back "liking" to people whom they believe have given "liking" to them (Backman & Secord, 1959; Kenny & La Voie, 1982). Furthermore, because of the way your beliefs can affect your behaviors, believing that someone likes or dislikes you can help bring that relationship about (Curtis & Miller, 1986). Can you predict how you would act toward someone you believe likes you? Toward someone you believe dislikes you? Suppose you act with hostility toward someone you think doesn't like you. Do you see how your belief could become a self-fulfilling prophecy? When we look out at the social world, our judgments about which acquaintances are united by a "liking" relationship tend to be heavily guided by reciprocity. That is, if we know that Person A particularly likes Person B, we infer that Person B has the same feelings toward Person A (Kenny et al., 1996).

The evidence we have reviewed suggests that most of your friends will be people you encounter frequently, and people with whom you share the bonds of similarity and reciprocity. But what have researchers found about more intense relationships people call "loving"?

Loving

Many of the same forces that lead to liking also get people started on the road to love—in most cases, you will first like the people you end up loving. (However, some people report loving certain relatives that they don't particularly like as individuals.) What special factors have social psychologists learned about loving relationships?

THE EXPERIENCE OF LOVE

What does it mean to experience *love?* You should take a moment to think how you would define this important concept. Do you think your definition would agree with your friends' definitions? Researchers have tried to answer this question in a variety of ways, and some consistency has emerged. People's conceptualizations of love cluster into three dimensions (Aron & Westbay, 1996):

- *Passion*—sexual passion and desire
- *Intimacy*—honesty and understanding
- *Commitment*—devotion and sacrifice

Would you characterize all your loving relationships as including all three dimensions? You're probably thinking, "not *all* of them." In fact, it is important to make a distinction between "loving" someone and being "in love" with someone (Meyers & Berscheid, 1997). Most people report themselves to "love" a larger category of people than the group with whom they are "in love"—who among us hasn't been heartbroken to hear the words, "I love you, but I'm not *in* love with you"? Being "in love" implies something more intense and special—this is the type of experience that includes sexual passion.

Although it is possible to state some general features of loving relationships, your knowledge of the world has probably led you to the correct generalization that there are individual differences in the way that people experience love. Researchers have been particularly interested in understanding individual differences in people's ability to sustain loving relationships over an extended period of time. In recent years, attention has often focused on *adult attachment style* (Fraley & Shaver, 2000; Shaver & Hazan, 1994). Recall from Chapter 11 the importance of the quality of a child's attachment to his or her parents for smooth social development. Researchers began to wonder how much impact that early attachment might have later in life, as the children grew up to have committed relationships and children of their own (Hazan & Shaver, 1987; Main et al., 1985).

What are the types of attachment style? **Table 17.2** provides three statements about close relationships (Hazan & Shaver, 1987; Shaver & Hazan, 1994). Please take a moment to note which statement fits you best. When asked which of these statements best describes them, the majority of people (55 percent) choose the first state-

ment; this is a *secure* attachment style. Sizable minorities select the second statement (25 percent, an *avoidant* style) and the third (20 percent, an *anxious-ambivalent* style). Attachment style has proven to be an accurate predictor of relationship quality (Feeney & Noller, 1990; Tidwell et al., 1996). Compared with individuals who chose the other two styles, securely attached individuals had the most enduring romantic relationships as adults. Attachment style also predicts the ways in which individuals experience jealousy in relationships (Sharpsteen & Kirkpatrick, 1997). For example, people with an anxious style tend to experience jealousy more frequently and more intensely than do people with a secure attachment style.

Let us make one final distinction. Many loving relationships start out with a period of great intensity and absorption, which is called *passionate love.* Over time, there is a tendency for relationships to migrate toward a state of lesser intensity but greater intimacy, called *companionate love* (Berscheid & Walster, 1978). When you find yourself in a loving relationship, you may do well to anticipate that transition—so that you don't misinterpret a natural change as a process of falling "out of love." Even so, the decline of passionate love may not be as dramatic as the stereotype of long-committed couples suggests. Researchers find a reasonable level of passionate love as much as 30 years into a relationship (Aron & Aron, 1994). When you enter a loving relationship, you can have high hopes that the passion will endure in some form, even as the relationship grows to encompass other needs.

Note that experiences of love are also influenced by cultural expectations. At various moments in this chapter, we've alluded to the cultural dimension of independence versus interdependence: Cultures with independent construals of self value the person over the collective; interdependent cultures put greater value on

TABLE 17.2

Styles of Adult Attachment for Close Relationships

Statement 1:

I find it relatively easy to get close to others and am comfortable depending on them. I don't often worry about being abandoned or about someone getting too close to me.

Statement 2:

I am somewhat uncomfortable being close to others; I find it difficult to trust them completely, difficult to allow myself to depend on them. I am nervous when anyone gets too close, and often, love partners want me to be more intimate than I feel comfortable being.

Statement 3:

I find that others are reluctant to get as close as I would like. I often worry that my partner doesn't really love me or won't want to stay with me. I want to get very close to my partner, and this sometimes scares people away.

Companionate feelings for someone you were once passionate about do not signal "falling out of love": On the contrary, they are a natural outgrowth of romance and a vital ingredient in most long-term partnerships.

shared cultural goals rather than on individual ones. How does this apply to your love life? If you choose a life partner based on your own feelings of love, you are showing preference for your personal goals; if you choose a partner with an eye to how that individual will mesh with your family's structure and concerns, you are being more attuned to collective goals. Cross-cultural research has led to the very strong generalization that members of independent cultures put much greater emphasis on love (Dion & Dion, 1993; Hatfield & Sprecher, 1995; Levine et al., 1995). Consider the question, "If a man (woman) had all the other qualities you desired, would you marry this person if you were not in love with him (her)?" Only 3.5 percent of a sample of male and female undergraduates in the United States answered "yes"; 49 percent of a comparable group of students in India answered "yes" (Levine et al., 1995).

Members of independent cultures are also more *demanding* of their potential partners. Because people in these cultures have stronger ideas about personal fulfillment within relationships, they also expect more from marriage partners (Hatfield & Sprecher, 1995).

WHAT FACTORS ALLOW RELATIONSHIPS TO LAST?

It seems likely that everyone reading this book—and certainly everyone *writing* this book—has been in a relationship that didn't last. What happened? Or, to put the question in a more positive light, what can researchers say about the types of situations, and people in those situations, that are more likely to lead to long-term loving relationships?

One theory conceptualizes people in close relationships as having a feeling that the "other" is included in their "self" (Aron et al., 1991; Aron & Aron, 1994). Consider the series of diagrams given in **Figure 17.7**. Each of the diagrams represents a way you could conceptualize a close relationship. If you are in a romantic relationship, can you say which of the diagrams seems to capture most effectively the extent of interdependence between you and your partner? Research has shown that people who perceive the most overlap between self and other—those people who come to view the other as included within the self—are most likely to remain committed to their relationships over time (Aron et al., 1992; Aron & Fraley, 1999).

What other factors contribute to the likelihood that someone will remain in a relationship? The *dependence model* suggests that commitment is based on a series of judgments (Drigotas & Rusbult, 1992, p. 65):

- The degree to which each of several needs is important in the individual's relationship. Important needs are intimacy, sex, emotional involvement, companionship, and intellectual involvement.

- The degree to which each of those needs is satisfied in that relationship.

Please circle the picture that best describes your relationship

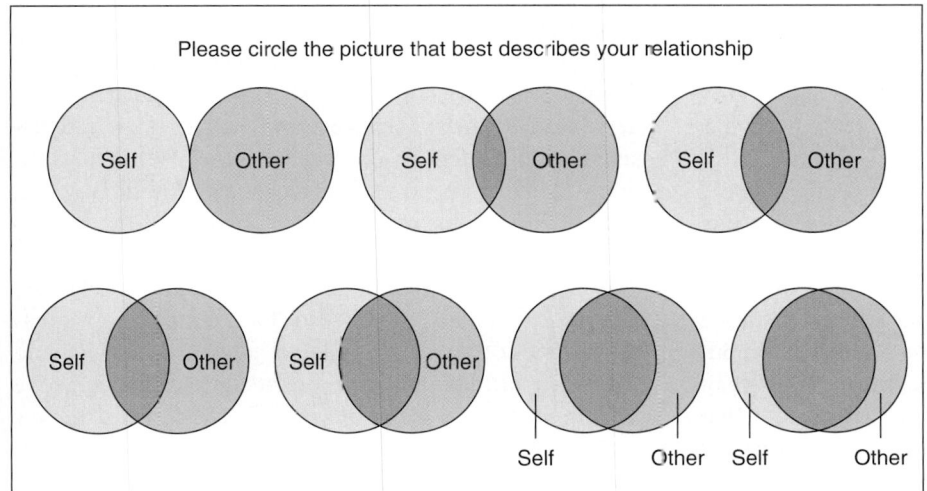

FIGURE 17.7

The Inclusion of Other in the Self (IOS) Scale

If you are in a romantic relationship, which diagram best captures the interdependence of you and your partner? Research with the IOS scale suggests that people who most perceive the other as included with the self are also most likely to stay committed to their relationships.

RELATIONSHIPS AND THE INTERNET

Does anyone doubt that the advent of the Internet has had a broad impact on how people initiate and conduct their close relationships? Consider a 13-year-old boy named Daniel from New York City whose "new girlfriend" is a 13-year-old named Rachel from South Carolina. Daniel and Rachel have not been able to exchange pictures over the Internet. When Daniel's mother suggested that they send photos through the U.S. mail, her son replied, "Mom, she's not going to give me her address" (Gardner, 2000, p. 40). Clearly, until late in the 20th century, this is not the type of relationship most boys would've had in mind for their "new girlfriend." Let's explore the impact of the Internet on relationships.

Studies have shown that social interaction is one of Internet users' most frequent activities. In one survey of roughly 4,100 people, 90 percent used the Internet to exchange e-mail and 24 percent participated in chat rooms (Nie & Erbing, 2000). Other research suggests that a good number of relationships forged in cyberspace make their way into the physical world. Consider a study that involved 563 individuals (59 percent women and 41 percent

men) who had made postings to newsgroups (McKenna et al., 2001). In that sample, 63 percent had spoken on the telephone with an acquaintance they'd made on the Internet; 54 percent had met face-to-face with an Internet acquaintance. A follow-up study two years later showed that many of the relationships formed over the Internet were still going strong. In fact, 15 percent of the sample had become engaged to someone they'd met on the Internet, and 10 percent had married an Internet partner.

We noted earlier that *proximity* is an important ingredient for liking: You need to meet people before they can become your friends or romantic partners. The studies we've just cited indicate that the Internet provides an important new mechanism to establish psychological proximity in the absence of geographic proximity. In fact, some evidence suggests that relationships get off to a better start when they begin on the Internet rather than face-to-face (Bargh et al., 2001). In one study using college students, participants interacted on two occasions with the same partner. For half of the pairs, both interactions were face-to-face. For the other half, an Internet

interaction preceded the face-to-face meeting. At the end of the second interaction, the participants were asked how much they liked their partners on a scale ranging from –7 (strong dislike) to +7 (strong like). Those participants whose first interaction had taken place over the Internet reported consistently greater liking for their partners (with a mean of 4.70) than did their peers who had only met face-to-face (with a mean of 2.45). Why might that be? The researchers speculated that the initial Internet interaction allowed participants to be less affected by surface features of their partners such as physical attractiveness. Furthermore, the momentary anonymity of the Internet likely encouraged people to be more self-disclosing, which also may increase liking.

Research attention has often focused on the lives of people whose use or overuse of the Internet decreases real-life social activity (Kraut et al., 1998; Nie & Erbing, 2000). However, the studies we've cited here suggest that the Internet may also be a positive force for many or most people's social and romantic lives. Perhaps someday Daniel may even get his girlfriend's address.

- For each need, whether there is anyone other than the current partner with whom the individual has an important relationship.

- The degree to which each need is satisfied by the alternative relationship.

As you might expect, this model predicts that people are more likely to stay in a relationship when the relationship satisfies important needs that cannot be satisfied by anyone else. Thus, if *companionship* is very important to you—you enjoy spending leisure time with other people—and a person with whom you share a relationship provides more companionship than anyone else you know, you're likely to feel committed to that relationship. This will be true even if your partner is not your first choice on dimensions that matter less. The dependence

model also offers insight into why people will stay in relationships in which they have been physically abused (Choice & Lamke, 1999). In a sample of 100 women at a shelter for battered women, the women who saw themselves as having few alternatives—often, for economic reasons—were still committed to returning to their relationships (Rusbult & Martz, 1995). Thus, people may be quite unhappy in a relationship and yet depend on the relationship.

Throughout this chapter, we've seen how social forces act on individuals. We've seen, for example, how situations function to constrain your personal behavior and how your attitudes are forged in the social cauldron. We've encouraged you to examine your behaviors, to see the way in which your social setting helps to explain important aspects of your day-to-day experiences. In the next chapter, we see how the same types of forces guide social behaviors at the personal level—to yield aggression and altruism—and at the cultural level—to yield war and peace.

SUMMING UP

Most people like other individuals who are in close proximity, physically attractive, similar, and who reciprocate liking. People characterize their love exp[...] spect to the dimensions of passion, int[...] mitment. Individual differences in love ex[...] predicted from adult attachment styles an[...] pectations. Loving relationships are closer if e[...] sees the other as included within the self. The dep[...] model suggests that people are more likely to stay in[...] lationship when it satisfies important needs that are not satisfied by anyone else.

RECAPPING
MAIN POINTS

The Power of the Situation

- Human thought and action are affected by situational influences.
- Being assigned to play a social role, even in artificial settings, can cause individuals to act contrary to their beliefs, values, and dispositions.
- Social norms shape the attitudes and behaviors of group members.
- Classic research by Sherif and Asch illustrated the informational and normative forces that lead to conformity.
- Minority influence may arise as a consequence of informational influence.

Constructing Social Reality

- Each person constructs his or her own social reality.
- Social perception is influenced by beliefs and expectations.
- Attribution theory describes the judgments people make about the causes of behaviors.
- Several biases, such as the fundamental attribution error, self-serving biases, and self-fulfilling prophecies, can creep into attributions and other judgments and behaviors.

- However, the influence of expectations is limited by accurate information you have about the world.

Attitudes, Attitude Change, and Action

- Attitudes are positive or negative evaluations of objects, events, or ideas.
- Not all attitudes accurately predict behaviors; they must be highly accessible or highly specific.
- According to the elaboration likelihood model, the central route to persuasion relies on careful analyses of arguments, whereas the peripheral route relies on superficial features of persuasive situations.
- The match between the basis for an attitude and the type of argument also affects the argument's effectiveness.
- Dissonance theory and self-perception theory consider attitude formation and change that arise from behavioral acts.
- To bring about compliance, people can exploit reciprocity, commitment, scarcity, and modeling.

Social Relationships

- Interpersonal attraction is determined in part by proximity, physical attractiveness, similarity, and reciprocity.
- Loving relationships are defined with respect to passion, intimacy, and commitment.
- Adult attachment style affects the quality of relationships.
- A person's commitment to a loving relationship is related to the level of closeness and dependence.

Key Terms

attitude (p. 550)
attribution theory (p. 545)
behavioral confirmation (p. 549)
cognitive dissonance (p. 554)
compliance (p. 556)
conformity (p. 539)
covariation principle (p. 545)
elaboration likelihood model (p. 552)
fundamental attribution error (FAE) (p. 546)
group polarization (p. 542)
groupthink (p. 542)
informational influence (p. 539)
normative influence (p. 539)
norm crystallization (p. 539)
persuasion (p. 552)
reciprocity norm (p. 557)
rules (p. 536)
self-fulfilling prophecy (p. 548)
self-perception theory (p. 556)
self-serving bias (p. 547)
social norms (p. 538)
social perception (p. 545)
social psychology (p. 535)
social role (p. 536)

social psychology, society, and culture

18

■ **ALTRUISM AND PROSOCIAL BEHAVIOR**
The Roots of Altruism •
Motives for Prosocial
Behavior • The Effects
of the Situation on
Prosocial Behavior

■ **AGGRESSION**
Evolutionary Perspectives •
Individual Differences •
Situational Influences •
Cultural Constraints

■ **PREJUDICE**
Origins of Prejudice • Effects
of Stereotypes • Reversing
Prejudice

■ **PSYCHOLOGY IN THE 21ST
CENTURY: THE WORLD
GROWS SMALLER**

■ **THE PSYCHOLOGY OF
CONFLICT AND PEACE**
Obedience to Authority •
The Psychology of Genocide
and War • Peace Psychology

■ **PSYCHOLOGY IN YOUR
LIFE: WHY DO PEOPLE
JOIN CULTS?**

■ **A PERSONAL ENDNOTE**

■ **RECAPPING MAIN POINTS**
Key Terms

In 1963, philosopher Hannah Arendt published *Eich-mann in Jerusalem*, a book-length account of the trial of Adolph Eichmann—a Nazi figure who helped arrange for the murder of millions of Jews. Eichmann's defense of his actions was familiar from the trials of other Nazis:

> *[Eichmann] remembered perfectly well that he would have had a bad conscience only if he had not done what he had been ordered to do—to ship millions of men, women, and children to their death with great zeal and the most meticulous care (p. 25).*

However, what is most striking in Arendt's account of Eichmann is all the ways in which he seemed absolutely ordinary:

> *Half a dozen psychiatrists had certified him as "normal"—"More normal, at any rate, than I am after having examined him," one of them was said to have exclaimed, while another had found that his whole psychological outlook, his attitude toward his wife and children, mother and father, brothers, sisters, and friends, was "not only normal but most desirable"…(pp. 25–26).*

Through her analysis of Eichmann, Arendt reached a famous conclusion:

> *The trouble with Eichmann was precisely that so many were like him, and that the many were neither perverted nor sadistic, that they were, and still are, terribly and terrifyingly normal. From the viewpoint of our legal institutions and our moral standards of judgment, this normality was much more terrifying than all the atrocities put together, for it implied… that this new type of criminal…commits his crimes under circumstances that make it well-nigh impossible for him to know or feel that he is doing wrong (p. 276).*
>
> *It was as though in those last minutes [of Eichmann's life] he was summing up the lesson that this long course in human wickedness had taught us—the lesson of the fearsome, word-and-thought-defying banality of evil (p. 252).*

Hannah Arendt's phrase the "banality of evil" resonates into the 21st century. In the 60 years since the Nazi Holocaust, several more waves of terror have been unleashed around the world. As we write these words in the fall of 2000, the Middle East has once again exploded into violence as Israelis and Palestinians clash in the West Bank. Elsewhere, a people's uprising in Yugoslavia has led to the ouster of the brutal dictator Slobodan Milosevic, but it seems that he and the members of his regime will escape trial for war crimes. In Nigeria, conflict between members of the Hausas and Yoruba tribes has left thousands dead over the last year and dozens in the last few days. There is a tendency to look at such circumstances and see madness: to search for characters who are insane or pure evil, such as Adolph Hitler. Arendt's phrase—the "banality of evil"—denies that analysis: She observes instead how easily social forces can prompt normal people to perform horrific acts.

We have come to the moment in *Psychology and Life* when we consider the most extreme consequences of the way in which social forces act on human behavior. Some of the content of this chapter will be quite disturbing with respect to the potential it reveals for destructive and inhumane acts. We consider aggressive behavior, prejudice, and the circumstances that can lead to acts of genocide. At the same time, we describe the innate drive of the human species to be prosocial—to perform altruistic acts of generosity with no expectation of reward. Ultimately, we hope that this chapter strikes an optimistic note by suggesting how the insights generated through social science research can help bring about world peace.

Students often find the topics discussed in this chapter both provocative and disconcerting. We hope you will have the opportunity to discuss and debate the full implications with your classmates. You should finish the chapter with an understanding of how the social psychological forces acting on each individual can, as individuals join together in groups, produce some of the most intimidating moments of world history.

■ Altruism and Prosocial Behavior

You see the same images after almost every tragedy: People risk their own lives to try to save the lives of others. Recall, for example, the horror of the Oklahoma City bombing. People from all the over the country converged on the gutted Alfred P. Murrah building with the hope of finding and aiding survivors. Such tragedies show the human species's potential for **prosocial behaviors,** behaviors that are carried out with the goal of helping other people. Beyond that, these tragedies often demonstrate **altruism**—the prosocial behaviors a person carries out without considering his or her own safety or interests. Much of what defines a *culture* or *society* is people's willingness to help each other. As members of a culture or society, people cooperate and make sacrifices for the good of other members. We begin this section by considering why it is that people are willing to perform acts of altruism.

■ The Roots of Altruism

Let's start with a concrete example of altruism, reported in a daily newspaper (Porstner, 1997):

> A Bay Shore man pulled in front of and stopped a swerving car on the Southern State Parkway in Lindenhurst Thursday, saving a Connecticut man whom police said may have suffered a seizure.
>
> "I just got up real close in front of him and just slowed down so he would hit me," said [the driver, age] 25. "That was the only way I could get his moving car to a stop."

What response do you have to this report? Can you imagine risking your own life—or, at least, your own car—to save someone else's life? As this event unfolded, what do you imagine the Bay Shore driver might have been thinking to himself? Do you believe he calculated costs and benefits before he acted?

When you consider examples like this courageous driver, it seems fairly natural to conclude that there is some basic human motive to be altruistic. In fact, the existence of altruism has sometimes been controversial. To

■ **Prosocial behaviors** Behaviors that are carried out with the goal of helping other people.

■ **Altruism** Prosocial behaviors a person carries out without considering his or her own safety or interests.

■ **Reciprocal altruism** The idea that people perform altruistic behaviors because they expect that others will perform altruistic behaviors for them in turn.

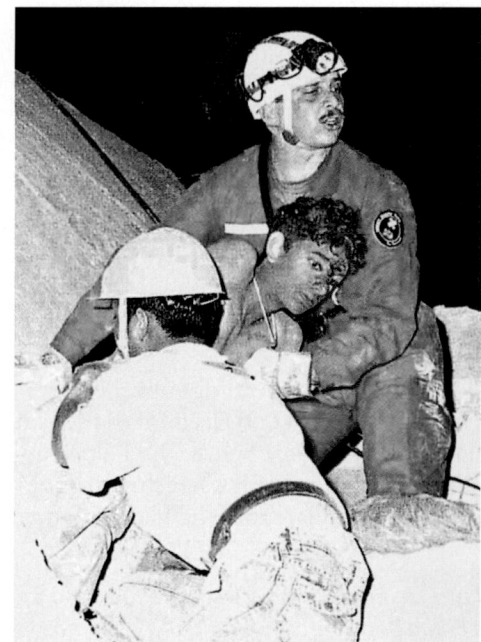

What social forces turn people like workers in India after the 2001 earthquake into heroes?

understand why, you must think back to the discussion of evolutionary forces we presented in Chapters 3 and 12. According to the evolutionary perspective, the main goal of life is to reproduce so that one can pass on one's genes. How, in that context, does altruism make sense? Why should you risk your life to aid others? There are two answers to this question, depending on whether the "others" are family members or strangers.

For family members, altruistic behaviors makes some sense because—even if you imperil your own survival— you aid the general survival of your gene pool. In fact, when asked about who they might aid in life-or-death situations, people are relatively sensitive to their genetic overlap.

HOW WE KNOW

ALTRUISM TOWARD KIN College students from the United States and Japan were asked to consider scenarios in which they could only save one of three individuals in grave peril. For example, in one scenario the three individuals were sleeping in a rapidly burning house. In each scenario, the individuals differed with respect to their imagined *kinship* with the students. Some were close relatives, such as brothers (.5 overlap in genes); others were more distant, such as cousins (.125 overlap). The students were asked to indicate which individual they would be most likely to save. As you can see in **Figure 18.1**, the closer the kinship, the more likely people were to "save" that individual. The figure also shows a comparison

Students in this study didn't actually have to rescue anyone from a burning house, yet you can see how kinship affected their choices. Although it's unlikely that anyone was explicitly reasoning "I have to protect the gene pool," if people follow the pattern represented in Figure 18.1, gene pool protection would emerge.

But how about non-kin? Why, for example, was the driver willing to risk his own survival to preserve someone else's genes? To explain altruism toward acquaintances and strangers, theorists have explored the concept of **reciprocal altruism** (Trivers, 1971). This concept suggests that people perform altruistic behaviors because they, in some sense, expect that others will perform altruistic behaviors for them: I will save you when you are drowning with the expectation that you would save me, in the future, when I am drowning. Thus, expectations of reciprocity endow altruism with survival value. You have already become acquainted with this concept in other guises. In Chapter 17, for example, we introduced the *norm of reciprocity* to explain one way in which people can bring about compliance. When someone does a favor for you, you are in a state of psychological distress until you can return the favor—this distress, apparently, has its roots in evolution because it helps increase survival. Because of these evolutionary underpinnings, altruism is not unique to the human species. In fact, anthropologists

have identified patterns of reciprocal altruism among a variety of species, such as vampire bats and chimpanzees, that function in social groups (Nielsen, 1994).

Note, however, that the concept of reciprocal altruism cannot explain all facets of cooperation in social species. Researchers have produced evidence that, in many situations, both human and nonhuman animals continue to cooperate and share resources without expectations of reciprocity (Matheson & Bernstein, 2000; Wedekind & Milinski, 2000; Widdig et al., 2000). For example, the small number of successful hunters among the !Kung people, hunter-gatherers who live in northwestern Botswana and neighboring parts of Namibia, share the meat from animals they kill with the other members of their camp even though they cannot expect to obtain comparable resources in return from the less skilled hunters (Hawkes, 1993). Based on these types of observations, researchers continue the search for a broader range of explanations for the existence of altruism.

Given that altruism appears to have an evolutionary basis, do individual differences in altruism affect a contemporary individual's ability to pass on his or her genes? Recall that in Chapter 12, we explored some of the factors evolutionary psychologists have suggested guide people's mate selections. Our discussion of altruism allows us to add another factor to this list.

HOW WE KNOW

WOMEN VALUE ALTRUISTIC MEN Female undergraduates watched a videotaped conversation between an experimenter and a male confederate. During the conversation, the confederate revealed his attitude toward altruistic behaviors. In the *high-altruism* condition, he talked about helping others and then volunteered to do a boring task, rather than allowing someone else to

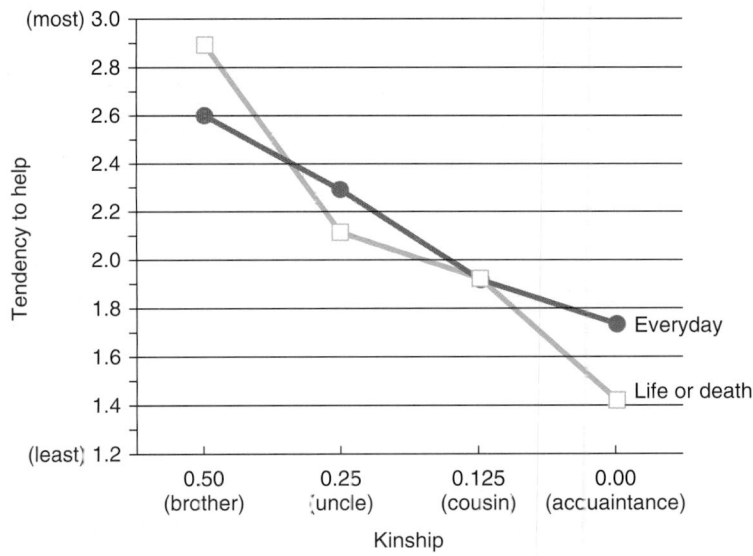

FIGURE 18.1

Tendency to Help Kin

Students were asked to indicate which relatives, of differing degrees of kinship, they were most likely to save in life-or-death and everyday circumstances. Although closeness had an effect on both types of judgments, it mattered more for life-or-death situations.

do it. In the *low-altruism* condition, the confederate talked about watching out for his own interests and opted to leave the boring task to someone else. After watching the conversation, the female participants were asked to rate the confederate on a number of dimensions, including physical and sexual attractiveness and social and dating desirability. Although the very same males appeared in the low- and high-altruism conditions, the women rated them as considerably more attractive and desirable when they were committed to altruistic behaviors (Jensen-Campbell et al., 1995).

Contrary to the old saying, in this study, nice guys finished first. In evolutionary terms, the results suggest that women prefer men who will actively share their resources to help nurture offspring. In this light, we have another reason why altruism remained part of the human genome: Women believed that men who provided evidence of altruistic behaviors would make better fathers.

Motives for Prosocial Behavior

In the last section, we suggested that altruism—a motive to sacrifice for others—has an innate basis. We now consider altruism in the context of other motives for prosocial behavior. Researcher **Daniel Batson** (1994) suggests that there are four forces that prompt people to act for the public good:

- *Altruism.* Acting in response to a motive to benefit others, as in the case of the driver who saved another person's life.

- *Egoism.* Performing prosocial behaviors ultimately in one's own self-interest; someone might perform a helping behavior to receive a similar favor in return (for example, compliance with a request) or to receive a reward (for example, money or praise).

- *Collectivism.* Performing prosocial behaviors to benefit a particular group; people might perform helping behaviors to improve circumstances for their families, fraternities or sororities, political parties, and so on.

- *Principlism.* Performing prosocial behaviors to uphold moral principles; someone might act in a prosocial manner because of a religious or civic principle.

You can see how each of these motives might apply in different situations.

Although each motive may lead people to perform behaviors in the service of others, they also sometimes can act in competition. Suppose, for example, that you must decide how to allocate a scarce resource to several people. You might be thinking, "I'd give the same amount to all individuals," because the principle of *justice* suggests

What prosocial motive explains why people band together to protect the environment?

that each person should have equal access to resources. Suppose, however, that other motives come into play that lead you to favor one individual over the others.

EMPATHY CAN LEAD TO INJUSTICE
Participants in an experiment were asked to allocate raffle tickets either to a whole group or to individuals within the group. If the tickets were given to the whole group, each member would get the same number of tickets—a *justice* outcome. However, in one condition of the experiment, the participants read an autobiographical message from someone they were led to believe was a group member; the message revealed that that person had just been dumped by a long-time romantic partner. How does this information affect people's distributions of raffle tickets? When the participants were encouraged to try to imagine how the student would feel, they gave extra tickets to the dumped individual. *Empathy*—the participants' emotional identification with the student—won out over *justice* (Batson et al., 1999).

Daniel Batson and his colleagues have provided several demonstrations in favor of the *empathy-altruism hypothesis:* When you feel empathy toward another individual, those feelings evoke an altruistic motive to provide help. In the experiment we just described, the immediate altruistic goal proved stronger for some participants than the more abstract goal of justice. In a similar fashion, empathy can give rise to altruistic behaviors that favor an individual over the collective good (Batson et al., 1995).

You can see why it's important to consider each behavior in light of the full situation: What looks at first like *anti*social behavior—for example, violating principles of justice—may turn out, from a different vantage point, to be *pro*social behavior. A social psychology lesson we emphasized in Chapter 17 was how much people's behaviors are constrained by situations. We have just had a first hint of such constraints for prosocial behavior. Next, we describe a classic program of research that demonstrated fully how much people's willingness to help—their ability to follow through on prosocial motives—depends on characteristics of the situation.

The Effects of the Situation on Prosocial Behavior

This program of research began with a tragedy. From the safety of their apartment windows, 38 respectable, law-abiding citizens in Queens, New York, for more than half an hour watched a killer stalk and stab a woman in three separate attacks. Two times the sound of the bystanders' voices and the sudden glow of their bedroom lights interrupted the assailant and frightened him off. Each time, however, he returned and stabbed the victim again. Not a single person telephoned the police during the assault; only one witness called the police after the woman was dead (Rosenthal, 1964). This newspaper account of the murder of Kitty Genovese shocked a nation that could not accept the idea of such apathy or hard-heartedness on the part of its responsible citizenry.

But is it fair to pin the label of "apathy" or "hard-hearted" on these bystanders? Or can we explain their inaction in terms of situational forces? To make the case for situational forces, **Bibb Latané** and **John Darley** (1970) carried out a classic series of studies. Their goal was

The murder of Kitty Genovese, in a pleasant Queens neighborhood, shocked the nation. Why did so many responsible citizens fail to intervene when they heard her cries for help?

to demonstrate that **bystander intervention**—people's willingness to help strangers in distress—was very sensitive to precise characteristics of the situation. They ingeniously created in the laboratory an experimental analogue of the bystander-intervention situation.

HOW WE KNOW

WHEN WILL PEOPLE HELP? The participants were male college students. Each student, placed in a room by himself with an intercom, was led to believe that he was communicating with one or more students in an adjacent room. During the course of a discussion about personal problems, he heard what sounded like one of the other students having an epileptic seizure and gasping for help. During the "seizure," it was impossible for the participant to talk to the other students or to find out what, if anything, they were doing about the emergency. The dependent variable was the speed with which the participant reported the emergency to the experimenter.

It turned out that the likelihood of intervention depended on the number of bystanders the participant thought were present. The more people he thought were present, the slower he was in reporting the seizure, if he did so at all. As you can see in **Figure 18.2**, everyone in a two-person situation intervened within 160 seconds, but nearly 40 percent of those who believed they were part of a larger group never bothered to inform the experimenter that another student was seriously ill (Darley & Latané, 1968).

This result arises from a **diffusion of responsibility.** When more than one person *could* help in an emergency situation, people often assume that someone else *will* or *should* help—so they back off and don't get involved.

Diffusion of responsibility is only one of the reasons that bystanders may fail to help. Let's explore more of the facets of many emergency situations.

BYSTANDERS MUST NOTICE THE EMERGENCY

In the seizure study, the situation was rigged so that participants had to notice what was going on. In many real-life circumstances, however, people who are pursuing their own agendas—they may, for example, be on their way to work or an appointment—may not even notice that there is a situation in which they can help. In one

Bystander intervention Willingness to assist a person in need of help.

Diffusion of responsibility In emergency situations, the larger the number of bystanders, the less responsibility any one bystander feels to help.

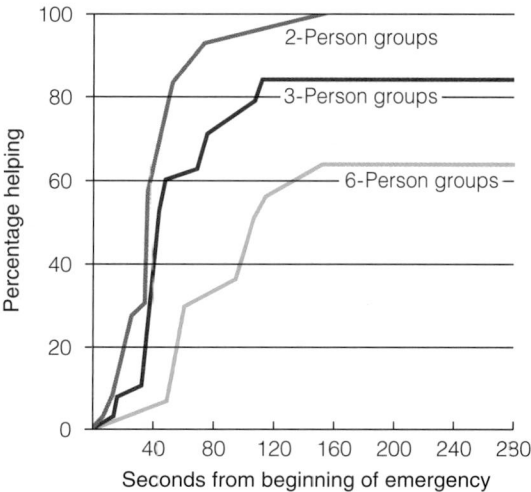

FIGURE 18.2

Bystander Intervention in an Emergency

The more people present, the less likely that any one bystander will intervene. Bystanders act most quickly in two-person groups.

dramatic experiment, students at the Princeton Theological Seminary thought they were going to be evaluated on their sermons, one of which was to be about the parable of the Good Samaritan—a New Testament figure who takes time to help a man lying injured by the roadside.

HOW WE KNOW

WHO NOTICES EMERGENCIES? The seminarians had to deliver their lectures in a different building from the one in which they were initially briefed. Some were randomly assigned to a *late* condition, in which they had to hurry to make the next session, others to an *on-time* condition, and a third group to an *early* condition. When each seminarian walked down an alley between the two buildings, he came upon a man slumped in a doorway, coughing and groaning. On their way to deliver a sermon about the Good Samaritan, these seminary students now had the chance to practice what they were about to preach. Did they? Of those who were in a hurry because they were late, only 10 percent helped. If they were on time, 45 percent helped the stranger. Most bystander intervention came from those who were early—63 percent of these seminarians acted as Good Samaritans (Darley & Batson, 1973).

How should we evaluate the "late" seminarians? Perhaps the seminarians were so caught up in their own concerns

that they failed to even "notice" the emergency situation. Perhaps they noticed, but in their hurry, they did not pay careful enough attention to determine how serious the situation was. In either case, you see that helping behavior depends on taking the time to evaluate a situation accurately.

BYSTANDERS MUST LABEL EVENTS AS AN EMERGENCY
Many situations in life are ambiguous. You don't want to embarrass yourself by trying to give mouth-to-mouth resuscitation to someone who is merely asleep. To decide if a situation is an emergency, you typically see how other people are responding (Latané & Darley, 1970). (You should recall the earlier discussion of informational influence in Chapter 17.) Consider this first-person account from one of your authors who was attending a lecture at which the speaker appeared to be on the brink of fainting:

> *The speaker is flustered and his rapid delivery is clearly slowing down. Is it to emphasize his final points or because he is about to collapse? Maybe he needs to sit down, but how can I tell without interrupting him? What if I am reading the situation wrong, and then everyone will think I'm a fool? But suppose I am right and he passes out before finishing, and falls off the stage? He will surely get hurt smashing down into the seats. I'll know that I could have prevented his accident and did not.*

You can see here how hard it is, even for someone with a firm grasp on the psychological forces at work in such a situation, to commit himself to action when no one else seems to be labeling the situation as an emergency. Here's how the situation ended:

> *I stood up in front of the speaker and put my arms up toward him. He looked down at me in total confusion. I imagined what my students and colleagues were thinking of my seemingly bizarre behavior as I wrapped my arms around the honored guest speaker, moments before he finished his distinguished lecture. Just then, the speaker went limp, unconscious, and fell on me. We crashed back into the first row seats.*

The decision to intervene, as you can see, proved to be prudent. However, from this brief account, you can see how very stressful it is to make a personal decision to define a situation as an emergency.

THE BYSTANDER MUST FEEL RESPONSIBILITY
We have already seen that an important factor in nonintervention is the diffusion of responsibility. If you find yourself in a situation in which you need help, you should do everything you can to cause bystanders to focus responsibility on themselves and overcome this force. You should point directly toward someone and say, "You! I need your help." Consider two studies that involved ap-

parent crimes. In the first study, New Yorkers watched as a thief snatched a women's suitcase in a fast-food restaurant when she left her table. In the second, beachgoers watched as a thief snatched a portable radio from a beach blanket when the owner left it for a few minutes.

HOW WE KNOW

CREATING A SENSE OF RESPONSIBILITY

In each experiment, the would-be theft victim (the experimenter's accomplice) asked the soon-to-be observer of the crime either, "Do you have the time?" or "Will you please keep an eye on my bag (radio) while I'm gone?" The first interaction elicited no personal responsibility, and the bystanders simply stood by idly as the thefts unfolded. However, of those who agreed to watch the victim's property, almost every bystander intervened. They called for help, and some even tackled the runaway thief on the beach (Moriarty, 1975).

These experiments suggest that the act of requesting a favor forges a special human bond that involves other people in ways that materially change the situation. This is another instance in which it would be wrong to make an attribution of apathy when people fail to stop the theft. The social psychological power of the small commitment—"Will you watch this for me?"—turned almost every bystander into someone who cared enough to help.

In this section, we have discussed prosocial behaviors—those circumstances in which people come to each others' aid. We suggested that the motivation to help may be part of each human's genetic inheritance. However, human nature presents a mixture of prosocial and antisocial impulses. In the next section, we move to another type of behavior—*aggression*—that may also be encoded in the human genome.

SUMMING UP

People carry out prosocial behaviors to help other individuals; they engage in altruism when those behaviors do not also serve their own interests. The evolutionary perspective suggests that people behave altruistically toward family members to preserve the gene pool; altruism toward strangers may rely, in part, on innate expectations that altruism will be reciprocated. Egoism, collectivism, and principlism are other motives for prosocial behavior. In some circumstances, the different motives may conflict. Several situational forces influence whether people will perform prosocial acts in particular circumstances. People are more likely to help when they don't experience a diffusion of responsibility, when they notice an emergency and label it as such, and when they feel responsibility in a situation.

■ Aggression

To introduce the concept of altruism, we quoted a newspaper article about a heroic act. Unfortunately, newspapers are much more likely to contain reports on acts of **aggression**: a person's behaviors that cause psychological or physical harm to another individual. These were some headlines from a single issue of *The New York Times*, October 13, 2000:

- Blast Kills Sailors on U.S. Ship in Yemen
- 2 Israeli Soldiers Slain by a Mob; Helicopters Hit Back
- Bomb Kills a Dozen People in Chechnya's Capital
- Colombian Rebels Said to Seize 10 Foreign Oil Workers

Just from this brief sample, you can see the many ways in which people aggress against one another. You can see why, consequently, it is so important to psychologists that they understand the causes of aggression. The ultimate goal, of course, is to try to use psychological knowledge to help reduce societal levels of aggression.

Evolutionary Perspectives

In the section on prosocial behavior, we posed a puzzle of evolution: Why is it that people would risk their own lives to benefit others? The existence of aggressive behaviors, however, has posed no similar puzzle. In evolutionary terms, animals commit aggressive behaviors to ensure themselves access to desired mates and to protect the resources that allow themselves and their offspring to survive. In his classic book *On Aggression*, **Karl Lorenz** (1966) documented a range of aggressive activity in the animal kingdom. In the course of his review, Lorenz also documented the mechanisms that keep aggression in check: "A raven can peck out the eye of another with one thrust of its beak, a wolf can rip the jugular vein of another with a single bite. There would be no more ravens and no more wolves if reliable inhibitions did not prevent such actions" (p. 240). On Lorenz's view, this is what sets the human species apart: He argued that humans do not have appropriately evolved mechanisms to *inhibit* their aggressive impulses. Lorenz believed that these inhibitory mechanisms failed to evolve because, until the invention of artificial weapons, humans could not do each other much harm. When weapons appeared, Lorenz suggested that the human species's "position was very nearly that of a dove which, by some

Aggression Behaviors that cause psychological or physical harm to another individual.

■ AGGRESSION

571

Why do so many species of animals engage in aggressive behaviors? What did Karl Lorenz believe makes human aggression unique?

unnatural trick of nature, has suddenly acquired the beak of a raven" (p. 241).

Research in response to Lorenz's work has contradicted his assessment of human aggression in two ways (Lore & Schultz, 1993). First, field research with a variety of animal species suggests that many other species commit the same range of aggressive acts as do humans. For example, even seemingly mild-mannered chimpanzees gang up on and kill their own kind (Goodall, 1986). Aggression in other species is not particularly good news for humans—it just seems that we're no worse—but it does suggest less of an evolutionary discontinuity. Second, research suggests that humans have more inhibitory control over their use of aggression than Lorenz suggested. In fact, humans make choices with respect to their display of aggression conditioned on their social environments. As we will see later in this section, cultures specify norms for circumstances in which aggression is acceptable or required. We will suggest there that cultures themselves play a critical role in determining the extent to which people are "able" to inhibit aggression.

Evolutionary analysis suggests that a drive for survival may have endowed many or most species with an innate predisposition toward some forms of violence. For humans, however, it is nonetheless the case that different members of the species are more or less likely to perform aggressive behaviors. We next consider those individual differences in aggression.

Individual Differences

Why are some individuals more aggressive than others? In the context of Lorenz's evolutionary claims, you can see why one hypothesis that researchers have pursued is that there is a genetic component to individual differences in rates of aggression. You will have no doubt observed that

some people seem more likely to commit aggressive acts than others. People often also believe that aggressive or violent behaviors run in families. We can't tell, however, if that pattern reflects shared genes or shared environments without turning to special research designs.

HOW WE KNOW

GENETIC AND ENVIRONMENTAL CONTRIBUTIONS TO AGGRESSION

Researchers have sought an answer to the genetics of aggression using many of the methodologies we've illustrated in earlier chapters. They have, for example, compared the similarity of identical (monozygotic) and fraternal (dizygotic) twins with respect to aggressive personalities; in other cases, they have estimated the contributions of nature and nurture by examining children raised in adoptive homes. One study used the statistical technique called *meta-analysis* to identify the important trends that emerged out of 24 previous studies on aggression, nature, and nurture. (Miles & Carey, 1997). (We described meta-analysis more fully in Chapter 16.) This meta-analysis revealed a consistent, strong contribution of genetic overlap between twins or between adopted-away children and biological parents. For example, monozygotic twins consistently showed higher correlations for aggressiveness than did dizygotic twins. Common environment exerted a smaller, but measurable, effect on patterns of aggression.

This meta-analysis suggests that some individuals may have a greater genetic predisposition toward aggression than others.

Researchers have also focused attention on brain and hormonal differences that may mark a predisposition

Here, students mourn the victims of the Columbine massacre. Why do people so often turn to aggression as a solution to their problems?

toward aggressive behavior. As we saw in Chapter 13, several brain structures, such as the amygydala and portions of cortex, play roles in the expression and regulation of emotion. With respect to aggression, it is critical that brain pathways function effectively so that individuals can control the expression of negative emotion. If, for example, people experience inappropriate levels of activation in the amygydala, they may not be able to inhibit the negative emotions that lead to aggressive behaviors (Davidson et al., 2000). Attention has also focused on the neurotransmitter serotonin; research suggests that inappropriate levels of serotonin may impair the brain's ability to regulate negative emotions and impulsive behavior (Enserink, 2000). Finally, studies suggest that some individual differences in aggression may reflect muted stress responses. For example, one project related levels of the stress hormone *cortisol* to the aggressive behavior of 7- to 12-year-old boys: The most aggressive boys had the most muted stress response (McBurnett et al., 2000). These results suggest that some individuals may not experience the type of physiological stress responses that inhibit most people from behaving in a dramatically aggressive fashion: Their bodies do not experience the negative consequences of negative behaviors and emotions.

Personality research on aggression has pointed to the importance of differentiating categories of aggressive behaviors: People with different personality profiles are likely to engage in different types of aggression. One important distinction separates *impulsive aggression* from *instrumental aggression* (Berkowitz, 1993; Caprara et al., 1996). **Impulsive aggression** is produced in reaction to situations and is emotion-driven: People respond with aggressive acts in the heat of the moment. If you see people get into a fistfight after a car accident, that is impulsive aggression. **Instrumental aggression** is goal-directed (the aggression serves as the *instrument* for some goal) and cognition-based: People carry out acts of aggression, with premeditated thought, to

achieve specific aims. If you see someone knock an elderly woman down to steal her purse, that is instrumental aggression. Research has confirmed that those individuals with high propensities toward one or the other of these types of violence have distinct sets of personality traits (Caprara et al., 1996). For example, individuals who reported a propensity toward impulsive aggression were likely, in general, to be characterized as high on the factor of *emotional responsivity.* That is, they were likely, in general, to report highly emotional responses to a range of situations. By contrast, individuals who reported a propensity toward instrumental aggression were likely to score high on the factor of *positive evaluation of violence.* These individuals believed that many forms of violence are justified, and they also did not accept moral responsibility for aggressive behaviors. You learn from this analysis that not all types of aggression arise from the same underlying personality factors.

Most people are not at the extremes of either impulsive or instrumental aggression: They do not lose their tempers at the least infraction or purposefully commit acts of violence. Even so, in some situations, even the most mild-mannered individuals will perform aggressive acts. We look now at the types of situations that may often provide the triggering conditions for aggression.

Situational Influences

Take a moment now to think back to the last time you engaged in aggressive behavior. It may not have been physical aggression: You may just have been verbally abusive toward some other individual, with the intent of causing psychological distress. How would you explain why that particular situation gave rise to aggression? Did you have a long history of conflict with the individual or was it just a one-time interaction? Were you inclined toward an aggressive act because of something very specific or were you just feeling frustrated at that moment? These are some of the questions researchers have asked when they've examined the links between situations and aggression. When we've asked our own students to think about their aggressive acts, they've given us a variety of answers, as you will see in what follows.

FRUSTRATION-AGGRESSION HYPOTHESIS

I'd been having a really bad day. I needed to register late for a course. I couldn't find anyone to help me. When I was told for the thousandth time, "You've got to go to a different office," I got so angry I practically kicked a hole in the door.

Impulsive aggression Emotion-driven aggression produced in reaction to situations in the "heat of the moment."

Instrumental aggression Cognition-based and goal-directed aggression carried out with premeditated thought, to achieve specific aims.

573

Why do some types of day-to-day experiences make even the calmest people contemplate aggressive acts?

This anecdote provides an instance of a general relationship captured by the **frustration-aggression hypothesis** (Dollard et al., 1939). According to this hypothesis, *frustration* occurs in situations in which people are prevented or blocked from attaining their goals; a rise in frustration then leads to a greater probability of aggression. The link between frustration and aggression has obtained a high level of empirical support (Berkowitz, 1993, 1998). For example, children who are frustrated in their expectation that they will be allowed to play with highly attractive toys act aggressively toward those toys when they finally have an opportunity to play (Barker et al., 1941). Researchers have used this relationship to explain aggression at both the personal and societal levels.

HOW WE KNOW

AGGRESSION AND THE ECONOMY Do you recognize this news story: A man gets fired from a job and goes back to kill the boss who fired him, as well as several coworkers. Could this count as an instance of frustration (that is, the frustrated goal of earning a living) leading to aggression? To provide a general answer to this question, a team of researchers examined the relationship between San Francisco's unemployment rate and the rate at which people in that city were committed for being "dangerous to others." This analysis allows for predictions across a whole community: What unemployment rate is likely to lead to the highest levels of violence? The researchers found that

violence increased as unemployment increased, but only to a certain point. When unemployment got too high, violence began to fall again. Why might that be? The researchers speculated that people's fears that they too might lose their jobs helped inhibit frustration-driven tendencies toward violence (Catalano et al., 1997).

This study suggests how individual and societal forces interact to produce a net level of violence. We can predict a certain level of aggression based on the frustration each individual experiences in an economy with rising unemployment. However, as people realize that expressions of aggression may imperil their own employment, violence is inhibited. You can probably recognize these own forces in your day-to-day experiences: There are many situations in which you might feel sufficiently frustrated to express aggression, but you also understand that an expression of aggression will work against your long-term best interest.

Frustration doesn't always lead to aggression. When, for example, the frustration is brought about unintentionally—suppose a child spills juice on his mother's new dress—people are less likely to become aggressive than when the action is intentional (Burnstein & Worchel, 1962). At the same time, other situations that are not frustrating with respect to goals, but bring about negative emotional states, can also lead to aggression. We see such a situation in another student anecdote.

TEMPERATURE AND AGGRESSION

It was a hot summer day, and the air conditioning in my car was broken. This guy cut me off. I chased after him and tried to run him off the road.

Is there a relationship between temperature and aggression? Consider the data plotted in **Figure 18.3**. This figure is taken from a study that examined the effects of temperature on assaults for a two-year period in Minneapolis, Minnesota; the plot is based on 36,617 reported assaults (Cohn & Rotton, 1997). As you can see, there is a strong relationship between how cold or hot it is and how likely it is that people will commit assaults. In fact, the figure doesn't tell quite the whole story: The relationship between temperature and assault is actually strongest in the late evening and early morning hours (that is, 9 P.M. to 3 A.M.).

Why might this be so? An explanation of these data relies on both societal and psychological forces. At a societal level, you probably guessed that it's more likely that

Frustration-aggression hypothesis According to this hypothesis, frustration occurs in situations in which people are prevented or blocked from attaining their goals; a rise in frustration then leads to a greater probability of aggression.

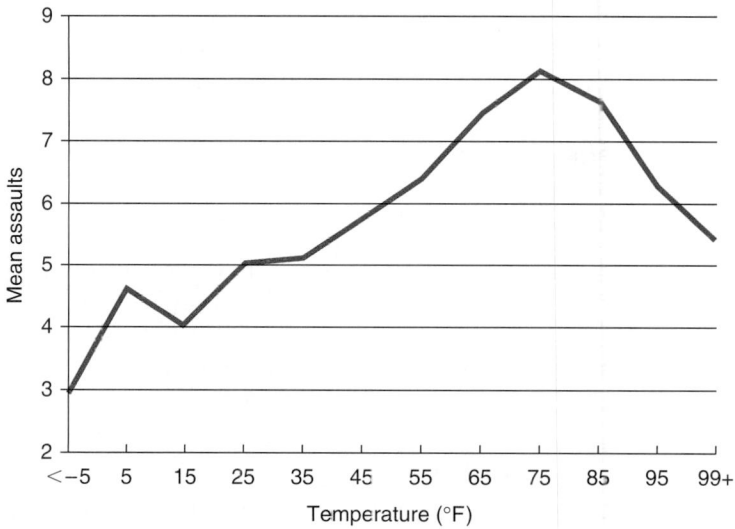

Temperature and Aggression

The figure presents average number of assaults (in a three-hour period) as a function of the temperature in that period. (°F = degrees Fahrenheit.) Aggression rises steadily as the temperature warms up to about 75°F.

people will commit assault when they are more likely to be out and about. That is, in warmer weather, people are more likely to be outdoors and, therefore, are also more likely to be "available" as assault victims. You can also provide the same analysis for time of day: In the 9 P.M. to 3 A.M. hours, people are typically less constrained by work or other responsibilities. Furthermore, by the late evening hours, people may have been drinking alcohol or using other substances that lower their inhibition for aggression (Ito et al., 1996).

Given all these societal explanations for increased aggression, do we also need to invoke psychology? The answer is "yes." Another important component of an explanation for the data in Figure 18.3 is the way in which people cope with and interpret the discomfort associated with high temperatures. Recall the discussion of appraisal and emotions in Chapter 13. Suppose on a 75-degree day you're having a conversation with someone that makes you feel hot and uncomfortable. Do you attribute the emotion to the temperature or to your adversary? To the extent that you misattribute your emotion to another person, rather than to the situation, you're more likely to become aggressive toward that person. (You might recognize this from Chapter 17 as a dangerous consequence of the fundamental attribution error.) Why does heat matter most in the late evening and early morning? As the day goes on, it may become harder to remember "I'm feeling this way because it's hot" and not just conclude "I'm feeling this way because this bozo is making me crazy." If all of this is true, why does Figure 18.3 show a decline in assaults when temperatures become very hot? Researchers have speculated that at very high temperatures, people might experience sufficient discomfort to withdraw from abrasive situations rather than stay and fight (Cohn & Rotton, 1997).

A third student anecdote illustrates how situations elicit hostility that gets amplified over time.

DIRECT PROVOCATION AND ESCALATION

I was sitting in the library trying to get some work done. These two women were having a really loud conversation that was bothering a lot of people. I asked them to quiet down, and they pretty much ignored me. I asked again about five minutes later, and they only started talking louder. Finally, I told them they were both stupid, ugly jerks and that if they didn't shut up I was going to pick them up and throw them out of the library. That worked.

It's not going to surprise you that *direct provocation* will also give rise to aggression. That is, when someone behaves in a way that makes you angry or upset—and you think that behavior was intentional—you are more likely to respond with some form of physical or verbal aggression (Johnson & Rule, 1986). The effects of direct provocation are consistent with the general idea that situations that produce negative affect will lead to aggression. The intentionality of the act matters because you are less likely to interpret an unintentional act in a negative way. (Recall that we made the similar observation that frustration is less likely to lead to aggression when it is brought about unintentionally.)

A second characteristic of this anecdote, beyond provocation, is *escalation:* Because less intense responses to the provocation had no effect, the student's response became more aggressive over time.

HOW WE KNOW

ESCALATION IN RESPONSE TO PERSISTENT ANNOYANCE In one study, two groups of individuals had to share resources to complete a task assigned to them by the experimenters. However, because the members of one group were, in actuality, the experimenters' confederates, they

refused to cooperate. The experimenters recorded the genuine participants' verbal attempts (via an intercom that connected the two rooms) to elicit resource sharing. Attempts began with *demanding statements* (for example, "We need it now"), and moved through *angry statements* (for example, "I'm really getting annoyed with you") all the way to *abusive statements* (for example, "You guys are total jerks"). In fact, the strength of the groups' responses followed a very orderly sequence of escalation. The experimenters suggested that people have learned an *escalation script*. This memory structure encodes cultural norms for the sequence with which people should ratchet up the aggressiveness of their responses to continuing provocation (Mikolic et al., 1997).

Can you see how the escalation script also refers back to the relationship between frustration and aggression? The failures of the initial attempts to change the situation likely lead to feelings of frustration that also will increase the likelihood of more intense aggression.

We've now considered some of the situational forces that may lead you to produce psychological or physical aggression. It's important to note that our examples all refer to impulsive aggression rather than to instrumental aggression. As we explained earlier, instrumental aggression refers to circumstances in which people use aggression to achieve an end—for example, when muggers use physical force to commit their crimes. That type of aggression must be explained as a component of a larger theory of criminality. We have been concerned here largely with circumstances in which ordinary individuals find themselves committing impulsive aggressive acts. In the next section, we will see, even so, that cultural differences constrain levels of both individual and criminal aggression.

Cultural Constraints

We have seen so far that aggressive behaviors are part of your evolutionary inheritance and that certain situations are more likely to evoke aggressive behavior. Even so, several types of data suggest that the probability that an individual will display aggression is highly constrained by cultural values and norms (Segall et al., 1997). To make this point, we need go no further than comparisons between the murder rate in the United States and other countries: You are seven to ten times more likely to be murdered in the United States than in most European countries (Lore & Schultz, 1993). What psychological forces give rise to such a vast difference in murder rates? If you are a citizen of the United States, you should have considerable interest in answers to this question.

CONSTRUALS OF THE SELF AND AGGRESSIVE BEHAVIOR

To begin an examination of culture and aggression, we return to a distinction in cultural construals of the self that has loomed large in several places in *Psychology and Life:* As explained earlier, most Western cultures embody *independent construals of self,* whereas most Eastern cultures embody *interdependent construals of self* (Markus & Kitayama, 1991). What are the consequences for aggressive behavior? Studies have shown that if you think of yourself as fundamentally interconnected with other members of your culture, you will be less likely to respond aggressively—an act of aggression, after all, would be an act against your "self."

HOW WE KNOW

AGGRESSION AMONG JAPANESE AND UNITED STATES CHILDREN One good way to gauge the effects of culture is to see how young children from different cultures have learned to respond to the same situation. Japanese and U.S. preschoolers, average age roughly 4½ years, were presented with stories including *conflict dilemmas* and were asked to use dolls to act out endings to the stories. For example, each child was asked to act out what might happen next after two children begin to argue and shove each other. The U.S. children scored considerably higher both on measures of aggressive verbalizations—U.S. children were more likely to say things such as "I hate you"—and aggressive behaviors—U.S. children were more likely to act out behaviors with the dolls such as pushing and hitting (Zahn-Waxler et al., 1996).

This experiment suggests that the Japanese children have already internalized the cultural norm of interdependence: They have already internalized the cultural sanctions against bringing harm to others. The United States children, by contrast, show evidence for a sense of independent self that must be protected from others' insults.

Although we have identified this major cultural divide between independence and interdependence, it is also possible to find more fine-grained cultural differences nested within this overarching perspective. For example, **Richard Nisbett** (Nisbett & Cohen, 1996) and his colleagues have extensively studied regional attitudes and behaviors within the United States with respect to uses of aggression. One consistent difference that has emerged is that southern behavior is guided by a *culture of honor,* in which "even small disputes become contests for reputation and social status" (Cohen et al., 1996, p. 945). The culture of honor doesn't sanction all forms of aggression—only those aggressive behaviors that are used to protect property or redress personal insults (Cohen & Nisbett, 1994).

Why might Gandhi's philosophy of nonviolent resistance have been particularly appropriate for the culture of India?

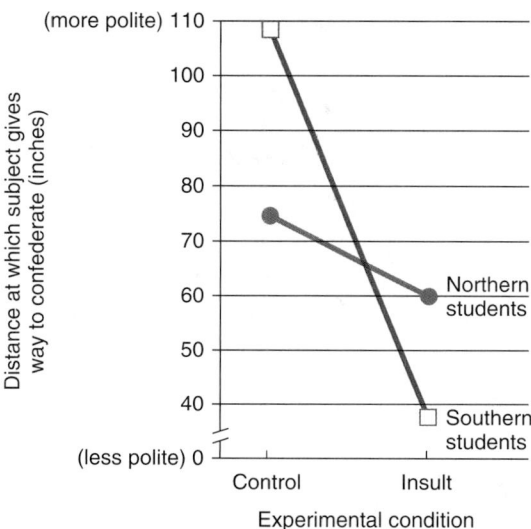

FIGURE 18.4

The Effects of Insults on Northerners and Southerners

Northern and southern students in the experimental group suffered a minor insult. Although southerners were more polite without an insult, they became considerably less likely to give way in a game of "chicken" after they had been insulted.

HOW WE KNOW

NORTHERN AND SOUTHERN RESPONSES TO INSULTS Researchers arranged for male college students—northerners and southerners—to endure a mild insult: While the participant walked down a hallway, an experimental confederate bumped each participant with his shoulder and called him an "asshole." (Students in the control group did not experience this event.) The researchers predicted that southerners would react more dramatically than their northern peers to the bump and insult. One measure the researchers used to gauge the students' reactions was based on the game of "chicken" in which two people drive toward each other until one swerves out of the way. In this case, a second confederate marched directly at each approaching participant. The researchers measured how close each participant got to the confederate before he changed path. As you can see in **Figure 18.4**, the mild insult had a dramatic effect on southern students' behavior. Without an insult, they were actually more polite than the northerners—they "gave way" sooner. However, when southerners had been bumped, they turned away considerably later (Cohen et al., 1996).

Many people in the United States share the general sense that southern culture is more polite than northern culture—you'd rather ask directions from someone in Richmond than someone in New York City. This experiment echos that belief, in the sense that southerners in the control group made way for the confederate earlier than did their northern peers. However, this general aura of politeness broke down quite quickly when an attack had been made on the students' sense of honor. Thus, even within the overarching independent construal of self that characterizes most United States citizens, southern males react more sharply when that sense of self is challenged and their "honor" is on the line (Nisbett & Cohen, 1996).

NORMS OF AGGRESSIVE BEHAVIOR

We have suggested so far that cultures that embody independent construals of self are more likely to give rise to aggressive behavior. This observation, however, doesn't explain the difference in murder rates we cited earlier: The European countries whose murder rates are vastly lower than that in the United States mostly share the same overarching independent culture. What other cultural forces are at work?

One major factor that has been identified for the United States is the availability of aggressive models in the environment. In Chapter 7, we discussed research suggesting that children very readily adapt aggressive behaviors from watching adult models. For example, children who watched adult models punching, hitting, and

kicking a large plastic BoBo doll later showed a greater frequency of the same behaviors than did children in control conditions who had not observed the aggressive models (Bandura et al., 1963). We also suggested in Chapter 7 that television in the United States beams an enormous number of aggressive models directly into children's homes—exposure to violence fosters imitation (Comstock & Scharrer, 1999). The effects of televised violence may be particularly salient in the United States. One study suggested that U.S. children are particularly "pro-TV"—dependent on TV—by comparison to children in Germany (Smith & Schutte, 1982). One way to decrease levels of aggression in the United States, then, would be to severely limit children's access to these aggressive models, both on television and in movies.

Of course, for many children models for aggression present themselves as part of day-to-day experience. Children may be exposed to aggressive acts in their homes: We noted in Chapter 7 that children who are physically punished often come themselves to use aggression as a tactic for controlling others' behaviors. Children may also be exposed to aggressive acts in their communities. For example, one study examined the stories produced by children who had experienced the riots in Los Angeles that followed the first Rodney King trial in 1992 (Farver & Frosch, 1996). Compared to children who had no exposure to riots, these L.A. children produced narratives with more unfriendly figures, more aggressive words, more physically aggressive characters, and more characters who used aggression to master situations.

It is important to note that all the children were merely playing with toys in the company of pleasant experimenters: Clearly, aggressive images loom large in the imaginations of children exposed to the riots. The L.A. riots were violent, but they occurred for a limited period of time. Unfortunately, many children in the United States grow up in inner-city communities in which violence is daily and chronic (Osofsky, 1997; Schwartz & Proctor, 2000). Researchers have only begun to explore the consequences of exposure to violence for children's mental health and their inclination to aggressive behavior.

We end this section on cultural norms for aggressive behavior by noting that those norms can be quite local and quite stable. Consider two adjacent Zapotec villages in the state of Oaxaca, Mexico (Scott, 1992). One of the villages is violent and the other nonviolent: The violent village has a murder rate five times as great as the nonviolent village. The villages have been on the same spots since at least the 1500s; they are highly similar with respect to religion and economics. More or less, the only explana-

tion for their differing characters is the stability of culture: One way or another each village has acquired a characteristic level of violence, and that has stayed stable over time. This is a salient real-world example of the processes of norm transmission and preservation we described in Chapter 17. Similarly, with its modern modes of mass communication, the United States has become a very large village that preserves norms of aggressive behavior.

In this section we have described forces that give rise to aggression, ranging from genetics to cultures. However, one idea that we have not yet touched on is that people sometimes commit aggression against other individuals for reasons of *prejudice*—just because those individuals are members of other racial or ethnic groups (or groups defined in any way as "other"). We turn now to the topic of prejudice and document both how it comes about and procedures that may be effective to reduce or eliminate it.

SUMMING UP

Evolutionary analyses suggest that the human propensity for aggressive behaviors arose so that, for example, people could protect themselves and their offspring. Research has revealed a genetic component to individual differences in aggression as well as biological and personality differences associated with propensities toward different types of aggression. When people experience frustration with respect to their goals, they are more likely to engage in aggressive behaviors. Features of the environment, like the temperature, also can change the likelihood of aggression. People will respond aggressively to direct, intentional provocation, and their aggressive behaviors will escalate when less intense responses have no effect. The prevalence of aggressive behavior in a culture is related to independent or interdependent construals of the self. Some cultures also provide models that support the appropriateness of aggressive behavior.

Prejudice

Of all human weaknesses, none is more destructive of the dignity of the individual and the social bonds of humanity than prejudice. Prejudice is the prime example of social reality gone awry—a situation created in the minds of people that can demean and destroy the lives of others. **Prejudice** is a learned attitude toward a target object, involving negative feelings (dislike or fear), negative beliefs (stereotypes) that justify the attitude, and a behavioral intention to avoid, control, dominate, or eliminate those in the target group. Nazi leaders, for example, passed laws to enforce their prejudiced beliefs that Jews were subhuman and trying

Prejudice A learned attitude toward a target object, involving negative affect (dislike or fear), negative beliefs (stereotypes) that justify the attitude, and a behavioral intention to avoid, control, dominate, or eliminate the target object.

How did Kenneth Clark contribute to the end of segregated schooling?

How does prejudice arise, and why is it so difficult to eradicate?

to bring about the downfall of Aryan culture. A false belief qualifies as prejudice when it resists change even in the face of appropriate evidence of its falseness. People display prejudice, for example, when they assert that African Americans are all lazy despite their hardworking African American colleagues. Prejudiced attitudes serve as biasing filters that influence the way individuals are perceived and treated once they are categorized as members of a target group.

Social psychology has always put the study of prejudice high on its agenda in an effort to understand its complexity and persistence and to develop strategies to change prejudiced attitudes and discriminatory behavior (Allport, 1954; Duckitt, 1992; Jones, 1997). Recall from Chapter 1 that the Supreme Court's 1954 decision to outlaw segregated public education was, in part, based on research, presented in federal court by social psychologist **Kenneth Clark,** that showed the negative impact on black children of their separate and unequal education (Clark & Clark, 1947). In this section, we will describe the progress social psychologists have made in their efforts to understand the origins and effects of prejudice, as well as their efforts to help reverse its effects.

Origins of Prejudice

One of the sad truths from the study of prejudice is that it is easy to get people to show negative attitudes

Social categorization The process by which people organize the social environment by categorizing themselves and others into groups.
In-groups The groups with which people identify as members.
Out-groups The groups with which people do not identify.
In-group bias An evaluation of one's own group as better than others.

toward people who do not belong to the same "group." **Social categorization** is the process by which people organize their social environment by categorizing themselves and others into groups. The simplest and most pervasive form of categorizing consists of an individual determining whether people are like him or her. This categorization develops from a "me versus not me" orientation to an "us versus them" orientation: People divide the world into **in-groups**—the groups with which they identify as members—and **out-groups**—the groups with which they do not identify. These cognitive distinctions result in an **in-group bias,** an evaluation of one's own group as better than others (Jones, 1997). People defined as part of the out-group almost instantly are candidates for hostile feelings and unfair treatment.

The most minimal of distinctive cues is sufficient to trigger the formation of bias and prejudice against those in an out-group.

HOW WE KNOW

RANDOM ASSIGNMENT CREATES GROUP SOLIDARITY In a series of experiments in Holland, participants were randomly divided into two groups: a blue group and a green group. According to the participants' group membership, they were given either blue or green pens and asked to write on either blue or green paper. The experimenter addressed participants in terms of their group color. Even though these color categories had no intrinsic psychological significance and assignment to the groups was

What is at work even in this "color" experiment is the
very swift action of social categorization.

Many experiments have examined the consequences
of *minimal groups,* like the "blue" versus "green" distinction (Tajfel, 1982; Tajfel & Billig, 1974). The members of
the different groups most often start out as strangers, but
almost instantly they show astonishing solidarity—they
believe the members of their in-group to be more pleasant and harder workers. When the time comes to share
resources, people do everything they can to deny benefits
to members of the out-group. These consequences develop regardless of limited exposure to the out-groups
and despite the positive experiences of individual in-
group members with particular members of the out-
group (Park & Rothbart, 1982; Quattrone, 1986).

If all these forces apply in these artificially constituted groups, you can begin to understand how prejudice can become so severe under situations of real-world
pressure. Prejudice easily leads to **racism**—discrimination against people based on their skin color or ethnic
heritage—and **sexism**—discrimination against people

■ **Racism** Discrimination against people based on their skin color or
ethnic heritage.
■ **Sexism** Discrimination against people because of their sex.

---

based on their sex. The instant tendency toward defining
"us" against "them" becomes even more powerful when
the perception grows that resources are scarce and
that goods can be given only to one group, at the expense of the other. In fact, people who express a high
degree of prejudice are much more careful about making judgments about who belongs to which categories of
humanity.

HOW WE KNOW

**PREJUDICE AND RACIAL CATEGORY
JUDGMENTS** A group of undergraduates
completed a scale that measured their attitudes
toward African Americans. Based on their
responses, half of the group was classified as
prejudiced and the other half nonprejudiced. Next,
all the students were asked to view a series of faces
and label them aloud as either "white" or "black."
Some of the faces were easily classified, whereas
other faces were ambiguous. The researchers
hypothesized that prejudiced individuals care more
about making "correct" racial judgments. Thus,
the researchers predicted that the prejudiced
students would take longer to provide answers
for the ambiguous faces. In fact, prejudiced
individuals took almost a second longer than
the nonprejudiced individuals when making
judgments of the ambiguous faces (Blascovich et
al., 1997).

This experiment suggests how important it is to individuals with prejudiced attitudes to define who qualifies as
"us" and who qualifies as "them." Recently, researchers

Why might prejudiced beliefs
affect individuals' ability to
categorize these racially
ambiguous faces?

have begun to develop an explicit measure of *nonprejudice* that captures the idea that people without prejudice are less likely to focus on the differences among individuals (Phillips & Ziller, 1997). People who fall high on the *universal orientation scale* tend to endorse statements such as "When I meet someone I tend to notice similarities between myself and the other person" and reject statements such as "I can tell a great deal about a person by knowing their gender." Thus, some people appear to have a fundamental ability to overcome the tendency to experience the world in terms of in-groups and out-groups.

We have seen so far that people's categorization of the world into "us" and "them" can swiftly lead to prejudice. Let's look at the way in which prejudice functions through applications of stereotypes.

Effects of Stereotypes

We can use the power of social categorization to explain the origins of many types of prejudice. To explain how prejudice affects day-to-day interactions, we must explore the memory structures that provide important support for prejudice, stereotypes. **Stereotypes** are generalizations about a group of people in which the same characteristics are assigned to all members of a group. You are no doubt familiar with a wide range of stereotypes. What beliefs do you have about men and women? Jews, Muslims, and Christians? Asians, African Americans, Native Americans, Hispanics, and Caucasians? How do those beliefs affect your day-to-day interactions with members of those groups? Do you avoid members of some of these groups based on your beliefs?

Because stereotypes so powerfully encode *expectations*, they frequently contribute to the types of situations we described in Chapter 17, in which people construct their own social reality. Consider the potential role stereotypes play to generate judgments about what "exists" in the environment. People are prone to fill in "missing data" with information from their stereotypes: "I'm not going to get in a car with Hiroshi—all Asians are terrible drivers." Similarly, people may knowingly or unknowingly use stereotypical information to produce *behavioral confirmation*. If, for example, you reason that Jewish friends are likely to be cheap, you may never give them opportunities to prove otherwise. Worse than that, to maintain consistency, people are likely to discount information that is inconsistent with their stereotyped beliefs.

classified students as having high or low prejudice toward homosexuals. Each student subsequently read a pair of scientific studies about homosexuality. One of those studies concluded that, consistent with the stereotype, homosexuality is associated with cross-gender behaviors. The other study came to the stereotype-inconsistent conclusion that homosexuality is not associated with cross-gender behaviors. When the high- and low-prejudice students evaluated the *quality* of each study, they gave consistently higher ratings to the study that supported their point of view. For example, high-prejudice students found more merit in the study that supported the cross-gender stereotype. Furthermore, as a consequence of reading a pair of studies that were intended to exactly balance each other out, the students on average reported that their beliefs had shifted further in the direction of their original attitudes (Munro & Ditto, 1997).

This experiment suggests why information alone can typically not reduce prejudice: People tend to devalue information that is inconsistent with their prior stereotype. (We will see in the next section more successful methods for overcoming prejudice.)

Let us remind you about another effect of stereotypes that we introduced in the context of intelligence testing. Recall that in Chapter 10, we discussed racial differences among IQ scores. In that section, we reviewed evidence that suggests that members of stereotyped groups suffer from what **Claude Steele** and his colleagues have called *stereotype threat* (Steele, 1997; Steele & Aronson, 1995, 1998). Stereotype threat occurs when people are placed in situations to which negative aspects of stereotypes are relevant. For example, in Chapter 10, we provided evidence that African Americans' performance on aptitude tests is impaired when they believe the outcome of the test is relevant to the stereotype of black underachievement. We remind you of this result here to emphasize the forces that sustain negative stereotypes—and the way they deform the lives of people who are stereotyped.

Even if you do not believe yourself to be a prejudiced person, you still are likely aware of the stereotypes that exist in contemporary society. Knowledge of these stereotypes might prompt you to use them in some ways, below the level of conscious awareness (Devine & Monteith, 1999). Even people whose explicit beliefs are not prejudiced may produce automatic acts of prejudice as a function of the messages they have unknowingly internalized from many sources in their current and earlier environments. Consider your best friends: Do they

Stereotypes Generalizations about a group of people in which the same characteristics are assigned to all members of a group.

belong to the same ethnic group as you do? If so, why might this be the case?

We have come to the rather troubling conclusion that prejudice is easy to create and difficult to remove. Even so, from the earliest days of social psychology, researchers have attempted to reverse the march of prejudice. Let's now sample some of those efforts.

Reversing Prejudice

One of the classic studies in social psychology was also the first demonstration that arbitrary "us" versus "them" divisions could lead to great hostility. In the summer of 1954, **Muzafer Sherif** and his colleagues (1961/1988) brought two groups of boys to a summer camp at Robbers Cave State Park in Oklahoma. The two groups were dubbed the "Eagles" and the "Rattlers." Each group forged its own camp bonds—for example, the boys hiked, swam, and prepared meals together—in ignorance of the other group for about a week. The groups' introduction to each other consisted of a series of competitive activities like baseball, football, and a tug-of-war. From this beginning, the rivalry between the groups grew violent. Group flags were burned, cabins were ransacked, and a near-riotlike food fight broke out. What could be done to reduce this animosity?

HOW WE KNOW

THE IMPORTANCE OF INTERDEPENDENCE
The experimenters tried a propaganda approach, by complimenting each group to the other. That did not work. The experimenters tried bringing the groups together in noncompetitive circumstances. That did not work either. Hostility seethed even when the groups were just watching a movie in the same place. Finally, the experimenters hit on a solution. What they did was to introduce problems that could be solved only through *cooperative action* on *shared goals*. For example, the experimenters arranged for the camp truck to break down. Both groups of boys were needed to pull it back up a steep hill. In the face of mutual dependence, hostility faded away. In fact, the boys started to make "best friends" across group boundaries.

The Robbers Cave experiment disproved the **contact hypothesis**—the idea that direct contact between hostile groups alone will reduce prejudice (Allport, 1954). The boys did not like each other any better just by being in each others' company. Instead, the experiment suggested that a program combating prejudice must foster personal interaction in the pursuit of shared goals. Take a moment to consider how you might apply these lessons to situations that matter to you. Suppose, for example, that you are managing employees who cannot get along. What intervention might you design?

More recently, social psychologist **Elliot Aronson** and his colleagues (1978) developed a program anchored in the Robbers Cave philosophy to tackle prejudice in newly desegregated classrooms in Texas and California. The research team created conditions in which fifth-grade students had to depend on one another rather than compete against one another to learn required material.

In the intergroup competition phase of the Robbers Cave experiment, the "Eagles" and "Rattlers" pulled apart—but in the end, they pulled together. What general conclusions about contact and prejudice can be drawn from this study?

Contact hypothesis The idea that direct contact between hostile groups alone will reduce prejudice.

In a strategy known as the *jigsaw technique,* each pupil is given part of the total material to master and then share with other group members. Performance is evaluated on the basis of the overall group presentation. Thus, every member's contribution is essential and valued.

Interracial conflict has decreased in **jigsaw classrooms**—classes in which jigsawing has united formerly hostile white, Latino, and African American students in a common-fate team (Aronson & Gonzalez, 1988; Gonzalez, 1983). Consider the story of one young boy named Carlos. Carlos, who had been ignored because his primary language was not English, was assigned a vital part of the team assignment on Joseph Pulitzer. The other teammates had to figure out how to get him to share the information he was responsible for providing. In response to his teammates' patience and encouraging comments, Carlos felt needed, developed affection for the group members, and also discovered that learning was fun. Both his self-esteem and his grades increased. (We are happy to report that Carlos went on to Harvard Law School after graduating from a Texas college.)

Although most of our examples have looked at prejudice within the United States, virtually every society defines in-groups and out-groups. To complete this section on reversing prejudice, we turn to a study that is international in scope—and one that is remarkably upbeat in its conclusions. **Thomas Pettigrew** (1997) examined data from nearly 4,000 people in France, the Netherlands, England, and the former West Germany to test hypotheses in the tradition of the Robbers Cave study: Specifically, he wished to further define the types of contact that lead to lower prejudice.

HOW WE KNOW

FRIENDSHIP REDUCES PREJUDICE In each country, participants were asked to provide their attitudes toward members of a particular minority (for example, English participants were asked about West Indians; German participants were asked about Turks). They were also asked to provide information about the types of contact they had had with people who belonged to other nationalities, races, religions, cultures, or social classes. Were they friends with members of other groups? Neighbors? Coworkers? The results of the study were quite dramatic. When people reported themselves to be *friends* with members of out-groups they showed reliably lower levels of prejudice.

With its cross-cultural scope, this study supports the very strong conclusion that friendship with out-group members can lead to the elimination of prejudice. Why is friendship so effective? Friendships allow people to learn about out-group members: They may come to identify and empathize with out-group members. Friendships may also foster a process of *deprovinicialization:* When people learn more about out-group social norms and customs, they may become less "provincial" about the correctness of their in-group processes.

Social psychology has no great solution to end prejudice all at once. It does, however, provide a set of ideas to eliminate prejudice's worst effects slowly but surely, in each small locality. It is worth taking a moment to contemplate the prejudices you have enforced or endured—to see how you might begin to make adjustments in your own small locality.

SUMMING UP

A sad reality of prejudice is that even the most minimal of distinctive cues is sufficient for the formation of harmful bias. Research shows that social categorization quickly turns strangers into cohesive groups that perceive their own in-group members more positively than out-group members. Stereotypes constrain people's experiences of "reality." Sherif's Robbers Cave experiment showed that prejudice can be reduced by programs that foster interaction in pursuit of shared goals. The technique of jigsawing puts this insight into practice in the classroom. Research generates the upbeat conclusion that prejudice is diminished when friendships form among members of different groups.

The Psychology of Conflict and Peace

We have seen in the last two sections that aggression and prejudice arise all too often in human experience. What is truly calamitous is the intersection of these two forces: In the 21st century, the globe is still littered with instances of catastrophic violence born from religious, racial, and cultural prejudice. What can be done? In the opening chapter of *Psychology and Life,* we characterized psychologists as a "rather optimistic group" because they believe that the theories and results of psychology can be used to better people's lives. In these final sections of *Psychology and Life,* we wish to carry through on that optimistic message. Although we will begin by documenting more of the psychological forces that can lead to devastating behaviors, that discussion will generate insights that can form the basis for

Jigsaw classrooms Classrooms that use a technique known as jigsawing, in which each pupil is given part of the total material to master and then share with other group members.

THE WORLD GROWS SMALLER

One of the most commonplace observations about the Internet is that it has made the world seem smaller. Many of us now trade e-mails or chat-room observations with individuals spread all across the globe. As even larger portions of the world's population obtain Web access, this practice will only grow. For example, one of the major nonsports stories that emerged from the 2000 Olympics in Sydney was about the Internet. The village in which the athletes were housed was heavily wired, allowing many of the worlds' athletes their first opportunity to cruise the Web. One media report noted that Cuban athletes—who previously had no Web experience—put up more than 160 home pages in a single week (Gordon, 2000). One of the questions psychologists and other social scientists will surely address in the 21st century is how the Web adapts to local culture and how local culture adapts to the Web.

Consider the way in which the introduction of Internet access has—and has not—affected life in Kuwait (Wheeler, 1998). As in many coun-

tries, the Web first became available to individuals in an academic setting, in this case at Kuwait University. However, in short order, the Web became more generally available. In some respects, Kuwaitis' use of the Web resembles Internet use the world over: People use the Internet largely to chat; users report having relationships and romances in cyberspace. However, there is one strong respect in which Kuwaitis are dissimilar from their peers: "Many surf the Internet, but few publish": "In Kuwait, information is more of a potential threat than a means for individual empowerment. It is a weapon to use against your enemies, a tool for keeping conformity, or a reinforcement of the regulations of daily life" (Wheeler, 1998, pp. 365–366). Given this cultural constraint, it is quite unlikely that Kuwaitis will use the Internet as an avenue for the self-exploration common among their peers in other countries.

Researchers have also explored more specific cultural differences with respect to people's preferences for different features of Web sites. Although the same site may be accessible to indi-

viduals all the world over, cultural constraints affect how comprehensible and appreciated the site will be (Sears et al., 2000). For example, the graphics on many Web sites provide a left-to-right, top-to-bottom flow of information that parallels the order in which people read languages such as English. However, readers of Chinese or Hebrew—which use a different spatial layout—may find such sites somewhat difficult to follow (O'Donnell, 1994). In general, Web site designers may discover that they need social science assistance to "internationalize" their products. A site that is highly appreciated by one group may be rejected by another group because it is, for example, too aggressive or complex in its design to suit local norms (Sears et al., 2000). To build sites that have truly cross-cultural appeal, Web designers will have to acquire knowledge of the types of cultural differences we've explored in *Psychology and Life*.

As a citizen of the 21st century, you are a participant in a shrinking world. What consequences do *you* foresee? What questions should psychologists address?

---

constructive change. Our endpoint will be a discussion of *peace psychology*, a multidisciplinary effort to use social science knowledge to further the cause of world peace. This is the note of optimism on which we wish you to end your first experience of psychology.

We begin with perhaps the most classic study in the social psychological canon—research carried out by **Stanley Milgram** in an effort to understand some of the vast horrors of World War II.

Obedience to Authority

What made thousands of Nazis willing to follow Hitler's orders and send millions of Jews to the gas chambers? Did character defects lead them to carry out orders blindly? Did they have no moral values? How can we explain the

willingness of cult members to take their own lives and the lives of others (a topic on which we elaborate in the Psychology in Your Life box on page 588)? How about you? Are there any conditions under which you would blindly obey an order from your religious leader to poison others and then commit suicide? Could you imagine being part of the massacre of hundreds of innocent citizens of the Vietnamese village of My Lai by U.S. soldiers who were following the orders of their superiors (Hersh, 1971; Opton, 1970, 1973)? Your answer—as ours used to be—is most likely, "No! What kind of person do you think I am?" After reading this section, we hope you may be more willing to answer, "Maybe. I don't know for sure." Depending on the power of the social forces operating, you might do what other human beings have done in those situations, however horrible and alien their actions may seem—to you and to them—outside that setting.

The most convincing demonstration of situational power over individual behavior was created by Stanley Milgram, a student of Solomon Asch. Milgram's research (1965, 1974) showed that the blind obedience of Nazis during World War II was less a product of dispositional characteristics (their unusual personality or German national character) than it was the outcome of situational forces that could engulf anyone. How did he demonstrate what Arendt had termed the "banality of evil"—that evil deeds could emerge from ordinary people who were not monstrous but simply following orders mindlessly, without thought (Arendt, 1963, 1971)? Milgram's program of obedience research is one of the most controversial because of its significant implications for real-world phenomena and the ethical issues it raises (Miller, 1986; Ross & Nisbett, 1991).

THE OBEDIENCE PARADIGM

To separate the variables of personality and situation, Milgram used a series of 19 separate controlled laboratory experiments involving more than 1,000 participants. Milgram's first experiments were conducted at Yale University, with male residents of New Haven and surrounding communities who received payment for their participation. In later variations, Milgram took his obedience laboratory away from the university. He set up a storefront research unit in Bridgeport, Connecticut, recruiting through newspaper ads a broad cross section of the population, varying widely in age, occupation, and education and including members of both sexes.

Milgram's basic experimental paradigm involved individual participants delivering a series of what they thought were extremely painful electric shocks to another person. These volunteers thought they were participating in a scientific study of memory and learning. They were led to believe that the educational purpose of the study was to discover how punishment affects memory, so that learning could be improved through the proper balance of reward and punishment. In their *so-cial roles* as *teachers,* the participants were to punish each error made by someone playing the role of *learner.* The major rule they were told to follow was to increase the level of shock each time the learner made an error until the learning was errorless. The white-coated experimenter acted as the *legitimate authority* figure—he presented the rules, arranged for the assignment of roles (by a rigged drawing of lots), and ordered the teachers to do their jobs whenever they hesitated or dissented. The dependent variable was the final level of shock—on a shock machine that went up to 450 volts in small, 15-volt steps—that a teacher gave before refusing to continue to obey the authority.

THE TEST SITUATION

The study was staged to make a participant think that, by following orders, he or she was causing pain and suffering and perhaps even killing an innocent person. Each teacher had been given a sample shock of 45 volts to feel the amount of pain it caused. The learner was a pleasant, mild-mannered man, about 50 years old, who mentioned something about a heart condition but was willing to go along with the procedure. He was strapped into an "electric chair" in the next room and communicated with the teacher via an intercom. His task was to memorize pairs of words, giving the second word in a pair when he heard the first one. The learner soon began making errors—according to a prearranged schedule—and the teacher began shocking the learner. The protests of the victim rose with the shock level. At 75 volts, he began to moan and grunt; at 150 volts, he demanded to be released from the experiment; at 180 volts, he cried out that he could not stand the pain any longer. At 300 volts, he insisted that he would no longer take part in the experiment and must be freed. He yelled out about his heart condition and screamed. If a teacher hesitated or protested delivering the next shock, the experimenter said, "The experiment requires that you continue" or "You have no other choice, you *must* go on."

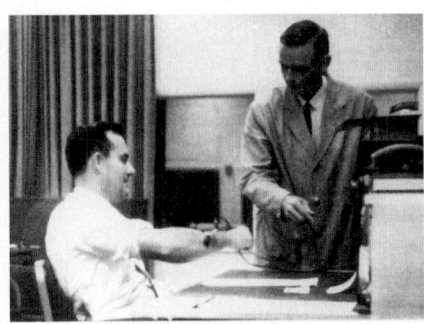  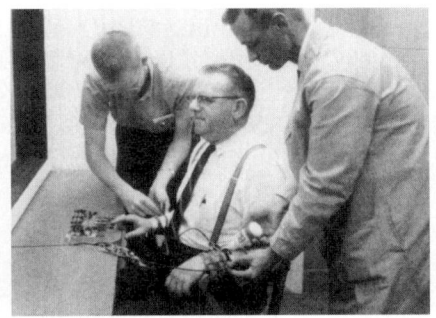

Milgram's obedience experiment: the "teacher" (participant) with experimenter (authority figure), the shock generator, and the "learner" (the experimenter's confederate). What aspects of the situation affected the likelihood that the teachers would continue to the maximum shock level?

As you might imagine, the situation was stressful for the participants. Most participants complained and protested, repeatedly insisting they could not continue. Women participants often were in tears as they dissented. That the experimental situation produced considerable conflict in the participants is readily apparent from their protests:

- 180 volts delivered: "He can't stand it! I'm not going to kill that man in there! You hear him hollering? He's hollering. He can't stand it. What if something happens to him?... I mean, who is going to take the responsibility if anything happens to that gentleman?" [The experimenter accepts responsibility.] "All right."

- 195 volts delivered: "You see he's hollering. Hear that. Gee, I don't know." [The experimenter says, "The experiment requires that you go on."] "I know it does, sir, but I mean—huh—he don't know what he's in for. He's up to 195 volts" (Milgram, 1965, p. 67).

Even when there was only silence from the learner's room, the teacher was ordered to keep shocking him more and more strongly, all the way up to the button that was marked "Danger: Severe Shock XXX (450 volts)."

TO SHOCK OR NOT TO SHOCK?

When 40 psychiatrists were asked by Milgram to predict the performance of participants in this experiment, they estimated that most would not go beyond 150 volts (based on a description of the experiment). In their professional opinions, fewer than 4 percent of the participants would still be obedient at 300 volts, and only about 0.1 percent would continue all the way to 450 volts. The psychiatrists presumed that only those few individuals who were *abnormal* in some way, sadists who enjoyed inflicting pain on others, would blindly obey orders to continue up to the maximum shock.

The psychiatrists based their evaluations on presumed *dispositional* qualities of people who would engage in such abnormal behavior; they were, however, overlooking the power of this special situation to influence the thinking and actions of most people caught up in its social context. The remarkable and disturbing conclusion is just how wrong these experts were: *The majority of participants obeyed the authority fully.* No participant quit below 300 volts. Sixty-five percent delivered the maximum 450 volts to the learner. Note that most people *dissented* verbally, but the majority did not *disobey* behaviorally. From the point of view of the victim, that's a critical difference. If you were the victim, would it matter much that the participants said they didn't want

to continue hurting you (they dissented), if they then shocked you repeatedly (they obeyed)?

The results of the Milgram studies were so unexpected that researchers worked hard to rule out alternative interpretations of the results. One possibility was that the participants did not really believe the "cover story" of the experiment. They might have believed that the victim was not really getting hurt. This alternative was ruled out by a study that made the effects of being obedient vivid, immediate, and direct for the participants. College students thought they were training a puppy by shocking him each time he made a mistake. The students actually saw the puppy jump and heard him squeal each time they pressed a button to activate an electrified grid beneath his paws. How many people would continue to shock the puppy and watch him suffer? Even under these vivid circumstances, three-fourths of all students delivered the maximum shock possible (Sheridan & King, 1972).

Another alternative explanation for participants' behavior is that the effect is limited to the *demand characteristics* of the experimental situation. **Demand characteristics** are cues in an experimental setting that influence participants' perceptions of what is expected of them and systematically influence their behavior. Suppose Milgram's participants guessed that his results would be more interesting if they kept giving shocks—so they played along. Further research showed that obedience to authority does not rely on the demands of an unusual experimental setting. It can happen in any natural setting.

HOW WE KNOW

OBEDIENCE IN A REAL-WORLD SETTING A team of researchers performed the following field study to test the power of obedience in the natural setting of a hospital. A nurse (the participant) received a call from a staff doctor whom she had not met. He told her to administer some medication to a patient so that it could take effect by the time he arrived. He would sign the drug order after he got to the ward. The doctor ordered a dose of 20 milligrams of a drug called *Astroten*. The label on the container of Astroten stated that 5 milligrams was the usual dose and warned that the maximum dose was 10 milligrams.

Would a nurse administer an excessive dose of a drug on the basis of a telephone call from an unfamiliar person when doing so was contrary to standard medical practice? When this dilemma was *described* to 12 nurses, 10 *said* they would disobey. However, what the nurses *did* was another, by now familiar, story. When another group of them was actually in the situation, almost every nurse obeyed. Twenty-one of 22 had started

Demand characteristics Cues in an experimental setting that influence the participants' perception of what is expected of them and that systematically influence their behavior within that setting.

to pour the medication (actually a harmless substance) before a physician researcher stopped them (Hofling et al., 1966).

These results suggest that Milgram's findings cannot be attributed solely to participants responding to the demands of the experiment.

WHY DO PEOPLE OBEY AUTHORITY?

Milgram's research suggests that, to understand why people obey authority, you need to look closely at the psychological forces at work in the situation. We saw in Chapter 17 how often situational factors constrain behaviors; in Milgram's research, we see an especially vivid instance of that general principal. Milgram and other researchers manipulated a number of aspects of the experimental circumstances to demonstrate that the obedience effect is overwhelmingly due to situational variables and not personality variables. **Figure 18.5** displays the level of obedience found in different situations. Obedience is quite high, for example, when a peer first models obedience, when a participant acts as an *intermediary bystander* assisting another person who actually delivers the shock, or when the victim (the learner) is physically remote from the teacher. Obedience is quite low when the

learner demands to be shocked, when two authorities give contradictory commands, or when the authority figure is the victim. These findings all point to the idea that the *situation,* and not differences among individual participants, largely controlled behavior.

Two reasons people obey authority in these situations can be traced to the effects of *normative* and *informational* sources of influence, which we discussed in Chapter 17: People want to be liked (normative influence), and they want to be right (informational influence). They tend to do what others are doing or requesting in order to be socially acceptable and approved. In addition, when in an ambiguous, novel situation—like the experimental situation—people rely on others for cues as to what is the appropriate and correct way to behave. They are more likely to do so when experts or credible communicators tell them what to do. A third factor in the Milgram paradigm is that participants were probably confused about *how* to *disobey;* nothing they said in dissent satisfied the authority. If they had a simple, direct way out of the situation—for example, by pressing a "quit" button—it is likely more would have disobeyed (Ross, 1988). Finally, obedience to authority in this experimental situation is part of an *ingrained habit* that is learned by children in many different settings—obey authority

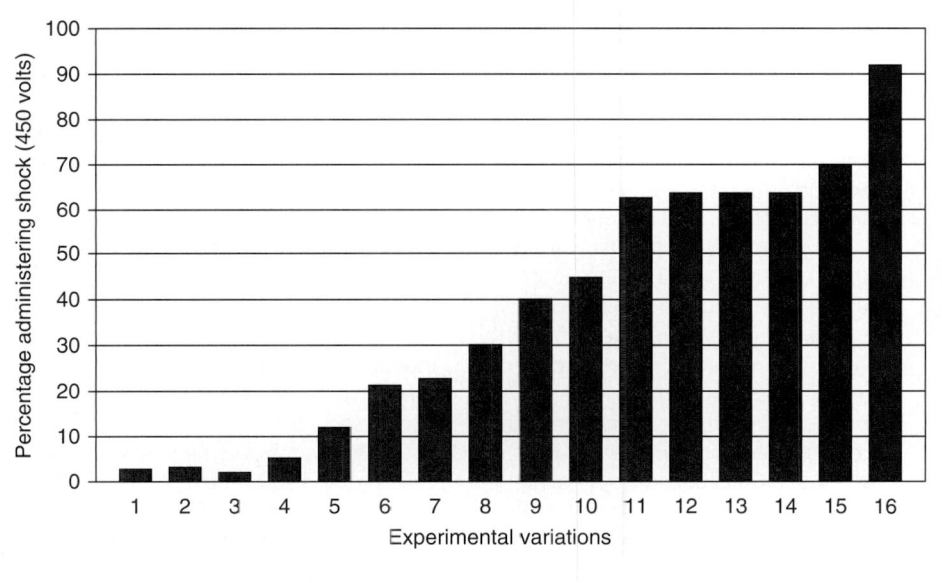

FIGURE 18.5

Obedience in Milgram's Experiments

The graph shows a profile of weak to strong obedience effects across Milgram's many experimental variations.

1. Learner demands to be shocked
2. Authority as victim—an ordinary man commanding
3. Two authorities— contradictory commands
4. Particpants free to choose shock level
5. Two peers rebel
6. An ordinary man gives orders
7. Remote authority
8. Touch proximity
9. Proximty
10. Institutional context
11. Voice feedback
12. Remote victim
13. Women as participants
14. Two authorities—one as victim
15. The participant as bystander
16. A peer administers shock

WHY DO PEOPLE JOIN CULTS?

Cults have no doubt forced themselves into your awareness in recent years because of the extreme, often bizarre behavior you read about and see in media accounts. In the United States, 39 members of Heaven's Gate committed suicide in March 1997 in an orderly ritual at the instigation of their leader. Nearly 20 years earlier, more than 900 American citizens committed mass suicide-murder in a jungle compound in Guyana at the persuasive urging of their charismatic leader, Reverend Jim Jones. In France, Canada, and Switzerland, members of The Order of the Solar Temple also took their lives in ritualized cult deaths, while in Japan, members of Aum Shin Rykyo gassed subway riders and had planned mass destruction in compliance with the dictates of their cult leader. Beyond these clearly dramatic instances, there are members of literally thousands of groups that qualify as cults who give total allegiance to their groups and leaders. Members obey every command, such as marrying a partner they have never met in mass ceremonies, begging, recruiting, working long hours for no pay, giving all their money and possessions to the group, or becoming celibate.

Can you imagine doing such things? Are there any circumstances under which you would join a cult and become subject to the pressures for conformity, compliance, and total obedience to authority that cults bring to bear on their members? Ob-viously, most of you would say, "No way!" But as psychologists, our task is to understand how such groups and leaders develop their coercive power, and to recognize the conditions that make many people vulnerable to their persuasive message.

So what exactly are cults? Cults vary considerably in their activities, structure, size, and ideology, but they typically are nontraditional religious groups led by an authoritarian leader who is the sole source of the group's ideology, doctrine, and primary reinforcements (Kramer & Alstad, 1993; Singer, 1995; Zimbardo & Andersen, 1993). This leader is often charismatic, filled with energy and intense dedication, and sometimes he or she claims special godlike powers of omnipotence, omniscience, and immortality. Despite the variations in the characteristics of particular cult groups, what is common are the recruiting promises, influence agendas, and group's coercive power that compromises the personal exercise of free will and critical thinking of its members (Hassan, 1988; Langone, 1993).

Why, then, would people want to join a cult? First of all, no one ever joins a *cult,* as such. People join interesting groups that promise to fulfill their pressing needs. They are perceived as cults later on when they are seen as deceptive, defective, dangerous, or as opposing basic values of society. Cults become appealing when they promise to fulfill an individual's personal needs, whether the need is for instant friendship, an identity, or an organized daily agenda. Cults also promise to compensate for a litany of societal failures: By eliminating people's feelings of isolation and alienation, cults make their slice of the world safe, healthy, caring, predictable, and controllable. Cult leaders offer simple solutions to an increasingly complex world by establishing a path to happiness, success, and salvation.

People are especially vulnerable to the persuasive power of cults when they are in a transitional phase in life, when they have moved to a new city or country, lost a job, dropped out of school, or given up traditional religion as personally irrelevant. Cults are also attractive to those who find their work tedious and trivial, who have an absent or inconsistent social life, and who have lost trust in government.

Although the mass suicides of cult members make media headlines, most cults operate quietly to achieve their goals. When they deliver on their promises, they can serve a valuable function for some individuals by helping to fill voids in their lives. But when they are deceptive, coercive, and distort basic values of freedom, independence, and critical thinking, they become dangerous to members and to society. One question worth raising is, Can society provide what cults promise so that they need not become an alternate lifestyle for so many people throughout the world?

---

without question (Brown, 1986). This heuristic usually serves society well when authorities are legitimate and deserving of obedience. The problem is that the rule gets overapplied. Blind obedience to authority means obeying any and all authority figures simply because of their ascribed status, regardless of whether they are unjust or just in their requests and commands.

THE MILGRAM EXPERIMENTS AND YOU

What is the personal significance to you of this obedience research? What choices will you make when faced with moral dilemmas throughout your life? Take a moment to reflect on the types of obedience to authority situations that might arise in your day-to-day experience. Suppose you were a salesclerk. Would you cheat custom-

Would you risk your life to defy authority in defense of your beliefs, as this young Chinese student did in a student-led rebellion?

ers if your boss encouraged such behavior? Suppose you were a member of Congress. Would you vote along party lines, rather than vote your conscience?

Milgram's obedience research challenges the myth that evil lurks in the minds of evil people—the bad "they" who are different from the good "us" or "you," who would never do such things. Our purpose in recounting these findings is not to debase human nature, but to make clear that even normal, well-meaning individuals are subject to the potential for frailty in the face of strong situational and social forces.

Finally, we wish to add a note on heroism. Suppose the majority of people who are comparable to you yield to powerful group forces. In our view, if you are able to resist, that qualifies you as heroic. The hero is the person who can act mindfully, out of conscience, when others are all conforming, or who can take the moral high road when others are standing by silently, allowing evil deeds to go unchallenged. Perhaps your knowledge of situational forces that make possible the "banality of evil" can nudge you in the direction of heroism.

The Psychology of Genocide and War

We have seen so far that the human species has a distinct predilection to obey authority. However, it takes more than an appreciation of this feature of human nature to explain why at some times and in some places one group undertakes the systematic destruction of another group—**genocide**—and why, far more often, one group goes to war or takes less formal aggressive action toward another group. In this section, we will analyze some of the historical and psychological forces that lead populations to pursue the path of highly organized aggression.

Psychologist **Ervin Staub** (1989, 2000) has studied campaigns of genocide throughout history and has offered an account of the sets of cultural and psychological forces that makes campaigns of terror possible:

- The starting point is often severely difficult life conditions for members of a society—harsh economic circumstances, political upheaval, and so on.

- Under these conditions of difficulty, people will intensify the ordinary impulse to define in-groups and out-groups. In this case, out-groups become *scapegoats* for the ills of society. In many instances, as in Nazi Germany, the scapegoating becomes part of the cultural or political ideology shared by the nation's leaders and citizens.

- Because the scapegoat group is blamed for society's ills, it becomes easy to justify violence against them. These incidents of violence lead to *just world thinking* (Lerner, 1980): Perpetrators and bystanders come to believe—because we live in a just world—that the victims must have done something to bring the violence upon themselves. Thus, Germans of the Nazi era came to believe that the Jews deserved their fate because of the imagined harm they had done to the German state.

- The violence also comes to justify itself—to stop the violence would mean to admit that it had been wrong to begin with. Furthermore, when regimes carry out organized violence without sanctions from other nations, the world community's passivity is taken as evidence of the justice of the regime's actions. This was the case with the "ethnic cleansing" massacres that followed the dissolution of Yugoslavia in 1991—although images of the massacres were widely transmitted, the world community took no action for several years.

Consider the case of Cambodia (Hinton, 1996). The situation began with difficult life conditions: Starting in the late 1960s, the country suffered economic hardships as well as bombings by the United States as war spread to Cambodia from its neighbor Vietnam. A new regime began to identify scapegoats, and the scapegoats became the targets of extreme violence: The Communists who captured the city of Phnom Penh in 1975 identified a number of ideological enemies who needed to be eliminated to put a new society into place. Former military and political leaders were arrested and often executed. The definition of "class enemies" swiftly became broader, however, as teachers, students, bureaucrats, and professionals were denounced as potential traitors. The killing gathered

Genocide The systematic destruction of one group of people, often an ethnic or racial group, by another.

A Cambodian man tends skulls from the "killing fields." What sequence of events may create a context for mass murders?

momentum because it was in service to such a powerful ideology and a clearly defined goal: The country must be rid of its internal enemies. Finally, as has most often been the case, the world community did not intervene.

CONCEPTS AND IMAGES OF THE "ENEMY"

We have suggested that an important way station on the path to genocide is scapegoating. We can see the same process at work, even when the endpoint is not systematic murder. Consider the attitudes of young adults in the former East Germany after the collapse of the socialist system. In national surveys, individuals aged 15 to 20 revealed themselves to hold, on average, quite negative attitudes to-

ward groups such as Poles and Turks. The major reason for these negative attitudes appears to be the threat of economic and cultural competition (Watts, 1996). That is, the Poles and Turks are suspected of contributing to the economic hardship of the transition from communism to democracy by taking jobs and income away from Germans. This perception of economic threat fits the model we described earlier: Prejudice and willingness to discriminate does not arise spontaneously; it requires societal circumstances that foster the belief that an "enemy" is consuming scarce resources. This sets the context for violence.

When regimes scapegoat the "enemy," they often also *dehumanize* them—they attempt to convince people to conceive of the group as nonhuman objects to be hated and destroyed. This process of dehumanization is also particularly critical to the conduct of war. Although most cultures oppose individual aggression as a crime, nations train millions of soldiers to kill. The challenge for leaders is to convert the act of murder into patriotism (Harle, 2000; Keen, 1986). Part of this mass social influence involves dehumanizing the soldiers of the other side into "the enemy." This dehumanization is accomplished by political rhetoric and by the media, in their vivid depictions of the enemy. According to army veterans, a soldier's most important weapon in war is not a gun but this internalized view of the hated "enemy" (see **Figure 18.6**). Thus, young soldiers become psychologically programmed to be wartime killers by these distorted images of anyone their government decides to label as the enemy.

In many cases, the images will not be literal representations but rather the mental images that politicians invoke to rally populations and send troops off to war. The most vivid example of this process in recent

This is the Enemy

FIGURE 18.6

Faces of the Enemy

How does military psychology convert killing into patriotism? Note how in each of these caricatures the designated enemy is given monstrous and dehumanized characteristics.

United States history was the regularity with which Saddam Hussein was likened to Adolph Hitler in the context of the 1990 Gulf War (Voss et al., 1992). By establishing this mapping in the public's mind, then President George Bush and other political leaders were able to call forth Americans' vast stores of anti-Hitler sentiment. When "Hussein" became "Hitler," it was much easier to argue for strenuous military action.

WHY WILL PEOPLE GO TO WAR?

When countries' leaders contemplate going to war, they do so with virtually certain knowledge that there will be negative consequences. Modern warfare no longer spares civilians—one of the great innovations of World War II was to target civilian populations to break "the will of the people." Even when a war is fought at great distance, as the Gulf War was for citizens of the United States, wars inevitably produce casualties on both sides. How does a country or other group determine that a cause is of sufficient importance that the loss of life is warranted? Most often this type of question is answered in a history class: Countries go to war, we have learned, to protect their territory, their people, or their economic interests. In this section, however, we briefly discuss some of the more psychological factors that lead individuals to choose to participate in war.

We can ask, for example, why it is that people will sacrifice their lives for their nations. That may be the ultimate act of altruism—to give up one's life in service of some cause. Recall from earlier in the chapter that the evolutionary perspective identifies the desire to protect family members (that is, to preserve one's genes) as one important root of altruism. Some researchers have suggested that people have internalized an association between "family" and "nation" (Stern, 1995): We talk about our "motherland" or "fatherland" and being "sons" or "daughters" of our country. Is this association sufficient to explain why people will die for their countries? Do people who march off to war construct a "social reality" in which they believe that, ultimately, they are protecting the interests of their literal family? You can see why this is an important question for psychologists to address.

We can acquire additional insight into psychological aspects of war making by examining the circumstances that prompted the Serbians to undertake the aggressive acts in 1992 that led to sustained war in Bosnia (White, 1996). The Serbians, apparently, feared that they would become a persecuted minority after the disintegration of Yugoslavia in 1991. We have already seen how reasonable a fear this may be for a minority in times of strife. Here is the testimony of one Bosnian Serb policeman, recorded by a British journalist (Glenny, 1994; cited in White, 1996, p. 111):

> He confirmed the countless observations I had made while talking with local fighters of all nationalities—he was not a man of evil. On the contrary, he explained how he found it very difficult to shoot at the other side of the village, because he knew everybody who lived there. But the war had somehow arrived and he had to defend his home. The man was confused and upset by events, but he now perceived the Green Berets [Muslims] and Ustashas [Croats] as a real threat to his family.
>
> "We can not let them form an Islamic state here," he said with genuine passion. "Are you sure they want to?" I asked him. "Of course they want to, I don't understand why you people outside don't see that we are fighting for Europe against a foreign religion."

In the context of this anticipated persecution, it was easy for Serbians to think of themselves as innocent even while they began to undertake aggressive action. From their psychological standpoint, they weren't the aggressors but the victims. As the conflict unfolded, Serbian leaders such as Slobodan Milosevic fanned the Serbian people's "persecution mania" to maintain the belief that they were right to make war. In the long run, the Serbians turned to massacres—"ethnic cleansing"—to remove all possible "persecutors" from their midst. We see how willing people are to go to war to protect themselves from enemies real, imagined, or created by their leaders.

What this analysis suggests is that, at least in modern times, countries rarely go to war with the goal of domination or conquest. Rather, countries come to believe—even when the rest of the world characterizes them as aggressors—that they are protecting interests that are important to their survival and identity. Countries, of course, are made of up of millions of individuals. Enough of those individuals must sufficiently internalize the values at stake to be willing to sacrifice their lives. Whatever the "real" causes of war revealed by historical analysis, it is these individual, psychological forces that prompt people to endure war's hardships.

In this section so far, we have seen some of the ways in which psychological forces create the context that makes war—and atrocities committed in the context of wars—seem entirely reasonable. As the last topic of *Psychology and Life*, we turn to the efforts *peace psychologists* make to use psychological forces to promote peaceful coexistence.

Peace Psychology

It is time now to turn these analyses around, to see how we can harness social psychology to wage peace instead of war. Psychology is uniquely equipped to study the question of how to help resolve the dilemmas of national and international disharmony. The American Psychological Association includes the division of **peace psychology.** The division works to promote peace within nations, communities, and families. It encourages research, education,

Peace psychology An interdisciplinary approach to the prevention of nuclear war and the maintenance of peace.

and training on issues concerning the causes, consequences, and prevention of violence and destructive conflict. We provide two examples of how applications of psychology can serve these goals.

ANALYZING FORMS OF LEADERSHIP AND GOVERNMENT

Some of the earliest research on what we now call peace psychology was inspired by world historical events culminating in World War II. Social psychologists sought to understand how leaders and forms of government emerge to exert considerable power on group behavior. What psychological constraints explain the emergence of Adolf Hitler in Germany and Benito Mussolini in Italy? These leaders forged individuals into mindless masses with unquestioning loyalty to fascist ideologies. Their authoritarian regimes threatened democracies and freedom everywhere. Modern social psychology developed out of this crucible of fear, prejudice, and war. Early social psychologists focused on understanding the nature of the *authoritarian personality* behind the fascist mentality (Adorno et al., 1950), the effects of propaganda and persuasive communications (Hovland et al., 1949), and the impact of group atmosphere and leadership styles on group members (Lewin et al., 1939).

The pioneering figure in social psychology was **Kurt Lewin,** a German refugee who escaped Nazi oppression. Lewin could not help but wonder how his nation could succumb totally to the tyranny of an autocratic, fascist dictator. He witnessed the spectacle of rallies of tens of thousands of people shouting allegiance to their *Führer.* This was a frightening testimony to the dynamic power of groups to transform the minds and actions of individuals and the power of an individual to affect the masses. Lewin investigated **group dynamics**—the ways in which leaders directly influenced their followers and the ways in which group processes changed the behavior of individuals.

In 1939, Lewin and his colleagues designed an experiment to investigate the effects of different leadership styles on group function. They wanted to find out if people are happier or more productive under autocratic or under democratic leadership. To assess the effects of different leadership styles, the researchers created three experimental groups, gave them different types of leaders, and observed the groups in action. The participants were four small groups of 10-year-old boys, who met after school. The group leaders were men trained to play each of the three leadership styles as they rotated from one to another group. When they acted as *autocratic leaders,* the men were to make all decisions and work assignments but not participate in the group activity. As *democratic leaders,* they were to encourage and assist group decision making and planning. Finally, when they acted as

laissez-faire leaders, their job was to allow complete freedom with little leader participation.

HOW   WE KNOW

THE EFFECTS OF LEADERSHIP STYLE The results of this experiment suggested a number of generalizations. First, *autocratic* leaders produced a mixed bag of effects on their followers—some positive and some quite negative. At times, the boys worked very hard, but typically only when the leader—acting as boss—was watching them. What most characterized the boys in the autocratic groups was their high level of aggression. These boys showed up to *30 times more hostility* when under autocratic leaders than they did under the other types of leaders. They demanded more attention, were more likely to destroy their own property, and showed more scapegoating behavior—using weaker individuals as displaced targets for their frustration and anger.

As for the *laissez-faire groups,* not much good resulted. They were the most inefficient of all, doing the least amount of work and of the poorest quality. In the absence of any social structure, they simply fooled around. However, when the same groups were *democratically run,* members worked the most steadily and were most efficient. The boys showed the highest levels of interest, motivation, and originality under democratic leadership. When discontent arose, it was likely to be openly expressed. Almost all the boys preferred the democratic group to the others. Democracy promoted more group loyalty and friendliness. There was more mutual praise, more friendly remarks, more sharing, and, overall, more playfulness (Lewin et al., 1939).

Democracy proved superior psychologically to the other forms of group atmosphere, as well as more productive. Democratic leaders also generated the most healthy reactions from group members, while autocratic-leader groups generated the most destructive individual reactions.

What was true in Lewin's classroom seems also to be true in the real world. Consider the finding that authoritarian leadership leads to increased hostility. We can find a real-world correlate to that finding in analyses that relate type of government to instances of *democide*—genocide and other forms of mass murder (Rummel, 1994). If you examine **Figure 18.7,** you see that totalitarian governments—such as Communist Russia and China—have been responsible for vast numbers of deaths; authoritarian governments—such as Idi Amin's reign in Uganda—have been responsible for fewer deaths, but democratic governments, though certainly not innocent of bloodshed, have produced fewest of all. Figure 18.7 also provides a comparison to the number of deaths caused by

Group dynamics The study of how group processes change individual functioning.

592

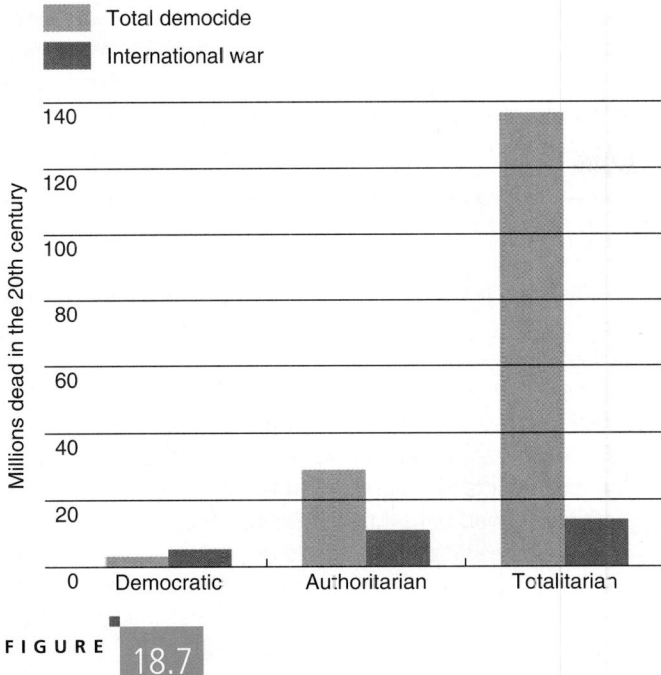

18.7

Types of Regimes and Democide

Totalitarian regimes are most likely to commit democide (genocide and other forms of mass murder). The comparison to war dead demonstrates that vastly more people are murdered by governments outside the context of war.

battles in war. You should note that the great majority of deaths caused by authoritarian and totalitarian regimes were victims not of war but of other programs of mass murder. Ideological considerations aside, the world suffers least when democratic systems of government are in place to ensure that power cannot be used according to the whims of a small elite, with deadly consequences.

Note, however, that it is *not* the case that democracies are less likely to go to war than other regimes, although one democracy rarely goes to a war with another democracy (Maoz & Abdolali, 1989). Research suggests that citizens of democracies disapprove of force used against other democracies but not against other forms of government.

HOW WE KNOW

SANCTIONING FORCE IN INTERNATIONAL CRISES Experimental participants read a description of an international crisis that was modeled after the crisis that led to the Gulf War: One nation had invaded another to resolve a conflict over the use of uranium. One version of the description indirectly identified the invading country as a democracy: The invasion was described as "a result of a democratic decision made by a vast majority of the parliament (including the opposition parties)." The other version indirectly identified the invading country as nondemocratic: The decision to invade was "undertaken by a military dictator of a police state with no need for public approval." Participants, drawn from two democracies, the United States and Israel, were asked to indicate how much they approved of the "use of force"—a naval invasion. Although the scenarios were otherwise the same, participants were much more reluctant to sanction the use of force (by the United States or Israel) when the action would be taken against a democratic regime (Mintz & Geva, 1993).

Living in a democratic society, you have certain expectations about other democratic societies that make it more difficult to contemplate using force against them. Politicians, in turn, hesitate to consider force in the face of probable opposition from their citizens.

The overall conclusion we can draw from research on forms of leadership is that democracy works best. We derive that insight from research on groups quite small (groups of young boys) and quite large (whole countries). You should also apply this insight to the smallest and largest groups in your own life!

FOSTERING CONTACT TO FACILITATE CONFLICT RESOLUTION

Many of the antagonisms that give rise to conflict and violence are quite ancient. The Serbs who waged war in Bosnia, for example, traced their fear of persecution back to the Battle of Kosovo Field in 1389. What can be done in these situations? The main approach peace psychologists take is the same one we described for healing other types of prejudices: People must be brought together in cooperative settings that can foster mutual trust and shared goals.

Such an approach is now being attempted, for example, in Northern Ireland. In an attempt to begin a healing process between Catholics and Protestants, the United Kingdom began in 1989 to fund Community Relations programs intended "to develop cross-community contact and cooperation; to promote greater mutual understanding; [and] to increase respect for other cultural traditions" (Knox, 1994, p. 600). Not every political unit in Northern Ireland undertook a community relations program, giving researchers the opportunity to make comparisons to assess the programs' effects. These comparisons indicate at least limited progress: After four years, the programs had succeeded, for example, in reducing participants' estimates of prejudice against Catholics (Knox, 1994). Other attempts to heal Northern Ireland are being made among schoolchildren (Cairns et al., 1995). Most children in this troubled region attend schools that are strictly segregated by religion. However, in the last 20 years, schools have been founded that bring Protestant and Catholic students and faculty together. These changes in schooling have yet to provide definitive data on whether cross-community

What psychological measures might allow Northern Ireland to continue its progress toward peace?

friendships can change political values. However, the important suggestion from both the community and school interventions is that governments can—and perhaps should—expend their resources to create situations of mutual contact in service of shared goals.

We turn to another of the world's major trouble spots, the Middle East, to describe the remarkable program of Israeli–Palestinian workshops conducted by psychologist **Herbert Kelman** (1997, 1999) and his colleagues. Over several years, Kelman's group has invited Palestinians and Israelis to participate in meetings in which they engaged in *interactive problem solving* with respect to the ongoing conflicts in their regions, such as the fate of settlements in occupied territories. The participants in this process were promised privacy and confidentiality as well as open and analytical discussion. They were encouraged to have appropriate expectations: No pressure was created to produce agreement among all the participants. Third-party members were present to facilitate conversation but did not mediate between the parties.

Kelman's group initiated these workshops at a time when it was still nearly unheard of for Palestinians and Israelis to meet at all. The workshops presented environments in which participants could have opportunities for direct interaction that could potentially foster mutual understanding. Moreover, graduates of the workshop could bring the insights they had gained into the broader, real-world political arena—along with a first approximation of the types of relationships and dialogue that are required for progress toward peace. In fact, Kelman (1997) reports that several participants in the workshops became directly involved in the efforts toward peace that eventuated in the 1993 Oslo Peace accord.

The violence in both Northern Ireland and the Middle East has, unfortunately, not come to an end. There are militant groups in each region with political, economic, and religious agendas that encourage violence and segre-gation over peace and integration. Even so, insights from psychological research have helped to produce some momentum toward peace. The results are sufficiently important and concrete to keep psychologists—that "rather optimistic group"—diligently at work.

SUMMING UP

The combination of prejudice and a government's resources for organized aggression can lead to devastating consequences. Milgram's studies on obedience were inspired by the events of World War II. His studies suggested that social forces—rather than dispositional factors—act powerfully to produce obedience to authority. Although many of the participants in Milgram's studies dissented verbally, the majority obeyed behaviorally. In times of economic distress, people create scapegoat groups that may, ultimately, become the targets for mass murder. Leaders often make attempts to dehumanize enemies. People who enter into war often do so out of the realistic or unrealistic belief that they are endangered. Peace psychologists are interested in exploring the individual and cultural forces that create war and promote peace. Research on forms of leadership and government supports the belief that an increase in democracies would benefit the world community. Strides toward peace have been made through programs that foster interaction and problem solving among long-standing enemies.

A Personal Endnote

We have come to the end of our journey through *Psychology and Life.* As you think back, we hope you will realize just how much you have learned on the way. Yet we have barely scratched the surface of the excitement and challenges that await the student of psychology. We hope you will pursue your interest in psychology and that you may even go on to contribute to this dynamic enterprise as a scientific researcher or a clinical practitioner, or by applying psychological knowledge to the solution of social and personal problems.

Playwright Tom Stoppard reminds us that "every exit is an entry somewhere else." We'd like to believe that the entry into the next phase of your life will be facilitated by what you have learned from *Psychology and Life* and from your introductory psychology course. In that next journey, may you infuse new life into the psychology of human endeavors while strengthening the connections among all the people you encounter.

Richard Gerrig

Phil Zimbardo

RECAPPING
MAIN POINTS

Altruism and Prosocial Behavior

- Researchers have tried to explain why people engage in prosocial behaviors, particularly altruistic behaviors that do not serve their own interests.

- Evolutionary explanations focus on kinship and reciprocity.

- People also engage in prosocial behaviors to serve their self-interest, to benefit particular communities, and to uphold social principles.

- Bystander intervention studies show that situations largely determine who is likely or unlikely to help in emergencies.

Aggression

- From an evolutionary perspective, aggressive behaviors arose because people needed to ensure their ability to preserve their genes.

- Individual differences in aggressive behavior are reflected both in genetic analyses and in brain and hormone function.

- Different personality profiles predict propensities toward either impulsive or instrumental aggression.

- Although there are inhibitions to aggressive behavior, situations arise that prompt people to respond aggressively.

- Frustration can lead to aggression; ongoing irritation will escalate the level of aggression.

- Different cultures provide different norms for aggressive behavior depending, in part, on cultural construals of the self.

Prejudice

- Even arbitrary, minimal cues can yield prejudice when they define an in-group and an out-group.

- Stereotypes affect the way in which people evaluate behaviors and information in the world.

- Researchers have eliminated some of the effects of prejudice by creating situations in which members of different groups must cooperate to reach shared goals.

- Cross-cultural studies also suggest that friendship plays an important role in eliminating prejudice.

The Psychology of Conflict and Peace

- Milgram's studies on obedience are a powerful testimony to the influence of the situational factors that can lead ordinary people to sanction and participate in organized aggression.

- Some of the same processes that foster prejudice can, in the long run, lead to mass murder and genocide.

- Leaders create images of the enemy as less than human.

- People sacrifice themselves for their country in response to fears and threats to their families and communities.

- Peace psychologists look for ways to help resolve competition and hostilities among nations.

- Democratic societies are least likely to commit mass murder.

- Programs fostering interaction between traditional "enemies" may help to prepare the way for peace.

Key Terms

aggression (p. 571)
altruism (p. 566)
bystander intervention (p. 569)
contact hypothesis (p. 582)
demand characteristics (p. 586)
diffusion of responsibility (p. 569)
frustration-aggression hypothesis (p. 574)
genocide (p. 589)
group dynamics (p. 592)
impulsive aggression (p. 573)
in-group bias (p. 579)
in-groups (p. 579)
instrumental aggression (p. 573)
jigsaw classrooms (p. 583)
out-groups (p. 579)
peace psychology (p. 591)
prejudice (p. 578)
prosocial behaviors (p. 566)
racism (p. 580)
reciprocal altruism (p. 566)
sexism (p. 580)
social categorization (p. 579)
stereotypes (p. 581)

Glossary

A-B-A design Experimental design in which participants first experience the baseline condition (A), then experience the experimental treatment (B), and then return to the baseline (A).

Abnormal psychology The area of psychological investigation concerned with understanding the nature of individual pathologies of mind, mood, and behavior.

Absolute threshold The minimum amount of physical energy needed to produce a reliable sensory experience; operationally defined as the stimulus level at which a sensory signal is detected half the time.

Accommodation 1. The process by which the ciliary muscles change the thickness of the lens of the eye to permit variable focusing on near and distant objects. 2. According to Piaget, the process of restructuring or modifying cognitive structures so that new information can fit into them more easily; this process works in tandem with assimilation.

Acquisition The stage in a classical conditioning experiment during which the conditioned response is first elicited by the conditioned stimulus.

Action potential The nerve impulse activated in a neuron that travels down the axon and causes neurotransmitters to be released into a synapse.

Acute stress A transient state of arousal with typically clear onset and offset patterns.

Addiction A condition in which the body requires a drug in order to function without physical and psychological reactions to its absence; often the outcome of tolerance and dependence.

Ageism Prejudice against older people, similar to racism and sexism in its negative stereotypes.

Aggression Behaviors that cause psychological or physical harm to another individual.

Agoraphobia An extreme fear of being in public places or open spaces from which escape may be difficult or embarrassing.

AIDS Acronym for acquired immune deficiency syndrome, a syndrome caused by a virus that damages the immune system and weakens the body's ability to fight infection.

Algorithm A step-by-step procedure that always provides the right answer for a particular type of problem.

All-or-none law The rule that the size of the action potential is unaffected by increases in the intensity of stimulation beyond the threshold level.

Altruism Prosocial behaviors a person carries out without considering his or her own safety or interests.

Alzheimer's disease A chronic organic brain syndrome characterized by gradual loss of memory, decline in intellectual ability, and deterioration of personality.

Amacrine cells Cells that integrate information across the retina; rather than sending signals toward the brain, amacrine cells link bipolar cells to other bipolar cells and ganglion cells to other ganglion cells.

Ambiguity A perceptual object that may have more than "one interpretation.

Amnesia A failure of memory caused by physical injury, disease, drug use, or psychological trauma.

Amygdala The part of the limbic system that controls emotion, aggression, and the formation of emotional memory.

Analytic psychology A branch of psychology that views the person as a constellation of compensatory internal forces in a dynamic balance.

Anchoring heuristic An insufficient adjustment up or down from an original starting value when judging the probable value of some event or outcome.

Animal cognition The cognitive capabilities of nonhuman animals; researchers trace the development of cognitive capabilities across species and the continuity of capabilities from nonhuman to human animals.

Anorexia nervosa An eating disorder in which an individual weighs less than 85 percent of her or his expected weight but still controls eating because of a self-perception of obesity.

Anticipatory coping Efforts made in advance of a potentially stressful event to overcome, reduce, or tolerate the imbalance between perceived demands and available resources.

Anxiety An intense emotional response caused by the preconscious recognition that a repressed conflict is about to emerge into consciousness.

Anxiety disorders Mental disorders marked by physiological arousal, feelings of tension, and intense apprehension without apparent reason.

Apparent motion A movement illusion in which one or more stationary lights going on and off in succession are perceived as a single moving light; the simplest form of apparent motion is the phi phenomenon.

Archetype A universal, inherited, primitive, and symbolic representation of a particular experience or object.

Assimilation According to Piaget, the process whereby new cognitive elements are fitted in with old elements or modified to fit more easily; this process works in tandem with accommodation.

Association cortex The parts of the cerebral cortex in which many high-level brain processes occur.

Attachment Emotional relationship between a child and the "regular caregiver.

Attention A state of focused awareness on a subset of the available perceptual information.

Attitude The learned, relatively stable tendency to respond to people, concepts, and events in an evaluative way.

Attribution theory A social-cognitive approach to describing the ways the social perceiver uses information to generate causal explanations.

Attributions Judgments about the causes of outcomes.

Audience design The process of shaping a message depending on the audience for which it is intended.

Auditory cortex The area of the temporal lobes that receives and processes auditory information.

Auditory nerve The nerve that carries impulses from the cochlea to the cochlear nucleus of the brain.

Automatic processes Processes that do not require attention; they can often be performed along with other tasks without interference.

Autonomic nervous system (ANS) The subdivision of the peripheral nervous system that controls the body's involuntary motor responses by connecting the sensory receptors to the central nervous system (CNS) and the CNS to the smooth muscle, cardiac muscle, and glands.

Availability heuristic A judgment based on the information readily available in memory.

Aversion therapy A type of behavioral therapy used to treat individuals attracted to harmful stimuli; an attractive stimulus is paired with a noxious stimulus in order to elicit a negative reaction to the target stimulus.

Axon The extended fiber of a neuron through which nerve impulses travel from the soma to the terminal buttons.

Basic level The level of categorization that can be retrieved from memory most quickly and used most efficiently.

Basilar membrane A membrane in the cochlea that, when set into motion, stimulates hair cells that produce the neural effects of auditory stimulation.

Behavior The actions by which an organism adjusts to its environment.

Behavior analysis The area of psychology that focuses on the environmental determinants of learning and behavior.

Behavior modification The systematic use of principles of learning to increase the frequency of desired behaviors and/or decrease the frequency of problem behaviors.

Behavior therapy See behavior modification.

Behavioral confirmation The process by which people behave in ways that elicit from others specific expected reactions and then use those reactions to confirm their beliefs.

Behavioral data Observational reports about the behavior of organisms and the conditions under which the behavior occurs or changes.

Behavioral measures Overt actions and reactions that are observed and recorded, exclusive of self-reported behavior.

Behavioral rehearsal Procedures used to establish and strengthen basic skills; as used in social-skills training programs, requires the client to rehearse a desirable behavior sequence mentally.

Behaviorism A scientific approach that limits the study of psychology to measurable or observable behavior.

Behaviorist perspective The psychological perspective primarily concerned with observable behavior that can be objectively recorded and with the relationships of observable behavior to environmental stimuli.

Belief-bias effect A situation that occurs when a person's prior knowledge, attitudes, or values distort the reasoning process by influencing the person to accept invalid arguments.

Between-subjects design A research design in which different groups of participants are randomly assigned to experimental conditions or to control conditions.

Biofeedback A self-regulatory technique by which an individual acquires voluntary control over nonconscious biological processes.

Biological constraints on learning Any limitations on an organism's capacity to learn that are caused by the inherited sensory, response, or cognitive capabilities of members of a given species.

Biological perspective The approach to identifying causes of behavior that focuses on the functioning of the genes, the brain, the nervous system, and the endocrine system.

Biomedical therapies Treatments for psychological disorders that alter brain functioning with chemical or physical interventions such as drug therapy, surgery, or electroconvulsive therapy.

Biopsychosocial model A model of health and illness that suggests that links among the nervous system, the immune system, behavioral styles, cognitive processing, and environmental factors can put people at risk for illness.

Bipolar cells Nerve cells in the visual system that combine impulses from many receptors and transmit the results to ganglion cells.

Bipolar disorder A mood disorder characterized by alternating periods of depression and mania

Blocking A phenomenon in which an organism does not learn a new stimulus that signals an unconditioned stimulus, because the new stimulus is presented simultaneously with a stimulus that is already effective as a signal.

Body image The subjective experience of the appearance of one's body.

Bottom-up processing Perceptual analyses based on the sensory data available in the environment; results of analyses are passed upward toward more abstract representations.

Brain stem The brain structure that regulates the body's basic life processes.

Brightness The dimension of color space that captures the intensity of light.

Broca's area The region of the brain that translates thoughts into speech or sign.

Bulimia nervosa An eating disorder characterized by binge eating followed by measures to purge the body of the excess calories.

Bystander intervention Willingness to assist a person in need of help.

Cannon–Bard theory of emotion A theory stating that an "emotional stimulus produces two co-occurring reactions—arousal "and experience of emotion—that do not cause each other.

Case study Intensive observation of a particular individual or small group of individuals.

Catharsis The process of expressing strongly felt but usually repressed emotions.

Central nervous system (CNS) The part of the nervous system consisting of the brain and spinal cord.

Centration A thought pattern common during the beginning of the preoperational stage of cognitive development; characterized by the child's inability to take more than one perceptual factor into account at the same time.

Cerebellum The region of the brain attached to the brain stem that controls motor coordination, posture, and balance as well as the ability to learn control of body movements.

Cerebral cortex The outer surface of the cerebrum.

Cerebral hemispheres The two halves of the cerebrum, connected by the corpus callosum.

Cerebrum The region of the brain that regulates higher cognitive and emotional functions.

Child-directed speech A special form of speech with an exaggerated and high-pitched intonation that adults use to speak to infants and young children.

Chronic stress A continuous state of arousal in which an individual perceives demands as greater than the inner and outer resources available for dealing with them.

Chronological age The number of months or years since an individual's birth.

Chunking The process of taking single items of information and recoding them on the basis of similarity or some other organizing principle.

Circadian rhythm A consistent pattern of cyclical body activities, usually lasting 24 to 25 hours and determined by an internal biological clock.

Classical conditioning A type of learning in which a behavior (conditioned response) comes to be elicited by a stimulus (conditioned stimulus) that has acquired its power through an association with a biologically significant stimulus (unconditioned stimulus).

Client The term used by clinicians who think of psychological disorders as problems in living, and not as mental illnesses, to describe those being treated.

Client-centered therapy A humanistic approach to treatment that emphasizes the healthy psychological growth of the individual; based on the assumption that all people share the basic tendency of human nature toward self-actualization.

Clinical ecology A field of psychology that relates disorders such as anxiety and depression to environmental irritants and sources of trauma.

Clinical psychologist An individual who has earned a doctorate in psychology and whose training is in the assessment and treatment of psychological problems.

Clinical social worker A mental health professional whose specialized training prepares him or her to consider the social context of people's problems.

Closure A perceptual organizing process that leads individuals to see incomplete figures as complete.

Cochlea The primary organ of hearing; a fluid-filled coiled tube located in the inner ear.

Cognition Processes of knowing, including attending, remembering, and reasoning; also the content of the processes, such as concepts and memories.

Cognitive appraisal With respect to emotions, the process through which physiological arousal is interpreted with respect to circumstances in the particular setting in which it is being experienced; also, the recognition and evaluation of a stressor to assess the demand, the size of the threat, the resources available for dealing with it, and appropriate coping strategies.

Cognitive appraisal theory of emotion A theory stating that the experience of emotion is the joint effect of physiological arousal and cognitive appraisal, which serves to determine how an ambiguous inner state of arousal will be labeled.

Cognitive behavior modification A therapeutic approach that combines the cognitive emphasis on the role of thoughts and attitudes influencing motivations and response with the behavioral emphasis on changing performance through modification of reinforcement contingencies.

Cognitive development The development of processes of knowing, including imagining, perceiving, reasoning, and problem solving.

Cognitive dissonance The theory that the tension-producing effects of incongruous cognitions motivate individuals to reduce such tension.

Cognitive map A mental representation of physical space.

Cognitive perspective The perspective on psychology that stresses human thought and the processes of knowing, such as attending, thinking, remembering, expecting, solving problems, fantasizing, and consciousness.

Cognitive processes Higher mental processes, such as perception, memory, language, problem solving, and abstract thinking.

Cognitive psychology The study of higher mental processes such as attention, language use, memory, perception, problem solving, and thinking.

Cognitive science The interdisciplinary field of study of the approach systems and processes that manipulate information.

Cognitive therapy A type of psychotherapeutic treatment that attempts to change feelings and behaviors by changing the way a client thinks about or perceives significant life experiences.

Collective unconscious The part of an individual's unconscious that is inherited, evolutionarily developed, and common to all members of the species.

Comorbidity The experience of more than one disorder at the same time.

Complementary colors Colors opposite each other on the color circle; when additively mixed, they create the sensation of white light.

Compliance A change in behavior consistent with a communication source's direct requests.

Concepts Mental representations of kinds or categories of items or ideas.

Conditioned reinforcers In classical conditioning, formerly neutral stimuli that have become reinforcers.

Conditioned response (CR) In classical conditioning, a response elicited by some previously neutral stimulus that occurs as a result of pairing the neutral stimulus with an unconditioned stimulus.

Conditioned stimulus (CS) In classical conditioning, a previously neutral stimulus that comes to elicit a conditioned response.

Conditioning The ways in which events, stimuli, and behavior become associated with one another.

Cones Photoreceptors concentrated in the center of the retina that are responsible for visual experience under normal viewing conditions and for all experiences of color.

Conformity The tendency for people to adopt the behaviors, attitudes, and values of other members of a reference group.

Confounding variable A stimulus other than the variable an experimenter explicitly introduces into a research setting that affects a participant's behavior.

Consciousness A state of awareness of internal events and of the external environment.

Consensual validation The mutual affirmation of conscious views of reality.

Conservation According to Piaget, the understanding that physical properties do not change when nothing is added or taken away, even though appearances may change.

Consistency paradox The observation that personality ratings across time and among different observers are consistent, while behavior ratings across situations are not consistent.

Contact comfort Comfort derived from an infant's physical contact with the mother or caregiver.

Contact hypothesis The idea that direct contact between hostile groups alone will reduce prejudice.

Context of discovery The initial phase of research, in which observations, beliefs, information, and general knowledge lead to a new idea or a different way of thinking about some phenomenon.

Context of justification The research phase in which evidence is brought to bear on hypotheses.

Contextual distinctiveness The assumption that the serial position effect can be altered by the context and the distinctiveness of the experience being recalled.

Contingency management A general treatment strategy involving changing behavior by modifying its consequences.

Control procedures Consistent procedures for giving instructions, scoring responses, and holding all other variables constant except those being systematically varied.

Controlled processes Processes that require attention; it is often difficult to carry out more than one controlled process at a time.

Convergence The degree to which the eyes turn inward to fixate on an object.

Coping The process of dealing with internal or external demands that are perceived to be threatening or overwhelming.

Corpus callosum The mass of nerve fibers connecting the two hemispheres of the cerebrum.

Correlation coefficient (r) A statistic that indicates the degree of relationship between two variables.

Correlational methods Research methodologies that determine to what extent two variables, traits, or attributes are related.

Counseling psychologist Psychologist who specializes in providing guidance in areas such as vocational selection, school problems, drug abuse, and marital conflict.

Counterconditioning A technique used in therapy to substitute a new response for a maladaptive one by means of conditioning procedures.

Countertransference Circumstances in which a psychoanalyst develops personal feelings about a client because of perceived similarity of the client to significant people in the therapist's life.

Covariation principle A theory that suggests that people attribute a behavior to a causal factor if that factor was present whenever the behavior occurred but was absent whenever it did not occur.

Creativity The ability to generate ideas or products that are both novel and appropriate to the circumstances.

Criterion validity The degree to which test scores indicate a result on a specific measure that is consistent with some other criterion of the characteristic being assessed; also known as predictive validity.

Cross-sectional design A research method in which groups of participants of different chronological ages are observed and compared at a given time.

Crystallized intelligence The facet of intelligence involving the knowledge a person has already acquired and the ability to access that knowledge; measures by vocabulary, arithmetic, and general information tests.

Cultural perspective The psychological perspective that focuses on cross-cultural differences in the causes and consequences of behavior.

Cutaneous senses The skin senses that register sensations of pressure, warmth, and cold.

Dark adaptation The gradual improvement of the eyes' sensitivity after a shift in illumination from light to near darkness.

Date rape Unwanted sexual violation by a social acquaintance in the context of a consensual dating situation.

Daytime sleepiness The experience of excessive sleepiness during daytime activities; the major complaint of patients evaluated at sleep disorder centers.

Debriefing A procedure conducted at the end of an experiment in which the researcher provides the participant with as much information about the study as possible and makes sure that no participant leaves feeling confused, upset, or embarrassed.

Decision aversion The tendency to avoid decision making; the tougher the decision, the greater the likelihood of decision aversion.

Decision making The process of choosing between alternatives; selecting or rejecting available options.

Declarative memory Memory for information such as facts and events.

Deductive reasoning A form of thinking in which one draws a conclusion that is intended to follow logically from two or more statements or premises.

Delusions False or irrational beliefs maintained despite clear evidence to the contrary.

Demand characteristics Cues in an experimental setting that influence the participants' perception of what is expected of them and that systematically influence their behavior within that setting.

Dendrites The branched fibers of neurons that receive incoming signals.

Dependent variable In an experimental setting, any variable whose values are the results of changes in one or more independent variables.

Descriptive statistics Statistical procedures that are used to summarize sets of scores with respect to central tendencies, variability, and correlations.

Determinism The doctrine that all events—physical, behavioral, and mental—are determined by specific causal factors that are potentially knowable.

Developmental age The chronological age at which most children show a particular level of physical or mental development.

Developmental psychology The branch of psychology concerned with interaction between physical and psychological processes and with stages of growth from conception throughout the entire life span.

Diathesis-stress hypothesis A hypothesis about the cause of certain disorders, such as schizophrenia, that suggests that genetic factors predispose an individual to a certain disorder, but that environmental stress factors must impinge in order for the potential risk to manifest itself.

Dichotic listening An experimental technique in which a different auditory stimulus is simultaneously presented to each ear.

Difference threshold The smallest physical difference between two stimuli that can still be recognized as a difference; operationally defined as the point at which the stimuli are recognized as different half of the time.

Diffusion of responsibility In emergency situations, the larger the number of bystanders, the less responsibility any one bystander feels to help.

Discriminative stimuli Stimuli that act as predictors of reinforcement, signaling when particular behaviors will result in positive reinforcement.

Dispositional variables The organismic variables, or inner determinants of behavior, that occur within human and nonhuman animals.

Dissociative amnesia The inability to remember important personal experiences, caused by psychological factors in the absence of any organic dysfunction.

Dissociative disorder A personality disorder marked by a disturbance in the integration of identity, memory, or consciousness.

Dissociative identity disorder (DID) A dissociative mental disorder in which two or more distinct personalities exist within the same individual; formerly known as multiple personality disorder.

Distal stimulus In the processes of perception, the physical object in the world, as contrasted with the proximal stimulus, the optical image on the retina.

Divergent thinking An aspect of creativity characterized by an ability to produce unusual but appropriate responses to problems.

DNA (deoxyribonucleic acid) The physical basis for the transmission of genetic information.

Double-blind control An experimental technique in which biased expectations of experimenters are eliminated by keeping both participants and experimental assistants unaware of which participants have received which treatment.

Dream analysis The psychoanalytic interpretation of dreams used to gain insight into a person's unconscious motives or conflicts.

Dream work In Freudian dream analysis, the process by which the internal censor transforms the latent content of a dream into manifest content.

Drives Internal states that arise in response to a disequilibrium in an animal's physiological needs.

DSM-IV-TR The current diagnostic and statistical manual of the American Psychiatric Association that classifies, defines, and describes mental disorders.

Echoic memory Sensory memory that allows auditory information to be stored for brief durations.

Ego The aspect of personality involved in self-preservation activities and in directing instinctual drives and urges into appropriate channels.

Ego defense mechanisms Mental strategies (conscious or unconscious) used by the ego to defend itself against conflicts experienced in the normal course of life.

Egocentrism In cognitive development, the inability of a young child at the preoperational stage to take the perspective of another person.

Elaboration likelihood model A theory of persuasion that defines how likely it is that people will focus their cognitive processes to elaborate upon a message and therefore follow the central and peripheral routes to persuasion.

Elaborative rehearsal A technique for improving memory by enriching the encoding of information.

Electroconvulsive therapy (ECT) The use of electroconvulsive shock as an effective treatment for severe depression.

Electroencephalogram (EEG) A recording of the electrical activity of the brain.

Emotion A complex pattern of changes, including physiological arousal, feelings, cognitive processes, and behavioral reactions, made in response to a situation perceived to be personally significant.

Emotional intelligence Type of intelligence defined as the abilities to perceive, appraise, and express emotions accurately and appropriately, to use emotions to facilitate thinking, to understand and analyze emotions, to use emotional knowledge effectively, and to regulate one's emotions to promote both emotional and intellectual growth.

Encoding The process by which a mental representation is formed in memory.

Encoding specificity The principle that subsequent retrieval of information is enhanced if cues received at the time of recall are consistent with those present at the time of encoding.

Endocrine system The network of glands that manufacture and secrete hormones into the bloodstream.

Engram The physical memory trace for information in the brain.

Environmental variables External influences on behavior.

Episodic memories Long-term memories for autobiographical events and the contexts in which they occurred.

EQ The emotional intelligence counterpart of IQ.

Equity theory A cognitive theory of work motivation that proposes that workers are motivated to maintain fair and equitable relationships with other relevant persons; also, a model that postulates that equitable relationships are those in which the participants' outcomes are proportional to their inputs.

Erogenous zones Areas of the skin surface that are especially sensitive to stimulation and that give rise to erotic or sexual sensations.

Estrogen The female sex hormone, produced by the ovaries, that is responsible for the release of eggs from the ovaries as well as for the development and maintenance of female reproductive structures and secondary sex characteristics.

Etiology The causes of, or factors related to, the development of a disorder.

Evolutionary perspective The approach to psychology that stresses the importance of behavioral and mental adaptiveness, based on the assumption that mental capabilities evolved over millions of years to serve particular adaptive purposes.

Excitatory inputs Information entering a neuron that signals it to fire.

Expectancy effects Results that occur when a researcher or observer subtly communicates to participants the kind of behavior he or she expects to find, thereby creating that expected reaction.

Expectancy theory A cognitive theory of work motivation that proposes that workers are motivated when they expect their efforts and job performance to result in desired outcomes.

Experience-sampling method An experimental method that assists researchers in describing the typical contents of consciousness; participants are asked to record what they are feeling and thinking whenever signaled to do so.

Experimental methods Research methodologies that involve the manipulation of independent variables in order to determine their effects on the dependent variables.

Explicit uses of memory Conscious efforts to recover information through memory processes.

Extinction In conditioning, the weakening of a conditioned association in the absence of a reinforcer or unconditioned stimulus.

Face validity The degree to which test items appear to be directly related to the attribute the researcher wishes to measure.

Fear A rational reaction to an objectively identified external danger that may induce a person to flee or attack in self-defense.

Fight-or-flight response A sequence of internal activities triggered when an organism is faced with a threat; prepares the body for combat and struggle or for running away to safety; recent evidence suggests that the response is characteristic only of males.

Figure Objectlike regions of the visual field that are distinguished from background.

Five-factor model A comprehensive descriptive personality system that maps out the relationships among common traits, theoretical concepts, and personality scales; informally called the Big Five.

Fixation A state in which a person remains attached to objects or activities more appropriate for an earlier stage of psychosexual development.

Fixed-interval schedule A schedule of reinforcement in which a reinforcer is delivered for the first response made after a fixed period of time.

Fixed-ratio schedule A schedule of reinforcement in which a reinforcer is delivered for the first response made after a fixed number of responses.

Flooding A therapy for phobias in which clients are exposed, with their permission, to the stimuli most frightening to them.

Fluid intelligence The aspect of intelligence that involves the ability to see complex relationships and solve problems.

Formal assessment The systematic procedures and measurement instruments used by trained professionals to assess an individual's functioning, aptitudes, abilities, or mental states.

Foundational theories Frameworks for initial understanding formulated by children to explain their experiences of the world.

Fovea Area of the retina that contains densely packed cones and forms the point of sharpest vision.

Frame A particular description of a choice; the perspective from which a choice is described or framed affects how a decision is made and which option is ultimately exercised.

Free association The therapeutic method in which a patient gives a running account of thoughts, wishes, physical sensations, and mental images as they occur.

Frequency distribution A summary of how frequently each score appears in a set of observations.

Frequency theory The theory that a tone produces a rate of vibration in the basilar membrane equal to its frequency, with the result that pitch can be coded by the frequency of the neural response.

Frontal lobe Region of the brain located above the lateral fissure and in front of the central sulcus; involved in motor control and cognitive activities.

Frustration-aggression hypothesis According to this hypothesis, frustration occurs in situations in which people are prevented or blocked from attaining their goals; a rise in frustration then leads to a greater probability of aggression.

Functional fixedness An inability to perceive a new use for an object previously associated with some other purpose; adversely affects problem solving and creativity.

Functional MRI (fMRI) A brain imaging technique that combines benefits of both MRI and PET scans by detecting magnetic changes in the flow of blood to cells in the brain.

Functionalism The perspective on mind and behavior that focuses on the examination of their functions in an organism's interactions with the environment.

Fundamental attribution error (FAE) The dual tendency of observers to underestimate the impact of situational factors and to overestimate the influence of dispositional factors on a person's behavior.

g According to Spearman, the factor of general intelligence underlying all intelligent performance.

Ganglion cells Cells in the visual system that integrate impulses from many bipolar cells in a single firing rate.

Gate-control theory A theory about pain modulation that proposes that certain cells in the spinal cord act as gates to interrupt and block some pain signals while sending others on to the brain.

Gender A psychological phenomenon that refers to learned sex-related behaviors and attitudes of males and females.

Gender identity One's sense of maleness or femaleness; usually includes awareness and acceptance of one's biological sex.

Gender roles Sets of behaviors and attitudes associated by society with being male or female and expressed publicly by the individual.

General adaption syndrome (GAS) The pattern of nonspecific adaptational physiological mechanisms that occurs in response to continuing threat by almost any serious stressor.

Generalized anxiety disorder An anxiety disorder in which an individual feels anxious and worried most of the time for at least six months when not threatened by any specific danger or object.

Generativity A commitment beyond one's self and one's partner to family, work, society, and future generations; typically, a crucial step in development in one's 30s and 40s.

Genes The biological units of heredity; discrete sections of chromosomes responsible for transmission of traits.

Genetics The study of the inheritance of physical and psychological traits from ancestors.

Genocide The systematic destruction of one group of people, often an ethnic or racial group, by another.

Genotype The genetic structure an organism inherits from its parents.s

Gestalt psychology A school of psychology that maintains that psychological phenomena can be understood only when viewed as organized, structured wholes, not when broken down into primitive perceptual elements.

Gestalt therapy Therapy that focuses on ways to unite mind and body to make a person whole.

Glia The cells that hold neurons together and facilitate neural transmission, remove damaged and dead neurons, and prevent poisonous substances in the blood from reaching the brain.

Goal-directed selection A determinant of why people select some parts of sensory input for further processing; it reflects the choices made as a function of one's own goals.

Ground The backdrop or background areas of the visual field, against which figures stand out.

Group dynamics The study of how group processes change individual functioning.

Group polarization The tendency for groups to make decisions that are more extreme than the decisions that would be made by the members acting alone.

Groupthink The tendency of a decision-making group to filter out undesirable input so that a consensus may be reached, especially if it is in line with the leader's viewpoint.

Guided search In visual perception, a parallel search of the environment for single, basic attributes that guides attention to likely locations of objects with more complex combinations of attributes.

Hallucinations False perceptions that occur in the absence of objective stimulation.

Health A general condition of soundness and vigor of body and mind; not simply the absence of illness or injury.

Health promotion The development and implementation of general strategies and specific tactics to eliminate or reduce the risk that people will become ill.

Health psychology The field of psychology devoted to understanding the ways people stay healthy, the reasons they become ill, and the ways they respond when they become ill.

Heredity The biological transmission of traits from parents to offspring.

Heritability estimate A statistical estimate of the degree of inheritance of a given trait or behavior, assessed by the degree of similarity between individuals who vary in their extent of genetic similarity.

Heuristics Cognitive strategies, or "rules of thumb," often used as short-cuts in solving a complex inferential task.

Hierarchy of needs Maslow's view that basic human motives form a hierarchy and that the needs at each level of the hierarchy must be satisfied before the next level can be achieved; these needs progress from basic biological needs to the need for transcendence.

Hippocampus The part of the limbic system that is involved in the acquisition of explicit memory.

HIV Human immunodeficiency virus, a virus that attacks white blood cells (T lymphocytes) in human blood, thereby weakening the functioning of the immune system; HIV causes AIDS.

Homeostasis Constancy or equilibrium of the internal conditions of the body.

Horizontal cells The cells that integrate information across the retina; rather than sending signals toward the brain, horizontal cells connect receptors to each other.

Hormones The chemical messengers, manufactured and secreted by the endocrine glands, that regulate metabolism and influence body growth, mood, and sexual characteristics.

Hozho A Navajo concept referring to harmony, peace of mind, goodness, ideal family relationships, beauty in arts and crafts, and health of body and spirit.

Hue The dimension of color space that captures the qualitative experience of the color of a light.

Human behavior genetics The area of study that evaluates the genetic component of individual differences in behaviors and traits.

Human-potential movement The therapy movement that encompasses all those practices and methods that release the potential of the average human being for greater levels of performance and greater richness of experience.

Humanistic perspective A psychological model that emphasizes an individual's phenomenal world and inherent capacity for making rational choices and developing to maximum potential.

Hypnosis An altered state of awareness characterized by deep relaxation, susceptibility to suggestions, and changes in perception, memory, motivation, and self-control.

Hypnotizability The degree to which an individual is responsive to standardized hypnotic suggestion.

Hypothalamus The brain structure that regulates motivated behavior (such as eating and drinking) and homeostasis.

Hypothesis A tentative and testable explanation of the relationship between two (or more) events or variables often stated as a prediction that a certain outcome will result from specific conditions.

Iconic memory Sensory memory in the visual domain; allows large amounts of information to be stored for very brief durations.

Id The primitive, unconscious part of the personality that operates irrationally and acts on impulse to pursue pleasure.

Identification and recognition Two ways of attaching meaning to percepts.

Illusion An experience of a stimulus pattern in a manner that is demonstrably incorrect but shared by others in the same perceptual environment.

Illusory contours Contours perceived in a figure when no contours are physically present.

Implicit uses of memory Availability of information through memory processes without the exertion of any conscious effort to encode or recover information.

Implosion therapy A behavioral therapeutic technique that exposes a client to anxiety-provoking stimuli, through his or her own imagination, in an attempt to extinguish the anxiety associated with the stimuli.

Imprinting A primitive form of learning in which some infant animals physically follow and form an attachment to the first moving object they see and/or hear.

Impulsive aggression Emotion-driven aggression produced in reaction to situations in the "heat of the moment."

Incentives External stimuli or rewards that motivate behavior although they do not relate directly to biological needs.

Independent construals of self Conceptualization of the self as an individual whose behavior is organized primarily by reference to one's own thoughts, feelings, and actions, rather than by reference to the thoughts, feelings, and actions of others.

Independent variable In experimental settings, the stimulus condition whose values are free to vary independently of any other variable in the situation.

Induced motion An illusion in which a stationary point of light within a moving reference frame is seen as moving and the reference frame is perceived as stationary.

Inductive reasoning A form of reasoning in which a conclusion is made about the probability of some state of affairs, based on the available evidence and past experience.

Inferences Missing information filled in on the basis of a sample of evidence or on the basis of prior beliefs and theories.

Inferential statistics Statistical procedures that allow researchers to determine whether the results they obtain support their hypotheses or can be attributed just to chance variation.

Informational influence Group effects that arise from individuals' desire to be correct and right and to understand how best to act in a given situation.

In-group bias An evaluation of one's own group as better than others.

In-groups The groups with which people identify as members.

Inhibitory inputs Information entering a neuron signaling it not to fire.

Insanity The legal (not clinical) designation for the state of an individual judged to be legally irresponsible or incompetent.

Insight therapy A technique by which the therapist guides a patient toward discovering insights between present symptoms and past origins.

Insomnia The chronic inability to sleep normally; symptoms include difficulty in falling asleep, frequent waking, inability to return to sleep, and early-morning awakening.

Instincts Preprogrammed tendencies that are essential to a species's survival.

Instinctual drift The tendency for learned behavior to drift toward instinctual behavior over time.

Instrumental aggression Cognition-based and goal-directed aggression carried out with premeditated thought, to achieve specific aims.

Intelligence The global capacity to profit from experience and to go beyond given information about the environment.

Intelligence quotient (IQ) An index derived from standardized tests of intelligence; originally obtained by dividing an individual's mental age by chronological age and then multiplying by 100; now directly computed as an IQ test score.

Interdependent construals of self Conceptualization of the self as part of an encompassing social relationship; recognizing that one's behavior is determined, contingent on, and, to a large extent organized by what the actor perceives to be the thoughts, feelings, and actions of others.

Interference A memory phenomenon that occurs when retrieval cues do not point effectively to one specific memory.

Internal consistency A measure of reliability; the degree to which a test yields similar scores across its different parts, such as on odd versus even items.

Internalization According to Vygotsky, the process through which children absorb knowledge from the social context.

Interneurons Brain neurons that relay messages from sensory neurons to other interneurons or to motor neurons.

Intimacy The capacity to make a full commitment—sexual, emotional, and moral—to another person.

Ion channels The portions of neurons' cell membranes that selectively permit certain ions to flow in and out.

James–Lange theory of emotion A peripheral-feedback theory of emotion stating that an eliciting stimulus triggers a behavioral response that sends different sensory and motor feedback to the brain and creates the feeling of a specific emotion.

Jigsaw classrooms Classrooms that use a technique known as jigsawing, in which each pupil is given part of the total material to master and then share with other group members.

Job burnout The syndrome of emotional exhaustion, depersonalization, and reduced personal accomplishment, often experienced by workers in high-stress jobs.

Judgment The process by which people form opinions, reach conclusions, and make critical evaluations of events and people based on available material; also, the product of that mental activity.

Just noticeable difference (JND) The smallest difference between two sensations that allows them to be discriminated.

Kinesthetic sense Sense concerned with bodily position and movement of the body parts relative to each other.

Language-making capacity The innate guidelines or operating principles that children bring to the task of learning a language.

Language production What people say, sign, and write, as well as the processes they go through to produce these messages.

Latent content In Freudian dream analysis, the hidden meaning of a dream.

Law of common fate A law of grouping that states that elements moving in the same direction at the same rate are grouped together.

Law of effect A basic law of learning that states that the power of a stimulus to evoke a response is strengthened when the response is followed by a reward and weakened when it is not followed by a reward.

Law of proximity A law of grouping that states that the nearest, or most proximal, elements are grouped together.

Law of similarity A law of grouping that states that the most similar elements are grouped together.

Learned helplessness A general pattern of nonresponding in the presence of noxious stimuli that often follows after an organism has previously experienced noncontingent, inescapable aversive stimuli.

Learning A process based on experience that results in a relatively permanent change in behavior or behavioral potential.

Learning-performance distinction The difference between what has been learned and what is expressed in overt behavior.

Lesions Injuries to or destruction of brain tissue.

Levels-of-processing theory A theory that suggests that the deeper the level at which information was processed, the more likely it is to be retained in memory.

Libido The psychic energy that drives individuals toward sensual pleasures of all types, especially sexual ones.

Life-change units (LCUs) In stress research, the measure of the stress levels of different types of change experienced during a given period.

Lightness constancy The tendency to perceive the whiteness, grayness, or blackness of objects as constant across changing levels of illumination.

Limbic system The region of the brain that regulates emotional behavior, basic motivational urges, and memory, as well as major physiological functions.

Longitudinal design A research design in which the same participants are observed repeatedly, sometimes over many years.

Long-term memory (LTM) Memory processes associated with the preservation of information for retrieval at any later time.

Loudness A perceptual dimension of sound influenced by the amplitude of a sound wave; sound waves with large amplitudes are generally experienced as loud and those with small amplitudes as soft.

Lucid dreaming The theory that conscious awareness of dreaming is a learnable skill that enables dreamers to control the direction and content of their dreams.

Magnetic resonance imaging (MRI) A technique for brain imaging that scans the brain using magnetic fields and radio waves.

Major depressive disorder A mood disorder characterized by intense feelings of depression over an extended time, without the manic high phase of bipolar depression.

Manic episode A component of bipolar disorder characterized by periods of extreme elation, unbounded euphoria without sufficient reason, and grandiose thoughts or feelings about personal abilities.

Manifest content In Freudian dream analysis, the surface content of a dream, which is assumed to mask the dream's actual meaning.

Maturation The continuing influence of heredity throughout development; the age-related physical and behavioral changes characteristic of a species.

Mean The arithmetic average of a group of scores; the most commonly used measure of central tendency.

Measure of central tendency A statistic, such as a mean, median, or mode, that provides one score as representative of a set of observations.

Measures of variability A statistic, such as a range or standard deviation, that indicates how tightly the scores in a set of observations cluster together.

Median The score in a distribution above and below which lie 50 percent of the other scores; a measure of central tendency.

Meditation A form of consciousness alteration designed to enhance self-knowledge and well-being through reduced self-awareness.

Medulla The region of the brain stem that regulates breathing, waking, and heartbeat.

Memory The mental capacity to encode, store, and retrieve information.

Menarche The onset of menstruation.

Mental age In Binet's measure of intelligence, the age at which a child is performing intellectually, expressed in terms of the average "age at which normal children achieve a particular score."

Mental retardation Condition in which individuals have IQ scores 70 to 75 or below and also demonstrate limitations in the ability to bring adaptive skills to bear on life tasks.

Mental set The tendency to respond to a new problem in the manner used to respond to a previous problem.

Meta-analysis A statistical technique for evaluating hypotheses by providing a formal mechanism for detecting the general conclusions found in data from many different experiments.

Metamemory Implicit or explicit knowledge about memory abilities and effective memory strategies; cognition about memory.

Mnemonics Strategies or devices that use familiar information during the encoding of new information to enhance subsequent access to the information in memory.

Mode The score appearing most frequently in a set of observations; a measure of central tendency.

Mood disorder A mood disturbance such as severe depression or depression alternating with mania.

Morality A system of beliefs and values that ensures that individuals will keep their obligations to others in society and will behave in ways that do not interfere with the rights and interests of others.

Motivation The process of starting, directing, and maintaining physical and psychological activities; includes mechanisms involved in preferences for one activity over another and the vigor and persistence of responses.

Motor cortex The region of the cerebral cortex that controls the action of the body's voluntary muscles.

Motor neurons The neurons that carry messages away from the central nervous system toward the muscles and glands.

Narcolepsy A sleep disorder characterized by an irresistible compulsion to sleep during the daytime.

Natural selection Darwin's theory that favorable adaptations to features of the environment allow some members of a species to reproduce more successfully than others.

Nature–nurture controversy The debate concerning the relative importance of heredity (nature) and learning or experience (nurture) in determining development and behavior.

Need for achievement (n Ach) An assumed basic human need to strive for achievement of goals that motivates a wide range of behavior and thinking.

Negative punishment A behavior is followed by the removal of an appetitive stimulus, decreasing the probability of that behavior.

Negative reinforcement A behavior is followed by the removal of an aversive stimulus, increasing the probability of that behavior.

Neuromodulator Any substance that modifies or modulates the activities of the postsynaptic neuron.

Neuron A cell in the nervous system specialized to receive, process, and/or transmit information to other cells.

Neuropathic pain Pain caused by abnormal functioning or overactivity of nerves; it results from injury or disease of nerves.

Neuroscience The scientific study of the brain and of the links between brain activity and behavior.

Neurotic disorders Mental disorders in which a person does not have signs of brain abnormalities and does not display grossly irrational thinking or violate basic norms but does experience subjective distress; a category dropped from *DSM-III*.

Neurotransmitters Chemical messengers released from neurons that cross the synapse from one neuron to another, stimulating the postsynaptic neuron.

Nociceptive pain Pain induced by a noxious external stimulus; specialized nerve endings in the skin send this pain message from the skin, through the spinal chord, into the brain.

Nonconscious Information not typically available to consciousness or memory.

Non-REM (NREM) sleep The period during which a sleeper does not show rapid eye movement; characterized by less dream activity than REM sleep.

Norm crystallization The convergence of the expectations of a group of individuals into a common perspective as they talk and carry out activities together.

Normal curve The symmetrical curve that represents the distribution of scores on many psychological attributes; allows researchers to make judgments of how unusual an observation or result is.

Normative influence Group effects that arise from individuals' desire to be liked, accepted, and approved of by others.

Normative investigations Research efforts designed to describe what is characteristic of a specific age or developmental stage.

Norms Standards based on measurements of a large group of people; used for comparing the scores of an individual with those of others within a well-defined group.

Object permanence The recognition that objects exist independently of an individual's action or awareness; an important cognitive acquisition of infancy.

Object relations theory Psychoanalytic theory that originated with Melanie Klein's view that the building blocks of how people experience the world emerge from their relations to loved and hated objects (significant people in their lives).

Observational learning The process of learning new responses by watching the behavior of another.

Observer bias The distortion of evidence because of the personal motives and expectations of the viewer.

Obsessive-compulsive disorder (OCD) A mental disorder characterized by obsessions—recurrent thoughts, images, or impulses that recur or persist despite efforts to suppress them—and compulsions—repetitive, purposeful acts performed according to certain rules or in a ritualized manner.

Occipital lobe Rearmost region of the brain; contains primary visual cortex

Olfactory bulb The center where odor-sensitive receptors send their signals, located just below the frontal lobes of the cortex.

Operant Behavior emitted by an organism that can be characterized in terms of the observable effects it has on the environment.

Operant conditioning Learning in which the probability of a response is changed by a change in its consequences.

Operant extinction When a behavior no longer produces predictable consequences, its return to the level of occurrence it had before operant conditioning.

Operational definition A definition of a variable or condition in terms of the specific operation or procedure used to determine its presence.

Opponent-process theory The theory that all color experiences arise from three systems, each of which includes two "opponent" elements (red versus green, blue versus yellow, and black versus white).

Optic nerve The axons of the ganglion cells that carry information from the eye toward the brain.

Organismic variables The inner determinants of an organism's behavior.

Organizational psychologists Psychologists who study various aspects of the human work environment such as communication among employees, socialization or enculturation of workers, leadership, job satisfaction, stress and burnout, and overall quality of life.

Orientation constancy The ability to perceive the actual orientation of objects in the real world despite their varying orientation in the retinal image.

Out-groups The groups with which people do not identify.

Overregularization A grammatical error, usually appearing during early language development, in which rules of the language are applied too widely, resulting in incorrect linguistic forms.

Pain The body's response to noxious stimuli that are intense enough to cause, or threaten to cause, tissue damage.

Panic disorder An anxiety disorder in which sufferers experience unexpected, severe panic attacks that begin with a feeling of intense apprehension, fear, or terror.

Parallel forms Different versions of a test used to assess test reliability; the change of forms reduces effects of direct practice, memory, or the desire of an individual to appear consistent on the same items.

Parallel processes Two or more mental processes that are carried out simultaneously.

Parasympathetic division The subdivision of the autonomic nervous system that monitors the routine operation of the body's internal functions and conserves and restores body energy.

Parental investment The time and energy parents must spend raising their offspring.

Parenting practices Specific parenting behaviors that arise in response to particular parental goals.

Parenting styles The manner in which parents rear their children; an authoritative parenting style, which balances demandingness and responsiveness, is seen as the most effective.

Parietal lobe Region of the brain behind the frontal lobe and above the lateral fissure; contains somatosensory cortex.

Partial reinforcement effect The behavioral principle that states that responses acquired under intermittent reinforcement are more difficult to extinguish than those acquired with continuous reinforcement.

Participant modeling A therapeutic technique in which a therapist demonstrates the desired behavior and a client is aided, through supportive encouragement, to imitate the modeled behavior.

Pastoral counselor A member of a religious order who specializes in the treatment of psychological disorders, often combining spirituality with practical problem solving.

Patient The term used by those who take a biomedical approach to the treatment of psychological problems to describe the person being treated.

Peace psychology An interdisciplinary approach to the prevention of nuclear war and the maintenance of peace.

Perceived control The belief that one has the ability to make a difference in the course or the consequences of some event or experience; often helpful in dealing with stressors.

Perception The processes that organize information in the sensory image and interpret it as having been produced by properties of objects or events in the external, three-dimensional world.

Perceptual constancy The ability to retain an unchanging percept of an object despite variations in the retinal image.

Perceptual organization The processes that put sensory information together to give the perception of a coherent scene over the whole visual field.

Peripheral nervous system (PNS) The part of the nervous system composed of the spinal and cranial nerves that connect the body's sensory receptors to the CNS and the CNS to the muscles and glands.

Personality The unique psychological qualities of an individual that influence a variety of characteristic behavior patterns (both overt and covert) across different situations and over time.

Personality disorder A chronic, inflexible, maladaptive pattern of perceiving, thinking, and behaving that seriously impairs an individual's ability to function in social or other settings.

Personality inventory A self-report questionnaire used for personality assessment that includes a series of items about personal thoughts, feelings, and behaviors.

Personality types Distinct patterns of personality characteristics used to assign people to categories; qualitative differences, rather than differences in degree, used to discriminate among people.

Persuasion Deliberate efforts to change attitudes.

PET scans Brain images produced by a device that obtains detailed pictures of activity in the living brain by recording the radioactivity emitted by cells during different cognitive or behavioral activities.

Phantom limb phenomenon As experienced by amputees, extreme or chronic pain in a limb that is no longer there.

Phenotype The observable characteristics of an organism, resulting from the interaction between the organism's genotype and its environment.

Pheromones Chemical signals released by organisms to communicate with other members of the species; often serve as long-distance sexual attractors.

Phi phenomenon The simplest form of apparent motion, the movement illusion in which one or more stationary lights going on and off in succession are perceived as a single moving light.

Phobia A persistent and irrational fear of a specific object, activity, or situation that is excessive and unreasonable, given the reality of the threat.

Phonemes Minimal units of speech in any given language that make a meaningful difference in speech production and reception; r and l are two distinct phonemes in English but variations of one in Japanese.

Photoreceptors Receptor cells in the retina that are sensitive to light.

Physical development The bodily changes, maturation, and growth that occur in an organism starting with conception and continuing across the life span.

Physiological dependence The process by which the body becomes adjusted to and dependent on a drug.

Pitch Sound quality of highness or lowness; primarily dependent on the frequency of the sound wave.

Pituitary gland Located in the brain, the gland that secretes growth hormone and influences the secretion of hormones by other endocrine glands.

Place theory The theory that different frequency tones produce maximum activation at different locations along the basilar membrane, with the result that pitch can be coded by the place at which activation occurs.

Placebo control An experimental condition in which treatment is not administered; it is used in cases where a placebo effect might occur.

Placebo effect A change in behavior in the absence of an experimental manipulation.

Placebo therapy A therapy independent of any specific clinical procedures that results in client improvement.

Pons The region of the brain stem that connects the spinal cord with the brain and links parts of the brain to one another.

Population The entire set of individuals to which generalizations will be made based on an experimental sample.

Positive punishment A behavior is followed by the presentation of an aversive stimulus, decreasing the probability of that behavior.

Positive reinforcement A behavior is followed by the presentation of an appetitive stimulus, increasing the probability of that behavior.

Possible selves The ideal selves that a person would like to become, the selves a person could become, and the selves a person is afraid of becoming; components of the cognitive sense of self.

Posttraumatic stress disorder (PTSD) An anxiety disorder characterized by the persistent reexperience of traumatic events through distressing recollections, dreams, hallucinations, or dissociative flashbacks; develops in response to rapes, life-threatening events, severe injuries, and natural disasters.

Preattentive processing Processing of sensory information that precedes attention to specific objects.

Preconscious memories Memories that are not currently conscious but that can easily be called into consciousness when necessary.

Predictive validity See criterion validity.

Prefrontal lobotomy An operation that severs the nerve fibers connecting the frontal lobes of the brain with the diencephalon, especially those fibers of the thalamic and hypothalamic areas; best-known form of psychosurgery.

Prejudice A learned attitude toward a target object, involving negative affect (dislike or fear), negative beliefs (stereotypes) that justify the attitude, and a behavioral intention to avoid, control, dominate, or eliminate the target object.

Primacy effect Improved memory for items at the start of a list.

Primary reinforcers Biologically determined reinforcers such as food and water.

Priming In the assessment of implicit memory, the advantage conferred by prior exposure to a word or situation.

Problem solving Thinking that is directed toward solving specific problems and that moves from an initial state to a goal state by means of a set of mental operations.

Problem space The elements that make up a problem: the initial state, the incomplete information or unsatisfactory conditions the person starts with; the goal state, the set of information or state the person wishes to achieve; and the set of operations, the steps the person takes to move from the initial state to the goal state.

Procedural memory Memory for how things get done; the way perceptual, cognitive, and motor skills are acquired, retained, and used.

Projective test A method of personality assessment in which an individual is presented with a standardized set of ambiguous, abstract stimuli and asked to interpret their meanings; the individual's responses are assumed to reveal inner feelings, motives, and conflicts.

Prosocial behaviors Behaviors that are carried out with the goal of helping other people.

Prototype The most representative example of a category.

Proximal stimulus The optical image on the retina; contrasted with the distal stimulus, the physical object in the world.

Psychiatrist An individual who has obtained an M.D. degree and also has completed postdoctoral specialty training in mental and emotional disorders; a psychiatrist may prescribe medications for the treatment of psychological disorders.

Psychic determinism The assumption that mental and behavioral reactions are determined by previous experiences.

Psychoactive drugs Chemicals that affect mental processes and behavior by temporarily changing conscious awareness of reality.

Psychoanalysis The form of psychodynamic therapy developed by Freud; an intensive and prolonged technique for exploring unconscious motivations and conflicts in neurotic, anxiety-ridden individuals.

Psychoanalyst An individual who has earned either a Ph.D. or an M.D. degree and has completed postgraduate training in the Freudian approach to understanding and treating mental disorders.

Psychobiography The use of psychological (especially personality) theory to describe and explain an individual's course through life.

Psychodynamic personality theories Theories of personality that share the assumption that personality is shaped by and behavior is motivated by powerful inner forces.

Psychodynamic perspective A psychological model in which behavior is explained in terms of past experiences and motivational forces; actions are viewed as stemming from inherited instincts, biological drives, and attempts to resolve conflicts between personal needs and social requirements.

Psychological assessment The use of specified procedures to evaluate the abilities, behaviors, and personal qualities of people.

Psychological dependence The psychological need or craving for a drug.

Psychological diagnosis The label given to psychological abnormality by classifying and categorizing the observed behavior pattern into an approved diagnostic system.

Psychology The scientific study of the behavior of individuals and their mental processes.

Psychometric function A graph that plots the percentage of detections of a stimulus (on the vertical axis) for each stimulus intensity (on the horizontal axis).

Psychometrics The field of psychology that specializes in mental testing.

Psychoneuroimmunology The research area that investigates interactions between psychological processes, such as responses to stress, and the functions of the immune system.

Psychopathological functioning Disruptions in emotional, behavioral, or thought processes that lead to personal distress or block one's ability to achieve important goals.

Psychopharmacology The branch of psychology that investigates the effects of drugs on behavior.

Psychophysics The study of the correspondence between physical stimulation and psychological experience.

Psychosocial stages Proposed by Erik Erikson, successive developmental stages that focus on an individual's orientation toward the self and others; these stages incorporate both the sexual and social aspects of a person's development and the social conflicts that arise from the interaction between the individual and the social environment.

Psychosomatic disorders Physical disorders aggravated by or primarily attributable to prolonged emotional stress or other psychological causes

Psychosurgery A surgical procedure performed on brain tissue to alleviate a psychological disorder.

Psychotherapy Any of a group of therapies, used to treat psychological disorders, that focus on changing faulty behaviors, thoughts, perceptions, and emotions that may be associated with specific disorders.

Psychotic disorders Severe mental disorders in which a person experiences impairments in reality testing manifested through thought, emotional, or perceptual difficulties; no longer used as a diagnostic category after *DSM-III*.

Puberty The attainment of sexual maturity; indicated for girls by menarche and for boys by the production of live sperm and the ability to ejaculate.

Punisher Any stimulus that, when made contingent upon a response, decreases the probability of that response.

Racism Discrimination against people based on their skin color or ethnic heritage.

Range The difference between the highest and the lowest scores in a set of observations; the simplest measure of variability.

Rapid eye movements (REM) A behavioral sign of the phase of sleep during which the sleeper is likely to be experiencing dreamlike mental activity.

Rational-emotive therapy (RET) A comprehensive system of personality change based on changing irrational beliefs that cause undesirable, highly charged emotional reactions such as severe anxiety.

Reasoning The process of thinking in which conclusions are drawn from a set of facts; thinking directed toward a given goal or objective.

Recall A method of retrieval in which an individual is required to reproduce the information previously presented.

Recency effect Improved memory for items at the end of a list.

Receptive field The visual area from which a given ganglion cell receives information.

Reciprocal altruism The idea that people perform altruistic behaviors because they expect that others will perform altruistic behaviors for them in turn.

Reciprocal determinism A concept of Albert Bandura's social-learning theory that refers to the notion that a complex reciprocal interaction exists among the individual, his or her behavior, and environmental stimuli and that each of these components affects the others.

Reciprocity norm Expectation that favors will be returned—if someone does something for another person, that person should do something in return.

Recognition A method of retrieval in which an individual is required to identify stimuli as having been experienced before.

Reconstructive memory The process of putting information together based on general types of stored knowledge in the absence of a specific memory representation.

Reflex An unlearned response elicited by specific stimuli that have biological relevance for an organism.

Refractory period The period of rest during which a new nerve impulse cannot be activated in a segment of an axon.

Reinforcement contingency A consistent relationship between a response and the changes in the environment that it produces.

Reinforcer Any stimulus that, when made contingent upon a response, increases the probability of that response.

Relative motion parallax A source of information about depth in which the relative distances of objects from a viewer determine the amount and direction of their relative motion in the retinal image.

Relaxation response A condition in which muscle tension, cortical activity, heart rate, and blood pressure decrease and breathing slows.

Reliability The degree to which a test produces similar scores each time it is used; stability or consistency of the scores produced by an instrument.

Representative sample A subset of a population that closely matches the overall characteristics of the population with respect to the distribution of males and females, racial and ethnic groups, and so on.

Representativeness heuristic A cognitive strategy that assigns an object to a category on the basis of a few characteristics regarded as representative of that category.

Repression The basic defense mechanism by which painful or guilt-producing thoughts, feelings, or memories are excluded from conscious awareness.

Residual stress pattern A chronic syndrome in which the emotional responses of posttraumatic stress persist over time.

Resistance The inability or unwillingness of a patient in psychoanalysis to discuss certain ideas, desires, or experiences.

Response bias The systematic tendency as a result of nonsensory factors for an observer to favor responding in a particular way.

Resting potential The polarization of cellular fluid within a neuron, which provides the capability to produce an action potential.

Reticular formation The region of the brain stem that alerts the cerebral cortex to incoming sensory signals and is responsible for maintaining consciousness and awakening from sleep.

Retina The layer at the back of the eye that contains photoreceptors and converts light energy to neural responses.

Retinal disparity The displacement between the horizontal positions of corresponding images in the two eyes.

Retrieval The recovery of stored information from memory.

Retrieval cues Internally or externally generated stimuli available to help with the retrieval of a memory.

Reversal theory Theory that explains human motivation in terms of reversals from one to the other opposing metamotivational states.

Ritual healing Ceremonies that infuse special emotional intensity and meaning into the healing process.

Rods Photoreceptors concentrated in the periphery of the retina that are most active in dim illumination; rods do not produce sensation of color.

Rules Behavioral guidelines for acting in certain ways in certain situations.

Sample A subset of a population selected as participants in an experiment.

Saturation The dimension of color space that captures the purity and vividness of color sensations.

Schedules of reinforcement In operant conditioning, the patterns of delivering and withholding reinforcement.

Schemas General conceptual frameworks, or clusters of knowledge, regarding objects, people, and situations; knowledge packages that encode generalizations about the structure of the environment.

Schemes Piaget's term for cognitive structures that develop as infants and young children learn to interpret the world and adapt to their environment.

Schizophrenic disorder Severe form of psychopathology characterized by the breakdown of integrated personality functioning, withdrawal from reality, emotional distortions, and disturbed thought processes.

Scientific method The set of procedures used for gathering and interpreting objective information in a way that minimizes error and yields dependable generalizations.

Selective optimization with compensation A strategy for successful aging in which one makes the most of gains while minimizing the impact of losses that accompany normal aging.

Selective social interaction theory The view that suggests that, as people age, they become more selective in choosing social partners who satisfy their emotional needs.

Self-actualization A concept in personality psychology referring to a person's constant striving to realize his or her potential and to develop inherent talents and capabilities.

Self-awareness The top level of consciousness; cognizance of the autobiographical character of personally experienced events.

Self-concept A person's mental model of his or her abilities and attributes.

Self-efficacy The set of beliefs that one can perform adequately in a particular situation.

Self-esteem A generalized evaluative attitude toward the self that influences both moods and behavior and that exerts a powerful effect on a range of personal and social behaviors.

Self-fulfilling prophecy A prediction made about some future behavior or event that modifies interactions so as to produce what is expected.

Self-handicapping The process of developing, in anticipation of failure, behavioral reactions and explanations that minimize ability deficits as possible attributions for the failure.

Self-perception theory The idea that people observe themselves in order to figure out the reasons they act as they do; people infer what their internal states are by perceiving how they are acting in a given situation.

Self-report measures The self-behaviors that are identified through a participant's own observations and reports.

Self-serving bias A class of attributional biases in which people tend to take credit for their successes and deny responsibility for their failures.

Semantic memories Generic, categorical memories, such as the meanings of words and concepts.

Sensation The process by which stimulation of a sensory receptor gives rise to neural impulses that result in an experience, or awareness of, conditions inside or outside the body.

Sensory adaptation A phenomenon in which receptor cells lose their power to respond after a period of unchanged stimulation; allows a more rapid reaction to new sources of information.

Sensory memory The initial memory processes involved in the momentary preservation of fleeting impressions of sensory stimuli.

Sensory neurons The neurons that carry messages from sense receptors toward the central nervous system.

Sensory physiology The study of the way in which biological mechanisms convert physical events into neural events.

Sensory receptors Specialized cells that convert physical signals into cellular signals that are processed by the nervous system.

Serial position effect A characteristic of memory retrieval in which the recall of beginning and end items on a list is often better than recall of items appearing in the middle.

Serial processes Two or more mental processes that are carried out in order, one after the other.

Set A temporary readiness to perceive or react to a stimulus in a particular way.

Sex chromosomes Chromosomes that contain the genes that code for the development of male or female characteristics.

Sex differences Biologically based characteristics that distinguish males from females.

Sexism Discrimination against people because of their sex.

Sexual arousal The motivational state of excitement and tension brought about by physiological and cognitive reactions to erotic stimuli.

Sexual scripts Socially learned programs of sexual responsiveness.

Shamanism A spiritual tradition that involves both healing and gaining contact with the spirit world.

Shape constancy The ability to perceive the true shape of an object despite variations in the size of the retinal image.

Shaping by successive approximations A behavioral method that reinforces responses that successively approximate and ultimately match the desired response.

Short-term memory (STM) Memory processes associated with preservation of recent experiences and with retrieval of information from long-term memory; short-term memory is of limited capacity and stores information for only a short length of time without rehearsal.

Shyness An individual's discomfort and/or inhibition in interpersonal situations that interferes with pursuing interpersonal or professional goals.

Signal detection theory (SDT) A systematic approach to the problem of response bias that allows an experimenter to identify and separate the roles of sensory stimuli and the individual's criterion level in producing the final response.

Significant difference A difference between experimental groups or conditions that would have occurred by chance less than an accepted criterion; in psychology, the criterion most often used is a probability of less than 5 times out of 100, or $p < .05$.

Situational variables External influences on behavior.

Size constancy The ability to perceive the true size of an object despite variations in the size of its retinal image.

Sleep apnea A sleep disorder of the upper respiratory system that causes the person to stop breathing while asleep.

Social categorization The process by which people organize the social environment by categorizing themselves and others into groups.

Social development The ways in which individuals' social interactions and expectations change across the life span.

Social intelligence A theory of personality that refers to the expertise people bring to their experience of life tasks.

Social-learning theory The learning theory that stresses the role of observation and the imitation of behaviors observed in others.

Social-learning therapy A form of treatment in which clients observe models' desirable behaviors being reinforced.

Social norms The expectation a group has for its members regarding acceptable and appropriate attitudes and behaviors.

Social perception The process by which a person comes to know or perceive the personal attributes of himself or herself and other people.

Social phobia A persistent, irrational fear that arises in anticipation of a public situation in which an individual can be observed by others.

Social psychology The branch of psychology that studies the effect of social variables on individual behavior, attitudes, perceptions, and motives; also studies group and intergroup phenomena.

Social role A socially defined pattern of behavior that is expected of a person who is functioning in a given setting or group.

Social support Resources, including material aid, socioemotional support, and informational aid, provided by others to help a person cope with stress.

Socialization The lifelong process whereby an individual's behavioral patterns, values, standards, skills, attitudes, and motives are shaped to conform to those regarded as desirable in a particular society.

Sociobiology A research field that focuses on evolutionary explanations for the social behavior and social systems of humans and other animal species.

Soma The cell body of a neuron, containing the nucleus and cytoplasm.

Somatic nervous system The subdivision of the peripheral nervous system that connects the central nervous system to the skeletal muscles and skin.

Somatosensory cortex The region of the parietal lobes that processes sensory input from various body areas.

Specific phobias Phobias that occur in response to specific types of objects or situations.

Split-half reliability A measure of the correlation between test takers' performance on different halves (e.g., odd- and even-numbered items) of a test.

Spontaneous recovery The reappearance of an extinguished conditioned response after a rest period.

Spontaneous-remission effect The improvement of some mental patients and clients in psychotherapy without any professional intervention; a baseline criterion against which the effectiveness of therapies must be assessed.

Standard deviation (SD) The average difference of a set of scores from their mean; a measure of variability.

Standardization A set of uniform procedures for treating each participant in a test, interview, or experiment or for recording data.

Stereotype threat The threat associated with being at risk for confirming a negative stereotype of one's group.

Stereotypes Generalizations about a group of people in which the same characteristics are assigned to all members of a group.

Stigma The negative reaction of people to an individual or group because of some assumed inferiority or source of difference that is degraded

Stimulus discrimination A conditioning process in which an organism learns to respond differently to stimuli that differ from the conditioned stimulus on some dimension.

Stimulus-driven capture A determinant of why people select some parts of sensory input for further processing; occurs when features of stimuli—objects in the environment—automatically capture attention, independent of the local goals of a perceiver.

Stimulus generalization The automatic extension of conditioned responding to similar stimuli that have never been paired with the unconditioned stimulus.

Storage The retention of encoded material over time.

Stress The pattern of specific and nonspecific responses an organism makes to stimulus events that disturb its equilibrium and tax or exceed its ability to cope.

Stress moderator variables Variables that change the impact of a stressor on a given type of stress reaction.

Stressor An internal or external event or stimulus that induces stress.

Structuralism The study of the structure of mind and behavior; the view that all human mental experience can be understood as a combination of simple elements or events.

Superego The aspect of personality that represents the internalization of society's values, standards, and morals.

Sympathetic division The subdivision of the autonomic nervous system that deals with emergency response and the mobilization of energy.

Synapse The gap between one neuron and another.

Synaptic transmission The relaying of information from one neuron to another across the synaptic gap.

Systematic desensitization A behavioral therapy technique in which a client is taught to prevent the arousal of anxiety by confronting the feared stimulus while relaxed.

Taste-aversion learning A biological constraint on learning in which an organism learns in one trial to avoid a food whose ingestion is followed by illness.

Temporal lobe Region of brain found below the lateral fissure; contains auditory cortex.

Tend-and-befriend response A response to stressors that is hypothesized to be typical for females; stressors prompt females to protect their offspring and join social groups to reduce vulnerability.

Terminal buttons The bulblike structures at the branched endings of axons that contain vesicles filled with neurotransmitters.

Testosterone The male sex hormone, secreted by the testes, that stimulates production of sperm and is also responsible for the development of male secondary sex characteristics.

Test–retest reliability A measure of the correlation between the scores of the same people on the same test given on two different occasions.

Thalamus The brain structure that relays sensory impulses to the cerebral cortex.

Thematic Apperception Test (TAT) A projective test in which pictures of ambiguous scenes are presented to an individual, who is encouraged to generate stories about them.

Theory An organized set of concepts that explains a phenomenon or set of phenomena.

Theory of ecological optics A theory of perception that emphasizes the richness of stimulus information and views the perceiver as an active explorer of the environment.

Think-aloud protocols Reports made by experimental participants of the mental processes and strategies they use while working on a task.

Three-term contingency The means by which organisms learn that, in the presence of some stimuli but not others, their behavior is likely to have a particular effect on the environment.

Timbre The dimension of auditory sensation that reflects the complexity of a sound wave.

Tolerance A situation that occurs with continued use of a drug in which an individual requires greater dosages to achieve the same effect.

Top-down processing Perceptual processes in which information from an individual's past experience, knowledge, expectations, motivations, and background influence the way a perceived object is interpreted and classified.

Traits Enduring personal qualities or attributes that influence behavior across situations.

Transduction Transformation of one form of energy into another; for example, light is transformed into neural impulses.

Transfer-appropriate processing The perspective that suggests that memory is best when the type of processing carried out at encoding matches the processes carried out at retrieval.

Transference The process by which a person in psychoanalysis attaches to a therapist feelings formerly held toward some significant person who figured in a past emotional conflict.

Trichromatic theory The theory that there are three types of color receptors that produce the primary color sensations of red, green, and blue.

Type A behavior pattern A complex pattern of behaviors and emotions that includes excessive emphasis on competition, aggression, impatience, and hostility; hostility increases the risk of coronary heart disease.

Type B behavior pattern As compared to Type A behavior pattern, a less competitive, less aggressive, less hostile pattern of behavior and emotion.

Type C behavior pattern A constellation of behaviors that may predict which individuals are more likely to develop cancer or to have their cancer progress quickly; these behaviors include passive acceptance and self-sacrifice.

Unconditional positive regard Complete love and acceptance of an individual by another person, such as a parent for a child, with no conditions attached.

Unconditioned response (UCR) In classical conditioning, the response elicited by an unconditioned stimulus without prior training or learning.

Unconditioned stimulus (UCS) In classical conditioning, the stimulus that elicits an unconditioned response.

Unconscious The domain of the psyche that stores repressed urges and primitive impulses.

Unconscious inference Helmholtz's term for perception that occurs outside of conscious awareness.

Validity The extent to which a test measures what it was intended to measure.

Variable In an experimental setting, a factor that varies in amount and kind.

Variable-interval schedule A schedule of reinforcement in which a reinforcer is delivered for the first response made after a variable period of time whose average is predetermined.

Variable-ratio schedule A schedule of reinforcement in which a reinforcer is delivered for the first response made after a variable number of responses whose average is predetermined.

Vestibular sense The sense that tells how one's own body is oriented in the world with respect to gravity.

Visual cortex The region of the occipital lobes in which visual information is processed.

Volley principle An extension of frequency theory which proposes that when peaks in a sound wave come too frequently for a single neuron to fire at each peak, several neurons fire as a group at the frequency of the stimulus tone.

Weber's law An assertion that the size of a difference threshold is proportional to the intensity of the standard stimulus.

Wellness Optimal health, incorporating the ability to function fully and actively over the physical, intellectual, emotional, spiritual, social, and environmental domains of health.

Wisdom Expertise in the fundamental pragmatics of life.

Within-subjects design A research design that uses each participant as his or her own control; for example, the behavior of an experimental participant before receiving treatment might be compared to his or her behavior after receiving treatment.

Working memory A memory resource that is used to accomplish tasks such as reasoning and language comprehension; consists of the phonological loop, visuospatial sketchpad, and central executive.

Yerkes–Dodson law A correlation between task performance and optimal level of arousal.

Zygote The single cell that results when a sperm fertilizes an egg.

References

Abelin, T., Muller, P., Buehler, A., Vesanen, K., & Imhof, P. R. (1989, January 7). Controlled trial of transdermal nicotine patch in tobacco withdrawal. *The Lancet*, pp. 7–10.

Abrams, R. (1992). *Electroconvulsive therapy*. New York: Oxford University Press.

Abramson, L. Y., Seligman, M. E. P., & Teasdale, J. D. (1978). Learned helplessness in humans: Critique and reformulation. *Journal of Abnormal Psychology, 87*, 32–48, 49–74.

Acierno, R., Resnick, H., Kilpatrick, D. G., Saunders, B., & Best, C. L. (1999). Risk factors for rape, physical assault, and posttraumatic stress disorder in women: Examination of differential multivariate relationships. *Journal of Anxiety Disorders, 13*, 541–563.

Adams, H. E., Wright, L. W., Jr., & Lohr, B. A. (1996). Is homophobia associated with homosexual arousal? *Journal of Abnormal Psychology, 105*, 440–445.

Adams, J. L. (1986). *Conceptual blockbusting* (3rd ed.). New York: Norton.

Adams, J. S. (1965). Inequity in social exchange. In L. Berkowitz (Ed.), *Advances in experimental social psychology* (Vol. 2, pp. 267–299). New York: Academic Press.

Addis, M. E., & Jacobson, N. S. (1996). Reasons for depression and the process and outcome of cognitive-behavioral psychotherapies. *Journal of Consulting and Clinical Psychology, 64*, 1417–1424.

Ader, R., & Cohen, N. (1981). Conditioned immunopharmacological responses. In R. Ader (Ed.), *Psychoneuroimmunology* (pp. 281–319). New York: Academic Press.

Ader, R., & Cohen, N. (1993). Psychoneuroimmunology: Conditioning and stress. *Annual Review of Psychology, 44*, 53–85.

Adler, A. (1929). *The practice and theory of individual psychology*. New York: Harcourt, Brace & World.

Adolphs, R., Tranel, D., Damasio, H., & Damasio, A. (1994). Impaired recognition of emotion in facial expressions following bilateral damage to the human amygdala. *Nature, 372*, 669–672.

Adolphs, R., Tranel, D., Hamann, S., Young, A. W., Calder, A. J., Phelps, E. A., Anderson, A., Lee, G. P., & Damasio, A. R. (1999). Recognition of facial emotion in nine individuals with bilateral amygdala damage. *Neuropsychologia, 37*, 1111–1117.

Adorno, T. W., Frenkel-Brunswick, E., Levinson, D. J., & Sanford, R. N. (1950). *The authoritarian personality*. New York: Harper.

Affleck, G., Tennen, H., Pfeiffer, C., & Fifield, J. (1987). Appraisals of control and predictability in adapting to a chronic disease. *Journal of Personality and Social Psychology, 53*, 273–279.

Aghajanian, G. K., & Marek, G. J. (1999). Serotonin and hallucinogens. *Neuropsychopharmacology, 21*, 16S–23S.

Ainsworth, M. D. S., Blehar, M., Waters, E., & Wall, S. (1978). *Patterns of attachment*. Hillsdale, NJ: Erlbaum.

Ajzen, I., & Sexton, J. (1999). Depth of processing, belief congruence, and attitude-behavior correspondence. In S. Chaiken & Y. Trope (Eds.), *Dual-process theories in social psychology* (pp. 117–138). New York: Guilford.

Akmajian, A., Demers, R. A., Farmer, A. K., & Harnish, R. M. (1990). *Linguistics*. Cambridge, MA: The MIT Press.

Alberti, R. E., & Emmons, M. L. (1990). *Your perfect right—A guide to assertive living*. San Luis Obispo, CA: Impact Publishers.

Aldrich, M. S. (1992). Narcolepsy. *Neurology, 42*(Suppl. 6), 34–43.

Alford, H. (1993). You'll never groom dogs in this town again. In *Municipal bondage: One man's anxiety-producing adventures in the big city* (pp. 61–83). New York: Random House.

Allen, D. J., & Olseon, T. (1999). Shame and internalized homophobia in gay men. *Journal of Homosexuality, 37*, 33–43.

Allen, J. P., & Land, D. (1999). Attachment in adolescence. In J. Cassidy & P. R. Shaver (Eds.), *Handbook of attachment: Theory, research, and clinical applications*. New York: The Guilford Press.

Allison, D. B., Heshka, S., Neale, M. C., Lykken, D. T., & Heymsfield, S. B. (1994). A genetic analysis of relative weight among 4,020 twin pairs, with an emphasis on sex effects. *Health Psychology, 13*, 362–365.

Allison, T., & Cicchetti, D. (1976). Sleep in mammals: Ecological and constitutional correlates. *Science, 194*, 732–734.

Allport, G. W., & Odbert, H. S. (1936). Trait-names, a psycholexical study. *Psychological Monographs, 47*(1, Whole No. 211).

Allport, G. W. (1937). *Personality: A psychological interpretation*. New York: Holt, Rinehart & Winston.

Allport, G. W. (1954). *The nature of prejudice*. Cambridge, MA: Addison-Wesley.

Allport, G. W. (1961). *Pattern and growth in personality*. New York: Holt, Rinehart & Winston.

Allport, G. W. (1965). *Letters from Jenny*. New York: Harcourt, Brace & World.

Allport, G. W. (1966). Traits revisited. *American Psychologist, 21*, 1–10.

Alvarez-Borda, B., Ramírez-Amaya, V., Pérez-Montfort, R., & Bermúdez-Rattoni, F. (1995). Enhancement of antibody production by a learning paradigm. *Neurobiology of Learning and Memory, 64*, 103–105.

Amabile, T. M. (1983). *The social psychology of creativity*. New York: Springer-Verlag.

American Association on Mental Retardation. (1992). *Mental retardation: Definition, classification, and systems of supports* (9th ed.). Washington, DC: American Association on Mental Retardation.

American Psychological Association. (1982). *Guidelines and ethical standards for researchers*. Washington, DC: American Psychological Association.

American Psychological Association. (1992). Ethical principles of psychologists and code of conduct. *American Psychologist, 47*, 1597–1611.

American Psychological Association. (1999). Summary report of journal operations, 1998. *American Psychologist, 54*, 715–716.

Ammerman, R. T., & Hersen, M. (1997). *Handbook of prevention and treatment with children and adolescents: Intervention in the real world context.* New York: Wiley.

Andersen, B., Kiecolt-Glaser, J. K., & Glaser, R. (1994). A biobehavioral model of cancer stress and disease course. *American Psychologist, 49,* 389–404.

Anderson, A. E., & DiDomenico, L. (1992). Diet vs. shape content of popular male and female magazines: A dose-response relationship to the incidence of eating disorders? *International Journal of Eating Disorders, 11,* 283–287.

Anderson, J. R. (1987). Skill acquisition: Compilation of weak-method problem-solutions. *Psychological Review, 94,* 192–210.

Anderson, J. R. (1996). ACT: A simple theory of complex cognition. *American Psychologist, 51,* 355–365.

Anderson, J. R., Fincham, J. M., & Douglass, S. (1999). Practice and retention: A unifying analysis. *Journal of Experimental Psychology: Learning, Memory, and Cognition, 25,* 1120–1136.

Anderson, N. B., McNeilly, M., & Myers, H. (1992). Toward understanding race difference in autonomic reactivity: A proposed contextual model. In J. R. Turner, A. Sherwood, & K. C. Light (Eds.), *Individual differences in cardiovascular response to stress* (pp. 125–145). New York: Plenum Press.

Anderson, V. L., Levinson, E. M., Barker, W., & Kiewra, K. R. (1999). The effects of meditation on teacher perceived occupational stress, state and trait anxiety, and burnout. *School Psychology Quarterly, 14,* 3–25.

Andrews, E. L. (1990, April 29). *A nicotine drug patch to end smoking. The New York Times Index* (Vol. 139, Section 1, Col. 1, p. 27, June 3, 1990).

Angier, N. (1999). *Woman: An intimate geography.* Boston, MA: Houghton Mifflin.

Anliker, J. A., Bartoshuk, L., Ferris, A. M., & Hooks, L. D. (1991). Children's food preferences and genetic sensitivity to the bitter taste of 6-*n*-propylthiouracil (PROP). *American Journal of Clinical Nutrition, 54,* 316–320.

Applebaum, P. S. (1994). *Almost a revolution: Mental health law and the limits of change.* New York: Oxford University Press.

Apter, M. J. (1989). *Reversal theory: Motivation, emotion, and personality.* London: Routledge.

Apter, M. J., & Batler, R. (1997). Gratuitous risk: A study of parachuting. In S. Svebak & M. J. Apter (Eds.), *Stress & health: A reversal theory perspective* (pp. 119–129). Washington, DC: Taylor & Francis.

Arendt, H. (1963). *Eichmann in Jerusalem: A report on the banality of evil.* New York: Viking Press.

Arendt, H. (1971). Organized guilt and universal responsibility. In R. W. Smith (Ed.), *Guilt: Man and society.* Garden City, NY: Doubleday Anchor Books.

Arkin, R. M. (Ed.). (1990). Centennial celebration of the principles of psychology. *Personality and Social Psychology Bulletin, 16*(4).

Aron, A., & Aron, E. N. (1994). Love. In A. L. Weber & J. H. Harvey (Eds.), *Perspectives on close relationships* (pp. 131–152). Boston: Allyn & Bacon.

Aron, A., Aron, E. N., & Smollan, D. (1992). Inclusion of other in the self scale and the structure of interpersonal closeness. *Journal of Personality and Social Psychology, 63,* 596–612.

Aron, A., Aron, E. N., Tudor, M., & Nelson, G. (1991). Close relationships as including other in the self. *Journal of Personality and Social Psychology, 60,* 241–253.

Aron, A., & Fraley, B. (1999). Relationship closeness as including other in the self: Cognitive underpinnings and measures. *Social Cognition, 17,* 140–160.

Aron, A., & Westbay, L. (1996). Dimensions of the prototype of love. *Journal of Personality and Social Psychology, 70,* 535–551.

Aronson, E. (1990). Applying social psychology to desegregation and energy conservation. *Personality and Social Psychology Bulletin, 16,* 118–132.

Aronson, E., Blaney, N., Stephan, C., Sikes, J., & Snapp, M. (1978). *The jigsaw classroom.* Beverly Hills, CA: Sage.

Aronson, E., & Gonzalez, A. (1988). Desegregation jigsaw, and the Mexican-American experience. In P. A. Katz & D. Taylor (Eds.), *Towards the elimination of racism: Profiles in controversy.* New York: Plenum Press.

Asch, S. E. (1940). Studies in the principles of judgments and attitudes: 11. Determination of judgments by group and by ego standards. *Journal of Social Psychology, 12,* 433–465.

Asch, S. E. (1952). *Social psychology.* Englewood Cliffs, NJ: Prentice Hall.

Asch, S. E. (1955). Opinions and social pressure. *Scientific American, 193*(5), 31–35.

Asch, S. E. (1956). Studies of independence and conformity: A minority of one against a unanimous majority. *Psychological Monographs, 70*(9, Whole No. 416).

Aserinsky, E., & Kleitman, N. (1953). Regularly occurring periods of eye mobility and concomitant phenomena during sleep. *Science, 118,* 273–274.

Ayllon, T., & Michael, J. (1959). The psychiatric nurse as a behavioral engineer. *Journal of the Experimental Analysis of Behavior, 2,* 323–334.

Ayres, T. J., Jonides, J., Reitman, J. S., Egan, J. C., & Howard, D. A. (1979). Differing suffix effects for the same physical stimulus. *Journal of Experimental Psychology: Human Learning and Memory, 5,* 315–321.

Baars, B. J. (1992). A dozen completing-plans techniques for inducing predictable slips in speech and action. In B. J. Baars (Ed.), *Experimental slips and human error: Exploring the architecture of volition* (pp. 129–150). New York: Plenum Press.

Baars, B. J. (1997). *In the theater of consciousness.* New York: Oxford University Press.

Baars, B. J., Cohen, J., Bower, G. H., & Berry, J. W. (1992). Some caveats on testing the Freudian slip hypothesis. In B. J. Baars (Ed.), *Experimental slips and human error: Exploring the architecture of volition* (pp. 289–313). New York: Plenum Press.

Baars, B. J., & McGovern, K. (1994). Consciousness. *Encyclopedia of Human Behavior, 1,* 687–699.

Baars, B. J., & McGovern, K. (1996). Cognitive views of consciousness: What are the facts? How can we explain them? In M. Velmans (Ed.), *The science of consciousness* (pp. 63–95). London: Routledge.

Baars, B. J., Motley, M. T., & MacKay, D. G. (1975). Output editing for lexical status in artificially elicited slips of the tongue. *Journal of Verbal Learning and Verbal Behavior, 14,* 382–391.

Bachar, E., Canetti, L., Bonne, O., Kaplan De-Nour, A., K., & Shalev, A. Y. (1997). Pre-adolescent chumship as a buffer against psychopathology in adolescents with weak family support and weak parental bonding. *Child Psychiatry and Human Development, 27,* 209–220.

Backman, C. W., & Secord, P. F. (1959). The effect of perceived liking on interpersonal attraction. *Human Relations, 12,* 379–384.

Baddeley, A. D. (1986). *Working memory.* New York: Oxford University Press.

Baddeley, A. D. (1992). Working memory. *Science, 255,* 556–559.

Baddeley, A. D. (1994). The magical number seven: Still magic after all these years? *Psychological Review, 101,* 353–356.

Baddeley, A. D., & Andrade, J. (2000). Working memory and the vividness of imagery. *Journal of Experimental Psychology: General, 129,* 126–145.

Bahrick, H. P., Bahrick, P. O., & Wittlinger, R. P. (1975). Fifty years of memory for names and faces: A cross-sectional approach. *Journal of Experimental Psychology: General, 104,* 54–75.

Bailey, J. M., & Pillard, R. C. (1991). A genetic study of male sexual orientation. *Archives of General Psychiatry, 48,* 1089–1096.

Bailey, J. M., Pillard, R. C., Dawood, K., Miller, M. B., Farrer, L. A., Trivedi, S., & Murphy, R. L. (1999). A family history study of male sexual orientation using three independent samples. *Behavior Genetics, 29,* 79–86.

Bailey, J. M., Pillard, R. C., Neale, M. C., & Agyei, Y. (1993). Heritable factors influence sexual orientation in women. *Archives of General Psychiatry, 50,* 217–223.

Bailey, M. B., & Bailey, R. E. (1993). "Misbehavior": A case history. *American Psychologist, 48,* 1157–1158.

Baillargeon, R. (1986). Representing the existence and the location of hidden objects: Object permanence. I. 6- and 8-month-old infants. *Cognition, 23,* 21–41.

Baillargeon, R. (1987a). Young infants reasoning about the physical and spatial properties of a hidden object. *Cognitive Development, 2,* 179–200.

Baillargeon, R. (1987b). Object permanence in 3½ and 4½-month-old infants. *Developmental Psychology, 23,* 655–664.

Baillargeon, R., & DeVos, J. (1991). Object permanence in young infants: Further evidence. *Child Development, 62,* 1227–1246.

Balch, W. R., & Lewis, B. S. (1996). Music-dependent memory: The roles of tempo change and mood mediation. *Journal of Experimental Psychology: Learning, Memory, and Cognition, 22,* 1354–1363.

Balda, R. P., Kamil, A. C., Bednekoff, P. A., & Hile, A. G. (1997). Species differences in spatial memory performance on a three-dimensional task. *Ethology, 103,* 47–55.

Baldwin, A. L., & Baldwin, C. P. (1973). Study of mother–child interaction. *American Scientist, 61,* 714–721.

Ballenger, J. C. (1999). Current treatments of the anxiety disorders in adults. *Biological Psychiatry, 46,* 1579–1594.

Baltes, P. B. (1993). The aging mind: Potential and limits. *The Gerontologist, 33,* 580–594.

Baltes, P. B., & Staudinger, U. M. (1993). The search for a psychology of wisdom. *Current Directions in Psychological Science, 2,* 75–80.

Baltes, P. B., Smith, J., & Staudinger, U. M. (1992). Wisdom and successful aging. In T. B. Sonderegger (Ed.), *The Nebraska Symposium on Motivation: Vol. 39. The psychology of aging* (pp. 123–167). Lincoln: University of Nebraska Press.

Baltes, P. B., & Staudinger, U. M. (2000). Wisdom: A metaheuristic (pragmatic) to orchestrate mind and virtue toward excellence. *American Psychologist, 55,* 122–136.

Banaji, M. R., & Prentice, D. A. (1994). The self in social contexts. *Annual Review of Psychology, 45,* 297–332.

Bancroft, J. (1978). The relationship between hormones and sexual behavior in humans. In J. B. Hutchinson (Ed.), *Biological determinants of sexual behavior* (pp. 493–519). New York: Wiley.

Bandura, A. (1970). Modeling therapy. In W. S. Sahakian (Ed.), *Psychopathology today: Experimentation, theory and research.* Itasca, IL: Peacock.

Bandura, A. (1977). *Social learning theory.* Englewood Cliffs, NJ: Prentice Hall.

Bandura, A. (1986). *Social foundations of thought and action: A social cognitive theory.* Englewood Cliffs, NJ: Prentice Hall.

Bandura, A. (1992). Exercise of personal agency through the self-efficacy mechanism. In R. Schwarzer (Ed.), *Self-efficacy: Thought control of action* (pp. 3–38). Washington, DC: Hemisphere.

Bandura, A. (1997). *Self-efficacy: The exercise of control.* New York: Freeman.

Bandura, A. (1999). Social cognitive theory of personality. In L. A. Pervin & O. P. John (Eds.), *Handbook of personality: Theory and research* (2nd ed.) (pp. 154–196). New York: Guilford Press.

Bandura, A., Barbaranelli, C., Caprara, G. V., & Pastorelli, C. (1996). Multifaceted impact of self-efficacy beliefs on academic functioning. *Child Development, 67,* 1206–1222.

Bandura, A., Ross, D., & Ross, S. A. (1963). Imitation of film-mediated aggressive models. *Journal of Abnormal and Social Psychology, 66,* 3–11.

Banks, M. S., & Bennet, P. J. (1988). Optical and photoreceptor immaturities limit the spatial and chromatic vision of human neonates. *Journal of the Optical Society of America, 5,* 2059–2079.

Banks, S. M., & Kerns, R. D. (1996). Explaining high rates of depression in chronic pain: A diathesis-stress framework. *Psychological Bulletin, 119,* 95–110.

Banks, W. C. (1990). *In Discovering Psychology, Program 16* [PBS video series]. Washington, DC: Annenberg/CPB Program.

Banuazizi, A., & Movahedi, S. (1975). Interpersonal dynamics in a simulated prison: A methodological analysis. *American Psychologist, 30,* 152–160.

Banyai, E. I., & Hilgard, E. R. (1976). Comparison of active-alert hypnotic induction with traditional relaxation induction. *Journal of Abnormal Psychology, 85,* 218–224.

Barbaranelli, C., Caprara, G. V., & Maslach, C. (1997). Individuation and the Five Factor Model of personality traits. *European Journal of Psychological Assessment, 13,* 75–84.

Bar-Hillel, M., & Neter, E. (1993). How alike is it versus how likely is it: A disjunction fallacy in probability judgments. *Journal of Personality and Social Psychology, 65,* 1119–1131.

Bargh, J. A., McKenna, K. Y. A., & Fitzsimmons, G. (2001). The self, online. In K. Y. A. McKenna & J. A. Bargh (Eds.), Interpersonal and group processes on the Internet: Is social life being transformed? *Journal of Social Issues.*

Barinaga, M. (1989). Can psychotherapy delay cancer deaths? *Science, 46,* 246, 249.

Barinaga, M. (1993). Carbon monoxide: Killer to brain messenger in one step. *Science, 259,* 309.

Barinaga, M. (1996). The cerebellum: Movement coordinator or much more? *Science, 272,* 482–433.

Barinaga, M. (1997). New imaging methods provide a better view into the brain. *Science, 276,* 1974–1976.

Barker, L. M., Best, M. R., & Domjan, M. (Eds.). (1978). *Learning mechanisms in food selection.* Houston: Baylor University Press.

Barker, R., Dembo, T., & Lewin, D. (1941). Frustration and aggression: An experiment with young children. *University of Iowa Studies in Child Welfare, 18*(1).

Barnett, W. S. (1998). Long-term cognitive and academic effects of early childhood education of children in poverty. *Preventive Medicine, 27,* 204–207.

Barondes, S. H. (1994). Thinking about Prozac. *Science, 263,* 1102–1103.

Bartlett, F. C. (1932). *Remembering: A study in experimental and social psychology.* Cambridge, U.K.: Cambridge University Press.

Bartoshuk, L. (1990, August–September). Psychophysiological insights on taste. *Science Agenda,* 12–13.

Bartoshuk, L. M. (1993). The biological basis of food perception and acceptance. *Food Quality and Preference, 4,* 21–32.

Bartoshuk, L. M., & Beauchamp, G. K. (1994). Chemical senses. *Annual Review of Psychology, 45,* 419–449.

Bartoshuk, L. M., Duffy, V. B., & Miller, I. J. (1994). PTC/PROP tasting: Anatomy, psychophysics, and sex effects. *Physiology and Behavior, 56,* 1165–1171.

Bassili, J. N. (1995). Response latency and the accessibility of voting intentions: What contributes to accessibility and how it affects vote choice. *Personality and Social Psychology Bulletin, 21,* 686–695.

Basso, E. B. (1987). The implications of a progressive theory of dreaming. In B. Tedlock (Ed.), *Dreaming: Anthropological and psychological interpretations* (pp. 86–104). Cambridge, U.K.: Cambridge University Press.

Batson, C. D. (1994). Why act for the public good? Four answers. *Personality and Social Psychology Bulletin, 20,* 603–610.

Batson, C. D., Ahmad, N., Yin, J., Bedell, S. J., Johnson, J. W., Templin, C. M., & Whiteside, A. (1999). Two threats to the common good: Self-interested egoism and empathy-induced altruism. *Personality and Social Psychology Bulletin, 25,* 3–16.

Batson, C. D., Klein, T. R., Highberger, L., & Shaw, L. L. (1995). Immorality from empathy-induced altruism: When compassion and justice conflict. *Journal of Personality and Social Psychology, 68,* 1042–1054.

Baumeister, R. F. (Ed.). (1994). Samples made of stories: Research using autobiographical narratives [Special issue]. *Personality and Social Psychology Bulletin, 20*(6).

Baumeister, R. F. (2000). Gender differences in erotic plasticity: The female sex drive as socially flexible and responsive. *Psychological Bulletin, 126,* 347–374.

Baumeister, R. F., Tice, D. M., & Hutton, D. G. (1989). Self-presentational motivations and personality differences in self-esteem. *Journal of Personality, 57,* 547–579.

Baumgardner, A. H. (1990). To know oneself is to like oneself: Self-certainty and self-affect. *Journal of Personality and Social Psychology, 58,* 1062–1072.

Baumrind, D. (1986). Sex differences in moral reasoning: Response to Walker's 1984 conclusion that there are none. *Child Development, 57,* 511–521.

Baxter, L. R., Schwartz, J. M., Bergman, K. S., Szuba, M. P., Guze, B. H., Mazziotta, J. C., Alazraki, A., Selin, C. E., Ferng, H. K., Munford, P., & Phelps, M. E. (1992). Caudate glucose metabolic rate changes with both drug and behavior therapy for obsessive-compulsive disorder. *Archives of General Psychiatry, 49,* 681–689.

Bayley, N. (1956). Individual patterns of development. *Child Development, 27,* 45–74.

Baylor, D. (1987). Photoreceptor signals and vision. *Investigative Opthalmology and Visual Science, 28,* 34–49.

Beattie, J., Baron, J., Hershey, J. C., & Spranca, M. D. (1994). Psychological determinants of decision attitude. *Journal of Behavioral Decision Making, 7,* 129–144.

Beck, A. T. (1976). *Cognitive therapy and emotional disorders.* New York: International Universities Press.

Beck, A. T. (1983). Cognitive theory of depression: New perspectives. In P. J. Clayton & J. E. Barrett (Eds.), *Treatment of depression: Old controversies and new approaches* (pp. 265–290). New York: Raven Press.

Beck, A. T. (1985). Cognitive therapy. In H. I. Kaplan & J. Sandock (Eds.), *Comprehensive textbook of psychiatry* (4th ed.). Baltimore: Williams & Wilkins.

Beck, A. T. (1988). Cognitive approaches to panic disorders: Theory and therapy. In S. Rachman & J. D. Maser (Eds.), *Panic: Psychological perspectives.* New York: Guilford Press.

Beck, A. T., & Emery, G. (1985). *Anxiety disorders and phobias: A cognitive perspective.* New York: Basic Books.

Beck, A. T., & Rush, A. J. (1989). Cognitive therapy. In H. I. Kaplan & B. Sadock (Eds.), *Comprehensive textbook of psychiatry* (Vol. 5). Baltimore: Williams & Wilkins.

Beck, A. T., Rush, A. J., Shaw, B. F., & Emery, G. (1979). *Cognitive therapy of depression.* New York: Guilford Press.

Beiser, M., & Gotowiec, A. (2000). Accounting for native/non-native differences in IQ scores. *Psychology in the Schools, 37,* 237–252.

Bell, A. P., & Weinberg, M. S. (1978). *Homosexualities: A study of diversity among men and women.* New York: Simon & Schuster.

Bell, I. R. (1982). *Clinical ecology.* Bolinas, CA: Common Knowledge Press.

Bell, S. T., Kuriloff, P. J., & Lottes, I. (1994). Understanding attributions of blame in stranger rape and date rape situations: An examination of gender, race, identification, and students' social perceptions of rape victims. *Journal of Applied Social Psychology, 24,* 1719–1734.

Bem, D. (2000). The exotic-becomes-erotic theory of sexual orientation. In J. Bancroft (Ed.), *The role of theory in sex research* (pp. 67–81). Bloomington: Indiana University Press.

Bem, D. J. (1972). Self-perception theory. In L. Berkowitz (Ed.), *Advances in experimental social psychology* (Vol. 6, pp. 1–62). New York: Academic Press.

Bem, D. J. (1996). Exotic becomes erotic: A developmental theory of sexual orientation. *Psychological Review, 103,* 320–335.

Bem, D. J., & Honorton, C. (1994). Does psi exist? Replicable evidence for an anomalous process of information transfer. *Psychological Bulletin, 115,* 4–18.

Bem, S. L. (1974). The measurement of psychological androgyny. *Journal of Consulting and Clinical Psychology, 42,* 155–162.

Bem, S. L. (1981). *The Bem Sex Role Inventory: Professional manual.* Palo Alto, CA: Consulting Psychology Press.

Benedict, R. (1938). Continuities and discontinuities in cultural conditioning. *Psychiatry, 1,* 161–167.

Benedict, R. (1959). *Patterns of culture.* Boston: Houghton Mifflin.

Benenson, J. F., Apostoleris, N. H., & Parnass, J. (1997). Age and sex differences in dyadic and group interaction. *Developmental Psychology, 33,* 538–543.

Benhamou, S., & Poucet, B. (1996). A comparative analysis of spatial memory processes. *Behavioural Processes, 35,* 113–126.

Benington, J. H., & Heller, H. C. (1994). Does the function of REM sleep concern non-REM sleep or waking? *Progress in Neurobiology, 44,* 433–449.

Benington, J. H., & Heller, H. C. (1995). Restoration of brain energy metabolism as the function of sleep. *Progress in Neurobiology, 45,* 347–360.

Benson, H., & Stuart, E. M. (Eds.). (1992). *The wellness book.* New York: Simon & Schuster.

Bergman, E. T., & Roediger, H. L., III. (1999). Can Bartlett's repeated reproduction experiments be replicated? *Memory & Cognition, 27,* 937–947.

Berkowitz, L. (1993). *Aggression: Its causes, consequences, and control.* New York: McGraw-Hill.

Berkowitz, L. (1998). Affective aggression: The role of stress, pain, and negative affect. In R. G. Geen & E. Donnerstein (Eds.), *Human aggression: Theories, research, and implications for public policy* (pp. 49–72). San Diego, CA: Academic Press.

Berlin, B., & Kay, P. (1969). *Basic color terms: Their universality and evolution.* Berkeley: University of California Press.

Berlyne, D. E. (1960). *Conflict, arousal, and curiosity.* New York: McGraw-Hill.

Berman, A. L., & Jobes, D. A. (1991). *Adolescent suicide: Assessment and intervention.* Washington, DC: American Psychological Association.

Berman, K. F., Torrey, E. F., Daniel, D. G., & Weinberger, D. R. (1992). Regional cerebral blood flow in monozygotic twins discordant and concordant for schizophrenia. *Archives of General Psychiatry, 49,* 927–934.

Bernard, L. L. (1924). *Instinct.* New York: Holt, Rinehart & Winston.

Berndt, T. J. (1992). Friendship and friends' influence in adolescence. *Current Directions in Psychological Science, 1,* 156–159.

Bernstein, I. L. (1988). What does learning have to do with weight loss and cancer? *Proceedings of the Science and Public Policy Seminar of the*

Federation of Behavioral, Psychological and Cognitive Sciences, Washington, DC.

Bernstein, I. L. (1990). Salt preferences and development. *Developmental Psychology, 26,* 552–554.

Bernstein, I. L. (1991). Aversion conditioning in response to cancer and cancer treatment. *Clinical Psychology Review, 11,* 185–191.

Berrettini, W. H., Ferraro, T. N., Goldin, L. R., Detera-Wadleigh, S. D., Choi, H., Muniec, D., Guroff, J. J., Kazuba, D. M., Nurnberger, J. I., Jr., Hsieh, W.-T., Hoehe, M. R., & Gershon, E. S. (1997). A linkage study of bipolar illness. *Archives of General Psychiatry, 54,* 27–35.

Berscheid, E., & Walster, E. H. (1978). *Interpersonal attraction* (2nd ed.). Reading, MA: Addison-Wesley.

Bertenthal, B. I., & Fischer, K. W. (1978). Development of self-recognition in the infant. *Developmental Psychology, 14,* 44–50.

Bexton, W. H., Heron, W., & Scott, T. H. (1954). Effects of decreased variation in the sensory environment. *Canadian Journal of Psychology, 8,* 70–76.

Bickerton, D. (1990). *Language and species.* Chicago: University of Chicago Press.

Biederman, I. (1987). Recognition by components. *Psychological Review, 94,* 115–147.

Biederman, I., & Cooper, E. E. (1991). Priming contour-deleted images: Evidence for intermediate representations in visual object recognition. *Cognitive Psychology, 23,* 393–419.

Biehl, M., Matsumoto, D., Ekman, P., Hearn, V., Heider, K., Kudoh, T., & Ton, V. (1997). Matsumoto and Ekman's Japanese and Caucasian facial expressions of emotion (JACFEE): Reliability data and cross-national differences. *Journal of Nonverbal Behavior, 21,* 3–21.

Biglan, A. (1991). Distressed behavior and its context. *Behavior Analyst, 14,* 157–169.

Billings, A. G., & Moos, R. H. (1982). Family environments and adaptation: A clinically applicable typology. *American Journal of Family Therapy, 20,* 26–38.

Binder, K. S., & Morris, R. K. (1995). Eye movements and lexical ambiguity resolution: Effects of prior encounter and discourse topic. *Journal of Experimental Psychology: Learning, Memory, and Cognition, 21,* 1186–1196.

Binet, A. (1911). *Les idées modernes sur les enfants.* Paris: Flammarion.

Bingham, C. R., Bennion, L. D., Openshaw, D. K., & Adams, G. R. (1994). An analysis of age, gender and racial differences in recent national trends of youth suicide. *Journal of Adolescence, 17,* 53–71.

Bitterman, M. E. (1975). The comparative analysis of learning. *Science, 188,* 699–709.

Blais, M. A., & Norman, D. K. (1997). A psychometric evaluation of the DSM-IV Personality Disorder criteria. *Journal of Personality Disorders, 11,* 168–176.

Blanchard, E. B., George, E., Vollmer, A., Payne, A., Gordon, M., Cornish, P., & Gilmore, L. (1996). Controlled evaluation of thermal biofeedback in treatment of elevated blood pressure in unmedicated mild hypertension. *Biofeedback and Self-Regulation, 21,* 167–190.

Blascovich, J., Wyer, N. A., Swart, L. A., & Kibler, J. L. (1997). Racism and racial categorization. *Journal of Personality and Social Psychology, 72,* 1364–1372.

Blau, G. L., McGinley, H., & Pasewark, R. (1993). Understanding the use of the insanity defense. *Journal of Clinical Psychology, 49,* 435–440.

Blehar, M. C., & Rosenthal, N. E. (1989). Seasonal affective disorders and phototherapy: Report of a National Institute of Mental Health-sponsored workshop. *Archives of General Psychiatry, 46,* 469–474.

Bleuler, M. (1978). The long-term course of schizophrenic psychoses. In L. C. Wynne, R. L. Cromwell, & S. Mattysse (Eds.), *The nature of schizophrenia: New approaches to research and treatment* (pp. 631–636). New York: Wiley.

Block, J. (1995). A contrarian view of the five-factor approach to personality description. *Psychological Bulletin, 117,* 187–215.

Bloom, K., Delmore-Ko, P., Masataka, N., & Carli, L. (1999). Possible self as parent in Canadian, Italian, and Japanese young adults. *Canadian Journal of Behavioural Science, 31,* 198–207.

Blos, P. (1965). *On adolescence: A psychoanalytic interpretation.* New York: The Free Press.

Bock, J. K. (1986). Meaning, sound, and syntax: Lexical priming in sentence production. *Journal of Experimental Psychology: Learning, Memory, and Cognition, 12,* 575–586.

Bock, K. (1990). Structure in language: Creating form in talk. *American Psychologist, 45,* 1221–1236.

Bock, K. (1996). Language production: Methods and methodologies. *Psychonomic Bulletin & Review, 3,* 395–421.

Bock, K., & Levelt, W. (1994). Language production: Grammatical encoding. In M. A. Gernsbacher (Ed.), *Handbook of psycholinguistics* (pp. 945–984). San Diego, CA: Academic Press.

Bohlin, G., Hagekull, B., & Rydell, A.-M. (2000). Attachment and social functioning: A longitudinal study from infancy to middle childhood. *Social Development, 9,* 24–39.

Boldizar, J. P., Wilson, K. L., & Deemer, D. K. (1989). Gender, life experiences, and moral judgment development: A process-oriented approach. *Journal of Personality and Social Psychology, 57,* 229–238.

Bond, C. F., Jr., Pitre, U., & van Leeuwen, M. D. (1991). Encoding operations and the next-in-line effect. *Personality and Social Psychology Bulletin, 17,* 435–441.

Bond, L. (1995). Unintended consequences of performance assessment: Issues of bias and fairness. *Educational Measurement: Issues and Practice, 14,* 21–24.

Boone, D. E. (1994). Validity of the MMPI-2 depression content scale with psychiatric in-patients. *Psychological Reports, 74,* 159–162.

Borman, W. C., Hanson, M. A., & Hedge, J. W. (1997). Personnel selection. *Annual Review of Psychology, 48,* 299–337.

Bornstein, P. A., & Quinna, K. (Eds.). (1988). *Teaching a psychology of people: Resources for gender and sociocultural awareness.* Washington, DC: American Psychological Association.

Bouchard, C., Tremblay, A., Nadeau, A., Despres, J. P. Theriault, G., Boulay, M. R., Lortie, G., Leblanc, C., & Fournier, G. (1989). Genetic effect in resting and exercise metabolic rates. *Metabolism, 38,* 364–370.

Bouchard, T. J. (1994). Genes, environment, and personality. *Science, 264,* 1700–1701.

Bourguignon, E. (1979). *Psychological anthropology: An introduction to human nature and cultural differences.* New York: Holt, Rinehart & Winston.

Bowd, A. D., & Shapiro, K. J. (1993). The case against laboratory animal research in psychology. *Journal of Social Issues, 49,* 133–142.

Bowden, E. M., & Beeman, M. J. (1998). Getting the right idea: Semantic activation in the right hemisphere may help solve insight problems. *Psychological Science, 9,* 435–440.

Bower, G. H. (1972). A selective review of organizational factors in memory. In E. Tulving & W. Donaldson (Eds.), *Organization of memory.* New York: Academic Press.

Bower, G. H. (1981). Mood and memory. *American Psychologist, 36,* 129–148.

Bower, G. H. (1991). Mood congruity of social judgements. In J. P. Forgas (Ed.), *Emotional & social judgments* (pp. 31–54). Oxford: Pergamon Press.

Bower, G. H., Thompson-Schill, S., & Tulving, E. (1994). Reducing retroactive interference: An interference analysis. *Journal of Experimental Psychology: Learning, Memory, and Cognition, 20,* 51–66.

Bower, S. A., & Bower, G. H. (1991). *Asserting yourself: A practical guide for positive change.* Reading, MA: Addison-Wesley. (Original work published 1976)

Bowers, K. S. (1976). *Hypnosis for the seriously curious.* New York: Norton.

Bowlby, J. (1969). *Attachment and loss, Vol 1. Attachment.* New York: Basic Books.

Bowlby, J. (1973). *Attachment and loss, Vol 2. Separation, anxiety and anger.* London: Hogarth.

Bradley, M. M. (1994). Emotional memory: A dimensional analysis. In S. H. M. van Goozen, N. E. Van de Poll, & J. A. Sergeant (Eds.), *Emotions: Essays on emotion theory* (pp. 97–134). Hillsdale, NJ: Erlbaum.

Braginsky, B., & Braginsky, D. (1967). Schizophrenic patients in the psychiatric interview: An experimental study of their effectiveness at manipulation. *Journal of Consulting Psychology, 31,* 543–547.

Brainerd, C. J. (1996). Piaget: A centennial celebration. *Psychological Science, 7,* 191–195.

Brakke, K. E., & Savage-Rumbaugh, E. S. (1995). The development of language skills in bonobo and chimpanzee—I. Comprehension. *Language & Communication, 15,* 121–148.

Brando, M. (1994). *Brando: Songs my mother taught me.* New York: Random House.

Breedlove, S. M. (1994). Sexual differentiation of the human nervous system. *Annual Review of Psychology, 45,* 389–418.

Breggin, P. R. (1979). *Electroshock: Its brain disabling effects.* New York: Springer.

Breggin, P. R. (1991). *Toxic psychiatry.* New York: St. Martin's Press.

Breggin, P. R., & Breggin, G. R. (1994). *Talking back to Prozac.* New York: St. Martin's Press.

Bregman, A. S. (1981). Asking the "what for" question in auditory perception. In M. Kobovy & J. Pomerantz (Eds.), *Perceptual organization* (pp. 99–118). Hillsdale, NJ: Erlbaum.

Breland, K., & Breland, M. (1951). A field of applied animal psychology. *American Psychologist, 6,* 202–204.

Breland, K., & Breland, M. (1961). A misbehavior of organisms. *American Psychologist, 16,* 681–684.

Brennan, S. E., & Williams, M. (1995). The feeling of another's knowing: Prosody and filled pauses as cues to listeners about the metacognitive states of speakers. *Journal of Memory and Language, 34,* 383–398.

Breslau, N. Davis, G. C., Andreski, P., Peterson, E. L., & Schultz, L. R. (1997). Sex differences in posttraumatic stress disorder. *Archives of General Psychiatry, 54,* 1044–1048.

Brewer, J. B., Zhao, Z., Desmond, J. E., Glover, G. H., & Gabrieli, J. D. E. (1998). Making memories: Brain activity that predicts how well visual experience will be remembered. *Science, 281,* 1185–1187.

Brewer, M. B., Dull, V., & Lui, L. (1981). Perceptions of the elderly: Stereotypes as prototypes. *Journal of Personality and Social Psychology, 41,* 656–670.

Brewer, M. B., & Lui, L. (1989). The primacy of age and sex in the structure of person categories. *Social Cognition, 7,* 262–274.

Briggs, C. L. (1996). The meaning of nonsense, the poetics of embodiment, and the production of power in Warao healing. In C. Laderman & M. Roseman (Eds.), *The performance of healing* (pp. 185–232). New York: Routledge.

Broadbent, D. E. (1958). *Perception and communication.* London: Pergamon Press.

Brody, L. R. (1997a). Gender and emotion: Beyond stereotypes. *Journal of Social Issues, 53,* 369–393.

Brody, N. (1997b). Intelligence, schooling, and society. *American Psychologist, 52,* 1046–1050.

Broman, S. H., Nichols, P. I., & Kennedy, W. A. (1975). *Preschool IQ: Prenatal and early developmental correlates.* Hillsdale, NJ: Erlbaum.

Bronfenbrenner, U. (1999). Environments in developmental perspective: Theoretical and operational models. In S. L. Friedman & T. D. Wachs (Eds.), *Measuring environment across the lifespan: Emerging methods and concepts* (pp. 3–28). Washington, DC: American Psychological Association.

Bronfenbrenner, U., & Ceci, S. J. (1994). Nature–nurture reconceptualized in developmental perspective: A bioecological model. *Psychological Review, 101,* 568–586.

Brooner, R. K., King. V. L., Kidorf, M., Schmidt, C. W., & Bigelow, G. E. (1997). Psychiatric and substance abuse comorbidity among treatment-seeking opioid abusers. *Archives of General Psychiatry, 54,* 71–80.

Broughton, W. A., & Broughton, R. J. (1994). Psychosocial impact of narcolepsy. *Sleep, 17*(Suppl. 8), S45–S49.

Broussard, C., & Northup, J. (1997). The use of functional analysis to develop peer interventions for disruptive classroom behavior. *School Psychology Quarterly, 12,* 65–76.

Brown, B. B. (1989). The role of peer groups in adolescents' adjustment to secondary school. In T. J. Berndt & G. W. Ladd (Eds.), *Peer relationships in child development* (pp. 188–215). New York: Wiley.

Brown, J. D. (1998). *The self.* New York: McGraw-Hill.

Brown, N. R., & Siegler, R. S. (1992). The role of availability in the estimation of national populations. *Memory & Cognition, 20,* 406–412.

Brown, R. (1976). Reference: In memorial tribute to Eric Lenneberg. *Cognition, 4,* 125–153.

Brown, R. (1986). *Social psychology: The second edition.* New York: The Free Press.

Brownell, K. D., & Rodin, J. (1994). The dieting maelstrom: Is it possible and advisable to lose weight? *American Psychologist, 49,* 781–791.

Bruner, J. S., Olver, R. R., & Greenfield, P. M. (1966). *Studies in cognitive growth.* New York: Wiley.

Brzustowicz, L. M., Hodgkinson, K. A., Chow, E. W. C., Honer, W. G., & Bassett, A. S. (2000). Location of a major susceptibility locus for familial schizophrenia on chromosome 1q21-q22. *Science, 288,* 678–682.

Buchner, A., & Wippich, W. (2000). On the reliability of implicit and explicit memory measures. *Cognitive Psychology, 40,* 227–259.

Bukowski, W. M., Newcomb, A. F., & Hartup, W. W. (Eds.). (1998). *The company they keep: Friendship in childhood and adolescence.* New York: Cambridge University Press.

Bulman, J. R., & Wortman, C. B. (1977). Attribution of blame and coping in the "real world": Severe accident victims react to their lot. *Journal of Personality and Social Psychology, 35,* 351–363.

Buntain-Ricklefs, J. J., Kemper, K. J., Bell, M., & Babonis, T. (1994). Punishments: What predicts adult approval. *Child Abuse & Neglect, 18,* 945–955.

Burchinal, M. R., Roberts, J. E., Riggins, R., Jr., Zeisel, S. A., Neebe, E., & Bryant, D. (2000). Relating quality of center-based child care to early cognitive and language development longitudinally. *Child Development, 71,* 338–357.

Burger, J. M., & Burns, L. (1988). The illusion of unique invulnerability and the use of effective contraception. *Personality and Social Psychology Bulletin, 14,* 264–270.

Burnstein, E., Crandall, C., & Kitayama, S. (1994). Some neo-Darwinian decision rules for altruism: Weighing cues for inclusive fitness as a function of the biological importance of the decision. *Journal of Personality and Social Psychology, 67,* 773–789.

Burnstein, E., & Worchel, P. (1962). Arbitrariness of frustration and its consequences for aggression in a social situation. *Journal of Personality, 30,* 528–540.

Buss, D. M. (1999). *Evolutionary psychology: The new science of mind.* Boston, MA: Allyn & Bacon.

Buss, D. M. (2000). The evolution of happiness. *American Psychologist, 55,* 15–23.

Buss, D. M., & Schmitt, D. P. (1993). Sexual strategies theory: An evolutionary perspective on human mating. *Psychological Review, 100,* 204–232.

Butcher, J. N., Dahlstrom, W. G., Graham, J. R., Tellegen, A., & Kaemmer, B. (1989). *Manual for the restandardized Minnesota Multiphasic Personality Inventory: MMPI-2. An administrative and interpretive guide.* Minneapolis: University of Minnesota Press.

Butcher, J. N., & Rouse, S. V. (1996). Personality: Individual differences and clinical assessment. *Annual Review of Psychology, 47,* 87–111.

Butcher, J. N., & Williams, C. L. (1992). *Essentials of MMPI-2 and MMPI-A interpretation.* Minneapolis: University of Minnesota Press.

Butler, L. D., & Nolen-Hoeksema, S. (1994). Gender differences in responses to depressed mood in a college sample. *Sex Roles, 30,* 331–346.

Bykov, K. M. (1957). *The cerebral cortex and the internal organs.* New York: Academic Press.

Byrne, D., & Clore, G. L. (1970). A reinforcement model of evaluative processes. *Personality: An International Journal, 1,* 103–128.

Cabeza, R., & Nyberg, L. (2000). Imaging cognition II: An empirical review of 275 PET and fMRI studies. *Journal of Cognitive Neuroscience, 12,* 1–47.

Cadoret, R. J., Yates, W. R., Troughton, E., Woodworth, G., & Stewart, M. A. (1995). Genetic-environmental interaction in the genesis of aggressivity and conduct disorders. *Archives of General Psychiatry, 52,* 916–924.

Cairns, E., Wilson, R., Gallagher, T., & Trew, K. (1995). Psychology's contribution to understanding conflict in Northern Ireland. *Peace and Conflict: Journal of Peace Psychology, 1,* 131–148.

Campbell, W. K., Sedikides, C., Reeder, G. D., & Elliot, A. J. (2000). Among friends? An examination of friendship and the self-serving bias. *British Journal of Social Psychology, 39,* 229–239.

Campfield, L. A., Smith, F. J., & Burn, P. (1998). Strategies and potential molecular targets for obesity treatment. *Science, 280,* 1383–1387.

Campos, J. J., Barrett, K. C., Lamb, M. E., Goldsmith, H. H., & Stenberg, C. (1983). *Socioemotional development* (Vol. 2). New York: Wiley.

Campos, J. J., Bertenthal, B. I., & Kermoian, R. (1992). Early experience and emotional development: The emergence of wariness of heights. *Psychological Science, 3,* 61–64.

Camras, L. A., Oster, H., Campos, J., Campos, R., Ujiie, T., Miyake, K., Wang, L., & Meng, Z. (1998). Production of emotional facial expressions in European American, Japanese, and Chinese infants. *Developmental Psychology, 34,* 616–628.

Camras, L. A., Oster, H., Campos, J. J., Miyake, K., & Bradshaw, D. (1992). Japanese and American infants' responses to arm restraint. *Developmental Psychology, 28,* 578–583.

Cannon, W. B. (1927). The James–Lange theory of emotion: A critical examination and an alternative theory. *American Journal of Psychology, 39,* 106–124.

Cannon, W. B. (1929). *Bodily changes in pain, hunger, fear, and rage* (2nd ed.). New York: Appleton-Century-Crofts.

Cannon, W. B. (1934). Hunger and thirst. In C. Murchison (Ed.) *A handbook of general experimental psychology.* Worcester, MA: Clark University Press.

Cannon, W. B., & Washburn, A. L. (1912). An explanation of hunger. *American Journal of Physiology, 29,* 441–454.

Cantor, N., & Kihlstrom, J. R. (1987). *Personality and social intelligence.* Englewood Cliffs, NJ: Prentice Hall.

Cantor, N., & Mischel, W. (1979). Traits as prototypes: Effects on recognition memory. *Journal of Personality and Social Psychology, 35,* 38–48.

Caplan, L. (1992, March 30). Not so nutty: The post-Dahmer insanity defense. *The New Republic,* pp. 18–20.

Caprara, G. V., Barbaranelli, C., Borgoni, L., & Perugini, M. (1993). The Big Five Questionnaire: A new questionnaire for the measurement of the five factor model. *Personality and Individual Differences, 15,* 281–288.

Caprara, G. V., Barbaranelli, C., & Zimbardo, P. G. (1996). Understanding the complexity of human aggression: Affective, cognitive, and social dimensions of individual differences in propensity toward aggression. *European Journal of Personality, 10,* 133–155.

Carducci, B. J., & Zimbardo, P. G. (1995, November/December). Are you shy? *Psychology Today, 28,* 34–40.

Carey, S. (1978). The child as word learner. In M. Hale, J. Bresnan, & G. A. Miller (Eds.), *Linguistic theory and psychological reality* (pp. 265–293). Cambridge, MA: The MIT Press.

Carey, S. (1985). *Conceptual change in childhood.* Cambridge, MA: The MIT Press.

Carlsmith, J. M., & Gross, A. (1969). Some effects of guilt on compliance. *Journal of Personality and Social Psychology, 11,* 232–240.

Carlson, M., Charlin, V., & Miller, N. (1988). Positive mood and helping behavior: A test of six hypotheses. *Journal of Personality and Social Psychology, 55,* 211–229.

Carlson-Radvansky, L. A., & Irwin, D. E. (1995). Memory for structural information across eye movements. *Journal of Experimental Psychology: Learning, Memory, and Cognition, 21,* 1441–1458.

Carmelli, D., & Swan, G. E. (1996). The relationship of Type A behavior and its components to all-cause mortality in an elderly subgroup of men from the Western Collaborative Group Study. *Journal of Psychosomatic Research, 40,* 475–483.

Carmichael, L. (1926). The development of behavior in vertebrates experimentally removed from the influence of external stimulation. *Psychological Review, 33,* 51–58.

Carmichael, L. (1970). The onset and early development of behavior. In P. H. Mussen (Ed.), *Carmichael's manual of child psychology* (3rd ed., Vol. 1). New York: Wiley.

Carstensen, L. L. (1991). Selectivity theory: Social activity in life-span context. In K. W. Schaie (Ed.), *Annual review of geriatrics and gerontology* (Vol. 11). New York: Springer.

Carstensen, L. L. (1998). A life-span approach to social motivation. In J. Heckhausen & C. S. Dweck (Eds.), *Motivation and self-regulation across the life span* (pp. 341–364). New York: Cambridge University Press.

Carstensen, L. L., & Freund, A. M. (1994). The resilience of the aging self. *Developmental Review, 14,* 81–92.

Carstensen, L. L., & Pasupathi, M. (1993). Women of a certain age. In S. Matteo (Ed.), *American women in the nineties: Today's critical issues* (pp. 66–78). Boston: Northeastern University Press.

Carter, J. H. (1982). The effects of aging on selected visual functions: Color vision, glare sensitivity, field of vision, and accommodation. In R. Sekuler, D. Kline, & K. Dismukes (Eds.), *Aging and human visual function* (pp. 121–130). New York: Liss.

Cartwright, R. D. (1978). *A primer on sleep and dreaming.* Reading, MA: Addison-Wesley.

Cartwright, R. D. (1982). The shape of dreams. In *1983 yearbook of science and the future.* Chicago: Encyclopaedia Britannica.

Catalan, J., Burgess, A., Pergami, A., Hulme, N., Gazzard, B., & Phillips, R. (1996). The psychological impact on staff of caring for people with serious diseases: The case of HIV infection and oncology. *Journal of Psychosomatic Research, 42,* 425–435.

Catalano, R., Novaco, R., & McConnell, W. (1997). A model of the net effect of job loss on violence. *Journal of Personality and Social Psychology, 72,* 1440–1447.

Catania, J. A., Coates, T. J., & Kegeles, S. (1994). A test of the AIDS risk reduction model: Psychosocial correlates of condom use in the AMEN cohort survey. *Health Psychology, 13,* 548–555.

Caterina, M. J., Leffler, A., Malmberg, A. B., Martin, W. J., Trafton, J., Petersen-Zeitz, K. R., Koltzenburg, M., Basbaum, A. I., & Julius, D.

(2000). Impaired nociception and pain sensation in mice lacking the capsaicin receptor. *Science, 288,* 306–313.

Catrambone, R., Jones, C. M., Jonides, J., & Seifert, C. (1995). Reasoning about curvilinear motion: Using principles of analogy. *Memory & Cognition, 23,* 368–373.

Cattell, R. B. (1963). Theory of fluid and crystallized intelligence: A critical experiment. *Journal of Educational Psychology, 54,* 1–22.

Cattell, R. B. (1979). *Personality and learning theory.* New York: Springer.

Cave, C. B., & Squire, L. R. (1992). Intact and long-lasting repetition priming in amnesia. *Journal of Experimental Psychology: Learning, Memory, and Cognition, 18,* 509–520.

Ceci, S. J. (1999). Schooling and intelligence. In S. J. Ceci & W. M. Williams (Eds.), *The nature-nurture debate: The essential readings* (pp. 168–175). Oxford, U.K.: Blackwell.

Ceci, S. J., & Liker, J. K. (1986). A day at the races: A study of IQ, expertise, and cognitive complexity. *Journal of Experimental Psychology: General, 115,* 255–266.

Centers for Disease Control and Prevention. (1997). Cigarette smoking among adults—United States, 1995. *Morbidity and Mortality Weekly Report, 46,* 1217–1220.

Cervone, D. (2000). Thinking about self-efficacy. *Behavior Modification, 24,* 30–56.

Cervone, D., & Shoda, Y. (Eds.). (1999). *The coherence of personality: Social-cognitive bases of consistency, variability, and organization.* New York: Guilford Press.

Chae, Y. M. (1998). Expert systems in medicine. In J. Liebowitz (Ed.), *The handbook of applied expert systems* (pp. 32-1–32-20). Boca Raton, FL: CRC Press.

Chamberlain, K., & Zika, S. (1990). The minor events approach to stress: Support for the use of daily hassles. *British Journal of Psychology, 81,* 469–481.

Champoux, M., Boyce, W. T., & Suomi, S. J. (1995). Biobehavioral comparisons between adopted and nonadopted rhesus monkey infants. *Journal of Developmental and Behavioral Pediatrics, 16,* 6–13.

Chan, A. Y., & Wethington, E. (1998). Factors promoting marital resilience among interracial couples. In H. I. McCubbin, E. A. Thompson, A. I. Thompson, & J. E. Fromer (Eds.), *Resiliency in Native American and immigrant families* (pp. 71–87). Thousand Oaks, CA: Sage.

Chandler, C. C., & Gargano, G. J. (1995). Item-specific interference caused by cue-dependent forgetting. *Memory & Cognition, 23,* 701–708.

Chandrasekaran, B., & Mittal, S. (1999). Deep versus compiled knowledge approaches to diagnostic problem-solving. *International Journal of Human-Computer Studies, 51,* 357–368.

Chapman, P. D. (1988). *Schools as sorters: Lewis M. Terman, applied psychology, and the intelligence testing movement, 1890–1930.* New York: New York University Press.

Chase, W. G., & Ericsson, K. A. (1981). Skilled memory. In J. R. Anderson (Ed.), *Cognitive skills and their acquisition.* Hillsdale, NJ: Erlbaum.

Chasnoff, I. J., Anson, A., Hatcher, R., Senson, H., Iaukea, K., & Randolph, L. (1998). Prenatal exposure to cocaine and other drugs: Outcome at four to six years. In J. A. Harvey & B. E. Kosofsky (Eds.), *Cocaine: Effects on the developing brain* (pp. 314–328). New York: New York Academy of Sciences.

Chaudhari, N., Landin, A. M., & Roper, S. D. (2000). A metabotropic glutamate receptor variant functions as a taste receptor. *Nature Neuroscience, 3,* 113–119.

Chaves, J. F. (1999). Applying hypnosis in pain management: Implications of alternative theoretical perspectives. In I. Kirsch, A. Capafons, E. Cardeña-Buelna, & S. Amigó (Eds.), *Clinical hypnosis and self-regulation: Cognitive-behavioral perspectives* (pp. 227–247). Washington, DC: American Psychological Association.

Cheek, J. (1989). *Conquering shyness: The battle anyone can win.* New York: Putnam.

Chen, I. (1990, July 13). Quake may have caused baby boom in Bay Area. *The San Francisco Chronicle,* p. A3.

Cheney, D. L., & Seyfarth, R. M. (1990). *How monkeys see the world.* Chicago: University of Chicago Press.

Cheng, P. W., & Holyoak, K. J. (1985). Pragmatic reasoning schemas. *Cognitive Psychology, 17,* 391–416.

Cherry, E. C. (1953). Some experiments on the recognition of speech, with one and with two ears. *Journal of the Acoustical Society of America, 25,* 975–979.

Chess, S., & Thomas, A. (1984). *Origins and evolution of behavior disorders.* New York: Brunner/Mazel.

Chicago Institute for Psychoanalysis. (1992). *The annual of psychoanalysis* (Vol. 20). Hillsdale, NJ: Analytic Press.

Choice, P., & Lamke, L. K. (1999). Stay/leave decision-making processes in abusive dating relationships. *Personal Relationships, 6,* 351–367.

Chomsky, N. (1965). *Aspects of a theory of syntax.* Cambridge, MA: The MIT Press.

Chomsky, N. (1975). *Reflections on language.* New York: Pantheon Books.

Chorover, S. (1981, June). *Organizational recruitment in "open" and "closed" social systems: A neuropsychological perspective.* Conference paper presented at the Center for the Study of New Religious Movements, Berkeley, California.

Christensen, A. J., Moran, P. J., Lawton, W. J., Stallman, D., & Voights, A. L. (1997). Monitoring attentional style and medical regimen adherence in hemodialysis patients. *Health Psychology, 16,* 256–262.

Christensen, A. J., Wiebe, J. S., Smith, T. W., Turner, C. W. (1994). Predictors of survival among hemodialysis patients: Effect of perceived family support. *Health Psychology, 13,* 521–525.

Cialdini, R. B. (2001). *Influence: Science and practice* (4th ed.), Boston, MA: Allyn & Bacon.

Cialdini, R. B., Vincent, J. E., Lewis, S. K., Catalan, J., Wheeler, D., & Darby, B. L. (1975). Reciprocal concessions procedure for inducing compliance: The door-in-the-face technique. *Journal of Personality and Social Psychology, 31,* 206–215.

Ciaranello, R. D., & Ciaranello, A. L. (1991). Genetics of major psychiatric disorders. *Annual Review of Medicine, 42,* 151–158.

Cici, S. J., & Liker, J. K. (1986). A day at the races: A study of IQ, expertise, and cognitive complexity. *Journal of Experimental Psychology: General, 115,* 225–266.

Clark, E. V. (1987). Principles of contrast: A constraint on language acquisition. In B. MacWhinney (Ed.), *Mechanisms of language acquisition* (pp. 1–33). Hillsdale, NJ: Erlbaum.

Clark, E. V. (1993). *The lexicon in acquisition.* Cambridge, U.K.: Cambridge University Press.

Clark, H. H. (1992). *Arenas of language use.* Chicago: University of Chicago Press.

Clark, H. H. (1996). *Using language.* Cambridge, U. K.: Cambridge University Press.

Clark, H. H., & Clark, E., V. (1977). *Psychology and language: An introduction to psycholinguisitics.* New York: Harcourt Brace Jovanovich.

Clark, H. H., & Gerrig, R. J. (1990). Quotations as demonstrations. *Language, 66,* 764–805.

Clark, H. H., & Marshall, C. R. (1981). Definite reference and mutual knowledge. In A. K. Joshi, B. Webber, & I. Sag (Eds.), *Elements of discourse understanding* (pp. 10–63). Cambridge, U. K.: Cambridge University Press.

Clark, K., & Clark, M. (1947). Racial indentification and preference in Negro children. In T. M. Newcomb & E. L. Hartley (Eds.), *Readings in social psychology* (pp. 169–178). New York: Holt.

Clark, N. M., & Becker, M. H. (1998). Theoretical models and strategies for improving adherence and disease management. In S. A. Shumaker & E. B. Schron (Eds.), *The handbook of health behavior change* (pp. 5–32). New York: Springer.

Clarke-Stewart, K. A. (1991). A home is not a school: The effects of child care on children's development. *Journal of Social Issues, 47,* 105–123.

Clarke-Stewart, K. A. (1993). *Daycare.* Cambridge, MA: Harvard University Press.

Clausen, J. A. (1981). Stigma and mental disorder: Phenomena and mental terminology. *Psychiatry, 44,* 287–296.

Clementz, B. A., & Sweeney, J. A. (1990). Is eye movement dysfunction a biological marker for schizophrenia? A methodological review. *Psychological Bulletin, 108,* 77–92.

Clopton, N. A., & Sorell, G. T. (1993). Gender differences in moral reasoning: Stable or situational? *Psychology of Women Quarterly, 17,* 85–101.

Coates, T. (1990). Strategies for modifying sexual behavior for primary and secondary prevention of HIV infection. *Journal of Consulting and Clinical Psychology, 58,* 57–69.

Coe, C. L. (1999). Psychosocial factors and psychoneuroimmunology within a lifespan perspective. In D. P. Keating & C. Hertzman (Eds.), *Developmental health and the wealth of nations: Social, biological, and educational dynamics* (pp. 201–219). New York: The Guilford Press.

Cogan, J. C., Bhalla, S. K., Sefa-Dedeh, A., & Rothblum, E. D. (1996). A comparison study of United States and African students on perceptions of obesity and thinness. *Journal of Cross-Cultural Psychology, 27,* 98–113.

Cohen, D., & Nisbett, R. E. (1994). Self-protection and the culture of honor: Explaining southern violence. *Personality and Social Psychology Bulletin, 20,* 551–567.

Cohen, D., Nisbett, R. E., Bowdle, B. R., & Schwarz, N. (1996). Insult, aggression, and the Southern culture of honor: An "experimental ethnography." *Journal of Personality and Social Psychology, 70,* 945–960.

Cohen, D., Taieb, O., Flament, M., Benoit, N., Chevret, S., Corcos, M., Fossati, P., Jeammet, P., Allilaire, J. F., & Basquin, M. (2000). Absence of cognitive impairment at long-term follow-up in adolescents treated with ECT for severe mood disorder. *American Journal of Psychiatry, 157,* 460–462.

Cohen, S., & McKay, G. (1983). Social support, stress, and the buffering hypotheses: A theoretical analysis. In A. Baum, S. E. Taylor, & J. Singer (Eds.), *Handbook of psychology and health* (Vol. 4). Hillsdale, NJ: Erlbaum.

Cohen, S., & Syme, S. L. (Eds.). (1985). *Social support and health.* Orlando, FL: Academic Press.

Cohen, S., Tyrrell, D. A. J., & Smith, A. P. (1993). Negative life events, perceived stress, negative affect, and susceptibility to the common cold. *Journal of Personality and Social Psychology, 64,* 131–140.

Cohn, E. G., & Rotton, J. (1997). Assault as a function of time and temperature: A moderator-variable time-series analysis. *Journal of Personality and Social Psychology, 72,* 1322–1334.

Coleman, L. (1987). *Suicide clusters.* Winchester, MA: Faber & Faber.

Coleman, R. M. (1986). *Wide awake at 3:00 A.M.: By choice or by chance?* New York: Freeman.

Coles, C. (1994). Critical periods for prenatal alcohol exposure. *Alcohol Health & Research World, 18,* 22–29.

Collaer, M. L., & Hines, M. (1995). Human behavioral sex differences: A role for gonadal hormones during early development? *Psychological Bulletin, 118,* 55–107.

Collins, A. M., & Quillian, M. R. (1969). Retrieval time from semantic memory. *Journal of Verbal Learning and Verbal Behavior, 8,* 240–247.

Collins, M. A., & Amabile, T. M. (1999). Motivation and creativity. In R. J. Sternberg (Ed.), *Handbook of creativity* (pp. 297–312). Cambridge, U.K.: Cambridge University Press.

Collins, W. A., Maccoby, E. E., Steinberg, L., Hetherington, E. M., & Bornstein, M. H. (2000). Contemporary research on parenting: The case for nature and nurture. *American Psychologist, 55,* 218–232.

Comstock, G., & Paik, H. (1991). *Television and the American child.* San Diego: Academic Press.

Comstock, G., & Scharrer, E. (1999). *Television: What's on, who's watching, and what it means.* San Diego, CA: Academic Press.

Comuzzie, A. G., & Allison, D. B. (1998). The search for human obesity genes. *Science, 280,* 1374–1377.

Conrad, C. D., Galea, L. A. M., Kuroda, Y., & McEwen, B. S. (1996). Chronic stress impairs rat spatial memory on the Y maze, and this effect is blocked by tianeptine treatment. *Behavioral Neuroscience, 110,* 1321–1334.

Contrada, R. J., Ashmore, R. D., Gary, M. L., Coups, E., Egeth, J. D., Sweell, A., Ewell, K., Goyal, T. M., & Chasse, V. (2000). Ethnicity-related sources of stress and their effects on well-being. *Current Directions in Psychological Science, 9,* 136–139.

Cook, T. D., Churck, M. B., Ajanaku, S., Shadish, W. R., Jr., Kim, J. R., & Cohen, R. (1996). The develoment of occupational aspirations and expectations among inner-city boys. *Child Development, 67,* 3368–3385.

Coren, S., Ward, L. M., & Enns, J. T. (1999). *Sensation and perception* (5th ed.). Fort Worth, TX: Harcourt Brace.

Corina, D. P. (1999). On the nature of left hemisphere specialization for signed language. *Brain & Language, 69,* 230–240.

Corr, P. J., & Gray, J. A. (1996). Attributional style as a personality factor in insurance sales performance in the UK. *Journal of Occupational and Organizational Psychology, 69,* 83–87.

Corso, J. F. (1977). Auditory perception and communication. In J. E. Birren & K. W. Schaie (Eds.), *Handbook of the psychology of aging* (pp. 535–553). New York: Van Nostrand Reinhold.

Costa, P. T., Jr., & McCrae, R. R. (1985). *The NEO Personality Inventory manual.* Odessa, FL: Psychological Assessment Resources.

Costa, P. T., Jr., & McCrae, R. R. (1992a). Four ways five factors are basic. *Personality and Individual Differences, 13,* 653–665.

Costa, P. T., Jr., & McCrae, R. R. (1992b). *Revised NEO Personality Inventory (NEO-PI-R) and NEO Five-factor Inventory (NEO-FFI) professional manual.* Odessa, FL: Psychological Assessment Resources.

Cowan, C. P., & Cowan, P. (2000). *When partners become parents: The big life change for couples.* Mahwah, NJ: Erlbaum.

Cowan, C. P., & Cowan, P. A. (1988). Changes in marriage during the transition to parenthood. In G. Y. Michaels & W. A. Goldberg (Eds.), *The transition to parenthood: Current theory and research.* Cambridge, U.K.: Cambridge University Press.

Cowan, C. P., Cowan, P. A., Heming, G., Garrett, E., Coysh, W. S., Curtis-Boles, H., & Boles, A. J., III. (1985). Transitions to parenthood: His, hers, and theirs. *Journal of Family Issues, 6,* 451–481.

Cowan, N. (1993). Acitvation, attention, and short-term memory. *Memory & Cognition, 21,* 162–167.

Cowan, P., & Cowan, C. P. (1998). New families: Modern couples as new pioneers. In M. A. Mason, A. Skolnick, & S. D. Sugarman (Eds.), *All our families: New policies for a new century.* New York: Oxford University Press.

Cowan, W. M. (1979, September). The development of the brain. *Scientific American, 241,* 106–117.

Cowles, J. T. (1937). Food tokens as incentives for learning by chimpanzees. *Comparative Psychology Monographs, 74,* 1–96.

Coyne, J. C., Wortman, C. B., & Lehman, D. R. (1988). The other side of support: Emotional overinvolvement and miscarried helping. In B. Gottlieb (Ed.), *Marshalling social support* (pp. 305–330). Newbury Park, CA: Sage.

Crago, M., Shisslak, C. M., & Estes, L. S. (1996). Eating disturbances among American minority groups: A review. *International Journal of Eating Disorders, 19,* 239–248.

Craik, F. I. M. (1994). Memory changes in normal aging. *Current Directions in Psychological Science, 3,* 155–158.

Craik, F. I. M. (1999). Age-related changes in human memory. In D. C. Park & N. Schwarz (Eds.), *Cognitive aging: A primer* (pp. 75–92). Philadelphia: Psychology Press.

Craik, F. I. M., & Lockhart, R. S. (1972). Levels of processing; A framework for memory research. *Journal of Verbal Learning and Verbal Behavior, 11,* 671–684.

Craik, K. (1943). *The nature of explanation.* Cambridge, U.K.: Cambridge University Press.

Cramer, P. (1997). Identity, personality, and defense mechanisms: An observer-based study. *Journal of Research in Personality, 31,* 58–77.

Cranson, R. W., Orme-Johnson, D. W., Gackenbach, J., Dillbeck, M. C., Jones, C. H., & Alexander, C. N. (1991). Transcendental meditation and improved performance on intelligence-related measures: A longitudinal study. *Personality and Individual Differences, 12,* 1105–1116.

Cranston, M. (1991). *The noble savage: Jean-Jacques Rousseau, 1754–1762.* Chicago: University of Chicago Press.

Crapo, L. (1985). *Hormones: The messengers of life.* Stanford, CA: Stanford Alumni Association Press.

Creasey, G., Mitts, N., & Catanzaro, S. (1995). Associations among daily hassles, coping, and behavior problems in nonreferred kindergartners. *Journal of Child Clinical Psychology, 24,* 311–319.

Crockett, L., J., & Silbereisen, R. K. (Eds.). (2000). *Negotiating adolescence in times of social change.* New York: Cambridge University Press.

Cronbach, L. J. (1975). Five decades of public controversy over mental testing. *American Psychologist, 30,* 1–14.

Crowder, R. G. (1976). *Principles of learning and memory.* Hillsdale, NJ: Erlbaum.

Crowder, R. G. (1992). Eidetic imagery. In L. R. Squire (Ed.), *Encyclopedia of learning and memory* (pp. 154–156). New York: Macmillan.

Crowder, R. G., & Morton, J. (1969). Precategorical acoustic storage (PAS). *Perception and Psychophysics, 8,* 815–820.

Csikszentmihalyi, M. (1990). *Flow: The psychology of optimal experience.* New York: Harper & Row.

Cummins, D. D. (1996). Evidence of deontic reasoning in 3- and 4-year-old children. *Memory & Cognition, 24,* 823–829.

Cummins, D. D. (1999). Cheater detection is modified by social rank: The impact of dominance on the evolution of cognitive functions. *Evolution and Human Behavior, 20,* 229–248.

Curtis, R. C., & Miller, K. (1986). Believing another likes or dislikes you: Behaviors making the beliefs come true. *Journal of Personality and Social Psychology, 51,* 284–290.

Cutler, W. B., Preti, G., Krieger, A., Huggins, G. R., Ramon Garcia, C., & Lawley, H. J. (1986). Human axillary secretions influence women's menstrual cycles: The role of donor extract from men. *Hormones and Behavior, 20,* 463–473.

Cutting, J. C., & Bock, K. (1997). That's the way the cookie bounces: Syntactic and semantic components of experimentally elicited idiom blends. *Memory & Cognition, 25,* 57–71.

Cutting, J. C., & Proffitt, D. (1982). The minimum principle and the perception of absolute, common and relative motions. *Cognitive Psychology, 14,* 211–246.

Cutting, J. E., Vishton, P. M., & Braren, P. A. (1995). How we avoid collisions with stationary and moving obstacles. *Psychological Review, 102,* 627–651.

Czeisler, C. A., Duffy, J. F., Shanahan, T. L., Brown, E. N., Mitchell, J. F., Rimmer, D. W., Ronda, J. M., Silva, E. J., Allan, J. S., Emens, J. S., Dijk, D.-J., & Kronauer, R. E. (1999). Stability, precision, and near-24-hour period of the human circadian pacemaker. *Science, 284,* 2177–2181.

Dahlstrom, W. G., Welsh, H. G., & Dahlstrom, L. E. (1975). *An MMPI handbook, Vol. 1: Clinical interpretation.* Minneapolis: University of Minnesota Press.

Dakof, G. A., & Taylor, S. E. (1990). Victims' perceptions of social support: What is helpful from whom? *Journal of Personality and Social Psychology, 58,* 80–89.

Damasio, H., Grabowski, T., Frank, R., Galaburda, A. M., & Damasio, A. R. (1994). The return of Phineas Gage: Clues about the brain from the skull of a famous patient. *Science, 264,* 1102–1105.

Daneman, M., & Carpenter, P. A. (1980). Individual differences in working memory and reading. *Journal of Verbal Learning and Verbal Behavior, 19,* 450–466.

Daneman, M., & Merikle, P. M. (1996). Working memory and language comprehension: A meta-analysis. *Psychonomic Bulletin & Review, 3,* 422–433.

Dannemiller, J. L., Babler, T. G., & Babler, B. L. (1996). On catching fly balls. *Science, 273,* 256–257.

Darley, J., & Latané, B. (1968). Bystander intervention in emergencies: Diffisuion of responsibility. *Journal of Personality and Social Psychology, 8,* 377–383.

Darley, J. M., & Batson, C. D. (1973). From Jerusalem to Jericho: A study of situational and dispositional variables in helping behavior. *Journal of Personality and Social Psychology, 27,* 100–108.

Darling, N., & Steinberg, L. (1993). Parenting style as context: An integrative model. *Psychological Bulletin, 113,* 487–496.

Darnton, R. (1968). *Mesmerism and the end of the Enlightenment in France.* Cambridge, MA: Harvard University Press.

Darwin, C. (1965). *The expression of emotions in man and animals.* Chicago: University of Chicago Press. (Original work published 1872)

Darwin, C. J., Turvey, M. T., & Crowder, R. G. (1972). The auditory analogue of the Sperling partial report procedure: Evidence for brief auditory stage. *Cognitive Psychology, 3,* 255–267.

D'Augelli, A. R. (1993). Preventing mental health problems among lesbian and gay college students. *The Journal of Primary Prevention, 13,* 245–261.

Davanagh, D. J. (1992). Recent developments in expressed emotion and schizophrenia. *British Journal of Psychiatry, 160,* 601–620.

Davidson, A. R., & Jaccard, J. J. (1979). Variables that moderate the attitude-behavior relation: Results of a longitudinal survey. *Journal of Personality and Social Psychology, 37,* 1364–1376.

Davidson, J. R. T., Hughes, D., Blazer, D. G., & George, L. K. (1991). Posttraumatic stress disorder in the community: An epidemiological study. *Psychological Medicine, 21,* 713–721.

Davidson, R. J., Putnam, K. M., & Larson, C. L. (2000). Dysfunction in the neural circuitry of emotion regulation? A possible prelude to violence. *Science, 289,* 591–594.

Davison, K. P., Pennebaker, J. W., & Dicerson, S. S. (2000). Who talks? The social psychology of illness support groups. *American Psychologist, 55,* 202–217.

Dawkins, K., Lieberman, J. A., Lebowitz, B. D., & Hsiao, J. K. (1999). Antipsychotics: Past and future. *Schizophrenia Bulletin, 25,* 395–405.

DeCasper, A. J., & Fifer, W. P. (1980). Of human bonding: Newborns prefer their mother's voices. *Science, 208,* 1174–1176.

DeCasper, A. J., & Prescott, P. A. (1984). Human newborns' perception of male voices: Preference, discrimination, and reinforcing value. *Developmental Psychology, 17,* 481–491.

Degreef, G., Ashari, M., Bogerts, B., Bilder, R. M., Jody, D. N., Alvir, J. M. J., & Lieberman, J. A. (1992). Volumes of ventricular system subdivisions measured from magnetic resonance images in first-episode schizophrenic patients. *Archives of General Psychiatry, 49,* 531–537.

Dehaene, S., & Akhavein, R. (1995). Attention, automaticity, and levels of representation in number processing. *Journal of Experimental Psychology: Learning, Memory, and Cognition, 21,* 314–326.

Dejin-Karlsson, E., Hsonson, B. S., Oestergren, P.-O., Sjoeberg, N.-O., & Karel, M. (1998). Does passive smoking in early pregnancy increase the risk of small-for-gestational age infants? *American Journal of Public Health, 88,* 1523–1527.

Delaney, A. J., & Sah, P. (1999). GABA receptors inhibited by benzodiazepines mediate fast inhibitory transmission in the central amygdala. *Journal of Neuroscience, 19,* 9698–9704.

Dell, G. S. (1986). A spreading-activation theory of retrieval in sentence production. *Psychological Review, 93,* 283–321.

Dell, G. S., Burger, L. K., & Svec, W. R. (1997). Language production and serial order: A functional analysis and a model. *Psychological Review, 104,* 123–147.

Delprato, D. J., & Midgley, B. D. (1992). Some fundamentals of B. F. Skinner's behaviorism. *American Psychologist, 47,* 1507–1520.

Dement, W. C. (1976). *Some watch while some must sleep.* San Francisco: San Francisco Book Co.

Dement, W. C., & Vaughan, C. (1999). *The promise of sleep.* New York: Delacorte Press.

Dennett, D. C. (1987). Consciousness. In R. L. Gregory (Ed.), *The Oxford companion to the mind* (pp. 160–164). New York: Oxford University Press.

Denton, K., & Zarbatany, L. (1996). Age differences in support processes in conversations between friends. *Child Development, 67,* 1360–1373.

de Rivera, J. (1997). The construction of false memory syndrome: The experience of retractors. *Psychological Inquiry, 8,* 271–292.

de Rivera, J. (2000). Understanding persons who repudiate false memories recovered in therapy. *Professional Psychology: Research and Practice, 31,* 378–386.

De Valois, R. L., & Jacobs, G. H. (1968). Primate color vision. *Science, 162,* 533–540.

Devanand, D. P., Verma, A. K., Tirumalasetti, F., & Sackeim, H. A. (1991). Absence of cognitive impairment after more than 100 lifetime ECT treatments. *American Journal of Psychiatry, 148,* 929–932.

Devereux, G. (1961). Mohave ethnopsychiatry and suicide: The psychiatric knowledge and psychic disturbances of an Indian tribe. *Bureau of American Ethnology (Bulletin 175).* Washington, DC: Smithsonian Institution.

Devine, P. G., & Monteith, M. J. (1999). Automaticity and control in stereotyping. In S. Chaiken & Y. Trope (Eds.), *Dual-process theories in social psychology* (pp. 339–360). New York: Guilford.

De Witte, P. (1996). The role of neurotransmitters in alcohol dependence: Animal research. *Alcohol & Alcoholism, 31*(Suppl. 1), 13–16.

Dewsbury, D. A. (1981). Effects of novelty on copulatory behavior: The Coolidge effect and related phenomena. *Psychological Bulletin, 89,* 464–482.

Dhawan, N., Roseman, I. J., Naidu, R. K., Thapa, K., & Rettek, S. I. (1995). Self-concepts across two cultures: India and the United States. *Journal of Cross-Cultural Psychology, 26,* 606–621.

DiClemente, C. C., Prochaska, J. O., Fairhurst, S. K., Velicer, W. F., Valesquez, M. M., & Rossi, J. S. (1991). The process of smoking cessation: An analysis of precontemplation, contemplation, and preparation stages of change. *Journal of Consulting and Clinical Psychology, 59,* 259–304.

Digman, J. M. (1990). Personality structure: Emergence of the five-factor model. *Annual Review of Psychology, 41,* 417–440.

Dillbeck, M. C., & Orme-Johnson, D. W. (1987). Physiological differences between transcendental meditation and rest. *American Psychologist, 42,* 879–881.

Di Marzo, V., Fontana, A., Cadas, H., Schinelli, S., Cimino, G., Schwartz, J.-C., & Piomelli, D. (1994). Formation and inactivation of endogenous cannabinoid anandamide in central neurons. *Nature, 372,* 686–691.

DiMatteo, M. R., & DiNicola, D. D. (1982). *Achieving patient compliance.* Elmsford, NY: Pergamon Press.

Dinges, M. M., & Oetting, E. R. (1993). Similarity in drug use patterns between adolescents and their friends. *Adolescence, 28,* 253–266.

Dion, K. K., & Dion, K. L. (1993). Individualistic and collectivist perspectives on gender and the cultural context of love and intimacy. *Journal of Social Issues, 49*(3), 53–69.

Dishman, R. K., & Buckworth, J. (1997). Adherence to physical activity. In W. P. Morgan (Ed.), *Physical activity and mental health* (pp. 63–80). Washington, DC: Taylor & Francis.

di Tomaso, E., Massimiliano, B., & Piomelli, D. (1996). Brain cannabinoids in chocolate. *Nature, 382,* 677–678.

Dixon, R. A. (1999). Concepts and mechanisms of gains in cognitive aging. In D. C. Park & N. Schwarz (Eds.), *Cognitive aging: A primer* (pp. 23–41). Philadelphia: Psychology Press.

Dollard, J., Doob, L. W., Miller, N., Mower, O. H., & Sears, R. R. (1939). *Frustration and aggression.* New Haven: Yale University Press.

Dollard, J., & Miller, N. E. (1950). *Personality and psychotherapy.* New York: McGraw-Hill.

Domhoff, G. W. (1996). *Finding meanings in dreams: A quantitative approach.* New York: Plenum.

Domhoff, G. W. (1999). Drawing theoretical implications from descriptive empirical findings on dream content. *Dreaming, 9,* 201–210.

Domjan, M., & Purdy, J. E. (1995). Animal research in psychology. *American Psychologist, 50,* 496–503.

Donald, M. (1995). The neurobiology of human consciousness: An evolutionary approach. *Neuropsychology, 33,* 1087–1102.

Dong, Q., Weisfeld, G., Boardway, R. H., & Shen, J. (1996). Correlates of social status among Chinese adolescents. *Journal of Cross-Cultural Psychology, 27,* 476–493.

Donnay, D. A. C., & Borgen, F. H. (1996). Validity, structure, and content of the 1994 Strong Interest Inventory. *Journal of Counseling Psychology, 43,* 275–291.

Dosher, B. A., & Corbett, A. T. (1982). Instrument inferences and verb schemata. *Memory & Cognition, 10,* 531–539.

Drigotas, S. M., & Rusbult, C. E. (1992). Should I stay or should I go? A dependence model of breakups. *Journal of Personality and Social Psychology, 62,* 62–87.

Drozd, J. F., & Goldfried, M. R. (1996). A critical evaluation of the state-of-the-art in psychotherapy outcome research. *Psychotherapy, 33,* 171–180.

Dryfoss, J. G. (1990). *Adolescents at risk: Prevalence and prevention.* New York: Oxford University Press.

DSM-IV. (1994). *Diagnostic and statistical manual of mental disorders* (4th ed.). Washington, DC: American Psychiatric Association.

DSM-IV-TR. (2000). *Diagnostic and statistical manual of mental disorders* (4th ed., Text revision). Washington, DC: American Psychiatric Association.

DuBois, P. H. (1970). *A history of psychological testing.* Boston: Allyn & Bacon.

Duckitt, J. (1992). Psychology and prejudice: A historical analysis and integrative framework. *American Psychologist, 47,* 1182–1193.

Dudycha, G. J. (1936). An objective study of punctuality in relation to personality and achievement. *Archives of Psychology, 204,* 1–53.

Dugatkin, L. A. (1996). Interface between culturally based preferences and genetic preferences: Female mate choice in *Poecilia reticulata. Proceedings of the National Academy of Sciences, 93,* 2770–2773.

Duker, P. C., & Seys, D. M. (1996). Long-term use of electrical aversion treatment with self-injurious behavior. *Research in Developmental Disabilities, 17,* 293–301.

Duman, R. S., Heninger, G. R., & Nestler, E. J. (1997). A molecular and cellular theory of depression. *Archives of General Psychiatry, 54,* 597–606.

Duncker, D. (1945). On problem solving. *Psychological Monographs, 58* (No. 270).

Dunegan, K. J. (1996). Fines, frames, and images: Examining formulation effects on punishment decisions. *Organizational Behavior and Human Decision Processes, 68,* 58–67.

Durlak, J. A., & Wells, A. M. (1997). Primary prevention mental health programs for children and adolescents: A meta-analytic review. *American Journal of Community Psychology, 25,* 115–152.

Dutton, D. G., & Aron, A. P. (1974). Some evidence for heightened sexual attraction under conditions of high anxiety. *Journal of Personality and Social Psychology, 30,* 510–517.

Dweck, C. S. (1975). The role of expectations and attributions in the alleviation of learned helplessness. *Journal of Personality and Social Psychology, 31,* 674–685.

Eagly, A. H., Ashmore, R. D., Makhijani, M. G., & Longo, L. C. (1991). What is beautiful is good, but . . . : A meta-analytic review of research on the physical attractiveness stereotype. *Psychological Bulletin, 110,* 109–128.

Eagly, A. H., & Chaiken, S. (1993). *The psychology of attitudes.* Fort Worth, TX: Harcourt Brace Jovanovich.

Ebbinghaus, H. (1973). *Psychology: An elementary text-book.* New York: Arno Press. (Original work published 1908)

Eckensberger, L. H., & Zimba, R. F. (1997). The development of moral judgment. In J. W. Berry, P. R. Dasen, & T. S. Saraswathi (Eds.), *Handbook of cross-cultural psychology: Vol. 2. Basic processes and human development* (pp. 299–338). Boston: Allyn & Bacon.

Edwards, A. E., & Acker, L. E. (1962). A demonstration of the long-term retention of a conditioned galvanic skin response. *Psychosomatic Medicine, 24,* 459–463.

Egeland, J. A., Gerhard, D. S., Pauls, D. L., Sussex, J. N., Kidd, K. K., Allen, C. R., Hostetter, A. M., & Housman, D. E. (1987). Bipolar affective disorder linked to DNA markers on chromosome 11. *Nature, 325,* 783–787.

Ehrlich, B. E., & Diamond, J. M. (1980). Lithium, membranes, and manic-depressive illness. *Journal of Membrane Biology, 52,* 187–200.

Eich, E. (1995). Searching for mood dependent memory. *Psychological Science, 6,* 67–75.

Eich, E., & Macaulay, D. (2000). Fundamental factors in mood-dependent memory. In J. P. Forgas (Ed.), *Feeling and thinking: The role of affect in social cognition* (pp. 109–130). New York: Cambridge University Press.

Eich, E., Macaulay, D., & Ryan, L. (1994). Mood dependent memory for events of the personal past. *Journal of Experimental Psychology: General, 123,* 201–215.

Eichenbaum, H. (1999). Conscious awareness, memory and the hippocampus. *Nature Neuroscience, 2,* 775–776.

Eisenberg, N., Cumberland, A., & Spinrad, T. L. (1998). Parental socialization of emotion. *Psychological Inquiry, 9,* 241–273.

Ekman, P. (1972). Universal and cultural differences in facial expressions of emotion. In J. Cole (Ed.), *Nebraska Symposium on Motivation.* Lincoln: University of Nebraska Press.

Ekman, P. (1984). Expression and the nature of emotion. In K. R. Scherer & P. Ekman (Eds.), *Approaches to emotion.* Hillsdale, NJ: Erlbaum.

Ekman, P. (1994). Strong evidence for universals in facial expressions: A reply to Russell's mistaken critique. *Psychological Bulletin, 115,* 268–287.

Ekman, P., & Friesen, W. V. (1971). Constants across cultures in the face and emotion. *Journal of Personality and Social Psychology, 17,* 124–129.

Ekman, P., & Friesen, W. V. (1986). A new pan-cultural facial expression of emotion. *Motivation and Emotion, 10,* 159–168.

Ekman, P., Levenson R. W., & Friesen, W. V. (1983). Autonomic nervous system activity distinguishes among emotions. *Science, 221,* 1208–1210.

Ekstrand, M. L., & Coates, T. J. (1990). Maintenance of safer sexual behaviors and predictors of risky sex: The San Francisco men's health survey. *American Journal of Public Health, 80,* 973–977.

Elbert, T., Pantev, C., Wienbruch, C., Rockstroh, B., & Taub, E. (1995). Increased cortical representation of the fingers of the left hand in string players. *Science, 270,* 305–307.

Elkin, I., Shea, M. T., Watkins, J. T., Imber, S. D., Sotsky, S. M., Collins, J. F., Glass, D. R., Pilkonis, P. A., Leber, W. R., Kocherty, J. P., Fiester, S. J., & Parloff, M. B. (1989). National Institutes of Mental Health treatment of depression collaborative research program: General effectiveness of treatments. *Archives of General Psychiatry, 46,* 971–982.

Ellis, A. (1962). *Reason and emotion in psychotherapy.* New York: Lyle Stuart.

Ellis, A. (1995). *Better, deeper, and more enduring brief therapy: The rational emotive behavior therapy approach.* New York: Brunner/Mazel.

Elms, A. C. (1988). Freud as Leonardo: Why the first psychobiography went wrong. *Journal of Personality, 56,* 19–40.

Emmelkamp, P. M. G. (1990). Anxiety and fear. In A. S. Bellack, M. Hersen, & A. E. Kazdin (Eds.), *International handbook of behavior modification and therapy* (2nd ed., pp. 283–305). New York: Plenum.

Emmelkamp, P. M. G., & Kuipers, A. (1979). Agoraphobia: A follow-up study four years after treatment. *British Journal of Psychology, 134,* 352–355.

Enserink, M. (1999). Can the placebo be the cure? *Science, 284,* 238–240.

Enserink, M. (2000). Searching for the mark of Cain. *Science, 289,* 575–579.

Erber, R., & Erber, M. W. (1994). Beyond mood and social judgment: Mood incongruent recall and mood regulation. *European Journal of Social Psychology, 24,* 79–88.

Ericsson, K. A., & Chase, W. G. (1982). Exceptional memory. *American Scientist, 70,* 607–615.

Ericsson, K. A., & Simon, H. A. (1993). *Protocol analysis: Verbal reports as data* (rev. ed.). Cambridge, MA: The MIT Press.

Esser, J. K. (1998). Alive and well after 25 years: A review of groupthink research. *Organizational Behavior and Human Decision Processes, 73,* 116–141.

Estrada, C. A., Isen, A. M., & Young, M. J. (1994). Positive affect improves creative problem solving and influences reported source of practice satisfaction in physicians. *Motivation and Emotion, 18,* 285–299.

Evans, D. A., Funkenstein, H. H., Albert, M. S., Scherr, P. A., Cook, N. R., Chown, M. J., Hebert, L. E., Hennekens, C. H., & Taylor, J. O. (1989). Prevalence of Alzheimer's disease in a community population of older persons. *Journal of the American Medical Association, 262,* 2251–2256.

Evans, J. S. B., Barston, J. L., & Pollard, P. (1983). On the conflict between logic and belief in syllogistic reasoning. *Memory and Cognition, 11,* 295–306.

Evans, J. St. B. T., Newstead, S. E., Allen, J. L., & Pollard, P. (1994). Debiasing by instruction: The case of belief bias. *European Journal of Cognitive Psychology, 6,* 263–285.

Evans-Pritchard, E. E. (1937). *Witchcraft, oracles and magic among the Azande.* Oxford: Oxford University Press.

Exner, J. E., Jr. (1974). *The Rorschach: A comprehensive system: Vol. 1.* New York: Wiley.

Exner, J. E., Jr. (1991). *The Rorschach: A comprehensive system: Vol. 2. Interpretation* (2nd ed.). New York: Wiley.

Exner, J. E., Jr. (1993). *The Rorschach: A comprehensive system: Vol. 1. Basic foundations* (3rd ed.). New York: Wiley.

Exner, J. E., Jr. (1996). A comment on "The comprehensive system for the Rorschach: A critical examination." *Psychological Science, 7,* 11–13.

Exner, J. E., Jr., & Weiner, I. B. (1994). *The Rorschach: A comprehensive system: Vol. 3. Assessment of children and adolescents* (2nd ed.). New York: Wiley.

Eysenck, H. J. (1952). The effects of psychotherapy: An evaluation. *Journal of Consulting Psychology, 16,* 319–324.

Eysenck, H. J. (1973). *The inequality of man.* London: Temple Smith.

Eysenck, H. J. (1990). Biological dimensions of personality. In L. A. Pervin (Ed.), *Handbook of personality theory and research* (pp. 244–276). New York: Guilford Press.

Eysenck, H. J. (1992). Four ways five factors are not basic. *Personality and Individual Differences, 13,* 667–673.

Eysenck, H. J. (1994). Cancer, personality, and stress: Prediction and prevention. *Advances in Behaviour Research and Therapy, 16,* 167–215.

Fagot, B. I., & Hagan, R. (1991). Observations of parent reactions to sex-stereotyped behaviors: Age and sex effects. *Child Development 62,* 617–628.

Fairbank, J. A., Schlenger, W. E., Caddell, J. M., & Woods, M. G. (1993). Post-traumatic stress disorder. In P. B. Sutker & H. E. Adams (Eds.), *Comprehensive handbook of psychopathology* (2nd ed., pp. 145–165). New York: Plenum Press.

Fantuzzo, J., Sutton-Smith, B., Atkins, M., Meyers, R., Stevenson, H., Coolahan, K., Weiss, A., & Manz, P. (1996). Community-based resilient peer treatment of withdrawn maltreated school children. *Journal of Consulting and Clinical Psychology, 64,* 1377–1386.

Fantz, R. L. (1963). Pattern vision in newborn infants. *Science, 140,* 296–297.

Farbman, A. I. (1992). *Cell biology of olfaction.* New York: Cambridge University Press.

Farina, A., Fischer, E. H., Boudreau, L. A., & Belt, W. E. (1996). Mode of target presentation in measuring the stigma of mental disorder. *Journal of Applied Social Psychology, 26,* 2147–2156.

Farina, A., Gliha, D., Boudreau, L. A., Allen, J. G., & Sherman, M. (1971). Mental illness and the impact of believing others know about it. *Journal of Abnormal Psychology, 77,* 1–5.

Farine, J. P., Everaerts, C., Abed, D., & Ntari, M. (1996). Pheromonal emission during the mating behavior of *Eurycotis floridana* (Walker) (Dictyoptera: Blattidea). *Journal of Insect Behavior, 9,* 197–213.

Farver, J. A. M., & Frosch, D. L. (1996). L.A. Stories: Aggression in preschoolers' spontaneous narratives after the riots of 1992. *Child Development, 67,* 19–32.

Fazio, R. H. (1987). Self-perception theory: A current perspective. In M. P. Zanna, J. M. Olson, & C. P. Herman (Eds.), *Social influence: The Ontario Symposium* (Vol. 5, pp. 129–150). Hillsdale, NJ: Erlbaum.

Fazio, R. H. (1995). Attitudes as object-evaluation associations: Determinants, consequences, and correlates of attitude accessibility. In R. E. Petty & J. A. Krosnick (Eds.), *Attitude strength: Antecedents and consequences* (pp. 247–282). Mahwah, NJ: Erlbaum.

Fazio, R. H., & Towles-Schwen, T. (1999). The MODE model of attitude-behavior processes. In S. Chaiken & Y. Trope (Eds.), *Dual-process theories in social psychology* (pp. 97–116). New York: Guilford.

Feather, N. T. (1961). The relationship of persistence at a task to expectation of success and achievement related motives. *Journal of Abnormal and Social Psychology, 63,* 552–561.

Featherstone, M., & Wernick, A. (Eds.) (1995). *Images of aging: Cultural representations of later life.* London: Routledge.

Fechner, G. T. (1966). *Elements of psychophysics* (H. E. Adler, Trans.). New York: Holt, Rinehart & Winston. (Original work published 1860).

Feeney, J. A., & Noller, P. (1990). Attachment style as a predictor of adult romantic relationships. *Journal of Personality and Social Psychology, 58,* 281–291.

Fernald, A., & Morikawa, H. (1993). Common themes and cultural variations in Japanese and American mothers' speech to infants. *Child Development, 64,* 637–656.

Fernald, A., Taeschner, T., Dunn, J., Papousek, M., De Boysson-Bardies, B., & Fukui, I. (1989). A cross-cultural study of prosodic modification in mothers' and fathers' speech to preverbal infants. *Journal of Child Language, 16,* 477–501.

Ferster, C. B., & Skinner, B. F. (1957). *Schedules of reinforcement.* New York: Appleton-Century-Crofts.

Festinger, L. (1957). *A theory of cognitive dissonance.* Stanford, CA: Stanford University Press.

Festinger, L., & Carlsmith, J. M. (1959). Cognitive conquences of forced compliance. *Journal of Abnormal and Social Psychology, 58,* 203–211.

Feynman, R. P. (1985). *"Surely you're joking, Mr. Feynman."* New York: W. W. Norton & Company.

Field, T. F., & Schanberg, S. M. (1990). Massage alters growth and catecholamine production in preterm newborns. In N. Gunzenhauser (Ed.), *Advances in touch* (pp. 96–104). Skillman, NJ: Johnson & Johnson.

Fields, H. L., & Levine, J. D. (1984). Placebo analgesia: A role for endorphins. *Trends in Neuroscience, 7,* 271–273.

Fink, J. (1999). *How to use computers and cyberspace in the clinical practice of psychotherapy.* Northvale, NJ: Jason Aronson Inc.

Fiorito, G., & Scotto, P. (1992). Observational learning in *Octopus vulgaris. Science, 256,* 545–547.

Fisher, J. D., Fisher, W. A., Misovich, S. J., Kimble, D. L., & Malloy, T. E. (1996). Changing AIDS risk behavior: Effects of an intervention emphasizing AIDS risk reduction information, motivation and behavioral skills in a college student population. *Health Psychology, 15,* 114–123.

Fisher, J. D., Fisher, W. A., Williams, S. S., & Malloy, T. E. (1994). Empirical tests of an information-motivation-behavioral skills model of AIDS-prevention behavior with gay men and heterosexual university students. *Health Psychology, 13,* 238–250.

Fisher, S., & Greenberg, R. (1996). *Freud scientifically appraised.* New York: Wiley.

Fishman, H. C. (1993). *Intensive structural therapy: Treating families in their social context.* New York: Basic Books.

Fiske, S. T., & Taylor, S. E. (1991). *Social cognition.* New York: McGraw-Hill.

Flavell, J. H. (1985). *Cognitive development* (2nd ed.). Englewood Cliffs, NJ: Prentice Hall.

Flavell, J. H. (1996). Piaget's legacy. *Psychological Science, 7,* 200–203.

Fleming, I. (1959). From a view to a kill. In *For your eyes only* (pp. 1–30). New York: Charter Books.

Foa, E. B., & Riggs, D. S. (1995). Posttraumatic stress disorder following assault: Theoretical considerations and empirical findings. *Current Directions in Psychological Science, 4,* 61–65.

Fobair, P. (1997). Cancer support groups and group therapies. *Journal of Psychosocial Oncology, 15,* 43–81.

Foley, V. D. (1979). Family therapy. In R. J. Corsini (Ed.), *Current psychotherapies* (2nd ed., pp. 460–469). Itasca, IL: Peacock.

Folkman, S. (1984). Personal control and stress and coping processes: A theoretical analysis. *Journal of Personality and Social Psychology, 46,* 839–852.

Ford, C. S., & Beach, F. A. (1951). *Patterns of sexual behavior.* New York: Harper & Row.

Forgas, J. P. (1995). Mood and judgment: The affect infusion model (AIM). *Psychological Bulletin, 117,* 39–66.

Forgas, J. P. (1999). Feeling and speaking: Mood effects on verbal communication strategies. *Personality and Social Psychology Bulletin, 25,* 850–863.

Forgas, J. P. (Ed.) (2000). *Feeling and thinking: The role of affect in social cognition.* New York: Cambridge University Press.

Foucault, M. (1975). *The birth of the clinic.* New York: Vintage Books.

Foulkes, D. (1962). Dream reports from different states of sleep. *Journal of Abnormal and Social Psychology, 65,* 14–25.

Fowler, H. (1965). *Curiosity and exploratory behavior.* New York: Macmillan.

Fowler, R. D. (1999). Report of the association. *American Psychologist, 54,* 539–558.

Frager, R., & Faciman, J. (1998). *Personality and personal growth.* New York: Longman.

Fraley, R. C., & Shaver, P. R. (2000). Adult romantic attachment: Theoretical developments, emerging controversies, and unanswered questions. *Review of General Psychology, 4,* 132–154.

Frank, J. D., & Frank, J. B. (1991). *Persuasion and healing: A comparative study of psychotherapy* (3rd ed.). Baltimore: Johns Hopkins University Press.

Frank, M. E., & Nowlis, G. H. (1989). Learned aversions and taste qualities in hamsters. *Chemical Senses, 14,* 379–394.

Franklin, N., & Tversky, B. (1990). Searching imagined environments. *Journal of Experimental Psychology: General, 119,* 63–76.

Fraser, S. C. (1974). *Deindividuation: Effects of anonymity on aggression in children.* Unpublished mimeograph report, University of Southern California.

Fredrickson, B. L., Maynard, K. E., Helms, M. J., Haney, T. L., Siegler, I. C., & Barefoot, J. C. (2000). Hostility predicts magnitude and duration of blood pressure response to anger. *Journal of Behavioral Medicine, 23,* 229–243.

Freedman, J. L., & Fraser, S. C. (1966). Compliance without pressure: The foot-in-the-door technique. *Journal of Personality and Social Psychology, 4,* 195–202.

Freedman, M. S., Lucas, R. J., Soni, B., von Schantz, M., Muñoz, M., David-Gray, Z., & Foster, R. (1999). Regulation of mammalian circadian behavior by non-rod, non-cone, ocular photoreceptors. *Science, 284,* 502–507.

Freud, A. (1946). *The ego and the mechanisms of defense.* New York: International Universities Press.

Freud, A. (1958). Adolescence. *Psychoanalytic Study of the Child, 13,* 255–278.

Freud, S. (1915). Instincts and their vicissitudes. In S. Freud, *The collected papers.* New York: Collier.

Freud, S. (1923). *Introductory lectures on psycho-analysis* (J. Riviera, Trans.). London: Allen & Unwin.

Freud, S. (1953). Three essays on the theory of sexuality. In J. Strachey (Ed.), *The standard edition of the complete psychological works of Sigmund Freud* (Vol. 7, pp. 135–243). London: Hogarth Press. (Original work published 1905)

Freud, S. (1957). Leonardo da Vinci and a memory of his childhood. In J. Strachey (Ed. and Trans.), *The standard edition of the complete psychological works of Sigmund Freud* (Vol. 11, pp. 59–137). London: Hogarth Press. (Original work published 1910)

Freud, S. (1965). *The interpretation of dreams.* New York: Avon. (Original work published 1900)

Freund, A. M., & Baltes, P. B. (1998). Selection, optimization, and compensation as strategies of life management: Correlations with subjective indicators of successful aging. *Psychology and Aging, 13,* 531–543.

Frey, K. P. (1997). About reversal theory. In S. Svebak & M. J. Apter (Eds.), *Stress & health: A reversal theory perspective* (pp. 3–19). Washington, DC: Taylor & Francis.

Friedman, M., & Rosenman, R. F. (1974). *Type A behavior and your heart.* New York: Knopf.

Friedman, M., Thoresen, C. E., Gill, J. J., Ulmer, D., Powell, L. H., Price, V. A., Brown, B., Thompson, L., Rabin, D. D., Breall, W. S., Bourg, E., Levy, R., & Dixon, T. (1986). Alteration of Type A behavior and its effect on cardiac recurrences in post-myocardial infarction patients: Summary results of the Recurrent Coronary Prevention Project. *American Heart Journal, 11,* 653–665.

Friedman, R., Myers, P., Krass, S., & Benson, H. (1996). The relaxation response: Use with cardiac patients. In R. Allan & S. S. Scheidt (Eds.), *Heart and mind: The practice of cardiac psychology* (pp. 363–384). Washington, DC: American Psychological Association.

Friend, R., Rafferty, Y., & Bramel, D. (1990). A puzzling misinterpretation of the Asch "conformity" study. *European Journal of Social Psychology, 20,* 29–44.

Fromkin, V. A. (1971). The non-anomalous nature of anomalous utterances. *Language, 47,* 27–52.

Fromkin, V. A. (Ed.). (1973). *Speech errors as linguistic evidence.* The Hague: Mouton.

Fromkin, V. A. (Ed.). (1980). *Errors in linguistic performance: Slips of the tongue, pen, and hand.* New York: Academic Press.

Fromm, E., & Shor, R. E. (Eds.). (1979). *Hypnosis: Developments in research and new perspectives* (2nd ed.). Hawthorne, NY: Aldine.

Fuhriman, A., & Burlingame, G. M. (Eds.) (1994). *Handbook of group psychotherapy: An empirical and clinical synthesis.* New York: Wiley.

Fuligni, A. J. (1997). The academic achievement of adolescents from immigrant families: The roles of family background, attitudes, and behavior. *Child Development, 68,* 351–363.

Fuller, B., Holloway, S. D., & Liang, X. (1996). Family selection of child-care centers: The influence of household support, ethnicity, and parental practices. *Child Development, 67,* 3320–3337.

Furman, W., Rahe, D., & Hartup, W. W. (1979). Rehabilitation of socially withdrawn preschool children through mixed-aged and same-sex socialization. *Child Development, 50,* 915–922.

Furnham, A., Crump, J., & Whelan, J. (1997). Validating the NEO Personality Inventory using assessor's ratings. *Personality & Individual Differences, 22,* 669–675.

Fussell, S. R., & Krauss, R. M. (1992). Coordination of knowledge in communication: Effects of speakers' assumptions about what others know. *Journal of Personality and Social Psychology, 62,* 378–391.

Gabrieli, J. D. E., Brewer, J. B., Desmond, J. E., & Glover, G. H. (1997). Separate neural bases of two fundamental memory processes in the human medial temporal lobe. *Science, 276,* 264–266.

Gabrieli, J. D. E., Desmond, J. E., Demb, J. B., Wagner, A. D., Stone, M. V., Vaidya, C. J., & Glover, G. H. (1996). Functional magnetic resonance imaging of semantic memory processes in the frontal lobes. *Psychological Science, 7,* 278–283.

Gackenbach, J., & LaBerge, S. (Eds.). (1988). *Conscious mind, sleeping brain: Perspectives on lucid dreaming.* New York: Plenum Press.

Gagnon, J. H. (1977). *Human sexualities.* Glenview, IL: Scott, Foresman.

Galton, F. (1869). *Hereditary genius.* London: Macmillan.

Galton, F. (1907). *Inquiries into human faculty and its development.* London: Dent Publishers. (Original work published 1883)

Garcia, J. (1990). Learning without memory. *Journal of Cognitive Neuroscience, 2,* 287–305.

Garcia, J. (1993). Misrepresentations of my criticisms of Skinner. *American Psychologist, 48,* 1158.

Garcia, J., & Koelling, R. A. (1966). The relation of cue to consequence in avoidance learning. *Psychonomic Science, 4,* 123–124.

Garcia, M. M., Shaw, D. S., Winslow, E. B., & Yaggi, K. E. (2000). Destructive sibling conflict and the development of conduct problems in young boys. *Developmental Psychology, 36,* 44–53.

Gardner, H. (1983). *Frames of mind.* New York: Basic Books.

Gardner, H. (1993). *Creating minds.* New York: Basic Books.

Gardner, H. (1999). *Intelligence reframed.* New York: Basic Books.

Gardner, R., Jr. (2000, June 12). Parenting: Is AOL worse than TV? *New York, 33,* 38–41.

Gardner, R. A., & Gardner, B. T. (1969). Teaching sign language to a chimpanzee. *Science, 165,* 664–672.

Garland, A. F., & Zigler, E. (1993). Adolescent suicide prevention. *American Psychologist, 48,* 169–182.

Garnsey, S. M. (1993). Event-related brain potentials in the study of language: An introduction. *Language and Cognitive Processes, 8,* 337–356.

Garrett, M. F. (1975). The analysis of sentence production. In G. H. Bower (Ed.), *The psychology of learning and motivation* (Vol. 9, pp. 133–177). New York: Academic Press.

Garrison, V. (1977). The "Puerto Rican syndrome" in psychiatry and Espiritismo. In V. Crapanzano & V. Garrison (Eds.), *Case studies in spirit possession.* New York: Wiley Interscience.

Gawin, F. H. (1991). Cocaine addiction: Psychology and neurophysiology. *Science, 251,* 1580–1586.

Gazzaniga, M. (1970). *The bisected brain.* New York: Appleton-Century-Crofts.

Gazzaniga, M. S. (1985). *The social brain.* New York: Basic Books.

Gazzaniga, M. S. (1990). In *Discovering Psychology,* Program 14 [PBS video series]. Washington, DC: Annenberg/CPB Program.

Gazzaniga, M. S., Fendrich, R., & Wessinger, C. M. (1994). Blindsight reconsidered. *Current Directions in Psychological Science, 3,* 93–96.

Gegenfurtner, K. R., & Sperling, G. (1993). Information transfer in iconic memory experiments. *Journal of Experimental Psychology: Human Perception and Performance, 19,* 845–866.

Gelman, S. A., & Wellman, H. M. (1991). Insides and essences: Early understandings of the non-obvious. *Cognition, 38,* 213–244.

George, M. S., Ketter, T. A., Parekh, P. I., Horwitz, B., Herscovitch, P., & Post, R. M. (1995). Brain activity during transient sadness and happiness in healthy women. *American Journal of Psychiatry, 152,* 341–351.

Gergen, K. J., Gulerce, A., Lock A., & Misra, G. (1996). Psychological science in a cultural context. *American Psychologist, 51,* 496–503.

Gerrig, R. J. (1993). *Experiencing narrative worlds.* New Haven, CT: Yale University Press.

Gerrig, R. J., & Banaji, M. R. (1994). Language and thought. In R. J. Sternberg (Ed.), *Handbook of perception and cognition: Vol 2. Thinking and problem solving* (pp. 233–261). Orlando, FL: Academic Press.

Gershon, E. S., Berrettini, W., Nurnberger, J., Jr., & Goldin, L. (1987). Genetics of affective illness. In H. Y. Meltzer (Ed.), *Psychopharmacology: The third generation of progress* (pp. 481–491). New York: Raven Press.

Ghadirian, A. M., & Lehmann, H. E. (1992). *Environment and psychopathology.* New York: Springer.

Giambra, L. M., & Arenberg, D. (1993). Adult age differences in forgetting sentences. *Psychology and Aging, 8,* 451–462.

Gibbs, R. W. (1986). Comprehension and memory for nonliteral utterances: The problem of sarcastic indirect requests. *Acta Psychologia, 62,* 41–57.

Gibbs, R. W. (1994). *The poetics of mind.* Cambridge, U. K.: Cambridge University Press.

Gibson, E. J., & Walk, R. D. (1960). The "visual cliff." *Scientific American, 202,* 64–71.

Gibson, J. J. (1966). *The senses considered as perceptual systems.* Boston: Houghton Mifflin.

Gibson, J. J. (1979). *An ecological approach to visual perception.* Boston: Houghton Mifflin.

Giesler, R. B., Josephs, R. A., & Swann, W. B., Jr. (1996). Self-verification in clinical depression: The desire for negative evaluation. *Journal of Abnormal Psychology, 105,* 358–368.

Gillespie, J. M., Byrne, B., & Workman, L. J. (1995). An intensive reunification program for children in foster care. *Child & Adolescent Social Work Journal, 12,* 213–228.

Gilligan, C. (1982). *In a different voice: Psychological theory and women's development.* Cambridge, MA: Harvard University Press.

Gilligan, S., & Bower, G. H. (1984). Cognitive consequences of emotional arousal. In C. Izard, J. Kagan, & R. Zajonc (Eds.), *Emotions, cognitions, and behavior* (pp. 547–588). Cambridge, U.K.: Cambridge University Press.

Gilovich, T. (1991). *How we know what isn't so: The fallibility of human reason in everyday life.* New York: The Free Press.

Ginns, E. I., Egland, J. A., Allen, C. R., Pauls, D. L., Falls, L., Keith, T. P., & Paul, S. M. (1992). Update on the search for DNA markers linked to manic-depressive illness in the Old Order Amish. *Journal of Psychiatric Research, 26,* 305–308.

Giron, M., & Gomez-Beneyto, M. (1998). Relationship between empathic family attitude and relapse in schizophrenia: A two-year follow-up prospective study. *Schizophrenia Bulletin, 24,* 619–627.

Giros, B., Jaber, M., Jones, S. R., Wightman, R. M., & Caron, M. G. (1996). Hyperlocomotion and indifference to cocaine and amphetamine in mice lacking the dopamine transporter. *Nature, 379,* 606–612.

Gitlin, M. J. (1990). *The psychotherapist's guide to psychopharmacology.* New York: The Free Press.

Gladue, B. A. (1994). The biopsychology of sexual orientation. *Current Directions in Psychological Science, 3,* 150–154.

Gleaves, D. H. (1996). The sociocognitive model of dissociative identity disorder: A reexamination of evidence. *Psychological Bulletin, 120,* 42–59.

Glenny, M. (1994). *The fall of Yugoslavia.* New York: Penguin.

Gobet, F., & Simon, H. A. (1996). The roles of recognition processes and look-ahead search in time-constrained expert problem solving: Evidence from grand-master-level chess. *Psychological Science, 7,* 52–55.

Goddard, H. H. (1914). *The Kallikak family: A study of the heredity of feeble-mindedness.* New York: Macmillan.

Goddard, H. H. (1917). Mental tests and immigrants. *Journal of Delinquency, 2,* 243–277.

Goldfried, M. R., Greenberg, L., & Marmar, C. (1990). Individual psychotherapy: Process and outcome. *Annual Review of Psychology, 41,* 659–688.

Goldfried, M. R., & Wolfe, B. E. (1996). Psychotherapy practice and research: Repairing a strained alliance. *American Psychologist, 51,* 1007–1016.

Goldin-Meadow, S., & Mylander, C. (1990). Beyond the input given: The child's role in the acquisition of language. *Language, 66,* 323–355.

Goldin-Meadow, S., & Mylander, C. (1998). Spontaneous sign systems created by deaf children in two cultures. *Nature, 391,* 279–281.

Goldsmith, S. K., Shapiro, R. M., & Joyce, J. N. (1997). Disrupted pattern of D$_2$ dopamine receptors in the temporal lobe in schizophrenia. *Archives of General Psychiatry, 54,* 649–658.

Goldstein, E. B. (1999). *Sensation & perception* (5th ed.). Pacific Grove, CA: Brooks/Cole Publishing Company.

Goleman, D. (1995). *Emotional intelligence.* New York: Bantam Books.

Gonzalez, A. (1983). Classroom cooperation and ethnic balance: The Chicanos and equal status contact. *La Red/The Net, 68,* 6–8.

Goodall, J. (1986). *The chimpanzees of Gombe: Patterns of behavior.* Cambridge, MA: Harvard University Press.

Goodall, J. (1990). *Through a window: My thirty years with the chimpanzees of Gombe.* Boston: Houghton Mifflin.

Gooden, D. R., & Baddeley, A. D. (1975). Context-dependent memory in two natural environments: On land and under water. *British Journal of Psychology, 66,* 325–331.

Goodison, T., & Siegel, S. (1995). Learning and tolerance to the intake suppressive effect of cholecystokinin in rats. *Behavioral Neuroscience, 109,* 62–70.

Goodlett, C. R., & Johnson, T. B. (1999). Temporal windows of vulnerability within the third trimester equivalent: Why "knowing when" matters. In J. H. Hannigan, L. P. Spear, N. E. Spear, & C. R. Goodlett (Eds.), *Alcohol and alcoholism: Effects on brain development* (pp. 59–91). Mahwah, NJ: Erlbaum.

Goodwillie, S. (Ed.). (1993). *Voices from the future: Our children tell us about violence in America.* New York: Crown.

Gordon, D. (2000, October 2). Castro's crew gets hooked up. *Newsweek, 136,* 64.

Gottesman, I. I. (1991). *Schizophrenia genesis: The origins of madness.* New York: Freeman.

Gottfredson, L. S. (1997a). Mainstream science on intelligence: An editorial with 52 signatories, history, and bibliography. *Intelligence, 24,* 13–23.

Gottfredson, L. S. (1997b). Why *g* matters: The complexity of everyday life. *Intelligence, 24,* 79–132.

Gottlieb, B. H. (Ed.). (1981). *Social networks and social support.* Beverly Hills, CA: Sage.

Gottman, J. M. (1994). *What predicts divorce?* Hillsdale, NJ: Erlbaum.

Gould, M. S., Fisher, P., Parides, M., Flory, M., & Shaffer, D. (1996). Psychosocial risk factors of child and adolescent completed suicide. *Archives of General Psychiatry, 53,* 1155–1162.

Gould, S. J. (1981). *The mismeasure of man.* New York: Norton.

Graesser, A. C., Singer, M., & Trabasso, T. (1994). Constructing inferences during narrative text comprehension. *Psychological Review, 101,* 371–395.

Graf, P., Squire, L. R., & Mandler, G. (1984). The information that amnesic patients do not forget. *Journal of Experimental Psychology: Learning, Memory, and Cognition, 10,* 164–178.

Grammer, K. (1993). 5-α-androst–16en–3α-on: A male pheromone? *Ethology & Sociobiology, 14,* 201–207.

Grant, B. R., & Grant, P. (1989). *Evolutionary dynamics of a natural population.* Princeton: Princeton University Press.

Grant, L., & Evans, A. (1994). *Principles of behavior analysis.* New York: HarperCollins.

Grant, P. R. (1986). *Ecology and evolution of Darwin's finches.* Princeton, NJ: Princeton University Press.

Gray, M. R., & Steinberg, L. (1999). Unpacking authoritative parenting: Reassessing a multidimensional construct. *Journal of Marriage and the Family, 61,* 574–587.

Green, B. L. (1994). Psychosocial research in traumatic stress: An update. *Journal of Traumatic Stress, 7,* 341–362.

Green, D. M., & Swets, J. A. (1966). *Signal detection theory and psychophysics.* New York: Wiley.

Greene, E., & Nelson, B. (1997). Evaluating Müller-Lyer effects using single fin-set configurations. *Perception & Psychophysics, 59,* 293–312.

Greene, R. L. (1991). *The MMPI-2/MMPI: An interpretive manual.* Boston: Allyn & Bacon.

Greene, R. L., Gwin, R., & Staal, M. (1997). Current status of MMPI–2 research: A methodologic overview. *Journal of Personality Assessment, 68,* 20–36.

Greenfield, P. M. (1997). You can't take it with you: Why ability assessments don't cross cultures. *American Psychologist, 52,* 1115–1124.

Greeno, C. G., & Wing, R. R. (1994). Stress-induced eating. *Psychological Bulletin, 115,* 444–464.

Greeno, J. G. (1994). Gibson's affordances. *Psychological Review, 101,* 336–342.

Greenwald, A. G., Spangenber, E. R., Pratkanis, A. R., & Eskenazi, J. (1991). Double-blind tests of subliminal self-help audiotapes. *Psychological Science, 2,* 119–122.

Grice, H. P. (1968). Utterer's meaning, sentence-meaning, and word-meaning. *Foundations of Language, 4,* 1–18.

Grice, H. P. (1975). Logic and conversation. In P. Cole & J. L. Morgan (Eds.), *Syntax and semantics: Vol. 3. Speech acts* (pp. 41–58). New York: Academic Press.

Grice, H. P. (1978). Further notes on logic and conversation. In P. Cole (Ed.), *Syntax and semantics: Vol. 9. Pragmatics* (pp. 113–128). New York: Academic Press.

Griffin, K., Friend, R., Eitel, P., & Lobel, M. (1993). Effects of environmental demands, stress, and mood on health practices. *Journal of Behavioral Medicine, 16,* 1–19.

Griffiths, M. (1998). Internet addiction: Does it really exist? In J. Gackenbach (Ed.), *Psychology and the Internet: Intrapersonal, interpersonal, and transpersonal implications* (pp. 61–75). San Diego, CA: Academic Press.

Grigorenko, E. L. (2000). Heritability and intelligence. In R. J. Sternberg (Ed.), *Handbook of intelligence* (pp. 53–91). Cambridge, England: Cambridge University Press.

Grohol, J. M. (1998). Future clinical directions: Professional development, pathology, and psychotherapy on-line. In J. Gackenbach (Ed.), *Psychology and the Internet: Intrapersonal, interpersonal, and transpersonal implications* (pp. 111–140). San Diego, CA: Academic Press.

Guilford, J. P. (1961). Factorial angles to psychology. *Psychological Review, 68,* 1–20.

Guilford, J. P. (1985). The Structure-of-Intellect model. In B. B. Wolman (Ed.), *Handbook of intelligence.* New York: Wiley.

Gumperz, J. J., & Levinson, S. C. (Eds.). (1996). *Rethinking linguistic relativity.* Cambridge, U.K.: Cambridge University Press.

Gur, R. E., & Pearlson, G. D. (1993). Neuroimaging in schizophrenia research. *Schizophrenia Bulletin, 19,* 337–353.

Gura, T. (2000). Tracing leptin's partners in regulating body weight. *Science, 287,* 1738–1741.

Haas, S. M., & Stafford, L. (1998). An initial examination of maintenance behaviors in gay and lesbian relationships. *Journal of Social and Personal Relationships, 15,* 846–855.

Haines, B. A., Metalsky, G. I., Cardamone, A. L., & Joiner, T. (1999). Interpersonal and cognitive pathways in to the origins of attributional style: A developmental perspective. In T. E. Joiner & J. C. Coyne (Eds.), *The interactional nature of depression; Advances in interpersonal approaches* (pp. 65–92). Washington, DC: American Psychological Association.

Halberstadt, J. B., Niedenthal, P. M., & Kushner, J. (1995). Resolution of lexical ambiguity by emotional state. *Psychological Science, 6,* 278–282.

Hall, D., & Suboski, M. D. (1995). Visual and olfactory stimuli in learned release of alarm reactions by zebra danio fish (*Brachydanio rerio*). *Neurobiology of Learning and Memory, 63*, 229–240.

Hall, G. S. (1904). *Adolescence: Its psychology and its relations to physiology, anthropology, sociology, sex, crime, religion and education* (Vols. 1 and 2). New York: D. Appleton.

Hamer, D. H. (1996). The heritability of happiness. *Nature Genetics, 14*, 125–126.

Hamer, D. H., Hu, S., Magnuson, V. L., Hu, N., & Pattatucci, A. M. L. (1993). A linkage between DNA markers on the X chromosome and male sexual orientation. *Science, 261*, 321–327.

Haney, C., & Zimbardo, P. G. (1977). The socialization into criminality: On becoming a prisoner and a guard. In J. L. Tapp & F. L. Levine (Eds.), *Law, justice and the individual in society: Psychological and legal issues* (pp. 198–223). New York: Holt, Rinehart & Winston.

Harder, J. W. (1991). Equity theory versus expectancy theory: The case of major league baseball free agents. *Journal of Applied Psychology, 76*, 458–464.

Hargadon, R., Bowers, K. S., & Woody, E. Z. (1995). Does counterpain imagery mediate hypnotic analgesia? *Journal of Abnormal Psychology, 104*, 508–516.

Harle, V. (2000). *The enemy with a thousand faces: The tradition of the other in western political thought and history.* Westport, CT: Praeger.

Harlow, H. F. (1965). Sexual behavior in the rhesus monkey. In F. Beach (Ed.), *Sex and behavior.* New York: Wiley.

Harlow, H. F., Harlow, M. K., & Meyer, D. R. (1950). Learning motivated by a manipulation drive. *Journal of Experimental Psychology, 40*, 228–234.

Harlow, H. F., & Zimmerman, R. R. (1958). The development of affectional responses in infant monkeys. *Proceedings of the American Philosophical Society, 102*, 501–509.

Harlow, J. M. (1868). Recovery from the passage of an iron bar through the head. *Publications of the Massachusetts Medical Society, 2*, 327–347.

Harmon, L. W., Hansen, J. C., Borgen, F. H., & Hammer, A. L. (1994). *Strong Interest Inventory applications and technical guide.* Palo Alto, CA: Consulting Psychologists Press.

Harris, B. (1979). Whatever happened to Little Albert? *American Psychologist, 34*, 151–160.

Harrison, L. M., Kastin, A. J., & Zadina, J. E. (1998). Opiate tolerance and dependence: Receptors, G-proteins, and antiopiates. *Peptides, 19*, 1603–1630.

Harrison, Y., & Horne, J. A. (1996). Long-term sleep extension—Are we really chronically sleep deprived? *Psychophysiology, 33*, 22–30.

Hart, J. T. (1965). Memory and the feeling-of-knowing experience. *Journal of Educational Psychology, 56*, 208–216.

Hartshorne, H., & May, M. A. (1928). *Studies in the nature of character, Vol. 1: Studies in deceit.* New York: Macmillan.

Hartup, W. H. (1996). The company they keep: Friendships and their developmental significance. *Child Development, 67*, 1–13.

Harvey, J. H., Weber, A. L., & Orbuch, T. L. (1990). *Interpersonal accounts: A social psychological perspective.* Oxford: Basil Blackwell.

Hassan, S. (1988). *Combatting cult mind control.* Rochester, VT: Park Street Press.

Hastorf, A. H., & Cantril, H. (1954). They saw a game: A case study. *Journal of Abnormal and Social Psychology, 49*, 129–134.

Hatcher, C., & Himelstein, P. (Eds.). (1996). *The handbook of Gestalt therapy.* Northvale, NJ: Jason Aronson.

Hatchett, L., Friend, R., Symister, P., & Wadhwa, N. (1997). Interpersonal expectations, social support, and adjustment to chronic illness. *Journal of Personality and Social Psychology, 73*, 560–573.

Hatfield, E., & Sprecher, S. (1995). Men's and women's preferences in marital partners in the United States, Russia, and Japan. *Journal of Cross-Cultural Psychology, 26*, 728–750.

Hathaway, S. R., & McKinley, J. C. (1940). A multiphasic personlaity schedule (Minnesota): I. Construction of the schedule. *Journal of Psychology, 10*, 249–254.

Hathaway, S. R., & McKinley, J. C. (1943). *Minnesota Multiphasic Inventory manual.* New York: Psychological Corporation.

Hauri, P. (1977). *The sleep disorders.* Kalamazoo, MI: Upjohn.

Hawkes, K. (1993). Why hunter-gatherers work. *Current Anthropology, 34*, 341–351.

Hayward, W. G., & Williams, P. (2000). Viewpoint dependence and object discriminability. *Psychological Science, 11*, 7–12.

Hazan, C., & Shaver, P. (1987). Romantic love conceptualized as an attachment process. *Journal of Personality and Social Psychology, 52*, 511–524.

Healy, A. F., & McNamara, D. S. (1996). Verbal learning and memory: Does the modal model still work? *Annual Review of Psychology, 47*, 143–172.

Hearst, E. (1988). Fundamentals of learning and conditioning. In R. C. Atkinson, R. J. Herrnstein, G. Lindzey, & R. D. Luce (Eds.), *Stevens' handbook of experimental psychology: Vol. 2. Learning and Cognition* (2nd ed., pp. 3–109). New York: Wiley.

Heatherton, T. F., Herman, C. P., & Polivy, J. (1991). Effects of physical threat and ego threat on eating behavior. *Journal of Personality and Social Psychology, 60*, 138–143.

Heatherton, T. F., Polivy, J., Herman, C. P., & Baumeister, R. F. (1993). Self-awareness, task failure, and disinhibition: How attentional focus affects eating. *Journal of Personality, 61*, 49–61.

Hebb, D. O. (1955). Drives and the CNS (conceptual nervous system). *Psychological Review, 62*, 243–254.

Hebl, M. R., & Heatherton, T. F. (1998). The stigma of obesity in women: The difference is black and white. *Personality and Social Psychology Bulletin, 24*, 417–426.

Heider, F. (1958). *The psychology of interpersonal relationships.* New York: Wiley.

Heine, S. J., & Lehman, D. R. (1997). Culture, dissonance, and self-affirmation. *Personality and Social Psychology Bulletin, 23*, 389–400.

Helgeson, V. S., & Cohen, S. (1996). Social support and adjustment to cancer: Reconciling descriptive, correlational, and intervention research. *Health Psychology, 15*, 135–148.

Helmes, E., & Reddon, J. R. (1993). A perspective on developments in assessing psychopathology: A critical review of the MMPI and MMPI–2. *Psychological Bulletin, 113*, 453–471.

Henderson, L., & Zimbardo, P. G. (1998). Shyness. In *Encyclopedia of Mental Health.* San Diego: Academic Press.

Henry, W. P., Strupp, H. H., Schacht, T. E., & Gaston, L. (1994). Psychodynamic approaches. In A. E. Bergin & S. L. Garfield (Eds.), *Handbook of psychotherapy and behavior change* (4th ed., pp. 467–508). New York: Wiley.

Hentschel, U., Smith, G., Ehlers, W., & Draguns, J. G. (Eds.). (1993). *The concept of defense mechanisms in contemporary psychology.* New York: Springer-Verlag.

Herek, G. M. (1994). Assessing heterosexuals' attitudes toward lesbians and gay men: A review of empirical research with the ATLG scale. In B. Greene & G. M. Herek (Eds.), *Lesbian and gay psychology: Theory, research, and clinical applications* (pp. 206–228). Thousand Oaks, CA: Sage.

Herek, G. M. (Ed.). (1998). *Stigma and sexual orientation: Understanding prejudice against lesbians, gay men, and bisexuals.* Newbury Park, CA: Sage.

REFERENCES

Herek, G. M., & Capitanio, J. P. (1996). "Some of my best friends": Intergroup contact, concealable stigma, and heterosexuals' attitudes toward gay men and lesbians. *Personality and Social Psychology Bulletin, 22,* 412–424.

Hernnstein, R. J., & Murray, C. (1994). *The bell curve.* New York: The Free Press.

Hersh, S. M. (1971). *My Lai 4: A report on the massacre and its aftermath.* New York: Random House.

Hertzog, C., Dixon, R. A., & Hultsch, D. F. (1990). Relationships between metamemory, memory predictions, and memory task performance in adults. *Psychology and Aging, 5,* 215–227.

Herz, R. S. (1997). The effects of cue distinctiveness on odor-based context-dependent memory. *Memory & Cognition, 25,* 375–380.

Hickok, G., Bellugi, U., & Klima, E. S. (1996). The neurobiology of sign language and its implications for the neural basis of language. *Nature, 381,* 699–702.

Higgins, R. L., Snyder, C. R., & Berglas, S. (Eds.). (1990). *Self-handicapping: The paradox that isn't.* New York: Plenum Press.

Higgins, S. T., Wong, C. J., Badger, G. J., Ogden, D. E. H., & Dantona, R. L. (2000). Contingent reinforcement increases cocaine abstinence during outpatient treatment and 1 year of follow-up. *Journal of Consulting and Clinical Psychology, 68,* 64–72.

Hilgard, E. R. (1968). *The experience of hypnosis.* New York: Harcourt Brace Jovanovich.

Hilgard, E. R. (1986). *Psychology in America: A historical survey.* San Diego: Harcourt Brace Jovanovich.

Hilgetag, C.-C., O'Neill, M. A., & Young, M. P. (1996). Indeterminate organization of the visual system. *Science, 271,* 776–777.

Hinton, A. L. (1996). Agents of death: Explaining the Cambodian genocide in terms of psychosocial dissonance. *American Anthropologist, 98,* 818–831.

Hintzman, D. L. (1986). "Schema abstraction" in a multiple-trace memory model. *Psychological Review, 93,* 411–428.

Hirschfeld, R. M. A. (1999). Efficacy of SSRIs and newer antidepressants in severe depression: Comparison with TCAs. *Journal of Clinical Psychiatry, 60,* 326–335.

Hobson, J. A. (1988). *The dreaming brain.* New York: Basic Books.

Hobson, J. A., & McCarley, R. W. (1977). The brain as a dream state generator: An activation-synthesis hypothesis of the dream process. *American Journal of Psychiatry, 134,* 1335–1348.

Hoffman, C., Lau, I., & Johnson, D. R. (1986). The linguistic relativity of person cognition: An English–Chinese comparison. *Journal of Personality and Social Psychology, 51,* 1097–1105.

Hoffman, L. W. (1989). Effects of maternal employment in the two-parent family. *American Psychologist, 44,* 283–292.

Hoffman, M. L. (1986). Affect, cognition, and motivation. In R. Sorrentino & E. Higgins (Eds.), *Handbook of motivation and cognition: Foundations of social behavior* (pp. 244–280). New York: Guilford Press.

Hofling, C. K., Brotzman, E., Dalrymple, S., Graves, N., & Pierce, C. M. (1966). An experimental study in nurse–physician relationships. *Journal of Nervous and Mental Disease, 143*(2), 171–180.

Holden, C. (1986). Depression research advances, treatment lags. *Science, 233,* 723–725.

Holden, C. (1998). No last word on language origins. *Science, 282,* 1455–1458.

Holen, M. C., & Oaster, T. R. (1976). Serial position and isolation effects in a classroom lecture simulation. *Journal of Educational Psychology, 68,* 723–725.

Holland, R. L., Musch, B. C., & Hindmarch, I. (1999). Specific effects of benzodiazepines and tricyclic antidepressants in panic disorder: Comparisons of clomipramine with alprazolam SR and adinaz-

olam SR. *Human Psychopharmacology: Clinical and Experimental, 14,* 119–124.

Holmbeck, G. N., & O'Donnell, D. (1991). Discrepancies between perceptions of decision making and behavioral autonomy. In R. L. Paikoff (Ed.), *Shared views in the family during adolescence* (pp. 51–69). San Francisco: Jossey-Bass.

Holmes, D. S. (1984). Mediation and somatic arousal: A review of the experimental evidence. *American Psychologist, 39,* 1–10.

Holmes, D. S. (1994). *Abnormal psychology.* New York: HarperCollins.

Holmes, T. H., & Rahe, R. H. (1967). The social readjustment rating scale. *Journal of Psychosomatic Research, 11*(2), 213–218.

Holtgraves, T., & Skeel, J. (1992). Cognitive biases in playing the lottery: Estimating the odds and choosing the numbers. *Journal of Applied Social Psychology, 22,* 934–952.

Holyoak, K. J., & Nisbett, R. E. (1988). Induction. In R. J. Sternberg & E. E. Smith (Eds.), *The psychology of human thought* (pp. 50–91). Cambridge, U. K.: Cambridge University Press.

Holyoak, K. J., & Spellman, B. A. (1993). Thinking. *Annual Review of Psychology, 44,* 265–315.

Holyoak, K. J., & Thagard, P. (1997). The analogical mind. *American Psychologist, 52,* 35–44.

Homme, L. E., de Baca, P. C., Devine, J. V., Steinhorst, R., & Rickert, E. J. (1963). Use of the Premack principle in controlling the behavior of nursery school children. *Journal of the Experimental Analysis of Behavior, 6,* 544.

Hopson, J. L. (1979). *Scent signals: The silent language of sex.* New York: Morrow.

Horne, J. A. (1988). *Why we sleep: The functions of sleep in humans and other mammals.* Oxford: Oxford University Press.

Horney, K. (1937). *The neurotic personality of our time.* New York: Norton.

Horney, K. (1939). *New ways in psychoanalysis.* New York: Norton.

Horney, K. (1945). *Our inner conflicts: A constructive theory of neurosis.* New York: Norton.

Horney, K. (1950). *Neurosis and human growth.* New York: Norton.

Houghton, J. (1980). One personal experience: Before and after mental illness. In J. G. Rabkin, L. Gelb, & J. B. Lazar (Eds.), *Attitudes toward the mentally ill: Research perspectives* (pp. 7–14). Rockville, MD: National Institutes of Mental Health.

Houlihan, D., Schwartz, C., Miltenberger, R., & Heuton, D. (1993). The rapid treatment of a young man's balloon (noise) phobia using *in vivo* flooding. *Journal of Behavior Therapy and Experimental Psychiatry, 24,* 233–240.

House, J. S., Landis, K. R., & Umberson, D. (1988). Social relationships and health. *Science, 241,* 540–545.

Hovland, C. I., Lumsdaine, A. A., & Sheffield, F. D. (1949). *Experiments on mass communication.* Princeton, NJ: Princeton University Press.

Howard, D. J. (1984). Drug related deaths in a major metropolitan area: A sixteen year review. *Journal of Applied Social Sciences, 8,* 235–248.

Hubel, D. H., & Wiesel, T. N. (1962). Receptive fields, binocular interaction, and functional architecture in the cat's visual cortex. *Journal of Physiology (London), 160,* 106–154.

Hubel, D. H., & Wiesel, T. N. (1979). Brain mechanisms of vision. *Scientific American, 241*(9), 150–168.

Hudson, D. L., & Cohen, M. E. (2000). *Neural networks and artificial intelligence for biomedical engineering.* New York: IEEE Press.

Huey, R. B., Gilchrist, G. W., Carlson, M. L., Berrigan, D., & Serra, L. (2000). Rapid evolution of a geographic cline in size in an introduced fly. *Science, 287,* 308–309.

Hull, C. L. (1943). *Principles of behavior: An introduction to behavior theory.* New York: Appleton-Century-Crofts.

Hull, C. L. (1952). *A behavior system: An introduction to behavior theory concerning the individual organism.* New Haven: Yale University Press.

Hultsch, D. F., Hertzog, C., Dixon, R. A., & Small, B. J. (1998). *Memory change in the aged.* Cambridge, U.K.: Cambridge University Press.

Hultsch, D. F., Hertzog, C., Small, B. J., & Dixon, R. A. (1999). Use it or lose it: Engaged lifestyle as a buffer of cognitive decline in aging? *Psychology and Aging, 14,* 245–263.

Hume, D. (1951). In L. A. Selby-Bigge (Ed.), *An enquiry concerning human understanding.* London: Oxford University Press. (Original work published 1748)

Hummel, J. E., & Biederman, I. (1992). Dynamic binding in a neural network for shape recognition. *Psychological Review, 99,* 480–517.

Humphrey, T. (1970). The development of human fetal activity and its relation to postnatal behavior. In H. W. Reese & L. P. Lipsitt (Eds.), *Advance in child development and behavior* (Vol. 5). New York: Academic Press.

Hunt, E., & Agnoli, F. (1991). The Whorfian hypothesis: A cognitive psychology perspective. *Psychological Review, 92,* 377–389.

Hurvich, L., & Jameson, D. (1974). Opponent processes as a model of neural organization. *American Psychologist, 29,* 88–102.

Huston, A. C., McLoyd, V. C., & Coll, C. G. (Eds.). (1994). Children and poverty: Issues in contemporary research [Special issue]. *Child Development, 65*(2).

Huxley, A. (1954). *The doors of perception.* New York: Harper & Brothers.

Hyde, J. S., & Durik, A. M. (2000). Gender differences in erotic plasticity—evolutionary or sociocultural forces? Comment on Baumeister (2000). *Psychological Bulletin, 126,* 375–379.

Ingram, D. (1995). The cultural basis of prosodic modifications to infants and children: A response to Fernald's universalist theory. *Journal of Child Language, 22,* 223–233.

Insko, C. A., Thibaut, J. W., Moehle, D., Wilson, M., Diamond, W. D., Gilmore, R., Solomon, M. R., & Lipsitz, A. (1980). Social evolution and the emergence of leadership. *Journal of Personality and Social Psychology, 39,* 431–448.

Irvine, J. T. (1990). Registering affect: Heteroglossia in the linguistic expression of emotion. In C. A. Lutz & L. Abu-Lughod (Eds.), *Language and the politics of emotions* (pp. 126–161). Cambridge, U. K.: Cambridge University Press.

Irwin, D. E. (1991). Information integration across saccadic eye movements. *Cognitive Psychology, 23,* 420–456.

Isaacs, E. A., & Clark, H. H. (1987). References in conversations between experts and novices. *Journal of Experimental Psychology: General, 116,* 26–37.

Isen, A. M. (1984). Toward understanding the role of affect in cognition. In R. Wyer & T. Srull (Eds.), *Handbook of social cognition* (pp. 174–236). Hillsdale, NJ: Erlbaum.

Isen, A. M., Daubman, D. A., & Nowicki, G. P. (1987). Positive affect facilitates creative problem solving. *Journal of Personality and Social Psychology, 52,* 1122–1131.

Ishii-Kuntz, M. (1990). Social interaction and psychological well-being: Comparison across stages of adulthood. *International Journal of Aging and Human Development, 30,* 15–36.

Itard, J. M. G. (1962). *The Wild Boy of Aveyron* (G. & M. Humphrey, Trans.). New York: Appleton-Century-Crofts. (Originally published in 1802)

Ito, T. A., Miller, N., & Pollock, V. E. (1996). Alcohol and aggression: A meta-analysis on the moderating effects of inhibitory cues, triggering events, and self-focused attention. *Psychological Bulletin, 120,* 60–82.

Izard, C. E. (1993). Four systems for emotion activation: Cognitive and noncognitive processes. *Psychological Review, 100,* 68–90.

Izard, C. E. (1994). Innate and universal facial expressions: Evidence from developmental and cross-cultural research. *Psychological Bulletin, 115,* 288–299.

Jackson, L. A., & McGill, O. D. (1996). Body type preferences and body characteristics associated with attractive and unattractive bodies by African Americans and Anglo Americans. *Sex Roles, 35,* 295–307.

Jackson, R. S., Creemers, J. W. M., Ohagi, S., Raffin-Sanson, M.-L., Sanders, L., Montague, C. T., Hutton, J. C., & O'Rahilly, S. (1997). Obesity and impaired prohormone processing associated with mutations in the human prohormone convertase 1 gene. *Nature Genetics, 16,* 303–306.

Jacob, S., & McClintock, M. K. (2000). Psychological state and mood effects of steroidal chemosignals in women and men. *Hormones and Behavior, 37,* 57–78.

Jacobs, R. C., & Campbell, D. T. (1961). The perpetuation of an arbitrary tradition through several generations of a laboratory microculture. *Journal of Abnormal and Social Psychology, 62,* 649–658.

Jacobs, T. M., Lawrence, M. D., Hong, K., Giordano, N., Jr., & Giordano, N., Sr. (1996). On catching fly balls. *Science, 273,* 257–258.

Jacobsen, P. B., Bovbjerg, D. H., Schwartz, M. D., Andrykowski, M. A., Futterman, A. D., Gilewski, T., Norton, L., & Redd, W. H. (1993). Formation of food aversions in cancer patients receiving repeated infusions of chemotherapy. *Behaviour Research and Therapy, 31,* 739–748.

Jacobson, N. S., Dobson, K. S., Truax, P. A., Addis, M. E., Koerner, K., Gollan, J. K., Gortner, E., & Prince, S. (1996). A component analysis of cognitive-behavioral treatment for depression. *Journal of Consulting and Clinical Psychology, 64,* 295–304.

Jacobson, S. W., Jacobson, J. L., Sokol, R. J., Martier, S. S., & Ager, J. W. (1993). Prenatal alcohol exposure and infant information processing ability. *Child Development, 64,* 1706–1721.

Jacoby, L. L., Kelley, C. M., & McElree, B. D. (1999). The role of cognitive control: Early selection versus late correction. In S. Chaiken & Y. Trope (Eds.), *Dual-process theories in social psychology* (pp. 383–400). New York: The Guilford Press.

Jacoby, L. L., Woloshyn, V., & Kelley, C. (1989). Becoming famous without being recognized: Unconscious influences of memory produced by divided attention. *Journal of Experimental Psychology: General, 118,* 115–125.

Jahnke, J. C. (1965). Primacy and recency effects in serial-position curves of immediate recall. *Journal of Experimental Psychology, 70,* 130–132.

James, S. E., & Murphy, B. C. (1998). Gay and lesbian relationships in a changing social context. In C. J. Patterson & A. R. D'Augelli (Eds.), *Lesbian, gay, and bisexual identities in families: Psychological perspectives* (pp. 99–121). New York: Oxford University Press.

James, W. (1882). Subjective effects of nitrous oxide. *Mind, 7,* 186–208.

James, W. (1892). *Psychology.* New York: Holt.

James, W. (1902). *The varieties of religious experience.* New York: Longmans, Green.

James, W. (1950). *The principles of psychology* (2 vols.). New York: Holt, Rinehart & Wilson. (Original work published 1890)

Janis, I. (1982). *Groupthink* (2nd ed.). Boston: Houghton Mifflin.

Janis, I. L., & Frick, F. (1943). The relationship between attitudes toward conclusions and errors in judging logical validity of syllogisms. *Journal of Experimental Psychology, 33,* 73–77.

Janofsky, J. S., Dunn, M. H., Roskes, E. J., Briskin, J. K., & Rudolph, M. S. L. (1996). Insanity defense pleas in Baltimore City: An analysis of outcome. *American Journal of Psychiatry, 153,* 1464–1468.

Janowitz, H. D., & Grossman, M. I. (1950). Hunger and appetite: Some definitions and concepts. *Journal of the Mount Sinai Hospital, 16,* 231–240.

Janz, N. K., & Becker, M. H. (1984). The health belief model: A decade later. *Health Education Quarterly, 11,* 1–47.

Jedrej, M. C. (1995). Ingessana: *The religious institutions of a people of the Sudan–Ethiopia borderland.* Leiden: Brill.

Jenike, M. A., Breiter, H. C., Baer, L., Kennedy, D. N., Savage, C. R., Olivares, M. J., O'Sullivan, R. L., Shera, D. M., Rauch, S. C., Keuthen, N., Rosen, B. R., Caviness, V. S., & Filipek, P. A. (1996). Cerebral structural abnomalities in obsessive-compulsive disorder. *Archives of General Psychiatry, 53,* 625–632.

Jenkins, C. D. (1976). Recent evidence supporting psychologic and social risk factors for coronary disease. *New England Journal of Medicine, 294,* 987–994, 1033–1038.

Jenkins, L., Myerson, J., Hale, S., & Fry, A. F. (1999). Individual and developmental differences in working memory across the life span. *Psychonomic Bulletin & Review, 6,* 28–40.

Jensen, A. R. (1962). Spelling errors and the serial position effect. *Journal of Educational Psychology, 53,* 105–109.

Jensen-Campbell, L. A., Graziano, W. G., & West, S. G. (1995). Dominance, prosocial orientation, and female preferences: Do nice guys really finish last? *Journal of Personality and Social Psychology, 68,* 427–440.

Johnson, J. R., & Vickers, Z. M. (1993). The effects of flavor and macronutrient composition of preloads on liking, hunger, and subsequent intake in humans. *Appetite, 21,* 15–31.

Johnson, M. K., Hashtroudi, S., & Lindsay, D. S. (1993). Source monitoring. *Psychological Bulletin, 114,* 3–28.

Johnson, T. D., & Gottlieb, G. (1981). Visual preferences of imprinted ducklings are altered by the maternal call. *Journal of Comparative and Physiological Psychology, 95*(5), 665–675.

Johnson, T. E., & Rule, B. G. (1986). Mitigating circumstances, information, censure, and aggression. *Journal of Personality and Social Psychology, 50,* 537–542.

Johnson-Laird, P. N., & Wason, P. C. (1977). A theoretical analysis of insight into a reasoning task. In P. N. Johnson-Laird & P. C. Wason (Eds.), *Thinking* (pp. 143–157). Cambridge, U.K.: Cambridge University Press.

Jones, E. (1953). *The life and works of Sigmund Freud.* New York: Basic Books.

Jones, E. E., & Berglas, S. (1978). Control of attributions about the self through self-handicapping strategies: The appeal of alcohol and the role of underachievement. *Personality and Social Psychology Bulletin, 4,* 200–206.

Jones, H. C., & Loninger, P. W. (1985). *The marijuana question: And science's search for an answer.* New York: Dodd, Mead.

Jones, J. M. (1997). *Prejudice and racism* (2nd ed.). New York: McGraw-Hill.

Jones, J. M., Levine, I. S., & Rosenberg, A. A. (Eds.). (1991). Homelessness [Special issue]. *American Psychologist, 46*(11).

Jones, M. C. (1924). A laboratory study of fear: The case of Peter. *Pedagogical Seminary and Journal of Genetic Psychology, 31,* 308–315.

Jones, W. H., Cheek, J. M., & Briggs, S. R. (Eds.). (1986). *Shyness: Perspectives on research and treatment.* New York: Plenum Press.

Joyce, L. (1990). Losing the connection. *Stanford Medicine,* pp. 19–21.

Judge, T. A., & Cable, D. M. (1997). Applicant personality, organizational culture, and organization attraction. *Personnel Psychology, 50,* 359–392.

Jung, C. G. (1959). The concept of the collective unconscious. In *The archetypes and the collective unconscious, collected works* (Vol. 9, Part 1, pp. 54–74.). Princeton, NJ: Princeton University Press. (Original work published 1936)

Jung, C. G. (1973). *Memories, dreams, reflections* (Rev. ed., A. Jaffe, Ed.). New York: Pantheon Books.

Jusczyk, P. W., & Aslin, R. N. (1995). Infants' detection of the sound patterns of words in fluent speech. *Cognitive Psychology, 29,* 1–23.

Jussim, L. (1986). Self-fulfilling prophecies: A theoretical and integrative review. *Psychological Review, 93,* 429–445.

Jussim, L. (1991). Social perception and social reality: A reflection-construction model. *Psychological Review, 98,* 54–73.

Jussim, L. (1993). Accuracy in interpersonal expectation: A reflection-construction analysis of current and classic research. *Journal of Personality, 61,* 637–668.

Just, N., & Alloy, L. B. (1997). The response styles theory of depression: Tests and an extension of the theory. *Journal of Abnormal Psychology, 106,* 221–229.

Kagan, J. (1994). *Galen's prophesy: Temperament in human nature.* New York: Basic Books.

Kahneman, D. (1973). *Attention and effort.* Englewood Cliffs, NJ: Prentice Hall.

Kahneman, D. (1991). Judgment and decision making: A personal view. *Psychological Science, 2,* 142–145.

Kahneman, D. (1992). Reference points, anchors, norms, and mixed feelings. *Organizational Behavior and Human Decision Processes, 51,* 296–312.

Kahneman, D., & Tversky, A. (1973). On the psychology of prediction. *Psychological Review, 80,* 237–251.

Kalat, J. W. (1974). Taste salience depends on novelty, not concentration in taste-aversion learning in the rat. *Journal of Comparative and Physiological Psychology, 86,* 47–50.

Kallmann, F. J. (1946). The genetic theory of schizophrenia: An analysis of 691 schizophrenic index families. *American Journal of Psychiatry, 103,* 309–322.

Kamil, A. C., & Balda, R. P. (1990). Spatial memory in seed-caching corvids. In G. H. Bower (Ed.), *The psychology of learning and motivation* (Vol. 26, pp. 1–25). San Diego: Academic Press.

Kamil, A. C., Balda, R. P., Olson, D. P., & Good, S. (1993). Returns to emptied cache sites by Clark's nutcrackers, *Nucifraga columbiana*: A puzzle revisited. *Animal Behaviour, 45,* 241–252.

Kamin, L. J. (1969). Predictability, surprise, attention, and conditioning. In B. A Campbell & R. M. Church (Eds.), *Punishment and aversive behavior* (pp. 279–296). New York: Appleton-Century-Crofts.

Kantrowitz, B., & McGinn, D. (2000, June 19). When teachers are cheaters. *Newsweek, 135,* 48–49.

Kaplan, C. A., & Simon, H. A. (1990). In search of insight. *Cognitive Psychology, 22,* 374–419.

Kaplan, R. M. (2000). Two pathways to prevention. *American Psychologist, 55,* 382–396.

Kappé, B., van Erp, J., & Korteling, J. E. (1999). Effects of head-slaved and peripheral displays on lane-keeping performance and spatial orientation. *Human Factors, 41,* 453–466.

Karney, B. R., & Bradbury, T. N. (1995). The longitudinal course of marital quality and stability: A review of theory, method, and research. *Psychological Bulletin, 118,* 3–34.

Kassebaum, N. L. (1994). Head Start: Only the best for America's children. *American Psychologist, 49,* 1123–1126.

Katsanis, J., Kortenkamp, S., Iacono, W. G., & Grove, W. M. (1997). Antisaccade performance in patients with schizophrenia. *Journal of Abnormal Psychology, 106,* 468–472.

Katz, R. (1982). *Boiling energy: Community healing among the Kalahari Kung.* Cambridge, MA: Harvard University Press.

Katz, R. (1993). *The straight path: A story of healing and transformation in Fiji.* Reading, MA: Addison-Wesley.

Kay, P., & Kempton, W. (1984). What is the Sapir-Whorf hypothesis? *American Anthropologist, 86,* 65–79.

Kazdin, A. E. (1982). The token economy: A decade later. *Journal of Applied Behavior Analysis, 15,* 431–445.

Kazdin, A. E. (1994). *Behavior modification in applied settings* (5th ed.). Pacific Grove, CA: Brooks/Cole.

Keen, S. (1986). *Faces of the enemy: Reflections of the hostile imagination.* New York: Harper & Row.

Kegeles, S. M., Hays, R. B., & Coates, T. J. (1996). The Mpowerment project: A community-level HIV prevention intervention for young gay men. *American Journal of Public Health, 86,* 1129–1136.

Keiger, D. (1993, November). Touched with fire. *Johns Hopkins Magazine,* pp. 38, 40–44.

Keller, H. (1990). *The story of my life.* New York: Bantam Books. (Original work published 1902)

Keller, M. B., McCullough, J. P., Klein, D. N., Arnow, B., Dunner, D. L., Gelenberg, A. J., Markowitz, J. C., Nemeroff, C. B., Russell, J. M., Thase, M. E., Trivedi, M. H., & Zajecka, J. (2000). A comparison of nefazodone, the cognitive behavioral-analysis system of psychotherapy, and their combination for the treatment of chronic depression. *New England Journal of Medicine, 342,* 1462–1470.

Kelley, H. H. (1967). Attribution theory in social psychology. In D. Levine (Ed.), *Nebraska Symposium on Motivation* (Vol. 15). Lincoln: University of Nebraska Press.

Kelley, J. E., Lumley, M. A., & Leisen, J. C. C. (1997). Health effects of emotional disclosure in rheumatoid arthritis patients. *Health Psychology, 16,* 331–340.

Kelman, H. C. (1997). Group processes in the resolution of international conflicts: Experiences from the Israeli–Palestinian case. *American Psychologist, 52,* 212–220.

Kelman, H. C. (1999). Interactive problem solving as a metaphor for international conflict resolution: Lessons for the policy process. *Peace & Conflict: Journal of Peace Psychology, 5,* 201–218.

Kelsoe, J. R., Ginns, E. I., Egeland, J. A., Gerhard, D. S., Goldstein, A. M., Bale, S. J., Pauls, D. L., Long, R. T., Kidd, K. K., Conte, G., Housman, D. E., & Paul, S. M. (1989). Re-evaluation of the linkage relationship between chromosome 11p loci and the gene for bipolar affective disorder in the Old Order Amish. *Nature, 342,* 238–243.

Kelsoe, J. R., Kristbjanarson, H., Bergesch, P., Shilling, P., Hirsch, S., Mirow, A., Moises, H. W., Helgason, T., Gillin, J. C., & Egeland, J. A. (1993). A genetic linkage study of bipolar disorder and 13 markers on chromosome 11 including the D2 dopamine receptor. *Neuropsychopharmacology, 9,* 293–301.

Kendler, H. H. (1987). *Historical foundations of modern psychology.* Chicago: Dorsey Press.

Kendler, K. S., & Diehl, S. R. (1993). The genetics of schizophrenia: A current, genetic-epidemiologic perspective. *Schizophrenia Bulletin, 19,* 261–285.

Kendler, K. S., Heath, A. C., Neale, M. C., Kessler, R. C., & Eaves, L. J. (1992). A population-based twin study of alcoholism in women. *Journal of the American Medical Association, 268,* 1877–1882.

Kendrick, T., Tylee, A., & Freeling (Eds.) (1996). *The prevention of mental illness in primary care.* Cambridge, U.K.: Cambridge University Press.

Kennedy, R. E., & Craighead, W. E. (1988). Differential effects of depression and anxiety on recall of feedback in a learning task. *Behavior Therapy, 19,* 437–454.

Kenny, D. A., Bond, C. F., Jr., Mohr, C. D., & Horn, E. M. (1996). Do we know how much people like one another? *Journal of Personality and Social Psychology, 71,* 928–936.

Kenny, D. A., & La Voie, L. (1982). Reciprocity of interpersonal attraction: A confirmed hypothesis. *Social Psychology Quarterly, 45,* 54–58.

Kenrick, D. T., Keefe, R. C., Gavrielidis, C., & Cornelius, J. S. (1996). Adolescents' age preferences for dating partners: Support for an evolutionary model of life-history strategies. *Child Development, 67,* 1499–1511.

Kesey, K. (1962). *One flew over the cuckoo's nest.* New York: Viking Press.

Kessel, N. (1989). Genius and mental disorder: A history of ideas concerning their conjunction. In P. Murray (Ed.), *Genius: The history of an idea* (pp. 196–212). London: Basil Blackwell.

Kessler, R. C., McGonagle, K. A., Zhao, S., Nelson, C. B., Hughes, M., Eshleman, S., Wittchen, H. U., & Kendler, K. S. (1994). Lifetime and 12-month prevalence of DSM-III-R psychiatric disorders in the United States. *Archives of General Psychiatry, 51,* 8–19.

Kessler, R. C., Mickelson, K. D., & Zhao, S. (1997). Patterns and correlates of self-help group membership in the United States. *Social Policy, 27,* 27–46.

Kety, S. S., Wender, P. H., Jacobsen, B., Ingraham, L. J., Jansson, L., Faber, B., & Kinney, D. K. (1994). Mental illness in the biological and adoptive relatives of schizophrenic adoptees: Replication of the Copenhagen study in the rest of Denmark. *Archives of General Psychiatry, 51,* 442–455.

Kihlstrom, J. F., & Cantor, N. (2000). Social intelligence. In R. J. Sternberg (Ed.), *Handbook of intelligence* (pp. 359–369). New York: Cambridge University Press.

Killen, M., & Hart, D. (Eds.). (1999). *Morality in everyday life: Developmental perspectives.* New York: Cambridge University Press.

Kim, M. S., & Cave, K. R. (1995). Spatial attention in visual search for features and feature conjunctions. *Psychological Science, 6,* 376–380.

Kimura, D. (1999). *Sex and cognition.* Cambridge, MA: MIT Press.

King, S., & Dixon, M. J. (1996). The influence of expressed emotion, family dynamics, and symptom type on the social adjustment of schizophrenic young adults. *Archives of General Psychiatry, 53,* 1098–1104.

King, S. A., & Moreggi, D. (1998). Internet therapy and self-help groups—The pros and cons. In J. Gackenbach (Ed.), *Psychology and the Internet: Intrapersonal, interpersonal, and transpersonal implications* (pp. 77–109). San Diego, CA: Academic Press.

Kinney, D. K., Holzman, P. S., Jacobsen, B., Jansson, L., Faber, B., Hildebrand, W., Kasell, E., & Zimbalist, M. E. (1997). Thought disorder in schizophrenic and control adoptees and their relatives. *Archives of General Psychiatry, 54,* 475–479.

Kinomura, S., Larsson, J., Gulyás, B., & Roland, P. E. (1996). Activation by attention of the human reticular formation and thalamic intralaminar nuclei. *Science, 271,* 512–515.

Kinsey, A. C., Martin, C. E., & Pomeroy, W. B. (1948). *Sexual behavior in the human male.* Philadelphia: Saunders.

Kinsey, A. C., Pomeroy, W. B., Martin, C. E., & Gebhard, R. H. (1953). *Sexual behavior in the human female.* Philadelphia: Saunders.

Kintsch, W. (1974). *The representation of meaning in memory.* Hillsdale, NJ: Erlbaum.

Kirsch, I., & Lynn, S. J. (1995). The altered state of hypnosis: Changes in the theoretical landscape. *American Psychologist, 50,* 846–858.

Kirsch, I., & Lynn, S. J. (1998). Dissociation theories of hypnosis. *Psychological Bulletin, 123,* 100–115.

Kitayama, S., Markus, H. R., & Lieberman, C. (1995). The collective construction of self-esteem: Implications for culture, self, and emotion. In J. A. Russell, J. Fernandez-Dols, T. Manstead, & J. Wellenkamp (Eds.), *Everyday conceptions of emotion* (pp. 523–550). Dordrecht: Kluwer.

Kitayama, S., Markus, H. R., Matsumoto, H., & Norasakkunkit, V. (1997). Individual and collective processes in the construction of the self: Self-enhancement in the United States and self-criticism in Japan. *Journal of Personality and Social Psychology, 72,* 1245–1267.

Kite, M. E., & Johnson, B. T. (1988). Attitudes toward older and younger adults: A meta-analysis. *Psychology and Aging, 3,* 233–244.

Klag, M. J., Whelton, P. K., Grim, C. E., & Kuller, L. H. (1991). The association of skin color with blood pressure in U.S. blacks with low socioeconomic status. *Journal of the American Medical Association, 265,* 599–602.

Klein, D. F., & Ross, D. C. (1993). Reanalysis of the National Institutes of Mental Health Treatment of Depression Collaborate Research Program General Effectiveness Report. *Neuropsychopharmacology, 8,* 241–251.

Klein, K. E., & Wegmann, H. M. (1974). The resynchronization of human circadian rhythms after transmeridian flights as a result of flight direction and mode of activity. In L. E. Scheving, F. Halberg, & J. E. Pauly (Eds.), *Chronobiology* (pp. 564–570). Tokyo: Igaku.

Klein, M. (1975). *The writings of Melanie Klein* (Vols. 1–4). London: Hogarth Press and the Institute of Psychoanalysis.

Klerman, G. L., Weissman, M. M., Markowitz, J. C., Glick, R., Wilner, P. J., Mason, B., & Shear, M. K. (1994). Medication and psychotherapy. In A. E. Bergin & S. L. Garfield (Eds.), *Handbook of psychotherapy and behavior change* (4th ed.) (pp. 734–782). New York: Wiley.

Kluckhohn, C. (1944). Navaho witchcraft. *Papers of the Yale University Peabody Museum* (Vol. 24, No. 2). New Haven: Yale University Press.

Knoedler, A. J., Hellwig, K. A., & Neath, I. (1999). The shift from recency to primacy with increasing delay. *Journal of Experimental Psychology: Learning, Memory, and Cognition, 25,* 474–487.

Knox, C. (1994). Conflict resolution at the microlevel: Community relations in Northern Ireland. *Journal of Conflict Resolution, 38,* 595–619.

Koffka, K. (1935). *Principles of Gestalt psychology.* New York: Harcourt Brace.

Kohlberg, L. (1964). Development of moral character and moral ideology. In M. L. Hoffman & L. W. Hoffman (Eds.), *Review of child development research* (Vol. 1). New York: Russell Sage Foundation.

Kohlberg, L. (1981). *The philosophy of moral development.* New York: Harper & Row.

Köhler, W. (1947). *Gestalt psychology.* New York: Liveright.

Kohut, H. (1977). *The restoration of the self.* New York: International Universities Press.

Kolb, B. (1989). Development, plasticity, and behavior. *American Psychologist, 44,* 1203–1212.

Kolodner, J. L. (1997). Educational implications of analogy: A view from case-based reasoning. *American Psychologist, 52,* 57–66.

Kondo, T., Antrobus, J., & Fein, G. (1989). Later REM activation and sleep mentation. *Sleep Research, 18,* 147.

Koopman, C., Classen, C., & Spiegel, D. (1996). Dissociative responses in the immediate aftermath of the Oakland/Berkeley firestorm. *Journal of Traumatic Stress, 9,* 521–540.

Koren, G., Nulman, I., Rovet, J., Greenbaum, R., Loebstein, M., & Einarson, T. (1998). Long-term neurodevelopmental risks in children exposed in utero to cocaine: The Toronto adoption study. In J. A. Harvey & B. E. Kosofsky (Eds.), *Cocaine: Effects on the developing brain* (pp. 306–313). New York: New York Academy of Sciences.

Koriat, A. (1993). How do we know that we know? The accessibility model of the feeling of knowing. *Psychological Review, 100,* 609–639.

Koriat, A. (1995). Dissociating knowing and the feeling of knowing: Further evidence for the accessibility model. *Journal of Experimental Psychology: General, 124,* 311–333.

Koriat, A., & Fischoff, B. (1974). What day is today? An inquiry into the process of time orientation. *Memory & Cognition, 2,* 201–205.

Koriat, A., & Levy-Sadot, R. (1999). Processes underlying metacognitive judgments: Information-based and experience-based monitoring of one's own knowledge. In S. Chaiken & Y. Trope (Eds.), *Dual-process theories in social psychology* (pp. 483–502). New York: Guilford.

Korn, J. (1987). Judgments of acceptability of deception in psychological research. *Journal of General Psychology, 114,* 205–216.

Kosslyn, S. M. (1980). *Image and mind.* Cambridge, MA: Harvard University Press.

Kosslyn, S. M., Pascual-Leone, A., Felician, O., Camposano, S., Keenan, J. P., Thompson, W. L., Ganis, G., Sukel, K. E., & Alpert, N. M. (1999). The role of Area 17 in visual imagery: Convergent evidence from PET and rTMS. *Science, 284,* 167–170.

Kotovsky, K., Hayes, J. R., & Simon, H. A. (1985). Why are some problems hard? Evidence from Tower of Hanoi. *Cognitive Psychology, 17,* 248–294.

Kotovsky, K., & Simon, H. A. (1990). What makes some problems really hard: Explorations in the problem space of difficulty. *Cognitive Psychology, 22,* 143–183.

Kraepelin, E. (1921). *Manic-depressive disorder and paranoia.* London: Churchill Livingstone.

Kramer, J., & Alstad, D. (1993). *The guru papers: Masks of authoritarian power.* Berkeley, CA: North Atlantic Books/Frog Ltd.

Kramer, P. D. (1993). *Listening to Prozac.* New York: Penguin Books.

Kraut, A. M. (1990). Healers and strangers: Immigrant attitudes toward the physician in America—A relationship in historical perspective. *Journal of the American Medical Association, 263,* 1807–1811.

Kraut, R., Patterson, M., Lundmark, V., Kiesler, S, Mukopadhyay, T, & Scherlis, W. (1998). Internet paradox: A social technology that reduces social involvement and psychological well being? *American Psychologist, 53,* 1017–1031.

Kristof, A. L. (1996). Person-organization fit: An integrative review of its conceptualizations, measurement, and implications. *Personnel Psychology, 49,* 1–49.

Krug, R. S., Nixon, S. J., & Vincent, R. (1996). Psychological response to the Oklahoma City bombing. *Journal of Clinical Psychology, 52,* 103–105.

Krupa, D. J., Thompson, J. K., & Thompson, R. F. (1993). Localization of a memory trace in the mammalian brain. *Science, 260,* 989–991.

Kubovy, M., Cohen, D. J., & Hollier, J. (1999). Feature integration that routinely occurs without focal attention. *Psychonomic Bulletin & Review, 6,* 183–203.

Kuhn, M. H., & McPartland, T. S. (1954). An empirical investigation of self-attitudes. *American Sociological Review, 19,* 68–76.

Kuijer, R. G., Ybema, J. F., Buunk, B. P., De Jon, G. M., Thijs-Boer, F., & Sanderman, R. (2000). Active engagement, protective buffering, and overprotection: Three ways of giving support by intimate partners of patients with cancer. *Journal of Social and Clinical Psychology, 19,* 256–275.

Kujawski, J. H., & Bower, T. G. R. (1993). Same-sex preferential looking during infancy as a function of abstract representation. *British Journal of Developmental Psychlogy, 11,* 201–209.

Kulik, J. A., & Mahler, H. I. M. (1989). Social support and recovery from surgery. *Health Psychology, 8,* 221–238.

Kuno, E., Rothbard, A. B., Averyt, J., & Culhane, D. (2000). Homelessness among persons with serious mental illness in an enhanced community-based mental health system. *Psychiatric Services, 51,* 1012–1016.

LaBerge, S., & DeGracia, D. J. (2000). Varieties of lucid dreaming experience. In R. G. Kunzendorf & B. Wallace (Eds.), *Individual differences in conscious experience* (pp. 269–307). Amsterdam: John Benjamins Publishing Company.

LaBerge, S., & Levitan, L. (1995). Validity established of DreamLight cues for eliciting lucid dreaming. *Dreaming: Journal of the Association for the Study of Dreams, 5,* 159–168.

LaBerge, S., Nagle, L., Dement, W., & Zarcone, V. (1981). Lucid dreaming verified by volitional communication during REM sleep. *Perceptual & Motor Skills, 52,* 727–732.

LaBerge, S., & Rheingold, H. (1990). *Exploring the world of lucid dreaming.* New York: Ballantine Books.

Lachman, R., Lachman, J. L., & Butterfield, E. C. (1979). *Cognitive psychology and information processing.* Hillsdale, NJ: Erlbaum.

Ladd, G. W., & Cairns, E. (1996). Children: Ethnic and political violence. *Child Development, 67,* 14–18.

LaFrance, M., & Banaji, M. (1992). Towards a reconsideration of the gender-emotion relationship. *Review of Personality and Social Psychology, 14,* 178–201.

LaFromboise, T. (1988, March 30). Suicide prevention. In *Campus Report* (p. 9). Stanford, CA: Stanford University Press.

Lal, S. K. L., Henderson, R. J., Carter, N., Bath, A., Hart, M. G., Langeluddecke, P., & Hunyor, S. N. (1998). Effect of feedback signal and psychological characteristics on blood pressure self-manipulation capability. *Psychophysiology. 35,* 405–412.

Lambo, T. A. (1978). Psychotherapy in Africa. *Human Nature, 1,* 32–39.

Lane, H. (1976). *The Wild Boy of Aveyron.* Cambridge, MA: Harvard University Press.

Lane, H. (1986). The Wild Boy of Aveyron and Dr. Jean-Marc Itard. *History of Psychology, 17,* 3–16.

Lang, F. R., & Carstensen, L. L. (1994). Close emotional relationships in late life: Further support for proactive aging in the social domain. *Psychology and Aging, 9,* 315–324.

Langone, M. D. (Ed.). (1993). *Recovery from cults.* New York: Norton.

Larner, A. J., Moss, J., Rossi, M. L., & Anderson, M. (1994). Congenital insensitivity to pain: A 20-year follow up. *Journal of Neurology, Neurosurgery & Psychiatry, 57,* 973–974.

Lashley, K. S. (1929). *Brain mechanisms and intelligence.* Chicago: University of Chicago Press.

Lashley, K. S. (1950). In search of the engram. In *Physiological mechanisms in animal behavior: Symposium of the Society for Experimental Biology.* New York: Academic Press.

Latané, B., & Darley, J. M. (1970). *The unresponsive bystander: Why doesn't he help?* New York: Appleton-Century-Crofts.

Laurent, J., Swerdlik, M., & Ryburn, M. (1992). Review of validity research on the Stanford–Binet intelligence scale. *Psychological Assessment, 4,* 102–112.

Lavond, D. G., Kim, J. J., & Thompson, R. F. (1993). Mammalian brain substrates of aversive classical conditioning. *Annual Review of Psychology, 44,* 317–342.

Lay, C. H. (1986). At last my research article on procrastination. *Journal of Research in Personality, 20,* 474–495.

Lazarus, R. S. (1981, July). Little hassles can be hazardous to your health. *Psychology Today,* pp. 58–62.

Lazarus, R. S. (1984a). On the primacy of cognition. *American Psychologist, 39,* 124–129.

Lazarus, R. S. (1984b). Puzzles in the study of daily hassles. *Journal of Behavioral Medicine, 7,* 375–389.

Lazarus, R. S. (1991). Cognition and motivation in emotion. *American Psychologist, 46,* 352–367.

Lazarus, R. S. (1993). From psychological stress to the emotions: A history of changing outlooks. *Annual Review of Psychology, 44,* 1–21.

Lazarus, R. S. (1995). Vexing research problems inherent in cognitive-mediational theories of emotion—and some solutions. *Psychological Inquiry, 6,* 183–196.

Lazarus, R. S., & Folkman, S. (1984). *Stress, appraisal, and coping.* New York: Springer.

Lazarus, R. S., & Lazarus, B. N. (1994). *Passion and reason: Making sense of our emotions.* New York: Oxford University Press.

Leaper, C. (2000). The social construction and socialization of gender during development. In P. H. Miller & E. K. Scholnick (Eds.), *Toward a feminist developmental psychology* (pp. 127–152). New York: Routledge.

Leary, M. R., Tchividjian, L. R., & Kraxberger, B. E. (1994). Self-presentation can be hazardous to your health: Impression management and health risk. *Health Psychology, 13,* 461–470.

LeCompte, D. C., & Watkins, M. J. (1995). Grouping in primary memory: The case of the compound suffix. *Journal of Experimental Psychology: Learning, Memory, and Cognition, 21,* 96–102.

LeDoux, J. E. (1989). Cognitive-emotional interactions in the brain. *Cognition and Emotion, 3,* 267–289.

LeDoux, J. E. (1995). Emotion: Clues from the brain. *Annual Review of Psychology, 46,* 209–235.

Lee, M., Zimbardo, P., & Bertholf, M. (1977, November). Shy murderers. *Psychology Today,* pp. 68–70, 76, 148.

Lee-Sammons, W. H., & Whitney, P. (1991). Reading perspectives and memory for text: An individual differences analysis. *Journal of Experimental Psychology: Learning, Memory, and Cognition, 17,* 1074–1081.

Leger, D. (1992). *Biological foundations of behavior: An integrative approach.* New York: HarperCollins.

LeGrand, L. E. (1991). United we cope: Support groups for the dying and bereaved. *Death Studies, 15,* 207–230.

Leiter, M. P., & Maslach, C. (1988). The impact of interpersonal environment on burnout and organizational commitment. *Journal of Organizational Behavior, 9,* 297–308.

Leiter, M. P., & Maslach, C. (2000). *Preventing burnout and building engagement: A complete program for organizational renewal.* San Francisco, CA: Jossey-Bass.

Lencer, R., Malchow, C. P., Trillenberg-Krecker, K., Schwinger, E., & Arolt, V. (2000). Eye-tracking dysfunction (ETD) in families with sporadic and familial schizophrenia. *Biological Psychiatry, 47,* 391–401.

Lennon, R. T. (1985). Group tests of intelligence. In B. B. Wolman (Ed.), *Handbook of intelligence* (pp. 825–847). New York: Wiley.

Lerner, M. (1980). *The belief in a just world: A fundamental delusion.* New York: Plenum Press.

Lesher, G. W. (1995). Illusory contours: Toward a neurally based perceptual theory. *Psychonomic Bulletin & Review, 2,* 279–321.

Leslie, R. F. (1985). *Lorenzo the Magnificent: The story of an orphaned blue jay.* New York: Norton.

LeVay, S. (1996). *Queer science: The use and abuse of research into homosexuality.* Cambridge, MA: The MIT Press.

Levenson, R. W., Carstensen, L. L., & Gottman, J. M. (1993). Long-term marriage: Age, gender, and satisfaction. *Psychology and Aging, 8,* 301–313.

Levenson, R. W., Ekman, P., Heider, K., & Friesen, W. V. (1992). Emotion and autonomic nervous system activity in the Minangkabau of West Sumatra. *Journal of Personality and Social Psychology, 62,* 972–988.

Leventhal, H. (1980). Toward a comprehensive theory of emotion. In L. Berkowitz (Ed.), *Advances in experimental social psychology* (Vol. 13, pp. 139–207). New York: Academic Press.

Leventhal, T., & Brooks-Gunn, J. (2000). The neighborhoods they live in: The effects of neighborhood on child and adolescent outcomes. *Psychological Bulletin, 126,* 309–337.

Levine, M. W., & Shefner, J. M. (1981). *Fundamentals of sensation and perception.* Reading, MA: Addison-Wesley.

Levine, R., Sato, S., Hashimoto, T., & Verma, J. (1995). Love and marriage in eleven cultures. *Journal of Cross-Cultural Psychology, 26,* 544–571.

Levine, S. B. (1998). *Sexuality in mid-life.* New York: Plenum.

Levi-Strauss, C. (1963). The effectiveness of symbols. In C. Levi-Strauss (Ed.), *Structural anthropology.* New York: Basic Books.

Levy, B., & Langer, E. (1994). Aging free from negative stereotypes: Successful memory in China and among the American deaf. *Journal of Personality and Social Psychology, 66,* 989–997.

Levy, G. D., & Fivush, R. (1993). Scripts and gender: A new approach for examining gender-role development. *Developmental Review, 13,* 126–146.

Levy, J. A. (1994). Sex and sexuality in later life stages. In A. Rossi (Ed.), *Sexuality across the life course* (pp. 287–309). Chicago: University of Chicago Press.

Levy, S. R., Plaks, J. E., & Dweck, C. S. (1999). Modes of social thought: Implicit theories and social understanding. In S. Chaiken & Y. Trope (Eds.), *Dual-process theories in social psychology* (pp. 179–202). New York: Guilford.

Lewin, K. (1936). *Principles of topological psychology.* New York: Mc-Graw-Hill.

Lewin, K. (1948). *Resolving social conflicts.* New York: Harper.

Lewin, K., Lippitt, R., & White, R. K. (1939). Patterns of aggressive behavior in experimentally created "social climates." *Journal of Social Psychology, 10,* 271–299.

Lewinsohn, P. M. (1975). The behavioral study and treatment of depression. In M. Hersen, R. M. Eisler, & P. M. Miller (Eds.), *Progress in behavior modification* (pp. 19–64). New York: Academic Press.

Lewinsohn, P. M., Hoberman, H. M., Teri, L., & Hautzinger, M. (1985). An integrative theory of depression. In S. Reiss & R. Bootzin (Eds.), *Theoretical issues in behavior therapy* (pp. 331–359). San Diego: Academic Press.

Lewis, J. R. (1995). *The dream encyclopedia.* Detroit: Visible Ink Press.

Lewis, M. (1991). Ways of knowing: Objective self-awareness or consciousness. *Developmental Review, 11,* 231–243.

Lewis, M. (1999). Social cognition and the self. In P. Rochat (Ed.), *Early social cognition: Understanding others in the first months of life* (pp. 81–98). Mahwah, NJ: Erlbaum.

Liittschwager, J. C., & Markman, E. M. (1994). Sixteen- and 24-month-olds' use of mutual exclusivity as a default assumption in second-label learning. *Developmental Psychology, 30,* 955–968.

Lilienfeld, S. O., Kirsch. I., Sarvin, T. R., Lynn, St. J., Chaves, J. F., Ganaway, G. K., & Powell, R. A. (1999). Dissociative identity disorder and the sociocognitive model: Recalling the lessons of the past. *Psychological Bulletin, 125,* 507–523.

Lindsay, D. S. (1990). Misleading suggestions can impair eyewitnesses' ability to remember event details. *Journal of Experimental Psychology: Learning, Memory, and Cognition, 16,* 1077–1083.

Lindsay, D. S. (1993). Eyewitness suggestibility. *Current Directions in Psychological Science, 2,* 86–89.

Link, B. G., Struening, E. L., Rahav, M., Phelan, J. C., & Nuttbrock, L. (1997). On stigma and its consequences: Evidence from a longitudinal study of men with dual diagnoses of mental illness and substance abuse. *Journal of Health and Social Behavior, 38,* 177–190.

Lipkus, I. M., Barefoot, J. C., Williams, R. B., & Siegler, I. C. (1994). Personality measures as predictors of smoking initiation and cessation in the UNC Alumni Heart Study. *Health Psychology, 13,* 149–155.

Lipsey, M. W., & Wilson, D. B. (1993). The efficacy of psychological, educational, and behavioral treatment: Confirmation from meta-analysis. *American Psychologist, 48,* 1181–1209.

Little, S. G. (1992). The WISC-III: Everything old is new again. *School Psychology Quarterly, 7,* 136–142.

Liu, J. H., & Latané, B. (1998). Extremitization of attitudes: Does thought- and discussion-induced polarization cumulate? *Basic and Applied Social Psychology, 20,* 103–110.

Liu, W., McGucken, E., Clements, M., DeMarco, C., Vichienchom, K., Hughes, C., Humayun, M., Weiland, J., Greenber, R., & de Juan, E. (2000). Multiple-unit artificial retina chipset system to benefit the visually impaired. *IEEE Transactions on Rehabilitation Engineering,* in press.

Livesley, W. J., Jang, K. L., Jackson, D. N., & Vernon, P. A. (1993). Genetic and environmental contributions to dimensions of personality disorder. *American Journal of Psychiatry, 150,* 1826–1831.

Livingstone, M., & Hubel, D. (1988). Segregation of form, color, movement, and depth: Anatomy, physiology, and perception. *Science, 240,* 740–749.

Lobel, M. (1994). Conceptualizations, measurement, and the effects of prenatal maternal stress on birth outcomes. *Journal of Behavioral Medicine, 17,* 225–272.

Lobel, M., Dunkel-Schetter, C., & Scrimshaw, S. C. M. (1992). Prenatal maternal stress and prematurity: A prospective study of socioeconomically disadvantaged women. *Health Psychology, 11,* 32–40.

Locke, J. (1975). *An essay concerning human understanding.* Oxford: P. H. Nidditch. (Original work published 1690)

Lockhart, R. S., & Craik, F. I. M. (1990). Levels of processing: A retrospective commentary on a framework for memory research. *Canadian Journal of Psychology, 44,* 87–122.

Loehlin, J. C. (1992). *Genes and environment in personality development.* Newbury Park, CA: Sage.

Loehlin, J. C. (2000). Group differences in intelligence. In R. J. Sternberg (Ed.), *Handbook of intelligence* (pp. 176–193). Cambridge, U.K.: Cambridge University Press.

Loehlin, J. C., McCrae, R. R., Costa, P. T., & John, O. P. (1998). Heritabilities of common and measure-specific components of the big five personality factors. *Journal of Research in Personality, 32,* 431–453.

Loftus, E. F. (1979). *Eyewitness testimony.* Cambridge, MA: Harvard University Press.

Loftus, E. F. (1992). When a lie becomes memory's truth: Memory distortion after exposure to misinformation. *Current Directions in Psychological Science, 1,* 121–123.

Loftus, E. F. (1993). The reality of repressed memories. *American Psychologist, 48,* 518–537.

Loftus, E. F., & Ketcham, K. (1994). *The myth of repressed memory: False memories and allegations of sexual abuse.* New York: St. Martin's Press.

Loftus, E. F., & Palmer, J. C. (1974). Reconstruction of automobile destruction: An example of the interaction between language and memory. *Journal of Verbal Learning and Verbal Behavior, 13,* 585–589.

Loftus, G. R., Duncan, J., & Gehrig, P. (1992). On the time course of perceptual information that results from a brief visual presentation. *Journal of Experimental Psychology: Human Perception and Performance, 18,* 530–549.

Logan, G. D. (1988). Toward an instance theory of automatization. *Psychological Review, 95,* 492–527.

Logan, G. D. (1992). Shapes of reaction-time distributions and shapes of learning curves: A test of the instance theory of automaticity. *Journal of Experimental Psychology: Learning, Memory, and Cognition, 18,* 883–914.

Logue, A. W. (1991). *The psychology of eating & drinking: An introduction* (2nd ed.). New York: Freeman.

Lombard, M., & Ditton, T. (1997). At the heart of it all: The concept of presence. *Journal of Computer-Mediated Communication, 3*(2).

Loomis, A. L., Harvey, E. N., & Hobart, G. A. (1937). Cerebral states during sleep as studied by human brain potentials. *Journal of Experimental Psychology, 21,* 127–144.

Lore, R. K., & Schultz, L. A. (1993). Control of human aggression: A comparative perspective. *American Psychologist, 48,* 16–25.

Lorenz, K. (1966). *On aggression.* New York: Harcourt, Brace, & World.

Los Angeles Times. (1988, February 23). Bullet in the brain cures man's mental problem.

Lourenço, O., & Machado, A. (1996). In defense of Piaget's theory: A reply to 10 common criticisms. *Psychological Review, 103,* 143–164.

Lovett, M. C., & Anderson, J. R. (1994). Effects of solving related proofs on memory and transfer in geometry problem solving. *Journal* of *Experimental Psychology: Learning, Memory, and Cognition, 20,* 366–378.

Lovibond, S. H., Adams, M., & Adams, W. G. (1979). The effects of three experimental prison environments on the behavior of nonconflict volunteer subjects. *Australian Psychologist, 14,* 273–285.

Lowenthal, M. F., & Chiriboga, D. (1972). Transition to the empty nest: Crisis, challenge, or relief? *Archives of General Psychiatry, 26,* 8–14.

Lubart, T. I. (1994). Creativity. In R. J. Sternberg (Ed.), *Handbook of perception and cognition: Vol. 2. Thinking and problem solving* (pp. 289–332). Orlando, FL: Academic Press.

Lubin, B., Larsen, R. M., & Matarazzo, J. D. (1984). Patterns of psychological test usage in the United States: 1935–1982. *American Psychologist, 39,* 451–455.

Lubow, R. E., Rifkin, B., & Alex, M. (1976). The context effect: The relationship between stimulus preexposure and environmental preexposure determines subsequent learning. *Journal of Experimental Psychology: Animal Behavior Processes, 2,* 38–47.

Luchins, A. S. (1942). Mechanization in problem solving. *Psychological Monographs, 54* (No. 248).

Luzzo, D. A., James, T., & Luna, M. (1996). Effects of attributional retraining on the career beliefs and career exploration behavior of college students. *Journal of Counseling Psychology, 43,* 415–422.

Lykken, D., & Tellegen, A. (1996). Happiness is a stochastic phenomenon. *Psychological Science, 7,* 186–189.

Lymburner, J. A., & Roesch, R. (1999). The insanity defense: Five years of research (1993–1997). *International Journal of Law and Psychiatry, 22,* 213–240.

Lynch, J. W., Kaplan, G. A., & Shema, S. J. (1997). Cumulative impact of sustained economic hardship on physical, cognitive, psychological, and social functioning. *New England Journal of Medicine, 337,* 1889–1895.

Lynn, R. (1996). Racial and ethnic differences in intelligence in the U.S. on the Differential Ability Scale. *Personality and Individual Differences, 20,* 271–273.

Lynn, S. J., & Payne, D. G. (Eds.) (1997). Memory as the theater of the past [Special issue]. *Current Directions in Psychological Science, 6*(3).

Lynn, S. J., Stafford, J., Malinoski, P., & Pintar, J. (1997). Memory in the hall of mirrors: The experience of "retractors" in psychotherapy. *Psychological Inquiry, 8,* 307–312.

Lyons, N. (1983). Two perspectives: On self, relationships, and morality. *Harvard Educational Review, 53,* 125–146.

Lytton, H., & Romney, D. M. (1991). Parents' differential socialization of boys and girls: A meta-analysis. *Psychological Bulletin, 109,* 267–296.

Ma, V., & Schoeneman, T. J. (1997). Individualism versus collectivism: A comparison of Kenyan and American self-concepts. *Basic and Applied Social Psychology, 19,* 261–273.

Maas, J. (1998). *Power sleep: The revolutionary program that prepares your mind for peak performance.* New York: Villard.

Maccoby, E. E. (1980). *Social development: Psychological growth and the parent–child relationship.* San Diego: Harcourt Brace Jovanovich.

Maccoby, E. E. (1998). *The two sexes: Growing up apart, coming together.* Cambridge, MA: Harvard University Press.

Maccoby, E. E. (2000). Parenting and its effects on children: On reading and misreading behavior genetics. *Annual Review of Psychology, 51,* 1–27.

Maccoby, E. E., & Martin, J. A. (1983). Socialization in the context of the family: Parent–child interaction. In E. M. Hetherington (Ed.), *Handbook of child psychology: Vol. 4. Socialization, personality, and social development* (pp. 1–101). New York: Wiley.

MacDonald, M. C. (1993). The interaction of lexical and syntactic ambiguity. *Journal of Memory and Language, 32,* 692–715.

Mace, W. M. (1977). James J. Gibson's strategy for perceiving: Ask not what's inside your head, but what your head's inside of. In R. Shaw & J. Bransford (Eds.), *Perceiving, acting, and knowing.* Hillsdale, NJ: Erlbaum.

MacLeod, C., & Campbell, L. (1992). Memory accessibility and probability judgments: An experimental evaluation of the availability heuristic. *Journal of Personality and Social Psychology, 63,* 890–902.

Madon, S., Jussim, L., & Eccles, J. (1997). In search of the powerful self-fulfilling prophecy. *Journal of Personality and Social Psychology, 72,* 791–809.

Magee, W. J., Eaton, W. W., Wittchen, H.-U., McConagle, K. A., & Kessler, R. C. (1996). Agoraphobia, simple phobia, and social phobia in the national comorbidity survey. *Archives of General Psychiatry, 53,* 159–168.

Magnusson, D. (1987). Adult delinquency in the light of conduct and physiology at an early age: A longitudinal study. In D. Magnusson & A. Ohman (Eds.), *Psychopathology* (pp. 221–234). Orlando, FL: Academic Press.

Magnusson, D., & Bergman, L. R. (1990). A pattern approach to the study of pathways from childhood to adulthood. In L. N. Robins & M. Rutter (Eds.), *Straight and devious pathways from childhood to adulthood* (pp. 101–115). Cambridge, England: Cambridge University Press.

Mahoney, A., Donnelly, W. O., Lewis, T., & Maynard, C. (2000). Mother and father self-reports of corporal punishment and severe physical aggression toward clinic-referred youth. *Journal of Clinical Child Psychology, 29,* 266–281.

Maier, N. R. F. (1931). Reasoning in humans: II. The solution of a problem and its appearance in consciousness. *Journal of Comparative Psychology, 12,* 181–194.

Maier, S. F., & Seligman, M. E. P. (1976). Learned helplessness: Theory and evidence. *Journal of Experimental Psychology, 105,* 3–46.

Main, M., & George, C. (1985). Responses of abused and disadvantaged toddler to distress in agemates: A study in the day care setting. *Developmental Psychology, 21,* 407–412.

Main, M., Kaplan, N., & Cassidy, J. (1985). Security in infancy, childhood, and adulthood: A move to the level of representation. In I. Bretherton & E. Waters (Eds.), *Growing points of attachment theory and research: Monographs of the Society of Research in Child Development, 4* (Serial No. 209, pp. 66–104).

Malinowski, B. (1927). *Sex and repression in savage society.* London: Routledge & Kegan Paul.

Malizia, A. L. (1999). What do brain imaging studies tell us about anxiety disorders? *Journal of Psychopharmacology, 13,* 372–378.

Malizia, A. L., Cunningham, V. J., Bell, C. J., Liddle, P. F., Jones, T., & Nutt, D. J. (1998). Decreased brain GABA-sub(A)-benzodiazepine receptor binding in panic disorder: Preliminary results from a quantitative PET study. *Archives of General Psychiatry, 55,* 715–720.

Malizia, A. L., & Nutt, D. J. (1995). Psychopharmacology of benzodiazepines: An update. *Human Psychopharmacology: Clinical and Experimental, 10*(Suppl. 1), S1–S14.

Mandel, D. R., Jusczyk, P. W., & Pisoni, D. B. (1995). Infants' recognition of the sound patterns of their own names. *Psychological Science, 5,* 314–317.

Maoz, Z., & Abdolali, N. (1989). Regime types and international conflict, 1816–1976. *Journal of Conflict Resolution, 33,* 3–35.

Marcel, A. J. (1983). Conscious and unconscious perception: An approach to the relation between phenomenal experience and perceptual processes. *Cognitive Psychology, 15,* 238–300.

Marcus, A. D. (1990, December 3). Mists of memory cloud some legal proceedings. *The Wall Street Journal*, p. B1.

Marcus, H., & Cross, S. (1990). The interpersonal self. In L. A. Pervin (Ed.), *Handbook of personality theory and research* (pp. 576–608). New York: Guilford Press.

Markman, E. M. (1989). *Categorization and naming in children: Problems of induction*. Cambridge, MA: The MIT Press.

Markman, E. M., & Wachtel, G. F. (1988). Children's use of mutual exclusivity to constrain meanings of words. *Cognitive Psychology, 20*, 121–157.

Markovitz, H., & Nantel, G. (1989). The belief-bias effect in the production and evaluation of logical conclusions. *Memory & Cognition, 17*, 11–17.

Markowitsch, H. J. (2000). Neuroanatomy of memory. In E. Tulving & F. I. M. Craik (Eds.), *The Oxford handbook of memory* (pp. 465–484). Oxford, U.K.: Oxford University Press.

Marks, A. R., & Crowder, R. G. (1997). Temporal distinctiveness and modality. *Journal of Experimental Psychology: Learning, Memory, and Cognition, 23*, 164–180.

Markus, H. (1977). Self-schemata and processing information about the self. *Journal of Personality and Social Psychology, 35*, 63–78.

Markus, H., Cross, S., & Wurf, E. (1990). The role of the self-system in competence. In R. J. Sternberg & J. Lollgian, Jr. (Eds.), *Competence considered* (pp. 205–225). New Haven: Yale University Press.

Markus, H., & Nurius, P. (1986). Possible selves. *American Psychologist, 41*, 954–969.

Markus, H., & Smith, J. (1981). The influence of self-schemas on the perception of others. In N. Cantor & J. F. Kihlstrom (Eds.), *Personality, cognition, and social interaction* (pp. 233–262). Hillsdale, NJ: Erlbaum.

Markus, H. R., & Kitayama, S. (1991). Culture and the self: Implications for cognition, emotion, and motivation. *Psychological Review, 98*, 224–253.

Markus, H. R., Mullally, P. R., & Kitayama, S. (1997). Selfways: Diversity in modes of cultural participation. In U. Neisser & D. A. Jopling (Eds.), *The conceptual self in context* (pp. 13–61). Cambridge, U.K.: Cambridge University Press.

Marr, D., & Nishihara, H. K. (1978). Representation and recognition of the spatial organization of three-dimensional shapes. *Proceedings of the Royal Society of London (Series B), 200*, 269–294.

Marsella, A. J. (1979). Cross-cultural studies of mental disorders. In A. J. Marsella, R. G. Sharp, & T. J. Ciborowski (Eds.), *Perspectives on cross-cultural psychology* (pp. 233–262). New York: Academic Press.

Marsh, L., Harris, D., Lim, K. O., Beal, M., Hoff, A. L., Minn, K., Csernansky, J. G., DeMent, S., Faustman, W. O., Sullivan, E. V., & Pfefferbaum, A. (1997). Structural magnetic resonance imaging abnormatilities in men with severe chronic schizophrenia and an early age at clinical onset. *Archives of General Psychiatry, 54*, 1104–1112.

Marshall, G. D., & Zimbardo, P. G. (1979). Affective consequences of inadequately explained physiological arousal. *Journal of Personality and Social Psychology, 37*, 970–988.

Martin, G., & Pear, J. (1999). *Behavior modification: What it is and how to do it* (6th ed.). Upper Saddle River, NJ: Prentice-Hall.

Martin, M. M., & Anderson, C. M. (1995). Roommate similarity: Are roommates who are similar in their communication traits more satisfied? *Communication Research Reports, 12*, 46–52.

Martin, R., Davis, G. M., Baron, R. S., Suls, J., & Blanchard, E. B. (1994). Specificity in social support: Perceptions of helpful and unhelpful provider behaviors among irritable bowel syndrome, headache, and cancer patients. *Health Psychology, 13*, 432–439.

Martin, R. J., White, B. D., & Hulsey, M. G. (1991). The regulation of body weight. *American Scientist, 79*, 528–541.

Marttunen, M. J., Henriksson, M. M., Isometsae, E. T., Heikkinen, M. E., Aro, H. M., & Loennqvist, J. K. (1998). Completed suicide among adolescents with no diagnosable psychiatric disorder. *Adolescence, 33*, 669–681.

Marx, B. P., & Gross, A. M. (1995). Date rape: An analysis of two contextual variables. *Behavior Modification, 19*, 451–463.

Maslach, C. (1979). Negative emotional biasing of unexplained arousal. *Journal of Personality and Social Psychology, 37*, 953–969.

Maslach, C. (1982). *Burnout: The cost of caring*. Englewood Cliffs, NJ: Prentice Hall.

Maslach, C., & Florian, V. (1988). Burnout, job setting, and self-evaluation among rehabilitation counselors. *Rehabilitation Psychology, 33*, 135–157.

Maslach, C., & Leiter, M. P. (1997). *The truth about burnout: How organizations cause personal stress and what to do about it*. San Francisco: Jossey-Bass.

Maslow, A. H. (1968). *Toward a psychology of being* (2nd ed.). Princeton, NJ: Van Nostrand.

Maslow, A. H. (1970). *Motivation and personality* (Rev. ed.). New York: Harper & Row.

Mason, L. E. (1997, August 4). Divided she stands. *New York, 30*, 42–49.

Mason, M. A., Skolnick, A., & Sugarman, S. D. (Eds.). (1998) *All our families: New policies for a new century*. New York: Oxford University Press.

Mason, W. A., & Kenney, M. D. (1974). Reduction of filial attachments in rhesus monkeys: Dogs as mother surrogates. *Science, 183*, 1209–1211.

Masters, W. H., & Johnson, V. E. (1966). *Human sexual response*. Boston: Little, Brown.

Masters, W. H., & Johnson, V. E. (1970). *Human sexual inadequacy*. Boston: Little, Brown.

Masters, W. H., & Johnson, V. E. (1979). *Homosexuality in perspective*. Boston: Little, Brown.

Matarazzo, J. D. (1984). Behavioral immunogens and pathogens in health and illness. In B. L. Hammonds & C. J. Scheirer (Eds.), *Psychology and health: The Master Lecture Series, Vol. 3* (pp. 9–43). Washington, DC: American Psychological Association.

Matheson, M. D., & Bernstein, I. S. (2000). Grooming, social bonding, and agonistic aiding in rhesus monkeys. *American Journal of Primatology, 51*, 177–186.

Matson, J. L., Esveldt-Dawson, K., Andrasik, F., Ollendick, T., Petti, T., & Hersen, M. (1980). Direct, observational, and generalization effects of social skills training with emotionally disturbed children. *Behavior Therapy, 11*, 522–531.

Maurer, D., Lewis, T. L., Brent, H. P., & Levin, A. V. (1999). Rapid improvement in the acuity of infants after visual input. *Science, 286*, 108–110.

Mauro, R., & Kubovy, M. (1992). Caricature and face recognition. *Memory & Cognition, 20*, 433–440.

May, R. (1975). *The courage to create*. New York: Norton.

Mayer, J. D., McCormick, L. J., & Strong, S. E. (1995). Mood-congruent memory and natural mood: New evidence. *Personality and Social Psychology Bulletin, 21*, 736–746.

Mayer, J. D., & Salovey, P. (1997). What is emotional intelligence? In P. Salovey & D. Sluyter (Eds.), *Emotional development and emotional intelligence: Educational implications* (pp. 3–31). New York: Basic Books.

Mayer, J. D., Salovey, P., & Caruso, D. (2000). Models of emotional intelligence. In R. J. Sternberg (Ed.), *Handbook of intelligence* (pp. 396–420). Cambridge, U.K.: Cambridge University Press.

Mayes, A. R. (2000). Selective memory disorders. In E. Tulving & F. I. M. Craik (Eds.), *The Oxford handbook of memory* (pp. 427–440). Oxford, U.K.: Oxford University Press.

McAdams, D. P. (1988). Biography, narrative, and lives: An introduction. *Journal of Personality, 56,* 1–18.

McAdams, D. P. (1996). Personality, modernity, and the storied self: A contemporary framework for studying persons. *Psychological Inquiry, 7,* 295–321.

McAdams, D. P., & de St. Aubin, E. (1992). A theory of generativity and its assessment through self-report, behavioral acts, and narrative themes in autobiography. *Journal of Personality and Social Psychology, 62,* 1003–1015.

McAdams, D. P., & de St. Aubin, E. (Eds.). (1998). *Generativity and adult development: How and why we care for the next generation.* Washington, DC: American Psychological Association.

McAllister, H. A. (1996). Self-serving bias in the classroom: Who shows it? Who knows it? *Journal of Educational Psychology, 88,* 123–131.

McBeath, M. K., Shaffer, D. M., & Kaiser, M. K. (1995). How baseball outfielders determine where to run to catch fly balls. *Science, 268,* 569–573.

McBeath, M. K., Shaffer, D. M., & Kaiser, M. K. (1996). On catching fly balls. *Science, 273,* 258–260.

McBurnett, K., Lahey, B. B., Rathouz, P. J., & Loeber, R. (2000). Low salivary cortisol and persistent aggression in boys referred for disruptive behavior. *Archives of General Psychiatry, 57,* 38–43.

McClelland, D. C. (1961). *The achieving society.* Princeton, NJ: Van Nostrand.

McClelland, D. C. (1971). *Motivational trends in society.* Morristown NJ: General Learning Press.

McClelland, D. C., Atkinson, J. W., Clark, R. A., & Lowell, E. L. (1953). *The achievement motive.* New York: Appleton-Century-Crofts.

McClelland, D. C., Atkinson, J. W., Clark, R. A., & Lowell, E. L. (1976). *The achievement motive* (2nd ed.). New York: Irvington.

McClelland, D. C., & Franz, C. E. (1992). Motivational and other sources of work accomplishments in mid-life: A longitudinal study. *Journal of Personality, 60,* 679–707.

McClelland, J. L., & Elman, J. L. (1986). The TRACE model of speech perception. *Cognitive Psychology, 18,* 1–86.

McClintock, M. K. (1971). Menstrual synchrony and suppression. *Nature, 229,* 244–245.

McCrae, R. R., & Costa, P. T., Jr. (1997). Personality trait structure as a human universal. *American Psychologist, 52,* 509–516.

McCrae, R. R., & Costa, P. T., Jr. (1999). A five-factor theory of personality. In L. A. Pervin & O. P. John (Eds.), *Handbook of personality: Theory and research* (2nd ed.) (pp. 139–153). New York: Guilford Press.

McCrae, R. R., Costa, P. T., Jr., Ostendorf, F., Angleitner, A., Hrebickova, M., Avia, M. D., Sanz, J., Sanchez-Bernardos, M. L., Kusdil, M. E., Woodfield, R., Saunders, P. R., & Smith, P. B. (2000). Nature over nurture: Temperament, personality, and life span development. *Journal of Personality and Social Psychology, 78,* 173–186.

McEwen, B. S. (1999). Stress and hippocampal plasticity. *Annual Review of Neuroscience, 22,* 105–122.

McGinnis, J. M. (1991). Health objectives for the nation. *American Psychologist, 46,* 520–524.

McGlashan, T. H., Evans, F. J., & Orne, M. T. (1978). The nature of hypnotic analgesia and placebo response to experimental pain. *Psychosomatic Medicine, 31,* 227–246.

McGrath, E., Keita, G. P., Strickland, B. R., & Russo, N. F. (1990). *Women and depression: Risk factors and treatment issues.* Hyattsville, MD: American Psychological Association.

McGue, M., & Christensen, K. (1997). Genetic and environmental contributions to depression symptomatology: Evidence from Danish twins 75 years of age and older. *Journal of Abnormal Psychology, 106,* 439–448.

McGuire, W. J., & McGuire, C. V. (1988). Content and process in the experience of self. In L. Berkowitz (Ed.), *Advances in experimental social psychology* (Vol. 21, pp. 97–144). New York: Academic Press.

McKenna, K. Y. A., & Bargh, J. A. (1998). Coming out in the age of the Internet: Identity "demarginalization" through virtual group participation. *Journal of Personality and Social Psychology, 75,* 681–694.

McKenna, K. Y. A., & Bargh, J. A. (2000). Plan 9 from cyberspace: The implications of the Internet for personality and social psychology. *Personality and Social Psychology Review, 4,* 57–75.

McKenna, K. Y. A., Green, A. S., & Gleason, M. (2001). Relationship formation on the Internet: What's the big attraction? In K. Y. A. McKenna & J. A. Bargh (Eds.), Interpersonal and group processes on the Internet: Is social life being transformed? *Journal of Social Issues.*

McKone, E., & Trynes, K. (1999). Acquisition of novel traces in short-term implicit memory: Priming for nonwords and new associations. *Memory & Cognition, 27,* 619–632.

McKoon, G., & Ratcliff, R. (1992). Inference during reading. *Psychological Review, 99,* 440–446.

McNally, R. J. (1990). Psychological approaches to panic disorder: A review. *Psychological Bulletin, 108,* 403–419.

McNeil, B. J., Pauker, S. G., Sox, H. C., Jr., & Tversky, A. (1982). On the elicitation of preferences for alternative therapies. *New England Journal of Medicine, 306,* 1259–1262.

Mcphail, E. M. (1998). *The evolution of consciousness.* Oxford, U.K.: Oxford University Press.

McPherson, K. S. (1985). On intelligence testing and immigration legislation. *American Psychologist, 40,* 242–243.

Mead, M. (1928). *Coming of age in Samoa.* New York: Morrow.

Mead, M. (1939). *From the South Seas: Studies of adolescence and sex in primitve societies.* New York: Morrow.

Meador, B. D., & Rogers, C. R. (1979). Person-centered therapy. In R. J. Corsini (Ed.), *Current psychotherapies* (2nd ed., pp. 131–184). Itasca, IL: Peacock.

Meany, M. J., Aitken, D. H., Van Berkel, C. Bhatnagar, S., & Sapolsky, R. M. (1988). Effect of neonatal handling on age-related impairments associated with the hippocampus. *Science, 239,* 766–768.

Medin, D. L., & Ross, B. H. (1992). *Cognitive psychology.* Fort Worth, TX: Harcourt Brace Jovanovich.

Meehan, P. J., Lamb, J. A., Saltzman, L. E., & O'Carroll, P. W. (1992). Attempted suicide among young adults: Progress toward a meaningful estimate of prevalence. *American Journal of Psychiatry, 149,* 41–44.

Meichenbaum, D. (1977). *Cognitive-behavior modification: An integrative approach.* New York: Plenum.

Meichenbaum, D. (1985). *Stress inoculation training.* New York: Pergamon Press.

Meichenbaum, D. (1993). Changing conceptions of cognitive behavior modification: Retrospect and prospect. *Journal of Consulting and Clinical Psychology, 61,* 202–204.

Meier, R. P. (1991). Language acquisition by deaf children. *American Scientist, 79,* 60–70.

Melzack, R. (1973). *The puzzle of pain.* New York: Basic Books.

Melzack, R. (1980). Psychological aspects of pain. In J. J. Bonica (Ed.), *Pain.* New York: Raven Press.

Melzack, R. (1992). Phantom limbs. *Scientific American, 266*(4), 120–126.

Melzack, R. (1999). Pain and stress: A new perspective. In R. J. Gatchel & D. C. Turk (Eds.), *Psychosocial factors in pain: Critical perspectives* (pp. 89–106). New York: Guilford Press.

Menon, T., Morris, M. W., Chiu, C., & Hong, Y. (1999). Culture and construal of agency: Attribution to individual versus group dispositions. *Journal of Personality and Social Psychology, 76,* 701–717.

Merigan, W. H., & Maunsell, J. H. R. (1993). How parallel are the primate visual pathways? *Annual Review of Neuroscience, 16,* 369–402.

Merton, R. K. (1957). *Social theory and social structures.* New York: The Free Press.

Mervis, C. B., & Rosch, E. (1981). Categorization of natural objects. *Annual Review of Psychology, 32,* 89–115.

Mesquita, B., & Frijda, N. H. (1992). Cultural variations in emotions: A review. *Psychological Bulletin, 112,* 179–204.

Metcalfe, J. (2000). Metamemory: Theory and data. In E. Tulving & F. I. M. Craik (Eds.), *The Oxford handbook of memory* (pp. 197–211). Oxford, U.K.: Oxford University Press.

Metcalfe, J., Schwartz, B. L., & Joaquim, S. G. (1993). The cue-familiarity heuristic in metacognition. *Journal of Experimental Psychology: Learning, Memory, and Cognition, 19,* 851–861.

Meyer, G. J. (2000). Incremental validity of the Rorschach Prognostic Rating scale over the MMPI Ego Strength Scale and IQ. *Journal of Personality Assessment, 74,* 356–370.

Meyers, S. A., & Berscheid, E. (1997). The language of love: The difference a preposition makes. *Personality and Social Psychology Bulletin, 23,* 347–362.

Michael, R. T., Gagnon, J. H., Laumann, E. O., & Kolata, G. (1994). *Sex in America: A definitive survey.* Boston: Little, Brown.

Middlebrooks, J. C., & Green, D. C. (1991). Sound localization by human listeners. *Annual Review of Psychology, 42,* 135–159.

Middleton, J. (Ed.). (1967). *Magic, witchcraft, and curing.* Garden City, NY: Natural History Press.

Mignot, E. (1998). Genetic and familial aspects of narcolepsy. *Neurology, 50,* S16–S22.

Mikolic, J. M., Parker, J. C., & Pruitt, D. G. (1997). Escalation in response to persistent annoyance: Groups versus individuals and gender effects. *Journal of Personality and Social Psychology, 72,* 151–163.

Miles, D. R., & Carey, G. (1997). Genetic and environmental architecture of human aggression. *Journal of Personality and Social Psychology, 72,* 207–217.

Milgram, S. (1965). Some conditions of obedience and disobedience to authority. *Human Relations, 18,* 56–76.

Milgram, S. (1974). *Obedience to authority.* New York: Harper & Row.

Milgram, S. (1977, October). Subject reaction: The neglected factor in the ethics of experimentation. *Hastings Center Report,* pp. 19–23.

Milkowitz, D. J. (1994). Family risk indicators in schizophrenia. *Schizophrenia Bulletin, 20,* 137–149.

Miller, A. G. (1986). *The obedience paradigm: A case study in controversy in social sceince.* New York: Praeger.

Miller, G. A. (1956). The magic number seven plus or minus two: Some limits in our capacity for processing information. *Psychological Review, 63,* 81–97.

Miller, J. B. (1986). *Toward a new psychology of women.* Boston: Beacon Press. (Originally published in 1976)

Miller, J. G. (1984). Culture and the development of everyday social explanation. *Journal of Personality and Social Psychology, 46,* 961–978.

Miller, J. G., & Bersoff, D. M. (1992). Culture and moral judgment: How are conflicts between justice and interpersonal responsibilities resolved? *Journal of Personality and Social Psychology, 62,* 541–554.

Miller, J. G., Bersoff, D. M., & Harwood, R. L. (1990). Perceptions of social responsibilities in India and in the United States: Moral imperatives or personal decisions? *Journal of Personality and Social Psychology, 58,* 33–47.

Miller, M. A., & Rahe, R. H. (1997). Life changes scaling for the 1990s. *Journal of Psychosomatic Research, 43,* 279–292.

Miller, M. E., & Bowers, K. S. (1993). Hypnotic analgesia: Dissociated experience or dissociated control? *Journal of Abnormal Psychology, 102,* 29–38.

Miller N. E. (1978). Biofeedback and visceral learning. *Annual Review of Psychology, 29,* 373–404.

Miller, N. E. (1985). The value of behavioral research on animals. *American Psychologist, 40,* 423–440.

Miller, N. E. (1992). Introducing and teaching much-needed understanding of the scientific process. *American Psychologist, 47,* 848–850.

Miller, N. S. (1999). Benzodiazepines: Behavioral and pharmacologic basis of addiction, tolerance, and dependence. In S. M. Powell (Ed.), *The Hatherleigh guide to pharmacology* (pp. 83–113). New York: Hatherleigh Press.

Minckely, R. L., Buchmann, S. L., & Wcislo, W. J. (1991). Bioassay evidence for a sex attractant pheromone in the large carpenter bee *Xylocopa varipuncta* (Anthophoridea: Hymenoptera). *Journal of Zoology, 224,* 285–291.

Mindell, J. A. (1997). Children and sleep. In M. R. Pressman & W. C. Orr (Eds.), *Understanding sleep: The evaluation and treatment of sleep disorders* (pp. 427–439). Washington, DC: American Psychological Association.

Mintz, A., & Geva, N. (1993). Why don't democracies fight each other? *Journal of Conflict Resolution, 37,* 484–503.

Mischel, W. (1968). *Personality and assessment.* New York: Wiley.

Mischel, W. (1973). Toward a cognitive social learning reconceptualization of personality. *Psychological Review, 80,* 252–283.

Mischel, W., & Shoda, Y. (1995). A cognitive-affective system theory of personality: Reconceptualizing situations, dispositions, dynamics, and invariance in personality structure. *Psychological Review, 102,* 246–268.

Mischel, W., & Shoda, Y. (1999). Integrating dispositions and processing dynamics within a unified theory of personality: The cognitive-affective personality system. In L. A. Pervin & O. P. John (Eds.), *Handbook of personality: Theory and research* (2nd ed.) (pp. 197–218). New York: Guilford Press.

Mitchell, K. J., & Zaragoza, M. S. (1996). Repeated exposure to suggestion and false memory: The role of contextual variability. *Journal of Memory and Language, 35,* 246–260.

Moffitt, A., Karmer, M., & Hoffmann, R. (Eds.). (1993). *The functions of dreaming.* Albany: State University of New York Press.

Molitor, F., & Hirsch, K. W. (1994). Children's tolerance of real-life aggression after exposure to media violence: A replication of the Drabman and Thomas studies. *Child Study Journal, 24,* 191–207.

Moloney, D. P., Bouchard, T. J., Jr., & Segal, N. L. (1991). A genetic and environmental analysis of the vocational interests of monozygotic and dizygotic twins reared apart. *Journal of Vocational Behavior, 39,* 76–109.

Moncrieff, R. W. (1951). *The chemical senses.* London: Leonard Hill.

Montague, A. (1986). *Touching: The human significance of the skin.* New York: Harper & Row.

Montague, C. T., Farooqi, I. S., Whitehead, J. P., Soos, M. A., Rau, H., Wareham, N. J., Sewter, C. P., Digby, J. E., Mohammed, S. N., Hurst, J. A., Cheetham, C. H., Earley, A. R., Barnett, A. H., Prins, J. B., & O'Rahilly, S. (1997). Congenital leptin deficiency is associated with severe early-onset obesity in humans. *Nature, 387,* 903–908.

Moore, E. G. J. (1986). Family socialization and the IQ test performance of traditionally and transracially adopted black children. *Developmental Psychology, 22,* 317–326.

Moore, P. (1990). In *Discovering Psychology,* Program 18 [PBS video series]. Washington, DC: Annenberg/CPB Program.

Moore-Ede, M. C. (1993). *The twenty-four-hour society: Understanding human limits in a world that never stops.* Reading, MA: Addison-Wesley.

Moore-Ede, M. C., Sulzman, F. M., & Fuller, C. A. (1982). *The clocks that time us: Physiology of the circadian timing system.* Cambridge, MA: Harvard University Press.

Morgan, A. H., Hilgard, E. R., & Davert, E. C. (1970). The heritability of hypnotic susceptibility of twins: A preliminary report. *Behavior Genetics, 1,* 213–224.

Morgan, A. H., Johson, D. L., & Hilgard, E. R. (1974). The stability of hypnotic susceptibility: A longitudinal study. *International Journal of Clinical and Experimental Hypnosis, 22,* 249–257.

Morgenstern, J., Labouvie, E., McCrady, B. S., Kahler, C. W., & Frey, R. M. (1997). Affiliation with Alcoholics Anonymous after treatment: A study of its therapeutic effects and mechanisms of action. *Journal of Consulting and Clinical Psychology, 65,* 768–777.

Moriarty, T. (1975). Crime, commitment and the responsive bystander: Two field experiments. *Journal of Personality and Social Psychology, 31,* 370–376.

Morin, S. F., & Rothblum, E. D. (1991). Removing the stigma: Fifteen years of progress. *American Psychologist, 46,* 947–949.

Morrell, E. M. (1986). Meditation and somatic arousal. *American Psychologist, 41,* 712–713.

Morris, J. S., Frith, C. D., Perrett, D. I., Rowland, D., Young, A. W., Calder, A. J., & Dolan, R. J. (1996). A differential neural response in the human amygdala to fearful and happy facial expressions. *Nature, 383,* 812–815.

Moscovici, S. (1976). *Social influence and social change.* New York: Academic Press.

Moscovici, S. (1980). Toward a theory of conversion behavior. In L. Berkowitz (Ed.), *Advances in experimental social psychology* (Vol. 13, pp. 209–239). New York: Academic Press.

Moscovici, S. (1985). Social influence and conformity. In G. Lindzey & E. Aronson (Eds.), *The handbook of social psychology* (3rd ed., pp. 347–412). New York: Random House.

Moscovici, S., & Faucheux, C. (1972). Social influence, conformity bias, and the study of active minorities. In L. Berkowitz (Ed.), *Advances in experimental social psychology* (Vol. 6). New York: Academic Press.

Moskowitz, B. A. (1978). The acquisition of language. *Scientific American, 239*(11), 92–108.

Motley, M. T., & Baars, B. J. (1979). Effects of cognitive set upon laboratory-induced verbal (Freudian) slips. *Journal of Speech and Hearing Research, 22,* 421–432.

Muehlenhard, C. L., & Cook, S. W. (1988). Men's self-reports of unwanted sexual activity. *The Journal of Sex Research, 24,* 58–72.

Muehlenhard, C. L., & Linton, M. A. (1987). Date rape and sexual aggression in dating situations: Incidence and risk factors. *Journal of Counseling Psychology, 34,* 186–196.

Munro, G. D., & Ditto, P. H. (1997). Biased assimilation, attitude polarization, and affect in reactions to stereotype-relevant scientific information. *Personality and Social Psychology Bulletin, 23,* 636–653.

Munsterberg, H. (1908). *On the witness stand.* New York: McClure.

Murata, P. J., McGlynn, E. A., Siu, A. L., & Brook, R. H. (1992). *Prenatal care.* Santa Monica, CA: The Rand Corporation.

Murphy, M. C., & Archer, J. (1996). Stressors on the college campus: A comparison of 1985–1993. *Journal of College Student Development, 37,* 20–28.

Murphy, S. L. (2000). Deaths: Final data for 1998. *National Vital Statistics Reports, 48*(11).

Murray, H. A. (1938). *Explorations in personality.* New York: Oxford University Press.

Murray, J. B. (1995). Evidence for acupuncture's analgesic effectiveness and proposals for the physiological mechanisms involved. *Journal of Psychology, 129,* 443–461.

Murray, J. P., & Kippax, S. (1977). Children's social behavior in three towns with differing television experience. *Journal of Communication, 28,* 19–29.

Murray, T. M., & Williams, S. (1999). *Analyses of data from graduate study in psychology.* Washington, DC: American Psychological Association.

Muskin, P. R., & Fyer, A. J. (1981). Treatment of panic disorder. *Journal of Clinical Psychopharmacology, 1,* 81–90.

Myers, R. S., & Roth, D. L. (1997). Perceived benefits of and barriers to exercise and stage of exercise adoption in young adults. *Health Psychology, 16,* 277–283.

Nakayama, K. (1994). James J. Gibson—An appreciation. *Psychological Review, 101,* 329–335.

Napier, A. Y. (2000). Making a marriage. In W. C. Nichols, M. A. Pace-Nichols, D. S. Becvar, & A. Y. Napier (Eds.), *Handbook of family development and intervention* (pp. 145–170). New York: Wiley.

Nash, E. B., Edwards, G. W., Thompson, J. A., & Barfield, W. (2000). A review of presence and performance in virtual environments. *International Journal of Human—Computer Interaction, 12,* 1–41.

National Institutes of Mental Health. (1977). *Lithium and the treatment of mood disorders* (DHEW Publication No. ADM 77–73). Washington, DC: U.S. Government Printing Office.

National Sleep Foundation. (2000). *2000 omnibus sleep in America poll* [On-line]. Available: www.sleepfoundation.org/publications/2000poll.html

Natsoulas, T. (1998). Consciousness and self-awareness. In M. Ferrari & R. J. Sternberg (Eds.), *Self-awareness: Its nature and development* (pp. 12–33). New York: The Guilford Press.

Nauta, W. J. H., & Feirtag, M. (1979). The organization of the brain. *Scientific American, 241*(9), 38–111.

Navon, D., & Gopher, D. (1979). On the economy of the human processing system. *Psychological Review, 86,* 214–255.

Neath, I. (1993). Contextual and distinctive processes and the serial position function. *Journal of Memory and Language, 32,* 820–840.

Neath, I. (1998). *Human memory: An introduction to research, data, and theory.* Pacific Grove, CA: Brooks/Cole.

Neath, I., & Crowder, R. G. (1990). Schedules of presentation and temporal distinctiveness in human memory. *Journal of Experimental Psychology: Learning, Memory, and Cognition, 16,* 316–327.

Neath, I., & Knoedler, A. J. (1994). Distinctiveness in serial position effects in recognition and sentence processing. *Journal of Memory and Language, 33,* 776–795.

Neath, I., Surprenant, A. M., & Crowder, R. G. (1993). The context-dependent stimulus suffix effect. *Journal of Experimental Psychology: Learning, Memory, and Cognition, 19,* 698–703.

Neisser, U. (1967). *Cognitive psychology.* New York: Appleton-Century-Crofts.

Neisser, U., Boodoo, G., Bouchard, T. J., Jr., Boykin, A. W., Brody, N., Ceci, S. J., Halpern, D. F., Loehlin, J. C., Perloff, R., Sternberg, R. J., & Urbina, S. (1996). Intelligence: Knowns and unknowns. *American Psychologist, 51,* 77–101.

Nelson, R. E., & Craighead, W. E. (1977). Selective recall of positive and negative feedback, self-control behaviors and depression. *Journal of Abnormal Psychology, 86,* 379–388.

Nelson, T. O. (1996). Consciousness and metacognition. *American Psychologist, 51,* 102–116.

Nelson, T. O., & Narens, L. (1980). Norms of 300 general-information questions: Accuracy of recall, latency of recall, and feeling-of-knowing ratings. *Journal of Verbal Learning and Verbal Behavior, 19,* 338–368.

Neumeister, A., Praschak-Rieder, N., Heßelmann, B., Rao, M.-L., Glück, J., & Kasper, S. (1997). Effects of tryptophan depletion on drug-free patients with seasonal affective disorder during a stable response to bright light therapy. *Archives of General Psychiatry, 54,* 133–138.

Newcomb, M. D., & Bentler, P. M. (1988). *Consequences of adolescent drug use: Impact on the lives of young adults.* Newbury Park, CA: Sage.

Newcomb, T. M. (1929). *The consistency of certain extrovert-introvert behavior traits in 50 problem boys* (Contributions to Education, No. 382). New York: Columbia University Press.

Newell, A., & Simon, H. A. (1972). *Human problem solving.* Englewood Cliffs, NJ: Prentice Hall.

Newman, M. G., Consoli, A. J., & Taylor, C. B. (1999). A palmtop computer program for the treatment of generalized anxiety disorder. *Behavior Modification, 23,* 597–619.

Newman, M. G., Kenardy, J., Herman, S., & Taylor, C. B. (1997). Comparison of palmtop-computer-assisted brief cognitive-behavioral treatment to cognitive-behavioral treatment for panic disorder. *Journal of Consulting and Clinical Psychology, 65,* 178–183.

Newstead, S. E., Pollard, P., Evans, J. St. B. T., & Allen, J. L. (1992). The source of belief bias effects in syllogistic reasoning. *Cognition, 45,* 257–284.

Nhat Hanh, T. (1991). *Peace is every step: The path of mindfulness in everyday life.* New York: Bantam.

Nichols, S., Haldane, C., & Wilson, J. R. (2000). Measurement of presence and its consequences in virtual environments. *International Journal of Human-Computer Studies, 52,* 471–491.

Nicoll, C., Russell, S., & Katz, L. (1988, May 26). Research on animals must continue. *San Francisco Chronicle,* p. A25.

Nie, N. H., & Erbring, L. (2000). *Internet and society: A preliminary report.* Stanford, CA: Stanford Institute for the Quantitative Study of Society.

Nielsen, F. (1994). Sociobiology and sociology. *Annual Review of Sociology, 20,* 267–303.

Nietzel, M. T., Bernstein, D. A., & Milich, R. (1991). *Introduction to clinical psychology.* Englewood Cliffs, NJ: Prentice Hall.

Nigg, J. T., & Goldsmith, H. H. (1994). Genetics of personality disorders: Perspectives from personality and psychopathology research. *Psychological Bulletin, 115,* 346–380.

Nisbett, R. E. (1995). Race, IQ, and scientism. In S. Fraser (Ed.), *The Bell Curve wars: Race, intelligence, and the future of America* (pp. 36–57). New York: Basic Books.

Nisbett, R. E. (1998). Race, genetics, and IQ. In C. Jencks & M. Phillips (Eds.), *The black–white test score gap* (pp. 86–102). Washington, DC: Brookings Institution Press.

Nisbett, R. E., & Cohen, D. (1996). *Culture of honor: The psychology of violence in the South.* Boulder, CO: Westview Press.

Nobles, W. W. (1976). Black people in white insanity: An issue for black community mental health. *Journal of Afro-American Issues, 4,* 21–27.

Nobles, W. W. (1980). African philosophy: Foundations for black psychology. In R. L. Jones (Ed.), *Black psychology* (2nd ed., pp. 23–36). New York: Harper & Row.

Nolen-Hoeksema, S. (1990). *Sex differences in depression.* Stanford, CA: Stanford University Press.

Nolen-Hoeksema, S., & Girgus, J. S. (1994). The emergence of gender differences in depression during adolescence. *Psychological Bulletin, 115,* 424–443.

Nolen-Hoeksema, S., Larson, J., & Grayson, C. (1999). Explaining the gender difference in depressive symptoms. *Journal of Personality and Social Psychology, 77,* 1061–1072.

Nolen-Hoeksema, S., Morrow, J., & Fredrickson, B. L. (1993). Response styles and the duration of episodes of depressed mood. *Journal of Abnormal Psychology, 102,* 20–28.

Norden, K. A., Klein, D. N., Donaldson, S. K., Pepper, C. M., & Klein, L. M. (1995). Reports of the early home environment in DSM-III-R personality disorders. *Journal of Personality Disorders, 9,* 213–223.

Norman, W. T. (1963). Toward an adequate taxonomy of personality attributes: Replicated factor structure in peer nomination personality ratings. *Journal of Abnormal and Social Psychology, 66,* 574–583.

Norman, W. T. (1967). *2,800 personality trait descriptors: Normative operating characteristics for a university population* (Research Rep. No. 08310–1-T). Ann Arbor: University of Michigan Press.

Nosofsky, R. M., Kruschke, J. K., & McKinley, S. C. (1992). Combining exemplar-based category representations and connectionist learning rules. *Journal of Experimental Psychology: Learning, Memory, and Cognition, 18,* 211–233.

Novick, L. R., & Holyoak, K. J. (1991). Mathematical problem solving by analogy. *Journal of Experimental Psychology: Learning, Memory, and Cognition, 17,* 398–415.

Nungesser, L. G. (1990). *Axioms for survivors: How to live until you say goodbye.* Santa Monica, CA: IBS Press.

Nurmi, J. E. (1991). How do adolescents see their future? A review of the development of future orientation and planning. *Developmental Review, 11,* 1–59.

Nyberg, L., & Cabeza, R. (2000). Brain imaging of memory. In E. Tulving & F. I. M. Craik (Eds.), *The Oxford handbook of memory* (pp. 501–519). Oxford, U.K.: Oxford University Press.

Nyberg, L., Cabeza, R., & Tulving, E. (1996). PET studies of encoding and retrieval: The HERA model. *Psychonomic Bulletin & Review, 3,* 135–148.

Oaksford, M., & Chater, N. (1994). A rational analysis of the selection task as optimal data selection. *Psychological Review, 101,* 608–631.

Oaksford, M., Chater, N., Grainger, B., & Larking, J. (1997). Optimal data selection in the reduced array selection task (RAST). *Journal of Experimental Psychology: Learning, Memory, and Cognition, 23,* 441–458.

Oden, S., & Asher, S. R. (1977). Coaching children in social skills for friendship making. *Child Development, 48,* 495–506.

O'Donnell, S. M. (1994). *Programming for the world: A guide to internationalization.* Englewood Cliffs, NJ: Prentice-Hall.

Offer, D., Kaiz, M., Howard, K. I., & Bennett, E. S. (1998). Emotional variables in adolescence, and their stability and contribution to the mental health of adult men: Implications for early intervention strategies. *Journal of Youth and Adolescence, 27,* 675–690.

Offer, D., Ostrov, E., & Howard, K. I. (1981a). *The adolescent: A psychological self-portrait.* New York: Basic Books.

Offer, D., Ostrov, E., & Howard, K. I. (1981b). The mental health professional's concept of the normal adolescent. *AMA Archives of General Psychiatry, 38,* 149–153.

Offer, D., Ostrov, E., Howard, K. I., & Atkinson, R. (1988). *The teenage world: Adolescents' self-image in ten countries.* New York: Plenum Medical.

Offer, D., & Schonert-Reichl, K. A. (1992). Debunking the myths of adolescence: Findings from recent research. *Journal of the American Academy of Child and Adolescent Psychiatry, 31,* 1003–1014.

Ogbu, J. (1987). *Minority education over caste: The American system in cross-cultural perspective.* New York: Academic Press.

O'Guinn, T. C., & Shrum, L. J. (1997). The role of television in the construction of consumer reality. *Journal of Consumer Research, 23,* 278–294.

Öhman, A. (1986). Face the beast and fear the face: Animal and social fears as prototypes for evolutionary analyses of emotion. *Psychophysiology, 23,* 123–145.

Okonjo, K. (1992). Aspects of continuity and change in mate-selection among the Igbo west of the River Niger. *Journal of Comparative Family Studies, 23,* 339–360.

Oldham, D. G. (1978a). Adolescent turmoil: A myth revisited. In S. C. Feinstein & P. L. Giovacchini (Eds.), *Adolescent psychiatry* (Vol. 6). Chicago: University of Chicago Press.

Oldham, D. G. (1978b). Adolescent turmoil and a myth revisited. In A. H. Esman (Ed.), *The psychology of adolescence.* New York: International University Press.

Olson, D. J., Kamil, A. C., Balda, R. P., & Nims, P. J. (1995). Performance of four seed-caching corvid species in operant tests of nonspatial and spatial memory. *Journal of Comparative Psychology, 109,* 173–181.

Olton, D. S. (1992). Tolman's cognitive analyses: Predecessors of current approaches in psychology. *Journal of Experimental Psychology: General, 121,* 427–428.

Opton, E. M., Jr. (1970). Lessons of My Lai. In N. Sanford & C. Comstock (Eds.), *Sanctions for evil.* San Francisco: Jossey-Bass.

Opton, E. M., Jr. (1973). "It never happened and besides they deserved it." In W. E. Henry & N. Stanford (Eds.), *Sanctions for evil* (pp. 49–70). San Francisco: Jossey-Bass.

O'Regan, J. K. (1992). Solving the "real" mysteries of visual perception: The world as an outside memory. *Canadian Journal of Psychology, 46,* 461–488.

Orne, M. T. (1980). Hypnotic control of pain: Toward a clarification of the different psychological processes involved. In J. J. Bonica (Ed.), *Pain* (pp. 155–172). New York: Raven Press.

Ornstein, R. E. (1991). *The evolution of consciousness.* New York: Simon & Schuster.

Orr, W. C. (1997). Obstructive sleep apnea: Natural history and varieties of clinical presentation. In M. R. Pressman & W. C. Orr (Eds.), *Understanding sleep: The evaluation and treatment of sleep disorders* (pp. 267–281). Washington, DC: American Psychological Association

Osofsky, J. D. (Ed.). (1997). *Children in a violent society.* New York: Guilford.

Owens, J., Bower, G. H., & Black, J. B. (1979). The "soap opera" effect in story recall. *Memory & Cognition, 7,* 185–191.

Ozer, D. J., & Reise, S. P. (1994). Personality assessment. *Annual Review of Psychology, 45,* 357–388.

Paikoff, R. L. (Ed.). (1991). *Shared views in the family during adolescence.* San Francisco: Jossey-Bass.

Paivio, A. (1986). *Mental representations: A dual coding approach.* New York: Oxford University Press.

Paran, E., Amir, M., & Yaniv, N. (1996). Evaluating the response of mild hypertensives to biofeedback-assisted relaxation using a mental stress test. *Journal of Behavior Therapy and Experimental Psychiatry, 27,* 157–167.

Paris, J. (1997). Childhood trauma as an etiological factor in the personality disorders. *Journal of Personality Disorders, 11,* 34–49.

Park, B., & Rothbart, M. (1982). Perception of out-group homogeneity and levels of social categorization: Memory for the subordinate attributes of in-group and out-group members. *Journal of Personality and Social Psychology, 42,* 1051–1068.

Park, S. M., & Gabrieli, J. D. E. (1995). Perceptual and nonperceptual components of implicit memory for pictures. *Journal of Experimental Psychology: Learning, Memory, and Cognition, 21,* 1583–1594.

Parker, S., Nichter, M., Nichter, M., Vuckovic, N., Sims, C., & Ritenbaugh, C. (1995). Body image and weight concerns among African American and White adolescent females: Differences that make a difference. *Human Organization, 54,* 103–114.

Parr, W. V., & Siegert, R. (1993). Adults' conceptions of everyday memory failures in others: Factors that mediate the effects of target age. *Psychology and Aging, 8,* 599–605.

Parson, E. R. (1995). Mass traumatic terror in Oklahoma City and the phases of adaptational coping. *Journal of Contemporary Psychotherapy, 25,* 155–184.

Pascalis, O., de Schonen, S., Morton, J., Deruelle, C., & Fabre-Grenet, M. (1995). Mother's face recognition by neonates: A replication and extension. *Infant Behavior & Development, 18,* 79–85.

Pashler, H. (1992). Attentional limitations in doing two tasks at the same time. *Current Directions in Psychological Science, 1,* 44–48.

Pashler, H. (1994). Dual-task interference in simple tasks: Data and theory. *Psychological Bulletin, 116,* 220–244.

Patterson, C. J. (1995). Lesbian mothers, gay fathers, and their children. In A. R. D'Augelli & C. J. Patterson (Eds.), *Lesbian, gay, and bisexual identities over the life span: Psychological perspectives* (pp. 262–290). New York: Oxford University Press.

Pattie, F. A. (1994). *Mesmer and animal magnetism: A chapter in the history of medicine.* New York: Edmonston.

Paul, S. M., Crawley, J. N., & Skolnick, P. (1986). The neurobiology of anxiety: The role of the GABA/benzodiazepine complex. In P. A. Berger & H. K. H. Brodie (Eds.), *American handbook of psychiatry: Biological psychology* (3rd ed.). New York: Basic Books.

Pauli, P., Dengler, W., Wiedemann, G., Montoya, P., Flor, H., Birbaumer, N., & Buchkremer, G. (1997). Behavioral and neuropsychological evidence for altered processing of anxiety-related words in panic disorder. *Journal of Abnormal Psychology, 106,* 213–220.

Pavlov, I. P. (1927). *Conditioned reflexes* (G. V. Anrep, Trans.). London: Oxford University Press.

Pavlov, I. P. (1928). *Lectures on conditioned reflexes: Twenty-five years of objective study of higher nervous activity (behavior of animals)* (Vol. 1, W. H. Gantt, Trans.). New York: International Publishers.

Pawlik, K., & d'Ydewalle, G. (1996). Psychology and the global commons: Perspectives on international psychology. *American Psychologist, 51,* 488–495.

Pederson, D. R., & Moran, G. (1996). Expressions of the attachment relationship outside of the strange situation. *Child Development, 67,* 915–927.

Penick, S., Smith, G., Wienske, K., & Hinkle, L. (1963). An experimental evaluation of the relationship between hunger and gastric motility. *American Journal of Physiology, 205,* 421–426.

Penn, D. L., Guynan, K., Daily, T., Spaulding, W. D., Garbin, C. P., & Sullivan, M. (1994). Dispelling the stigma of schizophrenia: What sort of information is best? *Schizophrenia Bulletin, 20,* 567–578.

Penn, D. L., Kommana, S., Mansfield, M., & Link, B. G. (1999). Dispelling the stigma of schizophrenia: II. The impact of information on dangerousness. *Schizophrenia Bulletin, 25,* 437–446.

Pennebaker, J. W. (1990). *Opening up: The healing power of confiding in others.* New York: Morrow.

Pennebaker, J. W. (1997). Writing about emotional experiences as a therapeutic process. *Psychological Science, 8,* 162–166.

Pennebaker, J. W., & Harber, K. D. (1993). A social stage model of collective coping: The Loma Prieta earthquake and the Persian Gulf War. *Journal of Social Issues, 49*(4), 125–145.

Pennisi, E. (2000). And the gene number is . . . ? *Science, 288,* 1146–1147.

Penton-Voak, I. S., & Perrett, D. I. (2000). Female preference for male faces changes cyclically: Further evidence. *Evolution and Human Behavior, 21,* 39–48.

Penton-Voak, I. S., Perrett, D. I., Castles, D. L., Kobayashi, T., Burt, D. M., Murray, L. K., & Minamisawa, R. (1999). Menstrual cycle alters face preference. *Nature, 399,* 741–742.

Perkins, D. N. (1988). Creativity and the quest for mechanism. In R. J. Sternberg & E. E. Smith (Eds.), *The psychology of human thought* (pp. 309–336). Cambridge, U.K.: Cambridge University Press.

Perls, F. S. (1969). *Gestalt therapy verbatim*. Lafayette, CA: Real People Press.

Pervin, L. A. (1994). A critical analysis of current trait theory. *Psychological Inquiry, 5*, 103–113.

Peterson, C., & Seligman, M. E. P. (1984). Causal explanations as a risk factor for depression: Theory and evidence. *Psychological Review, 91*, 347–374.

Peterson, C., Seligman, M. E. P., & Valliant, G. E. (1988). Pessimistic explanatory style is a risk factor for physical illness: A thirty-five year longitudinal study. *Journal of Personality and Social Psychology, 55*, 23–27.

Peterson, D., & Goodall, J. (1993). *Visions of Caliban: On chimpanzees and people*. Boston: Houghton Mifflin.

Peterson, L. R., & Peterson, M. J. (1959). Short-term retention of individual verbal items. *Journal of Experimental Psychology, 58*, 193–198.

Peterson, R. S., & Nemeth, C. J. (1996). Focus versus flexibility: Majority and minority influence can both improve performance. *Personality and Social Psychology Bulletin, 22*, 14–23.

Petrie, K. J., Booth, R. J., & Pennebaker, J. W. (1998). The immunological effects of thought suppression. *Journal of Personality and Social Psychology, 75*, 1264–1272.

Petrinovich, L. F. (1998). *Darwinian dominion: Animal welfare and human interests*. Cambridge, MA: The MIT Press.

Pettigrew, T. F. (1997). Generalized intergroup contact effects on prejudice. *Personality and Social Psychology Bulletin, 23*, 173–185.

Petty, R. E., & Cacioppo, J. T. (1986). *Communication and persuasion: Central and peripheral routes to attitude change*. New York: Springer-Verlag.

Petty, R. E., & Wegener, D. T. (1999). The elaboration likelihood model: Current status and controversies. In S. Chaiken & Y. Trope (Eds.), *Dual-process theories in social psychology* (pp. 41–72). New York: Guilford.

Pfiffner, L. J., & McBurnett, K. (1997). Social skills training with parent generalization: Treatment effects for children with attention deficit disorder. *Journal of Consulting and Clinical Psychology, 65*, 749–757.

Phillips, D. P. (1993). Representation of acoustic events in primary auditory cortex. *Journal of Experimental Psychology: Human Perception and Performance, 19*, 203–216.

Phillips, S. T., & Ziller, R. C. (1997). Toward a theory and measure of the nature of nonprejudice. *Journal of Personality and Social Psychology, 72*, 420–432.

Piaget, J. (1929). *The child's conception of the world*. New York: Harcourt, Brace.

Piaget, J. (1954). *The construction of reality in the child*. New York: Basic Books.

Piaget, J. (1965). *The moral judgment of the child* (M. Gabain, Trans.). New York: Macmillan.

Piaget, J. (1977). *The development of thought: Equilibrium of cognitive structures*. New York: Viking Press.

Piccione, C., Hilgard, E. R., & Zimbardo, P. G. (1989). On the degree of stability of measured hypnotizability over a 25-year period. *Journal of Personality and Social Psychology, 56*, 289–295.

Pich, E. M., Pagliusi, S. R., Tessari, M., Talabot-Ayer, D., van Juijsduijnen, R. H., & Chaimulera, C. (1997). Common neural substrates for the addictive properties of nicotine and cocaine. *Science, 275*, 83–85.

Pierce, J. P., & Gilpin, E. A. (1995). A historical analysis of tobacco marketing and the uptake of smoking by youth in the United States: 1890–1977. *Health Psychology, 14*, 500–508.

Pilisuk, M., & Parks, S. H. (1986). *The healing web: Social networks and human survival*. Hanover, NH: University Press of New England.

Pilkonis, P. A., & Zimbardo, P. G. (1979). The personal and social dynamics of shyness. In C. E. Izard (Ed.), *Emotions in personality and psychopathology* (pp. 131–160). New York: Plenum Press.

Pincus, H. A., Tanielian, T. L., Marcus, S. C., Olfson, M., Zarin, D. A., Thompson, J., & Zito, J. M. (1998). Prescribing trends in psychotropic medications. *Journal of the American Medical Association, 279*, 526–531.

Pines, A., & Zimbardo, P. G. (1978). The personal and cultural dynamics of shyness: A comparison between Israelis, American Jews and Americans. *Journal of Psychology and Judaism, 3*, 81–101.

Pinker, S. (1994). *The language instinct: How the mind creates language*. New York: Morrow.

Pion, G. M., Mednick, M. T., Astin, H. S., Hall, C. C. I., Kenkel, M. B., Keita, G. P., Hohout, J. L., & Kelleher, J. C. (1996). The shifting gender composition of psychology: Trends and implications for the discipline. *American Psychologist, 51*, 509–528.

Piotrowski, C., Keller, J. W., & Ogawa, T. (1993). Projective techniques: An international perspective. *Psychological Reports, 72*, 179–182.

Piotrowski, C., Sherry, D., & Keller, J. W. (1985). Psychodiagnostic test usage: A survey of the Society for Personality Assessment. *Journal of Personality Assessment, 49*, 115–119.

Pitts, D. G. (1982). The effects of aging on selected visual functions: Dark adaptation, visual acuity, stereopsis, and brightness contrast. In R. Sekuler, D. Kline, & K. Dismukes (Eds.), *Aging and human visual function* (pp. 131–159). New York: Liss.

Plante, T. G., & Sykora, C. (1994). Are stress and coping associated with WISC-III performance among children? *Journal of Clinical Psychology, 50*, 759–762.

Plomin, R., Owen, M. J., & McGuffin, P. (1994). The genetic basis of complex human behaviors. *Science, 264*, 1733–1739.

Plomin, R., & Petrill, S. A. (1997). Genetics and intelligence: What's new? *Intelligence, 24*, 53–77.

Plomin, R., & Rende, R. (1991). Human behavioral genetics. *Annual Review of Psychology, 42*, 161–190.

Plous, S. (1996a). Attitudes toward the use of animals in psychological research and education: Results from a national survey of psychology majors. *Psychological Science, 7*, 352–358.

Plous, S. (1996b). Attitudes toward the use of animals in psychological research and education: Results from a national survey of psychologists. *American Psychologist, 51*, 1167–1180.

Plutchik, R. (1980). *Emotion: A psychoevolutionary synthesis*. New York: Harper & Row.

Plutchik, R. (1984). Emotions: A general psychoevolutionary theory. In K. Scherer & P. Ekman (Eds.), *Approaches to emotion*. Hillsdale, NJ: Erlbaum.

Poizner, H., Bellugi, U., & Klima, E. S. (1991). Brain function for language: Perspectives from another modality. In I. G. Mattingly & M. Studdert-Kennedy (Eds.), *Modularity and the motor theory of speech perception* (pp. 145–169). Hillsdale, NJ: Erlbaum.

Polivy, J., & Herman, C. P. (1999). Distress and eating: Why do dieters overeat? *International Journal of Eating Disorders, 26*, 153–164.

Polivy, J., Herman, C. P., & McFarlane, T. (1994). Effects of anxiety on eating: Does palatability moderate distress-induced overeating in dieters? *Journal of Abnormal Psychology, 103*, 505–510.

Poppen, P. J. (1995). Gender and patterns of sexual risk taking in college students. *Sex Roles, 32*, 545–555.

Porkka-Heiskanen, T., Strecker, R. E., Thakkar, M., Bjørkum, A. A., Greene, R. W., & McCarley, R. W. (1997). Adenosine: A mediator of the sleep-inducing effects of prolonged wakefulness. *Science, 276*, 1265–1268.

Porstner, D. (1997, July 26). Man stops car with own. *Newsday*, p. A32.

Porter, L. W., & Lawler, E. E. (1968). *Managerial attitudes and performance*. Homewood, IL: Irwin.

Posner, M. I. (1993). Seeing the mind. *Science, 262,* 673–674.

Poucet, B. (1993). Spatial cognitive maps in animals: New hypotheses on their structure and neural mechanisms. *Psychological Review, 100,* 163–182.

Poulin, J. E. (1985). Long term foster care, natural family attachment and loyalty conflict. *Journal of Social Service Research, 9,* 17–29.

Poulos, C. X., & Cappell, H. (1991). Homeostatic theory of drug tolerance: A general model of physiological adaptation. *Psychological Review, 98,* 390–408.

Povinelli, D. J., Landau, K. R., & Perilloux, H. K. (1996). Self-recognition in young children using delayed versus live feedback: Evidence of a developmental asynchrony. *Child Development, 67,* 1540–1554.

Povinelli, D. J., & Prince, C. G. (1998). When self met other. In M. Ferrari & R. J. Sternberg (Eds.) *Self-awareness: Its nature and development.* New York: The Guilford Press.

Powley, T. (1977). The ventromedial hypothalamic syndrome, satiety, and a cephalic phase hypothesis. *Psychological Review, 84,* 89–126.

Pratt, M. W., Golding, G., Hunter, W., & Norris, J. (1988). From inquiry to judgment: Age and sex differences in patterns of adult moral thinking and information-seeking. *International Journal of Aging and Human Development, 27,* 109–124.

Premack, D. (1965). Reinforcement theory. In D. Levine (Ed.), *Nebraska Symposium on Motivation* (pp. 128–180). Lincoln: University of Nebraska Press.

Premack, D. (1971). Language in chimpanzee? *Science, 172,* 808–822.

Prentice, D. A., & Gerrig, R. J. (1999). Exploring the boundary between fiction and reality. In S. Chaiken & Y. Trope (Eds.), *Dual-process theories in social psychology* (pp. 529–546). New York: Guilford.

Prentice, D. A., Gerrig, R. J., & Bailis, D. S. (1997). What readers bring to the experience of fictional texts. *Psychonomic Bulletin & Review, 4,* 416–420.

Preti, G., Cutler, W. B., Huggins, G. R., Garcia, C. R., & Lawley, H. J. (1986). Human axillary secretions influence women's menstrual cycles: The role of donor extract from females. *Hormones and Behavior, 20,* 463–473.

Price, D. D. (2000). Psychological and neural mechanisms of the affective dimension of pain. *Science, 288,* 1769–1772.

Price, R. (1980). *Droodles.* Los Angeles: Price/Stern/Sloan. (Original work published 1953)

Prochaska, J. O., DiClemente, C. C., Velicer, W. F., & Rossi, J. S. (1993). Standardized, individualized, interactive, and personalized self-help programs for smoking cessation. *Health Psychology, 12,* 399–405.

Prosser, D., Johnson, S., Kuipers, E., Szmukler, G., Bebbington, P., & Thornicroft, G. (1997). Perceived sources of work stress and satisfaction among hospital and community mental health staff, and their relation to mental health, burnout, and job satisfaction. *Journal of Psychosomatic Research, 43,* 51–59.

Putnam, D. E., Finney, J. W., Barkley, P. L., & Bonner, M. J. (1994). Enhancing commitment improves adherence to a medical regimen. *Journal of Consulting and Clinical Psychology, 62,* 191–194.

Pyszczynski, T., Wicklund, R. A., Floresku, S., Koch, H., Gauch, G., Solomon, S., & Greenberg, J. (1996). Whistling in the dark: Exaggerated consensus estimates in response to incidental reminders of mortality. *Psychological Science, 7,* 332–336.

Quattrone, G. (1986). On the perception of a group's variability. In S. Worchell & W. Austin (Eds.), *The psychology of intergroup relations* (Vol. 2, pp. 25–48). New York: Nelson-Hall.

Quine, W. V. O. (1960). *Word and object.* Cambridge, MA: The MIT Press.

Rabbie, J. M (1981). The effects of intergroup competition and cooperation on intra- and intergroup relationships. In J. Grzelak & V. Derlega (Eds.), *Living with other people: Theory and research on cooperation and helping.* New York: Academic Press.

Rabins, P. V. (1992). Prevention of mental disorder in the elderly: Current perspectives and future prospects. *Journal of the American Geriatric Society, 40,* 727–733.

Rachlin, H. (1990). Why do people gamble and keep gambling despite heavy losses? *Psychological Science, 1,* 294–297.

Radowsky, M., & Siegel, L. J. (1997). The gay adolescent: Stressors, applications, and psychosocial interventions. *Clinical Psychology Review, 17,* 191–216.

Rainnie, D. G., Grunze, H. C. R., McCarley, R. W., & Greene, R. W. (1994). Adenosine inhibition of mesopontine cholinergic neurons: Implications for EEG arousal. *Science, 263,* 689–692.

Rajaram, S., & Coslett, H. B. (2000). New conceptual associative learning in amnesia: A case study. *Journal of Memory and Language, 43,* 291–315.

Rajaram, S., & Roediger, H. L., III (1993). Direct comparison of four implicit memory tests. *Journal of Experimental Psychology: Learning, Memory, and Cognition, 19,* 765–776.

Rajaram, S., Srinivas, K., & Roediger, H. L., III. (1998). A transfer-appropriate processing account of context effects in word-fragment completion. *Journal of Experimental Psychology: Learning, Memory, and Cognition, 24,* 993–1004.

Rand, C. S., & Kuldau, J. M. (1992). Epidemiology of bulimia and symptoms in a general population: Sex, age, race, and socioeconomic status. *International Journal of Eating Disorders, 11,* 37–44.

Rand, C. S. W., & Kuldau, J. M. (1990). The epidemiology of obesity and self-defined weight problem in the general population: Gender, race, age, and social class. *International Journal of Eating Disorders, 9,* 329–343.

Rao, S. C., Rainer, G., & Miller, E. K. (1997). Integration of what and where in the primate prefrontal cortex. *Science, 276,* 821–824.

Rapoport, J. L., Giedd, J., Kumra, S., Jacobsen, A. S., Lee, P., Nelson, J., & Hamburger, S. (1997). Childhood-onset schizophrenia: Progressive ventricular change during adolescence. *Archives of General Psychiatry, 54,* 897–903.

Rapoport, J. L. (1989, March). The biology of obsessions and compulsions. *Scientific American,* pp. 83–89.

Rapp, B., & Goldrick, M. (2000). Discreteness and interactivity in spoken word production. *Psychological Review, 107,* 460–499.

Rasmussen, T., & Milner, B. (1977). The role of early left-brain injury in determining lateralization of cerebral speech functions. *Annals of the New York Academy of Sciences, 299,* 355–369.

Ratcliff, R. (1978). A theory of memory retrieval. *Psychological Review, 85,* 59–108.

Ratcliff, R., & McKoon, G. (1978). Priming in item recognition: Evidence for the propositional structure of sentences. *Journal of Verbal Learning and Verbal Behavior, 17,* 403–418.

Ratner, C. (2000). A cultural-psychological analysis of emotions. *Culture and Psychology, 6,* 5–39.

Raymond, J. L., Lisberger, S. G., & Mauk, M. D. (1996). The cerebellum: A neuronal learning machine? *Science, 272,* 1126–1131.

Reder, L. M., & Ritter, F. E. (1992). What determines initial feelings of knowing? Familiarity with question terms, not with the answer. *Journal of Experimental Psychology: Learning, Memory, and Cognition, 18,* 435–452.

Redfern, P., Minors, D., & Waterhouse, J. (1994). Circadian rhythms, jet lag, and chronobiotics: An overview. *Chronobiology International, 11,* 253–265.

Reed, G. M., Kemeny, M. E., Taylor, S. E., Wang, H. Y. J., & Visscher, B. R. (1994). Realistic acceptance as a predictor of decreased survival time in gay men with AIDS. *Health Psychology, 13,* 299–307.

Reed, S. B., Kirsch, I., Wickless, C., Moffitt, K. H., & Taren, P. (1996). Reporting biases in hypnosis: Suggestion of compliance? *Journal of Abnormal Psychology, 105,* 142–145.

Regan, R. T. (1971). Effects of a favor and liking on compliance. *Journal of Experimental Social Psychology, 7,* 627–639.

Regier, D. A., Boyd, J. H., Burke, J. D., Rae, D. S., Myers, J. K., Kramer, M., Robins, L. N., George, L. K., Karno, M., & Locke, B. Z. (1988). One-month prevalence of mental disorders in the United States. *Archives of General Psychiatry, 45,* 977–986.

Regier, D. A., Farmer, M. E., Rae, D. S., Myers, J. K., Kramer, M., Robins, L. N., George, L. K., Karno, M., & Locke, B. Z. (1993a). One-month prevalence of mental disorders in the United States and sociodemographic characteristics: The Epidemiological Catchment Area Study. *Acta Psychiatrica Scandinavica, 88,* 35–47.

Regier, D. A., Narrow, W. E., Rae, D. S., Manderscheid, R. W., Locke, B. Z., & Goodwin, F. K. (1993b). The de facto US mental and addictive disorders service system: Epidemiologic Catchment Area prospective 1-year rates of disorders and services. *Archives of General Psychiatry, 50,* 85–94.

Reid, E. (1998). The self and the Internet: Variations on the illusion of one self. In J. Gackenbach (Ed.), *Psychology and the Internet: Intrapersonal, interpersonal, and transpersonal implications* (pp. 29–42). San Diego, CA: Academic Press.

Reiman, E. M., Lane, R. D., Ahern, G. L., Schwartz, G. E., Davidson, R. J., Friston, K. J., Yun, L.-S., & Chen, K. (1997). Neuroanatomical correlates of externally and internally generated human emotion. *American Journal of Psychiatry, 154,* 918–925.

Reisine, T. (1995). Opiate receptors. *Neuropharmacology, 34,* 463–472.

Reiss, D., & Price, R. H. (1996). National research agenda for prevention research: The National Institute of Mental Health report. *American Psychologist, 51,* 1109–1115.

Remafedi, G. (1999). Sexual orientation and youth suicide. *Journal of the American Medical Association, 282,* 1291–1292.

Rescorla, R. A. (1966). Predictability and number of pairings in Pavlovian fear conditioning. *Psychonomic Science, 4,* 383–384.

Rescorla, R. A. (1988). Pavlovian conditioning: It's not what you think it is. *American Psychologist, 43,* 151–160.

Restrepo, D., Miyamoto, T., Bryant, B. P., & Teeter, J. H. (1990). Odor stimuli trigger influx of calcium into olfactory neurons of the channel catfish. *Science, 249,* 1166–1168.

Rheingold, H. L., & Cook, K. V. (1974). The contents of boys' and girls' rooms as an index of parents' behavior. *Child Development, 46,* 459–463.

Rhodes, G. , Graham, B., Tremewan, T., & Kennedy, A. (1997). Facial distinctiveness and the power of caricatures. *Perception, 26,* 207–223.

Rhodewelt, F., & Hill, S. K. (1995). Self-handicapping in the classroom: The effects of claimed self-handicaps on responses to academic failure. *Basic and Applied Social Psychology, 16,* 397–416.

Rice, G., Anderson, C., Risch, N., & Ebers, G. (1999). Male homosexuality: Absence of linkage to microsatellite markers at Xq28. *Science, 284,* 665–667.

Richards, M. H., Crowe, P. A., Larson, R., & Swarr, A. (1998). Developmental patterns and gender differences in the experience of peer companionship during adolescence. *Child Development, 69,* 154–163.

Riemann, R., Angleitner, A., & Strelau, J. (1997). Genetic and environmental influences on personality: A study of twins reared together using the self- and peer report NEO-FFI scales. *Journal of Personality, 65,* 449–475.

Riessman, F. (1997). Ten self-help principles. *Social Policy, 27,* 6–11.

Riger, S. (1992). Epistemological debates, feminist voices: Science, social values, and the study of women. *American Psychologist, 47,* 730–740.

Rinck, M., Hähnel, A., Bower, G. H., & Glowalla, U. (1997). The metrics of spatial situation models. *Journal of Experimental Psychology: Learning, Memory, and Cognition, 23,* 622–637.

Rips, L. J. (1990). Reasoning. *Annual Review of Psychology, 41,* 321–353.

Roberts, A. H., Kewman, D. G., Mercier, L., & Hovell, M. (1993). The power of nonspecific effects in healing: Implications for psychosocial and biological treatments. *Clinical Psychology Review, 13,* 375–391.

Roberts, G., & McGrady, A. (1996). Racial and gender effects on the relaxation response: Implications for the development of hypertension. *Biofeedback and Self-Regulation, 21,* 51–62.

Rock, I. (1983). *The logic of perception.* Cambridge, MA: Bradford Books/The MIT Press.

Rock, I. (1986). The description and analysis of object and event perception. In K. R. Boff, L. Kaufman, & J. P. Thomas (Eds.), *Handbook of perception and human performance* (Vol. 2, pp. 33–71). New York: Wiley.

Rock, I., & Gutman, D. (1981). The effect of inattention on form perception. *Journal of Experimental Psychology: Human Perception and Performance, 7,* 275–285.

Rodin, J. (1981). Current status of the internal-external hypothesis for obesity: What went wrong? *American Psychologist, 26,* 361–372.

Roebuck, T. M., Mattson, S. N., & Riley, E. P. (1999). Prenatal exposure to alcohol: Effects on brain structure and neuropsychological functioning. In J. H. Hannigan, L. P. Spear, N. E. Spear, & C. R. Goodlett (Eds.), *Alcohol and alcoholism: Effects on brain development* (pp. 1–16). Mahwah: NJ: Erlbaum.

Roediger, H. L. (1990). Implicit memory. *American Psychologist, 45,* 1043–1056.

Roediger, H. L., III, Weldon, M. S., & Challis, B. H. (1989). Explaining dissociations between implicit and explicit measures of retention: A processing account. In H. L. Roediger & F. I. M. Craik (Eds.), *Varieties of memory and consciousness: Essays in honour of Endel Tulving* (pp. 3–14). Hillsdale, NJ: Erlbaum.

Rogers, C. R. (1947). Some observations on the organization of personality. *American Psychologist, 2,* 358–368.

Rogers, C. R. (1951). *Client-centered therapy: Its current practice, implications and theory.* Boston: Houghton Mifflin.

Rogers, C. R. (1959). A theory of therapy, personality, and interpersonal relationships, as developed in the client-centered framework. In S. Koch (Ed.), *Psychology: A study of a science* (Vol. 3). New York: McGraw-Hill.

Rogers, C. R. (1977). *On personal power: Inner strength and its revolutionary impact.* New York: Delacorte.

Rogers, M., & Smith, K. (1993). Public perceptions of subliminal advertising: Why practitioners shouldn't ignore this issue. *Journal of Advertising Research, 33*(2), 10–18.

Rogers, R. W. (1984). Changing health-related attitudes and behavior: The role of preventative health psychology. In J. H. Harver, J. E. Maddux, R. P. McGlynn, & C. D. Stolenberg (Eds.), *Social perception in clinical and consulting psychology* (Vol. 2, pp. 91–112). Lubbock: Texas Tech University Press.

Rogers, S. (1993). How a publicity blitz created the myth of subliminal advertising. *Public Relations Quarterly, 37,* 12–17.

Rogoff, B. (1990). *Apprenticeship in thinking: Cognitive development in social context.* New York: Oxford University Press.

Rogoff, B., & Chavajay, P. (1995). What's become of research on the cultural basis of cognitive development? *American Psychologist, 50,* 859–877.

Rohrer, J. H., Baron, S. H., Hoffman, E. L., & Swinder, D. V. (1954). The stability of autokinetic judgment. *Journal of Abnormal and Social Psychology, 49,* 595–597.

Rolls, B. J., Rowe, E. A., Rolls, E. T., Kingston, B., Megson, A., & Gunary, R. (1981). Variety in a meal enhances food intake in man. *Physiology & Behavior, 26,* 215–221.

Rolls, E. T. (1994). Neural processing related to feeding in primates. In C. R. Legg & D. Booth (Eds.), *Appetite: Neural and behavioural bases* (pp. 11–53). Oxford, U.K.: Oxford University Press.

Rolls, E. T. (2000). Memory systems in the brain. *Annual Review of Psychology, 51,* 599–630.

Rorschach, H. (1942). *Psychodiagnostics: A diagnostic test based on perception.* New York: Grune & Stratton.

Rosch, E. H. (1973). Natural categories. *Cognitive Psychology, 4,* 328–350.

Rosch, E. H. (1978). Principles of categorization. In E. Rosch & B. B. Lloyd (Eds.), *Cognition and categorization* (pp. 27–48). Hillsdale, NJ: Erlbaum.

Rosch, E. H., Mervis, C. B., Gray, W. D., Johnson, D. M., & Boyes-Braem, P. (1976). Basic objects in natural categories. *Cognitive Psychology, 8,* 382–439.

Rosen, H. S., & Rosen, L. A. (1983). Eliminating stealing: Use of stimulus control with an elementary student. *Behavior Modification, 7,* 56–63.

Rosenbaum, M. E. (1986). The repulsion hypothesis: On the nondevelopment of relationships. *Journal of Personality and Social Psychology, 51,* 1156–1166.

Rosenfarb, I. S., Goldstein, M. J., Mintz, J., & Nuechterlein, K. H. (1995). Expressed emotion and subclinical psychopathology observable within the transactions between schizophrenic patients and their family members. *Journal of Abnormal Psychology, 104,* 259–267.

Rosenfield, S. (1997). Labeling mental illness: The effects of received services and perceived stigma on life satisfaction. *American Sociological Review, 52,* 660–672.

Rosenhan, D. L. (1973). On being sane in insane places. *Science, 179,* 250–258.

Rosenhan, D. L. (1975). The contextual nature of psychiatric diagnoses. *Journal of Abnormal Psychology, 84,* 462–474.

Rosenhan, D. L., & Seligman, M. E. P. (1989). *Abnormal psychology* (2nd ed.). New York: Norton.

Rosenkoetter, L. I. (1999). The television situation comedy and children's prosocial behavior. *Journal of Applied Social Psychology, 29,* 979–993.

Rosenthal, A. M. (1964). *Thirty-eight witnesses.* New York: McGraw-Hill.

Rosenthal, D., Wender, P. H., Kety, S. S., Schulsinger, F., Weiner, J., & Rieder, R. (1975). Parent–child relationships and psychopathological disorder in the child. *Archives of General Psychiatry, 32,* 466–476.

Rosenthal, N. E., Sack, D. A., Gillin, J. C., Lewy, A. J., Goodwin, F. K., Davenport, Y., Mueller, P. S., Newsome, D. A., & Wehr, T. A. (1984). Seasonal affective disorder: A description of the syndrome and preliminary findings with light therapy. *Archives of General Psychiatry, 41,* 72–80.

Rosenthal, R. (1966). *Experimenter effects in behavioral research.* New York: Appleton-Century-Crofts.

Rosenthal, R. (1974). *On the social psychology of the self-fulfilling prophecy: Further evidence for Pygmalion effects and their mediating mechanisms.* New York: MSS Modular Publications.

Rosenthal, R. (1994). Science and ethics in conducting, analyzing, and reporting psychological research. *Psychological Science, 5,* 127–134.

Rosenthal, R., & Fode, K. L. (1963). The effect of experimenter bias on the performance of the albino rat. *Behavioral Science, 8,* 183–189.

Rosenthal, R., & Jacobson, L. F. (1968). *Pygmalion in the classroom: Teacher expectations and intellectual development.* New York: Holt.

Rosenwald, G. C., & Ochberg, R. L. (1992). *Storied lives: The cultural politics of self-understanding.* New Haven: Yale University Press.

Rosenzweig, M. R. (1996). Aspects of the search for neural mechanisms of memory. *Annual Review of Psychology, 47,* 1–32.

Rosenzweig, M. R. (1999a). Continuity and change in the development of psychology around the world. *American Psychologist, 54,* 252–259.

Rosenzweig, M. R. (1999b). Effects of differential experience on brain and cognition throughout the life span. In S. H. Broman & J. M. Fletcher (Eds.), *The changing nervous system: Neurobehavioral consequences of early brain disorders* (pp. 25–50). New York: Oxford University Press.

Ross, B. H., & Kennedy, P. T. (1990). Generalizing from the use of earlier examples in problem solving. *Journal of Experimental Psychology: Learning, Memory, and Cognition, 16,* 42–55.

Ross, L. (1988). Situational perspectives on the obedience experiments. [Review of the obedience experiments: A case study of controversy in social science]. *Contemporary Psychology, 33,* 101–104.

Ross, L., Amabile, T., & Steinmetz, J. (1977). Social roles, social control and biases in the social perception process. *Journal of Personality and Social Psychology, 37,* 485–494.

Ross, L., & Nisbett, R. E. (1991). *The person and the situation: Perspectives of social psychology.* New York: McGraw-Hill.

Ross, M. J., & Berger, R. S. (1996). Effects of stress inoculation training on athletes' postsurgical pain and rehabilitation after orthopedic injury. *Journal of Consulting and Clinical Psychology, 64,* 406–410.

Ross, M. W., & Rosser, B. R. S. (1996). Measurement and correlates of internalized homophobia: A factor analytic study. *Journal of Clinical Psychology, 52,* 15–21.

Rossi, A. (1984). Gender and parenthood. *American Sociological Review, 49,* 1–19.

Rothbaum, B. O., Hodges, L. F. Kooper, R., Opdyke, D., Williford, J. S., & North, M. (1995). Effectiveness of computer-generated (virtual reality) graded exposure in the treatment of acrophobia. *American Journal of Psychiatry, 152,* 626–628.

Rothenberg, A. (1990). *Creativity and madness.* Baltimore: The Johns Hopkins University Press.

Rothman, D. J. (1971). *The discovery of the asylum: Social order and disorder in the new republic.* Boston: Little, Brown.

Rotter, J. B. (1954). *Social learning and clinical psychology.* Englewood Cliffs, NJ: Prentice Hall.

Rouhana, N. N., & Kelman, H. C. (1994). Promoting joint thinking in international conflicts: An Israeli-Palestinian continuing workshop. *Journal of Social Issues, 50*(1), 157–168.

Rowe, D. C. (1997). A place at the policy table? Behavior genetics and estimates of family environmental effects on IQ. *Intelligence, 24,* 133–158.

Rozin, P., & Fallon, A. E. (1987). A perspective on disgust. *Psychological Review, 94,* 23–41.

Rozin, P., Millman, L., & Nemeroff, C. (1986). Operation of the laws of sympathetic magic in disgust and other domains. *Journal of Personality and Social Psychology, 50,* 703–712.

Rubin, D. C., & Kontis, T. C. (1983). A schema for common cents. *Memory & Cognition, 11,* 335–341.

Rubin, J. Z., Provenzano, F. J., & Luria, Z. (1974). The eye of the beholder: Parents' views on sex of newborns. *American Journal of Orthopsychiatry, 44,* 512–519.

Ruch, R. (1937). *Psychology and life.* Glenview, IL: Scott, Foresman.

Rucker, C. E., III, & Cash, T. F. (1992). Body images, body-size perceptions, and eating behaviors among African-American and White college women. *International Journal of Eating Disorders, 12,* 291–299.

Ruitenbeek, H. M. (1973). *The first Freudians.* New York: Jason Aronson.

Rumelhart, D. E., & McClelland, J. L. (1986). *Parallel distributed processing: Explorations in the microstructure of cognition* (2 vols.). Cambridge, MA: The MIT Press.

Rumelhart, D. E., Smolensky, P., McClelland, J. L., & Hinton, G. E. (1986). Schemata and sequential thought processes in PDP models. In J. L. McClelland & D. E. Rumelhart (Eds.), *Parallel distributed processing: Vol. 2. Psychological and biological models* (pp. 7–57). Cambridge, MA: The MIT Press.

Rummel, R. J. (1994). Power, genocide and mass murder. *Journal of Peace Research, 31,* 1–10.

Runco, M. A. (1991). *Divergent thinking.* Norwood, NJ: Ablex.

Rundle, H. D., Nagel, L., Boughman, J. W., & Schluter, D. (2000). Natural selection and parallel speciation in sympatric sticklebacks. *Science, 287,* 306–308.

Rusbult, C. E., & Martz, J. M. (1995). Remaining in an abusive relationship: An investment model analysis of nonvoluntary dependence. *Personality and Social Psychology Bulletin, 21,* 558–571.

Russo, N. F., & Denmark, F. L. (1987). Contributions of women to psychology. *Annual Review of Psychology, 38,* 279–298.

Ryckman, R. M., Graham, S. S., Thornton, B., Gold, J. A., & Lindner, M. A. (1998). Physical size stereotyping as a mediator of attributions of responsibility in an alleged date-rape situation. *Journal of Applied Social Psychology, 28,* 1876–1888.

Ryff, C. D. (1989). In the eye of the beholder: Views of psychological well-being among middle-aged and older adults. *Psychology and Aging, 4,* 195–210.

Saarinen, T. F. (1987). *Centering of mental maps of the world: Discussion paper.* Tucson: University of Arizona, Department of Geography and Regional Development.

Saberi, K. (1996). An auditory illusion predicted form a weighted cross-correlation model of binaural interaction. *Psychological Review, 103,* 137–142.

Sackheim, H. A., Prudic, J., Devanand, D. P., Nobler, M. S., Lisanby, S. H., Peyser, S., Fitzsimons, L., Moody, B. J., & Clark, J. (2000). A prospective, randomized, double-blind comparison of bilateral and right unilateral electroconvulsive therapy at different stimulus intensities. *Archives of General Psychiatry, 57,* 425–434.

Sacks, O. (1995). *An anthropologist on Mars.* New York: Knopf.

Salthouse, T. A. (1996). The processing-speed theory of adult age differences in cognition. *Psychological Review, 103,* 403–428.

Samuda, R. J. (1998). *Psychological testing of American minorities* (2nd ed.). Thousand Oaks, CA: Sage.

Samuel, A. G. (1981). Phonemic restoration: Insights from a new methodology. *Journal of Experimental Psychology: General, 110,* 474–494.

Samuel, A. G. (1991). A further examination of attentional effects in the phonemic restoration illusion. *Quarterly Journal of Experimental Psychology: Human Experimental Psychology, 43A,* 679–699.

Samuel, A. G. (1997). Lexical activation produces potent phonemic percepts. *Cognitive Psychology, 32,* 97–127.

Sanderson, C. A., & Cantor, N. (1995). Social dating goals in late adolescence: Implications for safer sexual activity. *Journal of Personality and Social Psychology, 68,* 1121–1134.

Sanderson, C. A., & Cantor, N. (1997). Creating satisfaction in steady dating relationships: The role of personal goals and situational affordances. *Journal of Personality and Social Psychology, 73,* 1424–1433.

Sapir, E. (1964). *Culture, language, and personality.* Berkeley: University of California Press. (Original work published 1941)

Sapolsky, R. M. (1994). *Why zebras don't get ulcers: A guide to stress, stress-related disease, and coping.* New York: Freeman.

Sapolsky, R. M. (1996). Why stress is bad for your brain. *Science, 273,* 749–750.

Sarbin, T. R. (1997). The power in believed-in imaginings. *Psychological Inquiry, 8,* 322–325.

Satir, V. (1967). *Conjoint family therapy* (Rev. ed.). Palo Alto, CA: Science and Behavior Books.

Sattler, J. M., & Atkinson, L. (1993). Item equivalence across scales: The WPPSI-R and WISC-III. *Psychological Assessment, 5,* 203–206.

Savage-Rumbaugh, S., Shanker, S. G., & Taylor, T. J. (1998). *Apes, language, and the human mind.* New York: Oxford University Press.

Scarborough, E., & Forumoto, L. (1987). *Untold lives: The first generation of women psychologists.* New York: Columbia University Press.

Scarr, S. (1998). American child care today. *American Psychologist, 53,* 95–108.

Scarr, S., & Eisenberg, M. (1993). Child care research: Issues, perspectives, and results. *Annual Review of Psychology, 44,* 613–644.

Scarr, S., Phillips, D., & McCartney, K. (1990). Facts, fantasies and the future of child care in the United States. *Psychological Science, 1,* 26–35.

Schab, F. R. (1990). Odors and the remembrance of things past. *Journal of Experimental Psychology: Learning, Memory, and Cognition, 16,* 648–655.

Schachter, S. (1971a). Some extraordinary facts about obese humans and rats. *American Psychologist, 26,* 129–144.

Schachter, S. (1971b). *Emotion, obesity and crime.* New York: Academic Press.

Schacter, D. L., Chiu, C.-Y., P., & Ochsner, K. N. (1993). Implicit memory: A selective review. *Annual Review of Neuroscience, 16,* 159–182.

Schaeken, W., De Booght, G., Vandierendonck, A., & d'Ydewalle, G. (Eds.). (2000). *Deductive reasoning and strategies.* Mahwah, NJ: Erlbaum.

Schaie, K. W. (1989). The hazards of cognitive aging. *The Gerontologist, 29,* 484–493.

Schaie, K. W. (1993). Ageist language in psychological research. *American Psychologist, 48,* 49–51.

Schaie, K. W. (1994). The course of adult intellectual development. *American Psychologist, 49,* 304–313.

Schaie, K. W., & Willis, S. L. (1986). Can decline in adult intellectual functioning be reversed? *Developmental Psychology, 22,* 223–232.

Schank, R. C., & Abelson, R. (1977). *Scripts, plans, goals and understanding: An inquiry into human knowledge and structures.* Hillsdale, NJ: Erlbaum.

Schaufeli, W. B., Maslach, C., & Marek, T. (1993). *Professional burnout: Recent developments in theory and research.* Washington, DC: Taylor & Francis.

Schiff, M., & Bargal, D. (2000). Helping characteristics of self-help and support groups: Their contribution to participants' subjective well-being. *Small Group Research, 31,* 275–304.

Schlitz, M. (1997). *Dreaming for the community: Subjective experience and collective action among the Anchuar Indians of Ecuador.* Research proposal. Marin, CA: Institute of Noetic Sciences.

Schmidt, D. F., & Boland, S. M. (1986). Structure of perceptions of older adults: Evidence for multiple stereotypes. *Psychology and Aging, 1,* 255–260.

Schmidt, N. B., Lerew, D. R., & Jackson, R. J. (1997). The role of anxiety sensitivity in the pathogenesis of panic: Prospective evaluation of spontaneous panic attacks during acute stress. *Journal of Abnormal Psychology, 106,* 355–364.

Schmidt, S. E., Liddle, H. A., & Dakof, G. A. (1996). Changes in parenting practices and adolescent drug abuse during multidimensional family therapy. *Journal of Family Psychology, 10,* 12–27.

Schneider, K., & May, R. (1995). *The psychology of existence: An integrative, clinical perspective.* New York: McGraw-Hill.

Scholnick, E. K., Nelson, K., Gelman, S. A., & Miller, P. H. (1999). Conceptual development: Piaget's legacy. Mahwah, NJ: Erlbaum.

Schooler, J. W., & Eich, E. (2000). Memory for emotional events. In E. Tulving & F. I. M. Craik (Eds.), The Oxford handbook of memory (pp. 379–392). Oxford, U.K.: Oxford University Press.

Schou, M. (1997). Forty years of lithium treatment. Archives of General Psychiatry, 54, 9–13.

Schreiber, T. A., & Sergent, S. D. (1998). The role of commitment in producing misinformation effects in eyewitness testimony. Psychonomic Bulletin & Review, 5, 443–448.

Schroeder, D. A., Penner, L. A., Dovido, J. F., & Piliavin, J. A. (1995). The psychology of helping and altruism. New York: McGraw-Hill.

Schultz, R., Braun, R. G., & Kluft, R. P. (1989). Multiple personality disorder: Phenomenology of selected variables in comparison to major depression. Dissociation, 2, 45–51.

Schwartz, B. L., & Metcalfe, J. (1992). Cue familiarity but not target retrievability enhances feeling-of-knowing judgments. Journal of Experimental Psychology: Learning, Memory, and Cognition, 18, 1074–1083.

Schwartz, D., & Proctor, L. J. (2000). Community violence exposure and children's social adjustment in the school peer group: The mediating roles of emotion regulation and social cognition. Journal of Consulting and Clinical Psychology, 68, 670–683.

Schwartz, J. M., Stoessel, P. W., Baxter, L. R., Martin, K. M., & Phelps, M. E. (1996). Systematic changes in cerebral glucose metabolic rate after successful behavior modification treatment of obsessive-compulsive disorder. Archives of General Psychiatry, 53, 109–113.

Schwarzer, R. (Ed.). (1992). Self-efficacy: Thought control of action. Washington, DC: Hemisphere.

Schwebel, A. I., & Fine, M. A. (1994). Understanding and helping families: A cognitive-behavioral approach. Hillsdale, NJ: Erlbaum.

Scott, J. P. (1963). The process of primary socialization in canine and human infants. Monographs of the Society for Research in Child Development, 28, 1–47.

Scott, J. P. (1992). Aggression: Functions and control in social systems. Aggressive Behavior, 18, 1–20.

Scott, K. K., Young, A. W., Calder, A. J., Hellawell, D. J., Aggleton, J. P., & Johnson, M. (1997). Impaired auditory recognition of fear and anger following bilateral amygdala lesions. Nature, 385, 254–257.

Scull, A. (1993). A most solitary of afflictions: Madness and society in Britain 1700–1900. London: Yale University Press.

Searle, J. R. (1979a). Metaphor. In A. Ortony (Ed.), Metaphor and thought (pp. 92–123). Cambridge, U.K.: Cambridge University Press.

Searle, J. R. (1979b). Literal meaning. In J. R. Searle (Ed.), Expression and meaning (pp. 117–136). Cambridge, U.K.: Cambridge University Press.

Sears, A., Jacko, J. A., & Dubach, E. M. (2000). International aspects of World Wide Web usability and the role of high-end graphical enhancements. International Journal of Human–Computer Interaction, 12, 241–261.

Segal, S. P., Bola, J. R., & Watson, M. A. (1996). Race, quality of care, and antipsychotic prescribing practices in psychiatric emergency services. Psychiatric Services, 47, 282–286.

Segall, M. H., Ember, C. E., & Ember, M. (1997). Aggression, crime, and warfare. In J. W. Berry, M. H. Segall, & C. Kagitçibasi (Eds.), Handbook of cross-cultural psychology: Vol. 3. Social behaviors and applications (pp. 213–254). Boston: Allyn & Bacon.

Segerstrom, S. C., Taylor, S. E., Kemeny, M. E., & Fahey, J. L. (1998). Optimism is associated with mood, coping and immune change in response to stress. Journal of Personality and Social Psychology, 74, 1646–1655.

Seidenberg, M. S., & Petitto, L. A. (1979). Signing behavior in apes: A critical review. Cognition, 7, 177–215.

Sekuler, R., & Blake, R. (1994). Perception (3rd ed.). New York: McGraw-Hill.

Self, E. A. (1990). Situational influences on self-handicapping. In R. L. Higgins, C. R. Snyder, & S. Berglas (Eds.), Self-handicapping: The paradox that isn't (pp. 37–68). New York: Plenum Press.

Selfridge, O. G. (1955). Pattern recognition and modern computers. Proceedings of the Western Joint Computer Conference. New York: Institute of Electrical and Electronics Engineers.

Seligman, M. E. P. (1971). Preparedness and phobias. Behavior Therapy, 2, 307–320.

Seligman, M. E. P. (1975). Helplessness: On depression, development, and death. San Francisco: Freeman.

Seligman, M. E. P. (1991). Learned optimism. New York: Norton.

Seligman, M. E. P. (1996). Science as an ally of practice. American Psychologist, 51, 1072–1079.

Seligman, M. E. P., & Maier, S. F. (1967). Failure to escape traumatic shock. Journal of Experimental Psychology, 74, 1–9.

Selye, H. (1956). The stress of life. New York: McGraw-Hill.

Selye, H. (1976a). Stress in health and disease. Reading, MA: Butterworth.

Selye, H. (1976b). The stress of life (2nd ed.). New York: McGraw-Hill.

Sereno, S. C. (1995). Resolution of lexical ambiguity: Evidence from an eye movement priming paradigm. Journal of Experimental Psychology: Learning, Memory, and Cognition, 21, 582–595.

Serpell, R. (2000). Intelligence and culture. In R. J. Sternberg (Ed.), Handbook of intelligence (pp. 549–577). Cambridge, U.K.: Cambridge University Press.

Serpell, R., & Boykin, A. W. (1994). Cultural dimensions of cognition: A multiplex, dynamic system of constraints and possibilities. In R. J. Sternberg (Ed.), Handbook of perception and cognition: Vol. 2. Thinking and problem solving (pp. 369–408). Orlando, FL: Academic Press.

Serrano, J. M., Iglesias, J., & Loeches, A. (1992). Visual discrimination and recognition of facial expressions of anger, fear, and surprise in 4- to 6-month-old infants. Developmental Psychobiology, 25, 411–425.

Serrano, J. M., Iglesias, J., & Loeches, A. (1995). Infants' responses to adult static facial expressions. Infant Behavior and Development, 18, 477–482.

Shadish, W. R., Matt, G. E., Navarro, A. M., Siegle, G., Crits-Christoph, P., Hazelrigg, M. D., Jorm, A. F., Lyons, L. C., Nietzel, M. T., Prout, H. T., Robinson, L., Smith, M. L., Svartberg, M., & Weiss, B. (1997). Evidence that therapy works in clinically representative conditions. Journal of Consulting and Clinical Psychology, 65, 355–365.

Shadish, W. R., Montgomery, L. M., Wilson, P., Wilson, M. R., Bright, I., & Okwumabua, T. (1993). Effects of family and marital psychotherapies: A meta-analysis. Journal of Consulting and Clinical Psychology, 61, 992–1002.

Shadish, W. R., Ragsdale, K., Glaser, R. R., & Montgomery, L. M. (1995). The efficacy and effectiveness of marital and family therapy: A perspective from meta-analysis. Journal of Marital and Family Therapy, 21, 345–360.

Shafii, M., Carrigan, S., Whittinghill, J. R., & Derrick, A. (1985). Psychological autopsy of completed suicide in children and adolescents. American Journal of Psychiatry, 142, 1061–1064.

Shafir, E. (1993). Choosing versus rejecting: Why some options are both better and worse than others. Memory & Cognition, 21, 546–556.

Shapiro, K. F. (1998). Animal models of human psychology: Critique of science, ethics, and policy. Seattle, WA: Hogrefe & Huber.

Shapiro, L. P., Nagel, H. N., & Levine, B. A. (1993). Preferences for a verb's complements and their use in sentence processing. Journal of Memory and Language, 32, 96–114.

Shapiro, S. L., Schwartz, G. E., & Bonner, G. (1998). Effects of mindfulness-based stress reduction on medical and premedical students. *Journal of Behavioral Medicine, 21,* 581–599.

Sharps, M., J., Price-Sharps, J. L., & Hanson, J. (1998). Attitudes of young adults toward older adults: Evidence from the United States and Thailand. *Educational Gerontology, 24,* 655–660.

Sharpsteen, D. J., & Kirkpatrick, L. A. (1997). Romantic jealousy and adult romantic attachment. *Journal of Personality and Social Psychology, 72,* 627–640.

Shatz, M., & Gelman, R. (1973). The development of communication skills: Modifications in the speech of young children as a function of listener. *Monographs of the Society for Research in Child Development, 38*(5, Serial No. 152).

Shaver, P. R., & Hazan, C. (1994). Attachment. In A. L. Weber & J. H. Harvey (Eds.), *Perspectives on close relationships* (pp. 110–130). Boston: Allyn & Bacon.

Shavitt, S. (1990). The role of attitude objects in attitude functions. *Journal of Experimental Social Psychology, 26,* 124–148.

Shaywitz, B. A., Shaywitz, S. E., Pugh, K. R., Constable, R. T., Skudlarski, P., Fulbright, K., Bronen, R. A., Fletcher, J. M., Shankweller, D. P., Katz, L., & Gore, J. C. (1995). Sex differences in the functional organization of the brain for language. *Nature, 373,* 607–609.

Shealy, C. N. (1995). From *Boys Town* to *Oliver Twist:* Separating fact from fiction in welfare reform and out-of-home placement for children and youth. *American Psychologist, 50,* 565–580.

Sheehan, E. P. (1993). The effects of turnover on the productivity of those who stay. *Journal of Social Psychology, 133,* 699–706.

Sheldon, W. (1942). *The varieties of temperament: A psychology of constitutional differences.* New York: Harper.

Shepard, R. N. (1978). Externalization of mental images and the act of creation. In B. S. Randhawa & W. E. Coffman (Eds.), *Visual learning, thinking, and communicating.* New York: Academic Press.

Shepard, R. N. (1984). Ecological constraints on internal representation: Resonant kinematics of perceiving, imagining, thinking and dreaming. *Psychological Review, 91,* 417–447.

Shepard, R. N., & Cooper, L. A. (1982). *Mental images and their transformations.* Cambridge, MA: The MIT Press.

Shepard, R. N., & Jordan, D. S. (1984). Auditory illusions demonstrating that tones are assimilated to an internalized musical scale. *Science, 226,* 1333–1334.

Shepp, B., & Ballisteros, M. (Eds.). (1989). *Object perception.* Hillsdale, NJ: Erlbaum.

Sheridan, C. L., & King, R. G. (1972). Obedience to authority with an authentic victim. Proceedings from the 80th Annual Convention, *American Psychological Association, Part I, 7,* 165–166.

Sherif, C. W. (1981, August). *Social and psychological bases of social psychology.* The G. Stanley Hall Lecture on social psychology, presented at the annual convention of the American Psychological Association, Los Angeles.

Sherif, M. (1935). A study of some social factors in perception. *Archives of Psychology, 27*(187).

Sherif, M., Harvey, O. J., White, B. J., Hood, W. R., & Sherif, C. W. (1988). *The Robbers Cave experiment: Intergroup conflict and cooperation.* Middletown, CT: Wesleyan University Press. (Original work published 1961)

Sherrod, K., Vietze, P., & Friedman, S. (1978). *Infancy.* Monterey, CA: Brooks/Cole.

Shettleworth, S. J. (1993). Where is the comparison in comparative cognition? *Psychological Science, 4,* 179–184.

Shiffrar, M. (1994). When what meets where. *Current Directions in Psychological Science, 3,* 96–100.

Shiffrin, R. M. (1993). Short-term memory: A brief commentary. *Memory & Cognition, 21,* 193–197.

Shiffrin, R. M., & Schneider, W. (1977). Controlled and automatic human information processing: II. Perceptual learning, automatic attending, and a general theory. *Psychological Review, 84,* 127–190.

Shimamura, A. P., Berry, J. M., Mangels, J. A., Rusting, C. L., & Jurica, P. J. (1995). Memory and cognitive abilities in university professors: Evidence for successful aging. *Psychological Science, 6,* 271–277.

Shirley, M. M. (1931). *The first two years.* Minneapolis: University of Minnesota Press.

Shneidman, E. S. (1985). *Definition of suicide.* New York: Wiley.

Shneidman, E. S. (1987, March). At the point of no return. *Psychology Today,* pp. 54–59.

Shneidman, E. S. (1999). *Lives and deaths: Selections from the works of Edwin S. Shneidman.* Philadelphia, PA: Brunner/Mazel.

Shoda, Y., & Mischel, W. (1993). Cognitive social approach to dispositional inferences: What if the perceiver is a cognitive social theorist? *Personality and Social Psychology Bulletin, 19,* 574–585.

Shoda, Y., Mischel, W., & Wright, J. C. (1993a). The role of situational demands and cognitive competencies in behavior organization and personality coherence. *Journal of Personality and Social Psychology, 65,* 1023–1035.

Shoda, Y., Mischel, W., & Wright, J. C. (1993b). Links between personality judgments and contextualized behavior patterns: Situation-behavior profiles of personality prototypes. *Social Cognition, 11,* 399–429.

Shortliffe, E. H. (1976). *Computer-based medical consultations—MYCIN.* New York: Elsevier/North Holland.

Shotter, J. (1984). *Social accountability and selfhood.* Oxford: Basil Blackwell.

Shulman, S. (1993). Close friendships in early and middle adolescence: Typology and friendship reasoning. In B. Laursen (Ed.), *Close friendships in adolescence* (pp. 55–71). San Francisco: Jossey-Bass.

Sia, T. L., Lord, C. G., Blessum, K. A., Ratcliff, C. D., & Lepper, M. R. (1997). Is a rose always a rose? The role of social category exemplar change in attitude stability and attitude-behavior consistency. *Journal of Personality and Social Psychology, 72,* 501–514.

Siegel, A. M. (1996). *Heniz Kohut and the psychology of the self.* New York: Routledge.

Siegel, B. (1988). *Love, medicine and miracles.* New York: Harper & Row.

Siegel, R. K. (1992). *Fire in the brain.* New York: Dutton.

Siegel, S. (1984). Pavlovian conditioning and heroin overdose: Reports by overdose victims. *Bulletin of the Psychonomic Society, 22,* 428–430.

Siegel, S. (1999). Drug anticipation and drug addiction: The 1998 H. David Archibald lecture. *Addiction, 94,* 1113–1124.

Siegel, S., Hinson, R. E., Krank, M. D., & McCully, J. (1982). Heroin "overdose" death: The contribution of drug-associated environmental cues. *Science, 216,* 436–437.

Siegelman, M. (1972). Adjustment of homosexual and heterosexual women. *British Journal of Psychiatry, 120,* 477–481.

Siegler, R. S., & Crowley, K. (1991). The microgenetic method: A direct means for studying cognitive development. *American Psychologist, 46,* 606–620.

Silver, E., Cirincione, C., & Steadman, H. J. (1994). Demythologizing inaccurate perceptions of the insanity defense. *Law & Human Behavior, 18,* 63–70.

Silver, R., & Wortman, E. (1980). Coping with undesirable life events. In J. Garber & M. E. P. Seligman (Eds.), *Human helplessness: Theory and application.* New York: Academic Press.

Silverman, A. B., Reinherz, H. Z., & Giaconia, R. M. (1996). The long-term sequelae of child and adolescent abuse: A longitudinal community study. *Child Abuse & Neglect, 20,* 709–723.

Simkin, L. R., & Gross, A. M. (1994). Assessment of coping with high-risk situations for exercise relapse among healthy women. *Health Psychology, 13,* 274–277.

Simmons, J. A., Ferragamo, M. J., & Moss, C. F. (1998). Echo-delay resolution in sonar images of the big brown bat, *Eptesicus fuscus. Proceedings of the National Academy of Sciences of the United States, 95*, 12647–12652.

Simon, H. A. (1973). The structure of ill-structured problems. *Artifical Intelligence, 4*, 181–202.

Simon, H. A. (1979). *Models of thought* (Vol. 1). New Haven: Yale University Press.

Simon, H. A. (1989). *Models of thought* (Vol. 2). New Haven: Yale University Press.

Simons, D. J. (1996). In sight, out of mind: When object representations fail. *Psychological Science, 7*, 301–305.

Simons, D. J. (2000). Current approaches to change blindness. *Visual Cognition, 7*, 1–15.

Sinclair, R. C., Hoffman, C., Mark, M. M., Martin, L. L., & Pickering, T. L. (1994). Construct accessibility and the misattribution of arousal: Schachter and Singer revisited. *Psychological Science, 5*, 15–19.

Singer, D. G., & Singer, J. L. (1990). *The house of make-believe.* Cambridge, MA: Harvard University Press.

Singer, J. L. (Ed.). (1990). *Repression and dissociation.* Chicago: University of Chicago Press.

Singer, M. (1995). *Cults in our midst.* San Francisco: Jossey-Bass.

Sireteanu, R. (1999). Switching on the infant brain. *Science, 286*, 59–61.

Skaar, K. L., Tsoh, J. Y., McClure, J. B., Cinciripini, P. M., Friedman, K., Wetter, D. W., & Gritz, E. R. (1997). Smoking cessation 1: An overview of research. *Behavioral Medicine, 23*, 5–13.

Skibinski, G. J. (1995). The influence of the family preservation model on child sexual abuse intervention strategies: Changes in child welfare worker tasks. *Child Welfare, 74*, 975–989.

Skinner, B. F. (1938). *The behavior of organisms.* New York: Appleton-Century-Crofts.

Skinner, B. F. (1953). *Science and human behavior.* New York: Macmillan.

Skinner, B. F. (1966). What is the experimental analysis of behavior? *Journal of the Experimental Analysis of Behavior, 9*, 213–218.

Skinner, B. F. (1972). *Beyond freedom and dignity.* Toronto: Bantam Books.

Skinner, B. F. (1990). Can psychology be a science of mind? *American Psychologist, 45*, 1206–1210.

Skre, I., Onstad, S., Torgersen, S., Kygren, S., & Kringlen, E. (1993). A twin study of DSM-III-R anxiety disorders. *Acta Psychiatrica Scandinavica, 88*, 85–92.

Sloane, R. B., Staples, F. R., Cristol, A. H., Yorkston, N. J., & Whipple, K. (1975). *Psychotherapy versus behavior therapy.* Cambridge, MA: Harvard University Press.

Slobin, D. I. (1982). Universal and particular in the acquisition of language. In E. Wanner & L. Gleitman (Eds.), *Language acquisition: The state of the art* (pp. 128–170). Cambridge, U.K.: Cambridge University Press.

Slobin, D. I. (1985). Crosslinguistic evidence for the language-making capacity. In D. Slobin (Ed.), *The crosslinguistic study of language acquisition: Vol. 2. Theoretical issues* (pp. 1157–1256). Hillsdale, NJ: Erlbaum.

Slobin, D. I., & Aksu, A. (1982). Tense, aspect, and modality in the use of the Turkish evidential. In P. J. Hopper (Ed.), *Tense-aspect: Between semantics & pragmatics* (pp. 185–200). Amsterdam: Benjamins.

Sloman, S. A., Hayman, C. A. G., Ohta, N., Law, J., & Tulving, E. (1988). Forgetting in primed fragment completion. *Journal of Experimental Psychology: Learning, Memory, and Cognition, 14*, 223–239.

Slovic, P. (1995). The construction of preference. *American Psychologist, 50*, 364–371.

Smith, J., & Baltes, P. B. (1990). Wisdom-related knowledge: Age/cohort differences in response to life-planning problems. *Developmental Psychology, 26*, 494–505.

Smith, M. V. (1996). Linguistic relativity: On hypotheses and confusions. *Communication & Cognition, 29*, 65–90.

Smith, R. J., & Schutte, N. S. (1982). Children's television experience in two cultures. *Educational Psychology, 2*, 137–146.

Smith, S. L., & Donnerstein, E. (1998). Harmful effects of exposure to media violence: Learning of aggression, emotional desensitization, and fear. In R. G. Geen & E. Donnerstein (Eds.), *Human aggression: Theories, research, and implications for public policy* (pp. 167–202). San Diego, CA: Academic Press.

Smith, T. W. (1992). Hostility and health: Current status of a psychosomatic hypothesis. *Health Psychology, 11*, 139–150.

Snyder, M. (1984). When beliefs create reality. In L. Berkowitz (Ed.), *Advances in experimental social psychology* (Vol. 18, pp. 247–305). New York: Academic Press.

Snyder, M., & Haugen, J. A. (1995). Why does behavioral confirmation occur? A functional perspective on the role of the target. *Personality and Social Psychology Bulletin, 21*, 963–974.

Snyder, M., & Swann, W. B., Jr. (1978). Hypothesis-testing processes in social interaction. *Journal of Personality and Social Psychology, 36*, 1202–1212.

Sokal, M. M. (Ed.). (1987). *Psychological testing and American society, 1890–1930.* New Brunswick, NJ: Rutgers University Press.

Solso, R. L., & McCarthy, J. E. (1981). Prototype formation of faces: A case study of pseudomemory. *British Journal of Psychology, 72*, 499–503.

Sommer, W., Heinz, A., Leuthold, H., Matt, J., & Schweinberger, S. R. (1995). Metamemory, distinctiveness, and event-related potentials in recognition memory for faces. *Memory & Cognition, 23*, 1–11.

Spangler, W. D. (1992). Validity of questionnaire and TAT measures of need for achievement: Two meta-analyses. *Psychological Bulletin, 112*, 140–154.

Spanos, N. P. (1994). Multiple identity enactments and multiple personality disorder: A sociocognitive perspective. *Psychological Bulletin, 116*, 143–165.

Spearman, C. (1927). *The abilities of man.* New York: Macmillan.

Spence, M. J., & DeCasper, A. J. (1987). Prenatal experience with low-frequency maternal-voice sounds influences neonatal perception of maternal voice samples. *Infant Behavior and Development, 10*, 133–142.

Spence, M. J., & Freeman, M. S. (1996). Newborn infants prefer the maternal low-pass filtered voice, but not the maternal whispered voice. *Infant Behavior and Development, 19*, 199–212.

Sperling, G. (1960). The information available in brief visual presentations. *Psychological Monographs, 74*, 1–29.

Sperling, G. (1963). A model for visual memory tasks. *Human Factors, 5*, 19–31.

Sperry, R. W. (1968). Mental unity following surgical disconnection of the cerebral hemispheres. *The Harvey Lectures*, Series 62. New York: Academic Press.

Spiegel, D., Bloom, J. R., Kraemer, H. C., & Gottheil, E. (1989, October 14). Effect of psychosocial treatment on survival of patients with metastatic breast cancer. *The Lancet*, pp. 888–891.

Spiegel, D., & Cardeña, E. (1991). Disintegrated experience: The dissociative disorders revisited. *Psychological Bulletin, 100*, 366–378.

Spiegel, D. A., Wiegel, M., Baker, S. L., & Greene, K. A. I. (2000). Pharmacological management of anxiety disorders. In D. I. Mostofsky & D. H. Barlow (Eds.), *The management of stress and anxiety in medical disorders* (pp. 36–65). Boston, MA: Allyn & Bacon.

Spiegler, M. D., & Guevremont, D. C. (1998). *Contemporary behavior therapy* (3rd ed.). Pacific Grove, CA: Brooks/Cole.

Spielman, A. J., & Glovinsky, P. B. (1997). The diagnostic interview and differential diagnosis for complaints of insomnia. In M. R. Pressman & W. C. Orr (Eds.), *Understanding sleep: The evaluation and treatment of sleep disorders* (pp. 125–160). Washington, DC: American Psychological Association.

Spitz, R. A., & Wolf, K. (1946). Anaclitic depression. *Psychoanalytic Study of Children, 2,* 313–342.

Squire, L. R. (1992). Memory and the hippocampus: A synthesis from findings with rats, monkeys, and humans. *Psychological Review, 99,* 195–231.

Squire, L. R., Amaral, D. G., Zola-Morgan, S., Kritchevsky, M., & Press, G. (1989). Description of brain injury in the amnesic patient N. A. based on magnetic resonance imaging. *Experimental Neurology, 105,* 23–35.

Srinivas, K. (1995). Representations of rotated objects in explicit and implicit memory. *Journal of Experimental Psychology: Learning, Memory, and Cognition, 21,* 1019–1036.

Srinivas, K., & Roediger, H. L., III. (1990). Classifying implicit memory tests: Category association and anagram solution. *Journal of Memory and Language, 29,* 389–412.

Stacy, A. W., Newcomb, M. D., & Bentler, P. M. (1991). Cognitive motivation and drug use: A 9-year longitudinal study. *Journal of Abnormal Psychology, 100,* 502–515.

Stahl, S. M. (1998). Getting stoned without inhaling: Anandamide is the brain's natural marijuana. *Journal of Clinical Psychiatry, 59,* 566–567.

Stampfl, T. G., & Levis, D. J. (1967). Essentials of implosive therapy: A learning theory-based psychodynamic behavioral therapy. *Journal of Abnormal Psychology, 72,* 496–503.

Stanford Daily. (1982, February 2, pp. 1, 3, 5). Rape is no accident, say campus assault victims.

Stattin, H., & Magnusson, D. (1996). Antisocial development: A holistic approach. *Development and Psychopathology, 8,* 617–645.

Staub, E. (1989). *The roots of evil: The origins of genocide and other group violence.* New York: Cambridge University Press.

Staub, E. (2000). Genocide and mass killing: Origins, prevention, healing and reconciliation. *Political Psychology, 21,* 367–382.

Steele, C. M. (1988). The psychology of self-affirmation: Sustaining the integrity of the self. In L. Berkowitz (Ed.), *Advances in experimental social psychology* (Vol. 21, pp. 261–302). New York: Academic Press.

Steele, C. M. (1997). A threat in the air: How stereotypes shape intellectual identity and performance. *American Psychologist, 6,* 613–629.

Steele, C. M., & Aronson, J. (1995). Stereotype threat and the intellectual test performance of African Americans. *Journal of Personality and Social Psychology, 69,* 797–811.

Steele, C. M., & Aronson, J. (1998). Stereotype threat and the test performance of academically successful African Americans. In C. Jencks & M. Phillips (Eds.), *The black–white test score gap* (pp. 401–427). Washington, DC: Brookings Institution Press.

Steinberg, L., Lamborn, S. D., Dornbusch, S. M., & Darling, N. (1992). Impact of parenting practices on adolescent achievement: Authoritative parenting, school involvement, and encouragement to succeed. *Child Development, 63,* 1266–1281.

Steininger, M., Newell, J. D., & Garcia, L. T. (1984). *Ethical issues in psychology.* Homewood, IL: Dorsey.

Stemberger, J. P. (1992). The reliability and replicability of naturalistic speech error data: A comparison with experimentally induced errors. In B. J. Baars (Ed.), *Experimental slips and human error: Exploring the architecture of volition* (pp. 195–215). New York: Plenum Press.

Stephan, W. G., Stephan, C. W., & de Vargas, M. C. (1996). Emotional expression in Costa Rica and the United States. *Journal of Cross-Cultural Psychology, 27,* 147–160.

Stephens, R. (1994). *On top of the world.* London: Macmillan.

Stern, K., & McClintock, M. K. (1998). Regulation of ovulation by human pheromones. *Nature, 392,* 177–179.

Stern, M., & Karraker, K. H. (1989). Sex stereotyping of infants: A review of gender labeling studies. *Sex Roles, 20,* 501–522.

Stern, P. C. (1995). Why do people sacrifice for their nations? *Political Psychology, 16,* 217–235.

Stern, W. (1914). The psychological methods of testing intelligence. *Educational Psychology Monographs* (No. 13).

Sternberg, R. J. (1985). *Beyond IQ.* Cambridge, MA: Cambridge University Press.

Sternberg, R. J. (1986). *Intelligence applied.* San Diego: Harcourt Brace Jovanovich.

Sternberg, R. J. (1988). *The triarchic mind: A new theory of human intelligence.* New York: Viking.

Sternberg, R. J. (1994). Intelligence. In R. J. Sternberg (Ed.), *Handbook of perception and cognition: Vol. 2. Thinking and problem solving* (pp. 263–288). Orlando, FL: Academic Press.

Sternberg, R. J., & Lubart, T. I. (1996). Investing in creativity. *American Psychologist, 51,* 677–688.

Sternberg, R. J., & Lubart, T. I. (1999). The concept of creativity: Prospects and paradigms. In R. J. Sternberg (Ed.), *Handbook of creativity* (pp. 3–15). Cambridge, U.K.: Cambridge University Press.

Sternberg, R. J., & O'Hara, L. A. (1999). Creativity and intelligence. In R. J. Sternberg (Ed.), *Handbook of creativity* (pp. 251–272). Cambridge, U.K.: Cambridge University Press.

Sternberg, S. (1966). High-speed scanning in human memory. *Science, 153,* 652–654.

Sternberg, S. (1969). Memory-scanning: Mental processes revealed by reaction time experiments. *American Scientist, 57,* 421–457.

Stevens, J. A., Fonlupt, P., Shiffrar, M., & Decety, J. (2000). New aspects of motion perception: Selective neural encoding of apparent human movements. *Neuroreport, 11,* 109–115.

Stevenson, H. W., Chen, C., & Lee, S. Y. (1993). Mathematics achievement of Chinese, Japanese, and American children: Ten years later. *Science, 259,* 53–58.

Stone, A. A., Neale, J. M., Cox, D. S., Napoli, A., Valdimarsdottir, H., & Kennedy-Moore, E. (1994). Daily events are associated with a secretory immune response to an oral antigen in men. *Health Psychology, 13,* 440–446.

Stone, R. (2000). Stress: The invisible hand in Eastern Europe's death rates. *Science, 288,* 1732–1733.

Strassberg, Z., Dodge, K. A., Pettit, G. S., & Bates, J. E. (1994). Spanking in the home and children's subsequent aggression toward kindergarten peers. *Development and Psychopathology, 6,* 445–461.

Strauch, I., & Lederbogen, S. (1999). The home dreams and waking fantasies of boys and girls between ages 9 and 15: A longitudinal study. *Dreaming, 9,* 153–161.

Straus, M. A., & Kantor, G. K. (1994). Corporal punishment of adolescents by parents: A risk factor in the epidemiology of depression, suicide, alcohol abuse, child abuse, and wife beating. *Adolescence, 29,* 543–561.

Straus, M. A., & Stewart, J. H. (1999). Corporal punishment by American parents: National data on prevalence, chronicity, severity, and duration, in relation to child and family characteristics. *Clinical Child and Family Psychology Review, 2,* 55–70.

Strickland, C. J. (1997). Suicide among American Indian, Alaskan Native, and Canadian aboriginal youth. Advancing the research agenda. *International Journal of Mental Health, 25,* 11–32.

Striegel-Moore, R. H., & Cachelin, F. M. (1999). Body image concerns and disordered eating in adolescent girls: Risk and protective factors. In N. G. Johnson, M. C. Roberts, & J. P. Worell (Eds.), *Beyond appearance: A new look at adolescent girls* (pp. 85–108). Washington, DC: American Psychological Association.

Striegel-Moore, R. H., Silberstein, L. R., & Rodin, J. (1993). The social self in bulimia nervosa: Public self-consciousness, social anxiety, and perceived fraudulence. *Journal of Abnormal Psychology, 102,* 297–303.

Strober, M. (1992). Family-genetic studies. In K. A. Halmi (Ed.), *Psychobiology and treatment of anorexia nervosa and bulimia nervosa* (pp. 61–76). Washington, DC: American Psychiatric Press.

Ström, L., Pettersson, R., & Andersson, G. (2000). A controlled trial of self-help treatment of recurrent headache conducted via the Internet. *Journal of Consulting and Clinical Psychology, 68,* 722–727.

Stunkard, A. J., Harris, J. R., Pedersen, N. L., & McClearn, G. E. (1990). The body mass index of twins who have been reared apart. *New England Journal of Medicine, 322,* 1483–1487.

Substance Abuse and Mental Health Services Administration. (1996). *Preliminary estimates from the 1995 national household survey on drug abuse.* Washington, DC: U.S. Department of Health and Human Services.

Substance Abuse and Mental Health Services Administration (1999). *Summary of findings from the 1998 national household survey on drug abuse* [On-line]. Available: www.samhsa.gov/OAS/NHSDA/98SummHtml/TOC.htm

Suchman, A. L., & Ader, R. (1989). Placebo response in humans can be shaped by prior pharmalogic experience. *Psychosomatic Medicine, 51,* 251.

Sullivan, H. S. (1953). *The interpersonal theory of psychiatry.* New York: Norton.

Sulloway, F. J. (1996). *Born to rebel: Birth order, family dynamics, and creative lives.* New York: Pantheon.

Suls, J., & Marco, C. A. (1990). Relationship between JAS- and FTAS-Type A behavior and non-CHD illness: A prospective study controlling for negative affectivity. *Health Psychology, 9,* 479–492.

Suomi, S. J. (1999). Developmental trajectories, early experiences, and community consequences: Lessons from studies with rhesus monkeys. In D. P. Keating & C. Hertzman (Eds.), *Developmental health and the wealth of nations: Social, biological, and educational dynamics* (pp. 185–200). New York: The Guilford Press.

Suzuki, L. A., & Valencia, R. R. (1997). Race-ethnicity and measured intelligence: Educational implications. *American Psychologist, 52,* 1103–1114.

Svanum, S., McGrew, J., & Ehrmann, L. (1994). Validity of the substance abuse scales of the MMPI-2 in college student sample. *Journal of Personality Assessment, 62,* 427–439.

Swann, W. B., Jr. (1990). To be adored or to be known? The interplay of self-enhancement and self-verification. In R. M. Sorrentino & E. T. Higgins (Eds.), *Handbook of motivation and cognition* (Vol. 2). New York: Guilford Press.

Swann, W. B., Jr. (1997). The trouble with change: Self-verification and allegiance to the self. *Psychological Science, 8,* 177–180.

Swann, W. B., Jr., & Ely, R. J. (1984). A battle of wills: Self-verification versus behavioral confirmation. *Journal of Personality and Social Psychology, 46,* 1287–1302.

Swazey, J. P. (1974). *Chlorpromazine in psychiatry: A study of therapeutic innovation.* Cambridge, MA: The MIT Press.

Sweeney, J. A., Clementz, B. A., Haas, G. L., Escobar, M. D., Drake, K., & Frances, A. J. (1994). Eye tracking dysfunction in schizophrenia: Characterization of component eye movement abnormalities, diagnostic specificity, and the role of attention. *Journal of Abnormal Psychology, 103,* 222–230.

Swim, J. K., Aikin, K. J., Hall, W. S., & Hunter, B. A. (1995). Sexism and racism: Old-fashioned and modern prejudices. *Journal of Personality and Social Psychology, 68,* 199–214.

Szasz, T. (1995). The origin of psychiatry: The alienist as nanny for troublesome adults. *History of Psychiatry, 6,* 1–19.

Szasz, T. S. (1961). *The myth of mental illness.* New York: Harper & Row.

Szasz, T. S. (1977). *The manufacture of models.* New York: Dell.

Szymanski, S., Kane, J. M., & Leiberman, J. A. (1991). A selective review of biological markers in schizophrenia. *Schizophrenia Bulletin, 17,* 99–111.

Tajfel, H. (Ed.). (1982). *Social identity and intergroup relations.* New York: Cambridge University Press.

Tajfel, H., & Billig, M. (1974). Familiarity and categorization in intergroup behavior. *Journal of Experimental Social Psychology, 10,* 159–170.

Tanofsky-Kraff, M., Wilfley, D. E., & Spurrell, E. (2000). Impact of interpersonal and ego-related stress on restrained eaters. *International Journal of Eating Disorders, 27,* 411–418.

Tarr, M. J. (1994). Visual representation: From features to objects. In V. S. Ramachandran (Ed.), *The encyclopedia of human behavior.* San Diego: Academic Press.

Tarr, M. J., & Pinker, S. (1989). Mental rotation and orientation-dependence in shape recognition. *Cognitive Psychology, 21,* 233–282.

Taylor, M., Cartwright, B. S., & Bowden, T. (1991). Perspective taking and theory of mind: Do children predict interpretive diversity as a function of differences in observers' knowledge? *Child Development, 62,* 1334–1351.

Taylor, M. G. (1996). The development of children's beliefs about social and biological aspects of gender differences. *Child Development, 67,* 1555–1571.

Taylor, S. E. (1986). *Health psychology.* New York: Random House.

Taylor, S. E. (1990). Health psychology: The science and the field. *American Psychologist, 45,* 40–50.

Taylor, S. E., & Armor, D. A. (1996). Positive illusions and coping with adversity. *Journal of Personality, 64,* 873–898.

Taylor, S. E., & Brown, J. D. (1988). Illusion and well-being: A social psychological perspective on mental health. *Psychological Bulletin, 103,* 193–210.

Taylor, S. E., & Brown, J. D. (1994). Positive illusions and well-being revisited: Separating fact from fiction. *Psychological Bulletin, 116,* 21–27.

Taylor, S. E., & Clark, L. F. (1986). Does information improve adjustment to noxious events? In M. J. Saks & L. Saxe (Eds.), *Advances in applied social psychology* (Vol. 3, pp. 1–28). Hillsdale, NJ: Erlbaum.

Taylor, S. E., Klein, L. C., Lewis, B. P., Gruenewald, T. L., Gurung, R. A. R., & Updegraff, J. A. (2000). Biobehavioral responses to stress in females: Tend-and-befriend, not fight-or-flight. *Psychological Review, 107,* 411–429.

Teasdale, J. D. (1985). Psychological treatments for depression: How do they work? *Behavior Research and Therapy, 23,* 157–165.

Teasdale, J. D., Segal, Z., & Williams, J. M. G. (1995). How does cognitive therapy prevent depressive relapse and why should attentional control (mindfulness) training help? *Behaviour Research and Therapy, 33,* 25–39.

Tedlock, B. (Ed.). (1987). *Dreaming: Anthropological and psychological interpretations.* Cambridge, U.K.: Cambridge University Press.

Tedlock, B. (1992). The role of dreams and visionary narratives in Mayan cultural survival. *Ethos, 20,* 453–476.

Temoshok, L. (1990). On attempting to articulate the biopsychosocial model: Psychological-psychophysiological homeostasis. In H. S. Friedman (Ed.), *Personality and disease* (pp. 203–225). New York: Wiley.

Temoshok, L., & Dreher, H. (1992). *The Type C connection: The mind–body link to cancer and your health.* New York: Plume.

Templin, M. (1957). Certain language skills in children: Their development and interrelationships. *Institute of Child Welfare Monograph,* Series No. 26. Minneapolis: University of Minnesota Press.

Tenopyr, M. L., & Oeltjen, P. D. (1982). Personnel selection and classification. *Annual Review of Psychology, 33,* 581–618.

Terman, L. M. (1916). *The measurement of intelligence.* Boston: Houghton Mifflin.

Terman, L. M., & Merrill, M. A. (1937). *Measuring intelligence.* Boston: Houghton Mifflin.

Terman, L. M., & Merrill, M. A. (1960). *The Stanford-Binet intelligence scale.* Boston: Houghton Mifflin.

Terman, L. M., & Merrill, M. A. (1972). *Stanford-Binet intelligence scale—manual for the third revision, Form L-M.* Boston: Houghton Mifflin.

Theeuwes, J., Kramer, A. F., Hahn, S., & Irwin, D. E. (1998). Our eyes do not always go where we want them to go: Capture of the eyes by new objects. *Psychological Science, 9,* 379–385.

Thomas, E., & Wingert, P. (2000, June 19). Bitter lessons. *Newsweek, 135,* 50, 51–52.

Thompson, R. F. (1986). The neurobiology of learning and memory. *Science, 233,* 941–944.

Thompson, S. C., Nanni, C., & Levine, A. (1994). Primary versus secondary and central versus consequence-related control in HIV-positive men. *Journal of Personality and Social Psychology, 67,* 540–547.

Thompson, T. (1995). *The beast: A journey through depression.* New York: Plume.

Thoresen, C. E., & Powell, L. H. (1992). Type A behavior pattern: New perspectives on theory, assessment, and intervention. *Journal of Consulting and Clinical Psychology, 60,* 595–604.

Thorndike, E. L. (1898). Animal intelligence. *Psychological Review Monograph Supplement, 2*(4, Whole No. 8).

Thorndike, R. L., Hagen, E. P., & Sattler, J. M. (1986). *Stanford-Binet intelligence scale* (4th ed.). Chicago: Riverside.

Tice, D. M., & Baumeister, R. F. (1990). Self-esteem, self-handicapping, and self-presentation: The strategy of inadequate practice. *Journal of Personality, 58,* 443–464.

Tice, D. M., & Baumeister, R. F. (1997). Longitudinal study of procrastination, performance, stress, and health: The costs and benefits of dawdling. *Psychological Science, 8,* 454–458.

Tidwell, M.-C. O., Reis, H. T., & Shaver, P. R. (1996). Attachment, attractiveness, and social interaction: A diary study. *Journal of Personality and Social Psychology, 71,* 729–745.

Titchener, E. B. (1898). The postulates of structural psychology. *Philosophical Review, 7,* 449–453.

Todd, J. T., & Morris, E. K. (1992). Case histories in the great power of steady misrepresentation. *American Psychologist, 47,* 1441–1453.

Todd, J. T., & Morris, E. K. (1993). Change and be ready to change again. *American Psychologist, 48,* 1158–1159.

Todrank, J., & Bartoshuk, L. M. (1991). A taste illusion: Taste sensation localized by touch. *Physiology & Behavior, 50,* 1027–1031.

Tolman, E. C. (1948). Cognitive maps in rats and men. *Psychological Review, 55,* 189–208.

Tolman, E. C., & Honzik, C. H. (1930). "Insight" in rats. *University of California Publications in Psychology, 4,* 215–232.

Tomkins, S. (1962). *Affect, imagery, consciousness* (Vol. 1). New York: Springer.

Tomkins, S. (1981). The quest for primary motives; Biography and autobiography of an idea. *Journal of Personality and Social Psychology, 41,* 306–329.

Tomoyasu, N., Bovbjerg, D. H., & Jacobsen, P. B. (1996). Conditioned reactions to cancer chemotherapy: Percent reinforcement predicts anticipatory nausea. *Physiology & Behavior, 59,* 273–276.

Torrance, E. P. (1974). *The Torrance tests of creative thinking: Technical-norms manual.* Bensenville, IL: Scholastic Testing Services.

Toth, J. P., Reingold, E. M., & Jacoby, L. L. (1994). Toward a redefinition of implicit memory: Process dissociations following elaborative processing and self-generation. *Journal of Experimental Psychology: Learning, Memory, and Cognition, 20,* 290–303.

Townsend, J. T. (1971). A note on the identifiability of parallel and serial processes. *Perception & Psychophysics, 10,* 161–163.

Townsend, J. T. (1990). Serial vs. parallel processing: Sometimes they look like Tweedledum and Tweedledee but they can (and should) be distinguished. *Psychological Science, 1,* 46–54.

Trainor, L. J., Austin, C. M., & Desjardins, R. N. (2000). Is infant-directed speech prosody a result of the vocal expression of emotion? *Psychological Science, 11,* 188–195.

Treisman, A. (1960). Contextual cues in selective listening. *Quarterly Journal of Experimental Psychology, 12,* 242–248.

Treisman, A., & Gormican, S. (1988). Feature analysis in early vision: Evidence from search asymmetries. *Psychological Review, 95,* 15–48.

Treisman, A., & Sato, S. (1990). Conjunction search revisited. *Journal of Experimental Psychology: Human Perception and Performance, 16,* 459–478.

Triandis, H. C. (1990). Cross-cultural studies of individualism and collectivism. In J. Berman (Ed.), *Nebraska Symposium on Motivation, 1989* (pp. 41–133). Lincoln: University of Nebraska Press.

Triandis, H. C. (1994). *Culture and social behavior.* New York: McGraw-Hill.

Triandis, H. C. (1995). *Individualism and collectivism.* Boulder, CO: Westview.

Trinder, J. (1988). Subjective insomnia without objective findings: A pseudodiagnostic classification. *Psychological Bulletin, 103,* 87–94.

Trivers, R. L. (1971). The evolution of reciprocal altruism. *Quarterly Review of Biology, 46,* 35–57.

Trivers, R. L. (1972). Parental investment and sexual selection. In B. Campbell (Ed.), *Sexual selection and the descent of man* (pp. 139–179). Chicago: Aldine.

Trueswell, J. C. (1996). The role of lexical frequency in syntactic ambiguity resolution. *Journal of Memory and Language, 35,* 566–585.

Tsoh, J. Y., McClure, J. B., Skaar, K. L., Wetter, D. W., Cinciripini, P. M., Prokhorov, A. V., Friedman, K., & Gritz, E. (1997). Smoking cessation 2: Components of effective intervention. *Behavioral Medicine, 23,* 15–27.

Tsuang, M. (2000). Schizophrenia: Genes and environment. *Biological Psychiatry, 47,* 210–220.

Tulving, E. (1972). Episodic and semantic memory. In E. Tulving & W. Donaldson (Eds.), *Organization of memory.* New York: Academic Press.

Tulving, E. (1985). Memory and consciousness. *Canadian Psychology, 26,* 1–12.

Tulving, E., Kapur, S., Craik, F. I. M., Moscovitch, M., & Houle, S. (1994). Hemispheric encoding/retrieval asymmetry in episodic memory: Positron emission tomography findings. *Proceedings of the National Academy of Sciences of the United States of America, 91,* 2016–2020.

Tulving, E., & Thompson, D. M. (1973). Encoding specificity and retrieval processes in episodic memory. *Psychological Review, 80,* 352–373.

Tupes, E. G., & Christal, R. C. (1961). *Recurrent personality factors based on trait ratings* (Tech. Rep. No. ASD-TR–61–97). Lackland Air Force Base, TX: U.S. Air Force.

Turk, D. C. (1994). Perspectives on chronic pain: The role of psychological factors. *Current Directions in Psychological Science, 3,* 45–48.

Turnbull, C. (1961). *The forest people.* New York: Simon & Schuster.

Turner, M. E., & Pratkanis, A. R. (1998). A social identity maintenance model of groupthink. *Organizational Behavior and Human Decision Processes, 73,* 210–235.

Tversky, A., & Kahneman, D. (1973). Availability: A heuristic for judging frequency and probability. *Cognitive Psychology, 5*, 207–232.

Tversky, A., & Kahneman, D. (1974). Judgment under uncertainty: Heuristics and biases. *Science, 185*, 1124–1131.

Tversky, A., & Kahneman, D. (1981). The framing of decisions and the psychology of choice. *Science, 211*, 453–458.

Tversky, A., & Shafir, E. (1992). Choice under conflict: The dynamics of deferred decision. *Psychological Science, 3*, 358–361.

Tyler, L. E. (1965). *The psychology of human differences* (3rd ed.). New York: Appleton-Century-Crofts.

Underwood, B. J. (1948). Retroactive and proactive inhibition after five and forty-eight hours. *Journal of Experimental Psychology, 38*, 28–38.

Underwood, B. J. (1949). Proactive inhibition as a function of time and degree of prior learning. *Journal of Experimental Psychology, 39*, 24–34.

U. S. Department of Health and Human Services. (2000). *Reducing tobacco use: A report of the Surgeon General.* Atlanta, GA: U.S. Department of Health and Human Services.

Urban, J., Carlson, E., Egeland, B., & Stroufe, L. A. (1991). Patterns of individual adaptation across childhood. *Development and Psychopathology, 3*, 445–460.

Uttal, D. H., & Perlmutter, M. (1989). Toward a broader conceptualization of development: The role of gains and losses across the life span. *Developmental Review, 9*, 101–132.

Vahtera, J., Kivimaeki, M., Uutela, A., & Pentti, J. (2000). Hostility and ill health: Role of psychosocial resources in two contexts of working life. *Journal of Psychosomatic Research, 48*, 89–98.

Vaillant, G. E. (1977). *Adaptation to life.* Boston: Little, Brown.

Valenstein, E. S. (Ed.). (1980). *The psychosurgery debate.* New York: Freeman.

Valenza, E., Simion, F., Cassia, V. M., & Umilta, C. (1996). Face preference at birth. *Journal of Experimental Psychology: Human Perception & Performance, 22*, 892–903.

Vandewater, K., & Vickers, Z. (1996). Higher-protein foods produce greater sensory-specific satiety. *Physiology & Behavior, 59*, 579–583.

Van Essen, D. C., Anderson, C. H., & Felleman, D. J. (1992). Information processing in the primate visual system: An integrated systems perspective. *Science, 255*, 419–422.

Van IJzendoorn, M. H., & Kroonenberg, P. M. (1988). Cross-cultural patterns of attachment: A meta-analysis of the Strange Situation. *Child Development, 59*, 147–156.

Van Vianen, A. E. M. (2000). Person-organization fit: The match between newcomers' and recruiters' preferences for organizational culture. *Personnel Psychology, 53*, 113–149.

Vasari, G. (1967). *Lives of the most eminent painters.* New York: Heritage. (Original work published 1568)

Vaughan, E. (1993). Chronic exposure to an environmental hazard: Risk perceptions and self-protective behaviors. *Health Psychology, 12*, 74–85.

Vaughan, E., & Seifert, M. (1992). Variability in the framing of risk issues. *Journal of Social Issues, 48*(4), 119–135.

Veith, I. (1965). *Hysteria: The history of the disease.* Chicago: University of Chicago Press.

Vinje, W. E., & Gallant, J. L. (2000). Sparse coding and decorrelation in primary visual cortex during natural vision. *Science, 287*, 1273–1276.

Vita, A., Dieci, M., Silenzi, C., Tenconi, F., Giobbio, G. M., & Invernizzi G. (2000). Cerebral ventricular enlargement as a generalized feature of schizophrenia: A distribution analysis on 502 subjects. *Schizophrenia Research, 44*, 25–34.

Vonnegut, M. (1975). *The Eden express.* New York: Bantam.

Voss, J. F., Kennet, J., Wiley, J., & Schooler, T. Y. E. (1992). Experts at debate: The use of metaphor in the U.S. Senate Debate on the Gulf Crisis. *Metaphor and Symbolic Activity, 7*, 197–214.

Vrana, S., & Lauterbach, D. (1994). Prevalence of traumatic events and post-traumatic psychological symptoms in a nonclinical sample of college students. *Journal of Traumatic Stress, 7*, 289–302.

Vroom, V. H. (1964). *Work and motivation.* New York: Wiley.

Vu, H., Kellas, G., Metcalf, K., & Herman, R. (2000). The influence of global discourse on lexical ambiguity resolution. *Memory & Cognition, 28*, 236–252.

Vu, H., Kellas, G., & Paul, S. T. (1998). Sources of constraint on lexical ambiguity resolution. *Memory & Cognition, 26*, 979–1001.

Wade, E., & Clark, H. H. (1993). Reproduction and demonstration in quotation. *Journal of Memory and Language, 32*, 805–819.

Wagner, A. D., Schacter, D. L., Rotte, M., Koutstaal, W., Maril, A., Dale, A. M., Rosen, B. R., & Buckner, R. L. (1998). Building memories: Remembering and forgetting of verbal experiences as predicted by brain activity. *Science, 281.* 1188–1191.

Walden, J., Normann, C., Langosch, J., Berger, M., & Grunze, H. (1998). Differential treatment of bipolar disorder with old and new antiepileptic drugs. *Neuropsychobiology, 38*, 181–184.

Walker, L. G., Hays, S. D., & Eremin, O. (1999). Surviving cancer: Do psychosocial factors count? *Journal of Psychosomatic Research, 47*, 497–503.

Walker, L. J. (1984). Sex differences in the development of moral reasoning: A critical review. *Child Development, 55*, 667–691.

Walker, L. J. (1986). Sex differences in the development of moral reasoning: A rejoinder to Baumrind. *Child Development, 57*, 522–526.

Wallace, S. T., & Alden, L. E. (1997). Social phobia and positive social events: The price of success. *Journal of Abnormal Psychology, 106*, 416–424.

Wallach, M. A., & Kogan, N. (1965). *Modes of thinking in young children.* New York: Holt, Rinehart & Winston.

Wallach, M. A., & Wallach, L. (1983). *Psychology's sanction for selfishness.* San Francisco: Freeman.

Wallis, C. (1984, June 11). Unlocking pain's secrets. *Time,* pp. 58–66.

Walsh, R. N. (1990). *The spirit of shamanism.* Los Angeles: J. P. Tarcher.

Walster, E., Aronson, V., Abrahams, D., & Rottman, L. (1966). Importance of physical attractiveness in dating behavior. *Journal of Personality and Social Psychology, 5*, 508–516.

Walters, C. C., & Grusec, J. E. (1977). *Punishment.* San Francisco: Freeman.

Wanous, J. P. (1980). *Organizational entry: Recruitment, selection and socialization of newcomers.* Reading, MA: Addison-Wesley.

Ward, C. D., & Cooper, R. P. (1999). A lack of evidence in 4-month-old human infants for paternal voice preference. *Developmental Psychobiology, 35*, 49–59.

Warren, R. M. (1970). Perceptual restoration of missing speech sounds. *Science, 167*, 392–393.

Washburn, M. (1908). *The animal mind.* New York: Macmillan.

Wasserman, E. A. (1993). Comparative cognition: Beginning the second century of study of animal intelligence. *Psychological Bulletin, 113*, 211–228.

Wasserman, E. A. (1994). Animal learning and comparative cognition. In I. P. Levin & J. V. Hinrichs (Eds.), *Experimental psychology: Contemporary methods and applications* (pp. 117–164). Dubuque, IA: Brown & Benchmark.

Wasserman, E. A., DeVolder, C. L., & Coppage, D. J. (1992). Non-similarity-based conceptualization in pigeons via secondary or mediated generalization. *Psychological Science, 3,* 374–379.

Wasserman, E. A., Hugart, J. A., & Kirkpatrick-Steger, K. (1995). Pigeons show same-different conceptualization after training with complex visual stimuli. *Journal of Experimental Psychology: Animal Behavior Processes, 21,* 248–252.

Watkins, L. R., & Mayer, D. J. (1982). Organization of the endogenous opiate and nonopiate pain control systems. *Science, 216,* 1185–1193.

Watson, J. B. (1913). Psychology as the behaviorist views it. *Psychological Review, 20,* 158–177.

Watson, J. B. (1919). *Psychology from the standpoint of a behaviorist.* Philadelphia: Lippincott.

Watson, J. B. (1924). *Behaviorism.* New York: Norton.

Watson, J. B., & Rayner, R. (1920). Conditioned emotional reactions. *Journal of Experimental Psychology, 3,* 1–14.

Watterlond, M. (1983). The holy ghost people. Reprinted in A. L. Hammond & P. G. Zimbardo (Eds.), *Readings on human behavior: The best of* Science *'80–'86* (pp. 48–55). Glenview, IL: Scott, Foresman.

Watts, M. W. (1996). Political xenophobia in the transition from socialism: Threat, racism and ideology among East German youths. *Political Psychology, 17,* 97–126.

Wearden, A. J., Tarrier, N., Barrowclough, C., Zastowny. T. R., & Rahill, A. A. (2000). A review of expressed emotion research in health care. *Clinical Psychology Review, 20,* 633–666.

Webb, W. B. (1974). Sleep as an adaptive response. *Perceptual and Motor Skills, 38,* 1023–1027.

Wechsler, D. (1981). *Manual for the Wechsler Adult Intelligence Scale—revised.* New York: Psychological Corporation.

Wechsler, D. (1989). *WPPSI-R manual.* New York: Psychological Corporation.

Wechsler, D. (1991). *WISC-III manual.* New York: Psychological Corporation.

Wedekind, C., & Milinski, M. (2000). Cooperation through image scoring in humans. *Science, 288,* 850–852.

Weinberger, M., Hiner, S. L., & Tierney, W. M. (1987). In support of hassles as a measure of stress in predicting health outcomes. *Journal of Behavioral Medicine, 10,* 19–31.

Weiner, J. (1994). *The beak of the finch.* New York: Knopf.

Weinfield, N. S., Ogawa, J. R., & Sroufe, L. A. (1997). Early attachment as a pathway to adolescent peer competence. *Journal of Research on Adolescence, 7,* 241–265.

Weingardt, K. R., Loftus, E. F., & Lindsay, D. S. (1995). Misinformation revisited: New evidence for the suggestibility of memory. *Memory & Cognition, 23,* 72–82.

Weisberg, R. W. (1986). *Creativity: Genius and other myths.* New York: Freeman.

Weisberg, R. W. (1994). Genius and madness? A quasi-experimental test of the hypothesis that manic-depression increases creativity. *Psychological Science, 5,* 361–367.

Weisberg, R. W. (1996). Causality, quality, and creativity: A reply to Repp. *Psychological Science, 7,* 123–124.

Weiskrantz, L. (1995). Blindsight—not an island unto itself. *Current Directions in Psychological Science, 4,* 146–151.

Weiskrantz, L., Warington, E. K., Sanders, M. D., & Marshall, J. (1974). Visual capacity in the hemianopic field following a restricted occipital ablation. *Brain, 97,* 709–728.

Weldon, M. S., Roediger, H. L., III, Beitel, D. A., Johnston, T. R. (1995). Perceptual and conceptual processes in implicit and explicit tests with picture fragment and word fragment cues. *Journal of Memory & Language, 34,* 268–285.

Wellman, H. M., & Gelman, S. A. (1992). Cognitive development: Foundational theories of core domains. *Annual Review of Psychology, 43,* 337–375.

Wellman, H. M., & Inagaki, K. (1997). *The emergence of core domains of thought.* San Francisco: Jossey-Bass.

Wells, S. (1869). *How to read character: A new illustrated handbook of phrenology and physiognomy.* New York: Fowler & Wells.

Werker, J. F. (1991). The ontogeny of speech perception. In I. G. Mattingly & M. Studdert-Kennedy (Eds.), *Modularity and the motor theory of speech perception* (pp. 91–109). Hillsdale, NJ: Erlbaum.

Werker, J. F., & Lalond, F. M. (1988). Cross-language speech perception: Initial capabilities and developmental change. *Developmental Psychology, 24,* 672–683.

Werker, J. F., & Tees, R. C. (1999). Influences on infant speech processing: Toward a new synthesis. *Annual Review of Psychology, 50,* 509–535.

Wertheim, E. H., Paxton, S. J., Schutz, H. K., & Muir, S. L. (1997). Why do adolescent girls watch their weight? An interview study examining sociocultural pressures to be thin. *Journal of Psychosomatic Research, 42,* 345–355.

Wertheimer, M. (1923). Untersuchungen zur lehre von der gestalt, II. *Psychologische Forschung, 4,* 301–350.

Westen, D. (1998). The scientific legacy of Sigmund Freud: Toward a psychodynamically informed psychological science. *Psychological Bulletin, 124,* 333–371.

Wever, E. G. (1949). *Theory of hearing.* New York: Wiley.

Wheeler, D. L. (1998). Global culture or culture clash: New information technologies in the Islamic world—A view from Kuwait. *Communication Research, 25,* 359–376.

Whitbourne, S. K., & Hulicka, I. M. (1990). Ageism in undergraduate psychology texts. *American Psychologist, 45,* 1127–1136.

White, J. L., & Mitler, M. M. (1997). The diagnostic interview and differential diagnosis for complaints of excessive daytime sleepiness. In M. R. Pressman & W. C. Orr (Eds.), *Understanding sleep: The evaluation and treatment of sleep disorders* (pp. 161–175). Washington, DC: American Psychological Association.

White, R. K. (1996). Why the Serbs fought: Motives and misperceptions. *Peace and Conflict: Journal of Peace Psychology, 2,* 109–128.

Whitman, M. (Ed.). (1993). *Removing the badge of slavery: The record of* Brown v. Board of Education. New York: Markus Wiener.

Whorf, B. L. (1956). In J. B. Carroll (Ed.), *Language, and reality: Selected writings of Benjamin Lee Whorf.* Cambridge, MA: The MIT Press.

Wicklund, R. A., & Brehm, J. W. (1976). *Perspectives on cognitive dissonance.* Hillsdale, NJ: Erlbaum.

Widdig, A., Streich, W. J., & Tembrock, G. (2000). Coalition formation among male Barbary macaques (*Macaca sylvanus*). *American Journal of Primatology, 51,* 37–51.

Wiggins, J. S. (1973). *Personality and prediction: Principles of personality and prediction: Principles of personality assessment.* Reading, MA: Addison-Wesley.

Wiggins, J. S., & Pincus, A. L. (1992). Personality: Structure and assessment. *Annual Review of Psychology, 43,* 473–504.

Williams, D. R. (1999). Race, socioeconomic status, and health: The added effects of racism and discrimination. *Annals of the New York Academy of Sciences, 896,* 173–188.

Williams, L. M. (1995). Recovered memories of abuse in women with documented child sexual victimization histories. *Journal of Traumatic Stress, 8,* 649–673.

Williams, W. M., & Ceci, S. J. (1997). Are Americans becoming more or less alike? Trends in race, class, and ability differences in intelligence. *American Psychologist, 52,* 1226–1235.

Williamson, G. M., Clark, M. S., Pegalis, L. J., & Behan, A. (1996). Affective consequences of refusing to help in communal and exchange relationships. *Personality and Social Psychology Bulletin, 22,* 34–47.

Wilson, D. S., & Jacobson, C. K. (1995). White attitudes towards black and white interracial marriage. In C. K. Jacobson (Ed.), *American families: Issues in race and ethnicity* (pp. 353–367). New York: Garland.

Wilson, F. A. W., Scalaidhe, S. P. O., & Goldman-Rakic, P. S. (1993). Dissociation of object and spatial processing domains in primate prefrontal cortex. *Science, 260,* 1955–1958.

Wilson, T. D., Houston, C. E., Etling, K. M., & Brekke, N. (1996). A new look at anchoring effects: Basic anchoring and its antecedents. *Journal of Experimental Psychology: General, 125,* 387–402.

Winarick, K. (1997). Visions of the future: The analyst's expectations and their impact on the analytic process. *American Journal of Psychoanalysis, 57,* 95–109.

Windy, D., & Ellis, A. (1997). *The practice of rational emotive behavior therapy.* New York: Springer.

Witt, S. D. (1997). Parental influence of children's socialization to gender roles. *Adolescence, 32,* 253–259.

Wolf, M., Risley, T., & Mees, H. (1964). Application of operant conditioning procedures to the behavior problems of an autistic child. *Behavior Research and Therapy, 1,* 305–312.

Wolfe, J. M. (1992). The parallel guidance of visual attention. *Current Directions in Psychological Science, 1,* 124–128.

Wolfe, J. M. (1994). A revised model of visual search. *Psychonomic Bulletin & Review, 1,* 202–238.

Wolfe, J. M., Friedman-Hill, S. R., & Bilsky, A. B. (1994). Parallel processing of part-whole information in visual search tasks. *Perception & Psychophysics, 55,* 537–550.

Wolfe, J. M., & Gancarz, G. (1996). Guided Search 3.0: A model of visual search catches up with Jay Enoch 40 years later. In V. Lakshminarayanan (Ed.), *Basic and clinical applications of vision science* (pp. 189–192). Dordrecht, Netherlands: Kluwer Academic.

Wolfson, A. R., & Carskadon, M. A. (1998). Sleep schedules and daytime functioning in adolescents. *Child Development, 69,* 875–887.

Wolman, C. (1975). Therapy and capitalism. *Issues in Radical Therapy, 3*(1).

Wolpe, J. (1958). *Psychotherapy by reciprocal inhibition.* Stanford, CA: Stanford University Press.

Wolpe, J. (1973). *The practice of behavior therapy* (2nd ed.). New York: Pergamon Press.

Wolpe, J. (1986). Misconceptions about behaviour therapy: Their sources and consequences. *Behaviour Change, 3,* 9–15.

Wood, J. M., & Bootzin, R. R. (1990). The prevalence of nightmares and their independence from anxiety. *Journal of Abnormal Psychology, 99,* 64–68.

Wood, J. M., Bootzin, R. R., Kihlstrom, J. F., & Schacter, D. L. (1992). Implicit and explicit memory for verbal information presented during sleep. *Psychological Science, 3,* 236–239.

Wood, J. M., Bootzin, R. R., Rosenhan, D., Nolen-Hoeksema, S., & Jourden, F. (1992). Effects of the 1989 San Francisco earthquake on frequency and content of nightmares. *Journal of Abnormal Psychology, 101,* 219–224.

Wood, J. M., Nezworski, M. T., & Stejskal, W. J. (1996a). The comprehensive system for the Rorschach: A critical examination. *Psychological Science, 7,* 3–10.

Wood, J. M., Nezworski, M. T., & Stejskal, W. J. (1996b). Thinking critically about the comprehensive system for the Rorschach: A reply to Exner. *Psychological Science, 7,* 14–17.

Wood, N., & Cowan, N. (1995a). The cocktail party phenomenon revisited: How frequent are attention shifts to one's name in an irrelevant auditory channel? *Journal of Experimental Psychology: Learning, Memory, and Cognition, 21,* 255–260.

Wood, N., & Cowan, N. (1995b). The cocktail party phenomenon revisited: Attention and memory in the classic selective listening procedure of Cherry (1953). *Journal of Experimental Psychology: General, 124,* 243–262.

Wood, R. E., & Bandura, A. (1989). Impact of conceptions of ability on self-regulatory mechanisms and complex decision making. *Journal of Personality and Social Psychology, 56,* 407–415.

Wood, W. (2000). Attitude change: Persuasion and social influence. *Annual Review of Psychology, 51,* 539–570.

Wood, W., Lundgren, S., Ouellette, J. A., Busceme, S., & Blackstone, T. (1994). Minority influence: A meta-analytic review of social influence processes. *Psychological Bulletin, 115,* 323–345.

Wood, W., Pool, G. J., Leck, K., & Purvis, D. (1996). Self-definition, defensive processing, and influence: The normative impact of majority and minority groups. *Journal of Personality and Social Psychology, 71,* 1181–1193.

Woods, C. J. P. (1996). Gender differences in moral development and acquisition: A review of Kohlberg's and Gilligan's models of justice and care. *Social Behavior and Personality, 24,* 375–384.

Woods, S. C., Seeley, R. J., Porte, D., Jr., & Schwartz, M. W. (1998). Signals that regulate food intake and homeostasis. *Science, 280,* 1378–1383.

Worchel, S., Lee, J., & Adewole, A. (1975). Effects of supply and demand on ratings of object value. *Journal of Personality and Social Psychology, 32,* 906–914.

Workman, B. (1990, December 1). Father guilty of killing daughter's friend, in '69. *San Francisco Examiner-Chronicle,* pp. 1, 4.

Worthington, E. L., Jr., Martin, G. A., Shumate, M., & Carpenter, J. (1983). The effect of brief Lamaze training and social encouragement on pain endurance in a cold pressor task. *Journal of Applied Social Psychology, 13,* 223–233.

Wortman, C. B., & Silver, R. C. (1989). The myths of coping with loss. *Journal of Consulting and Clinical Psychology, 57,* 349–357.

Wortman, C. B., Silver, R. C., & Kessler, R. C. (1993). The meaning of loss and adjustment to bereavement. In M. S. Stroebe, W. Stroebe, & R. O. Hansson (Eds.), *Handbook of bereavement: Theory, research, and intervention* (pp. 349–366). Cambridge: Cambridge University Press.

Wright, E. R., Gronfein, W. P., & Owens, T. J. (2000). Deinstitutionalization, social rejection, and the self-esteem of former mental patients. *Journal of Health and Social Behavior, 41,* 68–90.

Wright, R. (1994). *The moral animal.* New York: Pantheon Books.

Wundt, W. (1907). *Outlines of psychology* (7th ed., C. H. Judd, Trans.). Leipzig: Englemann. (Original work published 1896)

Yantis, S. (1993). Stimulus-driven attentional capture. *Current Directions in Psychological Science, 2,* 156–161.

Yantis, S., & Jonides, J. (1996). Attentional capture by abrupt onsets: New perceptual objects or visual masking? *Journal of Experimental Psychology: Human Perception and Performance, 22,* 1505–1513.

Yates, B. (1985). *Self-management.* Belmont, CA: Wadsworth.

Yau, J., & Smetana, J. G. (1996). Adolescent–parent conflict among Chinese adolescents in Hong Kong. *Child Development, 67,* 1262–1275.

Yerkes, R. M., & Dodson, J. D. (1908). The relation of strength of stimulus to rapidity of habit formation. *Journal of Comparative Neurology and Psychology, 18,* 459–482.

Young, K. (1998). *Caught in the net: How to recognize the signs of Internet addiction and a winning strategy for recovery.* New York: Wiley.

Young, M. A., Meaden, P. M., Fogg, L. F., Cherin, E. A., & Eastman, C. I. (1997). Which environmental variables are related to the onset of seasonal affective disorder? *Journal of Abnormal Psychology, 106,* 554–562.

Young, M. E., Wasserman, E. A., & Dalrymple R. M. (1997). Memory-based *same-different* conceptualization by pigeons. *Psychonomic Bulletin & Review, 4,* 552–558.

Youniss, J., & Smollar, J. (1985). *Adolescent relations with mothers, fathers, and friends.* Chicago: University of Chicago Press.

Yzer, M. C., Fisher, J. D., Bakker, A. B., Siero, F. W., & Misovich, S. J. (1998). The effects of information about AIDS risk and self-efficacy on women's intentions to engage in AIDS preventive behavior. *Journal of Applied Social Psychology, 28,* 1837–1852.

Zahn-Waxler, C., Friedman, R. J., Cole, P. M., Mizuta, I., & Hiruma, N. (1996). Japanese and United States preschool children's responses to conflict and distress. *Child Development, 67,* 2462–2477.

Zajonc, R. B. (1968). Attitudinal effects of mere exposure. *Journal of Personality and Social Psychology. Monograph Supplement, 9*(2, Part 2), 1–27.

Zajonc, R. B. (1980). Feeling and thinking: Preferences need no inferences. *American Psychologist, 35,* 151–175.

Zajonc, R. B. (2000). Feeling and thinking: Closing the debate over the independence of affect. In J. P. Forgas (Ed.), *Feeling and thinking: The role of affect in social cognition* (pp. 31–58). New York: Cambridge University Press.

Zaslow, M. J. (1991). Variation in child care quality and its implications for children. *Journal of Social Issues, 47,* 125–138.

Zeiss, R. A., & Dickman, H. R. (1989). PTSD 40 years later: Incidence and person-situation correlates in former POWs. *Journal of Clinical Psychology, 45,* 80–87.

Zelazo, P. D., Helwig, C. C., & Lau, A. (1996). Intention, act, and outcome in behavioral prediction and moral judgment. *Child Development, 67,* 2478–2492.

Zelinski, E. M., Gilewski, M. J., & Schaie, K. W. (1993). Individual differences in cross-sectional and 3-year longitudinal memory performance across the adult life span. *Psychology and Aging, 8,* 176–186.

Zentall, T. R., Sutton, J. E., & Sherburne, L. M. (1996). True imitative learning in pigeons. *Psychological Science, 7,* 343–346.

Zhang, Y., Proenca, R., Maffel, M., Barone, M., Leopold, L., & Friedman, J. M. (1994). Positional cloning of the mouse *obese* gene and its human homologue. *Nature, 372,* 425–432.

Zigler, E., & Muenchow, S. (1992). *Head Start: The inside story of America's most successful educational experiment.* New York: Basic Books.

Zigler, E., & Styfco, S. J. (1994). Head Start: Criticisms in a constructive context. *American Psychologist, 49,* 127–132.

Zilboorg, G., & Henry, G. W. (1941). *A history of medical psychology.* New York: Norton.

Zimbardo, P. G. (1975). On transforming experimental research into advocacy for social change. In M. Deutsch & H. Hornstein (Eds.), *Applying social psychology: Implications for research, practice and training.* Hillsdale, NJ: Erlbaum.

Zimbardo, P. G. (1991). *Shyness: What it is, what to do about it* (Rev. ed.). Reading, MA: Addison-Wesley. (Original book published 1977)

Zimbardo, P. G., & Andersen, S. A. (1993). Understanding mind control: Exotic and mundane mental manipulations. In M. Lagnone (Ed.), *Recovery from cults* (pp. 104–125). New York: Norton.

Zimbardo, P. G., & Leippe, M. (1991). *The psychology of attitude change and social influence.* New York: McGraw-Hill.

Zimbardo, P. G., & Montgomery, K. D. (1957). The relative strengths of consummatory responses in hunger, thirst, and exploratory drive. *Journal of Comparative and Physiological Psychology, 50,* 504–508.

Zimmerman, B. J., Bandura, A., & Martinez-Pons, M. (1992). Self-motivation for academic attainment: The role of self-efficacy beliefs and personal goal setting. *American Educational Research Journal, 29,* 663–676.

Zuckerman, M. (1988). Sensation seeking, risk taking, and health. In M. P. Janisse (Ed.), *Individual differences, stress, and health psychology* (pp. 72–88). New York: Springer-Verlag.

Zuckerman, M. (1990). Some dubious premises in research and theory on racial differences: Scientific, social, and ethical issues. *American Psychologist, 45,* 1297–1303.

Zwaan, R. A., & Radvansky, G. A. (1998). Situation models in language comprehension and memory. *Psychological Bulletin, 123,* 162–185.

Name Index

A

AAMR, 296
Abdolali, N., 593
Abelin, T., 25
Abrams, R., 525
Abramson, L. Y., 486
Acierno, R., 412
Acker, L. E., 191
Adams, H. E., 382
Adams, J. L., 269, 274
Adams, J. S., 387
Addis, M. E., 520
Ader, R., 193
Adolphs, R., 63
Adorno, T. W., 592
Affleck, G., 417
Aghajanian, G. K., 175
Agnoli, F., 267
Ainsworth, M., 343
Ainsworth, M. D. S., 343
Ajzen, I., 551, 554
Akhavein, R., 257
Akmajian, A., 262
Aksu, A., 265
Alberti, R. E., 516
Alden, L. E., 479
Aldrich, M. S., 165
Alford, Henry, 290
Allen, J. P., 348, 383
Allison, D. B., 371
Allison, T., 164
Alloy, L. B., 488
Allport, G. W., 579, 582
Alstad, D., 588
Alvarez-Borda, B., 194
Amabile, T. M., 312, 314
Ammerman, R. T., 532
Andersen, A. E., 373
Andersen, B., 412
Andersen, S. A., 588
Anderson, C. M., 559
Anderson, J. R., 172, 219, 225, 278
Anderson, N. B., 412
Andrade, J., 227
Andrews, E. L., 25
Angier, N., 379
Anliker, J. A., 112
Appelbaum, P. S., 476
Apter, M. J., 366
Archer, J., 166
Arenberg, D., 335
Arendt, H., 585
Arkin, R. M., 9
Aron, A., 560, 561

Aron, A. P., 400
Aron, E. N., 560, 561
Aronson, E., 557, 583
Aronson, J., 310, 581
Asch, S. E., 541
Aserinsky, E., 162
Asher, S. R., 516
Aslin, R. N., 337
Atkinson, L., 298
Ayllon, T., 515
Ayres, T. J., 223

B

Baars, B. J., 156, 157, 159, 261, 444
Bachar, E., 349
Backman, C. W., 559
Baddeley, A. D., 224, 225, 227, 229
Baddeley, Alan, 227
Bahrick, H. P., 335
Bailey, J. M., 382
Bailey, M. B., 206
Bailey, R. E., 206
Baillargeon, R., 331, 332
Balch, W. R., 229
Balda, R. P., 210
Baldwin, A. L., 211
Baldwin, C. P., 211
Ballenger, J. C., 78
Baltes, M., 335
Baltes, P. B., 334, 335, 360
Baltes, Paul, 335
Banaji, M., 303
Banaji, M. R., 267, 455
Bancroft, J., 376
Bandura, A., 211, 213, 416, 516, 519, 578
Banks, S. M., 111
Banks, W., 314
Banuazizi, A., 538
Banyai, E. I., 170
Bar-Hillel, M., 283
Barbaranelli, C., 462
Bargal, D., 524
Bargh, J. A., 459, 562
Barinaga, M., 57, 62, 80
Barker, L. M., 207
Barker, R., 574
Barnett, W. S., 309
Barondes, S. H., 79
Bartlett, F., 244–245
Bartoshuk, L., 108, 111
Bartoshuk, L. M., 108, 112, 123

Bassili, J. N., 551
Basso, E. B., 167
Batler, R., 366
Batson, C. D., 568, 570
Baumeister, R. F., 379, 410, 447, 455, 456
Baumgardner, A. H., 454
Baumrind, D., 358
Baxter, L. R., 528
Bayley, N., 324
Baylor, D., 98
Beach, F. A., 376
Beattie, J., 287
Beauchamp, G. K., 108
Beck, A. T., 482, 519
Becker, M. H., 422
Beeman, M. J., 68
Beiser, M., 307
Bell, A. P., 383
Bell, I. R., 532
Bell, S. T., 381
Bem, D. J., 20
Benedict, R., 347
Benenson, J. F., 356
Benhamou, S., 209
Benington, J. H., 164, 167
Benson, H., 424
Bentler, P. M., 175
Berger, R. S., 417
Berglas, S., 455
Bergman, E. T., 245
Bergman, L. R., 348
Berkowitz, L., 573, 574
Berlin, B., 265
Berlyne, D. E., 365
Berman, A. L., 488
Berman, K. F., 497
Bernard, L. L., 367
Berndt, T. J., 348
Bernstein, I. L., 208
Bernstein, I. S., 567
Berrettini, W. H., 485
Berscheid, E., 560
Bersoff, D. M., 359, 457
Bertenthal, B. I., 160
Bexton, W. H., 402
Bickerton, D., 52
Biderman, I., 146–147
Biederman, I., 147
Biehl, M., 396
Biglan, A., 486
Billig, M., 580
Billings, A. G., 415
Binder, K. S., 263
Binet, A., 295
Bingham, C. R., 488

Bitterman, M. E., 203
Blake, R., 109
Blascovich, J., 580
Blau, G. L., 476
Blehar, M. C., 485
Bleuler, M., 495
Block, J., 436
Blos, P., 347
Bock, K., 9, 261, 262
Bohlin, G., 344
Boland, S. M., 353
Boldizar, J. P., 358
Bond, C. F., 236
Bond, L., 314
Boone, D. E., 462
Bootzin, R. R., 168
Borgen, F. H., 389
Borman, W. C., 389
Bornstein, P. A., 6
Bouchard, C., 371
Bouchard, T. J., 437
Bourguignon, E., 507
Bowd, A. D., 33
Bowden, E. M., 68
Bower, 233
Bower, G. H., 236, 404, 516
Bower, S. A., 516
Bower, T. G. R., 355
Bowers, K. S., 172
Bowlby, J., 343, 346
Boykin, A. W., 333
Bradbury, T. N., 352
Bradley, M. M., 404
Braginsky, B., 293
Braginsky, D., 293
Brainerd, C. J., 328
Brakke, K. E., 266
Brando, M., 216
Breedlove, S. M., 69
Breggin, G. R., 527
Breggin, P. R., 526, 527
Bregman, A. S., 123
Brehm, J. W., 555
Breland, K., 206
Breland, M., 206
Breslau, N., 480
Brewer, J. B., 250
Brewer, M. B., 353
Briggs, C. L., 393, 419
Broadbent, D., 128
Broca, Paul, 56
Brody, L. R., 303, 309
Broman, S. H., 307
Bronfenbrenner, U., 319
Brooks-Gunn, J., 340
Brooner, R. K., 489

Broughton, R. J., 165
Broughton, W. A., 165
Broussard, C., 515
Brown, B. B., 348
Brown, N. R., 282
Brown, R., 265, 588
Brownell, K. D., 370
Brzustowicz, L. M., 496
Buchner, A., 219
Buckworth, J., 423
Bukowski, W. M., 348
Bulman, J. R., 417
Buntain-Ricklefs, J. J., 200
Burchinal, M. R., 346
Burlingame, G. M., 523
Burnstein, E., 567, 574
Buss, D. M., 55, 378, 379
Butcher, J. N., 461, 463
Butler, L. D., 488
Byrne, D., 559

C

Cabeza, R., 58, 249
Cable, D. M., 389
Cachelin, F. M., 326, 373
Cacioppo, J. T., 552
Cadoret, R. J., 490
Cairns, E., 340, 593
Cajal, S. R., 55
Calkins, Mary, 15
Campbell, D. T., 540
Campbell, L., 282
Campbell, W. K., 547
Campfield, L. A., 371
Campos, J. J., 324, 343
Camras, L. A., 395
Cannon, W. B., 369
Cantor, N., 243
Cantril, H., 544
Capitanio, J. P., 383
Caplan, L., 476
Cappell, H., 193
Caprara, G. V., 462, 573
Cardeña, E., 490
Carducci, B. J., 439
Carey, G., 572
Carey, S., 333, 337
Carlsmith, J. M., 403, 555
Carlson, M., 403
Carlson-Radvansky, L. A., 133
Carmelli, D., 427
Carmichael, L., 322
Carskadon, M. A., 166
Carstenen, L., 352

Carstensen, L. L., 340, 352, 353, 360
Carter, J. H., 327
Cartwright, R. D., 164
Cash, T. F., 374
Catalan, J., 426
Catalano, R., 574
Catania, J. A., 422
Caterina, M. J., 112
Catrambone, R., 278
Cattell, R., 300
Cave, C. B., 249
Cave, K. R., 129, 130
Ceci, S. J., 302, 306, 307, 319
Cervone, D., 438
Chae, Y. M., 280
Chaiken, S., 553, 554, 555
Chamberlain, K., 413
Champoux, M., 345
Chan, A. Y., 351
Chandler, C. C., 233
Chandrasekaran, B., 280
Chapman, P. D., 295
Chase, W. G., 225
Chasnoff, I. J., 322
Chater, N., 277
Chaudhari, N., 108
Chavajay, P., 333
Chaves, J. F., 171
Cheek, J., 6
Chen, I., 28
Cheney, D., 266
Cheney, D. L., 157
Cheng, P. W., 277
Cherry, E. C., 128
Chess, S., 200
Chiriboga, D., 352
Choice, P., 562
Chomsky, N., 338–339
Chorover, S., 470
Christal, R. C., 436
Christensen, A. J., 418, 423
Christensen, K., 484
Cialdini, R. B., 556, 557
Ciaranello, A. L., 484
Ciaranello, R. D., 484
Cicchetti, D., 164
Clark, E. V., 264, 338
Clark, H., 259
Clark, H. H., 245, 246, 258, 260, 264
Clark, K., 2, 579
Clark, L. F., 416
Clark, M., 579
Clark, N. M., 422
Clarke-Stewart, A., 346
Clarke-Stewart, K. A., 346
Clausen, J. A., 499
Clementz, B. A., 497
Clopton, N. A., 358
Clore, G. L., 559
Coates, T., 422
Coates, T. J., 422
Coe, C. L., 193
Cogan, J. C., 373, 374
Cohen, D., 526, 576, 577
Cohen, M. E., 280
Cohen, N., 193
Cohen, S., 410, 418
Cohn, E. G., 574, 575
Coleman, R. M, 161
Coles, C., 322
Collaer, M. L., 355
Collins, M. A., 314

Comstock, G., 212, 578
Comuzzie, A. G., 371
Conrad, C. D., 79
Contrada, R. J., 412
Cook, K. V., 356
Cook, T. D., 350
Cooper, E. E., 147
Cooper, L. A., 268
Cooper, R. P., 324
Corbett, A. T., 265
Coren, S., 97
Corina, D. P., 68
Corso, J. F., 327
Coslett, H. B., 249
Costa, P. T., 436
Costa, P. T., Jr., 436, 462
Cowan, C. P., 352
Cowan, C.P., 409
Cowan, N., 128, 129, 156, 223
Cowan, P. A., 409
Cowan, W. M., 322
Cowles, J. T., 201
Coyne, J. C., 418
Crago, M., 374
Craighead, W. E., 486
Craik, F. I. M., 234, 335
Cramer, P., 444
Cranson, R. W., 172
Crapo, L., 69
Creasey, G., 414
Crockett, L. J., 340
Cronbach, L. J., 304
Crowder, R. G., 223, 224, 230, 231
Crowley, K., 319
Csikszentmihalyi, M., 156
Cummins, D. D., 277
Curtis, R. C., 559
Cutler, W. B., 107
Cutting, J. C., 135, 262
Czeisler, C. A., 161

D

Dahlstrom, W. G., 461
Dakof, G. A., 418
Dali, S., 121
Damasio, H., 64
Daneman, M., 227
Dannemiller, J. L., 141
Darley, J., 569
Darley, J. M., 570
Darling, N., 344
Darnton, R., 472
Darwin, C. J., 223
D'Augelli, A. R., 383
Davidson, A. R., 552
Davidson, J. R. T., 480
Davidson, R. J., 573
Davison, K. P., 524
Dawkins, K., 527
DeCasper, A. J., 323
DeGracia, D. J., 169
Degreef, G., 496
Dehaene, S., 257
Dejin-Karlsson, E., 322
Delaney, A. J., 175
Delaney, N., 303
Delprato, D. J., 182
Dement, W. C., 164, 166
Denmark, F. L., 15
Dennett, D. C., 156
Denton, K., 320
De Rivera, J., 510

Descartes, R., 55
De St. Aubin, E., 353, 448
De Valois, R. L., 98
Devanand, D. P., 526
Devereux, G., 507
Devine, P. G., 581
DeVos, J., 331
Dewey, John, 9
De Witte, P., 176
Dewsbury, D. A., 376
Dhawan, N., 456
Di Marzo, V., 175
Di Tomaso, E., 175
Dickman, H. R., 412
DiClemente, C. C., 421
DiDomenico, L., 373
Diehl, S. R., 495
Digman, J. M., 436
Dillbeck, M. C., 172
Dinges, M. M., 348
Dion, K. K., 561
Dion, K. L., 561
Dishman, R. K., 423
Ditto, P. H., 581
Ditton, T., 124
Dixon, M. J., 498
Dixon, R. A., 319, 334
Dodson, J. D., 403
Dollard, J., 574
Domhoff, C. W., 168
Domhoff, G. W., 167
Domhoff, W., 168
Domjan, M., 33
Donald, M., 157
Donders, F.C., 254
Dong, Q., 559
Donnay, D. A. C., 389
Donnerstein, E., 212
Dosher, B. A., 265
Dreher, H., 427
Drigotas, S. M., 561
Drozd, J. F., 529
Dryfoss, J. G., 340
DuBois, P. H., 461
Duckitt, J., 579
Dudycha, G. J., 438
Dugatkin, L. A., 376
Duker, P. C., 514
Duman, R. S., 484
Duncker, D., 275
Dunegan, K. J., 286
Durik, A. M., 379
Durlak, J. A., 531
Dutton, D. G., 400
Dweck, C. S., 368

E

Eagly, A. H., 553, 554, 555, 559
Ebbinghaus, H., 8, 217–218
Eckensberger, L. H., 358
Edwards, A. E., 191
Egeland, J. A., 484
Eich, E., 404, 510
Eichenbaum, H., 62
Eisenberg, M., 341
Eisenberg, N., 303
Ekman, P., 395, 396
Ekstrand, M. L., 422
Elbert, T., 79
Elkin, I., 530
Ellis, A., 520
Elman, J. L., 145

Elms, A. C., 447
Ely, R. J., 550
Emery, G., 482
Emmelkamp, P. M. G., 513, 514
Emmons, M. L., 516
Enserink, M., 529, 573
Erbring, L., 439, 492, 562
Ericsson, K. A., 156, 225, 274
Erikson, E., 341
Esser, J. K., 542
Estrada, C. A., 404
Evans, A., 182, 201
Evans, D. A., 335
Evans, J. S. B., 276
Evans, J. St. B. T., 276
Evans-Pritchard, E. E., 507
Exner, J. E., Jr., 463
Eysenck, H. J., 427, 436

F

Fadiman, J., 446, 511
Fagot, B. I., 356
Fairbank, J. A., 480
Fallon, A. E., 191
Fantuzzo, J., 516
Fantz, R., 324
Farbman, A. I., 106
Farina, A., 499, 500
Farine, J. P., 107, 376
Farver, J. A. M., 578
Faucheux, C., 543
Fazio, R. H., 551, 556
Feather, N. T., 385
Featherstone, M., 353
Fechner, G., 84
Fechner, G. T., 84
Feeney, J. A., 560
Feirtag, M., 73
Fernald, A., 337
Ferster, C. B., 204
Festinger, L., 368, 555
Feynman, R., 19
Field, T. F., 110
Fields, H. G., 80
Fifer, W. P., 323
Fine, M. A., 523
Fink, J., 521
Fiorito, G., 211
Fischer, K. W., 160
Fischoff, B., 230
Fisher, J. D., 422
Fisher, S., 167
Fishman, H. C., 524
Fiske, S. T., 545
Fivush, R., 355
Flavell, J. H., 329, 331
Fleming, I., 270
Florian, V., 426
Foa, E. B., 412, 480
Fobair, P., 524
Fode, K. L., 24
Folkman, S., 414, 415
Ford, C. S., 376
Forgas, J. P., 403, 404
Foucault, M., 506
Foulkes, D., 165
Fowler, H., 365
Fowler, R. D., 15
Frager, R., 446, 511
Fraley, B., 561
Fraley, R. C., 560

Frank, J. B., 529
Frank, J. D., 529
Frank, M. E., 108
Franklin, N., 270
Franz, C. E., 385
Fraser, S. C., 26, 557
Fredrickson, B. L., 427
Freedman, J. L., 557
Freedman, M. S., 161
Freeman, M. S., 323
Freud, A., 15, 347
Freud, S., 10, 156, 166–167, 447
Freund, A. M., 335, 353, 360
Frey, K. P., 366
Frick, F., 276
Friedman, M., 427
Friedman, R., 424
Friend, R., 541
Friesen, W. V., 395, 396
Frijda, N. H., 396
Fromkin, V. A., 261
Fromm, E., 170
Frosch, D. L., 578
Fuhriman, A., 523
Fuligni, A. J., 349
Fuller, B., 346
Furman, W., 517
Furnham, A., 462
Furomoto, L., 15
Fussell, S. R., 261
Fyer, A. J., 478

G

Gabrieli, J. D. E., 235, 249
Gackenbach, J., 169
Gagnon, J. H., 380
Gallant, J. L., 98
Galton, F., 291
Gancarz, G., 130
Garcia, J., 188, 206, 207
Garcia, M. M., 28
Gardner, B. T., 266
Gardner, H., 302, 313, 448
Gardner, R. A., 266
Gardner, R., Jr., 562
Gargano, G. J., 233
Garland, A. F., 348, 488
Garrison, V., 507
Gawin, F. H., 177
Gazzaniga, M., 67
Gazzaniga, M. S., 67, 93
Gegenfurtner, K. R., 222
Gelman, R., 332
Gelman, S. A., 333
George, C., 347
George, M. S., 399
Gergen, K. J., 13
Gerrig, R. J., 245, 264, 267, 554
Gershon, E. S., 484
Geva, N., 593
Ghadirian, A. M., 532
Giambra, L. M., 335
Gibbs, R. W., 263
Gibson, E., 125, 324
Gibson, J., 125
Gibson, J. J., 126, 134
Giesler, R. B., 487
Gillespie, J. M., 347
Gilligan, Carol, 358
Gilligan, S., 404
Gilovich, T., 547

Gilpin, E. A., 177
Ginns, E. I., 485
Girgus, J. S., 488
Giron, M., 498
Giros, B., 177
Gitlin, M. J., 527
Gladue, B. A., 382
Gleaves, D. H., 492
Glenny, M., 591
Glovinsky, P. B., 164
Gobet, F., 274
Goddard, H., 304
Goddard, H. H., 305
Goldfried, M. R., 529, 531
Goldin-Meadow, S., 339
Goldrick, M., 261
Goldsmith, H. H., 490
Goldstein, E. B., 143, 144
Goleman, D., 303
Gomez-Beneyto, M., 498
Gonzalez, A., 583
Goodall, J., 31, 32, 572
Goodall, Jane, 31–32
Gooden, D. R., 229
Goodison, T., 193
Goodlett, C. R., 322
Goodwillie, S., 318
Gopher, D., 257
Gordon, D., 584
Gormican, S., 129, 130
Gotowiec, A., 307
Gottfredson, L. S., 295, 309
Gottlieb, B. H., 418
Gottlieb, G., 343
Gottman, J. M., 352
Gould, M. S., 488
Gould, S. J., 307
Graesser, A. C., 264
Graf, P., 249
Grammer, K., 107
Grant, B. R., 50
Grant, L., 182, 201
Grant, P., 50–51
Grant, P. R., 50
Grant, R., 50–51
Gray, M. R., 344
Green, B. L., 480
Green, D. C., 105
Green, D. M., 86
Greenberg, R., 167
Greene, E., 123
Greene, R. L., 461, 462
Greenfield, P. M., 310
Greeno, C. G., 372
Greeno, J. G., 126
Greenwald, A. G., 29
Grice, H. P., 258, 259, 263
Griffin, K., 423
Griffiths, M., 492
Grigorenko, E. L., 305
Grohol, J. M., 521
Gross, A., 403
Gross, A. M., 381, 423
Grossman, M. I., 369
Grusec, J. E., 201
Guevremont, D. C., 513
Guilford, J. P., 301
Guilford, J.P., 300
Gumperz, J. J., 265
Gur, R. E., 496
Gura, T., 371

H

Haas, S. M., 351
Hagan, R., 356
Haines, B. A., 386
Hall, D., 211
Hall, G. S., 8, 347
Hamer, D. H., 54, 382
Haney, C., 536
Hanh, N., 172
Harber, K. D., 411
Harder, J. W., 388
Hargadon, R., 171
Harle, V., 590
Harlow, H., 345
Harlow, H. F., 345, 365
Harlow, J. M., 48
Harmon, L. W., 389
Harris, B., 191
Harrison, L. M., 175
Harrison, Y., 163
Hart, D., 357
Hart, J.T., 237
Hartshorne, H., 438
Hartup, W. H., 348
Hassan, S., 588
Hastorf, A. H., 544
Hatcher, C., 522
Hatchett, L., 418
Hatfield, E., 561
Hathaway, S. R., 461
Haugen, J. A., 550
Hawkes, K., 567
Hayward, W. G., 147
Hazan, C., 560
Hazen, C., 560
Healy, A. F., 227
Hearst, E., 185
Heatherton, T. F., 372, 374, 559
Hebb, D., 55
Hebb, D. O., 402
Hebl, M. R., 374, 559
Heine, S. J., 556
Helgeson, V. S., 418
Heller, H. C., 164, 167
Helmes, E., 462
Henderson, L., 439
Henry, G. W., 471, 506
Henry, W. P., 508, 509
Hentschel, U., 444
Herek, G. M., 382, 383
Hering, E., 98
Herman, C. P., 372
Hernnstein, R. J., 306
Hersen, M., 532
Hersh, S. M., 584
Hertzog, C., 335
Herz, R. S., 229
Hess, W., 56
Hickok, G., 68
Higgins, R. L., 455
Higgins, S. T., 515
Hilgard, E. R., 8, 170
Hilgetag, C.-C., 93
Hill, S. K., 455
Himelstein, P., 522
Hines, M., 355
Hinton, A. L., 589
Hintzman, D. L., 240
Hirsch, K. W., 212
Hirschfeld, R. M. A., 527
Hobson, J. A., 167–168, 168
Hoffman, C., 244
Hoffman, L. W., 346

Hoffman, M. L., 403
Hofling, C. K., 587
Holden, C., 52, 483
Holen, M. C., 238
Holland, R. L., 481
Holmbeck, G. N., 348
Holmes, D. S., 172, 527
Holmes, T. H., 410
Holtgraves, T., 283
Holyoak, K. J., 277, 278
Homme, L. E., 202
Honerton, C., 20
Honzik, C. H., 209
Hopson, J. L., 376
Horne, J. A., 163
Horney, K., 445, 446
Houghton, J., 499
Houlihan, D., 513
House, J. S., 418
Hovland, C. I., 592
Howard, D. J., 175
Hubel, D., 98
Hubel, D. H., 99
Hudson, D. L., 280
Huey, R. B., 51
Hulicka, I. M., 354
Hultsch, D. F., 335
Humayun, M., 94
Hume, D., 205–206
Hummel, J. E., 147
Humphrey, T., 322
Hunt, E., 267
Hurvich, L., 98
Huston, A. C., 340
Huxley, A., 174
Hyde, J. S., 379

I

Inagaki, K., 333
Ingram, D., 337
Insko, C. A., 539
Irvine, J. T., 396
Irwin, D. E., 133
Isaacs, E. A., 260
Isen, A. M., 403, 404
Ishii-Kuntz, M., 351
Itard, J. M., 321
Itard, J. M. G., 321
Ito, T. A., 575
Izard, C. E., 394, 402

J

Jaccard, J. J., 552
Jackson, L. A., 559
Jackson, R. S., 371
Jacob, S., 107
Jacobs, G. H., 98
Jacobs, R. C., 540
Jacobs, T. M., 141
Jacobsen, P. B., 208
Jacobson, C. K., 351
Jacobson, L. F., 548
Jacobson, N. S., 520
Jacobson, S. W., 322
Jacoby, L. L., 159, 160
Jahnke, J. C., 230
James, S. E., 351, 352
James, W., 8, 173, 174, 399
Jameson, D., 98
Janis, I. L., 276
Janofsky, J. S., 476
Janowitz, H. D., 369
Jedrej, M. C., 167

Jenike, M. A., 481
Jenkins, C. D., 427
Jenkins, L., 227
Jensen, A. R., 238
Jensen-Campbell, L. A., 568
Jobes, D. A., 488
Johnson, B. T., 353
Johnson, J. R., 369
Johnson, M. K., 247, 510
Johnson, T. B., 322
Johnson, T. D., 343
Johnson, T. E., 575
Johnson-Laird, P. N., 277
Jones, E. E., 455
Jones, J. M., 343, 579
Jonides, J., 128
Jordan, D. S., 123
Joyce, L., 76
Judge, T. A., 389
Jung, C. G., 446
Jusczyk, P. W., 337
Jussim, L., 548, 549
Just, N., 488

K

Kagan, J., 439
Kahneman, D., 257, 281, 283, 285, 286
Kalat, J. W., 190
Kallmann, F. J., 495
Kamil, A. C., 210
Kamin, L., 188–189
Kantor, G. K., 200
Kantrowitz, B., 314
Kaplan, C. A., 274
Kaplan, R. M., 531
Kappé, B., 124
Karney, B. R., 352
Karraker, K. H., 355
Kassebaum, N. L., 309
Katsanis, J., 497
Katz, R., 507
Kay, P., 265, 267
Kazdin, A. E., 202, 512, 515, 517
Keen, S., 590
Kegeles, S. M., 422
Keiger, D., 313
Keller, H., 253
Keller, M. B., 530
Kelley, J.E., 425
Kelsoe, J. R., 485
Kempton, W., 267
Kendler, H. H., 8, 9
Kendler, K. S., 495
Kendrick, T., 532
Kennedy, P. T., 278
Kennedy, R. E., 486
Kenny, D. A., 559
Kerns, R. D., 111
Kessel, N., 313
Kessler, R. C., 467, 477, 478, 483, 484, 493, 498, 524
Ketcham, K., 510
Kety, S. S., 495
Killen, M., 357
Kim, M-S., 129, 130
Kimura, D., 69
King, R. G., 586
King, S., 498
King, S. A., 521
Kinney, D. K., 496
Kinomura, S., 61

Kintsch, W., 264
Kirkpatrick, L. A., 560
Kirsch, I., 170
Kitayama, S., 456, 458, 546, 576
Kite, M. E., 353
Klag, M. J., 412
Klein, D. F., 530
Klein, K. E., 162
Kleitman, N., 162
Klerman, G. L., 481
Kluckhohn, C., 507
Knoedler, A. J., 230
Knox, C., 593
Koelling, R. A., 207
Koffka, Kurt, 125
Kogan, N., 312
Kohlberg, L., 357–358
Köhler, W., 125
Kolb, B., 322
Kolodner, J. L., 278
Kondo, T., 165
Kontis, T. C., 243
Koopman, C., 490
Koren, G., 322
Koriat, A., 230, 238, 239
Korn, J., 33
Kosslyn, S., 72
Kosslyn, S. M., 72, 269
Kotovsky, K., 274
Kramer, J., 588
Kramer, P. D., 527
Krauss, R. M., 261
Kraut, A. M., 507
Kraut, R., 439, 492, 562
Kristof, A. L., 389
Kroonenberg, P. M., 343
Krug, R. S., 411
Kubovy, M., 129, 146
Kuhn, M. H., 456
Kuijer, R. G., 418
Kuipers, A., 514
Kujawski, J. H., 355
Kuldau, J. M., 373, 374
Kulik, J. A., 418
Kuno, E., 506

L

LaBerge, S., 169
Lachman, R., 255
Ladd, G. W., 340
LaFrance, M., 303
LaFromboise, T., 489
Lal, S. K. L., 424
Lalond, F. M., 337
Lambo, T. A., 507
Lamke, L. K., 562
Land, D., 348
Lang, F. R., 360
Langer, J., 335
Langone, M. D., 588
Larner, A. J., 111
Lashley, K., 247
Latané, B., 542, 569, 570
Laurent, J., 296
Lauterbach, D., 480
La Voie, L., 559
Lawler, E. E., 388
Lay, C. H., 410
Lazarus, B. N., 400, 414, 416
Lazarus, R. S., 400, 413, 414, 415, 416
Leaper, C., 356

Leary, M. R., 421, 422
LeCompte, D. C., 223
Lederbogen, S., 168
Lee-Sammons, W. H., 228
Leger, D., 206
LeGrand, L. E., 524
Lehman, D. R., 556
Lehmann, H. E., 532
Leippe, M., 424
Leiter, M. P., 426
Lencer, R., 497
Lennon, R. T., 296
Lerner, M., 589
Lesher, G. W., 132
Leslie, R. F., 180
LeVay, S., 382
Levelt, W., 261
Levenson, R. W., 352, 398, 401, 409
Leventhal, H., 399
Leventhal, T., 340
Levine, J. D., 80
Levine, M. W., 84
Levine, R., 561
Levine, S. B., 327
Levinson, S. C., 265
Levis, D. J., 513
Lévi-Strauss, C., 507
Levitan, L., 169
Levy, B., 335
Levy, G. D., 355
Levy, J. A., 327
Levy, S. R., 243
Levy-Sadot, R., 238
Lewin, K., 368, 592
Lewinsohn, P. M., 486
Lewis, B. S., 229
Lewis, J. R., 167
Lewis, M., 160
Liittschwager, J. C., 338
Liker, J. K., 302
Lilienfeld, S. O., 492
Lindsay, D. S., 246, 247
Link, B. G., 499, 500
Linton, M. A., 381
Lipkus, I. M., 421
Lipsey, M. W., 529
Little, S. G., 298
Liu, J. H., 542
Liu, W., 94
Livesley, W. J., 490
Livingstone, M., 98
Lobel, M., 412
Locke, John, 156, 321
Lockhart, R. S., 234
Loehlin, J. C., 307, 437
Loftus, E. F., 246, 247, 510
Loftus, G. R., 222
Logan, G. D., 257
Logue, A. W., 369
Lombard, M., 124
Loomis, A. L., 162
Lore, R. K., 572, 576
Lorenz, Konrad, 343
Lourenço, O., 331, 332, 333
Lovett, M. C., 278
Lovibond, S. H., 536
Lowenthal, M. F., 352
Lubart, T. I., 311, 312, 313
Lubin, B., 463, 464
Lubow, R. E., 190
Luchins, A. S., 279
Lui, L., 353
Luzzo, D. A., 387

Lykken, D., 54
Lymburner, J. A., 476
Lynch, J. W., 413
Lynn, R., 308
Lynn, S. J., 170, 510
Lyons, N., 358
Lytton, H., 356

M
Ma, V., 457
Maas, J., 165
Macaulay, D., 404
Maccoby, E., 356
Maccoby, E. E., 53, 344, 355
MacDonald, M. C., 263
Mace, W. M., 125
Machado, A., 331, 332, 333
MacLeod, C., 282
Madon, S., 549
Magee, W. J., 479, 480
Magnusson, D., 347, 348
Mahler, H. I. M., 418
Mahoney, A., 200
Maier, N. R. F., 275
Maier, S. F., 486
Main, M., 347, 560
Malinowski, B., 13
Malizia, A. L., 175, 481
Mandel, D. R., 337
Maoz, Z., 593
Marcel, A. J., 117
Marco, C. A., 427
Marcus, A. D., 510
Marek, G. J., 175
Markman, E. M., 338
Markovitz, H., 276
Markowitsch, H. J., 247
Marks, A. R., 230
Markus, H. R., 456, 546, 576
Marr, D., 146
Marsella, A. J., 507
Marsh, L., 496
Marshall, C., 259
Marshall, G. D., 401
Martin, A., 202, 515
Martin, J. A., 344
Martin, M. M., 559
Martin, R., 418
Martin, R. J., 370
Marttunen, M. J., 489
Martz, J. M., 562
Marx, B. P., 381
Maslach, C., 401, 426
Mason, L. E., 491
Mason, M. A., 351
Mass, J., 165
Matarazzo, J. D., 420
Matheson, M. D., 567
Matson, J. L., 517
Maunsell, J. H. R., 98
Maurer, D., 324
Mauro, R., 146
May, M. A., 438
May, R., 447, 520
Mayer, D. J., 80
Mayer, J. D., 302, 303
Mayes, A. R., 248
McAdams, D. P., 353, 447, 448
McAllister, H. A., 547
McBeath, M. K., 141
McBurnett, K., 516, 573

McCarley, Robert, 168
McCarthy, J. E., 240
McClelland, D. C., 384, 385, 463
McClelland, J. L., 145
McClintock, M. K., 107
McCrae, R. R., 436, 462
McEwen, B. S., 79
McGill, O. D., 559
McGinn, D., 314
McGlashan, T. H., 171
McGovern, K., 156, 157, 444
McGrady, A., 424
McGrath, E., 488
McGue, M., 484
McKay, G., 418
McKenna, K. Y. A., 459, 562
McKinley, J. C., 461
McKone, E., 224
McKoon, G., 264
McNamara, D. S., 227
McNeil, B. J., 286
McPartland, T. S., 456
Mcphail, E. M., 157
McPherson, K. S., 304, 305
Mead, M., 347
Meador, B. D., 522
Meany, M. J., 110, 355
Meehan, P. J., 488
Meichenbaum, D., 519
Meier, R. P., 336
Melzack, R., 111, 113
Menon, T., 547
Merigan, W. H., 98
Merikle, P. M., 227
Merrill, M. A., 296
Merton, R. K., 548
Mervis, C. B., 239
Mesquita, B., 396
Metcalfe, J., 238, 239
Meyer, G. J., 463
Meyers, S. A., 560
Michael, J., 515
Michael, R. T., 375, 379
Middlebrooks, J. C., 105
Middleton, J., 507
Midgley, B. D., 182
Mignot, E., 165
Mikolic, J. M., 576
Miles, D. R., 572
Milgram, S., 586
Milinski, M., 567
Milkowitz, D. J., 497
Miller, G., 224
Miller, J. G., 359, 457, 546
Miller, K., 559
Miller, M. A., 410
Miller, M. E., 172
Miller, N. E., 19, 33
Miller, N. S., 176
Milner, B., 68
Minckely, R. L., 107, 376
Mindell, J. A., 168
Mintz, A., 593
Mischel, W., 243, 438
Mitchell, K. J., 247
Mitler, M. M., 165
Mittal, S., 280
Moffitt, A., 164
Molitor, F., 212
Moloney, D. P., 389
Moncrieff, R. W., 106
Montague, A., 110
Montague, C. T., 371

Monteith, M. J., 581
Montgomery, K. D., 365
Moore, E. G. J., 308
Moore, P., 354
Moore-Ede, M. C., 161
Moos, R. H., 415
Moran, G., 343
Moreggi, D., 521
Morgan, A. H., 170
Morgenstern, J., 524
Moriarty, T., 571
Morikawa, H., 337
Morin, S. F., 383
Morrell, E. M., 172
Morris, E. K., 206, 208
Morris, J. S., 399
Morris, R. K., 263
Morton, J., 223
Moscovici, S., 543
Motley, M. T., 159
Movahedi, S., 538
Muehlenhard, C. L., 381
Muenchow, S., 309
Munro, G. D., 581
Murphy, B. C., 351, 352
Murphy, M. D., 166
Murphy, S. L., 488
Murray, C., 306
Murray, J. B., 80
Murray, T. M., 16
Muskin, P. R., 478
Myers, R. S., 423
Mylander, C., 339

N
Nakayama, K., 126
Nantel, G., 276
Napier, A. Y., 523
Nash, E. B., 124
Natsoulas, T., 154
Nauta, W. J. H., 73
Navon, D., 257
Neath, I., 223, 230, 231
Neisser, U., 222, 305, 310
Nelson, B., 123
Nelson, R. E., 486
Nelson, T. O., 159
Nemeth, C. J., 543
Neter, E., 283
Neumeister, A., 485
Newcomb, M. D., 175
Newcomb, T. M., 438
Newell, A., 272
Newman, M. G., 521
Newstead, S. E., 276
Nichols, S., 124
Nicoll, C., 33
Nie, N. H., 439, 492, 562
Nielsen, F., 567
Nietzel, M. T., 471
Nigg, J. T., 490
Nisbett, R. E., 278, 306, 307, 545, 576, 585
Nisbett, R.E., 576, 577
Nishihara, H. K., 146
Nobles, W. W., 6, 507
Nolen-Hoeksema, S., 487, 488
Noller, P., 560
Norden, K. A., 490
Norman, W. T., 436
Northup, J., 515
Nosofsky, R. M., 240

Novick, L. R., 278
Nowlis, G. H., 108
Nungesser, L. G., 524
Nurmi, J. -E., 349
Nutt, D. J., 175
Nyberg, L., 58, 249

O
Oaksford, M., 277
Oaster, T. R., 238
Ochberg, R. L., 447
Oden, S., 516
O'Donnell, D., 348
O'Donnell, S. M., 584
Oetting, E. R., 348
Offer, D., 326, 347
Ogbu, J., 308
O'Guinn, T. C., 282
O'Hara, L. A., 312
Öhman, A., 481
Olseon, T., 383
Olson, D. J., 210
Olton, D. S., 209
Oppel, J.J., 123
Opton, E. M., Jr., 584
O'Regan, J. K., 133
Orme-Johnson, D. W., 172
Orne, M. T., 170
Ornstein, R. E., 157
Orr, W. C., 165
Osofsky, J. D., 578
Owens, J., 245
Ozer, D. J., 436

P
Paikoff, R. L., 348
Paivio, A., 236
Palmer, J. C., 246
Paran, E., 424
Paris, J., 490
Park, B., 580
Park, S. M., 235
Parker, S., 374
Parks, S. H., 418
Parr, W. V., 334
Parson, E. R., 411
Pascalis, O., 324
Pashler, H., 258
Pasupathi, M., 340, 352
Patterson, C. J., 352
Pattie, F. A., 472
Paul, S. M., 78
Pauli, P., 482
Pavlov, I., 183–184
Pavlov, I. P., 183
Payne, D. G., 510
Pear, J., 202, 515
Pearlson, G. D., 496
Pederson, D. R., 343
Penick, S., 369
Penn, D. L., 500
Pennebaker, J. W., 411, 444, 459
Pennisi, E., 53
Penton-Voak, I. S., 379
Perkins, 312
Perlmutter, M., 319
Perrett, D. I., 379
Pervin, L. A., 436
Peterson, C., 385, 427, 486, 487
Peterson, D., 31
Peterson, L. R., 225

Peterson, M. J., 225
Peterson, R. S., 543
Petitto, L. A., 266
Petrie, K. J., 425, 444
Petrill, S. A., 305, 306
Petrinovich, L. F., 33
Petty, R. E., 552
Pfiffner, L. J., 516
Phillips, D. P., 105
Phillips, S. T., 581
Piccione, C., 170
Pich, E. M., 177
Pierce, J. P., 177
Pilkonis, P. A., 439
Pillard, R. C., 382
Pincus, A. L., 436
Pincus, H. A., 528
Pines, A., 439
Pinker, S., 148, 269, 336
Pion, G. M., 16
Piotrowski, C., 463, 464
Pitts, D. G., 327
Plante, T. G., 413
Plomin, R., 53, 305, 306
Plous, S., 33
Poizner, H., 68
Polivy, J., 372
Poppen, P. J., 381
Porkka-Heiskanen, T., 164
Porstner, D., 566
Porter, L. W., 388
Posner, M. I., 57
Poucet, B., 209
Poulin, J. E., 347
Poulos, C. X., 193
Povinelli, D. J., 160, 266
Powell, L. H., 427
Powley, T., 370
Pratkanis, A. R., 542
Pratt, M. W., 359
Premack, D., 202, 266
Prentice, D. A., 455, 553, 554
Prescott, P. A., 323
Preti, G., 107
Price, D. D., 111
Price, R., 145
Price, R. H., 531
Prince, C. G., 266
Prochaska, J. O., 421
Proctor, L. J., 578
Proffitt, D., 135
Prosser, D., 426
Purdy, J. E., 33
Putnam, D. E., 424
Pyszczynski, T., 158

Q

Quattrone, G., 580
Quina, K., 6
Quine, W. V. O., 337

R

Rabbie, J. M., 580
Rabins, P. V., 531
Rachlin, H., 204
Radowsky, M., 489
Radvansky, G. A., 270
Rahe, R. H., 410
Rainnie, D. G., 164
Rajaram, S., 234, 235, 249
Rand, C. S., 373

Rapoport, J. L., 480, 497
Rapp, B., 261
Rasmussen, T., 68
Ratcliff, R., 226, 264
Ratner, C., 396
Raymond, J. L., 62
Rayner, R., 191
Reddon, J. R., 462
Reder, L. M., 239
Redfern, P., 161
Reed, G. M., 427
Reed, S. B., 171
Regan, R. T., 556
Regier, D. A., 477, 483
Reid, E., 459
Reiman, E. M., 399
Reise, S. P., 436
Reisine, T., 175
Reiss, D., 531
Remafedi, G., 489
Rende, R., 53
Rescorla, R. A., 188
Restrepo, D., 106
Rheingold, H., 169
Rheingold, H. L., 356
Rhodes, G., 146
Rhodewelt, F., 455
Rice, G., 382
Richards, M. H., 157, 168
Riemann, R., 437
Riessman, F., 524
Riger, S., 6
Riggs, D. S., 412, 480
Rinck, M., 270
Rips, L. J., 276
Ritter, F. E., 239
Roberts, A. H., 24
Roberts, G., 424
Rock, I., 134, 143
Rodin, J., 370, 371
Roebuck, T. M., 322
Roediger, H. L., 219, 234
Roediger, H. L. III, 234, 235, 245
Roesch, R., 476
Rogers, C. R., 522
Rogers, M., 28
Rogers, S., 28, 34
Rogoff, B., 333
Rohrer, J. H., 539
Rolls, B. J., 369
Rolls, E. T., 247, 370
Romney, D. M., 356
Rorschach, H., 463
Rosch, E., 239
Rosch, E. H., 241, 242
Rosen, H. S., 517
Rosen, L. A., 517
Rosenbaum, M. E., 559
Rosenfarb, I. S., 498
Rosenfield, S., 499
Rosenhan, D. L., 468, 471
Rosenkoetter, L. I., 213
Rosenman, R. F., 427
Rosenthal, A. M., 569
Rosenthal, N. E., 485
Rosenthal, R., 24, 32, 548
Rosenwald, G. C., 447
Rosenzweig, M. R., 15, 79
Ross, B. H., 278
Ross, D. C., 530
Ross, L., 545, 585, 587
Ross, M. J., 417
Ross, M. W., 383

Rosser, B. R. S., 383
Ross, A., 355
Roth, D.L., 165, 423
Rothbart, M., 580
Rothbaum, B. O., 514
Rothblum, E. D., 383
Rothenberg, A., 313
Rothman, D. J., 506
Rotter, J. B., 385
Rotton, J., 574, 575
Rouse, S. V., 461
Rousseau, J.-J., 321
Rowe, D. C., 307
Rozin, P., 191
Rubin, D. C., 243
Rubin, J. Z., 356
Ruch, R., 304
Rucker, C. E. III, 374
Ruitenbeek, H. M., 509
Rule, B. G., 575
Rumelhart, D. E., 243
Rummel, R. J., 592
Runco, M. A., 312
Rundle, H. D., 51
Rusbult, C. E., 561, 562
Rush, A. J., 519
Russo, N. F., 15
Ryckman, R. M., 381
Ryff, C. D., 353

S

Saarinen, T. F., 270
Saberi, K., 123
Sackeim, H. A., 525
Sacks, C., 83
Sah, P., 175
Salovey, P., 302
Salthouse, 334
SAMHSA, 176, 177
Samuda, R. J., 310
Samuel, A. G., 145
Sapir, E., 265
Sapolsky, R. M., 79, 405
Sarbin, T. R., 510
Sato, S., 129
Sattler, J. M., 298
Savage-Rumbaugh, E. S., 266
Savage-Rumbaugh, S., 266
Scarborough, E., 15
Scarr, S., 341, 346
Schab, F. R., 229
Schachter, S., 371
Schacter, D. L., 234
Schaeken, W., 276
Schaie, K. W., 319, 335, 354
Schaie, W., 335
Schanberg, S. M., 110
Scharrer, E., 212, 578
Schaufeli, W. B., 426
Schiff, M., 524
Schlitz, M., 167
Schmidt, D. F., 353
Schmidt, N. B., 482
Schmidt, S. E., 524
Schmitt, D. P., 379
Schneider, K., 447, 520
Schneider, W., 257
Schoeneman, T. J., 457
Scholnick, E. K., 331
Schonert-Reichl, K. A., 347
Schooler, J. W., 510
Schou, M., 527

Schreiber, 491
Schreiber, T. A., 247
Schroeder, D. A., 403
Schultz, L. A., 572, 576
Schultz, R., 491
Schutte, N. S., 578
Schwartz, B. L., 239
Schwartz, D., 578
Schwartz, J. M., 528
Schwarzer, R., 519
Schwebel, A. I., 523
Scott, J. P., 578
Scott, K. K., 399, 403
Scotto, P., 211
Scull, A., 506
Searle, J. R., 263, 267
Sears, A., 584
Secord, P. F., 559
Segal, S., 528
Segall, M. H., 576
Segerstrom, S. C., 427
Seidenberg, M. S., 266
Seifert, M., 286
Sekuler, R., 109
Selfridge, O. G., 149
Seligman, M. E. P., 385, 386, 427, 468, 471, 481, 486, 487, 531
Selye, H., 408
Sereno, S. C., 263
Sergent, S. D., 247
Serpell, R., 310, 333
Serrano, J. M., 395
Sexton, J., 551, 554
Seyfarth, R., 266
Seyfarth, R. M., 157
Seys, D. M., 514
Shadish, W. R., 523, 529
Shafir, E., 284, 287
Shapiro, K. F., 33
Shapiro, K. J., 33
Shapiro, L. P., 263
Shapiro, S. L., 172
Sharps, M. J., 353
Sharpsteen, D. J., 560
Shatz, M., 332
Shaver, P., 560
Shaver, P. R., 560
Shavitt, S., 554
Shaywitz, B. A., 69
Shealy, C. N., 347
Sheehan, E. P., 388
Shefner, J. M., 84
Shepard, R. N., 123, 135, 168, 268
Sheridan, C. L., 586
Sherif, C. W., 535
Sherrington, C., 55
Sherrod, K., 346
Shettleworth, S. J., 209
Shiffrar, M., 135
Shiffrin, R. M., 223, 257
Shimamura, A. P., 334
Shirley, M. M., 326
Shneidman, E. S., 488
Shoda, Y., 438
Shor, R. E., 170
Shortliffe, E. H., 280
Shrum, L. J., 282
Shulman, S., 349
Siegel, A. M., 511
Siegel, B., 424
Siegel, L. J., 489
Siegel, R. K., 173

Siegel, S., 192, 193
Siegelman, M., 383
Siegert, R., 334
Siegler, R. S., 282, 319
Silbereisen, R. K., 340
Silver, E., 476
Silver, R., 412
Silver, R. C., 412
Silverman, A. B., 347
Simkin, L. R., 423
Simmons, J. A., 105
Simon, H., 280
Simon, H. A., 156, 272, 274
Simons, D. J., 133
Sinclair, R. C., 401
Singer, D. G., 213
Singer, J. L., 213
Singer, M., 444, 588
Sireteanu, R., 324
Skaar, K. L., 421
Skeel, J., 283
Skibinski, G. J., 347
Skinner, B. F., 182, 195, 197, 204
Skre, I., 481
Sloane, R. B., 512
Slobin, D., 339
Slobin, D. I., 265
Sloman, S. A., 235
Slovic, P., 285
Smetana, J. G., 349
Smith, J., 334
Smith, K., 28
Smith, M. V., 267
Smith, R. J., 578
Smith, S. L., 212
Smith, T. W., 427
Smollar, J., 348
Snyder, M., 549, 550
Sokal, M. M., 304
Solso, R. L., 240
Sommer, W., 57
Sorell, G. T., 358
Spangler, W. D., 463
Spanos, N. P., 492
Spearman, C., 300
Spellman, B. A., 277
Spence, M. J., 323
Sperling, G., 222, 242
Sperry, R., 67
Spiegel, D., 171, 425, 490
Spiegel, D. A., 528
Spiegler, M. D., 513
Spielman, A. J., 164
Spitz, R. A., 347
Sprecher, S., 561
Squire, L. R., 62, 248, 249
Srinivas, K., 235, 269
Stacy, A. W., 175
Stafford, L., 351
Stahl, S. M., 175
Stampfl, T. G., 513
Stattin, H., 347
Staudinger, U. M., 334
Steele, C. M., 310, 455, 581
Steinberg, L., 344
Steininger, M., 33
Stemberger, J. P., 261
Stephan, W. G., 397, 457
Stern, K., 107
Stern, M., 355
Stern, P. C., 591
Sternberg, R. J., 295, 301, 302, 311, 312, 313

Stevens, J. A., 135
Stevenson, H., 310
Stewart, J. H., 200
Stone, A. A., 414
Stone, R., 412
Strassberg, Z., 200
Strauch, I., 168
Straus, M. A., 200
Strickland, C. J., 489
Striegel-Moore, R. H., 326, 373
Strober, M., 373
Ström, L., 521
Stuart, E. M., 424
Stunkard, A. J., 371
Styfco, S. J., 309
Suboski, M. D., 211
Suchman, A. L., 193
Suls, J., 427
Suomi, S., 345
Suzuki, L. A., 307
Svanum, S., 462
Swan, G. E., 427
Swann, W. B., Jr., 487, 549, 550
Swazey, J. P., 526
Sweeney, J. A., 497
Swets, J. A., 86
Sykora, C., 413
Syme, S. L., 418
Szymanski, S., 497

T

Tajfel, H., 580
Tanofsky-Kraff, M., 372
Tarr, M. J., 147, 148, 269
Taylor, M., 332
Taylor, M. G., 355
Taylor, S. E., 416, 418, 419, 545
Teasdale, J. D., 520
Tedlock, B., 167
Tees, R. C., 337
Tellegen, A., 54
Temoshok, L., 427
Templin, M., 337
Terman, L. M., 296, 305
Thagard, P., 278
Theeuwes, J., 127
Thomas, A., 200
Thomas, E., 314

Thompson, S. C., 417
Thomson, D. M., 242
Thoresen, C. E., 427
Thorndike, E. L., 194
Thorndike, R. L., 296
Tice, D. M., 410, 456
Tidwell, M.-C. O., 560
Titchener, E., 8, 9
Todd, J. T., 206, 208
Todrank, J., 123
Tolman, E. C., 209
Tomoyasu, N., 208
Torrance, E. P., 312
Toth, J. P., 219
Towles-Schwen, T., 551
Townsend, J. T., 226
Trainor, L. J., 337
Treisman, A., 129, 130
Triandis, H. C., 6, 302, 397, 456, 507
Trinder, J., 164
Trivers, R. L., 379, 567
Trueswell, J. C., 263
Trynes, K., 224
Tsoh, J. Y., 421
Tsuang, M., 495
Tulving, E., 155, 232, 242, 249
Tupes, E. G., 436
Turk, D. C., 111
Turnbull, C., 116
Turner, M. E., 542
Tversky, A., 281, 283, 286, 287
Tversky, B., 270
Tyler, L. E., 433

U

Underwood, B. J., 234
Urban, J., 344
Uttal, D. H., 319

V

Vaillant, G., 353
Vaillant, G. E., 353
Valencia, R. R., 307
Valenza, E., 324
Vandewater, K., 369
Van Essen, D. C., 92
Van IJzendoorn, M. H., 343
Van Vianen, A. E. M., 389

Vasari, G., 138
Vaughan, C., 166
Vaughan, E., 286, 417
Veith, I., 471
Vickers, Z., 369
Vickers, Z. M., 369
Vinje, W. E., 98
Vita, A., 496
Von Békésy, G., 104
Von Helmholtz, H., 97, 125
Voss, J. F., 591
Vrana, S., 480
Vroom, V. H., 388
Vu, H., 156, 263
Vuhtrea, 427
Vygotsky, L., 333

W

Wachtel, G. F., 338
Wade, E., 246
Wagner, A. D., 250
Walden, J., 527
Walk, R., 324
Walker, L. G., 425
Walker, L. J., 358
Wallace, S. T., 479
Wallach, L., 511
Wallach, M. A., 312, 511
Walsh, R. N., 507
Walster, E., 559
Walster, E. H., 560
Walters, C. C., 201
Ward, C. D., 324
Warren, R. M., 145
Washburn, A. L., 369
Washburn, M., 15
Wason, P. C., 277
Wasserman, E. A., 209, 211
Watkins, L. R., 80
Watkins, M. J., 223
Watson, J., 182, 191
Watson, J. B., 182
Watterlond, M., 174
Watts, M. W., 590
Wearden, A. J., 497, 498
Webb, W. B., 164
Weber, E., 87
Wechsler, D., 296, 297, 298
Wedekind, C., 567
Wegener, D. T., 552
Wegmann, H. M., 162

Weinberg, M. S., 383
Weiner, I. B., 463
Weiner, J., 50
Weinfield, N. S., 344
Weingardt, K. R., 247
Weisberg, R. W., 313
Weiskrantz, L., 93
Weldon, M. S., 236
Wellman, H. M., 333
Wells, A. M., 531
Werker, J. F., 337
Wernick, A., 353
Wertheim, E. H., 373
Wertheimer, M., 9, 125, 132
Westbay, L., 560
Westen, D., 156, 159, 444
Wethington, E., 351
Wever, E. G., 105
Wheeler, D. L., 584
Whitbourne, S. K., 354
White, J. L., 165
White, R. K., 591
Whitney, P., 228
Whorf, B.L., 265
Wicklund, R. A., 555
Widdig, A., 567
Wiesel, T., 98–99
Wiesel, T. N., 99
Wiggins, J. S., 291, 436
Williams, C. L., 461
Williams, D. R., 412
Williams, L. M., 510
Williams, P., 147
Williams, S., 16
Williams, W. M., 306
Williamson, G. M., 403
Willis, S. L., 335
Wilson, D. B., 529
Wilson, D. S., 351
Wilson, F. A. W., 92
Wilson, T. D., 284
Winarick, K., 509
Windy, D., 520
Wing, R. R., 372
Wingert, P., 314
Wippich, W., 219
Witt, S. D., 356
Wolf, K., 347
Wolf, M., 204
Wolfe, B. E., 531
Wolfe, J. M., 129, 130
Wolfson, A. R., 166

Wolman, C., 531
Wolpe, J., 512
Wood, J. M., 168, 463
Wood, N., 128, 129, 156
Wood, R. E., 519
Wood, W., 541, 543, 555
Woods, C. J. P., 358
Woods, S. C., 370
Worchel, P., 574
Worchel, S., 557
Workman, B., 510
Wortman, C. B., 412, 417
Wortman, E., 412
Wright, E. R., 499
Wright, R., 378, 379
Wundt, W., 8

Y

Yantis, S., 127, 128
Yates, B., 516
Yau, J., 349
Yerkes, R. M., 403
Young, K., 492
Young, T., 97
Youniss, J., 348
Yzer, M. C., 422

Z

Zahn-Waxler, C., 576
Zajonc, R. B., 401, 558
Zaragoza, M. S., 247
Zarbatany, L., 320
Zaslow, M. J., 346
Zeiss, R. A., 412
Zelazo, P. D., 357
Zelinski, E. M., 335
Zentall, T. R., 211
Zhang, Y., 371
Zigler, E., 309, 348, 488
Zika, S., 413
Zilboorg, G., 471, 506
Ziller, R. C., 581
Zimba, R. F., 358
Zimbardo, P. G., 6, 165, 294, 365, 401, 424, 439, 494, 536, 588
Zimmerman, R. R., 345
Zuckerman, M., 307, 421
Zwaan, R. A., 270

Subject Index

Note: *f* after page reference denotes figure, *t* denotes tabular material.

A

AAMR (American Association of Mental Retardation), 296
A-B-A design, 26, 26*f*
Abnormal psychology, 468
Absolute threshold, for hearing test, 101
  calculation of, 84–85, 85*f*
  for familiar events, 85*t*
Abstract reasoning, *vs.* real-world reasoning, 276–277, 277*f*
Accessibility hypothesis, 239
Accommodation
  cognitive, 328–329
  visual, 90
Acetylcholine, 78
Achievement
  motivation for, 383–388, 386*f*
  need for, 384–385, 384*f*
  pressure, 385
Acoustical coding, 66*f*
Acquired immune deficiency syndrome (AIDS), 422–423
Acquisition, 184–185, 185*f*, 188–190, 188*f*–190*f*
ACTH (adrenocorticotrophic hormone), 407
Action potential
  biochemical basis of, 75–76, 75*f*
  properties, 76–77, 76*f*
  refractory period, 76–77, 76*f*
  self-propagation, 76
Acupuncture, pain-relieving effects, 80
Addiction
  drug, 174, 192–193, 515
  Internet, 492
Additive color mixture, 95–96, 96*f*
Adolescents
  aggressiveness, adult criminality and, 348, 348*f*
  college students (*See* College students)
  conflicts with parents, in Hong Kong, 349
  future goals and, 349–350, 350*f*
  physical development of, 326–327
  social development of, 347–350, 347*t*, 348*t*
  thoughts of, 157
Adrenal cortex, 407
Adrenal gland hormones, 71*t*
Adrenal medulla, 407

Adrenocorticotrophic hormone (ACTH), 407
Adult attachment style, 560, 560*t*
Adulthood
  cognitive development in, 334–335
  late, cultural construction of, 353–354
  physical changes in, 327–328
  social development in, 350–354
Advertisements
  attitudes and, 554, 554*f*
  classical conditioning and, 192
  subliminal messages and, 28, 29*f*
Aesthetic needs, 390
Ageism, 354
Age-related changes, accommodation, 90
Aggression, 571
  adolescent, 348, 348*f*
  anonymity-induced, 26, 26*f*
  childhood, parental discipline and, 200, 201*f*
  cultural constraints, 576–578, 577*f*
  economy and, 574
  environmental factors, 572
  escalation, direct provocation and, 575–576
  evolutionary perspectives, 571–572
  frustration and, 573–574
  genetic influences, 572
  impulsive, 573
  individual differences in, 572–573
  instrumental, 573
  norms, 577–578
  situational influences, 573–576
  temperature and, 574–575, 575*f*
  tolerance, media violence and, 212–213
Aging, successful, 360
Agoraphobia, 479
Agranulocytosis, 527
AIDS (acquired immune deficiency syndrome), 422–423
Alarm reactions, 408
Alcohol, 176, 176*t*
Algorithm, 272–273
All-or-none law, 76
Alternative explanations, 23
Altruism, 566–568, 567*f*
Alzheimer's disease, 335
Amacrine cells, 91*f*, 92
Ambiguity

lexical, 262–263
  perceptual, 120–121, 120*f*, 121*f*
  structural, 262, 262*t*
Ambiguous utterances, resolving, 262–263, 262*f*, 263*t*
American Association of Mental Retardation (AAMR), 296
American Psychological Association (APA), 15, 32, 33, 35
American Sign Language, 68, 266
Ames room illusion, 141–142, 142*f*
Amnesia, 248–249
  dissociative, 490
Amphetamines, 176–177, 176*t*
Amplitude, of sound, 100, 100*f*
Amygdala, 62–63, 247, 399
Anagrams, 234
Analogical problem solving, 278, 279*f*
Analytic psychology, 446
Anandamide, 175
Anchoring heuristic, 284
Androcentric bias, 444
Androgens, 376
Angel dust (PCP; phencyclidine), 175, 176*t*
Angular gyrus, 66*f*
Animal cognition, 209–211, 209*f*, 210*f*
Animal magnetism, 472
The Animal Mind (Washburn), 15
Animal research, ethical issues in, 33–34
Animal rights, 33
Animals, language learning and, 266
"Animal spirits," 55
Anonymity-induced aggression, 26, 26*f*
Anorexia, 327
Anorexia nervosa, 372–373
ANS. *See* Autonomic nervous system
Antecedent environmental conditions, 11
Anterior chamber, 90, 90*f*
Anterior pituitary, hormones, 71*t*
Antianxiety drugs, 528
Anticipatory coping, 415
Antidepressant drugs, 527
Antipsychotic drugs, 527
Antisocial personality disorder, 489–490
Anvil, 103, 103*f*, 104
Anxiety, 443–444
  effect on eating, 372, 372*f*
  excitement reversal and, 366

Anxiety disorders, 478
  causes, 481–482
  generalized, 478
  obsessive-compulsive, 480
  panic, 478–479
  phobias, 479–480, 479*t*
  posttraumatic stress disorder, 480–481
  processing of, 482
  treatment, GABA activity and, 78
Anxiety sensitivity, 482
APA (American Psychological Association), 15, 32, 33, 35
Apparent motion, 134–135
Appetitive, 196–197
Aqueous humor, 90, 90*f*
Archetype, 445–446
Arousal, motivation and, 402–403, 402*f*
Asch effect, 540–541, 540*f*
Aspirations, adolescent, 350, 350*f*
Assimilating, as reconstructive memory process, 245
Assimilation, 328–329
Association, between stimuli, 183
Association cortex, 66, 66*f*
Astrocytes, 74
Attachment, 343–344, 560, 560*t*
Attachment needs, 389
Attention, 126
  focus of, 127–128, 127*f*
  objects in environment and, 129–130, 129*f*, 130*f*
  selective, 126–129, 127*f*, 128*f*
  visual search and, 129–130, 129*f*
Attentional bottleneck, 258
Attentional processes, 126–130
Attitude, 550
  accessibility, 551
  behavior and, 550–552, 552*t*
Attribution
  about financial scandals, 546–547
  retraining, for career beliefs, 387
  of success and failure, 385–387, 386*f*
Attributional styles, 386
Attribution theory, origins of, 545
Audience design, 258–259
Auditory cortex, 65, 103, 103*f*, 104
Auditory nerve, 103*f*, 104
Authoritarian leaders, 592, 593*f*
Authoritative parents, 344
Authority, obedience and, 584–589, 587*f*

Autistic child, shaping with, 204
Autobiographical memory, mood and, 404
Autocratic leaders, 592
Auto-hypnosis, 171
Autokinetic effect, 539–540
Automatic processes, 257, 257t
Autonomic nervous system (ANS), 59–60, 60f
   emotions and, 398
   parasympathetic division, 60, 60f, 61
   stress response and, 406–407
   sympathetic division, 60, 60f, 61
Autonomy, 348–349
Autonomy vs. self-doubt, 341–342, 341t
Availability heuristic, 281–282
Aversion therapy, 514
Aversive, 196
Awareness, consciousness and, 154–155
Axon, 71f, 72

B

Backward conditioning, 186, 186f
"Banality of evil," 565
Barbiturates, 175, 176t
Basic level, 241–242
Basilar membrane, 103, 103f, 104
Behavior
   abnormal, determination of, 468–469
   attitude and, 550–552, 552t
   biology and, 55–71
   brain function and, 48
   characteristic patterns of, 431–432
   control of, 6
   definition of, 3
   experimental analysis of, 195
   external influences on, 5
   genes and, 53–55
   heredity and, 49
   inappropriate, punishment for, 498–500, 499f
   innate laws of, vs. learning process, 4460
   inner determinants of, 5
   modeling, 557–558
   observable, 182
   patterns of, 450
   prediction, personality traits and, 437–438, 440
   underlying cause of, 5–6
Behavioral confirmation, 549–550
Behavioral conformation, 581
Behavioral data, 4
Behavioral geneticists, 14t
Behavioral genetics, 437
Behavioral measures, 31
Behavioral rehearsal, 516–517
Behavioral response, 11
Behavioral theories
   of anxiety disorders, 481–482
   of mood disorders, 486
   of psychopathology, 473
Behavioral therapy. See Behavior modification
Behavior analysis, 182
Behavior analysts, 14t
Behavior change, learning and, 181

Behavior genetics research, on happiness, 53–54, 54f
Behaviorism, 11, 182
Behaviorist perspective, 11, 14, 13t
Behavior modification, 512
   brain changes from, 528
   cognitive, 518–519
   contingency management, 514–515
   counterconditioning, 512–514, 513t
   generalization techniques, 517
   social-learning therapy, 515–517, 516f
   vs. psychoanalysis, 518t
Behavior outcome
   attributions of, 385–387, 386f
   dispositional forces and, 368
   situational forces and, 368
Behavior therapy, 504
Behavior variability, 364
Belief-bias effect, 276
Bell-shaped curve, 291
Benzodiazepines, 78, 176t, 528
Between-subjects design, 25
Beyond Freedom and Dignity (Skinner), 182
BFQ (Big Five Questionnaire), 462
Bias
   androcentric, 444
   in-group, 579
   observer, 21–22, 22f
   response, 85–86
   self-serving, 547, 548f
Big Five Questionnaire (BFQ), 462
Binocular disparity, 136–137
Biofeedback, 424
Biological causes, of mood disorders, 484–486, 485f
Biological clock, 161–162
Biological constraints on learning
   instinctual drift, 205–206
   taste-aversion learning, 206–208, 207f
Biological determinism, 10
Biological etiology, of psychopathology, 472–473
Biological markers, of schizophrenia, 496–497
Biological perspective, 10, 13, 13t
Biological psychologists, 14t
Biological science, 3
Biological theories, of anxiety disorders, 481
Biology
   behavior and, 55–71
   learning and, 205–208
Biomedical therapies, 504, 525–528
Biopsychosocial model, of health, 419–420
Bipedalism, 52
Bipolar cells, 91, 91f
Bipolar disorder, 483–484, 484f
   biological causes of, 484–485
   creativity and, 313
Birth cohorts, 320
Birth-control pills, 70
Birthorder, personality and, 433–434, 434f
Blindsight, 92–93
Blind spot (optic disc), 92, 92f
Blocking, 190
Blood-brain barrier, 74
Bodily kinesthetic intelligence, 303t

Body image, 326–327
Body size, cross-cultural perceptions of, 373–374, 374f, 375f
Bottom-up processing, 145
Botulism, 78
Boufée delirante, 477
Bounded rationality, 280
Boyhood conduct disorder, destructive sibling conflict and, 28
Brain
   activity
      imaging, 57–58
      recording, 57–58
   biological potential and, 48–49
   changes, from behavioral modification, 528
   electrical stimulation of, 56
   function
      behavior and, 48
      schizophrenia and, 496–497
   growth, in utero, 322, 323f
   hemispheric lateralization, 66–69, 67f
   interventions, 56
   lesions, 56, 117
   life experiences and, 79
   pathways to eye, 92–93, 93f
   structures (See also specific brain structures)
      functions of, 60–66, 61f
      involved in memory, 247–248, 248f
Brain imaging, 249–250, 250f
   of brain activity, 57–58
   of life experience effects, 79
   PET scans, 57, 58f
Brain stem, 61, 61f, 62f, 104
Brain waves, during sleep, 162, 162f
Breast cancer patients, taste aversions in, 208
Brightness, 95
Broca's aphasia, 66
Broca's area, 56, 66f
Brown v. Board of Education of Topeka, 2
Bulimia nervosa, 327, 373
Bystander intervention, 569–571, 570f

C

Caffeine, 176t, 177
Calcium ions, 75
Cancer survival, social support and, 425
Cannabinoids, 175
Cannabis, 175, 176t
Cannon-Bard theory of central neural processes, 399–400, 401f
Capsaicin, 112
Carbon monoxide, 80
Case study, 32
Cataplexy, 165
Catastrophic events, stress from, 411–412
Catecholamines, 78–79
Categorization
   echoic memory and, 223
   long-term memory and, 239–240
Category association, 234

Catharsis, 508
Causal prediction, 6
Causation, correlation and, 27–28
Central cortex, 64f
Central executive, 227
Central nervous system (CNS), 58–59
Central sulcus, 63
Centration, 329–330
Cerebellum, 61f, 62, 62f, 247
Cerebral cortex, 61, 61f, 63, 247
Cerebral hemispheres, 63
Cerebrum, 61, 63–66
Change blindness, 133, 134f
Child development, day care and, 346
Child-directed speech, 337
Children
   academic achievement of, self-efficacy and, 451
   aggressive behavior, culture and, 576
   infants (See Infants)
   kindergartners, daily hassles of, 414
   physical development of, 324–325, 325f
   social development of, 342–347, 345f
   token economies and, 202
   understanding of sex differences by, 355
Chloride ions, 75
Chocolate, 175
Chromosomes, 53
Chronological age, 295, 319
Chunking, 225–226
Circadian rhythm, 161–162
Classical conditioning, 183–194
   acquisition, 188–190, 188f–190f
   applications, 190–194
   contingency in, 188, 188f, 189f
   informativeness in, 188–190, 190f
   usage of, 193–194
Client, 505–506
Client-centered therapy, 522
Clinical ecology, 532
Clinical psychologists, 14t, 505
Clinical social worker, 505
Closure, 132
CNS (central nervous system), 58–59
Cocaine
   addiction, 176–177, 176t
   in utero exposure, 322
Cochlea, 103, 103f, 104–105
Cochlear nucleus, of brain stem, 104
Cocktail party phenomenon, 128–129
Codeine, 176t
Cognition, 253
   animal, 209–211, 209f, 210f
   reappraising, 416
   studying, 254–258, 254f, 255t, 256f, 257t
   visual, 267, 268f
Cognitive-affective personality theory, 449–450, 449f
Cognitive appraisal, of stress, 414–415, 415t
Cognitive appraisal theory of emotion, 400–402

Cognitive behavior modification, 518–519
Cognitive development, 328
  in adulthood, 334–335
  contemporary perspectives, 331–334, 332f
  cultural influences on, 333–334
  moral reasoning and, 357
  social influences on, 333–334
  stages in, 328–331, 328t
Cognitive dissonance, 554–556
Cognitive functioning, emotional effects of, 403–405
Cognitive influences, on learning, 208–213, 209f, 210f
Cognitive maps, 209–210, 209f
Cognitive needs, 390
Cognitive perspective, 11–12, 14, 13t
Cognitive processes, 253
Cognitive psychologists, 14t
Cognitive psychology, 253, 254f
Cognitive restructuring, 518–519
Cognitive science, 3, 253–254, 254f
Cognitive scientists, 14t
Cognitive social-learning theory, 450–451, 450f, 452f
Cognitive theories
  of anxiety disorders, 482
  of mood disorders, 486
  of psychopathology, 473
Cognitive therapy, 504, 517–518
  for changing false beliefs, 519–520
  for depression, 519–520
Collective unconscious, 445
Collectivism, 568
Collectivistic cultures, 397, 398f, 456
College students
  self-handicapping by, 455
  sleep and, 166
Color afterimage, 96, 96f
Color blindness, 83, 97, 97f
Color circle, 95, 96f
Color judgments, language and, 267
Color vision, theories of, 97–98
Commitment, 557, 560
Common fate, law of, 132
Common ground, 259
Community membership, language production and, 259–260
Community psychologists, 14t
Community support groups, 524
Comorbidity, 477
Companionate love, 560
Compensation, 335, 360
Competence vs. inferiority, 342, 341t
Complementary colors, 96, 96f
Completion task, 249
Complex cells, 99
Complex visual analysis, 98–99, 99f
Compliance, 423, 556–558
Componential intelligence, 301, 301f
Comprehension, nonliteral meanings, context and, 263
Concept learning, in pigeons, 210–210, 210f
Conceptual behavior, of animals, 210–211, 210f
Concrete operations stage, 329t, 330–331

Conditioned compensatory response, 192
Conditioned enhancement, of immune response, 194
Conditioned reinforcers, 200–202
Conditioned response (CR), 184–186, 185f, 186f
Conditioned stimulus (CS), 184–186, 185f, 186f
Conditioned stimulus, contingent with unconditioned stimulus, 188
Conditioning, 180
  Palovian, 183–184, 184f
  processes of, 184–188, 185f–187f
Conduct disorder, destructive sibling conflict and, 28
Conduction deafness, 104
Cones, 91, 91f, 98
Confirmation, behavioral, 549–550
Conflict dilemmas, 576
Conflict resolution, facilitation, fostering contact for, 593–594
Conformity, 539–543, 540f
Confounding variable, 23
Consciousness, 153
  accessibility to, 155
  acquisition, 160
  altered levels of, 168–178
    hallucinations, 172–173, 173f
    hypnosis, 169–172, 170f
    lucid dreaming, 169
    meditation, 172
    mind-altering drugs and, 174–177, 176t
    religious ecstasy, 173–174
  awareness and, 154–155
  contents of, 154–157
  functions of, 157–161
    personal construction of reality, 158
    planning or execution control, 158
    restrictive, 158
    selective storage, 158
    studying, 159–161, 159f
  levels of, 154
  in opposition with unconscious, 159–160, 159f
  uses of, 157–159
  vs. unconsciousness, 460
Consensual validation, 158
Consensus, 545
Consequences, observable, 11
Conservation, 330–331, 331f
Consistency, 545
Consistency paradox, 438
Consumer, critical thinking skills for, 34
Contact comfort, social experience and, 344–346
Contact hypothesis, 582
Contemplation stage, 421, 422
Context
  language processes and, 263–264
  nonliteral meanings and, 263
Context of discovery, 19–20
Context of justification, 21–22, 22f
Contextual distinctiveness, 230
Contextual intelligence, 301–302
Contingency, 188, 188f, 189f
Contingency management, 514–515
Control, of behavior, 6
Controlled processes, 257

Control procedures, 24–25
Convergence, 13–138, 137f
Cooperative principle, 259
Coping
  responses, types of, 415–416, 416f
  self-statements for, 417, 417f
  strategies, 415–419, 416f
  with stress, 414–419
Cornea, 89, 90f
Corpus callosum, 63, 67f, 68f
Correlation, causation and, 27–28
Correlational coefficient, 27–29
Correlational methods, 27–29, 27f
Correlations, 291
  negative, 27f
  positive, 27f
Cortex, 399
Cortical cells
  receptive fields of, 99, 99f
  simple vs. complex, 99
Counseling psychologists, 14t, 505
Counterconditioning, 512–514, 513t
Countertransference, 509
Couples counseling, 523
Covariation principle, 545
CR (conditioned response), 184–186, 185f, 186f
Creativity, 311–314
  exceptional, 313–314
  link with intelligence, assessment of, 312, 312f
Criminality, adult, adolescent aggressiveness and, 348, 343f
Criterion preformance, 217
Criterion validity, 293
Critical thinking skills, 19, 34
Criticism, constructive, 426
Cross-cultural responses
  differences, 12–13
  in emotional recognition, 395–396, 395f
  similarities, of self-criticism, 457–458, 457t
Cross-sectional design, 320
Cross-twin, cross-time analysis, 54, 54f
Crystallized intelligence, 300, 334
CS (conditioned stimulus), 184–186, 185f, 186f
Cue familiarity hypothesis, 239
Cults, 588
Cultural anthropologists, 507
Cultural construction, of self, 456–458, 457t
Cultural constructions of reality, 158
Cultural perspective, 12–13, 14, 13t
Cultural symbols of treatment, 506–507
Culture
  cognitive dissonance and, 555–556
  collectivistic, 397, 398f
  constraints, on aggression, 576–578, 577f
  differences, on Internet, 584
  dream interpretation and, 167
  emotional expression and, 396–397, 398f
  hallucinations and, 173
  individualistic, 397, 398f
  IQ test validity and, 309–311

  language, thought and, 265–267
  love and, 561
  self-enhancement, self-criticism and, 457–458, 458f
Culture-bound syndromes, 473
Culture of honor, 576
Cupboard theory of attachment, 345
Curare, 78
Cutaneous senses, 108–110, 109f

D
Daily hassles, stress from, 413–414
Dark adaptation, 91
Darwin, Charles, 49, 50
Data, behavioral, 4
Date rape, 381
Dating relationships, intimacy and, 452
Day care, child development and, 346
Daytime sleepiness, 165
dB (decibels), 101, 101f
Death, causes of, 421t
Death instinct, 511
Debriefing, 33
Deception, intentional, 32, 33
Decibels (dB), 101, 101f
Decision aversion, 287, 287t
Decision making, 280–281
  framing in, 285–287, 286t, 287t
  group, 542
  psychology of, 284–285, 285t
Decision process, in signal detection theory, 86, 86f
Decision seeking, 287
Declarative memory, 219
Deductive reasoning, 276–277, 277f
Dehumanization, of enemy, 590, 590f
Deinstitutionalization, 506
Delayed conditioning, 185, 186
Delirium tremens (DTs), 173
Delusions, 493
Demand characteristics, 586
Demandingness, 344
Democide, 592, 593f
Democratic leaders, 592, 593f
Dendrites, 71f, 72
Deoxyribonucleic acid (DNA), 53
Dependent variable, 22
Depolarization, 76
Depressants, 175–176, 176t
Depression
  cognitive therapy for, 519–520
  cognitive triad of, 486
  gender differences in, 487–488
  self-verification and, 487, 487f
  treatment of, evaluation of, 530–531, 530f
Deprivation, human, 346–347
Depth cues, 136, 137f
Depth perception, 136–139, 136f–138f
  binocular cues, 136–138, 137f
  motion cues, 138
  pictorial cues, 138–139, 138f, 139f
  texture gradients, 138–139, 140f
Descriptions, 5
Desensitization, 212
Determinism, 20

Development
  documenting, 319–320
  explaining, 321
  studying/explaining, 319–321
Developmental age, 319
Developmental psychologists, 14t
Developmental psychology, 318
Diagnosis, 504
Diagnostic and Statistical Manual of Mental Disorders (DSM), 474–477, 475t
Diathesis-stress hypothesis, 496, 497
Dichotic listening, 128, 128f
DID (dissociative identity disorder), 490–491, 491t
Difference thresholds, 87–88, 87f
Diffusion of responsibility, 569
Discovery, 19
Discriminative stimuli, 197
Disinhibition, 372
Dispositional nature, of humanistic theories, 447
Dispositional variables, 5
Dissociative amnesia, 490
Dissociative disorder, 490–492, 491t
Dissociative identity disorder (DID), 490–491, 491t
Dissonance theory, 554–556
Distal stimulus, 118–119, 119f
Distinctiveness, 545
Divergent thinking, 312
Dizygotic twins, 53, 437, 381
DNA (deoxyribonucleic acid), 53
Door-in-the-face technique, 557
The Doors of Perception (Huxley), 174
Dopamine, 78–79
Double-blind control, 25
Drapetomania, 469–470
Dream analysis, 509
Dreaming, lucid, 169
Dreams, 165–168
  content, physiological theories of, 167–168
  Freudian analysis of, 166–167
  interpretation, non-Western approaches, 167
  problem-solving and, 168
Dream work, 166
Drives
  incentives and, 365
  psychosexual development and, 441–442, 441f
Droodles, 145, 145f
Drug abuse
  adolescent, family therapy for, 523–524
  consequences of, 175
Drug addiction
  behavioral treatment for, 515
  classical conditioning in, 192–193
Drug therapy, for psychological disorders, 526–528
DSM-IV-TR, 474–477, 475t
DTs (delirium tremens), 173
Dual-center model, 370

E

Ear, anatomic structure of, 102–104, 103f
Earthquake, psychological aftermath of, 411

Eating
  physiology of, 369–370
    central, 370
    peripheral responses, 369–370
  psychology of, 370–375
  restrained *vs.* unrestrained, 372, 372f
Eating disorders, body image and, 372–373
Echoic memory, 223
Echolocation, 105–106, 105f
Ecological optics, theory of, 125–126
Economy, aggression and, 574
ECT (electroconvulsive therapy), 525–526
Ectomorphic body build, 433
Education, psychological assessment and, 314
Educational psychologists, 14t
EEG (electroencephalogram), 57, 162, 162f
Effect, law of, 194–195, 195f
Ego, 442–443, 473, 508
Egocentrism, 332
Ego defense mechanisms, 443–444, 443t
  individual differences in, 444
  repression and, 443–444, 443t
Ego-integrity *vs.* despair, 342, 341t
Egoism, 568
Eidetic imagery, 222–223
Elaboration likelihood model, 552
Elaborative rehearsal, 236, 238
Electrical stimulation, of brain, 56
Electroconvulsive therapy (ECT), 525–526
Electroencephalogram (EEG), 57, 162, 162f
Electromagnetic spectrum, 94–95, 95, 95f
Elemental, structuralism as, 9
Emergency situation, bystander intervention in, 569–571, 570f
Emotion, 393, 394
  adaptive functions of, 394
  autonomic nervous system and, 398
  cross-cultural responses, in infants, 395
  culture and, 394–397
  functions of, 402–405, 402f, 404f
  innate, 394–395
  misinterpretation, arousal and, 400
  physiology of, 398
  sympathetic nervous system and, 398
  theories of, 397–402
  universality of, 394, 395–396, 395f
Emotional conditioning, 190–192
Emotional disclosure, health benefits of, 425
Emotional intelligence, 302–303
Emotional responsivity, 573
Empathy, 568
Empathy-altruism hypothesis, 568
Empiricism, 321
Employment, psychological assessment and, 314
Encephalization, 52

Encoding, 220, 249–250, 250f
Encoding specificity, 228–229, 238
Endocrine glands, hormones, 69, 70f, 71t
Endocrine system, 69–71
Endogenous morphine, 175
Endomorphic body build, 433
Endorphins, 79–80
Enemy, concepts/images of, 590–591, 590f
Engram, 247–248
Enlightenment, 172
Environment
  antisocial personality disorder and, 490
  behavior and, 49
  enriched, brain effects of, 79
  IQ and, 307–309, 308f
  natural selection and, 50–52
  vs. heredity, 4460
Environmental variables, 5
Epilepsy treatment, hemispheric differences in, 66–67
Episodic memories, 232
EQ, 302
Equity theory, 387–388
Erogenous zones, 109, 441
Eros, 441
Erotic plasticity, 379
An Essay Concerning Human Understanding (Locke), 156
Esteem needs, 390
Estrogen, 70, 376
Ethical issues
  in animal research, 33–34
  in human research, 32–33
Ethnicity, IQ scores and, 306–307
Etiology
  definition of, 472
  of psychopathology, 472–474, 504
    biological, 472–473
    psychological, 473
    sociocultural, 473–474
Eugenics movement, 291
Evolution
  human timeline, 52f
  natural selection and, 52
Evolutionary perspective, 12, 14, 13t
Excitatory inputs, 74
Excitatory processes, of nervous system, 55
Exemplars, 552
Existential-humanistic therapy, 504–505, 520–522
Existential perspective, 447
Existential terror, 158
Expectancy effects, 23–24
Expectancy theory, 388, 389
Expectations
  adjustment to chronic illness and, 418–419
  adolescent, 350, 350f
  changes in, 548
  in motivating behavior, 368
  of rejection, 500
  stereotypes and, 581
Experience
  learning and, 181
  perception and, 116
Experience-sampling method, 156
Experimental intelligence, 301
Experimental methods, 23–26
Experimental psychologists, 14t

Expert systems, in medicine, 280
Explanations, 5
Explicit uses of memory, 218–219, 218f
Expressed emotion, schizophrenia symptom relapse and, 498
Extension, 339
External of control orientation, 385
Extinction, 185f, 186
Extinction strategies, 515
Extraversion, 435, 435f
Eye
  anatomic structure of, 89–92, 90f
  pathways to brain, 92–93, 93f
Eyewitness memory, 246

F

Face validity, 293
Facial expressions, recognition, cross-cultural responses, 395–396, 395f
FAE (fundamental attribution error), 545–547, 546f
Failure, attributions of, 385–387, 386f
False beliefs, changing, 519–520
Families, genetically inferior, 304–305
Family therapy, 507, 523–524
Fear, 479
Fear conditioning, 191
Female, endocrine glands, 69–70, 70f
Fetus, 322
Fight-or-flight response, 60, 406
Figure, 131
Filter theory of attention, 128
Five-factor model, of personality traits, 436, 436t
Fixation, 133, 135f, 442
Fixed-interval schedule, 203f, 204
Fixed-ratio schedule, 203, 203f
Flooding, 513–514
Fluid intelligence, 300, 334
fMRI (Functional magnetic resonance imaging), 58, 249–250, 250f
Foot-in-the-door technique, 557
Forensic psychologists, 14t
Forgetting curve, 217–218, 218f
Formal assessment, 292–294
Formal operations stage, 329t, 331
Foundational theories, 332–333
Fovea, 91
Frame, for decision making, 285–287, 286t, 287t
Fraternal twins, 53
Free association, 508
Frequency, of sound, 100, 100f
Frequency theory, 104–105, 105f
Freudian dream analysis, 166–167
Freudian psychoanalysis, 508–509
  evaluation of, 444–445
  psychodynamic personality theories and, 440–444, 441t, 443t
Friendship
  in reducing prejudice, 583
  self-serving biases and, 547, 548f
Frontal lobe damage, 63–64
Frustration-aggression hypothesis, 573–574
Functional fixedness, 275

Functionalism, 9
Functional magnetic resonance
    imaging (fMRI), 58,
    249–250, 250*f*
Fundamental, 102
Fundamental attribution error
    (FAE), 545–547, 546*f*

G

g (general intelligence), 300
GABA (gamma-amino butyric
    acid), 78, 175, 528
GABA receptors, 78, 481
Gage, Phineas, 48, 56
Galton, Sir Francis, 291
Gamma-amino butyric acid
    (GABA), 78, 175, 528
Ganglion cells, 91–92, 91*f*, 98, 99*f*
Gate-control theory, 113
Gays, coming out, 383
Gender, 355
    development, 354–356
    differences
        in depression, 487–488
        in taste buds, 112
Gender identity, 355
Gender roles, 355, 356
General adaptation syndrome, 408,
    409*f*
General intelligence (g), 300
Generalization, 278
Generalization techniques, 517
Generalized anxiety disorder, 478
General Procrastination Scale, 410,
    411*f*
Generativity, 353–354, 353*t*
Generativity *vs.* stagnation, 342,
    341*t*
Genes, 53
    behavior and, 53–55
    obesity and, 371
Genetic inferiority, 304–305
Genetic risk, for schizophrenia, 495,
    495*f*
Genetics, 53
Genocide, 589
Genotype, 51
    in natural selection, 52
    natural selection and, 51, 51*f*
    variation in, 53–55
Geometrical optical illusions, 123
German measles (rubella), 322
Gestalt psychology, 9, 125
Gestalt therapy, 522
Glia (glial cells), 74
Goal-directed selection, 126, 127
Gonads, 376
Grammar, acquisition of, 338–339
Griots, 396
Ground, 131
Group comparisons, history of,
    304–305, 304*f*
Group dynamics, 592
Group polarization, 542
Group solidarity, random assign-
    ment and, 579–580
Group therapy, 523–524
Groupthink, 542
Growth, childhood, 324–325, 325*f*
Guided search, 130, 130*f*
Guppies, mate selection of, 376,
    377*t*
Gut, hormones, 71*t*

H

Habitats, natural selection and, 50
Habituation, 332, 332*f*
Hallucinations
    drug-induced, 122, 172–173,
        173*f*, 175
    in schizophrenia, 493
Hallucinogens, 175, 176*t*
Hammer, 103, 103*f*, 104
Hand-eye coordination, 69*f*
Happiness
    heritability of, 53–54, 54*f*
    operational definition of, 23*f*
    valid measure of, 30
Harmonics, 102, 102*f*
Hashish, 175
Head Start program, IQ scores and,
    309
Health, 419
    benefits, of emotional disclosure,
        425
    biopsychosocial model, 420
    personality and, 427
    year-round resolutions for, 426,
        428
Health-care system, job burnout
    and, 425–426
Health costs, of proscrastination,
    410, 411*f*
Health outcome, psychological
    impact on, 425
Health practices, traditional,
    419–420
Health promotion, 420–423, 421*t*
Health psychologists, 14*t*, 393
Health psychology, 419
Health science, 3
Healthy People 2010, 422
Hearing, 100–106
    age-related changes, 327
    names, attention and, 128
    physiology of, 102–106
        auditory system and,
        102–104, 103*f*
Hemispheric lateralization, 66–69
Hemodialysis patients, compliance
    for, 423
Heredity, 53
    behavior and, 49
    IQ and, 305–307, 306*f*
    vs. environment, 4460
Heredity versus environment con-
    troversy, 49
Heritability, of happiness, 53–54,
    54*f*
Heritability estimate, 304–307, 306*f*
Heroin, 175, 176*t*
Hertz, 100, 100*f*
Heuristics, 273, 281–284
Hierarchies, 241, 243*f*
Hierarchy of needs, 388–390, 390*f*
Hippocampus, 62, 79, 247
Hippocrates, 433
Histrionic personality disorder, 489
HIV (human immunodeficiency
    virus), 422–423
Holistic nature, of humanistic theo-
    ries, 447
Holy Ghost people of Appalachia,
    173
Homeostasis, 63, 365
Homonegativity, internalized, 383
Homophobia
    internalized, 383

masking homosexual interest,
    382
Homosexuality, 381–383
    DSM classification of, 476–477
    genetic factors and, 381–382
    society and, 382–383
Honor, culture of, 576
Horizontal cells, 91*f*, 92
Hormones, 69, 70*f*, 71*t*, 376
Hostility, health and, 427
Hozho, 419–420
Hue, 95
Human behavior genetics, 53
Human evolution
    natural selection and, 52
    timeline, 52*f*
Human factors psychologists, 14*t*
Human genotype, variation in,
    53–55
Human immunodeficiency virus
    (HIV), 422–423
Humanistic personality theories,
    446–448
Humanistic perspective, 11, 14, 13*t*
Human-potential movement, 521
Human research, ethical issues in,
    32–33
Hunger center, 370
Hunger sensations, 369–370
Hypercomplex cells, 99
Hypnosis
    definition of, 169–170
    effects of, 171–172
    induction, 170, 170*f*
    as mental illness treatment, 472
    for pain reduction, 171–172
    simulation of, 171
Hypnotic analgesia, 171
Hypnotizability, 170, 170*f*
Hypothalamus
    anatomy, 61*f*, 63, 69–70
    emotion and, 399
    hormones, 71*t*
    lateral, 370
    stress response and, 406
    ventromedial, 238, 370
Hypothesis, 20
Hysteria, 471

I

Iconic memory, 222–223, 222*f*
Id, 442, 473, 508
Identification and recognition pro-
    cesses, 118, 120*f*, 144–150
    bottom-up processing, 145
    contexts and, 148–149, 148*f*, 149*f*
    expectations and, 148–149,
        148*f*–150*f*
    object recognition, 146–148,
        147*f*
    top-down processing, 145, 145*f*,
        146*f*
Illusions, 122–124, 122*f*, 123*f*, 245
Illusory contours, 132, 132*f*
Immune response
    classical conditioning and, 193
    conditioned enhancement of,
        194
Implicit memory
    amnesia and, 249
    conceptual, 249
    perceptual, 249
    processes and, 234–235, 235*f*

Implicit uses of memory, 218–219,
    218*f*
Implosion therapy, 513
Imprinting, 343
Impulsive aggression, 573
Incentives, 365–366
Independent construals of self, 456
Independent variable, 22
Individualistic culture, 397, 398*f*,
    456
Induced motion, 134
Inductive reasoning, 277–279, 279*f*
Industrial psychologists, 14*t*
Infants
    newborn, physical development
        of, 322–324
    proximity-promoting signals,
        343
Inferences, 233–234, 264–265
Inferiority, 445
Information, unattended, 128–129,
    128*f*, 156
Informational influence, 539–540
Information explosion, psychologi-
    cal research and, 35
Information-influence model, 542
Information processing, memory
    and, 217
Informativeness, 188–190, 190*f*
Informed consent, 32–33
In-group bias, 579
In-groups, 579
Inhibitory processes, of nervous
    system, 55
Initiative *vs.* guilt, 342, 341*t*
Innate laws of behavior, *vs.* learning
    process, 460
Inner disposition, *vs.* outer situa-
    tion, 460
Inner ear, 103, 103*f*, 104
Insanity, 476
Insight therapy, 508
Insomnia, 164–165
Instincts, learning and, 367–368
Instinctual drift, 206
Instrumental aggression, 573
Instrumentality, 388
Insults, Northern *vs.* Southern re-
    sponses to, 577, 577*f*
Intellectualization defenses, 470
Intelligence, 334–335
    age-related changes in, 334–335
    link with creativity, assessment
        of, 312, 312*f*
    politics of, 304–311
    theories of, 299–303
        psychometric, 299–301, 300*f*
        triarchic, 301–302, 301*f*
Intelligence assessment, 295–299
Intelligence quotient (IQ), 296
Intelligence testing, origins of,
    295–296
Interactions perspective, of psycho-
    pathology, 473
Interactive problem solving, 594
Interdependence, importance of,
    582
Interdependent construes of self,
    456, 576
Internal consistency, 292
Internalization, 333
Internal of control orientation, 385
International crises, sanctioning
    force in, 593

Internet
  addiction, 492
  anonymity of, 459
  cultural differences on, 584
  romantic relationships and, 562
  sleep and, 166
Interneurons, 73
Interpersonal intelligence, 303t
Interpersonal responsibilities, vs.
  justice, 359, 359f
Interposition cues, for depth per-
  ception, 138, 138f
The Interpretation of Dreams
  (Freud), 166
Interventions, psychological, 6
Interview, 31
Interviewers, 31
Intimacy, 351–352, 351f
  dating relationships and, 452
  love and, 560
  vs. isolation, 342, 341t
Intrapersonal intelligence, 303t
Intrinsic motivation, 314
Introversion, 439
Invariant cues, 141
Ion channels, 75f, 76
Ions, 75
IQ
  environment and, 307–309, 308f
  heredity and, 305–307, 306f
  scores
    of adopted children, 308, 309f
    Head Start program and, 309
IQ tests, 296–298
  distribution of scores, 296, 297f
  on-line, 299
  scores, ethnicity and, 306–307
  validity, culture and, 309–311
Iris, 90, 90f
Irrationality, 468

J

James-Lange theory of body reac-
  tion, 399, 401f
Jet lag, 161–162
Jigsaw classrooms, 583
JND (just noticeable difference),
  87–88, 87f
Job burnout, 425–426
Job productivity/performance, cor-
  relation with stress, 27
Journals, psychological research in,
  35
Judgment, 280–281
  about bad business practice, 286
  heuristics and, 281–284
  in signal detection theory, 86, 86f
Juke family, 304–305
Justice
  prosocial behavior and, 568
  vs. interpersonal responsibilities,
    359, 359f
Justification, 19
Just noticeable difference (JND),
  87–88, 87f
Just world thinking, 589

K

Kallikak family, 304–305
Kapolo Indians, 167
Keller, Helen, 253
Kinesthetic sense, 110–111
Knowledge compilation, 219

Koro, 477
Korsakoff syndrome, 249

L

Labeling, psychological assessment
  and, 315
Laissez-faire, 592
Lamaze method of childbirth, 112
Lane keeping, 124
Language, 52, 258
  acquisition, 335–340
  color judgments and, 267
  cultural evolution and, 52
  differences, in stereotypes, 244
  learning, by animals, 266
  production, 258–262, 259f, 260t,
    261f
  structure of, 335t
  thought, culture and, 265–267
  understanding, 262–265, 262f,
    263t
  use, mood and, 403, 404f
Language-making capacity, 339
Latent content, 166
Lateral fissure, 63
Lateral hypothalamus, 370
Law of common fate, 132
Law of effect, 194–195, 195f
Law of proximity, 132
Law of similarity, 132
LCUs (life-change units), 409–410
Leadership styles, 592–593, 593f
Learned helplessness, 486–487
Learning
  biological constraints on,
    205–206
  capacity, 180–181
  cognitive influences on,
    208–213, 209f, 210f
  conservation across species, 182
  definition of, 181
  evolutionary perspective, 180
  instincts and, 367–368
  observational, 211–213
  study of, 181–182
  taste-aversion, 206–208, 207f
  variability in, 181
Learning-performance distinction,
  181
Learning process, vs. innate laws of
  behavior, 460
Left-handedness, 68–69
Lens, 90, 90f
Leptin, 371
Lesbians, coming out, 383
Lesion, 56
Leveling, as reconstructive memory
  process, 245
Level of analysis, 4–5, 5f
Levels-of-processing theory, 234
Lexical meaning, 336f
Libido, 441–442
Life-change units (LCUs), 409–410
Life events, major, 409–411, 410t
Life experiences, effects on brain, 79
Life span development, stages of,
  319t
Lightness constancy, 143–144, 144f
Liking, in social relationships,
  558–559
Limbic system, 61, 61f, 62–63, 63f,
  399

Linear perspective, for depth per-
  ception, 138, 139f
Linguistic copresence, 259
Linguistic determinism, 265
Linguistic intelligence, 303t
Linguistic relativity, 265
Literal statement, 263t
Lithium, 527
Locomotion, maturational timeta-
  ble for, 326f
Locus of control orientation, 385
Logical-mathematical intelligence,
  303t
Longitudinal design, 319–320
Long-term memory, encoding spec-
  ificity and, 228–229
Lorenzo the Magnificent (Leslie), 180
Loudness, of sound, 100–101, 101f
Love, 560–563, 560t
LSD, 173, 175, 176t
Lucid dreaming, 169

M

Magnetic resonance imaging
  (MRI), 57–58
Maintenance rehearsal, 224–225,
  225f
Major depressive disorder, 483, 483t
Maladaptiveness, 468
Male, endocrine glands, 69–70, 70f
Mania, creativity and, 313
Manic-depression, creativity and,
  313
Manic episode, 483
Manifest content, 166
MAOIs (monoamine oxidase inhib-
  itors), 527
MARC (multiple-unit artificial
  retina chipset), 94
Marijuana, 175, 176t
Marital therapy, 523–524
"Master gland" (pituitary gland), 70
Mate selection, of female guppies,
  376, 377t
Mating, short-term vs. long-term,
  379
Maturation, 324–325, 326f
Media violence, tolerance toward
  real-life aggression and,
  212–213
Medical model, emergence of, 471
Meditation, 172
Medulla, 61
Meissner corpuscles, 109, 109f
Memories, repressed, 510
Memory
  age-related changes, 335
  availability, mood and, 282
  biological aspects of, 247–250,
    248f, 250f
  declarative, 219
  definition of, 217
  earliest, 216
  echoic, 223
  explicit uses of, 218–219, 218f
  hippocampus damage and, 62
  iconic, 222–223, 222f
  implicit uses of, 218–219, 218f
  long-term, 228–239
    context and, 230–231
    encoding, 234–236, 235f
    encoding specificity and,
      228–229

flow of information and, 220,
    221f
  improving, for unstructured
    information, 236–237,
    237f
  retrieval, 234–236, 235f
  retrieval cues and, 231–234
  serial position effect and,
    229–231, 230f
  structures in, 239–247
photographic, 222–223
procedural, 219
processes, overview of, 220
quantification of, 217–218, 218f
reports, influence of postevent
  information on, 246
research, preparation for exams
  and, 233
sensory, 221–223, 221f, 222f
short-term, 223–224
  accommodating to capacity
    limitations of, 224–226,
    225f
  capacity limitations of, 224
  retrieval from, 226
  structure, propositions and, 264
subliminal message effects, 29
time anchors for, 216
types of, 218–220, 218f
usage, goal effects on, 245–246
working, 224, 226–228
Memory span, 224
Memory structures, 239–247
  using, 243–244, 244f
Men, altruistic, women and,
  567–568
Menarche, 326
Menopause, 327–328
Mental abilities, evolution of, 12
Mental age, 295
Mental health continuum, 469, 469f
Mental illness. See Psychological
  disorders
Mental images, visual scanning of,
  269, 269f
Mentalistic, structuralism as, 9
Mental operations, 330
Mental processes, 3
  analysis of, 254–255, 255t
  mental resources and, 255–258,
    256f, 257t
Mental resources, mental processes
  and, 255–258, 256f, 257t
Mental retardation, diagnosis of,
  29226, 297t
Mental rotation, physical rotation
  and, 268–269, 268f
Mental set, 149, 279
Mere exposure effect, 401
Merkel disks, 109, 109f
Mescaline (peyote), 175, 176t
Mesomorphic body build, 433
Meta-analysis, 529–530, 572
Metamemory, 237–239, 238
Metamotivational states, 366, 366t
Method of loci, 236, 237f
Mind-altering drugs, 174–177, 176t
Mind-body connection, 424–425
Minnesota Multiphasic Personality
  Inventory (MMPI), 461
Minnesota Multiphasic Personality
  Inventory-2 (MMPI-2),
  461–462, 461t, 462t
Minority influence, 542–543

Misattribution, 401
MMPI (Minnesota Multiphasic Personality Inventory), 461
MMPI-2 (Minnesota Multiphasic Personality Inventory-2), 461–462, 461t, 462t
M'Naghten rule, 476
Mnemonics, 236–237, 237f
Modeling, 557–558
Monk puzzle, 274–276, 274t, 275f
Monoamine oxidase inhibitors (MAOIs), 527
Monosodium glutamate (MSG), 108
Monozygotic twins, 53, 437, 381–382
Mood
    autobiographical memory and, 404
    availability of memories and, 282
    language use and, 403, 404f
Mood-congruent processing, 404
Mood-dependent memory, 404
Mood disorders, 482–483
    bipolar disorder, 483–484, 484f
    causes, 484–487, 485f
        behavioral, 486
        cognitive, 486–487
        psychodynamic, 486
    major depressive disorder, 483, 483t
    suicide and, 488–489
Moral development, 357–359, 357t, 359f
Morality, 357
Moral reasoning, 357–358, 357t
    cognitive development and, 357
    cultural perspectives on, 358–359, 359f
    gender and, 358–359
Morpheme, 336t, 339
Morphine, 175, 176t
Motherese, 337
Motion cues, 138
Motion perception, 133–135, 135f
    invariant cues, 141
Motion sickness, 110
Motivation, 364
    arousal and, 402–403, 402f
    cognitive approaches to, 368
    concepts, function of, 364
    for personal achievement, 383–388, 384f, 386f
    psychic energy and, 441
    sources of, 364–369
Motor cortex, 64, 65f
Motor neurons, 73
Motor set, 149
MRI (magnetic resonance imaging), 57–58
MSG (monosodium glutamate), 108
Müller-Lyer illusion, 123, 123f
Multiple intelligences, 302–303, 303f
Multiple personality disorder, 490–492, 491t
Multiple sclerosis, 76
Multiple-unit artificial retina chipset (MARC), 94
Musical intelligence, 303t
Mutual exclusivity, 338
MYCIN, 280
Myelin sheath, 74, 76

N
Names, hearing, 128
Naming explosion, 337
Nanometers, 95
Narcissistic personality disorder, 489
Narcolepsy, 165
Narcotics, 176t
National Sleep Foundation, 164, 165, 166
Nativist viewpoint, 321
Naturalistic observation, 31–32
Naturalist intelligence, 303t
Natural selection
    evolution and, 50–52, 52
    over short periods, 50–51
    process of, 51, 51f
Nature versus nurture controversy, 49, 321
Near point, 90
Necker cube, 121, 121f, 136
Need for achievement, 384–385, 384f
Needs, hierarchy of, 388–390, 390f
Negative afterimage, 96, 96f
Negative punishment, 197
Negative reinforcement, 196–197
Negative spin, 286
Neomatrix theory of pain, 113
NEO Personality Inventory (NEO-PI), 462
Nerve deafness, 104
Nervous system
    central, 58–59
        excitatory processes, 55
        hierarchical organization of, 59
        inhibitory processes, 55
        neuron, 71–74
    peripheral, 58–59
    physical organization of, 59
Neuromodulator, 79–80
Neurons, 71–74
    action potentials, 75–77, 75f
    excitatory inputs, 75
    functions of, 73–74, 74f
    inhibitory inputs, 75
    structures, 73f
    types of, 71–72, 71f
Neuropathic pain, 111
Neuroscience, 55–56
Neuroses, 475
Neurotic disorders, 475
Neuroticism, 435, 435f
Neurotransmitters, 472. See also specific neurotransmitters
    excitatory, 78
    functions, 78–80
    inhibitory, 78
    in synaptic transmission, 77–78, 77f
Newborns
    physical development of, 322–324
Newton, Sir Isaac, 93
Next-in-line effect, 236
Nicotine, 176t, 177
Nicotine replacement therapy, 421–422
Nightmares, 168
Nitric oxide, 80
Nociceptive pain, 111, 112
Nodes of Ranvier, 76
Noise, 102
Nonconformity, 542–543

Nonconscious, 155
Non-Freudian therapies, 509–511
Non-rapid-eye movement sleep (NREM sleep), 162, 167–168
    deprivation of, 164
    dreaming and, 165
Nontasters, 112
Norepinephrine, 78–79
Normal distribution, 291
Normative influence, 539, 540–51
Normative investigations, 319
Norm crystallization, 539
Norm of reciprocity, 567
Norms, 294
Nose dot test, 160
NREM sleep. See Non-rapid-eye movement sleep
Numbers, meaning of, 257, 257t

O
Obedience, authority and, 584–589, 587f
Obesity
    dieting and, 371–372
    genes and, 371
Objective personality tests, 460–462, 461t, 462t
Objective self, 160
Objectivity
    in behavioral measurement, 4, 5
    challenge to, 21–22
Object permanence, 329
Object recognition, 146–148, 147f
Object relations theory, 511
Observation, 31
    direct, 31
    naturalistic, 31
    standardized, 22
Observational learning, 211–213
Observer bias, 21–22, 22f
Obsessive-compulsive disorder (OCD), 480
Occipital lobe, 64
Occlusion cues, for depth perception, 138, 138f
OCD (obsessive-compulsive disorder), 480
ODC (ornithine decarboxylase), 110
Oedipus complex, 441–442
Oedipus conflict, 511
Olfactory bulb, 106, 107f
Olfactory cilia, 106, 107f
Open-mindedness, 20
Operant chamber, 195, 196f
Operant conditioning, 194–205, 195, 196f
Operant extinction, 196–197
Operating principles, for language learning, 339
Operational definition, 22, 23f, 30
Operationalism, 22
Opiates, 175, 176t
Opponent-process theory, 98
Optic chiasma, 92
Optic disc (blind spot), 92, 92f
Optic nerve, 92
Optic tracts, 92
Optimism, 386, 427
Optimization, 335, 360
Organismic variables, 5
Organizational psychologists, 387

Orgasm, sexual, 377
Orientation constancy, 142–143, 143f, 144f
Orienting response, 183
The Origin of Species (Darwin), 49
Ornithine decarboxylase (ODC), 110
Outcome-based experiences, 451, 452f
Out-groups, 579
Ovarian hormones, 71t
Overregulation, 339
Overtones, 102, 102f

P
Pain, 111–113
    mechanisms of, 111
    neuropathic, 111
    nociceptive, 111, 112
    perception, psychological aspects of, 113
    psychology of, 111–113
    reduction, hypnosis for, 171–172
Pain withdrawal reflex, 73–74, 74f
Palovian conditioning, 183–184
Pancreas, hormones, 71t
Panic attacks, 478–479
Panic disorder, 478–479, 482
Papillae, 108
Paradoxical sleep, 162, 162f
Parallel forms, 292
Parallel processes, 256
Paranoid delusions, 177
Paranoid personality disorder, 489
Parasympathetic division, of autonomic nervous system, 60, 60f, 61
Paratelic state, 366
Parathyroid hormones, 71t
Parent, possible selves as, 454
Parent conflicts with adolescents, in Hong Kong, 349
Parentese, 337
Parenting practices, 344
Parenting styles, 344, 345f
Parietal lobe, 64
Parkinson's disease, 79
Partial reinforcement effect, 203
Partial reinforcement schedule, 203
Participant modeling, 516, 516f
Passionate love, 560
Pastoral counselor, 505
Patient, 505
Pattern recognition, 92
Payoff matrix, 86–87, 86f
PCP (phencyclidine; angel dust), 175, 176t
Peace psychology, 591–594, 593f
Peer pressure, 348
Peer review, 35
Peg-word method, 236–237
Perceived control, 417–418
Percept, 131, 131f
Perception, 116–117
    ambiguity and, 120–121, 120f, 121f
    analytical stage of, 125
    catching a fly ball and, 141
    depth, 136–139, 136f–138f
    distal stimulus and, 118–119, 119f
    experience and, 116

Perception (*continued*)
    identification and recognition processes, 144–150
    illusions and, 122–124, 122f, 123f
    organizational processes in, 131–144
        grouping, 132–133, 133f
        motion perception, 133–135, 135f
        spatial integration, 133
        temporal integration, 133
    proximal stimulus and, 118–119, 119f
    studying, approaches for, 125–126, 126f
    synthetic stage of, 125
Perceptual constancy, 139–144
    of lightness, 143–144, 144f
    of orientation, 142–143, 143f, 144f
    of shape, 142, 143f
    of size, 139–142, 142f
Perceptual grouping, principles of, 132–133, 133f
Perceptual organization, 117–118
Perceptual set, 149
Peripheral nervous system (PNS), 58–59
Perpheralist theory, 399
Personality, 431–432
    assessment, 460–464
        objective tests, 460–462, 461t, 462t
        projective tests, 462–464, 463f, 464f
    health and, 427
    structure of, 442–443
    traits, 432
        behavior prediction and, 437–438, 440
        cardinal, 435
        central, 435
        descriptions of, 434–436, 435f
        evaluation of, 440
        five-factor model, 436, 436t
        heritability of, 436–437
        secondary, 435
    types, 427, 433–434, 434f
Personality disorders, 489–490
Personality inventory, 460–461
Personality psychologists, 14t
Personality theories, 433
    cognitive-affective, 449–450, 449f
    cognitive social-learning theory, 450–451, 450f, 452f
    comparison of, 459–460
    evaluation of, 440
    humanistic, 446–448
    post-Freudian, 445–446
    psychodynamic, 440
        Freudian psychoanalysis and, 440–444, 441f, 443t
    self view and (*See* Self theories)
    social intelligence, 452–453
    social-learning, 448–449
Personal relevance, persuasion and, 553, 553f
Personnel psychology, 389
Person-organization fit, 389
Persuasion, 552–554
    personal relevance and, 553, 553f
    subliminal, 28, 29f
    by your own actions, 554–556

Pessimism, 386
PET scans, 57, 58f, 72, 399
Peyote (mescaline), 175, 176t
Phantom limb phenomenon, 111
Phencyclidine (angel dust; PCP), 175, 176t
Phenomenological nature, of humanistic theories, 447
Phenomenologists, 11
Phenotype, in natural selection, 51, 51f, 52
Pheromones, 106–107, 376
Phi phenomenon, 134, 135
Phobias, 479–480, 479t
Phonemes, 145, 336–337
Phonemic restoration, 145, 146f
Phonetics, 336t
Phonological loop, 227
Phonology, 336t
Photographic memory, 222–223
Photoreceptors, 91, 91f
Physical attractiveness, liking and, 558–559
Physical copresence, 259
Physical development, 321
    in adolescence, 326–327
    in childhood, 324–325
    newborns/infants, 322–324, 325f
    prenatal, 322
Physiological dependence, 174
Piaget, Jean, 328, 357
    centration and, 329–330
    cognitive development stages, 328–331, 328t
Pictorial cues, for depth perception, 138–139, 138f, 139f
Pigeons, concept learning in, 210–211, 210f
Pinna (external ear), 103, 103f, 104
Pitch, 100
Pitch perception, theories of, 104–105, 105f
Pituitary gland, 70, 407
Pituitary hormones, 71t
Placebo control, 25
Placebo effect, 24, 29, 529
Place recognition, 92
Place theory, 104, 105
Plasticity, 181
Play, structure of, gender differences in, 356
Pleasure principle, 442
PNS (peripheral nervous system), 58–59
Polarized, 75
Politics, of intelligence, 304–311
Pons, 61
Ponzo illusion, for depth perception, 138, 139f
Population, 25
Positive punishment, 197
Positive reinforcement, 196–197, 514–515
Positive reinforcers, probable activities as, 202
Positive spin, 286
Possible selves, 454
Posterior pituitary hormones, 71t
Post-Freudian personality theories, 445–446
Postsynaptic membrane, 77
Posttraumatic stress disorder (PTSD), 412, 480–481
Potassium ions, 75

Poverty, stressful effects of, 413
Pragmatic reasoning schema, 277
Pragmatics, 336t
Preattentive processing, 129
Preconscious memories, 155–156
Precontemplation stage, 421, 422
Prediction, psychological, 6
Predictive validity, 293
Preferences, classical conditioning and, 190–192
Prefrontal lobotomy, 525
Prejudice, 578–579
    origins of, 579–581
    racial category judgments and, 580
    reversing, 582–583
    stereotypes and, 581–582
Premack principle, 202
Prenatal period, 322
Preoperational period, 332
Preoperational stage, 329–330, 329t
Preparedness hypothesis, 481
Prescriptions, for psychoactive drugs, 528
Presence, in virtual environment, 124
Presynaptic membrane, 77
Prevention
    primary, 531
    secondary, 531
    strategies, for psychological disorders, 531–532
    tertiary, 531
Primacy effect, 230
Primary reinforcers, 200
Priming, 234
Principlism, 568
Proactive inference, 233
Problem reasoning, 271–272
Problem solving, 270, 271–276, 273f
    deductive reasoning for, 276–277, 277f
    improving, 274–276, 274t, 275f
    inductive reasoning and, 277–279, 279f
Problem space, 272–274
Procedural memory, 219
Prognosis, 504
Progressive education, 9
Projective tests, 462–464, 463f, 464f
Propositions, 264
Proscrastination, health costs of, 410, 411f
Prosocial behavior, 566
    altruism, 566–568, 567f
    motives for, 568–569
    situation effect on, 569–571, 570f
Prototypes, 240–241, 241f
Provocation, direct, aggression escalation and, 575–576
Proximal stimulus, 118–119, 119f
Proximity
    law of, 132
    liking and, 558
Psilocybe mushroom (*teonanaacatl*), 174, 175, 176t
Psilocybin, 174, 175, 176t
Psychedelics (hallucinogens), 175
Psychiatric hospital, pseudopatients, 470
Psychiatrists, 14t, 505, 293
Psychic determinism, 442
Psychoactive drugs, 174
    hallucination and, 173

prescriptions for, 528
    types of, 526–528
    varieties of, 175–177, 176t
Psychoanalysis, 15–16, 508–509
    vs. behavioral approaches, 518t
Psychoanalyst, 505
Psychobiography, 447–448
Psychodynamic personality theories, 440
    of anxiety disorders, 481
    Freudian psychoanalysis and, 440–445, 441t, 443t
    of mood disorders, 486
    of psychopathology, 473
Psychodynamic perspective, 10, 14, 13t
Psychodynamic therapy, 504, 508–509
Psychological analysis, subjects of, 3
Psychological assessment, 290–291
    formal, basic features of, 292–294
    history of, 291
    society and, 314–315
Psychological dependence, 174
Psychological disorders, 467–468. *See also specific psychological disorders*
    classification of, 474
        DSM-IV-TR for, 474–477, 475t
        goals for, 474
    classification system for, 471–472
    historical perspectives, 470–472
    prevention strategies, 531–532
    stigma of, 498–500, 499f
    therapeutic process, 503–504
        goals of, 504–505
    treatment, 423–425, 504
        behavioral (*See* Behavior modification)
        cognitive (*See* Cognitive therapy)
        cultural symbols of, 506–507
        development of, 530–531, 531f
        effectiveness of, 529–532, 530f, 531f
        evaluation of, 530–531, 530f, 531f
        existential-humanistic, 520–522
        non-Freudian, 509–511
        psychodynamic, 508–509
        psychopharmacology, 526–528
        regimen, adherence to, 423–424
        rituals of curing and, 506–507
        Western, history of, 506
    types of, 477–478
        anxiety-related (*See* Anxiety disorders)
        mood-related (*See* Mood disorders)
        personality-related (*See* Personality disorders)
        schizophrenic (*See* Schizophrenic disorders)
Psychological etiology, of psychopathology, 473
Psychological inquiry, diversity of, 14t

Psychological measurement, 30–32
    behavioral, 31–32
    observations, 31–32
    reliability/validity of, 30
    self-reports, 30–31
Psychological models, emergence
    of, 472
Psychological research
    goals of, 4–7
    impact on society, 2, 7
    information explosion and, 35
Psychologists
    functions, diversity of, 14–15,
        14*t*, 16
    intuitive, 545
    work settings for, 15, 15*f*
Psychology
    current perspectives, 10–14, 13*t*
    definition of, 3, 154
    goals of, 4–7
    historical aspects of, 8–10
    modern, evolution of, 8–14, 13*t*
    scientific aspect of, 3
    in 21st century, 16
    studying, rationale for, 7
    uniqueness of, 3–4
    women in, 15–16, 15*f*
*Psychology from the Standpoint of a
    Behaviorist* (Watson), 182
Psychometric function, 84–85, 85*f*
Psychometrics, 299–301, 300*f*
Psychometric theories of intelli-
    gence, 299–301, 300*f*
Psychomotor behavior, 493
Psychoneuroimmunology, 193
Psychopathological functioning,
    468
Psychopathology, etiology of,
    472–474
Psychopharmacologists, 14*t*
Psychopharmacology, for psycho-
    logical disorders, 526–528
Psychophysics, 84–88
    absolute thresholds and, 84–85,
        85*f*, 85*t*
    difference thresholds and, 87–88,
        87*f*
    response bias and, 85–86
    sensory adaptation and, 85
    signal detection theory and,
        86–87, 86*f*
Psychoses, 475
Psychosexual development, drives
    and, 441–442, 441*f*
Psychosocial maturity, outcomes,
    353*t*
Psychosocial stages, of social devel-
    opment, 341–342, 341*t*
Psychosomatic disorders, 408
Psychosurgery, 525
Psychotherapy, 504
    with computers, 521
    group, 523–524
    psychoanalysis *vs.* behavioral
        approaches, 518*t*
Psychotic disorders, 475
PTSD (posttraumatic stress disor-
    der), 412, 480–481
Puberty, 326
Pubescent growth spurt, 326
Public verifiability, 20
Punisher, 197
Punishment
    negative, 197

    parental, childhood aggression
        and, 200, 201*f*
    positive, 197
Pupil, 90, 90*f*

Q
Questionnaire, 30–31
Questions, open-ended, 30–31

R
Racism, 580
Radical behaviorism, 182
Random assignment, 25
Rapid-eye movement sleep (REM),
    162, 167–168
    deprivation of, 164
    dreaming and, 165
    lucid dreaming, 169
Rational-emotive therapy (RET),
    520
Rats, maze-bright *vs.* maze-dull, 24
Reaction formation, 444
Reaction time, 255, 256
Reality
    cultural constructions of, 158
    personal construction of, 158
Reality principle, 443
Reasoning, 270
Recall
    by partial-report procedure, 222,
        222*f*
    by whole-report procedure, 222
Recency effect, 230
Receptive fields, 98–99, 99*f*
Receptor molecule, 78
Reciprocal altruism, 567
Reciprocal determinism, 450–451,
    450*f*
Reciprocal inhibition theory, 512
Reciprocity, liking and, 559
Reciprocity norm, 556–557
Recognition, 231–232
Reconstructive memory, 244–247
Reductionistic, structuralism as, 9
Reference point, for decision
    making, 285
Reflex, 184
Refractory period, 76–77
Rehearsal, short-term memory
    recall and, 224–225, 225*f*
Reinforcement
    differential, 204
    negative, 196
    positive, 196–197
    schedules of, 202–204, 203*f*
Reinforcement contingency,
    195–196
    discriminative stimuli and
        generalization, 197
    in everyday life, 198–199, 198*f*,
        199*f*
    punishers, 197
    reinforcers, 196–197
Reinforcement history, 448
Reinforcers, properties of, 199–202
Rejection, expectations of, 500
Relative motion parallax, 138
Relative refractory period, 77, 76*f*
Relatives, altruism toward, 566–567,
    567*f*
Relative size, for depth perception,
    138, 139*f*
Relaxation response, 424

Reliability, 30, 292
Religious experiences, hallucina-
    tions and, 173
REM. *See* Rapid-eye movement
    sleep
Repetitive transcranial magnetic
    stimulation (rTMS), 72
Representativeness heuristic,
    283–284, 283*f*
Representative sample, 25–26
Repressed memories, 510
Repressed thoughts, 156
Repression, ego defense and,
    443–444, 443*t*
Reproductive functioning, age-re-
    lated changes, 327–328
Research, informal, 19
Research project
    costs, 32
        potential gains, 32
Residual stress pattern, 412
Resistance, 509
Response bias, 85–86
Response selection, 255
Responsiveness, 344
Restful alertness, 172
Resting metabolic rate, 371
Resting potential, 75–76
Resting state, 75
RET (rational-emotive therapy),
    520
Retention interval, 231
Reticular formation, 61
Retina
    anatomy, 90, 90*f*, 90–92, 91*f*
    imaging, interpretation of,
        118–119, 119*f*
Retinal disparity, 137, 137*f*
Retrieval, 220, 226
Retrieval cues, long-term memory
    and, 232–234
Retroactive inference, 233
Reversal theory, 366–367
Review boards, 32
Right-handedness, 68
Risk/gain assessment, 33
Rituals healing, 506–507
Robbers Cave experiment, 582
Rods, 91, 91*f*
Romantic relationships, 560–563,
    560*t*
    Internet and, 562
    longevity of, 561–563, 561*f*
Rorschach test, 463, 463*f*
Rote learning, 217
Rubella (German measles), 322
Rules, social role and, 535–538
Rumination, depression and,
    487–488

S
Saccule, 110
SAD (seasonal affective disorder),
    485–486, 485*f*
Sample, 25
Sapir-Whorf hypothesis, 265
Sarcastic statement, 263*t*
Satiety cues, 369
Satiety needs, 389
Saturation, 95
Scapegoats, 589
Scarcity, 557

Schedules of reinforcement,
    202–204, 203*f*
Schemas, 242–243, 454
Schemes, 328
Schizophrenia
    biological markers of, 496–497
    brain function, 496–497
    causes, 494–495
    dopamine in, 79
    environmental stressor, family
        interaction as, 497–498
    genetic risk for, 495–496, 495*f*,
        496*f*
    symptom relapse, expressed
        emotion and, 498
    thought disorders in, 495–496,
        496*t*
    types, 493–498, 494*t*
        catatonic, 494, 494*t*
        disorganized, 494, 494*t*
        paranoid, 494, 494*t*
        residual, 494, 494*t*
        undifferentiated, 494, 494*t*
Schizophrenic disorders, 493
School psychologists, 14*t*
Scientific method, 3, 21
Scientific prediction, 6
SDT (signal detection theory),
    86–87, 86*f*
Season, birthrate and, 28
Seasonal affective disorder (SAD),
    485–486, 485*f*
Seconal, 176*t*
Segregation, psychological costs
    of, 2
Selective attention, 126–129, 127*f*,
    128*f*
Selective encoding, 544
Selective exclusion, 304–305, 304*f*
Selective optimization with com-
    pensation, 335, 360
Selective social interaction theory,
    352
Self
    construals, aggressive behavior
        and, 576–577
    cultural construction of,
        456–458, 457*t*
    independent construals of, 456,
        546
    interdependent construals of,
        456, 546
Self-actualization, 390, 446
Self-awareness, 154–155
    objective, 160
    subjective, 160
Self-concept, dynamic aspects of,
    453–454
Self-criticism, culture, self-en-
    hancement and, 457–458,
    458*f*
Self-destructive behavior, body
    image and, 326–327
Self-efficacy, 451, 519
Self-enhancement, culture, self-
    criticism and, 457–458,
    458*f*
Self-esteem, 454–455, 456*t*
    operational definition of, 22
    public face of, 455
    subliminal message effects, 29
Self-evaluations, 456–457
Self-fulfilling prophecy, 548–549
Self-handicapping, 455

Self-help groups, 524
Self-hypnosis, 171
Self-perception theory, 556
Self-preservation, 441
Self-report inventory, 460–461
Self-report measures, 30–31
Self-serving bias, 547, 548*f*
Self theories, 453–459
Self-verification, depression and, 487, 487*f*
Semantic memories, 232
Semantics, 336*t*
Semicircular canal, 110
Sensation, 83–84, 117
Sensation seeking, 421
Sense of self, 154, 158
Senses
 hearing, 100–106
 kinesthetic, 110–111
 taste, 107–108, 108*f*
 touch, 108–110, 109*f*
 vestibular, 110
Sensorimotor intelligence, 328
Sensorimotor period, 331–332
Sensorimotor stage, 329, 329*t*
Sensory adaptation, 85
Sensory memory, 221–223, 221*f*, 222*f*
Sensory neurons, 73
Sensory physiology, 88
Sensory process, in signal detection theory, 86, 86*f*
Sensory receptors, 83, 88, 89*t*
 olfactory, 106, 107*f*
 taste, 108*f*
Sensory-specific satiety, 369
Sensuality, survival and, 84
Sentence meaning, 258
Sentence structures, 262–263, 262*t*
Serial position, 229–231, 230*f*, 238
Serial processes, 256
Serotonin
 hallucinogenic drugs and, 175
 seasonal affective disorder and, 485–486, 485*f*
Serotonin neurons, 79
Set, 149
Sex chromosomes, 53, 97
Sex differences, 354–355
Sexism, 580
Sexual arousal
 hormones and, 376
 human, 376–378, 378*f*
 nonhuman, 376, 377*f*
Sexual behavior, 375
 evolution of, 378–379
 nonhuman, 375–376
 norms, 379–381, 380*f*
 sense of smell and, 107
Sexual disorders, 477
Sexual functioning, age-related changes, 327–328
Sexuality, in dream analysis, 167
Sexual response cycle, phases of, 377–378, 378*f*
Sexual risk taking, 381
Sexual scripts, 380
Shadowing, 128
Shamanism, 507
Shamans, 167
Shape constancy, 142, 143*f*
Shaping, 195, 204–205
Shaping by successive approximations, 204–205

Sharpening, as reconstructive memory process, 245
Shuttlebox, 188, 188*f*
Shyness, 435, 435*f*, 438, 439
Siblings, destructive conflict, conduct disorder and, 28
Signal detection theory (SDT), 86–87, 86*f*
Sign language, hemispheric lateralization and, 68
Similarity
 law of, 132
 liking and, 559
Simulation, of hypnosis, 171
Simultaneous conditioning, 186, 186*f*
Sine wave, 100, 100*f*
Situation
 effect on prosocial behavior, 569–571, 570*f*
 influence on aggression, 573–576
Situational power, 543–544
Situational variables, 5
Size constancy, 139–142, 142*f*
Size/distance relation, for depth perception, 138, 139*f*
Skin senses, 108–110, 109*f*
Slave Market with the Disappearing Bust of Voltaire (Dali), 121, 121*f*
Sleep, 161
 amount of, 162–163
 circadian rhythm and, 161–162
 cycle, 162–163
 functions of, 163–164
 lifestyle and, 166
 patterns, over lifetime, 163, 163*f*
 stages of, 162–163, 163*f*
 studying, 162–163, 162*f*
Sleep Alert (Mass), 165
Sleep apnea, 165
Sleep disorders, 164–165
Sleep spindles, 162
SLIP (Spoonerisms of Laboratory-Induced Predisposition), 159, 261
Smell, sense of, 106–107, 107*f*
Smoking
 cessation
  placebo control group, 25
  programs, 421–422
 nicotine effects, 176*t*, 177
 risks from, 421
Sociability, consciousness and, 157
Social assertiveness, learning, 517
Social categorization, 579
Social comparison model, 542
Social desirability, self-report measures and, 31
Social development, 340–341
 in adolescence, 347–350, 347*t*, 348*t*
 in adulthood, 350–354, 351*f*
 in childhood, 342–347, 345*f*
 human deprivation and, 346–347
 psychosocial stages of, 341–342, 341*t*
Social experience, contact comfort and, 344–346
Social functions, of emotion, 403
Social imitation, 448
Social intelligence theory, 452–453
Social-learning theory, 448–449

Social-learning therapy, 515–517, 516*f*
Social norms, 538–539
Social perception, 544–545
Social phobia, 479
Social psychologists, 14*t*
Social psychology, 535–536
Social Readjustment Rating Scale (SRRS), 409
Social reality, 538, 544–545
Social relationships
 adolescent, 348–349
 liking, 558–559
 loving, 560–563, 560*t*
Social role, 535–538
Social science, 3
Social-skills training, 516–517
Social support, 507
 cancer survival and, 425
 as coping resource, 418, 418*f*
Sociobiology, 54
Sociocultural etiology, of psychopathology, 473–474
Sodium ions, 75
Soma, 71*f*, 72
Somatic nervous system, 59
Somatoform disorders, 477
Somatosensory cortex, 65, 65*f*
Sophora seed (mescal bean), 174
Sound
 localization, 105–106, 105*f*
 physics of, 100, 100*f*
 psychological dimensions of, 100–102, 101*f*
Sound shadow, 105–106
Spatial integration, 133
Spatial intelligence, 303*t*
Spatial mental models, 270, 270*f*
Speaker's meaning, 258
Specificity, attitude-behavior correlations and, 551–552, 552*t*
Specific phobias, 479–480, 479*t*
Speech, 66, 66*f*
 children's, two-word stage of, 339
 perception, 336–337
 telegraphic, 339
Speech errors, 261–262, 261*t*
Speech execution, 261–262
Speech production
 processes, 261
 representations, 261–262
Speed of recognition, 226
Spinal cord, 58, 61*f*
Spiritualism, phenomenon of, 182
Split-brain patients, studies on, 67, 67*f*
Split-half reliability, 292
Spontaneous recovery, 186
Spontaneous-remission effect, 529
Spoonerism, 261
Sports psychologists, 14*t*
SRRS (Social Readjustment Rating Scale), 409
Standardization, 22, 294
Stanford-Binet Intelligence Scale, 296
Stanford Hypnotic Susceptibility Scale, 170, 170*f*
Stanford Prison Experiment, 535–538
Stereotyped sexual behavior, 376
Stereotype-inconsistent information, discounting, 581

Stereotypes, 549
 across languages, 244
 prejudice and, 581–582
Stereotype threat, 310, 311*f*, 581
Stigma, of mental illness, 498–500, 499*f*
Stigmatization, psychological assessment and, 315
Stimulants, 176–177, 176*t*
Stimulus
 conditioned, 184, 185*f*
 neutral, 184
Stimulus categorization, 255
Stimulus contrast, 98
Stimulus discrimination, 187–188
Stimulus-driven capture, 126, 127
Stimulus generation, 186–187, 187*f*
Stimulus generation gradients, 186–187, 187*f*
Stimulus-response connection, 194
Stirrup, 103, 103*f*, 104
Storage, 220
Strange Situation Test, 343
Stress, 405, 406*f*
 acute, 406
 appraisal of, 414–415, 415*t*
 from catastrophic/traumatic events, 411–412
 chronic, 406, 408, 409*f*
 coping with, 414–419
 physiological reactions to, 406–408, 407*f*
 psychological reactions, 408–414
Stress inoculation training, 417
Stress moderator variables, 415
Stressors, 405, 406*f*
 chronic, 412–413
 uncontrollable *vs.* controllable, 415
Striatum, 247
Strong Interest Inventory, 389
Structuralism, 9
Structure of intellect model, 300–301, 300*f*
Student Stress Scale, 410, 410*f*
Subjective reality, 12
Subjective self, 160
Subjective self-awareness, 160
Subjective viewpoint, 5
Subliminal messages, 28, 29*f*
Substance Abuse and Mental Health Services Administration (SAMHSA), 174
Substance-use disorders, 477
Subtractive color mixture, 96–97
Success, attributions of, 385–387, 386*f*
Suicide, depression and, 488–489
Superego, 442, 473, 508
Superiority, 445
Supertasters, 112
Survey, 30–31
Survival
 consciousness and, 157–158
 sense of touch and, 110
 sensuality and, 84
Sympathetic division, of autonomic nervous system, 60, 60*f*, 61
Sympathetic nervous system, emotions and, 398
Symptom substitution, 512
Synapse, 77
Synaptic cleft, 78
Synaptic transmission, 77–78, 77*f*

Synaptic vesicles, 77
Syntax, 336t
Synthesis, in perception, 117
Systematic desensitization, 512–513, 513t

T

Tabula rasa, 321
Taijin kyofusho, 477
Tardive dyskinesia, 527
Taste, sense of, 107–108, 108f
Taste-aversion learning, 206–208, 207f
Taste buds, 112
TAT (Thematic Apperception Test), 384, 384f, 463–464, 464f
Television violence, childhood aggression and, 20, 22, 23, 212–213
Telic state, 366
Temperaments, child, 344
Temperature, aggression and, 574–575, 575f
Temporal integration, 133
Temporal lobe, 64
Tend-and-befriend response, 407–408
Tension, 365
Tension reduction, 365, 448
Terminal buttons, 71f, 72–73
Testicular hormones, 71t
Testosterone, 70
Test-retest reliability, 292
Texture gradients, for depth perception, 138–139, 140f
Thalamus, 61f, 62, 62f
THC, 175
Thematic Apperception Test (TAT), 384, 384f, 463–464, 464f
Theory, 20
Theory of ecological optics, 125–126
Theory of mind, 333
Therapeutic settings, therapists and, 505–506
Therapists, types of, 505–506
Think-aloud protocols, 156, 274
Thorndike puzzle box, 194–195, 195f
Thought, language, culture and, 265–267
Thought disorders, in schizophrenia, 495–496, 496t
Three-term contingency, 197, 199f
Thyroid gland, 407
Thyroid hormones, 71t
Thyrotrophic hormone (TTH), 407
Timbre, 101–102, 102f

Time disparity, sound localization and, 105–106, 105f
Time perspective, balanced, 426
Timing, in classical conditioning, 184–185, 185f
Token economies, 202, 515
Token resistance, 381
Tolerance, 174
Top-down processing, 145, 145f, 146f
Totalitarianism, 592, 593f
Touch, sense of, 108–110, 109f
Trace conditioning, 185–186, 186f
Trance, hypnotic, 170
Transcendence, need for, 390
Transduction, 88
Transfer-appropriate processing, 234–235, 235f
Transference, 509
Transient psychoses, 166
Traumatic events, stress from, 411–412
Trial and error, 194
Triarchic theory of intelligence, 301–302, 301f
Trichromatic theory, 97–98
Tricyclic antidepressants, 527
Trust *vs.* mistrust, 341, 341t
TTH (thyrotrophic hormone), 407
Twins
    dizygotic, 53
    monozygotic, 53
Twin studies, of IQ, 305–307, 306f
Tympanic membrane, 103, 103f, 104
Type A behavior pattern, 427
Type B behavior pattern, 427
Type C behavior pattern, 427

U

UCR (unconditioned response), 184–186, 185f, 186f
UCS (unconditioned stimulus), 184–186, 185f, 186f
Ummami, 108
Unconditional positive regard, 446, 522
Unconditioned response (UCR), 184–186, 185f, 186f
Unconditioned stimulus (UCS), 184, 185f
Unconscious, 156, 442
Unconscious conflict, 473
Unconscious inference, 125
Unconsciousness, *vs.* consciousness, 460
Utricle, 110

V

Valence, 388
Validity, 30, 292–294
Valium, 78, 175–176, 176t
Variable, 22
Variable-interval schedule, 203f, 204
Variable-ratio schedule, 203–204, 203f
Variables, degree of correlation between, 27
Variation, individual, natural selection and, 50
Ventricle size, in schizophrenia, 496–497
Ventromedial hypothalamus (VMH), 238, 370
Verbal aggression, consistency in, 438
Verbal representations, combining with visual representations, 269–271, 270f, 271f
Vestibular sense, 110
Violence, positive evaluation of, 573
Virtual reality, 124
Vision
    age-related changes, 327
    brain pathways for, 92–93, 93f
    color, 93–98
    complex analysis, 98–99, 99f
    functions, separation of, 92–93
    neonatal, 324
Visual cliff, 324, 325f
Visual cognition, 267, 268f
Visual cortex, 65, 66f, 72, 92
Visual information
    brain localization, 72
    neural pathways for, 68f
Visual representations, 268–269, 268f
    combining with verbal representations, 269–271, 270f, 271f
Visual scanning, of mental images, 269, 269f
Visual system, 89–100. *See also* Eye
Visuospatial sketchpad, 227
Vitreous humor, 90, 90f
VMH (ventromedial hypothalamus), 238, 370
Vocational interest surveys, 380
Volley principle, 105, 105f

W

War, reasons for, 591
Wason selection task, 277
Wavelength, 94–95, 95f
    preferences, of cones, 98
Weber's constant, 88, 88t

Weber's Law, 87–88, 87f
Web search process, *vs.* human memory searches, 242
Web sites, IQ testing, 299
Wechsler Adult Intelligence Scale (WAIS), 297
Wechsler Adult Intelligence Scale-Revised (WAIS-R), 297–298, 298f
Wechsler Intelligence Scale for Children-Third Edition (WISC-III), 298
Wechsler Intelligence Scales, 296–298
Wechsler Preschool and Primary Scale of Intelligence (WPPSI-R), 298
Wellness, 420
Wernicke's area, 66, 66f
Western psychology, 6, 8–10
Wild Boy of Aveyron, 321
Wisdom, 334, 335
Within-subjects design, 26
Women
    preferences for males' faces, 379
    in psychology, 15–16, 15f
    valuing of altruistic men, 567–568
Woods, Tiger, 307
Word fragment completion, 234
Word identification, 234
Word meanings, learning, 337–338, 338t
Words, overextending, 338
Word stem completion, 234
Working memory span, 227–228
Work setting, organizational psychologists and, 387
World Wide Web
    information sources, legitimate, 35
    sleep and, 166

X

Xanax, 78, 175–176
X chromosome, 53, 97

Y

Y chromosome, 53
Yerkes-Dodson law, 402–403, 402f

Z

Zygote, 322

Credits

1, *Crowd #9,* Source: Diana Ong/SuperStock; 4 TL, © Elizabeth Crews/ The Image Works; 4 TR, © Joel Gordon 1987; 4 BL, Susan Kuklin/Photo Researchers, Inc.; 4 BR, Tom McCarthy/Index Stock; 5, National Gallery/London/© Eric Lessing/Art Resource; 7, © Matthew Neal McVay/Stock Boston; 8, Archives of the History of American Psychology/University of Akron; 11, The Granger Collection; 12, Courtesy American Museum of Natural History Library; 15, © Michael Grecco/Stock Boston; 18, *Businesswoman on Computer, Light Bulb,* Source: © Alexander Barsky/Stock Illustration Source, Inc.; 20, © 1995 Sidney Harris; 21, AP/Wide World Photos; 23L, © A. Gottfried/The Image Works; 23R, © Rob Crandall/The Image Works; 23B, Edouard Berne/Stone; 26, Marcia Weinstein; 27, © Larry Mulvehill/Photo Reseachers, Inc.; 31, © Jeff Greenberg/PhotoEdit; 32, Michael K. Nichols/National Geographic Image Collection; 34, © Richard T. Nowitz/PhotoTake NYC; 36, © *Jacksonville Journal Courier*/The Image Works; 47, *Body Electric,* Source: Diana Ong/SuperStock; 49, © Willie Hill/The Image Works; 53, Dan McCoy/Rainbow; 55, © Mary Kate Denny/ PhotoEdit; 56, Reprinted with permission from Damasio H, Grabowski T, Frank R, Galaburda AM, Damasio AR: The return of Phineas Gage: Clues about the brain from a famous patient. *Science, 264*:1102–1105, © 1994. American Association for the Advancement of Science. Photo courtesy of H. Damasio, Human Neuroanatomy and Neuroimaging Laboratory, Department of Neurology, University of Iowa; 57T, © Dan McCoy Rainbow; 57B, Roger Tully/Stone; 58, Courtesy of Marcus E. Raichle, M.D. Washington University School of Medicine; 68, © John Coletti/Stock Boston; 73, © D. W. Fawcett/Komuro/Photo Researchers, Inc.; 80, Tim Malyon and Paul Biddle/ SPL/Photo Reseachers, Inc.; 82, *Warm Wind,* Source: © Alexandra Rozenman; 83, David Lissy/Index Stock; 85, Alex von Kroscrembahr/Photo Researchers, Inc.; 89, W. E. Harvey/Photo Researchers, Inc.; 95, © Alan Levenson/Stock, Boston; 101, Spencer Grant/Photo Researchers, Inc.; 104, © Bob Daemmrich/Stock Boston; 106, Stephen Krasemann/Stone; 108, © Seth Resnick/Stock Boston; 110 T, David Ball/ Index Stock; 110 B, © Pic Tommy Hindley/Professional Sport/Topham/The Image Works; 112, Scott Foresman; 113, © Fuji Photos/The Image Works; 115, *Rhythm and colors,* 1939, Sonia Delaunay. Oil on canvas. © L & M Services. B. V. Amsterdam 20010210. Photo: R. G. Ojeda. Musee des Beaux-Arts, Lille, France. Source: Reunion des Musees Nationaux/Art Resource, NY; 118, © Innervisions 1994; 120, Scott Foresman; 121, Salvador Dali, *Slave Market with Disappearing Bust of Voltaire* (1940). Oil on canvas. 18¼ × 25⅜ inches. Collection of the Salvador Dali Museum, St. Petersburg, Florida. Copyright 1997 Salvador Dali Museum, Inc.; 126, Boyd Norton/ © 1995 Comstock, Inc.; 131, Mike Yamashita/Woodfin Camp & Associates; 136, Dennis O'Clair/Stone; 138, Andy Levin/Photo Researchers, Inc.; 139, © Michael Dwyer/Stock Boston; 140T, © Francis Lepine/Earth Scenes; 140BL, Duccio, *Maesta: Christ and St. Anne.* 1308–1311. Scala/Art Resource, New York; 140BR, Perugino: *Delivering the Keys of the Kingdom to St. Peter.* 1481–1483. Scala/Art Resource, New York; 141, AP/Wide World Photos; 142, © David Wells/The Image Works; 143, AP/ Wide World Photos; 144, Bob Rowan/Corbis; 146, Taylor Jones/© Los Angeles Times Syndicate. Reprinted by permission; 152, *Girl sleeping under a tent,* Pavel Kuznetsov. Tretyakov Gallery, Moscow, Russia. Source: Scala/Art Resource, NY; 154, © Rhoda Sidney/PhotoEdit; 155L, © Bonnie Kamin/PhotoEdit; 155TR, N. Durrell McKenna/ Photo Researchers, Inc; 155BR, © Ulrike Welsch/PhotoEdit; 158, David Hockney, "The Crossword Puzzle, Minneapolis, Jan. 1983" Photographic Collage, ED: 10, 33 × 46" © David Hockney; 161L, Jim Sugar/Corbis; 161R, Chuck Solomon/Sports Illustrated ©Time, Inc.; 164, © Bill Aron/PhotoEdit; 169, Courtesy of Dr. Phillip G. Zimbardo; 172, © Gary Conner/PhotoEdit; 173, Mike Maple/Woodfin Camp & Associates; 177, Chuck Savage/The Stock Market; 179, *Art Class,* ca. 1939-1940. Oil on plywood. William H. Johnson. Source: Smithsonian American Art Museum, Washington, DC/Art Resource, NY; 181, John Terence Turner/FPG; 182, © Joe McNally Photography; 183, © Bettmann/Corbis; 187, © Innervisions 1994; 191T, Archives of the History of American Psychology, University of Akron; 191B, Hulton/ Archive Photos; 192, © Billy E. Barnes/PhotoEdit; 193, © M. Abbey/Photo Researchers, Inc.; 199, Cindy Charles/PhotoEdit; 202, Yerkes Regional Primate Research Center, Emory University; 205T, © Gerald Davis/Woodfin Camp & Associates; 205B, Stephen Ferry/Liaison Agency, Inc.; 208, Courtesy Dr. Stuart R. Ellins, California State University, San Bernadino; 212, Courtesy Dr. Albert Bandura, Stanford University; 215, *Woman reading on black background,* Henri Matisse. © 2001 Succession H. Matisse, Paris/Artists Rights Society (ARS), New York. Musee National d'Art Moderne, Centre Georges Pompidou, Paris, France. Source: Giraudon/Art Resource, NY; 217, AP/Wide World Photos; 219, © Bill Gallery/Stock Boston; 226, Kevin Horan/ Stone; 227, © Joseph Nettis/Stock Boston; 229, Spencer Grant/Photo Researchers, Inc.; 233, © Michael Newman/PhotoEdit; 240, © Tom McCarthy/PhotoEdit; 245, ©1995 Comstock, Inc.; 246, © John Neubauer/PhotoEdit; 252, *Community* (study for mural, Jamaica, NY). 1986, Jacob Lawrence. Gouache on paper. Source: Smithsonian American Art Museum, Washington, DC/Art Resource, NY; 257, © David Young-Wolff/PhotoEdit; 257L, Stuart Cohen/©1995 Comstock, Inc.; 257R, Fred Bavendam/ Peter Arnold; 263, AP/Wide World Photos; 266, Steve Winter/Language Research Center/GSU; 267, Karl Muller/Woodfin Camp & Associates; 272, Hank Morgan/Photo Researchers, Inc.; 276, © 1995 Sidney Harris; 282, © 1995 Comstock, Inc.; 286, © David Frazier/The Image Works; 288, *Power Book Girl,* Source: Private collection/ Christian Pierre/SuperStock; 291, Science Library/Photo Researchers, Inc.; 293, © Bachman/Photo Researchers, Inc.; 298T, © Bob Daemmrich/Stock Boston; 298B, Courtesy of Riverside Publishing; 302, © J. Griffin/The Image Works; 304, Brown Brothers; 307, AP/Wide World Photos; 308L, Ed Clark/TimePix; 308R, Joan Clifford/ Index Stock; 312, Joel Gordon; 313, Granger; 314, © Tony Freeman/PhotoEdit; 317, *Children,* Kasimir Malevich. Pushkin Museum of Fine Arts, Moscow, Russia, Source: Scala/Art Resource, NY; 320L, Popperfoto/Hulton/Archive; 320M, Hulton/Archive; 320R, Topham/The Image Works; 320BL , Brown Brothers; 320BR, © Tom McCarthy/ PhotoEdit; 322, Lennart Nelson/*A Child Is Born*/Bonniers; 323, © Elizabeth Crews/ The Image Works; 324, © Alan Carey/The Image Works; 325T, Birnbach/Monkmeyer; 325B, © Mike Greenlar/The Image Works; 327, © Michael Newman/PhotoEdit; 328, Donna Day/Stone; 330T, Lew Merrim/Monkmeyer; 330B, Marcia Weinstein; 333, © McLaughlin/The Image Works; 334, AP/Wide World Photos; 338, © Robert Brenner/PhotoEdit; 342, Sarah Putnam/Index Stock; 343, © Nina Leen/Timepix; 344, © Bob Daemmrich/The Image Works; 345, Martin Rogers/Stone; 349, Caterine Karnow/Woodfin Camp & Associates; 351, © R. Sidney/The Image Works; 355, J. P. Williams/Stone; 356, © Tony Freeman/PhotoEdit; 362, *Moonlight Lovers.* Michael Escoffery. Private Collection. © 2001 Michael Escoffery/Artists Rights Society (ARS), New York. Source: Michael Escoffery/Art Resource, NY; 364, Jo McBride/Stone; 365, AP/Wide World Photos; 367, John Shaw/Bruce Coleman, Inc.; 370, © Jeff Greenberg/PhotoEdit; 373L, AP/Wide World Photos; 373R, AP/Wide World Photos; 378, © B. Bachman/The Image Works; 380, © Esbin/Anderson/The Image Works; 382, © Deborah Davis/PhotoEdit, 383, © Bob Daemmrich/Stock Boston; 384, © M. Antman/The Image Works; 385, © Steven Frame/Stock Boston; 388, Reuters/ Jeff Topping/Archive Photos; 390, Paul Avis/The Liaison Agency; 392, *Sprint,* Source: Gilbert Mayers/SuperStock; 394, Photography Collection Miriam and Ira D. Wallach Division of Art, Prints and Photographs. The New York Public Library, Astor, Lenox and Tilden Foundation; 395, Dr. Paul Ekman/Human Interaction Library/ University of California, San Francisco; 397L, © Burbank/The Image Works; 397R, © Barbara Alper/Stock Boston; 399, Sean Murphy/Stone; 400, © Bonnie Kamin/PhotoEdit; 403, © Robert Brenner/PhotoEdit; 405T, Damien Lovegrove/Science Photo Library/Photo Researchers, Inc.; 405B, Paula Lerner/Woodfin Camp & Associates; 408, © Esbin/ Anderson/The Image Works; 413, Jim West/Impact Visuals. 416, © Bob Daemmrich/ The Image Works; 420, © Terry Eiler/Stock Boston; 424, © Cotla/Liaison Agency; 425, © R Lord/The Image Works; 426, Chuck Nacke/Woodfin Camp and Associates; 430, *The Modern Idol,* Peter Blake. © 2001 Artists Rights Society (ARS), New York/DACS, London. Victoria and Albert Museum, London. Source: Victoria and Albert Museum, London/Art Resource, NY; 431, North Wind Picture Archives; 433, Courtesy of Zentralbibliothek, Zurich; 434L, Granger Collection; 434M, Bettmann/CORBIS; 34R, Reuters/Jonathan Evans/Archive Photos; 437, © Tony Freeman/PhotoEdit; 440L, Doug Armand/Stone; 440R, Gary Braasch/Woodfin Camp & Associates; 441, Jake Rais/Stone; 445, Art © Jim Berris/Photo Rafael Marcia/Photo Researchers, Inc.; 448, © Richard Hutchings/PhotoEdit; 450, © Richard Hutchings/PhotoEdit; 454, © Steve Rubin/The Image Works; 455, © Jeff Greenberg/Photo Researchers, Inc.; 456, © Steve Maines/Stock Boston; 464, Henry A. Murray, 1971, /Harvard University Press; 466, *Woman Meditating,* Alexei von Jawlensky. Fundacion Coleccion Thyssen-Bornemisza, Madrid, Spain, Source: Scala/Art Resource, NY; 468, Jack Rezmicki/The Stock Market; 470, Mihail Chemiakin/Memories of St. Petersburg, 1984, lithograph; 471, *The Trial of George Jacobs,* August 5, 1692, oil on canvas by T.H. Matenson, 1855, Peabody Essex Museum; 472, Granger Collection; 478, © David Grossman/The Image Works; 479, William Hubbell/Woodfin Camp & Associates; 483, *Melancholia,* 1998 Amy Wicherski/SuperStock; 485, © Jeff Greenberg/PhotoEdit; 487, © Esbin-Anderson/ The Image Works; 488, Reuters/Lee Celano/Archive Photos; 490, Photomondo/FPG International; 491, © Susan Greenwood/Liaison Agency; 497T, Lab of Psychology and Psychopathy, National Institute of Mental Health; reproduced by permission of Edna Morlock; 497B, © David Young-Wolff/PhotoEdit; 502, *Self Love,* Source: Gayle Ray/ SuperStock; 506, Granger Collection; 508, AP/Wide World Photos; 511, Wellcome Library. London; 514, AP/Wide World Photos; 516, Courtesy of Dr. Philip G. Zimbardo; 519, © Stephen Frisch/Stock Boston; 523, © Bob Daemmrich/The Image Works; 526L, James Wilson/Woodfin Camp and Associates; 526R, Will McIntyre/ Photo Researchers, Inc.; 527, Jim West/Impact Visuals; 529, © 1995 by Sidney Harris; 531, Stewart Cohen/Stone; 534, *Collage of People's Lives,* Source: © Jose Ortega/Stock Illustration Source, Inc.; 536, Michael S. Yamashita/Woodfin Camp & Associates; 537, Courtesy of Dr. Philip G. Zimbardo; 539, Kaku Kurita/Liaison Agency; 540, Courtesy of William Vandivert; 543, Everett Collection; 544, AP/ Wide World Photos; 549, Sandra Lousada/Woodfin Camp & Associates; 551, Photo: Francois Duhamel /Everett Collection; 552, © Bob Daemmrich/Stock Boston; 553, Tony Hawk ©1998 Courtesy of National Fluid Milk Processor Promotion Board; 555, AP/Wide World Photos; 558, © Susan Van Etten-Lawson/PhotoEdit; 559, Stone; 561, Bruce Ayers/Stone; 564, *Figure Holding Sun,* Source: © Jose Ortega/Stock Illustration Source, Inc.; 566, AP/Wide World Photos; 568, © David Young-Wolff/ PhotoEdit; 569, AP/Wide World Photos; 572L, © M. Reardon/Photo Researchers, Inc.; 572R, © Catherine Ursillo/Photo Researchers, I Inc.; 573; AP/Wide World Photos; 574, © B. Daemmrich/ The Image Works; 577, Hulton/Archive Photos; 579L, AP/ Wide World Photos; 579R, © Robert W. Ginn/PhotoEdit; 580L, © Bill Aron/PhotoEdit; 580R, © W. Hill, Jr./The Image Works; 582, Dr. O. J. Harvey, University of Colorado; 585, From the film *Obedience* © 1965 by Stanley Milgram, by permission of Alexandra Milgram; 589, AP/Wide World Photos, 590T, AP/Wide World Photos; 590B, S. Keen (1986) Faces of the Enemy; Reflections of the hostile imagination. © 1986 by Sam Keen. All rights reserved. Reprinted by permission of HarperCollins Publishers, Inc.; 594, AP/Wide World Photos.

Cookies

1,001 Mouthwatering Recipes

from around the World

Reader's Digest

THE READER'S DIGEST ASSOCIATION, INC.
PLEASANTVILLE, NEW YORK / MONTREAL

A READER'S DIGEST BOOK
This edition published by the Reader's Digest Association by arrangement with McRae Books Srl

Copyright © 2004 McRae Books Srl

This book was conceived, edited and designed by
McRae Books Srl
Borgo Santa Croce, 8,
50122 Florence, Italy
info@mcraebooks.com

FOR McRAE BOOKS:
Project Director: Anne McRae
Design Directors: Marco Nardi, Sara Mathews
Text: Pamela Egan, Brenda Moore, Ting Morris, Palma Rella, Mollie Thomson
Photography: Marco Lanza, Studio Cappelli
Pastry Cook for Photography: Masha Rinascente
Layouts and Cut-outs: Adina Stefania Dragomir, Filippo delle Monache
Project Editor: Helen Farrell

FOR READER'S DIGEST:
U.S. Project Editor: Andrea Chesman
Canadian Project Editor: Pamela Johnson
Project Designer: George McKeon
Executive Editor, Trade Publishing: Dolores York
Associate Publisher, Trade Publishing: Christopher T. Reggio
Vice President & Publisher, Trade Publishing: Harold Clarke

Library of Congress Cataloging-in-Publication Data
Cookies : 1,001 classic recipes from around the world.
    p. cm.
  ISBN: 0-7621-0593-3
  1. Cookies. 2. Cookery, International. I Reader's Digest Association.

TX772.C396415 2004
641.8'654--dc22   2004051138

Address any comments about *Cookies* to:
The Reader's Digest Association, Inc.
Adult Trade Publishing
Reader's Digest Road
Pleasantville, NY 10570-7000

For more Reader's Digest products and information, visit our website:
www.rd.com (in the United States)
www.readersdigest.ca (in Canada)

Printed and bound in Italy by Lito Terrazzi s.r.l.

1 3 5 7 9 10 8 6 4 2

contents

introduction 10

drop cookies 12 • rolled cookies 64

bars & brownies 118 • icebox cookies 160

shortbread cookies 182 • piped & shaped cookies 200

meringues & macaroons 226 • wafers & thins 246

italian biscotti 266 • dainty tea cakes 278

festive cookies 294 • no-bake cookies 320

fried cookies 330 • decorating & serving 338

index 350

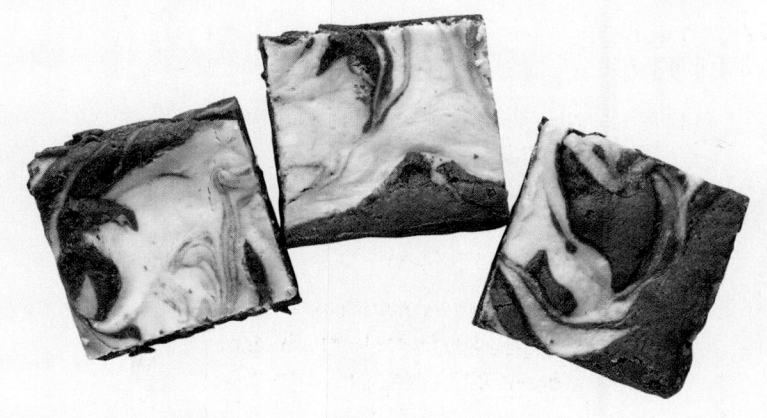

Introduction

Cookies—as we know them today—probably were created by accident. Dutch cooks used to test the temperature of their ovens by dropping a little cake batter onto the oven shelves to see if the batter would begin to bake. The name cookie derives from the Dutch word koekje, meaning "little cake."

The first cookie recipe is attributed to the Roman author, Apicius, who recorded a mixture of boiled wheat flour left to dry on a plate, which was then cut up and fried. Served with honey and pepper, this recipe is far removed from the delightful confections we enjoy today.

Butterflies (see page 70)

But it was in the Middle Ages that the cookie tradition began to flourish. Savoy cookies from France, made from egg whites, sugar, and flour—and the forerunners of meringues—date from this time. The basic method of creaming butter and sugar arrived in Europe and America in the 18th century as baking tools and techniques evolved. Shortly afterward, a drop in the price of sugar and flour made baking a pastime affordable to all.

In this book, we have gathered 1,001 recipes for cookies and their fillings and frostings from baking traditions around the world. There are classic recipes for peanut butter and chocolate chip cookies, as well as an entire chapter chock-full of bars and brownies, including the popular blondies and Canadian Nanaimo bars. For the more adventurous baker, there is an array of festive cookies, fried delicacies, and curved wafers to serve during the holiday season or as afterdinner treats. To provide the maximum variety of recipes, we have been as inclusive as possible with our definition of cookies.

Baking is a precise art, and to ensure your success with these recipes, you should follow the measurements given. We have attempted to list ingredients easily found in your local supermarkets or to provide alternatives where there may be difficulties. All of the recipes are ranked from 1 (easy) to 3 (complicated), but the majority are either easy or fairly easy (2). The recipes have been standardized to use measures and pans commonly found in North America. If you are baking outside of the United States, make sure you use the tables at the end of the book for easy substitutions.

Drop cookies, brownies, and no-bake cookies are by far the easiest to whip together. Icebox cookies and biscotti, while slightly more time-consuming, are also perfect for beginning bakers. Experienced bakers will enjoy the challenge of some of the more intricate wafers, rolled cookies, and piped cookies. With 1,001 recipes, there is sure to be something for everyone.

In the final chapter in this book, you will also find a selection of sumptuous frostings and butter-creams. We have included a range of flavored sugars and mixed spices, which are cross-referenced throughout the book.

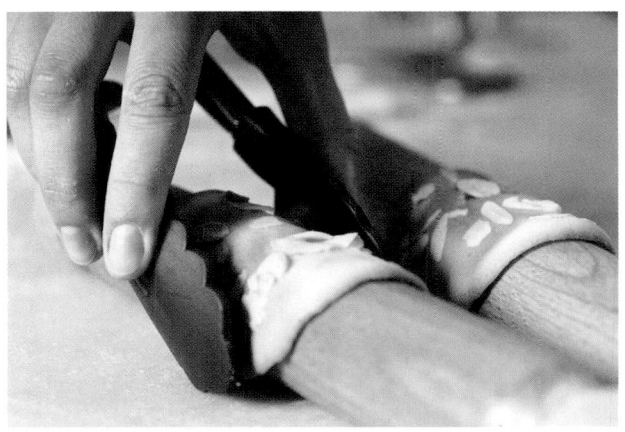

We recommend using rimless cookie sheets as they allow the hot air to circulate around the cookies, resulting in even baking. Aluminum or nonstick sheets are ideal for cookie baking. To prevent sticking, butter your cookie sheets or line them with parchment paper. Rolling pins, nylon pastry bags, and a variety of cookie cutters are useful items of equipment for baking the cookies in this book.

A maximum storage time has been given for all the cookies. Unless otherwise stated, this is the time during which your freshly baked cookies will stay fresh if kept in an airtight container.

drop
cookies

Quick and simple to make, these cookies are
easily dropped onto the cookie sheet using
two spoons or by first forming them into balls.
Prepare a butter-based dough and fold in
an array of delicious ingredients. Just
remember to leave space in between
the cookies as the butter will make them
spread during baking. We recommend
buttering your cookie sheets or lining them with
parchment paper so that the cookies do not
stick and are easily removed after baking.
Versatile and great-textured, drop cookies are
the ambassadors of home-baking.

above: Orange cookies with
chocolate chips (page 39)

right: Clockwise from top
left: Raspberry
thumbprints, Hazelnut
–citrus cookies, Bretzels,
and Chocolate–banana
cookies (see pages 16, 38,
214, and 29)

crunchy crags

1/2	cup (1 stick) butter, softened
2/3	cup firmly packed dark brown sugar
1	large egg, lightly beaten
2/3	cup all-purpose flour
1/3	cup old-fashioned rolled oats
1 1/2	tablespoons unsweetened cocoa powder
1/2	teaspoon baking powder
1/8	teaspoon salt
3	oz white chocolate, coarsely chopped
3	oz milk chocolate, coarsely chopped
1	cup coarsely chopped hazelnuts

Preheat the oven to 350°F. • Butter a cookie sheet. • Beat the butter and brown sugar in a large bowl with an electric mixer at high speed until creamy. • Add the egg, beating until just blended. • Mix in the flour, oats, cocoa, baking powder, and salt. • Stir in the white and milk chocolates and hazelnuts. • Drop teaspoons of the mixture 1/2 inch apart on the prepared baking sheet. • Bake for 10–15 minutes, or until risen and craggy. • Cool on the sheet until the cookies firm slightly. Transfer to racks and let cool completely.

Makes 16–20 cookies · Prep: 30 min. · Cooking: 10–15 min. · Level: 1 · Keeps: 5 days

lemon drop cookies

3	cups all-purpose flour
1	tablespoon baking powder
1/4	teaspoon salt
3	large eggs
1/2	cup milk
2	teaspoons lemon extract
1/2	cup granulated sugar
1/2	cup vegetable oil

Lemon frosting
2	cups confectioners' sugar
2	teaspoons lemon extract
1/2	cup water

Preheat the oven to 350°F. • Butter two cookie sheets. • Sift the flour, baking powder, and salt into a medium bowl. • Beat the eggs, milk, lemon extract, sugar, and oil in a large bowl with an electric mixer at high speed until well blended. • With mixer at low speed, gradually add the dry ingredients until the dough is soft and sticky. • Drop teaspoons of the dough 2 inches apart onto the prepared cookie sheets. • Bake for 6–8 minutes, or until just lightly browned at the edges, rotating the sheets halfway through for even baking. • Transfer the cookies to racks to cool. • Lemon frosting: Beat the confectioners' sugar, lemon extract, and water until smooth. Spread the frosting over the cookies.

Makes 35 cookies · Prep: 25 min. · Cooking: 6–8 min. · Level: 1 · Keeps: 5 days (without the frosting)

chocolate crumblies

1	cup all-purpose flour
2	tablespoons unsweetened cocoa powder
1	teaspoon baking powder
1/8	teaspoon ground cinnamon
1/8	teaspoon salt
1/2	cup (1 stick) butter, softened
1/2	cup granulated sugar
1	large egg yolk
2	oz semisweet chocolate, coarsely chopped

Preheat the oven to 350°F. • Butter two cookie sheets. • Sift the flour, cocoa, baking powder, cinnamon, and salt into a medium bowl. • Beat the butter and sugar in a large bowl with an electric mixer at high speed until creamy. • Add the egg yolk, beating until just blended. • Mix in the dry ingredients. • Drop teaspoons of the dough 1 inch apart onto the prepared cookie sheets. • Bake for 12–15 minutes, or until firm around the edges, rotating the sheets halfway through for even baking. • Transfer to racks to cool. • Melt the chocolate in a double boiler over barely simmering water. Drizzle the tops with the melted chocolate.

Makes 25–30 cookies · Prep: 20 min. · Cooking: 12–15 min. · Level: 1 · Keeps: 7 days

mocha chocolate cookies

1 1/4	cups all-purpose flour
1	teaspoon baking powder
1/8	teaspoon salt
1/2	cup (1 stick) butter, softened
2/3	cup granulated sugar
2	teaspoons coffee extract or 2 teaspoons freeze-dried coffee granules dissolved in 1 tablespoon boiling water
1	teaspoon vanilla extract
30	Hershey kisses

Preheat the oven to 325°F. • Butter two cookie sheets. • Sift the flour, baking powder, and salt into a large bowl. • Beat the butter and sugar in a large bowl with an electric mixer at high speed until creamy. • Add the coffee extract and vanilla. • Mix in the dry ingredients to form a smooth dough. • Roll into balls the size of walnuts and place 1 1/2 inches apart on the prepared baking sheet, pressing down lightly. • Press a Hershey kiss into the tops. • Bake for 15–20 minutes, or until firm to the touch, rotating the sheets halfway through for even baking. • Transfer to racks to cool.

Makes about 30 cookies · Prep: 15 min. · Cooking: 15–20 min. · Level: 1 · Keeps: 7 days

sunflower–bran cookies

1	cup whole-wheat flour
1/2	teaspoon baking soda
1/2	teaspoon salt
1/2	cup (1 stick) butter, softened
1/2	cup firmly packed light brown sugar
1	large egg
1/2	teaspoon vanilla extract
1/2	cup bran
1/2	cup old-fashioned rolled oats
1 1/4	cups carob chips
1/4	cup sunflower seeds

Preheat the oven to 375°F. • Butter two cookie sheets. • Sift the flour, baking soda, and salt into a medium bowl. • Beat the butter and brown sugar in a large bowl with an electric mixer at high speed until creamy. • Add the egg and vanilla, beating until just blended. • Mix in the dry ingredients, bran, oats, carob chips, and sunflower seeds. • Drop tablespoons of the dough 3 inches apart onto the prepared cookie sheets. • Bake for 8–10 minutes, or until just golden, rotating the sheets halfway through for even baking. • Transfer to racks to cool.

Makes 20–24 cookies · Prep: 20 min. · Cooking: 8–10 min. · Level: 1 · Keeps: 5 days

snickerdoodles

These cookies have German origins and were formerly called "Schneckenoodles." Hugely popular in the United States, the name has become Americanized through time.

2 1/3	cups all-purpose flour
1	teaspoon baking powder
1/4	teaspoon freshly grated nutmeg
1/8	teaspoon salt
1	cup (2 sticks) butter, softened
3/4	cup Vanilla Sugar (see page 341)
1/2	cup + 1/3 cup granulated sugar
1/2	teaspoon vanilla extract
2	large eggs
1/2	cup finely chopped walnuts
1	tablespoon ground cinnamon

Sift the flour, baking powder, nutmeg, and salt into a medium bowl. • Beat the butter, vanilla sugar, and 1/2 cup granulated sugar in a large bowl with an electric mixer at high speed until creamy. • Add the vanilla and eggs, beating until just blended. • Mix in the dry ingredients and walnuts. • Form the dough into four logs, about 1 inch in diameter, wrap in plastic wrap, and refrigerate for at least 30 minutes, or until firm. • Preheat the oven to 375°F. • Line two cookie sheets with parchment paper. • Mix the remaining $^1/3$ cup sugar and cinnamon in a small bowl. • Cut off small dough slices and roll into balls the size of walnuts. Roll in the cinnamon-sugar mixture. • Place on the prepared cookie sheets, about $1^1/2$ inches apart. • Bake for 12–15 minutes, or until golden brown around the edges, rotating the sheets halfway through for even baking. Cool the cookies on the cookie sheets for 1 minute. • Transfer to racks to finish cooling.

Makes about 45 cookies · Prep: 30 min. + 30 min. to chill · Cooking: 12–15 min. · Level: 2 · Keeps: 7 days

chocolate–nutmeg cookies

1   cup all-purpose flour
2   tablespoons unsweetened cocoa powder
1   teaspoon baking powder
$^1/8$ teaspoon freshly grated nutmeg
$^1/8$ teaspoon salt
$^1/2$ cup (1 stick) butter, softened
$^1/2$ cup granulated sugar
1   large egg yolk

Preheat the oven to 350°F. • Butter two cookie sheets. • Sift the flour, cocoa, baking powder, nutmeg, and salt into a medium bowl. • Beat the butter and sugar in a large bowl with an electric mixer at high speed until creamy. • Add the egg yolk, beating until just blended. • Mix in the dry ingredients. • Drop teaspoons of the dough 1 inch apart onto the prepared cookie sheets. • Bake for 12–15 minutes, or until firm around the edges, rotating the sheets halfway through for even baking. • Transfer to racks to cool.

Makes 25–30 cookies · Prep: 20 min. · Cooking: 12–15 min. · Level: 1 · Keeps: 7 days

cherry–chocolate crunchies

2   cups all-purpose flour
1   tablespoon unsweetened cocoa powder
1   teaspoon baking powder
$^1/8$ teaspoon salt
$^1/2$ cup corn flakes
2   tablespoons old-fashioned rolled oats
2   tablespoons finely chopped candied cherries
$^1/2$ cup (1 stick) butter, cut up
$^2/3$ cup superfine sugar
1   tablespoon light corn syrup
1   teaspoon baking soda dissolved in 1 tablespoon milk

Preheat the oven to 350°F. • Butter two cookie sheets. • Sift the flour, cocoa, baking powder, and salt into a large bowl. • Stir in the corn flakes, oats, and cherries. • Melt the butter, superfine sugar, and corn syrup in a small saucepan over low heat. • Add the baking soda mixture. • Stir the butter mixture into the dry ingredients. • Drop teaspoons of the dough $1^1/2$ inches apart onto the prepared cookie sheets, pressing down firmly with a fork. • Bake for 15–20 minutes, or until crisp, rotating the sheets halfway through for even baking. • Transfer to racks to cool.

Makes about 35 cookies · Prep: 15 min. · Cooking: 15–20 min. · Level: 1 · Keeps: 7 days

simple white chocolate chip cookies

1   cup all-purpose flour
$1^1/2$ teaspoons baking powder
$^1/2$ teaspoon salt
$^1/2$ cup (1 stick) butter, softened
$^1/4$ cup granulated sugar
1   large egg, lightly beaten
6   oz white chocolate, coarsely chopped

Preheat the oven to 350°F. • Butter two cookie sheets. • Sift the flour, baking powder, and salt into a large bowl. • Beat the butter and sugar in a large bowl with an electric mixer at high speed until creamy. • Add the egg, beating until just blended. • Mix in the dry ingredients and white chocolate. • Drop teaspoons of the mixture 1 inch apart onto the prepared cookie sheets. • Bake for 15–20 minutes, or until golden brown, rotating the sheets halfway through for even baking. • Cool on the sheets for 15 minutes. • Transfer to racks to cool.

Makes 30 cookies · Prep: 15 min. · Cooking: 15–20 min. · Level: 1 · Keeps: 4 days

strawberry thumbprints

$1^1/2$ cups all-purpose flour
1   teaspoon baking powder
$^1/8$ teaspoon salt
$^1/3$ cup butter, cut up
$^1/3$ cup granulated sugar
2   large eggs, lightly beaten
$^1/4$ cup strawberry preserves

Preheat the oven to 400°F. • Butter a cookie sheet. • Sift the flour, baking powder, and salt into a medium bowl. • Use a pastry blender to cut in the butter until the mixture resembles fine crumbs. • Stir in the sugar and make a well in the center. • Add the eggs to form a stiff dough. • Form the dough into balls the size of walnuts and place 2 inches apart on the prepared cookie sheet. • Use your thumb to make an indentation in each cookie and fill with the preserves. • Bake for 15–20 minutes, or until golden. • Cool on the sheet until the cookies firm slightly. • Transfer to racks to finish cooling.

Makes 10–12 cookies · Prep: 20 min. · Cooking: 15–20 min. · Level: 1 · Keeps: 5 days

chocolate hedgehogs

2   cups all-purpose flour
1   tablespoon unsweetened cocoa powder
1   teaspoon baking powder
$^1/8$ teaspoon salt
$^1/2$ cup corn flakes
2   tablespoons old-fashioned rolled oats
2   tablespoons shredded coconut
$^1/2$ cup (1 stick) butter, cut up
$^2/3$ cup superfine sugar
1   tablespoon light corn syrup
1   teaspoon baking soda dissolved in 1 tablespoon milk

Preheat the oven to 350°F. • Butter two cookie sheets. • Sift the flour, cocoa, baking powder, and salt into a large bowl. • Stir in the corn flakes, oats, and coconut. • Melt the butter, sugar, and corn syrup in a small saucepan over low heat. • Add the baking soda mixture. • Stir the butter mixture into the dry ingredients. • Drop teaspoons of the dough $1^1/2$ inches apart onto the prepared cookie sheets, pressing down firmly with a fork. • Bake for 15–20 minutes, or until crisp, rotating the sheets halfway through for even baking. • Transfer to racks to cool.

Makes about 35 cookies · Prep: 15 min. · Cooking: 15–20 min. · Level: 1 · Keeps: 7 days

Chocolate hedgehogs

vanilla-filled kisses

1¹/₃ cups all-purpose flour
2   tablespoons unsweetened cocoa powder
2   teaspoons baking powder
¹/₈   teaspoon salt
³/₄   cup (1¹/₂ sticks) butter, softened
³/₄   cup granulated sugar
¹/₄   cup milk

Vanilla filling
1   cup confectioners' sugar
¹/₄   cup (¹/₂ stick) butter, melted
¹/₂   teaspoon vanilla extract

Preheat the oven to 350°F. • Set out two cookie sheets. • Sift the flour, cocoa, baking powder, and salt into a medium bowl. • Beat the butter and sugar in a large bowl with an electric mixer at high speed until creamy. • Mix in the dry ingredients and milk. • Roll teaspoons of the mixture into balls the size of walnuts and place 2 inches apart on the cookie sheets. • Bake for 15–20 minutes, or until firm to the touch, rotating the sheets halfway through for even baking. • Transfer to racks to cool. • Vanilla filling: Beat the confectioners' sugar, butter, and vanilla in a small bowl until creamy • Stick the cookies together in pairs with the vanilla filling.

Makes 20–24 cookies · Prep: 10 min. · Cooking: 15–20 min. · Level: 1 · Keeps: 7 days

raspberry thumbprints

²/₃   cup butter, softened
¹/₂   cup granulated sugar
1   large egg yolk, lightly beaten
1²/₃ cups all-purpose flour
2   tablespoons fresh orange juice
¹/₂   cup raspberry preserves

Beat the butter and sugar in a large bowl with an electric mixer at high speed until creamy. • Add the egg yolk, beating until just blended. • Mix in the flour and orange juice. • Refrigerate for 30 minutes. • Preheat the oven to 375°F. • Butter three cookie sheets. • Form the dough into balls the size of walnuts and place 2 inches apart on the prepared cookie sheets. • Use your thumb to make an indentation in each cookie. • Bake for 8–10 minutes, or until lightly browned. • Fill the centers with the preserves. • Bake, one sheet at a time, for 5 minutes more, or until the preserves are bubbling. • Cool on the sheets until the cookies firm slightly. Transfer to racks to cool.

Makes 36 cookies · Prep: 45 min. + 30 min. to chill · Cooking: 13–15 min. per batch · Level: 1 · Keeps: 5 days

raspberry drops

Children-friendly and simple to make.

3   cups all-purpose flour
2   teaspoons baking powder
¹/₄   teaspoon salt
²/₃   cup butter, cut up
²/₃   cup granulated sugar
4   large eggs
¹/₂   cup raspberry preserves

Preheat the oven to 350°F. • Butter two cookie sheets. • Sift the flour, baking powder, and salt into a large bowl. • Use a pastry blender to cut in the butter until the mixture resembles fine crumbs. • Stir in the sugar and make a well in the center. • Add the eggs to form a stiff dough. • Form the dough into twenty equal-size balls and place them 2 inches apart on the prepared cookie sheets. • Make a hole in the center of each ball and fill with a little of the preserves. Close up the hole completely. • Bake for 15–20 minutes, or until golden brown, rotating the sheets halfway through for even baking. • Cool the cookies on the sheets for 5 minutes. • Transfer to racks to cool.

Makes 20 cookies · Prep: 25 min. · Cooking: 15–20 min. · Level: 1 · Keeps: 2–3 days

apricot thumbprints

1¹/₂ cups all-purpose flour
1   teaspoon baking powder
¹/₈   teaspoon salt
¹/₃   cup butter, cut up
¹/₃   cup granulated sugar
2   large eggs, lightly beaten
¹/₄   cup apricot preserves or jam

Preheat the oven to 400°F. • Butter a cookie sheet. • Sift the flour, baking powder, and salt into a medium bowl. • Use a pastry blender to cut in the butter until the mixture resembles fine crumbs. • Stir in the sugar and make a well in the center. • Add the eggs to form a stiff dough. • Form the dough into balls the size of walnuts and place 2 inches apart on the prepared cookie sheet. • Use your thumb to make an indentation in each cookie and fill with the preserves. • Bake for 15–20 minutes, or until golden. • Cool on the sheet until the cookies firm slightly. • Transfer to racks to cool.

Makes 10–12 cookies · Prep: 20 min. · Cooking: 15–20 min. · Level: 1 · Keeps: 5 days

raspberry kisses

²/₃   cup all-purpose flour
¹/₂   cup cornstarch
1   teaspoon baking powder
¹/₂   cup (1 stick) butter, softened
¹/₂   cup granulated sugar
2   large eggs
2–3   tablespoons raspberry preserves
¹/₃   cup confectioners' sugar, to dust

Preheat the oven to 400°F. • Butter two cookie sheets. • Sift the flour, cornstarch, and baking powder into a medium bowl. • Beat the butter and sugar in a large bowl with an electric mixer at high speed until creamy. • Add the eggs, beating until just blended. • Mix in the dry ingredients • Drop teaspoons of the dough 1 inch apart onto the prepared cookie sheets. • Bake for 8–10 minutes, or until golden brown, rotating the sheets halfway through for even baking. • Transfer to a rack to cool. • Stick the cookies together in pairs with the preserves. Dust with the confectioners' sugar just before serving.

Makes 15 cookies · Prep: 25 min. · Cooking: 8–10 min. · Level: 1 · Keeps: 4–5 days

date–oat cookies

³/₄   cup all-purpose flour
¹/₂   teaspoon baking powder
¹/₈   teaspoon salt
¹/₂   cup (1 stick) butter, cut up
1   large egg, lightly beaten
1   cup granulated sugar
¹/₂   cup old-fashioned rolled oats
¹/₂   cup coarsely chopped dates

Preheat the oven to 350°F. • Butter two cookie sheets. • Sift the flour, baking powder, and salt into a large bowl. • Use a pastry blender to cut in the butter until the mixture resembles fine crumbs. • Add the egg, beating until just blended. • Mix in the sugar, oats, and dates. • Drop tablespoons of the dough 2 inches apart onto the prepared cookie sheets. • Bake for 12–15 minutes, or until lightly browned, rotating the sheets halfway through for even baking. • Cool on the sheets until the cookies firm slightly. • Transfer to racks to cool.

Makes 20 cookies · Prep: 20 min. · Cooking: 12–15 min. · Level: 1 · Keeps: 5 days

Raspberry kisses (top)
and Vanilla-filled kisses (bottom)

hazelnut–cinnamon cookies

1¼ cups coarsely chopped hazelnuts
²/₃ cup granulated sugar
3 tablespoons all-purpose flour
1 tablespoon cornstarch
¹/₈ teaspoon salt
3 tablespoons butter, melted
1 teaspoon vanilla extract
1 teaspoon ground cinnamon
3 large egg whites, lightly beaten

Stir together the hazelnuts, sugar, flour, cornstarch, and salt in a large bowl. • Add the butter, vanilla, and cinnamon. • Stir in the egg whites. • Refrigerate for 30 minutes. • Preheat the oven to 400°F. • Line two cookie sheets with aluminum foil. • Drop ¹/₂ tablespoons of the dough 2 inches apart onto the prepared cookie sheets. • Bake for 5–7 minutes, or until golden brown, rotating the sheets halfway through for even baking. • Transfer to racks to cool.

Makes 25 cookies · Prep: 20 min. · Cooking: 5–7 min. · Level: 1 · Keeps: 3–4 days

walnut–date cookies

1 cup all-purpose flour
¹/₂ teaspoon ground cinnamon
¹/₄ teaspoon baking soda
2 tablespoons water
³/₄ cup finely chopped dates
³/₄ cup golden raisins
¹/₃ cup butter, softened
¹/₂ cup granulated sugar
1 large egg
¹/₂ cup finely chopped walnuts

Preheat the oven to 400°F. • Butter two cookie sheets. • Sift the flour and cinnamon into a medium bowl. • Mix the baking soda and water in a small bowl. Add the dates and raisins. • Beat the butter and sugar in a large bowl with an electric mixer at high speed until creamy. • Add the egg, beating until just blended. • Stir in the date and raisin mixture. • Mix in the dry ingredients and walnuts. • Drop tablespoons of the dough 1 inch apart onto the prepared cookie sheets. • Bake for 8–10 minutes, or until lightly browned, rotating the sheets halfway through for even baking. • Cool on the sheets until the cookies firm slightly. • Transfer to racks and let cool completely.

Makes 26 cookies · Prep: 20 min. · Cooking: 8–10 min. · Level: 1 · Keeps: 5 days

hazelnut puffs

²/₃ cup all-purpose flour
¹/₈ teaspoon salt
¹/₂ cup (1 stick) butter, softened
2 tablespoons granulated sugar
1 teaspoon vanilla extract
1 cup finely ground hazelnuts
¹/₃ cup unsweetened cocoa powder

Preheat the oven to 350°F. • Butter two cookie sheets. • Sift the flour and salt into a large bowl. • Beat the butter and sugar in a large bowl with an electric mixer at high speed until creamy. • Add the vanilla. • Stir the ground hazelnuts into the mixture. • Form the dough into balls the size of marbles and place 1 inch apart on the prepared cookie sheets. • Bake for 12–15 minutes, or until firm, rotating the sheets halfway through for even baking. • Transfer to racks to cool. • Roll in the cocoa until well coated.

Makes 24 cookies · Prep: 20 min. · Cooking: 12–15 min. · Level: 1 · Keeps: 5 days

pecan–date cookies

1 cup all-purpose flour
¹/₂ teaspoon ground cinnamon
¹/₄ teaspoon baking soda
2 tablespoons water
³/₄ cup finely chopped dates
³/₄ cup currants
¹/₃ cup butter, softened
¹/₂ cup granulated sugar
1 large egg
¹/₂ cup finely chopped pecans

Preheat the oven to 400°F. • Butter two cookie sheets. • Sift the flour and cinnamon into a medium bowl. • Mix the baking soda and water in a small bowl. Add the dates and currants. • Beat the butter and sugar in a large bowl with an electric mixer at high speed until creamy. • Add the egg, beating until just blended. • Stir in the date and currant mixture. • Mix in the dry ingredients and pecans. • Drop tablespoons of the dough 1 inch apart onto the prepared cookie sheets. • Bake for 8–10 minutes, or until lightly browned, rotating the sheets halfway through for even baking. • Cool on the sheets until the cookies firm slightly. • Transfer to racks and let cool completely.

Makes 26 cookies · Prep: 20 min. · Cooking: 8–10 min. · Level: 1 · Keeps: 5 days

almond–cinnamon cookies

1¼ cups coarsely chopped almonds
²/₃ cup granulated sugar
3 tablespoons all-purpose flour
1 tablespoon cornstarch
¹/₈ teaspoon salt
3 tablespoons butter, melted
1 teaspoon almond extract
1 teaspoon ground cinnamon
3 large egg whites, lightly beaten

Stir together the almonds, sugar, flour, cornstarch, and salt in a large bowl. • Add the butter, almond extract, and cinnamon. • Stir in the egg whites. • Refrigerate for 30 minutes. • Preheat the oven to 400°F. • Line two cookie sheets with aluminum foil. • Drop ¹/₂ tablespoons of the dough 2 inches apart onto the prepared cookie sheets. • Bake for 5–7 minutes, or until golden brown, rotating the sheets halfway through for even baking. • Transfer to racks to cool.

Makes 25 cookies · Prep: 20 min. · Cooking: 5–7 min. · Level: 1 · Keeps: 3–4 days

chocolate–hazelnut kisses

³/₄ cup all-purpose flour
¹/₈ teaspoon salt
¹/₃ cup butter, softened
³/₄ cup granulated sugar
1¼ cups finely ground hazelnuts
Filling
¹/₂ cup chocolate hazelnut cream (Nutella)
¹/₃ cup heavy cream

Preheat the oven to 300°F. • Butter three cookie sheets. • Sift the flour and salt into a medium bowl. • Beat the butter and sugar in a large bowl with an electric mixer at high speed until creamy. • Mix in the dry ingredients and hazelnuts to form a stiff dough. • Form into balls the size of walnuts and place 1 inch apart on the prepared cookie sheets. • Bake, one sheet at a time, for 25–30 minutes, or until lightly browned. • Transfer to racks to cool. • Filling: Heat the chocolate hazelnut cream in a double boiler over barely simmering water until liquid. Remove from the heat and mix in the cream until well blended. Let cool completely. • Stick the cookies together in pairs with the filling.

Makes 20–22 cookies · Prep: 20 min · Cooking: 25–30 min. per batch · Level: 1 · Keeps: 5 days in the refrigerator

Chocolate–hazelnut kisses

stem ginger cookies

Stem ginger is fresh ginger root preserved in syrup. It came to Britain from China in the 18th century, shipped in distinctive porcelain jars that were valued as decorative pieces when the ginger had long been eaten. Stem ginger is available in specialty stores.

1¼ cups all-purpose flour
1 tablespoon ground ginger
1 teaspoon baking powder
½ teaspoon baking soda
⅛ teaspoon salt
⅓ cup firmly packed light brown sugar
1 tablespoon finely chopped stem ginger
¼ cup (½ stick) butter, cut up
2 tablespoons dark corn syrup
1 tablespoon stem ginger syrup
1 large egg, lightly beaten

Preheat the oven to 350°F. • Butter two cookie sheets. • Sift the flour, ground ginger, baking powder, baking soda, and salt into a large bowl. • Stir in the brown sugar and stem ginger. • Melt the butter with the corn syrup and stem ginger syrup in a small saucepan over low heat. • Remove from the heat and let cool for 5 minutes. • Mix the melted butter mixture into the dry ingredients. • Add the egg to form a stiff dough. • Form the dough into balls the size of walnuts and place 2 inches apart on the prepared cookie sheets. • Dip a fork into flour and press lines onto the balls, flattening them slightly. • Bake for 12–15 minutes, or until golden, rotating the sheets halfway through for even baking. • Cool on the sheets until the cookies firm slightly. • Transfer to racks to cool.

Makes 18–24 cookies · Prep: 30 min. · Cooking: 12–15 min. · Level: 1 · Keeps: 7 days

glazed pineapple cookies

A taste of the tropics—these cookies are impressive with their concentrated pineapple flavor.

2 cups all-purpose flour
1½ teaspoons baking powder
¼ teaspoon salt
½ cup vegetable shortening
1 cup firmly packed light brown sugar
1 large egg
½ teaspoon vanilla extract
1 can (8 oz) crushed pineapple, drained (reserve the juice)

Pineapple glaze
3 cups confectioners' sugar
¼ cup pineapple juice (see above)

Preheat the oven to 400°F. • Butter three cookie sheets. • Sift the flour, baking powder, and salt into a medium bowl. • Beat the shortening and brown sugar in a large bowl with an electric mixer at high speed until creamy. • Add the egg and vanilla, beating until just blended. • Mix in the pineapple and dry ingredients. • Drop teaspoons of the dough 2 inches apart onto the prepared cookie sheets. • Bake, one sheet at a time, for 8–10 minutes, or until just golden at the edges. • Transfer to racks to cool. • Pineapple glaze: Mix the confectioners' sugar and pineapple juice in a small bowl. • Spread the glaze over the tops of the cookies and let set for 30 minutes.

Makes 32–36 cookies · Prep: 25 min. + 30 min. to set · Cooking: 8–10 min. per batch · Level: 1 · Keeps: 7 days

coffee-nut wafers

¼ cup (½ stick) butter, softened
¼ cup granulated sugar
1 tablespoon freeze-dried coffee granules
1 large egg, lightly beaten
⅓ cup all-purpose flour
⅛ teaspoon salt
¼ cup finely chopped walnuts
½ teaspoon vanilla extract

Preheat the oven to 350°F. • Butter a cookie sheet. • Beat the butter, sugar, and coffee granules in a large bowl with an electric mixer at high speed until creamy. • Add the egg, beating until just blended. • Mix in the flour and salt. • Mix in the walnuts and vanilla. • Drop teaspoons of the dough 1 inch apart onto the prepared cookie sheet. • Bake for 10–15 minutes, or until just golden. • Cool on the sheet until the cookies firm slightly. • Transfer to racks to cool.

Makes 10–12 cookies · Prep: 20 min. · Cooking: 10–15 min. · Level: 1 · Keeps: 7 days

pineapple–date drops

2 cups all-purpose flour
2 teaspoons baking powder
½ teaspoon baking soda
¼ teaspoon salt
1 cup coarsely chopped dates
⅓ cup butter, softened
¾ cup firmly packed light brown sugar
¼ cup granulated sugar
1 large egg
1 cup crushed pineapple, drained

Preheat the oven to 350°F. • Butter two cookie sheets. • Sift the flour, baking powder, baking soda, and salt into a medium bowl. Stir in the dates. • Beat the butter and both sugars in a large bowl with an electric mixer at high speed until creamy. • Add the egg, beating until just blended. • Add the pineapple. • Mix in the dry ingredients. • Drop teaspoons of the dough 1 inch apart onto the prepared cookie sheets. • Bake for 15–18 minutes, or until golden brown, rotating the sheets halfway through for even baking. • Transfer to racks to cool.

Makes 30–35 cookies · Prep: 10 min. · Cooking: 15–18 min. · Level: 1 · Keeps: 7 days

apricot sandwich cookies

¾ cup (1½ sticks) butter, softened
½ cup confectioners' sugar
1 teaspoon vanilla extract
2 cups all-purpose flour
⅛ teaspoon salt
½ cup apricot preserves or jam

Preheat the oven to 350°F. • Butter two cookie sheets. • Beat the butter, confectioners' sugar, and vanilla in a large bowl with an electric mixer at high speed until creamy. • Mix in the flour and salt. • Drop tablespoons of the dough 2 inches apart onto the prepared cookie sheets, flattening them slightly with a fork. • Bake for 15–20 minutes, or until just golden at the edges, rotating the sheets halfway through for even baking. • Transfer to racks to cool. • Warm the preserves in a small saucepan over low heat until liquid. • Stick the cookies together in pairs with the preserves.

Makes 12 cookies · Prep: 20 min. · Cooking: 15–20 min. · Level: 1 · Keeps: 4 days

soft apricot drops

2/3 cup all-purpose flour
1 teaspoon baking powder
1/3 cup butter, softened
2/3 cup firmly packed light brown sugar
1 tablespoon Vanilla Sugar (see page 341)
2 large eggs
1/3 cup Kix cereal (roasted and honey-coated corn puffs)
1/2 cup finely chopped dried apricots
3 tablespoons shredded coconut
3 oz bittersweet chocolate, coarsely chopped
2 tablespoons finely chopped Kix cereal, to decorate

Preheat the oven to 350°F. • Line two cookie sheets with parchment paper. • Sift the flour and baking powder into a large bowl. • Beat the butter, brown sugar, and vanilla sugar in a large bowl with an electric mixer at high speed until creamy. • Add the eggs, beating until just blended. • Mix in the dry ingredients, followed by the cereal, apricots, and coconut. • Drop heaping teaspoons of the mixture 1½ inches apart onto the prepared cookie sheets. • Bake for 10–12 minutes, or until lightly browned, rotating the sheets halfway through for even baking. • Transfer the cookies on the parchment paper to racks and let cool completely. • Melt the chocolate in a double boiler over barely simmering water. • Drizzle the chocolate over the cookies and sprinkle with the cereal.

Makes 35 cookies · Prep: 30 min. · Cooking: 10–12 min. · Level: 2 · Keeps: 4 days

apricot rocks

1¹/3 cups all-purpose flour
2 teaspoons baking powder
1/2 teaspoon salt
1/2 cup (1 stick) cold butter, cut up
1/4 cup granulated sugar
3 tablespoons coarsely chopped dried apricots
1 tablespoon coarsely chopped candied pineapple
1 tablespoon coarsely chopped candied cherries
1 large egg
1 tablespoon orange juice
1 teaspoon finely grated orange zest
2 tablespoons firmly packed light brown sugar, to sprinkle

Preheat the oven to 400°F. • Line two cookie sheets with parchment paper. • Sift the flour, baking powder, and salt into a large bowl. • Use a pastry blender to cut in the butter until the mixture resembles coarse crumbs. • Stir in the granulated sugar, apricots, pineapple, and cherries. • Beat the egg and orange juice and zest in a small bowl until pale. • Add the egg mixture to the dry ingredients and mix until well blended. • Drop teaspoons of the mixture 2 inches apart onto the prepared cookie sheets. • Sprinkle with the brown sugar. • Bake for 15–20 minutes, or until golden brown, rotating the sheets halfway through for even baking. • Cool the cookies on the cookie sheets for 5 minutes. • Transfer to racks to cool.

Makes 15–18 cookies · Prep: 20 min. · Cooking: 15–20 min. · Level: 1 · Keeps: 1–2 days

apricot–corn flake cookies

2/3 cup all-purpose flour
1 teaspoon baking powder
1/3 cup butter, softened
2/3 cup firmly packed light brown sugar
2 large eggs
1/3 cup corn flakes
1/2 cup finely chopped dried apricots
3 tablespoons shredded coconut

Preheat the oven to 350°F. • Line two cookie sheets with parchment paper. • Sift the flour and baking powder into a large bowl. • Beat the butter and brown sugar in a large bowl with an electric mixer at high speed until creamy. • Add the eggs, beating until just blended. • Mix in the dry ingredients, followed by the corn flakes, apricots, and coconut. • Drop heaping teaspoons of the mixture 1¹/2 inches apart onto the prepared cookie sheets. • Bake for 10–12 minutes, or until lightly browned, rotating the sheets halfway through for even baking. • Transfer the cookies on the parchment paper to racks to cool.

Makes 35 cookies · Prep: 30 min. · Cooking: 10–12 min. · Level: 2 · Keeps: 4 days

Apricot rocks

chocolate chip cookies

1   cup all-purpose flour
1¹/2 teaspoons baking powder
¹/2   teaspoon salt
¹/2   cup (1 stick) butter, softened
¹/4   cup granulated sugar
1   large egg, lightly beaten
6   oz semisweet chocolate, coarsely chopped

Preheat the oven to 350°F. • Butter two cookie sheets. • Sift the flour, baking powder, and salt into a large bowl. • Beat the butter and sugar in a large bowl with an electric mixer at high speed until creamy. • Add the egg, beating until just blended. • Mix in the dry ingredients and chocolate. • Drop teaspoons of the mixture 1 inch apart onto the prepared cookie sheets. • Bake for 15–20 minutes, or until golden brown, rotating the sheets halfway through for even baking. • Cool on the sheets for 15 minutes. • Transfer to racks to cool.

Makes 30 cookies · Prep: 15 min. · Cooking: 15–20 min. · Level: 1 · Keeps: 4 days

chocolate-filled creams

1   cup all-purpose flour
¹/8   teaspoon salt
¹/2   cup (1 stick) butter, softened
¹/4   cup granulated sugar
¹/2   teaspoon vanilla extract
¹/2   cup Chocolate Buttercream (see page 345)

Preheat the oven to 375°F. • Butter a cookie sheet. • Sift the flour and salt into a medium bowl. • Beat the butter, sugar, and vanilla in a large bowl with an electric mixer at high speed until creamy. • Mix in the dry ingredients. • Form the dough into balls the size of walnuts and place 1 inch apart on the prepared cookie sheet, flattening them slightly. • Bake for 10–15 minutes, or until lightly browned and firm. • Cool on the sheets until the cookies firm slightly. Transfer to racks to finish cooling. • Stick the cookies together in pairs with the buttercream.

Makes 12–15 cookies · Prep: 20 min. · Level: 1 · Cooking: 10–15 min. · Keeps: 7 days in an airtight container in the refrigerator

chocolate–vanilla drops

²/3   cup all-purpose flour
1   tablespoon unsweetened cocoa powder
¹/2   teaspoon baking powder
¹/8   teaspoon salt
¹/2   cup (1 stick) butter, softened
¹/4   cup granulated sugar
¹/2   teaspoon vanilla extract

Preheat the oven to 375°F. • Butter two cookie sheets. • Sift the flour, cocoa, baking powder, and salt into a medium bowl. • Beat the butter and sugar in a large bowl with an electric mixer at high speed until creamy. • Mix in the vanilla and dry ingredients. • Drop tablespoons of the dough 2 inches apart onto the prepared cookie sheets. • Bake for 15–18 minutes, or until firm to the touch, rotating the sheets halfway through for even baking. • Cool on the sheets until the cookies firm slightly. • Transfer to racks to finish cooling.

Makes 15–20 cookies · Prep: 20 min. · Cooking: 15–18 min. · Level: 1 · Keeps: 5 days

chocolate chip–walnut cookies

1¹/3 cups all-purpose flour
1   teaspoon baking powder
¹/8   teaspoon salt
¹/3   cup butter, softened
¹/2   cup granulated sugar
¹/2   cup firmly packed light brown sugar
¹/2   teaspoon vanilla extract
1   large egg, lightly beaten
¹/2   cup semisweet chocolate chips
²/3   cup coarsely chopped walnuts

Preheat the oven to 350°F. • Butter two cookie sheets. • Sift the flour, baking powder, and salt into a large bowl. • Beat the butter, granulated and brown sugars, and vanilla in a large bowl with an electric mixer at high speed until creamy. • Add the egg, beating until just blended. • Mix in the dry ingredients, chocolate chips, and walnuts. • Drop tablespoons of the dough 2 inches apart onto the prepared cookie sheets. • Bake for 12–15 minutes, or until just golden, rotating the sheets halfway through for even baking. • Cool on the sheets until the cookies firm slightly. • Transfer to racks to finish cooling.

Makes 18–20 cookies · Prep: 20 min. · Cooking: 12–15 min. · Level: 1 · Keeps: 7 days

oat crunchies

1   cup all-purpose flour
¹/2   teaspoon baking soda
¹/8   teaspoon salt
²/3   cup butter, softened
1¹/4 cups firmly packed dark brown sugar
1   large egg
1   teaspoon vanilla extract
1   cup old-fashioned rolled oats
1   tablespoon water, or more as needed

Preheat the oven to 350°F. • Line two cookie sheets with parchment paper. • Sift

the flour, baking soda, and salt into a large bowl. • Beat the butter and brown sugar in a large bowl with an electric mixer at high speed until creamy. • Add the egg, beating until just blended. Add the vanilla. • Mix in the dry ingredients, oats, and water. • Roll teaspoons of the mixture into balls and place on the prepared cookie sheets, about 1¹/2 inches apart, flattening them slightly. • Bake for 12–15 minutes, or until golden brown, rotating the sheets halfway through for even baking. • Transfer to racks to cool.

Makes 35–40 cookies · Prep: 30 min. · Cooking: 12–15 min. · Level: 1 · Keeps: 3–5 days

chocolate cookies with peanut butter topping

³/4   cup all-purpose flour
1   teaspoon salt
2   oz semisweet chocolate, coarsely chopped
¹/2   cup (1 stick) butter, softened
²/3   cup granulated sugar
1   teaspoon vanilla extract
1   large egg, lightly beaten

Peanut butter topping
6   tablespoons smooth peanut butter
2   tablespoons butter, softened
²/3   cup firmly packed dark brown sugar
2   tablespoons all-purpose flour

Preheat the oven to 325°F. • Butter three cookie sheets. • Sift the flour and salt into a medium bowl. • Melt the chocolate in a double boiler over barely simmering water. • Beat the butter and sugar in a large bowl with an electric mixer at high speed until creamy. • Add the vanilla and egg, beating until just blended. • Mix in the dry ingredients and chocolate. • Drop teaspoons of the dough 1 inch apart onto the prepared cookie sheets. • Peanut butter topping: With mixer at high speed, beat the peanut butter, butter, and brown sugar in a medium bowl. • Mix in the flour. • Top each cookie with the topping, pressing down with a fork. • Bake, one sheet at a time, for 10–12 minutes, or until browned. • Cool on the sheets until the cookies firm slightly. • Transfer to racks to finish cooling.

Makes 36 cookies · Prep: 25 min. · Cooking: 10–12 min. per batch · Level: 1 · Keeps: 5 days

Chocolate cookies
with peanut butter topping

Black pepper–chocolate chip cookies

black pepper–chocolate chip cookies

The black pepper gives a special bite to these delicious cookies.

- 1/2   cup all-purpose flour
- 1/2   teaspoon baking powder
- 1/2   teaspoon freshly ground black pepper
- 1/4   teaspoon salt
- 1/2   cup raisins
- 2   tablespoons coffee liqueur
- 8   oz bittersweet chocolate, coarsely chopped
- 1/4   cup (1/2 stick) butter, cut up
- 2   large eggs
- 3/4   cup granulated sugar
- 2   teaspoons vanilla extract
- 1   cup semisweet chocolate chips

Preheat the oven to 350°F. • Butter two cookie sheets. • Sift the flour, baking powder, pepper, and salt into a small bowl. • Heat the raisins with the coffee liqueur in a small saucepan over low heat. • Melt the chocolate with the butter in a double boiler over barely simmering water. Set aside to cool. • Beat the eggs and sugar in a large bowl with an electric mixer at high speed until very pale and creamy, about 5 minutes. • With mixer at medium speed, beat in the melted chocolate and vanilla. • With mixer at low speed, beat in the dry ingredients, followed by the raisin mixture and the chocolate chips. • Drop tablespoons of the dough 2 inches apart onto the prepared cookie sheets. • Bake for 10–12 minutes, or until set but still slightly soft, rotating the sheets halfway through for even baking. • Cool on the sheets until the cookies firm slightly. • Transfer to racks to finish cooling.

Makes 15–18 cookies · Prep: 20 min. · Cooking: 10–12 min. · Level: 1 · Keeps: 7 days

almond–chocolate chip cookies

- 1 2/3   cups all-purpose flour
- 3/4   cup confectioners' sugar
- 1   cup (2 sticks) butter, softened
- 1   large egg yolk, lightly beaten
- 1   teaspoon almond extract
- 1   cup finely chopped almonds
- 1/2   cup semisweet chocolate chips

Preheat the oven to 325°F. • Butter two cookie sheets. • Sift the flour and confectioners' sugar into a large bowl. • With an electric mixer at high speed, beat in the butter and egg yolk until well blended. • Mix in the almond extract, almonds, and chocolate chips. • Form the dough into balls the size of walnuts and place 1 inch apart on the prepared cookie sheets. • Bake for 20–25 minutes, or until just golden, rotating the sheets halfway through for even baking. • Cool on the sheets until the cookies firm slightly. • Transfer to racks to finish cooling.

Makes 30 cookies · Prep: 25 min. · Cooking: 20–25 min. · Level: 1 · Keeps: 5 days

white chocolate chip cookies

- 1 1/4   cups all-purpose flour
- 1/2   teaspoon baking soda
- 1/8   teaspoon salt
- 1/2   cup (1 stick) butter, softened
- 2/3   cup raw sugar (Demerara or Barbados)
- 1   teaspoon vanilla extract
- 1   large egg
- 5   oz white chocolate, finely chopped
- 1/2   cup finely chopped pecans

Preheat the oven to 350°F. • Butter a cookie sheet. • Sift the flour, baking soda, and salt into a medium bowl. • Beat the butter and raw sugar in a large bowl with an electric mixer at high speed until creamy. • Add the vanilla and egg, beating until just blended. • Mix in the dry ingredients, white chocolate,

and pecans. • Form the dough into balls the size of walnuts and place 2 inches apart on the prepared cookie sheet. • Bake for 10–12 minutes, or until just golden. • Cool on the sheet until the cookies firm slightly. • Transfer to racks and let cool completely.

Makes 16 cookies · Prep: 20 min. · Cooking: 10–12 min. · Level: 1 · Keeps: 10 days

brown sugar–chocolate chip cookies

- 2   cups all-purpose flour
- 1/4   teaspoon salt
- 1   cup (2 sticks) butter, softened
- 1 1/2   cups firmly packed dark brown sugar
- 1/4   cup granulated sugar
- 1   teaspoon vanilla extract
- 1   large egg + 1 large egg yolk
- 1   teaspoon baking soda dissolved in 1 tablespoon hot water
- 1 1/4   cups semisweet chocolate chips

Butter and flour two 12-cup muffin pans, or line with foil or paper baking cups. • Sift the flour and salt into a medium bowl. • Beat the butter and both sugars in a large bowl with an electric mixer at high speed until creamy. • Add the vanilla and egg and egg yolk, beating until just blended. • Mix in the baking soda mixture, followed by the dry ingredients. • Stir in the chocolate chips. • Spoon the cookie dough evenly into the prepared cups and refrigerate for 30 minutes. • Preheat the oven to 350°F. • Bake for 15–18 minutes, or until set, rotating the pans halfway through for even baking. • Cool the cookies completely in the pans. • Transfer to racks and let cool completely.

Makes 24 cookies · Prep: 20 min. + 30 min. to chill · Cooking: 15–18 min. · Level: 2 · Keeps: 5 days in an airtight container, wrapped individually in waxed paper

oatmeal cookies

- 1   cup all-purpose flour
- 1/2   teaspoon baking soda
- 1/8   teaspoon salt
- 1   cup shredded coconut
- 1   cup old-fashioned rolled oats
- 1/2   cup (1 stick) butter, cut up
- 3/4   cup granulated sugar
- 2   tablespoons light corn syrup

Preheat the oven to 350°F. • Butter two cookie sheets. • Sift the flour, baking soda, and salt into a large bowl. Stir in the coconut and oats. • Melt the butter with the sugar and corn syrup in a small saucepan over medium heat. • Mix in the dry ingredients until well blended. • Roll into balls the size of walnuts and place 1 inch apart on the prepared cookie sheets, flattening them slightly with a fork. • Bake for 15–20 minutes, or until golden brown, rotating the sheets halfway through the baking to ensure even browning. • Cool on the sheets until the cookies firm slightly. Transfer to racks to cool.

Makes 20 cookies · Prep: 20 min. · Cooking: 15–20 min. · Level: 1 · Keeps: 7 days

oat chips

2¹/₄ cups old-fashioned rolled oats
1   cup firmly packed light brown sugar
¹/₂   cup granulated sugar
2   tablespoons all-purpose flour
¹/₄   teaspoon salt
1¹/₃ cups butter, melted
1   large egg
1   teaspoon vanilla extract
¹/₂   cup semisweet chocolate chips

Preheat the oven to 350°F. • Set out two cookie sheets. • Stir together the oats, brown and granulated sugars, flour, and salt in a large bowl. • Make a well in the center and stir in the butter, egg, and vanilla. • Stir in the chocolate chips. • Drop teaspoons of the dough 3 inches apart onto the cookie sheets. • Bake for 5–8 minutes, or until lightly browned and the centers are bubbling, rotating the sheets halfway through for even baking. • Transfer to racks and let cool completely.

Makes 24 cookies · Prep: 20 min. · Cooking: 5–8 min. · Level: 1 · Keeps: 3 days

dreamy white chocolate chip cookies

1   cup all-purpose flour
1   tablespoon unsweetened cocoa powder
¹/₂   teaspoon baking soda
¹/₄   teaspoon salt
¹/₂   cup (1 stick) butter, softened
¹/₃   cup firmly packed light brown sugar
¹/₄   cup granulated sugar
1   large egg
¹/₂   teaspoon vanilla extract
4   oz best-quality white chocolate, finely chopped

Preheat the oven to 350°F. • Butter four cookie sheets. • Sift the flour, cocoa, baking soda, and salt into a medium bowl. • Beat the butter and brown sugar and granulated sugar in a large bowl with an electric mixer

at high speed until creamy. • Add the egg and vanilla, beating until just blended. • Mix in the dry ingredients and white chocolate. • Drop tablespoons of the dough 3 inches apart onto the prepared cookie sheets. Do not drop more than eight cookies onto each sheet. • Bake, one sheet at a time, for 10–12 minutes, or until pale gold, rotating the sheets halfway through for even baking. • Cool on the sheets until the cookies firm slightly. • Transfer to racks to finish cooling.

Makes 32 cookies · Prep: 20 min. · Cooking: 10–12 min. per batch · Level: 1 · Keeps: 2 weeks

italian hazelnut cookies

2¹/₂ cups finely chopped hazelnuts
1   large egg, lightly beaten
³/₄   cup granulated sugar
¹/₂   teaspoon orange liqueur
¹/₂   teaspoon fresh lemon juice
¹/₂   teaspoon vanilla extract
¹/₈   teaspoon salt
13   candied cherries, cut in half
26   coffee beans

Preheat the oven to 350°F. • Line two cookie sheets with parchment paper. • Use a wooden spoon to mix the hazelnuts, egg, sugar, orange liqueur, lemon juice, vanilla, and salt until a stiff dough has formed. • Form the dough into balls the size of walnuts and place 1 inch apart on the prepared cookie sheets. • Decorate with cherry halves and coffee beans. • Bake, one sheet at a time, for 15–20 minutes, or until just golden at the edges. • Transfer to racks and let cool completely.

Makes 26 cookies · Prep: 25 min. · Cooking: 15–20 min. per batch · Level: 1 · Keeps: 3 days

oatmeal–chocolate chip cookies

1¹/₄ cups all-purpose flour
¹/₂   teaspoon baking soda
¹/₂   teaspoon salt
¹/₂   cup (1 stick) butter, softened
¹/₂   cup granulated sugar
¹/₂   cup firmly packed dark brown sugar
¹/₂   teaspoon vanilla extract
1   large egg, lightly beaten
¹/₃   cup old-fashioned rolled oats
¹/₂   cup semisweet chocolate chips
²/₃   cup coarsely chopped peanuts

Preheat the oven to 350°F. • Butter three cookie sheets. • Sift the flour, baking soda, and salt into a medium bowl. • Beat the butter and granulated and brown sugars in a large bowl with an electric mixer at high speed until creamy. • Add the vanilla and egg, beating until just blended. • Mix in the dry ingredients, oats, chocolate chips, and peanuts. • Drop heaping teaspoons of the dough 2 inches apart onto the prepared cookie sheets. • Bake, one sheet at a time, for 12–15 minutes, or until lightly browned. • Transfer to racks and let cool completely.

Makes 45 cookies · Prep: 20 min. · Cooking: 12–15 min. per batch · Level: 1 · Keeps: 7 days

Oatmeal–chocolate chip cookies

chocolate–peanut cookies

1¼ cups firmly packed dark brown sugar
1 cup granulated sugar
½ cup (1 stick) butter, softened
3 large eggs
¾ cup smooth peanut butter
2 teaspoons baking soda
1 teaspoon vanilla extract
4½ cups old-fashioned rolled oats
½ cup coarsely chopped mixed nuts
⅛ teaspoon salt
½ cup M&Ms
½ cup semisweet chocolate chips

Preheat the oven to 350°F. • Butter two cookie sheets. • Beat the brown sugar, granulated sugar, and butter in a large bowl with an electric mixer at high speed until creamy. • Add the eggs, beating until just blended. • With mixer at medium speed, gradually add the peanut butter, baking soda, and vanilla. • Mix in the oats, nuts, salt, M&Ms, and chocolate chips. • Drop teaspoons of the dough 1 inch apart onto the prepared cookie sheets. • Bake for 12–15 minutes, or until just golden, rotating the sheets halfway through for even baking. • Cool on the sheets until the cookies firm slightly. • Transfer to racks to finish cooling.

Makes 48–50 cookies · Prep: 20 min. · Cooking: 12–15 min. · Level: 1 · Keeps: 3 days

peanut brownie cookies

1 cup all-purpose flour
2 tablespoons cocoa powder
1 teaspoon baking powder
⅛ teaspoon salt
½ cup (1 stick) butter, softened
½ cup granulated sugar
1 large egg, at room temperature
1 cup coarsely chopped salted peanuts

Preheat the oven to 325°F. • Butter a cookie sheet. • Sift the flour, cocoa, baking powder, and salt into a large bowl. • Beat the butter and sugar in a large bowl with an electric mixer at high speed until creamy. • Add the egg, beating until just blended. • Mix in the dry ingredients, followed by the peanuts. • Drop teaspoons of the dough 1 inch apart onto the prepared cookie sheet. • Bake for 20–25 minutes, or until crisp and golden brown. • Cool on the sheet until the cookies firm slightly. • Transfer to racks to cool.

Makes 15 cookies · Prep: 20 min. · Cooking: 20–25 min. · Level: 1 · Keeps: 5 days

chocolate–peanut butter cookies

1¼ cups all-purpose flour
½ teaspoon baking soda
¼ teaspoon salt
½ cup (1 stick) butter, softened
½ cup raw sugar (Demerara or Barbados)
½ cup smooth peanut butter
1 teaspoon vanilla extract
1 large egg
4 oz semisweet chocolate, coarsely chopped

Preheat the oven to 375°F. • Butter a cookie sheet. • Sift the flour, baking soda, and salt into a large bowl. • Beat the butter and sugar in a large bowl with an electric mixer at high speed until creamy. • Beat in the peanut butter. • Add the vanilla and egg, beating until just blended. • Mix in the dry ingredients, followed by the chocolate. • Drop tablespoons of the dough 2 inches apart onto the prepared cookie sheet. • Bake for 10–12 minutes, or until just golden at the edges. • Transfer to racks and let cool completely.

Makes 16 cookies · Prep: 20 min. · Cooking: 10–12 min. · Level: 1 · Keeps: 7 days

salted peanut cookies

1 cup all-purpose flour
2 teaspoons baking powder
½ cup (1 stick) butter, softened
¼ cup vegetable shortening
⅓ cup firmly packed light brown sugar
½ teaspoon vanilla extract
1 large egg
½ cup salted peanuts

Preheat the oven to 375°F. • Line two cookie sheets with parchment paper. • Sift the flour and baking powder into a large bowl. • Beat the butter, shortening, and brown sugar in a large bowl with an electric mixer at high speed until creamy. • Add the vanilla and egg, beating until just blended. • Mix in the dry ingredients and peanuts. • Drop teaspoons of the dough 2 inches apart onto the prepared cookie sheets. • Bake for 8–10 minutes, or until firm to the touch, rotating the sheets halfway through for even baking. • Transfer to racks to cool.

Makes 25–30 cookies · Prep: 20 min. · Cooking: 8–10 min. · Level: 1 · Keeps: 5 days

white chocolate drops

1⅓ cups all-purpose flour
1 teaspoon baking powder
¼ teaspoon salt
½ cup (1 stick) butter, softened
⅔ cup firmly packed light brown sugar
1 large egg, lightly beaten
4 oz white chocolate, finely chopped
½ cup coarsely chopped hazelnuts or macadamia nuts

Preheat the oven to 375°F. • Butter two cookie sheets. • Sift the flour, baking powder, and salt into a large bowl. • Beat the butter and brown sugar in a large bowl with an electric mixer at high speed until creamy. • Add the egg, beating until just blended. • Mix in the dry ingredients, chocolate, and nuts until well blended. • Drop teaspoons of the dough 2 inches apart onto the prepared cookie sheets. • Bake for 10–15 minutes, or until golden brown and firm to the touch, rotating the sheets halfway through for even baking. • Cool on the sheets until the cookies firm slightly. • Transfer to racks to finish cooling.

Makes 25 cookies · Prep: 20 min. · Cooking: 10–15 min. · Level: 1 · Keeps: 14 days

rice–olive oil cookies

Aromatic extra-virgin olive oil gives these cookies an unusual refreshing flavor.

1⅔ cups rice flour
½ teaspoon baking powder
⅛ teaspoon baking soda
⅛ teaspoon salt
⅓ cup granulated sugar
¼ cup best-quality extra-virgin olive oil
⅓–⅔ cup water

Preheat the oven to 350°F. • Butter two cookie sheets. • Sift the flour, baking powder, baking soda, and salt into a large bowl. • Stir in the sugar. • Mix in the olive oil and enough water to form a stiff dough. • Form the dough into balls the size of walnuts and place 1 inch apart on the prepared cookie sheets, flattening them slightly. • Bake for 20–25 minutes, or until just golden, rotating the sheets halfway through for even baking. • Transfer to racks and let cool completely.

Makes 24 cookies · Prep: 20 min. · Cooking: 20–25 min. · Level: 1 · Keeps: 7 days

*White chocolate drops (left) and
Chocolate peanut cookies (right)*

drop sugar cookies

1¹/₂ cups all-purpose flour
1 tablespoon unsweetened cocoa powder
¹/₄ teaspoon salt
¹/₂ cup (1 stick) butter, softened
²/₃ cup + 3 tablespoons granulated sugar
1 large egg

Preheat the oven to 350°F. • Butter two cookie sheets. • Sift the flour, cocoa, and salt into a medium bowl. • Beat the butter and ²/₃ cup sugar in a large bowl with an electric mixer at high speed until creamy. • Add the egg, beating until just blended. • Mix in the dry ingredients. • Pinch off small pieces of dough. Form into balls and roll in the remaining 3 tablespoons sugar. • Place 1 inch apart on the prepared cookie sheets, flattening them slightly with a fork. • Bake for 15–20 minutes, or until lightly cracked and browned, rotating the sheets halfway through for even baking. • Transfer to racks to cool.

Makes 30 cookies · Prep: 15 min. · Cooking: 15–20 min. · Level: 1 · Keeps: 2 weeks

sunflower–oat drops

1¹/₂ cups all-purpose flour
1 teaspoon baking soda
¹/₄ teaspoon salt
1 cup (2 sticks) butter, softened
1 cup firmly packed light brown sugar
1 cup granulated sugar
2 large eggs, lightly beaten
¹/₂ teaspoon vanilla extract
2 cups old-fashioned rolled oats
1 cup sunflower seeds

Preheat the oven to 350°F. • Butter three cookie sheets. • Sift the flour, baking soda, and salt into a medium bowl. • Beat the butter and brown and granulated sugars in a large bowl with an electric mixer at high speed until creamy. • Add the eggs and vanilla, beating until just blended. • Mix in the dry ingredients, oats, and sunflower seeds. • Drop tablespoons of the dough 2 inches apart onto the prepared cookie sheets. • Bake, one batch at a time, for 10–15 minutes, or until golden brown. • Cool on the sheets until the cookies firm slightly. Transfer to racks to finish cooling.

Makes 36–40 cookies · Prep: 20 min. · Cooking: 10–15 min. per batch · Level: 1 · Keeps: 10 days

butter drops

1¹/₄ cups all-purpose flour
¹/₂ teaspoon baking soda
¹/₈ teaspoon salt
¹/₂ cup (1 stick) butter, softened
3 tablespoons firmly packed light brown sugar
3 tablespoons granulated sugar
1 large egg, lightly beaten
¹/₂ teaspoon vanilla extract

Preheat the oven to 375°F. • Butter three cookie sheets. • Sift the flour, baking soda, and salt into a medium bowl. • Beat the butter and brown and granulated sugars in a large bowl with an electric mixer at high speed until creamy. • Add the egg and vanilla extract, beating until just blended. • Mix in the dry ingredients. • Drop teaspoons of the dough 2 inches apart onto the prepared cookie sheets. • Bake, one sheet at a time, for 7–10 minutes, or until golden. • Transfer to racks to cool.

Makes 40–45 cookies · Prep: 20 min. · Cooking: 7–10 min. per batch · Level: 1 · Keeps: 10 days

white chocolate–cherry cookies

³/₄ cup all-purpose flour
¹/₂ teaspoon baking powder
¹/₈ teaspoon salt
¹/₂ cup (1 stick) butter, softened
¹/₄ cup granulated sugar
¹/₂ teaspoon vanilla extract
¹/₃ cup finely chopped candied cherries
1 oz white chocolate, finely chopped

Preheat the oven to 375°F. • Butter two cookie sheets. • Sift the flour, baking powder, and salt into a large bowl. • Beat the butter, sugar, and vanilla in a large bowl with an electric mixer at high speed until creamy. • Mix in the dry ingredients, cherries, and white chocolate. • Drop rounded teaspoons of the dough 1 inch apart onto the prepared cookie sheets. • Bake for 15–20 minutes, or until just golden, rotating the sheets halfway through for even baking. • Cool on the sheets until the cookies firm slightly. Transfer to racks to finish cooling.

Makes 18–20 cookies · Prep: 20 min. · Cooking: 15–20 min. · Level: 1 · Keeps: 7 days

Double chocolate drops

double chocolate drops

1¹/₃ cups all-purpose flour
¹/₂ teaspoon baking soda
¹/₈ teaspoon salt
2 oz semisweet chocolate, coarsely chopped
¹/₂ cup (1 stick) butter, softened
1 cup granulated sugar
1 teaspoon vanilla extract
1 large egg, lightly beaten
2 tablespoons milk

Chocolate frosting
2 oz semisweet chocolate
¹/₄ cup (¹/₂ stick) butter, softened
1¹/₃ cups confectioners' sugar
¹/₂ cup pecans, halved

Preheat the oven to 400°F. • Butter three cookie sheets. • Sift the flour, baking soda, and salt into a large bowl. • Melt the chocolate in a double boiler over barely simmering water. • Beat the butter, sugar, and melted chocolate in a large bowl with an electric mixer at high speed until creamy. • Add the vanilla and egg, beating until just blended. • Mix in the dry ingredients and milk until well blended. • Drop teaspoons of the dough 1 inch apart onto the prepared cookie sheets. • Bake, one sheet at a time, for 8–10 minutes, or until slightly risen. • Cool on the sheets until the cookies firm slightly. Transfer to racks to finish cooling. • Chocolate frosting: Melt the chocolate in a double boiler over barely simmering water. • With mixer at high speed, beat the butter and melted chocolate in a medium bowl until creamy. • Beat in the confectioners' sugar until well blended. • Spread the frosting over the tops of the cookies and decorate with the pecans.

Makes 36 cookies · Prep: 25 min. · Cooking: 8–10 min. per batch · Level: 1 · Keeps: 5 days

chocolate–banana cookies

2¹/₃ cups all-purpose flour
1   teaspoon baking soda
¹/₈ teaspoon salt
1   cup (2 sticks) butter, softened
³/₄ cup firmly packed dark brown sugar
¹/₂ cup granulated sugar
1   teaspoon vanilla extract
2   large eggs
1   large banana, peeled and lightly mashed
³/₄ cup semisweet chocolate chips
¹/₃ cup coarsely chopped dried banana chips

Preheat the oven to 375°F. • Butter three cookie sheets. • Sift the flour, baking soda, and salt into a medium bowl. • Beat the butter and both sugars in a large bowl with an electric mixer at high speed until creamy. • Add the vanilla and eggs, beating until just blended. • Mix in the banana and dry ingredients, followed by the chocolate and banana chips. • Drop teaspoons of the dough 1 inch apart onto the prepared cookie sheets. • Bake, one sheet at a time, for 15–20 minutes, or until just golden. • Cool on the sheets until the cookies firm slightly. • Transfer to racks to finish cooling.

Makes 36 cookies · Prep: 20 min. · Cooking: 15–20 min. per batch · Level: 1 · Keeps: 2 weeks

nutty cherry–chocolate cookies

1   can (7 oz) pitted sour cherries, drained
¹/₂ cup kirsch
1¹/₂ cups all-purpose flour
¹/₂ teaspoon baking soda
¹/₄ teaspoon salt
¹/₂ cup (1 stick) butter, softened
¹/₂ cup granulated sugar
¹/₂ cup raw sugar (Demerara or Barbados)
1¹/₂ teaspoons vanilla extract
¹/₄ teaspoon almond extract
1   large egg
5   oz white chocolate, coarsely chopped
5   oz semisweet chocolate, coarsely chopped
¹/₂ cup finely chopped macadamia nuts

Preheat the oven to 350°F. • Line three cookie sheets with parchment paper. • Soak the cherries in the kirsch in a medium bowl for 15 minutes. • Drain well. • Sift the flour, baking soda, and salt into a medium bowl. • Beat the butter and granulated and raw sugars in a large bowl with an electric mixer at high speed until creamy. • Add the vanilla and almond extracts and egg, beating until just blended. • Mix in the dry ingredients, followed by the cherries, white and semisweet chocolates, and macadamia

nuts. • Drop heaping tablespoons of the dough 2 inches apart onto the prepared cookie sheets. • Bake, one sheet at a time, for 12–15 minutes, or until lightly browned. • Cool the cookies on the sheets for 15 minutes. • Transfer to racks and let cool completely.

Makes 36 cookies · Prep: 20 min. + 15 min. to soak the cherries · Cooking: 12–15 min. per batch · Level: 1 · Keeps: 7 days

chocolate cherry cookies

³/₄ cup all-purpose flour
¹/₂ teaspoon baking powder
¹/₈ teaspoon salt
¹/₂ cup (1 stick) butter, softened
¹/₄ cup granulated sugar
¹/₂ teaspoon vanilla extract
¹/₃ cup finely chopped candied cherries
1   oz semisweet chocolate, finely chopped

Preheat the oven to 375°F. • Butter two cookie sheets. • Sift the flour, baking powder, and salt into a large bowl. • Beat the butter, sugar, and vanilla in a large bowl with an electric mixer at high speed until creamy. • Mix in the dry ingredients, cherries, and chocolate. • Drop rounded teaspoons of the dough 1 inch apart onto the prepared cookie sheets. • Bake for 15–20 minutes, or until just golden, rotating the sheets halfway through for even baking. • Cool on the sheets until the cookies firm slightly. • Transfer to racks to finish cooling

Makes 18–20 cookies · Prep: 20 min. · Cooking: 15–20 min. · Level: 1 · Keeps: 7 days

cherry oat cookies

2   cups all-purpose flour
1   tablespoon baking powder
¹/₂ teaspoon salt
³/₄ cup (1¹/₂ sticks) butter, softened
³/₄ cup firmly packed light brown sugar
1   teaspoon vanilla extract
1   large egg, lightly beaten
¹/₄ cup old-fashioned rolled oats
10   candied cherries, halved, to decorate

Preheat the oven to 350°F. • Butter two cookie sheets. • Sift the flour, baking powder, and salt into a medium bowl. • Beat the butter, brown sugar, and vanilla in a large bowl with an electric mixer at high speed until creamy. • Add the egg, beating until just blended. • Mix in the dry ingredients and oats until well blended. • Form into balls the size of walnuts and place 2 inches apart on the prepared cookie

sheets, flattening them slightly. • Place half a cherry in the center of each cookie. • Bake for 15–20 minutes, or until lightly browned, rotating the sheets halfway through for even baking. • Cool completely on the cookie sheets.

Makes 20 cookies · Prep: 15 min. · Cooking: 15–20 min. · Level: 1 · Keeps: 4–5 days

sunflower drops

1¹/₂ cups all-purpose flour
1   teaspoon baking soda
¹/₄ teaspoon salt
1   cup (2 sticks) butter, softened
1   cup firmly packed light brown sugar
1   cup granulated sugar
2   large eggs, lightly beaten
¹/₂ teaspoon vanilla extract
2   cups corn flakes
1   cup sunflower seeds

Preheat the oven to 350°F. • Butter two cookie sheets. • Sift the flour, baking soda, and salt into a medium bowl. • Beat the butter and both sugars in a large bowl with an electric mixer at high speed until creamy. • Add the eggs and vanilla, beating until just blended. • Mix in the dry ingredients, corn flakes, and sunflower seeds. • Drop tablespoons of the dough 2 inches apart onto the prepared cookie sheets. • Bake for 10–15 minutes, or until golden brown, rotating the sheets halfway through for even baking. • Cool on the sheets until the cookies firm slightly. • Transfer to racks to cool.

Makes 36–40 cookies · Prep: 20 min. · Cooking: 10–15 min. · Level: 1 · Keeps: 10 days

Chocolate cherry cookies

coconut rock cakes

3/4 cup whole-wheat flour
1/8 teaspoon salt
1 cup shredded coconut
1/4 cup granulated sugar
   Grated zest and juice of 1/2 lemon
1/4 cup (1/2 stick) butter, cut up
2 large eggs, lightly beaten

Preheat the oven to 425°F. • Butter a cookie sheet. • Sift the flour and salt into a large bowl. Stir in the coconut, sugar, and lemon zest. • Use a pastry blender to cut in the butter until the mixture resembles coarse crumbs. • Add the lemon juice and eggs, mixing until a smooth dough has formed. • Drop heaping tablespoons of the dough 2 inches apart onto the prepared cookie sheet. • Bake for 8–10 minutes, or until lightly browned. • Transfer to racks to cool.

Makes 12 cookies · Prep: 20 min. · Cooking: 8–10 min. · Level: 1 · Keeps: 4–5 days

coconut cookies

3/4 cup all-purpose flour
1 teaspoon baking powder
1/8 teaspoon salt
1 cup (2 sticks) butter, softened
1 cup granulated sugar
1 large egg
1 cup shredded coconut

Preheat the oven to 400°F. • Butter two cookie sheets. • Sift the flour, baking powder, and salt into a medium bowl. • Beat the butter and sugar in a large bowl with an electric mixer at high speed until creamy. • Add the egg, beating until just blended. • Mix in the dry ingredients and coconut until well blended. • Drop tablespoons of the dough 2 inches apart onto the prepared cookie sheets, pressing down lightly with a fork. • Bake for 10–15 minutes, or until golden brown, rotating the sheets halfway through for even baking. • Cool on the cookie sheets for 15 minutes. • Transfer to racks to cool.

Makes 15 cookies · Prep: 20 min. · Cooking: 10–15 min. · Level: 1 · Keeps: 5 days

coconut thumbprints

11/4 cups all-purpose flour
2 teaspoons baking soda
1/4 teaspoon salt
2/3 cup shredded coconut
1/2 cup (1 stick) butter, softened
1/2 cup firmly packed light brown sugar

1 teaspoon vanilla extract
1 large egg
3 tablespoons raspberry or strawberry
   preserves

Preheat the oven to 350°F. • Set out two cookie sheets. • Sift the flour, baking soda, and salt into a medium bowl. Stir in the coconut. • Beat the butter, brown sugar, and vanilla in a large bowl with an electric mixer at high speed until creamy. • Add the egg, beating until just blended. • With mixer at low speed, gradually add the dry ingredients. • Form the dough into balls the size of walnuts and place 1 inch apart on the sheets. • Use your thumb to make a slight hollow in each center and fill with a small amount of preserves. • Bake for 12–15 minutes, or until golden brown, rotating the sheets halfway through for even baking. • Transfer to racks to cool.

Makes 25–30 cookies · Prep: 20 min. · Cooking: 12–15 min. · Level: 1 · Keeps: 7 days

carob-topped sunflower seed drops

2 cups all-purpose flour
1 teaspoon ground allspice
1 teaspoon baking soda
1/4 teaspoon salt
11/2 cups sunflower seeds
1 cup old-fashioned rolled oats
1/4 cup sesame seeds
1 cup (2 sticks) butter, cut up
2 tablespoons firmly packed dark
   brown sugar
1 tablespoon dark molasses
11/2 cups carob chips

Preheat the oven to 375°F. • Butter two cookie sheets. • Sift the flour, allspice, baking soda, and salt into a large bowl. • Stir in the sunflower seeds, oats, and sesame seeds. • Melt the butter with the brown sugar and molasses in a small saucepan over low heat until the sugar has dissolved completely. • Pour the melted butter mixture into the dry ingredients and mix well. • Drop teaspoons of the mixture 11/2 inches apart onto the prepared cookie sheets. • Bake for 8–10 minutes, or until just golden, rotating the sheets halfway through for even baking. • Transfer to racks to cool. • Melt the carob in a double boiler over barely simmering water. • Drizzle the carob over the cookies and let stand for 30 minutes until set.

Makes 20 cookies · Prep: 25 min. + 30 min. to set · Cooking: 8–10 min. · Level: 1 · Keeps: 5 days

melting moments

11/4 cups all-purpose flour
1 teaspoon baking powder
1/8 teaspoon salt
1/3 cup butter, softened
1/2 cup granulated sugar
1 large egg
1 teaspoon vanilla extract
11/4 cups finely chopped candied cherries

Preheat the oven to 350°F. • Butter two cookie sheets. • Sift the flour, baking powder, and salt into a large bowl. • Beat the butter and sugar in a large bowl with an electric mixer at high speed until creamy. • Add the egg and vanilla, beating until just blended. • Mix in the dry ingredients and cherries. • Form the dough into balls the size of walnuts and place 1 inch apart on the prepared cookie sheets. • Bake for 15–20 minutes, or until just golden, rotating the sheets halfway through for even baking. • Cool on the sheets until the cookies firm slightly. • Transfer to racks to finish cooling.

Makes 28–30 cookies · Prep: 20 min. · Level: 1 · Cooking: 15–20 min. · Keeps: 5 days

anzac cookies

These cookies from Down Under are named after the Australian and New Zealand Army Corps of World War I.

1/2 cup old-fashioned rolled oats
1 cup shredded coconut
1 cup all-purpose flour
1/3 cup superfine sugar
1/8 teaspoon salt
2/3 cup butter, melted
2 tablespoons boiling water
1 tablespoon light corn syrup
1 teaspoon baking soda

Preheat the oven to 300°F. • Set out two cookie sheets. • Stir together the oats, coconut, flour, sugar, and salt in a large bowl. • Stir in the butter. • Mix the water, corn syrup, and baking soda in a small bowl. • Stir into the dry ingredients. • Drop teaspoons of the dough 1 inch apart onto the cookie sheets. • Bake for 12–15 minutes, or until lightly browned, rotating the sheets halfway through for even baking. • Transfer to racks to cool.

Makes 40 cookies · Prep: 10 min. · Cooking: 12–15 min. · Level: 1 · Keeps: 2 weeks

Melting moments (left) and Anzac cookies (right)

sweet apple cookies

2	medium sweet cooking apples, peeled, cored, and finely chopped
3/4	cup granulated sugar
2	cups all-purpose flour
1	teaspoon baking powder
1	teaspoon ground cinnamon
1/8	teaspoon salt
3/4	cup (1 1/2 sticks) butter, softened
1	large egg
3/4	cup raisins
1	cup corn flakes

Cook the apples with 1 tablespoon of sugar in a small saucepan over low heat, stirring often, until the apples have softened. Remove from the heat and let cool completely. • Preheat the oven to 400°F. • Butter three cookie sheets. • Sift the flour, baking powder, cinnamon, and salt into a medium bowl. • Beat the butter and remaining sugar in a large bowl with an electric mixer at high speed until creamy. • Add the egg, beating until just blended. • Mix in alternating tablespoons of the dry ingredients and the cooked apples until well blended. • Stir in the raisins and corn flakes. • Drop teaspoons of the dough 1 inch apart onto the prepared cookie sheets. • Bake, one sheet at a time, for 10–15 minutes, or until golden brown. • Transfer to racks to cool.

Makes 40–45 cookies · Prep: 30 min. · Cooking: 10–15 min. per batch · Level: 1 · Keeps: 5 days

corn flake cookies

1	cup all-purpose flour
1/2	teaspoon baking powder
1/4	cup (1/2 stick) butter, softened
1/4	cup vegetable shortening
1/2	cup granulated sugar
1	large egg, lightly beaten
1	cup corn flakes

Preheat the oven to 350°F. • Butter two cookie sheets. • Sift the flour and baking powder into a medium bowl. • Beat the butter, shortening, and sugar in a large bowl with an electric mixer at high speed until creamy. • Mix in the dry ingredients. • Add the egg, beating until just blended. • Sprinkle the corn flakes onto a cookie sheet. • Drop tablespoons of the batter onto the corn flakes. • Use a spatula to flatten the cookies and turn until completely coated. • Transfer the cookies to the prepared cookie sheets, placing 1 inch apart. • Bake for

10–15 minutes, or until just golden, rotating the sheets halfway through for even baking. • Transfer to racks to cool.

Makes 20–24 cookies · Prep: 20 min. · Cooking: 10–15 min. · Level: 1 · Keeps: 2 days

maidstone cookies

Maidstone, the county town of Kent, in southeast England, is the original home of these crunchy little cookies.

1	cup all-purpose flour
1/8	teaspoon salt
1/2	cup (1 stick) butter, softened
2/3	cup granulated sugar
1/2	cup finely chopped almonds
1	teaspoon rose water

Preheat the oven to 350°F. • Butter two cookie sheets. • Sift the flour and salt into a medium bowl. • Use a wooden spoon to beat the butter and sugar in a medium bowl until creamy. • Mix in the dry ingredients, almonds, and rose water to form a stiff dough. • Drop teaspoons of dough 1 inch apart onto the prepared cookie sheets. • Bake for 12–15 minutes, or until golden, rotating the sheets halfway through for even baking. • Transfer to racks to cool.

Makes 16–20 cookies · Prep: 20 min. · Cooking: 12–15 min. · Level: 1 · Keeps: 7 days

brown sugar cookies

2 1/3	cups all-purpose flour
1	tablespoon baking soda
1	tablespoon ground ginger
1/4	teaspoon salt
1 1/4	cups firmly packed light brown sugar
3	tablespoons light corn syrup
1/4	cup water
1	large egg
1	cup finely chopped pecans

Preheat the oven to 375°F. • Butter three cookie sheets. • Sift the flour, baking soda, ginger, and salt into a medium bowl. • Beat the brown sugar, corn syrup, water, and egg in a large bowl with an electric mixer at high speed until well blended. • Stir in the dry ingredients and pecans. • Drop teaspoons of the dough 2 inches apart onto the prepared cookie sheets. • Bake, one sheet at a time, for 10–12 minutes, or until just golden at the edges. • Transfer to racks to cool.

Makes 36 cookies · Prep: 20 min. · Cooking: 10–12 min. per batch · Level: 1 · Keeps: 7 days

crunchy butterscotch cookies

1	cup all-purpose flour
1 1/2	teaspoons baking powder
1/8	teaspoon salt
1/2	cup (1 stick) butter, softened
1	cup firmly packed dark brown sugar
1	tablespoon light corn syrup
2	tablespoons corn flakes
24	pecan halves, to decorate

Preheat the oven to 350°F. • Butter two cookie sheets. • Sift the flour, baking powder, and salt into a medium bowl. • Beat the butter, brown sugar, and corn syrup in a large bowl with an electric mixer at high speed for 1 minute. • Mix in the dry ingredients and corn flakes until well blended. • Form the mixture into twenty-four balls the size of walnuts, flattening them slightly. Press the pecan halves into the tops. • Arrange the cookies 1 1/2 inches apart on the prepared cookie sheets. • Bake for 10–15 minutes, or until lightly browned, rotating the sheets halfway through for even baking. • Cool the cookies completely on the cookie sheets.

Makes 24 cookies · Prep: 20 min. · Cooking: 10–15 min. · Level: 1 · Keeps: 5 days

ginger–walnut cookies

2 1/3	cups all-purpose flour
1	tablespoon baking soda
1	tablespoon ground ginger
1/4	teaspoon salt
1 1/4	cups firmly packed light brown sugar
3	tablespoons light corn syrup
1/4	cup water
1	large egg
1/2	cup finely chopped candied cherries
1/2	cup finely chopped walnuts

Preheat the oven to 375°F. • Butter three cookie sheets. • Sift the flour, baking soda, ginger, and salt into a medium bowl. • Beat the brown sugar, corn syrup, water, and egg in a large bowl with an electric mixer at high speed until well blended. • Stir in the dry ingredients, cherries, and walnuts. • Drop teaspoons of the dough 2 inches apart onto the prepared cookie sheets. • Bake, one sheet at a time, for 10–12 minutes, or until just golden at the edges. • Transfer to racks to cool.

Makes 36 cookies · Prep: 20 min. · Cooking: 10–12 min. per batch · Level: 1 · Keeps: 7 days

Crunchy butterscotch cookies

peanut butter cookies

These all-American classics are grea___ ␣ a
glass of chilled milk to serve to your ␣␣␣ren
when they come home from scho␣
butter is made from ground pe ␣␣␣␣␣␣d
with vegetable oil and salt. Use ␣mo␣␣␣␣ion
for these cookies. Why not stick the coo␣
together in pairs with Italian Buttercream (page
345) for an extra delicious cookie?

Peanut oaties

$1^2/_3$ cups all-purpose flour
1   teaspoon baking powder
$1/_2$ teaspoon ground cinnamon
$1/_2$ teaspoon ground nutmeg
$1/_4$ teaspoon ground cloves
$1/_2$ teaspoon salt
$1/_3$ cup sunflower or canola oil
$1/_3$ cup honey
1   cup smooth peanut butter
$1/_2$ cup old-fashioned rolled oats
$1/_2$ cup raisins

Preheat the oven to 375°F. • Line two cookie
sheets with parchment paper. • Sift the flour,
baking powder, cinnamon, nutmeg, cloves,
and salt into a large bowl. • Beat the oil,

honey, and peanut butter in a large bowl
with an electric mixer at high speed until
well blended. • Mix in the dry ingredients,
oats, and raisins. • Drop tablespoons of the
dough 1 inch apart onto the prepared cookie
sheets. • Bake for 8–10 minutes, or until
golden brown, rotating the sheets halfway
through for even baking. • Cool on the
sheets until the cookies firm slightly. •
Transfer to racks to finish cooling.

Makes 30 cookies · Prep: 20 min. · Cooking: 8–10
min. · Level: 1 · Keeps: 10 days

peanut butter–bran cookies

1   cup whole-wheat flour
$1/_2$ teaspoon baking powder
$1/_8$ teaspoon salt
$1/_2$ cup (1 stick) butter, softened
$1/_2$ cup firmly packed dark brown sugar
1   cup smooth peanut butter
1   large egg
$1/_2$ teaspoon vanilla extract
1   cup bran

Preheat the oven to 375°F. • Butter two
cookie sheets. • Sift the flour, baking powder,
and salt into a medium bowl. • Beat the
butter and brown sugar in a large bowl with
an electric mixer at high speed until creamy. •
Beat in the peanut butter, egg, and vanilla. •

Mix in the dry ingredients and bran. • Form
the dough into balls the size of walnuts and
place $1^1/_2$ inches apart on the prepared
cookie sheets, flattening them slightly. • Bake
for 8–10 minutes, or until just golden,
rotating the sheets halfway through for even
baking. • Transfer to racks to cool.

Makes 20–25 cookies · Prep: 20 min. · Cooking:
8–10 min. · Level: 1 · Keeps: 5 days

peanut butter–chocolate kiss cookies

2   cups all-purpose flour
$1/_2$ teaspoon baking powder
$1/_2$ teaspoon baking soda
$1/_8$ teaspoon salt
$1/_2$ cup (1 stick) butter, softened
$1/_3$ cup smooth peanut butter
$2/_3$ cup confectioners' sugar
$1/_3$ cup firmly packed dark brown sugar
$1/_2$ teaspoon vanilla extract
1   large egg
35   Hershey kisses

Preheat the oven to 350°F. • Butter three
cookie sheets. • Sift the flour, baking powder,
baking soda, and salt into a large bowl. • Beat
the butter, peanut butter, confectioners'
sugar, and brown sugar in a large bowl with
an electric mixer at high speed until creamy. •
Add the vanilla and egg, beating until just
blended. • Mix in the dry ingredients to form a
stiff dough. • Form the dough into balls the
size of walnuts and press a Hershey kiss into
the center of each ball. Smooth the dough
around the kiss until only the tip is visible. •
Transfer the cookies to the prepared cookie
sheets, placing them 2 inches apart. • Bake,
one sheet at a time, for 8–10 minutes, or until
lightly browned. • Transfer to racks to cool.

Makes 35 cookies · Prep: 30 min. · Cooking: 8–10
min. per batch · Level: 1 · Keeps: 7 days

peanut oaties

1   cup all-purpose flour
$1/_2$ teaspoon baking powder
$1/_2$ teaspoon baking soda
$1/_2$ cup (1 stick) butter, softened
1   cup granulated sugar
1   large egg, lightly beaten
$1/_2$ cup salted peanuts
1   cup corn flakes
$2^1/_4$ cups old-fashioned rolled oats

Preheat the oven to 300°F. • Butter a cookie
sheet. • Sift the flour, baking powder, and
baking soda into a medium bowl. • Beat the
butter and sugar in a large bowl with an
electric mixer at high speed until creamy. •
Add the egg, beating until just blended. • Mix
in the dry ingredients, peanuts, corn flakes,
and oats to make a stiff dough. • Drop
teaspoons of the dough 1 inch apart onto the
prepared cookie sheet. • Bake for 10–15
minutes, or until lightly browned. • Cool on the
sheet until the cookies firm slightly. • Transfer
to racks and let cool completely.

Makes 14–16 cookies · Prep: 20 min. · Cooking:
10–15 min. · Level: 1 · Keeps: 5 days

queensland cookies

*These cookies are from Brisbane in the eastern
sunshine state of Queensland, Australia.*

$3/_4$ cup all-purpose flour
1   teaspoon baking powder
$1/_8$ teaspoon salt
$1/_2$ cup smooth peanut butter
$1/_2$ cup granulated sugar
1   tablespoon finely grated orange zest
1   large egg
$1/_2$ cup raisins

Preheat the oven to 325°F. • Butter three cookie sheets. • Sift the flour, baking powder, and salt into a medium bowl. • Beat the peanut butter, sugar, and orange zest in a large bowl with an electric mixer at high speed until creamy. • Add the egg, beating until just blended. • Mix in the raisins. • Mix in the dry ingredients. • Form the dough into balls the size of walnuts and place 2 inches apart on the prepared cookie sheets. • Dip a fork in flour and press lines into the tops. • Bake, one sheet at a time, for 12–15 minutes, or until golden brown. • Transfer to racks to cool.

Makes 30–35 cookies · Prep: 20 min. · Cooking: 12–15 min. per batch · Level: 1 · Keeps: 5 days

chocolate-filled coconut cookies

1¹/3	cups all-purpose flour
1	teaspoon baking powder
¹/8	teaspoon salt
³/4	cup (1¹/2 sticks) butter, softened
¹/3	cup granulated sugar
¹/2	teaspoon vanilla extract
1	large egg
3	tablespoons shredded coconut

Chocolate filling

1	cup confectioners' sugar
¹/4	cup (¹/2 stick) butter, melted
1	tablespoon unsweetened cocoa powder

Preheat the oven to 300°F. • Set out two cookie sheets. • Sift the flour, baking powder, and salt into a medium bowl. • Beat the butter, sugar, and vanilla in a large bowl with an electric mixer at medium speed until creamy. • Add the egg, beating until just blended. • Mix in the dry ingredients. • Place the coconut in a small bowl. • Roll teaspoons of the dough in the coconut and place 1 inch apart on the cookie sheets. • Bake for 18–20

minutes, or until lightly browned, rotating the sheets halfway through for even baking. • Transfer to racks to cool. • Chocolate filling: Beat the confectioners' sugar and melted butter in a small bowl. • Mix in the cocoa powder. • Stick the cookies together in pairs with the chocolate filling.

Makes 15–20 cookies · Prep: 25 min. · Cooking: 18–20 min. · Level: 1 · Keeps: 7 days

nutty cinnamon cookies

1¹/4	cups all-purpose flour
1	teaspoon baking powder
¹/8	teaspoon salt
¹/2	cup (1 stick) butter, softened
²/3	cup granulated sugar
1	large egg
³/4	cup finely chopped pecans
2	teaspoons ground cinnamon

Preheat the oven to 375°F. • Butter two cookie sheets. • Sift the flour, baking powder, and salt into a medium bowl. • Beat the butter and sugar in a large bowl with an electric mixer at high speed until creamy. • Add the egg, beating until just blended. • Mix in the dry ingredients to form a smooth dough. • Mix the pecans and cinnamon in a small bowl. • Form the dough into balls the size of walnuts and roll them in the nut mixture until well coated. • Place the cookies 2 inches apart on the prepared cookie sheets. • Bake for 10–15 minutes, or until golden, rotating the sheets halfway through for even baking. • Transfer to racks to cool.

Makes 20–25 cookies · Prep: 20 min. · Cooking: 10–15 min. · Level: 1 · Keeps: 7 days

pecan–sour cream cookies

2	cups all-purpose flour
2	teaspoons baking powder
¹/2	teaspoon baking soda
¹/2	teaspoon ground cinnamon
¹/8	teaspoon salt
¹/2	cup (1 stick) butter, softened
³/4	cup granulated sugar
1	large egg
¹/2	cup reduced-fat sour cream
¹/2	cup coarsely chopped pecans

Preheat the oven to 375°F. • Butter three cookie sheets. • Sift the flour, baking powder, baking soda, cinnamon, and salt into a medium bowl. • Beat the butter and sugar in a large bowl with an electric mixer at high speed until creamy. • Add the egg, beating until just blended. • Mix in the sour cream and dry ingredients. • Stir in the pecans. • Drop

teaspoons of the dough 1 inch apart onto the prepared cookie sheets. • Bake, one sheet at a time, for 10–15 minutes, or until golden brown. • Transfer to racks to cool.

Makes 30–35 cookies · Prep: 20 min. · Cooking: 10–15 min. per batch · Level: 1 · Keeps: 7 days

nutty cranberry cookies

1	cup all-purpose flour
¹/4	teaspoon baking soda
¹/8	teaspoon salt
2	tablespoons butter, softened
2	tablespoons vegetable shortening
¹/4	cup granulated sugar
¹/4	cup firmly packed light brown sugar
¹/2	teaspoon vanilla extract
1	large egg
¹/2	cup coarsely chopped dried cranberries
¹/4	cup finely chopped mixed candied peel
¹/4	cup finely chopped pecans

Preheat the oven to 375°F. • Line two cookie sheets with parchment paper. • Sift the flour, baking soda, and salt into a medium bowl. • Beat the butter, shortening, and granulated and brown sugars in a large bowl with an electric mixer at high speed until creamy. • Add the vanilla and egg, beating until just blended. • Mix in the dry ingredients, cranberries, candied peel, and pecans. • Drop tablespoons of the dough 1¹/2 inches apart onto the prepared cookie sheets. • Bake for 8–10 minutes, or until golden at the edges, rotating the sheets halfway through for even baking. • Cool on the sheets until the cookies firm slightly. • Transfer to racks to finish cooling.

Makes 25–30 cookies · Prep: 20 min. · Cooking: 8–10 min. · Level: 1 · Keeps: 7 days

three-ingredient cookies

This recipe is one of the simplest you'll ever encounter—and the cookies are oh-so-yummy.

1	large egg, lightly beaten
1	cup smooth peanut butter
1	cup granulated sugar

Preheat the oven to 350°F. • Butter a cookie sheet. • Mix the egg, peanut butter, and sugar in a large bowl until well blended. • Form the dough into balls the size of walnuts and place 2 inches apart on the prepared cookie sheet, flattening them slightly. • Bake for 8–10 minutes, or until just golden. • Transfer to racks to cool.

Makes 12 cookies · Prep: 20 min. · Cooking: 8–10 min. · Level: 1 · Keeps: 5 days

caribbean chocolate cookies

2 oz semisweet chocolate,
  coarsely chopped
1/3 cup butter, softened
1/3 cup granulated sugar
1 teaspoon coconut extract
2 tablespoons cream of coconut
1 teaspoon finely shredded lemon zest
1 teaspoon finely shredded lime zest
3/4 cup shredded coconut
1 3/4 cups all-purpose flour

Preheat the oven to 350°F. • Line two cookie sheets with parchment paper. • Melt the chocolate in a double boiler over barely simmering water. • Beat the butter and sugar in a medium bowl with an electric mixer at high speed until creamy. • Add the coconut extract, cream of coconut, melted chocolate, and the lemon and lime zests. • Mix in 1/2 cup of the shredded coconut and flour. • Turn the dough onto a lightly floured surface and knead until smooth. • Form the dough into balls the size of walnuts. Roll in the remaining 1/4 cup coconut and place 2 inches apart on the prepared cookie sheet, flattening them slightly. • Bake for 15–20 minutes, or until just golden, rotating the sheets halfway through for even baking. • Transfer to racks to cool.

Makes 25–30 cookies · Prep: 30 min. · Cooking: 15–20 min. · Level: 1 · Keeps: 2 days

crispy chocolate creams

1 1/2 cups all-purpose flour
1/4 cup unsweetened cocoa powder
1/2 teaspoon baking powder
1/8 teaspoon salt
1/2 cup (1 stick) butter, softened
1/2 cup lard or vegetable shortening, softened
1/2 cup granulated sugar
1 cup old-fashioned rolled oats
1/4 cup light corn syrup dissolved in
  1 tablespoon hot water

Chocolate filling
1/4 cup (1/2 stick) butter, softened
1/4 cup confectioners' sugar
1/4 cup unsweetened cocoa powder
1/2 teaspoon vanilla extract

Preheat the oven to 350°F. • Butter two cookie sheets. • Sift the flour, cocoa, baking powder, and salt into a medium bowl. • Beat the butter, lard, and sugar in a large bowl with an electric mixer at high speed until creamy. • Mix in the dry ingredients, followed by the oats and corn syrup mixture to form a smooth dough. • Form the dough into balls the size of walnuts, and place 1 inch apart on the prepared cookie sheets, flattening them slightly. • Bake for 20–25

minutes, or until firm to the touch, rotating the sheets halfway through for even baking. • Transfer to racks to cool. • Chocolate filling: Beat the butter and confectioners' sugar in a small bowl until creamy. • Mix in the cocoa and vanilla. • Stick the cookies together in pairs with the chocolate filling.

Makes 16 cookies · Prep: 25 min. · Cooking: 20–25 min. · Level: 1 · Keeps: 7 days

chocolate–nut crackles

2/3 cup all-purpose flour
1/2 teaspoon baking powder
1/8 teaspoon salt
12 oz bittersweet chocolate,
  coarsely chopped
1/2 cup (1 stick) butter, cut up
3 large eggs
1 cup granulated sugar
1 tablespoon freeze-dried coffee granules
1 teaspoon vanilla extract
1 1/2 cups coarsely chopped pecans
1 1/2 cups coarsely chopped hazelnuts
1 cup semisweet chocolate chips

Preheat the oven to 325°F. • Set out two cookie sheets. • Sift the flour, baking powder, and salt into a large bowl. • Melt the chocolate and butter in a double boiler over barely simmering water. • Beat the eggs and sugar in a large bowl with an electric mixer at high speed until pale and thick. • Beat in the chocolate mixture, coffee granules, and vanilla. • Mix in the dry ingredients, pecans, hazelnuts, and chocolate chips. • Drop tablespoons of the dough 3 inches apart onto the cookie sheets. • Bake for 20–25 minutes, or until lightly cracked on top, rotating the sheets halfway through for even baking. • Transfer to racks to cool.

Makes 20 cookies · Prep: 20 min. · Cooking: 20–25 min. · Level: 1 · Keeps: 7 days

death-by-chocolate cookies

1/2 cup all-purpose flour
2/3 cup unsweetened cocoa powder
1 1/2 teaspoons baking powder
1/4 teaspoon salt
9 oz semisweet chocolate,
  coarsely chopped
3/4 cup (1 1/2 sticks) butter, cut up
3 large eggs
1 cup granulated sugar
1/3 cup firmly packed light brown sugar
1 teaspoon vanilla extract
1 1/3 cups semisweet chocolate chips
1 1/2 cups coarsely chopped pecans
6 oz white chocolate, coarsely chopped

Preheat the oven to 325°F. • Butter four cookie sheets. • Sift the flour, cocoa, baking powder, and salt into a large bowl. • Melt the semisweet chocolate and butter in a double boiler over barely simmering water. • Beat the eggs and granulated and brown sugars in a large bowl with an electric mixer at high speed until creamy. • Beat in the chocolate mixture and vanilla. • Mix in the dry ingredients, chocolate chips, pecans, and white chocolate. • Drop tablespoons of the dough 4 inches apart onto the prepared cookie sheets. Use the bottom of a glass to flatten the cookies slightly. • Bake, one sheet at a time, for 8–10 minutes, or until cracked on top. • Transfer to racks to cool.

Makes 24 cookies · Prep: 20 min. · Cooking: 8–10 min. per batch · Level: 1 · Keeps: 5 days

double chocolate–almond cookies

2/3 cup all-purpose flour
1/2 teaspoon baking powder
1/8 teaspoon salt
6 oz semisweet chocolate,
  coarsely chopped
6 oz white chocolate, coarsely chopped
1/2 cup (1 stick) butter, cut up
3 large eggs
1 cup granulated sugar
1 tablespoon freeze-dried coffee granules
1 teaspoon almond extract
3 cups coarsely chopped almonds
1 cup white chocolate chips

Preheat the oven to 325°F. • Set out two cookie sheets. • Sift the flour, baking powder, and salt into a large bowl. • Melt the semisweet and white chocolates and butter in a double boiler over barely simmering water. • Beat the eggs and sugar in a large bowl with an electric mixer at high speed until pale and thick. • Beat in the chocolate mixture, coffee granules, and almond extract. • Mix in the dry ingredients, almonds, and white chocolate chips. • Drop tablespoons of the dough 3 inches apart onto the cookie sheets. • Bake for 20–25 minutes, or until lightly cracked on top, rotating the sheets halfway through for even baking. • Transfer to racks and let cool completely.

Makes 20 cookies · Prep: 20 min. · Cooking: 20–25 min. · Level: 1 · Keeps: 7 days

Death-by-chocolate cookies

Oatmeal–raisin cookies

oatmeal, raisin, and walnut cookies

- 1¼ cups all-purpose flour
- ½ teaspoon baking soda
- ½ teaspoon salt
- ½ cup (1 stick) butter, softened
- ½ cup granulated sugar
- ½ cup firmly packed dark brown sugar
- ½ teaspoon vanilla extract
- 1 large egg, lightly beaten
- ⅓ cup old-fashioned rolled oats
- ½ cup golden raisins
- ⅔ cup coarsely chopped walnuts

Preheat the oven to 350°F. • Butter three cookie sheets. • Sift the flour, baking soda, and salt into a medium bowl. • Beat the butter and both sugars in a large bowl with an electric mixer at high speed until creamy. • Add the vanilla and egg, beating until just blended. • Mix in the dry ingredients, oats, raisins, and walnuts. • Drop heaping teaspoons of the dough 2 inches apart onto the prepared cookie sheets. • Bake, one sheet at a time, for 12–15 minutes, or until lightly browned. • Transfer to racks and let cool completely.

Makes 45 cookies · Prep: 20 min. · Cooking: 12–15 min. per batch · Level: 1 · Keeps: 7 days

brandied spiced cookies

The raisins soften the texture of these spiced cookies.

- ⅓ cup raisins
- 2 tablespoons brandy
- 1½ cups all-purpose flour
- 1 teaspoon ground cinnamon
- 1 teaspoon freshly grated nutmeg
- ½ teaspoon baking soda
- ⅛ teaspoon salt
- ¾ cup (1½ sticks) butter, softened

- ⅔ cup granulated sugar
- ¼ cup firmly packed dark brown sugar
- ¼ cup milk
  Grated zest of 1 orange

Preheat the oven to 350°F. • Butter two cookie sheets. • Plump the raisins in the brandy in a small bowl for 15 minutes, or until almost all the liquid has been absorbed. • Sift the flour, cinnamon, nutmeg, baking soda, and salt into a medium bowl. • Beat the butter and granulated and brown sugars in a large bowl with an electric mixer at high speed until creamy. • Mix in the milk, raisin mixture, dry ingredients, and orange zest. • Drop teaspoons of the dough 1 inch apart onto the prepared cookie sheets. • Bake for 10–15 minutes, or until just golden, rotating the sheets halfway through for even baking. • Cool on the sheets until the cookies firm slightly. • Transfer to racks to finish cooling.

Makes 20 cookies · Prep: 20 min. + 15 min. to plump the raisins · Cooking: 10–15 min. · Level: 1 · Keeps: 7 days

soft raisin–walnut cookies

- 2 cups all-purpose flour
- ½ teaspoon ground cinnamon
- ½ teaspoon ground nutmeg
- ½ teaspoon baking soda
- ¼ teaspoon salt
- ½ cup vegetable shortening
- ⅔ cup firmly packed dark brown sugar
- 1 large egg
- 1 cup raisins
- ½ cup water
- ½ cup coarsely chopped walnuts

Preheat the oven to 350°F. • Butter two cookie sheets. • Sift the flour, cinnamon, nutmeg, baking soda, and salt into a medium bowl. • Beat the shortening and brown sugar in a large bowl with an electric mixer at high speed until well blended. • Add the egg, beating until just blended. • Stir in the raisins, water, and walnuts. • Mix in the dry ingredients. • Drop teaspoons of the dough 1 inch apart onto the prepared cookie sheets. • Bake for 8–10 minutes, or until just golden, rotating the sheets halfway through for even baking. • Transfer the cookies to racks to cool.

Makes 30 cookies · Prep: 20 min. · Cooking: 8–10 min. · Level: 1 · Keeps: 7 days

oatmeal–raisin cookies

- 1¼ cups all-purpose flour
- ½ teaspoon baking soda
- ½ teaspoon salt
- ½ cup (1 stick) butter, softened
- ½ cup granulated sugar
- ½ cup firmly packed dark brown sugar
- ½ teaspoon vanilla extract
- 1 large egg, lightly beaten
- ⅓ cup old-fashioned rolled oats
- ½ cup raisins
- ⅔ cup coarsely chopped peanuts

Preheat the oven to 350°F. • Butter three cookie sheets. • Sift the flour, baking soda, and salt into a large bowl. • Beat the butter and granulated and brown sugars in a large bowl with an electric mixer at high speed until creamy. • Add the vanilla and egg, beating until just blended. • Mix in the dry ingredients, oats, raisins, and peanuts. • Drop heaping teaspoons of the dough 2 inches apart onto the prepared cookie sheets. • Bake, one sheet at a time, for 12–15 minutes, or until lightly browned. • Transfer to racks and let cool completely.

Makes 45 cookies · Prep: 20 min. · Cooking: 12–15 min. per batch · Level: 1 · Keeps: 7 days

hazelnut–citrus cookies

- ½ cup (1 stick) butter, softened
- ¼ cup granulated sugar
- 1 large egg, separated
- 1 teaspoon finely grated orange zest
- ½ teaspoon finely grated lemon zest
- ¼ teaspoon salt
- ¾ cup all-purpose flour
- 1 cup finely ground hazelnuts

Beat the butter and sugar in a large bowl with an electric mixer at high speed until creamy. • Add the egg yolk, beating until just blended. • Beat in the orange and lemon zests and salt. • Mix in the flour until well blended. • Refrigerate for 30 minutes. • Preheat the oven to 350°F. • Butter two cookie sheets. • Form the dough into balls the size of walnuts. • Beat the egg white lightly in a small bowl. • Dip the balls first in the egg white, then in the hazelnuts until well coated. • Place 1 inch apart on the prepared cookie sheets. • Bake for 18–20 minutes, or until firm to the touch, rotating the sheets halfway through for even baking. • Transfer to racks and let cool completely.

Makes 24 cookies · Prep: 20 min. + 30 min. to chill · Cooking: 18–20 min. · Level: 1 · Keeps: 5 days

orange cookies with chocolate chips

Be sure to use a dark brown sugar in these cookies, or add 1 tablespoon of dark molasses. The orange and chocolate are enhanced by the deep, dark flavor of raw sugar.

2	cups all-purpose flour
1/2	cup whole-wheat flour
1	teaspoon baking soda
1/2	teaspoon salt
1	cup granulated sugar
1/2	cup firmly packed dark brown sugar
3/4	cup (1 1/2 sticks) butter, softened
2	tablespoons finely grated orange zest
2	large eggs
1	cup finely chopped walnuts
1	cup semisweet chocolate chips

Preheat the oven to 350°F. • Butter two cookie sheets. • Sift the all-purpose and whole-wheat flours, the baking soda, and salt into a medium bowl. • Beat the granulated and brown sugars, butter, and orange zest in a large bowl with an electric mixer at high speed until creamy. • With mixer at medium speed, add the eggs, beating until just blended. • With mixer at low speed, gradually beat in the dry ingredients, followed by the walnuts and the chocolate chips. • Drop tablespoons of the dough 2 inches apart onto the prepared cookie sheets. • Bake for 10–12 minutes, or until lightly browned, rotating the sheets halfway through for even baking. • Cool on the sheets until the cookies firm slightly. • Transfer to racks to finish cooling.

Makes 40 cookies · Prep: 20 min. · Cooking: 10–12 min. · Level: 1 · Keeps: 7 days

traditional coriander cookies

3/4	cup all-purpose flour
1	teaspoon ground coriander
1/2	teaspoon ground aniseeds
1/8	teaspoon salt
2	large eggs
2/3	cup granulated sugar

Preheat the oven to 350°F. • Butter two cookie sheets. • Sift the flour, coriander, aniseeds, and salt into a large bowl. • Beat the eggs and sugar in a medium bowl with an electric mixer at high speed until pale and thick. • Mix in the dry ingredients until well blended. • Drop teaspoons of the cookie dough 3 inches apart onto the prepared cookie sheets. • Bake for 8–12 minutes, or until faintly tinged with brown on top and slightly darker at the edges, rotating the sheets halfway through for even baking. • Use a spatula to turn the cookies over. • Bake for 3–5 minutes more, or until firm to the touch. • Transfer to racks and let cool completely.

Makes 25–30 cookies · Prep: 20 min. · Cooking: 11–17 min. · Level: 1 · Keeps: 5 days

orange–raisin cookies

1 1/3	cups all-purpose flour
1/2	teaspoon baking powder
1/2	teaspoon salt
1/2	cup (1 stick) butter, softened
2/3	cup granulated sugar
1	large egg, lightly beaten
1/2	teaspoon vanilla extract
2/3	cup raisins
1	tablespoon finely grated orange zest

Preheat the oven to 375°F. • Butter two cookie sheets. • Sift the flour, baking powder, and salt into a medium bowl. • Beat the butter and sugar in a large bowl with an electric mixer at high speed until creamy. • Add the egg and vanilla, beating until just blended. • Mix in the dry ingredients, followed by the raisins and orange zest. • Drop tablespoons of the dough 2 inches apart onto the prepared cookie sheets. • Bake for 12–15 minutes, or until just golden, rotating the sheets halfway through for even baking. • Cool on the sheets until the cookies firm slightly. • Transfer to racks to finish cooling.

Makes 25 cookies · Prep: 25 min. · Cooking: 12–15 min. · Level: 1 · Keeps: 2 weeks

viennese lemon cookies

1 1/2	cups all-purpose flour
1	tablespoon cornstarch
1/2	teaspoon baking powder
1/8	teaspoon salt
1	cup (2 sticks) butter, softened
2/3	cup confectioners' sugar + extra, to dust
	Grated zest of 2 lemons
	Confectioners' sugar, to dust

Preheat the oven to 350°F. • Butter two cookie sheets. • Sift the flour, cornstarch, baking powder, and salt into a large bowl. • Beat the butter and 2/3 cup confectioners' sugar in a large bowl with an electric mixer at high speed until creamy. • Mix in the dry ingredients and lemon zest. • Drop teaspoons of the mixture 2 inches apart onto the prepared cookie sheets. • Bake for 12–15 minutes, or until golden brown, rotating the sheets halfway through for even baking. • Cool completely on the sheets. • Dust with the confectioners' sugar.

Makes 25 cookies · Prep: 25 min. · Cooking: 12–15 min. · Level: 1 · Keeps: 4 days

Orange–raisin cookies

cracked ginger cookies

Rolling the cookies in sugar and baking them in a hot oven gives them a crackle-top finish.

2	cups all-purpose flour
1	tablespoon ground ginger
2	teaspoons baking powder
1 1/2	teaspoons ground cinnamon
1/4	teaspoon ground cloves
1/4	teaspoon salt
3/4	cup vegetable shortening
1 1/4	cups granulated sugar
1	large egg
1/4	cup dark molasses

Preheat the oven to 350°F. • Set out three cookie sheets. • Sift the flour, ginger, baking powder, cinnamon, cloves, and salt into a medium bowl. • Beat the shortening and 1 cup of the sugar in a large bowl with an electric mixer at high speed until creamy. • Add the egg and molasses, beating until just blended. • Mix in the dry ingredients to form a smooth dough. • Form the dough into balls the size of marbles, roll in the remaining 1/2 cup sugar, and place 2 inches apart on the cookie sheets. • Bake, one sheet at a time, for 10–12 minutes, or until just colored at the edges. • Cool on the sheets until the cookies firm slightly. • Transfer to racks to cool.

Makes 45–50 cookies · Prep: 25 min. · Cooking: 10–12 min. per batch · Level: 1 · Keeps: 2 weeks

chocolate–ginger cookies

2/3	cup all-purpose flour
1	tablespoon unsweetened cocoa powder
2	teaspoons ground ginger
1/2	teaspoon baking soda
1/4	cup crystallized ginger, finely chopped
1/4	cup (1/2 stick) butter
1 1/2	tablespoons golden syrup (sold with imported foods in many supermarkets, or substitute light corn syrup)
1/4	cup granulated sugar

Preheat the oven to 300°F. • Butter a cookie sheet. • Stir together the flour, cocoa, ground ginger, and baking soda in a medium bowl. Stir in the crystallized ginger. • Melt the butter and golden syrup in a medium saucepan over low heat, stirring constantly. • Add the sugar and continue stirring over very low heat until dissolved. • Remove from the heat. Use a large rubber spatula to fold in the dry ingredients and mix thoroughly. • Shape the mixture into balls the size of walnuts. • Place 1 1/2 inches apart on the prepared cookie sheet. • Use a fork to flatten them

slightly. • Bake for 12–15 minutes, or until golden brown. • Transfer to racks to cool.

Makes about 15 cookies · Prep: 10 min. · Cooking: 12–15 min. · Level: 1 · Keeps: about 7 days

tiny ginger cookies

In the 17th century, the Fens, bordering England's eastern coast, were desolate marshes. Drained by the ingenuity of Dutch engineers, they became one of the country's richest arable farming areas, famous for wheat, sugar beets, and fruit. These unusual pale ginger cookies are a specialty of the region.

1 2/3	cups all-purpose flour
1	teaspoon baking powder
1	teaspoon ground ginger
1/8	teaspoon salt
1/2	cup (1 stick) butter, softened
1 3/4	cups + 2 tablespoons granulated sugar
1	large egg, lightly beaten

Preheat the oven to 300°F. • Butter two cookie sheets. • Sift the flour, baking powder, ginger, and salt into a medium bowl. • Use a wooden spoon to beat the butter and 1 3/4 cups sugar in a large bowl until creamy. • Add the egg, beating until just blended. • Mix in the dry ingredients to form a stiff dough. • Form the dough into balls the size of walnuts and place 2 inches apart on the prepared cookie sheets. • Bake for 40–45 minutes, or until crisp and golden, rotating the sheets halfway through for even browning. • Transfer to racks to cool. • Dust with the remaining 2 tablespoons sugar.

Makes 28–32 cookies · Prep: 25 min. · Cooking: 40–45 min. · Level: 1 · Keeps: 5 days

cardamom cookies

Tiny aromatic cardamom seeds are found inside the small green or ivory seed-pods of a plant that grows in tropical climates. Traders first brought them to Europe from India and Southeast Asia, where they are widely used to flavor food and also chewed as a breath freshener. In Germany and the Netherlands, ground cardamom is a favorite flavoring for cookies.

3/4	cup all-purpose flour
3/4	cup cornstarch
1	tablespoon ground cardamom
1/8	teaspoon salt
3	large eggs
1	cup granulated sugar
1/2	teaspoon vanilla extract

Butter two cookie sheets. • Sift the flour, cornstarch, cardamom, and salt into a large bowl. • Beat the eggs, sugar, and vanilla in a large bowl with an electric mixer at high

speed until pale and thick. • Mix in the dry ingredients. • Drop teaspoons of the dough 2 inches apart onto the prepared cookie sheets. • Cover with a clean kitchen towel and let rest for 12 hours. • Preheat the oven to 300°F. • Bake for 25–35 minutes, or until golden brown, rotating the sheets halfway through for even baking. • Transfer to racks and let cool completely.

Makes 20–24 cookies · Prep: 20 min. + 12 hr. to rest Cooking: 25–35 min. · Level: 1 · Keeps: 2 weeks

sacher torte cookies

These cookies take their name from the rich Viennese chocolate cake that was first invented in 1832 by a 16-year-old apprentice chef, Franz Sacher.

2	cups all-purpose flour
1/4	cup Dutch-process cocoa powder
1/8	teaspoon salt
1	cup (2 sticks) butter, softened
1/4	cup granulated sugar
1	large egg
1/2	cup apricot preserves or jam

Rich chocolate glaze

7	oz semisweet chocolate, coarsely chopped
2	tablespoons butter

Preheat the oven to 350°F. • Butter three cookie sheets. • Sift the flour, cocoa, and salt into a medium bowl. • Beat the butter and sugar in a large bowl with an electric mixer at high speed until creamy. • Add the egg, beating until just blended. • Mix in the dry ingredients to form a smooth dough. • Form the dough into balls the size of walnuts and place 2 inches apart on the prepared cookie sheets. Press your thumb into each one to make a small hollow. • Bake, one batch at a time, for 12–15 minutes, or until firm to the touch. • Transfer to racks to cool. • Fill the hollows with a dab of preserves. • Rich chocolate glaze: Melt the chocolate and butter in a double boiler over barely simmering water. • Spoon the glaze into a small freezer bag and cut off a tiny corner. • Pipe over the cookies in a decorative manner and let stand for 30 minutes until set.

Makes 40–45 cookies · Prep: 25 min. + 30 min. to set · Cooking: 12–15 min. per batch · Level: 1 · Keeps: 3 days

Sacher torte cookies (center) and Cracked ginger cookies (edge)

two-tone cookies

1²/₃ cups all-purpose flour
1 teaspoon baking powder
¹/₈ teaspoon salt
¹/₃ cup butter, softened
¹/₄ cup granulated sugar
2 large eggs
1 tablespoon milk
¹/₄ cup confectioners' sugar
¹/₄ cup unsweetened cocoa powder

Preheat the oven to 350°F. • Butter two cookie sheets. • Sift the flour, baking powder, and salt into a large bowl and make a well in the center. • Add the butter, sugar, eggs, and milk. • Use your hands to knead the mixture into a smooth dough. • Form the dough into balls the size of walnuts and place 1 inch apart on the prepared cookie sheets. • Bake for 15–20 minutes, or until just golden, rotating the sheets halfway through for even baking. • Transfer to racks and let cool completely. • Dip half of each cookie in the confectioners' sugar and the remaining half in the cocoa.

Makes 26 cookies · Prep: 35 min. · Cooking: 15–20 min. · Level: 1 · Keeps: 5 days

butter drop cookies

These scrumptious cookies just melt in your mouth.

1 cup all-purpose flour
¹/₂ teaspoon baking powder
¹/₈ teaspoon salt
¹/₂ cup (1 stick) butter, cut up
²/₃ cup granulated sugar
2 large eggs, lightly beaten

Preheat the oven to 325°F. • Butter two cookie sheets. • Sift the flour, baking powder, and salt into a medium bowl. • Melt the butter in a medium saucepan over low heat. • Remove from the heat and let cool for 10 minutes. • Add the sugar and eggs, beating until just blended. • Mix in the dry ingredients until well blended. • Drop teaspoons of the dough 2 inches apart onto the prepared cookie sheets. • Bake for 15–20 minutes, or until just golden, rotating the sheets halfway through for even baking. • Transfer to racks to cool.

Makes 20 cookies · Prep: 20 min. · Cooking: 15–20 min. · Level: 1 · Keeps: 7 days

Two-tone cookies

whole-wheat orange cookies

These cookies are delicious filled with freshly whipped cream.

5 large eggs
1¹/₄ cups granulated sugar
1¹/₂ cups whole-wheat flour
¹/₈ teaspoon salt
 Grated zest of 1 orange

Preheat the oven to 350°F. • Butter two cookie sheets. • Beat the eggs and sugar in a large bowl with an electric mixer at high speed until pale and thick. • Use a large rubber spatula to fold in the flour, salt, and orange zest. • Drop tablespoons of the mixture 2 inches apart onto the cookie sheets. • Bake for 15–20 minutes, or until lightly browned, rotating the sheets halfway through for even baking. • Transfer to racks to cool.

Makes 25 cookies · Prep: 20 min. · Cooking: 15–20 min. · Level: 1 · Keeps: 5 days

hungarian sandwich cookies

³/₄ cup all-purpose flour
1 tablespoon unsweetened cocoa powder
¹/₂ teaspoon baking powder
¹/₈ teaspoon salt
¹/₂ cup (1 stick) butter, softened
¹/₄ cup granulated sugar
¹/₂ teaspoon vanilla extract
¹/₂ cup Coffee Buttercream (see page 345)

Preheat the oven to 375°F. • Butter two cookie sheets. • Sift the flour, cocoa, baking powder, and salt into a medium bowl. • Beat the butter, sugar, and vanilla in a large bowl with an electric mixer at high speed until creamy. • Mix in the dry ingredients to form a stiff dough. • Form the dough into balls the size of walnuts and place 1 inch apart on the prepared cookie

sheets. Use a fork to flatten them slightly. • Bake for 10–15 minutes, or until firm to the touch, rotating the sheets halfway through for even baking. • Cool on the sheets until the cookies firm slightly. • Transfer to racks to finish cooling. • Stick the cookies together in pairs with the buttercream.

Makes 12–15 cookies · Prep: 20 min. · Level: 1 · Cooking: 10–15 min. · Keeps: 7 days in the refrigerator

apple–walnut cookies

2 cups all-purpose flour
¹/₂ teaspoon baking powder
¹/₂ teaspoon baking soda
¹/₂ teaspoon ground cinnamon
¹/₄ teaspoon salt
¹/₂ cup (1 stick) butter, softened
¹/₂ cup granulated sugar
¹/₄ cup firmly packed dark brown sugar
1 large egg
1 cup Applesauce (see page 340)
1 tart apple, such as Granny Smith, peeled, cored, and finely chopped
1 cup finely chopped walnuts

Preheat the oven to 375°F. • Butter three cookie sheets. • Sift the flour, baking powder, baking soda, cinnamon, and salt into a medium bowl. • Beat the butter and granulated and brown sugars in a large bowl with an electric mixer at high speed until creamy. • Add the egg and applesauce, beating until just blended. • Mix in the dry ingredients, apple, and walnuts. • Drop tablespoons of the dough 2 inches apart onto the prepared cookie sheets. • Bake, one sheet at a time, for 15–20 minutes, or until just golden at the edges. • Transfer to racks to cool.

Makes 45–48 cookies · Prep: 20 min. · Cooking: 15–20 min. per batch · Level: 1 · Keeps: 3 days

date delights

1³/4   cups finely chopped pitted dates
1³/4   cups finely chopped walnuts
2   large egg whites
1   cup confectioners' sugar
1   tablespoon unsweetened cocoa powder
       Juice of 1 lemon

Preheat the oven to 325°F. • Butter two cookie sheets. • Chop the dates very finely and place in a large bowl. Add the walnuts. • Stir in the egg whites, confectioners' sugar, cocoa, and lemon juice and mix until well blended. • Drop teaspoons of the dough 1 inch apart onto the prepared cookie sheets. • Bake for 25–30 minutes, or until just golden at the edges, rotating the sheets halfway through for even baking. • Transfer to racks and let cool completely.

Makes 25 cookies · Prep: 20 min. · Cooking: 25–30 min. · Level: 1 · Keeps: 7 days

heavenly moments

Look for Bird's Custard Powder near the tapioca in your local supermarket.

2   cups all-purpose flour
¹/3   cup custard powder
²/3   cup butter, softened
¹/3   cup confectioners' sugar
2   teaspoons fresh orange juice

Filling
²/3   cup confectioners' sugar
1   tablespoon butter, melted
1   tablespoon custard powder
       Grated zest of ¹/2 orange

Preheat the oven to 325°F. • Butter two cookie sheets. • Sift the flour and custard powder into a large bowl. • Beat the butter and confectioners' sugar in a large bowl with an electric mixer at high speed until creamy. Beat in the orange juice. • Mix in the dry ingredients. • Form into balls the size of walnuts and place 2 inches apart on the prepared cookie sheets, flattening slightly with a fork. • Bake for 15–20 minutes, or until firm to the touch, rotating the sheets halfway through for even baking. • Transfer to racks to cool. • Filling: Use a fork to beat the confectioners' sugar, butter, custard powder, and orange zest until smooth. • Stick cookies together in pairs with a generous amount of the filling.

Makes 15 cookies · Prep: 15 min. · Cooking: 15–20 min. · Level: 1 · Keeps: 2 days

muesli drop cookies

2¹/4   cups all-purpose flour
2¹/2   teaspoons baking powder
2   teaspoons ground cinnamon
¹/2   teaspoon ground nutmeg
¹/2   teaspoon baking soda
¹/4   teaspoon salt
¹/2   cup (1 stick) butter, softened
1   cup granulated sugar
¹/4   cup fresh orange juice
1   large egg
1   cup muesli or granola-type cereal
¹/2   cup raisins
¹/2   cup finely chopped dates
¹/2   cup finely chopped dried apricots
¹/2   cup finely chopped walnuts
¹/2   cup old-fashioned rolled oats

Preheat the oven to 350°F. • Butter three cookie sheets. • Sift the flour, baking powder, cinnamon, nutmeg, baking soda, and salt into a medium bowl. • Beat the butter and sugar in a large bowl with an electric mixer at high speed until creamy. • Gradually add the orange juice and egg, beating until just blended. • Stir in the muesli, raisins, dates, apricots, walnuts, and oats. • Mix in the dry ingredients. • Drop tablespoons of the dough 2 inches apart onto the prepared cookie sheets. • Bake, one sheet at a time, for 12–15 minutes, or until just golden. • Transfer to racks to cool.

Makes 33–36 cookies · Prep: 20 min. · Cooking: 12–15 min. per batch · Level: 1 · Keeps: 3 days

viennese orange cookies

1¹/2   cups all-purpose flour
1   tablespoon cornstarch
¹/2   teaspoon baking powder
¹/8   teaspoon salt
1   cup (2 sticks) butter, softened
²/3   cup confectioners' sugar + extra, to dust
       Grated zest of 2 oranges
       Confectioners' sugar, to dust

Preheat the oven to 350°F. • Butter two cookie sheets. • Sift the flour, cornstarch, baking powder, and salt into a large bowl. • Beat the butter and ²/3 cup confectioners' sugar in a large bowl with an electric mixer at high speed until creamy. • Mix in the dry ingredients and orange zest. • Drop teaspoons of the mixture 2 inches apart onto the prepared cookie sheets. • Bake for 12–15 minutes, or until golden brown, rotating the sheets halfway through for even baking. • Cool completely on the sheets. • Dust with the confectioners' sugar.

Makes 25 cookies · Prep: 25 min. · Cooking: 12–15 min. · Level: 1 · Keeps: 4 days

date–almond cookies

1³/4   cups finely chopped pitted dates
1³/4   cups finely chopped almonds
2   large egg whites
1   cup confectioners' sugar
1   tablespoon unsweetened cocoa powder
       Juice of 1 lemon

Preheat the oven to 325°F. • Butter two cookie sheets. • Chop the dates very finely and place in a large bowl. Add the almonds. • Stir in the egg whites, confectioners' sugar, cocoa, and lemon juice and mix until well blended. • Drop teaspoons of the dough 1 inch apart onto the prepared cookie sheets. • Bake for 25–30 minutes, or until just golden at the edges, rotating the sheets halfway through for even baking. • Transfer to racks to cool.

Makes 25 cookies · Prep: 20 min. · Cooking: 25–30 min. · Level: 1 · Keeps: 7 days

date–pecan cookies

1³/4   cups finely chopped pitted dates
1³/4   cups finely chopped pecans
2   large egg whites
1   cup confectioners' sugar
1   tablespoon unsweetened cocoa powder
       Juice of 1 lemon

Preheat the oven to 325°F. • Butter two cookie sheets. • Chop the dates very finely and place in a large bowl. Add the pecans. • Stir in the egg whites, confectioners' sugar, cocoa, and lemon juice and mix until well blended. • Drop teaspoons of the dough 1 inch apart onto the prepared cookie sheets. • Bake for 25–30 minutes, or until just golden at the edges, rotating the sheets halfway through for even baking. • Transfer to racks to cool.

Makes 25 cookies · Prep: 20 min. · Cooking: 25–30 min. · Level: 1 · Keeps: 7 days

Viennese orange cookies

extra-large chocolate chip cookies

Bake a double batch of these great-tasting cookies and freeze them so you will always have them on hand for unexpected guests. Soft and chocolatey, these super-sized cookies look scrumptious in a cookie jar. Substitute walnuts for half the chocolate, if you want a crunchy texture, and mix them into the cookie dough just before dropping onto the sheets.

1¹/₂ cups all-purpose flour
³/₄ cup unsweetened cocoa powder
¹/₈ teaspoon salt
1¹/₂ cups firmly packed light brown sugar
³/₄ cup (1¹/₂ sticks) butter, softened
8 oz semisweet chocolate, coarsely chopped
3 large eggs, lightly beaten

Preheat the oven to 350°F. • Line four cookie sheets with parchment paper. • Sift the flour, cocoa, and salt into a large bowl. • Stir in the brown sugar and make a well in the center. • Melt the butter and 5 oz chocolate in a double boiler over barely simmering water. • Stir the chocolate mixture into the dry ingredients. • Add the eggs, beating until just blended. • Stir in the remaining 3 oz chocolate. • Drop two tablespoons of the cookie dough onto the prepared cookie sheets for each cookie, allowing no more than four cookies on each cookie sheet. • Bake, one batch at a time, for 12–15 minutes, or until well spread and firm to the touch. • Transfer to racks to cool. • Line the cookie sheets with fresh parchment paper and continue to bake in batches until all the cookie dough has been used.

Makes 20–25 cookies · Prep: 25 min. · Cooking: 12–15 min. per batch · Level: 2 · Keeps: 2 days

piquant chocolate cookies

Fiery but delicious.

³/₄ cup all-purpose flour
1 teaspoon ground red pepper
¹/₂ teaspoon baking powder
¹/₈ teaspoon salt
¹/₂ cup (1 stick) butter, softened
2 tablespoons granulated sugar
¹/₄ cup firmly packed dark brown sugar
1 large egg
¹/₂ teaspoon vanilla extract
3 oz semisweet chocolate, finely chopped

Preheat the oven to 350°F. • Butter two cookie sheets. • Sift the flour, red pepper, baking powder, and salt into a medium bowl. • Beat the butter and granulated and brown sugars in a large bowl with an electric mixer at high speed until creamy. • Add the egg and vanilla, beating until just blended. • Mix in the dry ingredients and chopped chocolate. • Drop teaspoons of the dough 1 inch apart onto the prepared cookie sheets. • Bake for 12–15 minutes, or until firm to the touch, rotating the sheets halfway through for even baking. • Transfer to racks to cool.

Makes 20–25 cookies · Prep: 20 min. · Cooking: 12–15 min. · Level: 1 · Keeps: 10 days

passionfruit crunchies

1 cup all-purpose flour
1 cup rice flour
1 teaspoon baking powder
¹/₄ teaspoon salt
³/₄ cup (1¹/₂ sticks) butter, softened
¹/₂ cup confectioners' sugar
1 teaspoon passionfruit extract or liqueur
¹/₃ cup Passionfruit Filling and Frosting (see page 349)

Preheat the oven to 350°F. • Set out two cookie sheets. • Sift the flour, rice flour, baking powder, and salt into a medium bowl. • Beat the butter, confectioners' sugar, and passionfruit extract in a large bowl with an electric mixer at high speed until creamy. • With mixer at low speed, gradually add the dry ingredients. • Form teaspoons of the dough into balls the size of walnuts and place 1 inch apart on the prepared cookie sheets, pressing down lightly with a fork. • Bake for 15–18 minutes, or until golden, rotating the sheets halfway through for even baking. • Transfer to racks to cool. • Stick the cooled cookies together in pairs with the filling.

Makes 15 cookies · Prep: 25 min. · Cooking 15–18 min. · Level 1 · Keeps: 7 days

nutmeg-topped cookies

²/₃ cup all-purpose flour
¹/₃ cup confectioners' sugar
1 teaspoon baking powder
¹/₄ teaspoon salt
¹/₂ cup (1 stick) butter, melted
1 tablespoon freshly grated nutmeg

Preheat the oven to 300°F. • Dust a cookie sheet with flour. • Sift the flour, confectioners' sugar, baking powder, and salt into a large bowl. • Stir in the butter to make a soft dough. • Form the dough into balls the size of walnuts, flattening them slightly, and place them 2 inches apart on the prepared cookie sheet. • Sprinkle with the nutmeg. • Bake for 15–20 minutes, or until pale but slightly cracked on top. • Transfer the cookies to racks to cool.

Makes 12 cookies · Prep: 25 min. · Cooking: 15–20 min. · Level: 1 · Keeps: 3 days

cinnamon–corn flake cookies

³/₄ cup all-purpose flour
1 teaspoon ground cinnamon
1 teaspoon ground ginger
¹/₂ teaspoon baking powder
¹/₈ teaspoon salt
¹/₄ cup (¹/₂ stick) butter, cut up
1¹/₄ cups corn flakes
²/₃ cup granulated sugar
5 tablespoons light molasses

Preheat the oven to 350°F. • Butter two cookie sheets. • Sift the flour, cinnamon, ginger, baking powder, and salt into a medium bowl. • Use a pastry blender to cut in the butter until the mixture resembles coarse crumbs. • Stir in the corn flakes and sugar. Stir in the molasses to make a stiff dough. • Form the dough into balls the size of walnuts and place 2 inches apart on the prepared cookie sheets. • Bake for 15–20 minutes, or until lightly browned, rotating the sheets halfway through for even baking. • Transfer to racks to cool.

Makes 20–24 cookies · Prep: 25 min. · Cooking: 15–20 min. · Level: 1 · Keeps: 5 days

Extra-large chocolate chip cookies

Ginger–cinnamon cookies

ginger–cinnamon cookies

2 cups all-purpose flour
2 teaspoons baking soda
1 teaspoon ground ginger
1 teaspoon ground cinnamon
1/4 teaspoon salt
1/2 cup (1 stick) butter, softened
2/3 cup granulated sugar
1/3 cup dark molasses
1 large egg, lightly beaten
1/4 cup water
1/3 cup golden raisins

Preheat the oven to 400°F. • Butter three cookie sheets. • Sift the flour, baking soda, ginger, cinnamon, and salt into a large bowl. • Beat the butter and sugar in a large bowl with an electric mixer at high speed until creamy. • Add the molasses and egg, beating until just blended. • Mix in the water and dry ingredients until well blended. • Drop tablespoons of the dough 2 inches apart onto the prepared cookie sheets. Sprinkle with the raisins. • Bake, one sheet at a time, for 6–8 minutes, or until lightly browned. • Cool on the sheets until the cookies firm slightly. Transfer to racks to finish cooling.

Makes 30 cookies · Prep: 20 min. · Cooking: 6–8 min. per batch · Level: 1 · Keeps: 7 days

gingernuts

1 1/2 cups all-purpose flour
2 teaspoons ground ginger
1 teaspoon baking powder
1/2 teaspoon ground cinnamon
1/8 teaspoon salt
1/3 cup butter, softened
1 1/4 cups granulated sugar
1 tablespoon light corn syrup
1 large egg

Preheat the oven to 350°F. • Butter two cookie sheets. • Sift the flour, ginger, baking powder, cinnamon, and salt into a large bowl. • Beat the butter, sugar, and corn syrup in a large bowl with an electric mixer at high speed until creamy. • Add the egg, beating until just blended. • Mix in the dry ingredients. • Drop teaspoons of the dough 2 inches apart onto the prepared cookie sheets, flattening them slightly. • Bake for 10–12 minutes, or until firm to the touch, rotating the sheets halfway through for even baking. • Transfer to racks to cool.

Makes 30 cookies · Prep: 15 min. · Cooking: 10–12 min. · Level: 1 · Keeps: 2 weeks

cinnamon crunchies

3/4 cup wheat germ, toasted
1/2 teaspoon baking soda
1 teaspoon ground cinnamon
1/8 teaspoon salt
1/4 cup old-fashioned rolled oats
1/3 cup granulated sugar
1/3 cup butter, cut up
1 tablespoon light corn syrup
1 tablespoon milk

Preheat the oven to 350°F. • Butter two cookie sheets. • Stir together the wheat germ, baking soda, cinnamon, and salt in a large bowl. Stir in the oats and sugar. • Melt the butter with the corn syrup and milk in a small saucepan over low heat. • Pour into the dry ingredients and mix until smooth. • Form into balls the size of walnuts and place 2 inches apart on the prepared cookie sheets, flattening them slightly. • Bake for 12–15 minutes, or until golden brown, rotating the trays halfway through for even baking. • Cool the cookies completely on the cookie sheets.

Makes 25 cookies · Prep: 15 min. · Cooking: 12–15 min. · Level: 1 · Keeps: 5 days

montecaos

These cinnamon-topped cookies are a Tunisian specialty.

2/3 cup all-purpose flour
1 teaspoon baking powder
1/4 teaspoon salt
1/3 cup confectioners' sugar
1/2 cup (1 stick) butter, melted
1 tablespoon ground cinnamon

Preheat the oven to 300°F. • Dust a cookie sheet with flour. • Sift the flour, baking powder, and salt into a large bowl. • Stir in the confectioners' sugar. Use your hands to mix in the butter to make a soft dough. • Form the dough into balls the size of walnuts, flattening them slightly, and place them 2 inches apart on the prepared cookie sheet. • Sprinkle with the cinnamon. • Bake for 15–20 minutes, or until pale but slightly cracked on top. • Transfer the cookies to racks to cool.

Makes 12 cookies · Prep: 25 min. · Cooking: 15–20 min. · Level: 1 · Keeps: 3 days

lebkuchen

2 cups all-purpose flour
1/2 cup rye flour
2 teaspoons baking powder
1 1/2 teaspoons ground cinnamon
1 teaspoon ground nutmeg
1 teaspoon ground cloves
1 teaspoon ground allspice
1/2 teaspoon salt
1/2 teaspoon freshly ground black pepper
1 large egg, lightly beaten
1 cup honey
3/4 cup firmly packed light brown sugar
    Grated zest of 1 lemon
1 tablespoon fresh lemon juice
1 cup finely chopped almonds
1 cup finely chopped candied lemon peel

Lemon glaze
1 1/2 cups confectioners' sugar
1 tablespoon fresh lemon juice
1–2 tablespoons water

Preheat the oven to 350°F. • Butter three cookie sheets. • Sift the all-purpose and rye flours, baking powder, cinnamon, nutmeg, cloves, allspice, and salt into a large bowl. Stir in the black pepper. • Make a well in the center and add the egg, beating until just blended. • Mix in the honey, brown sugar, lemon zest and juice, almonds, and candied lemon peel. • Drop tablespoons of the dough 2 inches apart onto the prepared cookie sheets. • Bake, one sheet at a time, for 15–20 minutes, or until lightly browned and firm to the touch. • Transfer to racks to cool. • Lemon glaze: Mix the confectioners' sugar, lemon juice, and enough water to make a spreading consistency. • Spread the glaze over the tops of the cookies.

Makes 36 cookies · Prep: 25 min. · Cooking: 15–20 min. per batch · Level: 1 · Keeps: 7 days

hermits

These spicy drop cookies were a favorite in both Britain and the United States in the 19th century. In some of older recipes, beef fat (suet) is used instead of butter.

2 1/3 cups all-purpose flour
2 teaspoons ground cinnamon
1 teaspoon baking powder
1 teaspoon ground cloves
1/2 teaspoon freshly grated nutmeg
1/4 teaspoon salt
1/2 cup (1 stick) butter, softened
3/4 cup firmly packed dark brown sugar
2 large eggs
1/2 cup raisins
1/2 cup flaked almonds

Sift the flour, cinnamon, baking powder, cloves, nutmeg, and salt into a medium bowl. • Beat the butter, brown sugar, and eggs in a large bowl with an electric mixer at medium speed until well combined. • Mix in the dry ingredients, followed by the raisins and almonds. • Cover with plastic wrap and refrigerate for 30 minutes. • Preheat the oven to 375°F. • Butter two cookie sheets. • Drop teaspoons of the cookie dough 2 inches apart onto the prepared cookie sheets. • Bake for 8–10 minutes, or until golden brown, rotating the sheets halfway through for even baking. • Transfer to racks and let cool completely.

Makes 24–30 cookies · Prep: 20 min. + 30 min. to chill · Cooking: 8–10 min. · Level: 1 · Keeps: 2 weeks

spicy cornish fairings

This crisp, spicy cookie comes from Cornwall in the southwest of England.

1 1/2 cups all-purpose flour
1 tablespoon ground ginger
2 teaspoons baking powder
2 teaspoons baking soda
2 teaspoons ground allspice
1 teaspoon ground cinnamon
1/8 teaspoon salt
1/2 cup (1 stick) butter, cut up
1/2 cup granulated sugar
1/4 cup light corn syrup

Preheat the oven to 400°F. • Butter two cookie sheets. • Sift the flour, ginger, baking powder, baking soda, allspice, cinnamon, and salt into a large bowl. • Use a pastry blender to cut in the butter until the mixture resembles fine crumbs. • Stir in the sugar and corn syrup until well blended. • Form the dough into balls the size of walnuts and place 2 inches apart on the prepared cookie sheets. • Bake for

10–15 minutes, or until just golden, rotating the sheets halfway through for even baking. • Watch them closely towards the end of the baking time as they darken very quickly. • Cool on the sheets until the cookies firm slightly. • Transfer to racks and let cool completely.

Makes 20–24 cookies · Prep: 25 min. · Cooking: 10–15 min. · Level: 1 · Keeps: 5 days

spicy hazelnut–lemon cookies

5 cups finely chopped toasted hazelnuts
1/2 cup granulated sugar
3 large eggs
1/2 teaspoon ground cinnamon
1/2 teaspoon ground cloves
Grated zest of 1/2 lemon
1/8 teaspoon salt

Preheat the oven to 350°F. • Line three cookie sheets with parchment paper. • Use a wooden spoon to mix the hazelnuts, sugar, eggs, cinnamon, cloves, lemon zest, and salt until a stiff dough has formed. • Form the dough into balls the size of walnuts and place 1 inch apart on the prepared cookie sheets, flattening them slightly. • Bake, one sheet at a time, for 15–20 minutes, or until just golden at the edges. • Cool the cookies completely on the cookie sheets.

Makes 40 cookies · Prep: 25 min. · Cooking: 15–20 min. per batch · Level: 1 · Keeps: 2 weeks

coffee–cherry cookies

1 cup all-purpose flour
1 tablespoon unsweetened cocoa powder
1/4 teaspoon salt
1/2 cup (1 stick) butter, softened
1/4 cup granulated sugar
1 teaspoon vanilla extract
2 teaspoons freeze-dried coffee granules
1/2 cup finely chopped pecans
1/4 cup finely chopped candied cherries
1/3 cup confectioners' sugar

Preheat the oven to 325°F. • Butter three cookie sheets. • Sift the flour, cocoa, and salt into a medium bowl. • Beat the butter, sugar, and vanilla in a large bowl with an electric mixer at high speed until creamy. • Mix in the dry ingredients, coffee granules, pecans, and cherries until well blended. • Form the dough into balls the size of walnuts and place 1 inch apart on the prepared cookie sheets. • Bake, one sheet at a time, for 15–18 minutes, or until firm

to the touch. • Transfer to racks and let cool completely. • Dust with the confectioners' sugar.

Makes 36 cookies · Prep: 20 min. · Cooking: 15–18 min. per batch · Level: 1 · Keeps: 7 days

amish spicy raisin cookies

The Amish community is a religious group that stresses humility, family, and abstinence from modern living. Amish baking and cooking is noted for its simplicity and delicious nature.

2 1/2 cups all-purpose flour
1 1/2 teaspoons baking powder
1/2 teaspoon ground cinnamon
1/4 teaspoon ground ginger
1/4 teaspoon salt
1/2 cup (1 stick) butter, softened
1/2 cup vegetable shortening
2 large eggs
1 cup firmly packed dark brown sugar
1/2 cup raisins
1/2 cup coarsely chopped walnuts

Milk Frosting
1 1/2 cups confectioners' sugar
1/2 cup milk, or more as needed

Preheat the oven to 375°F. • Butter two cookie sheets. • Sift the flour, baking powder, cinnamon, ginger, and salt into a large bowl. • Beat the butter, shortening, and brown sugar in a large bowl with an electric mixer at high speed until creamy. • Add the eggs, beating until just blended. • Mix in the dry ingredients, raisins, and walnuts. • Drop teaspoons of the dough 1 inch apart onto the prepared cookie sheets. • Bake for 8–10 minutes, or until just lightly browned at the edges, rotating the sheets halfway through for even baking. • Transfer the cookies to racks to cool. • Milk Frosting: Mix the confectioners' sugar and enough milk in a small bowl to make a drizzling consistency. Drizzle the frosting over the cookies.

Makes 40 cookies · Prep: 25 min. · Cooking: 8–10 min. · Level: 1 · Keeps: 3 days

Amish spicy raisin cookies

banana–sunflower seed cookies

1/3	cup sunflower seeds
1/3	cup old-fashioned rolled oats
2	tablespoons honey
1	tablespoon sunflower oil
1	large egg, lightly beaten
1	large ripe banana, mashed

Preheat the oven to 350°F. • Butter a cookie sheet. • Finely grind the sunflower seed and oats with a pestle and mortar or in a blender until they resemble flour. • Heat the honey and oil in a small saucepan over low heat. • Mix the honey mixture with the sunflower seed mixture in a medium bowl. • Add the egg, beating until just blended. Stir in the banana. • Drop teaspoons of the mixture 1 inch apart onto the prepared cookie sheet. • Bake for 12–15 minutes, or until golden brown. • Cool the cookies completely on the cookie sheets.

Makes 20 cookies · Prep: 20 min. · Cooking: 12–15 min. · Level: 1 · Keeps: 5 days

bavarian kisses

3/4	cup hazelnuts
1	cup granulated sugar
2	cups all-purpose flour
1	teaspoon baking powder
1/8	teaspoon salt
1	cup (2 sticks) butter, softened
1/2	cup firmly packed light brown sugar
2	large eggs, at room temperature
1	teaspoon vanilla extract
1–2	tablespoons fresh orange juice
7	oz semisweet chocolate, coarsely chopped

Preheat the oven to 325°F. • Set out three cookie sheets. • Spread the hazelnuts on a baking sheet. Toast for 7 minutes, or until lightly golden. • Let cool completely. Transfer to a food processor, add 1/2 cup of the granulated sugar and process until the nuts are coarsely chopped. • Sift the flour, baking powder, and salt into a medium bowl. • Beat the butter and remaining 1/2 cup granulated sugar and brown sugar in a large bowl with an electric mixer at high speed until creamy. • Add the eggs, beating until just blended. Add the vanilla. • Mix in the dry ingredients and enough orange juice to make a smooth dough. • Stir in the chocolate and hazelnuts. • Drop teaspoons of the dough 1 inch apart onto the cookie sheets. • Bake, one sheet at a time, for 10–12 minutes, or until golden brown. • Cool the cookies for 3 minutes on each cookie sheet. • Transfer to racks to finish cooling.

Makes 45 cookies · Prep: 40 min. · Cooking: 10–12 min. per batch · Level: 1 · Keeps: 3–4 days

mini cocoa–corn flake cookies

3/4	cup (11/2 sticks) butter, softened
1/2	cup granulated sugar
2	cups all-purpose flour
2	tablespoons unsweetened cocoa powder
1/4	cup corn flakes, lightly crushed

Frosting

1	cup confectioners' sugar
2	tablespoons butter, softened
1	tablespoon boiling water
1	tablespoon unsweetened cocoa powder
1	teaspoon vanilla extract
30	walnut halves, to decorate

Preheat the oven to 350°F. • Butter two cookie sheets. • Beat the butter and sugar in a large bowl with an electric mixer at high speed until creamy. • Sift in the flour and cocoa. Stir in the corn flakes until well mixed. • Drop teaspoons of the dough 1 inch apart onto the prepared cookie sheets. • Bake for 10–15 minutes, or until firm to the touch, rotating the sheets halfway through for even baking. • Transfer to racks to cool. • Frosting: Mix the confectioners' sugar, butter, water, cocoa, and vanilla in a small bowl until well blended. • Spread the frosting over the tops of the cooled cookies. Decorate with the walnut halves.

Makes 30 cookies · Prep: 15 min. · Cooking: 10–15 min. · Level: 1 · Keeps: 7 days

oat drops

The long soaking time allows the oats to develop a richer flavor.

2	cups old-fashioned rolled oats
1	cup firmly packed light brown sugar
1/2	cup vegetable oil
1	large egg, lightly beaten
1/2	teaspoon almond extract
1/8	teaspoon salt

Mix the oats, brown sugar, and oil in a medium bowl until well blended. • Set aside for 12 hours in a cool place. • Preheat the oven to 325°F. • Butter two cookie sheets. • Mix the egg, almond extract, and salt into the oat mixture. • Drop teaspoons of the dough 1 inch apart onto the prepared cookie sheets. • Bake for 15–18 minutes, or until golden, rotating the sheets halfway through for even baking. • Transfer to racks to cool.

Makes 16–18 cookies · Prep: 15 min. + 12 hr. to soak Cooking: 15–18 min. · Level: 1 · Keeps: 2 weeks

white chocolate–banana cookies

11/2	cups all-purpose flour
1/2	cup whole-wheat flour
1/4	cup unsweetened cocoa powder
2	teaspoons baking powder
1/4	teaspoon baking soda
1/4	teaspoon ground cinnamon
1/8	teaspoon salt
6	oz semisweet chocolate, coarsely chopped
1/4	cup (1/2 stick) butter, softened
1/2	cup granulated sugar
1/2	cup firmly packed light brown sugar
2	large firm-ripe bananas, peeled and mashed
1	teaspoon vanilla extract
2	large eggs
1/2	cup semisweet chocolate chips
6	oz white chocolate, coarsely chopped
1	cup coarsely chopped walnuts
1	cup raisins

Line three cookie sheets with parchment paper. • Sift the all-purpose and whole-wheat flours, cocoa, baking powder, baking soda, cinnamon, and salt into a medium bowl. • Melt the semisweet chocolate in a double boiler over barely simmering water. • Beat the butter and granulated and brown sugars in a large bowl with an electric mixer at high speed until creamy. • Beat in the bananas and vanilla until well blended. • Add the melted chocolate and eggs, beating until just blended. • Mix in the dry ingredients, chocolate chips, white chocolate, walnuts, and raisins. • Drop teaspoons of the dough 2 inches apart onto the prepared cookie sheets. • Preheat the oven to 375°F. • Bake, one sheet at a time, for 15–20 minutes, or until just golden at the edges. • Transfer to racks and let cool completely.

Makes 36 cookies · Prep: 20 min. · Cooking: 15–20 min. per batch · Level: 1 · Keeps: 7 days

White chocolate–banana cookies

Nuremberg spice cookies

nuremburg spice cookies

These rich and spicy cookies come from the old city of Nuremberg in Bavaria, southern Germany.

- 40 rice paper circles, cut 2 1/2 inches in diameter
- 2 large eggs
- 1 cup granulated sugar
- 1/2 teaspoon vanilla extract
- 1 1/3 cups finely ground almonds
- 3/4 cup finely chopped mixed candied peel
- 1 tablespoon dark rum
- 2 teaspoons grated lemon zest
- 1/4 teaspoon baking powder
- 1/4 teaspoon ground cloves
- 1/8 teaspoon salt
- 1 1/3 cups finely ground hazelnuts
- 1 1/3 cups confectioners' sugar
- 1/4 cup hot water

Preheat the oven to 300°F. • Butter three cookie sheets. • Place the rice paper circles on the cookie sheets. • Beat the eggs, granulated sugar, and vanilla in a large bowl with an electric mixer at high speed until pale and thick. • Mix in the almonds, candied peel, rum, lemon zest, baking powder, cloves, and salt. • Stir in the hazelnuts until well blended. • Drop teaspoons of the cookie dough onto each rice paper circle. Shape into a smooth dome. • Bake, one sheet at a time, for 25–35 minutes, or until golden brown. • Transfer to racks and let cool completely. • Mix the confectioners' sugar with enough hot water to make a spreadable frosting. • Drizzle the frosting over the cookies.

Makes 40 cookies · Prep: 25 min. · Cooking: 25–35 min. per batch · Level: 1 · Keeps: 7 days

apple–spice cookies

- 2 cups all-purpose flour
- 1 teaspoon ground cinnamon
- 1 teaspoon ground ginger
- 1/2 teaspoon ground cloves
- 1/2 teaspoon baking soda
- 1/2 teaspoon salt
- 1/2 cup (1 stick) butter, softened
- 1/2 cup firmly packed light brown sugar
- 1/3 cup granulated sugar
- 1 teaspoon vanilla extract
- 1 large egg
- 1 cup Applesauce (see page 340)
- 1 cup golden raisins
- 3/4 cup finely chopped walnuts

Preheat the oven to 350°F. • Butter three cookie sheets. • Sift the flour, cinnamon, ginger, cloves, baking soda, and salt into a medium bowl. • Beat the butter and brown and granulated sugars in a large bowl with an electric mixer at high speed until creamy. • Add the vanilla and egg, beating until just blended. • Stir in the applesauce. • Mix in the dry ingredients, followed by the raisins and walnuts. • Drop tablespoons of the dough 2 inches apart onto the prepared cookie sheets. • Bake, one sheet at a time, for 5–7 minutes, or until just golden. • Transfer to racks and let cool completely.

Makes 36 cookies · Prep: 20 min. · Cooking: 5–7 min. per batch · Level: 1 · Keeps: 5 days

spiced raisin cookies

- 1 cup golden raisins
- 2 cups all-purpose flour
- 1 teaspoon baking powder
- 1 teaspoon ground cinnamon
- 1/8 teaspoon freshly grated nutmeg
- 1/8 teaspoon salt
- 1/4 cup milk
- 1/8 teaspoon fresh lemon juice
- 1/2 cup (1 stick) butter, softened
- 1 cup raw sugar (Demerara or Barbados)
- 1/4 cup granulated sugar
- 2 large eggs

Preheat the oven to 350°F. • Butter two cookie sheets. • Plump the raisins in hot water to cover in a small bowl for 10 minutes. • Drain well and pat dry with paper towels. • Sift the flour, baking powder, cinnamon, nutmeg, and salt into a medium bowl. • Mix the milk and lemon juice in a small bowl. • Beat the butter and raw and granulated sugars in a large bowl with an electric mixer at high speed until creamy. • Add the eggs, beating until just blended. • Mix in the dry ingredients, milk mixture, and

raisins. • Drop teaspoons of the dough 1 inch apart onto the prepared cookie sheets. • Bake for 12–15 minutes, or until just golden, rotating the sheets halfway through for even baking. • Transfer to racks to cool.

Makes 32 cookies · Prep: 25 min. · Cooking: 12–15 min. · Level: 1 · Keeps: 7 days

spice, nut, and honey ginger rounds

- 1 1/2 cups all-purpose flour
- 1 teaspoon baking powder
- 1 teaspoon baking soda
- 1 teaspoon ground ginger
- 1/4 teaspoon ground cinnamon
- 1/8 teaspoon salt
- 1/2 cup firmly packed dark brown sugar
- 1/3 cup butter
- 3 tablespoons dark corn syrup
- 3 tablespoons dark molasses
- 1 large egg, lightly beaten
- 1/2 cup finely chopped crystallized ginger

Ginger frosting
- 1/2 cup confectioners' sugar
- 1/8 teaspoon ground ginger
- 1/4 teaspoon unsweetened cocoa powder
- 1 tablespoon hot water
- 1 teaspoon coconut oil or coconut extract

Preheat the oven to 325°F. • Line two cookie sheets with parchment paper. • Sift the flour, baking powder, baking soda, ground ginger, cinnamon, and salt into a large bowl. Stir in the brown sugar. • Heat the butter, corn syrup, and molasses over low heat until the butter has melted. • Remove from the heat and add the egg, beating until just blended. • Stir in the crystallized ginger. • Beat the butter mixture into the dry ingredients with an electric mixer at low speed until well blended. • Drop teaspoons of the dough 1 1/2 inches apart onto the prepared cookie sheets. Use a fork to flatten them slightly. • Bake for 15–20 minutes, or until golden brown, rotating the sheets halfway through for even baking. • Cool the cookies on the cookie sheets for 5 minutes. Use a metal spatula to transfer to racks and let cool completely. • Ginger frosting: Mix the confectioners' sugar, ginger, cocoa, water, and coconut oil to make a smooth paste. Spread the frosting over the cookies.

Makes 35 cookies · Prep: 30 min. · Cooking: 15–20 min. · Level: 2 · Keeps: 6 days

DROP COOKIES

ginger–fruit cookies

1¹/4 cups all-purpose flour
1 teaspoon baking powder
¹/8 teaspoon salt
¹/3 cup butter, softened
¹/3 cup firmly packed light brown sugar
1 large egg, lightly beaten
1 teaspoon almond extract
 Seeds of 8 cardamom pods, crushed
¹/2 cup finely chopped candied cherries
¹/2 cup finely chopped dried apricots
¹/2 cup finely chopped crystallized ginger

Preheat the oven to 350°F. • Butter two cookie sheets. • Sift the flour, baking powder, and salt into a medium bowl. • Beat the butter and brown sugar in a large bowl with an electric mixer at high speed until creamy. • Add the egg, beating until just blended. • Mix in the dry ingredients, almond extract, and crushed cardamom, followed by the cherries, apricots, and ginger. • Drop rounded teaspoons of the dough 1 inch apart onto the prepared cookie sheets. • Bake for 20–25 minutes, or until lightly browned, rotating the sheets halfway through for even baking. • Transfer to racks and let cool completely.

Makes 24 cookies · Prep: 20 min. · Cooking: 20–25 min. · Level: 1 · Keeps: 5 days

ginger puffs

1¹/4 cups all-purpose flour
2 teaspoons ground ginger
1 teaspoon baking powder
¹/2 teaspoon baking soda
¹/8 teaspoon salt
¹/3 cup firmly packed light brown sugar
¹/4 cup (¹/2 stick) butter, softened
3 tablespoons light corn syrup
1 large egg

Preheat the oven to 350°F. • Butter two cookie sheets. • Sift the flour, ginger, baking powder, baking soda, and salt into a large bowl. • Stir in the brown sugar. • Melt the butter with the corn syrup in a small saucepan over low heat. • Remove from the heat and let cool. • Stir the butter mixture into the dry ingredients. • Add the egg and mix to make a stiff dough. • Form the dough into twenty balls the size of walnuts and place 2 inches apart on the prepared cookie sheets. • Bake for 12–15 minutes, or until just golden and firm to the touch, rotating the sheets halfway through for even baking. • Cool the cookies

on the sheets for 5 minutes. • Transfer to racks and let cool completely.

Makes 20 cookies · Prep: 20 min. · Cooking: 12–15 min. · Level: 1 · Keeps: 5 days

turkish marmalade cookies

1 cup all-purpose flour
¹/8 teaspoon salt
¹/2 cup (1 stick) butter, softened
¹/2 cup granulated sugar
¹/2 teaspoon vanilla extract
1 large egg + 2 large egg yolks
1 teaspoon finely grated lemon zest
2 tablespoons orange marmalade
¹/3 cup confectioners' sugar, to dust

Preheat the oven to 350°F. • Butter a cookie sheet. • Sift the flour and salt into a medium bowl. • Beat the butter and sugar in a large bowl with an electric mixer at high speed until creamy. • Add the vanilla and egg and egg yolks, beating until just blended. • Mix in the lemon zest and dry ingredients. • Drop teaspoons of the dough 2 inches apart onto the prepared cookie sheet. • Bake for 10–15 minutes, or until just golden. • Transfer to racks to cool. • In a small saucepan or in a microwave, heat the marmalade until liquid. Brush the marmalade over the cookies and dust with the confectioners' sugar.

Makes 10–12 cookies · Prep: 20 min. · Cooking: 10–15 min. · Level: 1 · Keeps: 2 days

parkin

Parkin is the traditional cookie served on Bonfire Night (November 5), which commemorates a foiled attempt to blow up the Houses of Parliament in Great Britain.

³/4 cup all-purpose flour
1 teaspoon ground cinnamon
1 teaspoon ground ginger
¹/2 teaspoon baking powder
¹/8 teaspoon salt
¹/4 cup (¹/2 stick) butter, cut up
1¹/4 cups old-fashioned rolled oats
²/3 cup granulated sugar
5 tablespoons light molasses

Preheat the oven to 350°F. • Butter two cookie sheets. • Sift the flour, cinnamon, ginger, baking powder, and salt into a medium bowl. • Use a pastry blender to cut in the butter until the mixture resembles coarse crumbs. • Stir in the oats and sugar. Stir in the molasses to make a stiff dough. • Form the dough into balls the size of walnuts and place 2 inches apart on the prepared cookie sheets. • Bake for 15–20 minutes, or until lightly browned, rotating the sheets halfway through for even baking. • Transfer to racks and let cool completely.

Makes 20–24 cookies · Prep: 25 min. · Cooking: 15–20 min. · Level: 1 · Keeps: 5 days

Parkin

caraway crisps

3/4 cup all-purpose flour
1 teaspoon baking powder
1/8 teaspoon salt
1/3 cup butter, softened
1/4 cup + 1 teaspoon granulated sugar
1 teaspoon milk
1 teaspoon caraway seeds

Preheat the oven to 375°F. • Set out two cookie sheets. • Sift the flour, baking powder, and salt into a medium bowl. • Beat the butter and 1/4 cup sugar in a large bowl with an electric mixer at high speed until creamy. • Mix in the dry ingredients, followed by the milk to make a soft dough. • Form the dough into balls the size of walnuts and place 2 inches apart on the cookie sheets. • Sprinkle with the caraway seeds and remaining 1 teaspoon sugar. • Bake for 12–15 minutes, or until lightly browned, rotating the sheets halfway through for even baking. • Cool on the sheets until the cookies firm slightly. • Transfer to racks to finish cooling.

Makes 20 cookies · Prep: 30 min. · Cooking: 12–15 min. · Level: 1 · Keeps: 3–4 days

prairie cookies

These cookies hail from the level grasslands of central North America.

2 cups all-purpose flour
1 teaspoon baking powder
1/4 teaspoon freshly grated nutmeg
1/8 teaspoon salt
1/2 cup (1 stick) butter, cut up
1/2 cup firmly packed light brown sugar
2/3 cup finely chopped candied peel
1/3 cup raisins
1 large egg, lightly beaten
1 tablespoon confectioners' sugar, to dust

Preheat the oven to 400°F. • Butter a cookie sheet. • Sift the flour, baking powder, nutmeg, and salt into a large bowl. • Use a pastry blender to cut in the butter until the mixture resembles coarse crumbs. • Stir in the brown sugar, candied peel, raisins, and egg. • Drop tablespoons of the dough 2 inches apart onto the prepared cookie sheet. • Bake for 20–25 minutes, or until golden brown. • Transfer the cookies to racks to cool. • Dust with the confectioners' sugar.

Makes 15–20 cookies · Prep: 30 min. · Cooking: 20–25 min. · Level: 1 · Keeps: 5 days

hot and spicy cornmeal cookies

Spicy on the palate.

1/3 cup all-purpose flour
1/4 cup finely ground yellow cornmeal
1 1/2 teaspoons ground hot chile powder
1/8 teaspoon salt
1/4 cup (1/2 stick) butter, cut up
1/2 cup granulated sugar
3 tablespoons light corn syrup
1 tablespoon fresh lemon juice
1/2 cup hulled pumpkin seeds or sunflower seeds

Preheat the oven to 350°F. • Line two cookie sheets with parchment paper. • Sift the flour, cornmeal, chile powder, and salt into a medium bowl. • Melt the butter with the sugar and corn syrup in a large saucepan over medium heat until the sugar has dissolved completely. • Remove from the heat and stir in the dry ingredients, lemon juice, and pumpkin seeds. • Let cool completely. • Form the dough into balls the size of walnuts and place 2 inches apart on the prepared cookie sheets. • Bake for 8–10 minutes, or until just golden at the edges, rotating the sheets halfway through for even baking. • Transfer to racks to cool.

Makes 22–25 cookies · Prep: 25 min. · Cooking: 8–10 min. · Level: 1 · Keeps: 4 days

crisp cornmeal cookies

Great tasting—like a corn muffin.

1 1/2 cups all-purpose flour
1 cup finely ground yellow cornmeal
1 teaspoon baking powder
1/8 teaspoon salt
1/2 cup (1 stick) butter, cut up
2 large eggs, lightly beaten
2/3 cup granulated sugar

Preheat the oven to 325°F. • Butter two cookie sheets. • Sift the flour, cornmeal, baking powder, and salt into a large bowl. • Use a pastry blender to cut in the butter until the mixture resembles coarse crumbs. • Mix in the eggs and sugar to form a soft dough. • Form the dough into balls the size of walnuts and place 1 1/2 inches apart on the prepared cookie sheets. • Bake for 20–25 minutes, or until lightly browned, rotating the sheets halfway through for even baking. • Transfer to racks to cool.

Makes 28 cookies · Prep: 40 min. · Cooking: 20–25 min. · Level: 1 · Keeps: 7 days

pecan balls

1 1/4 cups all-purpose flour
1/8 teaspoon salt
1/2 cup (1 stick) butter, softened
1/3 cup confectioners' sugar
1/2 teaspoon vanilla extract
1/2 cup finely chopped pecans

Preheat the oven to 400°F. • Set out two cookie sheets. • Sift the flour and salt into a medium bowl. • Beat the butter, 1/4 cup confectioners' sugar, and vanilla in a large bowl with an electric mixer at high speed until creamy. • Mix in the dry ingredients and pecans to make a stiff dough. • Press the dough into a disk, wrap in plastic wrap, and refrigerate for 30 minutes. • Form the dough into balls the size of walnuts and place 1 inch apart on the cookie sheets. • Bake for 10–12 minutes, or until firm to the touch but not browned, rotating the sheets halfway through for even baking. • Transfer to racks to cool. • Dust with the remaining confectioners' sugar.

Makes 25–30 cookies · Prep: 25 min. + 30 min. to chill · Cooking: 10–12 min. · Level: 1 · Keeps: 10 days

brown sugar–cornmeal cookies

1 1/2 cups all-purpose flour
1 cup finely ground yellow cornmeal
1 teaspoon baking powder
1/8 teaspoon salt
1/2 cup (1 stick) butter, cut up
2 large eggs, lightly beaten
2/3 cup firmly packed dark brown sugar

Preheat the oven to 325°F. • Butter two cookie sheets. • Sift the flour, cornmeal, baking powder, and salt into a large bowl. • Use a pastry blender to cut in the butter until the mixture resembles coarse crumbs. • Mix in the eggs and brown sugar to form a soft dough. • Form the dough into balls the size of walnuts and place 1 1/2 inches apart on the prepared cookie sheets. • Bake for 20–25 minutes, or until lightly browned, rotating the sheets halfway through for even baking. • Transfer to racks to cool.

Makes 28 cookies · Prep: 25 min. · Cooking: 20–25 min. · Level: 1 · Keeps: 7 days

Hot and spicy cornmeal cookies (top) and Crisp cornmeal cookies (bottom)

Chocolate chip–pumpkin cookies

pumpkin cookies

1	cup all-purpose flour
1/2	teaspoon baking powder
1/2	teaspoon baking soda
1/2	teaspoon ground cinnamon
1/8	teaspoon salt
1/4	cup (1/2 stick) butter, cut up
1/2	cup granulated sugar
1/2	cup canned pumpkin puree
1/2	tablespoon finely grated orange zest
1/2	cup raisins
1/2	cup finely chopped pecans

Preheat the oven to 375°F. • Set out two cookie sheets. • Sift the flour, baking powder, baking soda, cinnamon, and salt into a large bowl. • Use a pastry blender to cut in the butter until the mixture resembles fine crumbs. • Stir in the sugar, pumpkin, and orange zest. • Stir in the raisins and pecans. • Drop teaspoons of the dough 2 inches apart onto the cookie sheets. • Bake for 8–10 minutes, or until golden, rotating the sheets halfway through for even browning. • Transfer to racks to cool.

Makes 18–24 cookies · Prep: 20 min. · Cooking: 8–10 min. · Level: 1 · Keeps: 7 days

norwegian cookies

2	cups all-purpose flour
3/4	teaspoon baking powder
1/8	teaspoon salt
1	cup (2 sticks) butter, cut up
1	large egg, separated
1/2	teaspoon vanilla extract
1	cup granulated sugar
1/2	cup finely chopped almonds

Preheat the oven to 350°F. • Butter two cookie sheets. • Sift the flour, baking powder, and salt into a large bowl. • Use a pastry blender to cut in the butter until the mixture resembles fine crumbs. • Add the egg yolk and vanilla, beating until just blended. • Set aside 1 tablespoon egg white. Beat the remaining egg white and sugar in a small bowl with an electric mixer at high speed until soft peaks form. Use a large rubber spatula to fold the egg white into the dough. • Form the dough into balls the size of walnuts and place 1 inch apart on the prepared cookie sheets. • Lightly beat the reserved 1 tablespoon egg white and brush over the tops of the cookies. Sprinkle with the almonds. • Bake for 10–15 minutes, or until golden brown, rotating the sheets halfway through for even browning. • Transfer to racks to cool.

Makes 25–30 cookies · Prep: 25 min. · Cooking: 10–15 min. · Level: 1 · Keeps: 7 days

chocolate chip–pumpkin cookies

1	cup all-purpose flour
1/2	teaspoon baking powder
1/2	teaspoon baking soda
1/2	teaspoon ground cinnamon
1/8	teaspoon salt
1/4	cup (1/2 stick) butter, softened
1/2	cup granulated sugar
1/2	cup canned pumpkin puree
1/2	tablespoon finely grated orange zest
1/2	cup semisweet chocolate chips

Preheat the oven to 375°F. • Set out two cookie sheets. • Sift the flour, baking powder, baking soda, cinnamon, and salt into a large bowl. • Use a pastry blender to cut in the butter until the mixture resembles fine crumbs. • Stir in the sugar, pumpkin, and orange zest. • Stir in the chocolate chips. • Drop teaspoons of the dough 2 inches apart onto the cookie sheets. • Bake for 8–10 minutes, or until golden, rotating the sheets halfway through for even browning. • Transfer to racks to cool.

Makes 18–24 cookies · Prep: 20 min. · Cooking: 8–10 min. · Level: 1 · Keeps: 7 days

sand dollars

1/2	cup all-purpose flour
1/8	teaspoon salt
1/4	cup (1/2 stick) butter, cut up
1/3	cup granulated sugar
1/4	cup dark corn syrup
1/2	teaspoon vanilla extract

Preheat the oven to 325°F. • Line two cookie sheets with parchment paper. • Sift the flour and salt into a large bowl. • Heat the butter, sugar, and corn syrup in a medium saucepan over medium heat, stirring often until the butter melts. • Remove from the heat and mix in the vanilla and dry ingredients until well blended. • Drop teaspoons of the dough 3 inches apart onto the prepared cookie sheets. • Bake for 7–10 minutes, or until golden brown, rotating the sheets halfway through to ensure even browning. • Cool on the sheets until the cookies firm slightly. • Transfer to racks to cool.

Makes 20–24 cookies · Prep: 20 min. · Cooking: 7–10 min. · Level: 1 · Keeps: 7 days

citrus cream cookies

12/3	cups all-purpose flour
1/8	teaspoon salt
1	cup (2 sticks) butter, softened
2/3	cup granulated sugar
2	large egg yolks
11/3	cups finely ground almonds
1	tablespoon finely grated lemon zest

Citrus cream filling

1/2	cup (1 stick) butter, softened
3/4	cup confectioners' sugar
1	tablespoon finely grated lemon zest
1	tablespoon finely grated orange zest

Preheat the oven to 350°F. • Butter three cookie sheets. • Sift the flour and salt into a medium bowl. • Beat the butter and sugar in a large bowl with an electric mixer at high speed until creamy. • Add the egg yolks, beating until just blended. • Mix in the dry ingredients, ground almonds, and lemon zest. • Form the dough into balls the size of walnuts and place 1 inch apart on the prepared cookie sheets. Use the back of a fork to flatten each cookie slightly. • Bake, one sheet at a time, for 8–10 minutes, or until pale gold. • Cool on the sheets until the cookies firm slightly. Transfer to racks to finish cooling. • <u>Citrus cream filling</u>: With mixer at high speed, beat the butter and confectioners' sugar in a medium bowl until creamy. • Mix in the lemon and orange zests. • Stick the cookies together in pairs with the filling.

Makes 16–18 cookies · Prep: 25 min. · Cooking: 8–10 min. per batch · Level: 1 · Keeps: 5 days

golden nuts

3/4 cup all-purpose flour
1 teaspoon baking powder
1/8 teaspoon salt
1/3 cup butter, softened
1/3 cup raw sugar (Demerara or Barbados)
1 tablespoon light corn syrup
1 tablespoon coarsely chopped walnuts
1 tablespoon milk
1 teaspoon white distilled vinegar

Preheat the oven to 350°F. • Butter two cookie sheets. • Sift the flour, baking powder, and salt into a medium bowl. • Beat the butter, raw sugar, and corn syrup in a large bowl with an electric mixer at high speed until well blended. • Mix in the dry ingredients and walnuts. • Mix in the milk and vinegar. • Drop teaspoons of the dough 2 inches apart on the prepared cookie sheets. • Bake for 15–20 minutes, or until golden brown, rotating the sheets halfway through for even baking. • Transfer to racks to cool.

Makes 30–35 cookies · Prep: 20 min. · Cooking: 15–20 min. · Level: 1 · Keeps: 7 days

fruity french drops

1 1/2 cups all-purpose flour
1/8 teaspoon salt
3 large eggs, separated
1 cup granulated sugar
1/2 cup very finely chopped mixed candied peel
1/4 cup confectioners' sugar, to sprinkle

Preheat the oven to 350°F. • Line three cookie sheets with parchment paper. • Sift the flour and salt into a medium bowl. • Beat the egg whites in a large bowl with an electric mixer at medium speed until frothy. • With mixer at high speed, gradually add the granulated sugar, beating until stiff, glossy peaks form. • Use a large rubber spatula to fold in the candied peel and dry ingredients. • With mixer at high speed, beat the egg yolks in a small bowl until frothy. • Fold the beaten egg yolks into the batter. • Drop teaspoons of the dough 2 inches apart onto the prepared cookie sheets. • Sprinkle with confectioners' sugar. • Bake, one batch at a time, for 10–12 minutes, or until pale gold. • Cool on the sheets until the cookies firm slightly. • Transfer to racks to finish cooling.

Makes 35–40 cookies · Prep: 25 min. · Cooking: 10–12 min. per batch · Level: 1 · Keeps: 10 days

citrus–mincemeat cookies

2/3 cup all-purpose flour
1 teaspoon baking soda
1/4 teaspoon ground cinnamon
1/4 teaspoon ground ginger
1/4 teaspoon freshly grated nutmeg
1/8 teaspoon salt
1/3 cup butter, softened
2 tablespoons granulated sugar
2 tablespoons firmly packed dark brown sugar
Grated zest and juice of 1 orange
1 large egg
1/2 teaspoon vanilla extract
1/2 cup Mincemeat (see page 340)
1/3 cup finely chopped pecans

Preheat the oven to 350°F. • Line two cookie sheets with parchment paper. • Sift the flour, baking soda, cinnamon, ginger, nutmeg, and salt into a medium bowl. • Beat the butter, granulated and brown sugars, and orange zest in a large bowl with an electric mixer at high speed until creamy. • Add the vanilla and egg, beating until just blended. • Mix in the dry ingredients and orange juice. • Stir in the mincemeat and pecans. • Drop teaspoons of the dough 2 inches apart onto the prepared cookie sheets. • Bake for 8–10 minutes, or until just golden at the edges, rotating the sheets halfway through for even baking. • Transfer to racks to cool.

Makes 25–30 cookies · Prep: 20 min. · Cooking: 8–10 min. · Level: 2 · Keeps: 2 weeks

mint pryaniki

1 1/4 cups all-purpose flour
1/2 teaspoon baking powder
1/8 teaspoon salt
1 tablespoon finely chopped mint leaves
3 large eggs
1 1/4 cups granulated sugar

Preheat the oven to 375°F. • Butter two cookie sheets. • Sift the flour, baking powder, and salt into a large bowl. Stir in the mint. • Beat the eggs and sugar in a large bowl until pale and thick. • Mix in the dry ingredients. • Drop teaspoons of the cookie dough 2 inches apart onto the prepared cookie sheets. • Bake for 15–20 minutes, or until golden brown, rotating the sheets halfway through for even baking. • Cool on the sheets until the cookies firm slightly. • Transfer to racks to finish cooling.

Makes 20–24 cookies · Prep: 20 min. · Cooking: 15–20 min. · Level: 1 · Keeps: 5 days

cranberry–prune cookies

3 cups raisins
1 cup dried cranberries
1 cup hot water
2 1/2 cups all-purpose flour
2 teaspoons ground cinnamon
1 1/2 teaspoons baking soda
1 teaspoon ground ginger
1/2 teaspoon baking powder
1/2 teaspoon ground allspice
1/2 teaspoon salt
3/4 cup (1 1/2 sticks) butter, softened
1 1/2 cups firmly packed light brown sugar
1 1/2 teaspoons vanilla extract
2 large eggs, lightly beaten
2 cups old-fashioned rolled oats
2 cups coarsely chopped walnuts
1 1/4 cups coarsely chopped pitted prunes
1 1/4 cups coarsely chopped pitted dates

Preheat the oven to 400°F. • Butter three cookie sheets. • Soak the raisins and cranberries in the water in a large bowl for 15 minutes. • Drain well, reserving 1/3 cup liquid, and set aside. • Sift the flour, cinnamon, baking soda, ginger, baking powder, allspice, and salt into a medium bowl. • Beat the butter and brown sugar in a large bowl with an electric mixer at high speed until creamy. • Add the vanilla and eggs, beating until just blended. • Mix in the dry ingredients and reserved liquid. • Stir in the oats, walnuts, prunes, dates, raisins, and cranberries until well blended. • Drop tablespoons of the dough 3 inches apart onto the prepared cookie sheets, flattening them slightly. • Bake, one sheet at a time, for 6–8 minutes, or until just golden at the edges and set. • Transfer to racks and let cool completely.

Makes 36 cookies · Prep: 20 min. + 15 min. to soak · Cooking: 6–8 min. per batch · Level: 1 · Keeps: 4 days

Citrus mincemeat cookies

lemon–almond bites

2   large egg whites
2   teaspoons water
3 1/2 cups finely chopped almonds
1 3/4 cups granulated sugar
2 1/3 cups all-purpose flour
1/2   teaspoon ground cinnamon
      Grated zest of 1 lemon

Preheat the oven to 300°F. • Line two cookie sheets with parchment paper. • Beat the egg whites and water in a large bowl with an electric mixer at high speed until frothy. • Use a large rubber spatula to fold in the almonds, sugar, flour, cinnamon, and lemon zest to make a soft dough. • Form the dough into balls the size of marbles and place 1 inch apart on the prepared cookie sheets. • Bake, one sheet at a time, for 20–25 minutes, or until just golden. • Transfer to racks on the parchment paper and let cool completely.

Makes 28 cookies · Prep: 20 min. · Cooking: 20–25 min. per batch · Level: 1 · Keeps: 3 days

pecan–oat clusters

1/2   cup all-purpose flour
1/2   teaspoon baking powder
1/8   teaspoon salt
1/2   cup (1 stick) butter, softened
1/2   cup firmly packed dark brown sugar
1   large egg
1/2   cup old-fashioned rolled oats
1/2   cup finely chopped pecans

Preheat the oven to 350°F. • Butter a cookie sheet. • Sift the flour, baking powder, and salt into a medium bowl. • Beat the butter and brown sugar in a large bowl with an electric mixer at high speed until creamy. • Add the egg, beating until just blended. • Stir in the oats and pecans. • Mix in the dry ingredients. • Drop heaping teaspoons of the dough 1 inch apart onto the prepared cookie sheet. • Bake for 15–20 minutes, or until just golden at the edges. • Transfer to racks and let cool completely.

Makes 16 cookies · Prep: 20 min. · Cooking: 15–20 min. · Level: 1 · Keeps: 7 days

rose pryaniki

1 1/4 cups all-purpose flour
1/2   teaspoon baking powder
1/8   teaspoon salt
3   large eggs
1 1/4 cups granulated sugar
2   tablespoons rose water

Preheat the oven to 375°F. • Butter two cookie sheets. • Sift the flour, baking powder, and salt into a large bowl. • Beat the eggs and sugar in a large bowl until pale and thick. • Mix in the dry ingredients and rose water. • Drop teaspoons of the cookie dough 2 inches apart onto the prepared cookie sheets. • Bake for 15–20 minutes, or until golden brown, rotating the sheets halfway through for even baking. • Cool on the sheets until the cookies firm slightly. • Transfer to racks to finish cooling.

Makes 20–24 cookies · Prep: 20 min. · Cooking: 15–20 min. · Level: 1 · Keeps: 5 days

coconut toasties

2   cups coarsely chopped pecans
1   cup coarsely chopped dried apricots
1   cup firmly packed light brown sugar
2   large eggs, lightly beaten
2 1/4 cups shredded coconut

Preheat the oven to 350°F. • Butter three cookie sheets. • Process the pecans, apricots, and brown sugar in a food processor to a finely ground paste. • Add the eggs and process until blended. • Transfer to a large bowl and mix in 1 1/2 cups coconut to form a stiff dough. • Place the remaining 3/4 cup coconut in a small bowl. • Form the dough into balls the size of walnuts and roll in the coconut. • Place the cookies 1 inch apart on the prepared cookie sheets. • Bake, one sheet at a time, for 10–12 minutes, or until golden brown, rotating the sheets halfway through for even baking. • Transfer to racks to cool.

Makes 30–40 cookies · Prep: 20 min. · Cooking: 10–12 min. per batch · Level: 1 · Keeps: 7 days

almond-coated sugar cookies

1 2/3 cups all-purpose flour
1/4   teaspoon salt
2/3   cup butter, softened
1/4   cup granulated sugar
1   tablespoon Vanilla Sugar (see page 341)
1/4   teaspoon vanilla extract
2   large egg yolks or 1 large egg, beaten

Coating
1/4   cup firmly packed light brown sugar or sugar crystals
3   tablespoons finely chopped almonds
1   egg yolk, beaten with 1 teaspoon milk
2–3   tablespoons orange marmalade or strawberry preserves

Frosting
1/3   cup confectioners' sugar, sifted
1   tablespoon brandy or fresh lemon juice

Sift the flour and salt into a large bowl. • Beat the butter and granulated and vanilla sugars in a large bowl with an electric mixer at high speed until creamy. • Add the vanilla and egg, beating until just blended. • With mixer at low speed, gradually beat in the dry ingredients to make a soft dough. • Turn the dough out onto a lightly floured surface and knead until smooth. • Wrap in plastic wrap and refrigerate for 30 minutes. • Preheat the oven to 350°F. • Set out two cookie sheets. • Form the dough into 35–40 balls the size of walnuts, pressing down with a teaspoon to create a dimple in the centers. • Coating: Sprinkle the sugar and almonds onto a plate. • Brush the cookies with the beaten egg yolk. Roll in the sugar mixture to cover. • Fill the dimple with marmalade. • Place 2 inches apart on the cookie sheets. • Bake for 15–20 minutes, or until golden brown, rotating the sheets halfway through the baking to ensure even browning. • Transfer to racks to cool. • Frosting: Mix the confectioners' sugar with the brandy into a smooth paste. • Spoon the frosting over the cookies.

Makes 35–40 cookies · Prep: 40 min. + 30 min. to chill · Cooking: 15–20 min. · Level: 2 · Keeps: 4 days

Convent kipferl (top, see page 214) and Almond-coated molded sugar cookies (bottom)

lime and sunflower seed cookies

- 3 1/2 cups all-purpose flour
- 1 teaspoon baking soda
- 1/2 teaspoon salt
- 1/2 cup sunflower seeds, toasted
- 1/2 cup (1 stick) butter, softened
- 2 1/4 cups granulated sugar
- 2 tablespoons extra-virgin olive oil
  Grated zest of 2 limes
- 2 large eggs
- 3 tablespoons fresh lime juice

Preheat the oven to 350°F. • Line three cookie sheets with parchment paper. • Sift the flour, baking soda, and salt into a medium bowl. • Stir in the sunflower seeds. • Beat the butter, 2 cups sugar, oil, and grated zest of 1 lime in a large bowl with an electric mixer at high speed until creamy. • Add the eggs, beating until just blended. • Mix in the dry ingredients and lime juice. • Mix the remaining 1/4 cup sugar and lime zest in a small bowl. • Form the dough into balls the size of walnuts and roll in the lime sugar. • Place the cookies 2 inches apart on the prepared cookie sheets, flattening them slightly. • Bake, one sheet at a time, for 8–10 minutes, or until just golden at the edges. • Transfer to racks and let cool completely.

Makes 36 cookies · Prep: 25 min. · Cooking: 8–10 min. per batch · Level: 1 · Keeps: 5 days

lime buttercream cookies

- 1 1/4 cups all-purpose flour
- 1/8 teaspoon salt
- 1/2 cup (1 stick) butter, softened
- 2/3 cup granulated sugar
- 1 large egg
- 1 tablespoon finely grated lime zest
- 3 tablespoons fresh lime juice

Lime buttercream
- 1 1/3 cups butter, softened
- 1 1/4 cups confectioners' sugar
- 1 tablespoon fresh lime juice

Preheat the oven to 350°F. • Line two cookie sheets with parchment paper. • Sift the flour and salt into a medium bowl. • Beat the butter and sugar in a large bowl with an electric mixer at high speed until creamy. • Add the egg and lime zest and juice, beating until just blended. • Mix in the dry ingredients to make a stiff dough. • Form the dough into balls the size of walnuts and place 1 inch apart on the prepared cookie sheets, flattening them slightly with a fork. • Bake for 12–15

minutes, or until pale gold, rotating the sheets halfway through for even baking. • Cool on the sheets until the cookies firm slightly. Transfer to racks to finish cooling. • Lime buttercream: With mixer at high speed, beat the butter and confectioners' sugar in a medium bowl until creamy. • Beat in the lime juice until well blended. • Stick the cookies together in pairs with the buttercream.

Makes 12–14 cookies · Prep: 25 min. · Cooking: 12–15 min. · Level: 1 · Keeps: 7 days

date cookies

- 1/2 cup (1 stick) butter, softened
- 1/4 cup granulated sugar
- 1/2 teaspoon vanilla extract
- 1/4 cup finely chopped dates
- 3/4 cup all-purpose flour

Preheat the oven to 375°F. • Butter two cookie sheets. • Beat the butter, sugar, and vanilla in a large bowl with an electric mixer at high speed until creamy. • Mix in the flour and dates. • Drop rounded teaspoons of the dough 1 inch apart onto the prepared cookie sheets. • Bake for 15–20 minutes, or until just golden, rotating the sheets halfway through for even baking. • Cool on the sheets until the cookies firm slightly. • Transfer to racks to finish cooling.

Makes 18–20 cookies · Prep: 20 min. · Cooking: 15–20 min. · Level: 1 · Keeps: 7 days

molasses bites

- 3/4 cup all-purpose flour
- 1 teaspoon baking powder
- 1/2 teaspoon salt
- 3/4 cup old-fashioned rolled oats
- 1/4 cup shredded coconut
- 1/2 cup (1 stick) butter, cut up
- 3/4 cup granulated sugar
- 2 tablespoons light molasses
- 1 teaspoon baking soda dissolved in 1 tablespoon milk

Preheat the oven to 350°F. • Set out a cookie sheet. • Sift the flour, baking powder, and salt into a large bowl. Stir in the oats and coconut. • Melt the butter with the sugar and molasses in a medium saucepan over medium heat. Bring to a boil, stirring constantly. • Remove from the heat and add the baking soda mixture. • Pour the butter mixture into the dry ingredients and mix until well blended. • Let stand for at least 30 minutes, or until firm. • Form the dough

Lime buttercream cookies

into balls the size of walnuts and place 1 1/2 inches apart on the cookie sheet. • Bake for 12–15 minutes, or until firm to the touch. • Cool the cookies on the cookie sheet for 15 minutes. • Transfer to racks to cool.

Makes 15 cookies · Prep: 15 min. + 30 min. to stand · Cooking: 12–15 min. · Level: 1 · Keeps: 3 days

corn flake–walnut cookies

- 2/3 cup all-purpose flour
- 1/2 teaspoon baking soda
- 1/8 teaspoon salt
- 1/2 cup (1 stick) butter, softened
- 1/4 cup granulated sugar
- 2/3 cup firmly packed light brown sugar
- 1/2 teaspoon vanilla extract
- 1 large egg, lightly beaten
- 1/3 cup corn flakes
- 2/3 cup coarsely chopped walnuts

Preheat the oven to 375°F. • Butter three cookie sheets. • Sift the flour, baking soda, and salt into a large bowl. • Beat the butter and granulated and brown sugars in a large bowl with an electric mixer at high speed until creamy. • Add the vanilla and egg, beating until just blended. • Mix in the dry ingredients, followed by the corn flakes and walnuts. • Drop teaspoons of the dough 1 inch apart onto the prepared cookie sheets. • Bake, one sheet at a time, for 12–15 minutes, or until lightly browned. • Cool on the sheets until the cookies firm slightly. • Transfer to racks to finish cooling.

Makes 36 cookies · Prep: 20 min. · Cooking: 12–15 min. per batch · Level: 1 · Keeps: 7 days

DROP COOKIES

oat–walnut cookies

2/3 cup all-purpose flour
1/2 teaspoon baking soda
1/8 teaspoon salt
1/2 cup (1 stick) butter, softened
1/4 cup granulated sugar
2/3 cup firmly packed light brown sugar
1/2 teaspoon vanilla extract
1 large egg, lightly beaten
1/3 cup old-fashioned rolled oats
2/3 cup coarsely chopped walnuts

Preheat the oven to 375°F. • Butter three cookie sheets. • Sift the flour, baking soda, and salt into a large bowl. • Beat the butter and granulated and brown sugars in a large bowl with an electric mixer at high speed until creamy. • Add the vanilla and egg, beating until just blended. • Mix in the dry ingredients, followed by the oats and walnuts. • Drop teaspoons of the dough 1 inch apart onto the prepared cookie sheets. • Bake, one sheet at a time, for 12–15 minutes, or until lightly browned. • Cool on the sheets until the cookies firm slightly. • Transfer to racks to finish cooling.

Makes 36 cookies · Prep: 20 min. · Cooking: 12–15 min. per batch · Level: 1 · Keeps: 7 days

walnut clusters

1/3 cup all-purpose flour
1/2 teaspoon salt
1/4 teaspoon baking powder
1/4 cup (1/2 stick) butter, softened
2/3 cup granulated sugar
11/2 teaspoons vanilla extract
1 large egg, lightly beaten
13/4 cups coarsely chopped walnuts
1/3 cup confectioners' sugar

Preheat the oven to 350°F. • Butter three cookie sheets. • Sift the flour, salt, and baking powder into a medium bowl. • Beat the butter and sugar in a large bowl with an electric mixer at high speed until creamy. • Add the vanilla and egg, beating until just blended. • Mix in the dry ingredients, followed by the walnuts. • Drop heaping teaspoons of the dough 1 inch apart onto the prepared cookie sheets. • Bake, one sheet at a time, for 8–10 minutes, or until lightly browned. • Transfer to racks and let cool completely. • Dust with the confectioners' sugar.

Makes 36 cookies · Prep: 20 min. · Cooking: 8–10 min. per batch · Level: 1 · Keeps: 7 days

canadian maple cookies

4 cups all-purpose flour
2 teaspoons baking soda
1/2 teaspoon salt
1 cup (2 sticks) butter, softened
1 cup firmly packed light brown sugar
1 cup maple syrup
1 large egg, lightly beaten
1/3 cup confectioners' sugar

Preheat the oven to 350°F. • Butter four cookie sheets. • Sift the flour, baking soda, and salt into a medium bowl. • Beat the butter and brown sugar in a large bowl with an electric mixer at high speed until creamy. • Add the maple syrup and egg, beating until just blended. • Mix in the dry ingredients. • Form the dough into balls the size of walnuts and place 2 inches apart on the prepared cookie sheets, flattening them slightly. • Bake, one sheet at a time, for 8–10 minutes, or until lightly browned. • Transfer to racks and let cool completely. • Dust with the confectioners' sugar.

Makes 60 cookies · Prep: 20 min. · Cooking: 8–10 min. per batch · Level: 1 · Keeps: 2 weeks

walnut–raisin cookies

31/4 cups all-purpose flour
1/2 teaspoon ground cinnamon
1/8 teaspoon salt
1 cup (2 sticks) butter, softened
11/2 cups firmly packed light brown sugar
3 large eggs
1 teaspoon baking soda dissolved in 11/2 tablespoons hot water
1 cup coarsely chopped walnuts
1 cup raisins

Preheat the oven to 350°F. • Butter four cookie sheets. • Sift the flour, cinnamon, and salt into a large bowl. • Beat the butter and brown sugar in a large bowl with an electric mixer at high speed until creamy. • Add the eggs, beating until just blended. • Stir in the baking soda mixture. • Mix in the dry ingredients, walnuts, and raisins. • Drop tablespoons of the dough 3 inches apart onto the prepared cookie sheets. • Bake, one sheet at a time, for 8–10 minutes, or until just golden at the edges. • Transfer to racks and let cool completely.

Makes 50 cookies · Prep: 20 min. · Cooking: 8–10 min. per batch · Level: 1 · Keeps: 7 days

marbled cookies

12/3 cups all-purpose flour
1/2 teaspoon baking powder
1/8 teaspoon salt
1/2 cup (1 stick) butter, softened
2/3 cup firmly packed light brown sugar
2/3 cup granulated sugar
1 large egg
1/2 cup sour cream
1/2 teaspoon vanilla extract
5 oz semisweet chocolate, coarsely chopped

Preheat the oven to 300°F. • Butter two cookie sheets. • Sift the flour, baking powder, and salt into a medium bowl. • Beat the butter and brown and granulated sugars in a large bowl with an electric mixer at high speed until creamy. • Add the egg, beating until just blended. • Beat in the sour cream and vanilla. • Mix in the dry ingredients. • Melt the chocolate in a double boiler over barely simmering water. • Use a large rubber spatula to fold the melted chocolate into the batter. Do not overmix; the batter should have streaks of chocolate. • Drop tablespoons of the mixture 2 inches apart onto the prepared cookie sheets. • Bake for 15–20 minutes, or until lightly browned, rotating the sheets halfway through for even baking. • Cool on the sheets until the cookies firm slightly. • Transfer to racks to finish cooling.

Makes 25–30 cookies · Prep: 20 min. · Cooking: 15–20 min. · Level: 1 · Keeps: 10 days

Marbled cookies

carrot cookies

During World War II, British cooks often adapted traditional recipes to accommodate the exigencies of butter and sugar rationing. This recipe, which uses carrots because of their natural sweetness, comes to us from that time. Use young, sweet carrots to achieve the maximum flavor in these cookies. Wash the carrots well and scrape off the outer skins. Grate the carrots finely just before adding them to the cookie dough.

1/2 cup all-purpose flour
1 teaspoon baking powder
1/8 teaspoon salt
1/4 cup granulated sugar
2 tablespoons margarine or butter, softened
1 2/3 cups very finely shredded carrots
1 tablespoon cold water (optional)

Preheat the oven to 350°F. · Butter a cookie sheet. · Sift the flour, baking powder, and salt into a medium bowl. · Reserve 2 teaspoons of the sugar. · Beat the margarine and remaining sugar in a medium bowl with an electric mixer at high speed until creamy.

· Use a wooden spoon to mix in the shredded carrot, followed by the dry ingredients to make a soft dough. · If the dough is stiff, add the water. · Drop tablespoons of the dough 2 inches apart onto the prepared cookie sheet. Sprinkle the tops of the cookies with the reserved sugar. · Bake for 15–20 minutes, or until golden and firm to the touch.

Makes 8–12 cookies · Prep: 40 min. · Cooking: 15–20 min. · Level: 1 · Keeps: 10 days

carrot and raisin drops

1 1/3 cups all-purpose flour
1 teaspoon baking soda
1 teaspoon ground cinnamon
1/2 teaspoon ground allspice
1/2 teaspoon freshly grated nutmeg
1/4 teaspoon ground ginger
1/4 teaspoon salt
1 cup (2 sticks) butter, softened
1 cup firmly packed light brown sugar
1 teaspoon finely grated orange zest
1 teaspoon vanilla extract
2 large eggs
1 1/2 cups finely shredded carrots
1/2 cup raisins
1/2 cup shredded coconut
1/4 cup old-fashioned rolled oats

Preheat the oven to 375°F. • Oil four cookie sheets. • Sift the flour, baking soda, cinnamon, allspice, nutmeg, ginger, and salt into a medium bowl. • Beat the butter and brown sugar in a large bowl with an electric mixer at high speed until creamy. • Add the orange zest and vanilla. • Add the eggs, carrots, raisins, coconut, and oats. • Mix in the dry ingredients. • Drop teaspoons of the dough 2 inches apart on the prepared cookie sheets. • Bake, one sheet at a time, for 8–10 minutes, or until golden brown. • Transfer to racks and let cool completely.

Makes about 60 cookies · Prep: 20 min. · Cooking: 8–10 min. per batch · Level: 1 · Keeps: 7 days

soldier cookies

1 cup all-purpose flour
1 cup shredded coconut
1/2 cup raisins
1 tablespoon light corn syrup
1/2 cup (1 stick) butter, softened
1 cup granulated sugar
1 teaspoon baking soda dissolved in 1 tablespoon boiling water

Preheat the oven to 300°F. • Set out a cookie sheet. • Stir together the flour and coconut in a large bowl. Mix in the raisins. • Beat the golden syrup, butter, and sugar in a large bowl with an electric mixer at high speed until creamy. • With mixer at low speed, beat in the baking soda mixture, followed by the dry ingredients. • Shape the mixture into balls the size of walnuts. Place 1 1/2 inches apart on the cookie sheet. • Use a fork to flatten them slightly. • Bake for 12–15 minutes, or until golden brown. • Transfer to racks to cool.

Makes 20–25 cookies · Prep: 10 min. · Cooking: 15 min. · Level: 1 · Keeps: 7 days

whole-wheat date cookies

3/4 cup all-purpose flour
3/4 cup whole-wheat flour
1 teaspoon baking powder
1/8 teaspoon salt
1 cup finely chopped pitted dates
3/4 cup (1 1/2 sticks) butter, softened
3/4 cup granulated sugar
1 large egg
1 tablespoon confectioners' sugar

Preheat the oven to 400°F. • Butter two cookie sheets. • Sift the all-purpose and whole-wheat flours, baking powder, and salt into a large bowl. • Beat the butter and granulated sugar in a large bowl with an electric mixer at high speed until creamy. • Add the egg, beating until just blended. • Mix in the dry ingredients and dates to make a stiff dough. • Form the dough into balls the size of walnuts and place 2 inches apart on the prepared cookie sheets, flattening them slightly. • Bake for 15–20 minutes, or until lightly browned, rotating the sheets halfway through for even baking. • Transfer to racks

and let cool completely. • Dust with the confectioners' sugar.

Makes 20–25 cookies · Prep: 20 min. · Cooking: 15–20 min. · Level: 1 · Keeps: 7 days

carrot–orange cookies

3 cups chopped carrots
1 1/4 cups all-purpose flour
1 teaspoon baking powder
1/8 teaspoon salt
2/3 cup butter, softened
2/3 cup granulated sugar
1 large egg
1/2 cup finely chopped walnuts

Orange glaze
2/3 cup confectioners' sugar
2 tablespoons fresh orange juice
Grated zest of 1/2 orange

Cook the carrots in a large pot of boiling water for 12–15 minutes, or until tender. • Drain well and run through a vegetable mill until pureed. • Preheat the oven to 350°F. • Butter two cookie sheets. • Sift the flour, baking powder, and salt into a medium bowl. • Beat the butter and sugar in a large bowl with an electric mixer at high speed until creamy. • Add the egg, beating until just blended. • Mix in the dry ingredients, followed by the pureed carrots and walnuts. • Drop teaspoons of the dough 1 inch apart onto the prepared cookie sheets. • Bake for 12–15 minutes, or until just golden, rotating the sheets halfway through for even baking. • Transfer the cookies to racks. • Orange glaze: Mix the confectioners' sugar, orange juice, and orange zest in a small bowl. • Spread the glaze over the warm cookies and let cool completely.

Makes 25 cookies · Prep: 40 min. · Cooking: 12–15 min. · Level: 1 · Keeps: 7 days (without the glaze)

Carrot–orange cookies

popcorn puffs

These little puffs are both tasty and easy to make—especially with the kids.

1   large egg white
1/4   teaspoon salt
1/3   cup firmly packed light brown sugar
3/4   cup coarsely chopped popped popcorn
1/2   teaspoon vanilla extract

Preheat the oven to 350°F. • Butter a cookie sheet. • Beat the egg white and salt in a large bowl with an electric mixer at medium speed until frothy. • With mixer at high speed, gradually add the brown sugar, beating until stiff peaks form. • Mix in the popcorn and vanilla. • Drop teaspoons of the mixture 2 inches apart onto the prepared cookie sheet. • Bake for 15–20 minutes, or until golden brown. • Transfer to racks to cool.

Makes 16–20 cookies · Prep: 20 min. · Cooking: 15–20 min. · Level: 1 · Keeps: 5 days

hazelnut–grape cookies

These cookies come from the south of Italy from the region of Apulia.

1   tablespoon baking soda
1/2   cup milk
31/3   cups all-purpose flour
1/3   cup extra-virgin olive oil
3/4   cup granulated sugar
1/2   cup coarsely chopped toasted hazelnuts
1/4   cup grape juice or vincotto

Preheat the oven to 350°F. • Butter three cookie sheets. • Mix the baking soda and milk in a small bowl. • Use a wooden spoon to mix the flour, olive oil, sugar, hazelnuts, grape juice, and baking soda mixture to make a soft dough. • Form the dough into balls the size of walnuts and place 1 inch apart on the prepared cookie sheets, flattening them slightly. • Bake, one sheet at a time, for 15–20 minutes, or until just golden. • Transfer to racks and let cool completely.

Makes 36 cookies · Prep: 25 min. · Cooking: 15–20 min. per batch · Level: 1 · Keeps: 10 days

glazed lemon–olive oil cookies

11/3   cups all-purpose flour
1/8   teaspoon salt
1/3   cup extra-virgin olive oil
4   large eggs, lightly beaten

Lemon syrup
11/4   cups granulated sugar
1/2   cup water
1/2   tablespoon grated lemon zest

Preheat the oven to 350°F. • Butter two cookie sheets. • Sift the flour and salt into a large bowl. • Mix in the olive oil and eggs to make a smooth dough. • Break off balls of dough the size of walnuts. Form the dough into 2-inch ropes and place 1 inch apart on the prepared cookie sheets. • Bake for 12–15 minutes, or until just golden at the edges, rotating the sheets halfway through for even baking. • Transfer to racks. • Lemon syrup: Mix the sugar and water in a medium saucepan. • Place over medium heat and cook until a thick syrup has formed. • Remove from the heat and stir in the lemon zest. • Dip the cookies in the syrup and let cool completely.

Makes 22–25 cookies · Prep: 25 min. · Cooking: 12–15 min. · Level: 1 · Keeps: 5 days

lemon–raisin cookies

11/2   cups all-purpose flour
1   teaspoon baking powder
1/8   teaspoon salt
1/2   cup (1 stick) butter, softened
1/2   cup granulated sugar
     Grated zest of 1 lemon
1   large egg
1/4   cup old-fashioned rolled oats
1   cup raisins

Preheat the oven to 375°F. • Butter a cookie sheet. • Sift the flour, baking powder, and salt into a large bowl. • Beat the butter, sugar, and lemon zest in a large bowl with an electric mixer at high speed until creamy. • Add the egg, beating until just blended. • Mix in the dry ingredients, oats, and raisins. • Drop tablespoons of the dough 3 inches apart onto the prepared cookie sheet. • Bake for 15–20 minutes, or until just golden at the edges. • Transfer to racks to cool.

Makes 16 cookies · Prep: 20 min. · Cooking: 15–20 min. · Level: 1 · Keeps: 7 days

fruit and nut rock cookies

1   cup all-purpose flour
1/2   teaspoon baking powder
1/2   teaspoon salt
1/2   teaspoon ground cinnamon
1/4   teaspoon freshly grated nutmeg
1/4   cup (1/2 stick) butter, softened
1/2   cup firmly packed dark brown sugar
1   large egg
1/4   cup finely chopped walnuts
3/4   cup golden raisins

Preheat the oven to 350°F. • Butter two cookie sheets. • Plump the raisins in hot water to cover in a small bowl for 10 minutes. • Drain well and pat dry with paper towels. • Sift the flour, baking powder, salt, cinnamon, and nutmeg into a medium bowl. • Beat the butter and brown sugar in a large bowl with an electric mixer at high speed until creamy. • Add the egg, beating until just blended. • Stir in the dry ingredients, walnuts, and raisins. • Drop heaping teaspoons of the dough 11/2 inches apart onto the prepared cookie sheets. • Bake for 15–20 minutes, or until lightly browned and firm to the touch, rotating the sheets halfway through for even baking. • Transfer to racks to cool.

Makes 20 cookies · Prep: 20 min. · Cooking: 15–20 min. · Level: 1 · Keeps: 5 days

lemon curd drops

Use the unused egg white from this recipe to make meringues or macaroons.

13/4   cups all-purpose flour
1/3   cup cornstarch
1/8   teaspoon salt
1   cup (2 sticks) butter, softened
1/4   cup granulated sugar
1   tablespoon fresh lemon juice
1   large egg yolk
1/3   cup Lemon Curd, Orange Curd, or
     Raspberry Curd (see page 340)
     Confectioners' sugar, to dust

Sift the flour, cornstarch, and salt into a medium bowl. • Beat the butter and granulated sugar in a large bowl with an electric mixer at high speed until creamy. • Add the lemon juice and egg yolk, beating until just blended. • Mix in the dry ingredients to make a soft, sticky dough. • Cover with plastic wrap and refrigerate for 30 minutes. • Preheat the oven to 350°F. • Line three cookie sheets with parchment paper. • Form the dough into balls the size of walnuts and place 1 inch apart on the prepared cookie sheets. Make a slight hollow in each center and fill with a small amount of Lemon Curd • Bake, one batch at a time, for 20–25 minutes, or until just golden. • Transfer to racks to cool. • Dust with the confectioners' sugar.

Makes 35–40 cookies · Prep: 20 min. + 30 min. to chill · Cooking: 20–25 min. per batch · Level: 1 · Keeps: 3 days

coffee–walnut cookies

3/4	cup all-purpose flour
1/2	teaspoon baking powder
1/8	teaspoon salt
1/2	cup (1 stick) butter, softened
1/4	cup granulated sugar
2/3	cup finely chopped walnuts
2	teaspoons freeze-dried coffee granules

Preheat the oven to 375°F. • Butter two cookie sheets. • Sift the flour, baking powder, and salt into a large bowl. • Beat the butter and sugar in a large bowl with an electric mixer at high speed until creamy. • Mix in the dry ingredients, walnuts, and coffee granules until well blended. • Drop tablespoons of the dough 1 inch apart onto the prepared cookie sheets. • Bake for 15–20 minutes, or until just golden, rotating the sheets halfway through for even baking. • Cool on the sheets until the cookies firm slightly. • Transfer to racks to finish cooling.

Makes 25–30 cookies · Prep: 20 min. · Cooking: 15–20 min. · Level: 1 · Keeps: 7 days

glazed lemon cookies

2	cups all-purpose flour
1/8	teaspoon salt
2	large eggs + 2 large egg yolks
3/4	cup granulated sugar
	Grated zest and juice of 1 1/2 lemons
1	teaspoon orange-flower water
2/3	cup confectioners' sugar
1/2	cup flaked almonds

Preheat the oven to 350°F. • Butter two cookie sheets. • Sift the flour and salt into a large bowl. • Beat the eggs and egg yolks in a large bowl with an electric mixer at high speed until pale and thick. • Beat in the granulated sugar, lemon zest and juice (reserving 2 tablespoons for the glaze), and orange-flower water until well blended. • Mix in the dry ingredients. • Drop heaping teaspoons 1 inch apart onto the prepared cookie sheets. • Bake for 15–20 minutes, or until lightly browned. • Transfer to racks and let cool completely. • Mix the confectioners' sugar with the reserved 2 tablespoons lemon juice in a small bowl. • Spread the tops of the cookies with the lemon glaze and sprinkle with the almonds.

Makes 25 cookies · Prep: 25 min. · Cooking: 15–20 min. · Level: 1 · Keeps: 5 days

hazelnut–fig cookies

2	large egg whites
1/2	cup raw sugar (Demerara or Barbados)
1	tablespoon Vanilla Sugar (see page 341)
1/2	cup old-fashioned rolled oats
1/2	cup finely ground hazelnuts
1	tablespoon very finely chopped dried figs
1	tablespoon fresh lemon juice
	Grated zest of 1 lemon
2	tablespoons sunflower seeds

Preheat the oven to 350°F. • Line three cookie sheets with parchment paper. • Beat the egg whites and 1 tablespoon raw sugar in a large bowl with an electric mixer at medium speed until soft peaks form. • With mixer at high speed, gradually add the remaining raw sugar, beating until stiff peaks form. • Use a large rubber spatula to fold in the vanilla sugar, oats, hazelnuts, and figs. • Drizzle with the lemon juice and sprinkle with the zest. • Drop teaspoons of the mixture 1 inch apart onto the prepared cookie sheets. Sprinkle with the sunflower seeds. • Bake, one sheet at a time, for 12–15 minutes, or until lightly browned. • Cool the cookies on the cookie sheet for 15 minutes. Transfer to racks and let cool completely.

Makes 45 cookies · Prep: 20 min. · Cooking: 12–15 min. per batch · Level: 1 · Keeps: 10 days

pink and pretty sugar-sprinkled gems

1 2/3	cups all-purpose flour
1	teaspoon baking powder
1/8	teaspoon salt
1/3	cup butter, cut up
1/2	cup granulated sugar
1/2	teaspoon Alchermes liqueur or red food coloring
1	large egg, lightly beaten
1	tablespoon milk
1/4	cup sugar crystals

Preheat the oven to 375°F. • Line two cookie sheets with parchment paper. • Sift the flour, baking powder, and salt into a large bowl. • Use a pastry blender to cut in the butter until the mixture resembles coarse crumbs. • Stir in the granulated sugar, Alchermes, and egg to form a soft dough. • Form the dough into balls the size of walnuts and place 2 inches apart on the prepared cookie sheets, flattening them slightly. • Brush with the milk and sprinkle with sugar crystals. • Bake for 15–20 minutes, or until just golden, rotating the

sheets halfway through for even baking. • Transfer to racks to cool.

Makes 25 cookies · Prep: 20 min. · Cooking: 15–20 min. · Level: 1 · Keeps: 4 days

coffee–pecan cookies

3/4	cup all-purpose flour
1/2	teaspoon baking powder
1/8	teaspoon salt
1/2	cup (1 stick) butter, softened
1/4	cup granulated sugar
2/3	cup finely chopped pecans
2	teaspoons freeze-dried coffee granules

Preheat the oven to 375°F. • Butter two cookie sheets. • Sift the flour, baking powder, and salt into a medium bowl. • Beat the butter and sugar in a large bowl with an electric mixer at high speed until creamy. • Mix in the dry ingredients, pecans, and coffee granules until well blended. • Drop tablespoons of the dough 1 inch apart onto the prepared cookie sheets. • Bake for 15–20 minutes, or until just golden, rotating the sheets halfway through for even baking. • Cool on the sheets until the cookies firm slightly. • Transfer to racks to finish cooling.

Makes 25–30 cookies · Prep: 20 min. · Cooking: 15–20 min. · Level: 1 · Keeps: 7 days

Pink and pretty sugar-sprinkled gems

rolled
cookies

Stars, animals, trees—rolled cookies are especially appropriate for themed parties and celebrations. One dough provides the opportunity to create a myriad of cookies of different shapes and sizes.

For even chilling, press the dough into a disk, wrap in plastic wrap, and refrigerate for 30 minutes.

For stickier doughs, roll out the dough on a lightly floured surface or between two sheets of plastic wrap. Transfer the cookies to sheets with a thin spatula so that the cookies do not lose their form. Drizzled with chocolate, dotted with silver balls, or simply dusted with confectioners' sugar, rolled cookies are welcome treats whatever the occasion.

above: Rolled white chocolate cookies (page 105)

right: Clockwise from top left: Shrewsbury cookies, Sablé cookies, Butter digestive cookies, and Multicolored sandwich cookies (pages 92, 86, 84, and 82)

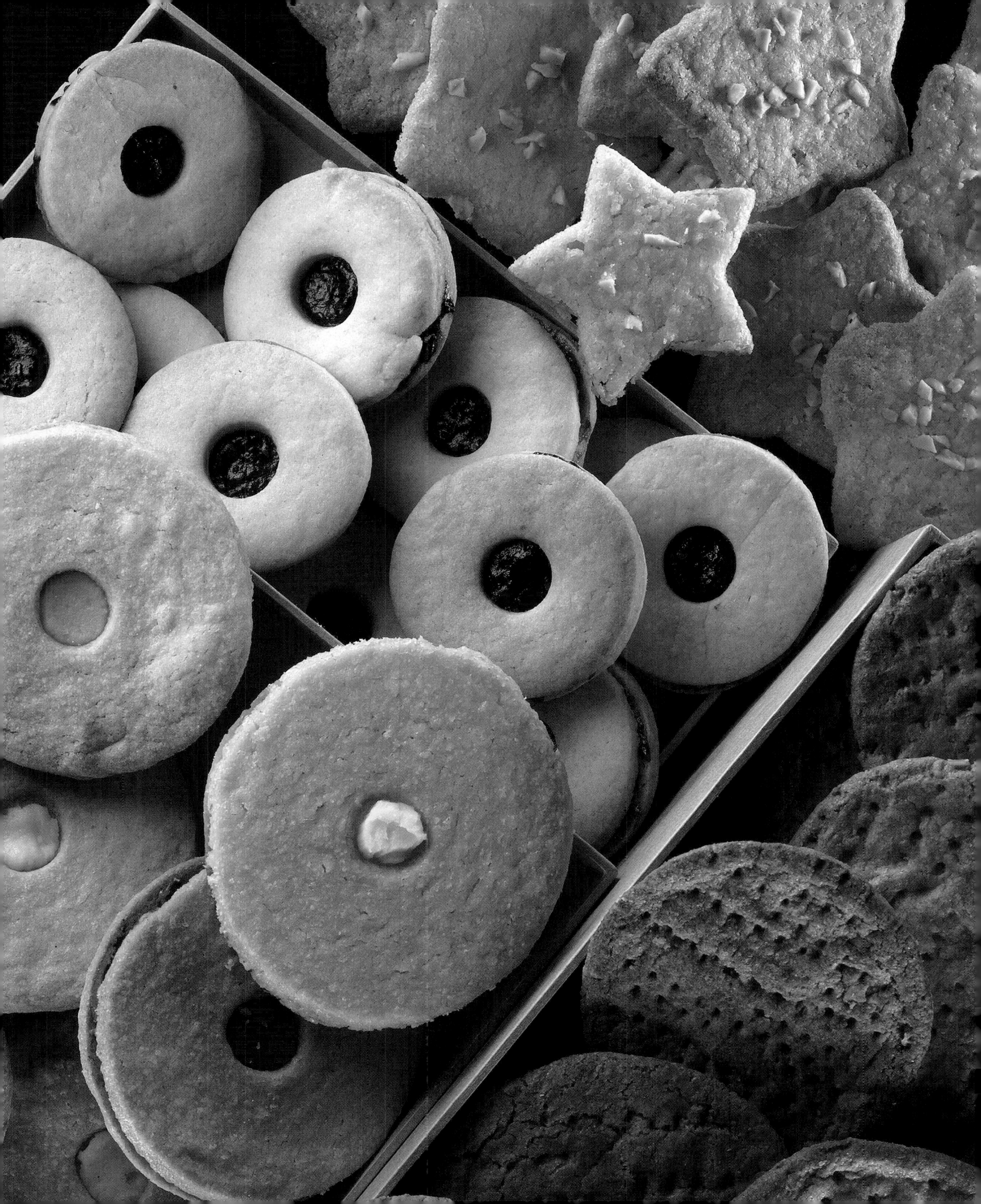

making rolled sugar cookies

1³/4 cups all-purpose flour
2 teaspoons baking powder
¹/4 teaspoon ground allspice
¹/8 teaspoon salt
¹/2 cup (1 stick) butter, softened
1 cup granulated sugar
1 teaspoon vanilla extract
2 large eggs
¹/4 cup confectioners' sugar or Vanilla
    Confectioners' Sugar (see page 341),
    to dust

Sift the flour, baking powder, allspice, and salt into a medium bowl. • Beat the butter, granulated sugar, and vanilla in a large bowl with an electric mixer at high speed until creamy. • Add the eggs, beating until just blended. • Mix in the dry ingredients to form a smooth dough. • Press the dough into a disk, wrap in plastic wrap, and refrigerate for at least 30 minutes, or until firm. • Preheat the oven to 350°F. • Butter two cookie sheets. • Roll out the dough on a lightly floured surface to a thickness of ¹/8 inch. Use a 2-inch round cutter to cut out the cookies. Gather the dough scraps, re-roll, and continue cutting out until all the dough is used. • Use a spatula to transfer the cookies to the prepared cookie sheets, placing them 1 inch apart. • Bake for 10–12 minutes, or until just lightly browned at the edges, rotating the sheets halfway through for even baking. • Cool on the sheets until the cookies firm slightly. Transfer to racks to finish cooling. • Dust with the confectioners' sugar.

Makes 36 cookies · Prep: 40 min. + 30 min. to chill · Cooking: 10–12 min. · Level: 1 · Keeps: 4–5 days

1. Make the cookie dough. Press it into a disk and wrap in plastic wrap.

2. Roll out the dough on a lightly floured surface to the required thickness.

3. Use your chosen cookie cutter to stamp out the cookies.

4. Use a metal spatula to transfer the cookies to the prepared cookie sheets.

chocolate-filled sugar cookies

1 cup all-purpose flour
¹/8 teaspoon salt
¹/3 cup butter, cut up
¹/4 cup light cream
¹/3 cup granulated sugar, to dust
Chocolate filling
2 oz semisweet chocolate, coarsely
    chopped
1 cup confectioners' sugar
1 tablespoon light cream

Sift the flour and salt into a large bowl. • Use a pastry blender to cut in the butter until the mixture resembles coarse crumbs. • Mix in the cream. • Press the dough into a disk, wrap in plastic wrap, and refrigerate for 30 minutes. • Preheat the oven to 375°F. • Line two cookie sheets with parchment paper. • Roll out the dough on a lightly floured surface to a thickness of ¹/8 inch. • Use a 1¹/2-inch cookie cutter to cut out the cookies. Gather the dough scraps, reroll, and continue cutting out cookies until all the dough is used. • Use a spatula to transfer the cookies to the cookie sheet, spacing them 1¹/2 inches apart. • Sprinkle with the sugar. • Bake for 8–10 minutes, or until just golden at the edges, rotating the sheets halfway through for even baking. • Transfer to racks to cool. • Chocolate filling: Melt the chocolate in a double boiler over barely simmering water. Remove from the heat and mix in the confectioners' sugar and cream. • Stick the cookies together in pairs with the filling. • Let the cookies stand for 30 minutes to set.

Makes 12–14 cookies · Prep: 40 min. + 60 min. to chill and set · Cooking: 8–10 min. · Level: 2 · Keeps: 2 days

coconut oat cookies

3/4 cup all-purpose flour
1/8 teaspoon salt
1/2 cup vegetable shortening
1 cup shredded coconut
1 cup old-fashioned rolled oats
1/2 cup granulated sugar
2 tablespoons cold water
1 tablespoon light molasses
1 teaspoon baking soda

Preheat the oven to 300°F. • Butter two cookie sheets. • Sift the flour and salt into a large bowl. • Use a pastry blender to cut in the shortening until the mixture resembles fine crumbs. • Stir in the coconut, oats, and sugar. • Mix the water, molasses, and baking soda in a small bowl. • Stir the baking soda liquid into the oat mixture to form a stiff dough. Press the dough into a disk, wrap in plastic wrap, and refrigerate for 30 minutes. • Roll out the dough on a lightly floured surface to a thickness of 1/4 inch. • Use a 3-inch cookie cutter to cut out the cookies. Gather the dough scraps, re-roll, and continue cutting out cookies until all the dough is used. • Use a spatula to transfer the cookies to the prepared cookie sheet, placing them 1 inch apart. • Bake for 25–30 minutes, or until just golden at the edges, rotating the sheets halfway through for even baking. • Transfer to racks and let cool completely.

Makes 25–30 cookies · Prep: 40 min. + 30 min. to chill · Cooking: 25–30 min. · Level: 1 · Keeps: 5 days

lemon–hazelnut sticks

2 1/4 cups hazelnuts
1 1/4 cups granulated sugar
1 2/3 cups all-purpose flour
1/8 teaspoon salt
   Grated zest and juice of 1/2 lemon
1 cup (2 sticks) butter, cut up
2 large eggs + 1 large egg yolk
1 teaspoon milk

Preheat the oven to 325°F. • Sprinkle the nuts onto a baking sheet. Toast for 7 minutes, or until lightly golden. • Transfer to a kitchen towel. Fold the towel over and gently rub the nuts to remove the skins. Pick out and discard the skins. • Place 1 1/2 cups of the nuts and 2 tablespoons sugar in a food processor and process until finely ground. Set aside. • Chop the remaining 3/4 cup nuts coarsely and set aside. • Sift the flour and salt into a large bowl. • Stir in the remaining sugar, finely ground hazelnuts, and lemon zest. • Use a pastry blender to cut in the butter until the mixture resembles coarse crumbs. • Use a fork to mix in the lemon juice and whole eggs to form a smooth dough. • Press the dough into a disk, wrap in plastic wrap, and refrigerate for 30 minutes. • Set out four cookie sheets. • Roll out the dough on a lightly floured surface to a thickness of 1/4 inch. • Cut into 1 x 2-inch sticks. • Use a spatula to transfer the cookies to the cookie sheets, placing them 1 inch apart. • Refrigerate for 20 minutes more. • Preheat the oven to 350°F. • Mix the egg yolk with the milk in a small bowl and brush over the cookies. • Sprinkle with the reserved coarsely chopped hazelnuts. • Bake, one sheet at a time, for 8–10 minutes, or until golden and firm around the edges. • Cool on sheets until the cookies firm slightly. • Transfer to racks and let cool completely.

Makes 55–60 cookies · Prep: 55 min. + 50 min. to chill · Cooking: 8–10 min. per batch · Level: 2 · Keeps: 3 weeks

york cookies

This recipe comes from York in the northeastern part of England. The chief city of its largest county, Yorkshire, York was the home of many rich merchants, whose wives would serve these cookies to their visitors with glasses of sweet Madeira wine.

1 1/2 cups all-purpose flour
1 teaspoon baking powder
1/8 teaspoon salt
1/3 cup butter
1/3 cup granulated sugar
1/4 cup milk, + more as needed

Preheat the oven to 325°F. • Butter two cookie sheets. • Sift the flour, baking powder, and salt into a medium bowl. • Use a wooden spoon to beat the butter and sugar together in a large bowl until creamy. • Mix in the dry ingredients and enough milk to form a stiff dough. Press the dough into a disk, wrap in plastic wrap, and refrigerate for 30 minutes. • Roll out the dough on a lightly floured surface to a thickness of 1/8 inch. • Use a 2-inch cookie cutter to cut out the cookies. Gather the dough scraps, re-roll, and continue cutting out cookies until all the dough is used. • Use a spatula to transfer the cookies to the prepared cookie sheets, placing them 1 inch apart. • Bake for 25–35 minutes, or until just golden, rotating the sheets halfway through for even baking. • Transfer to racks and let cool completely.

Makes 20–25 cookies · Prep: 40 min. + 30 min. to chill · Cooking: 25–35 min. · Level: 1 · Keeps: 2 weeks

coconut squares

1 1/3 cups all-purpose flour
1 teaspoon baking powder
1/4 teaspoon salt
3 tablespoons granulated sugar
1/2 cup (1 stick) butter, cut up
1 large egg yolk, lightly beaten with 2 tablespoons cold water

Frosting
1 large egg white
5 tablespoons confectioners' sugar, sifted
3 tablespoons shredded coconut
   Colored sprinkles, chopped Brazil nuts, or hazelnuts (optional)

Preheat the oven to 325°F. • Line two cookie sheets with parchment paper. • Sift the flour, baking powder, and salt into a large bowl. • Stir in the sugar. • Use a pastry blender to cut in the butter until the mixture resembles fine crumbs. • Stir the egg yolk mixture into the mixture and knead into a stiff dough, adding more water if needed. • Wrap in plastic wrap and refrigerate for 30 minutes. • Frosting: Beat the egg white with an electric mixer at medium speed until frothy. With mixer at high speed, gradually add the confectioners' sugar, beating until stiff. • Roll out the dough on a lightly floured surface to a thickness of 1/4 inch. Cut into 3 x 8-inch strips. • Spread the frosting over and sprinkle with coconut. Sprinkle with sprinkles or nuts, if using. • Cut the strips in half lengthwise and into 1 1/2-inch squares. • Gather the dough scraps, re-roll, and continue cutting out the cookies until all the dough is used. • Use a spatula to transfer the cookies to the prepared cookie sheets, placing them 1 inch apart. • Bake for 15–20 minutes, or until lightly golden, rotating the sheets halfway through for even baking. • Transfer to racks to cool.

Makes 35–40 cookies · Prep: 40 min. + 30 min. to chill · Cooking 15–20 min. · Level: 1 · Keeps: 10 days

ormskirk crisp gingerbread

Ormskirk, a small town in northwest England, is noted for this treasured recipe.

1²/3 cups all-purpose flour
2 teaspoons ground ginger
1/4 teaspoon baking soda
1/8 teaspoon salt
2/3 cup granulated sugar
1 cup finely chopped mixed candied peel
1/2 teaspoon grated lemon zest
1/2 cup (1 stick) butter, cut up
1/4 cup light molasses

Sift the flour, ginger, baking soda, and salt into a large bowl. • Stir in the sugar, candied peel, and lemon zest. • Heat the butter and molasses in a small saucepan over low heat until liquid. • Mix the molasses mixture into the dry ingredients to form a stiff dough. • Press the dough into a disk, wrap in plastic wrap, and refrigerate for 30 minutes. • Preheat the oven to 350°F. • Butter two cookie sheets. • Roll out the dough on a lightly floured surface to a thickness of 1/8 inch. • Use a 2-inch cookie cutter to cut out the cookies. Gather the dough scraps, re-roll, and continue cutting out cookies until all the dough is used. • Use a spatula to transfer the cookies to the prepared cookie sheets, placing them 2 inches apart. • Bake for 8–10 minutes, or until just golden, rotating the sheets halfway through for even baking. • Cool on the sheets until the cookies firm slightly. • Transfer to racks to cool.

Makes 24–30 cookies · Prep: 40 min. + 30 min. to chill · Cooking: 8–10 min. · Level: 1 · Keeps: 10 days

abernethy cookies

A healthy cookie that was believed to promote good digestion—abernethies were named after the small town in Scotland where they originated in the 18th century.

3¹/3 cups all-purpose flour
1/8 teaspoon salt
1/4 cup (1/2 stick) butter, cut up
2 tablespoons granulated sugar
2 tablespoons caraway seeds
2 large eggs, lightly beaten
2 tablespoons milk

Sift the flour and salt into a large bowl. • Use a pastry blender to cut in the butter until the mixture resembles fine crumbs. • Stir in the sugar and caraway seeds. • Mix in the beaten eggs and milk to form a stiff dough. Press the dough into a disk, wrap in plastic wrap, and refrigerate for 30 minutes. • Preheat the oven to 350°F. • Butter two cookie sheets. • Roll out the

dough on a lightly floured surface to a thickness of 1/4 inch. • Use a 3-inch cookie cutter to cut out the cookies. Gather the dough scraps, re-roll, and continue cutting out cookies until all the dough is used. • Use a spatula to transfer the cookies to the prepared cookie sheets, placing them 1 inch apart. • Prick all over with a fork. • Bake for 15–20 minutes, or until just golden, rotating the sheets halfway through for even baking. • Transfer to racks and let cool completely.

Makes 8–10 cookies · Prep: 20 min. + 30 min. to chill Cooking: 15–20 min. · Level: 1 · Keeps: 2 weeks

moravian spice squares

The Moravian Church is a religious group that attempts to fulfill the words of Christ in everyday living. It was founded in 1457 in Bohemia, then revived in the 18th century.

1¹/4 cups all-purpose flour
1 teaspoon ground ginger
1 teaspoon ground cinnamon
1/4 teaspoon ground cloves
1/2 teaspoon baking soda
1/8 teaspoon salt
1/4 cup (1/2 stick) butter, cut up
1/4 cup firmly packed dark brown sugar
2 tablespoons dark molasses
 Grated zest of 1 lemon
1/4 cup granulated sugar

Sift the flour, ginger, cinnamon, cloves, baking soda, and salt into a medium bowl. • Mix the butter, brown sugar, and molasses in a medium saucepan over low heat. • Cook, stirring constantly, until the sugar has dissolved completely. • Remove from the heat and mix in the dry ingredients and lemon zest to form a stiff dough. • Divide the dough in half. Press the dough into two disks, wrap in plastic wrap, and refrigerate for 1 hour. • Preheat the oven to 350°F. • Butter two cookie sheets. • Roll half the dough out on a lightly floured surface to 10-inch square. • Cut into 2-inch squares. • Use a spatula to transfer the cookies to the prepared cookie sheets, placing them 1 inch apart. • Prick all over with a fork. • Repeat with the remaining dough. • Sprinkle with the granulated sugar. • Bake for 5–7 minutes, or until lightly browned, rotating the sheets halfway through for even baking. • Transfer to racks and let cool completely.

Makes 30 cookies · Prep: 40 min. + 60 min. to chill · Cooking: 5–7 min. · Level: 1 · Keeps: 10 days

turkish yogurt cookies

This unusual cookie is cousin to the American biscuit and British scone with its firm top and soft interior.

1/2 cup plain yogurt
1/2 cup (1 stick) butter, softened
1 cup extra-virgin olive oil
2¹/2 cups all-purpose flour
1 large egg yolk, lightly beaten
2 tablespoons honey

Use a wooden spoon to beat the yogurt, butter, and olive oil in a medium bowl until well blended. • Mix in the flour to form a soft, smooth dough. • Press the dough into a disk, wrap in plastic wrap, and refrigerate for 30 minutes. • Preheat the oven to 375°F. • Butter a cookie sheet. • Roll out the dough very gently on a lightly floured surface to a thickness of 1/2 inch. • Use a 2-inch crescent-shaped cookie cutter to cut out the cookies. • Gather the dough scraps, re-roll, and continue cutting out cookies until all the dough is used. • Use a spatula to transfer the cookies to the prepared cookie sheet, placing them 2 inches apart. • Brush the tops of the cookies with the beaten egg yolk. • Bake for 20–25 minutes, or until just golden. • Transfer to racks to cool. • Warm the honey in a small saucepan over very low heat. • Drizzle the tops of the cookies with the honey.

Makes 15–18 cookies · Prep: 40 min. + 30 min. to chill · Cooking: 20–25 min. · Level: 1 · Keeps: 3 days

mazurek

These Russian cookies are eaten as an accompaniment to tea from the samovar, or tea urn, taken with lemon and a spoonful or two of "varenye"—homemade black currant or red currant preserves.

1 cup all-purpose flour
1/8 teaspoon salt
1/2 cup (1 stick) butter, softened
1/3 cup + 1 tablespoon granulated sugar
1/2 cup heavy cream
1 large egg, lightly beaten
3 tablespoons sweet white wine, such as Sauternes
1 teaspoon finely chopped mixed candied peel
1/3 cup finely chopped almonds

Preheat the oven to 400°F. • Butter a cookie sheet. • Sift the flour and salt into a large bowl. • Use a pastry blender to cut in the butter until the mixture resembles fine crumbs. • Stir in 1/3 cup sugar and make a well in the center. • Mix in the cream, egg, 2 tablespoons of the wine, and the candied peel to form a smooth dough. • Press the dough into a disk, wrap in plastic wrap, and refrigerate for 30 minutes. • Roll out the dough on a lightly floured surface to a large rectangle with a thickness of $1/4$ inch. • Use a rolling pin to transfer the dough to the prepared cookie sheet. • Brush the remaining 1 tablespoon of wine over the dough. Sprinkle with the remaining 1 tablespoon of sugar and almonds. • Bake for 12–15 minutes, or until just golden. • Cut into 2-inch triangles. • Bake for 3–5 minutes more, or until firm to the touch and golden brown. • Cool completely on the cookie sheet.

Makes 30–35 cookies · Prep: 30 min. + 30 min. to chill · Cooking: 15–18 min. · Level: 1 · Keeps: 3 days

honey-spiced pryaniki

- 3 cups all-purpose flour
- 1 teaspoon baking soda
- $1/2$ teaspoon ground cinnamon
- $1/2$ teaspoon ground cardamom
- $1/4$ teaspoon ground nutmeg
- $1/8$ teaspoon salt
- 2 large eggs
- 1 cup granulated sugar
- 1 cup honey
- $1/2$ teaspoon vanilla extract
- $1/4$ cup confectioners' sugar, to dust

Sift the flour, baking soda, cinnamon, cardamom, nutmeg, and salt into a medium bowl. • Beat the eggs and sugar in a large bowl with an electric mixer at high speed until pale and thick. • Heat the honey in a small saucepan over low heat until liquid. • Stir the honey and vanilla into the beaten egg mixture. • Mix in the dry ingredients to form a stiff dough. • Cover with plastic wrap and refrigerate for 1 hour. • Preheat the oven to 375°F. • Butter two cookie sheets. • Roll out the dough on a lightly floured surface to a thickness of $1/2$ inch. • Use a 2-inch cookie cutter to cut out the cookies. • Gather the dough scraps, re-roll, and continue cutting out cookies until all the dough is used. • Use a spatula to transfer the cookies to the prepared cookie sheets, placing them 2 inches apart. • Bake for 15–20 minutes, or until just golden, rotating the sheets halfway through for even baking. • Cool on the sheets until the cookies firm slightly. • Transfer to racks to finish cooling. • Dust with the confectioners' sugar.

Makes 24–30 cookies · Prep: 40 min. + 60 min. to chill · Cooking: 15–20 min. · Level: 1 · Keeps: 5 days

linzer cookies

This cookie is based on the classic Austrian recipe for Linzer Torte and uses the same rich, spicy pastry.

- $2/3$ cup all-purpose flour
- 2 teaspoons unsweetened cocoa powder
- $1/2$ teaspoon ground allspice
- $1/2$ teaspoon ground cinnamon
- $1/2$ teaspoon ground ginger
- $1/8$ teaspoon salt
- $3/4$ cup (1$1/2$ sticks) butter, softened
- $1/2$ cup granulated sugar
- 1 large egg yolk
- 1 tablespoon finely grated lemon zest
- 2 tablespoons fresh lemon juice
- 2 cups finely ground almonds
- $1/3$ cup raspberry preserves

Sift the flour, cocoa, allspice, cinnamon, ginger, and salt into a medium bowl. • Beat the butter and sugar in a large bowl with an electric mixer at high speed until creamy. • Add the egg yolk and lemon zest and juice, beating until just blended. • Mix in the dry ingredients and almonds to form a stiff dough. • Press the dough into a disk, wrap in plastic wrap, and refrigerate for 30 minutes. • Preheat the oven to 350°F. • Set out three cookie sheets. • Roll out the dough on a lightly floured surface to a thickness of $1/4$ inch. • Use a 2-inch cookie cutter to cut out the cookies. Gather the dough scraps, re-roll, and continue cutting out cookies until all the dough is used. • Use a spatula to transfer the cookies to the cookie sheets, placing them 1 inch apart. • Bake, one sheet at a time, for 25–35 minutes, or until lightly browned and firm to the touch. • Transfer to racks to cool. • Stick the cookies together in pairs with the preserves.

Makes 14–16 cookies · Prep: 25 min. + 30 min. to chill · Cooking: 25–35 min. per batch · Level: 1 · Keeps: 10 days

vanilla wafers

- 2 cups all-purpose flour
- 2 teaspoons baking powder
- $1/4$ teaspoon salt
- $1/3$ cup vegetable shortening
- 1 large egg
- 1 cup granulated sugar
- $1/4$ cup milk
- 2 teaspoons vanilla extract

Sift the flour, baking powder, and salt into a medium bowl. • Beat the shortening, egg, sugar, milk, and vanilla in a large bowl with an electric mixer at high speed until well

blended. • Mix in the dry ingredients. • Press the dough into a ball, wrap in plastic wrap, and refrigerate for 30 minutes. • Preheat the oven to 350°F. • Butter four cookie sheets. • Roll out the dough on a lightly floured surface to a thickness of $1/4$ inch. • Use a 1$1/2$-inch cookie cutter to cut out the cookies. Gather the dough scraps, reroll, and continue cutting out cookies until all the dough is used. • Use a spatula to transfer the cookies to the prepared cookie sheets, placing them 1 inch apart. • Bake, one sheet at a time, for 15–20 minutes, or until just golden at the edges. • Transfer to racks to cool.

Makes 42–46 cookies · Prep: 40 min. + 30 min. to chill · Cooking: 15–20 min. per batch · Level: 1 · Keeps: 7 days

lemon moon cookies

- 1$1/2$ cups all-purpose flour
- $1/8$ teaspoon salt
- $2/3$ cup butter, cut up
- $1/3$ cup granulated sugar
- 1 tablespoon finely grated lemon zest
- 2 tablespoons fresh lemon juice
- 2 large egg yolks
- 1 cup Lemon Curd (see page 340)
- 1 tablespoon confectioners' sugar

Sift the flour and salt into a large bowl. • Use a pastry blender to cut in the butter until the mixture resembles fine crumbs. • Stir in the granulated sugar, lemon zest and juice, and egg yolks to form a stiff dough. • Press the dough into a disk, wrap in plastic wrap, and refrigerate for 30 minutes. • Preheat the oven to 350°F. • Butter two cookie sheets. • Roll out the dough on a lightly floured surface to a thickness of $1/8$ inch. • Use a 3-inch fluted cookie cutter to cut out the cookies. • Use a 1-inch crescent-shaped cookie cutter to cut out the centers from half the cookies. Gather the dough scraps, re-roll, and continue cutting out cookies until all the dough is used. • Use a spatula to transfer the cookies to the prepared cookie sheets. • Bake for 6–8 minutes, or until golden brown, rotating the sheets halfway through for even baking. • Cool on the sheets until the cookies firm slightly. Transfer to racks to finish cooling. • Spread the cooled whole cookies with the lemon curd and place the cookies with holes on top. Dust with the confectioners' sugar.

Makes 12–15 cookies · Prep: 45 min. + 30 min. to chill · Cooking: 6–8 min. · Level: 1 · Keeps: 5 days

mint-chocolate sandwiches

1 cup all-purpose flour
1/4 cup unsweetened cocoa powder
1/8 teaspoon salt
1/2 cup (1 stick) butter, softened
1/4 cup granulated sugar
1 teaspoon mint extract
1 large egg

Mint–chocolate filling
1/2 cup heavy cream
7 oz white chocolate, coarsely chopped
1 teaspoon mint extract

Glaze
5 oz bittersweet chocolate, coarsely chopped
1/3 cup butter, cut up

Sift the flour, cocoa, and salt into a medium bowl. • Beat the butter and sugar in a large bowl with an electric mixer at high speed until creamy. • Add the mint extract and egg, beating until just blended. • Mix in the dry ingredients. • Press the dough into a disk, wrap in plastic wrap, and refrigerate for 30 minutes. • Preheat the oven to 350°F. • Butter two cookie sheets. • Roll out the dough on a lightly floured surface to a thickness of 1/8 inch. • Use a 2-inch cookie cutter to cut out the cookies. Gather the dough scraps, re-roll, and continue cutting out cookies until all the dough is used. • Use a spatula to transfer the cookies to the prepared cookie sheets, placing them 1 inch apart. • Bake for 6–8 minutes, or until just golden at the edges, rotating the sheets halfway through for even baking. • Transfer to racks and let cool completely. • Mint–chocolate filling: Bring the cream to a boil in a small saucepan over low heat. • Remove from the heat and stir in the white chocolate. Add the mint extract and transfer to a medium bowl. • Cool for 30 minutes, or until firm but not set. • Stick the cookies together in pairs with filling. • Glaze: Melt the chocolate and butter in a double boiler over barely simmering water. • Spread on top of the cookies and refrigerate for 30 minutes.

Makes 24 cookies · Prep: 40 min. + 90 min. to chill · Cooking: 6–8 min. · Level: 2 · Keeps: 3 days

chocolate–semolina cookies

2/3 cup all-purpose flour
1/2 cup semolina flour
1/4 cup unsweetened cocoa powder
1/8 teaspoon salt
1/3 cup butter, softened
1/2 cup granulated sugar
1 large egg, lightly beaten

Sift the flour, semolina, cocoa, and salt into a medium bowl. • Beat the butter and sugar in a large bowl until creamy. • Add the egg, beating until just blended. • Mix in the dry ingredients. • Press the dough into a disk, wrap in plastic wrap, and refrigerate for 30 minutes. • Preheat the oven to 375°F. • Set out two cookie sheets. • Roll out the dough on a lightly floured surface to a thickness of 1/4 inch. • Use a 2-inch cookie cutter to cut out the cookies. Gather the dough scraps, re-roll, and continue cutting out cookies until all the dough is used. Use a spatula to transfer the cookies to the cookie sheets. • Bake for 12–15 minutes, or until lightly browned, rotating the sheets halfway through to ensure even browning. • Transfer to racks to cool.

Makes 25–30 cookies · Prep: 40 min. + 30 min. to chill · Cooking: 12–15 min. · Level: 1 · Keeps: 10 days

chocolate-filled cookies

1 2/3 cups self-rising flour
2 tablespoons unsweetened cocoa powder
2/3 cup butter, softened
3/4 cup granulated sugar
1 large egg yolk
20 chocolate drops (buttons) or small squares of semisweet chocolate

Preheat the oven to 375°F. • Butter two cookie sheets. • Sift the flour and cocoa into a medium bowl. • Beat the butter and sugar in a large bowl with an electric mixer at medium speed until creamy. • Add the egg yolk, beating until just blended. • Mix in the dry ingredients. • Form the dough into three equal-size disks, wrap in plastic wrap, and refrigerate for 30 minutes. • Roll out the dough on a lightly floured surface to a thickness of 1/4 inch. • Use a 2-inch cutter to cut out twenty circles and use a 1 1/2-inch cutter to cut out another twenty circles, re-rolling the dough as necessary. • Place one of the larger circles on a cookie sheet. Place a piece of chocolate in the center. Cover with one of the smaller circles. • Working carefully, mold the smaller circle over the chocolate and turn the edges of the larger circle upward, sealing the chocolate completely. • Repeat with the rest of the circles, spacing 2 inches apart. • Bake for 8–10 minutes, or until the cookies have spread slightly, rotating the sheets halfway through for even baking. • Cool on the sheet for 5 minutes. • Transfer to racks to cool.

Makes about 20 cookies · Prep: 20 min. + 30 min. to chill · Cooking: 8–10 min. · Level: 2 · Keeps: 1 week

butterflies

These attractive cookies are great for children's birthday parties and bake sales.

1 1/3 cups all-purpose flour
2/3 cup confectioners' sugar
1/3 cup cornstarch
1 teaspoon baking powder
1/8 teaspoon salt
2/3 cup butter, softened
1 large egg
1 tablespoon unsweetened cocoa powder
1/4 teaspoon peppermint extract
2–3 drops pink food coloring

Cream filling
1/4 cup heavy cream
1/4 cup superfine sugar

Sift the flour, confectioners' sugar, cornstarch, baking powder, and salt into a large bowl. • Add the butter and egg, beating until just blended. • Knead on a lightly floured surface to form a smooth dough. • Divide the dough in half. • Knead the cocoa into one half. • Knead the peppermint extract and pink food coloring into the remaining half. • Press into eight differently sized balls, wrap in plastic wrap, and refrigerate for 30 minutes. • Preheat the oven to 350°F. • Line two cookie sheets with parchment paper. • Roll out six balls into 1/4-inch thick rounds and place the rounds close together so they are touching. • Continue rolling out the dough rounds to make one unbroken dappled sheet, about 1/8 inch thick. • Use a 3-inch butterfly-shaped cookie cutter to cut out the cookies. Gather the dough scraps, re-roll, and continue cutting out cookies until all the dough is used. • Use a spatula to transfer the cookies to the prepared cookie sheets, placing them 1 inch apart. • Roll out the remaining pink ball and brown ball of dough separately and place on the prepared cookie sheets. • Bake for 8–10 minutes, or until firm to the touch, rotating the sheets halfway through for even baking. • Cool on the sheets until the cookies firm slightly. • Transfer to racks to finish cooling. • Cream filling: Bring the cream and superfine sugar to a boil in a small saucepan, stirring constantly. • Simmer, uncovered, over low heat for about 3 minutes, or until thick and syrupy. • Remove from the heat and let cool for 15 minutes. • Spread half the cookies with the filling. Top with the remaining cookies.

Makes 15–16 cookies · Prep: 1 hr. + 60 min. to chill · Cooking: 8–10 min. · Level: 3 · Keeps: 2 days

Butterflies

Apricot–pecan cookies

marzipan-topped oat cookies

- 1 1/2 cups all-purpose flour
- 1/2 cup old-fashioned rolled oats
- 1/2 cup granulated sugar
- 1/4 teaspoon salt
- 1/2 cup (1 stick) butter, melted
- 1 tablespoon lukewarm water
- 1 recipe Homemade Marzipan (see page 346) or 1 lb store-bought marzipan
- 1/2 cup apricot preserves

Preheat the oven to 375°F. • Butter two cookie sheets. • Stir together the flour, oats, sugar, and salt in a medium bowl. • Mix in the melted butter and water. • Roll out the dough on a lightly floured surface to a thickness of 1/4 inch. • Use a 1 1/2-inch cookie cutter to cut out the cookies. Gather the dough scraps, re-roll, and continue cutting out cookies until all the dough is used. • Use a spatula to transfer the cookies to the prepared cookie sheets, placing them 1/2 inch apart. • Bake for 10–12 minutes, or until lightly browned, rotating the sheets halfway through for even baking. • Cool on the sheets until the cookies firm slightly. Transfer to racks to finish cooling. • Prepare the marzipan to the point where it is rolled out to a thickness of 1/4 inch. • Cut the marzipan to the same size as the cookies. • Warm the apricot preserves in a small saucepan over low heat until liquid. • Spread the preserves over the cookies and arrange the marzipan circles on top.

Makes 30 cookies · Prep: 40 min. · Cooking: 10–12 min. · Level: 2 · Keeps: 5 days

pecan sugar cookies

- 2 cups all-purpose flour
- 1/8 teaspoon salt
- 1 cup (2 sticks) butter, softened
- 1 1/4 cups granulated sugar
- 1 large egg + 1 large egg white, lightly beaten
- 1 cup finely chopped pecans

Sift the flour and salt into a medium bowl. • Beat the butter and sugar in a large bowl with an electric mixer at high speed until creamy. •

Add the egg, beating until just blended. • Mix in the dry ingredients. • Press the dough into four disks, wrap each in plastic wrap, and refrigerate for 30 minutes. • Preheat the oven to 350°F. • Butter three cookie sheets. • Roll out the dough on a lightly floured surface to a thickness of 1/4 inch. • Use a 2-inch cookie cutter to cut out the cookies. Gather the dough scraps, re-roll, and continue cutting out cookies until all the dough is used. • Use a spatula to transfer the cookies to the prepared cookie sheets, placing them 1 inch apart. • Brush with the beaten egg white and sprinkle with the pecans. • Bake, one sheet at a time, for 8–10 minutes, or until just golden. • Cool on the sheets until the cookies firm slightly. • Transfer to racks to cool completely.

Makes 35 cookies · Prep: 40 min. + 30 min. to chill · Cooking: 8–10 min. per batch · Level: 1 · Keeps: 5 days

apricot–pecan cookies

- 1/3 cup butter, softened
- 1/3 cup firmly packed light brown sugar
- 1 large egg yolk
- 1 1/4 cups whole-wheat flour
- Grated zest and juice of 1/2 lemon
- 1/2 cup finely chopped dried apricots
- 1/2 cup coarsely chopped pecans

Preheat the oven to 350°F. • Butter two cookie sheets. • Beat the butter and brown sugar in a large bowl with an electric mixer at high speed until creamy. • Add the egg yolk, beating until just blended. • Mix in the flour, lemon zest and juice, apricots, and pecans. • Press the dough into a disk, wrap in plastic wrap, and refrigerate for 30 minutes. • Roll out the dough on a lightly floured surface to a thickness of 1/4 inch. • Use a 2-inch cookie cutter to cut out the cookies. Gather the dough scraps, re-roll, and continue cutting out cookies until all the dough is used. • Use a spatula to transfer the cookies to the prepared cookie sheets. • Bake for 15–20 minutes, or until lightly browned, rotating the sheets halfway through for even baking. • Transfer to racks and let cool completely.

Makes 16 cookies · Prep: 40 min. + 30 min. to chill Cooking: 15–20 min. · Level: 1 · Keeps: 10 days

irish oat cookies

These crunchy delights come from Galway, a county in western Ireland.

- 1/3 cup golden raisins
- 1 1/4 cups all-purpose flour
- 1/2 teaspoon baking powder
- 1/8 teaspoon salt
- 1/2 cup old-fashioned rolled oats
- 1/2 cup coarsely chopped walnuts
- 2 tablespoons granulated sugar
- 1/3 cup butter, melted
- 1/4 cup milk
- 1 large egg, lightly beaten

Plump the raisins in hot water to cover in a small bowl for 10 minutes. • Drain well and pat dry with paper towels. • Sift the flour, baking powder, and salt into a large bowl. • Stir in the raisins, oats, walnuts, and sugar. • Mix in the butter, milk, and egg. Press the dough into a disk, wrap in plastic wrap, and refrigerate for 30 minutes. • Preheat the oven to 425°F. • Line two cookie sheets with parchment paper. • Roll out the dough on a lightly floured surface to a thickness of 1/2 inch. • Use a sharp knife to cut the dough into 2-inch diamonds. • Use a spatula to transfer the cookies to the prepared cookie sheets, placing them 1 inch apart. • Bake for 12–15 minutes, or until just golden at the edges, rotating the sheets halfway through for even baking. • Transfer to racks to cool.

Makes 22–25 cookies · Prep: 40 min. + 30 min. to chill · Cooking: 12–15 min. · Level: 1 · Keeps: 4 days

honey–oat cookies

- 2 cups old-fashioned rolled oats
- 2 large egg yolks, lightly beaten
- 3/4 cup honey
- 1/4 cup corn oil
- 1 cup whole-wheat flour
- 1/8 teaspoon salt

Preheat the oven to 400°F. • Sprinkle the oats onto a large baking sheet. Toast for 10 minutes, or until lightly browned. • Lower the oven temperature to 350°F. • Butter two cookie sheets. • Beat 1 egg yolk, the honey, and oil in a large bowl with an electric mixer at high speed until creamy. • Mix in the oats, flour, and salt. • Roll out the dough on a lightly floured surface to a thickness of 1/8 inch. • Use a 3-inch star cookie cutter to cut out the cookies. Gather the dough scraps, re-roll, and continue cutting out cookies until all the dough is used. • Use a spatula to transfer the cookies to the prepared cookie sheets. Brush with the remaining beaten egg yolk. • Bake for 10–15 minutes, or until just golden, rotating the sheets halfway through for even baking. • Transfer to racks and let cool completely.

Makes 30 cookies · Prep: 40 min. · Cooking: 10–12 min. · Level: 1 · Keeps: 7 days

cumberland rum–butter cookies

In Cumbria in the northwest of England, it was traditional to celebrate a baby's christening by serving homemade rum butter with freshly baked cookies.

Rum butter
- 1 cup (2 sticks) butter, softened
- 1/2 cup firmly packed light brown sugar
- 1/2 teaspoon freshly grated nutmeg
- 1 tablespoon fresh lemon juice
- 1/4 cup dark rum

Cookies
- 1 1/3 cups all-purpose flour
- 1/8 teaspoon salt
- 1/2 cup (1 stick) butter, at room temperature
- 1/2 cup granulated sugar
- 1 large egg, lightly beaten

<u>Rum butter</u>: Beat the butter, brown sugar, and nutmeg in a large bowl with an electric mixer at high speed until creamy. • Add the lemon juice. • Heat the rum in a small saucepan over very low heat until warmed. • Gradually beat the rum into the butter mixture. • Cover with plastic wrap and refrigerate for 1 hour, or until set. • <u>Cookies</u>: Sift the flour and salt into a medium bowl. • Use a pastry blender to cut in the butter until the mixture resembles fine crumbs. • Stir in the sugar and enough egg to form a stiff dough. • Press the dough into a disk, wrap in plastic wrap, and refrigerate for 30 minutes. • Preheat the oven to 375°F. • Butter two cookie sheets. • Roll out the dough on a lightly floured surface to a thickness of 1/4 inch. • Use a 2-inch fluted cookie cutter to cut out the cookies. Gather the dough scraps, re-roll, and continue cutting out cookies until all the dough is used. • Use a spatula to transfer the cookies to the prepared cookie sheets, placing them 1 inch apart. • Bake for 12–15 minutes, or until pale gold, rotating the sheets halfway through for even baking. • Cool on the sheets until the cookies firm slightly. Transfer to racks to finish cooling. • Spread the tops of the cookies with rum butter.

Makes 24–30 cookies · Prep: 40 min. + 90 min. to chill · Cooking: 12–15 min. · Level: 1 · Keeps: 2 days

berliners

These are called Berliner Brot *(Berlin bread) in German.*

- 3 cups all-purpose flour
- 1 teaspoon baking powder
- 1/8 teaspoon salt
- 5 large eggs
- 2 1/2 cups granulated sugar
- 1 tablespoon ground cinnamon
- 1 teaspoon ground cloves
- 5 cups blanched almonds or hazelnuts, coarsely chopped
- 2 tablespoons butter, melted
- 8 oz semisweet chocolate, grated

Frosting
- 1–2 tablespoons fresh lemon juice
- 1 tablespoon kirsch or rum (optional)
- 1 tablespoon cold water, or more as needed
- 1 1/2 cups confectioners' sugar

Butter and flour a large baking sheet. • Sift the flour, baking powder, and salt into a large bowl. • Beat the eggs and sugar in a large bowl with an electric mixer at high speed until pale and thick. • Add the cinnamon and cloves. • Use a large rubber spatula to fold in the nuts, butter, and grated chocolate, followed by the dry ingredients. • Shape into a ball, wrap in plastic wrap, and refrigerate for 1 hour. • Preheat the oven to 350°F. • Turn the dough out onto a lightly floured surface. Roll out the dough to a rectangle about 4 inches thick. Transfer to the prepared baking sheet. • Bake for 12–15 minutes, or until golden brown. • Use a sharp knife to cut the cookie into 2 x 3/4-inch fingers. Transfer to racks to cool. • <u>Frosting</u>: Mix 1 tablespoon lemon juice, kirsch, if using, and water in a small bowl. Stir in the confectioners' sugar to make a thick paste, adding more lemon juice or water if needed. • Spread the frosting over the tops of the cookies.

Makes 95 cookies · Prep: 45 min. + 60 min. to chill · Cooking: 12–15 min. · Level: 2 · Keeps: 14–20 days

rum and oat rings

- 2/3 cup all-purpose flour
- 1 tablespoon baking powder
- 1/8 teaspoon salt
- 1/3 cup butter, softened
- 1/2 cup granulated sugar
- 1 tablespoon Vanilla Sugar (see page 341)
- 2 tablespoons dark rum
- 1 large egg
- 3/4 cup old-fashioned rolled oats

Glaze
- 3/4 cup confectioners' sugar
- 2 tablespoons rum or orange juice
- 1 tablespoon red currant jelly

Sift the flour, baking powder, and salt into a medium bowl. • Beat the butter in a large bowl with an electric mixer at high speed until creamy. • Gradually beat in the granulated and vanilla sugars and rum. • Add the egg, beating until just blended. • Mix in the dry ingredients and oats. • Knead on a lightly floured surface to form a soft dough. • Divide the dough in half. Press the dough into disks, wrap in plastic wrap, and refrigerate for 30 minutes. • Preheat the oven to 350°F. • Line two cookie sheets with parchment paper. • Roll out half the dough on the floured surface to a thickness of 1/4 inch. Keep the remaining dough refrigerated. • Use a 2 1/2-inch round cookie cutter to cut out thirty cookies. • Use a small cutter to stamp out small circles in the center of each round to make rings. Repeat with the remaining dough. • Gather the dough scraps, re-roll, and continue cutting out the cookies until all the dough is used. • Use a spatula to transfer the cookies to the prepared cookie sheets, placing them 1 inch apart. • Bake for 10–12 minutes, or until pale golden, rotating the sheets halfway through the baking to ensure even browning. • <u>Glaze</u>: Sift the confectioners' sugar into a small bowl and add the rum. Stir in the jelly until a spreadable glaze is formed, adding more confectioners' sugar as needed. • Transfer the rings on the parchment paper to racks. • Brush with a thick layer of the glaze while they are still warm.

Makes 40 cookies · Prep: 60 min. + 30 min. to chill Cooking: 10–12 min. · Level: 2 · Keeps 3–4 weeks

Rum and oat rings

lepeshki

These cookies hail from Russia where sour cream is a commonly used ingredient.

- 1 1/2 cups all-purpose flour
- 1/8 teaspoon salt
- 1/2 cup granulated sugar
- 1 large egg, separated
- 1/2 cup sour cream
- 1 tablespoon milk
- 1/2 teaspoon vanilla extract
- 1/2 cup flaked almonds

Sift the flour and salt into a large bowl. Stir in the sugar. • Beat the egg white lightly in a medium bowl. Set aside 2 teaspoons of beaten egg white in a small bowl. • Mix the egg yolk, sour cream, milk, and vanilla into the remaining beaten egg white until well blended. • Make a well in the center of the dry ingredients and mix in the sour cream mixture to form a stiff dough. • Press the dough into a disk, wrap in plastic wrap, and refrigerate for 30 minutes. • Preheat the oven to 400°F. • Butter two cookie sheets. • Roll out the dough on a lightly floured surface to a thickness of 1/2 inch. • Use a 3-inch cookie cutter to cut out the cookies. Gather the dough scraps, re-roll, and continue cutting out cookies until all the dough is used. • Use a spatula to transfer the cookies to the prepared cookie sheets, placing them 2 inches apart. • Brush the tops of the cookies with the reserved egg white and sprinkle with the almonds. • Bake for 8–10 minutes, or until golden, rotating the sheets halfway through for even browning. • Transfer to racks to cool.

Makes 20–25 cookies · Prep: 40 min. + 30 min. to chill · Cooking: 8–10 min. · Level: 1 · Keeps: 10 days

filled sugar wafers

- 1 cup all-purpose flour
- 1/8 teaspoon salt
- 1/3 cup butter, cut up
- 1/4 cup light cream
- 1/3 cup granulated sugar, to dust

Pink filling
- 1 cup confectioners' sugar
- 1 tablespoon butter, softened
- 1 tablespoon light cream
- 1/2 teaspoon vanilla extract
  Few drops red food coloring

Sift the flour and salt into a large bowl. • Use a pastry blender to cut in the butter until the mixture resembles coarse crumbs. • Mix in the cream. • Press the dough into a disk, wrap in plastic wrap, and refrigerate for 30

minutes. • Preheat the oven to 375°F. • Line two cookie sheets with parchment paper. • Roll out the dough on a lightly floured surface to a thickness of 1/8 inch. • Use a 1 1/2-inch cookie cutter to cut out the cookies. Gather the dough scraps, reroll, and continue cutting out cookies until all the dough is used. • Use a spatula to transfer the cookies to the cookie sheet, spacing them 1 1/2 inches apart. • Sprinkle with the sugar. • Bake for 8–10 minutes, or until just golden at the edges, rotating the sheets halfway through for even baking. • Transfer to racks to cool. • Pink filling: Mix the confectioners' sugar, butter, cream, vanilla, and red food coloring in a small bowl. • Stick the cookies together in pairs with the filling.

Makes 12–14 cookies · Prep: 40 min. + 30 min. to chill · Cooking: 8–10 min. · Level: 2 · Keeps: 2 days

oxford johns

This easy-to-make cookie is traditionally made with lard and comes from the world-renowned university city of Oxford, in the United Kingdom.

- 3/4 cup all-purpose flour
- 1/2 teaspoon baking powder
- 1/8 teaspoon salt
- 1 tablespoon granulated sugar
- 1/3 cup vegetable shortening or lard
- 1/2 cup dried currants
- 2 tablespoons ice water, + more as needed

Sift the flour, baking powder, and salt into a medium bowl. Stir in the sugar. • Use a pastry blender to cut in the shortening until the mixture resembles fine crumbs. • Stir in the currants. • Mix in enough water to form a stiff dough. • Press the dough into a disk, wrap in plastic wrap, and refrigerate for 30 minutes. • Preheat the oven to 400°F. • Butter a cookie sheet. • Roll out the dough on a lightly floured surface to a thickness of 1/4 inch. • Use a sharp knife to cut the dough into 2-inch squares. Gather the dough scraps, re-roll, and continue cutting out cookies until all the dough is used. • Use a spatula to transfer the cookies to the prepared cookie sheet, placing them 1 inch apart. • Bake for 8–10 minutes, or until golden. • Transfer to racks to cool.

Makes 12–16 cookies · Prep: 40 min. + 30 min. to chill · Cooking: 8–10 min. · Level: 1 · Keeps: 10 days

animal cut-out cookies

- 1 2/3 cups all-purpose flour
- 1 teaspoon baking powder
- 1/8 teaspoon salt
- 3/4 cup (1 1/2 sticks) butter, softened
- 1/4 cup granulated sugar
- 3 tablespoons Vanilla Sugar (see page 341)
- 1/2 teaspoon vanilla extract
- 1/4 cup sour cream
- 1 large egg yolk
- 2 tablespoons milk
- 2 tablespoons sugar crystals or soft light brown sugar

Sift the flour, baking powder, and salt into a medium bowl. • Beat the butter and granulated and vanilla sugars in a large bowl with an electric mixer at high speed until creamy. • Beat in the vanilla and sour cream. • Mix in the dry ingredients to form a smooth dough. • Press the dough into a disk, wrap in plastic wrap, and refrigerate for 30 minutes. • Preheat the oven to 350°F. • Line four cookie sheets with parchment paper. • Roll out the dough on a lightly floured surface to a thickness of 1/4 inch. • Use 1 1/2- and 2-inch animal cookie cutters (such as fish, dog, elephant, etc.) to cut out the cookies. Gather the dough scraps, re-roll, and continue cutting out cookies until all the dough is used. • Use a spatula to transfer the cookies to the prepared cookie sheets, placing them 1 inch apart. • Mix the egg yolk and milk and brush over the cookies. Sprinkle with sugar crystals. • Bake, one sheet at a time, for 10–15 minutes, or until just golden. • Transfer on the parchment paper to racks and let cool completely.

Makes 50 cookies · Prep: 60 min. + 30 min. to chill · Cooking: 10–15 min. per batch · Level: 2 · Keeps: 15 days

Animal cut-out cookies

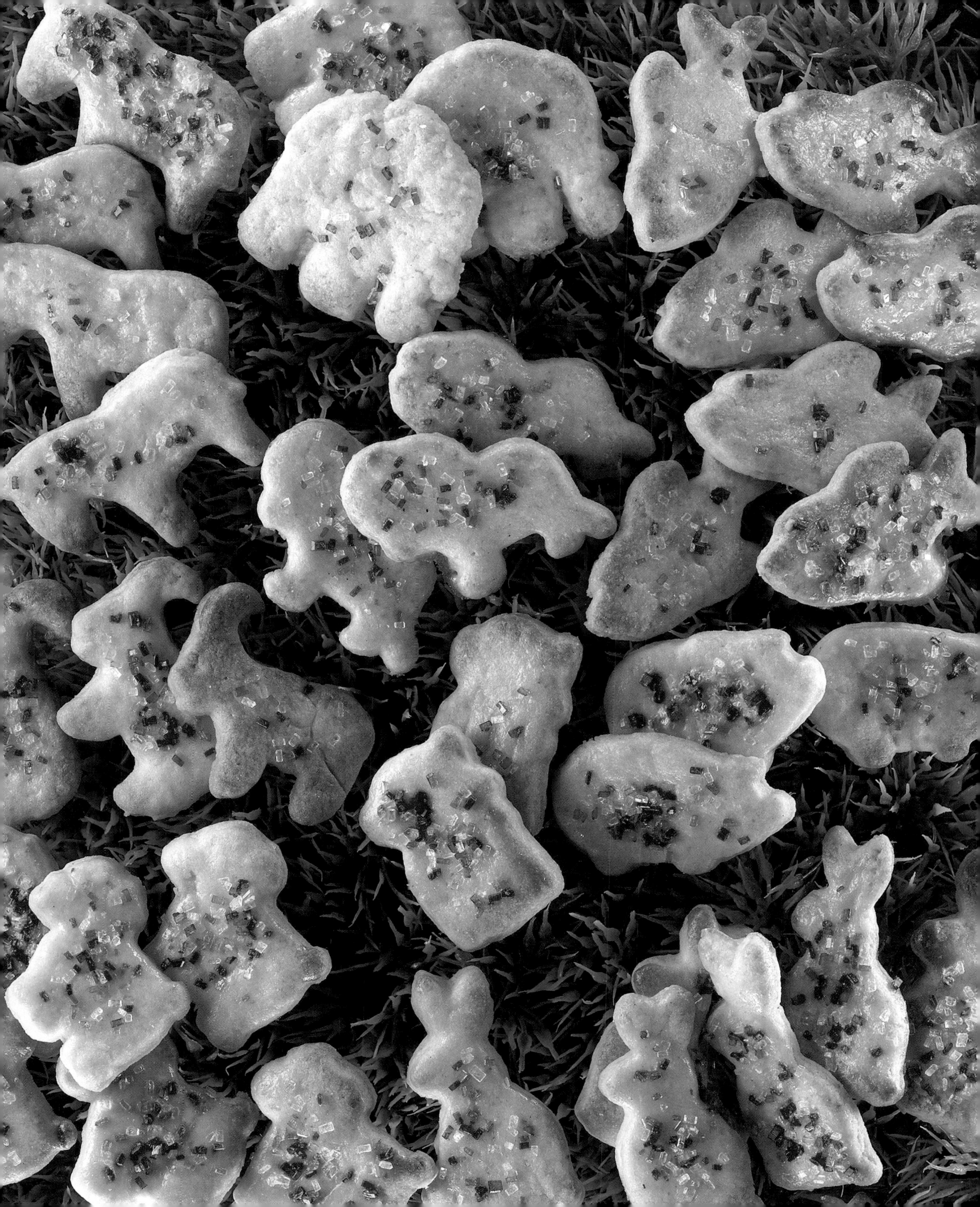

Maple walnut cookies

maple–walnut cookies

- 1/2 cup (1 stick) butter, softened
- 1/2 cup granulated sugar
- 2 teaspoons light brown sugar
- 2 teaspoons pure maple syrup
- 1 1/3 cups all-purpose flour
- 1 teaspoon freeze-dried coffee granules
- 2/3 cup finely chopped walnuts
- 1/8 teaspoon salt

Beat the butter, granulated and brown sugars, and maple syrup in a large bowl with an electric mixer at high speed until creamy. • Mix in the flour, coffee, walnuts, and salt to form a soft dough. • Turn the dough out onto a lightly floured surface and knead until smooth. • Press the dough into a disk, wrap in plastic wrap, and refrigerate for 30 minutes. • Preheat the oven to 375°F. • Butter and flour two cookie sheets. • Roll out the dough to a thickness of 1/8 inch. • Use a 3-inch cookie cutter to cut out the cookies. • Gather the dough scraps, re-roll, and continue cutting out cookies until all the dough is used. • Use a spatula to transfer the cookies to the prepared cookie sheets, placing them 1 inch apart. • Bake for 8–10 minutes, or until barely colored, rotating the sheets halfway through for even baking. • Cool on the sheets until the cookies firm slightly. • Transfer to racks to finish cooling.

Makes 30 cookies · Prep: 40 min. + 30 min. to chill · Cooking: 8–10 min. · Level: 1 · Keeps: 7 days

walnut half-moons

Pastry
- 1 1/2 cups all-purpose flour
- 1/8 teaspoon salt
- 1 teaspoon granulated sugar
- 1/2 teaspoon ground fennel seeds
- 1/2 cup (1 stick) cold butter, cut up
- 2 tablespoons ice water, or more as needed

Filling
- 2 teaspoons superfine sugar
- 1/2 teaspoon cardamom seeds, lightly crushed
- 1/4 teaspoon ground cinnamon
- 1/4 teaspoon ground allspice
- 2 cups walnuts, finely chopped
- 2 tablespoons honey
  Zest of 1 lemon, finely grated
- 1 large egg, lightly beaten
- 2 tablespoons confectioners' sugar, to dust

Pastry: Sift the flour and salt into a large bowl. Stir in the sugar and fennel seeds. • Use a pastry blender to cut in the butter until the mixture resembles fine crumbs. • Add enough water to form a soft, but not sticky, dough. • Turn the dough out onto a lightly floured surface and knead once or twice. Shape into a ball, wrap in plastic wrap, and refrigerate for 30 minutes. • **Filling**: Mix the superfine sugar, cardamom seeds, cinnamon, allspice, walnuts, honey, and lemon zest in a medium bowl. • Preheat the oven to 375°F. • Set out a cookie sheet. • Roll out the dough on a lightly floured surface to a thickness of 1/4 inch. Use a round cutter to stamp out 4-inch circles. • Fill each dough circle with 2 teaspoonfuls of the filling. Fold over to make a half moon, sealing the edges with a fork. • Brush with the beaten egg. • Place on the cookie sheet, spacing 1 inch apart. • Bake for 15–20 minutes, or until pale golden. Transfer to racks to cool. • Dust with the confectioners' sugar.

Makes 12 cookies · Prep: 30 min. + 30 min. to chill · Cooking: 15–20 min. · Level: 2 · Keeps: 4–6 days

cream-cheese crescents

Pastry
- 1 package (8 oz) cream cheese, softened
- 3/4 cup (1 1/2 sticks) butter, softened
- 1 tablespoon granulated sugar
- 1 2/3 cups all-purpose flour

Filling
- 1/3 cup firmly packed light brown sugar
- 3/4 cup walnuts, finely chopped
- 1 teaspoon ground cinnamon
- 1 large egg white, lightly beaten with 1 tablespoon water
- 1 teaspoon granulated sugar

Pastry: Beat the cream cheese, butter, and sugar in a large bowl with an electric mixer at low speed until creamy. • Sift the flour into the cream cheese mixture and mix to form a smooth dough. • Turn out onto a lightly floured surface. Knead the dough for 5–7 minutes, or until smooth and elastic. Shape into two balls, wrap in plastic wrap, and refrigerate for at least 30 minutes. • Preheat the oven to 375°F. • Set out two cookie sheets. • **Filling**: Mix the brown sugar, walnuts, and cinnamon in a small bowl. • Roll out one dough ball on a lightly floured surface to a 10-inch round. With a 10-inch round cake pan as a guide, use a sharp knife to cut around it. • Cut the round into sixteen equal wedges. • Brush the pastry wedges with 1/4 of the egg white mixture. • Sprinkle half the filling over the wedges. • Cover tightly with plastic wrap and press the filling into the dough. • Carefully roll up the slices starting at the base of each wedge. Curl into a crescent shape. • Place on the cookie sheets, spacing 1 inch apart. Brush with half the remaining egg white mixture and sprinkle with 1/2 teaspoon sugar. • Repeat with the remaining dough ball. • Bake for 10–20 minutes, or until golden brown, rotating the sheets halfway through for even baking. • Transfer to racks to cool.

Makes 32 crescents · Prep: 40 min. + 30 min. to chill · Cooking: 20 min. · Level: 3 · Keeps: 4 days

cinnamon-topped flower cookies

- 2 1/3 cups all-purpose flour
- 1/8 teaspoon salt
- 3/4 cup (1 1/2 sticks) butter, cut up
- 2/3 cup granulated sugar
- 2 tablespoons Vanilla Sugar (see page 341)
- 2–3 tablespoons dry white wine
- 2 large egg whites
- 1/4 cup superfine sugar
- 1/4 teaspoon ground cinnamon
- 2/3 cup finely chopped almonds or pistachio nuts

Sift the flour and salt into a large bowl. • Use a pastry blender to cut in the butter until the mixture resembles coarse crumbs. • Stir in the granulated and vanilla sugars. • Add enough wine to form a stiff dough. • Press the dough into a disk, wrap in plastic wrap, and refrigerate for 30 minutes. • Preheat the oven to 350°F. • Butter three cookie sheets. • Roll out the dough on a lightly floured surface to a thickness of 1/4 inch. • Use a 1 1/2-inch flower-shaped cookie cutter to cut out the cookies. Gather the dough scraps, re-roll, and continue cutting out cookies until all the dough is used. • Use a spatula to transfer the cookies to the prepared cookie sheets, placing them 1 inch apart. • Topping: Beat the egg whites in a large bowl with an electric mixer at high speed until stiff peaks form. • Mix the superfine sugar and cinnamon in a small bowl. • Spread the tops of the cookies with the egg white and sprinkle with cinnamon sugar and almonds. • Bake, one sheet at a time, for 10–15 minutes, or until golden brown. • Transfer to racks to cool.

Makes 35–40 cookies · Prep: 40 min. + 30 min. to chill · Cooking: 10–15 min. per batch · Level: 2 · Keeps: 7 days

orange-glazed nut cookies

1   large egg white
1/8   teaspoon salt
1/2   cup superfine sugar
1   cup finely ground hazelnuts
       + more as needed
1   cup finely ground almonds
       + more as needed
1/2   cup coarsely chopped pistachios
2   teaspoons finely chopped candied peel
2/3   cup Orange Glaze (see page 342)

Beat the egg white and salt in a large bowl with an electric mixer at medium speed until frothy. • With mixer at high speed, gradually add the superfine sugar, beating until stiff, glossy peaks form. • Use a large rubber spatula to fold in the hazelnuts, almonds, pistachios, and candied peel to form a stiff dough. Add more ground nuts if the dough is very sticky. • Press the dough into a disk, wrap in plastic wrap, and refrigerate for 30 minutes. • Preheat the oven to 300°F. • Line three cookie sheets with parchment paper. • Roll out the dough between sheets of waxed paper dusted with confectioners' sugar to a thickness of 1/4 inch. • Cut into 2 x 3/4-inch strips. • Gather the dough scraps, re-roll, and continue cutting out cookies until all the dough is used. • Use a spatula to transfer the cookies to the prepared cookie sheets, placing them 1 inch apart. • Bake, one sheet at a time, for 12–15 minutes, or until golden brown. • Transfer to racks to cool. • Dip the cookies halfway into the glaze and let stand for 30 minutes until set.

Makes 35–40 cookies · Prep: 45 min. + 60 min. to chill and set · Cooking: 12–15 min. per batch · Level: 2 · Keeps: 10 days

alberts

These delicate cookies have been known in Germany since the 19th century. They are most likely named after Prince Albert, Queen Victoria's German husband.

1 2/3   cups all-purpose flour
3/4   cup cornstarch
1   teaspoon baking powder
1/2   cup (1 stick) butter, cut up
1/8   teaspoon salt
3/4   cup granulated sugar
2   large eggs, lightly beaten
1   teaspoon vanilla extract

Sift the flour, cornstarch, baking powder, and salt into a large bowl. • Use a pastry blender to cut in the butter until the mixture resembles fine crumbs. • Mix in the sugar, eggs, and vanilla to form a smooth dough. • Wrap in plastic wrap and refrigerate for 30 minutes. • Preheat the oven to 375°F. • Set out two cookie sheets. • Roll out the dough on a lightly floured surface to a thickness of 1/4 inch. • Use a 2-inch cookie cutter to cut out the cookies. Gather the dough scraps, re-roll, and continue cutting out cookies until all the dough is used. • Use a spatula to transfer the cookies to the cookie sheets, placing them 1 inch apart. • Prick the cookies all over with a fork. • Bake, one sheet at a time, for 10–15 minutes, or until just golden at the edges. • Transfer to racks and let cool completely.

Makes 40-45 cookies · Prep: 40 min. + 30 min. to chill · Cooking: 10–15 min. per batch · Level: 1 · Keeps: 7 days

pistachio windmills

1 2/3   cups all-purpose flour
1   teaspoon baking powder
1/8   teaspoon salt
1/3   cup butter, softened
1/3   cup cream cheese, softened
1/2   cup granulated sugar
1/2   teaspoon vanilla extract
1   large egg
3-4   tablespoons peach or apricot preserves
2   tablespoons finely chopped pistachios
1-2   tablespoons butter, melted

Sift the flour, baking powder, and salt into a medium bowl. • Beat the butter, cream cheese, and sugar in a large bowl with an electric mixer at high speed until creamy. • Add the vanilla and egg, beating until just blended. • Mix in the dry ingredients to form a smooth dough. • Divide the dough in half. • Press the dough into disks, wrap in

plastic wrap, and refrigerate for 30 minutes. • Preheat the oven to 350°F. • Set out two cookie sheets. • Roll out each piece of dough on a lightly floured surface into a 10-inch square. • Cut each square into 2 1/2-inch squares. • Drop 1/2 teaspoon of the preserves into the center of each square. • Cut 1-inch diagonal slits from each corner to the center. • Fold every other corner to the center to make a windmill shape. • Sprinkle the preserves and corners with pistachios, pressing down to seal. • Use a spatula to transfer the cookies to the cookie sheets, placing them 1 1/2 inches apart. • Brush with melted butter. • Bake for 8–10 minutes, or until golden brown and the edges are firm, rotating the sheets halfway through for even baking. • Cool on the sheets until the cookies firm slightly. • Transfer to racks and let cool completely.

Makes 32 cookies · Prep: 50 min. + 30 min. to chill Cooking: 8–10 min. · Level: 3 · Keeps: 4 days

Pistachio windmills

chocolate–orange stars

- 2 1/4 cups all-purpose flour
- 1 1/2 teaspoons baking powder
- 1/4 teaspoon salt
- 3/4 cup (1 1/2 sticks) butter, softened
- 3/4 cup granulated sugar
- 1 teaspoon vanilla extract
  Grated zest of 1 orange
- 1 tablespoon fresh orange juice
- 1 large egg
- 2 oz semisweet chocolate, coarsely chopped
- 1/4 cup superfine sugar

Sift the flour, baking powder, and salt into a medium bowl. • Beat the butter and granulated sugar in a large bowl with an electric mixer at high speed until creamy. • Add the vanilla, orange zest and juice, and egg, beating until just blended. • Mix in the dry ingredients to form a soft dough. • Divide the dough in half. Press half the dough into a disk, wrap in plastic wrap, and refrigerate for 1 hour. • Melt the chocolate in a double boiler over barely simmering water. • Knead the chocolate into the remaining dough until no streaks remain. Press into a disk, wrap in plastic wrap, and refrigerate for 1 hour. • Preheat the oven to 350°F. • Butter three cookie sheets. • Roll out the plain dough on a lightly floured surface to a thickness of 1/4 inch. • Use a 3-inch star-shaped cookie cutter to cut out the cookies. • Use a spatula to transfer the cookies to the prepared cookie sheets, placing them 1 inch apart. • Repeat with the chocolate dough. • Use a 2-inch star-shaped cookie cutter to cut out the centers of the cookies. Place the small chocolate stars into the holes in the large orange cookies and vice versa to create alternating colors. • Sprinkle with the superfine sugar. • Bake, one sheet at a time, for 8–10 minutes, or until just golden at the edges. • Transfer to racks to cool.

Makes 30 cookies · Prep: 50 min. + 60 min. to chill · Cooking: 8–10 min. per batch · Level: 2 · Keeps: 5 days

chocolate–orange cookies

Potato starch, sometimes referred to as potato flour, can be found in health food stores.

- 1 1/4 cups whole-wheat flour
- 1/2 cup potato starch
- 1 teaspoon baking powder
- 1/8 teaspoon salt
- 1/2 cup (1 stick) butter, softened
- 2/3 cup granulated sugar
  Grated zest of 1 orange
- 1 large egg
- 3 oz semisweet chocolate, coarsely grated

Sift the flour, potato starch, baking powder, and salt into a medium bowl. • Beat the butter and sugar in a large bowl with an electric mixer at high speed until creamy. • Add the orange zest and egg, beating until just blended. • Mix in the dry ingredients and chocolate to form a smooth dough. • Press the dough into a disk, wrap in plastic wrap, and refrigerate for 30 minutes. • Preheat the oven to 400°F. • Butter three cookie sheets. • Roll out the dough on a lightly floured surface to a thickness of 1/4 inch. • Use a sharp knife to cut the dough into 2 x 1-inch rectangles. • Gather the dough scraps, re-roll, and continue cutting out cookies until all the dough is used. • Use a spatula to transfer the cookies to the prepared cookie sheets. • Bake, one sheet at a time, for 12–15 minutes, or until lightly browned. • Transfer to racks to cool.

Makes 40 cookies · Prep: 40 min. + 30 min. to chill · Cooking: 12–15 min. per batch · Level: 1 · Keeps: 10 days

sugar hearts

- 3 cups all-purpose flour
- 1/2 teaspoon baking powder
- 1/2 teaspoon salt
- 1 cup (2 sticks) butter, softened
- 1 cup granulated sugar
- 1 teaspoon vanilla extract
- 1/4 teaspoon almond extract
- 1/4 cup half-and-half
- 1 large egg + 1 large egg yolk
- 6 oz semisweet chocolate, coarsely chopped

Sift the flour, baking powder, and salt into a medium bowl. • Beat the butter and sugar in a large bowl with an electric mixer at high speed until creamy. • Add the vanilla and almond extracts and half-and-half. • Add the egg and egg yolk, beating until just blended. • Mix in the dry ingredients to form a soft dough. • Divide the dough in half. Press the dough into disks, wrap each in plastic wrap, and refrigerate for 30 minutes. • Preheat the oven to 350°F. • Line three cookie sheets with parchment paper. • Roll out one of the disks of dough on a lightly floured surface to a thickness of 1/4 inch. • Use a 2 1/2-inch heart cookie cutter to cut out the cookies. • Gather the dough scraps, re-roll, and continue cutting out cookies until all the dough is used. • Use a spatula to transfer the cookies to the prepared cookie sheets, placing them 2 inches apart. • Repeat with the remaining dough. • Bake, one sheet at a time, for 12–15 minutes, or until just golden. • Transfer to racks and let cool completely. • Melt the chocolate in a double boiler over barely simmering water. • Dip the hearts halfway into the chocolate and let stand for 30 minutes until set.

Makes 36 cookies · Prep: 40 min. + 60 min. to chill and set · Cooking: 12–15 min. per batch · Level: 1 · Keeps: 5 days

chocolate-coated party rings

- 1 2/3 cups all-purpose flour
- 1 tablespoon unsweetened cocoa powder
- 1/8 teaspoon salt
- 1/2 cup (1 stick) butter, softened
- 2/3 cup granulated sugar
- 1/4 teaspoon vanilla extract
- 1 large egg
- 8 oz semisweet chocolate, coarsely chopped

Sift the flour, cocoa, and salt into a medium bowl. • Beat the butter and sugar in a large bowl with an electric mixer at high speed until creamy. • Add the vanilla and egg, beating until just blended. • Mix in the dry ingredients and 2 oz of the chopped chocolate to form a firm dough. • Turn the dough out onto a lightly floured surface and knead until smooth. • Press the dough into a disk, wrap in plastic wrap, and refrigerate for 30 minutes. • Preheat the oven to 375°F. • Butter two cookie sheets. • Roll out the dough to a thickness of 1/4 inch. • Use a 2-inch cookie cutter to cut out the cookies. • Cut out the centers with a 1-inch cookie cutter. • Gather the dough scraps, re-roll, and continue cutting out cookies until all the dough is used. • Use a spatula to transfer the cookies to the prepared cookie sheets, placing them 1 inch apart. • Bake for 12–15 minutes, or until firm to the touch, rotating the sheets halfway through for even baking. • Cool until the cookies firm slightly. • Transfer to racks to finish cooling. • Set out a large sheet of parchment paper. • Melt the remaining 6 oz chocolate in a double boiler over barely simmering water. • Dip the cookies completely in the chocolate. • Place on the paper and let stand for 30 minutes until set.

Makes 22–24 cookies · Prep: 45 min. + 60 min. to chill and set · Cooking: 12–15 min. · Level: 2 · Keeps: 5 days

Chocolate-coated party rings
and Chocolate–orange stars

quark spirals

Quark is a high-protein, nonfat soft cheese with a smooth texture and creamy taste. It is one of the main ingredients in south German baking and cooking. If necessary, ricotta can be used as a substitute.

Quark Dough
- 1 cup quark or 2/3 cup ricotta cheese
- 2 cups all-purpose flour
- 1 teaspoon baking powder
- 1/8 teaspoon salt
- 1/3 cup vegetable oil
- 2 tablespoons milk
- 1/3 cup granulated sugar
- 1 large egg
- 1 teaspoon finely grated lemon zest

- 1/4 teaspoon vanilla extract

Filling
- 1/2 cup blanched hazelnuts
- 1/4 cup firmly packed light brown sugar
- 1/2 cup candied mixed peel, finely chopped
- 1/3 cup currants
- 1/4 teaspoon ground cinnamon
- 1/3 cup butter, melted and cooled

Glaze
- 3/4 cup confectioners' sugar
- 4 teaspoons fresh orange juice

Quark Dough: Spoon the quark onto a kitchen towel and wring out any excess moisture. • Sift the flour, baking powder, and salt into a large bowl. • Beat the quark, oil, milk, sugar, and egg in a large bowl with an electric mixer at medium speed until smooth. • Stir in the lemon zest and vanilla. • Mix in the dry ingredients. • Turn the dough out onto a lightly floured surface and knead for 5–7 minutes, or until smooth and elastic. • Place in a large bowl, cover with a clean kitchen towel, and set aside. • Filling: Toast the hazelnuts in a skillet over medium heat for 5–7 minutes, or until golden brown. Let cool completely. Transfer the nuts to a food processor, add the brown

coffee heart cookies

- 2/3 cup all-purpose flour
- 1/4 cup cornstarch
- 1 tablespoon unsweetened cocoa powder
- 1/2 teaspoon baking powder
- 1/8 teaspoon salt
- 1/4 cup (1/2 stick) butter
- 1/4 cup granulated sugar
- 1 teaspoon coffee extract
- 1 tablespoon milk, or more as needed
- 1/2 cup Chocolate Butter Frosting, Simple Chocolate Frosting, or Chocolate–Sour Cream Frosting (see pages 346, 346, and 348)

Preheat the oven to 375°F. • Butter two cookie sheets. • Sift the flour, cornstarch, cocoa, baking powder, and salt into a large bowl. • Use a pastry blender to cut in the butter until the mixture resembles coarse crumbs. • Stir in the sugar. • Add the coffee extract and enough milk to form a stiff dough. • Turn the dough out onto a lightly floured surface and knead until smooth. • Roll out the dough to a thickness of 1/4 inch. • Use a heart-shaped cookie cutter to cut out the cookies.

Coffee heart cookies

Gather the dough scraps, re-roll, and continue cutting out cookies until all the dough is used. • Use a spatula to transfer the cookies onto the prepared cookie sheets, placing them 1 inch apart. • Bake for 10–15 minutes, or until lightly browned, rotating the sheets halfway through for even baking. • Cool on the sheets until the cookies firm slightly. Transfer to racks to finish cooling. • Spread with the frosting. Draw the tines of a fork through the frosting to make decorative patterns.

Makes 25 cookies · Prep: 40 min. · Cooking: 10–15 min. · Level: 1 · Keeps: 7 days

coffee-time cookies

- 2 2/3 cups all-purpose flour
- 2/3 cup cornstarch
- 1/8 teaspoon salt
- 3/4 cup granulated sugar
- 1 tablespoon Vanilla Sugar (see page 341)
- 1/4 teaspoon vanilla extract
- 3 oz marzipan, cut up and softened
- 1 cup (2 sticks) cold butter, cut up
- 1 large egg, lightly beaten + 1 egg yolk, mixed with 1/2 cup water

Sift the flour, cornstarch, and salt into a bowl. Stir in the granulated sugar, vanilla sugar, and vanilla. • Dot the butter and marzipan evenly over the dry ingredients. Use a pastry blender to cut in the ingredients until the mixture resembles coarse crumbs. • Make a well in the center and add the egg. • Work the dough until combined and knead once or twice on a lightly floured surface into a smooth dough. • Wrap in plastic wrap and refrigerate for at least 30 minutes, or until firm. • Preheat the oven to 350°F. • Butter two cookie sheets. • Roll out the dough on a lightly floured

surface to a thickness of about 1/8 inch. Use small cookie cutters to stamp out different shapes. • Gather the dough scraps, re-roll, and continue cutting out cookies until all the dough is used. • Arrange on the prepared cookie sheets, spacing 1 inch apart. • Brush with the egg glaze. • Bake for 10–15 minutes, or until golden brown, rotating the sheets halfway through for even baking. • Cool on the cookie sheets for 5 minutes. • Transfer to racks to cool.

Makes 80–90 cookies · Prep: 30 min. + 30 min. to chill · Cooking: 10–15 min. · Level: 2 · Keeps: 14 days

coffee–hazelnut bars

- 1 2/3 cups all-purpose flour
- 1/8 teaspoon salt
- 3/4 cup (1 1/2 sticks) butter, softened
- 3/4 cup confectioners' sugar
- 1 1/4 cups finely chopped hazelnuts

Coffee glaze
- 1 large egg white, lightly beaten
- 1 tablespoon freeze-dried coffee granules dissolved in 2 teaspoons hot water

Sift the flour and salt into a large bowl. • Beat the butter and confectioners' sugar in a large bowl with an electric mixer at high speed until creamy. • Mix in the dry ingredients, followed by the hazelnuts to form a dough. • Press the dough into a disk, wrap in plastic wrap, and refrigerate for 30 minutes. • Preheat the oven to 375°F. • Butter two cookie sheets. • Roll out the dough on a lightly floured surface to a thickness of 1/4 inch. • Coffee glaze: Beat the egg white and coffee in a small bowl. Brush all over the dough. • Cut into 3 x 1 1/2-inch bars and use a spatula to transfer to the prepared cookie sheets, placing them 1 inch apart. • Bake for 12–15

sugar, and process until coarsely chopped. • Mix the hazelnuts, candied peel, currants, and cinnamon in a medium bowl. • Preheat the oven to 350°F. • Butter two cookie sheets. • Turn the dough out onto a lightly floured surface. Roll out to an 18 x 14-inch rectangle. • Brush with the melted butter and sprinkle with the filling. • Roll the dough up from the short side, sealing the edge with cold water. Use a sharp knife to cut it into 1/3-inch slices. • Place each slice 1 inch apart cut-side down on the prepared cookie sheets. Use a fork to flatten them

minutes, or until firm to the touch, rotating the sheets halfway through for even baking. • Transfer to racks and let cool completely.

Makes 30 cookies · Prep: 40 min. + 30 min. to chill Cooking: 12–15 min. · Level: 1 · Keeps: 7 days

mint-topped cookies

- 1 2/3 cups all-purpose flour
- 2/3 cup confectioners' sugar
- 1 tablespoon unsweetened cocoa powder
- 1 teaspoon baking powder
- 1/8 teaspoon salt
- 2/3 cup butter, softened
- 1 large egg, lightly beaten
- 1 tablespoon Vanilla Sugar (see page 341)

Mint topping

- 1 2/3 cups confectioners' sugar
- 3 tablespoons light corn syrup
- 1 tablespoon fresh lemon juice
- 1/2 teaspoon peppermint extract
- 2–3 drops green food coloring
- 2 oz semisweet chocolate, coarsely chopped

Sift the flour, confectioners' sugar, cocoa, baking powder, and salt into a large bowl. • Mix in the butter, egg, and vanilla sugar to form a smooth dough. • Divide the dough in half. • Press the dough into disks, wrap in plastic wrap, and refrigerate for 30 minutes. • Preheat the oven to 350°F. • Butter four cookie sheets. • Roll out the dough on a lightly floured surface to a thickness of 1/8 inch. • Use a 1 1/2-inch cookie cutter to cut out the cookies. Gather the dough scraps, re-roll, and continue cutting out cookies until the dough is used. • Use a spatula to transfer the cookies to the prepared cookie sheets, placing them 1 inch apart. • Bake, one sheet at a time, for 10–15 minutes, or until the edges are firm and the bottoms are lightly browned. • Transfer on the parchment paper to racks and let cool completely. • Mint topping:

slightly. • Bake for 25–30 minutes, or until golden brown, rotating the sheets halfway through for even baking. • Cool the cookies on the sheets for 2 minutes. • Transfer to racks to finish cooling. · Glaze: Mix the confectioners' sugar with enough orange juice to make a thick glaze. Drizzle over the cookies.

Makes 22 cookies · Prep: 1 hr. · Cooking: 25–30 min. · Level: 3 · Keeps: 5 days

Mix the confectioners' sugar, corn syrup, lemon juice, peppermint extract, and green food coloring in a medium bowl until a smooth dough has formed. • Roll the mint paste out on a surface lightly dusted with confectioners' sugar to a thickness of 1/8 inch. • Use 1 1/2-inch petit four cutters to cut out green shapes. • Melt the chocolate in a double boiler over barely simmering water. • Spoon the melted chocolate into a small freezer bag and cut off a tiny corner. • Pipe chocolate dots on top of the cookies and top with the mint shapes.

Makes 60 cookies · Prep: 60 min. + 30 min. to chill · Cooking: 10–15 min. per batch · Level: 3 · Keeps: 15 days stacked between layers of parchment paper

st john's alms

These round German cookies are called Johannistaler (St John's thalers—coins or alms). Currants are called Johannesbeeren ("St John's berries") in German because they supposedly ripen around the feast day of St John the Baptist (June 24).

- 1 2/3 cups all-purpose flour
- 2 tablespoons baking powder
- 1/8 teaspoon salt
- 1/2 cup (1 stick) butter
- 1/2 cup granulated sugar
- 2 tablespoons Vanilla Sugar (see page 341)
- 1 large egg

Light glaze

- 1 1/3 cups confectioners' sugar
- 1 tablespoon Marsala wine, rum, or lemon juice
- 2–3 tablespoons water

Dark glaze

- 1/2 cup confectioners' sugar
- 1 teaspoon unsweetened cocoa powder
- 1 tablespoon dark rum, lemon, or orange juice
- 1/2 cup red currant jelly

Sift the flour, baking powder, and salt into a

large bowl. • Beat the butter and granulated and vanilla sugars in a large bowl with an electric mixer at high speed until creamy. • Add the egg, beating until just blended. • Mix in the dry ingredients. • Turn the dough onto a lightly floured surface and knead until smooth. • Divide the dough into four portions. Press the dough into disks, wrap in plastic wrap, and refrigerate for 30 minutes. • Preheat the oven to 350°F. • Line two cookie sheets with parchment paper. • On the floured surface, roll out one portion of the dough to a thickness of 1/4 inch. • Use a 2-inch fluted round cutter to cut out about twelve cookies. • Use a small cutter to stamp out circles in the centers. • Gather the dough scraps, re-roll, and continue cutting out the cookies until all the dough is used. • Use a spatula to transfer the cookies to the prepared cookie sheets, placing them 1 inch apart. • Bake for 8–10 minutes, or until golden brown, rotating the sheets halfway through the baking to ensure even browning. • Transfer the cookies on the parchment paper to racks to cool. • Light glaze: Mix the confectioners' sugar with Marsala and water until smooth and thick. • Spread the glaze over each cookie. Set aside and let stand for 30 minutes until set. • Spread a thin layer of jelly over and top with a glazed ring. • Dark glaze: Sift the confectioners' sugar and cocoa into a small bowl. Add the rum and mix into a smooth paste. • Spoon the glaze into a pastry bag fitted with a plain tip. • Pipe dark arches onto the glazing and let set completely.

Makes 24–30 cookies · Prep: 2 hr. + 60 min. to chill and set · Cooking: 8–10 min. · Level: 3 · Keeps: 10 days

St John's alms

multicolored sandwich cookies

1²/₃ cups all-purpose flour
1/4 teaspoon salt
3/4 cup (1¹/₂ sticks) butter, softened
1 cup granulated sugar
2 tablespoons milk
1 teaspoon vanilla extract
2 large egg yolks, lightly beaten

Multicolored filling
1/4 cup (¹/₂ stick) butter, softened
1²/₃ cups confectioners' sugar
2 tablespoons milk
3 drops each red, green, and yellow
food coloring

Sift the flour and salt into a medium bowl. • Beat the butter and sugar in a large bowl with an electric mixer at high speed until creamy. • Add the milk, vanilla, and egg yolks, beating until just blended. • Mix in the dry ingredients to form a smooth dough. • Press the dough into a disk, wrap in plastic wrap, and refrigerate for 30 minutes. • Preheat the oven to 375°F. • Butter three cookie sheets. • Roll out the dough on a lightly floured surface to a thickness of ¹/₈ inch. • Use a 2¹/₂-inch cookie cutter to cut out the cookies. Cut the centers from half the cookies with a ¹/₂-inch cutter. Gather the dough scraps, re-roll, and continue cutting out cookies until all the dough is used. • Use a spatula to transfer the cookies to the cookie sheets, placing them ¹/₂ inch apart. • Bake, one sheet at a time, for 8–10 minutes, or until lightly browned. • Transfer to racks and let cool completely. • Multicolored filling: With mixer at high speed, beat the butter in a medium bowl until creamy. • Beat in the confectioners' sugar and milk to make a spreadable consistency. • Divide the filling among three small bowls and add a different color of food coloring to each one, stirring until well blended. • Spread the fillings over the whole cookies and place a ring cookie on top.

Makes 36 cookies · Prep: 45 min. + 30 min. to chill · Cooking: 8–10 min. per batch · Level: 2 · Keeps: 4 days

hazelnut scoundrels

3 cups all-purpose flour
1/8 teaspoon salt
1 cup superfine sugar
1¹/₃ cups finely ground hazelnuts
1 cup (2 sticks) cold butter, cut up
2 large eggs, lightly beaten
1/4 cup Vanilla Sugar (see page 341)
1/2 cup strawberry or raspberry preserves

Refrigerate three cookie sheets. • Sift the flour and salt into a large bowl. Stir in the superfine sugar and hazelnuts. • Dot the butter evenly over the mixture. • Use a pastry blender to cut in the butter until the mixture resembles coarse crumbs. • Add the eggs, beating until just blended. • Turn out onto a lightly floured surface and work into a smooth dough. Knead gently once or twice (too much kneading causes cracks when cutting out shapes). • Shape into a ball, wrap in plastic wrap, and refrigerate for at least 1 hour. • Roll out small portions of dough to a thickness of ¹/₄ inch. • Use a cutter to stamp into 1-inch circles. Gather the dough scraps, re-roll, and continue cutting out cookies until all the dough is used. • Use a metal spatula to transfer the cookies onto one of the chilled baking sheets, placing them 1¹/₂ inches apart. • Preheat the oven to 375°F. • Bake, one batch at a time, for 12–15 minutes, or until just golden. • Cool the cookies on the cookie sheets for 5 minutes. • Place the vanilla sugar in a small bowl. Turn the cookies in the sugar while they are still warm. • Spread each cookie with a little preserves and sandwich them together.

Makes 60 cookies · Prep: 40 min. + 60 min. to chill · Cooking: 12–15 min. per batch · Level: 2 · Keeps: 12 days

cornmeal–lemon cookies

2 cups finely ground yellow cornmeal
1 cup all-purpose flour
1 cup confectioners' sugar
1 teaspoon baking powder
1/8 teaspoon salt
1 large egg + 1 egg yolk
2/3 cup butter, cut up
1/4 cup lard or vegetable shortening
Grated zest of 1 lemon

Preheat the oven to 375°F. • Butter two cookie sheets. • Sift the cornmeal, flour, confectioners' sugar, baking powder, and salt onto a work surface and make a well in the center. • Add the egg and egg yolk, butter, lard, and lemon zest. • Use your hands to knead the mixture into a smooth dough. • Roll out the dough on a lightly floured surface to a thickness of ¹/₈ inch. • Use a 2-inch fluted cookie cutter to cut out the cookies. Gather the dough scraps, re-roll, and continue cutting out cookies until all the dough is used. • Use a spatula to

transfer the cookies to the prepared cookie sheets. • Bake for 12–15 minutes, or until just golden, rotating the sheets halfway through for even baking. • Transfer to racks and let cool completely.

Makes 25 cookies · Prep: 40 min. · Cooking: 12–15 min. · Level: 1 · Keeps: 7 days

marshmallow cookies

Cookie base
1¹/₃ cups all-purpose flour
2 teaspoons baking powder
1/4 teaspoon salt
1/4 cup (¹/₂ stick) butter, softened
1/2 cup granulated sugar
1 large egg

Marshmallow topping
3/4 cup coarsely chopped pink marshmallows
2 tablespoons butter
1/4 cup confectioners' sugar
1/2 cup shredded coconut

Cookie base: Sift the flour, baking powder, and salt into a medium bowl. • Beat the butter and sugar in a large bowl with an electric mixer at high speed until creamy. • Add the egg, beating until just blended. • Mix in the dry ingredients to form a stiff dough. • Turn the dough out onto a lightly floured surface and knead until smooth. • Press the dough into a disk, wrap in plastic wrap, and refrigerate for 30 minutes. • Preheat the oven to 350°F. • Line two cookie sheets with parchment paper. • Roll out the dough to a thickness of ¹/₄ inch. • Use a fluted pastry wheel to cut the dough into 1¹/₂ x 2¹/₂-inch rectangles. • Gather the dough scraps, re-roll, and continue cutting out cookies until all the dough is used. • Use a spatula to transfer the cookies to the prepared cookie sheets, placing them 1 inch apart. • Bake for 8–10 minutes, or until just golden at the edges, rotating the sheets halfway through for even baking. • Transfer to racks to cool. • Marshmallow topping: Mix the marshmallows and butter in a small saucepan over low heat until the marshmallows have melted. • Remove from the heat and stir in the confectioners' sugar. • Spread ¹/₂ teaspoon of the topping over each cookie top, spreading it smooth. • Sprinkle with the coconut.

Makes 28 cookies · Prep: 40 min. + 30 min. to chill Cooking: 8–10 min. · Level: 2 · Keeps: 2 days

Marshmallow cookies

jelly cookies

- 1/4 cup old-fashioned rolled oats
- 3/4 cup all-purpose flour
- 1/4 cup granulated sugar
- 1/4 cup (-/2 stick) butter
- 1 cup red currant jelly
- 1/3 cup confectioners' sugar

Stir together the oats, flour, and sugar in a medium bowl. • Use a pastry blender to cut in the butter. Knead until a dough has formed. Press the dough into a disk, wrap in plastic wrap, and refrigerate for 30 minutes. • Preheat the oven to 400°F. • Set out two cookie sheets. • Gather the dough into a ball and roll out on a lightly floured surface to a thickness of 1/4 inch. • Use an oval 2-inch cookie cutter to cut out the cookies. • Cut two tiny circles from half of the oval shapes with a sharp knife. • Gather the dough scraps, re-roll, and continue cutting out cookies until all the dough is used. • Use a spatula to transfer the cookies to the cookie sheets. • Bake for 10–12 minutes, or until lightly browned, rotating the sheets halfway through for even baking. • Cool on the sheets until the cookies firm slightly. Transfer to racks to finish cooling. • Warm the jelly in a small saucepan over low heat until liquid. • Spread the complete cookies with the jelly and stick together with a holed cookie. • Dust generously with the confectioners' sugar.

Makes 25–27 cookies · Prep: 40 min. + 30 min. to chill · Cooking: 10–12 min. · Level: 2 · Keeps: 7–9 days

uplands cookies

These tasty cookies come from villages in the northeast of England, where baking remains a popular community tradition.

- 2 cups all-purpose flour
- 1 1/2 teaspoons baking powder
- 1/8 teaspoon salt
- 1 cup (2 sticks) butter, softened
- 1 1/2 cups granulated sugar
- 1 large egg
- 1/2 teaspoon vanilla extract
- 1/2 cup raspberry preserves
- 1/3 cup confectioners' sugar
- 1 tablespoon water, or more as needed
- 10 candied cherries, cut in half

Sift the flour, baking powder, and salt into a large bowl. • Beat the butter and sugar in a large bowl with an electric mixer at high speed until creamy. • Add the egg and vanilla, beating until just blended. • Turn the dough out onto a lightly floured surface and knead until smooth. • Press the dough into a disk, wrap in plastic wrap, and refrigerate for 30

minutes. • Preheat the oven to 350°F. • Butter two cookie sheets. • Roll out the dough to a thickness of 1/4 inch. • Use a 1 1/2-inch cookie cutter to cut out the cookies. • Gather the dough scraps, re-roll, and continue cutting out cookies until all the dough is used. • Use a spatula to transfer the cookies to a cookie sheet, placing them 1 inch apart. • Bake for 8–10 minutes, or until lightly browned, rotating the sheets halfway through for even baking. • Cool on the sheets until the cookies firm slightly. Transfer to racks to finish cooling. • Warm the raspberry preserves in a small saucepan over low heat until liquid. • Stick the cookies together in pairs with the preserves. • Mix the confectioners' sugar with enough water to make a spreadable frosting. • Spread the tops of the cookies with the frosting and decorate with a half cherry.

Makes 20 cookies · Prep: 40 min. · Cooking: 8–10 min. · Level: 1 · Keeps: 3 days

tutti-frutti cookies

- 2 cups all-purpose flour
- 1/2 cup granulated sugar
- 1 tablespoon Vanilla Sugar (see page 341)
  Grated zest of 1/2 lemon
- 1/4 teaspoon salt
- 3/4 cup (1 1/2 sticks) cold butter, cut up
- 1 large egg, lightly beaten
- 1 tablespoon candied cherries, chopped
- 2 tablespoons mixed candied peel, chopped
- 2 tablespoons sugared nuts, crushed
- 1 large egg yolk, to brush
- 1/2 cup water

Stir together the flour, granulated sugar, vanilla sugar, lemon zest, and salt in a medium bowl. • Add the butter, distributing the pieces evenly over the mixture. Use a pastry blender to cut in the butter until the mixture resembles coarse crumbs. • Make a well in the center and add the egg, mixing until a dough is formed. • Turn out onto a lightly floured surface, working in the candied cherries, candied peel, and nuts. Knead until smooth. • Return to the bowl, cover with plastic wrap, and refrigerate for 30 minutes. • Preheat the oven to 350°F. • Line two cookie sheets with parchment paper. • Roll out the dough to a thickness of 1/2 inch. Use a 2 1/2-inch round or diamond-shaped cutter to stamp out shapes. • Use a metal spatula to transfer the cookies to the prepared cookie sheets, spacing 1 inch apart. • Mix the egg yolk and water in a small bowl. • Brush the cookies with the egg yolk

mixture. • Bake for 12–15 minutes, or until lightly browned, rotating the sheets halfway through for even baking. • Cool the cookies on the sheets for 10 minutes. Use a metal spatula to transfer to racks to cool.

Makes 40 cookies. · Prep: 45 min. + 30 min. to chill Cooking: 12–15 min. · Level: 2 · Keeps: 10 days

rustic aniseed cookies

- 2 cups all-purpose flour
- 1 cup granulated sugar
- 1/8 teaspoon salt
- 1/4 cup extra-virgin olive oil
- 1/4 cup Muscatel wine
- 2 tablespoons anisette
- 1 tablespoon aniseeds
- 1 large egg, lightly beaten
- 1 tablespoon Vanilla Sugar (see page 341)

Stir together the flour, sugar, and salt in a large bowl. • Gradually mix in the oil and wine until well blended. • Add the anisette and aniseeds and knead until a smooth dough has formed. • Press the dough into a disk, wrap in plastic wrap, and refrigerate for 30 minutes. • Preheat the oven to 350°F. • Butter and flour a cookie sheet. • Roll out the dough on a lightly floured surface to a thickness of 1/8 inch. • Use a 2-inch cookie cutter to cut out the cookies. • Gather the dough scraps, re-roll, and continue cutting out cookies until all the dough is used. • Use a spatula to transfer the cookies to the prepared cookie sheet. Prick all over with a fork. • Brush the cookies with the beaten egg and sprinkle with the vanilla sugar. • Bake for 12–15 minutes, or until just golden. • Transfer to racks and let cool completely.

Makes 16 cookies · Prep: 40 min. + 30 min. to chill Cooking: 12–15 min. · Level: 1 · Keeps: 5 days

butter digestive cookies

Quintessentially British—digestive, or sweetmeal, cookies are slightly sweet and made from whole-wheat flour. They are excellent coated with chocolate and dipped into freshly brewed tea.

- 1 1/3 cups whole-wheat flour
- 1/4 cup all-purpose flour
- 1 teaspoon baking powder
- 1/2 teaspoon salt
- 2 tablespoons old-fashioned rolled oats
- 1/3 cup butter
- 1 cup granulated sugar
- 1/3 cup milk

Sift the whole-wheat and all-purpose flours, baking powder, and salt into a large bowl. • Stir in the oats. • Use a pastry blender to cut in the butter until the mixture resembles coarse crumbs. • Stir in the sugar and enough milk to form a soft dough. • Turn the dough out onto a lightly floured surface and knead until smooth. • Press the dough into a disk, wrap in plastic wrap, and refrigerate for 30 minutes. • Preheat the oven to 375°F. • Butter two cookie sheets. • Roll out the dough to a thickness of $^1/_4$ inch. • Use a 2$^1/_2$-inch cookie cutter to cut out the cookies. Gather the dough scraps, re-roll, and continue cutting out cookies until all the dough is used. • Use a spatula to transfer the cookies to the prepared cookie sheets, placing them 1 inch apart. Prick all over with a fork. • Bake for 15–20 minutes, or until just golden, rotating the sheets halfway through for even baking. • Transfer to racks to cool.

Makes 24 cookies · Prep: 40 min. + 30 min. to chill
Cooking: 15–20 min. · Level: 1 · Keeps: 7 days

crunchy-topped almond butter cookies

1$^2/_3$ cups all-purpose flour
$^1/_8$ teaspoon salt
$^3/_4$ cup (1$^1/_2$ sticks) butter, softened
$^1/_3$ cup granulated sugar
1   teaspoon almond extract

Almond-cinnamon topping
$^1/_3$ cup superfine sugar
$^1/_2$ teaspoon ground cinnamon
$^2/_3$ cup coarsely chopped blanched almonds, toasted
1   large egg white, lightly beaten

Preheat the oven to 375°F. • Butter three cookie sheets. • Sift the flour and salt into a medium bowl. • Beat the butter and sugar in a large bowl with an electric mixer at high speed until creamy. • Mix in the dry ingredients and almond extract. The mixture should be slightly crumbly. • Refrigerate for at least 1 hour, or until the dough can be formed into a firm, smooth dough. • Roll out the dough on a lightly floured surface to a 12 x 8-inch rectangle. • Cut into 3 x 1-inch bars. • Transfer the cookies to the prepared cookie sheets, placing them $^1/_2$ inch apart. • Almond-cinnamon topping: Mix the superfine sugar, cinnamon, and almonds in a small bowl. • Brush the cookies with the beaten egg white and sprinkle with the topping. • Bake, one sheet at a time, for 12–15 minutes, or until just golden. • Cool on the sheet until the cookies firm slightly. Transfer to racks to cool.

Makes 32 cookies · Prep: 40 min. + 60 min. to chill · Cooking: 12–15 min. per batch · Level: 1 · Keeps: 7 days

bohemian caraway cookies

1$^1/_2$ cups all-purpose flour
1   teaspoon freshly grated nutmeg
$^1/_8$ teaspoon salt
$^1/_3$ cup cold butter, cut up
1   cup granulated sugar
1$^1/_2$ tablespoons firmly packed light brown sugar
2   large eggs, lightly beaten
2   tablespoons caraway seeds

Sift the flour, nutmeg, and salt into a large bowl • Use a pastry blender to cut in the butter until the mixture resembles fine crumbs. Stir in the granulated sugar and 1 tablespoon of the brown sugar. • Reserve 1$^1/_2$ tablespoons of the egg for the glaze. Add the remaining eggs and caraway seeds and mix well. • Turn the dough out onto a lightly floured surface. Knead for 5–7 minutes, or until smooth and elastic. Press the dough into a disk, wrap in plastic wrap, and refrigerate for 30 minutes. • Preheat the oven to 325°F. Butter two cookie sheets. • Roll out to a thickness of $^1/_4$ inch. Use a cookie cutter to stamp out 2-inch rounds. • Use a spatula to transfer the cookies to the prepared cookie sheets, placing them 1 inch apart. Brush the tops with the reserved egg and sprinkle with the remaining brown sugar. • Bake for 10–15 minutes or until golden brown and crisp, rotating the sheets halfway through for even baking. • Cool the cookies on the sheets for 2 minutes. Transfer to racks to finish cooling.

Makes about 40 cookies · Prep: 20 min. + 30 min. to chill · Cooking: 10–15 min. · Level: 1 · Keeps: 7 days

digestive biscuits

The backbone of British baking—digestive biscuits—are great with freshly brewed tea and have the perfect texture to make cookie bases for cheesecakes.

$^2/_3$ cup whole-wheat flour
$^1/_2$ teaspoon baking soda
$^1/_4$ teaspoon salt
$^1/_2$ cup (1 stick) butter, cut up
1   cup oat bran
$^1/_4$ cup granulated sugar
1   large egg, lightly beaten

Sift the whole-wheat flour, baking soda, and salt into a large bowl. • Use a pastry blender to cut in the butter until the mixture resembles fine crumbs. • Stir in the oat bran and sugar. • Mix in enough beaten egg to form a stiff dough. Press the dough into a disk, wrap in plastic wrap, and refrigerate for 30 minutes. • Preheat the oven to 375°F.

• Butter a cookie sheet. • Roll out the dough on a surface lightly dusted with oat bran to a thickness of $^1/_4$ inch. • Use a 2-inch cookie cutter to cut out the cookies. Gather the dough scraps, re-roll, and continue cutting out cookies until all the dough is used. • Use a spatula to transfer the cookies to the prepared cookie sheet, placing them 1 inch apart. • Bake for 10–15 minutes, or until lightly browned. • Transfer to racks and let cool completely.

Makes 16 cookies · Prep: 40 min. + 30 min. to chill
Cooking: 10–15 min. · Level: 1 · Keeps: 2 weeks

crispy butter cookies

1   large egg yolk
2   tablespoons milk
1$^1/_4$ cups all-purpose flour
$^1/_3$ cup granulated sugar
2   tablespoons butter, melted
$^1/_8$ teaspoon salt

Beat the egg yolk and milk in a small bowl until frothy. • Stir together the flour, sugar, butter, and salt in a medium bowl. • Use a wooden spoon to stir in the beaten egg mixture until well blended. Press the dough into a disk, wrap in plastic wrap, and refrigerate for 30 minutes. • Preheat the oven to 400°F. • Butter a cookie sheet. • Roll out the dough on a lightly floured surface to a thickness of $^1/_8$ inch. • Use a 2-inch cookie cutter to cut out the cookies. Gather the dough scraps, re-roll, and continue cutting out cookies until all the dough is used. • Use a spatula to transfer the cookies to the prepared cookie sheet, placing them 1 inch apart. • Bake for 5–8 minutes, or until lightly browned. • Cool on the sheet until the cookies firm slightly. • Transfer to a rack and let cool completely.

Makes 12–16 cookies · Prep: 40 min. + 30 min. to chill · Cooking: 5–8 min. · Level: 1 · Keeps: 10 days

Digestive biscuits

sablé cookies

These delicate almond cookies are a French classic, taking their name from the French word for sand.

1/2 cup all-purpose flour
1/3 cup cornstarch
1/8 teaspoon salt
2/3 cup granulated sugar
1/2 cup (1 stick) butter, cut up
1 large egg yolk
1/2 teaspoon almond extract
1/2 cup finely chopped almonds

Sift the flour, cornstarch, and salt into a large bowl. • Stir in the sugar and make a well in the center. • Use a pastry blender to cut in the butter until the mixture resembles coarse crumbs. • Add the egg yolk and almond extract and knead until a smooth dough has formed. • Press the dough into a disk, wrap in plastic wrap, and refrigerate for 30 minutes. • Preheat the oven to 350°F. • Butter two cookie sheets. • Roll out the dough on a lightly floured surface to a thickness of 1/4 inch. • Use a 2-inch star-shaped cookie cutter to cut out the cookies. Gather the dough scraps, re-roll, and continue cutting out cookies until the dough is used. • Use a spatula to transfer the cookies to the prepared cookie sheets. Sprinkle with the almonds. • Bake for 15–20 minutes, or until lightly browned, rotating the sheets halfway through for even baking. • Cool on the sheets until the cookies firm slightly. Transfer to racks to finish cooling.

Makes 20 cookies · Prep: 40 min. + 30 min. to chill Cooking: 15–20 min. · Level: 1 · Keeps: 2 weeks

cinnamon cookies

3/4 cup all-purpose flour
1 teaspoon ground cinnamon
1/4 teaspoon baking powder
1/4 teaspoon salt
1/4 cup (1/2 stick) butter, softened
2/3 cup granulated sugar
1 large egg yolk, lightly beaten
1 tablespoon milk

Sift the flour, cinnamon, baking powder, and salt into a medium bowl. • Beat the butter and sugar in a large bowl with an electric mixer at high speed until creamy. • Add the egg yolk, beating until just blended. • Mix in the dry ingredients and milk to form a smooth dough. • Press the dough into a disk, wrap in plastic wrap, and refrigerate for 30 minutes. • Preheat the oven to 350°F. • Butter three cookie sheets. • Divide the dough in half. Roll out each piece of dough on a lightly floured

surface to a thickness of 1/8 inch. • Use a 2-inch cookie cutter to cut out the cookies. Gather the dough scraps, re-roll, and continue cutting out cookies until all the dough is used. • Use a spatula to transfer the cookies to the prepared cookie sheets. • Bake, one sheet at a time, for 12–15 minutes, or until just golden. • Cool on the sheets until the cookies firm slightly. • Transfer to racks to finish cooling.

Makes 36 cookies · Prep: 40 min. + 30 min. to chill · Cooking: 12–15 min. per batch · Level: 1 · Keeps: 7 days

lovers' knots

2 cups all-purpose flour
1 teaspoon baking powder
1/4 teaspoon ground allspice
1/8 teaspoon salt
1/2 cup (1 stick) butter, softened
1/3 cup granulated sugar
1/2 teaspoon vanilla extract
1 large egg + 1 large egg yolk
1/4 cup milk
Grated zest of 1/2 lemon
1 tablespoon confectioners' sugar

Sift the flour, baking powder, allspice, and salt into a large bowl. • Beat the butter and sugar in a large bowl with an electric mixer at high speed until creamy. • Add the vanilla and egg and egg yolk, beating until just blended. • Stir in the milk and lemon zest. • Mix in the dry ingredients to form a smooth dough. Press the dough into a disk, wrap in plastic wrap, and refrigerate for 30 minutes. • Preheat the oven to 350°F. • Butter a cookie sheet. • Roll out the dough on a lightly floured surface to a thickness of 1/8 inch. Cut into 12 x 1/2-inch-long strips. • Carefully tie the dough strips into knots. • Place the cookies 1/2 inch apart on the prepared cookie sheet. • Bake for 15–20 minutes, or until lightly browned. • Transfer to racks and let cool completely. • Dust with the confectioners' sugar.

Makes 20 cookies · Prep: 40 min. + 30 min. to chill Cooking: 15–20 min. · Level: 1 · Keeps: 7 days

madeira bars

1 1/2 cups all-purpose flour
1/8 teaspoon salt
1/2 cup (1 stick) butter, cut up
1/2 cup granulated sugar
1/4 cup Madeira wine
1 large egg yolk, lightly beaten

Sift the flour and salt into a large bowl. • Use a pastry blender to cut in the butter until the mixture resembles fine crumbs. • Stir in the

sugar and Madeira to form a smooth dough. • Press the dough into a disk, wrap in plastic wrap, and refrigerate for 30 minutes. • Preheat the oven to 325°F. • Butter two cookie sheets. • Roll out the dough on a lightly floured surface to a thickness of 1/8 inch. • Cut into 1 x 3-inch bars. • Use a spatula to transfer the cookies to the prepared cookie sheets. • Brush with the beaten egg yolk. • Bake for 12–15 minutes, or until just golden, rotating the sheets halfway through for even baking. • Transfer to racks and let cool completely.

Makes 34 cookies · Prep: 40 min. + 30 min. to chill Cooking: 12–15 min. · Level: 1 · Keeps: 3 days

sugar cookies

The brightly colored sugar used to jazz up these cookies can be bought at Maid of Scandinavia or other specialty baking stores.

3/4 cup all-purpose flour
1/8 teaspoon salt
1/2 cup (1 stick) butter, cut up
1/3 cup granulated sugar
1 teaspoon finely grated lemon zest
1 large egg, lightly beaten
Raw sugar and colored coarse sugar, to decorate

Sift the flour and salt into a large bowl. • Use a pastry blender to cut in the butter until the mixture resembles fine crumbs. • Stir in the sugar and lemon zest. • Add half the beaten egg to form a stiff dough. • Turn the dough out onto a lightly floured surface and knead until smooth. • Press the dough into a disk, wrap in plastic wrap, and refrigerate for 30 minutes. • Preheat the oven to 375°F. • Butter two cookie sheets. • Roll the dough out to a thickness of 1/4 inch. • Use a 2-inch star-shaped cookie cutter to cut out the cookies. • Gather the dough scraps, re-roll, and continue cutting out until all the dough has been used. • Use a spatula to transfer the cookies to the prepared cookie sheets, placing them 1/2 inch apart. • Brush the tops of the cookies with the remaining beaten egg. Sprinkle half the cookies with the raw brown sugar and half with the colored sugar. • Bake for 10–12 minutes, or until just golden at the edges, rotating the sheets halfway through for even baking. • Transfer to racks to cool.

Makes 30 cookies · Prep: 40 min. + 30 min. to chill Cooking: 10–12 min. · Level: 1 · Keeps: 5 days

Sugar cookies

Karlsbad cookies

karlsbad cookies

These cookies are a traditional recipe from Karlsbad, the German name for Karlovy Vary, an old Czech spa with salty mineral springs. The cookies are not salty, however, but very sweet!

1	cup all-purpose flour
2/3	cup butter, softened
1/2	cup granulated sugar
1	cup finely ground almonds
1	teaspoon finely grated lemon zest
1	teaspoon fresh lemon juice

Glaze

2/3	cup confectioners' sugar
1	teaspoon fresh lemon juice, or more as needed
2	tablespoons seedless red currant or raspberry preserves

Refrigerate two cookie sheets. • Sift the flour into a medium bowl. • Beat the butter and sugar in a large bowl with an electric mixer at high speed until creamy. • Mix in the flour, almonds, and lemon zest and juice to form a soft dough. • Divide the dough in half. Press into disks, wrap in plastic wrap, and refrigerate for 30 minutes. • Roll out half the dough on a lightly floured surface to a thickness of $^1/8$ inch. • Use a $1^1/2$-inch cookie cutter to cut out the cookies. • Use a spatula to transfer the cookies to one of the prepared cookie sheets, placing them 1 inch apart. • Use a $^3/4$-inch fluted cutter to cut the centers out of half the cookies. • Re-roll the centers with the remaining dough and repeat the cutting out procedure. • Refrigerate for 30 minutes. • Preheat the oven to 375°F. • Bake for 6–8 minutes, or until just golden and the edges are firm, rotating the sheets halfway through for even baking. • Transfer the cookies to racks to cool. • Glaze: Mix the confectioners' sugar with enough lemon juice to make a thick paste. • Spread the tops of the cookies with cut-out centers with the glaze. • Set aside until the glaze has dried. • Stick the cookies together in pairs with the preserves, glazed-side up.

Makes 25–30 cookies · Prep: 45 min. + 60 min. to chill · Cooking: 6–8 min. · Level: 2 · Keeps: 10 days

poppy seed–cornmeal cookies

1$^1/3$	cups finely ground yellow cornmeal
1$^1/3$	cups all-purpose flour
2	teaspoons baking powder
$^1/8$	teaspoon salt
$^2/3$	cup granulated sugar
$^2/3$	cup butter, softened
3	large eggs, lightly beaten
2	teaspoons dry white wine
1	tablespoons milk
$^1/3$	cup poppy seeds
$^1/3$	cup confectioners' sugar

Sift the cornmeal, flour, baking powder, and salt into a large bowl. • Stir in the sugar, butter, and 2 eggs. • Add the wine and mix to form a smooth dough. • Press the dough into a disk, wrap in plastic wrap, and refrigerate for 30 minutes. • Preheat the oven to 400°F. • Butter two cookie sheets. • Roll out the dough on a lightly floured surface to a thickness of $^1/4$ inch. • Cut into 2-inch triangles and place 1 inch apart on the prepared cookie sheets. • Beat the remaining egg with the milk in a small bowl. Brush over the cookies. • Sprinkle with the poppy seeds and confectioners' sugar. • Bake for 15–20 minutes, or until just golden, rotating the sheets halfway through for even baking. • Transfer to racks to cool.

Makes 22 cookies · Prep: 40 min. + 30 min. to chill · Cooking: 15–20 min. · Level: 1 · Keeps: 10 days

glazed lemon cookie strips

1$^2/3$	cups all-purpose flour
$^1/8$	teaspoon salt
$^1/2$	cup (1 stick) butter, softened
$^1/3$	cup granulated sugar
1	large egg, lightly beaten
	Grated zest and juice of 1 lemon
$^1/2$	cup raspberry preserves
1	cup confectioners' sugar

Sift the flour and salt into a large bowl. • Mix in the butter, sugar, egg, and lemon zest to form a smooth dough. • Press the dough into a disk, wrap in plastic wrap, and refrigerate for 30 minutes. • Preheat the oven to 400°F. • Butter two cookie sheets. • Roll out the dough on a lightly floured surface to a thickness of $^1/8$ inch. • Use a sharp knife to cut the dough into 2 x $^3/4$-inch strips. • Use a spatula to transfer the cookies to the prepared cookie sheets. • Bake for 8–10 minutes, or until just golden at the edges, rotating the sheets halfway through for even baking. • Transfer to racks and let cool completely. • Reserve 1 teaspoon of the lemon juice. Combine the remaining juice with the preserves in a small saucepan and warm over low heat until liquid. Spread the cookies with the preserves. • Mix the confectioners' sugar with the reserved 1 teaspoon lemon juice until a thick frosting has formed. Spread over the cookies.

Makes 18 cookies · Prep: 40 min. + 30 min. to chill Cooking: 8–10 min. · Level: 1 · Keeps: 2 days

italian hearts

2$^2/3$	cups all-purpose flour
$^1/8$	teaspoon salt
1$^1/4$	cups granulated sugar
	Grated zest of 1 lemon
$^3/4$	cup (1$^1/2$ sticks) butter, cut up
1	large egg + 2 large egg yolks
$^1/2$	cup raspberry preserves
$^1/4$	cup Alchermes or cherry liqueur
1	cup confectioners' sugar

Sift the flour and salt into a large bowl. • Stir in the sugar and lemon zest. • Use a pastry blender to cut in the butter until the mixture resembles fine crumbs. • Add the egg and egg yolks, beating until just blended. Stir to form a smooth dough. Press the dough into a disk, wrap in plastic wrap, and refrigerate for 30 minutes. • Preheat the oven to 350°F. • Butter four cookie sheets. • Roll out the dough on a lightly floured surface to a thickness of $^1/4$ inch. • Use a 2-inch heart cookie cutter to cut out the cookies. Cut out the centers from half the cookies with an apple corer. • Gather the dough scraps, re-roll, and continue cutting out cookies until all the dough is used. • Use a spatula to transfer the cookies to the prepared cookie sheets, placing them 1 inch apart. • Bake, one sheet at a time, for 8–10 minutes, or until just golden at the edges. • Transfer to racks and let cool completely. • Heat the raspberry preserves in a small pan over low heat until liquid. • Spread the whole cookies with the preserves. • Place the liqueur in a small bowl and the confectioners' sugar in a separate bowl. • Dip the holed cookies first in the liqueur, then in the confectioners' sugar. • Place the holed cookies on top of the cookies spread with preserves.

Makes 25 cookies · Prep: 45 min. + 30 min. to chill · Cooking: 8–10 min. per batch · Level: 1 · Keeps: 3 days

apple turnovers

Apfeltaschen (apple bags) are a traditional German specialty made with yeast or quark dough. This recipe uses quark.

Quark dough
1	cup quark or 1⅓ cups ricotta cheese
2	cups all-purpose flour
1	teaspoon baking powder
1/8	teaspoon salt
1/3	cup vegetable oil
1–2	tablespoons milk
1/3	cup granulated sugar
1	large egg
1	teaspoon finely grated lemon zest
1/4	teaspoon vanilla extract
1/3	cup butter, melted

Filling
3	tablespoons golden raisins
3	medium apples, peeled, cored, and cut into small cubes
1	tablespoon butter
1/3	cup granulated sugar
	Zest of 1 lemon
1	teaspoon fresh lemon juice
1	large egg, lightly beaten Confectioners' sugar, to dust

Quark dough: Use the ingredients for the quark dough following the instructions on page 80 to the stage of setting the dough aside in a covered bowl. • Filling: Plump the raisins in hot water for 10 minutes. Drain well and pat dry with paper towels. • Preheat the oven to 350°F. • Set out a cookie sheet. • Mix the apples, butter, sugar, and lemon zest and juice in a large saucepan over low heat and stew for about 5 minutes, or until the apples begin to soften. • Stir in the raisins and let cool

completely • Discard the lemon zest. • Roll out to a thickness of ¼ inch. • Use a round cookie cutter to stamp out 3-inch circles. • Spread with a heaping teaspoonful of the apple filling, leaving a ½-inch border around the edge. • Brush the border with the beaten egg and fold over, pressing down firmly. • Brush the tops with the remaining egg. • Arrange on the cookie sheet about 1 inch apart. • Bake for 20–30 minutes, or until golden brown. • Cool on the sheet for 2 minutes. Transfer to racks to cool. • Dust with confectioners' sugar.

Makes 12–15 cookies · Prep: 60 min. · Cooking: 20–30 min · Level: 2 · Keeps: 2 days

canary cream cookies

Zesty with just a touch of coconut—these cookies hail from the Spanish Canary Islands 200 miles from the west coast of Africa.

1	cup all-purpose flour
1/4	teaspoon baking soda
1/4	teaspoon ground cinnamon
1/8	teaspoon ground aniseeds
1/3	cup butter, softened
1/4	cup + 2 tablespoons granulated sugar
1	large egg + 1 large egg yolk, lightly beaten
1	teaspoon finely grated lemon zest
1	teaspoon finely grated orange zest
2	tablespoons heavy cream
1	tablespoon shredded coconut

Preheat the oven to 350°F. • Set out a cookie sheet. • Sift the flour, baking soda, cinnamon, and aniseeds into a medium bowl. • Beat the butter and ¼ cup sugar in a large bowl with an electric mixer at high speed until creamy. • Add the egg yolk, beating until just blended. • Beat in the lemon and orange zests, cream, and coconut. • Mix in the dry ingredients to form a smooth dough. Press the dough into a disk, wrap in plastic wrap, and refrigerate for 30 minutes. • Roll out the dough on a lightly floured surface to a thickness of ¼ inch. • Use a 2½-inch cookie cutter to cut out the cookies. • Gather the dough scraps, re-roll, and continue cutting out cookies until all the dough is used. • Use a spatula to transfer the cookies to the cookie sheet, placing them 1 inch apart. • Brush the cookies with the beaten egg and sprinkle with the remaining 2 tablespoons sugar. • Bake for 10–12 minutes, or until just golden at the edges. • Transfer to racks to cool.

poppy seed cookies

2½	cups all-purpose flour
2½	teaspoons baking powder
1/4	teaspoon salt
1	large egg
1/2	cup granulated sugar
1/3	cup vegetable oil
1/3	cup cold water
1	tablespoon grated orange zest
1	tablespoon fresh orange juice
2	tablespoons poppy seeds

Sift the flour, baking powder, and salt into a medium bowl. • Beat the egg and sugar in a large bowl with an electric mixer at high speed until pale and thick. • Use a wooden spoon to beat the oil and water into the beaten egg. • Stir in the orange zest and juice and poppy seeds. • Mix in the dry ingredients. • Press the dough into a disk, wrap in plastic wrap, and refrigerate for 30 minutes. • Preheat the oven to 375°F. • Butter two cookie sheets. • Roll out the dough on a lightly floured surface to a thickness of ⅛ inch. • Use a 2-inch cookie cutter to cut out the cookies. Gather the dough scraps, re-roll, and continue cutting out cookies until all the dough is used. • Use a spatula to transfer the cookies to the prepared cookie sheets, placing them 1 inch apart. • Bake for 10–12 minutes, or until just golden at the edges, rotating the sheets halfway through for even baking. • Transfer to racks to cool.

Makes 30–35 cookies · Prep: 25 min. + 30 min. to chill · Cooking: 10–12 min. · Level: 1 · Keeps: 7 days

Poppy seed cookies

zesty citrus bars

2¼ cups all-purpose flour
1¾ cups granulated sugar
4 large egg whites, lightly beaten
1⅓ cups finely ground almonds
⅔ cup finely chopped candied orange peel
Grated zest of 1 lemon
1 teaspoon baking soda
⅛ teaspoon salt

Line a cookie sheet with parchment paper. • Use a wooden spoon to mix the flour, sugar, egg whites, almonds, candied orange peel, lemon zest, baking soda, and salt in a large bowl until a stiff dough has formed. • Press the dough into a disk, wrap in plastic wrap, and refrigerate for 30 minutes. • Roll out the dough on a lightly floured surface to a 12 x 3-inch rectangle. • Transfer to the prepared cookie sheet and refrigerate for 30 minutes. • Preheat the oven to 300°F. • Cut the dough in half lengthwise and slice into ½-inch strips. • Bake for 10–15 minutes, or until just golden. • Transfer to racks to cool.

Makes 48 cookies · Prep: 25 min. + 30 min. to chill
Cooking: 10–15 min. · Level: 1 · Keeps: 5 days

cinnamon tickets

1⅔ cups all-purpose flour
1 teaspoon ground cinnamon
⅛ teaspoon salt
½ cup granulated sugar
⅔ cup butter, cut up
2 large egg yolks + 1 large egg white, lightly beaten
½ cup flaked almonds

Sift the flour, cinnamon, and salt into a large bowl. • Stir in the sugar. • Use a pastry blender to cut in the butter until the mixture resembles coarse crumbs. • Mix in the egg yolks to form a smooth dough. • Press the dough into a disk, wrap in plastic wrap, and refrigerate for 30 minutes. • Set out three cookie sheets. • Roll out the dough on a lightly floured surface to a thickness of ⅛ inch. • Cut out 1½ x 2½-inch rectangles. • Use a spatula to transfer the cookies to the cookie sheets. • Refrigerate for 1 hour. • Preheat the oven to 350°F. • Brush the cookies with the egg white and sprinkle with almonds. • Bake, one sheet at a time, for 8–10 minutes, or until just golden at the edges. • Cool on the sheets until the cookies firm slightly. • Transfer to racks to cool.

Makes 40 cookies · Prep: 35 min. + 90 min. to chill · Cooking: 8–10 min. per batch · Level: 1 · Keeps: 2 weeks

almond-orange pockets

1⅓ cups all-purpose flour
⅓ cup cornstarch
½ teaspoon baking powder
⅛ teaspoon salt
⅓ cup granulated sugar
1 tablespoon Vanilla Sugar (see page 341)
1 teaspoon grated orange zest
¾ cup (1½ sticks) butter, cut up
1 large egg
Milk, to brush

Almond-orange filling
1 cup finely ground almonds
⅓ cup firmly packed light brown sugar
Grated zest and juice of 1 orange

Orange glaze
⅔ cup confectioners' sugar
1 tablespoon fresh orange juice
2–3 teaspoons hot water

Sift the flour, cornstarch, baking powder, and salt into a large bowl. • Stir in the granulated and vanilla sugars and the orange zest. • Use a pastry blender to cut in the butter until the mixture resembles coarse crumbs. • Use a fork to mix in the egg to form a smooth dough. • Press the dough into a disk, wrap in plastic wrap, and refrigerate for 30 minutes. • Set out two cookie sheets. • Roll out the dough on a lightly floured surface to a thickness of ⅛ inch. • Use a 1½-inch cookie cutter to cut out the cookies. Gather the dough scraps, re-roll, and continue cutting out cookies until all the dough is used. • Use a spatula to transfer the cookies to the cookie sheets, placing them 2 inches apart. • Almond-orange filling: Mix the almonds, brown sugar, and orange zest and juice in a small bowl. • Drop ½ teaspoon of the filling onto one half of each cookie. • Fold half of the cookie over the filling to make a crescent-shaped pocket. • Use a fork to seal the edges together and brush with a little milk. • Set aside for 30 minutes. • Preheat the oven to 350°F. • Bake for 8–10 minutes, or until just golden at the edges, rotating the sheets halfway through for even baking. • Transfer to racks to cool. • Orange glaze: Mix the confectioners' sugar with the orange juice. Add enough water to make a runny glaze. Drizzle over the cookies.

Makes 30–35 cookies · Prep: 40 min. + 60 min. to chill and rest · Cooking: 8–10 min. · Level: 2 · Keeps: 8 days

raspberry sandwiches

1¼ cups whole almonds +
½ cup flaked almonds
½ cup granulated sugar
1½ cups all-purpose flour
¾ cup (1½ sticks) butter, softened
1 large egg, separated
Grated zest of 1 lemon
1 teaspoon vanilla extract
½ teaspoon salt
1 cup raspberry preserves
1 tablespoon fresh lemon juice
⅓ cup confectioners' sugar

Process the 1¼ cups almonds, 2 tablespoons of the granulated sugar, and ¼ cup flour in a food processor or blender until very finely ground. • Beat the butter and remaining 6 tablespoons sugar in a large bowl with an electric mixer at high speed until creamy. • Add the egg yolk, lemon zest, and vanilla. • Mix in the almond mixture, remaining 1¼ cups flour, and salt to form a soft dough. • Divide the dough in half. Press the dough into two disks, wrap each in plastic wrap, and refrigerate for 30 minutes. • Preheat the oven to 350°F. • Line three cookie sheets with parchment paper. • Roll out half the dough on a lightly floured surface to a 12-inch square. • Cut into thirty-six 2-inch squares. • Use a ¾-inch cookie cutter to cut out the centers from half the squares. Gather the dough scraps, re-roll, and continue cutting out cookies until all the dough is used. • Use a spatula to transfer the cookies to the prepared cookie sheets, spacing them 1 inch apart. • Repeat with the remaining dough. • Beat the egg white in a small bowl until frothy and brush over the cookies. Sprinkle with the flaked almonds. • Bake, one sheet at a time, for 8–10 minutes, or until just golden. • Transfer to racks to cool. • Heat the raspberry preserves and lemon juice in a small saucepan over low heat until liquid. • Spoon over the whole squares and top with a holed cookie. • Dust with the confectioners' sugar.

Makes 36 cookies · Prep: 40 min. + 30 min. to chill · Cooking: 8–10 min. per batch · Level: 2 · Keeps: 5 days

Raspberry sandwiches

custard creams

These classically British cookies require custard powder, which is available as Bird's Custard Powder or Bird's Dessert Mix in the pudding section of most supermarkets.

1²/₃ cups all-purpose flour
1¹/₄ cups custard powder
1 cup granulated sugar
¹/₂ cup rice flour
1 teaspoon baking powder
¹/₈ teaspoon salt
³/₄ cup (1¹/₂ sticks) butter, cut up
¹/₄ cup milk
1 cup Italian Buttercream, Chocolate Buttercream, or Coffee Buttercream (see page 345)

Stir together the flour, custard powder, sugar, rice flour, baking powder, and salt in a large bowl. • Use a pastry blender to cut in the butter until the mixture resembles coarse crumbs. Pour in the milk to form a firm dough. • Press the dough into a disk, wrap in plastic wrap, and refrigerate for 30 minutes. • Preheat the oven to 350°F. · Set out two cookie sheets. • Transfer the dough to a lightly floured surface and roll out to a thickness of ¹/₄ inch. • Use a 1¹/₂-inch cookie cutter to cut out the cookies. • Gather the dough scraps, re-roll, and

until golden brown, rotating the sheets halfway through for even baking. • Transfer to racks to cool. • Melt the chocolate in a double boiler over barely simmering water. • Dip the cookies halfway into the melted chocolate and let stand for 30 minutes until set.

Makes 25–30 cookies · Prep: 45 min. + 60 min. to chill and set · Cooking: 10–15 min. · Level: 1 · Keeps: 5 days

sweet and spiced shapes

2 cups all-purpose flour
1 teaspoon baking powder
1 teaspoon ground cinnamon
¹/₂ teaspoon ground allspice
¹/₄ teaspoon ground cloves
¹/₈ teaspoon salt
3 large eggs
1¹/₂ cups granulated sugar
2¹/₂ cups finely ground almonds
4 oz semisweet chocolate, finely grated
¹/₂ cup finely chopped candied lemon peel
¹/₂ cup finely chopped candied orange peel
1 teaspoon finely grated lemon zest

Chocolate glaze
7 oz semisweet chocolate, coarsely chopped
3 tablespoons lukewarm water
2 tablespoons butter, cut up

Sift the flour, baking powder, cinnamon, allspice, cloves, and salt into a medium bowl. • Beat the eggs and sugar in a large bowl with an electric mixer at high speed until very pale and thick. • Mix in the dry ingredients, almonds, chocolate, candied lemon and orange peel, and lemon zest to form a smooth dough. • Press the dough into a disk, wrap in plastic wrap, and refrigerate for 30 minutes. • Preheat the oven to 325°F. • Line three cookie sheets with parchment paper. • Roll out the dough on a lightly floured surface to a thickness of ¹/₄ inch. • Cut into 2-inch squares and triangles. Gather the dough scraps, re-roll, and continue cutting out cookies until all the dough is used. • Use a spatula to transfer the cookies to the prepared cookie sheets, placing them 1 inch apart. • Bake, one sheet at a time, for 12–15 minutes, or until the edges are firm and the bottoms are

lightly browned. • Transfer to racks to cool. • Chocolate glaze: Melt the chocolate with the water in a double boiler over barely simmering water. • Stir in the butter until smooth. • Drizzle the glaze over the cookies and let stand on parchment paper for 30 minutes until completely set.

Makes 35–40 cookies · Prep: 50 min. + 60 min. to chill and set · Cooking: 12–15 min. per batch · Level: 2 · Keeps: 20 days, layered between parchment paper

chocolate-dipped orange cookies

1 cup all-purpose flour
¹/₈ teaspoon salt
¹/₃ cup butter, cut up
¹/₃ cup finely ground almonds
¹/₄ cup granulated sugar
1 tablespoon finely grated orange zest
1 large egg yolk, lightly beaten
2 tablespoons fresh orange juice
4 oz semisweet chocolate, coarsely chopped

Sift the flour and salt into a large bowl. • Use a pastry blender to cut in the butter until the mixture resembles fine crumbs. • Mix in the ground almonds, sugar, and orange zest. • Add the egg yolk and orange juice to form a smooth dough. • Press the dough into a disk, wrap in plastic wrap, and refrigerate for 30 minutes. • Preheat the oven to 350°F. • Line two cookie sheets with parchment paper. • Roll out the dough on a lightly floured surface to a thickness of ¹/₄ inch. • Use a 2-inch cookie cutter to cut out the cookies. Gather up the dough scraps, re-roll, and continue cutting out cookies until all the dough is used. • Use a spatula to transfer the cookies to the prepared cookie sheets, placing them 1 inch apart. • Bake for 10–15 minutes, or

shrewsbury cookies

These cookies take their name from a town on the English/Welsh border, where they have been enjoyed for centuries.

2¹/₂ cups all-purpose flour
1 teaspoon baking powder
¹/₈ teaspoon salt
¹/₂ cup (1 stick) butter
²/₃ cup granulated sugar
1 large egg
¹/₂ teaspoon almond extract
¹/₂ cup raspberry preserves

Sift the flour, baking powder, and salt into a medium bowl. • Beat the butter and sugar in a large bowl with an electric mixer at high speed until creamy. • Add the egg, beating until just blended. Add the almond extract. • Mix in the dry ingredients. Press the dough into a disk, wrap in plastic wrap, and refrigerate for 30 minutes. • Preheat the oven to 350°F. • Butter two cookie sheets. • Roll out the dough to a thickness of ¹/₄ inch. Use a 2-inch cookie cutter to stamp out rounds. • Use an apple corer to make a small hole in the center of half the rounds. • Gather the dough scraps, re-roll, and continue cutting out cookies until all the dough is used up. • Use a spatula to transfer the cookies to the prepared cookie

continue cutting out the cookies until all the dough is used. • Use a spatula to transfer the cookies to the cookie sheets, placing them 1 inch apart. • Bake for 12–15 minutes, or until lightly browned, rotating the sheets halfway through the baking to ensure even browning. • Transfer to racks to cool. • Stick pairs of cookies together with the buttercream.

Makes 15 cookies · Prep: 45 min. · Cooking: 12–15 min. · Level: 1 · Keeps: 2 days in the refrigerator

sheets. • Bake for 15–20 minutes, or until firm to the touch, rotating the sheets halfway through for even browning. • Transfer to racks to cool. • Spread the cookies without holes with the raspberry preserves. Top each one with a cookie that has a hole to make a sandwich, with preserves showing through the holes.

Makes 15 cookies · Prep: 30 min. + 30 min. to chill · Cooking: 15–20 min. · Level: 2 · Keeps: 7 days

citrus moons

- 1²/₃ cups all-purpose flour
- 1/8 teaspoon salt
- 1/2 cup (1 stick) butter, softened
- 3/4 cup confectioners' sugar
- 1 tablespoon Vanilla Sugar (see page 341)
- 1 large egg + 1 large egg yolk
- 1/2 teaspoon vanilla extract
  Grated zest of 1 orange
  Grated zest of 1/2 lemon

Topping
- 1 large egg yolk
- 1 tablespoon water
- 2 tablespoons flaked almonds

Sift the flour and salt into a medium bowl. • Beat the butter and confectioners' and vanilla sugars in a large bowl with an electric mixer at high speed until creamy. • Add the whole egg and egg yolk and vanilla, beating until just blended. • Mix in the dry ingredients to form a stiff dough. • Divide the dough in half. Knead the orange zest into one half and lemon zest into the other. • Press each dough into a disk, wrap in plastic wrap, and refrigerate for 30 minutes. • Preheat the oven to 350°F. • Set out three cookie sheets. • Roll out each dough half on a lightly floured surface to a thickness of 1/4 inch. • Use 2-inch crescent-shaped

cookie cutters to cut out the cookies. Gather the dough scraps, re-roll, and continue cutting out cookies until all the dough is used. • Use a spatula to transfer the cookies to the prepared cookie sheets, placing them 1 inch apart. • Topping: Beat the egg yolk with the water in a small bowl. Brush over the tops of the cookies and decorate with almonds. • Bake, one sheet at a time, for 8–10 minutes, or until firm to the touch and the edges are lightly golden. • Transfer to racks to cool.

Makes 20–25 cookies · Prep: 45 min. + 30 min. to chill · Cooking: 8–10 min. per batch · Level: 1 · Keeps: 1 month

chocolate cream sandwich cookies

- 1 cup all-purpose flour
- 1/3 cup custard powder
- 2 tablespoons unsweetened cocoa powder
- 1/8 teaspoon salt
- 1/2 cup (1 stick) butter, softened
- 1 cup granulated sugar
- 1 large egg, at room temperature
  superfine sugar, to sprinkle

Chocolate cream
- 3 tablespoons butter, softened
- 1/3 cup confectioners' sugar
- 2 tablespoons cocoa powder
- 1 teaspoon coffee extract

Sift the flour, custard powder, cocoa, and salt into a medium bowl. • Beat the butter and granulated sugar in a large bowl with an electric mixer at high speed until creamy. • Add the egg, beating until just blended. • Mix in the dry ingredients to form a stiff dough. Press the dough into a disk, wrap in plastic wrap, and refrigerate for 30 minutes. • Preheat the oven to 350°F. • Butter two cookie sheets. • Roll out to a thickness of 1/4 inch. Use a sharp knife to cut into 3 x 1-inch rectangles. • Arrange the cookies 1 inch apart on the prepared cookie sheets. Use a fork to prick all over and sprinkle with the superfine sugar. • Bake for 10–12 minutes, or until lightly browned rotating the sheets halfway through for even baking. • Cool the cookies completely on the sheets. • Chocolate cream: With mixer at high speed, beat the butter in a medium bowl until creamy. Gradually beat in the confectioners' sugar, cocoa, and coffee extract until well blended. • Stick the cookies together in pairs with the chocolate cream.

Makes 15 cookies · Prep: 45 min. · Cooking: 10–12 min. · Level: 1 · Keeps: 2 days in the refrigerator

pine nut and raisin cookies

- 1/3 cup golden raisins
- 2²/₃ cups all-purpose flour
- 2 teaspoons baking powder
- 1/8 teaspoon salt
- 1/2 cup granulated sugar
- 1/3 cup extra-virgin olive oil
- 1/3 cup water
- 1/3 cup pine nuts

Plump the raisins in hot water to cover in a small bowl for 10 minutes. • Drain well and pat dry with paper towels. • Sift the flour, baking powder, and salt into a large bowl and make a well in the center. • Mix in the sugar, olive oil, and water to form a smooth dough. • Knead in the raisins and pine nuts. Press the dough into a disk, wrap in plastic wrap, and refrigerate for 30 minutes. • Preheat the oven to 350°F. • Butter two cookie sheets. • Roll out the dough on a lightly floured surface to a thickness of 1/4 inch. • Use a 2-inch cookie cutter to cut out the cookies. Gather the dough scraps, re-roll, and continue cutting out cookies until all the dough is used. • Use a spatula to transfer the cookies to the prepared cookie sheets, placing them 1 inch apart. • Bake for 15–20 minutes, or until just golden, rotating the sheets halfway through for even baking. • Transfer to racks to cool.

Makes 30 cookies · Prep: 40 min. · Cooking: 15–20 min. · Level: 1 · Keeps: 10 days

Chocolate cream sandwich cookies

victorian almond jumbles

This English recipe dates from the 1870s. The first recipes for jumbles appeared in Elizabethan times, but today these cookies are more likely to be found in the United States, where they have been popular since the 18th century.

- 1/2   cup (1 stick) butter, softened
- 3/4   cup granulated sugar
- 1 1/2   cups all-purpose flour
- 2/3   cup finely ground almonds
- 1/8   teaspoon salt
-       Juice of 1 lemon

Beat the butter and sugar in a large bowl with an electric mixer at high speed until creamy. • Mix in the flour, almonds, and salt. • Add the lemon juice to form a stiff dough. • Press the dough into a disk, wrap in plastic wrap, and refrigerate for 30 minutes. • Preheat the oven to 375°F. • Butter a cookie sheet. • Roll out the dough on a lightly floured surface to a thickness of 1/4 inch. • Use a 2-inch cookie cutter to cut out the cookies. Gather the dough scraps, re-roll, and continue cutting out cookies until all the dough is used. • Use a spatula to transfer the cookies to the prepared cookie sheet, placing them 2 inches apart. • Bake for 12–15 minutes, or until pale golden. • Cool on the sheet until the cookies firm slightly. • Transfer to racks to cool.

Makes 12–16 cookies · Prep: 40 min. + 30 min. to chill · Cooking: 12–15 min. · Level: 1 · Keeps: 7 days

ginger cookies

- 2 1/3   cups all-purpose flour
- 2   teaspoons ground ginger
- 1   teaspoon baking powder
- 1   teaspoon baking soda
- 1/8   teaspoon salt
- 1   cup light corn syrup
- 1/2   cup (1 stick) butter, softened
- 3/4   cup granulated sugar

Sift the flour, ginger, baking powder, baking soda, and salt into a large bowl. • Heat the corn syrup in a small saucepan over low heat until liquid. • Beat the butter and sugar in a large bowl with an electric mixer at high speed until creamy. • Mix in the dry ingredients. • Make a well in the center and pour in the corn syrup to form a smooth dough. Press the dough into a disk, wrap in plastic wrap, and refrigerate for 30 minutes. • Preheat the oven to 350°F. • Butter four cookie sheets. • Turn the dough out onto a lightly floured surface and roll out to a thickness of 1/4 inch. • Use a 2-inch cookie

cutter to cut out the cookies. Gather the dough scraps, re-roll, and continue cutting out cookies until all the dough is used. • Use a spatula to transfer the cookies to the prepared cookie sheets, placing them 1 inch apart. • Bake, one batch at a time, for 15–20 minutes, or until lightly browned. • Transfer to racks to cool.

Makes 40 cookies · Prep: 40 min. · Cooking: 15–20 min. per batch · Level: 1 · Keeps: 5 days

golden raisin cookies

- 1/2   cup golden raisins
- 1 1/2   cups all-purpose flour
- 1   teaspoon baking powder
- 1/8   teaspoon salt
- 1/2   cup granulated sugar
- 1/3   cup butter, cut up
- 1   large egg, lightly beaten
- 3   tablespoons dry white wine
-       Grated zest of 1 lemon

Plump the raisins in hot water to cover in a small bowl for 10 minutes. • Drain well and pat dry with paper towels. • Sift the flour, baking powder, and salt into a large bowl. • Stir in the sugar. • Use a pastry blender to cut in the butter until the mixture resembles coarse crumbs. • Mix in the egg, wine, and lemon zest to form a smooth dough. Knead in the raisins until well blended. • Press the dough into a disk, wrap in plastic wrap, and refrigerate for 30 minutes. • Preheat the oven to 400°F. • Butter two cookie sheets. • Roll out the dough on a lightly floured surface to a thickness of 1/4 inch. • Use a 2-inch cookie cutter to cut out the cookies. Gather the dough scraps, re-roll, and continue cutting out cookies until all the dough is used. • Use a spatula to transfer the cookies to the prepared cookie sheets, spacing them 1 inch apart. • Bake for 12–15 minutes, or until just golden, rotating the sheets halfway through for even baking. • Transfer to racks to cool.

Makes 25 cookies · Prep: 40 min. + 30 min. to chill Cooking: 12–15 min. · Level: 1 · Keeps: 5 days

old english jumbles

- 1/3   cup rose water
- 1 1/2   cups finely ground almonds
- 1   cup all-purpose flour
- 1/3   cup butter, cut up
- 3/4   cup granulated sugar + more for sprinkling
- 2   tablespoons light cream
- 1   large egg white, lightly beaten

Mix 1 tablespoon rose water into the almonds in a small bowl to prevent them from becoming oily. • Sift the flour into a large bowl. • Use a pastry blender to cut in the butter until the mixture resembles fine crumbs. • Stir in the 3/4 cup sugar, almond mixture, and the cream. • Add the egg white and enough of the remaining rose water to form a stiff dough. • Press the dough into a disk, wrap in plastic wrap, and refrigerate for 30 minutes. • Preheat the oven to 325°F. • Set out two cookie sheets. • Roll out the dough on a lightly floured surface to a thickness of 1/4 inch. • Use a knife to cut out S-shaped cookies. Gather the dough scraps, re-roll, and continue cutting out cookies until all the dough is used. • Use a spatula to transfer the cookies to the cookie sheets, placing them 2 inches apart. • Bake for 10–15 minutes, or until just golden, rotating the sheets halfway through for even baking. • Sprinkle with a little sugar. • Transfer to racks to cool.

Makes 18–24 cookies · Prep: 25 min. + 30 min. to chill · Cooking: 10–15 min. · Level: 2 · Keeps: 7 days

jumble rings

- 1   cup all-purpose flour
- 1/3   cup finely ground almonds
- 1/2   cup granulated sugar
- 1/8   teaspoon salt
- 1/2   cup (1 stick) butter, cut up
- 1   large egg, lightly beaten

Stir together the flour, almonds, sugar, and salt in a medium bowl. • Use a pastry blender to cut in the butter until the mixture resembles coarse crumbs. • Add enough beaten egg to form a smooth dough. Press the dough into a disk, wrap in plastic wrap, and refrigerate for 30 minutes. • Preheat the oven to 350°F. • Butter a cookie sheet. • Roll out the dough on a lightly floured surface to a thickness of 1/4 inch. • Trim the edges into a square. Cut into 4-inch logs and form into rings. • Use a spatula to transfer the cookies to the prepared cookie sheet, placing them 1 inch apart. • Bake for 10–12 minutes, or until just golden. • Transfer to racks and let cool completely.

Makes 12–16 cookies · Prep: 40 min. + 30 min. to chill · Cooking: 10–12 min. · Level: 1 · Keeps: 2 weeks

Jumble rings and Old English jumbles

lavender lights

Throughout history, lavender has been used to calm and soothe. These cookies make an ideal treat after a stressful day.

1¼ cups all-purpose flour
1   teaspoon baking powder
⅛   teaspoon salt
⅓   cup butter
¼   cup granulated sugar
1   large egg yolk
2   tablespoons fresh lavender leaves, rinsed, dried, and chopped
1   teaspoon lavender flowers (heads only), rinsed and dried

Preheat the oven to 450°F. • Line two cookie sheets with parchment paper. • Sift the flour, baking powder, and salt into a large bowl. • Beat the butter and sugar in a large bowl with an electric mixer at high speed until creamy. • Add the egg yolk, beating until just blended. • Mix in the dry ingredients and lavender leaves. • Turn the dough out onto a lightly floured surface and knead to form a soft dough. • Roll out the dough to a thickness of ¼ inch. • Sprinkle the dough with the lavender flowers, pressing in the heads with a rolling pin. • Use 2-inch cookie cutters to cut out the cookies. Gather the dough scraps, re-roll, and continue cutting out cookies until all the dough is used. • Use a spatula to transfer the cookies to the prepared cookie sheets. • Bake for 10–12 minutes, or until firm to the touch and lightly browned, rotating the sheets halfway through for even baking. • Transfer to racks to cool.

Makes about 20 cookies · Prep: 20 min. · Cooking: 10–12 min. · Level: 1 · Keeps: 8 days

Flower cookies

tea leaves

3–4 tablespoons lukewarm water (105°–115°F)
1   package (½ oz each) active dry yeast or ¾ oz fresh yeast
1⅔   cups all-purpose flour
⅛   teaspoon salt
¼   cup (½ stick) cold butter, cut up
4–5 tablespoons granulated sugar

Preheat the oven to 325°F. • Line a cookie sheet with parchment paper. • Stir together the water and yeast. Set aside for 10 minutes, or until frothy. • Sift the flour and salt into a large bowl. • Use a pastry blender to cut in the butter. • Use a fork to stir in the yeast mixture. • Turn out onto a lightly floured surface and knead the mixture into a smooth dough. • Roll out the dough to a thickness of ⅛ inch. • Use a 2-inch leaf-shaped cookie cutter to cut out the cookies. • Gather the dough scraps, re-roll, and continue cutting out the cookies until all the dough is used. • Sprinkle a surface with sugar and place the rounds on top. Use a rolling pin to roll over both sides of the rounds to form very thin sugar-coated leaf shapes. • Use a spatula to transfer the cookies to the prepared baking sheet, placing them 1 inch apart. • Bake for 5–8 minutes, or until golden brown. Turn over and bake for 5 minutes more, or until golden brown. • Transfer to racks to cool.

Makes 24 cookies · Prep: 40 min. · Cooking: 10–13 min. · Level: 2 · Keeps: 3 days

flower cookies

Nesquik can be found in the instant drinks aisle of your local supermarket.

1⅓   cups all-purpose flour
⅔   cup chocolate or strawberry flavor powder, such as Nesquik
⅓   cup confectioners' sugar
1   teaspoon baking powder
⅛   teaspoon salt
⅔   cup butter, softened

Topping
⅓   cup strawberry preserves
1   tablespoon water
     Sugar confetti, chopped nuts, or chocolate flakes, to decorate

Frosting
¾   cup confectioners' sugar
1   tablespoon strawberry or cranberry juice, or more as needed

Sift the flour, Nesquik, confectioners' sugar, baking powder, and salt into a large bowl. •

Gradually beat in the butter with an electric mixer fitted with a dough hook at low speed until just blended. • Continue beating at high speed until well blended. • Turn the dough out onto a lightly floured surface and knead until smooth. • Press the dough into a disk, wrap in plastic wrap, and refrigerate for 30 minutes. • Preheat the oven to 350°F. • Line two cookie sheets with parchment paper. • Roll out the dough on a lightly floured surface to a thickness of ⅛ inch. • Use a 1½-inch flower cutter to cut out the cookies. Gather the dough scraps, re-roll, and continue cutting out cookies until all the dough is used. • Use a spatula to transfer the cookies to the prepared cookies sheets, placing them 1 inch apart. • Bake for 8–10 minutes, or until the edges are firm, rotating the sheets halfway through for even baking. • Using the parchment paper as handles, lift the cookies onto a rack. Carefully peel off the paper and let cool completely. • <u>Topping</u>: Strain the preserves into a small saucepan. • Add the water and bring to a boil, stirring constantly. Simmer for 3 minutes, or until thickened. • Spoon a little preserves in the center of each cookie. • Sprinkle with the sugar confetti, chopped nuts, or chocolate flakes. • <u>Frosting</u>: Mix the confectioners' sugar with just enough juice to make a thick frosting. • Spoon the frosting into a small freezer bag and cut off a tiny corner. • Pipe over the cookies in a decorative manner to resemble petals.

Makes 50–60 cookies · Prep: 55 min. + 30 min. to chill · Cooking: 8–10 min. · Level: 2 · Keeps: 8 days

jam-filled turnovers

4   cups all-purpose flour
1   tablespoon baking powder
⅛   teaspoon salt
1   cup granulated sugar
⅔   cup butter, cut up
3   large eggs, lightly beaten
3   tablespoons dark rum
⅓   cup cherry or plum preserves
     Confectioners' sugar, to dust

Preheat the oven to 375°F. • Butter and flour two cookie sheets. • Sift the flour, baking powder, and salt into a large bowl. Stir in the sugar. • Use a pastry blender to cut in the butter until the mixture resembles coarse crumbs. • Mix in the eggs and rum to form a smooth dough. • Shape into a ball, wrap in plastic wrap, and let stand for 1 hour. • Roll out the dough on a lightly floured surface to a thickness of $1/4$ inch. Use a 3-inch cookie cutter to cut out the cookies. • Place 1 teaspoon preserves in the center of each round. Fold over and form crescent shapes, sealing the edges. • Place the turnovers 1 inch apart on the prepared cookie sheets. • Bake for 25–30 minutes, or until lightly browned, rotating the sheets halfway through for even baking. • Transfer to racks to cool. Dust with confectioners' sugar before serving.

Makes about 15 cookies · Prep: 40 min. + 1 hr. to stand · Cooking: 25–30 min. · Level: 2 · Keeps: 7 days

cream crescents

4   cups all-purpose flour
1   tablespoon baking powder
1   cup granulated sugar
1   cup (2 sticks) butter, softened
    Grated zest of 1 lemon
2   large egg yolks
$1/8$ teaspoon salt

Filling
3   large egg yolks
3   tablespoons granulated sugar
3   tablespoons all-purpose flour
2   cups milk
$1/8$ teaspoon salt
$1/2$ teaspoon vanilla extract
$2/3$ cup confectioners' sugar

Sift the flour and baking powder into a large bowl and make a well in the center. Stir in the sugar, butter, lemon zest, egg yolks, and salt. Use your hands to work the dough together. Press the dough into a disk, wrap in plastic wrap, and refrigerate for 30 minutes. • Preheat the oven to 350°F. • Butter and flour a large baking sheet. • Roll out the dough on a lightly floured surface to $1/4$-inch thick. Use a pastry cutter to cut into 2-inch rounds. Gather the dough scraps, re-roll, and continue cutting out rounds until all the dough is used. • Filling: Beat the egg yolks and sugar in a large bowl with an electric mixer at high speed until pale and thick. Use a large rubber spatula to fold in the flour. • Bring the milk to a boil with the salt and vanilla. Stir the hot milk mixture into the beaten egg yolks. Cook over low heat, stirring constantly, until thick. • Press a piece of plastic wrap directly on the surface and set aside to cool completely. • Place spoonfuls of the filling on the pastry rounds. Fold in half to form crescent-shapes, sealing the edges. • Place on the prepared

baking sheet. • Bake for 15–20 minutes, or until lightly browned. • Cool the crescents completely on the baking sheet. • Dust with confectioners' sugar before serving.

Makes 15 filled cookies · Prep: 30 min. · Cooking: 15–20 min. · Level: 2 · Keeps: 2 days

peruvian cookies

$2^{1/4}$ cups all-purpose flour
$2/3$ cup confectioners' sugar
$1/8$ teaspoon salt
1   cup (2 sticks) butter, softened
1   tablespoon warm water, + more as needed

Spice honey
2   cups firmly packed dark brown sugar
1   stick cinnamon
2   cloves
    Zest of 1 orange, in one piece
1   cup water
$1/4$ teaspoon white vinegar

Sift the flour, confectioners' sugar, and salt into a large bowl. Use a pastry blender to cut in the butter until the mixture resembles coarse crumbs. Add the water to form a stiff dough. • Press the dough into a disk, wrap in plastic wrap, and refrigerate for 30 minutes. • Preheat the oven to 375°F. • Line two cookie sheets with parchment paper. • Roll out the dough on a lightly floured surface to a thickness of $1/8$ inch. • Use a $2^{1/2}$-inch cookie cutter to cut out the cookies. Gather the dough scraps, re-roll, and continue cutting out cookies until all the dough is used. • Use a spatula to transfer the cookies to the prepared cookie sheets, spacing them 1 inch apart. • Bake for 10–12 minutes, or until just golden, rotating the sheets halfway through for even baking. • Transfer to racks and let cool completely. • Spice honey: Place the brown sugar, cinnamon, cloves, orange zest, and water in a medium saucepan. • Wash down the sides of the pan with a pastry brush dipped in cold water to prevent sugar crystals from forming. Cook, without stirring, until the mixture reaches 238°F, or the soft-ball stage. • Stir in the vinegar, discard the cloves, cinnamon stick, and orange zest, and remove from the heat. • Let cool completely. • Stick the cookies together in pairs with the spice honey.

Makes 30 cookies · Prep: 55 min. + 30 min. to chill Cooking: 10–12 min. · Level: 2 · Keeps: 7 days

jelly-filled hearts

$2^{1/2}$ cups all-purpose flour
$1/4$ teaspoon salt
1   cup (2 sticks) butter, softened
1   cup finely ground almonds
$1/2$ cup granulated sugar
$1/4$ cup milk, + more as needed
1   large egg, lightly beaten
$1/4$ cup raspberry preserves

Sift the flour and salt into a large bowl. • Use a pastry blender to cut in the butter until the mixture resembles fine crumbs. • Mix in the almonds and sugar. • Stir in enough milk to form a stiff dough. • Press the dough into a disk, wrap in plastic wrap, and refrigerate for 30 minutes. • Preheat the oven to 350°F. • Butter two cookie sheets. • Roll out the dough on a lightly floured surface to a thickness of $1/4$ inch. • Use a 3-inch heart-shaped cookie cutter to cut out 48 cookies. • Use a spatula to transfer 24 of the cookies to the prepared cookie sheets, spacing them 1 inch apart. • Use a 2-inch heart-shaped cookie cutter to cut out the centers from twelve of the cookies. Set aside the cookies with cut-out centers. • Gather the dough scraps, including the leftover hearts, re-roll, and continue cutting out cookies and outlines until all the dough is used. • Brush the edges of the whole cookies with the beaten egg and place the hearts with the cut-out centers on top to raise the edges. • Bake for 15–20 minutes, or until golden brown, rotating the sheets halfway through for even baking. • Drop teaspoons of the preserves into the cookie centers. • Transfer to racks to cool.

Makes 24 cookies · Prep: 40 min. + 30 min. to chill Cooking: 15–20 min. · Level: 2 · Keeps: 10 days

Jelly-filled hearts

cookie hands

2 cups all-purpose flour
1 teaspoon baking powder
1/4 teaspoon salt
1/2 cup (1 stick) butter, softened
1/2 cup granulated sugar
1 tablespoon milk
1/2 teaspoon vanilla extract
1 large egg
1/4 cup confectioners' sugar
1 tablespoon hot water, + more as needed
Candy pieces, to decorate

Sift the flour, baking powder, and salt into a medium bowl. • Beat the butter and granulated sugar in a large bowl with an electric mixer at high speed until creamy. • Add the milk, vanilla, and egg. • Mix in the dry ingredients. • Divide the dough in half. Press the dough into disks, wrap in plastic wrap, and refrigerate for 30 minutes. • Preheat the oven to 350°F. • Butter two cookie sheets. • Roll out the dough on a lightly floured surface to a thickness of 1/4 inch. • Place outstretched hand, palm down, on the dough and use a knife to cut around the outline. • Gather the dough scraps, re-roll, and continue cutting out cookies until all the dough is used. • Arrange on the prepared cookie sheets, placing them 1/2 inch apart. • Bake for 10–12 minutes, or until just golden at the edges, rotating the sheets halfway through for even baking. • Transfer to racks to cool. • Mix the confectioners' sugar with enough water to form a paste. Attach the candies to the ends of the fingertips as nails.

Makes 6 cookies · Prep: 40 min. + 30 min. to chill · Cooking: 10–12 min. · Level: 2 · Keeps: 5 days

bran cookies

1 cup all-purpose flour
1 teaspoon baking powder
1/8 teaspoon salt
1/2 cup (1 stick) butter, softened
1/3 cup granulated sugar
1 large egg
1 cup bran flakes
1 cup whole-wheat flour

Sift the all-purpose flour, baking powder, and salt into a large bowl. • Beat the butter and sugar in a large bowl with an electric mixer at high speed until creamy. • Add the egg, beating until just blended. • Mix in the dry ingredients, followed by the bran flakes and whole-wheat flour. • Preheat the oven to 350°F. • Set out two cookie sheets. • Press the dough into a disk, wrap in plastic wrap, and

refrigerate for 30 minutes. • Roll out the dough on a lightly floured surface. Use a 2-inch cookie cutter to cut out the cookies. Gather the dough scraps, re-roll, and continue cutting out cookies until all the dough is used. • Use a spatula to transfer the cookies to the cookie sheets, placing them 1 inch apart. • Bake for 12–15 minutes, or until lightly browned, rotating the sheets halfway through for even baking. • Transfer to racks to cool.

Makes 30 cookies · Prep: 20 min. + 30 min. to chill Cooking: 12–15 min. · Level: 1 · Keeps: 2 weeks

easter currant cookies

1 1/4 cups all-purpose flour
1 teaspoon baking powder
1/8 teaspoon salt
1/3 cup butter, softened
1 cup granulated sugar
1 large egg, lightly beaten
1 tablespoon dried currants

Preheat the oven to 325°F. • Butter a cookie sheet. • Sift the flour, baking powder, and salt into a medium bowl. • Beat the butter and sugar in a large bowl with an electric mixer at high speed until creamy. • Add the egg, beating until just blended. • Mix in the flour to form a smooth dough. • Knead in the currants. • Transfer the dough to a lightly floured surface and roll out to a thickness of 1/4 inch. • Use a 3-inch cookie cutter to cut out the cookies. • Gather the dough scraps, re-roll, and continue cutting out the cookies until all the dough is used. • Arrange on the prepared cookie sheets, placing them 1 inch apart. • Bake for 10–15 minutes, or until lightly browned. • Transfer to racks to cool.

Makes 8 cookies · Prep: 40 min. · Cooking: 10–15 min. · Level: 1 · Keeps: 5 days

chocolate-flecked cookies

2 2/3 cups all-purpose flour
1/8 teaspoon salt
1 1/4 cups granulated sugar
3/4 cup (1 1/2 sticks) butter, softened
1 large egg + 2 large egg yolks
3 oz semisweet chocolate, coarsely grated

Sift the flour and salt into a large bowl. • Use a wooden spoon to mix in the sugar, butter, egg and egg yolks, and chocolate to form a smooth dough. Press the dough into a disk, wrap in plastic wrap, and refrigerate for 30 minutes. • Preheat the oven to 350°F. • Butter three cookie sheets. • Roll out the dough on a lightly floured surface to a thickness of 1/4

inch. • Use a 2-inch cookie cutter to cut out the cookies. Gather the dough scraps, re-roll, and continue cutting out cookies until all the dough is used. • Use a spatula to transfer the cookies to the prepared cookie sheets, placing them 1 inch apart. • Bake, one sheet at a time, for 10–15 minutes, or until just golden. • Transfer the cookies to racks to cool.

Makes 34 cookies · Prep: 40 min. + 30 min. to chill · Cooking: 10–15 min. per batch · Level: 1 · Keeps: 10 days

smiling face cookies

Strikingly decorated smiley cookies make ideal decorations on the table at children's birthday parties.

3 1/4 cups all-purpose flour
1/4 teaspoon salt
1 cup (2 sticks) butter, softened
1 1/3 cups granulated sugar
1 large egg, lightly beaten
1/2 teaspoon vanilla extract
14 oz ready-to-roll pink fondant icing
White candy writer, to decorate

Sift the flour and salt into a medium bowl. • Beat the butter and sugar in a large bowl with an electric mixer at high speed until creamy. • Add the egg and vanilla, beating until just blended. • Mix in the dry ingredients to form a soft dough. • Press the dough into a disk, wrap in plastic wrap, and refrigerate for 30 minutes. • Preheat the oven to 400°F. • Butter two cookie sheets. • Roll out the dough on a lightly floured surface to a thickness of 1/4 inch. • Use a 2-inch cookie cutter to cut out the cookies. Gather up the dough scraps, re-roll, and continue cutting out cookies until all the dough is used. • Use a spatula to transfer the cookies to the prepared cookie sheets, placing them 1 inch apart. • Bake for 6–8 minutes, or until golden brown, rotating the sheets halfway through for even baking. • Cool on the sheets until the cookies firm slightly. Transfer to racks to finish cooling. • Roll out the icing on a surface lightly dusted with confectioners' sugar. Cut out rounds using the same cutter as for the cookies. • Brush the cookies lightly with cold water and place an icing circle on top of each one, pressing down gently. • Pipe a happy face on top of each cookie.

Makes 20–25 cookies · Prep: 40 min. + 30 min. to chill · Cooking: 6–8 min. · Level: 1 · Keeps: 7 days

Smiling face cookies and Cookie hands

baseler leckerli

The word lecker *means delicious in German. In Switzerland, leckerli are special finger-length cookies that are baked for holidays and the pre-Lenten carnival. They are made with honey, nuts, and spices, and arguably the best and most famous come from Basel.*

4 cups all-purpose flour, or more as needed
1 teaspoon baking soda
1/8 teaspoon salt
1 cup honey
1 1/2 cups granulated sugar
1 tablespoon ground cinnamon
1 teaspoon cloves, very finely chopped
1 1/2 cups blanched almonds, coarsely chopped
1 1/2 cups unblanched almonds, coarsely chopped
2/3 cup candied lemon peel, finely chopped
2/3 cup candied orange peel, finely chopped
1/3 cup kirsch

Glaze
1 1/3 cups confectioners' sugar, or more as needed
1 tablespoon hot water, or more as needed
1 tablespoon fresh lemon juice
1 tablespoon dark rum

Preheat the oven to 350°F. • Butter and flour two cookie sheets. • Sift the flour, baking soda, and salt into a large bowl. • Heat the honey in a medium saucepan over low heat until liquid. Stir in the sugar, cinnamon, cloves, both almonds, and the candied lemon and orange peel. • Remove from the heat. • Mix in the dry ingredients and kirsch. • Shape the warm mixture into a ball and knead on a lightly floured surface until smooth. • If it is sticky, add more flour. • Roll out the dough to a thickness of 1/4 inch. Use a sharp knife to cut into 2-inch rectangles. • Place the rectangles closely together on the prepared baking sheets. • Bake for 15–20 minutes, or until lightly browned, rotating the sheets halfway through for even baking. Transfer the cookies to racks and let cool to warm. • Glaze: Mix the confectioners' sugar with the water in a small bowl. Add lemon juice and rum to make a pouring consistency. Add more water if needed. • Thinly brush the glaze on the hot cookies and let cool completely.

Makes 50 cookies · Prep: 45 min. · Cooking: 15–20 min. · Level: 2 · Keeps: 20 days

honey crisps

2 1/3 cups all-purpose flour
1/2 cup granulated sugar
1 large egg
1/3 cup butter, softened
2 tablespoons water

1 teaspoon baking soda
2 teaspoons honey
1/8 teaspoon salt
2 teaspoons milk

Use a wooden spoon to mix the flour, sugar, egg, butter, water, baking soda, honey, and salt in a large bowl to form a smooth dough. Press the dough into a disk, wrap in plastic wrap, and refrigerate for 30 minutes. • Preheat the oven to 350°F. • Butter two cookie sheets. • Roll out the dough on a lightly floured surface to a thickness of 1/4 inch. • Use a knife to cut out squares. Gather the dough scraps, re-roll, and continue cutting out cookies until all the dough is used. • Use a spatula to transfer the cookies to the prepared cookie sheets, placing them 1 inch apart. • Brush with the milk. • Bake for 10–15 minutes, or until just golden at the edges, rotating the sheets halfway through for even baking. • Transfer to racks to cool.

Makes 25 cookies · Prep: 35 min. + 30 min. to chill Cooking: 10–15 min. · Level: 1 · Keeps: 7 days

golden crisps

Substitute cornstarch for the arrowroot if unavailable.

1 1/3 cups all-purpose flour
1/4 cup arrowroot starch
1/2 cup (1 stick) butter, softened
2/3 cup granulated sugar
1 large egg + 1 large egg yolk, lightly beaten

Sift the flour and arrowroot into a large bowl. • Use a pastry blender to cut in the butter until the mixture resembles fine crumbs. • Stir in the sugar. • Add the egg and egg yolk to form a stiff dough. • Press the dough into a disk, wrap in plastic wrap, and refrigerate for 30 minutes. • Preheat the oven to 425°F. • Butter two cookie sheets. • Roll out the dough on a lightly floured surface to a thickness of 1/4 inch. • Use a 2-inch cookie cutter to cut out the cookies. • Gather the dough scraps, re-roll, and continue cutting out cookies until all the dough is used. • Use a spatula to transfer the cookies to the cookie sheets, placing them 1 inch apart. • Bake for 10–15 minutes, or until deep golden brown, rotating the sheets halfway through for even baking. • Transfer to racks to cool.

Makes 20–25 cookies · Prep: 40 min. + 30 min. to chill · Cooking: 10–15 min. · Level: 1 · Keeps: 5 days

buttermilk cookies

Buttermilk used to be the thin liquid left in the churn after the butter had been made. Today's buttermilk is a cultured, thick, slightly tangy milk that adds tenderness to baked goods.

1 cup all-purpose flour
1 teaspoon baking powder
1/2 teaspoon baking soda
1/8 teaspoon salt
1/3 cup butter, cut up
2 tablespoons granulated sugar
3/4 cup buttermilk

Preheat the oven to 350°F. • Butter a cookie sheet. • Sift the flour, baking powder, baking soda, and salt into a large bowl. Stir in the sugar. • Use a pastry blender to cut in the butter until the mixture resembles fine crumbs. • Stir in the buttermilk to form a smooth dough. • Roll out the dough on a lightly floured surface to a thickness of 1/2 inch. • Use a 2-inch cookie cutter to cut out the cookies. • Gather the dough scraps, re-roll, and continue cutting out cookies until all the dough is used. • Use a spatula to transfer the cookies to the prepared cookie sheet, placing them 1 inch apart. • Bake for 10–15 minutes, or until lightly browned. • Transfer to racks to cool.

Makes 12–16 cookies · Prep: 40 min. · Cooking: 10–15 min. · Level: 1 · Keeps: 5 days

rice flour cookies

1/2 cup (1 stick) butter, softened
2/3 cup granulated sugar
1 1/2 cups rice flour
2 large eggs, lightly beaten

Beat the butter and sugar in a large bowl with an electric mixer at high speed until creamy. • Mix in the rice flour. • Add the eggs, beating to form a smooth dough. • Press the dough into a disk, wrap in plastic wrap, and refrigerate for 30 minutes. • Preheat the oven to 300°F. • Butter two cookie sheets. • Roll out the dough on a lightly floured surface to a thickness of 1/4 inch. • Use a 2-inch cookie cutter to cut out the cookies. • Gather the dough scraps, re-roll, and continue cutting out cookies until all the dough is used. • Use a spatula to transfer the cookies to the cookie sheets, placing them 1 inch apart. • Bake for 15–20 minutes, or until just golden, rotating the sheets halfway through for even baking. • Transfer to racks to cool.

Makes 18–22 cookies · Prep: 40 min. + 30 min. to chill · Cooking: 10–15 min. · Level: 1 · Keeps: 5 days

sherry tea cakes

These cookies date from around 1780. This is an English recipe, but similar ones can be found in cookbooks used in the southern seaboard states of colonial America.

1/2   cup (1 stick) butter, cut up
1   tablespoon half-and-half
12/3   cups all-purpose flour
2/3   cup granulated sugar
11/2   teaspoons caraway seeds
1/2   teaspoon freshly grated nutmeg
1/8   teaspoon salt
1   large egg yolk
1   tablespoon sweet sherry

Melt the butter with the cream in a small saucepan over low heat. • Transfer to a large bowl. • Mix in the flour, sugar, caraway seeds, nutmeg, and salt. • Beat the egg yolk and sherry in a small bowl until frothy. • Stir the egg mixture into the dry ingredients to form a stiff dough. • Press the dough into a disk, wrap in plastic wrap, and refrigerate for 1 hour. • Preheat the oven to 325°F. • Butter two cookie sheets. • Roll out the dough on a lightly floured surface to a thickness of 1/4 inch. • Use a 2-inch cookie cutter to cut out the cookies. • Gather the dough scraps, re-roll, and continue cutting out cookies until all the dough is used. • Use a spatula to transfer the cookies to the cookie sheets, placing them 1 inch apart. • Bake for 10–15 minutes, or until just golden, rotating the sheets halfway through for even baking. • Transfer to racks to cool.

Makes 18–22 cookies · Prep: 40 min. + 1 hr. to chill Cooking: 10–15 min. · Level: 1 · Keeps: 3 days

tunbridge wells crisps

In 1606, the tutor to the Prince of Wales enjoyed the natural waters at the British village of Tunbridge in Kent. Since that time, Tunbridge Wells has developed into an elegant spa town.

11/4   cups all-purpose flour
1   teaspoon ground ginger
1/2   teaspoon baking powder
1/8   teaspoon salt
1/4   cup (1/2 stick) butter, cut up
1/4   cup firmly packed light brown sugar
1/4   cup light molasses

Sift the flour, ginger, baking powder, and salt into a medium bowl. • Melt the butter with the brown sugar and molasses in a medium saucepan over low heat. • Remove from the heat and mix in the dry ingredients to form a stiff dough. • Press the dough into a disk, wrap in plastic wrap, and refrigerate for 1 hour. • Preheat the oven to 325°F. • Butter

two cookie sheets. • Roll out the dough on a lightly floured surface to a thickness of 1/4 inch. • Use a 2-inch cookie cutter to cut out the cookies. • Gather the dough scraps, re-roll, and continue cutting out cookies until all the dough is used. • Use a spatula to transfer the cookies to the prepared cookie sheets, placing them 1 inch apart. • Bake for 10–15 minutes, or until firm to the touch and just golden, rotating the sheets halfway through for even baking. • Transfer to racks to cool.

Makes 18–22 cookies · Prep: 40 min. + 1 hr. to chill Cooking: 10–15 min. · Level: 1 · Keeps: 5 days

whetstone cookies

These cookies are named after the town of Whetstone in central England and date from 1741.

11/2   cups all-purpose flour
1/8   teaspoon salt
1   cup granulated sugar
1   teaspoon caraway seeds
1   large egg yolk + 3 large egg whites
1   tablespoon rose water

Sift the flour and salt into a medium bowl. • Stir in the sugar and caraway seeds. • Beat in the egg yolk and egg whites and rose water to form a stiff dough. • Press the dough into a disk, wrap in plastic wrap, and refrigerate for 30 minutes. • Preheat the oven to 325°F. • Butter two cookie sheets. • Roll out the dough on a lightly floured surface to a thickness of 1/8 inch. • Use a 2-inch cookie cutter to cut out the cookies. Gather the dough scraps, re-roll, and continue cutting out cookies until all the dough is used. • Use a spatula to transfer the cookies to the prepared cookie sheets, placing them 1 inch apart. • Bake for 10–15 minutes or until golden brown, rotating the sheets halfway through for even baking. • Cool on the sheets until the cookies firm slightly. • Transfer to racks to finish cooling.

Makes 24–30 cookies · Prep: 40 min. + 30 min. to chill · Cooking: 10–15 min. · Level: 1 · Keeps: 2 weeks

derwentwater cookies

These cookies are traditionally made around Lake Derwentwater, one of the most beautiful lakes in the United Kingdom.

12/3   cups all-purpose flour
1/8   teaspoon salt
1/2   cup (1 stick) butter, softened
1/2   cup granulated sugar
2   large eggs
2/3   cup currants

Sift the flour and salt into a medium bowl. • Beat the butter and sugar in a large bowl with an electric mixer at high speed until creamy. • Add the eggs, beating until just blended. • Mix in the dry ingredients and currants. • Press the dough into a disk, wrap in plastic wrap, and refrigerate for 30 minutes. • Preheat the oven to 325°F. • Butter two cookie sheets. • Roll the dough out on a lightly floured surface to a thickness of 1 inch. • Use a 2-inch cookie cutter to cut out the cookies. Gather the dough scraps, re-roll, and continue cutting out cookies until all the dough is used. • Use a spatula to transfer the cookies to the prepared cookie sheets, placing them 2 inches apart. • Bake for 12–15 minutes, or until golden, rotating the sheets halfway through for even baking. • Transfer to racks to cool.

Makes 20–24 cookies · Prep: 40 min. + 30 min. to chill · Cooking: 12–15 min. · Level: 1 · Keeps: 2 weeks

garibaldis

These cookies are named after Giuseppe Garibaldi, the 19th century Italian revolutionary, famous for his contribution to the unification of Italy.

21/3   cups all-purpose flour
2/3   cup confectioners' sugar
1/8   teaspoon salt
3/4   cup (11/2 sticks) butter, cut up
1 large egg + 1 large egg yolk, lightly beaten
1/3   cup dried currants

Sift the flour, confectioners' sugar, and salt into a large bowl. • Use a pastry blender to cut in the butter until the mixture resembles fine crumbs. • Add the whole egg to form a stiff dough. • Divide the dough in half. Press each half into a disk, wrap in plastic wrap, and refrigerate for 30 minutes. • Preheat the oven to 400°F. • Butter four cookie sheets. • Roll out one disk on a lightly floured surface to a thickness of 1/8 inch and to a 14 x 12-inch rectangle. Sprinkle with the currants. • Roll out the remaining dough to the same dimensions and place on top of the currants, pressing down lightly. • Cut into 2 x 11/2-inch strips. • Use a spatula to transfer the cookies to the prepared cookie sheets, placing them 1 inch apart. Brush with the remaining beaten egg yolk. • Bake, one sheet at a time, for 10–12 minutes, or until golden brown. • Transfer to racks to cool.

Makes 56 cookies · Prep: 40 min. + 30 min. to chill Cooking: 10–12 min. · Level: 1 · Keeps: 2 weeks

sweet jewel cookies

These pretty little cookies look almost too good to eat with their piped pink frosting and delicate decoration.

1¹/₃ cups all-purpose flour
¹/₄ cup cornstarch
¹/₈ teaspoon salt
¹/₂ cup (1 stick) butter, softened
¹/₃ cup granulated sugar
1 large egg
¹/₂ teaspoon vanilla extract

Pink buttercream frosting
¹/₃ cup butter, softened
1¹/₃ cups confectioners' sugar
2–3 drops red food coloring
 Silver balls, to decorate

Sift the flour, cornstarch, and salt into a medium bowl. • Beat the butter and sugar in a large bowl with an electric mixer at high speed until creamy. • Add the egg and vanilla, beating until just blended. • Mix in the dry ingredients to form a stiff dough. • Press the dough into a disk, wrap in plastic wrap, and refrigerate for 30 minutes. • Preheat the oven to 350°F. • Butter two cookie sheets. • Roll out the dough on a lightly floured surface to a thickness of ¹/₄ inch. • Use 1¹/₂-inch heart- and star-shaped cookie cutters to cut out the cookies. • Gather the dough scraps, re-roll, and continue cutting out cookies until all the dough is used. • Use a spatula to transfer the cookies to the prepared cookie sheets, placing them 1 inch apart. • Bake for 12–15 minutes, or until pale gold, rotating the sheets halfway through for even baking. • Cool on the sheets until the cookies firm slightly. Transfer to racks to finish cooling. Pink buttercream frosting: With mixer at high speed, beat the butter and confectioners' sugar in a medium bowl until creamy. • Mix in the food coloring to make an even pale pink frosting. • Fit a pastry bag with a ¹/₂-inch star tip. Fill the pastry bag, twist the opening tightly closed, and squeeze out small stars to form a border around each cookie. Decorate with silver balls.

Makes 20–24 cookies · Prep: 40 min. + 30 min. to chill · Cooking: 12–15 min. · Level: 2 · Keeps: 4 days

lemon cookies

¹/₃ cup butter, softened
2 tablespoons granulated sugar
1 tablespoon Vanilla Sugar (see page 341)
1 large egg yolk
 Finely grated zest of 1 lemon
1¹/₄ cups all-purpose flour

Glaze
²/₃ cup confectioners' sugar
1 tablespoon fresh lemon juice, or more as needed

Beat the butter, granulated sugar, and vanilla sugar in a large bowl with an electric mixer at medium speed until creamy. • Add the egg yolk and lemon zest, beating until just blended. • Mix in the flour to form a stiff dough. Press the dough into a disk, wrap in plastic wrap, and refrigerate for 30 minutes. • Preheat the oven to 350°F. • Butter and flour a cookie sheet. • Roll out the dough to a thickness of ¹/₈ inch. • Use a fluted cutter to stamp out small rounds. Gather the dough scraps, re-roll, and continue cutting out cookies until all the dough is used. • Use a spatula to transfer the cookies to the prepared cookie sheet. • Bake for 8–10 minutes, or until golden around the edges. • Cool the cookies on the sheet for 5 minutes. Transfer to racks to cool. • Glaze: Mix the confectioners' sugar with enough lemon juice to make a pourable consistency. • Drizzle the glaze in a decorative zigzag over the cookies.

Makes 20 cookies · Prep: 40 min. + 30 min. to chill · Cooking: 8–10 min. · Level: 1 · Keeps: 5–8 days

spice cookies

1²/₃ cups all-purpose flour
¹/₂ teaspoon baking powder
1 teaspoon ground cinnamon
¹/₂ teaspoon allspice
¹/₄ teaspoon freshly grated nutmeg
¹/₈ teaspoon salt
¹/₂ cup (1 stick) butter, softened
¹/₂ cup confectioners' sugar
1 large egg yolk

Sift the flour, baking powder, cinnamon, pumpkin pie spice, and salt into a large bowl. • Beat the butter and sugar in a large bowl with an electric mixer at high speed until creamy. • Add the egg yolk, beating until just blended. • Mix in the dry ingredients to form a smooth dough. • Press the dough into a disk, wrap in plastic wrap, and refrigerate for 30 minutes. • Preheat

the oven to 350°F. • Butter two cookie sheets. • Transfer the dough to a lightly floured surface and roll out to a thickness of ¹/₄ inch. • Use a 2-inch cookie cutter to cut out the cookies. • Gather the dough scraps, re-roll, and continue cutting out the cookies until all the dough is used. • Use a spatula to transfer the cookies to the prepared cookie sheets, placing them 1 inch apart. • Bake for 12–15 minutes, or until lightly browned, rotating the sheets halfway through the baking to ensure even browning. • Cool the cookies completely on the cookie sheets.

Makes 20 cookies · Prep: 40 min. + 30 min. to chill Cooking: 12–15 min. · Level: 1 · Keeps: 3 days

golden star cookies

1¹/₂ cups all-purpose flour
¹/₈ teaspoon salt
²/₃ cup butter, cut up
¹/₃ cup granulated sugar
1 tablespoon finely grated lemon zest
2 tablespoons fresh lemon juice
2 large egg yolks
1 cup Lemon Curd (see page 340)
1 tablespoon confectioners' sugar

Preheat the oven to 350°F. • Butter two cookie sheets. • Sift the flour and salt into a large bowl. • Use a pastry blender to cut in the butter until the mixture resembles fine crumbs. • Stir in the granulated sugar, lemon zest and juice, and egg yolks to form a stiff dough. • Press the dough into a disk, wrap in plastic wrap, and refrigerate for 30 minutes. • Roll out the dough on a lightly floured surface to a thickness of ¹/₈ inch. • Use a 3-inch fluted cookie cutter to cut out the cookies. • Use a 1-inch star-shaped cookie cutter to cut out the centers from half the cookies. Gather the dough scraps, re-roll, and continue cutting out cookies until all the dough is used. • Use a spatula to transfer the cookies to the prepared cookie sheets. • Bake for 6–8 minutes, or until golden brown, rotating the sheets halfway through for even baking. Cool on the sheets until the cookies firm slightly. Transfer to racks to finish cooling. • Spread the cooled whole cookies with the lemon curd and place the cookies with holes on top. Dust with the confectioners' sugar.

Makes 12–15 cookies · Prep: 45 min. + 30 min. to chill · Cooking: 6–8 min. · Level: 1 · Keeps: 5 days

*Golden star cookies
and Sweet jewel cookies*

ginger fairings

Fairings are so named because they used to be sold by the hundreds at the large fairs held once or twice a year in English towns from early medieval times. Fairs lasted up to a week. Farmers, cattle dealers, and merchants came from long distances to sell their wares. Among the most popular stalls were those selling spicy gingerbread fairings, which were sometimes highly decorated with gold leaf.

- 2/3 cup all-purpose flour
- 1 teaspoon ground ginger
- 1 teaspoon ground coriander
- 1/2 teaspoon ground cinnamon
- 1/8 teaspoon salt
- 1/4 cup dark molasses
- 2 tablespoons butter
- 2 tablespoons firmly packed dark brown sugar

Sift the flour, ginger, coriander, cinnamon, and salt into a medium bowl. • Heat the molasses, butter, and brown sugar in a small saucepan over low heat until the sugar has dissolved completely. • Mix the molasses mixture into the dry ingredients. • Knead the dough on a lightly floured surface until smooth. • Press the dough into a disk, wrap in plastic wrap, and refrigerate for 1 hour. • Preheat the oven to 350°F. • Butter a cookie sheet. • Roll out the dough to a thickness of 1/4 inch. • Use 1-inch cookie cutters to cut out the cookies. Gather the dough scraps, re-roll, and continue cutting out cookies until all the dough is used. • Use a spatula to transfer the cookies to the prepared cookie sheet, placing them 2 inches apart. • Bake for 15–20 minutes, or until golden brown. • Transfer the cookies to racks to cool.

Makes 10–15 cookies · Prep: 40 min. + 1 hr. to chill · Cooking: 15–20 min. · Level: 1 · Keeps: 2 days

st gallen honey drops

This time-consuming but scrumptious recipe comes from the eponymous northeastern region of Switzerland.

Sweet honey dough
- 1 cup all-purpose flour
- 2/3 cup rye flour
- 1 teaspoon baking soda
- 1 teaspoon ground cinnamon
- 1 teaspoon ground aniseeds
- 1/2 teaspoon finely grated nutmeg
- 1/4 teaspoon ground ginger
- 1/4 teaspoon salt
- 1 cup honey
- 1/4 cup granulated sugar

Marzipan filling
- 14 oz marzipan, softened
- 2/3 cup confectioners' sugar
- 1/2 teaspoon fresh lemon juice
- 1 teaspoon finely grated lemon zest
- 1 tablespoon cornstarch
- 1 tablespoon confectioners' sugar
- 3/4 cup hot water

Sweet honey dough: Sift the all-purpose and rye flours, the baking soda, cinnamon, aniseeds, nutmeg, ginger, and salt into a large bowl. • Heat the honey and sugar in a small saucepan over low heat until the sugar has dissolved completely. Cool for 15 minutes. • Use a wooden spoon to work the honey mixture into the dry ingredients to form a smooth dough. • Cover with a clean kitchen towel and let rest at room temperature for 3 days. • Preheat the oven to 350°F. • Line two cookie sheets with parchment paper. • Marzipan filling: Knead the marzipan, confectioners' sugar, and lemon juice and zest until smooth. • Roll the honey dough out on a lightly floured surface into three 12 x 4-inch strips. • Shape the marzipan filling into logs of the same length as the dough strips. • Place the marzipan logs on top of the dough strips and fold over the dough to seal. • Slice the filled dough 1 inch thick and place cut-side up 1 inch apart on the prepared cookie sheets. • Bake for 12–15 minutes, or until just golden at the edges, rotating the sheets halfway through for even baking. • Transfer to racks. • Toast the cornstarch in a skillet for 3–4 minutes, or until lightly golden, shaking the pan constantly. Add the confectioners' sugar and water and bring to a boil, stirring constantly. • Remove from the heat and drizzle over the cookies while warm. • Let cool completely.

Makes 35–40 cookies · Prep: 1 hr. + 3 days to rest · Cooking: 12–15 min. · Level: 3 · Keeps: 3 weeks

cream crisps

- 3 1/3 cups all-purpose flour
- 1/3 cup cornstarch
- 2 teaspoons baking powder
- 1/8 teaspoon salt
- 1 cup granulated sugar
- 3/4 cup (1 1/2 sticks) butter, melted
- 1 large egg
- 1/3 cup light cream
- 1/2 teaspoon vanilla extract

Preheat the oven to 350°F. • Butter three cookie sheets. • Sift the flour, cornstarch, baking powder, and salt into a large bowl. • Use a wooden spoon to mix in the sugar, butter, egg, cream, and vanilla to form a smooth dough. • Press the dough into a disk, wrap in plastic wrap, and refrigerate for 30 minutes. • Roll out the dough on a lightly floured surface to a thickness of 1/4 inch. • Use a 2 1/2-inch cookie cutter to cut out the cookies. Gather the dough scraps, re-roll, and continue cutting out cookies until all the dough is used. • Use a spatula to transfer the cookies to the prepared cookie sheets, placing them 1 inch apart. • Bake, one sheet at a time, for 10–15 minutes, or until just golden at the edges. • Transfer to racks and let cool completely.

Makes 36 cookies · Prep: 40 min. + 30 min. to chill · Cooking: 10–15 min. per batch · Level: 1 · Keeps: 10 days

nut crisps

- 1 cup whole almonds
- 1 cup superfine sugar
- 2 large egg whites
- 1/8 teaspoon salt
- 2 cups finely ground almonds
- 1/2 cup coarsely chopped cashew nuts
- 1 teaspoon finely grated lemon zest
- 1 teaspoon finely grated orange zest
- 2–3 tablespoons raw sugar (such as Barbados or Demerara), for rolling out

Toast the whole almonds in a skillet over medium heat for 5–7 minutes, or until lightly golden. • Transfer the almonds to a food processor, add 2 tablespoons of the superfine sugar, and process until finely ground. • Beat the egg whites and salt in a large bowl with an electric mixer at medium speed until frothy. • With mixer at high speed, gradually add the remaining superfine sugar, beating until stiff, glossy peaks form. • Use a large rubber spatula to fold in the toasted ground almond mixture, 2 cups finely ground almonds, cashews, and lemon and orange zests to form a stiff dough. • Press the dough into a disk, wrap in plastic wrap, and refrigerate for 30 minutes. • Preheat the oven to 300°F. • Line four cookie sheets with parchment paper. • Discard the plastic wrap. Roll out the dough on a surface lightly dusted with raw sugar to a thickness of $^1/_8$ inch. • Use a sharp knife to cut the dough into $1^1/_2$-inch squares. Gather the dough scraps, re-roll, and continue cutting out cookies until all the dough is used. • Use a spatula to transfer the cookies to the prepared cookie sheets, placing them 1 inch apart. • Bake, one sheet at a time, for 12–15 minutes, or until just golden around the edges. • Cool on the sheets until the cookies firm slightly. Transfer to racks to finish cooling.

Makes 60–70 cookies · Prep: 50 min. + 30 min. to chill · Cooking: 12–15 min. per batch · Level: 1 · Keeps: 2 weeks

rolled white chocolate cookies

Chocolate shavings can be made from any type of chocolate and are a versatile decoration that always looks spectacular.

- 6 oz white couverture chocolate, coarsely chopped
- 2 cups all-purpose flour
- $^1/_8$ teaspoon salt
- $^3/_4$ cup ($1^1/_2$ sticks) butter, cut up
- 2 large egg yolks, lightly beaten
- $^2/_3$ cup confectioners' sugar
- $^1/_4$ teaspoon almond extract

Melt 4 oz of the white chocolate in a double boiler over barely simmering water. Spread the chocolate in a thin layer over a cold marble surface. Let the chocolate set and cool completely. • When the chocolate has set, take a large sharp knife, a chocolate shaver, or a vegetable peeler and gently draw it toward you over the surface of the chocolate. Shavings of chocolate will form. • Preheat the oven to 400°F. • Butter two cookie sheets. • Sift the flour and salt into a medium bowl. • Use a pastry blender to cut in the butter until the mixture resembles fine crumbs. • Mix in the egg yolks, confectioners' sugar, and almond extract to form a smooth dough. • Press the dough into a disk, wrap in plastic wrap, and refrigerate for 30 minutes. • Roll out the dough on a lightly floured surface to a thickness of $^1/_4$ inch. • Use a 2-inch cookie cutter to cut out the cookies. Gather the dough scraps, re-roll, and continue cutting out cookies until all the dough is used. • Use a spatula to transfer the cookies to the prepared cookie sheets, placing them 1 inch apart. • Bake for 7–10 minutes, or until pale gold and slightly darker at the edges, rotating the sheets halfway through for even browning. • Transfer to racks to cool. • Melt

the remaining 2 oz chocolate in the double boiler over barely simmering water. Brush a little chocolate onto each cookie and press some chocolate shavings gently on top.

Makes 18–24 cookies · Prep: 45 min. + 30 min. to chill · Cooking: 7–10 min. · Level: 3 · Keeps: 10 days

cashew cookies

- $1^2/_3$ cups all-purpose flour
- $^1/_8$ teaspoon salt
- $^1/_4$ cup ($^1/_2$ stick) butter, cut up
- 3 large egg yolks, lightly beaten
- $^2/_3$ cup granulated sugar
- $^1/_4$ cup coarsely chopped cashew nuts
  Grated zest of $^1/_2$ lemon
- $^1/_3$ cup milk
- $^1/_3$ cup confectioners' sugar
- $^1/_3$ cup unsweetened cocoa powder

Sift the flour and salt into a large bowl. • Use a pastry blender to cut in the butter until the mixture resembles coarse crumbs. • Add the egg yolks, granulated sugar, cashew nuts, lemon zest, and milk to form a stiff dough. • Press the dough into a disk, wrap in plastic wrap, and refrigerate for 30 minutes. • Preheat the oven to 325°F. • Butter two cookie sheets. • Roll out the dough on a lightly floured surface to a thickness of $^1/_4$ inch. • Cut into $1^1/_2$-inch-wide strips, then cut the strips into $2^1/_2$-inch rectangles. • Use a spatula to transfer the cookies to the prepared cookie sheets, placing them 1 inch apart. • Bake for 12–15 minutes, or until just golden, rotating the sheets halfway through for even baking. • Transfer to racks to cool. • Dust one side of the cookie with the confectioners' sugar and the remaining half with cocoa.

Makes 30 cookies · Prep: 40 min. + 30 min. to chill Cooking: 12–15 min. · Level: 1 · Keeps: 5 days

almond cookies

- $1^2/_3$ cups all-purpose flour
- $^1/_8$ teaspoon salt
- $^1/_4$ cup ($^1/_2$ stick) butter, cut up
- 3 large egg yolks, lightly beaten
- $^2/_3$ cup granulated sugar
- $^1/_4$ cup coarsely chopped almonds
  Grated zest of $^1/_2$ lemon
- $^1/_3$ cup milk
- $^1/_3$ cup confectioners' sugar
- $^1/_3$ cup unsweetened cocoa powder

Sift the flour and salt into a large bowl. • Use a pastry blender to cut in the butter until the mixture resembles coarse crumbs. • Add the egg yolks, granulated sugar,

almonds, lemon zest, and milk to form a stiff dough. • Press the dough into a disk, wrap in plastic wrap, and refrigerate for 30 minutes. • Preheat the oven to 325°F. • Butter two cookie sheets. • Roll out the dough on a lightly floured surface to a thickness of $^1/_4$ inch. • Cut into $1^1/_2$-inch-wide strips, then cut the strips into $2^1/_2$-inch rectangles. • Use a spatula to transfer the cookies to the prepared cookie sheets, placing them 1 inch apart. • Bake for 12–15 minutes, or until just golden, rotating the sheets halfway through for even baking. • Transfer to racks to cool. • Dust one side of the cookie with the confectioners' sugar and the remaining half with cocoa.

Makes 30 cookies · Prep: 40 min. + 30 min. to chill Cooking: 12–15 min. · Level: 1 · Keeps: 5 days

korzhiki

These cookies, traditionally given to Russians embarking on long journeys, have a rich shortbread flavor.

- 1 cup all-purpose flour
- $^1/_2$ teaspoon baking powder
- $^1/_8$ teaspoon salt
- 2 tablespoons butter, cut up
- 3 tablespoons granulated sugar
- 5 tablespoons sour cream
- 2 large eggs

Sift the flour, baking powder, and salt into a large bowl. • Use a pastry blender to cut in the butter until the mixture resembles fine crumbs. • Stir together the sugar, sour cream, and 1 egg. Stir into the dry ingredients to form a smooth dough. • Press the dough into a disk, wrap in plastic wrap, and refrigerate for 30 minutes. • Preheat the oven to 425°F. • Line two cookie sheets with parchment paper. • Roll out the dough on a lightly floured surface to a thickness of $^1/_4$ inch. Use a 2-inch cookie cutter to cut out the cookies. Gather the dough scraps, re-roll, and continue cutting out until all the dough is used. • Use a spatula to transfer the cookies to the cookie sheets, spacing them 2 inches apart. Prick all over with a fork. • Beat the remaining egg and brush over the tops of the cookies. • Bake for 10–15 minutes, or until golden brown, rotating the sheets halfway through for even baking. • Transfer to racks to cool.

Makes 16–20 cookies · Prep: 40 min. + 30 min. to chill · Cooking: 10–15 min. · Level: 1 · Keeps: 2 weeks

Coffee-frosted walnut cookies

almond-studded playing cards

A popular cookie from Vienna, home of the most refined pastry cooks and coffeeshops.

1 1/3 cups all-purpose flour
1/8 teaspoon salt
2/3 cup butter, softened
1/2 cup granulated sugar
1 large egg
1 tablespoon finely grated lemon zest
1 teaspoon ice water
3/4 cup almond halves

Sift the flour and salt into a medium bowl. • Beat the butter and sugar in a large bowl with an electric mixer at high speed until creamy. • Add the egg and lemon zest, beating until just blended. • Mix in the dry ingredients to form a stiff dough. Press the dough into a disk, wrap in plastic wrap, and refrigerate for 30 minutes. • Preheat the oven to 350°F. • Set out two cookie sheets. • Roll out the dough on a lightly floured surface to a thickness of 1/4 inch. • Use a sharp knife to cut into 2 x 3-inch rectangles. Gather the dough scraps, re-roll, and continue cutting out cookies until all the dough is used. • Sprinkle the cookies lightly with the water. • Arrange the almond halves on top of the cookies in a diagonal line. • Use a spatula to transfer the cookies to the cookie sheets, placing them 1 inch apart. • Bake for 20–25 minutes, or until pale gold and firm to the touch, rotating the sheets halfway through for even browning. • Cool completely on the sheets.

Makes 20–25 cookies · Prep: 40 min. + 30 min. to chill · Cooking: 20–25 min. · Level: 1 · Keeps: 10 days

mocha–almond cookies

1 large egg + 1 large egg yolk
2/3 cup granulated sugar
1 tablespoon Vanilla Sugar (see page 341)

1 teaspoon freeze-dried coffee granules dissolved in 1 teaspoon warm water
1/8 teaspoon salt
2 oz semisweet chocolate, coarsely chopped
2 cups finely ground almonds, + more as needed
1/4 teaspoon baking powder
Glaze
1 large egg white
1/8 teaspoon salt
1/3 cup confectioners' sugar

Beat the whole egg and yolk, granulated and vanilla sugars, and salt in a large bowl with an electric mixer at high speed until creamy. • Melt the chocolate in a double boiler over barely simmering water. • Mix in the coffee. • Beat the chocolate mixture into the batter. • Mix in the almonds and baking powder to form a stiff dough, adding more almonds if needed. • Divide the dough in half. Press the dough into two disks, wrap each in plastic wrap, and refrigerate for 30 minutes. • Preheat the oven to 350°F. • Butter three cookie sheets. • Roll out each dough disk between sheets of waxed paper into an 8 x 5-inch rectangle. • Cut into 2 1/2 x 3/4-inch strips. • Use a spatula to transfer the cookies to the prepared cookie sheets, placing them 1 inch apart. • Glaze: With mixer at medium speed, beat the egg white and salt in a small bowl until frothy. • With mixer at high speed, gradually add the confectioners' sugar until stiff, glossy peaks form. • Spread the glaze evenly over the tops of the cookies. • Bake, one sheet at a time, for 10–12 minutes, or until golden at the edges and the bottoms are lightly browned. • Transfer to racks to cool.

Makes 40–45 cookies · Prep: 45 min. + 30 min. to chill · Cooking: 10–12 min. per batch · Level: 1 · Keeps: 10 days

coffee-frosted walnut cookies

1 1/2 cups all-purpose flour
1/8 teaspoon salt
1/2 cup (1 stick) butter, softened
1/3 cup granulated sugar
1 large egg, lightly beaten
1 tablespoon freeze-dried coffee granules
2 tablespoons milk, + more as needed
Coffee buttercream
1/4 cup (1/2 stick) butter, softened
3/4 cup confectioners' sugar
1/2 teaspoon coffee extract
Coffee frosting
3/4 cup confectioners' sugar
1 teaspoon lukewarm water (110°–115°F)

1 teaspoon hot strong coffee
10–12 walnut halves, to decorate

Sift the flour and salt into a medium bowl. • Beat the butter and sugar in a large bowl with an electric mixer at high speed until creamy. • Add the egg, beating until just blended. • Mix in the dry ingredients until well blended. • Dissolve the coffee granules in 2 tablespoons milk and mix in to form a smooth dough, adding more milk as needed. • Press the dough into a disk, wrap in plastic wrap, and refrigerate for 30 minutes. • Preheat the oven to 350°F. • Butter two cookie sheets. • Roll out the dough on a lightly floured surface to a thickness of 1/8 inch. • Use a 2-inch cookie cutter to cut out the cookies. Gather the dough scraps, re-roll, and continue cutting out cookies until all the dough is used. Prick lightly with a fork. Use a spatula to transfer the cookies to the prepared cookie sheets, placing them 1 inch apart. • Bake for 12–15 minutes, or until golden, rotating the sheets halfway through to ensure even browning. • Transfer to racks to cool. • Coffee buttercream: With mixer at high speed, beat the butter in a medium bowl until creamy. Beat in the confectioners' sugar and coffee extract until well blended. • Coffee frosting: Sift the confectioners' sugar into a double boiler placed over barely simmering water. Beat in enough water and coffee to make a glossy, spreadable frosting. Stick the cookies together in pairs with the buttercream. Spread the tops of the cookies with the coffee frosting and top with a half walnut.

Makes 10–12 cookies · Prep: 50 min. + 30 min. to chill · Cooking: 12–15 min. · Level: 2 · Keeps: 5 days

northern pepper stars

1/3 cup butter, cut up
2 tablespoons dark molasses
3 black peppercorns, crushed
 Seeds of 10 cardamom pods, crushed
1 1/2 cups all-purpose flour
1/2 teaspoon baking soda
1/2 teaspoon ground cinnamon
1/2 teaspoon ground ginger
1/2 teaspoon salt
1/4 cup granulated sugar
1 large egg, lightly beaten
1 cup Decorator's Frosting (see page 348)

Melt the butter with the molasses in a small saucepan. Remove from the heat and set aside to cool. • Mix the peppercorns and cardamom in a small bowl. • Sift the flour, baking soda, cinnamon, ginger, and salt into a large bowl. Stir in the peppercorns and cardamom. • Use a wooden spoon to stir in the sugar, molasses mixture, and egg. • Turn out onto a lightly floured surface and knead lightly until smooth. • Shape into a disk, wrap in plastic wrap, and refrigerate for 30 minutes. • Preheat the oven to 325°F. • Line two cookie sheets with parchment paper. • Roll out the dough on a lightly floured surface to a thickness of $^1/4$ inch. • Use a star-shaped cutter to stamp into shapes. • Gather the dough scraps, re-roll, and continue cutting out cookies until all the dough is used. Use a metal spatula to transfer to the prepared cookie sheets, spacing 1 inch apart. • Bake for 10–15 minutes, or until firm to the touch, rotating the sheets halfway through for even baking. • Cool the cookies completely on the cookie sheets. Transfer to a rack. • Spoon the frosting into a small freezer bag and cut off a tiny corner. Pipe over the cookies in a decorative manner.

Makes 35 cookies · Prep: 50 min. + 30 min. to chill · Cooking: 10–15 min. · Level: 1 · Keeps: 18–20 days

stars in the sky

To vary this recipe and prepare cinnamon stars, replace the vanilla extract with ground cinnamon.

3   large egg whites
1$^1/2$ cups confectioners sugar, sifted
$^1/8$ teaspoon cream of tartar
4   cups finely ground almonds
2   teaspoons Vanilla Sugar (see page 341)
$^1/4$ teaspoon vanilla extract

Line two cookie sheets with parchment paper. • Beat the egg whites in a large bowl with an electric mixer at medium speed until frothy. With mixer at high speed, gradually add the confectioners' sugar and lemon juice until stiff, glossy peaks form. • Spoon 1 cup beaten whites into a small bowl and set aside in the refrigerator as a glaze. • Use a large rubber spatula to fold 3 cups almonds, the vanilla sugar, and vanilla into the large bowl of beaten whites. Cover with plastic wrap and refrigerate for 30 minutes. • Preheat the oven to 275°F. •

Sprinkle a lightly floured surface with the remaining 1 cup ground almonds. Roll out the dough in small portions to a thickness of $^1/2$ inch. • D p a star cutter into cold water and stamp out star shapes. Gather the dough scraps, re-roll, and continue cutting out cookies until all the dough is used. Use a spatula to transfer the cookies to the cookie sheets, placing them 1 inch apart. Brush a thin layer of reserved chilled egg white over each star. • Bake for 25–30 minutes, or until firm to the touch, rotating the sheets halfway through for even baking. The glaze should remain white. • Cool the cookies completely on the cookie sheets.

Makes 40 cookies · Prep: 60 min. + 30 min. to chill Cooking: 25–30 min. · Level: 2 · Keeps: 5 days

fresh ginger cookies

This recipe caters to the British taste for ginger, which has been a popular feature in their cooking since it was brought from Asia by merchants in the Middle Ages.

$^1/2$ cup firmly packed light brown sugar
$^1/3$ cup butter, cut up
2   tablespoons milk
1$^1/3$ cups all-purpose flour
$^1/3$ cup finely grated fresh ginger
$^1/8$ teaspoon salt

Heat the brown sugar, butter, and milk in a small saucepan over low heat. • Cook, stirring constantly, until the butter has melted and the mixture is well blended. • Transfer to a large bowl. • Mix in the flour, ginger, and salt to form a stiff dough. • Press the dough into a disk, wrap in plastic wrap, and refrigerate for 1 hour. • Preheat the oven to 325°F. • Butter two cookie sheets. - Roll out the dough on a lightly floured surface to a thickness of $^1/4$ inch. • Use a 2$^1/2$-inch cookie cutter to cut out the cookies. Gather the dough scraps, re-roll, and continue cutting out cookies until all the dough is used. • Use a spatula to transfer the cookies to the prepared cookie sheets, placing them 1 inch apart. • Prick all over with a fork. • Bake for 10–15 minutes, or until just golden, rotating the sheets halfway through for even baking. • Cool on the sheets until the cookies firm slightly. • Transfer to racks to finish cooling.

Makes 25–30 cookies · Prep: 40 min. + 1 hr. to chill Cooking: 10–15 min. · Level: 1 · Keeps: 10 days

coconut–lime stars

1$^1/2$ cups all-purpose flour
$^1/3$ cup cornstarch
$^1/8$ teaspoon salt
$^3/4$ cup (1$^1/2$ sticks) butter, cut up
$^1/4$ cup granulated sugar
$^1/2$ cup shredded coconut
     Grated zest of 1 lime
2   tablespoons milk, + more as needed
$^1/2$ cup Vanilla Frosting (see page 348)

Sift the flour, cornstarch, and salt into a medium bowl. • Use a pastry blender to cut in the butter until the mixture resembles fine crumbs. • Stir in the sugar, coconut, lime zest, and enough milk to form a stiff dough. • Press the dough into a disk, wrap in plastic wrap, and refrigerate for 30 minutes. • Preheat the oven to 350°F. • Butter two cookie sheets. • Roll out the dough on a lightly floured surface to a thickness of $^1/4$ inch. • Use a 3-inch star-shaped cookie cutter to cut out the cookies. Gather the dough scraps, re-roll, and continue cutting out cookies until all the dough is used. • Use a spatula to transfer the cookies to the prepared cookie sheets, placing them 1 inch apart. • Bake for 12–15 minutes, or until pale gold, rotating the sheets halfway through for even baking. • Transfer to racks to cool. • Spoon the frosting into a small freezer bag. Pipe over the tops of the cookies in a decorative manner.

Makes 20–24 cookies · Prep: 40 min. + 30 min. to chill · Cooking: 12–15 min. · Level: 1 · Keeps: 7 days

Coconut–lime stars

belgian cookies

1	cup all-purpose flour
3/4	cup cornstarch
2	teaspoons unsweetened cocoa powder
1	teaspoon ground cinnamon
1/2	teaspoon allspice
1/2	teaspoon baking soda
1/4	teaspoon ground ginger
1/4	teaspoon freshly grated nutmeg
1/4	teaspoon salt
1/2	cup (1 stick) butter, softened
3/4	cup granulated sugar
1	tablespoon light corn syrup
2	large eggs
2–3	tablespoons raspberry preserves
3–4	tablespoons confectioners' sugar
3–4	teaspoons lukewarm water (105°–115°F)
2	drops red food coloring

Sift the flour, cornstarch, cocoa, cinnamon, allspice, baking soda, ginger, nutmeg, and salt into a medium bowl. • Beat the butter, sugar, and corn syrup in a large bowl with an electric mixer at high speed until creamy. • Add the eggs, beating until just blended. • Mix in the dry ingredients to form a smooth dough. Press the dough into a disk, wrap in plastic wrap, and refrigerate for 30 minutes. • Preheat the oven to 350°F. • Butter two cookie sheets. • Roll out the dough on a lightly floured surface to a thickness of 1/2 inch. • Use a 2-inch cutter to cut into rounds. • Transfer the cookies to the prepared cookie sheets, placing them 1 inch apart. • Bake for 8–10 minutes, or until firm, rotating the sheets halfway through for even baking. • Cool completely on the cookie sheets. • Stick the cookies together in pairs with the preserves. • Mix the confectioners' sugar, water, and food coloring to make a soft frosting. Spread the frosting over the tops.

Makes 20 cookies · Prep: 40 min. + 30 min. to chill Cooking: 8–10 min. · Level: 1 · Keeps: 5 days

cinnamon–orange cookies

2	cups all-purpose flour
1/2	teaspoon ground cinnamon
1/8	teaspoon salt
2/3	cup lard or vegetable shortening
1/3	cup butter, softened
1/2	cup granulated sugar
1	large egg yolk
1	teaspoon finely grated orange zest

Sift the flour, cinnamon, and salt into a medium bowl. • Beat the lard and butter in a large bowl with an electric mixer at high

speed until well blended. • Add the sugar, egg yolk, and orange zest. • Mix in the dry ingredients to form a smooth dough. Press the dough into a disk, wrap in plastic wrap, and refrigerate for 30 minutes. • Preheat the oven to 350°F. • Butter two cookie sheets. • Roll out the dough on a lightly floured surface to a thickness of 1/4 inch. • Use a 3-inch fluted cookie cutter to cut out the cookies. Gather the dough scraps, re-roll, and continue cutting out cookies until all the dough is used. • Use a spatula to transfer the cookies to the prepared cookie sheets, placing them 1 inch apart. • Bake for 8–10 minutes, or until just golden, rotating the sheets halfway through for even baking. • Transfer to racks to cool.

Makes 30 cookies · Prep: 40 min. + 30 min. to chill Cooking: 8–10 min. · Level: 1 · Keeps: 5 days

saffron cookies

Saffron is the most expensive spice in the world. If possible, buy saffron in threads—they should be intact and a deep red color—to make sure you are getting the real thing.

1 1/2	cups all-purpose flour
1	tablespoon cornstarch
1/2	teaspoon baking powder
1/8	teaspoon salt
1/3	cup corn oil
1/2	cup + 2 tablespoons raw sugar (Barbados or Demerara)
1/2	teaspoon crumbled saffron threads
1	large egg
1/3	cup finely ground almonds

Sift the flour, cornstarch, baking powder, and salt into a medium bowl. • Beat the oil, 1/2 cup raw sugar, and saffron in a large bowl with an electric mixer at high speed until creamy. • Add the egg, beating until just blended. • Mix in the dry ingredients and almonds to form a stiff dough. • Press the dough into a disk, wrap in plastic wrap, and refrigerate for 30 minutes. • Preheat the oven to 350°F. • Butter two cookie sheets. • Roll out the dough on a lightly floured surface to a thickness of 1/4 inch. Use a 2-inch cookie cutter to cut out the cookies. • Gather the dough scraps, re-roll, and continue cutting out cookies until all the dough is used. • Use a spatula to transfer the cookies to the prepared cookie sheets, spacing them 1 inch apart. Sprinkle with the remaining 2 tablespoons raw sugar. • Bake for 10–12 minutes, or until just

golden, rotating the sheets halfway through for even baking. • Transfer to racks to cool.

Makes 25–30 cookies · Prep: 40 min. + 30 min. to chill · Cooking: 10–12 min. · Level: 1 · Keeps: 7 days

cinnamon streusel cookies

1	cup all-purpose flour
1/8	teaspoon salt
2/3	cup butter, cut up
2/3	cup ricotta cheese
1	tablespoon Vanilla Sugar (see page 341)

Cinnamon–almond streusel

2/3	cup all-purpose flour
1	tablespoon finely ground almonds
1/4	teaspoon ground cinnamon
1/3	cup butter, cut up
1/3	cup strawberry preserves
1–2	teaspoons confectioners' sugar, to dust

Sift the flour and salt into a medium bowl. • Use a pastry blender to cut in the butter until the mixture resembles coarse crumbs. • Stir in the ricotta and vanilla sugar to form a stiff dough. • Press the dough into a disk, wrap in plastic wrap, and refrigerate for 30 minutes. • Preheat the oven to 400°F. • Line two cookie sheets with parchment paper. • Cinnamon–almond streusel: Mix the flour, almonds, and cinnamon in a small bowl. • Use a pastry blender to cut in the butter until the crumble resembles coarse crumbs. • Roll out the dough on a lightly floured surface to a thickness of 1/4 inch. • Use a 2 1/2-inch cookie cutter to cut out cookies. • Gather the dough scraps, re-roll, and continue cutting out cookies until all the dough is used. • Use a spatula to transfer the cookies to the prepared cookie sheets, placing them 1 inch apart. • Warm the preserves in a small saucepan over low heat until liquid. • Spread the preserves over the tops of the cookies and sprinkle with the streusel. • Bake for 15–20 minutes, or until the tops are golden and the edges are beginning to brown, rotating the sheets halfway through for even baking. • Transfer to racks to cool. Dust with the confectioners' sugar just before serving.

Makes 25–30 cookies · Prep: 45 min. + 30 min. to chill · Cooking: 15–20 min. · Level: 1 · Keeps: 5 days

Cinnamon streusel cookies (right) and Saffron cookies (left)

french butter cookies

Cherry-topped and buttery in flavor, these cookies are a welcome addition to any cookie jar.

1²/₃ cups all-purpose flour
¹/₄ teaspoon salt
¹/₃ cup pine nuts
¹/₄ cup granulated sugar
³/₄ cup (1¹/₂ sticks) butter, softened
²/₃ cup confectioners' sugar
3 large egg yolks
¹/₂ teaspoon vanilla extract
12 candied cherries, cut in half

Sift the flour and salt into a large bowl. • Process the pine nuts and granulated sugar in a food processor or blender until very finely ground. • Beat the butter and confectioners' sugar in a large bowl with an electric mixer at high speed until creamy. • Add the egg yolks and vanilla, beating until just blended. • Mix in the pine nut mixture and dry ingredients to form a stiff dough. • Press the dough into a disk, wrap in plastic wrap, and refrigerate for 30 minutes. • Preheat the oven to 350°F. • Butter two cookie sheets. • Roll out the dough on a lightly floured surface to a thickness of ¹/₄ inch. • Use a fluted pastry wheel to cut into 1-inch squares. • Gather the dough scraps, re-roll, and continue cutting out cookies until all the dough is used. • Use a spatula to transfer the cookies to the prepared cookie sheets, placing them 1 inch apart. Press a half cherry into each cookie top. • Bake for 12–15 minutes, or until just golden, rotating the sheets halfway through for even baking. • Transfer to racks to cool.

Makes 24 cookies · Prep: 40 min. + 30 min. to chill
Cooking: 12–15 min. · Level: 1 · Keeps: 5 days

French butter cookies

lancashire tea cakes

In Lancashire, in the north of England, these tea cakes were eaten between slices of bread and butter on special occasions, often to accompany a glass of homemade wine.

1¹/₂ cups all-purpose flour
¹/₄ teaspoon ground cinnamon
¹/₈ teaspoon salt
¹/₂ cup (1 stick) butter, softened
2 tablespoons granulated sugar

Sift the flour, cinnamon, and salt into a medium bowl. • Use a wooden spoon to beat the butter and sugar in a medium bowl until creamy. • Mix in the dry ingredients to form a smooth dough. Press the dough into a disk, wrap in plastic wrap, and refrigerate for 30 minutes. • Preheat the oven to 400°F. • Butter a cookie sheet. • Roll out the dough on a lightly floured surface to a thickness of ¹/₄ inch. • Use a 3-inch cookie cutter to cut out the cookies. Gather the dough scraps, re-roll, and continue cutting out cookies until all the dough is used. Use a spatula to transfer the cookies to the prepared cookie sheet, placing them 2 inches apart. • Bake for 15–20 minutes, or until just golden. • Transfer to racks to cool.

Makes 12–15 cookies · Prep: 40 min. + 30 min. to chill · Cooking: 15–20 min. · Level: 1 · Keeps: 7 days

honey–butter cookies

1³/₄ cups all-purpose flour
2 tablespoons cornstarch
1 teaspoon powdered milk
¹/₂ teaspoon baking soda
¹/₂ teaspoon cream of tartar
¹/₈ teaspoon salt
¹/₂ cup (1 stick) butter, softened
¹/₂ cup granulated sugar
1 large egg
1 tablespoon honey
¹/₄ teaspoon vanilla extract

Sift the flour, cornstarch, powdered milk, baking soda, cream of tartar, and salt into a medium bowl. • Beat the butter and sugar in a large bowl with an electric mixer at high speed until creamy. • Add the egg, honey, and vanilla, beating until just blended. • Mix in the dry ingredients to form a smooth dough. Press the dough into a disk, wrap in plastic wrap, and refrigerate for 30 minutes. • Preheat the oven to 300°F. • Line three cookie sheets with parchment paper. • Roll out the dough on a lightly floured surface to a thickness of ¹/₄

inch. • Dust a springerle pin with flour and firmly roll over the dough to imprint the patterns. Cut off any surplus dough and separate the printed squares with a knife. Use a spatula to transfer the cookies to the prepared cookie sheets, placing them 2 inches apart. • Bake, one sheet at a time, for 15–20 minutes, or until lightly browned. • Transfer to racks to cool.

Makes 36 cookies · Prep: 40 min. + 30 min. to chill · Cooking: 15–20 min. per batch · Level: 2 · Keeps: 7 days

ginger leaves

1²/₃ cups all-purpose flour
1 teaspoon ground ginger
¹/₈ teaspoon salt
¹/₃ cup butter, cut up
¹/₂ cup superfine sugar
Seeds of 1 vanilla pod
1 large egg + 1 large egg yolk, lightly beaten
1 tablespoon very finely chopped crystallized ginger

Sift the flour, ground ginger, and salt into a large bowl. • Use a pastry blender to cut in the butter until the mixture resembles coarse crumbs. • Stir in the superfine sugar and vanilla seeds. • Add the whole egg to form a smooth dough. • Press the dough into a disk, wrap in plastic wrap, and refrigerate for 30 minutes. • Preheat the oven to 375°F. • Line two cookie sheets with parchment paper. • Roll out the dough on a lightly floured surface to a thickness of ¹/₄ inch. • Use a fluted pastry wheel to cut out 1 x 2¹/₂-inch leaf shapes. Gather the dough scraps, re-roll, and continue cutting out cookies until all the dough is used. • Use a spatula to transfer the cookies to the prepared cookie sheets, placing them 1 inch apart. • Brush with the remaining beaten egg yolk and decorate with the crystallized ginger. • Bake for 8–10 minutes, or until golden, rotating the sheets halfway through for even baking. • Transfer to racks to cool.

Makes 25–30 cookies · Prep: 40 min. + 30 min. to chill · Cooking: 8–10 min. · Level: 1 · Keeps: 3 weeks

old english crisps

1²/₃ cups all-purpose flour
¹/₈ teaspoon salt
¹/₂ cup (1 stick) butter, cut up
2 tablespoons heavy cream
2 tablespoons honey

Sift the flour and salt into a medium bowl. • Use a pastry blender to cut in the butter until the mixture resembles fine crumbs. • Mix in the cream and honey to form a stiff dough. • Press the dough into a disk, wrap in plastic wrap, and refrigerate for 30 minutes. • Preheat the oven to 300°F. • Butter two cookie sheets. • Roll out the dough on a lightly floured surface to a thickness of $1/8$ inch. Use a 2-inch cookie cutter to cut out the cookies. • Gather the dough scraps, re-roll, and continue cutting out cookies until all the dough is used. • Use a spatula to transfer the cookies to the prepared cookie sheets, placing them 2 inches apart. • Bake for 15–20 minutes, or until golden, rotating the sheets halfway through for even baking. • Transfer to racks to cool.

Makes 20–24 cookies · Prep: 40 min. + 30 min. to chill · Cooking: 15–20 min. · Level: 1 · Keeps: 10 days

cinnamon curls

$2/3$ cup all-purpose flour
$1/8$ teaspoon salt
3 large eggs
$3^{1}/3$ cups confectioners' sugar
Grated zest of $1/2$ lemon
1 teaspoon ground cinnamon
5 cups finely ground hazelnuts

Sift the flour and salt into a medium bowl. • Beat the eggs and confectioners' sugar in a large bowl with an electric mixer at high speed until very pale and thick. • Set aside one-third of the mixture for the glaze. • Add the lemon zest and cinnamon to the remaining mixture. Stir in the hazelnuts. • Mix in the dry ingredients to form a smooth dough. Press the dough into a disk, wrap in plastic wrap, and refrigerate for 30 minutes. • Preheat the oven to 300°F. • Line two cookie sheets with parchment paper. • Lightly dust a surface with confectioners' sugar and roll out the dough to a thickness of $1/4$ inch. • Cut into 3 x $3/4$-inch strips and place 1 inch apart on the prepared cookie sheets. Bend the strips into curved shapes. • Brush with the reserved mixture to glaze the cookies. • Bake for 15–18 minutes, or until just golden at the edges. • Transfer to racks to cool.

Makes 25–30 cookies · Prep: 40 min. + 30 min. to chill · Cooking: 15–18 min. · Level: 2 · Keeps: 10 days

double-deckers

$1^{1}/2$ cups all-purpose flour
$1/4$ cup granulated sugar
$2^{1}/2$ tablespoons Vanilla Sugar (see page 341)
$1/8$ teaspoon salt
$1/2$ package (4 oz) cream cheese, softened
$1/3$ cup butter, softened

Filling and Glaze
$3/4$ cup hazelnuts
$2/3$ cup orange marmalade
7 oz marzipan, grated
2 large eggs, separated
2 tablespoons milk, or more as needed
Toasted hazelnuts, coarsely chopped, or slivered almonds

Sift together the flour, granulated sugar, vanilla sugar, and salt into a large bowl. • Gradually beat in the cream cheese and butter with an electric mixer fitted with a dough-hook attachment at medium speed until well blended. • Turn the dough out onto a lightly floured surface and knead lightly until smooth. • Press the dough into a disk, wrap in plastic wrap, and refrigerate for 30 minutes. • Filling: Preheat the oven to 325°F. • Sprinkle the hazelnuts onto a large baking sheet. Toast for 7 minutes, or until lightly golden. Increase the oven temperature to 375°F. • Line two cookie sheets with parchment paper. • Rub the skins off the hazelnuts with a kitchen towel. Set aside the nuts to cool. • Process the nuts in a food processor until finely chopped. • Stir together the nuts, marmalade, and marzipan in a small bowl. • Roll out the dough on a lightly floured surface to a thickness of $1/4$ inch. Use a $2^{1}/2$-inch cutter to stamp out about 80 rounds. • Lightly beat the egg whites in a small bowl • Brush the edge of half the dough rounds with a little egg white. • Fill the rounds with a spoonful of the nut mixture. • Press the other circle on top. Use a fork to press down, sealing the edges. • Glaze: Mix the egg yolks with the milk. • Brush over the tops and sprinkle with hazelnuts. • Place the cookies on the prepared cookie sheets, spacing 1 inch apart. • Bake for 10–15 minutes, or until golden brown, rotating the sheets halfway through for even baking. • Transfer to racks to cool.

Makes 40 cookies · Prep: 1 hr. 40 min. + 30 min to chill · Cooking: 10–15 min. · Level: 2 · Keep: 5 days

Maple leaves

maple leaves

3 cups all-purpose flour
$1/4$ teaspoon salt
1 cup (2 sticks) butter, softened
$3/4$ cup granulated sugar
$1/2$ cup pure maple syrup
1 large egg yolk
$1/2$ teaspoon vanilla extract

Sift the flour and salt into a medium bowl. • Beat the butter and sugar in a large bowl with an electric mixer at high speed until creamy. • Add the maple syrup, egg yolk, and vanilla, beating until just blended. • Mix in the dry ingredients. • Divide the dough in half. Press the dough into disks, wrap in plastic wrap, and refrigerate for 30 minutes. • Preheat the oven to 350°F. • Butter three cookie sheets. • Roll out the dough on a lightly floured surface to a thickness of $1/4$ inch. • Use a 3-inch leaf-shaped cookie cutter to cut out the cookies. Gather the dough scraps, re-roll, and continue cutting out cookies until all the dough is used. Use a spatula to transfer the cookies to the prepared cookie sheets, placing them 1 inch apart. • Bake, one sheet at a time, for 12–15 minutes, or until lightly browned. • Transfer to racks to cool.

Makes 25–30 cookies · Prep: 40 min. + 30 min. to chill · Cooking: 12–15 min. per batch · Level: 1 · Keeps: 5 days

fig rolls

1¹/₃ cups all-purpose flour
¹/₂ teaspoon ground cinnamon
¹/₂ teaspoon ground nutmeg
¹/₈ teaspoon salt
¹/₂ cup (1 stick) butter, softened
¹/₃ cup granulated sugar
1 large egg
¹/₂ cup finely ground almonds

Fig filling
1²/₃ cups finely chopped dried figs
¹/₂ cup water
¹/₂ cup granulated sugar
2 teaspoons finely grated orange zest

Sift the flour, cinnamon, nutmeg, and salt into a large bowl. • Beat the butter and sugar in a large bowl with an electric mixer at high speed until creamy. • Add the egg, beating until just blended. • Stir in the dry ingredients and almonds to form a smooth dough. • Divide the dough in four. • Press the dough into disks, wrap each in plastic wrap, and refrigerate for 30 minutes. • Fig filling: Cook the figs with the water, sugar, and orange zest in a medium saucepan over low heat for 15 minutes. • Preheat the oven to 350°F. • Butter two cookie sheets. • Roll out each disk of dough on a lightly floured surface to a 4 x 8-inch rectangle. • Spoon the filling onto the center of the rectangles, leaving a ¹/₂-inch border. • Roll up the rectangles from a long side, making sure they are well sealed. • Transfer to the prepared sheets, seam-side down. • Bake for 20–25 minutes, or until lightly browned, rotating the sheets halfway through for even baking. • Transfer to racks to cool. • Use a sharp knife to cut into ¹/₂-inch slices.

Makes 32 cookies · Prep: 30 min. + 30 min. to chill
Cooking: 20–25 min. · Level: 2 · Keeps: 5 days

rosemary–lemon hearts

1¹/₃ cups all-purpose flour
¹/₈ teaspoon salt
¹/₄ cup (¹/₂ stick) butter, softened
²/₃ cup firmly packed light brown sugar
1 large egg yolk
Grated zest and juice of 1 lemon
1 tablespoon finely chopped rosemary

Sift the flour and salt into a medium bowl. • Beat the butter and brown sugar in a large bowl with an electric mixer at high speed until creamy. • Add the egg yolk and lemon zest and juice, beating until just blended. • Mix in the dry ingredients and rosemary to form a stiff dough. • Press the dough into a

disk, wrap in plastic wrap, and refrigerate for 30 minutes. • Preheat the oven to 350°F. • Butter two cookie sheets. • Discard the plastic wrap. Roll out the dough on a lightly floured surface to a thickness of ¹/₄ inch. • Use a 3-inch heart-shaped cookie cutter to cut out the cookies. Gather the dough scraps, re-roll, and continue cutting out cookies until all the dough is used. • Use a spatula to transfer the cookies to the prepared cookie sheets, placing them 1 inch apart. • Bake for 12–15 minutes, or until pale gold, rotating the sheets halfway through for even baking. • Transfer to racks to cool.

Makes 25–30 cookies · Prep: 40 min. + 30 min. to chill · Cooking: 12–15 min. · Level: 1 · Keeps: 7 days

swiss hearts

These are a specialty of Basel, in northern Switzerland.

2 large egg whites
1¹/₄ cups superfine sugar
1 tablespoon Vanilla Sugar (see page 341)
1¹/₂ tablespoons dark rum
1 tablespoon butter, melted
2 teaspoons unsweetened cocoa powder
1¹/₂ teaspoons ground cinnamon
¹/₂ teaspoon ground cloves
2¹/₂ cups finely ground almonds + more as needed for rolling
¹/₂ teaspoon baking powder

Icing
1¹/₃ cups confectioners' sugar
2 tablespoons hot water, + more as needed

Beat the egg whites and superfine and vanilla sugars in a large bowl with an electric mixer at medium speed until thick and glossy. • Mix in the rum, butter, cocoa, cinnamon, and cloves. • Mix in the ground almonds and baking powder to form a stiff dough. • Press the dough into a disk, wrap in plastic wrap, and refrigerate for 30 minutes. • Preheat the oven to 350°F. • Line four cookie sheets with parchment paper. • Discard the plastic wrap. Roll out the dough between sheets of waxed paper to a thickness of ¹/₄ inch. • Use a 1¹/₂-inch heart-shaped cookie cutter to cut out the cookies. Gather the dough scraps, re-roll, and continue cutting out cookies until all the dough is used. • Bake, one sheet at a time, for 8–10 minutes, or until pale gold and firm at the edges. • Transfer to racks to cool. • Icing: Mix the confectioners' sugar with

enough water to make a thick, spreadable icing. Spread over the tops of the cookies.

Makes 45–50 cookies · Prep: 45 min. + 30 min. to chill · Cooking: 8–10 min. per batch · Level: 1 · Keeps: 1 month

dainty lime treats

2 cups all-purpose flour
1 cup confectioners' sugar
¹/₈ teaspoon salt
³/₄ cup (1¹/₂ sticks) butter, cut up
Grated zest and juice of 1 lime
1 tablespoon very finely chopped candied lime peel
1 large egg, lightly beaten

Lime glaze
1 cup confectioners' sugar
3 tablespoons butter, melted
1–2 tablespoons fresh lime juice
Few drops green food coloring (optional)
1–2 tablespoons finely chopped pistachios

Sift the flour, confectioners' sugar, and salt into a large bowl. • Use a pastry blender to cut in the butter until the mixture resembles coarse crumbs. • Stir in the lime zest and juice and candied lime peel. • Add enough egg to form a stiff dough. • Press the dough into a disk, wrap in plastic wrap, and refrigerate for 30 minutes. • Preheat the oven to 350°F. • Line three cookie sheets with parchment paper. • Roll out the dough on a lightly floured surface to a thickness of ¹/₄ inch. • Use 1¹/₂-inch fluted cookie cutters to cut out the cookies. Gather the dough scraps, re-roll, and continue cutting out cookies until all the dough is used. • Use a spatula to transfer the cookies to the prepared cookie sheets, placing them 1 inch apart. • Bake, one sheet at a time, for 10–12 minutes, or until golden around the edges. • Transfer to racks to cool. • Lime glaze: Mix the confectioners' sugar, butter, and enough lime juice in a small bowl to achieve a spreading consistency. • Add the food coloring and mix until no white streaks remain. • Spread the glaze over the tops of the cookies and sprinkle with pistachios. Let stand for 30 minutes until set.

Makes 45–50 cookies · Prep: 45 min. + 60 min. to chill and set · Cooking: 10–12 min. per batch · Level: 2 · Keeps: 8 days

Dainty lime treats (top)
and Fig rolls (bottom)

ROLLED COOKIES

alphabet cookies

These fun-to-make cookies are perfect for your toddler's birthday celebration.

1²/₃ cups all-purpose flour
1 teaspoon baking powder
1/8 teaspoon salt
1/2 cup (1 stick) butter, softened
1/2 cup granulated sugar
    Grated zest of 1 lemon
1 large egg, lightly beaten
2 tablespoons fresh lemon juice
1/4 teaspoon vanilla extract
1/4 cup apricot preserves or jam, warmed
    Sugar strands, jimmies, or sprinkles,
      to decorate

Sift the flour, cream of tartar, baking soda, and salt into a large bowl. • Beat the butter, sugar, and lemon zest in a large bowl with an electric mixer at high speed until creamy. • Add the egg, beating until just blended. Add the lemon juice and vanilla. Mix in the dry ingredients to form a soft dough. Press the dough into a disk, wrap in plastic wrap, and refrigerate for 30 minutes. • Preheat the oven to 350°F. • Butter three cookie sheets and line with parchment paper. • Use 1-inch cookie cutter to cut out the cookies. Gather the dough scraps, re-roll, and continue cutting out cookies until all the dough is used. • Place 1 inch apart on the prepared cookie sheets. • Bake for 15–20 minutes, or until lightly browned, rotating the sheets halfway through the baking to ensure even browning. • Transfer to racks to cool. • Brush the tops of the cookies with the preserves and sprinkle with the sugar strands.

Makes 35 cookies · Prep: 40 min. + 30 min. to chill
Cooking: 15–20 min. · Level: 1 · Keeps: 10 days

lemon–cinnamon cookies

2 cups all-purpose flour
1/2 teaspoon ground cinnamon
1/8 teaspoon salt
2/3 cup lard or vegetable shortening
1/3 cup butter, softened
1/2 cup granulated sugar
1 large egg yolk
1 teaspoon finely grated lemon zest

Sift the flour, cinnamon, and salt into a medium bowl. • Beat the lard and butter in a large bowl with an electric mixer at high speed until well blended. • Add the sugar, egg yolk, and lemon zest. • Mix in the dry ingredients to form a smooth dough. Press the dough into a disk, wrap in plastic wrap, and refrigerate for 30 minutes. • Preheat the oven to 350°F. • Butter two cookie sheets. • Roll

out the dough on a lightly floured surface to a thickness of 1/4 inch. • Use a 3-inch fluted cookie cutter to cut out the cookies. Gather the dough scraps, re-roll, and continue cutting out cookies until all the dough is used. • Use a spatula to transfer the cookies to the prepared cookie sheets, placing them 1 inch apart. • Bake for 8–10 minutes, or until just golden, rotating the sheets halfway through for even baking. • Transfer to racks to cool.

Makes 30 cookies · Prep: 40 min. + 30 min. to chill
Cooking: 8–10 min. · Level: 1 · Keeps: 5 days

orange cookies

1/3 cup butter, softened
3 tablespoons granulated sugar
1 large egg yolk
    Finely grated zest of 1 orange
1¼ cups all-purpose flour

Glaze
2/3 cup confectioners' sugar
1 tablespoon fresh orange juice, or
      more as needed

Beat the butter and sugar in a large bowl with an electric mixer at medium speed until creamy. • Add the egg yolk and orange zest, beating until just blended. • Mix in the flour to form a stiff dough. Press the dough into a disk, wrap in plastic wrap, and refrigerate for 30 minutes. • Preheat the oven to 350°F. • Butter and flour a cookie sheet. • Roll out the dough to a thickness of 1/8 inch. • Use a fluted cutter to stamp out small rounds. Gather the dough scraps, re-roll, and continue cutting out cookies until all the dough is used. • Use a spatula to transfer the cookies to the prepared cookie sheet. • Bake for 8–10 minutes, or until golden around the edges. • Cool the cookies on the sheet for 5 minutes. Transfer to racks to cool. • Glaze: Mix the confectioners' sugar with enough orange juice to make a pourable consistency. • Drizzle the glaze in a decorative zigzag over the cookies.

Makes 20 cookies · Prep: 40 min. + 30 min. to chill
Cooking: 8–10 min. · Level: 1 · Keeps: 5–8 days

orange star cookies

1½ cups all-purpose flour
1/8 teaspoon salt
2/3 cup butter, cut up
1/3 cup granulated sugar
1 tablespoon finely grated orange zest
2 tablespoons fresh orange juice
2 large egg yolks
1 cup Orange Curd (see page 340)
1 tablespoon confectioners' sugar

Sift the flour and salt into a large bowl. • Use a pastry blender to cut in the butter until the mixture resembles fine crumbs. • Stir in the granulated sugar, orange zest and juice, and egg yolks to form a stiff dough. • Press the dough into a disk, wrap in plastic wrap, and refrigerate for 30 minutes. • Preheat the oven to 350°F. • Butter two cookie sheets. • Roll out the dough on a lightly floured surface to a thickness of 1/8 inch. • Use a 3-inch fluted cookie cutter to cut out the cookies. • Use a 1-inch star-shaped cookie cutter to cut out the centers from half the cookies. Gather the dough scraps, re-roll, and continue cutting out cookies until all the dough is used. • Use a spatula to transfer the cookies to the prepared cookie sheets. • Bake for 6–8 minutes, or until golden brown, rotating the sheets halfway through for even baking. Cool on the sheets until the cookies firm slightly. Transfer to racks to finish cooling. • Spread the cooled whole cookies with the orange curd and place the cookies with holes on top. Dust with the confectioners' sugar.

Makes 12–15 cookies · Prep: 45 min. + 30 min. to chill · Cooking: 6–8 min. · Level: 1 · Keeps: 5 days

zesty lemon bars

2¼ cups all-purpose flour
1¾ cups granulated sugar
4 large egg whites, lightly beaten
1¹/₃ cups finely ground almonds
2/3 cup finely chopped candied lemon peel
    Grated zest of 1 lemon
1 teaspoon baking soda
1/8 teaspoon salt

Line a cookie sheet with parchment paper. • Mix the flour, sugar, egg whites, almonds, candied lemon peel, lemon zest, baking soda, and salt in a large bowl to form a stiff dough. Press the dough into a disk, wrap in plastic wrap, and refrigerate for 30 minutes. • Roll out the dough on a lightly floured surface to a 12 x 3-inch rectangle. • Transfer to the prepared cookie sheet and refrigerate for 30 minutes. • Preheat the oven to 300°F. • Cut the dough in half lengthwise and slice into 1/2-inch strips. • Bake for 10–15 minutes, or until just golden. • Transfer to racks to cool.

Makes 48 cookies · Prep: 25 min. + 30 min. to chill
Cooking: 10–15 min. · Level: 1 · Keeps: 5 days

Alphabet cookies

bars &
brownies

Great for snacking at breakfast or at any time of day, bar cookies are often packed with fiber and goodness to give you that burst of energy you require. Try using fresh fruit and whole grain bases for the best flavor and texture. Brownies, the all-American classic, are loaded with pecans and walnuts or are baked simply with cocoa. Deliciously moist, they will always leave you craving for more. Blondies are a no-chocolate version of the brownie.

above: Chocolate–orange squares (page 132)

right: Chewy oat and dried fruit bars, Apricot squares, Chocolate caramel squares, and Lemon and ginger cookies (pages 146, 120, 132, and 150)

apricot squares

Base

- 3/4 cup all-purpose flour
- 2/3 cup firmly packed light brown sugar
- 1/4 cup (1/2 stick) cold butter, cut up

Topping

- Zest and juice of 1 orange
- Zest and juice of 1/2 lemon
- Water
- 3/4 cup dried apricots
- 1/3 cup firmly packed light brown sugar
- 2 teaspoons cornstarch
- 1/2 cup finely chopped walnuts

Preheat the oven to 350°F. • Place a large baking sheet in the hot oven. • Butter an 8-inch baking pan. • <u>Base</u>: Mix the flour and brown sugar in a large bowl. • Use a pastry blender to cut in the butter until the mixture resembles coarse crumbs. • Firmly press the mixture into the prepared pan to form a smooth, even layer. • Place the pan on the heated baking sheet. • Bake for 12–15 minutes, or until lightly browned. • Cool the base completely in the pan. • <u>Topping</u>: Mix the orange and lemon juices with enough water to make 2/3 cup liquid. • Simmer the apricots in the liquid in a large saucepan for 15 minutes, or until they have softened. • Drain the apricots, reserving the liquid in a small bowl. • Finely chop the apricots and return to the saucepan. Add both zests, the brown sugar, cornstarch, and 1/4 cup apricot liquid. • Bring to the boil and boil for 1 minute, stirring constantly. Let cool, then spread it over the base. Sprinkle with walnuts. • Bake for 15–20 minutes, or until golden brown. • Cool completely before cutting into bars.

Makes 16–25 bars · Prep: 30 min. · Cooking: 30–35 min. · Level: 2 · Keeps: 5 days

banana brownies

A deliciously moist brownie.

- 3/4 cup all-purpose flour
- 1/4 cup unsweetened cocoa powder
- 1 teaspoon baking powder
- 1/8 teaspoon salt
- 6 oz semisweet chocolate, coarsely chopped
- 3/4 cup (1 1/2 sticks) butter, cut up
- 1 1/4 cups firmly packed dark brown sugar
- 1 cup coarsely chopped pecans
- 3 large eggs, lightly beaten
- 2 firm-ripe bananas, mashed

Preheat the oven to 325°F. • Butter an 11 x 7-inch baking pan. • Sift the flour, cocoa, baking powder, and salt into a medium bowl. • Melt the chocolate with the butter and brown sugar in a double boiler over barely simmering water. • Remove from the heat and stir in the pecans, eggs, and bananas. • Mix in the dry ingredients. • Spoon the mixture evenly into the prepared pan. • Bake for 25–35 minutes, or until dry on top and almost firm to the touch. Do not overbake. • Cool completely before cutting into bars.

Makes 22–33 bars · Prep: 20 min. · Cooking: 25–35 min. · Level: 1 · Keeps: 3 days

chester fingers

These elegant cookies hail from the city of Chester in the northwest of England, famous for its black-and-white Tudor buildings called The Rows.

- 1 1/4 cups all-purpose flour
- 1/2 teaspoon baking powder
- 1/8 teaspoon salt
- 1/2 cup (1 stick) butter, softened
- 1/2 cup granulated sugar
- 3 large eggs
- 1 cup finely ground almonds
- 1/4 cup raspberry preserves
- 1 1/4 cups confectioners' sugar
- 2 tablespoons lukewarm water (110°–115°F), + more as needed

Preheat the oven to 350°F. • Butter an 11 x 7-inch baking pan. • Sift the flour, baking powder, and salt into a medium bowl. • Beat the butter and sugar in a large bowl with an electric mixer at high speed until creamy. • Add the eggs, beating until just blended. • Mix in the dry ingredients and almonds. • Firmly press the dough into the prepared pan to form a smooth, even layer. Prick all over with a fork. • Bake for 25–35 minutes, or until golden. • Cool completely before cutting into bars. • Stick the bars together in pairs with the preserves. • Beat the confectioners' sugar with enough water in a small bowl to make a spreadable frosting. • Spread the tops of the bars with the frosting.

Makes 12–15 bars · Prep: 20 min. · Cooking: 25–35 min. · Level: 1 · Keeps: 7 days

banana fingers

- 4 firm-ripe bananas
- 1 tablespoon fresh lemon juice
- 1 2/3 cups whole-wheat flour
- 1 teaspoon baking powder
- 1/8 teaspoon salt
- 1 cup (2 sticks) butter, cut up
- 2 cups old-fashioned rolled oats
- 1 1/4 cups granulated sugar
- 2 large eggs, lightly beaten

Preheat the oven to 350°F. • Butter a 13 x 9-inch baking pan. • Peel the bananas and slice them thinly. • Drop the banana slices into a small bowl of cold water. Add the lemon juice to prevent them from turning brown. • Sift the whole-wheat flour, baking powder, and salt into a large bowl. • Use a pastry blender to cut in the butter until the mixture resembles fine crumbs. • Stir in the oats and sugar. • Mix in enough of the beaten eggs to form a stiff dough. • Divide the dough in two. • Firmly press one half of the dough into the prepared pan to form a smooth, even layer. • Drain the banana slices and arrange them over the dough. • Press the remaining dough on top. • Bake for 25–30 minutes, or until golden brown. • Cool completely before cutting into bars.

Makes 36–45 bars · Prep: 30 min. · Cooking: 25–30 min. · Level: 1 · Keeps: 2 days in the refrigerator

apple bars with orange glaze

- 2 2/3 cups all-purpose flour
- 1 teaspoon baking powder
- 1/2 teaspoon salt
- 1/2 cup finely chopped dried apples
- 3/4 cup (1 1/2 sticks) butter, cut up
- 1/3 cup granulated sugar
- 2 tablespoons Vanilla Sugar (see page 341)
- 1/3 cup light corn syrup
- 1 tablespoon orange-flower water or orange juice
- 1 large egg

Orange glaze

- 1 cup confectioners' sugar
- 1–2 tablespoons fresh orange juice
- 1 tablespoon warm water
- Grated zest of 1 orange

Preheat the oven to 350°F. • Butter an 11 x 7-inch baking pan. • Sift the flour, baking powder, and salt into a medium bowl. • Process the apples, butter, granulated and vanilla sugars, corn syrup, and orange-flower water in a food processor until pureed. • Add the egg, processing until just blended. • Mix in the dry ingredients. • Firmly press the mixture into the baking pan to form a smooth, even layer. • Bake for 15–20 minutes, or until firm to the touch. • Cool completely in the pan. • <u>Orange glaze</u>: Mix the confectioners' sugar with enough orange juice and water to form a runny glaze. • Drizzle over the cake and sprinkle with the orange zest. Cut into bars.

Makes 22–33 bars · Prep: 30 min. · Cooking: 15–20 min. · Level: 2 · Keeps: 8 days

Banana fingers

brownies

Brownies are rich, chocolate-flavored squares that have been eaten in America since the 19th century. The first printed reference to brownies appeared in the 1897 Sears, Roebuck and Company catalog named for their dark chocolatey appearance. Brownies should be moist and chewy, so make sure you don't overbake them. It's best to take the brownies out of the oven when they still seem a little underdone. They will firm up as they cool.

2/3   cup all-purpose flour
1/4   teaspoon baking powder
1/8   teaspoon salt
3   oz bittersweet chocolate, coarsely chopped
1/2   cup butter, cut up
1/3   cup firmly packed dark brown sugar
1   large egg, lightly beaten
1   teaspoon vanilla extract
3/4   cup coarsely chopped walnuts
1   tablespoon milk

Preheat the oven to 350°F. • Butter an 8-inch baking pan. • Sift the flour, baking powder, and salt into a large bowl. • Melt the chocolate with the butter in a double boiler over barely simmering water. • Add the egg, beating until just blended. • Remove from the heat and mix in the brown sugar and dry ingredients, followed by the vanilla and walnuts. • Add 1 tablespoon milk to soften the mixture slightly. • Pour the mixture into the prepared pan. • Bake for 20–25 minutes, or until dry on the top and almost firm to the touch. Do not overbake. • Cool completely before cutting into bars.

Makes 16–25 squares · Prep: 15 min. · Cooking: 20–25 min. · Level: 1 · Keeps: 6 days

marbled fudge brownies

Chocolate-walnut base
1   cup (2 sticks) butter, cut up
4   oz semisweet chocolate, coarsely chopped
2 1/2 cups granulated sugar
3   large eggs, lightly beaten
3/4   cup all-purpose flour
1 1/4 cups coarsely chopped walnuts
1   teaspoon vanilla extract
1/2   teaspoon salt

Topping
1   package (8 oz) cream cheese, softened
2/3   cup granulated sugar
1   large egg, lightly beaten
1   teaspoon vanilla extract

Preheat the oven to 350°F. • Butter a 13 x 9-inch baking pan. • Chocolate-walnut base: Melt the butter and chocolate in a double boiler over barely simmering water. • Remove from the heat and add the sugar and eggs, beating until just blended. • Mix in the flour, walnuts, vanilla, and salt. • Spoon the mixture into the prepared pan. • Topping: Beat the cream cheese, sugar, egg, and vanilla in a large bowl with an electric mixer at high speed until smooth. • Spoon the mixture over the chocolate base. • Use a knife to draw decorative lines across the topping. • Bake for 40–45 minutes, or until almost firm to the touch. Do not overbake. • Cool completely before cutting into bars.

Makes 36–45 bars · Prep: 30 min. · Cooking: 40–45 min. · Level: 1 · Keeps: 4 days in a refrigerator

mint and currant bars

Base
2   cups all-purpose flour
1/8   teaspoon salt
1/4   cup granulated sugar
3/4   cup (1 1/2 sticks) butter, cut up
1/3   cup ice water

Mint and currant filling
1 1/4 cups dried currants
1/4   cup (1/2 stick) butter, cut up
1/4   cup firmly packed light brown sugar
3   tablespoons finely chopped fresh mint
1   large egg, lightly beaten

Preheat the oven to 400°F. • Butter a 13 x 9-inch baking pan. • Base: Sift the flour and salt into a medium bowl. • Stir in the granulated sugar. • Use a pastry blender to cut in the butter until the mixture resembles fine crumbs. • Add enough water to form a stiff dough. • Divide the dough in half. • Roll out half on a lightly floured surface to a thickness of 1/8 inch and to the size of the cookie sheet. • Trim the edges and transfer to the prepared pan. • Mint and currant filling: Sprinkle the currants over the base, leaving a border of 1/2 inch. • Dot with the butter. • Mix the brown sugar and mint in a small bowl and sprinkle over the currants. • Roll out the remaining dough to the same size. • Place the dough on top of the currant filling. • Brush with the beaten egg. • Bake for 25–30 minutes, or until just golden. • Cool completely before cutting into bars.

Makes 30–35 bars · Prep: 40 min. · Cooking: 25–30 min. · Level: 1 · Keeps: 5 days

marbled mint brownies

Cream cheese-mint layer
3/4   package (6 oz) cream cheese, softened
1/4   cup (1/2 stick) butter, softened
1/2   cup granulated sugar
2   large eggs
2   tablespoons all-purpose flour
1   teaspoon mint extract

Brownie layer
1   cup all-purpose flour
1   teaspoon baking powder
1/8   teaspoon salt
1/2   cup (1 stick) butter, cut up
4   oz semisweet chocolate, coarsely chopped
4   large eggs
1 1/2 cups granulated sugar
1/2   cup finely chopped walnuts

Preheat the oven to 350°F. • Butter and flour a 13 x 9-inch baking pan. • Cream cheese-mint layer: Beat the cream cheese, butter, and sugar in a large bowl with an electric mixer at high speed until creamy. • Add the eggs, beating until just blended. • Mix in the flour and mint extract. • Brownie layer: Sift the flour, baking powder, and salt into a medium bowl. • Melt the butter and chocolate in a double boiler over barely simmering water. • With mixer at high speed, beat the eggs and sugar in a large bowl until pale and thick. • Mix in the dry ingredients, followed by the chocolate mixture and walnuts. • Pour half the brownie mixture into the prepared pan. • Use a thin metal spatula to spread the cream cheese layer on top. • Drop spoonfuls of the remaining brownie mixture on top. • Draw through the batter with a knife to create a marbled effect. • Bake for 40–45 minutes, or until dry on top and almost firm to the touch. Do not overbake. • Cool completely before cutting into bars.

Makes 36–45 bars · Prep: 30 min. · Cooking: 40–45 min. · Level: 1 · Keeps: 3 days

Brownies & Marbled mint brownies

Grasmere gingerbread

grasmere gingerbread

This traditional recipe comes from the picturesque village of Grasmere in the heart of one of England's national parks, the Lake District. It was once home to the Romantic poet, William Wordsworth.

2   cups whole-wheat flour
1   tablespoon ground ginger
1¹/2 teaspoons cream of tartar
³/4   teaspoon baking soda
¹/8   teaspoon salt
1¹/4 cups (2¹/2 sticks) butter, cut up
¹/3   cup old-fashioned rolled oats
1¹/2 cups firmly packed light brown sugar

Preheat the oven to 325°F. • Butter a 13 x 9-inch baking pan. • Sift the flour, ginger, cream of tartar, baking soda, and salt into a large bowl. • Use a pastry blender to cut in the butter until the mixture resembles coarse crumbs. • Stir in the oats and brown sugar. • Firmly press the mixture into the prepared pan to form a smooth, even layer, pressing down with a floured fork. • Bake for 20–30 minutes, or until lightly browned. • Cool completely before cutting into bars.

Makes 36–45 bars · Prep: 20 min. · Cooking: 20–30 min. · Level: 1 · Keeps: 4–5 days

scottish gingerbread

This traditional and delicious Scottish recipe for rich gingerbread comes from the Highlands in the far northeastern part of Scotland.

1¹/4 cups dark molasses
2¹/3 cups all-purpose flour
³/4   cup oat bran
1   cup (2 sticks) butter, softened
²/3   cup light cream
1¹/4 cups finely chopped candied lemon peel
2   tablespoons finely grated fresh ginger

Preheat the oven to 350°F. • Butter a 13 x 9-inch baking pan. • Heat the molasses in a small saucepan over low heat until liquid. • Stir together the flour and oat bran in a medium bowl. • Beat the butter in a large bowl with an electric mixer at high speed until creamy. • Mix in the dry ingredients, followed by the cream. • Stir in the molasses, candied peel, and ginger. • Spread the mixture in the prepared pan. • Bake for 45–50 minutes, or until lightly browned. • Cool completely before cutting into bars.

Makes 36–45 bars · Prep: 20 min. · Cooking: 45–50 min. · Level: 1 · Keeps: 5 days

rhubarb–ginger squares

2   cups all-purpose flour
1   teaspoon ground ginger
¹/8   teaspoon salt
1   cup (2 sticks) butter, softened
²/3   cup firmly packed soft brown sugar
1   large egg, lightly beaten
1   lb fresh rhubarb stalks, washed, trimmed, and finely chopped
¹/2   cup finely chopped crystallized ginger

Preheat the oven to 350°F. • Butter a 13 x 9-inch baking pan. • Sift the flour, ground ginger, and salt into a medium bowl. • Beat the butter and brown sugar in a large bowl with an electric mixer at high speed until creamy. • Use a wooden spoon to mix in the dry ingredients until the mixture resembles coarse crumbs. Transfer half the mixture to a small bowl and set aside. • Add the egg to the remaining mixture and mix to form a smooth dough. • Firmly press the dough into the prepared pan to form a smooth, even layer. • Place the rhubarb over the top and sprinkle with the remaining crumb mixture. • Sprinkle the crystallized ginger on top of the crumbs. • Bake for 45–50 minutes, or until golden. • Cool in the pan for 15 minutes and cut into bars. • Serve warm.

Makes 36–45 bars · Prep: 30 min. · Cooking: 45–50 min. · Level: 1 · Keeps: 5 days

molasses–currant bars

Sweet, sharp, fruity, and soft—an irresistible combination.

²/3   cup dried currants
5   tablespoons light molasses
2   tablespoons fresh lemon juice
1   cup all-purpose flour
¹/8   teaspoon salt
²/3   cup butter, softened
²/3   cup granulated sugar
2   large eggs
1   teaspoon finely grated lemon zest

Preheat the oven to 375°F. • Butter an 8-inch square baking pan. • Sprinkle the currants into the prepared pan. • Mix the molasses and lemon juice in a small bowl until well blended. Pour the mixture over the currants. • Sift the flour and salt into a medium bowl. • Use a wooden spoon to beat the butter and sugar in a large bowl until creamy. • Add the eggs, beating until just blended. • Mix in the dry ingredients and lemon zest until well blended. • Spread the mixture evenly in the pan. • Bake for 25–30 minutes, or until firm to the touch. • Cool completely before cutting into bars.

Makes 16–25 bars · Prep: 20 min. · Cooking: 25–30 min. · Level: 1 · Keeps: 7 days

coconut–walnut squares

³/4   cup all-purpose flour
¹/2   teaspoon baking powder
¹/4   teaspoon salt
¹/2   cup shredded coconut
¹/2   cup finely chopped walnuts
2   tablespoons finely ground almonds
¹/3   cup old-fashioned rolled oats
³/4   cup granulated sugar
¹/2   cup (1 stick) butter, cut up
1   tablespoon light corn syrup
1   tablespoon milk
1   large egg

Preheat the oven to 350°F. • Butter an 11 x 7-inch baking pan. • Sift the flour, baking powder, and salt into a large bowl. • Stir in the coconut, walnuts, almonds, oats, and sugar. • Use a pastry blender to cut in the butter until the mixture resembles fine crumbs. • Dissolve the corn syrup in the milk in a small saucepan over low heat. Add the egg, beating until just blended. • Pour the egg mixture into the dry ingredients and mix well. • Spread the mixture evenly in the baking pan. • Bake for 40–45 minutes, or until golden brown. • Cool completely before cutting into bars.

Makes 22–33 bars · Prep: 15 min. · Cooking: 40–45 min. · Level: 1 · Keeps: 5 days

walnut squares

- 2/3 cup all-purpose flour
- 1/4 teaspoon baking powder
- 1/4 teaspoon salt
- 2 1/2 oz semisweet chocolate, coarsely chopped
- 1/3 cup butter, softened
- 1/3 cup granulated sugar
- 1 large egg, lightly beaten, at room temperature
- 3/4 cup walnuts, coarsely chopped
- 1 teaspoon vanilla extract
- 1 tablespoon milk (optional)

Preheat the oven to 350°F. • Butter an 8-inch square baking pan. • Sift the flour, baking powder, and salt into a large bowl. • Melt the chocolate in a double boiler over barely simmering water. • Beat the butter and sugar in a large bowl with an electric mixer at high speed until creamy. • Add the egg, beating just until blended. • Mix in the dry ingredients, followed by the walnuts, melted chocolate, and vanilla. • If the batter is very stiff, add a little milk. • Pour the batter into the prepared pan. • Bake for 20–25 minutes, or until the top is lightly browned and springy to the touch. • Cool completely before cutting into squares.

Makes 16–25 squares · Prep: 35 min.· Cooking: 20–25 min.· Level: 1 · Keeps: 5–7 days

port wine–walnut squares

- 3/4 cup all-purpose flour
- 1/2 teaspoon baking powder
- 1/8 teaspoon salt
- 1/2 cup (1 stick) butter, softened
- 3/4 cup firmly packed dark brown sugar
- 1 large egg, lightly beaten
- 1/2 teaspoon vanilla extract
- 2 tablespoons milk
- 1/4 cup best-quality port wine
- 1 1/2 cups coarsely chopped walnuts

Preheat the oven to 350°F. • Butter and flour a 9-inch square baking pan. • Sift the flour, baking powder, and salt into a medium bowl.

• Beat the butter and brown sugar in a large bowl with an electric mixer at high speed until creamy. • Add the egg, beating until just blended. • Add the vanilla, milk, and 2 tablespoons port. • Mix in the dry ingredients, followed by 1 cup walnuts. • Spoon the mixture into the prepared pan. Sprinkle with the remaining 1/2 cup walnuts. • Bake for 15–20 minutes, or until a toothpick inserted into the center comes out clean. • Remove from the oven and brush with the remaining 2 tablespoons port. • Cool completely before cutting into squares.

Makes 16–25 squares · Prep: 20 min. · Cooking: 15–20 min. · Level: 1 · Keeps: 3 days

crunchy oatmeal bars

- 1 1/2 cups whole-wheat flour
- 2 teaspoons baking powder
- 1/4 teaspoon salt
- 1/3 cup butter, cut up
- 1/2 cup raw sugar (Barbados or Demerara)
- 1/2 cup old-fashioned rolled oats
- 1/2 cup milk

Preheat the oven to 375°F. • Butter an 11 x 7-inch baking pan. • Sift the whole-wheat flour, baking powder, and salt into a medium bowl. • Melt the butter with the raw sugar in a medium saucepan over low heat until the sugar has dissolved completely. • Remove from the heat and mix in the dry ingredients, oats, and milk. • Firmly press the mixture into the prepared pan to form a smooth, even layer. • Bake for 20–25 minutes, or until just golden and firm to the touch. • Cool completely before cutting into bars.

Makes 22–33 bars · Prep: 20 min. · Cooking: 20–25 min. · Level: 1 · Keeps: 3 days

meringue-topped butterscotch squares

- 1/2 cup all-purpose flour
- 1 teaspoon ground cinnamon
- 1/4 teaspoon salt
- 1/4 cup (1/2 stick) butter, cut up
- 1 cup firmly packed dark brown sugar
- 1 large egg
- 1/2 teaspoon vanilla extract

Meringue topping
- 1 large egg white
- 1/8 teaspoon salt
- 1 tablespoon light corn syrup
- 1/2 cup superfine sugar
- 1 cup finely chopped walnuts

Preheat the oven to 350°F. • Line an 8-inch square baking pan with aluminum foil, letting the edges overhang. • Sift the flour, cinnamon, and salt into a medium bowl. • Melt the butter with the brown sugar in a small saucepan over low heat until the sugar has dissolved completely. • Remove from the heat and let cool completely. • Add the egg and vanilla, beating until just blended. • Mix in the dry ingredients. • Spread the mixture in the prepared pan. • Meringue topping: Beat the egg white and salt in a medium bowl with an electric mixer at medium speed until soft peaks form. • With mixer at high speed, gradually add the corn syrup and superfine sugar, beating until stiff, glossy peaks form. • Use a large rubber spatula to fold in 1/2 cup of the walnuts. • Spread the topping over the base and sprinkle with the remaining 1/2 cup walnuts. • Bake for 25–30 minutes, or until just golden. • Using the foil as handles, lift onto a rack and let cool completely. • Remove the foil and cut into squares.

Makes 16 squares · Prep: 30 min. · Cooking: 25–30 min. · Level: 1 · Keeps: 2 days in the refrigerator

Meringue-topped butterscotch squares

irish cheese squares

The cheese used in these squares is curd cheese, a denser and drier cheese than cottage cheese. If cottage cheese must be substituted, it should be drained overnight in a colander lined with heavy-duty paper towels or cheesecloth.

1/3 cup butter, softened
3/4 cup granulated sugar
3 large eggs, separated
1 tablespoon cornstarch
1 2/3 cups curd cheese
1/3 cup golden raisins
1 teaspoon finely grated lemon zest
1/8 teaspoon salt

Preheat the oven to 375°F. • Butter an 11 x 7-inch baking pan. • Beat the butter and sugar in a large bowl with an electric mixer at high speed until creamy. • Add the egg yolks, beating until just blended. • Stir in the cornstarch, cheese, raisins, lemon zest, and salt. • With mixer at high speed, beat the egg whites in a medium bowl until stiff peaks form. • Use a large rubber spatula to fold the egg whites into the cheese mixture. • Spread the mixture in the prepared baking pan. • Bake for 30 minutes. • Reduce the oven temperature to 300°F. • Bake for 30–40 minutes more, or until firm to the touch and golden. • Cool completely in the pan and cut into squares.

Makes 22–33 bars · Prep: 25 min. · Cooking: 60–70 min. · Level: 1 · Keeps: 5 days

apple, raisin, and oat bars

Cookie base
1 1/3 cups all-purpose flour
2 teaspoons baking powder
1/4 teaspoon salt
1 cup shredded coconut
2/3 cup butter, cut up
3/4 cup firmly packed light brown sugar

Apple–oat topping
4 large tart apples, peeled, cored, and coarsely chopped
2 tablespoons butter
2 tablespoons water
1/4 cup golden raisins
1/3 cup old-fashioned rolled oats
1/4 teaspoon ground cinnamon
1/4 teaspoon freshly grated nutmeg

Preheat the oven to 350°F. • Butter an 11 x 7-inch baking pan. • Cookie base: Sift the flour, baking powder, and salt into a large bowl. Stir in the coconut. • Melt the butter with the brown sugar

in a small saucepan over low heat until the sugar has dissolved completely. • Stir the butter mixture into the dry ingredients until well blended. • Reserve 1 cup of the cookie mixture. Firmly press the remaining mixture into the prepared pan to form a smooth, even layer. • Bake for 8–10 minutes, or until lightly browned. • Apple-oat topping: Cook the apples with the butter and water in a skillet over medium heat for 15–20 minutes, stirring frequently, until the apples have softened. • Plump the raisins in hot water to cover in a small bowl for 10 minutes. • Drain well and pat dry with paper towels. • Spread the apple mixture over the cookie base. • Mix together the reserved cookie mixture, raisins, oats, cinnamon, and nutmeg. Sprinkle the mixture over the apples. • Bake for 25–30 minutes, or until golden brown. • Cool completely before cutting into bars.

Makes 22–33 bars · Prep: 40 min. · Cooking: 33–40 min. · Level: 1 · Keeps: 3 days

pumpkin–raisin bars with cream cheese frosting

2/3 cup all-purpose flour
1 teaspoon baking powder
1/2 teaspoon baking soda
1/2 teaspoon ground cinnamon
1/2 teaspoon ground nutmeg
1/8 teaspoon salt
2 large eggs
3/4 cup granulated sugar
1/2 cup sunflower oil
1 cup cooked or canned pumpkin puree
1/3 cup golden raisins

Cream cheese frosting
2 packages (3 oz each) cream cheese, softened
1 cup confectioners' sugar
1 tablespoon finely grated lemon zest
2–3 tablespoons fresh lemon juice

Preheat the oven to 350°F. • Butter and flour a 13 x 9-inch baking pan. • Sift the flour, baking powder, baking soda, cinnamon, and nutmeg into a medium bowl. • Beat the eggs and sugar in a large bowl with an electric mixer at high speed until pale and thick. • Beat in the oil and pumpkin until well blended. • Mix in the dry ingredients, followed by the raisins. • Pour the batter into the prepared pan. • Bake for 25–30 minutes, or until

a toothpick inserted into the center comes out clean. • Cool completely in the pan. • Cream cheese frosting: With mixer at medium speed, beat the cream cheese, confectioners' sugar, and lemon zest in a large bowl until fluffy. Add enough lemon juice to make a smooth, spreadable frosting. • Spread over the top and cut into bars.

Makes 36–45 bars · Prep: 25 min. · Cooking: 25–30 min. · Level: 1 · Keeps: 3 days in the refrigerator

apricot–raisin bars

2 cups dried apricots, soaked overnight
2 tablespoons sunflower oil
1 cup raisins
2/3 cup old-fashioned rolled oats
Grated zest of 1 lemon
1/2 teaspoon ground cardamom
1/8 teaspoon salt

Preheat the oven to 400°F. • Butter a 13 x 9-inch baking pan. • Bring the apricots and their soaking liquid to a boil in a small saucepan over low heat and simmer for 5 minutes, or until softened. • Drain and transfer to a food processor or blender. Process until smooth. • Transfer to a large bowl and add the oil. • Mix in the raisins, oats, lemon zest, cardamom, and salt until well blended. • Spread the mixture evenly in the prepared pan. • Bake for 40–45 minutes, or until firm to the touch. • Cool completely in the pan. • Cut into bars.

Makes 36–45 bars · Prep: 25 min. · Cooking: 40–45 min. · Level: 1 · Keeps: 3 days

Pumpkin–raisin bars
with cream cheese frosting

three-chocolate brownies

1 1/2 cups all-purpose flour
1/8 teaspoon salt
7 oz semisweet chocolate, coarsely chopped
1/2 cup (1 stick) butter, cut up
1 cup white chocolate chips
1 cup milk chocolate chips
1 cup coarsely chopped pecans
2 large eggs

Preheat the oven to 350°F. • Butter an 8-inch square baking pan. • Sift the flour and salt into a medium bowl. • Melt the semisweet chocolate with the butter in a double boiler over barely simmering water. • Transfer the chocolate mixture to a medium bowl and let cool for 5 minutes. • Mix in the white and milk chocolate chips and the pecans. • Add the eggs, beating until just blended. • Mix in the dry ingredients. • Spoon the batter evenly into the prepared pan. • Bake for 35–40 minutes, or until dry on top and almost firm to the touch. Do not overbake. • Cool completely before cutting into bars.

Makes 16–25 bars · Prep: 20 min. · Cooking: 35–40 min. · Level: 1 · Keeps: 5 days

new zealand honey–nut brownies

1 cup all-purpose flour
1/2 teaspoon baking powder
1/8 teaspoon salt
6 oz semisweet chocolate, coarsely chopped
1/2 cup (1 stick) butter, cut up
1/2 cup granulated sugar
1/2 cup honey
2 large eggs
1 cup finely chopped walnuts

Preheat the oven to 350°F. • Butter a 13 x 9-inch baking pan. • Sift the flour, baking powder, and salt into a medium bowl. • Melt the chocolate with the butter in a double boiler over barely simmering water. Transfer the chocolate mixture to a large bowl and let cool for 5 minutes. • Beat in the sugar and honey. • Add the eggs, beating until just blended. • Mix in the dry ingredients and walnuts. • Spoon the mixture evenly into the prepared pan. • Bake for 30–35 minutes, or until dry on top and almost firm to the touch. Do not overbake. • Cool completely before cutting into bars.

Makes 36–45 bars · Prep: 20 min. · Cooking: 30–35 min. · Level: 1 · Keeps: 5 days

coffee brownies

1 cup all-purpose flour
1 teaspoon baking powder
1/4 teaspoon salt
1/2 cup (1 stick) butter, cut up
1 1/3 cups firmly packed light or dark brown sugar
1 tablespoon freeze-dried coffee granules dissolved in 1 tablespoon hot water
1 teaspoon vanilla extract
2 large eggs, lightly beaten
5 oz semisweet chocolate, coarsely chopped
2 tablespoons coarsely chopped walnuts

Preheat the oven to 350°F. • Butter a 9-inch square baking pan. • Sift the flour, baking powder, and salt into a large bowl. • Melt the butter with the brown sugar in a medium saucepan over low heat, stirring constantly. • Stir in the coffee mixture. • Remove from the heat and let cool for 5 minutes. • Add the vanilla and eggs, beating until just blended. • Mix in the dry ingredients, chocolate, and walnuts until well blended. • Pour the mixture into the prepared pan. • Bake for 30–35 minutes, or until dry on the top and almost firm to the touch. Do not overbake. • Cool completely before cutting into bars.

Makes 16–25 bars · Prep: 15 min. · Cooking: 30–35 min. · Level: 1 · Keeps: 6 days

chocolate–hazelnut brownies

6 oz bittersweet chocolate, coarsely chopped
1/2 cup (1 stick) butter, cut up
2 large eggs
1 cup granulated sugar
3/4 cup finely chopped toasted hazelnuts
2/3 cup all-purpose flour
1/2 teaspoon baking powder
1/4 teaspoon salt
1 teaspoon vanilla extract

Preheat the oven to 350°F. • Butter an 8-inch baking pan. • Melt the chocolate with the butter in a double boiler over barely simmering water. Set aside to cool. • Transfer to a medium bowl. • With an electric mixer at medium speed, add the eggs, beating until just blended. • With mixer at low speed, gradually beat in the sugar, hazelnuts, flour, baking powder, salt, and vanilla. • Spoon the batter into the prepared pan. • Bake for 30–35 minutes, or until dry on top and almost firm to the touch. Do not overbake. • Cool completely before cutting into bars.

Makes 16–25 bars · Prep: 20 min. · Cooking: 30–35 min. · Level: 1 · Keeps. 5 days

Chocolate–hazelnut brownies

almond–toffee bars

Almond–toffee topping
- 1/3 cup butter
- 1/2 cup granulated sugar
- 2 tablespoons firmly packed light brown sugar
- 2 tablespoons milk
- 2 1/2 cups flaked almonds

Cookie base
- 1 1/3 cups all-purpose flour
- 1 teaspoon baking powder
- 1/4 teaspoon salt
- 1/2 cup (1 stick) butter, softened
- 2/3 cup granulated sugar
- 1 large egg
- 1 teaspoon finely grated lemon zest

Preheat the oven to 350°F. • Butter a 9-inch baking pan. • Almond-toffee topping: Melt the butter with the granulated and brown sugars in a small saucepan over low heat. • Add the milk and bring to a boil, stirring constantly. • Remove from the heat and stir in the almonds. • Cookie base: Sift the flour, baking powder, and salt into a medium bowl. • Beat the butter and sugar in a large bowl with an electric mixer at high speed until creamy. • Add the egg, beating until just blended. • Mix in the dry ingredients and lemon zest. • Firmly press the mixture into the prepared pan to form a smooth, even layer. • Spread the almond-toffee topping evenly over the cookie base. • Bake for 30–35 minutes, or until just golden. • Cut into bars while the topping is still warm.

Makes 15 bars · Prep: 30 min. · Cooking: 30–35 min. · Level: 1 · Keeps: 5 days

sticky toffee–walnut bars

- 3/4 cup all-purpose flour
- 1/8 teaspoon salt
- 1/2 cup (1 stick) butter, cut up
- 2 teaspoons fresh lemon juice
- 1–2 tablespoons ice water
- 5 tablespoons honey
- 1/2 cup firmly packed light brown sugar
- 1/2 teaspoon vanilla extract
- 2 large eggs, lightly beaten
- 1 cup finely chopped walnuts

Sift the flour and salt into a medium bowl. • Use a pastry blender to cut in 1/4 cup butter until the mixture resembles fine crumbs. • Mix in the lemon juice and enough water to form a soft dough. • Press the dough into a disk, wrap in plastic wrap,

and refrigerate for 30 minutes. • Preheat the oven to 375°F. • Butter an 8-inch baking pan. • Roll out the dough on a lightly floured surface to a thickness of 1/8 inch and to an 8-inch square. • Fit the dough into the prepared pan. • Melt the remaining 1/4 cup butter in a small saucepan over low heat. • Mix in the honey, brown sugar, and vanilla until well blended. • Add the eggs, beating until just blended. • Stir in the walnuts. • Spread the mixture evenly over the base. • Bake for 40–45 minutes, or until lightly browned and firm to the touch. • Cool completely before cutting into bars.

Makes 16–25 bars · Prep: 30 min. + 30 min. to chill · Cooking: 40–45 min. · Level: 1 · Keeps: 7 days

toffee–oat bars

- 3/4 cup all-purpose flour
- 1/8 teaspoon salt
- 1 cup (2 sticks) butter, softened
- 1 cup firmly packed light brown sugar
- 2 large egg yolks
- 3/4 cup old-fashioned rolled oats

Chocolate frosting
- 6 oz semisweet chocolate, coarsely chopped
- 2 tablespoons butter, cut up

Preheat the oven to 375°F. • Butter an 11 x 7-inch baking pan. • Sift the flour and salt into a medium bowl. • Beat the butter and brown sugar in a large bowl with an electric mixer at high speed until creamy. • Add the egg yolks, beating until just blended. • Mix in the dry ingredients and oats. • Firmly press the mixture into the prepared pan to form a smooth, even layer. • Bake for 15–20 minutes, or until firm to the touch. • Cool completely in the pan. • Chocolate frosting: Melt the chocolate and butter in a double boiler over barely simmering water. • Spread the chocolate mixture over and let stand for 30 minutes until set. • Cut into bars.

Makes 22–33 bars · Prep: 25 min. · Cooking: 15–20 min. · Level: 1 · Keeps: 5 days

toffee bars

- 1/2 cup (1 stick) butter, softened
- 2/3 cup firmly packed light brown sugar
- 1 large egg yolk
- 1/3 cup all-purpose flour
- 1/4 cup old-fashioned rolled oats
- 1/8 teaspoon salt

Chocolate-walnut topping
- 3 oz semisweet chocolate
- 1 tablespoon butter
- 1/2 cup finely chopped walnuts

Preheat the oven to 375°F. • Butter a 10 1/2 x 15 1/2-inch jelly-roll pan. • Beat the butter and brown sugar in a large bowl with an electric mixer at high speed until creamy. • Add the egg yolk, beating until just blended. • Mix in the flour, oats, and salt until well blended. • Firmly press the mixture into the prepared pan to form a smooth, even layer. • Bake for 15–20 minutes, or until just golden. • Chocolate-walnut topping: Melt the chocolate and butter in a double boiler over barely simmering water. • Spread the melted chocolate mixture over the oat base and sprinkle with the chopped walnuts. • Cool completely before cutting into bars.

Makes 25 bars · Prep: 25 min. · Cooking: 15–20 min. · Level: 1 · Keeps: 3 days

Toffee bars

paradise bars

2 cups all-purpose flour
1/8 teaspoon salt
1¼ cups (2½ sticks) butter, cut up
1/4 cup ice water
1/3 cup raspberry preserves
2/3 cup granulated sugar
1 large egg
2/3 cup finely ground almonds
1/2 cup rice flour
1/4 cup all-purpose flour
2 tablespoons coarsely chopped candied cherries
2 tablespoons coarsely chopped pecans
1/2 teaspoon almond extract

Preheat the oven to 350°F. • Line a 13 x 9-inch baking pan with aluminum foil, letting the edges overhang. Butter the foil. • Sift the flour and salt into a large bowl. • Use a pastry blender to cut in 3/4 cup of the butter until the mixture resembles fine crumbs. • Add enough ice water to form a stiff dough. • Roll out the dough on a lightly floured surface to a thickness of 1/4 inch and to a 13 x 9-inch rectangle. • Trim the edges and transfer to the prepared baking pan. • Warm the raspberry preserves in a small saucepan over low heat until liquid. • Brush the preserves over the base. • Beat the remaining 1/2 cup butter and sugar in a medium bowl with an electric mixer at high speed until creamy. • Add the egg, beating until just blended. • Mix in the almonds, the rice and all-purpose flours, cherries, pecans, and almond extract until well blended. • Spread the mixture over the preserves. • Bake for 40–45 minutes, or until lightly browned. • Cool completely in the pan on a rack. • Using the foil as handles, lift onto a cutting board. Peel off the foil. Cut into bars.

Makes 36–45 bars · Prep: 25 min. · Cooking: 40–45 min. · Level: 2 · Keeps: 5 days

pecan pie bars

Cookie base
1/4 cup finely chopped pecans
2/3 cup confectioners' sugar
2 cups all-purpose flour
1/8 teaspoon salt
1 cup (2 sticks) butter, cut up

Pecan pie filling
3 oz semisweet chocolate, coarsely chopped
1/2 cup (1 stick) butter, cut up
3/4 cup firmly packed dark brown sugar
3/4 cup dark corn syrup
1/2 teaspoon vanilla extract
1 tablespoon dark rum
3 cups coarsely chopped pecans

Preheat the oven to 350°F. • Set out a 13 x 9-inch baking pan. • Cookie base: Process the pecans, confectioners' sugar, flour, and salt in a food processor or blender until well blended. • Add the butter and process until a dough begins to form. • Firmly press the mixture into the prepared pan to form a smooth, even layer. • Bake for 15–20 minutes, or until lightly golden. • Pecan pie filling: Melt the chocolate and butter in a double boiler over barely simmering water. • Transfer to a large bowl and mix in the brown sugar, corn syrup, vanilla, and rum until well blended. • Stir in the nuts. • Spread the filling over the baked cookie base. • Bake for 20–25 minutes, or until the filling is bubbling. • Cool completely before cutting into bars.

Makes 36–45 bars · Prep: 40 min. · Cooking: 35–45 min. · Level: 1 · Keeps: 3 days in the refrigerator

toffee–walnut blondies with caramel frosting

1¼ cups all-purpose flour
1 teaspoon baking powder
1/8 teaspoon salt
1 cup (2 sticks) butter, cut up
1 cup firmly packed light brown sugar
1/4 cup light corn syrup
1/2 teaspoon vanilla extract
4 large eggs
1/2 cup coarsely chopped walnuts

Caramel frosting
1½ cups confectioners' sugar
2 tablespoons butter, melted
1 tablespoon light corn syrup
1/2 teaspoon vanilla extract

Preheat the oven to 350°F. • Butter an 11 x 7-inch baking pan. • Sift the flour, baking powder, and salt into a medium bowl. • Melt the butter with the brown sugar and corn syrup in a medium saucepan over low heat until the sugar has dissolved completely. • Add the vanilla and eggs, beating until just blended. • Mix in the dry ingredients and walnuts. • Pour the mixture into the prepared pan. • Bake for 25–30 minutes, or until dry on top and almost firm to the touch. Do not overbake. • Cool completely in the pan. • Caramel frosting: Beat the confectioners' sugar, butter, corn syrup, and vanilla extract in a medium bowl until well blended. • Spread the frosting over. • Cut into squares.

Makes 22–33 squares · Prep: 25 min. · Cooking: 25–30 min. · Level: 1 · Keeps: 5 days

date and pecan shortcakes

2/3 cup all-purpose flour
2/3 cup cornstarch
1/8 teaspoon salt
1/2 cup (1 stick) butter, softened
1/2 cup firmly packed light brown sugar
1 large egg
2/3 cup finely chopped pitted dates
1 cup coarsely chopped pecans
2 tablespoons milk
2 tablespoons granulated sugar

Preheat the oven to 375°F. • Line a 13 x 9-inch baking pan with aluminum foil, letting the edges overhang. Butter the foil. • Sift the flour, cornstarch, and salt into a large bowl. • Beat the butter, brown sugar, and egg in a large bowl with an electric mixer at high speed until well blended. • Mix in the dry ingredients, dates, and pecans to form a stiff dough. • Firmly press the mixture into the prepared pan to form a smooth, even layer. • Brush with the milk and sprinkle with the granulated sugar. • Bake for 20–30 minutes, or until just golden. • Cool completely in the pan on a rack. • Using the foil as handles, lift onto a cutting board. Peel off the foil. Cut into squares.

Makes 36–45 bars · Prep: 20 min. · Cooking: 20–30 min. · Level: 1 · Keeps: 7 days

Toffee–walnut blondies with caramel frosting (top) and Pecan pie bars (bottom)

Chocolate quickies

chocolate quickies

1   cup (2 sticks) butter, cut up
2   tablespoons unsweetened cocoa powder
1   tablespoon firmly packed light
     brown sugar
2   tablespoons light corn syrup
2   cups graham cracker crumbs
4   oz semisweet chocolate,
     coarsely chopped

Butter an 8-inch square baking pan. • Melt the butter in a small saucepan over low heat. Stir in the cocoa, brown sugar, and corn syrup. Bring to a boil and let boil for 1 minute. • Remove from the heat and stir in the crumbs. • Spoon the mixture into the prepared pan, pressing down lightly . • Melt the chocolate in a double boiler over barely simmering water. Pour the melted chocolate over the cookie base. Use a knife to swirl the chocolate in a decorative manner. • Refrigerate for 1 hour. • Cut into squares.

Makes 16–25 squares · Prep: 15 min. + 1 hr. to chill · Level: 1 · Keeps: 3 days

chocolate caramel squares

Cookie base
1   cup all-purpose flour
1   teaspoon baking powder
1/8   teaspoon salt
1/2   cup (1 stick) butter, softened
1/4   cup granulated sugar

Caramel topping
1/2   cup (1 stick) butter, cut up
1/2   cup granulated sugar
2   tablespoons light corn syrup
1   can (14 oz) sweetened condensed milk
8   oz semisweet chocolate, coarsely chopped

Preheat the oven to 325°F. • Line a 10^1/2 x 15^1/2-inch jelly-roll pan with aluminum foil. • Cookie base: Sift the flour, baking powder, and salt into a large bowl. • Beat the butter and sugar in a large bowl with an electric

mixer at high speed until creamy. • Mix in the dry ingredients. • Spread the mixture evenly in the prepared pan. • Bake for 10–15 minutes, or until golden brown. • Caramel topping: Melt the butter with the sugar, corn syrup, and condensed milk in a medium saucepan over low heat, stirring constantly. Bring to a boil and let boil for 5 minutes. Remove from the heat and let cool slightly. • Spread the caramel topping evenly over the cookie base. • Melt the chocolate in a double boiler over barely simmering water. Pour the chocolate over the caramel topping and let stand for 30 minutes until set. • Cut into bars.

Makes 15 bars · Prep: 20 min. + 30 min. to set · Cooking: 10 min. · Level: 2 · Keeps: 5 days

fudge brownies

3^1/3   cups all-purpose flour
2   teaspoons baking powder
1/4   teaspoon salt
1/2   cup (1 stick) butter, cut up
4   oz semisweet chocolate, coarsely chopped
2   cups granulated sugar
4   large eggs, lightly beaten
1   teaspoon vanilla extract
3/4   cup coarsely chopped pecans

Preheat the oven to 350°F. • Line a 13 x 9-inch baking pan with aluminum foil, letting the edges overhang. • Sift the flour, baking powder, and salt into a medium bowl. • Melt the butter and chocolate in a double boiler over barely simmering water. • Remove from the heat and stir in the sugar. • Add the eggs, beating until just blended. • Mix in the dry ingredients, vanilla, and pecans. • Pour the batter into the prepared pan. • Bake for 25–30 minutes, or until dry on top and almost firm to the touch. Do not overbake. • Cool completely in the pan. • Using the foil as handles, lift onto a cutting board. Peel off the foil. Cut into bars.

Makes 36–45 bars · Prep: 20 min. · Cooking: 25–30 min. · Level: 1 · Keeps: 4 days

coconut–cherry squares

10   oz semisweet chocolate, coarsely chopped
1/2   cup (1 stick) butter, softened
1^1/4   cups granulated sugar
2   large eggs, at room temperature
2/3   cup candied cherries, coarsely chopped
2   cups shredded coconut

Preheat the oven to 325°F. • Line a 10^1/2 x 15^1/2-inch jelly-roll pan with aluminum foil. • Melt the chocolate in a double boiler over

barely simmering water. Spread the chocolate over the foil and set aside to cool. • Beat the butter and sugar in a large bowl with an electric mixer at high speed until creamy. • Add the eggs, beating until just blended after each addition. • Use a large rubber spatula to fold in the cherries and coconut. • Spread over the cooled chocolate. • Bake for 15–20 minutes, or until a toothpick inserted into the center comes out clean. • Cool completely before cutting into squares.

Makes 15 squares · Prep: 15 min. · Cooking: 15–20 min. · Level: 1 · Keeps: 5 days

chocolate–orange squares

Chocolate cookie base
1   cup all-purpose flour
1/4   cup unsweetened cocoa powder
1/4   teaspoon salt
1   cup (2 sticks) butter, softened
1/3   cup granulated sugar
1/3   cup confectioners' sugar

Orange filling
     Grated zest of 1 orange
1/2   cup fresh orange juice
1/2   cup water
1/3   cup cornstarch
1   teaspoon fresh lemon juice
1   tablespoon butter, softened
1/2   cup orange marmalade

Chocolate cream glaze
3   tablespoons heavy cream
1^1/2   teaspoons light corn syrup
3   oz semisweet chocolate, coarsely chopped

Preheat the oven to 325°F. • Line an 8-inch square baking pan with aluminum foil, letting the edges overhang. • Chocolate cookie base: Sift the flour, cocoa, and salt into a medium bowl. • Beat the butter, granulated sugar, and confectioners' sugar in a large bowl with an electric mixer at high speed until creamy. • Mix in the dry ingredients. • Firmly press the mixture into the prepared pan to form a smooth, even layer. • Prick all over with a fork. • Bake for 25–30 minutes, or until firm to the touch. • Let cool for 10 minutes. • Orange filling: Mix the orange zest and juice, water, cornstarch, and lemon juice in a small saucepan over medium heat. • Bring to a boil and boil, stirring constantly, for 1 minute, or until thickened. • Remove from the heat and mix in the butter and marmalade until well blended. • Pour the filling evenly over the cookie base. • Bake for 5 minutes. • Cool completely in the pan. • Refrigerate for 1 hour, or until set. • Chocolate cream glaze: Bring the cream to a boil with the corn syrup in a small saucepan. • Remove from the heat and stir in the chocolate until melted and smooth. • Spoon the glaze into a small freezer bag and cut off a tiny corner. • Pipe over the filling in a decorative manner and refrigerate for 30 minutes. • Using the foil as handles, transfer to a cutting board. • Cut into squares.

Makes 16–25 squares · Prep: 40 min. + 90 min. to chill · Cooking: 30–35 min. · Level: 2 · Keeps: 2 days

sunshine bars

2/3 cup milk
1/2 cup finely chopped dates
3/4 cup whole-wheat flour
1/2 teaspoon baking powder
1/2 teaspoon ground cinnamon
1/8 teaspoon salt
1 large egg, lightly beaten
1/4 cup (1/2 stick) butter, melted
Grated zest and chopped flesh of 1 orange

Preheat the oven to 350°F. • Butter an 8-inch square baking pan. • Heat the milk in a small saucepan over low heat. • Pour the milk into a large bowl, add the dates, and let soak for 15 minutes. • Sift the flour, baking powder, cinnamon, and salt into a medium bowl. • Beat the egg, butter, and orange zest into the date mixture. • Mix in the dry ingredients, followed by the orange flesh until well blended. • Spoon the batter into the prepared pan. • Bake for 35–40 minutes, or until a toothpick inserted into the center comes out clean. • Cool completely before cutting into bars.

Makes 16–25 bars · Prep: 20 min. + 15 min. to soak the dates · Cooking: 35–40 min. · Level: 1 · Keeps: 2 days

date diamonds

12/3 cups all-purpose flour
1 teaspoon ground cinnamon
1 teaspoon baking powder
1/2 teaspoon baking soda
1/2 teaspoon salt
1 cup firmly packed dark brown sugar
2 large eggs, lightly beaten
1 cup (2 sticks) butter, melted
1/2 cup sour cream
11/3 cups finely chopped dates
3/4 cup finely chopped walnuts or pecans

Lemon glaze
11/3 cups confectioners' sugar
3 tablespoons butter, melted
1 tablespoon fresh lemon juice
1–2 tablespoons water

Preheat the oven to 350°F. • Butter a 13 x 9-inch baking pan. • Sift the flour, cinnamon,

baking powder, baking soda, and salt into a large bowl. • Stir in the brown sugar. • Add the eggs, beating until just blended. • Beat in the butter and sour cream. • Stir in the dates and walnuts. • Pour the mixture into the prepared pan. • Bake for 20–25 minutes, or until golden brown and a toothpick inserted into the center comes out clean. • Cool completely in the pan. • Lemon glaze: Mix the confectioners' sugar, butter, and lemon juice in a small bowl. • Add enough water to create a glazing consistency. • Spread the glaze over the cooled cake. • Cut lengthwise into long strips. • Cut the strips into diamonds by running the knife diagonally from one side of the pan to the other.

Makes 36–45 bars · Prep: 25 min. · Cooking: 20–25 min. · Level: 1 · Keeps: 10 days

white chocolate–oat squares

1 cup (2 sticks) butter
3/4 cup light corn syrup
1/2 cup firmly packed light brown sugar
1 cup old-fashioned rolled oats
2/3 cup all-purpose flour
1/8 teaspoon salt
1/2 cup currants
3 oz white chocolate, coarsely chopped

Preheat the oven to 325°F. • Butter a 9-inch square baking pan. • Melt the butter with the corn syrup and brown sugar in a small saucepan until smooth. • Stir together the oats, flour, salt, and currants in a large bowl. • Stir in the butter mixture until well blended. • Spoon the mixture into the prepared pan, pressing down firmly. • Bake for 25–30 minutes, or until lightly browned. • Cool completely in the pan. • Melt the white chocolate in a double boiler over barely simmering water. Use a thin metal spatula to spread the chocolate over and cut into squares.

Makes 16–25 squares · Prep: 20 min. · Cooking: 25–30 min. Level: 1 · Keeps: 5 days

cranberry squares

1 cup all-purpose flour
1/4 teaspoon salt
1/2 cup (1 stick) butter, softened
1/2 cup firmly packed dark brown sugar
21/2 cups old-fashioned rolled oats
1/2 cup store-bought cranberry sauce
1/2 cup coarsely chopped walnuts

Preheat the oven to 350°F. • Line an 8-inch baking pan with aluminum foil, letting the

edges overhang. • Sift the flour and salt into a medium bowl. • Beat the butter and brown sugar in a large bowl with an electric mixer at high speed until creamy. • Mix in the dry ingredients and oats. • Firmly press two-thirds of the mixture into the prepared pan to form a smooth, even layer. • Mix the cranberry sauce and walnuts in a small bowl and spread over the base. • Spoon the remaining oat mixture over the top, pressing down gently. • Bake for 15–20 minutes, or until lightly browned. • Cool completely in the pan. • Using the foil as handles, lift onto the cutting board. Peel off the foil. Cut into squares.

Makes 16–25 squares · Prep: 20 min. · Cooking: 15–20 min. · Level: 1 · Keeps: 4 days

carob–oat squares

4 oz carob, coarsely chopped
1/2 cup (1 stick) butter, cut up
1 tablespoon pure maple syrup
1 cup old-fashioned rolled oats
1 cup finely chopped dates
1/2 cup shredded coconut
1/8 teaspoon salt

Preheat the oven to 350°F. • Butter an 8-inch baking pan. • Melt the carob with the butter and maple syrup in a double boiler over barely simmering water. • Stir in the oats, dates, coconut, and salt until well coated. • Spread the mixture in the prepared pan, smoothing the top. • Bake for 25–30 minutes, or until firm to the touch. • Cool completely in the pan. • Cut into squares.

Makes 16–25 bars · Prep: 20 min. · Cooking: 25–30 min. · Level: 1 · Keeps: 5 days

White chocolate–oat squares

cherry–meringue bars

- 2/3 cup all-purpose flour
- 1/2 cup confectioners' sugar
- 1/3 cup butter, softened
- 1 large egg + 2 large egg whites
- 2/3 cup cherry preserves
- 1/2 cup superfine sugar
- 1 teaspoon freshly grated nutmeg
- 1/2 cup finely chopped candied cherries

Preheat the oven to 350°F. • Butter a 10-inch square baking pan. • Sift the flour and confectioners' sugar into a large bowl. • With an electric mixer at medium speed, beat in the butter and whole egg until well blended. • Firmly press the mixture into the prepared pan to form a smooth, even layer. • Bake for 10 minutes. • Reduce the oven temperature to 300°F. • Warm the preserves in a small saucepan over low heat until liquid. • Spread the preserves over the base. • With mixer at medium speed, beat the egg whites in a large bowl until soft peaks form. • With mixer at high speed, gradually add the superfine sugar and nutmeg, beating until stiff, glossy peaks form. • Gently fold in the cherries. • Spread the meringue on top of preserves. • Bake for 20–25 minutes, or until the meringue is lightly browned. • Cool in the pan for 15 minutes. • Cut into bars and let cool completely.

Makes 25 bars · Prep: 30 min. · Cooking: 30–35 min. · Level: 1 · Keeps: 3 days in the refrigerator

banana bars with cinnamon sugar topping

- 1 1/2 cups all-purpose flour
- 1 1/2 teaspoons baking powder
- 1/8 teaspoon salt
- 1/2 cup (1 stick) butter, softened
- 1 cup firmly packed light brown sugar
- 2 large bananas, peeled and mashed
- 1/2 teaspoon vanilla extract
- 1/2 cup finely chopped pecans
- 1 recipe Cinnamon Sugar (see page 341)

Preheat the oven to 350°F. • Butter an 11 x 7-inch baking pan. • Sift the flour, baking powder, and salt into a medium bowl. • Beat the butter, brown sugar, bananas, and vanilla in a large bowl with an electric mixer at high speed until well blended. • Mix in the dry ingredients, followed by the pecans. • Pour the mixture into the prepared pan. • Bake for 30–35

minutes, or until a toothpick inserted into the center comes out clean. Sprinkle with the cinnamon sugar. • Cool completely before cutting into bars.

Makes 22–33 bars · Prep: 20 min. · Cooking: 30–35 min. · Level: 1 · Keeps: 5 days

nutty cornmeal squares

- 1/2 cup all-purpose flour
- 1 1/2 tablespoons unsweetened cocoa powder
- 1 teaspoon baking powder
- 1/4 teaspoon ground cinnamon
- 1/8 teaspoon salt
- 2/3 cup butter, softened
- 3/4 cup firmly packed light brown sugar
- 1 teaspoon vanilla extract
- 2 large eggs
- 1/4 cup milk
- 1/3 cup finely ground yellow cornmeal
- 1/4 cup milk chocolate chips
- 1/2 cup coarsely chopped pecans
- 1/2 cup coarsely chopped Brazil nuts
- 2/3 cup finely chopped Brazil nuts

Preheat the oven to 350°F. • Butter an 11 x 7-inch baking pan. • Sift the flour, cocoa, baking powder, cinnamon, and salt into a medium bowl. • Beat the butter and brown sugar in a large bowl with an electric mixer at high speed until creamy. • Add the vanilla and eggs, beating until just blended. • Mix in the dry ingredients, followed by the milk and cornmeal. • Add the chocolate chips, pecans, and coarsely chopped Brazil nuts until well blended. • Spoon the mixture into the prepared pan. • Sprinkle with the finely chopped nuts. • Bake for 30 minutes. If the topping is browned, cover with aluminum foil. • Bake for 10–15 minutes more, or until a toothpick inserted into the center comes out clean. • Cool completely before cutting into squares.

Makes 22–33 bars · Prep: 45 min. · Cooking: 40–45 min. · Level: 1 · Keeps: 5 days

cinnamon–meringue bars

- 2/3 cup all-purpose flour
- 1/2 cup confectioners' sugar
- 1/8 teaspoon salt
- 1/3 cup butter, softened
- 1 large egg + 2 large egg whites
- 2/3 cup raspberry preserves
- 1/2 cup superfine sugar
- 1 teaspoon ground cinnamon

Preheat the oven to 350°F. • Butter a 10-inch square baking pan. • Sift the flour,

confectioners' sugar, and salt into a large bowl. • With an electric mixer at medium speed, beat in the butter and whole egg until well blended. • Firmly press the mixture into the prepared pan to form a smooth, even layer. • Bake for 10 minutes. • Reduce the oven temperature to 300°F. • Warm the preserves in a small saucepan over low heat until liquid. • Spread the preserves over the base. • With mixer at medium speed, beat the egg whites in a large bowl until soft peaks form. • With mixer at high speed, gradually add the superfine sugar and cinnamon, beating until stiff, glossy peaks form. • Spread the meringue on top of preserves. • Bake for 20–25 minutes, or until the meringue is lightly browned. • Cool in the pan for 15 minutes. • Cut into bars and let cool completely.

Makes 25 bars · Prep: 30 min. · Cooking: 30–35 min. Level: 1 · Keeps: 3 days in the refrigerator

chinese chews

- 1 cup all-purpose flour
- 1 teaspoon baking powder
- 1/8 teaspoon salt
- 1 cup mixed dried fruit, finely chopped
- 1/2 cup crystallized ginger, finely chopped
- 1/2 cup (1 stick) butter, softened
- 3/4 cup granulated sugar
- 1 large egg

Preheat the oven to 300°F. • Butter an 11 x 7-inch baking pan. • Sift the flour, baking powder, and salt into a medium bowl. • Stir in the dried fruit and ginger. • Beat the butter and sugar in a large bowl with an electric mixer at high speed until creamy. • Add the egg. • Mix in the dry ingredients. • Spoon the mixture into the prepared pan. • Bake for 40–45 minutes, or until golden brown. • Cool completely before cutting into bars.

Makes 22–33 bars · Prep: 10 min. · Cooking: 40–45 min. · Level: 1 · Keeps: 5 days

Nutty cornmeal squares (right) and
Curly cinnamon ducks
(left, see page 219)

Crispy mint squares

the prepared pan. • Bake for 20–25 minutes, or until a toothpick inserted into the center comes out clean. • Cool completely in the pan. • Melt the chocolate in a double boiler over barely simmering water. • Drizzle the chocolate over. • Let stand for 30 minutes until set. • Cut into bars.

Makes 16–25 bars · Prep: 25 min. + 30 min. to set
Cooking: 20–25 min. · Level: 1 · Keeps: 3 days

chocolate peppermint bars

Cookie base
2/3   cup all-purpose flour
1/4   cup unsweetened cocoa powder
1   teaspoon baking powder
1/4   teaspoon salt
1/3   cup granulated sugar
2   tablespoons butter, cut up
1   large egg, lightly beaten with
     1/3 cup water

Peppermint layer
2 1/4   cups confectioners' sugar
1   tablespoon mint liqueur
1–2   tablespoons milk

Chocolate frosting
4   oz semisweet chocolate,
     coarsely chopped
1/3   cup butter

Preheat the oven to 350°F. • Butter a 13 x 9-inch baking pan. • <u>Cookie base:</u> Sift the flour, cocoa, baking powder, and salt into a large bowl. Stir in the sugar. • Use a pastry blender to cut in the butter until the mixture resembles fine crumbs. • Mix in the beaten egg mixture. • Firmly press the mixture into the prepared pan to form a smooth, even layer. • Bake for 15–20 minutes, or until firm to the touch. • <u>Peppermint layer:</u> Mix the confectioners' sugar and mint liqueur in a medium bowl until well blended. • Stir in enough milk to achieve a spreadable consistency. • Spread the peppermint mixture evenly over the cookie base. • <u>Chocolate frosting:</u>

Melt the chocolate and butter in a double boiler over barely simmering water. • Pour the frosting evenly over the peppermint layer. • Let stand for 30 minutes until set. • Cut into bars.

Makes 36–45 bars · Prep: 40 min. + 30 min. to set
Cooking: 15–20 min. · Level: 1 · Keeps: 3 days

florentine squares

Tiny, crispy Florentine drop cookies are famous all over the world. These bar cookies have the same flavor with a brownielike texture.

1/2   cup golden raisins
1   cup all-purpose flour
1   teaspoon baking powder
1/8   teaspoon salt
2/3   cup butter, cut up
3/4   cup granulated sugar
3/4   cup flaked almonds
1/2   cup finely chopped candied cherries
3   oz semisweet chocolate, coarsely
     chopped

Preheat the oven to 350°F. • Butter an 8-inch square baking pan. • Plump the raisins in hot water to cover in a small bowl for 10 minutes. • Drain well and pat dry with paper towels. • Sift the flour, baking powder, and salt into a medium bowl. • Melt the butter with the sugar in a medium saucepan over low heat until the sugar has dissolved completely. • Remove from the heat and mix in the raisins, almonds, and cherries. • Mix in the dry ingredients. • Pour the mixture into

crispy mint squares

Crispy base
1   cup all-purpose flour
1   cup shredded coconut
1/4   cup granulated sugar
1   tablespoon unsweetened cocoa powder
1/2   teaspoon baking powder
1/8   teaspoon salt
1/2   cup (1 stick) butter, cut up

Mint topping
1 2/3   cups confectioners' sugar
1/2   teaspoon mint extract
1/2   teaspoon green food coloring
1/4   cup lukewarm water (105°–115°F),
     or more as needed

<u>Crispy base:</u> Preheat the oven to 350°F. • Set out a 10 1/2 x 15 1/2-inch jelly-roll pan. • Stir together the flour, coconut, sugar, cocoa, baking powder, and salt in a large bowl. • Use a pastry blender to cut in the butter until the mixture resembles fine crumbs. • Press the mixture evenly into the pan. • Bake for 25–30 minutes, or until lightly browned. • Cool completely in the pan on a rack. • <u>Mint topping:</u> Mix the confectioners' sugar, mint extract, and green food coloring in a small bowl. Add enough water to make a spreadable paste. • Spread the topping over the crispy base. • Cut into bars.

Makes 15 bars · Prep: 25 min. · Cooking: 25–30 min. · Level: 1 · Keeps: 4 days

cheesecake cookie bars

Cookie base
7   oz ladyfingers, crumbled
1/3   cup butter, melted

Cheesecake filling
2   packages (16 oz) cream cheese,
     softened
1/4   cup (1/2 stick) butter, softened
2/3   cup granulated sugar
2   tablespoons Vanilla Sugar
     (see page 341)
2   large eggs, lightly beaten
     Grated zest of 1/2 lemon

1 tablespoon fresh lemon juice
2 tablespoons cornstarch

Almond topping
2 tablespoons flaked almonds
2 teaspoons raw sugar
(Demerara or Barbados)

Preheat the oven to 350°F. • Butter a 13 x 9-inch baking pan. • Cookie base: Reserve 2 tablespoons of the crumbled ladyfingers. Mix the remaining ladyfingers and butter in a medium bowl. • Firmly press the mixture into the prepared pan to form a smooth, even layer. • Cheesecake filling: Beat the cream cheese, butter, granulated and vanilla sugars, eggs, lemon zest and juice, and cornstarch in a large bowl with an electric mixer at high speed until creamy. • Spread the filling over the cookie base. • Almond topping: Mix together the reserved 2 tablespoons ladyfingers, almonds, and raw sugar. Sprinkle the topping over the filling. • Bake for 40–45 minutes, or until the center has set. • Turn the oven off and cool the cheesecake for 40 minutes in the oven with the door ajar. • Refrigerate for at least 12 hours, or until well chilled. • Cut into bars.

Makes 36–45 bars · Prep: 25 min. + 12 hr. to chill Cooking: 40–45 min. · Level: 2 · Keeps: 4–5 days in the refrigerator

sunflower bars

These healthy bars are packed with fiber and are a high-energy snack on or off the road.

3/4 cup cashew nuts, shelled
1 teaspoon vegetable or sesame oil
4 cups sunflower seeds
1/3 cup apple juice concentrate or maple syrup
1 cup shredded coconut
1/2 teaspoon vanilla extract
1/4 teaspoon salt

Preheat the oven to 350°F. • Oil an 11 x 7-inch baking pan. • Process the cashew nuts and oil in a food processor or blender until smooth. (If you don't have a food processor or blender, grind the nuts with a pestle and mortar.) • Stir together the cashew nut mixture, sunflower seeds, apple juice, coconut, vanilla, and salt in a large bowl until well blended. • Press the mixture into the prepared pan, smoothing the top. • Bake for 25–30 minutes, or until golden brown. • Cool completely before cutting into bars.

Makes 22–33 bars · Prep: 15 min. · Cooking: 25–30 min. · Level: 1 · Keeps: 8–10 days

marbled cream cheese squares

Cream cheese mixture
1 cup cream cheese, softened
1/4 cup granulated sugar
2 tablespoons finely grated orange zest
3 tablespoons fresh orange juice
1 teaspoon cornstarch
1 large egg

Chocolate mixture
7 oz semisweet chocolate, coarsely chopped
1/4 cup (1/2 stick) cold butter, cut up
3/4 cup granulated sugar
2 teaspoons vanilla extract
2 large eggs, lightly beaten with 2 tablespoons cold water
1/2 cup all-purpose flour

Preheat the oven to 350°F. • Butter a 9-inch baking pan. • Cream cheese mixture: Beat the cream cheese and sugar in a large bowl with an electric mixer at high speed until creamy. • Beat in the orange zest and juice and cornstarch. Add the egg, beating until just blended. • Chocolate mixture: Melt the chocolate and butter in a double boiler over barely simmering water. Set aside to cool. • Stir in the sugar and vanilla. • Add the beaten egg mixture, followed by the flour. • Pour the chocolate mixture into the prepared pan. • Drop tablespoons of the cream cheese mixture over the chocolate base. • Use a thin metal spatula to swirl the mixtures together to create a marbled effect. • Bake for 25–30 minutes, or until slightly risen around the edges and set in the center. • Cool completely before cutting into squares.

Makes 16–25 squares · Prep: 35 min. · Cooking: 25–30 min. · Level: 2 · Keeps: 3 days in the refrigerator

cocoa, orange, and date squares

1 1/2 cups all-purpose flour
1/4 cup unsweetened cocoa powder
2 teaspoon baking powder
1/4 teaspoon salt
1/2 cup (1 stick) butter, softened
3/4 cup firmly packed light brown sugar
3 large eggs
1 tablespoon finely grated orange zest
3/4 cup fresh orange juice
1 cup finely chopped pitted dates
1/3 cup confectioners' sugar

Preheat the oven to 350°F. • Butter an 11 x 7-inch baking pan. • Sift the flour, cocoa, baking powder, and salt into a medium bowl. • Beat the butter and brown sugar in a large bowl with an electric mixer at high speed until creamy. • Add the eggs and orange zest, beating until just blended. • Mix in the dry ingredients, orange juice, and dates. • Pour the mixture into the prepared pan. • Bake for 30–35 minutes, or until a toothpick inserted into the center comes out clean. • Cool completely in the pan. • Dust with the confectioners' sugar and cut into bars.

Makes 22–33 bars · Prep: 20 min. · Cooking: 30–35 min. · Level: 1 · Keeps: 3 days

Marbled cream cheese squares

easy oat bars

- 1/3 cup old-fashioned rolled oats
- 1/3 cup butter, melted
- 1/2 cup firmly packed dark brown sugar
- 1/8 teaspoon salt

Preheat the oven to 350°F. • Butter an 8-inch square baking pan. • Mix the oats, butter, sugar, and salt in a medium bowl . • Firmly press the mixture into the pan. • Bake for 25–30 minutes, or until golden brown. • Cool completely before cutting into bars.

Makes 16–25 bars · Prep: 10 min. · Cooking: 25–30 min. · Level: 1 · Keeps: 7 days

whole-wheat aniseed bars

- 1 1/3 cups whole-wheat flour
- 1/2 teaspoon baking powder
- 1/8 teaspoon salt
- 2 large eggs
- 1 cup granulated sugar
- 1 tablespoon Vanilla Sugar (see page 341)
- 2 tablespoons aniseeds

Preheat the oven to 400°F. • Butter a 15 x 10-inch baking pan. • Sift the flour, baking powder, and salt into a medium bowl. • Beat the eggs, granulated sugar, and vanilla sugar in a large bowl with an electric mixer at high speed until pale and thick. • Mix in the dry ingredients to form a smooth dough. • Firmly press the dough into the prepared pan to form a smooth, even layer. • Sprinkle with the aniseeds. • Bake for 20–25 minutes, or until golden brown. • Cool completely before cutting into bars.

Makes 32 bars · Prep: 25 min. · Cooking: 20–25 min. · Level: 1 · Keeps: 5 days

frosted cappuccino bars

- 1 1/2 cups all-purpose flour
- 2 tablespoons unsweetened cocoa powder
- 1 teaspoon baking powder
- 1/8 teaspoon salt
- 2 tablespoons very strong hot coffee
- 1 cup (2 sticks) butter, softened
- 1 cup granulated sugar
- 4 large eggs
- 2 cups Coffee Buttercream or Chocolate Buttercream (see page 345)

Preheat the oven to 350°F. • Butter an 11 x 7-inch baking pan. • Sift the flour, cocoa, baking powder, and salt into a medium bowl. • Beat the butter and sugar in a large bowl with an electric mixer at high speed until creamy. • Beat in the eggs until just blended. • Mix in the dry ingredients and

coffee until well blended. • Pour the batter into the prepared pan. • Bake for 25–35 minutes, or until dry on top and almost firm to the touch. Do not overbake. • Cool completely in the pan. • Spread the frosting over and cut into bars.

Makes 22–33 bars · Prep: 30 min. · Cooking: 25–35 min. · Level: 1 · Keeps: 7 days

muesli bars

Also known as granola, muesli is a popular breakfast item made from cereal, dried fruit, and nuts.

- 1/2 cup (1 stick) butter, softened
- 2/3 cup smooth peanut butter
- 1/3 cup honey
- 1/2 cup shredded coconut
- 1/2 cup muesli
- 2 cups old-fashioned rolled oats
- 1/8 teaspoon salt

Preheat the oven to 350°F. • Set out 13 x 9-inch baking pan. • Mix the butter, peanut butter, and honey in a medium saucepan over low heat until well blended. • Stir in the coconut, muesli, oats, and salt. • Spoon the mixture onto the baking sheet and level with a spoon. • Bake for 15–20 minutes, or until just golden. • Cool completely before cutting into bars.

Makes 36–45 bars · Prep: 20 min. · Cooking: 15–20 min. · Level: 1 · Keeps: 10 days

nanaimo bars

These luxurious bar cookies take their name from the Canadian city of Nanaimo in British Columbia.

First layer
- 1 large egg
- 1/4 cup granulated sugar
- 1/2 cup (1 stick) butter, softened
- 1 teaspoon vanilla extract
- 3 tablespoons unsweetened cocoa powder
- 2 cups graham cracker crumbs
- 1 cup shredded coconut
- 1/2 cup finely chopped pecans

Second layer
- 1/4 cup (1/2 stick) butter, softened
- 3 tablespoons light cream
- 2 1/4 cups confectioners' sugar
- 1/2 teaspoon vanilla extract

Top layer
- 5 oz semisweet chocolate, coarsely chopped
- 2 tablespoons butter, cut up

Preheat the oven to 350°F. • Butter a 13 x 9-inch baking pan. • First layer: Beat the egg and sugar in a large bowl with an electric mixer at high speed until pale and thick. •

Use a wooden spoon to stir in the butter, vanilla, cocoa, graham cracker crumbs, coconut, and pecans. • Firmly press the mixture into the prepared pan to form a smooth, even layer. • Bake for 10–15 minutes, or until firm to the touch. • Let cool completely. • Second layer: Beat the butter, cream, confectioners' sugar, and vanilla in a large bowl with an electric mixer at high speed until well blended. • Spread the mixture over the first layer and freeze for 10 minutes. • Top layer: Melt the chocolate and butter in a double boiler over barely simmering water. • Spread over the second layer. • Refrigerate for at least 1 hour, or until set. • Cut into bars.

Makes 36–45 bars · Prep: 30 min. + 10 min. to freeze + 1 hr. to chill · Cooking: 10–15 min. · Level: 2 · Keeps: 3 days in the refrigerator

corn flake bars

- 1/3 cup corn flakes
- 1/3 cup butter, melted
- 1/2 cup firmly packed dark brown sugar
- 1/2 cup candied green cherries
- 1/8 teaspoon salt

Preheat the oven to 350°F. • Butter an 8-inch square baking pan. • Mix the corn flakes, butter, sugar, cherries, and salt in a medium bowl . • Firmly press the mixture into the pan. • Bake for 25–30 minutes, or until golden brown. • Cool completely before cutting into bars.

Makes 16–25 bars · Prep: 10 min. · Cooking: 25–30 min. · Level: 1 · Keeps: 7 days

bran flake and date bars

- 1/3 cup bran flake cereal
- 1/3 cup butter, melted
- 1/2 cup firmly packed dark brown sugar
- 1/2 cup coarsely chopped pitted dates
- 1/8 teaspoon salt

Preheat the oven to 350°F. • Butter an 8-inch square baking pan. • Mix the bran flakes, butter, sugar, dates, and salt in a medium bowl . • Firmly press the mixture into the pan. • Bake for 25–30 minutes, or until golden brown. • Cool completely before cutting into bars.

Makes 16–25 bars · Prep: 10 min. · Cooking: 25–30 min. · Level: 1 · Keeps: 7 days

Nanaimo bars

australian crunchies

These simple bar cookies are perfect for picnics in the park and to take on long walks. They will provide you with a continued source of energy. Oats have a slight nutty flavor and a crunchy texture.

- 1/2 cup (1 stick) butter, cut up
- 1 cup granulated sugar
- 1 tablespoon light corn syrup
- 1 tablespoon all-purpose flour
- 1/2 cup old-fashioned rolled oats

Preheat the oven to 325°F. • Butter a 9-inch square baking pan. • Melt the butter, sugar, and corn syrup in a small saucepan over medium heat. • Remove from the heat and stir in the flour and oats until well blended. • Spoon the mixture evenly into the prepared pan, pressing down lightly. • Bake for 15–20 minutes, or until golden brown. • Cool completely before cutting into bars.

Makes 16–25 bars · Prep: 15 min. · Cooking: 15–20 min. · Level: 1 · Keeps: 3 days

maraschino cherry bars

- 1 1/2 cups all-purpose flour
- 1/8 teaspoon salt
- 3/4 cup (1 1/2 sticks) butter, softened
- 1/2 cup firmly packed light brown sugar
- 1 tablespoon maraschino syrup (from a jar of maraschino cherries)
- 1/2 cup finely chopped maraschino cherries
- 2 cups Maraschino Frosting (see page 349) (optional)

Preheat the oven to 350°F. • Butter a 13 x 9-inch baking pan. • Sift the flour and salt into a medium bowl. • Beat the butter, brown sugar, and maraschino syrup in a large bowl with an electric mixer at high speed until creamy. • Mix in the dry ingredients and cherries until well blended. • Spread the mixture evenly in the baking pan. • Bake for 30–40 minutes, or until a toothpick inserted into the center comes out clean. • Cool completely in the pan. • If desired, spread the frosting over. Cut into bars.

Makes 36–45 bars · Prep: 20 min. · Cooking: 30–40 min. · Level: 1 · Keeps: 10 days

rocky road bars

- 1 3/4 cups all-purpose flour
- 1/4 cup unsweetened cocoa powder
- 1 teaspoon baking soda
- 1/4 teaspoon salt
- 1/2 cup (1 stick) butter, softened
- 1 cup firmly packed light brown sugar
- 2 large eggs
- 1/2 teaspoon vanilla extract
- 3/4 cup shredded coconut
- 3 cups semisweet chocolate chips
- 1 cup finely chopped almonds
- 1 cup mini marshmallows

Preheat the oven to 350°F. • Line a 13 x 9-inch baking pan with aluminum foil, letting the edges overhang. • Sift the flour, cocoa, baking soda, and salt into a medium bowl. • Beat the butter and brown sugar in a large bowl with an electric mixer at high speed until creamy. • Add the eggs and vanilla, beating until just blended. • Mix in the dry ingredients, coconut, 2 cups chocolate chips, and 3/4 cup almonds. • Pour the mixture into the prepared pan. • Bake for 12–15 minutes, or until set but slightly moist in the center. • Sprinkle with the remaining 1 cup chocolate chips, 1/4 cup almonds, and marshmallows. • Return to the oven and bake for 3–5 minutes, or until the chocolate and marshmallows have melted. • Using the foil as handles, lift onto a rack and let cool completely. • Remove the foil and cut into bars.

Makes 30 bars · Prep: 30 min. · Cooking: 15–20 min. · Level: 1 · Keeps: 3 days

date-filled oat bars

Date filling

- 1 lb pitted dates
- 1 cup firmly packed dark brown sugar
- 1 cup water
- 1/2 teaspoon vanilla extract
- 1/2 teaspoon ground cinnamon

Oat crust

- 1 1/2 cups all-purpose flour
- 1 cup firmly packed dark brown sugar
- 1 teaspoon ground cinnamon
- 1/2 teaspoon baking soda
- 1/8 teaspoon salt
- 1 cup (2 sticks) butter, cut up
- 2/3 cup old-fashioned rolled oats
- 1/2 cup finely chopped walnuts

Preheat the oven to 350°F. • Line a 13 x 9-inch baking pan with aluminum foil, letting the edges overhang. • Date filling: Cook the dates with the brown sugar and water in a saucepan over medium heat until the sugar has dissolved completely. • Remove from the heat and add the vanilla and cinnamon. • Transfer to a food processor or blender and process until pureed. • Return to the bowl and let cool completely. • Oat crust: Mix the flour, brown sugar, cinnamon, baking soda, and salt in a large bowl. • Use a pastry blender to cut in the butter until the mixture resembles coarse crumbs. Stir in the oats and walnuts. • Firmly press half the mixture into the prepared pan to form a smooth, even layer. • Pour the filling over the oat crust and sprinkle with the remaining oat crust mixture. • Bake for 30–35 minutes, or until lightly browned. • Using the foil as handles, lift onto a rack and let cool completely. • Cut into bars.

Makes 36–45 bars · Prep: 40 min. · Cooking: 30–35 min. · Level: 1 · Keeps: 4 days

almond coconut bars

Base

- 1/2 cup (1 stick) butter, softened
- 2/3 cup firmly packed light brown sugar
- 2/3 cup all-purpose flour
- 1/4 cup old-fashioned rolled oats
- 1/4 cup toasted wheat germ
- 1 tablespoon finely grated orange zest
- 1/8 teaspoon salt

Topping

- 2 large eggs, lightly beaten
- 1/4 cup firmly packed light brown sugar
- 3/4 cup blanched almonds, halved
- 1/2 cup shredded coconut

Preheat the oven to 350°F. • Butter an 8-inch square baking pan. • Base: Beat the butter and brown sugar in a large bowl with an electric mixer at high speed until creamy. • Mix in the flour, oats, wheat germ, orange juice, and salt until well blended. • Firmly press the mixture into the prepared pan to form a smooth, even layer. • Topping: With mixer at high speed, beat the eggs and brown sugar in a large bowl until pale and thick. • Stir in the almonds and coconut. • Spread the topping evenly over the base. • Bake for 30–35 minutes, or until just golden. • Cool completely before cutting into bars.

Makes 16–25 bars · Prep: 30 min. · Cooking: 30–35 min. · Level: 1 · Keeps: 5 days

energy bars

Great for hiking—these bars are packed with high-energy ingredients.

- $1/3$ cup butter, softened
- $1/3$ cup honey
- $1/2$ cup raw sugar (Demerara or Barbados)
- $1^1/2$ cups old-fashioned rolled oats
- $1/2$ cup coarsely chopped walnuts
- $1/2$ cup raisins
- 2 tablespoons pumpkin seeds
- 2 tablespoons sunflower seeds
- 2 tablespoons sesame seeds
- 2 tablespoons shredded coconut
- $3/4$ teaspoon ground cinnamon
- $1/8$ teaspoon salt

Preheat the oven to 375°F. • Butter an 11 x 7-inch baking pan. • Melt the butter with the honey and raw sugar in a large saucepan over low heat, stirring constantly. • Bring to a boil and cook until the sugar has dissolved completely. • Stir in the oats, walnuts, raisins, pumpkin seeds, sunflower seeds, sesame seeds, coconut, cinnamon, and salt. • Spoon the mixture evenly into the prepared pan. • Bake for 30–35 minutes, or until just golden. • Cool completely before cutting into bars.

Makes 22–33 bars · Prep: 20 min. · Cooking: 30–35 min. · Level: 1 · Keeps: 5 days, wrapped individually in waxed paper

german chocolate bars

- 4 large egg whites
- $1^1/4$ cups granulated sugar
- 3 cups finely ground almonds
- 2 oz bittersweet chocolate, finely grated
- 1 teaspoon vanilla extract
- 2 cups Chocolate–Pecan Frosting, Chocolate–Walnut Frosting, or Coconut–Walnut Frosting (see page 344) (optional)

Preheat the oven to 350°F. • Butter a 13 x 9-inch baking pan. • Beat 3 of the egg whites in a large bowl with an electric mixer at medium speed until soft peaks form. • With mixer at high speed, gradually

beat in 1 cup of the sugar, beating until stiff, glossy peaks form. • Use a large rubber spatula to fold in the almonds, chocolate, and vanilla. • Spread the mixture evenly in the prepared pan. • Beat the remaining egg white and remaining $1/4$ cup sugar until frothy. Brush over the top. • Bake for 20–25 minutes, or until lightly browned. • Cool completely in the pan. If desired, spread with the frosting. • Cut into bars.

Makes 36–45 bars · Prep: 30 min. · Level: 1 · Cooking: 20–25 min. · Keeps: 7 days

cherry marshmallow bars

- $1^3/4$ cups all-purpose flour
- $1/4$ cup unsweetened cocoa powder
- 1 teaspoon baking soda
- $1/4$ teaspoon salt
- $1/2$ cup (1 stick) butter, softened
- 1 cup firmly packed light brown sugar
- 2 large eggs
- $1/2$ teaspoon vanilla extract
- $3/4$ cup finely chopped candied cherries
- 3 cups semisweet chocolate chips
- 1 cup finely chopped hazelnuts
- 1 cup mini marshmallows

Preheat the oven to 350°F. • Line a 13 x 9-inch baking pan with aluminum foil, letting the edges overhang. • Sift the flour, cocoa, baking powder, and salt into a medium bowl. • Beat the butter and brown sugar in a large bowl with an electric mixer at high speed until creamy. • Add the eggs and vanilla, beating until just blended. • Mix in the dry ingredients, cherries, 2 cups

chocolate chips, and $3/4$ cup hazelnuts. • Pour the mixture into the prepared pan. • Bake for 12–15 minutes, or until set but slightly moist in the center. • Sprinkle with the remaining 1 cup chocolate chips, $1/4$ cup hazelnuts, and marshmallows. • Return to the oven and bake for 3–5 minutes, or until the chocolate and marshmallows have melted. • Using the foil as handles, lift onto a rack and let cool completely. • Remove the foil and cut into bars.

Makes 36–45 bars · Prep: 30 min. · Cooking: 15–20 min. · Level: 1 · Keeps: 3 days

coconut–corn flake squares

- $1/2$ cup (1 stick) butter, cut up
- $1/2$ cup granulated sugar
- 1 cup all-purpose flour
- $3/4$ cup corn flakes
- $1^1/2$ cups shredded coconut
- $1/3$ cup confectioners' sugar

Preheat the oven to 400°F. • Set out a 9-inch square baking pan. • Melt the butter with the sugar in a medium saucepan over low heat. • Stir in the flour, corn flakes, and 1 cup coconut until well coated. • Firmly press the mixture into the pan. • Bake for 10–15 minutes, or until just golden. • Dust with the confectioners' sugar and the remaining $1/2$ cup coconut. • Cool completely before cutting into squares.

Makes 16–25 squares · Prep: 20 min. · Level: 1 · Cooking: 10–15 min. · Keeps: 3 days

Coconut–corn flake squares

lucerne-style lebkuchen bars

These cookies come from the beautiful Swiss city of Lucerne, set on the banks of Vierwaldstaetter See, or Lake Lucerne.

3 1/3 cups all-purpose flour
1 tablespoon baking powder
1/8 teaspoon ground aniseeds
1/8 teaspoon ground cinnamon
1/8 teaspoon ground nutmeg
1/8 teaspoon ground cloves
1/8 teaspoon salt
3/4 cup heavy cream
1/2 cup light molasses
3/4 cup granulated sugar
1 tablespoon finely chopped candied lemon peel
1 tablespoon finely chopped candied orange peel
 scant 1 cup milk

Preheat the oven to 350°F. • Butter a 9-inch square baking pan. • Sift the flour, baking powder, aniseeds, cinnamon, nutmeg, cloves, and salt into a large bowl. • Beat the cream in a large bowl with an electric mixer at high speed until thick. • Mix in 1/4 cup molasses until well blended. • Mix in the dry ingredients, candied lemon and orange peel, and milk. • Pour the batter into the prepared pan, smoothing the top. • Bake for 15–20 minutes, or until a toothpick inserted into the center comes out clean. • Transfer to a rack to cool. • Warm the remaining 1/4 cup molasses in a small saucepan over medium heat until liquid. • Brush the molasses over and cut into bars.

Makes 16–25 bars · Prep: 25 min. · Cooking: 15–20 min. · Level: 1 · Keeps: 7 days

honey–cinnamon bars

Store these bars in an airtight container with an apple, changing the apple regularly, to help maintain freshness and texture.

1 1/4 cups all-purpose flour
1/2 teaspoon ground cinnamon
1/4 teaspoon ground nutmeg
1/8 teaspoon salt
1/4 cup honey
1/2 cup granulated sugar
1 large egg, lightly beaten
1/4 teaspoon baking soda dissolved in 1/2 tablespoon water

Preheat the oven to 350°F. • Butter a 9-inch square baking pan. • Sift the flour, cinnamon, nutmeg, and salt into a medium bowl. • Beat the honey and sugar in a large bowl with an electric mixer at high speed until well blended. • Add the egg, beating until just blended. • Mix in the baking soda

mixture and the dry ingredients until well blended. • Firmly press the mixture into the prepared pan to form a smooth, even layer. • Bake for 20–25 minutes, or until golden. • Cool completely before cutting into bars.

Makes 16–25 bars · Prep: 20 min. · Cooking: 20–25 min. · Level: 1 · Keeps: 4 weeks

banana–oat bars

3/4 cup (1 1/2 sticks) butter, softened
3/4 cup raw sugar (Barbados or Demerara)
1 large banana, peeled and mashed
1 1/2 cups old-fashioned rolled oats
1/8 teaspoon salt

Preheat the oven to 425°F. • Butter a 13 x 9-inch baking pan. • Beat the butter and raw sugar in a large bowl with an electric mixer at high speed until creamy. • Mix in the mashed banana, oats, and salt until well blended. • Firmly press the mixture into the prepared pan to form a smooth, even layer. • Bake for 18–25 minutes, or until lightly golden. • Cool completely before cutting into bars.

Makes 36–45 bars · Prep: 40 min. · Cooking: 18–25 min. · Level: 1 · Keeps: 5 days

chocolate and honey lebkuchen bars

3 cups all-purpose flour
1 1/2 teaspoons baking powder
1 teaspoon ground cinnamon
1/2 teaspoon ground cloves
1/4 teaspoon ground cardamom
1/8 teaspoon salt
2 large eggs
1 cup granulated sugar
1 cup honey
 Grated zest of 1/2 lemon
3 1/2 oz semisweet chocolate, finely grated
3/4 cup flaked almonds
1/2 cup coarsely chopped hazelnuts or almonds
1/2 cup finely chopped candied orange peel
1/2 cup finely chopped candied lemon peel
3 tablespoons orange flower water

Frosting
2 1/2 oz bittersweet chocolate
3/4 cup confectioners' sugar
1 teaspoon dark rum
1–2 tablespoons red currant jelly

Preheat the oven to 350°F. • Butter and flour a 9-inch baking pan. • Sift the flour, baking powder, cinnamon, cloves, cardamom, and salt into a medium bowl. • Heat the honey in a small saucepan over low heat until liquid. • Beat the eggs and

sugar in a large bowl with an electric mixer at high speed until very pale and thick. • Mix in the honey, lemon zest, chocolate, honey, almonds, hazelnuts, candied orange and lemon peel, and orange flower water. • Mix in the dry ingredients to form a smooth dough. • Spread the mixture in the prepared pan, smoothing the top. • Bake for 15–20 minutes, or until firm and the edges begin to crisp. • Cool completely in the pan. • Frosting: Melt the chocolate in a double boiler over barely simmering water. Mix in the confectioners' sugar and rum until smooth and spreadable. • Heat the jelly in a small saucepan over low heat until liquid. • Spread with jelly and then with the chocolate glaze. • Let stand for 30 minutes until set. • Cut into bars.

Makes 25 bars · Prep: 35 min. + 30 min. to set · Cooking: 15–20 min. · Level: 1 · Keeps: 4 weeks

apple–oat bars

1 large tart apple, peeled, cored, and finely chopped
3/4 cup (1 1/2 sticks) butter, softened
3/4 cup raw sugar (Barbados or Demerara)
1 1/2 cups old-fashioned rolled oats
1/8 teaspoon salt

Cook the apple in a small saucepan over medium heat for 10–15 minutes, or until the apple has broken down. Use a wooden spoon to beat the apple until smooth and let cool completely. • Preheat the oven to 425°F. • Butter a 13 x 9-inch baking pan. • Beat the butter and raw sugar in a large bowl with an electric mixer at high speed until creamy. • Mix in the apple puree, oats, and salt until well blended. • Firmly press the mixture into the prepared pan to form a smooth, even layer. • Bake for 18–25 minutes, or until lightly golden. • Cool completely before cutting into bars.

Makes 36–45 bars · Prep: 40 min. · Cooking: 18–25 min. · Level: 1 · Keeps: 5 days

Chocolate and honey lebkuchen bars

lemon bars

1 1/4 cups all-purpose flour
1/3 cup confectioners' sugar
1/8 teaspoon salt
1/2 cup (1 stick) cold butter, cut up

Filling
1/3 cup all-purpose flour
1/2 teaspoon baking powder
4 large eggs
1 1/2 cups superfine sugar
Grated zest and juice of 3 lemons
1 teaspoon finely grated lime zest
2 tablespoons confectioners' sugar, to dust

Preheat the oven to 325°F. • Butter a 9-inch square baking pan. • Sift the flour, confectioners' sugar, and salt into a large bowl. Use a pastry blender to cut in the butter until the mixture resembles fine crumbs. • Firmly press the mixture into the prepared pan. • Bake for 15–20 minutes, or until lightly browned. • Cool the base completely in the pan. • Lower the oven temperature to 300°F. • Filling: Sift the flour and baking powder into a large bowl. • Beat the eggs and superfine sugar in a large bowl with an electric mixer at high speed until pale and thick. • Stir in the lemon and lime zests and the juice. • Use a large rubber spatula to fold in the dry ingredients. • Pour the filling over the prepared base. • Bake for 30–40 minutes, or until the filling is set but still a little wobbly in the center. The mixture will continue to cook after it has been taken out of the oven. • Cool completely in the pan. • Dust with confectioners' sugar and cut into bars.

Makes 16–25 bars · Prep: 35 min. · Cooking: 45–60 min. · Level: 2 · Keeps: 4 days in the refrigerator

lemon cheesecake squares

Cookie base
1 1/4 cups graham cracker crumbs
1/3 cup butter, melted

Topping
2 packages (8 oz total) cream cheese, softened
1/2 cup granulated sugar
3 tablespoons Lemon Curd (see page 340)
3 tablespoons cornstarch
1 large egg, lightly beaten

Preheat the oven to 375°F. • Butter a 13 x 9-inch baking pan. • Cookie base: Mix the graham cracker crumbs and butter in a large bowl until well blended. • Firmly press the mixture into the prepared pan to form a smooth, even layer. • Topping: Beat the

Lemon cheesecake squares

cream cheese and sugar in a large bowl with an electric mixer at low speed until smooth. • Beat in the lemon curd, cornstarch, and egg. • Spoon the topping over the cookie base. • Bake for 25–30 minutes, or until firm to the touch. • Cool completely before cutting into bars.

Makes 24 bars · Prep: 30 min. · Cooking: 25–30 min. · Level: 1 · Keeps: 3 days in the refrigerator

almond slices

Rice flour can be found in the health- or natural-foods section of most supermarkets.

Short-crust pastry
2 cups all-purpose flour
1 1/2 teaspoons salt
1/4 cup (1/2 stick) butter, at room temperature, cut up
5–6 tablespoons cold water
1/2 cup apricot preserves

Almond topping
2/3 cup granulated sugar
3/4 cup confectioners' sugar
1 1/4 cups finely ground almonds
1/3 cup rice flour
1 large egg + 1 large egg white
1/2 cup finely chopped almonds

Preheat the oven to 375°F. • Set out a 10 1/2 x 15 1/2-inch jelly-roll pan. • Short-crust pastry: Sift the flour and salt into a large bowl. Use a pastry blender to cut in the butter until the mixture resembles coarse crumbs. • Stir in enough water to form a stiff dough. • Knead the dough on a lightly floured surface until smooth. • Shape into a rectangle and fold the short sides over. Roll into a rectangle once more, working in the opposite direction. • Fold the short side over

once more. Repeat once more. • Press the dough into a disk, wrap in plastic wrap, and refrigerate for 1 hour. • Roll out the dough on a lightly floured surface to a thickness of 1/4 inch and to a 10 x 15-inch rectangle. • Transfer the dough to the jelly-roll pan. • Warm the apricot preserves in a small saucepan over low heat until liquid. • Spread the preserves over the pastry base. • Almond topping: Mix the granulated sugar, confectioners' sugar, ground almonds, rice flour, and the egg and egg white in a medium bowl until well blended. • Spread the topping over the preserves, smoothing it out. • Sprinkle with the chopped almonds. • Bake for 15–20 minutes, or until lightly browned. • Cool completely before cutting into bars.

Makes 25 bars · Prep: 55 min. + 1 hour to chill · Cooking: 15–20 min. · Level: 2 · Keeps: 5 days

almond lattice bars

Rich pastry
2/3 cup butter
1/4 cup granulated sugar
1 2/3 cups all-purpose flour
1/8 teaspoon salt
1 large egg yolk

Almond paste
1 1/4 cups finely ground almonds
1 1/3 cups confectioners' sugar
1/4 cup superfine sugar
1/2 teaspoon almond extract
1 large egg, separated
1/4 cup raspberry preserves

Preheat the oven to 350°F. • Set out a 15 1/2 x 10 1/2-inch jelly-roll pan. • Rich pastry: Beat the butter and sugar in a large bowl with an electric mixer at high speed until creamy. •

Mix in the flour and salt. • Add the egg yolk and knead to form a stiff dough. • Firmly press the dough into the baking pan to form a smooth, even layer. • Bake for 25–30 minutes, or until firm to the touch. • Increase the oven temperature to 400°F. • Almond paste: Stir together the almonds, 1/3 cup of the confectioners' sugar, superfine sugar, and almond extract in a medium bowl. Add enough egg yolk to form a stiff paste. • Chop up the almond paste and place in a double boiler over barely simmering water. Cook, stirring constantly, until soft and malleable. • Remove from the heat and stir in the egg white and remaining 1 cup confectioners' sugar. • Return the saucepan to the heat and cook for 3 minutes more until well blended. • Fit a pastry bag with a small rose tip. Fill the pastry bag, twist opening tightly closed, and pipe a lattice pattern all over the pastry base, keeping the lines 1/2 inch apart. • Bake for 10 minutes. • Cool the pastry completely on the sheet. • Warm the raspberry preserves in a small saucepan over low heat until liquid. • Spoon into the empty spaces on the pastry. • Cool completely before cutting into bars.

Makes 36 bars · Prep: 50 min. · Cooking: 35–40 min. · Level: 2 · Keeps: 3 days

almond–walnut bars

1 cup whole almonds
1 2/3 cups all-purpose flour
1 teaspoon ground cinnamon
1/2 teaspoon ground cloves
1/2 teaspoon baking powder
1/8 teaspoon salt
3 large eggs
1 1/4 cups granulated sugar
1 cup coarsely chopped walnuts
1 cup coarsely chopped almonds
1/3 cup finely chopped candied lemon peel
1/3 cup finely chopped candied orange peel
1 tablespoon orange flower water

Glaze
1 1/3 cups confectioners' sugar
1 tablespoon fresh lemon juice
1 tablespoon rum or brandy
1–2 tablespoons lukewarm water

Preheat the oven to 325°F. • Spread the almonds on a large baking sheet. Toast for 7 minutes, or until lightly golden. • Let cool completely and chop coarsely. • Line a cookie sheet with parchment paper. • Sift the flour, cinnamon, cloves, baking powder,

and salt into a medium bowl. • Beat the eggs and sugar in a large bowl with an electric mixer at high speed until very pale and thick. • Mix in the dry ingredients, walnuts, almonds, candied lemon and orange peel, and orange flower water. • Spread the mixture over the prepared cookie sheet to a thickness of 1/2 inch. • Bake for 15–18 minutes, or until golden brown. • Cool completely before cutting into bars. • Glaze: Mix the confectioners' sugar, lemon juice, rum, and water in a small bowl until thick and glossy. • Spread over the bars and let stand for 30 minutes until set.

Makes 30–35 bars · Prep: 40 min. + 30 min. to set Cooking: 15–18 min. · Level: 1 · Keeps: 15 days, layered in parchment paper

chocolate–raspberry macaroon bars

Base
1 cup all-purpose flour
1/4 cup unsweetened cocoa powder
1/4 teaspoon salt
1/2 cup (1 stick) butter, softened
1/2 cup granulated sugar
1/2 teaspoon vanilla extract

Chocolate–raspberry filling
1/2 cup seedless raspberry preserves
1 tablespoon raspberry liqueur
1 cup semisweet chocolate chips
1 1/2 cups finely ground almonds
4 large egg whites
1 cup granulated sugar
1/2 teaspoon almond extract
1/4 cup flaked almonds

Preheat the oven to 325°F. • Line a 13 x 9-inch baking pan with aluminum foil, letting the edges overhang. • Base: Sift the flour, cocoa, and salt into a medium bowl. • Beat the butter, sugar, and vanilla in a large bowl with an electric mixer at high speed until creamy. • Mix in the dry ingredients. • Firmly press the mixture into the prepared pan to form a smooth, even layer. Prick all over with a fork. • Bake for 15–20 minutes, or until firm to the touch. • Increase the oven temperature to 375°F. • Chocolate–raspberry filling: Mix the preserves and liqueur in a small bowl and spread it evenly over the base. Sprinkle with the chocolate chips. • Process the finely ground almonds, egg whites, sugar, and almond extract in a food processor or blender until well blended. • Pour the mixture over the preserves and sprinkle with the flaked

almonds. • Bake for 20–25 minutes, or until lightly browned. • Using the foil as handles, lift onto a rack and let cool completely. • Remove the foil and cut into bars.

Makes 30 bars · Prep: 25 min. · Cooking: 35–45 min. · Level: 1 · Keeps: 4 days

orange cheesecake squares

Cookie base
1 1/4 cups graham cracker crumbs
1/3 cup butter, melted

Topping
2 packages (8 oz total) cream cheese, softened
1/2 cup granulated sugar
3 tablespoons Orange Curd (see page 340)
3 tablespoons cornstarch
1 large egg, lightly beaten

Preheat the oven to 375°F. • Butter a 13 x 9-inch baking pan. • Cookie base: Mix the graham cracker crumbs and butter in a large bowl until well blended. • Firmly press the mixture into the prepared pan to form a smooth, even layer. • Topping: Beat the cream cheese and sugar in a large bowl with an electric mixer at low speed until smooth. • Beat in the orange curd, cornstarch, and egg. • Spoon the topping over the cookie base. • Bake for 25–30 minutes, or until firm to the touch. • Cool completely before cutting into bars.

Makes 24 bars · Prep: 30 min. · Cooking: 25–30 min. · Level: 1 · Keeps: 3 days in the refrigerator

Almond–walnut bars

crusty lemon butter squares

1   cup all-purpose flour
1   teaspoon baking powder
1/8 teaspoon salt
     Grated zest and juice of 1 lemon
3/4 cup (1 1/2 sticks) butter, softened
3/4 cup firmly packed light brown sugar
2   large eggs
1/2 cup superfine sugar

Preheat the oven to 325°F. • Butter a 13 x 9-inch baking pan. • Sift the flour, baking powder, and salt into a medium bowl. Stir in the lemon zest. • Beat the butter and brown sugar in a large bowl with an electric mixer at high speed until creamy. • Add the eggs, one at a time, until just blended after each addition. • With mixer at low speed, gradually add the dry ingredients. • Pour the batter into the prepared pan, smoothing the top. • Bake for 30–35 minutes, or until set and lightly browned. • Mix the superfine sugar with enough lemon juice to make a thin glaze. • Spread over the top while warm. • Cool completely before cutting into squares.

Makes 36–45 squares · Prep: 20 min. · Cooking: 30–35 min. · Level: 1 · Keeps: 4–5 days

chewy oat and dried fruit bars

A sweet bar-type cookie full of goodness makes a healthy start to the day.

1 1/4 cups dried figs, coarsely chopped
1 1/4 cups pitted dates, coarsely chopped
       Grated zest and juice of 1 orange
1/2   cup cold water
1   cup all-purpose flour
1/4   teaspoon baking soda
1/8   teaspoon salt
1/2   cup firmly packed light brown sugar
1/2   cup old-fashioned rolled oats
1/2   cup pecans, toasted and coarsely chopped
1/2   cup sunflower seeds, coarsely chopped
1/3   cup butter, softened

Place the figs and dates in a small saucepan. • Cover with the orange juice and water. Bring the mixture to a boil over medium heat. Add half the orange zest. Simmer, covered, for 15–20 minutes, or until the figs and dates have softened. • Remove from the heat and let cool. • Preheat the oven to 325°F. • Butter an 11 x 7-inch baking pan. • Sift the flour, baking soda, and salt into a large bowl. Stir in the brown sugar, oats, pecans, sunflower seeds,

and remaining orange zest. • Use a pastry blender to cut in the butter until the mixture resembles coarse crumbs. • Place half the mixture into the prepared pan, patting down lightly. Fold the remaining flour mixture into the date mixture. Spread over the crumble base. • Bake for 25–30 minutes, or until lightly browned. • Cool completely before cutting into bars.

Makes 12 bars · Prep: 40 min. · Cooking: 25–30 min · Level: 1 · Keeps: 4 days

pear–cherry bars

1   cup all-purpose flour
1/4 cup unsweetened cocoa powder
1/2 teaspoon ground cinnamon
1/2 teaspoon baking soda
1/4 teaspoon salt
2   tablespoons butter, cut up
2   large firm-ripe pears, peeled, cored, and finely chopped
2   teaspoons fresh lemon juice
1   large egg, lightly beaten
2   tablespoons granulated sugar
1/2 cup dried sour cherries
1   tablespoon pear juice

Preheat the oven to 350°F. • Butter an 8-inch square baking pan. • Sift the flour, cocoa, cinnamon, baking soda, and salt into a large bowl. • Use a pastry blender to cut in the butter until the mixture resembles coarse crumbs. • Stir together the pears, lemon juice, egg, and sugar in a large bowl until well blended. • Mix in the dry ingredients, cherries, and pear juice. • Spread the mixture evenly in the prepared pan. • Bake for 20–25 minutes, or until firm to the touch. • Cool completely in the pan. • Cut into bars.

Makes 16–25 bars · Prep: 20 min. · Cooking: 20–25 min. · Level: 1 · Keeps: 4 days

classic brownies

2/3 cup all-purpose flour
1/2 teaspoon baking powder
1/4 teaspoon salt
1/3 cup butter, cut up
2   oz semisweet chocolate, coarsely chopped
1   cup granulated sugar
2   large eggs, lightly beaten
1/2 teaspoon vanilla extract
1/3 cup coarsely chopped walnuts

Preheat the oven to 350°F. • Butter an 8-inch square baking pan. • Sift the flour, baking powder, and salt into a large bowl. •

Melt the butter and chocolate in a double boiler over barely simmering water. • Remove from the heat and stir in the sugar. • Set aside to cool slightly. • Add the eggs, beating until just blended. • Mix in the dry ingredients, vanilla, and walnuts until well blended. • Pour the mixture into the prepared pan. • Bake for 35–40 minutes, or until dry on top and almost firm to the touch. Do not overbake. • Cool completely before cutting into bars.

Makes 16–25 bars · Prep: 25 min. · Cooking: 35–40 min. · Level: 1 · Keeps: 5 days

pumpkin bars

These scrumptious and colorful bars are the perfect sweet snack at Thanksgiving.

Oat crust
2   cups old-fashioned rolled oats
1   cup all-purpose flour
1/2 cup (1 stick) butter, melted
1/2 cup firmly packed light brown sugar
1/8 teaspoon salt

Pumpkin filling
1   can (15 oz) pumpkin puree
1   can (14 oz) sweetened condensed milk
3/4 cup granulated sugar
2   large eggs
1 1/2 teaspoons ground cinnamon

Brown sugar topping
2   tablespoons butter, softened
1/2 cup finely chopped walnuts
1/2 cup firmly packed dark brown sugar

Oat crust: Preheat the oven to 350°F. • Set out a 13 x 9-inch baking pan. • Mix the oats, flour, butter, brown sugar, and salt in a medium bowl until well blended. • Firmly press the mixture into the pan to form an even layer. • Bake for 15 minutes. • Pumpkin filling: Mix the pumpkin puree, condensed milk, sugar, eggs, and cinnamon in a large bowl until well blended. • Pour the mixture over the baked crust. • Bake for 20 minutes. • Brown sugar topping: Mix the butter, walnuts, and brown sugar in a small bowl. • Sprinkle the topping over the filling. • Bake for 20 minutes more. • Cool completely before cutting into bars.

Makes 36–45 bars · Prep: 40 min. · Cooking: 55 min. · Level: 2 · Keeps: 7 days

Pumpkin bars

blondies

The toffee flavor of these bars more than makes up for the absence of the chocolate. Use high-quality vanilla extract, which can be found in most supermarkets or in specialty stores, to enhance the delicious flavor of these brownies. The quality of the butter is also essential: use the best you can find.

1 1/3 cups all-purpose flour
1/2 teaspoon baking powder
1/8 teaspoon salt
2/3 cup butter, softened
3/4 cup firmly packed light brown sugar
2 large eggs
2 tablespoons light corn syrup
1 1/2 teaspoons vanilla extract
1 cup finely chopped walnuts

Preheat the oven to 350°F. • Butter an 8-inch square baking pan. • Sift the flour, baking powder, and salt into a medium bowl. • Beat the butter and brown sugar in a large bowl with an electric mixer at high speed until creamy. • Add the eggs, corn syrup, and vanilla, beating until just blended. • Mix in the dry ingredients and walnuts. • Pour the batter into the prepared pan, smoothing the top. • Bake for 25–30 minutes, or until dry on top and almost firm to the touch. Do not overbake. • Cool completely before cutting into bars.

Makes 16–25 bars · Prep: 20 min. · Cooking: 25–30 min. · Level: 1 · Keeps: 5 days

tyrolean chocolate fingers

1 1/2 cups self-rising flour
1/2 teaspoon ground cinnamon
1/2 teaspoon ground cloves
1/4 teaspoon ground cardamom
1/4 teaspoon salt
1/2 cup dark raisins
1/2 cup golden raisins
1/2 cup dark rum mixed with 1 tablespoon cold water
3/4 cup candied cherries, rinsed under cold water, dried, and halved
1 cup walnuts, coarsely chopped
1 cup blanched almonds, coarsely chopped
3 oz semisweet chocolate, coarsely chopped
3/4 cup (1 1/2 sticks) butter, softened
1 cup firmly packed light brown sugar
Grated zest of 1 orange
3 large eggs, lightly beaten
3 tablespoons fresh orange juice

Preheat the oven to 325°F. • Butter an 11 x 7-inch baking pan. Line with parchment paper, letting the edges overhang. • Sift the flour, cinnamon, cloves, cardamom, and salt into a large bowl. • Bring the dark raisins, golden raisins, and rum mixture to a boil in a large saucepan. Remove from the heat and set aside for 15 minutes to allow the raisins to soak up the liquid. • Mix the raisin mixture, cherries, walnuts, and almonds in a large bowl. Use a large rubber spatula to fold in 1 tablespoon of the dry ingredients and stir until well coated. • Melt the chocolate in a double boiler over barely simmering water. • Beat the butter and brown sugar in a large bowl with an electric mixer at high speed until creamy. • Add the orange zest and melted chocolate. • Add the eggs, beating until just blended, adding 1 tablespoon of the dry ingredients. • Use a large rubber spatula to fold in the remaining dry ingredients, followed by the raisin mixture and orange juice. • Spoon the batter into the prepared pan, smoothing the top. • Bake for 60–75 minutes, or until a toothpick inserted into the center comes out clean. • Cool completely before cutting into bars.

Makes 22–33 bars · Prep: 45 min. · Cooking: 60–75 min. · Level: 2 · Keeps: 10 days

lemon party cakes

1 cup all-purpose flour
1 teaspoon baking powder
1/8 teaspoon salt
1 tablespoon grated lemon zest
1/2 cup (1 stick) butter, softened
1/2 cup granulated sugar
2 large eggs
3/4 cup confectioners' sugar
Juice of 1 lemon
3–4 tablespoons apricot preserves or jam, warmed
1/2 cup walnuts, coarsely chopped

Preheat the oven to 350°F. • Butter an 11 x 7-inch baking pan. Line with waxed paper. • Sift the flour, baking powder, and salt into a medium bowl. Stir in the lemon zest. • Beat the butter and sugar in a large bowl with an electric mixer at high speed until creamy. • Add the eggs, one at a time, until just blended after each addition. • With mixer at low speed, gradually add the dry ingredients. • Spoon the mixture into the prepared pan, smoothing the top. • Bake for 15–20 minutes, or until golden brown and a toothpick inserted into the center comes out clean. • Cool in the pan for 5 minutes. Turn out onto a rack, carefully remove the waxed paper, and let cool completely. • Place the confectioners' sugar in a small bowl and add enough lemon juice to make a soft spreadable frosting. • Spread the frosting over the top. • Cut into bars and brush the sides with the jam and sprinkle with the walnuts.

Makes 22–33 bars · Prep: 20 min. · Cooking: 15–20 min. · Level: 1 · Keeps: 3 days

luxury chocolate brownies

1/2 cup all-purpose flour
1/2 teaspoon baking powder
1/8 teaspoon salt
6 oz bittersweet chocolate, coarsely chopped
1 1/2 cups (3 sticks) butter, cut up
5 large eggs
2 1/4 cups firmly packed light brown sugar
1 teaspoon vanilla extract

Preheat the oven to 325°F. • Butter and flour a 9-inch baking pan. • Sift the flour, baking powder, and salt into a large bowl. • Melt the chocolate and butter in a double boiler over barely simmering water. Remove from the heat and let cool. • Beat the eggs, brown sugar, and vanilla in a large bowl with an electric mixer at high speed until pale and thick. • Use a large rubber spatula to fold in the chocolate mixture, followed by the dry ingredients. • Pour the batter into the prepared pan. • Bake for 35–40 minutes, or until dry on top and almost firm to the touch. Do not overbake. • Cool completely before cutting into squares.

Makes 16–25 squares · Prep: 35 min. · Cooking: 35–40 min. · Level: 1 · Keeps: 5–7 days

Blondies

raspberry linzer squares

These bars take their name from the famous Austrian dessert, Linzertorte, which combines a raspberry filling with spiced pastry layers.

1   cup finely ground almonds
1   large egg, lightly beaten
1¼   cups granulated sugar
1⅔   cups all-purpose flour
¾   cup (1½ sticks) butter, softened
1   teaspoon ground cinnamon
1   teaspoon finely grated lemon zest
⅛   teaspoon ground cloves
½   cup raspberry preserves

Beat the almonds, egg, sugar, flour, butter, cinnamon, lemon zest, and cloves in a large bowl with an electric mixer at medium speed until well blended. • Press the dough into a disk and refrigerate for 30 minutes. • Preheat the oven to 350°F. • Butter an 11 x 7-inch baking pan. • Firmly press half the dough into the prepared pan to form a smooth, even layer. • Warm the raspberry preserves in a small saucepan over low heat until liquid. • Spread the jam over the dough. • Knead the remaining dough on a lightly floured surface and divide in half. • Cut one half of the dough into six portions. Roll each portion into an 11-inch rope. • Place the ropes lengthways on top of the preserves. • Cut the remaining dough into eight portions. Roll each portion into a 7-inch rope. • Place the ropes crosswise on top of the preserves to create a lattice pattern. • Bake for 35–40 minutes, or until the dough is lightly browned. • Cool completely before cutting into squares.

Makes 22–33 squares · Prep: 40 min. + 30 min. to chill · Cooking: 35–40 min. · Level: 2 · Keeps: 14 days

pear–apricot bars

1½   cups whole-wheat flour
1½   teaspoons baking powder
¼   teaspoon salt
3   large firm-ripe pears, peeled, cored, and finely chopped
1½   cups finely chopped dried apricots
2   tablespoons honey
1   tablespoon Applesauce (see page 340)
2   tablespoons vegetable oil
2   large eggs, lightly beaten
½   cup flaked almonds, to decorate

Preheat the oven to 375°F. • Line an 8-inch baking pan with aluminum foil, letting the edges overhang. • Sift the flour, baking powder, and salt into a medium bowl. • Mix the pears, apricots, honey, and applesauce in a large bowl. • Beat in the oil and eggs until well blended. • Mix in the dry ingredients. • Pour the mixture into the prepared pan. • Sprinkle with the almonds. • Bake for 25–30 minutes, or until just golden and a toothpick inserted into the center comes out clean. • Using the foil as handles, lift onto a rack to cool. • Cut into bars.

Makes 16–25 bars · Prep: 20 min. · Cooking: 20–25 min. · Level: 1 · Keeps: 3 days

milk chocolate-frosted bars

1½   cups all-purpose flour
1   tablespoon unsweetened cocoa powder
2   teaspoons baking powder
⅛   teaspoon salt
1   cup (2 sticks) butter, softened
1   cup granulated sugar
4   large eggs, lightly beaten
2   tablespoons milk
½   teaspoon vanilla extract

Milk chocolate frosting
¾   cup milk chocolate chips
¼   cup (½ stick) butter, cut up
2   tablespoons milk
1   cup confectioners' sugar

Preheat the oven to 350°F. • Butter an 11 x 7-inch baking pan. • Sift the flour, cocoa, baking powder, and salt into a medium bowl. • Beat the butter and sugar in a large bowl with an electric mixer at high speed until creamy. • Add the eggs, beating until just blended. • Mix in the dry ingredients, milk, and vanilla until well blended. • Spread the mixture evenly in the prepared pan. • Bake for 35–45 minutes, or until firm to the touch and a toothpick inserted into the center comes out clean. • Cool completely in the pan. • Milk chocolate frosting: Melt the chocolate chips and butter with the milk in a double boiler over barely simmering water until well blended. Remove from the heat and beat in the confectioners' sugar until thick and spreadable. • Spread the frosting over the cookie base. Let stand for 30 minutes, or until set. • Cut into bars.

Makes 22–33 bars · Prep: 40 min. + 30 min. to set Cooking: 35–45 min. · Level: 1 · Keeps: 10 days

apple–marzipan bars

1½   cups all-purpose flour
⅛   teaspoon salt
¾   cup (1½ sticks) butter, softened
2   large eggs, separated
1–2 tablespoons ice water
1½   lb tart apples, such as Granny Smiths, peeled and cored
4   oz ready-made marzipan
2   tablespoons granulated sugar

Butter an 11 x 7-inch baking pan. • Sift the flour and salt into a medium bowl. • Use a pastry blender to cut in ½ cup butter until the mixture resembles fine crumbs. • Add 1 egg yolk and enough water to form a soft dough. • Press the dough into a disk, wrap in plastic wrap, and refrigerate for 30 minutes. • Preheat the oven to 425°F. • Roll out the dough on a lightly floured surface to a thickness of ⅛ inch and to a 11 x 7-inch rectangle. • Gather the dough scraps and set aside. • Fit the dough rectangle into the prepared pan. Prick all over with a fork. Finely grate the apples. Place in a fine-mesh sieve and press with the back of a wooden spoon to remove as much juice as possible. • Coarsely grate the marzipan. Sprinkle the grated marzipan over the base. • Use a wooden spoon to beat the remaining ¼ cup butter and sugar in a medium bowl until creamy. Mix in the grated apple. • Beat the 2 egg whites in a medium bowl with an electric mixer at high speed until stiff peaks form. Use a large rubber spatula to fold them into the apple mixture. • Spread the mixture evenly over the base. • Gather the dough scraps and re-roll on a lightly floured surface to a thickness of ⅛ inch. Cut the dough into ¼-inch wide strips and arrange in a lattice pattern over the apple mixture. • Use a pastry brush to brush the remaining egg yolk over the strips. • Bake for 30–35 minutes, or until the pastry is golden and the apple mixture lightly browned on top. • Cool completely before cutting into bars.

Makes 22–33 bars · Prep: 50 min. + 30 min. to chill Cooking: 30–35 min. · Level: 1 · Keeps: 5 days

Raspberry linzer bars

Date and walnut squares

walnut bars

1 cup (2 sticks) butter, softened
1¼ cups granulated sugar
1⅓ cups all-purpose flour
⅛ teaspoon salt
1 large egg, separated
1 teaspoon vanilla extract
⅔ cup coarsely chopped walnuts

Preheat the oven to 350°F. • Butter a 13 x 9-inch baking pan. • Beat the butter and sugar in a large bowl with an electric mixer at high speed until creamy. • Mix in the flour, salt, egg yolk, and vanilla until well blended. • Firmly press the mixture into the prepared pan to form a smooth, even layer. • Use a fork to beat the egg white lightly and brush over the base. Sprinkle with the walnuts. • Bake for 30–35 minutes, or until just golden. • Cut into bars while warm.

Makes 36–45 bars · Prep: 30 min. · Cooking: 30–35 min. · Level: 1 · Keeps: 7 days

a-bit-of-everything bars

Chock-full of flavor and texture, these cookies will never make it as far as the cookie jar!

½ cup golden raisins
1¼ cups whole-wheat flour
1 teaspoon baking powder
⅛ teaspoon salt
2 large eggs
½ cup granulated sugar
¼ teaspoon vanilla extract
   Grated zest of ½ lemon
2 tablespoons milk
1 tablespoon dark rum
¾ cup finely chopped hazelnuts

½ cup finely chopped walnuts
3 oz bittersweet chocolate, finely grated

Chocolate frosting
⅔ cup confectioners' sugar
2 tablespoons unsweetened cocoa powder
¼ teaspoon vanilla extract
2 tablespoons water, or more as needed

Preheat the oven to 400°F. • Butter a 9-inch baking pan. • Plump the raisins in hot water to cover in a small bowl for 10 minutes. • Drain well and pat dry with paper towels. • Sift the flour, baking powder, and salt into a medium bowl. • Beat the eggs and sugar in a large bowl with an electric mixer at high speed until pale and thick. • Add the vanilla and lemon zest. • Mix in the dry ingredients, followed by the milk, rum, raisins, hazelnuts, walnuts, and chocolate. • Pour the mixture into the prepared pan. • Bake for 15–20 minutes, or until a toothpick inserted into the center comes out clean. • Cool completely in the pan. • Chocolate frosting: Mix the confectioners' sugar, cocoa, vanilla, and enough water to make a smooth frosting. • Spread with the frosting and cut into bars.

Makes 16–25 bars · Prep: 25 min. + 10 min. to plump the raisins · Cooking: 15–20 min. · Level: 1 · Keeps: 5 days

date and walnut squares

¾ cup all-purpose flour
½ teaspoon baking powder
⅛ teaspoon salt

½ cup (1 stick) butter, softened
¾ cup granulated sugar
1 large egg
2½ cups finely chopped pitted dates
1⅓ cups finely chopped walnuts
7 oz semisweet chocolate, coarsely chopped

Preheat the oven to 350°F. • Butter a 10½ x 15½-inch jelly-roll pan. • Sift the flour, baking powder, and salt into a medium bowl. • Beat the butter and sugar in a large bowl with an electric mixer at high speed until creamy. • Add the egg, beating until just blended. • Mix in the dry ingredients, dates, and walnuts until well blended. • Spoon the mixture into the prepared pan. • Bake for 25–30 minutes, or until firm to the touch. • Cool completely in the pan. • Melt the chocolate in a double boiler over barely simmering water. • Use a thin metal spatula to spread the chocolate evenly over the top. • Set aside for 30 minutes before cutting into squares.

Makes 25 squares · Prep: 25 min. + 30 min. to set · Cooking: 25–30 min. · Level: 1 · Keeps: 3 days

yorkshire curd bars

These cookie bars are based on one of the oldest cooked cheesecake recipes. Curd tarts are traditional fare for family celebrations and church festivals, such as Pentecost, in the county of Yorkshire in England. Farmers' wives used to make them from the creamy second milking of a newly calved cow (the first milking was thought to be too rich to use). English farmers still call this special milk by its Anglo-Saxon name of "beestings."

Curd filling
2½ cups milk
1 tablespoon fresh lemon juice
2 large eggs
⅔ cup granulated sugar
¼ cup raisins
2 teaspoons grated lemon zest
2 tablespoons butter, melted

Base
½ cup (1 stick) butter, cut up
1⅔ cups all-purpose flour
¼ cup ice water

Curd filling: To make curds, heat the milk in a small saucepan until almost boiling. Remove from the heat and add the lemon juice. • Pour into a large bowl and let stand for 12 hours. The milk will separate into solid curds and liquid whey. • Strain the mixture through a fine sieve, discarding the whey. • Preheat the oven to 350°F. • Line a 13 x 9-inch baking pan with aluminum foil, letting the edges overhang. Butter the foil. • Base: Use a pastry blender to cut the butter into the flour until the mixture resembles fine crumbs. • Use a wooden spoon to mix in enough ice water to form a stiff dough. • Firmly press the mixture into the prepared pan to form a smooth, even layer. • Beat the eggs in a large bowl with an electric mixer at high speed until frothy. • Mix in 1 cup curds, sugar, raisins, lemon zest, and butter. • Spread the mixture over the base. • Bake for 25–35 minutes, or until set and golden brown. • Cool completely in the pan. • Using the foil as handles, lift onto a cutting board and cut into bars.

Makes 36–45 bars · Prep: 40 min. + 12 hr. to stand Cooking: 25–35 min. · Level: 2 · Keeps: 2 days in the refrigerator

maple blondies

A variation of the traditional blondie, the yummy buttery alternative to chocolate-laden brownies.

- 2/3 cup almonds or macadamia nuts
- 1 1/4 cups all-purpose flour
- 1/4 teaspoon salt
- 3/4 cup (1 1/2 sticks) butter, cut up
- 3/4 cup granulated sugar
- 3/4 cup pure maple syrup
- 1 teaspoon vanilla extract
- 2 large eggs, lightly beaten

Preheat the oven to 325°F. • Butter an 8-inch baking pan. • Spread the nuts out on a large baking sheet. Toast for 7 minutes, or until lightly golden. • Increase the oven temperature to 375°F. • Let the nuts cool completely, then chop them coarsely. • Sift the flour and salt into a large bowl. • Melt the butter in a large saucepan over low heat. • Remove from the heat and stir in the sugar, maple syrup, and vanilla. • Add the eggs, beating until just blended. • Mix in the dry ingredients and nuts until well blended. • Pour the mixture into the prepared pan. • Bake for 25–30 minutes, or until dry on the top and barely firm to the touch. Do not overbake. • Cool completely before cutting into squares.

Makes 16–25 squares · Prep: 15 min. · Cooking: 25–30 min. · Level: 1 · Keeps: 6 days

hazelnut bars

- 1 cup (2 sticks) butter, softened
- 1 1/4 cups granulated sugar
- 1 1/3 cups all-purpose flour
- 1/8 teaspoon salt

- 1 large egg, separated
- 1 teaspoon vanilla extract
- 2/3 cup coarsely chopped hazelnuts

Preheat the oven to 350°F. • Butter a 13 x 9-inch baking pan. • Beat the butter and sugar in a large bowl with an electric mixer at high speed until creamy. • Mix in the flour, salt, egg yolk, and vanilla until well blended. • Firmly press the mixture into the prepared pans to form a smooth, even layer. • Use a fork to beat the egg white lightly and brush over the base. Sprinkle with the hazelnuts. • Bake for 30–35 minutes, or until just golden. • Cut into bars while warm.

Makes 36–45 bars · Prep: 30 min. · Cooking: 30–35 min. · Level: 1 · Keeps: 7 days

prune ribbon cookies

Cookie base
- 1 2/3 cups all-purpose flour
- 1 teaspoon baking powder
- 1/2 teaspoon salt
- 3/4 cup (1 1/2 sticks) butter, softened
- 1 1/2 cups firmly packed light brown sugar
- 1 teaspoon vanilla extract
- 1 large egg, lightly beaten

Prune filling
- 1 1/4 cups pitted prunes
- 2 cups water

- 1/4 cup honey
  Grated zest and juice of 1/4 lemon

Preheat the oven to 350°F. • Butter a 9-inch baking pan. • Cookie base: Sift the flour, baking powder, and salt into a large bowl. • Beat the butter and brown sugar in a large bowl with an electric mixer at high speed until creamy. • Add the vanilla and egg, beating until just blended. • Mix in the dry ingredients until well blended. • Prune filling: Bring the prunes and water to a boil in a large saucepan. • Reduce the heat and simmer for 3 minutes. • Drain well and transfer the prunes to a food processor or blender. Add the honey and lemon zest and juice and process until smooth. • Firmly press one third of the cookie base into the prepared pan to form a smooth, even layer. Spoon over half of the prune filling and spread it evenly. Sprinkle with half the remaining cookie base and spread with the remaining prune filling. Sprinkle with the remaining cookie base to finish. • Bake for 55–65 minutes, or until lightly browned. • Cool completely before cutting into squares.

Makes 16–25 squares · Prep: 30 min. · Cooking: 55–65 min. · Level: 1 · Keeps: 7 days

Prune ribbon cookies

coffee–almond squares

1 1/3   cups whole almonds
2   tablespoons water
3/4   cup granulated sugar
2   teaspoons freeze-dried coffee granules
2   large egg whites
1/8   teaspoon salt
1   tablespoon confectioners' sugar

Preheat the oven to 350°F. • Butter an 8-inch baking pan. • Place the almonds in a large bowl and pour over enough hot water to cover them completely. • Let stand for 5 minutes. • Use a slotted spoon to scoop the nuts out of the water and place on a kitchen towel. • Fold over the kitchen towel and gently rub the nuts to remove the skins. Pick out the skins and discard them. • Finely chop the almonds. • Bring 2 tablespoons water, the granulated sugar, and the coffee granules to a boil in a small saucepan until the sugar and coffee have dissolved completely. • Stir in the almonds. • Remove from the heat and set aside. • Beat the egg whites and salt in a large bowl with an electric mixer at high speed until stiff peaks form. • Use a large rubber spatula to fold in the almond mixture. • Pour the batter into the prepared pan. • Bake for 35–40 minutes, or until a toothpick inserted into the center comes out clean. • Cool completely before cutting into squares. • Dust with the confectioners' sugar.

Makes 16–25 squares · Prep: 40 min. · Cooking: 35–40 min. · Level: 2 · Keeps: 4 days

orange–pecan squares

1 1/2   cups coarsely chopped pitted dates
1   tablespoon finely grated orange zest
3   tablespoons fresh orange juice
1/2   cup (1 stick) butter, softened
1/4   cup granulated sugar
3/4   cup all-purpose flour
1/3   cup rice flour
1/3   cup coarsely chopped pecans, toasted
1/8   teaspoon salt

Topping
2   tablespoons all-purpose flour
2   tablespoons firmly packed light brown sugar
1/4   teaspoon freshly grated nutmeg
2   tablespoons butter, cut up
1/3   cup coarsely chopped pecans, toasted

Cook the dates, orange zest, and orange juice in a medium saucepan over low heat for 12–15 minutes, or until the dates have absorbed all the juice. • Use a wooden spoon to beat the mixture until smooth and let cool completely. • Preheat the oven to 350°F. • Butter an 8-inch baking pan. • Beat the butter and sugar in a large bowl with an electric mixer at high speed until creamy. • Mix in the all-purpose and rice flours, pecans, and salt until well blended. • Firmly press the mixture into the prepared pan to form a smooth, even layer. • Topping: Stir together the flour, brown sugar, and nutmeg in a small bowl. • Use a pastry blender to cut in the butter until the mixture resembles coarse crumbs. Stir in the pecans. • Spread the date mixture evenly over the base and sprinkle with the topping. • Bake for 35–45 minutes, or until lightly browned. • Cool completely before cutting into squares.

Makes 16–25 squares · Prep: 50 min. · Cooking: 35–45 min. · Level: 1 · Keeps: 5 days

indulgent chocolate brownies

The richness of the bittersweet chocolate is complemented by sour cream to create a decadent brownie.

1   cup all-purpose flour
1   teaspoon baking powder
1/8   teaspoon salt
1/2   cup (1 stick) butter, cut up
6   oz bittersweet chocolate, coarsely chopped
1   cup granulated sugar
1/2   teaspoon vanilla extract
2   large eggs
1/2   cup coarsely chopped pecans

Frosting
3   oz bittersweet chocolate, coarsely chopped
1/4   cup sour cream
1/4   cup pecan halves

Preheat the oven to 350°F. • Butter an 8-inch baking pan. • Sift the flour, baking powder, and salt into a medium bowl. • Melt the butter and chocolate in a double boiler over barely simmering water. • Transfer to a large bowl and beat in the sugar and vanilla. • Add the eggs, beating until just blended. • Mix in the dry ingredients and pecans. • Pour the batter into the prepared pan. • Bake for 25–30 minutes, or until dry on top and almost firm to the touch. Do not overbake. • Cool completely in the pan. • Frosting: Melt the chocolate in a double boiler over barely simmering water. • Stir in the sour cream until well blended. • Spread the frosting over the brownie and decorate with the pecan halves. Let stand for 30 minutes until set. • Cut into bars.

Makes 16–25 bars · Prep: 25 min. + 30 min. to set · Cooking: 25–30 min. · Level: 1 · Keeps: 3 days

swiss chocolate treats

This is a spicy Swiss specialty.

3   cups all-purpose flour, or more if needed
2   teaspoons baking powder
1/2   teaspoon ground cloves
1/4   teaspoon ground cardamom
1/8   teaspoon salt
1   cup honey
3   large eggs
1   cup granulated sugar
3   oz semisweet chocolate, grated
       Grated zest of 1/2 lemon
1/2   cup candied orange peel, finely chopped
1   cup candied lemon peel, finely chopped
1   cup blanched almonds, coarsely chopped
3–4   tablespoons kirsch

Glaze
5   oz semisweet chocolate, coarsely chopped
2   tablespoons butter

Preheat the oven to 350°F. • Line a rimmed baking sheet with parchment paper. • Sift the flour, baking powder, cloves, cardamom, and salt into a medium bowl. • Heat the honey in a small saucepan over low heat until liquid. Set aside. • Beat the eggs and sugar in a large bowl with an electric mixer at high speed until pale and thick. • Mix in the chocolate, lemon zest, orange and lemon peel, almonds, kirsch, and honey, followed by the dry ingredients. • You may need to mix in more flour to get a soft and spreadable consistency. • Spoon the mixture onto the prepared sheet. Use a thin metal spatula to spread it evenly to a thickness of 1/2 inch. • Bake for 15–20 minutes, or until firm to the touch. • Cool completely in the pan. • Glaze: Melt the chocolate and butter in a double boiler over barely simmering water. • Spread the glaze over and cut into bars.

Makes about 35 bars · Prep: 45 min. · Cooking: 15–20 min. · Level: 2 · Keeps: 20 days

Orange–pecan squares

marshmallow–peanut "pizza"

Eye-catching and fun-to-make, pizza cookies are ideal for children's parties and finger food gatherings. Create the cookie base, then decorate the top with the candies and frostings of your choice. For extra-special occasions, pipe a greeting over the cookie.

1³/4 cups all-purpose flour
1/4 teaspoon salt
1 cup (2 sticks) butter, softened
1/2 cup granulated sugar
1/2 cup firmly packed light brown sugar
1/2 teaspoon vanilla extract
1 large egg
1¹/4 cup coarsely chopped pink and/or white marshmallows
1 cup semisweet chocolate chips
1/2 cup roasted peanuts

Preheat the oven to 375°F. • Set out a 12-inch pizza pan. • Sift the flour and salt into a medium bowl. • Beat the butter and granulated and brown sugars in a large bowl with an electric mixer at high speed until creamy. • Add the vanilla and egg, beating until just blended. • Mix in the dry ingredients. • Spread the dough in the pan. • Bake for 12–15 minutes, or until just golden. • Cool completely in the pan. • Sprinkle with the marshmallows, chocolate chips, and peanuts. • Bake for 5 minutes more, or until the marshmallows are toasted. • Cut into wedges.

Makes 16 wedges · Prep: 20 min. · Cooking: 17–20 min. · Level: 1 · Keeps: 3 days

oatmeal "pizza"

3/4 cup all-purpose flour
1/2 teaspoon baking powder
1/4 teaspoon baking soda
1/8 teaspoon salt
3/4 cup old-fashioned rolled oats
1/3 cup butter, softened
1/3 cup granulated sugar
1/3 cup firmly packed light brown sugar
1/2 teaspoon vanilla extract
1 large egg

Preheat the oven to 375°F. • Set out a 12-inch pizza pan. • Sift the flour, baking powder, baking soda, and salt into a large bowl. Stir in the oats. • Beat the butter and granulated and brown sugars in a large bowl with an electric mixer at high speed until creamy. • Add the vanilla and egg, beating until just blended. • Mix in the dry ingredients. • Spread the dough in the pan. • Bake for 12–15 minutes, or until just golden. • Cool completely in the pan. • Cut into wedges.

Makes 16 wedges · Prep: 20 min. · Cooking: 12–15 min. · Level: 1 · Keeps: 3 days

pecan and chocolate chip "pizza"

2 cups all-purpose flour
1 teaspoon baking soda
1/2 teaspoon salt
1/2 cup (1 stick) butter, softened
1/3 cup granulated sugar
1/2 cup firmly packed light brown sugar
1/2 teaspoon vanilla extract
1 large egg
3/4 cup (4 oz) semisweet chocolate chips
1/2 cup finely chopped pecans
1/2 cup M&Ms

Preheat the oven to 350°F. • Set out a 12-inch pizza pan. • Sift the flour, baking soda, and salt into a medium bowl. • Beat the butter and granulated and brown sugars in a large bowl with an electric mixer at high speed until creamy. • Add the vanilla and egg, beating until just blended. • Mix in the dry ingredients, chocolate chips, pecans, and M&Ms. • Spread the mixture in the pan. • Bake for 12–15 minutes, or until lightly browned. • Cool completely in the pan. • Cut into wedges.

Makes 16 wedges · Prep: 20 min. · Cooking: 12–15 min. · Level: 1 · Keeps: 3 days

chocolate chip "pizza"

2¹/4 cups all-purpose flour
1 teaspoon baking soda
1/2 teaspoon salt
1 cup (2 sticks) butter, softened
3/4 cup granulated sugar
3/4 cup firmly packed light brown sugar
1/2 teaspoon vanilla extract
2 large eggs
1 cup semisweet chocolate chips

Preheat the oven to 375°F. • Set out a 14-inch pizza pan. • Sift the flour, baking soda, and salt into a medium bowl. • Beat the butter and granulated and brown sugars in a large bowl with an electric mixer at high speed until creamy. • Add the vanilla and eggs, beating until just blended. • Mix in the dry ingredients and chocolate chips. • Spread the mixture in the pan. • Bake for 20–25 minutes, or until lightly browned. • Cool completely in the pan. • Cut into wedges.

Makes 16 wedges · Prep: 20 min. · Cooking: 20–25 min. · Level: 1 · Keeps: 3 days

peanut butter "pizza"

1³/4 cups all-purpose flour
1/2 teaspoon baking soda
1/2 teaspoon salt
1/2 cup (1 stick) butter, softened
1¹/4 cups firmly packed light brown sugar
3/4 cup smooth peanut butter
1/4 cup milk
1/2 teaspoon vanilla extract
1 large egg
4 oz white chocolate, coarsely chopped
4 oz semisweet chocolate, coarsely chopped

Preheat the oven to 375°F. • Set out two 12-inch pizza pans. • Sift the flour, baking soda, and salt into a medium bowl. • Beat the butter, brown sugar, peanut butter, milk, and vanilla in a large bowl with an electric mixer at high speed until creamy. • Add the egg, beating until just blended. • Mix in the dry ingredients. • Divide the dough in half. • Spread the dough halves in the pans. • Bake for 10–12 minutes, or until lightly browned, rotating the sheets halfway through for even baking. • Cool completely in the pans. • Melt the white and semisweet chocolates in separate double boilers over barely simmering water. • Drizzle the chocolate over the cookies and let stand for 30 minutes to set. • Cut into wedges.

Makes 32 wedges · Prep: 20 min. + 30 min. to stand · Cooking: 10–12 min. · Level: 1 · Keeps: 3 days

Marshmallow–peanut "pizza" (top) and Pecan and chocolate chip "pizza" (bottom)

icebox
cookies

Icebox, or refrigerator, cookies have the advantage of being made in advance and stored in the icebox until just before baking. Form the dough into a log, wrap it up, and chill for at least 30 minutes. For perfectly formed cookies, pack the dough into a long buttered glass lined with plastic wrap and refrigerate. Try baking pinwheel and checkerboard cookies for patterned and colorful designs. If you're aiming for simplicity, follow the Sliced refrigerator cookie recipe on page 164, adding your desired ingredients and flavoring. Fresh-tasting cookies every time without the prolonged preparation!

above: Three color icebox cookies (page 164)

right: Clockwise from top left: Orange and chocolate icebox cookies, Coffee pinwheels, Citrus pinwheels, and Ginger sandwich cookies, (see pages 168, 163, 162, and 172)

making mocha pinwheels

- 3 1/3 cups all-purpose flour
- 1/4 teaspoon baking powder
- 1/8 teaspoon salt
- 1 cup (2 sticks) butter, softened
- 3/4 cup granulated sugar
- 3 tablespoons Vanilla Sugar (see page 341)
- 1 tablespoon brandy
- 1/2 teaspoon vanilla extract
- 2 large eggs
- 1/4 cup chocolate hazelnut spread (Nutella)
- 1 tablespoon coffee liqueur

Refrigerate four cookie sheets. • Sift the flour, baking powder, and salt into a medium bowl. • Beat the butter and granulated and vanilla sugars in a large bowl with an electric mixer at high speed until creamy. Add the brandy and vanilla. • Add the eggs, beating until just blended. •

Mix in the dry ingredients to form a soft dough. • Mix the chocolate hazelnut spread and coffee liqueur in a small bowl. • Roll out the dough into a large rectangle about 1/2 inch thick. • Spread evenly with the chocolate spread mixture and tightly roll up the dough from the long side. • Wrap in plastic wrap and refrigerate for 30 minutes. • Preheat the oven to 375°F. • Cut the dough into 1/2-inch thick slices. • Place 1 inch apart on the prepared cookie sheets. • Bake, one sheet at a time, for 8–10 minutes, or until lightly browned and firm to the touch. • Cool the cookies on the cookie sheets for 5 minutes. • Transfer to racks to cool.

Makes 60–65 cookies · Prep: 60 min. + 30 min. to chill · Cooking: 8–10 min. · Level: 2 · Keeps: 4 days

1. Roll out the dough into a rectangle.

2. Spread the dough with chocolate mixture, leaving a small border.

3. Roll it up tightly into a log.

4. Chill and slice. Arrange on a cookie sheet and bake the cookies.

citrus pinwheels

- 1 1/3 cups all-purpose flour
- 1 teaspoon baking powder
- 1/8 teaspoon salt
- 1/2 cup (1 stick) butter, softened
- 1/2 cup granulated sugar
- 1 teaspoon vanilla extract
- 1 large egg yolk, lightly beaten
- 1/4 teaspoon lemon extract
- 3 drops yellow food coloring
- 1/2 teaspoon orange extract
- 3 drops red food coloring

Sift the flour, baking powder, and salt into a medium bowl. • Beat the butter and sugar in a large bowl with an electric mixer at high speed until creamy. • Add the vanilla and egg yolk, beating until just blended. • Mix in the dry ingredients to form a smooth dough. • Dust two sheets of waxed paper with confectioners'

sugar. • Divide the dough in four and place each on a piece of waxed paper. • Roll out one dough portion to a 12 x 6-inch rectangle. • Knead the lemon extract and yellow food coloring into the second dough portion until well blended. • Roll out the dough to the same-sized rectangle as the plain dough. • Invert the lemon dough and place on top of the plain dough, peeling off the paper. • Roll the dough up tightly from the long side and refrigerate for at least 30 minutes. • Repeat with the remaining two dough portions, substituting the orange extract and red food coloring for the lemon extract and yellow food coloring. • Preheat the oven to 350°F. • Set out two cookie sheets. • Slice the dough 1/4 inch thick and place 1 inch apart on the cookie sheets. • Bake for 12–15 minutes, or until lightly

browned, rotating the sheets halfway through for even baking. • Cool on the sheets until the cookies firm slightly. Transfer to racks to cool. • Re-use the cookie sheets and continue until all the cookies are baked.

Makes 30–32 cookies · Prep: 60 min. + 30 min. to chill · Cooking: 12–15 min. per batch · Level: 2 · Keeps: 7 days

coffee pinwheels

- 1 2/3 cups all-purpose flour
- 1 teaspoon baking powder
- 1/8 teaspoon salt
- 1/2 cup (1 stick) butter, softened
- 1/3 cup granulated sugar
- 2 teaspoons freeze-dried coffee granules
- 1 teaspoon milk

Sift the flour, baking powder, and salt into a medium bowl. • Beat 1/4 cup butter and 2 tablespoons sugar in a medium bowl with an electric mixer at high speed until creamy. • Mix in ³/₄ cup of the dry ingredients. • Stir the coffee granules into the remaining flour. • Beat the remaining ¹/₄ cup butter and sugar until creamy. • Mix in the coffee mixture. • Roll out both doughs on a lightly floured surface into rectangles ¹/₄ inch thick. • Brush the plain dough with the milk. • Top with the coffee dough and roll up tightly from a long side. Wrap in plastic wrap and refrigerate for at least 30 minutes. • Preheat the oven to 350°F. • Butter a cookie sheet. • Slice the dough ¹/₄ inch thick and place 1 inch apart on the prepared cookie sheet. • Bake for 12–15 minutes, or until just golden. • Transfer to racks to cool.

Makes 30 cookies · Prep: 60 min. + 30 min. to chill Cooking: 12–15 min. · Level: 1 · Keeps: 9 days

chill-and-bake ginger nuts

²/₃	cup butter, cut up
¹/₃	cup light corn syrup
¹/₃	cup dark molasses
³/₄	cup firmly packed dark brown sugar
2	teaspoons finely grated fresh ginger root
2²/₃	cups all-purpose flour
1¹/₂	teaspoons baking soda
1	teaspoon ground allspice
¹/₈	teaspoon salt
2	tablespoons granulated sugar
2	large eggs, lightly beaten

Melt the butter with the corn syrup, molasses, and brown sugar in a small saucepan over low heat. • Mix in the ginger, remove from the heat, and let cool. • Sift the flour, baking powder, allspice, and salt into a large bowl. • Stir in the granulated sugar. Add the eggs, beating until just blended. • Mix in the corn syrup mixture to form a smooth dough. • Form the dough into four logs, each 8 inches long and 2 inches in diameter. • Wrap in plastic wrap and refrigerate for at least 30 minutes. • Preheat the oven to 325°F. • Line two cookie sheets with parchment paper. • Slice the dough ¹/₂ inch thick and place 1 inch apart on the prepared cookie sheets. • Bake for 15–20 minutes, or until the edges are firm but the center still gives a little to the touch, rotating the sheets halfway through for even baking. • Cool on the sheets until the cookies firm slightly. • Transfer to racks to cool completely.

Makes 64 cookies · Prep: 40 min. + 30 min. to chill · Cooking: 15–20 min. · Level: 2 · Keeps: 8–10 days

strawberry pinwheels

2	cups all-purpose flour
¹/₈	teaspoon salt
¹/₂	cup finely ground almonds
¹/₂	cup granulated sugar
¹/₃	cup butter, cut up
1	large egg, lightly beaten with 2 tablespoons cold water
¹/₄	cup strawberry preserves

Sift the flour and salt into a large bowl. Stir in the almonds and sugar. • Use a pastry blender to cut in the butter until the mixture resembles fine crumbs. • Mix in the egg mixture to form a firm dough. • Turn the dough out onto a lightly floured surface and knead until smooth. • Transfer to a large sheet of parchment paper and roll out to a 10 x 14-inch rectangle. Spread evenly with the strawberry preserves and tightly roll up the dough from the long side. • Wrap in plastic wrap and refrigerate for at least 30 minutes. • Preheat the oven to 350°F. • Line two cookie sheets with parchment paper. • Slice the dough ¹/₂ inch thick and place ¹/₂ inch apart on the prepared cookie sheets. • Bake for 12–15 minutes, or until just golden at the edges, rotating the sheets halfway through for even baking. • Transfer to racks to cool.

Makes 28 cookies · Prep: 60 min. + 30 min. to chill · Cooking: 12–15 min. · Level: 2 · Keeps: 1 week

chocolate rose leaf cookies

Rose leaf decorations
6	oz bittersweet chocolate, coarsely chopped
30–32	green rose leaves, washed and dried

Cookies
1¹/₂	cups all-purpose flour
1	tablespoon unsweetened cocoa powder
1	teaspoon baking powder
¹/₈	teaspoon salt
¹/₂	cup (1 stick) butter, softened
³/₄	cup granulated sugar
1	large egg

Rose leaf decorations: Melt the chocolate in a double boiler over barely simmering water. Use a small pastry brush to paint the melted chocolate onto the underside of each rose leaf. • Keep any remaining chocolate in the double boiler. Leave the decorations to set at room temperature for at least 30 minutes—do not refrigerate. When the chocolate has set, carefully peel off the rose leaves. • Cookies: Sift the flour, cocoa, baking powder, and salt into a

medium bowl. • Beat the butter and sugar in a large bowl with an electric mixer at high speed until creamy. • Add the egg, beating until just blended. • Mix in the dry ingredients to form a stiff dough. • Form the dough into two logs 1¹/₂ inches in diameter. Wrap in plastic wrap and refrigerate for at least 30 minutes. • Preheat the oven to 400°F. • Line two cookie sheets with parchment paper. • Slice the dough ¹/₄ inch thick and place 3 inches apart on the prepared cookie sheets. • Bake for 8–10 minutes, or until golden, rotating the sheets halfway through for even browning. • Transfer to racks to cool. • Melt the remaining chocolate in the double boiler over barely simmering water. Brush a little chocolate onto each cookie and lay a rose leaf decoration on top.

Makes 30–32 cookies · Prep: 60 min. + 30 min. to chill · Cooking: 8–10 min. · Level: 3 · Keeps: 10 days

Chocolate rose leaf cookies

sliced refrigerator cookies

A perfect recipe to keep on hand for unexpected guests. Make up the dough, form it into a log, wrap it in plastic wrap or waxed paper, and store in the refrigerator for up to a week (or in the freezer for up to a month). When an unexpected guest drops in, just slice off as much you need straight from the refrigerator or freezer and bake. The colder the dough, the thinner it slices. You can adapt this basic recipe for sliced cookies by flavoring the dough with orange, rum, peppermint, or other extracts; by adding chocolate chips, nuts, and fruit; or by sprinkling the cookie slices with chopped nuts or sugar before baking. You can roll the dough logs in chopped almonds or pistachios, or stack contrasting doughs for striped or checkered cookies. Very rich mixtures with a high proportion of fat are baked on ungreased baking sheets. Unless otherwise stated, nonstick baking sheets do not need to be greased.

- 3 cups all-purpose flour
- 1 teaspoon baking powder
- 1/2 teaspoon baking soda
- 1/2 teaspoon salt
- 1 cup (2 sticks) butter, softened
- 3/4 cup granulated sugar
- 2/3 cup firmly packed light brown sugar
- 2 tablespoons Vanilla Sugar (see page 341)
- 2 large eggs, lightly beaten
- 1 teaspoon vanilla extract
- 1 teaspoon finely grated lemon zest
- 1 teaspoon fresh lemon juice
- 2 tablespoons milk, or more as needed

Sift the flour, baking powder, baking soda, and salt into a medium bowl. • Beat the butter, granulated sugar, brown sugar, and vanilla sugar in a large bowl with an electric mixer at high speed until creamy. • Add the eggs, beating until just blended. • Stir in the vanilla and lemon zest and juice. • Mix in the

pecan slices

- 2 2/3 cups all-purpose flour
- 1/3 cup unsweetened cocoa powder
- 1 teaspoon baking soda
- 1/2 teaspoon ground cinnamon
- 1/2 teaspoon salt
- 1 1/4 cups (2 1/2 sticks) butter, softened
- 1 1/2 cups firmly packed light brown sugar
- 2 tablespoons granulated sugar
- 2 large eggs, lightly beaten
- 1 1/2 cups finely chopped pecans

Sift the flour, cocoa, baking soda, cinnamon, and salt into a medium bowl. • Beat the butter, brown sugar, and granulated sugar in a large bowl with an electric mixer at high speed until creamy. • Add the eggs, beating until just blended. • Mix in the dry ingredients and pecans to form a smooth dough. Divide the dough in half. Form each half into a log 2 inches in diameter, wrap in plastic wrap, and

Pecan slices

refrigerate for at least 30 minutes. • Preheat the oven to 375°F. • Line three baking sheets with parchment paper. • Slice the dough 1/4 inch thick and place 1 inch apart on the prepared cookie sheets. • Bake, one sheet at a time, for 8–10 minutes, or until lightly browned and firm around the edges. • Cool on the sheet until the cookies firm slightly. • Transfer to racks to finish cooling.

Makes 50 cookies · Prep: 40 min. + 30 min. to chill · Cooking: 8–10 min. per batch · Level: 2 · Keeps: 8 days

three-color icebox cookies

- 1 1/2 cups all-purpose flour
- 1/4 teaspoon baking soda
- 1/8 teaspoon salt
- 1/2 cup (1 stick) butter, softened
- 1/2 cup granulated sugar
- 1 large egg
- 1/2 teaspoon almond extract
- 1/4 cup finely chopped pistachios
  Few drops green and red food colorings
- 1/4 cup finely chopped red candied cherries

Line a 9 x 5-inch loaf pan with plastic wrap, letting the edges overhang. • Sift the flour, baking soda, and salt into a medium bowl. • Beat the butter and sugar in a large bowl with an electric mixer at high speed until creamy. • Add the egg and almond extract, beating until just blended. • Mix in the dry ingredients. • Transfer one third of the dough to a separate bowl and mix in the pistachios and green food coloring. • Transfer one third of the plain dough to a separate bowl and mix in the cherries and red food coloring. • Spoon the green cookie dough into the prepared pan, smoothing the top. Refrigerate for 30 minutes. • Remove from the refrigerator and spoon over the plain dough. Refrigerate for 30 minutes more. • Spoon the red dough over the top, cover with plastic wrap, and refrigerate for 30 minutes. • Preheat the oven to 350°F. • Set out three cookie sheets. • Turn the dough out of the pan, cut in half lengthwise, and slice 1/2 inch thick. • Use a spatula to transfer the cookies to the cookie sheets, placing them 1 inch apart. • Bake, one sheet at a time, for 10–12 minutes, or until just golden and firm to the touch. • Cool on the sheets until the cookies firm slightly. • Transfer to racks to cool.

Makes 36 cookies · Prep: 40 min. + 90 min. to chill · Cooking: 10–12 min. per batch · Level: 2 · Keeps: 5 days

white chocolate chip refrigerator cookies

- 1 2/3 cups all-purpose flour
- 1 1/2 teaspoons baking powder
- 1/4 teaspoon salt
- 1/2 cup (1 stick) butter, softened
- 1/4 cup sunflower or peanut oil
- 3/4 cup firmly packed light brown sugar
- 1 large egg, lightly beaten
- 1/2 teaspoon vanilla extract
- 1 cup white chocolate chips or 2 oz white chocolate, finely chopped
- 1 cup finely chopped walnuts

Sift the flour, baking powder, and salt into a medium bowl. • Beat the butter, oil, and brown sugar in a large bowl with an electric mixer at high speed until creamy. • Add the egg and vanilla, beating until just blended. • Mix in the dry ingredients, chocolate chips, and walnuts. • Form the dough into a 7-inch log, wrap in plastic wrap, and refrigerate for at least 30 minutes. • Preheat the oven to

dry ingredients until well blended. • Add enough milk to form a soft, but not sticky dough. • Turn the cookie dough onto a lightly floured surface and knead until smooth. • Divide the dough in half. Form each half into a 12-inch log, wrap in plastic wrap, and refrigerate for at least 30 minutes. • Preheat the oven to 400°F. • Butter two cookie sheets • Slice the dough 1/4 inch thick and place 1 inch apart on the prepared cookie sheets. • Bake for 6–8 minutes, or until lightly browned and firm around the edges, rotating the sheets halfway through for even baking. • Cool on the sheet until the cookies firm slightly. Transfer to racks to finish cooling.

Makes 30–35 cookies · Prep: 40 min. + 30 min. to chill · Cooking: 6–8 min. · Level: 1 · Keeps: 10 days

375°F. • Butter two cookie sheets. • Slice the dough 1/4 inch thick and place 2 inches apart on the prepared cookie sheets. • Bake for 8–10 minutes, or until just golden at the edges, rotating the sheets halfway through for even baking. • Transfer to racks to cool.

Makes 28 cookies · Prep: 40 min. + 30 min. to chill Cooking: 8–10 min. · Level: 1 · Keeps: 7 days

checkered cookies

- 1 1/3 cups all-purpose flour
- 1/2 teaspoon baking powder
- 1/8 teaspoon salt
- 2/3 cup butter, softened
- 1/3 cup Vanilla Sugar (see page 341)
- 1 tablespoon unsweetened cocoa powder
- 1 large egg white, lightly beaten

Sift the flour, baking powder, and salt into a medium bowl. • Beat the butter and vanilla sugar in a large bowl with an electric mixer at high speed until creamy. • Mix in the dry ingredients to form a stiff dough. • Lightly dust a surface with confectioners' sugar and divide the dough in half. • Knead the cocoa powder into one half of the dough until well blended. Wrap each dough portion in plastic wrap and refrigerate for at least 30 minutes. • Cut each chilled portion in thirds and form into long logs 1 inch in diameter. Press the edges of the logs to make them into even-sided oblongs. • Arrange the three chocolate logs and the three plain logs on top of each other in a checkerboard pattern. To do so, place one light log next to one dark log, then set a dark log on top of the light log to make a roll with alternating chocolate and plain sections. • Seal the sections together by brushing them with a little egg white. The dough will now be rectangular in shape. • Wrap in plastic wrap and refrigerate for at least 1 hour. • Preheat the oven to 375°F. • Butter two large cookie sheets. • Slice the dough 1/4 inch thick and place 1 1/2 inches apart on the prepared cookie sheets. • Bake for 10–15 minutes, or until lightly browned and the edges are firm, rotating the sheets halfway through for even baking. • Cool on the sheets until the cookies firm slightly. • Transfer to racks to finish cooling.

Makes 20 cookies · Prep: 50 min. + 90 min. to chill Cooking: 10–15 min · Level: 2 · Keeps: 10 days

black-and-white cookies

- 1 2/3 cups all-purpose flour
- 1 teaspoon baking powder
- 1/8 teaspoon salt
- 2/3 cup butter, cut up
- 3/4 cup firmly packed light brown sugar
- 1 large egg, lightly beaten
- 2 teaspoons rum extract
- 1 teaspoon vanilla extract
- 2 oz semisweet chocolate, coarsely chopped
- 2 tablespoons Vanilla Sugar (see page 341)
- 1 tablespoon unsweetened cocoa powder
- 1 tablespoon milk

Sift the flour, baking powder, and salt into a large bowl. • Use a pastry blender to cut in the butter until the mixture resembles fine crumbs. • Mix in the brown sugar, egg, and rum and vanilla extracts to form a stiff dough. Divide the dough in half. Press the dough into a disk, wrap each in plastic wrap, and refrigerate for 30 minutes. • Melt the chocolate in a double boiler over barely simmering water. Remove from the heat and mix in the vanilla sugar, cocoa, and milk. • Take one half of the dough and knead in the chocolate mixture until completely blended. • Form the chocolate dough into a 9-inch log and wrap in plastic wrap. • Refrigerate for 30 minutes. • Roll out the plain dough on a lightly floured surface to fit around the chocolate roll. Wrap the plain dough around the chilled chocolate dough to form a larger roll. • Wrap in plastic wrap and refrigerate for at least 20 minutes. • Preheat the oven to 350°F. • Line two cookie sheets with parchment paper. • Slice the dough 1/4 inch thick and place 1 inch apart on the prepared cookie sheets. • Bake for 12–15 minutes, or until the edges are firm and the bottoms are lightly browned, rotating the sheets halfway through for even baking. • Transfer to racks to cool.

Makes 36 cookies · Prep: 45 min.+ 80 min. to chill · Cooking: 12–15 min. · Level: 2 · Keeps: 12 days

chocolate–hazelnut pinwheels

Use this recipe as the basis for creating pinwheel cookies. Substitute finely ground almonds for the hazelnuts and spread the dough with apricot or strawberry preserves. Pinwheels are attractive cookies that are perfect for Halloween night celebrations. Rolled up, left to chill, and sliced, pinwheels are low-maintenance cookies. They are simple to prepare in advance and fun to make.

2   cups all-purpose flour
1/8   teaspoon salt
1/2   cup finely ground hazelnuts

1/2   cup granulated sugar
1/3   cup butter, cut up
1   large egg, lightly beaten with
        2 tablespoons cold water
1/4   cup chocolate hazelnut spread (Nutella)

Sift the flour and salt into a large bowl. Stir in the hazelnuts and sugar. • Use a pastry blender to cut in the butter until the mixture resembles fine crumbs. • Mix in the egg mixture to form a firm dough. • Turn the dough out onto a lightly floured surface and knead until smooth. • Transfer to a large sheet of parchment paper and roll out to a 10 x 14-inch rectangle. Spread evenly with the chocolate hazelnut spread and tightly roll up the dough from the long side. • Wrap in plastic wrap and refrigerate for 30 minutes. • Preheat the oven to 350°F. • Line two cookie sheets with parchment paper. • Slice the dough 1/2 inch thick and place 1/2 inch apart on the prepared cookie sheets. • Bake for 12–15 minutes, or until just golden at the edges, rotating the sheets halfway through for even baking. • Transfer to racks to cool.

Makes 28 cookies · Prep: 60 min. + 30 min. to chill · Cooking: 12–15 min. · Level: 2 · Keeps: 2 weeks

sour cream icebox cookies

1 1/3 cups all-purpose flour
1/8   teaspoon salt
1/3   cup granulated sugar
2/3   cup butter, cut up
3   tablespoons reduced-fat sour cream
1   large egg yolk, lightly beaten
1   cup finely chopped almonds

Sift the flour and salt into a large bowl. Stir in the sugar. • Use a pastry blender to cut in the butter until the mixture resembles fine crumbs. • Mix in the sour cream to form a stiff dough. • Form the dough into an 8-inch log. Wrap in plastic wrap and refrigerate for at least 30 minutes. • Preheat the oven to 400°F. • Set out two cookie sheets. • Slice the dough 1/2 inch thick and place 1 inch apart on the prepared cookie sheets. • Brush the tops of the cookies with the beaten egg yolk and sprinkle with the chopped almonds. • Bake for 10–15 minutes, or until golden brown and firm to the touch, rotating the sheets halfway through for even baking. • Transfer to racks to cool.

Makes 16 cookies · Prep: 40 min. + 30 min. to chill · Cooking: 10–15 min. · Level: 2 · Keeps: 7 days

sunflower seed cookies

1 2/3 cups all-purpose flour
1/8   teaspoon salt
3/4   cup butter, softened
1/4   cup granulated sugar
2   tablespoons Vanilla Sugar (see page 341)
1   cup ground sunflower seeds
1/2   teaspoon vanilla extract
2   tablespoons milk
4   tablespoons finely chopped
         sunflower seeds
1/3   cup confectioners' sugar

Preheat the oven to 350°F. • Line two cookie sheets with parchment paper. • Sift the flour and salt into a medium bowl. • Beat the butter and granulated and vanilla sugars until creamy. • Add the ground sunflower seeds and vanilla. • Mix in the dry ingredients and milk to form a stiff dough. • Divide the dough in half. Form the dough into two 8-inch logs and roll in the finely chopped sunflower seeds. Wrap each in plastic wrap, and refrigerate for at least 30 minutes. • Slice the dough 1/2 inch thick and place 1 inch apart on the prepared cookie sheets. • Bake for 10–15 minutes, or until golden and the edges are firm. • Cool on the sheet until the cookies firm slightly. • Transfer to racks and let cool completely. Dust with the confectioners' sugar.

Makes 32 cookies · Prep: 50 min. + 30 min. to chill Cooking: 10–15 min. · Level: 2 · Keeps: 10 days

espresso cookies

3   oz semisweet chocolate, coarsely
         chopped
1   cup all-purpose flour
2   tablespoons unsweetened cocoa powder
1   teaspoon freeze-dried espresso coffee
         powder
1   teaspoon baking soda
1/4   teaspoon salt
2/3   cup butter, softened
1/2   cup firmly packed light brown sugar
1   large egg, lightly beaten
1   teaspoon vanilla extract
Frosting
1 1/3 cups confectioners' sugar
1   teaspoon freeze-dried espresso coffee
         powder
1–2   tablespoons warm water

Melt the chocolate in a bowl set over simmering water. • Sift the flour, cocoa, espresso powder, baking soda, and salt into a medium bowl. • Beat the butter and brown sugar in a large bowl with an electric mixer at high speed until creamy. • Add the egg and vanilla and beat for 1 minute. • Stir in the melted chocolate. • Mix in the dry ingredients. • Divide the dough in half. Form the dough into two 9 x 2-inch logs, wrap in plastic wrap, and refrigerate for at least 2 hours. • Preheat the oven to 350°F. • Butter two cookie sheets. • Slice the dough 2/3 inch thick and place 1 inch apart on the prepared cookie sheets. • Bake for 12–15 minutes, or until the edges are firm and the bottoms are lightly browned, rotating the sheets halfway through for even baking. • Cool on the sheets until the cookies firm slightly. • Transfer to racks to cool. • Frosting: Mix the sugar and espresso powder in a small bowl. Stir in enough warm water to make a drizzling consistency. • Drizzle over the cookies and let set.

Makes 27 cookies · Prep: 45 min.+ 2 hr. to chill · Cooking: 12–15 min. · Level: 2 · Keeps: 6 days

Chocolate–hazelnut pinwheels

Chocolate drizzlers

chocolate drizzlers

These delicious cookies are easy and fun to make, especially for kids.

2¼ cups all-purpose flour
⅓ cup unsweetened cocoa powder
½ teaspoon baking powder
½ teaspoon baking soda
⅛ teaspoon salt
7 oz semisweet chocolate, coarsely chopped
¾ cup (1½ sticks) butter, softened
1 cup granulated sugar
1 large egg
1 teaspoon vanilla extract
3 oz white chocolate, coarsely chopped

Sift the flour, cocoa, baking powder, baking soda, and salt into a medium bowl. • Melt 4 oz of semisweet chocolate in a double boiler over barely simmering water. • Beat the butter and sugar in a large bowl with an electric mixer at high speed until creamy. • Add the egg, beating until just blended. • Beat in the melted chocolate and vanilla until well blended. • Mix in the dry ingredients. • Divide the dough in half. Form into two long logs each 2 inches in diameter, wrap in waxed paper, and freeze for at least 4 hours. • Preheat the oven to 350°F. • Line two cookie sheets with aluminum foil. Butter the foil. • Slice the dough ¼ inch thick and place 1 inch apart on the prepared cookie sheets. • Bake for 10–12 minutes, or until lightly browned, rotating the sheets halfway through for even baking. • Transfer the cookies to racks

to cool. • Melt the remaining 3 oz semisweet chocolate and white chocolate in separate double boilers over barely simmering water. Drizzle the chocolates over the cookies.

Makes 30 cookies · Prep: 40 min. + 4 hr. to freeze · Cooking: 10–12 min. · Level: 1 · Keeps: 3 days

banana kipferl

These Austrian crescent-shaped cookies have a distinctly exotic flavor.

1⅔ cups all-purpose flour
1 teaspoon baking powder
⅛ teaspoon salt
⅔ cup butter, softened
½ cup granulated sugar
2 tablespoons Vanilla Sugar (see page 341)
1 large egg yolk
1 vanilla pod
1 cup broken-up, dried unsweetened banana chips
3½ oz semisweet chocolate, coarsely chopped
3½ oz white chocolate, coarsely chopped

Sift the flour, baking powder, and salt into a medium bowl. • Beat the butter and granulated and vanilla sugars in a large bowl with an electric mixer at high speed. • Add the egg yolk, beating until just blended. • Scoop out the pulp from the vanilla pod and add to the mixture. • Stir in the banana chips and vanilla pulp. • Mix in the dry ingredients to form a smooth dough. • Divide the dough in half. • Form into 10-inch logs, wrap in plastic wrap, and refrigerate for at least 30 minutes. • Preheat the oven to 350°F. • Line three cookie sheets with parchment paper. • Slice the dough ½ inch thick. • Press the centers inward and taper the ends to form crescents and place 1 inch apart on the prepared cookie sheets. • Bake, one sheet at a time, for 10–12 minutes, or until just golden at the edges. • Transfer on the parchment paper to a rack and let cool completely. • Melt the chocolates separately in double boilers over barely simmering water. • Dip one cookie end into the white chocolate and the other end into the semisweet chocolate.

Makes 40 cookies · Prep: 45 min. + 30 min. to chill · Cooking: 10–12 min. per batch · Level: 2 · Keeps: 10 days

cashew butter cookies

1⅔ cups all-purpose flour
1 teaspoon baking soda
½ teaspoon salt
1 cup roasted whole cashew nuts + 1 cup
coarsely chopped roasted cashew nuts
2 tablespoons vegetable oil
½ cup (1 stick) butter, softened
½ cup granulated sugar
½ cup firmly packed light brown sugar
1 large egg, lightly beaten
1 teaspoon vanilla extract
½ teaspoon rum extract
1 cup old-fashioned rolled oats

Sift the flour, baking soda, and salt into a medium bowl. • Process 1 cup roasted whole cashew nuts with the oil in a food processor or blender until a thick paste has formed. • Beat the butter and granulated and brown sugars in a large bowl with an electric mixer at high speed until creamy. • Add the egg, beating until just blended. • Stir in the cashew paste and vanilla and rum extracts until well blended. • Mix in the dry ingredients, 1 cup chopped cashew nuts, and oats to form a soft dough. • Divide the dough in half. Form into two logs 2 inches in diameter, wrap in plastic wrap, and refrigerate for at least 30 minutes. • Preheat the oven to 350°F. • Butter four cookie sheets. • Slice the dough ¼ inch thick and place 1 inch apart on the prepared cookie sheets. • Bake, one sheet at a time, for 8–10 minutes, or until just golden. • Transfer to racks and let cool completely.

Makes 45 cookies · Prep: 40 min. + 30 min. to chill · Cooking: 8–10 min. per batch · Level: 1 · Keeps: 7 days

orange and chocolate icebox cookies

¾ cup (1½ sticks) butter, softened
1½ cups granulated sugar
1 large egg, lightly beaten
2⅓ cups all-purpose flour
⅛ teaspoon salt
2 oz bittersweet chocolate, coarsely chopped
1 tablespoon finely grated orange zest

Beat the butter and sugar in a large bowl with an electric mixer at high speed until creamy. • Add the egg, beating until just blended. • Mix in the flour and salt to form a soft dough. • Transfer half the cookie dough to a separate bowl. • Melt the chocolate in a double boiler over barely simmering water. • Mix the cooled chocolate into one half of the cookie dough until well blended. • Mix the orange zest into the plain cookie dough. • Roll out both cookie dough portions on a lightly floured surface to a thickness of ¼ inch. • Shape into rectangles of the same size. • Place the orange dough on top of the chocolate dough. • Tightly roll up the stacked rectangles into a log, starting from the long side. Wrap in plastic wrap and refrigerate for at least 30 minutes. • Preheat the oven to 375°F. • Butter and flour two cookie sheets. • Slice the dough $1/4$ inch thick and place 1 inch apart on the prepared baking sheets. • Bake for 10–12 minutes, or until lightly browned, rotating the sheets halfway through for even baking. • Cool on the sheets until the cookies firm slightly. Transfer to racks to finish cooling.

Makes 40 cookies · Prep: 1 hr. + 30 min. to chill · Cooking: 10–12 min. · Level: 2 · Keeps: 15 days

lemon icebox cookies

2	cups all-purpose flour
$1/4$	teaspoon baking powder
$1/4$	teaspoon salt
$3/4$	cup ($1^1/2$ sticks) butter, softened
$1/2$	cup granulated sugar
$1/2$	cup confectioners' sugar
1	tablespoon finely grated lemon zest
2	tablespoons fresh lemon juice
$1/2$	teaspoon vanilla extract

Sift the flour, baking powder, and salt into a medium bowl. • Beat the butter, granulated sugar, and confectioners' sugar in a large bowl with an electric mixer at high speed until creamy. • Add the lemon zest and juice and vanilla. • Mix in the dry ingredients to form a smooth dough. • Divide the dough in half. Form into two 6-inch logs, wrap in plastic wrap, and refrigerate for at least 30 minutes. • Preheat the oven to 350°F. • Set out three cookie sheets. • Slice the dough $1/4$ inch thick and place 1 inch apart on the cookie sheets. • Bake, one sheet at a time, for 10–12 minutes, or until just golden at the edges. • Cool on the sheets until the cookies firm slightly. • Transfer to racks and let cool completely.

Makes 48 cookies · Prep: 40 min. + 30 min. to chill · Cooking: 10–12 min. per batch · Level: 1 · Keeps: 7 days

butterscotch shorties

$1^1/2$	cups all-purpose flour
1	teaspoon baking powder
$1/8$	teaspoon salt
$3/4$	($1^1/2$ sticks) butter, softened
1	cup raw sugar (Demerara or Barbados)
1	large egg
$1/3$	cup bran

Sift the flour, baking powder, and salt into a medium bowl. • Beat the butter and raw sugar in a large bowl with an electric mixer at high speed until creamy. • Add the egg, beating until just blended. • Mix in the dry ingredients and bran to form a stiff dough. • Form the dough into two 8-inch logs, wrap in plastic wrap, and refrigerate for at least 30 minutes. • Preheat the oven to 400°F. • Set out four cookie sheets. • Slice the dough $1/4$ inch thick and place 1 inch apart on the cookie sheets. • Bake, one sheet at a time, for 7–10 minutes, or until pale gold. • Transfer to racks to cool.

Makes 64 cookies · Prep: 40 min. + 30 min. to chill · Cooking: 7–10 min. per batch · Level: 1 · Keeps: 2 weeks

chocolate chip refrigerator cookies

$1^2/3$	cups all-purpose flour
$1^1/2$	teaspoons baking powder
$1/4$	teaspoon salt
$1/2$	cup (1 stick) butter, softened
$1/4$	cup sunflower or peanut oil
$3/4$	cup firmly packed light brown sugar
1	large egg, lightly beaten
$1/2$	teaspoon vanilla extract
1	cup semisweet chocolate chips
1	cup finely chopped walnuts

Sift the flour, baking powder, and salt into a medium bowl. • Beat the butter, oil, and brown sugar in a large bowl with an electric mixer at high speed until creamy. • Add the egg and vanilla, beating until just blended. • Mix in the dry ingredients, chocolate chips, and walnuts. • Form the dough into a 7-inch log, wrap in plastic wrap, and refrigerate for at least 30 minutes. • Preheat the oven to 375°F. • Butter two cookie sheets. • Slice the dough $1/4$ inch thick and place 2 inches apart on the prepared cookie sheets. • Bake for 8–10 minutes, or until just golden at the edges, rotating the sheets halfway through for even baking. • Transfer to racks to cool.

Makes 28 cookies · Prep: 40 min. + 30 min. to chill Cooking: 8–10 min. · Level: 1 · Keeps: 7 days

chocolate caramel cookies

$2^2/3$	cups all-purpose flour
1	teaspoon baking powder
$1/2$	teaspoon baking soda
$1/4$	teaspoon salt
$3/4$	cup ($1^1/2$ sticks) butter, softened
$3/4$	cup firmly packed light brown sugar
2	tablespoons firmly packed dark brown sugar
2	large eggs, lightly beaten
7	oz caramel-filled chocolates, such as Rolos, cut into small chunks
3	oz dried banana chips, coarsely chopped
2	tablespoons milk

Sift the flour, baking powder, baking soda, and salt into a medium bowl. • Beat the butter and the brown sugars in a large bowl with an electric mixer at high speed until creamy. • Add the eggs, beating until just blended. • Mix in the dry ingredients, chocolates, banana chips, and milk. • Divide the dough in half. Form the dough into two 8-inch logs, wrap in plastic wrap, and refrigerate for at least 2 hours. • Preheat the oven to 350°F. • Line two cookie sheets with parchment paper. • Slice the dough $1/2$ inch thick and place 1 inch apart on the prepared cookie sheets. • Bake for 15–18 minutes, or until the edges are firm and the centers are still slightly soft, rotating the sheets halfway through for even baking. • Cool on the sheets until the cookies firm slightly. • Transfer to racks to cool.

Makes 30–32 cookies · Prep: 60 min. + 2 hr. to chill Cooking: 15–18 min. · Level: 2 · Keeps: 5 days

Chocolate chip refrigerator cookies

coconut and orange cookies

1/2 cup (1 stick) butter, softened
1/2 package (4 oz) cream cheese, softened
1 1/4 cups confectioners' sugar
1/4 teaspoon baking soda
1/4 teaspoon salt
1 large egg, lightly beaten
1 tablespoon finely grated orange zest
1 tablespoon fresh orange juice
1/2 teaspoon vanilla extract
2 1/4 cups all-purpose flour
1/2 cup shredded coconut

Beat the butter and cream cheese in a large bowl with an electric mixer at medium speed for 1 minute. • Beat in the confectioners' sugar, baking soda, and salt. • Add the egg, beating until just blended. • Beat in the orange zest, juice, and vanilla. • Mix in the flour to form a soft dough. • Turn the dough out on a lightly floured surface and knead until smooth. • Divide the dough in half. Form the dough into two 8-inch logs and roll each in the coconut. Wrap in plastic wrap, and refrigerate for at least 30 minutes. • Preheat the oven to 375°F. • Set out three cookie sheets. • Slice the dough 1/4 inch thick and place 1 inch apart on the cookie sheets. • Bake, one sheet at a time, for 6–8 minutes, or until just golden. • Cool on the sheet until the cookies firm slightly. • Transfer to racks to finish cooling.

Makes 64 cookies · Prep: 40 min. + 30 min. to chill · Cooking: 6–8 min. per batch · Level: 2 · Keeps: 10 days

three-citrus cookies

2 1/3 cups all-purpose flour
1 1/2 teaspoons baking powder
1/8 teaspoon salt
3/4 cup (1 1/2 sticks) butter, softened
1 cup granulated sugar
2 large eggs, lightly beaten
   Few drops each orange (or red and yellow), yellow, and green food colorings
1/4 teaspoon orange extract
1/4 teaspoon lemon extract
1/4 teaspoon lime extract

Sift the flour, baking powder, and salt into a medium bowl. • Beat the butter and sugar in a large bowl with an electric mixer at high speed until creamy. • Add the eggs, beating until well blended. • Divide the mixture into three small bowls. • Use a wooden spoon to mix the orange, yellow, and green food colorings alternately into

the mixtures. • Mix one-third of the dry ingredients into each mixture. • Mix the orange extract into the orange mixture, the lemon extract into the yellow mixture, and the lime extract into the green mixture until well blended. • Form the orange dough into a 2 x 6-inch log. Repeat with the yellow and green dough. Place two of the logs side-by-side, with the third on top, pressing down gently so that the logs stick together. Wrap in plastic wrap and refrigerate for at least 30 minutes. • Preheat the oven to 400°F. • Line two cookie sheets with parchment paper. • Slice the dough 1/4 inch thick and place 2 inches apart on the prepared cookie sheets. • Bake for 5–8 minutes, or until firm to the touch, rotating the sheets halfway through for even baking. • Transfer to racks to cool.

Makes 20–24 cookies · Prep: 30 min. + 30 min. to chill Cooking: 5–8 min. · Level: 2 · Keeps: 3 days

cream cheese sandwich cookies

2 2/3 cups all-purpose flour
1/3 cup unsweetened cocoa powder
1 teaspoon baking powder
1/2 teaspoon baking soda
1/4 teaspoon salt
1 cup (2 sticks) butter, softened
3/4 cup granulated sugar
1/2 cup firmly packed light brown sugar
1 teaspoon Vanilla Sugar (see page 341)
2 large eggs
1/2 cup white chocolate chips
2–3 tablespoons milk

Pecan–cream cheese filling

1 1/2 packages (12 oz total) cream cheese, softened
1/2 cup confectioners' sugar
1 teaspoon vanilla extract
2/3 cup finely chopped pecans
3 oz white chocolate, coarsely chopped

Sift the flour, cocoa, baking powder, baking soda, and salt into a medium bowl. • Beat the butter and granulated, brown, and vanilla sugars in a large bowl with an electric mixer at high speed until creamy. • Add the eggs, beating until just blended. • Mix in the dry ingredients, chocolate chips, and enough milk to form a soft, but non sticky dough. • Form the dough into two 10-inch logs, wrap in plastic wrap, and refrigerate for at least 30 minutes. • Preheat the oven to 375°F. • Set out four cookie sheets. • Slice the dough 1/4 inch

thick and place 1 inch apart on the cookie sheets. • Bake, one sheet at a time, for 8–10 minutes, or until the edges are firm and the bottoms are lightly browned. • Cool on the sheets until the cookies firm slightly. • Transfer to racks and let cool completely. • Pecan–cream cheese filling: With mixer at medium speed, beat the cream cheese, confectioners' sugar, and vanilla until well blended. • Stir in the pecans. • Stick the cookies together in pairs with the filling. • Melt the chocolate in a double boiler over barely simmering water. • Drizzle the chocolate over the cookies.

Makes 20 cookies · Prep: 45 min. + 30 min. to chill Cooking: 8–10 min. · Level: 2 · Keeps: 4 days in the refrigerator

orange–bran flake cookies

1 1/2 cups all-purpose flour
1 teaspoon baking powder
1/8 teaspoon salt
1/2 cup (1 stick) butter, softened
3/4 cup firmly packed light brown sugar
1 large egg
2 cups bran flakes, lightly crushed
2 teaspoons grated orange zest

Sift the flour, baking powder, and salt into a medium bowl. • Beat the butter and brown sugar in a large bowl with an electric mixer at high speed until creamy. • Add the egg, beating until just blended. • Stir in the bran flakes and orange zest. • Mix in the dry ingredients to form a stiff dough. • Form the dough into a 12 x 2-inch log, wrap in plastic wrap, and refrigerate for at least 30 minutes. • Preheat the oven to 425°F. • Butter three cookie sheets. • Slice the dough 1/4 inch thick and place 1 inch apart on the prepared cookie sheets. • Bake, one sheet at a time, for 8–10 minutes, or until just golden. • Transfer to racks and let cool completely.

Makes 40–44 cookies · Prep: 25 min. + 30 min. to chill · Cooking: 8–10 min. per batch · Level: 1 · Keeps: 7 days

*Cream cheese sandwich cookies (top)
and Orange–bran flake cookies (bottom)*

cherry stand-by cookies

Stand-by cookies are the best type to have on hand in your freezer for when friends unexpectedly drop by for coffee or an impromptu gathering. Make the basic dough and, instead of chilling the dough in the refrigerator, freeze it. Let it thaw for a hour before you want to bake the cookies. The dough can be frozen for up to 2 weeks. Prepare a variety of different doughs by adding chocolate chips, raisins, or nuts, or whatever takes your fancy!

1²/₃ cups all-purpose flour
1 teaspoon baking powder
¹/₈ teaspoon salt
¹/₂ cup (1 stick) butter, cut up
1 large egg, lightly beaten
³/₄ cup granulated sugar
¹/₂ cup finely chopped candied cherries
1 teaspoon vanilla extract

Sift the flour, baking powder, and salt into a large bowl. • Use a pastry blender to cut in the butter until the mixture resembles fine crumbs. • Add the egg, beating until just blended. • Stir in the sugar, cherries, and vanilla to form a soft dough. • Turn the dough out onto a lightly floured surface and knead until smooth. • Form the dough into a long log 2 inches in diameter, wrap in plastic wrap, and refrigerate for at least 30 minutes. • Preheat the oven to 375°F. • Butter three cookie sheets. • Slice the dough ¹/₂ inch thick and place 1 inch apart on the prepared cookie sheets. • Bake, one sheet at a time, for 8–10 minutes, or until just golden. • Cool on the sheets until the cookies firm slightly. • Transfer to racks to finish cooling.

Makes 35 cookies · Prep: 40 min. + 30 min. to chill
Cooking: 8–10 min. per batch · Level: 1 · Keeps: 3–4 days

ginger sandwich cookies

3 cups all-purpose flour
1 teaspoon ground ginger
1 teaspoon baking powder
¹/₂ teaspoon baking soda
¹/₄ teaspoon salt
1 cup (2 sticks) butter, softened
³/₄ cup granulated sugar
²/₃ cup firmly packed light brown sugar
2 tablespoons Vanilla Sugar
   (see page 341)
1 teaspoon vanilla extract
2 large eggs, lightly beaten
1 teaspoon finely grated fresh ginger
3 tablespoons milk, or more as needed

Filling
1¹/₂ packages (12 oz total) cream cheese, softened
²/₃ cup confectioners' sugar
1 teaspoon vanilla extract
1 teaspoon finely grated fresh ginger

Sift the flour, ground ginger, baking powder, baking soda, and salt into a medium bowl. • Beat the butter, granulated sugar, brown sugar, and vanilla sugar in a large bowl with an electric mixer at high speed until creamy. • Add the vanilla and eggs, beating until just blended. • Mix in the dry ingredients and fresh ginger. • Add enough milk to form a soft, but not sticky, dough. • Turn the dough out onto a lightly floured surface and knead until smooth. • Divide the dough in half. Form the dough into two 12-inch logs, wrap in plastic wrap, and refrigerate for at least 30 minutes. • Preheat the oven to 375°F. • Butter three baking sheets. • Slice the dough ¹/₄ inch thick and place 2 inches apart on the prepared cookie sheets. • Bake, one sheet at a time, for 8–10 minutes, or until lightly browned and firm around the edges. • Cool on the sheets until the cookies firm slightly. Transfer to racks to finish cooling. • Filling: With mixer at high speed, beat the cream cheese, confectioners' sugar, and vanilla in a large bowl until creamy. Stir in the ginger until well blended. • Stick the cookies together in pairs with the filling.

Makes 48 cookies · Prep: 45 min. + 30 min. to chill Cooking: 8–10 min. per batch · Level: 2 · Keeps: 3 days in the refrigerator

ginger icebox cookies

1²/₃ cups all-purpose flour
1 teaspoon baking powder
2 teaspoons ground ginger
¹/₈ teaspoon salt
¹/₂ cup (1 stick) butter, cut up
1 large egg, lightly beaten
³/₄ cup granulated sugar

Sift the flour, baking powder, ginger, and salt into a large bowl. • Use a pastry blender to cut in the butter until the mixture resembles fine crumbs. • Add the egg, beating until just blended. • Stir in the sugar to form a soft dough. • Turn the dough out onto a lightly floured surface and knead until smooth. • Form the dough into a long log 2 inches in diameter, wrap in plastic wrap, and refrigerate for at least 30 minutes. • Preheat the oven to 375°F. • Butter three cookie sheets. • Slice the dough ¹/₂ inch thick and place 1 inch apart on the prepared cookie sheets. • Bake, one sheet at a time, for 8–10 minutes, or until just golden. • Cool on the sheets until the cookies firm slightly. • Transfer to racks to finish cooling.

Makes 35 cookies · Prep: 40 min. + 30 min. to chill Cooking: 8–10 min. per batch · Level: 1 · Keeps: 3–4 days

Ginger icebox cookies

cinnamon–coffee cookies

1   cup all-purpose flour
1/2   teaspoon baking powder
1/2   teaspoon ground cinnamon
1/8   teaspoon salt
1/2   cup (1 stick) butter, softened
2   tablespoons vegetable shortening
1/2   cup + 2 tablespoons granulated sugar
1/4   cup firmly packed light brown sugar
1   tablespoon + 1 teaspoon freeze-dried
       coffee granules
1   large egg
2   teaspoons hot water
       coffee beans, to decorate

Sift the flour, baking powder, cinnamon, and salt into a medium bowl. • Beat the butter, vegetable shortening, 1/2 cup granulated sugar, and brown sugar in a large bowl with an electric mixer at high speed until creamy. • Dissolve 1 tablespoon of the coffee granules in the hot water. • Add the coffee mixture and egg, beating until just blended. • Mix in the dry ingredients to form a stiff dough. • Divide the dough in half. Form into two 7-inch logs, wrap in plastic wrap, and refrigerate for at least 1 hour. • Preheat the oven to 375°F. • Butter four cookie sheets. • Slice the dough 1/4 inch thick and place 1 inch apart on the prepared cookie sheets. • Mix the remaining 2 tablespoons granulated sugar and 1 teaspoon coffee granules in a small bowl. Sprinkle over the tops of the cookies and decorate with the coffee beans. • Bake, one sheet at a time, for 8–10 minutes, or until pale gold. • Cool on the sheets until the cookies firm slightly. • Transfer to racks to finish cooling.

Makes 56 cookies · Prep: 40 min. + 1 hr. to chill · Cooking: 8–10 min. per batch · Level: 1 · Keeps: 10 days

cherry–walnut cookies

2 3/4 cups all-purpose flour
1   teaspoon baking powder
1/2   teaspoon ground cinnamon
1/4   teaspoon baking soda
1/8   teaspoon salt
3/4   cup (1 1/2 sticks) butter, softened
1/2   cup granulated sugar
1/2   cup firmly packed light brown sugar
2   large eggs
1   cup finely chopped candied cherries
1   cup finely chopped walnuts

Sift the flour, baking powder, cinnamon, baking soda, and salt into a large bowl. • Beat the butter and granulated and brown sugars in a large bowl with an electric mixer at high speed until creamy. • Add the eggs, beating until just blended. • Mix in the dry ingredients, cherries, and walnuts to form a stiff dough. • Form the dough into a 14-inch log, wrap in plastic wrap, and refrigerate for at least 30 minutes. • Preheat the oven to 375°F. • Butter four cookie sheets. • Slice the dough 1/4 inch thick and place 1 inch apart on the prepared cookie sheets. • Bake, one sheet at a time, for 8–10 minutes, or until lightly browned. • Cool on the sheets until the cookies firm slightly. • Transfer to racks to finish cooling.

Makes 56 cookies · Prep: 40 min. + 30 min. to chill · Cooking: 8–10 min. per batch · Level: 1 · Keeps: 10 days

ginger–walnut icebox cookies

1 1/4 cups all-purpose flour
1   teaspoon ground ginger
1/8   teaspoon salt
1/2   cup (1 stick) butter, softened
1   cup firmly packed light brown sugar
1   large egg
1   cup finely chopped walnuts

Sift the flour, ginger, and salt into a medium bowl. • Beat the butter and 1/2 cup brown sugar in a large bowl with an electric mixer at high speed until creamy. • Add the egg, beating until just blended. • Mix in the dry ingredients and walnuts to form a stiff dough. • Form the dough into four logs, each 1 inch in diameter. Wrap in plastic wrap and refrigerate for at least 30 minutes. • Preheat the oven to 400°F. • Set out two cookie sheets. • Sprinkle the remaining 1/2 cup brown sugar onto a surface and roll the logs in the sugar until well coated. • Slice the dough 1/4 inch thick and place 1/2 inch apart on the cookie sheets. • Bake for 8–10 minutes, or until just golden at the edges, rotating the sheets halfway through for even baking. • Transfer to racks to cool.

Makes 20–25 cookies · Prep: 40 min. + 30 min. to chill · Cooking: 8–10 min. · Level: 1 · Keeps: 5 days

nutty icebox cookies

1 2/3 cups all-purpose flour
1   teaspoon baking powder
1/8   teaspoon salt
1/2   cup (1 stick) butter, cut up
1   large egg, lightly beaten
3/4   cup granulated sugar
1/2   cup finely chopped walnuts
1   teaspoon vanilla extract

Sift the flour, baking powder, and salt into a large bowl. • Use a pastry blender to cut in the butter until the mixture resembles fine crumbs. • Add the egg, beating until just blended. • Stir in the sugar, walnuts, and vanilla to form a soft dough. • Turn the dough out onto a lightly floured surface and knead until smooth. • Form the dough into a long log 2 inches in diameter, wrap in plastic wrap, and refrigerate for at least 30 minutes. • Preheat the oven to 375°F. • Butter three cookie sheets. • Slice the dough 1/2 inch thick and place 1 inch apart on the prepared cookie sheets. • Bake, one sheet at a time, for 8–10 minutes, or until just golden. • Cool on the sheets until the cookies firm slightly. • Transfer to racks to finish cooling.

Makes 35 cookies · Prep: 40 min. + 30 min. to chill · Cooking: 8–10 min. per batch · Level: 1 · Keeps: 3–4 days

potato–almond cookies

1¼ cups all-purpose flour
⅓ cup whole-wheat flour
1 teaspoon baking powder
½ teaspoon ground allspice
½ teaspoon ground cinnamon
½ teaspoon ground nutmeg
⅛ teaspoon salt
½ cup (1 stick) butter, softened
⅔ cup firmly packed light brown sugar
1 tablespoon dark corn syrup
1 cup peeled and finely grated potato
⅓ cup finely chopped flaked almonds
⅓ cup finely chopped candied cherries

Sift the all-purpose and whole-wheat flours, baking powder, allspice, cinnamon, nutmeg, and salt into a medium bowl. • Beat the butter and brown sugar in a large bowl with an electric mixer at high speed until creamy. • Stir in the corn syrup, grated potatoes, almonds, and cherries until well blended. • Mix in the dry ingredients to form a stiff dough. • Form the dough into an 8-inch log, wrap in plastic wrap, and refrigerate for at least 30 minutes. • Preheat the oven to 350°F. • Butter two cookie sheets. • Slice the dough ½ inch thick and place 1 inch apart on the prepared cookie sheets. • Bake for 18–20 minutes, or until just golden, rotating the sheets halfway through for even baking. • Cool on the sheets until the cookies firm slightly. • Transfer to racks to finish cooling.

Makes 16 cookies · Prep: 40 min. + 30 min. to chill
Cooking: 18–20 min. · Level: 1 · Keeps: 5 days

red-and-white cookies

2½ cups all-purpose flour
1½ teaspoons baking powder
⅛ teaspoon salt
1 cup (2 sticks) butter, cut up
1½ cups granulated sugar
1 large egg white, lightly beaten
½ teaspoon vanilla extract
Few drops red food coloring

Sift the flour, baking powder, and salt into a large bowl. • Cut in the butter until the mixture resembles fine crumbs. • Stir in the sugar, egg white, and vanilla to form a smooth dough. • Transfer one-third of the dough to a separate bowl. Knead in the red food coloring until no white streaks remain. • Form the dough into three logs 1 inch in diameter, wrap in plastic wrap, and refrigerate for at least 30 minutes. • Stack the logs in alternating order (white, red,

white) and press together firmly to form a rectangle. Wrap in plastic wrap and refrigerate for 30 minutes. • Preheat the oven to 350°F. • Set out three cookie sheets. • Slice the dough ¼ inch thick and place 1 inch apart on the cookie sheets. • Bake, one sheet at a time, for 12–15 minutes, or until just golden at the edges. • Cool on the sheets until the cookies firm slightly. • Transfer to racks and let cool completely.

Makes 48 cookies · Prep: 45 min. + 30 min. to chill · Cooking: 12–15 min. per batch · Level: 1 · Keeps: 2 weeks

nut cookies

1⅔ cups all-purpose flour
¼ teaspoon salt
¾ cup (1½ sticks) butter, softened
⅔ cup firmly packed light brown sugar
⅔ cup finely chopped almonds

Sift the flour and salt into a medium bowl. • Beat the butter and brown sugar in a large bowl with an electric mixer at high speed until creamy. • Mix in the dry ingredients until well blended. • Sprinkle the almonds onto a 6 x 18-inch piece of aluminum foil. • Form the dough into a 10-inch log and roll on the foil, pressing in the almonds. • Wrap in the foil and refrigerate for at least 30 minutes. • Preheat the oven to 325°F. • Butter three cookie sheets. • Slice the dough ¼ inch thick and place 1 inch apart on the prepared cookie sheets. • Bake, one sheet at a time, for 15–20 minutes, or until lightly browned. • Cool on the sheets until the cookies firm slightly. • Transfer to racks to finish cooling.

Makes 40 cookies · Prep: 40 min. + 30 min. to chill · Cooking: 10–20 min. per batch · Level: 1 · Keeps: 5 days

sherry butter cookies

1¼ cups all-purpose flour
¼ teaspoon freshly grated nutmeg
⅛ teaspoon salt
½ cup (1 stick) butter, softened
⅓ cup + 1 tablespoon granulated sugar
1 large egg, separated
1 tablespoon sweet sherry

Sift the flour, nutmeg, and salt into a medium bowl. • Beat the butter and ⅓ cup sugar in a large bowl with an electric mixer at high speed until creamy. • Add the egg yolk and sherry, beating until just blended. • Mix in the dry ingredients to form a stiff dough. • Form

the dough into an 8-inch long log, wrap in plastic wrap, and refrigerate for at least 30 minutes. • Preheat the oven to 375°F. • Set out two cookie sheets. • Slice the dough ¼ inch thick and place 1 inch apart on the cookie sheets. • Beat the egg white lightly in a small bowl and brush over the tops of the cookies. Sprinkle with the remaining 1 tablespoon of sugar. • Bake for 10–12 minutes, or until pale gold, rotating the sheets halfway through for even baking. • Cool on the sheets until the cookies firm slightly. • Transfer to racks and let cool completely.

Makes 32 cookies · Prep: 40 min. + 30 min. to chill
Cooking: 10–12 min. · Level: 1 · Keeps: 7 days

plain-and-fancy cookies

2⅓ cups all-purpose flour
⅛ teaspoon salt
1 cup (2 sticks) butter, softened
¾ cup granulated sugar
1 large egg yolk
½ teaspoon vanilla extract
1 cup coarsely chopped almonds
6 oz bittersweet chocolate, coarsely chopped
1¾ cups flaked almonds, toasted

Sift the flour and salt into a medium bowl. • Beat the butter and sugar in a large bowl with an electric mixer at high speed until creamy. • Add the egg yolk and vanilla, beating until just blended. • Mix in the dry ingredients and chopped almonds to form a stiff dough. • Form the dough into two logs 2 inches in diameter, wrap in plastic wrap, and refrigerate for at least 30 minutes. • Preheat the oven to 350°F. • Line two cookie sheets with parchment paper. • Slice the dough ½ inch thick and place 2 inches apart on the prepared cookie sheets. • Bake for 15–18 minutes, or until lightly browned, rotating the sheets halfway through for even browning. • Transfer to racks to cool. • Melt the chocolate in a double boiler over barely simmering water. • Dip the cookies halfway into the chocolate, then into the flaked almonds. • Return the cookies to racks until set.

Makes 20–25 cookies · Prep: 45 min. + 30 min. to chill · Cooking: 15–18 min. · Level: 1 · Keeps: 2 weeks

Plain-and-fancy cookies
and Checkered cookies (see page 165)

Orange creams

completely. • <u>Filling:</u> Process the pistachios and brown sugar in a food processor until very finely chopped. • Add the butter and process until smooth. Continue processing, adding enough orange juice to make a thick cream. • Stick the cookies together in pairs with the filling, pressing down gently.

Makes 25 cookies · Prep: 45 min. + 30 min. to chill · Cooking: 6–8 min. per batch · Level: 2 · Keeps: 4 days

norwegian brown cookies

2/3	cup all-purpose flour
1/8	teaspoon salt
1/2	cup (1 stick) butter, cut up
1/2	cup granulated sugar
1/4	cup light corn syrup
1/3	cup finely chopped almonds
1 1/2	teaspoons finely grated orange zest
1 1/2	teaspoons ground cinnamon
1/2	teaspoon ground cloves
1/2	teaspoon baking soda dissolved in 1 1/2 teaspoons hot water
1	teaspoon ice water
	25–30 almond halves, to decorate

Sift the flour and salt into a medium bowl. • Melt the butter with the sugar and corn syrup in a medium saucepan over low heat until the sugar has dissolved completely. • Remove from the heat and mix in the chopped almonds, orange zest, cinnamon, and cloves. • Mix in the baking soda mixture and dry ingredients to form a stiff dough. • Form the dough into a log 2 inches in diameter, wrap in plastic wrap, and refrigerate for at least 1 hour. • Preheat the oven to 300°F. • Butter two cookie sheets. • Slice the dough 1/4 inch thick and place 1 inch apart on the prepared cookie sheets. • Sprinkle the cookies with the water and decorate with the almond halves. • Bake for 8–10 minutes, or until lightly browned, rotating the sheets halfway through for even browning. • Transfer to racks to cool.

Makes 25–30 cookies · Prep: 40 min. + 60 min. to chill · Cooking: 8–10 min. · Level: 1 · Keeps: 2 weeks

black walnut cookies

Black walnuts are native to North America and more strongly flavored than English walnuts, which can be used instead.

2	cups all-purpose flour
1	teaspoon baking powder
1/8	teaspoon salt
1	cup (2 sticks) butter, softened
1	cup firmly packed dark brown sugar
1	teaspoon pure maple syrup
1	large egg
1 1/2	cups coarsely chopped black walnuts

Sift the flour, baking powder, and salt into a large bowl. • Beat the butter and brown sugar in a large bowl with an electric mixer at high speed until creamy. • Add the maple syrup and egg, beating until just blended. • Mix in the dry ingredients and walnuts until well blended. • Divide the dough in thirds. Form the dough into three long logs each 2 inches in diameter, wrap in plastic wrap, and refrigerate for at least 30 minutes. • Preheat the oven to 400°F. • Butter two cookie sheets. • Slice the dough 1/4 inch thick and place 1 inch apart on the prepared cookie sheets. • Bake for 8–10 minutes, or until lightly browned, rotating the sheets halfway through for even baking. • Transfer the cookies to racks to cool.

Makes 30 cookies · Prep: 40 min. + 30 min. to chill Cooking: 8–10 min. · Level: 1 · Keeps: 3 days

orange creams

2 1/3	cups all-purpose flour
2	teaspoons baking powder
1/8	teaspoon salt
1/3	cup butter, softened
1	cup raw sugar (Demerara or Barbados)
1	large egg
1	tablespoon fresh orange juice
1	teaspoon vanilla extract

Filling

1/4	cup pistachios
3/4	cup firmly packed light brown sugar
1/3	cup butter, softened
2	tablespoons fresh orange juice

Sift the flour, baking powder, and salt into a medium bowl. • Beat the butter and raw sugar in a large bowl with an electric mixer at high speed until creamy. • Add the egg, beating until just blended. • Beat in the orange juice and vanilla. • Mix in the dry ingredients. • Transfer to a lightly floured surface and knead the mixture into a smooth dough. Form into two logs about 2 inches in diameter, wrap in plastic wrap, and refrigerate for at least 30 minutes. • Preheat the oven to 375°F. • Butter four cookie sheets. • Slice the dough 1/8 inch thick. • Place the cookies on the prepared cookie sheets. • Bake, one batch at a time, for 6–8 minutes, or until golden brown. • Cool the cookies on the cookie sheets for 2 minutes. Transfer to racks and let cool

sesame–raisin cookies

1/3	cup golden raisins
1/2	cup brandy
1	cup all-purpose flour
1	cup cornstarch
2/3	cup granulated sugar
1	teaspoon baking powder
1/4	teaspoon ground cinnamon
1/8	teaspoon salt

2 tablespoons extra-virgin olive oil
2/3 cup butter, softened
1¼ cups sesame seeds, toasted
1/2 cup water, or more as needed

Plump the raisins in the brandy in a small bowl for 15 minutes. Drain and pat dry with paper towels. • Mix the flour, cornstarch, sugar, baking powder, cinnamon, and salt in a large bowl. • Stir in the oil, butter, sesame seeds, and raisins. • Add enough water to form a smooth dough. • Form the dough into a log 1 inch in diameter, wrap in plastic wrap, and refrigerate for at least 30 minutes. • Preheat the oven to 350°F. • Butter two cookie sheets. • Slice the dough 1/2 inch thick and place 1 inch apart on the prepared cookie sheets. • Bake for 15–20 minutes, or until lightly browned, rotating the sheets halfway through for even baking. • Transfer to racks and let cool completely.

Makes 25 cookies · Prep: 55 min. + 30 min. to chill Cooking: 15–20 min. · Level: 1 · Keeps: 10 days

pretty petal icebox cookies

1²/3 cups all-purpose flour
3/4 cup confectioners' sugar
1/8 teaspoon salt
1 cup (2 sticks) butter, cut up
    Petals from 2 red roses, well-washed and finely chopped

Sift the flour, confectioners' sugar, and salt into a large bowl. • Use a pastry blender to cut in the butter until the mixture resembles fine crumbs. • Mix in the rose petals. • Form the dough into an 8-inch log, wrap in plastic wrap, and refrigerate for at least 30 minutes. • Preheat the oven to 325°F. • Butter two cookie sheets. • Slice the dough 1/4 inch thick and place 1 inch apart on the prepared cookie sheets. • Bake for 8–10 minutes, or until pale gold, rotating the sheets halfway through for even baking. • Cool on the sheets until the cookies firm slightly. • Transfer to racks to finish cooling.

Makes 32 cookies · Prep: 40 min. + 30 min. to chill Cooking: 8–10 min. · Level: 1 · Keeps: 7 days

coconut–lime snaps

2¼ cups all-purpose flour
1/2 teaspoon salt
1 cup (2 sticks) butter, softened
1 cup granulated sugar
2 large eggs, lightly beaten
    Grated zest of 1 lime
1 tablespoon fresh lime juice

1/2 teaspoon vanilla extract
1/2 teaspoon almond extract
1 cup shredded coconut

Sift the flour and salt into a medium bowl. • Beat the butter and sugar in a large bowl with an electric mixer at high speed until creamy. • Add the eggs, beating until just blended. • Add the lime zest, lime juice, and vanilla and almond extracts. • Mix in the dry ingredients and 3/4 cup coconut to form a stiff dough. • Divide the dough in half. Form the dough into two logs 2 inches in diameter, wrap each in plastic wrap, and flatten slightly to form oblongs. • Refrigerate for at least 30 minutes. • Preheat the oven to 375°F. • Butter three cookie sheets. • Discard the plastic wrap. • Slice the dough 1/4 inch thick and place 1 inch apart on the prepared cookie sheets. • Sprinkle with the remaining 1/4 cup coconut. • Bake, one sheet at a time, for 10–12 minutes, or until just golden. • Transfer to racks and let cool completely.

Makes 36 cookies · Prep: 40 min. + 30 min. to chill · Cooking: 10–12 min. per batch · Level: 1 · Keeps: 3 days

cinnamon slices

These little cookies make an especially tasty nibble with an espresso or a glass of after-dinner wine.

1/2 cup all-purpose flour
3/4 cup cornstarch
1½ teaspoons ground cinnamon
1/8 teaspoon salt
1/2 cup butter, softened
2/3 cup confectioners' sugar
2 tablespoons Vanilla Sugar (see page 341)
1/4 teaspoon vanilla extract

Sift the flour, cornstarch, 1 teaspoon of cinnamon, and salt into a medium bowl. • Beat the butter, 1/3 cup of confectioners' sugar, vanilla sugar, and vanilla extract in a large bowl with an electric mixer at high speed until creamy. • Mix in the dry ingredients to form a stiff dough. • Form the dough into two 8-inch logs, wrap in plastic wrap, and refrigerate for at least 30 minutes. • Preheat the oven to 375°F. • Line two cookie sheets with parchment paper. • Slice the dough 1/2 inch thick and place them 2 inches on the prepared cookie sheets. • Bake, one sheet at a time, for 12–15 minutes, or until firm at the edges and lightly golden. • Transfer to racks and let cool completely. • Dust with the remaining 1/3 cup confectioners' sugar and remaining cinnamon.

Makes 32 cookies · Prep: 60 min. · Cooking: 12–15 min. · Level: 1 · Keeps: 5 days

angelica cookies

Angelica is a tall herb that grows in the northern United States, Canada, and northern Europe. Its hollow green stems are naturally sweet in flavor.

2 cups all-purpose flour
1 teaspoon baking powder
1/8 teaspoon salt
1/2 cup (1 stick) butter, softened
1 cup granulated sugar
1 large egg, lightly beaten
1 tablespoon finely grated orange zest
2 tablespoons fresh orange juice
1 cup finely chopped candied angelica

Sift the flour, baking powder, and salt into a medium bowl. • Beat the butter and sugar in a large bowl with an electric mixer at high speed until creamy. • Add the egg and orange zest and juice, beating until just blended. • Mix in the dry ingredients and angelica to form a stiff dough. • Form the dough into a log 2 inches in diameter, wrap in plastic wrap, and refrigerate for at least 30 minutes. • Preheat the oven to 375°F. • Butter three cookie sheets. • Slice the dough 1/4 inch thick and place 1 inch apart on the prepared cookie sheets. • Bake, one sheet at a time, for 12–15 minutes, or until golden brown. • Transfer to racks to cool.

Makes 40 cookies · Prep: 40 min. · Cooking: 12–15 min. per batch · Level: 1 · Keeps: 10 days

Coconut–lime snaps

Vanilla targets

vanilla refrigerator cookies

Vary the extract to create different flavored cookies. Try coffee or peppermint for a change of taste.

1^1/3 cups all-purpose flour
1 teaspoon baking powder
^{1}/8 teaspoon salt
^{1}/2 cup (1 stick) butter, softened
^{1}/2 cup granulated sugar
1 teaspoon vanilla extract
1 large egg yolk, lightly beaten

Sift the flour, baking powder, and salt into a medium bowl. • Beat the butter and sugar in a large bowl with an electric mixer at high speed until creamy. • Add the vanilla and egg yolk, beating until just blended. • Mix in the dry ingredients to form a smooth dough. • Form the dough into a log 1^1/2 inches in diameter, wrap in plastic wrap, and refrigerate for 30 minutes. • Preheat the oven to 400°F. • Butter three cookie sheets. • Slice the dough ^{1}/2 inch thick and place 1 inch apart on the prepared cookie sheets. • Bake, one sheet at a time, for 8–10 minutes, or until lightly browned. • Cool on the sheets until the cookies firm slightly. Transfer to racks to finish cooling.

Makes 45 cookies · Prep: 40 min. + 30 min. to chill · Cooking: 8–10 min. per batch · Level: 1 · Keeps: 5 days

peanut butter icebox slices

2 cups all-purpose flour, sifted
^{2}/3 cup rice flour
1^1/2 teaspoons baking powder
^{1}/8 teaspoon salt
^{3}/4 cup (1^1/2 sticks) butter, softened
1 cup firmly packed light brown sugar
^{1}/3 cup crunchy peanut butter
1 oz semisweet chocolate, coarsely chopped
2 tablespoons milk
2 cups Crunchy Peanut Butter Frosting (see page 348)

Sift the all-purpose and rice flours, baking powder, and salt into a large bowl. • Beat the butter, brown sugar, and peanut butter in a medium bowl with an electric mixer at high speed until creamy. • Mix in the dry ingredients and milk to form a smooth, firm dough. • Melt the chocolate in a double boiler over barely simmering water. Mix the chocolate into the dough. • Form the dough into two 8-inch logs, wrap in plastic wrap, and refrigerate for at least 2 hours. Slice the dough ^{1}/4 inch thick and place 2 inches apart on the prepared cookie sheets. • Preheat the oven to 350°F. • Line two cookie sheets with parchment paper. • Bake for 8–10 minutes, until golden brown and firm around the edges, rotating the sheets halfway through for even baking. • Transfer to racks to cool. If desired, spread the frosting over the cookies.

Makes 64 cookies · Prep: 60 min. + 2 hr. to chill · Cooking: 8–10 min. · Level: 2 · Keeps: 5 days

vanilla targets

1^2/3 cups all-purpose flour
1 teaspoon baking powder
^{1}/8 teaspoon salt
^{1}/2 cup (1 stick) butter, cut up
^{3}/4 cup granulated sugar
1 large egg, lightly beaten
1 teaspoon vanilla extract
2 tablespoons unsweetened cocoa powder
1 tablespoon milk

Sift the flour, baking powder, and salt into a large bowl. • Use a pastry blender to cut in the butter until the mixture resembles fine crumbs. • Mix in the sugar, egg, and vanilla to form a smooth dough. • Divide the dough in half. • Mix the cocoa and milk in a small bowl. • Knead the cocoa mixture into one half of the dough. • Form the plain dough into a 12-inch log. Brush with cold water. • Roll out the cocoa dough on a lightly floured surface into a 12 x 6-inch rectangle. • Place the plain dough log in the center of the cocoa rectangle and wrap the cocoa dough around it. Fold over the overhanging edges

and seal with water. • Wrap in plastic wrap and refrigerate for at least 30 minutes. • Preheat the oven to 375°F. • Butter three cookie sheets. • Slice the dough ^{1}/4 inch thick and place 2 inches apart on the prepared cookie sheets. • Bake, one sheet at a time, for 8–10 minutes, or until lightly browned. • Cool on the sheets until the cookies firm slightly. • Transfer to racks and let cool completely.

Makes 48 cookies · Prep: 40 min. + 30 min. to chill Cooking: 8–10 min. per batch · Level: 2 · Keeps: 7 days

almond–lemon swirls

1 cup finely chopped almonds
^{1}/2 cup orange marmalade
2 oz semisweet chocolate, finely grated
^{1}/2 teaspoon ground cinnamon
^{1}/4 teaspoon freshly grated nutmeg
 Grated zest of 1 lemon
1^1/2 cups firmly packed light brown sugar
^{1}/4 cup (^{1}/2 stick) butter, softened
^{1}/4 cup vegetable shortening
1 large egg
1^3/4 cups all-purpose flour
^{1}/8 teaspoon salt

Mix the almonds, marmalade, finely grated chocolate, cinnamon, nutmeg, 1 tablespoon lemon zest, and ^{1}/4 cup brown sugar in a large bowl. • Beat the butter, shortening, and remaining 1^1/4 cups brown sugar in a large bowl with an electric mixer at high speed until creamy. • Add the egg, beating until just blended. • Stir in the remaining lemon zest, flour, and salt to form a stiff dough. • Divide the dough in half. Press each half into a disk, wrap in plastic wrap, and refrigerate for 30 minutes. • Roll out half the dough on a lightly floured surface to make an 11 x 7-inch rectangle. • Spread with half the almond mixture, leaving a ^{1}/4-inch border. • Roll up the dough from a short side and wrap in plastic wrap. • Repeat with the remaining dough and hazelnut mixture. • Refrigerate for 30 minutes. • Preheat the oven to 350°F. • Butter four cookie sheets. • Slice the dough ^{1}/4 inch thick and place 1 inch apart on the prepared cookie sheets. • Bake, one sheet at a time, for 8–10 minutes, or until just golden. • Transfer to racks and let cool completely.

Makes 54 cookies · Prep: 40 min. + 60 min. to chill Cooking: 8–10 min. per batch · Level: 2 · Keeps: 5 days

sugar strand icebox cookies

- 1²/₃ cups all-purpose flour
- 1 teaspoon baking powder
- ¹/₈ teaspoon salt
- ¹/₈ cup (1 stick) butter, cut up
- 1 large egg, lightly beaten
- ³/₄ cup granulated sugar
- ¹/₂ cup sugar strands or jimmies, mixed colors
- 1 teaspoon vanilla extract

Sift the flour, baking powder, and salt into a large bowl. • Use a pastry blender to cut in the butter until the mixture resembles fine crumbs. • Add the egg, beating until just blended. • Stir in the sugar, sugar strands, and vanilla until a soft dough has formed. • Turn the dough out onto a lightly floured surface and knead until smooth. • Form the dough into a long log 2 inches in diameter, wrap in plastic wrap, and refrigerate for at least 30 minutes. • Preheat the oven to 375°F. • Butter three cookie sheets. • Discard the plastic wrap. Slice the dough ¹/₂ inch thick and place 1 inch apart on the prepared cookie sheets. • Bake, one sheet at a time, for 8–10 minutes, or until just golden. • Cool on the sheets until the cookies firm slightly. Transfer to racks to finish cooling.

Makes 35 cookies · Prep: 40 min. + 30 min. to chill · Cooking: 8–10 min. per batch · Level: 1 · Keeps: 3–4 days

lemon–corn flake cookies

- 1¹/₂ cups all-purpose flour
- 1 teaspoon baking powder
- ¹/₈ teaspoon salt
- ¹/₂ cup (1 stick) butter, softened
- ³/₄ cup granulated sugar
- 1 large egg
- 2 cups cornflakes, lightly crushed
- 2 teaspoons grated lemon zest

Sift the flour, baking powder, and salt into a medium bowl. • Beat the butter and sugar in a large bowl with an electric mixer at high speed until creamy. • Add the egg, beating until just blended. • Stir in the cornflakes and lemon zest. • Mix in the dry ingredients to form a stiff dough. • Form the dough into a 12 x 2-inch log, wrap in plastic wrap, and refrigerate for at least 30 minutes. • Preheat the oven to 425°F. • Butter three cookie sheets. • Slice the dough ¹/₄ inch thick and place 1 inch apart on the prepared cookie sheets. •

Bake, one sheet at a time, for 8–10 minutes, or until just golden. • Transfer to racks and let cool completely.

Makes 48 cookies · Prep: 40 min. + 30 min. to chill · Cooking: 8–10 min. per batch · Level: 1 · Keeps: 7 days

marmalade–hazelnut swirls

- 1 cup finely chopped hazelnuts
- ¹/₂ cup orange marmalade
- 2 oz semisweet chocolate, finely grated + 4 oz semisweet chocolate, coarsely chopped
- ¹/₂ teaspoon ground cinnamon
- ¹/₄ teaspoon freshly grated nutmeg
  Grated zest of 1 orange
- ¹/₄ cup (¹/₂ stick) butter, softened
- ¹/₄ cup vegetable shortening
- 1¹/₂ cups firmly packed light brown sugar
- 1 large egg
- 1³/₄ cups all-purpose flour
- ¹/₈ teaspoon salt

Mix the hazelnuts, marmalade, finely grated chocolate, cinnamon, nutmeg, 1 tablespoon orange zest, and ¹/₄ cup brown sugar in a large bowl. • Beat the butter, shortening, and remaining 1¹/₄ cups brown sugar in a large bowl with an electric mixer at high speed until creamy. • Add the egg, beating until just blended. • Stir in the remaining orange zest, flour, and salt to form a stiff dough. • Divide the dough in half. Press each half into a disk, wrap in plastic wrap, and refrigerate for 30 minutes. • Roll out half the dough on a lightly floured surface to a thickness of ¹/₄ inch and to an 11 x 7-inch rectangle. • Spread with half the hazelnut mixture, leaving a ¹/₄-inch border. • Roll up the dough from a short side and wrap in plastic wrap. • Repeat with the remaining dough and hazelnut mixture. • Refrigerate for 30 minutes. • Preheat the oven to 350°F. • Butter four cookie sheets. • Discard the plastic wrap. • Slice the dough ¹/₄ inch thick and place 1 inch apart on the prepared cookie sheets. • Bake, one sheet at a time, for 8–10 minutes, or until just golden. • Transfer to racks and let cool completely. • Melt the coarsely chopped chocolate in a double boiler over barely simmering water. • Spoon the chocolate into a small freezer bag and cut off a tiny corner. • Drizzle over the cookies.

Makes 56 cookies · Prep: 40 min. + 60 min. to chill · Cooking: 8–10 min. per batch · Level: 1 · Keeps: 5 days

walnut icebox cookies

- 2 cups all-purpose flour
- 1 teaspoon ground cinnamon
- ¹/₄ teaspoon baking soda
- ¹/₈ teaspoon salt
- ¹/₂ cup lightly crushed walnuts
- 1 cup (2 sticks) butter, softened
- ¹/₂ cup firmly packed dark brown sugar
- ¹/₂ cup granulated sugar
- 1 large egg

Sift the flour, cinnamon, baking soda, and salt into a large bowl. Stir in the walnuts. • Beat the butter and brown and granulated sugars in a large bowl with an electric mixer at high speed until creamy. • Add the egg, beating until just blended. • Mix in the dry ingredients to form a smooth dough. • Form the dough into logs 2 inches in diameter, wrap in plastic wrap, and refrigerate for at least 30 minutes. • Preheat the oven to 350°F. • Set out two cookie sheets. • Discard the plastic wrap. • Slice the dough ¹/₄ inch thick and place 1 inch apart on the cookie sheets. • Bake for 12–15 minutes, or until lightly browned, rotating the sheets halfway through the baking to ensure even browning. • Transfer to racks to cool.

Makes 30 cookies · Prep: 20 min. + 12 hr. to chill · Cooking: 12–15 min. · Level: 1 · Keeps: 5 days

Marmalade–hazelnut swirls

Sunflower seed surprises

sunflower seed surprises

- 2/3   cup all-purpose flour
- 1/2   teaspoon baking powder
- 1/4   teaspoon ground cinnamon
- 1/8   teaspoon salt
- 1/4   cup (1/2 stick) butter, softened
- 1/4   cup firmly packed light brown sugar
- 1   large egg
- 1/2   cup finely chopped raisins
- 1/4   cup finely chopped dried apricots
- 1/2   cup finely chopped almonds
- 1/4   cup finely chopped sunflower seeds

Peach glaze
- 1/2   cup peach preserves
- 2   tablespoons butter

Sift the flour, baking powder, cinnamon, and salt into a medium bowl. • Beat the butter and brown sugar in a large bowl with an electric mixer at high speed until creamy. • Add the egg, beating until just blended. • Mix in the raisins, apricots, almonds, and sunflower seeds. • Mix in the dry ingredients to form a soft dough. • Form the dough into a 14-inch log, wrap in plastic wrap, and refrigerate for at least 30 minutes. • Preheat the oven to 350°F. • Line two cookie sheets with parchment paper. • Slice the dough 1/2 inch thick and place 1 inch apart on the prepared cookie sheets. • Bake for 10–15 minutes, or until just golden, rotating the sheets halfway through for even baking. • Transfer to racks and let cool completely. • <u>Peach glaze</u>: Heat the preserves and butter in a small saucepan over low heat and simmer for 2 minutes. • Drizzle the glaze over the cookies.

Makes 28 cookies · Prep: 40 min. + 30 min. to chill
Cooking: 10–15 min. · Level: 2 · Keeps: 5 days

lemon–fig cookies

- 2 1/3   cups all-purpose flour
- 1/8   teaspoon salt
- 1   cup (2 sticks) butter, softened
- 1/3   cup confectioners' sugar
- 1/2   cup finely chopped dried figs
- 1   tablespoon finely grated lemon zest

Sift the flour and salt into a large bowl. • Beat the butter and confectioners' sugar in a large bowl with an electric mixer at medium speed until creamy. • Stir in the figs and lemon zest. • Mix in the dry ingredients to form a stiff dough. • Divide the dough in half. Form into two 6-inch logs, wrap in plastic wrap, and refrigerate for at least 30 minutes. • Preheat the oven to 350°F. • Butter three cookie sheets. • Slice the dough 1/4 inch thick and place 1 inch apart on the prepared cookie sheets. • Bake, one sheet at a time, for 10–12 minutes, or until pale gold. • Transfer to racks to cool.

Makes 48 cookies · Prep: 40 min. + 30 min. to chill · Cooking: 10–12 min. per batch · Level: 1 · Keeps: 7 days

fruits of the fall cookies

- 2 1/2   cups all-purpose flour
- 1/2   teaspoon baking soda
- 1/2   teaspoon ground cinnamon
- 1/2   teaspoon ground nutmeg
- 1/4   teaspoon ground cloves
- 1/8   teaspoon salt
- 3/4   cup (1 1/2 sticks) butter, softened
- 1   cup granulated sugar
- 1   large egg
- 1/2   cup finely chopped walnuts
- 1/2   cup Applesauce, store-bought or homemade (see page 340)

Sift the flour, baking soda, cinnamon, nutmeg, cloves, and salt into a medium bowl. • Beat the butter and sugar in a large bowl with an electric mixer at high speed until creamy. • Add the egg, beating until just blended. • Mix in the dry ingredients, walnuts, and applesauce to form a stiff dough. • Form the dough into a 10-inch log, wrap in plastic wrap, and refrigerate for at least 30 minutes. • Preheat the oven to 375°F. • Butter three cookie sheets. • Slice the dough 1/4 inch thick and place 1 inch apart on the prepared cookie sheets. • Bake, one sheet at a time, for 8–10 minutes, or until lightly browned. • Cool on the sheets until the cookies firm slightly. • Transfer to racks to finish cooling.

Makes 40 cookies · Prep: 40 min. + 30 min. to chill · Cooking: 8–10 min. per batch · Level: 1 · Keeps: 10 days

coconut-macadamia cookies

- 1   cup all-purpose flour
- 1/2   teaspoon baking soda
- 1/8   teaspoon salt
- 3/4   cup (1 1/2 sticks) butter, softened
- 2/3   cup granulated sugar
- 1/4   teaspoon vanilla extract
- 1   cup old-fashioned rolled oats
- 1   cup coarsely chopped macadamia nuts
- 1/2   cup shredded coconut

Sift the flour, baking soda, and salt into a medium bowl. • Beat the butter and sugar in a large bowl with an electric mixer at high speed until creamy. • Add the vanilla. • Mix in the dry ingredients, oats, macadamia nuts, and coconut. • Divide the dough in half. Form into two 4-inch logs, wrap in plastic wrap, and refrigerate for at least 30 minutes. Preheat the oven to 325°F. • Butter three cookie sheets. • Slice the dough 1/4 inch thick and place 1 inch apart on the prepared cookie sheets. • Bake, one sheet at a time, for 12–15 minutes, or until golden brown. • Cool on the sheets until the cookies firm slightly. • Transfer to racks to cool.

Makes 32 cookies · Prep: 40 min. + 30 min. to chill · Cooking: 12–15 min. per batch · Level: 1 · Keeps: 7 days

rum spice cookies

- 3   cups all-purpose flour
- 1/2   teaspoon baking soda
- 1/2   teaspoon baking powder
- 1/2   teaspoon salt
- 1   cup butter, softened
- 1   cup granulated sugar
- 2   large eggs
- 1   teaspoon rum extract
- 1/2   teaspoon almond extract
- 1/8   teaspoon freshly grated nutmeg

Sift the flour, baking soda, baking powder, nutmeg, and salt into a large bowl. • Use a pastry blender to cut in the butter until the mixture resembles coarse crumbs. • Stir in the sugar. • Add the eggs and rum and almond extracts to form a stiff dough. • Divide the dough in half. Form into two 6-inch logs, wrap in plastic wrap, and refrigerate for at least 30 minutes. • Preheat the oven to 350°F. • Butter three cookie sheets. • Slice the dough $1/4$ inch thick and place 1 inch apart on the prepared cookie sheets. • Bake for 12–15 minutes, or until lightly golden. • Cool on the sheets until the cookies firm slightly. Transfer to racks to cool completely.

Makes 48 cookies · Prep: 40 min. + 30 min. to chill · Cooking: 12–15 min. per batch · Level: 2 · Keeps: 10 days

date and corn flake cookies

1 cup all-purpose flour
$1/2$ teaspoon baking soda
$1/2$ teaspoon salt
$1/2$ cup vegetable shortening
$1/2$ cup firmly packed light brown sugar
$1/2$ cup granulated sugar
2 large eggs
1 cup old-fashioned rolled oats
$1/2$ cup corn flakes
$1/2$ cup finely chopped dates
$1/2$ cup semisweet chocolate chips

Sift the flour, baking soda, and salt into a large bowl. • Beat the shortening and brown and granulated sugars in a large bowl with an electric mixer at high speed until creamy. • Add the eggs, beating until just blended. • Mix in the dry ingredients, oats, corn flakes, dates, and chocolate chips to form a stiff dough. • Divide the dough in half. Form into two 8-inch logs, wrap in plastic wrap, and refrigerate for at least 30 minutes. • Preheat the oven to 375°F. • Butter two cookie sheets. • Slice the dough $1/4$ inch thick and place 2 inches apart on the prepared cookie sheets. • Bake for 10–12 minutes, or until lightly golden. • Cool on the sheets until the cookies firm slightly. • Transfer to racks to cool completely.

Makes 64 cookies · Prep: 45 min. + 30 min. to chill Cooking: 10–12 min. · Level: 2 · Keeps: 12 days

pecan-edged cookies

3 cups all-purpose flour
$1/8$ teaspoon salt
2 cups (4 sticks) butter, softened
1 cup confectioners' sugar
1 teaspoon vanilla extract
$1/2$ cup finely chopped pecans

Sift the flour and salt into a medium bowl. • Beat the butter, confectioners' sugar, and

vanilla in a large bowl with an electric mixer at high speed until creamy. • Mix in the dry ingredients. • Form the dough into two 10-inch logs and roll in the pecans until well coated. Wrap in plastic wrap and refrigerate for at least 30 minutes. • Preheat the oven to 350°F. • Set out four cookie sheets. • Slice the dough $1/4$ inch thick and place 1 inch apart on the cookie sheets. • Bake, one sheet at a time, for 7–9 minutes, or until lightly golden. • Transfer to racks to cool.

Makes 80 cookies · Prep: 40 min. + 30 min. to chill · Cooking: 7–9 min. per batch · Level: 1 · Keeps: 7 days

neapolitan cookies

$11/3$ cups all-purpose flour
1 teaspoon baking powder
$1/8$ teaspoon salt
$1/2$ cup (1 stick) butter, softened
$1/2$ cup granulated sugar
1 teaspoon vanilla extract
1 large egg yolk, lightly beaten
1 oz semisweet chocolate, coarsely chopped
$1/2$ teaspoon almond extract
2 drops red food coloring
$2/3$ cup coarsely chopped walnuts

Line an $81/2$ x $41/2$-inch loaf pan with waxed paper. • Sift the flour, baking powder, and salt into a medium bowl. • Beat the butter and sugar in a large bowl with an electric mixer at high speed until creamy. • Add the vanilla and egg yolk, beating until just blended. • Mix in the dry ingredients. • Divide the cookie dough into three small bowls. • Melt the chocolate in a double boiler over barely simmering water. • Add the almond extract to one bowl, the red food coloring and melted chocolate to the second bowl, and the walnuts to the third bowl, mixing each until well blended. • Spread the almond mixture in the prepared pan, followed by the walnut mixture. Finish with the chocolate mixture. • Cover with waxed paper and refrigerate for at least 4 hours, or until firm. • Preheat the oven to 350°F. • Butter four cookie sheets. • Turn the dough out of the pan and peel off the paper. • Slice the dough in half lengthwise, then cut into $1/4$-inch thick slices. • Place the cookies 1 inch apart on the prepared cookie sheets. • Bake, one sheet at a time, for 10–12 minutes, or until lightly browned. • Cool on the sheets until the cookies firm slightly. • Transfer to racks to finish cooling.

Makes 68 cookies · Prep: 40 min. + 4 hr. to chill · Cooking: 10–12 min. per batch · Level: 2 · Keeps: 5 days

coconut–cherry icebox cookies

$21/2$ cups all-purpose flour
$1/8$ teaspoon salt
1 cup (2 sticks) butter, softened
1 cup granulated sugar
1 tablespoon milk
1 teaspoon vanilla extract
1 cup finely chopped red and green candied cherries
$1/2$ cup finely chopped walnuts
1 cup shredded coconut

Sift the flour and salt into a large bowl. • Beat the butter and sugar in a large bowl with an electric mixer at high speed until creamy. • Add the milk and vanilla. • Mix in the dry ingredients, cherries, and pecans to form a stiff dough. • Form the dough into two 7-inch logs. Roll in the coconut until well coated. Wrap in plastic wrap and refrigerate for at least 30 minutes. • Preheat the oven to 375°F. • Set out three cookie sheets. • Slice the dough $1/4$ inch thick and place 1 inch apart on the cookie sheets. • Bake, one sheet at a time, for 12–15 minutes, or until lightly golden. • Transfer to racks to cool.

Makes 56 cookies · Prep: 35 min. + 30 min. to chill Cooking: 12–15 min. per batch · Level: 2 · Keeps: 12 days

Neapolitan cookies

shortbread
cookies

Of Scottish origin, shortbread was originally only eaten during the Christmas season. Nowadays it is enjoyed throughout the year. Traditionally made with one part sugar to two parts butter and three parts flour, its heavenly melt-in-the-mouth texture can be assured by using the highest quality butter. For a crispier textured cookie, substitute semolina or rice flour for the all-purpose flour. On special occasions, top your shortbread with melted chocolate or bake them in a variety of the rustic wooden molds available in specialty baking stores.

above: Jam-topped piped shortbread (page 192).

right: Clockwise from top left: Shortbread thumbprints, Ginger shortbread fingers, Caramel shortbread squares, and Pistachio shortbread (pages 192, 184, 185, and 188).

scottish shortbread

Shortbread dates from the 12th century and is regarded as a specialty of Scotland. Instructions for these simple cookies were included in a recipe book printed in 1594, and there have been many variations ever since. The only common ingredient is the use of shortening—butter or lard—to make the dough soft and crumbly. Shortbread with the traditional Scottish thistle pattern is made with special wooden shortbread molds that are pressed into the dough before baking.

2¹/₃ cups all-purpose flour
¹/₂   cup rice flour
¹/₂   cup cornstarch
¹/₈   teaspoon salt
1¹/₂ cups (3 sticks) butter, softened
¹/₃   cup superfine sugar
¹/₂   cup confectioners' sugar

Sift the flour, rice flour, cornstarch, and salt into a large bowl. • Beat the butter, superfine sugar, and confectioners' sugar in a large bowl with an electric mixer at high speed until creamy. • With mixer at low speed, gradually beat in the dry ingredients to form a smooth dough. • Form the dough into an 8-inch log about 2 inches in diameter. Wrap in plastic wrap and refrigerate for 30 minutes. • Line a cookie sheet with parchment paper. • Use a sharp knife to cut the dough into ²/₃-inch rounds. • Place the rounds on a lightly floured surface. • Lightly oil a shortbread mold and dust with flour. • Firmly press the mold onto the cookies. • Place the cookies on the prepared cookie sheet, spacing 2 inches apart. • Refrigerate for 20 minutes.

hazelnut shortbread rounds

Sandwich these cookies together with whipped cream and fresh raspberries for a spectacular—and delicious—presentation.

¹/₂   cup raw sugar (Demerara or Barbados)
1²/₃ cups finely ground hazelnuts
1¹/₂ cups all-purpose flour
¹/₈   teaspoon salt
²/₃   cup butter, cut up
1   large egg yolk, lightly beaten

Process the raw sugar, hazelnuts, flour, and salt in a food processor until well blended. • Add the butter and process briefly until the mixture resembles fine crumbs. • Add the egg and process briefly to mix. • Gather the dough together and press into a disk. Wrap in plastic wrap and refrigerate for 30 minutes. • Preheat the oven to 350°F. • Line two cookie sheets with parchment paper. • Roll out the dough on a lightly floured surface to a thickness of ¹/₈ inch. • Use a 2¹/₂-inch cookie cutter to cut out the cookies. Gather the dough scraps, re-roll, and continue cutting out cookies until all the dough is used. • Use a spatula to transfer the cookies to the prepared cookie sheets, spacing them 1 inch apart. • Bake for 12–15 minutes, or until lightly browned, rotating the sheets halfway through for even baking. • Cool on the sheets until the cookies firm slightly. • Transfer to racks to cool.

Makes 32–36 cookies · Prep: 40 min. + 30 min. to chill · Cooking: 12–15 min. · Level: 1 · Keeps: 7 days

peanut shortbread

Shortbread base
2¹/₃ cups all-purpose flour
¹/₈   teaspoon salt
1   cup (2 sticks) butter, softened
¹/₂   cup granulated sugar
Peanut topping
¹/₃   cup butter, softened
¹/₃   cup granulated sugar
1   cup finely ground peanuts
¹/₂   cup all-purpose flour
3   tablespoons coarsely chopped peanuts

Preheat the oven to 350°F. • Line a 9-inch round cake pan with parchment paper. • Shortbread base: Sift the flour and salt into a medium bowl. • Beat the butter and sugar in a large bowl with an electric mixer at high speed until creamy. • Mix in the dry ingredients. • Firmly press the dough into the prepared pan to form a smooth, even layer, pressing back the edges to make them thick. • Peanut topping: With mixer at high speed, beat the butter and sugar in a medium bowl until creamy. • Mix in the ground peanuts and flour. • Spread the topping over the shortbread base and sprinkle with the chopped peanuts. • Press the peanuts in slightly with a knife and score the round into 16 wedges. • Bake for 25–30 minutes, or until pale gold. • Cool completely before cutting along the scored lines.

Makes 16 cookies · Prep: 30 min. · Cooking: 25–30 min. · Level: 1 · Keeps: 7–10 days

ginger shortbread fingers

1   cup (2 sticks) butter, softened
¹/₂   cup superfine sugar
1   tablespoon Vanilla Sugar (see page 341)
2¹/₃ cups all-purpose flour
2   teaspoons ground ginger or 1-inch piece fresh ginger, peeled and finely grated
Ginger frosting
1¹/₃ cups confectioners' sugar
1   teaspoon ground ginger
2   tablespoons cold water, or more if needed

Preheat the oven to 300°F. • Butter an 11 x 7-inch baking pan. • Beat the butter, superfine sugar, and vanilla sugar in a large bowl with an electric mixer at high speed until creamy. • If you are using fresh ginger, add it to the butter mixture. • Sift the flour and ground ginger, if using, into a medium bowl. • Mix the dry ingredients into the butter mixture to form a smooth dough. • Turn the dough out onto a lightly floured surface and knead lightly until smooth. • Press the dough into the prepared pan and prick all over with a fork. • Bake for 45–50 minutes, or until lightly browned. • Cool the shortbread completely in the pan. • Ginger frosting: Sift the confectioners' sugar and ginger into a small bowl. Add enough water to make a spreadable paste. • Spread the frosting over the shortbread. • Let stand for 30 minutes until the frosting has set. • Use a sharp knife to cut the shortbread into fingers.

Makes 20 cookies · Prep: 35 min. + 30 min. to set Cooking: 45–50 min. · Level: 2 · Keeps: 10 days

ginger-frosted spiced shortbread

2   cups all-purpose flour
2   teaspoons baking powder
2   teaspoons ground ginger
¹/₈   teaspoon salt
1   cup (2 sticks) butter, softened
1   cup granulated sugar
Ginger frosting
¹/₂   cup (1 stick) butter, cut up
1   cup confectioners' sugar
1¹/₂ teaspoons ground ginger
1¹/₂ tablespoons light corn syrup

Preheat the oven to 375°F. • Butter a 10¹/₂ x 15¹/₂-inch jelly-roll pan. • Sift the flour, baking

• Preheat the oven to 325°F. • Bake for 20–25 minutes, or until the cookies are firm to the touch and lightly browned. • Cool on the cookie sheet for 15 minutes. • Transfer to racks to cool.

Makes 16 cookies · Prep: 40 min. + 50 min. to chill Cooking: 20–25 min. · Level: 2 · Keeps: 12 days

powder, ginger, and salt into a medium bowl. Beat the butter and sugar in a large bowl with an electric mixer at high speed until creamy. • Mix in the dry ingredients. • Spoon the mixture evenly into the prepared pan, pressing down lightly. • Bake for 30–35 minutes, or until golden brown. • Cool completely in the pan on a rack. • Ginger frosting: Melt the butter with the confectioners' sugar, ginger, and corn syrup in a small saucepan over low heat, stirring constantly. • Remove from the heat and stir until smooth. • Pour the frosting evenly over the shortbread and let stand for 15 minutes. • Use a sharp knife to cut into 30 bars.

Makes 30 bars · Prep: 20 min. · Cooking: 30–35 min. · Level: 1 · Keeps: 2 days in the refrigerator

ginger–brandy shortbread cookies

2 1/2 cups all-purpose flour
1/2 teaspoon baking powder
1/8 teaspoon salt
1 cup (2 sticks) butter, softened
2/3 cup + 2 tablespoons granulated sugar
2 large egg yolks
1 tablespoon light corn syrup
1 tablespoon brandy
1/2 cup finely chopped crystallized ginger

Preheat the oven to 325°F. • Butter an 11 x 7-inch baking pan. • Sift the flour, baking powder, and salt into a medium bowl. • Beat the butter and 2/3 cup sugar in a large bowl with an electric mixer at high speed until creamy. • Add the egg yolks, beating until just blended. • Beat in the corn syrup and brandy. • Mix in the dry ingredients to form a stiff dough. • Divide the dough in half. Firmly press one half into the

prepared pan to form a smooth, even layer. Sprinkle with the ginger. • Roll out the remaining dough on a lightly floured surface into an 11 x 7-inch rectangle. Place the dough on top of the ginger. • Sprinkle with the remaining 2 tablespoons sugar. • Bake for 35–40 minutes, or until pale gold. • Cool completely before cutting into bars.

Makes 22–33 bars · Prep: 30 min. · Cooking: 35–40 min. · Level: 1 · Keeps: 10 days

caramel shortbread squares

1 1/4 cups halved macadamia nuts or halved hazelnuts
Shortbread
1 1/2 cups all-purpose flour
1/8 teaspoon salt
1/3 cup firmly packed light brown sugar
3/4 cup (1 1/2 sticks) butter, softened
Caramel
1/2 cup (1 stick) butter, cut up
1/2 cup firmly packed light brown sugar
1 1/2 tablespoons all-purpose flour
1 tablespoon heavy cream
7 oz bittersweet chocolate, finely chopped
3/4 cup shredded coconut, to sprinkle

Preheat the oven to 325°F. • Butter a 9-inch baking pan and line with parchment paper. • Sprinkle the nuts onto a large baking sheet. Toast for 7 minutes, or until lightly golden. • Remove from the oven and set aside. • Shortbread: Sift the flour and salt into a large bowl. Stir in the sugar. • Use a pastry blender to cut in the butter until the mixture resembles fine crumbs. • Turn out onto a lightly floured surface and knead to form a smooth dough. • Press the mixture into the prepared pan. • Bake for 10–15 minutes, or until lightly browned. • Cool the shortbread in the pan while you prepare the Caramel: Melt the butter with the brown sugar, flour, and cream in a small saucepan over low heat. Bring to a boil, stirring constantly. • Remove from the heat and set aside. • Sprinkle the chocolate and coconut over the shortbread base. Top with the toasted nuts. • Pour the caramel over. • Return to the oven and bake for 15–20 minutes, or until the caramel is golden brown and bubbling. • Cool the shortbread completely in the pan. • Use a sharp knife to cut into squares.

Makes 16 squares · Prep: 40 min. · Cooking: 25–35 min. · Level: 2 · Keeps: 5 days in the refrigerator

chocolate-cinnamon shortbread

1/2 cup all-purpose flour
1/2 cup cornstarch
2 tablespoons unsweetened cocoa powder
1/4 teaspoon ground cinnamon
1/8 teaspoon salt
1/2 cup (1 stick) butter, softened
1/4 cup confectioners' sugar

Preheat the oven to 325°F. • Butter two cookie sheets. • Sift the flour, cornstarch, cocoa, cinnamon, and salt into a medium bowl. • Beat the butter and confectioners' sugar in a large bowl with an electric mixer at high speed until creamy. • With mixer at low speed, gradually add the dry ingredients. • Knead the mixture briefly on a lightly floured surface. • Form into an 11 x 1 1/2-inch log and slice 1/2 inch thick. • Use a spatula to transfer the cookies to the prepared cookie sheets, placing them 1 inch apart. • Bake for 15–20 minutes, or until firm, rotating the sheets halfway through for even baking. • Transfer to racks to cool.

Makes 22 cookies · Prep: 20 min. · Cooking: 15–20 min. · Level: 1 · Keeps: 2 weeks

Chocolate–cinnamon shortbread

white chocolate–passionfruit shortbread

Elegant and sumptuous—a perfect finish to a dinner party.

Shortbread
2¼ cups all-purpose flour
¼ cup rice flour
⅛ teaspoon salt
1 cup (2 sticks) butter, softened
⅓ cup granulated sugar

Passionfruit and white chocolate drizzle
1 cup confectioners' sugar
2 tablespoons passionfruit pulp
1 tablespoon butter, softened
1 tablespoon cold water
2 oz white chocolate, coarsely chopped

Shortbread: Sift the all-purpose and rice flours and salt into a medium bowl. • Beat the butter and sugar in a large bowl with an electric mixer at high speed until creamy. • Mix in the dry ingredients to form a soft dough. • Turn the dough out onto a lightly floured surface and knead until smooth. • Press the dough into a disk, wrap in plastic wrap, and refrigerate for 30 minutes. • Preheat the oven to 300°F. • Line four cookie sheets with parchment paper. • Roll out the dough on a lightly floured surface to a thickness of ¼ inch. • Cut into 1½-inch diamonds. • Use a spatula to transfer the cookies to the prepared cookie sheets, placing them 1 inch apart. • Bake for 12–15 minutes, or until just golden at the edges, rotating the sheets halfway through for even baking. • Transfer to racks to cool. • Passionfruit and white chocolate drizzle: Mix the confectioners' sugar, passionfruit pulp, butter, and water in a double boiler over barely simmering water until smooth. • Drizzle the tops of the cookies with the icing. • Let stand for 30 minutes until set. • Melt the white chocolate in a double boiler over barely simmering water and drizzle over the cookies. Let stand for 30 minutes.

Makes 35–40 cookies · Prep: 40 min. + 90 min. to chill and set · Cooking: 12–15 min. per batch · Level: 2 · Keeps: 2 days

passionfruit shortbread

1¼ cups all-purpose flour
⅓ cup cornstarch
⅛ teaspoon salt
¾ cup (1½ sticks) butter, softened
¼ cup granulated sugar
2 passionfruit

Sift the flour, cornstarch, and salt into a medium bowl. • Beat the butter and sugar in a large bowl with an electric mixer at high speed until creamy. • Mix in the dry ingredients. • Use a teaspoon to scoop the pulp from the passionfruit and stir into the mixture. • Press the dough into a 5-inch log, wrap in plastic wrap, and refrigerate for 30 minutes. • Preheat the oven to 350°F. • Butter two cookie sheets. • Slice the dough ¼ inch thick and place 1 inch apart on the prepared cookie sheets. • Bake for 15–20 minutes, or until pale gold, rotating the sheets halfway through for even baking. • Transfer to racks to cool.

Makes 20 cookies · Prep: 40 min. + 30 min. to chill Cooking: 15–20 min. · Level: 1 · Keeps: 10 days

chocolate–pecan shortbread

1¾ cups all-purpose flour
½ cup confectioners' sugar
¼ cup cornstarch
¼ teaspoon salt
1 cup (2 sticks) butter, cut up
1 cup semisweet chocolate chips
1 cup finely chopped pecans
2 oz semisweet chocolate, coarsely chopped

Preheat the oven to 325°F. • Butter two 9-inch springform pans. • Sift the flour, confectioners' sugar, cornstarch, and salt into a large bowl. • Use a pastry blender to cut in the butter until the mixture resembles coarse crumbs. • Stir in the chocolate chips and pecans. • Firmly press the mixture evenly into the prepared pans to form smooth, even layers. • Bake for 15–20 minutes, or until just golden, rotating the pans halfway through for even baking. • Cool for 5 minutes in the pan. • Loosen and remove the springform sides. Let cool completely. • Cut each round into sixteen wedges. • Melt the chocolate in a double boiler over barely simmering water. • Drizzle over the cookies and let stand for 30 minutes until set.

Makes 32 cookies · Prep: 20 min. + 30 min. to set · Cooking: 15–20 min. · Level: 1 · Keeps: 5 days

mincemeat-filled shortbread cookies

2 cups all-purpose flour
½ cup confectioners' sugar
⅛ teaspoon salt
¾ cup (1½ sticks) butter, cut up
2 large eggs, lightly beaten
¼ cup Mincemeat (see page 340)

Sift the flour, confectioners' sugar, and salt into a large bowl. • Use a pastry blender to cut in the butter until the mixture resembles fine crumbs. • Add half of the beaten eggs to form a stiff dough. • Turn the dough out onto a lightly floured surface and knead until smooth. • Divide the dough in half. Press the dough into disks, wrap in plastic wrap, and refrigerate for 30 minutes. • Preheat the oven to 350°F. • Line a cookie sheet with parchment paper. • Roll out half the dough on a lightly floured surface to a thickness of ¼ inch. • Use a 1½-inch cookie cutter to cut out the cookies. • Drop half-teaspoons of the mincemeat onto the centers of the cookies. Gather the dough scraps, re-roll, and continue cutting out cookies until the first half of dough is used. • Brush the edges with the remaining beaten egg. • Use a spatula to transfer the cookies to the prepared cookie sheet, placing them 1 inch apart. • Roll out the remaining dough to a thickness of ⅛ inch. • Use a 1½-inch cookie cutter to cut out the cookie tops. • Place the cookie tops over the filled bases, pinching the edges to seal. • Bake for 15–20 minutes, or until just golden. • Transfer to racks to cool.

Makes 15–18 cookies · Prep: 40 min. + 30 min. to chill · Cooking: 15–20 min. · Level: 2 · Keeps: 5 days

Mincemeat-filled shortbread cookies (left) and Chocolate–pecan shortbread (right)

pecan shortbread tails

The only nut native to North America, the pecan is a valuable species. Pecans have also been exported into Australia and South Africa. Pecan trees grow best on flood plains, requiring large amounts of water to achieve their optimum potential. Crunchy and buttery in flavor, pecans work best with a simple cookie base.

3/4 cup all-purpose flour
1/8 teaspoon salt
1/2 cup superfine sugar
2 tablespoons finely ground pecans, toasted
1/2 cup (1 stick) cold butter, cut up
1 teaspoon vanilla extract
16 pecan halves

Preheat the oven to 325°F. • Butter a cookie sheet. • Sift the flour and salt into a large bowl. • Stir in the superfine sugar and pecans. • Use a pastry blender to cut in the butter until the mixture resembles fine crumbs. • Turn out onto a lightly floured surface, add the vanilla, and knead lightly

pistachio shortbread

3/4 cup finely chopped pistachios
2 tablespoons granulated sugar
1 cup (2 sticks) butter, softened
1 1/3 cups confectioners' sugar
1 2/3 cups all-purpose flour
1/8 teaspoon salt

Preheat the oven to 350°F. • Butter and flour two cookie sheets. • Stir together the pistachios and granulated sugar in a small bowl. • Beat the butter and confectioners' sugar in a large bowl with an electric mixer at high speed until creamy. • With mixer at low speed, gradually beat in the flour and salt. • Scoop out a heaping tablespoon of dough and shape into a ball the size of a walnut. • Use your index finger to make a hollow in the center. • Fill with 1 teaspoon of the pistachio mixture. • Repeat until all the dough is used. • Place the cookies on the prepared cookie sheets, spacing them 1 inch apart. • Bake for 15–20 minutes, or until golden brown, rotating the trays halfway through for even baking. • Cool the cookies completely on the cookie sheets.

Makes 15 cookies · Prep: 15 min. · Cooking: 15–20 min. · Level: 1 · Keeps: 10 days

coconut–pecan shortbread

1/2 cup pecans
2 tablespoons granulated sugar
1 cup all-purpose flour
1/2 teaspoon baking powder
1/4 teaspoon salt
1/3 cup butter, softened
1/4 cup confectioners' sugar
1/2 cup shredded coconut

Preheat the oven to 325°F. • Set out a 9-inch springform pan. • Process the pecans

and granulated sugar in a food processor or blender until very finely ground. • Sift the flour, baking powder, and salt into a medium bowl. • Beat the butter and confectioners' sugar in a large bowl with an electric mixer at high speed until creamy. • Mix in the dry ingredients and 1/4 cup coconut to form a stiff dough. • Firmly press the dough into the pan to form a smooth, even layer. Sprinkle with the remaining 1/4 cup coconut. Use a sharp knife to score the shortbread into 16 wedges. • Bake for 25–30 minutes, or until golden brown. • Cool in the pan for 15 minutes. • Use a sharp knife to cut into wedges along the scored lines. • Loosen and remove the pan sides and let cool completely.

Makes 16 cookies · Prep: 25 min. · Cooking: 25–30 min. · Level: 1 · Keeps: 7 days

orange–lemon shortbread

1 cup all-purpose flour
1 tablespoon semolina flour
1/8 teaspoon salt
1/2 cup (1 stick) butter, softened
1/4 cup granulated sugar
1 teaspoon finely grated lemon zest
1 teaspoon finely grated orange zest
1/4 cup superfine sugar, to dust

Preheat the oven to 325°F. • Butter an 8-inch springform pan. • Sift the all-purpose and semolina flours and salt into a medium bowl. • Beat the butter and granulated sugar in a large bowl with an electric mixer at high speed until creamy. • Mix in the dry ingredients and lemon and orange zests. • Firmly press the mixture into the prepared pan, pinching the edges to make a decorative pattern. Use a sharp knife to

score the shortbread into 16 wedges. • Bake for 35–40 minutes, or until firm to the touch. • Dust with the superfine sugar. Use a sharp knife to cut into 16 wedges along the scored lines. • Loosen and remove the pan sides and bottom. Transfer to racks and let cool completely.

Makes 16 cookies · Prep: 20 min. · Cooking: 35–40 min. · Level: 1 · Keeps: 7 days

venetian fregolata

This crumbly Italian treat is eaten during the Carnival season in Venice.

2/3 cup all-purpose flour
2/3 cup finely ground yellow cornmeal
1/8 teaspoon salt
1/2 cup (1 stick) butter, cut up
1 cup finely ground almonds
1/2 cup granulated sugar
2 large egg yolks, lightly beaten
 Grated zest and juice of 1 lemon
1/2 teaspoon almond extract
1/4 cup finely chopped almonds
2 tablespoons raw sugar (Barbados or Demerara)

Preheat the oven to 350°F. • Butter a 9-inch springform pan. • Sift the flour, cornmeal, and salt into a medium bowl. • Use a pastry blender to cut in the butter until the mixture resembles coarse crumbs. • Stir in the ground almonds and granulated sugar. • Mix in the egg yolks, lemon zest and juice, and almond extract to form a stiff dough. • Firmly press the dough into the prepared pan to form a smooth, even layer. Sprinkle with the chopped almonds and raw sugar. • Use a sharp knife to score the fregolata into 16 wedges. • Bake for 20 minutes. • Reduce the oven temperature to 300°F. • Bake for 20–25 minutes more, or

until a smooth dough is formed. • Lightly grease an 8-inch springform pan with oil and dust with flour. • Bake for 25–30 minutes, or until golden brown. • Use a sharp knife to cut into 16 wedges. Press a pecan half into the center of each wedge. • Use a thin metal spatula to transfer the cookies to racks and let cool completely.

Makes 16 cookies · Prep: 20 min. · Cooking: 25–30 min. · Level: 2 · Keeps: 10 days

until pale gold and firm to the touch. • Use a sharp knife to cut into 16 wedges along the scored lines. • Loosen and remove the pan sides and bottom. Transfer to racks and let cool completely.

Makes 16 cookies · Prep: 35 min. · Cooking: 40–45 min. · Level: 1 · Keeps: 10 days

chocolate shortbread cookies

1²/₃ cups all-purpose flour
2 tablespoons unsweetened cocoa powder
1/4 teaspoon salt
1 cup (2 sticks) butter, softened
1 cup confectioners' sugar
1 teaspoon Vanilla Sugar (see page 341)
1/2 teaspoon vanilla extract
1 tablespoon confectioners' sugar, to dust

Sift the flour, cocoa, and salt into a medium bowl. • Beat the butter, confectioners' sugar, vanilla sugar, and vanilla in a large bowl with an electric mixer at high speed until creamy. • With mixer at low speed, gradually beat in the dry ingredients to form a smooth dough. • Spread out a large sheet of plastic wrap and turn the dough onto it. • Place a sheet of plastic wrap on top and roll out the dough to a thickness of about ²/₃ inch. • Refrigerate for 2 hours. • Preheat the oven to 325°F. • Butter two cookie sheets and line with parchment paper. • Remove the dough from the refrigerator and peel off the top sheet of plastic wrap. • Use a 2-inch cookie cutter to cut out cookies. • Transfer the rounds to the prepared baking sheets, spacing 1/2 inch apart. • Bake for 10–15 minutes, or until firm to the touch, rotating the sheets halfway through for even baking. • Cool the cookies on the cookie sheet for 15 minutes.

Use a thin metal spatula to transfer the cookies to racks and let cool completely. • Dust with the confectioners' sugar.

Makes 30 cookies · Prep: 40 min. + 2 hr. to chill · Cooking: 15–20 min. · Level: 2 · Keeps: 10 days

lemon shortbread fingers

1¹/₄ cups all-purpose flour
1/8 teaspoon salt
1/4 cup firmly packed light brown sugar
1/2 cup (1 stick) cold butter, cut up
2 teaspoons finely grated lemon zest
1/4 teaspoon lemon extract

Preheat the oven to 350°F. • Butter two cookie sheets. • Sift the flour and salt into a large bowl. Stir in the brown sugar. • Use a pastry blender to cut in the butter until the mixture resembles fine crumbs. • Turn out onto a lightly floured surface, add the lemon zest and extract, and knead into a smooth dough. • Roll out the dough to a 1/4-inch thick rectangle. Use a sharp knife to cut the dough into three ³/₄ x 1-inch bars. • Transfer the bars to the prepared cookie sheets, spacing them 1/2 inch apart. • Prick all over with a fork. • Bake for 15–20 minutes, or until golden, rotating the sheets halfway through for even baking. • Cool the shortbread completely on the cookie sheets.

Makes 25–30 bars · Prep: 40 min. · Cooking: 15–20 min. · Level: 1 · Keeps: 10 days

cherry–rum shortbread cookies

2¹/₂ cups all-purpose flour
1/2 teaspoon baking powder
1/8 teaspoon salt
1 cup (2 sticks) butter, softened
²/₃ + 2 tablespoons granulated sugar
2 large egg yolks
1 tablespoon light corn syrup
1 tablespoon dark rum
1/2 cup finely chopped candied cherries

Preheat the oven to 325°F. • Butter an 11 x 7-inch baking pan. • Sift the flour, baking powder, and salt into a medium bowl. • Beat the butter and ²/₃ cup sugar in a large bowl with an electric mixer at high speed until creamy. • Add the egg yolks, beating until just blended. • Beat in the corn syrup and rum. • Mix in the dry ingredients to form a stiff dough. • Divide the dough in half. Firmly press one half into the prepared pan to form a smooth, even layer. Sprinkle with the cherries. • Roll out the remaining dough on a lightly floured surface into an 11 x 7-inch rectangle. Place the dough on top of the cherries. • Sprinkle with the remaining 2 tablespoons sugar. • Bake for 35–40 minutes, or until pale gold. • Cool completely before cutting into bars.

Makes 22–33 cookies · Prep: 30 min. · Cooking: 35–40 min. · Level: 1 · Keeps: 10 days

Lemon shortbread fingers

jammy shortbread bars

- 1 cup all-purpose flour
- 1/8 teaspoon salt
- 2 tablespoons granulated sugar
- 1 tablespoon Vanilla Sugar (see page 341)
- 1 teaspoon finely grated orange zest
- 1/2 cup (1 stick) cold butter, cut up
- 1/4 cup strawberry or raspberry preserves
- 3–4 tablespoons slivered almonds or finely chopped pistachios, to decorate

Preheat the oven to 325°F. • Set out a cookie sheet. • Sift the flour and salt into a large bowl. Stir in the granulated sugar, vanilla sugar, and orange zest. • Use a pastry blender to cut in the butter until the mixture resembles fine crumbs. • Turn out onto a lightly floured surface and knead to form a smooth dough. • Divide the dough in half. • Form each half into an 8-inch log and roll into 2-inch wide strips. • Use a spatula to transfer the two strips to the cookie sheet, placing them 6 inches apart. • Use the back of a teaspoon to press a 3/4-inch wide groove down the center of each strip. • Bake for 20–25 minutes, or until golden brown. • Transfer the strips to racks. • Fill the grooves with jam. • Sprinkle with the nuts and let cool completely. • Use a sharp knife to cut the strips diagonally into 3/4-inch bars.

Makes 18 bars · Prep: 25 min. · Cooking: 20–25 min. · Level: 1 · Keeps: 5 days

spanish shortbread

All Spanish children hope to be given mantecados, *or lard cookies, on the morning of the Epiphany, January 6.*

- 3 1/3 cups all-purpose flour
- 1 teaspoon ground cinnamon
- 1/8 teaspoon salt
- 1 cup lard, softened
- 1 1/4 cups granulated sugar
- 2 large egg yolks
- Grated zest and juice of 1 lemon
- 2 1/2 cups finely ground almonds

Preheat the oven to 325°F. • Grease four cookie sheets with lard. • Sift the flour, cinnamon, and salt into a large bowl. • Beat the lard and sugar in a large bowl with an electric mixer at high speed until creamy. • Add the egg yolks, beating until just blended. • Mix in the dry ingredients and lemon zest. • Stir in the almonds and lemon juice until well blended. • Turn out onto a lightly floured surface and knead to form a smooth dough. Cover with a large piece of

parchment paper. Roll out the dough to a thickness of 1/2 inch. Remove the paper. • Use a 2 1/2-inch cookie cutter to cut out the cookies. • Use a spatula to transfer the cookies to the prepared cookie sheet, placing them 1 inch apart. • Bake, one batch at a time, for 20 minutes. • Lower the oven temperature to 300°F and bake for 5–10 minutes more, or until lightly golden. • Cool on the cookie sheets for 1 minute. Use a thin metal spatula to transfer the cookies to racks and let cool completely. • Wrap the cookies separately in colored tissue paper to serve.

Makes 40 cookies · Prep: 40 min. · Cooking: 25–30 min. · Level: 2 · Keeps: 8 days

millionaire's shortbread

Rich in flavor and high in calories—one small square is sure to satisfy.

Shortbread
- 3 cups all-purpose flour
- 1/8 teaspoon salt
- 1 cup (2 sticks) butter, softened
- 1/2 cup granulated sugar
- 2 tablespoons water, + more as needed

Topping
- 1/2 cup (1 stick) butter, cut up
- 2 tablespoons light molasses
- 2/3 cup granulated sugar
- 1 can (14 oz) sweetened condensed milk
- 7 oz semisweet chocolate, coarsely chopped

Shortbread: Preheat the oven to 350°F. • Butter a cookie sheet and dust lightly with flour. • Sift the flour and salt into a medium bowl. • Beat the butter and sugar in a large bowl with an electric mixer at high speed until creamy. • Mix in the dry ingredients and enough water to form a soft dough. Transfer to the prepared cookie sheet and use your hands to press the dough to a thickness of 1/2 inch. Prick all over with a fork. • Bake for 20–25 minutes, or until just golden. • Cool completely on the sheet. • Topping: Melt the butter with the molasses, sugar, and condensed milk in a medium saucepan over low heat. Bring the mixture to the boil, stirring constantly. Boil for 10 minutes, until it darkens and thickens. • Use a spatula to spread the topping over the shortbread. Let cool completely. • Melt the chocolate in a double boiler over barely simmering water. Spread the melted chocolate evenly over

the topping and let stand for 30 minutes, or until set. • Cut into bars.

Makes 40–45 bars · Prep: 40 min. + 60 min. to set and cool · Cooking: 20–25 min. · Level: 2 · Keeps: 5 days in the refrigerator

royal balmoral shortbread

Nine small holes were traditionally pricked into this shortbread cookie when it was served to Queen Victoria at her Highland castle of Balmoral. These delicate little cookies were originally cut out using the floured edge of a wine glass.

- 1 1/3 cups all-purpose flour
- 1/8 teaspoon salt
- 1/3 cup granulated sugar
- 1/2 cup (1 stick) butter, softened

Sift the flour and salt into a medium bowl. • Beat the butter and sugar in a large bowl until creamy. • Mix in the dry ingredients until well blended. • Press the dough into a disk, wrap in plastic wrap, and refrigerate for 30 minutes. • Preheat the oven to 350°F. • Butter a cookie sheet. • Roll out the dough on a lightly floured surface to a thickness of 1/8 inch. • Use a 2-inch cookie cutter to cut out the cookies. Gather the dough scraps, re-roll, and continue cutting out cookies until all the dough is used. • Use a skewer to prick each cookie with three rows of three dots. • Use a spatula to transfer the cookies to the prepared cookie sheets, placing them 1 inch apart. • Bake for 12–15 minutes, or until pale golden. • Transfer to racks to cool.

Makes 16–20 cookies · Prep: 40 min. + 30 min. to chill · Cooking: 12–15 min. · Level: 1 · Keeps: 2 weeks

Spanish shortbread (left)
and Jammy shortbread bars (right)

petticoat tails

Some say that these cookies got their name because they are baked in a round shape and scored into triangular sections to resemble an outspread petticoat for a hoop skirt. Others believe that the name derives from the French "*petites galettes,*" meaning little cakes. Whatever the etymology, these shortbread cookies are divinely buttery and attractive in presentation. Serve them on an old-fashioned silver platter with freshly brewed tea for resonances of Olde England.

shortbread thumbprints

3/4	cup all-purpose flour
1/4	cup cornstarch
1/4	cup unsweetened cocoa powder
1	teaspoon baking powder
1/2	teaspoon salt
1/4	cup granulated sugar
1/3	cup cold butter, cut up
1	oz lard, cut up (or substitute 2 tablespoons butter)
1/2	teaspoon vanilla extract

Cocoa frosting

3/4	cup confectioners' sugar
1	tablespoon unsweetened cocoa powder
1/4	cup (1/2 stick) butter, softened
1	tablespoon hot water, or more if needed
12	walnut halves, to decorate

Preheat the oven to 300°F. • Line a cookie sheet with parchment paper. • Sift the flour, cornstarch, cocoa, baking powder, and salt into a large bowl. Stir in the sugar. • Use a pastry blender to cut in the butter and lard until the mixture resembles fine crumbs. • Add the vanilla. • Turn out onto a lightly floured surface and knead to form a smooth dough. • Form into twelve balls the size of walnuts and place 1 1/2 inches apart on the prepared cookie sheet. • Press your thumb into each one to make a small hollow. • Bake for 15–20 minutes, or until firm to the touch. • Transfer to racks on the parchment paper and let cool completely. • Cocoa frosting: Sift the confectioners' sugar and cocoa into a medium bowl. Beat in the butter. • Add enough water to make a smooth frosting. • Spoon the frosting into a pastry bag and pipe in a decorative manner into the hollows. • Decorate with a walnut on top of each cookie.

Makes 12 cookies · Prep: 30 min. · Cooking: 15–20 min. · Level: 2 · Keeps: 3 days

jam-topped piped shortbread

1 1/4	cups all-purpose flour
1/8	teaspoon salt
3/4	cup (1 1/2 sticks) butter, softened
1/4	cup granulated sugar
1/2	teaspoon vanilla extract
2	teaspoons milk
2	tablespoons raspberry preserves
2	tablespoons confectioners' sugar, to dust

Preheat the oven to 325°F. • Set out twelve mini paper liners on a baking sheet. • Sift the flour and salt into a medium bowl. • Beat the butter, granulated sugar, and vanilla in a large bowl with an electric mixer at high speed until creamy. • Mix in the dry ingredients and milk. • Fit a pastry bag with a 1/2-inch star tip. Fill the pastry bag, twist the opening tightly closed, and squeeze rosettes into the paper liners. • Bake for 20–25 minutes, or until firm to the touch. • Transfer the cookies still in the liners to racks and let cool completely. • Dot the tops of the cookies with 1/2 teaspoon preserves and dust with the confectioners' sugar.

Makes 12 cookies · Prep: 25 min. · Cooking: 20–25 min. · Level: 1 · Keeps: 7 days

almond shortbread cookies

3/4	cup all-purpose flour
1/4	cup semolina flour
1/8	teaspoon salt
1/2	cup (1 stick) butter, softened
1/3	cup confectioners' sugar
1/2	cup finely ground almonds
1	large egg, lightly beaten
1/4	cup superfine sugar, to dust

Sift the all-purpose and semolina flours and salt into a medium bowl. • Beat the butter and confectioners' sugar in a large bowl with an electric mixer at high speed until creamy. • Mix in the dry ingredients and almonds to form a smooth dough. • Press the dough into a disk, wrap in plastic wrap, and refrigerate for 30 minutes. • Preheat the oven to 325°F. • Butter two cookie sheets. • Discard the plastic wrap. • Roll out the dough on a lightly floured surface to a thickness of 1/4 inch. • Use a 2-inch fluted cookie cutter to cut out the cookies. Gather the dough scraps, reroll, and continue cutting out cookies until all the dough is used. • Use a spatula to transfer the cookies to the prepared cookie sheets, placing them 1 inch apart. Brush the tops of the cookies with the beaten egg. • Bake for 20–25 minutes, or until just golden at the edges, rotating the sheets halfway through for even baking. • Dust with the superfine sugar and transfer to racks to cool.

Makes 18–20 cookies · Prep: 40 min. + 30 min. to chill · Cooking: 20–25 min. · Level: 1 · Keeps: 2 weeks

gold-top shortbread

You will apply an expensive finish to these rich-tasting cookies so you may wish to save them for special occasions.

2 1/4	cups all-purpose flour
1/2	cup unsweetened cocoa powder
1/4	teaspoon salt
1	cup (2 sticks) butter, softened
3/4	cup confectioners' sugar
1/2	teaspoon vanilla extract
2	tablespoons 24-carat gold dust or metallic luster dust (optional)

Sift the flour, cocoa, and salt into a medium bowl. • Beat the butter, confectioners' sugar, and vanilla in a large bowl with an electric mixer at high speed until creamy. • Mix in the

1¼ cups all-purpose flour
¼ cup superfine sugar
½ cup (1 stick) cold butter, cut up

Preheat the oven to 300°F. • Line a cookie sheet with parchment paper. • Sift the flour into a large bowl. Stir in the superfine sugar. • Use a pastry blender to cut in the butter until the mixture resembles fine crumbs. • Turn the dough out onto a lightly floured surface. Shape into a ball and knead until smooth. Roll out to a 7-inch circle, $^2/_3$ inch thick. • Place the dough on the prepared cookie sheet, fluting the edges and scoring into eight triangular sections. • Prick all over with a fork. • Bake for 40–50 minutes, or until lightly golden. • While the wedges are still warm, cut along the scored lines. • Use a thin metal spatula to transfer the cookies to racks and let cool completely.

Makes 8 cookies · Prep: 40 min. · Cooking: 40–50 min. · Level: 1 · Keeps: 10 days

dry ingredients to form a smooth dough. • Press the dough into a disk, wrap in plastic wrap, and refrigerate for 30 minutes. • Preheat the oven to 300°F. • Set out a cookie sheet. • Lightly dust a work surface with confectioners' sugar and roll out the dough to a thickness of $^1/_4$ inch. • Use a 3-inch cookie cutter to cut out the cookies. Gather the dough scraps, re-roll, and continue cutting out cookies until all the dough is used. • Use a spatula to transfer the cookies to the cookie sheet. • Lightly brush the tops with the gold dust. • Bake for 12–15 minutes, or until firm to the touch. • Transfer to racks to cool.

Makes 12–15 cookies · Prep: 40 min. + 30 min to chill · Cooking: 12–15 min. · Level: 1 · Keeps: 7 days

crunchy brown sugar shortbread

2½ cups all-purpose flour
¼ teaspoon salt
1 cup (2 sticks) butter, softened
1¼ cups firmly packed light brown sugar
½ teaspoon vanilla extract

Sift the flour and salt into a medium bowl. • Beat the butter, brown sugar, and vanilla in a large bowl with an electric mixer at high speed until creamy. • Mix in the dry ingredients to form a smooth dough. • Press the dough into a disk, wrap in plastic wrap, and refrigerate for 30 minutes. • Preheat the oven to 300°F. • Butter two cookie sheets. • Roll out the dough on a lightly floured surface to a thickness of $^1/_4$ inch. • Use a 2-inch cookie cutter to cut out the cookies. Gather the dough scraps, re-roll, and continue cutting out cookies until all the dough is used. • Use a spatula to transfer the cookies to the prepared cookie sheets, placing them 1 inch apart. • Bake for 35–40 minutes, or until just golden at the edges, rotating the sheets halfway through for even baking. • Transfer to racks to cool.

Makes 18–20 cookies · Prep: 40 min. + 30 min to chill · Cooking: 35–40 min. · Level: 1 · Keeps: 7 days

semolina shortbread

Pale yellow semolina flour is coarsely ground from hard wheats, such as durum. It can be found in most supermarkets and health-food stores.

1 cup all-purpose flour
$^1/_3$ cup semolina flour
$^1/_8$ teaspoon salt
$^1/_2$ cup (1 stick) butter, softened
$^1/_4$ cup + 2 tablespoons granulated sugar

Preheat the oven to 375°F. • Butter two cookie sheets. • Sift the all-purpose and semolina flours and salt into a medium bowl. • Beat the butter and $^1/_4$ cup sugar in a large bowl with an electric mixer at high speed until creamy. • Mix in the dry ingredients to form a soft dough. • Turn the dough out onto a lightly floured surface and knead until smooth. • Roll out the dough to a thickness of $^1/_4$ inch. • Use a 2-inch cookie cutter to cut out the cookies. Gather the dough scraps, reroll, and continue cutting out cookies until all the dough is used. Use a spatula to transfer the cookies to the prepared cookie sheets, placing them 1 inch apart. • Bake for 15–20 minutes, or until just golden, rotating the sheets halfway through for even baking. • Sprinkle with the remaining 2 tablespoons sugar. • Cool the cookies completely on the sheets.

Makes 24 cookies · Prep: 40 min. · Cooking: 12–15 min. · Level 1 · Keeps: 3–4 days

piped cherry-topped shortbread

1¼ cups all-purpose flour
$^1/_8$ teaspoon salt
$^3/_4$ cup (1½ sticks) butter, softened
$^1/_4$ cup granulated sugar
$^1/_2$ teaspoon vanilla extract
2 teaspoons milk
2 tablespoons finely chopped candied cherries

Preheat the oven to 325°F. • Set out twelve mini paper liners on a baking sheet. • Sift the flour and salt into a medium bowl. • Beat the butter, granulated sugar, and vanilla in a large bowl with an electric mixer at high speed until creamy. • Mix in the dry ingredients and milk. • Fit a pastry bag with a $^1/_2$-inch star tip. Fill the pastry bag, twist the opening tightly closed, and squeeze rosettes into the paper liners. Press a piece of cherry into the top of each cookie. • Bake for 20–25 minutes, or until firm to the touch. • Transfer the cookies still in the liners to racks to cool. •

Makes 12 cookies · Prep: 25 min. · Cooking: 20–25 min. · Level: 1 · Keeps: 7 days

Semolina shortbread

zesty almond shortbread

- 1 1/2 cups all-purpose flour
- 1/4 cup rice flour
- 1/8 teaspoon salt
- 3/4 cup (1 1/2 sticks) butter, cut up
- 1/3 cup granulated sugar
- 2 tablespoons finely chopped mixed candied peel
- 1 tablespoon coarsely chopped almonds
- 1 tablespoon superfine sugar, to dust

Preheat the oven to 325°F. • Butter a 9-inch round cake pan. • Sift the all-purpose and rice flours and salt into a medium bowl. Use a pastry blender to cut in the butter until the mixture resembles coarse crumbs. • Stir in the granulated sugar. • Mix in the candied peel and almonds. • Firmly press the dough into the prepared pan to form a smooth, even layer, using your thumb to press the dough into a raised, decorative edge. • Prick all over with a fork and sprinkle with superfine sugar. Use a sharp knife to score the shortbread into 16 wedges. • Bake for 35–40 minutes, or until pale gold. • Cool completely before cutting along the scored lines.

Makes 16 cookies · Prep: 30 min. · Cooking: 35–40 min. · Level: 1 · Keeps: 7–10 days

peach-filled shortbread

- 2 2/3 cups all-purpose flour
- 1/3 cup cornstarch
- 2 teaspoons baking powder
- 1/8 teaspoon salt
- 1 cup (2 sticks) butter, softened
- 1/2 cup firmly packed light brown sugar
- 1 large egg, lightly beaten
- 1/2 teaspoon almond extract

Peach filling
- 1/2 cup finely chopped dried peaches
- 1/4 cup fresh orange juice
- 1/3 cup peach preserves

Sift the flour, cornstarch, baking powder, and salt into a medium bowl. • Beat the butter and brown sugar in a large bowl with an electric mixer at high speed until creamy. • Add the egg and almond extract, beating until just blended. • Mix in the dry ingredients to form a stiff dough. • Divide the dough in quarters. Press into four disks, wrap in plastic wrap, and refrigerate for 30 minutes. • Preheat the oven to 300°F. • Butter two 8-inch round cake pans. • Peach filling: Cook the peaches with the orange juice in a small saucepan over medium heat for 5 minutes, or until the liquid has been mostly absorbed. • Remove from the heat

and mix in the preserves. • Firmly press one disk of the dough into each prepared pan to form a smooth, even layer. Spoon over the filling and press the remaining dough on top. • Bake for 35–45 minutes, or until the top is lightly browned, rotating the pans halfway through for even baking. • Cool completely before cutting into wedges.

Makes 32 cookies · Prep: 30 min. + 30 min. to chill Cooking: 35–45 min. · Level: 1 · Keeps: 3 days

brandy butter shortbread

A wonderfully rich Christmas treat.

- 3/4 cup all-purpose flour
- 1/2 cup rice flour
- 1/8 teaspoon salt
- 1/2 cup (1 stick) butter, softened
- 2/3 cup + 1 tablespoon granulated sugar
- 1 tablespoon brandy

Preheat the oven to 350°F. • Set out a 9-inch springform pan. • Sift the all-purpose and rice flours and salt into a medium bowl. • Beat the butter and 2/3 cup sugar in a large bowl with an electric mixer at high speed until creamy. • Mix in the dry ingredients and brandy. • Firmly press the mixture into the pan to form a smooth, even layer. Prick all over with a fork and sprinkle with the remaining 1 tablespoon sugar. • Use a sharp knife to score the shortbread into 16 wedges. • Bake for 20–25 minutes, or until pale gold. • Use a sharp knife to cut into 16 wedges along the scored lines. • Loosen and remove the pan sides and bottom. Transfer to racks to cool.

Makes 16 cookies · Prep: 20 min. · Cooking: 20–25 min. · Level: 1 · Keeps: 7 days

almond shortbread with blackberry topping

Almond shortbread
- 2 cups all-purpose flour
- 1/4 teaspoon salt
- 3/4 cup (1 1/2 sticks) butter, cut up
- 1/2 cup finely ground almonds
- 1/2 cup granulated sugar

Blackberry topping
- 1 cup blackberries
- 3 large eggs
- 1 1/2 cups granulated sugar
- 1 tablespoon fresh lemon juice
- 1/4 cup (1/2 stick) butter, cut up
- 1/3 cup confectioners' sugar, to dust

Preheat the oven to 350°F. • Butter a 13 x 9-inch baking pan. • Almond shortbread: Sift the flour and salt into a large bowl. •

Use a pastry blender to cut in the butter until the mixture resembles fine crumbs. • Stir in the almonds and sugar. • Firmly press the mixture into the prepared pan to form a smooth, even layer. • Bake for 15–20 minutes, or until just golden. • Cool completely in the pan. • Reduce the oven temperature to 325°F. • Blackberry topping: Process the blackberries in a food processor or blender until pureed. • Strain the puree, discarding the solids. • Whisk the eggs and sugar in a saucepan until well blended. • Cook over low heat, stirring constantly with a wooden spoon, until pale and thick. • Mix in the blackberry puree, lemon juice, and butter. • Immediately plunge the pan into a bowl of ice water and stir until the egg mixture has cooled. • Use a thin metal spatula to spread the topping evenly over the shortbread. • Bake for 25–30 minutes, or until the topping has set. • Cool completely in the pan. • Dust with the confectioners' sugar and cut into bars.

Makes 36–45 bars · Prep: 30 min. · Cooking: 40–50 min. · Level: 2 · Keeps: 3 days

chocolate chip shortbread

- 1 3/4 cups all-purpose flour
- 1/2 cup confectioners' sugar
- 1/4 cup cornstarch
- 1/4 teaspoon salt
- 1 cup (2 sticks) butter, cut up
- 2 cups semisweet chocolate chips

Preheat the oven to 325°F. • Butter two 9-inch springform pans. • Sift the flour, confectioners' sugar, cornstarch, and salt into a large bowl. • Use a pastry blender to cut in the butter until the mixture resembles coarse crumbs. • Stir in the chocolate chips. • Firmly press the mixture evenly into the prepared pans to form smooth, even layers. • Bake for 15–20 minutes, or until just golden, rotating the pans halfway through for even baking. • Cool for 5 minutes in the pan. • Loosen and remove the springform sides. Let cool completely. • Cut each round into sixteen wedges.

Makes 32 cookies · Prep: 20 min. + 30 min. to set · Cooking: 15–20 min. · Level: 1 · Keeps: 5 days

Almond shortbread with blackberry topping

yetholm bannock

In the wild, beautiful moors on the border between Scotland and England, sweet cookie bannocks have been enjoyed as a luxurious shortbread for centuries. Served at weddings and christenings, the yetholm bannock is eaten by people on the Scottish side of the border, near the town of Kelso.

honey–hazelnut shortbread

- 1¹/₂ cups all-purpose flour
- ¹/₈ teaspoon salt
- 1 cup (2 sticks) butter, cut up
- 1 cup finely ground hazelnuts
- ¹/₃ cup granulated sugar
- 2 large egg yolks, lightly beaten
- ³/₄ cup honey
- 2¹/₄ cups finely chopped hazelnuts

Preheat the oven to 325°F. • Butter a 9-inch springform pan. • Sift the flour and salt into a large bowl. • Use a pastry blender to cut in ³/₄ cup butter until the mixture resembles fine crumbs. • Mix in the ground hazelnuts, sugar, and egg yolks to form a stiff dough. • Firmly press the mixture into the prepared pan to form a smooth, even layer. • Melt the remaining ¹/₄ cup butter with the honey in a small saucepan over low heat. • Stir in the chopped hazelnuts and cook for 5 minutes, or until the hazelnuts are well coated. • Remove from the heat and spread evenly over the shortbread base. • Use a sharp knife to score the shortbread into 16 wedges. • Bake for 40–45 minutes, or until the topping is golden brown. • Use a sharp knife to cut into 16 wedges along the scored lines. • Loosen and remove the pan sides and bottom. Transfer to racks to cool.

Makes 16 cookies · Prep: 30 min. · Cooking: 40–45 min. · Level: 1 · Keeps: 7 days

coconut shortbread thins

- ²/₃ cup all-purpose flour
- ¹/₈ teaspoon salt
- ¹/₂ cup butter, softened
- ¹/₄ cup granulated sugar
- ¹/₂ teaspoon vanilla extract
- 2 tablespoons shredded coconut
- 8 candied cherries, cut in half

Preheat the oven to 375°F. • Set out a cookie sheet. • Sift the flour and salt into a medium bowl. • Beat the butter, sugar, and vanilla in a large bowl with an electric mixer at high speed until creamy. • Mix in the dry ingredients and coconut to form a smooth dough. • Form the dough into balls the size of walnuts and place 2 inches apart on the cookie sheet. • Press a half-cherry into each cookie. • Bake for 12–15 minutes, or until just golden at the edges. • Transfer to racks to cool.

Makes 16–18 cookies · Prep: 20 min. · Cooking: 12–15 min. · Level: 1 · Keeps: 7 days

apple shortbread

- 2¹/₃ cups all-purpose flour
- ¹/₄ teaspoon salt
- 1 cup (2 sticks) butter, softened
- ¹/₂ cup granulated sugar
- 2 large tart apples, peeled, cored, and thinly sliced
- 1 tablespoon confectioners' sugar, to dust

Preheat the oven to 325°F. • Butter two 9-inch round cake pans. • Sift the flour and salt into a medium bowl. • Beat the butter and granulated sugar in a large bowl with an electric mixer at high speed until creamy. • Mix in the dry ingredients. • Divide the dough into quarters. • Firmly press one quarter of the dough into each prepared pan to form a smooth, even layer. • Arrange the apple slices on top and press the remaining two dough quarters on top. • Bake for 45–55 minutes, or until pale gold, rotating the pans halfway through for even baking. • Cool completely before cutting into wedges. Dust with the confectioners' sugar.

Makes 32 cookies · Prep: 25 min. · Cooking: 45–55 min. · Level: 1 · Keeps: 7 days

cherry–walnut shortbread

- 2 cups all-purpose flour
- ¹/₈ teaspoon salt
- 1 cup (2 sticks) butter, softened
- 1 cup firmly packed dark brown sugar
- 1 large egg yolk
- ¹/₂ cup candied cherries, cut in half
- ¹/₂ cup finely chopped walnuts

Sift the flour and salt into a medium bowl. • Beat the butter and brown sugar in a large bowl with an electric mixer at high speed until creamy. • Add the egg yolk, beating until just blended. • Mix in the dry ingredients, cherries, and walnuts to form a smooth dough. • Divide the dough in half. Form into two 4-inch logs, wrap each in plastic wrap, and refrigerate for 30 minutes. • Preheat the oven to 375°F. • Butter two cookie sheets. • Slice the dough ¹/₄ inch thick and place 1 inch apart on the prepared cookie sheets. • Bake for 10–12 minutes, or until just golden at the edges, rotating the sheets halfway through for even baking. • Transfer to racks to cool.

Makes 32 cookies · Prep: 25 min. + 30 min. to chill Cooking: 10–12 min. · Level: 1 · Keeps: 2 weeks

simple shortbread cookies

- 1¹/₄ cups all-purpose flour
- ¹/₈ teaspoon salt
- ¹/₂ cup (1 stick) butter, softened
- ¹/₄ cup granulated sugar
- ¹/₄ cup superfine sugar, to dust

Sift the flour and salt into a medium bowl. • Beat the butter and granulated sugar in a large bowl with an electric mixer at high speed until creamy. • Mix in the dry ingredients to form a smooth dough. •

1½ cups all-purpose flour
1 teaspoon ground ginger
⅛ teaspoon salt
⅔ cup butter, softened
⅓ cup granulated sugar
2 large egg yolks
⅓ cup flaked almonds
⅓ cup finely chopped candied peel
1 tablespoon finely grated lemon zest
½ teaspoon vanilla extract
½ cup finely chopped stem ginger
Glaze
1 large egg yolk lightly beaten with
   1 tablespoon milk
2 tablespoons granulated sugar
⅓ cup slivered almonds

Sift the flour, ginger, and salt into a medium bowl. • Beat the butter and sugar in a large bowl with a wooden spoon until creamy. • Add the egg yolks, beating until just blended. • Mix in the dry ingredients, almonds, candied peel, lemon zest, and vanilla to form a soft dough. • Press the dough into a disk, wrap in plastic wrap, and refrigerate for 30 minutes. • Line a cookie sheet with parchment paper. • Divide the dough in half. • Roll out half the dough on a lightly floured surface into a 6 x 8-inch rectangle. • Use a spatula to transfer the dough to the prepared cookie sheet. Sprinkle with the stem ginger. • Roll the remaining

dough out to the same size and place over the first half. • <u>Glaze</u>: Use a pastry brush to coat the top of the dough with the egg mixture. • Sprinkle with the granulated sugar and almonds. • Refrigerate on the cookie sheet for 30 minutes. • Preheat the oven to 275°F. • Bake for 1 hour. Remove from the oven and coat with the remaining egg mixture. • Bake for 1 hour more, or until golden. • Transfer to racks to cool before cutting into squares.

Makes 16 squares · Prep: 40 min. + 60 min. to chill · Cooking: 2 hr. · Level: 1 · Keeps: 10 days

Press the dough into a disk, wrap in plastic wrap, and refrigerate for 30 minutes. • Preheat the oven to 300°F. • Butter a cookie sheet. • Roll out the dough on a lightly floured surface to a thickness of ¼-inch. • Use a 3-inch fluted cookie cutter to cut out the cookies. Gather the dough scraps, reroll, and continue cutting out cookies until all the dough is used. • Use a spatula to transfer the cookies to the prepared cookie sheet, placing them 1 inch apart. • Bake for 25–35 minutes, or until just golden at the edges. • Transfer to racks to cool and dust with the superfine sugar.

Makes 12–16 cookies · Prep: 40 min. + 30 min. to chill · Cooking: 25–35 min. · Level: 1 · Keeps: 7 days

lavender-scented shortbread

1 cup all-purpose flour
¼ cup cornstarch
⅛ teaspoon salt
1 teaspoon lavender flowers (heads only),
   rinsed and dried
½ cup (1 stick) butter, softened
¼ cup granulated sugar
½ teaspoon vanilla extract

Preheat the oven to 325°F. • Set out a 9-inch springform pan. • Sift the flour, cornstarch, and salt into a medium bowl. Stir in the lavender. • Beat the butter, sugar, and vanilla in a large bowl with an electric mixer at high speed until creamy. • Mix in the dry ingredients. • Firmly press the dough into the pan to form a smooth, even layer. Use a sharp knife to score the shortbread into 16 wedges. • Bake for 25–30 minutes, or until lightly browned. • Use a sharp knife to cut the shortbread into wedges along the scored lines. •

Loosen and remove the pan sides and bottom. Transfer to racks to cool.

Makes 16 cookies · Prep: 25 min. · Cooking: 25–30 min. · Level: 1 · Keeps: 5 days

coffee-frosted walnut shortbread cookies

¾ cup walnut halves
⅔ cup granulated sugar
2¼ cups all-purpose flour
⅛ teaspoon salt
½ teaspoon vanilla extract
1 cup (2 sticks) butter, cut up

Coffee frosting
1 tablespoon freeze-dried coffee granules
   dissolved in 3 tablespoons hot water
¼ cup (½ stick) butter, melted
2 cups confectioners' sugar
½ teaspoon vanilla extract
64 coffee beans, to decorate

Process the walnuts and 2 tablespoons of the sugar in a food processor or blender until very finely ground. • Sift the flour and salt into a large bowl. Stir in the remaining sugar, ground walnuts, and vanilla. • Use a pastry blender to cut in the butter until the mixture just holds together. • Divide the dough in half. Form the dough into two 8-inch logs, wrap each in plastic wrap, and refrigerate for 30 minutes. • Preheat the oven to 350°F. • Set out four cookie sheets. • Slice the dough ¼ inch thick and place 1 inch apart on the cookie sheets. • Bake, one sheet at a time, for 8–10 minutes, or until firm to the touch. • Cool on the sheets until the cookies firm slightly. • Transfer to racks to cool. • <u>Coffee frosting</u>: Beat the coffee mixture, butter, confectioners' sugar, and vanilla in a small bowl until well blended. •

Spread the frosting over the tops of the cookies and top each with a coffee bean. Let stand for 20 minutes until set.

Makes 64 cookies · Prep: 25 min. + 60 min. to chill and set · Cooking: 8–10 min. per batch · Level: 1 · Keeps: 3 days

Coffee-frosted walnut shortbread cookies

marzipan shortbread

12/3 cups all-purpose flour
1/8 teaspoon salt
1 cup (2 sticks) butter, softened
31/2 oz marzipan, softened
1/2 cup firmly packed light brown sugar
1 tablespoon raw sugar (Demerara or Barbados)

Sift the flour and salt into a medium bowl. • Use a wooden spoon to beat the butter and marzipan in a large bowl until well blended. • Beat in the brown sugar. • Mix in the dry ingredients to form a stiff dough. • Press the dough into a disk, wrap in plastic wrap, and refrigerate for 30 minutes. • Preheat the oven to 350°F. • Line two cookie sheets with parchment paper. • Discard the plastic wrap. Roll out the dough on a lightly floured surface to a thickness of 1/4 inch. • Cut into 3/4 x 21/2-inch strips. Gather the dough scraps, re-roll, and continue cutting out cookies until all the dough is used. • Use a spatula to transfer the cookies to the prepared cookie sheets, placing them 1 inch apart. • Use a fork to make lines over the tops of the cookies. Sprinkle with the raw sugar. • Bake for 10–12 minutes, or until golden brown, rotating the sheets halfway through for even baking. • Transfer to racks to cool.

Makes 25–30 cookies · Prep: 40 min. + 30 min. to chill · Cooking: 10–12 min. · Level: 1 · Keeps: 10 days

zesty lime petticoat tails

2 cups all-purpose flour
1/8 teaspoon salt
1 cup (2 sticks) butter, softened
3/4 cup granulated sugar
1 teaspoon finely grated lime zest
2 teaspoons fresh lime juice
1/2 teaspoon vanilla extract

Preheat the oven to 325°F. • Set out two 9-inch springform pans. • Sift the flour and salt into a medium bowl. • Beat the butter and sugar in a large bowl with an electric mixer at high speed until creamy. • Add the lime zest and juice and vanilla. • Mix in the dry ingredients. • Divide the dough in half. Firmly press each dough half into the pans to form smooth, even layers. Use a sharp knife to score each round into 16 wedges. Use a fork to draw decorative patterns around the edges. • Bake for 45–50 minutes, or until golden brown, rotating the

sheets halfway through for even baking. • Use a sharp knife to cut the shortbread into 16 wedges along the scored lines. • Loosen and remove the pan sides and bottom. Transfer to racks to cool.

Makes 32 cookies · Prep: 25 min. · Cooking: 45–50 min. · Level: 1 · Keeps: 7 days in the refrigerator

apricot-topped shortbread squares

2 cups all-purpose flour
1/8 teaspoon salt
1 cup firmly packed light brown sugar
2/3 cup butter, cut up
11/2 cups finely chopped dried apricots
11/2 cups water
11/2 cups granulated sugar
1 tablespoon cornstarch
1 cup finely chopped pecans

Preheat the oven to 350°F. • Set out a 13 x 9-inch baking pan. • Sift the flour and salt into a large bowl. Stir in the brown sugar. • Use a pastry blender to cut in the butter until the mixture resembles coarse crumbs. • Firmly press the mixture into the prepared pan to form a smooth, even layer. • Bake for 12–15 minutes, or until firm to the touch. • Cook the apricots in 11/4 cups water and the sugar in a medium saucepan over medium heat for 5–7 minutes, or until the apricots have softened. • Stir the cornstarch into the remaining 1/4 cup water until smooth. • Stir the cornstarch mixture into the apricots and continue cooking until the mixture starts to thicken. Remove from the heat and let cool completely. • Spread the apricot mixture over the cookie base and sprinkle with the pecans. • Bake for 20–25 minutes, or until lightly browned and firm to the touch. • Cool completely before cutting into squares.

Makes 36–45 squares · Prep: 40 min. · Cooking: 32–40 min. · Level: 1 · Keeps: 5 days

coffee shortbread

11/4 cups all-purpose flour
3/4 cup confectioners' sugar
1/8 teaspoon salt
1/2 cup finely ground almonds
2 tablespoons freeze-dried coffee granules
3/4 cup (11/2 sticks) butter, softened
1/3 cup granulated sugar, to dust

Sift the flour, confectioners' sugar, and salt into a large bowl. Stir in the almonds and coffee granules. • Use a pastry blender to

cut in the butter until the dough just holds together. • Press the dough into a disk, wrap in plastic wrap, and refrigerate for 30 minutes. • Preheat the oven to 350°F. • Set out two cookie sheets. • Roll out the dough on a lightly floured surface to a thickness of 1/4 inch. • Use a 2-inch fluted cookie cutter to cut out the cookies. Gather the dough scraps, re-roll, and continue cutting out cookies until all the dough is used. • Use a spatula to transfer the cookies to the cookie sheets, placing them 1 inch apart. • Bake for 10–12 minutes, or until just golden at the edges, rotating the sheets halfway through for even baking. • Transfer to racks to cool and dust with the granulated sugar.

Makes 30–35 cookies · Prep: 40 min. + 30 min. to chill · Cooking: 10–12 min. per batch · Level: 1 · Keeps: 7 days

pine nut shortbread

3/4 cup finely chopped pine nuts
2 tablespoons granulated sugar
1 cup (2 sticks) butter, softened
11/3 cups confectioners' sugar
12/3 cups all-purpose flour
1/8 teaspoon salt

Preheat the oven to 350°F. • Butter and flour two cookie sheets. • Stir together the pine nuts and granulated sugar in a small bowl. • Beat the butter and confectioners' sugar in a large bowl with an electric mixer at high speed until creamy. • With mixer at low speed, gradually beat in the flour and salt. • Scoop out a heaping tablespoon of dough and shape into a ball the size of a walnut. • Place the cookies on the prepared cookie sheets, spacing them 1 inch apart. • Sprinkle with the pine nut mixture. • Bake for 15–20 minutes, or until golden brown, rotating the trays halfway through for even baking. • Cool the cookies completely on the cookie sheets.

Makes 30 cookies · Prep: 20 min. · Cooking: 15–20 min. · Level: 1 · Keeps: 10 days

Coffee shortbread (left) and Apricot-topped shortbread squares (right)

piped & shaped cookies

above: Mint spritz cookies (page 208)

right: Chocolate-coated arches, Piped strawberry thumbprints, Lemon duchesses, and Orange fingers (pages 210, 210, 204, and 206)

Whether you use a pastry bag, a cookie press, or your hands, shaped cookies have that professional bakery finish. If using a pastry bag, choose from a variety of nozzles to pipe out an assortment of decorative cookies. If you own a cookie press, just insert your desired design plate, spoon in the dough, and press it out onto cookie sheets. Hand-shaped cookies can be just as attractive and require no gadgets. Decorated with candied cherries and angelica or drizzled with white or semisweet chocolate, piped and shaped cookies are perfect for afternoon tea or as after-dinner treats.

making fingers & rosettes

1. Spoon the dough into a pastry bag until it is half-full. Twist the bag tightly closed.

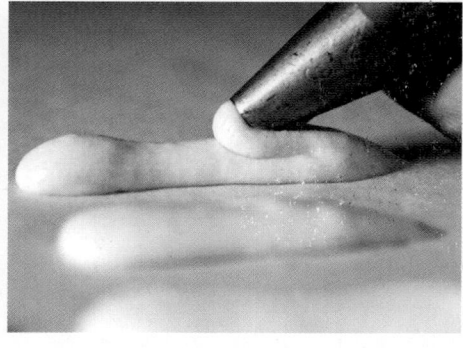

2. Pipe out the fingers with a smooth tip.

3. Pipe out rosettes in a circular manner with a star tip.

piped cookies

- 1¹/₃ cups all-purpose flour
- ¹/₃ cup cornstarch
- 1 cup (2 sticks) butter, softened
- ²/₃ cup confectioners' sugar
- 1 large egg
- ¹/₄ teaspoon vanilla extract
- ¹/₄ teaspoon lemon extract
- 2 tablespoons unsweetened cocoa powder
- 1 teaspoon vegetable oil
  Confectioners' sugar, to dust

Preheat the oven to 350°F. • Butter three cookie sheets. • Sift the flour and cornstarch into a medium bowl. • Beat the butter and confectioners' sugar in a large bowl with an electric mixer at high speed until creamy. • Add the egg, beating until just blended. Stir in the vanilla and lemon extracts. Continue beating until pale and fluffy. • Mix in the dry ingredients. • Divide the dough evenly between two bowls. • Mix the cocoa and oil in a small bowl. Stir the cocoa mixture into one bowl of the dough. • Fit a pastry bag with a ¹/₄-inch star tip. Fill the pastry bag with the plain batter, twist the opening tightly closed, and pipe out small rings, hearts, circles, and swirls spacing 1¹/₂ inches apart on the prepared cookie sheets. • Repeat with the chocolate batter. • Bake, one sheet at a time, for 10–15 minutes, or until the plain cookies are golden brown. • Cool the cookies on the cookie sheets for 2 minutes. • Transfer to racks to cool. • Dust some of the dark cookies with the confectioners' sugar.

Makes 50 cookies · Prep: 25 min. · Cooking: 10–15 min. per batch · Level: 2 · Keep: 8 days

parisian petits fours

French pastry-making is made easy with these simple petits fours.

- 1¹/₄ cups finely ground almonds
- ³/₄ cup confectioners' sugar
- 2 large egg whites
- ¹/₈ teaspoon salt
- 6 candied cherries, finely chopped

Dust two cookie sheets with rice flour. • Mix the almonds, confectioners' sugar, egg whites, and salt in a large bowl until smooth. • Fit a pastry bag with a ¹/₂-inch star tip. Fill the pastry bag, twist the opening tightly closed, and squeeze out rosettes, spacing 1 inch apart on the prepared cookie sheets. • Place a piece of candied cherry on top of each cookie. • Refrigerate for 30 minutes. • Preheat the oven to 475°F. • Bake for 3–5 minutes, or until lightly browned at the edges, rotating the sheets halfway through for even baking. • Transfer to racks to cool.

Makes 25 cookies · Prep: 25 min. + 30 min. to chill Cooking: 3–5 min. · Level: 2 · Keeps: 5 days

piped coconut treats

- 2 cups granulated sugar
- 1¹/₂ cups shredded coconut
- 5 large egg whites
  Grated zest of ¹/₂ lemon
- ¹/₄ teaspoon vanilla extract

Preheat the oven to 325°F. • Line three cookie sheets with parchment paper. • Mix the sugar, coconut, egg whites, lemon zest, and vanilla in a large shallow saucepan. • Cook over low heat, stirring constantly, for about 5 minutes, or until creamy. Do not bring to a boil. Remove from the heat and let cool for 15 minutes, or until thickened for piping. • Fit a pastry bag with a ¹/₄-inch star tip. Fill the pastry bag, twist the opening tightly closed, and pipe out hazelnut-sized rounds, spacing 1 inch apart on the prepared cookie sheets. • Bake, one batch at a time, for 8–10 minutes, or until firm to the touch and golden brown. • Cool the cookies on the cookie sheets for 5 minutes. • Transfer to racks to cool.

Makes 50 cookies · Prep: 40 min. · Cooking: 8–10 min. per batch · Level: 2 · Keep: 10 days

making sugar pretzels

Traditional German pretzels come in all sizes and flavors—dusted with sugar, chocolate-coated, glazed, or salted. The first pretzels were made by monks well over a thousand years ago as a tasty reward for children who had learned their prayers. Their special shape represented the arms of a child praying.

1 1/3 cups all-purpose flour
1/3 cup granulated sugar
2 tablespoons Vanilla Sugar (see page 341)
1/2 cup finely ground almonds
1/8 teaspoon salt
1/2 cup (1 stick) cold butter, cut up
1 large egg, lightly beaten
2/3 cup Vanilla Confectioners' Sugar (see page 341) or plain confectioners' sugar

Stir together the flour, granulated sugar, vanilla sugar, almonds, and salt in a large bowl. • Dot the butter over the dry ingredients. Use a pastry blender to cut in the butter until the mixture resembles coarse crumbs. • Make a well in the center, add the egg, and beat until just blended. • Turn out onto a lightly floured surface and knead into a soft dough. • Shape into two logs, wrap in plastic wrap, and refrigerate for at least 1 hour, or until firm. • Preheat the oven to 350°F. • Line two cookie sheets with parchment paper. • Slice the dough 1/2 inch thick. • Hand-roll each slice out on a lightly floured surface to a 10-inch long rope. • Make each rope into a pretzel shape by twisting the two ends around each other, then bringing both back near to the center of the strip, about 1 inch apart. • Place on the prepared cookie sheets, spacing 1 inch apart. • Bake for 12–15 minutes, or until golden brown, rotating the sheets halfway through for even baking. • Dust with the confectioners' sugar and let cool completely.

Makes 18–20 pretzels · Prep: 60 min. + 60 min. to chill · Cooking: 12–15 min. · Level: 2 · Keeps: 14 days

1. Make each rope into a pretzel shape by twisting the ends around each other.

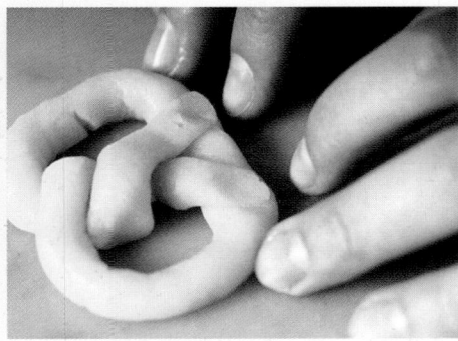

2. Bring both ends back to the center of the strip, about 1 inch apart.

3. Dust with confectioners' sugar while still warm.

piped mocha rosettes

1 3/4 cups all-purpose flour
1 1/2 tablespoons unsweetened cocoa powder
1/8 teaspoon salt
1 large egg yolk
1 teaspoon freeze-dried coffee granules
1 cup (2 sticks) butter, softened
3/4 cup confectioners' sugar
2 oz semisweet chocolate, finely grated

Preheat the oven to 350°F. • Butter four cookie sheets. • Sift the flour, cocoa, and salt into a medium bowl. • Beat the egg yolk and coffee granules in a small bowl until frothy. • Beat the butter and confectioners' sugar in a large bowl with an electric mixer at high speed until creamy. • Add the egg yolk mixture, beating until just blended. • Mix in the dry ingredients and grated chocolate. • Fit a pastry bag with a 1/2-inch star tip. Fill the pastry bag, twist the opening tightly closed, and squeeze out 1-inch rosettes, spacing 1 1/2 inches apart on the prepared cookie sheets. • Bake, one sheet at a time, for 8–10 minutes, or until firm to the touch. • Cool on the sheets until the cookies firm slightly. • Transfer to racks to finish cooling.

Makes 40–50 cookies · Prep: 25 min. · Cooking: 8–10 min. per batch · Level: 2 · Keeps: 5 days

Piped mocha rosettes

lemon hearts

Sugar confetti can be bought from specialty baking stores or Maid of Scandinavia.

3 large egg whites
3/4 cup superfine sugar
1 tablespoon fresh lemon juice
2 teaspoons lemonade powder
   or lemon sherbet
11/2 tablespoons instant pudding (vanilla or lemon flavor)
1/2 teaspoon lemon extract
2 tablespoons sugar confetti, to decorate

Line two cookie sheets with parchment paper. • Draw thirty 21/2-inch hearts on the paper, spacing 2 inches apart. • Beat the egg whites with an electric mixer at medium speed until frothy. With mixer at high speed, gradually add the superfine sugar and lemon juice until stiff, glossy peaks form. • Mix the lemonade, instant pudding, and lemon extract in a small bowl. Use a rubber spatula to fold into the beaten whites. • Fit a pastry bag with a plain 1/2-inch tip. Fill the pastry bag, twist the opening tightly closed, and pipe out hearts to fill in the outlines on the cookie sheets. • Preheat the oven to 200°F. • Sprinkle the hearts with the sugar confetti. • Bake for 80–90 minutes, or until pale golden. • Cool the hearts in the oven for 10 minutes. • Transfer to racks to cool.

Makes 30 hearts · Prep: 60 min. · Cooking: 80–90 min. · Level: 3 · Keeps: 5 days

lemon duchesses

2/3 cup all-purpose flour
1/8 teaspoon salt
1/4 cup (1/2 stick) + 2 tablespoons butter, softened
31/2 oz marzipan, softened
2 large eggs, separated
2/3 cup confectioners' sugar
1 tablespoon Vanilla Sugar (see page 341)
   Grated zest of 1 lemon
2 tablespoons milk
1/2 cup Lemon Curd (see page 340)
5 oz semisweet chocolate, coarsely chopped

Preheat the oven to 350°F. • Butter two cookie sheets. • Sift the flour and salt into a medium bowl. • Use a wooden spoon to beat the 1/4 cup butter and marzipan in a large bowl until well blended. • Add the egg yolks, beating until just blended. • Mix in the confectioners' and vanilla sugars and lemon zest. • Gradually mix in the dry ingredients and milk. • Beat the egg whites in a large

bowl with an electric mixer at high speed until stiff peaks form. • Use a large rubber spatula to fold the beaten whites into the batter. • Fit a pastry bag with a 1/2-inch plain tip. Fill the pastry bag, twist the opening tightly closed, and squeeze 1-inch rounds spacing them 1 inch apart on the prepared cookie sheets. • Bake for 10–12 minutes, or until lightly browned, rotating the sheets halfway through for even baking. • Cool on the sheets until the cookies firm slightly. Transfer to racks to cool. • Stick the cookies together in pairs with the lemon curd. • Melt the chocolate with the remaining 2 tablespoons butter in a double boiler over simmering water. • Dip the cookies halfway into the chocolate mixture and let stand for 30 minutes to set.

Makes 20–25 cookies · Prep: 35 min. + 30 min. to set · Cooking: 10–12 min. · Level: 2 · Keeps: 5 days, layered between parchment paper

whipped and piped cookies

1 cup (2 sticks) butter, softened
1/2 cup confectioners' sugar
11/4 cups all-purpose flour, sifted
1/8 teaspoon salt

Lemon glaze
1/3 cup confectioners' sugar
2–3 teaspoons fresh lemon juice
1 tablespoon sugar confetti (available from Maid of Scandinavia and other specialty baking stores)

Preheat the oven to 350°F. • Lightly oil two cookie sheets. • Beat the butter and confectioners' sugar in a large bowl with an electric mixer at high speed until creamy. • With mixer at low speed, gradually beat in the flour and salt. • Continue beating for 2–3 minutes until smooth and light. • Fit a pastry bag with a 3/4-inch star tip. Fill the pastry bag, twist the opening tightly closed, and squeeze 2-inch lines and rosettes spacing them 2 inches apart on the prepared cookie sheets. • Bake for 6–8 minutes, or until lightly browned, rotating the sheets halfway through for even baking. • Cool the cookies on the sheet for 1 minute. Transfer to racks to cool. • Lemon Glaze: Sift the confectioners' sugar into a small bowl and mix with the lemon juice until smooth. • Drizzle over the cookies. • Sprinkle with the confetti.

Makes 35 cookies · Prep: 25 min. · Cooking: 6–8 min. · Level: 1 · Keeps: 8 days

almond crescents

3/4 cup (11/2 sticks) butter, softened
1/3 cup granulated sugar
12/3 cups all-purpose flour
1 cup finely chopped almonds
1/2 teaspoon vanilla extract
1 tablespoon honey
1/2 cup finely chopped pistachios

Preheat the oven to 350°F. • Butter two cookie sheets. • Beat the butter and sugar in a large bowl with an electric mixer at high speed until creamy. • Mix in the flour, almonds, and vanilla to make a stiff dough. • Form teaspoons of the cookie dough into crescent shapes and place 1 inch apart on the prepared cookie sheets. • Bake for 15–20 minutes, or until faintly tinged with brown, rotating the sheets halfway through for even baking. • Transfer to racks to cool. • Melt the honey in a saucepan over low heat. • Dip both ends of the crescents in the honey, then in the pistachios.

Makes 25–30 cookies · Prep: 40 min. · Cooking: 15–20 min. · Level: 1 · Keeps: 4 days

viennese whirls

11/3 cups all-purpose flour
1/3 cup cornstarch
1/8 teaspoon salt
1 cup (2 sticks) butter, softened
1/2 cup confectioners' sugar, sifted
   Grated zest of 1 lemon
1/2 teaspoon vanilla extract

Topping
2 tablespoons raspberry preserves
2 tablespoons plum or gooseberry preserves

Preheat the oven to 375°F. • Arrange twelve paper baking cups on a baking sheet. • Sift the flour, cornstarch, and salt into a large bowl. • Beat the butter, confectioners' sugar, and vanilla in a large bowl with an electric mixer at high speed until creamy. • Use a large rubber spatula to fold in the dry ingredients. • Fit a pastry bag with a 1/4-inch star tip. Fill the pastry bag, twist the opening tightly closed, and pipe into the paper cups in a decorative manner to create whirls. • Bake for 20–25 minutes, or until golden brown. Transfer to racks to cool. • Topping: Spoon a small amount of both preserves in the center of each whirl.

Makes 12 cookies · Prep: 30 min. · Cooking: 20–25 min. · Level: 2 · Keeps: 10 days

Viennese whirls and Lemon hearts

ladyfingers

Also known as sponge fingers or boudoir fingers, these cookies are popular all around the world. Made from a simple mixture of beaten eggs, sugar, and flour, they are delicious dipped into sweet dessert wines and as a basis for creamy desserts. Their versatility allows them to be used as a sponge base for tiramisù, traditional English trifles, and charlottes. Soak them first in a syrup or liqueur, then layer them in the appropriate dish.

2/3 cup all-purpose flour
1/8 teaspoon salt
3 large eggs, separated
1/2 cup granulated sugar
   Confectioners' sugar, to dust

Preheat the oven to 350°F. • Line a baking sheet with parchment paper. • Sift the flour and salt into a medium bowl. • Beat the egg yolks and sugar in a large bowl with an electric mixer at high speed until pale and thick. • With mixer at high speed, beat the egg whites in a large bowl until stiff peaks form. • Use a large rubber spatula to gradually fold the dry ingredients into the

chocolate-dipped butter cookies

Butter cookies
1 cup all-purpose flour
1/8 teaspoon salt
1/3 cup butter, softened
1/4 cup granulated sugar
1 large egg yolk, lightly beaten
2 tablespoons sour cream
1/4 teaspoon almond extract

Chocolate glaze
1/2 cup granulated sugar
2 tablespoons water
1 tablespoon butter
2 teaspoons dark corn syrup
1/4 cup semisweet chocolate chips

Butter cookies: Preheat the oven to 375°F. • Set out two cookie sheets. • Sift the flour and salt into a medium bowl. • Beat the butter and sugar in a large bowl with an electric mixer at high speed until creamy. • Add the egg yolk, beating until just blended. • Beat in the sour cream and almond extract. • Mix in the dry ingredients to form a smooth dough. • Insert a Christmas tree design plate into a cookie press by sliding it into the head and locking in place. Press out the cookies, spacing about 1/2 inch apart on the cookie sheets. • Bake for 12–15 minutes, or until lightly browned, rotating the sheets halfway through for even baking. • Cool on the sheets until the cookies firm slightly. Transfer to racks to finish cooling. • Chocolate glaze: Cook the sugar, water, butter, and corn syrup in a small saucepan over low heat until the sugar has dissolved. • Remove from the heat and stir in the chocolate chips. • Return the saucepan to the heat and stir until the glaze is smooth. •

Dip the cookies halfway into the glaze, letting the excess drip off. • Let stand until the glaze has dried, about 30 minutes.

Makes 27 cookies · Prep: 45 min. + 30 min. to set · Cooking: 12–15 min. · Level: 2 · Keeps: 2–3 days

butter wreaths

1 1/4 cups all-purpose flour
1/2 teaspoon baking powder
1/8 teaspoon salt
1/2 cup (1 stick) butter, softened
2/3 cup granulated sugar
1/2 teaspoon vanilla extract
1 large egg
   Silver and colored balls, to decorate
2 tablespoons sugar strands, to decorate

Preheat the oven to 375°F. • Set out four cookie sheets. • Sift the flour, baking powder, and salt into a medium bowl. • Beat the butter and sugar in a large bowl with an electric mixer at high speed until creamy. • Add the vanilla and egg, beating until just blended. • Mix in the dry ingredients. • Fit a pastry bag with a 3/4-inch plain tip. Fill the pastry bag, twist the opening tightly closed, and squeeze out 1 1/2-inch wreaths, spacing 1 inch apart on the cookie sheets. • Press the sugar strands and balls in a decorative manner into the tops of the cookies. • Bake, one batch at a time, for 8–10 minutes, or until the edges are just golden. • Transfer to racks to cool.

Makes 35–40 cookies · Prep: 25 min. · Cooking: 8–10 min. per batch · Level: 2 · Keeps: 7 days

orange fingers

1 1/4 cups all-purpose flour
1/4 cup cornstarch
1/8 teaspoon salt
3 large eggs, lightly beaten

1 cup superfine sugar
2 teaspoons grated orange zest
2 tablespoons sugar crystals

Preheat the oven to 375°F. • Line two baking sheets with parchment paper. • Sift the flour, cornstarch, and salt into a medium bowl. • Use a whisk to beat the eggs, superfine sugar, and orange zest in a double boiler over barely simmering water until pale and very thick. • Transfer to a medium bowl. • Use a large rubber spatula to fold in the dry ingredients. • Fit a pastry bag with a 1/2-inch plain tip. Fill the pastry bag, twist the opening tightly closed, and squeeze out 3-inch lines, spacing 2 inches apart on the prepared cookie sheets. • Sprinkle with the sugar crystals. • Bake for 8–10 minutes, or until just golden, rotating the sheets halfway through for even baking. • Cool the cookies on the cookie sheets for 5 minutes. • Transfer to racks and let cool completely.

Makes 30–35 cookies · Prep: 40 min. · Cooking: 8–10 min. · Level: 1 · Keeps: 3 days

hazelnut arches

2 cups all-purpose flour
1/8 teaspoon salt
1 cup (2 sticks) butter, softened
2/3 cup granulated sugar
2 tablespoons Vanilla Sugar (see page 341)
1 large egg
1/4 teaspoon almond extract
1 cup finely ground hazelnuts or pecans
1/4 cup confectioners' sugar, to dust

Preheat the oven to 375°F. • Set out four cookie sheets. • Sift the flour and salt into a medium bowl. • Beat the butter and granulated and vanilla sugars in a large bowl with an electric mixer at high speed until creamy. • Add the egg and almond beaten yolks, followed by the beaten whites. • Fit a pastry bag with $^1/_2$-inch plain tip. Fill the pastry bag, twist the opening tightly closed, and squeeze out 3-inch lengths, spacing them 2 inches apart on the prepared baking sheet. • Dust lightly with the confectioners' sugar. • Bake for 10–12 minutes, or until firm to the touch and lightly browned. • Cool the ladyfingers completely on the baking sheet.

Makes 15 ladyfingers · Prep: 25 min. · Cooking: 10–12 min. · Level: 2 · Keeps: 3 days

extract, beating until just blended. • Mix in the dry ingredients and ground hazelnuts. • Fit a pastry bag with a $^1/_2$-inch star tip. Fill the pastry bag, twist the opening tightly closed, and squeeze out generous 1-inch tall arches (horseshoes), spacing 1 inch apart on the cookie sheets. • Bake, one sheet at a time, for 8–10 minutes, or until golden and firm at the edges. • Transfer to racks to cool and dust with confectioners' sugar.

Makes 60–65 cookies · Prep: 30 min. · Cooking: 8–10 min. per batch · Level: 2 · Keeps: 10 days

lemony cream stars

1$^2/_3$	cups all-purpose flour
$^1/_2$	teaspoon baking powder
$^1/_8$	teaspoon salt
$^1/_2$	cup granulated sugar
1	large egg
$^1/_3$	cup sunflower oil
$^1/_4$	cup light cream
1	teaspoon honey
	Grated zest of 1 lemon

Preheat the oven to 350°F. • Butter two cookie sheets. • Sift the flour, baking powder, and salt into a large bowl. • Stir in the sugar. • Add the egg, beating until just blended. • Stir in the oil, cream, honey, and lemon zest. • Fit a pastry bag with a $^1/_2$-inch star tip. Fill the pastry bag, twist the opening tightly closed, and squeeze out generous 1$^1/_2$-inch stars, spacing 1 inch apart onto the prepared cookie sheets. • Bake for 10–15 minutes, or until just golden at the edges, rotating the sheets halfway through for even baking. • Transfer to racks to cool.

Makes 25 cookies · Prep: 25 min. · Cooking: 10–15 min. · Level: 2 · Keeps: 5 days

ladies' delights
(*palais des dames*)

*These crisp, delicately flavored cookies are a traditional French specialty. As their name implies, they are considered a favorite with the ladies—*palais *means "palate" or "taste."*

2	tablespoons finely chopped mixed candied peel
2	tablespoons orange liqueur
1	cup all-purpose flour
$^1/_4$	teaspoon baking powder
$^1/_8$	teaspoon salt
$^1/_2$	cup (1 stick) butter, softened
$^2/_3$	cup granulated sugar
$^1/_2$	teaspoon lemon extract
2	egg whites, lightly beaten

Soak the candied peel in the orange liqueur for 1 hour. • Drain, reserving the liqueur. • Preheat the oven to 375°F. • Line two cookie sheets with parchment paper. • Sift the flour, baking powder, and salt into a medium bowl. • Beat the butter and sugar in a large bowl with an electric mixer at high speed until creamy. • Add the lemon extract. • With mixer at high speed, beat in the egg whites and the reserved orange liqueur. • Mix in the dry ingredients. • Fit a pastry bag with a $^1/_2$-inch plain tip. Fill the pastry bag, twist the opening tightly closed, and squeeze out 1$^1/_2$-inch mounds, spacing 2 inches apart on the prepared cookie sheets. • Lightly press a piece of candied peel into the top of each cookie. • Bake for 8–10 minutes, or until golden brown, rotating the sheets halfway through for even baking. • Cool on the sheets until the cookies firm slightly. • Transfer to racks and let cool completely.

Makes 30 cookies · Prep: 30 min. + 1 hr. to soak · Cooking: 8–10 min. · Level: 2 · Keeps: 5 days

butter whirls

1$^1/_4$	cups all-purpose flour
$^1/_2$	teaspoon baking powder
$^1/_8$	teaspoon salt
$^3/_4$	cup (1$^1/_2$ sticks) butter, softened
$^1/_3$	cup confectioners' sugar
$^1/_2$	teaspoon vanilla extract
8–9	candied cherries, cut in half

Preheat the oven to 325°F. • Butter a cookie sheet. • Sift the flour, baking powder, and salt into a medium bowl. • Beat the butter, confectioners' sugar, and vanilla in a large bowl with an electric mixer at high speed until creamy. • Mix in the dry ingredients until well blended. • Fit a pastry bag with a $^1/_2$-inch star tip. Fill the pastry bag, twist the

opening tightly closed, and squeeze out flat whirls, spacing 1 inch apart on the prepared cookie sheet. • Place a half cherry on top of each whirl. • Bake for 15–20 minutes, or until lightly browned. • Cool on the sheet until the cookies firm slightly. • Transfer to racks and let cool completely.

Makes 16–18 cookies · Prep: 25 min. · Cooking: 15–20 min. · Level: 2 · Keeps: 5–7 days

piped dreams

2	large egg whites
1	cup superfine sugar
1$^3/_4$	cups finely ground almonds
$^1/_2$	teaspoon almond extract
4	oz semisweet chocolate, coarsely chopped

Preheat the oven to 350°F. • Line two cookie sheets with rice paper. • Beat the egg whites in a large bowl with an electric mixer at high speed until stiff peaks form. • Use a large rubber spatula to fold in the superfine sugar, almonds, and almond extract. • Fit a pastry bag with a $^1/_2$-inch plain tip. Fill the pastry bag, twist the opening tightly closed, and pipe out 3 inch-long lines spacing 1$^1/_2$ inches apart on the prepared cookie sheets. • Bake for 15–20 minutes, or until golden brown. • Cool the cookies on the cookie sheets for 1 minute. • Transfer to racks to cool. • Tear away the excess rice paper from around the edges. • Melt the chocolate in a double boiler over barely simmering water. • Drizzle the chocolate in a zigzag pattern over the tops.

Makes 20 cookies · Prep: 30 min. · Cooking: 15–20 min. · Level: 2 · Keeps: 6 days

Butter wreaths

mint spritz cookies

1 cup all-purpose flour
1/8 teaspoon salt
1/2 cup (1 stick) butter, softened
1/3 cup granulated sugar
1/2 large egg, lightly beaten
1/2 teaspoon vanilla extract
1/2 teaspoon mint extract
 Few drops green food coloring
30 Hershey kisses

Preheat the oven to 400°F. • Butter two cookie sheets. • Sift the flour and salt into a medium bowl. • Beat the butter, sugar, egg, and vanilla and mint extracts in a large bowl with an electric mixer at high speed. • Mix in the dry ingredients, followed by the food coloring. • Refrigerate for 30 minutes. • Insert a star-shaped design plate into a cookie press by sliding it into the head and locking in place. Press out the cookies, spacing about 1 inch apart on the prepared cookie sheet. • Bake for 8–10 minutes, or until just golden at the edges, rotating the sheets halfway through for even baking. • Working quickly, press a chocolate into the center of each cookie. • Cool on the sheets until the cookies firm slightly. • Transfer to racks and let cool completely.

Makes 30 cookies · Prep: 25 min. + 30 min. to chill Cooking: 8–10 min. · Level: 2 · Keeps: 3 days

pineapple spritz cookies

2 1/4 cups all-purpose flour
1/2 teaspoon baking powder
1/4 teaspoon salt
1 cup (2 sticks) butter, softened
2/3 cup granulated sugar
1 large egg
1 tablespoon fresh or canned pineapple juice

Preheat the oven to 400°F. • Set out two cookie sheets. • Sift the flour, baking powder, and salt into a medium bowl. • Beat the butter and sugar in a large bowl with an electric mixer at high speed until creamy. • Add the egg, beating until just blended. • Mix in the dry ingredients, followed by the pineapple juice. • Insert a star-shaped design plate into a cookie press by sliding it into the head and locking it in place. Press out the cookies, spacing about 1 inch apart on the prepared cookie sheets. • Bake for 8–10 minutes, or until just golden at the edges, rotating the sheets halfway through for even baking. • Cool on the sheets until the cookies firm slightly. • Transfer to racks and let cool completely.

Makes 32–36 cookies · Prep: 25 min. · Cooking: 8–10 min. · Level: 2 · Keeps: 5 days

almond spritzers

3 1/3 cups all-purpose flour
1/8 teaspoon salt
1 1/2 cups (3 sticks) butter, softened
1 1/4 cups granulated sugar
2 tablespoons Vanilla Sugar (see page 341)
1 1/4 cups finely ground almonds

Preheat the oven to 375°F. • Butter four cookie sheets. • Sift the flour and salt into a medium bowl. • Beat the butter and granulated and vanilla sugars in a large bowl with an electric mixer at high speed until creamy. • Gradually mix in the dry ingredients and ground almonds to form a smooth dough. • Insert a flower or star design plate into a cookie press by sliding it into the head and locking in place. Press out the cookies, spacing about 1 inch apart on the prepared cookie sheets. • Bake, one batch at a time, for 10–15 minutes, or until golden brown and firm at the edges. • Transfer to racks to cool.

Makes 60–70 cookies · Prep: 30 min. · Cooking: 10–15 min. per batch · Level: 2 · Keeps: 2 weeks

lemon–ginger spritzers

3 1/3 cups all-purpose flour
1 teaspoon ground ginger
1/4 teaspoon ground cloves
1/8 teaspoon salt
1 1/2 cups (3 sticks) butter, softened
1 1/4 cups granulated sugar
2 tablespoons Vanilla Sugar (see page 341)
1 large egg
1 teaspoon finely grated lemon zest
1 tablespoon fresh lemon juice
1 tablespoon chopped crystallized ginger
1 tablespoon colored sugar crystals

Preheat the oven to 375°F. • Butter four cookie sheets. • Sift the flour, ginger, cloves, and salt into a medium bowl. • Beat the butter and granulated and vanilla sugars in a large bowl with an electric mixer at high speed until creamy. • Add the egg and lemon zest and juice, beating until just blended. • Mix in the dry ingredients to form a stiff dough. • Insert the chosen design plate into a cookie press by sliding it into the head and locking in place. Press out the cookies, spacing about 1 inch apart on the prepared cookie sheets. • Decorate each cookie with crystallized ginger and sprinkle with sugar crystals. • Bake, one sheet at a time, for 10–12 minutes, or until firm to the touch and golden at the edges. • Transfer to racks to cool.

Makes 60–70 cookies · Prep: 30 min. · Cooking: 10–12 min. per batch · Level: 2 · Keeps: 2 weeks

mascarpone spritzers

It is best to bake these spritzer cookies 2 or 3 days in advance and make the filling on the day you wish to serve them.

1 1/3 cups all-purpose flour
1/3 cup cornstarch
1 teaspoon baking powder
1/8 teaspoon salt
2/3 cup mascarpone cheese
1 cup granulated sugar
3 large egg yolks
1 tablespoon sunflower oil
1 tablespoon unsweetened cocoa powder
1 tablespoon milk

Lemon mascarpone filling
1/2 cup mascarpone cheese
1 tablespoon confectioners' sugar
1/2 teaspoon vanilla extract
1/2 teaspoon finely grated lemon zest

Lemon glaze
1/2 cup confectioners' sugar
2–3 tablespoons fresh lemon juice

Preheat the oven to 350°F. • Line two cookie sheets with parchment paper. • Sift the flour, cornstarch, baking powder, and salt into a large bowl. • Beat in the mascarpone, sugar, egg yolks, and oil with an electric mixer at medium speed until smooth. • Fit a pastry bag with a 1/2-inch star tip. Fill the pastry bag with half the dough and twist the opening tightly closed. Squeeze out ten 2-inch rings, spacing 1 1/2 inches apart, on one of the prepared cookie sheets. • Mix the cocoa and milk in a small bowl and stir into the remaining dough portion. • Clean the pastry bag. • Fill the pastry bag with the chocolate dough. Pipe rings onto the other prepared cookie sheet. • Bake for 15–20 minutes, or until just golden at the edges, rotating the sheets halfway through for even baking. • Transfer on the parchment paper to racks and let cool completely. • Lemon mascarpone filling: Beat the mascarpone, confectioners' sugar, vanilla, and lemon zest in a small bowl. • Spoon the frosting into a small freezer bag and cut off a tiny corner. • Pipe over the light cookies and top with the dark cookies. Pipe over ten dark cookies and top with the light cookies. • Lemon glaze: Mix the confectioners' sugar and lemon juice in a small bowl. Drizzle over the cookies.

Makes about 20 cookies · Prep: 1 hr. · Cooking: 15–20 min. · Level: 2 · Keeps: 2 days in the refrigerator

Mascarpone spritzers

multicolored shells

These shells use tiny amounts of food coloring to give them their multicolored look. Use pastes and gels rather than liquids for best color results and pipe them into a variety of shapes. This recipe is for plain cookies, but if you don't tint them, you could flavor them with 1½ teaspoons coffee extract, cocoa powder, or another extract.

- ²/₃ cup all-purpose flour
- 2 tablespoons cornstarch
- ¹/₈ teaspoon salt
- ¹/₂ cup (1 stick) butter, softened
- 2¹/₂ tablespoons confectioners' sugar
- ¹/₄ teaspoon lemon extract
- Few drops pink, blue, and green food coloring

Flaked almonds, chopped nuts, and candied cherries, to decorate

Preheat the oven to 350°F. • Line two cookie sheets with parchment paper. • Sift the flour, cornstarch, and salt into a medium bowl. • Beat the butter and confectioners' sugar in a large bowl with an electric mixer at high speed until creamy. • Mix in the dry ingredients and lemon extract. • Divide the mixture into three bowls. • Tint one with pink, one with blue, and the remaining dough with green. You will only need the tiniest dot of color from your jar or tube. • Fit a pastry bag with a ¹/₂-inch star tip. Spoon the mixture into the pastry bag, using a different bag for each color. Squeeze out 1-inch shells spacing 2 inches apart on the prepared cookie sheets. • Decorate with a flaked almond, chopped nut, or a piece of candied cherry. • Bake for 10–12 minutes, until firm, rotating the sheets halfway through for even baking. • Cool on the sheets until the cookies firm slightly. • Transfer to racks and let cool completely.

Makes 35 cookies · Prep: 25 min. · Cooking: 10–12 min · Level: 2 · Keeps: 5–7 days

chocolate-coated arches

From Piedmont in northern Italy, these decadent arches of butter dough are finished with a coating of high-quality chocolate—a great way to complete a dinner party.

- ³/₄ cup all-purpose flour
- ³/₄ cup finely ground yellow cornmeal
- ¹/₈ teaspoon salt
- ¹/₃ cup granulated sugar
- ¹/₂ teaspoon vanilla extract
- 2 large eggs
- ²/₃ cup butter, softened
- 7 oz semisweet chocolate, coarsely chopped

Sift the flour, cornmeal, and salt into a large bowl. • Stir in the sugar and vanilla. • Add the eggs, beating until just blended. • Stir in the butter to form a stiff dough. • Cover with a clean kitchen towel and let stand for 30 minutes. • Preheat the oven to 400°F. • Line two cookie sheets with parchment paper. • Fit a pastry bag with a ¹/₂-inch star tip. Fill the pastry bag, twist the opening tightly closed, and squeeze out 4-inch tall arches (horseshoes) spacing them 2 inches apart on the prepared cookie sheets. • Bake for 10–15 minutes, or until just golden, rotating the sheets halfway through for even baking. • Cool the cookies completely on the cookie sheet. • Melt the chocolate in a double boiler over barely simmering water. • Dip the cookies halfway into the chocolate and let stand until set, about 30 minutes.

Makes 26 cookies · Prep: 30 min. + 30 min. to set · Cooking: 10–15 min. · Level: 2 · Keeps: 3 days

double chocolate fingers

- 1 cup all-purpose flour
- ¹/₂ cup cornstarch
- ¹/₈ teaspoon salt
- ³/₄ cup (1¹/₂ sticks) butter, softened
- ¹/₃ cup confectioners' sugar
- ¹/₂ teaspoon vanilla extract
- 2 oz semisweet chocolate, coarsely chopped
- 2 oz white chocolate, coarsely chopped

Preheat the oven to 350°F. • Line two cookie sheets with parchment paper. • Sift the flour, cornstarch, and salt into a medium bowl. • Beat the butter, confectioners' sugar, and vanilla in a large bowl with an electric mixer at high speed until creamy. • Mix in the dry ingredients. • Fit the pastry bag with a ¹/₂-inch tip. Fill the pastry bag, twist opening tightly closed, and squeeze out 3-inch lines, spacing 2 inches apart on the prepared cookie sheets. • Bake for 12–15 minutes, or until just golden at the edges and firm to the touch, rotating the sheets halfway through for even baking. • Transfer to racks to cool. • Melt the semisweet and white chocolate separately in double boilers over barely simmering water. • Spoon the chocolates into separate small freezer bags and cut off tiny corners. • Drizzle over the cookies in a decorative manner. • Let stand for 30 minutes until set.

Makes 18–20 cookies · Prep: 30 min. + 30 min. to set · Cooking: 12–15 min. · Level: 1 · Keeps: 5 days

spiced clove cookies

These spiced, crunchy cookies, baked in a loaf and sliced, are known as Nussbrot *(nut bread) in Germany and Austria. Unglazed nut bread, cut into small cookies, is often served as a nibble with a glass of chilled white wine.*

- 1¹/₄ cups whole hazelnuts
- 1²/₃ cups all-purpose flour
- 1 teaspoon ground cinnamon
- ¹/₂ teaspoon ground cloves
- ¹/₈ teaspoon salt
- 2 large eggs + 1 egg yolk
- 1 cup granulated sugar
- Grated zest of 1 lemon
- ¹/₂ teaspoon vanilla extract

Preheat the oven to 325°F. • Spread the hazelnuts on a large baking sheet. Toast for 7 minutes, or until lightly golden. • Transfer to a large cotton kitchen towel. Fold the towel over the nuts and rub them in the towel to remove the thin inner skins. • Discard the skins and coarsely chop the nuts. • Butter a cookie sheet. • Sift the flour, cinnamon, cloves, and salt into a medium bowl. • Beat the eggs and egg yolk and sugar in a large bowl with an electric mixer at high speed until very pale and thick. • Mix in the dry ingredients, hazelnuts, lemon zest, and vanilla to form a smooth dough. • Divide the dough in half. Form the dough into two 12-inch-long logs about 1¹/₂ inches in diameter and place them 2 inches apart on the prepared sheet. • Bake for 30–40 minutes, or until firm to the touch. • Cool on the cookie sheet for 15 minutes. • Cut on the diagonal into 1¹/₂-inch slices and transfer to racks to cool completely.

Makes 16 cookies · Prep: 35 min. · Cooking: 30–40 min. · Level: 2 · Keeps: 15 days

piped strawberry thumbprints

- 2 cups all-purpose flour
- ¹/₂ teaspoon baking powder
- ¹/₂ teaspoon ground cinnamon
- ¹/₈ teaspoon salt
- ¹/₄ cup (¹/₂ stick) butter, softened
- ¹/₂ cup granulated sugar
- 2 large eggs
- ¹/₂ teaspoon vanilla extract
- ¹/₂ cup strawberry preserves

Preheat the oven to 400°F. • Butter three cookie sheets. • Sift the flour, baking powder, cinnamon, and salt into a medium bowl. • Beat the butter and sugar in a large bowl with an electric mixer at high speed until creamy. • Add the eggs and vanilla, beating until just blended. • Mix in the dry ingredients. • Fit the pastry bag with a $^1/_2$-inch plain tip. Fill the pastry bag, twist the opening tightly closed, and squeeze out 2-inch rounds, spacing 1 inch apart on the prepared cookie sheets. • Press your thumb into each cookie to make a small hollow. • Bake, one sheet at a time, for 8–10 minutes, or until just golden. • Transfer to racks to cool. • Heat the preserves in a small saucepan over low heat until liquid. • Fill each hollow with a little preserves and let stand for 20 minutes until set.

Makes 48 cookies · Prep: 25 min. + 20 min. to stand · Cooking: 8–10 min. per batch · Level: 2 · Keeps: 7 days

vanilla spritz cookies

1 cup (2 sticks) butter, softened
$^1/_2$ cup + 2 tablespoons granulated sugar
$1^1/_2$ teaspoons vanilla extract
1 large egg
2 cups all-purpose flour
$^1/_8$ teaspoon salt

Preheat the oven to 375°F. • Set out four cookie sheets. • Beat the butter and $^1/_2$ cup sugar in a large bowl with an electric mixer at high speed until creamy. • Add the vanilla and egg, beating until just blended. • Mix in the flour and salt to form a soft dough. • Insert the chosen design plate into the press by sliding it into the head and locking it in place. Press out the cookies, spacing 1 inch apart on the cookie sheets. • Sprinkle with the remaining 2 tablespoons sugar. • Bake, one sheet at a time, for 5–8 minutes, or until just golden at the edges. • Transfer to racks and let cool completely.

Makes 48 cookies · Prep: 40 min. · Cooking: 5–8 min. per batch · Level: 2 · Keeps: 7 days

chocolate–cherry spritz cookies

2 cups all-purpose flour
$^1/_4$ teaspoon salt
2 oz semisweet chocolate, coarsely chopped
$^1/_2$ cup (1 stick) butter, softened
1 cup granulated sugar
1 teaspoon vanilla extract

2 tablespoons milk
1 large egg, lightly beaten
24 candied cherries, cut in half

Preheat the oven to 350°F. • Butter four cookie sheets. • Sift the flour and salt into a medium bowl. • Melt the chocolate in a double boiler over barely simmering water. • Beat the butter and sugar in a large bowl with an electric mixer at high speed until creamy. • Add the vanilla, milk, and egg, beating until just blended. • Mix in the dry ingredients and chocolate. • Insert the chosen design plate into the press by sliding it into the head and locking in place. Press out the cookies, spacing about $1^1/_2$ inches apart on the prepared cookie sheets. • Place a cherry half into the center of each cookie. • Bake, one sheet at a time, for 8–10 minutes, or until just colored and crisp. • Transfer to racks to cool.

Makes 48 cookies · Prep: 50 min. · Cooking: 8–10 min. per batch · Level: 2 · Keeps: 7 days

piped butter s-shapes

$2^2/_3$ cups all-purpose flour
$^1/_8$ teaspoon salt
1 cup (2 sticks) butter, softened
$1^1/_4$ cups granulated sugar
3 large eggs
    Grated zest of $^1/_2$ lemon
$1^1/_4$ cups finely ground hazelnuts or almonds
5 tablespoons Vanilla Sugar (see page 341)

Sift the flour and salt into a medium bowl. • Beat the butter and granulated sugar in a large bowl with an electric mixer at high speed until creamy. • Add the eggs and lemon zest, beating until just blended. • Mix in the dry ingredients and hazelnuts to form a smooth, not sticky, dough. • Refrigerate for 30 minutes. • Set out four cookie sheets. • Fit a pastry bag with a $^1/_2$-inch round or star tip, twist the opening tightly closed, and squeeze out long strips of dough onto a sheet of parchment paper. • Cut into 3-inch lengths and press into S-shapes with your fingers. Use a long spatula to transfer to the prepared cookie sheets, spacing 2 inches apart. • Refrigerate for 1 hour. • Preheat the oven to 375°F. • Bake, one sheet at a time, for 7–10 minutes, or until golden and the edges are firm. • Cool on the sheets for 2 minutes until slightly firm. Dip in the vanilla sugar while still warm. • Transfer to racks and let cool completely.

Makes 60 cookies · Prep: 40 min. · Cooking: 7–10 min. + 90 min. to chill · Level: 2 · Keeps: 12 days

cinnamon spritz cookies

1 cup all-purpose flour
$^1/_4$ teaspoon ground cinnamon
$^1/_8$ teaspoon salt
$^1/_2$ cup (1 stick) butter, softened
$^1/_4$ package (2 oz) cream cheese, softened
$^1/_2$ cup granulated sugar
$^1/_2$ teaspoon vanilla extract
1 large egg yolk

Preheat the oven to 350°F. • Set out two cookie sheets. • Sift the flour, cinnamon, and salt into a medium bowl. • Beat the butter, cream cheese, and sugar in a large bowl with an electric mixer at high speed until creamy. • Add the vanilla and egg yolk, beating until just blended. • Mix in the dry ingredients until well blended. • Insert the chosen design plate into the press by sliding it into the head and locking in place. • Press out the cookies, spacing 1 inch apart on the cookie sheets. • Bake for 12–15 minutes, or until just golden, rotating the sheets halfway through for even baking. • Transfer to racks to cool.

Makes 34 cookies · Prep: 30 min. · Cooking: 12–15 min. · Level: 2 · Keeps: 10 days

Chocolate–cherry spritz cookies

Filled chocolate fingers

filled chocolate fingers

- 2 cups all-purpose flour
- 2 tablespoons unsweetened cocoa powder
- 1/8 teaspoon salt
- 2/3 cup butter, softened
- 1 cup granulated sugar
- 2 large eggs
- 1 cup Chocolate Buttercream or Coffee Buttercream (see page 345)

Preheat the oven to 375°F. • Butter two cookie sheets. • Sift the flour, cocoa, and salt into a large bowl. • Beat the butter and sugar in a large bowl with an electric mixer at high speed until creamy. • Add the eggs, beating until just blended. • Mix in the dry ingredients. • Fit a pastry bag with a star tip. Fill the pastry bag, twist the opening tightly closed, and pipe out 2-inch lengths, spacing 1 inch apart on the prepared cookie sheets. • Bake for 10–15 minutes, or until lightly browned, rotating the sheets halfway through for even baking. • Cool on the sheets until the cookies firm slightly. Transfer to racks and let cool completely. • Stick the cookies together in pairs with the buttercream.

Makes 20 cookies · Prep: 40 min. · Cooking: 10–15 min. · Level: 2 · Keeps: 5 days in the refrigerator

orange s-shapes

- 3/4 cup all-purpose flour
- 1/8 teaspoon salt
- 1 1/3 cups finely ground almonds
- 1 cup granulated sugar
- 1 tablespoon finely grated orange zest
- 1/2 cup (1 stick) butter, cut up
- 2 large egg whites, lightly beaten

Sift the flour and salt into a large bowl. • Stir in the ground almonds, sugar, and orange zest. • Use a pastry blender to cut in the butter until the mixture resembles fine crumbs. • Mix in the egg whites to form a stiff dough. • Divide the dough in half. Form the dough into two disks, wrap in plastic wrap, and refrigerate for 30 minutes. • Preheat the oven to 350°F. • Butter three cookie sheets. • Pinch off balls of dough the size of walnuts and shape into rounded S-shape cookies. • Use a spatula to transfer the cookies to the prepared cookie sheets, placing them 1 inch apart. • Bake, one sheet at a time, for 12–15 minutes, or until golden brown, rotating the sheets halfway through for even baking. • Transfer to racks to cool.

Makes 40 cookies · Prep: 25 min. + 30 min. to chill Cooking: 12–15 min. per batch · Level: 1 · Keeps: 10 days

butter teardrops

- 1 1/2 teaspoons active dry yeast
- 2 tablespoons granulated sugar
- 1/4 cup lukewarm water (105°–115°F)
- 1 2/3 cups all-purpose flour
- 1/8 teaspoon salt
- 1/3 cup butter, softened

Stir together the yeast, 1 tablespoon of the sugar, and water. Set aside for 10 minutes. • Sift the flour and salt into a large bowl. • Stir in the yeast mixture to make a smooth dough. • Cover with plastic wrap and let rise in a warm place for 1 hour, or until doubled in bulk. • Punch down the dough and let rise for 30 minutes more. • Preheat the oven to 350°F. • Butter three cookie sheets. • Break off small pieces of dough and form into 2 1/2-inch-long ropes, about 1/8 inch in diameter. Bend into teardrop shapes, pressing the ends together, and sprinkle with the remaining 1 tablespoon sugar. • Transfer to the prepared cookie sheets, placing 1 inch apart. • Cover with a kitchen towel and let rest for 15 minutes. • Bake, one sheet at a time, for 12–15 minutes, or until crisp and golden. • Transfer to racks to cool.

Makes 36 cookies · Prep: 30 min. + 1 hr. 45 min. to rise · Cooking: 12–15 min. per batch · Level: 2 · Keeps: 2 weeks

sweet ring cookies

- 2 cups all-purpose flour
- 1 cup granulated sugar
- 1 teaspoon baking powder
- 1 teaspoon ground cinnamon
- 1/4 teaspoon salt
  Grated zest of 1 lemon
- 3 tablespoons extra-virgin olive oil
- 1/2 teaspoon vanilla extract
- 2 large eggs

Stir together the flour, sugar, baking powder, cinnamon, salt, and lemon zest in a large bowl. • Stir in the oil and vanilla. • Add the eggs, beating until just blended. • With an electric mixer at high speed, beat the mixture until well blended. Cover with a clean kitchen cloth and let stand for 1 hour. • Preheat the oven to 400°F. • Butter and flour two cookie sheets. • Turn the dough out onto a lightly floured surface. Shape into long, thin ropes and cut into 4-inch lengths. Press the ends of each length together to form rings. • Place 1 inch apart on the prepared cookie sheets. • Bake for 20–25 minutes, or until lightly browned and firm to the touch, rotating the sheets halfway through for even baking. • Transfer to racks to cool.

Makes 20 cookies · Prep: 25 min. + 1 hr. to stand · Cooking: 20–25 min. · Level: 1 · Keeps: 2 weeks

ginger whole-wheat twists

- 1 cup all-purpose flour
- 1/2 cup whole-wheat flour
- 1 tablespoon ground ginger
- 1 teaspoon baking powder
- 1/4 teaspoon salt
- 1/2 cup (1 stick) butter, cut up
- 1/3 cup firmly packed light brown sugar
- 1/4 cup finely chopped walnuts
- 1 large egg, lightly beaten

Sift the all-purpose and whole-wheat flours, ginger, baking powder, and salt into a large bowl. • Use a pastry blender to cut in the butter until the mixture resembles coarse crumbs. • Stir in the brown sugar and walnuts. • Mix in the egg to form a smooth dough. • Cover with plastic wrap and refrigerate for 30 minutes. • Preheat the oven to 350°F. • Butter three cookie sheets. • Form tablespoons of the dough into 6-inch ropes and fold the ropes in half. • Twist the dough and place 1 1/2 inches apart on the prepared cookie sheets. • Bake, one sheet at a time, for 12–15 minutes, or until lightly browned and firm to the touch. • Transfer to racks to cool.

Makes 36–40 cookies · Prep: 30 min. + 30 min. to chill · Cooking: 12–15 min. per batch · Level: 1 · Keeps: 7 days

pine nut rings

2²/₃ cups all-purpose flour
2 teaspoons baking powder
¹/₈ teaspoon ground cinnamon
¹/₈ teaspoon salt
³/₄ cup granulated sugar
3 large eggs
¹/₃ cup butter, softened
 Grated zest of ¹/₂ lemon
2–4 tablespoons milk
2 tablespoons pine nuts

Preheat the oven to 350°F. • Butter two cookie sheets. • Sift the flour, baking powder, cinnamon, and salt into a medium bowl. • Stir in the sugar. • Use a wooden spoon to beat the eggs in a large bowl until pale and thick. • Beat in the butter and lemon zest until well blended. • Mix in the dry ingredients and enough milk to make a stiff dough. • Break off balls of dough the size of walnuts and form into 4-inch ropes. Form the ropes into rings and sprinkle with the pine nuts. • Use a spatula to transfer the cookies to the prepared cookie sheets, placing 1 inch apart. • Bake for 15–20 minutes, or until just golden, rotating the sheets halfway through for even baking. • Transfer to racks to cool.

Makes 25–30 cookies · Prep: 20 min. · Cooking: 15–20 min. · Keeps: 2 weeks

banana creams

1 cup all-purpose flour
1 cup cornstarch
1 teaspoon baking powder
¹/₈ teaspoon salt
¹/₂ cup (1 stick) butter, softened
¹/₂ cup granulated sugar
1 teaspoon banana extract or liqueur
1 large egg

Filling
2 tablespoons butter, cut up
2 tablespoons firmly packed light
 brown sugar
2 teaspoons milk
¹/₂ teaspoon banana extract or liqueur
4–6 tablespoons confectioners' sugar

Preheat the oven to 350°F. • Set out two cookie sheets. • Sift the flour, cornstarch, baking powder, and salt into a medium bowl. • Beat the butter, sugar, and banana extract in a large bowl with an electric mixer at high speed until creamy. • Add the egg, beating until just blended. • With mixer at low speed, gradually add the dry ingredients. • Form the cookie dough into 3-inch cylinders, making them slightly thicker

in the center. • Place 1 inch apart on the cookie sheets, pressing them down slightly. • Bake for 15–18 minutes, or until lightly browned, rotating the sheets halfway through for even baking. • Transfer to racks to cool. • Filling: Stir the butter, brown sugar, and milk in a small saucepan over low heat until the sugar has dissolved. • Bring to a boil for 2 minutes. Remove from the heat and add the banana extract. Beat in enough confectioners' sugar to make a stiff filling. Stick pairs of cookies together with the filling.

Makes about 20 cookies · Prep: 30 min. · Cooking: 15–18 min. · Level: 1 · Keeps: 7 days

cookie ringlets

²/₃ cup butter, softened
¹/₂ cup granulated sugar
2 large egg yolks, lightly beaten
1²/₃ cups all-purpose flour
2 tablespoons fresh orange juice

Beat the butter and sugar in a large bowl with an electric mixer at high speed until creamy. • Add 1 egg yolk, beating until just blended. • Mix in the flour and orange juice until well blended. • Divide the dough in four and form into long logs 2 inches in diameter. Wrap in plastic wrap and refrigerate for 30 minutes. • Preheat the oven to 375°F. • Butter two cookie sheets. • Discard the plastic wrap • Slice each dough log into sixteen portions and roll each portion into a 7-inch rope. • Twist the ropes together tightly in pairs and shape into rings. • Place the cookies 1 inch apart on the prepared baking sheets. • Brush with the remaining beaten egg yolk. • Bake for 10–12 minutes, or until just golden, rotating the sheets halfway through for even baking. • Transfer to racks and let cool completely.

Makes 32 cookies · Prep: 50 min. + 30 min. to chill Cooking: 10–12 min. · Level: 1 · Keeps: 5 days

sesame cookies

1 cup (2 sticks) butter, softened
1 cup granulated sugar
1 tablespoon finely grated lemon zest
2 cups all-purpose flour
¹/₈ teaspoon salt
1 large egg white, lightly beaten
2 tablespoons honey
1¹/₃ cups sesame seeds

Preheat the oven to 400°F. • Butter and flour two cookie sheets. • Beat the butter, sugar,

and lemon zest in a large bowl with an electric mixer at high speed until creamy. • With mixer at low speed, gradually beat in the flour and salt. • Mix the egg white, honey, and sesame seeds in a small bowl. • Place 2 teaspoons of the sesame mixture on a clean surface. • Scoop out 1 heaping tablespoon of dough and form into a ball about the size of a walnut. • Place over the sesame mixture and press down with your fingers until the cookie is about 3 inches in diameter. • Place the cookies, sesame seed-side up, on the prepared cookie sheets, spacing them 2 inches apart. Repeat until both mixtures are used up. • Bake for 10–15 minutes, or until golden brown, rotating the sheets halfway through for even baking. • Cool the cookies completely on the cookie sheets.

Makes 20 cookies · Prep: 30 min. · Cooking: 10–15 min. · Level: 1 · Keeps: 5 days

Banana creams

vanilla kipferl

Kipferl are crescent-shaped Austrian cookies. They are usually served with morning coffee or as a dessert.

1   cup all-purpose flour
1/2 cup (1 stick) cold butter, cut up
    Seeds of 1 vanilla pod
2/3 cup finely ground almonds
2   tablespoons Vanilla Sugar (see page 341)
4   tablespoons confectioners' sugar, to dust

Sift the flour into a large bowl. • Use a pastry blender to cut in the butter until the mixture resembles fine crumbs. • Add the vanilla seeds. • Work in the almonds and the vanilla sugar and knead to form a smooth dough. • Shape into a ball, wrap in plastic wrap, and refrigerate for 30 minutes. • Preheat the oven to 350°F. • Line two cookie sheets with parchment paper. • Cut the dough into thirty pieces and pinch each into a 3/4-inch thick crescent shape. • Place 1 1/2 inches apart on the prepared cookie sheets. • Bake for 7–10 minutes, or until firm to the touch, rotating the sheets halfway through for even baking. The kipferl should not turn brown. • Dust the cookies with the confectioners' sugar. • Cool completely on the cookie sheets.

Makes 30 cookies · Prep: 60 min. + 30 min. to chill Cooking: 7–10 min. · Level: 2 · Keeps: 10 days

convent kipferl

These cookies are a variation of the Vanilla Kipferl (above) and were originally concocted in a convent kitchen in Austria.

1 2/3 cups all-purpose flour
3/4   cup confectioners' sugar
1/4   cup unsweetened cocoa powder
1/8   teaspoon salt
2/3   cup butter, cut up
1   cup finely ground almonds
1   large egg + 1 large egg yolk, lightly beaten

Chocolate glaze
3 1/2 oz semisweet chocolate, coarsely chopped
1   teaspoon butter

Light glaze
1/4   cup fresh lemon juice + more as needed
1   tablespoon kirsch or white rum (optional)
1 1/3 cups confectioners' sugar

Sift the flour, confectioners' sugar, cocoa, and salt into a large bowl. • Use a pastry blender to cut in the butter until the mixture resembles fine crumbs. • Stir in the almonds. • Mix in the egg and egg yolk to form a stiff

dough. • Divide the dough in four. Press the dough into three disks, wrap in plastic wrap, and refrigerate for 30 minutes. • Preheat the oven to 375°F. • Line four cookie sheets with parchment paper. • Divide the dough into forty-five pieces. Pinch each piece into a 1/2-inch crescent shape and place 1 inch apart on the prepared cookie sheets. • Bake, one sheet at a time, for 10–12 minutes, or until pale golden. • Transfer to racks to cool. • Chocolate glaze: Melt the chocolate with the butter in a double boiler over barely simmering water. • Spread the chocolate glaze over half of the cookies and let stand for 30 minutes until set. • Light glaze: Beat the lemon juice and kirsch in a small bowl until well blended. • Mix in the confectioners' sugar to form a spreadable glaze. • Spread over the remaining cookies and let stand for 30 minutes until set.

Makes 45 cookies · Prep: 50 min. + 60 min. to chill and set · Cooking: 12–15 min. per batch · Level: 2 · Keeps: 10 days

bretzels

These German cookies are the softer equivalents of the more famous pretzels that are eaten all over the world.

1/2   cup (1 stick) butter, softened
1/4   cup firmly packed light brown sugar
1/4   teaspoon almond extract
1   large egg, lightly beaten
1/2   cup finely ground almonds
1 1/4 cups all-purpose flour
1/8   teaspoon salt

Preheat the oven to 425°F. • Butter two cookie sheets. • Beat the butter and brown sugar in a large bowl with an electric mixer at high speed until creamy. • Add the almond extract and three-quarters of the egg, beating until just blended. • Mix in the almonds, flour, and salt to make a stiff dough. • Divide the dough into eighteen portions. • Form each portion into an 8-inch long rope. • Shape each rope into a figure-of-eight and place 1 inch apart on the prepared cookie sheets. Brush with the remaining egg. • Bake for 12–15 minutes, or until lightly browned, rotating the sheets halfway through for even baking. • Transfer to racks and let cool completely.

Makes 18 cookies · Prep: 40 min. · Cooking: 12–15 min. · Level: 2 · Keeps: 7 days

chocolate pretzels

18–20 Sugar Pretzels (see page 203)
4   oz semisweet chocolate, coarsely chopped

Melt the chocolate in a double boiler over barely simmering water. • Dip one half of each pretzel into the melted chocolate. Set aside to dry on parchment paper.

Makes 18–20 pretzels · Prep: 10 min. · Level: 1 · Keeps: 14 days

glazed pretzels

18–20 Sugar Pretzels (see page 203)

Glaze
1   large egg, lightly beaten
2   tablespoons almonds, coarsely chopped
1   tablespoon granulated sugar
2   tablespoons sugar crystals

Prepare the sugar pretzels, following the instructions on page 203 to the stage that the pretzels have been shaped and are ready to bake. • Refrigerate for at least 1 hour, or until firm. Glaze: Brush with the beaten egg and sprinkle with the almonds, granulated sugar, and sugar crystals. • Bake for 12–15 minutes, or until golden brown. • Transfer to racks to cool.

Makes 18–20 pretzels · Prep: 60 min. + 60 min. to chill · Cooking: 12–15 min. · Level: 2 · Keeps: 14 days

chocolate crescents

1 1/3 cups finely chopped almonds
5   oz semisweet chocolate, coarsely chopped
2/3   cup butter
1 1/4 cups granulated sugar

Preheat the oven to 375°F. • Butter a cookie sheet. • Toast the almonds on a baking sheet for 5–7 minutes, or until lightly golden. • Melt the chocolate and butter in a double boiler over barely simmering water. • Transfer to a large bowl and mix in the sugar and almonds. • Cool for 15 minutes. • Form teaspoons of the dough into crescent shapes and place 1 inch apart on the prepared cookie sheet. • Bake for 15–20 minutes, or until firm to the touch. • Cool on the sheet until the cookies firm slightly. • Transfer to racks to finish cooling.

Makes 15–20 cookies · Prep: 25 min. · Cooking: 15–20 min. · Level: 1 · Keeps: 4 days

Sugar pretzels (see page 203) and Chocolate pretzels

apricot-chocolate pretzels

1   cup finely chopped dried apricots
1/3   cup fresh orange juice
1   tablespoon + 1/4 cup (1/2 stick) butter
1 1/3 cups all-purpose flour
1   teaspoon baking powder
1/4   teaspoon salt
1/4   cup granulated sugar
2   large egg yolks, lightly beaten
2   oz semisweet chocolate, finely grated

Preheat the oven to 350°F. • Line three cookie sheets with parchment paper. • Mix the apricots, orange juice, and 1 tablespoon butter in a small saucepan. Cook over low heat for 5 minutes, or until the apricots have softened. • Let cool completely. • Sift the flour, baking powder, and salt into a large bowl. Stir in the sugar. • Use a pastry blender to cut in the remaining 1/4 cup butter until the mixture resembles fine crumbs. • Add the egg yolks, chocolate, and apricot mixture to make a stiff dough. • Form tablespoons of the dough into 6-inch ropes. • Make each rope into a pretzel shape by twisting the two ends around each other, then bringing both back near to the center of the strip, about 1 inch apart. • Use a spatula to transfer the cookies to the cookie sheet, spacing 1 inch apart. • Bake, one sheet at a time, for 12–15 minutes, or until just golden. • Transfer to racks to cool.

Makes 35–40 cookies · Prep: 45 min. · Cooking: 12–15 min. per batch · Level: 2 · Keeps: 5 days

danish almond cookies

1   cup all-purpose flour
1/8   teaspoon salt
1/2   cup (1 stick) butter, cut up
1/4   cup granulated sugar
1/4   cup finely ground almonds
1/4   teaspoon vanilla extract
1   large egg, lightly beaten

Preheat the oven to 400°F. • Butter a cookie sheet. • Sift the flour and salt into a large bowl. • Use a pastry blender to cut in the butter until the mixture resembles fine crumbs. • Stir in the sugar and almonds. • Add the vanilla and egg, beating until just blended. • Fit a pastry bag with a 1/2-inch star tip. • Fill the pastry bag, twist the opening tightly closed, and squeeze out 2-inch rings, spacing 1 inch apart on the prepared cookie sheet. • Refrigerate for 30 minutes. • Bake for 8–10 minutes, or until just golden at the edges. • Transfer to racks to cool.

Makes 12–16 cookies · Prep: 25 min. + 30 min. to chill · Cooking: 8–10 min. · Level: 2 · Keeps: 10 days

orange-almond cookies

3   large egg whites
1/8   teaspoon salt
1 3/4 cups granulated sugar
3 1/3 cups finely ground almonds
1/4   cup orange marmalade
18   candied cherries, cut in half

Preheat the oven to 350°F. • Butter three cookie sheets. • Beat the egg whites and salt in a large bowl with an electric mixer at medium speed until soft peaks form. • With mixer at high speed, gradually add the sugar, beating until stiff, glossy peaks form. • Use a large rubber spatula to fold in the almonds. • Heat the marmalade in a small saucepan over low heat until liquid. Let cool slightly. • Carefully fold the marmalade into the batter. • Fit a pastry bag with a 1/2-inch star tip. Fill the pastry bag, twist the opening tightly closed. Squeeze out generous 1 1/2-inch stars spacing them 2 inches apart on the prepared cookie sheets. • Decorate with cherry halves. • Bake, one sheet at a time, for 10–15 minutes, or until just golden. • Transfer to racks to cool.

Makes 36 cookies · Prep: 25 min. · Cooking: 10–15 min. per batch · Level: 2 · Keeps: 5 days

mini marzipan mounds

This sweet almond delicacy is just right for Christmas day festivities.

7   oz marzipan, grated
2   large eggs
1/4   cup cornstarch
2   tablespoons superfine sugar
1   tablespoon Vanilla Sugar (see page 341)
1/4   teaspoon almond extract
4   tablespoons slivered almonds, toasted

Preheat the oven to 350°F. • Line two cookie sheets with parchment paper. • Beat the marzipan, eggs, cornstarch, superfine sugar, vanilla sugar, and almond extract in a large bowl with an electric mixer at medium speed until smooth. • Fit a pastry bag with a 3/4-inch plain tip. Fill the pastry bag, twist the opening tightly closed, and squeeze out 1 1/2-inch mounds spacing them 2 inches apart on the prepared cookie sheets. • Crush the almonds and sprinkle over the mounds. • Bake for 12–15 minutes, or until golden brown, rotating the sheets halfway through for even baking. • Cool on the cookie sheets for 15 minutes. • Transfer to racks and let cool completely.

Makes 40 cookies · Prep: 25 min. · Cooking: 12–15 min. · Level: 2 · Keeps: 10–14 days

cornmeal ribbons

1   cup all-purpose flour
1/4   teaspoon salt
2   cups finely ground yellow cornmeal
1   cup (2 sticks) butter, cut up
     Grated zest of 1/2 orange
2   large eggs + 1 large egg yolk
1   cup firmly packed light brown sugar

Preheat the oven to 375°F. • Butter three cookie sheets. • Sift the flour and salt in a large bowl. Stir in the cornmeal. • Use a pastry blender to cut in the butter until the mixture resembles fine crumbs. • Add the orange zest. • Beat the eggs and egg yolk and brown sugar in a medium bowl with an electric mixer at high speed until frothy. • Mix the beaten eggs into the dry ingredients to form a smooth, sticky dough. • Fit a pastry bag with a 1/2-inch star tip. Fill the pastry bag, twist the opening tightly closed, and squeeze out S-shaped ribbons, spacing 1 inch apart on the prepared cookie sheet. • Bake, one sheet at a time, for 15–20 minutes, or until golden brown. • Cool on the sheets until the cookies firm slightly. • Transfer to racks and let cool completely.

Makes 36–40 cookies · Prep: 35 min. · Cooking: 15–20 min. per batch · Level: 2 · Keeps: 10 days

lemon s-shapes

1 3/4 cups all-purpose flour
1/3   cup rice flour
1 1/4 teaspoons baking powder
1/8   teaspoon salt
1/4   cup (1 stick) butter, softened
3/4   cup granulated sugar
1   large egg
1   tablespoon finely grated lemon zest

Preheat the oven to 375°F. • Butter two cookie sheets. • Sift the all-purpose and rice flours, baking powder, and salt into a medium bowl. • Beat the butter and sugar in a large bowl with an electric mixer until creamy. • Add the egg and lemon zest, beating until just blended. • Mix in the dry ingredients to form a stiff dough. • Break off balls of dough the size of walnuts and shape into S-shape cookies. • Use a spatula to transfer the cookies to the prepared cookie sheets, placing them 1 inch apart. • Bake for 8–10 minutes, or until pale golden, rotating the sheets halfway through for even browning. • Transfer to racks to cool.

Makes 20–24 cookies · Prep: 25 min. · Cooking: 8–10 min. · Level: 1 · Keeps: 7 days

Cornmeal ribbons (left)
and Danish almond cookies (right)

kaffeehaus cookies

The Viennese kaffeehaus, or coffeehouse, culture thrived in the eighteenth century, when it was politic to frequent coffeehouses to be recognized as part of society. In Vienna today, coffeehouses are still the places to go to discuss poetry and philosophy alongside the art of gossip.

2/3   cup butter, softened
1/2   cup granulated sugar
1   large egg yolk, lightly beaten
12/3   cups all-purpose flour
1/8   teaspoon salt
2   tablespoons fresh orange juice

Beat the butter and sugar in a large bowl with an electric mixer at high speed until creamy. • Add the egg yolk, beating until just blended. • Mix in the flour, salt, and orange juice until well blended. • Refrigerate for 1 hour. • Preheat the oven to 375°F. • Butter two cookie sheets. • Fit a pastry bag with a 1-inch star tip. Fill the pastry bag, twist the opening tightly closed, and squeeze out four long strips on each sheet, spacing them at least 1 inch apart on the prepared cookie sheets. • Use a sharp knife to score each strip at 2 1/2-inch intervals. • Bake, one sheet at a time, for 8–10 minutes, or until just golden. • Cut up the cookies along the scored lines. • Cool on the sheet until the cookies firm slightly. • Transfer to racks to finish cooling.

Makes 36 cookies · Prep: 40 min. + 60 min. to chill · Cooking: 8–10 min. per batch · Level: 2 · Keeps: 5 days

Pineapple–almond cookies

orange–syrup spritzers

3   tablespoons all-purpose flour
1/8   teaspoon salt
11/3   cups finely ground hazelnuts
2/3   cup finely ground almonds
1   large egg, lightly beaten
1/4   cup fresh orange juice
1   tablespoon finely grated orange zest
1   tablespoon maple or corn syrup
3   tablespoons apricot preserves
2   tablespoons finely chopped pistachios or almonds

Preheat the oven to 300°F. • Line two cookie sheets with parchment paper. • Sift the flour and salt into a small bowl. • Stir the hazelnuts, almonds, and egg in a large bowl. • Mix in the orange juice, orange zest, and 1 tablespoon of maple syrup. • Gradually mix in the dry ingredients, 1 tablespoon at a time, to form a soft, smooth dough. • Fit a pastry bag with a plain 1-inch tip. Spoon half the mixture into the pastry bag and squeeze out half moons and wreaths spacing 2 inches apart on the prepared cookie sheets. • Fit a second pastry bag with an 1-inch star tip. Spoon the remaining dough into the pastry bag and squeeze out ridged moons and wreaths. • Bake for 12–15 minutes, or until lightly golden, rotating the sheets halfway through for even baking. • Transfer to racks to cool. • Warm the preserves in a small saucepan over low heat until melted. • Brush over the warm cookies and sprinkle with the chopped pistachios.

Makes 30 cookies · Prep: 30 min. · Cooking: 12–15 min. · Level: 2 · Keeps: 8 days

pineapple–almond cookies

11/4   cups finely ground almonds
2   large eggs, 1 separated
1   cup confectioners' sugar
2   tablespoons finely ground yellow cornmeal
1/3   cup butter, melted
1/2   cup pineapple chunks

Preheat the oven to 375°F. • Line a cookie sheet with parchment paper. • Mix the almonds, 1 egg white, and 3/4 cup confectioners' sugar in a large bowl. • Add the whole egg and egg yolk, beating until just blended. • Stir in the cornmeal and butter until well blended. • Fit a pastry bag with a 1/2-inch plain tip. Fill the pastry bag, twist the opening tightly closed, and squeeze out into 1-inch dots spacing 1 inch apart on the prepared cookie sheet. • Place a piece of pineapple on top of each cookie. • Dust with

the remaining 1/4 cup confectioners' sugar. • Bake for 10–12 minutes, or until lightly browned. • Transfer to racks to cool.

Makes 15 cookies · Prep: 40 min. · Cooking: 10–12 min. · Level: 2 · Keeps: 5 days

piped almond-topped cookies

11/3   cups all-purpose flour
1/8   teaspoon salt
2/3   cup butter, softened
1/3   cup granulated sugar
1   large egg white
    Grated zest of 1 lemon
1/2   teaspoon vanilla extract
24–26   whole almonds

Preheat the oven to 350°F. • Butter two cookie sheets. • Sift the flour and salt into a medium bowl. • Beat the butter and sugar in a large bowl with an electric mixer at high speed until creamy. • Add the egg white, lemon zest, and vanilla, beating until just blended. • Mix in the dry ingredients. • Fit a pastry bag with a 1/2-inch star tip. Fill the pastry bag and twist the opening tightly closed. Squeeze out 1 1/2-inch wide heaps, dragging the cookies forward to finish in a thin point, spacing 2 inches apart on the prepared cookie sheets. • Press an almond onto the thin point of the cookie. • Bake for 15–20 minutes, or until just golden, rotating the sheets halfway for even baking. • Cool on the sheets until the cookies firm slightly. Transfer to racks to finish cooling.

Makes 24–26 cookies · Prep: 25 min. · Cooking: 15–20 min. · Level: 2 · Keeps: 10 days

naples cookies

In the 18th and 19th centuries, these cookies were the standard accompaniment to trifles and other sweet dishes.

3/4   cup all-purpose flour
1/8   teaspoon salt
3   large eggs, separated
1/3   cup confectioners' sugar
1/4   teaspoon rose water

Preheat the oven to 350°F. • Line two cookie sheets with parchment paper. • Sift the flour and salt into a large bowl. • Beat the egg whites in a large bowl with an electric mixer at medium speed until soft peaks form. • With mixer at high speed, gradually add the confectioners' sugar, beating until stiff, glossy peaks form. • With mixer at medium speed, beat the egg yolks and rose water in a medium bowl until well blended. • Use a large rubber spatula to fold the beaten yolks into the beaten whites. • Fold in the dry ingredients. • Fit a pastry bag with a $^1/_2$-inch plain tip. Fill the pastry bag, twist the opening tightly closed, and squeeze out 3-inch fingers, spacing 2 inches apart on the prepared cookie sheets. • Bake for 8–10 minutes, or until lightly browned, rotating the sheets halfway through for even baking. • Cool on the sheets until the cookies firm slightly. • Transfer to racks and let cool completely.

Makes 24–30 cookies · Prep: 25 min. · Cooking: 8–10 min. · Level: 2 · Keeps: 7 days

coconut spritzers

3$^1/_3$	cups all-purpose flour
$^1/_8$	teaspoon salt
1	cup (2 sticks) butter, softened
1$^1/_4$	cups granulated sugar
1	large egg
$^1/_2$	teaspoon vanilla extract
	Grated zest of 1 lemon
7	oz semisweet chocolate, coarsely chopped
$^3/_4$	cup shredded coconut

Preheat the oven to 325°F. • Butter four cookie sheets. • Sift the flour and salt into a medium bowl. • Beat the butter and sugar in a large bowl with an electric mixer at high speed until creamy. • Add the egg and vanilla, beating until just blended. • Mix in the dry ingredients and lemon zest to form a stiff dough. • Insert the chosen design plate into a cookie press by sliding it into the head and locking in place. Press out the cookies, spacing about 1 inch apart on the prepared cookie sheets. • Bake, one sheet at a time, for 10–15 minutes, or until golden brown. • Transfer to racks to cool. • Melt the chocolate in a double boiler over barely simmering water. • Spread the melted chocolate over the tops of the cookies and sprinkle with the coconut. Let stand for 30 minutes until set.

Makes 60–70 cookies · Prep: 40 min. + 30 min. to set · Cooking: 10–15 min. per batch · Level: 2 · Keeps: 10 days, layered between parchment paper

honey whole-wheat cookies

1$^1/_4$	cups whole-wheat flour
$^1/_2$	teaspoon baking powder
$^1/_8$	teaspoon salt
2	tablespoons honey
$^1/_3$	cup extra-virgin olive oil
$^1/_2$	teaspoon vanilla extract
1	large egg
1–2	tablespoons milk (optional)
$^1/_3$	cup confectioners' sugar

Preheat the oven to 350°F. • Butter two cookie sheets. • Sift the flour, baking powder, and salt into a medium bowl. • Mix the honey and olive oil in a large bowl until well blended. • Add the vanilla and egg, beating until just blended. • Mix in the dry ingredients to form a soft dough. • If the dough is stiff, add the milk. • Fit a pastry bag with $^1/_2$-inch star tip. Fill the pastry bag, twist the opening tightly closed, and squeeze out small heaps, spacing 2 inches apart on the prepared cookie sheet. • Bake for 15–20 minutes, or until lightly browned, rotating the sheets halfway through for even baking. • Transfer to racks to cool. • Dust with the confectioners' sugar.

Makes 28 cookies · Prep: 25 min. · Cooking: 15–20 min. · Level: 2 · Keeps: 5 days

curly cinnamon ducks

2	cups all-purpose flour
1	teaspoon baking powder
1	teaspoon ground cinnamon
$^1/_8$	teaspoon salt
$^3/_4$	cup (1$^1/_2$ sticks) butter, softened
1	cup firmly packed light brown sugar
1	large egg

Cinnamon glaze
1	tablespoon granulated sugar
$^1/_2$	teaspoon ground cinnamon
1	large egg white, lightly beaten
40–45	miniature chocolate chips or currants
40–45	sunflower or pumpkin seeds

Sift the flour, baking powder, cinnamon, and salt into a medium bowl. • Beat the butter and brown sugar in a large bowl with an electric mixer at high speed until creamy. • Add the egg, beating until just blended. • Mix in the dry ingredients to form a smooth dough. • Divide the dough in half. • Form the dough into 12-inch logs, wrap in plastic wrap, and refrigerate for 30 minutes. • Preheat the oven to 375°F. • Line three cookie sheets with parchment paper. • Discard the plastic wrap. • Slice the dough $^1/_2$-inch thick. • Roll each slice into a 6-inch rope. • Coil the rope halfway into a spiral shape, with one end forming the duck's head. Coil the remaining length of the rope in the opposite direction to form a larger spiral for the body. • Use a spatula to transfer the cookies to the prepared cookie sheets, placing them 2 inches apart. • Cinnamon glaze: Mix the sugar and cinnamon in a small bowl. • Brush the cookies with egg white and sprinkle with the cinnamon sugar. • Stick a chocolate chip into each head to

resemble an eye and a sunflower seed to resemble a beak. • Bake, one sheet at a time, for 5–8 minutes, or until golden brown and firm to the touch. • Transfer on the parchment paper to racks to cool completely.

Makes 40–45 cookies · Prep: 30 min. + 30 min. to chill · Cooking: 6–8 min. per batch · Level: 2 · Keeps: 2 weeks in an airtight container

spiced piped cookies

1$^1/_2$	cups all-purpose flour
1	teaspoon ground cinnamon
$^1/_2$	teaspoon baking powder
$^1/_2$	teaspoon ground nutmeg
$^1/_2$	teaspoon ground ginger
$^1/_2$	teaspoon ground cardamom
$^1/_4$	teaspoon freshly ground black pepper
$^1/_8$	teaspoon salt
$^1/_3$	cup vegetable shortening
$^1/_3$	cup granulated sugar
$^1/_3$	cup dark molasses
1	large egg
2	tablespoons distilled white vinegar

Preheat the oven to 350°F. • Butter a cookie sheet. • Sift the flour, cinnamon, baking powder, nutmeg, ginger, cardamom, pepper, and salt into a medium bowl. • Beat the shortening and sugar in a large bowl with an electric mixer at high speed until creamy. • Add the molasses, egg, and vinegar, beating until just blended. • Mix in the dry ingredients. • Fit a pastry bag with a $^1/_4$-inch plain tip. Fill the pastry bag, twist the opening tightly closed, and squeeze out small rounds, spacing 2 inches apart on the prepared cookie sheet. • Bake for 8–10 minutes, or until firm to the touch. • Transfer to racks to cool.

Makes 12–15 cookies · Prep: 25 min. · Cooking: 8–10 min. · Level: 2 · Keeps: 5 days

Spiced piped cookies

marzipan arches

7	oz marzipan, diced and softened
2	large eggs
2	tablespoons superfine sugar
1	tablespoon Vanilla Sugar (see page 341)
1/3	cup cornstarch
1/2	teaspoon baking powder
1/4	teaspoon almond extract
1/8	teaspoon salt
1/2	cup slivered almonds, toasted and coarsely chopped

Preheat the oven to 350°F. • Line two cookie sheets with parchment paper. • Beat the marzipan, eggs, superfine and vanilla sugars, cornstarch, baking powder, almond extract, and salt in a large bowl with an electric mixer at low speed until smooth. • Fit a pastry bag with a plain 1/4-inch tip. Fill the pastry bag, twist the opening tightly closed, and squeeze about forty small arches spacing them 1 inch apart on the prepared cookie sheets. Sprinkle with the almonds, pressing them lightly into the tops. • Bake for 12–15 minutes, or until golden brown, rotating the sheets halfway through for even baking. • Cool the cookies on the sheet for 5 minutes. • Transfer to racks and let cool completely.

Makes 40 cookies · Prep: 50 min. · Cooking: 12–15 min. · Level: 1 · Keeps: 5 days

savoy fingers

These sugar-dusted ladyfingers are a variation on those served for afternoon tea at one of London's most exclusive hotels.

2/3	cup all-purpose flour
1/8	teaspoon salt
3	large eggs
1/2	cup + 2 tablespoons superfine sugar
1/2	teaspoon vanilla extract

Preheat the oven to 325°F. • Line two cookie sheets with parchment paper. • Sift the flour and salt into a medium bowl. • Beat the eggs, 1/2 cup superfine sugar, and vanilla in a double boiler over barely simmering water. Beat until the batter falls off the beaters in ribbons. • Use a large rubber spatula to fold in the dry ingredients. • Fit a pastry bag with a 1/2-inch star tip. Fill the pastry bag, twist the opening tightly closed, and squeeze out 3 x 3/4-inch lengths spacing them 1 inch apart on the prepared cookie sheets. • Sprinkle with the remaining 2 tablespoons superfine sugar. • Bake for 10–15 minutes, or until

crisp and dry to the touch, rotating the sheets halfway through for even baking. • Cool on the sheets until the cookies firm slightly. • Transfer to racks to finish cooling.

Makes 30–35 fingers · Prep: 30 min. · Cooking: 10–15 min. · Level: 2 · Keeps: 7 days

aniseed rounds

1/2	cup all-purpose flour
2	tablespoons cornstarch
1	tablespoon ground aniseeds
2	large eggs
1/2	cup granulated sugar
1/4	teaspoon salt
1	teaspoon water

Line two cookie sheets with parchment paper. • Sift the flour, cornstarch, and aniseed into a large bowl. • Beat the eggs, sugar, and salt in a double boiler over barely simmering water with an electric mixer at high speed until pale and thick. Remove from the heat and continue beating until the mixture has cooled. • Use a large rubber spatula to fold the dry ingredients into the batter, followed by the water. • Fit a pastry bag with a 1/4-inch plain tip. Fill the pastry bag, twist the opening tightly closed, and squeeze about 3/4 inch round cookies, spacing 1 1/2 inches apart on the prepared cookie sheets. • Set aside, covered, at room temperature for about 12 hours, or until a thin crust has formed. • Preheat the oven to 275°F. • Bake for 25–30 minutes, or until lightly browned, rotating the sheets halfway through for even baking. • Transfer to racks to cool.

Makes 20–25 cookies · Prep: 60 min. + 12 hr. to rest Cooking: 25–30 min. · Level: 2 · Keeps: 5–7 days

chocolate-dipped lime cookies

1/4	cup all-purpose flour
1/4	cup cornstarch
1/4	teaspoon baking powder
1/2	cup (1 stick) butter, softened
1/3	cup confectioners' sugar
1	large egg, separated
	Grated zest of 1 lime
1	tablespoon fresh lime juice
1/2	teaspoon vanilla extract
1/8	teaspoon salt
4	oz semisweet chocolate, coarsely chopped
2	tablespoons finely chopped pistachios

Preheat the oven to 350°F. • Butter two cookie sheets. • Sift the flour, cornstarch, and baking powder into a medium bowl. •

Beat the butter and confectioners' sugar in a large bowl with an electric mixer at high speed until creamy. • Add the egg yolk, lime zest and lime juice, and vanilla, beating until just blended. • Mix in the dry ingredients. • Beat the egg whites and salt in a large bowl with an electric mixer at high speed until stiff peaks form. • Use a large rubber spatula to fold the beaten whites into the lime mixture. • Fit a pastry bag with a 1/2-inch plain tip. Fill the pastry bag, twist the opening tightly closed, and squeeze out 2-inch lines, spacing 1 inch apart on the prepared cookie sheets. • Bake for 8–10 minutes, or until just golden, rotating the sheets halfway through for even baking. • Cool on the sheets until the cookies firm slightly. • Transfer to racks to cool. • Melt the chocolate in a double boiler over barely simmering water. • Dip the cookies halfway in the chocolate, sprinkle with the pistachios, and let stand on parchment paper for 30 minutes until set.

Makes 30 cookies · Prep: 25 min. + 30 min. to set · Cooking: 8–10 min. · Level: 2 · Keeps: 7 days

orange–hazelnut cookies

3	large egg whites
1/8	teaspoon salt
1 3/4	cups granulated sugar
3 1/3	cups finely ground hazelnuts
1/4	cup orange marmalade
18	candied cherries, cut in half

Preheat the oven to 350°F. • Butter three cookie sheets. • Beat the egg whites and salt in a large bowl with an electric mixer at medium speed until soft peaks form. • With mixer at high speed, gradually add the sugar, beating until stiff, glossy peaks form. • Fold in the hazelnuts. • Heat the marmalade in a small saucepan over low heat until liquid. Let cool slightly. • Carefully fold the marmalade into the batter. • Fit a pastry bag with a 1/2-inch star tip. Fill the pastry bag, twist the opening tightly closed. Squeeze out generous 1 1/2-inch stars spacing 2 inches apart on the prepared cookie sheets. • Decorate with cherry halves. • Bake, one sheet at a time, for 10–15 minutes, or until just golden. • Transfer to racks to cool.

Makes 36 cookies · Prep: 25 min. · Cooking: 10–15 min. per batch · Level: 2 · Keeps: 5 days

Chocolate-dipped lime cookies

candied spritzers

3¹/₃ cups all-purpose flour
2 teaspoons baking powder
¹/₈ teaspoon salt
1 cup (2 sticks) butter, softened
1¹/₄ cups granulated sugar
1 tablespoon Vanilla Sugar (see page 341)
3 large egg yolks
¹/₂ teaspoon vanilla extract
1 tablespoon grated lemon or orange zest
1 tablespoon milk, + more as needed
1–2 tablespoons very finely chopped candied orange, lemon, or lime peel, to decorate
7 oz semisweet chocolate, coarsely chopped
6 tablespoons coarsely chopped pistachios

Preheat the oven to 350°F. • Butter four cookie sheets. • Sift the flour, baking powder, and salt into a medium bowl. • Beat the butter and granulated and vanilla sugars in a large bowl with an electric mixer at high speed until creamy. • Add the egg yolks and vanilla, beating until just blended. • Mix in the dry ingredients, lemon zest, and enough milk to form a soft dough. • Insert a design plate into a cookie press by sliding it into the head and locking in place. Press out the cookies, spacing about 1 inch apart on the prepared cookie sheets. • Decorate the tops of the cookies with candied peel. • Bake, one sheet at a time, for 10–15 minutes, or until golden and firm at the edges. • Transfer to

Candied spritzers

racks to cool. • Melt the chocolate in a double boiler over barely simmering water. • Dip the cookies halfway into the chocolate and sprinkle with pistachios. Let stand for 30 minutes until set.

Makes 60–70 cookies · Prep: 35 min. + 30 min. to set · Cooking: 10–15 min. per batch · Level: 2 · Keeps: 2 weeks, layered between parchment paper

almond spritz cookies

1 cup (2 sticks) butter, softened
¹/₂ cup + 2 tablespoons granulated sugar
1¹/₂ teaspoons almond extract
1 large egg
2 cups all-purpose flour
¹/₈ teaspoon salt

Preheat the oven to 375°F. • Set out four cookie sheets. • Beat the butter and ¹/₂ cup sugar in a large bowl with an electric mixer at high speed until creamy. • Add the almond extract and egg, beating until just blended. • Mix in the flour and salt to form a soft dough. • Insert the chosen design plate into the press by sliding it into the head and locking it in place. Press out the cookies, spacing 1 inch apart on the cookie sheets. • Sprinkle with the remaining 2 tablespoons sugar. • Bake, one sheet at a time, for 5–8 minutes, or until just golden at the edges. • Transfer to racks to cool.

Makes 48 cookies · Prep: 40 min. · Cooking: 5–8 min. per batch · Level: 2 · Keeps: 7 days

chocolate angelica spritz cookies

2 cups all-purpose flour
¹/₄ teaspoon salt
2 oz semisweet chocolate, coarsely chopped
¹/₂ cup (1 stick) butter, softened
1 cup granulated sugar
1 teaspoon vanilla extract
2 tablespoons milk
1 large egg, lightly beaten
2 tablespoons chopped angelica

Preheat the oven to 350°F. • Butter four cookie sheets. • Sift the flour and salt into a medium bowl. • Melt the chocolate in a double boiler over barely simmering water. • Beat the butter and sugar in a large bowl with an electric mixer at high speed until creamy. • Add the vanilla, milk, and egg, beating until just blended. • Mix in the dry ingredients and chocolate. • Insert the chosen design plate into the press by sliding it into the head and locking in place. Press

out the cookies, spacing about 1¹/₂ inches apart on the prepared cookie sheets. • Place a piece of angelica into the center of each cookie. • Bake, one sheet at a time, for 8–10 minutes, or until just colored and crisp. • Transfer to racks to cool.

Makes 48 cookies · Prep: 50 min. · Cooking: 8–10 min. per batch · Level: 2 · Keeps: 7 days

red wine cookies

Use a full-bodied red wine to make these cookies.

2¹/₄ cups all-purpose flour
2 teaspoons baking powder
¹/₄ teaspoon salt
¹/₄ cup granulated sugar
¹/₂ cup vegetable oil
¹/₂ cup full-bodied red wine

Preheat the oven to 350°F. • Butter two cookie sheets. • Sift the flour, baking powder, and salt into a large bowl. • Stir in the sugar, oil, and wine to form a stiff dough. • Divide the dough into twenty portions. Form each piece into a 5-inch rope and bend into a ring, pinching the ends firmly together. • Use a spatula to transfer the cookies to the prepared cookie sheets, placing 2 inches apart. • Bake for 15–20 minutes, or until firm to the touch, rotating the sheets halfway through for even baking. • Reduce the oven temperature to 300°F. • Bake for 15–20 minutes more, or until golden and toasted. • Transfer to racks to cool.

Makes 20–24 cookies · Prep: 25 min. · Cooking: 30–40 min. · Level: 2 · Keeps: 2 weeks

butter cookies with orange glaze

Butter cookies
1 cup all-purpose flour
¹/₈ teaspoon salt
¹/₃ cup butter, softened
¹/₄ cup granulated sugar
1 large egg yolk, lightly beaten
2 tablespoons sour cream
¹/₄ teaspoon almond extract

Orange glaze
3 tablespoons confectioners' sugar
1 tablespoon fresh orange juice
¹/₄ cup apricot preserves

Butter cookies: Preheat the oven to 375°F. • Set out two cookie sheets. • Sift the flour and salt into a medium bowl. • Beat the butter and sugar in a large bowl with an electric mixer at high speed until creamy. •

Add the egg yolk, beating until just blended. • Beat in the sour cream and almond extract. • Mix in the dry ingredients to form a smooth dough. • Insert a Christmas tree design plate into a cookie press by sliding it into the head and locking in place. Press out the cookies, spacing about $1/2$ inch apart on the cookie sheets. • Bake for 8–10 minutes, or until lightly browned, rotating the sheets halfway through for even baking. • <u>Orange glaze</u>: Mix the confectioners' sugar and orange juice in a small bowl. • Warm the apricot preserves in a small saucepan over low heat until liquid. • Brush the cookies with a little preserves, followed by the orange glaze. • Bake for 5 minutes more, or until the glaze begins to crystallize. • Cool on the sheets until the cookies firm slightly. • Transfer to racks to finish cooling.

Makes 27 cookies · Prep: 45 min. · Cooking: 13–15 min. · Level: 2 · Keeps: 7 days

muesli rosettes

2	large egg whites
$1/8$	teaspoon salt
$3/4$	cup granulated sugar
1	teaspoon Vanilla Sugar (see page 341)
1	tablespoon all-purpose flour
2	teaspoons cornstarch
$1/2$	cup fine oat flakes or wheat flakes
	Finely chopped dates, nuts, and dried fruit (muesli or granola)

Preheat the oven to 275°F. • Line two cookie sheets with parchment or rice paper. • Beat the egg whites and salt in a large bowl with an electric mixer at medium speed until frothy. With mixer at high speed, gradually beat in the granulated and vanilla sugars, beating until stiff, glossy peaks form. • Mix in the flour, cornstarch, and oat flakes. • Fit a pastry bag with an 1-inch tip. Fill the pastry bag, twist the opening tightly closed, and squeeze out small rounds spacing them 1 inch apart on the prepared cookie sheets. • Sprinkle with the dates, nuts, and dried fruit. • Bake for 20–25 minutes, or until lightly golden, rotating the sheets halfway through for even baking. • Transfer on the parchment paper to racks and let cool completely.

Makes 20–25 cookies · Prep: 15 min. · Cooking: 20–25 min. · Level: 1 · Keeps: 3 days

peach–hazelnut cookies

$1^{1}/4$	cups finely ground hazelnuts
2	large eggs, 1 separated
1	cup confectioners' sugar
2	tablespoons all-purpose flour
$1/3$	cup butter, melted
$1/2$	cup finely chopped canned peaches

Preheat the oven to 375°F. • Line a cookie sheet with parchment paper. • Mix the hazelnuts, 1 egg white, and $3/4$ cup confectioners' sugar in a large bowl. • Add the whole egg and egg yolk, beating until just blended. • Stir in the flour and butter until well blended. • Fit a pastry bag with a $1/2$-inch plain tip. Fill the pastry bag, twist the opening tightly closed, and squeeze out into 1-inch dots spacing them 1 inch apart on the prepared cookie sheet. • Arrange a piece of peach on top of each cookie. • Sprinkle with the remaining $1/4$ cup confectioners' sugar. • Bake for 10–12 minutes, or until lightly browned. • Transfer to racks to cool.

Makes 15 cookies · Prep: 40 min. · Cooking: 10–12 min. · Level: 2 · Keeps: 2 days

nutmeg spritz cookies

1	cup all-purpose flour
$1/4$	teaspoon freshly grated nutmeg
$1/8$	teaspoon salt
$1/2$	cup (1 stick) butter, softened
$1/4$	package (2 oz) cream cheese, softened
$1/2$	cup granulated sugar
$1/2$	teaspoon almond extract
1	large egg yolk

Preheat the oven to 350°F. • Set out two cookie sheets. • Sift the flour, nutmeg, and salt into a medium bowl. • Beat the butter, cream cheese, and sugar in a large bowl with an electric mixer at high speed until creamy. • Add the almond extract and egg yolk, beating until just blended. • Mix in the dry ingredients until well blended. • Insert the chosen design plate into the press by sliding it into the head and locking in place. • Press out the cookies, spacing 1 inch apart on the cookie sheets. • Bake for 12–15 minutes, or until just golden, rotating the sheets halfway through for even baking. • Transfer to racks to cool.

Makes 34 cookies · Prep: 30 min. · Cooking: 12–15 min. · Level: 2 · Keeps: 10 days

aniseed puffs

3	cups all-purpose flour
$1/8$	teaspoon salt
4	large eggs
$1^{1}/2$	cups granulated sugar
$1/8$	teaspoon anisette
	Grated zest of 1 lemon
1	tablespoon aniseeds

Butter four cookie sheets. • Sift the flour and salt into a medium bowl. • Beat the eggs and sugar in a large bowl with an electric mixer at high speed until pale and very thick. • Beat in the anisette, lemon zest, and aniseeds. • Mix in the dry ingredients. • Fit a pastry bag with a $1/4$-inch plain tip. Fill the pastry bag, twist the opening tightly closed, and squeeze out 1-inch mounds spacing 2 inches apart onto the prepared cookie sheets. • Set aside for 12 hours. • Preheat the oven to 300°F. • Bake, one sheet at a time, for 15–20 minutes, or until puffed and just golden. • Transfer to racks and let cool completely.

Makes 48 cookies · Prep: 40 min. + 12 hr. to rest Cooking: 15–20 min. per batch · Level: 2 · Keeps: 7 days

Aniseed puffs

koulourakias

These Greek aniseed cookies are perfect when served with a cup of strong black coffee. Aniseed has been used in Greece since the 4th century B.C.

1^1/3 cups all-purpose flour
1   teaspoon baking powder
^{1}/8 teaspoon salt
^{1}/2 cup (1 stick) butter, softened
^{1}/2 cup granulated sugar
1   teaspoon ground aniseeds
1   teaspoon finely grated lemon zest
1   large egg + 1 large egg yolk + 1 large
       egg white
2   tablespoons + 1 teaspoon milk
4   tablespoons sesame seeds

Sift the flour, baking powder, and salt into a medium bowl. • Beat the butter and sugar in a large bowl with an electric mixer at high speed until creamy. • Add the aniseeds and lemon zest. • With mixer at high speed, beat the whole egg and egg yolk and 2 tablespoons milk until frothy in a large bowl. • Beat the egg mixture into the batter. • Mix in the dry ingredients to form a smooth dough. • Divide the dough in half. • Form into 8-inch logs, wrap in plastic wrap, and refrigerate for at least 30 minutes. • Preheat the oven to 375°F. • Line two cookie sheets with parchment paper. • Discard the plastic wrap. • Slice the dough ^{1}/2 inch thick. • Roll each slice into a 6-inch log and form into an S-shape, flattening it slightly. • Place the cookies 1 inch apart on the prepared cookie sheets. • Mix the egg white and remaining 1 teaspoon milk in a small bowl. • Brush over the cookies and sprinkle with sesame seeds. • Bake for

8–10 minutes, or until just golden at the edges, rotating the sheets halfway through for even baking. • Transfer to racks and let cool completely.

Makes 32 cookies · Prep: 40 min. + 30 min. to chill
Cooking: 8–10 min. · Level: 2 · Keeps: 10 days

s-shaped cookies

1^2/3 cups all-purpose flour
3   large egg yolks
^{1}/2 cup (1 stick) butter, softened
^{2}/3 cup granulated sugar
^{1}/8 teaspoon salt
Lemon glaze
1   cup confectioners' sugar
4–5 tablespoons fresh lemon juice
1^1/2 teaspoons finely grated lemon zest

Use a wooden spoon to mix the flour, egg yolks, butter, sugar, and salt in a large bowl to form a smooth dough. • Press the dough into a disk, wrap in plastic wrap, and refrigerate for 30 minutes. • Preheat the oven to 350°F. • Butter two cookie sheets. • Form the dough into 1-inch long logs and place 1 inch apart on the prepared cookie sheets. • Shape the logs into S-shapes. • Bake for 8–10 minutes, or until just golden, rotating the sheets halfway through for even baking. • Lemon glaze: Put the confectioners' sugar in a medium bowl. Beat in 4 tablespoons lemon juice and zest until smooth, adding the additional tablespoon of lemon juice as needed to make a good spreading consistency. • Drizzle the glaze over the cookies.

Makes 25 cookies · Prep: 35 min. + 30 min. to chill
Cooking: 8–10 min. · Level: 1 · Keeps: 5 days

white chocolate-coated pretzels

2   cups all-purpose flour
^{1}/4 cup unsweetened cocoa powder
1   teaspoon baking powder
^{1}/2 teaspoon salt
^{3}/4 cup (1^1/2 sticks) butter, softened
1   cup granulated sugar
1   large egg
^{1}/2 teaspoon almond extract
^{1}/2 cup finely ground almonds
8   oz white chocolate, coarsely chopped

Sift the flour, cocoa, baking powder, and salt into a medium bowl. • Beat the butter and sugar in a large bowl with an electric mixer at high speed until creamy. • Add the egg and almond extract, beating until just blended. • Mix in the dry ingredients and almonds to form a smooth dough. • Divide the dough in half. Press the dough into disks, wrap each in plastic wrap, and refrigerate for 30 minutes. • Preheat the oven to 350°F. • Butter two cookie sheets. • Form the dough into 1^1/2-inch balls and roll each into a 12-inch rope. • Make each rope into a pretzel shape by twisting the two ends around each other, then bringing both back near to the center of the strip, about 1 inch apart. • Place on the prepared cookie sheets, spacing 1 inch apart. • Bake for 10–12 minutes, or until golden brown, rotating the sheets halfway through to ensure even baking. • Transfer to racks to cool. • Melt the white chocolate in a double boiler over barely simmering water. • Dip the cookies halfway into the chocolate and let stand for 30 minutes until set.

Makes 20–25 cookies · Prep: 40 min. + 1 hr. to chill and set · Cooking: 10–12 min. · Level: 2 · Keeps: 7 days

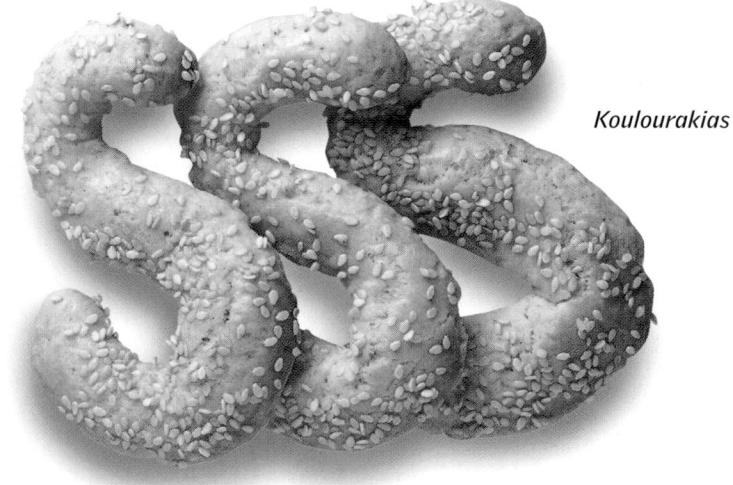

Koulourakias

lemon–vanilla rings

3¹/₃ cups all-purpose flour
³/₄ cup granulated sugar
2 large eggs
¹/₂ cup milk
1 teaspoon vanilla extract
¹/₃ cup butter, softened
Grated zest of 1 lemon
¹/₈ teaspoon salt

Preheat the oven to 350°F. • Line three cookie sheets with parchment paper. • Use a wooden spoon to mix the flour, sugar, eggs, milk, vanilla, butter, lemon zest, and salt in a large bowl to make a smooth dough. • Break off balls of dough the size of walnuts and form into 3-inch ropes. Form the ropes into 1¹/₂-inch rings and place 1 inch apart on the prepared cookie sheets. • Bake, one sheet at a time, for 15–20 minutes, or until just golden. • Cool the cookies completely on the cookie sheets.

Makes 38 cookies · Prep: 25 min. · Cooking: 15–20 min. per batch · Level: 1 · Keeps: 2 weeks

vanilla cookies

1¹/₃ cups all-purpose flour
¹/₈ teaspoon salt
²/₃ cup butter, cut up
¹/₃ cup granulated sugar
1 large egg yolk, lightly beaten
¹/₂ teaspoon vanilla extract
Grated zest of 1 lemon
¹/₃ cup confectioners' sugar

Preheat the oven to 350°F. • Line a cookie sheet with parchment paper. • Sift the flour and salt into a large bowl. • Use a pastry blender to cut in the butter until the mixture resembles coarse crumbs. • Mix in the granulated sugar, egg yolk, vanilla, and grated lemon zest to form a smooth dough. • Form the dough into 1¹/₂ x ¹/₂-inch logs and place 1 inch apart on the prepared cookie sheet, flattening them slightly. • Bake for 10–12 minutes, or until just golden. • Transfer to racks to cool. • Dust with the confectioners' sugar.

Makes 16 cookies · Prep: 25 min. · Cooking: 10–12 min. · Level: 1 · Keeps: 4 days

chocolate–orange twists

3 cups all-purpose flour
2 teaspoons baking powder
¹/₄ teaspoon salt
³/₄ cup (1¹/₂ sticks) butter, softened
¹/₂ cup granulated sugar
1 large egg
5 oz semisweet chocolate
1 tablespoon finely shredded orange zest

Preheat the oven to 350°F. • Line four cookie sheets with parchment paper. • Sift the flour, baking powder, and salt into a medium bowl. • Beat the butter and sugar in a large bowl with an electric mixer at high speed until creamy. • Add the egg, beating until just blended. • Finely grate 2 oz of the chocolate and beat into the mixture. • Beat in the orange zest. • Mix in the dry ingredients to form a soft dough. • Turn the dough out onto a lightly floured surface and knead until smooth. • Form tablespoons of the dough into 8-inch ropes. • Fold in half and twist, pressing the ends of the rope together. • Transfer to the prepared cookie sheets, placing them 2 inches apart. • Bake, one batch at a time, for 10–12 minutes, or until just firm. • Transfer to racks to cool. • Melt the remaining 3 oz chocolate in a double boiler over barely simmering water. • Dip in the tops of cookies and let set for 30 minutes.

Makes 40–45 cookies · Prep: 40 min. + 30 min. to set · Cooking: 10–12 min. per batch · Level: 2 · Keeps: 3 days

poppy seed s-shapes

1¹/₃ cups all-purpose flour
1 teaspoon baking powder
¹/₈ teaspoon salt
¹/₂ cup (1 stick) butter, softened
¹/₂ cup granulated sugar
1 teaspoon ground aniseeds
1 teaspoon finely grated lemon zest
1 large egg + 1 large egg yolk + 1 large egg white
2 tablespoons + 1 teaspoon milk
2 tablespoons poppy seeds

Sift the flour, baking powder, and salt into a medium bowl. • Beat the butter and sugar in a large bowl with an electric mixer at high speed until creamy. • Add the aniseeds and lemon zest. • With mixer at high speed, beat the whole egg and egg yolk and 2 tablespoons milk until frothy in a large bowl. • Beat the egg mixture into the batter. • Mix in the dry ingredients to form a

smooth dough. • Divide the dough in half. • Form into 8-inch logs, wrap in plastic wrap, and refrigerate for at least 30 minutes. • Preheat the oven to 375°F. • Line two cookie sheets with parchment paper. • Slice the dough ¹/₂ inch thick. • Roll each slice into a 6-inch log and form into an S-shape, flattening it slightly. • Place the cookies 1 inch apart on the prepared cookie sheets. • Mix the egg white and remaining 1 teaspoon milk in a small bowl. • Brush over the cookies and sprinkle with poppy seeds. • Bake for 8–10 minutes, or until just golden at the edges, rotating the sheets halfway through for even baking. • Transfer to racks to cool.

Makes 32 cookies · Prep: 40 min. + 30 min. to chill Cooking: 8–10 min. · Level: 2 · Keeps: 10 days

lime s-shapes

³/₄ cup all-purpose flour
¹/₈ teaspoon salt
1¹/₃ cups finely ground almonds
1 cup granulated sugar
1 tablespoon finely grated lime zest
¹/₂ cup (1 stick) butter, cut up
2 large egg whites, lightly beaten

Sift the flour and salt into a large bowl. • Stir in the ground almonds, sugar, and lime zest. • Use a pastry blender to cut in the butter until the mixture resembles fine crumbs. • Mix in the egg whites to form a stiff dough. • Divide the dough in half. Form the dough into two disks, wrap in plastic wrap, and refrigerate for 30 minutes. • Preheat the oven to 350°F. • Butter three cookie sheets. • Pinch off balls of dough the size of walnuts and shape into rounded S-shape cookies. • Use a spatula to transfer the cookies to the prepared cookie sheets, placing them 1 inch apart. • Bake, one sheet at a time, for 12–15 minutes, or until golden brown, rotating the sheets halfway through for even baking. • Transfer to racks to cool.

Makes 40 cookies · Prep: 25 min. + 30 min. to chill Cooking: 12–15 min. per batch · Level: 1 · Keeps: 10 days

meringues &
macaroons

above: Poppy seed
macaroons (page 234)

right: Orange macaroons,
Meringue date morsels,
Coconut meringue slices, and
Petite meringues (see pages
234, 236, 236, and 238)

Crisp and delicate, meringues are ideal for those with a sweet tooth but a small appetite. Drop or pipe the meringues onto a cookie sheet lined with parchment paper. They should always be baked in a slow oven for a long period of time. When dry to the touch, turn off the oven and let them cool with the oven door ajar. The lightness of the sweetened egg whites combines well with all nuts and spices to create crunchy or slightly chewy macaroons. Serve them with a bowl of fresh fruit coulis or compote or sandwiched together with a flavored whipped cream for a satisfying dessert.

chocolate-glazed macaroons

This traditional cookie is made by spreading a meringue-like batter on rice paper, which is available from specialty baking stores and wherever Vietnamese foods are sold.

- 1/4 cup all-purpose flour, or more as needed
- 1 teaspoon baking powder
- 1/8 teaspoon salt
- 4 large egg whites
- 1 teaspoon fresh lemon juice
- 1 1/2 cups superfine sugar
- 2 1/2 cups finely ground almonds
- 3 oz semisweet chocolate, coarsely grated
- 1 cup mixed candied peel, finely chopped
  Rice paper, cut into 2-inch rounds
- 3 oz semisweet chocolate, coarsely chopped
- 3 oz white chocolate, coarsely chopped

Sift the flour, baking powder, and salt into a large bowl. • Beat the egg whites in a large bowl with an electric mixer at medium speed until frothy. • With mixer at high speed, gradually add the lemon juice and superfine sugar, beating until stiff, glossy peaks form. • Use a large rubber spatula to fold in the almonds, grated chocolate, and candied peel, followed by the dry ingredients until well blended. • Drop spoonfuls of the mixture onto the rice paper circles. Use a thin metal spatula to spread the mixture to 1/2 inch thick and place on a baking sheet. • Refrigerate for at least 2 hours. • Preheat the oven to 300°F. • Bake for 20–25 minutes, or until firm to the touch. • Transfer to racks to cool. • Tear off any extra paper from around the cookies. • Melt each chopped chocolate in a separate double boiler over barely simmering water. • Drizzle the chocolates over the top of the macaroons, swirling with a knife to create a marbled effect.

Makes 15 cookies · Prep: 50 min. + 2 hr. to chill · Level: 2 · Keeps: 14 days

rich chocolate macaroons

- 1 1/4 lb bittersweet chocolate, coarsely chopped
- 1 1/3 cups finely ground almonds
- 2/3 cup granulated sugar
- 1/4 teaspoon almond extract
- 1/4 teaspoon vanilla extract
- 1 tablespoon unsweetened cocoa powder
- 2 large egg whites, lightly beaten
- 1 teaspoon water
- 1/4 cup confectioners' sugar

Preheat the oven to 350°F. • Line two cookie sheets with parchment paper. • Melt the chocolate in a double boiler over barely

simmering water. • Remove from the heat and let cool for 5 minutes. • Stir together the almonds, granulated sugar, almond and vanilla extract, and cocoa in a large bowl. • Make a well in the center and pour in the melted chocolate and three-quarters of the beaten whites. Mix well to make a smooth dough, adding more whites if the dough is too stiff to mold. • Dust your hands with a little confectioners' sugar. • Shape the dough into balls the size of walnuts. • Place 2 inches apart on the prepared cookie sheets. Use a fork to flatten them slightly. Brush with a little water. Dust with confectioners' sugar. • Bake for 10–12 minutes, or until firm to the touch. Cool the macaroons on the sheet for 1 minute. • Transfer to racks and let cool completely.

Makes 20 cookies · Prep: 20 min. · Cooking: 10–12 min. · Level: 1 · Keeps: 2 days

eliza's macaroons

German Elisenlebkuchen *are a kind of macaroon made with beaten egg whites and sugar. The most famous, called* Nürnberger Elisen, *or Eliza's macaroons, come from the city of Nuremberg, where the bakers still keep Eliza's recipe a secret.*

- 1 1/2 cups blanched whole almonds
- 3/4 cup all-purpose flour
- 1 teaspoon ground cinnamon
- 1/8 teaspoon ground cloves
- 1/8 teaspoon freshly grated nutmeg
- 5 large egg whites
- 2 cups confectioners' sugar
- 1/8 teaspoon cream of tartar
- 1/2 teaspoon baking soda
- 1 teaspoon hot water
- 1/2 cup candied lemon peel, finely chopped
- 1/2 cup candied orange peel, finely chopped

Lemon glaze
- 1 1/3 cups confectioners' sugar
- 2 tablespoons fresh lemon juice
- 1-2 tablespoons hot water

Preheat the oven to 325°F. • Line two baking sheets with rice paper. • Sprinkle the nuts on a large baking sheet. Toast for 7 minutes, or until lightly golden. • Chop finely in a food processor. • Sift the flour, cinnamon, cloves, and nutmeg into a medium bowl. • Beat the egg whites in a large bowl with an electric mixer at medium speed until frothy. With mixer at high speed, gradually add the confectioners' sugar and cream of tartar, beating until stiff, glossy peaks form. • Mix the baking soda and water in a small bowl. • Use a large rubber spatula to fold the baking

soda mixture into the egg whites, followed by the dry ingredients and lemon and orange peels. Fold in the almonds. • Drop heaped spoonfuls 1 inch apart onto the paper. Use the back of a wooden spoon to flatten them slightly. • Refrigerate for at least 2 hours. • Preheat the oven to 300°F. • Bake for 20–25 minutes, or until golden brown, rotating the sheets halfway through for even baking. • Cool the macaroons on the baking sheets for 5 minutes. Transfer to racks to cool. • Tear away any excess paper from around the edges. • Lemon glaze: Sift the confectioners' sugar into a medium bowl. Beat in the lemon juice and hot water, a teaspoon at a time, until thick. • Drizzle with the glaze.

Makes 30–35 cookies · Prep: 45 min. + 2 hr. to chill Cooking: 20–25 min. · Level: 2 · Keeps: 10 days

coconut and macadamia nut macaroons

- 2 large egg whites
- 1/8 teaspoon salt
- 3/4 cup granulated sugar
- 1 1/2 cups shredded coconut
- 1 cup coarsely chopped macadamia nuts

Preheat the oven to 350°F. • Butter a cookie sheet. • Beat the egg whites and salt in a large bowl with an electric mixer at medium speed until frothy. • With mixer at high speed, gradually add the sugar, beating until stiff, glossy peaks form. • Use a large rubber spatula to fold in the coconut and macadamia nuts. • Drop teaspoons of the mixture 1 inch apart onto the prepared cookie sheet. • Bake for 10–15 minutes, or until lightly golden. • Transfer to racks to cool.

Makes 15 cookies · Prep: 20 min. · Cooking: 10–15 min. · Level: 1

oatmeal macaroons

- 1 1/4 cups (2 1/2 sticks) butter, softened
- 2 cups old-fashioned rolled oats
- 1 1/3 cups all-purpose flour
- 1 teaspoon baking powder
- 1/4 teaspoon salt
- 1/2 cup firmly packed light brown sugar
- 1/2 cup raw sugar (Barbados or Demerara)
- 2 large eggs
- 1 1/4 cups shredded coconut
- 3 tablespoons heavy cream
- 1 teaspoon vanilla extract

Preheat the oven to 350°F. • Line two cookie sheets with parchment paper. • Melt 1/3 cup of the butter in a large skillet and toast the oats until lightly golden. • Sift the flour, baking powder, and salt into a large bowl. • Beat the remaining butter and the sugars in a large bowl with an electric mixer at high speed until creamy. • Add the eggs, coconut, cream, and vanilla, beating until just blended. • Mix in the dry ingredients. • Form into balls the size of walnuts and place 2 inches apart on the prepared cookie sheets, flattening them slightly. • Bake for 12–15 minutes, until firm to the touch and golden brown, rotating the sheets halfway through for even baking. • Cool on the sheets until the cookies firm slightly. • Transfer to racks and let cool completely.

Makes 35–40 cookies · Prep: 25 min. · Cooking: 12–15 min. · Level: 1 · Keeps: 8 days

convent almond macaroons

When the nuns of Nancy were evicted from their convent during the French Revolution, they set up their own bakery to earn a living. The sisters' macaroon recipes have been passed down through the centuries and are still made in the traditional way. To make the orange flavored sugar, follow the method for Vanilla Sugar on page 341, substituting the vanilla pods for orange zest and changing it at regular intervals.

- 1   cup blanched almonds, toasted and finely ground
- 1/2 cup Vanilla Sugar (see page 341)
- 1/4 cup orange-flavored sugar
- 2   large egg whites
- 1/4 teaspoon almond extract
- 15   blanched almonds or almond halves
- 1   teaspoon water
- 3   tablespoons confectioners' sugar

Preheat the oven to 375°F. • Line a cookie sheet with parchment paper. • Mix the almonds with the egg white in a food processor to form a smooth paste. • Mix the vanilla and orange sugars and gradually work the sugars into the almond paste until the mixture is soft. • Add the almond extract. • Form the mixture into balls the size of walnuts. • Place 2 inches apart on the prepared cookie sheet, flattening them slightly. • Lightly press an almond into the top of each cookie. Brush with the water and dust with the confectioners' sugar. • Bake for 15–20 minutes, or until golden and slightly firm to the touch. • Transfer the cookies on their parchment to racks and cool until they firm slightly. • Peel from the paper and let cool completely.

Makes 12–15 cookies · Prep: 40 min. · Cooking: 15–20 min. · Level: 2 · Keeps: 10 days

convent hazelnut macaroons

- 2   large egg whites
- 1/2 cup granulated sugar
- 2   tablespoons Vanilla Sugar (see page 341)
- 1   cup finely ground shelled hazelnuts, toasted, + 20 hazelnuts
- 1/8 teaspoon freshly grated nutmeg
- 1   teaspoon fresh lemon juice
- 1   teaspoon water
- 3   tablespoons confectioners' sugar

Preheat the oven to 300°F. • Line a cookie sheet with parchment paper. • Beat the egg whites in a medium bowl with an electric mixer at medium speed in a bowl over barely simmering water. With mixer at high speed, gradually beat in the granulated and vanilla sugars. • Mix in the ground hazelnuts, nutmeg, and lemon juice and beat until frothy. The mixture should remain just warm to the touch. • Remove from the water and beat with an electric mixer until stiff and glossy. • Mix in the nuts. • Drop teaspoons of the mixture 1 inch apart onto the prepared cookie sheets, flattening them slightly. Press a hazelnut into the center of each cookie. • Brush lightly with water and dust with the confectioners' sugar. • Bake for 15–20 minutes, or until lightly golden around the edges and just firm to the touch. • Transfer on their parchment to racks and cool until the cookies firm slightly. • Peel from the paper and let cool completely.

Makes 15 cookies · Prep: 50 min. · Cooking: 18–20 min. · Level: 2 · Keeps: 10 days

chocolate macaroons

- 3/4 cup almonds
- 2   large egg whites
- 1/2 cup superfine sugar
- 2   tablespoons Vanilla Sugar (see page 341)
- 1/8 teaspoon cream of tartar
- 1/8 teaspoon salt
- 2   oz bittersweet chocolate, grated

Preheat the oven to 325°F. • Line two cookie sheets with rice paper. • Sprinkle half the almonds on a large baking sheet. Toast for 7 minutes, or until lightly golden. Lower the oven temperature to 300°F. • Place the almonds on a clean kitchen towel and rub off the skins. • Coarsely chop half the peeled almonds. • Process the remaining almonds in a food processor until finely chopped. Set aside. • Beat the egg whites in a medium bowl with an electric mixer at medium speed until frothy. • With mixer at high

speed, gradually add the superfine sugar, vanilla sugar, cream of tartar, and salt, beating until glossy, stiff peaks form. • Use a rubber spatula to fold in all the almonds and chocolate. • Use two teaspoons to form domes the size of apricots. • Place 2 inches apart on the prepared baking sheets. • Bake for 20–30 minutes, or until golden, rotating the sheets halfway through for even baking. • Cool the macaroons completely on the cookie sheets. Tear the excess rice paper from around the macaroons.

Makes 20 cookies · Prep: 40 min. Cooking: 20–30 min. · Level: 1 · Keeps: 7–10 days

lemon lights

- 1/2 cup all-purpose flour
- 2   tablespoons cornstarch
- 1/4 teaspoon salt
- 1/3 cup butter, softened
- 1/2 cup granulated sugar
- 1   tablespoon finely grated lemon zest
- 3   large egg whites
- 1/2 cup finely chopped pitted dates
- 1   tablespoon fresh lemon juice
- 1   teaspoon rum extract

Sift the flour, cornstarch, and salt into a medium bowl. • Beat the butter and sugar in a large bowl with an electric mixer at high speed until creamy. • Add the lemon zest. • With mixer at high speed, beat the egg whites in a large bowl until soft peaks form. • Fold them into the butter mixture. • Mix in the dry ingredients, dates, lemon juice, and rum extract. Refrigerate for 30 minutes. • Preheat the oven to 375°F. • Butter two cookie sheets. • Drop teaspoons of the mixture 1 1/2 inches apart onto the prepared cookie sheets. • Bake for 8–10 minutes, or until golden brown, rotating the sheets halfway through for even baking. • Transfer to racks to cool.

Makes 30 cookies · Prep: 20 min. + 30 min. to chill Cooking: 10 min. · Level: 2 · Keeps: 5 days

Chocolate macaroons

pecan–coffee meringues

2   large egg whites
1/8   teaspoon salt
1   cup superfine sugar
1   teaspoon coffee extract
1/2   cup coarsely chopped pecans
1   tablespoon cornstarch
1/2   cup heavy cream, whipped

Preheat the oven to 300°F. • Line a cookie sheet with waxed paper. • Beat the egg whites and salt in a large bowl with an electric mixer at medium speed until frothy. • With mixer at high speed, gradually beat in the superfine sugar, beating until stiff, glossy peaks form. • Use a large rubber spatula to fold in the coffee extract, pecans, and cornstarch. • Fit a pastry bag with a 1/2-inch star tip. Fill the pastry bag, twist the opening tightly closed, and squeeze out 2-inch stars, spacing 2 inches apart on the prepared cookie sheet. • Bake for 80–90 minutes, or until the meringues are crisp and lightly browned. • Cool the meringues completely in the oven with the door ajar. • Fill with whipped cream just before serving.

Makes 15 cookies · Prep: 30 min. · Cooking: 80–90 min. · Level: 2 · Keeps: 7 days before filling

foolproof mini meringues

1   large egg white
1/8   teaspoon salt
2/3   cup superfine sugar
1   teaspoon white distilled vinegar
2   tablespoons boiling water

Preheat the oven to 250°F. • Butter a large cookie sheet. • Beat the egg white in a large bowl with an electric mixer at medium speed until soft peaks form. With mixer at high speed, gradually add the superfine sugar, beating until stiff, glossy peaks form. • Beat in the vinegar, followed by the water, until very stiff peaks are formed. • Drop teaspoons of the meringues 2 inches apart onto the prepared cookie sheet. • Bake for 80–90 minutes, or until the meringues are crisp and dry. • Cool in the oven with the door ajar.

Makes 12–14 cookies · Prep: 20 min. · Cooking: 80–90 min. · Level: 1 · Keeps: 1 week

chocolate cream-filled kisses

2   large egg whites
1/8   teaspoon salt
2   tablespoons superfine sugar
1/3   cup confectioners' sugar

1 1/4   cup finely chopped hazelnuts
1/3   cup Nutella (chocolate hazelnut cream)

Preheat the oven to 375°F. • Line two cookie sheets with parchment paper. • Beat the egg whites and salt in a large bowl with an electric mixer at medium speed until frothy. • With mixer at medium speed, gradually add the superfine sugar, beating until stiff, glossy peaks form. • Use a large rubber spatula to fold in the confectioners' sugar and hazelnuts. • Fit a pastry bag with a 1-inch star tip. Fill the pastry bag, twist the opening tightly closed, and squeeze out 1-inch stars spacing 1 inch apart onto the prepared cookie sheets. • Bake for 8–10 minutes, or until pale gold, rotating the sheets halfway through for even baking. • Transfer to racks to cool. • Stick the cookies together in pairs with the chocolate hazelnut cream.

Makes 18–22 cookies · Prep: 30 min. · Cooking: 8–10 min. · Level: 2 · Keeps: 7 days

hazelnut–coffee meringues

2   large egg whites
1/8   teaspoon salt
1   cup superfine sugar
1   teaspoon coffee extract
1/2   cup coarsely chopped hazelnuts
1   tablespoon cornstarch

Preheat the oven to 300°F. • Line a cookie sheet with waxed paper. • Beat the egg whites and salt in a large bowl with an electric mixer at medium speed until frothy. • With mixer at high speed, gradually add the superfine sugar, beating until stiff, glossy peaks form. • Use a large rubber spatula to fold in the coffee extract, hazelnuts, and cornstarch. • Fit a pastry bag with a 1/2-inch star tip. Fill the pastry bag, twist the opening tightly closed, and squeeze out 2-inch stars, spacing 2 inches apart on the prepared cookie sheet. • Bake for 80–90 minutes, or until the meringues are crisp and lightly browned. • Cool in the oven with the door ajar.

Makes 15 cookies · Prep: 30 min. · Cooking: 80–90 min. · Level: 2 · Keeps: 7 days

chocolate-filled macaroon kisses

2   large egg whites
1/8   teaspoon salt
2   tablespoons superfine sugar
1/3   cup confectioners' sugar
1/2   cup finely ground almonds

3/4   cup finely chopped hazelnuts
3   oz semisweet chocolate, coarsely chopped

Preheat the oven to 375°F. • Line two cookie sheets with parchment paper. • Beat the egg whites and salt in a large bowl with an electric mixer at medium speed until frothy. • With mixer at medium speed, gradually add the superfine sugar, beating until stiff, glossy peaks form. • Use a large rubber spatula to fold in the confectioners' sugar and almonds. • Fit a pastry bag with a 1-inch star tip. Fill the pastry bag, twist the opening tightly closed, and squeeze out 1-inch stars spacing 1 inch apart on the prepared cookie sheets. Sprinkle with the hazelnuts. • Bake for 8–10 minutes, or until pale gold, rotating the sheets halfway through for even baking. • Transfer to racks to cool. • Melt the chocolate in a double boiler over barely simmering water. • Stick the cookies together in pairs with the melted chocolate.

Makes 18–22 cookies · Prep: 30 min. · Cooking: 8–10 min. · Level: 1 · Keeps: 7 days

pistachio meringue drops

4   large egg whites
3/4   cup superfine sugar
1   tablespoon Vanilla Sugar (see page 341)
2 1/4   cups coarsely chopped pistachio nuts
1   cup finely chopped candied orange peel

Preheat the oven to 250°F. • Line two cookie sheets with parchment paper. • Beat the egg whites and superfine and vanilla sugars in a large bowl with an electric mixer at high speed until stiff peaks form. • Use a large rubber spatula to fold in the pistachios and candied peel. • Drop teaspoons of the batter 2 inches apart onto the prepared cookie sheets. • Bake for 12–15 minutes, or until crisp and dry to the touch, rotating the sheets halfway through for even baking. • Transfer to racks to cool.

Makes 16–20 cookies · Prep: 30 min. · Cooking: 12–15 min. · Level: 1 · Keeps: 5 days

Chocolate-filled macaroon kisses (top)
and Pistachio meringue drops (bottom)

passover macaroons

A light and delicious variation on the macaroon, perfect for serving at the Jewish Passover holiday.

- 2 teaspoons matzo meal
- 2 large egg whites
- 1/8 teaspoon salt
- 1/2 cup granulated sugar
- 1 cup finely ground almonds

Preheat the oven to 300°F. • Line two cookie sheets with parchment paper. Sprinkle with 1 teaspoon matzo meal. • Beat the egg whites and salt in a medium bowl with an electric mixer at medium speed until frothy. • With mixer at high speed, gradually add the sugar, beating until stiff, glossy peaks form. • Use a large rubber spatula to fold in the almonds and the remaining 1 teaspoon matzo meal. • Drop teaspoons of the batter 1 inch apart onto the prepared cookie sheets. • Bake for 15–20 minutes, or until lightly browned, rotating the sheets halfway through for even baking. • Transfer to racks to cool.

Makes 20–24 cookies · Prep: 20 min. · Cooking: 15–20 min. · Level: 1 · Keeps: 7 days

nutty meringues

- 2 large egg whites
- 1/8 teaspoon salt
- 1/2 cup superfine sugar
- 1/4 teaspoon fresh lemon juice
- 3 tablespoons finely ground almonds or hazelnuts, toasted
- 1 teaspoon cornstarch
- 2 tablespoons flaked almonds or crushed hazelnuts, to sprinkle
- 2 tablespoons confectioners' sugar, to dust

Preheat the oven to 250°F. • Line two cookie sheets with parchment paper. • Beat the egg whites and salt in a large bowl with an electric mixer at medium speed until soft peaks form. With mixer at high speed, gradually add the superfine sugar and lemon juice, beating until stiff, glossy peaks form. • Stir together the finely ground nuts and cornstarch and fold it into the mixture. • Fit a pastry bag with a 1/2-inch star tip. Fill the pastry bag, twist the opening tightly closed, and squeeze out small stars and shells, spacing 1 inch apart on the prepared cookie sheets. • Sprinkle with the flaked almonds and dust with the confectioners' sugar. • Bake for 50–60 minutes, or until

the meringues are dry to the touch, rotating the sheets halfway through for even baking. • Turn off the oven. Leave in the warm oven for 30 minutes more. • Using the parchment paper as handles, lift the meringues onto a rack. Carefully peel off the paper and let cool completely.

Makes 20–25 meringues · Prep: 30 min. · Cooking: 50–60 min. + 30 min. to rest · Level: 2 · Keeps: 10 days

nutty mini meringues

- 1 1/4 cups blanched almonds
- 4 large egg whites
- 1/8 teaspoon salt
- 2 cups confectioners' sugar
- 1/4 teaspoon almond extract

Preheat the oven to 300°F. • Line two cookie sheets with aluminum foil. • Process the almonds in a food processor or blender until finely chopped. • Beat the egg whites, confectioners' sugar, and salt in a large bowl placed over barely simmering water with an electric mixer at high speed until stiff peaks form. • Remove the bowl from the water. Stir in the almond extract and chopped almonds. • Drop teaspoons of the mixture 1 inch apart onto the prepared cookie sheets. • Bake for 20–30 minutes, or until crisp, rotating the sheets halfway through for even baking. • Transfer the meringues on the foil to racks and let cool completely.

Makes 25 cookies · Prep: 20 min. · Cooking: 20–30 min. · Level: 1 · Keeps: 5 days

hazelnut heaps

- 3 large egg whites
- 1/8 teaspoon salt
- 1 cup confectioners' sugar
- 1 cup toasted, finely chopped hazelnuts

Preheat the oven to 300°F. • Butter a cookie sheet. • Beat the egg whites and salt in a large bowl with an electric mixer at high speed until stiff peaks form. • Use a large rubber spatula to gradually fold in the confectioners' sugar, followed by the hazelnuts. • Place the bowl over barely simmering water and cook, stirring constantly with a wooden spoon, until the mixture starts to shrink from the sides. • Drop heaping teaspoons of the mixture 1/2 inch apart onto the prepared cookie sheet. • Bake for 15–20 minutes, or until just golden. • Transfer to racks and let cool completely.

Makes 16 cookies · Prep: 20 min. · Cooking: 15–20 min. · Level: 1 · Keeps: 5 days

brazil nut macaroons

- 1 cup coarsely chopped Brazil nuts
- 1/2 cup firmly packed light brown sugar
- 1/2 cup firmly packed dark brown sugar
- 1 large egg white
- 1/8 teaspoon salt
- 1/2 teaspoon vanilla extract

Preheat the oven to 325°F. • Line three cookie sheets with parchment paper. • Process the nuts with the light and dark brown sugars in a food processor or blender until the mixture resembles coarse crumbs. • Beat the egg white and salt in a medium bowl with an electric mixer at high speed until stiff peaks form. • Use a large rubber spatula to fold in the ground nut mixture and vanilla. • Drop teaspoons of the batter 1 inch apart onto the prepared cookie sheets. • Bake, one sheet at a time, for 8–10 minutes, or until lightly browned. • Transfer to racks to cool.

Makes 36 cookies · Prep: 20 min. · Cooking: 8–10 min. per batch · Level: 1 · Keeps: 7 days

pine nut meringues

- 3/4 cup pine nuts
- 1 1/2 cups finely chopped almonds
- 1 1/4 cups granulated sugar
- 1/2 teaspoon vanilla extract
- 2 large egg whites

Line a cookie sheet with parchment paper. • Place small heaps of pine nuts (about 10 pine nuts per heap) on the prepared cookie sheet. • Mix the almonds, sugar, and vanilla in a large bowl. • Beat the egg whites in a large bowl with an electric mixer at high speed until stiff peaks form. • Use a large rubber spatula to fold the beaten whites into the almond mixture. • Drop teaspoons of the mixture on top of the pine nuts to cover them completely. • Refrigerate for 30 minutes. • Preheat the oven to 300°F. • Bake for 18–20 minutes, or until set. • Turn off the oven. Cool the meringues completely in the oven with the door ajar.

Makes 16 cookies · Prep: 20 min. + 30 min. to chill Cooking: 18–20 min. · Level: 1 · Keeps: 3 days

Brazil nut macaroons (top) and Passover macaroons (bottom)

walnut macaroons

When buying walnuts in the shell, always pick small nuts with tightly closed shells. Once the walnuts are shelled, they do not keep very well and go rancid quickly, so always taste one before using them. Store in an airtight container in the refrigerator for no more than 3 months.

Cookies
- 1/3 cup all-purpose flour
- 2 cups finely ground walnuts
- 3 large egg whites
- 1/4 teaspoon salt
- 3/4 cup granulated sugar

Filling
- 7 oz white chocolate, coarsely chopped
- 1/4 cup light cream
- 2 tablespoons apricot brandy or orange liqueur
- 1–2 tablespoons finely chopped pistachios

Cookies: Preheat the oven to 275°F. • Butter two cookie sheets and line with parchment paper. • Sift the flour into a medium bowl.

walnut drops

- 2 1/3 cups walnut halves
- 1 1/3 cups granulated sugar
- 3 large eggs
  Grated zest and juice of 1/2 lemon

Preheat the oven to 325°F. • Line three cookie sheets first with parchment paper and then rice paper. • Spread the walnuts on a large baking sheet. Toast for 7 minutes, or until lightly golden. • Process in a food processor or blender with 1/3 cup of the sugar until finely ground. • Beat the eggs and the remaining 1 cup sugar in a large bowl with an electric mixer at high speed until pale and thick. • Mix in the lemon zest and juice and ground walnuts. • Drop rounded teaspoons of the mixture onto the prepared cookie sheets, spacing them 1 1/2 inches apart. • Bake, one sheet at a time, for 12–15 minutes, or until lightly browned. • Transfer the cookies still on the parchment paper to racks to cool. • Tear away the excess rice paper from around the cookies.

Makes 35–40 cookies · Prep: 20 min. · Cooking: 12–15 min. per batch · Level: 2 · Keeps: 3 weeks

poppy seed macaroons

- 3/4 cup blanched almonds
- 1 cup granulated sugar
- 1/4 cup all-purpose flour
- 2 large egg whites
- 1/8 teaspoon salt
- 1/4 teaspoon vanilla extract
- 1 tablespoon poppy seeds

Preheat the oven to 325°F. • Line a cookie sheet with rice paper. • Spread the nuts on a large baking sheet. • Toast for 7 minutes, or until lightly golden. • Increase the oven temperature to 375°F. • Transfer the almonds

to a food processor, add the sugar, and process until finely ground. • Stir together the almond mixture and flour in a medium bowl. • Beat the egg whites and salt in a large bowl with an electric mixer at high speed until stiff peaks form. • Use a large rubber spatula to fold in the dry ingredients and vanilla. • Fit a pastry bag with a 1-inch star tip. Fill the pastry bag, twist the opening tightly closed, and squeeze out 1-inch stars 1 inch apart on the prepared cookie sheet. Sprinkle with the poppy seeds. • Bake for 12–15 minutes, or until pale gold. • Cool on the sheets until the cookies firm slightly. • Transfer to racks on the rice paper, tearing away the excess paper, and let cool completely.

Makes 14–16 cookies · Prep: 30 min. · Cooking: 12–15 min. · Level: 2 · Keeps: 5 days

orange macaroons

- 1 1/4 cups blanched almonds
- 3 large egg whites
- 3/4 cup superfine sugar
- 1 tablespoon Vanilla Sugar (see page 341)
  Grated zest of 1 orange
- 1 tablespoon orange juice
- 1 cup fresh bread crumbs

Glaze
- 2 tablespoons orange marmalade
- 2 oz semisweet chocolate, coarsely chopped

Preheat the oven to 325°F. • Line three cookie sheets with parchment paper. • Sprinkle the almonds on a large baking sheet. Toast for 7 minutes, or until lightly golden. Lower the oven temperature to 275°F. • Process the almonds in a food processor until very finely chopped. • Beat the egg whites, superfine sugar, and vanilla sugar in a double boiler over

barely simmering water with an electric mixer at high speed until stiff peaks form. • Add the orange zest and juice. • Remove from the heat. Use a rubber spatula to fold the almonds and bread crumbs into the batter. • Drop teaspoons of the batter 1 inch apart onto the prepared cookie sheets. • Bake, one sheet at a time, for 20–25 minutes, or until pale golden. The macaroons should still be soft but will harden while cooling. • Transfer to racks to cool. • Glaze: Heat the marmalade in a small saucepan and drizzle over the cooled macaroons. Set aside. • Melt the chocolate in a double boiler over barely simmering water. • Drizzle the chocolate over the tops.

Makes 50 cookies · Prep: 50 min. · Cooking: 20–25 min. per batch · Level: 2 · Keeps: 7–14 days

hazelnut meringues

- 2 cups hazelnuts
- 1 cup superfine sugar
- 4 large egg whites
- 1/4 teaspoon salt

Preheat the oven to 325°F. • Line two cookie sheets with parchment paper. • Spread the hazelnuts on a large baking sheet. Toast for 7 minutes, or until lightly golden. • Reduce the oven temperature to 250°F. • Transfer the nuts to a food processor with 1/2 cup of the superfine sugar and process until finely ground. • Beat the egg whites and salt in a large bowl with an electric mixer at medium speed until soft peaks form. With mixer at high speed, gradually add the remaining 1/2 cup superfine sugar, beating until stiff, glossy peaks form. • Use a large rubber spatula to fold in the hazelnuts. • Drop

Stir in the walnuts. • Beat the egg whites and salt in a large bowl with an electric mixer at medium speed until frothy. • With mixer at high speed, gradually beat in the sugar, beating until stiff, glossy peaks form. • Use a large rubber spatula to fold in the dry ingredients. • Fit a pastry bag with a $3/4$-inch plain tip. Fill the pastry bag, twist the opening tightly closed, and squeeze out mounds the size of walnuts spacing them 1 inch apart on the prepared cookie sheets. • Bake for 20–25 minutes, or until the cookies are set and lightly browned, rotating the

teaspoons of the meringue 2 inches apart on the prepared cookie sheets. • Bake for 50–60 minutes, or until the meringues are dry and crisp, rotating the sheets halfway through for even baking. • Transfer while still on the parchment paper to a rack to cool.

Makes 30–35 cookies · Prep: 20 min. · Cooking: 50–60 min. · Level: 1 · Keeps: 5 days

chocolate meringues

1/2	cup superfine sugar
2/3	cup confectioners' sugar
1/4	cup unsweetened cocoa powder
4	large egg whites
1/8	teaspoon salt

Preheat the oven to 300°F. • Line two cookie sheets with parchment paper. • Stir together the superfine sugar, confectioners' sugar, and cocoa in a medium bowl. • Beat the egg whites and salt in a large bowl with an electric mixer at medium speed until soft peaks form. • With mixer at high speed, gradually beat in half the sugar mixture, beating until stiff, glossy peaks form. • Use a large rubber spatula to fold in the remaining sugar mixture. • Fit a pastry bag with a $1/2$-inch star tip. Fill the pastry bag, twist the opening tightly closed, and squeeze out small stars, spacing 1 inch apart on the prepared cookie sheets. • Bake for 40–50 minutes, or until the meringues are dry to the touch, rotating the sheets halfway through for even baking. • Turn off the oven. Leave in the warm oven for 30 minutes. • Using the parchment paper as handles, lift the meringues onto a rack. Carefully peel off the paper and let cool completely.

Makes 24 cookies · Prep: 25 min. + 30 min. to cool Cooking: 40–50 min. · Level: 2 · Keeps: 7 days

sheets halfway through for even baking. • Transfer the macaroons to racks on the parchment paper and let cool completely. • Filling: Melt the chocolate with the cream in a double boiler over barely simmering water. • Stir in the brandy. • Plunge the pan into a bowl of ice water and stir until the mixture has cooled. • With mixer at high speed, beat the mixture until creamy. • Stick the macaroons together in pairs with the filling. Roll the sides in the pistachios.

Makes 20 cookies · Prep: 55 min. · Cooking: 20–25 min. · Level: 2 · Keeps: 2–3 days in the refrigerator

coconut meringues

2	large egg whites
1/8	teaspoon salt
1/2	cup superfine sugar
1	cup shredded coconut
	Candied cherries, to decorate

Preheat the oven to 325°F. • Line a cookie sheet with parchment paper. • Beat the egg whites and salt in a large bowl with an electric mixer at medium speed until frothy. With mixer at high speed, gradually add the sugar, beating until stiff, glossy peaks form. • Use a large rubber spatula to fold in the coconut. • Drop teaspoons of the meringue 2 inches apart onto the prepared cookie sheet. • Decorate with the cherries. • Bake for 35–45 minutes, or until dry and crisp. • Turn the oven off and let the meringues cool in the oven with the door ajar.

Makes 15 cookies · Prep: 20 min. · Cooking: 35–45 min. · Level: 1 · Keeps: 5 days

pine nut macaroons

3	tablespoons dried currants
3	tablespoons Marsala
3/4	cup almonds
1 1/2	cups pine nuts
1/2	cup granulated sugar
1	tablespoon all-purpose flour
1/8	teaspoon salt
1	large egg white, lightly beaten
1/4	teaspoon almond extract

Preheat the oven to 325°F. • Butter two cookie sheets. • Soak the currants in the Marsala in a small bowl for 10 minutes. • Drain well and pat dry with paper towels. • Spread the almonds and $1/2$ cup pine nuts on a large baking sheet. • Toast for 7 minutes, or until lightly golden. • Increase the oven temperature to 350°F. • Process the toasted nuts, sugar, flour, and salt in a food processor or blender until very finely ground. • Transfer to a large bowl and mix in the egg white and almond extract. • Stir in the currants. • Form the dough into balls the size of marbles and roll in the remaining 1 cup pine nuts until well coated. • Place 2 inches apart on the prepared cookie sheets, flattening the cookies slightly. • Bake for 12–15 minutes, or until just golden, rotating the sheets halfway through for even baking. • Transfer the cookies to racks to cool.

Makes 24 cookies · Prep: 25 min. · Cooking: 12–15 min. · Level: 1 · Keeps: 7 days

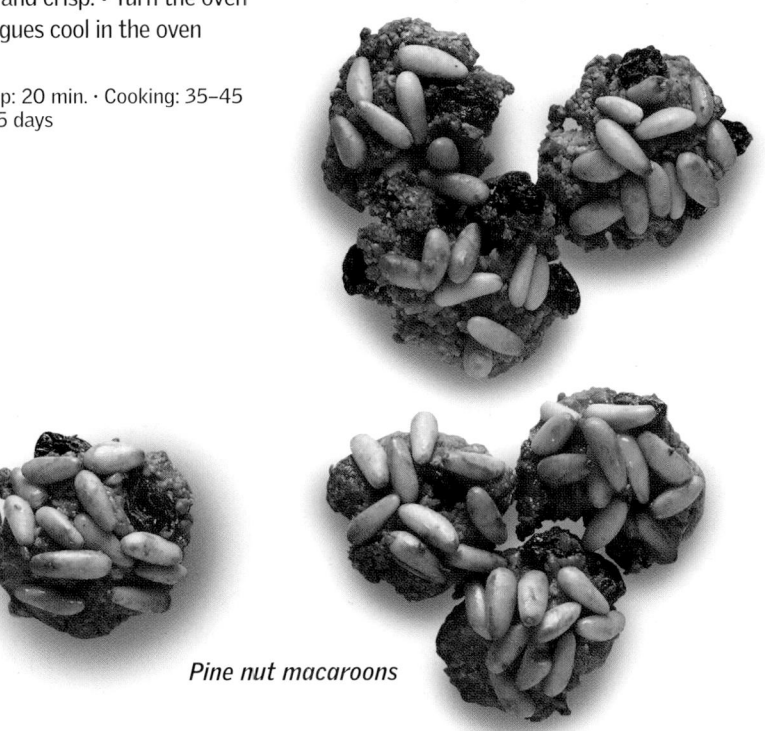

Pine nut macaroons

meringue date morsels

1²/₃ cups pitted dates
1¹/₃ cups walnuts
¹/₂ teaspoon finely grated orange zest
2 large egg whites
¹/₃ cup superfine sugar

Preheat the oven to 250°F. • Line two cookie sheets with waxed paper. • Process the dates and walnuts in a food processor until finely chopped. • Transfer to a large bowl and mix in the orange zest. • Shape into balls the size of walnuts. • Beat the egg whites in a large bowl with an electric mixer at medium speed until frothy. • With mixer at high speed, gradually add the sugar, beating until stiff, glossy peaks form. • Pierce the balls with a skewer and dip into the meringue, coating them completely. • Slide the balls off the skewers and place 2 inches apart on the prepared cookie sheets. • Bake for 45–60 minutes, or until the meringue is crisp, rotating the sheets halfway through for even baking. • Cool completely in the oven with the door ajar.

Makes 30–35 cookies · Prep: 35 min. · Cooking: 45–60 min. · Level: 2 · Keeps: 3 days

coconut meringue slices

Base
1¹/₄ cups all-purpose flour
1 teaspoon baking powder
¹/₈ teaspoon salt
¹/₃ cup butter, softened
²/₃ cup granulated sugar
2 tablespoons milk
2 large egg yolks

Coconut meringue topping
2 large egg whites
²/₃ cup granulated sugar
¹/₂ cup shredded coconut
¹/₃ cup finely chopped mixed nuts
¹/₃ cup finely chopped candied cherries

Preheat the oven to 350°F. • Butter a 15¹/₂ x 10¹/₂-inch jelly-roll pan. • Base: Sift the flour, baking powder, and salt into a medium bowl. • Beat the butter and sugar in a medium bowl with an electric mixer at high speed until creamy. • Add the milk and egg yolks, beating until just blended. • Mix in the dry ingredients. • Firmly press the mixture into the prepared baking sheet to form a smooth, even layer. • Coconut meringue topping: With mixer at high speed, beat the egg whites and sugar in a large bowl until stiff, glossy peaks form. • Fold in the coconut, nuts, and cherries. • Spread the topping over the base. • Bake for 20 minutes, or until lightly browned. • Cool

completely in the pan. • Cut into bars.

Makes 28 bars · Prep: 30 min. · Cooking: 20 min. · Level: 1 · Keeps: 2 days in the refrigerator

mocha meringues

1 tablespoon + 1 cup confectioners' sugar
1 teaspoon unsweetened cocoa powder
¹/₂ teaspoon freeze-dried coffee granules
2 large egg whites
¹/₈ teaspoon salt
¹/₂ teaspoon vanilla extract

Preheat the oven to 250°F. • Line two cookie sheets with parchment paper. • Sift 1 tablespoon of the confectioners' sugar and the cocoa into a small bowl. Stir in the coffee granules. • Beat the egg whites and salt in a large bowl with an electric mixer at medium speed until soft peaks form. • With mixer at high speed, gradually add the remaining 1 cup confectioners' sugar, beating until stiff, glossy peaks form. • Fold in the cocoa mixture and vanilla. • Fit a pastry bag with a ¹/₂-inch star tip. Fill the pastry bag, twist the opening tightly closed, and squeeze out 2¹/₂-inch rosettes, spacing 2 inches apart on the prepared cookie sheets. • Bake for 50–60 minutes, or until the meringues are dry to the touch, rotating the sheets halfway through for even baking. • Turn the oven off. Carefully lift the meringues off the paper, press in the bottoms slightly, and return to the warm oven for 30 minutes more. • Transfer the meringues to racks to cool completely.

Makes 18 cookies · Prep: 25 min. + 30 min. to cool Cooking: 50–60 min. · Level: 2 · Keeps: 5 days

pistachio and orange macaroons

¹/₃ cup all-purpose flour
¹/₈ teaspoon salt
²/₃ cup + 2 tablespoons pistachios
²/₃ cup granulated sugar
3 tablespoons finely chopped orange candied peel
1 tablespoon finely grated orange zest
3 large egg whites
¹/₄ cup superfine sugar
2 tablespoons confectioners' sugar

Preheat the oven to 350°F. • Line two cookie sheets with parchment paper and grease them with almond oil. • Sift the flour and salt into a medium bowl. • Process ²/₃ cup of pistachios in a food processor until finely chopped. • Transfer to a large bowl and mix in the granulated sugar, candied peel, and orange zest. • Mix in the dry ingredients. • Beat the egg whites in a large

bowl with an electric mixer at medium speed until frothy. With mixer at high speed, gradually beat in the superfine sugar, beating until stiff, glossy peaks form. • Mix in the pistachios. • Drop teaspoons of the mixture 1¹/₂ inches apart onto the prepared cookie sheets. • Sprinkle with the remaining 2 tablespoons pistachios. • Bake for 10–12 minutes, or until the cookies are lightly golden and the bottoms are firm and just browned. • Dust with the confectioners' sugar and let cool on the parchment. • Transfer to racks to cool completely.

Makes 25–30 cookies · Prep: 20 min. · Cooking: 10–12 min. · Level: 1 · Keeps: 5 days

meringue mushrooms

2 large egg whites
¹/₄ teaspoon cream of tartar
¹/₈ teaspoon salt
¹/₂ cup superfine sugar
2 oz semisweet chocolate, coarsely chopped
¹/₄ cup unsweetened cocoa powder

Preheat the oven to 250°F. • Line two cookie sheets with parchment paper. • Beat the egg whites, cream of tartar, and salt in a large bowl with an electric mixer at medium speed until frothy. • With mixer at high speed, gradually add the sugar, beating until stiff, glossy peaks form. • Fit a pastry bag with a ¹/₂-inch plain tip. Fill the pastry bag, twist the opening tightly closed, and squeeze out 1¹/₂-inch rounds with a height of 1 inch, spacing 2 inches apart on one of the prepared cookie sheets. • Pipe 1-inch cone shapes to resemble the mushroom stalks onto the remaining prepared cookie sheets, placing them 2 inches apart. • Bake for 50–60 minutes, or until the meringues are dry and crisp, rotating the sheets halfway through for even baking. • Transfer the meringues still on the parchment paper to a rack. • Melt the chocolate in a double boiler over barely simmering water. • Use a sharp knife to make a small incision in the center of the base of the mushroom caps. • Fill the holes with chocolate and carefully attach the mushroom stalks. • Return the mushrooms cap-side-down to the paper and let set for 10 minutes • Dust with the cocoa.

Makes 25–30 cookies · Prep: 40 min. + 10 min. to set · Cooking: 50–60 min. · Level: 2 · Keeps: 2 weeks

Meringue mushrooms

Carrot and orange meringues

cinnamon meringues

2	large egg whites
1/8	teaspoon salt
2/3	cup superfine sugar
1/3	cup unsweetened cocoa powder
1/2	teaspoon ground cinnamon
1/2	teaspoon almond extract

Preheat the oven to 250°F. • Line two cookie sheets with parchment paper. • Beat the egg whites and salt in a large bowl with an electric mixer at medium speed until frothy. • With mixer at high speed, gradually add the superfine sugar, beating until stiff, glossy peaks form. • Fold in the cocoa, cinnamon, and almond extract. • Fit a pastry bag with a 1 1/2-inch star tip. Fill the pastry bag, twist the opening tightly closed, and squeeze out generous rosettes spacing 1 inch apart on the prepared cookie sheets. • Bake for 50–60 minutes, or until crisp and dry to the touch, rotating the sheets halfway through for even baking. • Cool completely on the sheets.

Makes 25–30 cookies · Prep: 25 min. · Cooking: 50–60 min. · Level: 2 · Keeps: 7 days

white chocolate–nut meringues

3	large egg whites
1/8	teaspoon salt
1	cup superfine sugar
2	cups finely ground hazelnuts
2	teaspoons freeze-dried coffee granules
1	tablespoon Dutch-process cocoa powder
3	oz white chocolate, coarsely chopped
60	coffee beans, to decorate

Preheat the oven to 300°F. • Line four cookie sheets with parchment paper. • Beat the egg whites and salt in a large bowl with an electric mixer at medium speed until frothy. • With mixer at high speed, gradually add the superfine sugar, beating until stiff, glossy peaks form. • Use a large rubber spatula to fold in the hazelnuts, coffee granules, and cocoa. • Fit a pastry bag with a 1/2-inch tip. Fill the pastry bag, twist the opening tightly closed, and squeeze out mounds the size of walnuts, spacing them 1 inch apart on the prepared cookie sheets. • Bake, one sheet at a time, for 15–20 minutes, or until crisp and dry. • Transfer to racks on the parchment paper to cool. • Melt the white chocolate in a double boiler over barely simmering water. • Drizzle the chocolate over the meringues and decorate each top with a coffee bean.

Makes 60 cookies · Prep: 25 min. · Cooking: 15–20 min. per batch · Level: 2 · Keeps: 7 days

carrot and orange meringues

For best results, grate the carrots as finely as possible and squeeze out any excess water.

2	large egg whites
1/8	teaspoon salt
3/4	cup superfine sugar
1	teaspoon fresh orange juice
1/2	cup finely shredded carrot
3	oz semisweet chocolate, coarsely chopped
1	tablespoon finely grated orange zest

Preheat the oven to 300°F. • Line three cookie sheets with parchment paper. • Beat the egg whites and salt in a large bowl with an electric mixer at medium speed until soft peaks form. • With mixer at high speed, gradually add the superfine sugar and orange juice, beating until stiff, glossy peaks form. • Use a large rubber spatula to fold in the carrot. • Fit a pastry bag with a 1/2-inch star tip. Fill the pastry bag, twist the opening tightly closed, and squeeze out 2-inch rosettes, spacing 1 1/2 inches apart on the prepared cookie sheets. • Bake for 40–45 minutes, or until the meringues are crisp and dry, rotating the sheets halfway through for even baking. • Turn off the oven. Cool the meringues completely in the oven with the door ajar. • Melt the chocolate in a double boiler over barely simmering water. • Dip the cooled meringues halfway into the chocolate and sprinkle with the orange zest. • Let stand until set, about 30 minutes.

Makes 35 cookies · Prep: 30 min. + 30 min. to set · Cooking: 40–45 min. · Level: 2 · Keeps: 3 days

almond heaps

6	cups whole almonds
2 1/4	cups superfine sugar
6	large egg whites
1/8	teaspoon salt

Preheat the oven to 325°F. • Butter and flour a large cookie sheet. • Spread the almonds out on a separate baking sheet. Toast in the oven for 7 minutes, or until lightly golden. • Increase the oven temperature to 350°F. • Use a kitchen towel to rub off the skins. Transfer the nuts to a food processor, add 1 cup of the superfine sugar, and process until finely chopped. • Beat the egg whites and salt in a large bowl with an electric mixer at high speed until soft peaks form. • Fold in the ground almonds and remaining 1 1/4 cups superfine sugar. • Transfer to a large bowl over barely simmering water. Cook, covered, for 20 minutes, or until very thick. • Drop heaped tablespoons 2 inches apart onto the prepared cookie sheet. • Bake for 40–45 minutes, or until golden brown, rotating the sheets halfway through for even baking. • Cool completely on the cookie sheets.

Makes 25 cookies · Prep: 40 min. · Cooking: 40–45 min. · Level: 1 · Keeps: 3 days

petite meringues

These little meringues go well with coffee or tea. For a special treat, dip them in melted chocolate, sandwich them together with whipped cream, or fill them with chocolate ganache.

2	large egg whites
1/8	teaspoon salt
1/2	cup superfine sugar
1/4	teaspoon fresh lemon juice
2	tablespoons flaked almonds or crushed pistachios
1	tablespoon confectioners' sugar
2 1/2	oz semisweet chocolate, coarsely chopped

Filling

1/2	cup heavy cream
1–2	teaspoons Vanilla Sugar (see page 341)
1/2	cup Chocolate Buttercream (see page 345)

Preheat the oven to 250°F. • Line two cookie sheets with parchment paper. • Beat the egg whites and salt in a large bowl with an electric mixer at medium speed until soft peaks form. • With mixer at high speed, gradually add the superfine sugar and lemon juice, beating until stiff, glossy peaks form. • Fit a pastry bag with a 1/2-inch star tip. Fill the pastry bag, twist the opening tightly closed, and squeeze out small shapes, spacing them 1 inch apart on the prepared cookie sheets. • Sprinkle the meringues with flaked almonds and dust with the confectioners' sugar. • Bake for 50–60 minutes, or until the meringues are dry to the touch, rotating the sheets halfway through for even baking. • Turn the oven off. Carefully lift the meringues off the paper, press in the bottoms slightly, and return to the warm oven for 30 minutes more. • Transfer the meringues to racks to cool. • Melt the chocolate in a double boiler over barely simmering water. • Dip the bottoms of the meringues in the chocolate. • Place the meringues upside-down on a rack to dry. • Filling: With mixer at high speed, beat the cream and vanilla sugar in a small bowl until stiff. • Stick half the meringues together in pairs with the cream or fill them with the chocolate buttercream.

Makes 20–25 meringues · Prep: 30 min. · Cooking: 50–60 min. + 30 min. to rest · Level: 2 · Keeps: 15 days unfilled

piped and topped macaroons

1¼	cups finely ground almonds
1	tablespoon confectioners' sugar
1	teaspoon cornstarch
3	large egg whites
⅛	teaspoon salt
⅔	cup superfine sugar
1	tablespoon Vanilla Sugar (see page 341)
½	teaspoon almond extract
	Chopped candied cherries, angelica, and chopped nuts, to decorate

Preheat the oven to 275°F. • Line three cookie sheets with parchment paper. • Mix the almonds, confectioners' sugar, and cornstarch in a medium bowl. • Beat the egg whites and salt in a large bowl with an electric mixer at medium speed until frothy. • With mixer at high speed, gradually add the superfine and vanilla sugars until stiff, glossy peaks form. • Use a large rubber spatula to fold in the dry ingredients and almond extract. • Fit a pastry bag with a 1½-inch plain tip. Fill the pastry bag, twist the opening tightly closed, and squeeze out small lengths and rings, spacing them 1 inch apart on the prepared cookie sheets. • Top with the candied cherries, angelica, and nuts. • Bake, one sheet at a time, for 20–25 minutes, or until golden brown. • Transfer to racks to cool.

Makes 45–50 cookies · Prep: 30 min. · Cooking: 20–25 min. per batch · Level: 2 · Keeps: 8 days

milk chocolate macaroons

1	cup blanched almonds
6	oz milk chocolate, coarsely chopped
½	cup granulated sugar
1	tablespoon unsweetened cocoa powder
¼	teaspoon ground cinnamon
2	large egg whites, lightly beaten
1	teaspoon water
¼	cup confectioners' sugar

Preheat the oven to 325°F. • Spread the almonds on a large baking sheet. Toast for 7 minutes, or until lightly golden. • Let cool completely. • Transfer the nuts to a food processor and process until finely ground. • Melt 3 oz of chocolate in a double boiler over barely simmering water. • Mix the ground almonds, sugar, cocoa, and cinnamon in a large bowl and make a well in the center. • Mix in the melted chocolate and enough egg white to form a soft, but not sticky paste. • Refrigerate for 30 minutes. • Preheat the oven to 325°F. • Line two cookie sheets with parchment paper. • Spoon scant tablespoons of the mixture 1 inch apart onto the prepared cookie sheets, flattening them slightly. • Brush the tops with a little water and sprinkle with the confectioners' sugar. • Bake for 10–12 minutes, or until just firm to the touch. • Transfer to racks to cool. • Melt the remaining 3 oz of chocolate in a double boiler over barely simmering water. • Dip the macaroons halfway into the melted chocolate. • Let dry on parchment paper for 30 minutes.

Makes 20–24 cookies · Prep: 40 min.+ 60 min. to chill and set · Cooking: 10–12 min. · Level: 2 · Keeps: 5 days

white meringue mice

Ideal for your children's birthday parties. For a fun presentation, serve the mice swimming in a bowl of one of the purees, compotes, or coulis found on pages 342–344.

2	large egg whites
⅔	cup superfine sugar
24	almond halves, to decorate
24	silver balls, to decorate

Preheat the oven to 250°F. • Line a cookie sheet with parchment paper. • Beat the egg whites in a large bowl with an electric mixer at medium speed until frothy. With mixer at high speed, gradually beat in the superfine sugar, beating until stiff, glossy peaks form. • Fit a pastry bag with a ½-inch plain tip. • Fill the pastry bag, twist the

White meringue mice

opening tightly closed, and squeeze out generous mounds, wide at one end and finishing in a point at the other end, spacing them 1 inch apart on the prepared cookie sheets. • Press the almonds and silver balls into the wide end to resemble ears and eyes. • Bake for 1 hour and 20–30 minutes, or until crisp and dry to the touch. • Transfer to racks to cool.

Makes 12 cookies · Prep: 30 min. · Cooking: 80–90 min. · Level: 2 · Keeps: 7 days

brown sugar meringues

Professional bakers always measure egg whites by weight and use double the weight of sugar when they make meringues. So weigh your egg whites first to find out how much sugar you will need.

3½	oz egg whites (3½ large egg whites)
1	cup soft dark brown sugar
2	tablespoons coarsely chopped hazelnuts

Preheat the oven to 300°F. • Line two cookie sheets with parchment paper. • Mix the egg whites and brown sugar in a large bowl over barely simmering water, stirring until the sugar has dissolved and the mixture has become warm to the touch. • Remove the bowl from the heat and whisk with an electric mixer until thick and cool, about 15–20 minutes. • Fold in 1 tablespoon of the nuts. • Drop tablespoons of the mixture 2 inches apart onto the prepared cookie sheets. • Sprinkle with the remaining 1 tablespoon nuts. • Bake for 12–15 minutes, or until crisp and dry to the touch, rotating the sheets halfway through for even baking. • Cool completely in the oven.

Makes 12 cookies · Prep: 40 min. · Cooking: 15 min. · Level: 2 · Keeps: 5 days

Chestnut meringues

chestnut meringues

3   large egg whites
1/8 teaspoon salt
1   cup superfine sugar
1/4 teaspoon fresh lemon juice
1   oz semisweet chocolate, coarsely grated

Filling
1   cup finely chopped candied chestnuts
3/4 cup heavy cream
1   teaspoon vanilla extract

Preheat the oven to 250°F. • Line two cookie sheets with parchment paper. • Beat the egg whites and salt in a large bowl with an electric mixer at medium speed until soft peaks form. With mixer at high speed, gradually add the superfine sugar and lemon juice, beating until stiff, glossy peaks form. • Fold in the chocolate. • Fit a pastry bag with a 1/2-inch star tip. Fill the pastry bag, twist the opening tightly closed, and squeeze out small rosettes, spacing them 1 inch apart on the prepared cookie sheets. • Bake for 60–70 minutes, or until the meringues are dry to the touch. • Turn off the oven. Leave in the oven for 30 minutes. • Use the parchment paper as handles to lift the meringues onto a rack. Let cool completely. • Filling: Process the chestnuts in a food processor or blender until pureed. • With mixer at high speed, beat the cream and vanilla in a large bowl until stiff. • Fold in the puree. Stick the meringues together in pairs with the cream.

Makes 25–30 meringues · Prep: 30 min. + 30 min. to rest · Cooking: 60–70 min. · Level: 2 · Keeps: 10 days unfilled

tutti-frutti puffs

1   large egg white
1/8 teaspoon salt
1   cup granulated sugar
1/3 cup finely chopped crystallized ginger
1/3 cup finely chopped candied cherries
1/3 cup finely chopped seedless raisins
2/3 cup finely chopped almonds
1/3 cup finely chopped angelica

Preheat the oven to 325°F. • Line a cookie sheet with parchment paper. • Beat the egg white and salt in a medium bowl with an electric mixer at medium speed until frothy. • With mixer at high speed, gradually add the sugar, beating until stiff, glossy peaks form. • Fold in the ginger, candied cherries, raisins, and almonds. • Drop teaspoons of the batter 2 inches apart onto the prepared cookie sheets. • Bake for 10 minutes. • Remove from the oven and top with angelica. • Bake for 10–15 minutes more, or until firm to the touch. • Transfer to racks to cool.

Makes 13–18 cookies · Prep: 20 min. · Cooking: 20–25 min. · Level: 1 · Keeps: 5 days

cocoa–amaretti cookies

1   cup granulated sugar
1¼ cups finely ground almonds
1   tablespoon cornstarch
2   large egg whites
1   teaspoon unsweetened cocoa powder
1/8 teaspoon salt

Preheat the oven to 350°F. • Butter two cookie sheets. • Mix the sugar, almonds, cornstarch, egg whites, cocoa, and salt in a large bowl until well blended. • Drop heaping teaspoons of the dough 1 inch apart onto the prepared cookie sheets. • Bake for 10–12 minutes, or until firm to the touch, rotating the sheets halfway through for even baking. • Transfer to racks and let cool completely.

Makes 30 cookies · Prep: 20 min. · Cooking: 10–12 min. · Level: 1 · Keeps: 2 weeks

coconut heaps

1   large egg
1   cup superfine sugar
2   cups shredded coconut
1/8 teaspoon salt

Preheat the oven to 325°F. • Line two cookie sheets with parchment paper. • Beat the egg and superfine sugar in a medium bowl with an electric mixer at high speed until pale and thick. • Fold in the coconut and salt. • Drop teaspoons of the dough 1½ inches apart onto the prepared cookie sheets. • Bake for 12–15 minutes, or until lightly browned, rotating the sheets halfway

through for even baking. • Transfer to racks to cool.

Makes 25 cookies · Prep: 20 min. · Cooking: 12–15 min. · Level: 1 · Keeps: 5 days

aniseed and pine-nut cookies

2/3 cup blanched almonds
1/2 cup raw sugar (Barbados or Demerara)
1/2 teaspoon ground aniseeds
1/4 teaspoon almond extract
1   large egg white, lightly beaten
1   tablespoon finely chopped pine nuts

Preheat the oven to 325°F. • Line a cookie sheet with parchment paper. • Spread the almonds on a large baking sheet. Toast for 7 minutes, or until lightly browned. • Transfer the nuts to a food processor, add the raw sugar, and process until finely ground. • Transfer to a large bowl and stir in the aniseeds. • Beat the egg white and almond extract in a medium bowl until frothy. • Use a large spatula to fold in the nut mixture. • Form the dough into balls the size of walnuts and place 1 inch apart on the prepared cookie sheet, flattening them slightly. • Sprinkle the tops of the cookies with the pine nuts, pressing them into the dough. • Bake for 20–25 minutes, or until golden and dry to the touch. • Transfer to racks to cool.

Makes 15–18 cookies · Prep: 35 min. · Cooking 20–25 min. · Level: 1 · Keeps: 14 days

coconut macaroons

4   large egg whites
1/4 teaspoon cream of tartar
1   cup superfine sugar
1   tablespoon Vanilla Sugar (see page 341)
1/8 teaspoon salt
2   cups shredded coconut
1   teaspoon vanilla extract

Preheat the oven to 300°F. • Line two cookie sheets with rice paper or parchment paper. • Beat the egg whites and cream of tartar in a large bowl with an electric mixer at medium speed until frothy. With mixer at high speed, gradually beat in the superfine and vanilla sugars and salt until stiff, glossy peaks form. • Use a rubber spatula to fold in the coconut and vanilla. • Use two teaspoons to form domes the size of apricots. Place on the prepared cookie sheets, spacing 2 inches apart. • Bake for 20–30 minutes, or until firm to the touch and crispy, rotating the sheets halfway through for even baking. • Cool the macaroons on the sheets for 10 minutes. Transfer to racks to cool completely.

Makes 30–35 cookies · Prep: 40 min. · Cooking: 20–30 min. · Level: 1 · Keeps: 10–14 days

almond macaroons

Recipes for macaroons have been passed down since the late 17th century. Originally, macaroons were baked on wafers and were often served with wine or a liqueur. Macaroons taste best freshly baked, but they will keep for up to two weeks.

- 2/3 cup superfine sugar
- 1 cup finely ground almonds, or more as needed
- 1 teaspoon ground rice
- 1/4 teaspoon almond extract
- 1/2 teaspoon grated lemon zest
- 1 teaspoon fresh lemon juice
- 2 large egg whites
- 8 blanched almonds, halved

Preheat the oven to 300°F. • Line a cookie sheet with rice paper. • Stir together the superfine sugar, ground almonds, ground rice, almond extract, and lemon zest and juice in a large bowl. Set aside. • Beat the egg whites in a large bowl with an electric mixer at high speed until stiff peaks form. • Use a rubber spatula to fold in the almond mixture and mix to form a stiff paste. If the mixture is very sticky, add more ground almonds. • Place spoonfuls of the mixture the size of apricots on the prepared cookie sheet, spacing 1 1/2 inches apart. • Press half an almond into the center of each macaroon. • Bake for 20–25 minutes, or until golden brown. • Cool the macaroons on the cookie sheet. • Tear away the excess rice paper from around the macaroons.

Makes 16 cookies · Prep: 35 min. · Cooking: 20–25 min. · Level: 1 · Keeps: 2 weeks

coconut puffs

- 4 large egg whites
- 1 cup granulated sugar
- 1 1/2 cups shredded coconut
- 2 tablespoons all-purpose flour
- 1 teaspoon fresh lemon juice
- 1/8 teaspoon salt

Preheat the oven to 325°F. • Line two 12-cup mini muffin pans with mini paper liners. • Beat the egg whites in a large bowl with an electric mixer at medium speed until soft peaks form. • With mixer at high speed, gradually add the sugar, beating until stiff, glossy peaks form. • Use a large rubber

spatula to fold in the coconut, flour, lemon juice, and salt. • Drop teaspoons of the batter into the paper cups, filling them about two-thirds full. • Bake for 25–30 minutes, or until risen and a toothpick inserted into a center comes out clean. • Cool the cookies completely in the pans.

Makes 24 cookies · Prep: 30 min. · Cooking: 25–30 min. · Level: 1 · Keeps: 5 days

almond–brown sugar meringues

- 3 1/2 oz egg whites (3 1/2 large egg whites)
- 1 cup soft dark brown sugar
- 2 tablespoons coarsely chopped almonds

Preheat the oven to 300°F. • Line two cookie sheets with parchment paper. • Mix the egg whites and brown sugar in a large bowl over barely simmering water, stirring until the sugar has dissolved and the mixture is warm to the touch. • Remove the bowl from the heat and whisk with an electric mixer until thick and cool, about 15–20 minutes. • Fold in 1 tablespoon of the almonds. • Drop tablespoons of the mixture 2 inches apart onto the prepared cookie sheets. • Sprinkle with the remaining 1 tablespoon almonds. • Bake for 12–15 minutes, or until crisp and dry to the touch, rotating the sheets halfway through for even baking. • Cool completely in the oven.

Makes 12 cookies · Prep: 40 min. · Cooking: 15 min. Level: 2 · Keeps: 5 days

aniseed macaroons

- 3/4 cup blanched almonds
- 1 cup granulated sugar
- 1/4 cup all-purpose flour
- 2 large egg whites
- 1/8 teaspoon salt
- 1/4 teaspoon almond extract
- 1 tablespoon ground aniseeds

Preheat the oven to 325°F. • Spread the nuts on a large baking sheet. • Toast for 7 minutes, or until lightly golden. • Increase the oven temperature to 375°F. • Line a cookie sheet with rice paper. • Transfer the almonds to a food processor, add the sugar, and process until finely ground. • Stir together the almond mixture and flour in a medium bowl. • Beat the egg whites and salt in a large bowl with an electric mixer at high speed until stiff peaks form. • Use a large rubber spatula to fold in the dry

ingredients and almond extract. • Fit a pastry bag with a 1-inch plain tip. Fill the pastry bag, twist the opening tightly closed, and squeeze out 1-inch stars spacing 1 inch apart on the prepared cookie sheet. Sprinkle with the aniseeds. • Bake for 12–15 minutes, or until pale gold. • Cool on the sheets until the cookies firm slightly. • Transfer to racks on the rice paper, tearing away the excess paper, and let cool completely.

Makes 14–16 cookies · Prep: 30 min. · Cooking: 12–15 min. · Level: 1 · Keeps: 5 days

pineapple–cherry macaroons

- 3 large egg whites
- 1/8 teaspoon salt
- 1 cup finely ground almonds
- 3/4 cup granulated sugar
- 2/3 cup coarsely chopped candied pineapple
- 2/3 cup coarsely chopped candied cherries

Preheat the oven to 350°F. • Line two cookie sheets with parchment paper. • Beat the egg whites and salt in a large bowl with an electric mixer at high speed until stiff peaks form. • Use a large rubber spatula to fold in the almonds, sugar, pineapple, and 1/3 cup cherries. • Drop teaspoons of the batter 2 inches apart onto the prepared cookie sheets. • Decorate the tops of the cookies with the remaining 1/3 cup cherries. • Bake for 12–15 minutes, or until lightly browned and crisp, rotating the sheets halfway through for even baking. • Transfer to racks to cool.

Makes 16–20 cookies · Prep: 20 min. · Cooking: 12–15 min. · Level: 1 · Keeps: 7 days

Pineapple–cherry macaroons

orange–walnut meringues

- 3   large egg whites
- 1/4   teaspoon cream of tartar
- 1/8   teaspoon salt
- 1/2   teaspoon fresh orange juice
- 3/4   cup granulated sugar
- 1/2   cup finely chopped walnuts

Preheat the oven to 300°F. • Line two cookie sheets with parchment paper. • Beat the egg whites, cream of tartar, and salt in a large bowl with an electric mixer at medium speed until frothy. • Add the orange juice. • With mixer at high speed, gradually add the sugar, beating until stiff, glossy peaks form. • Use a large rubber spatula to fold in the walnuts. • Drop teaspoons of the mixture 1 inch apart onto the prepared cookie sheets. • Bake for 20–25 minutes, or until the meringues are dry and crisp, rotating the sheets halfway through for even baking • Transfer to racks to cool.

Makes 24 cookies · Prep: 20 min. · Cooking: 20–25 min. · Level: 1 · Keeps: 3 days

hazelnut rice-paper cookies

You will need rice paper, available from specialty baking stores as well as Asian food stores, to create these tasty nut cookies.

- 4   cups hazelnuts + 40 hazelnuts, halved
- 1 1/2   cups granulated sugar
- 4   large eggs
- 1   cup Vanilla Sugar (see page 341)

Preheat the oven to 325°F. • Spread the 4 cups hazelnuts on a large baking sheet. Toast for 7 minutes, or until lightly golden. • Transfer to a large cotton kitchen towel. Fold the towel over the nuts and rub them to remove the thin inner skins. • Discard the skins and process with 1/2 cup of the granulated sugar in a food processor or blender until finely ground. • Line three cookie sheets with rice paper. • Beat the eggs and remaining 1 cup granulated sugar and vanilla sugar in a large bowl with an electric mixer until very pale and thick. • Mix in the ground hazelnuts to form a smooth dough. • Moisten your hands with water and form the dough into balls the size of walnuts. • Place 2 inches apart on the rice paper, flattening each ball slightly and pressing a hazelnut half into the center. • Bake, one sheet at a time, for 10–12 minutes, or until firm to the touch. Transfer on the rice paper to racks to cool. • Tear away the excess rice paper from around the cookies.

Makes 60–70 cookies · Prep: 45 min. · Cooking: 10–12 min. per batch · Level: 2 · Keeps: 25 days

almond–poppy seed cookies

- 4   large egg whites
- 2   tablespoons all-purpose flour
- 1/4   cup superfine sugar
- 2   cups finely ground almonds
- 2   tablespoons poppy seeds
- 1   tablespoon almond oil

Preheat the oven to 350°F. • Line two cookie sheets with parchment paper. • Beat the egg whites in a large bowl with an electric mixer at high speed until soft peaks form. • Use a large rubber spatula to fold in the flour, superfine sugar, almonds, poppy seeds, and almond oil until smooth. • Drop teaspoons of the cookie dough 1 inch apart onto the prepared cookie sheets. • Bake for 6–8 minutes, or until golden brown around the edges, rotating the sheets halfway through for even baking. • Cool the cookies on the cookie sheet for 1 minute. Transfer to racks to finish cooling.

Makes about 24 cookies · Prep: 20 min. · Cooking: 6–8 min. · Level: 1 · Keeps: 5 days

peppermint meringues

- 3   large egg whites
- 1/2   teaspoon cream of tartar
- 1/8   teaspoon salt
- 3/4   cup granulated sugar
- 1/4   cup crushed peppermint candy
- 2   drops green food coloring

Preheat the oven to 300°F. • Line two cookie sheets with parchment paper. • Beat the egg whites, cream of tartar, and salt in a large bowl with an electric mixer at medium speed until frothy. • With mixer at high speed, gradually add the sugar, beating until stiff, glossy peaks form. • Use a large rubber spatula to fold in the crushed candy and food coloring. • Drop teaspoons of the batter 2 inches apart onto the prepared cookie sheets. • Bake for 20–25 minutes, or until the meringues are dry and crisp. • Transfer to racks to cool.

Makes 24 cookies · Prep: 20 min. · Cooking: 20–25 min. · Level: 1 · Keeps: 3 days

orange–peanut meringues

- 3   large egg whites
- 1/4   teaspoon cream of tartar
- 1/8   teaspoon salt
- 1/2   teaspoon fresh orange juice
- 3/4   cup granulated sugar
- 1/2   cup finely chopped peanuts

Preheat the oven to 300°F. • Line two cookie sheets with parchment paper. • Beat the egg whites, cream of tartar, and salt in a large bowl with an electric mixer at medium speed until frothy. • Add the orange juice. • With mixer at high speed, gradually add the sugar, beating until stiff, glossy peaks form. • Use a large rubber spatula to fold in the peanuts. • Drop teaspoons of the mixture 1 inch apart onto the prepared cookie sheets. • Bake for 20–25 minutes, or until the meringues are dry and crisp, rotating the sheets halfway through for even baking. • Transfer to racks to cool.

Makes 24 cookies · Prep: 20 min. · Cooking: 20–25 min. · Level: 1 · Keeps: 3 days

wasps' nests

- 2   cups slivered almonds
- 3   large egg whites
- 1   cup superfine sugar
- 1/8   teaspoon cream of tartar
- 1/4   teaspoon vanilla extract
- 1/8   teaspoon salt
- 4   oz semisweet chocolate, finely grated

Preheat the oven to 325°F. • Line three cookie sheets with rice paper. • Sprinkle the almonds onto a large baking sheet. Toast for 7 minutes, or until lightly golden. • Set aside to cool completely. Lower the oven to 275°F. • Beat the egg whites in a large bowl with an electric mixer at medium speed until frothy. • With mixer at high speed, gradually add the sugar, cream of tartar, vanilla, and salt, until stiff, glossy peaks form. • Use a large rubber spatula to fold in the chocolate and almonds. • Drop teaspoons of the batter 1 1/2 inches apart onto the rice paper. • Bake, one sheet at a time, for 20–25 minutes, or until lightly browned. • Cool the cookies completely on the cookie sheets. Tear away the excess paper from around the nests.

Makes 40 cookies · Prep: 40 min. · Cooking: 20–25 min. per batch · Level: 1 · Keeps: 4 days

Peppermint meringues (bottom) and Orange–walnut meringues (top)

amaretti cookies

These Italian cookies have been exported all over the world. They are often wrapped in brightly colored paper or served simply with a dusting of confectioners' sugar. If you have time available, it is best to toast the almonds in order to enhance their flavor. As soon as they have browned, remove from the oven and let cool completely. Transfer to a food processor and grind them finely. Serve these chewy cookies with coffee or with ice cream—delicious!

1	tablespoon all-purpose flour
1	tablespoon cornstarch
1/2	teaspoon ground cinnamon
1 1/4	cups finely ground almonds
2	large egg whites
1/8	teaspoon salt
2/3	cup granulated sugar
1/4	cup confectioners' sugar, to dust

Preheat the oven to 350°F. • Line three cookie sheets with parchment paper. • Sift the flour, cornstarch, and cinnamon into a small bowl. • Stir in the almonds. • Beat the egg whites and salt in a large bowl with an electric mixer at medium speed until frothy. With mixer at high speed, gradually add the granulated sugar, beating until stiff, glossy peaks form. • Use a large rubber spatula to fold in the dry ingredients to form a soft dough. • Dust your hands with confectioners' sugar. Form the dough into balls the size of walnuts and place 1 inch apart on the prepared cookie sheets. Dust with the confectioners' sugar. • Bake, one sheet at a time, for 15–20 minutes, or until pale gold. • Transfer to racks to cool.

Makes 35–40 cookies · Prep: 20 min. · Cooking: 15–20 min. per batch · Level: 1 · Keeps: 7 days

ratafia cookies

These tiny almond cookies differ from macaroons because they contain bitter almonds.

2	large egg whites
1/8	teaspoon salt
1 1/4	cups superfine sugar
1	cup finely ground almonds (use bitter almonds if available)
1/8	teaspoon almond extract

Preheat the oven to 300°F. • Line three cookie sheets with parchment paper. • Beat the egg whites and salt in a large bowl with an electric mixer at high speed until stiff peaks form. • Fold in the superfine sugar, almonds, and almond extract. • Fit a pastry bag with a plain 1/2-inch tip. Fill the pastry bag, twist the opening tightly closed, and squeeze out cookies the size of walnuts onto the prepared cookie sheets, spacing them 2 inches apart. • Bake, one sheet at a time, for 35–45 minutes, or until pale brown and crisp at the edges. • Cool completely on the sheet.

Makes 45–50 cookies · Prep: 25 min. · Cooking: 35–45 min. per batch · Level: 2 · Keeps: 1 month

lemon petits fours

1 3/4	cups whole almonds
1	cup superfine sugar
1	cup confectioners' sugar + extra to dust
2	tablespoons chopped candied lemon peel
1/2	teaspoon lemon extract
1	large egg white

Preheat the oven to 325°F. • Line a cookie sheet with rice paper. • Spread the almonds out on a large baking sheet. Toast in the oven for 7 minutes, or until lightly golden. Transfer to a food processor, add the superfine sugar, and process until finely chopped. • Transfer to a large bowl. Stir in the confectioners' sugar, lemon peel, and lemon extract. • Beat the egg white in a small bowl with an electric mixer at high speed until stiff peaks form. • Fold the beaten white into the almond mixture. • Spread the mixture into 1-inch squares on the prepared cookie sheet. • Cover with a clean kitchen towel and let stand in a cool place overnight. • Preheat the oven to 300°F. • Bake for 55–65 minutes, or until set. Cool completely on the cookie sheet. • Tear off any excess paper and dust with the confectioners' sugar.

Makes about 15 cookies · Prep: 25 min. + 12 hr. to rest · Cooking: 55–65 min. · Level: 2 · Keeps: 5 days

amarettini

1/2	cup blanched whole almonds
1	tablespoon granulated sugar
2/3	cup unblanched whole almonds
1/2	cup confectioners' sugar
2	large egg whites
1/2	cup superfine sugar
1/2	teaspoon vanilla extract
1	teaspoon almond extract

Preheat the oven to 325°F. • Spread out the blanched almonds on a large baking sheet. Toast for 7 minutes, or until lightly golden. • Let cool completely. Transfer to a food processor or blender with the granulated sugar and process until finely ground. • Lower the oven temperature to 300°F. • Butter four cookie sheets. • Process the unblanched whole almonds until finely ground. • Transfer to a large bowl and mix in the confectioners' sugar. • Beat the egg whites in a large bowl with an electric mixer at medium speed until frothy. • With mixer at high speed, gradually add the superfine sugar, beating until stiff, glossy peaks form. • Fold in the vanilla and almond extracts. • Fold in the almond sugar mixture and mix gently. • Fit a pastry bag with a plain 1-inch tip. Fill the pastry bag, twist the opening tightly closed, and squeeze out dots the size of hazelnuts, spacing 1 inch apart on the prepared cookie sheets. • Bake, one sheet at a time, for 12–15 minutes, or until lightly golden. • Turn the oven off and let dry in the oven for 20 minutes. Transfer to racks and let cool completely.

Makes 60 cookies · Prep: 45 min. · Cooking: 12–15 min. per batch + 20 min. to dry · Level: 2 · Keeps: 8 days

lemon amaretti cookies

2	large egg whites
2 1/2	cups finely chopped almonds
1 1/4	cups granulated sugar
1	tablespoon whole-wheat flour
	Grated zest of 1 lemon
1/2	teaspoon vanilla extract
1/8	teaspoon salt

Preheat the oven to 350°F. • Butter two cookie sheets. • Beat the egg whites in a large bowl with an electric mixer at high speed until stiff peaks form. • Use a large rubber spatula to fold the almonds, sugar, flour, lemon zest, vanilla, and salt into the beaten whites. • Fit a pastry bag with a 1/2-inch plain tip. Fill the pastry bag, twist the opening tightly closed, and squeeze out dots, spacing 1 inch apart on the prepared cookie sheets. • Bake for 20–25 minutes, or until lightly golden, rotating the sheets halfway through for even baking. • Cool on the sheets for 5 minutes. • Transfer to racks and let cool completely.

Makes 25 cookies · Prep: 25 min. · Cooking: 20–25 min. · Level: 2 · Keeps: 2 weeks

Amaretti cookies

wafers & thins

Florentines and French lace cookies—wafers are crisp and delicate. They are best served straight from the oven, wrapped around a smooth creamy filling. Preparation is the key to making wafer cookies because they harden quickly when removed from the oven. If you are creating curved or pirouette cookies, set out as many rolling pins or wooden spoons as you have on hand in your kitchen for shaping these challenging cookies.

above: Sesame thins
(page 252)

right: Ginger-filled brandy
snaps, Bavarian apple
cones, & Langues de chats
(pages 264, 258, and 262)

making french almond tiles (*tuiles aux amandes*)

These classic cookies are often served with Vanilla ice cream (see page 344)

- 1/4 cup (1/2 stick) butter, melted
- 1 cup confectioners' sugar
- 1/3 cup all-purpose flour
- 1/8 teaspoon salt
- 2 large egg whites
- 1/2 cup flaked almonds

Preheat the oven to 400°F. • Butter four cookie sheets. • Set out two rolling pins. • Place the melted butter in a large bowl. • Mix in 2/3 cup of the confectioners' sugar, the flour, salt, and egg whites. • Use a balloon whisk to beat the mixture until smooth. • Drop tablespoons of the mixture 2 inches apart onto the prepared cookie sheets. Do not place more than five cookies on one sheet. Spread the mixture out into thin circles. • Sprinkle with the almonds. • Bake, one sheet at a time, for 5–6 minutes, or until just golden at the edges. • Working quickly, use a spatula to lift each cookie from the sheet and drape it over a rolling pin. • Let cool completely. • Sprinkle the cooled tiles with the remaining 1/3 cup confectioners' sugar before serving.

Makes 20–24 cookies · Prep: 25 min. · Cooking: 5–6 min. per batch · Level: 3 · Keeps: 3 days

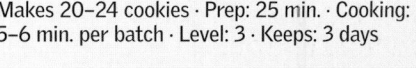

1. Grease rolling pins with butter.

2. Spread a tablespoon of the cookie mixture into a large circle, spacing them well apart. Bake the cookies.

3. Working quickly, remove the baked cookies from the sheets with a long, thin spatula.

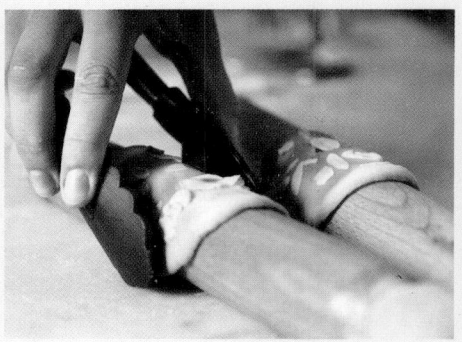

4. Press the cookies around the edges of the rolling pin and let cool completely.

white chocolate–hazelnut florentines

- 1 lb hazelnuts
- 1 cup granulated sugar
- 1 cup (2 sticks) butter, softened
- 1/2 cup honey
- 1/2 cup heavy cream
- 1/8 teaspoon salt
- 6 oz white chocolate, coarsely chopped
- 6 oz semisweet chocolate, coarsely chopped

Preheat the oven to 325°F. • Spread the hazelnuts on a large baking sheet. Toast for 7 minutes, or until lightly golden. • Transfer to a food processor or blender with 1/4 cup of the sugar and process until very finely chopped. • Increase the oven temperature to 375°F. • Set out three cookie sheets. • Melt the butter with the honey, cream, and the remaining 3/4 cup sugar in a small saucepan over low heat until the sugar has dissolved completely. • Bring to a boil and boil for 2 minutes. • Remove from the heat and stir in the nut mixture and salt. • Drop teaspoons of the mixture 3 inches apart onto the cookie sheets. • Bake, one sheet at a time, for 8–10 minutes, or until golden brown. • Cool on the sheets until the cookies firm slightly. • Transfer to racks to cool. • Melt the chocolate in a double boiler over barely simmering water. Dip the bottoms of the cookies into the chocolate and let stand for 30 minutes until set.

Makes 22–25 cookies · Prep: 40 min. + 30 min. to set · Cooking: 8–10 min. per batch · Level: 3 · Keeps: 5 days

chocolate pirouette lace cookies

- 1/2 cup (1 stick) butter, softened
- 1/2 cup granulated sugar
- 2 large egg whites
- 1/2 teaspoon vanilla extract
- 1/2 cup all-purpose flour
- 2 oz semisweet chocolate, coarsely grated

Preheat the oven to 400°F. • Butter four cookie sheets. • Butter the handles of two wooden spoons. • Beat the butter and sugar in a large bowl with an electric mixer at high speed until creamy. • With mixer at high speed, beat the egg whites in a large bowl until stiff peaks form. • Use a large rubber spatula to fold the beaten whites into the butter mixture. • Fold in the vanilla and flour until just blended. • Fold in the grated chocolate. • Spread the mixture into 2-inch rounds on the prepared cookie sheets. Do not spread more than four cookies on the sheet. • Bake, one sheet at a time, for 4–6 minutes, or until just golden at the edges. • Use a thin metal spatula to transfer the cookies individually to sheets of parchment paper. • Working quickly, roll the cookies around the prepared handles. • Slide off the handles and let cool completely on racks. • Butter the cookie sheets again and continue to bake in batches until all the batter has been used.

Makes 32–36 cookies · Prep: 40 min. · Cooking: 6–8 min. per batch · Level: 3 · Keeps: 2 weeks

making chocolate-dipped pirouette cookies

These delicacies are a challenge due to the speed at which you must work when they come out of the oven.

- 2 large egg whites
- 1/8 teaspoon salt
- 1/2 cup granulated sugar
- 1/3 cup all-purpose flour
- 3 tablespoons butter, melted
- 2 oz semisweet chocolate, coarsely chopped

Preheat the oven to 400°F. • Line four cookie sheets with parchment paper. • Use a pencil and ruler to draw four 4 x 3-inch rectangles on each sheet of paper, spaced well apart. • Butter the handles of two wooden spoons. • Beat the egg whites and salt in a large bowl with an electric mixer at high speed until stiff peaks form. • Use a large rubber spatula to fold in the sugar, flour, and melted butter. • Spread the mixture into the 4 x 3-inch rectangles on the prepared cookie sheets. • Bake, one sheet at a time, for 6–8 minutes, or until lightly browned. • Use a thin metal spatula to transfer the cookies individually to sheets of parchment paper. • Working quickly, roll the cookies one-by-one around the prepared skewer. • Slide off the skewer and let cool completely on racks. • Melt the chocolate in a double boiler over barely simmering water. • Dip both ends of the cookies in the chocolate and let stand on the long sides until dry, about 30 minutes.

Makes 16 cookies · Prep: 40 min. + 30 min. to set Cooking: 6–8 min. per batch · Level: 3 · Keeps: 10 days

1. Grease the handles of as many wooden spoons as you have in your kitchen.

2. While the cookies are still hot, begin to roll around the handles, pressing the ends under.

3. Roll the cookies up completely.

white florentines

Despite their Italian name, florentines are a German and Austrian specialty and are now made everywhere. Traditionally, these rich, chewy disks studded with flaked and chopped nuts, candied peel, and dried fruit are backed with dark chocolate. This version is brushed with white chocolate.

- 1/2 cup heavy cream
- 1/4 vanilla pod
- 2 tablespoons butter
- 1/2 cup granulated sugar
- 1/2 cup coarsely chopped almonds
- 1/4 cup coarsely chopped hazelnuts
- 1 cup finely chopped mixed candied peel
- 1/4 cup finely sliced red candied cherries
- 1 tablespoon finely chopped candied angelica
- 2 tablespoons all-purpose flour
- 7 oz white chocolate, coarsely chopped

Preheat the oven to 325°F. • Line four cookie sheets with parchment paper. • Heat the cream with the vanilla pod, butter, and sugar in a medium saucepan over medium heat, stirring constantly, until the sugar has dissolved. Bring to a boil and remove from the heat immediately. Discard the vanilla pod and let cool. • Mix the almonds, hazelnuts, candied peel, cherries, angelica, and flour in a large bowl. • Stir in the cooled cream mixture and mix well. • Drop heaping teaspoons of the mixture 4 inches apart onto the prepared cookie sheets, flattening them to make 2-inch circles. Do not place more than five cookies on one sheet. • Bake, one sheet at a time, for 10–12 minutes, or until golden around the edges. • Cool on the sheets until the cookies firm slightly. Transfer to racks and let cool completely. • Melt the white chocolate in a double boiler over barely simmering water. • Lay the cold florentines flat-side upwards on a sheet of waxed paper, and spread the chocolate over them with a pastry brush. For a thick coating, paint the cookies several times. • When they are nearly set, make swirly patterns with a fork on the white chocolate base.

Makes 18–20 cookies · Prep: 45 min. · Cooking: 10–12 min. per batch · Level: 3 · Keeps: 14 days

poppy seed and sesame wafers

- 2 tablespoons butter
- 1/4 cup raw sugar (Demerara or Barbados)
- 2 tablespoons honey
- 2 tablespoons poppy seeds
- 3 tablespoons sesame seeds

Preheat the oven to 400°F. • Butter a cookie sheet. • Melt the butter, raw sugar, and honey in a medium saucepan and bring to a boil. • Stir in the poppy and sesame seeds. Remove from the heat and let stand 15 minutes. • Form the mixture into balls the size of walnuts and place 2 inches apart on the prepared cookie sheet. • Bake for 5–7 minutes, or until slightly darker in color. • Transfer to racks to cool.

Makes 10 cookies · Prep: 20 min. · Cooking: 5–7 min. · Level: 1 · Keeps: 3 days

chinese fortune cookies

These cookies are homemade versions of the entertaining variety found in Chinese restaurants all around the world. Write out your messages on small pieces of paper before starting to bake the cookies.

3	large egg whites
3/4	cup granulated sugar
1	cup all-purpose flour
1/2	cup (1 stick) butter, melted
1/2	teaspoon vanilla extract
1/2	teaspoon almond extract
2	tablespoons cold water

Preheat the oven to 375°F. • Butter four cookie sheets. • Beat the egg whites and sugar in a large bowl with an electric mixer at high speed until frothy. • With mixer at low speed, beat in the flour, butter, vanilla and almond extracts, and water. • Drop teaspoons of the mixture onto the prepared cookie sheets, spreading it out to 3-inch circles. • Bake, one sheet at a time, for 5–7 minutes, or until just golden at the edges. • Use a spatula to remove the cookies, placing a message in the center. Fold the cookies in half, enclosing your message, to form a semicircle. Hold the rounded edges of the semicircle between your thumb and index finger. Place your other index finger at the center of the folded edge and push in. • Let cool completely.

Makes 40–50 cookies · Prep: 25 min. · Cooking: 5–7 min. · Level: 3 · Keeps: 2 weeks

chocolate–almond wafers

1	cup flaked almonds
1/4	cup all-purpose flour
1/4	cup unsweetened cocoa powder
1/8	teaspoon salt
1	large egg + 1 large egg white, lightly beaten
1/2	cup granulated sugar
2	tablespoons butter, softened

Preheat the oven to 325°F. • Spread the almonds on a large baking sheet. • Toast for 7 minutes, or until lightly golden. • Butter four cookie sheets. • Set out two rolling pins. • Sift the flour, cocoa, and salt into a medium bowl. • Use a wooden spoon to mix the egg and egg white and sugar in a large bowl. • Mix in the dry ingredients and butter. • Drop tablespoons of the mixture 2 inches apart onto the prepared cookie sheets. Do not place more than five cookies on one sheet. Spread the mixture out into thin circles. Sprinkle with the almonds. • Bake, one sheet at a time, for 8–10 minutes, or until firm at the edges. • Working quickly, use a spatula to lift each cookie from the sheet and drape it over a rolling pin. • Let cool completely.

Makes 20–22 cookies · Prep: 30 min. · Cooking: 8–10 min. per batch · Level: 3 · Keeps: 5 days

chocolate–almond tuiles

"Tiles" in French, the name defines their elongated, curved shape, reminiscent of Mediterranean-style roof tiles in the south of France.

1	tablespoon all-purpose flour
1	tablespoon unsweetened cocoa powder
2	large egg whites
1/8	teaspoon salt
1/4	cup superfine sugar
1	tablespoon heavy cream
1	tablespoon butter, melted
2	tablespoons flaked almonds

Preheat the oven to 425°F. • Line three cookie sheets with parchment paper. Set out two rolling pins. • Sift the flour and cocoa into a small bowl. • Beat the egg whites and salt in a large bowl with an electric mixer at medium speed until frothy. With mixer at high speed, gradually add the superfine sugar, beating until stiff, glossy peaks form. • Use a large rubber spatula to fold in the dry ingredients. • Fold in the cream and butter until well blended. • Drop tablespoons of the dough onto the cookie sheet, placing them 3 inches apart. Do not drop more than six cookies onto each sheet. Sprinkle with the almonds. • Bake, one sheet at a time, for 4–6 minutes, or until the cookies are faintly tinged with gold and slightly darker at the edges. • Working quickly, use a spatula to lift each cookie from the sheet and drape it over a rolling pin. Slide each cookie off the pin and onto racks to finish cooling.

Makes 12–15 cookies · Prep: 20 min. · Cooking: 4–6 min. per batch · Level: 3 · Keeps: 2 weeks

berry thins

1/4	cup (1/2 stick) butter
1/4	cup granulated sugar
2	teaspoons honey
1/3	cup finely ground pecans
1/3	cup silvered almonds
1/4	cup dried cranberries or cherries
1/4	cup all-purpose flour

Preheat the oven to 350°F. • Line two cookie sheets with parchment paper. • Melt the butter with the sugar and honey in a medium saucepan over low heat, stirring constantly, until the sugar has dissolved completely. • Remove from the heat and mix in the almonds, cranberries, and pecans. • Stir in the flour and mix well. • Drop teaspoons of the mixture 3 inches apart onto the prepared cookie sheets, spreading them out as thinly as possible. • Bake, one sheet at the time, for 8–10 minutes, or until they are golden brown at the edges. • Cool on the sheets until the cookies firm slightly. Transfer to racks and let cool completely.

Makes about 20 cookies · Prep: 15 min. per batch · Cooking: 8–10 min. · Level: 2 · Keeps: 8 days

French almond tiles (top and right) and Chinese fortune cookies (center)

dainty almond wafers

3/4 cup all-purpose flour
1/2 teaspoon baking powder
1/8 teaspoon salt
1/3 cup butter, softened
1/2 cup granulated sugar
2 large eggs
1/4 teaspoon vanilla extract
2 tablespoons flaked almonds

Preheat the oven to 350°F. • Butter four cookie sheets. • Sift the flour, baking powder, and salt into a medium bowl. • Beat the butter and sugar in a large bowl with an electric mixer at high speed until creamy. • Add the eggs and vanilla, beating until just blended. • Mix in the dry ingredients. • Drop teaspoons of the mixture 3 inches apart onto the prepared cookie sheets. Do not drop more than eight cookies onto each sheet. Use a metal spatula to spread the batter into 2-inch circles. • Sprinkle with the almonds. • Bake, one sheet at a time, for 8–10 minutes, or until golden brown. • Working quickly, use a spatula to lift each cookie from the sheet. • Transfer to racks to cool.

Makes 30–35 cookies · Prep: 25 min. · Cooking: 8–10 min. per batch · Level: 2 · Keeps: 10 days

curled ginger thins

2/3 cup all-purpose flour
1 teaspoon ground ginger
1/8 teaspoon salt
1/3 cup dark molasses
1/2 cup (1 stick) butter
1/2 cup firmly packed dark brown sugar
1 tablespoon fresh lemon juice

Preheat the oven to 350°F. • Butter four cookie sheets. • Butter a rolling pin. • Sift the flour, ginger, and salt into a medium bowl. • Heat the molasses, butter, and brown sugar in a small saucepan over low heat until the sugar has dissolved completely. • Mix the molasses mixture into the dry ingredients. • Stir in the lemon juice. • Drop teaspoons of the dough 3 inches apart onto the prepared cookie sheets. Do not bake more than five cookies on one sheet. • Bake, one sheet at a time, for 8–10 minutes, or until golden brown. • Cool on the sheets until the cookies firm slightly. • Working quickly, use a spatula to lift each cookie off the sheet and drape it over the rolling pin. • Let cool completely.

Makes 16–20 cookies · Prep: 40 min. · Cooking: 8–10 min. · Level: 3 · Keeps: 7 days

Curled ginger thins

sesame thins

1/2 cup sesame seeds
1 cup firmly packed light brown sugar
1/3 cup all-purpose flour
1 tablespoon butter, softened
1/8 teaspoon salt
1 large egg, lightly beaten
1 teaspoon vanilla extract

Preheat the oven to 350°F. • Butter three cookie sheets. • Toast the sesame seeds in a skillet for 3 minutes, or until golden brown and fragrant, shaking the pan constantly. • Transfer to a large bowl. • Mix in the brown sugar, flour, butter, salt, egg, and vanilla until well blended. • Drop teaspoons of the dough 3 inches apart onto the prepared cookie sheets. • Bake, one sheet at a time, for 5–7 minutes, or until just golden. • Cool on the sheets until the cookies firm slightly. • Use a thin metal spatula to transfer to racks to cool.

Makes 36 cookies · Prep: 20 min. · Cooking: 5–7 min. per batch · Level: 1 · Keeps: 3 days

honey–nutmeg wafers

1/3 cup all-purpose flour
1/4 teaspoon freshly ground nutmeg
1/8 teaspoon salt
1/4 cup (1/2 stick) butter, softened
1/4 cup firmly packed light brown sugar
3/4 cup honey
1 large egg
1/2 cup shredded coconut

Preheat the oven to 375°F. • Butter four cookie sheets. • Sift the flour, nutmeg, and salt into a medium bowl. • Beat the butter and brown sugar in a large bowl with an electric mixer at high speed until creamy. • Beat in the honey and egg, beating until just blended. • Mix in the dry ingredients and coconut. • Drop teaspoons of the batter 3 inches apart onto the prepared cookie sheets. Do not drop more than eight cookies onto each sheet. Spread the mixture out into thin circles. • Bake, one sheet at a time, for 8–10 minutes, or until faintly tinged with brown on top and slightly darker at the edges. • Working quickly, use a spatula to lift each cookie from the sheet. Transfer to racks to cool. • Butter the cookie sheets again and continue to bake in batches until all the batter has been used.

Makes 32–36 cookies · Prep: 20 min. · Cooking: 8–10 min. per batch · Level: 2 · Keeps: 5 days

almond lace cookies

These thin, crisp cookies also can be molded to hold a filling. If you are intending to mold them into a basket for fruit or whipped cream, bake just four cookies at a time, since they must be shaped quickly.

- 1/4 cup (1/2 stick) butter, cut up
- 1/2 cup Vanilla Sugar (see page 341)
- 1/2 cup finely ground almonds
- 3 tablespoons all-purpose flour
- 1/8 teaspoon salt
- 2 tablespoons heavy cream

Preheat the oven to 375°F. • Line two cookie sheets with parchment paper. • Melt the butter in a saucepan over low heat. • Stir in the vanilla sugar, almonds, flour, salt, and cream. • Drop teaspoons of the mixture 2 inches apart onto the prepared cookie sheets. Use a thin spatula to spread them thinly. Do not place more than four cookies on each sheet. • Bake, one batch at a time, for 5–7 minutes, or until golden brown. • Cool on the sheet for 1 minute. Use a thin metal spatula to transfer the cookies to a cool surface to crispen. • If you are making baskets, cool for 1 minute on the cookie sheet before lifting them off with a thin metal spatula. • Working quickly, drape over an upturned cup. Press the cookie down gently and pleat with your fingers to form a cup.

Makes 18 cookies · Prep: 15 min. · Cooking: 5–7 min. per batch · Level: 3 · Keeps: 2–3 days

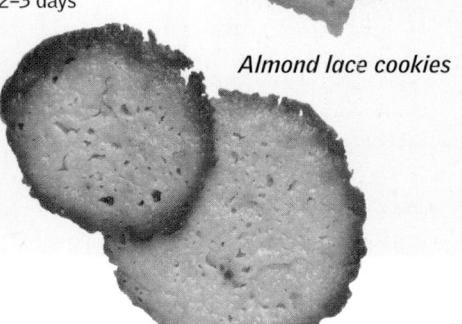

Almond lace cookies

filled almond wafers

- 1 2/3 cups blanched almonds
- 1 1/2 cups confectioners' sugar
- 4 large egg whites
- 1/8 teaspoon salt

Almond cream
- 4 large egg yolks
- 2 tablespoons granulated sugar
- 2 tablespoons water
- 2 tablespoons butter

Preheat the oven to 350°F. • Line a cookie sheet with parchment paper. • Process the almonds with the confectioners' sugar in a food processor or blender until very finely ground. • Beat the egg whites and salt in a large bowl with an electric mixer at high speed until stiff peaks form. • Set aside 2 tablespoons of the almond mixture. Use a large rubber spatula to fold the remaining almond mixture into the egg whites. • Spread the mixture onto the prepared baking sheet. • Bake for 10–12 minutes, or until lightly browned. • Cool completely on the baking sheet. • Cut into 2 x 1 1/2-inch bars. • Almond cream: Beat the egg yolks, sugar, and water in a double boiler until well blended. • Cook over low heat, stirring constantly with a wooden spoon, until the mixture lightly coats a metal spoon or registers 160°F on an instant-read thermometer. • Stir in the reserved almond mixture and butter until well blended. • Immediately plunge the pan into a bowl of ice water and stir until the egg mixture has cooled. • Stick the cookies together in pairs with the almond cream.

Makes 25 cookies · Prep: 40 min. · Cooking: 10–12 min. · Level: 2 · Keeps: 7 days

poppy-seed ice-cream baskets

These cookies make decorative and tasty ice cream bowls. If you prefer, top the ice cream with a Chocolate-fudge sauce (see page 342).

- 4 large egg whites
- 1/8 teaspoon salt
- 2 tablespoons poppy seeds
- 1/4 cup superfine sugar
- 1 tablespoon Vanilla Sugar (see page 341)
- 2 tablespoons all-purpose flour
- 2 1/4 cups finely ground almonds
  Vanilla Ice Cream (see page 344), to serve
  Red Berry Compote, Tropical Coulis, Strawberry Coulis, or Raspberry Coulis, (pages 342–344), to serve

Preheat the oven to 350°F. • Line three cookie sheets with parchment paper. • Beat the egg whites and salt in a large bowl with an electric mixer at high speed until soft peaks form. • Use a large rubber spatula to fold in the poppy seeds, superfine sugar, vanilla sugar, flour, and almonds. • Drop tablespoons of the mixture 2 inches apart onto the cookie sheets. Use a spatula to spread them thinly. Do not place more than four cookies on each sheet. • Bake, one batch at a time, for 5–7 minutes, or until golden brown. • Cool the cookies for 1 minute on the cookie sheet. • Use a thin metal spatula to lift up each cookie. • Working quickly, drape over an upturned glass or cup. Press the cookie down gently and pleat with your fingers to form a cup. • Cool the cookies completely. To serve, fill each basket with a scoop of ice cream. Top with a spoonful of compote.

Makes 12–15 cookie baskets · Prep: 15 min. · Cooking: 5–7 min. per batch · Level: 3 · Keeps: 2–3 days

almond–orange wafers

- scant 2 tablespoons all-purpose flour
- 1/8 teaspoon salt
- 2 large eggs
- 1/2 cup superfine sugar
- 1 1/2 tablespoons Vanilla Sugar (see page 352)
- 2 tablespoons butter, melted
- 1 teaspoon finely grated orange zest
- 1 1/4 cups slivered almonds
- 1–2 teaspoons milk

Preheat the oven to 350°F. • Line three cookie sheets with parchment paper. • Butter two rolling pins. • Sift the flour and salt into a small bowl. • Beat the eggs and superfine and vanilla sugars in a large bowl with an electric mixer until frothy. • Mix in the butter, orange zest, dry ingredients, and almonds. • Add enough milk to form a soft dough. • Drop rounded teaspoons of the mixture 4 inches apart on the prepared cookie sheets. Do not place more than four cookies on each sheet. Use a metal spatula to spread out the batter as thinly as possible into 3-inch discs. • Bake, one sheet at a time, for 8–10 minutes, or until faintly tinged with brown on top and slightly darker at the edges. • Working quickly, use a spatula to lift each cookie from the sheet and drape it over a rolling pin. • Transfer to racks to cool completely. • Butter the cookie sheets again and continue to bake in batches until all the batter has been used.

Makes 20–25 cookies · Prep: 25 min. · Cooking: 8–10 min. per batch · Level: 3 · Keeps: 3 days

walnut–cherry florentines

- 1/4 cup golden raisins
- 1/4 cup (1/2 stick) butter, cut up
- 1/3 cup raw sugar (Barbados or Demerara)
- 1 tablespoon light molasses
- 1/2 cup coarsely chopped candied cherries
- 1/4 cup finely chopped walnuts
- 1/4 cup finely chopped almonds
- 1/4 cup finely chopped mixed candied peel
- 1/4 cup all-purpose flour
- 1/8 teaspoon salt
- 1/4 cup flaked almonds
- 3 1/2 oz semisweet chocolate, coarsely chopped

Preheat the oven to 325°F. • Line four cookie sheets with parchment paper. • Plump the raisins in hot water to cover in a small bowl for 10 minutes. • Drain well and pat dry with paper towels. • Melt the butter with the raw sugar and molasses in a large saucepan over low heat until the sugar has dissolved completely. • Mix in the raisins, cherries, walnuts, chopped almonds, candied peel, flour, salt, and flaked almonds until well blended. • Drop teaspoons of the mixture 3 inches apart onto the prepared cookie sheets. Do not place more than five cookies on each sheet. • Bake, one sheet at a time, for 10–15 minutes, or until just golden. • Cool on the sheets until the cookies firm slightly. • Use a thin metal spatula to transfer the cookies to racks to finish cooling. • Butter the cookie sheets again and continue to bake in batches until all the batter has been used. • Melt the chocolate in a double boiler over barely simmering water. • Brush the bottoms of the cookies with the chocolate. • Draw the tines of a fork across the chocolate to form wavy lines. Let stand upside-down until set, about 30 minutes.

Makes 45 cookies · Prep: 40 min. + 40 min. to plump raisins and set · Cooking: 10–15 min. per batch · Level: 2 · Keeps: 3 days

summer berry florentines

These thin wafers are a variation on the chewy Florentine-style cookie theme.

- 3/4 cup all-purpose flour
- 1/8 teaspoon salt
- 1/2 cup (1 stick) butter, cut up
- 3/4 cup granulated sugar
- 2 teaspoons honey
- 1/2 cup flaked almonds, toasted
- 2/3 cup finely chopped dried blueberries
- 2/3 cup finely chopped dried cherries
- 2/3 cup finely chopped dried peaches

- 4 oz semisweet chocolate, coarsely chopped

Preheat the oven to 350°F. • Line four cookie sheets with parchment paper. • Sift the flour and salt into a medium bowl. • Melt the butter with the sugar and honey in a medium saucepan over low heat, stirring often, until the sugar has dissolved completely. • Increase the heat and bring the mixture almost to a boil. • Remove from the heat and mix in the almonds and dried fruit. • Add the dry ingredients all at once and stir until well blended. • Drop teaspoons of the dough 3 inches apart onto the prepared cookie sheets, flattening them slightly. • Bake, one sheet at a time, for 8–10 minutes, or until golden brown on top and slightly darker brown at the edges. • Cool on the sheets until the cookies firm slightly. Transfer to racks to finish cooling. • Melt the chocolate in a double boiler over barely simmering water. Arrange the cookies flat-side up on a sheet of waxed paper. • Brush with the melted chocolate and let stand for 30 minutes until set.

Makes 45 cookies · Prep: 25 min. + 30 min. to stand · Cooking: 8–10 min. per batch · Level: 1 · Keeps: 5 days

coffee-pecan wafers

- 1/4 cup (1/2 stick) butter, softened
- 1/4 cup granulated sugar
- 1 tablespoon freeze-dried coffee granules
- 1 large egg, lightly beaten
- 1/3 cup all-purpose flour
- 1/8 teaspoon salt
- 1/4 cup finely chopped pecans
- 1/2 teaspoon vanilla extract

Preheat the oven to 350°F. • Butter a cookie sheet. • Beat the butter, sugar, and coffee granules in a large bowl with an electric mixer at high speed until creamy. • Add the egg, beating until just blended. • Mix in the flour and salt until well blended. • Stir in the pecans and vanilla. • Drop rounded teaspoons of the cookie dough 1 inch apart onto the prepared cookie sheets. • Bake for 10–15 minutes, or until just golden. • Cool on the sheet until the cookies firm slightly. Transfer to racks to finish cooling.

Makes 10–12 cookies · Prep: 20 min. · Cooking: 10–15 min. · Level: 1 · Keeps: 7 days

florentines

- 1/2 cup heavy cream
- 1/2 vanilla pod
- 1 cup granulated sugar
- 1/4 cup (1/2 stick) butter
- 1 1/3 cups flaked almonds
- 1 1/3 cups hazelnuts, coarsely chopped
- 1 1/2 cups mixed candied peel, coarsely chopped
- 1/4 cup candied cherries, finely chopped
- 1/3 cup all-purpose flour
- 3 oz semisweet chocolate, coarsely chopped
- 3 oz white chocolate, coarsely chopped

Preheat the oven to 350°F. • Butter two cookie sheets. Bring the cream, vanilla pod, sugar, and butter to a boil in a medium saucepan over low heat, stirring constantly. • Remove from the heat. • Let cool completely and remove the vanilla pod. • Stir together the almonds, hazelnuts, candied peel, cherries, and flour in a medium bowl. Mix the dry ingredients into the cream mixture. • Use a tablespoon to drop 2-inch heaps of batter onto the prepared cookie sheets, spacing 2 inches apart. • Bake for 10–15 minutes, or until golden brown, rotating the sheets halfway through for even baking. • Cool the cookies on the cookie sheets for 3 minutes. • Use a thin metal spatula to transfer to racks and let cool completely. • Melt the chocolates separately in double boilers over barely simmering water. • Use the metal spatula to spread a thin layer of both chocolates on the smooth side of the cookies.

• Use a fork to make wavy lines across the chocolate.

Makes about 30 cookies · Prep: 50 min. · Cooking: 10–15 min. · Level: 3 · Keeps: 10–12 days

Florentines

darjeeling wafers

Darjeeling tea is a superior blend of black tea from high in the Himalayas in northern India. The first tea seeds were planted by an expatriate surgeon 150 years ago. Assisted by the government action of starting tea gardens in the area, Darjeeling tea turned the small hamlet into a thriving industrial town. Today over 10 million kilograms of Darjeeling tea are produced annually. Unusually flavored with an undertone of Muscat grapes, these wafers are delicious served in the late afternoon with delicate teas.

Tea leaves from 2 Darjeeling tea bags
1/2 cup boiling water
6 tablespoons firmly packed light brown sugar
1/2 cup all-purpose flour
1/8 teaspoon salt
2 tablespoons butter, softened
1 large egg
1/2 teaspoon vanilla extract

Steep half the tea leaves in the boiling water in a small bowl for 5 minutes. • Strain the brewed tea, discard the tea leaves, and let cool completely. • Process the remaining tea leaves and 2 tablespoons brown sugar in a food processor or blender until very finely ground. • Sift the flour and salt into a medium bowl. • Beat the butter, remaining 1/4 cup brown sugar, and the finely ground tea mixture in a large bowl with an electric mixer at high speed until creamy. • Add the egg, beating until just blended. • Beat in the cooled tea and vanilla. • Mix in the dry ingredients. • Cover with a clean kitchen towel and let stand for 30 minutes. • Preheat the oven to 350°F. • Butter three cookie sheets. • Drop teaspoons of the mixture 2 inches apart onto the prepared

chocolate and hazelnut wafers

2/3 cup hazelnuts
1/2 cup superfine sugar
1/4 cup (1/2 stick) butter, softened
1 1/2 tablespoons unsweetened cocoa powder
1 tablespoon light cream
2 teaspoons dark rum
2 large egg whites, lightly beaten
1/3 cup all-purpose flour
1/8 teaspoon salt

Preheat the oven to 425°F. • Line three cookie sheets with parchment paper. Butter two rolling pins. • Chop one-third of the hazelnuts coarsely. • Process the remaining hazelnuts with the superfine sugar in a food processor until very finely ground. • Beat the butter in a large bowl with an electric mixer at high speed until creamy. • Mix in the finely ground hazelnut mixture, cocoa, cream, and rum. • Stir in the egg whites, followed by the flour and salt. • Drop tablespoons of the mixture 2 inches apart onto the prepared cookie sheets. Do not place more than five cookies on one sheet. Spread the mixture out into 3-inch circles. • Sprinkle with the coarsely chopped hazelnuts. • Bake, one sheet at a time, for 5–6 minutes, or until just golden at the edges. • Working quickly, use a spatula to lift each cookie from the sheet and drape it over a rolling pin. Slide each cookie off the pin onto a rack to finish cooling. • Let cool completely.

Makes 15 cookies · Prep: 25 min. · Cooking: 5–6 min. per batch · Level: 3 · Keeps: 5 days

honey gingersnaps

3/4 cup all-purpose flour
1 teaspoon ground ginger
1/8 teaspoon salt
1/4 cup (1/2 stick) butter, cut up
1/2 cup honey
2/3 cup raw sugar (Demerara or Barbados)

Sift the flour, ginger, and salt into a medium bowl. • Melt the butter with the honey in a medium saucepan over low heat, stirring occasionally, until well blended. • Mix in the dry ingredients and sugar. Increase the heat and stir until the mixture boils. • Reduce to medium heat and simmer for 3 minutes, stirring constantly. • Pour the mixture into a medium bowl and let cool completely. • Preheat the oven to 350°F. • Line four cookie sheets with parchment paper. • Butter two rolling pins. • Form the dough into balls the size of walnuts and roll out on a lightly floured surface to a thickness of 1/8 inch. • Use a spatula to transfer the cookies to the prepared cookie sheets, placing them 2 inches apart. Do not bake more than six cookies on each sheet. • Bake, one sheet at a time, for 8–10 minutes, or until faintly tinged with brown on top and slightly darker at the edges. • Working quickly, use a spatula to lift each cookie from the sheet and drape it over a rolling pin. Slide each cookie off the pin onto a rack to finish cooling. • Butter the cookie sheets again and continue to bake in batches until all the batter has been used.

Makes 30–35 cookies · Prep: 25 min. · Cooking: 8–10 min. per batch · Level: 3 · Keeps: 10 days

cardamom krumkake wafer cones

Norwegian in origin, these wafer-thin cookies melt in your mouth and taste amazing served with ice cream.

1 1/2 cups all-purpose flour
2 teaspoons ground cardamom
1/2 teaspoon ground ginger
1/8 teaspoon salt
1 cup granulated sugar
Grated zest of 2 lemons
1/4 teaspoon freshly grated nutmeg
1/3 cup butter, softened
2 large eggs
2/3 cup light cream
1/3 cup confectioners' sugar
Vanilla Ice Cream (see page 344), to serve

Preheat a 7-inch krumkake or pizzelle iron. • Sift the flour, cardamom, ginger, and salt

Chocolate and hazelnut wafers

sheets. • Bake, one sheet at a time, for 8–10 minutes, or until the edges are just golden. • Cool the cookies on the baking sheets for 5 minutes. • Transfer to racks and let cool completely.

Makes 36 cookies · Prep: 25 min. + 30 min. to stand · Cooking: 8–10 min. per batch · Level: 1 · Keeps: 5 days

into a large bowl. Stir in the granulated sugar, lemon zest, and nutmeg. • Mix in the butter, eggs, and cream until well blended. • Drop 2 tablespoons of the batter onto the center of the iron. • Lower the top so that the batter spreads. • Cook for 30 seconds, or until just golden at the edges. • Lift up the top and remove the cookie from the iron. • Place the cookie on a rack and let cool for 10 seconds. Use a wooden krumkake roller to shape the cookie into a cone. • Repeat with the remaining cookie dough. • Dust with the confectioners' sugar just before serving with ice cream.

Makes 30–40 cookies · Prep: 20 min. · Cooking: 30 seconds per batch · Level: 3 · Keeps: 7 days

orange wafer thins

1³/4 cups all-purpose flour
1 teaspoon baking powder
1/8 teaspoon salt
3/4 cup (1¹/2 sticks) butter, softened
1 cup granulated sugar
1 large egg
1 teaspoon finely grated orange zest
1 tablespoon orange flower water
1 tablespoon light cream
 Granulated sugar, to sprinkle

Sift the flour, baking powder, and salt into a medium bowl. • Beat the butter and sugar in a large bowl with an electric mixer at high speed until creamy. • Add the egg and orange zest, beating until just blended. • Mix in the dry ingredients, orange flower water, and cream. • Form the dough into a log, wrap in plastic wrap, and refrigerate for at least 30 minutes. • Preheat the oven to 375°F. • Line two cookie sheets with parchment paper. •

Slice the dough ¹/8 inch thick and place on the prepared cookie sheets, spacing them 1 inch apart. Sprinkle with sugar. • Bake for 8–10 minutes, or until golden on top and light brown around the edges, rotating the sheets halfway through for even baking. • Transfer to racks to cool.

Makes 50–60 cookies · Prep: 15 min. + 30 min. to chill · Cooking: 8–10 min. · Level: 1 · Keeps: 14 days

maple syrup lace cookies

3/4 cup pure maple syrup
2/3 cup butter, cut up
1 cup all-purpose flour
1/4 teaspoon baking soda
1/8 teaspoon salt
1/4 cup granulated sugar
1 teaspoon vanilla extract
1 large egg

Preheat the oven to 375°F. • Butter four cookie sheets. • Bring the maple syrup to a boil in a small saucepan over medium heat and boil for 5 minutes. • Add the butter and boil for 2 minutes. • Let cool for 10 minutes. • Sift the flour, baking soda, and salt into a large bowl. Stir in the sugar. • Add the vanilla and egg to the maple syrup mixture, beating until just blended. • Pour into the dry ingredients and mix well. • Drop teaspoons of the batter 3 inches apart onto the prepared cookie sheets. Do not drop more than four cookies onto each cookie sheet. • Bake, one sheet at a time, for 5–8 minutes, or until faintly tinged with brown on top and slightly darker at the edges. • Cool on the sheets until the cookies firm slightly. • Transfer to racks to finish cooling. • Butter the cookie sheets again

and continue to bake in batches until all the batter has been used.

Makes 35–40 cookies · Prep: 40 min. · Cooking: 5–8 min. per batch · Level: 1 · Keeps: 7 days

coconut fortune cookies

Substitute almond extract for the coconut extract if it is unavailable. Write messages of wisdom on small rectangles of paper before you prepare the cookies.

2 large egg whites
1/3 cup granulated sugar
1/3 cup all-purpose flour
2 tablespoons butter, melted
1 teaspoon coconut extract
1/8 teaspoon salt
1/4 cup shredded coconut

Preheat the oven to 350°F. • Butter four cookie sheets. • Beat the egg whites and sugar in a large bowl with an electric mixer at high speed until frothy. • With mixer at low speed, beat in the flour, butter, coconut extract, and salt. • Use a large rubber spatula to fold in the melted butter, flour, and salt. • Drop teaspoons of the batter onto the prepared cookie sheets, spreading it out to 3-inch circles. • Sprinkle with the coconut. • Bake, one sheet at a time, for 5–7 minutes, or until lightly browned. • Use a spatula to remove the cookies, placing a message in the center. Fold the cookies in half, enclosing the message to form a semicircle. Hold the rounded edges of the semicircle between your thumb and index finger. Place your other index finger at the center of the folded edge and push in. • Let cool completely.

Makes 30–35 cookies · Prep: 25 min. · Cooking: 5–7 min. per batch · Level: 3 · Keeps: 7 days

orange lace cookies with coffee-cream filling

Coffee-cream filling
3   oz bittersweet chocolate, coarsely chopped
1/2   cup heavy cream
1   tablespoon freeze-dried coffee granules
1   teaspoon coffee liqueur

Orange lace cookies
1/3   cup all-purpose flour
1/8   teaspoon salt
1/4   cup granulated sugar
1   tablespoon butter, softened
1/2   teaspoon finely grated orange zest
1 1/2 tablespoons fresh orange juice

Coffee-cream filling: Melt the chocolate with the cream in a double boiler over barely simmering water. • Stir in the coffee granules and liqueur until well blended. • Transfer to a large bowl and let cool completely. • Cover with plastic wrap and refrigerate for 2 hours. • Orange lace cookies: Preheat the oven to 300°F. • Butter two cookie sheets. • Butter two rolling pins. • Sift the flour and salt into a medium bowl. • Use a wooden spoon to beat the sugar, butter, and orange zest and juice in a large bowl until well blended. • Mix in the dry ingredients. • Drop teaspoons of the mixture 3 inches apart onto the prepared cookie sheets. Do not drop more than five cookies on one sheet. • Bake, one sheet at a time, for 10–12 minutes, or until just golden at the edges. • Working quickly, use a spatula to lift each cookie from the sheet and drape it over a rolling pin. Remove from the rolling pin and overlap the edges to form a cone. Let cool completely. • Butter the cookie sheets again and continue to bake in batches until all the batter has been used. • Fit a pastry bag with a 1/4-inch star tip. Fill with the coffee-cream, twist the opening tightly closed, and squeeze the filling into the cookie cones.

Makes 10 cookies · Prep: 40 min. + 2 hr. to chill · Cooking: 10–12 min. per batch · Level: 3 · Keeps: 1 day in the refrigerator

double chocolate crisps

1   cup all-purpose flour
1/2   cup cornstarch
1/8   teaspoon salt
3/4   cup (1 1/2 sticks) butter, softened
1/3   cup confectioners' sugar
1/2   teaspoon vanilla extract
2   oz semisweet chocolate, coarsely chopped
2   oz white chocolate, coarsely chopped

Preheat the oven to 350°F. • Line two cookie sheets with parchment paper. • Sift the flour, cornstarch, and salt into a medium bowl. • Beat the butter, confectioners' sugar, and vanilla in a large bowl with an electric mixer at high speed until creamy. • Mix in the dry ingredients. • Fit the pastry bag with a 1/2-inch plain tip. Fill the pastry bag, twist the opening tightly closed, and squeeze out 3-inch lines, spacing 2 inches apart on the prepared cookie sheets. • Bake for 12–15 minutes, or until just golden at the edges and firm to the touch, rotating the sheets halfway through for even baking. • Transfer to racks to cool. • Melt the semisweet and white chocolate separately in double boilers over barely simmering water. • Spoon the chocolates into separate small freezer bags and cut off tiny corners. • Drizzle over the cookies in a decorative manner. • Let stand for 30 minutes until set.

Makes 18–20 cookies · Prep: 30 min. + 30 min. to set · Cooking: 12–15 min. · Level: 2 · Keeps: 5 days

bavarian apple cones

Apple filling
2   apples, cored, and coarsely chopped
1   tablespoon orange or lemon juice
1   cup heavy cream
1/2   cup Vanilla Sugar (see page 341)

Cones
2/3   cup all-purpose flour
1/2   teaspoon ground cinnamon
1/8   teaspoon salt
3   large eggs
1/2   cup granulated sugar
1   teaspoon finely grated lemon zest

Apple filling: Cook the apples with the juice in a medium saucepan over low heat for about 15 minutes, or until softened. • Transfer to a food processor and process until smooth. Transfer to a small bowl and refrigerate for 1 hour. • With mixer at high speed, beat the cream and vanilla sugar until stiff. • Beat in the apple mixture. • Cones: Preheat the oven to 375°F. • Line a cookie sheet with parchment paper. Draw four 4-inch squares on the paper. • Sift the flour, cinnamon, and salt into a medium bowl. • Beat the eggs and sugar in a large bowl with an electric mixer at high speed until pale and thick. • Mix in the dry ingredients and lemon zest. • Drop 1 tablespoon of the mixture onto each square on the prepared cookie sheet. Use a thin metal spatula to fill the 4-inch squares. • Bake for 5–7 minutes, or until lightly browned. • Peel each square away from the parchment paper and use a thin metal spatula to lift the cookies.

• Twist the squares into cones, smooth-side inward, working quickly. • Cool the cookies completely on racks. • Repeat to make twelve cones. • Fill the cones with the apple filling.

Makes 12 cookies · Prep: 55 min. + 1 hr. to chill · Cooking: 5–7 min. per batch · Level: 3 · Keeps: 1 day

cookie cones with hazelnut cream

2/3   cup all-purpose flour
1/8   teaspoon salt
1/3   cup butter, softened
2/3   cup confectioners' sugar
1/2   teaspoon vanilla extract
4   large egg whites, lightly beaten

Hazelnut cream
2/3   cup chocolate hazelnut cream (Nutella)
1   tablespoon dark rum
1   cup heavy cream

Preheat the oven to 400°F. • Butter four cookie sheets. • Butter two rolling pins. • Sift the flour and salt into a medium bowl. • Beat the butter and confectioners' sugar in a large bowl with an electric mixer at high speed until creamy. • Mix in the dry ingredients and vanilla. • Stir in the egg whites until well blended. • Fit a pastry bag with a 1/2-inch plain tip. Fill the pastry bag, twist the opening tightly closed, and squeeze out small ovals, spacing them 3 inches apart on the prepared cookie sheets. • Do not pipe more than 5 cookies on one sheet. • Bake, one sheet at a time, for 5–8 minutes, or until just golden at the edges. • Working quickly, use a spatula to lift each cookie from the sheet and drape it over a rolling pin. Remove from the rolling pin and overlap the edges to form a cone. Let cool completely. • Butter the cookie sheets again and continue to bake in batches until all the batter has been used. • Hazelnut cream: Heat the chocolate hazelnut cream in a double boiler over barely simmering water until liquid. • Mix in the rum and transfer to a large bowl. • Beat the cream in a large bowl with an electric mixer at high speed until thick. • Use a large rubber spatula to fold the cream into the chocolate mixture until well blended. • Fit a pastry bag with a 1/4-inch star tip. Fill the pastry bag and pipe the cream into the cones.

Makes 36 cookies · Prep: 40 min. · Cooking: 5–8 min. per batch · Level: 3 · Keeps: 3 days in the refrigerator

Orange lace cookies with coffee-cream filling (bottom) and Cookie cones with hazelnut cream (top)

Coconut crisps

coconut crisps

2	large egg whites
1/8	teaspoon salt
1/2	cup superfine sugar
1/3	cup all-purpose flour
1/4	cup (1/2 stick) butter, melted
1/2	teaspoon coconut extract
1/2	cup shredded coconut

Preheat the oven to 350°F. • Butter four cookie sheets. • Butter two rolling pins. • Beat the egg whites and salt in a large bowl with an electric mixer at medium speed until soft peaks form. • With mixer at high speed, gradually add the superfine sugar, beating until stiff, glossy peaks form. • Use a large rubber spatula to fold in the flour, butter, and coconut extract. • Drop heaped teaspoons of the mixture onto the prepared cookie sheets. Do not place more than four cookies on the sheet. Use a thin metal spatula to spread the mixture into 3-inch rounds. Sprinkle with the coconut. • Bake, one batch at a time, for 3–5 minutes, or until just golden. • Working quickly, use the spatula to lift each cookie from the sheet and drape it over a rolling pin. • Butter the cookie sheets again and continue to bake in batches until all the batter has been used.

Makes 30 cookies · Prep: 50 min. · Cooking: 3–5 min. per batch · Level: 3 · Keeps: 3 days

caribbean coconut wafers

1 3/4	cups shredded coconut
1/3	cup vegetable shortening
2	cups all-purpose flour
1	teaspoon baking powder
1	cup granulated sugar

1	large egg, lightly beaten
	Grated zest and juice of 1 lime

Preheat the oven to 350°F. • Butter four cookie sheets. • Sift the flour, baking powder, and salt into a medium bowl. • Beat the shortening and sugar in a large bowl with an electric mixer at high speed until creamy. • Mix in the coconut and lime zest and juice. • Add the egg, beating until just blended. Mix in the dry ingredients. • Drop teaspoons of the dough onto the prepared cookie sheets. Use a floured fork to press the cookies into thin wafers. • Bake, one sheet at a time, for 6–8 minutes, or until golden. • Cool on the sheets until the cookies firm slightly. • Transfer to racks to cool completely.

Makes 50 wafers · Prep: 30 min. · Cooking: 6–8 min. per batch · Level: 1 · Keeps: 8 days

sunny sesame snaps

1	cup sesame seeds
2/3	cup all-purpose flour
1/8	teaspoon salt
1/3	cup butter, softened
2/3	cup confectioners' sugar
2	tablespoons Vanilla Sugar (see page 341)
	Grated zest of 1 orange
3	large egg whites, lightly beaten

Toast the sesame seeds in a skillet over medium heat for 5–7 minutes until lightly browned. • Sift the flour and salt into a medium bowl. • Beat the butter, confectioners' sugar, and orange zest in a large bowl with an electric mixer at high speed until creamy. • Gradually beat in the egg whites. • Mix in the dry ingredients and sesame seeds. Refrigerate for 1 hour. • Preheat the oven to 350°F. • Butter four cookie sheets. • Butter two rolling pins. • Drop teaspoons of the mixture 2 inches apart onto the prepared cookie sheets. Use a thin spatula to spread out the mixture to about 3 inches in diameter. • Do not place more than five cookies on one sheet. • Bake, one sheet at a time, for 5–6 minutes, or until the edges are lightly golden. • Working quickly, use a spatula to place the cookies over a rolling pin. • Slide each cookie off the pin onto a rack to finish cooling. • Butter the cookie sheets again and continue to bake in batches until all the batter has been used.

Makes about 26 cookies · Prep: 50 min. + 1 hr. to chill · Cooking: 5–6 min. per batch · Level: 3 · Keeps: 3 days

almond cookie cups

1	cup blanched almonds
3/4	cup granulated sugar
1/3	cup all-purpose flour
1	large egg yolk + 2 egg whites, lightly beaten
3	tablespoons butter, melted
1/4	teaspoon almond extract
	Heavenly Cream, Zabaglione, Sweet Almond Zabaglione, or Passionfruit Cream (see pages 344–345), to serve

Preheat the oven to 350°F. • Line three cookie sheets with parchment paper. • Spread the almonds on a large baking sheet. Toast for 5–7 minutes, or until lightly golden. • Transfer the nuts to a food processor with 1/4 cup sugar and process until finely chopped. • Transfer to a large bowl and mix with the remaining 1/2 cup sugar, flour, egg yolk, egg whites, butter, and almond extract. • Drop tablespoons of the mixture 6 inches apart onto the prepared cookie sheets. Use a thin spatula to spread out to rounds about 4 inches in diameter. • Bake, one batch at a time, for 8–10 minutes, or until lightly golden at the edges. • Lift off the sheet with a palette knife and mold over an upturned, well-buttered jam jar or glass with a base of about 3 inches. • Pull the edges out to make frilly cups. • Transfer to racks and let cool completely. Repeat with the remaining batter. Fill the cooled cookies with Heavenly Cream just before serving.

Makes 12–15 cookies · Prep: 60 min. · Cooking: 8–10 min. per batch · Level: 3 · Keeps: 3 days

lemon pizzelles

These Italian-style cookies are scrumptious, especially when drizzled with maple syrup.

1 3/4	cups all-purpose flour
2	teaspoons baking powder
1/2	teaspoon salt
3	large eggs, lightly beaten
1/4	cup granulated sugar
1/2	cup (1 stick) butter, melted
	Grated zest of 1 lemon
1	tablespoon lemon extract

Preheat a 7-inch pizzelle iron. • Sift the flour, baking powder, and salt into a large bowl and make a well in the center. • Add the eggs, beating until just blended. • Stir in the sugar, butter, lemon zest, and lemon extract until well blended. • Drop 2 tablespoons of the batter onto the center of the iron. • Lower the top so that the batter spreads. • Cook for 1 minute, or until browned at the edges. • Lift

minute, or until browned at the edges. • Lift up the top and remove the cookie from the iron. and place on a rack to cool. • Repeat with the remaining batter.

Makes 12 cookies · Prep: 20 min. · Cooking: 1 min. per cookie · Level: 3 · Keeps: 2 days

orange–almond petits fours

1³/₄   cups whole almonds
1   cup superfine sugar
1   cup confectioners' sugar + extra to dust
2   tablespoons coarsely chopped candied orange peel
1/2   teaspoon almond extract
1   large egg white

Preheat the oven to 325°F. • Line a baking sheet with rice paper. • Spread the almonds out on a separate baking sheet. Toast in the oven for 7 minutes, or until lightly golden. Transfer to a food processor, add the superfine sugar, and process until finely chopped. • Transfer to a large bowl. Stir in the confectioners' sugar, orange peel, and almond extract. • Beat the egg white in a small bowl with an electric mixer at high speed until stiff peaks form. • Use a large rubber spatula to fold the beaten white into the almond mixture. • Spread the mixture into thin squares on the prepared baking sheet. • Cover with a clean kitchen towel and let stand in a cool place overnight. • Preheat the oven to 300°F. • Bake for 55–65 minutes, or until set. Cool the cookies completely on the baking sheet. Tear off any excess paper and dust with the confectioners' sugar.

Makes about 15 cookies · Prep: 25 min. + 12 hr. to rest · Cooking: 55–65 min. · Level: 2 · Keeps: 5 days

pecan lace cookies

1/2   cup finely chopped pecans
1/2   cup granulated sugar
1/4   cup all-purpose flour
1/4   cup (1/2 stick) butter, melted
2   large egg whites, lightly beaten
1/2   teaspoon vanilla extract
1/8   teaspoon salt

Preheat the oven to 350°F. • Butter four cookie sheets. • Butter two rolling pins. • Process the pecans and sugar in a food processor or blender until finely ground. • Transfer to a large bowl and stir in the flour, butter, egg whites, vanilla, and salt. • Drop teaspoons of the batter 3 inches apart onto the prepared cookie sheets. • Do not place more than five cookies on one sheet. Spread

the mixture out into thin circles. • Bake, one sheet at a time, for 8–10 minutes, or until just golden at the edges. • Use a spatula to lift each cookie off the sheet. Working quickly, drape it over a rolling pin to give it a rounded finish. • Let cool completely.

Makes 20–25 cookies · Prep: 30 min. · Cooking: 8–10 min. per batch · Level: 3 · Keeps: 2 weeks in the refrigerator

cashew–chocolate crisps

1/2   cup all-purpose flour
1/8   teaspoon salt
1/4   cup (1/2 stick) butter, softened
1/4   cup firmly packed light brown sugar
1/4   cup light corn syrup
1¹/₄   cups coarsely chopped cashews
1/2   teaspoon almond extract
7   oz semisweet chocolate, coarsely chopped

Preheat the oven to 350°F. • Butter two cookie sheets. • Sift the flour and salt into a medium bowl. • Melt the butter with the brown sugar and corn syrup in a medium saucepan over low heat until the sugar has dissolved completely. • Remove from the heat and mix in the dry ingredients, cashew nuts, and almond extract. • Drop teaspoons of the mixture 2 inches apart onto the prepared cookie sheets. • Bake for 8–10 minutes, or until faintly tinged with brown on top and slightly darker at the edges, rotating the sheets halfway through for even baking. • Cool on the sheets until the cookies firm slightly. Transfer to racks to finish cooling. • Melt the chocolate in a double boiler over barely simmering water. • Dip the cookies halfway into the melted chocolate and let stand for 30 minutes until set.

Makes 25–30 cookies · Prep: 30 min. + 30 min. to set · Cooking: 8–10 min. · Level: 1 · Keeps: 7 days

walnut lace cookies

1/2   cup finely chopped walnuts
1/2   cup granulated sugar
1/4   cup all-purpose flour
1/4   cup (1/2 stick) butter, melted
2   large egg whites, lightly beaten
1/2   teaspoon vanilla extract
1/8   teaspoon salt

Preheat the oven to 350°F. • Butter four cookie sheets. • Butter two rolling pins. • Process the walnuts and sugar in a food processor or blender until finely ground. • Transfer to a large bowl and stir in the flour, butter, egg whites, vanilla, and salt. • Drop

teaspoons of the batter 3 inches apart onto the prepared cookie sheets. • Do not place more than five cookies on one sheet. Spread the mixture out into thin circles. • Bake, one sheet at a time, for 8–10 minutes, or until just golden at the edges. • Use a spatula to lift each cookie off the sheet. Working quickly, drape it over a rolling pin to give it a rounded finish. • Slide each cookie off the pin onto a rack to finish cooling.

Makes 20–25 cookies · Prep: 30 min. · Cooking: 8–10 min. per batch · Level: 3 · Keeps: 2 weeks in the refrigerator

Cashew–chocolate crisps

langues de chats

Directly translated as cats' tongues, these delicate cookies have been the backbone of French patisserie for centuries.

1/3 cup all-purpose flour
1/8 teaspoon salt
1/4 cup (1/2 stick) butter, softened
1/4 cup granulated sugar
2 large egg whites
1/2 teaspoon vanilla extract

Preheat the oven to 400°F. • Butter and flour two cookie sheets. • Sift the flour and salt into a medium bowl. • Beat the butter and sugar in a large bowl with an electric mixer at high speed until creamy. • With mixer at high speed, beat the egg whites in a medium bowl until stiff peaks form. • Use a large rubber spatula to fold them into the butter mixture, followed by the dry ingredients and vanilla. • Fit a pastry bag with a 1/2-inch plain tip. Fill the pastry bag, twist the opening tightly closed, and squeeze out 3-inch lengths spacing 2 inches apart onto the prepared cookie sheets. • Bake for 8–10 minutes, or until lightly browned in the centers, rotating the sheets halfway through for even baking. • Transfer to racks to cool.

Makes 20 cookies · Prep: 20 min. · Cooking: 8–10 min. · Level: 2 · Keeps: 5 days

filled cats' tongues

2/3 cup all-purpose flour
1/8 teaspoon salt
1/3 cup butter, softened
1/3 cup granulated sugar
1 tablespoon Vanilla Sugar (see page 341)
2 large egg whites
1 teaspoon finely grated lemon zest
3 1/2 oz semisweet chocolate, coarsely chopped

Chocolate–nougat filling
2 oz nougat, broken into large pieces
2–3 tablespoons chocolate hazelnut spread (Nutella)
1 tablespoon confectioners' sugar

Preheat the oven to 350°F. • Line two cookie sheets with parchment paper. • Sift the flour and salt into a medium bowl. • Beat the butter and granulated and vanilla sugars in a large bowl with an electric mixer at high speed until creamy. • Add the egg whites and lemon zest, beating until pale and thick. • Mix in the dry ingredients. • Fit a pastry bag with a 2-inch plain tip. Fill the pastry bag, twist the opening tightly

closed, and squeeze out 2-inch lengths spacing 1 1/2 inches apart on the prepared cookie sheets. Make the cookies slightly wider at both ends. • Bake, one sheet at a time, for 5–7 minutes, or until faintly tinged with brown on top and slightly darker at the edges. • Working quickly, use a spatula to lift each cookie from the sheet and transfer to racks to cool. • Melt the chocolate in a double boiler over barely simmering water. Dip both ends of the cookies in the melted chocolate and let stand for 30 minutes to set. • Chocolate-nougat filling: Chop the nougat in a food processor until finely ground. • Transfer to a small bowl and mix in the chocolate spread and confectioners' sugar to form a stiff cream. • Stick the cookies together in pairs with the filling.

Makes 16 cookies · Prep: 40 min. + 30 min. to set Cooking: 5–7 min. per batch · Level: 3 · Keeps: 10 days

pecan lace snaps

1/2 cup all-purpose flour
1/4 teaspoon baking powder
1/8 teaspoon salt
1/4 cup (1/2 stick) butter, cut up
1/3 cup light corn syrup
1/4 cup firmly packed dark brown sugar
1/2 cup finely chopped pecans
1/2 cup heavy cream
1/4 teaspoon vanilla extract
1/4 cup confectioners' sugar

Preheat the oven to 375°F. • Line three to four cookie sheets with parchment paper. Butter two rolling pins. • Sift the flour, baking powder, and salt into a medium bowl. • Melt the butter with the corn syrup and brown sugar in a medium saucepan over low heat, stirring occasionally. Remove from the heat and let cool slightly. • Mix in the dry ingredients and pecans until well blended. • Drop teaspoons of the dough 3 inches apart onto the prepared cookie sheets. Do not drop more than six cookies onto each sheet. • Bake, one sheet at a time, for 5–7 minutes, or until lightly browned. • Working quickly, use a spatula to lift each cookie from the sheet and drape it over a rolling pin. Slide each cookie off the pin and onto racks to finish cooling. • Butter the cookie sheets again and continue to bake in batches until all the batter has been used. • Just before the cookies are served, beat the

cream with the vanilla and confectioners' sugar until stiff. Fit a pastry bag with a 1 1/2-inch star tip. Fill the pastry bag, twist the opening tightly closed, and squeeze out cream rosettes into the cookies.

Makes 18–24 cookies · Prep: 40 min. · Cooking: 5–7 min. per batch · Level: 3 · Keeps: 1 day in the refrigerator, 4 days, unfilled

dark cat tuiles

These wafer-thin cat faces make a crunchy decoration for ice cream or puddings. You can make your own acetate stencil, and you could cut other simple shapes to bake butterfly, apple, or pear tuiles.

2 tablespoons butter, softened
1/4 cup granulated sugar
1 tablespoon honey
3 tablespoons all-purpose flour
1 tablespoon unsweetened cocoa powder
1 large egg white
1/4 teaspoon rum extract
1/4 teaspoon lemon or vanilla extract

Beat the butter and sugar in a large bowl with an electric mixer at high speed until creamy. • Beat in the honey, flour, cocoa, and egg white. Add the rum and lemon extracts. • Refrigerate for 1–2 hours. • Draw the outline of a cat's face and ears (about 3 1/4 x 3 inches) on a acetate square or plastic lid. Cut along the outline to make a stencil. • Preheat the oven to 325°F. • Line three cookie sheets with parchment paper. • Place the stencil on the parchment at the top corner of the cookie sheet. • Hold the stencil in position and spread a thin layer of the mixture across it with a rubber spatula, making sure the ears are filled in! • Carefully lift the stencil and place on the parchment next to the cat face you just made, spacing 2 inches apart. • Do not place more than eight cookies on one sheet. • Bake, one sheet at a time, for 6–8 minutes, or until the edges are firm. • Cool on the sheets until the cookies firm slightly. • Transfer to racks to cool.

Makes 20–24 cookies · Prep: 30 min. + 2 hr. to chill · Cooking: 6–8 min. per batch · Level: 2 · Keeps: 4–5 days

Filled cat's tongue wafers

ginger-filled brandy snaps

- 2/3 cup all-purpose flour
- 1 teaspoon ground ginger
- 1/8 teaspoon salt
- 1/2 cup (1 stick) butter, cut up
- 1/2 cup firmly packed light brown sugar
- 1/2 cup light corn syrup
- 1 teaspoon fresh lemon juice
- 1 teaspoon brandy

Ginger cream
- 1 cup heavy cream
- 2 tablespoons finely chopped crystallized ginger

Preheat the oven to 325°F. • Line two cookie sheets with parchment paper. • Butter two rolling pins. • Sift the flour, ginger, and salt into a large bowl. • Melt the butter with the brown sugar and corn syrup in a small saucepan over low heat, stirring constantly until the sugar has dissolved. • Remove from the heat and let cool slightly. • Mix in the dry ingredients, followed by the lemon juice and brandy. • Drop 4–5 teaspoons of the mixture 2 inches apart onto the prepared baking sheets. • Bake, one batch at a time, for 8–10 minutes, or until golden brown. • Cool the cookies for 1 minute on the baking sheets. • Working quickly, use a spatula to lift each cookie from the sheet and drape it over a rolling pin. • Slide each cookie off the pin onto a rack to finish cooling. • If the cookies harden too quickly before they have been rolled, return the cookie sheets to the oven for 1–2 minutes, or until the cookies are soft again. • Repeat until all the batter is used. • Ginger cream: Beat the cream in a medium bowl with an electric mixer at high speed until stiff. Stir in the ginger. • Fill both ends of the cooled brandy snaps with the cream.

Makes 25 cookies · Prep: 25 min. · Cooking: 8–10 min. per batch · Level: 3 · Keeps: unfilled, 2–3 days

sweet russian cigarettes

- 1/3 cup all-purpose flour
- 1/8 teaspoon salt
- 2 large egg whites
- 3/4 cup Vanilla Confectioners' Sugar (see page 341)
- 1/3 cup butter, melted

Preheat the oven to 400°F. • Butter two cookie sheets. • Oil the handles of two wooden spoons. • Sift the flour and salt into a small bowl. • Beat the egg whites in a large bowl with an electric mixer at medium speed until frothy. • With mixer at high speed, gradually beat in the confectioners' sugar, beating until stiff, glossy peaks form. • Mix in the dry ingredients and melted butter. • Drop teaspoons of the mixture 3 inches apart onto the prepared cookie sheets. Use a thin spatula to spread out the mixture to about 3 inches in diameter. Do not place more than three cookies on one sheet. • Bake, one sheet at a time, for 5–6 minutes, or until the edges are lightly golden. • Working quickly, use a spatula to lift the cookies from the sheet. • Wrap each cookie around the wooden-spoon handle. Place the spoon near the edge of your worktop, so you can easily turn it. • Let cool completely. • Butter the cookie sheets again and continue to bake in batches until all the batter has been used.

Makes 18–20 cookies · Prep: 60 min. · Cooking: 5–6 min. per batch · Level: 3 · Keeps: 4 days

ginger–almond florentines

- 2/3 cup all-purpose flour
- 1/2 teaspoon ground ginger
- 1/8 teaspoon salt
- 1/2 cup (1 stick) butter, cut up
- 1/4 cup light corn syrup
- 1/2 cup granulated sugar
- 1 1/4 cups finely chopped almonds
- 1/2 cup finely chopped crystallized ginger
- 5 oz semisweet chocolate, coarsely chopped

Preheat the oven to 350°F. • Butter three to four cookie sheets. • Sift the flour, ground ginger, and salt into a medium bowl. • Melt the butter with the corn syrup and sugar in a small saucepan over low heat, stirring constantly, until the sugar has dissolved completely. • Remove from the heat and let cool for 5 minutes. • Mix in the dry ingredients, almonds, and crystallized ginger until well blended. • Drop teaspoons of the mixture 3 inches apart onto the prepared cookie sheets. Do not drop more than eight cookies onto each sheet. • Bake, one sheet at a time, for 8–10 minutes, or until faintly tinged with brown on top and slightly darker at the edges. • Cool on the sheets until the cookies firm slightly. Transfer to racks to finish cooling. • Butter the cookie sheets again and continue to bake in batches until all the batter has been used. • Melt the chocolate in a double boiler over barely simmering water. Brush the bottoms of the cookies with the chocolate. • Draw the tines of a fork across the chocolate to form wavy lines. • Let stand upside-down for 30 minutes until set.

Makes 18–24 cookies · Prep: 20 min. + 30 min. to set · Cooking: 8–10 min. per batch · Level: 2 · Keeps: 7 days

cherry florentines

- 1 cup all-purpose flour
- 1/8 teaspoon salt
- 1/2 cup (1 stick) butter, cut up
- 1/4 cup light corn syrup
- 1/2 cup granulated sugar
- 1 1/2 cups finely chopped red and green candied cherries
- 5 oz semisweet chocolate, coarsely chopped

Preheat the oven to 350°F. • Butter three cookie sheets. • Sift the flour and salt into a medium bowl. • Melt the butter with the corn syrup and sugar in a small saucepan over low heat, stirring constantly, until the sugar has dissolved completely. • Remove from the heat and let cool for 5 minutes. • Mix in the dry ingredients and candied cherries until well blended. • Drop teaspoons of the mixture 3 inches apart onto the prepared cookie sheets. Do not drop more than eight cookies onto each sheet. • Bake, one sheet at a time, for 8–10 minutes, or until faintly tinged with brown on top and slightly darker at the edges. • Cool on the sheets until the cookies firm slightly. Transfer to racks to finish cooling. • Melt the chocolate in a double boiler over barely simmering water. • Brush the bottoms of the cookies with the chocolate. • Draw the tines of a fork across the chocolate to form wavy lines. • Let stand upside-down for 30 minutes until set.

Makes 18–24 cookies · Prep: 20 min. + 30 min. to set · Cooking: 8–10 min. per batch · Level: 2 · Keeps: 7 days

Cherry florentines (top)
and Ginger–almond florentines (bottom)

Italian biscotti

Chunky in size and crunchy in texture, biscotti are the U.S. interpretation of this Italian-style cookie. Meaning "twice-baked," biscotti are ideal for dunking into sweet dessert wines or coffee. Biscotti store well and can be kept up to a month in an airtight container. Traditionally made with almonds, the biscotti trend has been modernized to include a selection of ingredients, from pistachios and poppy seeds to chocolate chips and cinnamon.

above: Pecan biscotti (page 268)

right: Double chocolate biscotti, Brown sugar–oat biscotti, Prato cookies, & Chocolate chip biscotti (pages 270, 274, 270, and 276)

making biscotti

1. Shape the dough into a rectangle and cut into lengths.

2. Roll the lengths into long logs.

3. Flatten the dough slightly.

4. Bake the logs until firm to the touch. Transfer to a board and slice on the diagonal.

5. Return the cookies to the sheets and bake until crisp and browned.

pecan biscotti

- 1¼ cups all-purpose flour
- 1 teaspoon baking powder
- ⅛ teaspoon salt
- ¼ cup (½ stick) butter, softened
- ½ cup granulated sugar
- 1 large egg
- ¼ cup finely ground yellow cornmeal
- ¾ cup finely chopped pecans

Preheat the oven to 350°F. • Butter a cookie sheet. • Sift the flour, baking powder, and salt into a medium bowl. • Beat the butter and sugar in a large bowl with an electric mixer at high speed until creamy. • Mix in the egg, dry ingredients, cornmeal, and pecans. • Form the dough into two logs 1 inch in diameter and place 3 inches apart on the prepared cookie sheet. • Bake for 25–30 minutes, or until firm to the touch. • Transfer to a cutting board to cool for 15 minutes. • Cut on the diagonal into ½-inch slices. • Arrange the slices cut-side up on two cookie sheets and bake, one sheet at a time, for 7–10 minutes, or until golden and toasted. • Transfer to racks to cool.

Makes 30 cookies · Prep: 20 min. · Cooking: 32–40 min. · Level: 2 · Keeps: 2 weeks

orange–hazelnut biscotti

- 2 cups all-purpose flour
- 1½ teaspoons baking powder
- ¾ teaspoon ground cinnamon
- ½ teaspoon ground ginger
- ¼ teaspoon salt
- ½ cup (1 stick) butter, softened
- 1¼ cups granulated sugar
- 2 large eggs
  - Grated zest of 1 orange
- ¼ cup fresh orange juice
- 1¾ cups finely chopped toasted hazelnuts
- 1 cup semisweet chocolate chips
- 1 lb semisweet chocolate, coarsely chopped

Preheat the oven to 350°F. • Butter a cookie sheet. • Sift the flour, baking powder, cinnamon, ginger, and salt into a medium bowl. • Beat the butter and sugar in a large bowl with an electric mixer at high speed until creamy. • Mix in the eggs, orange zest and juice, dry ingredients, hazelnuts, and chocolate chips. • Form into two 12-inch logs and place 2 inches apart on the prepared cookie sheet. • Bake for 25–35 minutes, or until firm to the touch. • Transfer to a cutting board to cool for 15 minutes. • Reduce the oven temperature to 325°F. • Cut on the diagonal into 1-inch slices. • Arrange the slices cut-side up on three cookie sheets and bake for 10–15 minutes more, or until golden and toasted. • Transfer to racks to cool. • Melt the chocolate in a double boiler over barely simmering water • Dip the biscotti halfway into the chocolate and let stand on parchment paper for 30 minutes until set.

Makes 24 cookies · Prep: 25 min. + 30 min. to stand · Cooking: 35–50 min. · Level: 2 · Keeps: 2 weeks

Orange–hazelnut biscotti

Chocolate–coffee biscotti

chocolate–coffee biscotti

2/3 cup hazelnuts
2 cups all-purpose flour
1/2 teaspoon baking powder
1/2 teaspoon baking soda
1/2 teaspoon ground cinnamon
1/4 teaspoon salt
1 cup granulated sugar
1/4 cup very strong coffee
2 tablespoons milk
1 large egg
1/2 teaspoon vanilla extract
1/2 cup (3 oz) semisweet chocolate chips

Preheat the oven to 325°F. • Spread the hazelnuts on a large baking sheet. • Toast for 7 minutes, or until lightly golden. • Transfer the nuts to a clean kitchen towel. Fold the kitchen towel over and gently rub the nuts to remove the skins. Pick out the nuts and chop coarsely. • Line a cookie sheet with parchment paper. • Sift the flour, baking powder, baking soda, cinnamon, and salt into a large bowl. Stir in the sugar. • Beat the coffee, milk, egg, and vanilla in a small bowl until well blended. • Mix the coffee mixture into the dry ingredients. • Stir in the hazelnuts and chocolate chips. • Turn the dough out onto a lightly floured surface and knead until smooth. • Divide the dough in half. Form the dough into two 12-inch logs and place 3 inches apart on the prepared cookie sheets, flattening the tops. • Bake for 25–35 minutes, or until firm to the touch. • Reduce the oven temperature to 300°F. • Transfer to a cutting board to cool for 15 minutes. • Cut on the diagonal into 1-inch slices. • Arrange the slices cut-side up on two cookie sheets and bake for 10–15 minutes more, or until golden and toasted. • Transfer to racks to cool.

Makes 25–30 cookies · Prep: 40 min. · Cooking: 35–50 min. · Level: 2 · Keeps: 2 weeks

prato cookies

2 cups whole almonds
4 large eggs, separated
2 1/2 cups granulated sugar
3 1/2 cups all-purpose flour
1/8 teaspoon salt

Preheat the oven to 325°F. • Butter and flour a large baking sheet. • Spread the almonds out on a separate baking sheet. Toast in the oven for 7 minutes, or until lightly golden. Increase the oven temperature to 375°F. • Use a kitchen towel to rub off the skins and coarsely chop. • Beat the egg yolks and sugar in a large bowl with an electric mixer at high speed until pale and thick. • Use a fork to stir in the flour, chopped almond mixture, and salt. • Beat the egg whites in a large bowl with an electric mixer at high speed until frothy. Fold them into the mixture to form a stiff dough. Turn the dough out onto a lightly floured surface and knead lightly. • Form into two 1/2-inch cylinders and place 2 inches apart on the prepared baking sheet. • Bake for 25 minutes, or until firm to the touch. • Transfer to a cutting board to cool for 15 minutes. • Increase the oven temperature to 400°F. • Cut on the diagonal into 1 1/2-inch slices. • Arrange the slices cut-side up on the cookie sheet and bake for 10–12 minutes more, or until golden and toasted. • Transfer to racks to cool.

Makes 20 cookies · Prep: 15 min. · Cooking: 35–37 min. · Level: 1 · Keeps: 2 weeks

double chocolate biscotti

3/4 cup shelled hazelnuts
1 1/3 cups all-purpose flour
1/2 cup unsweetened cocoa powder
1 1/2 teaspoons baking soda
1/8 teaspoon salt
3 large eggs
1 cup granulated sugar
1/2 teaspoon vanilla extract
2 teaspoons freeze-dried coffee granules
1/3 cup (2 oz) semisweet chocolate chips
8 oz white chocolate, coarsely chopped

Preheat the oven to 325°F. • Spread the hazelnuts on a large baking sheet. Toast for 7 minutes, or until lightly golden. Transfer to a large cotton kitchen towel. Fold the towel over the nuts and rub them to remove the skins. Pick out the nuts and chop coarsely. • Increase the oven temperature to 350°F. • Butter a cookie sheet. • Sift the flour, cocoa, baking soda, and salt into a medium bowl. • Beat the eggs, sugar, and vanilla in a large bowl with an electric mixer at high speed until pale and thick. • Mix in the dry ingredients, coffee granules, chocolate chips, and hazelnuts to form a stiff dough. • Divide the dough in half. Form into two 12-inch logs and place 2 inches apart on the prepared cookie sheet, flattening them slightly. • Bake for 25–30 minutes, or until firm to the touch. • Transfer to a cutting board to cool for 15 minutes. • Reduce the oven temperature to 325°F. • Cut on the diagonal into 1-inch slices. • Arrange the slices cut-side down on two cookie sheets and bake for 10–15 minutes, or until golden and toasted. • Transfer to racks to cool. • Melt the white chocolate in a double boiler over barely simmering water. Drizzle the chocolate over the biscotti and let stand for 30 minutes until set.

Makes 24 cookies · Prep: 40 min. + 30 min. to set · Cooking: 35–45 min. · Level: 2 · Keeps: 2 weeks

chocolate–walnut biscotti

2 1/2 cups all-purpose flour
3/4 cup unsweetened cocoa powder
2 teaspoons baking powder
1/4 teaspoon salt
1/2 cup (1 stick) butter, softened
1 1/3 cups granulated sugar
1/2 teaspoon vanilla extract
3 large eggs
1 cup coarsely chopped walnuts
4 oz semisweet chocolate, coarsely chopped

Preheat the oven to 325°F. • Line a cookie sheet with parchment paper. • Sift the flour, cocoa, baking powder, and salt into a medium bowl. • Beat the butter and sugar in a large bowl with an electric mixer at high speed until creamy. • Add the vanilla and eggs, beating until just blended. • Mix in the dry ingredients, walnuts, and chocolate to form a stiff dough. • Divide the dough in half. • Form the dough into two 12-inch logs and place 3 inches apart on the prepared cookie sheet, flattening the tops. • Bake for 25–35 minutes, or until firm to the touch. • Transfer to a cutting board to cool for 15 minutes. •

Reduce the oven temperature to 325°F. • Cut on the diagonal into 1-inch slices. • Arrange the slices cut-side up on two cookie sheets and bake for 10–15 minutes, or until golden and toasted. • Transfer to racks to cool.

Makes 48 cookies · Prep: 40 min. · Cooking: 35–50 min. · Level: 2 · Keeps: 2 weeks

maple cantuccini

1²/₃	cups bread flour
²/₃	cup finely ground cornmeal
1	teaspoon baking powder
¹/₄	teaspoon salt
2	large eggs + 1 large egg yolk
¹/₂	teaspoon vanilla extract
1	cup coarsely chopped pecans
¹/₂	cup pure maple syrup

Preheat the oven to 350°F. • Butter two cookie sheets. • Sift the flour, cornmeal, baking powder, and salt into a medium bowl. • Beat the eggs, egg yolk, and vanilla in a large bowl with an electric mixer at high speed until frothy. • Mix in the dry ingredients, pecans, and maple syrup to form a stiff dough. • Divide the dough in four. • Form into four logs about 1 inch in diameter and place 2 inches apart on the prepared cookie sheets, flattening them slightly. • Bake for 25–30 minutes, or until firm to the touch, rotating the sheets halfway through for even baking. • Transfer to a cutting board to cool for 15 minutes. • Reduce the oven temperature to 300°F. • Cut on the diagonal into 1-inch slices. • Arrange the slices cut-side down on the cookie sheets and bake for 15–20 minutes, or until golden and toasted. • Transfer to racks to cool.

Makes 35 cookies · Prep: 40 min. · Cooking: 40–50 min. · Level: 2 · Keeps: 1 month

choc-and-nut biscotti

¹/₃	cup shelled hazelnuts
2	cups all-purpose flour
2	tablespoons unsweetened cocoa powder
1	teaspoon baking powder
¹/₂	teaspoon ground cinnamon
¹/₄	teaspoon ground cloves
¹/₈	teaspoon salt
³/₄	cup granulated sugar
3	large eggs + 1 large egg white
1	teaspoon vanilla extract
2	teaspoons freeze-dried coffee granules dissolved in 1 tablespoon hot water
1–2	tablespoons slivered almonds
2	tablespoons semisweet chocolate chips
Glaze	
1	large egg yolk
1–2	tablespoons milk

Preheat the oven to 325°F. • Spread the hazelnuts on a large baking sheet. • Toast for 7 minutes, or until lightly golden. Transfer the nuts to a clean kitchen towel. Fold the kitchen towel over and gently rub the nuts to remove the skins. Pick out the nuts. • Increase the oven temperature to 350°F. • Butter two cookie sheets. • Sift the flour, cocoa, baking powder, cinnamon, cloves, and salt. Stir in the sugar. • Beat the eggs, egg white, and vanilla in a large bowl with an electric mixer at high speed until frothy. • Mix in the dry ingredients, coffee, hazelnuts, almonds, and chocolate chips to form a stiff dough. • Divide the dough in four. • Form into four logs about 1 inch in diameter and place 4 inches apart on the prepared cookie sheets, flattening them slightly. • Glaze: Beat the yolk and milk in a small bowl and brush it over the logs. • Bake for 25–30 minutes, or until firm to the touch, rotating the sheets halfway through for even baking. Transfer to a cutting board to cool for 15 minutes. • Reduce the oven temperature to 300°F. • Cut on the diagonal into 1-inch slices. • Arrange the slices cut-side up on the cookie sheets and bake for 8–10 minutes, or golden and toasted. • Transfer to racks to cool.

Makes 35 biscotti · Prep: 40 min. · Cooking: 33–40 min. · Level: 2 · Keeps: 2 weeks

aniseed biscotti

3	cups all-purpose flour
2	teaspoons baking powder
¹/₈	teaspoon salt
2	teaspoons ground aniseeds
²/₃	cup butter, softened
1	cup granulated sugar
	Grated zest of 2 lemons
3	large eggs

Preheat the oven to 375°F. • Set out a cookie sheet. • Sift the flour, baking powder, and salt into a medium bowl. Stir in the aniseeds. • Beat the butter and sugar in a large bowl with an electric mixer at high speed until creamy. • Add the lemon zest and eggs, beating until just blended. • Mix in the dry ingredients to form a stiff dough. • Divide the dough in half. Form the dough into two 11-inch logs and place 3 inches apart on the cookie sheet. • Bake for 25–35 minutes, or until firm to the touch. • Transfer to a cutting board to cool for 15 minutes. • Cut on the diagonal into 1-inch slices. • Arrange

the slices cut-side up on two cookie sheets and bake for 5–7 minutes more, or until golden and toasted. • Transfer to racks to cool.

Makes 25–30 cookies · Prep: 40 min. · Cooking: 30–42 min. · Level: 2 · Keeps: 7 days

chocolate–almond biscotti

³/₄	cup blanched almonds
2	cups all-purpose flour
1	teaspoon baking soda
¹/₂	teaspoon salt
1	cup granulated sugar
	Grated zest of ¹/₂ orange
2	large eggs + 2 large egg yolks + 1 large egg white
3	oz semisweet chocolate, coarsely chopped

Preheat the oven to 325°F. • Spread the almonds on a large baking sheet. Toast for 7 minutes, or until lightly golden. • Set out two cookie sheets. • Process half the almonds in a food processor until finely ground. • Chop the remaining almonds coarsely. • Sift the flour, baking soda, and salt into a large bowl. • Stir in the sugar, ground almonds, and orange zest. • Stir in the eggs and egg yolks. • Mix in the chopped almonds and chocolate to form a stiff dough. • Divide the dough in four. Form into four 1¹/₂-inch thick logs and brush with the egg white. • Transfer to the cookie sheets. • Bake for 15–20 minutes, or until firm to the touch, rotating the sheets halfway through for even baking. • Transfer to a cutting board to cool for 15 minutes. • Reduce the oven temperature to 275°F. • Cut on the diagonal into ¹/₂-inch slices. • Arrange the slices cut-side up on three cookie sheets and bake for 25–30 minutes more, or until golden and toasted. • Transfer to racks to cool.

Makes 40 cookies · Prep: 40 min. · Cooking: 45–50 min. · Level: 2 · Keeps: 2 weeks

Chocolate–almond biscotti

dried cherry–almond biscotti

1/4	cup dried cherries
1	tablespoon cherry brandy
1 1/2	cups all-purpose flour
1/2	teaspoon baking powder
1/8	teaspoon salt
1/4	cup (1/2 stick) butter, softened
1/2	cup granulated sugar
2	large eggs
1/2	teaspoon vanilla extract
1/2	cup coarsely chopped almonds

Soak the cherries in the cherry brandy in a small bowl for 15 minutes. Drain and pat dry with paper towels. • Preheat the oven to 375°F. • Butter a cookie sheet. • Sift the flour, baking powder, and salt into a large bowl. • Beat the butter and sugar in a large bowl with an electric mixer at high speed until creamy. • Add the eggs and vanilla, beating until just blended. • Mix in the dry ingredients, almonds, and cherries to form a stiff dough. • Divide the dough in half. Form the dough into two 12-inch logs and place 2 inches apart on the prepared cookie sheet, flattening them slightly. • Bake for 20–25 minutes, or until firm to the touch. • Transfer to a cutting board to cool for 15 minutes. • Reduce the oven temperature to 325°F. • Cut on the diagonal into 1-inch slices. • Arrange the slices cut-side up on two cookie sheets and bake for 10–15 minutes, or until golden and toasted. • Transfer to racks to cool.

Makes 30 cookies · Prep: 25 min. · Cooking: 35–45 min. · Level: 2 · Keeps: 3 weeks

candied cardamom biscotti

2	cups bread flour
1	teaspoon baking powder
1	teaspoon ground cardamom
1/4	teaspoon ground allspice
1/4	teaspoon salt
1 1/4	cups raw sugar (Barbados or Demerara)
2	large eggs + 1 egg white
1	teaspoon lemon extract
2	tablespoons finely chopped candied mixed peel
1	tablespoon finely grated lemon zest
1	tablespoon finely grated orange peel

Cardamom glaze

1	large egg yolk
1	tablespoon milk
1	teaspoon granulated sugar
1/4	teaspoon ground cardamom

Preheat the oven to 350°F. • Butter two cookie sheets. • Sift the flour, baking powder, cardamom, allspice, and salt into a medium bowl. • Stir in the sugar, candied peel, and lemon and orange zests. • Beat the eggs, egg white, and lemon extract in a large bowl with an electric mixer at high speed until frothy. • Mix in the dry ingredients to form a stiff dough. • Divide the dough in three. • Form into three 10-inch logs about 1 inch in diameter and place 4 inches apart on the prepared cookie sheets, flattening them slightly. • Cardamom glaze: Mix the egg yolk and milk in a small bowl and brush it over the logs. Sprinkle with the sugar and cardamom. • Bake for 25–30 minutes, or until firm to the touch, rotating the sheets halfway through for even baking. • Transfer to a cutting board to cool for 15 minutes. • Reduce the oven temperature to 300°F. • Cut on the diagonal into 1-inch slices. • Arrange the slices cut-side up on the cookie sheets and bake for 8–10 minutes, or golden and toasted. • Transfer to racks to cool.

Makes 35 cookies · Prep: 40 min. · Cooking: 33–40 min. · Level: 2 · Keeps: 1 month

ginger biscotti

1	cup whole almonds
3	cups all-purpose flour
2	teaspoons baking powder
1	tablespoon ground ginger
1	teaspoon ground nutmeg
1/2	teaspoon ground cloves
1/2	teaspoon ground allspice
1/8	teaspoon salt
1/2	cup (1 stick) butter, softened
3/4	cup granulated sugar
1/2	cup dark molasses
2	tablespoons minced fresh ginger
3	large eggs

Preheat the oven to 325°F. • Spread the almonds on a large baking sheet. • Toast for 7 minutes, or until lightly golden. • Increase the oven temperature to 350°F. • Butter two cookie sheets. • Sift the flour, baking powder, ground ginger, nutmeg, cloves, allspice, and salt into a medium bowl. • Beat the butter and sugar in a large bowl with an electric mixer at high speed until creamy. • Beat in the molasses and fresh ginger. • Add the eggs, beating until just blended. • Mix in the dry ingredients to form a stiff dough. • Divide the dough in four. Form the dough into four 12-inch logs and place 2 inches apart on the prepared cookie sheets, flattening them slightly. • Bake for 25–35 minutes, or until firm to the touch, rotating the sheets halfway through for even baking. • Transfer to a cutting board to cool for 15 minutes. • Reduce the oven temperature to 325°F. • Cut on the diagonal into 1-inch slices. • Arrange the slices cut-side up on three cookie sheets and bake for 10–15 minutes more, or until golden and toasted. • Transfer to racks to cool.

Makes 48 cookies · Prep: 25 min. · Cooking: 35–45 min. · Level: 2 · Keeps: 2 weeks

lemon–poppy seed biscotti

Low in fat and high in flavor.

2	cups all-purpose flour
1/2	teaspoon baking powder
1/2	teaspoon baking soda
1/8	teaspoon salt
3/4	cup granulated sugar
1/2	cup finely ground almonds
1	large egg + 2 large egg whites, lightly beaten
3	tablespoons poppy seeds
1	tablespoon finely grated lemon zest
1	teaspoon lemon extract

Preheat the oven to 350°F. • Butter a cookie sheet. • Sift the flour, baking powder, baking soda, and salt into a medium bowl. Stir in the sugar and almonds. • Mix the egg and egg whites, poppy seeds, lemon zest, and lemon extract in a large bowl. • Mix in the dry ingredients to form a smooth dough. • Divide the dough in half. Form into two 9-inch logs and place 2 inches apart on the prepared cookie sheet, flattening them slightly. • Bake for 25–30 minutes, or until firm to the touch. • Transfer to a cutting board to cool for 15 minutes. • Reduce the oven temperature to 325°F. • Cut on the diagonal into 1-inch slices. • Arrange the slices cut-side up on three cookie sheets and bake for 10–15 minutes, or until golden and toasted. • Transfer to racks to cool.

Makes 36 cookies · Prep: 25 min. · Cooking: 35–45 min. · Level: 2 · Keeps: 2 weeks

Ginger biscotti (top)
and Lemon-poppy seed biscotti (bottom)

pumpkin pie biscotti

These biscotti taste like Thanksgiving with their pumpkin and heavily spiced flavor. Use canned pumpkin puree, or prepare the puree yourself for extra flavor. Cut the pumpkin into thin slices and arrange them on a baking sheet. Bake the pumpkin for 30–45 minutes, or until softened. Discard the seeds and scrape out the flesh. Use a potato masher to mash the flesh until pureed. Season with nutmeg, sugar, and butter before using it in this recipe.

2¼ cups all-purpose flour
1 teaspoon baking powder
½ teaspoon ground cinnamon
¼ teaspoon ground ginger
¼ teaspoon salt
⅛ teaspoon ground allspice
⅛ teaspoon ground nutmeg
¾ cup firmly packed dark brown sugar
¼ cup pumpkin puree
1 large egg
½ teaspoon vanilla extract
1 cup finely chopped pecans
1 tablespoon butter

brown sugar–oat biscotti

2¾ cups all-purpose flour
1½ teaspoons baking powder
1½ teaspoons ground cinnamon
⅛ teaspoon salt
½ cup (1 stick) butter, softened
⅓ cup granulated sugar
⅔ cup firmly packed dark brown sugar
2 large eggs
2 tablespoons Irish cream liqueur
2 cups old-fashioned rolled oats

Preheat the oven to 350°F. • Butter a cookie sheet. • Sift the flour, baking powder, cinnamon, and salt into a medium bowl. • Beat the butter and granulated and brown sugars in a large bowl with an electric mixer at high speed until creamy. • Add the eggs and liqueur, beating until just blended. • Mix in the dry ingredients and oats to form a stiff dough. • Divide the dough in half. Form into two 12-inch logs and place 2 inches apart on the prepared cookie sheet, flattening them slightly. • Bake for 30–35 minutes, or until firm to the touch. • Transfer to a cutting board to cool for 15 minutes. • Reduce the oven temperature to 325°F. • Cut on the diagonal into 1-inch slices. • Arrange the slices cut-side up on two cookie sheets and bake for 10–15 minutes, or until golden and toasted. • Transfer to racks to cool.

Makes 24 cookies · Prep: 40 min. · Cooking: 40–50 min. · Level: 2 · Keeps: 2 weeks

espresso biscotti

1 cup almonds
½ cup coarsely chopped pistachios
5 tablespoons espresso coffee beans
2⅓ cups all-purpose flour
2 teaspoons baking powder
½ teaspoon salt
½ cup (1 stick) butter, cut up
1 cup granulated sugar
3 large eggs, lightly beaten
½ cup strong coffee
1 tablespoon unsweetened cocoa powder
⅛ teaspoon ground cinnamon

Preheat the oven to 350°F. • Line three cookie sheets with parchment paper. • Spread the almonds and pistachios on separate large baking sheets. Toast each for 7 minutes, or until lightly golden. • Transfer the almonds to a food processor and process until finely chopped. • Coarsely grind 2 tablespoons of the beans with a pestle and mortar or in a food processor. • Grind the remaining beans in a coffee grinder until very fine. • Sift the flour, baking powder, and salt into a large bowl. • Use a pastry blender to cut in the butter until the mixture resembles coarse crumbs. • Mix in the almonds, pistachios, coarsely and finely ground espresso beans, sugar, eggs, and coffee to form a stiff dough. • Divide the dough in three. Form into three logs about 2 inches in diameter and place 2 inches apart on the prepared cookie sheets, flattening them slightly. • Dust each log with cocoa powder and cinnamon. • Bake, one sheet at a time, for 25–30 minutes, or until firm to the touch. • Transfer to a cutting board to cool for 15 minutes. • Lower the oven temperature to 300°F. • Cut on the diagonal into 1-inch slices. • Arrange the slices cut-side up on the cookie sheets and bake for 15–20 minutes, or golden and toasted. • Transfer to racks to cool.

Makes 40 cookies · Prep: 40 min. · Cooking: 40–50 min. · Level: 2 · Keeps: 1 month

honey-almond biscotti

⅔ cup all-purpose flour
½ teaspoon allspice
⅛ teaspoon salt
2 large egg whites
¼ cup granulated sugar
1 tablespoon honey
½ cup blanched almonds, halved

Preheat the oven to 350°F. • Butter a cookie sheet. • Sift the flour, allspice, and salt into a medium bowl. • Beat the egg whites, sugar, and honey in a large bowl with an electric mixer at high speed until frothy. • Mix in the dry ingredients and almonds. • Spread the mixture into the prepared pan. • Bake for 25–30 minutes, or until lightly browned and firm to the touch. • Let cool completely and wrap in aluminum foil. Let stand for 12 hours. • Re-heat the oven to 300°F. • Discard the foil. Slice the dough ⅛ inch thick and arrange on cookie sheets. • Bake for 15–20 minutes, or until golden and toasted, rotating the sheets halfway through for even baking. • Let cool completely.

Makes 45 cookies · Prep: 40 min. + 12 hr. to rest · Cooking: 40–50 min. · Level: 2 · Keeps: 1 month

coconut-almond biscotti

1⅔ cups all-purpose flour
1 teaspoon baking powder
⅛ teaspoon salt
2 large eggs
1 cup superfine sugar
1 teaspoon finely grated lemon zest
½ cup shredded coconut
1 cup blanched almonds, halved

Preheat the oven to 350°F. • Butter a cookie sheet. • Sift the flour, baking powder, and salt into a medium bowl. • Beat the eggs, sugar, and lemon zest in a large bowl with an electric mixer at high speed until frothy. •

Preheat the oven to 350°F. • Butter a cookie sheet. • Sift the flour, baking powder, cinnamon, ginger, salt, allspice, and nutmeg into a medium bowl. • Beat the brown sugar, pumpkin puree, egg, and vanilla in a large bowl with an electric mixer at high speed until well blended. • Mix in the dry ingredients to form a stiff dough. • Sauté the pecans in the butter in a skillet over medium heat until well coated. • Knead the pecans into the dough. • Divide the dough in half. Form into two 12-inch logs and place 2 inches apart on

the prepared cookie sheet, flattening them slightly. • Bake for 25–35 minutes, or until firm to the touch. • Transfer to a cutting board to cool for 15 minutes. • Reduce the oven temperature to 325°F. • Cut on the diagonal into 1-inch slices. • Arrange the slices cut-side up on two cookie sheets and bake for 10–15 minutes more, or until golden and toasted. • Transfer to racks to cool.

Makes 24 cookies · Prep: 40 min. · Cooking: 35–50 min. · Level: 2 · Keeps: 2 weeks

ginger–almond biscotti

- 2 1/2 cups all-purpose flour
- 1 teaspoon ground ginger
- 1/2 teaspoon baking soda
- 1/2 teaspoon ground allspice
- 1/4 teaspoon salt
- 1/2 cup finely ground almonds
- 1 1/2 cups finely chopped almonds
- 3/4 cup pine nuts
- 2 large eggs
- 1 cup granulated sugar
- 1/2 cup firmly packed light brown sugar
- 1/4 cup (1/2 stick) butter, melted
  Grated zest of 1 lemon
- 2 tablespoons finely chopped fresh ginger
- 1/2 teaspoon almond extract

Preheat the oven to 375°F. • Butter a cookie sheet. • Sift the flour, ground ginger, baking soda, allspice, and salt into a medium bowl. Stir in the ground and chopped almonds and pine nuts. • Beat the eggs and granulated and brown sugars in a large bowl with an electric mixer at high speed until pale and thick. • Beat in the butter, lemon zest, chopped ginger, and almond extract until well blended. • Mix in the dry ingredients to form a stiff dough. • Divide the dough in half. Form into two 10-inch logs and place 2 inches apart on the prepared cookie sheet. • Bake for 20–25 minutes, or until firm to the touch. • Reduce the oven temperature to 325°F. • Transfer to a cutting board to cool for 15 minutes. • Cut on the diagonal into 1-inch slices. • Arrange the slices cut-side up on two cookie sheets and bake for 10–15 minutes, or until golden and toasted. • Transfer to racks to cool.

Makes 20 cookies · Prep: 40 min. · Cooking: 30–40 min. · Level: 2 · Keeps: 2 weeks

Mix in the dry ingredients, coconut, and almonds to form a stiff dough. • Divide the dough in two. Form into two 8-inch logs and place 4 inches apart on the prepared cookie sheet, flattening them slightly. • Bake for 30–35 minutes, or until firm to the touch. • Transfer to a chopping board and let cool completely. • Cut on the diagonal into 1-inch slices and arrange cut-side up on two cookie sheets. • Bake for 10–15 minutes, or until golden and toasted. • Transfer to racks to cool.

Makes 30 cookies · Prep: 40 min. · Cooking: 40–50 min. · Level: 1

fig–sesame biscotti

- 2 1/2 cups all-purpose flour
- 1 teaspoon baking powder
- 1/2 teaspoon baking soda
- 1/8 teaspoon salt
- 3/4 cup firmly packed light brown sugar
- 2 tablespoons sesame seeds
  Grated zest of 1 lemon
- 2 large eggs + 2 large egg whites, lightly beaten
- 1/2 cup finely chopped dried figs

Preheat the oven to 350°F. • Butter two cookie sheets. • Sift the flour, baking powder, baking soda, and salt into a large bowl. • Stir in the brown sugar, sesame seeds, and lemon zest. • Mix in the eggs and egg whites until well blended. • Add the figs to form a stiff dough. • Divide the dough in four. • Form the dough into four logs each 2 inches in diameter. • Transfer the logs to the prepared cookie sheets. • Bake for 15–20 minutes, or until firm to the touch, rotating the sheets halfway through for even baking. • Transfer to a cutting board to cool for 15

minutes • Cut on the diagonal into 1/2-inch slices. • Arrange the slices cut-side up on three cookie sheets and bake, one sheet at a time, for 7–10 minutes, or until golden and toasted. • Transfer to racks to cool.

Makes 40 cookies · Prep: 20 min. · Cooking: 22–30 min. · Level: 2 · Keeps: 10 days

ginger–chocolate biscotti

- 2 1/2 cups all-purpose flour
- 1/4 cup unsweetened cocoa powder
- 1 teaspoon baking soda
- 1/2 teaspoon salt
- 1/4 teaspoon ground cinnamon
- 1/4 teaspoon ground cloves
- 1 cup granulated sugar
- 1 1/4 cups finely chopped almonds
- 3 large eggs, lightly beaten
- 2 tablespoons freshly grated fresh ginger
- 1/2 teaspoon almond extract

Preheat the oven to 350°F. • Line a cookie sheet with parchment paper. • Sift the flour, cocoa, baking soda, salt, cinnamon, and cloves into a large bowl. • Stir in the sugar and almonds. • Mix in the eggs, ginger, and almond extract to form a stiff dough. • Divide the dough in half. • Form the dough into two 10-inch logs and place 3 inches apart on the prepared cookie sheet, flattening the tops. • Bake for 20–30 minutes, or until lightly browned and firm to the touch. • Transfer to a cutting board to cool for 15 minutes. • Reduce the oven temperature to 300°F. • Cut on the diagonal into 1-inch slices. • Arrange the slices cut-side up on two cookie sheets and bake for 10–15 minutes, or until golden and toasted. • Transfer to racks to cool.

Makes 20 cookies · Prep: 40 min. · Cooking: 30–45 min. · Level: 2 · Keeps: 2 weeks

Ginger–almond biscotti

chocolate chip biscotti

This is one of the many variations of the cantuccini cookies—almond cookies—found all over Tuscany in central Italy.

3/4	cup blanched almonds
1	cup granulated sugar
2	cups all-purpose flour
1	teaspoon baking soda
1/4	teaspoon salt
	Grated zest of 1 orange
2	large eggs + 2 large egg yolks + 1 large egg white, lightly beaten
3	oz semisweet chocolate, finely chopped

Preheat the oven to 325°F. • Butter and flour two cookie sheets. • Spread the almonds on a separate baking sheet. Toast for 7 minutes, or until lightly golden. • Let cool completely, then chop half the almonds coarsely. • Process the remaining almonds with the sugar in a food processor until very finely ground. • Sift the flour, baking soda, and salt into a large bowl. • Stir in the ground almond mixture and orange zest. • Make a well in the center and work in the whole egg and egg yolks to form a sticky dough. • Mix in the coarsely chopped almonds and chocolate. • Divide the dough in four. • Form the dough into four 6-inch logs and brush with the beaten egg white. • Place the logs 2 inches apart on the prepared cookie sheets. • Bake for 15–20 minutes, or until firm to the touch. • Transfer to a cutting board to cool for 15 minutes. • Cut on the diagonal into 1/2-inch slices. • Arrange the slices cut-side up on four cookie sheets and bake for 15–20 minutes, or until golden and toasted. • Transfer to racks to cool.

Makes 48 cookies · Prep: 25 min. · Cooking: 30–40 min. · Level: 2 · Keeps: 2 weeks

coconut–pecan biscotti

2 1/4	cups all-purpose flour
1 1/2	teaspoons baking powder
1/4	teaspoon salt
1/2	cup (1 stick) butter, softened
3/4	cup firmly packed dark brown sugar
2	large eggs
1/2	cup shredded coconut
1	cup finely chopped pecans

Sift the flour, baking powder, and salt into a medium bowl. • Beat the butter and brown sugar in a large bowl with an electric mixer at high speed until creamy. • Add the eggs, beating until just blended. • Mix in the dry ingredients, coconut, and pecans. • Preheat the oven to 350°F. • Line a cookie sheet with parchment paper. • Divide the dough in half. • Form the dough into two 12-inch logs and place 3 inches apart on the prepared cookie sheet, flattening the tops. • Bake for 25–35 minutes, or until lightly browned and firm to the touch. • Transfer to a cutting board to cool for 15 minutes. • Lower the oven temperature to 300°F. • Cut on the diagonal into 1-inch slices. • Arrange the slices cut-side up on two cookie sheets and bake for 10–15 minutes, or until golden and toasted. • Transfer to racks to cool.

Makes 24 cookies · Prep: 40 min. · Cooking: 35–50 min. · Level: 2 · Keeps: 2 weeks

pine nut biscotti

1/4	cup blanched almonds
1/2	cup pine nuts
2	cups all-purpose flour
1	teaspoon baking powder
1/4	teaspoon salt
1 1/4	cups granulated sugar
1/2	cup finely chopped pitted dates
1/4	cup finely chopped dried apricots
1/4	cup finely chopped pitted prunes
1/4	cup whole almonds with skins
	Grated zest of 1 orange
1	teaspoon grated lemon zest
3	large eggs, lightly beaten

Preheat the oven to 325°F. • Spread the blanched almonds on a large baking sheet. Toast for 7 minutes, or until lightly golden. • Let cool completely and cut the almonds in half. • Increase the oven temperature to 350°F. • Line a cookie sheet with parchment paper. • Toast the pine nuts in a skillet over medium heat for 5–7 minutes, or until lightly golden. • Sift the flour, baking powder, and salt into a large bowl. Stir in the sugar, dates, apricots, prunes, halved and whole almonds, pine nuts, and the orange and lemon zests. • Beat the eggs in a medium bowl with an electric mixer at high speed until frothy. • Add the beaten egg to the dry ingredients, reserving 1 tablespoon. • Divide the dough in half. Form the dough into two long logs about 1 1/4 inches in diameter. • Transfer the logs to the prepared cookie sheets, flattening them slightly. • Bake for 15–20 minutes, or firm to the touch. • Transfer to a cutting board to cool for 10 minutes. • Lower the oven temperature to 300°F. • Cut on the diagonal into 1/2 inch slices. • Arrange the slices cut-side up on the cookie sheet and bake for 7–10 minutes, or until golden and toasted. • Transfer to racks to cool.

Makes about 40 biscotti · Prep: 40 min. · Cooking: 22–30 min. · Level: 2 · Keeps: 2 weeks

polenta biscotti

1 1/2	cups all-purpose flour
1	teaspoon baking soda
1/8	teaspoon salt
2	large eggs
1	cup granulated sugar
2	tablespoons anisette
1/3	cup finely ground yellow cornmeal
	Grated zest of 1 lemon
1	teaspoon coarsely chopped cilantro
1/4	cup almonds

Glaze

1	egg yolk
2	tablespoons milk
1	tablespoon granulated sugar

Preheat the oven to 300°F. • Line two cookie sheets with parchment paper. • Sift the flour, baking soda, and salt into a medium bowl. • Beat the eggs and sugar in a large bowl with an electric mixer at high speed until thick and creamy. • Beat in the anisette, polenta flour, lemon zest, and cilantro. • Mix in the dry ingredients and nuts to form a sticky dough. • Form the dough into 3 flat logs, about 2 1/2 inches wide. • Transfer the logs to the prepared cookie sheets. • Glaze: Mix the egg yolk and milk in a small bowl and brush it over the logs. Sprinkle them with sugar. • Bake for 25–30 minutes, or until firm to the touch. • Transfer to a cutting board to cool for 10 minutes. • Lower the oven temperature to 300°F. • Cut on the diagonal into 1/2 inch slices. • Arrange the slices cut-side up on three cookie sheets and bake for 7–10 minutes, or until golden and toasted. • Transfer to racks to cool.

Makes 40 biscotti · Prep: 15 min. · Cooking: 32–40 min. · Level: 2 · Keeps: 1 month

Chocolate–walnut biscotti (top) and Coconut–pecan biscotti (bottom)

tea
cakes

Whether you want to set the tone at an elegant bridal shower, complement the menu for a luncheon among friends, or just have a fast snack with your espresso coffee break, you'll find the perfect tasty treat here. From elegant French madeleines to dainty tea cakes and nutritious mini tarts—any of these half-cake, half-cookie creations will fit the bill and satisfy your sweet tooth.

above: Mini jelly tarts (page 293)

right: Dainty tea cakes, Quick mini coconut cups, and Tiny pecan tarts (pages 290, 286, and 286)

Madeleines with pistachios

madeleines with pistachios

2/3 cup all-purpose flour
1²/3 cups confectioners' sugar
1/8 teaspoon salt
1/2 cup finely ground pistachios
4 large egg whites
3/4 cup (1¹/2 sticks) butter, melted
1 tablespoon honey
1 teaspoon almond extract

Preheat the oven to 375°F. • Butter two madeleine pans (for 20–24 madeleines). • Sift the flour, confectioners' sugar, and salt into a medium bowl. • Stir in the pistachios. • Beat the egg whites in a large bowl with an electric mixer at high speed until stiff peaks form. • Use a large rubber spatula to fold in the dry ingredients, followed by the butter, honey, and almond extract. • Spoon the batter evenly into the prepared pans. • Bake for 12–15 minutes, or until a toothpick inserted into one comes out clean, rotating the pans halfway through for even baking. • Cool the madeleines in the pans for 15 minutes. • Transfer to a rack and let cool completely.

Makes 20–24 cookies · Prep: 20 min. · Cooking: 12–15 min. · Level: 1 · Keeps: 4 days

old-fashioned madeleines with lavender honey

1/3 cup all-purpose flour
1/8 teaspoon salt
3 large eggs
Grated zest of 1 lemon
2 tablespoons lavender honey
1/2 cup (1 stick) butter, melted
Confectioners' sugar, to dust

Preheat the oven to 425°F. • Butter two madeleine pans (for 20–24 madeleines). • Sift the flour and salt into a large bowl. • Beat the eggs and lemon zest in a large bowl with an electric mixer at high speed until pale and thick. Add the honey and beat until creamy. • Fold in the dry ingredients, followed by the butter. • Spoon the batter evenly into the prepared pans. • Bake for 15–20 minutes, or until a toothpick inserted into one comes out clean, rotating the pans halfway through for even baking. • Cool the madeleines in the pans for 15 minutes. Transfer to racks to cool completely. • Dust with the confectioners' sugar.

Makes 20–24 cookies · Prep: 20 min. · Cooking: 15–20 min. · Level: 1· Keeps: 4 days

lemon madeleines

Tantalizingly tangy, these cookies are perfect on a summer's day served with homemade lemonade.

1/2 cup all-purpose flour
1 teaspoon baking powder
1/8 teaspoon salt
1/3 cup butter, softened
1/3 cup Vanilla Sugar (see page 341)
1 large egg, separated
Grated zest and juice of 1 lemon

Lemon drizzle
1 teaspoon butter
2–3 tablespoons fresh lemon juice
1/3 cup confectioners' sugar

Preheat the oven to 350°F. • Butter a madeleine pan (for 12 cookies). • Sift the flour, baking powder, and salt into a medium bowl. • Beat the butter and vanilla sugar in a large bowl with an electric mixer at high speed until creamy. • Add the egg yolk and lemon zest and juice, beating until just blended. • Mix in the dry ingredients. • With mixer at high speed, beat the egg white in a medium bowl until stiff peaks form. • Use a large rubber spatula to fold in the beaten white. • Spoon the batter into prepared pan, filling each cup three-quarters full. • Bake for 10–12 minutes, or until springy to the touch. • Cool the madeleines in the pan for 15 minutes. • Transfer to racks and let cool completely. • Lemon drizzle: Melt the butter with the lemon juice in a small saucepan over low heat. • Remove from the heat and beat in the confectioners' sugar. • Drizzle the frosting over the cookies and let stand for 30 minutes until set.

Makes 12 cookies · Prep: 20 min. + 30 min. to set · Cooking: 10–12 min. · Level: 1 · Keeps: 4 days

maple tarts

Pastry
1¹/4 cups all-purpose flour
1/8 teaspoon salt
1/2 cup (1 stick) butter, cut up
1–2 tablespoons milk

Syrup filling
1/2 cup pure maple syrup
2/3 cup all-purpose flour
1/2 teaspoon baking powder
1/4 cup (¹/2 stick) butter, softened
1/4 cup firmly packed light brown sugar
1 large egg, lightly beaten
1/2 teaspoon vanilla extract
1 tablespoon milk

Mascarpone–Vanilla Cream or Vanilla Whipped Cream (see pages 340), to serve

Pastry: Sift the flour and salt into a medium bowl. • Use a pastry blender to cut in the butter until the mixture resembles coarse crumbs. • Add enough milk to form a stiff dough. • Press the dough into a disk, wrap in plastic wrap, and refrigerate for 30 minutes. • Preheat the oven to 375°F. • Set out two 12-cup mini-muffin pans. • Roll out the dough on a lightly floured surface to a thickness of 1/8 inch. • Use a 2-inch fluted cookie cutter to cut out rounds. • Gather the dough scraps, re-roll, and continue cutting out rounds until all the dough is used. Press the dough rounds into the prepared cups. • Syrup filling: Drop teaspoons of the maple syrup into each pastry base. • Sift the flour and baking powder into a medium bowl. • Beat the butter and brown sugar in a medium bowl with an electric mixer at high speed until creamy. • Add the egg and vanilla, beating until just blended. • Mix in the dry ingredients and milk. • Spoon the mixture evenly into the prepared cups. • Bake for 15–20 minutes, or until golden brown, rotating the sheets halfway through for even baking. • Transfer to racks to cool. • Serve topped with a spoonful of Mascarpone–Vanilla Cream.

Makes 24 cookies · Prep: 45 min. + 30 min. to chill Cooking: 15–20 min. · Level: 2 · Keeps: 5 days

almond tarts

4 oz store-bought flaky pie pastry
1/4 cup cherry jelly or cherry jam
1/4 cup plain cake crumbs
1/2 cup finely ground almonds
1 teaspoon all-purpose flour
1/2 cup (1 stick) butter
1/2 cup granulated sugar

1   large egg, lightly beaten
1/2   teaspoon vanilla extract
3   tablespoons apricot preserves or jam
3/4   cup confectioners' sugar
1   teaspoon lukewarm water (105°–115°F), or more as needed

Preheat the oven to 350°F. • Set out a 12-cup mini muffin pan. • Roll out the pastry on a lightly floured surface to a thickness of 1/4 inch. Use a 2-inch cookie cutter to stamp out twelve rounds. • Line the cups with the pastry rounds. • Brush each pastry round with 1 teaspoon of cherry jelly. • Stir together the cake crumbs, almonds, and flour in a medium bowl. • Melt the butter in a small saucepan over low heat. • Stir in the sugar and remove from the heat. • Add the egg, beating until just blended. • Use a large rubber spatula to fold in the dry ingredients and vanilla. • Spoon the mixture evenly into the prepared cups. • Bake for 25–30 minutes, or until the pastry is golden brown and a toothpick inserted into a center comes out clean. • Turn out of the cups and transfer to racks to cool. • Brush the tops with the apricot jam. • Mix the confectioners' sugar with the water until thick. • Spread the tartlets with the frosting.

Makes 12 cookies · Prep: 30 min. · Cooking 25–30 min. · Level: 1 · Keeps: 4–5 days

plum–nutmeg friands

Originally French, friands were reinvented in Australia in the 1990s. For an oval finish, use a friand pan or oval aspic molds available in specialty food stores.

8   oz firm-ripe plums, halved and pitted
1/2   cup all-purpose flour
1 1/2   teaspoons finely grated nutmeg
1/4   teaspoon ground cinnamon
1/8   teaspoon salt
1 1/4   cups finely ground almonds
3/4   cup (1 1/2 sticks) butter, softened
1 2/3   cups confectioners' sugar
6   large egg whites

Preheat the oven to 350°F. • Butter a 12-cup mini muffin pan. • Cut each half-plum into three. • Sift the flour, nutmeg, cinnamon, and salt into a medium bowl. Stir in the almonds. • Beat the butter and confectioners' sugar in a large bowl with an electric mixer at high speed until creamy. • Mix in the dry ingredients and egg whites. • Pour the batter evenly into the prepared cups and place a piece of plum on top of each. • Bake for 25–30 minutes, or until a

toothpick inserted into the centers comes out clean. • Transfer to racks to cool.

Makes 12 cookies · Prep: 25 min. · Cooking: 25–30 min. · Level: 1 · Keeps: 1 week

strawberry–almond friands

1/2   cup all-purpose flour
1/8   teaspoon salt
1 1/4   cups finely ground almonds
3/4   cup (1 1/2 sticks) butter, softened
1 2/3   cups confectioners' sugar
6   large egg whites
1/2   cup thinly sliced strawberries

Preheat the oven to 350°F. • Butter a 12-cup mini muffin pan. • Sift the flour and salt into a medium bowl. Stir in the almonds. • Beat the butter and confectioners' sugar in a large bowl with an electric mixer at high speed until creamy. • Mix in the dry ingredients and egg whites. • Pour the batter evenly into the prepared cups and place a slice of strawberry on top of each. • Bake for 25–30 minutes, or until a toothpick inserted into one comes out clean. • Transfer to racks to cool.

Makes 12 cookies · Prep: 25 min. · Cooking: 25–30 min. · Level: 1 · Keeps: 1 week

raspberry–almond friands

1/2   cup all-purpose flour
1/8   teaspoon salt
1 1/4   cups finely ground almonds
3/4   cup (1 1/2 sticks) butter, softened
1 2/3   cups confectioners' sugar
6   large egg whites
1/2   cup raspberries

Preheat the oven to 350°F. • Butter a 12-cup mini muffin pan. • Sift the flour and salt into a large bowl. Stir in the almonds. • Beat the butter and confectioners' sugar in a large bowl with an electric mixer at high speed until creamy. • Mix in the dry ingredients and egg whites. • Pour the batter evenly into the prepared cups and place a raspberry on top of each. • Bake for 25–30 minutes, or until a toothpick inserted into the centers comes out clean. • Transfer to racks to cool.

Makes 12 cookies · Prep: 25 min. · Cooking: 25–30 min. · Level: 1 · Keeps: 1 week

macaroon tarts

Pastry
1 1/4   cups all-purpose flour
1/8   teaspoon salt
1/4   cup (1/2 stick) butter, cut up

1/4   cup lard, cut up, or vegetable shortening
1–2   tablespoons ice water
Filling
2–3   tablespoons raspberry jelly
1   large egg white
1/3   cup superfine sugar
2   tablespoons shredded coconut
2   tablespoons finely ground almonds

Pastry: Sift the flour and salt into a large bowl. • Use a pastry blender to cut in the butter and lard until the mixture resembles fine crumbs. • Mix in the ice water to form a smooth dough. • Shape into a ball, wrap in plastic wrap, and refrigerate for at least 30 minutes. • Preheat the oven to 350°F. • Butter twelve 2 x 3/4-inch tartlet pans. • Roll out the pastry on a lightly floured surface to a thickness of 1/4 inch. Use a pastry cutter to stamp out twelve rounds to slightly larger than the tartlet pans. Press the pastry rounds into the prepared pans. • Filling: Heat the raspberry jelly in a small saucepan until liquid. Brush 1/4 teaspoon jelly over each pastry base. • Beat the egg white in a medium bowl with an electric mixer at high speed until stiff peaks form. Use a rubber spatula to fold in the superfine sugar, coconut, and almonds. • Spoon the coconut mixture evenly into the pastry bases. • Bake for 20–25 minutes, or until golden brown. • Cool the tarts completely in the pans.

Makes 12 tarts · Prep: 40 min. + 30 min. to chill · Cooking: 20–25 min. · Level: 2 · Keeps: 5–8 days

blueberry–almond friands

1/2   cup all-purpose flour
1/8   teaspoon salt
1 1/4   cups finely ground almonds
3/4   cup (1 1/2 sticks) butter, softened
1 2/3   cups confectioners' sugar
6   large egg whites
1/2   cup blueberries

Preheat the oven to 350°F. • Butter a 12-cup mini muffin pan. • Sift the flour and salt into a medium bowl. Stir in the almonds. • Beat the butter and confectioners' sugar in a large bowl with an electric mixer at high speed until creamy. • Mix in the dry ingredients and egg whites. • Pour the batter evenly into the prepared cups and place some blueberries on top of each. • Bake for 25–30 minutes, or until a toothpick inserted into one comes out clean. • Transfer to racks to cool.

Makes 12 cookies · Prep: 25 min. · Cooking: 25–30 min. · Level: 1 · Keeps: 1 week

traditional madeleines

Madeleines are small spongelike cookies that are baked in special shell-shaped molds. They are associated with the small town of Commercy in Lorraine, France and probably originated in the 18th century. According to one story, Louis XV first tasted them at the Chateau de Commercy and named them after the pastry cook, Madeleine Paulmier. The French writer Marcel Proust made madeleines famous when he wrote about them in his novel *Remembrance of Things Past*.

- 2/3 cup all-purpose flour
- 1/8 teaspoon salt
- 2 large eggs
- 1/2 cup granulated sugar
- 1/3 cup butter, melted
- 1 teaspoon orange-flower water
- 1/2 teaspoon finely grated lemon zest
- 1/3 cup confectioners' sugar

Sift the flour and salt into a medium bowl. • Beat the eggs in a large bowl with an electric mixer at medium speed for 3 minutes. • Gradually add the granulated sugar, beating until the batter falls off the beater in ribbons. • Use a large rubber spatula to fold in the dry ingredients, followed by the butter, orange-flower water, and lemon zest. • Refrigerate for 30 minutes. • Let rest at room temperature for 15 minutes. • Preheat the oven to 375°F. • Butter two madeleine pans (for 20–24 madeleines). • Spoon the batter into the prepared pans. • Bake for 10–12 minutes, or until golden brown and springy to the touch, rotating the pans halfway through for even baking. • Cool in the pans for 15 minutes. • Transfer to racks and let cool completely. • Dust with confectioners' sugar just before serving.

Makes 20–24 cookies · Prep: 30 min. + 45 min. to chill and rest · Cooking: 10–12 min. · Level: 1 · Keeps: 4 days

bittersweet chocolate madeleines

- 3/4 cup all-purpose flour
- 1/2 teaspoon baking powder
- 1/8 teaspoon salt
- 3 large eggs
- 1/2 cup granulated sugar
- 2 tablespoons Vanilla Sugar (see page 341)
- 4 oz bittersweet chocolate, coarsely chopped
- 1/2 cup (1 stick) butter, cut up
- 1/3 cup confectioners' sugar

Sift the flour, baking powder, and salt into a medium bowl. • Beat the eggs in a large bowl with an electric mixer at high speed for 3 minutes. • Gradually add the granulated and vanilla sugars, beating until the batter falls off the beaters in ribbons. • Fold in the dry ingredients. • Melt the chocolate with the butter in a double boiler over barely simmering water. • Gently fold in the chocolate mixture. • Refrigerate for 30 minutes. • Let rest at room temperature for 15 minutes. • Preheat the oven to 375°F. • Butter two madeleine pans (for 20–24 madeleines). • Spoon the batter into the prepared pans. • Bake, one pan at a time, for 10–12 minutes, or until brown and springy to the touch. • Cool the madeleines in the pans for 15 minutes. • Transfer to racks to cool. • Dust with confectioners' sugar just before serving.

Makes 20–24 cookies · Prep: 30 min. + 45 min. to chill and rest · Cooking: 10–12 min. per batch · Level: 2 · Keeps: 4 days

mocha madeleines

- 1/2 cup all-purpose flour
- 1/4 cup unsweetened cocoa powder
- 1/8 teaspoon baking soda
- 1/8 teaspoon salt
- 2 large eggs
- 1 teaspoon freeze-dried coffee granules
- 1/2 teaspoon vanilla extract
- 1 cup confectioners' sugar
- 1/2 cup (1 stick) butter, melted
- 2 cups Mocha Icing (see page 346)

Preheat the oven to 375°F. • Butter two madeleine pans (for 20–24 madeleines). • Sift the flour, cocoa, baking soda, and salt into a medium bowl. • Beat the eggs, coffee granules, and vanilla in a large bowl with an electric mixer at high speed until blended. • Beat in the confectioners' sugar and continue beating until thick. • Mix in the dry ingredients and butter. • Spoon the batter into the prepared cups, filling each three-quarters full. • Bake for 10–12 minutes, or until springy to the touch, rotating the pans halfway through for even baking. • Cool the madeleines in the pans for 15 minutes. • Transfer to racks and let cool completely. Frost with the mocha icing.

Makes 20–24 cookies · Prep: 25 min. · Cooking: 10–12 min. · Level: 1 · Keeps: 2 days

hazelnut madeleines

- 1/2 cup all-purpose flour
- 1 2/3 cups confectioners' sugar
- 1/8 teaspoon salt
- 1/2 cup finely ground hazelnuts
- 6 large egg whites
- 3/4 cup (1 1/2 sticks) butter, melted
- 1 container (8 oz) chocolate hazelnut spread (Nutella), softened

Preheat the oven to 375°F. • Butter two madeleine pans (for 20–24 madeleines). • Sift the flour, confectioners' sugar, and salt into a large bowl. • Stir in the hazelnuts. • Beat the egg whites in a large bowl with an electric mixer at high speed until stiff peaks form. • Fold in the dry ingredients, followed by the butter and chocolate hazelnut spread. • Spoon the batter evenly into the prepared pan. • Bake for 12–15 minutes, or until a toothpick inserted into one comes out clean, rotating the pans halfway through for even baking. • Cool the madeleines in the pans for 15 minutes. Transfer to racks and let cool completely.

Makes 20–24 cookies · Prep: 20 min. · Cooking: 12–15 min. · Level: 1 · Keeps: 5 days

spiced madeleines

- 1 cup all-purpose flour
- 1 teaspoon ground cinnamon
- 1/2 teaspoon baking powder
- 1/4 teaspoon ground nutmeg
- 1/8 teaspoon salt
- 3 large eggs
- 1 teaspoon vanilla extract
- 2/3 cup granulated sugar
- 1/2 cup (1 stick) butter, melted
- 1/3 cup confectioners' sugar

Sift the flour, cinnamon, baking powder, nutmeg, and salt into a medium bowl. • Beat the eggs and vanilla in a large bowl with an electric mixer at high speed for 3 minutes. • Gradually add the granulated sugar, beating until the batter falls off the beater in ribbons. • Fold in the dry ingredients and butter. • Refrigerate for 30 minutes. • Let rest at room temperature for 15 minutes. • Preheat the oven to 375°F. • Butter two madeleine pans (for 20–24 madeleines). • Spoon the batter into the prepared pans. • Bake for 10–12 minutes, or until brown and springy to the touch, rotating the pans halfway through for even baking. • Cool the madeleines in the pans for 15 minutes. • Transfer to racks and let cool completely. • Dust with confectioners' sugar.

Makes 24 cookies · Prep: 30 min. + 45 min. to chill Cooking: 10–12 min. · Level: 2 · Keeps: 4 days

Traditional madeleines
and Bittersweet chocolate madeleines

almond–lemon madeleines

1/2 cup all-purpose flour
1/2 teaspoon baking powder
1/8 teaspoon baking soda
1/8 teaspoon salt
2 large eggs
1/2 cup granulated sugar
1/2 cup (1 stick) butter, melted
1/2 teaspoon finely grated lemon zest
1 tablespoon fresh lemon juice
1/2 teaspoon vanilla extract
1/4 cup finely chopped almonds

Preheat the oven to 375°F. • Butter two madeleine pans (for 24 madeleines). • Sift the flour, baking powder, baking soda, and salt into a medium bowl. • Beat the eggs and sugar in a large bowl with an electric mixer at medium speed until blended. • Mix in the dry ingredients, followed by the butter, lemon zest and juice, and vanilla. • Stir in the almonds. • Spoon the batter into the prepared pans, filling each one about three-quarters full. • Bake for 10–12 minutes, or until springy to the touch, rotating the pans halfway through for even baking. • Cool the madeleines in the pans for 15 minutes. • Transfer to racks and let cool completely.

Makes 24 cookies · Prep: 25 min. · Cooking: 10–12 min. · Level: 1 · Keeps: 2 days

Almond–lemon madeleines

honey and lemon madeleines

1 cup all-purpose flour
1 teaspoon baking powder
1/8 teaspoon salt
2 large eggs
1/2 cup honey
1/4 cup granulated sugar
   Grated zest of 1 lemon
1 tablespoon fresh lemon juice
1/2 teaspoon vanilla extract
1/3 cup butter, melted
1/3 cup confectioners' sugar

Sift the flour, baking powder, and salt into a medium bowl. • Beat the eggs, honey, and granulated sugar in a large bowl with an electric mixer at high speed until pale and thick. • Use a large rubber spatula to fold in the dry ingredients, lemon zest and juice, and vanilla, followed by the butter. • Refrigerate for 30 minutes. • Let rest at room temperature for 15 minutes. • Preheat the oven to 375°F. • Butter a madeleine pan (for 12 madeleines). • Spoon the batter into the prepared pan. • Bake for 10–12 minutes, or until golden brown and springy to the touch. • Cool the madeleines in the pan for 15 minutes. • Transfer to racks and let cool completely. • Dust with confectioners' sugar just before serving.

Makes 12 cookies · Prep: 40 min. + 45 min. to rest and chill · Cooking: 10–12 min. · Level: 1 · Keeps: 4 days

welsh scallop-shell cookies

If you are unable to obtain scallop shells, bake the dough in a madeleine pan.

3/4 cup all-purpose flour
1 teaspoon baking powder
1/8 teaspoon salt
1/2 cup (1 stick) butter, softened
1/2 cup granulated sugar
2 large eggs

Preheat the oven to 375°F. • Scrub eight scallop shells well, dry thoroughly, and butter them. Arrange on a cookie sheet. • Sift the flour, baking powder, and salt into a medium bowl. • Beat the butter and sugar in a large bowl with an electric mixer at high speed until creamy. • Add the eggs, beating until just blended. • Mix in the dry ingredients to form a soft dough. • Divide the mixture evenly among the shells. • Bake for 12–15 minutes, or until golden brown and firm to the touch. • Transfer to racks to cool.

Makes 8 cookies · Prep: 20 min. · Cooking: 12–15 min. · Level: 1 · Keeps: 7 days

shell cookies

1/2 cup all-purpose flour
1/8 teaspoon salt
2 large eggs
1/2 cup granulated sugar
1 teaspoon finely grated lemon zest
1/4 cup (1/2 stick) butter, melted

Preheat the oven to 400°F. • Butter and flour a madeleine pan. • Sift the flour and salt into a medium bowl. • Beat the eggs and sugar in a large bowl with an electric mixer at high speed until pale and thick. • Mix in the dry ingredients and lemon zest until well blended. • Stir in the melted butter. • Spoon the batter into the prepared pan, filling each cup three-quarters full. • Bake for 6–8 minutes, or until golden brown. • Transfer to racks to cool.

Makes 12 cookies · Prep: 20 min. · Cooking: 6–8 min. · Level: 1 · Keeps: 3 days

almond shell cookies

1/2 cup all-purpose flour
1/8 teaspoon salt
2 large eggs
1/2 cup granulated sugar
1/3 cup finely ground almonds
1/4 teaspoon almond extract
1/4 cup (1/2 stick) butter, melted

Preheat the oven to 400°F. • Butter and flour a madeleine pan (for 12 madeleines). • Sift the flour and salt into a medium bowl. • Beat the eggs and sugar in a large bowl with an electric mixer at high speed until pale and thick. • Mix in the dry ingredients, almonds, and almond extract until well blended. • Stir in the melted butter. • Spoon the batter into the prepared pan, filling each cup three-quarters full. • Bake for 6–8 minutes, or until golden brown. • Transfer to racks to cool.

Makes 12 cookies · Prep: 20 min. · Cooking: 6–8 min. · Level: 1 · Keeps: 3 days

petit-four fancies

1 cup all-purpose flour
1 cup cornstarch
1 teaspoon baking powder
1/8 teaspoon salt
6 large eggs, separated
3/4 cup granulated sugar
2 tablespoons Vanilla Sugar (see page 341)
1/4 cup unsweetened cocoa powder
1–2 tablespoons dark rum
2 teaspoons finely grated orange zest
2 teaspoons finely grated lemon zest
2/3–3/4 cup apricot preserves or jam
3 1/3 cups confectioners' sugar

3–4 tablespoons fresh lemon juice
     Chopped nuts, sweets, sugar flowers and petals, chocolate flakes, candied fruits and peel, colored sugar crystals, silver balls, or Homemade marzipan fruits (see pages 346), to decorate

Preheat the oven to 375°F. • Line two 13 x 9-inch baking pans with parchment paper. • Sift the flour, cornstarch, baking powder, and salt into a large bowl. • Beat the egg yolks and granulated and vanilla sugars in a large bowl with an electric mixer at high speed until pale and thick. • Mix in the dry ingredients. • With mixer at high speed, beat the egg whites in a large bowl until stiff peaks form. • Use a large rubber spatula to fold the beaten whites into the batter. • Spoon half the mixture into a separate bowl. Mix in the cocoa powder and rum. • Mix the orange and lemon zest into the remaining mixture. • Spoon one mixture evenly into each of the prepared pans. • Bake for 12–15 minutes, or until golden brown and springy to the touch, rotating the pans halfway through the baking. • Cool in the pans for 15 minutes. • Turn out onto a sheet of waxed paper dusted with confectioners' sugar. • Use 1-inch cookie cutters to cut out pairs of shapes from each cake. • Stick the cake shapes together in pairs with the preserves. • Mix the confectioners' sugar and lemon juice in a small bowl to make a spreadable icing. • Spoon the icing over the shapes, letting it run down the sides. • Decorate with a combination of the nuts, candies, and marzipan fruits.

Makes 35–40 cookies · Prep: 50 min. · Cooking: 12–15 min. · Level: 2 · Keeps: 10 days, layered between parchment paper

pine nut–pecan tarts

Pastry
1¼ cups all-purpose flour
1/8 teaspoon salt
1/4 cup granulated sugar
     Grated zest of 1 orange
1/4 cup (1/2 stick) butter, cut up
1 large egg yolk, lightly beaten

Pine nut–pecan filling
1/4 cup granulated sugar
1 tablespoons water
3/4 cup finely chopped pecans
1/4 cup pine nuts
2 tablespoons honey
1 tablespoon light cream

Pastry: Sift the flour and salt into a medium bowl. Stir in the sugar and orange zest. • Use a pastry blender to cut in the butter until the mixture resembles coarse crumbs. • Mix in the egg yolk to form a smooth dough. • Press the dough into a disk, wrap in plastic wrap, and refrigerate for 30 minutes. • Preheat the oven to 350°F. • Butter twenty-four mini-muffin cups. • Roll out the dough on a lightly floured surface to a thickness of 1/8 inch. • Use a fluted 2-inch cookie cutter to cut out twenty-four dough rounds. • Press the dough rounds into the prepared cups and prick all over with a fork. • Bake for 10–15 minutes, or until the pastry is just golden. • Transfer to racks to cool. • Pine nut–pecan filling: Mix the sugar with the water in a small saucepan. Wash down the sides of the pan with a pastry brush dipped in cold water to prevent sugar crystals from forming. Cook over low heat until the syrup is golden, about 10 minutes. • Mix in the pecans, pine nuts, honey, and cream until well blended. • Spoon the filling into the cups and let cool completely.

Makes 24 cookies · Prep: 45 min. · Cooking: 10–15 min. · Leve : 2 · Keeps: 5 days

chocolate buckwheat pixies

2/3 cup all-purpose flour
2/3 cup buckwheat flour
1 tablespoon unsweetened cocoa powder
1 teaspoon baking powder
1/8 teaspoon salt
1 tablespoon ground almonds
1/3 cup butter, softened
1/2 cup firmly packed soft brown sugar
3 large eggs
2 tablespoons milk
1/2 teaspoon vanilla or rum extract
2 oz semisweet chocolate, finely grated
2 oz white chocolate, coarsely chopped

Preheat the oven to 350°F. • Butter two 12-cup mini muffin pans. • Sift the all-purpose and buckwheat flours, cocoa, baking powder, and salt into a medium bowl. Stir in the almonds. - Beat the butter and brown sugar in a large bowl with an electric mixer at high speed until creamy. • Add the eggs, milk, and vanilla, beating until just blended. • Mix in the dry ingredients and semisweet chocolate. • Fit a pastry bag with a plain 1/2-inch tip. Fill the pastry bag, twist the opening tightly closed, and squeeze out small rounds into each prepared cup. • Bake for 20–25 minutes, or until lightly browned and a toothpick inserted in the centers comes out clean, rotating the pans halfway through for even baking. • Cool in the pans for 3 minutes. Transfer to racks and let cool completely. • Melt the white chocolate in a double boiler over barely simmering water. Spoon the chocolate into a small freezer bag and cut off a tiny corner. Pipe chocolate lines over the tops in a decorative manner. Let set for 30 minutes.

Makes 24–30 cookies · Prep: 25 min. + 30 min. to set · Cooking: 20–25 min. · Level: 2 · Keeps: 5 days

orange–walnut madeleines

1/2 cup all-purpose flour
1/2 teaspoon baking powder
1/4 teaspoon ground cardamom
1/8 teaspoon baking soda
1/8 teaspoon salt
2 large eggs
1/2 cup granulated sugar
1/2 cup (1 stick) butter, melted
1 teaspoon finely grated orange zest
1 tablespoon fresh orange juice
1/2 teaspoon vanilla extract
1/4 cup finely chopped walnuts

Preheat the oven to 375°F. • Butter two madeleine pans (for 24 madeleines). • Sift the flour, baking powder, cardamom, baking soda, and salt into a medium bowl. • Beat the eggs and sugar in a large bowl with an electric mixer at high speed until blended. • Mix in the dry ingredients, followed by the butter, orange zest and juice, and vanilla. • Stir in the walnuts. • Spoon the batter into the prepared cups, filling each cup about three-quarters full. • Bake for 10–12 minutes, or until springy to the touch, rotating the pans halfway through for even baking. • Cool the madeleines in the pans for 15 minutes. • Transfer to racks and let cool completely.

Makes 24 cookies · Prep: 25 min. · Cooking: 10–12 min. · Level: 1 · Keeps: 2 days

Orange–walnut madeleines

quick mini coconut cups

2	cups shredded coconut
1¼	cups granulated sugar
3	large eggs, lightly beaten
2	tablespoons finely grated orange zest
2	tablespoons all-purpose flour
½	teaspoon baking powder
⅛	teaspoon salt

Preheat the oven to 425°F. • Line 12 mini muffin cups with mini candy cups. • Stir together the coconut and sugar in a large bowl. • Add the eggs, beating until just blended. • Stir in the orange zest, flour, baking powder, and salt. • Drop heaped teaspoons of the mixture into the paper cups. • Bake for 10–12 minutes, or until golden brown and firm to the touch. • Cool the cookies for 10 minutes in the pan. • These are best still warm from the oven.

Makes 12 cookies · Prep: 20 min. · Cooking: 10–12 min. · Level: 1 · Keeps: 2–3 days

pecan–rum tarts

Pastry

1	cup all-purpose flour
¼	cup finely ground cornmeal
⅛	teaspoon salt
½	cup (1 stick) butter, softened
½	package (4 oz) cream cheese, softened

Pecan–rum filling

½	cup firmly packed dark brown sugar
¼	cup dark corn syrup
1	tablespoon dark rum
1	tablespoon butter, melted
1	large egg, lightly beaten
1	cup finely chopped pecans

Pastry: Sift the flour, cornmeal, and salt into a medium bowl. • Beat the butter and cream cheese in a large bowl with an electric mixer at high speed until creamy. • Mix in the dry ingredients to form a smooth dough. • Press the dough into a disk, wrap in plastic wrap, and refrigerate for 30 minutes. • Preheat the oven to 350°F. • Butter twenty-four mini-muffin cups. • Roll out the dough on a lightly floured surface to a thickness of ⅛ inch. • Use a 2-inch fluted cookie cutter to cut out twenty-four rounds. Press the rounds into the prepared cups. • Pecan–rum filling: Mix the brown sugar, corn syrup, rum, butter, and egg in a large bowl until well blended. Fold in the pecans. • Drop tablespoons of the filling into the cups. • Bake for 20–25 minutes, or until just golden. • Transfer to racks and let cool completely.

Makes 24 cookies · Prep: 30 min. + 30 min. to chill Cooking: 20–25 min. · Level: 2 · Keeps: 7 days

tiny pecan tarts

Pastry

½	package (4 oz) cream cheese, softened
½	cup (1 stick) butter, softened
¾	cup all-purpose flour

Filling

2	large eggs
½	cup firmly packed dark brown sugar
2	tablespoons butter, melted
½	teaspoon vanilla extract
⅛	teaspoon salt
1	cup coarsely chopped pecans

Preheat the oven to 350°F. • Butter twenty-four mini-muffin cups. • Pastry: Beat the cream cheese and butter in a large bowl with an electric mixer at high speed until creamy. • Mix in the flour to form a smooth dough. • Roll out the dough on a lightly floured surface to a thickness of ⅛ inch. • Use a 2-inch fluted cookie cutter to cut out 24 dough rounds. Press the dough rounds into the prepared cups. • Filling: With mixer at high speed, beat the eggs in a large bowl until frothy. • Beat in the brown sugar, butter, vanilla, and salt. • Stir in the pecans. • Spoon the filling into the cups. • Bake for 15–20 minutes, or until a toothpick inserted into one center comes out clean. • Transfer to racks and let cool completely.

Makes 24 cookies · Prep: 40 min. · Cooking: 15–20 min. · Level: 2 · Keeps: 5 days

lemon–cream tartlets

Pastry

1⅔	cups all-purpose flour
¼	cup confectioners' sugar
⅛	teaspoon salt
⅔	cup butter, cut up
1	large egg
1–2	tablespoons water

Lemon–cream filling

½	cup Lemon Curd (see page 340)
¼	cup heavy cream
1½	cups hazelnuts
	Curls of lemon zest, to decorate

Pastry: Sift the flour, confectioners' sugar, and salt into a medium bowl. • Use a pastry blender to cut in the butter until the mixture resembles coarse crumbs. • Add the egg and enough water to form a stiff dough. • Divide the dough in half. Press the dough into disks, wrap each in plastic wrap, and refrigerate for 30 minutes. • Preheat the oven to 325°F. • Spread the hazelnuts on a large baking sheet. Toast for 7 minutes, or until lightly golden. • Transfer to a large cotton kitchen towel. Fold the towel over the nuts and rub them through the towel to remove the thin inner skins. Pick out the nuts and coarsely chop. • Increase the oven temperature to 375°F. • Set out four 12-cup mini-muffin pans. • Roll out the dough on a lightly floured surface to a thickness of ⅛ inch. • Use a 2-inch round cookie cutter to cut out rounds. • Gather the dough scraps, re-roll, and continue cutting out rounds until there are at least 48 rounds. • Press the rounds into the muffin cups and prick all over with a fork. • Bake, one batch at a time, for 8–10 minutes, or until the pastry is pale gold. • Cool completely in the pans. • Lemon–cream filling: Mix the lemon curd and cream in a small bowl. Spoon the filling into the pastry bases. • Decorate with the chopped hazelnuts and lemon zest.

Makes 48 cookies · Prep: 40 min. + 30 min. to chill Cooking: 8–10 min. · Level: 2 · Keeps: 2 days in the refrigerator

lemon tartlets

1¾	cups all-purpose flour
⅛	teaspoon salt
½	cup (1 stick) butter, softened
½	cup granulated sugar
1	large egg yolk
	Grated zest of 1 lemon
½	teaspoon lemon extract
¾	cup Lemon Curd (see page 340)

Sift the flour and salt into a medium bowl. • Beat the butter and sugar in a large bowl with an electric mixer at high speed until creamy. • Add the egg yolk, lemon zest, and lemon extract, beating until just blended. • Mix in the dry ingredients. • Cover with plastic wrap and refrigerate for 30 minutes. • Preheat the oven to 350°F. • Set out three 12-cup mini muffin pans. • Form the dough into balls the size of walnuts and press into the cups. • Prick all over with a fork. • Bake, one pan at a time, for 12–15 minutes, or until just golden. • Transfer to racks to cool. • Fill with a teaspoon of lemon curd.

Makes 36 cookies · Prep: 30 min. + 30 min. to chill Cooking: 12–15 min. per batch · Level: 1 · Keeps: 3 days in the refrigerator

Lemon tartlets (top)
and Pecan–rum tarts (bottom)

maids of honor

These mini-tartlets are thought to date back to the 16th-century court of the English monarch, Henry VIII. Others believe that they originated during the rule of Elizabeth I in the mid 16th century. Rich and filling, there is little reason to wonder why they are only bite-sized. Traditionally served for afternoon tea at historic houses and gardens in the United Kingdom, Maids of Honor are occasionally topped with strawberries or other berry fruits in the summer months.

Pastry
3/4 cup all-purpose flour
1/8 teaspoon salt
2 tablespoons lard or vegetable shortening, cut up
2 tablespoons butter, cut up
2 tablespoons cold water, or more if needed

Filling
1/2 package (4 oz) cream cheese, softened
1/3 cup butter, softened
2 large egg yolks
1/3 cup granulated sugar
1/2 cup finely ground almonds
    Grated zest of 1/2 lemon
1/3 cup confectioners' sugar

orange meringue tartlets

Pastry
12/3 cups all-purpose flour
1/4 cup confectioners' sugar
1/8 teaspoon salt
2/3 cup butter, cut up
1 large egg, lightly beaten
1–2 tablespoons water
1/2 cup Orange Curd (see page 340)

Meringue topping
2 large egg whites
2 teaspoons water
1/8 teaspoon cream of tartar
1/8 teaspoon salt
1/2 cup superfine sugar
1 teaspoon finely grated orange zest
    curls of orange zest, to decorate
1 tablespoon confectioners' sugar, to dust

Pastry: Sift the flour, confectioners' sugar, and salt into a medium bowl. • Use a pastry blender to cut in the butter until the mixture resembles coarse crumbs. • Add the egg and enough water to form a stiff dough. • Divide the dough in half. Press the dough into disks, wrap each in plastic wrap, and refrigerate for 30 minutes. • Preheat the oven to 400°F. • Set out four 12-cup mini-muffin pans. • Roll out the dough on a lightly floured surface to a thickness of 1/8 inch. • Use a 2-inch round cookie cutter to cut out rounds. • Gather the dough scraps, re-roll, and continue cutting out rounds until there are at least 48 rounds. • Press the rounds into the prepared cups and prick all over with a fork. • Bake for 8–10 minutes, or until the pastry is pale gold, rotating the pans halfway through for even baking. • Cool completely in the pans. • Drop 1/2 teaspoon of the orange curd into each pastry base. • Meringue topping: Stir the egg whites, water, cream of tartar, and salt in a

double boiler until blended. Cook over low heat, beating constantly with a hand-held electric mixer at low speed until the mixture registers 160°F on an instant-read thermometer. Transfer to a bowl and beat at high speed with an electric mixer, gradually adding the superfine sugar until stiff peaks form. • Fit a pastry bag with a 1/2-inch star tip. Fill the pastry bag with the meringue and squeeze over the tarts in a decorative manner. • Bake for 6–8 minutes, or until the meringue is lightly browned. • Cool completely in the pans. • Decorate with the orange curls and dust with confectioners' sugar.

Makes 48 cookies · Prep: 40 min. + 30 min. to chill Cooking: 14–18 min. · Level: 3 · Keeps: 3 days in the refrigerator

lemon–vanilla ladyfingers

1/2 cup all-purpose flour
1/3 cup cornstarch
1 teaspoon baking powder
3 large eggs, separated
1/3 cup granulated sugar
1 tablespoon Vanilla Sugar (see page 341)
1 teaspoon finely grated lemon zest
1/2 teaspoon vanilla extract
1/8 teaspoon salt
2 tablespoons confectioners' sugar, to dust

Preheat the oven to 350°F. • Line two cookie sheets with parchment paper. • Sift the flour, cornstarch, and baking powder into a medium bowl. • Beat the egg yolks, 3 tablespoons of the granulated sugar, vanilla sugar, lemon zest, and vanilla in a large bowl with an electric mixer at medium speed until pale and thick. • With mixer at medium speed, beat the egg whites and salt in a large bowl until frothy. • With mixer at high speed, gradually add the remaining

granulated sugar, beating until stiff, glossy peaks form. • Use a large rubber spatula to fold the beaten whites into the batter. • Fold in the dry ingredients. • Fit a pastry bag with a 1/2-inch plain tip. Fill the pastry bag, twist the opening tightly closed, and squeeze out 3 x 3/4-inch strips, spacing them 11/2 inches apart on the prepared cookie sheets. • Dust with the confectioners' sugar. • Bake for 8–10 minutes, or until pale golden, rotating the sheets halfway through for even baking. • Cool on the sheets until the cookies firm slightly. • Transfer to racks to finish cooling.

Makes 25–30 cookies · Prep: 25 min. · Cooking: 8–10 min. · Level: 2 · Keeps: 2 weeks

orange ladyfingers

1/3 cup all-purpose flour
1/8 teaspoon salt
2 large eggs
1/3 cup superfine sugar
    Grated zest of 1 orange

Preheat the oven to 375°F. • Line two cookie sheets with parchment paper. • Sift the flour and salt into a medium bowl. • Beat the eggs, superfine sugar, and orange zest in a large bowl with an electric mixer at high speed until pale and very thick. • Use a large rubber spatula to gradually fold in the dry ingredients. • Fit a pastry bag with a 1/2-inch star tip. Fill the pastry bag, twist the opening tightly closed, and squeeze out 2-inch lines, spacing them 3 inches apart on the prepared cookie sheets. • Bake, one sheet at a time, for 5–10 minutes, or until just golden. • Transfer to racks to cool.

Makes 20 cookies · Prep: 15 min. · Cooking: 5–10 min. per batch · Level: 2 · Keeps: 1–2 days

Preheat the oven to 375°F. • Set out a pan with 12 mini muffin cups. • Pastry: Sift the flour and salt into a large bowl. • Use a pastry blender to cut in the lard and butter until the mixture resembles coarse crumbs. • Add enough water to form a smooth dough. • Roll out the dough on a lightly floured surface to a thickness of 1/8 inch. • Use a 2-inch fluted cookie cutter to cut out twelve rounds. • Press the rounds into the muffin cups. • Filling: Beat the cream cheese and butter in a large bowl with an electric mixer at high speed until creamy. • Add the egg

yolks, beating until just blended. • Mix in the sugar, almonds, and lemon zest. • Spoon the filling into the muffin pans. • Bake for 25–30 minutes, or until a toothpick inserted into one center comes out clean. • Transfer to racks and let cool completely. • Dust with confectioners' sugar.

Makes 12 tartlets · Prep: 40 min. · Cooking: 25–30 min. · Level 2 · Keeps: 5 days

Bake for 35–45 minutes, or until well risen and just golden, rotating the sheets halfway through for even baking. • Invert the molds and turn out onto racks. Let cool completely. • Butter the molds again and continue to bake until all the batter is used. • Dust with the confectioners' sugar just before serving.

Makes 25–30 cookies · Prep: 30 min. + 30 min. to cool + 12 hr. to chill · Cooking: 35–45 min. per batch · Level: 2 · Keeps: 5 days

mini mincemeat tartlets

Pastry

1 1/3	cups all-purpose flour
1/8	teaspoon salt
1/3	cup butter, cut up
1/4	cup finely ground almonds
1/4	cup granulated sugar
1/4	cup milk
1/4	teaspoon almond extract

Mincemeat topping

2	tablespoons butter
2/3	cup light corn syrup
2	tablespoons light molasses
1/3	cup golden raisins
1/4	cup cake crumbs
2	tablespoons finely chopped candied peel
1	tablespoon dried currants
1/2	teaspoon ground allspice
1	large egg, lightly beaten
5	tablespoons confectioners' sugar
2	tablespoons fresh lemon juice, + more as needed

Pastry: Sift the flour and salt into a large bowl. • Use a pastry blender to cut in the butter until the mixture resembles coarse crumbs. • Stir in the almonds and sugar. • Mix in the milk and almond extract to form a soft, but not sticky, dough. • Form the dough into two 9-inch logs, wrap in plastic wrap, and refrigerate for 30 minutes. • Mincemeat topping: Melt the butter with the corn syrup and molasses in a small saucepan over low heat. • Mix in the raisins, cake crumbs, candied peel, currants, and allspice. • Remove from the heat and add the egg, beating until just blended. • Preheat the oven to 375°F. • Butter and flour three 12-cup mini muffin pans. • Slice the dough 1/2 inch thick and press into the prepared cups. • Spoon the topping evenly into the cups. • Bake, one pan at a time,

for 12–15 minutes, or until the pastry is golden around the edges and the topping is bubbling. • Cool in the pans for 5 minutes. • Transfer to racks to finish cooling. • Mix the confectioners' sugar with enough lemon juice in a small bowl to make a pouring consistency. • Drizzle over the tops of the cookies.

Makes 36 cookies · Prep: 30 min. + 30 min. to chill Cooking: 12–15 min. per batch · Level: 2 · Keeps: 4–5 days

french cannelés

These attractive dainty tea cakes come from Bordeaux in western France. You will need cannelé molds, which are available from specialty baking stores.

1	cup milk
1	vanilla pod
1	large egg + 1 large egg yolk
1 1/2	cups confectioners' sugar + 1/3 cup, to dust
2	teaspoons dark rum
2	tablespoons butter, melted
1/2	cup all-purpose flour
1/8	teaspoon salt

Heat the milk with the vanilla pod in a small saucepan until it almost comes to a boil. • Remove the vanilla pod. Set aside for 30 minutes, or until cooled. • Beat the egg and egg yolk in a large bowl with an electric mixer at high speed until pale and thick. • Mix in the 1 1/2 cups confectioners' sugar, rum, butter, flour, and salt. • Stir in the cooled milk until well blended. • Cover with plastic wrap and refrigerate for 12 hours. • Preheat the oven to 400°F. • Butter eighteen 1-inch cannelé molds and place on two cookie sheets or butter and flour two 12-cup muffin pans. • Whisk the batter briefly. • Fill each mold three-quarters full. •

white chocolate tartlets

1 3/4	cups all-purpose flour
1/8	teaspoon salt
1/2	cup (1 stick) butter, softened
1/2	cup granulated sugar
1	large egg yolk
3	oz white chocolate, coarsely chopped

Sift the flour and salt into a medium bowl. • Beat the butter and sugar in a large bowl with an electric mixer at high speed until creamy. • Add the egg yolk, beating until just blended. • Mix in the dry ingredients. • Cover with plastic wrap and refrigerate for 30 minutes. • Preheat the oven to 350°F. • Set out three 12-cup mini muffin pans. • Form the dough into balls the size of walnuts and press into the cups. • Prick all over with a fork. • Bake, one pan at a time, for 12–15 minutes, or until just golden. • Transfer to racks to cool. • Melt the white chocolate in a double boiler over barely simmering water. Fill each tartlet with the melted chocolate and serve.

Makes 36 cookies · Prep: 30 min. + 30 min. to chill Cooking: 12–15 min. per batch · Level: 1 · Keeps: 3 days in the refrigerator

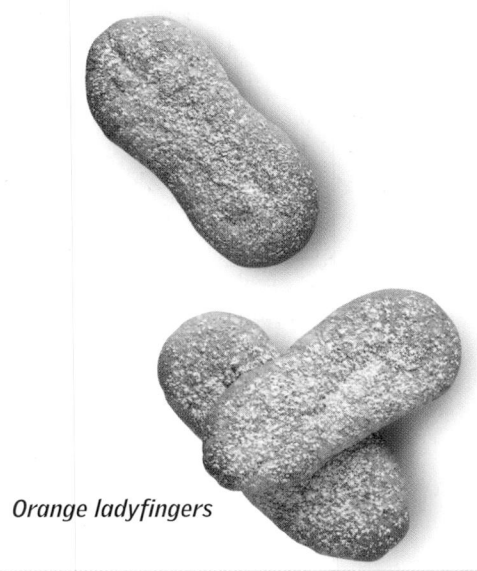

Orange ladyfingers

palmiers

For quickness, we recommend that you use thawed frozen puff pastry. Homemade puff pastry is difficult to make but easy to master if you attempt it a few times. It requires the layering of chilled butter and pastry sheets and continuous rolling until the butter is worked into the pastry and many layers have been created. These light-as-air cookies can burn easily, so be sure to watch them carefully during baking.

1 sheet frozen puff pastry (about 8 oz), thawed
1/4 cup superfine sugar

Preheat the oven to 400°F. • Butter two cookie sheets. • Sprinkle some sugar on a surface. • Unfold or unroll the pastry to make a 10-inch square. • Sprinkle with 1 tablespoon superfine sugar. • Fold in two opposite sides of the pastry to meet in the center. Sprinkle with 1 tablespoon sugar and fold in the same sides again. • Fold one half of the pastry over the other half. • Slice the pastry crosswise into 1/2-inch thick slices. Dip the cut sides into sugar and place the cookies cut-sides down 2 inches apart on the prepared cookie sheets. • Sprinkle with the remaining sugar. • Bake, one sheet at a time, for about 12 minutes, or until just golden on the bottom. • Remove from the oven and turn the pastries over. • Bake for 5–7 minutes more, or until golden. • Transfer to racks and let cool completely.

Makes 16 cookies · Prep: 30 min. · Cooking: 17–19 min. per batch · Level: 2 · Keeps: 5 days

---

mini redcurrant pies

Look for Bird's Custard Powder near the tapioca in your local supermarket.

Pastry
1 2/3 cups all-purpose flour
1/4 cup confectioners' sugar
1/8 teaspoon salt
2/3 cup butter, cut up
1 large egg
1–2 tablespoons water

Redcurrant filling
2 cups redcurrants
1 1/2 cups granulated sugar
1 1/3 cups water
2/3 cup custard powder
2–4 tablespoons water

Pastry: Sift the flour, confectioners' sugar, and salt into a medium bowl. • Use a pastry blender to cut in the butter until the mixture resembles coarse crumbs. • Add the egg and enough water to form a stiff dough. • Divide the dough in half. Press the dough into disks, wrap each in plastic wrap, and refrigerate for 30 minutes. • Preheat the oven to 375°F. • Set out four 12-cup mini-muffin pans. • Roll out the dough on a lightly floured surface to a thickness of 1/8 inch. • Use a 2-inch round cookie cutter to cut out rounds. Gather the dough scraps, re-roll, and continue cutting out until there are at least 48 rounds. • Press the rounds into the prepared cups and prick all over with a fork. • Bake, one pan at a time, for 8–10 minutes, or until the pastry is pale gold. • Cool completely in the pans. • Redcurrant filling: Bring the redcurrants, sugar, and water to a boil in a medium saucepan over medium heat. • Simmer for 5–7 minutes, or until tender. • Transfer to a food processor or blender and process until pureed. • Mix the custard powder with enough water to form a smooth paste and stir into the puree. • Return the mixture to the saucepan and bring to a boil over medium heat, stirring constantly. • Spoon the filling into the pastry bases and refrigerate for 1 hour.

Makes 48 cookies · Prep: 45 min. + 90 min. to chill Cooking: 8–10 min. per batch · Level: 2 · Keeps: 2 days in the refrigerator

---

dainty tea cakes

These bite-sized cakes, made with a basic sponge cake mixture, are easily made and great fun to decorate for artistic bakers! To give them a professional finish, we recommend you frost them with white ready-to-use icing, and follow the instructions on the package.

1/3 cup butter, softened
1/2 cup granulated sugar
1/2 teaspoon vanilla extract
2 large eggs, lightly beaten
2/3 cup all-purpose flour
1/8 teaspoon salt
1 tablespoon milk, or more as needed
1/3 package (8 oz) white ready-to-use icing
1/3 cup apricot preserves
Sugar flowers, fruit decorations, candied cherries, or sugar confetti, to decorate

Preheat the oven to 375°F. • Line 15 mini muffin cups with mini candy cups. • Beat the butter and sugar in a large bowl with an electric mixer at high speed until creamy. • Add the vanilla and eggs, beating until just blended. • Mix in the flour, salt, and add enough milk to form a soft, sticky dough. • Drop teaspoons of the mixture into the cups. • Bake for 10–15 minutes, or until lightly golden and a toothpick inserted into the centers comes out clean. • Transfer to racks to cool. • Lightly dust a surface with confectioners' sugar. Roll out the icing to a thickness of 1/4 inch. • Use a mini cookie cutter to cut out rounds of icing. • Warm the preserves in a small saucepan over low heat until liquid. • Brush the cakes with the preserves and place the icing rounds on top. Finish with the decorations of your choice.

Makes 15–20 cakes · Prep: 20 min. · Cooking: 10–15 min. · Level: 2 · Keeps: 3 days

---

cardamom–sugar palmiers

1/3 cup superfine sugar
1/2 teaspoon ground cardamom
1 sheet frozen puff pastry (about 8 oz), thawed

Preheat the oven to 350°F. • Butter a cookie sheet. • Stir together the superfine sugar and cardamom in a small bowl. Lightly sprinkle a surface with 1 tablespoon of the sugar mixture. • Unfold or unroll the pastry to an 10-inch square. • Sprinkle with 1 tablespoon of the sugar mixture. • Fold the long sides of the pastry over to meet in the center. Sprinkle with 1 tablespoon sugar mixture and fold in half lengthways. • Slice the pastry into 12 portions. • Place the cookies cut-side down 2 inches apart on the prepared cookie sheets. • Sprinkle with the remaining sugar mixture. •Bake for 10–12 minutes, or until just golden. • Transfer to racks to cool.

Makes 12 cookies · Prep: 30 min. · Cooking: 20–27 min. · Level: 2 · Keeps: 5 days

Palmiers

coffee–raisin cookie cakes

2/3   cup all-purpose flour
1   teaspoon baking powder
1/4   cup golden raisins
1/2   cup (1 stick) butter, softened
1/2   cup granulated sugar
1   tablespoon coffee extract
2   large eggs, at room temperature
1/2   cup confectioners' sugar
2–3   tablespoons boiling water

Preheat the oven to 400°F. • Set out about twenty-four mini-cupcake paper cups on a baking sheet. • Stir together the flour and baking powder in a medium bowl. Stir in the raisins. • Beat the butter, sugar, and 2 teaspoons of the coffee extract in a large bowl with an electric mixer at medium speed until creamy. • Add the eggs, one at a time, until just blended after each addition. • With mixer at low speed, gradually add the dry ingredients. • Drop heaping teaspoons of the mixture into the baking cups. • Bake for 12–15 minutes, or until a toothpick inserted into the centers comes out clean. • Cool the cookies completely on a rack. • Sift the confectioners' sugar into a medium bowl and add the remaining 1 teaspoon coffee extract and enough water to make a soft frosting. Frost the top of each cookie.

Makes 24 cookies · Prep: 10 min. · Cooking: 12–15 min. · Level: 1 · Keeps: 4–5 days

Meringue-topped mince pies

petits-fours

A petit-four is a tiny fancy cake, cookie, or sweet, typically made with marzipan and beautifully frosted. The name, which means "little oven" in French, probably comes from the small ovens that were used for baking such confections in the 18th century. It is best to make petits fours one or two days in advance.

2/3   cup all-purpose flour
1/8   teaspoon salt
4   large eggs
1/2   cup superfine sugar
1/4   cup (1/2 stick) butter, melted
1/3   cup apricot preserves, warmed
8   oz marzipan, softened

Frosting
2 1/3   cups confectioners' sugar
1–2   tablespoons hot water
1–2   teaspoons white rum or fruit liqueur
3   drops red food coloring
     Pistachios, marzipan roses, crystallized violets, or sugared rose petals, to decorate

Preheat the oven to 375°F. • Butter a 13 x 9-inch baking pan and line with parchment paper. • Sift the flour and salt into a small bowl. • Beat the eggs and superfine sugar in a double boiler over barely simmering water with an electric mixer at high speed until the mixture falls from the blades in ribbons. • Use a large rubber spatula to gradually fold in the flour and butter. • Pour the mixture into the prepared pan, spreading it out evenly. • Bake for 15–20 minutes, or until golden brown and a toothpick inserted into the center comes out clean. • Cool the cake in the pan for 15 minutes. • Sprinkle some superfine sugar onto a large sheet of waxed paper. Turn the cake out onto the paper. • Use a sharp knife to cut the cake horizontally into three equal pieces. • Brush the tops with apricot preserves. Place the three pieces on top of each other with a preserves layer on top. • Lightly dust a surface with confectioners' sugar. Roll out the marzipan to a thickness of 1/4 inch. Cut the marzipan to fit the top layer and place it on the sandwiched cake. • Cover with waxed paper and position a heavy cutting board on top. • Set aside for 5 hours, or until the cake is evenly pressed into shape. • Cut into 1-inch squares and triangles. • Frosting: Mix 1/4 cup confectioners' sugar and 1 tablespoon hot water in a small bowl. • Add the rum and stir in enough additional confectioners' sugar to make a smooth paste. • Spoon some of the frosting into a separate bowl and add the food coloring, keeping the colors pale. • Place the petits fours on waxed paper and spoon plain and colored frosting over them, letting it run down the sides. Set aside until the frosting has dried. • Use the remaining confectioners' sugar and water to make more frosting with a piping consistency. • Spoon into a small freezer bag and cut off a tiny corner. Pipe whirls and lines over the petits fours. • Decorate with pistachios, marzipan roses, violets, and rose petals.

Makes 20 cookies · Prep: 1 hr. + 5 hr. to press the cake · Cooking: 15–20 min. · Level: 3 · Keeps: 6 days in the refrigerator

meringue-topped mince pies

3/4   cup all-purpose flour
1/8   teaspoon salt
1/4   cup (1/2 stick) butter, cut up
1   tablespoon water, or more as needed
1/4   cup Mincemeat (see page 340)

Meringue topping
1   large egg white
1/4   cup superfine sugar
2   teaspoons water
1/8   teaspoon cream of tartar

Sift the flour and salt into a large bowl. • Use a pastry blender to cut in the butter until the mixture resembles fine crumbs. Gradually add 1 tablespoon water to form a smooth dough, adding more water if needed. • Press the dough into a disk, wrap in plastic wrap, and refrigerate for 30 minutes. • Preheat the oven to 400°F. • Set out a mini muffin pan (12 cups). • Roll out the pastry on a lightly floured surface to a thickness of 1/8 inch. Use a 2-inch cookie cutter to cut out rounds and use them to line the pans. Prick all over with a fork. • Bake for 12–15 minutes, or until just golden. • Lower the oven to 350°F. • Drop teaspoons of mincemeat into the bases. • Meringue topping: Stir the egg whites, superfine sugar, water, and cream of tartar in a double boiler until blended. Cook over low heat, beating constantly with a hand-held electric mixer at low speed until the whites register 160°F on an instant-read thermometer. Transfer to a bowl and beat at high speed until the whites form stiff, glossy peaks. • Fit a pastry bag with a 1/2-inch star tip. Fill the pastry bag, twist the opening tightly closed, and squeeze out generous stars on top of the mince pies. • Bake for 5 minutes, or until dry and crisp to the touch. • Transfer to racks to cool.

Makes 12 cookies · Prep: 50 min. · Cooking: 17–20 min. · Level: 2 · Keeps: 7 days

mini jelly tarts

- 1/2   package (4 oz) cream cheese, softened
- 1/2   cup (1 stick) butter, softened
- 3/4   cup all-purpose flour
- 1/2   cup raspberry preserves
- 1/3   cup confectioners' sugar, to dust

Preheat the oven to 350°F. • Butter twenty-four mini-muffin cups. • Beat the cream cheese and butter in a large bowl with an electric mixer at high speed until creamy. • Mix in the flour to form a smooth dough. • Roll out the dough on a lightly floured surface to a thickness of $^1/_8$ inch. • Use a 2-inch fluted cookie cutter to cut out twenty-four dough rounds. • Line the muffin cups with the dough. • Drop teaspoons of the raspberry preserves into the cups. • Bake for 15–20 minutes, or until the preserves are bubbling. • Transfer to racks and let cool completely. • Dust with the confectioners' sugar.

Makes 24 cookies · Prep: 30 min. · Cooking: 15–20 min. · Level: 1 · Keeps: 5 days

almond–raspberry tarts

Pastry
- 3/4   cup all-purpose flour
- 1/8   teaspoon salt
- 2   tablespoons lard or vegetable shortening
- 2   tablespoons butter, cut up
- 2   tablespoons cold water, or more as needed

Filling
- 2   tablespoons butter, softened
- 2   tablespoons granulated sugar
- 1/2   large egg, lightly beaten
- 1/4   cup finely ground almonds
- 1   tablespoon all-purpose flour
- 1/4   teaspoon baking powder
- 1/2   teaspoon almond extract
- 1/2   teaspoon vanilla extract
- 2   tablespoons raspberry preserves

Preheat the oven to 350°F. • Set out a 12-cup muffin pan. • Pastry: Sift the flour and salt into a medium bowl. • Use a pastry blender to cut in the lard and butter until the mixture resembles coarse crumbs. Add enough water to form a soft, but not sticky dough. • Turn the dough out onto a lightly floured surface and knead until smooth. • Roll out the dough to a thickness of $^1/_4$ inch. • Use a 3-inch pastry cutter to cut out circles. • Firmly press the dough circles into the muffin cups to form smooth, even crusts. • Filling: Beat the butter and sugar in a large bowl with an electric mixer at high speed until creamy. • Add the egg,

beating until just blended. • Mix in the almonds, flour, baking powder, and almond and vanilla extracts until well blended. • Spoon a little preserves onto each dough base and 1 tablespoon of the filling. • Bake for 25–30 minutes, or until lightly browned and a toothpick inserted into the center comes out clean. • Cool the tarts completely in the pan.

Makes 12 tarts · Prep: 50 min. · Cooking: 25–30 min. · Level: 2 · Keeps: 3 days in the refrigerator

leipzig tarts

This is a traditional recipe from the German city of Leipzig.

- 1 1/3   cups all-purpose flour
- 1/8   teaspoon salt
- 1/3   cup butter, cut up
- 1/3   cup finely ground hazelnuts
- 1/3   cup granulated sugar
- 1   tablespoon Vanilla Sugar (see page 341)
- 2–3   tablespoons water

Almond–rum filling
- 3   tablespoons butter, softened
- 1/4   cup firmly packed light brown sugar
- 1   large egg + 1 egg yolk
- 1/4   teaspoon almond extract
- 1/3   cup all-purpose flour
- 2/3   cup finely ground almonds
- 3   tablespoons milk
- 1   tablespoon rum
- 1/4   cup apricot preserves or jam

Sift the flour and salt into a medium bowl. • Use a pastry blender to cut in the butter until the mixture resembles coarse crumbs. • Mix in the hazelnuts and granulated and vanilla sugars. • Mix in enough water to form a soft, but not sticky, dough. • Press the dough into a disk, wrap in plastic wrap, and refrigerate for 30 minutes. • Preheat the oven to 375°F. • Set out two 12-cup mini-muffin pans. • Almond–rum filling: Beat the butter and brown sugar in a large bowl with an electric mixer at high speed until creamy. • Add the whole egg and almond extract, beating until just blended. • Mix in the flour, almonds, 2 tablespoons milk, and rum. • Roll out the dough on a lightly floured surface to a thickness of $^1/_8$ inch. • Use a 2$^1/_2$-inch fluted cookie cutter to cut out twenty-four rounds. Press the dough circles into the prepared cups. • Gather the dough scraps and re-roll. Use a 1-inch star-shaped cookie cutter to cut out twenty-four small stars. • Drop $^1/_2$ teaspoon of the apricot preserves into each pastry

base and spoon in the filling. • Place the pastry stars lightly on top of the filling. • Beat the remaining egg yolk with the remaining 1 tablespoon milk and brush over the stars. • Bake for 15–20 minutes, or until the pastry is pale golden and the filling has set, rotating the pans halfway through for even baking. • Cool completely before removing from the pans.

Makes 24 cookies · Prep: 1 hr. + 30 min. to chill · Cooking: 15–20 min. · Level: 2 · Keeps: 5 days

mini marshmallow tarts

- 3/4   cup all-purpose flour
- 1/8   teaspoon salt
- 1/4   cup (1/2 stick) butter, cut up
- 1   tablespoon water, + more as needed
- 1/4   cup raspberry or strawberry preserves
- 12   pink or white marshmallows, to decorate
- 12   almond halves, to decorate

Sift the flour and salt into a large bowl. • Use a pastry blender to cut in the butter until the mixture resembles fine crumbs. Gradually add 1 tablespoon water to form a smooth dough, adding more water if needed. • Press the dough into a disk, wrap in plastic wrap, and refrigerate for 30 minutes. • Preheat the oven to 400°F. • Set out a mini muffin pan (12 cups). • Roll out the pastry on a lightly floured surface to a thickness of $^1/_8$ inch. Use a 2-inch cookie cutter to cut out rounds and use them to line the pans. Prick all over with a fork. • Drop teaspoons of preserves into the bases. • Bake for 12–15 minutes, or until just golden. • Arrange the marshmallows on top of the preserves and bake for 2 minutes more, or until the marshmallows have melted. Top each tart with an almond half. • Transfer to racks to cool.

Makes 12 cookies · Prep: 40 min. + 30 min. to chill Cooking: 14–17 min. · Level: 2 · Keeps: 2 days

Mini marshmallow tarts

festive cookies

above: Christmas carollers
(page 297)
right: Christmas gift
cookies (page 298)

Stained glass cookies to hang on your tree at Christmas. Home-baked heart cookies for St. Valentine's Day. Cookie towers for bake sales. In this chapter, we have collected recipes to celebrate a wide range of religious festivals, as well as some favorites for special events such as birthdays, weddings, and even Mothers' Day. Serving fun and festive cookies such as these gives you the chance to personalize every party.

christmas stars

These Zimtsterne—cinnamon stars—are among the many cookies that form an important part of German Christmas celebrations. They were first introduced to the United States by immigrants in the 19th century.

3	large egg whites, at room temperature
1²/3	cups confectioners' sugar
1¹/2	cups finely ground almonds
2	tablespoons all-purpose flour
2	teaspoons ground cinnamon
1/4	teaspoon almond extract
1/8	teaspoon salt

Preheat the oven to 300°F. • Line three cookie sheets with parchment paper. • Beat the egg whites in a large bowl with an electric mixer at medium speed until frothy. • With mixer at high speed, gradually add in the confectioners' sugar, beating until stiff, glossy peaks form. Set aside two heaped tablespoons of the meringue in a small bowl. • Use a metal spoon to fold $3/4$ cup almonds, the flour, cinnamon, almond extract, and salt into the remaining meringue mixture to form a slightly sticky dough, adding more almonds if needed. • Sprinkle the remaining almonds in a thick layer onto a clean surface. • Roll out the dough over the almonds to a thickness of $1/4$ inch. Use a 2-inch star-shaped cookie cutter to cut out the cookies. Gather the dough scraps, re-roll, and continue cutting out the cookies until all the dough is used. Use a spatula to transfer the cookies to the prepared cookie sheets, placing them 1 inch apart. • Use a pastry brush to coat each cookie top with the reserved meringue. • Bake, one sheet at a time, for 30–40 minutes, or until just golden. • Cool on the sheets until the cookies firm slightly. Transfer to racks and let cool completely.

Makes 35–40 cookies · Prep: 50 min. · Cooking: 30–40 min. per batch · Level: 2 · Keeps: 5 days

christmas cranberry bars

1	cup all-purpose flour
1/2	teaspoon ground cinnamon
1/8	teaspoon salt
1/4	cup (¹/2 stick) butter, melted
3/4	cup granulated sugar
1	large egg, lightly beaten
2/3	cup finely chopped pecans
1/2	cup fresh or frozen cranberries
1/4	cup confectioners' sugar, to dust

Preheat the oven to 350°F. • Butter a 9-inch baking pan. • Sift the flour, cinnamon, and salt into a medium bowl. • Mix the butter and sugar in a medium bowl. • Add the egg, beating until just blended. • Mix in the dry ingredients, pecans, and cranberries until well blended. • Spread the mixture in the prepared pan. • Bake for 30–35 minutes, or until just golden and a toothpick inserted into the center comes out clean. • Cool completely in the pan. • Dust with the confectioners' sugar and cut into squares.

Makes 16–25 bars · Prep: 20 min. · Cooking: 30–35 min. · Level: 1 · Keeps: 3 days

chocolate turtles

1/2	cup all-purpose flour
1	tablespoon freeze-dried coffee granules
1/2	teaspoon baking powder
1/8	teaspoon salt
14	oz semisweet chocolate, coarsely chopped
1/4	cup (¹/2 stick) butter, cut up
1¹/2	cups granulated sugar
1	teaspoon vanilla extract
4	large eggs
2	cups finely chopped pecans + 2 cups pecan halves
1	cup (6 oz) semisweet chocolate chips

Preheat the oven to 350°F. • Line two cookie sheets with parchment paper. • Sift the flour, coffee granules, baking powder, and salt into a large bowl. • Melt the chocolate and butter in a double boiler over barely simmering water. • Stir in the sugar until completely dissolved. • Remove from the heat and mix in the vanilla and eggs. • Mix in the dry ingredients, finely chopped pecans, and chocolate chips. • Drop tablespoons of the dough 3 inches apart onto the prepared cookie sheets. • Press four pecan halves into each corner of the cookies to resemble the legs of a turtle and an additional one to resemble a head. • Bake for 8–10 minutes, or until just set, rotating the sheets halfway through for even baking. • Do not overbake. • Transfer to racks and let cool completely.

Makes 24 cookies · Prep: 20 min. · Cooking: 8–10 min. · Level: 1 · Keeps: 5 days

chocologs

Fabulous for a children's Christmas party garnished with a sugar craft robin or a sprig of holly.

3/4	cup all-purpose flour
1/3	cup unsweetened cocoa powder
1/8	teaspoon salt
1/3	cup butter, cut up
1/4	cup granulated sugar
1/2	teaspoon vanilla extract
2	tablespoons milk

Chocolate butter frosting
1	tablespoon unsweetened cocoa powder
2	teaspoons cold water
1/4	cup (¹/2 stick) butter, softened
1/2	cup confectioners' sugar

Sift the flour, cocoa, and salt into a large bowl. • Use a pastry blender to cut in the butter until the mixture resembles fine crumbs. • Stir in the sugar and vanilla. • Add the milk to form a stiff dough. • Form the dough into a log 1 inch in diameter, wrap in plastic wrap, and refrigerate for 30 minutes. • Preheat the oven to 400°F. • Butter a cookie sheet. • Slice the dough into 2-inch lengths and place 1 inch apart on the prepared cookie sheet. • Bake for 20–25 minutes, or until lightly browned and firm to the touch. • Transfer to racks to cool. • Chocolate butter frosting: Mix the cocoa with the water until smooth. • Beat the butter in a medium bowl until creamy. • Beat in $1/4$ cup confectioners' sugar and the cocoa mixture until smooth. • Use a thin metal spatula to spread the tops of the cookies with the frosting. • Draw the tines of a fork across the frosting to resemble the bark of a log. • Dust with the remaining $1/4$ cup confectioners' sugar.

Makes 14–16 cookies · Prep: 30 min. + 30 min. to chill · Cooking: 20–25 min. · Level: 1 · Keeps: 3 days

mexican chocolate pastelitos

These tasty little gems are traditionally served at Mexican weddings.

1¹/2	cups all-purpose flour
2/3	cup cornstarch
1/4	cup unsweetened cocoa powder
1/8	teaspoon salt
1	cup (2 sticks) butter, softened
1/4	cup granulated sugar
2/3	cup confectioners' sugar, to dust

Preheat the oven to 325°F. • Line three cookie sheets with parchment paper. • Sift the flour, cornstarch, cocoa, and salt into a medium bowl. • Beat the butter and granulated sugar in a large bowl with an electric mixer at high speed until creamy. • Mix in the dry ingredients to make a smooth dough. • Form heaping teaspoons of the dough into balls the size of walnuts and place 2 inches apart on the prepared cookie sheets. • Bake, one sheet at a time, for 35–40 minutes, or until pale gold. • Cool on the sheets until the cookies firm slightly. Transfer to racks to finish cooling. • Put the confectioners' sugar in a small bowl and dip in the cookies until well coated.

Makes 40–45 cookies · Prep: 20 min. · Cooking: 35–40 min. per batch · Level: 1 · Keeps: 7 days

pistachio chocolates

This is a traditional specialty from Legnica in Poland, where homemade chocolate cookies are a popular Christmas present.

Dough
- 2$^{1}/_{3}$ cups all-purpose flour
- 1 tablespoon Homemade Gingerbread Spice (see page 341)
- 2 teaspoons baking soda
- $^{1}/_{8}$ teaspoon salt
- 1 cup honey
- $^{2}/_{3}$ cup granulated sugar
- 2 cups finely ground almonds
- $^{3}/_{4}$ cup finely chopped mixed candied peel

Marzipan filling
- 7 oz marzipan, softened
- $^{3}/_{4}$ cup red currant jelly
- 1 cup coarsely chopped almonds
- $^{1}/_{2}$ cup finely chopped candied lemon peel
- $^{1}/_{2}$ cup dried currants, soaked overnight and drained

Chocolate glaze
- 5 tablespoons water
- $^{1}/_{4}$ cup dark corn syrup
- 1 cup superfine sugar
- 12 oz semisweet chocolate, coarsely chopped
- 3–4 tablespoons coarsely chopped pistachios
- 2 tablespoons finely chopped candied fruit

Dough: Sift the flour, gingerbread spice, baking soda, and salt into a medium bowl. • Heat the honey and sugar in a small saucepan over low heat until the sugar has dissolved completely. • Let cool for 5 minutes. • Use a wooden spoon to work in the dry ingredients, almonds, and candied peel to form a smooth dough. • Cover with a clean kitchen towel and let rest for 2 days. • Preheat the oven to 375°F. • Line four cookie sheets with parchment paper. •
Marzipan filling: Knead the marzipan and preserves in a medium bowl until smooth. Work in the almonds and candied lemon peel. Form the dough into two 6-inch logs. • Roll out each log on a lightly floured surface to a thickness of $^{1}/_{4}$ inch. • Cut into two 12 x 6-inch rectangles. • Spread the dough strips with the marzipan mixture and sprinkle with currants. • Roll the dough strips up

tightly to form logs 2 inches in diameter. Slice the dough $^{1}/_{2}$-inch thick. Use a spatula to transfer the slices to the prepared cookie sheets, placing them 1 inch apart, cut-side up. • Bake, one sheet at a time, for 15–20 minutes, or until just golden. • Cool on the sheets until the cookies firm slightly. • Transfer to racks and let cool completely. •
Chocolate glaze: Bring the water, corn syrup, and superfine sugar to a boil in a small saucepan. • Remove from the heat and stir in the chocolate. • Drizzle the glaze over the cookies, letting it run down the sides. • Decorate with pistachios and candied fruit.

Makes 30–35 cookies · Prep: 60 min. + 2 days to rest · Cooking: 15–20 min. per batch · Level: 2 · Keeps: 25 days stacked between layers of parchment paper

christmas carollers

- 2$^{1}/_{2}$ cups all-purpose flour
- $^{1}/_{2}$ teaspoon baking powder
- $^{1}/_{8}$ teaspoon salt
- $^{3}/_{4}$ cup (1$^{1}/_{2}$ sticks) butter, softened
- 1 cup granulated sugar
- 1 large egg, lightly beaten
- $^{1}/_{2}$ teaspoon vanilla extract
  Few drops red food coloring
- 2 tablespoons confectioners' sugar
- 2 teaspoons water, + more as needed
  Colored candies, to decorate

Sift the flour, baking powder, and salt into a medium bowl. • Beat the butter and granulated sugar in a large bowl with an electric mixer at high speed until creamy. • Add the egg and vanilla, beating until just blended. • Mix in the dry ingredients. • Divide the dough in half. Form into two 6-inch logs, wrap each in plastic wrap, and refrigerate for 30 minutes. • Preheat the oven to 375°F. • Butter three cookie sheets. • Slice the dough $^{1}/_{4}$ inch thick and place 1 inch apart on the prepared cookie sheets. Reserve three dough slices to form decorations. • Work the red food coloring into the reserved dough until there are no white streaks. • Roll out the red dough on a lightly floured surface and cut off small hat shapes. Gather the dough scraps and force through a garlic press to form hair. • Arrange the hats and hair on top of the cookies. • Bake, one sheet at a time, for 6–8 minutes, or until just golden at the edges. • Transfer to racks to cool. • Mix the confectioners' sugar and water in a small bowl to form a stiff paste. • Stick the candy on top of the cookies with the icing to form eyes, mouths, and noses.

Makes 45 cookies · Prep: 40 min. · Cooking: 6–8 min. per batch · Level: 2 · Keeps: 7 days

Pistachio chocolates

christmas gift cookies

This recipe allows you to create four types of cookies from the same basic dough, reducing the time required for baking during the hectic festive season. Arrange in brightly colored gift boxes to give to your friends and family.

1²/₃	cups all-purpose flour
1/4	teaspoon salt
3/4	cup (1¹/₂ sticks) butter
3/4	cup granulated sugar
1/3	cup semolina flour
2	tablespoons currants
1/2	teaspoon almond extract
1	teaspoon ground cinnamon
	Grated zest of 1/2 lemon
1	large egg yolk mixed with 2–3 tablespoons water
1/3	cup confectioners' sugar
1	tablespoon water, or more as needed
1/4	teaspoon green food coloring
	Candied cherries, cut in half
1/2	cup Chocolate Butter Frosting (see page 346)
	Silver balls, to decorate
1/2	cup raspberry preserves

Preheat the oven to 425°F. • Butter four cookie sheets. • Sift the flour and salt into a large bowl. • Use a pastry blender to cut in the butter until the mixture resembles fine crumbs. • Stir in the sugar and semolina flour. • Divide the mixture into four separate bowls. • Mix the currants into one bowl of the mixture, the almond extract into the second bowl, the cinnamon into the third, and the lemon zest into the remaining bowl. • Add enough of the egg yolk mixture to the bowls to form each into a stiff dough. • Christmas wreaths: Roll out the currant mixture on a lightly floured surface to a thickness of 1/4 inch. • Use a fluted cookie cutter to cut out ring-shaped cookies. • Star cookies: Roll out the almond extract mixture to the same thickness. • Use a star-shaped cookie cutter to cut out the cookies. • Bell cookies: Roll out the cinnamon mixture to the same thickness. • Use a bell-shaped cookie cutter to cut out cookies. • Christmas tree cookies: Roll out the lemon zest mixture to the same thickness. • Use a tree cookie cutter to cut out the cookies. • Gather the dough scraps separately, re-roll, and continue cutting out cookies until all the dough is used. • Use a spatula to transfer all the cookies to the prepared cookie sheets, placing 1 inch apart. • Bake, one sheet at a time, for 10–15 minutes, or until lightly browned. •

Cool on the sheets until the cookies firm slightly. • Transfer to racks to finish cooling. • Mix the confectioners' sugar with enough water to make a spreadable consistency. Stir in the green food coloring. Spread the tops of the star cookies with the frosting and decorate with a half cherry. • Stick the bell cookies together in pairs with the chocolate frosting and decorate the edges with silver balls. • Warm the raspberry preserves in a small saucepan over low heat until liquid. • Stick the Christmas tree cookies together in pairs with the preserves.

Makes 40 cookies · Prep: 1 hr. · Cooking: 10–15 min. per batch · Level: 2 · Keeps: 7 days

spekulatius

These crisp, spicy cookies are a Dutch specialty baked at Christmas, but they are tasty treats at any time of the year. The traditional recipe calls for the dough to be pressed into special wooden molds in order to create the traditional spekulatius pattern of the cut-out figures, but you can, of course, use cookie cutters and a toothpick to create the same effect.

3	cups all-purpose flour
1	teaspoon ground cinnamon
1/2	teaspoon ground nutmeg
1/4	teaspoon ground cardamom
1/8	teaspoon salt
1¹/₄	cups granulated sugar
1	cup finely ground almonds
1/2	cup coarsely chopped almonds
1/3	cup butter, cut up
1	large egg, lightly beaten
1/4	cup milk
1/2	teaspoon almond extract
	Flaked almonds, to sprinkle

Sift the flour, cinnamon, nutmeg, cardamom, and salt into a large bowl. • Stir in the sugar and finely ground and chopped almonds. • Use a pastry blender to cut in the butter until the mixture resembles coarse crumbs. • Beat the egg, milk, and almond extract in a small bowl until frothy. • Mix the beaten egg mixture into the dry ingredients to form a smooth dough. • Cover with a clean kitchen towel and refrigerate for 30 minutes. • Preheat the oven to 350°F. • Butter two cookie sheets and sprinkle with flaked almonds. • Form the dough into balls the size of walnuts. Roll out the dough balls on a lightly floured surface to a thickness of 1/8 inch. • Dust the spekulatius mold with flour and press a dough disk into it. Cut off any surplus

dough and tap the cookie out onto the prepared cookie sheet, placing them 1 inch apart. • Repeat until all the dough has been used. • If you do not have a mold, roll the dough out to a thickness of 1/4 inch. Use a cookie cutter to cut out cookies and use a toothpick to draw lines across the dough (see photo). • Bake for 8–10 minutes, or until just golden at the edges, rotating the sheets halfway through for even baking. • Transfer to racks to cool.

Makes 50 cookies · Prep: 50 min. + 30 min. to chill Cooking: 8–10 min. · Level: 3 · Keeps: 20 days in a container with air holes

candy cane cookies

1¹/₂	cups all-purpose flour
1/4	teaspoon salt
2/3	cups confectioners' sugar
2/3	cup butter, softened
1	large egg
1	teaspoon peppermint extract
1/2	teaspoon vanilla extract
1/4	cup crushed red-and-white candy canes
	Few drops red food coloring

Preheat the oven to 350°F. • Set out two cookie sheets. • Sift the flour and salt into a large bowl. • Beat the confectioners' sugar and butter in a large bowl with an electric mixer at high speed until creamy. • Add the egg and peppermint and vanilla extracts, beating until just blended. • Mix in the dry ingredients. • Divide the dough between two bowls. • Mix the crushed candy into one bowl and the food coloring into the other bowl until well blended. • Form tablespoons of the candy dough into 4-inch ropes. Repeat with the colored dough. • Twist one candy dough rope and one colored dough rope together to form a striped rope. • Shape one end of the rope into a curve to resemble a candy cane and place 2 inches apart on the prepared cookie sheets. • Bake for 10–12 minutes, or until firm to the touch. • Transfer to racks to cool.

Makes 20–25 cookies · Prep: 30 min. · Cooking: 10–12 min. per batch · Level: 1 · Keeps: 4 days

Spekulatius

cookie lollipops

To make these cookies into lollipops, you will need wooden craft sticks or lollipop sticks. These cookies are simple to make for children's birthday parties. Decorate them as you like with names piped in frosting, or candy and chocolate.

2³/4 cups all-purpose flour
1 teaspoon baking powder
¹/2 teaspoon baking soda
¹/4 teaspoon salt
1 cup (2 sticks) butter, softened
1¹/2 cups granulated sugar
¹/2 teaspoon vanilla extract
2 large eggs
2 cups M&Ms
¹/2 cup Vanilla Frosting (see page 348)

Sift the flour, baking powder, baking soda, and salt into a medium bowl. • Beat the butter and sugar in a large bowl with an electric mixer at high speed until creamy. • Add the vanilla and eggs, beating until just blended. • Mix in the dry ingredients and 1 cup M&Ms. • Press the dough into a disk, wrap in plastic wrap, and refrigerate for 30 minutes. • Preheat the oven to 375°F. • Line two cookie sheets with parchment paper. • Roll 2 tablespoons of dough into a ball and insert a wooden craft stick into the dough. Flatten the dough completely with the base of a glass. • Repeat with the remaining dough. • Place the cookies 2 inches apart on the prepared cookie sheets. • Bake for 10–12 minutes, or until just golden at the edges, rotating the sheets halfway through for even baking. • Cool on racks until the cookies firm slightly. • Transfer to racks to finish cooling. • Spoon the frosting into a small freezer bag and cut off a tiny corner. • Pipe lines of frosting over the cookies and press the remaining M&Ms on top.

Makes 25–30 cookies · Prep: 30 min. · Cooking: 10–12 min. · Level: 2 · Keeps: 1 day

greeting card cookies

Give these cookies to your friends for birthdays and Christmas. Or pipe on names and use them as place markers for a fun dinner party.

1¹/2 cups all-purpose flour
¹/3 cup unsweetened cocoa powder
¹/2 teaspoon baking powder
¹/2 teaspoon baking soda
¹/4 teaspoon salt
¹/2 cup (1 stick) butter, softened
³/4 cup granulated sugar
¹/2 teaspoon vanilla extract
1 large egg

Colored frosting
3 cups confectioners' sugar
¹/3 cup butter, softened
¹/4 cup milk
Few drops food coloring

Sift the flour, cocoa, baking powder, baking soda, and salt into a medium bowl. • Beat the butter and sugar in a large bowl with an electric mixer at high speed until creamy. • Add the vanilla and egg, beating until just blended. • Mix in the dry ingredients to form a stiff dough. • Press the dough into a disk, wrap in plastic wrap, and refrigerate for 30 minutes. • Preheat the oven to 350°F. • Butter four cookie sheets. • Roll out half the dough on a lightly floured surface to a thickness of ¹/4 inch. • Use a fluted pastry wheel and ruler to cut out 2 x 4-inch rectangles. • Repeat with the remaining dough. • Gather the dough scraps, re-roll, and continue cutting out cookies until all the dough is used. • Use a spatula to transfer the cookies to the prepared cookie sheets, placing them ¹/2 inch apart. • Bake, one sheet at a time, for 8–10 minutes, or until lightly browned. • Cool on racks until the cookies firm slightly. • Transfer to racks to finish cooling. • Use a sharp knife to trim the edges if the cookies have lost their shape during the baking. • Colored frosting: Beat the confectioners' sugar and butter in a medium bowl until well blended. • Gradually add the milk to form a thick paste. • Stir in the food coloring of your choice until no white streaks remain. • Spoon the frosting into a small freezer bag and cut off a tiny corner. • Pipe your greeting message over the cookies and pipe decorative lines around the edge of the cookies.

Makes 10–12 cookies · Prep: 40 min. · Cooking: 8–10 min. per batch · Level: 2 · Keeps: 5 days

st. catherine's cookies

These English cookies derive from the county of Bedfordshire, where Henry VIII's imprisoned first Queen, Catherine of Aragon, once visited and saved poor lacemakers from starvation by burning all of her own lace and commissioning more from the local women.

2¹/2 cups all-purpose flour
¹/2 teaspoon baking soda
1 teaspoon ground cinnamon
¹/8 teaspoon salt
1 cup (2 sticks) butter, softened
6 tablespoons granulated sugar
²/3 cup finely ground almonds
¹/2 cup dried currants
2 teaspoons caraway seeds (optional)
1 large egg, lightly beaten
2 teaspoons water

Sift the flour, baking soda, cinnamon, and salt into a large bowl. • Use a pastry blender to cut in the butter until the mixture resembles fine crumbs. • Stir in the ¹/2 cup sugar, almonds, currants, caraway seeds, if using. • Add the egg and mix to make a firm dough. • Press the dough into a disk, wrap in plastic wrap, and refrigerate for 30 minutes. • Preheat the oven to 400°F. • Butter two cookie sheets. • Roll out the dough on a lightly floured surface to an 8 x 6-inch rectangle. • Use a pastry brush to brush lightly with water. Sprinkle with the remaining 2 tablespoons sugar. • Cut the dough into ¹/2 x 6-inch long strips and shape into rounded ropes. Form each rope into a tight circular coil. Use a spatula to transfer the cookies to the prepared cookie sheets, flattening them slightly. • Bake for 10–12 minutes, or until golden brown, rotating the sheets halfway through for even baking. • Transfer to racks to cool.

Makes 24 cookies · Prep: 40 min. + 30 min. to chill Cooking: 10–12 min. · Level: 1 · Keeps: 2 weeks

christmas walnut–cranberry bars

1 cup all-purpose flour
¹/8 teaspoon salt
¹/4 cup (¹/2 stick) butter, melted
³/4 cup granulated sugar
1 large egg, lightly beaten
²/3 cup finely chopped walnuts
¹/2 cup fresh or frozen cranberries

Preheat the oven to 350°F. • Butter a 9-inch baking pan. • Sift the flour and salt into a medium bowl. • Mix the butter and sugar in a medium bowl. • Add the egg, beating until just blended. • Mix in the dry ingredients, walnuts, and cranberries. • Spread the mixture in the prepared pan. • Bake for 30–35 minutes, or until golden and a toothpick inserted into the center comes out clean. • Cool completely in the pan. • Cut into squares.

Makes 16–25 bars · Prep: 20 min. · Cooking: 30–35 min. · Level: 1 · Keeps: 3 days

Cookie lollipops (top) and Greeting card cookies (bottom)

czech christmas hearts

A traditional Christmas cookie from the Czech Republic.

1³/4	cups all-purpose flour
1/4	teaspoon ground allspice
1/4	teaspoon baking soda
1/4	teaspoon ground cinnamon
1/4	teaspoon ground cloves
1/4	teaspoon ground ginger
1/4	teaspoon freshly grated nutmeg
1/8	teaspoon salt
1/2	cup light molasses, warmed
1/2	cup firmly packed light brown sugar
1/4	cup (1/2 stick) butter, melted

Sift the flour, allspice, baking soda, cinnamon, cloves, ginger, nutmeg, and salt into a medium bowl. • Use a wooden spoon to beat the molasses, brown sugar, and butter in a large bowl until well blended. • Mix in the dry ingredients to form a stiff dough. • Press the dough into a disk, wrap in plastic wrap, and refrigerate for 30 minutes. • Preheat the oven to 375°F. • Butter two cookie sheets. • Roll out the dough on a lightly floured surface to a thickness of 1/4 inch. • Use a 1¹/2-inch heart-shaped cookie cutter to cut out the cookies. Gather the dough scraps, re-roll, and continue cutting out cookies until all the dough is used. • Use a spatula to transfer the cookies to the prepared cookie sheets, placing them 1 inch apart. • Bake for 7–10 minutes, or until golden brown, rotating the sheets halfway through for even baking. • Transfer to racks to cool.

Makes 20–25 cookies · Prep: 40 min. + 30 min. to chill · Cooking: 7–10 min. · Level: 1 · Keeps: 10 days

chocolate–hazelnut valentines

1¹/3	cups all-purpose flour
1/3	cup unsweetened cocoa powder
1/8	teaspoon salt
1/2	cup (1 stick) butter, softened
2/3	cup firmly packed light brown sugar
2	large eggs, 1 separated
2/3	cup finely ground hazelnuts
1/2	cup finely chopped hazelnuts

Sift the flour, cocoa, and salt into a medium bowl. • Beat the butter and brown sugar in a large bowl with an electric mixer at high speed until creamy. • Add 1 whole egg and 1 egg yolk, beating until just blended. • Mix in the dry ingredients and ground hazelnuts to form a smooth dough. • Press the dough into a disk, wrap in plastic wrap, and refrigerate for 30 minutes. • Preheat the oven to 350°F. •

Line two cookie sheets with parchment paper. • Discard the plastic wrap. Roll out the dough on a lightly floured surface to a thickness of 1/4 inch. • Use a 1¹/2-inch heart-shaped cookie cutter to cut out the cookies. Gather the dough scraps, re-roll, and continue cutting out cookies until all the dough is used. • Use a spatula to transfer the cookies to the prepared cookie sheets, placing them 1 inch apart. • Use a wire whisk to beat the remaining egg white in a small bowl until frothy and brush over the tops of the cookies. Sprinkle with the chopped hazelnuts. • Bake for 10–15 minutes, or until golden brown, rotating the sheets halfway through for even baking. • Transfer to racks to cool.

Makes 25–30 cookies · Prep: 40 min. + 30 min. to chill · Cooking: 10–15 min. · Level: 1 · Keeps: 10 days

mother's day hearts

2	cups all-purpose flour
1	teaspoon baking powder
1/8	teaspoon salt
2/3	cup cream cheese or quark, softened
1/3	cup butter, softened
1	large egg
1/4	cup unsweetened cocoa powder
3¹/2	oz nougat, cut into small pieces

Frosting

1	cup confectioners' sugar
1/4	teaspoon vanilla extract
1	tablespoon milk, + more as needed
2–3	drops each red and green food coloring
	Colored candy writers, to decorate
	Sugar flowers, to decorate

Sift the flour, baking powder, and salt into a medium bowl. • Beat the cream cheese and butter in a large bowl with an electric mixer at high speed until creamy. • Process the egg, cocoa, and nougat in a food processor until well blended. • Mix the nougat mixture into batter. • Mix in the dry ingredients to form a smooth, and not sticky, dough. • Press the dough into a disk, wrap in plastic wrap, and refrigerate for 30 minutes. • Preheat the oven to 375°F. • Line two cookie sheets with parchment paper. • Roll out the dough on a lightly floured surface to a thickness of 1/2 inch. • Use a 3-inch heart-shaped cookie cutter to cut out the cookies. Gather the dough scraps, re-roll, and continue cutting out cookies until all the dough is used. • Use a spatula to transfer the cookies to the prepared cookie sheets, placing them 1 inch apart. • Bake for 12–15 minutes, or until lightly browned and the edges are firm, rotating the

sheets halfway through for even baking. • Cool on the sheets until the cookies firm slightly. Transfer to racks to finish cooling. • Frosting: Mix the confectioners' sugar, vanilla, and enough milk to form a thick paste. • Divide into three bowls. Leave one mixture plain and tint the remaining mixtures with the red and green food coloring. • Spread each cookie top with the frosting, making some pink, some green, and others white. • Use a contrasting colored candy writer to pipe a special message or design on top of the cookies. • Decorate with the sugar flowers.

Makes 12–16 cookies · Prep: 40 min. + 30 min. to chill · Cooking: 12–15 min. · Level: 2 · Keeps: 2 weeks

valentine message cookies

2¹/3	cups all-purpose flour
2	teaspoons ground cinnamon
1	teaspoon baking soda
1/2	teaspoon ground cloves
1/8	teaspoon salt
1/2	cup (1 stick) butter, cut up
2/3	cup granulated sugar
1/4	cup light molasses
1	tablespoon finely grated lemon zest
1	large egg, lightly beaten
	Colored candy writers, to decorate

Sift the flour, cinnamon, baking soda, cloves, and salt into a medium bowl. • Use a pastry blender to cut in the butter until the mixture resembles fine crumbs. • Stir in the sugar, molasses, lemon zest, and egg to form a stiff dough. • Press the dough into a disk, wrap in plastic wrap, and refrigerate for 30 minutes. • Preheat the oven to 375°F. • Butter a cookie sheet. • Roll out the dough on a lightly floured surface to a thickness of 1/4 inch. • Use a 4-inch heart-shaped cookie cutter to cut out the cookies. Gather the dough scraps, re-roll, and continue cutting out cookies until all the dough is used. • Use a spatula to transfer the cookies to the prepared cookie sheet, placing them 1 inch apart. • Bake for 10–15 minutes, or until lightly browned. • Transfer to racks to cool. • Use various colored candy writers to pipe a message onto each cookie.

Makes 6–8 cookies · Prep: 45 min. + 30 min. to chill · Cooking: 10–15 min. · Level: 1 · Keeps: 7 days

Mother's day hearts

spiced black pepper cookies

These cookies are one of seven traditional cookies eaten during the Christmas period in Norway.

3¼ cups all-purpose flour
1 teaspoon baking powder
1 teaspoon baking soda
1 teaspoon ground cinnamon
1 teaspoon ground allspice
⅛ teaspoon salt
1 cup (2 sticks) butter
1 cup granulated sugar
¼ cup heavy cream
1 teaspoon freshly ground black pepper

Sift the flour, baking powder, baking soda, cinnamon, allspice, and salt into a medium bowl. • Beat the butter and sugar in a large bowl with an electric mixer at high speed until creamy. • Beat in the cream. • Mix in the dry ingredients and black pepper to form a smooth dough. • Form the dough into a log 2½ inches in diameter. Wrap in plastic wrap and refrigerate for 30 minutes. • Preheat the oven to 375°F. • Butter four cookie sheets. • Slice the dough ¼ inch thick and place the cookies 1 inch apart on the prepared cookie sheets. • Bake, one sheet at a time, for 5–7 minutes, or until just golden. • Transfer to racks and let cool completely.

Makes 55 cookies · Prep: 40 min. + 30 min. to chill · Cooking: 5–7 min. per batch · Level: 1 · Keeps: 10 days

party peppermint windmills

These cookies are ideal for children to take home at the end of a birthday party.

2 cups all-purpose flour
1½ teaspoons baking powder
¼ teaspoon salt
⅓ cup butter, softened
⅓ cup vegetable shortening
¾ cup granulated sugar
1 large egg, lightly beaten
1 tablespoon milk
½ teaspoon vanilla extract
½ cup crushed peppermint candies

Sift the flour, baking powder, and salt into a medium bowl. • Beat the butter, shortening, and sugar in a large bowl with an electric mixer at high speed until creamy. • Add the egg, milk, and vanilla, beating until just blended. • Mix in the dry ingredients to form a smooth dough. • Divide the dough in half. Press into two disks, wrap in plastic wrap, and refrigerate for 30 minutes. • Preheat the oven to 350°F. • Set out four cookie sheets. • Roll out the dough on a lightly floured surface into a 12 x 9-inch rectangle. • Use a fluted pastry wheel to cut into twelve 3-inch squares. • Repeat with the remaining dough. • Use a spatula to transfer the cookies to the cookie sheets. Do not place more than six cookies on each sheet as there must be space for the craft sticks. • Sprinkle with the crushed candies, pressing them lightly into the dough. • Cut 1-inch slits in each corner toward the center of the square. Fold every other

corner into the center to make a windmill shape. • Press craft sticks into the base of the squares, pressing the dough around them so that they are firmly held. • Bake, one sheet at a time, for 6–8 minutes, or until just golden at the edges. • Cool on the sheets until the cookies firm slightly. • Transfer to racks to cool.

Makes 24 cookies · Prep: 30 min. + 30 min. to chill · Cooking: 6–8 min. per batch · Level: 2 · Keeps: 7 days

pepperkakor

Spicy, but sweet, these cookies are traditional Christmas treats in Sweden.

2 cups all-purpose flour
2 tablespoons ground cinnamon
2 teaspoons ground cloves
1½ teaspoons ground ginger
1 teaspoon baking powder
¼ teaspoon salt
⅔ cup butter, cut up
⅔ cup granulated sugar
½ cup light corn syrup
⅓ cup coarsely chopped almonds
1 tablespoon finely grated lemon zest
1 tablespoon finely chopped mixed candied peel
1 tablespoon flaked almonds

Sift the flour, cinnamon, cloves, ginger, and baking powder into a large bowl. • Melt the butter with the sugar and corn syrup in a medium saucepan over low heat. • Remove from the heat and let cool for 10 minutes. • Stir in the almonds, lemon zest, and candied peel. • Mix in the dry ingredients to form a stiff dough. • Turn the dough out onto a lightly floured surface and knead until smooth. • Return to the bowl, cover with plastic wrap, and refrigerate for at least 1 hour, or until firm. • Preheat the oven to 375°F. • Butter two cookie sheets. • Roll out the dough on a lightly floured surface to a thickness of ¼ inch. • Use a 2-inch cookie cutter to cut out the cookies. Gather the dough scraps, re-roll, and continue cutting out cookies until all the dough is used. • Use a spatula to transfer the cookies to the prepared cookie sheets, placing them 1 inch apart. • Place a flaked almond piece on top of each cookie. • Bake for 8–10 minutes, or until just golden, rotating the sheets halfway through for even baking. • Cool on the sheets until the cookies firm slightly. • Transfer to racks to finish cooling.

Makes 28–32 cookies · Prep: 40 min. + 1 hr. to chill · Level: 1 · Cooking: 8–10 min. · Keeps: 10–14 days

Pepperkakor

color-your-own cookies

Paint your own special designs on these iced cookies to make them perfect for every occasion.

- 1/2 cup all-purpose flour
- 1/4 teaspoon baking soda
- 1/8 teaspoon salt
- 2 tablespoons butter, softened
- 1/4 cup firmly packed light brown sugar
- 1 tablespoon honey
- 1 large egg, lightly beaten
- 1/4 cup apricot preserves or jam
- 7 oz ready-to-roll fondant icing
  Few drops various food colorings

Sift the flour, baking soda, and salt into a medium bowl. • Use a pastry blender to cut in the butter until the mixture resembles fine crumbs. • Stir in the brown sugar. • Add the honey and enough egg to form a stiff dough. • Press the dough into a disk, wrap in plastic wrap, and refrigerate for 30 minutes. • Preheat the oven to 375°F. • Butter two cookie sheets. • Roll out the dough on a lightly floured surface to a thickness of 1/4 inch. • Use various shaped cookie cutters to cut out the cookies. • Gather the dough scraps, re-roll, and continue cutting out cookies until all the dough is used. • Use a spatula to transfer the cookies to the prepared cookie sheets, placing them 1 inch apart. • Bake for 7–10 minutes, or until pale gold, rotating the sheets halfway through for even baking. • Transfer to racks to cool. • Spread the tops of the cookies with the preserves. • Roll out the fondant on a surface lightly dusted with confectioners' sugar to a thickness of 1/4 inch. • Cut out the same shapes to top the cookies with the fondant. Place the matching shape of icing on top of each cookie. • Use a paint brush to decorate the tops of the cookies with the food colorings.

Makes 25–30 cookies · Prep: 50 min. + 30 min. to chill · Cooking: 7–10 min. · Level: 2 · Keeps: 7 days

jam cookie towers

A cookie showpiece—these cookie towers will steal the show at a bake sale.

- 3 cups all-purpose flour
- 1/8 teaspoon salt
- 1 cup granulated sugar
- 1/4 cup Vanilla Sugar (see page 341)
- 1/2 cup (1 stick) butter, cut up
- 1 large egg + 3 large egg yolks
- 1 teaspoon vanilla extract

- 3 tablespoons damson plum or raspberry preserves
- 1/2 cup confectioners' sugar

Sift the flour and salt into a large bowl. • Stir in the granulated and vanilla sugars. • Use a pastry blender to cut in the butter until the mixture resembles coarse crumbs. • Use a fork to mix in the egg and egg yolks and vanilla to form a smooth dough. • Divide the dough in half. • Press the dough into disks, wrap in plastic wrap, and refrigerate for 30 minutes. • Preheat the oven to 350°F. • Set out three cookie sheets. • Roll out the dough on a lightly floured surface to a thickness of 1/8 inch. • Use differently sized (e.g. 1-, 1 1/2-, and 2-inch) star cutters to cut out the cookies. Gather the dough scraps, re-roll, and continue cutting out cookies until all the dough is used. • Use a spatula to transfer the cookies to the cookie sheets, placing them 1 inch apart. • Refrigerate for 10 minutes. • Bake for 8–12 minutes, or until just golden at the edges, rotating the sheets halfway through for even baking. • Cool on the sheets until the cookies firm slightly. • Transfer to racks and let cool completely. • Stick the differently sized cookies together with the preserves—the largest at the bottom, the smallest at the top. • Dust the cookie towers with confectioners' sugar.

Makes 24–35 cookie towers · Prep: 50 min. + 30 min. to chill   Cooking: 8–10 min. · Level: 2 · Keeps: 2 weeks

austrian christmas butter cookies

- 1 1/2 cups all-purpose flour
- 1/2 teaspoon ground cinnamon
- 1/8 teaspoon salt
- 2/3 cup + 2 tablespoons granulated sugar
- 2 teaspoons freeze-dried coffee granules, dissolved in 1 tablespoon hot water
- 1 cup (2 sticks) butter, cut up
- 2 cups coarsely chopped toasted hazelnuts

Preheat the oven to 325°F. • Set out two cookie sheets. • Sift the flour, cinnamon, and salt into a large bowl. • Use a pastry blender to cut in the butter until the mixture resembles coarse crumbs. • Stir in 2/3 cup sugar and the coffee. • Press the dough into a disk and knead it lightly. • Place the hazelnuts on a large plate. • Form the dough into balls the size of walnuts and roll in the hazelnuts until well coated. • Place the cookies 1 inch apart on the cookie sheets, flattening them slightly. Sprinkle with the remaining 2 tablespoons sugar. • Bake for 20–25 minutes, or until faintly tinged with brown on top and slightly darker at the edges, rotating the sheets halfway through for even baking. • Cool on the sheets until the cookies firm slightly. • Transfer to racks to finish cooling.

Makes 30–34 cookies · Prep: 25 min. · Cooking: 20–25 min. · Level: 1 · Keeps: 10 days

Jam cookie towers

currant spice cookies

For special Christmas cookies, use an angel-shaped cookie cutter to stamp out these cookies.

1 2/3   cups all-purpose flour
1   teaspoon baking soda
1   teaspoon ground cinnamon
1/4   teaspoon ground nutmeg
1/8   teaspoon ground cloves
1/8   teaspoon salt
1/2   cup (1 stick) butter, softened
1   cup granulated sugar
2   teaspoons milk
1   large egg, lightly beaten
1/2   cup currants

Sift the flour, baking soda, cinnamon, nutmeg, and cloves into a medium bowl. • Beat the butter and 3/4 cup sugar in a large bowl with an electric mixer at high speed until creamy. • Add the milk and egg, beating until just blended. • Mix in the dry ingredients, followed by the currants. • Press the dough into a disk, wrap in plastic wrap, and refrigerate for 30 minutes. • Preheat the oven to 375°F. • Set out three cookie sheets. • Roll out the dough on a lightly floured surface to a thickness of 1/8 inch. • Sprinkle with the remaining 1/4 cup sugar. • Use a 2-inch diamond-shaped cookie cutter to cut out the cookies. Gather the dough scraps, re-roll, and continue cutting out until all the dough is used. Use a spatula to transfer the cookies to the cookie sheets. • Bake, one sheet at a time, for 5–8 minutes, or until lightly browned. • Cool on the sheets until the cookies firm slightly. Transfer to racks to finish cooling.

Makes 36 cookies · Prep: 40 min. + 30 min. to chill · Cooking: 5–8 min. per batch · Level: 1 · Keeps: 7 days

rugelach

These delicious cookies are a Hannukkah tradition.

2   cups (4 sticks) butter, softened
2   packages (1 lb) cream cheese, softened
2   cups all-purpose flour
1/2   cup golden raisins
2   tablespoons granulated sugar
1   tablespoon ground cinnamon
4   tablespoons confectioners' sugar, to dust

Beat the butter and cream cheese in a large bowl with an electric mixer at high speed until creamy. • Mix in the flour to form a smooth dough. Divide the dough in half and press each half into a disk. Wrap in plastic wrap and refrigerate for 30 minutes. • Preheat the oven to 375°F. • Set out two cookie sheets. •

Combine the raisins, sugar, and cinnamon in a small bowl. • Roll out one piece of the dough on a lightly floured surface to a circle with a thickness of 1/4 inch. • Cut the circle into sixteen wedges. • Sprinkle half the raisin mixture over the entire surface, leaving a 1/4-inch border. • Roll up each wedge from the wide end to the point, tucking the point under. Repeat with the remaining dough and filling. • Use a spatula to transfer the cookies to the cookie sheets. • Bake for 10–15 minutes, or until the bottoms are lightly browned, rotating the sheets halfway through for even baking. • Transfer to racks and let cool completely. • Dust with the confectioners' sugar.

Makes 32 cookies · Prep: 30 min. · Cooking: 10–15 min. · Level: 2 · Keeps: 3 days

snake's tongue cookie

A unique-looking cookie—perfect for children's themed parties.

1/3   cup butter, softened
3/4   cup confectioners' sugar
4   large egg whites, lightly beaten
1/2   cup all-purpose flour
1/8   teaspoon salt
1   tablespoon unsweetened cocoa powder

Preheat the oven to 400°F. • Butter a cookie sheet. • Use a pencil and ruler to draw a 12 x 8-inch rectangle on a sheet of parchment paper. Draw triangles, points facing inward, at each end of the rectangle to resemble a double-pronged snake's tongue. Cut out the template. • Place the template on the prepared cookie sheet. • Beat the butter and confectioners' sugar in a large bowl with an electric mixer at high speed until creamy. • Stir in the egg whites, followed by the flour and salt. • If the mixture separates, place over barely simmering water and mix. • Set aside 2 tablespoons of the mixture. Stir the cocoa into the remaining batter. • Use a thin metal spatula to spread a small amount of plain cookie batter around the inside edge of the template to form a border. • Spread the remaining plain batter in the center of the template. • Spoon the cocoa batter into a small plastic freezer bag. Cut off the corner and pipe over the edges. • Bake for 8–10 minutes, or until just golden. • Use a spatula to loosen the edges and transfer to a rack to cool completely.

Makes 1 large cookie · Prep: 30 min. · Cooking: 8–10 min. · Level: 2 · Keeps: 3 days

easter cookies

These crisp cookies provide an alternative to chocolate eggs as your indulgent Easter treat.

1 1/4   cups all-purpose flour
1   teaspoon baking powder
1/2   teaspoon ground allspice
1/8   teaspoon salt
1/3   cup butter, softened
1/3   cup + 2 teaspoons granulated sugar
1   large egg, separated
1/3   cup currants
1   tablespoon finely chopped mixed candied peel
1/4   teaspoon brandy
2   tablespoons milk, or more as needed

Preheat the oven to 375°F. • Butter two cookie sheets. • Sift the flour, baking powder, allspice, and salt into a medium bowl. • Beat the butter and 1/3 cup sugar in a large bowl with an electric mixer at high speed until creamy. • Add the egg yolk, beating until just blended. • Mix in the dry ingredients, currants, candied peel, and brandy until well blended. • Add enough milk to form a soft, but not sticky, dough. • Cover with plastic wrap and refrigerate for 30 minutes. • Roll out the dough to a thickness of 1/4 inch. • Use a 2-inch cookie cutter to cut out the cookies. Gather the dough scraps, re-roll, and continue cutting out cookies until all the dough is used. Use a spatula to transfer the cookies to a cookie sheet, placing them 1 inch apart. Prick all over with a fork. • Bake, one sheet at a time, for 10 minutes. • Beat the egg white lightly in a small bowl. • Remove the cookie sheet from the oven and brush the cookies with the beaten egg white. Sprinkle with the remaining 2 teaspoons sugar. • Bake for 5–10 minutes more, or until lightly browned, rotating the sheets halfway through for even baking. • Cool on the sheets until the cookies firm slightly. Transfer to racks to finish cooling.

Makes 24 cookies · Prep: 40 min. + 30 min. to chill Cooking: 15–20 min. · Level: 1 · Keeps: 7 days

Rugelach

pfeffernuesse

These tasty cookies are a traditional Christmas offering throughout Germany.

3/4 cup all-purpose flour
1 teaspoon ground cinnamon
1/2 teaspoon ground cloves
1/2 teaspoon ground mace
1/8 teaspoon salt
1/2 teaspoon grated lemon zest
1/8 teaspoon ground aniseeds
1/8 teaspoon ground black pepper
1/3 cup honey
1/3 cup light molasses
1/4 cup granulated sugar
2 tablespoons butter
1 large egg, lightly beaten
2 tablespoons confectioners' sugar

Preheat the oven to 375°F. • Butter two cookie sheets. • Sift the flour, cinnamon, cloves, mace, and salt into a large bowl. • Stir in the lemon zest, aniseeds, and black pepper. • Mix the honey, molasses, and granulated sugar in a medium saucepan over low heat. • Cook, stirring constantly, until the sugar has dissolved completely. • Add the butter and remove from the heat. • Add the egg, beating until just blended. • Mix in the dry ingredients to form a stiff dough. • Drop teaspoons of the dough 2 inches apart onto the prepared sheets. • Bake for 12–15 minutes, or until firm and golden brown, rotating the sheets halfway through for even baking. • Cool on the sheets until the cookies firm slightly. • Transfer to racks and let cool completely. • Dust with the confectioners' sugar.

Makes 30–35 cookies · Prep: 40 min. · Cooking: 12–15 min. · Level: 1 · Keeps: 10 days

bonfire cookies

Guy Fawkes' Night, November 5, is a national bank holiday in the United Kingdom. The date commemorates an attempt by Guy Fawkes and a band of conspirators to blow up the Houses of Parliament when the monarch arrived to open the session in 1605. The plan was foiled by a night watchman who found barrels of gunpowder hidden beneath the Parliament buildings.

3/4 cup all-purpose flour
3/4 cup whole-wheat flour
3/4 cup confectioners' sugar
1 teaspoon ground cinnamon
1/8 teaspoon ground cloves
1/8 teaspoon salt
1/3 cup butter, cut up
1 large egg yolk, lightly beaten
1/4 teaspoon vanilla extract
1 tablespoon raw sugar (Barbados or Demerara)

Preheat the oven to 400°F. • Butter two cookie sheets. • Sift the all-purpose and whole-wheat flours, confectioners' sugar, cinnamon, cloves, and salt into a large bowl. • Use a pastry blender to cut in the butter until the mixture resembles coarse crumbs. • Add the egg yolk and vanilla and mix to form a smooth dough. • Press the dough into a disk, wrap in plastic wrap, and refrigerate for 30 minutes. • Roll out the dough on a lightly floured surface to a thickness of 1/8 inch. • Use a 3-inch cookie cutter to cut out the cookies. Gather the dough scraps, re-roll, and continue cutting out cookies until all the dough is used. • Use a spatula to transfer the cookies to the prepared cookie sheets, placing them 1 inch apart. • Sprinkle with the raw sugar. • Bake

for 12–15 minutes, or until golden, rotating the sheets halfway through for even baking. • Transfer to racks to cool.

Makes 30–35 cookies · Prep: 40 min. · Cooking: 12–15 min. · Level: 1 · Keeps: 10 days

spooky cookies

These cookies are great served at a Halloween party or handed out to trick-or-treaters at the door. Candy writers, used for decorating, can be located at confectionery specialists, such as Maid of Scandinavia.

1 1/2 cups all-purpose flour
1/4 teaspoon baking soda
1/4 teaspoon salt
1/2 cup (1 stick) butter, softened
1/2 cup firmly packed light brown sugar
1 large egg
2 oz semisweet chocolate, coarsely chopped
7 oz store-bought ready-to-roll white fondant
2 drops orange food coloring (or red and yellow)

Sift the flour, baking soda, and salt into a medium bowl. • Beat the butter and brown sugar in a large bowl with an electric mixer until creamy. • Add the egg, beating until just blended. • Melt the chocolate in a double boiler over barely simmering water. • Stir the melted chocolate into the butter mixture. • Mix in the dry ingredients to form a stiff dough. • Press the dough into a disk, wrap in plastic wrap, and refrigerate for 30 minutes. • Preheat the oven to 350°F. • Butter two cookie sheets. • Roll out the dough on a lightly floured surface to a thickness of 1/4 inch. • Use a 3-inch cookie cutter to cut out the cookies. Gather the dough scraps, re-roll, and continue cutting out cookies until all the dough is used. • Use a spatula to transfer the cookies to the prepared cookie sheets, placing them 1 inch apart. • Bake for 10–15 minutes, or until just golden, rotating the sheets halfway through for even baking. • Transfer to racks and let cool completely. • Knead the white fondant frosting until malleable. • Divide the fondant into two portions. • Place one portion in a bowl and mix in the orange food coloring until no white streaks remain. • Roll out the plain fondant on a surface lightly dusted with confectioners' sugar to a thickness of 1/8 inch. • Use the cookie cutter to cut out enough fondant rounds to cover half the cookies. • Brush the fondant rounds with

Bonfire cookies

water. • Place wet-side down on top of half the cookies. • Repeat with the orange fondant and place on top of the remaining cookies. • Use an edible black candy writer to draw spooky designs over the fondant.

Makes 12–16 cookies · Prep: 25 min. + 30 min. to chill · Cooking: 10–15 min. · Level: 2 · Keeps: 3 days

spider's web cookies

If you can find ready-to-roll white fondant, you will speed up the decorating time for these impressive Halloween cookies.

30   Rolled Sugar Cookies (see page 66)

Fondant
2   cups granulated sugar
3/4   cup cold water
1/4   teaspoon cream of tartar
1/4   cup confectioners' sugar, to dust
1/2   cup apricot preserves
4   oz bittersweet chocolate, coarsely chopped

Prepare the cookies and let cool completely on racks. • <u>Fondant</u>: Bring the sugar, water, and cream of tartar to a boil in a medium saucepan over medium heat. Wash down the sides of the pan with a pastry brush dipped in cold water to prevent sugar crystals from forming. Cook, without stirring, until the mixture reaches 238°F, or the soft-ball stage. • Sprinkle a marble slab or lightly oiled baking sheet with cold water. Pour the fondant syrup onto the slab or sheet and let cool until lukewarm, 10–15 minutes. When ready, the fondant should hold an indentation made with a fingertip. • Use a large spatula to work the fondant, lifting from the edges toward the center, folding it until it begins to thicken, lose its gloss, and turn pure white. • Dust your hands with confectioners' sugar and knead the fondant until smooth and creamy. Place in a bowl and cover with a clean cloth. Let stand overnight. • Knead the fondant until malleable. Roll out on a surface lightly dusted with confectioners' sugar to a thickness of 1/4 inch. • Using a rolling pin, drape the fondant over the cookies and cut out the fondant to fit the tops of the cookies. Set aside. • Warm the preserves in a small saucepan over low heat until liquid. • Spread the preserves over the cookies and place the fondant layers on top. • Melt the chocolate in a double boiler over barely simmering water. • Spoon the chocolate into a small freezer bag and cut off a tiny

Christmas cookies

corner. • Pipe over the cookies in concentric circles. • Let stand for 5 minutes until set. • Use a toothpick to draw through the lines from the center outward to create a spider's web effect.

Makes 30 cookies · Prep: 1 hr. · Cooking: 8–10 min. Level: 3 · Keeps: 1–2 days

christmas cookies

11/4   cups all-purpose flour
1/3   cup confectioners' sugar
1/8   teaspoon salt
1/2   cup (1 stick) butter, softened
1   tablespoon heavy cream
1/2   teaspoon vanilla extract
25   lightly crushed hard candies, mixed colors

Stir together the confectioners' sugar, flour, salt, butter, cream, and vanilla in a large bowl to form a smooth dough. • Press into a disk, cover with plastic wrap and refrigerate for 30 minutes. • Preheat the oven to 400°F. • Line two cookie sheets with parchment paper. • Roll out the dough on a lightly floured surface to a thickness of 1/8 inch. • Use Christmas-shaped cookie cutters, such as holly, stars, and snowmen, to cut out the cookies. Gather the dough scraps, re-roll, and continue cutting out cookies until all the dough is used. Use a spatula to transfer the cookies to the prepared cookie sheets, placing them 1 inch apart. • Use a sharp knife to cut a small hole in each cookie. Place a candy piece in each hole. • Bake for 5–7 minutes, or until the cookies are lightly browned and the candies have melted, rotating the sheets halfway through

for even baking. • Cool the cookies completely on the cookie sheet.

Makes 25 cookies · Prep: 40 min. + 30 min. to chill Cooking: 5–7 min. · Level: 2 · Keeps: 5 days

czech christmas diamonds

11/2   cups all-purpose flour
1/8   teaspoon salt
1/4   cup (1/2 stick) butter, softened
1/4   cup granulated sugar
1   large egg
1   teaspoon caraway seeds
2   tablespoons colored sugar crystals

Sift the flour and salt into a medium bowl. • Beat the butter and granulated sugar in a large bowl with an electric mixer at high speed until creamy. • Add the egg, beating until just blended. • Mix in the dry ingredients and caraway seeds to form a stiff dough. Press the dough into a disk, wrap in plastic wrap, and refrigerate for 30 minutes. • Preheat the oven to 325°F. • Butter three cookie sheets. • Roll out the dough on a lightly floured surface to a thickness of 1/8 inch. Cut the dough into 2-inch diamonds. Gather the dough scraps, re-roll, and continue cutting out cookies until all the dough is used. • Use a spatula to transfer the cookies to the prepared cookie sheets, placing them 1 inch apart. Sprinkle the tops of the cookies with the sugar crystals. • Bake, one sheet at a time, for 10–12 minutes, or until pale gold. • Transfer to racks to cool.

Makes 38–42 cookies · Prep: 40 min. + 30 min. to chill · Cooking: 10–12 min. per batch · Level: 1 · Keeps: 7 days

all souls' cookies

Halloween takes its name from a corrupted version of the Catholic celebration of All Hallows Eve. This day is dedicated to all the saints of the Catholic Church. On this day in the past, it was traditional for children to go "souling" on November 1 and 2—singing and asking for treats from neighbors. This is the origin of the American "trick or treat" custom.

3/4 cup all-purpose flour
1/2 teaspoon ground cinnamon
1/4 teaspoon ground cloves
1/8 teaspoon salt
1/3 cup butter, softened
1/3 cup granulated sugar
1 large egg yolk
2 tablespoons milk, + more as needed

Sift the flour, cinnamon, cloves, and salt into a medium bowl. • Beat the butter and sugar in a large bowl until creamy. • Add the egg yolk, beating until just blended. • Mix in the dry ingredients and enough milk to form a soft dough. • Press the dough into a disk, wrap in plastic wrap, and refrigerate for 30 minutes. • Preheat the oven to 350°F. • Butter a cookie sheet. • Roll out the dough on a lightly floured surface to thickness of 1/2 inch. • Use a 2-inch cookie cutter to cut out the cookies. Gather the dough scraps, re-roll, and continue cutting out cookies until all the dough is used. • Use a sharp knife to mark a cross on top of each cookie. • Use a spatula to transfer the cookies to the prepared cookie sheet. • Bake for 10–15 minutes, or until deep golden. • Transfer to racks to cool.

Makes 12–16 cookies · Prep: 40 min. + 30 min. to chill · Cooking: 10–15 min. · Level: 1 · Keeps: 10 days

belgian pressed cookies

If you are using a nonstick krumkake iron, it is not necessary to butter the iron before use.

1/2 cup (1 stick) butter, softened
1 cup firmly packed light brown sugar
3 large eggs
1/4 teaspoon vanilla extract
1/4 teaspoon salt
4 cups all-purpose flour

Beat the butter and brown sugar in a large bowl with an electric mixer at high speed until creamy. • Add the eggs, vanilla, and salt, beating until just blended. • Gradually mix in the flour, a little at a time, to form a smooth dough. • Refrigerate for 12 hours. • Lightly butter a krumkake iron and place over medium heat. • The iron is ready to use when a drop of water holds its shape on the surface of the iron. • Use a wooden spoon to stir the batter well and drop a tablespoon (or enough batter to fit your iron) of the batter onto the center of the hot iron. Lower the top so that the batter spreads. • Cook for 1 minute, or until browned at the edges. • Lift up the top and, working quickly, remove the cookie from the iron with a krumkake roller. The cookie should be cone-shaped. • Repeat with the remaining cookie dough. • Let cool completely. • If you are using an electric krumkake iron, follow the manufacturer's directions for preheating and baking.

Makes 12 cookies · Prep: 20 min. + 12 hr. to chill · Cooking: 1 min. per cookie · Level: 3 · Keeps: 2 weeks

italian easter cookies

These delicate cookies are eaten in Apulia, a region in southern Italy.

1/4 cup milk
1 teaspoon baking soda
3 1/3 cups all-purpose flour
2 teaspoons baking powder
1/8 teaspoon salt
1 cup granulated sugar
1 teaspoon vanilla extract
2 large eggs + 1 large egg white, lightly beaten
1/3 cup sunflower oil
7 oz semisweet chocolate, finely grated

Heat the milk in a small saucepan over low heat. Remove from the heat and mix in the baking soda. • Sift the flour, baking powder, and salt into a large bowl. • Stir in the sugar. • Add the vanilla and 2 eggs, beating until just blended. • Pour in the oil and baking soda mixture and mix to form a smooth dough. Press the dough into a disk, wrap in plastic wrap, and refrigerate for 30 minutes. • Preheat the oven to 350°F. • Butter three cookie sheets. • Roll out the dough on a lightly floured surface to a thickness of 1/4 inch. • Use a 2 1/2-inch diamond-shaped cookie cutter to cut out the cookies. Gather the dough scraps, re-roll, and continue cutting out cookies until all the dough is used. • Use a spatula to transfer the cookies to the prepared cookie sheets, placing them 1 inch apart. • Brush with the beaten egg white and sprinkle with the chocolate. • Bake for 15–20 minutes, or until just golden, rotating the sheets halfway through for even baking. • Transfer to racks and let cool completely.

Makes 32 cookies · Prep: 40 min. + 30 min. to chill Cooking: 15–20 min. · Level: 1 · Keeps: 2 weeks

halloween cookies

1 1/3 cups all-purpose flour
1/3 cup confectioners' sugar
1/4 teaspoon teaspoon baking powder
1/4 teaspoon teaspoon ground ginger
1/8 teaspoon ground paprika
1/8 teaspoon salt
1/2 cup (1 stick) butter
1 cup finely ground pecans
1 tablespoon finely ground almonds
1 large egg yolk, lightly beaten
2 tablespoons light corn syrup

Glaze
1 2/3 cups confectioners' sugar
1–2 tablespoons fresh lemon juice
1–2 drops red and yellow food coloring
      Few drops black food coloring gel
1 teaspoon warm water
1/2 teaspoon unsweetened cocoa powder

Sift the flour, confectioners' sugar, baking powder, ginger, paprika, and salt into a large bowl. • Use a pastry blender to cut in the butter until the mixture resembles coarse crumbs. • Stir in the pecans, almonds, egg yolk, and corn syrup to form a smooth dough. • Press the dough into a disk, wrap in plastic wrap, and refrigerate for 30 minutes. • Preheat the oven to 350°F. • Line three cookie sheets with parchment paper. • Roll out the dough on a lightly floured surface to a thickness of 1/4 inch. • Use ghost-shaped, bat-shaped, and round cookie cutters to cut out the cookies. Gather the dough scraps, re-roll, and continue cutting out cookies until all the dough is used. • Use a spatula to transfer the cookies to the prepared cookie sheets, placing them 1 inch apart. • Bake, one sheet at a time, for 10–12 minutes, or until just golden at the edges. • Cool on the sheets until the cookies firm slightly. • Transfer to racks and let cool completely. • <u>Glaze</u>: Mix 1 1/3 cups confectioners' sugar with the lemon juice. • Divide the glaze in three and tint with the food colorings. • Keep white for ghosts, use black for bats, and mix red and yellow food coloring to make pumpkins. • Spread the glaze over the cookies. • Mix the remaining confectioners' sugar with the water and cocoa to make a spreading consistency. • Spoon the frosting into a small freezer bag and cut off a tiny corner. • Pipe over the cookies in a decorative manner to add eerie details.

Makes 50 cookies · Prep: 1 hr. + 30 min. to chill · Cooking: 10–12 min. per batch · Level: 2 · Keeps: 15 days

Halloween cookies

Mexican wedding cakes

mexican wedding cakes

These cookies are baked all year-round, not just for wedding celebrations.

1   cup (2 sticks) butter, softened
1³/4 cups confectioners' sugar
2¹/2 cups all-purpose flour
1   teaspoon vanilla extract
1   teaspoon almond extract
1   cup finely chopped pecans

Beat the butter and ³/4 cup confectioners' sugar in a large bowl with an electric mixer at high speed until creamy. • Mix in the flour, vanilla and almond extracts, and pecans. • Refrigerate for 30 minutes. • Preheat the oven to 350°F. • Butter three cookie sheets. • Form the dough into balls the size of walnuts and place 2 inches apart on the prepared cookie sheets. • Use the bottom of a glass to flatten them slightly. • Bake, one sheet at a time, for 12–15 minutes, or until lightly browned. • Transfer to racks and let cool completely. • Roll in the remaining 1 cup confectioners' sugar until well coated.

Makes 36 cookies · Prep: 35 min. + 30 min. to chill · Cooking: 12–15 min. per batch · Level: 1 · Keeps: 7 days

norwegian cardamom cookies

1¹/4 cups all-purpose flour
1/2   teaspoon ground cardamom
1/8   teaspoon salt
2   large eggs
³/4   cup granulated sugar
³/4   cup heavy cream

Sift the flour, cardamom, and salt into a medium bowl. • Beat the eggs and sugar in a large bowl with an electric mixer at high speed until pale and thick. • With mixer at high speed, beat the cream in a medium bowl until stiff. • Mix the dry ingredients into the egg batter, followed by folding in the cream, until well blended. • Lightly butter a krumkake iron and place over medium heat. • The iron is ready to use when a drop of water holds its shape on the surface of the iron. • Drop a tablespoon (or enough dough to fit your iron) of the cookie dough onto the center of the iron. • Lower the top so that the cookie dough spreads. • Cook for 1 minute, or until browned at the edges. • Lift up the top and, working quickly, remove the cookie from the iron with a krumkake roller. The cookie should be cone-shaped. • Repeat with the remaining cookie batter. • Let cool completely.

Makes 12 cookies · Prep: 20 min. · Cooking: 1 min. per cookie · Level: 3 · Keeps: 2 weeks

hansel and gretel lebkuchen

In Germany, Hansel and Gretel's gingerbread house is called a Lebkuchenhaus. It is traditionally made at Christmas and is kept on display until the feast of the Epiphany (January 6), when at last it can be devoured. These cookies have been developed from the original gingerbread house recipe.

12   cloves
1   piece (3-inch) cinnamon stick
      Seeds from 8 cardamom pods
1   blade mace
1/4   teaspoon freshly grated nutmeg
2   cups whole almonds
1/2   cup finely chopped candied lemon peel
1/2   cup finely chopped candied orange peel
      Grated zest of ¹/2 lemon
2¹/3 cups all-purpose flour
1   teaspoon baking powder
1/8   teaspoon salt
3   large eggs
1   cup granulated sugar
2   tablespoons honey
1   teaspoon kirsch

Light rum glaze
1   cup confectioners' sugar
1   tablespoon warm water
1/2   teaspoon white rum

Preheat the oven to 325°F. • Pound the cloves, cinnamon, cardamom seeds, mace, and nutmeg in a pestle and mortar until finely ground. • Spread the almonds on a large baking sheet. Toast for 7 minutes, or until lightly golden. • Finely chop the almonds. • Increase the oven temperature to 350°F. • Line three cookie sheets with rice paper. • Let the almonds cool completely and transfer to a medium bowl. • Stir in the candied lemon and orange peel, lemon zest, and ground spices. • Sift the flour, baking powder, and salt into a medium bowl. • Beat the eggs and sugar in a large bowl with an electric mixer at high speed until pale and thick. • Beat in the honey and almond mixture. • Add the kirsch. • Mix in the dry ingredients. • Drop rounded tablespoons of the mixture 2 inches apart onto the prepared cookie sheets. • Bake, one sheet at a time, for 15–20 minutes, or until lightly browned. • Cool on the sheets until the cookies firm slightly. • Transfer the cookies still on the rice paper to racks and let cool completely. • Tear away the excess rice paper from around the cookies. • Light rum glaze: Mix the confectioners' sugar, water, and rum in a small bowl until smooth. • Spread the glaze over the cookies and let stand for 30 minutes until set.

Makes 35–40 cookies · Prep: 50 min. + 30 min. to set · Cooking: 15–20 min. per batch · Level: 2 · Keeps: 4 weeks in a cool place

pizzelle cookies

1¹/4 cups all-purpose flour
1   teaspoon baking powder
1/8   teaspoon salt
2   large eggs
1³/4 cups granulated sugar
1   teaspoon vanilla extract
1/3   cup butter, melted

Preheat a pizzelle iron. • Sift the flour, baking powder, and salt into a medium bowl. • Beat the eggs and ³/4 cup sugar in a large bowl with an electric mixer at high speed until pale and thick. • Add the vanilla and butter. • Mix in the dry ingredients until well blended. • Drop 1¹/2 tablespoons of the batter onto the center of the iron. • Lower the top so that the batter spreads. • Cook for 1 minute, or until browned at the edges. • Lift up the top and remove the cookie from the iron. • Repeat with the remaining batter, stacking the cookies between sheets of waxed paper. • Let cool completely. • If you are using an electric pizzelle iron, follow the manufacturer's directions for preheating and baking.

Makes 22 cookies · Prep: 20 min. · Cooking: 1 min. per cookie · Level: 3 · Keeps: 2 weeks

prune hamantaschen

These cookies are made by Jewish families all over the world to enjoy during the festival of Purim. This holiday celebrates the biblical story of Esther, a virtuous girl who defeated the villainous Haman and saved the life of her uncle, Mordecai. The name of these triangular cookies is variously said to represent Haman's ears, pockets, and hat.

1½ cups vegetable shortening
1 cup granulated sugar
3 large eggs
3 tablespoons honey
2 tablespoons fresh lemon juice
1/3 cup cold water
1/2 teaspoon vanilla extract
4 cups all-purpose flour
1 lb dried pitted prunes, soaked overnight and drained
1¼ cups coarsely chopped walnuts
2 teaspoons ground cinnamon

Beat the shortening and 1/2 cup sugar in a large bowl with an electric mixer at high speed until creamy. • Add 2 eggs, beating until just blended. • Stir in the honey, 1 tablespoon lemon juice, water, and vanilla. • Mix in the flour to form a smooth dough. Press into a disk, cover with plastic wrap, and refrigerate for 30 minutes. • Preheat the oven to 375°F. • Butter three cookie sheets. • Chop the prunes coarsely. • Mix the prunes, walnuts, remaining 1 tablespoon lemon juice, 1 teaspoon cinnamon, and 1 tablespoon sugar in a small bowl. • Roll out the dough on a lightly floured surface to a thickness of 1/4 inch. • Use a 3-inch cookie cutter to cut out the cookies. Gather the dough scraps, re-roll, and continue cutting out cookies until all the dough is used. • Drop teaspoons of the prune mixture into the center of the cookies. • Lift up three sides of each circle to form a triangular shape, pinching the edges of the dough together to seal. • Beat the remaining egg and brush over the cookies. Mix the remaining 7 tablespoons sugar and 1 teaspoon cinnamon and sprinkle over the cookies. • Use a spatula to transfer the cookies to the cookie sheets, placing them 2 inches apart. • Bake, one sheet at a time, for 12–15 minutes, or until just golden at the edges. • Transfer to racks and let cool completely.

Makes 40–45 cookies · Prep: 25 min. + 30 min. to chill · Cooking: 12–15 min. per batch · Keeps: 7 days

christmas ball cookies

1 large egg, lightly beaten
1/2 cup granulated sugar
1/2 cup coarsely chopped pecans
1/2 cup coarsely chopped crystallized pineapple
1/2 cup shredded coconut, toasted
1/2 teaspoon vanilla extract
1/3 cup confectioners' sugar, to dust

Preheat the oven to 350°F. • Set out a 9 x 5-inch loaf pan. • Beat the egg and sugar in a large bowl with an electric mixer at high speed until creamy. • Mix in the pecans, pineapple, coconut, and vanilla until well blended. • Turn the mixture into the pan, smoothing the top. • Bake for 25–30 minutes, or until lightly browned. • Use a wooden spoon to mix the mixture after removing t from the oven. • Cool completely in the pan. • Form the mixture into balls the size of walnuts and roll in the confectioners' sugar.

Makes 18–20 cookies · Prep: 25 min. · Cooking: 25–30 min. · Level: 1 · Keeps: 3 days

ukrainian christmas cookies

In the Ukraine, it is traditional to decorate Christmas trees with cookies. You may vary the recipe by substituting colored sugar crystals for the candied cherries.

1/4 cup (1/2 stick) butter, cut up
1 tablespoon honey
1/3 cup firmly packed light brown sugar
1½ cups all-purpose flour
2 teaspoons ground cinnamon
1 teaspoon ground ginger
1/2 teaspoon baking soda
1/8 teaspoon salt
3 tablespoons milk
1 large egg, separated
2 tablespoons very finely chopped candied red and green cherries
Colored ribbons, to decorate

Melt the butter with the honey and brown sugar in a small saucepan over medium heat until the sugar has dissolved completely. Remove from the heat and let cool for 15 minutes. • Sift the flour, cinnamon, ginger, baking soda, and salt into a medium bowl and make a well in the center. Mix in the melted butter mixture, milk, and the egg yolk to form a stiff dough. Press the dough into a disk, wrap in plastic wrap, and refrigerate for 1 hour. • Preheat the oven to 350°F. • Line two cookie sheets with parchment paper. • Roll out the dough on a lightly floured surface to a thickness of 1/4 inch. • Use a 2-inch star-shaped cookie cutter to cut out the cookies. Gather the dough scraps, re-roll, and continue cutting out cookies until all the dough is used. • Use a spatula to transfer the cookies to the cookie sheets, placing them 1 inch apart. • Lightly beat the egg white in a small bowl and brush over the tops of the cookies. Sprinkle each cookie with the cherries. • Use a toothpick to make a hole in one point of each cookie. • Bake for 10–15 minutes, or until golden brown, rotating the sheets halfway through for even baking. • Cool on the sheets until the cookies firm slightly. Transfer to racks to cool. • Thread colored ribbons through the holes and hang on the Christmas tree.

Makes 25–30 cookies · Prep: 1 hr. + 1 hr. to chill · Cooking: 10–15 min. · Level: 1 · Keeps: 2 weeks

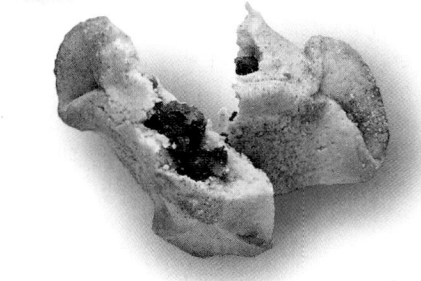

Prune hamantaschen

christmas mincemeat cookies

1¼ cups all-purpose flour
¼ teaspoon baking soda
⅛ teaspoon salt
⅓ cup butter, softened
¼ cup granulated sugar
¼ cup firmly packed light brown sugar
1 large egg
¾ cup Mincemeat (see page 340)
2 teaspoons brandy

Preheat the oven to 375°F. • Butter three cookie sheets. • Sift the flour, baking soda, and salt into a medium bowl. • Beat the butter and granulated and brown sugars in a large bowl with an electric mixer at high speed until creamy. • Add the egg, beating until just blended. • Mix in the dry ingredients, mincemeat, and brandy. • Drop heaped teaspoons of the dough 2 inches apart onto the prepared cookie sheets. • Bake, one sheet at a time, for 10–12 minutes, or until golden brown. Transfer to racks to cool.

Makes 40–50 cookies · Prep: 40 min. · Cooking: 10–12 min. per batch · Level: 1 · Keeps: 7 days

spritskransar

This Swedish Christmas cookie tastes like an almond shortbread. The dough can either be pressed out from a cookie press or piped.

1½ cups all-purpose flour
½ teaspoon baking powder
⅛ teaspoon salt
1 cup (2 sticks) butter, softened
½ cup granulated sugar
1 large egg yolk
½ teaspoon almond extract
⅓ cup finely ground almonds

Preheat the oven to 350°F. • Set out three cookie sheets. • Sift the flour, baking powder, and salt into a medium bowl. • Beat the butter and sugar in a large bowl with an electric mixer at high speed until creamy. • Add the egg yolk and almond extract, beating until just blended. • Mix in the dry ingredients and almonds until well blended. • Fit a pastry bag with a ½-inch star tip. Fill the pastry bag, twist the opening tightly closed, and squeeze out 2-inch rings onto the cookie sheets, spacing them 1 inch apart. • Bake, one sheet at a time, for 8–10 minutes, or until golden brown. • Cool on the sheets until the cookies firm slightly. Transfer to racks and let cool completely.

Makes 40–45 cookies · Prep: 25 min. · Cooking: 8–10 min. per batch · Level: 1 · Keeps: 2 weeks

traffic lights

These cookies, popular with young children, represent the international traffic-light sequence of red (stop), amber (caution), and green (go).

2⅓ cups all-purpose flour
⅛ teaspoon salt
¾ cup (1½ sticks) butter, softened
⅔ cup granulated sugar
1 large egg, lightly beaten
¾ cup confectioners' sugar
1 tablespoon warm water
   Few drops each red, green, and orange (red and yellow) food colorings
2 tablespoons raspberry preserves

Sift the flour and salt into a large bowl. • Beat the butter and granulated sugar in a large bowl with an electric mixer at high speed until creamy. • Add the egg, beating until just blended. • Mix in the dry ingredients to form a stiff dough. • Press the dough into a disk, wrap in plastic wrap, and refrigerate for 30 minutes. • Preheat the oven to 400°F. • Butter two cookie sheets. • Roll out the dough on a lightly floured surface to a thickness of ¼ inch. • Use a sharp knife to cut out forty 1 x 3-inch rectangles. • Use an apple corer to make three circular holes in half of the rectangles. • Use a spatula to transfer the cookies to the prepared cookie sheets, placing them ½ inch apart. • Bake for 15–20 minutes, or until just golden, rotating the sheets halfway through for even baking. • Transfer to racks to cool. • Mix the confectioners' sugar with the water in a small bowl to achieve a thick, spreading consistency. • Divide the icing into three bowls. • Use a wooden spoon to mix the red, green, and orange (or red and yellow) food colors alternately into the icings until no white streaks remain. • Warm the preserves in a small saucepan over low heat until liquid. • Use a thin metal spatula to spread the plain rectangles with the preserves. Place the rectangles with holes on top of the preserves. • Use a teaspoon to fill the three holes in each cookie with the red, orange, and green icing.

Makes 20 cookies · Prep: 40 min. + 30 min. to chill Cooking: 15–20 min. · Level: 2 · Keeps: 2 days

dominoes

¾ cup all-purpose flour
2 teaspoons unsweetened cocoa powder
⅛ teaspoon salt

¼ cup (½ stick) butter, cut up
⅓ cup granulated sugar
1 large egg, lightly beaten
Vanilla filling
¼ cup (½ stick) butter, softened
½ cup confectioners' sugar
½ teaspoon vanilla extract
Chocolate frosting
2 oz bittersweet chocolate, coarsely chopped
1 tablespoon milk
1 tablespoon water
¾ cup confectioners' sugar
Decorating frosting
⅓ cup confectioners' sugar
1 tablespoon lukewarm water

Preheat the oven to 375°F. • Butter a cookie sheet. • Sift the flour, cocoa, and salt into a medium bowl. • Use a pastry blender to cut in the butter until the mixture resembles fine crumbs. • Stir in the sugar. • Add the egg to form a stiff dough. Press into a disk, cover with plastic wrap, and refrigerate for 30 minutes. • Roll out the dough on a lightly floured surface to a thickness of ¼ inch. • Use a sharp knife to cut the dough into 2½ x 1½-inch rectangles. • Use a spatula to transfer the cookies to the prepared cookie sheet, placing them ½ inch apart. • Bake for 12–15 minutes, or until just colored at the edges. • Transfer to racks to cool. • Vanilla filling: Beat the butter, confectioners' sugar, and vanilla in a small bowl with an electric mixer at high speed until creamy. • Chocolate frosting: Melt the chocolate with the milk and water in a double boiler over barely simmering water, stirring often, until well blended. • Remove from the heat and beat in ¾ cup confectioners' sugar. • Stick the cookies together in pairs with the filling. • Use a thin metal spatula to spread the tops of the cookies with the chocolate frosting. Let stand for 30 minutes until set. • Decorating frosting: Beat ⅓ cup confectioners' sugar with the water to make a thick frosting. • Spoon the frosting into a small freezer bag and cut off a tiny corner. • Pipe a horizontal line across the center of each cookie and domino dots in each half square.

Makes 8–10 cookies · Prep: 40 min. + 60 min. to chill and set · Cooking: 12–15 min. · Level: 2 · Keeps: 2 days

Dominoes (top) and Traffic lights (bottom)

cherry christmas cookies

- 1¹/2 cups all-purpose flour
- ¹/2 teaspoon baking soda
- ¹/8 teaspoon salt
- ¹/2 cup (1 stick) butter, softened
- ³/4 cups firmly packed light brown sugar
- 2 large eggs
- 1¹/2 cups coarsely chopped pitted dates
- 1¹/2 cups coarsely chopped walnuts
- ¹/2 cup golden raisins
- ¹/4 cup whiskey
- 18 maraschino cherries, drained and cut in half

Preheat the oven to 350°F. • Butter two cookie sheets. • Sift the flour, baking soda, and salt into a large bowl. • Beat the butter and brown sugar in a large bowl with an electric mixer until creamy. • Add the eggs, beating until just blended. • Mix in the dry ingredients. • Stir in the dates, walnuts, raisins, and whiskey to form a stiff dough. • Drop teaspoons of the dough 2 inches apart onto the prepared cookie sheets. Top each cookie with a half cherry. • Bake for 8–10 minutes, or until lightly browned, rotating the sheets halfway through for even baking. • Transfer the cookies to racks to cool.

Makes 35 cookies · Prep: 20 min. · Cooking: 8–10 min. · Level: 1 · Keeps: 5 days

filled christmas trees

- 2 cups all-purpose flour
- ¹/4 teaspoon salt
- 1 cup (2 sticks) butter, softened
- ¹/3 cup milk
- ³/4 cup granulated sugar

Filling
- ¹/2 cup (1 stick) butter, softened
- ¹/2 teaspoon vanilla extract
- 2 cups confectioners' sugar
- 1¹/2 tablespoons milk
- Few drops green food coloring

Sift the flour and salt into a medium bowl. • Beat the butter in a large bowl with an electric mixer at high speed until creamy. • Mix in the dry ingredients and milk to form a smooth dough. • Press the dough into a disk, wrap in plastic wrap, and refrigerate for 30 minutes. • Preheat the oven to 375°F. • Set out three cookie sheets. • Roll out the dough on a lightly floured surface to a thickness of ¹/4 inch. • Use a 2-inch tree-shaped cookie cutter to cut out the cookies. Gather the dough scraps, re-roll, and continue cutting out cookies until all the dough is used. • Dip the cookies in the sugar and use a spatula to

transfer to the cookie sheets, placing them 1 inch apart. • Bake, one sheet at a time, for 8–10 minutes, or until just golden at the edges. • Cool on the sheets until the cookies firm slightly. Transfer to racks and let cool completely. • Filling: With mixer at high speed, beat the butter and vanilla in a medium bowl until creamy. • Beat in the confectioners' sugar and milk until well blended. • Add the green food coloring until no white streaks remain. • Stick the cookies together in pairs with the filling.

Makes 24 cookies · Prep: 45 min. + 30 min. to chill · Cooking: 8–10 min. per batch · Level: 1 · Keeps: 4 days

passover brownies

Passover is a Jewish festival celebrated in the spring, commemorating the freedom of the Jewish slaves from Egypt.

- 5 large eggs
- 2¹/2 cups granulated sugar
- 1¹/4 cups vegetable oil
- 1¹/4 cups matzo meal
- 1¹/2 cups unsweetened cocoa powder
- 1¹/4 cups finely chopped pecans

Preheat the oven to 325°F. • Oil a 13 x 9-inch baking pan. • Beat the eggs and sugar in a large bowl with an electric mixer at high speed until pale and thick. • Beat in the oil until well blended. • Mix in the matzo meal and cocoa. • Pour the batter into the prepared pan and sprinkle with the pecans. • Bake for 30–35 minutes, or until dry on top and almost firm to the touch. Do not overbake. • Cool completely before cutting into bars.

Makes 36–45 bars · Prep: 25 min.· Cooking: 30–35 min. · Level: 1 · Keeps: 4 days

dutch butter diamonds

- 2 cups all-purpose flour
- 1 teaspoon ground cinnamon
- 1 teaspoon ground ginger
- ¹/8 teaspoon salt
- 1 cup (2 sticks) butter, softened
- 1 cup granulated sugar
- 1 teaspoon almond extract
- 1 large egg, separated
- 1 tablespoon cold water
- 1 cup finely chopped walnuts

Preheat the oven to 350°F. • Butter a 10¹/2 x 15¹/2-inch jelly-roll pan. • Sift the flour, cinnamon, ginger, and salt into a medium bowl. • Beat the butter and sugar in a large bowl with an electric mixer at high speed until creamy. • Add the almond extract and

egg yolk, beating until just blended. • Mix in the dry ingredients to form a smooth dough. • Firmly press the dough into the prepared pan to form a smooth, even layer. • Beat the egg white and water in a small bowl and brush it over the dough. Sprinkle with walnuts. • Score the dough into 1-inch diamonds. • Bake for 15–20 minutes, or until lightly browned. • Cool completely in the pan. • Cut along the lines and divide into diamonds.

Makes 18 cookies · Prep: 20 min. · Cooking: 15–20 min. · Level: 1 · Keeps: 2 weeks

stained glass cookies

Pierce a small hole in these cookies before baking them so you can thread them with colored ribbon and hang them on your Christmas tree.

- 1¹/4 cups all-purpose flour
- ¹/8 teaspoon salt
- ¹/2 cup (1 stick) butter, softened
- ¹/3 cup confectioners' sugar
- 1 tablespoon milk
- ¹/2 teaspoon vanilla extract
- 1¹/4 cups (5 oz) assorted clear, hard, colored candies, such as lollipops

Mix the flour, salt, butter, confectioners' sugar, milk, and vanilla in a large bowl. • Turn out the dough onto a lightly floured surface and knead until smooth. • Return to the bowl, cover with plastic wrap, and refrigerate for 30 minutes. • Preheat the oven to 400°F. • Line two cookie sheets with parchment paper. • Roll out the dough on a lightly floured surface to a thickness of ¹/8 inch. • Use a 2-inch star-shaped cookie cutter to cut out the cookies. Use a 1-inch star-shaped cutter to cut out the centers. • Gather the dough scraps, re-roll, and continue cutting out cookies until all the dough is used. • Use a spatula to transfer the cookies to the prepared sheets, placing them ¹/2 inch apart. • Bake for 8–10 minutes, or until just golden, rotating the sheets halfway through for even baking. • Lightly crush the candy and arrange the candy into the cookie centers. • Bake for 3–5 minutes, or until the candy has melted. • Cool on the sheets for 10 minutes. • Transfer to racks and let cool completely.

Makes 16–20 cookies · Prep: 50 min. + 30 min. to chill · Cooking: 11–15 min · Level: 3 · Keeps: 2 weeks

Stained glass cookies

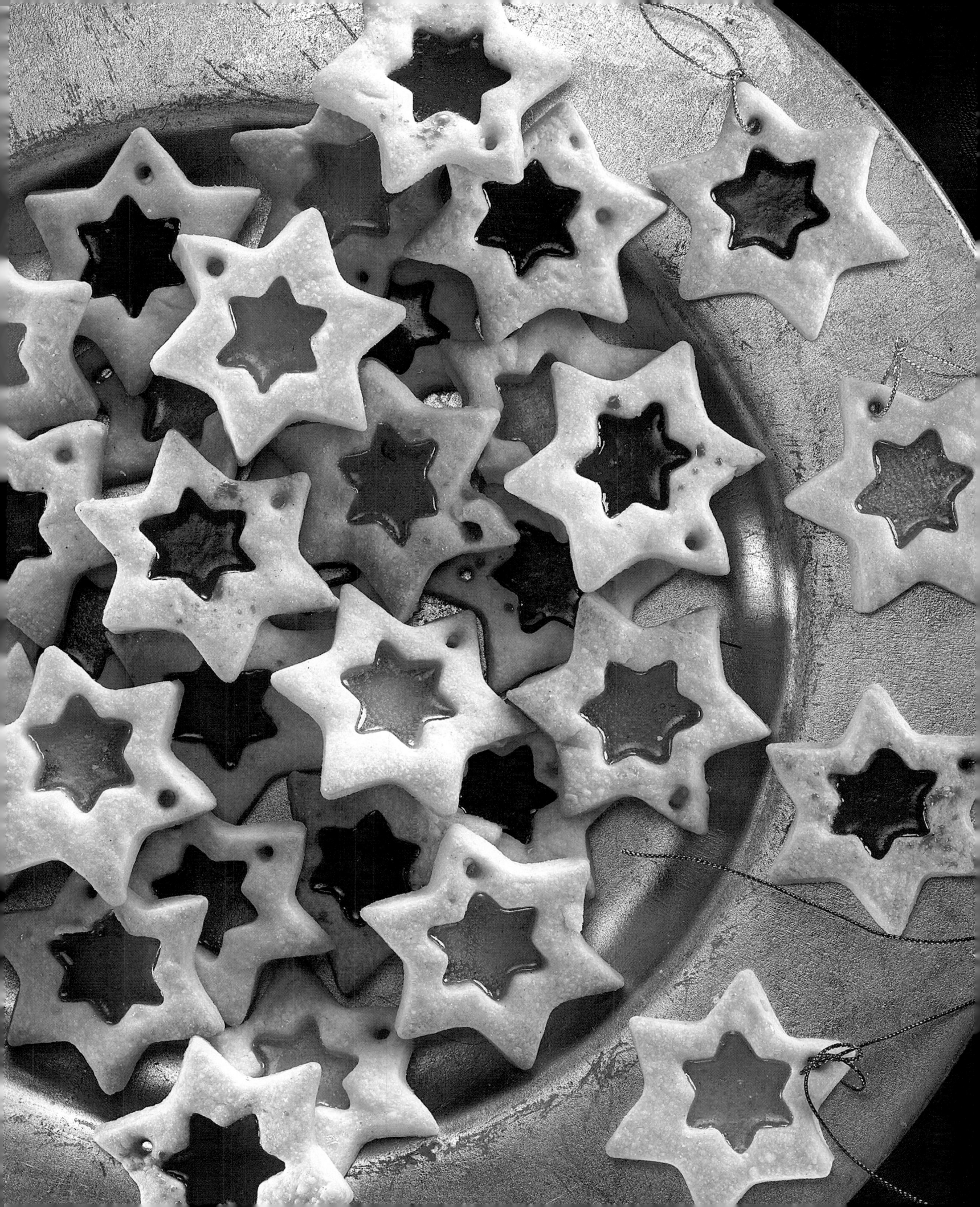

marmalade gingerbread squares

1¹/₂ cups all-purpose flour
2 teaspoons ground ginger
1 teaspoon baking powder
1 teaspoon ground cinnamon
¹/₈ teaspoon salt
1 cup light corn syrup
¹/₄ cup (¹/₂ stick) butter
1 cup orange marmalade
I large egg, lightly beaten
2 tablespoons hot water

Preheat the oven to 325°F. • Line a 13 x 9-inch baking pan with aluminum foil, letting the edges overhang. Butter the foil. • Sift the flour, ginger, baking powder, cinnamon, and salt into a medium bowl. • Heat the corn syrup and butter in a small saucepan over low heat. Cook, stirring constantly until the butter has melted. • Mix into the dry ingredients until well blended. • Stir in the marmalade, egg, and enough hot water to form a soft dough. • Spread the mixture in the prepared pan. • Bake for 45–55 minutes, or until a toothpick inserted into the center comes out clean. • Cool completely in the pan on a rack. • Using the foil as handles, lift onto a cutting board. Peel off the foil. • Cut into squares.

Makes 36–45 squares · Prep: 20 min. · Cooking: 45–55 min. · Level: 1 · Keeps: 5 days

springerle

These traditional Christmas cookies from Germany and Switzerland are beautifully detailed. Springerle pins, which are patterned rolling pins, can be bought from the mail-order specialists, Maid of Scandinavia.

1¹/₂ cups confectioners' sugar
1¹/₂ cups all-purpose flour
¹/₄ teaspoon baking powder
¹/₈ teaspoon salt
2 large eggs
2 teaspoons butter, softened
1 tablespoon ground aniseeds

Butter two cookie sheets. • Sift the confectioners' sugar into a medium bowl. • Sift the flour, baking powder, and salt into a separate medium bowl. • Beat the eggs in a large bowl with an electric mixer at medium speed until frothy. • Gradually beat in the confectioners' sugar, butter, and aniseeds until pale and thick. • Mix in the dry ingredients to form a stiff dough. • Knead the dough on a lightly floured surface until smooth. Roll out the dough on a lightly floured surface to a thickness of ¹/₄ inch. • Dust a springerle pin with flour and firmly roll over the dough to imprint the patterns. Cut off any surplus dough and separate the printed squares with a knife. • Use a spatula to transfer the cookies to the prepared cookie sheets, placing them 2 inches apart. • Let stand in a cool place for 24 hours. • Preheat the oven to 300°F. • Bake, one sheet at a time, for 15–25 minutes, or until just golden. • Transfer to racks and let cool completely.

Makes 25 cookies · Prep: 40 min. + 24 hr. to rest · Cooking: 15–25 min. per batch · Level: 2 · Keeps: 5 days

christmas ginger cookies

2¹/₃ cups all-purpose flour
1 teaspoon baking powder
1 teaspoon unsweetened cocoa powder
1 teaspoon ground ginger
1 cup raw sugar (Demerara or Barbados)
1 large egg
¹/₂ cup (1 stick) butter, melted
2 tablespoons milk
¹/₂ teaspoon vanilla extract

Sift the flour, baking powder, cocoa, ginger, and salt into a large bowl. Use a wooden spoon to mix in the raw sugar, egg, butter, milk, and vanilla to form a soft dough. • Press the dough into a disk, wrap in plastic wrap, and refrigerate for 30 minutes. • Preheat the oven to 350°F. • Butter two cookie sheets. • Roll out the dough on a lightly floured surface to a thickness of ¹/₄ inch. • Use Christmas cookie cutters to cut out the cookies. Use a spatula to transfer the cookies to the prepared cookie sheets, placing them 1 inch apart. Prick all over with a fork. • Bake for 8–10 minutes, or until just golden, rotating the sheets halfway for even baking. • Transfer to racks and let cool completely.

Makes 25 cookies · Prep: 40 min. + 30 min. to chill Cooking: 8–10 min. · Level: 1 · Keeps: 10 days

christmas wreaths

1¹/₃ cups all-purpose flour
¹/₈ teaspoon salt
¹/₂ cup (1 stick) butter, softened
6 tablespoons granulated sugar
1 large egg, separated
1 teaspoon finely grated orange zest
3 green candied cherries and 3 red candied cherries, finely chopped, to decorate

Preheat the oven to 400°F. • Butter two cookie sheets. • Sift the flour and salt into a medium bowl. • Beat the butter and ¹/₄ cup sugar in a large bowl with an electric mixer at high speed until creamy. • Add the egg yolk, beating until just blended. • Mix in the dry ingredients and orange zest. • Form tablespoons of the dough into 6-inch ropes. • Shape into circles with slightly overlapping ends and place 1 inch apart on the prepared cookie sheets. • Brush with the egg white and sprinkle with the remaining 2 tablespoons sugar. • Decorate with the cherries. • Bake for 10–12 minutes, or until lightly browned, rotating the sheets halfway through for even baking. • Cool on the sheets until the cookies firm slightly. Transfer to racks and let cool completely.

Makes 24 cookies · Prep: 40 min. · Cooking: 10–12 min. · Level: 1 · Keeps: 7 days

chocolate-drizzled almond cookies

2 cups all-purpose flour
³/₄ teaspoon ground cinnamon
¹/₂ teaspoon baking powder
¹/₄ teaspoon salt
3 tablespoons butter
¹/₄ cup milk
2 tablespoons brandy
1 cup finely ground almonds + 1 cup finely chopped almonds
¹/₂ cup firmly packed light brown sugar
6 oz semisweet chocolate, coarsely chopped

Sift the flour, cinnamon, baking powder, and salt into a medium bowl. • Melt the butter in a medium saucepan over low heat. • Remove from the heat and stir in the milk and brandy. • Mix in the dry ingredients, finely ground almonds, and brown sugar. • Form the dough into a log 2 inches in diameter, wrap in plastic wrap, and refrigerate for 15 minutes. • Unwrap and roll in the finely chopped almonds. • Rewrap the log and refrigerate for 30 minutes. • Preheat the oven to 375°F. • Butter three cookie sheets. • Slice the dough ¹/₄ inch thick and place 1 inch apart on the prepared cookie sheets. • Bake, one sheet at a time, for 8–10 minutes, or until just golden. • Transfer to racks and let cool completely. • Melt the chocolate in a double boiler over barely simmering water. • Spoon the chocolate into a small freezer bag and cut off a tiny corner. • Drizzle over the cookies.

Makes 36 cookies · Prep: 40 min. + 45 min. to chill · Cooking: 8–10 min. per batch · Level: 1 · Keeps: 7 days

Chocolate-drizzled almond cookies (top) and Marmalade gingerbread squares (bottom)

no-bake cookies

For those with limited cooking facilities, these no-bake recipes provide a happy alternative. Chilled or made at room temperature, these cookies are loaded with fruit and candy, tasting as great as their oven-baked counterparts. Pack these simple treats for picnics and your children's lunchboxes.

above: No-bake date–banana squares (page 324)

right: No-bake pistachio moons, No-bake chocolate–raisin bars, and Chocolate corn flake cakes (pages 329, 328, and 328)

no-bake crunchy peanut bars

1¼ cups light corn syrup
1 cup smooth peanut butter
1 cup bran flakes
2 cups coarsely chopped peanuts
8 oz semisweet chocolate,
  coarsely chopped

Butter an 11 x 7-inch baking pan. • Bring the corn syrup to a boil with the peanut butter in a medium saucepan over low heat, stirring constantly. • Remove from the heat and mix in the bran flakes and peanuts until well coated. • Spoon the mixture into the prepared pan. • Refrigerate for at least 1 hour, or until set. • Melt the chocolate in a double boiler over barely simmering water. • Drizzle the melted chocolate over the peanut base and let stand for 30 minutes until set. • Cut into bars.

Makes 22–33 bars · Prep: 25 min. + 90 min. to chill and set · Level: 1 · Keeps: 5 days in the refrigerator

mallow macadamia crunchies

7 oz milk chocolate, coarsely chopped
3½ oz semisweet chocolate,
  coarsely chopped
3 tablespoons butter, cut up
2½ oz mini marshmallows
½ cup graham cracker crumbs
1 cup coarsely chopped macadamia nuts
½ cup coarsely chopped Brazil nuts

Melt the milk and semisweet chocolates and butter in a double boiler over barely

simmering water. • Remove from the heat and let cool for 15 minutes. • Mix in the marshmallows, graham cracker crumbs, and macadamia and Brazil nuts until well coated. • Set out two large sheets of plastic wrap and place a 10-inch square piece of parchment paper on top of each. • Pour half of the mixture onto the center of one piece of parchment paper. • Wrap up tightly in the paper and plastic wrap, squeezing it into a log. • Repeat with the remaining mixture. • Refrigerate for 1 hour, or until firm. • Leave at room temperature for 10 minutes. • Cut the mixture into ½-inch thick slices.

Makes 40 cookies · Prep: 40 min. + 60 min. to chill Level: 1 · Keeps: 10 days

chocolate crunch wedges

¼ cup (½ stick) butter, cut up
4 oz semisweet chocolate,
  coarsely chopped
¼ cup light corn syrup
⅓ cup corn flakes
2 tablespoons shredded coconut

Butter an 8-inch round cake pan and line with waxed paper. • Melt the butter and chocolate with the corn syrup in a medium saucepan over low heat. • Stir in the corn flakes and coconut until well blended. • Spoon into the prepared pan, pressing down lightly. • Refrigerate for 3 hours. • Use a sharp knife to cut into wedges.

Makes 8 cookies · Prep: 15 min. + 3 hr. to chill · Level: 1 · Keeps: 2 days

Chocolate crunch wedges

coffee–pecan wedges

⅓ cup butter, cut up
2 tablespoons granulated sugar
1¾ cups graham cracker crumbs
1 cup coarsely chopped pecans
1 tablespoon freeze-dried coffee granules
  dissolved in 1 tablespoon hot water
2 tablespoons plain yogurt

Set out an 8-inch springform pan. • Melt the butter with the sugar in a small saucepan over low heat until the sugar has dissolved completely. • Remove from the heat and mix in the graham cracker crumbs, pecans, coffee, and yogurt. • Firmly press the mixture into the prepared pan to form a smooth, even layer. • Refrigerate for at least 1 hour, or until set. • Loosen and remove the pan sides and cut into wedges.

Makes 16 cookies · Prep: 20 min. + 60 min. to chill Level: 1 · Keeps: 3 days in the refrigerator

carob truffle squares

½ cup (1 stick) butter, cut up
1 tablespoon dark brown sugar
⅓ cup carob powder
2 tablespoons light corn syrup
2 cups graham cracker crumbs
1 cup raisins
8 oz carob, coarsely chopped

Set out an 8-inch square baking pan. • Melt the butter with the brown sugar, carob powder, and corn syrup in a small saucepan over low heat until the sugar has dissolved completely. • Mix in the graham cracker crumbs and raisins. • Spread the mixture evenly into the pan. • Melt the carob in a double boiler over barely simmering water. • Use a thin metal spatula to spread the carob over the mixture. • Refrigerate for 4 hours, or until firm. • Cut into squares.

Makes 16–25 squares · Prep: 25 min. + 4 hr. to chill · Level: 1 · Keeps: 2 days in the refrigerator

fruity praline squares

¾ cup granulated sugar
1 tablespoon Vanilla Sugar (see page 341)
⅓ cup butter
1 tablespoon honey
2 oz marzipan, grated
¾ cup toasted hazelnuts, finely chopped
1 cup toasted almonds, coarsely chopped
⅔ cup candied cherries, finely chopped
3 tablespoons candied lemon peel,
  finely chopped
1 tablespoon pistachios, crushed
⅛ teaspoon salt
3 oz dark chocolate, coarsely chopped

Line a large baking sheet with aluminum foil. Oil the foil. • Melt both sugars in a medium saucepan over low heat. Stir in the butter, honey, and marzipan. • Add the hazelnuts, almonds, candied cherries, lemon peel, pistachios, and salt. Cook, stirring constantly, for 3–5 minutes until well mixed. • Pour the mixture onto the foil. • Flatten the mixture and spread it out to a thickness of $1/2$ inch. • Set aside to cool. • Use a sharp knife to cut into $3/4$-inch squares. • Melt the chocolate in a double boiler over barely simmering water. • Dip the praline squares into the chocolate to half coat.

Makes 50–60 squares · Prep: 60 min. · Level: 1 · Keeps: 15–20 days

chocolate–pistachio squares

$2^{1/4}$ cups granulated sugar
$2/3$ cup milk
$2/3$ cup butter, cut up
3 oz semisweet chocolate, coarsely chopped
2 tablespoons honey
$1/3$ cup pistachios, crushed
1 cup old-fashioned rolled oats

Butter an 8-inch square baking pan. • Stir the sugar, milk, butter, chocolate, and honey in a large saucepan over low heat until the ingredients have blended. • Wash down the sides of the pan with a pastry brush dipped in cold water to prevent sugar crystals from forming. Cook, without stirring, until the mixture reaches 238°F, or the soft-ball stage. • Remove from the heat and let cool for 5 minutes. • Stir in the pistachios and oats until creamy. • Pour the mixture into the prepared pan. • Use a sharp knife to score into 36 squares. • Let stand for at least 4 hours, or until firm to the touch.

Makes 36 squares · Prep: 45 min. + 4 hr. to set · Level: 1 · Keeps: 20–30 days if stored lined with waxed paper

no-bake chocolate fruit squares

$1/2$ cup (1 stick) butter, cut up
3 tablespoons light corn syrup
2 tablespoons unsweetened cocoa powder
$2/3$ cup golden raisins
$1/3$ cup candied cherries, coarsely chopped
10 oz plain, fine-textured cookies, broken into small pieces
10 oz semisweet chocolate, coarsely chopped

Set out a 9-inch baking pan. • Melt the butter with the corn syrup and cocoa in a small saucepan over medium heat. • Stir in the raisins and cherries until well blended. • Add the broken cookies and stir until well mixed. • Spread the mixture evenly in the pan, pressing down lightly. • Melt the chocolate in a double boiler over barely simmering water. Pour the melted chocolate over the cookie mixture and use a fork to create a swirly decorative effect. • Set aside for 12 hours in a cool place to set completely. • Use a long sharp knife to cut into squares.

Makes 10 squares · Prep: 15 min. + 12 hr. to set · Level: 1 · Keeps: 3 days in the refrigerator

chocolate-fruit chewies

$1/2$ cup (1 stick) butter, cut up
$1/2$ cup granulated sugar
$1^{3/4}$ cups finely chopped pitted dates
$2/3$ cup finely chopped candied cherries
$1/3$ cup golden raisins
2 cups rice krispies
8 oz semisweet chocolate, coarsely chopped

Set out a $10^{1/2}$ x $15^{1/2}$-inch jelly-roll pan. • Melt the butter and sugar in a large saucepan over medium heat. • Remove from the heat and stir in the dates, cherries, raisins, and rice krispies until well coated. •

Spoon the mixture evenly into the pan, pressing down firmly. • Refrigerate for 2 hours, or until set. • Melt the chocolate in a double boiler over barely simmering water. Pour the chocolate over and let stand for 20 minutes until set. • Use a sharp knife to cut into squares.

Makes 16 squares · Prep: 40 min. + 2 hr. 20 min. to chill and set · Level: 1 · Keeps: 2 days

chocolate–cherry squares

$1/4$ cup ($1/2$ stick) butter, cut up
7 oz semisweet chocolate, coarsely chopped
3 tablespoons light corn syrup
2 cups graham cracker crumbs
1 cup coarsely chopped walnuts

Line an 8-inch baking pan with waxed paper. • Melt the butter and chocolate with the corn syrup in a double boiler over barely simmering water. • Stir in the graham cracker crumbs and walnuts and mix until well blended. • Firmly press the mixture into the prepared pan. • Refrigerate for 3 hours. • Use a sharp knife to cut into bars, peeling off the paper.

Makes 16–25 bars · Prep: 15 min. + 3 hr. to chill · Level: 1 · Keeps: 2 days

No-bake chocolate fruit squares

no-bake date–banana squares

Simple yet nutritious—your family will love these.

2 tablespoons fresh lemon juice
2 tablespoons honey
2/3 cup water
2 1/4 cups coarsely chopped pitted dates
2 1/4 cups coarsely chopped bananas
1/3 cup butter, cut up
1 cup firmly packed light brown sugar
1 1/4 cups old-fashioned rolled oats

Bring the lemon juice, honey, and water to a boil with the dates and banana in a medium saucepan over medium heat. • Reduce the heat and simmer over low heat for 25–30 minutes, or until the fruit has softened. • Remove from the heat and let cool for 15 minutes. • Butter an 8-inch baking pan. • Melt the butter with the brown sugar in a medium saucepan over low heat until the sugar has dissolved completely. • Mix in the oats until well coated. • Firmly press half the oat mixture into the prepared pan to form a smooth, even layer. Spoon the date mixture evenly over the base and cover with the remaining oat mixture. • Cool completely before cutting into squares.

Makes 16–25 squares · Prep: 50–55 min. · Level: 1 Keeps: 3 days

no-bake chocolate mice

These easy-to-make novelty cookies look extra-special on the table for your children's birthday parties.

4 oz semisweet chocolate, coarsely chopped
1/3 cup heavy cream
1 cup chocolate wafer crumbs
1/3 cup confectioners' sugar
24 silver balls, to decorate
24 flaked almonds, to decorate
Red licorice whips, to decorate

Melt the chocolate with the cream in a double boiler over barely simmering water. • Mix in the chocolate wafer crumbs until well blended. • Cover with plastic wrap and refrigerate for 1 hour, or until firm. • Form the dough into balls the size of tangerines, tapering one end to resemble the nose. • Roll half the balls in the confectioners' sugar until well coated. • Decorate all with the silver balls to resemble the eyes, almonds for ears, and a small length of licorice for the tail. • Refrigerate for 2 hours.

Makes 12 cookies · Prep: 20 min. + 3 hr. to chill · Level: 1 · Keeps: 2 days in the refrigerator

no-bake carob brownies

These crumbly squares are delicious with herbal tea.

1 cup honey
3/4 cup old-fashioned rolled oats
1/2 cup carob powder
1/4 cup sesame seeds
1/4 cup sunflower seeds
1 cup finely chopped walnuts

Line an 8-inch baking pan with aluminum foil. • Warm the honey in a small saucepan over low heat until liquid. • Mix the oats, carob powder, sesame seeds, sunflower seeds, honey, and walnuts in a large bowl. • Firmly press the mixture into the prepared pan to form a smooth, even layer. • Refrigerate for 1 hour, or until set. • Cut into squares.

Makes 16–25 squares · Prep: 20 min. + 60 min. to chill · Level: 1 · Keeps: 4 days

no-bake apricot–banana squares

2 tablespoons fresh lemon juice
2 tablespoons honey
2/3 cup water
2 1/4 cups coarsely chopped dried apricots
2 1/4 cups coarsely chopped bananas
1/3 cup butter, cut up
1 cup firmly packed light brown sugar
1 1/4 cups corn flakes

Bring the lemon juice, honey, and water to a boil with the apricots and bananas in a medium saucepan over medium heat. • Reduce the heat and simmer over low heat for 25–30 minutes, or until the fruit has softened. • Remove from the heat and let cool for 15 minutes. • Butter an 8-inch baking pan. • Melt the butter with the brown sugar in a medium saucepan over low heat until the sugar has dissolved completely. • Mix in the corn flakes until well coated. • Firmly press half the corn flake mixture into the prepared pan to form a smooth, even layer. Spoon the apricot mixture evenly over the base and cover with the remaining corn flake mixture. • Cool completely before cutting into squares.

Makes 16–25 squares · Prep: 50–55 min. · Level: 1 Keeps: 3 days

crunchy cereal and fruit squares

1 cup light cream
1/3 cup pure maple syrup
2/3 cup firmly packed dark brown sugar

1 tablespoon butter
1 cup corn flakes
1/2 cup flaked almonds
1/4 cup shredded coconut
3/4 cup finely chopped dried unsweetened banana chips
1/2 cup coarsely chopped dried apricots

Butter an 11 x 7-inch baking pan. • Cook the cream, maple syrup, brown sugar, and butter in a medium saucepan over low heat, stirring often, until the sugar has dissolved completely. • Bring to a boil and boil for 10 minutes. • Stir in the corn flakes, almonds, coconut, banana chips, and apricots. • Firmly press the mixture into the prepared pan to form an even layer. • Refrigerate for at least 2 hours. • Cut into squares.

Makes 22 squares · Prep: 25 min. + 2 hr. to chill · Level: 1 · Keeps: 2 days in the refrigerator

crunchy snowmen

To create a unique decorative effect, order festive-shaped sprinkles, such as snowflakes or Christmas trees, from a specialty baking store.

1/2 cup (1 stick) butter, cut up
3 cups mini marshmallow pieces
6 cups rice krispies cereal
8 oz white chocolate, coarsely chopped
1/4 cup snowflake sprinkles (optional)
Black and red licorice, to decorate

Line a 10 1/2 x 15 1/2-inch jelly-roll pan with aluminum foil. • Melt the butter with the marshmallows in a small saucepan over low heat. • Remove from the heat and stir in the rice krispies. • Lightly press the mixture into the prepared pan. • Refrigerate for 30 minutes, or until firmly set. • Use a snowman-shaped cookie cutter or 2-inch and 3-inch cookie cutters to cut out the cookies. • Press craft sticks into the base of the cookies to form handles. • Melt the white chocolate in a double boiler over barely simmering water. • Spread the chocolate over the tops of the cookies and decorate with the snowflakes, if using, and licorice to form eyes and mouths. • Let stand for 30 minutes until set.

Makes 10–12 cookies · Prep: 25 min. + 60 min. to chill and stand · Level: 1 · Keeps: 7 days

Crunchy cereal and fruit bars

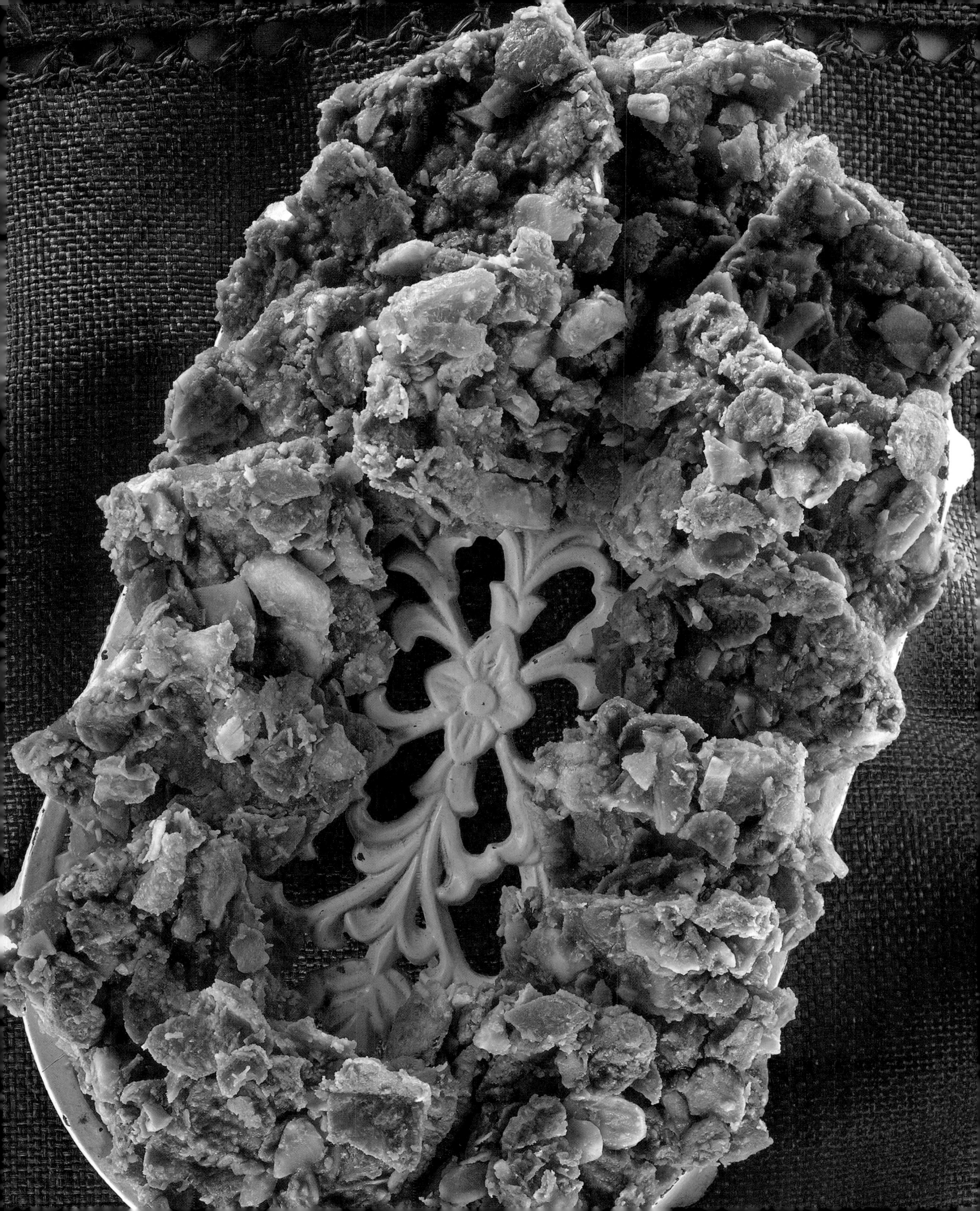

No-bake multicolored squares

no-bake multicolored squares

Bursting with color and goodness—these squares are ideal for packed lunches.

10 oz semisweet chocolate, coarsely chopped
2 cups graham cracker crumbs
1/2 cup finely chopped green and red candied cherries
1/2 cup finely chopped pitted dates
1/2 cup finely chopped dried apricots
2 oz white chocolate, finely chopped
1/2 cup coarsely chopped almonds

Butter a 9-inch square baking pan. • Melt the semisweet chocolate in a double boiler over barely simmering water. • Transfer to a large bowl and mix in the graham cracker crumbs, 1/4 cup candied cherries, 1/4 cup dates, and 1/4 cup apricots. • Firmly press the mixture into the prepared pan to form a smooth layer. • Sprinkle with the remaining 1/4 cup candied cherries, 1/4 cup dates, 1/4 cup apricots, white chocolate, and almonds. • Refrigerate for 1 hour, or until firm to the touch. • Cut into squares.

Makes 16–25 squares · Prep: 20 min. + 60 min. to chill · Level: 1 · Keeps: 5 days in the refrigerator

no-bake chocolate squares

6 oz semisweet chocolate, coarsely chopped
1/4 cup (1/2 stick) butter, cut up
2 tablespoon light corn syrup
2 cups graham cracker crumbs

Butter an 8-inch baking pan. • Melt the chocolate and butter with the corn syrup in a double boiler over barely simmering water. • Mix in the graham cracker crumbs. • Firmly press the mixture into the prepared pan. • Refrigerate for 2 hours, or until set. • Cut into squares.

Makes 16–25 bars · Prep: 20 min. + 2 hr. to chill · Level: 1 · Keeps: 5 days in the refrigerator

no-bake smilies and spookies

Smiley cookies are fun for children to make for birthday parties. They can be easily adapted to create spooky horrors at Halloween.

1 3/4 cups graham cracker crumbs
3/4 cup granulated sugar
1/4 cup unsweetened cocoa powder
1/2 cup finely ground almonds
1/3 cup butter, melted
2 tablespoons milk, + more as needed

Colored butter icing
1/2 cup (1 stick) butter, softened
1 2/3 cups confectioners' sugar
1/2 teaspoon vanilla extract (optional)
Few drops each blue, yellow, or red food coloring
Small candies, licorice whips, and candied cherries, to decorate

Mix the graham cracker crumbs, sugar, cocoa, and almonds in a large bowl. • Stir in the melted butter and enough milk to form a stiff dough. • Divide the mixture into 15 pieces and form into balls the size of walnuts. • Flatten into 1-inch thick rounds. • Colored butter icing: Beat the butter, confectioners' sugar, and vanilla in a large bowl with an electric mixer at high speed until creamy. • Divide into three small bowls. Add the food coloring to each bowl. Mix pale colors for smiley faces and deep blue and red icing for a spooky design. • Spread the icing over the tops of the cookies. • Decorate with candies or candied cherries to resemble eyes and noses. • Cut up the licorice whips into short lengths to resemble smiley mouths, hair, and other decorative details.

Makes 15 cookies · Prep: 25 min. · Level: 1 · Keeps: 4 days in the refrigerator

no-bake hazelnut–chocolate squares

1/2 cup whole hazelnuts
5 oz semisweet chocolate, coarsely chopped
2/3 cup butter, cut up
1/8 teaspoon salt
1 1/4 cups graham cracker crumbs

Preheat the oven to 325°F. • Butter an 8-inch square baking pan. • Spread the nuts on a large baking sheet. Toast for 7 minutes, or until lightly golden. • Transfer to a large cotton kitchen towel. Fold the towel over the nuts and rub these through the towel to remove the thin inner skins. Pick out the nuts and chop coarsely. • Melt the chocolate with the butter and salt in a double boiler over barely simmering water. • Remove from the heat and mix in the graham cracker crumbs and chopped hazelnuts until well coated. • Firmly press the mixture into the prepared pan to form a smooth, even layer. • Refrigerate for at least 1 hour, or until set. • Cut into bars.

Makes 16–25 bars · Prep: 25 min. + 60 min. to chill Level: 1 · Keeps: 5 days in the refrigerator

no-bake chocolate crumb drops

3 oz semisweet chocolate, coarsely chopped
1/4 cup (1/2 stick) butter, cut up
1 tablespoon dark rum
1 1/2 cups cake crumbs
3/4 cup coarsely chopped red and green candied cherries
1/4 cup golden raisins

Line a cookie sheet with parchment paper. • Melt the chocolate with the butter and rum in a double boiler over barely simmering water. • Mix in the cake crumbs, candied cherries, and golden raisins to form a soft dough. • Drop tablespoons of the mixture onto the prepared cookie sheet. • Refrigerate for at least 1 hour, or until firm to the touch.

Makes 15–18 cookies · Prep: 25 min. + 60 min. to chill · Level: 1 · Keeps: 5 days in the refrigerator

no-bake peanut–orange squares

- 1/4 cup (1/2 stick) butter, cut up
- 1/4 cup firmly packed light brown sugar
- 3 tablespoons honey
- 1/4 cup smooth peanut butter
  Grated zest of 1 orange
- 1 cup rice krispies

Butter an 8-inch square baking pan. • Melt the butter with the brown sugar, honey, and peanut butter in a large saucepan over low heat until the sugar has dissolved completely. • Remove from the heat and mix in the orange zest and rice krispies until well coated. • Press the mixture lightly into the prepared pan. • Let set for 30 minutes before cutting into squares.

Makes 16–25 squares · Prep: 20 min. + 30 min. to set · Level: 1 · Keeps: 7 days

white chocolate and amaretti crunch

- 10 oz white chocolate, coarsely chopped
- 2/3 cup butter, cut up
- 1/4 cup heavy cream
- 3 oz amaretti cookies, crushed
- 2 tablespoons shredded coconut
- 1 cup coarsely chopped candied cherries
- 1/2 cup flaked almonds, toasted

Line an 8-inch square baking pan with parchment paper. • Melt the white chocolate with the butter and cream in a double boiler over barely simmering water. • Mix in the amaretti cookies, coconut, cherries, and almonds until well coated. • Spoon into the prepared pan, spreading it evenly. • Refrigerate for 4 hours, or until set. • Use a knife dipped in hot water to cut into bars.

Makes 20 bars · Prep: 30 min. + 4 hr. to chill · Level: 1 · Keeps: 1 week in the refrigerator

coffee–walnut wedges

- 1/3 cup butter, cut up
- 2 tablespoons granulated sugar
- 1 3/4 cups graham cracker crumbs
- 1 cup coarsely chopped walnuts
- 1 tablespoon freeze-dried coffee granules dissolved in 1 tablespoon hot water
- 2 tablespoons plain yogurt

Set out an 8-inch springform pan. • Melt the butter with the sugar in a small saucepan over low heat until the sugar has dissolved completely. • Remove from the heat and mix in the graham cracker crumbs, walnuts, coffee, and yogurt. • Firmly press the mixture into the prepared pan to form a smooth, even layer. • Refrigerate for at least 1 hour, or until set. • Loosen and remove the pan sides and cut into wedges.

Makes 16 cookies · Prep: 20 min. + 60 min. to chill · Level: 1 · Keeps: 3 days in the refrigerator

no-bake chocolate–date cookies

- 2/3 cup graham cracker crumbs
- 1 cup finely chopped pitted dates
- 1/2 cup coarsely chopped candied cherries
- 5 oz semisweet chocolate, coarsely chopped
- 1/4 cup (1/2 stick) butter, cut up
- 2 oz white chocolate, coarsely chopped

Stir together the graham cracker crumbs, dates, and candied cherries in a large bowl. • Melt the semisweet chocolate with the butter in a double boiler over barely simmering water. Remove from the heat and let cool for 5 minutes. • Pour the chocolate mixture over the graham cracker mixture and mix well. • Turn the mixture onto a sheet of plastic wrap and form into a 10-inch log. • Wrap in the plastic wrap and refrigerate for 12 hours. • Slice the log 1/2 inch thick. • Melt the white chocolate in a double boiler over barely simmering water and drizzle over the tops of the cookies.

Makes 20 cookies · Prep: 20 min. + 12 hr. to chill · Level: 1 · Keeps: 3 days

no-bake chocolate–apricot cookies

- 2/3 cup graham cracker crumbs
- 1/2 cup coarsely chopped toasted almonds
- 1/2 cup finely chopped dried apricots
- 1/2 cup coarsely chopped candied cherries
- 1/3 cup white chocolate chips
- 5 oz semisweet chocolate, coarsely chopped
- 1/4 cup (1/2 stick) butter, cut up
- 2 oz white chocolate, coarsely chopped

Stir together the graham cracker crumbs, almonds, apricots, candied cherries, and chocolate chips in a large bowl. • Melt the semisweet chocolate with the butter in a double boiler over barely simmering water. Remove from the heat and let cool for 5 minutes. • Pour the chocolate mixture over the graham cracker mixture and mix well. • Turn the mixture onto a sheet of plastic wrap and form into a 10-inch log. • Wrap in the plastic wrap and refrigerate for 12 hours. •

Slice the log 1/2 inch thick. • Melt the white chocolate in a double boiler over barely simmering water and drizzle over the tops of the cookies.

Makes 20 cookies · Prep: 20 min. + 12 hr. to chill · Level: 1 · Keeps: 3 days

no-bake chocolate–prune cookies

- 2/3 cup graham cracker crumbs
- 1/2 cup coarsely chopped toasted almonds
- 1/2 cup finely chopped prunes
- 1/2 cup coarsely chopped candied cherries
- 1/3 cup white chocolate chips
- 5 oz semisweet chocolate, coarsely chopped
- 1/4 cup (1/2 stick) butter, cut up
- 2 oz white chocolate, coarsely chopped

Stir together the graham cracker crumbs, almonds, prunes, apricots, candied cherries, and chocolate, dates in a large bowl. • Melt the semisweet chocolate with the butter in a double boiler over barely simmering water. Remove from the heat and let cool for 5 minutes. • Pour the chocolate mixture over the graham cracker mixture and mix well. • Turn the mixture onto a sheet of plastic wrap and form into a 10-inch log. • Wrap in the plastic wrap and refrigerate for 12 hours. • Slice the log 1/2 inch thick. • Melt the white chocolate in a double boiler over barely simmering water and drizzle over the tops of the cookies.

Makes 20 cookies · Prep: 20 min. + 12 hr. to chill · Level: 1 · Keeps: 3 days

No-bake chocolate–apricot cookies

no-bake chocolate–peanut bars

These no-bake delights are flavorful and crispy. Peanuts are the dominant ingredient, making it a popular treat to pack in your children's lunchboxes, reserving a few squares for yourself to nibble on. High in protein and full of B vitamins, peanuts are a healthy snack. However, many people are allergic to peanuts, so avoid this recipe for parties and bake sales.

1	cup smooth peanut butter
2/3	cup firmly packed light brown sugar
1	tablespoon butter
1/3	cup light corn syrup
4	cups lightly crushed corn flakes
1 1/4	cups coarsely chopped peanuts
1/2	cup shredded coconut
1/2	teaspoon vanilla extract
1	cup semisweet chocolate chips

Butter a 13 x 9-inch baking pan. • Mix the peanut butter, brown sugar, corn syrup, and butter in a large saucepan. Bring to a boil and boil for 1 minute. • Remove from the heat and stir in the corn flakes, 1 cup

chocolate corn flake cakes

1/4	cup (1/2 stick) butter, cut up
2	tablespoons light corn syrup
2	tablespoons unsweetened cocoa powder
2	tablespoons granulated sugar
3/4	cup corn flakes

Set out 25 paper baking cases. • Melt the butter with the corn syrup in a medium saucepan over low heat. • Remove from the heat and stir in the cocoa and sugar. • Mix in the corn flakes until well coated. • Spoon the mixture into the paper cases. • Refrigerate for 2 hours, or until set.

Makes 25 cookies · Prep: 20 min. + 2 hr. to chill · Level: 1 · Keeps: 3 days

no-bake chocolate-raisin bars

This classic English recipe is rich and satisfying.

1/2	cup (1 stick) butter, cut up
1 1/2	tablespoons light corn syrup
2	tablespoons unsweetened cocoa powder
1	cup golden raisins
2	cups graham cracker crumbs
6	oz semisweet chocolate, coarsely chopped

Set out a 10 1/2 x 15 1/2-inch jelly-roll pan. • Melt the butter with the corn syrup and cocoa in a medium saucepan over low heat. • Remove from the heat and stir in the raisins and graham cracker crumbs. • Firmly press the mixture onto the baking pan. • Melt the chocolate in a double boiler over barely simmering water. • Pour the melted chocolate evenly over the cookie base. • Let stand until set and cut into small bars.

Makes 15 bars · Prep: 20 min. · Level: 1 · Keeps: 3 days in the refrigerator

no-bake chocolate caramel squares

3/4	cup sweetened condensed milk
12	oz semisweet chocolate, coarsely grated
2	tablespoons butter, softened
2	cups rice krispies

Grease an 11 x 7-inch baking pan with sunflower oil. • Heat the condensed milk in a medium saucepan over low heat for 3 minutes, stirring constantly. • Stir in the chocolate and butter and cook until smooth and well blended. • Remove from the heat and stir in the rice krispies until well coated. • Pour the mixture into the pan, smoothing the top. • Let cool for 5 minutes. Use a sharp knife to score the mixture into bars. • When set, cut into bars.

Makes 35 bars · Prep: 25 min. · Level: 1 · Keeps: 20 days lined with waxed paper

chocolate-covered coconut bars

3/4	cup (1 1/2 sticks) butter, softened
1	cup confectioners' sugar
1	cup shredded coconut
1	cup graham cracker crumbs
1	teaspoon vanilla extract
8	oz semisweet chocolate, coarsely chopped

Line a 10 1/2 x 15 1/2-inch jelly-roll pan with aluminum foil. • Beat the butter and confectioners' sugar in a large bowl with an electric mixer at high speed until creamy. • Use a large rubber spatula to fold in the coconut, graham cracker crumbs, and vanilla. • Dust your hands lightly with confectioners' sugar. • Press into a disk, wrap in plastic wrap, and refrigerate for 30 minutes. • Divide into

ten equal portions. Form each portion into a rectangle. • Melt the chocolate in a double boiler over barely simmering water. Use tongs to dip the bars into the chocolate to cover completely. • Place the bars on the prepared baking sheet and let stand for 30 minutes until set.

Makes 10 bars · Prep: 30 min. + 60 min. to chill and set · Level: 1 · Keeps: 3 days

rocky roads

5	oz white chocolate, coarsely chopped
2	tablespoons lightly crushed vanilla wafers
1/2	cup coarsely chopped pecans
1/2	cup coarsely chopped dried apricots
1/2	cup mini marshmallows
4	candied cherries, coarsely chopped
3	oz semisweet chocolate, coarsely chopped
	Silver balls or sugar strands, jimmies, sprills, or sprinkles, to decorate

Line a cookie sheet with waxed paper. • Melt the white chocolate in a double boiler over barely simmering water. • Remove from the heat and mix in the vanilla wafers, pecans, apricots, marshmallows, and candied cherries until well coated. • Drop heaped tablespoons onto the cookie sheet. • Refrigerate for 1 hour, or until set. • Melt the semisweet chocolate in a double boiler over barely simmering water. Remove from the heat and dip the cookies halfway into the semisweet chocolate. • Decorate with the silver balls or sprinkle with sugar strands. • Let stand for 30 minutes until set.

Makes 18–20 cookies · Prep: 20 min. + 90 min. to chill and set · Level: 1 · Keeps: 5 days

peanuts, coconut, and vanilla. • Spread the mixture into the prepared pan, smoothing the top. Sprinkle with the chocolate chips and remaining $^1/4$ cup peanuts. • Refrigerate for 30 minutes, or until firmly set. • Use a sharp knife to cut into bars.

Makes 36–45 bars · Prep: 20 min. + 30 min. to chill · Level: 1 · Keeps: 7 days

marshmallow pops

2 oz semisweet chocolate, coarsely chopped
2 oz milk chocolate, coarsely chopped
2 tablespoons butter, cut up
2 tablespoons light corn syrup
$^1/2$ cup mini marshmallows
$^1/2$ cup rice krispies

Set out 15–20 mini paper cases on a cookie sheet. • Melt the semisweet and milk chocolates with the butter and corn syrup in a double boiler over barely simmering water. • Remove from the heat and mix in the marshmallows and rice krispies until well coated. • Spoon evenly into the paper cases. • Refrigerate for 2 hours, or until set.

Makes 15–20 cookies · Prep: 20 min. + 2 hr. to set
Level: 1 · Keeps: 4 days in the refrigerator

no-bake ball cookies

The decorative red licorice whips make these cookies resemble the all-American baseball.

2 oz semisweet chocolate, coarsely chopped
$2^1/2$ cups vanilla wafer crumbs
$^1/2$ cup finely chopped pecans
1 can (14 oz) sweetened condensed milk
10 oz white chocolate, coarsely chopped
Red licorice whips, to decorate

Line four cookie sheets with parchment paper. • Melt the semisweet chocolate in a double boiler over barely simmering water. • Mix the vanilla wafer crumbs, pecans, condensed milk, and melted semisweet chocolate in a large bowl until well blended. • Form the mixture into balls the size of walnuts and place 1 inch apart on the prepared cookie sheets, flattening them slightly. • Refrigerate for 30 minutes until firm to the touch. • Melt the white

chocolate in the double boiler over barely simmering water. • Spread the white chocolate over the tops of the cookies and decorate with the licorice to resemble ball threads. • Let stand for 30 minutes until set.

Makes 45–50 cookies · Prep: 25 min. + 60 min. to chill and set · Level: 1 · Keeps: 5 days in the refrigerator

no-bake pistachio moons

14 oz marzipan
$^1/3$ cup finely chopped pistachios
$^2/3$ cup old-fashioned rolled oats
7 oz bittersweet chocolate, coarsely chopped
15 almond or pistachio halves, toasted (optional)

Lightly dust a surface with confectioners' sugar. • Roll the marzipan out to a thickness of about $^1/2$ inch. • Sprinkle the chopped pistachios and oats evenly over the marzipan and press down lightly with a rolling pin. • Use a 1-inch round cutter to stamp out small circles. • Re-roll the leftovers and stamp out more circles until all the marzipan has been used. • Melt the chocolate in a double boiler over barely simmering water. Dip one half of each full moon in the melted chocolate. • Decorate with the almond halves.

Makes 35–40 cookies · Prep: 50 min. · Level: 1 · Keeps: 14–20 days

mint liqueur balls

1 cup vanilla wafer crumbs
$3/4$ cup finely chopped walnuts
$1^1/4$ cups confectioners' sugar
2 tablespoons light corn syrup
$^1/3$ cup green-colored mint liqueur

Mix the wafer crumbs, walnuts, 1 cup confectioners' sugar, corn syrup, and mint liqueur in a large bowl to form a stiff dough. • Form the dough into balls the size of walnuts and roll in the remaining $^1/4$ cup confectioners' sugar. • Arrange in mini paper liners and serve.

Makes 24–28 cookies · Prep: 20 min. · Level: 1 · Keeps: 4 days

coffee liqueur balls

1 cup vanilla wafer crumbs
$3/4$ cup finely chopped walnuts
$1^1/4$ cups confectioners' sugar
2 tablespoons light corn syrup
$^1/3$ cup coffee liqueur

Mix the wafer crumbs, walnuts, 1 cup confectioners' sugar, corn syrup, and coffee liqueur in a large bowl to form a stiff dough. • Form the dough into balls the size of walnuts and roll in the remaining $^1/4$ cup confectioners' sugar. • Arrange in mini paper liners and serve.

Makes 24–28 cookies · Prep: 20 min. · Level: 1 · Keeps: 4 days

Mint liqueur balls

fried cookies

Fried cookies are reminiscent of the Italian pre-Lenten carnival season in spring, when freshly fried cookie twists and rosettes, dusted with confectioners' sugar, are served at market stalls. When making these cookies, be sure that the oil reaches its optimum temperature before adding the cookies—this can be tested by dipping a toothpick into the hot oil; if the oil froths, it is ready for frying.

above: Welsh bakestones
(page 337)

right: Fried cookie rosettes,
Polish diamonds, Sweet
pumpkin fried cookies, and
Sweet ricotta fritters
(pages 332, 336, and 337)

making carnival cookies

Springtime in Italy is a time of celebration and carnival. These crisp cookies can be found in pasticcerie, *or pastry shops, and bought at festival stands.*

3¹/₃ cups all-purpose flour
¹/₈ teaspoon salt
2 tablespoons granulated sugar
4 large eggs
2 tablespoons butter, softened
¹/₂ cup brandy
2 cups vegetable oil, for frying
¹/₃ cup confectioners' sugar, to dust

Sift the flour and salt into a large bowl. Stir in the granulated sugar. • Add the eggs, beating until just blended. • Mix in the butter and brandy to form a stiff dough. Set aside to rest for 2 hours. • Roll out the dough on a lightly floured surface to a thickness of ¹/₈ inch. Cut into 3 x 1-inch strips and tie each strip into a knot. • Heat the oil in a large deep skillet until very hot (365°F). Fry the cookies in small batches for 5–7 minutes, or until just golden. • Drain well on paper towels. • Dust with the confectioners' sugar just before serving.

Makes 50–60 cookies · Prep: 20 min. + 2 hr. to rest · Cooking: 5–7 min. per batch · Level: 3 · Keeps: 1 day

1. Test the hot oil with a toothpick.

2. Use a spatula to transfer the cookies to the hot oil.

3. Remove the cookies with a slotted spoon and drain well on paper towels.

4. Dust the cookies with confectioners' sugar.

fried cardamom cookies

These spicy fried delicacies will tantalize your taste buds with their Eastern flavor.

2²/₃ cups all-purpose flour
¹/₈ teaspoon salt
3 large egg yolks + 1 large egg white
¹/₄ cup rose water
¹/₂ cup milk
¹/₂ teaspoon ground cardamom
2 cups corn oil, for frying
¹/₃ cup confectioners' sugar, to dust

Sift the flour and salt into a large bowl. • Beat the egg yolks and egg white, rose water, milk, and cardamom in a large bowl with an electric mixer at high speed until well blended. • Mix in the dry ingredients to form a smooth dough. • Turn the dough out onto a lightly floured surface and knead until smooth. • Cover with a clean kitchen towel and let stand for 2 hours. • Form into balls the size of walnuts. • Roll the balls out to a thickness of ¹/₈ inch and a diameter of 3 inches. • Carefully fold the dough over, using a fork to press down the edges. • Cover with a kitchen towel and let stand for 5 minutes. • Heat the corn oil to 325°F in a large deep skillet. • Fry the cookies in batches for 1 minute, or until lightly browned all over. • Drain well on paper towels. • Dust with the confectioners' sugar.

Makes 10 cookies · Prep: 30 min. + 2 hr. 5 min. to stand · Cooking: 1 min. per batch · Level: 3 · Keeps: 2 days

fried cookie rosettes

3 cups all-purpose flour
¹/₈ teaspoon salt
1 tablespoon vegetable shortening
3 large eggs, lightly beaten
¹/₄ cup Champagne
1 tablespoon granulated sugar
2 cups vegetable oil, for frying
Sugar strands, jimmies, sprills, or sprinkles, to decorate

Sift the flour and salt into a large bowl. • Use a pastry blender to cut in the shortening until the mixture resembles fine crumbs. • Make a well in the center and mix in the eggs, Champagne, and sugar to form a stiff dough. • Press the dough into a disk, wrap in plastic wrap, and refrigerate for 30 minutes. • Heat the oil in a large deep skillet until very hot (365°F). • Roll out the dough on a lightly floured surface to a thickness of ¹/₄ inch. • Use a fluted pastry cutter to cut the dough into 15 x ¹/₂-inch strips. • Fold the strips in half lengthways and roll up, pinching the bottom together to open the top into a ruffled flower shape. • Fry the cookies in small batches, turning them with a slotted spoon, for 3–5 minutes, or until golden and crisp. • Drain well on paper towels. • Sprinkle with the sugar strands.

Makes 20–25 cookies · Prep: 40 min. + 30 min. to chill · Cooking: 3–5 min. per batch · Level: 3 · Keeps: 1 day

neapolitan christmas fritters

These tiny fried cookies are popular all over southern Italy during the holiday season.

3¹/2 cups all-purpose flour
¹/8 teaspoon salt
4 large eggs, lightly beaten
¹/2 cup anisette
2 tablespoons superfine sugar
2 cups vegetable oil, for frying
³/4 cup honey
1 cup finely chopped candied orange
1 cup finely chopped candied lemon peel
¹/4 cup sugar confetti

Sift the flour and salt into a large bowl. • Mix in the eggs, anisette, and superfine sugar until well blended. Set aside to rest for 2 hours. • Form tablespoonfuls of the dough into sticks about the thickness of a pencil. Cut into ¹/2-inch pieces. • Heat the oil in a large deep skillet until very hot (365°F). • Fry the cookies in small batches for 5–7 minutes, or until just golden all over. • Drain well on paper towels. • Heat the honey in a large saucepan over low heat until liquid. Add the cookies and candied peel and stir until well coated. • Transfer to a serving plate and decorate with the sugar confetti.

Makes over 100 cookies · Prep: 30 min. + 2 hr. to rest · Cooking: 5–7 min. per batch · Level: 3 · Keeps: 1 day

oast house cookies

Oast houses are distinctive circular "towers" set beside hop farms in Kent, the southern county known as "the garden of England". Until the Second World War, the poor of London's East End used to trek to Kent for a summer holiday, picking the hops grown to flavor beer. When the hops were safely in the oast house, the pickers used to fry these tasty cookies over their outdoor cooking fires to serve at tea time.

1¹/2 cups all-purpose flour
¹/2 teaspoon baking powder
¹/8 teaspoon salt
¹/4 cup vegetable shortening
¹/4 cup + 2 tablespoons granulated sugar
¹/2 cup dried currants
2 tablespoons water, + more as needed
1 cup peanut oil, for frying

Sift the flour, baking powder, and salt into a large bowl. • Use a pastry blender to cut in the shortening until the mixture resembles fine crumbs. • Stir in the ¹/4 cup sugar and the currants. • Mix in 2 tablespoons water to form a smooth dough, adding more water as needed. • Press the dough into a disk, wrap in plastic wrap, and

refrigerate for 30 minutes. • Roll out the dough on a lightly floured surface to a thickness of ¹/2 inch. • Use a 2-inch cookie cutter to cut out the cookies. • Heat the oil in a large deep skillet until very hot (365°F). • Fry the cookies in small batches for 5–7 minutes, or until golden brown. • Drain well on paper towels. • Sprinkle with the remaining 2 tablespoons sugar and serve hot.

Makes 10–12 cookies · Prep: 40 min. + 30 min. to chill · Cooking: 5–7 min. per batch · Level: 3 · Keeps: 2 days

aebleskiver cookies

These Danish ball cookies require a special aebleskiver pan, which can be bought at specialty baking stores.

1 cup all-purpose flour
1 teaspoon baking powder
¹/4 teaspoon baking soda
¹/4 teaspoon salt
1 tablespoon granulated sugar
2 tablespoons butter, melted
1 cup buttermilk
1 large egg white
scant 1 cup vegetable oil, for frying

Sift the flour, baking powder, baking soda, and salt into a large bowl. • Beat in the sugar, butter, and buttermilk until smooth. • Beat the egg white in a large bowl with an electric mixer at high speed until stiff peaks form. • Use a large rubber spatula to fold the beaten white into the batter. • Heat a 7-hole aebleskiver pan over medium heat and spoon 1 tablespoon of the oil into each hole. • Spoon 2 tablespoons of the batter into each hole and fry for about 3 minutes, or until the oil begins to bubble at the edges. • Use a long-handled fork to turn the cookies and fry for about 3 minutes, or until golden brown. • Use the fork to remove the cookies from the pan. Drain well on paper towels. • Repeat with the remaining oil and batter until all the batter has been used.

Makes 14 cookies · Prep: 25 min. · Cooking: 6 min. per batch · Level: 3 · Keeps: 1 day

fried cookie bows

1¹/2 cups all-purpose flour
¹/4 teaspoon baking powder
¹/4 teaspoon salt
5 large egg yolks
2 tablespoons granulated sugar
2 tablespoons sour cream

1¹/2 teaspoons dark rum
¹/2 teaspoon vanilla extract
1 cup vegetable oil, for frying
¹/2 cup confectioners' sugar, to dust

Sift the flour, baking powder, and salt into a medium bowl. • Beat the egg yolks and granulated sugar in a large bowl with an electric mixer at high speed until pale and thick. • Beat in the sour cream, rum, and vanilla. • Mix in the dry ingredients to form a stiff dough. • Turn the dough out onto a lightly floured surface and knead until smooth. • Press the dough into a disk, wrap in plastic wrap, and refrigerate for 30 minutes. • Roll out the dough to a thickness of ¹/8 inch. Cut into 4 x 1¹/2-inch strips. • Gather the dough scraps, reroll, and continue cutting out strips until all the dough is used. • Make a slit at one end of the strip and thread the other end of the strip through it to make a bow. • Heat the oil in a large deep skillet until very hot (365°F). • Fry the cookies in small batches for 5–7 minutes, or until just golden all over. • Drain well on paper towels. • Dust with the confectioners' sugar just before serving.

Makes 30 cookies · Prep: 40 min. + 30 min. to chill · Cooking: 5–7 min. per batch · Level: 3 · Keeps: 1 day

Fried cookie bows

sweet pumpkin fried cookies

1 cup golden raisins
2/3 cup all-purpose flour
1 tablespoon baking powder
1/8 teaspoon salt
2 lb pie pumpkin or winter squash
1/4 cup granulated sugar + 1/3 cup, to dust
    grated zest of 1 lemon
2 cups vegetable oil, for frying

Plump the raisins in hot water to cover in a small bowl for 10 minutes. • Drain well and pat dry with paper towels. • Sift the flour, baking powder, and salt into a medium bowl. • Peel the pumpkin and remove the seeds and fibrous matter. Slice the flesh and place in a large saucepan with enough cold water to cover. • Bring to a boil and cook over medium heat for 25–30 minutes, or until very tender. • Drain well and pat dry with a clean kitchen cloth to absorb any excess moisture. • Transfer to a large bowl and use a potato masher to puree the pumpkin. • Mix in the dry ingredients, raisins, 1/4 cup of the sugar, and lemon zest. • Form the dough into balls the size of walnuts. • Heat the oil in a large deep skillet until very hot (365°F). • Fry the cookies in small batches for 5–7 minutes, or until golden brown all over. • Drain well on paper towels. • Dust with the remaining 1/3 cup of sugar just before serving.

Makes 20 cookies · Prep: 65 min. · Cooking: 5–7 min. per batch · Level: 3 · Keeps: 1 day

crisp cookie petals

2 cups all-purpose flour
1/8 teaspoon salt
2 large eggs
2 tablespoons granulated sugar
1/3 cup light cream
1/3 cup dry white wine
2 cups peanut oil, for frying
1/4 cup confectioners' sugar, to dust

Sift the flour and salt into a medium bowl. • Use a wooden spoon to mix the eggs and granulated sugar in a large bowl. • Stir in the cream and white wine until well blended. • Mix in the dry ingredients to form a smooth dough. • Press the dough into a disk, wrap in plastic wrap, and refrigerate for 30 minutes. • Roll out the dough on a lightly floured surface until it is paper-thin. • Use a 3-inch fluted round cookie cutter to cut out the cookies. Gather the dough scraps, re-roll, and

continue cutting out cookies until all the dough is used. • Pinch the center of the cookies to crinkle them slightly. • Heat the oil in a large deep skillet until very hot (365°F). • Fry the cookies in small batches for about 3 minutes, or until crisp and golden brown. • Drain well on paper towels. • Dust with the confectioners' sugar just before serving.

Makes 25–30 cookies · Prep: 40 min. + 30 min. to chill · Cooking: 3 min. per batch · Level: 3 · Keeps: 1 day

jelly-filled fried cookies

3 1/3 cups all-purpose flour
1 tablespoon baking powder
1/8 teaspoon salt
1/4 cup (1/2 stick) butter, cut up
1 cup granulated sugar
3 large eggs, lightly beaten
3 tablespoons dark rum
1/2 cup black cherry or sweet cherry jelly
2 cups vegetable oil, for frying
1/3 cup confectioners' sugar

Sift the flour, baking powder, and salt into a large bowl. • Use a pastry blender to cut in the butter until the mixture resembles coarse crumbs. • Stir in the granulated sugar. Add the eggs and rum to form a smooth dough. • Press the dough into a disk, wrap in plastic wrap, and refrigerate for 30 minutes. • Roll out the dough on a lightly floured surface to a thickness of 1/4 inch. • Use a 2-inch cookie cutter to cut out the cookies. • Gather the dough scraps, re-roll, and continue cutting out cookies until all the dough is used. • Place a little jelly on one half of each cookie, then fold the other half over. Seal the edges well. • Heat the oil in a large deep skillet until very hot (365°F). • Fry the cookies in small batches for 5–7 minutes, or until golden brown. • Drain well on paper towels. • Dust with confectioners' sugar just before serving.

Makes 30 cookies · Prep: 40 min. + 30 min. to chill · Cooking: 5–7 min. per batch · Level: 3 · Keeps: 2 days

fried amaretti cookies

These succulent treats have a delicate almond flavor.

Batter
1 1/3 cups all-purpose flour
1/8 teaspoon salt
3/4 cup milk
2 large eggs, separated
2 tablespoons butter, melted
2 tablespoons granulated sugar
48 Amaretti cookies (store-bought or see page 244)
2 tablespoons raspberry preserves
1/4 cup light rum
2 cups peanut oil, for frying
1/3 cup confectioners' sugar

Batter: Sift the flour and salt into a large bowl. • Stir together the milk, egg yolks, butter, and sugar. • Mix into the dry ingredients, beating gently to ensure no lumps form. • Set aside in a warm place for 2 hours. • Stick the cookies together in pairs with the preserves. • Brush the cookies with the rum. • Beat the egg whites in a large bowl with an electric mixer at high speed until stiff peaks form. • Use a large rubber spatula to fold the beaten whites into the rested batter. • Heat the oil in a large deep skillet until very hot (365°F). • Dip the cookies in the batter and fry in small batches for 5–7 minutes, or until golden brown all over. • Drain well on paper towels. • Dust with the confectioners' sugar just before serving.

Makes 24 cookies · Prep: 25 min. + 2 hr. to rest · Cooking: 5–7 min. per batch · Level: 3 · Keeps: 1 day

*Crisp cookie petals (right and below)
and Fried amaretti cookies (left)*

*Norwegian christmas
cardamom cookies*

fattigmann

*Crisp and spicy treats from Norway—these
cookies are a Christmas specialty.*

3/4 cup all-purpose flour
1/2 teaspoon ground cardamom
1/8 teaspoon salt
3 large egg yolks
2 tablespoons granulated sugar
2 tablespoons light cream
2 teaspoons butter, melted
2 teaspoons brandy
2 teaspoons finely grated lemon zest
2 cups lard or vegetable oil, for frying
2 tablespoons confectioners' sugar, to dust

Sift the flour, cardamom, and salt into a
medium bowl. • Beat the egg yolks and
granulated sugar in a large bowl with an
electric mixer at high speed until pale and
thick. • Beat in the cream, butter, and
brandy until well blended. • Mix in the dry
ingredients and lemon zest to form a stiff
dough. Divide the dough into four. Press
each into a disk, wrap in plastic wrap, and
refrigerate for 30 minutes. • Heat the lard in
a large deep skillet until very hot (365°F). •
Discard the plastic wrap from one-quarter
of the dough. Keep the remainder chilled.
Roll out the dough on a lightly floured
surface to a thickness of 1/8 inch. Cut the
dough into 3-inch diamonds. Gather the
dough scraps, re-roll, and continue cutting
out cookies until all the dough is used. • Cut

a 1-inch slit in the center of each cookie.
Gently pull one corner through the slit to
form a "knot." • Fry the cookies in small
batches for 2–3 minutes, turning halfway
through with a slotted spoon, until golden
brown. • Drain well on paper towels. Repeat
with the remaining dough. • Dust with the
confectioners' sugar just before serving.

Makes 35–40 cookies · Prep: 40 min. + 30 min. to
chill · Cooking: 2–3 min. per batch · Level: 3 ·
Keeps: 2 days

polish diamonds

11/4 cups all-purpose flour
1/8 teaspoon salt
6 large egg yolks + 1 small egg,
lightly beaten
1 tablespoon granulated sugar
2 teaspoons dark rum
1/2 teaspoon vanilla extract
2 cups vegetable oil, for frying
1/3 cup confectioners' sugar, to dust

Sift the flour and salt into a large bowl. •
Make a well in the center and mix in the
egg yolks and whole egg, sugar, rum, and
vanilla to form a stiff dough. • Press the
dough into a disk, wrap in plastic wrap,
and refrigerate for 30 minutes. • Heat the
oil in a large deep skillet until very hot
(365°F). • Roll out the dough on a lightly
floured surface until paper thin. • Use a
fluted pastry cutter to cut the dough into
2-inch diamonds. Gather the dough scraps,
re-roll, and continue cutting out cookies.
Make a slit in the center of each cookie
and pull one point of the diamond through
the slit. • Fry the cookies in small batches,
turning halfway through with a slotted
spoon, for 2–3 minutes, or until crisp. •
Drain well on paper towels. • Dust with the
confectioners' sugar.

Makes 20–25 cookies · Prep: 40 min. + 30 min. to
chill · Cooking: 2–3 min. per batch · Level: 3 ·
Keeps: 1 day

norwegian christmas
cardamom cookies

*These Norwegian cookies are traditionally
fried in lard. If you want a lighter option,
substitute oil for the lard.*

1 large egg + 3 large egg yolks
1 tablespoon granulated sugar
1/4 cup heavy cream
1 tablespoon butter, melted
1/4 teaspoon ground cardamom
11/2 cups all-purpose flour

1/8 teaspoon salt
2 cups lard or vegetable oil, for frying

Beat the egg and egg yolks and sugar in a
large bowl with an electric mixer at high
speed until pale and thick. • Beat in the
cream, butter, and cardamom. • Mix in the
flour and salt to form a stiff dough. • Press
the dough into a disk, wrap in plastic wrap,
and refrigerate for 30 minutes. • Roll out
the dough on a lightly floured surface to a
thickness of 1/8 inch. • Cut into 2-inch
diamonds. • Gather the dough scraps, reroll,
and continue cutting out diamonds until all
the dough is used. • Heat the oil in a large
deep skillet until very hot (365°F). • Fry the
cookies in small batches for 5–7 minutes, or
until golden brown all over. • Drain well on
paper towels.

Makes 45–50 cookies · Prep: 40 min. + 30 min. to
chill · Cooking: 5–7 min. per batch · Level: 1 · Keeps:
1 day

st. joseph's day fritters

*Many Italian foods are associated with
festivals. These delicious lemon and egg
fritters are served on March 19, St. Joseph's
feast day.*

1 cup water
1/2 cup (1 stick) butter, cut up
1/4 cup granulated sugar
1/8 teaspoon salt
Grated zest of 1 lemon
2 cups all-purpose flour
8 large eggs
2 cups olive oil, for frying
1 cup confectioners' sugar, to dust

Bring the water, butter, granulated sugar,
salt, and lemon zest to a boil in a medium
saucepan. • Add the flour all at once and
stir with a wooden spoon. Continue
cooking, stirring constantly, until the dough
is thick and starts to come away from the
sides of the saucepan. Remove from the
heat and set aside to cool. • When cool, add
the eggs, one at a time, beating until just
blended. The dough should be soft, but not
runny. • Set aside to rest for 1 hour. • Heat
the oil in a large deep skillet until very hot
(365°F). • Fry teaspoons of the dough in
small batches for 5–7 minutes, or until
golden brown. • Drain well on paper towels.
• Dust with the confectioners' sugar just
before serving.

Makes 50 cookies · Prep: 25 min. + 1 hr. to rest
Cooking: 5–7 min. per batch · Level: 1 ·
Keeps: 1 day

sweet ricotta fritters

1/4	cup raisins
2	tablespoons dark rum
1 1/2	cups all-purpose flour
1/8	teaspoon baking soda
1/8	teaspoon salt
1 2/3	cups ricotta cheese
3	large eggs
1/3	cup granulated sugar
	Grated zest of 1 orange
2	cups vegetable oil, for frying
3/4	cup confectioners' sugar, to dust

Soak the raisins in the rum overnight. Drain and pat dry. • Sift the flour, baking soda, and salt into a medium bowl. • Strain the ricotta into a large bowl. • Add the eggs, granulated sugar, orange zest, and raisins. • Mix in the dry ingredients until smooth. Set aside to rest for 1 hour. • Heat the oil in a large deep skillet until very hot (365°F). • Fry tablespoons of the dough in batches of six to eight for 5–7 minutes, or until lightly browned. • Drain well on paper towels. • Dust with the confectioners' sugar just before serving.

Makes 18–24 cookies · Prep: 15 min. + 12 hr. to soak raisins + 1 hr. to rest batter · Cooking: 5–7 min. per batch · Level: 1 · Keeps: 1 day in the refrigerator

welsh bakestones

Bakestones are a Welsh treat. They are quick to make and are best fresh off the griddle, served with a cup of tea or coffee. Prepare the dough in advance and keep it chilled in the refrigerator until needed.

1 2/3	cups all-purpose flour
1	teaspoon baking powder
1/4	teaspoon ground allspice
1/8	teaspoon salt
1/2	cup (1 stick) butter, cut up
1/3	cup firmly packed light brown sugar
1/2	cup dried currants
1 1/2	tablespoons finely chopped mixed peel
1	large egg, lightly beaten
1–3	tablespoons milk
1–2	tablespoons superfine sugar, for sprinkling

Sift the flour, baking powder, allspice, and salt into a large bowl. • Use a pastry blender to cut in the butter until the mixture resembles coarse crumbs. • Mix in the brown sugar, currants, and mixed peel. • Add the egg and enough milk to form a smooth dough. • Press the dough into a disk, wrap in plastic wrap, and refrigerate for 30 minutes. • Roll out the dough on a lightly floured surface to a thickness of 1/4 inch. •

Use a 2-inch cookie cutter to cut out the cookies. • Gather the dough scraps, re-roll, and continue cutting out cookies until all the dough is used. • Preheat a griddle or cast-iron skillet and grease lightly with butter. • Fry the cookies for 4 minutes. • Use a spatula to turn the cookies over and cook for 3–4 minutes on the other side, or until golden brown on both sides. • Sprinkle with sugar just before serving.

Makes 18–20 cookies · Prep: 20 min. + 30 min. to chill · Cooking: 7–8 min. · Level: 2 · Keeps: 3 days

currant cookies

4	cups all-purpose flour
1	tablespoon baking powder
3/4	teaspoon ground nutmeg
1/8	teaspoon salt
1	cup vegetable shortening
1 1/2	cups granulated sugar
1	cup dried currants
3	large eggs, lightly beaten
1/4	cup milk, + more as needed

Sift the flour, baking powder, nutmeg, and salt into a large bowl. • Use a pastry blender to cut in the shortening until the mixture resembles coarse crumbs. • Stir in the sugar and currants. • Add the eggs and enough milk to form a stiff dough. • Press the dough into a disk, wrap in plastic wrap, and refrigerate for 30 minutes. • Roll out the dough on a lightly floured surface to a thickness of 1/4 inch. Use a 1 1/2-inch fluted

cookie cutter to cut out the cookies. • Gather the dough scraps, re-roll, and continue cutting out cookies until all the dough is used. • Grease a heavy skillet with oil and place over medium heat until very hot. • Fry four cookies, turning them over halfway through the cooking, for 7–10 minutes, or until golden brown. • Drain well on paper towels. • Wipe the skillet clean with paper towels, grease with more oil, and continue frying in batches until all the cookies are cooked.

Makes 34–38 cookies · Prep: 40 min. + 30 min. to chill · Cooking: 7–10 min. per batch · Level: 2 · Keeps: 1 day

sweet tortillas

These authentic Mexican specialties are delicious served on their own or with vanilla ice cream. Or set out bowls of Tropical Coulis (see page 342) for dipping into.

4	small wheat flour tortillas
1	cup vegetable oil, for frying
2/3	cup granulated sugar
4	teaspoons ground cinnamon

Cut the tortillas into quarters. • Heat the oil in a deep skillet over medium heat until very hot (365°F). • Carefully place the tortillas in the pan. • Fry the tortillas in batches of four for 5–7 minutes, or until golden all over. • Drain well on paper towels. Sprinkle with the sugar and cinnamon.

Makes 16 cookies · Prep: 5 min. · Cooking: 5–7 min. per batch · Level: 1 · Keeps: 1 day

Sweet tortillas

decorating &
serving

By decoratively piping with chocolate
frosting or sandwiching them together with
a buttercream, you can transform your
cookies into delicious morsels. And, by
pairing brownies with ice cream or
cookies with fruit compotes and coulis,
a simple dessert becomes festive enough for
a special occasion or sufficiently elegant for the
most formal of dinner parties.

above: Chocolate–fudge
sauce (see page 342)

right: Cinnamon sugar and
Vanilla sugar (see page 341)

Orange curd

applesauce

2¹/2   lb tart cooking apples (Granny Smiths are ideal), peeled, cored, and chopped
1   cup cold water
1   cup granulated sugar
¹/3   cup fresh lemon juice
1   teaspoon vanilla extract

Cook the apples, water, and sugar in a large saucepan over low heat until the apples are mushy, about 20 minutes. • Remove from the heat and stir in the lemon juice and vanilla. • Strain the mixture in a food mill or puree in a food processor or blender.

Makes about 2¹/2 cups · Prep: 30 min. · Level: 1 · Keeps: 1 week in the refrigerator

mincemeat

A flavor of Christmas—this sweet British filling originally included lean ground, or minced, meat. Use it to fill short-crust pastry tartlets.

4   large tart apples, peeled, cored, and finely chopped
1³/4   cups finely chopped almonds
²/3   cup finely chopped dried apricots
1   cup raisins
³/4   cup dried currants
1¹/2   cups finely chopped candied cherries
1¹/2   cups finely chopped mixed candied peel
  Grated zest and juice of 2 lemons
  Grated zest and juice of 1 orange
1   cup firmly packed dark brown sugar
2   teaspoons ground cinnamon
1   teaspoon freshly grated nutmeg
¹/2   teaspoon ground cloves
1   cup brandy

Mix all the ingredients, except the brandy, in a large bowl. • Stir in the brandy. • Cover with plastic wrap and refrigerate for 2 days.

Makes 3 cups · Prep: 20 min. + 2 days to chill · Level: 1 · Keeps: 4 months in sterilized jars in the refrigerator

raspberry curd

2   cups raspberries
¹/2   cup (1 stick) butter
¹/2   cup granulated sugar
4   large eggs

Process the raspberries in a food processor or blender until pureed. Transfer to a medium saucepan with the butter and sugar. • Cook over low heat, stirring constantly, until the mixture is well blended. Remove from the heat and let cool to lukewarm. • Add the eggs, beating until well blended. • Return the saucepan to the heat and cook over very low heat, stirring constantly, until the curd thickens enough to coat the back of the spoon, and registers 160°F on an instant-read thermometer, 20–25 minutes.

Makes 2 cups · Prep: 20 min. · Cooking: 30–35 min. Level: 2 · Keeps: 5 days in the refrigerator

lemon curd

3   large eggs
¹/2   cup granulated sugar
3   tablespoons finely grated lemon zest
¹/3   cup fresh lemon juice
¹/2   cup (1 stick) butter, cut up

Beat the eggs, sugar, and lemon zest and juice in a saucepan until well blended. Cook over low heat, stirring constantly with a wooden spoon, until the mixture lightly coats a wooden spoon and registers 160°F on an instant-read thermometer. • Add a piece of the butter, stirring until it has melted before adding more. When all the butter has been added, immediately plunge the pan into a bowl of ice water and stir until the mixture has cooled. • Transfer to a bowl, cover with plastic wrap, and refrigerate.

Makes about 1¹/2 cups · Prep: 25 min. · Level: 1 · Keeps: 5 days in the refrigerator

mascarpone–vanilla cream

¹/2   cup mascarpone cheese
1   cup heavy cream
1   teaspoon vanilla extract
1   tablespoon granulated sugar

Place all the ingredients in a large bowl and beat with an electric mixer at high speed until stiff. Refrigerate until ready to use.

Makes 1¹/2 cups · Prep: 5 min. · Level: 1 · Keeps: 3 days in the refrigerator

vanilla whipped cream

1   cup heavy cream
1   tablespoon granulated sugar
¹/2   teaspoon vanilla extract

Beat the cream, sugar, and vanilla in a large bowl with an electric mixer at high speed until stiff. Refrigerate for 30 minutes.

Makes about 3 cups · Prep: 15 min. + 30 min. to chill · Level: 2 · Keeps: 1 day

orange curd

2   large eggs, lightly beaten
1   cup granulated sugar
  Grated zest and juice of 2 oranges
  Grated zest and juice of 1 lemon
¹/4   cup (¹/2 stick) butter, cut up

Beat the eggs, superfine sugar, and citrus zest and juice in a saucepan until well blended. Cook over low heat, stirring constantly with a wooden spoon, until the mixture lightly coats a wooden spoon and registers 160°F on an instant-read thermometer. • Add the butter, a few pieces at a time, stirring until it has melted before adding more. Immediately plunge the pan into a bowl of ice water and stir until the mixture has cooled. • Transfer to a bowl, cover with plastic wrap, and refrigerate.

Makes 1¹/2 cups · Prep: 25 min. · Level: 1 · Keeps: 5 days in the refrigerator

making flavored sugars

Flavored sugars add a touch of authenticity to your baking. Always keep a supply of these sugars, refreshing the vanilla pods and cinnamon sticks frequently to retain the taste.

vanilla confectioners' sugar

- 2 cups confectioners' sugar
- 1 vanilla pod, cut into 2 or 3 pieces

Process the confectioners' sugar and vanilla pods in a food processor or blender until the vanilla is finely chopped. Spoon into an airtight container and set aside for 7 days.

Makes 2 cups · Prep: 7 days · Level: 1 · Keeps: up to 1 month

vanilla sugar

- 2¹/₂ cups granulated sugar
- 2 vanilla pods, cut into 2 or 3 pieces

Fill a glass jar with the sugar. • Add the vanilla pods, seal tightly, and set aside for 7–10 days. When you open the jar, the sugar will be flavored with vanilla. • As the pods have a long aromatic life, just add more sugar as needed.

Makes 2¹/₂ cups · Prep: 7–10 days · Level: 1 · Keeps: up to 6 months

cinnamon sugar

No baker should be without a ready supply of cinnamon sugar.

- 2¹/₂ cups granulated sugar
- 3 cinnamon sticks, broken into halves
- 4 cloves

Fill a glass jar with sugar and place the cinnamon sticks and cloves in it. • Let stand for 1 week and use as needed. Add more sugar when necessary.

chocolate whipped cream

- 1 cup heavy cream
- 1¹/₂ tablespoons Dutch process cocoa powder
- 2¹/₂ tablespoons granulated sugar
- ¹/₂ teaspoon vanilla extract

Beat the cream, cocoa, sugar, and vanilla in a large bowl with an electric mixer at high speed until stiff. Refrigerate for 30 minutes.

Makes about 3 cups · Prep: 15 min. + 30 min. to chill · Level: 2 · Keeps: 1 day

mock cream

This looks like the real thing but lasts longer.

- ¹/₂ cup (1 stick) butter, softened
- ¹/₂ cup granulated sugar
- ¹/₂ cup boiling water
- 1 teaspoon vanilla extract

Beat the butter, sugar, water, and vanilla in a medium bowl with an electric mixer at high speed until creamy. • The mixture may curdle as you beat; continue beating until smooth.

Makes 1 cup · Prep: 5 min. · Level: 1 · Keeps: 2–3 days

kahlua mousse

Serve with delicate cookies, such as the Almond lace cookies (page 253) or spoon into the Poppy seed ice cream baskets (page 253)

- 1 lb semisweet chocolate, coarsely chopped
- ¹/₃ cup butter, cut up
- ¹/₂ cup confectioners' sugar
- 3 large eggs, separated
- ¹/₄ cup Kahlua liqueur
- 1 teaspoon freeze-dried coffee granules
- 2 cups heavy cream

Melt the chocolate and butter in a double boiler over barely simmering water. • Mix the confectioners' sugar, egg yolks, Kahlua, and coffee granules in a large bowl. • Stir in the chocolate mixture. • Beat the cream in a large bowl with an electric mixer at high speed until stiff. Fold it into the chocolate mixture. • Beat the egg whites until just stiff (do not overbeat). Fold them into the mixture. • Spoon the mixture into individual serving bowls. • Refrigerate for 4 hours before serving.

Serves: 8 · Prep: 15 min + 4 hr. to chill · Cooking: 10 min · Level: 1 · Keeps: 2 days in the refrigerator

colored sprinkling sugars

- 1–2 drops food coloring of your choice
- 3 tablespoons granulated sugar

Place the sugar in a small freezer bag and drizzle with the food coloring. Close the bag and use your fingers to work the coloring into the sugar by squeezing the bag. Use more coloring if you want a bright sugar. Keep squeezing until the sugar is evenly colored.

Makes 3 tablespoons of sugar · Prep: 15 min. · Level: 1 · Keeps: 1 week

homemade gingerbread spice

The seven gingerbread spices included in the traditional Lebkuchen dough commemorate the seven days of Creation. This seven-spice mixture is aromatic and can be adjusted to suit your own taste.

- 1 tablespoon ground aniseeds
- 1 tablespoon ground cinnamon
- 1 tablespoon ground coriander seeds
- 1 tablespoon ground fennel
- 1 teaspoon ground cloves
- 1 teaspoon ground ginger
- ¹/₄ teaspoon ground nutmeg

Mix the aniseeds, cinnamon, coriander, fennel, cloves, ginger, and nutmeg in a small bowl until well blended. Transfer to a screw-top jar.

Makes ¹/₃ cup spice · Prep: 10 min. · Level: 1 · Keeps: 1 month

Applesauce

making brownie sundaes

There's no better way to enjoy a brownie than served with ice cream. Add a sauce and whipped cream and you have a sundae. Any brownie, sauce, and ice cream flavor will work, but here are some of our favorite combinations. Cherry sauce is an unusual choice, but the combination of chocolate and cherries is perfect.

1   recipe Three-Chocolate Brownies (page 128) or Chocolate–Hazelnut Brownies (page 128)
1   recipe Vanilla Ice Cream (page 344)
1   recipe Cherry Sauce, Caramel Sauce, Warm Chocolate Sauce, Chocolate–Fudge Sauce, or Raspberry Puree (see below)
1   recipe Vanilla Whipped Cream (page 340), Chocolate Whipped Cream (page 341), or Mock Cream (page 341)

Divide the brownies into 6 bars and place each on a dessert plate. Top with a scoop of ice cream. Pour over a few spoons of sauce and top with a dollop of whipped cream. Serve immediately.

Makes 6 servings · Prep: 5 min. · Level: 1

tropical coulis

1   (7 oz) mango, peeled and coarsely chopped
1–2 bananas, peeled
2   passionfruit, pulped
3/4 cup granulated sugar
1/4 cup dark rum

Process the mango, bananas, passionfruit, sugar, and rum in a food processor or blender until smooth, about 1 minute.

Makes about 2 cups · Prep: 15 min. · Level: 1 · Keeps: 2–3 days in the refrigerator

raspberry puree

1   lb fresh raspberries
1/4 cup fresh lemon juice
2–4 tablespoons granulated sugar

Place the raspberries, lemon juice, and 2 tablespoons sugar in a blender or food processor. Process until very finely chopped. • Taste and add the additional sugar as needed. • Pass the mixture through a sieve before serving. • If not using immediately, place in a suitable container and freeze for use later in the year.

Makes about 5 cups · Prep: 10 min · Keeps: 5 days

cherry sauce

    Zest and juice of 1/4 orange
1   cup + 1 tablespoon cold water
2 1/2 tablespoons granulated sugar
1/2 teaspoon ground cinnamon
2   cups frozen pitted cherries
1 1/2 teaspoons cornstarch
1/4 teaspoon vanilla extract

Bring the orange juice and zest, 1 cup of water, the sugar, and cinnamon in a medium saucepan over medium heat. Stir in the cherries and return the mixture to a boil.

Dissolve the cornstarch in the remaining 1 tablespoon of water and stir it into the sauce. As soon as the sauce begins to thicken, remove from the heat. Stir in the vaniilla. Let cool completely. Refrigerate for 12 hours before serving

Makes 2 cups · Prep: 15 min. + 12 hr. to chill · Cooking: 20 min. · Level: 1 · Keeps: 5 days in the refrigerator

cranberry sauce

2   cups fresh or frozen cranberries
1 1/4 cups granulated sugar
3/4 cup water

Place the cranberries and 2 tablespoons of water in large saucepan. Bring to a boil over low heat and cook for 30–35 minutes, or until the cranberries have softened. • Mix the sugar and the remaining water in a small saucepan and bring to a boil. • Pour the boiling syrup over the cranberries and let cool completely.

Makes 2 cups · Prep: 20 min. · Cooking: 35–40 min. Level: 1 · Keeps: 2 weeks

warm chocolate sauce

1/2 cup (1 stick) butter
1/2 cup water
5   oz bittersweet chocolate, coarsely chopped
1 1/4 cups granulated sugar
1/4 cup light corn syrup
1/8 teaspoon salt
1   teaspoon vanilla extract

Melt the butter in the water in a medium saucepan over medium heat. Bring to a boil, stirring constantly. • Add the chocolate and stir carefully until melted. • Add the sugar, corn syrup, and salt. Bring to a boil and

simmer for 5 minutes. Remove from the heat and stir in the vanilla. • Serve hot or warm.

Makes 2 cups · Prep: 20 min. · Cooking: 5 min. · Level: 1 · Keeps: 3 days in the refrigerator

chocolate–fudge sauce

2   oz semisweet chocolate
1/4 cup (1/2 stick) butter
2   tablespoons unsweetened cocoa powder
3/4 cup firmly packed dark brown sugar
2/3 cup heavy cream
1/2 cup finely chopped nuts, toasted (optional)

Melt the chocolate and butter in a double boiler over barely simmering water, then beat in the cocoa. • Add the sugar and stir well before adding the cream. • Cook for 15–20 minutes, stirring frequently, until it looks thick and shiny. • Remove from the heat. • Mix in the nuts, if using.

Makes 1 cup · Prep: 20 min. · Cooking: 15–20 min. · Level: 1 · Keeps: 3 days in the refrigerator

caramel sauce

1/3 cup butter
1/2 cup firmly packed light brown sugar
1 2/3 cups heavy cream

Cook the butter and brown sugar in a small saucepan over low heat, stirring constantly, until melted. • Stir in the cream. Bring to a boil and cook for 5 minutes, or until the sauce has thickened.

Makes about 1 cup · Prep: 30 min. · Level: 1 · Keeps: 1 week in the refrigerator

Mincemeat

making a traditional red berry compote

Rote Grütze is a traditional German berry compote thickened with cornstarch. It makes a good filling for cookies and mini tarts. If summer berries are not available, use frozen mixed summer fruits (thawed). It is best to prepare the compote a day in advance. When using to fill your baked tartlets or mini pies, sprinkle the base with flaked almonds before spooning in the compote.

26–28 oz summer berries, such as sliced strawberries, raspberries, red currants, black currants, blueberries, or pitted cherries (weight after hulling and stripping from the stalks)

- 3/4 cup granulated sugar
  Zest of 1 orange and 1 lemon
  Juice of 1 lemon
- 1/4 cup cornstarch
- 1–2 teaspoons water

Mix the berries, sugar, orange and lemon zest, and lemon juice in a large bowl. • Cover with plastic wrap and refrigerate for 6 hours. • Mix the cornstarch and enough water to achieve a smooth paste. • Strain the fruit juices into a saucepan and bring to a boil over medium heat. • Remove from the heat and gradually stir in the cornstarch mixture. Continue stirring until the mixture thickens. • Place the saucepan over very low heat and mix in the fruit. • Simmer for 5–10 minutes, or until thickened. • Remove from the heat and let cool completely. • Transfer to a bowl, cover with plastic wrap, and refrigerate.

Makes 1½ cups · Prep: 25 min. + 6 hr. to chill · Level: 1 · Keeps: 7 days in the refrigerator

raspberry coulis

- 1 lb fresh raspberries
- 3/4 cup granulated sugar
- 2 tablespoons fresh lemon juice
- 2 tablespoons kirsch or raspberry liqueur

Process the raspberries, sugar, lemon juice, and kirsch in a food processor or blender until smooth, about 1 minute.

Makes about 2 cups · Prep: 15 min. · Level: 1 · Keeps: 2–3 days in the refrigerator

berry coulis

- 1 lb fresh berries, such as blueberries, strawberries, raspberries, blackberries, in any combination
- 3/4 cup granulated sugar
- 2 tablespoons fresh lemon juice
- 2 tablespoons kirsch or raspberry liqueur

Process the berries, sugar, and wine in a food processor or blender until smooth.

Makes about 2 cups · Prep: 15 min. · Level: 1 · Keeps: 2–3 days in the refrigerator

strawberry coulis

- 1 lb fresh strawberries, hulled
- 1/2 cup granulated sugar
- 1/4 cup fresh lemon juice

Process the strawberries, sugar, and juice in a food processor or blender until smooth, about 1 minute.

Makes about 2 cups · Prep: 15 min. · Level: 1 · Keeps: 2–3 days in the refrigerator

kiwi coulis

- 1 lb ripe kiwifruit, peeled and roughly chopped
- 3/4 cup granulated sugar
- 2 tablespoons strong sweet dessert wine

Process the kiwifruit, sugar, and wine in a food processor or blender until smooth.

Makes about 2 cups · Prep: 15 min. · Level: 1 · Keeps: 2–3 days in the refrigerator

lemon glaze

- 2/3 cup confectioners' sugar
- 3 tablespoons fresh lemon juice, + more as needed

Mix the confectioners' sugar with enough lemon juice to form a smooth, thick consistency.

Makes 2/3 cup · Prep: 5 min. · Level: 1 · Keeps: 1 days

orange glaze

- 2/3 cup confectioners' sugar
- 3 tablespoons fresh orange juice, + more as needed

Mix the confectioners' sugar with enough orange juice to form a smooth, thick consistency.

Makes 2/3 cup · Prep: 5 min. · Level: 1 · Keeps: 1 days

vanilla ice cream

- 4 large egg yolks
- 1 scant cup granulated sugar
- 2 cups milk
- 1 cup light or heavy cream
- 1 teaspoon finely grated vanilla bean

Beat the egg yolks and sugar until pale and thick. • Bring the milk, cream, and vanilla to a boil in a saucepan. Remove from the heat and let cool slightly. Gradually stir into the egg and sugar. • Cook over low heat, beating constantly with a wooden spoon, until the mixture lightly coats a metal spoon or registers 160°F on an instant-read thermometer. Immediately plunge the pan into a bowl of ice water and stir until the egg mixture has cooled. · If you have an ice cream maker, pour the mixture into it and follow the instructions. · If you don't have an ice cream maker, pour into a large bowl and freeze. After 3 hours, stir the mixture well. After another 3 hours, stir for a few minutes and freeze for 3 hours more.

Makes 1 quart · Prep: 30 min. + 9 hr. to freeze (without ice cream maker) · Level: 2

heavenly cream

- 1 cup milk
- 4 large egg yolks
- 1/3 cup granulated sugar
- 1/3 cup sweet white dessert wine

Bring the milk to a boil in a saucepan over medium heat. Remove from the heat. • Beat the egg yolks and sugar in a large bowl with an electric mixer at high speed until pale and thick. • Pour the milk into the eggs. • Transfer to a double boiler over barely simmering water. Stir until the mixture lightly coats a metal spoon and registers 160°F on an instant-read thermometer. Remove from the heat and stir in the wine.

Makes 1½ cups · Prep: 15 min. · Level: 1 · Keeps: 2–3 days

sweet almond zabaglione

- 6 large egg yolks
- 1 cup granulated sugar
- 1/2 cup Champagne
- 1/2 cup almond liqueur
- 1/3 cup whipped cream

Beat the egg yolks and sugar in a double boiler with an electric mixer at high speed until pale and thick. • Cook over barely simmering water, gradually beating in the Champagne and liqueur. Continue cooking until the mixture lightly coats a metal spoon and registers 160°F on an instant-read thermometer. • Remove from heat and set aside to cool. • Use a large rubber spatula to fold in the whipped cream.

Makes about 2 cups · Prep: 25 min. + 25 min. to cool · Level: 1 · Keeps: 1 day

passionfruit cream

10 large passionfruit
2   tablespoons fresh lemon juice
2 1/2 cups granulated sugar
3   tablespoons butter
4   large eggs, lightly beaten

Cut the passionfruit in half and scoop out the pulp. • Beat the pulp, lemon juice, sugar, butter, and eggs in a double boiler until well blended. Cook over barely simmering water, stirring constantly with a wooden spoon, until the sauce lightly coats a metal spoon and registers 160°F on an instant-read thermometer. Set aside to cool.

Makes about 2 cups · Prep: 20 min. · Level: 1 · Keeps: 1–2 days in the refrigerator

chocolate buttercream

1/2 cup water
3/4 cup granulated sugar
3   large egg yolks
1   cup (2 sticks) butter, softened
8   oz bittersweet chocolate, coarsely chopped

Stir the water and sugar in a saucepan over medium heat until the sugar has dissolved. • With a pastry brush dipped in cold water, wash down the sides of the pan to prevent sugar crystals from forming. Cook, without stirring, until the mixture reaches 238°F, or the soft-ball stage. • Beat the egg yolks in a double boiler with an electric mixer at high speed until pale. • Gradually beat the syrup into the beaten yolks. • Place over barely simmering water, stirring constantly with a wooden spoon, until the mixture lightly coats a metal spoon and registers 160°F on an instant-read thermometer. • Immediately plunge the pan into a bowl of ice water and stir until cooled. • Beat the butter in a large bowl until creamy. Beat into the egg mixture. • Melt the chocolate in a double boiler over barely simmering water and stir into the buttercream until well blended.

Makes about 2 cups · Prep: 25 min. · Level: 1 · Keeps: 5–6 days in the refrigerator

italian buttercream

Add 1 teaspoon vanilla extract for vanilla buttercream or 1/2 teaspoon almond extract for an almond buttercream.

1/2 cup water
3/4 cup granulated sugar
3   large egg yolks
1   cup (2 sticks) butter, softened

Stir the water and sugar in a saucepan over medium heat until the sugar has dissolved. • With a pastry brush dipped in cold water, wash down the sides of the pan to prevent sugar crystals from forming. Cook, without stirring, until the mixture reaches 238°F, or the soft-ball stage. • Beat the egg yolks in a double boiler with an electric mixer at high speed until pale. • Gradually beat the syrup into the beaten yolks. • Place over barely simmering water, stirring constantly with a wooden spoon, until the mixture lightly coats a metal spoon and registers 160°F on an instant-read thermometer. • Immediately plunge the pan into a bowl of ice water and stir until cooled. • Beat the butter in a large bowl until creamy. Beat into the egg mixture.

Makes about 2 cups · Prep: 25 min. · Level: 1 · Keeps: 5–6 days in the refrigerator

coffee buttercream

2   tablespoons very strong coffee, lukewarm
3/4 cup granulated sugar
3   large egg yolks
1   cup (2 sticks) butter, softened

Stir the coffee and sugar in a saucepan over medium heat until the sugar has dissolved. • With a pastry brush dipped in cold water, wash down the sides of the pan to prevent sugar crystals from forming. Cook, without stirring, until the mixture reaches 238°F, or the soft-ball stage. • Beat the egg yolks in a double boiler with an electric mixer at high speed until pale. • Gradually beat the syrup into the beaten yolks. • Place over barely simmering water, stirring constantly with a wooden spoon, until the mixture lightly coats a metal spoon or registers 160°F on an instant-read thermometer. • Immediately plunge the pan into a bowl of ice water and stir until cooled. • Beat the butter in a large bowl until creamy. Beat into the egg mixture.

Makes about 2 cups · Prep: 25 min. · Level: 1 · Keeps: 5–6 days in the refrigerator

zabaglione

Serve this with freshly baked Langues de Chat (see page 262) or other wafer cookies.

4   large egg yolks
1/4 cup granulated sugar
1/2 cup dry Marsala wine or dry sherry or vin santo (a Tuscan sweet dessert wine)

Beat the egg yolks and sugar in a double boiler with an electric mixer at high speed until pale and very thick. • Gradually add the Marsala. • Place over low heat and cook, beating constantly, until very thick, about 10 minutes, making sure that the mixture cooks to 160°F. Serve right away or place plastic wrap directly on the surface and refrigerate until you are ready to serve.

Makes 1 1/2 cups · Prep: 20 min. · Level: 1 · Keeps: 1 day

Coffee buttercream

making homemade marzipan

Try making these decorative gems to finish your cookies off to perfection. Colorful and attractive, create any fruit or vegetable to highlight the dominant flavor in your cookies. Or serve these homemade marzipan shapes as they are as an after-dinner treat. You can buy packages of white and colored marzipan for molding candies and mini cookies. This recipe is almost as quick to make as a trip to the supermarket.

4 1/2   cups finely ground almonds
3   cups confectioners' sugar + extra for kneading and dusting
3   tablespoons rose water or orange-flower water
   Red, yellow, green, and orange food coloring

Use your hands to work together the almonds, confectioners' sugar, and rose water to form a firm dough. • Divide the dough into small pieces. • Add 1 or 2 drops of food coloring to each piece and work in the color. Dust your hands and work surface with confectioners' sugar to prevent the marzipan from becoming too sticky. • Roll the marzipan out to a thickness of 1/4 inch. Use very small cookie cutters to stamp out shapes. • Make oranges and lemons with small balls of marzipan. Pit the "peel" by rolling the marzipan against a fine grater. • Shape green and red marzipan into apples and strawberries, and yellow marzipan into bananas. Paint brown lines with food coloring down the banana skins. Short pieces of crystallized angelica make good fruit stalks. • Let harden for 24 hours.

Makes 50 shapes · Prep: 10 min. + 20–50 min for shapes · Level: 1 · Keeps: 30 days

coconut–walnut frosting

1   cup granulated sugar
3/4   cup milk
3   large eggs
1/3   cup butter
1   cup shredded coconut
1   cup finely chopped walnuts

Place the sugar, milk, eggs, and butter in a large saucepan. Cook over medium heat, stirring constantly until the mixture begins to thicken and reaches 160°F on an instant-read thermometer. • Remove from the heat and transfer to a large bowl. • Stir in the coconut and walnuts and beat with mixer at high speed until thick and spreadable. Refrigerate for 1 hour before using.

Makes about 1 cup · Prep: 20 min. · Level: 1 · Keeps: 3 days in the refrigerator

chocolate–walnut frosting

4   oz semisweet chocolate, coarsely chopped
1/3   cup butter, cut up
2 1/2   cups confectioners' sugar
1   teaspoon vanilla extract
1   tablespoon fresh lemon juice
1   cup walnuts, coarsely chopped

Melt the chocolate and butter in a double boiler over barely simmering water. Set aside to cool. • Beat in the confectioners' sugar, vanilla, and lemon juice. Add the walnuts. Use immediately.

Makes 2 cups · Prep: 10 min. · Level: 1 · Keeps: 2–3 days

chocolate–pecan frosting

4   oz semisweet chocolate, coarsely chopped
1/3   cup butter, cut up
2 1/2   cups confectioners' sugar
1   teaspoon vanilla extract
1   tablespoon fresh lemon juice
1   cup pecans, coarsely chopped

Melt the chocolate and butter in a double boiler over barely simmering water. Set aside to cool. • Beat in the confectioners' sugar, vanilla, and lemon juice. Add the pecans. Use immediately.

Makes 2 cups · Prep: 10 min. · Level: 1 · Keeps: 2–3 days

chocolate butter frosting

1/3   cup butter, softened
2/3   cup confectioners' sugar
1/4   cup unsweetened cocoa powder

Beat the butter in a medium bowl with an electric mixer at high speed until creamy. • Beat in the confectioners' sugar and cocoa until well blended.

Makes 1 1/4 cups · Prep: 5 min. · Level: 1 · Keeps: 2 days in the refrigerator

simple chocolate frosting

2   cups confectioners' sugar
1/4   cup unsweetened cocoa powder
2   tablespoons butter, softened
1   teaspoon vanilla extract
   About 2 tablespoons boiling water

Stir together the confectioners' sugar and cocoa in a double boiler. Add the butter, vanilla, and enough of the water to make a firm paste. Stir over simmering water until the frosting has a spreadable consistency, about 3 minutes.

Makes about 1 1/2 cups · Prep: 5 min. · Level: 1 · Keeps: 2–3 days

white chocolate frosting

8   oz white chocolate, coarsely chopped
1   cup milk
1   cup granulated sugar
1   cup (2 sticks) butter, softened
1   teaspoon vanilla extract

Melt the chocolate in a double boiler over barely simmering water. • Gradually beat in the milk until well blended. Cook over medium heat, stirring constantly, until very thick. Remove from the heat and let cool completely. • Beat the butter, sugar, and vanilla in a large bowl with an electric mixer at high speed until creamy. • With mixer at high speed, gradually beat in the cooled chocolate mixture until stiff.

Makes about 1 1/2 cups · Prep: 5 min. · Level: 1 · Keeps: 2–3 days

mocha icing

3   tablespoons butter, softened
3   cups confectioners' sugar
1   teaspoon vanilla extract
1/3   cup strong cold coffee
1/4   cup unsweetened cocoa powder

Beat the butter and confectioners' sugar in a large bowl with an electric mixer at high speed until creamy. Gradually beat in the cocoa until no white streaks remain. Stir in the coffee and vanilla to make a spreading consistency.

Makes 2 cups · Prep: 15 min. · Level: 1 · Keeps: 2 days in the refrigerator

Homemade marzipan

chocolate–sour cream frosting

- 8   oz semisweet chocolate, coarsely chopped
- 1/4 cup (1/2 stick) butter, softened
- 1/2 cup sour cream
- 2 2/3 cups confectioners' sugar

Melt the chocolate in a double boiler over barely simmering water. Add the butter and set aside to cool for 5 minutes. • Stir in the sour cream. Beat in the confectioners' sugar until smooth and spreadable.

Makes 2 1/2 cups · Prep: 15 min. + 5 min. to cool · Level: 1 · Keeps: 1–2 days

cream cheese–coconut frosting

- 1   package (8 oz) cream cheese, softened
- 3   cups confectioners' sugar
- 1/3 cup butter, softened
- 1/2 cup shredded coconut
- 1   tablespoon milk
- 1   teaspoon vanilla extract

Beat the cream cheese, confectioners' sugar, butter, coconut, milk, and vanilla in a large bowl with an electric mixer at high speed until creamy.

Makes 1 cup · Prep: 15 min. · Level: 1 · Keeps: 2 days in the refrigerator

cream cheese–vanilla frosting

- 1/2 package (4 oz) cream cheese, softened
- 3   cups confectioners' sugar
- 1/3 cup butter, softened
- 1   teaspoon vanilla extract
- 1   tablespoon milk

Beat the cream cheese, confectioners' sugar, butter, milk, and vanilla in a large bowl with an electric mixer at high speed until creamy.

Makes 1 cup · Prep: 15 min. · Level: 1 · Keeps: 2 days in the refrigerator

cocoa–almond frosting

- 3   cups confectioners' sugar
- 1   package (8 oz) cream cheese, softened
- 1/2 cup (1 stick) butter, softened
- 1/4 cup unsweetened cocoa powder
- 1/2 cup finely chopped almonds

Beat the confectioners' sugar, cream cheese, butter, and cocoa in a large bowl with an electric mixer at high speed until creamy. Stir in the almonds.

Makes 2 cups · Prep: 15 min. · Level: 1 · Keeps: 2 days in the refrigerator

applesauce–cinnamon frosting

- 1   cup Applesauce (see page 340)
- 1   cup fresh ricotta cheese
- 1   teaspoon ground cinnamon
- 2   tablespoons granulated sugar
- 1   teaspoon vanilla extract
- 1   cup heavy cream

Beat the applesauce, ricotta, and cinnamon in a large bowl with an electric mixer at high speed until well blended. • Add the sugar and vanilla. • With mixer at high speed, beat the cream in a medium bowl until stiff. • Use a large rubber spatula to

Lemon butter frosting

fold the applesauce mixture into the whipped cream. Refrigerate for 1 hour.

Makes 2 cups · Prep: 20 min. + 60 min. to chill · Level: 1 · Keeps: 5 days in the refrigerator

crunchy peanut butter frosting

- 1/3 cup butter, softened
- 1   cup firmly packed dark brown sugar
- 2/3 cup crunchy peanut butter
- 1/4 cup milk
- 2/3 cup finely chopped peanuts

Beat the butter, sugar, and peanut butter in a medium bowl with an electric mixer at high speed until creamy. Beat in the milk until smooth. • Stir in the peanuts.

Makes 2 cups · Prep: 20 min. · Level: 1 · Keeps: 2 weeks in the refrigerator

lemon butter frosting

- 2   cups confectioners' sugar
- 1/4 cup (1/2 stick) butter, softened
- 2   tablespoons fresh lemon juice

Beat the confectioners' sugar, butter, and lemon juice in a medium bowl with an electric mixer at medium speed until fluffy.

Makes 1 cup · Prep: 5 min. · Level: 1 · Keeps: 2–3 days

vanilla frosting

- 2/3 cup confectioners' sugar
- 1 1/2 tablespoons water
- 1/2 teaspoon vanilla extract

Sift the confectioners' sugar into a medium bowl. • Stir in the water and vanilla until smooth.

Makes 1/2 cup · Prep: 5 min. · Level: 1 · Keeps: 1 day in the refrigerator

decorators' frosting

- 2 1/3 cups confectioners' sugar
- 1/3 cup light corn syrup
- 1/4 cup water
       Food colorings (optional)

Cook the confectioners' sugar, corn syrup, and water in a double boiler over barely simmering water, stirring until the sugar is melted and smooth, about 5 minutes. Remove from the heat.   Stir in the food coloring, if using, until no white streaks remain. If the icing is too thick to spread, add a few drops of water until it is a spreadable consistency.

Makes about 3 cups · Prep: 15 min. · CooKing: 5 min. · Level: 2 · Keeps: 1 day

chocolate and ricotta cream

Serve with Chocolate pirouette lace cookies (page 248).

2   large egg yolks
1/2 cup granulated sugar
1¼ cups ricotta cheese
1   tablespoon dry Marsala wine
4   oz semisweet chocolate, coarsely chopped
2½ tablespoons milk

Whisk the egg yolks and sugar in a heavy saucepan until well blended. Cook over low heat, stirring constantly with a wooden spoon, until the mixture lightly coats a metal spoon and registers 160°F on an instant-read thermometer. Immediately plunge the pan into a bowl of ice water and stir until the egg mixture has cooled. • Beat the egg yolks and sugar until very pale and creamy. Mix in the ricotta and Marsala. • Melt the chocolate in the milk over very low heat. Let cool. • Mix the chocolate and milk with half of the ricotta mixture. • Pour the ricotta and chocolate mixtures into serving dishes. • Blend the surfaces of the two mixtures with a knife to give a marbled effect, or leave them separate, as preferred. • Refrigerate for 2 hours.

Makes about 2 cups · Prep: 25 min. + 2 hr. to chill · Level: 1 · Keeps: 1 day in the refrigerator

zesty lemon frosting

4   cups confectioners' sugar
1/2 cup (1 stick) butter, softened
1   tablespoon grated lemon zest
4–6 tablespoons fresh lemon juice

Beat the confectioners' sugar, butter, lemon zest, and 4 tablespoons lemon juice in a large bowl with an electric mixer at medium speed until smooth. Add enough of the remaining lemon juice, a tablespoon at a time, to make a thick spreadable frosting.

Makes 2 cups · Prep: 10 min. · Level: 1 · Keeps: 1–2 days

maraschino frosting

4   cups confectioners' sugar
1/4 cup (1/2 stick) butter, softened
1/2 cup milk
2   tablespoons maraschino cherry syrup
16 maraschino cherries, finely chopped

Beat the confectioners' sugar, butter, and milk in a large bowl with an electric mixer at high speed until smooth. Beat in the cherry syrup and cherries until well blended.

Makes 2 cups · Prep: 20 min. · Level: 1 · Keeps: 1 week in the refrigerator

passionfruit filling and frosting

1   tablespoon passionfruit pulp
2   teaspoons butter, softened
1/2 cup confectioners' sugar
1   tablespoon water (optional)

Beat the passionfruit pulp and butter in a medium bowl with an electric mixer at high speed until creamy. Beat in the confectioners' sugar until smooth. To make a spreadable frosting, beat in the water as needed.

Makes about 1/3 cup · Prep: 10 min. · Level: 1 · Keeps: 1–2 days

seven-minute frosting

1½ cups granulated sugar
2   large egg whites
1/3 cup water
1/4 teaspoon salt
1/4 teaspoon cream of tartar
1   teaspoon vanilla extract

Stir the sugar, egg whites, water, salt, and cream of tartar in a saucepan until blended. Cook over low heat, beating constantly with an electric mixer at low speed until the whites register 160°F on an instant-read thermometer. Transfer to a bowl and beat at high speed until the frosting forms stiff peaks. • Remove from the heat and stir in the vanilla. • Beat until smooth and spreadable.

Makes about 4 cups · Prep: 10 min. · Level: 1 · Keeps: 2–3 days in the refrigerator

chocolate and mascarpone cream

2   large egg yolks
1/2 cup granulated sugar
1¼ cups mascarpone cheese
1   tablespoon dry Marsala wine
4   oz semisweet chocolate, coarsely chopped
2½ tablespoons milk

Whisk the egg yolks and sugar in a heavy saucepan until well blended. Cook over low heat, stirring constantly with a wooden spoon, until the mixture lightly coats a metal spoon and registers 160°F on an instant-read thermometer. Immediately plunge the pan into a bowl of ice water and stir until the egg mixture has cooled. •• Beat the egg yolks and sugar until very pale and creamy. Mix in the Mascarpone gently and flavor with the Marsala. • Melt the chocolate in the milk over very low heat. Set aside to cool. •• Mix the chocolate and milk with half of the Mascarpone mixture. • Pour the Mascarpone and chocolate mixtures into individual serving dishes. •• Blend the surfaces of the two mixtures with a knife to give a marbled effect, or leave them separate, as preferred. • Refrigerate for 2 hours before serving.

Makes about 2 cups · Prep: 25 min. + 2 hr. to chill · Level: 1 · Keeps: 1 day in the refrigerator

Seven minute frosting

index

A

Almonds
-Almond–brown sugar meringues, 241
-Almond–chocolate chip cookies, 24
-Almond cinnamon cookies, 18
-Almond-coated sugar cookies, 56
-Almond coconut bars, 140
-Almond cookie cups, 260
-Almond cookies, 105
-Almond crescents, 204
-Almond heaps, 238
-Almond lace cookies, 253
-Almond lattice bars, 144
-Almond–lemon madeleines, 284
-Almond–lemon swirls, 178
-Almond macaroons, 241
-Almond orange pockets, 90
-Almond orange wafers, 253
-Almond poppy seed cookies, 242
-Almond raspberry tarts, 293
-Almond shell cookies, 284
-Almond shortbread cookies, 192
-Almond shortbread with blackberry topping, 194
-Almond slices, 144
-Almond spritz cookies, 222
-Almond spritzers, 208
-Almond-studded playing cards, 106
-Almond tarts, 280
-Almond–toffee bars, 129
-Almond–walnut bars, 145
-Augsburg mellow yellows, 114
-Baseler leckerli, 100
-Berliners, 73
-Blueberry–almond friands, 281
-Caramel–nut bars, 150
-Chester fingers, 120
-Chocolate almond biscotti, 271
-Chocolate almond tuiles, 250
-Chocolate almond wafers, 250
-Chocolate crescents, 214
-Chocolate-drizzled almond cookies, 318
-Cinnamon tickets, 90
-Citrus cream cookies, 54
-Clove cut-out cookies, 114
-Cocoa–almond frosting, 348
-Cocoa–amaretti cookies, 240
-Coconut–almond biscotti, 274
-Coffee–almond squares, 156
-Convent almond macaroons, 229
-Convent kipfeln, 214

-Crunchy-topped almond butter cookies, 85
-Dainty almond wafers, 252
-Danish almond cookies, 216
-Date–almond cookies, 43
-Double chocolate–almond cookies, 36
-Dried cherry–almond biscotti, 272
-Eliza's macaroons, 228
-Filled almond wafers, 253
-Florentine squares, 136
-Ginger–almond biscotti, 275
-Ginger–almond florentines, 264
-Honey–almond biscotti, 274
-Jumble rings, 94
-Karlsbad cookies, 88
-Lebkuchen, 46
-Leipzig tarts, 293
-Lemon–almond bites, 56
-Maidstone cookies, 32
-Making french almond tiles, 248
-Maple blondies, 155
-Mazurek, 68
-Mocha–almond cookies, 106
-Norwegian cookies, 54
-Nuremberg spice cookies, 50
-Nut cookies, 174
-Nut crisps, 104
-Nutty mini meringues, 232
-Old English jumbles, 94
-Orange–almond cookies, 216
-Orange-glazed nut cookies, 77
-Paradise bars, 130
-Petticoat tails, 192
-Pineapple–almond cookies, 218
-Piped almond-topped cookies, 218
-Piped and topped macaroons, 239
-Piped dreams, 207
-Plain-and-fancy cookies, 174
-Potato–almond cookies, 174
-Prato biscotti, 270
-Raspberry–almond friands, 281
-Rich chocolate macaroons, 228
-Rocky road bars, 140
-Sablé cookies, 86
-Shortbread thumbprints, 192
-Spanish shortbread, 190
-Stars in the sky, 107
-Strawberry–almond friands, 281
-Sweet almond zabaglione, 344
-Sweet and spiced shapes, 92
-Swiss hearts, 112
-Victorian almond jumbles, 94
-Wasps' nests, 242
-Zesty almond shortbread, 194
-Zesty citrus bars, 90

Aniseeds
-Aniseed and pine nut cookies, 240
-Aniseed biscotti, 271
-Aniseed macaroons, 241
-Aniseed puffs, 223
-Aniseed rounds, 220
-Rustic anise cookies, 84
-Traditional coriander cookies, 39
-Whole-wheat aniseed bars, 138
Apples
-Apple bars, 151
-Apple bars with orange glaze, 120
-Apple–marzipan bars, 152
-Apple–oat bars, 142
-Apple, raisin, and oat bars, 126
-Applesauce, 340
-Applesauce-cinnamon frosting, 348
-Apple shortbread, 196
-Apple–spice cookies, 50
-Apple turnovers, 89
-Apple–walnut cookies, 42
-Bavarian apple cones, 258
-Fruits of the fall cookies, 180
-Sweet apple cookies, 32
Apricots
-Apricot–chocolate pretzels, 216
-Apricot corn flake cookies, 21
-Apricot pecan cookies, 72
-Apricot–raisin bars, 126
-Apricot rocks, 21
-Apricot sandwich cookies, 20
-Apricot squares, 120
-Apricot thumbprints, 16
-Apricot-topped shortbread squares, 198
-Coconut toasties, 56
-Ginger–fruit cookies, 51
-Muesli drop cookies, 43
-No-bake apricot–banana squares, 324
-No-bake chocolate–apricot cookies, 327
-Pear–apricot bars, 152
-Soft apricot drops, 21

B

Bananas
-Banana bars with cinnamon sugar topping, 134
-Banana brownies, 120
-Banana creams, 213
-Banana fingers, 120
-Banana kipfeln, 168
-Banana–oat bars, 142

-Banana–sunflower seed cookies, 48
-Chocolate–banana cookies, 29
-No-bake apricot–banana squares, 324
-No-bake date–banana squares, 324
-White chocolate–banana cookies, 48
Bars
-A-bit-of-everything bars, 154
-Almond coconut bars, 140
-Almond lattice bars, 144
-Almond slices, 144
-Almond–toffee bars, 129
-Almond–walnut bars, 145
-Apple bars, 151
-Apple bars with orange glaze, 120
-Apple–marzipan bars, 152
-Apple–oat bars, 142
-Apple, raisin, and oat bars, 126
-Apricot–raisin bars, 126
-Apricot squares, 120
-Australian crunchies, 140
-Banana bars with cinnamon sugar topping, 134
-Banana fingers, 120
-Banana–oat bars, 142
-Blondies, 148
-Bran flake and date bars, 138
-Caramel–nut bars, 150
-Carob–oat squares, 133
-Cheesecake cookie bars, 136
-Cherry marshmallow bars, 141
-Cherry–meringue bars, 134
-Chester fingers, 120
-Chewy oat and dried fruit bars, 146
-Chinese chews, 134
-Chocolate and honey lebkuchen bars, 142
-Chocolate caramel squares, 132
-Chocolate–orange squares, 132
-Chocolate peppermint bars, 136
-Chocolate quickies, 132
-Chocolate–raspberry macaroon bars, 145
-Cinnamon–meringue bars, 134
-Cocoa, orange, and date squares, 137
-Coconut–cherry squares, 132
-Coconut–corn flake squares, 141
-Coconut–walnut squares, 124
-Coffee–almond squares, 156
-Corn flake bars, 138
-Cranberry squares, 133

-Crispy mint squares, 136
-Crunchy oatmeal bars, 125
-Crusty lemon butter squares, 146
-Czech cookies, 150
-Date and pecan shortcakes, 130
-Date and walnut squares, 154
-Date diamonds, 133
-Date-filled oat bars, 140
-Easy oat bars, 138
-Energy bars, 141
-Florentine squares, 136
-Frosted cappuccino bars, 138
-German chocolate bars, 141
-Grasmere gingerbread, 124
-Hazelnut bars, 155
-Honey–cinnamon bars, 142
-Irish cheese squares, 126
-Lemon and ginger cookies, 150
-Lemon bars, 144
-Lemon cheesecake squares, 144
-Lemon meringue bars, 151
-Lemon party cakes, 148
-Lucerne-style lebkuchen bars, 142
-Maple blondies, 155
-Maraschino cherry bars, 140
-Marbled cream cheese squares, 137
-Meringue-topped butterscotch squares, 125
-Milk chocolate-frosted bars, 152
-Mint and currant bars, 122
-Molasses–currant bars, 124
-Muesli bars, 138
-Nanaimo bars, 138
-Nutty cornmeal squares, 134
-Orange cheesecake squares, 145
-Orange meringue bars, 151
-Orange–pecan squares, 156
-Paradise bars, 130
-Pear–apricot bars, 152
-Pear–cherry bars, 146
-Pecan pie bars, 130
-Port wine–walnut squares, 125
-Prune ribbon cookies, 155
-Pumpkin bars, 146
-Pumpkin–raisin bars with cream cheese frosting, 126
-Raspberry linzer squares, 152
-Raspberry–oat squares, 150
-Rhubarb–ginger squares, 124
-Rocky road bars, 140
-Scottish gingerbread, 124
-Sticky toffee–walnut bars, 129
-Sunflower bars, 137
-Sunshine bars, 133
-Swiss chocolate treats, 156
-Toffee bars, 129
-Toffee–oat bars, 129
-Toffee–walnut blondies with caramel frosting, 130
-Tyrolean chocolate fingers, 148
-Walnut squares, 125

-White chocolate–oat squares, 133
-Whole-wheat aniseed bars, 138
-Yogurt–cocoa bars, 151
-Yorkshire curd bars, 154
Biscotti
-Aniseed biscotti, 271
-Brown sugar–oat biscotti, 274
-Candied cardamom biscotti, 272
-Choc-and-nut biscotti, 271
-Chocolate–almond biscotti, 271
-Chocolate chip biscotti, 276
-Chocolate–coffee biscotti, 270
-Chocolate–walnut biscotti, 270
-Coconut–almond biscotti, 274
-Coconut–pecan biscotti, 276
-Double chocolate biscotti, 270
-Dried cherry–almond biscotti, 272
-Espresso biscotti, 274
-Fig–sesame biscotti, 275
-Ginger–almond biscotti, 275
-Ginger biscotti, 272
-Ginger–chocolate biscotti, 275
-Honey–almond biscotti, 274
-Lemon–poppy seed biscotti, 272
-Making biscotti, 268
-Maple cantuccini, 271
-Orange–hazelnut biscotti, 268
-Pecan biscotti, 268
-Pine nut biscotti, 276
-Polenta biscotti, 276
-Prato biscotti, 270
-Pumpkin pie biscotti, 274
Blackberries
-Almond shortbread with blackberry topping, 194
Black pepper
-Black pepper chocolate chip cookies, 24
-Lebkuchen, 46
-Northern pepper stars, 106
-Spiced black pepper cookies, 304
Blueberries
-Blueberry–almond friands, 281
Bran
-Bran cookies, 98
-Bran flake and date bars, 138
-Orange–bran flake cookies, 170
-Peanut butter–bran cookies, 34
-Sunflower–bran cookies, 14
Brandy
-Brandied spiced cookies, 38
Brazil nuts
-Brazil nut macaroons, 232
Brownies
-Banana brownies, 120
-Brownies, 122
-Chocolate–hazelnut brownies, 128
-Classic brownies, 146
-Coffee brownies, 128
-Fudge brownies, 132
-Indulgent chocolate brownies, 156
-Luxury chocolate brownies, 148
-Making brownie sundaes, 342

-Marbled fudge brownies, 122
-Marbled mint brownies, 122
-New Zealand honey–nut brownies, 128
-Three-chocolate brownies, 128
Buckwheat
-Chocolate buckwheat pixies, 285
Buttercreams
-Chocolate buttercream, 345
-Coffee buttercream, 345
-Italian buttercream, 345

C
Candied peel
-Augsburg mellow yellows, 114
-Baseler leckerli, 100
-Candied spritzers, 222
-Eliza's macaroons, 228
-Fruity French drops, 55
-Ladies' delights, 207
-Ormskirk crisp gingerbread, 68
-Prairie cookies, 52
-Tutti-frutti cookies, 84
-Zesty citrus bars, 90
Caraway seeds
-Abernethy cookies, 68
-Bohemian caraway cookies, 85
-Caraway crisps, 52
-Sherry tea cakes, 100
-Whetstone cookies, 101
Cardamom
-Candied cardamom biscotti, 272
-Cardamom cookies, 40
-Cardamom krumkake wafer cones, 256
-Fried cardamom cookies, 332
-Ginger–fruit cookies, 51
-Norwegian cardamom cookies, 312
-Northern pepper stars, 106
-Norwegian Christmas cardamom cookies, 336
Carob
-Carob–oat squares, 133
-Carob-topped sunflower seed drops, 30
-Carob truffle squares, 323
-No-bake carob brownies, 324
-Sunflower–bran cookies, 14
Carrots
-Carrot and orange meringues, 238
-Carrot and raisin drops, 60
-Carrot cookies, 60
-Carrot–orange cookies, 60
Cashew nuts
-Caramel–nut bars, 150
-Cashew butter cookies, 168
-Cashew–chocolate crisps, 261
-Cashew cookies, 105
-Sunflower bars, 137
Cheese
-Irish cheese squares, 126
Cherries

-Cherry–chocolate crunchies, 15
-Cherry Christmas cookies, 316
-Cherry florentines, 264
-Cherry marshmallow bars, 141
-Cherry–meringue bars, 134
-Cherry oat cookies, 29
-Cherry–rum shortbread cookies, 189
-Cherry sauce, 342
-Cherry stand-by cookies, 172
-Cherry–walnut cookies, 173
-Cherry–walnut shortbread, 196
-Chocolate cherry cookies, 29
-Chocolate cherry spritz cookies, 211
-Coconut–cherry icebox cookies, 181
-Coconut–cherry squares, 132
-Coffee–cherry cookies, 47
-Dried cherry–almond biscotti, 272
-Florentine squares, 136
-Ginger–fruit cookies, 51
-Italian hazelnut cookies, 25
-Maraschino cherry bars, 140
-Maraschino frosting, 349
-Melting moments, 30
-Nutty cherry–chocolate cookies, 29
-Pear–cherry bars, 146
-Pineapple–cherry macaroons, 241
-Piped cherry-topped shortbread, 193
-Walnut–cherry florentines, 254
-White chocolate–cherry cookies, 28
Chestnuts
-Chestnut meringues, 240
Chocolate
-A-bit-of-everything bars, 154
-Almond–chocolate chip cookies, 24
-Apricot–chocolate pretzels, 216
-Bavarian kisses, 48
-Berliners, 73
-Bittersweet chocolate madeleines, 282
-Black-and-white cookies, 165
-Black pepper chocolate chip cookies, 24
-Brownies, 122
-Brown sugar chocolate chip cookies, 24
-Butterflies, 70
-Caramel shortbread squares, 185
-Caribbean chocolate cookies, 36
-Cashew–chocolate crisps, 261
-Cherry–chocolate crunchies, 15
-Choc-and-nut biscotti, 271
-Chocolate–almond biscotti, 271
-Chocolate–almond tuiles, 250
-Chocolate–almond wafers, 250
-Chocolate and hazelnut wafers, 256
-Chocolate and honey lebkuchen bars, 142

-Chocolate and mascarpone cream, 349
-Chocolate and ricotta cream, 349
-Chocolate angelica spritz cookies, 222
-Chocolate–banana cookies, 29
-Chocolate buckwheat pixies, 285
-Chocolate buttercream, 345
-Chocolate butter frosting, 346
-Chocolate caramel cookies, 169
-Chocolate caramel squares, 132
-Chocolate-coated party rings, 78
-Chocolate cherry cookies, 29
-Chocolate cherry spritz cookies, 211
-Chocolate–cherry squares, 323
-Chocolate chip biscotti, 276
-Chocolate chip cookies, 22
-Chocolate chip "pizza," 158
-Chocolate chip pumpkin cookies, 54
-Chocolate chip refrigerator cookies, 169
-Chocolate chip shortbread, 194
-Chocolate chip–walnut cookies, 22
-Chocolate–cinnamon shortbread, 185
-Chocolate-coated arches, 210
-Chocolate–coffee biscotti, 270
-Chocolate cookies with peanut butter topping, 22
-Chocolate corn flake cakes, 328
-Chocolate-covered coconut bars, 328
-Chocolate cream-filled kisses, 230
-Chocolate cream sandwich cookies, 93
-Chocolate crescents, 214
-Chocolate crumblies, 14
-Chocolate crunch wedges, 323
-Chocolate-dipped butter cookies, 206
-Chocolate-dipped lime cookies, 220
-Chocolate-dipped orange cookies, 92
-Chocolate-drizzled almond cookies, 318
-Chocolate drizzlers, 168
-Chocolate-filled coconut cookies, 35
-Chocolate-filled cookies, 70
-Chocolate-filled creams, 22
-Chocolate-filled macaroon kisses, 230
-Chocolate-filled sugar cookies, 66
-Chocolate-flecked cookies, 98
-Chocolate–fruit chewies, 322
-Chocolate–fudge sauce, 342
-Chocolate–ginger cookies, 40
-Chocolate–hazelnut brownies, 128
-Chocolate–hazelnut kisses, 18
-Chocolate–hazelnut pinwheels, 166
-Chocolate–hazelnut valentines, 302

-Chocolate hedgehogs, 15
-Chocolate macaroons, 229
-Chocolate meringues, 235
-Chocolate nut crackles, 36
-Chocolate nutmeg cookies, 15
-Chocolate–orange cookies, 78
-Chocolate–orange squares, 132
-Chocolate–orange stars, 78
-Chocolate–orange twists, 225
-Chocolate–peanut butter cookies, 26
-Chocolate peanut cookies, 26
-Chocolate–pecan frosting, 346
-Chocolate–pecan shortbread, 186
-Chocolate peppermint bars, 136
-Chocolate pirouette lace cookies, 248
-Chocolate–pistachio squares, 323
-Chocolate pretzels, 214
-Chocolate quickies, 132
-Chocolate–raspberry macaroon bars, 145
-Chocolate rose leaf cookies, 163
-Chocolate–semolina cookies, 70
-Chocolate shortbread cookies, 188
-Chocolate–sour cream frosting, 348
-Chocolate turtles, 296
-Chocolate vanilla drops, 22
-Chocolate–walnut biscotti, 270
-Chocolate–walnut frosting, 346
-Chocolate whipped cream, 341
-Chocologs, 296
-Classic brownies, 146
-Cocoa–almond frosting, 348
-Cocoa, orange, and date squares, 137
-Coconut–cherry squares, 132
-Coconut spritzers, 218
-Coffee brownies, 128
-Convent kipfeln, 214
-Crispy chocolate creams, 26
-Crunchy crags, 14
-Death-by-chocolate cookies, 36
-Double chocolate–almond cookies, 36
-Double chocolate biscotti, 270
-Double chocolate crisps, 258
-Double chocolate drops, 28
-Double chocolate fingers, 210
-Dreamy white chocolate chip cookies, 25
-Extra-large chocolate chip cookies, 44
-Filled cats' tongues, 262
-Filled chocolate fingers, 212
-Fudge brownies, 132
-German chocolate bars, 141
-Ginger–chocolate biscotti, 275
-Hungarian sandwich cookies, 42
-Indulgent chocolate brownies, 156
-Kahlua mousse, 341
-Linzer cookies, 69

-Luxury chocolate brownies, 148
-Making chocolate-dipped pirouette cookies, 249
-Marbled cookies, 59
-Marbled fudge brownies, 122
-Marbled mint brownies, 122
-Milk chocolate-frosted bars, 152
-Milk chocolate macaroons, 239
-Millionaire's shortbread, 190
-Mini cocoa–corn flake cookies, 48
-Mint–chocolate sandwiches, 70
-Mint-topped cookies, 81
-Mocha chocolate cookies, 14
-Mocha pinwheels, 162
-Nanaimo bars, 138
-New Zealand honey–nut brownies, 128
-No-bake chocolate–apricot cookies, 327
-No-bake chocolate caramel squares, 328
-No-bake chocolate crumb drops, 326
-No-bake chocolate–date cookies, 327
-No-bake chocolate fruit squares, 323
-No-bake chocolate mice, 324
-No-bake chocolate–peanut bars, 328
-No-bake chocolate–prune cookies, 327
-No-bake chocolate–raisin bars, 328
-No-bake chocolate squares, 326
-No-bake hazelnut–chocolate squares, 326
-Nutty cherry–chocolate cookies, 29
-Piquant chocolate cookies, 44
-Plain-and-fancy cookies, 174
-Oat chips, 25
-Oatmeal–chocolate chip cookies, 25
-Oatmeal "pizza," 158
-Orange and chocolate icebox cookies, 168
-Orange cookies with chocolate chips, 39
-Peanut butter–chocolate kiss cookies, 34
-Peanut butter "pizza," 158
-Pecan and chocolate chip "pizza," 158
-Piped mocha rosettes, 203
-Rich chocolate macaroons, 228
-Rolled white chocolate cookies, 105
-Sacher torte cookies, 40
-Simple chocolate frosting, 346
-Simple white chocolate chip cookies, 15
-Sugar hearts, 78

-Sweet and spiced shapes, 92
-Swiss chocolate treats, 156
-Three-chocolate brownies, 128
-Tyrolean chocolate fingers, 148
-Vanilla-filled kisses, 16
-Walnut bars, 154
-Warm chocolate sauce, 342
-White chocolate and amaretti crunch, 327
-White chocolate–banana cookies, 48
-White chocolate–cherry cookies, 28
-White chocolate chip cookies, 24
-White chocolate chip refrigerator cookies, 164
-White chocolate coated pretzels, 224
-White chocolate drops, 26
-White chocolate frosting, 346
-White chocolate–hazelnut florentines, 248
-White chocolate–nut meringues, 238
-White chocolate–passionfruit shortbread, 186
-White chocolate tartlets, 289
-Yogurt–cocoa bars, 151
Christmas cookies
-Austrian Christmas butter cookies, 305
-Candy cane cookies, 298
-Cherry Christmas cookies, 316
-Christmas ball cookies, 313
-Christmas carollers, 297
-Christmas cookies, 309
-Christmas cranberry bars, 296
-Christmas gift cookies, 298
-Christmas ginger cookies, 318
-Christmas mincemeat cookies, 314
-Christmas stars, 296
-Christmas walnut–cranberry bars, 300
-Christmas wreaths, 318
-Currant spice cookies, 306
-Czech Christmas diamonds, 309
-Czech Christmas hearts, 302
-Filled Christmas trees, 316
-Hansel and Gretel lebkuchen, 312
-Neapolitan Christmas fritters, 333
-Norwegian cardamom cookies, 312
-Norwegian Christmas cardamom cookies, 336
-Spekulatius, 298
-Spiced black pepper cookies, 304
-Springerle, 318
-Spritskransar, 314
-Stained glass cookies, 316
-Ukrainian Christmas cookies, 313
Cinnamon
-Almond cinnamon cookies, 18
-Applesauce–cinnamon frosting, 348

-Augsburg mellow yellows, 114
-Belgium cookies, 108
-Chocolate–cinnamon shortbread, 185
-Cinnamon–coffee cookies, 173
-Cinnamon cookies, 86
-Cinnamon corn flake cookies, 44
-Cinnamon crunchies, 46
-Cinnamon curls, 111
-Cinnamon–meringue bars, 134
-Cinnamon meringues, 238
-Cinnamon–orange cookies, 108
-Cinnamon slices, 177
-Cinnamon spritz cookies, 211
-Cinnamon streusel cookies, 109
-Cinnamon sugar, 341
-Cinnamon tickets, 90
-Cinnamon-topped flower cookies, 76
-Curly cinnamon ducks, 219
-Ginger–cinnamon cookies, 46
-Hazelnut cinnamon cookies, 18
-Hermits, 47
-Honey–cinnamon bars, 142
-Lemon–cinnamon cookies, 116
-Montecaos, 46
-Moravian spice squares, 68
-Norwegian brown cookies, 176
-Nutty cinnamon cookies, 35
-Peruvian cookies, 97
-Snickerdoodles, 14
Cloves
-Clove cut-out cookies, 114
Coconut
-Almond coconut bars, 140
-Anzac cookies, 30
-Canary cream cookies, 89
-Caribbean chocolate cookies, 36
-Caribbean coconut wafers, 260
-Chocolate-covered coconut bars, 328
-Chocolate-filled coconut cookies, 35
-Coconut–almond biscotti, 274
-Coconut and macadamia nut macaroons, 228
-Coconut and orange cookies, 170
-Coconut–cherry icebox cookies, 181
-Coconut–cherry squares, 132
-Coconut cookies, 30
-Coconut–corn flake squares, 141
-Coconut crisps, 260
-Coconut fortune cookies, 257
-Coconut heaps, 240
-Coconut–lime snaps, 177
-Coconut–lime stars, 107
-Coconut–macadamia cookies, 180
-Coconut macaroons, 240
-Coconut meringues, 235
-Coconut meringue slices, 236
-Coconut oat cookies, 67
-Coconut–pecan biscotti, 276

-Coconut–pecan shortbread, 188
-Coconut puffs, 241
-Coconut rock cakes, 30
-Coconut shortbread thins, 196
-Coconut spritzers, 218
-Coconut squares, 67
-Coconut thumbprints, 50
-Coconut toasties, 56
-Coconut–walnut frosting, 346
-Coconut–walnut squares, 124
-Cream cheese–coconut frosting, 348
-Marshmallow cookies, 32
-Piped coconut treats, 202
-Quick mini coconut cups, 286
-Soldier cookies, 60
Coffee
-Chocolate–coffee biscotti, 270
-Chocolate nut crackles, 36
-Cinnamon–coffee cookies, 173
-Coffee–almond squares, 156
-Coffee brownies, 128
-Coffee buttercream, 345
-Coffee–cherry cookies, 47
-Coffee-frosted walnut cookies, 106
-Coffee-frosted walnut shortbread cookies, 197
-Coffee–hazelnut bars, 80
-Coffee heart cookies, 80
-Coffee liqueur balls, 329
-Coffee–nut wafers, 20
-Coffee–pecan cookies, 63
-Coffee–pecan wafers, 254
-Coffee–pecan wedges, 322
-Coffee pinwheels, 163
-Coffee–raisin cookie cakes, 292
-Coffee shortbread, 198
-Coffee–walnut cookies, 63
-Coffee–walnut wedges, 327
-Double chocolate–almond cookies, 36
-Espresso biscotti, 274
-Espresso cookies, 166
-Frosted cappuccino bars, 138
-Hazelnut–coffee meringues, 230
-Kahlua mousse, 341
-Mocha–almond cookies, 106
-Mocha chocolate cookies, 14
-Mocha icing, 346
-Mocha madeleines, 282
-Mocha meringues, 236
-Mocha pinwheels, 162
-Orange lace cookies with coffee-cream filling, 258
-Pecan–coffee meringues, 230
-Piped mocha rosettes, 203
Cookie presses. See Piped
Coriander
-Traditional coriander cookies, 39
Corn flakes
-Apricot corn flake cookies, 21
-Cherry–chocolate crunchies, 15

-Chocolate corn flake cakes, 328
-Chocolate hedgehogs, 15
-Cinnamon corn flake cookies, 44
-Coconut–corn flake squares, 141
-Corn flake bars, 138
-Corn flake cookies, 32
-Corn flake–walnut cookies, 58
-Crunchy butterscotch cookies, 32
-Date and corn flake cookies, 181
-Lemon–corn flake cookies, 179
-Mini cocoa–corn flake cookies, 48
Cornmeal
-Brown sugar cornmeal cookies, 52
-Cornmeal–lemon cookies, 82
-Cornmeal ribbons, 215
-Crisp cornmeal cookies, 52
-Hot and spicy cornmeal cookies, 52
-Nutty cornmeal squares, 134
-Polenta biscotti, 276
-Poppy seed–cornmeal cookies, 88
-Venetian fregolata, 188
Coulis. See Purees
Cranberries
-Berry thins, 250
-Christmas cranberry bars, 296
-Cranberry–prune cookies, 55
-Cranberry sauce, 342
-Cranberry squares, 133
-Cranberry-topped hearts, 114
-Christmas walnut–cranberry bars, 300
-Nutty cranberry cookies, 35
Cream cheese
-Cheesecake cookie bars, 136
-Cream cheese–coconut frosting, 348
-Cream–cheese crescents, 76
-Cream cheese sandwich cookies, 170
-Cream cheese–vanilla frosting, 348
-Double-deckers, 111
-Lemon cheesecake squares, 144
-Maids of honor, 288
-Marbled cream cheese squares, 137
-Orange cheesecake squares, 145
-Pumpkin–raisin bars with cream cheese frosting, 126
Creams
-Chocolate and mascarpone cream, 349
-Chocolate and ricotta cream, 349
-Chocolate whipped cream, 341
-Heavenly cream, 344
-Mascarpone–vanilla cream, 340
-Mock cream, 341
-Passionfruit cream, 345
-Sweet almond zabaglione, 344
-Vanilla whipped cream, 340
-Zabaglione, 345
Currants

-Currant cookies, 337
-Derwentwater cookies, 101
-Easter currant cookies, 98
-Garibaldis, 101
-Mint and currant bars, 122
-Molasses–currant bars, 124
Custard powder
-Custard creams, 92

D

Dates
-Bran flake and date bars, 138
-Chewy oat and dried fruit bars, 146
-Cocoa, orange, and date squares, 137
-Date–almond cookies, 43
-Date and corn flake cookies, 181
-Date and pecan shortcakes, 130
-Date and walnut squares, 154
-Date cookies, 58
-Date delights, 43
-Date diamonds, 133
-Date-filled oat bars, 140
-Date–oat cookies, 16
-Date–pecan cookies, 43
-Meringue date morsels, 236
-Muesli drop cookies, 43
-No-bake chocolate–date cookies, 327
-No-bake date–banana squares, 324
-Pecan–date cookies, 18
-Pineapple date drops, 20
-Sunshine bars, 133
-Walnut–date cookies, 18
-Whole-wheat date cookies, 60
Drop cookies
-Almond–chocolate chip cookies, 24
-Amish spicy raisin cookies, 47
-Apple–spice cookies, 50
-Apple–walnut cookies, 42
-Apricot corn flake cookies, 21
-Apricot rocks, 21
-Apricot sandwich cookies, 20
-Apricot thumbprints, 16
-Almond cinnamon cookies, 18
-Almond-coated sugar cookies, 56
-Anzac cookies, 30
-Banana–sunflower seed cookies, 48
-Bavarian kisses, 48
-Black pepper chocolate chip cookies, 24
-Brandied spiced cookies, 38
-Brown sugar chocolate chip cookies, 24
-Brown sugar cookies, 32
-Brown sugar cornmeal cookies, 52
-Butter drop cookies, 42
-Butter drops, 28
-Canadian maple cookies, 59

-Caraway crisps, 52
-Cardamom cookies, 40
-Caribbean chocolate cookies, 36
-Carob-topped sunflower seed drops, 30
-Carrot and raisin drops, 60
-Carrot cookies, 60
-Carrot–orange cookies, 60
-Cherry–chocolate crunchies, 15
-Cherry oat cookies, 29
-Chocolate–banana cookies, 29
-Chocolate cherry cookies, 29
-Chocolate chip cookies, 22
-Chocolate chip pumpkin cookies, 54
-Chocolate chip–walnut cookies, 22
-Chocolate cookies with peanut butter topping, 22
-Chocolate crumblies, 14
-Chocolate-filled coconut cookies, 35
-Chocolate-filled creams, 22
-Chocolate–ginger cookies, 40
-Chocolate–hazelnut kisses, 18
-Chocolate hedgehogs, 15
-Chocolate nut crackles, 36
-Chocolate nutmeg cookies, 15
-Chocolate–peanut butter cookies, 26
-Chocolate peanut cookies, 26
-Chocolate vanilla drops, 22
-Cinnamon corn flake cookies, 44
-Cinnamon crunchies, 46
-Citrus cream cookies, 54
-Citrus mincemeat cookies, 55
-Coconut cookies, 30
-Coconut rock cakes, 30
-Coconut thumbprints, 30
-Coconut toasties, 56
-Coffee–cherry cookies, 47
-Coffee–nut wafers, 20
-Coffee–pecan cookies, 63
-Coffee–walnut cookies, 63
-Corn flake cookies, 32
-Corn flake–walnut cookies, 58
-Cracked ginger cookies, 40
-Cranberry–prune cookies, 55
-Crisp cornmeal cookies, 52
-Crispy chocolate creams, 26
-Crunchy butterscotch cookies, 32
-Crunchy crags, 14
-Date–almond cookies, 43
-Date cookies, 58
-Date delights, 43
-Date–oat cookies, 16
-Date–pecan cookies, 43
-Death-by-chocolate cookies, 36
-Double chocolate–almond cookies, 36
-Double chocolate drops, 28
-Double chocolate fingers, 210
-Dreamy white chocolate chip cookies, 25

-Drop sugar cookies, 28
-Extra-large chocolate chip cookies, 44
-Fruit and nut rock cookies, 62
-Fruity French drops, 55
-Ginger–cinnamon cookies, 46
-Ginger–fruit cookies, 51
-Gingernuts, 46
-Ginger puffs, 51
-Ginger–walnut cookies, 32
-Glazed lemon cookies, 63
-Glazed lemon–olive oil cookies, 62
-Glazed pineapple cookies, 20
-Golden nuts, 55
-Hazelnut cinnamon cookies, 18
-Hazelnut–citrus cookies, 38
-Hazelnut–fig cookies, 63
-Hazelnut–grape cookies, 62
-Hazelnut puffs, 18
-Heavenly moments, 43
-Hermits, 47
-Hot and spicy cornmeal cookies, 52
-Hungarian sandwich cookies, 42
-Italian hazelnut cookies, 25
-Lebkuchen, 46
-Lemon–almond bites, 56
-Lemon curd drops, 62
-Lemon drop cookies, 14
-Lemon–raisin cookies, 62
-Lime and sunflower seed cookies, 58
-Lime buttercream cookies, 58
-Maidstone cookies, 32
-Marbled cookies, 59
-Melting moments, 30
-Mini cocoa–corn flake cookies, 48
-Mint pryaniki, 55
-Mocha chocolate cookies, 14
-Molasses bites, 58
-Montecaos, 46
-Muesli drop cookies, 43
-Norwegian cookies, 54
-Nuremberg spice cookies, 50
-Nutmeg-topped cookies, 44
-Nutty cherry–chocolate cookies, 29
-Nutty cinnamon cookies, 35
-Nutty cranberry cookies, 35
-Oat chips, 25
-Oat crunchies, 22
-Oat drops, 48
-Oatmeal–chocolate chip cookies, 25
-Oatmeal cookies, 24
-Oatmeal, raisin, and walnut cookies, 38
-Oatmeal–raisin cookies, 38
-Oat–walnut cookies, 59
-Orange cookies with chocolate chips, 39
-Orange–raisin cookies, 39
-Orange viennese cookies, 43

-Parkin, 51
-Passionfruit crunchies, 44
-Peanut brownie cookies, 26
-Peanut butter–bran cookies, 34
-Peanut butter–chocolate kiss cookies, 34
-Peanut butter cookies, 34
-Peanut oaties, 34
-Pecan balls, 52
-Pecan–date cookies, 18
-Pecan–oat clusters, 56
-Pecan–sour cream cookies, 35
-Pineapple date drops, 20
-Pink and pretty sugar-sprinkled gems, 63
-Piquant chocolate cookies, 44
-Popcorn puffs, 62
-Prairie cookies, 52
-Pumpkin cookies, 54
-Queensland cookies, 34
-Raspberry drops, 16
-Raspberry kisses, 16
-Raspberry thumbprints, 16
-Rose pryaniki, 56
-Sacher torte cookies, 40
-Salted peanut cookies, 26
-Sand dollars, 54
-Simple white chocolate chip cookies, 15
-Snickerdoodles, 14
-Soft apricot drops, 21
-Soft raisin–walnut cookies, 38
-Soldier cookies, 60
-Spiced raisin cookies, 50
-Spice, nut, and honey ginger rounds, 50
-Spicy cornish fairings, 47
-Spicy hazelnut–lemon cookies, 47
-Stem ginger cookies, 20
-Strawberry thumbprints, 15
-Sunflower–bran cookies, 14
-Sunflower drops, 29
-Sunflower oat drops, 28
-Sweet apple cookies, 32
-Rice–olive oil cookies, 26
-Three-ingredient cookies, 35
-Tiny ginger cookies, 40
-Traditional coriander cookies, 39
-Turkish marmalade cookies, 51
-Two tone cookies, 42
-Vanilla-filled kisses, 16
-Viennese lemon cookies, 39
-Viennese orange cookies, 43
-Walnut clusters, 59
-Walnut–date cookies, 18
-Walnut–raisin cookies, 59
-White chocolate–banana cookies, 48
-White chocolate–cherry cookies, 28
-White chocolate chip cookies, 24
-White chocolate drops, 26
-Whole-wheat date cookies, 60

-Whole-wheat orange cookies, 42

E

Easter cookies. *See* Festive cookies

F

Festive cookies
-All Souls' cookies, 310
-Austrian Christmas butter cookies, 305
-Belgian pressed cookies, 310
-Bonfire cookies, 308
-Candy cane cookies, 298
-Cherry Christmas cookies, 316
-Chocolate-drizzled almond cookies, 318
-Chocolate–hazelnut valentines, 302
-Chocolate turtles, 296
-Chocologs, 296
-Christmas ball cookies, 313
-Christmas carollers, 297
-Christmas cookies, 309
-Christmas cranberry bars, 296
-Christmas gift cookies, 298
-Christmas ginger cookies, 318
-Christmas mincemeat cookies, 314
-Christmas stars, 296
-Christmas walnut–cranberry bars, 300
-Christmas wreaths, 318
-Color-your-own cookies, 305
-Cookie lollipops, 300
-Currant spice cookies, 306
-Czech Christmas diamonds, 309
-Czech Christmas hearts, 302
-Dominoes, 314
-Dutch butter diamonds, 316
-Easter cookies, 306
-Filled Christmas trees, 316
-Greeting card cookies, 300
-Halloween cookies, 310
-Hansel and Gretel lebkuchen, 312
-Italian Easter cookies, 310
-Jam cookie towers, 305
-Marmalade gingerbread squares, 318
-Mexican chocolate pastelitos, 296
-Mexican wedding cakes, 312
-Mother's Day hearts, 302
-Norwegian cardamom cookies, 312
-Party peppermint windmills, 304
-Passover brownies, 316
-Pepperkakor, 304
-Pistachio chocolates, 297
-Pizzelle cookies, 312
-Pfeffernuesse, 308
-Prune hamantaschen, 313
-Rugelach, 306
-Snake's tongue cookie, 306
-Spekulatius, 298
-Spiced black pepper cookies, 304
-Spider's web cookies, 309

-Spooky cookies, 308
-Springerle, 318
-Spritskransar, 314
-Stained glass cookies, 316
-St. Catherine's cookies, 300
-Traffic lights, 314
-Ukrainian Christmas cookies, 313
-Valentine message cookies, 302
Figs
-Chewy oat and dried fruit bars, 146
-Fig rolls, 112
-Fig–sesame biscotti, 275
-Hazelnut–fig cookies, 63
-Lemon–fig cookies, 180
Fillings
-Applesauce, 340
-Lemon curd, 340
-Mincemeat, 340
-Orange curd, 340
-Passionfruit filling and frosting, 349
-Raspberry curd, 340
-Traditional red berry compote, 344
Friands
-Blueberry–almond friands, 281
-Plum–nutmeg friands, 281
-Raspberry–almond friands, 281
-Strawberry–almond friands, 281
Fried cookies
-Aebleskiver cookies, 333
-Carnival cookies, 332
-Crisp cookie petals, 334
-Currant cookies, 337
-Fattigmann, 336
-Fried amaretti cookies, 334
-Fried cardamom cookies, 332
-Fried cookie bows, 333
-Jelly-filled fried cookies, 334
-Making fried cookies, 332
-Neapolitan Christmas fritters, 333
-Norwegian Christmas cardamom cookies, 336
-Oast house cookies, 333
-Polish diamonds, 336
-St. Joseph's day fritters, 336
-Sweet pumpkin fried cookies, 334
-Sweet ricotta fritters, 337
-Sweet tortillas, 337
-Welsh bakestones, 337
Frostings
-Applesauce–cinnamon frosting, 348
-Chocolate butter frosting, 346
-Chocolate–pecan frosting, 346
-Chocolate–sour cream frosting, 348
-Chocolate–walnut frosting, 346
-Cocoa–almond frosting, 348
-Coconut–walnut frosting, 346
-Cream cheese–coconut frosting, 348

-Cream cheese–vanilla frosting, 348
-Crunchy peanut butter frosting, 348
-Decorator's frosting, 348
-Lemon butter frosting, 348
-Maraschino frosting, 349
-Mocha icing, 346
-Passionfruit filling and frosting, 349
-Seven minute frosting, 349
-Vanilla frosting, 348
-White chocolate frosting, 346
-Zesty lemon frosting, 349

G
Ginger
-Chill-and-bake ginger nuts, 163
-Chinese chews, 134
-Chocolate–ginger cookies, 40
-Christmas ginger cookies, 318
-Cracked ginger cookies, 40
-Curled ginger thins, 252
-Fresh ginger cookies, 107
-Ginger–almond biscotti, 275
-Ginger–almond florentines, 264
-Ginger biscotti, 272
-Ginger–brandy shortbread cookies, 185
-Ginger–chocolate biscotti, 275
-Ginger–cinnamon cookies, 46
-Ginger cookies, 94
-Ginger fairings, 104
-Ginger-filled brandy snaps, 264
-Ginger-frosted spiced shortbread, 184
-Ginger–fruit cookies, 51
-Ginger icebox cookies, 172
-Ginger leaves, 110
-Gingernuts, 46
-Ginger puffs, 51
-Ginger sandwich cookies, 172
-Ginger shortbread fingers, 184
-Ginger–walnut cookies, 32
-Ginger–walnut icebox cookies, 173
-Ginger whole-wheat twists, 212
-Grasmere gingerbread, 124
-Homemade gingerbread spice, 341
-Honey gingersnaps, 256
-Lemon and ginger cookies, 150-
-Lemon–ginger spritzers, 208
-Marmalade gingerbread squares, 318
-Moravian spice squares 68
-Ormskirk crisp gingerbread, 68
-Rhubarb–ginger squares, 124
-Scottish gingerbread, 124
-Spice, nut, and honey ginger rounds, 50
-Spicy cornish fairings, 47
-Stem ginger cookies, 20
-Tiny ginger cookies, 40
-Yetholm bannock, 196

Glazes
-Lemon glaze, 344
-Orange glaze, 344
Granola
-Muesli bars, 138
-Muesli drop cookies, 43
-Muesli rosettes, 223
Grapes
-Hazelnut–grape cookies, 62

H
Halloween cookies. See Festive cookies
Hazelnuts
-A-bit-of-everything bars, 154
-Bavarian kisses, 48
-Chocolate and hazelnut wafers, 256
-Chocolate cream-filled kisses, 230
-Chocolate–hazelnut brownies, 128
-Chocolate–hazelnut kisses, 18
-Chocolate–hazelnut pinwheels, 166
-Chocolate–hazelnut valentines, 302
-Chocolate nut crackles, 36
-Cinnamon curls, 111
-Coffee–hazelnut bars, 80
-Convent hazelnut macaroons, 229
-Cookie cones with hazelnut cream, 258
-Crunchy crags, 14
-Hazelnut arches, 206
-Hazelnut bars, 155
-Hazelnut cinnamon cookies, 18
-Hazelnut–citrus cookies, 38
-Hazelnut–coffee meringues, 230
-Hazelnut–fig cookies, 63
-Hazelnut–grape cookies, 62
-Hazelnut heaps, 232
-Hazelnut–honey cookies, 115
-Hazelnut madeleines, 282
-Hazelnut meringues, 234
-Hazelnut puffs, 18
-Hazelnut rice-paper cookies, 242
-Hazelnut scoundrels, 82
-Hazelnut shortbread rounds, 184
-Honey–hazelnut shortbread, 196
-Italian hazelnut cookies, 25
-Lemon–hazelnut sticks, 67
-Marmalade–hazelnut swirls, 179
-No-bake hazelnut–chocolate squares, 326
-Nuremberg spice cookies, 50
-Orange-glazed nut cookies, 77
-Orange–hazelnut biscotti, 268
-Orange–hazelnut cookies, 220
-Orange–syrup spritzers, 218
-Peach–hazelnut cookies, 223
-Piped butter S-shapes, 211
-Spicy hazelnut–lemon cookies, 47
-White chocolate–hazelnut florentines, 248

-White chocolate–nut meringues, 238
Honey
-Chocolate and honey lebkuchen bars, 142
-Old English crisps, 110
-Hazelnut–honey cookies, 115
-Honey–almond biscotti, 274
-Honey and lemon madeleines, 284
-Honey–butter cookies, 110
-Honey–cinnamon bars, 142
-Honey crisps, 100
-Honey gingersnaps, 256
-Honey–hazelnut shortbread, 196
-Honey–nutmeg wafers, 252
-Honey–oat cookies, 72
-Honey-spiced pryaniki, 69
-Honey whole-wheat cookies, 219
-New Zealand honey–nut brownies, 128
-Old-fashioned madeleines with lavender honey, 280
-St. Gallen honey drops, 104

I
Icebox cookies
-Almond–lemon swirls, 178
-Angelica cookies, 177
-Banana kipfeln, 168
-Black-and-white cookies, 165
-Black walnut cookies, 176
-Butterscotch shorties, 168
-Cashew butter cookies, 168
-Checkered cookies, 165
-Cherry stand-by cookies, 172
-Cherry–walnut cookies, 173
-Chill-and-bake ginger nuts, 163
-Chocolate caramel cookies, 169
-Chocolate chip refrigerator cookies, 169
-Chocolate drizzlers, 168
-Chocolate–hazelnut pinwheels, 166
-Chocolate rose leaf cookies, 163
-Cinnamon–coffee cookies, 173
-Cinnamon slices, 177
-Citrus pinwheels, 162
-Coconut and orange cookies, 170
-Coconut–cherry icebox cookies, 181
-Coconut–lime snaps, 177
-Coconut–macadamia cookies, 180
-Coffee pinwheels, 163
-Cream cheese sandwich cookies, 170
-Date and corn flake cookies, 181
-Espresso cookies, 166
-Fruits of the fall cookies, 180
-Ginger icebox cookies, 172
-Ginger sandwich cookies, 172
-Ginger–walnut icebox cookies, 173
-Lemon–corn flake cookies, 179
-Lemon–fig cookies, 180

-Lemon icebox cookies, 169
-Marmalade–hazelnut swirls, 179
-Mocha pinwheels, 162
-Neapolitan cookies, 181
-Norwegian brown cookies, 176
-Nut cookies, 174
-Nutty icebox cookies, 173
-Orange and chocolate icebox
  cookies, 168
-Orange–bran flake cookies, 170
-Orange creams, 176
-Peanut butter icebox slices, 178
-Pecan-edged cookies, 181
-Pecan slices, 164
-Plain-and-fancy cookies, 174
-Potato–almond cookies, 174
-Pretty petal icebox cookies, 177
-Red-and-white cookies, 174
-Rum spice cookies, 180
-Sesame–raisin cookies, 176
-Sherry butter cookies, 174
-Sliced refrigerator cookies, 164
-Sour cream icebox cookies, 166
-Strawberry pinwheels, 163
-Sugar strand icebox cookies, 179
-Sunflower seed cookies, 166
-Sunflower seed surprises, 180
-Three-citrus cookies, 170
-Three-color icebox cookies, 164
-Vanilla refrigerator cookies, 178
-Vanilla targets, 178
-Walnut icebox cookies, 179
-White chocolate chip refrigerator
  cookies, 164
Ice cream
-Vanilla ice cream, 344
Icings. *See* Frostings

K
Kiwis
-Kiwi coulis, 344

L
Lavender
-Lavender lights, 96
-Lavender-scented shortbread, 197
Lemons
-Almond–lemon madeleines, 284
-Almond–lemon swirls, 178
-Citrus cream cookies, 54
-Citrus moons, 92
-Citrus pinwheels, 162
-Cornmeal–lemon cookies, 82
-Crusty lemon butter squares, 146
-Glazed lemon cookies, 63
-Glazed lemon cookie strips, 88
-Glazed lemon–olive oil cookies, 62
-Golden star cookies, 102
-Honey and lemon madeleines, 284
-Lebkuchen, 46
-Lemon–almond bites, 56
-Lemon amaretti cookies, 244
-Lemon and ginger cookies, 150

-Lemon bars, 144
-Lemon butter frosting, 348
-Lemon cheesecake squares, 144
-Lemon–cinnamon cookies, 116
-Lemon cookies, 102
-Lemon–corn flake cookies, 179
-Lemon–cream tartlets, 286
-Lemon curd, 340
-Lemon curd drops, 62
-Lemon drop cookies
-Lemon duchesses, 204
-Lemon–fig cookies, 180
-Lemon–ginger spritzers, 208
-Lemon glaze, 344
-Lemon–hazelnut sticks, 67
-Lemon hearts, 204
-Lemon icebox cookies, 169
-Lemon lights, 229
-Lemon madeleines, 280
-Lemon meringue bars, 151
-Lemon moon cookies, 69
-Lemon party cakes, 148
-Lemon petits fours, 244
-Lemon pizzelles, 260
-Lemon–poppy seed biscotti, 272
-Lemon–raisin cookies, 62
-Lemon shortbread fingers, 189
-Lemon s-shapes, 216
-Lemon–vanilla ladyfingers, 288
-Lemon–vanilla rings, 225
-Lemon viennese cookies, 39
-Lemon tartlets, 286
-Lemony cream stars, 207
-Orange–lemon shortbread, 188
-Rosemary–lemon hearts, 112
-Spicy hazelnut–lemon cookies, 47
-Viennese lemon cookies, 39
-Zesty lemon bars, 116
-Zesty lemon frosting, 349
Limes
-Chocolate-dipped lime cookies,
  220
-Coconut–lime snaps, 177
-Coconut–lime stars, 107
-Dainty lime treats, 112
-Lime and sunflower seed cookies,
  58
-Lime buttercream cookies, 58
-Lime s-shapes, 225
-Zesty lime petticoat tails, 198

M
Macadamia nuts
-Coconut and macadamia nut
  macaroons, 228
-Coconut–macadamia cookies, 180
-Mallow macadamia crunchies,
  322
-Nutty cherry–chocolate cookies,
  29
Macaroons
-Almond macaroons, 241
-Almond–poppy seed cookies, 242

-Amaretti cookies, 244
-Amarettini, 244
-Aniseed and pine nut cookies, 240
-Aniseed macaroons, 241
-Brazil nut macaroons, 232
-Chocolate-filled macaroon kisses,
  230
-Chocolate macaroons, 229
-Cocoa–amaretti cookies, 240
-Coconut and macadamia nut
  macaroons, 228
-Coconut heaps, 240
-Coconut macaroons, 240
-Convent almond macaroons, 229
-Convent hazelnut macaroons, 229
-Eliza's macaroons, 228
-Hazelnut rice-paper cookies, 242
-Lemon amaretti cookies, 244
-Lemon petits fours, 244
-Light and spiced macaroons, 228
-Milk chocolate macaroons, 239
-Oatmeal macaroons, 228
-Orange macaroons, 234
-Passover macaroons, 232
-Pineapple–cherry macaroons, 241
-Pine nut macaroons, 235
-Piped and topped macaroons, 239
-Pistachio and orange macaroons,
  236
-Poppy seed macaroons, 234
-Ratafia cookies, 244
-Rich chocolate macaroons, 228
-Walnut drops, 234
-Walnut macaroons, 234
-Wasps' nests, 242
Madeleines
-Almond–lemon madeleines, 284
-Almond shell cookies, 284
-Bittersweet chocolate madeleines,
  282
-Hazelnut madeleines, 282
-Honey and lemon madeleines, 284
-Lemon madeleines, 280
-Madeleines with pistachios, 280
-Mocha madeleines, 282
-Old-fashioned madeleines with
  lavender honey, 280
-Orange–walnut madeleines, 285
-Shell cookies, 284
-Spiced madeleines, 282
-Traditional madeleines, 282
-Welsh scallop-shell cookies, 284
Maple syrup
-Canadian maple cookies, 59
-Maple blondies, 155
-Maple cantuccini, 271
-Maple leaves, 111
-Maple syrup lace cookies, 257
-Maple tarts, 280
-Maple walnut cookies, 76
Marshmallows
-Cherry marshmallow bars, 141
-Marshmallow cookies, 82

-Marshmallow–peanut "pizza," 158
-Marshmallow pops, 329
-Marshmallow sandwich cookies,
  115
-Mini marshmallow tarts, 293
-Rocky road bars, 140
Marzipan
-Apple–marzipan bars, 152
-Coffee-time cookies, 80
-Making homemade marzipan, 346
-Marzipan arches, 220
-Marzipan shortbread, 198
-Marzipan-topped oat cookies, 72
-Mini marzipan mounds, 216
Mascarpone
-Chocolate and mascarpone cream,
  349
-Mascarpone spritzers, 208
-Mascarpone–vanilla cream, 340
Meringues
-Almond–brown sugar meringues,
  241
-Almond heaps, 238
-Brown sugar meringues, 239
-Carrot and orange meringues, 238
-Chestnut meringues, 240
-Chocolate cream-filled kisses, 230
-Chocolate meringues, 235
-Cinnamon meringues, 238
-Coconut meringues, 235
-Coconut meringue slices, 236
-Coconut puffs, 241
-Foolproof mini meringues, 230
-Hazelnut–coffee meringues, 230
-Hazelnut heaps, 232
-Hazelnut meringues, 234
-Lemon lights, 229
-Meringue date morsels, 236
-Meringue mushrooms, 236
-Meringue-topped mince pies, 292
-Mocha meringues, 236
-Nutty meringues, 232
-Nutty mini meringues, 232
-Orange meringue tartlets, 288
-Orange–peanut meringues, 242
-Orange–walnut meringues, 242
-Pecan–coffee meringues, 230
-Peppermint meringues, 242
-Petite meringues, 238
-Pine nut meringues, 232
-Pistachio meringue drops, 230
-Tutti-frutti puffs, 240
-White chocolate–nut meringues,
  238
-White meringue mice, 239
Mint
-Butterflies, 70
-Chocolate peppermint bars, 136
-Crispy mint squares, 136
-Marbled mint brownies, 122
-Mint–chocolate sandwiches, 70
-Mint and currant bars, 122
-Mint liqueur balls, 329

-Mint pryaniki, 55
-Mint spritz cookies, 208
-Mint-topped cookies, 81
-Party peppermint windmills, 304
-Peppermint meringues, 242
Mother's Day cookies. *See* Festive
  cookies
Mousse
-Kahlua mousse, 341
Muesli. *See* Granola

N
No-bake cookies
-Carob truffle squares, 323
-Chocolate caramel squares, 328
-Chocolate–cherry squares, 323
-Chocolate corn flake cakes, 328
-Chocolate-covered coconut bars,
  328
-Chocolate crunch wedges, 323
-Chocolate–fruit chewies, 322
-Chocolate–pistachio squares, 323
-Coffee liqueur balls, 329
-Coffee–pecan wedges, 322
-Coffee–walnut wedges, 327
-Crunchy cereal and fruit squares,
  324
-Crunchy snowmen, 324
-Fruity praline squares, 322
-Mallow macadamia crunchies,
  322
-Marshmallow pops, 329
-Mint liqueur balls, 329
-No-bake apricot–banana squares,
  324
-No-bake ball cookies, 329
-No-bake carob brownies, 324
-No-bake chocolate–apricot
  cookies, 327
-No-bake chocolate crumb drops,
  326
-No-bake chocolate–date cookies,
  327
-No-bake chocolate fruit squares,
  323
-No-bake chocolate mice, 324
-No-bake chocolate–peanut bars,
  328
-No-bake chocolate–prune cookies,
  327
-No-bake chocolate–raisin bars,
  328
-No-bake chocolate squares, 326
-No-bake crunchy peanut bars, 322
-No-bake date–banana squares,
  324
-No-bake hazelnut–chocolate
  squares, 326
-No-bake multicolored squares, 326
-No-bake peanut–orange squares,
  327
-No-bake pistachio moons, 329
-No-bake smilies and spookies, 326

-Rocky roads, 328
-White chocolate and amaretti
  crunch, 327
Nutmeg
-Chocolate nutmeg cookies, 15
-Honey–nutmeg wafers, 252
-Nutmeg spritz cookies, 223
-Nutmeg-topped cookies, 44
-Plum–nutmeg friands, 231
Nuts. *See* specific kind of nut

O
Oats
-Anzac cookies, 30
-Apple–oat bars, 142
-Apple, raisin, and oat bars, 126
-Australian crunchies, 140
-Banana fingers, 120
-Banana–oat bars, 142
-Brown sugar–oat biscotti, 274
-Carob–oat squares, 133
-Carob-topped sunflower seed
  drops, 30
-Cherry–chocolate crunchies, 15
-Cherry oat cookies, 29
-Chewy oat and dried fruit bars,
  146
-Coconut oat cookies, 67
-Crispy chocolate creams, 26
-Crunchy oatmeal bars, 125
-Date-filled oat bars, 140
-Date–oat cookies, 16
-Easy oat bars, 138
-Energy bars, 141
-Honey–oat cookies, 72
-Irish oat cookies, 72
-Marzipan-topped oat cookies, 72
-Molasses bites, 58
-Muesli drop cookies, 43
-Oat chips, 25
-Oat crunchies, 22
-Oat drops, 48
-Oatmeal cookies, 24
-Oatmeal macaroons, 228
-Oatmeal "pizza," 158
-Oatmeal, raisin, and walnut
  cookies, 38
-Oatmeal–raisin cookies, 38
-Oat–walnut cookies, 59
-Parkin, 51
-Peanut oaties, 34
-Pecan–oat clusters, 56
-Raspberry–oat squares, 150
-Rum and oat rings, 73
-Sunflower–bran cookies, 14
-Sunflower drops, 29
-Sunflower oat drops, 28
-Toffee–oat bars, 129
-White chocolate–oat squares,
  133
Oranges
-Almond–orange pockets, 90
-Almond–orange wafers, 253

-Butter cookies with orange glaze,
  222
-Carrot and orange meringues, 238
-Carrot–orange cookies, 60
-Chocolate-dipped orange cookies,
  92
-Chocolate–orange cookies, 78
-Chocolate–orange squares, 132
-Chocolate–orange stars, 78
-Chocolate–orange twists, 225
-Cinnamon–orange cookies, 108
-Citrus cream cookies, 54
-Citrus mincemeat cookies, 55
-Citrus moons, 92
-Citrus pinwheels, 162
-Cocoa, orange, and date squares,
  137
-Coconut and orange cookies, 170
-Cookie ringlets, 213
-Hazelnut–citrus cookies, 38
-Heavenly moments, 43
-Kaffeehaus cookies, 218
-No-bake peanut–orange squares,
  327
-Orange–almond cookies, 216
-Orange–almond petits fours,
  261
-Orange and chocolate icebox
  cookies, 168
-Orange–bran flake cookies, 170
-Orange cheesecake squares, 145
-Orange cookies, 116
-Orange cookies with chocolate
  chips, 39
-Orange creams, 176
-Orange curd, 340
-Orange fingers, 206
-Orange glaze, 344
-Orange-glazed nut cookies, 77
-Orange–hazelnut biscotti, 268
-Orange–hazelnut cookies, 220
-Orange lace cookies with coffee-
  cream filling, 258
-Orange ladyfingers, 288
-Orange–lemon shortbread, 188
-Orange macaroons, 234
-Orange meringue bars, 151
-Orange meringue tartlets, 288
-Orange–peanut meringues, 242
-Orange–pecan squares, 156
-Orange–raisin cookies, 39
-Orange s-shapes, 212
-Orange star cookies, 116
-Orange viennese cookies, 43
-Orange wafer thins, 257
-Orange–walnut madeleines, 285
-Orange–walnut meringues, 242
-Pistachio and orange macaroons,
  236
-Three-citrus cookies, 170
-Turkish marmalade cookies, 51
-Viennese orange cookies, 43
-Whole-wheat orange cookies, 42

P
Passionfruit
-Passionfruit cream, 345
-Passionfruit crunchies, 44
-Passionfruit filling and frosting, 349
-Passionfruit shortbread, 186
-White chocolate–passionfruit
  shortbread, 186
Passover cookies
-Passover brownies, 316
-Rugelach, 306
Peanut butter
-Chocolate cookies with peanut
  butter topping, 22
-Chocolate–peanut butter cookies,
  26
-Chocolate peanut cookies, 26
-Crunchy peanut butter frosting,
  348
-Peanut butter–bran cookies, 34
-Peanut butter–chocolate kiss
  cookies, 34
-Peanut butter cookies, 34
-Peanut butter icebox slices, 178
-Peanut butter "pizza," 158
-Queensland cookies, 34
-Three-ingredient cookies, 35
Peanuts
-Chocolate peanut cookies, 26
-Oatmeal–chocolate chip cookies,
  25
-Orange–peanut meringues, 242
-Marshmallow–peanut "pizza," 158
-No-bake chocolate–peanut bars,
  328
-No-bake crunchy peanut bars, 322
-No-bake peanut–orange squares,
  327
-Peanut brownie cookies, 26
-Peanut oaties, 34
-Peanut shortbread, 184
-Salted peanut cookies, 26
Peaches
-Peach-filled shortbread, 194
-Peach–hazelnut cookies, 223
Pears
-Pear–apricot bars, 152
-Pear–cherry bars, 146
Pecans
-Apricot pecan cookies, 72
-Brown sugar cookies, 32
-Chocolate nut crackles, 36
-Chocolate–pecan frosting, 346
-Chocolate–pecan shortbread, 186
-Coconut–pecan biscotti, 276
-Coconut–pecan shortbread, 188
-Coconut toasties, 56
-Coffee–pecan cookies, 63
-Coffee–pecan wafers, 254
-Coffee–pecan wedges, 322
-Date and pecan shortcakes, 130
-Date–pecan cookies, 43
-Death-by-chocolate cookies, 36

-Maple cantuccini, 271
-Nutty cinnamon cookies, 35
-Nutty cranberry cookies, 35
-Orange–pecan squares, 156
-Pecan and chocolate chip "pizza," 158
-Pecan balls, 52
-Pecan biscotti, 268
-Pecan–coffee meringues, 230
-Pecan–date cookies, 18
-Pecan-edged cookies, 181
-Pecan lace cookies, 261
-Pecan lace snaps, 262
-Pecan–oat clusters, 56
-Pecan pie bars, 130
-Pecan–rum tarts, 286
-Pecan shortbread tails, 188
-Pecan slices, 164
-Pecan–sour cream cookies, 35
-Pecan sugar cookies, 72
-Pine nut–pecan tarts, 285
-Tiny pecan tarts, 286
Pineapple
-Glazed pineapple cookies, 20
-Pineapple–almond cookies, 218
-Pineapple–cherry macaroons, 241
-Pineapple date drops, 20
-Pineapple spritz cookies, 208
Pine nuts
-Aniseed and pine nut cookies, 240
-French butter cookies, 110
-Pine nut and raisin cookies, 93
-Pine nut biscotti, 276
-Pine nut macaroons, 235
-Pine nut meringues, 232
-Pine nut–pecan tarts, 285
-Pine nut rings, 213
-Pine nut shortbread, 198
Piped cookies
-Almond spritz cookies, 222
-Aniseed puffs, 223
-Aniseed rounds, 220
-Butter cookies with orange glaze, 222
-Butter whirls, 207
-Butter wreaths, 206
-Candied spritzers, 222
-Chocolate angelica spritz cookies, 222
-Chocolate-coated arches, 210
-Chocolate-dipped lime cookies, 220
-Coconut spritzers, 218
-Cornmeal ribbons, 216
-Danish almond cookies, 216
-Double chocolate fingers, 210
-Filled chocolate fingers, 212
-Hazelnut arches, 206
-Honey whole-wheat cookies, 219
-Ladies' delights, 207
-Ladyfingers, 206
-Lemon duchesses, 204
-Lemon hearts, 204

-Lemony cream stars, 207
-Kaffeehaus cookies, 218
-Making fingers and rosettes, 202
-Marzipan arches, 220
-Mini marzipan mounds, 216
-Muesli rosettes, 223
-Multicolored shells, 210
-Naples cookies, 218
-Nutmeg spritz cookies, 223
-Orange–almond cookies, 216
-Orange fingers, 206
-Orange–hazelnut cookies, 220
-Orange–syrup spritzers, 218
-Parisian petits fours, 202
-Peach–hazelnut cookies, 223
-Pineapple–almond cookies, 218
-Piped almond-topped cookies, 218
-Piped butter s-shapes, 211
-Piped coconut treats, 202
-Piped cookies, 202
-Piped dreams, 207
-Piped mocha rosettes, 203
-Piped strawberry thumbprints, 210
-Savoy fingers, 220
-Sesame cookies, 213
-Spiced piped cookies, 219
-Viennese whirls, 204
-Whipped and piped cookies, 204
Pistachios
-Chocolate–pistachio squares, 323
-Madeleines with pistachios, 280
-No-bake pistachio moons, 329
-Pistachio and orange macaroons, 236
-Pistachio chocolates, 297
-Pistachio meringue drops, 230
-Pistachio shortbread, 188
-Pistachio windmills, 77
-Three-color icebox cookies, 164
Pizza pan cookies
-Chocolate chip "pizza," 158
-Marshmallow–peanut "pizza," 158
-Peanut butter "pizza," 158
-Pecan and chocolate chip "pizza," 158
Plums
-Plum–nutmeg friands, 281
Popcorn
-Popcorn puffs, 62
Poppy seeds
-Almond–poppy seed cookies, 242
-Lemon–poppy seed biscotti, 272
-Poppy seed and sesame wafers, 249
-Poppy seed cookies, 89
-Poppy seed–cornmeal cookies, 88
-Poppy-seed ice-cream baskets, 253
-Poppy seed macaroons, 234
-Poppy seed s-shapes, 225
Potatoes
-Potato–almond cookies, 174

Prunes
-Cranberry–prune cookies, 55
-No-bake chocolate–prune cookies, 327
-Prune ribbon cookies, 155
Puff pastry
-Cardamom-sugar palmiers, 290
-Palmiers, 290
Pumpkin
-Chocolate chip pumpkin cookies, 54
-Pumpkin bars, 146
-Pumpkin cookies, 54
-Pumpkin pie biscotti, 274
-Pumpkin–raisin bars with cream cheese frosting, 126
-Sweet pumpkin fried cookies, 334
Purees
-Berry coulis, 344
-Kiwi coulis, 344
-Raspberry coulis, 344
-Raspberry puree, 342
-Strawberry coulis, 344
-Tropical coulis, 342

Q
Quark
-Apple turnovers, 89
-Quark spirals, 80

R
Raisins
-Amish spicy raisin cookies, 47
-Apple, raisin, and oat bars, 126
-Apricot–raisin bars, 126
-Brandied spiced cookies, 38
-Carrot and raisin drops, 60
-Coffee–raisin cookie cakes, 292
-Fruit and nut rock cookies, 62
-Golden raisin cookies, 94
-Hermits, 47
-Lemon–raisin cookies, 62
-No-bake chocolate–raisin bars, 328
-Oatmeal, raisin, and walnut cookies, 38
-Oatmeal–raisin cookies, 38
-Orange–raisin cookies, 39
-Pine nut and raisin cookies, 93
-Pumpkin–raisin bars with cream cheese frosting, 126
-Sesame–raisin cookies, 176
-Soft raisin–walnut cookies, 38
-Spiced raisin cookies, 50
-Tyrolean chocolate fingers, 148
-Walnut–raisin cookies, 59
Raspberries
-Almond–raspberry tarts, 293
-Chocolate–raspberry macaroon bars, 145
-Jam-topped piped shortbread, 192
-Jelly-filled hearts, 97

-Raspberry–almond friands, 281
-Raspberry coulis, 344
-Raspberry curd, 340
-Raspberry drops, 16
-Raspberry kisses, 16
-Raspberry linzer squares, 152
-Raspberry–oat squares, 150
-Raspberry puree, 342
-Raspberry sandwiches, 90
-Raspberry thumbprints, 16
-Shrewsbury cookies, 92
-Syltkakor, 115
-Uplands cookies, 84
Rhubarb
-Rhubarb–ginger squares, 124
Rice
-Rice flour cookies, 100
-Rice–olive oil cookies, 26
Rice paper
-Nuremberg spice cookies, 50
Rolled cookies
-Abernethy cookies, 68
-Alberts, 77
-Almond cookies, 105
-Almond–orange pockets, 90
-Almond-studded playing cards, 106
-Alphabet cookies, 116
-Apple turnovers, 89
-Apricot pecan cookies, 72
-Animal cut-out cookies, 74
-Augsburg mellow yellows, 114
-Baseler leckerli, 100
-Belgium cookies, 108
-Berliners, 73
-Bohemian caraway cookies, 85
-Bran cookies, 93
-Butter digestive cookies, 84
-Butterflies, 70
-Buttermilk cookies, 100
-Canary cream cookies, 89
-Cashew cookies, 105
-Chocolate-coated party rings, 78
-Chocolate cream sandwich cookies, 93
-Cinnamon curls, 111
-Chocolate-dipped orange cookies, 92
-Chocolate-filled cookies, 70
-Chocolate-filled sugar cookies, 66
-Chocolate-flecked cookies, 98
-Chocolate–orange cookies, 78
-Chocolate–orange stars, 78
-Chocolate–semolina cookies, 70
-Cinnamon cookies, 86
-Cinnamon–orange cookies, 108
-Cinnamon streusel cookies, 109
-Cinnamon tickets, 90
-Cinnamon-topped flower cookies, 76
-Citrus moons, 92
-Clove cut-out cookies, 114
-Coconut–lime stars, 107

-Coconut oat cookies, 67
-Coconut squares, 67
-Coffee-frosted walnut cookies, 106
-Coffee–hazelnut bars, 80
-Coffee heart cookies, 80
-Coffee-time cookies, 80
-Cookie hands, 98
-Cornmeal–lemon cookies, 82
-Cranberry-topped hearts, 114
-Cream crisps, 104
-Cream–cheese crescents, 76
-Cream crescents, 96
-Cream crisps, 104
-Crispy butter cookies, 85
-Crunchy-topped almond butter cookies, 85
-Cumberland rum–butter cookies, 72
-Custard creams, 92
-Dainty lime treats, 112
-Derwentwater cookies, 101
-Digestive biscuits, 85
-Double-deckers, 111
-Easter currant cookies, 98
-Fig rolls, 112
-Filled sugar wafers, 74
-Finnish cookies, 115
-Flower cookies, 96
-French butter cookies, 110
-Fresh ginger cookies, 107
-Garibaldis, 101
-Ginger cookies, 94
-Ginger fairings, 104
-Ginger leaves, 110
-Glazed lemon cookie strips, 88
-Golden crisps, 100
-Golden raisin cookies, 94
-Golden star cookies, 102
-Hazelnut–honey cookies, 115
-Hazelnut scoundrels, 82
-Honey–butter cookies, 110
-Honey crisps, 100
-Honey–oat cookies, 72
-Honey-spiced pryaniki, 69
-Irish oat cookies, 72
-Italian hearts, 88
-Jam-filled turnovers, 96
-Jelly cookies, 84
-Jelly-filled hearts, 97
-Jumble rings, 94
-Karlsbad cookies, 88
-Korzhiki, 105
-Lancashire tea cakes, 110
-Lavender lights, 96
-Lemon–cinnamon cookies, 116
-Lemon cookies, 102
-Lemon–hazelnut sticks, 67
-Lemon moon cookies, 69
-Lepeshki, 74
-Linzer cookies, 69
-Lovers' knots, 86
-Madeira bars, 86
-Maple leaves, 111

-Maple walnut cookies, 76
-Marsala cookies, 114
-Marshmallow cookies, 82
-Marshmallow sandwich cookies, 115
-Marzipan-topped oat cookies, 72
-Mazurek, 68
-Mint–chocolate sandwiches, 70
-Mint-topped cookies, 81
-Mocha–almond cookies, 106
-Moravian spice squares, 68
-Multicolored sandwich cookies, 82
-Northern pepper stars, 106
-Nut crisps, 104
-Old English crisps, 110
-Old English jumbles, 94
-Orange cookies, 116
-Orange-glazed nut cookies, 77
-Orange star cookies, 116
-Ormskirk crisp gingerbread, 68
-Oxford johns, 74
-Pecan sugar cookies, 72
-Peruvian cookies, 97
-Pine nut and raisin cookies, 93
-Pistachio windmills, 77
-Poppy seed cookies, 89
-Poppy seed–cornmeal cookies, 88
-Quark spirals, 80
-Raspberry sandwiches, 90
-Rice flour cookies, 100
-Rolled sugar cookies, 66
-Rolled white chocolate cookies, 105
-Rosemary–lemon hearts, 112
-Rum and oat rings, 73
-Rustic anise cookies, 84
-Sablé cookies, 86
-Saffron cookies, 108
-Sherry tea cakes, 100
-Shrewsbury cookies, 92
-Smiling face cookies, 98
-Spice cookies, 102
-Stars in the sky, 107
-St. Gallen honey drops, 104
-St. John's alms, 81
-Sugar cookies, 86
-Sugar hearts, 78
-Sweet and spiced shapes, 92
-Sweet jewel cookies, 102
-Swiss hearts, 112
-Syltkakor, 115
-Tea leaves, 96
-Tunbridge Wells crisps, 101
-Turkish yogurt cookies, 68
-Tutti-frutti cookies, 84
-Uplands cookies, 84
-Vanilla wafers, 69
-Victorian almond jumbles, 94
-Whetstone cookies, 101
-York cookies, 67
-Zesty citrus bars, 90
-Zesty lemon bars, 116

Rosemary
-Rosemary–lemon hearts, 112
Rose water
-Old English jumbles, 94
-Maidstone cookies, 32
-Rose pryaniki, 56
-Whetstone cookies, 101
Rum
-Cumberland rum–butter cookies, 72
-Leipzig tarts, 293
-Pecan–rum tarts, 286
-Rum and oat rings, 73

S
Saffron
-Saffron cookies, 108
Sauces
-Caramel sauce, 342
-Cherry sauce, 342
-Chocolate–fudge sauce, 342
-Cranberry sauce, 342
-Warm chocolate sauce, 342
Semolina
-Chocolate–semolina cookies, 70
-Semolina shortbread, 193
Sesame seeds
-Fig–sesame biscotti, 275
-Koulourakias, 224
-Poppy seed and sesame wafers, 249
-Sesame cookies, 213
-Sesame–raisin cookies, 176
-Sesame thins, 252
-Sunny sesame snaps, 260
Shaped cookies
-Almond crescents, 204
-Apricot–chocolate pretzels, 216
-Banana creams, 213
-Bretzels, 214
-Butter teardrops, 212
-Chocolate crescents, 214
-Chocolate–orange twists, 225
-Chocolate pretzels, 214
-Convent kipfeln, 214
-Cookie ringlets, 213
-Curly cinnamon ducks, 219
-Ginger whole-wheat twists, 212
-Glazed pretzels, 214
-Koulourakias, 224
-Lemon s-shapes, 216
-Lemon–vanilla rings, 225
-Lime s-shapes, 225
-Making sugar pretzels, 203
-Orange s-shapes, 212
-Pine nut rings, 213
-Poppy seed s-shapes, 225
-Red wine cookies, 222
-Spiced clove cookies, 210
-S-shaped cookies, 224
-Sweet ring cookies, 212
-Vanilla cookies, 225
-Vanilla kipfeln, 214

-White chocolate-coated pretzels, 224
Shortbread
-Almond shortbread cookies, 192
-Almond shortbread with blackberry topping, 194
-Apple shortbread, 196
-Apricot-topped shortbread squares, 198
-Brandy butter shortbread, 194
-Caramel shortbread squares, 185
-Cherry–rum shortbread cookies, 189
-Cherry–walnut shortbread, 196
-Chocolate chip shortbread, 194
-Chocolate–cinnamon shortbread, 185
-Chocolate–pecan shortbread, 186
-Chocolate shortbread cookies, 188
-Coconut–pecan shortbread, 188
-Coconut shortbread thins, 196
-Coffee-frosted walnut shortbread cookies, 197
-Coffee shortbread, 198
-Crunchy brown sugar shortbread, 193
-Ginger–brandy shortbread cookies, 185
-Ginger-frosted spiced shortbread, 184
-Ginger shortbread fingers, 184
-Gold-top shortbread, 192
-Hazelnut shortbread rounds, 184
-Honey–hazelnut shortbread, 196
-Jammy shortbread bars, 190
-Jam-topped piped shortbread, 192
-Lavender-scented shortbread, 197
-Lemon shortbread fingers, 189
-Marzipan shortbread, 198
-Millionaire's shortbread, 190
-Mincemeat-filled shortbread cookies, 186
-Orange–lemon shortbread, 188
-Passionfruit shortbread, 186
-Peach-filled shortbread, 194
-Peanut shortbread, 184
-Pecan shortbread tails, 188
-Pine nut shortbread, 198
-Piped cherry-topped shortbread, 193
-Pistachio shortbread, 188
-Royal Balmoral shortbread, 190
-Semolina shortbread, 193
-Scottish shortbread, 184
-Simple shortbread cookies, 196
-Spanish shortbread, 190
-Venetian fregolata, 188
-White chocolate–passionfruit shortbread, 186
-Yetholm bannock, 196
-Zesty almond shortbread, 194
-Zesty lime petticoat tails, 198
Sour cream

-Chocolate–sour cream frosting, 348
-Korzhiki, 105
-Lepeshki, 74
-Marbled cookies, 59
-Pecan–sour cream cookies, 35
-Sour cream icebox cookies, 166
Spritz cookies
-Almond spritzers, 208
-Chocolate cherry spritz cookies, 211
-Cinnamon spritz cookies, 211
-Lemon–ginger spritzers, 208
-Mascarpone spritzers, 208
-Mint spritz cookies, 208
-Pineapple spritz cookies, 208
-Vanilla spritz cookies, 211
Strawberry
-Flower cookies, 96
-Piped strawberry thumbprints, 210
-Strawberry–almond friands, 281
-Strawberry coulis, 344
-Strawberry pinwheels, 163
-Strawberry thumbprints, 15
Sugars
-Cinnamon sugar, 341
-Colored sprinkling sugars, 341
-Vanilla confectioners' sugar, 341
-Vanilla sugar, 341
Sunflower seeds
-Banana–sunflower seed cookies, 48
-Carob-topped sunflower seed drops, 30
-Lime and sunflower seed cookies, 58
-Sunflower bars, 137
-Sunflower–bran cookies, 14
-Sunflower drops, 29
-Sunflower oat drops, 28
-Sunflower seed cookies, 166
-Sunflower seed surprises, 180

T
Tartlets
-Almond–raspberry tarts, 293
-Almond tarts, 280
-Leipzig tarts, 293
-Lemon–cream tartlets, 286
-Lemon tartlets, 286
-Macaroon tarts, 281
-Maids of honor, 288
-Maple tarts, 280
-Meringue-topped mince pies, 292
-Mini jelly tarts, 293
-Mini marshmallow tarts, 293
-Mini mincemeat tartlets, 289
-Mini redcurrant pies, 290
-Orange meringue tartlets, 288
-Pecan–rum tarts, 286
-Pine nut–pecan tarts, 285
-Quick mini coconut cups, 286

-Tiny pecan tarts, 286
-White chocolate tartlets, 289
Tea cakes
-Chocolate buckwheat pixies, 285
-Coffee–raisin cookie cakes, 292
-Dainty tea cakes, 290
-French cannelés, 289
-Orange–almond petits fours, 261
-Petit-four fancies, 284
-Petits-fours, 292
Techniques
-Making biscotti, 268
-Making chocolate-dipped pirouette cookies, 249
-Making fingers and rosettes, 202
-Making french almond tiles, 248
-Making fried cookies, 332
-Making mocha pinwheels, 162
-Making rolled sugar cookies, 66
-Making sugar pretzels, 203

V
Vanilla
-Chocolate vanilla drops, 22
-Cream cheese–vanilla frosting, 348
-Mascarpone–vanilla cream, 340
-Lemon–vanilla ladyfingers, 288
-Lemon–vanilla rings, 225
-Vanilla confectioners' sugar, 341
-Vanilla cookies, 225
-Vanilla-filled kisses, 16
-Vanilla frosting, 348
-Vanilla ice cream, 344
-Vanilla kipfeln, 214
-Vanilla refrigerator cookies, 178
-Vanilla spritz cookies, 211
-Vanilla sugar, 341
-Vanilla targets, 178
-Vanilla wafers, 69
-Vanilla whipped cream, 340
Valentine's Day cookies. *See* Festive cookies

W
Wafers
-Almond cookie cups, 260
-Almond lace cookies, 253
-Almond–orange wafers, 253
-Bavarian apple cones, 258
-Berry thins, 250
-Cardamom krumkake wafer cones, 256
-Caribbean coconut wafers, 260
-Cashew–chocolate crisps, 261
-Cherry florentines, 264
-Chinese fortune cookies, 250
-Chocolate–almond tuiles, 250
-Chocolate–almond wafers, 250
-Chocolate and hazelnut wafers, 256
-Chocolate pirouette lace cookies, 248

-Coconut crisps, 260
-Coconut fortune cookies, 257
-Coffee–pecan wafers, 254
-Cookie cones with hazelnut cream, 258
-Curled ginger thins, 252
-Dainty almond wafers, 252
-Dark cat tuiles, 262
-Darjeeling wafers, 256
-Double chocolate crisps, 258
-Filled almond wafers, 253
-Filled cats' tongues, 262
-Florentines, 254
-Ginger–almond florentines, 264
-Ginger-filled brandy snaps, 264
-Honey gingersnaps, 256
-Honey–nutmeg wafers, 252
-Langues de chat, 262
-Lemon pizzelles, 260
-Making chocolate-dipped pirouette cookies, 249
-Making french almond tiles, 248
-Maple syrup lace cookies, 257
-Orange lace cookies with coffee-cream filling, 258
-Orange wafer thins, 257
-Pecan lace cookies, 261
-Pecan lace snaps, 262
-Poppy seed and sesame wafers, 249
-Poppy-seed ice-cream baskets, 253
-Sesame thins, 252
-Summer berry florentines, 254
-Sunny sesame snaps, 260
-Sweet russian cigarettes, 264
-Walnut–cherry florentines, 254
-Walnut lace cookies, 261
-White chocolate–hazelnut florentines, 248
-White florentines, 249
Walnuts
-Almond–walnut bars, 145
-Apple–walnut cookies, 42
-Black walnut cookies, 176
-Cherry–walnut cookies, 173
-Cherry–walnut shortbread, 196
-Chocolate chip–walnut cookies, 22
-Chocolate–walnut biscotti, 270
-Chocolate–walnut frosting, 346
-Christmas walnut–cranberry bars, 300
-Coconut–walnut frosting, 346
-Coconut–walnut squares, 124
-Coffee-frosted walnut cookies, 106
-Coffee-frosted walnut shortbread cookies, 197
-Coffee–nut wafers, 20
-Coffee–walnut cookies, 63
-Coffee–walnut wedges, 327
-Corn flake–walnut cookies, 58
-Czech cookies, 150

-Date and walnut squares, 154
-Date delights, 43
-Fruit and nut rock cookies, 62
-Fruits of the fall cookies, 180
-Ginger–walnut cookies, 32
-Ginger–walnut icebox cookies, 173
-Golden nuts, 55
-Maple walnut cookies, 76
-Muesli drop cookies, 43
-New Zealand honey–nut brownies, 128
-Nutty icebox cookies, 173
-Oatmeal, raisin, and walnut cookies, 38
-Oat–walnut cookies, 59
-Orange–walnut madeleines, 285
-Orange–walnut meringues, 242
-Port wine–walnut squares, 125
-Snickerdoodles, 14
-Soft raisin–walnut cookies, 38
-Sticky toffee–walnut bars, 129
-Toffee–walnut blondies with caramel frosting, 130
-Walnut bars, 154
-Walnut–cherry florentines, 254
-Walnut clusters, 59
-Walnut–date cookies, 18
-Walnut drops, 234
-Walnut half-moons, 76
-Walnut icebox cookies, 179
-Walnut lace cookies, 261
-Walnut macaroons, 234
-Walnut–raisin cookies, 59
-Walnut squares, 125
Wine
-Madeira bars, 86
-Marsala cookies, 114
-Port wine–walnut squares, 125
-Red wine cookies, 222
-Sherry butter cookies, 174

Y
Yogurt
-Turkish yogurt cookies, 68
-Yogurt–cocoa bars, 151